Familiar Quotations

Familiar Quotations

*A collection of passages, phrases and
proverbs traced to their sources in
ancient and modern literature*

by JOHN BARTLETT

Fourteenth Edition
REVISED AND ENLARGED

EMILY MORISON BECK, *Editor*

Little, Brown and Company · Boston · Toronto

LIBRARY OF CONGRESS CATALOGUE CARD NO. 68-15664

00004

First Edition Published 1855
Fourteenth Edition Published 1968

Eleventh Printing

Published simultaneously in Canada
by Little, Brown & Company (Canada) Limited

PRINTED IN THE UNITED STATES OF AMERICA

Preface

TO THE FOURTEENTH EDITION

"BARTLETT" has now entered into our language, itself a "familiar quotation," not associated with either pears or trees, but a source book nearly as indispensable as the dictionary: "Look it up in *Bartlett!*" Sir Winston Churchill thought it an "admirable work" and studied it intently, he tells us in *My Early Life.* "The quotations when engraved upon the memory give you good thoughts. They also make you anxious to read the authors and look for more." Readers and editors of *Bartlett* have done just this—and found more. In more than a century of life *Bartlett* has grown prodigiously and its sales increase steadily each year. So, why now a new edition?

The most obvious reason, of course, is the number of quotations that have become memorable since the last edition in 1955. Historical events, the growth of philosophy and science, the eminence of certain statesmen, writers, poets, and others who use words effectively, strongly influence our use of language and choice of expressions. An appendix to *Bartlett* might have taken care of these addenda; this had been done in some earlier editions. But today there are important additional reasons for a thorough revision—if, like a dictionary, this collection of historical and living sayings is to keep abreast of the times.

Literary tastes and popular expressions change from one generation to another, and the facility of communication has accelerated this process. Figures of the past emerge from the shadow of neglect and begin to be quoted; others fade from fashion, or their words lose their relevance to the times. Fads create catchy phrases, some of them lasting. And all the while there is an accretion of sayings which, one supposes, will provide a ballast for civilization for as long as men continue to communicate with one another.

As the two postwar editions of *Bartlett*, the twelfth and thirteenth, record the advent of the atomic age, so the fourteenth bears the particular imprint of the last decade. Since the publication of the last edition, a large number of world-renowned figures now "belong to the ages," leaving their mark upon our culture—men like Churchill, Kennedy, Adlai Stevenson, Pope John XXIII, Nehru, Oppenheimer, Hammarskjöld, Albert Schweitzer; distinguished men of letters like Robert Frost, Hemingway, T. S. Eliot, Faulkner, Aldous Huxley, E. E. Cummings, Roethke, Pasternak, Thurber, Carl Sandburg, Camus. It is interesting to speculate, furthermore, whether this edition that bears their death dates for the first time will carry more of their quotations than will future editions, affected as they will be by historical perspective.

Some phenomena of recent years are crystallized in a word or phrase: beat generation, brinkmanship, the Great Society, the affluent society, the multiversity, cybernetics, racism, the revolution of rising expectations, the American Establishment, poverty—the other America.

The nature and the size of the *Bartlett* audience provide another reason for a new edition. The vastly increased number of students, the expanding interests of the intellectually curious, as evidenced by the tremendous variety of paperbacks and inexpensive editions on every subject, demand a broader reach into other fields of literature and an amplification of authors hitherto inadequately represented.

Outdated translation is another reason for revision. The classics for the most part have been heretofore represented by translations unchanged since the nineteenth century, some of them clearly archaic. Until now Homer has appeared in Pope's translation, of which even his contemporary, the classicist Richard Bentley, remarked, "It is a pretty poem, Mr. Pope, but you must not call it Homer." True enough; those "familiar quotations" like "Welcome the coming, speed the parting guest" are more Pope than Homer. They now appear appropriately under Pope, while well-known Homeric lines, like "All strangers and beggars are from Zeus, and a gift, though small, is precious," are here included for the first time.

As our range of reference expands inversely with the shrinkage of space on this earth, expressions and sayings from the cultures and literatures of Asia, Europe and South America are assimilated into our common heritage. Increasing interest in science, and the recognition that

vi

Freud, for example, in Auden's phrase is now "a whole climate of opinion," insist on greater representation from scientists and psychiatrists.

A number of figures besides Freud and Jung have never appeared in *Bartlett* before, perhaps because they were not thought to have said anything actually "familiar," or perhaps because they have not occurred to the editors as natural sources of quotations. But it was astonishing to find among the missing Confucius, Columbus, Chekhov, Bolívar, Brandeis, Bergson, Sir Thomas Malory, Cotton Mather, John Marshall, Pushkin, Flaubert, Gandhi, Lao Tzu, Kant, Kierkegaard. . . . Other important figures like St. Augustine or Julius Caesar formerly were credited with a single quote, not necessarily the most famous one.

An amazing number of famous quotations have been overlooked in previous editions. Here are a few: Man is the measure of all things (Protagoras); The greatest reverence is due the young (Juvenal); There is always something new out of Africa (Pliny); But it does move (Galileo); There go the ships (Psalm 104); When I am dead and opened, you shall find "Calais" lying in my heart (Mary Tudor); But that was in another country; and besides, the wench is dead (Marlowe); One man with courage makes a majority (Andrew Jackson); Surprised by joy (Wordsworth); Not Angles, but Angels (Gregory I); Praise the sea, on shore remain (John Florio); $E = mc^2$ (Einstein); Q.E.D. (Euclid); War is much too serious a matter to be entrusted to the military (Clemenceau); Hypocrite lecteur—mon semblable—mon frère (Baudelaire); A journey of a thousand miles must begin with a single step (Lao Tzu); I beseech you, in the bowels of Christ, think it possible you may be mistaken (Cromwell), a saying which Judge Learned Hand would like to have "written over the portals of every church, every school, every courthouse, and . . . of every legislative body in the United States."

Errors persist—one for over a hundred years: the misquotation of the title of Gray's *Elegy* in omitting the word *Written* before *in a Country Churchyard.*

The inescapable conclusion is that a collection of this kind must be thoroughly overhauled from time to time. Today a single editor, or a brace of editors, is no longer adequate for what to John Bartlett in 1891 was still "this very agreeable pursuit." It is one thing to carry on the tradition of "familiar" and "worthy of perpetuation," to recognize in the sifting of hoary sayings the line that still persists as vital or pertinent. But to assume authority on the well-known quotations in all the fields and among all the authors now represented in this edition would be presumptuous. Thus, for the first time, the editor of *Familiar Quotations* has had a staff of consulting scholars who have spent many hours helping to compile well-known material from the classics, from Chinese, Japanese, Sanskrit, Russian, German, French, and Spanish sources, from Latin America, and from the sciences, psychology, medicine, American history, political science, American and English literature. They have also scanned the existing text for errors, and recommended what to eliminate as "dead wood" or no longer relevant. At least a fourth of these experts are under thirty, to give proper representation to the younger generation.

The editor of the fourteenth edition gratefully acknowledges the contributions of the following: Elizabeth Perkins Aldrich, Peter Anastas, George Basalla, William J. Courtenay, Bernard De Voto (for Mark Twain in the thirteenth and fourteenth editions), Admiral E. M. Eller USN, Dudley Fitts, Arthur Freeman, Paul Freund, Richard Gombrich, Stanley Kunitz, Elena Levin, Louis Lyons, David McCord, Robert Minshall, Samuel Eliot Morison, Henry A. Murray, Gregory Rabassa, John Paul Russo, Alain Seznec, Zeph Stewart, Maurice B. Strauss, M.D., John L. Sweeney, Prescott B. Wintersteen, Jr., Philip Young.

In addition to the countless friends and the faithful readers of *Bartlett* who write in to point out errors and omissions, the following are to be especially thanked for help and advice: Judge Bailey Aldrich, Catharine Cooper, John Kenneth Galbraith, Donald Gallup, Seymour Harris, James Laughlin, Robert Lescher, Henry F. Pommer, Arthur Schlesinger, Jr., Robert Sussman, Michael des Tombe, Alexander Williams, the Reverend Prescott B. Wintersteen, D.D.

It is impossible to exaggerate what the thirteenth and fourteenth editions of *Familiar Quotations* owe to Mary Rackliffe, head of the copyediting department at Little, Brown and Company. Her mastery of complex styling problems is matched by her exceptional memory and ear for the elusive line. In judgment and taste she is without peer. Moreover, she is responsible for the index, which is the largest and most thorough that *Bartlett* has ever had.

*   *   *

"We come too late to say anything which has not been said already," observed La Bruyère in 1688. But anyone looking at the quotations after that date will know that there will always be new ways to bring home old truths. "Poetry reminds man of his limitations . . . of the richness and diversity of his existence," John F. Kennedy remarked. It has always been evident too that, as he said, "Art establishes the basic human truths which must serve as the touchstone of our judgment." The great lines and passages from the ancients make us recognize, with reassurance—or resignation—how little man changes down the ages. Seneca, in the first century, could be speaking of us at this very hour when he writes, "We are mad, not only individually, but nationally. We check manslaughter and isolated murders; but what of war and the much vaunted crime of slaughtering whole peoples?" We can take comfort from Solon in the sixth century B.C.—"I grow old ever learning many things."

Books "are the voices of the distant and the dead," William Ellery Channing tells us, "and make us heirs of the spiritual life of past ages." Quotations, like books, "are true levelers. They give to all, who will faithfully use them, the society, the spiritual presence, of the best and greatest of our race."

Bartlett provides a distillation of this heritage, a guide to the manifold ways in which man has tried to express the basic human truths.

EMILY MORISON BECK, *Editor*

Canton, Massachusetts

Historical Note

THE University Book Store in Cambridge, Massachusetts, was college for John Bartlett. He went to work there at the age of sixteen after attending the Plymouth public schools, and in 1849 when he was twenty-nine he bought the store. It had become a meeting place for book-loving Harvard professors and students, and through them developed John Bartlett's reputation for knowing a quotation, author and source. From his commonplace book of the most popular passages evolved *Familiar Quotations*, which he published himself and had printed in an edition of a thousand copies by the "printers to the university" in 1855.

It was a modest brown paperbound volume of two hundred and fifty-eight pages, representing a hundred and sixty-nine authors, many by a single quotation or, like his friend James Russell Lowell, by two. The Bible and Shakespeare took up about a third of the book; the balance was chiefly English poetry—Milton, Pope, Byron, and Wordsworth claiming the greatest number of entries. There was a small selection of prose from Milton, Bacon, Ben Franklin, Tom Paine, Macaulay, and one maxim from La Rochefoucauld, "Hypocrisy is the homage that vice pays to virtue." No Chaucer, Blake, Shelley, nor several other authors who could not have been much upon the tongue in the midnineteenth century. A mere handful of Americans were included: Longfellow, Irving, Bryant, Lowell, and a line each from "Hail Columbia," "The Star-Spangled Banner," and "The Old Oaken Bucket." People then, it seems, were not given to quoting Washington, Adams, Jefferson, Patrick Henry, Daniel Webster, or even Emerson (who made *Bartlett* by the third edition in 1858).

The Gettysburg Address had not yet been delivered. Walt Whitman published *Leaves of Grass* that same year, and Thoreau *Walden* the year before. Both writers were so in advance of their time, it seems, that neither was to be included in *Familiar Quotations* until the tenth edition in 1914, nine years after Bartlett's death.

The little book, one of the earliest collections of quotations, was a success, and in 1863 Little, Brown and Company became the publisher of the fourth edition. John Bartlett joined the firm that same year, becoming senior partner fifteen years later. He continued to edit *Familiar Quotations* until his death at the age of eighty-five in 1905, having also published *The Shakespeare Phrase Book*, a *Catalogue of Books on Angling*, and a *Complete Concordance to Shakespeare's Dramatic Works and Poems*.

In 1914 Nathan Haskell Dole, poet, editor, and translator from the French and Russian, edited the tenth edition, now grown twice the size and three times the thickness of the first. Dole's purpose, as he put it, was "to incorporate in the work quotations from those writers whose place in literature has been achieved since the issue of the ninth edition in 1891," and to add selections from other "best writers of their day." His criterion was that passages should have "the seal of popular approval" and be "distinctly worthy of perpetuation." He paid respectful homage to John Bartlett's "impeccable judgment," declaring, "It is not always easy for Elisha to wear the mantle of Elijah; but it is Elisha's business to carry on his predecessor's work in the same spirit."

Either because of contemporary tastes in literature or oversight, there were some rather surprising omissions in the tenth edition. No Blake, Pindar, Hawthorne, William or Henry James, or Emily Dickinson, to pick at random, but William Butler Yeats made it with, oddly enough, the one poem he himself refused to include in his *Collected Poems*, "The Land of Heart's Desire." There was a large section of "miscellaneous, translations, appendix," and the Bible, for some reason, now appeared at the end of the book. In the present edition it has been restored once more to the front, a fitting opening to quotations from our Judaeo-Christian culture.

No new edition appeared until 1937, a few years after Dole's death. Elijah's mantle passed to Christopher Morley, author, poet, editor, dubbed an "angloliterophile" for his love of the English language for its own sake. Louella D. Everett joined forces as associate editor.

Morley's preface to the eleventh edition is a lively essay which at the outset asks the question which every *Bartlett* editor, we feel, must try to answer: "What makes words memorable?" His broad literary background made him an ideal editor, and Miss Everett's ear for the popular line or verse gave that edition a more topical quality than the book had had hitherto.

For the first time the editors weeded out quotations no longer in currency. Some of the quainter lines by Miss Fannie Steers, Sir Samuel Tuke, and Captain Charles Morris ("Solid men of Boston, make no long orations; Solid men of Boston, drink no deep potations") had seen their day. The flowery descriptive verse and the sugary sentiments of the last half of the nineteenth century were sharply cut, though a great deal still remained. Furthermore, Miss Everett combed over the favorite poetry of the Nineties, and added such versifiers as Mary Artemisia Lathbury, "the Chatauqua Laureate"; and Julia Moore, "the Sweet Singer of Michigan," of whom Mark Twain wrote: "The one and unfailing great quality which distinguishes her poetry from Shakespeare's and makes it precious to us is its stern and simple irrelevancy." They still persevere into this edition of the 1960's.

Morley not only added to the twentieth-century quotations, he culled every period from ancient times on, reflecting perhaps a broadening cultural outlook on the part of the average American. The chronological order of authors remained, but otherwise the change in the eleventh edition was more striking than in any other, and the innovation of the two-column page allowed a vast increment of new quotations within a single volume.

Morley's theory of selection was broader than John Bartlett's. "Previous editions adhered, almost with pedantry, to the touchstone of familiarity," he wrote. "Only phrases or quotations that had gained wide recognition, become hypodermic, were admitted. . . . In the matter of new inclusions this edition is not so stringent: we have tried to make literary power the criterion rather than width and vulgarity of fame."

"Literary power" is so much more a matter of personal opinion than "familiarity" that this new approach opened up for future *Bartlett* editors the temptation to exploit their literary passions. Restraint has

xiii

been necessary to keep the volume from becoming idiosyncratic or growing into an anthology.

World War II and the atomic age required an updating of *Bartlett*, and in 1948 Morley and Everett published the twelfth edition with quotations from Churchill, Hitler, Einstein, the Charter of the United Nations, William Laurence, Douglas MacArthur, Truman, Lippmann, and others. There was also a catchall section for quotations omitted in previous editions, like "I have not yet begun to fight" (John Paul Jones); Article III, section 3 on treason from the Constitution of the United States; Donne's "No man is an island," famous as the source of the title of Hemingway's novel *For Whom the Bell Tolls*; Lord Acton's "Power tends to corrupt"; Emerson's "Four snakes gliding up and down . . . not to eat, not for love . . ."

The year 1955 marked the centennial of *Familiar Quotations,* and it was altogether appropriate for a new revised edition to appear, this time issued by the Little, Brown editors themselves. They continued the tradition of adding new quotations throughout and of eliminating the no-longer familiar, thus improving the work, which increases steadily in popularity.

The fourteenth edition is discussed in the Preface.

EMILY MORISON BECK, *Editor*

xiv

Guide to the Use
of FAMILIAR QUOTATIONS

For the sections of the book see the *Contents*, page xix.
The *Preface*, p. v, discusses the fourteenth edition.
The *Historical Note*, p. xi, tells of the different editions of
Familiar Quotations from the first edition of 1855 on.

The Quotations

The arrangement is not by topics or subject matter, nor is it by authors alphabetically, as in some collections. It is by authors chronologically with selections from their works in chronological order. Birth and death dates as well as pseudonyms accompany the author's name, and each work is dated wherever possible. Quotations give chapter and verse of their sources, or similarly, act, scene and line from dramatic works.

The chronological arrangement lends historical value to the collection of authors and quotations. One becomes quickly aware that Pericles, Sophocles, Euripides, Thucydides and Plato were contemporaries, as were Confucius, Lao Tzu, Aesop, Heraclitus, and the *Suttapitaka* a century earlier. The great poets of the Middle Ages—Dante, Petrarch, and Chaucer—follow one upon another. One discovers that Columbus, Sir Thomas Malory, and Machiavelli were contemporaries. Shakespeare appropriately is in the midst of the Elizabethans. Ben Franklin, Samuel Johnson, William Pitt, and John Adams were contemporaries; so were Jefferson, Goethe, and Talleyrand, while Kipling and Yeats were born in the same year and lived, actively writing, into their seventies.

The chronological selections of an author show his development, and in some instances provide a distillation of his work. Students have found this helpful in studying an author, both as a review and as an incentive to read more of the work quoted.

Footnotes and Cross-References

When the quotation is a translation the original language if familiar in itself appears in a footnote. For example, "The people are a many-headed beast," from Horace, on page 123a, has a footnote quoting the Latin, with cross-references to variations, and examples of derivative versions.

In cases where the familiar quotation differs from the original whence it derives, as in the case of the Latin mottoes of the Great Seal of the United States from Virgil, footnotes (on pages 116b, 117a, and 119b) provide full information. The footnotes also cross-reference. For example, a quotation from Horace's *Epode XIV* has a footnote cross-referring to Keats's *Ode to a Nightingale*, which it inspired. Under Keats we find a footnote to the *Ode* which cross-refers back to Horace.

Suppose you wish to find out who first used the expression "iron curtain." You look up either "iron" or "curtain" in the index, which sends you to page 924b. Here, under Churchill, you find the quotation that made the expression famous, in his speech at Fulton, Missouri, on March 5, 1946, together with a lengthy footnote which relates the other ways people used it before he did.

Franklin D. Roosevelt is usually credited with having first expressed the idea that "The only thing we have to fear is fear itself." Both the index and the footnote for the Roosevelt quotation indicate its derivation from earlier writers, some in languages other than English.

Index of Authors (page 1107)

Authors are listed alphabetically with their birth and death dates. Page numbers are given for both the author's main entry and for his quotations in footnotes throughout the text.

Index (page 1155)

In this edition we have continued and expanded the *Bartlett* tradition of thorough indexing of the quotations. The result is voluminous —more than 117,000 entries.

This thoroughness is aimed first of all at facilitating the location of remembered or half-remembered or almost forgotten or topical

("Let's see what *Bartlett* has about morning") quotations. The index plays another role as a browsing book of unusual proportions. The pursuit of an evocative index entry noticed almost at random may lead to renewed pleasures or to the discovery of hitherto unsuspected sources of illumination and enjoyment.

Keep the following in mind when using the index:

(1) Spelling follows American (Webster) forms, but there are occasional exceptions; for example, *burnt* (not *burned*) *offerings*.

(2) Hyphenation also occasionally varies from Webster; for example, we index *drop-scenes* (in Webster *drop scenes*) to isolate it from other *drop* entries.

(3) Dialect and other significantly variant spellings are generally indexed in Webster forms as well as in the original (*'ammer/hammer*).

(4) Alphabetization is (we hope) strict, which means that entries for inflected forms of a word may be widely separated from entries for the word itself; for example, *nightcap, nightingale, nightmare* and other entries separate *night* from *night's*. The standard order of plural and possessive forms is: *lover's, lovers, lovers'*.

(5) When an important word in a very familiar phrase is in a contracted form (*Beauty's* but skin deep; An honest *man's* the noblest work of God) it is indexed also in the singular (*Beauty* skin deep; Honest *man* noblest work). But most such contractions are indexed only in the original form (What *cat's* averse to fish).

(6) When entries under one keyword continue to another column of the index, the keyword is repeated at the top of the new column. If you find your keyword at the top of a column, check the foot of the previous column—or page if necessary—to be sure of covering all the entries under the keyword.

(7) The words of each entry are in the same order as in the quotation, with the keyword abbreviated in the correct position except when it starts the quotation (*a* and *b* with the page number indicate left and right columns on the page):

> Hope, all h. abandon who enter here, 159b
> beautiful Evelyn H., 663b
> deferred maketh the heart sick, 24a
> feed on h., 201a
> is the thing with feathers, 735a

When the keyword occurs both at the start and in the body of the entry it is not abbreviated:

> Alps, beyond A. lies Italy, 125a
> on Alps arise, 403a

(8) There are so many familiar ways of indexing one familiar phrase under one keyword (Love, *one* jot of former l.; Love, *jot* of former l.; Intellect, *monuments* of unaging i.; Intellect, *unaging* i.), that you should look for your quotation in all possible alphabetical locations under the keyword. Several columns of entries may come between one possibility and another (as in the first example above).

(9) In checking a two-word term of which one word is the keyword (for example, *old age*), note that retention of the quotation's original order means that all entries about the term will not necessarily appear grouped together:

> Age, dance attention upon old a., 885a
> green old a., 367b
> old a. and experience, 382b
> old a. should burn, 1070b
> 'tis well an old a. is out, 372a

(10) If you don't find your quotation under one keyword, try another. The first word of a quotation, moreover, is not necessarily a keyword. If you think Milton said *fresh fields and pastures new*, you will not find it under *fields* but you will (with its original *fresh woods*) under *fresh, pastures,* and *new*. We have, however, tried to include in footnotes and in the index such popular misquotations as A *poor thing but mine own* as well as the originals—in this case An *ill-favored thing, sir, but mine own*, from Shakespeare's As *You Like It*.

(11) If your quotation does not emerge under any of the remembered keywords, try synonyms or related words. A quotation about *valor* is often remembered as about *courage; dullness* as *boredom; approbation* as *praise*; and so on.

(12) If you are using the index as a topical source (looking for all the quotations you can find about *nature* or *bravery* or *wisdom* or *love* or whatever), think of all the synonyms and related words you can —and then, in addition, browse, eat, enjoy. You'll find more.

Emily Morison Beck
Mary Rackliffe

Contents

Familiar Quotations

ANCIENT EGYPT[1]

Mine is yesterday, I know tomorrow.
*Book of the Dead [c. 3500 B.C.
and after]*

Be a craftsman in speech that thou mayest be strong, for the strength of one is the tongue, and speech is mightier than all fighting.[2]
*Maxims of Ptahhotep
[c. 3400 B.C.]*

More acceptable is the virtue of the upright man than the ox of him that doeth iniquity.
Instruction to Prince Merikere from his father, a pharaoh of Heracleopolis [c. 2200 B.C.]

A man's virtue is his monument, but forgotten is the man of evil repute.
*Egyptian tombstone inscription
[c. 2100 B.C.]*

None cometh from thence
That he may tell us how they fare.
Lo, no man taketh his goods with him.
Yea, none returneth again that is gone thither.[3]
*The Song of the Harp-Player
[c. 2100 B.C.]*

To whom do I speak today?
Brothers are evil,
Friends of today are not of love. . . .
To whom do I speak today?
There are no righteous,
The land is left to those who do iniquity.
*Papyrus [4] by an unknown author
[c. 2000 B.C.]. Second Poem*

Death is before me today
As a man longs to see his house
When he has spent many years in captivity.
*Papyrus by an unknown author.
Third Poem*

Creator of all and giver of their sustenance.
Hymn to the Sun by Suti and Hor, architects to Amenhotep III [c. 1400 B.C.]

Valiant herdman who drives his cattle,
Their refuge and giver of their sustenance. *Ib.*

Sole lord taking captive all lands every day,
As one beholding them that walk therein;
Shining in the sky, a being as the sun.
He makes the seasons by the months,
Heat when he desires,
Cold when he desires. *Ib.*

Every land is in rejoicing
At his rising every day, in order to praise him. *Ib.*

IKHNATON
c. 1385 – 1358 B.C.

Thou dawnest beautifully in the horizon of the sky,
O living Aton who wast the Beginning of life! *Hymn to the Sun*

When thou settest in the western horizon of the sky,
The earth is in darkness like death.[1]
Ib.

Every lion cometh forth from his den,
All serpents, they sting.

[1] From JAMES HENRY BREASTED, *The Dawn of Civilization* [1933].
[2] The pen is mightier than the sword. — EDWARD BULWER-LYTTON, *Richelieu*, act II, sc. 2
[3] See *Ecclesiastes 5:15*, p. 28a; *I Timothy 6:7*, p. 55a; Theognis, p. 77a; and Shakespeare, p. 262a.
[4] Preserved in the Berlin Museum.

[1] See *Psalm 104:20*, p. 21b.

Darkness broods,
The world is in silence,
He that made them resteth in his
horizon.[1]   *Hymn to the Sun*

Bright is the earth when thou risest in
the horizon;
When thou shinest as Aton by day
Thou drivest away the darkness. . . .
Men waken and stand upon their
feet
When thou hast raised them up. . . .
Then in all the world they do their
work.[2]   *Ib.*

The barks sail upstream and down-
stream alike.
Every highway is open because thou
dawnest.
The fish in the river leap up before
thee.
Thy rays are in the midst of the great
green sea.[3]   *Ib.*

How manifold are thy works!
They are hidden before men,
O sole God, beside whom there is no
other.
Thou didst create the earth according
to thy heart.[4]   *Ib.*

AMENEMOPE[5]
Tenth century B.C.

In order to return a report to the one
that sent him.[6]
The Wisdom of Amenemope, I

Incline thine ears to hear my sayings,

[1] See *Psalm 104:21*, p. 21b.
[2] See *Psalm 104:22, 23*, p. 21b.
[3] See *Psalm 104:25, 26*, p. 21b.
[4] See *Psalm 104:24*, p. 21b.
[5] The Wisdom of Amenemope was translated into Hebrew, it was read by Hebrews, and an important part of it found its way into the Old Testament. . . . This whole section of about a chapter and a half of the Book of Proverbs (22:17–23:11) is largely drawn verbatim from The Wisdom of Amenemope; that is, the Hebrew version is practically a literal translation from the Egyptian. — JAMES HENRY BREASTED, *The Dawn of Civilization* [1933]
[6] See *Proverbs 22:21*, p. 25b.

And apply thine heart to their compre-
hension.
For it is a profitable thing to put them
in thy heart.[1]
The Wisdom of Amenemope, III

The truly prudent man, who putteth
himself aside,
Is like a tree growing in a garden,
He flourisheth and multiplieth his
fruit,
He abideth in the presence of his
lord,
His fruit is sweet, his shade is pleasant,
And he findeth his end in the garden.[2]
Ib. VI

Remove not the landmark on the
boundary of the fields.[3]   *Ib. VII*

Better is poverty in the hand of
God
Than riches in the storehouse.
Better are loaves when the heart is
joyous
Than riches in unhappiness.[4]   *Ib. IX*

Weary not thyself to seek for more.[5]
Ib.

They [riches] have made themselves
wings like geese,
And they have flown to heaven.[6]
Ib. X

Consider for thyself these thirty chapters,
That they are satisfaction and instruction.[7]   *Ib. XXVII*

A scribe skillful in his office,
He shall find himself worthy of being a
courtier.[8]   *Ib.*

[1] See *Proverbs 22:17–18*, p. 25b.
[2] See *Psalm 1*, p. 166, and *Jeremiah 17:5–8*, p. 34b.
[3] See *Proverbs 22:28*, p. 25b.
[4] See *Proverbs 15:16–17*, p. 24b.
[5] See *Proverbs 23:4*, p. 25b.
[6] See *Proverbs 23:5*, p. 25b.
[7] See *Proverbs 22:20*, p. 25b, the direct reference to Amenemope and his sayings.
[8] See *Proverbs 22:29*, p. 25b.

THE HOLY BIBLE
THE KING JAMES VERSION[1]
1611

THE OLD TESTAMENT

In the beginning God created the heaven and the earth.

And the earth was without form, and void; and darkness was upon the face of the deep. And the Spirit of God moved upon the face of the waters.

And God said, Let there be light:[2] and there was light.

Genesis[3] 1:1–3[4]

And the evening and the morning were the first day. 1:5

And God saw that it was good. 1:10

And God said, Let us make man in our image, after our likeness. 1:26

Male and female created he them. 1:27

Be fruitful, and multiply, and replenish the earth, and subdue it: and have dominion over the fish of the sea, and over the fowl of the air, and over every living thing that moveth upon the earth. 1:28

And on the seventh day God ended his work which he had made. 2:2

And the Lord God formed man of the dust of the ground, and breathed into his nostrils the breath of life; and man became a living soul.

Genesis 2:7

And the Lord God planted a garden eastward in Eden. 2:8

The tree of life also in the midst of the garden. 2:9

But of the tree of the knowledge of good and evil, thou shalt not eat of it: for in the day that thou eatest thereof thou shalt surely die. 2:17

It is not good that the man should be alone; I will make him an help meet for him. 2:18

And the Lord God caused a deep sleep to fall upon Adam, and he slept: and he took one of his ribs, and closed up the flesh instead thereof.

And the rib, which the Lord God had taken from man, made he a woman. 2:21–22

Bone of my bones, and flesh of my flesh. 2:23

Therefore shall a man leave his father and his mother, and shall cleave unto his wife: and they shall be one flesh.

And they were both naked, the man and his wife, and were not ashamed. 2:24–25

Now the serpent was more subtile than any beast of the field. 3:1

Your eyes shall be opened, and ye shall be as gods, knowing good and evil. 3:5

And they sewed fig leaves together, and made themselves aprons.[1]

And they heard the voice of the Lord God walking in the garden in the cool of the day. 3:7–8

---

[1] Among all our joys, there was no one that more filled our hearts, than the blessed continuance of the preaching of God's sacred Word among us; which is that inestimable treasure, which excelleth all the riches of the earth; because the fruit thereof extendeth itself, not only to the time spent in this transitory world, but directeth and disposeth men unto that eternal happiness which is above in heaven. — *The Translators' Dedication to James I*

[2] Fiat lux. — *The Vulgate*

[3] The First Book of Moses, first of the five books of the Pentateuch.

[4] Numbers in Bible citations represent chapter and verse.

[1] The Geneva Bible of 1557–1560 was known sometimes as the Breeches Bible because in this passage "aprons" is rendered as "breeches."

The woman whom thou gavest to be with me, she gave me of the tree, and I did eat.   *Genesis* 3:12

What is this that thou hast done? And the woman said, The serpent beguiled me, and I did eat.

And the Lord God said unto the serpent, Because thou hast done this, thou art cursed above all cattle, and above every beast of the field; upon thy belly shalt thou go, and dust shalt thou eat all the days of thy life.   3:13–14

It shall bruise thy head, and thou shalt bruise his heel.   3:15

In sorrow thou shalt bring forth children.   3:16

In the sweat of thy face shalt thou eat bread, till thou return unto the ground; for out of it wast thou taken: for dust thou art, and unto dust shalt thou return.

And Adam called his wife's name Eve; because she was the mother of all living.   3:19–20

So he drove out the man: and he placed at the east of the garden of Eden cherubims, and a flaming sword which turned every way, to keep the way of the tree of life.   3:24

And Abel was a keeper of sheep, but Cain was a tiller of the ground.   4:2

Am I my brother's keeper?   4:9

The voice of thy brother's blood crieth unto me from the ground.   4:10

A fugitive and a vagabond shalt thou be in the earth.   4:12

My punishment is greater than I can bear.   4:13

And the Lord set a mark upon Cain.   4:15

And Cain went out from the presence of the Lord, and dwelt in the land of Nod.   4:16

Jabal: he was the father of such as dwell in tents.   4:20

Jubal: he was the father of all such as handle the harp and organ.
    Genesis 4:21

And Enoch walked with God.
    5:24

And all the days of Methuselah were nine hundred sixty and nine years.
    5:27

And Noah begat Shem, Ham, and Japheth.   5:32

There were giants in the earth in those days . . . mighty men which were of old, men of renown.   6:4

Make thee an ark of gopher wood.
    6:14

And of every living thing of all flesh, two of every sort shalt thou bring into the ark.   6:19

And the rain was upon the earth forty days and forty nights.   7:12

But the dove found no rest for the sole of her foot.   8:9

And, lo, in her mouth was an olive leaf pluckt off.   8:11

For the imagination of man's heart is evil from his youth.   8:21

While the earth remaineth, seedtime and harvest, and cold and heat, and summer and winter, and day and night shall not cease.   8:22

Whoso sheddeth man's blood, by man shall his blood be shed: for in the image of God made he man.   9:6

I do set my bow in the cloud, and it shall be for a token of a covenant between me and the earth.   9:13

Even as Nimrod the mighty hunter before the Lord.   10:9

Therefore is the name of it called Babel; because the Lord did there confound the language of all the earth.   11:9

Let there be no strife, I pray thee, between me and thee . . . for we be brethren.   13:8

Abram dwelled in the land of Canaan, and Lot dwelled in the cities of the plain, and pitched his tent toward Sodom. *Genesis 13:12*

In a good old age. *15:15*

His [Ishmael's] hand will be against every man, and every man's hand against him. *16:12*

Thy name shall be Abraham; for a father of many nations have I made thee. *17:5*

My Lord, if now I have found favour in thy sight, pass not away, I pray thee, from thy servant. *18:3*

But his [Lot's] wife looked back from behind him, and she became a pillar of salt. *19:26*

My son, God will provide himself a lamb for a burnt offering. *22:8*

Behold behind him a ram caught in a thicket by his horns. *22:13*

Esau was a cunning hunter, a man of the field; and Jacob was a plain man, dwelling in tents. *25:27*

And he [Esau] sold his birthright unto Jacob.
Then Jacob gave Esau bread and pottage of lentiles. *25:33–34*

The voice is Jacob's voice, but the hands are the hands of Esau. *27:22*

Thy brother came with subtilty, and hath taken away thy blessing. *27:35*

He [Jacob] dreamed, and behold a ladder set up on the earth, and the top of it reached to heaven: and behold the angels of God ascending and descending on it. *28:12*

Surely the Lord is in this place; and I knew it not. *28:16*

This is none other but the house of God, and this is the gate of heaven. *28:17*

Jacob served seven years for Rachel; and they seemed unto him but a few days, for the love he had to her. *29:20*

Mizpah; for he said, The Lord watch between me and thee, when we are absent one from another. *Genesis 31:49*

And Jacob was left alone; and there wrestled a man with him until the breaking of the day. *32:24*

I will not let thee go, except thou bless me. *32:26*

And Jacob called the name of the place Peniel: for I have seen God face to face, and my life is preserved.[1] *32:30*

Behold, this dreamer cometh. *37:19*

They stript Joseph out of his coat, his coat of many colours. *37:23*

The Lord made all that he did to prosper in his hand. *39:3*

And she caught him by his garment, saying, Lie with me: and he left his garment in her hand, and fled, and got him out. *39:12*

And the seven thin and ill favoured kine that came up after them are seven years; and the seven empty ears blasted with the east wind shall be seven years of famine. *41:27*

Then shall ye bring down my gray hairs with sorrow to the grave. *42:38*

But Benjamin's mess was five times so much as any of theirs. *43:34*

Wherefore have ye rewarded evil for good? *44:4*

The man in whose hand the cup is found, he shall be my servant. *44:17*

And he fell upon his brother Benjamin's neck, and wept; and Benjamin wept upon his neck. *45:14*

And ye shall eat the fat of the land. *45:18*

And they came into the land of Goshen. *46:28*

But I will lie with my fathers, and thou shalt carry me out of Egypt, and bury me in their buryingplace. And he said, I will do as thou hast said. *47:30*

[1] See *1 Corinthians 13:12*, p. 52b.

Unstable as water, thou shalt not excel. *Genesis 49:4*

I have waited for thy salvation, O Lord. 49:18

Unto the utmost bound of the everlasting hills. 49:26

Now there arose up a new king over Egypt, which knew not Joseph.
Exodus[1] 1:8

She took for him an ark of bulrushes, and daubed it with slime and with pitch. 2:3

I have been a stranger in a strange land.[2] 2:22

Behold, the bush burned with fire, and the bush was not consumed.

3:2

Put off thy shoes from off thy feet, for the place whereon thou standest is holy ground. 3:5

And Moses hid his face; for he was afraid to look upon God. 3:6

A land flowing with milk and honey.[3] 3:8

And God said unto Moses, I AM THAT I AM. 3:14

I am slow of speech, and of a slow tongue. 4:10

Let my people go. 5:1

Ye shall no more give the people straw to make brick. 5:7

Thou shalt say unto Aaron, Take thy rod, and cast it before Pharaoh, and it shall become a serpent. 7:9

And he hardened Pharaoh's heart.
7:13

This is the finger of God. 8:19

Darkness which may be felt. 10:21

Yet will I bring one plague more upon Pharaoh, and upon Egypt. 11:1

Your lamb shall be without blemish.
12:5

[1] The Second Book of Moses, second of the five books of the Pentateuch.
[2] See Sophocles, p. 82b.
[3] Also in *Exodus 33:3* and *Jeremiah 11:5*.

And thus shall ye eat it; with your loins girded, your shoes on your feet, and your staff in your hand; and ye shall eat it in haste: it is the Lord's passover.

For I will pass through the land of Egypt this night, and will smite all the firstborn in the land of Egypt, both man and beast; and against all the gods of Egypt I will execute judgment: I am the Lord. *Exodus 12:11–12*

This day [Passover] shall be unto you for a memorial; and ye shall keep it a feast to the Lord throughout your generations. 12:14

Seven days shall ye eat unleavened bread. 12:15

There was a great cry in Egypt; for there was not a house where there was not one dead. 12:30

Remember this day, in which ye came out from Egypt, out of the house of bondage. 13:3

And the Lord went before them by day in a pillar of a cloud, to lead them the way; and by night in a pillar of fire, to give them light. 13:21

And the children of Israel went into the midst of the sea upon the dry ground: and the waters were a wall unto them on their right hand, and on their left. 14:22

I will sing unto the Lord, for he hath triumphed gloriously: the horse and his rider hath he thrown into the sea.

The Lord is my strength and song, and he is become my salvation. 15:1–2

The Lord is a man of war. 15:3

Thy right hand, O Lord, is become glorious in power: thy right hand, O Lord, hath dashed in pieces the enemy.
15:6

Thou sentest forth thy wrath, which consumed them as stubble. 15:7

Would to God we had died by the hand of the Lord in the land of Egypt, when we sat by the fleshpots, and when we did eat bread to the full. 16:3

It is manna. *Exodus* 16:15

Thou shalt have no other gods before me.

Thou shalt not make unto thee any graven image. 20:3–4

For I the Lord thy God am a jealous God, visiting the iniquity of the fathers upon the children unto the third and fourth generation of them that hate me.[1] 20:5

Thou shalt not take the name of the Lord thy God in vain. 20:7

Remember the sabbath day, to keep it holy.
Six days shalt thou labour, and do all thy work:
But the seventh day . . . thou shalt not do any work. 20:8–10

Honour thy father and thy mother: that thy days may be long upon the land which the Lord thy God giveth thee.[2]
Thou shalt not kill.
Thou shalt not commit adultery.
Thou shalt not steal.
Thou shalt not bear false witness against thy neighbour.
Thou shalt not covet thy neighbour's house, thou shalt not covet thy neighbour's wife, nor his manservant, nor his maidservant, nor his ox, nor his ass, nor any thing that is thy neighbour's. 20:12–17

But let not God speak with us, lest we die. 20:19

He that smiteth a man, so that he die, shall be surely put to death. 21:12

Eye for eye, tooth for tooth,[3] hand for hand, foot for foot. 21:24

Behold, I send an Angel before thee, to keep thee in the way. 23:20

A stiffnecked people. 32:9

Who is on the Lord's side? let him come unto me. 32:26

[1] See Euripides, p. 86a.
[2] See Aeschylus, p. 78a.
[3] Also in *Matthew* 5:38.

Thou canst not see my face: for there shall no man see me, and live. *Exodus* 33:20

And he [Moses] was there with the Lord forty days and forty nights; he did neither eat bread, nor drink water. And he wrote upon the tables the words of the covenant, the ten commandments. 34:28

Whatsoever parteth the hoof, and is clovenfooted, and cheweth the cud, among the beasts, that shall ye eat. *Leviticus* [1] 11:3

And the swine . . . is unclean to you.
Of their flesh shall ye not eat. 11:7–8

Let him go for a scapegoat into the wilderness. 16:10

And when ye reap the harvest of your land, thou shalt not wholly reap the corners of thy field, neither shalt thou gather the gleanings of thy harvest.
And thou shalt not glean thy vineyard, neither shalt thou gather every grape of thy vineyard; thou shalt leave them for the poor and stranger: I am the Lord your God. 19:9–10

Thou shalt not go up and down as a talebearer among thy people. 19:16

Thou shalt love thy neighbour as thyself.[2] 19:18

The Lord bless thee, and keep thee:
The Lord make his face shine upon thee, and be gracious unto thee:
The Lord lift up his countenance upon thee, and give thee peace. *Numbers* [3] 6:24–26

Sent to spy out the land. 13:16

And your children shall wander in the wilderness forty years. 14:33

He whom thou blessest is blessed. 22:6

[1] The Third Book of Moses, third of the five books of the Pentateuch.
[2] Also in *Matthew 19:19* and *22:39, Mark 12:31* and *33, Romans 13:9, Galatians 5:14, James 2:8.*
[3] The Fourth Book of Moses, fourth of the five books of the Pentateuch.

The Lord opened the mouth of the ass, and she said unto Balaam, What have I done unto thee?

Numbers 22:28

Let me die the death of the righteous, and let my last end be like his! 23:10

God is not a man, that he should lie.[1] 23:19

What hath God wrought! [2] 23:23

How goodly are thy tents, O Jacob, and thy tabernacles, O Israel! 24:5

Be sure your sin will find you out. 32:23

Thou shalt love the Lord thy God with all thine heart, and with all thy soul, and with all thy might.

And these words, which I command thee this day, shall be in thine heart:

And thou shalt teach them diligently unto thy children.

Deuteronomy [3] *6:5–7*

Ye shall not tempt the Lord your God.[4] 6:16

The Lord thy God hath chosen thee to be a special people unto himself.

7:6

Man doth not live by bread only,[5] but by every word that proceedeth out of the mouth of the Lord doth man live. 8:3

For the Lord thy God bringeth thee into a good land. 8:7

A land of wheat, and barley, and vines, and fig trees, and pomegranates; a land of oil olive, and honey;

A land wherein thou shalt eat bread without scarceness, thou shalt not lack any thing in it; a land whose stones are iron, and out of whose hills thou mayest dig brass. 8:8–9

[1] See Aeschylus, p. 78b.
[2] Quoted by Samuel F. B. Morse in the first telegraph message he sent to his partner, Alfred Vail, from Washington to Baltimore, May 24, 1844.
[3] The Fifth Book of Moses, last of the five books of the Pentateuch.
[4] Also in *Matthew 4:7*.
[5] Man shall not live by bread alone. — *Matthew 4:4*

A dreamer of dreams.

Deuteronomy 13:1

The wife of thy bosom. 13:6

The poor shall never cease out of the land.[1] 15:11

And thou shalt become an astonishment, a proverb, and a byword, among all nations. 28:37

In the morning thou shalt say, Would God it were even! and at even thou shalt say, Would God it were morning! 28:67

The secret things belong unto the Lord our God. 29:29

I have set before you life and death, blessing and cursing: therefore choose life, that both thou and thy seed may live. 30:19

He is the Rock, his work is perfect: for all his ways are judgment: a God of truth. 32:4

He kept him as the apple of his eye. 32:10

Jeshurun waxed fat, and kicked.

32:15

As thy days, so shall thy strength be. 33:25

The eternal God is thy refuge, and underneath are the everlasting arms.

33:27

No man knoweth of his [Moses'] sepulchre unto this day. 34:6

Be strong and of a good courage; [2] be not afraid, neither be thou dismayed: for the Lord thy God is with thee whithersoever thou goest.

The Book of Joshua 1:9

And the priests that bare the ark of the covenant of the Lord stood firm on dry ground in the midst of Jordan, and all the Israelites passed over on dry ground, until all the people were passed clean over Jordan. 3:17

Mighty men of valour. 6:2

And it came to pass, when the people heard the sound of the trumpet, and

[1] See *Matthew 26:11*, p. 44a.
[2] Also in *Deuteronomy 31:6, 7, 23*.

the people shouted with a great shout, that the wall fell down flat, so that the people went up into the city [Jericho].
Joshua 6:20

His fame was noised throughout all the country. 6:27

Hewers of wood and drawers of water. 9:21

Sun, stand thou still upon Gibeon; and thou, Moon, in the valley of Ajalon. 10:12

Old and stricken in years.[1] 13:1

I am going the way of all the earth. 23:14

They shall be as thorns in your sides.[2] *The Book of Judges 2:3*

Then Jael, Heber's wife, took a nail of the tent, and took an hammer in her hand, and went softly unto him, and smote the nail into his temples, and fastened it into the ground; for he was fast asleep, and weary: so he died.
4:21

I Deborah arose . . . I arose a mother in Israel. 5:7

The stars in their courses fought against Sisera. 5:20

She brought forth butter in a lordly dish. 5:25

At her feet he bowed, he fell, he lay down: at her feet he bowed, he fell: where he bowed, there he fell down dead. 5:27

Why tarry the wheels of his chariots?
5:28

Have they not divided the prey; to every man a damsel or two? 5:30

The sword of the Lord, and of Gideon. 7:18

Is not the gleaning of the grapes of Ephraim better than the vintage of Abiezer? 8:2

Say now Shibboleth: and he said Sibboleth: for he could not frame to pronounce it right. 12:6

[1] Also in *I Kings 1:1.*
[2] See *II Corinthians 12:7*, p. 53b.

There was a swarm of bees and honey in the carcase of the lion.
Judges 14:8

Out of the eater came forth meat, and out of the strong came forth sweetness. 14:14

If ye had not plowed with my heifer, ye had not found out my riddle.
14:18

He smote them hip and thigh.
15:8

With the jawbone of an ass . . . have I slain a thousand men. 15:16

The Philistines be upon thee, Samson. 16:9

Strengthen me, I pray thee, only this once, O God, that I may be . . . avenged of the Philistines for my two eyes. 16:28

So the dead which he slew at his death were more than they which he slew in his life. 16:30

From Dan even to Beersheba.
20:1

All the people arose as one man.
20:8

In those days there was no king in Israel: every man did that which was right in his own eyes. 21:25

Entreat me not to leave thee, or to return from following after thee: for whither thou goest, I will go; and where thou lodgest, I will lodge: thy people shall be my people, and thy God my God. *The Book of Ruth 1:16*

Let me glean and gather after the reapers among the sheaves. 2:7

Go not empty unto thy mother in law. 3:17

In the flower of their age.
The First Book of Samuel 2:33

The Lord called Samuel: and he answered, Here am I. 3:4

Speak, Lord; for thy servant heareth.
3:9

11

Be strong, and quit yourselves like men.[1]   *I Samuel* 4:9

The glory is departed from Israel: for the ark of God is taken.   4:22

Is Saul also among the prophets?   10:11

God save the king.   10:24

A man after his own heart.   13:14

Every man's sword was against his fellow.   14:20

But Jonathan heard not when his father charged the people with the oath: wherefore he put forth the end of the rod that was in his hand, and dipped it in an honeycomb, and put his hand to his mouth; and his eyes were enlightened.   14:27

For the Lord seeth not as man seeth; for man looketh on the outward appearance, but the Lord looketh on the heart.   16:7

I know thy pride, and the naughtiness of thine heart.   17:28

Let no man's heart fail because of him [Goliath].   17:32

Go, and the Lord be with thee.   17:37

And he [David] . . . chose him five smooth stones out of the brook.   17:40

So David prevailed over the Philistine with a sling and with a stone.   17:50

Saul hath slain his thousands, and David his ten thousands.   18:7

And Jonathan . . . loved him [David] as he loved his own soul.   20:17

Wickedness proceedeth from the wicked.   24:13

I have played the fool.   26:21

Tell it not in Gath, publish it not in the streets of Askelon.
The Second Book of Samuel 1:20

Saul and Jonathan were lovely and

pleasant in their lives, and in their death they were not divided: they were swifter than eagles, they were stronger than lions.   *II Samuel* 1:23

How are the mighty fallen in the midst of the battle!   1:25

Thy love to me was wonderful, passing the love of women.
How are the mighty fallen, and the weapons of war perished!   1:26–27

Abner . . . smote him under the fifth rib.   2:23

Know ye not that there is a prince and a great man fallen this day in Israel?   3:38

And David and all the house of Israel played before the Lord on all manner of instruments made of fir wood, even on harps, and on psalteries, and on timbrels, and on cornets, and on cymbals.   6:5

David danced before the Lord.   6:14

Tarry at Jericho until your beards be grown.[1]   10:5

Set ye Uriah in the forefront of the hottest battle.   11:15

The poor man had nothing, save one little ewe lamb.   12:3

Thou art the man.   12:7

Now he is dead, wherefore should I fast? Can I bring him back again? I shall go to him, but he shall not return to me.   12:23

For we must needs die, and are as water spilt on the ground, which cannot be gathered up again.   14:14

Would God I had died for thee, O Absalom, my son, my son!   18:33

The Lord is my rock, and my fortress, and my deliverer.   22:2

David the son of Jesse . . . the sweet psalmist of Israel.   23:1

Went in jeopardy of their lives.   23:17

[1] See *I Corinthians 16:13*, p. 53a.

[1] Also in *I Chronicles 19:5*.

A wise and an understanding heart.
The First Book of the Kings 3:12

Many, as the sand which is by the sea in multitude.   4:20

Judah and Israel dwelt safely, every man under his vine and under his fig tree.   4:25

He [Solomon] spake three thousand proverbs: and his songs were a thousand and five.   4:32

The wisdom of Solomon.   4:34

A proverb and a byword among all people.   9:7

When the queen of Sheba heard of the fame of Solomon . . . she came to prove him with hard questions.   10:1

The half was not told me: thy wisdom and prosperity exceedeth the fame which I heard.   10:7

Once in three years came the navy of Tharshish, bringing gold, and silver, ivory, and apes, and peacocks.   10:22

King Solomon loved many strange women.   11:1

My father hath chastised you with whips, but I will chastise you with scorpions.   12:11

To your tents, O Israel.   12:16

He went and dwelt by the brook Cherith, that is before Jordan.   17:5

And the ravens brought him bread and flesh in the morning, and bread and flesh in the evening; and he drank of the brook.   17:6

An handful of meal in a barrel, and a little oil in a cruse.   17:12

And the barrel of meal wasted not, neither did the cruse of oil fail.   17:16

How long halt ye between two opinions?   18:21

Either he is talking, or he is pursuing, or he is in a journey, or peradventure he sleepeth, and must be awaked.   18:27

There ariseth a little cloud out of the sea, like a man's hand.   *I Kings* 18:44

And he girded up his loins, and ran before Ahab.   18:46

But the Lord was not in the wind: and after the wind an earthquake; but the Lord was not in the earthquake:
And after the earthquake a fire; but the Lord was not in the fire: and after the fire a still small voice.   19:11-12

Let not him that girdeth on his harness boast himself as he that putteth it off.   20:11

Hast thou found me, O mine enemy?   21:20

The dogs shall eat Jezebel by the wall of Jezreel.   21:23

But there was none like unto Ahab, which did sell himself to work wickedness in the sight of the Lord, whom Jezebel his wife stirred up.   21:25

I saw all Israel scattered upon the hills, as sheep that have not a shepherd.   22:17

Feed him with bread of affliction, and with water of affliction, until I come in peace.   22:27

There appeared a chariot of fire, and horses of fire, and parted them both asunder; and Elijah went up by a whirlwind into heaven.
The Second Book of the Kings 2:11

The chariot of Israel, and the horsemen thereof. And he saw him no more.   2:12

There is death in the pot.   4:40

Is thy servant a dog, that he should do this great thing?   8:13

What hast thou to do with peace? turn thee behind me.   9:18

The driving is like the driving of Jehu the son of Nimshi; for he driveth furiously.   9:20

Jezebel heard of it; and she painted her face, and tired her head, and looked out at a window.   9:30

Set thine house in order.

II Kings 20:1

I will wipe Jerusalem as a man wipeth a dish, wiping it, and turning it upside down. 21:13

His mercy endureth for ever.

The First Book of the Chronicles 16:41

The Lord searcheth all hearts, and understandeth all the imaginations of the thoughts. 28:9

For all things come of thee, and of thine own have we given thee.[1] 29:14

Our days on the earth are as a shadow. 29:15

He [David] died in a good old age, full of days, riches, and honour.

29:28

Thou art a God ready to pardon, gracious and merciful, slow to anger, and of great kindness.

The Book of Nehemiah 9:17

Mordecai rent his clothes, and put on sackcloth with ashes.

The Book of Esther 4:1

The man whom the king delighteth to honour. 6:6

They hanged Haman on the gallows.

7:10

One that feared God, and eschewed evil. *The Book of Job* 1:1

Satan came also. 1:6

And the Lord said unto Satan, Whence comest thou? Then Satan answered the Lord, and said, From going to and fro in the earth, and from walking up and down in it. 1:7

Doth Job fear God for nought?

1:9

Naked came I out of my mother's womb, and naked shall I return thither: the Lord gave, and the Lord hath taken away; blessed be the name of the Lord. 1:21

Skin for skin, yea, all that a man hath will he give for his life. 2:4

Curse God, and die. 2:9

[1] See Marcus Aurelius, p. 142a.

Let the day perish wherein I was born, and the night in which it was said, There is a man child conceived.[1]

Job 3:3

For now should I have lain still and been quiet, I should have slept: then had I been at rest,

With kings and counsellors of the earth, which built desolate places for themselves. 3:13–14

There the wicked cease from troubling; and there the weary be at rest. 3:17

Who ever perished, being innocent? or where were the righteous cut off?

4:7

Fear came upon me, and trembling.

4:14

Then a spirit passed before my face; the hair of my flesh stood up. 4:15

Shall mortal man be more just than God? shall a man be more pure than his maker? 4:17

Wrath killeth the foolish man, and envy slayeth the silly one. 5:2

Man is born unto trouble, as the sparks fly upward. 5:7

He taketh the wise in their own craftiness. 5:13

For thou shalt be in league with the stones of the field: and the beasts of the field shall be at peace with thee.

5:23

Thou shalt come to thy grave in a full age, like as a shock of corn cometh in in his season. 5:26

How forcible are right words!

6:25

My days are swifter than a weaver's shuttle, and are spent without hope.

7:6

He shall return no more to his house, neither shall his place know him any more.[2] 7:10

[1] See Euripides, p. 84a.

[2] When a few years are come, then I shall go the way whence I shall not return. — *Job* 16:22

The place thereof shall know it no more. — *Psalm* 103:16

I would not live alway: let me alone; for my days are vanity.   *Job 7:16*

But how should man be just with God?   9:2

The land of darkness and the shadow of death.   10:21

Canst thou by searching find out God?   11:7

And thine age shall be clearer than the noonday.   11:17

No doubt but ye are the people, and wisdom shall die with you.   12:2

The just upright man is laughed to scorn.   12:4

But now ask the beasts, and they shall teach thee; and the fowls of the air, and they shall tell thee:
Or speak to the earth, and it shall teach thee; and the fishes of the sea shall declare unto thee.   12:7–8

With the ancient is wisdom; and in length of days understanding.   12:12

He discovereth deep things out of darkness, and bringeth out to light the shadow of death.   12:22

Man that is born of a woman is of few days, and full of trouble.
He cometh forth like a flower, and is cut down: he fleeth also as a shadow, and continueth not.   14:1–2

But man dieth, and wasteth away: yea, man giveth up the ghost, and where is he?   14:10

If a man die, shall he live again?   14:14

Should a wise man utter vain knowledge, and fill his belly with the east wind?   15:2

Miserable comforters are ye all.   16:2

My days are past.   17:11

I have said to corruption, Thou art my father: to the worm, Thou art my mother, and my sister.   17:14

The king of terrors.   18:14

I am escaped with the skin of my teeth.   19:20

Oh that my words were now written! oh that they were printed in a book!   *Job 19:23*

I know that my redeemer liveth, and that he shall stand at the latter day upon the earth: [1]
And though, after my skin, worms destroy this body, yet in my flesh shall I see God.   19:25–26

Seeing the root of the matter is found in me.   19:28

Though wickedness be sweet in his mouth, though he hide it under his tongue.   20:12

Suffer me that I may speak; and after that I have spoken, mock on.   21:3

Shall any teach God knowledge?   21:22

They are of those that rebel against the light.   24:13

The womb shall forget him; the worm shall feed sweetly on him; he shall be no more remembered.   24:20

Yea, the stars are not pure in his sight.
How much less man, that is a worm? and the son of man, which is a worm?   25:5–6

But where shall wisdom be found? and where is the place of understanding?   28:12

The land of the living.   28:13

The price of wisdom is above rubies.[2]   28:18

Behold, the fear of the Lord, that is wisdom; and to depart from evil is understanding.   28:28

I caused the widow's heart to sing for joy.   29:13

I was eyes to the blind, and feet was I to the lame.   29:15

The house appointed for all living.   30:23

[1] Also in *Book of Common Prayer, Burial of the Dead.*
[2] [Wisdom] is more precious than rubies. — *Proverbs 3:15*
See Sophocles, p. 82b.

I am a brother to dragons, and a companion to owls.   *Job* 30:29

My desire is, that the Almighty would answer me, and that mine adversary had written a book.   31:35

Great men are not always wise.   32:9

For I am full of matter, the spirit within me constraineth me.   32:18

One among a thousand.   33:23

Far be it from God, that he should do wickedness.   34:10

He multiplieth words without knowledge.   35:16

Fair weather cometh out of the north.   37:22

Then the Lord answered Job out of the whirlwind, and said,
Who is this that darkeneth counsel by words without knowledge?
Gird up now thy loins like a man.   38:1–3

Where wast thou when I laid the foundations of the earth? declare, if thou hast understanding.   38:4

The morning stars sang together, and all the sons of God shouted for joy.   38:7

Hitherto shalt thou come, but no further: and here shall thy proud waves be stayed?   38:11

Hast thou entered into the springs of the sea? or hast thou walked in the search of the depth?   38:16

Hath the rain a father? or who hath begotten the drops of dew?   38:28

Canst thou bind the sweet influences of Pleiades, or loose the bands of Orion?   38:31

Canst thou guide Arcturus with his sons?   38:32

Who can number the clouds in wisdom? or who can stay the bottles of heaven.   38:37

Hast thou given the horse strength?

hast thou clothed his neck with thunder?   *Job* 39:19

He paweth in the valley, and rejoiceth in his strength: he goeth on to meet the armed men.   39:21

He swalloweth the ground with fierceness and rage; neither believeth he that it is the sound of the trumpet.

He saith among the trumpets, Ha, ha; and he smelleth the battle afar off, the thunder of the captains, and the shouting.   39:24–25

Behold, I am vile; what shall I answer thee?   40:4

Behold now behemoth, which I made with thee; he eateth grass as an ox.   40:15

Canst thou draw out leviathan with a hook?   41:1

Hard as a piece of the nether millstone.   41:24

He maketh the deep to boil like a pot.   41:31

Upon earth there is not his like, who is made without fear.   41:33

He is a king over all the children of pride.   41:34

I have heard of thee by the hearing of the ear: but now mine eye seeth thee.   42:5

So the Lord blessed the latter end of Job more than his beginning.   42:12

Blessed is the man that walketh not in the counsel of the ungodly, nor standeth in the way of sinners, nor sitteth in the seat of the scornful.

But his delight is in the law of the Lord; and in his law doth he meditate day and night.

And he shall be like a tree planted by the rivers of water, that bringeth forth his fruit in his season; his leaf also shall not wither; and whatsoever he doeth shall prosper.

The ungodly are not so: but are like the chaff which the wind driveth away.   *The Book of Psalms* 1:1–4 [1]

[1] See Amenemope, VI, p. 4b, and *Jeremiah* 17:5–8, p. 34 a–b.

Why do the heathen rage, and the people imagine a vain thing?

Psalms 2:1

Blessed are all they that put their trust in him.   2:12

Lord, lift thou up the light of thy countenance upon us.   4:6

I will both lay me down in peace, and sleep.[1]   4:8

Out of the mouth of babes and sucklings hast thou ordained strength, because of thine enemies; that thou mightest still the enemy and the avenger.   8:2

What is man, that thou art mindful of him? and the son of man, that thou visitest him?   8:4

Thou hast made him a little lower than the angels.   8:5

How excellent is thy name in all the earth.   8:9

Flee as a bird to your mountain.
                                  11:1

How long wilt thou forget me, O Lord?   13:1

The fool hath said in his heart, There is no God.   *14:1 and 53:1*

Lord, who shall abide in thy tabernacle? who shall dwell in thy holy hill?   15:1

He that sweareth to his own hurt, and changeth not.   15:4

The lines are fallen unto me in pleasant places;[2] yea, I have a goodly heritage.   16:6

Keep me as the apple of the eye,[3] hide me under the shadow of thy wings.   17:8

He rode upon a cherub, and did fly: yea, he did fly upon the wings of the wind.   18:10

The heavens declare the glory of God; and the firmament showeth his handiwork.   *Psalms 19:1*

Day unto day uttereth speech, and night unto night showeth knowledge.
                                  19:2

Their line is gone out through all the earth, and their words to the end of the world. In them hath he set a tabernacle for the sun,

Which is as a bridegroom coming out of his chamber, and rejoiceth as a strong man to run a race.

His going forth is from the end of the heaven, and his circuit unto the ends of it: and there is nothing hid from the heat thereof.   19:4-6

The judgments of the Lord are true and righteous altogether.

More to be desired are they than gold, yea, than much fine gold: sweeter also than honey and the honeycomb.
                                19:9-10

Cleanse thou me from secret faults.
                                  19:12

Let the words of my mouth, and the meditation of my heart, be acceptable in thy sight, O Lord, my strength, and my redeemer.   19:14

Thou hast given him his heart's desire.   21:2

My God, my God, why hast thou forsaken me?[1] why art thou so far from helping me, and from the words of my roaring?   22:1

They part my garments among them, and cast lots upon my vesture.   22:18

The Lord is my shepherd; I shall not want.

He maketh me to lie down in green pastures: he leadeth me beside the still waters.

He restoreth my soul: he leadeth me in the paths of righteousness for his name's sake.

Yea, though I walk through the valley of the shadow of death, I will

---

[1] I will lay me down in peace, and take my rest. — *Book of Common Prayer, Psalm 4:9*
[2] The lot is fallen unto me in a fair ground. — *Book of Common Prayer, Psalm 16:7*
[3] Also in *Deuteronomy 32:10* and *Proverbs 7:2.*

[1] This was the psalm Christ recited on the cross. See *Matthew 27:46,* p. 45a.

fear no evil: for thou art with me; thy rod and thy staff they comfort me.

Thou preparest a table before me in the presence of mine enemies: thou anointest my head with oil; my cup runneth over.

Surely goodness and mercy shall follow me all the days of my life: and I will dwell in the house of the Lord for ever. 　　　　*Psalms* 23

The earth is the Lord's, and the fulness thereof; the world, and they that dwell therein.

For he hath founded it upon the seas, and established it upon the floods.

Who shall ascend into the hill of the Lord? or who shall stand in his holy place?

He that hath clean hands, and a pure heart; who hath not lifted up his soul unto vanity, nor sworn deceitfully.
　　　　24:1–4

Lift up your heads, O ye gates; and be ye lift up, ye everlasting doors; and the King of glory shall come in.
　　　　24:7

Who is this King of glory? The Lord of hosts, he is the King of glory.
　　　　24:10

The Lord is my light[1] and my salvation; whom shall I fear? the Lord is the strength of my life; of whom shall I be afraid? 　　　　27:1

Though an host should encamp against me, my heart shall not fear: though war should rise against me, in this will I be confident. 　　　　27:3

The Lord is my strength and my shield. 　　　　28:7

Worship the Lord in the beauty of holiness. 　　　　29:2

Weeping may endure for a night, but joy cometh in the morning.
　　　　30:5

I am forgotten as a dead man out of mind: I am like a broken vessel.
　　　　31:12

[1] Dominus illuminatio mea. — *The Vulgate.* Motto of Oxford University.

My times are in thy hand.
　　　　Psalms 31:15
From the strife of tongues. 　　31:20

Sing unto him a new song; play skilfully with a loud noise. 　　33:3

O taste and see that the Lord is good. 　　　　34:8

Keep thy tongue from evil, and thy lips from speaking guile.
Depart from evil, and do good; seek peace, and pursue it. 　　34:13–14

Rescue my soul from their destructions, my darling from the lions.
　　　　35:17

How excellent is thy lovingkindness, O God! 　　　　36:7

The meek shall inherit the earth.[1]
　　　　37:11

I have been young, and now am old; yet have I not seen the righteous forsaken, nor his seed begging bread.
　　　　37:25

I have seen the wicked in great power, and spreading himself[2] like a green bay tree. 　　　　37:35

Mark the perfect man, and behold the upright: for the end of that man is peace.[3] 　　　　37:37

For thine arrows stick fast in me, and thy hand presseth me sore. 　　38:2

I said, I will take heed to my ways, that I sin not with my tongue. 　　39:1

My heart was hot within me, while I was musing the fire burned. 　　39:3

Lord, make me to know mine end, and the measure of my days, what it is; that I may know how frail I am.
　　　　39:4
Every man at his best state is altogether vanity. 　　　　39:5

Surely every man walketh in a vain show: surely they are disquieted in

[1] See *Matthew* 5:5, p. 40a.
[2] Flourishing. — *Book of Common Prayer,* Psalm 37:36
[3] For that shall bring a man peace at the last. — *Book of Common Prayer, Psalm 37:38*

vain: he heapeth up riches, and knoweth not who shall gather them.
Psalms 39:6

For I am a stranger with thee, and a sojourner, as all my fathers were.
O spare me, that I may recover strength, before I go hence, and be no more.   *39:12–13*

As the hart panteth after the water brooks, so panteth my soul after thee, O God.
My soul thirsteth for God, for the living God.   *42:1–2*

Why art thou cast down, O my soul? and why art thou disquieted in me?
42:5, 11 and 43:5

Deep calleth unto deep.   *42:7*

My tongue is the pen of a ready writer.   *45:1*

The king's daughter is all glorious within.   *45:13*

God is our refuge and strength, a very present help in trouble.
Therefore will we not fear, though the earth be removed, and though the mountains be carried into the midst of the sea.   *46:1–2*

Be still, and know that I am God.
46:10

Every beast of the forest is mine, and the cattle upon a thousand hills.
50:10

I was shapen in iniquity; and in sin did my mother conceive me.   *51 [1]:5*

Purge me with hyssop, and I shall be clean: wash me, and I shall be whiter than snow.   *51:7*

Create in me a clean heart, O God; and renew a right spirit within me.
51:10

And take not thy holy spirit from me.   *51:11*

Open thou my lips; and my mouth shall show forth thy praise.   *51:15*

A broken and a contrite heart, O God, thou wilt not despise.
Psalms 51:17

Oh that I had wings like a dove! for then would I fly away, and be at rest.[1]   *55:6*

We took sweet counsel together.
55:14

The words of his mouth were smoother than butter, but war was in his heart: [2] his words were softer than oil, yet were they drawn swords.
55:21

They are like the deaf adder that stoppeth her ear;
Which will not hearken to the voice of charmers, charming never so wisely.
58:4–5

Moab is my washpot; over Edom will I cast out my shoe: Philistia, triumph thou because of me.   *60:8*

Lead me to the rock that is higher than I.   *61:2*

He only is my rock and my salvation: he is my defence; I shall not be moved.   *62:6*

Thou renderest to every man according to his work.   *62:12*

My soul thirsteth for thee, my flesh longeth for thee in a dry and thirsty land, where no water is.   *63:1*

Thou crownest the year with thy goodness.   *65:11*

Make a joyful noise unto God, all ye lands.   *66:1*

We went through fire and through water.   *66:12*

God setteth the solitary in families.
68:6

Cast me not off in the time of old age; forsake me not when my strength faileth.   *71:9*

He shall come down like rain upon

---

[1] This Psalm is known as the Miserere from its opening word in the Vulgate. The first line is: Have mercy upon me, O God.

[2] The words of his mouth were softer than butter, having war in his heart. — *Book of Common Prayer, Psalm 50:22*

the mown grass: as showers that water the earth.   *Psalms 72:6*

His enemies shall lick the dust.
72:9

His name shall endure for ever.
72:17

A stubborn and rebellious generation.
78:8

But ye shall die like men, and fall like one of the princes.   82:7

How amiable are thy tabernacles, O Lord of hosts!   84:1

They go from strength to strength.
84:7

A day in thy courts is better than a thousand. I had rather be a doorkeeper in the house of my God, than to dwell in the tents of wickedness.   84:10

Mercy and truth are met together; righteousness and peace have kissed each other.   85:10

Lord, why castest thou off my soul? why hidest thou thy face from me?
88:14

Lord, thou hast been our dwelling place in all generations.
Before the mountains were brought forth, or ever thou hadst formed the earth and the world, even from everlasting to everlasting, thou art God.
Thou turnest man to destruction; and sayest, Return, ye children of men.
For a thousand years in thy sight are but as yesterday when it is past, and as a watch in the night.
Thou carriest them away as with a flood; they are as a sleep: in the morning they are like grass which groweth up.
In the morning it flourisheth, and groweth up; in the evening it is cut down, and withereth.[1]   90:1–6

We spend our years as a tale that is told.[2]
90:9

The days of our years are threescore years and ten; and if by reason of strength they be fourscore years, yet is their strength labour and sorrow; for it is soon cut off, and we fly away.[1]
Psalms 90:–10

So teach us to number our days, that we may apply our hearts unto wisdom.
90:12

Establish thou the work of our hands upon us; yea, the work of our hands establish thou it.   90:17

He that dwelleth in the secret place of the most High shall abide under the shadow of the Almighty.
I will say of the Lord, He is my refuge and my fortress: my God; in him will I trust.
Surely he shall deliver thee from the snare of the fowler, and from the noisome pestilence.
He shall cover thee with his feathers, and under his wings shalt thou trust: his truth shall be thy shield and buckler.
Thou shalt not be afraid for the terror by night; nor for the arrow that flieth by day.
Nor for the pestilence that walketh in darkness; nor for the destruction that wasteth at noonday.
A thousand shall fall at thy side, and ten thousand at thy right hand; but it shall not come nigh thee.   91:1–7

He shall give his angels charge over thee, to keep thee in all thy ways.
They shall bear thee up in their hands, lest thou dash thy foot against a stone.[2]
Thou shalt tread upon the lion and adder: the young lion and the dragon shalt thou trample under feet.
91:11–13

The righteous shall flourish like the

---

[1] See *Isaiah 40:6, 8,* p. 32b, and *1 Peter 1:24,* p. 56b.

[2] We bring our years to an end, as it were a tale that is told. — *Book of Common Prayer, Psalm 90:9*

[1] The days of our age are threescore years and ten; and though men be so strong that they come to fourscore years, yet is their strength then but labour and sorrow; so soon passeth it away, and we are gone. — *Book of Common Prayer, Psalm 90:10*

[2] Also in *Matthew 4:6.*

palm tree: he shall grow like a cedar in Lebanon.   *Psalms* 92:12

Mightier than the noise of many waters.   93:4

In his hand are the deep places of the earth: the strength of the hills is his also.

The sea is his, and he made it: and his hands formed the dry land.
                                          95:4–5

We are the people of his pasture, and the sheep of his hand.   95:7

O sing unto the Lord a new song.
                                          96:1

The Lord reigneth; let the earth rejoice.   97:1

Make a joyful noise unto the Lord, all ye lands.

Serve the Lord with gladness: come before his presence with singing.

Know ye that the Lord he is God: it is he that hath made us, and not we ourselves; we are his people, and the sheep of his pasture.

Enter into his gates with thanksgiving, and into his courts with praise: be thankful unto him, and bless his name.

For the Lord is good; his mercy is everlasting; and his truth endureth to all generations.   100

My days are consumed like smoke.
                                          102:3

I watch, and am as a sparrow alone upon the house top.   102:7

As the heaven is high above the earth, so great is his mercy toward them that fear him.   103:11

As for man, his days are as grass: as a flower of the field, so he flourisheth.

For the wind passeth over it, and it is gone; and the place thereof shall know it no more.[1]   103:15–16

Who layeth the beams of his chambers in the waters: who maketh the clouds his chariot: who walketh upon the wings of the wind.   104:3

[1] See Homer, p. 67a.

Wine that maketh glad the heart of man.   *Psalms* 104:15

The cedars of Lebanon.   104:16

He appointeth the moon for seasons: the sun knoweth his going down.

Thou makest darkness, and it is night: wherein all the beasts of the forest do creep forth.

The young lions roar after their prey, and seek their meat from God.

The sun ariseth, they gather themselves together, and lay them down in their dens.

Man goeth forth unto his work and to his labor until the evening.

O Lord, how manifold are thy works! in wisdom hast thou made them all: the earth is full of thy riches.

So is this great and wide sea, wherein are things creeping innumerable, both small and great beasts.

There go the ships: there is that leviathan, whom thou hast made to play therein.

These wait all upon thee; that thou mayest give them their meat in due season.   104:19–27 [1]

Such as sit in darkness and in the shadow of death.   107:10

They that go down to the sea in ships, that do business in great waters.
                                          107:23

They mount up to the heaven, they go down again to the depths.   107:26

They reel to and fro, and stagger like a drunken man, and are at their wit's end.   107:27

For I am poor and needy, and my heart is wounded within me.

I am gone like the shadow when it declineth: I am tossed up and down as the locust.   109:22–23

Thou hast the dew of thy youth.
                                          110:3

The fear of the Lord is the beginning of wisdom.   111:10

From the rising of the sun unto the

[1] See Ikhnaton, p. 3b.

going down of the same the Lord's name is to be praised.   *Psalms* 113:3

The mountains skipped like rams, and the little hills like lambs.   114:4

They have mouths, but they speak not: eyes have they, but they see not.
They have ears, but they hear not.[1]   115:5–6

I said in my haste, All men are liars.   116:11

Precious in the sight of the Lord is the death of his saints.   116:15

The stone which the builders refused is become the head stone of the corner.[2]   118:22

This is the day which the Lord hath made.   118:24

Blessed be he that cometh in the name of the Lord.[3]   118:26

Thy word is a lamp unto my feet, and a light unto my path.   119:105

I am for peace: but when I speak, they are for war.   120:7

I will lift up mine eyes unto the hills, from whence cometh my help.[4]
My help cometh from the Lord, which made heaven and earth.
He will not suffer thy foot to be moved: he that keepeth thee will not slumber.
Behold, he that keepeth Israel shall neither slumber nor sleep.
The Lord is thy keeper: the Lord is thy shade upon thy right hand.
The sun shall not smite thee by day, nor the moon by night.
The Lord shall preserve thee from all evil: he shall preserve thy soul.
The Lord shall preserve thy going out and thy coming in from this time forth, and even for evermore.   121

I was glad when they said unto me,

Let us go into the house of the Lord.   *Psalms* 122:1

Peace be within thy walls, and prosperity within thy palaces.   122:7

They that sow in tears shall reap in joy.
He that goeth forth and weepeth, bearing precious seed, shall doubtless come again with rejoicing, bringing his sheaves with him.   126:5–6

Except the Lord build the house, they labour in vain that build it: except the Lord keep the city, the watchman waketh but in vain.   127:1

He giveth his beloved sleep.   127:2

As arrows are in the hand of a mighty man; so are children of the youth.
Happy is the man that hath his quiver full of them.   127:4–5

Out of the depths have I cried unto thee, O Lord.   130:1

My soul waiteth for the Lord more than they that watch for the morning.   130:6

I will not give sleep to mine eyes, or slumber to mine eyelids.[1]   132:4

Behold, how good and how pleasant it is for brethren to dwell together in unity!   133:1

By the rivers of Babylon, there we sat down, yea, we wept, when we remembered Zion.[2]
We hanged our harps upon the willows in the midst thereof.
For there they that carried us away captive required of us a song; and they that wasted us required of us mirth, saying, Sing us one of the songs of Zion.
How shall we sing the Lord's song in a strange land?
If I forget thee, O Jerusalem, let my right hand forget her cunning.
If I do not remember thee, let my

---

[1] Also in *Psalm 135:16–17.*

[2] Also in *Matthew 21:42.*

[3] Also in *Matthew 21:9, 23:39,* Mark *11:9,* and *Luke 13:35.*

[4] I lift up my eyes to the hills. From whence does my help come? — *Revised Standard Version*

[1] Also in *Proverbs 6:4.*

[2] By the waters of Babylon we sat down and wept: when we remembered thee, O Sion. — *Book of Common Prayer, Psalm 137:1*

tongue cleave to the roof of my mouth. *Psalms* 137:1–6

O Lord, thou hast searched me, and known me.

Thou knowest my downsitting and mine uprising, thou understandest my thought afar off. 139:1–2

Whither shall I go from thy spirit? or whither shall I flee from thy presence?

If I ascend up into heaven, thou art there: if I make my bed in hell, behold, thou art there.

If I take the wings of the morning, and dwell in the uttermost parts of the sea;

Even there shall thy hand lead me, and thy right hand shall hold me. 139:7–10

The darkness and the light are both alike to thee. 139:12

I am fearfully and wonderfully made. 139:14

They have sharpened their tongues like a serpent. 140:3

Thou openest thine hand, and satisfiest the desire of every living thing. 145:16

The Lord is nigh unto all them that call upon him, to all that call upon him in truth. 145:18

Put not your trust in princes. 146:3

He telleth the number of the stars; he calleth them all by their names. 147:4

Let every thing that hath breath praise the Lord. 150:6

To give subtilty to the simple, to the young man knowledge and discretion. *The Proverbs* 1:4

My son, if sinners entice thee, consent thou not. 1:10

Wisdom crieth without; she uttereth her voice in the streets. 1:20

Length of days is in her right hand; and in her left hand riches and honor. 3:16

Her ways are ways of pleasantness, and all her paths are peace. *Proverbs* 3:17

Be not afraid of sudden fear. 3:25

Wisdom is the principal thing; therefore get wisdom: and with all thy getting get understanding. 4:7

The path of the just is as the shining light, that shineth more and more unto the perfect day. 4:18

Keep thy heart with all diligence; for out of it are the issues of life. 4:23

For the lips of a strange woman drop as an honeycomb, and her mouth is smoother than oil:

But her end is bitter as wormwood, sharp as a two-edged sword. 5:3–4

Go to the ant, thou sluggard; consider her ways, and be wise:

Which having no guide, overseer, or ruler,

Provideth her meat in the summer, and gathereth her food in the harvest. 6:6–8

Yet a little sleep, a little slumber, a little folding of the hands to sleep: [1]

So shall thy poverty come as one that travelleth, and thy want as an armed man. 6:10–11

Lust not after her beauty in thine heart; neither let her take thee with her eyelids. 6:25

Can a man take fire in his bosom, and his clothes not be burned?

Can one go upon hot coals, and his feet not be burned? 6:27–28

Jealousy is the rage of a man: therefore he will not spare in the day of vengeance. 6:34

He goeth after her straightway, as an ox goeth to the slaughter. 7:22

I love them that love me; and those that seek me early shall find me. 8:17

Wisdom hath builded her house, she hath hewn out her seven pillars. 9:1

[1] Also in *Proverbs* 24:33.

Reprove not a scorner, lest he hate thee: rebuke a wise man, and he will love thee.   *Proverbs* 9:8

Stolen waters are sweet, and bread eaten in secret is pleasant.   9:17

A wise son maketh a glad father: but a foolish son is the heaviness of his mother.   10:1

Blessings are upon the head of the just: but violence covereth the mouth of the wicked.
The memory of the just is blessed: but the name of the wicked shall rot.   10:6–7

Hatred stirreth up strifes: but love covereth all sins.   10:12

In the multitude of counsellors there is safety.[1]
He that is surety for a stranger shall smart for it.   11:14–15

As a jewel of gold in a swine's snout, so is a fair woman which is without discretion.   11:22

He that trusteth in his riches shall fall.   11:28

A virtuous woman is a crown to her husband.   12:4

A righteous man regardeth the life of his beast: but the tender mercies of the wicked are cruel.   12:10

The way of a fool is right in his own eyes.   12:15

Hope deferred maketh the heart sick.   13:12

The way of transgressors is hard.
                                  13:15

The desire accomplished is sweet to the soul.   13:19

He that spareth his rod hateth his son: but he that loveth him chasteneth him betimes.[2]   13:24

Fools make a mock at sin.   14:9

The heart knoweth his own bitter-

ness; and a stranger doth not intermeddle with his joy.   *Proverbs* 14:10

Even in laughter the heart is sorrowful.   14:13

The prudent man looketh well to his going.   14:15

In all labor there is profit: but the talk of the lips tendeth only to penury.
                                  14:23

Righteousness exalteth a nation.
                                  14:34

A soft answer turneth away wrath.
                                  15:1

A merry heart maketh a cheerful countenance: but by sorrow of the heart the spirit is broken.   15:13

He that is of a merry heart hath a continual feast.
Better is little with the fear of the Lord than great treasure and trouble therewith.
Better is a dinner of herbs where love is, than a stalled ox and hatred therewith.[1]   15:15–17

A wrathful man stirreth up strife: but he that is slow to anger appeaseth strife.   15:18

A word spoken in due season, how good is it!   15:23

Before honour is humility.
                          15:33 *and* 18:12

A man's heart deviseth his way: but the Lord directeth his steps.   16:9

Pride goeth before destruction, and an haughty spirit before a fall.[2]
                                  16:18

The hoary head is a crown of glory, if it be found in the way of righteousness.
He that is slow to anger is better than the mighty; and he that ruleth his spirit than he that taketh a city.
                                  16:31–32

Whoso mocketh the poor reproacheth his Maker.   17:5

---

[1] Also in *Proverbs* 24:6.
[2] See Menander, p. 102a, and note.

[1] See Amenemope, IX, p. 4b.
[2] See Sophocles, p. 81b, and note.

He that repeateth a matter separateth very friends.   *Proverbs 17:9*

Whoso rewardeth evil for good, evil shall not depart from his house.   17:13

A merry heart doeth good like a medicine.   17:22

He that hath knowledge spareth his words: and a man of understanding is of an excellent spirit.
Even a fool, when he holdeth his peace, is counted wise.   17:27–28

A fool's mouth is his destruction.   18:7

A wounded spirit who can bear?   18:14

A brother offended is harder to be won than a strong city: and their contentions are like the bars of a castle.   18:19

Whoso findeth a wife findeth a good thing.   18:22

A man that hath friends must show himself friendly: and there is a friend that sticketh closer than a brother.   18:24

Wealth maketh many friends.   19:4

A foolish son is the calamity of his father: and the contentions of a wife are a continual dropping.   19:13

He that hath pity upon the poor lendeth unto the Lord.   19:17

Wine is a mocker, strong drink is raging.   20:1

It is an honour for a man to cease from strife: but every fool will be meddling.   20:3

Even a child is known by his doings, whether his work be pure, and whether it be right.
The hearing ear, and the seeing eye, the Lord hath made even both of them.   20:11–12

It is naught, it is naught, saith the buyer: but when he is gone his way, then he boasteth.   20:14

Bread of deceit is sweet to a man; but afterwards his mouth shall be filled with gravel.   *Proverbs 20:17*

Meddle not with him that flattereth with his lips.   20:19

It is better to dwell in a corner of the housetop, than with a brawling woman in a wide house.   21:9 *and* 25:24

A good name is rather to be chosen than great riches.   22:1

Train up a child in the way he should go: and when he is old, he will not depart from it.   22:6

The borrower is servant to the lender.   22:7

Bow down thine ear, and hear the words of the wise, and apply thine heart unto my knowledge.
For it is a pleasant thing if thou keep them within thee; they shall withal be fitted in thy lips.[1]   22:17–18

Have I not written to thee excellent things in counsels and knowledge,[2]
That I might make thee know the certainty of the words of truth; that thou mightest answer the words of truth to them that send unto thee?[3]   22:20–21

Remove not the ancient landmark.[4]   22:28

Seest thou a man diligent in his business? He shall stand before kings.[5]   22:29

Put a knife to thy throat, if thou be a man given to appetite.   23:2

Labor not to be rich: cease from thine own wisdom.[6]   23:4

Riches certainly make themselves wings.[7]   23:5

As he thinketh in his heart, so is he.   23:7

[1] See Amenemope, III, p. 4b.
[2] See Amenemope, XXVII, p. 4b.
[3] See Amenemope, I, p. 4a.
[4] Also in *Proverbs 23:10.* See Amenemope, VII, p. 4b.
[5] See Amenemope, XXVII, p. 4b.
[6] See Amenemope, IX, p. 4b.
[7] See Amenemope, X, p. 4b.

The drunkard and the glutton shall come to poverty: and drowsiness shall clothe a man with rags.
Proverbs 23:21

Despise not thy mother when she is old.   23:22

Look not thou upon the wine when it is red, when it giveth his colour in the cup, when it moveth itself aright.
At the last it biteth like a serpent, and stingeth like an adder.   23:31–32

A wise man is strong; yea, a man of knowledge increaseth strength.   24:5

If thou faint in the day of adversity, thy strength is small.   24:10

A word fitly spoken is like apples of gold in pictures of silver.   25:11

If thine enemy be hungry, give him bread to eat; and if he be thirsty, give him water to drink:
For thou shalt heap coals of fire upon his head.[1]   25:21–22

As cold waters to a thirsty soul, so is good news from a far country.   25:25

For men to search their own glory is not glory.   25:27

Answer a fool according to his folly.   26:5

As a dog returneth to his vomit, so a fool returneth to his folly.
Seest thou a man wise in his own conceit? There is more hope of a fool than of him.
The slothful man saith, There is a lion in the way; a lion is in the streets.   26:11–13

Whoso diggeth a pit shall fall therein: and he that rolleth a stone, it will return upon him.   26:27

Boast not thyself of tomorrow; for thou knowest not what a day may bring forth.[2]   27:1

Let another man praise thee, and not thine own mouth.   27:2

[1] See *Romans* 12:20 and Marcus Aurelius, p. 142b.
[2] See Sophocles, p. 82b.

Open rebuke is better than secret love.
Faithful are the wounds of a friend; but the kisses of an enemy are deceitful.
Proverbs 27:5–6

To the hungry soul every bitter thing is sweet.   27:7

Better is a neighbour that is near than a brother far off.   27:10

Iron sharpeneth iron; so a man sharpeneth the countenance of his friend.   27:17

The wicked flee when no man pursueth: but the righteous are bold as a lion.   28:1

He that maketh haste to be rich shall not be innocent.   28:20

He that trusteth in his own heart is a fool.   28:26

He that giveth unto the poor shall not lack.   28:27

A fool uttereth all his mind.
29:11

Where there is no vision, the people perish.   29:18

A man's pride shall bring him low: but honour shall uphold the humble in spirit.   29:23

Give me neither poverty nor riches.
30:8

Accuse not a servant unto his master.
30:10

The horseleach hath two daughters, crying, Give, give.   30:15

There be three things which are too wonderful for me, yea, four which I know not:
The way of an eagle in the air; the way of a serpent upon a rock; the way of a ship in the midst of the sea; and the way of a man with a maid.
30:18–19

Give strong drink unto him that is ready to perish, and wine unto those that be of heavy hearts.   31:6

Who can find a virtuous woman? for her price is far above rubies.

The heart of her husband doth safely trust in her.   *Proverbs 31:10–11*

Her husband is known in the gates, when he sitteth among the elders of the land.   *31:23*

Strength and honour are her clothing.   *31:25*

In her tongue is the law of kindness. She looketh well to the ways of her household, and eateth not the bread of idleness.

Her children arise up, and call her blessed.   *31:26–28*

Many daughters have done virtuously, but thou excellest them all.

Favour is deceitful, and beauty is vain: but a woman that feareth the Lord, she shall be praised.

Give her of the fruit of her hands; and let her own works praise her in the gates.   *31:29–31*

Vanity of vanities, saith the Preacher, vanity of vanities; all is vanity.

What profit hath a man of all his labour which he taketh under the sun?

One generation passeth away, and another generation cometh: but the earth abideth for ever.

The sun also ariseth.   *Ecclesiastes 1:2–5*

All the rivers run into the sea; yet the sea is not full.   *1:7*

The eye is not satisfied with seeing, nor the ear filled with hearing.   *1:8*

There is no new thing under the sun.   *1:9*

There is no remembrance of former things; neither shall there be any remembrance of things that are to come with those that shall come after.   *1:11*

I have seen all the works that are done under the sun; and, behold, all is vanity and vexation of spirit.

That which is crooked cannot be made straight: and that which is wanting cannot be numbered.   *Ecclesiastes 1:14–15*

In much wisdom is much grief: and he that increaseth knowledge increaseth sorrow.   *1:18*

Wisdom excelleth folly, as far as light excelleth darkness.   *2:13*

One event happeneth to them all.   *2:14*

How dieth the wise man? as the fool.   *2:16*

To every thing there is a season, and a time to every purpose under the heaven.

A time to be born, and a time to die; a time to plant, and a time to pluck up that which is planted;

A time to kill, and a time to heal; a time to break down, and a time to build up;

A time to weep, and a time to laugh; a time to mourn, and a time to dance;

A time to cast away stones, and a time to gather stones together; a time to embrace, and a time to refrain from embracing;

A time to get, and a time to lose; a time to keep, and a time to cast away;

A time to rend, and a time to sew; a time to keep silence, and a time to speak; [1]

A time to love, and a time to hate; a time of war, and a time of peace.   *3:1–8*

Wherefore I praised the dead which are already dead more than the living which are yet alive.   *4:2*

Better is an handful with quietness, than both the hands full with travail and vexation of spirit.   *4:6*

A threefold cord is not quickly broken.   *4:12*

Better is a poor and a wise child than an old and foolish king.   *4:13*

[1] See Homer, p. 66a.

God is in heaven, and thou upon earth: therefore let thy words be few.
Ecclesiastes 5:2

Better is it that thou shouldest not vow, than that thou shouldest vow and not pay.   5:5

The sleep of a labouring man is sweet . . . but the abundance of the rich will not suffer him to sleep.
5:12

As he came forth of his mother's womb, naked shall he return to go as he came,[1] and shall take nothing of his labour, which he may carry away in his hand.[2]   5:15

A good name is better than precious ointment; and the day of death than the day of one's birth.[3]   7:1

It is better to go to the house of mourning, than to go to the house of feasting.   7:2

As the crackling of thorns under a pot, so is the laughter of the fool.
7:6

Better is the end of a thing than the beginning thereof.   7:8

In the day of prosperity be joyful, but in the day of adversity consider.
7:14

Be not righteous over much.   7:16

There is not a just man upon earth, that doeth good, and sinneth not.
7:20

And I find more bitter than death the woman, whose heart is snares and nets, and her hands as bands.   7:26

One man among a thousand have I found; but a woman among all those have I not found.   7:28

God hath made man upright; but they have sought out many inventions.
7:29

There is no discharge in that war.
8:8

[1] See *Job 1:21*, p. 14a.
[2] See *The Song of the Harp-Player*, p. 3a.
[3] See Publilius Syrus, p. 125a.

A man hath no better thing under the sun, than to eat, and to drink, and to be merry.[1]   *Ecclesiastes* 8:15

A living dog is better than a dead lion.

For the living know that they shall die: but the dead know not any thing, neither have they any more a reward; for the memory of them is forgotten.
9:4–5

Whatsoever thy hand findeth to do, do it with thy might; for there is no work, nor device, nor knowledge, nor wisdom, in the grave, whither thou goest.   9:10

The race is not to the swift, nor the battle to the strong.   9:11

A feast is made for laughter, and wine maketh merry: but money answereth all things.   10:19

A bird of the air shall carry the voice, and that which hath wings shall tell the matter.   10:20

Cast thy bread upon the waters: for thou shalt find it after many days.
11:1

He that observeth the wind shall not sow; and he that regardeth the clouds shall not reap.   11:4

In the morning sow thy seed, and in the evening withhold not thine hand.
11:6

Rejoice, O young man, in thy youth.
11:9

Remember now thy Creator in the days of thy youth, while the evil days come not, nor the years draw nigh, when thou shalt say, I have no pleasure in them.

While the sun, or the light, or the moon, or the stars, be not darkened, nor the clouds return after the rain:

In the day when the keepers of the house shall tremble, and the strong men shall bow themselves, and the grinders cease because they are few, and those that look out of the windows be darkened,

[1] See *Luke 12:19*, p. 46b.

And the doors shall be shut in the streets, when the sound of the grinding is low, and he shall rise up at the voice of the bird, and all the daughters of music shall be brought low.
Ecclesiastes 12:1–4

The almond tree shall flourish, and the grasshopper shall be a burden, and desire shall fail; because man goeth to his long home, and the mourners go about the streets:

Or ever the silver cord be loosed, or the golden bowl be broken, or the pitcher be broken at the fountain, or the wheel broken at the cistern.

Then shall the dust return to the earth as it was: and the spirit shall return unto God who gave it.   *12:5–7*

The words of the wise are as goads, and as nails fastened by the masters of assemblies.   *12:11*

Of making many books there is no end; and much study is a weariness of the flesh.

Let us hear the conclusion of the whole matter: Fear God, and keep his commandments: for this is the whole duty of man.

For God shall bring every work into judgment, with every secret thing, whether it be good, or whether it be evil.   *12:12–14*

The song of songs, which is Solomon's.   *The Song of Solomon 1:1*

I am black, but comely, O ye daughters of Jerusalem, as the tents of Kedar, as the curtains of Solomon.
1:5

O thou fairest among women.
1:8

I am the rose of Sharon, and the lily of the valleys.   *2:1*

As the apple tree among the trees of the wood, so is my beloved among the sons.   *2:3*

His banner over me was love.
Stay me with flagons, comfort me with apples: for I am sick of love.
2:4–5

Rise up, my love, my fair one, and come away.

For, lo, the winter is past, the rain is over and gone;

The flowers appear on the earth; the time of the singing of birds is come, and the voice of the turtle is heard in our land.   *Song of Solomon 2:10–12*

The little foxes, that spoil the vines.
2:15

Until the day break, and the shadows flee away.   *2:17 and 4:6*

By night on my bed I sought him whom my soul loveth: I sought him, but I found him not.   *3:1*

Thy two breasts are like two young roes that are twins, which feed among the lilies.   *4:5*

Thou art all fair, my love; there is no spot in thee.   *4:7*

How much better is thy love than wine!   *4:10*

Awake, O north wind; and come, thou south; blow upon my garden, that the spices thereof may flow out. Let my beloved come into his garden, and eat his pleasant fruits.   *4:16*

My beloved put in his hand by the hole of the door, and my bowels were moved for him.   *5:4*

His mouth is most sweet: yea, he is altogether lovely. This is my beloved, and this is my friend, O daughters of Jerusalem.   *5:16*

Who is she that looketh forth as the morning, fair as the moon, clear as the sun, and terrible as an army with banners?   *6:10*

Return, return, O Shulamite.
6:13

Thy belly is like a heap of wheat set about with lilies.   *7:2*

Thy neck is as a tower of ivory.
7:4

Like the best wine . . . that goeth down sweetly, causing the lips of those that are asleep to speak.   *7:9*

I am my beloved's, and his desire is toward me. *Song of Solomon* 7:10

Set me as a seal upon thine heart, as a seal upon thine arm: for love is strong as death; jealousy is cruel as the grave. 8:6

Many waters cannot quench love, neither can the floods drown it. 8:7

Make haste, my beloved, and be thou like to a roe or to a young hart upon the mountains of spices. 8:14

The ox knoweth his owner, and the ass his master's crib. *The Book of the Prophet Isaiah* 1:3

The whole head is sick, and the whole heart faint. 1:5

As a lodge in a garden of cucumbers. 1:8

Bring no more vain oblations. 1:13

Learn to do well; seek judgment, relieve the oppressed, judge the fatherless, plead for the widow.
Come now, and let us reason together . . . though your sins be as scarlet, they shall be as white as snow. 1:17–18

They shall beat their swords into plowshares, and their spears into pruninghooks: nation shall not lift up sword against nation, neither shall they learn war any more.[1] 2:4

In that day a man shall cast his idols . . . to the moles and to the bats. 2:20

Cease ye from man, whose breath is in his nostrils. 2:22

The stay and the staff, the whole stay of bread, and the whole stay of water. 3:1

What mean ye that ye beat my people to pieces and grind the faces of the poor? 3:15

---

[1] Also in *Joel 3:10* and *Micah 4:3*.

Walk with stretched forth necks and wanton eyes, walking and mincing as they go, and making a tinkling with their feet. *Isaiah* 3:16

In that day seven women shall take hold of one man. 4:1

My wellbeloved hath a vineyard in a very fruitful hill. 5:1

And he looked for judgment, but behold oppression; for righteousness, but behold a cry.
Woe unto them that join house to house, that lay field to field, till there be no place, that they may be placed alone in the midst of the earth! 5:7–8

Woe unto them that rise up early in the morning, that they may follow strong drink. 5:11

Woe unto them that draw iniquity with cords of vanity, and sin as it were with a cart rope. 5:18

Woe unto them that call evil good, and good evil. 5:20

I saw also the Lord sitting upon a throne, high and lifted up, and his train filled the temple.
Above it stood the seraphims: each one had six wings; with twain he covered his face, and with twain he covered his feet, and with twain he did fly. 6:1–2

Holy, holy, holy, is the Lord of hosts: the whole earth is full of his glory. 6:3

Woe is me! for I am undone; because I am a man of unclean lips, and I dwell in the midst of a people of unclean lips: for mine eyes have seen the King, the Lord of hosts. 6:5

I heard the voice of the Lord, saying, Whom shall I send, and who will go for us? Then said I, Here am I; send me. 6:8

Then said I, Lord, how long? 6:11

Behold, a virgin shall conceive, and

bear a son, and shall call his name Immanuel. *Isaiah* 7:14

For a stone of stumbling and for a rock of offence. 8:14

The people that walked in darkness have seen a great light: they that dwell in the land of the shadow of death, upon them hath the light shined.
9:2

For unto us a child is born, unto us a son is given: and the government shall be upon his shoulder: and his name shall be called Wonderful, Counsellor, The mighty God, The everlasting Father, The Prince of Peace.
Of the increase of his government and peace there shall be no end.
9:6–7

The ancient and honorable, he is the head. 9:15

And there shall come forth a rod out of the stem of Jesse, and a Branch shall grow out of his roots:
And the Spirit of the Lord shall rest upon him, the spirit of wisdom and understanding, the spirit of counsel and might, the spirit of knowledge and of the fear of the Lord. 11:1–2

The wolf also shall dwell with the lamb, and the leopard shall lie down with the kid; and the calf and the young lion and the fatling together; and a little child shall lead them.
And the cow and the bear shall feed; their young ones shall lie down together: and the lion shall eat straw like the ox.
And the suckling child shall play on the hole of the asp, and the weaned child shall put his hand on the cockatrice' den.
They shall not hurt nor destroy in all my holy mountain: for the earth shall be full of the knowledge of the Lord, as the waters cover the sea. 11:6–9

For the Lord JEHOVAH is my strength and my song; he also is become my salvation. 12:2

And I will punish the world for their evil, and the wicked for their iniquity; and I will cause the arrogancy of the proud to cease, and will lay low the haughtiness of the terrible.
Isaiah 13:11

How art thou fallen from heaven, O Lucifer, son of the morning! 14:12

Is this the man that made the earth to tremble, that did shake kingdoms.
14:16

The nations shall rush like the rushing of many waters. 17:13

And they shall fight every one against his brother. 19:2

The burden of the desert of the sea. As whirlwinds in the south pass through; so it cometh from the desert, from a terrible land. 21:1

Babylon is fallen, is fallen; [1] and all the graven images of her gods he hath broken unto the ground. 21:9

Watchman, what of the night?
21:11

Let us eat and drink; for tomorrow we shall die. 22:13

I will fasten him as a nail in a sure place. 22:23

Whose merchants are princes.
23:8

As with the maid, so with her mistress. 24:2

For thou hast been a strength to the poor, a strength to the needy in his distress. 25:4

A feast of fat things, a feast of wines on the lees. 25:6

He will swallow up death in victory;[2] and the Lord God will wipe away tears from off all faces.[3] 25:8

Open ye the gates, that the righteous nation which keepeth the truth may enter in.
Thou wilt keep him in perfect peace, whose mind is stayed on thee.
26:2–3

[1] See *Revelation 14:8*, p. 58b.
[2] See *I Corinthians 15:54*, p. 53a.
[3] See *Revelation 21:4*, p. 58b.

Awake and sing.   *Isaiah 26:19*

Hide thyself as it were for a little moment, until the indignation be overpast.   *26:20*

Leviathan, that crooked serpent . . . the dragon that is in the sea.   *27:1*

For precept must be upon precept, precept upon precept; line upon line, line upon line; here a little, and there a little.   *28:10*

We have made a covenant with death, and with hell are we at agreement.   *28:15*

It shall be a vexation only to understand the report.   *28:19*

They are drunken, but not with wine; they stagger, but not with strong drink.   *29:9*

Their strength is to sit still.

Now go, write it before them in a table, and note it in a book, that it may be for the time to come for ever and ever.   *30:7–8*

The bread of adversity, and the water of affliction.   *30:20*

This is the way, walk ye in it.   *30:21*

Behold, a king shall reign in righteousness.   *32:1*

And a man shall be as an hiding place from the wind, and a covert from the tempest; as rivers of water in a dry place, as the shadows of a great rock in a weary land.   *32:2*

An habitation of dragons, and a court for owls.   *34:13*

The desert shall rejoice, and blossom as the rose.   *35:1*

Then the eyes of the blind shall be opened, and the ears of the deaf shall be unstopped.

Then shall the lame man leap as an hart, and the tongue of the dumb sing.   *35:5–6*

Sorrow and sighing shall flee away.   *35:10*

Thou trustest in the staff of this broken reed.   *Isaiah 36:6*

Incline thine ear, O Lord, and hear.   *37:17*

I shall go softly all my years in the bitterness of my soul.   *38:15*

Comfort ye, comfort ye my people.   *40:1*

Speak ye comfortably to Jerusalem, and cry unto her, that her warfare is accomplished, that her iniquity is pardoned: for she hath received of the Lord's hand double for all her sins.

The voice of him that crieth in the wilderness, Prepare ye the way of the Lord, make straight in the desert a highway for our God.[1]   *40:2–3*

Every valley shall be exalted, and every mountain and hill shall be made low: and the crooked shall be made straight, and the rough places plain.   *40:4*

All flesh is grass, and all the goodliness thereof is as the flower of the field.   *40:6*

The grass withereth, the flower fadeth:[2] but the word of our God shall stand for ever.   *40:8*

Get thee up into the high mountain . . . say unto the cities of Judah, Behold your God!   *40:9*

He shall feed his flock like a shepherd: he shall gather the lambs with his arm, and carry them in his bosom, and shall gently lead those that are with young.   *40:11*

The nations are as a drop of a bucket, and are counted as the small dust of the balance.   *40:15*

Have ye not known? have ye not heard? hath it not been told you from the beginning?   *40:21*

They that wait upon the Lord shall

[1] See *Matthew 3:3*, p. 39b. Also in *Mark 1:3*, *Luke 3:4* and *John 1:23*.
[2] See *Psalm 90:5–6*, p. 20a, and note.

renew their strength; they shall mount up with wings as eagles; they shall run, and not be weary; and they shall walk, and not faint. *Isaiah* 40:31

They helped every one his neighbour; and every one said to his brother, Be of good courage. 41:6

A bruised reed shall he not break, and the smoking flax shall he not quench. 42:3

Shall the clay say to him that fashioneth it, What makest thou? 45:9

O that thou hadst hearkened to my commandments! then had thy peace been as a river, and thy righteousness as the waves of the sea. 48:18

There is no peace, saith the Lord, unto the wicked. 48:22

Therefore the redeemed of the Lord shall return, and come with singing unto Zion. 51:11

Thou hast drunken the dregs of the cup of trembling. 51:17

Therefore hear now this. 51:21

How beautiful upon the mountains are the feet of him that bringeth good tidings, that publisheth peace. 52:7

They shall see eye to eye. 52:8

He is despised and rejected of men; a man of sorrows, and acquainted with grief. 53:3

Surely he hath borne our griefs, and carried our sorrows. 53:4

All we like sheep have gone astray. 53:6

He is brought as a lamb to the slaughter.[1] 53:7

Ho, everyone that thirsteth, come ye to the waters. 55:1

Behold, I have given him for a witness to the people, a leader and commander to the people. 55:4

Let the wicked forsake his way, and the unrighteous man his thoughts. *Isaiah* 55:7

For my thoughts are not your thoughts, neither are your ways my ways, saith the Lord. 55:8

Peace to him that is far off, and to him that is near. 57:19

Arise, shine; for thy light is come, and the glory of the Lord is risen upon thee. 60:1

A little one shall become a thousand, and a small one a strong nation. 60:22

Give unto them beauty for ashes, the oil of joy for mourning, the garment of praise for the spirit of heaviness. 61:3

I have trodden the winepress alone; and of the people there was none with me: for I will tread them in mine anger, and trample them in my fury; and their blood shall be sprinkled upon my garments, and I will stain all my raiment. 63:3

All our righteousnesses are as filthy rags; and we all do fade as a leaf. 64:6

We all are the work of thy hand. 64:8

I am holier than thou. 65:5

For, behold, I create new heavens and a new earth.[1] 65:17

And they shall build houses, and inhabit them; and they shall plant vineyards, and eat the fruit of them. They shall not build, and another inhabit; they shall not plant, and another eat. 65:21–22

As one whom his mother comforteth, so will I comfort you. 66:13

They were as fed horses in the morning: every one neighed after his neighbour's wife.
The Book of the Prophet Jeremiah 5:8

---

[1] Also in *Acts 8:32.*

[1] See *Revelation 21:1,* p. 58b.

Hear now this, foolish people, and without understanding; which have eyes, and see not; which have ears, and hear not. *Jeremiah 5:21*

But this people hath a revolting and a rebellious heart. 5:23

Saying, Peace, peace; when there is no peace. 6:14 *and* 8:11

Stand ye in the ways, and see, and ask for the old paths, where is the good way, and walk therein.[1] 6:16

Amend your ways and your doings. 7:3 *and* 26:13

The harvest is past, the summer is ended, and we are not saved. 8:20

Is there no balm in Gilead? 8:22

Oh that I had in the wilderness a lodging place of wayfaring men! 9:6

I will feed them . . . with wormwood, and give them water of gall to drink.[2] 9:15

Can the Ethiopian change his skin, or the leopard his spots? 13:23

Her sun is gone down while it was yet day. 15:9

A man of strife and a man of contention. 15:10

The sin of Judah is written with a pen of iron, and with the point of a diamond. 17:1

Cursed be the man that trusteth in man, and maketh flesh his arm, and whose heart departeth from the Lord.
For he shall be like the heath in the desert, and shall not see when good cometh; but shall inhabit the parched places in the wilderness, in a salt land and not inhabited.
Blessed is the man that trusteth in the Lord, and whose hope the Lord is.
For he shall be as a tree planted by the waters, and that spreadeth out her roots by the river, and shall not see

when heat cometh, but her leaf shall be green; and shall not be careful in the year of drought, neither shall cease from yielding fruit.[1] *Jeremiah 17:5–8*

The heart is deceitful above all things, and desperately wicked: who can know it? 17:9

As the partridge sitteth on eggs, and hatcheth them not; so he that getteth riches, and not by right, shall leave them in the midst of his days, and at his end shall be a fool. 17:11

Thou art my hope in the day of evil. 17:17

O earth, earth, earth, hear the word of the Lord. 22:29

The fathers have eaten a sour grape, and the children's teeth are set on edge.[2] 31:29

With my whole heart and with my whole soul. 32:41

And seekest thou great things for thyself? seek them not. 45:5

How doth the city sit solitary, that was full of people! how is she become as a widow!
The Lamentations of Jeremiah 1:1

She weepeth sore in the night, and her tears are on her cheeks: among all her lovers she hath none to comfort her. 1:2

Is it nothing to you, all ye that pass by? behold, and see if there be any sorrow like unto my sorrow. 1:12

It is good for a man that he bear the yoke in his youth. 3:27

As it were a wheel in the middle of a wheel.
The Book of the Prophet Ezekiel 1:16

As is the mother, so is her daughter. 16:44

---

[1] Stare super vias antiquas. — *The Vulgate*
[2] I will feed them with wormwood, and make them drink the water of gall. — *Jeremiah 23:15*

[1] See Amenemope, VI, p. 4b; see also *Psalm 1*, p. 16b.
[2] Also in *Ezekiel 18:2*.

The king of Babylon stood at the parting of the way.   *Ezekiel* 21:21

Can these bones live?   37:3

O ye dry bones, hear the word of the Lord.   37:4

Every man's sword shall be against his brother.   38:21

His legs of iron, his feet part of iron and part of clay.
The Book of Daniel 2:33

Shadrach, Meshach, and Abednego, fell down bound into the midst of the burning fiery furnace.   3:23

Nebuchadnezzar . . . was driven from men, and did eat grass as oxen.   4:33

Belshazzar the king made a great feast to a thousand of his lords.   5:1

And this is the writing that was written, MENE, MENE, TEKEL, UPHARSIN.
This is the interpretation of the thing: MENE; God hath numbered thy kingdom, and finished it.
TEKEL; Thou art weighed in the balances, and art found wanting.
PERES; Thy kingdom is divided, and given to the Medes and Persians.   5:25–28

According to the law of the Medes and Persians, which altereth not.   6:12

They brought Daniel, and cast him into the den of lions.   6:16

So Daniel was taken up out of the den, and no manner of hurt was found upon him, because he believed in his God.   6:23

The Ancient of days.   7:9 *and* 7:13

Many shall run to and fro, and knowledge shall be increased.   12:4

Ye are the sons of the living God.   *Hosea* 1:10

Like people, like priest.   4:9

After two days will he revive us: in the third day he will raise us up, and we shall live in his sight.   *Hosea* 6:2

He shall come unto us as the rain, as the latter and former rain unto the earth.   6:3

For I desired mercy, and not sacrifice; and the knowledge of God more than burnt offerings.   6:6

They have sown the wind, and they shall reap the whirlwind.   8:7

Ye have plowed wickedness, ye have reaped iniquity.   10:13

I drew them with . . . bands of love.   11:4

I have multiplied visions, and used similitudes, by the ministry of the prophets.   12:10

I will ransom them from the power of the grave; I will redeem them from death: O death, I will be thy plagues; O grave, I will be thy destruction.[1]   13:14

Your old men shall dream dreams, your young men shall see visions.
Joel 2:28

Multitudes in the valley of decision.   3:14

They sold the righteous for silver, and the poor for a pair of shoes.
Amos 2:6

Can two walk together, except they be agreed?   3:3

And Jonah was in the belly of the fish three days and three nights.
Jonah 1:17

What doth the Lord require of thee, but to do justly, and to love mercy, and to walk humbly with thy God?
Micah 6:8

The faces of them all gather blackness.[2]   *Nahum* 2:10

Write the vision, and make it plain

[1] See *I Corinthians* 15:54–55, p. 53a.
[2] The faces of them all are as the blackness of a kettle. — *Douay Bible* [1609], *Nahum* 2:10. The English version of the Roman Catholic Bible was first printed in Douay, France.

upon tables, that he may run that readeth it.   *Habakkuk 2:2*

The Lord is in his holy temple: let all the earth keep silence before him.
                                    2:20

Your fathers, where are they? And the prophets, do they live forever?
                        Zechariah 1:5

I have spread you abroad as the four winds of the heaven.   2:6

Not by might, nor by power, but by my spirit, saith the Lord of hosts.   4:6

For who hath despised the day of small things?   4:10

Behold, thy King cometh unto thee . . . lowly, and riding upon an ass.
                                    9:9

Prisoners of hope.   9:12

So they weighed for my price thirty pieces of silver.[1]   11:12

What are these wounds in thine hands? . . . Those with which I was wounded in the house of my friends.
                                    13:6

Have we not all one father? hath not one God created us?   *Malachi 2:10*

Behold, I will send my messenger, and he shall prepare the way before me.   3:1

Behold, the day cometh.   4:1

Healing in his wings.   4:2

Behold, I will send you Elijah the prophet before the coming of the great and dreadful day of the Lord.   4:5

THE APOCRYPHA[2]

And when they are in their cups, they forget their love both to friends

[1] See *Matthew 26:15*, p. 44b.
[2] These books form part of the sacred literature of the Alexandrian Jews, and with the exception of *II Esdras* are found interspersed with the Hebrew Scriptures in the ancient copies of the Septuagint, or Greek Version of the Old Testament. — *The Apocrypha According to the Authorized Version, Preface* (Oxford University Press)

and brethren, and a little after draw out swords.   *I Esdras 3:22*

Great is Truth, and mighty above all things.[1]   4:41

What is past I know, but what is for to come I know not.   *II Esdras 4:46*

Now therefore keep thy sorrow to thyself, and bear with a good courage that which hath befallen thee.   10:15

I shall light a candle of understanding in thine heart, which shall not be put out.   14:25

If thou hast abundance, give alms accordingly: if thou have but a little, be not afraid to give according to that little.   *Tobit 4:8*

Put on her garments of gladness.
                        Judith 10:3

The ear of jealousy heareth all things.
           The Wisdom of Solomon 1:10

Our time is a very shadow that passeth away.   2:5

Let us crown ourselves with rosebuds, before they be withered.   2:8

For God created man to be immortal, and made him to be an image of his own eternity.
Nevertheless through envy of the devil came death into the world.
                                 2:23-24

The souls of the righteous are in the hand of God, and there shall no torment touch them.
In the sight of the unwise they seemed to die: and their departure is taken for misery,
And their going from us to be utter destruction: but they are in peace.
For though they be punished in the sight of men, yet is their hope full of immortality.
And having been a little chastised, they shall be greatly rewarded: for God proved them, and found them worthy for himself.   3:1-5

[1] Magna est veritas et praevalet. — *The Vulgate, Book III* (uncanonical)

They that put their trust in him shall understand the truth.

The Wisdom of Solomon 3:9

Even so we in like manner, as soon as we were born, began to draw to our end.   5:13

For the hope of the ungodly is like dust that is blown away with the wind . . . and passeth away as the remembrance of a guest that tarrieth but a day.   5:14

For the very true beginning of her [wisdom] is the desire of discipline; and the care of discipline is love.
6:17

And when I was born, I drew in the common air, and fell upon the earth, which is of like nature; and the first voice which I uttered was crying, as all others do.   7:3

All men have one entrance into life, and the like going out.   7:6

The light that cometh from her [wisdom] never goeth out.   7:10

Who can number the sand of the sea, and the drops of rain, and the days of eternity?

The Wisdom of Jesus the Son of Sirach, or Ecclesiasticus, 1:2

To whom hath the root of wisdom been revealed?   1:6

For the Lord is full of compassion and mercy, longsuffering, and very pitiful, and forgiveth sins, and saveth in time of affliction.   2:11

The greater thou art, the more humble thyself.   3:18

Many are in high place, and of renown: but mysteries are revealed unto the meek.   3:19

Seek not out the things that are too hard for thee, neither search the things that are above thy strength.   3:21

Be not curious in unnecessary matters: for more things are shewed unto thee than men understand.   3:23

Profess not the knowledge . . . that thou hast not.

A stubborn heart shall fare evil at the last.   *Ecclesiasticus* 3:25–26

Wisdom exalteth her children, and layeth hold of them that seek her.

He that loveth her loveth life.
4:11–12

Observe the opportunity.   4:20

Be not as a lion in thy house, nor frantick among thy servants.

Let not thine hand be stretched out to receive, and shut when thou shouldest repay.   4:30–31

Set not thy heart upon thy goods; and say not, I have enough for my life.   5:1

Winnow not with every wind, and go not into every way.   5:9

Let thy life be sincere.   5:11

Be not ignorant of any thing in a great matter or a small.   5:15

If thou wouldest get a friend, prove him first.   6:7

A faithful friend is a strong defence: and he that hath found such an one hath found a treasure.   6:14

A faithful friend is the medicine of life.   6:16

If thou seest a man of understanding, get thee betimes unto him, and let thy foot wear the steps of his door.
6:36

Whatsoever thou takest in hand, remember the end, and thou shalt never do amiss.   7:36

Rejoice not over thy greatest enemy being dead, but remember that we die all.   8:7

Miss not the discourse of the elders.
8:9

Forsake not an old friend; for the new is not comparable to him: a new friend is as new wine; when it is old, thou shalt drink it with pleasure.
9:10

Pride is hateful before God and man. *Ecclesiasticus* 10:7

He that is to day a king to morrow shall die. 10:10

Pride was not made for men, nor furious anger for them that are born of a woman. 10:18

Be not overwise in doing thy business. 10:26

Many kings have sat down upon the ground; and one that was never thought of hath worn the crown. 11:5

In the day of prosperity there is a forgetfulness of affliction: and in the day of affliction there is no more remembrance of prosperity. 11:25

Judge none blessed before his death.[1] 11:28

A friend cannot be known in prosperity: and an enemy cannot be hidden in adversity. 12:8

How agree the kettle and the earthen pot together? 13:2

A rich man beginning to fall is held up of his friends: but a poor man being down is thrust also away by his friends. 13:21

The heart of a man changeth his countenance, whether it be for good or evil. 13:25

So is a word better than a gift. 18:16

Be not made a beggar by banqueting upon borrowing. 18:33

He that contemneth small things shall fall by little and little. 19:1

Whether it be to friend or foe, talk not of other men's lives. 19:8

A man's attire, and excessive laughter, and gait, shew what he is. 19:30

A tale out of season [is as] musick in mourning. 22:6

I will not be ashamed to defend a friend. 22:25

[1] See Solon, p. 69a, and note.

All wickedness is but little to the wickedness of a woman.
Ecclesiasticus 25:19

The discourse of fools is irksome. 27:13

Many have fallen by the edge of the sword: but not so many as have fallen by the tongue. 28:18

Better is the life of a poor man in a mean cottage, than delicate fare in another man's house. 29:22

There is no riches above a sound body. 30:16

Gladness of the heart is the life of a man, and the joyfulness of a man prolongeth his days. 30:22

Envy and wrath shorten the life, and carefulness bringeth age before the time. 30:24

Watching for riches consumeth the flesh, and the care thereof driveth away sleep. 31:1

Let thy speech be short, comprehending much in few words. 32:8

Consider that I laboured not for myself only, but for all them that seek learning. 33:17

Leave not a stain in thine honour. 33:22

Let the counsel of thine own heart stand. 37:13

Honour a physician with the honour due unto him for the uses which ye may have of him: for the Lord hath created him. 38:1

When the dead is at rest, let his remembrance rest; and be comforted for him, when his spirit is departed from him. 38:23

How can he get wisdom . . . whose talk is of bullocks? 38:25

Let us now praise famous men, and our fathers that begat us. 44:1

All these were honoured in their generations, and were the glory of their times.

There be of them, that have left a name behind them, that their praises might be reported.

And some there be, which have no memorial; who are perished, as though they had never been; and are become as though they had never been born; and their children after them.

Ecclesiasticus 44:7–9

Their bodies are buried in peace; but their name liveth for evermore.

44:14

His word burned like a lamp.

48:1

O all ye works of the Lord, bless ye the Lord: praise him and exalt him above all [1] for ever.

The Song of the Three Holy Children 35

Daniel had convicted them of false witness by their own mouth.

The History of Susanna 61

It is a foolish thing to make a long prologue, and to be short in the story itself. *The Second Book of the Maccabees* 2:32

When he was at the last gasp.

7:9

Speech finely framed delighteth the ears. *15:39*

THE NEW TESTAMENT

Behold, a virgin shall be with child, and shall bring forth a son, and they shall call his name Emmanuel, which being interpreted is, God with us.

The Gospel According to St. Matthew 1:23

Now when Jesus was born in Bethlehem of Judaea in the days of Herod the king, behold, there came wise men from the east to Jerusalem,

Saying, Where is he that is born King of the Jews? for we have seen his star in the east, and are come to worship him. *2:1–2*

[1] In the Book of Common Prayer (The Benedicite): "magnify him."

They saw the young child with Mary his mother, and fell down, and worshipped him: and . . . they presented unto him gifts; gold, and frankincense, and myrrh.

And being warned of God in a dream that they should not return to Herod, they departed into their own country another way. *Matthew 2:11–12*

Out of Egypt have I called my son. *2:15*

Rachel weeping for her children, and would not be comforted, because they are not.[1] *2:18*

He shall be called a Nazarene.

2:23

Repent ye: for the kingdom of heaven is at hand. *3:2*

The voice of one crying in the wilderness, Prepare ye the way of the Lord, make his paths straight.[2]

3:3

And his meat was locusts and wild honey. *3:4*

O generation of vipers, who hath warned you to flee from the wrath to come? *3:7*

Now also the axe is laid unto the root of the trees: therefore every tree which bringeth not forth good fruit is hewn down, and cast into the fire. *3:10*

The Spirit of God descending like a dove. *3:16*

This is my beloved Son, in whom I am well pleased. *3:17*

And when he had fasted forty days and forty nights, he was afterward an hungred. *4:2*

Follow me, and I will make you fishers of men. *4:19*

Blessed are the poor in spirit: for theirs is the kingdom of heaven. *5:3*

[1] Rahel weeping for her children refused to be comforted . . . because they were not. — *Jeremiah 31:15*
[2] See *Isaiah 40:3*, p. 32b.

Blessed are they that mourn: for they shall be comforted.

Blessed are the meek: for they shall inherit the earth.[1]

Blessed are they which do hunger and thirst after righteousness: for they shall be filled.

Blessed are the merciful: for they shall obtain mercy.

Blessed are the pure in heart: for they shall see God.

Blessed are the peacemakers: for they shall be called the children of God.

Blessed are they which are persecuted for righteousness' sake: for theirs is the kingdom of heaven.[2]

Matthew 5:4–10

Ye are the salt of the earth: but if the salt have lost his savour, wherewith shall it be salted?   5:13

Ye are the light of the world. A city that is set on an hill cannot be hid.

Neither do men light a candle, and put it under a bushel, but on a candlestick; and it giveth light unto all that are in the house.

Let your light so shine before men, that they may see your good works, and glorify your Father which is in heaven.

Think not that I am come to destroy the law, or the prophets: I am not come to destroy, but to fulfil.

5:14–17

Till heaven and earth pass, one jot or one tittle shall in no wise pass from the law, till all be fulfilled.   5:18

Whosoever looketh on a woman to lust after her hath committed adultery with her already in his heart.

And if thy right eye offend thee, pluck it out, and cast it from thee: for it is profitable for thee that one of thy members should perish, and not that thy whole body should be cast into hell.

And if thy right hand offend thee, cut it off.   5:28–30

[1] See *Psalm 37:11*, p. 18b.
[2] The Sermon on the Mount.
See Lao-Tzu, p. 74a.

Swear not at all; neither by heaven; for it is God's throne:

Nor by the earth; for it is his footstool.   *Matthew 5:34–35*

Resist not evil: but whosoever shall smite thee on thy right cheek, turn to him the other also.   5:39·

Love your enemies, bless them that curse you, do good to them that hate you, and pray for them which despitefully use you, and persecute you.

5:44

He maketh his sun to rise on the evil and on the good, and sendeth rain on the just and on the unjust.   5:45

Be ye therefore perfect, even as your Father which is in heaven is perfect.

5:48

When thou doest alms, let not thy left hand know what thy right hand doeth.   6:3

After this manner therefore pray ye: Our Father which art in heaven,[1] Hallowed be thy name.

Thy kingdom come. Thy will be done in earth, as it is in heaven.

Give us this day our daily bread.

And forgive us our debts, as we forgive our debtors.[2]

And lead us not into temptation, but deliver us from evil: For thine is the kingdom, and the power, and the glory, for ever. Amen.   6:9–13

Lay not up for yourselves treasures upon earth, where moth and rust doth corrupt, and where thieves break through and steal:

But lay up for yourselves treasures in heaven.   6:19–20

For where your treasure is, there will your heart be also.   6:21

The light of the body is the eye.

6:22

If therefore the light that is in thee

[1] Our Father, who art in heaven. — *Book of Common Prayer, Morning Prayer*
[2] And forgive us our trespasses, As we forgive those who trespass against us. — *Book of Common Prayer, Morning Prayer*

be darkness, how great is that darkness!　　　　　*Matthew 6:23*

No man can serve two masters: for either he will hate the one, and love the other; or else he will hold to the one, and despise the other. Ye cannot serve God and mammon.　　6:24

Is not the life more than meat, and the body than raiment?
Behold the fowls of the air: for they sow not, neither do they reap, nor gather into barns.　　　　6:25–26

Which of you by taking thought can add one cubit unto his stature?　　6:27

Consider the lilies of the field, how they grow; they toil not, neither do they spin.　　　　　　　　　6:28

Even Solomon in all his glory was not arrayed like one of these.　　6:29

Take therefore no thought for the morrow: for the morrow shall take thought for the things of itself. Sufficient unto the day is the evil thereof.
6:34

Judge not, that ye be not judged.
7:1

With what measure ye mete, it shall be measured to you again.
And why beholdest thou the mote that is in thy brother's eye, but considerest not the beam that is in thine own eye?　　　　　7:2–3

Thou hypocrite, first cast out the beam out of thine own eye.　　7:5

Neither cast ye your pearls before swine.　　　　　　　　　7:6

Ask, and it shall be given you; seek, and ye shall find; knock, and it shall be opened unto you.　　　　7:7

Or what man is there of you, whom if his son ask bread, will he give him a stone?　　　　　　　　　7:9

Therefore all things whatsoever ye would that men should do to you, do ye even so to them: for this is the law and the prophets.[1]　　　　7:12

[1] See Confucius, p. 72b.

Wide is the gate, and broad is the way, that leadeth to destruction.
Matthew 7:13

Strait is the gate, and narrow is the way, which leadeth unto life, and few there be that find it.　　　7:14

Beware of false prophets, which come to you in sheep's clothing, but inwardly they are ravening wolves.
7:15

By their fruits ye shall know them.
7:20

Not every one that saith unto me, Lord, Lord, shall enter into the kingdom of heaven; but he that doeth the will of my Father which is in heaven.
7:21

[The house] fell not: for it was founded upon a rock.　　　7:25

But the children of the kingdom shall be cast out into outer darkness: there shall be weeping and gnashing of teeth.　　　　　　　　　8:12

The foxes have holes, and the birds of the air have nests; but the Son of man hath not where to lay his head.
8:20

Follow me; and let the dead bury their dead.　　　　　　　8:22

Why are ye fearful, O ye of little faith?　　　　　　　　　8:26

The whole herd of swine ran violently down a steep place into the sea, and perished in the waters.　　8:32

He saw a man, named Matthew, sitting at the receipt of custom.
9:9

They that be whole need not a physician, but they that are sick.
9:12

I am not come to call the righteous, but sinners to repentance.　　9:13

Can the children of the bridechamber mourn, as long as the bridegroom is with them?　　　　　　　9:15

Neither do men put new wine into old bottles.   *Matthew* 9:17

The maid is not dead, but sleepeth. 9:24

The harvest truly is plenteous, but the labourers are few.   9:37

Go rather to the lost sheep of the house of Israel.   10:6

Freely ye have received, freely give. 10:8

Whosoever shall not receive you, nor hear your words, when ye depart out of that house or city, shake off the dust of your feet.   10:14

Be ye therefore wise as serpents, and harmless as doves.   10:16

Ye shall be hated of all men for my name's sake.   10:22

The disciple is not above his master, nor the servant above his lord. 10:24

Are not two sparrows sold for a farthing? and one of them shall not fall on the ground without your Father.
But the very hairs of your head are all numbered.   10:29–30

I came not to send peace, but a sword.   10:34

He that findeth his life shall lose it: and he that loseth his life for my sake shall find it.[1]   10:39

He that hath ears to hear, let him hear.   11:15

The Son of man came eating and drinking, and they say, Behold a man gluttonous, and a winebibber, a friend of publicans and sinners. But wisdom is justified of her children.   11:19

Come unto me, all ye that labour and are heavy laden, and I will give you rest.
Take my yoke upon you, and learn of me; for I am meek and lowly in heart: and ye shall find rest unto your souls.
For my yoke is easy, and my burden is light.   11:28–30

[1] See *Matthew 16:25*, p. 43a.

He that is not with me is against me.   *Matthew* 12:30

The tree is known by his fruit. 12:33

Out of the abundance of the heart the mouth speaketh.   12:34

Behold, a greater than Solomon is here.   12:42

Some seeds fell by the way side. 13:4

Because they had no root, they withered away.   13:6

But other fell into good ground, and brought forth fruit, some an hundredfold, some sixtyfold, some thirtyfold. 13:8

The care of this world, and the deceitfulness of riches.   13:22

The kingdom of heaven is like to a grain of mustard seed.   13:31

Pearl of great price.   13:46

Is not this the carpenter's son? 13:55

A prophet is not without honour, save in his own country.   13:57

The daughter of Herodias danced before them, and pleased Herod. 14:6

Give me here John Baptist's head in a charger.   14:8

We have here but five loaves, and two fishes.   14:17

And they did all eat, and were filled: and they took up of the fragments that remained twelve baskets full.   14:20

And in the fourth watch of the night Jesus went unto them, walking on the sea.   14:25

Be of good cheer; it is I; be not afraid.   14:27

O thou of little faith, wherefore didst thou doubt?   14:31

Of a truth thou art the Son of God.   14:33

Not that which goeth into the mouth defileth a man; but that which cometh out of the mouth, this defileth a man. *Matthew 15:11*

They be blind leaders of the blind. And if the blind lead the blind, both shall fall into the ditch. 15:14

The dogs eat of the crumbs which fall from their masters' table. 15:27

When it is evening, ye say, It will be fair weather: for the sky is red. 16:2

The signs of the times. 16:3

Thou art the Christ, the Son of the living God. 16:16

Thou art Peter, and upon this rock I will build my church; and the gates of hell shall not prevail against it.
And I will give unto thee the keys of the kingdom of heaven. 16:18–19

Get thee behind me, Satan. 16:23

Whosoever will save his life shall lose it: and whosoever will lose his life for my sake shall find it.[1]
For what is a man profited, if he shall gain the whole world, and lose his own soul? 16:25–26

Except ye be converted, and become as little children, ye shall not enter into the kingdom of heaven. 18:3

He rejoiceth more of that sheep, than of the ninety and nine which went not astray. 18:13

Where two or three are gathered together in my name, there am I in the midst of them.[2] 18:20

Until seventy times seven. 18:22

What therefore God hath joined together, let not man put asunder.[3] 19:6

If thou wilt be perfect, go and sell that thou hast, and give to the poor, and thou shalt have treasure in heaven. 19:21

[1] See *Matthew 10:39*, p. 42a.
[2] See *Book of Common Prayer, A Prayer of St. Chrysostom*, p. 60b.
[3] See *Book of Common Prayer, Solemnization of Matrimony*, p. 61b.

It is easier for a camel to go through the eye of a needle, than for a rich man to enter into the kingdom of God. *Matthew 19:24*

Many that are first shall be last; and the last shall be first. 19:30

Borne the burden and heat of the day. 20:12

Is it not lawful for me to do what I will with mine own? 20:15

Overthrew the tables of the money-changers. 21:12

My house shall be called the house of prayer; but ye have made it a den of thieves. 21:13

They made light of it. 22:5

Many are called, but few are chosen. 22:14

Render therefore unto Caesar the things which are Caesar's; and unto God the things that are God's. 22:21

Whosoever shall exalt himself shall be abased; and he that shall humble himself shall be exalted. 23:12

Woe unto you, scribes and Pharisees, hypocrites! for ye pay tithe of mint and anise and cummin. 23:23

Blind guides, which strain at a gnat, and swallow a camel. 23:24

Whited sepulchres, which indeed appear beautiful outward, but are within full of dead men's bones. 23:27

O Jerusalem, Jerusalem, thou that killest the prophets, and stonest them which are sent unto thee, how often would I have gathered thy children together, even as a hen gathereth her chickens under her wings, and ye would not! 23:37

Ye shall hear of wars and rumours of wars: see that ye be not troubled: for all these things must come to pass, but the end is not yet.
For nation shall rise against nation. 24:6–7

Abomination of desolation.
Matthew 24:15

Wheresoever the carcase is, there will the eagles be gathered together.
24:28

Heaven and earth shall pass away, but my words shall not pass away.
24:35

The one shall be taken, and the other left. 24:40

Then shall the kingdom of heaven be likened unto ten virgins, which took their lamps, and went forth to meet the bridegroom.
And five of them were wise, and five were foolish. 25:1–2

Well done, thou good and faithful servant . . . Enter thou into the joy of thy lord. 25:21

Unto every one that hath shall be given, and he shall have abundance: but from him that hath not shall be taken away even that which he hath.
25:29

And before him shall be gathered all nations: and he shall separate them one from another, as a shepherd divideth his sheep from the goats. 25:32

For I was an hungred, and ye gave me meat: I was thirsty, and ye gave me drink: I was a stranger, and ye took me in:
Naked, and ye clothed me: I was sick, and ye visited me: I was in prison, and ye came unto me. 25:35–36

Inasmuch as ye have done it unto one of the least of these my brethren, ye have done it unto me. 25:40

An alabaster box of very precious ointment. 26:7

To what purpose is this waste?
26:8

For ye have the poor always with you; but me ye have not always.[1]
26:11

What will ye give me, and I will deliver him unto you? And they covenanted with him for thirty pieces of silver.[1] *Matthew* 26:15

My time is at hand. 26:18

Verily I say unto you, that one of you shall betray me. 26:21

Lord, is it I? 26:22

It had been good for that man if he had not been born. 26:24

Jesus took bread, and blessed it, and brake it, and gave it to the disciples, and said, Take, eat; this is my body.
And he took the cup, and gave thanks, and gave it to them, saying, Drink ye all of it;
For this is my blood of the new testament, which is shed for many for the remission of sins. 26:26–28

This night, before the cock crow, thou shalt deny me thrice. 26:34

O my Father, if it be possible, let this cup pass from me: nevertheless, not as I will, but as thou wilt. 26:39

Could ye not watch with me one hour?
Watch and pray, that ye enter not into temptation: the spirit indeed is willing, but the flesh is weak.
26:40–41

He came to Jesus, and said, Hail, Master; and kissed him. 26:49

All they that take the sword shall perish with the sword. 26:52

Thy speech bewrayeth thee. 26:73

Then began he to curse and to swear, saying, I know not the man. And immediately the cock crew. 26:74

The potter's field, to bury strangers in. 27:7

Have thou nothing to do with that just man. 27:19

Let him be crucified. 27:22

[Pilate] took water, and washed his hands before the multitude, saying, I

[1] See *Deuteronomy 15:11*, p. 10b.

[1] See *Zechariah 11:12*, p. 36a.

am innocent of the blood of this just person: see ye to it. *Matthew* 27:24

His blood be on us, and on our children. 27:25

A place called Golgotha, that is to say, a place of a skull. 27:33

This is Jesus the King of the Jews. 27:37

He saved others; himself he cannot save. 27:42

Eli, Eli, lama sabachthani? that is to say, My God, my God, why hast thou forsaken me? [1] 27:46

And, behold, the veil of the temple was rent in twain from the top to the bottom; and the earth did quake, and the rocks rent. 27:51

His countenance was like lightning, and his raiment white as snow. 28:3

Go ye therefore, and teach all nations, baptizing them in the name of the Father, and of the Son, and of the Holy Ghost. 28:19

Lo, I am with you alway, even unto the end of the world. 28:20

There cometh one mightier than I after me, the latchet of whose shoes I am not worthy to stoop down and unloose.
The Gospel According to St. Mark 1:7

Arise, and take up thy bed, and walk. 2:9

The sabbath was made for man, and not man for the sabbath. 2:27

If a house be divided against itself, that house cannot stand. 3:25

The earth bringeth forth fruit of herself; first the blade, then the ear, after that the full corn in the ear. 4:28

What manner of man is this? 4:41

My name is Legion: for we are many. 5:9

[1] See *Psalm 22:1*, p. 17b.

Clothed, and in his right mind. *Mark* 5:15

My little daughter lieth at the point of death. 5:23

Knowing in himself that virtue had gone out of him. 5:30

I see men as trees, walking. 8:24

Lord, I believe; help thou mine unbelief. 9:24

Suffer the little children to come unto me, and forbid them not: for of such is the kingdom of God. 10:14

Which devour widows' houses, and for a pretense make long prayers. 12:40

And there came a certain poor widow, and she threw in two mites. 12:42

Watch ye therefore: for ye know not when the master of the house cometh, at even, or at midnight, or at the cockcrowing, or in the morning:
Lest coming suddenly he find you sleeping. 13:35–36

Go ye into all the world, and preach the gospel to every creature. 16:15

Hail, thou that art highly favoured, the Lord is with thee: blessed art thou among women.
The Gospel According to St. Luke 1:28

For with God nothing shall be impossible. 1:37

Blessed is the fruit of thy womb. 1:42

My soul doth magnify the Lord. 1:46

For he hath regarded the low estate of his handmaiden: for, behold, from henceforth all generations shall call me blessed. 1:48

He hath scattered the proud in the imagination of their hearts.
He hath put down the mighty from their seats, and exalted them of low degree. 1:51–52

He hath filled the hungry with good things; and the rich he hath sent empty away.　　　*Luke 1:53*

Blessed be the Lord God of Israel; for he hath visited and redeemed his people.　　　*1:68*

As he spake by the mouth of his holy prophets, which have been since the world began:
That we should be saved from our enemies, and from the hand of all that hate us.　　　*1:70–71*

Through the tender mercy of our God; whereby the dayspring from on high hath visited us,
To give light to them that sit in darkness and in the shadow of death.　　　*1:78–79*

And she brought forth her firstborn son, and wrapped him in swaddling clothes, and laid him in a manger; because there was no room for them in the inn.　　　*2:7*

There were in the same country shepherds abiding in the field, keeping watch over their flock by night.
And, lo, the angel of the Lord came upon them, and the glory of the Lord shone round about them: and they were sore afraid.
And the angel said unto them, Fear not: for, behold, I bring you good tidings of great joy, which shall be to all people.
For unto you is born this day in the city of David a Saviour, which is Christ the Lord.　　　*2:8–11*

Glory to God in the highest, and on earth peace, good will toward men.[1]
　　　2:14

Lord, now lettest thou thy servant depart in peace.　　　*2:29*

A light to lighten the Gentiles, and the glory of thy people Israel.　　　*2:32*

Wist ye not that I must be about my Father's business?　　　*2:49*

[1] The Douay Bible has "peace to men of good will."

Jesus increased in wisdom and stature, and in favour with God and man.　　　*Luke 2:52*

[The devil] shewed unto him all the kingdoms of the world in a moment of time.　　　*4:5*

Physician, heal thyself.　　　*4:23*

Woe unto you, when all men shall speak well of you!　　　*6:26*

Her sins, which are many, are forgiven; for she loved much.　　　*7:47*

Nothing is secret, that shall not be made manifest.　　　*8:17*

No man, having put his hand to the plow, and looking back, is fit for the kingdom of God.　　　*9:62*

Nor scrip, nor shoes.　　　*10:4*

Peace be to this house.　　　*10:5*

The labourer is worthy of his hire.
　　　10:7

I beheld Satan as lightning fall from heaven.　　　*10:18*

Many prophets and kings have desired to see those things which ye see, and have not seen them; and to hear those things which ye hear, and have not heard them.　　　*10:24*

A certain man went down from Jerusalem to Jericho, and fell among thieves.　　　*10:30*

A certain Samaritan . . . had compassion on him.　　　*10:33*

Go, and do thou likewise.　　　*10:37*

But Martha was cumbered about much serving.　　　*10:40*

But one thing is needful: and Mary hath chosen that good part, which shall not be taken away from her.　　　*10:42*

This is an evil generation: they seek a sign.　　　*11:29*

Soul, thou hast much goods laid up for many years; take thine ease, eat, drink, and be merry.[1]　　　*12:19*

Thou fool, this night thy soul shall be required of thee.　　　*12:20*

[1] See *Ecclesiastes 8:15*, p. 28b.

Let your loins be girded about, and your lights burning.   *Luke* 12:35

For unto whomsoever much is given, of him shall be much required: and to whom men have committed much, of him they will ask the more.   12:48

The poor, and the maimed, and the halt, and the blind.   14:21

Which of you, intending to build a tower, sitteth not down first, and counteth the cost, whether he have sufficient to finish it?   14:28

Rejoice with me; for I have found my sheep which was lost.   15:6

Wasted his substance with riotous living.   15:13

Bring hither the fatted calf, and kill it.   15:23

For this my son was dead, and is alive again; he was lost, and is found.   15:24

Son, thou art ever with me, and all that I have is thine.   15:31

The children of this world are in their generation wiser than the children of light.   16:8

He that is faithful in that which is least is faithful also in much: and he that is unjust in the least is unjust also in much.   16:10

The beggar died, and was carried by the angels into Abraham's bosom.   16:22

Between us and you there is a great gulf fixed.   16:26

It were better for him that a millstone were hanged about his neck, and he cast into the sea.   17:2

Remember Lot's wife.   17:32

God, I thank thee, that I am not as other men are.   18:11

God be merciful to me a sinner.   18:13

Out of thine own mouth will I judge thee.   19:22

If these should hold their peace, the stones would immediately cry out.   *Luke* 19:40

God forbid.   20:16

He is not a God of the dead, but of the living.   20:38

In your patience possess ye your souls.   21:19

The Son of man coming in a cloud with power and great glory.   21:27

This do in remembrance of me.   22:19

Not my will, but thine, be done.   22:42

For if they do these things in a green tree, what shall be done in the dry?   23:31

The place, which is called Calvary.   23:33

Father, forgive them; for they know not what they do.   23:34

Lord, remember me when thou comest into thy kingdom.   23:42

To day shalt thou be with me in paradise.   23:43

Father, into thy hands I commend my spirit.   23:46

He gave up the ghost.   *Ib.*

He was a good man, and a just.   23:50

Why seek ye the living among the dead?   24:5

Their words seemed to them as idle tales.   24:11

Did not our heart burn within us, while he talked with us?   24:32

In the beginning was the Word, and the Word was with God, and the Word was God.   *The Gospel According to St. John* 1:1

And the light shineth in darkness; and the darkness comprehended it not.   1:5

There was a man sent from God, whose name was John.　　*John 1:6*

The true Light, which lighteth every man that cometh into the world.
1:9

The Word was made flesh, and dwelt among us . . . full of grace and truth.　　1:14

No man hath seen God at any time.　　1:18

Behold the Lamb of God, which taketh away the sin of the world.
1:29

Can there any good thing come out of Nazareth?　　1:46

Hereafter ye shall see heaven open, and the angels of God ascending and descending upon the Son of man.
1:51

Woman, what have I to do with thee? mine hour is not yet come.
2:4

The water that was made wine.
2:9

When he had made a scourge of small cords, he drove them all out of the temple.　　2:15

Make not my Father's house an house of merchandise.　　2:16

Except a man be born again, he cannot see the kingdom of God.
3:3

The wind bloweth where it listeth, and thou hearest the sound thereof, but canst not tell whence it cometh, and whither it goeth: so is every one that is born of the Spirit.　　3:8

How can these things be?　　3:9

God so loved the world, that he gave his only begotten Son, that whosoever believeth in him should not perish, but have everlasting life.　　3:16

The hour cometh, and now is, when the true worshippers shall worship the Father in spirit and in truth.　　4:23

He was a burning and a shining light.　　*John 5:35*

Search the scriptures.　　5:39

What are they among so many?
6:9

Gather up the fragments that remain, that nothing be lost.　　6:12

I am the bread of life.　　6:35

It is the spirit that quickeneth.
6:63

Judge not according to the appearance.　　7:24

Never man spake like this man.
7:46

He that is without sin among you, let him first cast a stone at her.　　8:7

Neither do I condemn thee: go, and sin no more.　　8:11

I am the light of the world: he that followeth me shall not walk in darkness, but shall have the light of life.　　8:12

The truth shall make you free.
8:32

Ye are of your father the devil . . . there is no truth in him. . . . he is a liar, and the father of it.　　8:44

I must work the works of him that sent me, while it is day: the night cometh, when no man can work.
9:4

Whether he be a sinner or no, I know not: one thing I know, that, whereas I was blind, now I see.　　9:25

I am the door.　　10:9

I am come that they might have life, and that they might have it more abundantly.　　10:10

I am the good shepherd: the good shepherd giveth his life for the sheep.
10:11

Other sheep I have, which are not of this fold.　　10:16

I am the resurrection, and the life: he that believeth in me, though he were dead, yet shall he live:

And whosoever liveth and believeth in me shall never die.[1]

John 11:25–26

Jesus wept. *11:35*

It is expedient for us, that one man should die for the people. *11:50*

Yet a little while is the light with you. Walk while ye have the light, lest darkness come upon you. *12:35*

That thou doest, do quickly.

13:27

A new commandment I give unto you, That ye love one another.

13:34

Let not your heart be troubled: ye believe in God, believe also in me.
In my Father's house are many mansions: if it were not so, I would have told you. I go to prepare a place for you. *14:1–2*

I will come again, and receive you unto myself; that where I am, there ye may be also. *14:3*

I am the way, the truth, and the life. *14:6*

I will not leave you comfortless.

14:18

Peace I leave with you, my peace I give unto you: not as the world giveth, give I unto you. Let not your heart be troubled, neither let it be afraid.

14:27

Greater love hath no man than this, that a man lay down his life for his friends. *15:13*

Ye have not chosen me, but I have chosen you. *15:16*

Whither goest thou? [2] *16:5*

Ask, and ye shall receive, that your joy may be full. *16:24*

Be of good cheer; I have overcome the world. *16:33*

[1] Also in *Book of Common Prayer, Burial of the Dead.*
[2] Quo vadis? — *The Vulgate*

Pilate saith unto him, What is truth? *John 18:38*

Now Barabbas was a robber.

18:40

Behold the man! [1] *19:5*

Woman, behold thy son! *19:26*

It is finished. *19:30*

Touch me not.[2] *20:17*

Then saith he to Thomas . . . be not faithless, but believing. *20:27*

Blessed are they that have not seen, and yet have believed. *20:29*

Suddenly there came a sound from heaven as of a rushing mighty wind.
The Acts of the Apostles 2:2

There appeared unto them cloven tongues like as of fire, and it sat upon each of them.
And they were all filled with the Holy Ghost, and began to speak with other tongues. *2:3–4*

Silver and gold have I none; but such as I have give I thee. *3:6*

If this counsel or this work be of men, it will come to nought:
But if it be of God, ye cannot overthrow it. *5:38–39*

Thy money perish with thee.

8:20

In the gall of bitterness, and in the bond of iniquity. *8:23*

Saul, yet breathing out threatenings and slaughter against the disciples of the Lord. *9:1*

Saul, Saul, why persecutest thou me? *9:4*

It is hard for thee to kick against the pricks. *9:5*

He is a chosen vessel unto me.

9:15

Immediately there fell from his eyes as it had been scales. *9:18*

[1] Ecce homo. — *The Vulgate*
[2] Noli me tangere. — *The Vulgate*

What God hath cleansed, that call not thou common. *Acts* 10:15

God is no respecter of persons.[1]
10:34

The gods are come down to us in the likeness of men. 14:11

We also are men of like passions with you. 14:15

Come over into Macedonia, and help us. 16:9

Certain lewd fellows of the baser sort. 17:5

Ye men of Athens, I perceive that in all things ye are too superstitious.

For as I passed by, and beheld your devotions, I found an altar with this inscription, TO THE UNKNOWN GOD. 17:22–23

God that made the world, and all things therein, seeing that he is Lord of heaven and earth, dwelleth not in temples made with hands;
Neither is worshipped with men's hands, as though he needed any thing, seeing he giveth to all life, and breath, and all things;
And hath made of one blood all nations of men for to dwell on all the face of the earth. 17:24–26

For in him we live, and move, and have our being; as certain also of your own poets have said, For we are also his offspring.[2] 17:28

Your blood be upon your own heads. 18:6

Mighty in the Scriptures. 18:24

We have not so much as heard whether there be any Holy Ghost.
19:2

All with one voice about the space of two hours cried out, Great is Diana of the Ephesians. 19:34

It is more blessed to give than to receive. 20:35

[1] For there is no respect of persons with God. — *Romans* 2:11
[2] See Aeschylus, p. 78b; Cleanthes, p. 103b; Aratus, p. 104a; and Dante, p. 161b.

I am . . . a Jew of Tarsus, a city in Cilicia, a citizen of no mean city.
Acts 21:39

Brought up in this city at the feet of Gamaliel. 22:3

And the chief captain answered, With a great sum obtained I this freedom. And Paul said, But I was free born. 22:28

God shall smite thee, thou whited wall. 23:3

Revilest thou God's high priest?
23:4

I am a Pharisee, the son of a Pharisee. 23:6

A conscience void of offence toward God, and toward men. 24:16

When I have a convenient season, I will call for thee. 24:25

I appeal unto Caesar. 25:11

Paul, thou art beside thyself; much learning doth make thee mad.
26:24

I am not mad . . . but speak forth the words of truth and soberness.
26:25

For this thing was not done in a corner. 26:26

Almost thou persuadest me to be a Christian. 26:28

Wherein thou judgest another, thou condemnest thyself.
*The Epistle of Paul the Apostle
to the Romans* 2:1

These, having not the law, are a law unto themselves. 2:14

Where no law is, there is no transgression. 4:15

Who against hope believed in hope.
4:18

Where sin abounded, grace did much more abound. 5:20

Death hath no more dominion over him. 6:9

I speak after the manner of men.
                              Romans 6:19

The wages of sin is death; but the gift of God is eternal life.   6:23

The good that I would I do not: but the evil which I would not, that I do.[1]   7:19

Who shall deliver me from the body of this death?   7:24

Heirs of God, and joint-heirs with Christ.   8:17

For we know that the whole creation groaneth and travaileth in pain together until now.   8:22

All things work together for good to them that love God.   8:28

If God be for us, who can be against us?   8:31

Who shall separate us from the love of Christ?   8:35

Neither death, nor life, nor angels, nor principalities, nor powers, nor things present, nor things to come,

Nor height, nor depth, nor any other creature, shall be able to separate us from the love of God, which is in Christ Jesus our Lord.   8:38–39

Hath not the potter power over the clay, of the same lump to make one vessel unto honour, and another unto dishonour?   9:21

For who hath known the mind of the Lord?   11:34

Let love be without dissimulation.
                              12:9

Be kindly affectioned one to another with brotherly love.   12:10

Given to hospitality.   12:13

Be not wise in your own conceits. Recompense to no man evil for evil.   12:16–17

If it be possible, as much as lieth in you, live peaceably with all men.
                              12:18

Vengeance is mine; I will repay, saith the Lord.   *Romans* 12:19

Be not overcome of evil, but overcome evil with good.   12:21

The powers that be are ordained of God.   13:1

Render therefore to all their dues: tribute to whom tribute is due; custom to whom custom; fear to whom fear; honour to whom honour.

Owe no man anything, but to love one another.   13:7–8

Love is the fulfilling of the law.
                              13:10

The night is far spent, the day is at hand: let us therefore cast off the works of darkness, and let us put on the armour of light.

Let us walk honestly, as in the day; not in rioting and drunkenness, not in chambering and wantonness, not in strife and envying.

But put ye on the Lord Jesus Christ, and make not provision for the flesh, to fulfil the lusts thereof.[1]   13:12–14

Doubtful disputations.   14:1

Let every man be fully persuaded in his own mind.   14:5

For none of us liveth to himself, and no man dieth to himself.

For whether we live, we live unto the Lord; and whether we die, we die unto the Lord: whether we live therefore, or die, we are the Lord's.   14:7–8

Let us therefore follow after the things which make for peace.   14:19

We then that are strong ought to bear the infirmities of the weak, and not to please ourselves.   15:1

God hath chosen the foolish things of the world to confound the wise; and God hath chosen the weak things of the world to confound the things which are mighty.
          The First Epistle of Paul the Apostle to the Corinthians 1:27

---

[1] See Euripides, p. 84b, and Ovid, p. 129a.

[1] See St. Augustine, p. 147a, note 1.

As it is written,[1] Eye hath not seen, nor ear heard.   *I Corinthians 2:9*

I have planted, Apollos watered; but God gave the increase.   *3:6*

We are labourers together with God: ye are God's husbandry.   *3:9*

Every man's work shall be made manifest: for the day shall declare it, because it shall be revealed by fire; and the fire shall try every man's work of what sort it is.   *3:13*

For the temple of God is holy, which temple ye are.   *3:17*

We are made a spectacle unto the world, and to angels, and to men.   *4:9*

Absent in body, but present in spirit.   *5:3*

A little leaven leaveneth the whole lump.   *5:6*

It is better to marry than to burn.   *7:9*

The fashion of this world passeth away.   *7:31*

Knowledge puffeth up, but charity edifieth.   *8:1*

I am made all things to all men.   *9:22*

Know ye not that they which run in a race run all, but one receiveth the prize?   *9:24*

Let him that thinketh he standeth take heed lest he fall.   *10:12*

All things are lawful for me, but all things are not expedient.   *10:23*

The earth is the Lord's, and the fulness thereof.   *10:26*

If a woman have long hair, it is a glory to her.   *11:15*

Though I speak with the tongues of men and of angels, and have not charity,[1] I am become as sounding brass, or a tinkling cymbal.   *I Corinthians 13:1*

Though I have all faith, so that I could remove mountains, and have not charity, I am nothing.

And though I bestow all my goods to feed the poor, and though I give my body to be burned, and have not charity, it profiteth me nothing.

Charity suffereth long, and is kind; charity envieth not; charity vaunteth not itself, is not puffed up.   *13:2-4*

Beareth all things, believeth all things, hopeth all things, endureth all things.

Charity never faileth.   *13:7-8*

We know in part, and we prophesy in part.

But when that which is perfect is come, then that which is in part shall be done away.

When I was a child, I spake as a child, I understood as a child, I thought as a child: but when I became a man, I put away childish things.[2]

For now we see through a glass, darkly; but then face to face:[3] now I know in part; but then shall I know even as also I am known.

And now abideth faith, hope, charity, these three; but the greatest of these is charity.   *13:9-13*

If the trumpet give an uncertain sound, who shall prepare himself to the battle?   *14:8*

Let all things be done decently and in order.   *14:40*

And last of all he was seen of me also, as of one born out of due time.

For I am the least of the apostles, that am not meet to be called an apostle, because I persecuted the church of God.

---

[1] Men have not heard, nor perceived by the ear, neither hath the eye seen. — *Isaiah 64:4*

[1] In the Revised Standard Version *charity* throughout this chapter is translated as *love* — the love of mankind in the sense of the Greek *agapé* and the Latin *caritas*.

[2] See Homer, p. 65a.

[3] See *Genesis 32:30*, p. 7b.

But by the grace of God I am what I am.   *I Corinthians 15:8–10*

But now is Christ risen from the dead, and become the firstfruits of them that slept.

For since by man came death, by man came also the resurrection of the dead.

For as in Adam all die, even so in Christ shall all be made alive.
15:20–22

The last enemy that shall be destroyed is death.   15:26

Evil communications corrupt good manners.   15:33

Thou fool, that which thou sowest is not quickened, except it die.   15:36

One star differeth from another star in glory.   15:41

It is sown in corruption; it is raised in incorruption.   15:42

The first man is of the earth, earthy.
15:47

Behold, I show you a mystery; We shall not all sleep, but we shall all be changed,

In a moment, in the twinkling of an eye, at the last trump: for the trumpet shall sound, and the dead shall be raised incorruptible, and we shall be changed.

For this corruptible must put on incorruption, and this mortal must put on immortality.   15:51–53

Death is swallowed up in victory.[1]

O death, where is thy sting? O grave, where is thy victory?   15:54–55

Watch ye, stand fast in the faith, quit you like men, be strong.[2]   16:13

If any man love not the Lord Jesus Christ, let him be Anathema Maranatha.   16:22

Not of the letter, but of the spirit: for the letter killeth, but the spirit giveth life.

The Second Epistle of Paul the Apostle to the Corinthians 3:6

[1] See *Isaiah 25:8*, p. 31b, and *Hosea 13:14*, p. 35b.

[2] See *I Samuel 4:9*, p. 12a.

Seeing then that we have such hope, we use great plainness of speech.
II Corinthians 3:12

The things which are seen are temporal; but the things which are not seen are eternal.   4:18

We walk by faith, not by sight.
5:7

Now is the accepted time.   6:2

By honour and dishonour, by evil report and good report.   6:8

As having nothing, and yet possessing all things.[1]   6:10

God loveth a cheerful giver.   9:7

Though I be rude in speech.   11:6

For ye suffer fools gladly, seeing ye yourselves are wise.   11:19

Forty stripes save one.   11:24

A thorn in the flesh.[2]   12:7

My strength is made perfect in weakness.   12:9

The grace of the Lord Jesus Christ, and the love of God, and the communion of the Holy Ghost, be with you all.[3]   13:14

The right hands of fellowship.
The Epistle of Paul the Apostle to the Galatians 2:9

Weak and beggarly elements.
4:9

It is good to be zealously affected always in a good thing.   4:18

Ye are fallen from grace.   5:4

For the flesh lusteth against the Spirit, and the Spirit against the flesh: and these are contrary the one to the other: so that ye cannot do the things that ye would.   5:17

The fruit of the Spirit is love, joy, peace, longsuffering, gentleness, goodness, faith,

Meekness, temperance.   5:22–23

[1] Terence, p. 109a, and Wotton, p. 300b.

[2] See *Judges 2:3*, p. 11a.

[3] Also in *Book of Common Prayer, Morning Prayer* [end].

Every man shall bear his own burden.   *Galatians 6:5*

Be not deceived; God is not mocked: for whatsoever a man soweth, that shall he also reap.   6:7

Let us not be weary in well doing.   6:9

To be strengthened with might by his Spirit in the inner man.
The Epistle of Paul the Apostle to the Ephesians 3:16

Carried about with every wind of doctrine.   4:14

We are members one of another. Be ye angry, and sin not: let not the sun go down upon your wrath.   4:25–26

Speaking to yourselves in psalms and hymns and spiritual songs, singing and making melody in your heart to the Lord.[1]   5:19

Put on the whole armour of God.   6:11

For we wrestle not against flesh and blood, but against principalities, against powers, against the rulers of the darkness of this world, against spiritual wickedness in high places.
Wherefore take unto you the whole armour of God, that ye may be able to withstand in the evil day, and having done all, to stand.   6:12–13

To live is Christ, and to die is gain.
The Epistle of Paul the Apostle to the Philippians 1:21

Work out your own salvation with fear and trembling.   2:12

For it is God which worketh in you both to will and to do of his good pleasure.   2:13

This one thing I do, forgetting those things which are behind, and reaching forth unto those things which are before,
I press toward the mark.   3:13–14

[1] See *Book of Common Prayer, Morning Prayer (Venite)*, p. 59b.

Whose end is destruction, whose God is their belly, and whose glory is in their shame, who mind earthly things.   *Philippians 3:19*

The peace of God, which passeth all understanding, shall keep your hearts and minds through Christ Jesus.[1]   4:7

Whatsoever things are true, whatsoever things are honest, whatsoever things are just, whatsoever things are pure, whatsoever things are lovely, whatsoever things are of good report; if there be any virtue, and if there be any praise, think on these things.   4:8

I have learned, in whatsoever state I am, therewith to be content.   4:11

By him were all things created, that are in heaven, and that are in earth, visible and invisible . . . all things were created by him, and for him:
And he is before all things, and by him all things consist.
The Epistle of Paul the Apostle to the Colossians 1:16–17

Touch not; taste not; handle not.   2:21

Set your affection on things above, not on things on the earth.   3:2

Where there is neither Greek nor Jew, circumcision nor uncircumcision, Barbarian, Scythian, bond nor free: but Christ is all, and in all.   3:11

Fathers, provoke not your children to anger, lest they be discouraged.   3:21

Let your speech be alway with grace, seasoned with salt.   4:6

Luke, the beloved physician.   4:14

Labour of love.
The First Epistle of Paul the Apostle to the Thessalonians 1:3

Study to be quiet, and to do your own business.   4:11

The day of the Lord so cometh as a thief in the night.   5:2

[1] Also in *Book of Common Prayer, Holy Communion (Blessing)*.

Ye are all the children of light, and the children of the day: we are not of the night, nor of darkness.

I Thessalonians 5:5

Putting on the breastplate of faith and love; and for an helmet, the hope of salvation. 5:8

Pray without ceasing. 5:17

Prove all things; hold fast that which is good. 5:21

The law is good, if a man use it lawfully.

The First Epistle of Paul the Apostle to Timothy 1:8

Christ Jesus came into the world to save sinners; of whom I am chief.

1:15

For if a man know not how to rule his own house, how shall he take care of the church of God? [1] 3:5

Not greedy of filthy lucre. 3:8

Speaking lies in hypocrisy; having their conscience seared with a hot iron. 4:2

Every creature of God is good, and nothing to be refused, if it be received with thanksgiving. 4:4

Refuse profane and old wives' fables. 4:7

But if any provide not for his own, and specially for those of his own house, he hath denied the faith, and is worse than an infidel. 5:8

They learn to be idle, wandering about from house to house; and not only idle, but tattlers also and busybodies, speaking things which they ought not. 5:13

Drink no longer water, but use a little wine for thy stomach's sake.

5:23

We brought nothing into this world, and it is certain we can carry nothing out.[2] 6:7

The love of money is the root of all evil.[1] *I Timothy* 6:10

Fight the good fight of faith, lay hold on eternal life. 6:12

Rich in good works. 6:18

Science falsely so called. 6:20

For God hath not given us the spirit of fear; but of power, and of love, and of a sound mind.

The Second Epistle of Paul the Apostle to Timothy 1:7

A workman that needeth not to be ashamed. 2:15

Be instant in season, out of season.

4:2

I have fought a good fight, I have finished my course, I have kept the faith. 4:7

The Lord reward him according to his works. 4:14

Unto the pure all things are pure.

The Epistle of Paul to Titus 1:15

Making mention of thee always in my prayers.

The Epistle of Paul to Philemon 1:4

Who maketh his angels spirits, and his ministers a flame of fire.

The Epistle of Paul the Apostle to the Hebrews 1:7

The word of God is quick, and powerful, and sharper than any two-edged sword, piercing even to the dividing asunder of soul and spirit, and of the joints and marrow, and is a discerner of the thoughts and intents of the heart. 4:12

Strong meat belongeth to them that are of full age. 5:14

They crucify to themselves the Son of God afresh, and put him to an open shame. 6:6

---

[1] See Sophocles, p. 82a.

[2] Also in *Book of Common Prayer, Burial of the Dead.* See also *The Song of the Harp-Player,* p. 3a, and *Ecclesiastes 5:15,* p. 28a.

[1] See Sophocles, p. 82a, and Plato, p. 94a. Radix malorum est cupiditas. — CHAUCER, *The Canterbury Tales* [c. 1387], *The Pardoner's Prologue, l. 6*

Without shedding of blood is no remission.   *Hebrews 9:22*

Faith is the substance of things hoped for, the evidence of things not seen.   11:1

Wherefore seeing we also are compassed about with so great a cloud of witnesses . . . let us run with patience the race that is set before us,
Looking unto Jesus the author and finisher of our faith.   12:1–2

Whom the Lord loveth he chasteneth.   12:6

The spirits of just men made perfect.   12:23

Let brotherly love continue.
Be not forgetful to entertain strangers: for thereby some have entertained angels unawares.   13:1–2

The Lord is my helper, and I will not fear what man shall do unto me.   13:6

Jesus Christ the same yesterday, and to day, and for ever.   13:8

For here have we no continuing city, but we seek one to come.   13:14

To do good and to communicate forget not: for with such sacrifices God is well pleased.   13:16

Let patience have her perfect work, that ye may be perfect and entire, wanting nothing.
If any of you lack wisdom, let him ask of God.   *The General Epistle of James 1:4–5*

Blessed is the man that endureth temptation: for when he is tried, he shall receive the crown of life.   1:12

Every good gift and every perfect gift is from above, and cometh down from the Father of lights, with whom is no variableness, neither shadow of turning.   1:17

Be swift to hear, slow to speak, slow to wrath:

For the wrath of man worketh not the righteousness of God.   *James 1:19–20*

Be ye doers of the word, and not hearers only.   1:22

Unspotted from the world.   1:27

As the body without the spirit is dead, so faith without works is dead also.   2:26

How great a matter a little fire kindleth!   3:5

The tongue can no man tame; it is an unruly evil.   3:8

This wisdom descendeth not from above, but is earthly, sensual, devilish.   3:15

Resist the devil, and he will flee from you.   4:7

What is your life? It is even a vapour, that appeareth for a little time, and then vanisheth away.   4:14

Be patient therefore, brethren, unto the coming of the Lord. Behold, the husbandman waiteth for the precious fruit of the earth, and hath long patience for it, until he receive the early and latter rain.   5:7

Ye have heard of the patience of Job.   5:11

The effectual fervent prayer of a righteous man availeth much.   5:16

Hope to the end.   *The First Epistle General of Peter 1:13*

All flesh is as grass, and all the glory of man as the flower of grass. The grass withereth, and the flower thereof falleth away:
But the word of the Lord endureth for ever.[1]   1:24–25

Abstain from fleshly lusts, which war against the soul.   2:11

Honour all men. Love the brotherhood. Fear God. Honour the king.   2:17

---

[1] See *Isaiah 40:6, 8*, p. 32b.

Ornament of a meek and quiet spirit.   *I Peter* 3:4

Giving honour unto the wife, as unto the weaker vessel.   3:7

Charity shall cover the multitude of sins.   4:8

A crown of glory that fadeth not away.   5:4

Be sober, be vigilant; because your adversary the devil, as a roaring lion, walketh about, seeking whom he may devour.   5:8

And the day star arise in your hearts.
The Second Epistle General of Peter 1:19

The dog is turned to his own vomit again.   2:22

God is light, and in him is no darkness at all.
The First Epistle General of John 1:5

If we say that we have no sin, we deceive ourselves, and the truth is not in us.   1:8

He is antichrist, that denieth the Father and the Son.   2:22

Whoso hath this world's good, and seeth his brother have need, and shutteth up his bowels of compassion from him, how dwelleth the love of God in him?   3:17

He that loveth not knoweth not God; for God is love.   4:8

There is no fear in love; but perfect love casteth out fear.   4:18

Raging waves of the sea, foaming out their own shame; wandering stars, to whom is reserved the blackness of darkness for ever.
The General Epistle of Jude 13

I John, who also am your brother, and companion in tribulation, and in the kingdom and patience of Jesus Christ, was in the isle that is called Patmos, for the word of God, and for the testimony of Jesus Christ.
The Revelation of St. John the Divine 1:9

What thou seest, write in a book, and send it unto the seven churches which are in Asia.   1:11

And being turned, I saw seven golden candlesticks.   1:12

His feet like unto fine brass, as if they burned in a furnace; and his voice as the sound of many waters.   1:15

When I saw him, I fell at his feet as dead.   1:17

I am he that liveth, and was dead; and, behold, I am alive for evermore, Amen; and have the keys of hell and of death.   1:18

I have somewhat against thee, because thou hast left thy first love.   2:4

To him that overcometh will I give to eat of the tree of life.   2:7

Be thou faithful unto death, and I will give thee a crown of life.   2:10

He shall rule them with a rod of iron.   2:27

I will give him the morning star.   2:28

I will not blot out his name out of the book of life.   3:5

I know thy works, that thou art neither cold nor hot: I would thou wert cold or hot.
So then because thou art lukewarm, and neither cold nor hot, I will spew thee out of my mouth.   3:15–16

Behold, I stand at the door, and knock.   3:20

The first beast was like a lion, and the second beast like a calf, and the third beast had a face as a man, and the fourth beast was like a flying eagle.
And the four beasts had each of them six wings about him; and they were full of eyes within: and they rest

not day and night, saying, Holy, holy, holy, Lord God Almighty, which was, and is, and is to come.

Revelation 4:7–8

Thou hast created all things, and for thy pleasure they are and were created.

4:11

A book . . . sealed with seven seals.

5:1

He went forth conquering, and to conquer.

6:2

Behold a pale horse: and his name that sat on him was Death, and Hell followed with him.

6:8

Four angels standing on the four corners of the earth, holding the four winds of the earth.

7:1

Hurt not the earth, neither the sea, nor the trees.

7:3

All nations, and kindreds, and people, and tongues.

7:9

These are they which came out of great tribulation, and have washed their robes, and made them white in the blood of the lamb.

7:14

They shall hunger no more, neither thirst any more; neither shall the sun light on them, nor any heat.

7:16

The name of the star is called Wormwood.

8:11

The kingdoms of this world are become the kingdoms of our Lord and of his Christ.

11:15

There was war in heaven: Michael and his angels fought against the dragon; and the dragon fought and his angels,

And prevailed not.

12:7–8

The great dragon was cast out, that old serpent, called the Devil, and Satan, which deceiveth the whole world.

12:9

No man might buy or sell, save that

he had the mark, or the name of the beast.

Revelation 13:17

Babylon is fallen, is fallen, that great city.[1]

14:8

Blessed are the dead which die in the Lord . . . that they may rest from their labours.[2]

14:13

And he gathered them together into a place called in the Hebrew tongue Armageddon.

16:16

He is Lord of lords, and King of kings.

17:14

Another book was opened, which is the book of life.

20:12

I saw a new heaven and a new earth:[3] for the first heaven and the first earth were passed away; and there was no more sea.

And I John saw the holy city, new Jerusalem, coming down from God out of heaven, prepared as a bride adorned for her husband.

21:1–2

God shall wipe away all tears[4] from their eyes; and there shall be no more death, neither sorrow, nor crying, neither shall there be any more pain: for the former things are passed away.

21:4

There shall be no night there.

22:5

He that is unjust, let him be unjust still: and he which is filthy, let him be filthy still: and he that is righteous, let him be righteous still: and he that is holy, let him be holy still.

And, behold, I come quickly.

22:11–12

I am Alpha and Omega, the beginning and the end, the first and the last.

22:13

[1] See *Isaiah 21:9*, p. 31b.
[2] Also in *Book of Common Prayer, Burial of the Dead.*
[3] See *Isaiah 65:17*, p. 33b.
[4] See *Isaiah 25:8*, p. 31b.

THE MISSAL

Dominus vobiscum.
The Lord be with you.

Blessing

Mea culpa, mea culpa, mea maxima culpa.
Through my fault, through my fault, through my most grievous fault.

The Confiteor

Kyrie, eleison.
Lord, have mercy on us.

The Kyrie

Gloria in excelsis Deo. Et in terra pax hominibus bonae voluntatis.
Glory to God in the highest. And on earth peace to men of good will.[1]

The Gloria

Agnus Dei, qui tollis peccata mundi, miserere nobis.
O Lamb of God, who takest away the sins of the world, have mercy on us.[2]

Prayer

O felix culpa, quae talem ac tantum meruit habere Redemptorem.
O happy fault, which has deserved to have such and so mighty a Redeemer.[3]

Exsultet on Holy Saturday

THE BOOK OF
COMMON PRAYER[4]

Movable feasts.

Tables and Rules, p. xxxi

[1] See *Luke 2:14,* and note p. 46a.
[2] See *John 1:29,* p. 48a.
[3] This dates from the seventh century at the latest, and may be much older. It has been attributed to St. Augustine and St. Ambrose.
[4] It is a most invaluable part of that blessed "liberty wherewith Christ hath made us free," that in his worship different forms and usages may without offence be allowed, provided the substance of the Faith be kept entire; and that, in every Church, what cannot be clearly determined to belong to Doctrine must be referred to Discipline; and therefore, by common consent and authority, may be altered, abridged, enlarged, amended, or otherwise disposed of, as may seem most convenient for the edification

He is risen. The Lord is risen indeed.[1]

Morning Prayer, Easter, p. 5

The Scripture moveth us, in sundry places, to acknowledge and confess our manifold sins and wickedness.

Ib. Minister's Opening Words, p. 5

We have erred, and strayed from thy ways like lost sheep.

Ib. A General Confession, p. 6

We have left undone those things which we ought to have done; And we have done those things which we ought not to have done.   *Ib.*

Have mercy upon us, miserable offenders.   *Ib.*

Who desireth not the death of a sinner, but rather that he may turn from his wickedness and live.

*Ib. The Declaration of
Absolution, p. 7*

Let us come before his presence with thanksgiving; and show ourselves glad in him with psalms.[2]

Ib. Venite, p. 9

In his hand are all the corners of the earth; and the strength of the hills is his also.
The sea is his, and he made it; and his hands prepared the dry land.

Ib.

Glory be to the Father, and to the Son, and to the Holy Ghost;
As it was in the beginning, is now, and ever shall be, world without end.
Amen.   *Ib. Gloria Patri, p. 9*

of the people, "according to the various exigency of times and occasions." — *Preface to the edition for the Protestant Episcopal Church in the United States of America* [1789]
Also in *The Book of Common Prayer* is the prayer by Cardinal Newman on p. 598a.
Page numbers cited are for any printing of *The Book of Common Prayer.*
[1] He is risen. — *Mark 16:6*
The Lord is risen indeed. — *Luke 24:34*
[2] See *Ephesians 5:19,* p. 54a.

The noble army of Martyrs.
Morning Prayer, Te Deum, p. 10

I believe in God the Father Almighty, Maker of Heaven and earth: And in Jesus Christ his only Son our Lord: Who was conceived by the Holy Ghost, Born of the Virgin Mary: Suffered under Pontius Pilate, Was crucified, dead, and buried: He descended into hell; The third day he rose again from the dead: He ascended into heaven, And sitteth on the right hand of God the Father Almighty: From thence he shall come to judge the quick and the dead.

I believe in the Holy Ghost: The holy Catholic Church; The Communion of Saints: The Forgiveness of sins: The Resurrection of the body: And the Life everlasting.
Ib. Apostles' Creed, p. 15

Begotten of his Father before all worlds, God of God, Light of Light, Very God of very God; Begotten, not made; Being of one substance with the Father; By whom all things were made: Who for us men and for our salvation came down from heaven, And was incarnate by the Holy Ghost of the Virgin Mary, And was made man.
Ib. Nicene Creed, p. 16

O God, who art the author of peace and lover of concord, in knowledge of whom standeth our eternal life, whose service is perfect freedom; Defend us thy humble servants in all assaults of our enemies.
Ib. A Collect for Peace, p. 17

O God, the Creator and Preserver of all mankind, we humbly beseech thee for all sorts and conditions of men; that thou wouldest be pleased to make thy ways known unto them, thy saving health unto all nations.
Ib. A Prayer for All Conditions of Men, p. 18

We commend to thy fatherly goodness all those who are any ways afflicted, or distressed, in mind, body, or estate.
Ib. p. 19

We, thine unworthy servants, do give thee most humble and hearty thanks for all thy goodness and loving-kindness to us, and to all men; We bless thee for our creation, preservation, and all the blessings of this life; but above all, for thine inestimable love in the redemption of the world by our Lord Jesus Christ; for the means of grace, and for the hope of glory.
Morning Prayer, A General Thanksgiving, p. 19

Almighty God, who . . . dost promise that when two or three are gathered together in thy Name [1] thou wilt grant their requests; Fulfil now, O Lord, the desires and petitions of thy servants, as may be most expedient for them.
Ib. A Prayer of St. Chrysostom, p. 20

Lighten our darkness, we beseech thee, O Lord; and by thy great mercy defend us from all perils and dangers of this night.
Evening Prayer, A Collect for Aid against Perils, p. 31

From pride, vainglory, and hypocrisy; from envy, hatred, and malice, and all uncharitableness,
Good Lord, deliver us.
The Litany, p. 54

From all the deceits of the world, the flesh, and the devil. *Ib.*

From battle and murder, and from sudden death. *Ib.*

Give to all nations unity, peace, and concord. *Ib. p. 56*

The kindly fruits of the earth.
Ib. p. 57

Almighty God, unto whom all hearts are open, all desires known, and from whom no secrets are hid; Cleanse the thoughts of our hearts by the inspiration of thy Holy Spirit, that we may perfectly love thee, and worthily magnify thy holy Name.
Holy Communion, Collect, p. 67

---

[1] See *Matthew 18:20*, p. 43a.

We acknowledge and bewail our manifold sins and wickedness, Which we, from time to time, most grievously have committed, By thought, word, and deed, Against thy Divine Majesty, Provoking most justly thy wrath and indignation against us. We do earnestly repent, And are heartily sorry for these our misdoings; The remembrance of them is grievous unto us; The burden of them is intolerable.

> *Holy Communion, General Confession, p. 75*

Therefore with Angels and Archangels, and with all the company of heaven, we laud and magnify thy glorious Name; evermore praising thee.

> *Ib. Proper Preface, p. 77*

Miserable sinners.

> *Ib. The Exhortations, p. 86*

Read, mark, learn, and inwardly digest [the Scriptures].

> *Collect for the Second Sunday in Advent, p. 92*

Dost thou . . . renounce the devil and all his works, the vain pomp and glory of the world, with all covetous desires of the same, and the sinful desires of the flesh, so that thou wilt not follow, nor be led by them?

> *Holy Baptism, p. 276*

An outward and visible sign of an inward and spiritual grace.

> *Offices of Instruction, Questions on the Sacraments, p. 292*

Is not by any to be entered into unadvisedly or lightly; but reverently, discreetly, advisedly, soberly, and in the fear of God.

> *Solemnization of Matrimony, p. 300*

If any man can show just cause, why they may not lawfully be joined together, let him now speak, or else hereafter for ever hold his peace.

> *Ib.*

Wilt thou . . . forsaking all others, keep thee only unto her, so long as ye both shall live?   *Ib. p. 301*

To have and to hold from this day forward, for better for worse, for richer for poorer, in sickness and in health, to love and to cherish, till death us do part.

> *Solemnization of Matrimony, p. 301*

With this Ring I thee wed.

> *Ib. p. 302*

Those whom God hath joined together let no man put asunder.[1]

> *Ib. p. 303*

In the midst of life we are in death.[2]   *Burial of the Dead, p. 332*

Earth to earth, ashes to ashes, dust to dust; in sure and certain hope of the Resurrection unto eternal life.

> *Ib. p. 333*

The iron entered into his soul.

> *The Psalter, Psalm 105:18, p. 471*

THE BOOK OF COMMON PRAYER, ENGLISH

Grant that the old Adam in this Child may be so buried, that the new man may be raised up in him.

> *Public Baptism of Infants, Blessing on the Child*

To love, cherish, and to obey.

> *Solemnization of Matrimony*

With all my worldly goods I thee endow.   *Ib.*

THE UPANISHADS
800–500 B.C. [3]

Thou art that.[4]

> *Chandogya Upanishad 6.8.7, etc.*

---

[1] See *Matthew 19:6*, p. 43a.

[2] This is derived from a Latin antiphon, said to have been composed by Notker, a monk of St. Gall, in 911, while watching some workmen building a bridge at Martinsbrücke, in peril of their lives. It forms the groundwork of Luther's antiphon *De Morte*.

[3] Ancient Indian literary chronology is conjectural. The dates given are approximate.

[4] Tat tvam asi (Sanskrit). The context: That which is that subtle essence is the self of this All; it is the true; it is the Self. "Thou art that, O Svetaketu."

Lead me from the unreal to the real!

Lead me from darkness to light!

Lead me from death to immortality! [1]
Brihadaranyaka Upanishad 1.3.28

Not thus, not thus.[2] *Ib. 2.3.6*

This Self is the honey of all beings, and all beings are the honey of this Self. *Ib. 2.5.14*

The gods love the obscure and hate the obvious.[3] *Ib. 4.2.2*

Da da da [4] (that is) Be subdued, Give, Be merciful.[5]

If the slayer thinks he slays,
If the slain thinks he is slain,
Both these do not understand:
He slays not, is not slain.[6]
Katha Upanishad 2.19

Om.[7] *Passim*

Santi.[8] *Passim*

HOMER
C. 700 B.C.

Sing, goddess, the wrath of Peleus' son Achilles, a destroying wrath which brought upon the Achaeans myriad woes, and sent forth to Hades many valiant souls of heroes.
The Iliad, bk. I, l. 1

And the plan of Zeus was being accomplished. *I, 5*

---

[1] Translated by F. MAX MÜLLER.

[2] Neti neti. The only possible description of the world soul self. The context: Not thus, not thus; for there is nothing else higher than this "not thus."

[3] Translated by R. C. ZAEHNER.

[4] The voice of the thunder. The full Sanskrit is: Da da da iti. Damyata datta dayadhvamiti. See T. S. Eliot, *The Waste Land,* lines 400–433, and note.

[5] Translated by F. MAX MÜLLER.

[6] See Emerson, *Brahma,* p. 604a. *Bhagavad-Gītā 2.19* is almost identical.

[7] Om is a sacred syllable used especially to begin and end a scriptural recitation.

[8] Santi means "peace." T. S. Eliot, in his note to line 434 of *The Waste Land,* says, " 'The Peace which passeth understanding' is our equivalent to this word."

A dream, too, is from Zeus.
The Iliad, bk. I, l. 63

He knew the things that were and the things that would be and the things that had been before. *I, 70*

If you are very valiant, it is a god, I think, who gave you this gift.
I, 178

Speaking, he addressed her winged words. *I, 201 and elsewhere*

Whoever obeys the gods, to him they particularly listen. *I, 218*

From his tongue flowed speech sweeter than honey. *I, 249*

Rosy-fingered dawn appeared, the early-born. *I, 477 and elsewhere*

The son of Kronos [Zeus] spoke, and nodded with his darkish brows, and immortal locks fell forward from the lord's deathless head, and he made great Olympus tremble. *I, 528*

The Olympian is a difficult foe to oppose. *I, 589*

Uncontrollable laughter arose among the blessed gods.[1] *I, 599*

A councilor ought not to sleep the whole night through, a man to whom the populace is entrusted, and who has many responsibilities. *II, 24*

Proud is the spirit of Zeus-fostered kings — their honor comes from Zeus, and Zeus, god of council, loves them.
II, 196

A multitude of rulers is not a good thing. Let there be one ruler, one king. *II, 204*

He [Thersites] was the ugliest man who came to Ilium. *II, 216*

Yet with his powers of augury he [Chromis] did not save himself from dark death. *II, 859*

The glorious gifts of the gods are not to be cast aside. *III, 65*

Young men's minds are always changeable, but when an old man is

---

[1] Also in *Odyssey VIII: 326.*

concerned in a matter, he looks both before and after.
The Iliad, bk. III, l. 108

Like cicadas, which sit upon a tree in the forest and pour out their piping voices, so the leaders of Trojans were sitting on the tower.   III, 151

There is no reason to blame the Trojans and the well-greaved Achaeans that for such a woman they long suffer woes.   III, 156

Words like winter snowflakes.
III, 222

The sun, which sees all things and hears all things.   III, 277

Son of Atreus, what manner of speech has escaped the barrier of your teeth?   IV, 350

Far away in the mountains a shepherd hears their thundering.
IV, 455

He lives not long who battles with the immortals, nor do his children prattle about his knees when he has come back from battle and the dread fray.[1]   V, 407

Not at all similar are the race of the immortal gods and the race of men who walk upon the earth.[2]   V, 441

Great-hearted Stentor with brazen voice, who could shout as loud as fifty other men.   V, 785

He was a wealthy man, and kindly to his fellow men; for dwelling in a house by the side of the road, he used to entertain all comers.   VI, 14

A generation of men is like a generation of leaves: the wind scatters some leaves upon the ground, while others the burgeoning wood brings forth — and the season of spring comes on. So of men one generation springs forth and another ceases.[3]   VI, 146

Always to be bravest and to be preeminent above others.   VI, 208

[1] See Thomas Gray, p. 440a.
[2] See Xenophanes, p. 70b.
[3] See Pindar, p. 79b, and Aristophanes, p. 91b.

Victory shifts from man to man.
The Iliad, bk. VI, l. 339

May men say, "He is far greater than his father," when he returns from battle.   VI, 479

Smiling through tears.   VI, 484

Attach a golden chain from heaven, and all of you take hold of it, you gods and goddesses, yet would you not be able to drag Zeus the most high from heaven to earth.   VIII, 19

Hades is relentless and unyielding.
IX, 158

Hateful to me as the gates of Hades is that man who hides one thing in his heart and speaks another.   IX, 312

Even when someone battles hard, there is an equal portion for one who lingers behind, and in the same honor are held both the coward and the brave man; the idle man and he who has done much meet death alike.
IX, 318

To be both a speaker of words and a doer of deeds.[1]   IX, 443

Prayers are the daughters of mighty Zeus, lame and wrinkled and slanting-eyed.   IX, 502

A companion's words of persuasion are effective.   XI, 793

It was built against the will of the immortal gods, and so it did not last for long.   XII, 8

The single best augury is to fight for one's country.   XII, 243

There is a strength in the union even of very sorry men.   XIII, 237

There is a fullness of all things, even of sleep and of love.   XIII, 636

You will certainly not be able to take the lead in all things yourself, for to one man a god has given deeds of war, and to another the dance, to another the lyre and song, and in another wide-sounding Zeus puts a good mind.
XIII, 729

[1] See *James 1:22,* p. 56b.

It is not possible to fight beyond your strength, even if you strive.

The Iliad, bk. XIII, l. 787

She [Aphrodite] spoke and loosened from her bosom the embroidered girdle of many colors into which all her allurements were fashioned. In it was love and in it desire and in it blandishing persuasion which steals the mind even of the wise. XIV, 214

There she met sleep, the brother of death.[1] XIV, 231 *and* XVI, 672

Ocean, who is the source of all.

XIV, 246

The hearts of the noble may be turned [by entreaty]. XV, 203

It is not unseemly for a man to die fighting in defense of his country.[2]

XV, 496

Of men who have a sense of honor, more come through alive than are slain, but from those who flee comes neither glory nor any help. XV, 563

The outcome of the war is in our hands; the outcome of words is in the council. XVI, 630

But he, mighty man, lay mightily in the whirl of dust, forgetful of his horsemanship. XVI, 775

Once harm has been done, even a fool understands it. XVII, 32

The most preferable of evils.[3]

XVII, 105

Surely there is nothing more wretched than a man, of all the things

which breathe and move upon the earth.[1] *The Iliad, bk. XVII, l. 446*

Sweeter it [wrath] is by far than the honeycomb dripping with sweetness, and spreads through the hearts of men. XVIII, 109

I too shall lie in the dust when I am dead, but now let me win noble renown. XVIII, 120

Zeus does not bring all men's plans to fulfillment. XVIII, 328

The Erinyes, who exact punishment of men underground if one swears a false oath. XIX, 259

Not even Achilles will bring all his words to fulfillment. XX, 369

Miserable mortals who, like leaves, at one moment flame with life, eating the produce of the land, and at another moment weakly perish. XXI, 463

It is entirely seemly for a young man killed in battle to lie mangled by the bronze spear. In his death all things appear fair. But when dogs shame the gray head and gray chin and nakedness of an old man killed, it is the most piteous thing that happens among wretched mortals. XXII, 71

Then the father held out the golden scales, and in them he placed two fates of dread death. XXII, 209

There are no compacts between lions and men, and wolves and lambs have no concord. XXII, 262

By the ships there lies a dead man, unwept, unburied: Patroclus.[2]

XXII, 386

Remembering this, he wept bitterly, lying now on his side, now on his back, now on his face. XXIV, 9

The fates have given mankind a patient soul. XXIV, 49

Thus have the gods spun the thread for wretched mortals: that they live in

[1] Sleep, the brother of Death. — HESIOD [c. 700 B.C.], *The Theogony, l. 756*

See Virgil, p. 119a; Daniel, p. 210b; Shakespeare, p. 284a; and Shelley, p. 568a.

Sleep, Death's twin brother. — TENNYSON, *In Memoriam* [1850], *pt. LXVIII*

[2] See Horace, p. 121b.

[3] See Aristotle, p. 97b.

Of two evils, the least should be chosen. — CICERO [106–43 B.C.], *De Officiis III, 1*

Of harmes two, the lesse is for to chese. — CHAUCER, *Troilus and Criseyde* [1372–1386], *bk. II, l. 470*

Of two evils the less is always to be chosen. — THOMAS À KEMPIS [1380–1471], *Imitation of Christ, bk. III, ch. 12*

[1] See Aristophanes, p. 91b.

[2] See Horace, p. 122b; Chaucer, p. 164b; Shakespeare, p. 260a; Milton, p. 343b; Scott, p. 519a; and Byron, p. 557b.

grief while they themselves are without cares; for two jars stand on the floor of Zeus of the gifts which he gives, one of evils and another of blessings.

The Iliad, bk. XXIV, l. 525

Tell me, muse, of the man of many resources who wandered far and wide after he sacked the holy citadel of Troy, and he saw the cities and learned the thoughts of many men, and on the sea he suffered in his heart many woes.

The Odyssey, bk. I, l. 1

By their own follies they perished, the fools.   I, 7

Look now how mortals are blaming the gods, for they say that evils come from us, but in fact they themselves have woes beyond their share because of their own follies.   I, 32

Surely these things lie on the knees of the gods.   I, 267

You ought not to practice childish ways, since you are no longer that age.[1]   I, 296

For rarely are sons similar to their fathers: most are worse, and a few are better than their fathers.   II, 276

Gray-eyed Athena sent them a favorable breeze, a fresh west wind, singing over the wine-dark sea.   II, 420

A young man is embarrassed to question an older one.   III, 24

All men have need of the gods.
       III, 48

The minds of the everlasting gods are not changed suddenly.   III, 147

A small rock holds back a great wave.   III, 296

No mortal could vie with Zeus, for his mansions and his possessions are deathless.   IV, 78

She [Helen] threw into the wine which they were drinking a drug which takes away grief and passion and brings forgetfulness of all ills.   IV, 220

[1] See *I Corinthians 13:11*, p. 52b.

The immortals will send you to the Elysian plain at the ends of the earth, where fair-haired Rhadamanthys is. There life is supremely easy for men. No snow is there, nor ever heavy winter storm, nor rain, and Ocean is ever sending gusts of the clear-blowing west wind to bring coolness to men.

The Odyssey, bk. IV, l. 563

Olympus, where they say there is an abode of the gods, ever unchanging: it is neither shaken by winds nor ever wet with rain, nor does snow come near it, but clear weather spreads cloudless about it, and a white radiance stretches above it.[1]   VI, 42

May the gods grant you all things which your heart desires, and may they give you a husband and a home and gracious concord, for there is nothing greater and better than this — when a husband and wife keep a household in oneness of mind, a great woe to their enemies and joy to their friends, and win high renown.   VI, 180

All strangers and beggars are from Zeus, and a gift, though small, is precious.[2]   VI, 207

Their ships are swift as a bird or a thought.   VII, 36

We are quick to flare up, we races of men on the earth.   VII, 307

So it is that the gods do not give all men gifts of grace — neither good looks nor intelligence nor eloquence.
       VIII, 167

Evil deeds do not prosper; the slow man catches up with the swift.
       VIII, 329

Even if you gods, and all the goddesses too, should be looking on, yet

[1] The majesty of the gods is revealed, and their peaceful abodes, which neither the winds shake nor clouds soak with showers, nor does the snow congealed with biting frost besmirch them with its white fall, but an ever cloudless sky vaults them over, and smiles with light bounteously spread abroad. — LUCRETIUS [95–55 B.C.], *De Rerum Natura III, 18*

[2] See *Theocritus*, p. 104a.

would I be glad to sleep with golden Aphrodite.

    The Odyssey, bk. VIII, l. 341

Among all men on the earth bards have a share of honor and reverence, because the muse has taught them songs and loves the race of bards.

    VIII, 479

Thus she spoke; and I longed to embrace my dead mother's ghost. Thrice I tried to clasp her image, and thrice it slipped through my hands, like a shadow, like a dream.[1]   *XI, 204*

They strove to pile Ossa on Olympus, and on Ossa Pelion with its leafy forests, that they might scale the heavens.[2]   *XI, 315*

There is a time for many words, and there is also a time for sleep.[3]

    XI, 379

There is nothing more dread and more shameless than a woman who plans such deeds in her heart as the foul deed which she plotted when she contrived her husband's murder.

    XI, 427

In the extravagance of her evil she has brought shame both on herself and on all women who will come after her, even on one who is virtuous.

    XI, 432

Therefore don't you be gentle to your wife either. Don't tell her everything you know, but tell her one thing and keep another thing hidden.

    XI, 441

There is no more trusting in women.   *XI, 456*

I should rather labor as another's serf, in the home of a man without for-

tune, one whose livelihood was meager, than rule over all the departed dead.

    The Odyssey, bk. XI, l. 489

Friends, we have not till now been unacquainted with misfortunes.

    XII, 208

It is tedious to tell again tales already plainly told.[1]   *XII, 452*

The wine urges me on, the bewitching wine, which sets even a wise man to singing and to laughing gently and rouses him up to dance and brings forth words which were better unspoken.

    XIV, 463

It is equally wrong to speed a guest who does not want to go, and to keep one back who is eager. You ought to make welcome the present guest, and send forth the one who wishes to go.[2]

    XV, 72

Even his griefs are a joy long after to one that remembers all that he wrought and endured.[3]   *XV, 400*

God always pairs off like with like.[4]

    XVII, 218

Bad herdsmen ruin their flocks.

    XVII, 246

Wide-sounding Zeus takes away half a man's worth on the day when slavery comes upon him.   *XVII, 322*

Then dark death seized Argus, as soon as he had seen Odysseus in the twentieth year.   *XVII, 326*

The gods, likening themselves to all kinds of strangers, go in various disguises from city to city, observing the wrongdoing and the righteousness of men.   *XVII, 485*

Nothing feebler than a man does the earth raise up, of all the things which breathe and move on the earth, for he believes that he will never suffer evil in the future, as long as the gods give him success and he flourishes in his

---

[1] See Virgil, p. 118b.

[2] See Virgil, p. 117a.

Then the omnipotent Father with his thunder made Olympus tremble, and from Ossa hurled Pelion. — OVID [43 B.C.–A.D. 17], *Metamorphoses I, l. 154*

I would have you call to mind the strength of the ancient giants, that undertook to lay the high mountain Pelion on the top of Ossa, and set among those the shady Olympus. — RABELAIS, *Works, bk. IV* [1548], *ch. 38*

[3] See *Ecclesiastes 3:7*, p. 27b.

---

[1] See Shakespeare, p. 236b.

[2] See Pope, p. 405b.

[3] See Virgil, p. 117b.

[4] See Heywood, p. 183a.

strength; but when the blessed gods bring sorrows too to pass, even these he bears, against his will, with steadfast spirit, for the thoughts of earthly men are like the day which the father of gods and men brings upon them.

The Odyssey, bk. XVIII, l. 130

Men flourish only for a moment.[1]

XIX, 328

Dreams surely are difficult, confusing, and not everything in them is brought to pass for mankind. For fleeting dreams have two gates: one is fashioned of horn and one of ivory. Those which pass through the one of sawn ivory are deceptive, bringing tidings which come to nought, but those which issue from the one of polished horn bring true results when a mortal sees them.[2]   *XIX,* 560

Endure, my heart: you once endured something even more dreadful.

XX, 18

Your heart is always harder than a stone.   *XXIII,* 103

Therefore the fame of her excellence will never perish, and the immortals will fashion among earthly men a gracious song in honor of faithful Penelope.   *XXIV,* 196

HESIOD
c. 700 B.C.

With the muses of Helicon let us begin our singing.

The Theogony, l. 1

They once taught Hesiod beauteous song, when he was shepherding his sheep below holy Helicon.   *Ib.* 22

We know how to speak many falsehoods which resemble real things, but we know, when we will, how to speak true things.   *Ib.* 27

On his tongue they pour sweet dew, and from his mouth flow gentle words.

Ib. 83

Love, who is most beautiful among the immortal gods, the melter of limbs, overwhelms in their hearts the intelligence and wise counsel of all gods and all men.   *The Theogony, l.* 120

From their eyelids as they glanced dripped love.   *Ib.* 910

There was not after all a single kind of strife, but on the earth there are two kinds: one of them a man might praise when he recognized her, but the other is blameworthy.

Works and Days, l. 11

Potter bears a grudge against potter, and craftsman against craftsman, and beggar is envious of beggar, and bard of bard.[1]   *Ib.* 25

Fools, they do not even know how much more is the half than the whole.[2]

Ib. 40

Often an entire city has suffered because of an evil man.   *Ib.* 240

He harms himself who does harm to another, and the evil plan is most harmful to the planner.   *Ib.* 265

Badness you can get easily, in quantity: the road is smooth, and it lies close by. But in front of excellence the immortal gods have put sweat, and long and steep is the way to it, and rough at first. But when you come to the top, then it is easy, even though it is hard.[3]

Ib. 287

A bad neighbor is a misfortune, as much as a good one is a great blessing.

Ib. 346

Do not seek evil gains; evil gains are the equivalent of disaster.   *Ib.* 352

If you should put even a little on a little, and should do this often, soon this too would become big.[4]   *Ib.* 361

At the beginning of a cask and at the end take your fill; in the middle be sparing.   *Ib.* 368

---

[1] See Gay, p. 401b, and Meredith, p. 730a.
[2] See Browning, p. 664b, and note.
[3] See *Matthew 7:13–14*, p. 41b.
[4] See Chaucer, p. 169b.

[1] See *Psalm 103:15*, p. 21a.
[2] See Virgil, p. 119a.

The dawn speeds a man on his journey, and speeds him too in his work.
Works and Days, l. 579

Observe due measure, for right timing is in all things the most important factor.   *Ib.* 694

Gossip is mischievous, light and easy to raise, but grievous to bear and hard to get rid of. No gossip ever dies away entirely, if many people voice it: it too is a kind of divinity.   *Ib.* 761

ARCHILOCHUS
c. 680 B.C.

Some Saian glories in the shield which I left beside a bush, poor blameless weapon, against my will. But I have saved myself — what care I for that shield? Away with it! I'll get another one no worse.   *Fragment* 6

Old women should not seek to be perfumed.   *Fragment* 27

The fox knows many things, but the hedgehog knows one great thing.[1]
Fragment 103

THE SEVEN SAGES[2]
c. 650 – c. 600 B.C.

Know thyself.
Inscription at the Delphic Oracle. From PLUTARCH, *Morals*

Hesiod might as well have kept his breath to cool his pottage.[3]
PERIANDER. *From* PLUTARCH, *The Banquet of the Seven Wise Men, sec.* 14

Every one of you hath his particular

---

plague, and my wife is mine; and he is very happy who hath this only.
PITTACUS. *From* PLUTARCH, *Morals, On the Tranquillity of the Mind*

Nothing too much.[1]
From DIOGENES LAERTIUS, *bk. I, sec.* 63

Do not speak ill of the dead.[2]
Ib. 70

Not even the gods fight against necessity.   *Ib.* 77

Know the right timing.   *Ib.* 79

Rule will show the man.
BIAS. *From* ARISTOTLE, *Nichomachean Ethics* V, 1

MIMNERMUS
c. 650 – c. 590 B.C.

What life is there, what delight, without golden Aphrodite?
Fragment 1

SOLON
c. 638 – c. 559 B.C.

Many evil men are rich, and good men poor, but we shall not exchange with them our excellence for riches.
Fragment 4

Poets tell many lies.
Fragment 21

I grow old ever learning many things.   *Fragment* 22

Speech is the image of actions.
From DIOGENES LAERTIUS, *bk. I, sec.* 58

Laws are like spiders' webs, which stand firm when any light, yielding object falls upon them, while a larger

---

[1] The fox has many tricks, and the hedgehog has only one, but that is the best of all. — ERASMUS, *Adagia* [1500]

[2] Sayings throughout antiquity were variously attributed to the figures known as the "seven sages." The list is commonly given as Thales, Solon, Periander, Cleobulus, Chilon, Bias, Pittacus. (See Solon, column *b*.)

[3] Spare your breath to cool your porridge. — RABELAIS, *Works, bk. V* [1552], *ch.* 28

[1] See Terence, p. 108a; Horace, p. 120a; and Anonymous, p. 151a.

[2] The Latin form: De mortuis nil nisi bonum [Of the dead, nothing but good].
See Propertius, p. 128a.

thing breaks through them and escapes.[1]

From PLUTARCH, *The Banquet of the Seven Wise Men*

Let us sacrifice to the Muses.   *Ib.*

Until he is dead, do not yet call a man happy, but only lucky.[2]

From HERODOTUS [3] *I, 32*

STESICHORUS
c. 630 – c. 555 B.C.

This tale is not true: you [Helen] did not even board the well-benched ships, and you did not go to the citadel of Troy.   *Fragment 11*

ALCAEUS
c. 625 – c. 575 B.C.

Wine, dear boy, and truth.[4]
          Fragment 66

Wine is a peep-hole on a man.[4]
          Fragment 104

Let us run into a safe harbor.[5]
          Fragment 120

ANACHARSIS
fl. c. 600 B.C.

[On learning that the sides of a ship were four fingers thick] The passengers are just that distance from death.[6]

From DIOGENES LAERTIUS, *Anacharsis 5*

[1] See Zincgref, p. 321a, and Swift, p. 388b.
[2] See *Ecclesiasticus 11:28*, p. 38a; Aeschylus, p. 78b; Sophocles p. 81b; and Horace, p. 120a.
[3] Herodotus attributed these words to Solon.
[4] Earliest references to what became the proverb *In vino veritas* (In wine is truth) which was known to Plato (*Symposium 217*) and to Pliny the Elder [A.D. 23–79], *Natural History XIV, 141.*
[5] Part of what is probably the oldest poem using the image of the "ship of state." See Sophocles, p. 81b.
[6] "How thick do you judge the planks of our ship to be?" "Some two good inches and upward," returned the pilot. "It seems, then, we are within two fingers' breadth of damnation." — RABELAIS, *Works, bk. IV* [1548], *ch. 23*

SAPPHO
c. 612 B.C.

Deathless Aphrodite on your rich-wrought throne.[1]   *Fragment 1*

Equal to the gods seems to me that man who sits facing you and hears you nearby sweetly speaking and softly laughing. This sets my heart to fluttering in my breast, for when I look on you a moment, then can I speak no more, but my tongue falls silent, and at once a delicate flame courses beneath my skin, and with my eyes I see nothing, and my ears hum, and a cold sweat bathes me, and a trembling seizes me all over, and I am paler than grass, and I feel that I am near to death.[2]

Fragment 2

The stars about the lovely moon hide their shining forms when it lights up the earth at its fullest.   *Fragment 4*

I loved you once long ago, Athis . . . you seemed to me a small, ungainly child.   *Fragments 40–41*

The moon has set, and the Pleiades; it is midnight, and time passes, and I sleep alone.[3]   *Fragment 94*

Sweet mother, I cannot ply the loom, vanquished by desire for a youth through the work of soft Aphrodite.
          Fragment 114

As an apple reddens on the high bough; high atop the highest bough the apple pickers passed it by — no, not passed it by, but they could not reach it.   *Fragment 116*

As shepherds trample underfoot a hyacinth on the mountainside, and on the ground the purple flower.
          Fragment 117

Evening star, you bring all things which the bright dawn has scattered: you bring the sheep, you bring the goat, you bring the child back to its mother.[4]
          Fragment 120

[1] Or "with your intricate charms."
[2] See Catullus, p. 115a.
[3] See Housman, p. 854b.
[4] See Meleager, p. 110a, and Housman, p. 854a.

IBYCUS[1]
c. 580 B.C.

There is no medicine to be found for a life which has fled.   *Fragment 23*

An argument needs no reason, nor a friendship.   *Fragment 40*

PHEIDIPPIDES
d. 490 B.C.

Rejoice, we are victorious.
From LUCIAN, *Pro Lapsu in Salutando* 3

ANACREON
c. 570 – c. 480 B.C.

Bring water, bring wine, boy! Bring flowering garlands to me! Yes, bring them, so that I may try a bout with love.   *Fragment 27*

I both love and do not love, and am mad and am not mad.[2]
Fragment 79

War spares not the brave, but the cowardly.[3]
Fragment 101. From The Palatine Anthology VII, 160

HIPPONAX
c. 570 – 520 B.C.

There are two days when a woman is a pleasure: the day one marries her and the day one buries her.   *Fragment*

XENOPHANES
c. 570 – c. 475 B.C.

Homer and Hesiod attributed to the gods everything that is a shame and a reproach among men.   *Fragment 11*

If cattle and horses, or lions, had hands, or were able to draw with their feet and produce the works which men do, horses would draw the forms of gods like horses, and cattle like cattle, and they would make the gods' bodies the same shape as their own.[1]
Fragment 15

One god, greatest among gods and men, similar to mortals neither in shape nor even in thought.[2]
Fragment 23

It takes a wise man to recognize a wise man.
From DIOGENES LAERTIUS, *Xenophanes IX*

SIMONIDES
c. 556 – 468 B.C.

It is hard to be truly excellent, four-square in hand and foot and mind, formed without blemish.   *Fragment 4*

The city is the teacher of the man.
Fragment 53

Fighting in the forefront of the Greeks, the Athenians crushed at Marathon the might of the gold-bearing Medes.   *Fragment 88*

Go tell the Spartans, thou who passest by,
That here, obedient to their laws, we lie.[3]   *Fragment 92*

If the greatest part of excellence is nobly to die, this to us of all men has fortune given: for struggling to clothe Greece in freedom, we lie in unaging glory.[4]   *Fragment 118*

Painting is silent poetry, and poetry painting that speaks.
From PLUTARCH, *De Gloria Atheniensium III, 346*

---

[1] Associated with Ibycus is the phrase "the cranes of Ibycus." It derives from the legend that Ibycus was murdered at sea and his murderers were discovered through cranes that followed the ship. Hence, "the cranes of Ibycus" became a proverb for the agency of the gods in revealing crime.
[2] See Catullus, p. 115a.
[3] See Sophocles, p. 82b.

[1] See Montesquieu, p. 414b.
[2] See Homer, p. 63a.
[3] Translated by W. L. BOWLES.
Ruskin said of this epitaph that it was the noblest group of words uttered by man.
[4] See Thucydides, p. 90a.

CONFUCIUS[1]
551–479 B.C.

Fine words and an insinuating appearance are seldom associated with true virtue.
The Confucian Analects, bk. 1:3

A youth, when at home, should be filial, and, abroad, respectful to his elders. 1:6

If a man withdraws his mind from the love of beauty, and applies it as sincerely to the love of the virtuous; if, in serving his parents, he can exert his utmost strength; if, in serving his prince, he can devote his life; if, in his intercourse with his friends, his words are sincere — although men say that he has not learned, I will certainly say that he has. 1:7

Hold faithfulness and sincerity as first principles. 1:8, *ii*

Have no friends not equal to yourself. 1:8, *iii*

When you have faults, do not fear to abandon them. 1:8, *iv*

He who exercises government by means of his virtue may be compared to the north polar star, which keeps its place and all the stars turn towards it. 2:1

[The superior man] acts before he speaks, and afterwards speaks according to his actions. 2:13

Learning without thought is labor lost; thought without learning is perilous.[2] 2:15

When you know a thing, to hold that you know it; and when you do not know a thing, to allow that you do not know it — this is knowledge.[3]
2:17

Things that are done, it is needless to speak about . . . things that are past, it is needless to blame. 3:21, *ii*

[1] Sayings attributed to Confucius and his followers from *The Chinese Classics, Vol. I: The Confucian Analects,* translated by JAMES LEGGE.
[2] See Lao Tzu, p. 75b; Heraclitus, p. 77b; and Cardinal Newman, p. 598a.
[3] See Lao Tzu, p. 75a.

I have not seen a person who loved virtue, or one who hated what was not virtuous. He who loved virtue would esteem nothing above it.
The Confucian Analects,
bk. 4:6, *i*

If a man in the morning hear the right way, he may die in the evening without regret. 4:8

The superior man . . . does not set his mind either for anything, or against anything; what is right he will follow.
4:10

When we see men of worth, we should think of equaling them; when we see men of a contrary character, we should turn inwards and examine ourselves. 4:17

The cautious seldom err. 4:23

Virtue is not left to stand alone. He who practices it will have neighbors.
4:25

Man is born for uprightness. If a man lose his uprightness, and yet live, his escape from death is the effect of mere good fortune. 6:16

The man of virtue makes the difficulty to be overcome his first business, and success only a subsequent consideration. 6:20

With coarse rice to eat, with water to drink, and my bended arm for a pillow — I have still joy in the midst of these things. Riches and honors acquired by unrighteousness are to me as a floating cloud. 7:15

I am not one who was born in the possession of knowledge; I am one who is fond of antiquity, and earnest in seeking it there. 7:19

Is virtue a thing remote? I wish to be virtuous, and lo! virtue is at hand.
7:29

The superior man is satisfied and composed; the mean man is always full of distress. 7:36

The people may be made to follow a path of action, but they may not be made to understand it. 8:9

If a superior man dwelt among [barbarians], what rudeness would there be?

The Confucian Analects, bk. 9:13, ii

While you are not able to serve men, how can you serve spirits [of the dead]? . . . While you do not know life, how can you know about death?

11:11

To go beyond is as wrong as to fall short. *11:15, iii*

He with whom neither slander that gradually soaks into the mind, nor statements that startle like a wound in the flesh, are successful may be called intelligent indeed. *12:6*

In carrying on your government, why should you use killing [the unprincipled for the good of the unprincipled] at all? Let your evinced desires be for what is good, and the people will be good. The relation between superiors and inferiors is like that between the wind and the grass. The grass must bend when the wind blows across it.

12:19

Good government obtains when those who are near are made happy, and those who are far off are attracted.

13:16, ii

The firm, the enduring, the simple, and the modest are near to virtue.

13:27

The scholar who cherishes the love of comfort is not fit to be deemed a scholar. *14:3*

The man who in the view of gain thinks of righteousness; who in the view of danger is prepared to give up his life; and who does not forget an old agreement however far back it extends — such a man may be reckoned a complete man. *14:13, ii*

He who speaks without modesty will find it difficult to make his words good. *14:21*

In ancient times, men learned with a view to their own improvement. Nowadays, men learn with a view to the approbation of others.

The Confucian Analects, bk. 14:25

The superior man is modest in his speech, but exceeds in his actions.

14:29

Recompense injury with justice, and recompense kindness with kindness.

14:36, iii

The determined scholar and the man of virtue will not seek to live at the expense of injuring their virtue. They will even sacrifice their lives to preserve their virtue complete. *15:8*

If a man take no thought about what is distant, he will find sorrow near at hand. *15:11*

The superior man is distressed by his want of ability. *15:18*

What the superior man seeks is in himself. What the mean man seeks is in others. *15:20*

What you do not want done to yourself, do not do to others.[1] *15:23*

When a man's knowledge is sufficient to attain, and his virtue is not sufficient to enable him to hold, whatever he may have gained, he will lose again. *15:32, i*

The superior man cannot be known in little matters, but he may be entrusted with great concerns. The small man may not be entrusted with great concerns, but he may be known in little matters. *15:33*

Virtue is more to man than either water or fire. I have seen men die from treading on water and fire, but I have never seen a man die from treading the course of virtue. *15:34*

By nature, men are nearly alike; by practice, they get to be wide apart.

17:2

To be able to practice five things everywhere under heaven constitutes perfect virtue. . . . [They are] gravity,

[1] The Golden Rule. See *Matthew 7:12*, p. 41a.

generosity of soul, sincerity, earnestness, and kindness.

The Confucian Analects,
bk. 17:6

There are three things which the superior man guards against. In youth . . . lust. When he is strong . . . quarrelsomeness. When he is old . . . covetousness. 17:8

Without recognizing the ordinances of Heaven, it is impossible to be a superior man. 20:3, *i*

Without an acquaintance with the rules of propriety, it is impossible for the character to be established.
20:3, *ii*

Without knowing the force of words, it is impossible to know men.
20:3, *iii*

LAO TZU[1]
Sixth century[?] B.C.

The Tao [Way] that can be told of is
not the eternal Tao;
The name that can be named is not the
eternal name.
The Nameless is the origin of Heaven
and Earth;
The Named is the mother of all
things.
Therefore let there always be non-
being, so we may see their sub-
tlety,
And let there always be being, so we
may see their outcome.
The two are the same,
But after they are produced, they have
different names.
They both may be called deep and pro-
found.
Deeper and more profound,
The door of all subtleties!
The Way of Lao Tzu 1

When the people of the world all know
beauty as beauty,
There arises the recognition of ugliness.
When they all know the good as good,

[1] From *The Way of Lao Tzu*, translated by
WING-TSIT CHAN.

There arises the recognition of evil.
The Way of Lao Tzu 2

In the government of the sage,
He keeps their hearts vacuous,
Fills their bellies,
Weakens their ambitions,
And strengthens their bones,
He always causes his people to be with-
out knowledge [cunning] or de-
sire,
And the crafty to be afraid to act.
Ib. 3

Heaven and Earth are not humane.[1]
They regard all things as straw dogs.[2]
Ib. 5

The spirit of the valley never dies.
It is called the subtle and profound
female.
The gate of the subtle and profound
female
Is the root of Heaven and Earth.
It is continuous, and seems to be always
existing.
Use it and you will never wear it out.
Ib. 6

The best [man] is like water.
Water is good; it benefits all things and
does not compete with them.
It dwells in [lowly] places that all dis-
dain.
This is why it is so near to Tao.
Ib. 8

To produce things and to rear them,
To produce, but not to take possession
of them,
To act, but not to rely on one's own
ability,
To lead them, but not to master
them —
This is called profound and secret virtue. *Ib. 10*

He who loves the world as his body may
be entrusted with the empire.
Ib. 13

We look at it [Tao] and do not see
it;

[1] I.e., they are impartial.
[2] Straw dogs were used in sacrifices and then discarded.

Its name is The Invisible.
We listen to it and do not hear it;
Its name is The Inaudible.
We touch it and do not find it;
Its name is The Subtle [formless].
The Way of Lao Tzu 14

It is The Vague and Elusive.
Meet it and you will not see its head.
Follow it and you will not see its back.
Ib.

Manifest plainness,
Embrace simplicity,
Reduce selfishness,
Have few desires.   *Ib. 19*

Abandon learning and there will be no
    sorrow.   *Ib. 20*

To yield is to be preserved whole.
To be bent is to become straight.
To be empty is to be full.
To be worn out is to be renewed.
To have little is to possess.
To have plenty is to be perplexed.[1]
                          Ib. 22

He who knows others is wise;
He who knows himself is enlightened.
                          Ib. 33

[The sage] never strives himself for the
    great, and thereby the great is
    achieved.   *Ib. 34*

Tao invariably takes no action, and yet
    there is nothing left undone.
Reversion is the action of Tao.
Weakness is the function of Tao.
All things in the world come from be-
    ing.
And being comes from non-being.
                          Ib. 40

When the highest type of men hear
    Tao,
    They diligently practice it.
When the average type of men hear
    Tao,
    They half believe in it.
When the lowest type of men hear
    Tao,
    They laugh heartily at it.   *Ib. 41*

The softest things in the world over-

come the hardest things in the
    world.
Non-being penetrates that in which
    there is no space.
Through this I know the advantage of
    taking no action.
The Way of Lao Tzu 43

There is no calamity greater than lavish
    desires.
There is no greater guilt than discon-
    tentment.
And there is no greater disaster than
    greed.   *Ib. 46*

One may know the world without going
    out of doors.
One may see the Way of Heaven with-
    out looking through the windows.
The further one goes, the less one
    knows.[1]
Therefore the sage knows without going
    about,
Understands without seeing,
And accomplishes without any action.
                          Ib. 47

He who possesses virtue in abundance
May be compared to an infant.
                          Ib. 55

He who knows does not speak.
He who speaks does not know.
                          Ib. 56

The more laws and order are made
    prominent,
The more thieves and robbers there will
    be.   *Ib. 57*

Ruling a big country is like cooking a
    small fish.[2]   *Ib. 60*

Tao is the storehouse of all things.
It is the good man's treasure and the
    bad man's refuge.   *Ib. 62*

A journey of a thousand miles must
begin with a single step.[3]   *Ib. 64*

People are difficult to govern because
    they have too much knowledge.
                          Ib. 65

I have three treasures. Guard and keep
    them:

---

[1] See the Sermon on the Mount, *Matthew 5*,
p. 40a.

[1] I.e., the more one studies, the further one
is from the Tao.
[2] I.e., too much handling will spoil it.
[3] Traditional translation.

The first is deep love,
The second is frugality,
And the third is not to dare to be
ahead of the world.
Because of deep love, one is coura-
geous.
Because of frugality, one is generous.
Because of not daring to be ahead of
the world, one becomes the leader
of the world.
The Way of Lao Tzu 67

When armies are mobilized and issues
joined,
The man who is sorry over the fact will
win.　　　　　*Ib. 69*

To know that you do not know is the
best.
To pretend to know when you do not
know is a disease. [1]　　*Ib. 71*

Heaven's net is indeed vast.
Though its meshes are wide, it misses
nothing.[2]　　　　*Ib. 73*

To undertake executions for the master
executioner [Heaven] is like hewing wood for the master carpenter.
Whoever undertakes to hew wood for
the master carpenter rarely escapes
injuring his own hands.　*Ib. 74*

The Way of Heaven has no favorites.
It is always with the good man.
　　　　　　　Ib. 79

Let there be a small country with few
people. . . .
Though neighboring communities overlook one another and the crowing
of cocks and barking of dogs can
be heard,
Yet the people there may grow old and
die without ever visiting one another.　　　　*Ib. 80*

True words are not beautiful; [3]
Beautiful words are not true.
A good man does not argue;
He who argues is not a good man.

[1] See Confucius, p. 71a.
[2] The kingdom of heaven is like unto a net,
that was cast into the sea, and gathered of
every kind. — *Matthew 13:47*
[3] I.e., they are not "fine-sounding."

A wise man has no extensive knowledge;
He who has extensive knowledge is not
a wise man.[1]
The sage does not accumulate for himself.
The more he uses for others, the more
he has himself.
The more he gives to others, the more
he possesses of his own.
The Way of Heaven is to benefit others
and not to injure.
The Way of the sage is to act but not
to compete.
The Way of Lao Tzu 81

AESOP [2]
fl. c. 550 B.C.

The lamb . . . began to follow the
wolf in sheep's clothing.
The Wolf in Sheep's Clothing

Appearances often are deceiving.
　　　　　　　Ib.

Do not count your chickens before
they are hatched.[3]
The Milkmaid and Her Pail

I am sure the grapes are sour.[4]
The Fox and the Grapes

No act of kindness, no matter how
small, is ever wasted.
The Lion and the Mouse

Slow and steady wins the race.
The Hare and the Tortoise

[1] See Confucius, p. 71a; Heraclitus, p. 77b; and
Cardinal Newman, p. 598a.
[2] Animal fables from before Aesop's time and
after were attributed to him. The first collection
was made two hundred years after his death.
See also La Fontaine, p. 359a.
[3] To swallow gudgeons ere they're catch'd,
　And count their chickens ere they're
　hatched.
　　　SAMUEL BUTLER, *Hudibras,*
　　　pt. II [1664], *canto 3, l. 923*
[4] The fox, when he cannot reach the grapes,
says they are not ripe. — GEORGE HERBERT,
Jacula Prudentum [1640]
"They are too green," he said, "and only
good for fools." — LA FONTAINE, *bk. III* [*1668*],
fable 11, The Fox and the Grapes

Familiarity breeds contempt.[1]
The Fox and the Lion

The boy cried "Wolf, wolf!" and the villagers came out to help him.
The Shepherd Boy and the Wolf

A crust eaten in peace is better than a banquet partaken in anxiety.
The Town Mouse and the Country Mouse

Borrowed plumes.
The Jay and the Peacock

It is not only fine feathers that make fine birds. *Ib.*

Self-conceit may lead to self-destruction. *The Frog and the Ox*

People often grudge others what they cannot enjoy themselves.
The Dog in the Manger

It is thrifty to prepare today for the wants of tomorrow.
The Ant and the Grasshopper

Be content with your lot; one cannot be first in everything.
Juno and the Peacock [2]

A huge gap appeared in the side of the mountain. At last a tiny mouse came forth.[3]
The Mountain in Labor

Any excuse will serve a tyrant.
The Wolf and the Lamb

Beware lest you lose the substance by grasping at the shadow.
The Dog and the Shadow

Who shall bell the cat?
The Rats and the Cat

I will have nought to do with a man who can blow hot and cold with the same breath.
The Man and the Satyr

Thinking to get at once all the gold

the goose could give, he killed it and opened it only to find — nothing.
The Goose with the Golden Eggs

Put your shoulder to the wheel.
Hercules and the Wagoner

The gods help them that help themselves.[1] *Ib.*

We would often be sorry if our wishes were gratified.[2]
The Old Man and Death

Union gives strength.[3]
The Bundle of Sticks

While I see many hoof marks going in, I see none coming out. It is easier to get into the enemy's toils than out again.
The Lion, the Fox, and the Beasts

The haft of the arrow had been feathered with one of the eagle's own plumes. We often give our enemies the means of our own destruction.[4]
The Eagle and the Arrow

---

[1] God loves to help him who strives to help himself. — AESCHYLUS [525–456 B.C.], *Fragment 223*

Heaven helps not the men who will not act. — SOPHOCLES [495–405 B.C.]. *Fragment 288*

Try first thyself, and after call in God;
For to the worker God himself lends aid.
EURIPIDES [485–406 B.C.], *Hippolytus, frag. 435*

Help thyself, and God will help thee. — GEORGE HERBERT, *Jacula Prudentum* [1640]

God helps those who help themselves. — ALGERNON SIDNEY, *Discourses on Government* [1698], *sec. 23*, and BENJAMIN FRANKLIN, *Poor Richard's Almanac* [1733–1758]

[2] Granting our wish one of Fate's saddest jokes is! — J. R. LOWELL [1819–1891], *Two Scenes from the Life of Blondel, sc. II, st. 2*

Beware, my lord! Beware lest stern Heaven hate you enough to hear your prayers! — ANATOLE FRANCE, *The Crime of Sylvestre Bonnard* [1881], *pt. II, ch. 4*

When the gods wish to punish us they answer our prayers. — OSCAR WILDE, *An Ideal Husband* [1895], *act II*

[3] See John Dickinson, p. 460b, and G. P. Morris, p. 600a.

[4] So in the Libyan fable it is told
That once an eagle, stricken with a dart,
Said, when he saw the fashion of the shaft,
"With our own feathers, not by others' hands,
Are we now smitten."
AESCHYLUS [525–456 B.C.], *Fragment 135* (Plumptre's translation)

---

[1] See Mark Twain, p. 764b.

[2] See Sean O'Casey, p. 981a.

[3] A mountain was in labor, sending forth dreadful groans, and there was in the region the highest expectation. After all, it brought forth a mouse. — PHAEDRUS [C. A.D. 8] *IV, 22:1*
See Horace, p. 124a.

THEOGNIS
fl. c. 545 B.C.

One finds many companions for food and drink, but in a serious business a man's companions are very few.

Elegies, l. 115

Even to a wicked man a divinity gives wealth, Cyrnus, but to few men comes the gift of excellence.

Ib. 149

Surfeit begets insolence, when prosperity comes to a bad man.   *Ib.* 153

Adopt the character of the twisting octopus, which takes on the appearance of the nearby rock. Now follow in this direction, now turn a different hue.

Ib. 215

The best of all things for earthly men is not to be born and not to see the beams of the bright sun; but if born, then as quickly as possible to pass the gates of Hades, and to lie deep buried.[1]

Ib. 425

No man takes with him to Hades all his exceeding wealth.[2]   *Ib.* 725

Bright youth passes swiftly as a thought.   *Ib.* 985

HERACLITUS
c. 540 – c. 480 B.C.

All is flux, nothing stays still.

From DIOGENES LAERTIUS, *bk. IX, sec. 8, and* PLATO, *Cratylus,* 402A

Nothing endures but change.[1]

From DIOGENES LAERTIUS, *bk. IX, sec. 8, and* PLATO, *Cratylus,* 402A

Although the logos is common to all, the many live as if they had private understanding.   *Fragment* 2

Much learning does not teach a man to have intelligence.[2]   *Fragment* 40

Strife is the source and the master of all things.   *Fragment* 53

The path up and down is one and the same.   *Fragment* 60

Everything comes about by way of strife and necessity.   *Fragment* 80

It is not possible to step twice into the same river.   *Fragment* 91

Character is a man's guiding destiny.   *Fragment* 119

THEMISTOCLES
c. 528 – c. 462 B.C.

Tuning the lyre and handling the harp are no accomplishments of mine, but rather taking in hand a city that was small and inglorious and making it glorious and great.

From PLUTARCH, *Lives, Themistocles, sec.* 2

The wooden wall is your ships.[3]

Ib. 10

Strike, but hear me.[4]   *Ib.* 11

[Of his son] The boy is the most powerful of all the Hellenes; for the Hellenes are commanded by the Athenians, the Athenians by myself, myself by the boy's mother, and the mother by her boy.   *Ib.* 18

[1] See Honorat de Bueil, p. 318b; Swift, p. 388b; and Shelley, p. 568a.

[2] See Confucius, p. 71a; Lao Tzu, p. 75b; and Cardinal Newman, p. 598a.

[3] This was Themistocles' interpretation to the Athenians in 480 B.C. of the second oracle at Delphi: "Safe shall the wooden wall continue for thee and thy children." The account appears in full in Herodotus, Book VII, sec. 141–143.

[4] Said in reply to Eurybiades, commander of the Spartan fleet, when he raised his staff as though to strike.

That eagle's fate and mine are one,
  Which on the shaft that made him die
Espied a feather of his own,
  Wherewith he wont to soar so high.
    EDMUND WALLER [1605–1687], *To a Lady Singing a Song of His Composing*
Like a young eagle, who has lent his plume
To fledge the shaft by which he meets his doom,
See their own feathers pluck'd to wing the dart
Which rank corruption destines for their heart.
    THOMAS MOORE [1780–1852], *Corruption*
See Byron, p. 555a.

[1] See Sophocles, p. 83a; Bacon, p. 210a; Heine, p. 588b; and Yeats, p. 883b.

[2] See *The Song of the Harp-Player,* p. 3a; *Ecclesiastes 5:15,* p. 28a; and *I Timothy 6:7,* p. 55a.

[Of two suitors for his daughter's hand] I choose the likely man in preference to the rich man; I want a man without money rather than money without a man.

> From PLUTARCH, *Lives, Themistocles, sec.* 18

I have with me two gods, Persuasion and Compulsion.[1]　　　*Ib.* 21

The speech of man is like embroidered tapestries, since like them this too has to be extended in order to display its patterns, but when it is rolled up it conceals and distorts them.　　*Ib.* 29

He who commands the sea has command of everything.[2]

> From CICERO, *Ad Atticum* X, 8

[Upon being asked whether he would rather be Achilles or Homer] Which would you rather be — a victor in the Olympic games, or the announcer of the victor?

> From PLUTARCH, *Apothegms, Themistocles*

AESCHYLUS
525–456 B.C.

I would far rather be ignorant than knowledgeable of evils.

> *The Suppliants, l.* 453

"Reverence for parents" stands written among the three laws of most revered righteousness.[3]　　*Ib.* 707

Myriad laughter of the ocean waves.

> *Prometheus Bound, l.* 89

For somehow this is tyranny's disease, to trust no friends.　　*Ib.* 224

Words are the physicians of a mind diseased.[4]　　　　　*Ib.* 378

Time as he grows old teaches all things.　　　　　　　*Ib.* 981

God's mouth knows not how to speak falsehood, but he brings to pass every word.[1]

> *Prometheus Bound, l.* 1030

On me the tempest falls. It does not make me tremble. O holy Mother Earth, O air and sun, behold me. I am wronged.[2]　　　　　*Ib.* 1089

I pray the gods some respite from the weary task of this long year's watch that lying on the Atreidae's roof on bended arm, dog-like, I have kept, marking the conclave of all the night's stars, those potentates blazing in the heavens that bring winter and summer to mortal men, the constellations, when they wane, when they rise.

> *Agamemnon, l.* 1

A great ox stands on my tongue.[3]
> *Ib.* 36

Wisdom comes through suffering.
> *Ib.* 177

She [Helen] brought to Ilium her dowry, destruction.　　*Ib.* 406

It is in the character of very few men to honor without envy a friend who has prospered.　　　　　*Ib.* 832

Only when man's life comes to its end in prosperity can one call that man happy.[4]　　　　　　*Ib.* 928

Alas, I am struck a deep mortal blow!
> *Ib.* 1343

Death is better, a milder fate than tyranny.[5]　　　　*Ib.* 1364

Zeus, first cause, prime mover; for what thing without Zeus is done among mortals?[6]　　　　*Ib.* 1485

Do not kick against the pricks.[7]
> *Ib.* 1624

---

[1] Said to the Andrians, when demanding money from them, to which they replied that they already had two great gods, Penury and Powerlessness, who hindered them from giving him money.

[2] See Bacon, p. 209b; Mahan, p. 785b; and Morison, p. 998a.

[3] See *Exodus 20:12*, p. 9a.

[4] See Milton, p. 349a.

[1] See *Numbers 23:19*, p. 10a.

[2] Translated by EDITH HAMILTON.

[3] A proverbial expression of uncertain origin for enforced silence.

[4] See Solon, p. 69a, and note.

[5] See Patrick Henry, p. 465b.

[6] See *Acts 17:28*, p. 50a; Cleanthes, p. 103b; and Aratus, p. 104a.

[7] Also in PINDAR, *Pythian Odes* II, l. 174, and EURIPIDES, *Bacchae*, l. 795. See *Acts 9:5*, p. 49b.

I know how men in exile feed on dreams of hope.

Agamemnon, l. 1668

Good fortune is a god among men, and more than a god.

The Libation Bearers, l. 59

Destiny waits alike for the free man as well as for him enslaved by another's might. *Ib. 103*

For a deadly blow let him pay with a deadly blow: it is for him who has done a deed to suffer. *Ib. 312*

What is pleasanter than the tie of host and guest? *Ib. 702*

His resolve is not to seem, but to be, the best.

The Seven Against Thebes, l. 592

PINDAR
c. 518 – c. 438 B.C.

Water is best. But gold shines like fire blazing in the night, supreme of lordly wealth.

Olympian Odes I, l. 1

The days that are still to come are the wisest witnesses. *Ib. 51*

If any man hopes to do a deed without God's knowledge, he errs.

Ib. 104

Do not peer too far.[1]   *Ib. 184*

I have many swift arrows in my quiver which speak to the wise, but for the crowd they need interpreters. The skilled poet is one who knows much through natural gift, but those who have learned their art chatter turbulently, vainly, against the divine bird of Zeus. *Ib. II, 150*

I will not steep my speech in lies; the test of any man lies in action.[2]

Ib. IV, 27

The issue is in God's hands.

Ib. XIII, 147

Zeus, accomplisher, to all grant grave restraint and attainment of sweet delight.[1] *Olympian Odes XIII, last line*

Seek not, my soul, the life of the immortals; but enjoy to the full the resources that are within thy reach.[2]

Pythian Odes III, l. 109

They say that this lot is bitterest: to recognize the good but by necessity to be barred from it.[3]   *Ib. IV, 510*

Creatures of a day, what is a man? What is he not? Mankind is a dream of a shadow. But when a god-given brightness comes, a radiant light rests on men, and a gentle life.[4]

Ib. VIII, 135

When toilsome contests have been decided, good cheer is the best physician, and songs, the sage daughters of the Muses, soothe with their touch.

Nemean Odes IV, l. 1

Words have a longer life than deeds.   *Ib. 10*

Not every truth is the better for showing its face undisguised; and often silence is the wisest thing for a man to heed.   *Ib. V, 30*

One race there is of men, one of gods, but from one mother we both draw our breath.   *Ib. VI, 1*

If one but tell a thing well, it moves on with undying voice, and over the fruitful earth and across the sea goes the bright gleam of noble deeds ever unquenchable.

Isthmian Odes IV, l. 67

It is not possible with mortal mind to search out the purposes of the gods.

Fragment 61

O bright and violet-crowned and famed in song, bulwark of Greece, famous Athens, divine city!

Fragment 76

---

[1] Do not set your eyes on things far off. — *Pythian Odes III, 39*
See Euripides, p. 84a.
[2] Translated by RICHMOND LATTIMORE.

[1] Translated by RICHMOND LATTIMORE.
[2] See Euripides, p. 84a.
[3] See Boethius, p. 148a; Dante, p. 160a; Chaucer, p. 165a; and Tennyson, p. 647a.
[4] See Homer, pp. 63a and 64b, and Aristophanes, p. 91b.

Unsung, the noblest deed will die.
Fragment 120

What is God? Everything.
Fragment 140d

Convention is the ruler of all.
Fragment 169

Hope, which most of all guides the changeful mind of mortals.
Fragment 214

ANAXAGORAS
c. 500 – 428 B.C.

The descent to Hades is the same from every place.
From DIOGENES LAERTIUS,
Anaxagoras 2

SUTTAPITAKA[1]
c. 500 – c. 250 B.C.[2]

All that is is the result of what we have thought.   *Dhammapada 1.1*

Hatreds never cease by hatred; they cease by non-hatred; this is the primeval law.   *Ib. 1.5*

The scent of flowers does not go against the wind, not sandal, rosebay or jasmine; but the scent of the good goes against the wind; a good man is wafted to all quarters.   *Ib. 4.54*

If one conquer a thousand thousand men in battle, and if one conquer himself alone, he is in battle supreme.
Ib. 8.103

If one live a hundred years idle, without energy, better to live one day of steadfast energy.   *Ib. 8.112*

Think not lightly of evil, "It will not come to me." A waterpot is filled by the fall of waterdrops; a fool is filled with evil, amassing it bit by bit.
Ib. 9.121

If in the hand there be no wound one may hold poison in the hand. No poison follows where there is no wound;

[1] Means "basket of discourses." It is one of the three "baskets" which form the Pali canon, the sacred scriptures of Theravada Buddhists.
[2] Ancient Indian literary chronology is conjectural.

there is no evil for one who commits none.   *Dhammapada 9.124*

All tremble at the rod, all fear death; making yourself the exemplar, do not kill or cause to kill.   *Ib. 10.129*

This man of little learning grows old like an ox: his flesh increases, but not his wisdom.   *Ib. 11.152*

Who have not lived a holy life, have not acquired wealth in their youth, brood like decrepit herons in a pond where the fish have died.   *Ib. 11.155*

Extract yourself from bad ways like an elephant stuck in the mud.
Ib. 23.327

Better to live alone; with a fool there is no companionship. With few desires live alone and do no evil, like an elephant in the forest roaming at will.
Ib. 23.330

Decay is inherent in all component things! Work out your salvation with diligence! [1]
Mahaparinibbanasutta 6.7 [2]

I go for refuge to the Buddha.
I go for refuge to the Doctrine.
I go for refuge to the Order [of monks].
Traditional (liturgical), passim

PERICLES[3]
c. 495 – 429 B.C.

Wait for that wisest of all counselors, Time.
From PLUTARCH, *Lives,*
PERICLES, *sec. 18*

Trees, though they are cut and lopped, grow up again quickly,[4] but if men are destroyed, it is not easy to get them again.   *Ib. 33*

[1] Translated by T. RHYS DAVIDS. The last words of the Buddha. Quoted by T. S. ELIOT, *The Cocktail Party* [1950], *act II,* by Sir Henry Harcourt-Reilly.
[2] Pali Text Society, *Digh Nikaya,* vol. 2, p. 156, and *Samyutta Nikaya,* vol. 1, p. 158.
[3] See THUCYDIDES, *Funeral Speech of Pericles,* p. 89b.
[4] The lopped tree in time may grow again. — ROBERT SOUTHWELL [1561–1595], *Times Go by Turns*

SOPHOCLES[1]
c. 495 – 405 B.C.

Silence gives the proper grace to women. *Ajax, l. 293*

Nobly to live, or else nobly to die,
Befits proud birth.[2] *Ib. 480*

Of all human ills, greatest is fortune's wayward tyranny. *Ib. 486*

For kindness begets kindness evermore,
But he from whose mind fades the memory
Of benefits, noble is he no more.
  Ib. 522

Sleep that masters all. *Ib. 675*

I, whom proof hath taught of late
How so far only should we hate our foes
As though we soon might love them, and so far
Do a friend service as to one most like
Some day to prove our foe, since oftenest men
In friendship but a faithless haven find.[3] *Ib. 678*

Men of ill judgment oft ignore the good
That lies within their hands, till they have lost it. *Ib. 964*

It is not righteousness to outrage
A brave man dead, not even though you hate him. *Ib. 1344*

Ships are only hulls, high walls are nothing,
When no life moves in the empty passageways.[4]
  Oedipus Rex,[5] l. 56

How dreadful knowledge of the truth can be
When there's no help in truth!
  Oedipus Rex, l. 316

The tyrant is a child of Pride
Who drinks from his great sickening cup
Recklessness and vanity,
Until from his high crest headlong
He plummets to the dust of hope.[1]
  Ib. 872

The greatest griefs are those we cause ourselves. *Ib. 1230*

Let every man in mankind's frailty
Consider his last day; and let none
Presume on his good fortune until he find
Life, at his death, a memory without pain.[2] *Ib. 1529*

For God hates utterly
The bray of bragging tongues.
  Antigone[3] *[c. 442 B.C.], l. 123*

Our ship of State, which recent storms have threatened to destroy, has come safely to harbor at last.[4]
  Ib. 163

I have nothing but contempt for the kind of governor who is afraid, for whatever reason, to follow the course that he knows is best for the State; and as for the man who sets private friendship above the public welfare — I have no use for him, either. *Ib. 181*

---

[1] Sophocles said he drew men as they ought to be, and Euripides as they were. — ARISTOTLE, *Poetics, ch. 25*

[2] See Euripides, p. 85b, and note.

[3] They love as though they will some day hate and hate as though they will some day love. — ARISTOTLE quoting BIAS [c. 650 B.C.], *Rhetoric II, 13*
  See Publilius Syrus, p. 126a.

[4] See Thucydides, p. 90b, and Shakespeare, *Coriolanus III, i, 198*, p. 289b.

[5] Translated by DUDLEY FITTS and ROBERT FITZGERALD.

[1] See *Proverbs 16:18*, p. 24b.
  Pride will have a fall. — *English proverb* [c. 1509]. A variant is "Pride goeth before a fall."
  Pride goeth before, and shame cometh behynde. — *Treatise of a Gallant* [c. 1510]
    Pryde will have a fall;
  For pryde goeth before and shame cometh after.
    JOHN HEYWOOD, *Proverbs* [1546], *pt. I, ch. 10*

[2] See Solon, p. 69a, and note.
  There is a saying among men, put forth of old, that you cannot rightly judge whether a mortal's lot is good or evil, until he dies. — SOPHOCLES, *Trachiniae, l. 1*

[3] Translated by DUDLEY FITTS and ROBERT FITZGERALD.

[4] See Alcaeus, p. 69a.

Nobody likes the man who brings bad news.[1]   *Antigone, l.* 277

Money: There's nothing in the world so demoralizing as money.[2]   *Ib.* 295

How dreadful it is when the right judge judges wrong!   *Ib.* 323

Numberless are the world's wonders, but none
More wonderful than man.
          Ib. 333 *(Ode I)*

It is a good thing
To escape from death, but it is not great pleasure
To bring death to a friend.   *Ib.* 437

Grief teaches the steadiest minds to waver.   *Ib.* 563

All that is and shall be,
And all the past, is his [Zeus's].
          Ib. 611 *(Ode II)*

Show me the man who keeps his house in hand,
He's fit for public authority.[3]
          Ib. 660

Anarchy, anarchy! Show me a greater evil!
This is why cities tumble and the great houses rain down,
This is what scatters armies!
          Ib. 672

Reason is God's crowning gift to man.
          Ib. 684

The ideal condition
Would be, I admit, that men should be right by instinct;
But since we are all likely to go astray,
The reasonable thing is to learn from those who can teach.   *Ib.* 720

Love, unconquerable [4]
Waster of rich men, keeper
Of warm lights and all-night vigil
In the soft face of a girl:
Sea-wanderer, forest-visitor!

Even the pure immortals cannot escape you,
And mortal man, in his one day's dusk,
Trembles before your glory.
          Antigone, l. 781 *(Ode III)*

Wisdom outweighs any wealth.[1]
          Ib. 1050

There is no happiness where there is no wisdom; [2]
No wisdom but in submission to the gods.
Big words are always punished,
And proud men in old age learn to be wise.   *Ib.* 1347, *closing lines*

Death is not the worst; rather, in vain
To wish for death, and not to compass it.   *Electra, l.* 1008

A prudent mind can see room for misgiving, lest he who prospers should one day suffer reverse.[3]
          Trachiniae, l. 296

They are not wise, then, who stand forth to buffet against Love; for Love rules the gods as he will, and me.[4]
          Ib. 441

Knowledge must come through action; you can have no test which is not fanciful, save by trial.   *Ib.* 592

Rash indeed is he who reckons on the morrow, or haply on days beyond it; for tomorrow is not, until today is past.[5]   *Ib.* 943

War never slays a bad man in its course,
But the good always! [6]
          Philoctetes, l. 436

Stranger in a strange country.[7]
          Oedipus at Colonus [8] [406 B.C.], *l.* 184

---

[1] See *Job 28:18*, p. 15b.
[2] See Epicurus, p. 103a.
[3] See *Proverbs 16:18*, p. 24b.
[4] See Sophocles, *Antigone*, p. 82a.
[5] See *Proverbs 27:1*, p. 26a.
[6] Translated by Sir George Young.
          See Anacreon, p. 70a.
[7] See *Exodus 2:22*, p. 8a.
[8] Translated by Robert Fitzgerald.

[1] See Shakespeare, pp. 241b and 288a.
[2] See *I Timothy 6:10*, p. 55b, and Plato, p. 94a.
[3] See *I Timothy 3:5*, p. 55a.
[4] See Sophocles, *Trachiniae*, p. 82b; Virgil, p. 117a; and Chaucer, p. 166a.

The good befriend themselves.
Oedipus at Colonus, l. 309

The immortal
Gods alone have neither age nor death!
All other things almighty Time dis-
quiets.　　*Ib.* 607

Athens, nurse of men.　　*Ib.* 701

Not to be born surpasses thought and
speech.
The second best is to have seen the
light
And then to go back quickly whence we
came.[1]　　*Ib.* 1224

One word
Frees us of all the weight and pain of
life:
That word is love.　　*Ib.* 1616

It made our hair stand up in panic
fear.[2]　　*Ib.* 1625

A remedy too strong for the disease.
Tereus, frag. 514 [3]

Truly, to tell lies is not honorable;
But when the truth entails tremendous
ruin,
To speak dishonorably is pardonable.
Creusa, frag. 323

Sons are the anchors of a mother's life.
Phaedra, frag. 612

To him who is in fear everything rustles.　　*Acrisius, frag.* 58

No falsehood lingers on into old age.
Ib. frag. 59

No man loves life like him that's growing old.[4]　　*Ib. frag.* 64

A woman's vows I write upon the
wave.[5]
Unknown Dramas, frag. 694

[1] See Theognis, p. 77a, and note.
[2] See Robert Graves, p. 1034b.
[3] The fragments are from the Everyman Edition of *The Dramas of Sophocles.*
[4] See Euripides, p. 83b.
[5] See Catullus, p. 115a; More, p. 178b; Bacon,
p. 210a; Shakespeare, p. 299a; and Keats,
p. 586a.

EMPEDOCLES
c. 490 – c. 430 B.C.

At one time through love all things
come together into one, at another time
through strife's hatred they are borne
each of them apart.　　*Fragment* 17

The blood around men's heart is
their thinking.　　*Fragment* 105

EURIPIDES[1]
c. 485 – 406 B.C.

Never say that marriage has more of
joy than pain.
Alcestis [2] [438 B.C.], *l.* 238

A second wife
is hateful to the children of the first;
a viper is not more hateful.　　*Ib.* 309

A sweet thing, for whatever time,
to revisit in dreams the dear dead we
have lost.　　*Ib.* 355

Oh, if I had Orpheus' voice and poetry
with which to move the Dark Maid and
her Lord,
I'd call you back, dear love, from the
world below.
I'd go down there for you. Charon or
the grim
King's dog could not prevent me
then
from carrying you up into the fields of
light.　　*Ib.* 358

Light be the earth upon you, lightly
rest.[3]　　*Ib.* 462

God, these old men!
How they pray for death! How heavy
they find this life in the slow drag of
days!
And yet, when Death comes near
them,
You will not find one who will rise and
walk with him,

[1] Sophocles said he drew men as they ought
to be, and Euripides as they were. — ARISTOTLE,
Poetics, ch 25
[2] Translated by DUDLEY FITTS and ROBERT
FITZGERALD.
[3] See Anonymous, p. 151b; Beaumont and
Fletcher, p. 316b; and Robert Richardson,
p. 822a.

not one whose years are still a burden
to him.[1]   *Alcestis, l.* 669

You love the daylight: do you think
your
father does not?   *Ib.* 691

Dishonor will not trouble me, once I
am dead.   *Ib.* 726

Today's today. Tomorrow, we may be
ourselves gone down the drain of Eternity.[2]   *Ib.* 788

O mortal man, think mortal thoughts! [3]
                              Ib. 799

My mother was accursed the night she
bore me,
and I am faint with envy of all the
dead.[4]   *Ib.* 865

You were a stranger to sorrow: therefore Fate
has cursed you.   *Ib.* 927

I have found power in the mysteries of
thought,
exaltation in the chanting of the
Muses;
I have been versed in the reasonings of
men;
but Fate is stronger than anything I
have known.   *Ib.* 962

Time cancels young pain.   *Ib.* 1085

Slight not what's near through aiming
at
what's far.[5]
          Rhesus [*c.* 435 *B.C.*], *l* 482

There is no benefit in the gifts of a bad
man.
          Medea [431 *B.C.*], *l.* 618

When love is in excess it brings a man
nor honor
nor any worthiness.   *Ib.* 627

What greater grief than the loss of
one's
native land.   *Ib.* 650

---

[1] See Sophocles, p. 83a.
[2] See Edward Fitzgerald, p. 630a.
[3] See Pindar, p. 79b.
[4] See *Job 3:3*, p. 14a.
[5] See Pindar, p. 79a, and note.

I know indeed what evil I intend to
do,
but stronger than all my afterthoughts
is my fury,
fury that brings upon mortals the greatest evils.   *Medea, l.* 1078

We know the good, we apprehend it
clearly,
but we can't bring it to achievement.[1]
          Hippolytus [2] [428 *B.C.*], *l.* 380

There is one thing alone
that stands the brunt of life throughout
its course:
a quiet conscience.   *Ib.* 426

In this world second thoughts, it seems,
are best.[3]   *Ib.* 435

Love distills desire upon the eyes,
love brings bewitching grace into the
heart
of those he would destroy.
I pray that love may never come to me
with murderous intent,
in rhythms measureless and wild.
Not fire nor stars have stronger bolts
than those of Aphrodite sent
by the hand of Eros, Zeus's child.
                              Ib. 525

My tongue swore, but my mind was
still unpledged.[4]   *Ib.* 612

Would that I were under the cliffs, in
the secret
hiding-places of the rocks,
that Zeus might change me to a winged
bird.[5]   *Ib.* 732

I would win my way to the coast,
apple-bearing Hesperian coast
of which the minstrels sing,
where the Lord of the Ocean
denies the voyager further sailing,
and fixes the solemn limit of Heaven
which giant Atlas upholds.

---

[1] See *Romans 7:19*, p. 51a, and Ovid, p. 129a.
[2] Translated by DAVID GRENE.
[3] Second thoughts, they say, are best. —
DRYDEN, *The Spanish Friar* [1681], *act* II, *sc.* 2
Is it so true that second thoughts are best?
— TENNYSON, *Sea Dreams* [1864]
[4] See Sallust, p. 115b.
[5] See *Psalm 55:6*, p. 19b.

There the streams flow with ambrosia
by Zeus's bed of love,
and holy Earth, the giver of life,
yields to the Gods rich blessedness.[1]
Hippolytus, l. 742

I care for riches, to make gifts
To friends, or lead a sick man back to
health
With ease and plenty. Else small aid is
wealth
For daily gladness; once a man be
done
With hunger, rich and poor are all as
one.
Electra [1] [413 B.C.], *l. 427*

A coward turns away, but a brave
man's choice is danger.
Iphigenia in Tauris [c. 412
B.C.], *l. 114*

The day is for honest men, the night
for thieves. *Ib. 1026*

Mankind . . . possesses two supreme blessings. First of these is the
goddess Demeter, or Earth — which-
ever name you choose to call her by.
It was she who gave to man his nourishment of grain. But after her there came
the son of Semele, who matched her
present by inventing liquid wine as
his gift to man. For filled with that
good gift, suffering mankind forgets its
grief; from it comes sleep; with it
oblivion of the troubles of the day.
There is no other medicine for misery.[2]
The Bacchae [c. 407 B.C.], *l. 274*

Talk sense to a fool and he calls
you foolish. *Ib. 480*

Slow but sure moves the might of
the gods.[3] *Ib. 882*

What is wisdom? What gift of the
gods
is held in glory like this:

---

[1] Translated by GILBERT MURRAY.
[2] Translated by WILLIAM ARROWSMITH.
[3] See George Herbert, p. 325a, and von Logau,
p. 329a.

to hold your hand victorious
over the heads of those you hate?
Glory is precious forever.
The Bacchae, l. 877

Humility, a sense of reverence before
the sons of heaven —
of all the prizes that a mortal man
might win,
these, I say, are wisest; these are best.
Ib. 1150

Yet do I hold that mortal foolish
who strives against the stress of necessity. *Mad Heracles, l. 281*

The company of just and righteous
men is better than wealth and a rich
estate. *Aegeus,*[1] *frag. 7*

A bad beginning makes a bad ending. *Aeolus,*[1] *frag. 32*

Time will explain it all. He is a
talker, and needs no questioning before
he speaks. *Ib. frag. 38*

Waste not fresh tears over old griefs.
Alexander,[1] *frag. 44*

The nobly born must nobly meet his
fate.[2] *Alcymene,*[3] *frag. 100*

Man's best possession is a sympathetic wife. *Antigone,*[3] *frag. 164*

When good men die their goodness
does not perish,
But lives though they are gone. As for
the bad,
All that was theirs dies and is buried
with them.[4]
Temenidae,[5] *frag. 734*

---

[1] Translated by MORRIS HICKEY MORGAN.
[2] See Sophocles, p. 81a.
  If there be any good in nobility, I trow it
to be only this, that it imposeth a necessity
upon those which are noble, that they should
not suffer their nobility to degenerate from
the virtues of their ancestors. — BOETHIUS
[A.D. 470–525], *De Consolatione Philosophiae III,*
6:25
  Noblesse oblige. — DUC DE LEVIS [1764–1830]
[3] Translated by MORRIS HICKEY MORGAN.
[4] See Shakespeare, *Julius Caesar III, ii, 79,*
p. 255b.
[5] Translated by MORRIS HICKEY MORGAN.

An old man weds a tyrant, not a wife.
Phoenix (*quoted by* ARISTOPH-
ANES,   *Thesmophoriazusae*),
frag. 413

Every man is like the company he is
wont to keep.   *Ib.*[1] *frag. 809*

Who knows but life be that which men
call death,
And death what men call life? [2]
Phrixus,[3] *frag. 830*

Whoso neglects learning in his youth,
Loses the past and is dead for the future.   *Ib. frag. 927*

The gods
Visit the sins of the fathers upon the
children.[4]   *Ib. frag. 970*

In a case of dissension, never dare to
judge till you've heard the other side.
Heracleidae [5] (*quoted by* ARIS-
TOPHANES, *The Wasps*)

Those whom God wishes to destroy,
he first makes mad.[6]   *Fragment*

These men won eight victories over

[1] Translated by MORRIS HICKEY MORGAN.
[2] See Aristophanes, p. 92a, and Montaigne,
p. 190b.
[3] Translated by MORRIS HICKEY MORGAN.
[4] See *Exodus 20:5*, p. 9a.
For the sins of your fathers you, though
guiltless, must suffer. — HORACE, *Odes III, 6:1*
The sins of the fathers are to be laid upon
the children. — SHAKESPEARE, *Merchant of Venice* [1596–1597], *III, v, 1*
[5] Translated by MORRIS HICKEY MORGAN.
[6] The anonymous Latin version is: Quos [or
Quem] deus vult perdere prius dementat.
In Boswell's *Life of Dr. Johnson* [1791]
(Everyman ed.), *vol. 2, pp. 442–443,* this is
quoted as a saying which everybody repeats but
nobody knows where to find.
Whom Fortune wishes to destroy she first
makes mad. — PUBLILIUS SYRUS [c. 42 B.C.],
Maxim 911
When falls on man the anger of the gods,
First from his mind they banish under-
    standing.   LYCURGUS [fl. 820 B.C.]
For those whom God to ruin has designed,
He fits for fate, and first destroys their mind.
     DRYDEN, *The Hind and the Panther*
         [1687], *pt. III, l. 1093*
Whom the Gods would destroy they first
make mad. — LONGFELLOW, *The Masque of
Pandora* [1875], *VI*

the Syracusans when the favor of the
gods was equal for both sides.
*Epitaph for the Athenians Slain
in Sicily*

HERODOTUS
c. 485 – c. 425 B.C.

Men trust their ears less than their
eyes.   *Book I, ch. 8*

A woman takes off her claim to respect along with her garments.[1]   *Ib.*

In peace, children inter their parents;
war violates the order of nature and
causes parents to inter their children.
I, 87

[The Persians] are accustomed to
deliberate about the most important
matters when they are drunk.   *I, 133*

It was a kind of Cadmean victory.[2]
I, 166

For great wrongdoing there are great
punishments from the gods.
II, 120

If a man insisted always on being
serious, and never allowed himself a bit
of fun and relaxation, he would go mad
or become unstable without knowing
it.   *II, 173*

It is better to be envied than pitied.[3]
III, 52

Envy is born in a man from the
start.   *III, 80*

Force has no place where there is
need of skill.   *III, 127*

From the foot, Hercules.[4]   *IV, 82*

[1] See Chaucer, p. 168a.
[2] Polyneices and Eteocles, sons of Oedipus
and descendants of Cadmus, fought for the
possession of Thebes and killed each other.
Hence, a Cadmean victory means one where
victor and vanquished suffer alike.
See also Pyrrhus, p. 103b ("Pyrrhic victory").
[3] Also in PINDAR, *Pythian Odes I, 164.*
[4] Ex pede, Herculem. From AULUS GELLIUS
(*Noctes Atticae I, 1*), who tells how Pythagoras
deduced the stature of Hercules from the
length of his foot.
See Anonymous, p. 150b.

It is the gods' custom to bring low all things of surpassing greatness.[1]
Book VII, ch. 10

Haste in every business brings failures.   *VII, 10*

When life is so burdensome, death has become for man a sought-after refuge.   *VII, 46*

Circumstances rule men; men do not rule circumstances.   *VII, 49*

Great deeds are usually wrought at great risks.   *VII, 50*

Not snow, no, nor rain, nor heat, nor night keeps them from accomplishing their appointed courses with all speed.[2]
VIII, 98

The king's might is greater than human, and his arm is very long.
VIII, 140

This is the bitterest pain among men, to have much knowledge but no power.   *IX, 16*

In soft regions are born soft men.
IX, 122

PROTAGORAS
c. 485 – c. 410 B.C.

Man is the measure of all things.
Fragment 1

There are two sides to every question.
*From DIOGENES LAERTIUS,
Protagoras IX, 51*

[1] It is the lofty pine that by the storm
Is oftener tossed; towers fall with heavier crash
Which higher soar.
Horace [65–8 B.C.], Odes II, 10:9
The bigger they come, the harder they fall.
— ROBERT FITZSIMMONS [1862–1917] before his bout with James J. Jeffries, a heavier man, in San Francisco [June 9, 1899]

[2] Neither snow, nor rain, nor heat, nor gloom of night stays these couriers from the swift completion of their appointed rounds. — *Inscription on the Main Post Office, New York City, adapted from Herodotus*

AGIS
fifth century B.C.

The Lacedemonians are not wont to ask how many the enemy are, but where they are.
From PLUTARCH, Apothegms, Agis

SOCRATES[1]
469–399 B.C.

Often when looking at a mass of things for sale, he would say to himself, "How many things I have no need of!"
*From DIOGENES LAERTIUS,
bk. 2, sec. 25*

Having the fewest wants, I am nearest to the gods.
Ib. 27

There is only one good, knowledge, and one evil, ignorance.   *Ib. 31*

My divine sign indicates the future to me.   *Ib. 32*

I know nothing except the fact of my ignorance.   *Ib.*

Bad men live that they may eat and drink, whereas good men eat and drink that they may live.[2]
*From PLUTARCH, How a Young
Man Ought to Hear Poems, 4*

I am not an Athenian or a Greek, but a citizen of the world.[3]
From PLUTARCH, Of Banishment

[1] Much of Plato, especially in the *Apology* and *Phaedo,* is thought to be direct quotation from Socrates. See Plato, p. 93b.
[2] He used to say that other men lived to eat, but that he ate to live. — DIOGENES LAERTIUS [c. A.D. 200], *Socrates 14*
See Molière, p. 361a.
We must eat to live and live to eat. — FIELDING [1707–1754], *The Miser, act III, sc. iii*
[3] See Bacon, p. 208b; Thomas Paine, p. 467b; and William Lloyd Garrison, p. 615b.
Diogenes, when asked from what country he came, replied, "I am a citizen of the world." — DIOGENES LAERTIUS [c. A.D. 200], *Diogenes 6*
Citizen of the world, as I hold myself to be. — BOSWELL, *Life of Dr. Johnson* [1791], *Everyman Edition, vol. I, p. 521*

Crito, I owe a cock to Asclepius; will you remember to pay the debt?

From PLATO, *Phaedo* (*Socrates'*
last words)

DEMOCRITUS
c. 460 – c. 400 B.C.

Whatever a poet writes with enthusiasm and a divine inspiration is very fine.[1]   *Fragment 18*

In truth we know nothing, for truth lies in the depth.   *Fragment 117*

By convention there is color, by convention sweetness, by convention bitterness, but in reality there are atoms and space.   *Fragment 125*

Word is a shadow of deed.
   Fragment 145

HIPPOCRATES
c. 460 – 400 B.C.

I swear by Apollo Physician, by Asclepius, by Health, by Panacea, and by all the gods and goddesses, making them my witnesses, that I will carry out, according to my ability and judgment, this oath and this indenture. To hold my teacher in this art equal to my own parents; to make him partner in my livelihood; when he is in need of money to share mine with him; to consider his family as my own brothers, and to teach them this art, if they want to learn it, without fee or indenture . . . I will use treatment to help the sick according to my ability and judgment, but never with a view to injury and wrongdoing . . . I will keep pure and holy both my life and my art . . . In whatsoever houses I enter, I will enter to help the sick, and I will abstain from all intentional wrongdoing and harm, especially from abusing the bodies of man or woman, bond or free. And whatsoever I shall see or hear in the course of my profession in my intercourse with men, if it be what should not be published abroad, I will never

[1] Apparently the earliest reference to the madness or divine inspiration of poets.

divulge, holding such things to be holy secrets. Now if I carry out this oath, and break it not, may I gain forever reputation among all men for my life and for my art; but if I transgress it and forswear myself, may the opposite befall me.   *The Physician's Oath* [1]

Healing is a matter of time, but it is sometimes also a matter of opportunity.
   Precepts,[1] *ch. 1*

Sometimes give your services for nothing, calling to mind a previous benefaction or present satisfaction. And if there be an opportunity of serving one who is a stranger in financial straits, give full assistance to all such. For where there is love of man, there is also love of the art. For some patients, though conscious that their condition is perilous, recover their health simply through their contentment with the goodness of the physician. And it is well to superintend the sick to make them well, to care for the healthy to keep them well, also to care for one's own self, so as to observe what is seemly.
   Ib. ch. 6

In all abundance there is lack.
   Ib. ch. 8

If for the sake of a crowded audience you do wish to hold a lecture, your ambition is no laudable one, and at least avoid all citations from the poets, for to quote them argues feeble industry.
   Ib. ch. 12

Life is short, the art long, timing is exact, experience treacherous, judgment difficult.[2]   *Aphorisms, sec. I, 1*

For extreme illnesses extreme treatments are most fitting.[3]   *Ib. 6*

[1] Translated by W. H. S. JONES.
[2] Vita brevis est, ars longa. — SENECA, *De Brevitate Vitae I, 1*
   The lyf so short, the craft so long to lerne. — CHAUCER, *The Parliament of Fowls* [1380–1386], *l. 1*
   Art's long, though time is short. — BROWNING, *The Ring and the Book* [1868–1869], *IX, Juris Doctor Johannes-Baptista Bottinius*
   See Goethe, p. 477b, and Longfellow, p. 620b.
[3] See Shakespeare, *Hamlet IV, iii, 9*, p. 264b.

THUCYDIDES[1]
c. 460 – 400 B.C.

Thucydides, an Athenian, wrote the history of the war between the Peloponnesians and the Athenians; he began at the moment that it broke out, believing that it would be a great war, and more memorable than any that had preceded it.

> *The History of the Peloponnesian War* [431–413 B.C.], bk. I, sec. 1

With reference to the narrative of events, far from permitting myself to derive it from the first source that came to hand, I did not even trust my own impressions, but it rests partly on what I saw myself, partly on what others saw for me, the accuracy of the report being always tried by the most severe and detailed tests possible. My conclusions have cost me some labor from the want of coincidence between accounts of the same occurrences by different eyewitnesses, arising sometimes from imperfect memory, sometimes from undue partiality for one side or the other. The absence of romance in my history will, I fear, detract somewhat from its interest; but I shall be content if it is judged useful by those inquirers who desire an exact knowledge of the past as an aid to the interpretation of the future, which in the course of human things must resemble if it does not reflect it. My history has been composed to be an everlasting possession, not the showpiece of an hour.[2]   *Ib.* 22

The great wish of some is to avenge themselves on some particular enemy, the great wish of others to save their own pocket. Slow in assembling, they devote a very small fraction of the time to the consideration of any public object, most of it to the prosecution of their own objects. Meanwhile each fancies that no harm will come of his neglect, that it is the business of somebody else to look after this or that for him; and so, by the same notion being entertained by all separately, the common cause imperceptibly decays.[1]

> *The History of the Peloponnesian War, bk. I, sec. 141*

Our constitution is named a democracy, because it is in the hands not of the few but of the many. But our laws secure equal justice for all in their private disputes, and our public opinion welcomes and honors talent in every branch of achievement, not for any sectional reason but on grounds of excellence alone. And as we give free play to all in our public life, so we carry the same spirit into our daily relations with one another. We have no black looks or angry words for our neighbor if he enjoys himself in his own way, and we abstain from the little acts of churlishness which, though they leave no mark, yet cause annoyance to whoso notes them. Open and friendly in our private intercourse, in our public acts we keep strictly within the control of law. We acknowledge the restraint of reverence; we are obedient to whomsoever is set in authority, and to the laws, more especially to those which offer protection to the oppressed and those unwritten ordinances whose transgression brings admitted shame.

> *Ib.* II (*Funeral Oration of Pericles*), 37

We are lovers of beauty without extravagance, and lovers of wisdom without unmanliness. Wealth to us is not mere material for vainglory but an opportunity for achievement; and poverty we think it no disgrace to acknowledge but a real degradation to make no effort to overcome.   *Ib.* 40

But the bravest are surely those who have the clearest vision of what is before them, glory and danger alike, and yet notwithstanding go out to meet it.
> *Ib.*

---

[1] Translated by SIR RICHARD LIVINGSTONE.
[2] See Ranke, p. 586a.

[1] Quoted by President John F. Kennedy in Frankfurt [June 25, 1963].

We secure our friends not by accepting favors but by doing them.[1]
> *The History of the Peloponnesian War, bk. II (Funeral Oration of Pericles), sec. 40*

In a word I claim that our city as a whole is an education to Greece.
> *Ib. 41*

Fix your eyes on the greatness of Athens as you have it before you day by day, fall in love with her, and when you feel her great, remember that this greatness was won by men with courage, with knowledge of their duty, and with a sense of honor in action . . . So they gave their bodies to the commonwealth and received, each for his own memory, praise that will never die, and with it the grandest of all sepulchers, not that in which their mortal bones are laid, but a home in the minds of men, where their glory remains fresh to stir to speech or action as the occasion comes by. For the whole earth is the sepulcher of famous men; and their story is not graven only on stone over their native earth, but lives on far away, without visible symbol, woven into the stuff of other men's lives. For you now it remains to rival what they have done and, knowing the secret of happiness to be freedom and the secret of freedom a brave heart, not idly to stand aside from the enemy's onset.[2]
> *Ib. 43*

Great is the glory of the woman who occasions the least talk among men, whether of praise or of blame.
> *Ib. 45*

For human nature is as surely made arrogant by consideration as it is awed by firmness.
> *Ib. III, 39*

[1] Rather by conferring than by accepting favors, they [the Romans] established friendly relations. — SALLUST, *The War with Catiline* [c. 40 B.C.], *6*

[2] See Simonides, p. 70b, and Brandeis, p. 832b.

Men make the city, and not walls or ships without men in them.[1]
> *The History of the Peloponnesian War, bk. VII, 77 (Address of Nicias to the Athenians at Syracuse)*

This or the like was the cause of the death of a man [Nicias] who, of all the Greeks in my time, least deserved such a fate, for he had lived in the practice of every virtue.
> *Ib. VIII, 86*

This was the greatest event in the war, or, in my opinion, in Greek history; at once most glorious to the victors and most calamitous to the conquered. They were beaten at all points and altogether; their sufferings in every way were great. They were totally destroyed — their fleet, their army, everything — and few out of many returned home. So ended the Sicilian expedition.
> *Ib. VIII, 87*

All Hellas is the monument of Euripides, but the Macedonian land holds his bones, for it sheltered the end of his life. His country was Athens, the Hellas of Hellas, and as by his verse he gave exceeding delight, so for many he receiveth praise.
> *Epitaph. Greek Anthology [Loeb Classical Library], bk. VII, no. 45*

ARISTOPHANES
c. 450 – 385 B.C.

For then, in wrath, the Olympian Pericles
Thundered and lightened, and confounded Hellas
Enacting laws which ran like drinking songs.[2]
> *Acharnians [425 B.C.], l. 530*

When men drink, then they are rich and successful and win lawsuits and are happy and help their friends.
Quickly, bring me a beaker of wine, so

[1] See Sophocles, p. 81a.

[2] Translated by B. B. ROGERS.

that I may wet my mind and say something clever.
　　　　Knights [424 B.C.], *l. 92*

You have all the characteristics of a popular politician: a horrible voice, bad breeding, and a vulgar manner.　　　　*Ib. 217*

To make the worse appear the better reason.[1]
　　Clouds [423 B.C.], *l. 114 and elsewhere*

Haven't you sometimes seen a cloud that looked like a centaur?
Or a leopard perhaps? Or a wolf? Or a bull? [2]　　　　*Ib. 346*

Old men are children for a second time.[3]　　　　*Ib. 1417*

This is what extremely grieves us, that a man who never fought
Should contrive our fees to pilfer, one who for his native land
Never to this day had oar, or lance, or blister in his hand.
　　　　Wasps [4] [422 B.C.], *l. 1117*

Let each man exercise the art he knows.　　　　*Ib. 1431*

You cannot teach a crab to walk straight.
　　　　Peace [421 B.C.], *l. 1083*

[On the nightingale] Lord Zeus, listen to the little bird's voice; he has filled the whole thicket with honeyed song.
　　　　Birds [414 B.C.], *l. 223*

Bringing owls to Athens.[5]　　　*Ib. 301*

The wise learn many things from their enemies.　　　　*Ib. 375*

Full of wiles, full of guile, at all times, in all ways,
Are the children of Men.[6]　　*Ib. 451*

[1] See Milton, p. 343b.
[2] Translated by DUDLEY FITTS.
See Shakespeare, *Hamlet III, ii, 400,* p. 263b, and *Antony and Cleopatra IV, xii, 2,* p. 288b.
[3] See Shakespeare, p. 261a.
[4] Translated by B. B. ROGERS.
[5] See Horace, p. 120a.
[6] Translated by B. B. ROGERS.

Mankind, fleet of life, like tree leaves, weak creatures of clay, unsubstantial as shadows, wingless, ephemeral, wretched, mortal and dreamlike.[1]　　　　*Birds, l. 685*

Somewhere, what with all these clouds, and all this air,
There must be a rare name, somewhere . . . How do you like "Cloud-Cuckoo-Land"? [2]
　　　　Ib. 817

Halcyon days.[3]　　　　*Ib. 1594*

A woman's time of opportunity is short, and if she doesn't seize it, no one wants to marry her, and she sits watching for omens.
　　　Lysistrata [411 B.C.], *l. 596*

There is no animal more invincible than a woman, nor fire either, nor any wildcat so ruthless.
　　　　Ib. 1014

These impossible women! How they do get around us!
The poet was right: can't live with them, or without them! [4]
　　　　Ib. 1038

Under every stone lurks a politician.[5]
　　　Thesmophoriazusae [410 B.C.], *l. 530*

There's nothing worse in the world than shameless woman — save some other woman.　　　*Ib. l. 531*

Shall I crack any of those old jokes, master,
At which the audience never fail to laugh?　　*Frogs* [6] [405 B.C.], *l. 1*

[1] See Homer, p. 64b, and Pindar, p. 79b.
[2] Translated by DUDLEY FITTS.
[3] See Shakespeare, *Henry VI, Pt. I, I, ii, 131,* p. 214a.
　The appellation of Halcyon days, which was applied to a rare and bloodless week of repose.
—GIBBON: *Decline and Fall of the Roman Empire* [1776–1788], *ch. 48*
[4] Translated by DUDLEY FITTS.
Imitated by Martial (see p. 135b).
[5] A play on the proverb "Under every stone lurks a scorpion."
[6] Translated by B. B. ROGERS.

Brekekekex, ko-ax, ko-ax.[1]
> *Frogs, l. 209 and elsewhere*

A savage-creating stubborn-pulling fellow,
Uncurbed, unfettered, uncontrolled of speech,
Unperiphrastic, bombastiloquent.[2]
> *Ib. 837*

High thoughts must have high language.[3] *Ib. 1058*

Who knows whether living is dying, and breathing
Is eating, and sleeping is a wool blanket?[4] *Ib. 1477*

Blest the man who possesses a
Keen intelligent mind. *Ib. 1482*

I am amazed that anyone who has made a fortune should send for his friends.
> *Plutus [c. 388 B.C.], l. 340*

We say that poverty is the sister of beggary. *Ib. 549*

Even if you persuade me, you won't persuade me. *Ib. 600*

A man's homeland is wherever he prospers. *Ib. 1151*

AGATHON
c. 448 – 400 B.C.

This only is denied to God: the power to undo the past.
> *From* ARISTOTLE, *Nicomachean Ethics, bk. VI, ch. 2*

AGESILAUS
444–400 B.C.

If all men were just, there would be no need of valor.
> *From* PLUTARCH, *Lives, Agesilaus, sec. 23*

It is circumstance and proper timing that give an action its character and make it either good or bad. *Ib. 36*

---

[1] Adopted as a Yale College cheer.
[2] Refers to Aeschylus.
[3] Translated by DUDLEY FITTS.
[4] See Euripides, p. 86a, and Montaigne, p. 190b.

XENOPHON
c. 430 – 355 B.C.

Apollo said that everyone's true worship was that which he found in use in the place where he chanced to be.
> *Recollections of Socrates, bk. I, ch. 3, sec. 1*

The sea! The sea! [1]
> *Anabasis IV, 7, 24*

I knew my son was mortal.[2]
> *From* DIOGENES LAERTIUS, *Xenophon II, 55*

ZEUXIS
fl. 400 B.C.

Criticism comes easier than craftsmanship.
> *From* PLINY THE ELDER, *Natural History*

PLATO[3]
c. 428 – 348 B.C.

We who of old left the booming surge of the Aegean lie here in the midplain of Ecbatana: farewell, renowned Eretria once our country; farewell, Athens nigh to Euboea; farewell, dear sea.[4] *Greek Anthology III, 10*[5]

Beloved Pan, and all ye other gods who haunt this place, give me beauty in the inward soul; and may the outward and inward man be at one. May I reckon the wise to be the wealthy, and may I have such a quantity of gold as none but the temperate can carry.
> *Dialogues, Phaedrus, sec. 279*

Friends have all things in common.[6]
> *Ib.*

---

[1] Thalatta! Thalatta!
 Hail to thee, O Sea, ageless and eternal!
   HEINRICH HEINE [1797–1856], *Thalatta! Thalatta!, st. 1*
[2] When his son was killed in battle.
[3] Translated by BENJAMIN JOWETT.
[4] On the Eretrian exiles settled in Persia by Darius.
[5] Edited by J. W. MACKAIL.
[6] According to Timaios, he [Pythagoras, 582–500 B.C.] originated the saying "Friends share all things." — DIOGENES LAERTIUS *VIII, 10*
 Also in Euripides, *Orestes, l. 735.*
 See Sallust, p. 115b.

And the true order of going, or being led by another, to the things of love, is to begin from the beauties of earth and mount upwards for the sake of that other beauty, using these steps only, and from one going on to two, and from two to all fair forms to fair practices, and from fair practices to fair notions, until from fair notions he arrives at the notion of absolute beauty, and at last knows what the essence of beauty is.

Dialogues, Symposium 211

Beholding beauty with the eye of the mind, he will be enabled to bring forth, not images of beauty, but realities (for he has hold not of an image but of a reality), and bringing forth and nourishing true virtue to become the friend of God and be immortal, if mortal man may. *Ib.* 212

Socrates is a doer of evil, who corrupts the youth; and who does not believe in the gods of the state, but has other new divinities of his own. Such is the charge. *Ib. Apology* 24

The life which is unexamined is not worth living. *Ib. 38*

Either death is a state of nothingness and utter unconsciousness, or, as men say, there is a change and migration of the soul from this world to another.[1] . . . Now if death be of such a nature, I say that to die is to gain; for eternity is then only a single night.

Ib. 40

No evil can happen to a good man, either in life or after death. *Ib. 41*

The hour of departure has arrived, and we go our ways — I to die, and you to live. Which is better God only knows. *Ib. 42*

Man is a prisoner who has no right to open the door of his prison and run

[1] Either the soul is immortal and we shall not die, or it perishes with the flesh and we shall not know that we are dead. Live, then, as if you were eternal. — ANDRÉ MAUROIS [1885–1967]. From WILL DURANT, *On the Meaning of Life* [1932], *p. 53*.

away. . . . A man should wait, and not take his own life until God summons him.

Dialogues, Phaedo.[1] 62

Must not all things at the last be swallowed up in death? *Ib. 72*

Will you not allow that I have as much of the spirit of prophecy in me as the swans? For they, when they perceive that they must die, having sung all their life long, do then sing more lustily than ever, rejoicing in the thought that they are going to the god they serve.[2] *Ib. 85*

The partisan, when he is engaged in a dispute, cares nothing about the rights of the question, but is anxious only to convince his hearers of his own assertions. *Ib. 91*

False words are not only evil in themselves, but they infect the soul with evil. *Ib.*

The soul takes nothing with her to the other world but her education and culture; and these, it is said, are of the greatest service or of the greatest injury to the dead man, at the very beginning of his journey thither. *Ib. 107*

He who is of a calm and happy nature will hardly feel the pressure of age, but to him who is of an opposite disposition youth and age are equally a burden. *The Republic, bk. I, 329–D*

No physician, insofar as he is a physician, considers his own good in what he prescribes, but the good of his patient; for the true physician is also a ruler having the human body as a sub-

[1] See Socrates, p. 87b.
[2] The jalous swan, ayens his deth that singeth. — CHAUCER, *The Parliament of Fowls* [1380–1386], *l. 342*
> Makes a swan-like end,
> Fading in music.

SHAKESPEARE, *The Merchant of Venice* [1596–1597], *III, 2, 44*
I will play the swan and die in music. — *Othello* [1604–1605] *V, 2, 245*
See Shakespeare, p. 237a, and Byron, p. 561a.
See Socrates, p. 88a, for his last words.

ject, and is not a mere moneymaker.[1]
The Republic, bk. I, 342–D

When there is an income tax, the just man will pay more and the unjust less on the same amount of income.
Ib. 343–D

Mankind censure injustice fearing that they may be the victims of it, and not because they shrink from committing it.
Ib. 344–C

The beginning is the most important part of the work.[2]
Ib. 377–B

The judge should not be young; he should have learned to know evil, not from his own soul, but from late and long observation of the nature of evil in others: knowledge should be his guide, not personal experience.
Ib. III, 409–B

Everything that deceives may be said to enchant.
Ib. 413–C

How, then, might we contrive . . . one noble lie to persuade if possible the rulers themselves, but failing that the rest of the city? [3]
Ib. 414–C

Wealth is the parent of luxury and indolence, and poverty of meanness and viciousness, and both of discontent.[4]
Ib. IV, 422–A

The direction in which education starts a man will determine his future life.
Ib. 425–B

What is the prime of life? May it not be defined as a period of about twenty years in a woman's life, and thirty in a man's?
Ib. V, 460–E

Until philosophers are kings, or the kings and princes of this world have the spirit and power of philosophy, and political greatness and wisdom meet in one, and those commoner natures who pursue either to the exclusion of the other are compelled to stand aside, cities will never have rest from their

evils — no, nor the human race, as I believe — and then only will this our State have a possibility of life and behold the light of day.
The Republic, bk. V, 473–C

Let there be one man who has a city obedient to his will, and he might bring into existence the ideal polity about which the world is so incredulous.
Ib. 502–B

Behold! human beings living in an underground den . . . Like ourselves . . . they see only their own shadows, or the shadows of one another, which the fire throws on the opposite wall of the cave.
Ib. VII, 515–B

Astronomy compels the soul to look upwards and leads us from this world to another.
Ib. 529

I have hardly ever known a mathematician who was capable of reasoning.
Ib. 531–E

Solon was under a delusion when he said that a man when he grows old may learn many things [1] — for he can no more learn much than he can run much; youth is the time for any extraordinary toil.
Ib. 536–D

Bodily exercise, when compulsory, does no harm to the body; but knowledge which is acquired under compulsion obtains no hold on the mind.
Ib. 536–E

Let early education be a sort of amusement; you will then be better able to find out the natural bent.
Ib. 537

Oligarchy: A government resting on a valuation of property, in which the rich have power and the poor man is deprived of it.
Ib. VIII, 550–C

Democracy, which is a charming form of government, full of variety and disorder, and dispensing a sort of equality to equals and unequals alike.[2]
Ib. 558–C

---

[1] See Hippocrates, p. 88b.
[2] Proverbial. Also in *Laws VI*, 2. See Aristotle, p. 98b; Horace, p. 123a; and Heywood, p. 183b.
[3] *Loeb Classical Library* translation.
[4] See *I Timothy 6:10, p. 55b*, and Sophocles, p. 82a.

[1] See Solon, p. 68b.
[2] See Aristotle, p. 98b.

Democracy passes into despotism.[1]
The Republic, bk. VIII, 562–A

The people have always some champion whom they set over them and nurse into greatness. . . . This and no other is the root from which a tyrant springs; when he first appears he is a protector.   *Ib.* 565–C

In the early days of his power, he is full of smiles, and he salutes everyone whom he meets.   *Ib.* 566–D

When the tyrant has disposed of foreign enemies by conquest or treaty, and there is nothing to fear from them, then he is always stirring up some war or other, in order that the people may require a leader.   *Ib.* 566–E

There are three arts which are concerned with all things: one which uses, another which makes, a third which imitates them.   *Ib.* X, 601–D

No human thing is of serious importance.   *Ib.* 604–C

The soul of man is immortal and imperishable.   *Ib.* 608–D

If a person shows that such things as wood, stones, and the like, being many are also one, we admit that he shows the coexistence of the one and many, but he does not show that the many are one or the one many; he is uttering not a paradox but a truism.
Dialogues, Parmenides 129

The absolute natures or kinds are known severally by the absolute idea of knowledge.   *Ib.* 134

If a man, fixing his attention on these and the like difficulties, does away with ideas of things and will not admit that every individual thing has its own determinate idea which is always one and the same, he will have nothing on which his mind can rest; and so he will utterly destroy the power of reasoning.   *Ib.* 135

You cannot conceive the many without the one.   *Ib.* 166

[1] Translated by F. M. Cornford.

Let us affirm what seems to be the truth, that, whether one is or is not, one and the others in relation to themselves and one another, all of them, in every way, are and are not, and appear to be and appear not to be.
Dialogues, Parmenides 166

Well, my art of midwifery is in most respects like theirs; but differs, in that I attend men and not women, and I look after their souls when they are in labor, and not after their bodies: and the triumph of my art is in thoroughly examining whether the thought which the mind of the young man brings forth is a false idol or a noble and true birth.
Ib. Theaetetus 150

He [the philosopher] does not hold aloof in order that he may gain a reputation; but the truth is, that the outer form of him only is in the city: his mind, disdaining the littlenesses and nothingnesses of human beings, is "flying all abroad" as Pindar says, measuring earth and heaven and the things which are under and on the earth and above the heaven, interrogating the whole nature of each and all in their entirety, but not condescending to anything which is within reach.
Ib. 173

I would have you imagine, then, that there exists in the mind of man a block of wax, which is of different sizes in different men; harder, moister, and having more or less of purity in one than another, and in some of an intermediate quality. . . . Let us say that this tablet is a gift of Memory, the mother of the Muses; and that when we wish to remember anything which we have seen, or heard, or thought in our own minds, we hold the wax to the perceptions and thoughts, and in that material receive the impression of them as from the seal of a ring; and that we remember and know what is imprinted as long as the image lasts; but when the image is effaced, or cannot be taken, then we forget and do not know.
Ib. 191

Let us now suppose that in the mind of each man there is an aviary of all sorts of birds — some flocking together apart from the rest, others in small groups, others solitary, flying anywhere and everywhere. . . . We may suppose that the birds are kinds of knowledge, and that when we were children, this receptacle was empty; whenever a man has gotten and detained in the enclosure a kind of knowledge, he may be said to have learned or discovered the thing which is the subject of the knowledge: and this is to know.

Dialogues, Theaetetus 197

The greatest penalty of evildoing — namely, to grow into the likeness of bad men. *Laws* 728

Of all the animals, the boy is the most unmanageable. *Ib.* 808

You are young, my son, and, as the years go by, time will change and even reverse many of your present opinions. Refrain therefore awhile from setting yourself up as a judge of the highest matters. *Ib.* 888

And this which you deem of no moment is the very highest of all: that is whether you have a right idea of the gods, whereby you may live your life well or ill. *Ib.*

Not one of them who took up in his youth with this opinion that there are no gods ever continued until old age faithful to his conviction. *Ib.*

IPHICRATES
419–348 B.C.

My family history begins with me, but yours ends with you.[1]

From PLUTARCH, *Apothegms, Iphicrates*

[1] Iphicrates, a shoemaker's son who became a famous general, said this to Harmodius of distinguished ancestry when he reviled him for his mean birth.

Curtius Rufus seems to be descended from himself. — TIBERIUS. From TACITUS, *Annals XI, 21*

I am my own ancestor [Moi, je suis mon ancêtre.] — ANDOCHE JUNOT [1771–1813]

PHOCION
c. 402 – 317 B.C.

Have I inadvertently said some evil thing?[1]

From PLUTARCH, *Apothegms, Phocion, sec. 10*

The good have no need of an advocate. *Ib.*

DIOGENES THE CYNIC
c. 400 – c. 325 B.C.

[When asked by Alexander if he wanted anything] Stand a little out of my sun.

From PLUTARCH, *Lives, Alexander, sec. 14*

Plato having defined man to be a two-legged animal without feathers, Diogenes plucked a cock and brought it into the Academy, and said, "This is Plato's man."[2] On which account this addition was made to the definition: "With broad flat nails."

From DIOGENES LAERTIUS, *Diogenes 6*

[When asked what was the proper time for supper] If you are a rich man, whenever you please; and if you are a poor man, whenever you can.[3]

Ib.

I am looking for an honest man.[4] *Ib.*

The sun too penetrates into privies, but is not polluted by them.[5] *Ib.*

[1] Said when an opinion he delivered pleased the people.

[2] Seeing that the human race falls into the same classification as the feathered creatures, we must divide the biped class into featherless and feathered. — PLATO [c. 428 – c. 348 B.C.], *The Statesman 266–E*

[3] The rich when he is hungry, the poor when he has anything to eat. — RABELAIS, *Works, bk. IV* [1548], *ch. 64*

[4] Attributed also to Aesop.

[5] The spiritual virtue of a sacrament is like light: although it passes among the impure, it is not polluted. — ST. AUGUSTINE [A.D. 354–430], *Tract on St. John, ch. 5:15*

The sun shineth upon the dunghill, and is not corrupted. — LYLY, *Euphues* [1579]

The sun, which passeth through pollutions and itself remains as pure as before. — BACON,

ANTIPHANES
c. 388 – c. 311 B.C.

We must have richness of soul.
Greek Comic Fragments, no. 570

ARISTOTLE[1]
384–322 B.C.

Liars when they speak the truth are not believed.
From DIOGENES LAERTIUS,
bk. V, sec. 17

Hope is a waking dream. *Ib. 18*

What soon grows old? Gratitude.
Ib.

Beauty is the gift of God. *Ib. 19*

Educated men are as much superior to uneducated men as the living are to the dead.[2] *Ib.*

What is a friend? A single soul dwelling in two bodies.[3] *Ib. 20*

I have gained this by philosophy: that I do without being commanded what others do only from fear of the law.[4] *Ib. 21*

We should behave to our friends as we would wish our friends to behave to us.[5] *Ib.*

Education is the best provision for old age. *Ib.*

Time wastes things away, and all things grow old through time.
Physics, bk. IV, ch. 12

The least initial deviation from the truth is multiplied later a thousand-fold. *On the Heavens, bk. I, ch. 5*

In all things of nature there is something of the marvelous.
Parts of Animals, bk. I, ch. 5

All men by nature desire knowledge.
Metaphysics, bk. I, ch. 1

The final cause, then, produces motion through being loved.[1] *Ib. ch. 7*

The actuality of thought is life.
Ib. XII, ch. 7

It is of itself that the divine thought thinks (since it is the most excellent of things), and its thinking is a thinking on thinking. *Ib. ch. 9*

Every science and every inquiry, and similarly every activity and pursuit, is thought to aim at some good.
Nicomachean Ethics, bk. I, ch. 1

While both [Plato and truth] are dear, piety requires us to honor truth above our friends.[2] *Ib. ch. 6*

One swallow does not make a summer.[3] *Ib. ch. 7*

For the things we have to learn before we can do them, we learn by doing them. *Ib. II, ch. 1*

It is possible to fail in many ways . . . while to succeed is possible only in one way (for which reason also one is easy and the other difficult — to miss the mark easy, to hit it difficult).
Ib. ch. 6

We must as second best . . . take the least of the evils.[4] *Ib. ch. 9*

Advancement of Learning [1605], *bk. II*
Truth is as impossible to be soiled by any outward touch as the sunbeam. — MILTON, *The Doctrine and Discipline of Divorce* [1643]

[1] Chiefly from *The Basic Works of Aristotle,* edited by RICHARD MCKEON.

[2] This used to be quoted "with great warmth" by Dr. Johnson, according to BOSWELL in his *Life of Johnson* [1791].

[3] Andrágathos, my soul's half. — MELEAGER [fl. 80 B.C.]. From *The Greek Anthology XII, 52*
See Zeno, p. 103a; Cicero, p. 111b; Horace, p. 120b; and Donne, p. 306a.

[4] Also attributed to Xenocrates [396–314 B.C.] by Cicero.

[5] See *Matthew 7:12,* p. 41a, and Lord Chesterfield, p. 415a.

[1] See Dante, p. 162a.

[2] Amicus Plato, sed magis amica veritas [Plato is dear to me, but dearer still is truth]. Adapted from a medieval life of Aristotle.

[3] One swallow maketh not summer. — JOHN HEYWOOD, *Proverbs* [1546], *pt. II, ch. 5*
One swallow proveth not that summer is near. — NORTHBROOKE, *Treatise Against Dancing* [1577]
One swallow never makes a summer. — CERVANTES, *Don Quixote, pt. I* [1605], *bk. II, ch. 4*
One swallow makes a summer. — ROBERT LOWELL, *Fall, 1961*

[4] See Homer, p. 64a, and note.

97

A man is the origin of his action.[1]
Nicomachean Ethics,
bk. III, ch. 3

Without friends no one would choose to live, though he had all other goods. *Ib. VIII, ch.* 1

To enjoy the things we ought and to hate the things we ought has the greatest bearing on excellence of character.
Ib. X, ch. 1

If happiness is activity in accordance with excellence, it is reasonable that it should be in accordance with the highest excellence. *Ib. ch.* 7

We make war that we may live in peace. *Ib.*

With regard to excellence, it is not enough to know, but we must try to have and use it. *Ib. ch.* 9

Man is by nature a political animal.
Politics, bk. I, ch. 2

Nature does nothing uselessly.[2]
Ib.

He who is unable to live in society, or who has no need because he is sufficient for himself, must be either a beast or a god. *Ib.*

The two qualities which chiefly inspire regard and affection [are] that a thing is your own and that it is your only one. *Ib. II, ch.* 4

It is the nature of desire not to be satisfied, and most men live only for the gratification of it. The beginning of reform is not so much to equalize property as to train the noble sort of natures not to desire more, and to prevent the lower from getting more. *Ib. ch.* 7

Even when laws have been written down, they ought not always to remain unaltered. *Ib. ch.* 8

Again, men in general desire the good, and not merely what their fathers had. *Ib.*

They should rule who are able to rule best. *Ib. ch.* 11

[1] See Sallust, p. 116a.
[2] God and nature do nothing uselessly. —
On the Heavens, bk. I, ch. 4

A state is not a mere society, having a common place, established for the prevention of mutual crime and for the sake of exchange. . . . Political society exists for the sake of noble actions, and not of mere companionship.
Politics, bk. III, ch. 9

If liberty and equality, as is thought by some, are chiefly to be found in democracy, they will be best attained when all persons alike share in the government to the utmost.[1]
Ib. IV, ch. 4

The best political community is formed by citizens of the middle class.
Ib. ch. 11

Democracy arises out of the notion that those who are equal in any respect are equal in all respects; because men are equally free, they claim to be absolutely equal. *Ib. V, ch.* 1

Inferiors revolt in order that they may be equal, and equals that they may be superior. Such is the state of mind which creates revolutions. *Ib. ch.* 2

In revolutions the occasions may be trifling but great interests are at stake.
Ib. ch. 3

Well begun is half done.[2] *Ib. ch.* 4

The basis of a democratic state is liberty. *Ib. VI, ch.* 2

Law is order, and good law is good order. *Ib. VII, ch.* 4

Evils draw men together.[3]
Rhetoric, bk. I, ch. 6

It is this simplicity that makes the uneducated more effective than the educated when addressing popular audiences. *Ib. II, ch.* 22

A tragedy is the imitation of an action that is serious and also, as having magnitude, complete in itself . . . with incidents arousing pity and fear,

[1] See Plato, p. 94b.
[2] Aristotle is quoting a proverb.
See Plato, p. 94a, and note.
[3] Aristotle is quoting a proverb.

wherewith to accomplish its catharsis of such emotions. *Poetics, ch. 6*

A whole is that which has beginning, middle, and end. *Ib. ch. 7*

Poetry is something more philosophic and of graver import than history, since its statements are of the nature of universals, whereas those of history are singulars. *Ib. ch. 9*

A likely impossibility is always preferable to an unconvincing possibility. *Ib. ch. 24*

Misfortune shows those who are not really friends.[1] *Eudemian Ethics, bk. VII, ch. 2*

DEMOSTHENES
c. 384 – 322 B.C.

Every advantage in the past is judged in the light of the final issue. *First Olynthiac, sec. 11*

Nothing is easier than self-deceit. For what each man wishes, that he also believes to be true.[2] *Third Olynthiac, sec. 19*

You cannot have a proud and chivalrous spirit if your conduct is mean and paltry; for whatever a man's actions are, such must be his spirit. *Ib. 33*

I decline to buy repentance at the cost of ten thousand drachmas.[3] *From* AULUS GELLIUS, *Noctes Atticae, bk. I, ch. 8*

ANTIGONUS
c. 382 – 301 B.C.

But how many ships do you reckon my presence to be worth?[4] *From* PLUTARCH, *Apothegms, Antigonus*

[1] In prosperity it is very easy to find a friend, but in adversity it is the most difficult of all things. — EPICTETUS, *Fragment 127*
See Cicero, p. 111b; Publilius Syrus, p. 127a; Ovid, p. 129a; and John Heywood, p. 184b.
[2] See Caesar, p. 112a.
[3] In reply to the courtesan Laïs.
[4] His pilot had told him that the enemy outnumbered him in ships.

[When described by Hermodotus as "Son of the Sun"] My valet is not aware of this.[1] *From* PLUTARCH, *Apothegms, Antigonus*

MENCIUS[2]
372–289 B.C.

When one by force subdues men, they do not submit to him in heart. They submit, because their strength is not adequate to resist. *Book II, 1:3.2*

There is no attribute of the superior man greater than his helping men to practice virtue. *II, 1:8.5*

The superior man will not manifest either narrow-mindedness or the want of self-respect. *II, 1:9.3*

To give the throne to another man would be easy; to find a man who shall benefit the kingdom is difficult. *III, 1:4.10*

Never has a man who has bent himself been able to make others straight. *III, 2:1.5*

If you know that [a] thing is unrighteous, then use all dispatch in putting an end to it — why wait till next year? *III, 2:8.3*

The compass and square produce perfect circles and squares. By the sages, the human relations are perfectly exhibited. *IV, 1:2.1*

The root of the kingdom is in the state. The root of the state is in the family. The root of the family is in the person of its head. *IV, 1:5*

[1] See Montaigne, p. 190b.
The phrase "No man is a hero to his valet" has often been attributed to Madame de Sévigné, but on the authority of MADAME AÏssÉ (*Letters*, edited by Jules Ravenal, 1853) it belongs to Madame Cornuel [1614–1694].
It is said that no man is a hero to his valet. That is because a hero can be recognized only by a hero. The valet will probably be able to appreciate his like — that is, his fellow-valet. — GOETHE [1749–1832], *Sprüche in Prosa, vol. III, p. 204*
[2] From *The Chinese Classics, Vol. II: The Works of Mencius,* translated by JAMES LEGGE.

The people turn to a benevolent rule as water flows downwards, and as wild beasts fly to the wilderness.

Book IV, 1:9.2

Benevolence is the tranquil habitation of man, and righteousness is his straight path. IV, 1:10.2

The path of duty lies in what is near, and man seeks for it in what is remote.

IV, 1:11

Sincerity is the way of Heaven.

IV, 1:12.2

There are three things which are unfilial, and to have no posterity is the greatest of them.[1] IV, 1:26.1

Men must be decided on what they will not do, and then they are able to act with vigor in what they ought to do. IV, 2:8

The great man does not think beforehand of his words that they may be sincere, nor of his actions that they may be resolute — he simply speaks and does what is right. IV, 2:11

The great man is he who does not lose his child's-heart.[2] IV, 2:12

Friendship with a man is friendship with his virtue, and does not admit of assumptions of superiority.

IV, 2:13.1

If you must do violence and injury to the willow in order to make cups and bowls with it . . . you must in the same way do violence and injury to humanity in order to fashion from it benevolence and righteousness! [This,] alas! would certainly lead all men on to reckon benevolence and righteousness to be calamities. VI, 1:1.2

[1] To be without posterity . . . is an offense against the whole line of ancestors, and terminates the sacrifices to them. — MENCIUS, *Ib.*

[2] "Except ye be converted, and become as little children, ye shall not enter into the kingdom of heaven." But Christ speaks of the child's-heart as a thing to be regained; Mencius speaks of it as a thing not to be lost. — JAMES LEGGE

See *Book VI, 1:11.4.*

Water indeed will flow indifferently to the east or west, but will it flow indifferently up or down? The tendency of man's nature to good is like the tendency of water to flow downwards. There are none but have this tendency to good, just as all water flows downwards. *Book VI*, 1:2.2

From the feelings proper to it, [man's nature] is constituted for the practice of what is good.

VI, 1:6.5–6

Benevolence, righteousness, propriety, and knowledge are not infused into us from without. VI, 1:6.7

Benevolence is man's mind, and righteousness is man's path.

VI, 1:11.1

The great end of learning is nothing else but to seek for the lost mind.[1]

VI, 1:11.4

All men have in themselves that which is truly honorable. Only they do not think of it. VI, 1:17.1

If a scholar have not faith [in his principles], how shall he take a firm hold of things? VI, 2:12

When Heaven is about to confer a great office on any man, it first exercises his mind with suffering, and his sinews and bones with toil. VI, 2:15.2

There is no greater delight than to be conscious of sincerity on self-examination. VII, 1:4.2

Kindly words do not enter so deeply into men as a reputation for kindness.

VII, 1:14.1

Is it only the mouth and belly which are injured by hunger and thirst? Men's minds are also injured by them.

VII, 1:27.1

The people are the most important element in a nation; the spirits of the land and grain are next; the sovereign is the lightest. VII, 2:14.1

[1] The Chinese sages always end with the recovery of "the old heart"; the idea of "a new heart" is unknown to them. — JAMES LEGGE

See *Book IV, 2:12.*

CHUANG TZU[1]
369–286 B.C.

Great wisdom is generous; petty wisdom is contentious. Great speech is impassioned, small speech cantankerous.
On Leveling All Things

Take, for instance, a twig and a pillar, or the ugly person and the great beauty, and all the strange and monstrous transformations. These are all leveled together by Tao. Division is the same as creation; creation is the same as destruction.   *Ib.*

I do not know whether I was then a man dreaming I was a butterfly, or whether I am now a butterfly dreaming I am a man.   *Ib.*

All men know the utility of useful things; but they do not know the utility of futility.   *This Human World*

He who pursues fame at the risk of losing his self is not a scholar.
The Great Supreme

Those who seek to satisfy the mind of man by hampering it with ceremonies and music and affecting charity and devotion have lost their original nature.   *Joined Toes*

In the days of perfect nature, man lived together with birds and beasts, and there was no distinction of their kind. Who could know of the distinctions between gentlemen and common people? Being all equally without knowledge, their virtue could not go astray. Being all equally without desires, they were in a state of natural integrity, the people did not lose their [original] nature.
And then when Sages appeared, crawling for charity and limping with duty, doubt and confusion entered men's minds. They said they must make merry by means of music and enforce distinctions by means of ceremony, and the empire became divided

[1] From *The Wisdom of China and India*, edited by LIN YUTANG.

against itself. . . . Were Tao and virtue not destroyed, what use would there be for charity and duty? Were men's natural instincts not lost, what need would there be for music and ceremonies? . . . Destruction of the natural integrity of these things for the production of articles of various kinds — this is the fault of the artisan. Destruction of Tao and virtue in order to introduce charity and duty — this is the error of the Sages.   *Horses' Hoofs*

Banish wisdom, discard knowledge, and gangsters will stop!
Opening Trunks, or A Protest Against Civilization

For all men strive to grasp what they do not know, while none strive to grasp what they already know; and all strive to discredit what they do not excel in, while none strive to discredit what they do excel in. This is why there is chaos.   *Ib.*

Cherish that which is within you, and shut off that which is without; for much knowledge is a curse.
On Tolerance

"The prince keeps [a] tortoise carefully enclosed in a chest in his ancestral temple. Now would this tortoise rather be dead and have its remains venerated, or would it rather be alive and wagging its tail in the mud?"
"It would rather be alive . . . and wagging its tail in the mud."
"Begone!" cried Chuangtse. "I too will wag my tail in the mud."
Autumn Floods

PYTHEAS[1]
fl. 330 B.C.

They smell of the lamp.[2]
From PLUTARCH, *Lives, Demosthenes*

[1] See Virgil, p. 117a, and note.
[2] Pytheas refers to the orations of Demosthenes, who worked in an underground cave lighted only by a lamp.
See Cardozo, p. 902b.

APELLES
fl. 325 B.C.

Not a day without a line.[1]
Proverbial from PLINY THE
ELDER, *Natural History*
XXXV, *36*

A cobbler should not judge above his
last.[2]   *Ib. 85*

ALEXANDER
THE GREAT
356–323 B.C.

[At Achilles' tomb] O fortunate
youth, to have found Homer as the
herald of your glory!
From CICERO, *Pro Archia 24*

If I were not Alexander, I would be
Diogenes.
From PLUTARCH, *Lives*,
Alexander 14

MENANDER[3]
c. 342 – 292 B.C.

We live, not as we wish to, but as we
can.   *Lady of Andros, frag. 50*

Riches cover a multitude of woes.
The Boeotian Girl, frag. 90

Whom the gods love dies young.[4]
The Double Deceiver, frag. 125

At times discretion should be thrown
aside, and with the foolish we should
play the fool.[5]
Those Offered for Sale, frag. 421

The man who has never been flogged
has never been taught.[6]
The Girl Who Gets Flogged,
frag. 422

[1] Nulla dies sine linea.
[2] Ne supra crepidam sutor iudicaret.
The more common rendering is: Cobbler,
stick to your last.
[3] *Loeb Classical Library* translation.
[4] Also in PLAUTUS, *Bacchides IV, 7:18.*
Those that God loves do not live long. —
GEORGE HERBERT, *Jacula Prudentum* [2nd ed.
1651]
See Wordsworth, p. 516a.
Heaven gives its favorites — early death. —
BYRON, *Childe Harold, canto IV* [1818], st. *102*
[5] See Horace, p. 122b, and note.
[6] See *Proverbs 13:24*, p. 24a, and Samuel
Butler, p. 353a.

The truth sometimes not sought for
comes forth to the light.
The Girl Who Gets
Flogged, frag. 433

This is living, not to live unto oneself
alone.
The Brothers in Love, frag. 508

A god from the machine.[1]
The Woman Possessed with a
Divinity, frag. 227

I call a fig a fig, a spade a spade.[2]
Unidentified fragment 545

Even God lends a hand to honest
boldness.[3]   *Ib. 572*

Marriage, if one will face the truth, is
an evil, but a necessary evil.[4]
Ib. 651

It is not white hair that engenders
wisdom.   *Ib. 639*

Health and intellect are the two
blessings of life.
Monostikoi [Single Lines]

The man who runs may fight again.[5]
Ib.

They spare the rod and spoil the child. —
RALPH VENNING, *Mysteries and Revelations*
[1649]
[1] The Latin form is usually quoted: Deus ex
machina.
Also in LUCIAN, *Hermotimus, sec. 86.*
[2] Also attributed to Aristophanes by LUCIAN,
De Conscribend. Hist. 41.
The Macedonians are a rude and clownish
people that call a spade a spade. — PLUTARCH,
Apothegms, Philip of Macedon
I think it good plain English, without fraud,
To call a spade a spade, a bawd a bawd.
JOHN TAYLOR, The Water Poet
[1580–1653], *A Kicksey Winsey*
[3] See Terence, p. 109a and Propertius, p. 127b.
[4] Marriage is an evil that most men welcome.
— *Monostikoi [Single Lines] Motto of The Spec-*
tator, December 29, 1711
[5] He who flees will fight again. — TERTULLIAN
[c. 155–225], *De Fuga in Persecutione 10*
That same man that runnith awaie
Maie again fight an other daie.
ERASMUS, *Apothegms* [1542], translat-
ed by NICHOLAS UDALL [1505–1556]
Celuy qui fuit de bonne heure
Peut combattre derechef.
(Who flies in good time
Can fight anew.)
Satyre Menippée [1594]

Conscience is a God to all mortals.
Monostikoi [Single Lines]

EPICURUS
341–270 B.C.

Death is nothing to us, since when
we are, death has not come, and when
death has come, we are not.
From DIOGENES LAERTIUS,
bk. X, sec. 125

Pleasure is the beginning and the end
of living happily.　　　*Ib. 128*

It is impossible to live pleasurably
without living wisely, well, and justly,
and impossible to live wisely, well, and
justly without living pleasurably.[1]
Ib. 140

ZENO
335–263 B.C.

[When asked, "What is a friend?"]
Another I.[2]
From DIOGENES LAERTIUS,
bk. VII, sec. 23

Qui fuit peut revenir aussi;
Qui meurt, il n'en est pas ainsi.
(Who flies can also return;
Not so with him who dies.)
　　　　PAUL SCARRON [1610–1660]
For those that fly may fight again,
Which he can never do that's slain.
　　　SAMUEL BUTLER, *Hudibras, pt. III*
　　　　　　[1678], *canto 3, l. 243*
He that fights and runs away
May turn and fight another day;
But he that is in battle slain
Will never rise to fight again.
　　　JAMES RAY, *History of the*
　　　　　　Rebellion [1752]
For he who fights and runs away
May live to fight another day;
But he who is in battle slain
Can never rise and fight again.
　　　GOLDSMITH, *The Art of Poetry*
　　　　　　on a New Plan [1761]
But since the man that runs away
Lives to die another day,
And cowards' funerals, when they come,
Are not wept so well at home,
Therefore, though the best is bad,
Stand and do the best, my lad.
　　　A. E. HOUSMAN [1859–1936],
　　　　　　The Day of Battle

[1] See Sophocles, p. 82b.
[2] In Latin: Alter ego. See Aristotle p. 97a.

The goal of life is living in agreement
with nature.
From DIOGENES LAERTIUS,
bk. VII, sec. 87

CLEANTHES
c. 330–232 B.C.

For we are your offspring.[1]
Hymn to Zeus, l. 4

Lead me, Zeus, and you, Fate, wherever you have assigned me. I shall follow without hesitation; but even if I am
disobedient and do not wish to, I shall
follow no less surely.
From EPICTETUS, *Enchiridion,*
sec. 53

EUCLID
fl. 300 B.C.

Q.E.D. [Which it was necessary to
demonstrate.] [2]
Elements, bk. I, proposition 5

The bridge of asses.[3]　　　*Ib.*

[To Ptolemy I] There is no royal
road to geometry.[4]
From PROCLUS, *Commentary on*
Euclid, Prologue

PYRRHUS
c. 318 – 272 B.C.

Another such victory over the Ro-
mans, and we are undone.[5]
From PLUTARCH, *Lives,*
Pyrrhus, sec. 21

ARATUS
c. 315 – 240 B.C.

From Zeus let us begin, whom we
mortals never leave unnamed: full of

[1] Possibly the source of *Acts 17:28*, p. 50a.
See also Aratus, p. 104a.
[2] Translated into Latin as: Quod erat demonstrandum.
[3] Pons asinorum (i.e., too difficult for asses,
or stupid boys, to get over).
[4] Often misquoted as "learning" rather than
"geometry."
[5] Pyrrhus, king of Epirus, refers to the dearly
bought victory at Asculum, 280 B.C. Hence the
phrase "Pyrrhic victory." See also Herodotus,
p. 86b ("Cadmean victory").

Zeus are all streets and all gathering places of men, and full are the sea and harbors. Everywhere we all have need of Zeus. For we are also his offspring.[1]

Phaenomena, sec. 1

THEOPHRASTUS
d. 278 B.C.

Time is the most valuable thing a man can spend.[2]

From DIOGENES LAERTIUS, *Theophrastus V, sec. 40*

LACYDES
fl. c. 241 B.C.

[When asked late in life why he was studying geometry] If I should not be learning now, when should I be?

From DIOGENES LAERTIUS, *Lacydes, sec. V*

THEOCRITUS[3]
c. 310 − 250 B.C.

'Tis peace of mind, lad, we must find, and have a beldame nigh
To sit for us and spit for us and bid all ill go by.

The Harvest Home, l. 126

Oh cricket is to cricket dear, and ant for ant doth long,
The hawk's the darling of his fere, and o' me the Muse and her song.

The Third Country Singing Match, l. 31

Oh to be a frog, my lads, and live aloof from care. *The Reapers, l. 52*

Thou'lt cut thy finger, niggard, a-splitting caraway. *Ib. l. 55*

A great love goes here with a little gift.[4]

The Distaff, l. 24

---

[1] Probably the source of *Acts 17:28*, p. 50a. See also Aeschylus, p. 78b; Cleanthes, p. 103b; and Dante, p. 161b.

[2] Nothing is so dear and precious as time. — RABELAIS, *Works, bk. V* [1564], *ch. 5*
Remember that time is money. — BENJAMIN FRANKLIN, *Advice to a Young Tradesman* [1748]
See Hemingway, p. 1045a.

[3] Translated by J. M. EDMONDS.

[4] See Homer, p. 65b.

CALLIMACHUS
c. 305 − 240 B.C.

Great book, great evil.

Fragment 359

One told me of thy fate, Heraclitus, and wrung me to tears.[1]

Greek Anthology, J. W. MAC-KAIL, *ed.* [1906], *sec. 4, no. 31*

This is the tomb of Callimachus that thou art passing. He could sing well, and laugh well at the right time over the wine.

His Own Epitaph. Greek Anthology [*Loeb Classical Library*], *bk. VII, no. 415*

BION
fl. 280 B.C.

Old age is the harbor of all ills.

From DIOGENES LAERTIUS, *bk. IV, sec. 47*

Wealth is the sinews of affairs.[2]

Ib. 48

The road to Hades is easy to travel.[3]

Ib. 49

He has not acquired a fortune; the fortune has acquired him.[4] *Ib. 50*

Though boys throw stones at frogs in sport, the frogs do not die in sport, but in earnest.[5]

From PLUTARCH, *Water and Land Animals 7*

---

[1] See W. J. Cory, p. 719b.

[2] Endless money forms the sinews of war. — CICERO, *Philippics V, 2:5*
He who first called money the sinews of affairs seems to have spoken with special reference to the affairs of war. — PLUTARCH, *Lives, Cleomenes 27*
Neither is money the sinews of war (as it is trivially said). — FRANCIS BACON, *Essays* [1625], *Of the True Greatness of Kingdoms*
Money is the sinew of love as well as of war. — THOMAS FULLER, *Gnomologia, no. 3442*
See Rabelais, p. 181a.

[3] See Virgil p. 118b; *Matthew 7:13, 14,* p. 41b; Shakespeare, pp. 258b and 283b.
    A passage broad,
Smooth, easy, inoffensive, down to Hell.
MILTON, *Paradise Lost II, 432*

[4] See Robert Burton, p. 310b, and Ingersoll, p. 749a.

[5] See L'Estrange, p. 357a.

LEONIDAS OF TARENTUM
fl. 274 B.C.

Now is the season of sailing; for already the chattering swallow is come and the pleasant west wind; the meadows flower, and the sea tossed up with waves and rough blasts has sunk to silence. Weigh thine anchors and unloose thy hawsers, O mariner, and sail with all thy canvas set: this I Priapus of the harbor bid thee, O man, that thou mayest sail forth to all thy trafficking.

Greek Anthology, J. W. MAC-KAIL, *ed.* [1906], *sec. 6, no. 26*

ARCHIMEDES
c. 287 – 212 B.C.

I have found it! [1]

From VITRUVIUS POLLIO, *De Architectura, bk. IX, 215*

Give me where to stand, and I will move the earth.[2]

From PAPPUS OF ALEXANDRIA, *Collectio, bk. VIII, prop. 10, sec. 11*

FABIUS MAXIMUS
c. 275–203 B.C.

To be turned from one's course by men's opinions, by blame, and by misrepresentation shows a man unfit to hold an office.[3]

From PLUTARCH, *Lives, Fabius Maximus, sec. 5*

TITUS MACCIUS PLAUTUS
254–184 B.C.

What is yours is mine, and all mine is yours.[4]

Trinummus, act II, sc. ii, l. 48

---

[1] Eureka! (Said when he found the principle of specific gravity.)
[2] Said with reference to the lever.
[3] See Horace, p. 122a.
[4] See Shakespeare, *Measure for Measure V, i, 529,* p. 272a.

Not by age but by capacity is wisdom acquired.

Trinummus, act II, sc. ii, l. 88

You are seeking a knot in a bulrush.[1]

Menaechmi, act II, sc. i, l. 22

In the one hand he is carrying a stone, while he shows the bread in the other.[2]

Aulularia, act II, sc. ii, l. 18

There are occasions when it is undoubtedly better to incur loss than to make gain.

Captivi, act II, sc. ii, l. 77

Patience is the best remedy for every trouble. *Rudens, act II, sc. v, l. 71*

Consider the little mouse, how sagacious an animal it is which never entrusts its life to one hole only.[3]

Truculentus, act IV, sc. iv, l. 15

No guest is so welcome in a friend's house that he will not become a nuisance after three days.[4]

Miles Gloriosus, act III, sc. i

No man is wise enough by himself.

Ib. iii

Nothing is there more friendly to a man than a friend in need.[5]

Epidicus, act III, sc. iii, l. 44

---

[1] A proverbial expression implying a desire to create doubts and difficulties where there really are none. It occurs in TERENCE, *Andria V, 4:38;* also in ENNIUS, *Saturae 46.*
[2] See *Matthew 7:9,* p. 41a.
[3] I holde a mouses herte nat worth a leek,
That hath but oon hole for to sterte to,
And if that faille, thanne is al y-do.
    CHAUCER, *The Canterbury Tales* [c. 1387],
    The Wife of Bath's Prologue, l. 572
The mouse that hath but one hole is quickly taken. — GEORGE HERBERT, *Jacula Prudentum* [1640]
    The mouse that always trusts to one
        poor hole
    Can never be a mouse of any soul.
    POPE, *Paraphrase of the Prologue*
    [1714], l. 298
[4] Fish and guests in three days are stale. — JOHN LYLY, *Euphues* [1579]
Fish and visitors smell in three days. — BENJAMIN FRANKLIN, *Poor Richard's Almanac for 1735*
[5] A friend in need is a friend indeed. — HAZLITT, *English Proverbs*

Things which you do not hope happen more frequently than things which you do hope.[1]

> *Mostellaria, act I, sc. iii, l. 40*

To blow and swallow at the same moment is not easy.   *Ib. III, ii, 104*

Practice yourself what you preach.[2]
> *Asinaria, act III, sc. iii, l. 644*

MAHARBAL
[BARCA
THE CARTHAGINIAN]
fl. 210 B.C.

You know how to win a victory, Hannibal, but not how to use it.[3]
> *From* LIVY, *History XXII, 51*

BHAGAVAD GITA[4]
250 B.C. — A.D. 250 [5]

For certain is death for the born
And certain is birth for the dead;
Therefore over the inevitable
Thou shouldst not grieve.[6]
> *Gita, ch. 2, sec. 27*

Let not the fruit of action be thy motive,
Nor be thy attachment to inaction.[7]
> *Ib. 2, 47*

Better one's own duty, [though] imperfect,

---

[1] The unexpected always happens. — *Common saying*

[2] Facias ipse quod faciamus suades.
See St. Jerome, p. 145b.

[3] Vincere scis, Hannibal, victoria uti nescis.
See Polybius, p. 107b.

[4] Sanskrit: The Lord's Song.

[5] Ancient Indian literary chronology is conjectural. The dates given are approximate.

[6] Translated by ANNIE BESANT.

[7] Translated by F. EDGERTON.
At the moment which is not of action or inaction
You can receive this: "on whatever sphere of being
The mind of a man may be intent
At the time of death" — that is the one action
(And the time of death is every moment)
Which shall fructify in the lives of others:
And do not think of the fruit of action,
Fare forward.
     T. S. ELIOT, *Four Quartets* [*1943*].
     The Dry Salvages, pt. III

Than another's duty well performed.[1]
> *Gita 3, 35 and 18, 47*

In whatsoever way any come to Me,
In that same way I grant them favor.[1]
> *Ib. 4, 11*

Who sees Me in all,
And sees all in Me,
For him I am not lost,
And he is not lost for Me.[1]   *Ib. 6, 30*

Whatsoever state [of being] meditating upon
He leaves the body at death,[2]
To just that he goes, son of Kunti,
Always being made to be in the condition of that.[3]   *Ib. 8, 6*

If the radiance of a thousand suns
were to burst forth at once in the sky,
that would be like the splendor of the
Mighty One.[4]   *Ib. 11, 12*

QUINTUS ENNIUS
239–169 B.C.

No sooner said than done — so acts your man of worth.
> *Annals, bk. 9 (quoted by* PRISCIANUS)

I never indulge in poetics
Unless I am down with rheumatics.
> *Fragment of a satire (quoted by* PRISCIANUS)

By delaying he preserved the state.[5]
> *From* CICERO, *De Senectute IV*

Let no one pay me honor with tears, nor celebrate my funeral rites with weeping.[6]   *Ib. XX*

---

[1] Translated by F. EDGERTON.

[2] See Eliot's lines from *The Dry Salvages* quoted in the note to *Gita 2:47* above.

[3] Translated by F. EDGERTON.

[4] Translated by SWAMI NIKHILANANDA.
Quoted by J. Robert Oppenheimer when the first atomic bomb exploded on July 16, 1945, near Alamogordo, New Mexico.

[5] This refers to Quintus Fabius Maximus, "Cunctator." Hence the "Fabian policy" of waiting.

[6] See Tennyson, p. 655a.
No funeral gloom, my dears, when I am gone,

The ape, vilest of beasts, how like to us.[1]

> *From* CICERO, De Natura
> Deorum, bk. I, ch. 35

No one regards what is before his feet; we all gaze at the stars.

> *Iphigenia. From* CICERO, De
> Divinatione, bk. II, ch. 13

The idle mind knows not what it is it wants.   *Ib.*

Whom they fear they hate.

> *Thyestes. From* CICERO, De
> Officiis II, 7

MARCUS PORCIUS CATO, THE ELDER
234–149 B.C.

It is a hard matter, my fellow citizens, to argue with the belly, since it has no ears.[2]

> *From* PLUTARCH, Lives, Cato,
> sec. 8

Wise men profit more from fools than fools from wise men; for the wise men shun the mistakes of fools, but fools do not imitate the successes of the wise.   *Ib.* 9

I would much rather have men ask why I have no statue, than why I have one.   *Ib.* 19

Carthage must be destroyed.[3]
      Ib. 27

Grasp the subject, the words will follow.[4]

> *From* CAIUS JULIUS VICTOR, Ars
> Rhetorica I [4th century A.D.]

Corpse-gazings, tears, black raiment, graveyard grimness.
     WILLIAM ALLINGHAM [1828–1889],
                       Diary
[1] Simia quam similis, turpissima bestia, nobis!
[2] The belly has no ears nor is it to be filled with fair words. — RABELAIS, *Works IV* [1548], 67
   See LaFontaine, p. 359b, and Adlai Stevenson, p. 1048b.
[3] Delenda est Carthago. These words were added to everything Cato said or wrote on any question whatsoever, and were always preceded by "ceterum censeo" (in my opinion).
[4] Rem tene; verba sequentur.

An orator is a good man who is skilled in speaking.

> *From* SENECA THE ELDER
> [c. 45 B.C. – A.D. 40],
> *Controversiae I, Preface,*
> *and elsewhere*

CAECILIUS STATIUS
220–168 B.C.

He plants trees to benefit another generation.[1]

> *Synephebi. Quoted by* CICERO
> *in De Senectute VII*

POLYBIUS
c. 208 – c. 126 B.C.

For peace, with justice and honor, is the fairest and most profitable of possessions, but with disgrace and shameful cowardice it is the most infamous and harmful of all.

> *History, bk. IV, sec. 31*

Those who know how to win are much more numerous than those who know how to make proper use of their victories.[2]   *Ib. X, 36*

That historians should give their own country a break, I grant you; but not so as to state things contrary to fact. For there are plenty of mistakes made by writers out of ignorance, and which any man finds it difficult to avoid. But if we knowingly write what is false, whether for the sake of our country or our friends or just to be pleasant, what difference is there between us and hack-writers? Readers should be very attentive to and critical of historians, and they in turn should be constantly on their guard.[3]   *Ib. XVI*

---

[1] Serit arbores quae alteri seculo prosint. John Quincy Adams used *Alteri seculo* for his seal [c. 1830].
   He that plants trees loves others beside himself. — THOMAS FULLER, *Gnomologia* [1732]
   A man does not plant a tree for himself; he plants it for posterity. — ALEXANDER SMITH, *Dreamthorp* [1863], ch. 11
[2] See Maharbal, p. 106a.
[3] Translated by S. E. MORISON.
   See Cicero, p. 110b.

There is no witness so dreadful, no accuser so terrible as the conscience that dwells in the heart of every man.
History, bk. XVIII, sec. 43

MARCUS LICINIUS CRASSUS
fl. 70 B.C.

Those who aim at great deeds must also suffer greatly.
From PLUTARCH, *Lives, Crassus, ch. 26*

TERENCE[1]
[PUBLIUS TERENTIUS AFER]
C. 190 – 159 B.C.

Moderation in all things.[2]
Andria (The Lady of Andros), l. 61

Obsequiousness begets friends, truth hatred.[3]   *Ib. 68*

Hence these tears.[4]   *Ib. 126*

I am Davos, not Oedipus.[5]
Ib. 194

Lovers' quarrels are the renewal of love.[6]   *Ib. 555*

[1] Loeb Classical Library edition, with occasional changes in the translation.
[2] Ne quid nimis.
See The Seven Sages, p. 68b, Horace, p. 120a, and note.
[3] Obsequium amicos, veritas odium parit.
[4] Hinc illae lacrimae. The phrase is proverbial for "That's the cause of it," and was often quoted, by Horace in *Epistles I, xix, 41* and others.
Hence rage and tears [Inde irae et lacrimae].
— JUVENAL, *Satires, bk, I, l. 168*
[5] Davos sum, non Oedipus.
[6] Amantium irae amoris integratio est. This was quoted by Winston Churchill in a message to Roosevelt.
The anger of lovers renews the strength of love. — PUBLILIUS SYRUS [c. 42 B.C.], *Maxim 24*
The fallyng out of faithful friends renuyng is of love. — RICHARD EDWARDS, *The Paradise of Dainty Devices* [1576]
Let the falling out of friends be a renewing of affection. — LYLY, *Euphues* [1579]
The falling out of lovers is the renewing of love. — ROBERT BURTON, *Anatomy of Melancholy* [1621–1651], *pt. III, sec. 2*

Charity begins at home.[1]
Andria (The Lady of Andros), l. 635

I am a man: nothing human is alien to me.[2]
Heauton Timoroumenos (The Self-Tormentor), l. 77

Draw from others the lesson that may profit yourself.[3]   *Ib. 221*

Time removes distress.[4]   *Ib. 421*

Nothing is so difficult but that it may be found out by seeking.[5]
Ib. 675

Some people ask, "What if the sky were to fall?"[6]   *Ib. 719*

Extreme law is often extreme injustice.[7]   *Ib. 796*

There is nothing so easy but that it becomes difficult when you do it reluctantly.   *Ib. 805*

While there's life, there's hope.[8]
Ib. 981

[1] Proxumus sum egomet mihi.
Let them learn first to show piety at home. —
I Timothy 5:4
See Sir Thomas Browne, p. 330a.
[2] Homo sum: humani nil a me alienum puto.
Quoted by CICERO in *De Officiis I, 30.*
[3] Periclum ex aliis facito tibi quod ex usu siet. (A saying.)
Profit by the folly of others. — PLINY THE ELDER [A.D. 23–79], *Natural History XVIII, 31*
[4] Diem adimere aegritudinem hominibus. (A saying: Time heals all wounds.)
[5] Nil tam difficile est quin quaerendo investigari possiet.
[6] Quid si nunc caelum ruat?
Some ambassadors from the Celtae, being asked by Alexander what in the world they dreaded most, answered, that they feared lest the sky should fall upon them. — ARRIANUS [c. A.D. 100–170], *bk. I, 4*
[7] Ius summum saepe summa est malitia. See Anonymous Latin, p. 151b.
Extreme law, extreme injustice, is now become a stale proverb in discourse. — CICERO [106–43 B.C.], *De Officiis I, 33*
Extreme justice is often injustice. — RACINE, *La Thébaïde* [1664], *act IV, sc. 3*
Mais l'extrême justice est une extrême injure. — VOLTAIRE, *Oedipe* [1718], *act III, sc. 3*
[8] Modo liceat vivere, est spes.
See Cicero, p. 111a, Gay, p. 401b, and Goldsmith, p. 447a.

In fact, nothing is said that has not been said before.[1]

> *Eunuchus, l. 41 (Prologue)*

I have everything, yet have nothing; and although I possess nothing, still of nothing am I in want.[2]   *Ib. 243*

There are vicissitudes in all things.
Ib. 276

I don't care one straw.[3]   *Ib. 411*

Take care and say this with presence of mind.[4]   *Ib. 769*

He is wise who tries everything before arms.   *Ib. 789*

I know the disposition of women: when you will, they won't; when you won't, they set their hearts upon you of their own inclination.   *Ib. 812*

I took to my heels as fast as I could.
Ib. 844

Many a time . . . from a bad beginning great friendships have sprung up.   *Ib. 873*

Fortune helps the brave.[5]
> *Phormio, l. 203*

So many men, so many opinions; every one his own way.[6]   *Ib. 454*

As they say, I have got a wolf by the ears.[7]   *Ib. 506*

---

[1] See *Ecclesiastes 1:9*, p. 27a, and Robert Burton, p. 310a.

[2] See *II Corinthians 6:10*, p. 53b, and Wotton, p. 300b.

[3] Ego non flocci pendere.
Nor do they care a straw. — CERVANTES, *Don Quixote, pt. I* [1605], *bk. III, ch. 9*

[4] Fac animo haec praesenti dicas. Literally, "with a present mind" — equivalent to CAESAR's *praesentia animi* (*De Bello Gallico V, 43, 4*).

[5] See Menander, p. 102b, and Virgil, p. 119b.
PLINY THE YOUNGER says (*bk. VI, letter 16*) that PLINY THE ELDER said this during the eruption of Vesuvius: "Fortune favors the brave."

[6] Quot homines tot sententiae: suo quoque mos.
So many heads so many wits. — JOHN HEYWOOD, *Proverbs* [1546], *pt. I, ch. 2*
So many men so many minds. — GEORGE GASCOIGNE, *The Glass of Government* [1575]

[7] A proverbial expression which, according to SUETONIUS, was frequently in the mouth of Tiberius Caesar.

I bid him look into the lives of men as though into a mirror, and from others to take an example for himself.

> *Adelphoe (The Brothers), l. 415*

According as the man is, so must you humor him.   *Ib. 431*

It is the common vice of all, in old age, to be too intent upon our interests.[1]   *Ib. 833*

TUNG CHUNG-SHU[2]
C. 179 – C. 104 B.C.

He who is the ruler of men takes nonaction as his way and considers impartiality as his treasure. He sits upon the throne of non-action and rides upon the perfection of his officials.

> *Ch'un-ch'iu fan-lu*

When the first indications of error begin to appear in the state, Heaven sends forth ominous portents and calamities to warn men and announce the fact.   *Ib.*

LUCIUS ACCIUS
170–86 B.C.

Let them hate, so long as they fear.[3]

LUCIUS ANNAEUS FLORUS
fl. A.D. 125

Each year new consuls and proconsuls are made; but not every year is a king or a poet born.[4]

> *De Qualitate Vitae, frag. 8*

---

[1] CICERO quotes this in *Tusculan Disputations, bk. III*. The maxim was a favorite with the Stoic philosophers.

[2] From *Sources of Chinese Tradition*, edited by WILLIAM THEODORE DE BARY.

[3] Oderint dum metuant.
From a lost tragedy. Frequently cited by Cicero and others. SUETONIUS (*Gaius Caligula 30*) says that the Emperor Caligula was fond of quoting it.
See Machiavelli, p. 177a.

[4] From this derived the proverb: Poeta nascitur, non fit (The poet is born, not made).
See Ben Jonson, p. 303b.

HAN WU-TI[1]
157–87 B.C.

The sound of her silk skirt has
stopped.
On the marble pavement dust grows.
Her empty room is cold and still.
Fallen leaves are piled against the
doors.
Longing for that lovely lady
How can I bring my aching heart to
rest?
       On the death of his mistress [2]

HUAI-NAN TZU[3]
Second century B.C.

Before heaven and earth had taken
form all was vague and amorphous.
Therefore it was called the Great Beginning. The Great Beginning produced
emptiness and emptiness produced the
universe. . . . The combined essences
of heaven and earth became the yin
and yang, the concentrated essences of
the yin and yang became the four seasons, and the scattered essences of the
four seasons became the myriad creatures of the world.

MELEAGER
fl. 95 B.C.

Farewell, Morning Star, herald of
dawn, and quickly come as the Evening
Star, bringing again in secret her whom
thou takest away.[4]
       Greek Anthology, J. W. MAC-
       KAIL, *ed.* [1906], *sec. 1, no. 21*

MARCUS TERENTIUS VARRO
116–27 B.C.

A sick man dreams nothing so dreadful that some philosopher isn't saying
it.[5]   *Satires, frag. 122*

MARCUS TULLIUS CICERO
106–43 B.C.

How long, Catiline, will you abuse
our patience? [1]   *In Catilinam I, 1*

Oh what times! Oh what standards! [2]   *Ib.*

He has departed, withdrawn, gone
away, broken out.[3]   *Ib, II, 1*

I am a Roman citizen.[4]
       In Verrem V, 57

Law stands mute in the midst of
arms.[5]   *Pro Milone IV, 11*

Who gained by it? [6]
       Ib. XII, 32

These studies are a spur to the
young, a delight to the old; an ornament in prosperity, a consoling refuge
in adversity; they are pleasure for us at
home, and no burden abroad; they stay
up with us at night, they accompany us
when we travel, they are with us in our
country visits.
       Pro Archia Poeta I, 2

Leisure with dignity.[7]
       De Oratore II, 62

History is the witness that testifies to
the passing of time; it illumines reality,
vitalizes memory, provides guidance in
daily life, and brings us tidings of antiquity.   *Ib. II, 36*

The first law for the historian is that
he shall never dare utter an untruth.
The second is that he shall suppress
nothing that is true. Moreover, there

---

[1] Sixth emperor of the Han dynasty.
[2] From *Chinese Poems,* ARTHUR WALEY, translator.
[3] An anonymous work compiled at the court
of Liu An (d. 122 B.C.).
From *Sources of Chinese Tradition,* edited by
WILLIAM THEODORE DE BARY.
[4] See Sappho, p. 69b, and Housman, p. 854a.
[5] See Cicero, p. 111a; and Descartes, p. 327b.

[1] Quo usque, Catilina, abutere patientia nostra?
[2] O tempora! O mores!
[3] Abiit, excessit, evasit, erupit.
Me wretched! Let me curr to quercine shades!
Effund your albid hausts, lactiferous maids!
Oh, might I vole to some umbrageous clump, —
Depart, — be off, — excede, — evade, — erump!
       OLIVER WENDELL HOLMES, *The Auto-*
       crat of the Breakfast Table [*1858*]
       Aestivation, ch. II
[4] Civis Romanus sum.
[5] Silent enim leges inter arma.
[6] Cui bono [fuerit]?
[7] Otium cum dignitate.

shall be no suspicion of partiality in his writing, or of malice.[1]

De Oratore II, 62

The freedom of poetic license.[2]

Ib. III, 153

If a man aspires to the highest place, it is no dishonor to him to halt at the second, or even at the third.

Orator ad M. Brutum 4

For just as some women are said to be handsome though without adornment, so this subtle manner of speech, though lacking in artificial graces, delights us.[3]

Ib. 78

Nothing quite new is perfect.

Brutus 71

There were poets before Homer.

Ib.

The aim of forensic oratory is to teach, to delight, to move.

De Optimo Genere Oratorum 16

The dregs of Romulus.[4]

Ad Atticum II, 1

While there's life, there's hope.[5]

Ib. IX, 10

What is more agreeable than one's home? [6] *Ad Familiares IV, 8*

I like myself, but I won't say I'm as handsome as the bull that kidnapped Europa.

De Natura Deorum I, 78

It was ordained at the beginning of the world that certain signs should prefigure certain events.[7]

De Divinatione I, 118

There is nothing so ridiculous but some philosopher has said it.[8]

Ib. II, 119

I would rather be wrong with Plato than right with such men as these [the Pythagoreans].

Tusculanae Disputationes I, 17

O philosophy, you leader of life.[1]

Ib. V, 2

Socrates was the first to call philosophy down from the heavens and to place it in cities, and even to introduce it into homes and compel it to inquire about life and standards and goods and evils. *Ib. V, 4*

The highest good.[2]

De Officiis I, 2

Let arms yield to the toga, the laurel crown to praise.[3] *Ib. I, 22*

Never less idle than when wholly idle, nor less alone than when wholly alone.[4] *Ib. III, 1*

Rome, fortunately natal 'neath my consulship! [5] *De Consultatu Suo*

The people's good is the highest law.[6] *De Legibus III, 3*

He used to raise a storm in a teapot.[7]

Ib. 16

The shifts of Fortune test the reliability of friends.[8]

De Amicitia XVII

A friend is, as it were, a second self.[9]

Ib. XXI

Give me a young man in whom there is something of the old, and an old man

---

[1] See Polybius, p. 107b.

[2] Poetarum licentiae liberiora.

[3] See Milton, p. 345b, and Thomson, p. 419b.

[4] In Romuli faece. That is, the lowest order of society.

[5] Dum anima est, spes est.
See Terence, p. 108b; Gay, p. 401b; and Goldsmith, p. 447a.

[6] Quae est domestica sede iucundior?

[7] See Thomas Campbell, p. 538a, and note.

[8] See Varro, p. 110a, and Descartes, p. 327b.

[1] O vitae philosophia dux.
Adapted [1776] as the motto of Phi Beta Kappa, rendered in Greek as: Philosophia biou Kybernetes (Philosophy the guide to life).

[2] Summum bonum.
See Lucretius, p. 114a.
The nature of the good and the highest good. — Horace, *Satires II, 6, 76*

[3] Cedant arma togae, concedat laurea laudi.
He is quoting from his own poem *De suis temporibus, bk. III.*

[4] See Samuel Rogers, p. 500b.

[5] O fortunatam natam me consule Romam!
The verse is quoted disparagingly by Juvenal (*X, 122*), Quintilian (*XI, 1, 24*), and others.

[6] Salus populi suprema est lex.

[7] Excitabat enim fluctus in simpulo.
A tempest in a teapot. — *Proverb*

[8] See Aristotle, p. 99a, and note.

[9] See Aristotle, p. 97a.

with something of the young: guided so, a man may grow old in body, but never in mind.   *De Senectute XI*

Old men are garrulous by nature.   *Ib. XVI*

Old age: the crown of life, our play's last act.   *Ib. XXIII*

POMPEY
[CNEIUS POMPEIUS]
106–48 B.C.

More worship the rising than the setting sun.[1]
From PLUTARCH, *Lives, Pompey, sec. 14*

A dead man cannot bite.   *Ib. 77*

JULIUS CAESAR
100–44 B.C.

All Gaul is divided into three parts.[2]
De Bello Gallico I, 1

Men willingly believe what they wish.[3]   *Ib. III, 18*

I love treason but hate a traitor.[4]
From PLUTARCH, *Lives, Romulus, sec. 17*

I wished my wife to be not so much as suspected.[5]   *Ib. Caesar, sec. 10*

I had rather be the first man among these fellows than the second man in Rome.   *Ib. 11*

[1] Addressed to Sulla.
See David Garrick, p. 439a.
[2] Gallia est omnis divisa in partes tres.
[3] Fere libenter homines id quod volunt credunt.
See Demosthenes, p. 99a.
[4] Princes in this case do hate the traitor, though they love the treason. — SAMUEL DANIEL, *Tragedy of Cleopatra* [1594], *act IV, sc. i*
This principle is old, but true as fate,
Kings may love treason, but the traitor hate.
DEKKER, *The Honest Whore* [1604], *pt. I, act IV, sc. iv*
Though I love the treason, I hate the traitor.
— PEPYS, *Diary* [March 7, 1667]
See Dryden, p. 370b.
[5] Caesar's wife must be above suspicion. — *Traditional saying*

The die is cast.[1]
From PLUTARCH, *Lives, Caesar, sec. 32*

Go on, my friend, and fear nothing; you carry Caesar and his fortune in your boat.   *Ib. 38*

The Ides of March have come.[2]   *Ib. 63*

[In answer to a question as to what sort of death was the best] A sudden death.   *Ib.*

I came, I saw, I conquered.[3]
From SUETONIUS, *Lives of the Caesars, Julius, sec. 37*

You also, Brutus my son.[4]   *Ib. 82*

It is not these well-fed long-haired men that I fear, but the pale and the hungry-looking.[5]
From PLUTARCH, *Lives, Antony, sec. 11*

LUCRETIUS[6]
[TITUS LUCRETIUS CARUS]
99–55 B.C.

Mother of Aeneas and his race, darling of men and gods, nurturing Venus.
De Rerum Natura (On the Nature of Things), bk. I, l. 1 (Invocation)

For thee the wonder-working earth puts forth sweet flowers.   *Ib. 7*

So potent was religion in persuading to evil deeds.[7]   *Ib. 101*

[1] Iacta alea est. Proverb quoted by Caesar as he crossed the Rubicon.
Also in SUETONIUS, *Lives of the Caesars, Julius.*
[2] See Shakespeare, *Julius Caesar I, ii, 18*, p. 253a.
[3] Veni, vidi, vici. Inscription displayed in Caesar's Pontic triumph.
Also in PLUTARCH, *Apothegms, Caesar.*
[4] Et tu, Brute. Suetonius reports that Caesar said this in Greek.
See Shakespeare, p. 255a.
[5] The reference is to Brutus and Cassius.
See Shakespeare, p. 253b.
[6] Translated by W. H. D. ROUSE.
[7] Tantum religio potuit suadere malorum. (He is referring to Agamemnon's sacrifice of his daughter Iphigenia.)

Nothing can be created from nothing.[1]

De Rerum Natura, bk. I, l. 155

The ring on the finger becomes thin beneath by wearing, the fall of dripping water hollows the stone.[2]   *Ib. 314*

Material objects are of two kinds, atoms and compounds of atoms. The atoms themselves cannot be swamped by any force, for they are preserved indefinitely by their absolute solidity.[3]   *Ib. 518*

On a dark theme I trace verses full of light, touching all the muses' charm.[4]   *Ib. 933*

Pleasant it is, when over a great sea the winds trouble the waters, to gaze from shore upon another's tribulation: not because any man's troubles are a delectable joy, but because to perceive from what ills you are free yourself is pleasant.[5]   *Ib. II, 1*

---

[1] Nil posse creari de nilo.
See Shakespeare, p. 276b.
[2] Anulus in digito subter tenuatur habendo,
Stilicidi casus lapidem cavat.
See also the concluding lines of *Book IV:*
Nonne vides etiam guttas in saxa cadentis
Umoris longo in spatio pertundere saxa?
(Do you not see that even drops of water falling upon a stone in the long run beat a way through the stone?)
Drops of water hollow out a stone, a ring is worn thin by use. — OVID, *Ex Ponto IV, 10:5*
Also in PLUTARCH, *Of the Training of Children.*
The drop of rain maketh a hole in the stone, not by violence, but by oft falling. — HUGH LATIMER, *Seventh Sermon Before Edward VI* [1549]
The soft droppes of rain perce the hard marble. — JOHN LYLY, *Euphues* [1579]
And drizling drops that often doe redound,
The firmest flint doth in continuance wear.
       EDMUND SPENSER, *Amoretti* [1595],
                           sonnet 18
[3] Translated by R. E. LATHAM.
[4] Translated by CYRIL BAILEY.
[5] It is a pleasure to stand upon the shore, and to see ships tost upon the sea: a pleasure to stand in the window of a castle, and to see a battle and the adventures thereof below: but no pleasure is comparable to the standing upon the vantage ground of truth . . . and to see the errors, and wanderings, and mists, and tempests, in the vale below. — FRANCIS BACON, *Essays [1625], Of Truth*

O miserable minds of men! O blind hearts! In what darkness of life, in what great dangers ye spend this little span of years! [1]

De Rerum Natura, bk. II, l. 14

Thus the sum of things is ever being renewed, and mortals live dependent one upon another. Some races increase, others diminish, and in a short space the generations of living creatures are changed and like runners hand on the torch of life.[2]   *Ib. 75*

Never trust her at any time, when the calm sea shows her false alluring smile.   *Ib. 558*

That fear of Acheron be sent packing which troubles the life of man from its deepest depths, suffuses all with the blackness of death, and leaves no delight clean and pure.   *Ib. III, 37*

For as children tremble and fear everything in the blind darkness, so we in the light sometimes fear what is no more to be feared than the things children in the dark hold in terror and imagine will come true.[3]   *Ib. 87*

Therefore death is nothing to us, it matters not one jot, since the nature of the mind is understood to be mortal.[4]   *Ib. 831*

When immortal Death has taken mortal life.[5]   *Ib. 869*

Why dost thou not retire like a guest sated with the banquet of life, and with calm mind embrace, thou fool, a rest that knows no care? [6]   *Ib. 938*

---

[1] Translated by CYRIL BAILEY.
Insensate care of mortals! Oh how false the argument which makes thee downward beat thy wings. — DANTE, *Divine Comedy* [c. 1300], *Paradiso XI, 1*
[2] Et quasi cursores vitae lampada tradunt.
[3] See Bacon, p. 208a.
[4] Nil igitur mors est ad nos neque pertinet hilum,
Quandoquidem natura animi mortalis habetur.
[5] Translated by CYRIL BAILEY.
Mortalem vitam mors cum immortalis ademit.
[6] Translated by CYRIL BAILEY.
See Horace, p. 120a, and Bryant, p. 574b.

No less long a time will he be no more, who has made an end of life with today's light.

De Rerum Natura, bk. III, l. 1092

What is food to one, is to others bitter poison.[1]   *Ib. IV, 637*

From the heart of this fountain of delights wells up some bitter taste to choke them even amid the flowers.[2]

Ib. 1133

But if one should guide his life by true principles, man's greatest wealth is to live on a little with contented mind; for a little is never lacking.

Ib. V, 1117

[Epicurus] set forth what is the highest good, towards which we all strive, and pointed out the past, whereby along a narrow track we may strain on towards it in a straight course.[3]   *Ib. VI, 26*

GAIUS VALERIUS CATULLUS[4]
87 – c. 54 B.C.

To whom am I to present my pretty new book, freshly smoothed off with dry pumice stone? To you, Cornelius: for you used to think that my trifles were worth something, long ago.

Carmina I, l. 1

May it live and last for more than one century.   *Ib. 10*

Mourn, ye Graces and Loves, and all you whom the Graces love. My lady's sparrow is dead, the sparrow, my lady's pet.[5]   *III, 1*

Now he goes along the dark road, thither whence they say no one returns.   *Carmina III, l. 11*

But these things are past and gone.[1]

IV, 25

Let us live and love, my Lesbia, and value at a penny all the talk of crabbed old men. Suns may set and rise again: for us, when our brief light has set, there's the sleep of one everlasting night. Give me a thousand kisses.[2]

V, 1

Poor Catullus, you should cease your folly.   *VIII, 1*

But you, Catullus, be resolved and firm.   *Ib. 19*

And let her not look to find my love, as before; my love, which by her fault has dropped like a flower on the meadow's edge, when it has been touched by the plow passing by.   *XI, 21*

Over head and heels.[3]   *XX, 9*

Ah, what is more blessed than to put cares away!   *XXXI, 7*

Whatever it is, wherever he is, whatever he is doing, he smiles: it is a malady he has, neither an elegant one as I think, nor in good taste.   *XXXIX, 6*

There is nothing more silly than a silly laugh.   *Ib. 16*

Oh this age! How tasteless and ill-bred it is!   *XLIII, 8*

Now spring brings back balmy warmth.[4]   *XLVI, 1*

Catullus, the worst of all poets, gives you [Marcus Tullius] his warmest thanks; he being as much the worst of all poets as you are the best of all patrons.   *XLIX, 4*

---

[1] Ut quod ali cibus est aliis fuat acre venenum.
   What's one man's poison, signor,
   Is another's meat or drink.
      BEAUMONT AND FLETCHER, *Love's Cure* [1647], *act III, sc. ii*
[2] Translated by CYRIL BAILEY.
See Byron, p. 555a.
[3] Translated by CYRIL BAILEY.
The highest good [summum bonum]. See Cicero, p. 111b.
[4] Translated by F. W. CORNISH.
[5] Passer, deliciae meae puellae.
This is also the opening line of *Carmina II*.

[1] Sed haec prius fuere.
[2] Vivamus, mea Lesbia, atque amemus . . .
   Soles occidere et redire possunt:
   Nobis cum semel occidit brevis lux
   Nox est perpetua una dormienda.
   Da mi basia mille.
See Campion, p. 300a; Jonson, p. 302b; Herrick, p. 320a and 321a; and Fouché, p. 500a.
[3] Per caputque pedesque.
[4] Iam ver egelidos refert tepores.

He seems to me to be equal to a god, he, if it may be, seems to surpass the very gods, who sitting opposite you again gazes at you and hears you sweetly laughing.[1]   *Carmina LI, 1*

What an eloquent manikin![2]
LIII, 5

I would see a little Torquatus, stretching his baby hands from his mother's lap, smile a sweet smile at his father with lips half parted.
LXI, 209

The evening is come; rise up, ye youths. Vesper from Olympus now at last is just raising his long-looked-for light.   *LXII, 1*

What is given by the gods more desirable than the fortunate hour?[3]
Ib. 30

Not unknown am I to the goddess [Venus] who mingles with her cares a sweet bitterness.   *LXVIII, 17*

It is not fit that men should be compared with gods.   *Ib. 141*

What a woman says to her ardent lover should be written in wind and running water.[4]   *LXX*

Leave off wishing to deserve any thanks from anyone, or thinking that anyone can ever become grateful.
LXXIII, 1

If a man can take any pleasure in recalling the thought of kindnesses done.   *LXXVI, 1*

It is difficult suddenly to lay aside a long-cherished love.   *Ib. 13*

O ye gods, grant me this in return for my piety.   *Ib. 26*

I hate and I love. Why I do so, perhaps you ask. I know not, but I feel it and I am in torment.[5]   *LXXXV, 1*

---

[1] See Sappho, p. 69b.
[2] Salaputtium disertum!
[3] Quid datur a divis felici optatius hora?
[4] See Sophocles, p. 83a.
[5] Odi et amo. Quare id faciam, fortasse requiris.
    Nescio, sed fieri sentio et excrucior.
    See Anacreon, p. 70a.

Wandering through many countries and over many seas, I come, my brother, to these sorrowful obsequies, to present you with the last guerdon of death, and speak, though in vain, to your silent ashes.   *Carmina CI, 1*

And forever, O my brother, hail and farewell![1]   *Ib. 10*

But you shall not escape my iambics.[2]   *Fragment*

SALLUST
[GAIUS SALLUSTIUS CRISPUS]
86–34 B.C.

All our power lies in both mind and body; we employ the mind to rule, the body rather to serve; the one we have in common with the Gods, the other with the brutes.

*The War with Catiline
[c. 40 B.C.], sec. 1*

The renown which riches or beauty confer is fleeting and frail; mental excellence is a splendid and lasting possession.   *Ib.*

Covetous of others' possessions, he [Catiline] was prodigal of his own.[3]
Ib. 5

Ambition drove many men to become false; to have one thought locked in the breast, another ready on the tongue.[4]   *Ib. 10*

In truth, prosperity tries the souls even of the wise.[5]   *Ib. 11*

To like and dislike the same things, that is indeed true friendship.[6]
Ib. 20

Thus in the highest position there is the least freedom of action.[7]   *Ib. 51*

---

[1] Atque in perpetuum, frater, ave atque vale.
[2] At non effugies meos iambos.
[3] Alieni appetens, sui profusus.
[4] See Euripides, p. 84b.
[5] Quippe secundae res sapientium animos fatigant.
[6] Idem velle atque idem nolle, ea demum firma amicitia est.
    See Plato, p. 92b.
[7] Ita in maxima fortuna minima licentia est.

On behalf of their country, their children, their altars, and their hearths.[1]
The War with Catiline
[*c. 40 B.C.*], *sec. 59*

The soul is the captain and ruler of the life of mortals.[2]
The War with Jugurtha
[*c. 41 B.C.*], *sec 1*

The splendid achievements of the intellect, like the soul, are everlasting.
Ib. 2

A city for sale and soon to perish if it finds a buyer![3]   *Ib. 35*

Punic faith.[4]   *Ib. 108*

Experience has shown that to be true which Appius[5] says in his verses, that every man is the architect of his own fortune.[6]
Speech to Caesar on the State, sec. 1

VIRGIL
[PUBLIUS VIRGILIUS MARO]
70–19 B.C.

A god has brought us this peace.
Eclogues I, l. 6

To compare great things with small.
Ib. 23

Happy old man![7]   *Ib. 46*

[1] Pro patria, pro liberis, pro aris atque focis suis.
[2] Dux atque imperator vitae mortalium animus est.
See *Speech to Caesar on the State* (below). See also Shakespeare, p. 253b; Tennyson, p. 653a; and Henley, p. 816a.
Be the proud captain still of thine own fate. — J. B. Kenyon [1858–1924], *The Black Camel*
[3] Jugurtha's remark as he looked back at Rome upon being ordered by the senate to leave Italy.
[4] Punica fide (treachery).
[5] Appius Claudius Caecus, consul in 307 B.C., the earliest Roman writer known to us.
[6] See *The War with Jugurtha 1* (above) and Aristotle, p. 98a.
His own character is the arbiter of everyone's fortune. — Publilius Syrus [c. 42 B.C.], *Maxim 283*
The brave man carves out his fortune, and every man is the son of his own works. — Cervantes, *Don Quixote, pt. I* [1605], *bk. I, ch. 4*
See Bacon, p. 209a.
[7] Fortunate senex!

Ah Corydon, Corydon, what madness has caught you?
Eclogues II, 69

With Jove I begin.[1]   *Ib. III, 60*

A sad thing is a wolf in the fold, rain on ripe corn, wind in the trees, the anger of Amaryllis.   *Ib. 80*

A snake lurks in the grass.   *Ib. 93*

Let us raise a somewhat loftier strain.[2]   *Ib. IV, 1*

The great cycle of the ages is renewed. Now the Maiden returns, returns the Golden Age; a new generation now descends from heaven.[3]   *Ib. 5*

We have made you [Priapus] of marble for the time being.
Ib. VII, 35

We are not all capable of everything.[4]   *Ib. VIII, 63*

Draw Daphnis from the town, my songs, draw Daphnis home.   *Ib. 68*

Hylax barks in the doorway.
Ib. 107

Your descendants shall gather your fruits.[5]   *Ib. IX, 50*

Time bears away all things, even our minds.   *Ib. 51*

Let us go singing as far as we go: the road will be less tedious.   *Ib. 64*

This last labor grant me, O Arethusa.   *Ib. X, 1*

What if Amyntas is dark? Violets are dark, too, and hyacinths.   *Ib. 38*

[1] Ab Iove principium.
[2] Paulo maiora canamus!
[3] Magnus ab integro saeculorum nascitur ordo.
Iam redit et Virgo, redeunt Saturnia regna;
Iam nova progenies caelo demittitur alto.
Interpreted by the Middle Ages as a prophecy of the birth of Christ. Dante cites the lines in *Purgatorio*, canto 22, l. 70.
A phrase altered from the first line (Novus ordo seclorum) appears on the reverse of the Great Seal of the United States of America (first used on the silver dollar certificates, series of 1935). Virgil supplied the Latin for other phrases of the Great Seal. See p. 117a and p. 119b.
See Shelley, p. 570b.
[4] Non omnia possumus omnes.
[5] Carpent tua poma nepotes.

Love conquers all things; let us too surrender to Love.[1] *Ib. 69*

Utmost [farthest] Thule.[2]
Georgics I, l. 30

Look with favor upon a bold beginning.[3] *Ib. 40*

O farmers, pray that your summers be wet and your winters clear.
Ib. 100

Practice and thought might gradually forge many an art. *Ib. 133*

Thrice they tried to pile Ossa on Pelion, yes, and roll up leafy Olympus upon Ossa; thrice the Father of Heaven split the mountains apart with his thunderbolt.[4] *Ib. 281*

Frogs in the marsh mud drone their old lament. *Ib. 378*

Not every soil can bear all things.
Ib. II, 109

Ah too fortunate farmers, if they knew their own good fortune!
Ib. 458

May the countryside and the gliding valley streams content me. Lost to fame, let me love river and woodland.
Ib. 485

Happy the man who could search out the causes of things.[5] *Ib. 490*

And no less happy he who knows the

rural gods — Pan, and old Sylvanus, and the sisterhood of Nymphs.
Georgics II, l. 493

This life the old Sabines knew long ago; Remus knew it, and his brother.
Ib. 532

Years grow cold to love.
Ib. III, 97

Time is flying never to return.[1]
Ib. 284

All aglow is the work.[2]
Ib. IV, 169

A sudden madness came down upon the unwary lover [Orpheus] — forgivable, surely, if Death knew how to forgive. *Ib. 488*

I who once played shepherds' songs and in my brash youth sang of you, O Tityrus, beneath the spreading beech.[3]
Ib. 565

Arms and the man I sing.[4]
Aeneid, bk. I, l. 1

Can heavenly minds yield to such rage? *Ib. 11*

So vast was the struggle to found the Roman state. *Ib. 33*

Night, pitch-black, lies upon the deep.[5] *Ib. 89*

O thrice four times blessed![6]
Ib. 94

Fury provides arms. *Ib. 150*

You have suffered worse things; God will put an end to these also.
Ib. 199

Perhaps some day it will be pleasant to remember even this.[7] *Ib. 203*

The organizer a woman.[8] *Ib. 364*

---

[1] Omnia vincit amor: et nos cedamus amori.
See Sophocles, pp. 82a and 82b, and Chaucer, p. 166a.
[2] Ultima Thule.
The phrase, designating a far-off land, has been in use since the Greek mariner Pytheas discovered in the fourth century B.C. an island he named Thule six days north of England, thought to be Iceland. See Seneca, p. 131a, and Thomson, p. 419b.
[3] Audacibus annue coeptis.
This phrase also (see note p. 116b) was adapted for use on the reverse of the Great Seal of the United States of America: Annuit coeptis. See p. 119b for the Latin on the face of the Great Seal.
[4] See Homer, p. 66a.
[5] Felix qui potuit rerum cognoscere causas.
The reference is apparently to the scientist-philosopher-poet Lucretius.

---

[1] Fugit inreparabile tempus.
[2] Fervet opus.
[3] Tityrus is also referred to in *Eclogues I, 1.*
[4] Arma virumque cano.
[5] See *Genesis 1:2*, p. 5a.
[6] O terque quaterque beati!
[7] Forsan et haec olim meminisse iuvabit.
See Homer, p. 66b.
[8] Dux femina facti.

Her walk revealed her as a true goddess. *Aeneid, bk. I, l. 405*

How happy those whose walls already rise! *Ib. 437*

Here are the tears of things; mortality touches the heart.[1] *Ib. 462*

I make no distinction between Trojan and Tyrian. *Ib. 574*

A mind aware of its own rectitude.[2] *Ib. 604*

As long as rivers shall run down to the sea, or shadows touch the mountain slopes, or stars graze in the vault of heaven, so long shall your honor, your name, your praises endure. *Ib. 607*

I have known sorrow and learned to aid the wretched. *Ib. 630*

Unspeakable, O Queen, is the sorrow you bid me renew. *Ib. II, 3*

Whatever it is, I fear Greeks even when they bring gifts.[3] *Ib. 49*

From a single crime know the nation. *Ib. 65*

I shudder to say it.[4] *Ib. 204*

O fatherland, O Ilium home of the gods, O Troy walls famed in battle! *Ib. 241*

Ucalegon's afire next door.[5] *Ib. 311*

We have been Trojans; Troy has been. *Ib. 325*

There is but one safety to the vanquished — to hope not safety. *Ib. 354*

Our foes will provide us with arms. *Ib. 391*

[1] Sunt lacrimae rerum et mentem mortalia tangunt.
[2] The mind, conscious of rectitude, laughed to scorn the falsehood of report. — OVID [43 B.C.–A.D. 18], *Fasti, bk. IV, l. 311*
[3] Quidquid id est, timeo Danaos et dona ferentis.
[4] Horresco referens.
[5] Iam proximus ardet Ucalegon.

The gods thought otherwise.[1] *Aeneid, bk. II, l. 428*

Thrice would I have thrown my arms about her neck, and thrice the ghost embraced fled from my grasp: like a fluttering breeze, like a fleeting dream.[2] *Ib. 793*

O accurst craving for gold! *Ib. III, 57*

Rumor flies.[3] *Ib. 121*

I feel again a spark of that ancient flame.[4] *Ib. IV, 23*

Deep in her breast lives the silent wound. *Ib. 67*

A woman is always a fickle, unstable thing.[5] *Ib. 569*

Arise from my bones, avenger of these wrongs! *Ib. 625*

Thus, thus, it is joy to pass to the world below.[6] *Ib. 660*

Naked in death upon an unknown shore. *Ib. V, 871*

Yield not to evils, but attack all the more boldly. *Ib. VI, 95*

It is easy to go down into Hell; night and day, the gates of dark Death stand wide; but to climb back again, to retrace one's steps to the upper air — there's the rub, the task.[7] *Ib. 126*

[1] Dis aliter visum.
[2] Virgil here translates HOMER, *Odyssey, bk. XI, l. 204*. See p. 66a.
[3] Fama volat.
[4] Agnosco veteris vestigia flammae. See Dante, p. 161b.
[5] Varium et mutabile semper femina. Woman often changes; foolish the man who trusts her. — FRANCIS I OF FRANCE [1494–1547], written by him with his ring on a window of the château of Chambord (BRANTÔME, *Œuvres VII, 395*)
La donna è mobile. — PIAVE, *Libretto of* VERDI's *Rigoletto*, Duke's song See Scott, p. 519b.
[6] Sic, sic, iuvat ire sub umbras.
[7] Facilis descensus Averni:
Noctes atque dies patet atri ianua Ditis;
Sed revocare gradum superasque evadere ad auras,
Hoc opus, hic labor est.
See Bion, p. 104b, and note.

Faithful Achates.[1]
> *Aeneid, bk.* VI, *l.* 158
> *and elsewhere*

Death's brother, Sleep.[2]   *Ib.* 278

Had I a hundred tongues, a hundred lips, a throat of iron and a chest of brass, I could not tell men's countless sufferings.   *Ib.* 298

The swamp of Styx, by which the gods take oath.   *Ib.* 323

Unwillingly I left your land, O Queen.[3]   *Ib.* 460

That happy place, the green groves of the dwelling of the blest.   *Ib.* 638

The spirit within nourishes, and the mind, diffused through all the members, sways the mass and mingles with the whole frame.   *Ib.* 726

Each of us bears his own Hell.[4]
> *Ib.* 743

Others, I take it, will work better with breathing bronze and draw living faces from marble; others will plead at law with greater eloquence, or measure the pathways of the sky, or forecast the rising stars. Be it your concern, Roman, to rule the nations under law (this is your proper skill) and establish the way of peace; to spare the conquered and put down the mighty from their seat.[5]
> *Ib.* 847

Give me handfuls of lilies to scatter.[6]
> *Ib.* 883

There are two gates of Sleep. One is of horn, easy of passage for the shades of truth; the other, of gleaming white ivory, permits false dreams to ascend to the upper air.[7]   *Ib.* 893

Prayed to the Genius of the place.
> *Ib.* VII, 136

[1] Fidus Achates. Proverbial for a trusty friend; Achates was the faithful comrade of Aeneas.
[2] See Homer, p. 64a.
[3] Aeneas to the ghost of Dido, who had killed herself when he left her.
[4] See Marlowe, p. 213a, and note.
[5] See Milton, p. 339b.
[6] Quoted by DANTE in *The Divine Comedy, Purgatorio, canto 30, l. 21.*
[7] See Homer, p. 67a.

We descend from Jove; in ancestral Jove Troy's sons rejoice.
> *Aeneid, bk.* VII, *l.* 219

If I cannot bend Heaven, I shall move Hell.   *Ib.* 312

An old story, but the glory of it is forever.   *Ib.* IX, 79

To have died once is enough.
> *Ib.* 140

I cannot bear a mother's tears.
> *Ib.* 289

Good speed to your youthful valor, boy! So shall you scale the stars! [1]
> *Ib.* 641

Fortune favors the brave.[2]
> *Ib.* X, 284

Dying dreams of his sweet Argos.[3]
> *Ib.* 782

Believe one who has proved it. Believe an expert.[4]   *Ib.* XI, 283

His limbs were cold in death; his spirit fled with a groan, indignant, to the shades below.   *Ib.* XII, 951

One composed of many.[5]
> *Minor Poems, Moretum, l.* 104

Death twitches my ear. "Live," he says; "I am coming." [6]
> *Minor Poems, Copa, l.* 38

[1] Macte nova virtute, puer, sic itur ad astra.
See Dante, p. 161b.
[2] Audentes fortuna iuvat.
See Menander, p. 102b, and Terence, p. 109a.
[3] Dulces moriens reminiscitur Argos.
[4] Experto credite.
Believe an expert; believe one who has had experience. — ST. BERNARD, *Epistle 106*
Believe the experienced Robert. Believe Robert, who has tried it. — ROBERT BURTON, *Anatomy of Melancholy* [1621–1651], *Introduction*
[5] E pluribus unus.
Adapted (E pluribus unum) for the motto on the face of the Great Seal of the United States, adopted June 20, 1782. For the Latin Virgil supplied for the reverse of the Great Seal, see p. 116b and p. 117a.
[6] Quoted by Justice Oliver Wendell Holmes in a radio address on his ninetieth birthday, March 8, 1931.

HORACE
[QUINTUS HORATIUS FLACCUS]
65 – 8 B.C.

How comes it, Maecenas, that no man living is content with the lot that either his choice has given him, or chance has thrown in his way, but each has praise for those who follow other paths?

> *Satires, bk. I* [35 B.C.], *satire i, l. 1*

The story's about you.[1]   *Ib. 69*

There is measure in all things.[2]
         Ib. 106

We rarely find anyone who can say he has lived a happy life, and who, content with his life, can retire from the world like a satisfied guest.[3]   *Ib. 117*

And all that tribe.[4]   *Ib. ii, 2*

The limbs of a dismembered poet.[5]
         Ib. iv, 62

A man without a flaw.[6]   *Ib. v, 32*

Life grants nothing to us mortals without hard work.   *Ib. ix, 59*

As crazy as hauling timber into the woods.[7]   *Ib. x, 34*

Simplicity and charm.[8]   *Ib. 44*

This used to be among my prayers.[9] — a piece of land not so very large, which would contain a garden, and near the house a spring of ever-flowing water, and beyond these a bit of wood.
   Ib. bk. II [30 B.C.], *satire vi, l. 1*

O nights and suppers of the gods! [10]
         Ib. 65

[1] De te fabula.

[2] Est modus in rebus. See The Seven Sages, p. 68b.

[3] See Solon, p. 69a; Aeschylus, p. 78b; Sophocles, p. 81b; Lucretius, p. 113b; and Bryant, p. 574b.

[4] Hoc genus omne.

[5] Disiecti membra poetae. The reference is to Orpheus torn apart by the Maenads.

[6] Ad unguem factus homo.

[7] Carrying coals to Newcastle. — *Proverb*
Bringing owls to Athens. — ARISTOPHANES, *Birds, l. 301*

[8] Molle atque facetum. This refers to Virgil's poetry.

[9] Hoc erat in votis.

[10] O noctes cenaeque deum!

In Rome you long for the country; in the country — oh inconstant! — you praise the distant city to the stars.
> *Satires, bk. II, satire vii, l. 28*

Happy the man who far from schemes of business, like the early generations of mankind, works his ancestral acres with oxen of his own breeding, from all usury free.[1]
> *Epodes* [c. 29 B.C.], *II, st. 1*

You ask me why a soft numbness diffuses all my inmost senses with deep oblivion, as though with thirsty throat I'd drained the cup that brings the sleep of Lethe.[2]   *Ib. XIV, 1*

But if you name me among the lyric bards, I shall strike the stars with my exalted head.
> *Odes, bk. I* [23 B.C.], *ode i, last lines*

The half of my own soul.[3]
         Ib. iii, 8

No ascent is too steep for mortals. Heaven itself we seek in our folly.
         Ib. 37

Pale Death with impartial tread beats at the poor man's cottage door and at the palaces of kings.   *Ib. iv, 13*

Life's brief span forbids us to enter on far-reaching hopes.[4]   *Ib. 15*

What slender youth, bedewed with liquid odors,
Courts thee on roses in some pleasant cave,
Pyrrha? For whom bind'st thou
In wreaths thy golden hair,
Plain in thy neatness? [5]   *Ib. v, 1*

Never despair.[6]   *Ib. vii, 27*

[1] See Pope, p. 402a.

[2] See Keats, p. 582a.

[3] Animae dimidium meae. The reference is to Virgil.
See Aristotle, p. 97a, and note.

[4] Vitae summa brevis spem nos vetat incohare longam.
See Dowson, p. 890a.

[5] Translated by JOHN MILTON [1608–1674].

[6] Nil desperandum.

Tomorrow once again we sail the Ocean Sea.[1]

Odes, bk. I, ode vii, last line

Leave all else to the gods.[2]

Ib. ix, 9

Cease to ask what the morrow will bring forth, and set down as gain each day that Fortune grants.[3] *Ib. 13*

Seize the day, put no trust in the morrow![4]

Ib. xi, last line

Happy, thrice happy and more, are they whom an unbroken bond unites and whose love shall know no sundering quarrels so long as they shall live.

Ib. xiii, 17

O fairer daughter of a fair mother![5]

Ib. xvi, 1

The pure in life and free from sin.[6]

Ib. xxii, 1

What restraint or limit should there be to grief for one so dear?

Ib. xxiv, 1

Grant me, sound of body and of mind, to pass an old age lacking neither honor nor the lyre.[7]

Ib. xxxi, last lines

A grudging and infrequent worshipper of the gods.[8] *Ib. xxxiv, 1*

Now is the time for drinking, now the time to beat the earth with unfettered foot.[9] *Ib. xxxvii, 1*

Persian luxury, boy, I hate.[10]

Ib. xxxviii, 1

Cease your efforts to find where the last rose lingers.[1]

Odes, bk. I, ode xxxviii, l. 3

In adversity remember to keep an even mind.[2]

Ib. bk. II [23 B.C.], *ode iii, l. 1*

We are all driven into the same fold.[3] *Ib. 25*

Whoever cultivates the golden mean [4] avoids both the poverty of a hovel and the envy of a palace. *Ib. x, 5*

It is the mountaintop that the lightning strikes. *Ib. 11*

Nor does Apollo always stretch the bow.[5] *Ib. 19*

Alas, Postumus, Postumus, the fleeting years slip by.[6] *Ib. xiv, 1*

No lot is altogether happy.[7]

Ib. xvi, 27

I hate the common herd of men and keep them afar. Let there be sacred silence: I, the Muses' priest, sing for girls and boys songs not heard before.

Ib. bk. III [23 B.C.], *ode i, l. 1*

Dark Care sits enthroned behind the Knight.[8] *Ib. 40*

It is sweet and honorable to die for one's country.[9] *Ib. ii, 13*

The man who is tenacious of purpose in a rightful cause is not shaken from his firm resolve by the frenzy of his fel-

---

[1] Cras ingens iterabimus aequor.
Translated by S. E. MORISON.
[2] Permitte divis cetera.
[3] See *Matthew 6:34*, p. 41a, and Publilius Syrus, p. 126b.
[4] Carpe diem, quam minimum credula postero.
See Ronsard, p. 188a; Spenser, p. 200a; and Herrick, p. 320b.
[5] O matre pulchra filia pulchrior.
[6] Integer vitae scelerisque purus.
[7] Not to be tuneless in old age! — DOBSON [1840–1921], *Henry Wadsworth Longfellow*
[8] Parcus deorum cultor et infrequens.
[9] Nunc est bibendum, nunc pede libero puisanda tellus. Ode on the death of Cleopatra.
[10] Persicos odi, puer, apparatus.

[1] Mitte sectari, rosa quo locorum
Sera moretur.
[2] Aequam memento rebus in arduis
Servare mentem.
[3] Omnes eodem cogimur.
[4] Auream quisquis mediocritatem
Diliget.
Keep the golden mean. — PUBLILIUS SYRUS [c. 42 B.C.], *Maxim 1072*
See The Seven Sages, p. 68b; Terence, p. 108a; and Voltaire, p. 417b.
[5] Neque semper arcum
Tendit Apollo.
[6] Eheu fugaces, Postume, Postume,
Labuntur anni.
[7] Nihil est ab omni
Parte beatum.
[8] Post equitem sedet atra cura.
[9] Dulce et decorum est pro patria mori.
See Homer, p. 64a.

low citizens clamoring for what is wrong, or by the tyrant's threatening countenance.[1]

　　　Odes, bk. III, ode iii, l. 1

Force without wisdom falls of its own weight.　　　　　*Ib. iv, 65*

Our sires' age was worse than our grandsires'. We their sons are more worthless than they: so in our turn we shall give the world a progeny yet more corrupt.　　　　　　*Ib. vi, 46*

Skilled in the works of both languages.　　　　　　　*Ib. viii, 5*

With you I should love to live, with you be ready to die.[2]

　　　　　　Ib. ix, last line

Gloriously perjured, a maiden famous to all time.[3]　　*Ib. xi, 35*

O fount Bandusian, more sparkling than glass.[4]　　　*Ib. xiii, 1*

I would not have borne this in my hot youth when Plancus was consul.[5]

　　　　　　Ib. xiv, 27

A pauper in the midst of wealth.[6]

　　　　　　Ib. xvi, 28

He will through life be master of himself and a happy man who from day to day can have said, "I have lived: tomorrow the Father may fill the sky with black clouds or with cloudless sunshine."[7]　　　*Ib. xxix, 41*

---

[1] See Fabius Maximus, p. 105a.

[2] Tecum vivere amem, tecum obeam libens.

[3] Hypermnestra.

Swift chose Splendide mendax (Gloriously perjured) as Gulliver's motto.

[4] O fons Bandusiae splendidior vitro.

[5] In my hot youth, when George the Third was king. — BYRON, *Don Juan* [1819–1824], *canto 1, st. 212*

[6] Magnus inter opes inops.

[7]　　Ille potens sui

Laetusque deget, cui licet in diem

Dixisse "Vixi: cras vel atra

Nube polum pater occupato

Vel sole puro."

Tomorrow let my sun his beams display

Or in clouds hide them; I have lived my day.

　　COWLEY, *Discourse XI, Of Myself* [1661], *st. 11*

See Dryden, p. 369b, and Sydney Smith, p. 523b.

I have built a monument more lasting than bronze.

　　　Odes, bk. III, ode xxx, l. 1

I shall not wholly die.[1]　　*Ib. 6*

I am not what I was in the reign of the good Cinara. Forbear, cruel mother of sweet loves.[2]

　　　Odes, bk. IV [13 B.C.], ode i, l. 3

The centuries roll back to the ancient age of gold.[3]　　*Ib. ii, 39*

We are but dust and shadow.

　　　　　　Ib. vii, 16

Many brave men lived before Agamemnon; but all are overwhelmed in eternal night, unwept, unknown, because they lack a sacred poet.[4]

　　　　　　Ib. ix, 25

It is not the rich man you should properly call happy, but him who knows how to use with wisdom the blessings of the gods, to endure hard poverty, and who fears dishonor worse than death, and is not afraid to die for cherished friends or fatherland.

　　　　　　Ib. 45

It is sweet to let the mind unbend on occasion.[5]　　*Ib. xii, 27*

---

[1] Non omnis moriar.

[2] Non sum qualis eram bonae

Sub regno Cinarae. Desine, dulcium

Mater saeva Cupidinum.

Mater saeva Cupidinum. — *Odes, bk. I, xix, l. 1*

See Dowson, p. 890a.

[3] See Milton, p. 334a, and Macaulay, p. 596b.

The golden age, which a blind tradition has hitherto placed in the past, is before us. — C. H. SAINT-SIMON [1760–1825], quoted by CARLYLE in *Sartor Resartus, bk. III, ch. 5*

[4] How many, famous while they lived, are utterly forgotten for want of writers! — BOETHIUS [A.D. c. 480–524], *De Consolatione Philosophiae II, 7*

See Homer, p. 64b; Scott, p. 519a; and Byron, p. 557b.

Brave men were living before Agamemnon

And since, exceeding valorous and sage,

A good deal like him too, but quite the same none;

But then they shone not on the poet's page.

　　BYRON, *Don Juan, canto I, st. 5*

[5] See Menander, p. 102a; Montaigne, p. 191a: and Bacon, p. 209a.

I am not bound over to swear allegiance to any master; where the storm drives me I turn in for shelter.

Epistles, bk. I, epistle i, l. 14

To flee vice is the beginning of virtue, and to have got rid of folly is the beginning of wisdom.   *Ib. 41*

Make money, money by fair means if you can, if not, by any means money.[1]

Ib. 66

The people are a many-headed beast.[2]   *Ib. 76*

He who has begun has half done. Dare to be wise; begin! [3]   *Ib. ii. 40*

The covetous man is ever in want.

Ib. 56

Anger is a short madness.   *Ib. 62*

Think to yourself that every day is your last; the hour to which you do not look forward will come as a welcome surprise. As for me, when you want a good laugh, you will find me, in a fine state, fat and sleek, a true hog of Epicurus' herd.[4]   *Ib. iv, 13*

You may drive out Nature with a pitchfork, yet she still will hurry back.

Epistles, bk. I, epistle x, l. 24

They change their clime, not their disposition, who run across the sea.

Ib. xi, 27

He is not poor who has enough of things to use. If it is well with your belly, chest and feet, the wealth of kings can give you nothing more.

Ib. xii, 4

Harmony in discord.[1]   *Ib. 19*

For joys fall not to the rich alone, nor has he lived ill, who from birth to death has passed unknown.

Ib. xvii, 9

It is not everyone that can get to Corinth.[2]   *Ib. 36*

Once a word has been allowed to escape, it cannot be recalled.[3]

Ib. xviii, 71

It is your concern when your neighbor's wall is on fire.   *Ib. 84*

No poems can please for long or live that are written by water-drinkers.

Ib. xix, 2

O imitators, you slavish herd!

Ib. 19

---

[1] Get money; still get money, boy, no matter by what means. — BEN JONSON, *Every Man in His Humor* [1598], *act II, sc. iii*

[2] Belua multorum es capitum.

PLATO [c. 429–347 B.C.] describes the multitude as a "great strong beast." — *The Republic*, bk. VI, 493–B

The multitude of the gross people, being a beast of many heads. — ERASMUS [1465–1536], *Adagia, no. 122*

O weak trust of the many-headed multitude. — SIR PHILIP SIDNEY, *Arcadia* [1590], bk. II

See Machiavelli, p. 177b, and Shakespeare, pp. 241a, and 289b.

The beast of many heads, the staggering multitude. — MARSTON AND WEBSTER, *The Malcontent* [1604], *act III, sc. iii*

If there be any among those common objects of hatred I do contemn and laugh at, it is that great enemy of reason, virtue, and religion, the multitude . . . one great beast and a monstrosity more prodigious than Hydra. — SIR THOMAS BROWNE, *Religio Medici* [1643], II, 1

Sir, your people is a great beast. — *Attributed to* ALEXANDER HAMILTON [1757–1804]

[3] See Plato, p. 94a, and note.

[4] See Chaucer, p. 166b.

[1] Concordia discors.

[2] A rendering of a Greek proverb, "It's not everyone that can make the voyage to Corinth," which referred to the expense of the life there. There is but one road that leads to Corinth. — WALTER PATER, *Marius the Epicurean* [1885], ch. 24

[3] Semel emissum volat irrevocabile verbum.

The written word, unpublished, can be destroyed, but the spoken word can never be recalled. — HORACE, *Ars Poetica* [c. 8 B.C.], l. 389

It is as easy to recall a stone thrown violently from the hand as a word which has left your tongue. — MENANDER [343–292 B.C.], *Fragment 1092K*

Four things come not back: the spoken word; the sped arrow; time past; the neglected opportunity. — OMAR IBN AL-HALIF, *Aphorism*

A word once spoken revoked cannot be. — ALEXANDER BARCLAY, *Shyp of Folys* [1509], *p. 108*

Thoughts unexpressed may sometimes fall
    back dead;
But God Himself can't kill them when
    they're said.

WILL CARLETON [1845–1912], *The First Settler's Story, st. 21*

And seek for truth in the groves of Academe.[1]

> *Epistles, bk. II* [14 B.C.],
> *epistle ii, l. 45*

Barefaced poverty drove me to writing verses.   *Ib. 51*

The years as they pass plunder us of one thing after another.   *Ib. 55*

I have to submit to much in order to pacify the touchy tribe of poets.[2]
     Ib. 102

"Painters and poets," you say, "have always had an equal license in bold invention." We know; we claim the liberty for ourselves and in turn we give it to others.

> *Ib. bk. III* (*Ars Poetica*)
> [c. 8 B.C.], *l. 9*

It was a wine jar when the molding began: as the wheel runs round why does it turn out a water pitcher?
     Ib. 21

It is when I struggle to be brief that I become obscure.   *Ib. 25*

Scholars dispute and the case is still before the courts.[3]   *Ib. 78*

Foot and a half long words.[4]
     Ib. 97

Taught or untaught, we all scribble poetry.   *Ib. 117*

The mountains will be in labor, and a ridiculous mouse will be brought forth.[5]   *Ib. 139*

From the egg.[6]   *Ib. 147*

In the midst of things.[7]   *Ib. 148*

A praiser of past time.[8]   *Ib. 173*

---

[1] Atque inter silvas Academi quaerere verum.
[2] Genus irritabile vatum.
[3] Grammatici certant et adhuc sub iudice lis est.
[4] Sesquipedalia verba.
[5] Parturient montes, nascetur ridiculus mus. See Aesop, p. 76a, and note.
[6] Ab ovo.
Helen, the cause of the Trojan War, sprang from an egg engendered by Leda and the Swan (Zeus).
[7] In medias res.
[8] Laudator temporis acti.

Let a play have five acts, neither more nor less.

> *Epistles, bk. III* (*Ars Poetica*),
> *l. 189*

Turn the pages of your Greek models night and day.[1]   *Ib. 268*

He wins every hand who mingles profit with pleasure, by delighting and instructing the reader at the same time.   *Ib. 343*

Sometimes even good old Homer nods.[2]   *Ib. 359*

As in painting, so in poetry.[3]
     Ib. 361

He has defiled his father's grave.
     Ib. 471

AUGUSTUS CAESAR
63 B.C. — A.D. 14

Quintilius Varus, give me back my legions! [4]

> *From* SUETONIUS, *Augustus, sec. 23*

More haste, less speed.[5]   *Ib. 25*

Well done is quickly done.[6]   *Ib.*

I found Rome a city of bricks and left it a city of marble.   *Ib. 28*

After this time I surpassed all others in authority, but I had no more power than the others who were also my colleagues in office.   *Res Gestae 34*

Young men, hear an old man to whom old men hearkened when he was young.

> *From* PLUTARCH, *Apothegms,*
> *Caesar Augustus*

---

[1] See Hsieh Ho, p. 148a.
[2] Quandoque bonus dormitat Homerus.
Homer himself, in a long work, may sleep. — ROBERT HERRICK, *Hesperides* [1648], *no. 95*
See Pope, p. 402b.
[3] Ut pictura poesis.
[4] Quintili Vare, legiones redde!
[5] A Greek proverb, a familiar rendering of which is: Festina lente.
[6] A Latin proverb: Sat celeriter fieri quidquid fiat satis bene. See Publilius Syrus, p. 125a, and Anonymous, p. 150a.

LIVY
[TITUS LIVIUS]
59 B.C. — A.D. 17

We can endure neither our evils nor their cures.[1] *History, Prologue*

Better late than never.[2]
Ib. bk. IV, sec. 23

Woe to the vanquished.[3]
Ib. V, 48

Beyond the Alps lies Italy.[4]
Ib. XXI, 30

PUBLILIUS SYRUS[5]
fl. first century B.C.

As men, we are all equal in the presence of death. *Maxim 1*

He doubly benefits the needy who gives quickly.[6] *Maxim 6*

To do two things at once is to do neither. *Maxim 7*

A god could hardly love and be wise.[7] *Maxim 25*

The loss which is unknown is no loss at all.[8] *Maxim 38*

A good reputation is more valuable than money.[9] *Maxim 108*

It is well to moor your bark with two anchors. *Maxim 119*

Many receive advice, few profit by it. *Maxim 149*

While we stop to think, we often miss our opportunity. *Maxim 185*

Whatever you can lose, you should reckon of no account. *Maxim 191*

For a good cause, wrongdoing is virtuous.[1] *Maxim 244*

You should hammer your iron when it is glowing hot.[2] *Maxim 262*

What is left when honor is lost?
Maxim 265

A fair exterior is a silent recommendation. *Maxim 267*

Fortune is not satisfied with inflicting one calamity. *Maxim 274*

When Fortune is on our side, popular favor bears her company.
Maxim 275

When Fortune flatters, she does it to betray.[3] *Maxim 277*

Fortune is like glass — the brighter the glitter, the more easily broken.
Maxim 280

It is more easy to get a favor from Fortune than to keep it.
Maxim 282

There are some remedies worse than the disease.[4] *Maxim 301*

A cock has great influence on his own dunghill.[5] *Maxim 357*

---

[1] The two reasons for writing a history.
[2] Potius sero quam numquam.
It is better to learn late than never. — PUBLILIUS SYRUS, *Maxim 864*
[3] Vae victis.
[4] In conspectu Alpes habeant, quarum alterum latus Italiae sit.
Au-delà des Alpes est l'Italie. — NAPOLEON [1797]
[5] Commonly called Publius, but spelled Publilius by PLINY in his *Natural History, 35, sec. 199.* Translated mainly by DARIUS LYMAN. The numbers are those of the translator.
[6] See Augustus Caesar, p. 124b, and Anonymous, p. 150a.
[7] It is impossible to love and be wise. — FRANCIS BACON, *Essays* [1597–1625], *Of Love*
[8] See Shakespeare, p. 274b.
[9] See *Ecclesiastes 7:1*, p. 28a, and Bacon, p. 208b.
A good name is better than riches. — CERVANTES, *Don Quixote, pt. II* [1615], *bk. II, ch. 33*

[1] Honesta turpitudo est pro causa bona.
[2] When the iron is hot, strike. — JOHN HEYWOOD, *Proverbs* [1546], *pt. I, ch. 2*
Strike whilst the iron is hot. — RABELAIS, *bk. II* [1534], *ch. 31*
Nothing like striking while the iron is hot. — CERVANTES, *Don Quixote, pt. II* [1615], *bk. IV, ch. 71*
[3] See Shakespeare, p. 236b.
[4] Marius said, "I see the cure is not worth the pain." — PLUTARCH [A.D. 46–120], *Lives, Caius Marius*
The remedy is worse than the disease. — FRANCIS BACON, *Essays* [1597–1625], *Of Seditions*
I find the medicine worse than the malady. — BEAUMONT AND FLETCHER, *Love's Cure* [1647], *act III, sc. ii*
[5] Every cocke is proud on his owne dunghill. — JOHN HEYWOOD, *Proverbs* [1546], *pt. I, ch. 11*

Anyone can hold the helm when the sea is calm.[1] *Maxim 358*

The bow too tensely strung is easily broken. *Maxim 388*

Treat your friend as if he might become an enemy.[2] *Maxim 402*

No pleasure endures unseasoned by variety.[3] *Maxim 406*

The judge is condemned when the criminal is absolved.[4] *Maxim 407*

Practice is the best of all instructors.[5] *Maxim 439*

He who is bent on doing evil can never want occasion. *Maxim 459*

Never find your delight in another's misfortune. *Maxim 467*

It is a bad plan that admits of no modification. *Maxim 469*

It is an unhappy lot which finds no enemies. *Maxim 499*

The fear of death is more to be dreaded than death itself.[6] *Maxim 511*

A rolling stone gathers no moss.[7] *Maxim 524*

Never promise more than you can perform. *Maxim 528*

No one should be judge in his own case.[8] *Maxim 545*

Necessity knows no law except to prevail.[1] *Maxim 553*

Nothing can be done at once hastily and prudently.[2] *Maxim 557*

We desire nothing so much as what we ought not to have. *Maxim 559*

It is only the ignorant who despise education. *Maxim 571*

Do not turn back when you are just at the goal.[3] *Maxim 580*

It is not every question that deserves an answer. *Maxim 581*

No man is happy who does not think himself so.[4] *Maxim 584*

Never thrust your own sickle into another's corn.[5] *Maxim 593*

You cannot put the same shoe on every foot. *Maxim 596*

Every day should be passed as if it were to be our last.[6] *Maxim 633*

Money alone sets all the world in motion. *Maxim 656*

You should go to a pear tree for pears, not to an elm.[7] *Maxim 674*

[1] See Shakespeare, p. 267b.
[2] Treat your friend as if he will one day be your enemy, and your enemy as if he will one day be your friend. — LABERIUS [105–43 B.C.], *Fragment*
See Sophocles, p. 81a.
[3] See Cowper, p. 458a.
[4] Iudex damnatur ubi nocens absolvitur — motto adopted for the *Edinburgh Review.*
[5] Practice makes perfect. — *Proverb*
The saying "Practice is everything" is Periander's. — DIOGENES LAERTIUS [C. 200 A.D.], *Periander 6*
[6] See Shakespeare, p. 271a.
[7] The rolling stone never gathereth mosse. — JOHN HEYWOOD, *Proverbs* [1546], *pt. I, ch. 11*
The stone that is rolling can gather no moss. — THOMAS TUSSER, *Five Hundred Points of Good Husbandry* [1557]
[8] It is not permitted to the most equitable of men to be a judge in his own cause. — PASCAL [1623–1662], *Pensées, ch. 4, 1*

[1] Proverbial — attributed to Syrus.
Necessity gives the law and does not itself receive it. — *Maxim 399*
See St. Augustine, p. 147a, and note.
    And with necessity,
The tyrant's plea, excused his devilish deeds.
    MILTON, *Paradise Lost* [1667], *bk. IV, l. 393*
See William Pitt, p. 496b.
[2] See Chaucer, p. 168b.
[3] When men are arrived at the goal, they should not turn back. — PLUTARCH [A.D. 46–120], *Of the Training of Children*
[4] No man can enjoy happiness without thinking that he enjoys it. — SAMUEL JOHNSON [1709–1784], *The Rambler*
[5] Did thrust as now in others' corn his sickle. — DU BARTAS, *Divine Weeks and Works* [1578], *pt. II, Second Week*
Not presuming to put my sickle in another man's corn. — NICHOLAS YONGE, *Musica Transalpina, Epistle Dedicatory* [1588]
[6] See Horace, p. 121a, and Marcus Aurelius, p. 141b.
[7] You may as well expect pears from an elm. — CERVANTES, *Don Quixote, pt. II* [1615], *bk. IV, ch. 40*

It is a very hard undertaking to seek to please everybody.   *Maxim 675*

Look for a tough wedge for a tough log.   *Maxim 723*

Pardon one offense, and you encourage the commission of many.   *Maxim 750*

In every enterprise consider where you would come out.[1]   *Maxim 777*

It takes a long time to bring excellence to maturity.   *Maxim 780*

No one knows what he can do till he tries.   *Maxim 786*

It is vain to look for a defense against lightning.   *Maxim 835*

Everything is worth what its purchaser will pay for it.[2]   *Maxim 847*

Better be ignorant of a matter than half know it.[3]   *Maxim 865*

Prosperity makes friends, adversity tries them.[4]   *Maxim 872*

Let a fool hold his tongue and he will pass for a sage.   *Maxim 914*

You need not hang up the ivy branch over the wine that will sell.[5]   *Maxim 968*

It is a consolation to the wretched to have companions in misery.[6]   *Maxim 995*

[1] In every affair, consider what precedes and what follows and then undertake it. — EPIC-TETUS [c. A.D. 60]: *That Everything Is to be Undertaken with Circumspection, ch. 15*
[2]   What is worth in anything
But so much money as 'twill bring?
          BUTLER, *Hudibras, pt. I* [1663],
                              canto 1, l. 465
[3] See Pope, p. 402b.
[4] See Aristotle, p. 99a, and note.
[5] Good wine needs no bush. — SHAKESPEARE, *As You Like It* [1598–1600], *Epilogue, l. 4*
Good wine needs neither bush nor preface
To make it welcome.
          SIR WALTER SCOTT, *Peveril of the Peak* [1822], *ch. 4*
Bush: a shrub or branch, especially of ivy (perhaps as sacred to Bacchus) hung out at vintners' doors, or as a tavern sign. — WEBSTER, *New International Dictionary, 2nd ed.* [1945]. I.e., good wine needs no advertising.
[6] 'Tis the only comfort of the miserable to have partners in their woes. — CERVANTES, *Don Quixote, pt. I* [1605], *bk. III, ch. 10*

Unless degree is preserved, the first place is safe for no one.[1]   *Maxim 1042*

Confession of our faults is the next thing to innocence.   *Maxim 1060*

I have often regretted my speech, never my silence.[2]   *Maxim 1070*

Speech is a mirror of the soul: as a man speaks, so is he.   *Maxim 1073*

DIONYSIUS OF HALICARNASSUS
c. 54 – c. 7 B.C.

The contact with manners then is education; and this Thucydides appears to assert when he says history is philosophy learned from examples.
          Ars Rhetorica XI, 2

SEXTUS AURELIUS PROPERTIUS
54 B.C. – A.D. 2

Never change when love has found its home.   *Elegies I, i, 36*

The seaman's story is of tempest, the plowman's of his team of bulls; the soldier tells his wounds, the shepherd his tale of sheep.   *Ib. II, i, 43*

Let each man pass his days in that wherein his skill is greatest.   *Ib. 46*

What though strength fails? Boldness is certain to win praise. In mighty enterprises, it is enough to have had the determination.[3]   *Ib. x, 5*

Misery loves company. — JOHN RAY, *English Proverbs* [1670]
It is a comfort to the unhappy to have companions in misery. — SPINOZA, *Ethics* [1677], *pt. 4, proposition 57, note*
[1] See Shakespeare, p. 267b.
[2] Simonides said that "he never repented that he held his tongue, but often that he had spoken." — PLUTARCH [A.D. 46–120], *Rules for the Preservation of Health*
[3] Quod si deficiant vires, audacia certe
          Laus erit: in magnis et voluisse sat est.
See Menander, p. 102b.

Let no one be willing to speak ill of the absent.[1]   *Elegies II, xix, 32*

Let each man have the wit to go his own way.[2]   *Ib. xxv, 38*

Absence makes the heart grow fonder.[3]   *Ib. xxxiii, 43*

There is something beyond the grave; death does not end all, and the pale ghost escapes from the vanquished pyre.[4]   *Ib. IV, vii, 1*

ALBIUS TIBULLUS
c. 54 – c. 19 B.C.

May I look on you when my last hour comes; may I hold you, as I sink, with my failing hand.[5]
          Elegies I, i, 59

Jupiter laughs at the perjuries of lovers.[6]   *Ib. III, vi, 49*

Jove the Rain-giver.   *Ib. vii, 26*

OVID
[PUBLIUS OVIDIUS NASO]
43 B.C. – A.D. C. 18

Mine is good faith that will yield to none, and ways without reproach, and unadorned simplicity, and blushing modesty.   *Amores I, iii, 13*

The rest who does not know?[7]
          Ib. v, 25

Every lover is a warrior, and Cupid has his camps.[1]   *Amores I, ix, 1*

Stay far hence, far hence, you prudes![2]   *Ib. II, i, 3*

They come to see; they come that they themselves may be seen.[3]
          Ars Amatoria I, 99

It is convenient that there be gods, and, as it is convenient, let us believe there are.[4]   *Ib. 637*

To be loved, be lovable.
          Ib. II, 107

Nothing is stronger than habit.
          Ib. 345

Perhaps too my name will be joined to theirs[5] [the names of famous poets].   *Ib. III, 339*

Now are fields of corn where Troy once was.   *Heroides I, i, 2*

[Chaos] A rough, unordered mass of things.[6]   *Metamorphoses I, 7*

Your lot is mortal: not mortal is what you desire.   *Ib. II, 56*

You will be safest in the middle.[7]
          Ib. 137

I am Actaeon: recognize your master![8]   *Ib. III, 230*

The cause is hidden, but the result is well known.[9]   *Ib. IV, 287*

[1] Absenti nemo non nocuisse velit.
See The Seven Sages, p. 68b.
[2] Paddle your own canoe. — ANONYMOUS, *Harper's Monthly* [May 1854]
[3] Semper in absentes felicior aestus amantes.
[4] Our souls survive this death. — OVID, *Metamorphoses XV, l. 158*
[5] Te spectem, suprema mihi cum venerit hora, Te teneam moriens deficiente manu.
[6] Periuria ridet amantum Iupiter.
Also in OVID [43 B.C.–A.D. c. 18], *Ars Amatoria I, 633*
See Shakespeare, p. 223b.
And Jove but laughs at lovers' perjury. — DRYDEN, *Palamon and Arcite* [1680], bk. II, l. 758, and *Amphitryon* [1690], act I, sc. ii
[7] Cetera quis nescit?

[1] Love is a kind of warfare. — OVID, *Ars Amatoria II, 233*
A batallas de amor campo de pluma [A field of feathers for the strife of love]. — LUIS DE GÓNGORA [1571–1627], *Soledad I*
[2] Procul hinc, procul este, severi!
[3] Spectatum veniunt, veniunt spectentur ut ipsae.
And for to se, and eek for to be seye. — CHAUCER, *The Canterbury Tales* [c. 1387], *The Wife of Bath's Prologue*, l. 552
To see and to be seen. — BEN JONSON [1572–1637], *Epithalamion III, 4*
[4] See Tillotson, p. 366b, and Voltaire, p. 418a.
[5] Forsitan et nostrum nomen miscebitur istis.
[6] Rudis indigestaque moles.
[7] Medio tutissimus ibis.
[8] Actaeon ego sum, dominum cognoscite vestrum!
[9] Causa latet, vis est notissima.

We can learn even from our enemies.[1]   *Metamorphoses IV, 428*

I see and approve better things, but
follow worse.[2]   *Ib. VII, 20*

The gods have their own rules.[3]
      Ib. IX, 500

Time the devourer of all things.[4]
      Ib. XV, 234

And now I have finished a work that
neither the wrath of love, nor fire, nor
the sword, nor devouring age shall be
able to destroy.   *Ib. 871*

Resist beginnings; the prescription
comes too late when the disease has
gained strength by long delays.[5]
      Remedia Amoris 91

Love yields to business. If you seek a
way out of love, be busy; you'll be safe
then.[6]   *Ib. 143*

Poetry comes fine-spun from a mind
at peace.   *Tristia I, i, 39*

So long as you are secure you will
count many friends; if your life becomes clouded you will be alone.[7]
      Ib. ix, 5

Whatever I tried to write was verse.
      Ib. IV, x, 26

It is annoying to be honest to no
purpose.   *Ex Ponto II, iii, 14*

Note too that a faithful study of
the liberal arts humanizes character
and permits it not to be cruel.
      Ib. ix, 47

---

[1] Fas est et ab hoste doceri. Imitated from
Aristophanes, *The Birds, l. 370:* People before
this have learned from their enemies.

[2] Video meliora, proboque, deteriora sequor.
See *Romans 7:19,* p. 51a, and Euripides,
p. 84b.
I know and love the good, yet, ah! the worst
pursue. — Petrarch, *Sonnet 225, Canzone 21,
To Laura in Life* [c. 1327]

[3] Sunt superis sua iura.

[4] Tempus edax rerum.

[5] See Persius, p. 133b.

[6] Qui finem quaeris amoris
  Cedit amor rebus; res age, tutus eris.

[7] See Aristotle, p. 99a, and note.

PHAEDRUS[1]
fl. c. A.D. 8

Submit to the present evil, lest a
greater one befall you.
      Fables, bk. I, fable 2, l. 31

He was the author, our hand finished
it.   *Ib. 6, 20*

That it is unwise to be heedless ourselves while we are giving advice to others, I will show in a few lines.
      Ib. 9, 1

No one returns with good will to the
place which has done him a mischief.
      Ib. 18, 1

It has been related that dogs drink at
the river Nile running along, that they
may not be seized by the crocodiles.[2]
      Ib. 25, 3

Everyone is bound to bear patiently
the results of his own example.
      Ib. 26, 12

Come of it what may, as Sinon said.
      Ib. III, prologue, l. 27

Things are not always what they
seem.[3]   *Ib. IV, 2, 5*

To add insult to injury.   *Ib. V, 3*

LUCIUS ANNAEUS
SENECA[4]
8 B.C. — A.D. 65

What fools these mortals be.[5]
      Epistles 1, 3

It is not the man who has too little,
but the man who craves more, that is
poor.   *Ib. 2, 2*

---

[1] Translated by Henry Thomas Riley [1816–
1878].

[2] Pliny the Elder in his *Natural History*
(*bk. VIII, sec. 148*) and Aelian in his *Various
Histories* relate the same fact as to the dogs
drinking from the Nile. "To treat a thing as the
dogs do the Nile" was a common proverb,
signifying superficial treatment.

[3] Non semper ea sunt quae videntur.
See Longfellow, p. 620b, and W. S. Gilbert,
p. 766a.

[4] Loeb Classical Library.

[5] Tanta stultitia mortalium est.
See Shakespeare, p. 230a.

Love of bustle is not industry.
Epistles 3, 5

Live among men as if God beheld you; speak to God as if men were listening. *Ib.* 10, 5

The best ideas are common property. *Ib.* 12, 11

Men do not care how nobly they live, but only how long, although it is within the reach of every man to live nobly, but within no man's power to live long. *Ib.* 22, 17

A great pilot can sail even when his canvas is rent. *Ib.* 30, 3

Man is a reasoning animal.
Ib. 41, 8

That most knowing of persons — gossip. *Ib.* 43, 1

It is quality rather than quantity that matters.[1] *Ib.* 45, 1

You can tell the character of every man when you see how he receives praise. *Ib.* 52, 12

Nothing is so certain as that the evils of idleness can be shaken off by hard work. *Ib.* 56, 9

Not lost, but gone before.[2]
Ib. 63, 16

All art is but imitation of nature.
Ib. 65, 3

It is a rough road that leads to the heights of greatness. *Ib.* 84, 13

The pilot . . . who has been able to say, "Neptune, you shall never sink this ship except on an even keel," has fulfilled the requirements of his art.[3]
Ib. 85, 33

I was shipwrecked before I got aboard. *Epistles* 87, 1

It is better, of course, to know useless things than to know nothing.
Ib. 88, 45

Do not ask for what you will wish you had not got. *Ib.* 95, 1

We are mad, not only individually, but nationally. We check manslaughter and isolated murders; but what of war and the much vaunted crime of slaughtering whole peoples? *Ib.* 95, 30

A great step towards independence is a good-humored stomach, one that is willing to endure rough treatment.
Ib. 123, 3

Fire is the test of gold; adversity, of strong men.[1]
Moral Essays. On Providence 5, 9

Time discovers truth.[2]
Ib. On Anger 2, 22

Whom they have injured they also hate.[3] *Ib.* 33

I do not distinguish by the eye, but by the mind, which is the proper judge of the man.
Ib. On the Happy Life 2, 2

There is no great genius without some touch of madness.[4]
Ib. On Tranquillity of the Mind
17, 10

[1] See Beaumont and Fletcher, p. 316b.
[2] Veritatem dies aperit. Omnia tempus revelat [Time reveals all]. — TERTULLIAN [A.D. C. 155-c. 225], *Apologeticus* 7
Time reveals all things. — ERASMUS [1465-1536], *Adagia*
[3] It is human nature to hate those whom you have injured. — TACITUS [A.D. 54-119], *Agricola* 42, 15
Chi fa ingiuria non perdona mai [He never pardons those he injures]. — *Italian proverb*
The offender never pardons. — GEORGE HERBERT, *Jacula Prudentum* [1640]
Forgiveness to the injured does belong;
But they ne'er pardon who have done the wrong.
DRYDEN, *The Conquest of Granada* [1670], *pt. II, act I, sc. ii*
[4] An ancient commonplace, which Seneca says he quotes from ARISTOTLE, *Problemata 30, 1*: "No excellent soul is exempt from a mixture of madness." It is also in PLATO, *Phaedrus 245A*.

[1] See Anonymous, p. 151a.
[2] Non amittuntur, sed praemittuntur.
Not dead, but gone before. — SAMUEL ROGERS, *Human Life* [1819]
See Masefield, p. 947b-948a.
[3] The mariner of old said thus to Neptune in a great tempest, "O God! thou mayest save me if thou wilt, and if thou wilt, thou mayest destroy me; but whether or no, I will steer my rudder true." — MONTAIGNE, *Essays* [1580-1595], *bk. II, ch. 16*

A great fortune is a great slavery.
*Moral Essays. To Polybius on
Consolation 6, 5*

Wherever the Roman conquers, there
he dwells.
Ib. To Helvia on Consolation 7, 7

He who receives a benefit with gratitude repays the first installment on his
debt.   *On Benefits, bk. II, 22, 1*

You roll my log, and I will roll
yours.   *Apocolocyntosis, sec. 9*

Do you seek Alcides' equal? None is,
except himself.[1]
Hercules Furens 1, 1, 84

Successful and fortunate crime is
called virtue.[2]   *Ibid. 255*

An age will come after many years
when the Ocean will loose the chains of
things, and a huge land lie revealed;
when Tiphys [3] will disclose new worlds
and Thule [4] no more be the ultimate.[5]
Medea, l. 374

Good sense travels on the well-worn paths;
genius, never. And that is why the crowd, not
altogether without reason, is so ready to treat
great men as lunatics. — CESARE LOMBROSO
[1836–1909], *The Man of Genius, preface*
    See Dryden, p. 368a.
    [1] None but himself can be his parallel. —
LEWIS THEOBALD [1688–1744], *The Double Falsehood*
    And but herself admits no parallel. — MAS-
SINGER [1583–1640], *Duke of Milan, act IV, sc. iii*
    [2] See Harington, p. 210a.
    [3] Jason's pilot.
    [4] See Virgil, p. 117a, and Thomson, p. 419b.
    [5] Venient annis
    Saecula seris, quibus Oceanus
    Vincula rerum laxet, et ingens
    Pateat tellus, Tiphysque novos
    Detegat orbes nec sit terris
    Ultima Thule.
    Translated by S. E. MORISON.
    As one much addicted to prophesies, and who
had already voyaged beyond Thule (Iceland),
Columbus was much impressed by the passage in
Seneca's *Medea.* — S. E. MORISON, *Admiral of
the Ocean Sea* [1942], *vol. I, ch. 6.*
    Next to these lines from *Medea* in an early
edition of Seneca's tragedies that belonged to
Columbus's son Ferdinand, there is this anno-
tation in the son's hand: Haec profetia impleta
est per patrem meum . . . almirantem anno
1492 [The prophecy was fulfilled by my father
the Admiral in the year 1492]. *Ib. I, 5*

A good mind possesses a kingdom.[1]
Thyestes 380

Light griefs are loquacious, but the
great are dumb.[2]
Hippolytus II, 3, 607

CALIGULA
[GAIUS CAESAR]
A.D. 12–41

Would that the Roman people had a
single neck [to cut off their head].
From SUETONIUS, *Gaius
Caligula, sec. 30*

MANILIUS
fl. first century A.D.

He snatched the thunderbolt from
heaven, then the scepter from tyrants.[3]
Astronomica I, l. 104

As soon as we are born we begin to
die, and the end depends upon the beginning.[4]   *Ib. IV, 16*

ONASANDER
fl. A.D. 49

Vigor is found in the man who has
not yet grown old, and discretion in the
man who is not too young.
The General, ch. 1, sec. 10

Envy is a pain of mind that successful men cause their neighbors.
Ib. ch. 42, par. 25

PLINY THE ELDER[5]
A.D. 23–79

In comparing various authors with
one another, I have discovered that

---

    [1] See Dyer, p. 192a.
    [2] See Raleigh, p. 199a.
    [3] Eripuit Jovi fulmen viresque tonandi.
    Adapted by A. R. J. TURGOT for the inscrip-
tion on the Houdon bust of Franklin [1778] as:
Eripuit coelo fulmen, mox sceptra tyrannis.
    See Franklin, p. 421a, note 3.
    [4] See *The Wisdom of Solomon 5:13*, p. 37a.
    [5] With some alterations, translated by JOHN
BOSTOCK [1773–1846] and HENRY THOMAS RILEY
[1816–1878].
    See also Pliny the Younger, p. 140b.

some of the gravest and latest writers have transcribed, word for word, from former works, without making acknowledgment.

Natural History, bk. I, dedication, sec. 22

Everything is soothed by oil, and this is the reason why divers send out small quantities of it from their mouths, because it smooths every part which is rough.[1] *Ib. II, 234*

It is far from easy to determine whether she [Nature] has proved to man a kind parent or a merciless stepmother.[2] *Ib. VII, 1*

Man alone at the very moment of his birth, cast naked upon the naked earth, does she abandon to cries and lamentations.[3] *Ib. 2*

To laugh, if but for an instant only, has never been granted to man before the fortieth day from his birth, and then it is looked upon as a miracle of precocity.[4] *Ib.*

Man is the only one that knows nothing, that can learn nothing without being taught. He can neither speak nor

walk nor eat, and in short he can do nothing at the prompting of nature only, but weep.[1]

Natural History, bk. VII, sec. 4

With man, most of his misfortunes are occasioned by man.[2] *Ib. 5*

Indeed, what is there that does not appear marvelous when it comes to our knowledge for the first time?[3] How many things, too, are looked upon as quite impossible until they have been actually effected? *Ib. 6*

The human features and countenance, although composed of but some ten parts or little more, are so fashioned that among so many thousands of men there are no two in existence who cannot be distinguished from one another.[4] *Ib. 8*

All men possess in their bodies a poison which acts upon serpents; and the human saliva, it is said, makes them take to flight, as though they had been touched with boiling water. The same substance, it is said, destroys them the moment it enters their throat.[5]

Ib. 15

It has been observed that the height of a man from the crown of the head to the sole of the foot is equal to the distance between the tips of the middle

---

[1] Why does pouring oil on the sea make it clear and calm? Is it for that the winds, slipping the smooth oil, have no force, nor cause any waves? — PLUTARCH [A.D. 46–120], *Natural Questions IX*

Bishop Adain [A.D. 651] gave to a company about to take a journey by sea "some holy oil, saying, 'I know that when you go abroad you will meet with a storm and contrary wind; but do you remember to cast this oil I give you into the sea, and the wind shall cease immediately.' " — BEDE [673–735], *Eccesiastical History, bk. III, ch. 14*

In JARED SPARKS's edition of BENJAMIN FRANKLIN's *Works, vol. VI, p. 354,* there are letters between Franklin, Brownrigg, and Parish on the stilling of waves by means of oil.

[2] To man the earth seems altogether
No more a mother, but a step-dame rather.
    DU BARTAS [1544–1590], *Divine Weeks and Works, First Week, Third Day*

[3] See *The Wisdom of Solomon 7:3,* p. 37a.
He is born naked, and falls a-whining at the first. — ROBERT BURTON, *Anatomy of Melancholy* [1621–1651], *pt. I, sec. 2, member 3, subsec. 10*

[4] This term of forty days is mentioned by ARISTOTLE in his *Natural History.*

[1] See Tennyson, p. 650b.
[2] See Burns, p. 492b.
[3] See Tacitus, *Agricola 30,* p. 140a.
[4] It is the common wonder of all men, how among so many millions of faces there should be none alike. — SIR THOMAS BROWNE, *Religio Medici* [1642], *pt. II, sec. 2*
Of a thousand shavers. two do not shave so much alike as not to be distinguished. — SAMUEL JOHNSON [1777]; from BOSWELL. *Life of Dr. Johnson* [1791], *vol. II, p. 120* [Everyman ed.]
See Montaigne, p. 190b.
[5] MADAME D'ABRANTES relates that when Bonaparte was in Cairo he sent for a serpent-detector (Psylli) to remove two serpents that had been seen in his house. He, having enticed one of them from his hiding place, caught it in one hand, just below the jawbone, in such a manner as to oblige the mouth to open, when, spitting into it, the effect was like magic: the reptile appeared struck with instant death. — *Memoirs, vol. I, ch. 59*

fingers of the two hands when extended in a straight line.
Natural History, bk. VII, *sec.* 77

There is always something new out of Africa.[1]   *Ib.* VIII, 17

When a building is about to fall down, all the mice desert it.[2]
Ib. 103

Bears when first born are shapeless masses of white flesh a little larger than mice, their claws alone being prominent. The mother then licks them gradually into proper shape.[3]
Ib. 126

The agricultural population, says Cato, produces the bravest men, the most valiant soldiers, and a class of citizens the least given of all to evil designs.   *Ib.* XVIII, 26

The best plan is to profit by the folly of others.   *Ib.* 31

A grain of salt being added.[4]
Ib. XXIII, 8

Why is it that we entertain the belief that for every purpose odd numbers are the most effectual? [5]
Ib. XXVIII, 23

---

[1] Ex Africa semper aliquid novi.
Quoted as a Greek proverb.
[2] This is alluded to by CICERO in his letters to Atticus, and is mentioned by AELIAN (*Animated Nature, bk. VI, ch. 41*). Compare the modern proverb: Rats desert a sinking ship.
[3] Not unlike the bear which bringeth forth
In the end of thirty days a shapeless birth;
But after licking, it in shape she draws,
And by degrees she fashions out the paws,
The head, and neck, and finally doth bring
To a perfect beast that first deformed thing.
DU BARTAS, *Divine Weeks and Works* [1578], *First Week, First Day*
I had not time to lick it into form, as a bear doth her young ones. — ROBERT BURTON, *Anatomy of Melancholy* [1621–1651], *Democritus to the Reader*
[4] Cum grano salis [With a grain of salt].
Pompey's antidote against poison was "to be taken fasting, a grain of salt being added."
[5] The god delights in an odd number. — VIRGIL [70–19 B.C.], *Eclogues VIII, 75*
See Shakespeare, p. 267b, and Samuel Lover, p. 589a.

PERSIUS
[AULUS PERSIUS FLACCUS]
A.D. 34–62

The stomach is the teacher of the arts and the dispenser of invention.[1]
Satires, prologue, l. 10

Tell, priests, what is gold doing in a holy place?   *Ib.* II, 69

Let them look upon virtue and pine because they have lost her.
Ib. III, 38

Meet the disease at its first stage.[2]
Ib. 64

GAIUS PETRONIUS
[PETRONIUS ARBITER[3]]
d. A.D. c. 66

He has joined the great majority.[4]
Satyricon, sec. 42

A man who is always ready to believe what is told him will never do well.
Ib. 43

One good turn deserves another.
Ib. 45

A man must have his faults.   *Ib.*

Not worth his salt.   *Ib.* 57

My heart was in my mouth.
Ib. 62

Beauty and wisdom are rarely conjoined.[5]   *Ib.* 94

---

[1] Magister artis ingenique largitor venter.
See Anonymous Latin, p. 151a.
Necessity, mother of invention. — WYCHERLEY, *Love in a Wood* [1671], *act III, sc. iii*
Art imitates Nature, and necessity is the mother of invention. — RICHARD FRANCK, *Northern Memoirs* [written 1658, published 1694]
Sheer necessity — the proper parent of an art so nearly allied to invention. — SHERIDAN, *The Critic* [1779], *act I, sc. ii*
[2] Venienti occurrite morbo.
A stitch in time saves nine. — *Proverb*
See Ovid, p. 129a.
Also in Publilius Syrus, *Maxim 866*.
[3] Pliny calls Petronius Titus in *Natural History XXXVII, 8.*
See Tacitus, p. 140a.
[4] Abiit ad plures.
[5] See Petrarch, p. 163a.

The studied spontaneity of Horace.[1]
Satyricon, sec. 118

Natural curls.[2]   *Ib. 126*

NERO
A.D. 37–68

What an artist dies with me! [3]
From SUETONIUS, *Nero, sec. 49*

LUCAN
A.D. 39–65

If the victor had the gods on his side, the vanquished had Cato.[4]
The Civil War, bk. I, 128

There stands the shadow of a glorious name.[5]   *Ib. 135*

Pigmies placed on the shoulders of giants see more than the giants themselves.[6]   *Ib. II, 10 (Didacus Stella)*

Thinking nothing done while anything remained to be done.[7]
Ib. 657

More was lost than mere life and existence.[8]   *Ib. VII, 639*

We all praise fidelity; but the true friend pays the penalty when he supports those whom Fortune crushes.[9]
Ib. VIII, 485

---

[1] Horatii curiosa felicitas.
[2] Crines ingenio suo flexi.
[3] Qualis artifex pereo!
[4] Victrix causa deis placuit, sed victa Catoni.
[5] Stat magni nominis umbra.
[6] Pigmei gigantum humeris impositi plusquam ipsi gigantes vident.
See Robert Burton, p. 310a, and Sir Isaac Newton, p. 379b.
The dwarf sees farther than the giant, when he has the giant's shoulder to mount on. — COLERIDGE, *The Friend* [1828]
[7] The reference is to Caesar.
[8] Plus est quam vita salusque
Quod perit.
[9] "Dat poenas laudata fides, dum sustinet," inquit,
"Quos fortuna premit."
A praised faith
Is her own scourge, when it sustains their states
Whom fortune hath depressed.
BEN JONSON, *Anglia 39, 247*

A name illustrious and revered by nations.[1]
The Civil War, bk. IX, 203

Is the dwelling place of God anywhere but in the earth and sea, the air and sky, and virtue? Why seek we further for deities? Whatever you see, whatever you touch, that is Jupiter.
Ib. 578

The very ruins have been destroyed.[2]
Ib. 969

DIO CHRYSOSTOM [3]
A.D. C. 40 – C. 120

Diogenes: The man I know not, for I am not acquainted with his mind.
Fourth Discourse, On Kingship, ch. 17

Idleness and lack of occupation are the best things in the world to ruin the foolish.
Tenth Discourse, On Servants, ch. 7

Most men are so completely corrupted by opinion that they would rather be notorious for the greatest calamities than suffer no ill and be unknown.   *Ib. ch. 6*

MARTIAL [4]
[MARCUS VALERIUS MARTIALIS]
A.D. C. 40 – C. 104

My poems are naughty, but my life is pure.[5]   *Epigrams I, 4*

"I'll live." — Yes, but no sensible man would say so. Tomorrow's life is too late. Live today.   *Ib. 15*

And faith though prais'd, is punish'd, that supports
Such as good fate forsakes.
FLETCHER, *The False One* [1647], *act I, sc. i, l. 303*

[1] Clarum et venerabile nomen
Gentibus.
Cato's tribute to the fallen Pompey.
[2] Etiam periere ruinae.
The reference is to Troy.
[3] Translated by J. W. COHOON.
[4] Translated by DUDLEY FITTS.
[5] Lasciva est nobis pagina, vita proba.

Some good, some so-so, and lots plain bad: that's how a book of poems is made, my friend.   *Epigrams I, 16*

I don't like you, Sabidius, I can't say why; But I can say this: I don't like you, Sabidius.[1]   *Ib. 32*

Stop abusing my verses, or publish some of your own.   *Ib. 91*

You complain, friend Swift, of the length of my epigrams, but you yourself write nothing. Yours are shorter.   *Ib. 110*

Conceal a flaw, and the world will imagine the worst.   *Ib. III, 42*

The bee is enclosed, and shines preserved in amber, so that it seems enshrined in its own nectar.[2]   *Ib. IV, 32*

They praise those verses, yes, but read something else.   *Ib. 49*

You ask what a nice girl will do? She won't give an inch, but she won't say no.   *Ib. 71*

Our days pass by, and are scored against us.[3]   *Ib. V, 20*

What's a wretched man? A man whom no man pleases.   *Ib. 28*

A man who lives everywhere lives nowhere.   *Ib. 73*

You puff the poets of other days,
  The living you deplore.
Spare me the accolade: your praise
  Is not worth dying for.[4]
     Ib. VIII, 69

Virtue extends our days: he lives two

lives who relives his past with pleasure.[1]
     Epigrams X, 23

Neither fear your death's day nor long for it.[2]   *Ib. 47*

Lucretia blushed, and put my book aside. Brutus was there. — Exit Brutus. — Now she'll read.   *Ib. XI, 16*

You'll get no laurel crown for outrunning a burro.   *Ib. XII, 36*

You're obstinate, pliant, merry, morose, all at once. For me there's no living with you, or without you.[3]
     Ib. 47

The country in town.[4]   *Ib. 57*

I know these are nothing.[5]   *Ib. XIII, 2*

TITUS VESPASIANUS
A.D. C. 41 – 81

Friends, I have lost a day.[6]
     From SUETONIUS, *Titus, sec.* 8

QUINTILIAN
[MARCUS FABIUS
QUINTILIANUS]
A.D. 42 – 118

We give to necessity the praise of virtue.[7]

     De Institutione Oratoria,
     bk. I, 8, 14

---

[1] See Tom Brown, p. 386b.

[2] Whence we see spiders, flies, or ants entombed preserved forever in amber, a more than royal tomb. — FRANCIS BACON, *Historia Vitae et Mortis* [1623], *Sylva Sylvarum, cent. I, exper. 100*
  I saw a flie within a beade
  Of amber cleanly buried.
     HERRICK [1591–1674], *On a Fly
     Buried in Amber*
See Pope, p. 410b.

[3] Nobis pereunt et imputantur.

[4] See Louis Edwin Thayer, p. 949a.

[1] Thus would I double my life's fading space;
For he that runs it well, runs twice his race.
     COWLEY [1618–1667], *Discourse XI, Of
     Myself, st. 11*
For he lives twice who can at once employ
The present well, and ev'n the past enjoy.
     POPE [1688–1744], *Imitation of Martial*

[2] See Milton, p. 348a.

[3] Difficilis facilis fucundus acerbus es idem:
Nec tecum possum vivere nec sine te.
See Aristophanes, p. 91b.

[4] Rus in urbe.

[5] Nos haec novimus esse nihil.
Said of his own poems. The phrase was used by John Gay as epigraph for *The Beggar's Opera* [1728].

[6] Amici, diem perdidi.

[7] In the additions of Hadrianus Julius to the *Adages* of ERASMUS, he remarks, under the head of *Necessitatem edere,* that a very familiar proverb was current among his countrymen: Necessitatem in virtutem commutare [To make necessity a virtue].

A liar should have a good memory.[1]
De Institutione Oratoria,
bk. IV, 2, 91

Vain hopes are often like the dreams of those who wake.   *Ib. VI, 2, 30*

For it is feeling and force of imagination that make us eloquent.[2]
Ib. X, 7, 15

Those who wish to appear wise among fools, among the wise seem foolish.[3]   *Ib. 21*

PLUTARCH
A.D. 46–120

As geographers, Sosius, crowd into the edges of their maps parts of the world which they do not know about, adding notes in the margin to the effect that beyond this lies nothing but sandy deserts full of wild beasts, and unapproachable bogs.[4]
Lives, Aemilius Paulus, sec. 5

About Theseus began the saying, "He is a second Hercules."   *Ib. 29*

Thus maketh vertue of necessitee. — CHAUCER, *Troilus and Criseyde* [1372–1386], *bk. IV, l. 1586*
Others made a virtue of necessity. — RABELAIS, *Works, bk. V* [1552], *ch. 23*
See Shakespeare, p. 226a.
Make a virtue of necessity. — ROBERT BURTON, *Anatomy of Melancholy* [1621–1651], *pt. III, sec. 3, member 4, subsec. I*
[1] He who has not a good memory should never take upon him the trade of lying. — MONTAIGNE, *Essays* [1580–1595], *bk. I, ch. 9, Of Liars*
Il faut bonne mémoire, après qu'on a menti. — CORNEILLE, *Le Menteur* [1642], *act IV, sc. v*
Liars ought to have good memories. — ALGERNON SIDNEY, *Discourses on Government* [1698], *ch. 2, sec. 15*
[2] Pectus est enim, quod disertos facit.
[3] A wit with dunces, and a dunce wit.. wits. — POPE, *Dunciad* [1728], *bk. IV, l. 90*
A fool with judges, amongst fools a judge. — COWPER, *Conversation* [1782], *l. 298*
This man [Chesterfield], I thought, had been a lord among wits; but I find he is only a wit among lords. — SAMUEL JOHNSON; from BOSWELL, *Life of Dr. Johnson* [1791], *vol. II, p. 159* [*Everyman ed.*]
[4] So geographers, in Afric maps,
With savage pictures fill their gaps,
And o'er unhabitable downs
Place elephants for want of towns.
SWIFT, *On Poetry, A Rhapsody* [1733]

A Roman divorced from his wife, being highly blamed by his friends, who demanded, "Was she not chaste? Was she not fair? Was she not fruitful?" holding out his shoe, asked them whether it was not new and well made. "Yet," added he, "none of you can tell where it pinches me." [1]
Lives, Aemilius Paulus, sec. 5

Where the lion's skin will not reach, you must patch it out with the fox's.[2]
Ib. Lysander, sec. 7

Moral habits, induced by public practices, are far quicker in making their way into men's private lives, than the failings and faults of individuals are in infecting the city at large.   *Ib. 17*

As it is in the proverb, played Cretan against Cretan.[3]   *Ib. 20*

Perseverance is more prevailing than violence; and many things which cannot be overcome when they are together, yield themselves up when taken little by little.   *Ib. Sertorius, sec. 16*

Good fortune will elevate even petty minds, and give them the appearance of a certain greatness and stateliness, as from their high place they look down upon the world; but the truly noble and resolved spirit raises itself, and becomes more conspicuous in times of disaster and ill fortune.   *Ib. Eumenes, sec. 9*

Authority and place demonstrate and try the tempers of men, by moving every passion and discovering every frailty.
Ib. Demosthenes and Cicero, sec. 3

Medicine, to produce health, has to

---

[1] The wearer knows where the shoe wrings. — GEORGE HERBERT, *Jacula Prudentum* [1640]
I can tell where my own shoe pinches me. — CERVANTES, *Don Quixote, pt. I* [1605], *bk. IV, ch. 5*
[2] The prince must be a lion, but he must also know how to play the fox. — NICCOLÒ MACHIAVELLI, *The Prince* [1532]
[3] Cheat against cheat. The Cretans were considered notorious liars.

examine disease; and music, to create harmony, must investigate discord.

Lives, Demetrius, sec. 1

It is a true proverb, that if you live with a lame man you will learn to limp.

Morals. Of the Training of Children

The very spring and root of honesty and virtue lie in good education.

Ib.

It is indeed desirable to be well descended, but the glory belongs to our ancestors.   *Ib.*

Nothing made the horse so fat as the king's eye.   *Ib.*

It is wise to be silent when occasion requires, and better than to speak, though never so well.[1]   *Ib.*

An old doting fool, with one foot already in the grave.   *Ib.*

He is a fool who leaves things close at hand to follow what is out of reach.[2]

Ib. Of Garrulity

All men whilst they are awake are in one common world; but each of them, when he is asleep, is in a world of his own.[3]   *Ib. Of Superstition*

That proverbial saying, "Bad news travels fast and far."[4]

Ib. Of Inquisitiveness

Spintharus, speaking in commendation of Epaminondas, says he scarce ever met with any man who knew more and spoke less.

Ib. Of Hearing, sec. 6

[1] Closed lips hurt no one, speaking may. — CATO THE CENSOR [234–149 B.C.], *bk. I, distich 12*
[2] Better one bird in hand than ten in the wood. — JOHN HEYWOOD, *Proverbs* [1546], *pt. I, ch. 11*
One bird in the hand is worth two in the wood. — THOMAS LODGE, *Rosalyne* [1590]
A bird in hand is worth two in the bush. — CERVANTES, *Don Quixote, pt. I* [1605], *bk. IV, ch. 4*
A feather in hand is better than a bird in the air. — GEORGE HERBERT, *Jacula Prudentum* [1640]
[3] A saying attributed to Heraclitus.
[4] Evil news fly faster still than good. — THOMAS KYD, *Spanish Tragedy* [1594], *act I*
See Milton, p. 350a.

Antiphanes said merrily that in a certain city the cold was so intense that words were congealed as soon as spoken, but that after some time they thawed and became audible; so that the words spoken in winter were articulated next summer.[1]

Morals. Of Man's Progress in Virtue

When the candles are out all women are fair.[2]   *Ib. Conjugal Precepts*

Like watermen, who look astern while they row the boat ahead.[3]

Ib. Whether 'Twas Rightfully Said, Live Concealed

The great god Pan is dead.[4]

Ib. Why the Oracles Cease to Give Answers

I am whatever was, or is, or will be; and my veil no mortal ever took up.[5]

Ib. Of Isis and Osiris

For to err in opinion, though it be not the part of wise men, is at least human.[6]   *Ib. Against Colotes*

Pythagoras, when he was asked what time was, answered that it was the soul of this world.

Ib. Platonic Questions

[1] Rabelais gives a somewhat similar account, referring to Antiphanes, in *Works, bk. IV* [1548], *chs. 55–56*.
See Raspe (Baron Munchausen), p. 468a.
[2] When all candles be out, all cats be gray. — JOHN HEYWOOD, *Proverbs* [1546], *pt. I, ch. 5*
[3] Like rowers, who advance backward. — MONTAIGNE, *Essays* [1580–1595], *Of Profit and Honor, bk. III, ch. 1*
Like the watermen that row one way and look another. — ROBERT BURTON, *Anatomy of Melancholy* [1621–1651], *Democritus to the Reader*
[4] PLUTARCH says in *Of Isis and Osiris* that a ship well laden with passengers drove with the tide near the Isles of Paxi, when a loud voice was heard by most of the passengers calling one Thanus. The voice then said aloud to him, "When you are arrived at Palodes, take care to make it known that the great god Pan is dead."
Great Pan is dead. — ELIZABETH BARRETT BROWNING [1806–1861], *The Dead Pan, st. 26*
[5] I am the things that are, and those that are to be, and those that have been. No one ever lifted my skirts; the fruit which I bore was the sun. — PROCLUS [A.D. c. 411–485], *On Plato's Timaeus* (inscription in the temple of Neith at Sais, in Egypt)
[6] See Anonymous, p. 150b, and Pope, p. 403b.

EPICTETUS[1]
A.D. C. 50 – 120

To the rational being only the irrational is unendurable, but the rational is endurable.   *Discourses, bk. I, ch. 2*

When you close your doors, and make darkness within, remember never to say that you are alone, for you are not alone;[2] nay, God is within, and your genius is within. And what need have they of light to see what you are doing?   *Ib. 14*

No thing great is created suddenly, any more than a bunch of grapes or a fig. If you tell me that you desire a fig, I answer you that there must be time. Let it first blossom, then bear fruit, then ripen.   *Ib. 15*

Any one thing in the creation is sufficient to demonstrate a Providence to a humble and grateful mind.   *Ib. 16*

Were I a nightingale, I would sing like a nightingale; were I a swan, like a swan. But as it is, I am a rational being, therefore I must sing hymns of praise to God.   *Ib.*

Practice yourself, for heaven's sake, in little things; and thence proceed to greater.   *Ib. 18*

It is difficulties that show what men are.   *Ib. 24*

The good or ill of man lies within his own will.   *Ib. 25*

In theory there is nothing to hinder our following what we are taught; but in life there are many things to draw us aside.   *Ib. 26*

Appearances to the mind are of four kinds. Things either are what they appear to be; or they neither are, nor appear to be; or they are, and do not appear to be; or they are not, and yet appear to be. Rightly to aim in all these cases is the wise man's task.   *Ib. 27*

[1] Loeb Classical Library.
[2] Though in a wilderness, a man is never alone. — SIR THOMAS BROWNE, *Religio Medici* [1642], *Everyman ed, p. 82*

Only the educated are free.
  Discourses, bk. II, ch. 1

The materials are indifferent, but the use we make of them is not a matter of indifference.   *Ib. 5*

Shall I show you the sinews of a philosopher? "What sinews are those?" — A will undisappointed; evils avoided; powers daily exercised; careful resolutions; unerring decisions.   *Ib. 8*

What is the first business of one who practices philosophy? To get rid of self-conceit. For it is impossible for anyone to begin to learn that which he thinks he already knows.   *Ib. 17*

Whatever you would make habitual, practice it; and if you would not make a thing habitual, do not practice it, but accustom yourself to something else.
  Ib. 18

Be not swept off your feet by the vividness of the impression, but say, "Impression, wait for me a little. Let me see what you are and what you represent. Let me try you."   *Ib.*

There are some faults which men readily admit, but others not so readily.
  Ib. 21

Two principles we should always have ready — that there is nothing good or evil save in the will; and that we are not to lead events, but to follow them.   *Ib. III, 10*

First say to yourself what you would be; and then do what you have to do.
  Ib. 23

Remember that you ought to behave in life as you would at a banquet. As something is being passed around it comes to you; stretch out your hand, take a portion of it politely. It passes on; do not detain it. Or it has not come to you yet; do not project your desire to meet it, but wait until it comes in front of you. So act toward children, so toward a wife, so toward office, so toward wealth.   *The Encheiridion, 15*

Where do you suppose he got that high brow?   *The Encheiridion, 22*

Everything has two handles — by one of which it ought to be carried and by the other not.[1]   *Ib. 43*

DECIMUS JUNIUS JUVENAL
A.D. C. 50 – C. 130

Honesty is praised and starves.[2]
          Satires I, l. 74

If nature refuses, indignation will produce verses.[3]   *Ib. 79*

All the doings of mankind, their wishes, fears, anger, pleasures, joys, and varied pursuits, form the motley subject of my book.   *Ib. 85*

Censure pardons the raven, but is visited upon the dove.[4]   *Ib. II, 63*

No one becomes depraved in a moment.[5]   *Ib. 83*

Grammarian, rhetorician, geometrician, painter, trainer, soothsayer, ropedancer, physician, magician — he knows everything. Tell the hungry little Greek to go to heaven; he'll go.[6]   *Ib. III, 76*

Bitter poverty has no harder pang than that it makes men ridiculous.[7]
          Ib. 152

It is not easy for men to rise whose qualities are thwarted by poverty.
          Ib. 164

We all live in a state of ambitious poverty.   *Ib. 182*

A rare bird on earth, comparable to a black swan.[8]   *Ib. VI, 165*

I wish it, I command it. Let my will take the place of reason.[1]
          Satires VI, l. 223

We are now suffering the evils of a long peace. Luxury, more deadly than war, broods over the city, and avenges a conquered world.[2]   *Ib. 292*

But who is to guard the guards themselves?[3]   *Ib. 347*

An inveterate and incurable itch for writing besets many, and grows old in their sick hearts.   *Ib. VII, 51*

Nobility is the one and only virtue.[4]
          Ib. VIII, 20

Count it the greatest sin to prefer life to honor, and for the sake of living to lose what makes life worth having.[5]
          Ib. 83

The people that once bestowed commands, consulships, legions, and all else, now concerns itself no more, and longs eagerly for just two things — bread and circuses![6]   *Ib. X, 79*

Put Hannibal in the scales.[7]
          Ib. 147

You should pray for a sound mind in a sound body.[8]   *Ib. 356*

For revenge is always the delight of a mean spirit, of a weak and petty mind! You may immediately draw proof of this — that no one rejoices more in revenge than a woman.
          Ib. XIII, 189

---

[1] Hoc volo, sic iubeo, sit pro ratione voluntas.
[2] Nunc patimur longae pacis mala, saevior armis
Luxuria incubuit victumque ulciscitur orbem.
[3] Sed quis custodiet ipsos Custodes?
What an absurd idea — a guardian to need a guardian! — PLATO [c. 429-347 B.C.], *The Republic, bk. III, 403–E*
[4] Nobilitas sola est atque unica virtus.
[5] Summum crede nefas animam praeferre pudori,
Et propter vitam vivendi perdere causas.
[6] Panem et circenses.
[7] Expende Hannibalem.
[8] Mens sana in corpore sano.
See John Locke, p. 373a.

---

[1] There is a right and wrong handle to everything. — RASPE, *Travels of Baron Munchausen* [1785], *ch. 30*
[2] Probitas laudatur et alget.
A favorite quotation of Linnaeus.
[3] Si natura negat, facit indignatio versum.
[4] Dat veniam corvis, vexat censura columbas.
[5] Nemo repente fuit turpissimus.
Translated by GILBERT HIGHET. See Racine, p. 378b.
[6] See Dryden, p. 368b.
[7] Nil habet infelix paupertas durius in se, quam quod ridiculos homines facit.
[8] Rara avis in terris nigroque simillima cycno.

The greatest reverence is due the young.[1]   *Satires XIV, l.* 47

CAIUS CORNELIUS TACITUS
A.D. C. 55 – C. 117

The images of the most illustrious families . . . were carried before it [the bier of Julia]. Those of Brutus and Cassius were not displayed; but for that reason they shone with preeminent luster.[2]   *Annals, bk. III,* 76

He had talents equal to business, and aspired no higher.   *Ib. VI,* 39

What is this day supported by precedents will hereafter become a precedent.[3]   *Ib. XI,* 24

[Of Petronius] Arbiter of taste.[4]   *Ib. XVI,* 18

It is the rare fortune of these days that a man may think what he likes and say what he thinks.
        Histories, bk. I, 1

[Of Servius Galba] He seemed more important than a private citizen while he was a private citizen, and in the opinion of all he was capable of rule — if he had not ruled.   *Ib.* 49

The desire for glory clings even to the best men longer than any other passion.[5]   *Ib. IV,* 6

The gods are on the side of the stronger.[6]   *Ib.* 17

Whatever is unknown is taken for marvelous;[7] but now the limits of Britain are laid bare.
        Agricola, sec. 30

Where they make a desert, they call it peace.[1]   *Agricola, sec.* 30

Fortune favored him . . . in the opportune moment of his death.
        Ib. 45

PLINY THE YOUNGER[2]
A.D. 61–105

Modestus said of Regulus that he was "the biggest rascal that walks upon two legs."   *Letters,*[3] *bk. I, letter* 5

There is nothing to write about, you say. Well then, write and let me know just this — that there *is* nothing to write about; or tell me in the good old style if you are well. That's right. I am quite well.[4]   *Ib.* 11

An object in possession seldom retains the same charm that it had in pursuit.[5]   *Ib. II,* 15

He [Pliny the Elder] used to say that "no book was so bad but some good might be got out of it."[6]
        Ib. III, 5

This expression of ours, "Father of a family."[7]   *Ib. V,* 19

That indolent but agreeable condition of doing nothing.[8]   *Ib. VIII,* 9

---

[1] Maxima debetur puero reverentia.
See Locke, p. 373a.
[2] See Lord John Russell, p. 567b.
[3] One precedent creates another. They soon accumulate and become law. — JUNIUS, *Letters* [1769–1771], *Dedication*
[4] Elegantiae arbiter.
[5] See Milton, p. 338a.
[6] Deos fortioribus adesse.
See Bussy-Rabutin, p. 357a; Boileau, p. 377b; Frederick the Great, p. 435a; and Gibbon, p. 466a.
[7] Omne ignotum pro magnifico.

[1] Calgacus, addressing the Britons at the Battle of the Grampians, referring to the Romans.
See Byron, p. 558b.
[2] Translated [1746] by WILLIAM MELMOTH.
[3] *Book VI, letter 16*, contains the description of the eruption of Vesuvius, A.D. 79, as witnessed by Pliny the Elder.
[4] This comes to inform you that I am in a perfect state of health, hoping you are in the same. Ay, that's the old beginning. — GEORGE COLMAN THE YOUNGER, *The Heir at Law* [1797], *act III, sc. ii*
[5] It has been a thousand times observed, and I must observe it once more, that the hours we pass with happy prospects in view are more pleasing than those crowned with fruition. — GOLDSMITH, *The Vicar of Wakefield* [1766], *ch. 10*
[6] "There is no book so bad," said the bachelor, "but something good may be found in it." — CERVANTES, *Don Quixote, pt. II* [1615], *ch. 3*
[7] Paterfamilias.
[8] Dolce far niente [Sweet doing-nothing]. — *Italian proverb*

Objects which are usually the motives of our travels by land and by sea are often overlooked and neglected if they lie under our eye. . . . We put off from time to time going and seeing what we know we have an opportunity of seeing when we please.

Letters, bk. VIII, letter 20

His only fault is that he has no fault.[1]   *Ib. IX, 26*

SUETONIUS
A.D. C. 70 – C. 140

Hail, Emperor, we who are about to die salute you.[2]   *Life of Claudius 21*

HADRIAN
[PUBLIUS AELIUS HADRIANUS]
A.D. 76–138

Little soul, wandering, gentle guest and companion of the body, into what places will you now go, pale, stiff, and naked, no longer sporting as you did![3]

Ad Animam Suam

CHANG HENG[4]
A.D. 78–139

Heaven is like an egg, and the earth is like the yolk of the egg.

Saying

[1] The greatest of faults, I should say, is to be conscious of none. — CARLYLE, *Heroes and Hero-Worship* [1841], *The Hero as Prophet*

[2] Ave, Caesar, morituri te salutamus.
Also rendered "te salutant": those about to die salute you.

[3] Animula vagula blandula,
Hospes comesque corporis,
Quae nunc abibis in loca
Pallidula rigida nudula,
Nec ut soles dabis iocos!

Amelette Ronsardelette,
mignonelette doucelette,
trèschère hostesse de mon corps,
tu descens là bas foibelette,
pasle, maigrelette, seulette,
dans le froid Royaulme des mors.
RONSARD, *A son âme* [dictated on his deathbed, December 27, 1585]

See Pope, p. 404a.

[4] From *Sources of Chinese Tradition*, edited by WILLIAM THEODORE DE BARY.

MARCUS AURELIUS ANTONINUS[1]
A.D. 121–180

This Being of mine, whatever it really is, consists of a little flesh, a little breath, and the part which governs.

Meditations II, 2

Thou wilt find rest from vain fancies if thou doest every act in life as though it were thy last.[2]   *Ib. 5*

Remember that no man loseth other life than that which he liveth, nor liveth other than that which he loseth.

Ib. 14

Each thing is of like form from everlasting and comes round again in its cycle.   *Ib.*

The longest-lived and the shortest-lived man, when they come to die, lose one and the same thing.   *Ib.*

As for life, it is a battle and a sojourning in a strange land; but the fame that comes after is oblivion.   *Ib. 17*

Waste not the remnant of thy life in those imaginations touching other folk, whereby thou contributest not to the common weal.   *Ib. III, 4*

A man should *be* upright, not be *kept* upright.   *Ib. 5*

Never esteem anything as of advantage to thee that shall make thee break thy word or lose thy self-respect.

Ib. 7

By a tranquil mind I mean nothing else than a mind well ordered.

Ib. IV, 3

The universe is change; our life is what our thoughts make it.   *Ib.*

Death, like birth, is a secret of Nature.   *Ib. 5*

Whatever happens at all happens as it should; thou wilt find this true, if thou shouldst watch narrowly.

Ib. 10

[1] Translated by MORRIS HICKEY MORGAN [1859–1910].

[2] See Horace, p. 121a, and Publilius Syrus, p. 126b.

How much time he gains who does not look to see what his neighbor says or does or thinks, but only at what he does himself, to make it just and holy.
Meditations IV, 18

Whatever is in any way beautiful hath its source of beauty in itself, and is complete in itself; praise forms no part of it. So it is none the worse nor the better for being praised.   *Ib. 20*

All that is harmony for thee, O Universe, is in harmony with me as well. Nothing that comes at the right time for thee is too early or too late for me. Everything is fruit to me that thy seasons bring, O Nature. All things come of thee, have their being in thee, and return to thee.[1]   *Ib. 23*

"Let thine occupations be few," saith the sage,[2] "if thou wouldst lead a tranquil life."   *Ib. 24*

Love the little trade which thou hast learned, and be content therewith.
Ib. 31

There is a proper dignity and proportion to be observed in the performance of every act of life.   *Ib. 32*

All is ephemeral — fame and the famous as well.   *Ib. 35*

Search men's governing principles, and consider the wise, what they shun and what they cleave to.   *Ib. 38*

Time is a sort of river of passing events, and strong is its current; no sooner is a thing brought to sight than it is swept by and another takes its place, and this too will be swept away.[3]
Ib. 43

All that happens is as usual and familiar as the rose in spring and the crop in summer.   *Ib. 44*

Mark how fleeting and paltry is the estate of man — yesterday in embryo, tomorrow a mummy or ashes. So for the hairsbreadth of time assigned to

thee, live rationally, and part with life cheerfully, as drops the ripe olive, extolling the season that bore it and the tree that matured it.
Meditations IV, 48

In the morning, when thou art sluggish at rousing thee, let this thought be present: "I am rising to a man's work."   *Ib. V, 1*

A man makes no noise over a good deed, but passes on to another as a vine to bear grapes again in season.[1]
Ib. 6

Nothing happens to anybody which he is not fitted by nature to bear.
Ib. 18

Live with the gods.   *Ib. 27*

Look beneath the surface; let not the several quality of a thing nor its worth escape thee.   *Ib. VI, 3*

The controlling intelligence understands its own nature, and what it does, and whereon it works.   *Ib. 5*

Do not think that what is hard for thee to master is impossible for man; but if a thing is possible and proper to man, deem it attainable by thee.
Ib. 19

What is not good for the swarm is not good for the bee.   *Ib. 54*

One universe made up of all that is; and one God in it all, and one principle of being, and one law, the reason, shared by all thinking creatures, and one truth.   *Ib. VII, 9*

It is man's peculiar duty to love even those who wrong him.[2]   *Ib. 22*

Very little is needed to make a happy life.   *Ib. 67*

To change thy mind and to follow him that sets thee right is to be none the less the free agent that thou wast before.   *Ib. VIII, 16*

Look to the essence of a thing,

---

[1] See *I Chronicles 29:14*, p. 14a.
[2] Seneca, *De Ira III, 6; De Animi Tranquillitate 13.*
[3] See Isaac Watts, p. 397a.

[1] See *Matthew 6:3*, p. 40a.
[2] See *Proverbs 25:21*, p. 26a.

whether it be a point of doctrine, of practice, or of interpretation.
Meditations VIII, 22

Be not careless in deeds, nor confused in words, nor rambling in thought. *Ib. 51*

Think not disdainfully of death, but look on it with favor; for even death is one of the things that Nature wills.
Ib. IX, 3

A wrongdoer is often a man that has left something undone, not always he that has done something.[1] *Ib. 5*

Blot out vain pomp; check impulse; quench appetite; keep reason under its own control. *Ib. 7*

All things are the same — familiar in enterprise, momentary in endurance, coarse in substance. All things now are as they were in the day of those whom we have buried. *Ib. 14*

Whatever may befall thee, it was preordained for thee from everlasting.
Ib. X, 5

DIOGENES LAERTIUS
fl. A.D. C. 200

Ignorance plays the chief part among men, and the multitude of words.[2]
Cleobulus 4

Time is the image of eternity.
Plato 41

There is a written and an unwritten law. The one by which we regulate our constitutions in our cities is the written law; that which arises from custom is the unwritten law. *Ib. 51*

QUINTUS SEPTIMIUS TERTULLIAN
A.D. C. 155 – 225

O witness of the soul naturally Christian. *Apologeticus 17*

[1] See *Book of Common Prayer*, p. 59b.
[2] In the multitude of words there wanteth not sin. — *Proverbs 10:19*

See how these Christians love one another.[1] *Apologeticus 39*

We multiply whenever we are mown down by you; the blood of Christians is seed.[2] *Ib. 50*

Man is one name belonging to every nation upon earth. In them all is one soul though many tongues. Every country has its own language, yet the subjects of which the untutored soul speaks are the same everywhere.
Testimony of the Soul

Mother Church.[3] *Ad Martyras 1*

Truth persuades by teaching, but does not teach by persuading.
Adversus Valentinianos 1

Truth does not blush.[4] *Ib. 3*

The virtues of the heathen, being devoid of grace, can only be looked upon as splendid vices.
De Carne Christi 1

It is to be believed because it is absurd.[5] *Ib. 5*

It is certain because it is impossible.[6]
Ib.

[1] Tertullian is sarcastically repeating what the enemies of Christianity are saying.
See Emerson, p. 606b.
[2] Plures efficimur, quoties metimur a vobis; semen est sanguis christianorum.
This is often rendered as: The blood of the martyrs is the seed of the Church.
The Church of Christ has been founded by shedding its own blood, not that of others; by enduring outrage, not by inflicting it. Persecutions have made it grow; martyrdoms have crowned it. — St. Jerome [A.D. c. 340–420], *letter 82*
The blood of martyrs is the seed of Christians. — Beyerlinck, *Magnum Theatrum Vitae Humanorum* [1665]
The seed of the Church, I mean the blood of primitive martyrs. — Thomas Fuller, *Church History of Britain* [1665], *pt. IV, bk. I*
[3] Domina mater ecclesia.
See St. Cyprian, p. 144a.
[4] Veritas non erubescit.
[5] Prorsus credibile est, quia ineptum est.
[6] Certum est, quia impossibile est.
This is called "Tertullian's rule of faith." It is sometimes rendered as: Credo quia impossibile [I believe because it is impossible]. St. Augustine expresses the same idea in *Confessions VI, 5, 7.*

Out of the frying pan into the fire.[1]
De Carne Christi 6

One man's religion neither harms nor helps another man.
Ad Scapulam 2

It is certainly no part of religion to compel religion.   *Ib.*

I must dispel vanity with vanity.
Adversus Marcionem IV, 30

ST. CYPRIAN
d. A.D. 258

He cannot have God for his father who has not the Church for his Mother.[2]
De Unitate Ecclesiae [251], *ch. 6*

There is no salvation outside the Church.[3]   *Letter* 73 [*c.* 256]

LONGINUS
A.D. C. 210 – 273

It frequently happens that where the second line is sublime, the third, in which he meant to rise still higher, is perfect bombast.[4]
On the Sublime, sec. 3

Sublimity is the echo of a noble mind.   *Ib.* 9

In the Odyssey one may liken Homer to the setting sun, of which the grandeur remains without the intensity.
Ib.

CONSTANTINE
A.D. C. 288 – 337

In this sign shalt thou conquer.[5]
From EUSEBIUS, *Life of Constantine I, 28*

[1] De calcaria in carbonarium.
Leap out of the frying pan into the fire. — JOHN HEYWOOD, *Proverbs* [1546], *pt. II, ch. 5*
[2] Habere non potest deum patrem qui ecclesiam non habet matrem.
See Tertullian, p. 143b.
[3] Salus extra ecclesiam non est.
Quoted by St. Augustine in *De Baptismo*, hence sometimes attributed to him.
[4] The reference is to Lucan's style.
[5] In hoc signo vinces.
The alleged words of Constantine's vision be-

ST. JOHN CHRYSOSTOM
A.D. 327 – 407

No one can harm the man who does himself no wrong.[1]
Letter to Olympia

AMMIANUS
MARCELLINUS
A.D. C. 330 – 395

Rose among thorns.
History, bk. XVI, ch. 17

JULIAN
[THE APOSTATE]
A.D. 332 – 363

You have conquered, Galilean.[2]
From THEODORET, *Church History III, 20*

ST. AMBROSE
A.D. C. 340 – 397

When you are at Rome live in the Roman style; when you are elsewhere live as they live elsewhere.[3]
Advice to St. Augustine. From JEREMY TAYLOR, *Ductor Dubitantium* [1660] *I, 1, 5*

fore his battle with Maxentius at Saxa Rubra, near Rome, A.D. 312.
[1] No one is injured save by himself. — ERASMUS [1465–1536], *Adagia*
[2] Vicisti, Galilaee.
The Latin translation of the alleged dying words of the Emperor.
See Swinburne, p. 774a.
[3] Si fueris Romae, Romano vivito more; Si fueris alibi, vivito sicut ibi.
My mother, having joined me at Milan, found that the church there did not fast on Saturdays as at Rome, and was at a loss what to do. I consulted St. Ambrose, of holy memory, who replied, "When I am at Rome, I fast on a Saturday; when I am at Milan, I do not. Follow the custom of the church where you are." — ST. AUGUSTINE [A.D. 354–430], *Epistle to Januarius* (*Epistle* 2), *sec. 18.* Also *Epistle to Casualanus* (*Epistle 36*), *sec. 32*
When in Rome, do as the Romans do. — *Proverb*

ST. JEROME[1]
A.D. C. 342 – 420

A friend is long sought, hardly found, and with difficulty kept.
Letter 1

Love is not to be purchased, and affection has no price.   *Letter 3*

The friendship that can cease has never been real.   *Ib.*

It is easier to mend neglect than to quicken love.   *Letter 7*

Love knows nothing of order.   *Ib.*

The fact is that my native land is a prey to barbarism, that in it men's only God is their belly,[2] that they live only for the present, and that the richer a man is the holier he is held to be.
Ib.

An unstable pilot steers a leaking ship, and the blind is leading the blind straight to the pit.[3] The ruler is like the ruled.   *Ib.*

No athlete is crowned but in the sweat of his brow.   *Letter 14*

If there is but little water in the stream, it is the fault, not of the channel, but of the source.   *Letter 17*

You are a Ciceronian, not a Christian.[4]   *Letter 22*

It is idle to play the lyre for an ass.[5]
Letter 27

Everything must have in it a sharp seasoning of truth.   *Letter 31*

While truth is always bitter, pleasantness waits upon evildoing.
Letter 40

The line, often adopted by strong men in controversy, of justifying the means by the end.[6]   *Letter 48*

Do not let your deeds belie your words, lest when you speak in church someone may say to himself, "Why do you not practice what you preach?"[1]
Letter 48

Avoid, as you would the plague, a clergyman who is also a man of business.   *Letter 52*[2]

A fat paunch never breeds fine thoughts.[3]   *Ib.*

No one cares to speak to an unwilling listener. An arrow never lodges in a stone: often it recoils upon the sender of it.   *Ib.*

That clergyman soon becomes an object of contempt who being often asked out to dinner never refuses to go.
Ib.

The best almoner is he who keeps back nothing for himself.   *Ib.*

It is worse still to be ignorant of your ignorance.   *Letter 53*

Even brute beasts and wandering birds do not fall into the same traps or nets twice.[4]   *Letter 54*

Sometimes the character of the mistress is inferred from the dress of her maids.   *Ib.*

The face is the mirror of the mind, and eyes without speaking confess the secrets of the heart.   *Ib.*

The scars of others should teach us caution.   *Ib.*

When the stomach is full, it is easy to talk of fasting.   *Letter 58*

Small minds can never handle great themes.[5]   *Letter 60*

The Roman world is falling, yet we

---

1 Translated by W. H. FREMANTLE.
2 See *Philippians 3:19*, p. 54b.
3 See *Matthew 15:14*, p. 43a.
4 This was addressed to Jerome in a dream by Christ the Judge, censuring him for loving the classics more than the Fathers.
5 A Greek proverb frequently quoted by Jerome.
6 See Matthew Prior, p. 387b.

---

1 Cur ergo haec ipse non facis?
See Plautus, p. 106a.
2 Translated by F. A. WRIGHT.
3 This is a Greek proverb.
Fat paunches have lean pates, and dainty bits
Make rich the ribs, but bankrupt quite the wits.
      SHAKESPEARE, *Love's Labour's Lost, act I, sc. i, l. 26*
4 Translated by F. A. WRIGHT.
5 Translated by W. J. COURTENAY.

hold our heads erect instead of bowing our necks.[1]　　　　　　*Letter 60*

Every day we are changing, every day we are dying, and yet we fancy ourselves eternal.　　　　　　*Ib.*

Early impressions are hard to eradicate from the mind. When once wool has been dyed purple, who can restore it to its previous whiteness?
　　　　　　Letter 107

The tired ox treads with a firmer step.[2]　　　　　　*Letter 112*

Athletes as a rule are stronger than their backers; yet the weaker presses the stronger to put forth all his efforts.
　　　　　　Letter 118

For they wished to fill the winepress of eloquence not with the tendrils of mere words but with the rich grape juice of good sense.　　*Letter 125*

It is no fault of Christianity that a hypocrite falls into sin.　　　*Ib.*

The charges we bring against others often come home to ourselves; we inveigh against faults which are as much ours as theirs; and so our eloquence ends by telling against ourselves.　*Ib.*

Preferring to store her money in the stomachs of the needy rather than hide it in a purse.[3]　　　　　*Letter 127*

The privileges of a few do not make common law.[4]　　*Exposition on Jona*

Never look a gift horse in the mouth.[5]
　　On the Epistle to the Ephesians

---

[1] Romanus orbis ruit.

[2] An old Roman proverb quoted by St. Jerome to St. Augustine after the latter criticized the elder Jerome.

[3] Translated by F. A. WRIGHT.

[4] Privilegia paucorum non faciunt legem.
The exception proves the rule.

[5] Noli equi dentes inspicere donati.
No man ought to look a given horse in the mouth. — JOHN HEYWOOD, *Proverbs* [1546], *pt. I, ch. 5*
A gift horse should not be looked in the mouth. — CERVANTES, *Don Quixote, pt. II* [1615], *bk. IV, ch. 62*

KU K'AI-CHIH[1]
A.D. C. 344 – 406

Of all kinds of painting, figure painting is the most difficult; then comes landscape painting, and next dogs and horses. High towers and pavilions are definite things; they are difficult to execute, but easy to handle since they do not demand insight.
　　　　Discussion of Painting

VEGETIUS
[FLAVIUS VEGETIUS RENATUS]
fl. A.D. C. 375

Let him who desires peace prepare for war.[2]
　　De Rei Militari III, prologue

ST. AUGUSTINE
A.D. 354–430

Will is to grace as the horse is to the rider.[3]
　　De Libero Arbitrio [388–395]

The weakness of little children's limbs is innocent, not their souls.
　　Confessions [397–401] *I, 7*

To Carthage I came, where all about me resounded a caldron of dissolute loves.[4]　　　　　*Ib. III, 1*

I was in love with loving.　　*Ib.*

He ne'er considered it, as loth
To look a gift horse in the mouth.
　　SAMUEL BUTLER, *Hudibras, pt. I* [1663], *canto 1, l. 489*

[1] From *The Spirit of the Brush*, translated by SHIO SAKANISHI [*Wisdom of the East Series,* 1957].

[2] Qui desiderat pacem, praeparet bellum.
In peace, like a wise man, he has provided for the needs of war. — HORACE, *Satires, bk. II* [30 B.C.], *ii, 111*
We should provide in peace what we need in war. — PUBLILIUS SYRUS [1st century B.C.], *Maxim 709*
See Robert Burton, p. 311b; Fénélon, p. 383a; and George Washington, p. 461b.

[3] This is considered the most important definition of the relation of grace to free will in the Middle Ages.

[4] To Carthage then I came. — T. S. ELIOT, *The Waste Land* [1922], *III, l. 307 and note.*

In the usual course of study I had come to a book of a certain Cicero.
Confessions III, 4

Give me chastity and continence, but not just now. *Ib. VIII, 7*

Take up, read! Take up, read! [1]
Ib. 12

Too late I loved you, O Beauty so ancient yet ever new! Too late I loved you! And, behold, you were within me, and I out of myself, and there I searched for you. *Ib. X, 27*

Give what you command, and command what you will. *Ib. 29*

Hear the other side.[2]
De Duabus Animabus XIV, 2

I would not have believed the gospel had not the authority of the Church moved me.
Contra Epistulam Fundamenti [c. 410], ch. 5

Necessity has no law.[3]
Soliloquiorum. Animae ad Deum [c. 410], 2

We make a ladder of our vices, if we trample those same vices underfoot.
Sermons 3

Anger is a weed; hate is the tree.
Ib. 58

The dove loves when it quarrels; the wolf hates when it flatters. *Ib. 64*

Rome has spoken; the case is concluded.[4] *Ib. 131*

He who created you without you will not justify you without you. *Ib. 169*

The most glorious city of God.
City of God [415], I, preface

ST. VINCENT OF LERINS
d. A.D. C. 450

[That faith is catholic] which has been believed always, everywhere, and by all.[1] *Commonitorium, ch. 2*

Every word almost was a sentence; every sentence a victory.[2] *Ib. 18*

TSUNG PING[3]
A.D. 375–443

The virtuous man follows the Way by spiritual insight; the wise man takes this same approach. But the lovers of landscapes are led into the Way by a sense of form. The virtuous man also takes pleasure in this. Then, are not the pleasures of the virtuous and the wise similar to those of the lovers of landscapes?
Introduction to Landscape Painting

LONGUS
A.D. third century

There was never any yet that wholly could escape love, and never shall there be any, never so long as beauty shall be, never so long as eyes can see.
Daphnis and Chloe, proem, ch. 2

He is so poor that he could not keep a dog. *Ib. 15*

CLOVIS
A.D. 465–511

God of Clotilda,[4] if you grant me victory I shall become a Christian.
Legendary vow before battle

---

[1] Tolle lege, tolle lege. What the bell seemed to say to Augustine at the moment of his conversion. When he opened the Bible, his eyes fell on *Romans 13:12–14* (p. 51b).
[2] Audi partem alteram.
[3] See Publilius Syrus, p. 126b, and note, and Oliver Cromwell, p. 328a.
[4] Roma locuta est; causa finita est.

[1] Quod semper, quod ubique, quod ab omnibus creditum est.
The definition of the traditional articles of faith.
[2] This refers to Tertullian.
[3] From *The Spirit of the Brush*, translated by SHIO SAKANISHI [*Wisdom of the East Series* 1957].
[4] St. Clotilda, wife of Clovis.

BOETHIUS
A.D. C. 470 – 525

In every adversity of fortune, to have been happy is the most unhappy kind of misfortune.[1]

De Consolatione Philosophiae,
bk. II, 4, 4

Who hath so entire happiness that he is not in some part offended with the condition of his estate?   *Ib. 41*

Nothing is miserable but what is thought so, and contrariwise, every estate is happy if he that bears it be content.   *Ib. 64*

From thee, great God, we spring, to thee we tend —
Path, motive, guide, original and end.[2]
Ib. III, 9, 27

Who can give law to lovers? Love is a greater law to itself.   *Ib. 12, 47*

HSIEH HO[3]
fl. A.D. 500

[Concerning the Six Principles of painting]

The first is, that through a vitalizing spirit, a painting should possess the movement of life.

The second is, that by means of the brush, the structural basis should be established.

The third is, that the representation should so conform with the objects as to give their likenesses.

The fourth is, that the coloring should be applied according to their characteristics.

The fifth is, that through organization, place and position should be determined.

The sixth is, that by copying the ancient models should be perpetuated.[4]

Notes Concerning the Classi-
fication of Old Paintings

[1] See Pindar, p. 79b; Dante, p. 160a; Chaucer, p. 165a; and Tennyson, p. 647a.
[2] Translated by SAMUEL JOHNSON, and used as motto to *The Rambler, no. 7* [1750].
[3] From *The Spirit of the Brush,* translated by SHIO SAKANISHI [*Wisdom of the East Series,* 1957].
[4] See Horace, p. 124b; Ching Hao, p. 153a; and Fujiwara no Teika, p. 156b.

ST. BENEDICT[1]
A.D. 480–543

We are therefore about to establish a school of the Lord's service in which we hope to introduce nothing harsh or burdensome.

Rule of St. Benedict, prologue

MAGNUS AURELIUS CASSIODORUS
A.D. C. 487 – 583

He receives hope in future benefits who recognizes a benefit that has already taken place.   *Institutiones*

He is invited to great things who receives small things greatly.   *Ib.*

GREGORY I
A.D. 540–604

[They answered that they were called Angles.] It is well, for they have the faces of angels, and such should be the co-heirs of the angels in heaven.[2]

From BEDE, *Ecclesiastical History of the English People II, 1*

ALI IBN-ABU-TALIB[3]
A.D. C. 602 – 661

He who has a thousand friends has
    not a friend to spare,
And he who has one enemy will meet
    him everywhere.[4]

A Hundred Sayings

THE KORAN[5]
A.D. C. 610 – 632

Turn, therefore, thy face towards the holy temple of Mecca; and wherever ye

[1] Founder of Western monasticism.
[2] Traditionally quoted "Non Angli sed Angeli" (Not Angles but angels), these were the words of the Pope when he beheld two English slaves in a Roman slave market.
[3] Ali ibn-abu-Talib, son-in-law of Mohammed and fourth caliph, who was for his courage called the Lion of God, was murdered A.D. 661.
[4] Translated by EMERSON.
[5] Translated [1734] by GEORGE SALE [1697–1736].

be, turn your faces towards that place.
Ch. 2

Wherever ye be, God will bring you all back at the resurrection.   *Ib.*

As for him who voluntarily performeth a good work, verily God is grateful and knowing.   *Ib.*

Your God is one God; there is no God but He, the most merciful.   *Ib.*

O true believers, take your necessary precautions against your enemies, and either go forth to war in separate parties, or go forth all together in a body.   *Ch. 4*

Fight for the religion of God.   *Ib.*

O men, respect women who have borne you.   *Ib.*

Wheresoever ye be, death will overtake you, although ye be in lofty towers.   *Ib.*

God loveth not the speaking ill of anyone in public.   *Ib.*

Of his mercy he hath made for you the night and the day, that ye may rest in the one, and may seek to obtain provision for yourself of his abundance, by your industry, in the other.   *Ch. 28*

If God should punish men according to what they deserve, he would not leave on the back of the earth so much as a beast.   *Ch. 35*

God obligeth no man to more than he hath given him ability to perform.   *Ch. 65*

Woe be unto those who pray, and who are negligent at their prayer: who play the hypocrites, and deny necessaries to the needy.   *Ch. 107*

O unbelievers, I will not worship that which ye worship; nor will ye worship that which I worship. . . . Ye have your religion, and I my religion.   *Ch. 109*

ANONYMOUS MISCELLANEOUS [EARLY]

Whatever kind of word thou speakest the like shalt thou hear.
Greek Anthology [Loeb Classical Library], bk. IX, 382

Envy slays itself by its own arrows.
Ib. X, 111

Give me today, and take tomorrow.
Quoted, and condemned, by St. Chrysostom

One picture is worth more than ten thousand words.[1]   *Chinese proverb*

On the day of victory no one is tired.
Arab proverb

Death is afraid of him because he has the heart of a lion.   *Arab proverb*

I came to the place of my birth, and cried, "'The friends of my youth, where are they?" And echo answered, "Where are they?"   *Arab saying*

If only, when one heard
That Old Age was coming
One could bolt the door,
Answer "Not at home"
And refuse to meet him!
Kokinshu (Collection of Ancient and Modern Poems) [905][2]

Can this world
From of old
Always have been so sad,
Or did it become so for the sake
Of me alone?   *Ib.[2]*

ANONYMOUS LATIN

Ab urbe condita.
Since the founding of the city [Rome].   *Saying*

Absit omen.
May it not be an omen.   *Saying*

[1] See Turgenev, p. 688a.
[2] Translated by ARTHUR WALEY in *Anthology of Japanese Literature,* edited by Donald Keene [1955].

Acta est fabula.
The play is over.
>Said at ancient dramatic performances and quoted by Augustus on his deathbed

Actus non facit reum, nisi mens sit rea.
The act is not criminal unless the intent is criminal.   *Legal maxim*

Ad astra per aspera.
To the stars through hardships.
>*Motto of Kansas*

Adeste, fideles,
Laeti triumphantes;
Venite, venite in Bethlehem.

O come, all ye faithful,
Joyful and triumphant,
O come ye, O come ye to Bethlehem.
>*Hymn, eighteenth century*

Anno aetatis suae . . .
In the year of his age . . .   *Phrase*

Bis dat qui cito dat.
He gives twice who gives promptly.[1]
>*Saying*

Caveat emptor.
Let the buyer beware.   *Proverb*

Cave canem.
Beware of the dog.   *Proverb*

Cras amet qui nunquam amavit quique amavit cras amet.
Tomorrow let him love who has never loved and tomorrow let him who has loved love.[2]
>*Pervigilium Veneris* [A.D. *c.* 350], *refrain*

Cucullus non facit monachum.
The cowl does not make a monk.[3]
>*Medieval proverb*

Cuius regio eius religio.
He who controls the area controls the religion.   *Proverb*

De gustibus non disputandum.

There is no accounting for tastes.
>*Proverb*

De minimis non curat lex.
The law is not concerned with trifles.   *Legal maxim*

Deus vult.
God wills it.
>*Motto of the Crusades* [1095]

Dis manibus sacrum [abbreviation DMS].
Sacred to the departed spirit(s).
>*Inscription on tombstones*

Divide et impera.
Divide and rule.
>*Ancient political maxim cited by* MACHIAVELLI

Errare humanum est.
To err is human.[1]   *Saying*

Et in Arcadia ego.
I too have lived in Arcadia.[2]
>*Inscription on a tomb in a painting by* GUERCINO [*c.* 1623]

Ex ungue leonem.
From his toenail [one can tell] a lion.[3]   *Saying*

Finis coronat opus.
The ending crowns the work [in a good or bad sense].   *Saying*

Flagrante delicto.
"Red-handed."   *Saying*

Fluctuat nec mergitur.
It tosses but doesn't sink.
>*Motto of Paris*

Gaudeamus igitur,
Iuvenes dum sumus.

---

[1] See Publilius Syrus, p. 125a, and Augustus Caesar, p. 124b.

[2] See Parnell, p. 398a.

[3] It takes more than a hood and sad eyes to make a monk. — *Albanian proverb*

[1] See Plutarch, p. 137b, and Pope, p. 403b.

[2] This translation is now usually considered erroneous. The accepted translation is: I too am in Arcadia — that is, Even in Arcadia there am I [Death].
SCHIDONI [1560–1616] wrote: "Et ego in Arcadia vixi," which Poussin, Reynolds, and others used in their paintings. E. PANOFSKY discusses the phrase in *Philosophy and History: Essays Presented to E. Cassirer* [1936].

[3] See Herodotus, p. 86b.

Let us live then and be glad
While young life is before us.
Students' song [c. 1267]

Habeas corpus.
You are to produce the person [of
the accused].   *Legal maxim*

Hannibal ad portas!
Hannibal is at the gates!   *Saying*

In vino veritas.
In wine is truth.[1]
Proverb quoted by PLATO,
Symposium 217

Ipse dixit.
He himself [the Master] said it.
Saying

Ius est ars boni et aequi.
Legal justice is the art of the good
and the fair.   *Saying*

Mater artium necessitas.
Necessity is the mother of invention.[2]
Saying

Mors ultima ratio.
Death is the final accounting.
Saying

Nemo me impune lacessit.
No one provokes me with impunity.
Motto of the Crown of Scotland

Nihil [or Ne quid] nimis.
Nothing in excess.[3]   *Saying*

Non multa sed multum.
Not quantity but quality [Not many
but much].[4]   *Proverb*

Orare est laborare, laborare est
orare.
To pray is to work, to work is to
pray.
*Ancient motto of the
Benedictine Monks*

Parvis e glandibus quercus.
Tall oaks from little acorns grow.[5]

Pereant qui nostra ante nos dixerunt.
May they perish who have used our
words before us.   *Saying*

[1] See Alcaeus, p. 69a.
[2] See Persius, p. 133b, and note.
[3] See The Seven Sages, p. 68b.
[4] See Seneca, p. 130a.
[5] See David Everett, p. 507a.

Piscem natare doces.
You're teaching a fish to swim.
Saying

Post hoc, ergo propter hoc.
After this, therefore because of this.
Definition of fallacy in logic

Primus inter pares.
The first among equals.   *Saying*

Pro bono publico.
For the public good.   *Saying*

Requiescat in pace [abbreviation
RIP].
May he rest in peace.   *Saying*

Res iudicata pro veritate habetur.
A matter which has been [legally]
decided is considered true.
Legal maxim

Salus populi suprema lex.
The people's safety is the highest law.
Legal and political maxim.

Semper fidelis.
Ever faithful.
Motto of the U.S. Marine Corps

Sic semper tyrannis.[1]
Thus always to tyrants.
Motto of Virginia

Sit tibi terra levis [abbreviation
STTL].
May the earth rest lightly on you.[2]
Inscription on tombstones

Summum ius summa iniuria.
Extreme [legal] justice is extreme in-
justice.[3]
*Legal maxim cited by Cicero,
De Officiis* 1. 10. 33

Testis unus testis nullus.
A single witness is no witness.
Legal maxim

Ubi bene ibi patria.
Where one is happy, there's one's
homeland.   *Saying*

[1] See John Wilkes Booth, p. 778a.
[2] See Euripides, p. 83b; Beaumont and
Fletcher, p. 316b; and Richardson, p. 822a.
[3] See Terence, p. 108b, and note.

Urbi et orbi.
To the city [Rome] and to the world.　　　*Apostolic blessing*

Vade in pace.
Go in peace.
　　　End of confessional absolution

Vae victis!
Woe to the conquered!
　　　Quoted by LIVY, *5, 48, as said by Brennus to the Romans*

Volenti non fit iniuria.
To a person who consents no injustice is done.　　　*Legal maxim*

CAEDMON
fl. 670

Light was first
Through the Lord's word
Named day:
Beauteous, bright creation!
　　　Creation.[1] *The First Day*

The fiend with all his comrades
Fell then from heaven above,
Through as long as three nights and days,
The angels from heaven into hell;
And them all the Lord transformed to devils,
Because they his deed and word
Would not revere.
　　　Ib. The Fall of the Rebel Angels

BEDE
[VENERABLE BEDE]
c. 672 – c. 735

It is better never to begin a good work than, having begun it, to stop.
　　　Ecclesiastical History of the English People, bk. I, ch. 23

ST. JOHN OF DAMASCUS
c. 700 – c. 760

God is a sea of infinite substance.[2]
　　　De Fide Orthodoxa, bk. I, ch. 9

[1] From the text of BENJAMIN THORPE [1782–1870].
[2] This is the most frequently quoted definition of God in the Middle Ages. It is based on ST. GREGORY OF NAZIANZUS [c. 330–390], *Oration 38*.

ALCUIN
735–804

The voice of the people is the voice of God.[1]
　　　Letter to Charlemagne
　　　[A.D. 800]

Here halt, I pray you, make a little stay,
O wayfarer, to read what I have writ,
And know by my fate what thy fate shall be.
What thou art now, wayfarer, world-renowned,
I was: what I am now, so shall thou be.
The world's delight I followed with a heart
Unsatisfied: ashes am I, and dust.
　　　His Own Epitaph [2]

Alcuin was my name: learning I loved.　　　*Ib.*

LOTHAIR I
795–855

The times change and we change with them.[3]
　　　From OWEN's *Epigrammata*
　　　[1615]

ONO NO KOMACHI
Ninth century

The flowers withered,
Their color faded away,
While meaninglessly
I spent my days in the world
And the long rains were falling.
　　　Kokinshu [905] [4]

This night of no moon
There is no way to meet him.
I rise in longing —

[1] Vox populi, vox Dei.
See Pope, p. 412a.
[2] Translated by HELEN WADDELL.
[3] Tempora mutantur, nos et mutamur in illis.
Also quoted in HOLINSHED, *Chronicles of England* [1577].
See Spenser, p. 200b.
[4] Translated by DONALD KEENE. From *Anthology of Japanese Literature*, edited by Donald Keene.

My breast pounds, a leaping flame,
My heart is consumed in fire.
Kokinshu

So lonely am I
My body is a floating weed
Severed at the roots.
Were there water to entice me,
I would follow it, I think.　　　*Ib.*

CHANG YEN-YUAN
fl. c. 850

The painters of today mix their
brushes and ink with dust and dirt, and
their colors with mud, and in vain
smear the silk. How can this be called
painting?
Discussion of the Six Principles
of Painting [1]

CHING HAO
fl. 925

A youth who likes to study will in the
end succeed. To begin with he should
know that there are Six Essentials in
painting. The first is called *spirit*; the
second, *rhythm*; the third, *thought*; the
fourth, *scenery*; the fifth, the *brush*,
and the last is the *ink*.
Notes on Brushwork [1,2]

Resemblance reproduces the formal
aspect of objects, but neglects their
spirit; truth shows the spirit and substance in like perfection. He who tries
to transmit the spirit by means of the
formal aspect and ends by merely obtaining the outward appearance, will
produce a dead thing.　　　*Ib.*

SEI SHONAGON
b. 966

One writes a letter, taking particular
trouble to get it up as prettily as possi-

ble; then waits for the answer, making
sure every moment that it cannot be
much longer before something comes.
At last, frightfully late, is brought in
— one's own note, still folded or tied
exactly as one sent it, but so finger-
marked and smudged that even the address is barely legible. "The family is
not in residence," the messenger says,
giving one back the note.
Makura no Soshi [c. 1002] [1]

If someone with whom one is having
an affair keeps on mentioning some
woman whom he knew in the past,
however long ago it is since they separated, one is always irritated.　　　*Ib.*

MURASAKI SHIKIBU
c. 978 – 1031

[The art of the novel] does not simply consist in the author's telling a story
about the adventures of some other person. . . . It happens because the
storyteller's own experience of men and
things, whether for good or ill — not
only what he has passed through himself, but even events which he has only
witnessed or been told of — has moved
him to an emotion so passionate that
he can no longer keep it shut up in his
heart. . . . There must never come a
time, he feels, when men do not know
about it. . . .

Clearly then, it is no part of the
storyteller's craft to describe only what
is good or beautiful. Sometimes, of
course, virtue will be his theme, and he
may then make such play with it as he
will. But he is just as likely to have been
struck by numerous examples of vice
and folly in the world around him, and
about them he has exactly the same
feelings as about the preeminently good
deeds which he encounters: they are
important and must all be garnered in.
Thus anything whatsoever may become
the subject of a novel, provided only
that it happens in this mundane life

---

[1] From *The Spirit of the Brush*, translated by
SHIO SAKANISHI [*Wisdom of the East Series*,
1957].
[2] See Hsieh Ho, p. 148a.

[1] Translated by DONALD KEENE. From *Anthology of Japanese Literature*, edited by Donald Keene.

and not in some fairyland beyond our human ken.

The Tale of Genji [*c. 1000*] [1]

ST. ANSELM
c. 1033 – 1109

God is that, the greater than which cannot be conceived.[2]

Proslogion, ch. 3

ABU MOHAMMED KASIM BEN ALI HARIRI
1054–1122

We praise Thee, O God,
For whatever perspicuity of language
    Thou hast taught us
And whatever eloquence Thou hast inspired us with.

Makamat. Prayer

PETER ABELARD
1079–1142

O what their joy and their glory must
    be,
Those endless sabbaths the blessed ones
    see! [3]   *Hymnus Paraclitensis*

Against the disease of writing one must take special precautions, since it is a dangerous and contagious disease.

Letter 8, Abelard to Héloise [4]

ST. BERNARD
1091–1153

You will find something more in woods than in books. Trees and stones will teach you that which you can never learn from masters.[5]   *Epistle 106*

I have liberated my soul.[6]   *Ib. 371*

[1] Translated by ARTHUR WALEY. See Motoori, p. 455b.
[2] This is commonly referred to as the ontological argument for the existence of God, and derives from ST. AUGUSTINE, *De Doctrina Christiana, bk. I, ch. 7.* It is also to be found in DESCARTES, *Third Meditation.*
[3] O quanta qualia sunt illa sabbata,
  Quae semper celebrat superna curia.
Translated by JOHN MASON NEALE [1884].
[4] See Héloise, p. 154b.
[5] See Shakespeare, *As You Like It*, pp. 247b and 249b, and Wordsworth, p. 509a.
[6] Liberavi animam meam.

Hell is full of good intentions or desires.[1]

Attributed. From ST. FRANCIS DE SALES, *Letter 74*

SONG OF ROLAND
Eleventh century

Friend Roland, sound your oliphant.[2]

La Chanson de Roland, l. 1070

Roland is valorous and Oliver is wise.[3]   *Ib. 1093*

HÉLOISE[4]
c. 1101 – c. 1164

Riches and power are but gifts of blind fate, whereas goodness is the result of one's own merits.

Letter 2, Héloise to Abelard

ARCHPOET[5]
Twelfth century

When the hour is nigh me,
Let me in the tavern die,
With a tankard by me.[6]   *Confessio*

Sweeter tastes the wine to me in a tavern tankard
Than the watered stuff my Lord Bishop
    hath decanted.   *Ib.*

[1] Hell is full of good meanings and wishings. — GEORGE HERBERT, *Jacula Prudentum* [1651], *no. 170*
Hell is paved with good intentions. — JOHN RAY, *English Proverbs* [1670]
Quoted by SAMUEL JOHNSON [1775]; from BOSWELL, *Life of Dr. Johnson* [1791], *vol. I, p. 555* [*Everyman ed.*]
Hell is paved with good intentions, not with bad ones. — GEORGE BERNARD SHAW [1856–1950], *Maxims for Revolutionists*
[2] Compagnon Roland sonnez de votre oliphant.
[3] Roland est preux et Oliver est sage.
A Roland for an Oliver. I.e., a blow for a blow, tit for tat, referring to the drawn combat between Roland and Oliver.
[4] See Peter Abelard, p. 154a.
[5] Translated by HELEN WADDELL.
[6] In taberna mori
  ut sint vina proxima
  morientis ori.
See Walter Map, p. 155b.

Down the broad way do I go,
    Young and unregretting,
Wrap me in my vices up,
    Virtue all forgetting,
Greedier for all delight
    Than heaven to enter in:
Since the soul in me is dead,
    Better save the skin.
                Estuans Intrinsecus

GRATIAN
Twelfth century

Paintings are the Bible of the laity.[1]
                Decretum, pt. III

POEM OF THE CID[2]
Twelfth century

Were his lord but worthy, God, how
fine a vassal.   *l. 20*

Thus parted the one from the others
as the nail from the flesh.   *l. 375*

Who serves a good lord lives always
in luxury.   *l. 850*

One would grow poor staying in one
place always.   *l. 948*

FREDERICK I
[BARBAROSSA]
1122–1190

An emperor is subject to no one but
God and Justice.
                From ZINCGREF,
                Apophthegmata,
                bk. I [1626]

AVERROËS
1126–1198

Knowledge is the conformity of the
object and the intellect.[3]
                Destructio Destructionum

[1] Also attributed by Gratian to GREGORY
SERENO, Bishop of Massilio, *Letter 9.*
[2] Translated by W. S. MERWIN.
[3] The classic definition of epistemology, still
commented on today and used by the Neo-
Thomists.

HENRY II
1133–1189

Who will free me from this turbulent priest? [1]   *Attributed*

MOSES BEN MAIMON
[MAIMONIDES]
1135–1204

Anticipate charity by preventing poverty; assist the reduced fellowman, either by a considerable gift, or a sum of
money, or by teaching him a trade, or
by putting him in the way of business,
so that he may earn an honest livelihood, and not be forced to the dreadful
alternative of holding out his hand for
charity. This is the highest step and the
summit of charity's golden ladder.[2]
                Charity's Eight Degrees

WALTER MAP [MAPES]
c. 1140 – c. 1210

I intend to die in a tavern; let the
wine be placed near my dying mouth,[3]
so that when the choirs of angels come,
they may say, "God be merciful to this
drinker!"   *De Nugis Curialium*

ALAIN DE LILLE
[ALANUS DE INSULIS]
d. 1202

Do not hold as gold all that shines as
gold.[4]   • *Parabolae*

[1] Thomas à Becket.
[2] See Andrew Carnegie, p. 757a.
[3] Meum est propositum in taberna mori;
Vinum sit appositum morientis ori.
See Archpoet, p. 154b.
[4] Non teneas aurum totum quod splendet ut
aurum [All that glitters is not gold].
This was considered a common proverb which
had its roots in a Latin translation from ARIS-
TOTLE: Yellow-colored objects appear to be gold.
— *Elenchi, bk. I, ch. 1*
Hyt is not al gold that glareth. — CHAUCER,
The House of Fame [1374–1385], *bk. I, l. 272*
    But al thyng which that shineth as the
        gold
    Nis nat gold, as that I have herd it told.
        The Canterbury Tales [c. 1387]. *The
            Canon's Yeoman's Tale, l. 962*
All is not golde that outward shewith bright.
— LYDGATE [c. 1370–c. 1451], *On the Mutability
of Human Affairs*
                (*note continues p. 156*)

KAMO NO CHOMEI
1153–1216

The flow of the river is ceaseless and its water is never the same. The bubbles that float in the pools, now vanishing, now forming, are not of long duration: so in the world are man and his dwellings. . . . [People] die in the morning, they are born in the evening, like foam on the water.

Hojoki (An Account of My Hut) [1] [1212]

He who complies with the ways of the world may be impoverished thereby; he who does not, appears deranged. Wherever one may live, whatever work one may do, is it possible even for a moment to find a haven for the body or peace for the mind? *Ib.*

Only in a hut built for the moment can one live without fears. *Ib.*

My body is like a drifting cloud — I ask for nothing, I want nothing.
Ib.

WALTHER VON DER VOGELWEIDE
c. 1160 – 1230

Now the summer came to pass
And flowers through the grass
Joyously sprang,

Non omne quod fulget est aurum. — GABRIEL
BIEL [d. 1495], *Expositio Canonis Messe, lecture
77*, derived from WILLIAM OF AUVERGNE [d.
1249]. This is the Latin version closest to the
proverb as commonly known.
  Gold all is not that doth golden seem. —
SPENSER, *Faerie Queene, bk. II* [1590], *canto 8,
st. 14*
    All that glisters is not gold —
    Often have you heard that told.
      SHAKESPEARE, *Merchant of Venice*
      [1596–1597], *act II, sc. vii, l. 65*
All is not gold that glisters. — CERVANTES,
Don Quixote, pt. II [1615], *bk. III, ch. 33*
  All is not gold that glisteneth. — MIDDLETON,
A Fair Quarrel [1617], *act V, sc. i*
  All, as they say, that glitters is not gold. —
DRYDEN, *The Hind and the Panther* [1687],
l. 215
  [1] Translated by DONALD KEENE. From *An-
thology of Japanese Literature*, edited by Don-
ald Keene.

While all the tribes of birds sang.[1]
Dream Song, st. 1 [2]

This was ever the world's distempered will:
Fools have always mocked and spurned the wise.
These shall be judged according to their lies.[3]   *Lament, st.* 2

The sun no longer shows
His face; and treason sows
His secret seeds that no man can detect;
Fathers by their children are undone;
The brother would the brother cheat;
And the cowled monk is a deceit . . .
Might is right, and justice there is none.[4]   *Millennium*

FUJIWARA NO TEIKA
1162–1241

In the expression of the emotions originality merits the first consideration. . . . The words used, however, should be old ones. . . .

The style should imitate the great poems of the masters of former times. One must discard every last phrase of the sentiments and expressions written by men of recent times. . . .

One should impregnate one's mind with a constant study of the forms of expression of ancient poetry.[5]

There are no teachers of Japanese poetry. But they who take the old poems as their teachers, steep their minds in the old style, and learn their words from the masters of former time —who of them will fail to write poetry?
Guide to the Composition of Poetry [6]

[1] Dô der sumer komen was,
  Und die blumen dur daz gras
  Wünneclâchen sprungen,
  Aedâ die vogele sungen.
[2] See *Sumer is icumen in*, p. 1083a.
[3] Translated by MARGARET F. RICHEY.
[4] Translated by JETHRO BITHELL.
[5] See Horace, p. 124b, and Hsieh Ho, p. 148a.
[6] From *Sources of Japanese Tradition*, edited
by WILLIAM THEODORE DE BARY [1958].

HARTMANN VON AUE
c. 1170 – 1215

He who helps in the saving of others,
Saves himself as well.   *Poor Henry*

HERBERT
VON FRITZLAR
fl. c. 1210

The cart has no place where a fifth
wheel could be used.   *Saying*

EIKE VON REPKOW
fl. c. 1220

He who comes first, eats first.
        Sachsenspiegel [1219–1233]

ST. FRANCIS OF ASSISI[1]
c. 1181 – 1226

Praise to thee, my Lord, for all thy
    creatures,
Above all Brother Sun
Who brings us the day and lends us his
    light.
        The Song of Brother Sun and of
        All His Creatures [1225]

Love is he, radiant with great splen-
    dor,
And speaks to us of Thee, O Most
High.   *Ib.*

Where there is charity and wisdom,
there is neither fear nor ignorance.
Where there is patience and humility,
there is neither anger nor vexation.
Where there is poverty and joy, there is
neither greed nor avarice. Where there
is peace and meditation, there is neither
anxiety nor doubt.
        The Counsels of the Holy Father
        St. Francis. Admonition 27

Lord,
    make me an instrument of Your
        peace.
    Where there is hatred let me sow
        love;
    Where there is injury, pardon;
    Where there is doubt, faith;
    Where there is despair, hope;

[1] Translated by LEO SHERLEY-PRICE.

Where there is darkness, light; and
Where there is sadness, joy.
O divine Master,
    grant that I may not so much
    Seek to be consoled as to console;
    To be understood as to understand;
    To be loved as to love;
    For it is in giving that we receive;
    It is in pardoning that we are par-
        doned; and
    It is in dying that we are born to
        eternal life.   *Attributed*

I have sinned against my brother the
ass.   *Dying words*

MAGNA CARTA
1215

No freeman shall be taken, or imprisoned, or outlawed, or exiled, or in
any way harmed, nor will we go upon
him nor will we send upon him, except
by the legal judgment of his peers or by
the law of the land.   *Clause* 39

To none will we sell, to none deny or
delay, right or justice.   *Clause* 40

TOMMASO DI CELANO
c. 1185 – c. 1255

Day of wrath and doom impending,
David's word with Sibyl's blending,
Heaven and earth in ashes ending![1]
        Dies Irae

ALFONSO X
[ALFONSO THE WISE]
1221–1284

Had I been present at the creation, I
would have given some useful hints for
the better ordering of the universe.[2]
        Attributed

[1] Dies irae, dies illa
    Solvet saeclum in favilla,
    Teste David cum Sibylla.
Translated by W. J. IRONS. This has been attributed also to St. Gregory and St. Bernard.
[2] CARLYLE says, in his *History of Frederick
the Great, bk. II, ch.* 7, that this saying of
Alfonso about Ptolemy's astronomy, "that it
seemed a crank machine; that it was pity the
Creator had not taken advice," is still remembered by mankind — this and no other of his
many sayings.

RUTEBEUF
d. 1280

What became of the friends I had
With whom I was always so close
And loved so dearly?
La Complainte Rutebeuf

Friendship is dead:
They were friends who go with the
    wind,[1]
And the wind was blowing at my door.
                                        Ib.

ST. THOMAS AQUINAS
1227–1274

Sing, my tongue, the Savior's glory,
Of His Flesh the mystery sing;
Of the Blood, all price exceeding,
Shed by our immortal King.[2]
    Pange, Lingua (hymn for Ves-
    pers on the Feast of Corpus
    Christi), st. 1

Down in adoration falling,
Lo! the sacred Host we hail;
Lo! o'er ancient forms departing,
Newer rites of grace prevail;
Faith for all defects supplying,
Where the feeble senses fail.
    Ib. st. 5 (Tantum Ergo)

Thus Angels' Bread is made
The Bread of man today:
The Living Bread from Heaven
With figures doth away:
O wondrous gift indeed!
The poor and lowly may

---

[1] See Dowson, p. 890a.
[2] Pange, lingua, gloriosi
    Corporis mysterium
    Sanguinisque pretiosi,
    Quem in mundi pretium
    Fructus ventris generosi
    Rex effudit gentium.
    Translated by EDWARD CASWALL [1814–1878].
      Now, my tongue, the mystery telling
      Of the glorious Body sing.
          The Hymnal of the Protestant
                    Episcopal Church
    Pange, lingua, gloriosi proelium certaminis
    [Sing, my tongue, the glorious battle]. — VE-
    NANTIUS HONORIUS CLEMENTIANUS FORTUNATUS,
    Bishop of Poitiers [fl. c. 600].

Upon their Lord and Master feed.[1]
    Sacris Solemniis Juncta Sint
    Gaudia (Matins hymn for
    Corpus Christi), st. 6 (Panis
    Angelicus)

O saving Victim, opening wide
The gate of heaven to man below,
Our foes press on from every side,
Thine aid supply, Thy strength be-
    stow.[2]
    Verbum Supernum Prodiens
    (hymn for Lauds on Corpus
    Christi), st. 5 (O Salutaris
    Hostia)

Lord Jesu, blessed Pelican.
    Adoro Te Devote (hymn ap-
    pointed for the Thanksgiving
    after Mass), st. 6 (Pie Pellicane
    Jesu Domine)

Three things are necessary for the
salvation of man: to know what he
ought to believe; to know what he ought
to desire; and to know what he ought
to do.
    Two Precepts of Charity [1273]

Law: an ordinance of reason for the
common good, made by him who has
care of the community.
    Summa Theologica [1273]

Concerning   perfect   blessedness
which consists in a vision of God.[3]
                                        Ib.

Reason in man is rather like God in
the world.
    Opuscule 11, *De Regno*

Beware the man of one book.[4]
    Quoted by ISAAC D'ISRAEL *in*
    Curiosities of Literature [1791–
    1793]

FREIDANK
fl. c. 1250

New brooms sweep well.   *Saying*

---

[1] Translated by J. D. CHAMBERS [1805–1893].
Man did eat angels' food. — *Psalm 78:25*
[2] Translated by EDWARD CASWALL.
[3] Probably the origin of the phrase "beatific
vision."
[4] Cave ab homine unius libri.

MEISTER ECKHART
c. 1260 – 1327

In silence man can most readily preserve his integrity.

Directions for the
Contemplative Life

The more wise and powerful a master, the more directly is his work created, and the simpler it is.

Of the Eternal Birth

One must not always think so much about what one should do, but rather what one should be. Our works do not ennoble us; but we must ennoble our works.   *Work and Being*

DANTE ALIGHIERI
1265–1321

In that part of the book of my memory before which is little that can be read, there is a rubric, saying, "Incipit Vita Nova."

La Vita Nuova [1293] [1]

Love hath so long possess'd me for his
     own
And made his lordship so familiar.
                    Ib.

Love with delight discourses in my
     mind
Upon my lady's admirable gifts . . .
Beyond the range of human intellect.
Il Convito.[2] *Trattato Terzo, l. 1*

In the middle of the journey of our life I came to myself within a dark wood where the straight way was lost.[3]
The Divine Comedy [c. 1310–
1320]. *Inferno,*[4] *canto I, l. 1*

And as he, who with laboring breath has escaped from the deep to the shore, turns to the perilous waters and gazes.
                Ib. 22

Thou [1] art my master and my author; thou art he from whom alone I took the style whose beauty has done me honor.
The Divine Comedy. Inferno,
canto I, l. 85

All hope abandon, ye who enter here! [2]   *Ib. III, 9*

Here must all distrust be left behind; all cowardice must be ended.   *Ib. 14*

There sighs, lamentations and loud wailings resounded through the starless air, so that at first it made me weep; strange tongues, horrible language, words of pain, tones of anger, voices loud and hoarse, and with these the sound of hands, made a tumult which is whirling through that air forever dark, as sand eddies in a whirlwind.
                Ib. 22

This miserable state is borne by the wretched souls of those who lived without disgrace and without praise.
                Ib. 34

Let us not speak of them; but look, and pass on.[3]   *Ib. 51*

These wretches, who never were alive.   *Ib. 64*

Into the eternal darkness, into fire and into ice.[3, 4]   *Ib. 87*

Without hope we live in desire.
               Ib. IV, 42

I came into a place void of all light, which bellows like the sea in tempest, when it is combated by warring winds.[5]
               Ib. V, 28

As in the cold season their wings bear the starlings along in a broad, dense flock, so does that blast the wicked spir-

---

[1] Translated by DANTE GABRIEL ROSSETTI.
[2] Translated by CHARLES LYELL. The first line is also in *The Divine Comedy, Purgatorio II, 112.*
[3] Nel mezzo del cammin di nostra vita
     Mi ritrovai per una selva oscura,
     Che la diritta via era smarrita.
[4] Translated by JOHN D. SINCLAIR [1958], unless otherwise noted.

[1] Virgil.
[2] Lasciate ogni speranza, voi ch'entrate.
Traditional translation.
[3] Translated by JOHN AITKEN CARLYLE, *The Temple Classics* [1900].
[4] See Housman, p. 853a, and Frost, p. 927a.
[5] Translated by JOHN AITKEN CARLYLE, *The Temple Classics* [1900].

its. Hither, thither, downward, upward, it drives them.[1]

> The Divine Comedy. Inferno, canto V, l. 40

Love, which is quickly kindled in the gentle heart, seized this man for the fair form that was taken from me, and the manner still hurts me. Love, which absolves no beloved one from loving, seized me so strongly with his charm that, as thou seest, it does not leave me yet.[2]   *Ib. 100*

What sweet thoughts, what longing led them to the woeful pass.[3]

> *Ib. 113*

There is no greater sorrow
Than to be mindful of the happy time
In misery.[4]   *Ib. 121*

A Galeotto was the book and he that wrote it; that day we read in it no farther.[5]   *Ib. 137*

I fell as a dead body falls.

> *Ib. Last line*

Pride, Envy, and Avarice are the three sparks that have set these hearts on fire.   *Ib. VI, 74*

But when thou shalt be in the sweet world, I pray thee bring me to men's memory.[6]   *Ib. 88*

Ye that are of good understanding, note the doctrine that is hidden under the veil of the strange verses!

> *Ib. IX, 61*

Already I had fixed my look on his; and he rose upright with breast and countenance, as if he entertained great scorn of Hell.[1]

> The Divine Comedy. Inferno, canto X, l. 34

Necessity brings him [Dante] here, not pleasure.   *Ib. XII, 87*

If thou follow thy star, thou canst not fail of a glorious haven.

> *Ib. XV, 55*

So my conscience chide me not, I am ready for Fortune as she wills.

> *Ib. 91*

He listens well who takes notes.

> *Ib. 99*

A fair request should be followed by the deed in silence.   *Ib. XXIV, 77*

Consider your origin; you were not born to live like brutes, but to follow virtue and knowledge.

> *Ib. XXVI, 118*

If I thought my answer were to one who would ever return to the world, this flame should stay without another movement; but since none ever returned alive from this depth, if what I hear is true, I answer thee without fear of infamy.[2]   *Ib. XXVII, 60*

And thence we came forth, to see again the stars.[3]   *Ib. XXXIV, 139*

To run over better waters the little vessel of my genius now hoists her sails, as she leaves behind her a sea so cruel.

> *Ib. Purgatorio,*[4] *canto I, l. 1*

He goes seeking liberty, which is so dear, as he knows who for it renounces life.   *Ib. 71*

---

[1] Di qua, di là, di giù, di su li mena.

[2] Francesca of Rimini tells of the love she and Paolo, her brother-in-law, bore one another and of its tragic end when her husband surprised and stabbed them.

[3] Translated by JOHN AITKEN CARLYLE, *The Temple Classics* [1900].

[4] Translated by LONGFELLOW.
> Nessun maggior dolore
> Che ricordarsi del tempo felice
> Nella miseria.

See Pindar, p. 79b; Boethius, p. 148a; Chaucer, p. 165a; and Tennyson, p. 647a.

[5] Galeotto fu il libro e chi lo scrisse:
> Quel giorno più non vi leggemmo avante.

[6] Ciacco (Hog), noted for his gluttony, entreats Dante.

[1] Translated by JOHN AITKEN CARLYLE, *The Temple Classics* [1901]
Dante speaks of Farinata, head of the Uberti family, leaders of the Ghibelline faction in Florence.

[2] Count Guido da Montefeltro, the famous Ghibelline warrior, addresses Dante.
This passage in Italian is the epigraph for T. S. ELIOT, *The Love Song of J. Alfred Prufrock* [1917].

[3] E quindi uscimmo a riveder le stelle.

[4] Translated by CHARLES ELIOT NORTON [1902], unless otherwise noted.

O conscience, upright and stainless, how bitter a sting to thee is a little fault!
The Divine Comedy. Purgatorio, canto III, l. 8

For to lose time is most displeasing to him who knows most. *Ib.* 78

The Infinite Goodness has such wide arms that it takes whatever turns to it. *Ib.* 121

Unless, before then, the prayer assist me which rises from a heart that lives in grace: what avails the other, which is not heard in heaven? *Ib. IV, 133*

"Why is thy mind so entangled," said the Master,[1] "that thou slackenest thy pace? What is it to thee what they whisper there? Come after me and let the people talk. Stand like a firm tower that never shakes its top for blast of wind." *Ib. V,[2] 10*

Go right on and listen as thou goest. *Ib. 45*

[Beatrice] who shall be a light between truth and intellect. *Ib. VI, 45*

It was now the hour that turns back the longing of seafarers and melts their hearts, the day they have bidden dear friends farewell, and pierces the new traveler with love if he hears in the distance the bell that seems to mourn the dying day.[2] *Ib. VIII, 1*

Give us this day the daily manna,[3] without which, in this rough desert, he backward goes, who toils most to go on. *Ib. XI, 13*

Worldly renown is naught but a breath of wind, which now comes this way and now comes that, and changes name because it changes quarter. *Ib. 100*

O human race, born to fly upward, wherefore at a little wind dost thou so fall? *Ib. XII, 95*

[1] Virgil.
[2] Translated by JOHN D. SINCLAIR.
[3] See *Matthew, 6:11*, p. 40b.

To a greater force, and to a better nature, you, free, are subject, and that creates the mind in you, which the heavens have not in their charge. Therefore if the present world go astray, the cause is in you, in you it is to be sought.
The Divine Comedy. Purgatorio, canto XVI, l. 79

Everyone confusedly conceives of a good in which the mind may be at rest, and desires it; wherefore everyone strives to attain to it. *Ib. XVII, 127*

Love kindled by virtue always kindles another, provided that its flame appear outwardly. *Ib. XXII, 10*

Less than a drop of blood remains in me that does not tremble; I recognize the signals of the ancient flame.[1] *Ib. XXX, 46*

But so much the more malign and wild does the ground become with bad seed and untilled, as it has the more of good earthly vigor. *Ib. 118*

Pure and disposed to mount unto the stars.[2] *Ib. XXXIII, 145*

The glory of Him who moves everything penetrates through the universe, and is resplendent in one part more and in another less.[3]
Ib. Paradiso,[4] canto I, l. 1

A great flame follows a little spark. *Ib. 34*

And in His will is our peace.[5] *Ib. III, 85*

The greatest gift that God in His bounty made in creation, and the most conformable to His goodness, and that which He prizes the most, was the freedom of the will, with which the crea-

[1]   Men che dramma
   Di sangue m'è rimaso, che no tremi;
   Conosco i segni dell' antica fiamma.
See Virgil, p. 118b.
[2] *Puro e disposto a salire alle stelle.*
See Virgil, p. 119b.
[3] See *Acts 17:28*, p. 50a, and Aratus, p. 104a.
[4] Translated by JOHN D. SINCLAIR.
[5] *E'n la sua volontade e nostra pace.*
See T. S. Eliot, p. 1004a.

tures with intelligence, they all and they alone, were and are endowed.
The Divine Comedy. Paradiso, canto V, l. 19

Thou shalt prove how salt is the taste of another's bread and how hard is the way up and down another man's stairs.
Ib. XVII, 58

Overcoming me with the light of a smile, she [Beatrice] said to me: "Turn and listen, for not only in my eyes is Paradise." [1]
Ib. XVIII, 19

Therefore the sight that is granted to your world penetrates within the Eternal Justice as the eye into the sea; for though from the shore it sees the bottom, in the open sea it does not, and yet the bottom is there but the depth conceals it.
Ib. XIX, 73

The experience of this sweet life.[2]
Ib. XX, 47

Like the lark that soars in the air, first singing, then silent, content with the last sweetness that satiates it, such seemed to me that image, the imprint of the Eternal Pleasure.
Ib. 73

The night that hides things from us.
Ib. XXIII, 3

With the color that paints the morning and evening clouds that face the sun I saw then the whole heaven suffused.
Ib. XXVII, 28

The Love that moves the sun and the other stars.[3]
Ib. XXXIII, 145

YOSHIDA KENKO
1283–1350

To while away the idle hours, seated the livelong day before the ink slab, by jotting down without order or purpose whatever trifling thoughts pass through

my mind, verily this is a queer and crazy thing to do!
Tsurezure-Gusa (Essays in Idleness) [c. 1340] [1]

One should write not unskillfully in the running hand, be able to sing in a pleasing voice and keep good time to music; and, lastly, a man should not refuse a little wine when it is pressed upon him.
Ib.

However gifted and accomplished a young man may be, if he has no fondness for women, one has a feeling of something lacking, as of a precious wine cup without a bottom.
Ib.

To sit alone in the lamplight with a book spread out before you, and hold intimate converse with men of unseen generations — such is a pleasure beyond compare.
Ib.

A certain recluse, I know not who, once said that no bonds attached him to this life, and the only thing he would regret leaving was the sky.
Ib.

PHILIP VI
[PHILIP OF VALOIS]
1293–1350

He who loves me, let him follow me.[2]

WILLIAM OF OCKHAM
1300–1348

A plurality must not be asserted without necessity.[3]
Quodlibeta Septem [c. 1320]

---

[1] See Chaucer, p. 165a.
[2] L'esperienza di questa dolce vita.
[3] L'amor che muove il sole e l'altre stelle. See Aristotle, p. 97b.

[1] Translated by DONALD KEENE. From *Anthology of Japanese Literature*, edited by Donald Keene.
[2] Qui m'aime me suive.
[3] Translated by A. C. CROMBIE. This is the original statement of "Ockham's razor." The more familiar form, "Entities should not be multiplied beyond necessity," was introduced in the seventeenth century by John Ponce of Cork.

PETRARCH [1]
[FRANCESCO
PETRARCA]
1304–1374

Who overrefines his argument brings himself to grief.
> *To Laura in Life, canzone* 11

A good death does honor to a whole life.
> *To Laura in Death, canzone* 16

To be able to say how much you love is to love but little.　　*Ib.* 137

Rarely do great beauty and great virtue dwell together.[2]
> *De Remedies, bk.* II

EDWARD III
1312–1377

Honi soit qui mal y pense.[3]
> *Motto of the Order of the Garter*
> [1349]

Let the boy win his spurs.
> *Said of the Black Prince at the*
> *Battle of Crécy* [1345]

JOHN BARBOUR
c. 1316 – 1395

Ah! Freedom is a noble thing!
Freedom makes man to have liking.
Freedom all solace to man gives;
He lives at ease that freely lives.
> *The Bruce* [c. 1375], *l.* 225

JOHN WYCLIFFE
c. 1320 – 1384

I believe that in the end the truth will conquer.
> *To the Duke of Lancaster*
> [1381]. *From* J. R. GREEN,
> *A Short History of the English*
> *People, ch.* 5

By hook or by crook.[1]
> *Controversial Tracts* [c. 1380]

This Bible is for the government of the People, by the People, and for the People.[2]　　*Attributed* [1382]

WILLIAM
OF WYKEHAM
1324–1404

Manners maketh man.
> *Motto of his two foundations,*
> *Winchester College and New*
> *College, Oxford*

CHARLES V OF FRANCE
1337–1380

I speak Spanish to God, Italian to women, French to men, and German to my horse.[3]　　*Attributed*

GEOFFREY CHAUCER [4]
c. 1343 – 1400

To rede, and drive the night away.
> *The Book of the Duchess* [1369],
> *l.* 49

Soun ys noght but eyr ybroken,
And every speche that ys spoken,

---

[1] The phrase has been said to derive from the custom of some manors where tenants were authorized to take firebote *by hook or by crook;* that is, so much of the underwood as may be cut with a crook, and so much of the loose timber as may be collected from the boughs by means of a hook. Quoted by Skelton, Heywood, Spenser, and others.

[2] Supposedly, Wycliffe used this phrase in the general prologue of his translation of the Bible [1382]. However, this editor could not find it in the 1850 edition collated from all the Wycliffe MSS. by Josiah Forshall and Sir Frederick Madden. The closest sentence is: If this book be wel understanden, it is profitable bothe to goostly governours and bodily lordis, and iustisis and comyns also.
See Webster, p. 547a; Garrison, p. 616a; Lincoln, p. 639a; and Parker, p. 657b.

[3] Je parle espagnol à Dieu, italien aux femmes, français aux hommes, et allemand à mon cheval.

[4] From the text of F. N. ROBINSON, *The Works of Geoffrey Chaucer, 2nd ed.* [1957].

---

[1] Chaucer translated *Sonnet 88* [*In Vita*], *S'amor non è.* See p. 164b.
[2] See Petronius, p. 133b.
[3] Evil to him who evil thinks.

Lowd or pryvee, foul or fair,
In his substaunce ys but air.
> *The House of Fame* [1374–
> 1385], *bk. II, l.* 765

Venus clerk, Ovide,
That hath ysowen wonder wide
The grete god of Loves name.
> *Ib. III,* 1487

Hard is the herte that loveth nought
In May.
> *The Romaunt of the Rose* [1]
> [*c.* 1380], *l.* 85

The tyme, that may not sojourne,
But goth, and may never retourne,
As watir that doun renneth ay,
But never drope retourne may.
> *Ib.* 381

Nakid as a worm was she.   *Ib.* 454

As round as appil was his face.
> *Ib.* 819

So that the more she yaf awey,
The more, ywis, she hadde alwey.
> *Ib.* 1159

A ful gret fool is he, ywis,
That bothe riche and nygard is.
> *Ib.* 1171

The lyf so short, the craft so long to
lerne,[2]
Th' assay so hard, so sharp the con-
queryinge.
> *The Parliament of Fowls*
> [1380–1386], *l.* 1

For out of olde feldes, as men seyth,
Cometh al this newe corn fro yer to
yere;[3]
And out of olde bokes, in good feyth,
Cometh al this newe science that men
lere.   *Ib.* 22

Nature, the vicaire of the almyghty
lorde.   *Ib.* 379

---

[1] Chaucer, and probably others, translated the French *Roman de la Rose* by Guillaume de Lorris (begun in 1237) and Jean de Meun (continued c. 1277).

[2] See Hippocrates, p. 88b, and note.

[3] John Bartlett quoted this line at the head of his preface to the Ninth Edition of *Familiar Quotations* [1891].

A fol can not be stille.[1]
> *The Parliament of Fowls,*
> *l.* 574

Now welcome, somer, with thy sonne
softe,[2]
That hast this wintres weders overshake.
> *Ib.* 680

But the Troian gestes, as they felle,
In Omer, or in Dares, or in Dite,
Whoso that kan may rede hem as they
write.
> *Troilus and Criseyde* [*c.* 1385],
> *bk. I, l.* 145

If no love is, O God, what fele I so?
And if love is, what thing and which is
he?
If love be good, from whennes cometh
my woo? [3]
> *Ib.* 400 (*Canticus Troili*)

A fool may ek a wys-man ofte gide.
> *Ib.* 630

Ek som tyme it is craft to seme fle
Fro thyng whych in effect men hunte
faste.   *Ib.* 747

Unknowe, unkist, and lost, that is unsought.[4]   *Ib.* 809

O wynd, o wynd, the weder gynneth
clere.   *Ib. II,* 2

Til crowes feet be growen under youre
yë.   *Ib.* 403

    Lord, this is an huge rayn!
This were a weder for to slepen inne!
> *Ib. III,* 656

It is nought good a slepyng hound to
wake.[5]   *Ib.* 764

For I have seyn, of a ful misty morwe
Folowen ful often a myrie someris day.
> *Ib.* 1060

Right as an aspes leef she gan to
quake.   *Ib.* 1200

---

[1] See *Proverbs 29:11*, p. 26b.

[2] In a somer sesun, whan softe was the sonne.
—WILLIAM LANGLAND [c. 1330–c. 1400], *The Vision of Piers Plowman, prologue*

[3] The *Canticus Troili (Song of Troilus)* is a fairly close rendering of Petrarch's *Sonnet 88 (In Vita), S'amor non è.*

[4] See Homer, p. 64b, and note.

[5] See Dickens, p. 672a.

For of fortunes sharpe adversitee
The worste kynde of infortune is this,
A man to han ben in prosperitee,
And it remembren, whan it passed is.[1]
Troilus and Criseyde,
bk. III, l. 1625

Oon ere it herde, at tothir out it
wente.[2] *Ib. IV, 434*

Ek wonder last but nyne nyght nevere
in towne. *Ib. 588*

But manly sette the world on six and
sevene;[3]
And if thow deye a martyr, go to
hevene! *Ib. 622*

For tyme ylost may nought recovered
be. *Ib. 1283*

They take it wisly, faire, and softe.[4]
Ib. V, 347

For he that naught n' assaieth, naught
n' acheveth.[5] *Ib. 784*

Paradis stood formed in her yën.[6]
Ib. 817

Trewe as stiel. *Ib. 831*

This sodeyn Diomede. *Ib. 1024*

Ye, fare wel al the snow of ferne yere![7]
Ib. 1176

Ek gret effect men write in place lite;
Th' entente is al, and nat the lettres
space. *Ib. 1629*

Go, litel bok, go, litel myn tragedye.[1]
Troilus and Criseyde,
bk. V, l. 1786

O yonge, fresshe folkes, he or she,
In which that love up groweth with
youre age,
Repeyreth hom fro worldly vanyte.
Ib. 1835

O moral Gower, this book I directe
To the. *Ib. 1856*

Whan that the month of May
Is comen, and that I here the foules
synge,
And that the floures gynnen for to
sprynge,
Farewel my bok, and my devocioun!
The Legend of Good Women
[c. 1386], l. 36

That, of al the floures in the mede,
Thanne love I most thise floures white
and rede,
Swiche as men callen daysyes in our
toun. *Ib. 41*

Whan that Aprill with his shoures
soote

[1] See Pindar, p. 79b; Boethius, p. 148a;
Dante, p. 160a; and Tennyson, p. 647a.
[2] Went in at the tone eare and ont at tother.
— JOHN HEYWOOD, *Proverbs* [1546], *pt. II, ch. 9*
[3]   All is uneven,
And everything is left at six and seven.
SHAKESPEARE, *Richard II* [1595–1596],
act II, sc. ii, l. 120
Let things go at sixes and sevens. — CERVANTES,
Don Quixote, pt. I [1605], *bk. IV, ch. 3*
Things going on at sixes and sevens. — GOLD-
SMITH, *The Good-Natured Man* [1768], *act I*
     Say, why is everything
     Either at sixes or at sevens?
W.S. GILBERT, *H.M.S. Pinafore*
[1878], *act II, Fair Moon*
[4] The proverb is: Fair and softly goes far.
See Shakespeare, p. 224b.
[5] See Heywood, p. 184b, and note.
[6] See Dante, p. 162a.
[7] See Villon, p. 171a.

[1] Off with you down where you want to go. —
HORACE [65–8 B.C.], *Epistles I, xx, 5*
Little book, you will go without me — I
don't mind — to the city. — OVID [43 B.C.–A.D.
18], *Tristia I, i, 1*
Vade salutatem pro me, liber [Go forth, my
book, to bear my greetings]. — MARTIAL [A.D. C.
40–c. 104], *Epigrams I, 70*
Go now, my little book, to every place
Where my first pilgrim has but shown his face.
JOHN BUNYAN, *Pilgrim's Progress* [1678],
Apology
Go, little Book! From this my solitude
I cast thee on the Waters — go thy ways.
ROBERT SOUTHEY, *Lay of the Laureate*
[1815], *L'Envoi*
These lines of Southey's and the next two
were quoted by BYRON in *Don Juan* [1818],
canto I, stanza 222, which ends: The four first
rhymes are Southey's, every line:/ For God's sake,
reader! take them not for mine!
Go forth, my little book! pursue thy way;
Go forth, and please the gentle and the good.
WORDSWORTH, *Memorials of a Tour on
the Continent* [1820]
Go, little book, and wish to all
Flowers in the garden, meat in the hall.
R. L. STEVENSON, *Underwoods* [1887],
Envoy

The droghte of March hath perced to the roote.
The Canterbury Tales [c. 1387].
Prologue, l. 1

And smale foweles maken melodye,
That slepen al the nyght with open yë,
(So priketh hem nature in hir cor-
ages);
Thanne longen folk to goon on pil-
grimages. *Ib. 9*

He was a verray, parfit gentil knight.
Ib. 72

He was as fressh as is the month of
May. *Ib. 92*

He koude songes make, and wel endyte. *Ib. 95*

Curteis he was, lowely, and servysable,
And carf beforn his fader at the table.
Ib. 99

Ful weel she soong the service dyvyne,
Entuned in hir nose ful semely;
And Frenssh she spak ful faire and
fetisly,
After the scole of Stratford atte Bowe
For Frenssh of Parys was to hir un-
knowe. *Ib. 122*

She wolde wepe, if that she saugh a
mous
Kaught in a trappe, if it were deed or
bledde. *Ib. 144*

And theron heng a brooch of gold ful
sheene,
On which ther was first write a crowned
A,
And after *Amor vincit omnia.*[1]
Ib. 160

His palfrey was as broun as is a berye.
Ib. 207

A Frere ther was, a wantowne and a
merye. *Ib. 208*

He knew the tavernes wel in every
toun. *Ib. 240*

Somwhat he lipsed, for his wantown-
esse,
To make his Englissh sweete upon his
tonge. *Ib. 264*

[1] See Virgil, p. 117a.

A Clerk ther was of Oxenford also.
The Canterbury Tales.
Prologue, l. 285

As leene was his hors as is a rake.
Ib. 287

For hym was levere have at his beddes
heed
Twenty bookes, clad in blak or reed,
Of Aristotle and his philosophie,
Than robes riche, or fithele, or gay
sautrie,
But al be that he was a philosophre,
Yet hadde he but litel gold in cofre.
Ib. 293

And gladly wolde he lerne, and gladly
teche.[1] *Ib. 308*

Nowher so bisy a man as he ther nas,
And yet he semed bisier than he was.
Ib. 321

For he was Epicurus owene sone.[2]
Ib. 336

It snewed in his hous of mete and
drynke. *Ib. 345*

He was a good felawe.[3] *Ib. 395*

His studie was but litel on the Bible.
Ib. 438

For gold in phisik is a cordial,
Therefore he lovede gold in special.
Ib. 443

She was a worthy womman al hir lyve,
Housbondes at chirche dore she hadde
fyve. *Ib. 459*

This noble ensample to his sheep he
yaf,
That first he wroghte, and afterward he
taughte. *Ib. 496*

If gold ruste, what shal iren do?
Ib. 500

But Cristes loore and his apostles
twelve
He taughte, but first he folwed it hym-
selve. *Ib. 527*

[1] See Pope, p. 404a.
[2] See Horace, *Epistles iv, 13*, p. 123a.
[3] If he be not fellow with the best king, thou shalt find him the best king of good fellows. — SHAKESPEARE, *King Henry V* [1598–1600], *act V, sc. ii, l. 259*

And yet he hadde a thombe of gold.[1]
The Canterbury Tales.
Prologue, l. 563

That hadde a fyr-reed cherubynnes
face.   *Ib. 624*

Wel loved he garleek, oynons, and eek
lekes,
And for to drynken strong wyn, reed as
blood.   *Ib. 634*

And whan that he wel dronken hadde
the wyn,
Than wolde he speke no word but
Latyn.   *Ib. 637*

Whoso shal telle a tale after a man,
He moot reherce as ny as evere he kan
Everich a word, if it be in his charge,
Al speke he never so rudeliche and
large,
Or ellis he moot telle his tale untrewe,
Or feyne thyng, or fynde wordes new.
       Ib. 731

For May wol have no slogardie anyght.
The sesoun priketh every gentil herte,
And maketh hym out of his slep to
sterte.
       Ib. The Knight's Tale, l. 1042

Ech man for hymself.   *Ib. 1182*

The bisy larke, messager of day.
       Ib. 1491

May, with alle thy floures and thy
grene,
Welcome be thou, faire, fresshe May.
       Ib. 1510

That "feeld hath eyen, and the wode
hath eres."[2]   *Ib. 1522*

---

[1] In allusion to the proverb: An honest miller
hath a golden thumb.

[2] The proverb also occurs in the Latin form:
Campus habet lumen, et habet nemus auris
acumen.

Fieldes have eies and woodes have eares. —
JOHN HEYWOOD, *Proverbs* [1546], *pt. II, ch. 5*

Wode has erys, felde has sigt. — *King Edward
and the Shepherd, MS* [c. 1300]

Walls have ears. — CERVANTES, *Don Quixote,
pt. II* [1615], *ch. 48*

    Woods have tongues
    As walls have ears.
    TENNYSON, *Idylls of the King.
Balin and Balan* [1885], *l. 522*

Now up, now doun, as boket in a
welle.
       *The Canterbury Tales. The
Knight's Tale, l. 1533*

For pitee renneth soone in gentil
herte.   *Ib. 1761*

    Cupido,
Upon his shuldres wynges hadde he
two;
And blynd he was, as it is often seene;
A bowe he bar and arwes brighte and
kene.   *Ib. 1963*

The smylere with the knyf under the
cloke.   *Ib. 1999*

Up roos the sonne, and up roose
Emelye.   *Ib. 2273*

Myn be the travaille, and thyn be the
glorie!   *Ib. 2406*

And was al his chiere, as in his herte.
       Ib. 2683

What is this world? what asketh men
to have?
Now with his love, now in his colde
grave
Allone, withouten any compaignye.
       Ib. 2777

This world nys but a thurghfare ful of
wo,
And we been pilgrymes, passing to and
fro.
Deeth is an ende of every worldly
soore.   *Ib. 2847*

Jhesu Crist, and seiynte Benedight,
Blesse this hous from every wikked
wight.
       Ib. The Miller's Tale, l. 3483

And broghte of myghty ale a large
quart.   *Ib. 3497*

"Tehee!" quod she, and clapte the
wyndow to.   *Ib. 3740*

Yet in our asshen olde is fyr yreke.[1]
       Ib. The Reeve's Prologue, l. 3882

The gretteste clerkes been noght the
wisest men.[2]
       Ib. The Reeve's Tale, l. 4054

[1] See Thomas Gray, p. 441a.
[2] This proverb goes back to Heraclitus.
The greatest Clerkes be not the wisest men.
— JOHN HEYWOOD, *Proverbs* [1546], *pt. II, ch. 5*

Thurgh thikke and thurgh thenne.[1]
*The Canterbury Tales. The
Reeve's Tale. l. 4066*

So was hir joly whistle wel ywet.
Ib. 4155

She is mirour of alle curteisye.[2]
Ib. The Man of Law's Tale, l. 166

For in the sterres, clerer than is glas,
Is writen, God woot, whoso koude it
rede,
The deeth of every man.   *Ib. 194*

Sathan, that evere us waiteth to bigile.
Ib. 582

In his owene grece I made hym frye.[3]
*Ib. The Wife of Bath's
Prologue, l. 487*

What thyng we may nat lightly have,
Therafter wol we crie alday and crave.
Ib. 517

Greet prees at market maketh deere
ware,
And to greet cheep is holde at litel
prys.   *Ib. 522*

And for to se, and eek for be seye.[4]
Ib. 552

But yet I hadde alwey a coltes tooth.
Gat-toothed I was, and that bicam me
weel.   *Ib. 601*

A womman cast hir shame away,
Whan she cast of hir smok.[5]   *Ib. 782*

As thikke as motes in the sonne-beem.
Ib. The Wife of Bath's Tale, l. 868

"My lige lady, generally," quod he,
"Wommen desiren have sovereynetee

As well over hir housbond as hir love."
*The Canterbury Tales. The
Wife of Bath's Tale, l. 1037*

Looke who that is moost vertuous
alway,
Pryvee and apert, and most entendeth
ay
To do the gentil dedes that he kan;
Taak hym for the grettest gentil man.
Ib. 1113

That he is gentil that dooth gentil
dedis.[1]   *Ib. 1170*

For thogh we slepe or wake, or rome, or
ryde,
Ay fleeth the tyme, it nyl no man
abyde.[2]
Ib. The Clerk's Tale, l. 118

Love is noght oold as whan that it is
newe.   *Ib. 857*

This flour of wyfly pacience.   *Ib. 919*

O stormy peple! unsad and evere untrewe!   *Ib. 995*

No wedded man so hardy be t'assaille
His wyves pacience, in trust to fynde
Grisildis, for in certein he shal faille!
Ib. 1180

It is no childes pley
To take a wyf withoute avysement.
Ib. The Merchant's Tale, l. 1530

Love is blynd.[3]   *Ib. 1598*

My wit is thynne.   *Ib. 1682*

Ther nys no werkman, whatsoevere he
be,
That may bothe werke wel and hast-
ily;[4]
This wol be doon at leyser parfitly.[5]
Ib. 1832

Therfore bihoveth hire a ful long
spoon

---

[1] Through thicke and thin. — DU BARTAS,
Divine Weeks and Works [1578], *Second Week,
Fourth Day*

[2]   Call him bounteous Buckingham,
    The mirror of all courtesy.
        SHAKESPEARE, *Henry VIII* [1613], *act II,
                       sc. i, l. 53*

[3] Proverbial.
Frieth in her own grease. — JOHN HEYWOOD,
Proverbs [1546], *pt. I, ch. 11*
   The best way were to entertain him with hope,
till the wicked fire of lust have melted him in
his own grease. — SHAKESPEARE, *Merry Wives of
Windsor* [1601], *act II, sc. i, l. 60*

[4] See Ovid, p. 128b.

[5] See Herodotus *I, 8,* p. 86b.

---

[1] See Goldsmith, p. 448a.

[2] See John Heywood, p. 182b, and note.

[3] Proverbial. See Shakespeare, p. 228b, and
note.

[4] See Publilius Syrus, p. 126b, and John Heywood, p. 182a.

[5] Ease and speed in doing a thing do not give
the work lasting solidity or exactness of beauty.
— PLUTARCH [A.D. 46–120], *Life of Pericles*

That shal ete with a feend.[1]
> *The Canterbury Tales. The Squire's Tale, l.* 602

Men loven of propre kynde newefangelnesse.   *Ib.* 610

Fy on possessioun
But if a man be vertuous withal.
     Ib. 686

Pacience is an heigh vertu, certeyn.
> *Ib. The Franklin's Tale, l.* 773

Servant in love, and lord in mariage.
     Ib. 793

It is agayns the proces of nature.
     Ib. 1345

Trouthe is the hyeste thyng that men may kepe.   *Ib.* 1479

For dronkenesse is verray sepulture
Of mannes wit and his discrecioun.
> *Ib. The Pardoner's Tale, l.* 558

Mordre wol out, certeyn, it wol nat faille.[2]
> *Ib. The Prioress's Tale, l.* 1776

This may wel be rym dogerel.
> *Ib. Chaucer's Tale of Sir Thopas, l.* 2115

---

[1] Proverbial.
Hee must have a long spoon, shall eat with the devill. — JOHN HEYWOOD, *Proverbs* [1546], *pt. II, ch. 5*
He must have a long spoon that must eat with the devil. — SHAKESPEARE, *Comedy of Errors* [1592–1593], *act IV, sc. iii, l. 64*
[2] Proverbial. Also in *The Nun's Priest's Tale, ll. 4242 and 4247.*
How easily murder is discovered! — SHAKESPEARE, *Titus Andronicus* [1593–1594], *act II, sc. iii, l. 28*
Truth will come to light; murder cannot be hid long. — SHAKESPEARE: *Merchant of Venice* [1596–1597], *act II, sc. ii, l. 86*
Murder, though it have no tongue, will speak With most miraculous organ.
     SHAKESPEARE, *Hamlet* [1600–1601], *act II, sc. ii, l. 630*
Murder will out. — CERVANTES, *Don Quixote, pt. I* [1605], *bk. III, ch. 8*
Carcasses bleed at the sight of the murderer. — ROBERT BURTON, *Anatomy of Melancholy* [1621–1651], *pt. I, sec. 1 member 2, subsec. 5*
Other sins only speak; murder shrieks out. — JOHN WEBSTER, *Duchess of Malfi* [1623], *act IV, sc. ii*

Ful wys is he that kan hymselven knowe! [1]
> *The Canterbury Tales. The Monk's Tale, l.* 3329

He was of knyghthod and of fredom flour.   *Ib.* 3832

For whan a man hath over-greet a wit,
Ful oft hym happeth to mysusen it.
> *Ib. The Canon Yeoman's Prologue, l.* 648

My sone, keep wel thy tonge, and keep thy freend.
> *Ib. The Manciple's Tale, l.* 319

Thing that is seyd, is seyd; and forth it gooth.   *Ib.* 355

For the proverbe seith that "manye smale maken a greet." [2]
> *Ib. The Parson's Tale, l.* 361

Reule wel thyself, that other folk canst rede.
And trouthe thee shal delivere, it is no drede.   *Truth* [c. 1390], *l.* 6

The wrastling for this world axeth a fal.   *Ib.* 16

EUSTACHE DESCHAMPS
c. 1345 – c. 1406

Who will bell the cat? [3]
> *Ballad refrain*

Better honor than shameful wealth.[4]
     Ib.

JOHN HUSS
1373–1415

O holy simplicity! [5]
> *Last words, at the stake*

---

[1] See The Seven Sages, p. 68a.
[2] The proverb goes back to St. Augustine. See also Hesiod, p. 67b.
Many small make a great. — JOHN HEYWOOD, *Proverbs* [1546], *pt. I, ch. 11*
[3] Qui pendra la sonnette au chat?
Copied by La Fontaine.
[4] Mieux vaut honneur que honteuse richesse.
[5] O sancta simplicitas!

THE PRIMARY CHRONICLE[1]

1377

The Chuds, the Slavs and the Krivchians then said to the peoples of Rus: "Our whole land is great and rich, but there is no order in it. Come to rule and reign over us."

> *Annal for the years 860–862: Invitation of the Varangians to Novgorod*

Then we went to Greece, and the Greeks led us to the edifices where they worship their God, and we knew not whether we were in heaven or on earth. For on earth there is no such splendor or such beauty, and we are at a loss how to describe it. We only know that God dwells there among men, and their service is fairer than the ceremonies of other nations.

> *Annal for the year 987: Vladimir's Christianization of Russia*

It is the Russians' joy to drink; we cannot do without it.   *Ib.*

THOMAS À KEMPIS

1380–1471

How swiftly passes the glory of the world.[2]

> *Imitation of Christ [c. 1420], bk. I, ch. 3*

Be not angry that you cannot make others as you wish them to be, since you cannot make yourself as you wish to be.   *Ib. 16*

Man proposes, but God disposes.[3]

> *Ib. 19*

What canst thou see elsewhere which thou canst not see here? Behold the heaven and the earth and all the elements; for of these are all things created.

> *Imitation of Christ, bk. I, ch. 20*

No man ruleth safely but he that is willingly ruled.   *Ib.*

And when he is out of sight, quickly also is he out of mind.[1]   *Ib. 23*

First keep the peace within yourself, then you can also bring peace to others.   *Ib. II, 3*

Love is swift, sincere, pious, pleasant, gentle, strong, patient, faithful, prudent, long-suffering, manly and never seeking her own; for wheresoever a man seeketh his own, there he falleth from love.[2]   *Ib. III, 5*

CHARLES D'ORLÉANS

1394–1465

I am dying of thirst by the side of the fountain.[3]   *Ballades, 2*

The season has shed its mantle of wind and chill and rain.[4]

> *Rondeaux, 63*

All by myself, wrapped in my thoughts,

---

lation), and in *The Vision of Piers Plowman, l. 13994*, ed. 1550.

Man appoints, and God disappoints. — CERVANTES, *Don Quixote, pt. II* [1615], *bk. IV, ch. 55*

See *Proverbs 16:9*, p. 24b.

[1] Out of syght, out of mynd. — GOOGE, *Eglogs* [1563]

And out of mind as soon as out of sight. — FULKE GREVILLE [1554–1628], *Sonnet 56*

Fer from eze, fer from herte,
Quoth Hendyng.

HENDYNG, *Proverbs, MS* [c. 1320]

I do perceive that the old proverbis be not alwaies trew, for I do finde that the absence of my Nath. doth breede in me the more continuall remembrance of him. — LADY ANN BACON, *letter to Lady Jane Cornwallis* [1613]

[2] See *I Corinthians 13:4* and 7, p. 52b.

[3] Je meurs de soif en cousté la fontaine. See Wilbur, p. 1080a.

[4] Le temps a laissé son manteau
De vent, de froidure et de pluie.

[1] The earliest of the Russian chronicles or annals, begun in 1040 and continued through 1118 by various annalists, gives the record of Russian history since A.D. 852. It was copied several times and incorporated into later chronicles as the beginning. These quotations are from the Laurentian version, copied in 1377, translated by Samuel Cross.

[2] O quam cito transit [usual form: sic transit] gloria mundi.

The words addressed to the Pope in the ceremony of his elevation.

[3] This expression appears earlier in *The Chronicle of Battel Abbey, p. 27* (Lower's trans-

And building castles in Spain and in
France.[1]   *Rondeaux, 109*

JOHN FORTESCUE
c. 1395 – 1476

Moche crye and no wull.[2]
*De Laudibus Legum Angliae
[1471], ch. 10*

Comparisons are odious.[3]   *Ib. 19*

HENRY VI
1421–1471

Kingdoms are but cares,
State is devoid of stay;
Riches are ready snares,
And hasten to decay.
From SIR JOHN HARINGTON,
*Nugae Antiquae [published
1769]*

FRANÇOIS VILLON
1431 – c. 1465

Ah God! Had I but studied
In the days of my foolish youth.[4]
Le Grand Testament, 26

But where are the snows of yester-
year? [5]
*Ib. Ballade des Dames du
Temps Jadis*

In this faith I will to live and die.
*Ib. Ballade de l'Homage à
Notre Dame*

There's no good speech save in Paris.[1]
*Le Grand Testament, Ballade
des Femmes de Paris*

But pray God that he absolve us all! [2]
Codicile

I know all except myself.[3]
Ballade des Menus Propres

GABRIEL BIEL
d. 1495

To be crushed in the winepress of
passion.
*Expositio Canonis Missae,
lectio 52*

Always in these matters desiring
rather to be taught than to teach.
Ib. 53

No one conquers who doesn't fight.
Ib. 78

You get what you pay for.[4]
Ib. 86

ALDUS MANUTIUS
1450–1515

Talk of nothing but business, and
dispatch that business quickly.
*Placard on the door of the
Aldine Press, Venice, es-
tablished about 1490 [5]*

CHRISTOPHER COLUMBUS
1451–1506

The Admiral [Columbus] says here
that today and ever thereafter they had
very mild breezes, that the savor of the
mornings was a great delight, that the
only thing wanting was to hear night-

---

[1] Translated by NORBERT GUTERMAN.
  Thou shalt make castels thanne in Spayne,
  And dreme of joye, all but in vayne.
    JEAN DE MEUN, *The Romaunt of the
    Rose* [c. 1277], *frag. B, l. 2573,* trans-
    lated by CHAUCER
[2] A great cry, but little wool. — CERVANTES,
Don Quixote, pt. II [1615], *bk. III, ch. 13*
  All cry and no wool. — SAMUEL BUTLER,
Hudibras, pt. I [1663], *canto 1, l. 852*
[3] This was a well-known phrase in the four-
teenth century, and has been repeated by many,
including Lydgate, Shakespeare, and Swift.
[4] Hé Dieu! si j'eusse étudié
  Au temps de ma jeunesse folle.
[5] Mais où sont les neiges d'antan?
  See Chaucer, p. 165a.

---

[1] Il n'est bon bec que de Paris.
[2] Mais priez Dieu que tous nous veuille ab-
  soudre.
[3] Je connais tout, fors moi-même.
[4] Pro tali numismate tales merces.
[5] Quoted by THOMAS FROGNALL DIBDIN [1776–
1847] in *Introduction to the Knowledge of Rare
and Valuable Editions of the Greek and Latin
Classics* [1802], *vol. I, p. 436.*

ingales. Says he, "The weather was like April in Andalusia."

Journal of the First Voyage,[1]
September 16, 1492

"Thanks be to God," says the Admiral; "the air is soft as in April in Seville, and it is a pleasure to be in it, so fragrant it is."

Ib. October 8, 1492

Here the people could stand it no longer and complained of the long voyage; but the Admiral cheered them as best he could, holding out good hope of the advantages they would have. He added that it was useless to complain, he had come [to go] to the Indies, and so had to continue it until he found them, with the help of Our Lord.

Ib. October 10, 1492

At two hours after midnight appeared the land, at a distance of 2 leagues. They handed all sails and set the *treo*, which is the mainsail without bonnets, and lay-to waiting for daylight Friday, when they arrived at an island of the Bahamas that was called in the Indians' tongue Guanahaní.

Ib. October 12, 1492

The Admiral says that he never beheld so fair a thing: trees all along the river, beautiful and green, and different from ours, with flowers and fruits each according to their kind, many birds and little birds which sing very sweetly.

Ib. October 28, 1492

The two Christians met on the way many people who were going to their towns, women and men, with a firebrand in the hand, [and] herbs to drink the smoke thereof, as they are accustomed.[2]   *Ib. November 6, 1492*

It is certain, Lord Princes, that when there are such lands there should be profitable things without number; but I tarried not in any harbor, because I sought to see the most countries that I could, to give the story of them to Your Highnesses.

Journal of the First Voyage,
November 27, 1492

And I say that Your Highnesses ought not to consent that any foreigner does business or sets foot here, except Christian Catholics, since this was the end and the beginning of the enterprise, that it should be for the enhancement and glory of the Christian religion, nor should anyone who is not a good Christian come to these parts.[1]
Ib.

The Admiral ordered the lord to be given some things, and he and all his folk rested in great contentment, believing truly that they had come from the sky, and to see the Christians they held themselves very fortunate.

Ib. December 22, 1492

I declared to Your Highnesses that all the gain of this my Enterprise should be spent in the conquest of Jerusalem; and Your Highnesses smiled and said that it pleased you, and that even without this you had that strong desire.   *Ib. December 26, 1492*

The eternal God had given him [Columbus] strength and courage against all, and other things of much wonder which God had showed forth

ed. I 231) describes the process. The Indians made cigars which they called *tobacos,* and inhaled the smoke. He says that the Spaniards are taking it up in Hispaniola, "though I don't know what taste or profit they find in it." Esquemeling's *Buccaneers,* chap. xxvii (on **Cuba**) says "with uncut tobacco leaves they make little bullets that the Spaniards call *gigarros,* and which are smoked without a pipe." — SAMUEL ELIOT MORISON, *Journals and Other Documents on the Life and Voyages of Christopher Columbus*
[1] Here may be found the first suggestion of the exclusive colonial policy that Spain and other nations followed. — SAMUEL ELIOT MORISON, *Journals and Other Documents on the Life and Voyages of Christopher Columbus*

---

[1] BARTOLOMÉ DE LAS CASAS [1474–1566] made an abstract of Columbus's Journal of the First Voyage (*El Libro de la Primera Navegación*) which is the nearest thing to an original journal that we have. The quotations have been selected by SAMUEL ELIOT MORISON from his translation and edition of *Journals and Other Documents on the Life and Voyages of Christopher Columbus* [1963].
[2] The first certain reference in history to smoking tobacco. Las Casas, *Historia* ch. 46 (1951

towards him and for him on that voyage.

*Journal of the First Voyage,
February 14, 1493*

"Of this voyage, I observe," says the Admiral, "that it has miraculously been shown, as may be understood by this writing, by the many signal miracles that He has shown on the voyage, and for me, who for so great a time was in the court of Your Highnesses with the opposition and against the opinion of so many high personages of your household, who were all against me, alleging this undertaking to be folly, which I hope in Our Lord will be to the greater glory of Christianity, which to some slight extent already has happened."

Ib. March 15, 1493

All are most beautiful, of a thousand shapes, and all accessible, and filled with trees of a thousand kinds and tall, and they seem to touch the sky; and I am told that they never lose their foliage, which I can believe, for I saw them as green and beautiful as they are in Spain.

Letter to the Sovereigns on the First Voyage, February 15–March 4, 1493 [1]

It is true that after they have been reassured and have lost this fear, they are so artless and so free with all they possess, that no one would believe it without having seen it. Of anything they have, if you ask them for it, they never say no; rather they invite the person to share it, and show as much love as if they were giving their hearts.

Ib.

And they know neither sect nor idolatry, with the exception that all believe that the source of all power and goodness is in the sky, and they believe very firmly that I, with these ships and people, came from the sky, and in this belief they everywhere received me, after they had overcome their fear. *Ib.*

Your Highnesses will leave no greater memorial; and may they ponder this, that no prince of Castile is to be found, nor have I found one in word or writing, who has ever gained any land outside of Spain; and Your Highnesses have won these vast lands.

*Journal of the Third Voyage,
May 30–August 31, 1498* [1]

I have come to believe that this is a mighty continent which was hitherto unknown. I am greatly supported in this view by reason of this great river [Ozama], and by this sea which is fresh. *Ib.*

I have always read that the world, both land and water, was spherical, as the authority and researches of Ptolemy and all the others who have written on this subject demonstrate and prove, as do the eclipses of the moon and other experiments that are made from east to west, and the elevation of the North Star from north to south.

Letter to the Sovereigns on the Third Voyage, October 18, 1498

Your Highnesses have an Other World here, by which our holy faith can be so greatly advanced and from which such great wealth can be drawn. *Ib.*

I should be judged as a captain who went from Spain to the Indies to conquer a people numerous and warlike, whose manners and religion are very different from ours, who live in sierras and mountains, without fixed settlements, and where by divine will I have placed under the sovereignty of the King and Queen our Lords, an Other World, whereby Spain, which was reckoned poor, is become the richest of countries.

*Letter to Doña Juana de Torres,
October 1500* [2]

[1] This letter, the first and rarest of all printed Americana, describes the scenery and the natives of Hispaniola.

[1] The abstract of the Third Voyage by Bartolomé de Las Casas is less detailed than that of the First. Translated by SAMUEL ELIOT MORISON and MILTON ANASTOS.

[2] Columbus is coming from the Indies as a prisoner to Cadiz.

The tempest was terrible and separated me from my [other] vessels that night, putting every one of them in desperate straits, with nothing to look forward to but death. Each was certain the others had been destroyed. What man ever born, not excepting Job, who would not have died of despair, when in such weather seeking safety for my son, my brother, shipmates, and myself, we were forbidden [access to] the land and the harbors which I, by God's will and sweating blood, had won for Spain?

Lettera Rarissima to the Sovereigns, July 7, 1503 (Fourth Voyage)[1]

I came to serve you at the age of 28 and now I have not a hair on me that is not white, and my body is infirm and exhausted. All that was left to me and my brothers has been taken away and sold, even to the cloak that I wore, without hearing or trial, to my great dishonor.   *Ib.*

Weep for me, whoever has charity, truth and justice! I did not come on this voyage for gain, honor or wealth, that is certain; for then the hope of all such things was dead. I came to Your Highnesses with honest purpose and sincere zeal; and I do not lie. I humbly beseech Your Highnesses that, if it please God to remove me hence, you will help me to go to Rome and on other pilgrimages.   *Ib.*

LEONARDO DA VINCI
1452–1519

Iron rusts from disuse, stagnant water loses its purity, and in cold weather becomes frozen: even so does inaction sap the vigors of the mind.

Notebooks [c. 1500]

Whoever in discussion adduces authority uses not intellect but memory.   *Ib.*

Intellectual passion drives out sensuality.   *Ib.*

Let the street be as wide as the height of the houses.   *Notebooks*

No member needs so great a number of muscles as the tongue; this exceeds all the rest in the number of its movements.   *Ib.*

As a well-spent day brings happy sleep, so life well used brings happy death.   *Ib.*

SEBASTIAN BRANT
1457–1521

The world wants to be deceived.
Ship of Fools [Narrenschiff; 1494]

SIR THOMAS MALORY
fl. 1470

The noble history of the Sangreal,[1] and of the most renowned Christian king, first and chief of the three best Christian and worthy, King Arthur, which ought most to be remembered among us English men tofore all other Christian kings. For it is notoriously known through the universal world that there be nine worthy and the best that ever were. That is to wit three paynims, three Jews, and three Christian men. As for the paynims they were . . . the first Hector of Troy . . . the second Alexander the Great; and the third Julius Caesar. . . . And as for the three Jews . . . the first was Duke Joshua . . . the second David . . . and the third Judas Maccabaeus . . . And sith the said Incarnation have been three noble Christian men . . . of whom was first the noble Arthur. . . . The second was Charlemagne . . . and the third and last was Godfrey of Bouillon.

Le Morte d'Arthur. Preface [1485] *by* WILLIAM CAXTON [c. 1422–1491], *the first English printer*

For herein may be seen noble chivalry, courtesy, humanity, friendliness,

---

[1] Translated by MILTON ANASTOS.

[1] The Holy Grail.

hardiness, love, friendship, cowardice, murder, hate, virtue, and sin. Do after the good and leave the evil, and it shall bring you to good fame and renown.

Le Morte d' Arthur, preface

Whoso pulleth out this sword of this stone and anvil, is rightwise king born of all England.   *Ib. bk. I, ch. 5*

And with that the king saw coming toward him the strangest beast that ever he saw or heard of; so the beast went to the well and drank, and the noise was in the beast's belly like unto the questing of thirty couple hounds; but all the while the beast drank there was no noise in the beast's belly: and therewith the beast departed with a great noise, whereof the king had great marvel. . . . Pellinore, that time king, followed the questing beast.   *Ib. 19*

In the midst of the lake Arthur was ware of an arm clothed in white samite, that held a fair sword in that hand.   *Ib. 25*

Always Sir Arthur lost so much blood that it was marvel he stood on his feet, but he was so full of knighthood that knightly he endured the pain.   *Ib. IV, 9*

What, nephew, said the king, is the wind in that door? [1]   *Ib. VII, 34*

The joy of love is too short, and the sorrow thereof, and what cometh thereof, dureth over long.   *Ib. X, 56*

It is his day.   *Ib. 70*

The month of May was come, when every lusty heart beginneth to blossom, and to bring forth fruit; for like as herbs and trees bring forth fruit and flourish in May, in likewise every lusty heart that is in any manner a lover, springeth and flourisheth in lusty deeds. For it giveth unto all lovers courage, that lusty month of May.

Ib. XVIII, 25

[1] See Shakespeare, p. 246a.

Wherefore I liken love nowadays unto summer and winter; for like as the one is hot and the other cold, so fareth love nowadays; therefore all ye that be lovers call unto your remembrance the month of May, like as did Queen Guenever, for whom I make here a little mention, that while she lived she was a true lover, and therefore she had a good end.

*Le Morte d' Arthur,
bk. XVIII, ch. 25*

And therefore, said the king, wit you well my heart was never so heavy as it is now, and much more I am sorrier for my good knights' loss than for the loss of my fair queen; for queens I might have enow, but such a fellowship of good knights shall never be together in no company.   *Ib. XX, 9*

I shall curse you with book and bell and candle.[1]   *Ib. XXI, 1*

Through this man [Launcelot] and me [Guenever] hath all this war been wrought, and the death of the most noblest knights of the world; for through our love that we have loved together is my most noble lord slain.   *Ib. 9*

For as well as I have loved thee, mine heart will not serve me to see thee, for through thee and me is the flower of kings and knights destroyed.   *Ib.*

Then Sir Launcelot saw her visage, but he wept not greatly, but sighed.   *Ib. 11*

Thou Sir Launcelot, there thou liest, that thou were never matched of earthly knight's hand. And thou were the courteoust knight that ever bare shield. And thou were the truest friend to thy lover that ever bestrad horse. And thou were the truest lover of a sinful man that ever loved woman. And thou were the kindest man that ever struck with sword. And thou were the

[1] The reference is to the ceremony of excommunication, current since the eighth century, performed with bell, book, and candle. See Shakespeare, p. 236b.

goodliest person that ever came among press of knights. And thou were the meekest man and the gentlest that ever ate in hall among ladies. And thou were the sternest knight to thy mortal foe that ever put spear in the rest.
Le Morte d' Arthur,
bk. XXI, ch. 13

JOHN SKELTON
c. 1460 – 1529

I say, thou mad March hare.[1]
Replication Against Certain
Young Scholars

He ruleth all the roost.[2]
Why Come Ye Not to Court,
l. 198

The wolf from the door.[3]   *Ib.* 1531

     Old proverb says,
That bird is not honest
That filleth his own nest.[4]
Poems Against Garnesche

Maid, widow, or wife.
Philip Sparrow

WILLIAM DUNBAR
c. 1465 – c. 1530

London, thou art the flower of Cities all.   *London, refrain*

Gem of all joy, jasper of jocundity.
Ib. st. 3

Timor Mortis conturbat me.[5]
Lament for the Makers [6]
(Makaris) [c. 1508] *refrain*

---

[1] Mad as a March hare. — JOHN HEYWOOD, *Proverbs* [1546], *pt. II, ch. 5*
[2] Rule the rost. — JOHN HEYWOOD, *Proverbs* [1546], *pt. I, ch. 5*
Her that ruled the rost. — THOMAS HEYWOOD, *History of Women* [ed. 1624]
Rules the roast. — JONSON, CHAPMAN, MARSTON, *Eastward Ho* [1605], *act II, sc. ii*
[3] To Keepe the woolfe from the durre. — JOHN HEYWOOD, *Proverbs* [1546], *pt. II, ch. 7*
[4] It is a foul bird that filleth his own nest. — JOHN HEYWOOD, *Proverbs* [1546], *pt. II, ch. 5*
[5] Fear of Death hath me in thrall.
[6] Makers: poets.

Our plesance here is all vain glory,
This false world is but transitory.
Lament for the Makers, st. 2

DESIDERIUS ERASMUS
1465–1536

It is folly alone that stays the fugue of Youth and beats off louring Old Age.   *The Praise of Folly* [1509]

They may attack me with an army of six hundred syllogisms; and if I do not recant, they will proclaim me a heretic.
Ib.

A peck of troubles.
Apothegms [1542]

FERNANDO DE ROJAS
c. 1465 – c. 1538

Goods which are not shared are not goods.   *La Celestina, act I*

The use of riches is better than their possession.   *Ib. II*

The first step towards madness is to think oneself wise.   *Ib.*

Riches do not make one rich but busy.   *Ib. IV*

No one is so old that he cannot live yet another year, nor so young that he cannot die today.   *Ib.*

When God wounds from on high he will follow with the remedy.   *Ib. X*

When one door closes, fortune will usually open another.   *Ib. XV*

NICCOLÓ MACHIAVELLI[1]
1469–1527

There is nothing more difficult to take in hand, more perilous to conduct,

---

[1] Every Country hath its Machiavel. — SIR THOMAS BROWNE, *Religio Medici* [1642], *p. 24* [Everyman ed.]
Out of his surname they have coined an epithet for a knave, and out of his Christian name a synonym for the Devil. — MACAULAY, *Machiavelli* [1827]
See Butler, p. 353a.

or more uncertain in its success, than to take the lead in the introduction of a new order of things.
The Prince,[1] *ch. 6*

From this arises the question whether it is better to be loved rather than feared, or feared rather than loved. It might perhaps be answered that we should wish to be both: but since love and fear can hardly exist together, if we must choose between them, it is far safer to be feared than loved.[2]　*Ib. 8*

The chief foundations of all states, new as well as old or composite, are good laws and good arms; and as there cannot be good laws where the state is not well armed, it follows that where they are well armed they have good laws.　*Ib. 12*

A prince should therefore have no other aim or thought, nor take up any other thing for his study, but war and its organization and discipline, for that is the only art that is necessary to one who commands.　*Ib. 14*

Among other evils which being unarmed brings you, it causes you to be despised.　*Ib.*

But my intention being to write something of use to those who understand, it appears to me more proper to go to the real truth of the matter than to its imagination; and many have imagined republics and principalities which have never been seen or known to exist in reality; for how we live is so far removed from how we ought to live, that he who abandons what is done for what ought to be done, will rather bring about his own ruin than his preservation.　*Ib. 15*

The prince who relies upon their words, without having otherwise provided for his security, is ruined; for friendships that are won by awards, and not by greatness and nobility of soul, although deserved, yet are not real, and

cannot be depended upon in time of adversity.　　*The Prince, ch.* 17

A prince being thus obliged to know well how to act as a beast must imitate the fox and the lion, for the lion cannot protect himself from traps, and the fox cannot defend himself from wolves. One must therefore be a fox to recognize traps, and a lion to frighten wolves.　*Ib.*

When neither their property nor their honor is touched, the majority of men live content.　*Ib. 19*

There are three classes of intellects: one which comprehends by itself; another which appreciates what others comprehend; and a third which neither comprehends by itself nor by the showing of others; the first is the most excellent, the second is good, the third is useless.　*Ib. 22*

There is no other way of guarding oneself against flattery than by letting men understand that they will not offend you by speaking the truth; but when everyone can tell you the truth, you lose their respect.　*Ib. 23*

Where the willingness is great, the difficulties cannot be great.　*Ib. 26*

God is not willing to do everything, and thus take away our free will and that share of glory which belongs to us.　*Ib.*

Whoever desires to found a state and give it laws, must start with assuming that all men are bad and ever ready to display their vicious nature, whenever they may find occasion for it.
Discourse Upon the First Ten Books of Livy, bk. I, ch. 3

The people resemble a wild beast,[1] which, naturally fierce and accustomed to live in the woods, has been brought up, as it were, in a prison and in servitude, and having by accident got its liberty, not being accustomed to search for its food, and not knowing where to

---

[1] Translated by W. K. MARRIOTT.
[2] See Accius, p. 109b.

[1] See Horace, p. 123a, and note.

conceal itself, easily becomes the prey of the first who seeks to incarcerate it again.

> *Discourse Upon the First Ten Books of Livy, bk. I, ch. 16*

CHARLES VIII
1470–1498

This is our gracious will.[1]

> *Royal Order of March 12, 1497*

NICHOLAS COPERNICUS
1473–1543

Finally we shall place the Sun himself at the center of the Universe. All this is suggested by the systematic procession of events and the harmony of the whole Universe, if only we face the facts, as they say, "with both eyes open."

> *De Revolutionibus Orbium Coelestium* [1543][2]

LUDOVICO ARIOSTO
1474–1533

Nature made him, and then broke the mold.[3]

> *Orlando Furioso* [1532], canto X, st. 84

MICHELANGELO (BUONARROTI)
1474–1564

The more the marble wastes, the more the statue grows.   *Sonnet*

If it be true that any beautiful thing raises the pure and just desire of man from earth to God, the eternal fount of all, such I believe my love.   *Sonnet*

The power of one fair face makes my love sublime, for it has weaned my heart from low desires.   *Sonnet*

I live and love in God's peculiar light.   *Ib.*

---

[1] Tel est notre bon plaisir.
[2] Translated by JOHN F. DOBSON.
[3] Natura il fece, e poi ruppe la stampa.
See Byron, p. 559a.

SIR THOMAS MORE[1]
1478–1535

They wonder much to hear that gold, which in itself is so useless a thing, should be everywhere so much esteemed, that even men for whom it was made, and by whom it has its value, should yet be thought of less value than it is.

> *Utopia* [1516]. *Of Jewels and Wealth*

They have no lawyers among them, for they consider them as a sort of people whose profession it is to disguise matters.

> *Ib. Of Law and Magistrates*

Plato by a goodly similitude declareth, why wise men refrain to meddle in the commonwealth. For when they see the people swarm into the streets, and daily wet to the skin with rain, and yet cannot persuade them to go out of the rain, they do keep themselves within their houses, seeing they cannot remedy the folly of the people.[2]

> *Ib. Concerning the Best State of a Commonwealth*

A little wanton money, which burned out the bottom of his purse.

> *Works* [c. 1530], *p. 195*

This is a fair tale of a tub told of his election.[3]

> *Confutation of Tyndale's Answers* (1532)

For men use, if they have an evil turn, to write it in marble: and whoso doth us a good turn we write it in dust.[4]

> *Richard III and His Miserable End* [1543]

---

[1] Canonized by Pope Pius XI [1935].
See Robert Whittinton, p. 179a.
[2] In the modern phrase, "not sense enough to come in out of the rain."
[3] A tale of a tub is a cock-and-bull story. Jonson used it as the title of a comedy [1633] and Swift as the title of a satire [1696].
[4] See Sophocles, p. 83a, and note.
Words writ in waters. — GEORGE CHAPMAN [c. 1559–c. 1634], *Revenge for Honor, act. V, sc. ii*
L'injure se grave en métal; et le bienfait

See me safe up: for my coming down, I can shift for myself.
> *On ascending the scaffold. From* FROUDE, *History of England* [1856–1870]

This hath not offended the king.
> *As he drew his beard aside upon placing his head on the block. From* BACON, *Apothegms, no. 22*

ROBERT WHITTINTON
c. 1480 – c. 1530

More [1] is a man of angel's wit and singular learning; I know not his fellow. For where is the man of that gentleness, lowliness and affability? And as time requireth, a man of marvelous mirth and pastimes; and sometimes of as sad a gravity; a man for all seasons.[2]
> *Passage composed for schoolboys to put into Latin*

MARTIN LUTHER
1483–1546

If it were an art to overcome heresy with fire, the executioners would be the most learned doctors on earth.
> *To the Christian Nobility of the German States* [1520]

Here I stand, I cannot do otherwise.[3]
> *Speech at the Diet of Worms, April 18, 1521*

The mad mob does not ask how it could be better, only that it be different. And when it then becomes worse, it must change again. Thus they get bees for flies, and at last hornets for bees.
> *Whether Soldiers Can Also Be in a State of Grace* [1526]

A mighty fortress is our God,
A bulwark never failing.
Our helper He amid the flood
Of mortal ills prevailing.[1]
> *Hymn, Ein' Feste Burg* [1529]

What can only be taught by the rod and with blows will not lead to much good; they will not remain pious any longer than the rod is behind them.
> *The Great Catechism. Second Command* [1529]

Peace is more important than all justice; and peace was not made for the sake of justice, but justice for the sake of peace.   *On Marriage* [1530]

Justice is a temporary thing that must at last come to an end; but the conscience is eternal and will never die.   *Ib.*

Superstition, idolatry, and hypocrisy have ample wages, but truth goes a-begging.   *Table Talk* [1569], 53

For where God built a church, there the Devil would also build a chapel [2] . . . Thus is the Devil ever God's ape.   *Ib.* 67

The Mass is the greatest blasphemy of God, and the highest idolatry upon earth, an abomination the like of which has never been in Christendom since the time of the Apostles.   *Ib.* 171

There is no more lovely, friendly and charming relationship, communion or company than a good marriage.
     Ib. 292

---

s'escrit en l'onde [An injury is engraved in metal, but a benefit is written in water]. — JEAN BERTAUT [c. 1611]

All your better deeds shall be in water writ, but this in marble. — BEAUMONT AND FLETCHER, *Philaster* [1620], act V, sc. iii

[1] Sir Thomas More.
[2] See Ben Jonson, p. 303b.
[3] Hier steh' ich, ich kann nicht anders.
Inscribed on his monument at Worms.

[1] Ein' feste burg is unser Gott,
   ein gute wehr und waffen.
   Er hilft uns frei aus aller not,
   die uns itzt hat betroffen.
Translated by FREDERICK HENRY HEDGE [1853].
Great God! there is no safety here below;
Thou art my fortress, thou that seem'st my foe.
     FRANCIS QUARLES [1592–1644], *Divine Poems*

See *Psalm 46:1*, p. 19a.
[2] Where God hath a temple, the Devil will have a chapel. — ROBERT BURTON, *Anatomy of Melancholy* [1621–1651], *pt. III, sec. 4, member 1, subsec. 1*
No sooner is a temple built to God but the Devil builds a chapel hard by. — GEORGE HERBERT, *Jacula Prudentum* [1640]
See Defoe, p. 385a.

A theologian is born by living, nay dying and being damned, not by thinking, reading, or speculating.
Table Talk, 352

Reason is the greatest enemy that faith has: it never comes to the aid of spiritual things, but — more frequently than not — struggles against the divine Word, treating with contempt all that emanates from God. *Ib.* 353

If I had heard that as many devils would set on me in Worms as there are tiles on the roofs, I should none the less have ridden there.
Luthers Sammtliche Schriften [1745], XVI, 14

He remains a fool his whole life long Who loves not women, wine, and song. *Attributed* [1]

It makes a difference whose ox is gored.[2]
Works [1854 ed.], vol. LXII, *p. 449*

HUGH LATIMER
1485–1555

Play the man, Master Ridley; we shall this day light such a candle, by God's grace, in England, as I trust shall never be put out.[3]
Addressed to Nicholas Ridley [1500–1555] as they were being burned alive at Oxford for heresy, October 16, 1555.[4] From J. R. GREEN, A Short History of the English People, ch. 7

[1] First mentioned in *Wandsbecker Bothen, no. 75* [1775].
[2] This is the moral of the fable of the lawyer, the farmer, and the farmer's ox, which was included in NOAH WEBSTER, *American Spelling Book* [1802], entitled *The Partial Judge*.
[3] See *II Esdras 14:25*, p. 36b, and note 1, p. 981b.
[4] See Latimer and Ridley in the might
Of Faith stand coupled for a common flight!
WORDSWORTH [1770–1850], *Ecclesiastical Sonnets, pt. II, no. 34, Latimer and Ridley*

ST. IGNATIUS LOYOLA [1]
1491–1556

Teach us, good Lord, to serve Thee as Thou deservest:
To give and not to count the cost;
To fight and not to heed the wounds;
To toil and not to seek for rest;
To labor and not ask for any reward
Save that of knowing that we do Thy will.
Prayer for Generosity [1548]

PHILIPPUS AUREOLUS PARACELSUS
c. 1493 – 1541

Every experiment is like a weapon which must be used in its particular way — a spear to thrust, a club to strike. Experimenting requires a man who knows when to thrust and when to strike, each according to need and fashion.[2] *Chirurgische Bucher* [1605]

FRANCIS I OF FRANCE
1494–1547

All is lost save honor.[3]
Letter to his mother after defeat at Pavia, February 23, 1525

FRANÇOIS RABELAIS
c. 1494 – 1553

Break the bone and suck out the substantific marrow.
Gargantua and Pantagruel,[4] bk. I [1532], prologue

To laugh is proper to man.[5]
Ib. Rabelais to the Reader

Appetite comes with eating [6] . . . but the thirst goes away with drinking.
Ib. ch. 5

[1] Founder of the Society of Jesus.
[2] Translated by HENRY M. PACHTER.
[3] Tout est perdu fors l'honneur.
The actual words written were: De toutes choses ne m'est demeuré que l'honneur et la vie qui est saulvé. The letter is in DULAURE, *Histoire Civile, Physique et Morale de Paris* [1821–1825].
[4] Translated by SIR THOMAS URQUHART and PETER ANTHONY MOTTEUX [1653–1694].
[5] Pour ce que rire est le propre de l'homme.
[6] My appetite comes to me while eating. — MONTAIGNE, *Essays* [1580–1595], *III, 9*

War begun without good provision of money beforehand for going through with it is but as a breathing of strength and blast that will quickly pass away. Coin is the sinews of war.[1]
Gargantua and Pantagruel bk. I, Rableais to the Reader, ch. 46

How shall I be able to rule over others, that have not full power and command of myself? [2]   *Ib. 52*

Do what thou wilt.[3]   *Ib. 57*

Wisdom entereth not into a malicious mind, and science without conscience is but the ruin of the soul.
          Ib. II [1534], 8

Subject to a kind of disease, which at that time they called lack of money.[4]
          Ib. II, 16

So much is a man worth as he esteems himself.   *Ib. 29*

A good crier of green sauce.   *Ib. 31*

Then I began to think that it is very true which is commonly said, that the one half of the world knoweth not how the other half liveth.[5]   *Ib. 32*

This flea which I have in mine ear.
          Ib. III [1545], 31

Oh thrice and four times happy those who plant cabbages! [6]
          Ib. IV [1548], 18

Which was performed to a T.[7]
          Ib. 41

[1] See Bion, p. 104b, and note.
[2] He is most powerful who has power over himself. — SENECA [8 B.C.–A.D. 65] *Epistles 90, 34*
See Massinger, p. 315b.
[3] Fais ce que voudras.
[4] See Shakespeare, p. 241b.
Or that eternal want of pence,
Which vexes public men.
     TENNYSON, *Will Waterproof's Lyrical Monologue* [1842], st. 6
[5] See Herbert, p. 325a.
[6] See Montaigne, p. 189b, and Voltaire, p. 417a.
[7] We could manage this matter to a T. — STERNE, *Tristram Shandy, bk. II* [1760], *ch. 5*
You see they'd have fitted him to a T. — SAMUEL JOHNSON; from BOSWELL, *Life* [1791]
You will find it shall echo my speech to a T. — THOMAS MOORE [1779–1852], *Address for the Opening of the New Theatre of St. Stephen*

He that has patience may compass anything.
Gargantua and Pantagruel bk. IV, Rabelais to the Reader, ch. 48

We will take the good will for the deed.[1]   *Ib. 49*

Speak the truth and shame the Devil.[2]
          Ib. V [1552], author's prologue

Plain as a nose in a man's face.[3]
          Ib.

Like hearts of oak.[4]   *Ib.*

Go hang yourselves [critics] . . . you shall never want rope enough.[5]
          Ib.

Looking as like . . . as one pea does like another.[6]   *Ib. ch. 2*

And thereby hangs a tale.[7]   *Ib. 4*

It is meat, drink, and cloth to us.
          Ib. 7

[1] The will for deed I do accept. — DU BARTAS, *Divine Weeks and Works* [1578], *Second Week, Third Day, pt. II*
You must take the will for the deed. — SWIFT, *Polite Conversation* [1738], *Dialogue 2*
[2] While you live, tell truth and shame the devil! — SHAKESPEARE, *Henry IV, pt. I, act III, sc. i, l. 58*
I'd tell the truth, and shame the devil. — SAMUEL JOHNSON; from BOSWELL, *Boswell's Life of Johnson* [1791], *vol. I, p. 460* [Everyman ed.]
Truth being truth,
Tell it and shame the devil.
     BROWNING, *The Ring and the Book* [1868–1869], *III, The Other Half-Rome*
[3] See Shakespeare, p. 220b.
As clear and as manifest as the nose in a man's face. — ROBERT BURTON, *Anatomy of Melancholy* [1621–1651], *pt. III, sec. 3, member 4, subsec. 1*
[4] See Garrick, p. 439a.
[5] They were suffered to have rope enough till they had haltered themselves. — THOMAS FULLER, *The Historie of the Holy Warre* [1639], *bk. 5, ch. 7*
Give a man enough rope and he'll hang himself.   *Proverb*
[6] As lyke as one pease is to another. — LYLY, *Euphues* [1579]
They say we are
Almost as like as eggs.
     SHAKESPEARE, *The Winter's Tale* [1608–1611], *act I, sc. ii, l. 130*
As one egg is like another. — CERVANTES, *Don Quixote, pt. II* [1615], *bk. III, ch. 14*
[7] Also in Shakespeare, *Taming of the Shrew IV, i, 60, p. 219b.*

I am going to seek a grand perhaps;
draw the curtain, the farce is played.[1]
> *Alleged last words. From*
> MOTTEUX, *Life of Rabelais*

JOHN HEYWOOD[2]
c. 1497 – c. 1580

All a green willow, willow, willow,
All a green willow is my garland.[3]
> *The Green Willow*

The loss of wealth is loss of dirt,
As sages in all times assert;
The happy man's without a shirt.[4]
> *Be Merry Friends*

Let the world slide,[5] let the world go;
A fig for care, and a fig for woe!
If I can't pay, why I can owe,
And death makes equal the high and
    low.   *Ib.*

Haste maketh waste.[6]
> *Proverbs* [1546], *pt. I, ch. 2*

Good to be merry and wise.   *Ib.*

Beaten with his own rod.   *Ib.*

Look ere ye leap.[7]   *Ib.*

[1] Je m'en vais chercher un grand peut-être;
tirez le rideau, la farce est jouée.
His religion, at best, is an anxious wish; like
that of Rabelais, "a great Perhaps." — CARLYLE,
Essays, Burns.
The grand perhaps. — BROWNING, *Bishop
Blougram's Apology*
[2] JOHN HEYWOOD's *Proverbs,* first printed in
1546, is the earliest collection of English col-
loquial sayings. The selection here given is
from the edition of 1874 (a reprint of 1598),
edited by JULIAN SHARMAN. See also *Oxford
Dictionary of English Proverbs,* compiled by
WILLIAM G. SMITH and revised by PAUL HARVEY
[2nd ed., 1948], and *A Dictionary of the Proverbs
in English in the 16th and 17th Centuries,* compiled by MORRIS PALMER TILLEY [1950].
[3] The earliest known of the "willow" songs.
See Shakespeare, p. 276a.
[4] This line is the theme of many poems.
[5] Let the world slide. — *Towneley Mysteries*
[1420].
Let the world slide. — SHAKESPEARE, *Taming
of the Shrew* [1593–1594], *Induction, sc. i, l. 6*
[6] In wikked haste is no profit. — CHAUCER,
Canterbury Tales [c. 1387], *Melibee, 2240*
[7] Thou shouldst have looked before thou hadst
leapt. — JONSON, CHAPMAN, MARSTON, *Eastward
Ho* [1605], *act V, sc. i*
See Samuel Butler, p. 353a.

While between two stools my tail go
to the ground.[1]
> *Proverbs, pt. I, ch. 2*

He that will not when he may,
When he would he shall have nay.[2]
> *Ib.* 3

The fat is in the fire.   *Ib.*

When the sun shineth, make hay.
                        Ib.

The tide tarrieth no man.[3]   *Ib.*

Fast bind, fast find.[4]   *Ib.*

And while I at length debate and beat
    the bush,
There shall step in other men and catch
    the birds.[5]   *Ib.*

Wedding is destiny,
And hanging likewise.[6]   *Ib.*

Happy man, happy dole.[7]   *Ib.*

[1] Between two stools one sits on the ground.
— *Les Proverbes del Vilain,* MS Bodleian [c.
1303]
[2] He that will not when he may,
When he will he shall have nay.
     ROBERT BURTON, *Anatomy of Melan-
     choly* [1621–1651], *pt. III, sec. 2, mem-
     ber 5, subsec. 5*
[3] See Chaucer, p. 168b.
Time nor tide tarrieth no man. — ROBERT
GREENE, *Disputations* [1592]
    Hoist up sail while gale doth last,
    Tide and wind stay no man's pleasure.
         ROBERT SOUTHWELL, *St. Peter's
                   Complaint* [1595]
    Nae man can tether time or tide. — BURNS,
Tam O'Shanter [1787]
[4] Dry sun, dry wind;
    Safe bind, safe find.
         THOMAS TUSSER, *A Hundred Points
         of Good Husbandry* [1557] *October's
         Abstract, Washing*
    Fast bind, fast find;
    A proverb never stale in thrifty mind.
         SHAKESPEARE, *Merchant of Venice*
         [1596–1597], *act II, sc. v, l. 54*
[5] It is this proverb which Henry V is reported
to have uttered at the siege of Orleans: Shall
I beat the bush and another take the bird?
[6] Hanging and wiving go by destiny. — *The
Schole-hous for Women* [1541]
Marriage and hanging go by destiny; matches
are made in heaven. — ROBERT BURTON, *Anatomy of Melancholy* [1621–1651], *pt. III, sec. 2,
member 5, subsec. 5*
[7] Happy man be his dole. — SHAKESPEARE,
Merry Wives of Windsor [1600–1601], *act III,
sc. iv, l. 68* and *Winter's Tale* [1609–1611], *act I,
sc. ii, l. 163*

God never send'th mouth but he sendeth meat.[1]

Proverbs, pt. I, ch. 4

A hard beginning maketh a good ending.   *Ib.*

Like will to like.[2]   *Ib.*

When the sky falleth we shall have larks.   *Ib.*

More frayd then hurt.   *Ib.*

Nothing is impossible to a willing heart.   *Ib.*

Let the world wag, and take mine ease in mine inn.[3]   *Ib. 5*

Hold their noses to grindstone.[4]
     Ib.

A sleeveless errand.[5]   *Ib. 7*

Reckoners without their host must reckon twice.[6]   *Ib. 8*

Cut my coat after my cloth.[7]   *Ib.*

The nearer to the church, the further from God.[8]   *Ib. 9*

Now for good luck, cast an old shoe after me.   *Proverbs, pt. I, ch. 9*

Better is to bow than break.[1]   *Ib.*

It hurteth not the tongue to give fair words.[2]   *Ib.*

Two heads are better than one.
     Ib.

A short horse is soon curried.
     Ib. 10

To tell tales out of school.   *Ib.*

To hold with the hare and run with the hound.   *Ib.*

Neither fish nor flesh, nor good red herring.   *Ib.*

All is well that ends well.[3]   *Ib.*

Of a good beginning cometh a good end.[4]   *Ib.*

When the steed is stolen, shut the stable door.[5]   *Ib.*

She looketh as butter would not melt in her mouth.   *Ib.*

Ill weed groweth fast.[6]   *Ib.*

---

[1] God sendeth and giveth both mouth and the meat. — THOMAS TUSSER, *Five Hundred Points of Good Husbandry* [1557]
God sends meat, and the Devil sends cooks. — JOHN TAYLOR, *Works* [1630], vol. II, p. 85
     The holy prophet Zoroaster said,
     The Lord who made thy teeth shall give
         thee bread.   *Persian couplet*

[2] See Homer, p. 66b.
"Like to like" is quoted by Aristotle in *Rhetoric I, 11, 25.*
See Robert Burton, p. 311b.

[3] Shall I not take mine ease in mine inn? — SHAKESPEARE, *Henry IV, pt. I* [1597–1598], *act III, sc. iii, l. 91*

[4] And hold one another's noses to the grindstone hard. — ROBERT BURTON, *Anatomy of Melancholy* [1621–1651], *pt. III, sec. 1, member 3*

[5] Chaucer and Shakespeare use the phrase.
Sending every one of her children upon some sleeveless errand, as she terms it. — JOSEPH ADDISON, *The Spectator, no. 47* [April 24, 1711] (referring to April Fool errands)

[6] He reckoneth without his Hostesse. Love knoweth no lawes. — LYLY, *Euphues* [1579]

[7] A relic of the Sumptuary Laws. One of the earliest [1530] instances occurs in the interlude of *Godly Queene Hester.*

[8] Qui est près de l'église est souvent loin de Dieu [He who is near the Church is often far from God]. — *Les Proverbes Communs* [c. 1500]
     To Kerke the narre, from God more farre,
     Has bene an old sayd sawe.

     And he that strives to touch the starre,
     Oft stombles at a strawe.
         SPENSER, *The Shepheardes Calender*
             [1579], *July, l. 97*

[1] Rather to bow than break is profitable; Humility is a thing commendable.
     The Moral Proverbs of Cristyne [1390]

[2] Fair words never hurt the tongue. — JONSON, CHAPMAN, MARSTON, *Eastward Ho* [1605], *act IV, sc. i*

[3] Si finis bonus est, totum bonum erit [If the end is good, all will be good]. — *Gesta Romanorum* [1472], *tale 67*
See Shakespeare, *Troilus and Cressida, act IV, sc. v, l. 223,* p. 269b, and *All's Well That Ends Well, act IV, sc. iv, l. 35,* p. 270a, and note.

[4] See Plato, p. 94a; Aristotle, p. 98b; and Horace, p. 123a.
     Who that well his warke beginneth,
     The rather a good ende he winneth.
         GOWER, *Confessio Amantis*
             [c. 1386–1390]

[5] Quant le cheval est emblé dounke ferme fols l'estable [When the horse has been stolen, the fool shuts the stable]. — *Les Proverbes del Vilain* [c. 1303]

[6] Ewyl weed ys sone y-growe. — *MS Harleian* [c. 1490]

(*note continues p. 184*)

It is a dear collop
That is cut out of th' own flesh.[1]
Proverbs, pt. I, ch. 10

Beggars should be no choosers.
Ib.

Merry as a cricket. *Ib.* 11

To rob Peter and pay Paul.[2] *Ib.*

A man may well bring a horse to the
water,
But he cannot make him drink without
he will.[3] *Ib.*

Kinde will creep where it may not
go.[4] *Ib.*

The cat would eat fish, and would
not wet her feet.[5] *Ib.*

Rome was not built in one day.
Ib.

Ye have many strings to your bow.[6]
Ib.

Children learn to creep ere they can
learn to go. *Ib.*

Great weeds do grow apace. — SHAKESPEARE,
Richard III [1592–1593], act II, sc. iv, l. 13
An ill weed grows apace. — GEORGE CHAPMAN,
An Humorous Day's Mirth [1599]
[1] God knows thou art a collop of my flesh. —
SHAKESPEARE, *Henry VI* [1591], *pt. I, act V,
sc. iv, l. 18*
[2] Rob Peter, and pay Paul. — ROBERT BUR-
TON, *Anatomy of Melancholy* [1621–1651], *Democritus to the Reader*
Give not Saint Peter so much, to leave Saint
Paul nothing. — GEORGE HERBERT, *Jacula Prudentum* [1640]
"To rob Peter and pay Paul" is said to have
had its origin in the reign of Edward VI when
the lands of St. Peter at Westminster were ap-
propriated to raise money for the repair of St.
Paul's in London.
The French form of the proverb is: Découvrir
saint Pierre pour couvrir saint Paul.
[3] You may bring a horse to the river, but he
will drink when and what he pleaseth. — GEORGE
HERBERT, *Jacula Prudentum* [1640]
[4]   You know that love
Will creep in service when it cannot go.
SHAKESPEARE, *Two Gentlemen of Verona* [1594–1595], act IV, sc. ii, l. 19
[5] Cat lufat visch, ac he nele his feth wete. —
MS Trinity College, Cambridge [c. 1250]
See Shakespeare, *Macbeth I, vii, 44,* p. 282b.
[6] Two strings to his bow. — RICHARD HOOKER,
Laws of Ecclesiastical Polity, bk. V [1597]*, ch. 80*

Better is half a loaf than no bread.
Proverbs, pt. I, ch. 11

Nought venture nought have.[1]
Ib.

Children and fools cannot lie.[2]
Ib.

All is fish that cometh to net.[3]
Ib.

Who is worse shod than the shoemaker's wife? [4] *Ib.*

One good turn asketh another.
Ib.

A dog hath a day. *Ib.*

A hair of the dog that bit us.[5]
Ib.

But in deed,
A friend is never known till a man have
need.[6] *Ib.*

New broom sweepeth clean.
Ib. II, 1

Burnt child fire dreadeth.[7] *Ib.* 2

There is no fool to the old fool.[8]
Ib.

All is not gospel that thou dost
speak. *Ib.*

A fool's bolt is soon shot.[9] *Ib.* 3

[1] See Chaucer, p. 165a and W. S. Gilbert, p.
768a.
[2] 'Tis an old saw, Children and fooles speake
true. — LYLY, *Endymion* [1591]
[3] All's fish they get that cometh to net. —
TUSSER, *Five Hundred Points of Good Husbandry* [1557]*, February Abstract*
[4] Him that makes shoes go barefoot himself.
— ROBERT BURTON, *Anatomy of Melancholy*
[1621–1651]*, Democritus to the Reader*
[5] Old receipt books advised that an inebriate
should drink sparingly in the morning some of
the same kind of liquor which he had drunk
to excess the night before.
[6] See Aristotle, p. 99a.
[7] Brend child fur dredth,
Quoth Hendyng.
Proverbs of Hendyng, MS [c. 1320]
[8] There is no fool like an old fool. — JOHN
LYLY, *Mother Bombie* [1592]*, act IV, sc. ii,* and
in frequent use thereafter.
[9] Sottes bolt is sone shote. — *Proverbs of
Hendyng, MS* [c. 1320]

A woman hath nine lives like a cat.
        Proverbs, pt. II, ch. 4

A penny for your thought.   *Ib.*

You cannot see the wood for the trees.   *Ib.*

You stand in your own light.   *Ib.*

Tit for tat.[1]   *Ib.*

Three may keep counsel, if two be away.[2]   *Ib. 5*

Small pitchers have wide ears.[3]   *Ib.*

Many hands make light work.   *Ib.*

Out of God's blessing into the warm sun.[4]   *Ib.*

There is no fire without some smoke.[5]   *Ib.*

A cat may look on a king.   *Ib.*

Have ye him on the hip.[6]   *Ib.*

        Much water goeth by the mill
That the miller knoweth not of.[7]
        Ib.

He must needs go whom the devil doth drive.   *Ib. 7*

Set the cart before the horse.   *Ib.*

The more the merrier.
        Proverbs, pt. II, ch. 7

    It is better to be
An old man's darling than a young man's warling.   *Ib.*

    Be the day never so long,
Evermore at last they ring to evensong.[1]   *Ib.*

The moon is made of a green cheese.[2]   *Ib.*

I know on which side my bread is buttered.   *Ib.*

The wrong sow by th' ear.   *Ib. 9*

An ill wind that bloweth no man to good.[3]   *Ib.*

For when I gave you an inch, you took an ell.[4]   *Ib.*

Would ye both eat your cake and have your cake?[5]   *Ib.*

Every man for himself and God for us all.[6]   *Ib.*

Though he love not to buy the pig in the poke.[7]   *Ib.*

---

[1] This is a corruption of *Tant pour tant.*
[2] Two may keep counsel when the third's away. — SHAKESPEARE, *Titus Andronicus* [1593–1594], act IV, sc. ii, l. *145*
    Three can hold their peace if two be away. — GEORGE HERBERT, *Jacula Prudentum* [1640]
[3] Pitchers have ears. — SHAKESPEARE, *The Taming of the Shrew* [1593–1594], act IV, sc. iv, l. *52*, and *Richard III* [1592–1593], II, iv, *37*
    Little pitchers have wide ears. — GEORGE HERBERT, *Jacula Prudentum* [1640]
[4] Thou shalt come out of a warme sunne into Gods blessing. — LYLY, *Euphues* [1579]
    Thou out of Heaven's benediction comest
    To the warm sun.
        SHAKESPEARE, *King Lear* [1605–1606], act II, sc. ii, l. *168*
[5] There can no great smoke arise, but there must be some fire. — LYLY, *Euphues* [1579]
[6] See Shakespeare, p. 232a.
[7]   More water glideth by the mill
    Than wots the miller of.
        SHAKESPEARE, *Titus Andronicus* [1593–1594], act II, sc. i, l. *85*
    The miller sees not all the water that goes by his mill. — ROBERT BURTON, *Anatomy of Melancholy* [1621–1651], pt. III, sec. 3, member 4, subsec. *1*

[1] Be the day short or never so long,
    At length it ringeth to evensong.
        Quoted at the stake by George Tankerfield [1555] (FOXE, *Book of Martyrs* [1563], *ch. 7*)
[2] They wold make me believe that the moon was made of greene cheese. — JOHN FRITH, *A Pistle to the Christian Reader* [1529]
[3] Except wind stands as never it stood,
    It is an ill wind turns none to good.
        THOMAS TUSSER [1524–1580], *A Description of the Properties of Winds*
    Ill blows the wind that profits nobody. — SHAKESPEARE, *King Henry VI* [1591], pt. III, act II, sc. v, l. *55*
    Falstaff. What wind blew you hither, Pistol?
    Pistol. Not the ill wind which blows no man to good.
        SHAKESPEARE, *Henry IV* [1597–1598], pt. II, act V, sc. iii, l. *87*
[4] Give an inch, he'll take an ell. — JOHN WEBSTER [1580–1625], *Sir Thomas Wyatt*
[5] Wouldst thou both eat thy cake and have it? — GEORGE HERBERT, *The Size* [1633]
[6] Every man for himself, his own ends, the Devil for all. — ROBERT BURTON, *Anatomy of Melancholy* [1621–1651], pt. III, sec. *1*, member 3
[7] For buying or selling of pig in a poke. — TUSSER, *Five Hundred Points of Good Husbandry* [1557], *September Abstract*

This hitteth the nail on the head.
Proverbs, pt. II, ch. 11

Enough is as good as a feast. *Ib.*

JULIUS III[1]
d. 1555

Do you not know, my son, with what little understanding the world is ruled? [2]

> *To a Portuguese monk who sympathized with the Pope's burdens of office*

CHARLES V[3]
1500–1558

Fortune hath somewhat the nature of a woman; if she be too much wooed, she is the farther off.

> *From* FRANCIS BACON, *Advancement of Learning, bk. II*

Iron hand in a velvet glove.

> *Attributed to Charles V by* THOMAS CARLYLE, *Latter-Day Pamphlets, 11*

I make war on the living, not on the dead.

> *Said when advised to hang Luther's corpse on the gallows* [1546]

GREGORY XIII[4]
1502–1585

To the greater glory of God.[5]

> *Quoted in The Canons and Decrees of the Council of Trent* [1542–1560]

FERDINAND I
1503–1564

Let justice be done, though the world perish.[6]

> *From* MANLIUS, *Loci Communes, II, 290*

---

[1] Pope from 1550 to 1555.
[2] An nescis, mi fili, quantilla prudentia mundus regatur?
[3] See Lomonosov, p. 434b.
[4] Pope from 1572 to 1585.
[5] Ad maiorem Dei gloriam. Motto of the Society of Jesus.
[6] Fiat iustitia, et pereat mundus.
See Sir Thomas Browne, p. 330b.

SIR THOMAS WYATT
c. 1503 – 1542

Forget not yet the tried intent
Of such a truth as I have meant;
My great travail so gladly spent,
Forget not yet!

> *Forget Not Yet*

And wilt thou leave me thus?
Say nay, say nay, for shame!

> *The Appeal*

My lute, awake! perform the last
Labor that thou and I shall waste,
And end that I have now begun;
For when this song is sung and past,
My lute, be still, for I have done.

> *The Lover Complaineth the Unkindness of His Love*

They flee from me that sometime did me seek.

> *The Lover Showeth How He Is Forsaken of Such as He Sometime Enjoyed*

JOHN KNOX
1505–1572

A man with God is always in the majority.[1]

> *Inscription on Reformation Monument, Geneva, Switzerland*

JOHN BRADFORD
1510–1555

The familiar story, that, on seeing evildoers taken to the place of execution, he was wont to exclaim: "But for the grace of God there goes John Bradford," is a universal tradition, which has overcome the lapse of time.[2]

> *Biographical notice, Parker Society edition, The Writings of John Bradford* [1853]

---

[1] Un homme avec Dieu est toujours dans la majorité.
See Phillips, p. 659a.
[2] There but for the grace of God goes God.
— *Anonymous saying, attributed to* ORSON WELLES, *among others*

SIR THOMAS VAUX
1510–1556

Companion none is like
Unto the mind alone;
For many have been harmed by
speech,
Through thinking, few or none.
Of a Contented Mind [1557]

I loathe that I did love,
In youth that I thought sweet,
As time requires for my behove,
Methinks they are not meet.
*The Aged Lover Renounceth
Love, st. 1*

But age, with his stealing steps,
Hath claw'd me in his clutch.[1]
Ib. 3

RICHARD GRAFTON
d. 1572

Thirty days hath November,
April, June, and September,
February hath twenty-eight alone,
And all the rest have thirty-one.[2]
Chronicles of England [1562]

[1] Quoted by First Clown in SHAKESPEARE, *Hamlet, act V, sc. i, l. 77*
[2] Junius, Aprilis, Septémq; Nouemq; tricenos, Unum plus reliqui, Februs tenet octo vicenos, At si bissextus fuerit superadditur unus.
   WILLIAM HARRISON, *Description of Britain, prefixed to* HOLINSHED'S *Chronicles* [1577]
Thirty days hath September,
April, June, and November,
February has twenty-eight alone,
All the rest have thirty-one;
Excepting leap year — that's the time
When February's days are twenty-nine.
   The Return from Parnassus [1606]
Thirty days hath September,
April, June, and November,
All the rest have thirty-one,
Excepting February alone,
Which hath but twenty-eight, in fine,
Till leap year gives it twenty-nine.
   Common in the New England states
Fourth, eleventh, ninth, and sixth,
Thirty days to each affix;
Every other thirty-one
Except the second month alone.
   Common in Chester County, Pennsylvania, among the Friends
Compare the old Latin class mnemonic:
In March, July, October, May,

MARY TUDOR
1516–1558

When I am dead and opened, you
shall find "Calais" lying in my heart.[1]
From HOLINSHED, *Chronicles*
[1577], III, 1160

AMBROISE PARÉ
1517–1590

I treated him, God cured him.[2]
His favorite saying

JOACHIM DU BELLAY
1522–1560

France, mother of the arts, of arms,
and of laws.[3]
Les Regrets [1559], IX

Happy he who like Ulysses a glorious
voyage made.[4] *Ib. XXXI*

PIERRE DE RONSARD
1524–1585

When you are old, at evening candle-
lit,
Beside the fire bending to your wool,
Read out my verse and murmur, "Ron-
sard writ
This praise for me when I was beau-
tiful." [5]
Sonnets pour Hélène, I, 43

The Ides are on the fifteenth day,
The Nones the seventh: all other months besides
Have two days less for Nones and Ides.
[1] See Browning, p. 663b.
[2] Je le soignay, Dieu le guérit.
[3] France, mère des arts, des armes et des lois.
[4] Heureux qui, comme Ulysse, a fait un beau voyage.
[5] Quand vous serez bien vieille, au soir à la chandelle,
   Assise auprès du feu, devidant et filant,
   Direz, chantant mes vers, en vous émerveillant:
   "Ronsard me célébrait du temps que j'étais belle."
Translated by HUMBERT WOLFE.
See the adaptation by YEATS: When you are old and gray and full of sleep (p. 879b).

Live now, believe me, wait not till tomorrow;
Gather the roses of life today.[1]
> *Sonnets pour Hélène, I, 43*

Gather, gather your youth:
Just like this flower, old age
Your beauty will wither.[2]
> *Odes I, 17. À Cassandre*

THOMAS TUSSER
c. 1524 – 1580

At Christmas play and make good
cheer,
For Christmas comes but once a year.
> *A Hundred Points of Good
> Husbandry* [1557], *The Farm-
> er's Daily Diet*

Such mistress, such Nan,
Such master, such man.[3]
> *Ib. April's Abstract*

Sweet April showers
Do spring May flowers.
> *Ib. April's Husbandry*

Who goeth a-borrowing
Goeth a-sorrowing.
> *Ib. June's Abstract*

'Tis merry in hall
Where beards wag all.[4]
> *Ib. August's Abstract*

PIETER BRUEGEL
c. 1525 – 1569

Because the world is so faithless,
I go my way in mourning.[5]
> *Inscription in* MOLIÈRE, *The
> Misanthrope* [1568]

---

[1] Vivez, si m'en croyez, n'attendez à demain:
   Cueillez des aujourd'hui les roses de la vie.
See Horace, p. 121a; Spenser, p. 200a; and
Herrick, p. 320b.
[2] Cueillez, cueillez votre jeunesse:
   Comme à cette fleur, la vieillesse
   Fera ternir votre beauté.
[3] Tel maître, tel valet. Attributed to CHEVA-
LIER BAYARD by Cimber.
[4] Merry swithe it is in halle,
   When the beards waveth alle.
> *Life of Alexander* [1312]
[5] Om dat de werelt is soe ongetru
   Daer om gha ic in den ru.

GABRIEL MEURIER
1530–1601

He who excuses himself accuses himself.[1]
> *Trésor des Sentences*

WILLIAM STEVENSON
c. 1530 – 1575

I cannot eat but little meat,
My stomach is not good;
But sure I think that I can drink
With him that wears a hood.
> *Gammer Gurton's Needle
> [c. 1573], drinking song,
> act II*

Back and side go bare, go bare,
Both foot and hand go cold;
But, belly, God send thee good ale
enough,
Whether it be new or old.
> *Ib. refrain*

HENRI ESTIENNE
1531–1598

If youth but knew, and old age only
could.[2]
> *Les Prémices* [1594]

God tempers the wind to the shorn
lamb.[3]
> *Ib.*

ELIZABETH I
1533–1603

The use of the sea and air is common
to all; neither can a title to the ocean
belong to any people or private persons,
forasmuch as neither nature nor public
use and custom permit any possession
thereof.
> *To the Spanish Ambassador* [1580]

My care is like my shadow in the
sun —
Follows me flying — flies when I pursue
it.
> *On the departure of Alençon
> [1582]*

---

[1] Qui s'excuse, s'accuse.
See Shakespeare, pp. 231a and 237a.
[2] Si jeunesse savait, si vieillesse pouvait.
Translated by NORBERT GUTERMAN.
[3] Dieu mesure le froid à la brebis tondue.
See Laurence Sterne, p. 438b.

I know I have the body of a weak and feeble woman, but I have the heart and stomach of a king, and of a king of England too; and think foul scorn that Parma or Spain, or any prince of Europe, should dare to invade the borders of my realm.

Speech to the troops at Tilbury on the approach of the Armada [1588]

I am your anointed Queen. I will never be by violence constrained to do anything. I thank God I am endued with such qualities that if I were turned out of the Realm in my petticoat I were able to live in any place in Christendom.

From CHAMBERLIN, *Sayings of Queen Elizabeth*

I will make you shorter by the head.
Ib.

The daughter of debate, that eke discord doth sow.[1] *Ib.*

[To the Countess of Nottingham] God may forgive you, but I never can.
From HUME, *History of England Under the House of Tudor, vol. II, ch. 7*

Though God hath raised me high, yet this I count the glory of my crown: that I have reigned with your loves.
The Golden Speech [1601]

Semper eadem [Ever the same].
Motto

I am no lover of pompous title, but only desire that my name may be recorded in a line or two, which shall briefly express my name, my virginity, the years of my reign, the reformation of religion under it, and my preservation of peace.
To her ladies, discussing her epitaph

'Twas God the word that spake it, He took the Bread and brake it;

---

[1] Mary Queen of Scots.

And what the word did make it, That I believe, and take it.[1]
From S. CLARKE, *Marrow of Ecclesiastical History [ed. 1675], pt. II, Life of Queen Elizabeth*

MICHEL EYQUEM DE MONTAIGNE[2]
1533–1592

Man in sooth is a marvelous vain, fickle, and unstable subject.
Essays,[3] bk. I [1580], ch. 1

The thing of which I have most fear is fear.[4] *Ib.* 17

He who should teach men to die would at the same time teach them to live.[5] *Ib.* 19

I would let death seize upon me whilst I am setting my cabbages.[6]
Ib. 20

The value of life lies not in the length of days, but in the use we make of them: a man may live long, yet get little from life. Whether you find satisfaction in life depends not on your tale of years, but on your will. *Ib.*

My desire is therefore that the parent be very circumspect in choosing a direc-

---

[1] Answer on being asked her opinion of Christ's presence in the Sacrament.

[2] Translated by CHARLES COTTON [1636–1687], revised by HAZLITT and WIGHT.

[3] This book of Montaigne the world has endorsed by translating it into all tongues. — EMERSON, *Representative Men* [1850], *Montaigne*

[4] C'est de quoy j'ay le plus de peur que la peur.

See *Proverbs 3:25*, p. 23b; Bacon, p. 207b; Wellington, p. 506a; Thoreau, p. 681b; and Roosevelt, p. 971a.

[5] I have taught you, my dear flock, for above thirty years how to live, and I will show you in a very short time how to die. — SIR EDWIN SANDYS [1561–1629], *Anglorum Speculum*
See Tickell, p. 400b.

Teach him how to live,
And, oh still harder lesson! how to die.
BEILBY PORTEUS [1731–1808], *Death, l. 316*

In teaching me the way to live
It taught me how to die.
GEORGE POPE MORRIS [1802–1864],
My Mother's Bible, st. 4

[6] Je veux que la mort me trouve plantant mes choux.
Translated by FLORIO [1603].
See Rabelais, p. 181a, and Voltaire, p. 417a.

tor whom I would rather commend for having a well-composed and temperate brain than a full-stuffed head.[1]

Essays, bk. I, ch. 25

If you press me to say why I loved him, I can say no more than it was because he was he and I was I.[2]

Ib. 27

Nothing is so firmly believed as what we least know.   *Ib.* 31

A wise man never loses anything if he have himself.   *Ib.* 38

We should reserve a storehouse for ourselves, altogether ours,[3] and wholly free, wherein we may hoard up and establish our true liberty, and principal retreat and solitude.   *Ib.* 39

The greatest thing in the world is to know how to be sufficient unto oneself.[4]   *Ib.*

To know how to live is all my calling and all my art.[5]   *Ib. II* [1580], 6

Virtue can have naught to do with ease . . . It craves a steep and thorny path.   *Ib.* 11

When I play with my cat, who knows whether I do not make her more sport than she makes me?   *Ib.* 12

The souls of emperors and cobblers are cast in the same mold. . . . The same reason that makes us wrangle with a neighbor causes a war betwixt princes.   *Ib.*

This idea is more clearly conceived by a question, "What do I know?"[6] which I employ, with the device of a pair of scales.   *Ib.*

Man is certainly stark mad; he cannot make a worm, and yet he will be making gods by dozens.   *Ib.*

What truth is that, which these mountains bound, and is a lie in the world beyond them?[1]

Essays, bk. II, ch. 12

Life is a dream . . . we sleeping wake and waking sleep.[2]   *Ib.*

How many worthy men have we known to survive their own reputation![3]   *Ib.* 16

One may be humble out of pride.

Ib. 17

I find that the best virtue I have has in it some tincture of vice.   *Ib.* 20

Saying is one thing, and doing is another.   *Ib.* 31

There never were in the world two opinions alike, no more than two hairs or two grains; the most universal quality is diversity.[4]   *Ib.* 37

I will follow the right side even to the fire, but excluding the fire if I can.

Ib. III [1595], 1

I speak truth, not so much as I would, but as much as I dare; and I dare a little the more, as I grow older.

Ib. 2

Few men have been admired by their own domestics.[5]   *Ib.*

Every man bears the whole stamp of the human condition.[6]   *Ib.*

It [marriage] happens as with cages: the birds without despair to get in, and those within despair of getting out.[7]

Ib. 5

[1] Plutôt la tête bien faite que bien pleine. Translated by FLORIO.
[2] Parce que c'était lui; parce que c'était moi.
[3] Il se faut réserver une arrière boutique toute notre.
[4] La plus grande chose du monde, c'est de savoir être à soi.
[5] Mon métier et mon art, c'est vivre.
[6] Que sais-je?

[1] Quelle vérité que ces montagnes bornent, qui est mensonge qui se tient au delà?
[2] La vie est un songe . . . nous veillons dormants et veillants dormons.
See Euripides, p. 86b, and Aristophanes, p. 92a.
[3] See Bentley, p. 386a.
[4] See Pliny, p. 132b.
[5] See Antigonus, p. 99b.
[6] Chaque homme porte la form entière de l'humaine condition.
[7] I myself have loved a lady and pursued her with a great deal of under-age protestation, whom some three or four gallants that have en-

All the world knows me in my book, and my book in me.
Essays, bk. III, ch. 5

'Tis so much to be a king, that he only is so by being so. The strange luster that surrounds him conceals and shrouds him from us; our sight is there broken and dissipated, being stopped and filled by the prevailing light.[1]
Ib. 7

I moreover affirm that our wisdom itself, and wisest consultations, for the most part commit themselves to the conduct of chance.[2]　　*Ib.* 8

Not because Socrates said so,[3] but because it is in truth my own disposition — and perchance to some excess — I look upon all men as my compatriots, and embrace a Pole as a Frenchman, making less account of the national than of the universal and common bond.[4]　　　　　　*Ib.* 9

There is no man so good, who, were he to submit all his thoughts and actions to the laws, would not deserve hanging ten times in his life.　*Ib.*

A little folly is desirable in him that will not be guilty of stupidity.[5]　*Ib.*

I have never seen a greater monster or miracle in the world than myself.
Essays, bk. III, ch. 11

Men are most apt to believe what they least understand.　　　*Ib.*

I have here only made a nosegay of culled flowers, and have brought nothing of my own but the thread that ties them together.[1]　　　*Ib.* 12

There is more ado to interpret interpretations than to interpret the things, and more books upon books than upon all other subjects; we do nothing but comment upon one another.　*Ib.* 13

For truth itself has not the privilege to be spoken at all times and in all sorts.　　　　　　　　*Ib.*

Sits he on never so high a throne, a man still sits on his bottom.　*Ib.*

Let us a little permit Nature to take her own way; she better understands her own affairs than we.　　*Ib.*

I have ever loved to repose myself, whether sitting or lying, with my heels as high or higher than my head.
Ib.

I do not understand; I pause; I examine.　*Inscription for his library*

WILLIAM I
[WILLIAM THE SILENT]
1533–1584

My God, have mercy on my soul and on my poor people.[2]
Last words as he fell under an assassin's bullets

---

joyed would with all their hearts have been glad to have been rid of. 'Tis just like a summer bird-cage in a garden: the birds that are without despair to get in, and the birds that are within despair and are in a consumption for fear they shall never get out. — John Webster, *The White Devil* [1612], *act I, sc. ii*

Wedlock, indeed, hath oft compared been
To public feasts, where meet a public rout —
Where they that are without would fain go in,
And they that are within would fain go out.
　　　Sir John Davies [1569–1626], *Contention Betwixt a Wife, etc.*

See Emerson, p. 608a.

[1] See Shakespeare, p. 265a, and Tennyson, p. 653a.

[2] Although men flatter themselves with their great actions, they are not so often the result of great design as of chance. — La Rochefoucauld [1613–1680], *Maxim 57*

[3] See Socrates, p. 87b.

[4] See de Montesquieu, p. 414b.

[5] See Menander, p. 102b, Horace, p. 122b, and note.

[1] I am but a gatherer and disposer of other men's stuff, at my best value. — Sir Henry Wotton, *preface to The Elements of Architecture* [1624]

John Bartlett used this passage as an epigraph for the fourth edition of *Familiar Quotations* [1864]. It was the only quotation from Montaigne in that edition.

[2] Mon Dieu, ayez pitié de mon âme et de mon pauvre peuple.

SIR HUMPHREY GILBERT
c. 1539–1583

We are as near to heaven by sea as by land! [1]
> *From* HAKLUYT, *Voyages,*
> *vol. III* [1600], *p. 159*

SIR EDWARD DYER
c. 1540–1607

My mind to me a kingdom is;
  Such present joys therein I find
That it excels all other bliss
  That earth affords or grows by kind:
Though much I want which most
  would have,
Yet still my mind forbids to crave.
> *Rawlinson Poetry*
> *MS 85, p. 17* [2]

Some have too much, yet still do
  crave;
  I little have, and seek no more:
They are but poor, though much they
  have,
  And I am rich with little store:
They poor, I rich; they beg, I give;
They lack, I have; they pine, I live.
> *Ib.*

[1] The way to heaven out of all places is of like length and distance. — SIR THOMAS MORE, *Utopia* [1516]

Gilbert, on the last day of his life, was seen in his tiny pinnace *Squirrel* with a book in hand, probably More's *Utopia* which inspired his last utterance. He was homeward bound from Newfoundland, which he had just taken possession of in the name of the Queen [August 1583].

> "Do not fear! Heaven is as near,"
> He said, "by water as by land!"
> LONGFELLOW, *Sir Humphrey Gilbert*
> [1849], *st. 6*

See James T. Fields, p. 679b.

[2] This poem became popular as a song, altered thus:

My mind to me a kingdom is;
  Such perfect joy therein I find,
As far exceeds all earthly bliss
  That God and Nature hath assigned.
Though much I want that most would have,
Yet still my mind forbids to crave.
> BYRD, *Psalms, Sonnets, etc.* [1588]

My mind to me an empire is,
  While grace affordeth health.
> ROBERT SOUTHWELL [c. 1561–1595],
> *Content and Rich*

See Seneca, p. 131b.

Fain would I, but I dare not; I dare,
  and yet I may not;
I may, although I care not, for pleasure
  when I play not.
> *Fain Would I* [*attributed*]

WILLIAM GILBERT
1540–1603

In the discovery of secret things and in the investigation of hidden causes, stronger reasons are obtained from sure experiments and demonstrated arguments than from probable conjectures and the opinions of philosophical speculators of the common sort. [1]
> *De Magnete* [1600]

JAN ZAMOYSKI
1541–1605

The king reigns, but does not govern. [2]
> *Speech in the Polish Parliament*
> [1605], *referring to King Sigismund III*

MARY STUART
[MARY QUEEN OF SCOTS]
1542–1587

In my end is my beginning.
> *Motto*

O Lord my God, I have trusted in
  thee;
O Jesu my dearest one, now set me
  free.
In prison's oppression, in sorrow's obsession,
I weary for thee.
With sighing and crying bowed down
  as dying,
I adore thee, I implore thee, set me
  free! [3]
> *Prayer written in her Book of*
> *Devotion before her execution*

[1] Translated by P. F. MOTTELAY.
[2] Thiers adopted the epigram as the motto for his journal *Nationale*, which he established with Mignet and Carrel in 1830.
[3] Translated by SWINBURNE.
O Domine Deus! speravi in te;

GUILLAUME DE SALLUSTE, SEIGNEUR DU BARTAS
1544–1590

Oft seen in forehead of the frowning skies.[1]
> *Divine Weeks and Works [1578], First Week, Second Day*

For where's the state beneath the firmament
That doth excel the bees for government? [2]   *Ib. Fifth Day, pt. 1*

These lovely lamps, these windows of the soul.[3]   *Ib. Sixth Day*

Or almost like a spider, who, confin'd
In her web's center, shakt with every wind,
Moves in an instant if the buzzing fly
Stir but a string of her lawn canapie.[4]
> *Ib.*

Living from hand to mouth.
> *Ib. Second Week, First Day, pt. 4*

In the jaws of death.[5]   *Ib.*

O care mi Jesu! nunc libera me.
In dura catena, in misera poena,
Disidero te.
Languendo, gemendo, et genuflectendo,
Adore, imploro, ut liberes me!
[1] See Milton, p. 339a.
[2]   So work the honeybees,
Creatures that by a rule in Nature teach
The act of order to a peopled kingdom.
  SHAKESPEARE, *King Henry V* [1598–1600], *act I, sc. ii, l. 187*
[3] The windows of mine eyes. — SHAKESPEARE, *King Richard III* [1592–1593], *act V, sc. iii, l. 117*
[4] Much like a subtle spider which doth sit
In middle of her web, which spreadeth wide;
If aught do touch the utmost thread of it
She feels it instantly on every side.
  SIR JOHN DAVIES, *The Immortality of the Soul* [1599]
Our souls sit close and silently within,
And their own webs from their own entrails spin;
And when eyes meet far off, our sense is such
That, spider-like, we feel the tenderest touch.
  DRYDEN, *Marriage à la Mode* [1673], *act II, sc. i*
The spider's touch, how exquisitely fine!
Feels at each thread, and lives along the line.
  POPE, *An Essay on Man* [1733–1734], *epistle I, l. 217*
[5] Out of the jaws of death. — SHAKESPEARE, *Twelfth Night* [1598–1600], *act III, sc. iv, l. 396*
See Tennyson, p. 652a.

Only that he may conform
To tyrant custom.
> *Divine Weeks and Works, Second Week, Third Day, pt. 2*

Who breaks his faith, no faith is held with him.
> *Ib. Fourth Day, bk. 2*

Who well lives, long lives; for this age of ours
Should not be numbered by years, days, and hours.   *Ib.*

My lovely living boy,
My hope, my hap, my love, my life, my joy.[1]   *Ib.*

Out of the book of Nature's learned breast.[2]   *Ib.*

Flesh of thy flesh, nor yet bone of thy bone.   *Ib.*

MIGUEL DE CERVANTES
1547–1616

You are a King by your own Fireside, as much as any Monarch in his Throne.
> *Don Quixote de la Mancha*[3] *[1605–1615] author's preface, p. xix*

I was so free with him as not to mince the matter.[4]   *p. xx*

They can expect nothing but their labor for their pains.[5]   *p. xxiii*

---

[1]   My fair son!
My life, my joy, my food, my all the world.
  SHAKESPEARE, *King John* [1596–1597], *act III, sc. iv, l. 103*
[2] The book of Nature is that which the physician must read; and to do so he must walk over the leaves. — PARACELSUS [1493–1541]. From *Encyclopaedia Britannica* (*11th ed.*), *vol. XX, p. 749*
[3] Translated in 1700–1703 by PETER ANTHONY MOTTEUX [1660–1718]. Page numbers are those of the Modern Library Giant edition.
[4] See Shakespeare, p. 273b.
You mince matters. — MOLIÈRE, *Tartuffe* [1667], *act I, sc. i*
[5] Nothing is to be gotten without pains (labor). — *Old Proverb*
See Shakespeare, p. 267b.

Time out of mind.[1]
> Don Quixote, pt. I [1605],
> 　　bk. I, ch. 1, p. 4

Which I have earned with the sweat of my brows.[2]　　　*I, 4, p. 22*

By a small sample we may judge of the whole piece.　　　*p. 25*

Put you in this pickle.[3]
> *I, 5, p. 30*

Can we ever have too much of a good thing?　　　*I, 6, p. 37*

The charging of his enemy was but the work of a moment.　　*I, 8, p. 50*

I don't know that ever I saw one in my born days.　　　*II, 2, p. 57*

Those two fatal words, Mine and Thine.[4]　　　*II, 3, p. 63*

The eyes those silent tongues of Love.　　　*p. 65*

And had a face like a benediction.[5]
> *II, 4, p. 69*

There's not the least thing can be said or done, but people will talk and find fault.[6]　　　*p. 70*

Without a wink of sleep.[7]　　*p. 72*

It is a true saying, that a man must eat a peck of salt with his friend, before he knows him.　　*III, 1, p. 92*

Thank you for nothing.　　*p. 94*

No limits but the sky.[8]
> *III, 3, p. 110*

To give the devil his due.　*p. 111*

You're leaping over the hedge before you come to the stile.
> *Don Quixote, pt. I, bk. III,*
> 　　*ch. 4, p. 117*

Paid him in his own coin.　*p. 119*

The famous Don Quixote de la Mancha, otherwise called The Knight of the Woeful Figure.[1]
> *III, 5, p. 126*

You are come off now with a whole skin.　　　*p. 127*

Fear is sharp-sighted, and can see things underground, and much more in the skies.　　　*III, 6, p. 131*

A finger in every pie.[2]　　*p. 133*

No better than she should be.[3]
> *Ib.*

That's the nature of women . . . not to love when we love them, and to love when we love them not.[4]　　*Ib.*

You may go whistle for the rest.
> *p. 134*

Ill luck, you know, seldom comes alone.[5]　　　*p. 135*

Why do you lead me a wild-goose chase?　　　*p. 136*

Experience, the universal Mother of Sciences.　　　*III, 7, p. 140*

Give me but that, and let the world rub, there I'll stick.　　*p. 148*

Sing away sorrow, cast away care.
> *III, 8, p. 153*

Of good natural parts, and of a liberal education.　　　*p. 154*

---

[1] Time out o' mind. — SHAKESPEARE, *Romeo and Juliet* [1594–1595], *act I, sc. iv, l. 70*
[2] See *Genesis 3:19*, p. 6a.
[3] How cam'st thou in this pickle? — SHAKESPEARE, *The Tempest* [1611], *act V, sc. i, l. 281*
[4] See Boileau, p. 377b.
[5] The more familiar translation.
[6] Take wife, or cowl; ride you, or walk:
Doubt not but tongues will have their talk.
　　LA FONTAINE, *The Miller, His Son, and
　　　　　　the Donkey* [1694]
Do you think you could keep people from talking? — MOLIÈRE, *Tartuffe* [1667], *act I, sc. 1*
[7] See Shakespeare, *Cymbeline III, iv, 103*, p. 291a.
[8] Modern saying: The sky's the limit.

[1] El Caballero de la Triste Figura. More accurately translated by TOBIAS SMOLLETT as The Knight of the Sorrowful Countenance.
[2] No pie was baked at Castlewood but her little finger was in it. — THACKERAY, *The Virginians* [1857–1859], *ch. 5*
[3] An old proverb.
You are no better than you should be.
　　BEAUMONT AND FLETCHER, *The Coxcomb*
　　　　　　[1647], *act IV, sc. 3*
[4] See George Bernard Shaw, p. 836a.
[5] See Shakespeare, p. 265a.

Let every man mind his own business.   *Don Quixote, pt. I, bk. III, ch. 8, p. 157*

Those who'll play with cats must expect to be scratched.   *p. 159*

Raise a hue and cry.   *Ib.*

'Tis the part of a wise man to keep himself today for tomorrow, and not venture all his eggs in one basket.   *III, 9, p. 162*

The ease of my burdens, the staff of my life.   *p. 163*

Within a stone's throw of it.   *p. 170*

The very remembrance of my former misfortune proves a new one to me.   *III, 10, p. 174*

Absence, that common cure of love.   *p. 177*

From pro's and con's they fell to a warmer way of disputing.   *p. 181*

Little said is soon amended.[1]   *p. 184*

A close mouth catches no flies.   *Ib.*

Thou hast seen nothing yet.   *III, 11, p. 190*

Between jest and earnest.   *Ib.*

My love and hers have always been purely Platonic.   *p. 192*

'Tis ill talking of halters in the house of a man that was hanged.   *p. 195*

My memory is so bad that many times I forget my own name!   *Ib.*

'Twill grieve me so to the heart that I shall cry my eyes out.   *p. 197*

Ready to split his sides with laughing.   *III, 13, p. 208*

My honor is dearer to me than my life.   *IV, 1, p. 226*

On the word of a gentleman, and a Christian.   *p. 236*

Think before thou speakest.   *IV, 3, p. 252*

[1] Often rendered: Least said soonest mended.

Let us forget and forgive injuries.   *Don Quixote, pt. I, bk. IV, ch. 3, p. 254*

I must speak the truth, and nothing but the truth.   *p. 255*

More knave than fool.   *IV, 4, p. 261*

Here's the devil-and-all to pay.   *IV, 10, p. 319*

I begin to smell a rat.   *Ib.*

The proof of the pudding is in the eating.   *p. 322*

Let none presume to tell me that the pen is preferable to the sword.[1]   *p. 325*

There's no striving against the stream; and the weakest still goes to the wall.   *IV, 20, p. 404*

The bow cannot always stand bent, nor can human frailty subsist without some lawful recreation.   *IV, 21, p. 412*

It is not the hand but the understanding of a man that may be said to write.[2]   *Pt. II [1615], bk. III, author's preface, p. 441*

When the head aches, all the members partake of the pains.[3]   *III, 2, p. 455*

Youngsters read it, grown men understand it, and old people applaud it.   *III, 3, p. 464*

History is in a manner a sacred thing, so far as it contains truth; for where truth is, the supreme Father of it may

[1] See Edward Bulwer-Lytton, p. 601b.
Scholars' pens carry farther, and give a louder report than thunder. — SIR THOMAS BROWNE, *Religio Medici* [1642], *Everyman ed., p. 70*
[2] Cervantes's left hand was maimed for life by gunshot wounds in the battle of Lepanto.
[3] When the head is not sound, the rest cannot be well. — DU BARTAS, *Divine Weeks and Works* [1578]
For let our finger ache, and it indues
Our other healthful members even to that sense
Of pain.
   SHAKESPEARE, *Othello* [1604–1605], *act III, sc. iv, l. 145*

also be said to be, at least, in as much as concerns truth.

> *Don Quixote, pt. II, bk. III, ch. 3, p. 465*

Every man is as Heaven made him, and sometimes a great deal worse.

> *III, 4, p. 468*

There's no sauce in the world like hunger.   *III, 5, p. 473*

He casts a sheep's eye at the wench.

> *p. 474*

I ever loved to see everything upon the square.   *p. 475*

Neither will I make myself anybody's laughingstock.   *Ib.*

Journey over all the universe in a map, without the expense and fatigue of traveling, without suffering the inconveniences of heat, cold, hunger, and **thirst.**   *III, 6, p. 479*

Presume to put in her oar.   *p. 480*

The fair sex.[1]   *Ib.*

A little in one's own pocket is better than much in another man's purse. 'Tis good to keep a nest egg. Every little makes a mickle.[2]   *III, 7, p. 486*

Remember the old saying, "Faint heart ne'er won fair lady."

> *III, 10, p. 501*

Forewarned forearmed.   *p. 502*

As well look for a needle in a bottle of hay.[3]   *Ib.*

Are we to mark this day with a white or a black stone?[4]   *p. 503*

The very pink of courtesy.

> *III, 13, p. 521*

I'll turn over a new leaf.   *p. 524*

He's[5] a muddled fool, full of lucid intervals.   *III, 18, p. 556*

---

[1] That sex which is therefore called fair. — STEELE, *The Spectator, no. 302, February 15, 1712*

[2] See Hesiod p. 67b, and note.

[3] A needle in a haystack.

[4] A red-letter day.

[5] Don Quixote.

Marriage is a noose.

> *Don Quixote, pt. II, bk. III, ch. 19, p. 564*

There are only two families in the world, the Haves and the Have-Nots.

> *III, 20, p. 574*

He preaches well that lives well, quoth Sancho; that's all the divinity I understand.   *p. 575*

Love and War are the same thing, and stratagems and policy are as allowable in the one as in the other.

> *III, 21, p. 580*

A private sin is not so prejudicial in this world as a public indecency.

> *III, 22, p. 582*

There is no love lost, sir.[1]   *Ib.*

Come back sound, wind and limb.

> *p. 587*

Patience, and shuffle the cards.[2]

> *III, 23, p. 592*

Tell me thy company, and I'll tell thee what thou art.[3]   *p. 594*

Tomorrow will be a new day.

> *III, 26, p. 618*

I can see with half an eye.

> *III, 29, p. 632*

Great persons are able to do great kindnesses.   *III, 32, p. 662*

---

[1] There is no hate lost between us. — MIDDLETON [1580–1627], *The Witch, act IV, sc. ii.*

[2] But patience, cousin, and shuffle the cards, till our hand is a stronger one. — SIR WALTER SCOTT, *Quentin Durward* [1823], *ch. 8*
    Cut the fiercest quarrels short
    With "Patience, gentlemen, and shuffle."
    W. M. PRAED [1802–1839], *Quince, st. 5*
Men disappoint me so, I disappoint myself so, yet courage, patience, shuffle the cards. — MARGARET FULLER OSSOLI [1810–1850], *letter to the Reverend W. H. Channing*

[3] Tell me what you eat, and I will tell you what you are. — ANTHELME BRILLAT-SAVARIN [1755–1826], *La Physiologie du Goût, aphorism 4*
Show me your garden and I shall tell you what you are. — ALFRED AUSTIN, *The Garden That I Love* [1905]

Honesty's the best policy.[1]
Don Quixote, pt. II, bk. III,
ch. 33, p. 666

An honest man's word is as good as
his bond. *IV, 34, p. 674*

A blot in thy scutcheon to all futurity. *IV, 35, p. 681*

They had best not stir the rice,
though it sticks to the pot.
IV, 37, p. 691

Good wits jump;[2] a word to the wise
is enough. *p. 692*

Diligence is the mother of good fortune. *IV, 38, p. 724*

What a man has, so much he's sure
of. *p. 725*

The pot calls the kettle black.
Ib. p. 727

Mum's the word.[3] *IV, 44, p. 729*

I shall be as secret as the grave.
IV, 62, p. 862

Now blessings light on him that first
invented this same sleep! It covers a
man all over, thoughts and all, like a
cloak; 'tis meat for the hungry, drink
for the thirsty, heat for the cold, and
cold for the hot. 'Tis the current coin
that purchases all the pleasures of the
world cheap; and the balance that sets
the king and the shepherd, the fool and
the wise man even. *IV, 68, p. 898*

The ass will carry his load, but not a
double load; ride not a free horse to
death. *IV, 71, p. 917*

I thought it working for a dead
horse, because I am paid beforehand.[4]
Ib.

He . . . got the better of himself,
and that's the best kind of victory one
can wish for.
Don Quixote, pt. II, bk. IV,
ch. 72, p. 924

Every man was not born with a silver
spoon in his mouth. *IV, 73, p. 926*

Ne'er look for birds of this year in
the nests of the last.[1] *IV, 74, p. 933*

There is a strange charm in the
thoughts of a good legacy, or the hopes
of an estate, which wondrously allevi-
ates the sorrow that men would otherwise feel for the death of friends.
p. 934

For if he like a madman lived,
At least he like a wise one died.
p. 935 (Don Quixote's epitaph)

Don't put too fine a point to your
wit for fear it should get blunted.
The Little Gypsy (La Gitanilla)

My heart is wax molded as she
pleases, but enduring as marble to retain.[2] *Ib.*

CHARLES IX
1550–1574

Horses and poets should be fed, not
overfed.[3] *Saying*

WILLIAM CAMDEN
1551–1623

My friend, judge not me,
Thou seest I judge not thee.
Betwixt the stirrup and the ground
Mercy I asked, and mercy found.
Remains Concerning Britain.
Epitaph for a man killed by
falling from his horse

[1] I hold the maxim no less applicable to public
than to private affairs, that honesty is always
the best policy. — GEORGE WASHINGTON, *Farewell Address* [1796]
[2] Great wits jump. — LAURENCE STERNE, *Tristram Shandy, vol. III* [1761–1762], *ch. 9*
[3] Cry "mum." — SHAKESPEARE, *The Merry
Wives of Windsor* [1600–1601], *act V, sc. ii, l. 6*
[4] It is a heartrending delusion and a cruel
snare to be paid for your work before you accomplish it. As soon as once your work is finished you ought to be promptly paid; but to

receive your lucre one minute before it is due
is to tempt Providence to make a Micawber
of you. — EDMUND GOSSE, *Gossip in a Library*
[1891], *Beau Nash*
[1] For Time will teach thee soon the truth,
There are no birds in last year's nest!
LONGFELLOW [1807–1882], *It Is Not
Always May, st. 6*

[2] See Byron, p. 559b.
[3] Equi et poetae alendi, non saginandi.

THÉODORE AGRIPPA D'AUBIGNÉ
1552–1630

Each of us aspires to worth,
Each of us desires it
And desires it for himself.[1]
Pièces Épigrammatiques 49

More exquisite than any other is the autumn rose.[2]
Les Tragiques. Les Feux

SIR EDWARD COKE
1552–1634

Reason is the life of the law; nay, the common law itself is nothing else but reason. . . . The law, which is perfection of reason.[3]
First Institute [1628]

The gladsome light of jurisprudence.
Ib. epilogue

For a man's house is his castle, *et domus sua cuique tutissimum refugium.*[4]
Third Institute [1644]

The house of everyone is to him as his castle and fortress, as well for his defense against injury and violence as for his repose.
Semayne's Case. 5 Report 91

They [corporations] cannot commit treason, nor be outlawed nor excommunicate, for they have no souls.
Case of Sutton's Hospital. 10 Report 32

[1] Chacun au bien aspire,
Chacun le bien désire,
Et le désire sien.
[2] Une rose d'automne est plus qu'une autre exquise.
[3] Let us consider the reason of the case. For nothing is law that is not reason. — SIR JOHN POWELL, *Coggs v. Bernard, 2 Ld. Raym. Rep.* p. *911*
[4] One's home is the safest refuge to everyone. — *Pandects* [6th century], *lib. II, tit. IV, De in Ius Vocando*

I in mine own house am an emperor
And will defend what's mine.
MASSINGER, *The Roman Actor* [1629], act I, sc. ii

Magna Carta is such a fellow that he will have no sovereign.
Debate in the Commons [May 17, 1628]

Six hours in sleep, in law's grave study six,
Four spend in prayer, the rest on Nature fix.[1]
Translation quoted by COKE; *from The Pandects (Digests of Roman Civil Law, sixth century). De in Ius Vocando*

SIR WALTER RALEGH
c. 1552 – 1618

Like to an hermit poor in place obscure,
I mean to spend my days of endless doubt,
To wail such woes as time cannot recure,
Where none but Love shall ever find me out.
The Phoenix Nest [1593]. *Sonnet*

As you came from the holy land
Of Walsinghame,
Met you not with my true Love
By the way as you came?
As You Came from the Holy Land [c. 1599], *st. 1*

But true love is a durable fire,
In the mind ever burning,
Never sick, never old, never dead,
From itself never turning.
Ib. st. 11

If all the world and love were young,
And truth in every shepherd's tongue,
These pretty pleasures might me move
To live with thee, and be thy love.
The Nymph's Reply to the Passionate Shepherd[2] *(printed in England's Helicon, 1600), st. 1*

[1] Seven hours to law, to soothing slumber seven;
Ten to the world allot, and all to heaven.
SIR WILLIAM JONES [1746–1794]
[2] An answer to CHRISTOPHER MARLOWE, *The Passionate Shepherd to His Love* (see p. 212a).

Fain would I climb, yet fear I to fall.
Written on a windowpane [1]

Our passions are most like to floods and
  streams,
The shallow murmur, but the deep are
  dumb.[2]
Sir Walter Ralegh to the Queen
[c. 1599], st. 1

Silence in love bewrays more woe
Than words, though ne'er so witty;
A beggar that is dumb, you know,
Deserveth double pity.   *Ib. st. 5*

Go, Soul, the body's quest,
  Upon a thankless arrant:
Fear not to touch the best,
  The truth shall be thy warrant:
Go, since I needs must die,
And give the world the lie.
The Lie (printed in FRANCIS
DAVISON, *Poetical Rhapsody,*
1608; manuscript copy traced
to 1595), st. 1

Give me my scallop shell of quiet,
  My staff of faith to walk upon,
My scrip of joy, immortal diet,
  My bottle of salvation,
My gown of glory, hope's true gage
And thus I'll take my pilgrimage.
Diaphantus [1604]. The Pas-
sionate Man's Pilgrimage

Methought I saw the grave where
  Laura lay.
Verses to Edmund Spenser

Shall I, like a hermit, dwell
On a rock or in a cell?   *Poem*

What is our life? a play of passion,

---

[1] Under this Queen Elizabeth wrote, "If thy
heart fails thee, climb not at all." — THOMAS
FULLER, *Worthies of England* [1662]

[2] See Seneca, p. 131b.
Altissima quaeque flumina minimo sono labi
[The deepest rivers flow with the least sound].
— QUINTUS CURTIUS [1st century A.D.], *VII, 4, 13*
Where the stream runneth smoothest, the
water is deepest. — LYLY, *Euphues and his Eng-*
land [1580]
Smooth runs the water where the brook is
deep. — SHAKESPEARE, *Henry VI* [1591], *pt. II,*
act III, sc. i, l. 53
Take heed of still waters, the quick pass
away. — GEORGE HERBERT, *Jacula Prudentum*
[1640]

Our mirth the music of division,
Our mothers' wombs the tiring houses
  be
Where we are dressed for this short
  comedy.
From ORLANDO GIBBONS, *The*
First Set of Madrigals and Mo-
tets [1612]. On the Life of Man

[History] hath triumphed over time,
which besides it nothing but eternity
hath triumphed over.
History of the World [1614],
preface

Whosoever, in writing a modern history, shall follow truth too near the
heels, it may haply strike out his teeth.
Ib.

O eloquent, just, and mighty Death!
whom none could advise, thou hast persuaded; what none hath dared, thou
hast done; and whom all the world hath
flattered, thou only hast cast out of the
world and despised. Thou hast drawn
together all the far-stretched greatness,
all the pride, cruelty, and ambition of
man, and covered it all over with these
two narrow words, *Hic jacet!*
Ib. bk. V, pt. I, ch. 6, conclusion

Even such is time, that takes in trust
Our youth, our joys, our all we have,
And pays us but with age and dust;
Who in the dark and silent grave,
When we have wandered all our ways,
Shuts up the story of our days.
And from which earth, and grave, and
  dust,
The Lord shall raise me up, I trust.
A version of one of his earlier
poems, found at his death in his
Bible in the Gatehouse at West-
minster.

EDMUND SPENSER
1552–1599

He that strives to touch the stars
Oft stumbles at a straw.
The Shepheardes Calender
[1579]. July, l. 99

Fierce wars and faithful loves shall moralize my song.[1]

> *The Faerie Queene* [1590], *introduction, st. 1*

A gentle knight was pricking on the plain.   *Ib. bk. I, canto 1, st. 1*

A bold bad man.   *Ib. 37*

> Her angel's face
> As the great eye of heaven shined bright,
> And made a sunshine in the shady place.   *Ib. 3, 4*

Ay me, how many perils do enfold
The righteous man, to make him daily fall.[2]   *Ib. 8, 1*

Sleep after toil, port after stormy seas,
Ease after war, death after life does greatly please.[3]   *Ib. 9, 40*

All for love, and nothing for reward.   *Ib. II, 8, 2*

Gather therefore the Rose, whilst yet is prime,
For soon comes age, that will her pride deflower:
Gather the Rose of love, whilst yet is time.[4]   *Ib. 12, 75*

Her birth was of the womb of morning dew.[5]   *Ib. III, 6, 3*

> Roses red and violets blew,
> And all the sweetest flowers, that in the forest grew.   *Ib. 6*

All that in this delightful garden grows,
Should happy be, and have immortal bliss.   *Ib. 41*

That Squire of Dames.   *Ib. 8, 44*

And painful pleasure turns to pleasing pain.

> *The Faerie Queene, bk. III, canto 10, st. 60*

How over that same door was likewise writ,
Be bold, be bold, and everywhere *Be bold*.[1]   *Ib. 11, 54*

Another iron door, on which was writ,
Be not too bold.[2]   *Ib.*

Dan Chaucer, well of English undefiled,
On Fame's eternal beadroll worthy to be filed.   *Ib. IV [1596], 2, 32*

For all that nature by her mother wit
Could frame in earth.   *Ib. 10, 21*

Ill can he rule the great, that cannot reach the small.   *Ib. V, 2, 43*

Who will not mercy unto others show,
How can he mercy ever hope to have?[3]   *Ib. VI, 1, 42*

The gentle mind by gentle deeds is known.
For a man by nothing is so well bewrayed,
As by his manners.   *Ib. 3, 1*

That here on earth is no sure happiness.   *Ib. 11, 1*

> The ever-whirling wheel
> Of Change; the which all mortal things doth sway.   *Ib. VII, 6, 1*

Wars and alarums unto nations wide.   *Ib. 3*

But times do change and move continually.[4]   *Ib. 47*

For deeds do die, however nobly done,

---

[1] And moralized his song. — POPE, *Epistle to Dr. Arbuthnot* [1735], *l. 340*

[2] Ay me! what perils do environ
The man that meddles with cold iron!
SAMUEL BUTLER: *Hudibras, pt. I* [1663], *canto III, l. 1*

[3] These lines are cut on Joseph Conrad's gravestone at Canterbury.

[4] See Horace, p. 121a; Ronsard, p. 188a; and Herrick, p. 320b.

[5] The dew of thy birth is of the womb of the morning. — *Book of Common Prayer, Psalter, Psalm 110:3*

[1] See Danton, p. 496b, and Channing, p. 544a.

[2] Jockey of Norfolk, be not too bold,
For Dickon thy master is bought and sold.
SHAKESPEARE, *Richard III, act V, sc. iii, l. 305*

Forbear, said I; be not too bold.
Your fleece is white but 'tis too cold.
CRASHAW, *Hymn of the Nativity, l. 50*
Write on your doors the saying wise and old,
"Be bold! be bold!" and everywhere — "Be bold;
Be not too bold!"
LONGFELLOW, *Morituri Salutamus* [1875]

[3] See *Matthew 5:7*, p. 40a, and Pope, p. 412b.

[4] See Lothair I, p. 152b.

And thoughts of men do as themselves
  decay,
But wise words taught in numbers for
  to run,
Recorded by the Muses, live for ay.
    The Ruines of Time [1591], *l. 400*

Full little knowest thou that hast not
  tried,
What hell it is, in suing long to bide:
To lose good days, that might be better spent;
To waste long nights in pensive discontent;
To speed today, to be put back tomorrow;
To feed on hope, to pine with fear and
  sorrow.
    Mother Hubberds Tale [1591],
              l. 895

To fret thy soul with crosses and with
  cares;
To eat thy heart through comfortless
  despairs;
To fawn, to crouch, to wait, to ride, to
  run,
To spend, to give, to want, to be undone.
Unhappy wight, born to disastrous
  end,
That doth his life in so long tendance
  spend.   *Ib. 903*

What more felicity can fall to creature,
Than to enjoy delight with liberty.
    *Muiopotmos; or, The Fate of
    the Butterflie* [1591], *l. 209*

I hate the day, because it lendeth light
To see all things, and not my love to
  see.   *Daphnaida* [1591], *l. 407*

Death slew not him, but he made death
  his ladder to the skies.
    *An Epitaph upon Sir Philip
    Sidney* [1591], *l. 20*

Though last not least.[1]
    Colin Clouts Come Home Again
            [1595], *l. 144*

---

[1] See Shakespeare, pp. 255a and 276b.
  The last, not least in honor or applause. —
Pope, *The Dunciad* [1728], *bk. IV, l. 577*

Tell her the joyous time will not be
  stayed
Unlesse she do him by the forelock
  take.[1]
    Amoretti [1595]. *Sonnet 70*

The woods shall to me answer, and my
  Echo ring.
    Epithalamion [1595], *l. 18*

Behold whiles she before the altar
  stands
Hearing the holy priest that to her
  speaks
And blesseth her with his two happy
  hands.   *Ib. 223*

Ah! when will this long weary day have
  end,
And lend me leave to come unto my
  love?   *Ib. 278*

For of the soul the body form doth
  take:
For soul is form, and doth the body
  make.
    An Hymne in Honour of Beautie
           [1596], *l. 132*

For all that fair is, is by nature good;[2]
That is a sign to know the gentle
  blood.   *Ib. 139*

Sweet Thames! run softly, till I end my
  Song.[3]
    Prothalamion [1596], *refrain*

I was promised on a time
To have reason for my rhyme;
From that time unto this season,
I received nor rhyme nor reason.
    *Lines on his promised pension.
    From* Thomas Fuller, *Wor-
    thies of England* [1662]

JOHN FLORIO
c. 1553 – 1625

England is the paradise of women,
the purgatory of men, and the hell of
horses.[4]   *Second Frutes* [1591]

---

[1] Take Time by the forelock. — Thales [c. 636–
c. 546 B.C.]
[2] See Shakespeare, p. 271b.
[3] Sweet Thames, run softly till I end my song,
  Sweet Thames, run softly, for I speak not
  loud or long.
    T. S. Eliot, *The Waste Land* [1922], *pt. III*
[4] See Robert Burton, p. 312a.

Praise the sea; on shore remain.
Second Frutes

HENRI IV OF FRANCE
1553–1610

I want there to be no peasant in my realm so poor that he will not have a chicken in his pot every Sunday.
Attributed

Paris is well worth a Mass.[1]
Attributed

Let my white panache be your rallying point.[2]   *Attributed battle cry*

The wisest fool in Christendom.
Of James I of England; attributed to HENRI IV *or* SULLY

GEORGE KEITH, FIFTH EARL MARISCHAL
1553–1623

Thai half said. Quhat say thai? Let thame say.[3]
Family motto, Mitchell Tower, Marischal College, Aberdeen, Scotland, founded in 1593

FULKE GREVILLE, LORD BROOKE
1554–1628

Oh wearisome condition of humanity! Born under one law, to another bound.
Mustapha [1609], V, 4

RICHARD HOOKER
1554–1600

Of Law there can be no less acknowledged than that her seat is the bosom of God, her voice the harmony of the world. All things in heaven and earth do her homage — the very least

as feeling her care, and the greatest as not exempted from her power.
Laws of Ecclesiastical Polity
[1594], *bk. 1*

That to live by one man's will became the cause of all men's misery.
Ib.

JOHN LYLY
c. 1554 – 1606

Be valiant, but not too venturous. Let thy attire be comely, but not costly.[1]
Euphues: The Anatomy of Wit [1579], *Arber's reprint, p. 39*

The finest edge is made with the blunt whetstone.   *Ib. p. 47*

Delays breed dangers.[2]   *Ib. p. 65*

It seems to me (said she) that you are in some brown study.   *Ib. p. 80*

Many strokes overthrow the tallest oaks.[3]   *Ib. p. 81*

Let me stand to the main chance.[4]
Ib. p. 104

It is a world to see.   *Ib. p. 116*

A clear conscience is a sure card.
Ib. p. 207

Go to bed with the lamb, and rise with the lark.[5]
Euphues and His England,
[1580], *p. 229*

A comely old man as busy as a bee.
Ib. p. 252

---

[1] Paris vaut bien une messe.
Attributed also to Henri's minister Sully.
[2] Ralliez-vous à mon panache blanc.
[3] They say. What say they? Let them say. — *Motto over the fireplace in George Bernard Shaw's home*

[1] See Shakespeare, p. 258b.
[2] Periculum in mora. — *Latin proverb*
See Shakespeare, p. 214a.
All delays are dangerous in war. — DRYDEN, *Tyrannic Love* [1669], *act I, sc. i*
[3] Many strokes, though with a little axe,
Hew down and fell the hardest-timber'd oak.
SHAKESPEARE, *Henry VI* [1591], *pt. III, act II, sc. i, l. 54*
See Franklin, p. 422a.
[4] See Butler, p. 353a.
[5] To rise with the lark and go to bed with the lamb. — BRETON, *Court and Country* [1618]
Rise with the lark, and with the lark to bed.
— JAMES HURDIS [1763–1801], *The Village Curate*

Maidens, be they never so foolish, yet being fair they are commonly fortunate.

Euphues and His England
p. 279

Your eyes are so sharp that you cannot only look through a millstone, but clean through the mind.   *Ib. p. 289*

I am glad that my Adonis hath a sweet tooth in his head.   *Ib. p. 308*

A rose is sweeter in the bud than full-blown.[1]   *Ib. p. 314*

Cupid and my Campaspe play'd
At cards for kisses: Cupid paid.

Alexander and Campaspe
[1584], act III, sc. v

How at heaven's gates she claps her wings,
The morn not waking till she sings.[2]
Ib. V, i

Night hath a thousand eyes.[3]
Maides Metamorphosis III, 1

Marriages are made in heaven and consummated on earth.[4]

Mother Bombie [1590], *act IV, sc. i*

SIR PHILIP SIDNEY
1554–1586

High-erected thoughts seated in the heart of courtesy.[5]
The Arcadia [written 1580], *bk. I*

They are never alone that are accompanied with noble thoughts.[6]   *Ib.*

---

[1] The rose is fairest when 'tis budding new. — SCOTT, *Lady of the Lake* [1810], *canto III, st. 1*

[2] See Shakespeare, p. 290b.

[3] On the stars thou gazest, my star; would I were heaven to look at thee with many eyes. — *Greek Anthology*, edited by J. W. MACKAIL, 8, 7
See Bourdillon, p. 826a.

[4] Les mariages se font au ciel, et se consomment sur la terre. — *French proverb*
See Heywood, p. 182b.
If marriages
Are made in heaven, they should be happier.
THOMAS SOUTHERNE, *The Fatal Marriage* [1694]

[5] Great thoughts come from the heart. — VAUVENARGUES [1715–1747], *Maxim 127*

[6] He never is alone that is accompanied with noble thoughts. — BEAUMONT AND FLETCHER, *Love's Cure* [1647], *act III, sc. iii*

My dear, my better half.
The Arcadia, bk. III

My true-love hath my heart, and I have his,
By just exchange one for the other given:
I hold his dear, and mine he cannot miss,
There never was a better bargain driven.   *Ib. Sonnet*

Ring out your bells! Let mourning shows be spread!
For Love is dead.   *Ib. Song*

Leave me, O Love, which reachest but to dust,
And thou, my mind, aspire to higher things;
Grow rich in that which never taketh rust:
Whatever fades, but fading pleasure brings.   *Ib. Sonnet*

Sweet food of sweetly uttered knowledge.

The Defense of Poesy [written c. 1580]

He cometh unto you with a tale which holdeth children from play, and old men from the chimney corner.
Ib.

I never heard the old song of Percy and Douglas that I found not my heart moved more than with a trumpet.
Ib.

"Fool!" said my muse to me, "look in thy heart, and write." [1]
Astrophel and Stella [1591]

With how sad steps, O Moon, thou climb'st the skies!
How silently, and with how wan a face! [2]   *Ib.*

Have I caught my heav'nly jewel.[3]
Ib. Second Song

---

[1] Look, then, into thine heart and write. — LONGFELLOW, *Voices of the Night* [1839], *prelude*

[2] Wordsworth begins a sonnet with these two lines [1802].

[3] Quoted by SHAKESPEARE in *Merry Wives of Windsor, act III, sc. iii, l. 45*

Thy necessity [1] is yet greater than mine.

> *Said on the battlefield of Zutphen [September 22, 1586] on giving his water bottle to a dying soldier*

FRANÇOIS DE MALHERBE [2]
1555–1628

And a rose, she lived as roses do, the space of a morn. [3]

> *Consolation à Monsieur du Périer* [1599]

And the fruits will outdo what the flowers have promised. [4]

> *Prière pour le roi Henri le Grand* [1605]

What Malherbe writes will endure forever.　*Sonnet à Louis XIII* [1624]

THOMAS KYD
1558–1594

What outcries call me from my naked bed?

> *The Spanish Tragedy* [5] [1594], *act II, sc. v, l. 1*

O eyes, no eyes, but fountains fraught with tears;
O life, no life, but lively form of death;
O world, no world, but mass of public wrongs,
Confused and filled with murder and misdeeds.　　*Ib. III, ii, 1*

Hieronymo, beware: go by, go by.
> *Ib. III, xii, 31*

Why then I'll fit you, [6] say no more.
When I was young, I gave my mind
And plied myself to fruitless poetry:

---

[1] More often quoted as "Thy need."
[2] See Boileau, p. 377a.
[3] Et rose, elle a vécu ce que vivent les roses, L'espace d'un matin.
[4] Et les fruits passeront la promesse des fleurs.
[5] This play was undoubtedly the most popular drama of its time, outstripping Shakespeare and the other Elizabethans.
[6] Quoted by T. S. Eliot in *The Waste Land*, *l. 431*, followed by "Hieronymo's mad againe."

Which though it profit the professor naught
Yet it is passing pleasing to the world.
> *The Spanish Tragedy, act IV, sc. ii, l. 70*

THOMAS LODGE
c. 1558 – 1625

Love in my bosom like a bee
Doth suck his sweet.

> *Rosalind* [1590]

GEORGE PEELE
c. 1558 – c. 1597

Fair and fair, and twice so fair,
　As fair as any may be.
> *The Arraignment of Paris* [1584]

My merry, merry, merry roundelay
　Concludes with Cupid's curse:
They that do change old love for new,
　Pray gods, they change for worse!
> *Ib.*

His golden locks time hath to silver turned;
O time too swift, O swiftness never ceasing!
His youth 'gainst time and age hath ever spurned,
But spurned in vain; youth waneth by increasing.
> *Polyhymnia* [1590]. *The Aged Man-at-Arms, st. 1*

His helmet now shall make a hive for bees,
And lovers' sonnets turned to holy psalms,
A man-at-arms must now serve on his knees,
And feed on prayers, which are age his alms.　　*Ib. 2*

CHIDIOCK TICHBORNE [1]
c. 1558 – 1586

My prime of youth is but a frost of cares;
My feast of joy is but a dish of pain;
My crop of corn is but a field of tares;

---

[1] He was executed for an attempt on Queen Elizabeth's life.

And all my good is but vain hope of
  gain:
The day is past, and yet I saw no sun;
And now I live, and now my life is
  done.
                Tichborne's Elegy [1586]

GEORGE CHAPMAN
c. 1559 – 1634

Promise is most given when the least is
  said.
            Hero and Leander [1598]

Love calls to war;
  Sighs his alarms,
Lips his swords are,
  The field his arms.
    Ib. Epithalamion Teratos, refrain

Young men think old men are fools;
but old men know young men are
fools.
            All Fools [1605], *act V, sc. i*

Keep thy shop, and thy shop will
keep thee. Light gains make heavy
purses.[1]
    Eastward Ho [2] [1605], *act I, sc. i*

Why, do nothing, be like a gentleman, be idle . . . Make ducks and
drakes with shillings.   *Ib.*

Only a few industrious Scots perhaps, who indeed are dispersed over the
face of the whole earth. But as for
them, there are no greater friends to
Englishmen and England, when they
are out on't, in the world, than they
are. And for my own part, I would a
hundred thousand of them were there
[Virginia]; for we are all one countrymen now, ye know, and we should find
ten times more comfort of them there
than we do here.[3]   *Ib. III, ii*

I will neither yield to the song of the
siren nor the voice of the hyena, the
tears of the crocodile [1] nor the howling
of the wolf.
            Eastward Ho, act V, sc. i

For one heat, all know, doth drive out
  another,
One passion doth expel another still.[2]
            Monsieur d'Olive [1606],
                        act V, sc. i

To put a girdle round about the
  world.[3]
            Bussy d'Ambois [1607],
                        act I, sc. i

Speed his plow.   *Ib.*

    So our lives
In acts exemplary, not only win
Ourselves good names, but doth to oth-
  ers give
Matter for virtuous deeds, by which we
  live.   *Ib.*

Who to himself is law no law doth
  need,
Offends no law, and is a king indeed.
            Ib. II, i

Give me a spirit that on this life's
  rough sea
Loves t' have his sails fill'd with a lusty
  wind,
Even till his sail-yards tremble, his
  masts crack,
And his rapt ship run on her side so
  low
That she drinks water, and her keel
  plows air.
    *Conspiracy of Charles, Duke of
        Byron* [1608], *act III, sc. i*

We have watered our horses in Helicon.
            May-Day [1611], *act III, sc. iii*

---

[1] Quoted by BENJAMIN FRANKLIN in *Poor
Richard's Almanac* [1735].

[2] By Chapman, Jonson, and Marston.

[3] This is the famous passage that gave offense
to James I and caused the imprisonment of the
authors. The leaves containing it were canceled
and reprinted, and it only occurs in a few of
the original copies. — RICHARD HERNE SHEPHERD

[1] These crocodile tears. — ROBERT BURTON,
Anatomy of Melancholy [1621–1651], *pt. III,
sec. 2, member 2, subsec. 4*

She's false, false as the tears of crocodiles. —
SIR JOHN SUCKLING [1609–1642], *The Sad One,
act IV, sc. v*

[2] See Shakespeare, p. 223a.

[3] See Shakespeare, p. 229b.

MAXIMILIEN
DUC DE SULLY[1]
1559–1641

Tilling and grazing are the two
breasts that feed France.[2]

Economies Royales, III

ROBERT GREENE
1560–1592

Sweet are the thoughts that savor of
content;
The quiet mind is richer than a crown.

Farewell to Folly [1591], *st. 1*

A mind content both crown and
kingdom is.   *Ib. 2*

For there is an upstart crow, beautified with our feathers, that with his
tiger's heart wrapped in a player's
hide,[3] supposes he is as well able to
bumbast out a blank verse as the best
of you; and being an absolute *Johannes
fac totum*, is in his own conceit the
only Shake-scene in a country.[4]

The Croatsworth of Wit [1592]

Hangs in the uncertain balance of
proud time.

*Friar Bacon and Friar Bungay
[acted 1594], act III*

Hell's broken loose.[5]   *Ib. IV*

FRANCIS BACON[6]
1561–1626

I have taken all knowledge to be my
province.

Letter to Lord Burleigh [1592]

The monuments of wit survive the
monuments of power.

Essex's Device [1595]

---

[1] See Henri IV of France, p. 202a.

[2] Labourage et pâturage sont les deux ma-
melles dont la France est alimentée.

[3] See Shakespeare, p. 215b.

[4] First known literary reference to Shakespeare.

[5] See Milton, p. 346a.

[6] If parts allure thee, think how Bacon shined,
The wisest, brightest, meanest of mankind.
POPE, *Essay on Man*, epistle IV, l. 281
See Walton, p. 326b.

Knowledge is power [Nam et ipsa
scientia potestas est].[1]

Meditationes Sacrae [1597].
De Haeresibus

For all knowledge and wonder
(which is the seed of knowledge) is an
impression of pleasure in itself.

The Advancement of Learning
[1605], *bk. I, i, 3*

Time, which is the author of authors.   *Ib. iv, 12*

If a man will begin with certainties,
he shall end in doubts; but if he will be
content to begin with doubts he shall
end in certainties.   *Ib. v, 8*

Antiquitas saeculi juventus mundi.
These times are the ancient times,
when the world is ancient, and not
those which we account ancient *ordine
retrogrado*, by a computation backward
from ourselves.[2]   *Ib.*

[Knowledge] is a rich storehouse for
the glory of the Creator and the relief
of man's estate.   *Ib., 11*

It [Poesy] was ever thought to have

---

[1] See *Proverbs 24:5*, p. 26a.
Knowledge is more than equivalent to force.
— SAMUEL JOHNSON, *Rasselas* [1759], *ch. 13*

[2] As in the little, so in the great world, reason will tell you that old age or antiquity is
to be accounted by the farther distance from
the beginning and the nearer approach to the
end — the times wherein we now live being
in propriety of speech the most ancient since
the world's creation. — GEORGE HAKEWILL, *An
Apologie or Declaration of the Power and Providence of God in the Government of the World*
[1627]
For as old age is that period of life most
remote from infancy, who does not see that
old age in this universal man ought not to be
sought in the times nearest his birth, but in
those most remote from it? — PASCAL [1623–
1662], *Preface to the Treatise on Vacuum*
It is worthy of remark that a thought which
is often quoted from Francis Bacon occurs in
[Giordano] Bruno's *Cena di Cenere*, published
in 1584: I mean the notion that the later times
are more aged than the earlier. — WHEWELL,
Philosophy of the Inductive Sciences [1847],
vol. II, p. 198
    We are Ancients of the earth,
    And in the morning of the times.
TENNYSON, *The Day Dream* [1842],
L'Envoi

some participation of divineness, because it doth raise and erect the mind by submitting the shews of things to the desires of the mind.

The Advancement of Learning,
bk. II, iv, 2

They are ill discoverers that think there is no land, when they can see nothing but sea.   *Ib. vii, 5*

But men must know that in this theatre of man's life it is reserved only for God and angels to be lookers on.
Ib. xx, 8

We are much beholden to Machiavel and others, that write what men do, and not what they ought to do.
Ib. xxi, 9

All good moral philosophy is but the handmaid to religion.   *Ib. xxii, 14*

There are and can be only two ways of searching into and discovering truth. The one flies from the senses and particulars to the most general axioms . . . this way is now in fashion. The other derives axioms from the senses and particulars, rising by a gradual and unbroken ascent, so that it arrives at the most general axioms last of all. This is the true way, but as yet untried.

Novum Organum [1620]

There are four classes of Idols which beset men's minds. To these for distinction's sake I have assigned names — calling the first class, Idols of the Tribe; the second, Idols of the Cave; the third, Idols of the Market-Place; the fourth, Idols of the Theatre.
Ib. Aphorism 39

Nature, to be commanded, must be obeyed.   *Ib. 129*

I do plainly and ingenuously confess that I am guilty of corruption, and do renounce all defense. I beseech your Lordships to be merciful to a broken reed.[1]

On being charged by Parliament with corruption in the exercise of his office [1621]

[1] See *Isaiah 36:6,* p. 32b.

Lucid intervals and happy pauses.
History of King Henry VII
[1622], *III*

Nothing is terrible except fear itself.[1]
De Augmentis Scientiarum,
bk. II, Fortitudo [1623]

Riches are a good handmaid, but the worst mistress.   *Ib. Antitheta*

Hope is a good breakfast, but it is a bad supper.
Apothegms [1624], *no. 36*

Like strawberry wives, that laid two or three great strawberries at the mouth of their pot, and all the rest were little ones.   *Ib. 54*

Sir Amice Pawlet, when he saw too much haste made in any matter, was wont to say, "Stay a while, that we may make an end the sooner."   *Ib. 76*

Alonso of Aragon was wont to say in commendation of age, that age appears to be best in four things — old wood best to burn, old wine to drink, old friends to trust, and old authors to read.[2]   *Ib. 97*

Cosmus, Duke of Florence, was wont to say of perfidious friends, that "We read that we ought to forgive our enemies; but we do not read that we ought to forgive our friends."   *Ib. 206*

Cato said the best way to keep good acts in memory was to refresh them with new.   *Ib. 247*

My essays . . . come home to men's business and bosoms.
Essays, dedication [1625 edition]

What is truth? said jesting Pilate,[3] and would not stay for an answer.
Ib. Of Truth

[1] Nil terribile nisi ipse timor.
See Montaigne, p. 189b and note.
[2] See Webster, p. 314b.
Old friends are best. King James used to call for his old shoes; they were easiest for his feet.
— SELDEN, *Table Talk* [1689], *Friends*
See Goldsmith, p. 450b.
Old books, old wine, old Nankin blue. —
HENRY AUSTIN DOBSON [1840–1921], *Rondeau, To Richard Watson Gilder*
[3] See *John 18:38,* p. 49b.

No pleasure is comparable to the standing upon the vantage-ground of truth."

Essays, Of Truth

Men fear death as children fear to go in the dark; and as that natural fear in children is increased with tales, so is the other.[1]   *Ib. Of Death*

Revenge is a kind of wild justice, which the more man's nature runs to, the more ought law to weed it out.

Ib. Of Revenge

It was a high speech of Seneca (after the manner of the Stoics), that "The good things which belong to prosperity are to be wished, but the good things that belong to adversity are to be admired."   *Ib. Of Adversity*

Prosperity is the blessing of the Old Testament; adversity is the blessing of the New.   **Ib.**

Prosperity is not without many fears and distastes; and adversity is not without comforts and hopes.   **Ib.**

Prosperity doth best discover vice, but adversity doth best discover virtue.   *Ib.*

Virtue is like precious odors — most fragrant when they are incensed or crushed.[2]   **Ib.**

He that hath wife and children hath given hostages to fortune; for they are impediments to great enterprises, either of virtue or mischief.

Ib. Of Marriage and Single Life

Wives are young men's mistresses, companions for middle age, and old men's nurses.   **Ib.**

A good name is like a precious ointment; it filleth all around about, and will not easily away; for the odors of

[1] See Lucretius, p. 113b.
[2] As aromatic plants bestow
No spicy fragrance while they grow;
But crushed or trodden to the ground,
Diffuse their balmy sweets around.
     GOLDSMITH, *The Captivity* [1764], *act I*
The good are better made by ill,
As odors crushed are sweeter still.
     SAMUEL ROGERS, *Jacqueline* [1814], *st. 3*

ointments are more durable than those of flowers.[1]

Essays, Of Praise

In charity there is no excess.
Ib. Of Goodness and Goodness of Nature

If a man be gracious and courteous to strangers, it shows he is a citizen of the world,[2] and that his heart is no island cut off from other lands, but a continent that joins to them.[3]   *Ib.*

The desire of power in excess caused the angels to fall; the desire of knowledge in excess caused man to fall.[4]

Ib.

I had rather believe all the fables in the legends and the Talmud and the Alcoran, than that this universal frame is without a mind.   *Ib. Of Atheism*

A little philosophy inclineth man's mind to atheism, but depth in philosophy bringeth men's minds about to religion.[5]   *Ib.*

Travel, in the younger sort, is a part of education; in the elder, a part of experience. He that traveleth into a country before he hath some entrance into the language, goeth to school, and not to travel.   *Ib. Of Travel*

Princes are like to heavenly bodies, which cause good or evil times, and which have much veneration but no rest.[6]   *Ib. Of Empire*

[1] See *Ecclesiastes 7:1*, p. 28a, and Publilius Syrus, p. 125a.
[2] See Socrates, p. 87b.
[3] See Donne, p. 308b.
[4] Pride still is aiming at the blest abodes;
Men would be angels, angels would be gods.
Aspiring to be gods if angels fell,
Aspiring to be angels men rebel.
     ALEXANDER POPE, *Essay on Man,*
           epistle I [1733], *l. 125*
[5] A little skill in antiquity inclines a man to Popery; but depth in that study brings him about again to our religion. — THOMAS FULLER, *The Holy State and the Profane State* [1642], *The True Church Antiquary*
[6] See Shelley, p. 570b.

Fortune is like the market, where many times, if you can stay a little, the price will fall.

Essays, Of Delays

Nothing doth more hurt in a state than that cunning men pass for wise.

Ib. Of Cunning

Be so true to thyself, as thou be not false to others.[1]

Ib. Of Wisdom for a Man's Self

It is the nature of extreme self-lovers, as they will set an house on fire, and it were but to roast their eggs.　　　**Ib.**

Cure the disease and kill the patient.　　　*Ib. Of Friendship*

Riches are for spending.

Ib. Of Expense

There is a wisdom in this beyond the rules of physic. A man's own observation, what he finds good of and what he finds hurt of, is the best physic to preserve health.

Ib. Of Regimen of Health

Intermingle . . . jest with earnest.[2]

Ib. Of Discourse

Nature is often hidden; sometimes overcome; seldom extinguished.

Ib. Of Nature in Men

If a man look sharply and attentively, he shall see Fortune; for though she is blind, she is not invisible.[3]

Ib. Of Fortune

Chiefly the mold of a man's fortune is in his own hands.[4]　　　**Ib.**

Young men are fitter to invent than to judge, fitter for execution than for counsel, and fitter for new projects than for settled business.

Ib. Of Youth and Age

Virtue is like a rich stone — best plain set.　　　*Ib. Of Beauty*

[1] See Shakespeare, p. 259a.

[2] See Menander, p. 102a, Horace, p. 122b, and note.

[3] Fortune is painted blind, with a muffler afore her eyes, to signify to you that Fortune is blind. — SHAKESPEARE, *Henry V* [1598–1600], *act III, sc. vi, l. 31*

[4] See Sallust, p. 116a, and note.

There is no excellent beauty that hath not some strangeness in the proportion.

Essays, Of Beauty

God Almighty first planted a garden.[1]　　　*Ib. Of Gardens*

He that commands the sea is at great liberty, and may take as much and as little of the war as he will.[2]

Ib. Of the True Greatness of Kingdoms

Some books are to be tasted, others to be swallowed, and some few to be chewed and digested.　　*Ib. Of Studies*

Reading maketh a full man, conference a ready man, and writing an exact man.　　　**Ib.**

Histories make men wise; poets, witty; the mathematics, subtile; natural philosophy, deep; moral, grave; logic and rhetoric, able to contend.　　**Ib.**

The greatest vicissitude of things amongst men is the vicissitude of sects and religions.

Ib. Of Vicissitude of Things

I bequeath my soul to God. . . . My body to be buried obscurely. For my name and memory, I leave it to men's charitable speeches, and to foreign nations, and the next age.

From his will [1626]

The world's a bubble, and the life of man

[1] See *Genesis 2:8*, p. 5b.

Divina natura dedit agros, ars humana aedificavit urbes [Divine Nature gave the fields, human art built the cities]. — VARRO [116–27 B.C.], *De Re Rustica III, 1*

See Shakespeare, p. 265b.

Gardens were before gardeners, and but some hours after the earth. — SIR THOMAS BROWNE, *The Garden of Cyrus* [1658], *ch. I*

See Cowley, p. 358a, and Cowper, p. 457b.

[2] See Themistocles, p. 78a; Mahan, p. 785b; and Morison, p. 998a.

He that is master of the sea, may, in some sort, be said to be Master of every country; at least such as are bordering on the sea. For he is at liberty to begin and end War, where, when, and on what terms he pleaseth, and extend his conquests even to the Antipodes. — JOSEPH GANDER, *The Glory of Her Sacred Majesty Queen Anne in the Royal Navy* [1703]

Less than a span.[1]
The World [1629]

Who then to frail mortality shall trust
But limns on water, or but writes in
dust.[2] *Ib.*

What then remains but that we still
should cry
For being born, and, being born, to
die? [3] *Ib.*

Books must follow sciences, and not
sciences books.
*Proposition touching amend-
ment of laws*

SIR JOHN HARINGTON
1561–1612

Treason doth never prosper: what's the
reason?
For if it prosper, none dare call it treason.[4] *Epigrams. Of Treason*

The readers and the hearers like my
books,
But yet some writers cannot them
digest;
But what care I? for when I make a
feast
I would my guests should praise it, not
the cooks.
*Ib. Of Writers Who Carp at
Other Men's Books*

ROBERT SOUTHWELL
c. 1561 – 1595

Times go by turns, and chances change
by course,

From foul to fair, from better hap to
worse.
Times Go by Turns [c. 1595],
st. 1

May never was the month of love,
For May is full of flowers;
But rather April, wet by kind,
For love is full of showers.
Love's Servile Lot

As I in hoary winter night stood shivering in the snow,
Surprised was I with sudden heat which
made my heart to glow;
And lifting up a fearful eye to view
what fire was near
A pretty Babe all burning bright did in
the air appear.
The Burning Babe [written
c. 1595]

With this he vanished out of sight, and
swiftly shrunk away,
And straight I called unto mind that it
was Christmas Day. *Ib.*

SAMUEL DANIEL
1562–1619

Care-charmer Sleep, son of the sable
Night,
Brother to Death, in silent darkness
born.[1]
Sonnets to Delia [1592]

Make me to say, when all my griefs are
gone,
"Happy the heart that sighed for such a
one!"
Ib. Sonnet: I Must Not Grieve

Let others sing of knights and paladins
In aged accents and untimely words,
Paint shadows in imaginary lines

---

[1] Whose life is a bubble, and in length a
span. — WILLIAM BROWNE, *Britannia's Pastorals*
[1613], *bk. I, song*
See Sir John Davies, p. 301a, and *The New
England Primer,* p. 1089b.
[2] See Sophocles, p. 83a; Catullus, p. 115a;
More, p. 178b; Shakespeare, p. 299a; and Keats,
p. 586a.
[3] This line frequently occurs in almost exactly the same shape among the minor poems
of the time: "Not to be born, or, being born, to
die." — WILLIAM DRUMMOND, *Poems* [1656]
See Theognis, p. 77a, and note.
[4] See Seneca, p. 131a.

[1] Care-charmer sleep, sweet ease in restless
misery,
The captive's liberty, and his freedom's
song,
Balm of the bruised heart, man's chief
felicity,
Brother of quiet death, when life is too,
too long!
BARTHOLOMEW GRIFFIN, *Fidessa More
Chaste Than Kind* [1596]
See Homer, p. 64a; Virgil, p. 119a; Shakes-
peare, p. 284a; and Shelley, p. 568a.

Which well the reach of their high wits
    record.
> *Sonnets to Delia. Sonnet:*
> *I Must Not Grieve*

These are the arks, the trophies, I
    erect,
That fortify thy name against old age.
> *Ib.*

And for the few that only lend their
    ear,
That few is all the world.
> *Musophilus* [1599], *st. 97*

This is the thing that I was born to
    do.   *Ib. st. 100*

Unless above himself he can
Erect himself, how poor a thing is man!
> *To the Countess of Cumberland*
> [*c. 1600*], *st. 12*

Love is a sickness full of woes,
All remedies refusing.
> *Hymen's Triumph* [1615]

LOPE DE VEGA
1562–1632

Harmony is pure love, for love is
complete agreement.
> *Fuente Ovejuna,* [1] *act I, l. 381*

Except for God, the King's our only
lord.   *Ib. 1701*

MICHAEL DRAYTON
1563–1631

Fair stood the wind for France.
> *The Ballad of Agincourt* [1606],
> *st. 1*

O, when shall Englishmen
With such acts fill a pen,
Or England breed again
Such a King Harry?   *Ib. 15*

Since there's no help, come let us kiss
    and part —
Nay, I have done: you get no more of
    me,
And I am glad, yea glad with all my
    heart,
That thus so cleanly I myself can free.

---

[1] Translated by ANGEL FORES and MURIEL KITTEL. From *Spanish Drama* [1962].

Shake hands forever, cancel all our
    vows,
And when we meet at any time again,
Be it not seen in either of our brows
That we one jot of former love retain.
Now at the last gasp of love's latest
    breath,
When his pulse failing, Passion speech-
    less lies,
When Faith is kneeling by his bed of
    death,
And Innocence is closing up his eyes,
Now if thou wouldst, when all have
    given him over,
From death to life thou might'st him
    yet recover.
> *Poems* [1619]. *Idea*

The coast was clear.
> *Nymphidia* [1627]

Had in him those brave translunary
    things
That the first poets had.
> *Said of* MARLOWE. *To Henry*
> *Reynolds, Of Poets and Poesy*
> [1627]

For that fine madness still he did re-
    tain
Which rightly should possess a poet's
    brain.   *Ib.*

GALILEO GALILEI
1564–1642

Philosophy is written in this grand
book — I mean the universe — which
stands continually open to our gaze, but
it cannot be understood unless one first
learns to comprehend the language and
interpret the characters in which it is
written. It is written in the language of
mathematics, and its characters are triangles, circles, and other geometrical
figures, without which it is humanly
impossible to understand a single word
of it; without these, one is wandering
about in a dark labyrinth.
> *Il Saggiatore* [1623] [1]

---

[1] *The Assayer* in *The Controversy on the Comets of 1618* [1960], translated by STILLMAN DRAKE and C. D. O'MALLEY.

But it does move! [1]
From ABBÉ IRAILH, *Ouerelles litteraires* [1761], *vol. III, p. 49*

CHRISTOPHER MARLOWE
1564–1593

Our swords shall play the orators for us.
Tamburlaine the Great [c. 1587], *pt. I, l. 328*

Accurst be he that first invented war.
Ib. 664

And ride in triumph through Persepolis.
Ib. 759

Nature that framed us of our elements,
Warring within our breasts for regiment,
Doth teach us all to have aspiring minds:
Our souls, whose faculties can comprehend
The wondrous Architecture of the world:
And measure every wandering planet's course,
Still climbing after knowledge infinite,
And always moving as the restless Spheres,
Will us to wear ourselves and never rest,
Until we reach the ripest fruit of all,
That perfect bliss and sole felicity,
The sweet fruition of an earthly crown.
Ib. 869

Tamburlaine, the Scourge of God, must die.   *Ib. 4641*

Come live with me, and be my love;
And we will all the pleasures prove
That valleys, groves, hills, and fields,
Woods or steepy mountain yields.[2]
The Passionate Shepherd to his Love [c. 1589]

By shallow rivers, to whose falls
Melodious birds sing madrigals.[1]
The Passionate Shepherd to his Love

And I will make thee beds of roses
And a thousand fragrant posies.[1]
Ib.

I count religion but a childish toy,
And hold there is no sin but ignorance.[2]
The Jew of Malta [c. 1589], *prologue*

Infinite riches in a little room.[3]
Ib. act I, sc. 1

Excess of wealth is cause of covetousness.   *Ib. 2*

Now will I show myself to have more of the serpent than the dove; [4] that is, more knave than fool.   *Ib. II, 3*

Friar Barnadine: Thou hast committed—
Barabas: Fornication—but that was in another country;
And besides, the wench is dead.
Ib. IV, 1

My men, like satyrs grazing on the lawns,
Shall with their goat feet dance the antic hay.
Edward II [1593], *act I, sc. i*

Who ever loved that loved not at first sight? [5]
Hero and Leander [1598]

---

[1] E pur si muove!
The remark attributed to Galileo immediately after he was forced to recant his views on the earth's motion before the Inquisition in 1633.
[2] See Ralegh, p. 198b, and Donne, p. 306a.

[1] To shallow rivers, to whose falls
Melodious birds sing madrigals;
There will we make our peds of roses,
And a thousand fragrant posies.
SHAKESPEARE, *Merry Wives of Windsor* [1600–1601], *act III, sc. i, l. 17* [sung by Evans]
[2] See Wilde, p. 839a.
[3] Here lyeth muche rychnesse in lytell space.
— JOHN HEYWOOD, *The Foure PP* [1521–1525]
[4] See *Matthew 10:16*, p. 42a.
[5] Quoted in SHAKESPEARE, *As You Like It*, act III, sc. v, l. 82
None ever loved but at first sight they loved.
— GEORGE CHAPMAN, *The Blind Beggar of Alexandria* [1598]
I saw and loved. — GIBBON, *Memoirs* [1796]

Like untuned golden strings all women
are,
Which long time lie untoucht, will
harshly jar.
Vessels of brass oft handled brightly
shine.

Hero and Leander

Live and die in Aristotle's works.
*The Tragical History of Doctor
Faustus [published 1604], sc. i*

Unhappy spirits that fell with Lucifer,
Conspired against our God with Luci-
fer,
And are forever damned with Lucifer.
Ib. iii

Why this is hell, nor am I out of it:[1]
Think'st thou that I who saw the face
of God,
And tasted the eternal joys of Heaven,
Am not tormented with ten thousand
hells,
In being deprived of everlasting bliss?
Ib.

Hell hath no limits, nor is circum-
scribed
In one self place; for where we are is
hell,
And where hell is there must we ever
be.[1] *Ib. v*

When all the world dissolves,
And every creature shall be purified,
All places shall be hell that is not
Heaven. *Ib.*

Have not I made blind Homer sing to
me? *Ib. vi*

Was this the face that launched a thousand ships,
And burnt the topless towers of Ilium?[2]
Sweet Helen, make me immortal with a
kiss.

Her lips suck forth my soul;[1] see,
where it flies!
*The Tragical History of Doctor
Faustus, sc. xiv*

Oh, thou art fairer than the evening
air
Clad in the beauty of a thousand stars.
Ib.

Pray for me! and what noise soever
ye hear, come not unto me, for nothing
can rescue me. *Ib. xvi*

Now hast thou but one bare hour to
live,
And then thou must be damned per-
petually!
Stand still, you ever-moving spheres of
Heaven,
That time may cease, and midnight
never come. *Ib.*

O lente, lente currite noctis equi:[2]
The stars move still, time runs, the
clock will strike,
The Devil will come, and Faustus must
be damned.
O, I'll leap up to my God! Who pulls
me down?
See, see where Christ's blood streams
in the firmament!
One drop would save my soul—half a
drop: ah, my Christ! *Ib.*

O soul, be changed into little waterdrops,
And fall into the ocean—ne'er to be
found.
My God! my God! look not so fierce on
me! *Ib.*

I'll burn my books! *Ib.*

Cut is the branch that might have
grown full straight,
And burnèd is Apollo's laurel bough,[3]
That sometime grew within this
learnèd man. *Ib.*

---

[1] See Virgil, p. 119a; Browne, p. 330a; Milton,
p. 342a and p. 345a; Eliot, p. 1007a; Sartre, p.
1058b; and Robert Lowell, p. 1076b.
[2] Was this fair face the cause, quoth she,
Why the Grecians sacked Troy?
SHAKESPEARE, *All's Well that Ends Well*
[1601–1603], *act I, sc. iii, l. 75*

[1] Once he drew
With one long kiss my whole soul through
My lips.
TENNYSON, *Fatima* [1833], *st. 3*
[2] Run slowly, slowly, horses of the night.
At si, quem malis, Cephalum complexa
teneres,
Clamares "lente currite noctis equi."
OVID [43 B.C.–A.D. 18], *Amores I, xiii, 39*
[3] See Shakespeare, p. 288b.

WILLIAM
SHAKESPEARE[1]
1564–1616

Hung be the heavens with black, yield day to night!
King Henry VI [1591], *Part I, act I, sc. i, l. 1*

Fight till the last gasp. I, ii, 127

Expect Saint Martin's summer, halcyon days.[2] I, ii, 131

Glory is like a circle in the water,
Which never ceaseth to enlarge itself,
Till by broad spreading it disperse to nought. I, ii, 133

　Unbidden guests
Are often welcomest when they are gone. II, ii, 55

Between two hawks, which flies the higher pitch;
Between two dogs, which hath the deeper mouth;
Between two blades, which bears the better temper;
Between two horses, which doth bear him best;
Between two girls, which hath the merriest eye;
I have, perhaps, some shallow spirit of judgment;
But in these nice sharp quillets of the law,
Good faith, I am no wiser than a daw. II, iv, 12

I'll note you in my book of memory. II, iv, 101

Just death, kind umpire of men's miseries. II, v, 29

Chok'd with ambition of the meaner sort. II, v, 123

Delays have dangerous ends.[3] III, ii, 33

---

[1] From the text of W. J. Craig, Oxford University Press. The dates and order, about which there is much conjecture, are those which Sir Edmund Chambers (*William Shakespeare*, 1930) thinks most probable.
[2] See Aristophanes, p. 91b.
[3] See Lyly, p. 202b.
　All delays are dangerous in war. — Dryden, *Tyrannic Love* [1669], *act I, sc. i*

Of all base passions, fear is most accurs'd.
Henry VI, Part I, V, ii, 18

She's beautiful and therefore to be woo'd,
She is a woman, therefore to be won.[1]
V, iii, 78

For what is wedlock forced, but a hell,
An age of discord and continual strife?
Whereas the contrary bringeth bliss,
And is a pattern of celestial peace.
V, v, 62

　Whose large style
Agrees not with the leanness of his purse.
King Henry VI, Part II, act I, sc. i, l. 112

'Tis not my speeches that you do mislike,
But 'tis my presence that doth trouble ye.
Rancor will out. I, i, 141

Could I come near your beauty with my nails
I'd set my ten commandments in your face. I, iii, 144

Blessed are the peacemakers on earth.[2]
II, i, 34

Now, God be prais'd, that to believing souls
Gives light in darkness, comfort in despair! II, i, 66

God defend the right! II, iii, 55

　Sometimes hath the brightest day a cloud;
And after summer evermore succeeds
Barren winter, with his wrathful nipping cold:
So cares and joys abound, as seasons fleet. II, iv, 1

Now 'tis the spring, and weeds are shallow-rooted;
Suffer them now and they'll o'ergrow the garden. III, i, 31

---

[1] See *Titus Andronicus*, p. 218b.
[2] See *Matthew* 5:9, p. 40a.

In thy face I see
The map of honor, truth, and loyalty.
Henry VI, Part II, III, i, 202

What stronger breastplate than a heart
untainted!
Thrice is he arm'd that hath his quarrel just,
And he but naked, though locked up in
steel,
Whose conscience with injustice is corrupted.[1]   *III, ii, 232*

He dies, and makes no sign.
                                III, iii, 29

Forbear to judge, for we are sinners
all.[2]

Close up his eyes and draw the curtain
close;
And let us all to meditation.
                                III, iii, 31

The gaudy, blabbing, and remorseful
day
Is crept into the bosom of the sea.
                                IV, i, 1

Small things make base men proud.
                                IV, i, 106

True nobility is exempt from fear.
                                IV, i, 129

I will make it felony to drink small
beer.[3]   *IV, ii, 75*

The first thing we do, let's kill all the
lawyers.   *IV, ii, 86*

Is not this a lamentable thing, that
of the skin of an innocent lamb should
be made parchment? that parchment,
being scribbled o'er, should undo a
man?   *IV, ii, 88*

And Adam was a gardener.[4]
                                IV, ii, 146

Sir, he made a chimney in my father's house, and the bricks are alive at
this day to testify it.
Henry VI, Part II, IV, ii, 160

Thou hast most traitorously corrupted the youth of the realm in erecting a grammar-school; and whereas, before, our forefathers had no other books
but the score and the tally, thou hast
caused printing to be used; and, contrary to the king, his crown, and dignity, thou hast built a paper-mill.
                                IV, vii, 35

Beggars mounted run their horse to
death.[1]
King Henry VI, Part III, act I,
sc. iv, l. 127

O tiger's heart wrapp'd in a woman's
hide! [2]   *I, iv, 137*

To weep is to make less the depth of
grief.   *II, i, 85*

The smallest worm will turn being
trodden on.   *II, ii, 17*

Didst thou never hear
That things ill got had ever bad suc-
cess?
And happy always was it for that son
Whose father for his hoarding went to
hell?   *II, ii, 45*

Thou setter up and plucker down of
kings.[3]   *II, iii, 37*

And what makes robbers bold but too
much lenity?   *II, vi, 22*

My crown is in my heart, not on my
head;
Not deck'd with diamonds and Indian
stones,
Nor to be seen: my crown is call'd content;
A crown it is that seldom kings enjoy.
                                III, i, 62

---

[1] See Milton, p. 337a.
[2] See *Matthew 7:1*, p. 41a.
[3] Doth it not show vilely in me to desire small
beer? — *King Henry IV* [1597–1598], *pt. II, I, ii, 7*
   See *Othello*, p. 273b.
   That questionable superfluity — small beer.
— DOUGLAS JERROLD [1803–1857], *The Tragedy
of the Till*
   [4] See *Hamlet V, i, 32*, p. 265b; Bacon, p. 209b;
and Kipling, p. 877b.

[1] Set a beggar on horseback and he will ride
a gallop. — ROBERT BURTON, *Anatomy of Melancholy* [1621–1651], *pt. II, sec. 2, member 2*
   Set a beggar on horseback, and he'll outride
the Devil. — BOHN, *Foreign Proverbs, German*
[1855]
   [2] See Robert Greene, p. 206a.
   [3] Proud setter up and puller down of kings.
—*Ib. III, iii, 157*

'Tis a happy thing
To be the father unto many sons.
Henry VI, Part III, III, ii, 104

Like one that stands upon a promontory,
And spies a far-off shore where he would tread,
Wishing his foot were equal with his eye.   *III, ii,* 135

Yield not thy neck
To fortune's yoke, but let thy dauntless mind
Still ride in triumph over all mischance.   *III, iii,* 16

For how can tyrants safely govern home,
Unless abroad they purchase great alliance?   *III, iii,* 69

Having nothing, nothing can he lose.
III, iii, 152

Lives like a drunken sailor on a mast,
Ready with every nod to tumble down.
III, iv, 98

Hasty marriage seldom proveth well.
IV, i, 18

Let us be back'd with God and with the seas
Which he hath given for fence impregnable,
And with their helps only defend ourselves:
In them and in ourselves our safety lies.   *IV, i,* 43

What fates impose, that men must needs abide;
It boots not to resist both wind and tide.   *IV, iii,* 57

Now join your hands, and with your hands your hearts.   *IV, vi,* 39

For many men that stumble at the threshold
Are well foretold that danger lurks within.   *IV, vii,* 11

A little fire is quickly trodden out,
Which, being suffer'd, rivers cannot quench.   *IV, viii,* 7

When the lion fawns upon the lamb,
The lamb will never cease to follow him.
Henry VI, Part III, IV, viii, 49

What is pomp, rule, reign, but earth and dust?
And, live we how we can, yet die we must.   *V, ii,* 27

Every cloud engenders not a storm.
V, iii, 13

What though the mast be now blown overboard,
The cable broke, the holding anchor lost,
And half our sailors swallow'd in the flood?
Yet lives our pilot still.   *V, iv,* 3

So part we sadly in this troublous world
To meet with joy in sweet Jerusalem.
V, v, 7

Men ne'er spend their fury on a child.
V, v, 57

He's sudden if a thing comes in his head.   *V, v,* 86

Suspicion always haunts the guilty mind;
The thief doth fear each bush an officer.   *V, vi,* 11

This word "love," which greybeards call divine.   *V, vi,* 81

Now is the winter of our discontent
Made glorious summer by this sun of York.
King Richard III [1592–1593],
act I, sc. i, l. 1

Grim-visaged war hath smoothed his wrinkled front.   *I, i,* 9

He capers nimbly in a lady's chamber
To the lascivious pleasing of a lute.
I, i, 12

This weak piping time of peace.
I, i, 24

No beast so fierce but knows some touch of pity.   *I, ii,* 71

Look, how my ring encompasseth thy finger,

Even so thy breast encloseth my poor
heart;
Wear both of them, for both of them
are thine.
　　　Richard III, I, ii, 204

Was ever woman in this humor
woo'd?
Was ever woman in this humor won?
　　　I, ii, 229

Fram'd in the prodigality of nature.
　　　I, ii, 245

　　The world is grown so bad,
That wrens make prey where eagles
dare not perch.[1]　　　*I, iii, 70*

And thus I clothe my naked villany
With odd old ends stol'n forth of holy
writ,
And seem a saint when most I play the
devil.　　　*I, iii, 336*

Talkers are no good doers.
　　　I, iii, 351

O, I have passed a miserable night,
So full of ugly sights, of ghastly
dreams,
That, as I am a Christian faithful
man,
I would not spend another such a
night,
Though 'twere to buy a world of happy
days.　　　*I, iv, 2*

Lord, Lord! methought, what pain it
was to drown:
What dreadful noise of waters in mine
ears!
What ugly sights of death within mine
eyes!
Methought I saw a thousand fearful
wracks;
A thousand men that fishes gnaw
upon.　　　*I, iv, 21*

The kingdom of perpetual night.
　　　I, iv, 47

Sorrow breaks seasons and reposing
hours,
Makes the night morning, and the
noontide night.　　　*I, iv, 76*

A parlous boy.　　　*II, iv, 35*

[1] See Pope, p. 404a.

So wise so young, they say, do never live
long.[1]
　　　Richard III, III, i, 79

Off with his head! [2]　　　*III, iv, 75*

I am not in the giving vein today.
　　　IV, ii, 115

The sons of Edward sleep in Abraham's
bosom.[3]　　　*IV, iii, 38*

A grievous burden was thy birth to
me;
Tetchy and wayward was thy infancy.
　　　IV, iv, 168

An honest tale speeds best being plainly
told.　　　*IV, iv, 359*

Harp not on that string.　　　*IV, iv, 365*

Relenting fool, and shallow changing
woman!　　　*IV, iv, 432*

Is the chair empty? is the sword un-
sway'd?
Is the king dead? the empire unpos-
sess'd?　　　*IV, iv, 470*

Thus far into the bowels of the land
Have we march'd on without impedi-
ment.　　　*V, ii, 3*

True hope is swift, and flies with swallow's wings;
Kings it makes gods, and meaner creatures kings.　　　*V, ii, 23*

The king's name is a tower of strength.
　　　V, iii, 12

Give me another horse! bind up my
wounds!　　　*V, iii, 178*

O coward conscience, how dost thou
afflict me!　　　*V, iii, 180*

My conscience hath a thousand several
tongues,
And every tongue brings in a several
tale,
And every tale condemns me for a villain.　　　*V, iii, 194*

[1] A little too wise, they say, do ne'er live long.
— MIDDLETON [1580–1627], *The Phoenix, act I,
sc. i*

[2] See Colley Cibber, p. 392b, and Lewis Carroll, p. 744a.

[3] See *Luke 16:22*, p. 47a.

By the apostle Paul, shadows tonight
Have struck more terror to the soul of
Richard
Than can the substance of ten thou-
sand soldiers.
            Richard III, V, *iii*, 217

Conscience is but a word that cowards
use,
Devis'd at first to keep the strong in
awe.   V, *iii*, 310

A horse! a horse! my kingdom for a
horse!   V, *iv*, 7

        I have set my life upon a cast,
And I will stand the hazard of the die.
I think there be six Richmonds in the
field.   V, *iv*, 9

The pleasing punishment that women
bear.
        The Comedy of Errors [1592–
        1593], *act I, sc. i, l. 46*

We may pity, though not pardon thee.
            I, *i*, 97

Why, headstrong liberty is lash'd with
woe.
There's nothing situate under heaven's
eye
But hath his bound, in earth, in sea, in
sky.   II, *i*, 15

Every why hath a wherefore.[1]
            II, *ii*, 45

        There's no time for a man to recover
his hair that grows bald by nature.
            II, *ii*, 74

        What he hath scanted men in hair,
he hath given them in wit.   II, *ii*, 83

Small cheer and great welcome makes a
merry feast.   III, *i*, 26

There is something in the wind.
            III, *i*, 69

We'll pluck a crow together.
            III, *i*, 83

For slander lives upon succession,
Forever housed where it gets possession.   III, *i*, 105

Be not thy tongue thy own shame's
orator.
        The Comedy of Errors III, ii, 10

Ill deeds are doubled with an evil
word.   III, *ii*, 20

A back-friend, a shoulder-clapper.
            IV, *ii*, 37

Give me your hand and let me feel your
pulse.   IV, *iv*, 54

The venom clamors of a jealous
woman
Poison more deadly than a mad dog's
tooth.   V, *i*, 69

Unquiet meals make ill digestions.
            V, *i*, 74

    One Pinch, a hungry lean-fac'd vil-
lain,
A mere anatomy, a mountebank,
A threadbare juggler, and a fortune-
teller,
A needy, hollow-ey'd, sharp-looking
wretch,
A living-dead man.   V, *i*, 238

Sweet mercy is nobility's true badge.
        Titus Andronicus [1593–1594],
            act I, sc. i, l. 119

These words are razors to my wounded
heart.   I, *i*, 314

He lives in fame that died in virtue's
cause.   I, *i*, 390

These dreary dumps.[1]   I, *i*, 391

She is a woman, therefore may be
woo'd;
She is a woman, therefore may be
won.[2]   II, *i*, 82

    What you cannot as you would
achieve,
You must perforce accomplish as you
may.   II, *i*, 106

The eagle suffers little birds to sing.
And is not careful what they mean
thereby.   IV, *iv*, 82

Tut! I have done a thousand dreadful
things

---

[1] See *King Henry V*, p. 245a.
    For every why he had a wherefore. — SAMUEL
BUTLER, *Hudibras, pt. I* [1663], *canto 1, l. 132*

[1] And doleful dumps the mind oppress. —
Romeo and Juliet, act IV, sc. v, l. 129
[2] See *King Henry VI, Part I*, p. 214b.

As willingly as one would kill a fly.
>*Titus Andronicus* V, *i, 141*

I'll not budge an inch.
>*The Taming of the Shrew*
>[*1593–1594*], *Induction, i,*
>*13*

And if the boy have not a woman's
gift
To rain a shower of commanded tears,
An onion will do well for such a shift.
>*Ib. 124*

No profit grows where is no pleasure
ta'en;
In brief, sir, study what you most
affect. *Act I, sc. i, l. 39*

There's small choice in rotten apples. *I, i, 137*

To seek their fortunes further than at
home,
Where small experience grows.
>*I, ii, 51*

Nothing comes amiss, so money
comes withal. *I, ii, 82*

And do as adversaries do in law,
Strive mightily, but eat and drink as
friends. *I, ii, 281*

I must dance barefoot on her wedding
day,
And, for your love to her, lead apes in
hell. *II, i, 33*

Asses are made to bear, and so are you.
>*II, i, 200*

Kiss me, Kate, we will be married o'
Sunday. *II, i, 318*

Old fashions please me best.
>*III, i, 81*

Who woo'd in haste and means to wed
at leisure.[1] *III, ii, 11*

Such an injury would vex a saint.
>*III, ii, 28*

A little pot and soon hot.[2]
>*IV, i, 6*

And thereby hangs a tale.[1]
>*The Taming of the Shrew*
>*IV, i, 60*

It was the friar of orders grey,
As he forth walked on his way.[2]
>*IV, i, 148*

Sits as one new-risen from a dream.
>*IV, i, 189*

This is a way to kill a wife with kindness. *IV, i, 211*

Kindness in women, not their beauteous looks,
Shall win my love. *IV, ii, 41*

Our purses shall be proud, our garments poor:
For 'tis the mind that makes the body
rich;
And as the sun breaks through the
darkest clouds,
So honor peereth in the meanest
habit. *IV, iii, 173*

Forward, I pray, since we have come so
far,
And be it moon, or sun, or what you
please:
An if you please to call it a rush-
candle,
Henceforth I vow it shall be so for
me. *IV, v, 12*

He that is giddy thinks the world turns
round. *V, ii, 20*

A woman mov'd is like a fountain troubled,
Muddy, ill-seeming, thick, bereft of
beauty. *V, ii, 143*

Such duty as the subject owes the
prince,
Even such a woman oweth to her husband. *V, ii, 156*

Bid me discourse, I will enchant thine
ear.
>*Venus and Adonis* [*1593*], *l. 145*

Love is a spirit all compact of fire,

---

[1] See Congreve, p. 391b, and Cabell, p. 949b.
[2] He is a little chimney, and heated hot in a
moment. — LONGFELLOW, *The Courtship of Miles
Standish* [1858]

[1] See Rabelais, p. 181b. Elsewhere in Shakespeare.
[2] THOMAS PERCY [1728-1811] composed *The
Friar of Orders Grey* of various fragments of
ancient ballads found in Shakespeare's plays.
See Anonymous, p. 1084b.

Not gross to sink, but light, and will aspire.
> *Venus and Adonis, l.* 149

O! What a war of looks was then between them.   *l.* 355

Like a red morn, that ever yet betoken'd
Wrack to the seaman, tempest to the field.   *l.* 453

The owl, night's herald.   *l.* 531

Love comforteth like sunshine after rain.   *l.* 799

The text is old, the orator too green.
l. 806

For he being dead, with him is beauty slain,
And, beauty dead, black chaos comes again.[1]   *l.* 1019

The grass stoops not, she treads on it so light.   *l.* 1028

Beauty itself doth of itself persuade
The eyes of men without an orator.
> *The Rape of Lucrece* [1594], *l.* 29

This silent war of lilies and of roses,
Which Tarquin view'd in her fair face's field.   *l.* 71

Those that much covet are with gain so fond,
For what they have not, that which they possess
They scatter and unloose it from their bond,
And so, by hoping more, they have but less.   *l.* 134

One for all, or all for one we gage.[2]
l. 144

Who buys a minute's mirth to wail a week?
Or sells eternity to get a toy?
For one sweet grape who will the vine destroy?   *l.* 213

Extreme fear can neither fight nor fly.
l. 230

All orators are dumb when beauty pleadeth.   *l.* 268

[1] See *Othello*, p. 274a.
[2] See *Dumas*, p. 598b.

Time's glory is to calm contending kings,
To unmask falsehood, and bring truth to light.
> *The Rape of Lucrece, l.* 939

For greatest scandal waits on greatest state.   *l.* 1006

To see sad sights moves more than hear them told.   *l.* 1324

Cloud-kissing Ilion.   *l.* 1370

Lucrece swears he did her wrong.[1]
l. 1462

Home-keeping youth have ever homely wits.
> *The Two Gentlemen of Verona*
> [1594–1595], *act* I, *sc.* i, *l.* 2

I have no other but a woman's reason:
I think him so, because I think him so.   I, ii, 23

Julia: They do not love that do not show their love.
Lucetta: O! they love least that let men know their love.   I, ii, 31

Since maids, in modesty, say "No" to that
Which they would have the profferer construe "Ay."   I, ii, 53

O! how this spring of love resembleth
The uncertain glory of an April day!
I, iii, 84

O jest unseen, inscrutable, invisible,
As a nose on a man's face,[2] or a weathercock on a steeple!   II, i, 145

He makes sweet music with th' enamell'd stones.   II, vii, 28

That man that hath a tongue, I say, is no man,
If with his tongue he cannot win a woman.   III, i, 104

Except I be by Silvia in the night,
There is no music in the nightingale.
III, i, 178

[1] Some villain hath done me wrong. — *King Lear* [1605–1606], I, ii, 186
See *Frankie and Johnny*, p. 1101b.
[2] See *Rabelais*, p. 181b.

Much is the force of heaven-bred poesy.
The Two Gentlemen of Verona
III, ii, 72

Who is Silvia? what is she,
That all our swains commend her?
Holy, fair, and wise is she;
The heaven such grace did lend her,
That she might admired be.
IV, ii, 40

Alas, how love can trifle with itself!
IV, iv, 190

Black men are pearls in beauteous
ladies' eyes. V, ii, 12

How use doth breed a habit in a man! [1]
V, iv, 1

Spite of cormorant devouring Time.
Love's Labour's Lost [1594–
1595], *act I, sc. i, l. 4*

Make us heirs of all eternity. I, i, 7

Why, all delights are vain; but that
most vain
Which, with pain purchas'd doth inherit pain. I, i, 72

Light seeking light doth light of light
beguile. I, i, 77

Study is like the heaven's glorious sun,
That will not be deep-search'd with
saucy looks;
Small have continual plodders ever
won,
Save base authority from others'
books.
These earthly godfathers of heaven's
lights
That give a name to every fixed star,
Have no more profit of their shining
nights
Than those that walk and wot not what
they are. I, i, 84

At Christmas I no more desire a rose
Than wish a snow in May's newfangled
mirth;
But like of each thing that in season
grows. I, i, 105

[1] Custom is almost second nature. — PLUTARCH
[A.D. 46–120], *Rules for the Preservation of
Health, 18*

And men sit down to that nourishment which is called supper.
Love's Labour's Lost I, i, 237

That unlettered small-knowing soul.
I, i, 251

A child of our grandmother Eve, a
female; or, for thy more sweet understanding, a woman. I, i, 263

Affliction may one day smile again;
and till then, sit thee down, sorrow!
I, i, 312

Devise, wit; write, pen; for I am for
whole volumes in folio. I, ii, 194

Beauty is bought by judgment of the
eye,
Not utter'd by base sale of chapmen's
tongues. II, i, 15

A man of sovereign parts he is esteem'd;
Well fitted in arts, glorious in arms:
Nothing becomes him ill that he would
well. II, i, 44

A merrier man,
Within the limit of becoming mirth,
I never spent an hour's talk withal.
II, i, 66

Your wit's too hot, it speeds too fast,
'twill tire. II, i, 119

Warble, child; make passionate my
sense of hearing. III, i, 1

Remuneration! O! that's the Latin
word for three farthings. III, i, 143

A very beadle to a humorous sigh.
III, i, 185

This wimpled, whining, purblind, way-
ward boy,
This senior-junior, giant-dwarf, Dan
Cupid;
Regent of love-rimes, lord of folded
arms,
The anointed sovereign of sighs and
groans,
Liege of all loiterers and malcontents.
III, i, 189

He hath not fed of the dainties that
are bred of a book; he hath not eat

paper, as it were; he hath not drunk ink.

Love's Labour's Lost IV, ii, 25

Many can brook the weather that love not the wind. IV, ii, 34

You two are book-men. IV, ii, 35

These are begot in the ventricle of memory, nourished in the womb of pia mater, and delivered upon the mellowing of occasion. IV, ii, 70

By heaven, I do love, and it hath taught me to rime, and to be melancholy. IV, iii, 13

The heavenly rhetoric of thine eye.
IV, iii, 60

Young blood doth not obey an old decree:
We cannot cross the cause why we were born. IV, iii, 217

For where is any author in the world
Teaches such beauty as a woman's eye?
Learning is but an adjunct to ourself.
IV, iii, 312

But love, first learned in a lady's eyes,
Lives not alone immured in the brain.
IV, iii, 327

It adds a precious seeing to the eye.
IV, iii, 333

As sweet and musical
As bright Apollo's lute, strung with his hair;
And when Love speaks, the voice of all the gods
Makes heaven drowsy with the harmony. IV, iii, 342

From women's eyes this doctrine I derive:
They sparkle still the right Promethean fire;
They are the books, the arts, the academes,
That show, contain, and nourish all the world. IV, iii, 350

He draweth out the thread of his verbosity finer than the staple of his argument. V, i, 18

Moth: They have been at a great feast of languages, and stolen the scraps.

Costard: O! they have lived long on the alms-basket of words. I marvel thy master hath not eaten thee for a word; for thou art not so long by the head as *honorificabilitudinitatibus*; thou art easier swallowed than a flap-dragon.

Love's Labour's Lost V, i, 39

In the posteriors of this day, which the rude multitude call the afternoon.
V, i, 96

Taffeta phrases, silken terms precise,
Three-pil'd hyperboles, spruce affectation,
Figures pedantical. V, ii, 407

Let me take you a button-hole lower. V, ii, 705

The naked truth of it is, I have no shirt. V, ii, 715

A jest's prosperity lies in the ear
Of him that hears it, never in the tongue
Of him that makes it. V, ii, 869

When daisies pied and violets blue,
And lady-smocks all silver-white,
And cuckoo-buds of yellow hue
Do paint the meadows with delight,
The cuckoo then, on every tree,
Mocks married men; for thus sings he,
Cuckoo;
Cuckoo, cuckoo: O word of fear,
Unpleasing to a married ear.
V, ii, 902

When icicles hang by the wall,
And Dick, the shepherd, blows his nail,
And Tom bears logs into the hall,
And milk comes frozen home in pail,
When blood is nipp'd and ways be foul,
Then nightly sings the staring owl,
Tu-who;
Tu-whit, tu-who — a merry note,
While greasy Joan doth keel the pot.
V, ii, 920

When all aloud the wind doth blow,
And coughing drowns the parson's
saw,
And birds sit brooding in the snow,
And Marian's nose looks red and raw,
When roasted crabs hiss in the bowl.
    Love's Labour's Lost V, *ii*, 929

The words of Mercury are harsh after
the songs of Apollo.   V, *ii*, 938

A pair of star-cross'd lovers.
    Romeo and Juliet [1594–1595],
        prologue, *l.* 6

Saint-seducing gold.
        act I, sc. *i, l.* 220

One fire burns out another's burning,[1]
One pain is lessen'd by another's anguish.   I, *ii*, 47

I will make thee think thy swan a
crow.   I, *ii*, 92

For I am proverb'd with a grandsire
phrase.   I, *iv*, 37

We burn daylight.   I, *iv*, 43

Mercutio: O! then, I see Queen Mab
hath been with you! . . .
She is the fairies' midwife, and she
comes
In shape no bigger than an agate-stone
On the forefinger of an alderman,
Drawn with a team of little atomies
Athwart men's noses as they lie asleep.
        I, *iv*, 53

True, I talk of dreams,
Which are the children of an idle
brain,
Begot of nothing but vain fantasy.
        I, *iv*, 97

For you and I are past our dancing
days.[2]   I, *v*, 35

It seems she hangs upon the cheek of
night
Like a rich jewel in an Ethiop's ear;
Beauty too rich for use, for earth too
dear!   I, *v*, 49

[1] See Chapman, p. 205b.
[2] My dancing days are done. — BEAUMONT
AND FLETCHER, *The Scornful Lady* [1616], act V,
sc. *iii*

My only love sprung from my only
hate!
Too early seen unknown, and known
too late!
        Romeo and Juliet I, *v*, 142

Young Adam Cupid, he that shot so
trim
When King Cophetua lov'd the beggarmaid.[1]   II, *i*, 13

He jests at scars, that never felt a
wound.
But, soft! what light through yonder
window breaks?
It is the east, and Juliet is the sun!
        II, *ii*, 1

She speaks, yet she says nothing.
        II, *ii*, 12

See! how she leans her cheek upon her
hand:
O! that I were a glove upon that hand,
That I might touch that cheek.
        II, *ii*, 23

O Romeo, Romeo! wherefore art thou
Romeo? [2]
Deny thy father, and refuse thy name;
Or, if thou wilt not, be but sworn my
love,
And I'll no longer be a Capulet.
        II, *ii*, 33

What's in a name? That which we call
a rose
By any other name would smell as
sweet.   II, *ii*, 43

For stony limits cannot hold love out.
        II, *ii*, 67

At lovers' perjuries,
They say, Jove laughs.[3]   II, *ii*, 92

In truth, fair Montague, I am too
fond.   II, *ii*, 98

[1] See *Ballads,* p. 1087b, and Tennyson, p. 648a.
[2] HENRY FIELDING burlesqued this in Life and
Death of Tom Thumb the Great [1730] as follows:
Huncamunca: O Tom Thumb! Tom Thumb!
wherefore art thou Tom Thumb? — Act II, sc. *iii*
[3] See Tibullus, p. 128a.

And Jove but laughs at lovers' perjury. —
DRYDEN, *Palamon and Arcite* [1680], bk. II,
l. 758, and *Amphitryon* [1690], act I, sc. *ii*

I'll prove more true
Than those that have more cunning to
   be strange.
      Romeo and Juliet II, ii, 100

Romeo: Lady, by yonder blessed moon
   I swear
That tips with silver all these fruit-tree
   tops —
Juliet: O! swear not by the moon, the
   inconstant moon,
That monthly changes in her circled
   orb,
Lest that thy love prove likewise vari-
   able.   *II, ii, 107*

   Do not swear at all;
Or, if thou wilt, swear by thy gracious
   self,
Which is the god of my idolatry.
      II, ii, 112

It is too rash, too unadvis'd, too sudden;
Too like the lightning, which doth
   cease to be
Ere one can say it lightens.
      II, ii, 118

This bud of love, by summer's ripening
   breath,
May prove a beauteous flower when
   next we meet.   *II, ii, 121*

Love goes toward love, as schoolboys
   from their books;
But love from love, toward school with
   heavy looks.   *II, ii, 156*

   O! for a falconer's voice,
To lure this tassel-gentle back again.
      II, ii, 158

How silver-sweet sound lovers' tongues
   by night,
Like softest music to attending ears!
      II, ii, 165

   I would have thee gone;
And yet no further than a wanton's
   bird,
Who lets it hop a little from her hand,
Like a poor prisoner in his twisted
   gyves,
And with a silk thread plucks it back
   again,

So loving-jealous of his liberty.
      Romeo and Juliet II, ii, 176

Good night, good night! parting is such
   sweet sorrow,
That I shall say good night till it be
   morrow.   *II, ii, 184*

Virtue itself turns vice, being misap-
   plied;
And vice sometime's by action dignified.   *II, iii, 21*

Care keeps his watch in every old man's
   eye,
And where care lodges, sleep will never
   lie.   *II, iii, 35*

Wisely and slow; they stumble that run
   fast.[1]   *II, iii, 94*

   One, two, and the third in your
bosom.   *II, iv, 24*

O flesh, flesh, how art thou fishified!
      II, iv, 41

The very pink of courtesy.
      II, iv, 63

   A gentleman, nurse, that loves to
hear himself talk, and will speak more
in a minute than he will stand to in a
month.   *II, iv, 156*

These violent delights have violent
   ends.   *II, vi, 9*

Therefore love moderately; long love
   doth so; [2]
Too swift arrives as tardy as too slow.
      II, vi, 14

Here comes the lady: O! so light a
   foot
Will ne'er wear out the everlasting
   flint.   *II, vi, 16*

Thy head is as full of quarrels as an
egg is full of meat.[3]   *III, i, 23*

A word and a blow.[4]   *III, i, 44*

No, 'tis not so deep as a well, nor so

[1] See Chaucer, p. 165a.
[2] See Anonymous, p. 1084b, and Herrick, p. 320a.
[3] It's as full of good-nature as an egg's full of meat. — RICHARD BRINSLEY SHERIDAN, *A Trip to Scarborough* [1777], *act III, sc. iv*
[4] Word and a blow. — BUNYAN, *Pilgrim's Progress* [1678], *pt. I*

wide as a church-door; but 'tis enough,
'twill serve: ask for me tomorrow, and
you shall find me a grave man.
                    Romeo and Juliet III, i, 101

A plague o' both your houses!
They have made worms' meat of me.
                                    III, i, 112

O! I am Fortune's fool.   *III, i, 142*

Gallop apace, you fiery-footed steeds,
Towards Phoebus' lodging.   *III, ii, 1*

When he shall die,
Take him and cut him out in little
    stars,
And he will make the face of heaven so
    fine
That all the world will be in love with
    night,
And pay no worship to the garish sun.
                                    III, ii, 21

He was not born to shame:
Upon his brow shame is asham'd to
    sit.   *III, ii, 91*

Romeo, come forth; come forth, thou
    fearful man:
Affliction is enamor'd of thy parts,
And thou art wedded to calamity.
                                    III, iii, 1

Adversity's sweet milk, philosophy.
                                    III, iii, 54

Hang up philosophy!
Unless philosophy can make a Juliet.
                                    III, iii, 56

The lark, the herald of the morn.
                                    III, v, 6

Night's candles are burnt out, and
    jocund day
Stands tiptoe on the misty mountain-
    tops.   *III, v, 9*

Villain and he be many miles asunder.
                                    III, v, 82

Thank me no thankings, nor proud me
    no prouds.   *III, v, 153*

Is there no pity sitting in the clouds,
That sees into the bottom of my grief?
                                    III, v, 198

Past hope, past cure, past help!
                    Romeo and Juliet IV, i, 45

'Tis an ill cook that cannot lick his
own fingers.   *IV, ii, 6*

Apothecary: My poverty, but not my
    will, consents.
Romeo: I pay thy poverty, and not thy
    will.   *V, i, 75*

The strength
Of twenty men.   *V, i, 78*

The time and my intents are savage-
    wild,
More fierce and more inexorable far
Than empty tigers or the roaring sea.
                                    V, iii, 39

Tempt not a desperate man.
                                    V, iii, 59

One writ with me in sour misfortune's
    book.   *V, iii, 82*

How oft when men are at the point of
    death
Have they been merry!   *V, iii, 88*

Beauty's ensign yet
Is crimson in thy lips and in thy
    cheeks,
And death's pale flag is not advanced
    there.   *V, iii, 94*

O! here
Will I set up my everlasting rest,
And shake the yoke of inauspicious
    stars
From this world-wearied flesh. Eyes,
    look your last!
Arms, take your last embrace!
                                    V, iii, 109

O true apothecary!
Thy drugs are quick.   *V, iii, 119*

See what a scourge is laid upon your
    hate,
That heaven finds means to kill your
    joys with love.   *V, iii, 292*

For never was a story of more woe
Than this of Juliet and her Romeo.
                                    V, iii, 309

The purest treasure mortal times afford
Is spotless reputation.
King Richard II [1595–1596],
act I, sc. i, l. 177

Mine honor is my life; both grow in one;
Take honor from me, and my life is done. *I, i, 182*

We were not born to sue, but to command. *I, i, 196*

The daintiest last, to make the end most sweet. *I, iii, 68*

Truth hath a quiet breast. *I, iii, 96*

How long a time lies in one little word! *I, iii, 213*

Things sweet to taste prove in digestion sour. *I, iii, 236*

Must I not serve a long apprenticehood
To foreign passages, and in the end,
Having my freedom, boast of nothing else
But that I was a journeyman to grief? *I, iii, 271*

All places that the eye of heaven visits
Are to a wise man ports and happy havens.
Teach thy necessity to reason thus;
There is no virtue like necessity.[1]
Think not the king did banish thee,
But thou the king. *I, iii, 275*

For gnarling sorrow hath less power to bite
The man that mocks at it and sets it light. *I, iii, 292*

O! who can hold a fire in his hand
By thinking on the frosty Caucasus?
Or cloy the hungry edge of appetite
By bare imagination of a feast?
Or wallow naked in December snow
By thinking on fantastic summer's heat?
O, no! the apprehension of the good
Gives but the greater feeling to the worse. *I, iii, 294*

[1] See Quintilian, p. 1356, and note.

Where'er I wander, boast of this I can,
Though banish'd, yet a true-born Englishman.[1]
Richard II, I, iii, 308

The tongues of dying men
Enforce attention like deep harmony.
II, i, 5

The setting sun, and music at the close,
As the last taste of sweets, is sweetest last,
Writ in remembrance more than things long past. *II, i, 12*

Report of fashions in proud Italy,
Whose manners still our tardy apish nation
Limps after in base imitation.
II, i, 21

For violent fires soon burn out themselves;
Small showers last long, but sudden storms are short. *II, i, 34*

This royal throne of kings, this scepter'd isle,
This earth of majesty, this seat of Mars,
This other Eden, demi-paradise,
This fortress built by Nature for herself
Against infection and the hand of war,
This happy breed of men, this little world,
This precious stone set in the silver sea,
Which serves it in the office of a wall,
Or as a moat defensive to a house,
Against the envy of less happier lands,
This blessed plot, this earth, this realm, this England,
This nurse, this teeming womb of royal kings,
Fear'd by their breed and famous by their birth. *II, i, 40*

[1] A stern, a true-born Englishman. — SAMUEL JOHNSON; from BOSWELL, *Life of Dr. Johnson* [1791]
The True-born Englishman [1701]. Title of satire by Daniel Defoe.

England, bound in with the triumphant sea,
Whose rocky shore beats back the envious siege
Of watery Neptune.
Richard II, II, i, 61

That England, that was wont to conquer others,
Hath made a shameful conquest of itself.　　*II, i, 65*

A lunatic-lean-witted fool,
Presuming on an ague's privilege.
II, i, 115

The ripest fruit first falls.　　*II, i, 154*

Each substance of a grief hath twenty shadows.　　*II, ii, 14*

I count myself in nothing else so happy
As in a soul remembering my good friends.　　*II, iii, 46*

Evermore thanks, the exchequer of the poor.　　*II, iii, 65*

Grace me no grace, nor uncle me no uncle.　　*II, iii, 87*

The caterpillars of the commonwealth,
Which I have sworn to weed and pluck away.　　*II, iii, 166*

Things past redress are now with me past care.　　*II, iii, 171*

I see thy glory like a shooting star
Fall to the base earth from the firmament.　　*II, iv, 19*

Eating the bitter bread of banishment.[1]
III, i, 21

Not all the water in the rough rude sea
Can wash the balm from an anointed king.　　*III, ii, 54*

O! call back yesterday, bid time return.[2]　　*III, ii, 69*

The worst is death, and death will have his day.　　*III, ii, 103*

Of comfort no man speak:

Let's talk of graves, of worms, and epitaphs;
Make dust our paper, and with rainy eyes
Write sorrow on the bosom of the earth;
Let's choose executors and talk of wills.　　*Richard II, III, ii, 144*

And nothing can we call our own but death,
And that small model of the barren earth
Which serves as paste and cover to our bones.
For God's sake, let us sit upon the ground
And tell sad stories of the death of kings:
How some have been depos'd, some slain in war,
Some haunted by the ghosts they have depos'd,
Some poison'd by their wives, some sleeping kill'd;
All murder'd: for within the hollow crown
That rounds the mortal temples of a king
Keeps Death his court.　　*III, ii, 152*

Comes at the last, and with a little pin
Bores through his castle wall, and farewell king!　　*III, ii, 169*

He is come to open
The purple testament of bleeding war.
III, iii, 93

O! that I were as great
As is my grief, or lesser than my name,
Or that I could forget what I have been,
Or not remember what I must be now.
III, iii, 136

And my large kingdom for a little grave,
A little little grave, an obscure grave.
III, iii, 153

And there at Venice gave
His body to that pleasant country's earth,

---

[1] See *Isaiah 30:20*, p. 32a.
[2] See Thomas Heywood, p. 301b.

And his pure soul unto his captain
   Christ,
Under whose colors he had fought so
   long.   *Richard II, IV, i, 97*

Peace shall go sleep with Turks and infidels.   *IV, i, 139*

So Judas did to Christ: but he, in
   twelve,
Found truth in all but one; I, in twelve
   thousand, none.

God save the king! Will no man say,
   amen?   *IV, i, 170*

Now is this golden crown like a deep
   well
That owes two buckets filling one an-
   other;
The emptier ever dancing in the
   air,
The other down, unseen and full of
   water:
That bucket down and full of tears am
   I,
Drinking my griefs, whilst you mount
   up on high.   *IV, i, 184*

You may my glories and my state depose,
But not my griefs; still am I king of
   those.   *IV, i, 192*

   Some of you with Pilate wash your
      hands,
Showing an outward pity.[1]
                    IV, i, 239

A mockery king of snow.   *IV, i, 260*

As in a theatre, the eyes of men,
After a well-grac'd actor leaves the
   stage,
Are idly bent on him that enters next,
Thinking his prattle to be tedious.
                    V, ii, 23

   How sour sweet music is
When time is broke and no proportion
   kept!
So is it in the music of men's lives.
                    V, v, 42

I wasted time, and now doth time
   waste me;

[1] See *Matthew 27:24*, p. 44b.

For now hath time made me his numbering clock;
My thoughts are minutes.
                    Richard II, V, v, 49

This music mads me: let it sound no
   more.   *V, v, 61*

Mount, mount, my soul! thy seat is
   up on high,
Whilst my gross flesh sinks downward,
   here to die.   *V, v, 112*

To live a barren sister all your life,
Chanting faint hymns to the cold fruitless moon.
   A Midsummer-Night's Dream
   [*1595–1596*], *act I, sc. i, l. 72*

But earthlier happy is the rose distill'd,
Than that which withering on the virgin thorn [1]
Grows, lives and dies, in single blessedness.   *I, i, 76*

   For aught that I could ever read,
Could ever hear by tale or history,
The course of true love never did run
   smooth.   *I, i, 132*

Swift as a shadow, short as any dream,
Brief as the lightning in the collied
   night,
That, in a spleen, unfolds both heaven
   and earth,
And ere a man hath power to say, "Be-
   hold!"
The jaws of darkness do devour it up:
So quick bright things come to confu-
   sion.   *I, i, 144*

Love looks not with the eyes, but with
   the mind,
And therefore is wing'd Cupid painted
   blind.[2]   *I, i, 234*

   The most lamentable comedy, and
most cruel death of Pyramus and
Thisby.   *I, ii, 11*

[1] See Wordsworth, p. 515b.
[2] See Chaucer, p. 168b, and *Merchant of
Venice*, p. 233a.
   I have heard of reasons manifold
      Why Love must needs be blind,
   But this the best of all I hold —
      His eyes are in his mind.
         COLERIDGE, *Reason for Love's
                    Blindness* [1828]

Masters, spread yourselves.
> *A Midsummer-Night's Dream*
> I, ii, 16

This is Ercles' vein, a tyrant's vein.
> I, ii, 43

I'll speak in a monstrous little voice.
> I, ii, 55

I am slow of study.   I, ii, 70

That would hang us, every mother's son.   I, ii, 81

I will aggravate my voice so that I will roar you as gently as any sucking dove; I will roar you as 'twere any nightingale.   I, ii, 85

A proper man, as one shall see in a summer's day; a most lovely, gentleman-like man.   I, ii, 89

Over hill, over dale,[1]
> Thorough bush, thorough brier,
> Over park, over pale,
> Thorough flood, thorough fire.
> II, i, 2

I must go seek some dew drops here,
And hang a pearl in every cowslip's ear.   II, i, 14

I am that merry wanderer of the night.
I jest to Oberon, and make him smile
When I a fat and bean-fed horse beguile,
Neighing in likeness of a filly foal:
And sometimes lurk I in a gossip's bowl,
In very likeness of a roasted crab.
> II, i, 43

Since once I sat upon a promontory,
And heard a mermaid on a dolphin's back
Uttering such dulcet and harmonious breath,
That the rude sea grew civil at her song,
And certain stars shot madly from their spheres
To hear the sea-maid's music.
> II, i, 149

And the imperial votaress passed on,
In maiden meditation, fancy-free.

[1] See Gruber, p. 952a.

Yet mark'd I where the bolt of Cupid fell:
It fell upon a little western flower,
Before milk-white, now purple with love's wound,
And maidens call it, Love-in-idleness.
> *A Midsummer-Night's Dream*
> II, i, 163

I'll put a girdle round about the earth
In forty minutes.[1]   II, i, 175

For you in my respect are all the world:
Then how can it be said I am alone,
When all the world is here to look on me?   II, i, 224

I know a bank whereon the wild thyme blows,
Where oxlips and the nodding violet grows
Quite over-canopied with luscious woodbine,
With sweet musk-roses, and with eglantine:
There sleeps Titania some time of the night,
Lull'd in these flowers with dances and delight;
And there the snake throws her enamell'd skin,
Weed wide enough to wrap a fairy in.
> II, i, 249

Some to kill cankers in the musk-rose buds,
Some war with rere-mice for their leathern wings,
To make my small elves coats.
> II, ii, 3

The clamorous owl, that nightly hoots, and wonders
At our quaint spirits.   II, ii, 6

You spotted snakes with double tongue,
Thorny hedge-hogs, be not seen;
Newts, and blind-worms, do no wrong;
Come not near our fairy queen.
> II, ii, 9

Night and silence! who is here?
Weeds of Athens he doth wear.
> II, ii, 70

[1] See Chapman, p. 205b.

As a surfeit of the sweetest things
The deepest loathing to the stomach
    brings.[1]
        A Midsummer-Night's Dream
                    II, ii, 137

To bring in — God shield us! — a
lion among ladies, is a most dreadful
thing, for there is not a more fearful
wild-fowl than your lion living.
                    III, i, 32

A calendar, a calendar! look in the
almanack; find out moonshine.
                    III, i, 55

Bless thee, Bottom! bless thee! thou
art translated.   III, i, 124

Lord, what fools these mortals be! [2]
                    III, ii, 115

        So we grew together,
Like to a double cherry, seeming
    parted,
But yet an union in partition;
Two lovely berries molded on one
    stem.   III, ii, 208

Though she be but little, she is fierce.
                    III, ii, 325

I have a reasonable good ear in music: let us have the tongs and the
bones.   IV, i, 32

Truly, a peck of provender: I could
munch your good dry oats. Methinks I
have a great desire to a bottle of hay:
good hay, sweet hay, hath no fellow.
                    IV, i, 36

I have an exposition of sleep come
upon me.   IV, i, 44

My Oberon! what visions have I seen!
Methought I was enamor'd of an ass.
                    IV, i, 82

        I never heard
So musical a discord, such sweet thun-
    der.   IV, i, 123

I have had a dream, past the wit of
man to say what dream it was.
                    IV, i, 211

The eye of man hath not heard, the

ear of man hath not seen,[1] man's hand
is not able to taste, his tongue to conceive, nor his heart to report, what my
dream was.
        A Midsummer-Night's Dream
                    IV, i, 218

Eat no onions nor garlic, for we are
to utter sweet breath.   IV, ii, 44

The lunatic, the lover, and the poet,
Are of imagination all compact:
One sees more devils than vast hell can
    hold,
That is, the madman; the lover, all as
    frantic,
Sees Helen's beauty in a brow of
    Egypt:
The poet's eye, in a fine frenzy rolling,
Doth glance from heaven to earth,
    from earth to heaven;
And, as imagination bodies forth
The forms of things unknown, the
    poet's pen
Turns them to shapes, and gives to airy
    nothing
A local habitation and a name.
Such tricks hath strong imagination,
That, if it would but apprehend some
    joy,
It comprehends some bringer of that
    joy;
Or in the night, imagining some fear,
How easy is a bush suppos'd a bear!
                    V, i, 7

Very tragical mirth.   V, i, 57

The true beginning of our end.[2]
                    V, i, 111

The best in this kind are but shadows.   V, i, 215

A very gentle beast, and of a good
conscience.   V, i, 232

All that I have to say, is, to tell you
that the lanthorn is the moon; I, the
man in the moon; this thorn-bush, my
thorn-bush; and this dog, my dog.
                    V, i, 263

Well roared, Lion!   V, i, 272

This passion, and the death of a dear

---

[1] See *King Henry IV*, p. 240a.
[2] See Seneca, p. 129b.

[1] See *I Corinthians* 2:9, p. 52a.
[2] I see the beginning of my end. — MASSINGER,
The Virgin Martyr [1622], act III, sc. iii

friend, would go near to make a man look sad.
> *A Midsummer-Night's Dream*
> V, i, 295

With the help of a surgeon, he might yet recover, and prove an ass.
> V, i, 318

No epilogue, I pray you, for your play needs no excuse. Never excuse.[1]
> V, i, 363

The iron tongue of midnight hath told twelve;
Lovers, to bed; 'tis almost fairy time.
> V, i, 372

If we shadows have offended,
Think but this, and all is mended,
That you have but slumber'd here
While these visions did appear.
> V, ii, 54

Your mind is tossing on the ocean.
> *The Merchant of Venice* [1596–1597], *act I, sc. i, l. 8*

My ventures are not in one bottom trusted,
Nor to one place.
> I, i, 42

Nature hath fram'd strange fellows in her time.
> I, i, 51

You have too much respect upon the world:
They lose it that do buy it with much care.
> I, i, 74

I hold the world but as the world, Gratiano;
A stage, where every man must play a part,[2]
And mine a sad one.
> I, i, 77

Let me play the fool.
> I, i, 79

Why should a man, whose blood is warm within,
Sit like his grandsire cut in alabaster?
> I, i, 83

There are a sort of men whose visages
Do cream and mantle like a standing pond.
> I, i, 88

---

[1] See Meurier, p. 188b, and *King John*, p. 237a.
[2] See *As You Like It*, p. 248b.

I am Sir Oracle,
And when I ope my lips let no dog bark!
> *The Merchant of Venice* I, i, 93

I do know of these,
That therefore only are reputed wise
For saying nothing.
> I, i, 95

Fish not, with this melancholy bait,
For this fool-gudgeon, this opinion.
> I, i, 101

Gratiano speaks an infinite deal of nothing, more than any man in all Venice. His reasons are as two grains of wheat hid in two bushels of chaff: you shall seek all day ere you find them, and, when you have them, they are not worth the search.
> I, i, 114

In my school-days, when I had lost one shaft,
I shot his fellow of the selfsame flight
The selfsame way with more advised watch,
To find the other forth, and by adventuring both,
I oft found both.
> I, i, 141

They are as sick that surfeit with too much as they that starve with nothing.
> I, ii, 5

Superfluity comes sooner by white hairs, but competency lives longer.
> I, ii, 9

If to do were as easy as to know what were good to do, chapels had been churches, and poor men's cottages princes' palaces.
> I, ii, 13

The brain may devise laws for the blood, but a hot temper leaps o'er a cold decree.
> I, ii, 19

He doth nothing but talk of his horse.
> I, ii, 43

I fear he will prove the weeping philosopher when he grows old, being so full of unmannerly sadness in his youth.
> I, ii, 51

God made him, and therefore let him pass for a man.
> I, ii, 59

When he is best, he is a little worse than a man, and when he is worst, he is little better than a beast.

The Merchant of Venice I, ii, 93

I dote on his very absence.

I, ii, 118

My meaning in saying he is a good man is to have you understand me that he is sufficient. I, iii, 15

Ships are but boards, sailors but men: there be land-rats and water-rats, land-thieves and water-thieves.

I, iii, 22

Yes, to smell pork; to eat of the habitation which your prophet the Nazarite [1] conjured the devil into. I will buy with you, sell with you, talk with you, walk with you, and so following; but I will not eat with you, drink with you, nor pray with you. What news on the Rialto? I, iii, 34

How like a fawning publican he looks! I hate him for he is a Christian.

I, iii, 42

If I can catch him once upon the hip,[2] I will feed fat the ancient grudge I bear him. I, iii, 47

Cursed be my tribe,
If I forgive him. I, iii, 52

The devil can cite Scripture for his purpose. I, iii, 99

A goodly apple rotten at the heart.
O, what a goodly outside falsehood hath! I, iii, 102

For sufferance is the badge of all our tribe.
You call me misbeliever, cut-throat dog,
And spit upon my Jewish gaberdine.

I, iii, 111

Shall I bend low, and in a bondman's key,

---

[1] That hee shall be called a Nazarite. — *The Geneva Bible* [1557–1560], *Matthew* 2:23
The Geneva version of the Bible is the one Shakespeare was familiar with.
[2] See Heywood, p. 185a, and *The Merchant of Venice* IV, i, 334, p. 235a.

With bated breath and whispering humbleness,
Say this.
The Merchant of Venice I, iii, 124

I'll seal to such a bond,
And say there is much kindness in the Jew. I, iii, 153

O father Abram! what these Christians are,
Whose own hard dealing teaches them suspect
The thoughts of others. I, iii, 161

I like not fair terms and a villain's mind. I, iii, 180

Mislike me not for my complexion,
The shadow'd livery of the burnish'd sun. II, i, 1

If Hercules and Lichas play at dice
Which is the better man, the greater throw
May turn by fortune from the weaker hand. II, i, 32

O heavens! this is my true-begotten father. II, ii, 36

An honest, exceeding poor man.
II, ii, 54

The very staff of my age, my very prop. II, ii, 71

It is a wise father that knows his own child. II, ii, 83

And the vile squealing of the wry-neck'd fife. II, v, 30

Who riseth from a feast
With that keen appetite that he sits down? II, vi, 8

All things that are,
Are with more spirit chased than enjoy'd.
How like a younker or a prodigal
The scarfed bark puts from her native bay,
Hugg'd and embraced by the strumpet wind!
How like the prodigal doth she return,
With over-weather'd ribs and ragged sails,

Lean, rent, and beggar'd by the strumpet wind!
 The Merchant of Venice II, *vi, 12*

But love is blind,[1] and lovers cannot see
The pretty follies that themselves commit. *II, vi, 36*

Must I hold a candle to my shames?
 II, vi, 41

 Men that hazard all
Do it in hope of fair advantages:
A golden mind stoops not to show of dross. *II, vii, 18*

Young in limbs, in judgment old.
 II, vii, 71

My daughter! O my ducats! O my daughter!
Fled with a Christian! O my Christian ducats!
Justice! the law! my ducats, and my daughter!
A sealed bag, two sealed bags of ducats,
Of double ducats, stol'n from me by my daughter! *II, viii, 15*

The fool multitude, that choose by show. *II, ix, 26*

 I will not jump with common spirits
And rank me with the barbarous multitude. *II, ix, 32*

 Let none presume
To wear an undeserved dignity.
O! that estates, degrees, and offices
Were not deriv'd corruptly, and that clear honor
Were purchas'd by the merit of the wearer. *II, ix, 39*

Some there be that shadows kiss;
Such have but a shadow's bliss.
 II, ix, 66

 Let him look to his bond.
 III, i, 49

I am a Jew. Hath not a Jew eyes?

[1] See Chaucer, p. 168b; *Midsummer-Night's Dream,* p. 228b, and note.

hath not a Jew hands, organs, dimensions, senses, affections, passions?
 The Merchant of Venice III, *i, 62*

If you prick us, do we not bleed? if you tickle us, do we not laugh? if you poison us, do we not die? and if you wrong us, shall we not revenge?
 III, i, 65

The villainy you teach me I will execute, and it shall go hard but I will better the instruction. *III, i, 76*

I would not have given it for a wilderness of monkeys. *III, i, 130*

There's something tells me, but it is not love,
I would not lose you; and you know yourself,
Hate counsels not in such a quality.
 III, ii, 4

 Makes a swan-like end,
Fading in music.[1] *III, ii, 44*

Tell me where is fancy bred,
Or in the heart or in the head?
How begot, how nourished?
 Reply, reply. *III, ii, 63*

In law, what plea so tainted and corrupt
But, being season'd with a gracious voice,
Obscures the show of evil?
 III, ii, 75

There is no vice so simple but assumes
Some mark of virtue on his outward parts. *III, ii, 81*

Thus ornament is but the guiled shore
To a most dangerous sea. *III, ii, 97*

The seeming truth which cunning times put on
To entrap the wisest. *III, ii, 100*

How all the other passions fleet to air,
As doubtful thoughts, and rash-embrac'd despair,
And shuddering fear, and green-ey'd jealousy. *III, ii, 108*

[1] See Plato, p. 93b, and note.

An unlesson'd girl, unschool'd, unprac-
tis'd;
Happy in this, she is not yet so old
But she may learn.
            The Merchant of Venice
                        III, ii, 160

Here are a few of the unpleasant'st
words
That ever blotted paper.   *III, ii, 252*

Thou call'dst me dog before thou hadst
a cause,
But, since I am a dog, beware my
    fangs.   *III, iii, 6*

    Thus when I shun Scylla, your fa-
ther, I fall into Charybdis, your
mother.[1]   *III, v, 17*

Some men there are love not a gaping
pig;
Some, that are mad if they behold a
cat.   *IV, i, 47*

A harmless necessary cat.   *IV, i, 55*

Bassanio: Do all men kill the things
they do not love? [2]
Shylock: Hates any man the thing he
would not kill?   *IV, i, 66*

What! wouldst thou have a serpent
sting thee twice?   *IV, i, 69*

     The weakest kind of fruit
Drops earliest to the ground.
               IV, i, 115

To hold opinion with Pythagoras
That souls of animals infuse them-
selves
Into the trunks of men.[3]   *IV, i, 131*

    I never knew so young a body with so
old a head.[4]   *IV, i, 163*

[1] Scylla to port, and on our starboard beam
Charybdis, dire gorge of the salt sea tide. —
HOMER, *Odyssey, bk. XII, l. 232*

Scylla guards the right side; implacable Charybdis the left. — VIRGIL, *Aeneid, bk. III, l. 420*

Incidis in Scyllam cupiens vitare Charybdim
[You fall into Scylla in seeking to avoid Charyb-
dis]. — PHILIPPE GUALTIER, *Alexandreis* [c. 1300],
bk. V, l. 301

[2] See Oscar Wilde, p. 840b.

[3] *Clown:* What is the opinion of Pythagoras
concerning wild-fowl?

    Malvolio: That the soul of our grandam
might haply inhabit a bird.

       Twelfth-Night [1598–1600], *IV, ii, 55*

[4] He is young, but take it from me, a very
staid head. — THOMAS WENTWORTH, EARL OF

The quality of mercy is not strain'd,
It droppeth as the gentle rain from
heaven
Upon the place beneath: it is twice
bless'd;
It blesseth him that gives and him that
takes:
'Tis mightiest in the mightiest; it be-
comes
The throned monarch better than his
crown;
His scepter shows the force of temporal
power,
The attribute to awe and majesty,
Wherein doth sit the dread and fear of
kings;[1]
But mercy is above this scepter'd sway,
It is enthroned in the hearts of kings,
It is an attribute to God himself,
And earthly power doth then show
likest God's
When mercy seasons justice. Therefore,
Jew,
Though justice be thy plea, consider
this,
That in the course of justice, none of
us
Should see salvation: we do pray for
mercy,
And that same prayer doth teach us all
to render
The deeds of mercy.
        The Merchant of Venice
              IV, i, 184

To do a great right, do a little wrong.
               IV, i, 216

A Daniel come to judgment! yea, a
Daniel!   *IV, i, 223*

How much more elder art thou than
thy looks!   *IV, i, 251*

Is it so nominated in the bond?
               IV, i, 260

'Tis not in the bond.   *IV, i, 263*

For herein Fortune shows herself more
kind
Than is her custom: it is still her use

STRAFFORD [1593–1641], *letter commending the
Earl of Ormond to Charles I for appointment as
councilor*

[1] See *Measure for Measure II, ii, 59,* p. 270b.

To let the wretched man outlive his wealth,
To view with hollow eye and wrinkled brow
An age of poverty.
The Merchant of Venice
IV, i, 268

I have a daughter;
Would any of the stock of Barabbas
Had been her husband rather than a
Christian!   IV, i, 296

An upright judge, a learned judge!
IV, i, 324

A second Daniel, a Daniel, Jew!
Now, infidel, I have thee on the hip.[1]
IV, i, 334

A Daniel, still say I; a second Daniel!
I thank thee, Jew, for teaching me that word.   IV, i, 341

You take my house when you do take the prop
That doth sustain my house; you take my life
When you do take the means whereby I live.   IV, i, 376

He is well paid that is well satisfied.
IV, i, 416

Lorenzo: The moon shines bright: in such a night as this . . .
Troilus methinks mounted the Troyan walls,
And sigh'd his soul toward the Grecian tents,
Where Cressid lay that night.
Jessica: In such a night
Did Thisbe fearfully o'ertrip the dew,
And saw the lion's shadow ere himself,
And ran dismay'd away.
Lorenzo: In such a night
Stood Dido with a willow in her hand
Upon the wild sea-banks, and waft her love
To come again to Carthage.
Jessica: In such a night
Medea gather'd the enchanted herbs
That did renew old Aeson.   V, i, 1

How sweet the moonlight sleeps upon this bank!

Here we will sit, and let the sounds of music
Creep in our ears: soft stillness and the night
Become the touches of sweet harmony.
Sit, Jessica: look, how the floor of heaven
Is thick inlaid with patines of bright gold:
There's not the smallest orb which thou behold'st
But in his motion like an angel sings,
Still quiring to the young-eyed cherubins.
Such harmony is in immortal souls;
But, whilst this muddy vesture of decay
Doth grossly close it in, we cannot hear it.
The Merchant of Venice
V, i, 54

I am never merry when I hear sweet music.   V, i, 69

The man that hath no music in himself,
Nor is not mov'd with concord of sweet sounds,
Is fit for treasons, stratagems, and spoils;
The motions of his spirit are dull as night,
And his affections dark as Erebus:
Let no such man be trusted.
V, i, 83

How far that little candle throws his beams!
So shines a good deed in a naughty world.[1]   V, i, 90

How many things by season season'd are
To their right praise and true perfection!   V, i, 107

This night methinks is but the daylight sick.   V, i, 124

A light wife doth make a heavy husband.   V, i, 130

These blessed candles of the night.
V, i, 220

[1] See Heywood, p. 185a, and *The Merchant of Venice I, iii, 47,* p. 232a.

[1] See *Matthew 5:15,* p. 40a, and William Bradford, p. 319a.

For new-made honor doth forget men's names.
King John [1596–1597], *act I, sc. i, l. 187*

Sweet, sweet, sweet poison for the age's tooth. *I, i, 213*

Bearing their birthrights proudly on their backs,
To make a hazard of new fortunes here. *II, i, 70*

For courage mounteth with occasion. *II, i, 82*

The hare of whom the proverb goes,
Whose valor plucks dead lions by the beard.[1] *II, i, 137*

A woman's will. *II, i, 194*

Saint George, that swing'd the dragon, and e'er since
Sits on his horse back at mine hostess' door. *II, i, 288*

He is the half part of a blessed man,
Left to be finished by such a she;
And she a fair divided excellence,
Whose fullness of perfection lies in him. *II, i, 437*

'Zounds! I was never so bethump'd with words
Since I first call'd my brother's father dad. *II, i, 466*

Mad world! mad kings! mad composition! *II, i, 561*

That smooth-fac'd gentleman, tickling Commodity,
Commodity, the bias of the world. *II, i, 573*

I will instruct my sorrows to be proud;
For grief is proud and makes his owner stoop. *III, i, 68*

Thou wear a lion's hide! doff it for shame,
And hang a calf's-skin on those recreant limbs. *III, i, 128*

The sun's o'ercast with blood: fair day, adieu!

Which is the side that I must go withal?
I am with both: each army hath a hand;
And in their rage, I having hold of both,
They whirl asunder and dismember me. *King John III, i, 326*

Bell, book and candle shall not drive me back.[1] *III, iii, 12*

Look, who comes here! a grave unto a soul. *III, iv, 17*

Death, death: O, amiable lovely death! [2] *III, iv, 25*

Grief fills the room up of my absent child,
Lies in his bed, walks up and down with me,
Puts on his pretty looks, repeats his words,
Remembers me of all his gracious parts,
Stuffs out his vacant garments with his form. *III, iv, 93*

Life is as tedious as a twice-told tale,[3]
Vexing the dull ear of a drowsy man. *III, iv, 108*

When Fortune means to men most good,
She looks upon them with a threatening eye.[4] *III, iv, 119*

A scepter snatch'd with an unruly hand
Must be as boisterously maintain'd as gain'd;
And he that stands upon a slippery place
Makes nice of no vile hold to stay him up. *III, iv, 135*

As quiet as a lamb. *IV, i, 80*

To gild refined gold, to paint the lily,
To throw a perfume on the violet,
To smooth the ice, or add another hue
Unto the rainbow, or with taper-light

[1] So hares may pull dead lions by the beard.
— KYD, *The Spanish Tragedy* [1594] *I. ii, 172*

[1] See Malory, p. 175b, and note.
[2] See Whitman, p. 702a.
[3] See Homer, p. 66b.
[4] See Publilius Syrus, p. 125b.

To seek the beauteous eye of heaven to
garnish,
Is wasteful and ridiculous excess.
King John IV, ii, 11

And oftentimes excusing of a fault
Doth make the fault the worse by the
excuse.[1]   *IV, ii, 30*

We cannot hold mortality's strong
hand.   *IV, ii, 82*

There is no sure foundation set on
blood,
No certain life achiev'd by others'
death.   *IV, ii, 104*

Make haste; the better foot before.[2]
IV, ii, 170

Another lean unwash'd artificer.
IV, ii, 201

How oft the sight of means to do ill
deeds
Makes ill deeds done!   *IV, ii, 219*

Heaven take my soul, and England
keep my bones!   *IV, iii, 10*

I am amaz'd, methinks, and lose my
way
Among the thorns and dangers of this
world.   *IV, iii, 140*

Unthread the rude eye of rebellion,
And welcome home again discarded
faith.   *V, iv, 11*

The day shall not be up so soon as I,
To try the fair adventure of tomorrow.
V, v, 21

'Tis strange that death should
sing.
I am the cygnet to this pale faint
swan,
Who chants a doleful hymn to his own
death.[3]   *V, vii, 20*

Now my soul hath elbow-room.
V, vii, 28

[1] See Meurier, p. 188b, and *A Midsummer-Night's Dream*, p. 231a.
[2] Put forward your best foot! — BROWNING, *Respectability* [1855], *st. 3*
[3] See Plato, p. 93b, and note.

I do not ask you much:
I beg cold comfort.[1]
King John V, vii, 41

This England never did, nor never
shall,
Lie at the proud foot of a conqueror.
V, vii, 112

Come the three corners of the world in
arms,
And we shall shock them. Nought shall
make us rue,
If England to itself do rest but true.
V, vii, 116

So shaken as we are, so wan with care.
King Henry IV [1597–1598],
Part I, act I, sc. i, l. 1

In those holy fields
Over whose acres walk'd those blessed
feet
Which fourteen hundred years ago
were nail'd
For our advantage on the bitter cross.
I, i, 24

Unless hours were cups of sack, and
minutes capons, and clocks the tongues
of bawds, and dials the signs of leaping
houses, and the blessed sun himself a
fair hot wench in flame-color'd taffeta, I
see no reason why thou shouldst be so
superfluous to demand the time of the
day.   *I, ii, 7*

Diana's foresters, gentlemen of the
shade, minions of the moon.
I, ii, 29

A purse of gold most resolutely
snatched on Monday night and most
dissolutely spent on Tuesday morning.
I, ii, 38

Thy quips and thy quiddities.
I, ii, 51

So far as my coin would stretch; and
where it would not, I have used my
credit.   *I, ii, 61*

Old father antick the law.   *I, ii, 69*

I am as melancholy as a gib cat, or a
lugged bear.   *I, ii, 82*

[1] See *The Tempest*, II, i, 10, p. 296b, and William Bradford, p. 319a.

I would to God thou and I knew where a commodity of good names were to be bought.

> *Henry IV, Part I, I, ii, 92*

O! thou hast damnable iteration, and art indeed able to corrupt a saint.

> *I, ii, 101*

Now am I, if a man should speak truly, little better than one of the wicked.   *I, ii, 105*

'Tis my vocation, Hal; 'tis no sin for a man to labor in his vocation.

> *I, ii, 116*

There's neither honesty, manhood, nor good fellowship in thee.

> *I, ii, 154*

I know you all, and will a while uphold
The unyok'd humor of your idleness:
Yet herein will I imitate the sun,
Who doth permit the base contagious clouds
To smother up his beauty from the world,
That when he please again to be himself,
Being wanted, he may be more wonder'd at,
By breaking through the foul and ugly mists
Of vapors that did seem to strangle him.
If all the year were playing holidays,
To sport would be as tedious as to work.   *I, ii, 217*

You tread upon my patience.

> *I, iii, 4*

Came there a certain lord, neat, and trimly dress'd,
Fresh as a bridegroom; and his chin new-reap'd,
Show'd like a stubble-land at harvest-home.
He was perfumed like a milliner,
And 'twixt his finger and his thumb he held
A pouncet-box, which ever and anon
He gave his nose and took 't away again.   *I, iii, 33*

And as the soldiers bore dead bodies by,
He call'd them untaught knaves, unmannerly,
To bring a slovenly unhandsome corpse
Betwixt the wind and his nobility.

> *Henry IV, Part I, I, iii, 42*

So pester'd with a popinjay.

> *I, iii, 50*

God save the mark!   *I, iii, 56*

And but for these vile guns,
He would himself have been a soldier.

> *I, iii, 63*

To put down Richard, that sweet lovely rose,
And plant this thorn, this canker, Bolingbroke.   *I, iii, 176*

Sink or swim.   *I, iii, 194*

O! the blood more stirs
To rouse a lion than to start a hare!

> *I, iii, 197*

By heaven methinks it were an easy leap
To pluck bright honor from the pale-fac'd moon,
Or dive into the bottom of the deep,
Where fathom-line could never touch the ground,
And pluck up drowned honor by the locks.   *I, iii, 201*

Why, what a candy deal of courtesy
This fawning greyhound then did proffer me!   *I, iii, 251*

I know a trick worth two of that.

> *II, i, 40*

If the rascal have not given me medicines to make me love him, I'll be hanged.   *II, ii, 20*

I'll starve ere I'll rob a foot further.

> *II, ii, 24*

It would be argument for a week, laughter for a month, and a good jest forever.   *II, ii, 104*

Falstaff sweats to death
And lards the lean earth as he walks along.   *II, ii, 119*

Out of this nettle, danger, we pluck this flower, safety.
Henry IV, Part I, II, iii, 11

I could brain him with his lady's fan. *II, iii, 26*

Constant you are,
But yet a woman: and for secrecy,
No lady closer; for I well believe
Thou wilt not utter what thou dost not know;
And so far will I trust thee, gentle Kate. *II, iii, 113*

A Corinthian, a lad of mettle, a good boy. *II, iv, 13*

I am not yet of Percy's mind, the Hotspur of the North; he that kills me some six or seven dozen of Scots at a breakfast, washes his hands, and says to his wife, "Fie upon this quiet life! I want work." *II, iv, 116*

A plague of all cowards, I say.
II, iv, 129

There live not three good men unhanged in England, and one of them is fat and grows old. *II, iv, 146*

You care not who sees your back: call you that backing of your friends? A plague upon such backing!
II, iv, 168

I have peppered two of them. . . . I tell thee what, Hal, if I tell thee a lie, spit in my face; call me horse.
II, iv, 216

Give you a reason on compulsion! If reasons were as plenty as blackberries, I would give no man a reason upon compulsion, I. *II, iv, 267*

Mark now, how a plain tale shall put you down. *II, iv, 285*

What doth gravity out of his bed at midnight? *II, iv, 328*

A plague of sighing and grief! It blows a man up like a bladder.
II, iv, 370

I must speak in passion, and I will do it in King Cambyses' vein.
II, iv, 429

That reverend vice, that grey iniquity, that father ruffian, that vanity in years. *Henry IV, Part I, II, iv, 505*

If sack and sugar be a fault, God help the wicked! If to be old and merry be a sin, then many an old host that I know is damned: if to be fat be to be hated, then Pharaoh's lean kine are to be loved. *II, iv, 524*

Banish plump Jack, and banish all the world. *II, iv, 534*

Play out the play. *II, iv, 539*

O, monstrous! but one half-penny-worth of bread to this intolerable deal of sack! *II, iv, 597*

Diseased nature oftentimes breaks forth
In strange eruptions. *III, i, 27*

I am not in the roll of common men.
III, i, 43

Glendower: I can call spirits from the vasty deep.
Hotspur: Why, so can I, or so can any man;
But will they come when you do call for them? *III, i, 53*

I had rather be a kitten and cry mew,
Than one of these same metre ballad-mongers. *III, i, 128*

Mincing poetry:
'Tis like the forc'd gait of a shuffling nag. *III, i, 133*

But in the way of bargain, mark you me,
I'll cavil on the ninth part of a hair.
III, i, 138

A deal of skimble-skamble stuff.
III, i, 153

I understand thy kisses and thou mine,
And that's a feeling disputation.
III, i, 204

Lady Percy: . . . Lie still, ye thief, and hear the lady sing in Welsh.
Hotspur: I had rather hear Lady, my brach, howl in Irish. *III, i, 238*

A good mouth-filling oath.
Henry IV, Part I, III, i, 258

They surfeited with honey and began
To loathe the taste of sweetness,
whereof a little
More than a little is by much too
much.[1]   *III, ii, 71*

He was but as the cuckoo is in June,
Heard, not regarded.   *III, ii, 75*

My near'st and dearest enemy.[2]
     III, ii, 123

The end of life cancels all bands.
     III, ii, 157

An I have not forgotten what the inside of a church is made of, I am a
peppercorn, a brewer's horse.
     III, iii, 8

Company, villanous company, hath
been the spoil of me.   *III, iii, 10*

I have more flesh than another man,
and therefore more frailty.
     III, iii, 187

The very life-blood of our enterprise.
     IV, i, 28

     Were it good
To set the exact wealth of all our
states
All at one cast? to set so rich a main
On the nice hazard of one doubtful
hour?   *IV, i, 45*

Baited like eagles having lately
bath'd; . . .
As full of spirit as the month of May,
And gorgeous as the sun at midsummer.   *IV, i, 99*

I saw young Harry, with his beaver on.
     IV, i, 104

     Worse than the sun in March
This praise doth nourish agues.
     IV, i, 110

Doomsday is near; die all, die merrily.
     IV, i, 134

The cankers of a calm world and a long
peace.   *IV, ii, 32*

[1] See *A Midsummer-Night's Dream,* p. 230a.
[2] See *Hamlet I, ii, 180,* p. 258a.

To the latter end of a fray and the beginning of a feast
Fits a dull fighter and a keen guest.
     Henry IV, Part I, IV, ii, 86

Greatness knows itself.   *IV, iii, 74*

     I could be well content
To entertain the lag-end of my life
With quiet hours.   *V, i, 23*

Rebellion lay in his way, and he found
it.   *V, i, 28*

Never yet did insurrection want
Such water-colors to impaint his cause.
     V, i, 79

I would it were bed-time, Hal, and
all well.   *V, i, 126*

Honor pricks me on. Yea, but how if
honor prick me off when I come on?
how then? Can honor set to a leg? No.
Or an arm? No. Or take away the grief
of a wound? No. Honor hath no skill in
surgery, then? No. What is honor? a
word. What is that word, honor? Air. A
trim reckoning! Who hath it? he that
died o' Wednesday. Doth he feel it?
No. Doth he hear it? No. It is insensible then? Yea, to the dead. But will it
not live with the living? No. Why? Detraction will not suffer it. Therefore I'll
none of it: honor is a mere scutcheon;
and so ends my catechism.   *V, i, 131*

Suspicion all our lives shall be stuck full
of eyes;
For treason is but trusted like the fox.
     V, ii, 8

Let me tell the world.[1]   *V, ii, 65*

     The time of life is short;
To spend that shortness basely were too
long.   *V, ii, 81*

Two stars keep not their motion in one
sphere.   *V, iv, 65*

But thought's the slave of life, and life
time's fool;
And time, that takes survey of all the
world,

[1] I'll tell the world. — SHAKESPEARE, *Measure
for Measure* [1604–1605], *II, iv, 154*
Ay, tell the world! — BROWNING, *Paracelsus*
[1835], *pt. II*

Must have a stop. O! I could prophesy,
But that the earthy and cold hand of
death
Lies on my tongue.
      Henry IV, Part I, V, iv, 81

This earth, that bears thee dead,
Bears not alive so stout a gentleman.
      V, iv, 92

Thy ignominy sleep with thee in the
grave,
But not remember'd in thy epitaph!
      V, iv, 100

I could have better spar'd a better man.
      V, iv, 104

The better part of valor is discretion.[1]   *V, iv, 120*

Full bravely hast thou flesh'd
Thy maiden sword.   *V, iv, 132*

Lord, Lord, how this world is given
to lying!   *V, iv, 148*

I'll purge, and leave sack, and live
cleanly.   *V, iv, 168*

Rumor is a pipe
Blown by surmises, jealousies, conjec-
tures,
And of so easy and so plain a stop
That the blunt monster with un-
counted heads,
The still-discordant wavering multi-
tude,[2]
Can play upon it.
      King Henry IV [1597–1598],
      Part II, induction, l. 15

Even such a man, so faint, so spiritless,
So dull, so dead in look, so woe-begone,
Drew Priam's curtain in the dead of
night,
And would have told him half his Troy
was burn'd.   *Act I, sc. i, l. 70*

Yet the first bringer of unwelcome
news
Hath but a losing office, and his
tongue
Sounds ever after as a sullen bell,

Remember'd knolling a departing
friend.[1]
      Henry IV, Part II, I, i, 100

I am not only witty in myself, but
the cause that wit is in other men.[2]
      I, ii, 10

A rascally yea-forsooth knave.
      I, ii, 40

You lie in your throat.   *I, ii, 97*

Your lordship, though not clean past
your youth, hath yet some smack of age
in you, some relish of the saltness of
time.   *I, ii, 112*

It is the disease of not listening, the
malady of not marking, that I am troubled withal.   *I, ii, 139*

I am as poor as Job, my lord, but not
so patient.   *I, ii, 145*

We that are in the vaward of our
youth.   *I, ii, 201*

Have you not a moist eye, a dry
hand, a yellow cheek, a white beard, a
decreasing leg, an increasing belly?
      I, ii, 206

Every part about you blasted with
antiquity.   *I, ii, 210*

For my voice, I have lost it with hol-
laing and singing of anthems.
      I, ii, 215

It was always yet the trick of our
English nation, if they have a good
thing, to make it too common.
      I, ii, 244

I were better to be eaten to death
with rust than to be scoured to nothing
with perpetual motion.   *I, ii, 249*

I can get no remedy against this consumption of the purse: borrowing only
lingers and lingers it out, but the disease is incurable.[3]   *I, ii, 267*

Who lin'd himself with hope,
Eating the air on promise of supply.
      I, iii, 27

---

[1] It show'd discretion the best part of valor.
— BEAUMONT AND FLETCHER, *A King and No King* [1619], *act II, sc. iii*
[2] See Horace, p. 123a, and note.

[1] See Sophocles, p. 82a, and *Antony and Cleopatra II, v, 85*, p. 288a.
[2] See Samuel Johnson, p. 433b.
[3] See Rabelais, p. 181a.

A habitation giddy and unsure
Hath he that buildeth on the vulgar
   heart.
       Henry IV, Part II, I, iii, 89

Past and to come seem best; things
   present worst.   *I, iii,* 108

A poor lone woman.   *II, i,* 37

Away, you scullion! you rampallian!
you fustilarian! I'll tickle your catastrophe.   *II, i,* 67

He hath eaten me out of house and
home.   *II, i,* 82

Let the end try the man.
       II, ii, 52

Thus we play the fools with the time,
and the spirits of the wise sit in the
clouds and mock us.   *II, ii,* 155

     He was indeed the glass
Wherein the noble youth did dress
   themselves.   *II, iii,* 21

And let the welkin roar.   *II, iv,* 181

Is it not strange that desire should so
many years outlive performance?
       II, iv, 283

   O sleep! O gentle sleep! [1]
Nature's soft nurse, how have I frighted
   thee,
That thou no more wilt weigh my eye-
   lids down
And steep my senses in forgetfulness?
       III, i, 5

With all appliances and means to
   boot.   *III, i,* 29

Uneasy lies the head that wears a
   crown.   *III, i,* 31

O God! that one might read the book
   of fate.   *III, i,* 45

There is a history in all men's lives.
       III, i, 80

Death, as the Psalmist saith, is certain to all; all shall die.   *III, ii,* 41

Most forcible Feeble.   *III, ii,* 181

We have heard the chimes at midnight.   *III, ii,* 231

[1] Sleep, most gentle sleep. — OVID [43 B.C.–A.D.
18], *Metamorphoses, bk. II, l.* 624

   A man can die but once; we owe God
a death.
       Henry IV, Part II, III, ii, 253

We see which way the stream of time
   doth run
And are enforc'd from our most quiet
   sphere
By the rough torrent of occasion.
       IV, i, 70

We ready are to try our fortunes
To the last man.   *IV, ii,* 43

I may justly say, with the hook-nosed
fellow of Rome, "I came, saw, and
overcame." [1]   *IV, iii,* 44

O polish'd perturbation! golden care!
That keep'st the ports of slumber open
   wide
To many a watchful night!
       IV, v, 22

     See, sons, what things you are!
How quickly nature falls into revolt
When gold becomes her object!
       IV, v, 63

Thy wish was father, Harry, to that
   thought.[2]   *IV, v,* 91

Before thy hour be ripe.[3]   *IV, v,* 95

   Commit
The oldest sins the newest kind of
   ways.   *IV, v,* 124

His cares are now all ended.   *V, ii,* 3

This is the English, not the Turkish
   court;
Not Amurath an Amurath succeeds,
But Harry Harry.   *V, ii,* 47

How ill white hairs become a fool and
   jester!   *V, v,* 53

   Master Shallow, I owe you a thousand pound.   *V, v,* 78

O! for a Muse of fire, that would ascend

[1] See Julius Caesar, p. 112b.
[2] Men's thoughts are much according to their
inclination, their discourse and speeches according to their learning and infused opinions. —
FRANCIS BACON, *Essays* [1597–1625], *Of Custom
and Education*
[3] See Blake, p. 488b.

The brightest heaven of invention!
  King Henry V [1598–1600],
    Chorus, l. 1

 Or may we cram
Within this wooden O the very
 casques
That did affright the air at Agincourt?
       l. 12

Consideration like an angel came,
And whipp'd the offending Adam out
 of him.   *act I, sc. i, l. 28*

Hear him debate of commonwealth
 affairs,
You would say it hath been all in all his
 study.   *I, i, 41*

Turn him to any cause of policy,
The Gordian knot of it he will un-
 loose,
Familiar as his garter; that, when he
 speaks,
The air, a charter'd libertine, is still.
       I, i, 45

  Therefore doth heaven divide
The state of man in divers functions,
Setting endeavor in continual motion;
To which is fixed, as an aim or butt,
Obedience: for so work the honey-
 bees,
Creatures that by a rule in nature
 teach
The act of order to a peopled king-
 dom.   *I, ii, 183*

The singing masons building roofs of
 gold.   *I, ii, 198*

 Many things, having full reference
To one consent, may work contrari-
 ously;
As many arrows, loosed several ways,
Fly to one mark; as many ways meet
 in one town;
As many fresh streams meet in one salt
 sea;
As many lines close in the dial's cen-
 ter;
So may a thousand actions, once afoot,
End in one purpose, and be all well
 borne
Without defeat.   *I, ii, 205*

  'Tis ever common
That men are merriest when they are
 from home.
    Henry V, I, ii, 271

Now all the youth of England are on
 fire,
And silken dalliance in the wardrobe
 lies.   *II, Chorus, 1*

O England! model to thy inward great-
 ness,
Like little body with a mighty heart,
What mightst thou do, that honor
 would thee do,
Were all thy children kind and natural!
    II, Chorus, 16

That's the humor of it. *II, i, 63*

 He's in Arthur's bosom, if ever man
went to Arthur's bosom. A' made a
finer end and went away an it had been
any christom child; a' parted even just
between twelve and one, even at the
turning o' the tide: for after I saw him
fumble with the sheets and play with
flowers and smile upon his fingers' ends,
I knew there was but one way; for his
nose was as sharp as a pen, and a' babbled of green fields. *II, iii, 11*

 As cold as any stone. *II, iii, 26*

Trust none;
For oaths are straws, men's faiths are
 wafer-cakes,
And hold-fast is the only dog, my
 duck.   *II, iii, 53*

Once more unto the breach, dear
 friends, once more;
Or close the wall up with our English
 dead!
In peace there's nothing so becomes a
 man
As modest stillness and humility:
But when the blast of war blows in our
 ears,
Then imitate the action of the tiger;
Stiffen the sinews, summon up the
 blood,
Disguise fair nature with hard-favor'd
 rage;
Then lend the eye a terrible aspect.
      III, i, 1

And sheath'd their swords for lack of argument.   *Henry V, III, i, 21*

I see you stand like greyhounds in the slips,
Straining upon the start. The game's afoot:
Follow your spirit; and upon this charge
Cry "God for Harry! England and Saint George!"   *III, i, 31*

I would give all my fame for a pot of ale, and safety.   *III, ii, 14*

Men of few words are the best men.
    III, ii, 40

He will maintain his argument as well as any military man in the world.
    III, ii, 89

I know the disciplines of wars.
    III, ii, 156

I thought upon one pair of English legs
Did march three Frenchmen.
    III, vi, 161

We are in God's hand.   *III, vi, 181*

That island of England breeds very valiant creatures: their mastiffs are of unmatchable courage.   *III, vii, 155*

Give them great meals of beef and iron and steel, they will eat like wolves and fight like devils.   *III, vii, 166*

The hum of either army stilly sounds,
That the fix'd sentinels almost receive
The secret whispers of each other's watch:
Fire answers fire, and through their paly flames
Each battle sees the other's umber'd face:
Steed threatens steed, in high and boastful neighs
Piercing the night's dull ear; and from the tents
The armorers, accomplishing the knights,
With busy hammers closing rivets up,
Give dreadful note of preparation.
    IV, Chorus, 5

A little touch of Harry in the night.
    Henry V, IV, Chorus, 47

There is some soul of goodness in things evil,
Would men observingly distill it out.
    IV, i, 4

When blood is their argument.
    IV, i, 151

Every subject's duty is the king's; but every subject's soul is his own.
    IV, i, 189

    What infinite heart's ease
Must kings neglect that private men enjoy!
And what have kings that privates have not too,
Save ceremony, save general ceremony?
And what art thou, thou idol [1] ceremony?
What kind of god art thou, that suffer'st more
Of mortal griefs than do thy worshippers?
What are thy rents? what are thy comings-in?
O ceremony! show me but thy worth.
    IV, i, 256

'Tis not the balm, the scepter and the ball,
The sword, the mace, the crown imperial,
The intertissued robe of gold and pearl,
The farced title running 'fore the king,
The throne he sits on, nor the tide of pomp
That beats upon the high shore of this world,
No, not all these, thrice-gorgeous ceremony,
Not all these, laid in bed majestical,
Can sleep so soundly as the wretched slave,
Who with a body fill'd and vacant mind
Gets him to rest, cramm'd with distressful bread.   *IV, i, 280*

[1] Sometimes rendered: idle.

O God of battles! steel my soldiers'
hearts;
Possess them not with fear; take from
them now
The sense of reckoning, if the opposed
numbers
Pluck their hearts from them.
Henry V, IV, i, 309

But if it be a sin to covet honor,
I am the most offending soul alive.
IV, iii, 28

This day is call'd the feast of Crispian:
He that outlives this day, and comes
safe home,
Will stand a-tip-toe when this day is
nam'd.
And rouse him at the name of Crispian. *IV, iii, 40*

We few, we happy few, we band of
brothers;
For he today that sheds his blood with
me
Shall be my brother. *IV, iii, 60*

The saying is true, "The empty vessel makes the greatest sound."
IV, iv, 72

There is occasions and causes why
and wherefore [1] in all things.
V, i, 3

By this leek, I will most horribly revenge. I eat and eat, I swear.
V, i, 49

All hell shall stir for this. *V, i, 72*

The naked, poor, and mangled Peace,
Dear nurse of arts, plenties, and joyful
births. *V, ii, 34*

Grow like savages — as soldiers will,
That nothing do but meditate on
blood. *V, ii, 59*

For these fellows of infinite tongue,
that can rime themselves into ladies' favors, they do always reason themselves
out again. *V, ii, 162*

My comfort is, that old age, that ill
layer-up of beauty, can do no more
spoil upon my face. *V, ii, 246*

[1] See *The Comedy of Errors*, p. 218a.

Nice customs curtsy to great kings.
Henry V, V, ii, 291

He hath indeed better bettered expectation than you must expect of me
to tell you how.
Much Ado About Nothing
[1598–1600], act I, sc. i, l. 15

How much better is it to weep at joy
than to joy at weeping. *I, i, 28*

A very valiant trencher-man.
I, i, 52

There's a skirmish of wit between
them. *I, i, 64*

He wears his faith but as the fashion
of his hat. *I, i, 76*

I see, lady, the gentleman is not in
your books. *I, i, 79*

What! my dear Lady Disdain, are
you yet living? *I, i, 123*

Shall I never see a bachelor of threescore again? *I, i, 209*

In time the savage bull doth bear the
yoke. *I, i, 271*

Benedick the married man.
I, i, 278

I could not endure a husband with a
beard on his face: I had rather lie in
the woollen. *II, i, 31*

As merry as the day is long.
II, i, 52

Would it not grieve a woman to be
over-mastered with a piece of valiant
dust? to make an account of her life to
a clod of wayward marl? *II, i, 64*

I have a good eye, uncle: I can see a
church by daylight. *II, i, 86*

Speak low, if you speak love.
II, i, 104

Friendship is constant in all other
things
Save in the office and affairs of love:
Therefore all hearts in love use their
own tongues;

Let every eye negotiate for itself
And trust no agent.[1]

Much Ado About Nothing
II, i, 184

She speaks poniards, and every word
stabs: if her breath were as terrible as
her terminations, there were no living
near her; she would infect to the north
star.　　　　　　　　　　　II, i, 257

Silence is the perfectest herald of joy:
I were but little happy, if I could say
how much.　　　　　　　　II, i, 319

It keeps on the windy side of care.[2]
II, i, 328

There was a star danced, and under
that was I born.　　　　　　II, i, 351

I will tell you my drift.[3]　　II, i, 406

He was wont to speak plain and to
the purpose.　　　　　　　II, iii, 19

Sigh no more, ladies, sigh no more,
　Men were deceivers ever;
One foot in sea, and one on shore;
　To one thing constant never.
II, iii, 65

Sits the wind in that corner? [4]
II, iii, 108

Bait the hook well: this fish will
bite.　　　　　　　　　　　II, iii, 121

Shall quips and sentences and these
paper bullets of the brain awe a man
from the career of his humor? No; the
world must be peopled. When I said I
would die a bachelor, I did not think I
should live till I were married.
II, iii, 260

From the crown of his head to the
sole of his foot, he is all mirth.
III, ii, 9

He hath a heart as sound as a bell,
and his tongue is the clapper; for what
his heart thinks his tongue speaks.
III, ii, 12

Everyone can master a grief but he
that has it.

Much Ado About Nothing
III, ii, 28

Are you good men and true?
III, iii, 1

To be a well-favored man is the gift
of fortune; but to write and read comes
by nature.　　　　　　　　III, iii, 14

If they make you not then the better
answer, you may say they are not the
men you took them for.　　III, iii, 49

They that touch pitch will be defiled.[1]　　　　　　　　　　III, iii, 61

The fashion wears out more apparel
than the man.　　　　　　III, iii, 147

A good old man, sir; he will be talking: as they say, When the age is in,
the wit is out.　　　　　　　III, v, 36

O! what men dare do! what men
may do! what men daily do, not knowing what they do!　　　　　IV, i, 19

O! what authority and show of truth
Can cunning sin cover itself withal.
IV, i, 35

　　　For it so falls out
That what we have we prize not to the
　worth
Whiles we enjoy it, but being lack'd
　and lost,
Why, then we rack the value, then we
　find
The virtue that possession would not
　show us
Whiles it was ours.　　　　IV, i, 219

Masters, it is proved already that you
are little better than false knaves, and it
will go near to be thought so shortly.
IV, ii, 23

Flat burglary as ever was committed.
IV, ii, 54

Thou wilt be condemned into everlasting redemption for this.
IV, ii, 60

---

[1] See Longfellow, p. 623a.
[2] The windy side of the law. — *Twelfth-Night*
[1598–1600], *III, iv, 183*
[3] We know your drift. — *Coriolanus* [1607–
1608], *III, iii, 114*
[4] See Malory, p. 175a.

[1] He that toucheth pitch shall be defiled therewith. — *Apocrypha: Ecclesiasticus 13:1*
　This pitch, as ancient writers do report, doth
defile; so doth the company thou keepest. —
King Henry IV [1597–1598], *pt. I, II, iv, 460*

O that he were here to write me down an ass!
Much Ado About Nothing
IV, ii, 80

Patch griefs with proverbs. V, i, 17

Charm ache with air, and agony with words. V, i, 26

For there was never yet philosopher
That could endure the toothache patiently. V, i, 35

Some of us will smart for it.
V, i, 108

What though care killed a cat,[1] thou hast mettle enough in thee to kill care.
V, i, 135

I was not born under a riming planet. V, ii, 40

The trumpet of his own virtues.
V, ii, 91

Done to death by slanderous tongues.
V, iii, 3

Fleet the time carelessly, as they did in the golden world.
As You Like It [1598–1600], *act I, sc. i, l.* 126

Always the dullness of the fool is the whetstone of the wits. I, ii, 59

The little foolery that wise men have makes a great show. I, ii, 97

Well said: that was laid on with a trowel. I, ii, 113

Your heart's desires be with you!
I, ii, 214

One out of suits with fortune.
I, ii, 263

My pride fell with my fortunes.
I, ii, 269

Hereafter, in a better world than this, I shall desire more love and knowledge of you. I, ii, 301

Heavenly Rosalind! I, ii, 306

[1] Let care kill a cat,
We'll laugh and grow fat.
Shirburn Ballads [1585], *91*
Hang sorrow, care'll kill a cat. — JONSON: *Every Man in His Humour* [1598], I, i

O, how full of briers is this working-day world!
As You Like It I, iii, 12

Beauty provoketh thieves sooner than gold. I, iii, 113

We'll have a swashing and a martial outside,
As many other mannish cowards have.
I, iii, 123

Hath not old custom made this life more sweet
Than that of painted pomp? Are not these woods
More free from peril than the envious court? II, i, 2

Sweet are the uses of adversity,
Which, like the toad, ugly and venomous,
Wears yet a precious jewel in his head;
And this our life, exempt from public haunt,
Finds tongues in trees, books in the running brooks,
Sermons in stones, and good in every thing.[1] II, i, 12

The big round tears
Cours'd one another down his innocent nose
In piteous chase. II, i, 38

"Poor deer," quoth he, "thou mak'st a testament
As worldlings do, giving thy sum of more
To that which had too much."
II, i, 47

Sweep on, you fat and greasy citizens.
II, i, 55

And He that doth the ravens feed,
Yea, providently caters for the sparrow,
Be comfort to my age! II, iii, 43

Though I look old, yet I am strong and lusty;
For in my youth I never did apply
Hot and rebellious liquors in my blood. II, iii, 47

[1] See St. Bernard, p. 154a, *As You Like It III, ii, 5;* and Wordsworth, p. 509a.

Therefore my age is as a lusty winter,
Frosty, but kindly.
　　　　　As You Like It II, *iii,* 52

Thou art not for the fashion of these
　　times,
Where none will sweat but for promo-
　　tion.　　　　　II, *iii,* 59

Ay, now am I in Arden; the more
fool I: when I was at home, I was in a
better place: but travelers must be content.　　　　　II, *iv,* 16

If you remember'st not the slightest
　　folly
That ever love did make thee run into,
Thou hast not lov'd.　　　II, *iv,* 34

We that are true lovers run into
strange capers.　　　　II, *iv,* 53

Thou speakest wiser than thou art
ware of.　　　　　II, *iv,* 57

I shall ne'er be ware of mine own
wit, till I break my shins against it.
　　　　　　　　　II, *iv,* 59

　　Under the greenwood tree
　　Who loves to lie with me,
　　And turn his merry note
　　Unto the sweet bird's throat,
Come hither, come hither, come hither:
　　Here shall he see
　　No enemy
But winter and rough weather.
　　　　　　　　　II, *v,* 1

I can suck melancholy out of a song
as a weasel sucks eggs.　　II, *v,* 12

Who doth ambition shun,
And loves to live i' the sun,
Seeking the food he eats,
And pleas'd with what he gets.
　　　　　　　　　II, *v,* 38

　　I met a fool i' the forest,
A motley fool.　　　　II, *vii,* 12

And then he drew a dial from his
　　poke,
And looking on it with lack-luster eye,
Says, very wisely, "It is ten o'clock;
Thus may we see," quoth he, "how the
　　world wags."[1]　　　II, *vii,* 20

[1] So wags the world. — SIR WALTER SCOTT,
Ivanhoe [1819], *ch.* 37

And so, from hour to hour we ripe and
　　ripe,
And then from hour to hour we rot and
　　rot;
And thereby hangs a tale.[1]
　　　　　As You Like It II, *vii,* 26

My lungs began to crow like chanti-
　　cleer,
That fools should be so deep-contem-
　　plative,
And I did laugh sans intermission
An hour by his dial.　　II, *vii,* 30

Motley's the only wear.　II, *vii,* 34

　　If ladies be but young and fair,
They have the gift to know it.
　　　　　　　　　II, *vii,* 37

　　I must have liberty
Withal, as large a charter as the wind,
To blow on whom I please.
　　　　　　　　　II, *vii,* 47

The "why" is plain as way to parish
　　church.　　　　II, *vii,* 52

　　But whate'er you are
That in this desert inaccessible,
Under the shade of melancholy
　　boughs,
Lose and neglect the creeping hours of
　　time;
If ever you have look'd on better days,
If ever been where bells have knoll'd to
　　church,
If ever sat at any good man's feast,
If ever from your eyelids wip'd a tear,
And know what 'tis to pity, and be
　　pitied,
Let gentleness my strong enforcement
　　be.　　　　　II, *vii,* 109

True is it that we have seen better
　　days.　　　　II, *vii,* 120

Oppress'd with two weak evils, age and
　　hunger.　　　　II, *vii,* 132

　　All the world's a stage,
And all the men and women merely
　　players: [2]

[1] See Rabelais, p. 181b.
[2] See *The Merchant of Venice*, p. 231a.
The world's a theatre, the earth a stage,
Which God and Nature do with actors fill.
　　THOMAS HEYWOOD, *Apology for Actors*
　　　　　　　　　[1612]

They have their exits and their en-
trances;
And one man in his time plays many
parts,
His acts being seven ages. At first the
infant,
Mewling and puking in the nurse's
arms.
And then the whining school-boy, with
his satchel,
And shining morning face, creeping like
snail
Unwillingly to school. And then the
lover,
Sighing like furnace, with a woful bal-
lad
Made to his mistress' eyebrow. Then a
soldier,
Full of strange oaths, and bearded like
the pard,
Jealous in honor, sudden and quick in
quarrel,
Seeking the bubble reputation
Even in the cannon's mouth. And then
the justice,
In fair round belly with good capon
lin'd,
With eyes severe and beard of formal
cut,
Full of wise saws and modern in-
stances;
And so he plays his part. The sixth age
shifts
Into the lean and slipper'd pantaloon,
With spectacles on nose and pouch on
side,
His youthful hose well sav'd, a world
too wide
For his shrunk shank; and his big
manly voice,
Turning again toward childish treble,
pipes
And whistles in his sound. Last scene of
all,
That ends this strange eventful history,
Is second childishness, and mere oblivion,

Sans teeth, sans eyes, sans taste, sans
everything.
As You Like It II, vii, 139

Blow, blow, thou winter wind!
Thou art not so unkind
As man's ingratitude.   *II, vii, 174*

These trees shall be my books.[1]
III, ii, 5

The fair, the chaste, and unexpressive
she.   *III, ii, 10*

It goes much against my stomach.
Hast any philosophy in thee, shepherd?   *III, ii, 21*

He that wants money, means, and
content, is without three good friends.
III, ii, 25

I am a true laborer: I earn that I eat,
get that I wear, owe no man hate, envy
no man's happiness, glad of other
men's good, content with my harm.
III, ii, 78

From the east to western Ind,
No jewel is like Rosalind.   *III, ii, 94*

This is the very false gallop of
verses.   *III, ii, 120*

Let us make an honorable retreat;
though not with bag and baggage, yet
with scrip and scrippage.   *III, ii, 170*

O, wonderful, wonderful, and most
wonderful, wonderful! and yet again
wonderful! and after that out of all
whooping.   *III, ii, 202*

Answer me in one word.
III, ii, 238

Do you not know I am a woman?
when I think, I must speak.
III, ii, 265

I do desire we may be better strangers.   *III, ii, 276*

Jacques: What stature is she of?
Orlando: Just as high as my heart.
III, ii, 286

Time travels in divers paces with
divers persons. I'll tell you who Time

The world's a stage on which all the parts
are played. — MIDDLETON, *A Game of Chess*
[1624], *V, i*

[1] See St. Bernard, p. 154a; *As You Like It II,
i, 12;* and Wordsworth, p. 509a.

ambles withal, who Time trots withal, who Time gallops withal, and who he stands still withal.

As You Like It III, ii, 328

Every one fault seeming monstrous till his fellow fault came to match it.

III, ii, 377

Everything about you demonstrating a careless desolation.   III, ii, 405

Truly, I would the gods had made thee poetical.   III, iii, 16

The wounds invisible
That love's keen arrows make.

III, v, 30

Down on your knees,
And thank heaven, fasting, for a good
     man's love.   III, v, 57

I am falser than vows made in wine.

III, v, 73

It is a melancholy of mine own, compounded of many simples, extracted from many objects, and indeed the sundry contemplation of my travels, which, by often rumination, wraps me in a most humorous sadness.

IV, i, 16

I had rather have a fool to make me merry than experience to make me sad.   IV, i, 28

Farewell, Monsieur Traveler: look you lisp and wear strange suits, disable all the benefits of your own country, be out of love with your nativity, and almost chide God for making you that countenance you are; or I will scarce think you have swam in a gondola.

IV, i, 35

I'll warrant him heart-whole.

IV, i, 51

Very good orators, when they are out, they will spit; and for lovers lacking — God warn us! — matter, the cleanliest shift is to kiss.   IV, i, 77

Men have died from time to time, and worms have eaten them, but not for love.   IV, i, 110

Forever and a day.   IV, i, 151

Men are April when they woo, December when they wed: maids are May when they are maids, but the sky changes when they are wives.

As You Like It IV, i, 153

My affection hath an unknown bottom, like the bay of Portugal.

IV, i, 219

The horn, the horn, the lusty horn
Is not a thing to laugh to scorn.

IV, ii, 17

Chewing the food of sweet and bitter fancy.   IV, iii, 103

"So so" is good, very good, very excellent good: and yet it is not; it is but so so.   V, i, 30

The fool doth think he is wise, but the wise man knows himself to be a fool.   V, i, 35

No sooner met, but they looked; no sooner looked but they loved; no sooner loved but they sighed; no sooner sighed but they asked one another the reason; no sooner knew the reason but they sought the remedy.   V, ii, 37

But, O! how bitter a thing it is to look into happiness through another man's eyes!   V, ii, 48

It was a lover and his lass,
     With a hey, and a ho, and a hey
          nonino,
That o'er the green corn-field did pass,
     In the spring time, the only pretty
          ring time,
When birds do sing, hey ding a ding,
     ding;
Sweet lovers love the spring.

V, iii, 18

Here comes a pair of very strange beasts, which in all tongues are called fools.   V, iv, 36

An ill-favored thing, sir, but mine own.[1]   V, iv, 60

Rich honesty dwells like a miser, sir, in a poor house, as your pearl in your foul oyster.   V, iv, 62

[1] "A poor thing but mine own" is the popular version.

"The retort courteous." . . . "the quip modest." . . . "the reply churlish." . . . "the reproof valiant" . . . "the countercheck quarrelsome." . . . "the lie circumstantial," and "the lie direct." *As You Like It* V, *iv*, 75

Your "if" is the only peacemaker; much virtue in "if." V, *iv*, 108

He uses his folly like a stalking horse, and under the presentation of that he shoots his wit. V, *iv*, 112

If music be the food of love,[1] play on; Give me excess of it, that, surfeiting, The appetite may sicken, and so die. That strain again! it had a dying fall: O! it came o'er my ear like the sweet sound That breathes upon a bank of violets, Stealing and giving odor!
Twelfth-Night [1598–1600], *act I, sc. i, l. 1*

O spirit of love! how quick and fresh art thou, That, notwithstanding thy capacity Receiveth as the sea, nought enters there, Of what validity and pitch soe'er, But falls into abatement and low price, Even in a minute: so full of shapes is fancy, That it alone is high fantastical.
I, *i*, 9

When my tongue blabs, then let mine eyes not see. I, *ii*, 61

I am sure care's an enemy to life.
I, *iii*, 2

Let them hang themselves in their own straps.[2] I, *iii*, 13

I am a great eater of beef, and I believe that does harm to my wit.
I, *iii*, 92

Wherefore are these things hid?
I, *iii*, 135

[1] See *Antony and Cleopatra II, v, 1*, p. 288a. Is not music the food of love? — RICHARD BRINSLEY SHERIDAN, *The Rivals* [1775], *II, i*
[2] See Rabelais, p. 181b, and note.

Is it a world to hide virtues in?
Twelfth-Night I, *iii*, 142

God give them wisdom that have it; and those that are fools, let them use their talents. I, *v*, 14

One draught above heat makes him a fool, the second mads him, and a third drowns him. I, *v*, 139

'Tis beauty truly blent, whose red and white Nature's own sweet and cunning hand laid on: Lady, you are the cruel'st she alive, If you will lead these graces to the grave And leave the world no copy.
I, *v*, 259

Make me a willow cabin at your gate, And call upon my soul within the house. I, *v*, 289

Holla your name to the reverberate hills, And make the babbling gossip of the air Cry out, "Olivia!" I, *v*, 293

Farewell, fair cruelty. I, *v*, 309

O mistress mine! where are you roaming? II, *iii*, 42

Journeys end in lovers meeting, Every wise man's son doth know.
II, *iii*, 46

What is love? 'tis not hereafter; Present mirth hath present laughter. What's to come is still unsure: In delay there lies no plenty; Then come kiss me, sweet and twenty, Youth's a stuff will not endure.
II, *iii*, 50

He does it with a better grace, but I do it more natural. II, *iii*, 91

Is there no respect of place, persons, nor time, in you?[1] II, *iii*, 100

Sir Toby: Dost thou think, because thou art virtuous, there shall be no more cakes and ale?

[1] See *Acts 10:34*, p. 50a, and note.

Clown: Yes, by Saint Anne; and ginger shall be hot i' the mouth too.
Twelfth-Night II, iii, 124

My purpose is, indeed, a horse of that color.   *II, iii, 184*

These most brisk and giddy-paced times.   *II, iv, 6*

If ever thou shalt love,
In the sweet pangs of it remember me;
For such as I am all true lovers are:
Unstaid and skittish in all motions else
Save in the constant image of the creature
That is belov'd.   *II, iv, 15*

Let still the woman take
An elder than herself, so wears she to him,
So sways she level in her husband's heart:
For, boy, however we do praise ourselves,
Our fancies are more giddy and unfirm,
More longing, wavering, sooner lost and worn,
Than women's are.   *II, iv, 29*

Then, let thy love be younger than thyself,
Or thy affection cannot hold the bent;
For women are as roses, whose fair flower
Being once display'd, doth fall that very hour.   *II, iv, 36*

The spinsters and the knitters in the sun,
And the free maids that weave their thread with bones,
Do use to chant it: it is silly sooth,
And dallies with the innocence of love,
Like the old age.   *II, iv, 44*

Come away, come away, death,
    And in sad cypress let me be laid;
Fly away, fly away, breath;
    I am slain by a fair cruel maid.
       II, iv, 51

Duke: And what's her history?
Viola: A blank, my lord. She never told her love,

But let concealment, like a worm i' the bud,
Feed on her damask cheek: she pin'd in thought,
And with a green and yellow melancholy,
She sat like Patience on a monument,
Smiling at grief.
Twelfth-Night II, iv, 112

I am all the daughters of my father's house,
And all the brothers too.   *II, iv, 122*

Here comes the trout that must be caught with tickling.   *II, v, 25*

I may command where I adore.
       II, v, 116

Be not afraid of greatness: some are born great, some achieve greatness, and some have greatness thrust upon them.
       II, v, 159

Remember who commended thy yellow stockings, and wished to see thee ever cross-gartered.   *II, v, 168*

Foolery, sir, does walk about the orb like the sun; it shines everywhere.
       III, i, 44

This fellow's wise enough to play the fool,
And to do that well craves a kind of wit.   *III, i, 68*

Music from the spheres.[1]   *III, i, 122*

How apt the poor are to be proud.
       III, i, 141

Then westward-ho!   *III, i, 148*

O! what a deal of scorn looks beautiful In the contempt and anger of his lip.
       III, i, 159

Love sought is good, but giv'n unsought is better.   *III, i, 170*

You will hang like an icicle on a Dutchman's beard.   *III, ii, 30*

---

[1] The music of the spheres. — *Pericles V, i, 231.*
A phrase that stems from the Pythagorean Theory (sixth century B.C.) of the music or harmony of the spheres.
See Sir Thomas Browne, p. 330a.

Let there be gall enough in thy ink.
    Twelfth-Night III, ii, 54

Laugh yourselves into stitches.
                 III, ii, 75

I think we do know the sweet Roman
hand.   III, iv, 31

This is very midsummer madness.
                 III, iv, 62

More matter for a May morning.
              III, iv, 158

He's a very devil.   III, iv, 304

Out of my lean and low ability
I'll lend you something.   III, iv, 380

I hate ingratitude more in a man
Than lying, vainness, babbling drunk-
    enness,
Or any taint of vice whose strong cor-
    ruption
Inhabits our frail blood.   III, iv, 390

As the old hermit of Prague, that
never saw pen and ink, very wittily said
to a niece of King Gorboduc, "That
that is, is."   IV, ii, 14

Thus the whirligig of time brings in
his revenges.   V, i, 388

When that I was and a little tiny boy,
    With hey, ho, the wind and the
    rain;
A foolish thing was but a toy,
    For the rain it raineth every day.[1]
                 V, i, 404

A surgeon to old shoes.
    Julius Caesar [1598–1600],
        act I, sc. i, l. 26

As proper men as ever trod upon
neat's leather.   I, i, 27

Have you not made a universal shout,
That Tiber trembled underneath her
    banks,
To hear the replication of your sounds
Made in her concave shores?
                  I, i, 48

Beware the ides of March.[2]   I, ii, 18

Set honor in one eye and death i' the
    other,
And I will look on both indifferently.
        Julius Caesar I, ii, 86

Well, honor is the subject of my story.
I cannot tell what you and other men
Think of this life; but, for my single
    self,
I had as lief not be as live to be
In awe of such a thing as I myself.
                 I, ii, 92

Stemming it with hearts of contro-
    versy.   I, ii, 109

Why, man, he doth bestride the narrow
    world
Like a Colossus; and we petty men
Walk under his huge legs, and peep
    about
To find ourselves dishonorable graves.
Men at some time are masters of their
    fates: [1]
The fault, dear Brutus, is not in our
    stars,
But in ourselves, that we are under-
    lings.   I, ii, 134

Upon what meat doth this our Caesar
    feed,
That he is grown so great?   I, ii, 148

Let me have men about me that are
    fat;
Sleek-headed men, and such as sleep o'
    nights.
Yond Cassius has a lean and hungry
    look; [2]
He thinks too much: such men are
    dangerous.   I, ii, 191

        He reads much;
He is a great observer, and he looks
Quite through the deeds of men.
                 I, ii, 200

Seldom he smiles, and smiles in such a
    sort
As if he mock'd himself, and scorn'd
    his spirit
That could be moved to smile at any-
    thing.   I, ii, 204

---

[1] Parodied by the Fool in *King Lear*, p. 278a.
[2] See Julius Caesar, p. 112a.

[1] See Sallust, p. 116a.
[2] See Julius Caesar, p. 112b.

But, for my own part, it was Greek to
me.[1]
Julius Caesar I, ii, 288

Yesterday the bird of night did sit,
Even at noonday, upon the market-
place,
Hooting and shrieking.　　　I, iii, 26

So every bondman in his own hand
bears
The power to cancel his captivity.
I, iii, 101

O! he sits high in all the people's
hearts:
And that which would appear offense in
us,
His countenance, like richest alchemy,
Will change to virtue and to worthiness.　　　I, iii, 157

The abuse of greatness is when it disjoins
Remorse from power.　　　II, i, 18

'Tis a common proof,
That lowliness is young ambition's lad-
der,
Whereto the climber-upward turns his
face;
But when he once attains the upmost
round,
He then unto the ladder turns his
back,
Looks in the clouds, scorning the base
degrees
By which he did ascend.　　　II, i, 21

Therefore think him as a serpent's egg
Which, hatch'd, would, as his kind,
grow mischievous,
And kill him in the shell.　　　II, i, 32

Between the acting of a dreadful thing
And the first motion, all the interim
is
Like a phantasma, or a hideous dream:
The genius and the mortal instru-
ments
Are then in council; and the state of
man,
Like to a little kingdom, suffers then
The nature of an insurrection.
II, i, 63

O conspiracy!
Sham'st thou to show thy dangerous
brow by night,
When evils are most free?
Julius Caesar II, i, 77

Let's carve him as a dish fit for the
gods,
Not hew him as a carcass fit for
hounds.　　　II, i, 173

But when I tell him he hates flatterers,
He says he does, being then most flattered.　　　II, i, 207

Enjoy the honey-heavy dew of slumber.　　　II, i, 230

You are my true and honorable wife,
As dear to me as are the ruddy drops
That visit my sad heart.[1]　　　II, i, 288

Think you I am no stronger than my
sex,
Being so father'd and so husbanded?
II, i, 296

When beggars die, there are no comets
seen;
The heavens themselves blaze forth the
death of princes.　　　II, ii, 30

Cowards die many times before their
deaths;
The valiant never taste of death but
once.
Of all the wonders that I yet have
heard,
It seems to me most strange that men
should fear;
Seeing that death, a necessary end,
Will come when it will come.
II, ii, 32

Antony, that revels long o' nights.
II, ii, 116

How hard it is for women to keep
counsel!　　　II, iv, 9

But I am constant as the northern
star,
Of whose true-fix'd and resting quality
There is no fellow in the firmament.
III, i, 60

Speak, hands, for me!　　　III, i, 76

---

[1] This geare is Greeke to me. — GASCOIGNE,
Supposes I [1573]

[1] Dear as the ruddy drops that warm my heart.
— THOMAS GRAY, *The Bard* [1757], I, iii, 12

Et tu, Brute! [1]
> *Julius Caesar III, i, 77*

Some to the common pulpits, and cry
out,
"Liberty, freedom, and enfranchise-
ment."   *III, i, 79*

> How many ages hence
Shall this our lofty scene be acted o'er,
In states unborn and accents yet un-
known!   *III, i, 111*

O mighty Caesar! dost thou lie so low?
Are all thy conquests, glories, triumphs,
spoils,
Shrunk to this little measure?
> *III, i, 148*

The choice and master spirits of this
age.   *III, i, 163*

Though last, not least in love.[2]
> *III, i, 189*

O! pardon me, thou bleeding piece of
earth,
That I am meek and gentle with these
butchers;
Thou art the ruins of the noblest man
That ever lived in the tide of times.
> *III, i, 254*

Cry "Havoc!" and let slip the dogs of
war.   *III, i, 273*

> Romans, countrymen, and lovers!
hear me for my cause; and be silent,
that you may hear.   *III, ii, 13*

Not that I loved Caesar less, but that
I loved Rome more.   *III, ii, 22*

> As he was valiant, I honor him; but,
as he was ambitious, I slew him.
> *III, ii, 27*

If any, speak; for him have I offended. I pause for a reply.
> *III, ii, 36*

Friends, Romans, countrymen, lend me
your ears;
I come to bury Caesar, not to praise
him.
The evil that men do lives after them,

The good is oft interred with their
bones.[1]
> *Julius Caesar III, ii, 79*

For Brutus is an honorable man;
So are they all, all honorable men.
> *III, ii, 88*

When that the poor have cried, Caesar
hath wept;
Ambition should be made of sterner
stuff.   *III, ii, 97*

O judgment! thou art fled to brutish
beasts,
And men have lost their reason.
> *III, ii, 110*

But yesterday the word of Caesar
might
Have stood against the world; now lies
he there,
And none so poor to do him reverence.
> *III, ii, 124*

If you have tears, prepare to shed them
now.   *III, ii, 174*

See what a rent the envious Casca
made.   *III, ii, 180*

This was the most unkindest cut of all.
> *III, ii, 188*

> Great Caesar fell.
O! what a fall was there, my countrymen;
Then I, and you, and all of us fell
down,
Whilst bloody treason flourish'd over
us.   *III, ii, 194*

What private griefs they have, alas! I
know not.   *III, ii, 217*

I come not, friends, to steal away your
hearts:
I am no orator, as Brutus is;
But, as you know me all, a plain blunt
man.   *III, ii, 220*

For I have neither wit, nor words, nor
worth,
Action, nor utterance, nor the power of
speech,
To stir men's blood: I only speak right
on.   *III, ii, 225*

---

[1] See Julius Caesar, p. 112b.
[2] See Spenser, p. 201a, and *King Lear*, p. 276b.   [1] See Euripides, p. 85b.

Put a tongue
In every wound of Caesar, that should move
The stones of Rome to rise and mutiny.
    Julius Caesar III, *ii*, 232

When love begins to sicken and decay,
It useth an enforced ceremony.
There are no tricks in plain and simple faith.   *IV*, *ii*, 20

An itching palm.   *IV*, *iii*, 10

I had rather be a dog, and bay the moon,
Than such a Roman.   *IV*, *iii*, 27

I'll use you for my mirth, yea, for my laughter,
When you are waspish.   *IV*, *iii*, 49

There is no terror, Cassius, in your threats;
For I am arm'd so strong in honesty
That they pass by me as the idle wind,
Which I respect not.   *IV*, *iii*, 66

A friend should bear his friend's infirmities,
But Brutus makes mine greater than they are.   *IV*, *iii*, 85

All his faults observ'd,
Set in a notebook, learn'd, and conn'd by rote.   *IV*, *iii*, 96

There is a tide in the affairs of men,
Which, taken at the flood, leads on to fortune;
Omitted, all the voyage of their life
Is bound in shallows and in miseries.
    IV, *iii*, 217

We must take the current when it serves,
Or lose our ventures.   *IV*, *iii*, 222

The deep of night is crept upon our talk,
And nature must obey necessity.
    IV, *iii*, 225

But for your words, they rob the Hybla bees,
And leave them honeyless.   *V*, *i*, 34

Forever, and forever, farewell, Cassius!
If we do meet again, why, we shall smile;

If not, why then, this parting was well made.   *Julius Caesar* V, *i*, 117

O! that a man might know
The end of this day's business, ere it come.   *V*, *i*, 123

O Julius Caesar! thou art mighty yet!
Thy spirit walks abroad, and turns our swords
In our own proper entrails.
    V, *iii*, 94

The last of all the Romans, fare thee well!   *V*, *iii*, 99

This was the noblest Roman of them all.   *V*, *v*, 68

His life was gentle, and the elements
So mix'd in him that Nature might stand up
And say to all the world, "This was a man!" [1]   *V*, *v*, 73

For this relief much thanks; 'tis bitter cold,
And I am sick at heart.
    Hamlet [1600–1601], *act I, sc. i, l. 8*

Not a mouse stirring.[2]   *I*, *i*, 10

Thou art a scholar; speak to it, Horatio.   *I*, *i*, 42

But in the gross and scope of my opinion,
This bodes some strange eruption to our state.   *I*, *i*, 68

Whose sore task
Does not divide the Sunday from the week.   *I*, *i*, 75

This sweaty haste
Doth make the night joint-laborer with the day.   *I*, *i*, 77

In the most high and palmy state of Rome,
A little ere the mightiest Julius fell,
The graves stood tenantless and the sheeted dead
Did squeak and gibber in the Roman streets.   *I*, *i*, 113

---

[1] See *Hamlet I, ii, 187*, p. 258a.
[2] See Clement Clarke Moore, p. 541a.

The moist star
Upon whose influence Neptune's empire stands
Was sick almost to doomsday with eclipse. *Hamlet* I, i, 118

And then it started like a guilty thing
Upon a fearful summons. I, i, 148

The cock, that is the trumpet to the morn. I, i, 150

Whether in sea or fire, in earth or air,
The extravagant and erring spirit hies
To his confine. I, i, 153

It faded on the crowing of the cock.
Some say that ever 'gainst that season comes
Wherein our Saviour's birth is celebrated,
The bird of dawning singeth all night long;
And then, they say, no spirit can walk abroad;
The nights are wholesome; then no planets strike,
No fairy takes, nor witch hath power to charm,
So hallow'd and so gracious is the time. I, i, 157

But, look, the morn in russet mantle clad,
Walks o'er the dew of yon high eastern hill. I, i, 166

The memory be green.[1] I, ii, 2

With one auspicious and one dropping eye,
With mirth in funeral and with dirge in marriage,
In equal scale weighing delight and dole. I, ii, 11

So much for him. I, ii, 25

A little more than kin, and less than kind. I, ii, 65

Thou know'st 'tis common; all that live must die,
Passing through nature to eternity. I, ii, 72

Seems, madam! Nay, it is; I know not "seems."

[1] See Thomas Moore, p. 541b.

'Tis not alone my inky cloak, good mother,
Nor customary suits of solemn black. *Hamlet* I, ii, 76

But I have that within which passeth show;
These but the trappings and the suits of woe. I, ii, 85

To persever
In obstinate condolement is a course
Of impious stubbornness; 'tis unmanly grief:
It shows a will most incorrect to heaven,
A heart unfortified, a mind impatient. I, ii, 92

O! that this too too solid [1] flesh would melt,
Thaw and resolve itself into a dew;
Or that the Everlasting had not fix'd
His canon 'gainst self-slaughter! O God! O God!
How weary, stale, flat, and unprofitable
Seem to me all the uses of this world. I, ii, 129

Things rank and gross in nature
Possess it merely. That it should come to this! I, ii, 136

So excellent a king; that was, to this,
Hyperion to a satyr; so loving to my mother
That he might not beteem the winds of heaven
Visit her face too roughly. I, ii, 139

Why, she would hang on him,
As if increase of appetite had grown
By what it fed on. I, ii, 143

Frailty, thy name is woman! I, ii, 146

Like Niobe, all tears. I, ii, 149

A beast, that wants discourse of reason. I, ii, 150

It is not nor it cannot come to good. I, ii, 158

[1] Alternative readings are "sallied" and "sullied."

A truant disposition.
                    Hamlet I, ii, 169

Thrift, thrift, Horatio! the funeral
    bak'd meats
Did coldly furnish forth the marriage
    tables.

Would I had met my dearest foe [1] in
    heaven
Ere I had ever seen that day.
                    I, ii, 180

In my mind's eye, Horatio.   I, ii, 185

He was a man, take him for all in all,[2]
I shall not look upon his like again.
                    I, ii, 187

Season your admiration for a while.
                    I, ii, 192

In the dead vast and middle of the
    night.   I, ii, 198

Arm'd at points exactly, cap-a-pe.
                    I, ii, 200

        Distill'd
Almost to jelly with the act of fear.
                    I, ii, 204

A countenance more in sorrow than in
    anger.   I, ii, 231

While one with moderate haste might
    tell a hundred.   I, ii, 237

Hamlet: His beard was grizzled, no?
Horatio: It was, as I have seen it in his
    life,
A sable silver'd.   I, ii, 239

Give it an understanding, but no
    tongue.   I, ii, 249

        All is not well;
I doubt some foul play.   I, ii, 254

        Foul deeds will rise,
Though all the earth o'erwhelm them,
    to men's eyes.   I, ii, 256

The chariest maid is prodigal enough
If she unmask her beauty to the
    moon;
Virtue itself 'scapes not calumnious
    strokes;
The canker galls the infants of the
    spring

[1] See *Henry IV, pt. I, III, ii, 123,* p. 240a.
[2] See *Julius Caesar V, v, 73,* p. 256b.

Too oft before their buttons be dis-
    clos'd,
And in the morn and liquid dew of
    youth
Contagious blastments are most immi-
    nent.   *Hamlet* I, iii, 36

Do not, as some ungracious pastors do,
Show me the steep and thorny way to
    heaven,
Whiles, like a puff'd and reckless liber-
    tine,
Himself the primrose path of dalliance
    treads,[1]
And recks not his own rede.[2]
                    I, iii, 47

Give thy thoughts no tongue.
                    I, iii, 59

Be thou familiar, but by no means vul-
    gar;
Those friends thou hast, and their
    adoption tried,
Grapple them to thy soul with hoops of
    steel.   I, iii, 61

        Beware
Of entrance to a quarrel, but, being in,
Bear 't that th' opposed may beware of
    thee.
Give every man thy ear, but few thy
    voice;
Take each man's censure, but reserve
    thy judgment.
Costly thy habit as thy purse can buy,
But not express'd in fancy; rich, not
    gaudy; [3]
For the apparel oft proclaims the man.
                    I, iii, 65

Neither a borrower, nor a lender be;
For loan oft loses both itself and
    friend,

[1] See Bion, p. 104b, and *Macbeth II, iii, 22,*
p. 283b.
[2] Wel oghte a preest ensample for to yive,
    By his clennesse, how that his sheep shold
    live.
            CHAUCER, *Canterbury Tales* [c. 1387],
                        prologue, l. 504
And may you better reck the rede,
    Than ever did the adviser.
            ROBERT BURNS [1759–1796], *Epistle to
                        a Young Friend*
[2] See Lyly, p. 202b.
    Neat, not gaudy. — CHARLES LAMB, *letter to
Wordsworth* [1806]

And borrowing dulls the edge of hus-
　bandry.

This above all: to thine own self be
　true,
And it must follow, as the night the
　day,
Thou canst not then be false to any
　man.[1]　　　　*Hamlet I, iii, 75*

'Tis in my memory lock'd,
And you yourself shall keep the key of
　it.　　　　　　　*I, iii, 85*

You speak like a green girl,
Unsifted in such perilous circum-
　stance.　　　　　*I, iii, 101*

Springes to catch woodcocks.
　　　　　　　　　I, iii, 115

When the blood burns, how prodigal
　the soul
Lends the tongue vows.　*I, iii, 116*

Be somewhat scanter of your maiden
　presence.　　　　*I, iii, 121*

The air bites shrewdly.　*I, iv, 1*

But to my mind — though I am native
　here
And to the manner born — it is a cus-
　tom
More honor'd in the breach than the
　observance.　　　*I, iv, 14*

Angels and ministers of grace defend
　us!　　　　　　　*I, iv, 39*

Be thy intents wicked or charitable,
Thou com'st in such a questionable
　shape
That I will speak to thee.　*I, iv, 42*

What may this mean,
That thou, dead corse, again in com-
　plete steel
Revisit'st thus the glimpses of the
　moon,
Making night hideous;[2] and we fools
　of nature
So horridly to shake our disposition
With thoughts beyond the reaches of
　our souls?　　　*I, iv, 51*

[1] See Bacon, p. 209a.
[2] And makes night hideous. — ALEXANDER
POPE, *The Dunciad, bk. III* [1728], *l. 166*

I do not set my life at a pin's fee.
　　　　　　　Hamlet I, iv, 65

The dreadful summit of the cliff
That beetles o'er his base into the sea.
　　　　　　　　　I, iv, 70

My fate cries out,
And makes each petty artery in this
　body
As hardy as the Nemean lion's nerve.
　　　　　　　　　I, iv, 81

Unhand me, gentlemen,
By heaven! I'll make a ghost of him
　that lets me.　　　*I, iv, 84*

Something is rotten in the state of
　Denmark.　　　　*I, iv, 90*

I could a tale unfold whose lightest
　word
Would harrow up thy soul, freeze thy
　young blood,
Make thy two eyes, like stars, start from
　their spheres,
Thy knotted and combined locks to
　part,
And each particular hair to stand an
　end,
Like quills upon the fretful porpen-
　tine.　　　　　　*I, v, 15*

And duller shouldst thou be than the
　fat weed
That rots itself in ease on Lethe wharf.
　　　　　　　　　I, v, 32

O my prophetic soul!
My uncle!
　　　　　　　　　I, v, 40

O Hamlet! what a falling-off was there.
　　　　　　　　　I, v, 47

But virtue, as it never will be mov'd,
Though lewdness court it in a shape of
　heaven,
So lust, though to a radiant angel
　link'd,
Will sate itself in a celestial bed,
And prey on garbage.　　*I, v, 53*

In the porches of mine ears.
　　　　　　　　　I, v, 63

Cut off even in the blossoms of my
　sin,
Unhousel'd, disappointed, unanel'd,

No reckoning made, but sent to my account
With all my imperfections on my head.[1]   *Hamlet I, v, 76*

Leave her to heaven,
And to those thorns that in her bosom lodge,
To prick and sting her.   *I, v, 86*

The glowworm shows the matin to be near,
And 'gins to pale his uneffectual fire.
            I, v, 89

While memory holds a seat
In this distracted globe. Remember thee!
Yea, from the table of my memory
I'll wipe away all trivial fond records.
            I, v, 96

Within the book and volume of my brain.   *I, v, 103*

O villain, villain, smiling, damned villain!
My tables — meet it is I set it down,
That one may smile, and smile, and be a villain;
At least I'm sure it may be so in Denmark.   *I, v, 106*

There's ne'er a villain dwelling in all Denmark,
But he's an arrant knave.   *I, v, 123*

There are more things in heaven and earth, Horatio,
Than are dreamt of in your philosophy.   *I, v, 166*

To put an antic disposition on.
            I, v, 172

Rest, rest, perturbed spirit!   *I, v, 182*

The time is out of joint; O cursed spite,
That ever I was born to set it right!
            I, v, 188

Your bait of falsehood takes this carp of truth;
And thus do we of wisdom and of reach,
With windlasses and with assays of bias,

[1] See Homer, p. 64b, and note.

By indirections find directions out.
            Hamlet II, i, 63

Ungarter'd, and down-gyved to his ankle.   *II, i, 80*

This is the very ecstasy of love.
            II, i, 102

Brevity is the soul of wit.   *II, ii, 90*

More matter, with less art.   *II, ii, 95*

That he is mad, 'tis true; 'tis true 'tis pity;
And pity 'tis 'tis true.   *II, ii, 97*

Find out the cause of this effect,
Or rather say, the cause of this defect,
For this effect defective comes by cause.   *II, ii, 101*

Doubt thou the stars are fire;
    Doubt that the sun doth move;
Doubt truth to be a liar;
    But never doubt I love.
            II, ii, 115

Polonius: Do you know me, my lord?
Hamlet: Excellent well; you are a fishmonger.   *II, ii, 173*

To be honest, as this world goes, is to be one man picked out of ten thousand.   *II, ii, 179*

Hamlet: For if the sun breed maggots in a dead dog, being a god[1] kissing carrion — Have you a daughter?
Polonius: I have, my lord.
Hamlet: Let her not walk i' the sun.   *II, ii, 183*

Still harping on my daughter.
            II, ii, 190

Polonius: What do you read, my lord?
Hamlet: Words, words, words.
            II, ii, 195

They have a plentiful lack of wit.
            II, ii, 204

Though this be madness, yet there is method in 't.   *II, ii, 211*

These tedious old fools!
            II, ii, 227

[1] In some editions, good.

The indifferent children of the earth.   *Hamlet II, ii, 235*

Happy in that we are not over happy.   *II, ii, 236*

There is nothing either good or bad, but thinking makes it so.   *II, ii, 259*

O God! I could be bounded in a nut-shell, and count myself a king of infinite space, were it not that I have bad dreams.   *II, ii, 263*

Beggar that I am, I am even poor in thanks.   *II, ii, 286*

This goodly frame, the earth, seems to me a sterile promontory; this most excellent canopy, the air, look you, this brave o'erhanging firmament, this majestical roof fretted with golden fire, why, it appears no other thing to me but a foul and pestilent congregation of vapors. What a piece of work is a man! How noble in reason! how infinite in faculty! in form, in moving, how express and admirable! in action how like an angel! in apprehension how like a god!   *II, ii, 317*

And yet, to me, what is this quintessence of dust? man delights not me; no, nor woman neither.   *II, ii, 328*

There is something in this more than natural, if philosophy could find it out.   *II, ii, 392*

I am but mad north-northwest: when the wind is southerly I know a hawk from a handsaw.[1]   *II, ii, 405*

They say an old man is twice a child.[2]   *II, ii, 413*

One fair daughter and no more,
The which he loved passing well.
       II, ii, 435

Come, give us a taste of your quality.   *II, ii, 460*

The play, I remember, pleased not the million; 'twas caviare to the general.   *II, ii, 465*

[1] A heron.
[2] See Aristophanes, p. 91a.

They are the abstracts and brief chronicles of the time: after your death you were better have a bad epitaph than their ill report while you live.   *Hamlet II, ii, 555*

Use every man after his desert, and who should 'scape whipping?   *II, ii, 561*

O! what a rogue and peasant slave am I.   *II, ii, 584*

What's Hecuba to him or he to Hecuba,
That he should weep for her?
       II, ii, 593

Who calls me villain? breaks my pate across?
Plucks off my beard and blows it in my face?   *II, ii, 607*

But I am pigeon-liver'd, and lack gall
To make oppression bitter.
       II, ii, 613

    The play's the thing
Wherein I'll catch the conscience of the king.   *II, ii, 641*

    With devotion's visage
And pious action we do sugar o'er
The devil himself.   *III, i, 47*

To be, or not to be: that is the question:
Whether 'tis nobler in the mind to suffer
The slings and arrows of outrageous fortune,
Or to take arms against a sea of troubles,
And by opposing end them? To die: to sleep;
No more; and, by a sleep to say we end
The heartache and the thousand natural shocks
That flesh is heir to, 'tis a consummation
Devoutly to be wish'd. To die, to sleep;
To sleep: perchance to dream: ay, there's the rub;
For in that sleep of death what dreams may come,

When we have shuffled off this mortal
    coil,
Must give us pause. There's the re-
    spect
That makes calamity of so long life;
For who would bear the whips and
    scorns of time,
The oppressor's wrong, the proud
    man's contumely,
The pangs of dispriz'd love, the law's
    delay,
The insolence of office, and the spurns
That patient merit of the unworthy
    takes,
When he himself might his quietus
    make
With a bare bodkin? who would fardels
    bear,
To grunt and sweat under a weary life,
But that the dread of something after
    death,
The undiscover'd country from whose
    bourn
No traveler returns,[1] puzzles the will,
And makes us rather bear those ills we
    have
Than fly to others that we know not
    of?
Thus conscience does make cowards of
    us all;
And thus the native hue of resolution
Is sicklied o'er with the pale cast of
    thought,
And enterprises of great pith and mo-
    ment
With this regard their currents turn
    awry,
And lose the name of action.
                    Hamlet III, i, 56

Nymph, in thy orisons
Be all my sins remember'd.
                            III, i, 89

To the noble mind
Rich gifts wax poor when givers prove
    unkind.   *III, i, 100*

Get thee to a nunnery.   *III, i, 124*

What should such fellows as I do
crawling between heaven and earth?
We are arrant knaves, all.   *III, i, 128*

[1] See *Song of The Harp-Player,* p. 3a, and
note.

Be thou as chaste as ice, as pure as
snow, thou shalt not escape calumny.
                        Hamlet III, i, 142

I have heard of your paintings too,
well enough; God has given you one
face, and you make yourselves another.
                            III, i, 150

O! what a noble mind is here o'er-
    thrown:
The courtier's, soldier's, scholar's, eye,
    tongue, sword.   *III, i, 159*

The glass of fashion and the mould of
    form,
The observ'd of all observers!
                            III, i, 162

Now see that noble and most sovereign
    reason,
Like sweet bells jangled, out of tune
    and harsh.   *III, i, 166*

    O! woe is me,
To have seen what I have seen, see
    what I see!   *III, i, 169*

Speak the speech, I pray you, as I
pronounced it to you, trippingly on the
tongue; but if you mouth it, as many of
your players do, I had as lief the town-
crier spoke my lines. Nor do not saw
the air too much with your hand, thus;
but use all gently: for in the very torrent, tempest, and — as I may say —
whirlwind of passion, you must acquire
and beget a temperance, that may give
it smoothness. O! it offends me to the
soul to hear a robustious periwig-pated
fellow tear a passion to tatters, to very
rags, to split the ears of the groundlings, who for the most part are capable
of nothing but inexplicable dumbshows and noise: I would have such a
fellow whipped for o'erdoing Terma-
gant; it out-herods Herod.   *III, ii, 1*

Suit the action to the word, the word
to the action; with this special observance, that you o'erstep not the modesty
of nature.   *III, ii, 20*

To hold, as 'twere, the mirror up to
nature; to show virtue her own feature,
scorn her own image, and the very age

and body of the time his form and pressure. *Hamlet III, ii, 25*

I have thought some of nature's journeymen had made men and not made them well, they imitated humanity so abominably. *III, ii, 38*

No; let the candied tongue lick absurd pomp,
And crook the pregnant hinges of the knee
Where thrift may follow fawning. *III, ii, 65*

A man that fortune's buffets and rewards
Hast ta'en with equal thanks. *III, ii, 72*

They are not a pipe for fortune's finger
To sound what stop she please. Give me that man
That is not passion's slave, and I will wear him
In my heart's core, ay, in my heart of heart,
As I do thee. Something too much of this. *III, ii, 75*

My imaginations are as foul
As Vulcan's stithy. *III, ii, 88*

The chameleon's dish: I eat the air, promise-crammed; you cannot feed capons so. *III, ii, 98*

Nay, then, let the devil wear black, for I'll have a suit of sables. *III, ii, 138*

There's hope a great man's memory may outlive his life half a year. *III, ii, 141*

Marry, this is miching mallecho; it means mischief. *III, ii, 148*

Ophelia: 'Tis brief, my lord.
Hamlet: As woman's love. *III, ii, 165*

Where love is great, the littlest doubts are fear;
When little fears grow great, great love grows there. *III, ii, 183*

Wormwood, wormwood. *III, ii, 193*

The lady doth protest too much, methinks. *Hamlet III, ii, 242*

Let the galled jade wince, our withers are unwrung. *III, ii, 256*

Why, let the stricken deer go weep,[1]
The hart ungalled play;
For some must watch, while some must sleep:
So runs the world away. *III, ii, 287*

You would pluck out the heart of my mystery. *III, ii, 389*

Do you think I am easier to be played on than a pipe? *III, ii, 393*

Hamlet: Do you see yonder cloud that's almost in shape of a camel?
Polonius: By the mass, and 'tis like a camel, indeed.
Hamlet: Methinks it is like a weasel.
Polonius: It is backed like a weasel.
Hamlet: Or like a whale?
Polonius: Very like a whale.[2] *III, ii, 400*

They fool me to the top of my bent. *III, ii, 408*

By and by is easily said. *III, ii, 411*

'Tis now the very witching time of night,
When churchyards yawn and hell itself breathes out
Contagion to this world. *III, ii, 413*

I will speak daggers to her, but use none. *III, ii, 421*

O! my offense is rank, it smells to heaven;
It hath the primal eldest curse upon 't,
A brother's murder! *III, iii, 36*

Now might I do it pat, now he is praying;
And now I'll do 't: and so he goes to heaven;
And so I am reveng'd. *III, iii, 73*

[1] See Cowper, p. 458a.
[2] See Aristophanes, p. 91a, and *Antony and Cleopatra IV, xii, 2*, p. 288b.

With all his crimes broad blown, as
  flush as May.
                  Hamlet III, iii, 81

My words fly up, my thoughts remain
  below:
Words without thoughts never to
  heaven go.   *III, iii, 97*

  How now! a rat? Dead, for a ducat,
dead!   *III, iv, 23*

False as dicers' oaths.   *III, iv, 45*

A rhapsody of words.   *III, iv, 48*

See, what a grace was seated on this
  brow;
Hyperion's curls; the front of Jove him-
  self,
An eye like Mars, to threaten and com-
  mand,
A station like the herald Mercury
New-lighted on a heaven-kissing hill.
A combination and a form indeed,
Where every god did seem to set his
  seal,
To give the world assurance of a man.
                    III, iv, 55

      At your age
The heyday in the blood is tame, it's
  humble.   *III, iv, 68*

O shame! where is thy blush? Rebel-
  lious hell,
If thou canst mutine in a matron's
  bones,
To flaming youth let virtue be as wax,
And melt in her own fire: proclaim no
  shame
When the compulsive ardor gives the
  charge,
Since frost itself as actively doth burn,
And reason panders will.   *III, iv, 82*

A king of shreds and patches.[1]
                    III, iv, 102

Lay not that flattering unction to your
  soul.   *III, iv, 145*

    Confess yourself to heaven;
Repent what's past; avoid what is to
  come.   *III, iv, 149*

[1] A wandering minstrel I —
  A thing of shreds and patches.
    W. S. GILBERT, *The Mikado* [1885], *act I*

For in the fatness of these pursy times
Virtue itself of vice must pardon beg.
               Hamlet III, iv, 153

Assume a virtue, if you have it not.
                 III, iv, 160

    Refrain tonight;
And that shall lend a kind of easiness
To the next abstinence: the next more
  easy;
For use almost can change the stamp of
  nature.   *III, iv, 165*

I must be cruel, only to be kind.
                 III, iv, 178

For 'tis the sport to have the enginer
Hoist with his own petar.
                 III, iv, 206

   Diseases desperate grown
By desperate appliance are reliev'd,
Or not at all.[1]   *IV, iii, 9*

  A man may fish with the worm that
hath eat of a king, and eat of the fish
that hath fed of that worm.
                 IV, iii, 29

We go to gain a little patch of ground,
That hath in it no profit but the
  name.   *IV, iv, 18*

How all occasions do inform against
  me,
And spur my dull revenge! What is a
  man,
If his chief good and market of his
  time
Be but to sleep and feed? a beast, no
  more.[2]
Sure he that made us with such large
  discourse,
Looking before and after, gave us not
That capability and godlike reason
To fust in us unus'd.   *IV, iv, 32*

    Some craven scruple
Of thinking too precisely on the event.
                 IV, iv, 40

    Rightly to be great
Is not to stir without great argument,

[1] See Hippocrates, p. 88b.
[2] The unmotived herd that only sleep and
feed. — JAMES RUSSELL LOWELL [1819–1891],
Under the Old Elm, pt. VII, st. 3

But greatly to find quarrel in a straw
When honor's at the stake.
        Hamlet IV, iv, 53

So full of artless jealousy is guilt,
It spills itself in fearing to be spilt.
        IV, v, 19

How should I your true love know
  From another one?
By his cockle hat and staff,
  And his sandal shoon.[1]   *IV, v,* 23

He is dead and gone, lady,
  He is dead and gone;
At his head a grass-green turf,
  At his heels a stone.   *IV, v,* 29

We know what we are, but know not
what we may be.   *IV, v,* 43

Come, my coach! Good night, ladies;
good night, sweet ladies; good night,
good night.   *IV, v,* 72

When sorrows come, they come not
    single spies,
But in battalions.[2]   *IV, v,* 78

We have done but greenly,
In hugger-mugger to inter him.
        IV, v, 84

There's such divinity doth hedge a
    king,
That treason can but peep to what it
    would.[3]
        IV, v, 123

There's rosemary, that's for remembrance . . . and there is pansies, that's
for thoughts.   *IV, v,* 174

O! you must wear your rue with a
difference. There's a daisy; I would give
you some violets, but they withered all
when my father died.   *IV, v,* 181

[1] Ophelia is quoting a version of a poem by
Sir Walter Ralegh.
[2] See Cervantes, p. 194b.
One woe doth tread upon another's heel,
So fast they follow.
        Hamlet IV, vii, 164
Thus woe succeeds a woe, as wave a wave. —
HERRICK, *Sorrows Succeed* [1648]

Woes cluster; rare are solitary woes;
They love a train, they tread each other's heel.
    EDWARD YOUNG, *Night Thoughts* [1742–
        1745], *Night III, l. 63*
[3] See Montaigne, p. 191a, and Tennyson,
p. 653a.

A very riband in the cap of youth.
        Hamlet IV, vii, 77

Nature her custom holds,
Let shame say what it will.
        IV, vii, 188

There is no ancient gentlemen but
gardeners, ditchers, and grave-makers;
they hold up Adam's profession.[1]
        V, i, 32

Cudgel thy brains no more about it.
        V, i, 61

Has this fellow no feeling of his business, that he sings at grave-making?
        V, i, 71

Custom hath made it in him a property of easiness.   *V, i,* 73

A politician . . . one that would
circumvent God.   *V, i,* 84

Why may not that be the skull of a
lawyer? Where be his quiddities now,
his quillets, his cases, his tenures, and
his tricks?   *V, i,* 104

One that was a woman, sir; but, rest
her soul, she's dead.   *V, i,* 145

How absolute the knave is! we must
speak by the card, or equivocation will
undo us.   *V, i,* 147

The age is grown so picked that the
toe of the peasant comes so near the
heel of the courtier, he galls his kibe.
        V, i, 150

Alas! poor Yorick. I knew him, Horatio; a fellow of infinite jest, of most
excellent fancy; he hath borne me on
his back a thousand times; and now,
how abhorred in my imagination it is!
my gorge rises at it. Here hung those
lips that I have kissed I know not how
oft. Where be your gibes now? your
gambols? your songs? your flashes of
merriment, that were wont to set the
table on a roar? Not one now, to mock
your own grinning? quite chapfallen?
Now get you to my lady's chamber, and
tell her, let her paint an inch thick, to

[1] See Francis Bacon, p. 209b, and *King Henry
VI, pt. II, IV, ii, 146*, and note, p. 215a.

this favor she must come; make her laugh at that.   *Hamlet* V, i, 201

To what base uses we may return, Horatio! Why may not imagination trace the noble dust of Alexander, till he find it stopping a bung-hole?
                                    V, i, 222

Imperious Caesar, dead and turn'd to clay,
Might stop a hole to keep the wind away.   V, i, 235

           Lay her i' the earth;
And from her fair and unpolluted flesh
May violets spring! [1]   V, i, 260

A ministering angel shall my sister be. [2]
                                    V, i, 263

Sweets to the sweet: farewell!
                                    V, i, 265

I thought thy bride-bed to have deck'd, sweet maid,
And not have strew'd thy grave.
                                    V, i, 267

Though I am not splenetive and rash
Yet have I in me something danger-ous.   V, i, 283

I lov'd Ophelia: forty thousand broth-ers
Could not, with all their quantity of love,
Make up my sum.   V, i, 291

           Nay, an thou'lt mouth,
I'll rant as well as thou.   V, i, 305

Let Hercules himself do what he may,
The cat will mew and dog will have his day.   V, i, 313

There's a divinity that shapes our ends,
Rough-hew them how we will.
                                    V, ii, 10

I once did hold it, as our statists do,
A baseness to write fair.   V, ii, 33

It did me yeoman's service.
                                    V, ii, 36

[1] See FitzGerald, p. 629b, and Tennyson, p. 650a.
[2] See Sir Walter Scott, p. 519b.

Not a whit, we defy augury; there's a special providence in the fall of a spar-row. [1] If it be now, 'tis not to come; if it be not to come, it will be now; if it be not now, yet it will come: the readiness is all.
                    Hamlet V, ii, 232

A hit, a very palpable hit.   V, ii, 295

           This fell sergeant, death,
Is strict in his arrest.   V, ii, 350

Report me and my cause aright.
                                   V, ii, 353

I am more an antique Roman than a Dane.   V, ii, 355

O God! Horatio, what a wounded name,
Things standing thus unknown, shall live behind me.
If thou didst ever hold me in thy heart,
Absent thee from felicity awhile,
And in this harsh world draw thy breath in pain,
To tell my story.   V, ii, 358

The rest is silence.   V, ii, 372

Now cracks a noble heart. Good night, sweet prince,
And flights of angels sing thee to thy rest!   V, ii, 373

           O proud death! [2]
What feast is toward in thine eternal cell?   V, ii, 378

I will make a Star Chamber matter of it.
      The Merry Wives of Windsor
      [1600–1601], act I, sc. i, l. 2

She has brown hair, and speaks small like a woman.   I, i, 48

Seven hundred pounds and possibili-ties is goot gifts.   I, i, 65

I had rather than forty shillings I had my Book of Songs and Sonnets here.
                                    I, i, 205

"Convey," the wise it call. "Steal!" foh! a fico for the phrase!   I, iii, 30

[1] See *Matthew 10:29*, p. 42a, and Alexander Pope, p. 408a.
[2] See Donne, p. 308a.

I am almost out at heels.
The Merry Wives of Windsor
I, iii, 32

Thou art the Mars of malcontents.
I, iii, 111

Here will be an old abusing of God's patience and the king's English.
I, iv, 5

Dispense with trifles. II, i, 47

Faith, thou hast some crotchets in thy head now. II, i, 158

Why, then the world's mine oyster,
Which I with sword will open.
II, ii, 2

This is the short and the long of it.
II, ii, 62

Like a fair house built upon another man's ground. II, ii, 229

Better three hours too soon than a minute too late. II, ii, 332

I cannot tell what the dickens his name is. III, ii, 20

He capers, he dances, he has eyes of youth, he writes verses, he speaks holiday, he smells April and May.
III, ii, 71

O, what a world of vile ill-favor'd faults
Looks handsome in three hundred pounds a year! III, iv, 32

A woman would run through fire and water for such a kind heart.
III, iv, 106

I have a kind of alacrity in sinking.
III, v, 13

As good luck would have it.[1]
III, v, 86

A man of my kidney. III, v, 119

[He] curses all Eve's daughters, of what complexion soever. IV, ii, 24

Wives may be merry, and yet honest too. IV, ii, 110

This is the third time; I hope good

[1] As ill luck would have it. — CERVANTES, *Don Quixote*, pt. I [1605], bk. I, ch. 2

luck lies in odd numbers. . . . There is divinity in odd numbers, either in nativity, chance, or death.[1]
The Merry Wives of Windsor
V, i, 2

Better a little chiding than a great deal of heartbreak. V, iii, 10

Property was thus appall'd,
That the self was not the same;
Single nature's double name
Neither two nor one was call'd.
The Phoenix and the Turtle
[1601], l. 37

Reason, in itself confounded,
Saw division grow together. l. 41

The chance of war.
Troilus and Cressida [1601–1603], *prologue, l.* 31

I have had my labor for my travail.[2]
Act I, sc. i, l. 73

Women are angels, wooing:
Things won are done; joy's soul lies in the doing. I, ii, 310

Men prize the thing ungain'd more than it is. I, ii, 313

The sea being smooth,
How many shallow bauble boats dare sail
Upon her patient breast.[3] I, iii, 34

The heavens themselves, the planets, and this center,
Observe degree, priority, and place,
Insisture, course, proportion, season, form,
Office, and custom, in all line of order.
I, iii, 85

O! when degree is shak'd,
Which is the ladder to all high designs,
The enterprise is sick.[4] I, iii, 101

Take but degree away, untune that string,
And, hark! what discord follows; each thing meets

[1] See Pliny, p. 133a, and Samuel Lover, p. 589a.
[2] See Cervantes, p. 193b.
[3] See Publilius Syrus, p. 126a.
[4] See Publilius Syrus, p. 127b.

In mere oppugnancy: the bounded waters
Should lift their bosoms higher than the shores
And make a sop of all this solid globe.
Troilus and Cressida I, iii, 109

Then everything includes itself in power,
Power into will, will into appetite;
And appetite, an universal wolf,
So doubly seconded with will and power,
Must make perforce a universal prey,
And last eat up himself.   *I, iii, 119*

Like a strutting player, whose conceit
Lies in his hamstring, and doth think it rich
To hear the wooden dialogue and sound
'Twixt his stretch'd footing and the scaffoldage.   *I, iii, 153*

And in such indexes, although small pricks
To their subsequent volumes, there is seen
The baby figure of the giant mass
Of things to come.[1]   *I, iii, 343*

Who wears his wit in his belly, and his guts in his head.   *II, i, 78*

Modest doubt is call'd
The beacon of the wise, the tent that searches
To the bottom of the worst.
II, ii, 15

'Tis mad idolatry
To make the service greater than the god.   *II, ii, 56*

He that is proud eats up himself; pride is his own glass, his own trumpet, his own chronicle.   *II, iii, 165*

I am giddy, expectation whirls me round.
The imaginary relish is so sweet
That it enchants my sense.
III, ii, 17

Words pay no debts.   *III, ii, 56*

[1] See Cicero, p. 111a, and Thomas Campbell, p. 538a, and note.

To fear the worst oft cures the worse.
Troilus and Cressida III, ii, 77

All lovers swear more performance than they are able, and yet reserve an ability that they never perform; vowing more than the perfection of ten, and discharging less than the tenth part of one.   *III, ii, 89*

For to be wise, and love,
Exceeds man's might; that dwells with gods above.   *III, ii, 163*

If I be false, or swerve a hair from truth,
When time is old and hath forgot itself,
When waterdrops have worn the stones of Troy,
And blind oblivion swallow'd cities up,
And mighty states characterless are grated
To dusty nothing, yet let memory,
From false to false, among false maids in love
Upbraid my falsehood! when they have said "as false
As air, as water, wind, or sandy earth,
As fox to lamb, as wolf to heifer's calf,
Pard to the hind, or stepdame to her son";
Yea, let them say, to stick the heart of falsehood,
"As false as Cressid."   *III, ii, 191*

Time hath, my lord, a wallet at his back,
Wherein he puts alms for oblivion.
III, iii, 145

Perseverance, dear my lord,
Keeps honor bright: to have done, is to hang
Quite out of fashion, like a rusty mail
In monumental mockery.
III, iii, 150

For honor travels in a strait so narrow
Where one but goes abreast.
III, iii, 154

Time is like a fashionable host,
That slightly shakes his parting guest by the hand,

And with his arms outstretch'd, as he
  would fly,
Grasps in the comer: welcome ever
  smiles,
And farewell goes out sighing.
  Troilus and Cressida III, iii, 168

  Beauty, wit,
High birth, vigor of bone, desert in
  service,
Love, friendship, charity, are subjects
  all
To envious and calumniating time.
One touch of nature makes the whole
  world kin. *III, iii, 171*

And give to dust that is a little gilt
More laud than gilt o'er-dusted.
  III, iii, 178

My mind is troubled, like a fountain
  stirr'd;
And I myself see not the bottom of
  it. *III, iii, 314*

  You do as chapmen do,
Dispraise the thing that you desire to
  buy. *IV, i, 75*

As many farewells as be stars in heaven.
  IV, iv, 44

And sometimes we are devils to our-
  selves
When we will tempt the frailty of our
  powers,
Presuming on their changeful potency.
  IV, iv, 95

The kiss you take is better than you
  give. *IV, v, 38*

  Fie, fie upon her!
There's language in her eye, her cheek,
  her lip,
Nay, her foot speaks; her wanton spirits
  look out
At every joint and motive of her body.
  IV, v, 54

What's past and what's to come is
  strew'd with husks
And formless ruin of oblivion.
  IV, v, 165

  The end crowns all,[1]
And that old common arbitrator,
  Time,
Will one day end it.
  Troilus and Cressida IV, v, 223

Words, words, mere words, no matter
  from the heart. *V, iii, 109*

Hector is dead; there is no more to
  say. *V, x, 22*

  O world! world! world! thus is the
poor agent despised. *V, x, 36*

  Love all, trust a few,
Do wrong to none: be able for thine
  enemy
Rather in power than use, and keep thy
  friend
Under thy own life's key: be check'd
  for silence,
But never tax'd for speech.
  All's Well That Ends Well [2]
  [1601–1603], *act I, sc. i, l. 74*

  It were all one
That I should love a bright particular
  star
And think to wed it, he is so above
  me. *I, i, 97*

The hind that would be mated by the
  lion
Must die for love. *I, i, 103*

My friends were poor, but honest.[3]
  I, iii, 203

Oft expectation fails, and most oft
  there
Where most it promises. *II, i, 145*

  They say miracles are past.
  II, iii, 1

A young man married is a man that's
  marr'd. *II, iii, 315*

  The web of our life is of a mingled
yarn, good and ill together.
  IV, iii, 83

[1] See Anonymous, p. 150b; *All's Well That
Ends Well IV, iv, 35* and note, p. 270a; and
Herrick, p. 320a.
[2] See *IV, iv, 35,* p. 270a.
[3] Though I be poor, I'm honest. — THOMAS
MIDDLETON, *The Witch* [c. 1627], *III, 2*
See Anonymous, p. 1103a.

There's place and means for every man alive.

> *All's Well That Ends Well*
> IV, iii, 379

All's well that end's well: still the fine's the crown;
Whate'er the course, the end is the renown.[1] IV, iv, 35

I am a man whom Fortune hath cruelly scratched. V, ii, 28

Praising what is lost
Makes the remembrance dear.
V, iii, 19

The inaudible and noiseless foot of time.[2] V, iii, 41

Love that comes too late,
Like a remorseful pardon slowly carried. V, iii, 57

All impediments in fancy's course
Are motives of more fancy. V, iii, 216

Spirits are not finely touch'd
But to fine issues.

> *Measure for Measure* [1604–1605], act I, sc. i, l. 35

Good counselors lack no clients.
I, ii, 115

And liberty plucks justice by the nose.
I, iii, 29

I hold you as a thing ensky'd and sainted. I, iv, 34

A man whose blood
Is very snow-broth; one who never feels
The wanton stings and motions of the sense. I, iv, 57

Our doubts are traitors,
And make us lose the good we oft might win,
By fearing to attempt.[3] I, iv, 78

We must not make a scarecrow of the law,

[1] See Anonymous, p. 150b; Heywood, p. 183b; and *Troilus and Cressida* IV, v, 223, 269b.
All's well that ends well yet.— *All's Well That Ends Well* V, i, 25
[2] How noiseless falls the foot of time! — W. R. SPENCER [1769–1834], *Lines to Lady A. Hamilton*
[3] See *Macbeth* I, vii, 44, p. 282b.

Setting it up to fear the birds of prey,
And let it keep one shape, till custom make it
Their perch, and not their terror.

> *Measure for Measure* II, i, 1

The jury, passing on the prisoner's life,
May in the sworn twelve have a thief or two
Guiltier than him they try. II, i, 19

Some rise by sin, and some by virtue fall. II, i, 38

Great with child, and longing . . .
for stewed prunes. II, i, 94

This will last out a night in Russia,
When nights are longest there.
II, i, 144

His face is the worst thing about him. II, i, 167

Condemn the fault, and not the act of it? II, ii, 37

No ceremony that to great ones 'longs,
Not the king's crown, nor the deputed sword,
The marshal's truncheon, nor the judge's robe,
Become them with one half so good a grace
As mercy does.[1] II, ii, 59

Why, all the souls that were were forfeit once;
And He that might the vantage best have took,
Found out the remedy. How would you be,
If He, which is the top of judgment, should
But judge you as you are? II, ii, 73

The law hath not been dead, though it hath slept. II, ii, 90

O! it is excellent
To have a giant's strength; but it is tyrannous
To use it like a giant. II, ii, 107

But man, proud man,
Drest in a little brief authority,
Most ignorant of what he's most assur'd,

[1] See *The Merchant of Venice* IV, i, 184, p. 234b.

His glassy essence, like an angry ape,
Plays such fantastic tricks before high
  heaven
As make the angels weep.
> *Measure for Measure* II, *ii*, 117

That in the captain's but a choleric
  word,
Which in the soldier is flat blasphemy.
> II, *ii*, 130

It oft falls out,
To have what we would have, we speak
  not what we mean.   II, *iv*, 118

The miserable have no other medicine
But only hope.   III, *i*, 2

Be absolute for death.   III, *i*, 5

A breath thou art,
Servile to all the skyey influences.
> III, *i*, 8

Thou hast nor youth nor age;
But, as it were, an after-dinner's sleep,
Dreaming on both; for all thy blessed
  youth
Becomes as aged, and doth beg the
  alms
Of palsied eld; and when thou art old
  and rich,
Thou hast neither heat, affection, limb,
  nor beauty,
To make thy riches pleasant.
> III, *i*, 32

The sense of death is most in apprehen-
  sion,[1]
And the poor beetle, that we tread upon,
In corporal sufferance finds a pang as
  great
As when a giant dies.   III, *i*, 76

If I must die,
I will encounter darkness as a bride,
And hug it in my arms.   III, *i*, 81

The cunning livery of hell.
> III, *i*, 93

Ay, but to die, and go we know not
  where;
To lie in cold obstruction and to rot;
This sensible warm motion to become

[1] See Publilius Syrus, p. 126a.

A kneaded clod; and the delighted
  spirit
To bathe in fiery floods, or to reside
In thrilling region of thick-ribbed ice;
To be imprison'd in the viewless
  winds,
And blown with restless violence round
  about
The pendant world.
> *Measure for Measure* III, *i*, 116

The weariest and most loathed worldly
  life
That age, ache, penury, and imprison-
  ment
Can lay on nature, is a paradise
To what we fear of death.   III, *i*, 127

The hand that hath made you fair
hath made you good.[1]   III, *i*, 182

Virtue is bold, and goodness never
  fearful.   III, *i*, 214

There, at the moated grange, resides
this dejected Mariana.[2]   III, *i*, 279

This news is old enough, yet it is
every day's news.   III, *ii*, 249

He who the sword of heaven will bear
Should be as holy as severe.
> III, *ii*, 283

O, what may man within him hide,
Though angel on the outward side!
> III, *ii*, 293

Take, O take those lips away,
  That so sweetly were forsworn;
And those eyes, the break of day,
  Lights that do mislead the morn:
But my kisses bring again, bring again;
Seals of love, but seal'd in vain, seal'd
  in vain [3]   IV, *i*, 1

[1] See Spenser, p. 201b.
[2] "Mariana in the moated grange" — motto
used by TENNYSON for the poem *Mariana* [1830].
[3] This song occurs in *act V, sc. ii*, of FLETCH-
ER's *Bloody Brother* [c. 1616], with an additional
stanza:
  Hide, O hide those hills of snow,
    Which thy frozen bosom bears,
  On whose tops the pinks that grow
    Are of those that April wears!
  But first set my poor heart free,
  Bound in those icy chains by thee.

Music oft hath such a charm
To make bad good, and good provoke
to harm.[1]
Measure for Measure IV, i, 16

Every true man's apparel fits your
thief. *IV, ii, 46*

I am a kind of burr; I shall stick.
IV, iii, 193

We would, and we would not.
IV, iv, 37

A forted residence 'gainst the tooth of
time
And razure of oblivion. *V, i, 12*

Truth is truth
To the end of reckoning. *V, i, 45*

Neither maid, widow, nor wife.
V, i, 173

They say best men are molded out of
faults,
And, for the most, become much more
the better
For being a little bad. *V, i, 440*

What's mine is yours, and what is yours
is mine.[2] *V, i, 539*

Horribly stuff'd with epithets of war.
*Othello [1604–1605], act I, sc. i,
l. 14*

A fellow almost damn'd in a fair wife.
I, i, 21

The bookish theoric. *I, i, 24*

We cannot all be masters. *I, i, 43*

And when he's old, cashier'd.
I, i, 48

In following him, I follow but myself.
I, i, 58

But I will wear my heart upon my
sleeve
For daws to peck at. *I, i, 64*

An old black ram
Is tupping your white ewe. *I, i, 88*

You are one of those that will not
serve God if the devil bid you.
I, i, 108

---

[1] See Congreve, p. 391b, and note.
[2] See Plautus, p. 105a.

Your daughter and the Moor are now
making the beast with two backs.
Othello I, i, 117

Keep up your bright swords, for the
dew will rust them. *I, ii, 59*

The wealthy curled darlings of our nation. *I, ii, 68*

The bloody book of law
You shall yourself read in the bitter let-
ter
After your own sense. *I, iii, 67*

Rude am I in my speech,
And little bless'd with the soft phrase
of peace. *I, iii, 81*

Little shall I grace my cause
In speaking for myself. Yet, by your
gracious patience,
I will a round unvarnish'd tale deliver
Of my whole course of love.
I, iii, 88

A maiden never bold;
Of spirit so still and quiet, that her mo-
tion
Blush'd at herself. *I, iii, 94*

Still question'd me the story of my
life
From year to year, the battles, sieges,
fortunes
That I have pass'd. *I, iii, 129*

Wherein I spake of most disastrous
chances,
Of moving accidents by flood and
field,
Of hair-breadth 'scapes i' the imminent
deadly breach. *I, iii, 134*

Hills whose heads touch heaven.
I, iii, 141

And of the Cannibals that each other
eat,
The Anthropophagi, and men whose
heads
Do grow beneath their shoulders.
I, iii, 143

My story being done,
She gave me for my pains a world of
sighs:
She swore, in faith, 'twas strange, 'twas
passing strange,

'Twas pitiful, 'twas wondrous pitiful:
She wish'd she had not heard it, yet she
  wish'd
That heaven had made her such a man;
  she thank'd me,
And bade me, if I had a friend that
  lov'd her,
I should but teach him how to tell my
  story,
And that would woo her. Upon this
  hint I spake:
She lov'd me for the dangers I had
  pass'd,
And I loved her that she did pity
  them.
This only is the witchcraft I have us'd.
            Othello I, iii, 158

I do perceive here a divided duty.
                 I, iii, 181

To mourn a mischief that is past and
  gone
Is the next way to draw new mischief
  on.   *I, iii, 204*

The robb'd that smiles steals something
  from the thief.   *I, iii, 208*

Our bodies are our gardens, to the
which our wills are gardeners.
                 I, iii, 324

Put money in thy purse.
                 I, iii, 345

The food that to him now is as luscious as locusts, shall be to him shortly
as bitter at coloquintida. *I, iii, 354*

Framed to make women false.
                 I, iii, 404

The enchafed flood.   *II, i, 17*

One that excels the quirks of blazoning
  pens.   *II, i, 63*

You are pictures out of doors,
Bells in your parlors, wildcats in your
  kitchens,
Saints in your injuries, devils being
  offended,
Players in your housewifery, and housewives in your beds.   *II, i, 109*

For I am nothing if not critical.
                 II, i, 119

I am not merry, but I do beguile
The thing I am, by seeming otherwise.
           Othello II, i, 122

She that was ever fair and never
  proud,
Had tongue at will and yet was never
  loud.   *II, i, 148*

Iago: To suckle fools and chronicle
  small beer.[1]
Desdemona: O most lame and impotent conclusion!   *II, i, 160*

You may relish him more in the soldier than in the scholar. *II, i, 165*

If it were now to die,
'Twere now to be most happy.
                 II, i, 192
Base men being in love have then a
nobility in their natures more than is
native to them.   *II, i, 218*

Egregiously an ass.   *II, i, 321*

I have very poor and unhappy brains
for drinking.   *II, iii, 34*

Potations pottle deep. *II, iii, 57*

Well, God's above all; and there be
souls must be saved, and there be souls
must not be saved.   *II, iii, 106*

Silence that dreadful bell! it frights the
  isle
From her propriety.   *II, iii, 177*

But men are men; the best sometimes
  forget.   *II, iii, 243*

Thy honesty and love doth mince this
  matter.[2]   *II, iii, 249*

Reputation, reputation, reputation!
O! I have lost my reputation. I have
lost the immortal part of myself, and
what remains is bestial. *II, iii, 264*

Reputation is an idle and most false
imposition; oft got without merit, and
lost without deserving. *II, iii, 270*

O thou invisible spirit of wine! if
thou hast no name to be known by, let
us call thee devil!   *II, iii, 285*

[1] See *King Henry VI, pt. II, IV, ii, 75*, p. 215a.
[2] See Cervantes, p. 193b.

O God! that men should put an enemy in their mouths to steal away their brains; that we should, with joy, pleasance, revel, and applause, transform ourselves into beasts. *Othello II, iii, 293*

Good wine is a good familiar creature if it be well used. II, iii, 315

Play the villain. II, iii, 345

How poor are they that have not patience!

What wound did ever heal but by degrees? II, iii, 379

Excellent wretch! Perdition catch my soul
But I do love thee! and when I love thee not,
Chaos is come again.[1] III, iii, 99

Men should be what they seem.
III, iii, 126

Speak to me as to thy thinkings,
As thou dost ruminate, and give thy worst of thoughts
The worst of words. III, iii, 131

Good name in man and woman, dear my lord,
Is the immediate jewel of their souls:
Who steals my purse steals trash; 'tis something, nothing;
'Twas mine, 'tis his, and has been slave to thousands;
But he that filches from me my good name
Robs me of that which not enriches him,
And makes me poor indeed.
III, iii, 155

O! beware, my lord, of jealousy;
It is the green-ey'd monster which doth mock
The meat it feeds on; that cuckold lives in bliss
Who, certain of his fate, loves not his wronger;
But, O! what damned minutes tells he o'er
Who dotes, yet doubts; suspects, yet soundly loves! III, iii, 165

[1] See *Venus and Adonis,* p. 220a.

Poor and content is rich, and rich enough. *Othello III, iii, 172*

Think'st thou I'd make a life of jealousy,
To follow still the changes of the moon
With fresh suspicions? No; to be once in doubt
Is once to be resolved. III, iii, 177

I humbly do beseech you of your pardon
For too much loving you.
III, iii, 212

If I do prove her haggard,
Though that her jesses were my dear heart-strings,
I'd whistle her off and let her down the wind,
To prey at fortune. III, iii, 260

I am declin'd
Into the vale of years. III, iii, 265

O curse of marriage!
That we can call these delicate creatures ours,
And not their appetites. I had rather be a toad,
And live upon the vapor of a dungeon,
Than keep a corner in the thing I love
For others' uses. III, iii, 268

Trifles light as air
Are to the jealous confirmations strong
As proofs of holy writ. III, iii, 323

Not poppy, nor mandragora,[1]
Nor all the drowsy syrups of the world,
Shall ever medicine thee to that sweet sleep
Which thou ow'dst yesterday.
III, iii, 331

I swear 'tis better to be much abus'd
Than but to know 't a little.
III, iii, 337

He that is robb'd, not wanting what is stol'n,
Let him not know 't and he's not robb'd at all.[2] III, iii, 343

[1] See *Antony and Cleopatra I, v, 4,* p. 287a.
[2] See Publilius Syrus, p. 125a.

O! now, forever
Farewell the tranquil mind; farewell
content!
Farewell the plumed troop and the big
wars
That make ambition virtue! O, farewell!
Farewell the neighing steed, and the
shrill trump,
The spirit-stirring drum, the ear-piercing
fife,
The royal banner, and all quality,
Pride, pomp, and circumstance of glori-
ous war!
And, O you mortal engines, whose rude
throats
The immortal Jove's dread clamors
counterfeit,
Farewell! Othello's occupation's gone!
Othello III, iii, 348

Be sure of it; give me the ocular proof.
III, iii, 361

No hinge nor loop
To hang a doubt on. *III, iii, 366*

On horror's head horrors accumulate.
III, iii, 371

Take note, take note, O world!
To be direct and honest is not safe.
III, iii, 378

But this denoted a foregone conclusion. *III, iii, 429*

Swell, bosom, with thy fraught,
For 'tis of aspics' tongues!
III, iii, 450

Like to the Pontick sea,
Whose icy current and compulsive
course
Ne'er feels retiring ebb, but keeps due
on
To the Propontic and the Hellespont,
Even so my bloody thoughts, with vi-
olent pace,
Shall ne'er look back, ne'er ebb to
humble love,
Till that a capable and wide revenge
Swallow them up. *III, iii, 454*

Our new heraldry is hands not hearts.
III, iv, 48

But jealous souls will not be answer'd
so;
They are not ever jealous for the
cause,
But jealous for they are jealous; 'tis a
monster
Begot upon itself, born on itself.
Othello III, iv, 158

'Tis the strumpet's plague
To beguile many and be beguil'd by
one. *IV, i, 97*

They laugh that win. *IV, i, 123*

My heart is turn'd to stone; I strike
it, and it hurts my hand. O! the world
hath not a sweeter creature; she might
lie by an emperor's side and command
him tasks. *IV, i, 190*

O, she will sing the savageness out of
a bear. *IV, i, 198*

But yet the pity of it, Iago! O! Iago,
the pity of it, Iago! *IV, i, 205*

Is this the noble nature
Whom passion could not shake? whose
solid virtue
The shot of accident nor dart of chance,
Could neither graze nor pierce?
IV, i, 276

I understand a fury in your words,
But not the words. *IV, ii, 31*

Steep'd me in poverty to the very lips.
IV, ii, 49

But, alas! to make me
A fixed figure for the time of scorn
To point his slow and moving finger
at. *IV, ii, 52*

Patience, thou young and rose-lipp'd
cherubin. *IV, ii, 62*

O thou weed!
Who art so lovely fair and smell'st so
sweet
That the sense aches at thee, would
thou hadst ne'er been born.
IV, ii, 66

O heaven! that such companions
thou'dst unfold,
And put in every honest hand a whip

To lash the rascals naked through the world. *Othello* IV, *ii*, 141

Unkindness may do much;
And his unkindness may defeat my life,
But never taint my love. IV, *ii*, 159

The poor soul sat sighing by a sycamore tree,
Sing all a green willow; [1]
Her hand on her bosom, her head on her knee,
Sing willow, willow, willow.
IV, *iii*, 41

It makes us, or it mars us. V, *i*, 4

Every way makes my gain. V, *i*, 14

He hath a daily beauty in his life.
V, *i*, 19

This is the night
That either makes me or fordoes me quite. V, *i*, 128

And smooth as monumental alabaster.
V, *ii*, 5

Put out the light, and then put out the light:
If I quench thee, thou flaming minister,
I can again thy former light restore,
Should I repent me; but once put out thy light,
Thou cunning'st pattern of excelling nature,
I know not where is that Promethean heat
That can thy light relume. V, *ii*, 7

It is the very error of the moon;
She comes more near the earth than she was wont,
And makes men mad. V *ii*, 107

She was as false as water.[2] V, *ii*, 132

Curse his better angel from his side,
And fall to reprobation.. V, *ii*, 206

Here is my journey's end, here is my butt,
And very sea-mark of my utmost sail.
V, *ii*, 266

An honorable murderer, if you will;
For naught I did in hate, but all in honor. *Othello* V, *ii*, 293

I have done the state some service, and they know 't;
No more of that. I pray you, in your letters,
When you shall these unlucky deeds relate,
Speak of me as I am; nothing extenuate,
Nor set down aught in malice: then, must you speak
Of one that lov'd not wisely but too well;
Of one not easily jealous, but, being wrought,
Perplex'd in the extreme; of one whose hand,
Like the base Indian, threw a pearl away
Richer than all his tribe; of one whose subdu'd eyes
Albeit unused to the melting mood,
Drop tears as fast as the Arabian trees
Their med'cinable gum. V, *ii*, 338

In Aleppo once,
Where a malignant and a turban'd Turk
Beat a Venetian and traduc'd the state,
I took by the throat the circumcised dog,
And smote him thus. V, *ii*, 354

My love's
More richer than my tongue.
King Lear [1605–1606], *act* I,
sc. 1, *l.* 79

Now, our joy,
Although our last, not least.[1] I, *i*, 84

Nothing will come of nothing.[2]
I, *i*, 92

Mend your speech a little,
Lest you may mar your fortunes.
I, *i*, 96

---

[1] See John Heywood, p. 182a.
[2] See *Troilus and Cressida* III, *ii*, 191, p. 268b.

[1] See Spenser, p. 201a, and *Julius Caesar* III, *i*, 189, p. 255a.
[2] See Lucretius, p. 113a.

Lear: So young, and so untender?
Cordelia: So young, my lord, and true. *King Lear I, i, 108*

Come not between the dragon and his wrath. *I, i, 124*

Kill thy physician, and the fee bestow Upon the foul disease. *I, i, 166*

I want that glib and oily art, To speak and purpose not. *I, i, 227*

A still-soliciting eye. *I, i, 234*

Time shall unfold what plighted cunning hides; Who covers faults, at last shame them derides. *I, i, 282*

The infirmity of his age. *I, i, 296*

Who in the lusty stealth of nature take More composition and fierce quality Than doth, within a dull, stale, tired bed, Go to the creating a whole tribe of fops. *I, ii, 11*

We have seen the best of our time: machinations, hollowness, treachery, and all ruinous disorders, follow us disquietly to our graves. *I, ii, 125*

This is the excellent foppery of the world, that, when we are sick in fortune — often the surfeit of our own behavior — we make guilty of our disasters the sun, the moon, and the stars; as if we were villains by necessity, fools by heavenly compulsion, knaves, thieves, and teachers by spherical predominance, drunkards, liars, and adulterers by an enforced obedience of planetary influence. *I, ii, 129*

Edgar —

[*Enter Edgar*]
and pat he comes, like the catastrophe of the old comedy: my cue is villainous melancholy, with a sigh like Tom o' Bedlam. *I, ii, 149*

That which ordinary men are fit for, I am qualified in, and the best of me is diligence. *I, iv, 36*

Truth's a dog must to kennel; he must be whipped out, when Lady the brach may stand by the fire and stink. *King Lear I, iv, 125*

Have more than thou showest, Speak less than thou knowest, Lend less than thou owest. *I, iv, 132*

Ingratitude, thou marble-hearted fiend, More hideous, when thou show'st thee in a child, Than the sea-monster. *I, iv, 283*

How sharper than a serpent's tooth it is To have a thankless child! *I, iv, 312*

Striving to better, oft we mar what's well. *I, iv, 371*

The son and heir of a mongrel bitch. *II, ii, 23*

I have seen better faces in my time Than stands on any shoulder that I see Before me at this instant. *II, ii, 99*

A good man's fortune may grow out at heels. *II, ii, 164*

Fortune, good night, smile once more; turn thy wheel! *II, ii, 180*

Hysterica passio! down, thou climbing sorrow! Thy element's below. *II, iv, 57*

That sir which serves and seeks for gain, And follows but for form, Will pack when it begins to rain, And leave thee in the storm. *II, iv, 79*

Nature in you stands on the very verge Of her confine. *II, iv, 149*

Necessity's sharp pinch! *II, iv, 214*

Our basest beggars Are in the poorest thing superfluous: Allow not nature more than nature needs, Man's life is cheap as beast's. *II, iv, 267*

Let not women's weapons, waterdrops,
Stain my man's cheeks!
                              King Lear II, iv, 280

I have full cause of weeping, but this
      heart
Shall break into a hundred thousand
      flaws
Or e'er I'll weep. O fool! I shall go
      mad.   *II, iv, 287*

Blow, winds, and crack your cheeks!
      rage! blow!
You cataracts and hurricanoes, spout
Till you have drench'd our steeples,
      drown'd the cocks!
You sulphurous and thought-executing
      fires,
Vaunt-couriers to oak-cleaving thunder-
      bolts,
Singe my white head! And thou, all-
      shaking thunder,
Strike flat the thick rotundity o' the
      world!
Crack nature's molds, all germens spill
      at once
That make ingrateful man!
                              III, ii, 1

I tax not you, you elements, with un-
      kindness.   *III, ii, 16*

A poor, infirm, weak, and despis'd old
      man.   *III, ii, 20*

There was never yet fair woman but
she made mouths in a glass.
                              III, ii, 35

I will be the pattern of all patience.
                              III, ii, 37

      I am a man
More sinn'd against than sinning.
                              III, ii, 59

The art of our necessities is strange,
That can make vile things precious.
                              III, ii, 70

He that has and a little tiny wit,
      With hey, ho, the wind and the
      rain.
Must make content with his fortunes
      fit,
      Though the rain it raineth every
      day.[1]   *III, ii, 76*

[1] See *Twelfth-Night V, i, 404,* p. 253a.

O! that way madness lies; let me shun
      that.   *King Lear III, iv, 21*

Poor naked wretches, wheresoe'er you
      are,
That bide the pelting of this pitiless
      storm,
How shall your houseless heads and un-
      fed sides,
Your loop'd and window'd raggedness,
      defend you
From seasons such as these?
                              III, iv, 28

      Take physic, pomp;
Expose thyself to feel what wretches
      feel.   *III, iv, 33*

Pillicock sat on Pillicock-hill:
Halloo, halloo, loo, loo!   *III, iv, 75*

      Out-paramoured the Turk.
                              III, iv, 91

      Is man no more than this? Consider
him well. Thou owest the worm no silk,
the beast no hide, the sheep no wool,
the cat no perfume. Ha! here's three
on 's are sophisticated; thou art the
thing itself; unaccommodated man is
no more but such a poor, bare, forked
animal as thou art. Off, off, you
lendings! Come; unbutton here.
                              III, iv, 105

'Tis a naughty night to swim in.
                              III, iv, 113

      The green mantle of the standing
pool.   *III, iv, 137*

But mice and rats and such small deer
Have been Tom's food for seven long
      year.   *III, iv, 142*

The prince of darkness is a gentleman.[1]
                              III, iv, 147

Poor Tom's a-cold.   *III, iv, 151*

Child Rowland to the dark tower came,[2]

[1] The Devil is a gentleman. — SHELLEY, *Peter
Bell the Third* [1819], *pt. II, st. 2*
[2] Child Roland to the dark tower came. —
SIR WALTER SCOTT, *The Bridal of Triermain*
[1813]
      Dauntless the slug-horn to my lips I set,
      And blew. "*Childe Roland to the Dark Tower
      came.*"
            BROWNING, *Childe Roland to the Dark
                  Tower Came* [1855], *st. 34*

His word was still, Fie, foh, and fum,
I smell the blood of a British man.
          King Lear III, iv, 185

He's mad that trusts in the tameness
of a wolf, a horse's health, a boy's love,
or a whore's oath.   III, vi, 20

    The little dogs and all,
Tray, Blanch, and Sweetheart, see, they
    bark at me.   III, vi, 65

Is there any cause in nature that
makes these hard hearts?   III, vi, 81

I am tied to the stake, and I must stand
    the course.   III, vii, 54

Out, vile jelly!   III, vii, 83

The lowest and most dejected thing of
    fortune.   IV, i, 3

    The worst is not,
So long as we can say, "This is the
    worst."   IV, i, 27

As flies to wanton boys, are we to the
    gods;
They kill us for their sport.
          IV, i, 36

You are not worth the dust which the
    rude wind
Blows in your face.   IV, ii, 30

She that herself will sliver and dis-
    branch
From her material sap, perforce must
    wither
And come to deadly use.   IV, ii, 34

Wisdom and goodness to the vile seem
    vile;
Filths savor but themselves.
          IV, ii, 38

Tigers, not daughters.   IV, ii, 39

    It is the stars,
The stars above us, govern our condi-
    tions.   IV, iii, 34

Our foster-nurse of nature is repose.
          IV, iv, 12

    How fearful
And dizzy 'tis to cast one's eyes so low!
The crows and choughs that wing the
    midway air

Show scarce so gross as beetles; halfway
    down
Hangs one that gathers samphire,
    dreadful trade!
Methinks he seems no bigger than his
    head.
The fishermen that walk upon the
    beach
Appear like mice, and yond tall anchor-
    ing bark
Diminish'd to her cock, her cock a
    buoy
Almost too small for sight. The mur-
    muring surge,
That on the unnumber'd idle pebbles
    chafes,
Cannot be heard so high.
          King Lear IV, vi, 12

Nature's above art in that respect.
          IV, vi, 87

Ay, every inch a king.   IV, vi, 110

The wren goes to 't, and the small
    gilded fly
Does lecher in my sight.
Let copulation thrive.   IV, vi, 115

Give me an ounce of civet, good
apothecary, to sweeten my imagination.   IV, vi, 133

A man may see how this world goes
with no eyes. Look with thine ears: see
how yond justice rails upon yon simple
thief. Hark, in thine ear: change places;
and, handy-dandy, which is the justice,
which is the thief?   IV, vi, 154

Through tatter'd clothes small vices do
    appear;
Robes and furr'd gowns hide all. Plate
    sin with gold,
And the strong lance of justice hurtless
    breaks;
Arm it in rags, a pigmy's straw does
    pierce it.   IV, vi, 169

    Get thee glass eyes;
And, like a scurvy politician, seem
To see the things thou dost not.
          IV, vi, 175

When we are born, we cry that we are
    come

To this great stage of fools.

> *King Lear IV, vi,* 187

Then, kill, kill, kill, kill, kill, kill!

> *IV, vi,* 192

Mine enemy's dog,
Though he had bit me, should have stood that night
Against my fire.   *IV, vii,* 36

Thou art a soul in bliss; but I am bound
Upon a wheel of fire, that mine own tears
Do scald like molten lead.

> *IV, vii,* 46

I am a very foolish fond old man,
Fourscore and upward, not an hour more or less;
And, to deal plainly,
I fear I am not in my perfect mind.

> *IV, vii,* 60

Pray you now, forget and forgive.[1]

> *IV, vii,* 84

Men must endure
Their going hence, even as their coming hither:
Ripeness is all.   *V, ii,* 9

Come, let's away to prison;
We two alone will sing like birds i' the cage:
When thou dost ask me blessing, I'll kneel down,
And ask of thee forgiveness: so we'll live,
And pray, and sing, and tell old tales, and laugh
At gilded butterflies, and hear poor rogues
Talk of court news; and we'll talk with them too,
Who loses and who wins; who's in, who's out;
And take upon's the mystery of things,
As if we were God's spies: and we'll wear out,
In a wall'd prison, packs and sets of great ones

[1] All our great fray . . . is forgiven and forgotten between us quite. — HEYWOOD, *Proverbs* [1546], *pt. II, ch. 3*

That ebb and flow by the moon.

> *King Lear V, iii,* 8

Upon such sacrifices, my Cordelia,
The gods themselves throw incense.

> *V, iii,* 20

The gods are just, and of our pleasant vices
Make instruments to plague us.

> *V, iii,* 172

The wheel is come full circle.

> *V, iii,* 176

Howl, howl, howl, howl! O! you are men of stones:
Had I your tongues and eyes, I'd use them so
That heaven's vaults should crack.
She's gone forever.   *V, iii,* 259

Her voice was ever soft,
Gentle, and low, an excellent thing in woman.   *V, iii,* 274

And my poor fool is hang'd! No, no, no life!
Why should a dog, a horse, a rat, have life,
And thou no breath at all? Thou'lt come no more,
Never, never, never, never, never!
Pray you, undo this button.

> *V, iii,* 307

Vex not his ghost: O! let him pass; he hates him
That would upon the rack of this tough world
Stretch him out longer.   *V, iii,* 315

The weight of this sad time we must obey;
Speak what we feel, not what we ought to say.
The oldest hath borne most: we that are young,
Shall never see so much, nor live so long.   *V, iii,* 325

First Witch: When shall we three meet again
In thunder, lightning, or in rain?
Second Witch: When the hurlyburly's done,

When the battle's lost and won.
> *Macbeth* [1605–1606], *act I,
sc. i, l. 1*

Fair is foul, and foul is fair:
Hover through the fog and filthy air.
> *I, i, 12*

Banners flout the sky.   *I, ii, 50*

A sailor's wife had chestnuts in her
lap,
And munch'd, and munch'd, and
munch'd: "Give me," quoth I:
"Aroint thee, witch!" the rump-fed
ronyon cries.   *I, iii, 4*

Sleep shall neither night nor day
Hang upon his pent-house lid.
> *I, iii, 19*

Dwindle, peak, and pine.   *I, iii, 23*

So foul and fair a day I have not seen.
> *I, iii, 38*

If you can look into the seeds of time,
And say which grain will grow and
which will not,
Speak.   *I, iii, 58*

> And to be king
Stands not within the prospect of belief.   *I, iii, 73*

The earth hath bubbles, as the water
has,
And these are of them.   *I, iii, 79*

Or have we eaten on the insane root
That takes the reason prisoner?
> *I, iii, 84*

And oftentimes, to win us to our
harm,
The instruments of darkness tell us
truths,
Win us with honest trifles, to betray 's
In deepest consequence.   *I, iii, 123*

As happy prologues to the swelling act
Of the imperial theme.   *I, iii, 128*

> I am Thane of Cawdor:
If good, why do I yield to that suggestion
Whose horrid image doth unfix my
hair

And make my seated heart knock at my
ribs,
Against the use of nature? Present
fears
Are less than horrible imaginings.
> *Macbeth I, iii, 134*

If chance will have me king, why,
chance may crown me,
Without my stir.   *I, iii, 143*

> Come what come may,
Time and the hour runs through the
roughest day.   *I, iii, 146*

> Nothing in his life
Became him like the leaving it; he died
As one that had been studied in his
death
To throw away the dearest thing he
ow'd,
As 'twere a careless trifle.   *I, iv, 7*

> There's no art
To find the mind's construction in the
face:
He was a gentleman on whom I built
An absolute trust.   *I, iv, 11*

Glamis thou art, and Cawdor; and shalt
be
What thou art promis'd. Yet do I fear
thy nature;
It is too full o' the milk of human
kindness [1]
To catch the nearest way.   *I, v, 16*

> The raven himself is hoarse
That croaks the fatal entrance of Duncan
Under my battlements. Come, you spirits
That tend on mortal thoughts! unsex
me here,
And fill me from the crown to the toe
top full
Of direst cruelty; make thick my
blood,
Stop up the access and passage to remorse,
That no compunctious visitings of nature

---

[1] The thunder of your words has soured the
milk of human kindness in my heart. — RICHARD
BRINSLEY SHERIDAN, *The Rivals* [1775], *act III,
sc. iv*

Shake my fell purpose, nor keep peace between
The effect and it! Come to my woman's breasts,
And take my milk for gall, you murdering ministers.
      Macbeth I, v, 38

Nor heaven peep through the blanket of the dark,
To cry, "Hold, hold!"   *I, v, 54*

Your face, my thane, is as a book where men
May read strange matters.   *I, v, 63*

     Look like the innocent flower,
But be the serpent under 't.
      I, v, 66

Duncan: This castle hath a pleasant seat; the air
Nimbly and sweetly recommends itself
Unto our gentle senses.
Banquo: This guest of summer,
The temple-haunting martlet, does approve
By his lov'd mansionry that the heaven's breath
Smells wooingly here: no jutty, frieze,
Buttress, nor coign of vantage, but this bird
Hath made his pendent bed and procreant cradle:
Where they most breed and haunt, I have observed
The air is delicate.   *I, vi, 1*

If it were done when 'tis done, then 'twere well
It were done quickly; if the assassination
Could trammel up the consequence, and catch
With his surcease success; that but this blow
Might be the be-all and the end-all here,
But here, upon this bank and shoal of time,
We'd jump the life to come.
      I, vii, 1

This even-handed justice.   *I, vii, 10*

Besides, this Duncan
Hath borne his faculties so meek, hath been
So clear in his great office, that his virtues
Will plead like angels trumpet-tongu'd [1] against
The deep damnation of his taking-off;
And pity, like a naked new-born babe,
Striding the blast, or heaven's cherubin, hors'd
Upon the sightless couriers of the air,
Shall blow the horrid deed in every eye,
That tears shall drown the wind. I have no spur
To prick the sides of my intent, but only
Vaulting ambition, which o'erleaps itself
And falls on the other.
      Macbeth I, vii, 16

     I have bought
Golden opinions from all sorts of people.   *I, vii, 32*

Letting "I dare not" wait upon "I would,"
Like the poor cat i' the adage.[2]
      I, vii, 44

I dare do all that may become a man;
Who dares do more is none.   *I, vii, 46*

     Nor time nor place
Did then adhere.   *I, vii, 51*

     I have given suck, and know
How tender 'tis to love the babe that milks me:
I would, while it was smiling in my face,
Have pluck'd my nipple from his boneless gums,
And dash'd the brains out, had I so sworn as you
Have done to this.   *I, vii, 54*

Macbeth: If we should fail —
Lady Macbeth: We fail!

[1] And he shall send his angels with a great sound of a trumpet. — *Matthew 24:31*
[2] See John Heywood, p. 184a, and *Measure for Measure I, iv, 78*, p. 270a.

But screw your courage to the sticking-
place,
And we'll not fail.

　　　　　Macbeth I, vii, 59

Memory, the warder of the brain.

　　　　　I, vii, 65

Away, and mock the time with fairest
show:
False face must hide what the false
heart doth know.　　*I, vii, 81*

The moon is down.　　*II, i, 2*

　　There's husbandry in heaven;
Their candles are all out.　　*II, i, 4*

　　Merciful powers!
Restrain in me the cursed thoughts that
nature
Gives way to in repose.　　*II, i, 7*

　　Shut up
In measureless content.　　*II, i, 16*

Is this a dagger which I see before me,
The handle toward my hand? Come,
let me clutch thee:
I have thee not, and yet I see thee still.
Art thou not, fatal vision, sensible
To feeling as to sight? or art thou but
A dagger of the mind, a false creation,
Proceeding from the heat-oppressed
brain?　　*II, i, 33*

　　Now o'er the one half-world
Nature seems dead; and wicked dreams
abuse
The curtain'd sleep; witchcraft cele-
brates
Pale Hecate's offerings.　　*II, i, 49*

　　Thou sure and firm-set earth,
Hear not my steps, which way they
walk, for fear
The very stones prate of my whereabout.[1]　　*II, i, 56*

　　The bell invites me.
Hear it not, Duncan; for it is a knell
That summons thee to heaven or to
hell.　　*II, i, 62*

It was the owl that shriek'd, the fatal
bellman,

[1] For the stone shall cry out of the wall. —
Habakkuk 2:11
　See *Luke 19:40*, p. 47b.

Which gives the stern'st good-night.
　　　　　Macbeth II, ii, 4

　　The attempt and not the deed
Confounds us.　　*II, ii, 12*

　　Had he not resembled
My father as he slept I had done 't.
　　　　　II, ii, 14

I had most need of blessing, and
"Amen"
Stuck in my throat.　　*II, ii, 33*

Methought I heard a voice cry, "Sleep
no more!
Macbeth does murder sleep!" the inno-
cent sleep,
Sleep that knits up the ravel'd sleave of
care,
The death of each day's life, sore la-
bor's bath,
Balm of hurt minds, great nature's sec-
ond course,
Chief nourisher in life's feast.
　　　　　II, ii, 36

Glamis hath murder'd sleep, and
therefore Cawdor
Shall sleep no more, Macbeth shall
sleep no more!　　*II, ii, 43*

　　Infirm of purpose!
Give me the daggers. The sleeping and
the dead
Are but as pictures; 'tis the eye of
childhood
That fears a painted devil.　　*II, ii, 53*

Will all great Neptune's ocean wash
this blood
Clean from my hand? No, this my
hand will rather
The multitudinous seas incarnadine,
Making the green one red.
　　　　　II, ii, 61

　　The primrose way to the everlasting
bonfire.[1]　　*II, iii, 22*

　　It [drink] provokes the desire, but it
takes away the performance.
　　　　　II, iii, 34

The labor we delight in physics pain.
　　　　　II, iii, 56

[1] See Bion, p. 104b, and *Hamlet I, iii, 47*,
p. 258b.

Confusion now hath made his master-
piece!
Most sacrilegious murder hath broke
ope
The Lord's anointed temple, and stole
thence
The life o' the building!
Macbeth II, iii, 72

Shake off this downy sleep, death's
counterfeit.[1] II, iii, 83

Had I but died an hour before this
chance
I had liv'd a blessed time; for, from this
instant,
There's nothing serious in mortality,
All is but toys; renown and grace is
dead,
The wine of life is drawn, and the mere
lees
Is left this vault to brag of.
II, iii, 98

Who can be wise, amaz'd, temperate
and furious,
Loyal and neutral, in a moment? No
man. II, iii, 115

In the great hand of God I stand, and
thence
Against the undivulg'd pretense I fight
Of treasonous malice. II, iii, 137

To show an unfelt sorrow is an office
Which the false man does easy.
II, iii, 143

A falcon, towering in her pride of
place,
Was by a mousing owl hawk'd at and
kill'd. II, iv, 12

I must become a borrower of the night
For a dark hour or twain. III, i, 27

To be thus is nothing;
But to be safely thus. III, i, 48

Murderer: We are men, my liege.
Macbeth: Ay, in the catalogue ye go
for men. III, i, 91

I am one, my liege,
Whom the vile blows and buffets of the
world

1 See Homer, p. 64a, and note.

Have so incens'd that I am reckless
what
I do to spite the world.
Macbeth III, i, 108

So weary with disasters, tugg'd with
fortune,
That I would set my life on any
chance,
To mend it or be rid on 't.
III, i, 112

Things without all remedy
Should be without regard: what's done
is done. III, ii, 11

We have scotch'd the snake, not kill'd
it. III, ii, 13

Duncan is in his grave;
After life's fitful fever he sleeps well;
Treason has done his worst: nor steel,
nor poison,
Malice domestic, foreign levy, nothing
Can touch him further. III, ii, 22

Then be thou jocund. Ere the bat hath
flown
His cloister'd flight, ere, to black Hecate's summons
The shard-borne beetle with his drowsy
hums
Hath rung night's yawning peal, there
shall be done
A deed of dreadful note. III, ii, 40

Come, seeling night,
Scarf up the tender eye of pitiful day,
And with thy bloody and invisible
hand
Cancel and tear to pieces that great
bond
Which keeps me pale! Light thickens,
and the crow
Makes wing to the rooky wood.
III, ii, 46

Now spurs the lated traveler apace
To gain the timely inn. III, iii, 6

But now I am cabin'd, cribb'd, con-
fined, bound in
To saucy doubts and fears.
III, iv, 24

Now good digestion wait on appetite,
And health on both! III, iv, 38

Thou canst not say I did it: never shake
Thy gory locks at me.
                    Macbeth III, *iv, 50*

The air-drawn dagger.   III, *iv, 62*

I drink to the general joy of the whole
table.   III, *iv, 89*

    What man dare, I dare:
Approach thou like the rugged Russian
bear,
The arm'd rhinoceros, or the Hyrcan
tiger,
Take any shape but that, and my firm
nerves
Shall never tremble.   III, *iv, 99*

    Hence, horrible shadow!
Unreal mockery, hence!   III, *iv, 106*

Stand not upon the order of your
going,
But go at once.   III, *iv, 119*

It will have blood, they say; blood will
have blood:
Stones have been known to move and
trees to speak.   III, *iv, 122*

Macbeth: What is the night?
Lady Macbeth: Almost at odds with
morning, which is which.
            III, *iv, 126*

    I am in blood
Stepp'd in so far, that, should I wade
no more,
Returning were as tedious as go o'er.
            III, *iv, 136*

Double, double toil and trouble;
Fire burn and cauldron bubble.
            IV, *i, 10*

Eye of newt, and toe of frog,
Wool of bat, and tongue of dog.
            IV, *i, 14*

Finger of birth-strangled babe,
Ditch-deliver'd by a drab.   IV, *i, 30*

By the pricking of my thumbs,
Something wicked this way comes.
    Open, locks,
      Whoever knocks!   IV, *i, 44*

How now, you secret, black, and midnight hags!   IV, *i, 48*

A deed without a name.[1]
        Macbeth IV, *i, 49*

Be bloody, bold, and resolute; laugh to
scorn
The power of man, for none of woman
born
Shall harm Macbeth.   IV, *i, 79*

But yet I'll make assurance double
sure,
And take a bond of fate.   IV, *i, 83*

Macbeth shall never vanquish'd be until
Great Birnam wood to high Dunsinane
hill
Shall come against him.[2]   IV, *i, 92*

Show his eyes, and grieve his heart;
Come like shadows, so depart.
            IV, *i, 110*

What! will the line stretch out to the
crack of doom?   IV, *i, 117*

The weird sisters.   IV, *i, 136*

    When our actions do not,
Our fears do make us traitors.
            IV, *ii, 3*

He wants the natural touch.
            IV, *ii, 9*

Angels are bright still, though the
brightest fell.   IV, *iii, 22*

Pour the sweet milk of concord into
hell,
Uproar the universal peace, confound
All unity on earth.   IV, *iii, 98*

Give sorrow words; the grief that does
not speak
Whispers the o'er-fraught heart and
bids it break.   IV, *iii, 209*

    All my pretty ones?
Did you say all? O hell-kite! All?
What! all my pretty chickens and their
dam
At one fell swoop?   IV, *iii, 216*

Malcolm: Dispute it like a man.
Macbeth: I shall do so;
But I must also feel it as a man:

[1] See Ann Radcliffe, p. 501a.
[2] Till Birnam wood remove to Dunsinane
    I cannot taint with fear.
          Macbeth V, iii, 2

I cannot but remember such things
were
That were most precious to me.
                    Macbeth IV, iii, 219

Out, damned spot! out, I say!
                    V, *i*, 38

Fie, my lord, fie! a soldier, and
afeard?   V, *i*, 40

Who would have thought the old
man to have had so much blood in
him?   V, *i*, 42

The Thane of Fife had a wife: where
is she now?   V, *i*, 46

All the perfumes of Arabia will not
sweeten this little hand.   V, *i*, 56

Those he commands move only in
    command,
Nothing in love; now does he feel his
    title
Hang loose about him, like a giant's
    robe
Upon a dwarfish thief.   V, *ii*, 19

The devil damn thee black, thou cream-
    fac'd loon
Where gott'st thou that goose look?
                    V, *iii*, 11

Thou lily-liver'd boy.   V, *iii*, 15

I have liv'd long enough: my way of
    life
Is fall'n into the sere, the yellow leaf; [1]
And that which should accompany old
    age,
As honor, love, obedience, troops of
    friends,
I must not look to have; but, in their
    stead,
Curses, not loud but deep, mouth-
    honor, breath,
Which the poor heart would fain deny,
    and dare not.   V, *iii*, 22

Macbeth: Canst thou not minister to
    a mind diseas'd,
Pluck from the memory a rooted sor-
    row,
Raze out the written troubles of the
    brain,

[1] See Byron, p. 563a.

And with some sweet oblivious anti-
    dote
Cleanse the stuff'd bosom of that peril-
    ous stuff
Which weighs upon the heart?
Doctor: Therein the patient
Must minister to himself.
Macbeth: Throw physic to the dogs;
    I'll none of it.
                    Macbeth V, *iii*, 40

I would applaud thee to the very echo,
That should applaud again.   V, *iii*, 53

Hang out our banners on the outward
    walls;
The cry is still, "They come"; our cas-
    tle's strength
Will laugh a siege to scorn.   V, *v*, 1

        My fell of hair
Would at a dismal treatise rouse and
    stir
As life were in 't. I have supp'd full
    with horrors.   V, *v*, 11

She should have died hereafter;
There would have been a time for such
    a word.
Tomorrow, and tomorrow, and tomor-
    row,
Creeps in this petty pace from day to
    day,
To the last syllable of recorded time;
And all our yesterdays have lighted
    fools
The way to dusty death. Out, out, brief
    candle!
Life's but a walking shadow, a poor
    player
That struts and frets his hour upon the
    stage,
And then is heard no more; it is a tale
Told by an idiot, full of sound and
    fury,
Signifying nothing.   V, *v*, 17

I 'gin to be aweary of the sun,
And wish the estate o' the world were
    now undone.   V, *v*, 49

    Blow, wind! come, wrack!
At least we'll die with harness on our
    back.   V, *v*, 51

Why should I play the Roman fool, and die
On mine own sword?
Macbeth V, vii, 30

I bear a charmed life. V, vii, 41

And be these juggling fiends no more believ'd,
That palter with us in a double sense;
That keep the word of promise to our ear
And break it to our hope. V, vii, 48

Live to be the show and gaze o' the time. V, vii, 53

Lay on, Macduff,
And damn'd be him that first cries, "Hold, enough!" V, vii, 62

You shall see in him
The triple pillar of the world transform'd
Into a strumpet's fool.
Antony and Cleopatra [1606–1607], act I, sc. i, l. 12

There's beggary in the love that can be reckon'd. I, i, 15

Let Rome in Tiber melt, and the wide arch
Of the rang'd empire fall! Here is my space.
Kingdoms are clay. I, i, 33

In nature's infinite book of secrecy
A little I can read. I, ii, 11

I love long life better than figs.
I, ii, 34

On the sudden
A Roman thought hath struck him.
I, ii, 90

Eternity was in our lips and eyes,
Bliss in our brows bent. I, iii, 35

O! my oblivion is a very Antony,
And I am all forgotten. I, iii, 90

Give me to drink mandragora.[1] . . .
That I might sleep out this great gap of time
My Antony is away. I, v, 4

O happy horse, to bear the weight of Antony! I, v, 21

[1] See Othello III, iii, 331, p. 274b.

The demi-Atlas of this earth, the arm
And burgonet of men.
Antony and Cleopatra I, v, 23

Where's my serpent of old Nile?
I, v, 25

A morsel for a monarch. I, v, 31

My salad days,
When I was green in judgment.
I, v, 73

We, ignorant of ourselves,
Beg often our own harms, which the wise powers
Deny us for our good; so find we profit
By losing of our prayers. II, i, 5

Epicurean cooks
Sharpen with cloyless sauce his appetite. II, i, 24

No worse a husband than the best of men. II, ii, 135

The barge she sat in, like a burnish'd throne,
Burn'd on the water; the poop was beaten gold,
Purple the sails, and so perfumed, that
The winds were love-sick with them; the oars were silver,
Which to the tune of flutes kept stroke, and made
The water which they beat to follow faster,
As amorous of their strokes. For her own person,
It beggar'd all description.
II, ii, 199

Age cannot wither her, nor custom stale
Her infinite variety; other women cloy
The appetites they feed, but she makes hungry
Where most she satisfies; for vilest things
Become themselves in her, that the holy priests
Bless her when she is riggish.
II, ii, 243

I have not kept my square; but that to come

Shall all be done by the rule.
　　　Antony and Cleopatra II, iii, 6

　　Music, moody food
Of us that trade in love.[1]　　*II, v, 1*

Though it be honest, it is never good
To bring bad news.[2]　　*II, v, 85*

Come, thou monarch of the vine,
Plumpy Bacchus, with pink eyne!
　　　　　II, vii, 120

　　Ambition,
The soldier's virtue.　　*III, i, 22*

Celerity is never more admir'd
Than by the negligent.　　*III, vii, 24*

　　We have kiss'd away
Kingdoms and provinces.
　　　　III, viii, 17

　　He wears the rose
Of youth upon him.　　*III, xi, 20*

　　Men's judgments are
A parcel of their fortunes, and things
　　outward
Do draw the inward quality after
　　them,
To suffer all alike.　　*III, xi, 31*

I found you as a morsel, cold upon
Dead Caesar's Trencher.
　　　　III, xi, 116

Let's have one other gaudy night.
　　　　III, xi, 182

Now he'll outstare the lightning. To be
　　furious
Is to be frightened out of fear.
　　　　III, xi, 194

To business that we love we rise be-
　　time,
And go to 't with delight.
　　　　IV, iv, 20

O infinite virtue! com'st thou smiling
　　from
The world's great snare uncaught?
　　　　IV, viii, 17

The shirt of Nessus is upon me.
　　　　IV, x, 56

Sometimes we see a cloud that's drag-
　　onish;
A vapor sometime like a bear or lion,
A tower'd citadel, a pendant rock,
A forked mountain, or blue promon-
　　tory
With trees upon 't.[1]
　　　Antony and Cleopatra IV, xii, 2

Unarm, Eros; the long day's task is
　　done,
And we must sleep.　　*IV, xii, 35*

　　But I will be
A bridegroom in my death, and run
　　into 't
As to a lover's bed.　　*IV, xii, 99*

　　O sun!
Burn the great sphere thou mov'st in;
　　darkling stand
The varying shore [2] o' the world.
　　　　IV, xiii, 10

I am dying, Egypt, dying; only
I here importune death awhile, until
Of many thousand kisses the poor last
I lay upon thy lips.　　*IV, xiii, 18*

O! wither'd is the garland of the war,
The soldier's pole is fall'n; young boys
　　and girls
Are level now with men; the odds is
　　gone,
And there is nothing left remarkable
Beneath the visiting moon.
　　　　IV, xiii, 64

Let's do it after the high Roman fash-
　　ion,
And make death proud to take us.
　　　　IV, xiii, 87

　　And it is great
To do that thing that ends all other
　　deeds,
Which shackles accidents, and bolts up
　　change.　　*V, ii, 4*

His legs bestrid the ocean; his rear'd
　　arm
Crested the world; his voice was proper-
　　tied
As all the tuned spheres, and that to
　　friends;

---

[1] See *Twelfth-Night, I, i, 1*, p. 251a.
[2] See Sophocles, p. 82a, and *King Henry IV,
pt. II, I, i, 100*, p. 241b.

[1] See Aristophanes, p. 91a, and *Hamlet III,
ii, 400*, p. 263b.
[2] In some editions, star.

But when he meant to quail and shake
　　the orb,
He was as rattling thunder. For his
　　bounty,
There was no winter in 't, an autumn
　　'twas
That grew the more by reaping; his de-
　　lights
Were dolphin-like, they show'd his
　　back above
The element they liv'd in; in his livery
Walk'd crowns and crownets, realms
　　and islands were
As plates dropp'd from his pocket.
　　　　Antony and Cleopatra V, ii, 82

The bright day is done,
And we are for the dark.　　V, ii, 192

　　　　Antony
Shall be brought drunken forth, and I
　　shall see
Some squeaking Cleopatra boy my
　　greatness
I' the posture of a whore.　　V, ii, 217

A woman is a dish for the gods, if
the devil dress her not.　　V, ii, 274

　　　　I have
Immortal longings in me.　　V, ii, 282

If thou and nature can so gently part,
The stroke of death is as a lover's
　　pinch,
Which hurts, and is desir'd.
　　　　　　　　　　　　V, ii, 296

Dost thou not see my baby at my
　　breast,
That sucks the nurse asleep?
　　　　　　　　　　　　V, ii, 311

Now boast thee, death, in thy posses-
　　sion lies
A lass unparallel'd.　　V, ii, 317

First Guard: . . . Charmian, is this
　　well done?
Charmian: It is well done, and fitting
　　for a princess
Descended of so many royal kings.[1]
　　　　　　　　　　　　V, ii, 327

[1] One of the soldiers seeing her, angrily said
unto her: Is that well done Charmian? Very well
said she again, and meet for a princess descended
of so many noble kings. — SIR THOMAS NORTH,
Plutarch's "Lives" [1579]

As she would catch another Antony
In her strong toil of grace.
　　　　Antony and Cleopatra V, ii, 348

　　　　The gods sent not
Corn for the rich men only.
　　　　Coriolanus [1607–1608], *act* I,
　　　　　　　　　　sc. i, l. 213

　　　　They threw their caps
As they would hang them on the horns
　　o' the moon,
Shouting their emulation.　　I, i, 218

All the yarn she spun in Ulysses' absence did but fill Ithaca full of moths.
　　　　　　　　　　　　I, iii, 93

Nature teaches beasts to know their
friends.　　　　　　　　II, i, 6

A cup of hot wine with not a drop of
allaying Tiber in 't.[1]　　II, i, 52

My gracious silence, hail!　　II, i, 194

He himself stuck not to call us the
many-headed multitude.[2]　　II, iii, 18

　　　　Bid them wash their faces,
And keep their teeth clean.
　　　　　　　　　　　　II, iii, 65

I thank you for your voices, thank you,
Your most sweet voices.　　II, iii, 179

The mutable, rank-scented many.
　　　　　　　　　　　　III, i, 65

Hear you this Triton of the minnows?
　　mark you
His absolute "shall"?　　III, i, 88

What is the city but the people?[3]
　　　　　　　　　　　　III, i, 198

His nature is too noble for the world:
He would not flatter Neptune for his
　　trident,
Or Jove for 's power to thunder. His
　　heart's his mouth:
What his breast forges, that his tongue
　　must vent.　　　　　III, i, 254

　　　　The beast
With many heads butts me away.[4]
　　　　　　　　　　　　IV, i, 1

[1] See Lovelace, p. 358b.
[2] See Horace, p. 123a, and note.
[3] See Sophocles, p. 81a.
[4] See Horace, p. 123a, and note.

O! a kiss
Long as my exile, sweet as my revenge! [1]   *Coriolanus* V, iii, 44

Chaste as the icicle
That's curdied by the frost from purest
  snow,
And hangs on Dian's temple.
            V, iii, 65

He wants nothing of a god but eternity and a heaven to throne in.
            V, iv, 25

They'll give him death by inches.
            V, iv, 43

If you have writ your annals true, 'tis
  there,
That, like an eagle in a dovecote, I
Flutter'd your Volscians in Corioli:
Alone I did it.   V, v, 114

Thou hast done a deed whereat valor
  will weep.   V, v, 135

He shall have a noble memory.
            V, v, 155

'Tis not enough to help the feeble up,
But to support him after.
     Timon of Athens [1607–1608],
           act I, sc. i, l. 108

I call the gods to witness.[2]
            I, i, 138

I wonder men dare trust themselves
  with men.   I, ii, 45

Here's that which is too weak to be a
  sinner,
Honest water, which ne'er left man i'
  the mire.[3]   I, ii, 60

Immortal gods, I crave no pelf;
I pray for no man but myself;
Grant I may never prove so fond,
To trust man on his oath or bond.
            I, ii, 64

Men shut their doors against a setting
  sun.   I, ii, 152

Every man has his fault, and honesty
is his.   III, i, 30

---

[1] See Byron, p. 560a.
[2] I call heaven and earth to witness. —
Deuteronomy 4:26
[3] Inscribed on the drinking fountain in the
market square of Stratford-on-Avon.

Nothing emboldens sin so much as
  mercy.
     Timon of Athens III, v, 3

You fools of fortune, trencher-friends,
  time's flies.   III, vi, 107

We have seen better days.   IV, ii, 27

O! the fierce wretchedness that glory
  brings us.   IV, ii, 30

I am Misanthropos, and hate mankind.[1]   IV, iii, 53

Life's uncertain voyage.   V, i, 207

See, where she comes apparel'd like the
  spring.
     Pericles [1608–1609], *act I,*
          sc. i, l. 12

Few love to hear the sins they love to
  act.   I, i, 92

The sad companion, dull-eyed melancholy.   I, ii, 2

Third Fisherman: . . . Master, I
marvel how the fishes live in the sea.
First Fisherman: Why, as men do a-
land; the great ones eat up the little
ones.[2]   II, i, 29

Lest the bargain should catch cold
and starve.
     Cymbeline [1609–1610], *act I,*
          sc. iv, l. 186

Hath his bellyful of fighting.
            II, i, 24

Hark! hark! the lark at heaven's gate
  sings,
And Phoebus 'gins arise,[3]
His steeds to water at those springs
  On chalic'd flowers that lies;
And winking Mary-buds begin
  To ope their golden eyes:
With everything that pretty is,
  My lady sweet, arise.   II, iii, 22

As chaste as unsunn'd snow.   II, v, 13

Some griefs are med'cinable.
            III, ii, 33

---

[1] See Molière, p. 361a.
[2] Men lived like fishes; the great ones devoured
the small. — ALGERNON SIDNEY, *Discourses on
Government* [1698], *ch. 2, sec. 18*
[3] See Lyly, p. 203a.

O! for a horse with wings!
                    Cymbeline III, ii, 49

The game is up.   *III, iii, 107*

    Slander,
Whose edge is sharper than the sword, whose tongue
Outvenoms all the worms of Nile, whose breath
Rides on the posting winds and doth belie
All corners of the world.   *III, iv, 35*

I have not slept one wink.[1]
                         III, iv, 103

    Weariness
Can snore upon the flint when resty sloth
Finds the down pillow hard.
                         III, vi, 33

        An angel! or, if not,
An earthly paragon!   *III, vi, 42*

        Society is no comfort
To one not sociable.   *IV, ii, 12*

        I wear not
My dagger in my mouth.   *IV, ii, 78*

Fear no more the heat o' the sun,
    Nor the furious winter's rages;
Thou thy worldly task hast done,
    Home art gone, and ta'en thy wages.
Golden lads and girls all must,
As chimney-sweepers, come to dust.
                         IV, ii, 258

Quiet consummation have;
And renowned be thy grave!
                         IV, ii, 280

Fortune brings in some boats that are not steer'd.   *IV, iii, 46*

Hang there like fruit, my soul,
Till the tree die!   *V, v, 264*

From fairest creatures we desire increase,
That thereby beauty's rose might never die.
    Sonnets [2] *[published 1609], 1, l. 1*

[1] See Cervantes, p. 194a.
[2] The sonnets were written definitely before 1598, according to Meres's *Palladis Tamia*, and according to Leslie Hotson in *Mr. W. H.* [1964]

When forty winters shall besiege thy brow,
And dig deep trenches in thy beauty's field.   *Sonnet 2, l. 1*

Thou art thy mother's glass, and she in thee
Calls back the lovely April of her prime.   *Sonnet 3, l. 9*

Music to hear, why hear'st thou music sadly?
Sweets with sweet war not, joy delights in joy.   *Sonnet 8, l. 1*

        Everything that grows
Holds in perfection but a little moment.   *Sonnet 15, l. 1*

Shall I compare thee to a summer's day?
Thou art more lovely and more temperate:
Rough winds do shake the darling buds of May,
And summer's lease hath all too short a date.   *Sonnet 18, l. 1*

But thy eternal summer shall not fade.
                                   l. 9

The painful warrior famoused for fight,
After a thousand victories, once foil'd,
Is from the books of honor razed quite,
And all the rest forgot for which he toil'd.   *Sonnet 25, l. 9*

When in disgrace with fortune and men's eyes
I all alone beweep my outcast state,
And trouble deaf heaven with my bootless cries.   *Sonnet 29, l. 1*

they bear strong evidence of all being written in 1588–1589. They were published [1609] by Thomas Thorpe, who wrote the dedication:

TO THE ONLIE BEGETTER OF
THESE INSUING SONNETS
MR. W. H., ALL HAPPINESSE
AND THAT ETERNITIE
PROMISED
BY
OUR EVER-LIVING POET
WISHETH
THE WELL-WISHING
ADVENTURER IN
SETTING
FORTH
T. T.

Desiring this man's art, and that man's scope,
With what I most enjoy contented least;
Yet in these thoughts myself almost despising,
Haply I think on thee.
Sonnet 29, l. 7

For thy sweet love remember'd such wealth brings
That then I scorn to change my state with kings. *l. 13*

When to the sessions of sweet silent thought
I summon up remembrance of things past,
I sigh the lack of many a thing I sought,
And with old woes new wail my dear times' waste. *Sonnet 30, l. 1*

But if the while I think on thee, dear friend,
All losses are restor'd and sorrows end. *l. 13*

Full many a glorious morning have I seen. *Sonnet 33, l. 1*

Roses have thorns, and silver fountains mud;
Clouds and eclipses stain both moon and sun,
And loathsome canker lives in sweetest bud.
All men make faults. *Sonnet 35, l. 2*

Be thou the tenth Muse. *Sonnet 38, l. 9*

For nimble thought can jump both sea and land. *Sonnet 44, l. 7*

Against that time when thou shalt strangely pass,
And scarcely greet me with that sun, thine eye,
When love, converted from the thing it was,
Shall reasons find of settled gravity. *Sonnet 49, l. 5*

Not marble, nor the gilded monuments

Of princes, shall outlive this powerful rime. *Sonnet 55, l. i.*

Like as the waves make towards the pebbled shore,
So do our minutes hasten to their end. *Sonnet 60, l. 1*

Time doth transfix the flourish set on youth
And delves the parallels in beauty's brow. *l. 9*

When I have seen by Time's fell hand defac'd
The rich-proud cost of outworn buried age. *Sonnet 64, l. 1*

When I have seen the hungry ocean gain
Advantage on the kingdom of the shore,
And the firm soil win of the watery main,
Increasing store with loss, and loss with store. *l. 5*

Tir'd with all these, for restful death I cry. *Sonnet 66, l. 1*

And art made tongue-tied by authority. *l. 9*

And simple truth miscall'd simplicity,
And captive good attending captain ill. *l. 11*

No longer mourn for me when I am dead
Than you shall hear the surly sullen bell
Give warning to the world that I am fled
From this vile world, with vilest worms to dwell. *Sonnet 71, l. 1*

That time of year thou mayst in me behold
When yellow leaves, or none, or few, do hang
Upon those boughs which shake against the cold,[1]
Bare ruin'd choirs, where late the sweet birds sang. *Sonnet 73, l. 1*

Clean starved for a look. *Sonnet 75, l. 10*

[1] See Byron, p. 563a.

Who is it that says most? which can say
   more
Than this rich praise — that you alone
   are you?   *Sonnet 84, l. 1*

Farewell! thou art too dear for my possessing,
And like enough thou know'st thy estimate.   *Sonnet 87, l. 1*

In sleep a king, but, waking, no such
   matter.   *l. 14*

Ah! do not, when my heart hath 'scap'd
   this sorrow,
Come in the rearward of a conquer'd
   woe;
Give not a windy night a rainy mor-
   row,
To linger out a purpos'd overthrow.
   Sonnet 90, l. 5

They that have power to hurt and will
   do none,
That do not do the thing they most do
   show,
Who, moving others, are themselves as
   stone,
Unmoved, cold, and to temptation
   slow.   *Sonnet 94, l. 1*

They are the lords and owners of their
   faces,
Others but stewards of their excellence.
The summer's flower is to the summer
   sweet,
Though to itself it only live and die.
   l. 7

Lilies that fester smell far worse than
   weeds.[1]   *l. 14*

The hardest knife ill-used doth lose his
   edge.   *Sonnet 95, l. 14*

How like a winter hath my absence
   been.   *Sonnet 97, l. 1*

From you have I been absent in the
   spring,

[1] As in the nature of things, those which most admirably flourish, most swiftly fester or putrefy, as roses, lilies, violets, while others last: so in the lives of men, those that are most blooming, are soonest turned into the opposite. — PLINY [A.D. 23–79], *Natural History, bk. XVI, ch. 15*

When proud-pied April, dress'd in all
   his trim,
Hath put a spirit of youth in everything.   *Sonnet 98, l. 1*

Sweets grown common lose their dear
   delight.   *Sonnet 102, l. 12*

To me, fair friend, you never can be
   old,
For as you were when first your eye I
   ey'd,
Such seems your beauty still.
   Sonnet 104, l. 1

When in the chronicle of wasted time
I see descriptions of the fairest wights,
And beauty making beautiful old rime,
In praise of ladies dead and lovely
   knights,
Then, in the blazon of sweet beauty's
   best,
Of hand, of foot, of lip, of eye, of
   brow,
I see their antique pen would have ex-
   press'd
Even such a beauty as you master
   now.   *Sonnet 106, l. 1*

Not mine own fears, nor the prophetic
   soul
Of the wide world dreaming on things
   to come,
Can yet the lease of my true love control,
Suppos'd as forfeit to a confin'd doom.
The mortal moon hath her eclipse en-
   dur'd,
And the sad augurs mock their own
   presage;
Incertainties now crown themselves assur'd,
And peace proclaims olives of endless
   age.   *Sonnet 107, l. 1*

O! never say that I was false of heart,
Though absence seem'd my flame to
   qualify.   *Sonnet 109, l. 1*

That is my home of love: if I have
   rang'd,
Like him that travels, I return again.
   l. 5

Alas! 'tis true I have gone here and
   there,

And made myself a motley to the view,
Gor'd mine own thoughts, sold cheap
what is most dear,
Made old offenses of affections new.
Sonnet 110, l. 1

My nature is subdu'd
To what it works in, like the dyer's
hand.   *Sonnet 111, l. 6*

Let me not to the marriage of true
minds
Admit impediments. Love is not love
Which alters when it alteration finds,
Or bends with the remover to remove:
O, no! it is an ever-fixed mark,
That looks on tempests and is never
shaken;
It is the star to every wandering bark,
Whose worth's unknown, although his
height be taken.
Love's not Time's fool, though rosy lips
and cheeks
Within his bending sickle's compass
come;
Love alters not with his brief hours and
weeks,
But bears it out even to the edge of
doom.
If this be error, and upon me prov'd,
I never writ, nor no man ever lov'd.
Sonnet 116

What potions have I drunk of Siren
tears,
Distill'd from limbecks foul as hell
within.   *Sonnet 119, l. 1*

O benefit of ill!   *l. 9*

And ruin'd love, when it is built anew,
Grows fairer than at first, more strong,
far greater.   *l. 11*

'Tis better to be vile than vile esteem'd,
When not to be receives reproach of
being.   *Sonnet 121, l. 1*

The expense of spirit in a waste of
shame
Is lust in action; and till action, lust
Is perjur'd, murderous, bloody, full of
blame,
Savage, extreme, rude, cruel, not to
trust;

Enjoy'd no sooner but despised
straight;
Past reason hunted; and no sooner
had,
Past reason hated, as a swallow'd bait,
On purpose laid to make the taker
mad:
Mad in pursuit, and in possession so;
Had, having, and in quest to have, ex-
treme;
A bliss in proof — and prov'd, a very
woe;
Before, a joy propos'd; behind, a
dream.
All this the world well knows; yet none
knows well
To shun the heaven that leads men to
this hell.   *Sonnet 129*

My mistress' eyes are nothing like the
sun;
Coral is far more red than her lips'
red:
If snow be white, why then her breasts
are dun;
If hairs be wires, black wires grow on
her head.   *Sonnet 130, l. 1*

When my love swears that she is made
of truth,
I do believe her, though I know she
lies.   *Sonnet 138, l. 1*

Two loves I have of comfort and despair,
Which like two spirits do suggest me
still.   *Sonnet 144, l. 1*

Poor soul, the center of my sinful
earth.   *Sonnet 146, l. 1*

So shalt thou feed on Death, that feeds
on men,
And Death once dead, there's no more
dying then.   *l. 13*

Past cure I am, now Reason is past
care,
And frantic-mad with evermore unrest.
Sonnet 147, l. 9

For I have sworn thee fair, and thought
thee bright,
Who art as black as hell, as dark as
night.   *l. 13*

You pay a great deal too dear for what's given freely.
The Winter's Tale [1610–1611],
act I, sc. i, l. 18

Two lads that thought there was no more behind
But such a day tomorrow as today,
And to be boy eternal.   I, ii, 63

We were as twinn'd lambs that did frisk i' the sun,
And bleat the one at the other: what we chang'd
Was innocence for innocence.
I, ii, 67

Paddling palms and pinching fingers.
I, ii, 116

Affection! thy intention stabs the center:
Thou dost make possible things not so held,
Communicat'st with dreams.
I, ii, 139

He makes a July's day short as December.   I, ii, 169

A sad tale's best for winter. I have one of sprites and goblins.
II, i, 24

The silence often of pure innocence
Persuades when speaking fails.
II, ii, 41

It is a heretic that makes the fire,
Not she which burns in 't.
II, iii, 115

I am a feather for each wind that blows.   II, iii, 153

What's gone and what's past help
Should be past grief.   III, ii, 223

Exit, pursued by a bear.[1]
III, iii, 57

This is fairy gold, boy, and 'twill prove so.   III, iii, 127

Then comes in the sweet o' the year.
IV, ii, 3

A snapper-up of unconsidered trifles.   IV, ii, 26

[1] This is perhaps the most famous stage direction in English.

For the life to come, I sleep out the thought of it.
The Winter's Tale IV, ii, 30

Jog on, jog on, the footpath way,
And merrily hent the stile-a:
A merry heart goes all the day,
Your sad tires in a mile-a.
IV, ii, 133

For you there's rosemary and rue; these keep
Seeming and savor all the winter long.   IV, iii, 74

Daffodils,
That come before the swallow dares, and take
The winds of March with beauty.
IV, iii, 118

What you do
Still betters what is done.
IV, iii, 135

When you do dance, I wish you
A wave o' the sea, that you might ever do
Nothing but that.   IV, iii, 140

Lawn as white as driven snow.
IV, iii, 220

I love a ballad in print, a-life, for then we are sure they are true.
IV, iii, 262

The self-same sun that shines upon his court
Hides not his visage from our cottage, but
Looks on alike.   IV, iii, 457

I'll queen it no inch further,
But milk my ewes and weep.
IV, iii, 462

Prosperity's the very bond of love,
Whose fresh complexion and whose heart together
Affliction alters.   IV, iii, 586

Let me have no lying; it becomes none but tradesmen.   IV, iii, 747

To purge melancholy.
IV, iii, 792

There's time enough for that.
V, iii, 128

He hath no drowning mark upon him; his complexion is perfect gallows.
The Tempest [1611–1612], act I, sc. i, l. 33

Now would I give a thousand furlongs of sea for an acre of barren ground.   I, i, 70

I would fain die a dry death.
I, i, 73

What seest thou else
In the dark backward and abysm of time?   I, ii, 49

By telling of it,
Made such a sinner of his memory,
To credit his own lie.   I, ii, 100

Your tale, sir, would cure deafness.
I, ii, 106

My library
Was dukedom large enough.
I, ii, 109

The very rats
Instinctively have quit it.   I, ii, 147

Knowing I lov'd my books, he furnish'd me,
From mine own library with volumes that
I prize above my dukedom.
I, ii, 166

From the still-vexed Bermoothes.
I, ii, 229

I will be correspondent to command,
And do my spiriting gently.
I, ii, 297

You taught me language; and my profit on 't
Is, I know how to curse: the red plague rid you,
For learning me your language!
I, ii, 363

Come unto these yellow sands,
And then take hands:
Curtsied when you have, and kiss'd —
The wild waves whist —
Foot it featly here and there.
I, ii, 375

This music crept by me upon the waters,

Allaying both their fury, and my passion,
With its sweet air.
The Tempest I, ii, 389

Full fathom five thy father lies;
Of his bones are coral made:
Those are pearls that were his eyes:
Nothing of him that doth fade,
But doth suffer a sea-change
Into something rich and strange.[1]
I, ii, 394

The fringed curtains of thine eye advance.   I, ii, 405

Lest too light winning
Make the prize light.   I, ii, 448

There's nothing ill can dwell in such a temple:
If the ill spirit have so fair a house,
Good things will strive to dwell with 't.
I, ii, 454

He receives comfort like cold porridge.[2]   II, i, 10

I' the commonwealth I would by contraries
Execute all things; for no kind of traffic
Would I admit; no name of magistrate;
Letters should not be known; riches, poverty,
And use of service, none; contract, succession,
Bourn, bound of land, tilth, vineyard, none;
No use of metal, corn, or wine, or oil;
No occupation; all men idle, all;
And women too, but innocent and pure.[3]   II, i, 154

[1] The last three lines are inscribed on Shelley's gravestone.
[2] See *King John,* V, vii, 41, p. 237b, and William Bradford, p. 319a.
[3] It is a nation, would I answer Plato, that hath no kinde of traffike, no knowledge of Letters, no intelligence of numbers, no name of magistrate, nor of politike superioritie; no use of service, of riches or povertie; no contracts, no successions, no partitions, no occupation but idle; no respect of kindred, but common, no apparel but naturall, no manuring of lands, no use of wine, corne, or mettle. — MONTAIGNE, *Essays, bk. I* [1580], *ch. 30, Of the Canniballes*

What's past is prologue.
>*The Tempest* II, i, 261

Open-eyed Conspiracy
His time doth take.   II, i, 309

A very ancient and fish-like smell.
>II, ii, 27

Misery acquaints a man with strange
bedfellows.   II, ii, 42

I shall laugh myself to death.
>II, ii, 167

'Ban, 'Ban, Ca — Caliban,
Has a new master — Get a new man.
>II, ii, 197

>For several virtues
Have I lik'd several women.
>III, i, 42

Ferdinand: . . . Here's my hand.
Miranda: And mine, with my heart
in't.   III, i, 89

Moon-calf.   III, ii, 25

Thou deboshed fish thou.
>III, ii, 30

Keep a good tongue in your head.
>III, ii, 41

Flout 'em, and scout 'em; and scout
'em, and flout 'em;
Thought is free.[1]   III, ii, 133

He that dies pays all debts.
>III, ii, 143

>The isle is full of noises,
Sounds and sweet airs, that give de-
light, and hurt not.
Sometimes a thousand twangling in-
struments
Will hum about mine ears; and some-
times voices,
That, if I then had wak'd after long
sleep,
Will make me sleep again.
>III, ii, 146

>A kind
Of excellent dumb discourse.
>III, iii, 38

>Do not give dalliance
Too much the rein.   IV, i, 51

[1] Thought is free. — *Twelfth-Night* I, iii, 73

Our revels now are ended. These our
actors,
As I foretold you, were all spirits and
Are melted into air, into thin air;
And, like the baseless fabric of this vi-
sion,
The cloud-capp'd towers, the gorgeous
palaces,
The solemn temples, the great globe it-
self,
Yea, all which it inherit, shall dissolve;
And, like this insubstantial pageant
faded,
Leave not a rack behind. We are such
stuff
As dreams are made on, and our little
life
Is rounded with a sleep.
>*The Tempest* IV, i, 148

With foreheads villainous low.
>IV, i, 252

>I'll break my staff,
Bury it certain fathoms in the earth,
And, deeper than did ever plummet
sound,
I'll drown my book.   V, i, 54

Where the bee sucks, there suck I
In a cowslip's bell I lie;
There I couch when owls do cry.
On the bat's back I do fly
After summer merrily:
Merrily, merrily shall I live now
Under the blossom that hangs on the
bough.   V, i, 88

>O brave new world,
That has such people in't!
>V, i, 183

Let us not burden our remembrances
With a heaviness that's gone.
>V, i, 199

My ending is despair.
>*Epilogue, l.* 15

>No man's pie is freed
From his ambitious finger.
>*King Henry VIII* [1] [1613], *act* I,
>*sc.* i, *l.* 52

The force of his own merit makes his
way.   I, i, 64

[1] Written by Shakespeare and Fletcher.

Heat not a furnace for your foe so hot
That it do singe yourself.
        Henry VIII, I, i, 140

If I chance to talk a little wild, forgive
me;
I had it from my father.   *I, iv, 26*

The mirror of all courtesy.   *II, i, 53*

Go with me, like good angels, to my
end;
And, as the long divorce of steel falls on
me,
Make of your prayers one sweet sacrifice,
And lift my soul to heaven.   *II, i, 75*

This bold bad man.   *II, ii, 44*

        'Tis better to be lowly born,
And range with humble livers in con-
tent,
Than to be perk'd up in a glist'ring
grief
And wear a golden sorrow.
        II, iii, 19

        I would not be a queen
For all the world.   *II, iii, 45*

Orpheus with his lute made trees,
And the mountain-tops that freeze,
Bow themselves when he did sing.
        III, i, 3

Heaven is above all yet; there sits a
judge
That no king can corrupt.   *III, i, 99*

        'Tis well said again;
And 'tis a kind of good deed to say
well:
And yet words are no deeds.
        III, ii, 153

        And then to breakfast with
What appetite you have.   *III, ii, 203*

I have touch'd the highest point of all
my greatness;
And from that full meridian of my
glory,
I haste now to my setting: I shall fall
Like a bright exhalation in the eve-
ning,
And no man see me more.
        III, ii, 224

Press not a falling man too far.[1]
        Henry VIII, III, ii, 334

Farewell! a long farewell, to all my
greatness!
This is the state of man: today he puts
forth
The tender leaves of hopes; tomorrow
blossoms,
And bears his blushing honors thick
upon him;
The third day comes a frost, a killing
frost;
And, when he thinks, good easy man,
full surely
His greatness is a-ripening, nips his
root,
And then he falls, as I do. I have ven-
tur'd,
Like little wanton boys that swim on
bladders,
This many summers in a sea of glory,
But far beyond my depth: my high-
blown pride
At length broke under me, and now has
left me,
Weary and old with service, to the
mercy
Of a rude stream, that must forever
hide me.
Vain pomp and glory of this world, I
hate ye:
I feel my heart new open'd. O! how
wretched
Is that poor man that hangs on princes'
favors!
There is, betwixt that smile we would
aspire to,
That sweet aspect of princes, and their
ruin,
More pangs and fears than wars or
women have;
And when he falls, he falls like Luci-
fer,
Never to hope again.   *III, ii, 352*

A peace above all earthly dignities,
A still and quiet conscience.
        III, ii, 380

A load would sink a navy.   *III, ii, 384*

[1]   'Tis a cruelty
To load a falling man.
        Henry VIII, V, iii, 76

298

And sleep in dull cold marble.
Henry VIII, III, ii, 434

Cromwell, I charge thee, fling away
ambition:
By that sin fell the angels.
III, ii, 441

Love thyself last: cherish those hearts
that hate thee;
Corruption wins not more than hon-
esty.
Still in thy right hand carry gentle
peace,
To silence envious tongues: be just, and
fear not.
Let all the ends thou aim'st at be thy
country's,
Thy God's, and truth's; then if thou
fall'st, O Cromwell!
Thou fall'st a blessed martyr!
III, ii, 444

Had I but serv'd my God with half the
zeal [1]
I serv'd my king, he would not in mine
age
Have left me naked to mine enemies.
III, ii, 456

An old man, broken with the storms of
state,
Is come to lay his weary bones among
ye;
Give him a little earth for charity.
IV, ii, 21

He gave his honors to the world again,
His blessed part to heaven, and slept in
peace.   *IV, ii, 29*

So may he rest; his faults lie gently on
him!   *IV, ii, 31*

     He was a man
Of an unbounded stomach.
IV, ii, 33

Men's evil manners live in brass; their
virtues
We write in water.[2]   *IV, ii, 45*

[1] Had I served God as well in every part
  As I did serve my king and master still,
  My scope had not this season been so short,
  Nor would have had the power to do me ill.
    THOMAS CHURCHYARD, *Death of Morton*
                                    [1593]

[2] See Sophocles, p. 83a; Sir Thomas More,
p. 178b; Bacon, p. 210a; and Keats, p. 586a.

He was a scholar, and a ripe and good
one;
Exceeding wise, fair-spoken, and persuading;
Lofty and sour to them that lov'd him
not;
But, to those men that sought him
sweet as summer.
Henry VIII, IV, ii, 51

To dance attendance on their lordships'
pleasures.   *V, ii, 30*

Nor shall this peace sleep with her; but
as when
The bird of wonder dies, the maiden
phoenix,
Her ashes new-create another heir
As great in admiration as herself.
V, v, 40

Wherever the bright sun of heaven
shall shine,
His honor and the greatness of his
name
Shall be, and make new nations.
V, v, 51

     Some come to take their ease
And sleep an act or two.
Epilogue, l. 2

Good friend, for Jesus' sake forbear
To dig the dust enclosed here;
Blest be the man that spares these
stones,
And curst be he that moves my bones.
Shakespeare's epitaph

JOHN DAVIES
OF HEREFORD
c. 1565 – 1618

Beauty's but skin deep.[1]
*A Select Second Husband for
Sir Thomas Overburie's Wife
[1616], VI*

[1] All the beauty of the world, 'tis but skin
deep. — RALPH VENNING, *Orthodox Paradoxes*
[3d ed., 1650], *The Triumph of Assurance*, p. 41
  Many a dangerous temptation comes to us
in fine gay colors that are but skin-deep. —
MATHEW HENRY [1662–1714], *Commentaries,
Genesis, III*

THOMAS CAMPION
1567–1620

My sweetest Lesbia let us live and
  love,
And though the sager sort our deeds
  reprove,
Let us not weigh them. Heaven's great
  lamps do dive
Into their west, and straight again revive,
But soon as once set is our little light,
Then must we sleep one ever-during
  night.[1]
> *From* ROSSETER'S *A Book of Airs*
> [1601]. *My Sweetest Lesbia,*
> *st. 1*

Never love unless you can
Bear with all the faults of man.
> *Never Love* [c. 1617], *st. 1*

There is a garden in her face
  Where roses and white lilies grow;
A heavenly paradise is that place
  Wherein all pleasant fruits do flow.
There cherries grow which none may
  buy,
Till "cherry-ripe" themselves do cry.
> *Cherry-Ripe* [2] [c. 1617], *st. 1*

Those cherries fairly do enclose
Of orient pearl a double row,[3]
Which when her lovely laughter
  shows,
  They look like rosebuds fill'd with
    snow.   *Ib. st. 2*

The summer hath his joys,
  And winter his delights;
Though love and all his pleasures are
  but toys,
  They shorten tedious nights.
> *Winter Nights* [c. 1617], *st. 2*

THOMAS NASHE
1567–1601

Spring, the sweet spring, is the year's
  pleasant king;

Then blooms each thing, then maids
  dance in a ring,
Cold doth not sting, the pretty birds do
  sing.
Cuckoo, jug-jug, pu-we, to-witta-woo!
> *Summer's Last Will and Testa-*
> *ment* [1600]. *Spring, st. 1*

From winter, plague and pestilence,
  good Lord, deliver us!
> *Ib. Autumn, refrain*

Brightness falls from the air;
Queens have died young and fair;
Dust hath closed Helen's eye.
I am sick, I must die.
  Lord, have mercy on us!
> *Ib. Adieu! Farewell Earth's Bliss!*

SIR HENRY WOTTON
1568–1639

Love lodged in a woman's breast
Is but a guest.
> *A Woman's Heart* [1651]

How happy is he born and taught,
  That serveth not another's will;
Whose armour is his honest thought,
  And simple truth his utmost skill!
> *The Character of a Happy Life*
> [1614], *st. 1*

Who God doth late and early pray,
  More of his grace than gifts to send,
And entertains the harmless day
  With a well-chosen book or friend.
> *Ib. st. 5*

Lord of himself, though not of lands;
And having nothing, yet hath all.[1]
> *Ib. st. 6*

You meaner beauties of the night,
  That poorly satisfy our eyes
More by your number than your light;
  You common people of the skies,
  What are you when the sun shall
    rise?
> *On His Mistress, the Queen of*
> *Bohemia,* [2] *st. 1*

---

[1] See Catullus, p. 114b, and note.
[2] "Cherry-ripe" was a familiar street cry of
the time.
  See Herrick, p. 320a.
[3] See Herrick, p. 320a.

[1] See *II Corinthians 6:10,* p. 53b, and Terence, p. 109a.
[2] This was printed with music as early as 1624,
in East's *Sixth Set of Books,* and is found
in many manuscripts.

He first deceased; she for a little tried
To live without him, liked it not, and
died.
*Upon the Death of Sir Albert
Morton's Wife* [1651]

Hanging was the worst use a man
could be put to.
*The Disparity Between Buck-
ingham and Essex* [1651]

An ambassador is an honest man sent
to lie abroad for the commonwealth.[1]
Reliquiae Wottonianae [1651]

The itch of disputing will prove the
scab of churches.[2]
A Panegyric to King Charles [1651]

SIR JOHN DAVIES
1569–1626

What can we know? or what can we
discern,
When error chokes the windows of the
mind?
Nosce Teipsum [1599], *st. 15*

I know my soul hath power to know all
things,
Yet is she blind and ignorant in all:
I know I'm one of Nature's little
kings,
Yet to the least and vilest things am
thrall.   *Ib. st. 44*

I know my life's a pain, and but a
span;[3]
I know my sense is mock'd in ev'ry
thing:
And to conclude, I know myself a
man,
Which is a proud, and yet a wretched
thing.   *Ib. st. 45*

[1] In a letter to Velserus [1612] Wotton says
that this "merry definition of an ambassador
. . . I had chanced to set down at my friend's,
Mr. Christopher Fleckmore, in his Album."
[2] He directed that the stone over his grave be
inscribed: Hic jacet hujus sententiae primus auc-
tor: DISPUTANDI PRURITUS ECCLESIARUM SCABIES.
Nomen alias quaere [Here lies the author of this
phrase: "The itch for disputing is the sore of
churches." Seek his name elsewhere]. — IZAAK
WALTON, *Life of Wotton* [1651]
[3] See Bacon, p. 210a, and note.

THOMAS HEYWOOD
c. 1570 – 1641

Within the red-leaved table of my
heart.
A Woman Killed with Kindness
[1607], *act II, sc. 3*

I will walk on eggs.   *Ib. IV, 6*

O God! O God! that it were possible
To undo things done; to call back yesterday![1]
That Time could turn up his swift
sandy glass,
To untell the days, and to redeem these
hours.   *Ib.*

Pack clouds away, and welcome day,
With night we banish sorrow.
Pack Clouds Away [1630], *st. 1*

I hold he loves me best that calls me
Tom.
Hierarchie of the Blessed Angels
[1635]

Seven cities warred for Homer being
dead,
Who living had no roof to shroud his
head.[2]   *Ib.*

THOMAS DEKKER
1572–1632

This age thinks better of a gilded fool
Than of a threadbare saint in wisdom's
school.   *Old Fortunatus* [1600]

Honest labor bears a lovely face.
Patient Grissell [1603], *act I, sc. 1*

The best of men
That e'er wore earth about him, was a
sufferer,
A soft, meek, patient, humble, tranquil spirit,

[1] See Shakespeare, p. 227a.
[2] Seven cities strive for the learned root of
Homer:
Smyrna, Chios, Colophon, Ithaca, Pylos,
Argos, Athens.
UNKNOWN (*Greek Anthology, bk. VI,
epigram 298*)
Seven wealthy towns contend for Homer dead,
Through which the living Homer begged his
bread.
THOMAS SEWARD [1708–1790], *On Homer*

The first true gentleman that ever breathed.

> *The Honest Whore, pt. I [1604] (in collaboration with* THOMAS MIDDLETON), *act I, sc. 2*

We are ne'er like angels till our passion dies. *Ib. pt. II [1630], I, 2*

Cast away care, he that loves sorrow
Lengthens not a day, nor can buy to-morrow;
Money is trash, and he that will spend it,
Let him drink merrily, fortune will send it.

> *The Sun's Darling [1656] (in collaboration with* JOHN FORD)

BEN JONSON[1]
1572–1637

As sure as death.

> *Every Man in his Humour [1598], act II, sc. 1*

As he brews, so shall he drink. *Ib.*

It must be done like lightning.

> *Ib. IV, 5*

Art hath an enemy called Ignorance.

> *Every Man Out of His Humour [1599], act I, sc. 1*

There shall be no love lost. *Ib. II, 1*

True happiness
Consists not in the multitude of friends,
But in the worth and choice.

> *Cynthia's Revels [1600], act III, sc. 2*

Queen and huntress, chaste and fair,
Now the sun is laid to sleep,
Seated in thy silver chair,
State in wonted manner keep:
    Hesperus entreats thy light,
    Goddess, excellently bright.

> *Ib. V, 3*

[1] O rare Ben Jonson! — SIR JOHN YOUNG, *Epitaph.* (Which was done at the charge of Jack Young, who, walking there when the grave was covering, gave the fellow 18 pence to cut it. — JOHN AUBREY [1626–1697], *Brief Lives*)

That old bald cheater, Time.

> *The Poetaster [1601], act I, sc. 1*

Farewell, thou child of my right hand, and joy!
My sin was too much hope of thee, lov'd boy.

> *On My First Son [written c. 1603]; in Epigrams [1616]*

Rest in soft peace, and, ask'd, say here doth lie
Ben Jonson his best piece of poetry:
For whose sake, henceforth, all his vows be such,
As what he loves may never like too much. *Ib.*

Of all wild beasts preserve me from a tyrant; and of all tame, a flatterer.

> *Sejanus [1603], act I*

Calumnies are answered best with silence.

> *Volpone [1606], act II, sc. 2*

Come my Celia, let us prove,
While we can, the sports of love;
Time will not be ours forever,
He at length our good will sever.
Spend not then his gifts in vain;
Suns that set may rise again,
But if once we lose this light,
'Tis with us perpetual night.[1]

> *Song, To Celia [1607]*

Still to be neat, still to be drest,
As you were going to a feast.

> *Epicene; or, The Silent Woman [1609], act I, sc. 1*

Give me a look, give me a face,
That makes simplicity a grace;
Robes loosely flowing, hair as free,
Such sweet neglect more taketh me
Than all the adulteries of art:
They strike mine eyes, but not my heart.[2] *Ib.*

The dignity of truth is lost with much protesting.

> *Catiline's Conspiracy [1611], act III, sc. 2*

[1] See Catullus, p. 114b, and note.
[2] See Herrick, p. 320a.

Truth is the trial of itself
  And needs no other touch,
And purer than the purest gold,
  Refine it ne'er so much.
             On Truth [1616], *st. 1*

Preserving the sweetness of proportion and expressing itself beyond expression.
      The Masque of Hymen [1616]

Underneath this stone doth lie
As much beauty as could die;
Which in life did harbor give
To more virtue than doth live.
      Epitaph on Elizabeth, Lady
      H——, Epigrams [1616]

Follow a shadow, it still flies you;
  Seem to fly it, it will pursue:
So court a mistress, she denies you;
  Let her alone, she will court you.
      The Forest [1616]. *Follow a*
             Shadow, st. 1

Whilst that for which all virtue now is
  sold,
And almost every vice — almighty
  gold.[1]
      Ib. Epistle to Elizabeth,
        Countess of Rutland

God wisheth none should wreck on a
  strange shelf:
To him man's dearer than to himself.
      Ib. To Sir Robert Wroth

Drink to me only with thine eyes,
  And I will pledge with mine;
Or leave a kiss but in the cup
  And I'll not look for wine.[2]
The thirst that from the soul doth rise
  Doth ask a drink divine;
But might I of Jove's nectar sup,
  I would not change for thine.
      Ib. To Celia, st. 1

I sent thee late a rosy wreath,
  Not so much honoring thee
As giving it a hope that there

It could not wither'd be.
But thou thereon didst only breathe,
  And sent'st it back to me;
Since when it grows and smells, I
  swear,
Not of itself, but thee.
      The Forest. To Celia, st. 2

Reader, look,
Not at his picture, but his book.
      On the portrait of Shakespeare
      prefixed to the First Folio
      [1623]

Soul of the age!
The applause, delight, the wonder of
  our stage!
My Shakespeare, rise; I will not lodge
  thee by
Chaucer or Spenser, or bid Beaumont
  lie
A little further, to make thee a room;
Thou art a monument, without a
  tomb,
And art alive still, while thy book doth
  live,
And we have wits to read, and praise to
  give.[1]
      To the Memory of My Beloved,
      the Author, Mr. William Shake-
      speare [1623]

Marlowe's mighty line.   *Ib.*

And though thou hadst small Latin and
  less Greek.   *Ib.*

Call forth thundering Aeschylus.   *Ib.*

He was not of an age but for all time.[2]
                  Ib.

Who casts to write a living line, must
  sweat.   *Ib.*

For a good poet's made, as well as
  born.[3]   *Ib.*

Sweet Swan of Avon!   *Ib.*

Those that merely talk and never
  think,

---

[1] The flattering, mighty, nay, almighty gold.
— WOLCOT, *To Kien Long* [1782–1785], *ode IV*
  See Irving, p. 550b.
[2] Drink to me with your eyes alone. . . . And if you will, take the cup to your lips and fill it with kisses, and give it so to me. — PHILOSTRATUS [C. A.D. 181–250], *letter 24*

[1] See William Basse, p. 319b.
[2] See Robert Whittinton, p. 179a.
[3] See Florus, p. 109b.

That live in the wild anarchy of drink.[1]
Underwoods [1640]. *An Epistle,*
answering to One that asked to
be sealed of the Tribe of Ben

In small proportions we just beauties
see,
And in short measures life may perfect
be.
> *Ib. To the Immortal Memory of*
> *Sir Lucius Cary and Sir Henry*
> *Morison*

The players have often mentioned it
as an honor to Shakespeare that in his
writing (whatsoever he penned) he
never blotted out a line. My answer
hath been, "Would he had blotted a
thousand."
> *Timber; or, Discoveries Made*
> *Upon Men and Matter* [1640]

I loved the man [Shakespeare] and
do honor his memory, on this side idolatry, as much as any.   *Ib.*

Greatness of name in the father oft-
times overwhelms the son; they stand
too near one another. The shadow kills
the growth: so much, that we see the
grandchild come more and oftener to
be heir of the first.   *Ib.*

Though the most be players, some
must be spectators.   *Ib.*

Talking and eloquence are not the
same: to speak, and to speak well, are
two things. A fool may talk, but a wise
man speaks.   *Ib.*

JOHN DONNE[2]
1572–1631

I wonder by my troth, what thou,
and I
Did, till we lov'd? were we not wean'd
till then?
But suck'd on country pleasures, child-
ishly?

---

[1] See Dryden, p. 368b.
> They never taste who always drink;
> They always talk who never think.
> MATTHEW PRIOR [1664–1721], *Upon a*
> *Passage in the Scaligerana*

[2] See Izaak Walton, p. 325b, and Carew, p.
326b.

Or snorted we in the seven sleepers'
den?
> *The Good Morrow, st.* 1 [1]

And now good morrow to our waking
souls,
Which watch not one another out of
fear;
For love, all love of other sights controls,
And makes one little room, an everywhere.
Let sea-discoverers to new worlds have
gone,
Let maps to other, worlds on worlds
have shown,
Let us possess one world, each hath
one, and is one.   *Ib. st.* 2

My face in thine eye, thine in mine
appears,
And true plain hearts do in the faces
rest,
Where can we find two better hemi-
spheres
Without sharp North, without declin-
ing West?   *Ib. st.* 3

Go, and catch a falling star,
  Get with child a mandrake root,
Tell me, where all past years are,
  Or who cleft the Devil's foot.
Teach me to hear mermaids singing.[2]
          Song, st. 1

  And swear
  No where
Lives a woman true, and fair.
          Ib. st. 2

Though she were true, when you met
her,
And last, till you write your letter,
  Yet she
  Will be
False, ere I come, to two, or three.
          Ib. st. 3

---

[1] Quotations through *Farewell to Love* (p.
307a) are from *Songs and Sonnets*, composed
c. 1590–1601, published posthumously.
The *Songs and Sonnets* were written by
Donne before the turn of the century, according
to Ben Jonson "ere he was twenty-five years
old," but there is no evidence to show the exact
date of their composition. — JOHN HAYWARD,
John Donne, Complete Poetry and Selected Prose
[1936]

[2] See T. S. Eliot, p. 1001a.

I have done one braver thing
  Than all the Worthies did;
And yet a braver thence doth spring,
  Which is, to keep that hid.
            The Undertaking, st. 1

But he who loveliness within
  Hath found, all outward loathes,
For he who color loves, and skin,
  Loves but their oldest clothes.
            Ib. st. 4

And dare love that, and say so too,
And forget the He and She. *Ib. st.* 5

    Busy old fool, unruly Sun,
    Why dost thou thus,
Through windows, and through curtains call on us?
Must to thy motions lovers' seasons
  run?   *The Sun Rising, st.* 1

Love, all alike, no season knows, nor
  clime,
Nor hours, days, months, which are the
  rags of time.   *Ib.*

She is all states, and all princes, I,
Nothing else is.   *Ib. st.* 3

For God sake hold your tongue, and let
  me love.
            The Canonization, st. 1

The Phoenix riddle hath more wit
By us, we two being one, are it.
So to one neutral thing both sexes fit,
We die and rise the same, and prove
Mysterious by this love.   *Ib. st.* 3

As well a well-wrought urn becomes
The greatest ashes, as half-acre tombs.
            Ib. st. 4

I am two fools, I know,
For loving, and for saying so
In whining poetry.
            The Triple Fool, st. 1

Who are a little wise, the best fools
  be.   *Ib. st.* 2

Sweetest love, I do not go,
  For weariness of thee,
Nor in hope the world can show
  A fitter love for me;
    But since that I

Must die at last, 'tis best,
To use my self in jest
  Thus by feign'd deaths to die.
            Song, st. 1

Yesternight the sun went hence,
And yet is here today.   *Ib. st.* 2

But think that we
Are but turn'd aside to sleep.
            Ib. st. 5

When I died last, and dear, I die
As often as from thee I go.
            The Legacy, st. 1

Oh do not die, for I shall hate
All women so, when thou art gone.
            The Fever, st. 1

Twice or thrice had I loved thee,
Before I knew thy face or name.
            Air and Angels, st. 1

'Tis true, 'tis day; what though it be?
O wilt thou therefore rise from me?
Why should we rise, because 'tis light?
Did we lie down, because 'twas night?
Love which in spite of darkness brought
  us hether
Should in despite of light keep us to-
  gether.
            Break of Day, st. 1

All Kings, and all their favorites,
All glory of honors, beauties, wits,
The sun itself, which makes times, as
  they pass,
Is elder by a year, now, than it was
When thou and I first one another
  saw:
All other things, to their destruction
  draw,
Only our love hath no decay;
This, no tomorrow hath, nor yester-
  day,
Running, it never runs from us away,
But truly keeps his first, last, everlasting
  day.
            The Anniversary, st. 1

Send home my long strayed eyes to
  me,
Which (Oh) too long have dwelt on
  thee.   *The Message, st.* 1

'Tis the year's midnight, and it is the day's.

> A *Nocturnal Upon St. Lucy's Day, being the shortest day,* st. 1

The world's whole sap is sunk:
The general balm th' hydroptic earth
  hath drunk,
Whither, as to the bed's-feet, life is
  shrunk,
Dead and enterr'd; yet all these seem to
  laugh,
Compared with me, who am their epitaph.   *Ib.*

For I am every dead thing,
In whom love wrought new alchemy.
For his art did express
A quintessence even from nothingness,
From dull privations, and lean empti-
  ness
He ruin'd me, and I am re-begot
Of absence, darkness, death; things
  which are not.   *Ib. st. 2*

Come live with me, and be my love,
And we will some new pleasures prove
Of golden sands, and crystal brooks,
With silken lines, and silver hooks.

> The Bait,[1] st. 1

Dull sublunary lovers' love
  (Whose soul is sense) cannot admit
Absence, because it doth remove
  Those things which elemented it.

> A *Valediction Forbidding Mourning,* st. 4

Our two souls therefore which are one,[2]
  Though I must go, endure not yet
A breach, but an expansion,
  Like gold to airy thinness beat.

> *Ib. st. 6*

If they be two, they are two so
  As stiff twin compasses are two,
Thy soul the fixt foot, makes no show
To move, but doth, if the other do.

> *Ib. st. 7*

[1] Included by Izaak Walton in *The Compleat Angler* [1653], *ch. 9,* as "made by Dr. Donne, and made to shew the world that he could make soft verses, when he thought them fit and worth his labor."
  See Marlowe, p. 212a, and Ralegh, p. 198b.
[2] See Aristotle, p. 97a.

Our eye-beams twisted, and did thread
  Our eyes, upon one double string;
So to entergraft our hands, as yet
  Was all the means to make us one,
And pictures in our eyes to get
  Was all our propagation.

> *The Extasy, l.* 7

That subtle knot, which makes us
  man.   *Ib. l. 64*

Else a great Prince in prison lies.
> *Ib. l. 68*

Love's mysteries in souls do grow,
  But yet the body is his book.
> *Ib. l. 71*

I long to talk with some old lover's
  ghost,
Who died before the god of love was
  born.   *Love's Deity, st. 1*

To rage, to lust, to write to, to commend,
All is the purlieu of the god of love.
> *Ib. st. 3*

Who ever comes to shroud me, do not
  harm
    Nor question much
That subtle wreath of hair, which
  crowns my arm;
The mystery, the sign you must not
  touch,
    For 'tis my outward soul,
Viceroy to that, which then to heaven
  being gone,
    Will leave this to control,
And keep these limbs, her provinces,
  from dissolution.
> *The Funeral, st. 1*

A bracelet of bright hair about the
  bone.   *The Relic, st. 1*

Take heed of loving me.
> *The Prohibition, st. 1*

So, so, break off this last lamenting
  kiss,
Which sucks two souls, and vapors
  both away.
> *The Expiration, st. 1*

    Ah cannot we
As well as cocks and lions jocund be,

After such pleasures? [1]
> *Farewell to Love, st. 3*

Love built on beauty, soon as beauty,
dies.
> *Elegy II, The Anagram, l. 27*

Nature's lay idiot, I taught thee to
love.
> *Elegy VII, Nature's Lay
> Idiot, l. 1*

The Alphabet
Of flowers.   *Ib. l. 9*

She, and comparisons are odious.[2]
> *Elegy VIII, The Comparison,
> l. 54*

Sir, more than kisses, letters mingle
souls;
For, thus friends absent speak.
> *Verse Letter to Sir Henry
> Wotton, l. 1*

John Donne, Anne Donne, Un-done.
> *Letter to His Wife* [1602]

No spring, nor summer beauty hath
such grace,
As I have seen in one autumnal face.
> *Elegy IX, The Autumnal, l. 1*

The heavens rejoice in motion, why
should I
Abjure my so much lov'd variety.
> *Elegy XVII, Variety, l. 1*

Who ever loves, if he do not propose
The right true end of love, he's one
that goes
To sea for nothing but to make him
sick.
> *Elegy XVIII, Love's
> Progress, l. 1*

The Sestos and Abydos of her breasts
Not of two lovers, but two loves the
nests.   *Ib. l. 61*

Those set our hairs, but these our flesh
upright.
> *Elegy XIX, To His Mistress
> Going to Bed, l. 24*

O my America! my new-found land.
> *Ib. l. 27*

Full nakedness! All joys are due to
thee,

[1] See Gogarty, p. 945a.
[2] See Fortescue, p. 171a.

As souls unbodied, bodies unclothed
must be,
To taste whole joys.
> *Elegy XIX, To His Mistress
> Going to Bed l. 33*

And new philosophy calls all in doubt,
The element of fire is quite put out;
The sun is lost, and the earth, and no
man's wit
Can well direct him where to look for
it.
And freely men confess that this
world's spent,
When in the planets, and the firma-
ment
They seek so many new; then see that
this
Is crumbled out again to his atomies.
'Tis all in pieces, all coherence gone;
All just supply, and all relation:
Prince, subject, Father, Son, are things
forgot.
> *An Anatomy of the World. The
> First Anniversary of the Death of
> Mistress Elizabeth Drury* [1611],
> *l. 205*

Her pure, and eloquent blood
Spoke in her cheeks, and so distinctly
wrought,
That one might almost say, her body
thought.
> *The Progress of the Soul. The
> Second Anniversary of the
> Death of Mistress Elizabeth
> Drury* [1612], *l. 244*

I am a little world made cunningly
Of elements, and an angelic sprite.
> *Holy Sonnets* [written after
> 1610], V, *l. 1*

At the round earth's imagin'd corners,
blow
Your trumpets, angels, and arise, arise
From death, you numberless infinities
Of souls.   *Ib. VII, l. 1*

All whom war, dearth, age, agues,
tyrannies,
Despair, law, chance, hath slain.
> *Ib. l. 6*

If poisonous minerals, and if that tree,

Whose fruit threw death on else immortal us,
If lecherous goats, if serpents envious
Cannot be damn'd; alas; why should I
be?   *Holy Sonnets IX, l. 1*

Death be not proud, though some have
called thee
Mighty and dreadful, for thou art not
so,
For those whom thou think'st thou
dost overthrow,
Die not, poor death, nor yet canst thou
kill me.   *Ib. X, l. 1*

Thou art slave to fate, chance, kings,
and desperate men.   *Ib. l. 9*

One short sleep past, we wake eternally,
And death shall be no more; death,
thou shalt die.   *Ib. l. 13*

What if this present were the world's
last night?   *Ib. XIII, l. 1*

Batter my heart, three-person'd God;
for you
As yet but knock, breathe, shine, and
seek to mend.   *Ib. XIV, l. 1*

Show me, dear Christ, Thy spouse, so
bright and clear.
          Ib. XVIII, l. 1

Since I am coming to that holy room,
Where, with thy choir of saints forever-
more,
I shall be made thy music; as I come
I tune the instrument here at the door,
And what I must do then, think here
before.
          *Hymn to God My God, in My
          Sickness [written after 1610],
          st. 1*

Whilst my physicians by their love are
grown
Cosmographers, and I their map, who
lie
Flat on this bed.   *Ib. st. 2*

I observe the physician with the same
diligence as he the disease.
          Devotions [written 1623], VI

I do nothing upon myself, and yet
am mine own executioner.
          Devotions XII

The flea, though he kill none, he
does all the harm he can.   *Ib.*

No man is an island, entire of itself;
every man is a piece of the continent,[1] a
part of the main; if a clod be washed
away by the sea, Europe is the less, as
well as if a promontory were, as well as
if a manor of thy friends or of thine
own were; any man's death diminishes
me, because I am involved in mankind;
and therefore never send to know for
whom the bell tolls; it tolls for thee.
          Ib. XVII

Now God comes to thee, not as in
the dawning of the day, not as in the
bud of the spring, but as the sun at
noon to illustrate all shadows, as the
sheaves in harvest, to fill all penuries,
all occasions invite his mercies, and all
times are his seasons.
          Sermon III [1625]

Poor intricated soul! Riddling, perplexed, labyrinthical soul!
          Sermon XLVIII [1628/9]

And what is so intricate, so entangling as death? Who ever got out of a
winding sheet?   *Sermon LIV [1628]*

What gnashing is not a comfort,
what gnawing of the worm is not a tickling, what torment is not a marriage
bed to this damnation, to be secluded
eternally, eternally, eternally from the
sight of God?
          Sermon LXXVI [after 1622]

I throw myself down in my chamber,
and I call in and invite God and his
angels thither, and when they are there,
I neglect God and his angels, for the
noise of a fly, for the rattling of a
coach, for the whining of a door.
          *Sermon LXXX, At the Funeral
          of Sir William Cokayne [1626]*

When my mouth shall be filled with

[1] See Bacon, p. 208b.

dust, and the worm shall feed, and feed sweetly upon me, when the ambitious man shall have no satisfaction if the poorest alive tread upon him, nor the poorest receive any contentment in being made equal to princes, for they shall be equal but in dust.

Death's Duel (last sermon) [1]
[1630]

RICHARD BARNFIELD
1574–1627

The waters were his winding sheet, the
    sea was made for his tomb;
Yet for his fame the ocean sea, was not
    sufficient room.

Epitaph on Hawkins [1595]

As it fell upon a day
In the merry month of May,
Sitting in a pleasant shade
Which a grove of myrtles made.

Poems: In Divers Humours
[1598], *Ode*

King Pandion he is dead,
All thy friends are lapp'd in lead.

Ib.

Every one that flatters thee
Is no friend in misery.
Words are easy, like the wind;
Faithful friends are hard to find.
Every man will be thy friend
Whilst thou hast wherewith to spend;
But if store of crowns be scant,
No man will supply thy want.   *Ib.*

He that is thy friend indeed,
He will help thee in thy need.   *Ib.*

If music and sweet poetry agree.
Ib. To His Friend, Mr. R. L.

JOSEPH HALL,
BISHOP OF NORWICH
1574–1656

So little in his purse, so much upon his
    back.

Portrait of a Poor Gallant

[1] Called by his Majesty's household the Doctor's Own Funeral Sermon. — *Preface to the first edition* [1632]

'Mongst all these stirs of discontented
    strife,
O, let me lead an academic life;
To know much, and to think for nothing, know
Nothing to have, yet think we have
    enow.

*Discontent of Men with Their
Condition*

Moderation is the silken string running through the pearl chain of all virtues.

*Christian Moderation,
introduction*

Death borders upon our birth, and our cradle stands in the grave.[1]

Epistles. Decade III, epistle 2

There is many a rich stone laid up in the bowels of the earth, many a fair pearl laid up in the bosom of the sea, that never was seen, nor never shall be.[2]

*Contemplations, bk. IV, The
Veil of Moses*

JOHN MARSTON
c. 1575 – c. 1634

Oblivioni sacrum.[3]

Epitaph

HENRY PEACHAM
c. 1576 – c. 1643

Affect not as some do that bookish ambition to be stored with books and have well-furnished libraries, yet keep their heads empty of knowledge; to desire to have many books, and never to use them, is like a child that will have a candle burning by him all the while he is sleeping.

The Compleat Gentleman
[1622]

[1] See *The Wisdom of Solomon 5:13*, p. 37a.
They give birth astride a grave, the light gleams an instant, then it's night once more. — SAMUEL BECKETT, *Waiting for Godot* [1952]
[2] See Thomas Gray, p. 440b.
[3] Sacred to oblivion.

ROBERT BURTON
1577–1640

All my joys to this are folly,
Naught so sweet as melancholy.[1]
Anatomy of Melancholy [2] [1621–1651]. *The Author's Abstract*

I would help others, out of a fellow-feeling.[3]
Ib. Democritus to the Reader

They lard their lean books with the fat of others' works.[4] *Ib.*

We can say nothing but what hath been said.[5] Our poets steal from Homer. . . . Our story-dressers do as much; he that comes last is commonly best. *Ib.*

I say with Didacus Stella, a dwarf standing on the shoulders of a giant may see farther than a giant himself.[6]
Ib.

It is most true, *stylus virum arguit,* — our style bewrays us.[7] *Ib.*

Old friends become bitter enemies on a sudden for toys and small offenses.[8]
Ib.

Penny wise, pound foolish. *Ib.*

Women wear the breeches . . . in a word, the world turned upside downward.
Anatomy of Melancholy. Democritus to the Reader

Like Aesop's fox, when he had lost his tail, would have all his fellow foxes cut off theirs. *Ib.*

All poets are mad. *Ib.*

Every man hath a good and a bad angel attending on him in particular, all his life long.
Ib. pt. I, sec. 2, member 1, subsec. 2

That which Pythagoras said to his scholars of old, may be forever applied to melancholy men, A *fabis abstinete,* eat no beans.
Ib. member 2, subsec. 1

Cookery is become an art, a noble science; cooks are gentlemen.
Ib. subsec. 2

No rule is so general, which admits not some exception. *Ib. subsec. 3*

Idleness is an appendix to nobility.
Ib. subsec. 6

Why doth one man's yawning make another yawn?
Ib. member 3, subsec. 2

They do not live but linger.
Ib. subsec. 10

[Desire] is a perpetual rack, or horsemill, according to Austin [St. Augustine], still going round as in a ring.
Ib. subsec. 11

[The rich] are indeed rather possessed by their money than possessors.[1]
Ib. subsec. 12

Were it not that they are loath to lay out money on a rope, they would be hanged forthwith, and sometimes die to save charges. *Ib.*

A mere madness, to live like a wretch and die rich. *Ib.*

[1] See Fletcher, p. 313b.
There's not a string attuned to mirth
But has its chord in melancholy.
HOOD [1799–1845], *Ode to Melancholy*
[2] Burton's *Anatomy of Melancholy,* he said, was the only book that ever took him out of bed two hours sooner than he wished to rise. — SAMUEL JOHNSON; from BOSWELL, *Life of Dr. Johnson* [1791]
If the reader has patience to go through his volumes, he will be more improved for literary conversation than by the perusal of any twenty other works with which I am acquainted. — BYRON [1807], in MOORE'S *Life.*
[3] A fellow-feeling makes one wondrous kind. — GARRICK, *Prologue on Quitting the Stage* [1776]
[4] See Shakespeare, *King Henry IV, pt. I, II, ii, 119,* p. 238b.
[5] See Terence, p. 109a.
[6] See Lucan, p. 134a, and Newton, p. 379b.
[7] Le style c'est l'homme même [The style is the man himself]. — GEORGE-LOUIS LECLERC DE BUFFON, *Discours sur le Style,* on admission to the French Academy [1753]
[8] See Pope, p. 404a.

[1] See Bion, p. 104b.

I may not here omit those two main plagues and common dotages of human kind, wine and women, which have infatuated and besotted myriads of people; they go commonly together.

Anatomy of Melancholy, pt. I, sec. 2, member 3, subsec. 13

All our geese are swans.[1]

Ib. subsec. 14

They are proud in humility; proud in that they are not proud.[2]   *Ib.*

We can make majors and officers every year, but not scholars.

Ib. subsec. 15

Hinc quam sic calamus saevior ense, patet. The pen worse than the sword.[3]

Ib. member 4, subsec. 4

See one promontory (said Socrates of old), one mountain, one sea, one river, and see all.[4]   *Ib. subsec. 7*

One was never married, and that's his hell; another is, and that's his plague.   *Ib.*

Aristotle said melancholy men of all others are most witty.

Ib. sec. 3, member 1, subsec. 3

Seneca thinks the gods are well pleased when they see great men contending with adversity.

Ib. pt. II, sec. 2, member 1, subsec. 1

Machiavel says virtue and riches seldom settle on one man.

Ib. member 2

As he said in Machiavel, *omnes eodem patre nati,* Adam's sons, conceived all and born in sin, etc. "We are by nature all as one, all alike, if you see us naked; let us wear theirs and they our clothes, and what is the difference?"

Anatomy of Melancholy, pt. II, sec. 2, member 2

Who cannot give good counsel? 'Tis cheap, it costs them nothing.

Ib. member 3

Many things happen between the cup and the lip.[1]   *Ib.*

All places are distant from heaven alike.[2]   *Ib. member 4*

The commonwealth of Venice in their armory have this inscription: "Happy is that city which in time of peace thinks of war."[3]

Ib. member 6

Every man, as the saying is, can tame a shrew but he that hath her.   *Ib.*

Tobacco, divine, rare, superexcellent tobacco, which goes far beyond all the panaceas, potable gold, and philosopher's stones, a sovereign remedy to all diseases . . . but as it is commonly abused by most men, which take it as tinkers do ale, 'tis a plague, a mischief, a violent purger of goods, lands, health, hellish, devilish and damned tobacco, the ruin and overthrow of body and soul.

Ib. sec. 4, member 2, subsec. 2

"Let me not live," said Aretine's Antonia, "if I had not rather hear thy discourse than see a play."

Ib. pt. III, sec. 1, member 1, subsec. 1

Birds of a feather will gather together.[4]   *Ib. subsec. 2*

---

[1] Every man thinks his own geese swans. — DICKENS, *The Cricket on the Hearth* [1845], *Chirp the Second*

See Matthew Arnold, p. 715a.

[2] See Coleridge, p. 526a.

[3] See Bulwer-Lytton, p. 601b.

Pyrrhus was used to say that Cineas had taken more towns with his words than he with his arms. — PLUTARCH [A.D. 46–120], *Pyrrhus*

[4] See Sir Thomas Browne, p. 330a.

A blade of grass is always a blade of grass, whether in one country or another. — SAMUEL JOHNSON, in MRS. PIOZZI's *Anecdotes of Johnson* [1786]

[1] There is many a slip 'twixt the cup and the lip. — PALLADAS [fl. A.D. 400], *Greek Anthology, bk. X, epigram 32.* A very ancient proverb, sometimes attributed to Homer.

Though men determine, the gods do dispose; and ofttimes many things fall out between the cup and the lip. — ROBERT GREENE, *Perimedes the Blacksmith* [1588]

[2] See Gilbert, p. 192a, and note.

[3] See Vegetius, p. 146b, and note.

[4] See Homer, p. 66b.

Birds of a feather flock together. — GEORGE WITHER, *Abuses* [1613], *72*

No cord nor cable can so forcibly draw, or hold so fast, as love can do with a twined thread.[1]

Anatomy of Melancholy, pt. III, sec. 2, member 1, subsec. 2

To enlarge or illustrate this power and effect of love is to set a candle in the sun.[2]   *Ib.*

[Quoting Seneca] Cornelia kept her in talk till her children came from school, "and these," said she, "are my jewels."   *Ib.*

Diogenes struck the father when the son swore.   *Ib. subsec. 5*

England is a paradise for women and hell for horses; Italy a paradise for horses, hell for women, as the diverb goes.[3]

Ib. sec. 3, member 1, subsec. 2

For "ignorance is the mother of devotion," as all the world knows.   *Ib.*

The fear of some divine and supreme powers keeps men in obedience.[4]
     Ib.

One religion is as true as another.
     Ib.

Be not solitary, be not idle.[5]
     Last Words

---

[1] One hair of a woman can draw more than a hundred pair of oxen. — JAMES HOWELL, *Letters* [1621], *bk. II, 4*
She knows her man, and when you rant and swear,
Can draw you to her with a single hair.
     DRYDEN, *Persius* [1693], *satire V, l. 246*
See Pope, p. 404b.
[2] Like his that lights a candle to the sun. — ANDREW FLETCHER [1655–1716], *Letter to Sir Walter Aston*
And hold their farthing candle to the sun. — EDWARD YOUNG, *Satire VII* [1725–1728], *l. 56*
And hold their glimmering tapers to the sun. — GEORGE CRABBE, *The Parish Register* [1807], *pt. I, Introduction*
See Algernon Sidney, p. 362a.
[3] See Florio, p. 201b.
[4] The fear o' hell's a hangman's whip
To haud the wretch in order.
     ROBERT BURNS [1759–1796], *Epistle to a Young Friend*
[5] See Johnson, p. 433a.

THOMAS WARD
1577–1639

Where to elect there is but one,
'Tis Hobson's choice — take that or none.[1]
     England's Reformation [1630], *ch. 4*

WILLIAM HARVEY
1578–1657

I profess both to learn and to teach anatomy, not from books but from dissections; not from positions of philosophers but from the fabric of nature.
     De Motu Cordis et Sanguinis [1628] [2]

JOHN FLETCHER[3]
1579–1625

Drink today, and drown all sorrow;
You shall perhaps not do't tomorrow.
     Rollo, Duke of Normandy [1639] (*in collaboration with* JONSON *and others*), *act II, sc. 2*

And he that will to bed go sober
Falls with the leaf in October.[4]   *Ib.*

---

[1] Thomas Hobson [1544–1631], of whom Steele wrote in *The Spectator, no. 509* [October 14, 1712]:
Mr. Tobias Hobson, from whom we have the expression . . . was a carrier . . . the first in this Island who let out hackney-horses. He lived in Cambridge, and observing that the scholars rid hard, his manner was to keep a large stable of horses, with boots, bridles, and whips. . . . When a man came for an horse, he was led into the stable, where there was great choice, but he obliged him to take the horse which stood next to the stable-door; so that every customer was alike well served according to his chance, and every horse ridden with the same justice. From whence it became a proverb, when what ought to be your election was forced upon you, to say Hobson's Choice.
[2] *An Anatomical Disquisition on the Motion of the Heart and Blood in Animals,* translated from the Latin by ROBERT WILLIS [1847].
[3] See also BEAUMONT AND FLETCHER, p. 316a.
[4] The following well-known catch, or glee, is formed on this song:
He who goes to bed, and goes to bed sober,
Falls as the leaves do, and dies in October;
But he who goes to bed, and goes to bed mellow,
Lives as he ought to do, and dies an honest fellow.

Three merry boys, and three merry
　　boys,
And three merry boys are we.[1]
As ever did sing in a hempen string
Under the gallows tree.
　　　　Rollo, Duke of Normandy,
　　　　　　　act III, sc. 3

O woman, perfect woman! what dis-
　　traction
Was meant to mankind when thou
　　wast made a devil!
　　　　Monsieur Thomas [1639],
　　　　　　　act III, sc. 1

Man is his own star, and the soul that
　　can
Render an honest and a perfect man
Commands all light, all influence, all
　　fate.
Nothing to him falls early, or too late.
Our acts our angels are, or good or ill,
Our fatal shadows that walk by us still.
　　　　The Honest Man's Fortune
　　　　[1647] (*in collaboration with
　　　　three other authors*), *epilogue*

That soul that can
Be honest is the only perfect man.[2]
　　　　　　　　　　Ib.

Weep no more, nor sigh, nor groan,
Sorrow calls no time that's gone;
Violets plucked, the sweetest rain
Makes not fresh nor grow again.[3]
　　　　The Queen of Corinth [1647]
　　　　(*in collaboration with* MASSINGER
　　　　and a third author), *act III, sc. 2*

Of all the paths lead to a woman's
　　love
Pity's the straightest.[4]
　　　　The Knight of Malta [1647] (*in
　　　　collaboration with* MASSINGER),
　　　　act I, sc. 1

[1] Three merry men be we. — PEELE, *Old
Wives' Tale* [1595]
[2] See Pope, p. 409b.
[3] See *The Friar of Orders Gray*, p. 1085a.
[4] Pity's akin to love. — THOMAS SOUTHERNE,
Oroonoko [1696], *act II, sc. 1*
　For pity melts the mind to love. — DRYDEN,
Alexander's Feast [1697], *l. 96*
　Pity swells the tide of love. — EDWARD YOUNG,
Night Thoughts [1742–1745], *Night III, l. 107*

Go to grass.
　　　　The Little French Lawyer [1647]
　　　　(*in collaboration with* MASSIN-
　　　　GER), *act IV, sc. 7*

There is no jesting with edge tools.
　　　　　　　　　　Ib.

Let's meet, and either do or die.[1]
　　　　The Island Princess [1647],
　　　　　　　act II, sc. 4

Hence, all you vain delights,
As short as are the nights
Wherein you spend your folly!
There's naught in this life sweet
But only melancholy;
O sweetest melancholy!
　　　　Melancholy [2] [*The Nice Valour*,
　　　　　　　1647]

THOMAS MIDDLETON
1580–1627

Better the day, better the deed.[3]
　　　　Michaelmas Term [1607],
　　　　　　　act III, sc. 1

Since the worst comes to the worst.[4]
　　　　　　　Ib. III, 4

What is got over the Devil's back
(that's by knavery), is spent under the
belly (that's by lechery).[5]　*Ib. IV, 1*

[1] See Burns, p. 496a.
　This expression is a kind of common property,
being the motto, we believe, of a Scottish family.
— SIR WALTER SCOTT [1771–1832], review of
THOMAS CAMPBELL's *Gertrude of Wyoming,*
where it appears (*pt. III, l. 37*): Tomorrow let
us do or die!
[2] This poem is frequently and with some
likelihood attributed to WILLIAM STRODE [1602–
1645].
　See Robert Burton, p. 310a, and Milton,
p. 334b.
[3] The better the day, the worse deed. —
MATHEW HENRY [1662–1714], *Commentaries,
Genesis, III*
　The better the day the better the deed. —
DICKENS, *Edwin Drood* [1870], *ch. 10*
[4] If the worst comes to the worst. — *Discovery
of the Knights of the Poste* [1597]
[5] What is got over the Devil's back is spent
under the belly. — RABELAIS, *Works, bk. V* [1552],
ch. 11

Isocrates was in the right to insinuate that
what is got over the Devil's back is spent under
his belly. — LE SAGE, *Gil Blas* [1715–1735],
bk. 8, ch. 9

As true as I live.
> *The Family of Love* [1608],
> *act V, sc. 3*

Have you summoned your wits from
woolgathering?[1] *Ib. V, 5*

By my faith the fool has feathered
his nest well.[2]
> *The Roaring Girl* [1611], *act I,*
> *sc. 1*

That disease of which all old men
sicken — avarice.[3] *Ib.*

Beat all your feathers as flat down as
> pancakes. *Ib.*

As the case stands.
> *The Old Law* [1656], *act II, sc. 1*

On his last legs. *Ib. V, 1*

As old Chaucer was wont to say, that
broad famous English poet.
> *More Dissemblers Besides*
> *Women* [1657], *act I, sc. 4*

'Tis a stinger.[4] *Ib. III, 2*

How many honest words have suffered corruption since Chaucer's days!
> *No Wit, No Help, Like a*
> *Woman's* [1657], *act II, sc. 1*

By many a happy accident.
> *Ib. IV, 1*

Anything for a Quiet Life.
> *Title of play* [1662]

This was a good week's labor.
> *Anything for a Quiet Life, act V,*
> *sc. 3*

There's no hate lost between us.
> *The Witch* [written c. 1627],
> *act IV, sc. 2*

Black spirits and white, red spirits and
gray,

Mingle, mingle, mingle, you that
mingle may.[1]
> *The Witch, act V, sc. 2*

MATTHEW ROYDON
c. 1580 – 1622

You knew — who knew not Astrophil?
(That I should live to say I knew,
And have not in possession still!)
Things known permit me to renew;
Of him you know his merit such,
I cannot say, you hear, too much.
> *The Phoenix Nest* [1593]; *An*
> *Elegy, or Friend's Passion for His*
> *Astrophil* (*on the death of Sir*
> *Philip Sidney*)

A sweet attractive kind of grace,
A full assurance given by looks,
Continual comfort in a face,
The lineaments of Gospel books;
I trow that countenance cannot lie.
Whose thoughts are legible in the eye.
> *Ib.*

Was never eye, did see that face,
Was never ear, did hear that tongue,
Was never mind, did mind his grace,
That ever thought the travel long,
But eyes, and ears, and ev'ry thought,
Were with his sweet perfections caught.
> *Ib.*

JOHN WEBSTER
1580–1625

Is not old wine wholesomest, old pip-
pins toothsomest, old wood burn
brightest, old linen wash whitest? Old
soldiers, sweethearts, are surest, and old
lovers are soundest.[2]
> *Westward Hoe* [1607], *in colla-*
> *boration with* DEKKER, *act II,*
> *sc. 2*

I saw him now going the way of all
flesh.[3] *Ib.*

Call for the robin redbreast and the
wren,

---

[1] My understanding has forsook me, and is
gone a-woolgathering. — CERVANTES, *Don Qui-*
xote, pt. II [1605–1615], *bk. IV, ch. 38*

[2] We will feather oure nestes ere tyme may us
espie. — *A Merye Enterlude Entitled Respublica*
[1553], *III, 6*

[3] So for a good old-gentlemanly vice
I think I must take up with avarice.
> BYRON, *Don Juan* [1819–1824],
> *canto 1, st. 216*

[4] He 'as had a stinger. — FLETCHER, *Wit With-*
out Money [1639], *act IV, sc. 1*

[1] These lines are introduced into *Macbeth,*
act IV, sc. 1. According to Steevens, "the song
was, in all probability, a traditional one."

[2] See Bacon, p. 207b.

[3] See Samuel Butler, p. 755b.

Since o'er shady groves they hover,
And with leaves and flowers do cover
The friendless bodies of unburied
   men.
     The White Devil [1612], *act* V,
                    sc. 4

But keep the wolf far thence, that's foe
   to men,
For with his nails he'll dig them up
   again.   *Ib.*

Prosperity doth bewitch men, seeming
   clear;
But seas do laugh, show white, when
   rocks are near.   *Ib.* V, 6

Glories, like glowworms, afar off shine
   bright,
But look'd to near have neither heat
   nor light.
     Duchess of Malfi [1623], *act* IV,
                    sc. 2

Of what is't fools make such vain keep-
   ing?
Sin their conception, their birth, weep-
   ing:
Their life, a general mist of error,
Their death, a hideous storm of terror.
                     Ib.

I know death hath ten thousand several
   doors
For men to take their exits.[1]   *Ib.*

Heaven-gates are not so highly arch'd
As princes' palaces; they that enter
   there
Must go upon their knees.   *Ib.*

Ferdinand: Cover her face; mine eyes
   dazzle; she died young.
Bosola: I think not so; her infelicity
Seem'd to have years too many. *Ib.*

Vain the ambition of kings
Who seek by trophies and dead things
To leave a living name behind,

And weave but nets to catch the wind.[1]
     The Devil's Law Case [1623],
                   song

SIR THOMAS OVERBURY
1581–1613

Give me, next good, an understanding
   wife,
By nature wise, not learned much by
   art.   *A Wife* [1614]

He disdains all things above his
reach, and preferreth all countries before his own.[2]
    An Affectate Traveller [1614]

BISHOP RICHARD CORBET
1582–1635

Farewell, rewards and fairies,[3]
Good housewives now may say.
    Farewell to the Fairies, st. 1

Who of late for cleanliness,
Finds sixpence in her shoe?   *Ib.*

Nor too much wealth nor wit come to
   thee,
So much of either may undo thee.
    To His Son, Vincent Corbet

PHILIP MASSINGER
1583–1640

Be wise;
Soar not too high to fall; but stoop to
   rise.[4]
    Duke of Milan [1623], *act* I, *sc.* 2

He that would govern others, first
   should be
Master of himself.[5]
    The Bondman [1624], *act* I, *sc.* 3

To be nobly born
Is now a crime.
    The Roman Actor [1629], *act* I,
                    sc. 1

---

[1] Death hath a thousand doors to let out life.
—MASSINGER, *A Very Woman* [1655], *act* V,
sc. 4

  Death hath so many doors to let out life.
— FLETCHER AND MASSINGER, *The Custom of the
Country* [1647], *act* II, *sc.* 2

  The thousand doors that lead to death. —
SIR THOMAS BROWNE, *Religio Medici* [1642],
pt. I, sec. 44

[1] Since in a net I seek to hold the wind. —
WYATT, *Sonnet, Whoso List to Hunt* [c. 1557]

[2] See Shakespeare, *As You Like It* IV, i, 35,
p. 250a; Canning, p. 506b; and W.S. Gilbert,
p. 768a.

[3] See Kipling, p. 877a.

[4] See Mather, p. 387a.

[5] See Rabelais, p. 181a, and note.

Whose wealth
Arithmetic cannot number.
>   *The Roman Actor, act I, sc. 3*

Grim death.[1]   *Ib. IV, 2*

A New Way to Pay Old Debts.
>   *Title of Play* [1632]

JACQUES DU LAURENS
1583–1650

I do not attack fools, but foolishness.   *Satires* [1624]

FRANCIS BEAUMONT[2]
1584–1616

What things have we seen
Done at the Mermaid! heard words
that have been
So nimble, and so full of subtle flame,
As if that everyone from whence they
came,
Had meant to put his whole wit in a
jest,
And resolv'd to live a fool, the rest
Of his dull life.
>   *Letter to Ben Jonson* [1640]

BEAUMONT AND
FLETCHER[3]
FRANCIS BEAUMONT 1584–1616
JOHN FLETCHER 1579–1625[4]

It is always good
When a man has two irons in the fire.
>   *The Faithful Friends* [c. 1608],
>   *act I, sc. 2*

As cold as cucumbers.
>   *Cupid's Revenge* [1615], *act I,*
>   *sc. 1*

Kiss till the cow comes home.
>   *Scornful Lady* [1616], *act III,*
>   *sc. 1*

There is a method in man's wickedness —
It grows up by degrees.[1]
>   *A King and No King* [1619],
>   *act V, sc. 4*

Upon my buried body lie lightly, gentle
earth.[2]
>   *The Maid's Tragedy* [1619],
>   *act I, sc. 2*

The devil take the hindmost!
>   *Philaster* [1620], *act V*

Whistle, and she'll come to you.[3]
>   *Wit Without Money* [1639],
>   *act IV, sc. 4*

Calamity is man's true touchstone.[4]
>   *Four Plays in One. The Triumph*
>   *of Honour* [1647], *sc. 1*

Though I say it that should not say
it.
>   *Wit at Several Weapons* (*prob-*
>   *ably in collaboration with*
>   WILLIAM ROWLEY [c. 1585–
>   c. 1642]), *act II, sc. 2*

TIRSO DE MOLINA
[FRAY GABRIEL
TÉLLEZ]
1584–1648

Through his honor I conquered him.
For these peasants carry their honor in
their hands so that they may constantly
consult it; this same honor that once
felt so much at home in the city but
now has taken refuge in a more rural
setting.
>   *El Burlador de Sevilla* (*The*
>   *Rogue of Seville*) *act III,*
>   *sc. 3*[5]

---

[1] See Milton, p. 344a.
[2] See also Beaumont and Fletcher below.
[3] Of whose partnership JOHN AUBREY [1626–1697] said, "There was a wonderful consimility of fancy. They lived together not far from the playhouse, had one wench in the house between them, the same clothes and cloak, &c."
[4] Also on p. 312b.

[1] See Juvenal, p. 139a, and Racine, p. 378b.
[2] See Euripides, p. 83b, and note.
[3] Whistle, and I'll come to ye. — ROBERT BURNS [1759–1796], *Whistle, etc.*
[4] See Seneca, p. 130b.
[5] Translated by ROBERT O'BRIEN in *Spanish Drama* [1962]. This is the original Don Juan play.

JOHN SELDEN
1584–1654

Equity is a roguish thing. For Law we have a measure, know what to trust to; Equity is according to the conscience of him that is Chancellor, and as that is larger or narrower, so is Equity. 'Tis all one as if they should make the standard for the measure we call a "foot" a Chancellor's foot; what an uncertain measure would this be! One Chancellor has a long foot, another a short foot, a third an indifferent foot. 'Tis the same thing in the Chancellor's conscience.
Table Talk [1689]. *Equity*

Humility is a virtue all preach, none practice; and yet everybody is content to hear. *Ib. Humility*

'Tis not the drinking that is to be blamed, but the excess. *Ib.*

Commonly we say a judgment falls upon a man for something in him we cannot abide. *Ib. Judgments*

Ignorance of the law excuses no man; not that all men know the law, but because 'tis an excuse every man will plead, and no man can tell how to refute him. *Ib. Law*

No man is the wiser for his learning.
Ib. Learning

Wit and wisdom are born with a man. *Ib.*

Few men make themselves masters of the things they write or speak. *Ib.*

Take a straw and throw it up into the air — you may see by that which way the wind is. *Ib. Libels*

Philosophy is nothing but discretion. *Ib. Philosophy*

Marriage is a desperate thing.
Ib. Marriage

Thou little thinkest what a little foolery governs the world.[1]
Ib. Pope

[1] Behold, my son, with how little wisdom the world is governed. — AXEL OXENSTIERN [1583–1654]

They that govern the most make the least noise.
Table Talk. Power

Syllables govern the world. *Ib.*

Never tell your resolution beforehand. *Ib. Wisdom*

Wise men say nothing in dangerous times. *Ib.*

Pleasure is nothing else but the intermission of pain. *Ib. Pleasure*

Preachers say, Do as I say, not as I do. *Ib. Preaching*

A king is a thing men have made for their own sakes, for quietness' sake. Just as in a family one man is appointed to buy the meat. *Ib. Of a King*

JOHN FORD
1586–1639

Diamond cut diamond.
The Lover's Melancholy [1629], *act I, sc. 1*

'Tis Pity She's a Whore.
Title of Play [1633]

THOMAS RAINBOROUGH
d. 1648

The poorest he that is in England hath a life to live as the greatest he.
In the Army debates at Putney [*October 29, 1647*]

THOMAS HOBBES
1588–1679

The condition of man . . . is a condition of war of everyone against everyone.
Leviathan [1651], *pt. I, ch. 4*

Words are wise men's counters, they do but reckon with them, but they are the money of fools. *Ib.*

The privilege of absurdity; to which no living creature is subject but man only. *Ib. 5*

Sudden glory is the passion which maketh those grimaces called laughter.
Leviathan, pt. I, ch. 6

The secret thoughts of a man run over all things, holy, profane, clean, obscene, grave, and light, without shame or blame. *Ib. 8*

[In a state of nature] No arts; no letters; no society; and which is worst of all, continual fear and danger of violent death; and the life of man, solitary, poor, nasty, brutish, and short.
Ib. 13

The Papacy is not other than the Ghost of the deceased Roman Empire, sitting crowned upon the grave thereof.
Ib. pt. IV, ch. 47

The praise of ancient authors proceeds not from the reverence of the dead, but from the competition and mutual envy of the living.
Ib. Review and Conclusion

Such truth as opposeth no man's profit nor pleasure is to all men welcome. *Ib.*

I am about to take my last voyage, a great leap in the dark. *Last words*

JOHN WINTHROP
1588–1649

For we must consider that we shall be a city upon a hill.[1] The eyes of all people are upon us, so that if we shall deal falsely with our God in this work we have undertaken, and so cause Him to withdraw His present help from us, we shall be made a story and a byword through the world.
A Model of Christian Charity [1630], a sermon delivered on board the Arbella

GEORGE WITHER
1588–1667

Shall I wasting in despair
Die because a woman's fair?

[1] See *Matthew 5:14*, p. 40a.

Or make pale my cheeks with care
'Cause another's rosy are?
Be she fairer than the day,
Or the flow'ry meads in May,
 If she be not so to me,
 What care I how fair she be?
Fair Virtue [1622]. Sonnet 4, st. 1

If she love me, this believe,
I will die ere she shall grieve;
If she slight me when I woo,
I can scorn and let her go;
 For if she be not for me,
 What care I for whom she be?
Ib. st. 5

'Twas I that beat the bush,
The bird to others flew.
A Love Sonnet [1622], st. 11

Though I am young, I scorn to flit
On the wings of borrowed wit.
The Shepherd's Hunting [1622]

HONORAT DE BUEIL,
MARQUIS DE RACAN
1589–1650

Nothing in the world lasts
Save eternal change.[1]
Odes. The Coming of Spring

The good effect of Fortune may be short-lived. To build on it is to build on sand.[2] *Poésies Diverses*

WILLIAM BRADFORD
1590–1657

They knew they were pilgrims.[3]
Of Plymouth Plantation [1620–1647], ch. 7

So they committed themselves to the will of God and resolved to proceed.
Ib. 9

Being thus arrived in a good harbor, and brought safe to land, they fell upon

[1] Rien au monde ne dure
Qu'un éternel changement.
See Heraclitus, p. 77b, and note.
[2] Le bien de la fortune est un bien périssable: quand on bâtit sur elle, on bâtit sur le sable.
[3] It was owing to this passage, first printed in 1669, that the *Mayflower's* company came eventually to be called the Pilgrim Fathers.

their knees and blessed the God of Heaven who had brought them over the vast and furious ocean, and delivered them from all the perils and miseries thereof, again to set their feet on the firm and stable earth, their proper element.

Of Plymouth Plantation, ch. 9

Our fathers were Englishmen which came over this great ocean, and were ready to perish in this wilderness.

Ib.

The loss of . . . honest and industrious men's lives cannot be valued at any price.   *Ib.* 12

But it pleased God to visit us then with death daily, and with so general a disease that the living were scarce able to bury the dead.   *Ib.*

Cold comfort to fill their hungry bellies.[1]   *Ib.* 13

Behold, now, another providence of God. A ship comes into the harbor.

Ib.

Thus out of small beginnings greater things have been produced by His hand that made all things of nothing,[2] and gives being to all things that are; and, as one small candle may light a thousand, so the light here kindled hath shone unto many, yea in some sort to our whole nation.[3]   *Ib.* 21

WILLIAM BASSE
died c. 1653

Renowned Spenser, lie a thought more nigh
To learned Chaucer; and rare Beaumont, lie
A little nearer Spenser; to make room
For Shakespeare in your three-fold fourfold tomb.
To lodge all four in one bed make a shift
Until Doomsday; for hardly will a fift,

Betwixt this day and that, by fate be slain,
For whom your curtains may be drawn again.[1]
On Mr. Wm. Shakespeare
[c. 1616]

WILLIAM BROWNE
1591–1643

Underneath this sable hearse
Lies the subject of all verse:
Sidney's sister, Pembroke's mother.
Death, ere thou hast slain another
Fair and learn'd and good as she,
Time shall throw a dart at thee.
Epitaph on the Countess of
Pembroke [1621]

There is no season such delight can bring,
As summer, autumn, winter, and the spring.   *Variety*

ROBERT HERRICK
1591–1674

I sing of brooks, of blossoms, birds, and bowers:
Of April, May, of June, and July flowers.
I sing of Maypoles, Hock-carts, wassails, wakes,
Of bridegrooms, brides, and of their bridal cakes.
Hesperides [1648]. *Argument of*
His Book

What is a kiss? Why this, as some approve:
The sure, sweet cement, glue, and lime of love.   *Ib. A Kiss*

Bid me to live, and I will live
Thy Protestant to be,
Or bid me love, and I will give
A loving heart to thee.
Ib. To Anthea

Cherry ripe, ripe, ripe, I cry,
Full and fair ones; come and buy!
If so be you ask me where

---

[1] See Shakespeare, pp. 237b and 296b.
[2] See Dryden, p. 367a.
[3] See *Matthew 5:15*, p. 40a, and Shakespeare, *Merchant of Venice V, i, 90*, p. 235b.

[1] See Ben Jonson, p. 303b.

They do grow, I answer, there,
Where my Julia's lips do smile;
There's the land, or cherry-isle.
          Hesperides. Cherry Ripe [1]

It is the end that crowns us, not the
fight.[2]   *Ib. The End*

Some asked how pearls did grow, and
where?
Then spoke I to my girl
To part her lips, and showed them
there
The quarelets of pearl.[3]
      *Ib. The Rock of Rubies, and the
                    Quarrie of Pearls*

A sweet disorder in the dress
Kindles in clothes a wantonness.
          Ib. Delight in Disorder

A winning wave, deserving note,
In the tempestuous petticoat,
A careless shoestring, in whose tie
I see a wild civility,
Do more bewitch me than when art
Is too precise in every part.[4]   *Ib.*

You say to me-wards your affection's
strong;
Pray love me little, so you love me
long.[5]
      Ib. Love Me Little, Love Me Long

Night makes no difference 'twixt the
Priest and Clerk;
Joan as my Lady is as good i' the dark.[6]
      Ib. No Difference i' th' Dark

Give me a kiss, and to that kiss a
score;
Then to that twenty, add a hundred
more:
A thousand to that hundred: so kiss
on,[7]
To make that thousand up a million.
Treble that million, and when that is
done,

---

[1] See Campion, p. 300a.
[2] See Shakespeare, *Troilus and Cressida IV,
v; 223*, p. 269b, and note.
  See Anonymous, p. 150b.
[3] See Campion, p. 300a.
[4] See Jonson, p. 302b.
[5] See Anonymous, p. 1084b.
[6] See Plutarch, p. 137b.
[7] See Catullus, p. 114b.

Let's kiss afresh, as when we first begun.
          *Hesperides. To Anthea: Ah,
                    My Anthea!*

Gather ye rosebuds while ye may,
Old Time is still a-flying,
And this same flower that smiles today
Tomorrow will be dying.[1]
          *Ib. To the Virgins to Make
                    Much of Time*

Fair daffodils, we weep to see
You haste away so soon.
          Ib. To Daffodils

Her pretty feet, like snails, did creep
A little out, and then,[2]
As if they played at bo-peep,
Did soon draw in again.
      Ib. To Mistress Susanna Southwell

Her eyes the glowworm lend thee,
The shooting stars attend thee;
      And the elves also,
      Whose little eyes glow
Like the sparks of fire, befriend thee.
          Ib. The Night Piece to Julia

Thus times do shift, each thing his turn
does hold;
New things succeed, as former things
grow old.
          Ib. Ceremonies for Candlemas Eve

Made us nobly wild, not mad.
          Ib. Ode for Ben Jonson

Outdid the meat, outdid the frolic
wine.   *Ib.*

Attempt the end, and never stand to
doubt;
Nothing's so hard but search will find it
out.   *Ib. Seek and Find*

Get up, sweet Slug-a-bed, and see
The dew bespangling herb and tree.
          Ib. Corinna's Going a-Maying

      'Tis sin,
Nay, profanation to keep in.   *Ib.*

So when or you or I are made
A fable, song, or fleeting shade,
All love, all liking, all delight

---

[1] See *Wisdom of Solomon*, p. 36b; Horace,
p. 121a; Spenser, p. 200a; and Ronsard, p. 188a.
[2] See Suckling, p. 350b.

Lies drowned with us in endless night.[1]
> *Hesperides. Corinna's Going*
> *a-Maying*

Whenas in silks my Julia goes,
Then, then (methinks) how sweetly
  flows
That liquefaction of her clothes.
> *Ib. Upon Julia's Clothes*

Here a little child I stand
Heaving up my either hand.
Cold as paddocks though they be,
Here I lift them up to Thee,
For a benison to fall
On our meat, and on us all.
> *Noble Numbers* [1648]. *A Child's*
> *Grace*

JULIUS WILHELM ZINCGREF
1591–1635

One who longs for death is miserable, but more miserable is he who fears
it.   *Apophthegmata* [1628], *bk. II*

Laws and police regulations can be
compared to a spider's web that lets the
big mosquitoes through and catches the
small ones.[2]   *Ib.*

HENRY KING, BISHOP OF CHICHESTER
1592–1669

Thou art the book,
The library whereon I look.
> *The Exequy* [1657]

Then we shall rise
And view ourselves with clearer eyes
In that calm region where no night
Can hide us from each other's sight.
>   *Ib.*

Sleep on, my Love, in thy cold bed,
Never to be disquieted!
My last good-night! Thou wilt not
  wake,
Till I thy fate shall overtake;
Till age, or grief, or sickness, must
Marry my body to that dust
It so much loves, and fill the room

---

[1] See Catullus, p. 114b, and note.
[2] See Solon, p. 68b, and Swift, p. 388b.

My heart keeps empty in thy tomb.
Stay for me there; I will not fail
To meet thee in that hollow vale.
> *The Exequy*

I am content to live
Divided, with but half a heart.   *Ib.*

FRANCIS QUARLES
1592–1644

Death aims with fouler spite
At fairer marks.[1]
> *Divine Fancies* [1632]

We spend our midday sweat, our midnight oil;
We tire the night in thought, the day
  in toil.
> *Emblems* [1635], *bk. II, no.* 2

Be wisely worldly, be not worldly wise.
>   *Ib.*

This house is to be let for life or years;
Her rent is sorrow, and her income
  tears.
Cupid, 't has long stood void; her bills
  make known,
She must be dearly let, or let alone.
> *Ib.* 10, *Epigram*

The slender debt to Nature's quickly
  paid,[2]
Discharged, perchance, with greater
  ease than made.   *Ib.* 13

The road to resolution lies by doubt:
The next way home's the farthest way
  about.[3]
> *Ib. IV,* 2, *Epigram*

It is the lot of man but once to die.
> *Ib. V,* 7

My soul, sit thou a patient looker-on;
Judge not the play before the play is
  done:
Her plot hath many changes; every day

---

[1] See Edward Young, p. 399b.
[2] To die is a debt we must all of us discharge. — EURIPIDES, *Alcestis, l.* 418
[3] The longest way round is the shortest way
home. — BOHN, *Foreign Proverbs, Italian*

Speaks a new scene; the last act crowns
the play.[1]
Epigram. Respice Finem

And what's a life? — a weary pilgrimage,
Whose glory in one day doth fill the
stage
With childhood, manhood, and decrepit age. *What Is Life?*

Let all thy joys be as the month of
May,
And all thy days be as a marriage day:
Let sorrow, sickness, and a troubled
mind
Be stranger to thee. *To a Bride*

No man is born unto himself alone;[2]
Who lives unto himself, he lives to
none.
Esther, sec. 1, Meditation 1

The way to bliss lies not on beds of
down,
And he that has no cross deserves no
crown.[3] *Ib. sec. 9, Meditation 9*

THOMAS RAVENSCROFT
c. 1592 – 1635
Nose, nose, nose, nose!
And who gave thee this jolly red nose?
Nutmegs and ginger, cinnamon and
cloves,
And they gave me this jolly red nose.
Deuteromelia [1609]. *Song no.* 7 [4]

GEORGE HERBERT
1593–1633
A verse may find him who a sermon
flies.[5]
The Temple [1633]. *The Church
Porch, st.* 1

Drink not the third glass,[1] which thou
canst not tame
When once it is within thee.
*The Temple. The Church
Porch, st.* 5

Dare to be true: nothing can need a
lie:
A fault, which needs it most, grows two
thereby.[2] *Ib. st.* 13

By all means use sometimes to be
alone. *Ib. st.* 25

By no means run in debt: take thine
own measure.
Who cannot live on twenty pound a
year,
Cannot on forty. *Ib. st.* 30

Wit's an unruly engine, wildly striking
Sometimes a friend, sometimes the engineer. *Ib. st.* 41

Be useful where thou livest.
Ib. st. 55

Man is God's image; but a poor man
is
Christ's stamp to boot: both images regard. *Ib. st.* 64

Was ever grief like mine?
*Ib. The Church. The Sacrifice,
refrain*

For thirty pence he did my death devise,[3]
Who at three hundred did the ointment prize.[4] *Ib. st.* 5

Man stole the fruit, but I must climb
the tree. *Ib. st.* 51

I got me flowers to strew Thy way,
I got me boughs off many a tree:

---

[1] See Herrick, p. 320a, and Shakespeare,
Troilus and Cressida IV, v, 223, p. 269b, and
note.
[2] See *Romans 14:8*, p. 51b, and Donne, p.
308b.
[3] See William Penn, p. 380b.
[4] Quoted by Beaumont and Fletcher, *The
Knight of the Burning Pestle* [1613], act I, sc. 3.
Ravenscroft's *Deuteromelia* was a supplement to
his *Pammelia*, which was the earliest collection
of rounds, catches, and canons printed in
England.
[5] That many people read a song

Who will not read a sermon.
WINTHROP MACKWORTH PRAED [1802–
1839], *The Chant of the Brazenhead,
st. 1*
[1] See Victor Hugo, p. 599a.
[2] And he that does one fault at first,
And lies to hide it, makes it two.
ISAAC WATTS [1674–1748], *Song 15*
[3] See *King John and the Abbott of Canterbury*, p. 1088a.
[4] Then saith one of his disciples, Judas Iscariot,
Simon's son, which should betray him, Why
was not this ointment sold for three hundred
pence, and given to the poor? — *John 12:4*

But Thou wast up by break of day,
And brought'st Thy sweets along with
    Thee.
         The Temple. Easter, st. 4

Who says that fictions only and false
    hair
Become a verse? Is there in truth no
    beauty? [1]   *Ib. Jordan, st.* 1

Sweet day, so cool, so calm, so bright,
The bridal of the earth and sky.
         Ib. Virtue, st. 1

Sweet spring, full of sweet days and
    roses,
A box where sweets compacted lie.
         Ib. st. 3

Only a sweet and virtuous soul,
Like season'd timber, never gives.
         Ib. st. 4

Who goes to bed and does not pray,
Maketh two nights to every day.
         Ib. Charms and Knots, st. 4

Nothing wears clothes, but Man; noth-
    ing doth need
But he to wear them.
         Ib. Providence, st. 28

Most things move th' under-jaw, the
    crocodile not.[2]
Most things sleep lying, th' elephant
    leans or stands.[3]   *Ib. st.* 35

I struck the board, and cried, No
    more:
         I will abroad.
What? shall I ever sigh and pine?
My lines and life are free; free as the
    road,
Loose as the wind, as large as store.
         Shall I be still in suit?
Have I no harvest but a thorn
To let me blood, and not restore
What I have lost with cordial fruit?
         Sure there was wine
Before my sighs did dry it; there was
    corn

[1] See Keats, p. 583b.
[2] The crocodile does not move the lower jaw,
but is the only animal that brings down its
upper jaw to the under one. — HERODOTUS [484–
424 B.C.], *Customs of the Egyptians*
[3] Leans the huge elephant. — JAMES THOM-
SON, *The Seasons, Summer* [1727], *l.* 725

Before my tears did drown it;
Is the year only lost to me?
Have I no bays to crown it?
         The Temple. The Collar

Call in thy death's head there: tie up
    thy fears.   *Ib.*

But as I raved and grew more fierce and
    wild
         At every word,
Methought I heard one calling, *Child!*
    And I replied, *My Lord.*
         Ib.

He would adore my gifts instead of
    me,
And rest in Nature, not the God of
    Nature:
    So both should losers be.
         Ib. The Pulley, st. 3

Let him be rich and weary, that at
    least,
If goodness lead him not, yet weariness
May toss him to my breast.
         Ib. st. 4

      Grief melts away
      Like snow in May,
As if there were no such cold thing.
         Ib. The Flower, st. 1

Who would have thought my shrivel'd
    heart
Could have recover'd greenness?
         Ib. st. 2

And now in age I bud again,
After so many deaths I live and write;
    I once more smell the dew and rain,
And relish versing: O my only light,
         It cannot be
         That I am he
On whom thy tempests fell all night.
         Ib. st. 6

The harbingers are come. See, see their
    mark;
White is their color, and behold my
    head.
         Ib. The Forerunners, st. 1

Teach me, my God and King,
In all things thee to see.

And what I do in any thing,
To do it as for thee.
> *The Temple. The Elixir,*
> *st. 1*

A servant with this clause
Makes drudgery divine:
Who sweeps a room, as for thy laws,
Makes that and th' action fine.
> *Ib. st. 5*

Love bade me welcome: yet my soul
　　drew back,
　　Guilty of dust and sin.
But quick-ey'd Love, observing me grow
　　slack
From my first entrance in,
Drew nearer to me, sweetly question-
　　ing,
　　If I lack'd anything.
> *Ib. Love, st. 1*

You must sit down, says Love, and taste
　　my meat:
So I did sit and eat.　　　*Ib. st. 3*

Religion stands on tiptoe in our land,
Ready to pass to the American strand.
> *The Church Militant* [1633], *l. 235*

Love, and a cough, cannot be hid.
> *Jacula Prudentum* [1651], 49

Ill ware is never cheap. Pleasing ware
is half sold.　　　　　　*Ib. 61*

When a dog is drowning, everyone
offers him drink.　　　　*Ib. 77*

Deceive not thy physician, confessor,
nor lawyer.　　　　　　*Ib. 105*

Who would do ill ne'er wants occasion.　　　　　　　　*Ib. 116*

A snow year, a rich year.　*Ib. 125*

Well may he smell fire, whose gown
burns.　　　　　　　*Ib. 138*

Love your neighbor, yet pull not
down your hedge.[1]　　　*Ib. 141*

Marry your son when you will; your
daughter when you can.　*Ib. 149*

The mill cannot grind with the water
that's past.　　　　　*Ib. 153*

Good words are worth much, and
cost little.　　　　　*Ib. 155*

[1] See Robert Frost, p. 926a.

Hell is full of good meanings and
wishings.[1]
> *Jacula Prudentum,* 170

Where the drink goes in, there the
wit goes out.　　　　*Ib. 187*

Whose house is of glass, must not
throw stones at another.　*Ib. 196*

By suppers more have been killed
than Galen ever cured.　*Ib. 272*

The lion is not so fierce as they paint
him.[2]　　　　　　*Ib. 289*

Go not for every grief to the physician, nor for every quarrel to the lawyer, nor for every thirst to the pot.
> *Ib. 290*

The best mirror is an old friend.
> *Ib. 296*

When you are an anvil, hold you
still; when you are a hammer, strike
your fill.[3]　　　　　*Ib. 338*

He that lies with the dogs, riseth
with fleas.　　　　　*Ib. 343*

He that is not handsome at twenty,
nor strong at thirty, nor rich at forty,
nor wise at fifty, will never be handsome, strong, rich, or wise.　*Ib. 349*

The buyer needs a hundred eyes, the
seller not one.[4]　　　*Ib. 390*

My house, my house, though thou
art small, thou art to me the Escurial.
> *Ib. 413*

Trust not one night's ice.　*Ib. 453*

For want of a nail the shoe is lost,

[1] Sir, Hell is paved with good intentions.
— SAMUEL JOHNSON [1775]; from BOSWELL, *Life of Dr. Johnson* [1791], *vol. I, p. 555* [Everyman ed.]
[2] The lion is not so fierce as painted. — THOMAS FULLER [1608–1661], *Expecting Prefer-ment*
[3] Stand like an anvil when it is beaten upon. — ST. IGNATIUS THEOPHORUS, Bishop of Antioch [A.D. 104]
> When you are the anvil, bear —
> When you are the hammer, strike.
> EDWIN MARKHAM [1852–1940],
> *Preparedness*
[4] Caveat emptor [Buyer, beware]. — *Proverb*

for want of a shoe the horse is lost, for want of a horse the rider is lost.[1]
Jacula Prudentum, 499

Pension never enriched young man.
Ib. 515

One enemy is too much.[2]   *Ib.* 523

Thursday come, and the week is gone.   *Ib.* 587

Time is the rider that breaks youth.
Ib. 615

Show me a liar, and I'll show thee a thief.   *Ib.* 652

One father is more than a hundred schoolmasters.   *Ib.* 686

Reason lies between the spur and the bridle.   *Ib.* 711

One sword keeps another in the sheath.   *Ib.* 725

God's mill grinds slow, but sure.[3]
Ib. 747

He that lends, gives.   *Ib.* 787

Words are women, deeds are men.[4]
Ib. 842

Poverty is no sin.   *Ib.* 844

None knows the weight of another's burthen.   *Ib.* 880

One hour's sleep before midnight is worth three after.   *Ib.* 882

He hath no leisure who useth it not.
Ib. 897

Half the world knows not how the other half lives.[5]   *Ib.* 907

Life is half spent before we know what it is.   *Ib.* 917

Every mile is two in winter.
Ib. 949

[1] See Benjamin Franklin, p. 422a.
[2] See Ali Ibn-abu-Taleb, p. 148b.
[3] See Euripides, p. 85a, and von Logau, p. 329a.
[4] See Samuel Johnson, p. 427b.
Fatti maschii parole femine [Deeds are masculine, words are feminine]. — *State motto of Maryland*
[5] See Rabelais, p. 181a.

The eye is bigger than the belly.
Jacula Prudentum, 1018

His bark is worse than his bite.
Ib. 1090

There is an hour wherein a man might be happy all his life, could he find it.   *Ib.* 1143

Woe be to him that reads but one book.   *Ib.* 1146

IZAAK WALTON
1593–1683

But God, who is able to prevail, wrestled with him, as the Angel did with Jacob, and marked him; marked him for his own.[1]
Life of Donne [1640]

I have laid aside business, and gone a-fishing.
The Compleat Angler [1653–1655]. *Epistle to the Reader*

Angling may be said to be so like the mathematics that it can never be fully learnt.   *Ib.*

As no man is born an artist, so no man is born an angler.   *Ib.*

I shall stay him no longer than to wish him a rainy evening to read this following discourse; and that if he be an honest angler, the east wind may never blow when he goes a-fishing.
Ib.

I am, Sir, a brother of the Angle.
Ib. pt. I, ch. 1

Doubt not but angling will prove to be so pleasant that it will prove to be, like virtue, a reward to itself.[2]

[1] See *Genesis 32:24,* p. 7b, and Thomas Gray, p. 441a.
[2] Ipsa quidem virtus sibimet pulcherrima merces [Virtue herself is her own fairest reward]. — SILIUS ITALICUS [A.D. c. 25–99], *Punica, bk. XIII, l. 663*
Virtue was sufficient of herself for happiness. — DIOGENES LAERTIUS [c. A.D. 200], *Plato XLII*
That virtue is her own reward, is but a cold principle. — SIR THOMAS BROWNE, *Religio Medici* [1642], *pt. I, sec. 47*
Virtue is its own reward. — PRIOR [1664–1721], *Imitations of Horace, bk. III, ode 2*

Sir Henry Wotton . . . was a most dear lover, and a frequent practicer of the art of angling; of which he would say, "it was an employment for his idle time, which was then not idly spent . . . a rest to his mind, a cheerer of his spirits, a diverter of sadness, a calmer of unquiet thoughts, a moderator of passions, a procurer of contentedness; and that it begat habits of peace and patience in those that professed and practiced it."

The Compleat Angler, pt.
I, ch. 1

You will find angling to be like the virtue of humility, which has a calmness of spirit and a world of other blessings attending upon it.[1]   *Ib.*

I remember that a wise friend of mine did usually say, "That which is everybody's business is nobody's business."   *Ib. 2*

An honest ale-house where we shall find a cleanly room, lavender in the windows, and twenty ballads stuck about the wall.   *Ib.*

Good company and good discourse are the very sinews of virtue.   *Ib.*

The Chavender or Chub.   *Ib. 3*

An excellent angler, and now with God.   *Ib. 4*

Old-fashioned poetry, but choicely good.   *Ib.*

I love such mirth as does not make friends ashamed to look upon one another next morning.   *Ib. 5*

No man can lose what he never had.
Ib.

We may say of angling as Dr. Boteler [2] said of strawberries: "Doubtless God could have made a better berry,

[1] There is certainly something in angling . . . that tends to produce a gentleness of spirit, and a pure serenity of mind. — WASHINGTON IRVING, *The Sketch-Book, The Angler*

[2] William Butler [1535–1618], styled by THOMAS FULLER in his *Worthies of England* the "Aesculapius of our age." This praise of the strawberry first appeared in the second edition of *The Angler*, 1655.

but doubtless God never did"; and so, if I might be judge, God never did make a more calm, quiet, innocent recreation than angling.

The Compleat Angler, pt.
I, ch. 5

Thus use your frog. . . . Put your hook through his mouth, and out at his gills; . . . and then with a fine needle and silk sew the upper part of his leg, with only one stitch, to the arming-wire of your hook; or tie the frog's leg, above the upper joint, to the armed-wire; and in so doing use him as though you loved him.[1]   *Ib. 8*

This dish of meat is too good for any but anglers, or very honest men.
Ib.

Look to your health; and if you have it, praise God, and value it next to a good conscience; for health is the second blessing that we mortals are capable of; a blessing that money cannot buy.   *Ib. 21*

Let the blessing of St. Peter's Master be . . . upon all that are lovers of virtue, and dare trust in his Providence, and be quiet and go a-angling.   *Ib.*

The great secretary of Nature and all learning, Sir Francis Bacon.[2]
Life of Herbert [1670]

THOMAS CAREW
c. 1595 – c. 1639

Here lies a King that rul'd, as he thought fit
The universal monarchy of wit;
Here lies two flamens, and both those the best:
Apollo's first, at last the true God's priest.
Elegy on the Death of Donne
[1633]

Ask me no more where Jove bestows,
When June is past, the fading rose;

[1] See Blunden, p. 1036a.

[2] Plato, Aristotle, and Socrates are secretaries of Nature. — JAMES HOWELL [1594–1666], *Letters, bk. II, letter 11*

For in your beauty's orient deep
These flowers, as in their causes, sleep.
   Poems [1640]. *To Celia, st.* 1

Ask me no more whither doth haste
The nightingale when May is past;
For in your sweet dividing throat
She winters and keeps warm her note.
   Ib. st. 3

Ask me no more if east or west
The Phoenix builds her spicy nest;
For unto you at last she flies,
And in your fragrant bosom dies.
   Ib. st. 5

Give me more love or more disdain;
  The torrid or the frozen zone:
Bring equal ease unto my pain;
  The temperate affords me none.
   Ib. Mediocrity in Love
    Rejected, st. 1

Thou shalt confess the vain pursuit
Of human glory yields no fruit
  But an untimely grave.
   Ib. On the Duke of Buckingham

He that loves a rosy cheek,
  Or a coral lip admires,
Or, from star-like eyes, doth seek
  Fuel to maintain his fires;
As old Time makes these decay,
So his flames must waste away.
   Ib. Disdain Returned, st. 1

The firstling of the infant year.
   Ib. The Primrose

Then fly betimes, for only they
Conquer Love that run away.
   Ib. Conquest by Flight

The magic of a face.
  Ib. Epitaph on the Lady S——

RENÉ DESCARTES
1596–1650

Good sense is of all things in the world the most equally distributed, for everybody thinks he is so well supplied with it, that even those most difficult to please in all other matters never desire more of it than they already possess.
   Le Discours de la Méthode
    [1637], I

It is not enough to have a good mind. The main thing is to use it well.
   Le Discours de la Méthode, I

The greatest minds are capable of the greatest vices as well as of the greatest virtues.
   Ib.

The first precept was never to accept a thing as true until I knew it as such without a single doubt.
   Ib.

One cannot conceive anything so strange and so implausible that it has not already been said by one philosopher or another.[1]
   Ib. II

I think, therefore I am.[2]
   Ib. IV

JAMES SHIRLEY
1596–1666

How little room
Do we take up in death that, living, know
No bounds!   *The Wedding* [1626]

I presume you're mortal, and may err.[3]
   The Lady of Pleasure [1635]

Only the actions of the just
Smell sweet and blossom in their dust.[4]
   Ib.

Death calls ye to the crowd of common
  men.   *Cupid and Death* [1653]

The glories of our blood and state
  Are shadows, not substantial things;
There is no armor against fate;
  Death lays his icy hand on kings.[5]
   Contention of Ajax and Ulysses
    [1659], *sc.* 3

OLIVER CROMWELL
1599–1658

A few honest men are better than numbers.
   Letter to Sir W. Spring [*September* 1643]

---

[1] See Varro, p. 110a, and Cicero, p. 111a.
[2] Cogito, ergo sum.
  Je pense, donc je suis.
[3] See Pope, p. 403b, and note.
[4] The sweet remembrance of the just
  Shall flourish when he sleeps in dust.
   NAHUM TATE and NICHOLAS BRADY,
    Psalm 132 [1696], *st.* 6
[5] See Horace, p. 120b.

The State, in choosing men to serve it, takes no notice of their opinions. If they be willing faithfully to serve it, that satisfies.

Before the Battle of Marston Moor [July 2, 1644]

I beseech you, in the bowels of Christ, think it possible you may be mistaken.[1]

Letter to the Church of Scotland [August 3, 1650]

It is not fit that you sit here any longer! . . . you shall now give place to better men.

To the Rump Parliament [January 22, 1654]

Necessity hath no law.[2] Feigned necessities, imaginary necessities . . . are the greatest cozenage that men can put upon the Providence of God, and make pretenses to break known rules by.

To Parliament [September 12, 1654]

I would have been glad to have lived under my woodside, and to have kept a flock of sheep, rather than to have undertaken this government.

To Parliament [1658]

Mr. Lely, I desire you would use all your skill to paint my picture truly like me, and not flatter me at all; but remark all these roughnesses, pimples, warts, and everything as you see me, otherwise I will never pay a farthing for it.[3]

From HORACE WALPOLE, *Anecdotes of Painting in England [1762–1771]*

It is not my design to drink or to sleep, but my design is to make what haste I can to be gone.

Dying words

PEDRO CALDERÓN DE LA BARCA
1600–1681

What is life? A madness. What is life? An illusion, a shadow, a story. And the greatest good is little enough: for all life is a dream, and dreams themselves are only dreams.

Life Is a Dream,[1] act II, l. 1195

But whether it be dream or truth, to do well is what matters. If it be truth, for truth's sake. If not, then to gain friends for the time when we awaken.

Ib. III, 236

The treason past, the traitor is no longer needed. *Ib. III, 1109*

What surprises you, if a dream taught me this wisdom, and if I still fear I may wake up and find myself once more confined in prison? And even if this should not happen, merely to dream it is enough. For this I have come to know, that all human happiness finally ceases, like a dream.

Ib. III, 1114

MARTIN PARKER
1600–1656

Ye gentlemen of England
That live at home at ease,
Ah! little do you think upon
The dangers of the seas. *Song*

When the stormy winds do blow.[2]
Ib.

JULES, CARDINAL MAZARIN
1602–1661

I must leave all that! Farewell, dear paintings that I have loved so much and which have cost me so much.[3]

Remark shortly before his death.

SIR KENELM DIGBY
1603–1665

The hot water is to remain upon it [the tea] no longer than whiles you can

---

[1] See Hand, p. 912a.

[2] See Publilius Syrus, p. 126b, and St. Augustine, p. 147a.

[3] Warts and all. — *Saying*

[1] Translated by EDWARD and ELIZABETH HUBERMAN in *Spanish Drama* [1962].

[2] When the battle rages loud and long,
And the stormy winds do blow.
THOMAS CAMPBELL [1777–1884],
Ye Mariners of England

[3] Il faut quitter tout cela! Adieu, chers tableaux que j'ai tant aimés et qui m'ont tant coûté.

say the Miserere Psalm [1] very leisurely.
The Closet Opened. Tea with Eggs

All matter is indifferent to form.
Of the Vegetation of Plants

ROGER WILLIAMS
c. 1603 – 1683

There goes many a ship to sea, with many hundred souls in one ship, whose weal and woe is common, and is a true picture of a commonwealth or a human combination or society. It hath fallen out sometimes that both papists and Protestants, Jews and Turks may be embarked in one ship; upon which supposal I affirm that all the liberty of conscience that ever I pleaded for turns upon these two hinges — that none of the papists, Protestants, Jews or Turks be forced to come to the ship's prayers or worship, nor compelled from their own particular prayers or worship, if they practice any. I further add that I never denied that, notwithstanding this liberty, the commander of this ship ought to command the ship's course, yea, and also command that justice, peace, and sobriety be kept and practiced, both among the seamen and all the passengers.
Letter to the Town of Providence
[January 1655]

FRIEDRICH VON LOGAU
1604–1655

Armed peace.
Poetic Aphorisms [2] *[1654]*

This month is a kiss
Which heaven gives the earth
That she now become a bride
And then a future mother.
Ib. Characteristics of May

Though the mills of God grind slowly, yet they grind exceeding small.[3]
Ib. Retribution

---

[1] Psalm 51.
[2] Sinngedichten
[3] Translated by LONGFELLOW.
See Euripides, p. 85a, and Herbert, p. 325a.

SIR THOMAS BROWNE
1605–1682

I dare, without usurpation, assume the honorable style of a Christian.
Religio Medici [1642], *pt. I, sec. 1*

I could never divide myself from any man upon the difference of an opinion, or be angry with his judgment for not agreeing with me in that from which perhaps within a few days I should dissent myself. 　　　*Ib. 6*

Many . . . have too rashly charged the troops of error, and remain as trophies unto the enemies of truth.
　　　Ib.

A man may be in as just possession of truth as of a city, and yet be forced to surrender.[1] 　　　*Ib.*

As for those wingy mysteries in divinity, and airy subtleties in religion, which have unhinged the brains of better heads, they never stretched the pia mater of mine. 　　　*Ib. 9*

I love to lose myself in a mystery, to pursue my Reason to an *O altitudo!*
　　　Ib.

Rich with the spoils of Nature.[2]
　　　Ib. 13

We carry with us the wonders we seek without us: There is all Africa and her prodigies in us. 　　　*Ib. 15*

All things are artificial, for nature is the art of God.[3] 　　　*Ib. 16*

Obstinacy in a bad cause is but constancy in a good. 　　　*Ib. 25*

Persecution is a bad and indirect way to plant religion. 　　　*Ib.*

Not picked from the leaves of any author, but bred amongst the weeds and tares of mine own brain. 　　*Ib. 35*

This reasonable moderator, and equal piece of justice, Death. 　　*Ib. 38*

I am not so much afraid of death, as ashamed thereof. 'Tis the very disgrace

---

[1] See Euripides, p. 84b, and Ovid, p. 129a.
[2] See Thomas Gray, p. 440b.
[3] The course of Nature is the art of God. — EDWARD YOUNG, *Night Thoughts* [1742–1745], *Night IX, l. 1267*

and ignominy of our natures, that in a moment can so disfigure us, that our nearest friends, wife, and children, stand afraid and start at us.
Religio Medici, pt. I, sec. 40

Whosoever enjoys not this life, I count him but an apparition, though he wear about him the sensible affections of flesh. In these moral acceptions, the way to be immortal is to die daily.
Ib. 45

How shall the dead arise, is no question of my faith; to believe only possibilities, is not faith, but mere philosophy.
Ib. 48

The heart of man is the place the devils dwell in: I feel sometimes a hell within myself.[1]
Ib. 51

There is no road or ready way to virtue.
Ib. 54

All places, all airs make unto me one country; I am in England, everywhere, and under any meridian.[2]
Ib. II, 1

They that endeavor to abolish vice, destroy also virtue; for contraries, though they destroy one another, are yet the life of one another.
Ib. 4

But how shall we expect charity towards others, when we are uncharitable to ourselves? *Charity begins at home*,[3] is the voice of the world; yet is every man his greatest enemy, and, as it were, his own executioner.
Ib.

Sure there is music even in the beauty, and the silent note which Cupid strikes, far sweeter than the sound of an instrument. For there is a music wherever there is a harmony, order proportion; and thus far we may maintain the music of the spheres.
Ib. 9

For the world, I count it not an inn, but an hospital; and a place not to live, but to die in.
Ib. 11

[1] See Virgil, p. 199a, Marlowe, p. 213a, and note.
[2] See Burton, p. 311a.
[3] See Terence, p. 108b.

There is surely a piece of divinity in us, something that was before the elements, and owes no homage unto the sun.
Religio Medici, pt. II, sec. 11

Ruat coelum, fiat voluntas tua [Though the heaven falls, let Thy will be done].[1]
Ib.

Sleep is a death; O, make me try,
By sleeping what it is to die,
And as gently lay my head
On my grave, as now my bed.[2]
Ib. 12

When we desire to confine our words, we commonly say they are spoken under the rose.[3]
Vulgar Errors [1645]

An old and gray-headed error. **Ib.**

Times before you, when even living men were antiquities; when the living might exceed the dead, and to depart this world could not be properly said to go unto the greater number.[4]
Urn-Burial; or Hydriotaphia [1658]. Dedication

With rich flames, and hired tears, they solemnized their obsequies.
Ib. ch. 3

Were the happiness of the next world as closely apprehended as the felicities of this, it were a martyrdom to live.
Ib. 4

These dead bones have . . . quietly rested under the drums and tramplings of three conquests.
Ib. 5

[1] Fiat iustitia et ruant coeli [Let justice be done though the heavens fall]. — WILLIAM WATSON, *Ten Quodlibetical Questions Concerning Religion and State* [1601]
See Ferdinand I, p. 186a.
[2] See Thomas Ken, p. 377b.
[3] Sub rosa. This phrase, meaning secretly, is of unknown origin. With the ancients the rose was emblematic of secrecy, and when a host hung a rose above his tables, his guests understood that all words spoken under it were to remain secret. Later, roses were carved as decorations on the ceilings of council chambers and confessionals, with the same significance.
[4] 'Tis long since Death had the majority. — ROBERT BLAIR, *The Grave* [1743], *pt. II, l. 449*

Time which antiquates antiquities, and hath an art to make dust of all things.

Urn-Burial; or Hydriotaphia, ch. 5

What song the Sirens sang, or what name Achilles assumed when he hid himself among women, though puzzling questions, are not beyond all conjecture. *Ib.*

The long habit of living indisposeth us for dying. *Ib.*

The iniquity of oblivion blindly scattereth her poppy, and deals with the memory of men without distinction to merit of perpetuity. *Ib.*

Herostratus lives that burnt the Temple of Diana — he is almost lost that built it.[1] *Ib.*

Oblivion is not to be hired: the greater part must be content to be as though they had not been, to be found in the register of God, not in the record of man. *Ib.*

The night of time far surpasseth the day, and who knows when was the equinox? *Ib.*

Man is a noble animal, splendid in ashes, and pompous in the grave. *Ib.*

That unextinguishable laugh in heaven.

Garden of Cyrus [1658], ch. 2

Life itself is but the shadow of death, and souls departed but the shadows of the living. All things fall under this name. The sun itself is but the dark simulacrum, and light but the shadow of God. *Ib. 4*

To keep our eyes open longer were but to act our Antipodes. The huntsmen are up in America, and they are already past their first sleep in Persia. But who can be drowsy at that hour which freed us from everlasting sleep?

or have slumbering thoughts at that time, when sleep itself must end, and, as some conjecture, all shall awake again?

Garden of Cyrus, ch. 5

The created world is but a small parenthesis in eternity.

Christian Morals, III, 29 [1716]

PIERRE CORNEILLE
1606–1684

To conquer without risk is to triumph without glory.

Le Cid [1636], act II, sc. 2

Brave men are brave from the very first. *Ib. II, 3*

And the combat ceased for want of combatants. *Ib. IV, 3*

Do your duty, and leave the rest to heaven. *Horace [1639], act II, sc. 8*

All evils are equal when they are extreme. *Ib. III, 4*

The worst of all states is the people's state. *Cinna [1640], act II, sc. 1*

Who is all-powerful should fear everything. *Ib. IV, 2*

By speaking of our misfortunes we often relieve them.

Polyeucte [1640], act I, sc. 3

The manner of giving is worth more than the gift.

Le Menteur [1642], act I, sc. 1

A liar is always lavish of oaths. *Ib. III, 5*

A good memory is needed after one has lied.[1] *Ib. IV, 5*

The fire which seems extinguished often slumbers beneath the ashes.

Rodogune [1644], act III, sc. 4

Guess if you can, choose if you dare.

Héraclius [1646], act IV, sc. 4

---

[1] The aspiring youth that fired the Ephesian dome
Outlives in fame the pious fool that raised it.
COLLEY CIBBER [1671–1757], *Richard III, act III, sc. 1*

[1] Liars ought to have good memories. — ALGERNON SIDNEY, *Discourses on Government* [1698], *ch. 2, sec. 15*

A service beyond all recompense
Weighs so heavy that it almost gives
offense.
      Suréna [1674], *act III, sc.* 1

I owe my fame only to myself.
      Poésies Diverses, 23

SIR WILLIAM DAVENANT
1606–1668

The lark now leaves his wat'ry nest
And, climbing, shakes his dewy wings.
      Song [1637], *st.* 1

For angling-rod he took a sturdy oak;
For line, a cable that in storm ne'er
broke.
      Britannia Triumphans [1637]

The hook was baited with a dragon's
tail —
And then on rock he stood to bob for
whale.
      Ib.

I shall ask leave to desist, when I am
interrupted by so great an experiment
as dying.
      *His apology, in illness, for not
having finished Gondibert*

How much pleasure they lose (and
even the pleasures of heroic poesy are
not unprofitable) who take away the
liberty of a poet, and fetter his feet in
the shackles of a historian.
      *Prefatory letter to Thomas
Hobbes. From* S. T. COLE-
RIDGE, *Biographia Literaria*
[1817], *ch.* 22

EDMUND WALLER
1606–1687

Illustrious acts high raptures do infuse,
And every conqueror creates a muse.
      Panegyric to My Lord Protector

Under the tropic is our language
spoke,
And part of Flanders hath receiv'd our
yoke.
      *Upon the Death of the Lord
Protector* [1658]

Guarded with ships, and all our sea our
own.[1]   *To My Lord of Falkland*

The yielding marble of her snowy
breast.
      *On a Lady Passing Through a
Crowd of People* [1664]

To man, that was in th' evening made,
  Stars gave the first delight;
Admiring, in the gloomy shade,
  Those little drops of light.
      *An Apology for Having Loved
Before* [1664]

That which her slender waist confin'd
Shall now my joyful temples bind;
No monarch but would give his crown
His arms might do what this has done.
      On a Girdle [1664], *st.* 1

My joy, my grief, my hope, my love,
Did all within this circle move!
      Ib. st. 2

A narrow compass! and yet there
Dwelt all that's good, and all that's
fair;
Give me but what this riband bound,
Take all the rest the sun goes round!
      Ib. st. 3

Go, lovely rose! [2]
Tell her that wastes her time and me
  That now she knows,
When I resemble her to thee,
How sweet and fair she seems to be.
      Go, Lovely Rose [1664], *st.* 1

So all we know
Of what they do above
Is that they happy are, and that they
love.
      *Upon the Death of
My Lady Rich* [1664]

Poets that lasting marble seek
Must come in Latin or in Greek.
      Of English Verse [1668]

---

[1] See Sir Francis Bacon, p. 209b, and note.
[2] Most of all I envy the octogenarian poet
who joined three words — "Go, lovely Rose"
—so happily together, that he left his name
to float down through Time on the wings of a
phrase and a flower. — LOGAN PEARSALL SMITH,
Afterthoughts [1931]

And keeps the palace of the soul.[1]
> *Of Tea*

Poets lose half the praise they should
have got,
Could it be known what they discreetly
blot.
> *Upon Roscommon's Translation
> of* HORACE, *De Arte Poetica*

The soul's dark cottage, batter'd and
decay'd,
Lets in new light through chinks that
Time has made; [2]
Stronger by weakness, wiser, men be-
come
As they draw near to their eternal
home.
Leaving the old, both worlds at once
they view,
That stand upon the threshold of the
new.
> *On the Divine Poems* [1686]

PAUL GERHARDT
1607–1676

O sacred head, now wounded,
With grief and shame bowed down;
Now scornfully surrounded
With thorns, thy only crown.[3]
> *Passion Chorale, based on
> twelfth-century Latin hymn,
> st. 1*

THOMAS FULLER
1608–1661

Drawing near her death, she sent
most pious thoughts as harbingers to
heaven; and her soul saw a glimpse of
happiness through the chinks of her
sickness-broken body.
> *Life of Monica* [1642]

He was one of a lean body and vis-

---

[1] See Byron, p. 555b.
[2] To vanish in the chinks that Time has made.
— SAMUEL ROGERS, *Italy* [1822], *Paestum*
[3] O Haupt vol Blut und Wunden
Vol Schmerz und voller Hohn!
O Haupt zum Spott gebunden
Mit einer Dornen Krohn!
Translated by JAMES WADDELL ALEXANDER
[1861].

age, as if his eager soul, biting for anger
at the clog of his body, desired to fret a
passage through it.[1]
> *Life of the Duke of Alva* [1642]

He knows little who will tell his wife
all he knows.[2]
> *The Holy State and the Profane
> State* [1642]. *The Good Husband*

One that will not plead that cause
wherein his tongue must be confuted
by his conscience.
> *Ib. The Good Advocate*

Their heads sometimes so little that
there is no room for wit; sometimes so
long that there is no wit for so much
room.   *Ib. Of Natural Fools*

Light, God's eldest daughter, is a
principal beauty in a building.
> *Ib. Of Building*

Learning hath gained most by those
books by which the printers have lost.
> *Ib. Of Books*

Deceive not thyself by overexpecting
happiness in the married estate. Remember the nightingales which sing
only some months in the spring, but
commonly are silent when they have
hatched their eggs.   *Ib. Of Marriage*

They that marry ancient people,
merely in expectation to bury them,
hang themselves in hope that one will
come and cut the halter.   *Ib.*

Fame sometimes hath created something of nothing.   *Ib. Fame*

Anger is one of the sinews of the
soul; he that wants it hath a maimed
mind.   *Ib. Of Anger*

It is always darkest just before the
day dawneth.
> *Pisgah Sight* [1650], *bk. II, ch 2*

JOHN MILTON[3]
1608–1674

This is the month, and this the happy
morn,

---

[1] See Dryden, p. 368a.
[2] See *Odyssey XI, 441,* p. 66a.
[3] See Wordsworth, *London,* p. 512b.

Wherein the Son of Heav'n's eternal King,
Of wedded maid and virgin mother born,
Our great redemption from above did bring;
For so the holy sages once did sing,
That He our deadly forfeit should release,
And with His Father work us a perpetual peace.
> *On the Morning of Christ's Nativity* [1629], *st.* 1, *l.* 1

It was the winter wild
While the Heav'n-born child
All meanly wrapt in the rude manger lies.   *Ib. Hymn, st.* 1, *l.* 29

No war, or battle's sound
Was heard the world around.
The idle spear and shield were high up hung.   *Ib. st.* 4, *l.* 53

Time will run back and fetch the Age of Gold.[1]   *Ib. st.* 14, *l.* 135

The Oracles are dumb.
> *Ib. st.* 19, *l.* 173

From haunted spring and dale
Edg'd with poplar pale
The parting genius is with sighing sent.   *Ib. st.* 20, *l.* 184

Peor and Baalim
Forsake their temples dim.
> *Ib. st.* 22, *l.* 197

What needs my Shakespeare for his honor'd bones
The labor of an age in piled stones?
Or that his hallow'd relics should be hid
Under a star-y-pointing pyramid?
Dear son of memory, great heir of fame,
What need'st thou such weak witness of thy name?
> *On Shakespeare* [1630]

How soon hath Time, the subtle thief of youth,

[1] See Horace, p. 122b.

Stol'n on his wing my three-and-twentieth year.
> *On His Having Arrived at the Age of Twenty-three* [1631]

As ever in my great Taskmaster's eye.
> *Ib.*

Such sweet compulsion doth in music lie.
> *Arcades* [1630–1634], *l.* 68

Hence, loathed Melancholy,
Of Cerberus and blackest Midnight born,
In Stygian cave forlorn,
'Mongst horrid shapes, and shrieks, and sights unholy.
> *L'Allegro* [1631], *l.* 1

So buxom, blithe, and debonair.
> *Ib. l.* 24

Haste thee, Nymph, and bring with thee
Jest, and youthful jollity,
Quips and cranks and wanton wiles,
Nods and becks and wreathed smiles.
> *Ib. l.* 25

Sport, that wrinkled Care derides,
And Laughter, holding both his sides.
Come, and trip it, as you go,
On the light fantastic toe.   *Ib. l.* 31

The mountain nymph, sweet liberty.
> *Ib. l.* 36

Mirth, admit me of thy crew,
To live with her, and live with thee,
In unreproved pleasures free.
> *Ib. l.* 38

While the cock with lively din
Scatters the rear of darkness thin,
And to the stack, or the barn door,
Stoutly struts his dames before,
Oft list'ning how the hounds and horn
Cheerly rouse the slumb'ring morn.
> *Ib. l.* 49

And every shepherd tells his tale
Under the hawthorn in the dale.
> *Ib. l.* 67

Meadows trim, with daisies pied,
Shallow brooks, and rivers wide;
Towers and battlements it sees

Bosom'd high in tufted trees,
Where perhaps some beauty lies,
The cynosure of neighboring eyes.
L'Allegro, l. 75

And the jocund rebecks sound
To many a youth, and many a maid,
Dancing in the checkered shade.
And young and old come forth to play
On a sunshine holiday. *Ib. l.* 94

Then to the spicy nut-brown ale.
Ib. l. 100

Then lies him down the lubber fiend,
And stretch'd out all the chimney's
length,
Basks at the fire his hairy strength.
Ib. l. 110

Tower'd cities please us then,
And the busy hum of men.
Ib. l. 117

Ladies, whose bright eyes
Rain influence, and judge the prize.
Ib. l. 121

And pomp, and feast, and revelry,
With mask, and antique pageantry,
Such sights as youthful poets dream
On summer eves by haunted stream.
Then to the well-trod stage anon,
If Jonson's learned sock be on,
Or sweetest Shakespeare, Fancy's
child,
Warble his native wood-notes wild,
And ever, against eating cares,
Lap me in soft Lydian airs,
Married to immortal verse [1]
Such as the meeting soul may pierce,
In notes with many a winding bout
Of linked sweetness long drawn out.
Ib. l. 127

Untwisting all the chains that tie
The hidden soul of harmony.
Ib. l. 143

Such strains as would have won the ear
Of Pluto, to have quite set free
His half-regain'd Eurydice.
These delights, if thou canst give,
Mirth, with thee, I mean to live.
Ib. l. 148

[1] Wisdom married to immortal verse. —
WORDSWORTH, *The Excursion* [1814], *bk. VII*

Hence vain deluding Joys,
The brood of Folly without father
bred!
Il Penseroso [1631], *l.* 1

The gay motes that people the sunbeams. *Ib. l.* 8

Hail divinest Melancholy. *Ib. l.* 12

Sober, steadfast, and demure.
Ib. l. 32

And looks commercing with the skies,
Thy rapt soul sitting in thine eyes.
Ib. l. 39

Forget thyself to marble. *Ib. l.* 42

And join with thee, calm Peace and
Quiet,
Spare Fast, that oft with gods doth
diet. *Ib. l.* 45

And add to these retired Leisure,
That in trim gardens takes his pleasure. *Ib. l.* 49

Sweet bird, that shunn'st the noise of
folly,
Most musical, most melancholy!
Ib. l. 61

I walk unseen
On the dry smooth-shaven green,
To behold the wandering moon,
Riding near her highest noon,
Like one that had been led astray
Through the heav'n's wide pathless
way,
And oft, as if her head she bow'd,
Stooping through a fleecy cloud.
Ib. l. 65

Oft, on a plat of rising ground,
I hear the far-off curfew sound
Over some wide-watered shore,
Swinging low with sullen roar.
Ib. l. 73

Where glowing embers through the
room
Teach light to counterfeit a gloom,
Far from all resort of mirth,
Save the cricket on the hearth.
Ib. l. 79

Sometime let gorgeous Tragedy
In sceptered pall come sweeping by,

Presenting Thebes, or Pelops' line,
Or the tale of Troy divine.
                    Il Penseroso, l. 97

Or bid the soul of Orpheus sing
Such notes as, warbled to the string,
Drew iron tears down Pluto's cheek.
                    Ib. l. 105

Or call up him that left half told
The story of Cambuscan bold.
                    Ib. l. 109

Where more is meant than meets the
      ear.   *Ib. l.* 120

Hide me from day's garish eye,
While the bee with honied thigh,
That at her flowery work doth sing,
And the waters murmuring
With such consort as they keep,
Entice the dewy-feather'd sleep.
                    Ib. l. 141

And storied windows richly dight,
Casting a dim religious light.
There let the pealing organ blow,
To the full-voiced choir below,
In service high, and anthems clear
As may, with sweetness, through mine
      ear
Dissolve me into ecstasies,
And bring all Heaven before mine
      eyes.   *Ib. l.* 159

Till old experience do attain
To something like prophetic strain.
                    Ib. l. 173

Before the starry threshold of Jove's
      Court [1]
My mansion is.   *Comus* [1634], *l.* 1

Above the smoke and stir of this dim
      spot
Which men call earth.   *Ib. l.* 5

Yet some there be that by due steps
      aspire
To lay their just hands on that golden
      key
That opes the palace of Eternity.
                    Ib. l. 12

An old, and haughty nation proud in
      arms.   *Ib. l.* 33

[1] See William Blake, p. 488b.

What never yet was heard in tale or
      song,
From old or modern bard, in hall or
      bower.
                    Comus, l. 44

Bacchus, that first from out the purple
      grape
Crush'd the sweet poison of misused
      wine.   *Ib. l.* 46

These my sky-robes, spun out of Iris'
      woof.   *Ib. l.* 83

The star that bids the shepherd fold.
                    Ib. l. 93

And the gilded car of day,
His glowing axle doth allay
In the steep Atlantic stream.
                    Ib. l. 95

Midnight shout and revelry,
Tipsy dance and jollity.   *Ib. l.* 103

What hath night to do with sleep?
                    Ib. l. 122

Ere the blabbing eastern scout,
The nice morn on th' Indian steep,
From her cabin'd loop-hole peep.
                    Ib. l. 138

Come, knit hands, and beat the
      ground,
In a light fantastic round.   *Ib. l.* 143

      When the gray-hooded Even,
Like a sad votarist in palmer's weed,
Rose from the hindmost wheels of
      Phoebus' wain.   *Ib. l.* 188

      A thousand fantasies
Begin to throng into my memory,
Of calling shapes, and beck'ning shad-
      ows dire,
And airy tongues that syllable men's
      names
On sands and shores and desert wilder-
      nesses.   *Ib. l.* 205

Was I deceiv'd or did a sable cloud
Turn forth her silver lining on the
      night?   *Ib. l.* 221

Sweet Echo, sweetest nymph, that liv'st
      unseen
      Within thy airy shell

By slow Meander's margent green,
  And in the violet-embroider'd vale.
              Comus, l. 230

How sweetly did they float upon the
  wings
Of silence, through the empty-vaulted
  night,
At every fall smoothing the raven
  down
Of darkness till it smil'd!   *Ib. l.* 249

Such sober certainty of waking bliss.
                 Ib. l. 263

With thy long level'd rule of streaming
  light.   *Ib. l.* 340

Virtue could see to do what Virtue
  would
By her own radiant light, though sun
  and moon
Were in the flat sea sunk. And Wisdom's self
Oft seeks to sweet retired solitude,
Where, with her best nurse Contemplation,
She plumes her feathers, and lets grow
  her wings.   *Ib. l.* 373

     The unsunn'd heaps
Of miser's treasure.   *Ib. l.* 398

'Tis Chastity, my brother, Chastity:
She that has that, is clad in complete
  steel.[1]   *Ib. l.* 420

How charming is divine philosophy!
Not harsh and crabbed, as dull fools
  suppose,
But musical as is Apollo's lute,[2]
And a perpetual feast of nectar'd
  sweets
Where no crude surfeit reigns.
                 Ib. l. 476

Fill'd the air with barbarous dissonance.   *Ib. l.* 550

    I was all ear,
And took in strains that might create a
  soul
Under the ribs of Death.   *Ib. l.* 560

[1] See Shakespeare, p. 215a.
[2]   As sweet and musical
As bright Apollo's lute.
    SHAKESPEARE, *Love's Labour's Lost*
    [1594–1595], *act IV, sc. 3, l. 342*

     That power
Which erring men call Chance.
              Comus, l. 587

Thou canst not touch the freedom of
  my mind.   *Ib. l.* 663

Praising the lean and sallow abstinence.   *Ib. l.* 709

Beauty is Nature's coin, must not be
  hoarded,
But must be current, and the good
  thereof
Consists in mutual and partaken bliss.
                 Ib. l. 739

Beauty is Nature's brag, and must be
  shown
In courts, at feasts, and high solemni-
  ties,
Where most may wonder at the workmanship;
It is for homely features to keep
  home —
They had their name thence; coarse
  complexions
And cheeks of sorry grain will serve to
  ply
The sampler, and to tease the huswife's
  wool.
What need a vermeil-tinctur'd lip for
  that,
Love-darting eyes, or tresses like the
  morn?   *Ib. l.* 745

Enjoy your dear wit, and gay rhetoric,
That hath so well been taught her dazzling fence.   *Ib. l.* 790

Sabrina fair,
  Listen where thou art sitting
Under the glassy, cool, translucent
  wave,
  In twisted braids of lilies knitting
The loose train of thy amber-dropping
  hair;
  Listen for dear honor's sake,
  Goddess of the silver lake,
      Listen and save.   *Ib. l.* 859

But now my task is smoothly done:
I can fly, or I can run.   *Ib. l.* 1012

Love Virtue, she alone is free,
She can teach ye how to climb

Higher than the sphery chime;
Or, if Virtue feeble were,
Heav'n itself would stoop to her.
Comus, l. 1019

Yet once more, O ye laurels, and once
   more
Ye myrtles brown, with ivy never sere,
I come to pluck your berries harsh and
   crude,
And with forc'd fingers rude
Shatter your leaves before the mellow-
   ing year.   *Lycidas* [1637], *l.* 1

      He knew
Himself to sing, and build the lofty
   rhyme.   *Ib. l.* 10

Without the meed of some melodious
   tear.   *Ib. l.* 14

Hence with denial vain, and coy excuse.   *Ib. l.* 18

Under the opening eyelids of the
   morn,
We drove afield; and both together
   heard
What time the gray-fly winds her sultry
   horn,
Batt'ning our flocks with the fresh dews
   of night.   *Ib. l.* 26

But O the heavy change, now thou art
   gone,
Now thou art gone and never must return!   *Ib. l.* 37

The gadding vine.   *Ib. l.* 40

As killing as the canker to the rose.
                     Ib. l. 45

Whom universal Nature did lament.
                     Ib. l. 60

Alas! what boots it with incessant
   care
To tend the homely slighted shepherd's
   trade,
And strictly meditate the thankless
   Muse?
Were it not better done as others use,
To sport with Amaryllis in the shade,
Or with the tangles of Neaera's hair?
Fame is the spur that the clear spirit
   doth raise [1]

[1] See Tacitus, p. 140a.

(That last infirmity of noble mind) [1]
To scorn delights, and live laborious
   days;
But the fair guerdon when we hope to
   find,
And think to burst out into sudden
   blaze,
Comes the blind Fury with th' ab-
   horred shears,
And slits the thin-spun life.
                   Lycidas, l. 64

Fame is no plant that grows on mortal
   soil.   *Ib. l.* 78

That strain I heard was of a higher
   mood.   *Ib. l.* 87

It was that fatal and perfidious bark,
Built in th' eclipse, and rigg'd with
   curses dark,
That sunk so low that sacred head of
   thine.   *Ib. l.* 100

Last came, and last did go,
The Pilot of the Galilean lake;
Two massy keys he bore of metals
   twain,
(The golden opes, the iron shuts
   amain).   *Ib. l.* 108

     Such as for their bellies' sake,
Creep and intrude, and climb into the
   fold.   *Ib. l.* 114

Blind mouths! That scarce themselves
   know how to hold
A sheep-hook.   *Ib. l.* 119

The hungry sheep look up, and are not
   fed,
But swoln with wind and the rank mist
   they draw,
Rot inwardly, and foul contagion
   spread:
Besides what the grim wolf with privy
   paw
Daily devours apace, and nothing said;
But that two-handed engine at the
   door

[1] That thirst [for applause], if the last infirmity of noble minds, is also the first infirmity
of weak ones; and on the whole, the strongest
impulsive influence of average humanity. —
Ruskin, *Sesame and Lilies* [1865], *Of Kings'
Treasuries, sec. 3*

Stands ready to smite once, and smite
no more.

Lycidas, l. 123

Throw hither all your quaint enamel'd
eyes,
That on the green turf suck the honied
showers,
And purple all the ground with vernal
flowers.
Bring the rathe primrose that forsaken
dies.   *Ib. l.* 139

Whether beyond the stormy Hebrides,[1]
Where thou perhaps under the whelming tide
Visit'st the bottom of the monstrous
world.   *Ib. l.* 156

Look homeward, Angel, now, and melt
with ruth.   *Ib. l.* 163

For Lycidas your sorrow is not dead,
Sunk though he be beneath the watery
floor;
So sinks the day-star in the ocean bed;
And yet anon repairs his drooping
head,
And tricks his beams, and with new-
spangled ore
Flames in the forehead of the morning
sky.
So Lycidas sunk low, but mounted
high,
Through the dear might of him that
walk'd the waves.   *Ib. l.* 166

He touch'd the tender stops of various
quills,
With eager thought warbling his Doric
lay.   *Ib. l.* 188

At last he rose, and twitch'd his mantle
blue:
Tomorrow to fresh woods and pastures
new.   *Ib. l.* 192

The lazy leaden-stepping Hours,

Whose speed is but the heavy plummet's pace.   *On Time* [*c.* 1637]

O nightingale, that on yon bloomy
spray

[1] See Thomson, p. 420a.

Warbl'st at eve, when all the woods are
still.

Sonnet, To the Nightingale
[*c.* 1637]

Thy liquid notes that close the eye of
day.   *Ib.*

Where the bright seraphim in burning
row
Their loud up-lifted angel trumpets
blow.

At a Solemn Music [*c.* 1637]

A poet soaring in the high reason of
his fancies, with his garland and singing
robes about him.

The Reason of Church Govern-
ment [1641], *bk. II, introduc-*
tion

By labor and intent study (which I
take to be my portion in this life),
joined with the strong propensity of nature, I might perhaps leave something
so written to after-times, as they should
not willingly let it die.   *Ib.*

Beholding the bright countenance of
truth in the quiet and still air of delightful studies.   *Ib.*

He who would not be frustrate of his
hope to write well hereafter in laudable
things ought himself to be a true
poem.

Apology for Smectymnuus [1642]

His words . . . like so many nimble
and airy servitors trip about him at
command.   *Ib.*

Truth . . . never comes into the
world but like a bastard, to the ignominy of him that brought her forth.[1]

The Doctrine and Discipline of
Divorce [1643], *introduction*

Let not England forget her precedence of teaching nations how to live.[2]

Ib.

[1] Still rule those minds on earth
  At whom sage Milton's wormwood words
    were hurled:
  "Truth like a bastard comes into the world
  Never without ill-fame to him who gives
    her birth"?

THOMAS HARDY, *Lausanne* [1897]

[2] See Virgil, p. 119a.

Litigious terms, fat contentions, and flowing fees.

Tractate of Education [1644]

Inflamed with the study of learning and the admiration of virtue; stirred up with high hopes of living to be brave men and worthy patriots, dear to God, and famous to all ages. ***Ib.***

Ornate rhetoric taught out of the rule of Plato. . . . To which poetry would be made subsequent, or indeed rather precedent, as being less subtle and fine, but more simple, sensuous, and passionate. ***Ib.***

In those vernal seasons of the year, when the air is calm and pleasant, it were an injury and sullenness against Nature not to go out, and see her riches, and partake in her rejoicing with heaven and earth. ***Ib.***

Books are not absolutely dead things, but do contain a potency of life in them to be as active as that soul was whose progeny they are; nay they do preserve as in a vial the purest efficacy and extraction of that living intellect that bred them. *Areopagitica* [1644]

As good almost kill a man as kill a good book: who kills a man kills a reasonable creature, God's image; but he who destroys a good book kills reason itself. ***Ib.***

A good book is the precious lifeblood of a master spirit, embalmed and treasured up on purpose to a life beyond life. ***Ib.***

I cannot praise a fugitive and cloistered virtue, unexercised and unbreathed, that never sallies out and sees her adversary, but slinks out of the race, where that immortal garland is to be run for, not without dust and heat. ***Ib.***

Where there is much desire to learn, there of necessity will be much arguing, much writing, many opinions; for opinion in good men is but knowledge in the making. ***Ib.***

Methinks I see in my mind a noble and puissant nation rousing herself like a strong man after sleep, and shaking her invincible locks. Methinks I see her as an eagle mewing her mighty youth, and kindling her undazzled eyes at the full midday beam.

Areopagitica

Give me the liberty to know, to utter, and to argue freely according to conscience, above all liberties. ***Ib.***

Though all the winds of doctrine [1] were let loose to play upon the earth, so Truth be in the field, we do injuriously, by licensing and prohibiting, to misdoubt her strength. Let her and Falsehood grapple; who ever knew Truth put to the worse, in a free and open encounter? [2] ***Ib.***

Men of most renowned virtue have sometimes by transgressing most truly kept the law.

Tetrachordon [1644–1645]

That old man eloquent.

To the Lady Margaret Ley [c. 1644]

That would have made Quintilian stare and gasp.

On the Detraction Which Followed Upon My Writing Certain Treatises [1645]

In mirth, that after no repenting draws.

To Cyriack Skinner [1646–1647?]

For other things mild Heav'n a time ordains,
And disapproves that care, though wise in show,
That with superfluous burden loads the day,
And, when God sends a cheerful hour, refrains. ***Ib.***

For such kind of borrowing as this, if it be not bettered by the borrower, among good authors is accounted Plagiarè. *Eikonoklastes* [1649], 23

[1] See *Ephesians 4:14*, p. 54a.
[2] Error of opinion may be tolerated where reason is left free to combat it. — JEFFERSON, *Inaugural Address* [March 4, 1801]

None can love freedom heartily, but
good men; the rest love not freedom,
but license.
> *Tenure of Kings and Magistrates*
> . [1649]

No man who knows aught, can be so
stupid to deny that all men naturally
were born free.   *Ib.*

Peace hath her victories
No less renown'd than war.
> *To the Lord General Cromwell*
> [1652]

When I consider how my light is
    spent,
Ere half my days, in this dark world
    and wide,
And that one talent which is death to
    hide
Lodg'd with me useless.
> *On His Blindness* [1652]

Doth God exact day-labor, light de-
    nied?   *Ib.*

       Who best
Bear his mild yoke, they serve him best:
    his state
Is kingly; thousands at his bidding
    speed,
And post o'er land and ocean without
    rest;
They also serve who only stand and
    wait.   *Ib.*

Avenge, O Lord, thy slaughter'd saints,
    whose bones
Lie scatter'd on the Alpine mountains
    cold;
Ev'n them who kept thy truth so pure
    of old
When all our fathers worship'd stocks
    and stones
Forget not.
> *On the Late Massacre in*
> *Piedmont* [1655]

      Yet I argue not
Against Heav'n's hand or will, nor bate
    one jot
Of heart or hope; but still bear up, and
    steer
Right onward.
> *To Cyriack Skinner, Upon his*
> *Blindness* [c. 1655]

Methought I saw my late espoused
    saint
Brought to me like Alcestis from the
    grave.
> *On his Deceased Wife* [c. 1658]

But oh! as to embrace me she inclin'd,
I wak'd, she fled, and day brought back
    my night.   *Ib.*

Of Man's first disobedience, and the
    fruit
Of that forbidden tree whose mortal
    taste
Brought death into the world, and all
    our woe,
With loss of Eden.
> *Paradise Lost* [1667], bk. I, l. 1

Things unattempted yet in prose or
    rhyme.   *Ib. l. 16*

      What in me is dark
Illumine, what is low raise and sup-
    port;
That to the highth of this great argu-
    ment
I may assert eternal Providence,
And justify the ways of God to men.[1]
>   *Ib. l. 22*

The infernal serpent; he it was, whose
    guile,
Stirr'd up with envy and revenge, de-
    ceiv'd
The mother of mankind.   *Ib. l. 34*

      Him the Almighty Power
Hurl'd headlong flaming from th' ethe-
    real sky [2]
With hideous ruin and combustion
    down
To bottomless perdition, there to
    dwell
In adamantine chains and penal fire,
Who durst defy th' Omnipotent to
    arms.   *Ib. l. 44*

As far as angels ken.   *Ib. l. 59*

No light, but rather darkness visible.
>   *Ib. l. 63*

Regions of sorrow, doleful shades,
    where peace

---

[1] See *Samson Agonistes*, p. 349a; Pope, p.
407b; and A. E. Housman, p. 853b.
[2] See *Luke 10:18*, p. 46b.

And rest can never dwell, hope never
comes
That comes to all.
Paradise Lost, bk. I, l. 65

What though the field be lost?
All is not lost; th' unconquerable will,
And study of revenge, immortal hate,
And courage never to submit or yield.
Ib. l. 105

Vaunting aloud, but rack'd with deep
despair. *Ib. l. 126*

To be weak is miserable,
Doing or suffering. *Ib. l. 157*

And out of good still to find means of
evil. *Ib. l. 165*

The seat of desolation, void of light.
Ib. l. 181

A mind not to be chang'd by place or
time.
The mind is its own place, and in itself
Can make a heav'n of hell, a hell of
heav'n.[1] *Ib. l. 253*

To reign is worth ambition though in
hell:
Better to reign in hell than serve in
heav'n. *Ib. l. 262*

His spear, to equal which the tallest
pine
Hewn on Norwegian hills, to be the
mast
Of some great ammiral, were but a
wand,
He walk'd with, to support uneasy
steps
Over the burning marle. *Ib. l. 292*

Thick as autumnal leaves that strow the
brooks
In Vallombrosa. *Ib. l. 302*

Awake, arise, or be forever fallen!
Ib. l. 330

Spirits, when they please,
Can either sex assume, or both.
Ib. l. 423

[1] See Virgil, p. 199a, Marlowe, p. 213a, and
note.

When night
Darkens the streets, then wander forth
the sons
Of Belial, flown with insolence and
wine.
Paradise Lost, bk. I, l. 500

Th' imperial ensign, which, full high
advanc'd,
Shone like a meteor, streaming to the
wind.[1] *Ib. l. 536*

Sonorous metal blowing martial sounds:
At which the universal host up sent
A shout that tore hell's concave, and
beyond
Frighted the reign of Chaos and old
Night. *Ib. l. 540*

Anon they move
In perfect phalanx, to the Dorian
mood
Of flutes and soft recorders.
Ib. l. 549

His form had yet not lost
All her original brightness, nor ap-
pear'd
Less than archangel ruin'd, and th' ex-
cess
Of glory obscur'd. *Ib. l. 591*

The sun . . .
In dim eclipse, disastrous twilight
sheds
On half the nations, and with fear of
change
Perplexes monarchs. *Ib. l. 594*

Care
Sat on his faded cheek, but under
brows
Of dauntless courage. *Ib. l. 601*

Thrice he assay'd, and thrice, in spite
of scorn,
Tears, such as angels weep, burst
forth. *Ib. l. 619*

Who overcomes
By force hath overcome but half his
foe. *Ib. l. 648*

Mammon, the least erected spirit that
fell

[1] Stream'd like a meteor to the troubled air.
— THOMAS GRAY, *The Bard* [1757], *sec. I, st. 2,
l. 6*

From heaven; for ev'n in heaven his
    looks and thoughts
Were always downward bent, admiring
    more
The riches of heaven's pavement, trod-
    den gold,
Than aught divine or holy else enjoy'd
In vision beatific.
           Paradise Lost, bk. I, l. 679

      Let none admire
That riches grow in hell; that soil may
    best
Deserve the precious bane.
                  Ib. l. 690

      From morn
To noon he fell, from noon to dewy
    eve,
A summer's day; and with the setting
    sun
Dropp'd from the zenith like a falling
    star.   *Ib. l.* 742

High on a throne of royal state, which
    far
Outshone the wealth of Ormus and of
    Ind,
Or where the gorgeous East with rich-
    est hand
Showers on her kings barbaric pearl and
    gold,
Satan exalted sat, by merit rais'd
To that bad eminence; and from de-
    spair
Thus high uplifted beyond hope, as-
    pires
Beyond thus high, insatiate to pursue
Vain war with heav'n.   *Ib. II, l.* 1

    Moloch, scepter'd king,
Stood up, the strongest and the fiercest
    spirit
That fought in heav'n; now fiercer by
    despair.   *Ib. l.* 44

    Rather than be less
Car'd not to be at all.   *Ib. l.* 47

My sentence is for open war.
                      Ib. l. 51

Which if not victory is yet revenge.
                    Ib. l. 105

But all was false and hollow; though his
    tongue
Dropp'd manna, and could make the
    worse appear
The better reason.[1]
          Paradise Lost, bk. II, l. 112

    For who would lose,
Though full of pain, this intellectual
    being,
Those thoughts that wander through
    eternity,
To perish rather, swallow'd up and lost
In the wide womb of uncreated night,
Devoid of sense and motion?
                  Ib. l. 146

His red right hand.[2]   *Ib. l.* 174

Unrespited, unpitied, unrepriev'd.[3]
                  Ib. l. 185

    The never-ending flight
Of future days.   *Ib. l.* 221

Thus Belial with words cloth'd in rea-
    son's garb
Counsel'd ignoble ease, and peaceful
    sloth,
Not peace.   *Ib. l.* 226

    With grave
Aspect he rose, and in his rising
    seem'd
A pillar of state; deep on his front en-
    graven
Deliberation sat and public care;
And princely counsel in his face yet
    shone,
Majestic though in ruin.   *Ib. l.* 300

    To sit in darkness here
Hatching vain empires.   *Ib. l.* 377

The palpable obscure.   *Ib. l.* 406

    Long is the way
And hard, that out of hell leads up to
    light.[4]   *Ib. l.* 432

Their rising all at once was as the
    sound
Of thunder heard remote.   *Ib. l.* 476

[1] See Aristophanes, p. 91a.
[2] Rubente   dextera. — HORACE [65–8 B.C.].
Odes I, ii, 2, To Caesar Augustus
[3] See Homer, p. 64b, and note.
[4] See Virgil, p. 118b.

Others apart sat on a hill retir'd,
In thoughts more elevate, and reason'd
  high
Of Providence, foreknowledge, will, and
  fate,
Fix'd fate, free will, foreknowledge absolute,
And found no end, in wand'ring mazes
  lost.
          Paradise Lost, bk. II, l. 557

Vain wisdom all, and false philosophy.
                              Ib. l. 565

    Arm th' obdur'd breast
With stubborn patience as with triple
  steel.[1]   *Ib. l.* 568

Far off from these a slow and silent
  stream,
Lethe the river of oblivion rolls.
                              Ib. l. 582

At certain revolutions all the damn'd
Are brought: and feel by turns the bitter change
Of fierce extremes, extremes by change
  more fierce.   *Ib. l.* 597

    The other shape,
If shape it might be call'd.
                              Ib. l. 666

Whence and what art thou, execrable
  shape?   *Ib. l.* 681

Before mine eyes in opposition sits
Grim Death [2] my son and foe.
                              Ib. l. 803

Hot, cold, moist, and dry, four champions fierce,[3]
Strive here for mast'ry.   *Ib. l.* 898

    To compare
Great things with small.   *Ib. l.* 921

With ruin upon ruin, rout on rout,
Confusion worse confounded.
                              Ib. l. 995

And fast by hanging in a golden chain,
This pendent world, in bigness as a
  star

[1] See Shakespeare, p. 215a.
[2] See Massinger, p. 316a.
[3] Hot and cold, and moist and dry. — DU
BARTAS, *Divine Weeks and Works* [1578], *Second Day*
See Dryden, p. 369b.

Of smallest magnitude close by the
  moon.
          Paradise Lost, bk. II, l. 1051

Hail, holy light! offspring of heav'n firstborn.[1]   *Ib. III, l.* 1

    Thus with the year
Seasons return; but not to me returns
Day, or the sweet approach of ev'n or
  morn,
Or sight of vernal bloom, or summer's
  rose,
Or flocks, or herds, or human face di-
  vine; [2]
But cloud instead, and ever-during
  dark
Surrounds me, from the cheerful ways
  of men
Cut off, and for the book of knowledge
  fair
Presented with a universal blank
Of Nature's works to me expung'd and
  raz'd,
And wisdom at one entrance quite shut
  out.   *Ib. l.* 40

See golden days, fruitful of golden
  deeds,
With Joy and Love triumphing.
                              Ib. l. 337

Dark with excessive bright.
                              Ib. l. 380

Into a limbo large and broad, since
  called
The Paradise of Fools, to few unknown.   *Ib. l.* 495

The hell within him.   *Ib. IV, l.* 20

    At whose sight all the stars
Hide their diminish'd heads.[3]
                              Ib. l. 34

    A grateful mind
By owing owes not, but still pays, at
  once
Indebted and discharg'd.   *Ib. l.* 55

[1] God's first creature, which was light. —
BACON, *The New Atlantis* [1626]
Light, the prime work of God. — MILTON,
Samson Agonistes (*1671*), l. 70
[2] See Blake, pp. 487a and 489b.
[3] Ye little stars! hide your diminished rays.
— POPE: *Moral Essays* [1731–1735], *Epistle III,
l.* 282

Me miserable! which way shall I fly
Infinite wrath, and infinite despair?
Which way I fly is hell; myself am
hell; [1]
And in the lowest deep a lower deep,
Still threat'ning to devour me, opens
wide,
To which the hell I suffer seems a
heaven.
Paradise Lost, bk. IV, l. 73

So farewell hope, and with hope farewell fear,
Farewell remorse: all good to me is
lost;
Evil, be thou my good. *Ib. l. 108*

And on the Tree of Life,
The middle tree and highest there that
grew,
Sat like a cormorant. *Ib. l. 194*

A heaven on earth. *Ib. l. 208*

Flowers of all hue, and without thorn
the rose. *Ib. l. 256*

Two of far nobler shape erect and tall,
Godlike erect, with native honor clad
In naked majesty seem'd lords of all.
Ib. l. 288

For contemplation he and valor.
form'd,
For softness she and sweet attractive
grace;
He for God only, she for God in him.
Ib. l. 297

Implied
Subjection, but requir'd with gentle
sway,
And by her yielded, by him best re-
ceiv'd,
Yielded with coy submission, modest
pride,
And sweet reluctant amorous delay.
Ib. l. 307

Adam the goodliest man of men since
born
His sons, the fairest of her daughters
Eve. *Ib. l. 323*

So spake the Fiend, and with necessity,

[1] See Virgil, p. 199a, Marlowe, p. 213a, and
note.

The tyrant's plea,[1] excus'd his devilish
deeds.
Paradise Lost, bk. IV, l. 393

Imparadis'd in one another's arms.
Ib. l. 506

Live while ye may,
Yet happy pair. *Ib. l. 533*

Now came still evening on, and twilight
gray
Had in her sober livery all things clad.
Ib. l. 598

The wakeful nightingale,
She all night long her amorous descant
sung;
Silence was pleas'd: now glow'd the
firmament
With living sapphires: Hesperus, that
led
The starry host, rode brightest, till the
moon,
Rising in clouded majesty, at length
Apparent queen unveil'd her peerless
light,
And o'er the dark her silver mantle
threw. *Ib. l. 602*

The timely dew of sleep. *Ib. l. 614*

With thee conversing I forget all time,
All seasons, and their change; all please
alike.
Sweet is the breath of morn, her rising
sweet,
With charm of earliest birds. *Ib. l. 639*

Sweet the coming on
Of grateful ev'ning mild, then silent
night
With this her solemn bird, and this fair
moon,
And these the gems of heaven, her
starry train. *Ib. l. 646*

Millions of spiritual creatures walk the
earth
Unseen, both when we wake, and when
we sleep. *Ib. l. 677*

In naked beauty more adorn'd,

[1] See William Pitt, p. 496b.

More lovely, than Pandora.[1]
> *Paradise Lost*, bk. IV, l. 713

Eas'd the putting off
These troublesome disguises which we
wear.   *Ib. l.* 739

Hail wedded love, mysterious law, true
source
Of human offspring.   *Ib. l.* 750

Squat like a toad, close at the ear of
Eve.   *Ib. l.* 800

Not to know me argues yourselves unknown.   *Ib. l.* 830

Abash'd the Devil stood,
And felt how awful goodness is, and
saw
Virtue in her shape how lovely.
> *Ib. l.* 846

All hell broke loose.[2]   *Ib. l.* 918

Like Teneriff or Atlas unremoved.
> *Ib. l.* 987

The starry cope
Of heaven.   *Ib. l.* 992

His sleep
Was airy light from pure digestion
bred.   *Ib. V, l.* 3

My latest found,
Heaven's last, best gift, my ever new
delight!   *Ib. l.* 18

Good, the more
Communicated, more abundant grows.
> *Ib. l.* 71

These are thy glorious works, Parent of
good.   *Ib. l.* 153

Him first, him last, him midst, and
without end.   *Ib. l.* 165

A wilderness of sweets.   *Ib. l.* 294

So saying, with dispatchful looks in
haste
She turns, on hospitable thoughts intent.   *Ib. l.* 331

Nor jealousy
Was understood, the injur'd lover's
hell.   *Ib. l.* 449

[1] See Cicero, p. 111a, and James Thomson, p. 419b.
[2] See Robert Greene, p. 206a.

Freely we serve,
Because we freely love, as in our will
To love or not; in this we stand or fall.
> *Paradise Lost*, bk. V, l. 538

What if earth
Be but the shadow of heaven, and
things therein
Each to other like, more than on earth
is thought?   *Ib. l.* 574

Hear all ye Angels, progeny of light,
Thrones, Dominations, Princedoms,
Virtues, Powers.   *Ib. l.* 600

All seem'd well pleas'd, all seem'd but
were not all.   *Ib. l.* 617

Among the faithless, faithful only he.
> *Ib. l.* 897

Morn,
Wak'd by the circling hours, with rosy
hand [1]
Unbarr'd the gates of light.
> *Ib. VI, l.* 2

Servant of God, well done,[2] well hast
thou fought
The better fight, who single hast maintained
Against revolted multitudes the cause
Of truth, in word mightier than they in
arms.   *Ib. l.* 29

He onward came; far off his coming
shone.   *Ib. l.* 768

More safe I sing with mortal voice, un-
chang'd
To hoarse or mute, though fall'n on
evil days,
On evil days though fall'n, and evil
tongues;
In darkness, and with dangers compass'd round,
And solitude.   *Ib. VII, l.* 24

Out of one man a race
Of men innumerable.   *Ib. l.* 155

There Leviathan
Hugest of living creatures, on the deep
Stretch'd like a promontory sleeps or
swims,

[1] See Homer, p. 62b.
[2] See *Matthew* 25:21, p. 44a.

And seems a moving land, and at his
gills
Draws in, and at his trunk spouts out a
sea.
Paradise Lost, bk. VII, *l.* 412

Endued
With sanctity of reason. *Ib. l.* 507

The planets in their stations list'ning
stood,
While the bright pomp ascended jubilant.
Open, ye everlasting gates, they sung,
Open, ye heavens, your living doors; [1]
let in
The great Creator from his work return'd
Magnificent, his six days' work, a
world. *Ib. l.* 563

The angel ended, and in Adam's ear
So charming left his voice that he
awhile
Thought him still speaking, still stood
fix'd to hear. *Ib.* VIII, *l.* 1

To know
That which before us lies in daily life
Is the prime wisdom. *Ib. l.* 192

Liquid lapse of murmuring streams.
Ib. l. 263

And feel that I am happier than I
know. *Ib. l.* 282

Her virtue and the conscience of her
worth,
That would be woo'd, and not unsought be won. *Ib. l.* 502

The sum of earthly bliss. *Ib. l.* 522

So absolute she seems
And in herself complete, so well to
know
Her own, that what she wills to do or
say,
Seems wisest, virtuousest, discreetest,
best. *Ib. l.* 547

Accuse not Nature, she hath done her
part;
Do thou but thine. *Ib. l.* 561

[1] See *Psalm 24:7*, p. 18a.

Ofttimes nothing profits more
Than self-esteem, grounded on just and
right
Well manag'd.
Paradise Lost, bk. VIII, *l.* 571

My unpremeditated verse.
Ib. IX, *l.* 24

Pleas'd me long choosing, and beginning late. *Ib. l.* 26

Unless an age too late, or cold
Climate, or years damp my intended
wing. *Ib. l.* 44

The serpent subtlest beast of all the
field.[1] *Ib. l.* 86

For solitude sometimes is best society,
And short retirement urges sweet return. *Ib. l.* 249

At shut of evening flowers.
Ib. l. 278

As one who long in populous city
pent.[2] *Ib. l.* 445

God so commanded, and left that command
Sole daughter of his voice; [3] the rest,
we live
Law to ourselves, our reason is our law.
Ib. l. 652

Her rash hand in evil hour
Forth reaching to the fruit, she pluck'd,
she eat:
Earth felt the wound, and Nature from
her seat,
Sighing through all her works, gave
signs of woe
That all was lost. *Ib. l.* 780

So dear I love him, that with him all
deaths
I could endure, without him live no
life. *Ib. l.* 832

In her face excuse
Came prologue, and apology too
prompt. *Ib. l.* 853

O fairest of creation! last and best
Of all God's works! creature in whom
excell'd

[1] See *Genesis 3:1*, p. 5b.
[2] See Keats, p. 579a.
[3] See Wordsworth, p. 514b.

Whatever can to sight or thought be form'd,
Holy, divine, good, amiable, or sweet!
How art thou lost, how on a sudden lost,
Defac'd, deflower'd, and now to Death devote?
Paradise Lost, bk. IX, l. 896

I feel
The link of nature draw me: flesh of flesh,
Bone of my bone thou art,[1] and from thy state
Mine never shall be parted, bliss or woe.   *Ib. l.* 913

Our state cannot be sever'd; we are one,
One flesh; to lose thee were to lose myself.   *Ib. l.* 958

I shall temper so
Justice with mercy.   *Ib. X, l.* 77

Pandemonium, city and proud seat
Of Lucifer.   *Ib. l.* 424

A dismal universal hiss, the sound
Of public scorn.   *Ib. l.* 508

Death . . . on his pale horse.[2]
Ib. l. 588

Demoniac frenzy, moping melancholy,
And moon-struck madness.
Ib. XI, l. 485

Nor love thy life, nor hate; but what thou liv'st
Live well; how long or short permit to Heaven.[3]   *Ib. l.* 553

A bevy of fair women.   *Ib. l.* 582

The evening star,
Love's harbinger.   *Ib. l.* 588

The brazen throat of war.
Ib. l. 713

For now I see
Peace to corrupt no less than war to waste.   *Ib. l.* 783

An olive leaf he brings, pacific sign.
Ib. l. 860

In me is no delay; with thee to go,
Is to stay here; without thee here to stay,
Is to go hence unwilling; thou to me
Art all things under heaven, all places thou,
Who for my willful crime art banished hence.
Paradise Lost, bk. XII, l. 615

The world was all before them, where to choose
Their place of rest, and Providence their guide:
They hand in hand with wand'ring steps and slow
Through Eden took their solitary way.
Ib. l. 646

Most men admire
Virtue who follow not her lore.
Paradise Regained [1671], *bk. I, l.* 482

Skill'd to retire, and in retiring draw
Hearts after them tangled in amorous nets.   *Ib. II, l.* 161

Beauty stands
In the admiration only of weak minds
Led captive.   *Ib. l.* 220

Rocks whereon greatest men have oftest wreck'd.   *Ib. l.* 228

Of whom to be disprais'd were no small praise.   *Ib. III, l.* 56

Elephants endorsed with towers.
Ib. l. 329

Dusk faces with white silken turbans wreath'd.   *Ib. IV, l.* 76

The childhood shows the man,
As morning shows the day.[1]
Ib. l. 220

Athens, the eye of Greece, mother of arts
And eloquence.   *Ib. l.* 240

The olive grove of Academe,[2]
Plato's retirement, where the Attic bird
Trills her thick-warbled notes the summer long.   *Ib. l.* 244

---

[1] See *Genesis 2:23*, p. 5b.
[2] See *Revelation 6:8*, p. 58a.
[3] See Martial, p. 134b.

[1] See Wordsworth, p. 511b.
[2] See Horace, p. 124a.

Socrates . . .
Whom well inspir'd the oracle pronounc'd
Wisest of men.
>*Paradise Regained,*
>*bk. IV, l. 274*

The first and wisest of them all professed
To know this only, that he nothing knew.[1]   *Ib. l. 293*

Deep vers'd in books and shallow in himself.   *Ib. l. 327*

Till morning fair
Came forth with pilgrim steps, in amice gray.   *Ib. l. 426*

Eyeless in Gaza, at the mill with slaves.
>*Samson Agonistes* [1671], *l. 41*

O dark, dark, dark, amid the blaze of noon,
Irrecoverably dark, total eclipse
Without all hope of day!   *Ib. l. 80*

The sun to me is dark
And silent as the moon,
When she deserts the night,
Hid in her vacant interlunar cave.
>*Ib. l. 86*

To live a life half dead, a living death.
>*Ib. l. 100*

Ran on embattled armies clad in iron,
And, weaponless himself,
Made arms ridiculous.   *Ib. l. 129*

Apt words have power to suage
The tumors of a troubled mind.[2]
>*Ib. l. 184*

Wisest men
Have err'd, and by bad women been deceiv'd.   *Ib. l. 210*

Just are the ways of God,
And justifiable to men;[3]
Unless there be who think not God at all.   *Ib. l. 293*

A grain of manhood.   *Ib. l. 408*

What boots it at one gate to make defense,

[1] See Socrates, p. 87b.
[2] See Aeschylus, p. 78a.
[3] See *Paradise Lost, bk. I, l. 22,* p. 341b.

And at another to let in the foe?
>*Samson Agonistes, l. 560*

My race of glory run, and race of shame,
And I shall shortly be with them at rest.   *Ib. l. 597*

But who is this, what thing of sea or land?
Female of sex it seems,
That so bedeck'd, ornate, and gay,
Comes this way sailing
Like a stately ship
Of Tarsus, bound for th' isles
Of Javan or Gadire,
With all her bravery on, and tackle trim,
Sails fill'd, and streamers waving,
Courted by all the winds that hold them play;
An amber scent of odorous perfume
Her harbinger?   *Ib. l. 710*

Dalila: In argument with men a woman ever
Goes by the worse, whatever be her cause.
Samson: For want of words, no doubt, or lack of breath!   *Ib. l. 903*

Fame, if not double-faced, is double-mouthed,
And with contrary blast proclaims most deeds;
On both his wings, one black, the other white,
Bears greatest names in his wild airy flight.   *Ib. l. 971*

Yet beauty, though injurious, hath strange power,
After offense returning, to regain
Love once possess'd.   *Ib. l. 1003*

Love-quarrels oft in pleasing concord end;
Not wedlock-treachery.   *Ib. l. 1008*

Boast not of what thou would'st have done, but do
What then thou would'st.
>*Ib. l. 1104*

He's gone; and who knows how he may report

Thy words by adding fuel to the flame?
         Samson Agonistes, l. 1350

For evil news rides post, while good
   news baits.[1]   *Ib. l. 1538*

Suspense in news is torture.
         Ib. l. 1569

Nothing is here for tears, nothing to
   wail
Or knock the breast, no weakness, no
   contempt,
Dispraise, or blame, nothing but well
   and fair,
And what may quiet us in a death so
   noble.   *Ib. l. 1721*

All is best, though we oft doubt,
What the unsearchable dispose
Of highest Wisdom brings about.
         Ib. l. 1745

Calm of mind, all passion spent.
         Ib. l. 1758

    Such bickerings to recount, met
often in these our writers, what more
worth is it than to chronicle the wars of
kites or crows flocking and fighting in
the air?
     The History of England [1670],
                   bk. IV

SIR JOHN SUCKLING
1609–1642

Why so pale and wan, fond lover?
   Prithee, why so pale?
Will, when looking well can't move
   her,
   Looking ill prevail?
     Aglaura [1638]. *Song, st. 1*

Quit, quit, for shame, this will not
   move,
   This cannot take her.
If of herself she will not love,
   Nothing can make her.
The devil take her!   *Ib. st. 3*

But as when an authentic watch is
   shown,
Each man winds up and rectifies his
   own,

[1] See Plutarch, p. 137a.

So in our very judgments.[1]
         Aglaura, epilogue

High characters (cries one), and he
   would see
Things that ne'er were, nor are, nor
   ne'er will be.[2]
     The Goblins [1639], *epilogue*

Her feet beneath her petticoat
Like little mice, stole in and out,[3]
   As if they feared the light;
But oh, she dances such a way!
No sun upon an Easter-day
   Is half so fine a sight.
     A Ballad Upon a Wedding
              [1641], *st. 8*

Her lips were red, and one was thin,
Compared with that was next her chin,
   Some bee had stung it newly.
         Ib. st. 11

I prithee send me back my heart,
   Since I cannot have thine;
For if from yours you will not part,
   Why then shouldst thou have mine?
     Fragmenta Aurea [1646]. *Song,*
                   st. 1

'Tis not the meat, but 'tis the appetite
Makes eating a delight.
     Ib. Of Thee, Kind Boy, st. 3

Out upon it, I have loved
   Three whole days together;
And am like to love three more,
   If it prove fair weather.
     Ib. A Poem with the Answer,
                   st. 1

'Tis expectation makes a blessing dear,
Heaven were not heaven, if we knew
   what it were.
     Ib. Against Fruition, st. 4

[1] See Pope, p. 402b.
[2] See Pope, p. 403a.
There's no such thing in Nature, and you'll
   draw
A faultless monster which the world ne'er saw.
     JOHN SHEFFIELD, DUKE OF BUCKING-
     HAM AND NORMANBY [1648–1721], *Es-*
     say on Poetry
[3] See Herrick, p. 320b.

NAKAE TOJU[1]
1608–1648

Filial piety is the root of man. When it is lost from one's heart, then one's life becomes like a rootless plant, and if one does not expire instantly, it is nothing but sheer luck.

Toju Sensei Zenshu (Collected Works), vol. 1

SIR MATTHEW HALE[2]
1609–1676

Be not biased with compassion to the poor, or favor to the rich, in point of justice.

Things Necessary to Be Continually Had in Remembrance

Not to be solicitous what men will say or think. *Ib.*

WILLIAM CARTWRIGHT
1611–1643

Love makes those young whom age doth chill,
And whom he finds young, keeps young still. *To Chloe* [1651]

ARCHBISHOP ROBERT LEIGHTON
1611–1684

Deliver me, O Lord, from the errors of wise men, yea, and of good men.

Saying

ISAAC DE BENSERADE
1612–1691

In bed we laugh, in bed we cry;
And, born in bed, in bed we die.
The near approach a bed may show
Of human bliss to human woe.

À Son Lit (Translated by SAMUEL JOHNSON)

---

1 From *Sources of Japanese Tradition*, edited by William Theodore de Bary [1958].
2 Lord Chief Justice of England.

ANNE BRADSTREET
c. 1612–1672

Youth is the time of getting, middle age of improving, and old age of spending; a negligent youth is usually attended by an ignorant middle age, and both by an empty old age. He that hath nothing to feed on but vanity and lies must needs lie down in the bed of sorrow. *Thirty-three Meditations, 3*

Authority without wisdom is like a heavy axe without an edge, fitter to bruise than polish. *Ib.* 12

If we had no winter, the spring would not be so pleasant: if we did not sometimes taste of adversity, prosperity would not be so welcome. *Ib.* 14

Iron till it be thoroughly heated is uncapable to be wrought; so God sees good to cast some men into the furnace of affliction, and then beats them on his anvil into what frame he pleases.

Ib. 31

If ever two were one, then surely we.
If ever man were lov'd by wife, then thee;
If ever wife was happy in a man,
Compare with me ye women if you can.

To My Dear and Loving Husband [1678]

SAMUEL BUTLER
1612–1680

When civil fury first grew high,
And men fell out they knew not why.
Hudibras, pt. I [1663], *canto I, l. 1*

And pulpit, drum ecclesiastic,[1]
Was beat with fist, instead of a stick.
Ib. l. 11

Beside, 'tis known he could speak Greek

---

1 This is the first we hear of the "drum ecclesiastic" beating up for recruits in worldly warfare in our country. — WASHINGTON IRVING, *Knickerbocker's History of New York* [1809], *bk. V, ch.* 7

As naturally as pigs squeak: [1]
That Latin was no more difficile
Than to a blackbird 'tis to whistle.
Hudibras, pt. I, canto I, l. 51

He could distinguish and divide
A hair 'twixt south and southwest side,
On either which he would dispute,
Confute, change hands, and still confute. *Ib. l. 67*

He'd run in debt by disputation,
And pay with ratiocination.
Ib. l. 77

For rhetoric, he could not ope
His mouth, but out there flew a trope.
Ib. l. 81

For all a rhetorician's rules
Teach nothing but to name his tools.
Ib. l. 89

A Babylonish dialect
Which learned pedants much affect.
Ib. l. 93

For he by geometric scale,
Could take the size of pots of ale.
Ib. l. 121

And wisely tell what hour o' th' day
The clock doth strike, by algebra.
Ib. l. 125

Where entity and quiddity,
The ghosts of defunct bodies, fly.
Ib. l. 145

'Twas Presbyterian true blue.
Ib. l. 189

Such as do build their faith upon
The holy text of pike and gun.
Ib. l. 193

And prove their doctrine orthodox,
By apostolic blows and knocks.
Ib. l. 197

Compound for sins they are inclined to,
By damning those they have no mind
to. *Ib. l. 213*

[1] He Greek and Latin speaks with greater
ease
Than hogs eat acorns, and tame pigeons peas.
LIONEL CRANFIELD, EARL OF MIDDLE-
SEX [1575–1645], *Panegyric on Tom
Coriate*

The trenchant blade, Toledo trusty,
For want of fighting was grown rusty,
And ate into itself, for lack
Of somebody to hew and hack.
*Hudibras, pt. I,
canto I, l. 357*

For rhyme the rudder is of verses,
With which like ships they steer their
courses. *Ib. l. 457*

And force them, though it was in spite
Of Nature and their stars, to write.
Ib. l. 647

Great actions are not always true sons
Of great and mighty resolutions.
Ib. l. 885

I'll make the fur
Fly 'bout the ears of the old cur.
Ib. canto III, l. 277

These reasons made his mouth to
water. *Ib. l. 379*

I am not now in fortune's power:
He that is down can fall no lower.[1]
Ib. l. 871

Cheer'd up himself with ends of verse,
And sayings of philosophers.
Ib. l. 1011

Cleric before, and Lay behind;
A lawless linsey-woolsey brother,
Half of one order, half another.
Ib. l. 1226

Some have been beaten till they know
What wood a cudgel's of by th' blow;
Some kick'd, until they can feel
whether
A shoe be Spanish or neat's leather.
Ib. pt. II [1664], canto I, l. 221

Such great achievements cannot fail,
To cast salt on a woman's tail.
Ib. l. 277

For what is worth in anything
But so much money as 'twill bring?
Ib. l. 465

She that with poetry is won
Is but a desk to write upon.
Ib. l. 591

[1] He that is down needs fear no fall. —
BUNYAN, *Pilgrim's Progress* [1678], *pt. II*

Love is a boy by poets styl'd;
Then spare the rod, and spoil the child.[1]

*Hudibras, pt. II,
canto I, l. 843*

The sun had long since in the lap
Of Thetis, taken out his nap,
And like a lobster boil'd, the morn
From black to red began to turn.

Ib. canto II, l. 29

Oaths are but words, and words but wind. *Ib. l. 107*

For truth is precious and divine —
Too rich a pearl for carnal swine.

Ib. l. 257

He that imposes an oath makes it,
Not he that for convenience takes it;
Then how can any man be said
To break an oath he never made?

Ib. l. 377

As the ancients
Say wisely, have a care o' th' main chance,[2]
And look before you ere you leap;[3]
For as you sow, ye are like to reap.[4]

Ib. l. 501

Doubtless the pleasure is as great
Of being cheated as to cheat.

Ib. canto III, l. 1

He made an instrument to know
If the moon shine at full or no.

Ib. l. 261

As men of inward light are wont
To turn their optics in upon 't.

Ib. pt. III [1678], canto I, l. 481

What makes all doctrines plain and clear?
About two hundred pounds a year.
And that which was prov'd true before,
Prove false again? Two hundred more.

Ib. l. 1277

Nick Machiavel had ne'er a trick,

Though he gave his name to our Old Nick.

*Hudibras, pt. III,
canto I, l. 1313*

With crosses, relics, crucifixes,
Beads, pictures, rosaries, and pixes —
The tools of working our salvation
By mere mechanic operation.

Ib. l. 1495

The saints engage in fierce contests
About their carnal interests.

Ib. canto II, introduction

True as the dial to the sun,[1]
Although it be not shin'd upon.

Ib. l. 175

He that complies against his will
Is of his own opinion still.

Ib. canto III, l. 547

Neither have the hearts to stay,
Nor wit enough to run away.

Ib. l. 569

And poets by their sufferings grow,[2]
As if there were no more to do,
To make a poet excellent,
But only want and discontent.

Fragments

JAMES GRAHAM
FIRST MARQUESS OF
MONTROSE
1612–1650

He either fears his fate too much,
  Or his deserts are small,
That puts it not unto the touch
  To win or lose it all.

My Dear and Only Love, st. 2

I'll make thee glorious by my pen,
And famous by my sword.[3]

Ib. st. 5

---

[1] See *Proverbs, 13:24*, p. 24a, and Menander, p. 102a.
[2] See Lyly, p. 202b.
[3] See Heywood, p. 182a.
[4] See *Galatians 6:7*, p. 54a.

[1] True as the needle to the pole,
  Or as the dial to the sun.
    BARTON BOOTH [1681–1733], *Song*
[2] See Shelley, p. 569b.
[3] I'll make thee famous by my pen,
  And glorious by my sword.
    SCOTT, *Legend of Montrose* [1819], *ch. 15*

RICHARD CRASHAW
c. 1613 – 1649

The conscious water saw its God, and blushed.[1]
> *Epigrammata Sacra* [1634].
> *Aquae in Vinum Versae*

Two went to pray? Oh, rather say
One went to brag, the other to pray.
> *Steps to the Temple* [1648].
> *Two Went Up into the Temple to Pray*[2]

Whoe'er she be,
That not impossible she
That shall command my heart and me.
> *Ib. Wishes to His Supposed Mistress, l. 1*

Where'er she lie,
Locked up from mortal eye,
In shady leaves of destiny.   *Ib. l. 4*

Life that dares send
A challenge to his end,
And when it comes, say, Welcome, friend!   *Ib. l. 85*

Sidnaeian showers
Of sweet discourse, whose powers
Can crown old Winter's head with flowers.   *Ib. l. 88*

I would be married, but I'd have no wife,
I would be married to a single life.
> *Ib. On Marriage*

All is Caesar's, and what odds
So long as Caesar's self is God's?
> *Ib. Mark XII*

All those fair and flagrant things.
> *The Flaming Heart Upon the Book of Saint Teresa* [1652], *l. 34*

Love's passives are his activ'st part.
The wounded is the wounding heart.
> *Ib. l. 73*

O thou undaunted daughter of desires!
> *Ib. l. 93*

By all the eagle in thee, all the dove.
> *Ib. l. 95*

Poor world (said I) what wilt thou do
To entertain this starry stranger?
Is this the best thou canst bestow?
A cold, and not too cleanly, manger?
Contend, ye powers of heav'n and earth,
To fit a bed for this huge birth.
> *Hymn of the Nativity* [1652], *st. 6*

Proud world, said I, cease your contest,
And let the mighty babe alone.
The phoenix builds the phoenix' nest.
Love's architecture is his own.
The babe whose birth embraves this morn,
Made his own bed ere he was born.
> *Ib. st. 7*

Welcome, all wonders in one sight!
Eternity shut in a span.
> *Ib. Full Chorus*

The modest front of this small floor,
Believe me, reader, can say more
Than many a braver marble can —
"Here lies a truly honest man!"
> *Epitaph Upon Mr. Ashton*

---

[1] Nympha pudica Deum vidit, et erubuit. — Quoted by SAMUEL JOHNSON [1778]; from BOSWELL, *Life of Dr. Johnson* [1791], *vol. II, p. 218* [Everyman ed.]. A footnote states that this line has frequently been attributed to Dryden, but appeared in Crashaw's *Epigrammata Sacra* [1634].
  The bashful stream hath seen its God and blushed. — AARON HILL [1685–1750]
    The water hears thy faintest word,
    And blushes into wine.
      JOHN SAMUEL BEWLEY MONSELL [1811–1875], *Mysterious Is Thy Presence, Lord, st. 1*
[2] Two men went up into the temple to pray, the one a Pharisee, and the other a publican. — *Luke 18:10*

FRANÇOIS, DUC DE LA ROCHEFOUCAULD[1]
1613–1680

Our virtues are most frequently but vices in disguise.[2]
> *Reflections; or, Sentences and Moral Maxims. Epigraph*

[1] The fifth edition [1678] is the standard one.
[2] This epigraph, which is the key to the system of La Rochefoucauld, is found in another form as no. 179 of the Maxims of the first edition, 1665; it is omitted from the second and

Self-love is the greatest of all flatterers.

Reflections 2

We all have strength enough to endure the misfortunes of others.[1]

Ib. 19

Philosophy triumphs easily over past evils and future evils; but present evils triumph over it.[2]

Ib. 22

We need greater virtues to sustain good fortune than bad.

Ib. 25

If we had no faults of our own, we would not take so much pleasure in noticing those of others.

Ib. 31

Jealousy feeds upon suspicion, and it turns into fury or it ends as soon as we pass from suspicion to certainty.

Ib. 32

Self-interest speaks all sorts of tongues, and plays all sorts of roles, even that of disinterestedness.

Ib. 39

We are never so happy nor so unhappy as we imagine.

Ib. 49

To succeed in the world, we do everything we can to appear successful.

Ib. 56

There is no disguise which can for long conceal love where it exists or simulate it where it does not.

Ib. 70

There are very few people who are not ashamed of having been in love when they no longer love each other.

Ib. 71

True love is like ghosts, which everybody talks about and few have seen.

Ib. 76

The love of justice in most men is simply the fear of suffering injustice.

Ib. 78

Silence is the best tactic for him who distrusts himself.

Ib. 79

It is more ignominious to mistrust our friends than to be deceived by them.

Reflections 84

Everyone complains of his memory, and no one complains of his judgment.

Ib. 89

Old people like to give good advice, as solace for no longer being able to provide bad examples.

Ib. 93

A man who is ungrateful is sometimes less to blame for it than his benefactor.

Ib. 96

The mind is always the dupe of the heart.[1]

Ib. 102

Nothing is given so profusely as advice.

Ib. 110

The true way to be deceived is to think oneself more clever than others.

Ib. 127

We would rather speak ill of ourselves than not talk about ourselves at all.

Ib. 138

Usually we praise only to be praised.

Ib. 146

Our repentance is not so much regret for the ill we have done as fear of the ill that may happen to us in consequence.

Ib. 180

Who lives without folly is not so wise as he thinks.

Ib. 209

Most people judge men only by their success or their good fortune.

Ib. 212

Hypocrisy is the homage that vice pays to virtue.

Ib. 218

Too great haste in paying off an obligation is a kind of ingratitude.

Ib. 226

There is great skill in knowing how to conceal one's skill.

Ib. 245

The pleasure of love is in loving. We

---

third, and reappears for the first time in the fourth edition at the head of the Reflections. — Aimé Martin

[1] See Pope, p. 413a.
[2] See Goldsmith, p. 448b.

[1] The mind lives on the heart
Like any parasite.
Emily Dickinson, *The Mind Lives on the Heart* [c. 1876]

are happier in the passion we feel than in that we arouse.[1]

Reflections 259

Absence diminishes mediocre passions and increases great ones, as the wind blows out candles and fans fire.

Ib. 276

We always like those who admire us; we do not always like those whom we admire.   *Ib. 294*

The gratitude of most men is merely a secret desire to receive greater benefits.[2]   *Ib. 298*

We frequently forgive those who bore us, but cannot forgive those whom we bore.   *Ib. 304*

Lovers never get tired of each other, because they are always talking about themselves.   *Ib. 312*

In jealousy there is more self-love than love.   *Ib. 324*

We confess to little faults only to persuade ourselves that we have no great ones.   *Ib. 327*

We pardon to the extent that we love.   *Ib. 330*

We rarely find that people have good sense unless they agree with us.[3]

Ib. 347

Jealousy is always born together with love, but it does not always die when love dies.   *Ib. 361*

Mediocre minds usually dismiss anything which reaches beyond their own understanding.[4]   *Ib. 375*

The greatest fault of a penetrating wit is to go beyond the mark.

Reflections 377

We may give advice, but we do not inspire conduct.   *Ib. 378*

The veracity which increases with old age is not far from folly.   *Ib. 416*

Few people know how to be old.

Ib. 423

Nothing prevents our being natural so much as the desire to appear so.

Ib. 431

In their first passion women love their lovers, in the others they love love.[1]   *Ib. 471*

Quarrels would not last long if the fault were only on one side.   *Ib. 496*

In the misfortune of our best friends we often find something that is not displeasing.[2]   *Ib. 583*

BISHOP JEREMY TAYLOR
1613–1667

Desperate by too quick a sense of constant infelicity.

Holy Dying [1650–1651]

Every schoolboy knows it.

On the Real Presence, V

The union of hands and hearts.

Sermons [1653], *The Marriage Ring, pt. I*

No man ever repented that he arose from the table sober, healthful, and with his wits about him.   *Ib.*

---

[1] See Shelley, p. 569a.
[2] Sir Robert Walpole's [1676–1745] definition of the gratitude of place-expectants, "That it is a lively sense of *future* favors." — WILLIAM HAZLITT, *English Comic Writers* [1819], *Wit and Humor*
[3] "That was excellently observed," say I when I read a passage in another where his opinion agrees with mine. When we differ, then I pronounce him to be mistaken. — SWIFT [1667–1745]. *Thoughts on Various Subjects*
[4] See Schopenhauer, p. 564a.

[1] See Byron, p. 560b.
[2] In all distresses of our friends
We first consult our private ends;
While Nature, kindly bent to ease us,
Points out some circumstance to please us.
    SWIFT [1667–1745], *A Paraphrase of Rochefoucauld's Maxim*
See Burke, p. 451b.
Maxim 583 is one of the "maximes supprimées" discarded before the 1678 edition.

THOMAS ADY
fl. 1655

Matthew, Mark, Luke, and John,
The bed be blest that I lie on.
Four angels to my bed,
Four angels round my head,
One to watch, and one to pray,
And two to bear my soul away.

A Candle in the Dark [1655]

RICHARD BAXTER
1615–1691

I preached as never sure to preach
    again,
And as a dying man to dying men.

Love Breathing Thanks and
Praise

SIR JOHN DENHAM
1615–1669

Oh, could I flow like thee,[1] and make
    thy stream
My great example, as it is my theme!
Though deep yet clear, though gentle
    yet not dull;
Strong without rage, without o'erflow-
    ing full.

Cooper's Hill [1642], *l. 189*

SIR ROGER L'ESTRANGE
1616–1704

Though this may be play to you,
'Tis death to us.[2]

Fables from Several Authors,
Fable 398

ROGER DE BUSSY-RABUTIN
1618–1693

God is usually on the side of the big
squadrons and against the small ones.[3]

Letter to the Comte de Limoges
[*October 18, 1677*]

---

[1] The river Thames.
[2] See Bion, p. 104b.
[3] It is said that God is always for the big
battalions. — VOLTAIRE, *letter to M. le Riche,*
February 6, 1770

ABRAHAM COWLEY
1618–1667

What shall I do to be forever known,
And make the age to come my own?

The Motto

This only grant me, that my means
    may lie
Too low for envy, for contempt too
    high.   *The Vote* [1636]

Well then; I now do plainly see
This busy world and I shall ne'er
    agree;
The very honey of all earthly joy
Does of all meats the soonest cloy,
    And they (methinks) deserve my
      pity,
Who for it can endure the stings,
The crowd, and buzz and murmurings,
    Of this great hive, the city.

The Wish [1647]

Ah yet, ere I descend to the grave
May I a small house and large garden
    have;
And a few friends, and many books,
    both true,
Both wise, and both delightful too!
    Ib.

A mistress moderately fair.   *Ib.*

The world's a scene of changes, and to
    be
Constant, in Nature were inconstancy.

Inconstancy [1647]

The thirsty earth soaks up the rain,
And drinks, and gapes for drink again.
The plants suck in the earth, and are
With constant drinking fresh and fair.

Anacreon [1656], *II, Drinking*

Fill all the glasses there, for why
Should every creature drink but I,
Why, man of morals, tell me why?
    Ib.

A mighty pain to love it is,
And 'tis a pain that pain to miss;

Providence is always on the side of the last
reserve. — *Attributed to* NAPOLEON
  See Tacitus, p. 140a; Boileau, p. 377b; Frederick the Great, p. 435a; and Gibbon, p. 466a.

But of all pains, the greatest pain
It is to love, but love in vain.
> *Anacreon VII, Gold*

His time is forever, everywhere his
place.   *Friendship in Absence*

Nothing is there to come, and nothing
past,
But an eternal now does always last.[1]
> *Davideis* [1656], *bk. I, l.* 25

Life is an incurable disease.
> *To Dr. Scarborough* [1656]

Ye fields of Cambridge, our dear Cambridge, say,
Have ye not seen us walking every
day?
Was there a tree about which did not
know
   The love betwixt us two?
> *On the Death of Mr. William*
> *Harvey* [1657] [2]

Let but thy wicked men from out thee
go,
And all the fools that crowd thee so,
Even thou, who dost thy millions
boast,
A village less than Islington wilt grow,
A solitude almost.
> *Of Solitude, XII*

God the first garden made, and the first
city [3]
> *The Garden* [1664], *essay* 5

Hence ye profane! I hate ye all,
Both the great vulgar and the small.[4]
> *Horace, bk. III, ode* 1

Charm'd with the foolish whistling of a
name.[5]
> *Virgil, Georgics, bk. II, l.* 72

Words that weep and tears that speak.[6]
> *The Prophet*

---

[1] One of our poets (which is it?) speaks of an
everlasting now. — ROBERT SOUTHEY, *The Doctor* [1834–1847], *ch.* 25
[2] See William Harvey, p. 312b.
[3] See Bacon, p. 209b, and note.
[4] Odi profanum vulgus.
[5] See Pope, p. 410a.
[6] Thoughts that breathe, and words that burn.
— THOMAS GRAY, *Progress of Poesy* [1754], *III,*
3, 4

Poet and Saint! to thee alone are given
The two most sacred names of earth
and Heaven.
> *On the Death of Mr. Crashaw* [1]
> [1668]

His faith, perhaps, in some nice tenets
might
Be wrong; his life, I'm sure, was in the
right.[2]   *Ib.*

RICHARD LOVELACE
1618–1658

Oh, could you view the melody
   Of every grace
And music of her face,[3]
You'd drop a tear;
   Seeing more harmony
   In her bright eye
Than now you hear.
> *Lucasta* [1649]. *Orpheus to*
> *Beasts*

Tell me not, sweet, I am unkind,
   That from the nunnery
Of thy chaste breast and quiet mind,
   To war and arms I fly.
> *Ib. To Lucasta: Going to the*
> *Wars, st.* 1

I could not love thee, dear, so much,
Lov'd I not honor more.   *Ib. st.* 3

When I lie tangled in her hair,
   And fettered to her eye,
The gods that wanton in the air
   Know no such liberty.
> *Ib. To Althea: From Prison, st.* 1

When flowing cups pass swiftly round
With no allaying Thames.[4]
> *Ib. st.* 2

Stone walls do not a prison make,[5]
   Nor iron bars a cage;
Minds innocent and quiet take
   That for an hermitage;
If I have freedom in my love,

---

[1] See Crashaw, p. 354a.
[2] See Pope, p. 409b.
[3] The mind, the music breathing from her
face. — BYRON, *Bride of Abydos* [1813], *canto 1,*
st. 6
[4] See Shakespeare, p. 289b.
[5] Stone walls a prisoner make, but not a slave.
— WORDSWORTH [1770–1850], *Humanity*

And in my soul am free,
Angels alone that soar above
Enjoy such liberty.[1]

> *Lucasta. To Althea:*
> *From Prison, st. 4*

If to be absent were to be
Away from thee;
Or that when I am gone,
You and I were alone;
Then, my Lucasta, might I crave
Pity from blust'ring wind, or swallow-
ing wave.

> *Ib. To Lucasta: Going Beyond*
> *the Seas, st. 1*

NINON DE L'ENCLOS
1620–1705

Old age is woman's hell.[2]

> *Attributed saying*

JEAN DE LA FONTAINE
1621–1695

We believe no evil till the evil's
done.   *Fables, bk. I [1668], fable 8*

We heed no instincts but our own.
Ib.

The opinion of the strongest is always the best.   *Ib. 10*

Better to suffer than to die: that is
mankind's motto.   *Ib. 16*

By the work one knows the workman.   *Ib. 21*

I bend but do not break.   *Ib. 22*

It is a double pleasure to deceive the
deceiver.   *Ib. II [1668], fable 15*

It is impossible to please all the
world and one's father.

> *Ib. III [1668], fable 1*

In everything one must consider the
end.[1]

> *Fables, bk. III, fable 5*

Beware, as long as you live, of judging people by appearances.

> *Ib. VI [1668], fable 5*

On the wings of Time grief flies
away.   *Ib. 21*

The sign brings customers.

> *Ib. VII [1678–1679], fable 15*

People who make no noise are dangerous.

> *Ib. VIII [1678–1679], fable 23*

He knows the universe, and himself
he does not know.   *Ib. 26*

A hungry stomach cannot hear.[2]

> *Ib. IX [1678–1679], fable 17*

ANDREW MARVELL
1621–1678

The inglorious arts of peace.

> *Upon Cromwell's Return from*
> *Ireland [1650]*

He[3] nothing common did or mean
Upon that memorable scene,
But with his keener eye
The axe's edge did try.   *Ib.*

But bowed his comely head
Down as upon a bed.   *Ib.*

So much one man can do,
That does both act and know.   *Ib.*

Had we but world enough, and time,
This coyness, lady, were no crime.

> *To His Coy Mistress [1650–1652]*

I would
Love you ten years before the Flood,
And you should, if you please, refuse
Till the conversion of the Jews.
My vegetable love should grow
Vaster than empires, and more slow.

> *Ib.*

---

[1] But though my wing is closely bound,
My heart's at liberty;
My prison walls cannot control
The flight, the freedom of the soul.
    JEANNE GUYON [1648–1717], *A Prison-
    er's Song, Castle of Vincennes, France,
    st. 4*
[2] La vieillesse est l'enfer des femmes.

[1] Whatsoever thou takest in hand, remember
the end, and thou shalt never do amiss. — *Apocrypha, Ecclesiasticus 3:36*
[2] Ventre affamé n'a point d'oreilles.
See Cato the Elder, p. 107a, and note, and
Adlai Stevenson, p. 1048b.
[3] King Charles I.

But at my back I always hear
Time's winged chariot hurrying near;
And yonder all before us lie
Deserts of vast eternity.
            To His Coy Mistress

Then worms shall try
That long preserved virginity,
And your quaint honor turn to dust,
And into ashes all my lust.
The grave's a fine and private place,[1]
But none, I think, do there embrace.
            Ib.

Though we cannot make our sun
Stand still, yet we will make him run.
            Ib.

Annihilating all that's made
To a green thought in a green shade.[2]
            The Garden [1650–1652]

Casting the body's vest aside,
My soul into the boughs does glide.
            Ib.

The world in all doth but two nations
    bear —
The good, the bad; and these mixed
    everywhere.
            The Loyal Scot [1650–1652]

My love is of a birth as rare
    As 'tis for object strange and high;
It was begotten by despair
    Upon impossibility.
            The Definition of Love [1650–
                        1652], *st. 1*

As lines, so loves oblique, may well
    Themselves in every angle greet;
But ours, so truly parallel,
    Though infinite, can never meet.
            Ib. st. 7

Where the remote Bermudas ride,
In th' ocean's bosom unespied.
            Bermudas [1657]

Orange bright,
Like golden lamps in a green light.
            Ib.

And all the way, to guide their chime,
With falling oars they kept the time.[1]
            Bermudas

MOLIÈRE
[JEAN BAPTISTE POQUELIN]
1622–1673

To pull the chestnuts out of the fire
with the cat's paw.[2]
            L'Étourdi [1655], *act III, sc. 6*

We die only once, and for such a
long time!
            Le Dépit Amoureux [1656], *act V,
                        sc. 3*

I always make the first verse well, but
I have trouble making the others.
            Les Précieuses Ridicules [1659],
                        act I, sc. 11

The world, dear Agnes, is a strange
affair.
            L'École des Femmes [1662], *act II,
                        sc. 6*

There is no rampart that will hold
out against malice.
            Tartuffe [1664], *act I, sc. 1*

Those whose conduct gives room for
talk are always the first to attack their
neighbors.
            Ib.

You are a fool in four letters, my
son.[3]
            Ib.

She is laughing up her sleeve at you.
            Ib. 6

A woman always has her revenge
ready.
            Ib. II, 2

Cover that bosom that I must not
see.[4]
            Ib. III, 2

Although I am a pious man, I am
not the less a man.
            Ib. III, 3

To create a public scandal is what's
wicked; to sin in private is not a sin.
            Ib. IV, 5

---

[1] A grave is such a quiet place. — EDNA ST. VINCENT MILLAY, *Renascence* [1912]
[2] The same phrase is in VIRGIL, *Eclogues, IX,*
20

[1] See Thomas Moore, p. 541b.
[2] Tirer les marrons du feu avec la patte du chat. — *Proverb in many languages*
See Becker, p. 913b.
[3] Vous êtes un sot en trois lettres, mon fils.
[4] Couvrez ce sein que je ne saurais voir.

I saw him, I say, saw him with my own eyes.

Tartuffe, act V, sc. 3

There are fagots and fagots.

Le Médecin Malgré Lui [1666], *act I, sc. 6*

We have changed all that.[1]

Ib. II, 6

On some preference esteem is based; to esteem everything is to esteem nothing.

Le Misanthrope [1666], *act I, sc. 1*

He's a wonderful talker, who has the art of telling you nothing in a great harangue.

Ib. II, 5

He makes his cook his merit, and the world visits his dinners and not him.

Ib.

You see him laboring to produce *bons mots.*

Ib.

The more we love our friends, the less we flatter them; it is by excusing nothing that pure love shows itself.

Ib.

Doubts are more cruel than the worst of truths.

Ib. III, 7

Anyone may be an honorable man, and yet write verse badly.

Ib. IV, 1

If everyone were clothed with integrity, if every heart were just, frank, kindly, the other virtues would be well-nigh useless, since their chief purpose is to make us bear with patience the injustice of our fellows.

Ib. V, 1

It is a wonderful seasoning of all enjoyments to think of those we love.

Ib. 4

I prefer an accommodating vice to an obstinate virtue.

Amphitryon [1666], *act I, sc. 4*

One must eat to live, and not live to eat.[2]

Ib. III, 1

[1] Nous avons changé tout cela.
[2] See Socrates, p. 87b, and note.

The true Amphitryon is the Amphitryon who gives dinners.[1]

Amphitryon, act III, sc. 5

My Lord Jupiter knows how to sugarcoat the pill.

Ib. III, 10

You've asked for it, Georges Dandin, you've asked for it.[2]

Georges Dandin [1668], *act I, sc. 9*

Good Heavens! For more than forty years I have been speaking prose without knowing it.

Le Bourgeois Gentilhomme [1670], *act II, sc. 4*

All that is not prose is verse; and all that is not verse is prose.

Ib.

My fair one, let us swear an eternal friendship.[3]

Ib. IV, 1

I will maintain it before the whole world.

Ib. IV, 5

What the devil was he doing in that galley?[4]

Les Fourberies de Scapin [1671], *act II, sc. 11*

Grammar, which knows how to control even kings.[5]

Les Femmes Savantes [1672], *act II, sc. 6*

[1] Le véritable Amphitryon est l'Amphitryon où l'on dine.
See Dryden, p. 371a.
[2] Vous l'avez voulu, Georges Dandin, vous l'avez voulu.
[3] A sudden thought strikes me — let us swear an eternal friendship. — FRERE, *The Rovers* [1798]
Madam, I have been looking for a person who disliked gravy all my life; let us swear eternal friendship. — SYDNEY SMITH [1771–1845], *Lady Holland's Memoir, vol. I, ch. 9*
[4] Que diable allait-il faire dans cette galère?
Que diable aller faire aussi dans la galère d'un Turc? d'un Turc! [What the deuce did he want on board a Turk's galley? A Turk!] — CYRANO DE BERGERAC, *Le Pédant Joué* [1654], *act II, sc. 4*
The saying of Molière came into his head: "But what the devil was he doing in that galley?" and he laughed at himself. — TOLSTOI, *War and Peace* [1865–1872], *pt. IV, ch. 6*
Often misquoted "in that gallery," as in DICKENS, *A Tale of Two Cities* [1859], *bk. I, ch. 5:* What the devil do you do in that gallery there!
[5] Sigismund [1361–1437], Emperor of the Holy Roman Empire, at the Council of Constance

It is seasoned throughout with Attic salt.

> *Les Femmes Savantes,*
> *act III, sc. 2*

A learned fool is more foolish than an ignorant one. *Ib. IV, 3*

Ah, there are no longer any children!

> *Le Malade Imaginaire* [1673],
> *act II, sc. 11*

Nearly all men die of their remedies, and not of their illnesses.

> *Ib. III, 3*

RICHARD RUMBOLD
1622–1685

I never could believe that Providence had sent a few men into the world, ready booted and spurred to ride, and millions ready saddled and bridled to be ridden.

> *On the scaffold* [1685]. *From*
> MACAULAY, *History of England,*
> *ch. 1*

ALGERNON SIDNEY
1622–1683

This hand, unfriendly to tyrants,
Seeks with the sword placid repose
under liberty.[1]

> *Life and Memoirs of Algernon*
> *Sidney*

It is not necessary to light a candle to the sun.[2]

> *Discourses on Government*
> [1698], *sec. 23*

HENRY VAUGHAN
1622–1695

Dear Night! this world's defeat;
The stop to busy fools; care's check and
curb;

[1414], said to a prelate who had objected to his Majesty's grammar: Ego sum rex Romanus, et supra grammaticam [I am the Roman king, and am above grammar].
   [1]   Manus haec, inimica tyrannis,
  Ense petit placidam sub libertate quietem.
  The second line is the motto of the Commonwealth of Massachusetts.
  [2] See Robert Burton, p. 312a.

The day of spirits; my soul's calm retreat
  Which none disturb!
Christ's progress, and His prayer-time;
The hours to which high Heaven doth chime.

> *Silex Scintillans* [1655].
> *The Night, l. 25*

There is in God, some say,
A deep but dazzling darkness.

> *Ib. l. 49*

Happy those early days, when I
Shin'd in my angel-infancy! [1]
Before I understood this place
Appointed for my second race.

> *Ib. The Retreat, l. 1*

But felt through all this fleshly dress
Bright shoots of everlastingness.

> *Ib. l. 19*

Some men a forward motion love,
But I by backward steps would move.

> *Ib. l. 29*

I cannot reach it, and my striving eye
Dazzles at it, as at eternity.

> *Ib. Childhood*

I saw Eternity the other night
Like a great ring of pure and endless
light.
  All calm, as it was bright;
And round beneath it, Time in hours,
days, years,
  Driv'n by the spheres
Like a vast shadow mov'd; in which the
world
  And all her train were hurl'd.

> *Ib. The World*

They are all gone into the world of
light!
  And I alone sit lingering here;
Their very memory is fair and bright,
  And my sad thoughts doth clear.

> *Ib. They Are All Gone, st. 1*

I see them walking in an air of glory
  Whose light doth trample on my
days,
My days, which are at best but dull and
hoary,

---

[1] See Traherne, p. 378a, and Wordsworth, p. 513b.

Mere glimmering and decays.
            Silex Scintillans. They Are
                        All Gone, st. 3

Dear, beauteous death, the jewel of the
      just!
Shining nowhere but in the dark;
What mysteries do lie beyond thy
      dust,
Could man outlook that mark!
                        Ib. st. 5

My soul, there is a country
      Far beyond the stars
Where stands a winged sentry
      All skillful in the wars:
There, above noise and danger,
      Sweet Peace is crown'd with smiles,
And One born in a manger
      Commands the beauteous files.
                  Ib. Peace, st. 1

YAMAGA SOKO[1]
1622–1685

The business of the samurai consists
in reflecting on his own station in life,
in discharging loyal service to his master if he has one, in deepening his fidelity in associations with friends, and,
with due consideration of his own position, in devoting himself to duty above
all.   *The Way of the Samurai*

BLAISE PASCAL
1623–1662

Things are always at their best in
their beginning.
            Lettres Provinciales [1656–
                        1657], *no. 4*

True eloquence takes no heed of eloquence, true morality takes no heed of
morality. . . . To take no heed of philosophy is truly to philosophize.
            Pensées [1670], *no. 4*

Do you wish people to think well of
you? Don't speak well of yourself.
                        Ib. 44

[1] From *Sources of Japanese Tradition* edited
by William Theodore de Bary [1958].

What is man in nature? Nothing in
relation to the infinite, everything in relation to nothing, a mean between
nothing and everything.[1]
            Pensées, no. 72

I lay it down as a fact that if all men
knew what others say of them, there
would not be four friends in the world.
                        Ib. 101

The state of man: inconstancy, boredom, anxiety.[2]   *Ib. 127*

I have discovered that all human evil
comes from this, man's being unable to
sit still in a room.[3]   *Ib. 139*

Cleopatra's nose, had it been shorter,
the whole face of the world would have
been changed.   *Ib. 162*

The eternal silence of these infinite
spaces terrifies me.   *Ib. 206*

We shall die alone.[4]   *Ib. 211*

The heart has its reasons which reason knows nothing of.[5]   *Ib. 277*

We know the truth, not only by the
reason, but by the heart.   *Ib. 282*

Justice without strength is helpless,
strength without justice is tyrannical. . . . Unable to make what is just
strong, we have made what is strong
just.   *Ib. 298*

Man is but a reed, the weakest in
nature, but he is a thinking reed.[6]
                        Ib. 347

Man is neither angel nor beast; and
the misfortune is that he who would act
the angel acts the beast.[7]   *Ib. 358*

Evil is easy, and has infinite forms.
                        Ib. 408

[1] Qu'est-ce que l'homme dans la nature? Un
néant a l'égard de l'infini, un tout a l'égard du
néant, un milieu entre rien et tout.
[2] Condition de l'homme: inconstance, ennui,
inquiétude.
[3] See Walter Bagehot, p. 726b.
[4] On mourra seul.
[5] Le coeur a ses raisons que la raison ne con-
naît point.
[6] L'homme n'est qu'un roseau, le plus faible
de la nature, mais c'est un roseau pensant.
[7] L'homme n'est ni ange ni bête; et le malheur veut que qui veut faire l'ange fait la bête.

To ridicule philosophy is really to philosophize.[1]

> *Pensées, no. 430*

What a chimera then is man! What a novelty! What a monster, what a chaos, what a contradiction, what a prodigy! Judge of all things, feeble earthworm, depository of truth, a sink of uncertainty and error, the glory and the shame of the universe.[2] *Ib. 434*

Self is hateful.[3] *Ib. 455*

Men never do evil so completely and cheerfully as when they do it from religious conviction. *Ib. 894*

"The God of Abraham, the God of Isaac, the God of Jacob," not of philosophers and scholars.

> *Writing found in Pascal's effects after his death*

WILLIAM WALKER
1623–1684

Learn to read slow: all other graces
Will follow in their proper places.[4]

> *The Art of Reading*

GEORGE FOX[5]
1624–1691

The Lord showed me, so that I did see clearly, that he did not dwell in these temples which men had commanded and set up, but in people's hearts . . . his people were his temple, and he dwelt in them.[6]

> *Journal* [1694]

When the Lord sent me forth into the world, He forbade me to put off my hat to any, high or low. *Ib.*

Justice Bennet of Derby, was the first that called us Quakers, because I bid

them tremble at the word of the Lord. This was in the year 1650.

> *Journal*

He [Oliver Cromwell] said: "I see there is a people risen, that I cannot win either with gifts, honors, offices or places; but all other sects and people I can." *Ib.*

ANGELUS SILESIUS
[JOHANN SCHEFFLER]
1624–1677

God lives not without me.
I know that without me God cannot live at all;
Were I to go, he also to his death must fall.

> *The Cherubic Wanderer* [1657–1675]

I am like God, and God like me.
I am as large as God, he is as small as I:
He cannot above me, nor I beneath him be. *Ib.*

Everyone to his own.
The bird is in the sky, the stone rests on the land,
In water lives the fish, my spirit in God's hand. *Ib.*

THOMAS SYDENHAM
1624–1689

Fever itself is Nature's instrument.

> *Quoted in Bulletin of the New York Academy of Medicine, vol. IV* [1928], *p. 922*

Gout, unlike any other disease, kills more rich men than poor, more wise men than simple. Great kings, emperors, generals, admirals and philosophers have all died of gout. *Ib. 993*

A man is as old as his arteries.

> *Ib.*

JOHN AUBREY
1626–1697

He [Hobbes] had read much, but his contemplation was much more than

---

[1] Se moquer de la philosophie, c'est vraiment philosopher.
[2] See Pope, p. 408b–409a.
[3] Le moi est haïssable.
[4] Take time enough; all other graces
    Will soon fill up their proper places.
       JOHN BYROM [1692–1763], *Advice to Preach Slow*
[5] Founder of the Society of Friends (Quakers).
[6] See *I Corinthians 3:17*, p. 52a.

his reading. He was wont to say that if he had read as much as other men, he should have known no more than other men.   *Brief Lives* [ed. 1898], I, 349

He [John Milton] was so fair that they called him *the lady of* Christ's College.   *Ib.*

Mr. William Shakespeare was born at Stratford upon Avon in the county of Warwick. His father was a butcher, and I have been told heretofore by some of the neighbors, that when he was a boy he exercised his father's trade, but when he killed a calf he would do it in a high style and make a speech.

Ben Johnson and he did gather humors of men daily wherever they came.   *Ib.* II, 225

MARIE DE RABUTIN-CHANTAL, MARQUISE DE SÉVIGNÉ
1626–1696

True friendship is never serene.
      Lettres. À Madame de Grignan [*September 10, 1671*]

Racine will go out of style like coffee.   *Attributed saying*

JACQUES BÉNIGNE BOSSUET
1627–1704

The greatest weakness of all weaknesses is to fear too much to appear weak.

Politique Tirée de l'Écriture Sainte

The inexorable boredom that is at the core of life.
      From M. A. COUTURIER, *Se Garder Libre*

JOHN BUNYAN
1628–1688

Some said, "John, print it"; others said, "Not so."

Some said, "It might do good"; others said, "No."
      Pilgrim's Progress [1678].
      Apology for His Book

As I walked through the wilderness of this world.   *Ib. pt. I*

I saw a man clothed with rags . . . a book in his hand, and a great burden upon his back.   *Ib.*

The name of the one was Obstinate and the name of the other was Pliable.   *Ib.*

The name of the slough was Despond.   *Ib.*

Every fat [vat] must stand upon his bottom.[1]   *Ib.*

The gentleman's name was Mr. Worldly-Wise-Man.   *Ib.*

Set down my name, Sir.   *Ib.*

A very stately palace before him, the name of which was Beautiful.   *Ib.*

The valley of Humiliation.   *Ib.*

A foul Fiend coming over the field to meet him; his name is Apollyon.   *Ib.*

I will talk of things heavenly, or things earthly; things moral, or things evangelical; things sacred, or things profane; things past, or things to come; things foreign, or things at home; things more essential, or things circumstantial.   *Ib.*

It beareth the name of Vanity Fair, because the town where 'tis kept is lighter than vanity.   *Ib.*

Hanging is too good for him, said Mr. Cruelty.   *Ib.*

My great-grandfather was but a water-man, looking one way, and rowing another.[2]   *Ib.*

A castle called Doubting Castle, the owner whereof was Giant Despair.   *Ib.*

[1] Every tub must stand upon its bottom. — CHARLES MACKLIN, *The Man of the World* [1781], act I, sc. 2
[2] See Plutarch, p. 137b, and note.

They came to the Delectable Mountains.
> *Pilgrim's Progress, pt. I*

A great horror and darkness fell upon Christian.   *Ib.*

So I awoke, and behold it was a dream.   *Ib.*

A man that could look no way but downwards with a muckrake in his hand.   *Ib. pt. II*

He that is down needs fear no fall,
He that is low no pride.
> *Ib. Shepherd Boy's Song*

Who would true valor see,
  Let him come hither;
One here will constant be,
  Come wind, come weather.
There's no discouragement
Shall make him once relent
His first avow'd intent
  To be a pilgrim.   *Ib.*

My sword I give to him that shall succeed me in my pilgrimage, and my courage and skill to him that can get it. My marks and scars I carry with me, to be a witness for me, that I have fought His battle who now will be my rewarder.   *Ib.*

So he passed over, and all the trumpets sounded for him on the other side.   *Ib.*

The captain of all these men of death that came against him to take him away, was the Consumption, for it was that that brought him down to the grave.
> *The Life and Death of Mr. Badman* [1680]

JOHN RAY
1628–1705

In a calm sea every man is a pilot.
> *English Proverbs* [1670]

If wishes were horses, beggars might ride.   *Ib.*

SIR WILLIAM TEMPLE
1628–1699

Books, like proverbs, receive their chief value from the stamp and esteem of ages through which they have passed.
> *Miscellanea, pt. II* [1690]. *Ancient and Modern Learning*

When all is done, human life is, at the greatest and the best, but like a froward child, that must be played with and humored a little to keep it quiet till it falls asleep, and then the care is over.   *Ib. Of Poetry*

CHARLES II
1630–1685

This is very true: for my words are my own, and my actions are my ministers'.   *Reply to Lord Rochester* [1]

Let not poor Nelly starve.
> *On his deathbed. From* BURNET, *History of My Own Times, vol. I, bk. 2, ch. 17*

He had been, he said, an unconscionable time dying; he hoped that they would excuse it.
> *From* MACAULAY, *History of England* [1849], *vol. I, ch. 4*

JOHN TILLOTSON
1630–1694

If God were not a necessary Being of Himself, He might almost seem to be made for the use and benefit of men.[2]
> *Sermon*

They who are in highest places, and have the most power, have the least liberty, because they are most observed.
> *Reflections*

WALTER POPE
c. 1630 – 1714

May I govern my passions with absolute sway,

[1] See Rochester, p. 382a.
[2] See Ovid, p. 128b, and Voltaire, p. 418a.

And grow wiser and better, as strength
wears away,
Without gout or stone, by a gentle decay.
    The Old Man's Wish [1685]

BISHOP RICHARD CUMBERLAND
1631–1718

It is better to wear out than to rust
out.
    From Bishop George Horne
    [1730–1792], *Sermon on the
    Duty of Contending for the
    Truth*

JOHN DRYDEN
1631–1700

By viewing Nature, Nature's handmaid
Art,
Makes mighty things from small begin-
nings grow.[1]
    Annus Mirabilis [1667], *st. 155*

He [Shakespeare] was the man who
of all modern, and perhaps ancient
poets, had the largest and most comprehensive soul.
    Essay of Dramatic Poesy [1668]

He was naturally learned; he needed
not the spectacles of books to read Nature; he looked inwards, and found her
there.   *Ib.*

Pains of love be sweeter far
Than all other pleasures are.
    Tyrannic Love [1669], *act IV, sc. 1*

I am as free as Nature first made man,
Ere the base laws of servitude began,
When wild in woods the noble savage
ran.
    *The Conquest of Granada
    [1669–1670], pt. I, act I,
    sc. 1*

Death in itself is nothing; but we fear
To be we know not what, we know not
where.
    Aureng-Zebe [1676], *act IV, sc. 1*

[1] See William Bradford, p. 319a.

When I consider life, 'tis all a cheat;
Yet, fool'd with hope, men favor the
deceit;
Trust on, and think tomorrow will repay.
Tomorrow's falser than the former
day;
Lies worse, and while it says we shall be
blest
With some new joys, cuts off what we
possest.
Strange cozenage! None would live past
years again,
Yet all hope pleasure in what yet remain;
And from the dregs of life think to receive
What the first sprightly running could
not give.
    Aureng-Zebe, act IV, sc. 1

The wretched have no friends.
    All for Love [1678], *act III, sc. 1*

Your Cleopatra; Dolabella's Cleopatra;
every man's Cleopatra.
    Ib. IV, 1

With how much ease believe we what
we wish! [1]
Whatever is, is in its causes just.[2]
    Oedipus [1679] (*with* Nathaniel
    Lee), *act III, sc. 1*

    His hair just grizzled,
As in a green old age.[3]   *Ib.*

Of no distemper, of no blast he died,
But fell like autumn fruit that mellow'd
long —
Even wonder'd at, because he dropp'd
no sooner.
Fate seem'd to wind him up for fourscore years,
Yet freshly ran he on ten winters
more;
Till like a clock worn out with eating
time,
The wheels of weary life at last stood
still.   *Ib. IV, 1*

[1] Men freely believe that which they desire. —
Caesar [c. 102–44 b.c.], *De Bello Gallico, bk. III,
sec. 18*
[2] See Pope, p. 408b.
[3] A green old age, unconscious of decays. —
Pope, *Translation of the Iliad, XXIII, 929*

In pious times, ere priestcraft did
　begin,
Before polygamy was made a sin.
　　　　Absalom and Achitophel, pt. I
　　　　　　　　[*1680*], *l. 1*

Whate'er he did was done with so
　much ease,
In him alone, 'twas natural to please.
　　　　　　　　Ib. l. 27

Plots, true or false, are necessary
　things,
To raise up commonwealths and ruin
　kings.　　　　　*Ib. l. 83*

Of these the false Achitophel was first,
A name to all succeeding ages curs'd.
For close designs and crooked counsels
　fit,
Sagacious, bold, and turbulent of wit,
Restless, unfix'd in principles and place,
In power unpleas'd, impatient of dis-
　grace;
A fiery soul, which working out its
　way,
Fretted the pygmy-body to decay:
And o'er-inform'd the tenement of
　clay.[1]
A daring pilot in extremity;
Pleas'd with the danger, when the
　waves went high
He sought the storms; but for a calm
　unfit,
Would steer too nigh the sands to
　boast his wit.
Great wits are sure to madness near al-
　lied,
And thin partitions do their bounds di-
　vide.[2]　　　　　*Ib. l. 150*

Bankrupt of life, yet prodigal of ease.
　　　　　　　　Ib. l. 168

And all to leave what with his toil he
　won
To that unfeather'd two-legg'd thing,[3] a
　son.　　　　　*Ib. l. 169*

[1] See Thomas Fuller, p. 333b.
[2] Remembrance and reflection how allied!
　What thin partitions sense from thought
　divide!
　　　　POPE, *Essay on Man* [*1733–1734*],
　　　　　　　epistle I, l. 225
See Seneca, p. 130b, and note.
[3] See Diogenes the Cynic, p. 96b.

In friendship false, implacable in hate,
Resolv'd to ruin or to rule the state.
　　　　　　Absalom and Achitophel,
　　　　　　　　　pt. I, l. 173

And Heaven had wanted one immortal
　song.　　　　　*Ib. l. 197*

The people's prayer, the glad diviner's
　theme,
The young men's vision, and the old
　men's dream! [1]　　*Ib. l. 238*

His courage foes, his friends his truth
　proclaim.　　　　*Ib. l. 357*

All empire is no more than power in
　trust.　　　　　*Ib. l. 411*

Better one suffer, than a nation grieve.
　　　　　　　　Ib. l. 416

Who think too little, and who talk too
　much.[2]　　　　*Ib. l. 534*

A man so various that he seem'd to be
Not one, but all mankind's epitome:
Stiff in opinions, always in the wrong;
Was everything by starts, and nothing
　long:
But, in the course of one revolving
　moon,
Was chemist, fiddler, statesman, and
　buffoon.[3]　　　*Ib. l. 545*

So over violent, or over civil,
That every man with him was God or
　Devil.　　　　　*Ib. l. 557*

His tribe were God Almighty's gentle-
　men.　　　　　*Ib. l. 645*

Nor is the people's judgement always
　true:
The most may err as grossly as the
　few.　　　　　*Ib. l. 781*

Large was his wealth, but larger was his
　heart.　　　　　*Ib. l. 826*

Of ancient race by birth, but nobler
　yet
In his own worth.　　*Ib. l. 900*

Beware the fury of a patient man.
　　　　　　　　Ib. l. 1005

[1] See *Joel 2:28*, p. 35b.
[2] See Jonson, p. 304a.
[3] See Juvenal, p. 139a.

Made still a blund'ring kind of melody;
Spurr'd boldly on, and dashed through thick and thin,
Through sense and nonsense, never out nor in.
Free from all meaning, whether good or bad,
And in one word, heroically mad.
Absalom and Achitophel,
pt. II [1] [1682], *l. 413*

For every inch that is not fool is rogue.
Ib. l. 463

There is a pleasure sure
In being mad which none but madmen know.[2]
The Spanish Friar [1681],
act II, sc. 1

And, dying, bless the hand that gave the blow.[3]
Ib.

He's a sure card.
Ib.

They say everything in the world is good for something.
Ib. III, 2

Or break the eternal Sabbath of his rest.
Ib. V, 2

All human things are subject to decay,
And, when fate summons, monarchs must obey.
Mac Flecknoe [1682], *l. 1*

The rest to some faint meaning make pretense,
But Shadwell [4] never deviates into sense.
Some beams of wit on other souls may fall,
Strike through and make a lucid interval;
But Shadwell's genuine night admits no ray,
His rising fogs prevail upon the day.
Ib. l. 19

And torture one poor word ten thousand ways.
Mac Flecknoe, l. 208

Wit will shine
Through the harsh cadence of a rugged line.
To the Memory of Mr. Oldham
[1684], *l. 15*

Happy the man, and happy he alone,
He who can call today his own;
He who, secure within, can say,
Tomorrow, do thy worst, for I have liv'd today.[1]
Imitation of Horace, bk. III,
ode 29 [1685], *l. 65*

Not heaven itself upon the past has power;
But what has been, has been, and I have had my hour.
Ib. l. 71

I can enjoy her [Fortune] while she's kind;
But when she dances in the wind,
And shakes the wings and will not stay,
I puff the prostitute away.
Ib. l. 81

And virtue, though in rags, will keep me warm.
Ib. l. 87

Men met each other with erected look,
The steps were higher that they took;
Friends to congratulate their friends made haste,
And long inveterate foes saluted as they pass'd.
Threnodia Augustalis [1685], *l. 124*

Since heaven's eternal year is thine.
To the Pious Memory of Mrs.
Anne Killegrew [1686], *l. 15*

O gracious God! how far have we
Profan'd thy heavenly gift of poesy!
Ib. l. 56

Her wit was more than man, her innocence a child.[2]
Ib. l. 70

Then cold, and hot, and moist, and dry,[3]

---

[1] In collaboration with NAHUM TATE. See p. 383b.
[2] There is a pleasure in poetic pains
Which only poets know.
COWPER [1731–1800], *The Timepiece, l. 285*
[3] Adore the hand that gives the blow. —
JOHN POMFRET [1667–1702], *Verses to His Friend*
[4] See Shadwell, p. 380a.

[1] See Horace, p. 122a.
[2] Of manners gentle, of affections mild,
In wit a man; simplicity a child.
POPE, *Epitaph on Gay* [1730]
[3] See Milton, *Paradise Lost, bk. II, l. 898,*
p. 344a.

In order to their stations leap,
And Music's power obey.
From harmony, from heavenly har-
mony,
This universal frame began:
From harmony to harmony
Through all the compass of the notes it
ran,
The diapason closing full in Man.
> *A Song for St. Cecilia's Day*
> [1687], st. 1

What passion cannot Music raise and
quell?   *Ib. st. 2*

The trumpet's loud clangor
Excites us to arms.   *Ib. st. 3*

The soft complaining flute,
In dying notes, discovers
The woes of hopeless lovers.
> *Ib. st. 4*

The trumpet shall be heard on high
The dead shall live, the living die,
And Music shall untune the sky!
> *Ib. Grand Chorus*

She fear'd no danger, for she knew no
sin.
> *The Hind and the Panther*
> [1687], pt. I, l. 4

And doom'd to death, though fated not
to die.   *Ib. l. 8*

For truth has such a face and such a
mien
As to be lov'd needs only to be seen.[1]
> *Ib. l. 33*

Of all the tyrannies on human kind
The worst is that which persecutes the
mind.   *Ib. l. 239*

Reason to rule, mercy to forgive:
The first is law, the last prerogative.
> *Ib. l. 261*

And kind as kings upon their coronation day.   *Ib. l. 271*

And leaves the private conscience for
the guide.   *Ib. l. 478*

All have not the gift of martyrdom.
> *Ib. II, l. 59*

[1] See Pope, p. 409a.

War seldom enters but where wealth
allures.[1]
> *The Hind and the Panther,*
> *pt. II, l. 706*

Much malice mingled with a little wit.
> *Ib. III, l. 1*

Jealousy, the jaundice of the soul.
> *Ib. l. 73*

For present joys are more to flesh and
blood
Than a dull prospect of a distant good.
> *Ib. l. 364*

T' abhor the makers, and their laws approve,
Is to hate traitors and the treason love.[2]
> *Ib. l. 706*

Secret guilt by silence is betrayed.
> *Ib. l. 763*

Possess your soul with patience.[3]
> *Ib. l. 839*

Our vows are heard betimes! and
Heaven takes care
To grant, before we can conclude the
prayer:
Preventing angels met it half the way,
And sent us back to praise, who came
to pray.[4]
> *Britannia Rediviva* [1688], l. 1

Three poets, in three distant ages born,
Greece, Italy, and England did adorn.
The first in loftiness of thought sur-
pass'd;
The next, in majesty; in both the last.
The force of Nature could no further
go.
To make a third, she join'd the former
two.
> *Under Mr. Milton's Picture* [1688]

This is the porcelain clay of humankind.[5]
> *Don Sebastian* [1690], act I, sc. 1

A knockdown argument: 'tis but a
word and a blow.
> *Amphitryon* [1690], act I, sc. 1

[1] See Bion, p. 1046, and note.
[2] See Caesar, p. 112a.
[3] See *Luke 21:19*, p. 47b.
[4] See Goldsmith, p. 449b.
[5] The precious porcelain of human clay. —
BYRON, *Don Juan* [1819–1824], *canto 4, st. 11*

Whistling to keep myself from being afraid.[1]

> *Amphitryon, act III, sc. III, 1*

I am the true Amphitryon.[2]

> *Ib. V, 1*

Fairest Isle, all isles excelling,
Seat of pleasures, and of loves;
Venus here will choose her dwelling,
And forsake her Cyprian groves.

> *King Arthur* [1691], *act II, sc. 5,*
> *Song of Venus*

Theirs was the giant race, before the flood.[3]

> *Epistle to Congreve* [1693], *l. 5*

Genius must be born, and never can be taught. *Ib. l. 60*

Be kind to my remains; and oh defend,
Against your judgment, your departed friend! *Ib. l. 72*

Look round the habitable world: how few
Know their own good, or knowing it, pursue.

> *Juvenal, Satire X* [1693]

Arms, and the man I sing, who, forced by fate,
And haughty Juno's unrelenting hate.

> *Virgil, Aeneid, bk. I, l. 1* [1697]

None but the brave deserves the fair.

> *Alexander's Feast* [1697], *l. 15*

With ravish'd ears
The monarch hears;
Assumes the god,
Affects to nod,
And seems to shake the spheres.

> *Ib. l. 37*

Sound the trumpets; beat the drums . . .
Now give the hautboys breath; he comes, he comes.[4] *Ib. l. 50*

Bacchus, ever fair and ever young.

> *Ib. l. 54*

---

[1] Whistling aloud to bear his courage up. — BLAIR, *The Grave* [1743], *l. 58*
[2] See Molière, p. 361b.
[3] See *Genesis 6:4*, p. 6b.
[4] See Morell, p. 420b.

Rich the treasure,
Sweet the pleasure —
Sweet is pleasure after pain.

> *Alexander's Feast, l. 58*

The king grew vain;
Fought all his battles o'er again;
And thrice he routed all his foes, and thrice he slew the slain.

> *Ib. l. 68*

Fallen from his high estate,
And welt'ring in his blood;
Deserted, at his utmost need,
By those his former bounty fed,
On the bare earth expos'd he lies,
With not a friend to close his eyes.

> *Ib. l. 78*

Softly sweet, in Lydian measures,
Soon he sooth'd his soul to pleasures.
War, he sung, is toil and trouble;
Honor but an empty bubble;
Never ending, still beginning,
Fighting still, and still destroying.
If all the world be worth thy winning,
Think, oh think it worth enjoying:
Lovely Thaïs sits beside thee,
Take the good the gods provide thee. *Ib. l. 97*

Sigh'd and look'd, and sigh'd again.

> *Ib. l. 120*

And, like another Helen, fir'd another Troy. *Ib. l. 154*

Could swell the soul to rage, or kindle soft desire. *Ib. l. 160*

He rais'd a mortal to the skies,
She drew an angel down. *Ib. l. 169*

Words, once my stock, are wanting to commend
So great a poet and so good a friend.

> *Epistle to Peter Antony Motteux*
> [1698], *l. 54*

Lord of yourself, uncumber'd with a wife.

> *Epistle to John Driden of Chesterton* [1700], *l. 18*

Better to hunt in fields, for health unbought,

Than fee the doctor for a nauseous
draught.
The wise, for cure, on exercise depend;
God never made his work for man to
mend.
> *Epistle to John Driden
> of Chesterton, l. 92*

A very merry, dancing, drinking,
Laughing, quaffing, and unthinking
time.
> *The Secular Masque* [1700], *l. 38*

The sword within the scabbard keep,
And let mankind agree.   *Ib. l. 61*

All, all of a piece throughout:
Thy chase had a beast in view;
Thy wars brought nothing about;
Thy lovers were all untrue.
'Tis well an old age is out,
And time to begin a new.[1]
> *Ib. l. 86*

Ill habits gather by unseen degrees —
As brooks make rivers, rivers run to
seas.
> *Ovid, Metamorphoses* [1700],
> *bk. XV, The Worship of Aes-
> culapius, l. 155*

[Of Chaucer's *Canterbury Tales*]
Here is God's plenty.
> *Fables Ancient and Modern
> [1700], preface*

For Art may err, but Nature cannot
miss.
> *Ib. The Cock and the Fox, l. 452*

Old as I am, for ladies' love unfit,
The power of beauty I remember yet.
> *Ib. Cymon and Iphigenia, l. 1*

He trudg'd along unknowing what he
sought,
And whistled as he went, for want of
thought.   *Ib. l. 84*

She hugg'd the offender, and forgave
the offense:
Sex to the last.[2]   *Ib. l. 367*

Of seeming arms to make a short essay,
Then hasten to be drunk — the business of the day.   *Ib. l. 407*

[1] See Tennyson, p. 651a.
[2] And love the offender, yet detest the offense.
— POPE, *Eloisa to Abelard* [1717], *l. 192*

He was exhal'd; his great Creator drew
His spirit, as the sun the morning
dew.[1]
> *On the Death of a Very Young
> Gentleman* [1700]

Here lies my wife: here let her lie!
Now she's at rest, and so am I.
> *Epitaph intended for his wife*

WILLIAM STOUGHTON
1631–1701

God hath sifted a nation that he
might send choice grain into this wilderness.[2]
> *Election Sermon at Boston
> [April 29, 1669]*

JOHN LOCKE
1632–1704

New opinions are always suspected,
and usually opposed, without any other
reason but because they are not already
common.
> *Essay Concerning Human
> Understanding* [1690], *dedi-
> catory epistle*

No man's knowledge here can go beyond his experience.
> *Ib. bk. II, ch. 1, sec. 19*

It is one thing to show a man that he
is in error, and another to put him in
possession of truth.   *Ib. IV, 7, 11*

All men are liable to error; and most
men are, in many points, by passion or
interest, under temptation to it.
> *Ib. 20, 17*

Wherever Law ends, Tyranny begins.[3]
> *Second Treatise of Government
> [1690], sec. 202*

[1] Early, bright, transient, chaste as morning
dew,
She sparkled, was exhal'd, and went to
heaven.
EDWARD YOUNG, *Night Thoughts* [1742–
1745], *Night V, l. 600*
[2] God had sifted three kingdoms to find the
wheat for this planting. — LONGFELLOW, *Courtship of Miles Standish* [1858], *IV*
[3] See William Pitt, p. 426a.

A sound mind in a sound body,[1] is a short but full description of a happy state in this world.

Some Thoughts on Education [1693], *sec. 1*

Virtue is harder to be got than knowledge of the world; and, if lost in a young man, is seldom recovered.

Ib. 64

He that will have his son have a respect for him and his orders, must himself have a great reverence for his son.[2]

Ib. 65

The only fence against the world is a thorough knowledge of it.   *Ib. 88*

BENEDICT [BARUCH] SPINOZA[3]
1632–1677

Peace is not an absence of war, it is a virtue, a state of mind, a disposition for benevolence, confidence, justice.

Theological-Political Treatise [1670]

Nature abhors a vacuum.

Ethics [1677],[4] *pt. I, proposition 15: note*

God and all the attributes of God are eternal.   *Ib. 19*

Nothing exists from whose nature some effect does not follow.   *Ib. 36*

He who would distinguish the true from the false must have an adequate idea of what is true and false.

Ib. II, 42: proof

---

[1] See Juvenal, p. 139b.

[2] See Juvenal, p. 140a.

[3] Ein Gottbetrunkener Mensch [A God-intoxicated man]. — NOVALIS (FRIEDRICH VON HARDENBERG) [1772–1801]

The Lord blot out his name under heaven. The Lord set him apart for destruction from all the tribes of Israel, with all the curses of the firmament which are written in the Book of the Law. . . . There shall no man speak to him, no man write to him, no man show him any kindness, no man stay under the same roof with him, no man come nigh him. — *Amsterdam Synagogue's curse on Spinoza* [1656]

[4] Everyman edition, translated by ANDREW BOYLE.

Will and Intellect are one and the same thing.

Ethics, pt. II, proposition 49: corollary

He that can carp in the most eloquent or acute manner at the weakness of the human mind is held by his fellows as almost divine.

Ib. III: preface

Surely human affairs would be far happier if the power in men to be silent were the same as that to speak. But experience more than sufficiently teaches that men govern nothing with more difficulty than their tongues.

Ib. 2: note

Pride is therefore pleasure arising from a man's thinking too highly of himself.   *Ib. 26: note*

It may easily come to pass that a vain man may become proud and imagine himself pleasing to all when he is in reality a universal nuisance.

Ib. 30: note

Self-complacency is pleasure accompanied by the idea of oneself as cause.

Ib. 51: note

It therefore comes to pass that everyone is fond of relating his own exploits and displaying the strength both of his body and his mind, and that men are on this account a nuisance one to the other.   *Ib. 54: note*

I refer those actions which work out the good of the agent to courage, and those which work out the good of others to nobility. Therefore temperance, sobriety, and presence of mind in danger, etc., are species of courage; but modesty, clemency, etc., are species of nobility.   *Ib. 59: note*

Fear cannot be without hope nor hope without fear.

Ib. definition 13: explanation

So long as a man imagines that he cannot do this or that, so long is he determined not to do it: and consequently, so long it is impossible to him that he should do it.

Ib. 28: explanation

Those who are believed to be most abject and humble are usually most ambitious and envious.

Ethics, pt. III, proposition
29: explanation

One and the same thing can at the same time be good, bad, and indifferent, e.g., music is good to the melancholy, bad to those who mourn, and neither good nor bad to the deaf.

Ib. IV: preface

Man is a social animal.[1]

Ib. proposition 35: note

Men will find that they can prepare with mutual aid far more easily what they need, and avoid far more easily the perils which beset them on all sides, by united forces.   *Ib.*

Avarice, ambition, lust, etc., are nothing but species of madness.[2]

Ib. 44: note

He whose honor depends on the opinion of the mob must day by day strive with the greatest anxiety, act and scheme in order to retain his reputation. For the mob is varied and inconstant, and therefore if a reputation is not carefully preserved it dies quickly.

Ib. 58: note

In refusing benefits caution must be used lest we seem to despise or to refuse them for fear of having to repay them in kind.   *Ib. 70: note*

To give aid to every poor man is far beyond the reach and power of every man. . . . Care of the poor is incumbent on society as a whole.[3]

Ib. appendix, 17

None are more taken in by flattery than the proud, who wish to be the first and are not.   *Ib. 21*

Those are most desirous of honor

and glory who cry out the loudest of its abuse and the vanity of the world.

Ethics, pt. V, proposition
10: note

We feel and know that we are eternal.   *Ib. 23: note*

All excellent things are as difficult as they are rare.   *Ib. 42: note*

The things which . . . are esteemed as the greatest good of all . . . can be reduced to these three headings: to wit, Riches, Fame, and Pleasure. With these three the mind is so engrossed that it cannot scarcely think of any other good.

Tractatus de Intellectus
Emendatione [1677], *I, 3*

SIR CHRISTOPHER WREN
1632–1723

Si monumentum requiris circumspice [If you would see the man's monument, look around].

Inscription in St. Paul's Ca-
thedral, London. Written by
Wren's son

WENTWORTH DILLON, EARL OF ROSCOMMON
1633–1685

Choose an author as you choose a
  friend.

Essay on Translated Verse
[1684], *l. 96*

Immodest words admit of no defense,
For want of decency is want of sense.

Ib. l. 113

The multitude is always in the wrong.

Ib. l. 183

My God, my Father, and my Friend,
Do not forsake me in my end.

Translation of Dies Irae

SAMUEL PEPYS
1633–1703

I pray God to keep me from being proud.   *Diary, March 22, 1660*

[1] See Blackstone, p. 444b.
[2] To me, avarice seems not so much a vice, as a deplorable piece of madness. — SIR THOMAS BROWNE, *Religio Medici* [1642]
[3] See Samuel Johnson, p. 431a, and Andrew Carnegie, p. 757b.

This morning came home my fine camlet cloak, with gold buttons, and a silk suit, which cost me much money, and I pray God to make me able to pay for it.   *Diary, July 1, 1660*

And so to bed.   *July 22, 1660, etc.*

I am unwilling to mix my fortune with him that is going down the wind.
          September 6, 1660

A good honest and painful sermon.
          March 17, 1661

One, by his own confession to me, that can put on two several faces, and look his enemies in the face with as much love as his friends. But, good God! what an age is this, and what a world is this! that a man cannot live without playing the knave and dissimulation.   *September 1, 1661*

Though he be a fool, yet he keeps much company, and will tell all he sees or hears, so a man may understand what the common talk of the town is.
          September 2, 1661

My wife, poor wretch.
          September 18, 1661, etc.

Thanks be to God, since my leaving drinking of wine, I do find myself much better, and do mind my business better, and do spend less money, and less time lost in idle company.
          January 26, 1662

As happy a man as any in the world, for the whole world seems to smile upon me.   *October 31, 1662*

Bought Hudibras again, it being certainly some ill humor to be so against that which all the world cries up to be the example of wit; for which I am resolved once more to read him, and see whether I can find it or no.[1]
          February 6, 1663

To the Trinity House, where a very good dinner among the old soakers.
          February 15, 1665

[1] Pepys had bought *Hudibras* December 26, 1662, but thought it "so silly an abuse of the Presbyter Knight going to the wars" that he sold it the same day.

But Lord! how everybody's looks, and discourse in the street, is of death, and nothing else; and few people going up and down, that the town is like a place distressed and forsaken.[1]
          Diary, August 30, 1665

Strange to see how a good dinner and feasting reconciles everybody.
          November 9, 1665

Saw a wedding in the church; and strange to see what delight we married people have to see these poor fools decoyed into our condition.
          December 25, 1665

Musick and women I cannot but give way to, whatever my business is.
          March 9, 1666

The truth is, I do indulge myself a little the more in pleasure, knowing that this is the proper age of my life to do it; and, out of my observation that most men that do thrive in the world do forget to take pleasure during the time that they are getting their estate, but reserve that till they have got one, and then it is too late for them to enjoy it.   *March 10, 1666*

Home, and, being washing-day, dined upon cold meat.
          April 4, 1666

Musick is the thing of the world that I love most.   *July 30, 1666*

Busy till night, pleasing myself mightily to see what a deal of business goes off a man's hands when he stays by it.   *January 14, 1667*

Did satisfy myself mighty fair in the truth of the saying that the world do not grow old at all, but is in as good condition in all respects as ever it was.
          February 3, 1667

This day I am, by the blessing of God, 34 years old, in very good health and mind's content, and in condition of estate much beyond whatever my friends could expect of a child of theirs, this day 34 years. The Lord's

[1] The time of the Great Plague.

name be praised! and may I be thankful for it.   *Diary, February 23, 1667*

But it is pretty to see what money will do.   *March 21, 1667*

To church; and with my mourning, very handsome, and new periwig, make a great show.   *March 31, 1667*

But to think of the clatter they make with his coach, and their own fine clothes, and yet how meanly they live within doors, and nastily, and borrowing everything of neighbors.
April 1, 1667

Whose red nose makes me ashamed to be seen with him.   *May 3, 1667*

Gives me some kind of content to remember how painful it is sometimes to keep money, as well as to get it.
October 11, 1667

I find my wife hath something in her gizzard, that only waits an opportunity of being provoked to bring up; but I will not, for my content-sake, give it.
June 17, 1668

In appearance, at least, he being on all occasions glad to be at friendship with me, though we hate one another, and know it on both sides.
September 22, 1668

I do hate to be unquiet at home.
January 22, 1669

And so I betake myself to that course, which is almost as much as to see myself go into my grave; for which, and all the discomforts that will accompany my being blind, the good God prepare me!
May 31, 1669 (final entry)

GEORGE SAVILE, MARQUESS OF HALIFAX
1633–1695

Children and fools want everything, because they want wit to distinguish; there is no stronger evidence of a crazy

understanding than the making too large a catalogue of things necessary.
Advice to a Daughter [1688]

Popularity is a crime from the moment it is sought; it is only a virtue where men have it whether they will or no.
Political, Moral, and Miscellaneous Reflections [1750]

Misspending a man's time is a kind of self-homicide.   *Ib.*

Men are not hanged for stealing horses, but that horses may not be stolen.   *Ib.*

ROBERT SOUTH
1634–1716

Speech was given to the ordinary sort of men whereby to communicate their mind; but to wise men, whereby to conceal it.[1]   *Sermon* [1676]

ROBERT HOOKE
1635–1703

The truth is, the science of Nature has been already too long made only a work of the brain and the fancy: It is now high time that it should return to the plainness and soundness of observations on material and obvious things.
Micrographia [1665]

NICOLAS BOILEAU-DESPRÉAUX
1636–1711

Happy who in his verse can gently steer

[1] Speech was made to open man to man, and not to hide him; to promote commerce, and not betray it. — DAVID LLOYD [1635–1692], *The Statesmen and Favorites of England Since the Reformation* [1665, edited by Whitworth], *vol. I, p. 503*
Men talk only to conceal the mind. — EDWARD YOUNG, *Love of Fame* [1725–1728], satire II, l. 208
The true use of speech is not so much to express our wants as to conceal them. — GOLDSMITH, *The Bee, no. 3* [October 20, 1759]
See Voltaire, p. 417b.

From grave to light, from pleasant to severe.[1]
> *The Art of Poetry* [1674],
> *canto I, l. 75*

At last comes Malherbe [2] and, the first to do so in France, brings to his verse a smooth cadence.   *Ib. l. 131*

Whate'er is well conceived is clearly said,
And the words to say it flow with ease.
> *Ib. l. 153*

Every age has its pleasures, its style of wit, and its own ways.
> *Ib. III, l. 374*

The wisest man is he who does not fancy that he is so at all.
> *Satire 1, l. 46*

A Cat's a cat, and Rolet is a knave.
> *Ib. l. 52*

He [Molière] pleases all the world, but cannot please himself.   *Ib. l. 94*

In spite of every sage whom Greece can show,
Unerring wisdom never dwelt below;
Folly in all of every age we see,
The only difference lies in the degree.
> *Satire 4, l. 37*

Greatest fools are oft most satisfied.
> *Ib. l. 128*

If your descent is from heroic sires,
Show in your life a remnant of their fires.   *Satire 5, l. 43*

Of all the creatures that creep, swim, or fly,
Peopling the earth, the waters, and the sky,
From Rome to Iceland, Paris to Japan,
I really think the greatest fool is man.
> *Satire 8, l. 1*

But satire, ever moral, ever new,
Delights the reader and instructs him, too.
She, if good sense refine her sterling page,

Oft shakes some rooted folly of the age.   *Satire 8, l. 257*

Honor is like an island, rugged and without a beach; once we have left it, we can never return.
> *Satire 10, l. 167*

Now two punctilious envoys, Thine and Mine,
Embroil the earth about a fancied line;
And, dwelling much on right and much on wrong,
Prove how the right is chiefly with the strong.[1]   *Satire 11, l. 141*

Nothing but truth is lovely, nothing fair.   *Epistle 9*

The terrible burden of having nothing to do.   *Epistle 11*

BISHOP THOMAS KEN
1637–1711

Teach me to live, that I may dread
The grave as little as my bed.[2]
> *Morning and Evening Hymn,*
> *st. 3*

Praise God, from whom all blessings flow!
Praise Him, all creatures here below!
Praise Him above, ye heavenly host!
Praise Father, Son, and Holy Ghost!
> *Ib. st. 10 (Doxology)*

THOMAS TRAHERNE
c. 1637 – 1674

You never enjoy the world aright, till the sea itself floweth in your veins, till you are clothed with the heavens, and crowned with the stars: and perceive yourself to be the sole heir of the whole world.
> *Centuries of Meditations* [1908],
> *Century I, sec. 29*

The corn was orient and immortal wheat, which never should be reaped,

---

[1] See Pope, p. 410a.
   Translated by Dryden.
[2] Enfin Malherbe vint.

[1] See Tacitus, p. 140a; Bussy-Rabutin, p. 357a; Frederick the Great, p. 435a; and Gibbon, p. 466a.
[2] See Browne, p. 330b.

nor was ever sown. I thought it had stood from everlasting to everlasting.[1]
Centuries of Meditations,
Century III, sec. 3

How like an angel came I down! [2]
Wonder [1910], *st. 1*

I within did flow
With seas of life like wine.
Ib. st. 3

LOUIS XIV
1638–1715

I am the state.[3]
Attributed remark before the parliament in 1651

Has God forgotten all I have done for him? [4]
Attributed remark upon hearing the news of the French defeat at Malplaquet [1709]

I almost had to wait.[5]
Attributed remark when a coach he had ordered arrived just in time.

JEAN RACINE
1639–1699

I loved him too much not to hate him at all!
Andromaque [1667], *act II*

You are Emperor, my lord, and yet you weep?
Bérénice [1670], *act IV, sc. 5*

My only hope lies in my despair.
Bajazet [1672], *act I, sc. 4*

You have named him, not I.[6]
Phèdre [1677], *act I, sc. 3*

It is no longer a passion hidden in my heart: it is Venus herself fastened to her prey.[1]
Phèdre, act I, sc. 3

Innocence has nothing to dread.
Ib. III, 6

Crime like virtue has its degrees; and timid innocence was never known to blossom suddenly into extreme license.[2]
Ib. IV, 2

To repair the irreparable ravages of time.
Athalie [1691], *act II, sc. 5*

SIR CHARLES SEDLEY
c. 1639 – 1701

When change itself can give no more,
'Tis easy to be true.
Reasons for Constancy, st. 4

Phyllis is my only joy,
Faithless as the winds or seas;
Sometimes coming, sometimes coy,
Yet she never fails to please.
Song [1702], *st. 1*

IHARA SAIKAKU
1642–1693

Heaven says nothing, and the whole earth grows rich beneath its silent rule. Men, too, are touched by heaven's virtue; yet, in their greater part, they are creatures of deceit. They are born, it seems, with an emptiness of soul, and must take their qualities wholly from things without. To be born thus empty into this modern age, this mixture of good and ill, and yet to steer through life on an honest course to the splendors of success — this is a feat reserved for paragons of our kind, a task beyond the nature of the normal man.
The Japanese Family Storehouse; or, The Millionaires' Gospel,[3] *bk. I, 1*

The first consideration for all, throughout life, is the earning of a living. *Ib.*

---

[1] See *Psalm 90:2*, p. 20a.
[2] See Vaughan, p. 362b, and Wordsworth, p. 513b.
[3] L'état c'est moi.
See Napoleon Bonaparte, p. 504a.
[4] Dieu a donc oublié tout ce que j'ai fait pour lui?
[5] J'ai failli attendre.
[6] C'est toi qui l'a nommé.

[1] Ce n'est plus une ardeur dans mes veines cachée:
C'est Vénus toute entière à sa proie attachée.
[2] See Juvenal, p. 139a.
[3] Edited and translated by G. W. SARGENT.

Though mothers and fathers give us life, it is money alone which preserves it.

> The Japanese Family Storehouse; or, The Millionaires' Gospel, bk. I, 1

In life it is training rather than birth which counts.   *Ib.* 3

Ancient simplicity is gone . . . the people of today are satisfied with nothing but finery.   *Ib.* 4

Take care! Kingdoms are destroyed by bandits, houses by rats, and widows by suitors.[1]   *Ib.* 5

There is always something to upset the most careful of human calculations.[2]   *Ib. II,* 2

When you send a clerk on business to a distant province, a man of rigid morals is not your best choice.   *Ib.* 5

To think twice in every matter and follow the lead of others is no way to make money.   *Ib.*

For each of the four hundred and four bodily ailments celebrated physicians have produced infallible remedies, but the malady which brings the greatest distress to mankind — to even the wisest and cleverest of us — is the plague of poverty.   *Ib. III,* 1

To make a fortune some assistance from fate is essential. Ability alone is insufficient.   *Ib.* 4

If we live by subhuman means we might as well never have had the good fortune to be born human.   *Ib.*

Like ice beneath the sun's rays — to such poverty did he fall . . . his fortune melted to water.   *Ib.* 5

If making money is a slow process, losing it is quickly done.   *Ib.*

Harshness is for the good of a boy, softheartedness will ruin him.[3]

Ib. V, 5

1 See *Matthew 6:19,* p. 40b.
2 See Robert Burns, p. 492b.
3 See *Proverbs 13:24,* p. 24a.

SIR ISAAC NEWTON
1642–1727

If I have seen further (than you and Descartes) it is by standing upon the shoulders of Giants.[1]

> Letter to Robert Hooke, February 5, 1675/6

I frame no hypotheses; for whatever is not deduced from the phenomena is to be called an hypothesis; and hypotheses, whether metaphysical or physical, whether of occult qualities or mechanical, have no place in experimental philosophy.   *Ib.*

Every body continues in its state of rest, or of uniform motion in a right line, unless it is compelled to change that state by forces impressed upon it.

> Philosophiae Naturalis Principia Mathematica [1687].[2] Laws of Motion, I

The change of motion is proportional to the motive force impressed; and is made in the direction of the right line in which that force is impressed.[3]

Ib. II

To every action there is always opposed an equal reaction: or, the mutual actions of two bodies upon each other are always equal, and directed to contrary parts.   *Ib. III*

God in the beginning formed matter in solid, massy, hard, impenetrable, movable particles, of such sizes and figures, and with such other properties, and in such proportion to space, as most conduced to the end for which he formed them.   *Optics* [1704]

I do not know what I may appear to the world; but to myself I seem to have been only like a boy playing on the seashore, and diverting myself in now and then finding a smoother pebble or a prettier shell than ordinary, whilst the

1 See Lucan, p. 134a, and Robert Burton, p. 310a.
2 *Mathematical Principles of Natural Philosophy.* Translated by ANDREW MOTTE [1729].
3 In modern terms, acceleration is directly proportional to applied force.

great ocean of truth lay all undiscovered before me.

> From BREWSTER, *Memoirs of Newton* [1855], *vol. II, ch. 27*

O Diamond! Diamond! thou little knowest the mischief done!

> *Said to a pet dog who knocked over a candle and set fire to his papers*

THOMAS SHADWELL[1]
c. 1642 – 1692

And wit's the noblest frailty of the mind.   *A True Widow, act II, sc. 1*

The haste of a fool is the slowest thing in the world.   *Ib. III, 1*

I am, out of the ladies' company, like a fish out of the water.   *Ib.*

Every man loves what he is good at.   *Ib. V, 1*

MATSUO BASHO
1644–1694

The months and days are the travelers of eternity. The years that come and go are also voyagers. . . . I too for years past have been stirred by the sight of a solitary cloud drifting with the wind to ceaseless thoughts of roaming.

> *The Narrow Road of Oku (Oku no Hosomichi)* [2]

Such stillness —
The cries of the cicadas
Sink into the rocks.   *Ib.*

My body, now close to fifty years of age, has become an old tree that bears bitter peaches, a snail which has lost its shell, a bagworm separated from its bag; it drifts with the winds and clouds that know no destination. Morning and night I have eaten traveler's fare, and have held out for alms a pilgrim's wallet.

> *Prose Poem on The Unreal Dwelling (Genjuan no Fu)* [1]

My poetry is like a stove in the summer or a fan in the winter. It runs against the popular tastes and has no practical use.[2]

> *The Rustic Gate. From the collection titled Basho Bunshu*

Do not seek to follow in the footsteps of the men of old; seek what they sought.   *Ib.*

The white chrysanthemum
Even when lifted to the eye
Remains immaculate.[2]

> *Conversations with Basho. From the collection Kyoraisho Hyokai*

Clear cascades!
Into the waves scatter
Blue pine needles.   *Ib.*

An old pond —
A frog leaping in —
The sound of water.[3]   *Poem*

A rough sea!
Stretched out over Sado
The Milky Way.[3]   *Poem*

WILLIAM PENN
1644–1718

No cross, no crown.[4]
> *Title of Pamphlet* [1669]

Any government is free to the people under it where the laws rule and the people are a party to the laws.
> *Frame of Government* [1682]

Truth often suffers more by the heat of its defenders than from the arguments of its opposers.
> *Some Fruits of Solitude* [5] [1693]

---

[1] Shadwell was at open feud with Dryden from 1682, and the two poets repeatedly attacked one another in satires, the most famous of which is Dryden's *Mac Flecknoe.* See Dryden, p. 369a.

[2] From *Anthology of Japanese Literature,* edited by Donald Keene [1955].

[1] From *Anthology of Japanese Literature,* edited by Donald Keene [1955].

[2] From *Sources of Japanese Tradition,* edited by William Theodore de Bary [1960].

[3] Translated by DANA B. YOUNG.

[4] See Quarles, p. 322a.

[5] A copy of this little book, wrote ROBERT LOUIS STEVENSON, "I carried in my pocket all

It is a reproach to religion and government to suffer so much poverty and excess.

Some Fruits of Solitude

They that love beyond the world cannot be separated by it. Death is but crossing the world, as friends do the seas; they live in one another still.

Ib.

Men are generally more careful of the breed of their horses and dogs than of their children. *Ib.*

It were endless to dispute upon everything that is disputable. *Ib.*

Have a care where there is more sail than ballast. *Ib.*

Passion is a sort of fever in the mind, which ever leaves us weaker than it found us. *Ib.*

The public must and will be served.
Ib.

Much reading is an oppression of the mind, and extinguishes the natural candle, which is the reason of so many senseless scholars in the world.

Advice to His Children [1699]

EDWARD TAYLOR
c. 1644 – 1729

Who spread its canopy? Or curtains spun?
Who in this bowling alley bowled the sun?

Poetical Works [1939]. *God's Determinations Touching His Elect, preface*

For in Christ's coach saints sweetly sing
As they to glory ride therein.
Ib. The Joy of Church Fellowship Rightly Attended

Make me, O Lord, Thy spinning-wheel complete. *Ib. Housewifery*

about the San Francisco streets, read in streetcars and ferry-boats when I was sick unto death, and found in all times and places a peaceful and sweet companion."

Its food too fine for angels; yet come, take
And eat thy fill! It's Heaven's sugar cake.

Poetical Works. Preparatory Meditations, 8

This bread of life dropt in thy mouth doth cry:
Eat, eat me, soul, and thou shalt never die. *Ib.*

Is Christ thy advocate to plead thy cause?
Art thou his client? Such shall never slide.
He never lost his case. *Ib. 38*

My case is bad. Lord, be my advocate.
My sin is red: I'm under God's arrest.
Ib.

JEAN DE LA BRUYÈRE
1645–1696

We come too late to say anything which has not been said already.
Les Caractères [1688]. *Des Ouvrages de l'Esprit*

Liberality consists less in giving a great deal than in gifts well timed.
Ib. Du Coeur

Time, which strengthens friendship, weakens love. *Ib.*

We must laugh before we are happy, for fear we die before we laugh at all.[1]
Ib.

To laugh at men of sense is the privilege of fools. *Ib. De la Société*

There are but three events in a man's life: birth, life and death. He is not conscious of being born, he dies in pain, and he forgets to live.
Ib. De l'Homme

Most men make use of the first part of their life to render the last part miserable. *Ib.*

[1] See Beaumarchais, p. 46oa, and note.

Women run to extremes; they are either better or worse than men.
>   *Les Caractères. Des Femmes*

BARON GOTTFRIED WILHELM VON LEIBNITZ
1646–1716

I often say a great doctor kills more people than a great general.[1]
>   *Quoted in Bulletin of The New York Academy of Medicine, vol. V [1929], p. 152*

HENRY ALDRICH
1647–1710

If all be true that I do think,
There are five reasons we should drink:
Good wine — a friend — or being dry —
Or lest we should be by and by —
Or any other reason why.
>   *Five Reasons for Drinking*

JOHN WILMOT, EARL OF ROCHESTER
1647–1680

Here lies our sovereign lord the King,
  Whose promise none relies on;
He never said a foolish thing,
  Nor ever did a wise one.
>   *Written on the bedchamber door of Charles II* [2]

For pointed satire I would Buckhurst choose,
The best good man with the worst-natured muse.[3]
>   *An Allusion to Horace. Satire X, bk. I*

A merry monarch, scandalous and poor.
>   *A Satire on King Charles II*

The world appears like a great family,

Whose lord, oppressed with pride and poverty,
(That to the few great bounty he may show)
Is fain to starve the numerous train below.
>   *Like a Great Family*

There's not a thing on earth that I can name,
So foolish, and so false, as common fame.
>   *Did E'er This Saucy World*

Reason, which fifty times to one does err,
Reason, an ignis fatuus of the mind.
>   *A Satire Against Mankind [1675], l. 11*

Books bear him up a while, and make him try
To swim with bladders of philosophy.
>   *Ib. l. 20*

Then Old Age and Experience, hand in hand,
Lead him to death, and make him understand,
After a search so painful and so long,
That all his life he has been in the wrong.
>   *Ib. l. 25*

Dead, we become the lumber of the world.
>   *After Death*

JOHN SHEFFIELD, DUKE OF BUCKINGHAM AND NORMANBY
1648–1721

Of all those arts in which the wise excel,
Nature's chief masterpiece is writing well.
>   *Essay on Poetry [1682]*

Read Homer once, and you can read no more;
For all books else appear so mean, so poor,
Verse will seem prose; but still persist to read,
And Homer will be all the books you need.
>   *Ib.*

---

[1] See Prior, p. 387b.
[2] See Charles II, p. 366b.
[3] Thou best-humor'd man with the worst-humor'd muse! — GOLDSMITH, *Retaliation* [1774], *Postscript*

And when I feigned an angry look,
Alas! I loved you best.
> *The Reconcilement* [1701]

SIR THOMAS POPE BLOUNT
1649–1697

Every flower of the field, every fiber of a plant, every particle of an insect, carries with it the impress of its Maker, and can — if duly considered — read us lectures of ethics or divinity.[1]
> *A Natural History* [1693]

WILLIAM III, PRINCE OF ORANGE
1650–1702

There is one certain means by which I can be sure never to see my country's ruin: I will die in the last ditch.
> *From* HUME, *History of England* [1754–1757], *ch.* 65

Every bullet has its billet.
> *From* JOHN WESLEY, *Journal* [June 6, 1765]

FRANÇOIS DE SALIGNAC DE LA MOTHE FÉNELON
1651–1715

Do not men die fast enough without being destroyed by each other? Can any man be insensible of the brevity of life? and can he who knows it, think life too long!   *Télémaque* [1699], *bk.* VII

To be always ready for war, said Mentor, is the surest way to avoid it.[2]
> *Ib.* X

Some of the most dreadful mischiefs that afflict mankind proceed from wine; it is the cause of disease, quarrels, sedition, idleness, aversion to labor, and every species of domestic disorder.
> *Ib.*

The blood of a nation ought never to be shed except for its own preservation in the utmost extremity.
> *Télémaque, bk.* XIII

Mankind, by the perverse depravity of their nature, esteem that which they have most desired as of no value the moment it is possessed, and torment themselves with fruitless wishes for that which is beyond their reach.
> *Ib.* XVIII

THOMAS OTWAY
1651–1685

What mighty ills have not been done by woman!
Who was 't betrayed the Capitol? — A woman!
Who lost Mark Antony the world? — A woman!
Who was the cause of a long ten years' war,
And laid at last old Troy in ashes? — Woman!
Destructive, damnable, deceitful woman!
> *The Orphan* [1680], *act* III, *sc.* 1

Let us embrace, and from this very moment vow an eternal misery together.   *Ib.* IV, 2

O woman! lovely woman! Nature made thee
To temper man: we had been brutes without you;
Angels are painted fair, to look like you.
> *Venice Preserved* [1682], *act* I, *sc.* 1

NAHUM TATE
1652–1715
AND
NICHOLAS BRADY
1659–1726

When I am laid in earth.
> *Dido and Aeneas* [c. 1690] [1]

---

[1] See Tennyson, p. 654b.
[2] See Vegetius, p. 146b, and note.

[1] Tate wrote the libretto for the famous opera by Henry Purcell.

As pants the hart for cooling streams
When heated in the chase.
Version of Psalm 42 [1696]

Through all the changing scenes of
life.   *Hymn*

While shepherds watch'd their flocks
by night,
All seated on the ground,
The Angel of the Lord came down,
And glory shone around.
Christmas Hymn [1700]

CHIKAMATSU MONZAEMON[1]
1653–1725

In writing *joruri*,[2] one attempts first
to describe facts as they really are, but
in so doing one writes things which are
not true, in the interest of art.
Preface to HOZUMI IKAN,
Naniwa Miyage

I take pathos to be entirely a matter
of restraint. . . . When one says of
something which is sad that it is sad,
one loses the implications, and in the
end, even the impression of sadness is
slight. It is essential that one not say of
a thing that 'it is sad,' but that it be sad
of itself.   *Ib.*

[Literary composition] should have
stylization; this makes it art, and is
what delights men's minds.   *Ib.*

THOMAS D'URFEY
1653–1723

O'er the hills and far away.[3]
Pills to Purge Melancholy

RANSETSU
1653–1708

Against the blue stands
A pine tree etched
By tonight's moon.[4]   *Harvest Moon*

[1] From *Sources of Japanese Tradition*, edited
by William Theodore de Bary [1960].
[2] Plays for life-size puppets.
[3] See Gay, p. 401b.
[4] Translated by PRESCOTT B. WINTERSTEEN, JR.

ANDREW FLETCHER OF SALTOUN
1655–1716

If a man were permitted to make all
the ballads, he need not care who
should make the laws of a nation.
*Conversation Concerning a
Right Regulation of Governments for the Common Good
of Mankind* [1704]

NATHANIEL LEE[1]
1655–1692

Then he will talk — good gods! how he
will talk!
*The Rival Queens; or, The
Death of Alexander the Great*
[1677], *act I, sc. 3*

When Greeks joined Greeks, then was
the tug of war.   *Ib. IV, 2*

'Tis beauty calls, and glory shows the
way.   *Ib.*

Man, false man, smiling, destructive
man!
Theodosius [1680], *act III, sc. 2*

JOHN DENNIS
1657–1734

A man who could make so vile a pun
would not scruple to pick a pocket.
*The Gentleman's Magazine,
vol. LI* [1781], *p.* 324

They will not let my play run; and
yet they steal my thunder.[2]   *Remark*

[1] Lee collaborated with Dryden on *Oedipus*
(see p. 367b).
[2] For his play *Appius and Virginia* [1709].
Dennis had invented a new species of thunder.
"The tragedy however was coldly received, notwithstanding such assistance, and was acted
but a short time. Some nights after, Mr. Dennis,
being in the pit at the representation of
Macbeth, heard his own thunder made use of;
upon which he rose in a violent passion, and
exclaimed, with an oath, that it was his thunder.
'See,' said he, 'how the rascals use me! They
will not let my play run, and yet they steal my
thunder!' " — *Biographia Britannica, vol. V,
p. 103*

BERNARD LE BOVIER DE FONTENELLE
1657–1757

The geometrical mind is not so closely bound to geometry that it cannot be drawn aside and transferred to other departments of knowledge. A work of morality, politics, criticism, perhaps even eloquence will be more elegant, other things being equal, if it is shaped by the hand of geometry.[1]

Préface sur l'Utilité des Mathématiques et la Physique [1729]

JOHN NORRIS
1657–1711

How fading are the joys we dote upon!
Like apparitions seen and gone.
But those which soonest take their flight
Are the most exquisite and strong —
Like angels' visits, short and bright;[2]
Mortality's too weak to bear them
long.   *The Parting* [1678]

DANIEL DEFOE
c. 1661 – 1731

Wherever God erects a house of prayer,
The Devil always builds a chapel there;[3]
And 'twill be found, upon examination,
The latter has the largest congregation.

The True-Born Englishman [1701], *pt. I, l.* 1

From this amphibious ill-born mob began
That vain, ill-natur'd thing, an Englishman.   *Ib. l.* 132

Great families of yesterday we show,
And lords whose parents were the Lord knows who.   *Ib. l.* 374

[1] Translated by F. CAJORI.
[2] Like those of angels, short and far between.
— ROBERT BLAIR, *The Grave* [1743], *l.* 588
See Campbell, p. 537b.
[3] See Luther, p. 179b, and note.

In their religion they are so uneven,
That each man goes his own byway to heaven.

The True-Born Englishman, pt. II, l. 104

And of all plagues with which mankind are curs'd,
Ecclesiastic tyranny's the worst.
Ib. l. 299

When kings the sword of justice first lay down,
They are no kings, though they possess the crown.
Titles are shadows, crowns are empty things,
The good of subjects is the end of kings.   *Ib. l.* 313

All men would be tyrants if they could.
The Kentish Petition [1712–1713]

The best of men cannot suspend their fate:
The good die early, and the bad die late.

Character of the Late Dr. S. Annesley [1715]

He bade me observe it, and I should always find that the calamities of life were shared among the upper and lower part of mankind; but that the middle station had the fewest disasters.
Robinson Crusoe [1719]

One day, about noon, going towards my boat, I was exceedingly surprised with the print of a man's naked foot on the shore, which was very plain to be seen on the sand.   *Ib.*

I takes my man Friday with me.
Ib.

SIR SAMUEL GARTH
1661–1719

A barren superfluity of words.
The Dispensary [1699], *canto II, l.* 95

Hard was their lodging, homely was their food;

For all their luxury was doing good.[1]
Claremont, l. 148

KIKAKU
1661–1707

A harvest moon!
And on the mats —
Shadows of pine boughs.
Harvest Moon [2]

RICHARD BENTLEY
1662–1742

No man was ever written out of reputation but by himself.[3]
From J. H. Monk, *Life of Bentley* [1831]

It is a pretty poem, Mr. Pope, but you must not call it Homer. [4]
From Johnson, *Life of Pope*

MATHEW HENRY
1662–1714

He rolls it under his tongue as a sweet morsel.
Commentaries [1708–1710], *Psalm 36*

Our creature comforts.
Ib. Psalm 37

They that die by famine die by inches.
Ib. Psalm 59

To fish in troubled waters.
Ib. Psalm 60

Here is bread, which strengthens man's heart, and therefore called the staff of life.[5]
Ib. Psalm 104

---

[1] And learn the luxury of doing good. — Goldsmith, *The Traveller* [1764], *l.* 22
[2] Translated by Prescott B. Wintersteen, Jr.
[3] See Montaigne, p. 190b.
[4] The reference is to Pope's translation of the *Iliad*. See Pope, p. 405a.
[5] For, behold, the Lord, the Lord of hosts, doth take away from Jerusalem and from Judah the stay and the staff, the whole stay of bread, and the whole stay of water. — *Isaiah 3:1*
Bread is the staff of life. — Swift, *Tale of a Tub* [1704]
Corn, which is the staff of life. — Edward Winslow, *Good News from New England* [1624]

Hearkeners, we say, seldom hear good of themselves.
Commentaries, Ecclesiastes 7

It was a common saying among the Puritans, "Brown bread and the Gospel is good fare."
Ib. Isaiah 30

None so blind as those that will not see.[1]
Ib. Jeremiah 20

Judas had given them the slip.
Ib. Matthew 22

After a storm comes a calm.
Ib. Acts 9

Men of polite learning and a liberal education.
Ib. 10

It is good news, worthy of all acceptation! and yet not too good to be true.
Ib. Timothy 1

It is not fit the public trusts should be lodged in the hands of any, till they are first proved and found fit for the business they are to be entrusted with.[2]
Ib. 3

All this and heaven too.
Life of Philip Henry

THOMAS (TOM) BROWN
1663–1704

I do not love thee, Doctor Fell.
The reason why I cannot tell;
But this alone I know full well,
I do not love thee, Doctor Fell.[3]
Written while a student at Christ Church, Oxford

To treat a poor wretch with a bottle of Burgundy, and fill his snuffbox, is like giving a pair of laced ruffles to a man that has never a shirt on his back.[4]
Laconics [1707]

---

[1] See *Jeremiah 5:21*, p. 34a.
[2] See Burke, p. 454b; Jefferson, p. 472b; Clay, p. 538b; Calhoun, p. 545b; Sumner, p. 659b; and Cleveland, p. 771a.
[3] See Martial, p. 135a.
Je ne vous aime pas, Hylas;
Je n'en saurois dire la cause,
Je sais seulement une chose;
C'est que je ne vous aime pas.
Comte de Bussy-Rabutin [1618–1693]
[4] See Goldsmith, p. 451b.

COTTON MATHER
1663–1728

I write the wonders of the Christian religion, flying from the depravations of Europe, to the American strand: and, assisted by the Holy Author of that religion, I do, with all conscience of truth, required therein by Him, who is the Truth itself, report the wonderful displays of His infinite power, wisdom, goodness, and faithfulness, wherewith his Divine Providence hath irradiated an Indian wilderness.

> *Magnalia Christi Americana*
> [1702], *introduction*

You are young and have the world before you; stoop as you go through it, and you will miss many hard bumps.

> *Advice to Benjamin Franklin upon approaching a low-hanging beam in his parsonage* [1]

WILLIAM WALSH
1663–1708

Of all the plagues a lover bears,
Sure rivals are the worst.   *Song, st.* 1

I can endure my own despair,
But not another's hope.   *Ib. st.* 2

MATTHEW PRIOR
1664–1721

All jargon of the schools. [2]
> *I Am That I Am, An Ode* [1688]

Our hopes, like towering falcons, aim
   At objects in an airy height;
The little pleasure of the game
   Is from afar to view the flight.
> *To the Honorable Charles*
> *Montague*

Odds life! must one swear to the truth
   of a song?   *A Better Answer*

Be to her virtues very kind;
Be to her faults a little blind;

---

[1] From S. E. MORISON, *Vistas of History* [*1964*], *ch.* 4
   See Massinger, p. 315b.
[2] Noisy jargon of the schools. — JOHN POMFRET [1667–1702], *Reason*
   The sounding jargon of the schools. — COWPER, *Truth* [1782], *l. 367*

Let all her ways be unconfin'd;
And clap your padlock — on her mind!
> *An English Padlock* [1707]

The end must justify the means.[1]
> *Hans Carvel*

And thought the nation ne'er would
   thrive
Till all the whores were burnt alive.
> *Paulo Purganti*

He rang'd his tropes, and preach'd up
   patience;
Back'd his opinion with quotations.
> *Ib.*

Cured yesterday of my disease,
I died last night of my physician.[2]
> *The Remedy Worse Than the*
> *Disease*

And often took leave, but was loth to
   depart.[3]
> *The Thief and the Cordelier*

Nobles and heralds, by your leave,
   Here lies what once was Matthew
      Prior;
The son of Adam and of Eve:
   Can Bourbon or Nassau claim
      higher? [4]   *Epitaph*

Lays the rough paths of peevish Nature
   even,
And opens in each heart a little
   heaven.   *Charity*

His noble negligences teach
What others' toils despair to reach.
> *Alma, canto II, l.* 7

Till their own dreams at length deceive
   'em,
And oft repeating, they believe 'em.
> *Ib. III,* 13

---

[1] See St. Jerome, p. 145a.
[2] See Leibnitz, p. 382a.
[3] As men that be lothe to departe do often take their leff [JOHN CLERK TO WOLSEY]. — HENRY ELLIS [1777–1869], *Letters, Third Series, vol. I, p. 262*
   "A loth to depart" was the common term for a song, or a tune played, on taking leave of friends.
[4] The following epitaph was written long before the time of Prior:
> Johnnie Carnegie lais heer.
>   Descendit of Adam and Eve.
> Gif ony con gang hieher,
>   Ise willing give him leve.

Abra was ready ere I called her name;
And though I called another, Abra
came.
> *Solomon on the Vanity of the
> World* [1718], bk. II, l. 364

To John I ow'd great obligation;
  But John, unhappily, thought fit
To publish it to all the nation:
Sure John and I are more than quit.
> *Epigram* [1718]

Venus, take my votive glass;
Since I am not what I was,
What from this day I shall be,
Venus, let me never see.
> *The Lady Who Offers Her
> Looking-Glass to Venus. From
> The Greek Anthology*

SIR JOHN VANBRUGH
1664–1726

Once a woman has given you her
heart you can never get rid of the rest
of her.
> *The Relapse* [1697], *act II, sc. 1*

No man worth having is true to his
wife, or can be true to his wife, or ever
was, or ever will be so.   *Ib. III, 2*

Belinda: Ay, but you know we must
return good for evil.
Lady Brute: That may be a mistake
in the translation.
> *The Provoked Wife* [1698],
> *act I, sc. 1*

He laughs best who laughs last.[1]
> *The Country House* [1706],
> *act II, sc. 5*

Much of a muchness.
> *The Provoked Husband* [1728]
> (*completed by* COLLEY CIBBER)
> *act I, sc. 1*

JOHN POMFRET
1667–1702

We live and learn, but not the wiser
grow.[2]   *Reason, l. 112*

[1] Better the last smile than the first laughter.
— JOHN RAY, *Proverbs* [1670]
[2] It is good to live and learn. — CERVANTES,
Don Quixote, pt. II [1615], *ch. 32*

JONATHAN SWIFT
1667–1745

Books, like men their authors, have
no more than one way of coming into
the world, but there are ten thousand
to go out of it, and return no more.
> *A Tale of a Tub* [1704], *dedication*

Books, the children of the brain.
> *Ib. sec. 1*

As boys do sparrows, with flinging
salt upon their tails.   *Ib. 7*

Satire is a sort of glass, wherein beholders do generally discover everybody's face but their own.
> *The Battle of the Books* [1704],
> *preface*

The two noblest of things, which are
sweetness and light.[1]   *Ib.*

Laws are like cobwebs, which may
catch small flies, but let wasps and hornets break through.[2]
> *A Critical Essay Upon the Fac-
> ulties of the Mind* [1707]

There is nothing in this world constant, but inconstancy.[3]   *Ib.*

'Tis very warm weather when one's
in bed.
> *Journal to Stella* [*November 8,
> 1710*]

With my own fair hands.
> *Ib.* [*January 4, 1711*]

We are so fond of one another, because our ailments are the same.
> *Ib.* [*February 1, 1711*]

I love good creditable acquaintance; I
love to be the worst of the company.
> *Ib.* [*May 17, 1711*]

We were to do more business after
dinner; but after dinner is after din-

Live and learn,
Not first learn and then live.
> BROWNING, *Parleyings with Certain
> People. With Christopher Smart*
> [1887], *IX*
[1] See Matthew Arnold, p. 716a.
[2] See Solon, p. 68b, and Zincgref, p. 321a.
[3] See Heraclitus, p. 77b, and note.

ner — an old saying and a true, "much drinking, little thinking." [1]

> Journal to Stella
> [February 26, 1712]

We have just enough religion to make us hate, but not enough to make us love one another.

> Thoughts on Various Subjects
> [1711]

Censure is the tax a man pays to the public for being eminent.   *Ib.*

Every man desires to live long, but no man would be old.   *Ib.*

A nice man is a man of nasty ideas.
   Ib.

Party is the madness of many, for the gain of a few.[2]   *Ib.*

'Tis an old maxim in the schools,
That flattery's the food of fools;
Yet now and then your men of wit
Will condescend to take a bit.

> Cadenus and Vanessa [3] [1713]

Proper words in proper places, make the true definition of a style.

> Letter to a Young Clergyman
> [January 9, 1720]

If Heaven had looked upon riches to be a valuable thing, it would not have given them to such a scoundrel.

> Letter to Miss Vanhomrigh
> [August 12, 1720]

He [the Emperor] is taller by almost the breadth of my nail, than any of his court, which alone is enough to strike an awe into the beholders.

> Gulliver's Travels [1726].
> Voyage to Lilliput, ch. 2

[1] See Addison, p. 394b.
[2] See Pope, p. 405a.
[3] When the poem of "Cadenus and Vanessa" was the general topic of conversation, someone said, "Surely that Vanessa must be an extraordinary woman that could inspire the Dean to write so finely upon her." Mrs. Johnson smiled, and answered that "she thought that point not quite so clear; for it was well known the Dean could write finely upon a broomstick." — SAMUEL JOHNSON, *Lives of the Poets* [1779–1781], *Life of Swift*

I cannot but conclude the bulk of your natives to be the most pernicious race of little odious vermin that nature ever suffered to crawl upon the surface of the earth.

> Gulliver's Travels. Voyage to
> Brobdingnag, ch. 6

And he gave it for his opinion, that whoever could make two ears of corn or two blades of grass to grow upon a spot of ground where only one grew before, would deserve better of mankind, and do more essential service to his country, than the whole race of politicians put together.[1]   *Ib.*

He had been eight years upon a project for extracting sunbeams out of cucumbers, which were to be put in vials hermetically sealed, and let out to warm the air in raw inclement summers.

> Ib. Voyage to Laputa, ch. 5

I said the thing which was not.

> Ib. Voyage to the Houyhnhnms,
> ch. 3

I told him . . . that we ate when we were not hungry, and drank without the provocation of thirst.   *Ib. 6*

A set of phrases learnt by rote;
A passion for a scarlet coat;
When at a play to laugh, or cry,
Yet cannot tell the reason why:
Never to hold her tongue a minute;
While all she prates has nothing in it.

> The Furniture of a Woman's
> Mind [1727]

For conversation well endu'd;
She calls it witty to be rude;
And, placing raillery in railing,
Will tell aloud your greatest failing.
   Ib.

In party, furious to her pow'r;
A bitter Whig, or Tory sour;
Her arguments directly tend

[1] He who makes two blades of grass grow in place of one renders a service to the state. — VOLTAIRE, *Letter to M. Moreau* [1765]

Against the side she would defend.
*The Furniture of a
Woman's Mind*

Not die here in a rage, like a poisoned rat in a hole.
*Letter to Bolingbroke
[March 21, 1729]*

Yet malice never was his aim;
He lash'd the vice but spar'd the name.
No individual could resent,
Where thousands equally were meant.
His satire points at no defect
But what all mortals may correct;
For he abhorr'd that senseless tribe
Who call it humor when they gibe.
*Verses on the Death of Dr. Swift
[1731], l. 459*

Hobbes clearly proves that every creature
Lives in a state of war by nature.[1]
On Poetry. A Rhapsody [1733]

So, naturalists observe, a flea
Hath smaller fleas that on him prey;
And these have smaller still to bite
'em;
And so proceed *ad infinitum*.
Thus every poet, in his kind,
Is bit by him that comes behind.
Ib.

Conversation is but carving!
Give no more to every guest
Than he's able to digest.
Give him always of the prime,
And but little at a time.
Carve to all but just enough,
Let them neither starve nor stuff,
And that you may have your due,
Let your neighbor carve for you.
Conversation

Under this window in stormy weather
I marry this man and woman together;
Let none but Him who rules the thunder
Put this man and woman asunder.
*Marriage Service from His
Chamber Window*

[1] See Hobbes, p. 317b.

The sight of you is good for sore eyes.[1]
*Polite Conversation [1738?],
dialogue 1*

'Tis as cheap sitting as standing.
Ib.

I hate nobody: I am in charity with the world. *Ib.*

You were half seas over. *Ib.*

I won't quarrel with my bread and butter. *Ib.*

She's no chicken; she's on the wrong side of thirty, if she be a day. *Ib.*

She wears her clothes, as if they were thrown on her with a pitchfork.
Ib.

He was a bold man that first eat an oyster. *Ib.* 2

That's as well said, as if I had said it myself. *Ib.*

Fingers were made before forks, and hands before knives. *Ib.*

She has more goodness in her little finger, than he has in his whole body.
Ib.

Lord, I wonder what fool it was that first invented kissing! *Ib.*

The best doctors in the world are Doctor Diet, Doctor Quiet, and Doctor Merryman.[2] *Ib.*

I'll give you leave to call me anything, if you don't call me spade.
Ib.

May you live all the days of your life. *Ib.*

I always love to begin a journey on Sundays, because I shall have the prayers of the church to preserve all that travel by land, or by water. *Ib.*

[1] What a sight for sore eyes that would be!
— WILLIAM HAZLITT [1778–1830], *Of Persons
One Would Have Seen*
[2] Use three physicians —
First, Dr. Quiet;
Next, Dr. Merryman,
And Dr. Dyet.
Regimen Sanitatis Salernitanum [1607]

I know Sir John will go, though he was sure it would rain cats and dogs.
Polite Conversation, dialogue 2

I thought you and he were hand-in-glove.   *Ib.*

She watches him, as a cat would watch a mouse.   *Ib. dialogue* 3

She pays him in his own coin.
Ib.

There was all the world and his wife.   *Ib.*

Hail, fellow, well met,
All dirty and wet:
Find out if you can,
Who's master, who's man.
My Lady's Lamentation [1765],
l. 171

I shall be like that tree, I shall die at the top.
From SIR WALTER SCOTT, *Life of Swift* [1814]

Ubi saeva indignatio ulterius cor lacerare nequit.[1]
Epitaph. Inscribed on Swift's Grave, St. Patrick's, Dublin

SUSANNAH CENTLIVRE
c. 1667 – 1723

The real Simon Pure.
A Bold Stroke for a Wife [1718],
act V, *sc. 1*

ALAIN RENÉ LE SAGE
1668–1747

It may be said that his wit shines at the expense of his memory.[2]
Gil Blas [1715–1735], *bk. III, ch. 11*

A flatterer can risk everything with great personages.   *Ib.* IV, 7

Pride and conceit were the original sin of man.   *Ib.* VII, 3

I wish you all sorts of prosperity with a little more taste.   *Ib.* 4

[1] Where savage indignation can no longer tear the heart. See Yeats, p. 884a.
[2] See Sheridan, p. 482a.

The pleasure of talking is the inextinguishable passion of a woman, coeval with the act of breathing.
Gil Blas, bk. VII, *ch.* 7

Facts are stubborn things.[1]
Ib. X, 1

WILLIAM CONGREVE
1670–1729

Eternity was in that moment.
The Old Bachelor [1693],
act IV, *sc.* 7

Marry'd in haste, we may repent at leisure.[2]   *Ib.* V, 8

It is the business of a comic poet to paint the vices and follies of human kind.
The Double Dealer [1694],
epistle dedicatory

Retired to their tea and scandal, according to their ancient custom.[3]
Ib. act I, *sc.* 1

Though marriage makes man and wife one flesh, it leaves 'em still two fools.   *Ib.* II, 3

No mask like open truth to cover lies,
As to go naked is the best disguise.
Ib. V, 4

Thou liar of the first magnitude.
Love for Love [1695], *act* II, *sc.* 2

I warrant you, if he danced till doomsday, he thought I was to pay the piper.   *Ib.*

O fie, miss, you must not kiss and tell.   *Ib.* 10

Women are like tricks by sleight of hand,
Which, to admire, we should not understand.   *Ib.* IV, 3

Music has charms to soothe a savage breast,[4]

[1] Facts are contrary 'z mules. — JAMES RUSSELL LOWELL, *Biglow Papers, ser. II* [1862], *no. 4*
[2] See Shakespeare, p. 219a, and Cabell, p. 949b.
[3] See Fielding, p. 424b.
[4] Music hath charms, we all may find,
Ingratiate deeply with the mind.
MATTHEW GREEN [1696–1737], *The Spleen, l. 141*

To soften rocks, or bend a knotted oak.
> *The Mourning Bride* [1697],
> *act I, sc. 1*

By magic numbers and persuasive sound.   *Ib.*

Heaven has no rage like love to hatred turned,
Nor hell a fury like a woman scorned.[1]
> *Ib. III, 8*

Love's but a frailty of the mind,
When 'tis not with ambition joined.
> *The Way of the World* [1700],
> *act III, sc. 12*

I nauseate walking; 'tis a country diversion, I loathe the country.
> *Ib. IV, 5*

Let us be very strange and well-bred:
Let us be as strange as if we had been married a great while; and as well-bred as if we were not married at all.
> *Ib.*

Thou art a retailer of phrases, and dost deal in remnants of remnants.
> *Ib. 9*

O, she is the antidote to desire.
> *Ib. 14*

Careless she is with artful care,
Affecting to seem unaffected.
> *Amoret*

Defer not till tomorrow to be wise,
Tomorrow's sun to thee may never rise.[2]   *Letter to Cobham*

RICHARD LEVERIDGE
1670–1758

When mighty roast beef was the Englishman's food,
It ennobled our hearts, and enriched our blood,

Our soldiers were brave and our courtiers were good.
Oh! the roast beef of old England![1]
> *The Roast Beef of Old England,*
> *st. 1*

COLLEY CIBBER
1671–1757

As good be out of the world as out of the fashion.
> *Love's Last Shift* [1696], *act II*

Possession is eleven points in the law.   *Woman's Wit* [1697], *act I*

Words are but empty thanks.
> *Ib. V*

Off with his head [2] — so much for Buckingham.
> *Richard III (altered)* [1700],
> *act IV, sc. 3*

Perish the thought!   *Ib. V, 5*

This business will never hold water.
> *She Wou'd and She Wou'd Not*
> [1703], *act IV*

Old houses mended,
Cost little less than new before they're ended.
> *The Double Gallant* [1707],
> *prologue*

Oh, how many torments lie in the small circle of a wedding ring!
> *Ib. act I, sc. 2*

Stolen sweets are best.
> *The Rival Fools* [1709], *act I*

JOSEPH ADDISON
1672–1719

For wheresoe'er I turn my ravish'd eyes,
Gay gilded scenes and shining prospects rise,
Poetic fields encompass me around,

See Shakespeare, *Measure for Measure IV,*
i, 16, p. 372a.

[1] We shall find no fiend in hell can match the fury of a disappointed woman. — COLLEY CIBBER, *Love's Last Shift* [1696], *act IV*

[2] See Euripides, p. 84a, and Edward Young. p. 399a.

[1] Oh, the roast beef of England,
And old England's roast beef!
> FIELDING [1707–1754], *The Grub Street*
> *Opera, act III, sc. 2*

[2] See Shakespeare, p. 217b, and Lewis Carroll, p. 744a.

And still I seem to tread on classic
  ground.
          A Letter from Italy [1703]

And, pleas'd the Almighty's orders to
  perform,
Rides in the whirlwind and directs the
  storm.[1]
          The Campaign [1704], *l. 91*

The spacious firmament on high,
With all the blue ethereal sky,
And spangled heavens, a shining frame,
Their great Original proclaim.[2]
      Ode [*in The Spectator, no. 465,*
            August 23, 1712]

Soon as the evening shades prevail,
The moon takes up the wondrous tale,
And nightly to the listening earth
Repeats the story of her birth;
While all the stars that round her
  burn,
And all the planets in their turn,
Confirm the tidings as they roll,
And spread the truth from pole to
  pole.   *Ib.*

Forever singing as they shine,
"The Hand that made us is divine."
                    Ib.

Should the whole frame of Nature
  round him break,
In ruin and confusion hurled,
He, unconcerned, would hear the
  mighty crack,
And stand secure amidst a falling world.
          Horace, ode 3, bk. III

'Tis not in mortals to command success,
But we'll do more, Sempronius; we'll
  deserve it.
          Cato [3] [1713], *act I, sc. 2*

Blesses his stars and thinks it luxury.
                   Ib. 4

[1] This line is frequently ascribed to Pope, as
it is repeated in his *Dunciad, bk. III* [1728],
l. 264.

[2] See *Psalm 19*, p. 17a-b.

[3] The *Massachusetts Spy* used the following
lines from *Cato* as its motto from November 22,
1771 to April 6, 1775:

Do thou Great Liberty inspire our Souls —
And make our Lives in thy Possession happy —
Or, our Deaths glorious in thy just Defense.

'Tis pride, rank pride, and haughtiness
  of soul;
I think the Romans call it stoicism.
          Cato, act I, sc. 4

Were you with these, my prince, you'd
  soon forget
The pale, unripened beauties of the
  north.   *Ib.*

Beauty soon grows familiar to the
  lover,
Fades in his eye, and palls upon the
  sense.   *Ib.*

    My voice is still for war.
Gods! can a Roman senate long debate
Which of the two to choose, slavery or
  death?   *Ib. II, 1*

The woman that deliberates is lost.
                Ib. IV, 1

Curse on his virtues! they've undone his
  country.   *Ib. 4*

    What pity is it
That we can die but once to serve our
  country! [1]   *Ib.*

When vice prevails, and impious men
  bear sway,
The post of honor is a private station.[2]
                    Ib.

It must be so — Plato, thou reasonest
  well!
Else whence this pleasing hope, this
  fond desire,
This longing after immortality?
Or whence this secret dread, and in-
  ward horror,
Of falling into naught? Why shrinks
  the soul
Back on herself, and startles at destruc-
  tion?
'Tis the divinity that stirs within us;
'Tis heaven itself, that points out an
  hereafter,
And intimates eternity to man.

[1] See Nathan Hale, p. 484b.

[2] Give me, kind Heaven, a private station,
A mind serene for contemplation!
Title and profit I resign;
The post of honor shall be mine.
      GAY, *Fables, pt. II* [1738], *The Vulture,*
         The Sparrow, and Other Birds

Eternity! thou pleasing, dreadful thought!
Cato, act V, sc. 1

Sweet are the slumbers of the virtuous man.   *Ib. 4*

From hence, let fierce contending nations know
What dire effects from civil discord flow.   *Ib.*

Round-heads and Wooden-shoes are standing jokes.
The Drummer, prologue, l. 8

If I can any way contribute to the diversion or improvement of the country in which I live, I shall leave it, when I am summoned out of it, with the secret satisfaction of thinking that I have not lived in vain.[1]
The Spectator, no. 1
[March 1, 1711]

Thus I live in the world rather as a spectator of mankind than as one of the species.   *Ib.*

I shall endeavor to enliven morality with wit, and to temper wit with morality.   *Ib. 10 [March 11, 1711]*

True happiness is of a retired nature, and an enemy to pomp and noise; it arises, in the first place, from the enjoyment of one's self; and, in the next, from the friendship and conversation of a few select companions.
Ib. 15 [March 17, 1711]

In all thy humors, whether grave or mellow,
Thou'rt such a touchy, testy, pleasant fellow;
Hast so much wit, and mirth, and spleen about thee,
There is no living with thee, nor without thee. [2]
Ib. 68 [May 18, 1711]

There is not a more unhappy being than a superannuated idol.
Ib. 73 [May 24, 1711]

[1] See Étienne de Grellet, p. 531a.
[2] A translation of MARTIAL [A.D. 40–102] *XII, 47,* who imitated OVID [43 B.C.–A.D. 18], *Amores III, 11, 39.*

A man that has a taste of music, painting, or architecture, is like one that has another sense, when compared with such as have no relish of those arts.   *The Spectator, no. 93*
[June 16, 1711]

There is no defense against reproach but obscurity.
Ib. 101 [June 26, 1711]

Much might be said on both sides.
Ib. 122 [July 20, 1711]

Authors have established it as a kind of rule, that a man ought to be dull sometimes; as the most severe reader makes allowances for many rests and nodding-places in a voluminous writer.
Ib. 124 [July 23, 1711]

Books are the legacies that a great genius leaves to mankind, which are delivered down from generation to generation, as presents to the posterity of those who are yet unborn.
Ib. 166 [September 10, 1711]

Good nature is more agreeable in conversation than wit, and gives a certain air to the countenance which is more amiable than beauty.
Ib. 169 [September 13, 1711]

Were I to prescribe a rule for drinking, it should be formed upon a saying quoted by Sir William Temple: the first glass for myself, the second for my friends, the third for good humor, and the fourth for mine enemies.[1]
Ib. 195 [October 13, 1711]

A true critic ought to dwell rather upon excellencies than imperfections, to discover the concealed beauties of a writer, and communicate to the world such things as are worth their observation.   *Ib. 291 [February 2, 1712]*

These widows, sir, are the most perverse creatures in the world.
Ib. 335 [March 25, 1712]

Mirth is like a flash of lightning, that breaks through a gloom of clouds, and glitters for a moment; cheerfulness keeps up a kind of daylight in the

[1] See Swift, p. 389a.

mind, and fills it with a steady and perpetual serenity.

> *The Spectator, no.* 381
> [*May 17, 1712*]

Sir Roger made several reflections on the greatness of the British Nation; as, that one Englishman could beat three Frenchmen; that we could never be in danger of Popery so long as we took care of our fleet; that the Thames was the noblest river in Europe . . . with many other honest prejudices which naturally cleave to the heart of a true Englishman.

> *Ib.* 383 [*May 20, 1712*]

Our disputants put me in mind of the skuttle fish, that when he is unable to extricate himself, blackens all the water about him, till he becomes invisible.   *Ib.* 476 [*September 5, 1712*]

The fraternity of the henpecked.[1]

> *Ib.* 482 [*September 12, 1712*]

A man should always consider how much he has more than he wants, and how much more unhappy he might be than he really is.

> *Ib.* 574 [*July 30, 1714*]

We are always doing something for Posterity, but I would fain see Posterity do something for us.

> *Ib.* 587 [*August 20, 1714*]

See in what peace a Christian can die.

> *Dying words* [1719]. *From* Young, *Conjectures on Original Composition* [1759]

SIR RICHARD STEELE
1672–1729

I am come to a tavern alone to eat a steak, after which I shall return to the office.

> *Letters to His Wife*
> [*October 28, 1707*]

I was going home two hours ago, but was met by Mr. Griffith, who has kept me ever since. I will come within a pint of wine.

> *Letters to His Wife* [*Eleven at night, January 5, 1708*]

A little in drink, but at all times yr faithful husband.

> *Ib.* [*September 27, 1708*]

The finest woman in nature should not detain me an hour from you; but you must sometimes suffer the rivalship of the wisest men.

> *Ib.* [*September 17, 1712*]

Though her mien carries much more invitation than command, to behold her is an immediate check to loose behavior; to love her is a liberal education.[1]   *Tatler* [1709–1711], *no.* 49

Reading is to the mind what exercise is to the body.   *Ib. no.* 147

When you fall into a man's conversation, the first thing you should consider is, whether he has a greater inclination to hear you, or that you should hear him.

> *The Spectator, no.* 49
> [*April 26, 1711*]

Of all the affections which attend human life, the love of glory is the most ardent.   *Ib.* 139 [*August 9, 1711*]

Age in a virtuous person, of either sex, carries in it an authority which makes it preferable to all the pleasures of youth.

> *Ib.* 153 [*August 25, 1711*]

Among all the diseases of the mind there is not one more epidemical or more pernicious than the love of flattery.   *Ib.* 238 [*December 3, 1711*]

Will Honeycomb calls these overoffended ladies the outrageously virtuous.   *Ib.* 266 [*January 4, 1712*]

A favor well bestowed is almost as great an honor to him who confers it as to him who receives it.

> *Ib.* 497 [*September 30, 1712*]

---

[1] See Byron, p. 560a.

[1] Lady Elizabeth Hastings [1682–1739].

EDMOND HOYLE [1]
1672–1769

When in doubt, win the trick.
> *Twenty-four Rules for Learners,*
> *rule 12*

FRANÇOIS GOYOT DE PITAVALS
1673–1743

Causes Célèbres.
> *Title of book recounting famous*
> *trials and judgments*

NICHOLAS ROWE
1673–1718

As if Misfortune made the throne her
seat,
And none could be unhappy but the
great.[2]
> *The Fair Penitent* [1703], *prologue*

At length the morn and cold indifference came.   *Ib. act I, sc. 1*

Is this that haughty gallant, gay Lo-
thario?   *Ib.* V, 1

ISAAC WATTS
1674–1748

Were I so tall to reach the pole,
  Or grasp the ocean with my span,
I must be measured by my soul;
  The mind's the standard of the man.
> *Horae Lyricae* [1706], *bk. II,*
> *False Greatness*

Let dogs delight to bark and bite,
  For God hath made them so;
Let bears and lions growl and fight,
  For 'tis their nature too.
> *Divine Songs* [1715], 16,
> *Against Quarreling and*
> *Fighting*

---

[1] Hoyle published [1742] a *Short Treatise on
Whist,* which in subsequent editions added
rules for playing piquet, backgammon, chess,
and other games. His *Laws* [1760] ruled whist
playing until 1864, hence the saying, "according
to Hoyle."

[2] None think the great unhappy, but the great.
— EDWARD YOUNG, *The Love of Fame* [1725–
1728], *satire 1, l. 238*

But, children, you should never let
  Such angry passions rise;
Your little hands were never made
  To tear each other's eyes.
> *Divine Songs. Against*
> *Quarreling and Fighting*

Birds in their little nests agree;
  And 'tis a shameful sight,
When children of one family
  Fall out, and chide, and fight.
> *Ib.* 17, *Love Between Brothers*
> *and Sisters*

How doth the little busy bee
  Improve each shining hour,[1]
And gather honey all the day
  From every opening flower!
> *Ib.* 20, *Against Idleness and*
> *Mischief*

For Satan finds some mischief still
  For idle hands to do.   *Ib.*

Let me be dress'd fine as I will,
Flies, worms, and flowers, exceed me
  still.
> *Ib.* 22, *Against Pride in Clothes*

Hush! my dear, lie still and slumber,
  Holy angels guard thy bed!
Heavenly blessings without number
  Gently falling on thy head.
> *Ib.* 35, *A Cradle Hymn*

'Tis the voice of the sluggard; I heard
  him complain,
"You have wak'd me too soon, I must
  slumber again." [2]
> *Ib. The Sluggard*

Lord, in the morning thou shalt hear
My voice ascending high.
> *Psalm 5* [1719]

O God, our help in ages past,
  Our hope for years to come,
Our shelter from the stormy blast,
  And our eternal home.
> *Psalm 90* [1719], *st. 1*

A thousand ages in Thy sight
  Are like an evening gone;
Short as the watch that ends the night
  Before the rising sun.   *Ib. st. 4*

---

[1] See Lewis Carroll, p. 743a.
[2] See Lewis Carroll, p. 744b.

Time, like an ever-rolling stream,
　Bears all its sons away;
They fly forgotten, as a dream
　Dies at the opening day.[1]
　　　　　　Psalm 90, st. 5

Joy to the world! the Lord is come;
　Let earth receive her King.
Let ev'ry heart prepare Him room,
　And heav'n and nature sing.
　　　　　Psalm 98 [1719], st. 1

When I can read my title clear
　To mansions in the skies,
I'll bid farewell to every fear,
　And wipe my weeping eyes.
　　　　　Hymns and Spiritual Songs,
　　　　　bk. II, hymn 65

There is a land of pure delight,
　Where saints immortal reign;
Infinite day excludes the night,
　And pleasures banish pain.　　*Ib. 66*

WILLIAM SOMERVILLE[2]
1675–1742

Let all the learned say what they can,
'Tis ready money makes the man.
　　　　　Ready Money [1727]

There is something in a face,
An air, and a peculiar grace,
Which boldest painters cannot trace.
　　　　　The Lucky Hit [1727]

The chase, the sport of kings;
Image of war, without its guilt.
　　　　　The Chase [1735], I, 13

JOHN PHILIPS
1676–1709

Happy the man who, void of care and
　　strife,
In silken or in leathern purse retains
A Splendid Shilling.
　　　　The Splendid Shilling [1701], l. 1

---

[1] See Marcus Aurelius, p. 142a.
[2] Of whom SAMUEL JOHNSON, in his *Lives of the Poets*, made the famous remark, "He writes very well for a gentleman." See Johnson, p. 433b.

SIR ROBERT WALPOLE
1676–1745

The balance of power.
　　　Speech in the House of Com-
　　　mons [February 13, 1741]

All those men have their price.
　　　From WILLIAM COXE, *Memoirs*
　　　of Walpole [1798], vol. IV,
　　　p. 369

Anything but history, for history
must be false.　　*Walpoliana, no. 141*

HENRY ST. JOHN,
VISCOUNT
BOLINGBROKE
1678–1751

Truth lies within a little and certain
compass, but error is immense.
　　　Reflections Upon Exile [1716]

Nations, like men, have their infancy.
　　　On the Study and Use of History
　　　　　[1752], letter 4

They [Thucydides and Xenophon]
maintained the dignity of history.
　　　　　　　　　　Ib. 5

It is the modest, not the presumptuous, inquirer who makes a real and safe
progress in the discovery of divine
truths. One follows Nature and Nature's God; that is, he follows God in
his works and in his word.[1]
　　　　Letter to Alexander Pope

GEORGE FARQUHAR
1678–1707

Reason still keeps its throne, but it
nods a little, that's all.
　　　The Recruiting Officer [1706],
　　　　　act III, sc. 2

I have fed purely upon ale; I have eat
my ale, and I always sleep upon ale.
　　　The Beaux' Stratagem [1707],
　　　　　act I, sc. 1

My Lady Bountiful.　　　　　*Ib.*

---

[1] See Pope, p. 410a, and Jefferson, p. 470b.

I believe they talked of me, for they laughed consumedly.
The Beaux' Stratagem,
act III, sc. 1

'Twas for the good of my country that I should be abroad.[1] — Anything for the good of one's country — I'm a Roman for that. *Ib. III, 2*

How a little love and good company improves a woman! *Ib. IV, 1*

Spare all I have, and take my life.
Ib. V, 2

THOMAS PARNELL
1679–1718

My days have been so wondrous free,
The little birds that fly
With careless ease from tree to tree,
Were but as bless'd as I.
Song[2] *[1714], st. 1*

Still an angel appear to each lover beside,
But still be a woman to you.
When Thy Beauty Appears
[1722], st. 3

We call it only pretty Fanny's way.
An Elegy to an Old Beauty
[1722], st. 4

Let those love now who never loved before;
Let those who always loved, now love the more.
Translation of the Pervigilium
Veneris[3]

[1] Leaving his country for his country's sake. — CHARLES FITZ-GEFFREY, *The Life and Death of Sir Francis Drake* [1596], *st. 213*
True patriots all; for, be it understood,
We left our country for our country's good.
GEORGE BARRINGTON, *Prologue written for the opening of the playhouse at New South Wales* [*January 16, 1796*]
(According to *The Oxford Companion to English Literature,* Barrington was the adopted name of a notorious pickpocket who was transported to the penal settlement at Botany Bay.)
[2] Set to music by Francis Hopkinson; one of the earliest American songs.
[3] See Anonymous Latin, p. 150a.

DESTOUCHES
[PHILIPPE NÉRICAULT]
1680–1754

Those not present are always wrong.[1]
L'Obstacle Imprévu [1717],
act I, sc. 6

Criticism is easy, art is difficult.
Le Glorieux [1732], *act II, sc. 5*

EDWARD YOUNG
1683–1765

The love of praise, howe'er conceal'd by art,
Reigns more or less, and glows in ev'ry heart.
Love of Fame [1725–1728],
satire I, l. 51

Some for renown, on scraps of learning dote,
And think they grow immortal as they quote. *Ib. l. 89*

Be wise with speed;
A fool at forty is a fool indeed.
Ib. II, l. 282

Forever most divinely in the wrong.
Ib. VI, l. 105

For her own breakfast she'll project a scheme,
Nor take her tea without a stratagem.
Ib. l. 187

One to destroy, is murder by the law;
And gibbets keep the lifted hand in awe;
To murder thousands takes a specious name,
War's glorious art, and gives immortal fame.[2] *Ib. VII, l. 55*

The man that makes a character makes foes.
To Mr. Pope, epistle I, l. 28

In records that defy the tooth of time.
The Statesman's Creed

Tired nature's sweet restorer, balmy sleep!
Night Thoughts [1742–1745].
Night I, l. 1

[1] Les absents ont toujours tort.
[2] See Porteus, p. 460a.

Night, sable goddess! from her ebon
throne,
In rayless majesty, now stretches forth
Her leaden scepter o'er a slumbering
world.
Night Thoughts. Night I,
l. 18

Creation sleeps! 'Tis as the general
pulse
Of life stood still, and Nature made a
pause;
An awful pause! prophetic of her end.
Ib. l. 23

The bell strikes one. We take no
note of time
But from its loss. *Ib. l. 55*

Be wise today; 'tis madness to defer.[1]
Ib. l. 390

Procrastination is the thief of time.
Ib. l. 393

At thirty, man suspects himself a fool;
Knows it at forty, and reforms his
plan;
At fifty chides his infamous delay,
Pushes his prudent purpose to resolve;
In all the magnanimity of thought
Resolves, and re-resolves; then dies the
same. *Ib. l. 417*

All men think all men mortal but
themselves. *Ib. l. 424*

"I've lost a day!" — the prince who
nobly cried,
Had been an emperor without his
crown.[2] *Ib. II, l. 99*

Man wants but little, nor that little
long.[3] *Ib. IV, l. 118*

A God all mercy is a God unjust.
Ib. l. 233

By night an atheist half believes a
God.[4] *Ib. V, l. 177*

Like our shadows,

Our wishes lengthen as our sun declines.
Night Thoughts. Night V,
l. 661

Death loves a shining mark, a signal
blow.[1] *Ib. l. 1011*

Too low they build, who build beneath
the stars. *Ib. VIII, l. 215*

Final Ruin fiercely drives
Her plowshare o'er creation.[2]
Ib. IX, l. 167

An undevout astronomer is mad.
Ib. l. 771

SIR WILLIAM
PULTENEY,[3]
EARL OF BATH
1684–1764

Since twelve honest men have decided
the cause,
And were judges of facts, though not
judges of laws.
The Honest Jury [1731], *III*

GEORGE BERKELEY,
BISHOP OF CLOYNE
1685–1753

And what are these fluxions? The
velocities of evanescent increments.
And what are these same evanescent increments? They are neither finite quantities, nor quantities infinitely small,
nor yet nothing. May we not call them
ghosts of departed quantities?
The Analyst [1734], *sec. 4*

[Tar water] is of a nature so mild
and benign and proportioned to the
human constitution, as to warm without heating, to cheer but not inebriate.[4] *Siris* [1744], *par. 217*

Truth is the cry of all, but the game
of the few. *Ib. par. 368*

---

[1] See Congreve, p. 392a.
[2] See Anonymous, p. 1090a.
See Vespasian, p. 135b.
[3] See Goldsmith, p. 448a.
[4] See W. T. Cummings, p. 1053a.

[1] See Quarles, p. 321b.
[2] See Burns, p. 493a.
[3] One of "the three grand allies," the others
being Stanhope and Walpole. Walpole said that
he feared Pulteney's tongue more than another
man's sword.
[4] See Cowper, p. 458a.

He who says there is no such thing as an honest man, you may be sure is himself a knave.

> *Maxims Concerning Patriotism*

Westward the course of empire takes its way; [1]
The four first acts already past,
A fifth shall close the drama with the day:
Time's noblest offspring is the last.

> *On the Prospect of Planting Arts and Learning in America* [1752], st. 6

JANE BRERETON
1685–1740

The picture placed the busts between,
Adds to the thought much strength,
Wisdom, and Wit are little seen,
But Folly's at full length.

> *On Beau Nash's Picture at Full Length between the Busts of Sir Isaac Newton and Mr. Pope* [2]

AARON HILL
1685–1750

First, then, a woman will or won't, depend on 't;
If she will do 't she will; and there's an end on 't.
But if she won't, since safe and sound your trust is,
Fear is affront, and jealousy injustice.

> *Zara, epilogue*

Tender-handed stroke a nettle,
And it stings you for your pains;
Grasp it like a man of mettle,
And it soft as silk remains. [3]

> *Verses Written on a Window in Scotland*

---

[1] Westward the star of empire takes its way.
— JOHN QUINCY ADAMS, *Oration at Plymouth* [1802]

[2] In ALEXANDER DYCE [1798–1869], *Specimens of British Poetesses*. This epigram is generally ascribed to Chesterfield.

[3] The world's a nettle; disturb it, it stings:
Grasp it firmly, it stings not.
> OWEN MEREDITH [E. R. BULWER-LYTTON],
> *Lucile* [1860], *pt. I, canto 3, st. 2*

SAMUEL MADDEN
1686–1765

In an orchard there should be enough to eat, enough to lay up, enough to be stolen, and enough to rot upon the ground.

> *Quoted by* SAMUEL JOHNSON [1783]. *From* BOSWELL, *Life of Dr. Johnson, vol. II, p. 457* [Everyman edition]

ALLAN RAMSAY
1686–1758

Farewell to Lochaber, farewell to my Jean.

> *Lochaber No More* [1724], st. 1

THOMAS TICKELL
1686–1740

There taught us how to live; and (oh! too high
The price for knowledge) taught us how to die. [1]

> *On the Death of Mr. Addison* [1719], *l. 81*

HENRY CAREY
c. 1687 – 1743

Namby Pamby's little rhymes,
Little jingle, little chimes.

> *Namby Pamby* [2]

Aldiborontiphoscophornio!
Where left you Chrononhotonthologos?

> *Chrononhotonthologos, act I, sc. 1*

His cogitative faculties immersed
In cogibundity of cogitation.   *Ib.*

Of all the girls that are so smart,
There's none like pretty Sally.
She is the darling of my heart,
And she lives in our alley.

> *Sally in Our Alley* [1729], st. 1

---

[1] See Montaigne, p. 189b, and note.

[2] Ambrose Phillips . . . who had the honor of bringing into fashion a species of composition which has been called, after his name, Namby Pamby. — MACAULAY, *Review of Aikin's Life of Addison* [1843]

Of all the days that's in the week
   I dearly love but one day,
And that's the day that comes betwixt
   A Saturday and Monday.
           Sally in Our Alley, st. 4

God save our gracious king!
Long live our noble king!
   God save the king!
           God Save the King [c. 1740]

JOHN GAY [1]
1688–1732

'Twas when the seas were roaring
With hollow blasts of wind,
A damsel lay deploring,
All on a rock reclin'd.
       The What D'ye Call It [1715],
               act II, sc. 8

All in the Downs the fleet was moor'd.
       Sweet William's Farewell to
         Black-eyed Susan [1720]

Adieu! she cries; and wav'd her lily
   hand.   *Ib.*

My lodging is on the cold ground,
   And hard, very hard, is my fare,
But that which grieves me more
   Is the coldness of my dear.
       My Lodging Is on the Cold
           Ground [1720], *st. 1*

Whence is thy learning? Hath thy toil
O'er books consum'd the midnight oil?
       Fables, pt. I [1727]. *The Shep-*
       herd and the Philosopher

Where yet was ever found a mother
Who'd give her booby for another?
       Ib. The Mother, the Nurse, and
                  the Fairy

When we risk no contradiction,
It prompts the tongue to deal in fiction.
       Ib. The Elephant and the
                  Bookseller

Is there no hope? the sick man said;
The silent doctor shook his head.
       Ib. The Sick Man and the Angel

[1] See Pope's *Epitaph on Gay*, p. 407b.

While there is life there's hope, he
   cried.[1]
       Fables, pt. I. The Sick Man
               and the Angel

Those who in quarrels interpose
Must often wipe a bloody nose.
           Ib. The Mastiffs

I hate the man who builds his name
On ruins of another's fame.
           Ib. The Poet and the Rose

And when a lady's in the case,
You know all other things give place.
       Ib. The Hare and Many Friends

In every age and clime we see
Two of a trade can never agree.[2]
       Ib. The Rat-catcher and Cat

From wine what sudden friendship
   springs!
       Ib. II [1738]. *The Squire and*
               His Cur

O Polly, you might have toy'd and
   kiss'd,
By keeping men off, you keep them
   on.
       The Beggar's Opera [1728],
               act I, sc. 4, air 9

If with me you'd fondly stray.
Over the hills and far away.[3]
            Ib. 13, air 16

Fill ev'ry glass, for wine inspires us,
   And fires us
With courage, love and joy.
Women and wine should life employ.
Is there ought else on earth desirous?
            Ib. II, 1, air 19

If the heart of a man is depress'd with
   cares,
The mist is dispell'd when a woman
   appears.   *Ib. 3, air 21*

Youth's the season made for joys,
Love is then our duty.   *Ib. 4, air 22*

Man may escape from rope and gun;
Nay, some have outliv'd the doctor's
   pill:

[1] See Terence, p. 108b; Cicero, p. 111a; and Goldsmith, p. 447a.
[2] See Hesiod, p. 67b, and Meredith, p. 730a.
[3] See D'Urfey, p. 384a.

Who takes a woman must be undone,
That basilisk is sure to kill.
The fly that sips treacle is lost in the
sweets,
So he that tastes woman, woman,
woman,
He that tastes woman, ruin meets.
The Beggar's Opera,
act II, sc. 8, air 26

How happy could I be with either,
Were t'other dear charmer away!
Ib. 13, air 35

The charge is prepar'd; the lawyers are
met;
The Judges all ranged (a terrible
show!) *Ib. III, 11, air 57*

Life is a jest; and all things show it.
I thought so once; but now I know it.[1]
My Own Epitaph

PIERRE CARLET DE CHAMBLAIN DE MARIVAUX
1688–1763

In this world, you must be a bit too
kind in order to be kind enough.
Le Jeu de l'Amour et du Hasard
[1730], act I, sc. 2

ALEXANDER POPE[2]
1688–1744

Happy the man whose wish and care
A few paternal acres bound,
Content to breathe his native air
In his own ground.[3]
Ode on Solitude [c. 1700], st. 1

Thus let me live, unseen, unknown,
Thus unlamented let me die,
Steal from the world, and not a stone
Tell where I lie. *Ib. st. 5*

[1] Life is an empty dream. — BROWNING,
Paracelsus II [1835]
Life seems a jest of Fate's contriving. —
J. R. LOWELL, *Harvard Commemoration Ode*
[1865], *IV*
[2] A thousand years may elapse before there
shall appear another man with a power of
versification equal to that of Pope. — SAMUEL
JOHNSON [1781]; *from* BOSWELL, *Life of Dr.
Johnson* [1791]
[3] See Horace, p. 120b.

Where'er you walk, cool gales shall fan
the glade,
Trees, where you sit, shall crowd into a
shade:
Where'er you tread, the blushing flow'rs
shall rise,
And all things flourish where you turn
your eyes.
*Pastorals [written 1704]. Sum-
mer, l. 73*

Nor Fame I slight, nor for her favors
call;
She comes unlook'd for, if she comes at
all.
*The Temple of Fame [1711],
l. 513*

How vast a memory has Love!
Sappho to Phaon [1712], l. 52

'Tis with our judgments as our watches,
none
Go just alike, yet each believes his
own.[1]
*An Essay on Criticism [1711],
pt. I, l. 9*

Let such teach others who themselves
excel,
And censure freely who have written
well. *Ib. l. 15*

Some are bewilder'd in the maze of
schools,
And some made coxcombs nature
meant but fools. *Ib. l. 26*

Those oft are stratagems which errors
seem,
Nor is it Homer nods, but we that
dream.[2] *Ib. l. 177*

Of all the causes which conspire to
blind
Man's erring judgment, and misguide
the mind,
What the weak head with strongest
bias rules,
Is pride, the never-failing vice of fools.
Ib. II, l. 1

A little learning is a dangerous thing;[3]

[1] See Suckling, p. 350a.
[2] See Horace, p. 124b.
[3] See Publilius Syrus, p. 127a.

Drink deep, or taste not the Pierian
    spring:
There shallow draughts intoxicate the
    brain,
And drinking largely sobers us again.
            An Essay on Criticism,
                    pt. II, l. 15

Hills peep o'er hills, and Alps on Alps
    arise!   *Ib. l. 32*

'Tis not a lip, or eye, we beauty call,
But the joint force and full result of
    all.   *Ib. l. 45*

Whoever thinks a faultless piece to see,
Thinks what ne'er was, nor is, nor e'er
    shall be.[1]   *Ib. l. 53*

True wit is nature to advantage
    dress'd,
What oft was thought, but ne'er so
    well express'd.   *Ib. l. 97*

Words are like leaves; and where they
    most abound,
Much fruit of sense beneath is rarely
    found.   *Ib. l. 109*

Such labor'd nothings, in so strange a
    style,
Amaze th' unlearn'd, and make the
    learned smile.   *Ib. l. 126*

Be not the first by whom the new are
    tried,
Nor yet the last to lay the old aside.
                   Ib. l. 135

    As some to church repair,
Not for the doctrine, but the music
    there.
These equal syllables alone require,
Though oft the ear the open vowels
    tire;
While expletives their feeble aid do
    join,
And ten low words oft creep in one dull
    line.   *Ib. l. 142*

Then, at the last and only couplet
    fraught
With some unmeaning thing they call a
    thought,
A needless Alexandrine ends the song,
That, like a wounded snake, drags its
    slow length along.   *Ib. l. 156*

[1] See Suckling, p. 350b, and note.

True ease in writing comes from art,
    not chance,
As those move easiest who have learn'd
    to dance.[1]
'Tis not enough no harshness gives
    offense;
The sound must seem an echo to the
    sense.
            An Essay on Criticism,
                   pt. II, l. 162

At ev'ry trifle scorn to take offense.
                   Ib. l. 186

Yet let not each gay turn thy rapture
    move;
For fools admire, but men of sense
    approve.   *Ib. l. 190*

Some judge of authors' names, not
    works, and then
Nor praise nor blame the writings, but
    the men.   *Ib. l. 212*

What woeful stuff this madrigal would
    be,
In some starv'd hackney sonneteer, or
    me!
But let a lord once own the happy
    lines,
How the wit brightens! how the style
    refines!   *Ib. l. 218*

Some praise at morning what they
    blame at night,
But always think the last opinion
    right.   *Ib. l. 230*

To err is human, to forgive divine.[2]
                   Ib. l. 325

All seems infected that th' infected
    spy,
As all looks yellow to the jaundic'd
    eye.   *Ib. l. 358*

Be silent always when you doubt your
    sense.   *Ib. III, l. 6*

Men must be taught as if you taught
    them not,

[1] Also in *Imitations of Horace* [1737]. *Epistle II, bk. II, l. 178.*
[2] See Plutarch, p. 137b, and Shirley, p. 327b.
    Then gently scan your brother man,
      Still gentler sister woman;
    Though they may gang a kennin' wrang,
      To step aside is human.
      ROBERT BURNS, *Address to the Unco
                      Guid* [1787]

And things unknown proposed as things forgot.
> *An Essay on Criticism,*
> *pt. III, l. 15*

The bookful blockhead ignorantly read,
With loads of learned lumber in his head,
With his own tongue still edifies his ears,
And always list'ning to himself appears.
All books he reads, and all he reads assails. *Ib. l. 53*

For fools rush in where angels fear to tread.[1] *Ib. l. 66*

But where's the man who counsel can bestow,
Still pleas'd to teach, and yet not proud to know?[2] *Ib. l. 72*

Careless of censure, nor too fond of fame,
Still pleas'd to praise, yet not afraid to blame,
Averse alike to flatter or offend,
Not free from faults, nor yet too vain to mend. *Ib. l. 182*

Vital spark of heav'nly flame!
Quit, oh quit, this mortal frame:
Trembling, hoping, ling'ring, flying,
Oh the pain, the bliss of dying![3]
> *The Dying Christian to His Soul*
> *[1712], st. 1*

What dire offense from amorous causes springs,
What mighty contests rise from trivial things![4]
> *The Rape of the Lock [1712],*
> *canto I, l. 1*

On her white breast a sparkling cross she wore,
Which Jews might kiss, and infidels adore. *Ib. II, l. 7*

If to her share some female errors fall,
Look on her face, and you'll forget 'em all. *Ib. l. 17*

[1] See Shakespeare, *Richard III, I, iii, 70,* p. 217a.
[2] See Chaucer, p. 166b.
[3] See Hadrian, p. 141a.
[4] See Robert Burton, p. 310a.

Fair tresses man's imperial race ensnare,
And beauty draws us with a single hair.[1]
> *The Rape of the Lock,*
> *canto II, l. 27*

Here thou, great Anna![2] whom three realms obey,
Dost sometimes counsel take — and sometimes tea. *Ib. III, l. 7*

At every word a reputation dies. *Ib. l. 16*

The hungry judges soon the sentence sign,
And wretches hang that jurymen may dine. *Ib. l. 21*

Let spades be trumps! she said, and trumps they were. *Ib. l. 46*

Coffee, which makes the politician wise. *Ib. l. 117*

But when to mischief mortals bend their will,
How soon they find fit instruments of ill! *Ib. l. 125*

The meeting points the sacred hair dissever
From the fair head, forever, and forever!
Then flash'd the living lightning from her eyes,
And screams of horror rend th' affrighted skies. *Ib. l. 153*

Charms strike the sight, but merit wins the soul. *Ib. V, l. 34*

To wake the soul by tender strokes of art,
To raise the genius, and to mend the heart;
To make mankind, in conscious virtue bold,
Live o'er each scene, and be what they behold:
For this the Tragic Muse first trod the stage.
> *Prologue to Mr. Addison's Cato*
> *[1713], l. 1*

A brave man struggling in the storms of fate,

[1] See Robert Burton, p. 312a.
[2] Queen Anne [1665–1714].

And greatly falling with a falling state.
Prologue to Mr. Addison's
Cato, l. 21

Ignobly vain, and impotently great.
Ib. l. 29

Here hills and vales, the woodland and
the plain,
Here earth and water seem to strive
again,
Not chaos-like together crush'd and
bruis'd,
But, as the world, harmoniously con-
fus'd:
Where order in variety we see,
And where, though all things differ, all
agree.
Windsor Forest [1713], *l. 11*

Oft, as in airy rings they skim the
heath,
The clam'rous lapwings feel the leaden
death;
Oft, as the mounting larks their notes
prepare,
They fall, and leave their little lives in
air. *Ib. l. 131*

Party-spirit, which at best is but the
madness of many for the gain of a
few.[1]
Letter to E. Blount [*August 27*,
1714]

The wrath of Peleus' son, the direful
spring
Of all the Grecian woes, O goddess
sing![2]
Translation of Iliad[3] [1715] *I, 1*

She moves a goddess, and she looks a
queen. *Ib. III, 1*

Tell me, Muse, of the man of many
wiles.
Translation of Odyssey [1725–
1756] *I, 1*

So perish all who do the like again.
Ib. I, 37

True friendship's laws are by this rule
express'd,
Welcome the coming, speed the parting guest.[1]
Translation of Odyssey XV, 83

Dear, damn'd, distracting town, fare-
well!
Thy fools no more I'll tease:
This year in peace, ye critics, dwell,
Ye harlots, sleep at ease!
A Farewell to London [1715], *st. 1*

Luxurious lobster-nights, farewell,
For sober, studious days! *Ib. st. 12*

Oh name forever sad! forever dear!
Still breath'd in sighs, still usher'd with
a tear.
Eloisa to Abelard [1717], *l. 31*

Now warm in love, now with'ring in my
bloom,
Lost in a convent's solitary gloom!
Ib. l. 37

Speed the soft intercourse from soul to
soul,
And waft a sigh from Indus to the
Pole. *Ib. l. 57*

No, make me mistress to the man I
love;
If there be yet another name more
free,
More fond than mistress, make me that
to thee! *Ib. l. 88*

And if I lose thy love, I lose my all.
Ib. l. 118

How happy is the blameless vestal's lot!
The world forgetting, by the world forgot. *Ib. l. 207*

One thought of thee puts all the pomp
to flight,
Priests, tapers, temples, swim before my
sight.[2] *Ib. l. 273*

He best can paint them who shall feel
them most. *Ib. l. 366*

What beck'ning ghost, along the moonlight shade

---

[1] See Swift, p. 389a.
[2] Another version is:
Achilles' wrath, to Greece the direful spring
Of woes unnumber'd, heavenly goddess, sing!
[3] See Bentley, p. 386a.

[1] See Pope, *Epistle to Dr. Arbuthnot*, p. 411b.
[2] Priests, altars, victims, swam before my
sight. — EDMUND SMITH, *Phaedra and Hippolytus, adapted from* RACINE [1707], *act I, sc. I.*

Invites my steps, and points to yonder
   glade?
> *Elegy to the Memory of an*
> *Unfortunate Lady* [1717], *l. 1*

Is it, in Heav'n, a crime to love too
   well?
To bear too tender, or too firm a
   heart,
To act a lover's or a Roman's part?
Is there no bright reversion in the sky,
For those who greatly think, or bravely
   die?   *Ib. l. 6*

Ambition first sprung from your blest
   abodes;
The glorious fault of Angels and of
   Gods.   *Ib. l. 13*

By foreign hands thy dying eyes were
   clos'd,
By foreign hands thy decent limbs
   compos'd,
By foreign hands thy humble grave
   adorn'd,
By strangers honor'd, and by strangers
   mourn'd!   *Ib. l. 51*

How lov'd, how honor'd once, avails
   thee not,
To whom related, or by whom begot;
A heap of dust alone remains of thee;
'Tis all thou art, and all the proud shall
   be!   *Ib. l. 71*

  The fate of all extremes is such,
Men may be read, as well as books, too
   much.
To observations which ourselves we
   make,
We grow more partial for th' observer's
   sake.
> *Moral Essays* [1720–1735].
> *Epistle I, To Lord Cobham*
> [1734], *l. 9*

Like following life through creatures
   you dissect,
You lose it in the moment you detect.
                Ib. l. 29

Not always actions show the man: we
   find
Who does a kindness is not therefore
   kind.   *Ib. l. 109*

'Tis education forms the common
   mind:
Just as the twig is bent, the tree's inclined.
> *Moral Essays. Epistle I,*
> *To Lord Cobham, l. 149*

Give this cheek a little red.
                Ib. l. 251

And you, brave Cobham! to the latest
   breath
Shall feel your ruling passion strong in
   death.   *Ib. l. 262*

Most women have no characters at all.
      Ib. II, To Mrs. M. Blount
              [1735], *l. 2*

Choose a firm cloud before it fall, and
   in it
Catch, ere she change, the Cynthia of
   this minute.   *Ib. l. 19*

Chaste to her husband, frank to all beside,
A teeming mistress, but a barren bride.
                Ib. l. 71

Wise wretch! with pleasures too refin'd
   to please;
With too much spirit to be e'er at
   ease;
With too much quickness ever to be
   taught;
With too much thinking to have common thought.
You purchase pain with all that joy can
   give,
And die of nothing but a rage to live.
                Ib. l. 95

"With ev'ry pleasing, ev'ry prudent part,
Say, what can Chloe want?" — She
   wants a heart.   *Ib. l. 159*

In men, we various ruling passions
   find;
In women, two almost divide the
   kind;
Those, only fixed, they first or last
   obey,
The love of pleasure, and the love of
   sway.   *Ib. l. 207*

Men, some to business, some to pleasure take;

But every woman is at heart a rake.
> *Moral Essays. Epistle II, To Mrs. M. Blount, l. 215*

She who ne'er answers till a husband cools,
Or, if she rules him, never shows she rules;
Charms by accepting, by submitting, sways,
Yet has her humor most, when she obeys. *Ib. l. 261*

And mistress of herself, though china fall. *Ib. l. 268*

Woman's at best a contradiction still. *Ib. l. 270*

Who shall decide when doctors disagree? [1]
> *Ib. III, To Lord Bathurst [1732], l. 1*

But thousands die, without or this or that,
Die, and endow a college, or a cat. *Ib. l. 95*

The ruling passion, be it what it will,
The ruling passion conquers reason still. *Ib. l. 153*

Satan now is wiser than of yore,
And tempts by making rich, not making poor. *Ib. l. 351*

Good sense, which only is the gift of Heaven,
And though no science, fairly worth the seven.
> *Ib. IV, To Lord Burlington [1731], l. 43*

Statesman, yet friend to truth! of soul sincere,
In action faithful, and in honor clear;
Who broke no promise, serv'd no private end,
Who gain'd no title, and who lost no friend.
> *Ib. VII, To Mr. Addison [1720], l. 67*

[1] When doctors differ who decides amid the milliard-headed throng? — SIR RICHARD FRANCIS BURTON [1821–1890], *The Kasidah of Haji Abdu El-Yazdi VIII, 29*

Blessed is he who expects nothing, for he shall never be disappointed. [1]
> *Letter to Gay [October 6, 1727]*

You beat your pate, and fancy wit will come:
Knock as you please, there's nobody at home. [2]
> *Epigram: An Empty House [1727]*

Ye Gods! annihilate but space and time,
And make two lovers happy.
> *Martinus Scriblerus on the Art of Sinking in Poetry [1728], ch. 11*

In wit a man, simplicity a child.
> *Epitaph on Gay [1732]* [3]

Awake, my St. John! leave all meaner things
To low ambition, and the pride of kings.
Let us, since life can little more supply
Than just to look about us, and to die,
Expatiate free o'er all this scene of man;
A mighty maze! but not without a plan.
> *An Essay on Man [1733–1734]. Epistle I, l. 1*

Eye Nature's walks, shoot folly as it flies,
And catch the manners living as they rise:
Laugh where we must, be candid where we can;
But vindicate the ways of God to man. [4] *Ib. l. 13*

Say first, of God above or man below,
What can we reason but from what we know? *Ib. l. 17*

[1] Pope calls this the eighth beatitude (Roscoe's edition of Pope, *vol. X, p. 184*).
> Blessed are those that nought expect,
> For they shall not be disappointed.
> JOHN WOLCOT ("Peter Pindar") [1738–1819], *Ode to Pitt*

[2] His wit invites you by his looks to come,
But when you knock, it never is at home.
> COWPER, *Conversation* [1782], *l. 303*

[3] See Gay, p. 401a.
[4] See Milton, p. 341b.

Pleased to the last, he crops the flowery
    food,
And licks the hand just raised to shed
    his blood.
                An Essay on Man.
                Epistle I, l. 83

Who sees with equal eye, as God of
    all,
A hero perish or a sparrow fall,[1]
Atoms or systems into ruin hurl'd,
And now a bubble burst, and now a
    world.   *Ib. l. 87*

Hope springs eternal in the human
    breast:
Man never is, but always to be blest.
                      Ib. l. 95

Lo, the poor Indian! whose untutor'd
    mind
Sees God in clouds, or hears him in the
    wind;
His soul proud Science never taught to
    stray
Far as the solar walk or milky way;
Yet simple nature to his hope has giv'n,
Behind the cloud-topped hill, an hum-
    bler heav'n.   *Ib. l. 99*

But thinks, admitted to that equal sky,
His faithful dog shall bear him com-
    pany.   *Ib. l. 111*

In pride, in reas'ning pride, our error
    lies;
All quit their sphere, and rush into the
    skies!
Pride still is aiming at the bless'd
    abodes,
Men would be Angels, Angels would be
    Gods.
Aspiring to be Gods if Angels fell,
Aspiring to be Angels men rebel.
                     Ib. l. 123

Seas roll to waft me, suns to light me
    rise;
My footstool earth, my canopy the
    skies.[2]   *Ib. l. 139*

Die of a rose in aromatic pain?
                     Ib. l. 200

[1] See Shakespeare, *Hamlet V, ii, 232*, p. 266b,
and note.
[2] See *Matthew 5:35*, p. 40b; H. G. Wells,
p. 888b; and Clarence Day, p. 925b.

All are but parts of one stupendous
    whole,
Whose body Nature is, and God the
    soul.
                An Essay on Man.
                Epistle I, l. 267

As full, as perfect, in vile man that
    mourns
As the rapt seraph that adores and
    burns.
To Him no high, no low, no great, no
    small; [1]
He fills, he bounds, connects, and
    equals all!   *Ib. l. 277*

All nature is but art unknown to thee,
All chance, direction which thou canst
    not see;
All discord, harmony not understood;
All partial evil, universal good;
And, spite of pride, in erring reason's
    spite,
One truth is clear, Whatever is, is
    right.[2]   *Ib. l. 289*

Know then thyself, presume not God to
    scan;
The proper study of mankind is man.[3]
Placed on this isthmus of a middle
    state,
A being darkly wise and rudely great:
With too much knowledge for the
    sceptic side,
With too much weakness for the stoic's
    pride,
He hangs between; in doubt to act or
    rest;
In doubt to deem himself a god, or
    beast;
In doubt his mind or body to prefer;
Born but to die, and reas'ning but to
    err;
Alike in ignorance, his reason such,

[1] There is no great and no small
   To the Soul that maketh all.
        EMERSON [1803–1882], *Epigraph to
                            History*
[2] See Dryden, p. 367b.
[3] See The Seven Sages, p. 68a.
    La vraie science et la vraie étude de l'homme,
c'est l'homme [The true science and the true
study of man is man]. — PIERRE CHARRON,
Traité de la Sagesse [1601], *bk. I, preface*
    Trees and fields tell me nothing: men are
my teachers. — PLATO [427–347 B.C.], *Phaedrus*

Whether he thinks too little or too much;
Chaos of thought and passion, all confused;
Still by himself abused, or disabused;
Created half to rise, and half to fall;
Great lord of all things, yet a prey to all;
Sole judge of truth, in endless error hurled;
The glory, jest, and riddle of the world! [1]
An Essay on Man.
Epistle II, l. 1

Fix'd like a plant on his peculiar spot,
To draw nutrition, propagate, and rot.
Ib. l. 63

And hence one master-passion in the breast,
Like Aaron's serpent, swallows up the rest.[2]   *Ib. l. 131*

Vice is a monster of so frightful mien,
As to be hated needs but to be seen;[3]
Yet seen too oft, familiar with her face,
We first endure, then pity, then embrace.   *Ib. l. 217*

The learn'd is happy Nature to explore,
The fool is happy that he knows no more;
The rich is happy in the plenty giv'n,
The poor contents him with the care of Heav'n.   *Ib. l. 263*

Behold the child, by Nature's kindly law,
Pleased with a rattle, tickled with a straw:
Some livelier plaything gives his youth delight,
A little louder, but as empty quite:
Scarfs, garters, gold, amuse his riper stage,
And beads and prayer-books are the toys of age!
Pleased with this bauble still, as that before;

[1] See Pascal, p. 364a.
[2] For they cast down every man his rod, and they became serpents: but Aaron's rod swallowed up their rods. — *Exodus 7:12*
[3] See Dryden, p. 370a.

Till tired he sleeps, and life's poor play is o'er.
An Essay on Man.
Epistle II, l. 274

Learn of the little nautilus to sail,
Spread the thin oar, and catch the driving gale.   *Ib. III, l. 177*

For forms of government let fools contest;
Whate'er is best administer'd is best:
For modes of faith let graceless zealots fight;
His can't be wrong whose life is in the right.[1]
In faith and hope the world will disagree,
But all mankind's concern is charity.
Ib. l. 303

O happiness! our being's end and aim!
Good, pleasure, ease, content! whate'er thy name:
That something still which prompts the eternal sigh,
For which we bear to live, or dare to die.   *Ib. IV, l. 1*

Worth makes the man, and want of it the fellow;
The rest is all but leather or prunella.
Ib. l. 203

What's Fame? a fancy'd life in others' breath,
A thing beyond us, ev'n before our death.   *Ib. l. 237*

A wit's a feather, and a chief a rod;
An honest man's the noblest work of God.[2]   *Ib. l. 247*

One self-approving hour whole years outweighs
Of stupid starers and of loud huzzas:
And more true joy Marcellus exil'd feels
Than Caesar with a senate at his heels.
Ib. l. 255

If parts allure thee, think how Bacon shin'd,
The wisest, brightest, meanest of mankind!

[1] See Cowley, p. 358b.
[2] See Fletcher, p. 313a, and Burns, p. 492b.

Or ravish'd with the whistling of a
    name,[1]
See Cromwell, damn'd to everlasting
    fame!
           An Essay on Man.
           Epistle IV, l. 281

Slave to no sect, who takes no private
    road,
But looks through Nature up to Na-
    ture's God.[2]   *Ib. l.* 331

Form'd by thy converse, happily to
    steer
From grave to gay, from lively to
    severe.[3]   *Ib. l.* 379

Say, shall my little bark attendant sail,
Pursue the triumph and partake the
    gale? [4]   *Ib. l.* 385

Thou wert my guide, philosopher, and
    friend.[5]   *Ib. l.* 390

That true self-love and social are the
    same.   *Ib. l.* 396

Shut, shut the door, good John! fa-
    tigued, I said;
Tie up the knocker! say I'm sick, I'm
    dead.
    The Dog-star rages!
           Epistle to Dr. Arbuthnot [1735].
           Prologue to Imitations of Hor-
           ace, l. 1

Fire in each eye, and papers in each
    hand,
They rave, recite, and madden round
    the land.   *Ib. l.* 5

Is there a parson, much bemused in
    beer,
A maudlin poetess, a rhyming peer,
A clerk foredoom'd his father's soul to
    cross,
Who pens a stanza when he should en-
    gross?

           Ib. l. 15

---

[1] See Cowley, p. 358a.
[2] See Bolingbroke, p. 397b.
[3] See Boileau, p. 377a.
[4] See Dante, *Purgatorio, canto I, l. 1,* p. 160b.
[5] Is this my guide, philosopher, and friend?
— POPE, *Imitations of Horace* [1733–1738]. *Epis-*
tle I, bk. I, l. 177

Fired that the house [1] reject him,
    " 'Sdeath, I'll print it,
And shame the fools."
           Epistle to Dr. Arbuthnot, l. 61

No creature smarts so little as a fool.
           Ib. l. 84

Destroy his fib, or sophistry — in vain!
The creature's at his dirty work again.
           Ib. l. 91

As yet a child, nor yet a fool to fame,
I lisp'd in numbers, for the numbers
    came.   *Ib. l.* 127

This long disease, my life.   *Ib. l.* 132

Pretty! in amber to observe the forms
Of hairs, or straws, or dirt, or grubs, or
    worms! [2]
The things, we know, are neither rich
    nor rare,
But wonder how the devil they got
    there.   *Ib. l.* 169

Means not, but blunders round about a
    meaning;
And he whose fustian's so sublimely
    bad,
It is not poetry, but prose run mad.
           Ib. l. 186

         Were there one whose fires
True Genius kindles, and fair Fame in-
    spires,
Bless'd with each talent, and each art
    to please,
And born to write, converse, and live
    with ease;
Should such a man, too fond to rule
    alone,
Bear, like the Turk, no brother near the
    throne; [3]
View him with scornful, yet with jeal-
    ous eyes,
And hate for arts that caus'd himself to
    rise;

---

[1] The theater.
[2] See Martial, p. 135a.
[3] Nor is thy fame on lesser ruins built;
    Nor needs thy juster title the foul guilt
    Of Eastern kings, who, to secure their reign,
    Must have their brothers, sons, and kindred
    slain.
         SIR JOHN DENHAM, *On Mr. John*
               Fletcher's Works [1668]

Damn with faint praise, assent with
civil leer,
And, without sneering, teach the rest to
sneer; [1]
Willing to wound, and yet afraid to
strike,
Just hint a fault, and hesitate dislike;
Alike reserv'd to blame or to com-
mend,
A tim'rous foe, and a suspicious friend;
Dreading e'en fools, by flatterers be-
sieged,
And so obliging that he ne'er obliged;
Like Cato, give his little Senate laws,[2]
And sit attentive to his own applause.
Epistle to Dr. Arbuthnot, l. 193

Who but must laugh, if such a man
there be?
Who would not weep, if Atticus were
he! *Ib. l.* 213

Oh let me live my own, and die so too
(To live and die is all I have to do)!
Maintain a poet's dignity and ease,
And see what friends, and read what
books I please. *Ib. l.* 261

Curs'd be the verse, how well soe'er it
flow,
That tends to make one worthy man
my foe. *Ib. l.* 283

Let Sporus tremble — "What? that
thing of silk,
Sporus, that mere white curd of ass's
milk?
Satire or sense, alas! can Sporus feel?
Who breaks a butterfly upon a wheel?"
Ib. l. 305

Yet let me flap this bug with gilded
wings,
This painted child of dirt, that stinks
and stings;
Whose buzz the witty and the fair
annoys,

[1] When needs he must, yet faintly then he
praises;
Somewhat the deed, much more the means he
raises:
So marreth what he makes, and praising
most, dispraises.
PHINEAS FLETCHER, *The Purple Island*
[1633], *canto* 7
[2] While Cato gives his little senate laws. —
Prologue to Mr. Addison's Cato [1713], *l.* 23

Yet wit ne'er tastes, and beauty ne'er
enjoys.
Epistle to Dr. Arbuthnot, l. 309

Eternal smiles his emptiness betray,
As shallow streams run dimpling all the
way. *Ib. l.* 315

And he himself one vile antithesis.
Ib. l. 325

Wit that can creep, and pride that licks
the dust. *Ib. l.* 333

Unlearn'd, he knew no schoolman's
subtle art,
No language, but the language of the
heart. *Ib. l.* 398

I cannot sleep a wink.[1]
Imitations of Horace [1733–
1738], *satire I, bk. II, l.* 12

Satire's my weapon, but I'm too dis-
creet
To run amuck, and tilt at all I meet.
Ib. l. 69

But touch me, and no minister so sore.
Ib. l. 76

There St. John mingles with my
friendly bowl
The feast of reason and the flow of
soul. *Ib. l.* 127

For I, who hold sage Homer's rule the
best,
Welcome the coming, speed the going
guest.[2] *Ib. II, II, l.* 159

I've often wish'd that I had clear,
For life, six hundred pounds a year;
A handsome house to lodge a friend,
A river at my garden's end,
A terrace walk, and half a rood
Of land set out to plant a wood.[3]
Ib. VI, II, l. 1

Give me again my hollow tree,
A crust of bread, and liberty.
Ib. l. 220

A patriot is a fool in ev'ry age.
*Ib. Epilogue to the Satires,
Dialogue I, l.* 41

[1] See Cervantes, p. 194a.
[2] See Pope, *Odyssey XV, 83,* p. 405b.
[3] See Horace, p. 120a.

Laugh then at any but at fools or foes;
These you but anger, and you mend
    not those.
Laugh at your friends, and if your
    friends are sore,
So much the better, you may laugh the
    more.
        Imitations of Horace, Epilogue
        to the Satires, Dialogue I, l. 53

Let humble Allen, with an awkward
    shame,
Do good by stealth, and blush to find it
    fame.   *Ib. l. 135*

Never gallop Pegasus to death.
        Ib. Epistle I, bk. I, l. 14

When the brisk minor pants for twenty-
    one.   *Ib. l. 38*

Not to go back is somewhat to advance,
And men must walk, at least, before
    they dance.   *Ib. l. 53*

He's arm'd without that's innocent
    within.   *Ib. l. 94*

Get place and wealth, if possible with
    grace;
If not, by any means get wealth and
    place.[1]   *Ib. l. 103*

Above all Greek, above all Roman
    fame.   *Ib. II, l. 26*

    The people's voice is odd,
It is, and it is not, the voice of God.[2]
            Ib. l. 89

In quibbles angel and archangel join,
And God the Father turns a school-
    divine.
        Ib. l. 101 [on Paradise Lost]

The mob of gentlemen who wrote with
    ease.   *Ib. l. 108*

One simile that solitary shines
In the dry desert of a thousand lines.
            Ib. l. 111

Who says in verse what others say in
    prose.   *Ib. l. 202*

What will a child learn sooner than a
    song?   *Ib. l. 205*

Ev'n copious Dryden wanted, or forgot,

---

[1] See Horace, p. 123a.
[2] See Alcuin, p. 152b.

The last and greatest art — the art to
    blot.
        Imitations of Horace,
        Epistle I, bk. II, l. 280

There still remains, to mortify a wit,
The many-headed monster of the pit.[1]
            Ib. l. 304

We poets are (upon a poet's word)
Of all mankind the creatures most ab-
    surd:
The season when to come, and when to
    go,
To sing, or cease to sing, we never
    know.[2]   *Ib. l. 358*

Call, if you will, bad rhyming a
    disease,
It gives men happiness, or leaves them
    ease.   *Ib. II, II, l. 182*

The worst of madmen is a saint run
    mad.   *Ib. VI, I, l. 27*

Vain was the chief's, the sage's pride!
They had no poet, and they died.
        Ib. Odes, bk. IV, ode 9, st. 4

Father of all! in every age,
    In every clime ador'd,
By saint, by savage, and by sage,
    Jehovah, Jove, or Lord!
    The Universal Prayer [1738], st. 1

And binding Nature fast in fate,
Left free the human will.   *Ib. st. 3*

And deal damnation round the land.
            Ib. st. 7

Teach me to feel another's woe,
    To hide the fault I see;
That mercy I to others show,
    That mercy show to me.[3]
            Ib. st. 10

I am his Highness'[4] dog at Kew;
Pray tell me, sir, whose dog are you?
        On the collar of a dog

Nature and Nature's laws lay hid in
    night:
God said, Let Newton be! and all was
    light.
    Epitaph intended for Sir Isaac
                  Newton

---

[1] See Horace, p. 123a, and note.
[2] See Robert Frost, p. 926a.
[3] See Spenser, p. 200b.
[4] Frederick, Prince of Wales.

Who dare to love their country, and be poor.

> *On his grotto at Twickenham*
> [1740]

This is the Jew
That Shakespeare drew.

> *Of Macklin's performance in 1741 of Shylock in The Merchant of Venice. (Attributed to Pope)*

I never knew any man in my life who could not bear another's misfortunes perfectly like a Christian.[1]

> *Thoughts on Various Subjects*
> [1741]

A man should never be ashamed to own he has been in the wrong, which is but saying, in other words, that he is wiser today than he was yesterday.

> *Ib.*

It is with narrow-souled people as with narrow-necked bottles; the less they have in them the more noise they make in pouring out. *Ib.*

When men grow virtuous in their old age, they only make a sacrifice to God of the devil's leavings.[2] *Ib.*

True disputants are like true sportsmen, their whole delight is in the pursuit. *Ib.*

There, take (says Justice), take ye each a shell:
We thrive at Westminster on fools like you;
'Twas a fat oyster — live in peace — adieu.[3]

> *Verbatim from Boileau*

Whether thou choose Cervantes' serious air,

---

[1] See La Rochefoucauld, p. 355a.
[2] See La Rochefoucauld, p. 355b.
[3] "Tenez voilà," dit-elle, "à chacun une écaille,
Des sottises d'autrui nous vivons au Palais;
Messieurs, l'huître étoit bonne. Adieu. Vivez en paix."
> BOILEAU [1636–1711], *Epître II (à M. l'Abbé des Roches)*

Or laugh and shake in Rabelais' easy chair.

> *The Dunciad* [1728–1743],
> bk. I, l. 21

Poetic Justice, with her lifted scale,
Where, in nice balance, truth with gold she weighs,
And solid pudding against empty praise. *Ib. l. 52*

While pensive poets painful vigils keep,
Sleepless themselves to give their readers sleep. *Ib. l. 93*

Next o'er his books his eyes begin to roll,
In pleasing memory of all he stole.

> *Ib. l. 127*

Or where the pictures for the page atone,
And Quarles is sav'd by beauties not his own. *Ib. l. 139*

And gentle Dullness ever loves a joke.

> *Ib. II, l. 34*

A brain of feathers, and a heart of lead.

> *Ib. l. 44*

Peel'd, patch'd, and piebald, linsey-woolsey brothers,
Grave mummers! sleeveless some, and shirtless others.
That once was Britain.

> *Ib. III, l. 115*

And proud his mistress' order to perform,
Rides in the whirlwind and directs the storm.[1] *Ib. l. 263*

A wit with dunces, and a dunce with wits.[2] *Ib. IV, l. 90*

The Right Divine of Kings to govern wrong. *Ib. l. 188*

Stuff the head
With all such reading as was never read:
For thee explain a thing till all men doubt it,
And write about it, Goddess, and about it. *Ib. l. 249*

---

[1] See Addison, p. 393a.
[2] See Quintilian, p. 136a, and note.

To happy convents, bosom'd deep in
vines,
Where slumber abbots, purple as their
wines.
The Dunciad, bk. IV, l. 301

Led by my hand, he saunter'd Europe
round,
And gather'd every vice on Christian
ground. *Ib. l.* 311

Religion blushing veils her sacred fires,
And unawares Morality expires.
Nor public flame, nor private, dares to
shine;
Nor human spark is left, nor glimpse
divine!
Lo! thy dread empire Chaos! is restor'd:
Light dies before thy uncreating word;
Thy hand, great Anarch! lets the cur-
tain fall,
And universal darkness buries all.
Ib. l. 649

LADY MARY WORTLEY MONTAGU
1689–1762

And we meet, with champagne and a
chicken, at last.
The Lover [1748]

Be plain in dress, and sober in your
diet;
In short, my deary, kiss me, and be
quiet.
A Summary of Lord Lyttelton's
Advice

Satire should, like a polished razor
keen,
Wound with a touch that's scarcely felt
or seen.
*To the Imitator of the First
Satire of Horace, bk. II*

This world consists of men, women,
and Herveys.[1]
Letters [1763], *vol. I*

But the fruit that can fall without shak-
ing
Indeed is too mellow for me.
Letters and Works [1837]. *The
Answer*

[1] See Sydney Smith, p. 523a.

CHARLES DE SECONDAT, BARON DE MONTESQUIEU[1]
1689–1755

How can anyone be Persian?
Lettres Persanes [1721], *no.* 30

A man should be mourned at his
birth, not at his death. *Ib.* 40

If triangles had a god, he would have
three sides.[2] *Ib.* 59

Liberty is the right of doing whatever
the laws permit.
De l'Esprit des Lois [1748],
XI, 3

Useless laws weaken the necessary
laws. *Ib. XXIX, 16*

If I knew of something that could
serve my nation but would ruin another, I would not propose it to my
prince, for I am first a man and only
then a Frenchman . . . because I am
necessarily a man, and only accidentally
am I French.[3]
Pensées et Jugements

You have to study a great deal to
know a little. *Ib.*

CHARLES MACKLIN
1690–1797

The law is a sort of hocus-pocus science.[4]
Love à la Mode [1759], *act II, sc.* 1

JOHN BYROM
1692–1763

God bless the King, I mean the Faith's
Defender;
God bless — no harm in blessing — the
Pretender;

[1] See Carlyle, p. 578a, note 3.
[2] See Xenophanes, p. 70b.
[3] See Montaigne, p. 191a.
[4] Hocus was an old cunning attorney. — DR.
JOHN ARBUTHNOT, *Law Is a Bottomless Pit; or,
History of John Bull* [1712], *ch.* 5
  The words of consecration, "Hoc est corpus,"
were travestied into a nickname for jugglery, as
"Hocus-pocus." — JOHN RICHARD GREEN, *A Short
History of the English People* [1874], *ch.* 7.

But who Pretender is, or who is King,
God bless us all — that's quite another
thing.[1]

> *Miscellaneous Poems* [1773]. *To
> an officer of the Army, extempore*

Some say, that Signor Bononcini,
Compar'd to Handel's a mere ninny;
Others aver, to him, that Handel
Is scarcely fit to hold a candle.[2]
Strange! that such high dispute should
be
'Twixt Tweedledum and Tweedledee.

> *Ib. On the Feuds between
> Handel and Bononcini*

As clear as a whistle.

> *Epistle to Lloyd*

PHILIP DORMER STANHOPE, EARL OF CHESTERFIELD
1694–1773

Measures not men.[3]

> *Letters* [*March 6, 1742*]

Whatever is worth doing at all, is
worth doing well.

> *Ib.* [*March 10, 1746*]

The knowledge of the world is only
to be acquired in the world, and not in
a closet. *Ib.* [*October 4, 1746*]

An injury is much sooner forgotten
than an insult.

> *Ib.* [*October 9, 1746*]

Do as you would be done by, is the
surest method of pleasing.[4]

> *Ib.* [*October 9, 1747*]

Take the tone of the company that
you are in. *Ib.*

I knew once a very covetous, sordid
fellow,[5] who used to say, "Take care of
the pence, for the pounds will take care
of themselves."

> *Letters* [*November 6, 1747*]

Advice is seldom welcome; and those
who want it most always like it least.

> *Ib.* [*January 29, 1748*]

Speak of the moderns without contempt, and of the ancients without
idolatry. *Ib.* [*February 22, 1748*]

Wear your learning, like your watch,
in a private pocket: and do not pull it
out and strike it, merely to show that
you have one. *Ib.*

Manners must adorn knowledge, and
smooth its way through the world. Like
a great rough diamond, it may do very
well in a closet by way of curiosity, and
also for its intrinsic value.

> *Ib.* [*July 1, 1748*]

Women, then, are only children of a
larger growth.

> *Ib.* [*September 5, 1748*]

Women who are either indisputably
beautiful, or indisputably ugly, are best
flattered upon the score of their under-
standings; but those who are in a state
of mediocrity are best flattered upon
their beauty, or at least their graces; for
every woman who is not absolutely ugly
thinks herself handsome. *Ib.*

Without some dissimulation no business can be carried on at all.

> *Ib.* [*May 22, 1749*]

Idleness is only the refuge of weak
minds. *Ib.* [*July 20, 1749*]

Style is the dress of thoughts.

> *Ib.* [*November 24, 1749*]

Dispatch is the soul of business.

> *Ib.* [*February 5, 1750*]

Knowledge may give weight, but
accomplishments give luster, and many
more people see than weigh.

> *Ib.* [*May 8, 1750*]

---

[1] Quoted by SIR WALTER SCOTT in *Redgauntlet*, vol. II, ch. *1* [Edinburgh edition, 1832].
[2] See Lamb, p. 535b.
[3] See Goldsmith, p. 449a, and Burke, p. 452a.
[4] See Kingsley, p. 691b.
[5] William Lowndes [1652–1724], Secretary of the Treasury in the reigns of William III, Queen Anne, and George I.

Let blockheads read what blockheads write. *Letters [November . 1, 1750]*

Is it possible to love such a man? [1] No. The utmost I can do for him is to consider him as a respectable Hottentot. *Ib. [February 28, 1751]*

It is commonly said, and more particularly by Lord Shaftesbury,[2] that ridicule is the best test of truth.
  Ib. [February 6, 1752]

Every woman is infallibly to be gained by every sort of flattery, and every man by one sort or other.
  Ib. [March 16, 1752]

A chapter of accidents.[3]
  Ib. [February 16, 1753]

I assisted at the birth of that most significant word "flirtation," which dropped from the most beautiful mouth in the world.
  The World, no. 101

Unlike my subject will I frame my song,
It shall be witty, and it shan't be long.
  Epigram on ["Long"] Sir Thomas Robinson

The dews of the evening most carefully shun —
Those tears of the sky for the loss of the sun.
  Advice to a Lady in Autumn

He adorned whatever subject he either spoke or wrote upon, by the most splendid eloquence.[4]
  Character of Bolingbroke

[1] Lord Lyttelton.
[2] Truth, 'tis supposed, may bear all lights; and one of those principal lights or natural mediums by which things are to be viewed in order to a thorough recognition is ridicule itself. — ANTHONY ASHLEY COOPER, LORD SHAFTESBURY, *Essay on the Freedom of Wit and Humor* [1709], *pt. I, sec. 1*
[3] The Chapter of Accidents is the longest chapter in the book. — *Attributed to* JOHN WILKES by SOUTHEY in *The Doctor* [1837], *ch. 118*
[4] See Johnson, p. 430a.
Il embellit tout ce qu'il touche [He adorns whatever he touches]. — FÉNELON [1651–1715]. *Lettre sur les Occupations de l'Académie Française, sec. 4*

Give Dayrolles a chair.
  Last words

FRANCIS HUTCHESON
1694–1746

That action is best which procures the greatest happiness for the greatest numbers.[1]
  Inquiry Concerning Moral Good and Evil [1720], sec. 3

FRANÇOIS QUESNAY
1694–1774

Laissez faire, laissez passer.[2]
  Attributed

VOLTAIRE
[FRANÇOIS MARIE AROUET]
1694–1778

Virtue debases itself in justifying itself. *Oedipe [1718], act I, sc. 4*

O what fine times, this age of iron!
  Le Mondain [1736]

Paradise is where I am. *Ib.*

The superfluous, a very necessary thing.[3] *Ib.*

The secret of being a bore is to tell everything.
  Sept Discours en Vers sur l'Homme [1738]

Love truth, but pardon error. *Ib.*

He who is merely just is severe.
  Letter to Frederick the Great [1740]

[1] Priestley was the first (unless it was Beccaria) who taught my lips to pronounce this sacred truth — that the greatest happiness of the greatest number is the foundation of morals and legislation. — JEREMY BENTHAM [1748–1832], *Works, vol. X, p. 142*
[2] Let it be, let it pass. The phrase is not readily translatable, and also appears as "Laissez faire, laissez aller." It has also been attributed to PIERRE LE PESANT BOISGUILBERT [1676–1714] and JEAN CLAUDE GOURNAY [1712–1759]. It was widely used by the Physiocrats in urging freedom from government interference, and was adopted by ADAM SMITH [1723–1790].
[3] See Holmes, p. 788b.

The first who was king was a fortunate soldier:
Who serves his country well has no need of ancestors.[1]
Mérope [1743], *act I, sc. 3*

It is better to risk saving a guilty person than to condemn an innocent one.[2]
Zadig [1747], *ch. 6*

They squeeze the orange and throw away the skin.
Letter to Madame Denis [September 2, 1751] referring to his quarrel with Frederick the Great

This agglomeration which was called and which still calls itself the Holy Roman Empire is neither holy, nor Roman, nor an Empire.
Essai sur les Moeurs [1756]

All is for the best in the best of possible worlds.[3] *Candide* [1759], *ch. 1*

If this is the best of possible worlds, what then are the others? *Ib. 6*

Optimism, said Candide, is a mania for maintaining that all is well when things are going badly. *Ib. 19*

In this country [England] it is good to kill an admiral from time to time, to encourage the others.[4] *Ib. 23*

This is the happiest of mortals, for he is above everything he possesses.
Ib. 26

Work helps to preserve us from three great evils — weariness, vice, and want.
Ib. 30

We must cultivate our garden.[5]
Ib.

There are truths which are not for all men, nor for all times.
Letter to Cardinal de Bernis [April 23, 1761]

One feels like crawling on all fours after reading your work.
Letter to Rousseau [August 31, 1761]

Whatever you do, crush the infamous thing [superstition], and love those who love you.[1]
Letter to d'Alembert [November 28, 1762]

Common sense is not so common.
Dictionnaire Philosophique [1764]. Self-Love

In general, the art of government consists in taking as much money as possible from one class of citizens to give to the other. *Ib. Money*

The best is the enemy of the good.[2]
Ib. Dramatic Art

Very learned women are to be found, in the same manner as female warriors; but they are seldom or never inventors.
Ib. Women

The proper mean.[3]
Letter to Count d'Argental [November 28, 1765]

Men use thought only to justify their wrongdoings, and speech only to conceal their thoughts.[4]
Dialogue 14. Le Chapon et la Poularde [1766]

I have never made but one prayer to God, a very short one: "O Lord, make my enemies ridiculous." And God granted it.
Letter to M. Damiliville [May 16, 1767]

History is little else than a picture of human crimes and misfortunes.[5]
L'Ingénu [1767], *ch. 10*

---

[1] What can they see in the longest kingly line in Europe, save that it runs back to a successful soldier? — SIR WALTER SCOTT, *Woodstock* [1826], *ch. 37*
[2] See Blackstone, p. 444b.
[3] Tout est pour le mieux dans le meilleur des mondes possibles (referring to the philosophy of Leibnitz and his followers).
[4] Pour encourager les autres.
The reference is to Admiral Byng, who was executed in 1756 for failing to relieve Minorca.
[5] Il faut cultiver notre jardin.
See Rabelais, p. 181a, and Montaigne, p. 189b.

[1] Quoi que vous fassiez, écrasez l'infâme, et aimez qui vous aime.
[2] Le mieux est l'ennemi du bien.
[3] Le juste milieu. See Horace, p. 121b, and note.
[4] See Robert South, p. 376b.
[5] See Gibbon, p. 465b.

Thought depends absolutely on the stomach, but in spite of that, those who have the best stomachs are not the best thinkers.

Letter to d'Alembert
[August 20, 1770]

If God did not exist, it would be necessary to invent him.[1]

Épître á l'Auteur du Livre des Trois Imposteurs [November 10, 1770]

Change everything, except your loves.   *Sur l'Usage de la Vie*

I am very fond of truth, but not at all of martyrdom.

Letter to d'Alembert [February 1776]

The embarrassment of riches.
Le Droit du Seigneur, act II, sc. 6

He who thinks himself wise, O heavens! is a great fool.   *Ib. IV, 1*

Who has not the spirit of his age,
Of his age has all the unhappiness.[2]
Letter to Madame du Châtelet

I advise you to go on living solely to enrage those who are paying your annuities. It is the only pleasure I have left.
Letter to Madame du Deffand

Liberty of thought is the life of the soul.
Essay on Epic Poetry (written in English)

Whoe'er thou art, behold thy master,
He is, or was, or has to be.[3]
On a statuette of Cupid in the Cirey Gardens

I disapprove of what you say, but I will defend to the death your right to say it.   *Attributed* [4]

---

[1] See Ovid, p. 128b, and Tillotson, p. 366b.
[2] Qui n'a pas l'esprit de son âge,
   De son âge a tout le malheur.
[3] Qui que tu sois, voici ton maître;
   Il l'est — le fut — ou le doit être.
[4] This sentence is not Voltaire's, but was first used in quoting a letter from Voltaire to

MATTHEW GREEN
1696–1737

They politics like ours profess,
The greater prey upon the less.
The Grotto, l. 69

Fling but a stone, the giant dies.
Laugh and be well.
The Spleen [1737], l. 92

By happy alchemy of mind
They turn to pleasure all they find.
Ib. l. 610

WILLIAM OLDYS
1696–1761

Busy, curious, thirsty fly,
Drink with me, and drink as I.
On a Fly Drinking Out of a Cup of Ale, st. 1

MARIE DE VICHY-CHAMROND, MARQUISE DU DEFFAND
1697 – 1780

[Of Voltaire] He has invented history.

From FOURNIER, *L'Esprit dans l' Histoire [1857]*

The first step is the hardest.[1]
Letter to d'Alembert [July 7, 1763]

Helvétius in *The Friends of Voltaire* [1906] by S. G. TALLENTYRE (E. Beatrice Hall). She claims it was a paraphrase of Voltaire's words in the *Essay on Tolerance:* "Think for yourselves and let others enjoy the privilege to do so too."

Norbert Guterman, in *A Book of French Quotations* [1963], suggests that the probable source for the quotation is from a line in a letter to M. le Riche [*February 6, 1770*]: "Monsieur l'abbé, I detest what you write, but I would give my life to make it possible for you to continue to write."

[1] This remark refers to the legend that Saint Denis, carrying his head in his hands, walked from Montmartre to St. Denis, a few miles north of Paris. Voltaire wrote to Madame du Deffand [January 1764] that one of her bon mots was quoted in the notes of *La Pucelle, canto 1:* Il n'y a que le premier pas qui coûte.

KAMO MABUCHI[1]
1697–1769

Japanese poetry has as its subject the human heart. It may seem to be of no practical use and just as well left uncomposed, but when one knows poetry well, one understands also without explanation the reasons governing order and disorder in the world.   *Writings*

I need not recite again how troublesome, evil, turbulent a country China is. To mention just one instance — there is the matter of their picture-writing.   *Ib.*

RICHARD SAVAGE
1698–1743

No tenth transmitter of a foolish face.
          The Bastard [1728], *l. 8*

May see thee now, though late, redeem thy name,
And glorify what else is damn'd to fame.
          Character of the Reverend James Foster

WILLIAM WARBURTON, BISHOP OF GLOUCESTER
1698–1779

Orthodoxy is my doxy; heterodoxy is another man's doxy.[2]
          From JOSEPH PRIESTLEY [1733– 1804], *Memoirs, vol. I, p. 572*

JOHN DYER
c. 1700 – 1758

A little rule, a little sway,
A sunbeam in a winter's day,
Is all the proud and mighty have
Between the cradle and the grave.
          Grongar Hill [1726], *l. 89*

[1] From *Sources of Japanese Tradition,* edited by William Theodore de Bary [1960].

[2] Priestley relates that in a debate on the Test Laws, Lord Sandwich said: "I have heard frequent use of the words 'orthodoxy' and 'heterodoxy' but I confess myself at a loss to know precisely what they mean." Bishop Warburton whispered his definition to him.

See Carlyle, p. 577a.

JAMES THOMSON
1700–1748

See, Winter comes to rule the varied year,[1]
Sullen and sad.
          The Seasons. Winter [1726], *l. 1*

Welcome, kindred glooms!
Congenial horrors, hail!   *Ib. l. 5*

Cruel as death, and hungry as the grave.   *Ib. l. 393*

There studious let me sit,
And hold high converse with the mighty dead.   *Ib. l. 431*

Ships dim-discover'd dropping from the clouds.
          Ib. Summer [1727], *l. 946*

Sigh'd and look'd unutterable things.
          Ib. l. 1188

Come, gentle Spring! ethereal mildness, come.
          Ib. Spring [1728], *l. 1*

Delightful task! to rear the tender thought,
To teach the young idea how to shoot.
          Ib. l. 1149

An elegant sufficiency, content,
Retirement, rural quiet, friendship, books.   *Ib. l. 1158*

Crown'd with the sickle, and the wheaten sheaf,
While Autumn, nodding o'er the yellow plain,
Comes jovial on.
          Ib. Autumn [1730], *l. 1*

For loveliness
Needs not the foreign aid of ornament,
But is when unadorn'd adorn'd the most.[2]   *Ib. l. 208*

Or where the Northern ocean, in vast whirls,
Boils round the naked melancholy isles
Of farthest Thulè,[3] and th' Atlantic surge

[1] See Cowper, p. 458b.
[2] See Cicero, p. 111a, and Milton, p. 346a.
[3] See Virgil, p. 117a, and Seneca, p. 131a.

Pours in among the stormy Hebrides.[1]
The Seasons. Autumn, l. 871

Come then, expressive silence, muse
His praise.
Hymn [1730], *l. 118*

O Sophonisba! Sophonisba, O![2]
Sophonisba [1730], *act III, sc. 2*

Forever, Fortune, wilt thou prove
An unrelenting foe to love,
And, when we meet a mutual heart,
Come in between and bid us part?
To Fortune

When Britain first, at Heaven's com-
mand,
  Arose from out of the azure main,
This was the charter of the land,
  And guardian angels sung this strain:
Rule, Britannia, rule the waves;
Britons never will be slaves.
Alfred [1740], *act II, sc. 5*

A pleasing land of drowsyhead it was.
The Castle of Indolence [1748],
canto I, st. 6

A bard here dwelt, more fat than bard
  beseems,
Who, void of envy, guile, and lust of
  gain,
On virtue still, and nature's pleasing
  themes,
Pour'd forth his unpremeditated strain.
Ib. st. 68

A little round, fat, oily man of God.
Ib. st. 69

PHILIP DODDRIDGE
1702–1751

Awake my soul! stretch every nerve,
  And press with vigor on;
A heavenly race demands thy zeal,
  And an immortal crown.
Hymns [1755]. *Zeal and Vigor
in the Christian Race, st. 1*

[1] See Milton, p. 339a.
[2] This line was parodied by Fielding in his
Tom Thumb [acted 1730]: O Huncamunca,
Huncamunca, O.

JONATHAN EDWARDS
1703–1758

Resolved, never to do anything which
I should be afraid to do if it were the
last hour of my life.[1]
Seventy Resolutions

Intend to live in continual mortification, and never to expect or desire any
worldly ease or pleasure.
Diary [1723]

A little, wretched, despicable creature; a worm, a mere nothing, and less
than nothing; a vile insect that has
risen up in contempt against the majesty of Heaven and earth.
*The Justice of God in the Dam-
nation of Sinners* [1734]

I assert that nothing ever comes to
pass without a cause.
The Freedom of the Will [1754]

This dictate of common sense.
Ib.

THOMAS MORELL
1703–1784

See, the conquering hero comes!
Sound the trumpet, beat the drums![2]
Joshua [1748], *pt. III*

JOHN WESLEY
1703–1791

I look upon the world as my parish.
Journal [June 11, 1739]

That execrable sum of all villainies,
commonly called the Slave Trade.
Ib. [February 12, 1772]

Though I am always in haste, I am
never in a hurry.
Letters [December 10, 1777]

Let it be observed, that slovenliness
is no part of religion; that neither this
nor any text of Scripture, condemns

[1] See Gellert, p. 438b.
[2] Handel used this in his oratorios *Judas Maccabaeus* [April 1, 1747] and *Joshua* [March 9,
1748], the libretti of which were written by
Morell.
See Dryden, p. 371a.

neatness of apparel. Certainly this is a duty, not a sin. "Cleanliness is, indeed, next to godliness."[1]

Sermon 93, On Dress

Do all the good you can,
By all the means you can,
In all the ways you can,
In all the places you can,
At all the times you can,
To all the people you can,
As long as ever you can.

John Wesley's Rule

NATHANIEL COTTON
1705–1788

Yet still we hug the dear deceit.

Content. Vision IV

Hold the fleet angel fast until he bless thee.[2] *Tomorrow*

BENJAMIN FRANKLIN[3]
1706–1790

The body of Benjamin Franklin, Printer (like the cover of an old book, its contents torn out and stripped of its

lettering and gilding), lies here, food for worms; but the work shall not be lost, for it will (as he believed) appear once more in a new and more elegant edition, revised and corrected by the Author.[1]

Epitaph on Himself [*composed in 1728*]

Eat to live, and not live to eat.[2]

Poor Richard's Almanac [*for 1733*]

Where there's marriage without love, there will be love without marriage.

Ib. [*1734*]

Avarice and happiness never saw each other, how then should they become acquainted. *Ib.*

A little house well filled, a little field well tilled, and a little wife well willed, are great riches. *Ib.* [*1735*]

Some are weatherwise, some are otherwise. *Ib.*

Necessity never made a good bargain. *Ib.*

Three may keep a secret, if two of them are dead. *Ib.*

Opportunity is the great bawd. *Ib.*

Early to bed and early to rise, makes a man healthy, wealthy, and wise. *Ib.*

God helps them that help themselves.[3] *Ib.*

Don't throw stones at your neighbors', if your own windows are glass. *Ib.*

There are three faithful friends — an old wife, an old dog, and ready money. *Ib.* [*1738*]

If you would not be forgotten, as soon as you are dead and rotten, either write things worth reading, or do things worth the writing. *Ib.*

---

[1] According to Rabbi A. S. Bettelheim, this is found in the Hebrew fathers. He cites PHINEHAS BEN YAIR as follows: "The doctrines of religion are resolved into carefulness; carefulness into vigorousness; vigorousness into guiltlessness; guiltlessness into abstemiousness; abstemiousness into cleanliness; cleanliness into godliness" — literally, next to godliness.

[2] See *Genesis 32:26*, p. 7b, and Whittier, p. 625b.

[3] Eripuit coelo fulmen mox sceptra tyrannis [He snatched the thunderbolt from heaven, then the scepter from tyrants]. — *Attributed to* TURGOT
This line was inscribed on Houdon's bust of Franklin in 1778. FREDERICK VON DER TRENCK [1726–1794] asserted in 1794 that he was the author of the line.
See Manilius, p. 131b.
Antiquity would have raised altars to this mighty genius, who, to the advantage of mankind, compassing in his mind the heavens and the earth, was able to restrain alike thunderbolts and tyrants. — MIRABEAU, *Address Upon the Death of Franklin*
I succeed him; no one could replace him. — THOMAS JEFFERSON [to the Comte de Vergennes, who had remarked, "You replace Mr. Franklin" as envoy to France]
See Byron, p. 563a.

[1] See Clare, p. 573b.
[2] See Socrates, p. 87b, and note.
[3] See Aesop, p. 76b, and note.

Keep your eyes wide open before marriage, half shut afterwards.
Poor Richard's Almanac [1738]

None but the well-bred man knows how to confess a fault, or acknowledge himself in an error. *Ib.*

An empty bag cannot stand upright.
Ib. [1740]

He that riseth late must trot all day.
Ib. [1742]

Experience keeps a dear school, but fools will learn in no other.[1]
Ib. [1743]

The used key is always bright.
Ib. [1744]

When the well's dry, we know the worth of water.[2] *Ib.* [1746]

Dost thou love Life? Then do not squander Time; for that's the stuff Life is made of. *Ib.*

Lost time is never found again.
Ib. [1748]

Little strokes fell great oaks.[3]
Ib. [1750]

The cat in gloves catches no mice.
Ib. [1754]

Work as if you were to live a hundred years, pray as if you were to die tomorrow. *Ib.* [1757]

A word to the wise is enough, and many words won't fill a bushel.
Ib. [1758]

He that lives upon hope will die fasting. *Ib.*

Three removes is as bad as a fire.
Ib.

A little neglect may breed great mischief . . . for want of a nail the shoe was lost; for want of a shoe the horse

was lost; and for want of a horse the rider was lost.[1]
Poor Richard's Almanac [1758]

We are a kind of posterity in respect to them.
Letter to William Strahan [1745]

Eighth and lastly. They are so grateful!!
Reasons for Preferring an Elderly Mistress [1745]

Remember that time is money.[2]
Advice to a Young Tradesman [1748]

They that can give up essential liberty to obtain a little temporary safety deserve neither liberty nor safety.
Historical Review of Pennsylvania [1759]

Idleness and pride tax with a heavier hand than kings and parliaments. If we can get rid of the former, we may easily bear the latter.
Letter on the Stamp Act [July 11, 1765]

The grand leap of the whale up the Fall of Niagara is esteemed, by all who have seen it, as one of the finest spectacles in nature.
To the editor of a London newspaper [1765], *intended to chaff the English for their ignorance of America*

Here Skugg lies snug
As a bug in a rug.
Letter to Miss Georgiana Shipley [September 1772]

There never was a good war or a bad peace.[3]
Letter to Josiah Quincy [September 11, 1773]

---

[1] See Burke, p. 455a.
[2] Do not let your chances like sunbeams pass you by,
For you never miss the water till the well runs dry.
ROWLAND HOWARD, *You Never Miss the Water* [1876]
[3] See Lyly, p. 202b.

[1] See Herbert, pp. 324b–325a.
[2] We reckon hours and minutes to be dollars and cents. — T. C. HALIBURTON [1796–1865], *The Clockmaker*
[3] I cease not to advocate peace; even though unjust it is better than the most just war. — CICERO [106–43 B.C.], *Epistolae ad Atticum*, bk. *VII, epistle 14*
It hath been said that an unjust peace is to be preferred before a just war. — SAMUEL BUTLER, *Butler's Remains* [1759]. *Speeches in the Rump Parliament*

You and I were long friends: you are now my enemy, and I am

Yours,
B. Franklin
Letter to William Strahan
[July 5, 1775]

We must all hang together, or assuredly we shall all hang separately.
At the signing of the Declaration of Independence [July 4, 1776]

Poor man, said I, you pay too much for your whistle.   *The Whistle* [1779]

Here you would know and enjoy what posterity will say of Washington. For a thousand leagues have nearly the same effect with a thousand years.
Letter to Washington
[March 5, 1780]

George Washington, Commander of the American armies, who, like Joshua of old, commanded the sun and the moon to stand still, and they obeyed him.
A toast at a dinner in Versailles [1]

No nation was ever ruined by trade.
Thoughts on Commercial Subjects

I wish the bald eagle had not been chosen as the representative of our country; he is a bird of bad moral character; like those among men who live by sharping and robbing, he is generally poor, and often very lousy.

The turkey is a much more respectable bird, and withal a true original native of America.
Letter to Sarah Bache
[January 26, 1784]

He [the sun] gives light as soon as he rises.
An Economical Project [2] [1784]

Our Constitution is in actual operation; everything appears to promise that it will last; but in this world nothing is certain but death and taxes.
Letter to M. Leroy [1789]

The next thing most like living one's life over again seems to be a recollection of that life, and to make that recollection as durable as possible by putting it down in writing.
Autobiography [1771–1867],[1]
ch. 1

Eat not to dullness; drink not to elevation.   *Ib.* 6

I shall never ask, never refuse, nor ever resign an office.   *Ib.* 8

Human felicity is produced not so much by great pieces of good fortune that seldom happen, as by little advantages that occur every day.
Ib. 9

When men are employed, they are best contented; for on the days they worked they were good-natured and cheerful, and, with the consciousness of having done a good day's work, they spent the evening jollily; but on our idle days they were mutinous and quarrelsome.   *Ib.* 10

GEORGES LOUIS LECLERC DE BUFFON

1707–1788

[Of the horse] The noblest conquest man has ever made.
L'Histoire des Mammifères.
Le Cheval

The style is the man himself.[2]
Discourse [on his admission to the French Academy, 1753]

Genius is nothing but a greater aptitude for patience.

Attributed [3]

---

[1] The British Minister had proposed a toast to George III, in which he likened him to the sun, and the French Minister had toasted Louis XVI, comparing him with the moon.

[2] Letter to the *Journal de Paris* advocating daylight saving.

[1] The *Autobiography,* begun in 1771, was published in complete and accurate form in 1867.

[2] Le style c'est l'homme même.

[3] Le génie n'est qu'une plus grande aptitude à la patience.
Hérault de Séchelles, in *Voyage à Montbard,* first attributed this to Buffon. It is quoted by Matthew Arnold in *Essays in Criticism, A French Coleridge* [1865]. There is also a popular proverb: Genius is patience. LORD SYDENHAM [1799–1841] defined genius as a consummate sense of proportion.
See Carlyle, p. 578a; Butler, p. 756b; and Jane Ellice Hopkins, p. 770a.
(*note continued p.* 424)

HENRY FIELDING
1707–1754

All Nature wears one universal grin.
> *Tom Thumb the Great* [1730],
> *act I, sc. 1*

Today it is our pleasure to be drunk;
And this our queen shall be as drunk as
we. *Ib. 2*

When I'm not thank'd at all, I'm
thank'd enough;
I've done my duty, and I've done no
more. *Ib. 3*

I am as sober as a judge.
> *Don Quixote in England* [1734],
> *act III, sc. 14*

This story will never go down.
> *Tumble-Down Dick*

The dusky night rides down the sky,
And ushers in the morn;
The hounds all join in glorious cry,
The huntsman winds his horn,
And a-hunting we will go.[1]
> *A-Hunting We Will Go* [1734],
> *st. 1*

To whom nothing is given, of him
can nothing be required.[2]
> *Joseph Andrews* [1742], *bk. II,
> ch. 8*

I describe not men, but manners; not
an individual, but a species.
> *Ib. III, 1*

They are the affectation of affectation. *Ib. 3*

Public schools are the nurseries of all
vice and immorality. *Ib. 5*

Patience is a necessary ingredient of genius.
— DISRAELI, *The Young Duke* [1831]
Genius is capacity for taking trouble. —
LESLIE STEPHEN [1832–1904]
Genius is an intuitive talent for labor. —
JAN WALAEUS
[1] It's of three jovial huntsmen, and a-hunting
they did go;
And they hunted, and they hollo'd, and they
blew their horns also;
Look ye there!
> *The Three Jovial Huntsmen* (old
> English ballad), *st. 1*
[2] See *Luke 12:48,* p. 47a.

Some folks rail against other folks,
because other folks have what some
folks would be glad of.
> *Joseph Andrews, bk. IV, ch. 6*

Love and scandal are the best sweeteners of tea.[1]
> *Love in Several Masques* [1743]

Every physician almost hath his favorite disease.
> *Tom Jones* [2] [1749], *bk. II, ch. 9*

Thwackum was for doing justice, and
leaving mercy to heaven. *Ib. III, 10*

Can any man have a higher notion of
the rule of right and the eternal fitness
of things? *Ib. IV, 4*

Distinction without a difference.
> *Ib. VI, 13*

O! more than Gothic ignorance.
> *Ib. VII, 3*

An amiable weakness.[3] *Ib. X, 8*

His designs were strictly honorable,
as the phrase is; that is, to rob a lady of
her fortune by way of marriage.
> *Ib. XI, 4*

Hairbreadth missings of happiness
look like the insults of Fortune.
> *Ib. XIII, 2*

The republic of letters.
> *Ib. XIV, 1*

It hath been often said, that it is not
death, but dying which is terrible.
> *Amelia* [1751], *bk. III, ch. 4*

These are called the pious frauds of
friendship. *Ib. VI, 6*

When widows exclaim loudly against
second marriages, I would always lay a
wager that the man, if not the wedding
day, is absolutely fixed on. *Ib. 8*

---

[1] See Congreve, p. 391b.
[2] See Gibbon, p. 466a.
[3] Amiable weaknesses of human nature. —
GIBBON, *Decline and Fall of the Roman Empire*
[1776–1788], *ch. 14*
It was an amiable weakness. — SHERIDAN,
The School for Scandal [1777]

There is not in the universe a more ridiculous, nor a more contemptible animal, than a proud clergyman.
>> *Amelia, bk. VI, ch. 10*

One of my illustrious predecessors.[1]
>> *Covent Garden Journal*
>> [*January 11, 1752*]

LINNAEUS
[CARL VON LINNÉ]
1707–1778

To live by medicine is to live horribly.
>> *Diaeta Naturalis, introduction*

Nature does not proceed by leaps.[2]
>> *Philosophia Botanica, sec. 77*

Mingle your joys sometimes with your earnest occupation.[3]
>> *From biography of Linnaeus by*
>> BENJAMIN DAYDON JONES, *ch. 9*

A professor can never better distinguish himself in his work than by encouraging a clever pupil, for the true discoverers are among them, as comets amongst the stars.   *Ib.*

Live innocently; God is here.
>> *Ib. 15 (inscribed over the door of Linnaeus's bedchamber)*

If a tree dies, plant another in its place.   *Ib.*

CHARLES WESLEY
1707–1788

"Christ, the Lord, is risen today,"
Sons of men and angels say,
Raise your joys and triumphs high,
Sing, ye heavens, and earth reply.
>> *Hymns and Sacred Poems*
>> [1739]. *Christ, the Lord, Is Risen Today*

Jesus, lover of my soul,
  Let me to Thy bosom fly,
While the waters nearer roll,
  While the tempest still is high;
Hide me, O my Savior, hide,
  Till the storm of life is past;
Safe into the haven glide,
  O receive my soul at last.
>> *Hymns and Sacred Poems.*
>> [1740]. *Jesus, Lover of My Soul*

Gentle Jesus, meek and mild,
Look upon a little child;
Pity my simplicity,
Suffer me to come to thee.
>> *Ib.* [1742]. *Gentle Jesus, Meek and Mild*

Soldiers of Christ, arise,
And put your armor on.
>> *Ib.* [1749]. *Soldiers of Christ, Arise*

Hark! the herald angels sing
Glory to the newborn King;
Peace on earth, and mercy mild,
God and sinners reconciled!
Joyful all ye nations rise,
Join the triumph of the skies;
With th' angelic host proclaim
Christ is born in Bethlehem.[1]
>> *Ib.* [1753]. *Christmas Hymn: Hark! the Herald Angels Sing*

WILLIAM PITT, EARL
OF CHATHAM
1708–1778

The atrocious crime of being a young man, which the honorable gentleman [Walpole] has with such spirit and decency charged upon me, I shall neither attempt to palliate nor deny; but content myself with wishing that I may be one of those whose follies may cease with their youth, and not of that num-

---

[1] Illustrious predecessor. — BURKE, *The Present Discontents* [1770]
I tread in the footsteps of illustrious men. . . . In receiving from the people the sacred trust twice confined to my illustrious predecessor [Andrew Jackson]. — MARTIN VAN BUREN, *Inaugural Address* [March 4, 1837]
[2] Natura non facit saltus.
[3] See Horace, p. 122b, and note.

[1] George Whitefield [1714–1770] altered lines 1 and 2, 7 and 8 from Wesley's original:
Hark, how all the welkin rings,
  "Glory to the King of kings." . . .
Universal nature say,
  "Christ the Lord is born today."

ber who are ignorant in spite of experience.

> *Speech in the House of Commons* [1] [*March 6, 1741*]

I rejoice that America has resisted. Three millions of people, so dead to all the feelings of liberty, as voluntarily to submit to be slaves, would have been fit instruments to make slaves of the rest.

> *Ib.* [*January 14, 1766*]

Confidence is a plant of slow growth in an aged bosom; youth is the season of credulity.

> *Speech in the House of Commons* [*January 14, 1766*]

Unlimited power is apt to corrupt the minds of those who possess it; [2] and this I know, my lords, that where laws end, tyranny begins. [3]

> *Case of Wilkes. Speech* [*January 9, 1770*]

There is something behind the throne greater than the King himself.

> *Speech in the House of Lords* [*March 2, 1770*]

I love the Americans because they love liberty, and I love them for the noble efforts they made in the last war.

> *Ib.*

Reparation for our rights at home, and security against the like future violations. [4]

> *Letter to the Earl of Shelburne* [*September 29, 1770*]

If I were an American, as I am an Englishman, while a foreign troop was landed in my country, I never would

---

[1] This is the composition of Johnson, founded on some note or statement of the actual speech. Johnson said, "That speech I wrote in a garret, in Exeter Street." — BOSWELL, *Life of Johnson* [1791]

[2] See Lord Acton, p. 750a.

[3] See John Locke, p. 372b.

[4] Indemnity for the past and security for the future. — LORD JOHN RUSSELL, *Life and Times of Charles James Fox* [1859–1860], vol. III, p. 345, letter to the Hon. T. Maitland

lay down my arms, — never — never — never! You cannot conquer America.

> *Speech* [*November 18, 1777*]

I invoke the genius of the Constitution.

> *Ib.*

The poorest man may in his cottage bid defiance to all the forces of the Crown. It may be frail — its roof may shake — the wind may blow through it — the storm may enter — the rain may enter — but the King of England cannot enter — all his force dares not cross the threshold of the ruined tenement!

> *Speech on the Excise Bill*

SAMUEL JOHNSON
1709–1784

Of all the griefs that harass the distrest,
Sure the most bitter is a scornful jest.

> *London* [1738] (*An imitation of the Third Satire of Juvenal*), *l. 166*

This mournful truth is ev'rywhere confess'd —
Slow rises worth, by poverty depress'd. [1]

> *Ib. l. 176*

When learning's triumph o'er her barb'rous foes
First rear'd the stage, immortal Shakespeare rose;
Each change of many-color'd life he drew,
Exhausted worlds, and then imagin'd new:
Existence saw him spurn her bounded reign,
And panting Time toil'd after him in vain.

> *Prologue at the Opening of Drury Lane Theatre* [1747]

Cold approbation gave the ling'ring bays,
For those who durst not censure, scarce could praise.

> *Ib.*

Declamation roar'd, while Passion slept.

> *Ib.*

---

[1] Three years later Johnson wrote, "Mere unassisted merit advances slowly, if — what is not very common — it advances at all."

The wild vicissitudes of taste.
> *Prologue at the Opening of*
> *Drury Lane Theatre*

For we that live to please must please
to live. 　　　　*Ib.*

Studious to please, yet not ashamed to
fail.
> *Prologue to the Tragedy of Irene*
> [1749]

Let observation with extensive view
Survey mankind, from China to Peru.[1]
> *Vanity of Human Wishes*
> [1749], *l. 1*

Deign on the passing world to turn
thine eyes,
And pause a while from learning to be
wise.
There mark what ills the scholar's life
assail —
Toil, envy, want, the patron, and the
jail. 　　　　*Ib. l. 157*

A frame of adamant, a soul of fire,
No dangers fright him, and no labors
tire. 　　　　*Ib. l. 191*

He left the name at which the world
grew pale,
To point a moral, or adorn a tale.
　　　　Ib. l. 221

"Enlarge my life with multitude of
days!"
In health, in sickness, thus the sup-
pliant prays:
Hides from himself his state, and shuns
to know
That life protracted is protracted woe.
　　　　Ib. l. 255

Superfluous lags the vet'ran on the
stage. 　　　　*Ib. l. 308*

Must helpless man, in ignorance sedate,
Roll darkling down the torrent of his
fate? 　　　　*Ib. l. 345*

Secure, whate'er he gives, he gives the
best. 　　　　*Ib. l. 356*

---

[1] DE QUINCEY quotes with approval, but
without naming him, the criticism of a writer
who contends that this couplet amounts in
effect to this: "Let observation with extensive
observation observe mankind extensively." —
Rhetoric [1828]

With these celestial Wisdom calms the
mind,
And makes the happiness she does not
find.
> *Vanity of Human Wishes,*
> *l. 367*

Curiosity is one of the permanent
and certain characteristics of a vigorous
mind.
> *The Rambler* [1] [*March 12, 1751*]

No place affords a more striking conviction of the vanity of human hopes
than a public library.
　　　　Ib. [*March 23, 1751*]

I am not so lost in lexicography as to
forget that *words are the daughters of
earth, and that things are the sons of
heaven.*[2]
> *Dictionary* [1755], *preface*

CLUB — An assembly of good fellows, meeting under certain conditions.
　　　　Ib.

ESSAY — A loose sally of the mind;
an irregular indigested piece; not a regular and orderly composition. 　　*Ib.*

EXCISE — A hateful tax levied upon
commodities, and adjudged not by the
common judges of property, but
wretches hired by those to whom excise
is paid. 　　　　*Ib.*

GRUBSTREET — The name of a
street near Moorsfield, London, much
inhabited by writers of small histories,
dictionaries, and temporary poems.
　　　　Ib.

LEXICOGRAPHER — A writer of dictionaries, a harmless drudge. 　　*Ib.*

OATS — A grain which in England is
generally given to horses, but in Scotland supports the people.[3] 　　*Ib.*

---

[1] For the *Rambler* motto, see Johnson's translation of BOETHIUS, *De Consolatione Philosophiae III, 9, 27,* p. 148a.

[2] See Herbert, p. 325a.

[3] It was pleasant to me to find, that "oats,"
the "food of horses," were so much used as
the food of the people in Dr. Johnson's own
town. — BOSWELL, *Life of Dr. Johnson* [1791],
vol. I, p. 628 [Everyman ed.]

I own that by my definition of *oats* I meant
to vex them [the Scotch]. — SAMUEL JOHNSON;
from Ib. II, 434

The joy of life is variety; the tenderest love requires to be renewed by intervals of absence.

The Idler [1758–1760], *no.* 39

He is no wise man that will quit a certainty for an uncertainty. *Ib.* 57

Ye who listen with credulity to the whispers of fancy, and pursue with eagerness the phantoms of hope; who expect that age will perform the promises of youth, and that the deficiencies of the present day will be supplied by the morrow; attend to the history of Rasselas, Prince of Abyssinia.

Rasselas [1759], *ch.* 1

To a poet nothing can be useless.
Ib. 10

Human life is everywhere a state in which much is to be endured and little to be enjoyed. *Ib.* 11

Marriage has many pains, but celibacy has no pleasures. *Ib.* 26

Example is always more efficacious than precept. *Ib.* 29

The endearing elegance of female friendship. *Ib.* 45

How small, of all that human hearts endure,
That part which laws or kings can cause or cure!
Still to ourselves in every place consign'd,
Our own felicity we make or find.
Lines added to GOLDSMITH'S
Traveller [1763–1764]

That man is little to be envied whose patriotism would not gain force upon the plain of Marathon, or whose piety would not grow warmer among the ruins of Iona.
Journey to the Western Islands
[1775]. *Inch Kenneth*

Whoever wishes to attain an English style, familiar but not coarse, and elegant but not ostentatious, must give his

days and nights to the volumes of Addison.
Lives of the Poets [1779–1781].
Addison

To be of no church is dangerous. Religion, of which the rewards are distant, and which is animated only by faith and hope, will glide by degrees out of the mind unless it be invigorated and reimpressed by external ordinances, by stated calls to worship, and the salutary influence of example. *Ib. Milton*

The father of English criticism.
Ib. Dryden

He delighted to tread upon the brink of meaning. *Ib.*

The *Churchyard* abounds with images which find a mirror in every mind, and with sentiments to which every bosom returns an echo. *Ib. Gray* [1]

His [Garrick's] death has eclipsed the gaiety of nations, and impoverished the public stock of harmless pleasure.
Ib. Edmund Smith

New things are made familiar, and familiar things are made new.
Ib. Pope

Tomorrow I purpose to regulate my room.
Prayers and Meditations [*published* 1785]. [1764]

Preserve me from unseasonable and immoderate sleep. *Ib.* [1767]

Every man naturally persuades himself that he can keep his resolutions, nor is he convinced of his imbecility but by length of time and frequency of experiment. *Ib.* [1770]

This world, where much is to be done and little to be known.
*Ib. Against Inquisitive and
Perplexing Thoughts*

I have, all my life long, been lying till noon; yet I tell all young men, and tell them with great sincerity, that nobody

[1] See Gray, p. 440a.

who does not rise early will ever do any good.

> From BOSWELL, *Journal of a Tour to the Hebrides* [*published* 1785], [*September 14,* 1773]

Wickedness is always easier than virtue; for it takes the short cut to everything. **Ib.** [*September 17, 1773*]

Gratitude is a fruit of great cultivation; you do not find it among gross people. **Ib.** [*September 20, 1773*]

Here closed in death th' attentive eyes
That saw the manners in the face.
> *Epitaph on Hogarth* [1786]

When the hoary Sage replied,
"Come, my lad, and drink some beer."
> From MRS. PIOZZI, *Anecdotes of Samuel Johnson* [1786]

If the man who turnips cries,
Cry not when his father dies,
'Tis a proof that he had rather
Have a turnip than his father.[1] **Ib.**

He was a very good hater. **Ib.**

The law is the last result of human wisdom acting upon human experience for the benefit of the public. **Ib.**

The use of traveling is to regulate imagination by reality, and instead of thinking how things may be, to see them as they are. **Ib.**

Dictionaries are like watches; the worst is better than none, and the best cannot be expected to go quite true. **Ib.**

Books that you may carry to the fire, and hold readily in your hand, are the most useful after all.
> *Apothegms from* HAWKINS, *Life of Johnson* [1787]

As with my hat [2] upon my head
I walk'd along the Strand,

[1] Burlesque of Lope de Vega's lines, "Se acquien los leones vence," etc.
[2] Elsewhere found, "I put my hat."

I there did meet another man
With his hat in his hand.[1]
> *Anecdotes of Johnson by* GEORGE STEEVENS

Abstinence is as easy to me as temperance would be difficult.
> *Anecdotes of Johnson by* HANNAH MORE

Boswell: That, sir, was great fortitude of mind.
Johnson: No, sir; stark insensibility.
> From BOSWELL, *Life of Johnson* [2] [*published* 1791], [*November 5, 1728*]

Sir, we are a nest of singing birds.[3]
> **Ib.** [1730]

Tom Birch is as brisk as a bee in conversation; but no sooner does he take a pen in his hand than it becomes a torpedo to him, and benumbs all his faculties. **Ib.** [1743]

I'll come no more behind your scenes, David; [4] for the silk stockings and white bosoms of your actresses excite my amorous propensities. **Ib.** [1750]

A man may write at any time, if he will set himself doggedly to it.
> **Ib.** [*March 1750*]

Wretched un-idea'd girls.
> **Ib.** [1753]

Is not a patron, my lord, one who looks with unconcern on a man struggling for life in the water, and when he has reached ground encumbers him with help? The notice which you have been pleased to take of my labors, had it been early, had been kind; but it has been delayed till I am indifferent, and

[1] A parody on the ballad *The Hermit of Warkworth.*
[2] Edited by G. B. Hill and revised by L. F. Powell [1934].
The *Life of Johnson* is assuredly a great, a very great work. Homer is not more decidedly the first of heroic poets, Shakespeare is not more decidedly the first of dramatists, Demosthenes is not more decidedly the first of orators, than Boswell is the first of biographers. He has no second. — MACAULAY, *Samuel Johnson* [1831]
[3] Of Pembroke College.
[4] David Garrick.

cannot enjoy it; till I am solitary, and cannot impart it; till I am known, and do not want it.[1]

From BOSWELL, *Life of Johnson*
[*Letter to Lord Chesterfield, February 7, 1754*]

[Of Lord Chesterfield] This man, I thought, had been a Lord among wits; but, I find, he is only a wit among Lords!   *Ib.* [*1754*]

Sir, he [Bolingbroke] was a scoundrel, and a coward: a scoundrel, for charging a blunderbuss against religion and morality; a coward, because he had not resolution to fire it off himself, but left half a crown to a beggarly Scotchman to draw the trigger at his death.
Ib. [*March 6, 1754*]

Ignorance, madame, pure ignorance.[2]
Ib. [*1755*]

If a man does not make new acquaintances as he advances through life, he will soon find himself left alone. A man, sir, should keep his friendship in a constant repair.[3]   *Ib.* [*1755*]

Towering in the confidence of twenty-one.   *Ib.* [*January 9, 1758*]

Being in a ship is being in a jail, with the chance of being drowned.
Ib. [*March 1759*]

Nothing is little to him that feels it with great sensibility.
Ib. [*July 20, 1762*]

A man of genius has been seldom ruined but by himself.
Ib. [*December 21, 1762*]

Sir, I think all Christians, whether Papists or Protestants, agree in the essential articles, and that their differences are trivial, and rather political than religious.[1]

From BOSWELL, *Life of Johnson*
[*1763*]

The noblest prospect which a Scotchman ever sees is the high-road that leads him to England!
Ib. [*July 6, 1763*]

A man ought to read just as inclination leads him; for what he reads as a task will do him little good.[2]
Ib. [*July 14, 1763*]

If he does really think that there is no distinction between virtue and vice, why, sir, when he leaves our houses let us count our spoons.   *Ib.*

Sir, your levelers wish to level *down* as far as themselves; but they cannot bear leveling *up* to themselves.
Ib. [*July 21, 1763*]

Sherry[3] is dull, naturally dull; but it must have taken him a great deal of pains to become what we now see him. Such an excess of stupidity, sir, is not in Nature.   *Ib.* [*July 28, 1763*]

Sir, a woman preaching is like a dog's walking on his hind legs. It is not done well; but you are surprised to find it done at all.   *Ib.* [*July 31, 1763*]

I look upon it, that he who does not mind his belly will hardly mind anything else.   *Ib.* [*August 5, 1763*]

[1] See first excerpt for 1772.
I do not find that the age or country makes the least difference; no, nor the language the actor spoke, nor the religion which they professed — whether Arab in the desert, or Frenchman in the Academy. I see that sensible men and conscientious men all over the world were of one religion of well-doing and daring. — EMERSON, *Lectures and Biographical Sketches* [1884]. *The Preacher*
See Disraeli, p. 613a.
[2] The book which you read from a sense of duty, or because for any reason you must, does not commonly make friends with you. — WILLIAM DEAN HOWELLS, *My Literary Passions* [1895], ch. 7
[3] Thomas Sheridan [1719–1788], actor, lecturer, and author.

[1] What is a Patron? Johnson knew,
And well that lifelike portrait drew.
He is a Patron who looks down
With careless eye on men who drown;
But if they chance to reach the land,
Encumbers them with helping hand.
AUSTIN DOBSON [1840–1921], *The Noble Patron*
[2] When asked by a lady why he defined "pastern" as the "knee" of a horse in his Dictionary.
[3] Keep your friendships in repair. — EMERSON, *Uncollected Lectures: Table Talk*

This was a good dinner enough, to be sure, but it was not a dinner to *ask* a man to.
> From BOSWELL, *Life of Johnson* [*August 5, 1763*]

The gloomy calm of idle vacancy.[1]
> *Ib.* [*December 8, 1763*]

[Of Sir John Hawkins] A very unclubable man.   *Ib.* [*1764*]

It matters not how a man dies, but how he lives.
> *Ib.* [*October 26, 1769*]

That fellow seems to me to possess but one idea, and that is a wrong one.[2]
> *Ib.* [*1770*]

A gentleman who had been very unhappy in marriage, married immediately after his wife died: Johnson said, it was the triumph of hope over experience.   *Ib.*

A decent provision for the poor is the true test of civilization.[3]   *Ib.*

All denominations of Christians have really little difference in point of doctrine, though they may differ widely in external forms.[4]   *Ib.* [*1772*]

Nobody can write the life of a man, but those who have eat and drunk and lived in social intercourse with him.[5]
> *Ib.* [*March 31, 1772*]

I am a great friend to public amusements; for they keep people from vice.
> *Ib.*

A cow is a very good animal in the field; but we turn her out of a garden.
> *Ib.* [*April 15, 1772*]

Much may be made of a Scotchman if he be caught young.[1]
> From BOSWELL, *Life of Johnson* [*Spring 1772*]

It is a foolish thing well done.[2]
> *Ib.* [*April 3, 1773*]

No, sir, do *you* read books *through?* [3]
> *Ib.* [*April 19, 1773*]

An old tutor of a college said to one of his pupils: Read over your compositions, and wherever you meet with a passage which you think is particularly fine, strike it out.[4]
> *Ib.* [*April 30, 1773*]

You are the most unscottified of your countrymen.   *Ib.* [*May 1, 1773*]

The woman's a whore, and there's an end on 't.[5]   *Ib.* [*May 7, 1773*]

Was ever poet so trusted before? [6]
> *Ib.* [*July 4, 1774*]

Attack is the re-action; I never think I have hit hard unless it rebounds.
> *Ib.* [*April 2, 1775*]

Most vices may be committed very genteelly: a man may debauch his friend's wife genteelly: he may cheat at cards genteelly.   *Ib.* [*April 6, 1775*]

A man will turn over half a library to make one book.   *Ib.*

Patriotism is the last refuge of a scoundrel.   *Ib.* [*April 7, 1775*]

That is the happiest conversation where there is no competition, no vanity, but a calm quiet interchange of sentiments.   *Ib.* [*April 14, 1775*]

Knowledge is of two kinds. We know a subject ourselves, or we know where we can find information upon it.
> *Ib.* [*April 18, 1775*]

In lapidary inscriptions a man is not upon oath.   *Ib.* [*1775*]

---

[1] See Cowper, p. 458b.
[2] See Disraeli, p. 612a.
[3] See Spinoza, p. 374a, and Andrew Carnegie, p. 757b.
[4] See first entry for 1763.
[5] They only who live with a man can write his life with any genuine exactness and discrimination; and few people who have lived with a man know what to remark about him. — *vol. I, 617* (Everyman ed.)

[1] Of Lord Mansfield, educated in England.
[2] Of Goldsmith's apology in the *London Chronicle* for beating Evans the bookseller.
[3] Upon being asked by Elphinstone if he had read a new book through.
[4] See Sydney Smith, p. 523b.
[5] Of Lady Diana Beauclerk, divorced.
[6] Of Oliver Goldsmith.

There is nothing which has yet been contrived by man by which so much happiness is produced as by a good tavern or inn.[1]

From Boswell, *Life of Johnson* [March 21, 1776]

No man but a blockhead ever wrote except for money. *Ib.* [April 5, 1776]

Life is a progress from want to want, not from enjoyment to enjoyment.
Ib. [May 1776]

Sir, you have but two topics, yourself and me. I am sick of both. *Ib.*

Olivarii Goldsmith, Poetae, Physici, Historici, qui nullum fere scribendi genus non tetigit, Nullum quod tetigit non ornavit [To Oliver Goldsmith, Poet, Naturalist, Historian, who left scarcely any style of writing untouched, and touched nothing that he did not adorn].
Ib. Epitaph on Goldsmith [June 22, 1776]

Life admits not of delays; when pleasure can be had, it is fit to catch it. Every hour takes away part of the things that please us, and perhaps part of our disposition to be pleased.
Ib. [September 1, 1777]

Depend upon it, sir, when a man knows he is to be hanged in a fortnight, it concentrates his mind wonderfully.
Ib. [September 19, 1777]

When a man is tired of London, he is tired of life; for there is in London all that life can afford.
Ib. [September 20, 1777]

---

[1] Whoe'er has travel'd life's dull round,
Whate'er his various tour has been,
May sigh to think how oft he found
His warmest welcome at an inn.
William Shenstone [1714–1763];
written on a window of an inn at Henley. Quoted not quite correctly by Johnson following his remark.
Robert Leighton [1611–1684], Archbishop of Glasgow, often said that if he were to choose

It is a man's own fault, it is from want of use, if his mind grows torpid in old age.
From Boswell, *Life of Johnson* [April 9, 1778]

Johnson had said that he could repeat a complete chapter of *The Natural History of Iceland*, from the Danish of Horrebow, the whole of which was exactly thus: "Ch. LXXII. *Concerning snakes.* There are no snakes to be met with throughout the whole island." [1]
Ib. [April 13, 1778]

Every state of society is as luxurious as it can be. Men always take the best they can get. *Ib.* [April 14, 1778]

A country governed by a despot is an inverted cone. *Ib.*

I am willing to love all mankind, except an American.
Ib. [April 15, 1778]

Pleasure of itself is not a vice.
Ib.

As the Spanish proverb says, "He, who would bring home the wealth of the Indies, must carry the wealth of the Indies with him," so it is in traveling, a man must carry knowledge with him if he would bring home knowledge.
Ib. [April 17, 1778]

It is better to live rich, than to die rich.[2] *Ib.*

Were it not for imagination, sir, a man would be as happy in the arms of a chambermaid as a duchess.
Ib. [May 9, 1778]

I would rather be attacked than unnoticed. For the worst thing you can do to an author is to be silent as to his works. *Ib.* [March 26, 1779]

---

a place to die in, it should be an inn. — *Works, vol. I, p. 76*
See the Archpoet, p. 154b.
[1] Chapter XLII is still shorter: "There are no owls of any kind in the whole island."
[2] See Robert Frost, p. 928b.

I remember a passage in Goldsmith's *Vicar of Wakefield*, which he was afterwards a fool enough to expunge: "I do not love a man who is zealous for nothing."

From BOSWELL, *Life of Johnson* [March 26, 1779]

Claret is the liquor for boys; port for men; but he who aspires to be a hero must drink brandy.

Ib. [April 7, 1779]

Worth seeing? yes; but not worth going to see.   *Ib.* [October 12, 1779]

If you are idle, be not solitary; if you are solitary, be not idle.[1]

Ib. [October 27, 1779]

A Frenchman must be always talking, whether he knows anything of the matter or not; an Englishman is content to say nothing, when he has nothing to say.   *Ib.* [1780]

Greek, sir, is like lace; every man gets as much of it as he can.   *Ib.*

[Of Oliver Goldsmith] No man was more foolish when he had not a pen in his hand, or more wise when he had.   *Ib.*

The applause of a single human being is of great consequence.   *Ib.*

Come to me, my dear Bozzy, and let us be as happy as we can.

Ib. [March 14, 1781]

There are people whom one should like very well to drop, but would not wish to be dropped by.

Ib. [March 1781]

We are not here to sell a parcel of boilers and vats, but the potentiality of growing rich beyond the dreams of avarice.[2]   *Ib.* [April 4, 1781]

Classical quotation is the *parole* of literary men all over the world.

From BOSWELL, *Life of Johnson* [May 8, 1781]

My friend was of opinion that when a man of rank appeared in that character [as an author], he deserved to have his merit handsomely allowed.[1]

Ib. [May 1781]

A jest breaks no bones.

Ib. [June 4, 1781]

Officious, innocent, sincere,
Of every friendless name the friend.

Ib. [January 20, 1782; on the death of Robert Levett]

To let friendship die away by negligence and silence, is certainly not wise. It is voluntarily to throw away one of the greatest comforts of this weary pilgrimage.   *Ib.* [March 20, 1782]

Whatever you have, spend less.

Ib. [December 7, 1782]

I never have sought the world; the world was not to seek me.[2]

Ib. [March 23, 1783]

He is not only dull himself, but the cause of dullness in others.[3] *Ib.* [1783]

Clear your mind of cant.[4]

Ib. [May 15, 1783]

Who drives fat oxen should himself be fat.[5]   *Ib.* [June 1784]

I have found you an argument; I am not obliged to find you an understanding.   *Ib.*

Blown about by every wind of criticism.[6]   *Ib.*

Don't attitudenize.   *Ib.*

---

[1] "The great direction which Burton has left to men disordered like you, is this: Be not solitary, be not idle." — *Ib.*
See Burton, p. 312a.
[2] See Edward Moore, p. 435b.

[1] Usually quoted as: When a nobleman writes a book, he ought to be encouraged. See Somerville, p. 397a.
[2] See Byron, p. 556b, and Emerson, p. 601b.
[3] See Shakespeare, p. 241b.
[4] See Carlyle, p. 576b.
[5] Parody on: Who rules o'er freemen should himself be free. — BROOKE, *Gustavus Vasa* [1739]
[6] See *Ephesians 4:14*, p. 54a.

I look upon every day to be lost, in which I do not make a new acquaintance.

> From BOSWELL, *Life of Johnson* [*November 1784*]

God bless you, my dear!

> *Ib.* [*December 13, 1784; his last words*]

JULIEN OFFRAY DE LA METTRIE
1709–1751

The human body is a watch, a large watch constructed with . . . skill and ingenuity.

> *L'Homme Machine* [1748] [1]

GEORGE, LORD LYTTELTON
1709–1773

Women, like princes, find few real friends.

> *Advice to a Lady*

What is your sex's earliest, latest care, Your heart's supreme ambition? To be fair. *Ib.*

The lover in the husband may be lost. *Ib.*

Where none admire, 'tis useless to excel;
Where none are beaux, 'tis vain to be a belle.

> *Soliloquy on a Beauty in the Country*

THEODORE TRONCHIN
1709–1781

In medicine, sins of commission are mortal, sins of omission venial.

> *Quoted in Bulletin of New York Academy of Medicine*, V [1929], 151

---

[1] *Man a Machine.* Translated by M. W. CALKINS, 1912.

OLIVER EDWARDS
1711–1791

I have tried too in my time to be a philosopher; but I don't know how, cheerfulness was always breaking in.

> [*April 17, 1778*] From BOSWELL, *Life of Johnson* [1791]

DAVID HUME
1711–1776

Avarice, the spur of industry.

> *Essays* [1741–1742]. *Of Civil Liberty*

Beauty in things exists in the mind which contemplates them.[1]

> *Ib. Of Tragedy*

Custom, then, is the great guide of human life.

> *An Enquiry Concerning Human Understanding* [1748], *pt. 1*

No testimony is sufficient to establish a miracle, unless the testimony be of such a kind that its falsehood would be more miraculous than the fact which it endeavors to establish.

> *Ib. Of Miracles*

Opposing one species of superstition to another, set them a-quarreling; while we ourselves, during their fury and contention, happily make our escape into the calm, though obscure, regions of philosophy.

> *The Natural History of Religion* [1757]

Never literary attempt was more unfortunate than my Treatise of Human Nature. It fell dead-born from the press. *My Own Life* [1777], *ch. 1*

MIKHAIL LOMONOSOV[2]
1711–1765

Carolus V,[3] Emperor of Rome, was wont to say that the Hispanic tongue was seemly for converse with God, the

---

[1] See Wallace, p. 729b, and Hungerford, p. 831b.
[2] Lomonosov created our first university. To put it better, he himself was our first university. — ALEXANDER PUSHKIN, *The Trip from Moscow to Petersburg* [1834]
[3] See Charles V, p. 186a.

French with friends, the German with enemies, the Italian with the feminine sex. Had he been versed in the Russian tongue, however, he would of a certainty have added to this that it is appropriate to converse with all of the above, inasmuch as he would have found in it the magnificence of the Hispanic tongue, the sprightliness of the French, the sturdiness of the German, the tenderness of the Italian and, over and above all that, the richness and conciseness of powerful imagery, of the Greek and Latin tongues.

Russian Grammar [1] [1755]

FREDERICK THE GREAT
1712–1786

By push of bayonets, no firing till you see the whites of their eyes.[2]

At Prague [May 6, 1757]

Rascals, would you live forever? [3]

When the Guards hesitated at Kolin [June 18, 1757]

The prince is the first servant of his state.

Memoirs of the House of Brandenburg [1758]

God is always with the strongest battalions.[4]

Letter to the Duchess Luise Dorothea von Gotha [May 8, 1760]

I am tired of ruling over slaves.

Last words [April 1, 1786]

GEORGE GRENVILLE
1712–1770

A wise government knows how to enforce with temper or to conciliate with dignity.

Speech against expulsion of John Wilkes, in Parliament [1769]

[1] Translated by B. G. GUERNEY.
[2] See William Prescott, p. 446b.
[3] Ihr Racker, wollt ihr ewig leben?
  That sergeant at Belleau Woods . . .
  "Come on, you . . . Do you want to live forever?"
        SANDBURG, *Losers* [*1921*]
[4] See Bussy-Rabutin, p. 357a, and note.

EDWARD MOORE
1712–1757

This is adding insult to injury.[1]

The Foundling [1748], *act V, sc. 2*

I am rich beyond the dreams of avarice.[2]

The Gamester [1753], *act II, sc. 2*

JEAN JACQUES ROUSSEAU
1712–1778

The first man who, having fenced in a piece of land, said, "This is mine," and found people naïve enough to believe him, that man was the true founder of civil society.

Discours sur l'Origine et le Fondement de l'Inégalité parmi les Hommes [1754]

Never exceed your rights, and they will soon become unlimited.   *Ib.*

Money is the seed of money, and the first guinea is sometimes more difficult to acquire than the second million.
        Ib.

Man is born free, and everywhere he is in chains.[3]

Du Contrat Social [1762], I, ch. 1

The strongest is never strong enough to be always the master, unless he transforms his strength into right, and obedience into duty.   *Ib. 3*

The right of conquest has no foundation other than the right of the strongest.   *Ib. 4*

In the strict sense of the term, a true democracy has never existed, and never will exist.   *Ib. III, 4*

The body politic, like the human body, begins to die from its birth, and bears in itself the causes of its destruction.   *Ib. 11*

[1] See Phaedrus, p. 129b.
[2] See Johnson, p. 433a.
[3] L'homme est né libre, et partout il est dans les fers.
  See Bliss, p. 468b, and Schiller, p. 497b.

Good laws lead to the making of better ones; bad ones bring about worse.
> *Du Contrat Social*, III, 15

Everything is good when it leaves the hands of the Creator; everything degenerates in the hands of man.
> *Émile, ou de l'education* [1762], I

I shall always maintain that whoso says in his heart, "There is no God," while he takes the name of God upon his lips, is either a liar or a madman.
> *Ib.*

People who know little are usually great talkers, while men who know much say little.   *Ib.*

What wisdom can you find that is greater than kindness?   *Ib. II*

Nature never deceives us; it is always we who deceive ourselves.   *Ib. III*

There exists one book, which, to my taste, furnishes the happiest treatise of natural education. What then is this marvelous book? Is it Aristotle? Is it Pliny, is it Buffon? No — it is *Robinson Crusoe*.   *Ib.*

Self-love makes more libertines than love.   *Ib. IV*

Provided a man is not mad, he can be cured of every folly but vanity.
> *Ib.*

A man says what he knows, a woman says what will please.   *Ib. V*

Where is the man who owes nothing to the land in which he lives? Whatever that land may be, he owes to it the most precious thing possessed by man, the morality of his actions and the love of virtue.[1]   *Ib.*

I have entered on an enterprise which is without precedent, and will have no imitator. I propose to show my

[1] See John F. Kennedy, p. 1073a, and note.

fellows a man as nature made him, and this man shall be myself.
> *Les Confessions* [1781–1788], I

Remorse sleeps during a prosperous period but wakes up in adversity.
> *Ib. II*

It is too difficult to think nobly when one only thinks to get a living.
> *Ib. II*

Hatred, as well as love, renders its votaries credulous.   *Ib. V*

At length I recollected the thoughtless saying of a great princess, who, on being informed that the country people had no bread, replied, "Let them eat cake." [1]   *Ib. VI*

The thirst after happiness is never extinguished in the heart of man.
> *Ib. IX*

He [2] thinks like a philosopher, but governs like a King.   *Ib. XII*

JOSIAH TUCKER, DEAN OF GLOUCESTER
1712–1799

What is true of a shopkeeper is true of a shopkeeping nation.[3]
> *Tract Against Going to War for the Sake of Trade* [1763]

ALISON COCKBURN
1713–1794

I've seen the smiling of Fortune beguiling,

[1] Qu'ils mangent de la brioche.
This remark is usually attributed to Marie Antoinette, after her arrival in France in 1770, but the sixth book of the *Confessions* was written two or three years before that date.
[2] Frederick the Great, King of Prussia [1740–1786]
[3] See Adam Smith, p. 445a.
Let Pitt then boast of his victory to his nation of shopkeepers. — BERTRAND BARÈRE, *Speech* [June 11, 1794]
But it may be said as a rule, that every Englishman in the Duke of Wellington's army paid his way. The remembrance of such a fact surely becomes a nation of shopkeepers. — THACKERAY, *Vanity Fair* [1847–1848], *vol. I*, *ch. 28*

I've felt all its favors and found its decay.

> *The Flowers of the Forest*

The flowers of the forest are withered away.[1]

> *Ib.*

DENIS DIDEROT
1713–1784

My thoughts are my trollops.[2]
> *Le Neveu de Rameau, ch.* 1

I can be expected to look for truth but not to find it.
> *Pensées Philosophiques* [1746], *no. 29*

L'esprit de l'escalier [staircase wit].[3]
> *Paradoxe sur le Comédien*

From fanaticism to barbarism is only one step.
> *Essai sur le Mérite de la Vertu*

LAURENCE STERNE
1713–1768

Only the brave know how to forgive. . . . A coward never forgave; it is not in his nature.
> *Sermons, vol. I* [1760], *no. 12*

This sad vicissitude of things.[4]
> *Ib.* 15

I wish either my father or my mother, or indeed both of them, as they were in duty both equally bound to it, had minded what they were about when they begot me.
> *Tristram Shandy, bk. I* [1760], *ch.* 1

"Pray, my dear," quoth my mother, "have you not forgot to wind up the clock?" — "Good G—!" cried my father, making an exclamation, but taking care to moderate his voice at the same time — "Did ever woman, since the creation of the world, interrupt a man with such a silly question?"
> *Tristram Shandy, bk. I, ch.* 1

So long as a man rides his hobby-horse peaceably and quietly along the king's highway, and neither compels you or me to get up behind him — pray, sir, what have either you or I to do with it?
> *Ib.* 7

For every ten jokes, thou hast got an hundred enemies.
> *Ib.* 12

He was within a few hours of giving his enemies the slip forever.
> *Ib.*

Whistled up to London, upon a Tom Fool's errand.
> *Ib.* 16

'Tis known by the name of perseverance in a good cause — and of obstinacy in a bad one.
> *Ib.* 17

Persuasion hung upon his lips.
> *Ib.* 19

Digressions, incontestably, are the sunshine — they are the life, the soul of reading; take them out of this book for instance — you might as well take the book along with them.
> *Ib.* 22

The history of a soldier's wound beguiles the pain of it.
> *Ib.* 25

The desire of knowledge, like the thirst of riches, increases ever with the acquisition of it.
> *Ib. II* [1760], *ch.* 3

Writing, when properly managed (as you may be sure I think mine is), is but a different name for conversation.
> *Ib.* 11

Go, poor devil, get thee gone! Why should I hurt thee? This world surely is wide enough to hold both thee and me.[1]
> *Ib.* 12

That's another story,[2] replied my father.
> *Ib.* 17

---

[1] See Jane Elliott, p. 446b.

[2] Mes pensées sont mes catins.

[3] The witty retort thought up after the conversation is finished and one is on one's way downstairs.

[4] See Bacon, p. 209b.
Revolves the sad vicissitude of things. — REV. RICHARD GIFFORD [1725–1807], *Contemplation*

[1] Uncle Toby to the fly.

[2] But that is another story. — KIPLING, *Plain Tales from the Hills* [1888], *Three and — An Extra*

Trust that man in nothing who has not a conscience in everything.
Tristram Shandy, bk. II, ch. 17

Good — bad — indifferent.
Ib. III [1761–1762], *ch.* 2

"Our armies swore terribly in Flanders," cried my uncle Toby — "but nothing to this." *Ib.* 11

Of all the cants which are canted in this canting world, though the cant of hypocrites may be the worst, the cant of criticism is the most tormenting!
Ib. 12

'Twould be as much as my life was worth. *Ib.* 20

One of the two horns of my dilemma. *Ib. IV* [1761–1762], *ch.* 26

The feather put into his cap of having been abroad. *Ib.* 31

Now or never was the time. *Ib.*

There is a Northwest Passage to the intellectual world.
Ib. V [1761–1762], *ch.* 42

The Accusing Spirit, which flew up to heaven's chancery with the oath, blushed as he gave it in; and the Recording Angel, as he wrote it down, dropped a tear upon the word and blotted it out forever.[1]
Ib. VI [1761–1762], *ch.* 8

A man should know something of his own country, too, before he goes abroad. *Ib. VII* [1765], *ch.* 2

Ho! 'tis the time of salads. *Ib.* 17

L — d! said my mother, what is all this story about? — A Cock and a Bull, said Yorick. *Ib. IX* [1767], *ch.* 33

They order, said I, this matter better in France.
A Sentimental Journey [1768],
l. 1

I pity the man who can travel from

Dan to Beersheba and cry, 'Tis all barren!
A Sentimental Journey. In the Street, Calais

Tant pis and *tant mieux*, being two of the great hinges in French conversation, a stranger would do well to set himself right in the use of them before he gets to Paris. *Ib. Montreuil*

Hail, ye small, sweet courtesies of life! for smooth do ye make the road of it. *Ib. The Pulse, Paris*

God tempers the wind, said Maria, to the shorn lamb.[1] *Ib. Maria*

CHRISTIAN FÜRCHTEGOTT GELLERT
1715–1769

Live as you will have wished to have lived when you are dying.[2]
Of Death, st. 2

CLAUDE ADRIEN HELVÉTIUS
1715–1771

Truth is a torch that gleams through the fog without dispelling it.
De l'Esprit [1758],[3] *preface*

What makes men happy is liking what they have to do. This is a principle on which society is not founded. *Ib.*

We don't call a man mad who believes that he eats God, but we do the one who says he is Jesus Christ. *Ib.*

LUC DE CLAPIERS, MARQUIS DE VAUVENARGUES
1715–1747

Great thoughts come from the heart.
Réflexions et Maximes, [*c.* 1747]
no. 127

[1] See Henri Estienne, p. 188b.
[2] See Jonathan Edwards, p. 420b.
[3] Voltaire, when he read *De l'Esprit*, wrote the author: "Your book is dictated by the soundest reason. You had better get out of France as quickly as you can." The book was condemned by the *parlement* and burned.

[1] But sad as angels for the good man's sin,
Weep to record, and blush to give it in.
CAMPBELL, *Pleasures of Hope* [1799],
pt. II, l. 357

Lazy people are always looking for something to do.
Réflexions et Maximes, no. 458

The things we know best are those we have not learned. *Ib. 479*

WILLIAM WHITEHEAD
1715–1785

Yes, I'm in love, I feel it now
And Caelia has undone me;
And yet I swear I can't tell how
The pleasing plague stole on me.
The Je ne sçay quoi song

An old tale which every schoolboy knows.
The Roman Father, prologue

DAVID GARRICK
1716–1779

Let others hail the rising sun:
I bow to that whose course is run.[1]
On the Death of Mr. Pelham

Heart of oak are our ships,
Heart of oak are our men:
 We always are ready;
 Steady, boys, steady;
We'll fight, and we'll conquer again and again.
Heart of Oak [c. 1770]

Here lies Nolly Goldsmith, for shortness called Noll,
Who wrote like an angel, but talk'd like poor Poll.
Impromptu epitaph on Goldsmith

THOMAS GRAY
1716–1771

Ye distant spires, ye antique towers,
That crown the wat'ry glade.
On a Distant Prospect of Eton College [1742], st. 1

Still as they run they look behind,
They hear a voice in every wind,
And snatch a fearful joy. *Ib. st. 4*

Alas, regardless of their doom,
The little victims play!

[1] See Pompey, p. 112a.

No sense have they of ills to come,
Nor care beyond today.
On a Distant Prospect of Eton College, st. 6

Grim-visag'd comfortless Despair.
Ib. st. 7

To each his suff'rings: all are men,
Condemn'd alike to groan,
The tender for another's pain,
Th' unfeeling for his own.
Yet ah! why should they know their fate,
Since sorrow never comes too late,
And happiness too swiftly flies?
Thought would destroy their paradise.
No more; where ignorance is bliss,
'Tis folly to be wise.[1] *Ib. st. 10*

Daughter of Jove, relentless power,
Thou tamer of the human breast,
Whose iron scourge and tort'ring hour
The bad affright, afflict the best!
Hymn to Adversity [1742], st. 1

What sorrow was, thou bad'st her know,
And from her own she learn'd to melt at others' woe. *Ib. st. 2*

What female heart can gold despise?
What cat's averse to fish?
On the Death of a Favorite Cat [1747], st. 4

A fav'rite has no friend! *Ib. st. 6*

As sickly plants betray a niggard earth,
Whose barren bosom starves her gen'rous birth.
The Alliance of Education and Government [c. 1748], l. 1

The social smile, the sympathetic tear.
Ib. l. 37

When love could teach a monarch to be wise,
And gospel-light first dawn'd from Bullen's eyes.[2] *Ib. l. 108*

The curfew tolls the knell of parting day,

[1] See *Ecclesiastes 1:18*, p. 27b.
[2] The monarch is Henry VIII; Anne Boleyn's name is here spelled (as it is in Shakespeare's *Henry VIII*) as it is pronounced.

The lowing herd wind slowly o'er the lea,
The plowman homeward plods his weary way,
And leaves the world to darkness and to me.
Elegy Written in a Country Churchyard [1750], *st.* 1

Now fades the glimmering landscape on the sight,
And all the air a solemn stillness holds,
Save where the beetle wheels his droning flight,
And drowsy tinklings lull the distant folds.   *Ib. st. 2*

Save that from yonder ivy-mantled tow'r
The moping owl does to the moon complain.   *Ib. st. 3*

Each in his narrow cell forever laid,
The rude forefathers of the hamlet sleep.   *Ib. st. 4*

The breezy call of incense-breathing Morn.   *Ib. st. 5*

For them no more the blazing hearth shall burn,
Or busy housewife ply her evening care.[1]   *Ib. st. 6*

Let not ambition mock their useful toil,
Their homely joys, and destiny obscure;
Nor grandeur hear with a disdainful smile,
The short and simple annals of the poor.   *Ib. st. 8*

The boast of heraldry, the pomp of pow'r,
And all that beauty, all that wealth e'er gave,
Awaits alike the inevitable hour:
The paths of glory lead but to the grave.   *Ib. st. 9*

Where thro' the long-drawn aisle and fretted vault
The pealing anthem swells the note of praise.   *Ib. st. 10*

Can storied urn, or animated bust
Back to its mansion call the fleeting breath?

[1] See Homer, p. 63a.

Can honor's voice provoke the silent dust,
Or flatt'ry soothe the dull cold ear of death?
Elegy Written in a Country Churchyard, st. 11

Hands, that the rod of empire might have sway'd,
Or wak'd to ecstasy the living lyre.   *Ib. st. 12*

But knowledge to their eyes her ample page
Rich with the spoils of time did ne'er unroll; [1]
Chill penury repress'd their noble rage,
And froze the genial current of the soul.   *Ib. st. 13*

Full many a gem of purest ray serene,[2]
The dark unfathom'd caves of ocean bear:
Full many a flower is born to blush unseen,
And waste its sweetness on the desert air.   *Ib. st. 14*

Some village Hampden, that with dauntless breast
The little tyrant of his fields withstood;
Some mute inglorious Milton here may rest,
Some Cromwell guiltless of his country's blood.   *Ib. st. 15*

To scatter plenty o'er a smiling land,
And read their hist'ry in a nation's eyes.   *Ib. st. 16*

Forbade to wade through slaughter to a throne,
And shut the gates of mercy on mankind.   *Ib. st. 17*

Far from the madding crowd's ignoble strife,
Their sober wishes never learn'd to stray;
Along the cool sequester'd vale of life

[1] See Sir Thomas Browne, p. 329b.
[2] Every single phrase is a string of perfect gems, of purest ray serene, strung together on a loose golden thread. — GEORGE DU MAURIER, *Trilby, pt. VI* [1894]
See Joseph Hall, p. 309b.

They kept the noiseless tenor of their way.[1]
> *Elegy Written in a Country Churchyard, st. 19*

Implores the passing tribute of a sigh.
> *Ib. st. 20*

For who to dumb forgetfulness a prey,
This pleasing anxious being e'er resign'd,
Left the warm precincts of the cheerful day,
Nor cast one longing ling'ring look behind?
> *Ib. st. 22*

E'en from the tomb the voice of nature cries,
E'en in our ashes live their wonted fires.[2]
> *Ib. st. 23*

Mindful of th' unhonor'd dead.
> *Ib. st. 24*

Here rests his head upon the lap of Earth
A youth to fortune and to fame unknown.
Fair Science frown'd not on his humble birth,
And Melancholy mark'd him for her own.[3]
> *Ib. The Epitaph, st. 1*

Large was his bounty, and his soul sincere,
Heav'n did a recompense as largely send:
He gave to mis'ry all he had, a tear,
He gained from Heav'n ('twas all he wish'd) a friend.
> *Ib. st. 2*

No farther seek his merits to disclose,
Or draw his frailties from their dread abode,
(There they alike in trembling hope repose,)
The bosom of his Father and his God.
> *Ib. st. 3*

The meanest floweret of the vale,
The simplest note that swells the gale,
The common sun, the air, the skies,

---

[1]   In sober state,
Through the sequestered vale of rural life,
The venerable patriarch guileless held
The tenor of his way.
        Porteus [1731–1808], *Death, l. 108*
[2] See Chaucer, p. 167b.
[3] See Walton, p. 325b.

To him are opening paradise.
> *Ode on the Pleasure Arising from Vicissitude* [1754], *l. 49*

O'er her warm cheek and rising bosom move
The bloom of young Desire and purple light of Love.
> *The Progress of Poesy* [1754], I. 3, *l. 16*

Far from the sun and summer-gale,
In thy green lap was Nature's Darling [1] laid.
> *Ib. III. 1, l. 1*

Or ope the sacred source of sympathetic tears.
> *Ib. l. 12*

He [2] pass'd the flaming bounds of place and time:
The living throne, the sapphire-blaze,
Where angels tremble, while they gaze,
He saw; but blasted with excess of light,
Closed his eyes in endless night.
> *Ib. 2, l. 4*

Thoughts that breathe, and words that burn.
> *Ib. 3, l. 4*

Ruin seize thee, ruthless King!
Confusion on thy banners wait,
Though fann'd by Conquest's crimson wing
They mock the air with idle state.
> *The Bard* [1757], I. 1, *l. 1*

Weave the warp, and weave the woof,
The winding-sheet of Edward's race.
Give ample room and verge enough,
The characters of hell to trace.
> *Ib. II. 1, l. 1*

Fair laughs the morn, and soft the zephyr blows,
While proudly riding o'er the azure realm
In gallant trim the gilded vessel goes;
Youth on the prow, and Pleasure at the helm;
Regardless of the sweeping whirlwind's sway,
That, hush'd in grim repose, expects his evening prey.
> *Ib. 2, l. 9*

---

[1] Shakespeare.
[2] Milton.

Visions of glory, spare my aching sight,
Ye unborn ages, crowd not on my soul!
The Bard III. 1, l. 11

And truth severe, by fairy fiction drest.
Ib. 3, l. 3

Now my weary lips I close;
Leave me, leave me to repose!
Descent of Odin [1761], *l.* 71

Iron sleet of arrowy shower
Hurtles in the darken'd air.
The Fatal Sisters [1761]

Too poor for a bribe, and too proud to
importune,
He had not the method of making a
fortune.
On His Own Character [1761]

I shall be but a shrimp of an author.
Letter to Horace Walpole
[*February* 25, 1768]

Sweet is the breath of vernal shower,
The bee's collected treasures sweet,
Sweet music's melting fall, but sweeter
yet
The still small voice [1] of gratitude.
Ode for Music [1769]

HORACE WALPOLE
1717–1797

Our supreme governors, the mob.
Letters. To Horace Mann
[*September* 7, 1743]

Every drop of ink in my pen ran
cold.
Ib. To George Montagu
[*July* 3, 1752]

It is charming to totter into vogue.
Ib. To G. A. Selwyn
[*December* 2, 1765]

The next Augustan age will dawn on
the other side of the Atlantic. There
will, perhaps, be a Thucydides at Boston, a Xenophon at New York, and, in
time, a Virgil at Mexico, and a Newton
at Peru. At last, some curious traveler
from Lima will visit England and give a
description of the ruins of St. Paul's,

like the editions of Balbec and Pal-
myra.[1]
Ib. To Mann [*November* 24,
1774]

This world is a comedy to those that
think, a tragedy to those that feel.
*Ib. To the Countess of Upper
Ossory* [*August* 16, 1776]

Prognostics do not always prove
prophecies — at least the wisest prophets make sure of the event first.
Ib. To Thomas Walpole
[*February* 19, 1785]

All his [Sir Joshua Reynolds's] own
geese are swans, as the swans of others
are geese. *Ib.* [*December* 1, 1786]

JOHANN ELIAS SCHLEGEL
1719–1749

Busy leisure.
Der Geschäftige Müssiggänger
[1743]

SAMUEL FOOTE
1720–1777

Born in a cellar . . . and living in a
garret.[2] *The Author, act II*

Matt Minikin won't set fire to the
Thames though he lives near the
Bridge.
Trip to Calais [1776]

So she went into the garden to cut a
cabbage leaf to make an apple pie; and
at the same time a great she-bear, coming up the street, pops its head into the
shop. "What! no soap?" So he died,
and she very imprudently married the
barber; and there were present the Pic-
ninnies, and the Joblillies, and the
Garyalies, and the grand Panjandrum
himself, with the little round button at
top, and they all fell to playing the
game of catch as catch can, till the

---

[1] See *I Kings 19:12*, p. 13b.

[1] See Macaulay, p. 595b.
[2] Born in the garret, in the kitchen bred. —
BYRON, *A Sketch* [1816]

gunpowder ran out at the heels of their boots.

> *Nonsense written to test the boasted memory of Charles Macklin, The Quarterly Review [1854]. Credited to Foote by* MARIA EDGEWORTH, *Harry and Lucy Concluded, vol. II*

DENNIS O'KELLY
1720–1787

It will be Eclipse first, the rest no-where.

> *Declaration at Epsom [May 3, 1769] when the great race horse Eclipse was to run his first race. Annals of Sporting, vol. II, p. 271*

JOHN WOOLMAN
1720–1772

Though I felt uneasy at the thought of writing an instrument of slavery . . . through weakness I gave way and wrote it; but . . . said before my master and the Friend that I believed slave-keeping to be a practice inconsistent with the Christian religion. This, in some degree, abated my uneasiness; yet . . . I should have been clearer if I had desired to be excused from it, as a thing against my conscience.

> *Journal [published 1774]*

WILLIAM COLLINS
1721–1759

How sleep the brave, who sink to rest,
By all their country's wishes bless'd!

> *Ode Written in the Year 1746,*
> *st. 1*

By fairy hands their knell is rung,
By forms unseen their dirge is sung;
There Honor comes, a pilgrim gray,
To bless the turf that wraps their clay,
And Freedom shall awhile repair,
To dwell a weeping hermit there!

> *Ib. st. 2*

In numbers warmly pure and sweetly strong.

> *Ode to Simplicity [1747], st. 1*

If aught of oaten stop or pastoral song
May hope, O pensive Eve, to soothe thine ear.

> *Ode to Evening [1747], l. 1*

Now air is hush'd, save where the weak-ey'd bat,
With short shrill shriek flits by on leathern wing,
Or where the beetle winds
His small but sullen horn. *Ib. l. 9*

'Twas sad by fits, by starts 'twas wild.

> *The Passions [1747], l. 28*

With eyes uprais'd, as one inspir'd,
Pale Melancholy sate retir'd,
And from her wild sequester'd seat,
In notes by distance made more sweet,
Pour'd through the mellow horn her pensive soul *Ib. l. 57*

In hollow murmurs died away.

> *Ib. l. 68*

O Music, sphere-descended maid,
Friend of Pleasure, Wisdom's aid!

> *Ib. l. 95*

JEANNE, MARQUISE DE POMPADOUR
1721–1764

Après nous le déluge [After us the deluge].[1]

> *Reputed reply to Louis XV [November 5, 1757] after the defeat of the French and Austrian armies by Frederick the Great in the battle of Rossbach*

TOBIAS SMOLLETT
1721–1771

He was formed for the ruin of our sex.

> *Roderick Random [1748], ch. 22*

[1] The attribution to Mme. de Pompadour is made by DESPRÉS, *Mémoires de Madame de Hausset;* also by SAINTE-BEUVE and LA TOUR. LAROUSSE, *Fleurs Historiques,* attributes the saying to the King. It was original with neither, for it is an old French proverb.

SAMUEL ADAMS
1722–1803

Let us contemplate our forefathers, and posterity, and resolve to maintain the rights bequeathed to us from the former, for the sake of the latter. The necessity of the times, more than ever, calls for our utmost circumspection, deliberation, fortitude and perseverance. Let us remember that "if we suffer tamely a lawless attack upon our liberty, we encourage it, and involve others in our doom." It is a very serious consideration . . . that millions yet unborn may be the miserable sharers of the event. *Speech* [**1771**]

What a glorious morning for America! [1]
> *Upon hearing the gunfire at Lexington* [*April* 19, 1775]

Driven from every other corner of the earth, freedom of thought and the right of private judgment in matters of conscience direct their course to this happy country as their last asylum.[2]
> *Speech, Philadelphia* [*August* 1, 1776]

CHRISTOPHER SMART
1722–1771

Tell them I Am, Jehovah said
To Moses; while earth heard in dread,
  And smitten to the heart,
At once above, beneath, around,
All nature, without voice or sound,
  Replied, O Lord, Thou art.
> *A Song to David* [1763], *st. 40*

For adoration all the ranks
Of angels yield eternal thanks,
  And David in the midst.
> *Ib. st. 51*

Where ask is have, where seek is find,
Where knock is open wide.[3]
> *Ib. st. 77*

---

[1] The phrase was adopted by the town of Lexington as a legend for the town seal.
[2] See Thomas Paine, p. 466b.
[3] See *Matthew 7:7*, p. 41a.

And now the matchless deed's achiev'd,
Determin'd, dar'd, and done.
> *A Song to David, st. 86*

For I bless God in the libraries of the learned and for all the booksellers in the world.
> *Jubilate Agno, frag. B1, l. 79*

Let James rejoice with the Skuttle-Fish who foils his foe by the effusion of his ink.   *Ib. l. 125*

For the Mouse (mus) prevails in Latin.
For   Edi-mus,   bibi-mus,   vivi-mus, oremus.   *Ib. frag. B2, l. 638*

For I will consider my Cat Jeoffry,
For he is the servant of the Living God, duly and daily serving him.
> *Ib. l. 697*

For he counteracts the Devil, who is Death, by brisking about the life.
> *Ib. l. 722*

SIR WILLIAM BLACKSTONE
1723–1780

Man was formed for society.[1]
> *Commentaries* [1765–1769], *introduction*

The royal navy of England hath ever been its greatest defense and ornament; it is its ancient and natural strength; the floating bulwark of our island.
> *Ib. bk. I, ch. 13*

Time whereof the memory of man runneth not to the contrary.[2]   *Ib. 18*

That the king can do no wrong is a necessary and fundamental principle of the English constitution.   *Ib. III, 17*

It is better that ten guilty persons escape than one innocent suffer.[3]
> *Ib. IV, 27*

---

[1] See Spinoza, p. 374a.
[2] The favorite phrase of their law is "a custom whereof the memory of man runneth not back to the contrary." — EMERSON, *English Traits* [1856]
[3] See Voltaire, p. 417a.

ADAM SMITH
1723–1790

To found a great empire for the sole purpose of raising up a people of customers, may at first sight appear a project fit only for a nation of shopkeepers. It is, however, a project altogether unfit for a nation of shopkeepers; but extremely fit for a nation whose Government is influenced by shopkeepers.[1]

> *Wealth of Nations* [1776],
> *vol. II, bk. IV, ch. 7, pt.* 3

JOHN HOME
1724–1808

In the first days
Of my distracting grief, I found myself
As women wish to be who love their lords.

> *Douglas* [1756], *act I, sc.* 1

I'll woo her as the lion woos his brides.

> *Ib.*

My name is Norval; on the Grampian hills
My father feeds his flocks; a frugal swain,
Whose constant cares were to increase his store,
And keep his only son, myself, at home.

> *Ib. III,* 1

Like Douglas conquer, or like Douglas die.   *Ib. V,* 1

IMMANUEL KANT
1724–1804

Two things fill the mind with ever-increasing wonder and awe, the more often and the more intensely the mind of thought is drawn to them: the starry heavens above me and the moral law within me.

> *Critique of Pure Reason* [1781],
> *conclusion*

Morality is not properly the doctrine of how we may make ourselves happy,

but how we may make ourselves worthy of happiness.

> *Critique of Practical Reason* [1788]

There is . . . only a single categorical imperative and it is this: Act only on that maxim through which you can at the same time will that it should become a universal law.

> *The Metaphysic of Morals* [1]
> [1797], *ch.* 11

FRIEDRICH GOTTLIEB KLOPSTOCK
1724–1803

Worth the sweat of noblemen.

> *Lake Zurich* [1750]

ROBERT, LORD CLIVE
1725–1774

By God, Mr. Chairman, at this moment I stand astonished at my own moderation!

> *Reply During Parliamentary Inquiry* [1773]

LOGAN, MINGO CHIEF
1725–1780

I appeal to any white man to say if he ever entered Logan's cabin hungry and he gave him not meat; if ever he came cold and naked and he clothed him not? [2]

> *Message to Lord Dunmore, Governor of Virginia* [*November 11, 1774*]. *From* THOMAS JEFFERSON, *Notes on Virginia*

GEORGE MASON
1725–1792

That all men are by nature equally free and independent, and have certain inherent rights, of which, when they enter into a state of society, they can-

---

[1] See Josiah Tucker, p. 436b.

[1] Translated by A. D. LINDSAY.
Categorical imperative. — KANT, *Fundamental Principles of Ethics* [*1785*], *Part* 2
[2] See *Matthew 25:35-36*, p. 44a.

not by any compact deprive or divest their posterity; namely, the enjoyment of life and liberty, with the means of acquiring and possessing property, and pursuing and obtaining happiness and safety.

Virginia Bill of Rights [1]
[June 12, 1776], art. 1

Government is, or ought to be instituted for the common benefit, protection, and security of the people, nation, or community; of all the various modes and forms of government, that is best which is capable of producing the greatest degree of happiness and safety, and is most effectually secured against the danger of maladministration.[2]

Ib. 3

The freedom of the press is one of the great bulwarks of liberty, and can never be restrained but by despotic governments.   *Ib. 12*

JOHN NEWTON
1725–1807

Glorious things of thee are spoken,
Zion, city of our God.
Olney Hymns [1779], *Glorious
Things*

JAMES OTIS
1725–1783

An act against the Constitution is void; an act against natural equity is void.

*Argument Against the Writs of
Assistance* [3] *[1761]*

Taxation without representation is tyranny.[4]   *Attributed* [1763]

---

[1] The parent of all American bills of rights. — SAMUEL ELIOT MORISON, *The Oxford History of the American People* [1965]
See Patrick Henry, p. 465b. Henry drafted Article 16 on religious freedom.
[2] See Jefferson, p. 472b–473a.
[3] [Otis arguing] was a flame of fire . . . the seeds of patriots and heroes were then and there sown. — JOHN ADAMS, *Works* [1850–1856], vol. II, *p. 522*
[4] This maxim was the guide and watchword of all the friends of liberty. Otis actually said: No parts of His Majesty's dominions can be

Ubi libertas ibi patria [Where liberty is, there is my country].   *His motto*

JAMES HUTTON
1726–1797

The result, therefore, of this physical inquiry [into the age of the earth] is, that we find no vestige of a beginning — no prospect of an end.
The Theory of the Earth [1795]

WILLIAM PRESCOTT
1726–1795

Don't one of you fire until you see the whites of their eyes.[1]
At Bunker Hill [June 17, 1775]

JANE ELLIOT
1727–1805

I've heard them lilting, at the ewe milk-
ing,
Lasses a' lilting, before dawn of day;
But now they are moaning, on ilka
green loaning;
The flowers of the forest are a' wede
away.
The Flowers of the Forest [2]

ANNE ROBERT JACQUES TURGOT, BARON DE L'AULNE
1727–1781

They [the Americans] are the hope of this world. They may become its model.[3]

*Letter to Dr. Richard Price
[March 22, 1778]*

---

taxed without their consent. — *Rights of the Colonies* [1764], *p. 64.*
[1] Also attributed to ISRAEL PUTNAM [1718–1790].
See Frederick the Great, p. 435a.
Silent till you see the whites of their eyes. — PRINCE CHARLES OF PRUSSIA, at Jagerndorf, May 23, 1745
[2] Sir Walter Scott in *Minstrelsy of the Scottish Border* says that *The Flowers of the Forest* was written to an ancient tune and that the last line, the refrain, is indisputably ancient. The air was also used for verses by Alison Cockburn. See p. 437a.
[3] This is the origin of "America the hope of the world."

JOHN WILKES
1727–1797

Earl of Sandwich: 'Pon my honor, Wilkes, I don't know whether you'll die on the gallows or of the pox.

Wilkes: That must depend, my Lord, upon whether I first embrace your Lordship's principles, or your Lordship's mistresses.

> From Sir Charles Petrie, *The Four Georges* [1935]

OLIVER GOLDSMITH
1728–1774

One writer, for instance, excels at a plan or a title page, another works away the body of the book, and a third is a dab at an index.

> *The Bee* [1759], *no. 1*

As writers become more numerous, it is natural for readers to become more indolent.

> *Ib. 175. Upon Unfortunate Merit*

Good people all, with one accord,
Lament for Madame Blaize,
Who never wanted a good word —
From those who spoke her praise.

> *Ib. Elegy on Mrs. Mary Blaize* [1759], *st. 1*

A nightcap deck'd his brows instead of bay,
A cap by night — a stocking all the day!

> *Description of an Author's Bedchamber* [1760]

That strain once more; it bids remembrance rise.

> *The Captivity, An Oratorio* [1764], *act I*

O Memory! thou fond deceiver. *Ib.*

To the last moment of his breath
On hope the wretch relies;
And e'en the pang preceding death
Bids expectation rise.[1] *Ib. II*

Hope, like the gleaming taper's light,
Adorns and cheers our way;

[1] See Terence, p. 108b; Cicero, p. 111a; and Gay, p. 401b.

And still, as darker grows the night,
Emits a brighter ray.

> *The Captivity, An Oratorio,* *act II*

Remote, unfriended, melancholy, slow,
Or by the lazy Scheldt, or wandering Po. *The Traveller* [1764], *l. 1*

Where'er I roam, whatever realms to see,
My heart untravel'd fondly turns to thee;
Still to my brother turns with ceaseless pain,
And drags at each remove a lengthening chain. *Ib. l. 7*

Such is the patriot's boast, where'er we roam,
His first, best country ever is, at home.
 Ib. l. 73

Where wealth and freedom reign contentment fails,
And honor sinks where commerce long prevails. *Ib. l. 91*

Man seems the only growth that dwindles here.[1] *Ib. l. 126*

But winter ling'ring chills the lap of May. *Ib. l. 172*

They please, are pleas'd, they give to get esteem,
Till, seeming blest, they grow to what they seem.[2] *Ib. l. 265*

To men of other minds my fancy flies,
Embosom'd in the deep where Holland lies.
Methinks her patient sons before me stand,
Where the broad ocean leans against the land. *Ib. l. 281*

Pride in their port, defiance in their eye,
I see the lords of human kind[3] pass by.
 Ib. l. 327

The land of scholars, and the nurse of arms.[4] *Ib. l. 356*

[1] Italy.
[2] The character of the French.
[3] The British.
[4] England.

For just experience tells; in every soil,
That those that think must govern
those that toil.
                    The Traveller, l. 371

Laws grind the poor,[1] and rich men rule
the law.   *Ib. l. 386*

Vain, very vain, my weary search to
find
That bliss which only centers in the
mind.   *Ib. l. 423*

A book may be very amusing with
numerous errors, or it may be very dull
without a single absurdity.
          The Vicar of Wakefield [1766],
                                    preface

I . . . chose my wife, as she did her
wedding gown, not for a fine glossy surface, but such qualities as would wear
well.   *Ib. ch. 1*

We sometimes had those little rubs
which Providence sends to enhance the
value of its favors.   *Ib.*

Handsome is that handsome does.[2]
                                    Ib.

That virtue which requires to be ever
guarded is scarce worth the sentinel.
                                    Ib. 5

I find you want me to furnish you
with argument and intellects too.
                                    Ib. 7

Man wants but little here below,
Nor wants that little long.[3]
          *Ib. 8 [The Hermit (Edwin and
                    Angelina), st. 8]*

She was all of a muck of sweat.
                                    Ib. 9

They would talk of nothing but high
life, and high-lived company, with
other fashionable topics, such as pictures, taste, Shakespeare, and the musical glasses.[4]   *Ib.*

[1] See *Isaiah 3:15*, p. 30a.
[2] See Chaucer, p. 168b.
[3] See Edward Young, p. 339a, and Oliver
Wendell Holmes, p. 634a.
[4] "Shall we talk about Shakespeare?" he
asked sarcastically. "Or the musical glasses?"
— ALDOUS HUXLEY, *Point Counter Point* [1928],
ch. 21

Conscience is a coward, and those
faults it has not strength enough to
prevent it seldom has justice enough to
accuse.
          The Vicar of Wakefield, ch. 13

The naked every day he clad
When he put on his clothes.
          *Ib. 17. An Elegy on the Death
                    of a Mad Dog, st. 3*

And in that town a dog was found,
As many dogs there be,
Both mongrel, puppy, whelp, and
          hound,
And curs of low degree.   *Ib. st. 4*

The dog, to gain some private ends,
Went mad, and bit the man.
                                    Ib. st. 5

The man recovered of the bite,
The dog it was that died.   *Ib. st. 8*

When lovely woman stoops to folly,
And finds too late that men betray,
What charm can soothe her melan-
          choly?
What art can wash her guilt away? [1]
          Ib. 29. Song, st. 1

The only art her guilt to cover,
To hide her shame from every eye,
To give repentance to her lover,
And wring his bosom, is — to die.
                                    Ib. st. 2

This same philosophy is a good horse
in the stable, but an arrant jade on a
journey.[2]
          The Good-Natur'd Man [1768],
                                    act I

He calls his extravagance, generosity;
and his trusting everybody, universal
benevolence.   *Ib.*

All his faults are such that one loves
him still the better for them.   *Ib.*

Friendship is a disinterested commerce between equals; love, an abject
intercourse between tyrants and slaves.
                                    Ib.

Silence gives consent.   *Ib. II*

[1] See T. S. Eliot, p. 1002b.
[2] See La Rochefoucauld, p. 355a.

Measures, not men, have always been my mark.[1]

> *The Good-Natur'd Man,*
> *act II*

Sweet Auburn! loveliest village of the plain.

> *The Deserted Village* [1770], *l. 1*

The bashful virgin's sidelong looks of love,
The matron's glance that would those looks reprove.   *Ib. l. 29*

Ill fares the land, to hastening ills a prey,
Where wealth accumulates, and men decay;
Princes and lords may flourish, or may fade;
A breath can make them, as a breath has made;
But a bold peasantry, their country's pride,
When once destroy'd, can never be supplied.   *Ib. l. 51*

His best companions, innocence and health;
And his best riches, ignorance of wealth.   *Ib. l. 61*

How happy he who crowns in shades like these,
A youth of labor with an age of ease.   *Ib. l. 99*

Bends to the grave with unperceiv'd decay,
While resignation gently slopes the way;
And, all his prospects brightening to the last,
His heaven commences ere the world be past.   *Ib. l. 109*

The watchdog's voice that bay'd the whispering wind,
And the loud laugh that spoke the vacant mind.[2]   *Ib. l. 121*

---

[1] See Chesterfield, p. 415a, and Burke, p. 452a.

[2] Frequent and loud laughter is the characteristic of folly and ill manners: it is the manner in which the mob express their silly joy at silly things, and they call it being merry. In my mind there is nothing so illiberal

A man he was to all the country dear,
And passing rich with forty pounds a year.

> *The Deserted Village, l. 141*

Careless their merits or their faults to scan,
His pity gave ere charity began.
Thus to relieve the wretched was his pride,
And e'en his failings lean'd to Virtue's side.   *Ib. l. 161*

And, as a bird each fond endearment tries
To tempt its new-fledg'd offspring to the skies,
He tried each art, reprov'd each dull delay,
Allur'd to brighter worlds, and led the way.   *Ib. l. 167*

Truth from his lips prevail'd with double sway,
And fools, who came to scoff, remain'd to pray.[1]   *Ib. l. 179*

Even children follow'd with endearing wile,
And pluck'd his gown, to share the good man's smile.   *Ib. l. 183*

A man severe he was, and stern to view;
I knew him well, and every truant knew:
Well had the boding tremblers learn'd to trace
The day's disasters in his morning face;
Full well they laugh'd with counterfeited glee,
At all his jokes, for many a joke had he;
Full well the busy whisper, circling round,
Convey'd the dismal tidings when he frown'd;
Yet he was kind; or if severe in aught,
The love he bore to learning was in fault;
The village all declar'd how much he knew;

---

and so ill-bred as audible laughter. — LORD CHESTERFIELD, *Letters* [March 9, 1748]
See *Ecclesiastes* 7:6, p. 28a.

[1] See Dryden, p. 470b.

'Twas certain he could write, and cipher too.
>> *The Deserted Village, l.* 197

In arguing too, the parson own'd his skill,
For e'en though vanquish'd, he could argue still;
While words of learned length, and thundering sound
Amaz'd the gazing rustics rang'd around;
And still they gaz'd, and still the wonder grew,
That one small head could carry all he knew.   *Ib. l.* 211

Where village statesmen talk'd with looks profound,
And news much older than their ale went round.   *Ib. l.* 223

The whitewash'd wall, the nicely sanded floor,
The varnish'd clock that click'd behind the door;
The chest contriv'd a double debt to pay,
A bed by night, a chest of drawers by day.[1]   *Ib. l.* 227

The twelve good rules, the royal game of goose.[2]   *Ib. l.* 232

To me more dear, congenial to my heart,
One native charm, than all the gloss of art.   *Ib. l.* 253

And, ev'n while fashion's brightest arts decoy,
The heart distrusting asks, if this be joy.   *Ib. l.* 263

[1] See *Description of an Author's Bedchamber,* p. 447a.

[2] The twelve good rules were ascribed to Charles I: (1) Urge no healths; (2) profane no divine ordinances; (3) touch no state matters; (4) reveal no secrets; (5) pick no quarrels; (6) make no comparisons; (7) maintain no ill opinions; (8) keep no bad company; (9) encourage no vice; (10) make no long meals; (11) repeat no grievances; (12) lay no wagers.

Goose. A game played with counters on a board divided into compartments, in some of which a goose was depicted. — *Oxford English Dictionary*

Her modest looks the cottage might adorn,
Sweet as the primrose peeps beneath the thorn.
>> *The Deserted Village, l.* 329

In all the silent manliness of grief.
>> *Ib. l.* 384

Thou source of all my bliss, and all my woe,
That found'st me poor at first, and keep'st me so.   *Ib. l.* 413

In my time, the follies of the town crept slowly among us, but now they travel faster than a stagecoach.
>> *She Stoops to Conquer* [1775], *act I*

I love everything that's old: old friends, old times, old manners, old books, old wines.[1]   *Ib.*

The very pink of perfection.   *Ib.*

Let schoolmasters puzzle their brain,
With grammar, and nonsense, and learning;
Good liquor, I stoutly maintain,
Gives genius a better discerning.
>> *Ib.*

I'll be with you in the squeezing of a lemon.   *Ib.*

A modest woman, dressed out in all her finery, is the most tremendous object of the whole creation.   *Ib. II*

This is Liberty Hall, gentlemen.
>> *Ib.*

The first blow is half the battle.
>> *Ib.*

We are the boys
That fear no noise
Where the thundering cannons roar.
>> *Ib.*

They liked the book the better the more it made them cry.   *Ib.*

Ask me no questions, and I'll tell you no fibs.[2]   *Ib. III*

[1] See Bacon, p. 207b, and note.

[2] Them that asks no questions isn't told a lie. — KIPLING [1865–1936], *A Smuggler's Song,* st. 6

Our Garrick's a salad; for in him we see
Oil, vinegar, sugar, and saltness agree!
Retaliation [1774], *l. 11*

Here lies our good Edmund,[1] whose genius was such,
We scarcely can praise it, or blame it too much;
Who, born for the universe, narrow'd his mind,
And to party gave up what was meant for mankind . . .
Who, too deep for his hearers, still went on refining,
And thought of convincing, while they thought of dining;
Though equal to all things, for all things unfit;
Too nice for a statesman, too proud for a wit.   *Ib. l. 29*

His conduct still right, with his argument wrong.   *Ib. l. 46*

Here lies David Garrick, describe me, who can,
An abridgment of all that was pleasant in man.   *Ib. l. 93*

As a wit, if not first, in the very first line.   *Ib. l. 96*

On the stage he was natural, simple, affecting;
'Twas only that when he was off he was acting.   *Ib. l. 101*

He cast off his friends as a huntsman his pack,
For he knew when he pleas'd he could whistle them back.   *Ib. l. 107*

Who pepper'd the highest was surest to please.   *Ib. l. 112*

When they talk'd of their Raphaels, Correggios, and stuff,
He shifted his trumpet and only took snuff.[2]   *Ib. l. 145*

Such dainties to them, their health it might hurt;

[1] Edmund Burke.
[2] Sir Joshua Reynolds, who was exceedingly deaf.

It's like sending them ruffles, when wanting a shirt.[1]
The Haunch of Venison [1776]

There is no arguing with Johnson: for if his pistol misses fire, he knocks you down with the butt end of it.
From BOSWELL, *Life of Johnson* [1791] [*October 26, 1769*]

[To Dr. Johnson] If you were to make little fishes talk, they would talk like whales.   *Ib.* [*April 27, 1773*]

You may all go to pot.
Verses in reply to an invitation to dine at Dr. Baker's

JOHN STARK
1728–1822

My men, yonder are the Hessians. They were bought for seven pounds and ten pence a man. Are you worth more? Prove it. Tonight, the American flag floats from yonder hill or Molly Stark sleeps a widow!
Before the Battle of Bennington [*August 16, 1777*]

EDMUND BURKE[2]
1729–1797

The writers against religion, whilst they oppose every system, are wisely careful never to set up any of their own.
A Vindication of Natural Society [1756]

I am convinced that we have a degree of delight, and that no small one, in the real misfortunes and pains of others.[3]

On the Sublime and Beautiful [1756], *sec. 14*

[1] See Tom Brown, p. 386b.
[2] You could not stand five minutes with that man [Burke] beneath a shed while it rained, but you must be convinced you had been standing with the greatest man you had ever seen. — SAMUEL JOHNSON, *Johnsonian Miscellanies*, edited by G. B. Hill [1897], *vol. I, p. 290*
[3] See La Rochefoucauld, p. 356b.

Custom reconciles us to everything.[1]
*On the Sublime and
Beautiful, sec. 18*

There is, however, a limit at which
forbearance ceases to be a virtue.
*Observations on a Late Publication on the Present State of
the Nation* [1769]

The wisdom of our ancestors.[2]
Ib.

When bad men combine, the good
must associate; else they will fall one by
one, an unpitied sacrifice in a contemptible struggle.
*Thoughts on the Cause of the
Present Discontents* [April 23,
1770]

Of this stamp is the cant of, Not
men, but measures;[3] a sort of charm
by which many people get loose from
every honorable engagement.   *Ib.*

So to be patriots as not to forget we
are gentlemen.   *Ib.*

Public life is a situation of power and
energy; he trespasses against his duty
who sleeps upon his watch, as well as he
that goes over to the enemy.   *Ib.*

Reflect how you are to govern a people who think they ought to be free,
and think they are not. Your scheme
yields no revenue; it yields nothing but
discontent, disorder, disobedience; and
such is the state of America, that after
wading up to your eyes in blood, you
could only end just where you begun;
that is, to tax where no revenue is to be
found, to — my voice fails me; my inclination indeed carries me no farther
— all is confusion beyond it.
*First Speech on Conciliation
with America. American Taxation* [April 19, 1774]

[1] See Pushkin, p. 593b.
[2] *De Sapienta Veterum* [The Wisdom of the
Ancients]. — *Title of work* by FRANCIS BACON
[1609]. The phrase is also in Burke's *Discussion
on the Traitorous Correspondence Bill* [1793].
[3] See Chesterfield, p. 415a, and Goldsmith,
p. 449a.

Your representative owes you, not his
industry only, but his judgment; and he
betrays instead of serving you if he sacrifices it to your opinion.
Speech to the Electors of Bristol
[*November 3, 1774*]

I have in general no very exalted
opinion of the virtue of paper government.
*Second Speech on Conciliation
with America. The Thirteen
Resolutions* [*March 22, 1775*]

The concessions of the weak are the
concessions of fear.   *Ib.*

Young man, there is America
— which at this day serves for little
more than to amuse you with stories of
savage men and uncouth manners; yet
shall, before you taste of death, show
itself equal to the whole of that commerce which now attracts the envy of
the world.   *Ib.*

When we speak of the commerce
with our colonies, fiction lags after
truth; invention is unfruitful, and
imagination cold and barren.   *Ib.*

A people who are still, as it were, but
in the gristle, and not yet hardened into
the bone of manhood.   *Ib.*

Through a wise and salutary neglect
[of the colonies], a generous nature has
been suffered to take her own way to
perfection; when I reflect upon these
effects, when I see how profitable they
have been to us, I feel all the pride of
power sink and all presumption in the
wisdom of human contrivances melt
and die away within me. My rigor
relents. I pardon something to the spirit
of liberty.   *Ib.*

The use of force alone is but *temporary*. It may subdue for a moment; but
it does not remove the necessity of subduing again: and a nation is not governed, which is perpetually to be conquered.   *Ib.*

Nothing less will content me, than
whole America.   *Ib.*

Abstract liberty, like other mere abstractions, is not to be found.
Second Speech on Conciliation with America. The Thirteen Resolutions

The religion most prevalent in our northern colonies is a refinement on the principles of resistance: it is the dissidence of dissent, and the protestantism of the Protestant religion. ***Ib.***

In no country perhaps in the world is law so general a study [as in America]. . . . This study renders men acute, inquisitive, dexterous, prompt in attack, ready in defense, full of resources. . . . They augur misgovernment at a distance, and snuff the approach of tyranny in every tainted breeze. ***Ib.***

I do not know the method of drawing up an indictment against an' whole people. ***Ib.***

It is not, what a lawyer tells me I *may* do; but what humanity, reason, and justice, tell me I ought to do. ***Ib.***

The march of the human mind is slow. ***Ib.***

Freedom and not servitude is the cure of anarchy; as religion, and not atheism, is the true remedy for superstition. ***Ib.***

All government — indeed, every human benefit and enjoyment, every virtue and every prudent act — is founded on compromise and barter. ***Ib.***

Instead of a standing revenue, you will have therefore a perpetual quarrel. ***Ib.***

Slavery they can have anywhere. It is a weed that grows in every soil. ***Ib.***

Deny them this participation of freedom, and you break that sole bond, which originally made, and must still preserve the unity of the empire. ***Ib.***

It is the love of the [British] people; it is their attachment to their govern-ment, from the sense of the deep stake they have in such a glorious institution, which gives you both your army and your navy, and infuses into both that liberal obedience, without which your army would be a base rabble, and your navy nothing but rotten timber.
Second Speech on Conciliation with America. The Thirteen Resolutions

Magnanimity in politics is not seldom the truest wisdom; and a great empire and little minds go ill together. ***Ib.***

By adverting to the dignity of this high calling our ancestors have turned a savage wilderness into a glorious empire: and have made the most extensive, and the only honorable conquests, not by destroying, but by promoting the wealth, the number, the happiness of the human race. ***Ib.***

Corrupt influence, which is itself the perennial spring of all prodigality, and of all disorder; which loads us, more than millions of debt; which takes away vigor from our arms, wisdom from our councils, and every shadow of authority and credit from the most venerable parts of our constitution.
Speech on the Economical Reform [1780]

He was not merely a chip of the old block, but the old block itself.
On Pitt's first speech [February 26, 1781]

A rapacious and licentious soldiery.
Speech on Fox's East India Bill [1783]

The people never give up their liberties but under some delusion.
Speech at County Meeting of Buckinghamshire [1784]

There never was a bad man that had ability for good service.
Impeachment of Warren Hastings [February 15, 1788]

Religious persecution may shield it-

self under the guise of a mistaken and over-zealous piety.
Impeachment of Warren Hastings [February 17, 1788]

An event has happened, upon which it is difficult to speak, and impossible to be silent.   *Ib. [May 5, 1789]*

Resolved to die in the last dike of prevarication.   *Ib. [May 7, 1789]*

There is but one law for all, namely, that law which governs all law, the law of our Creator, the law of humanity, justice, equity — the law of nature, and of nations.   *Ib. [May 28, 1794]*

They made and recorded a sort of institute and digest of anarchy, called the Rights of Man.
On the Army Estimates [1790]

People will not look forward to posterity who never look backward to their ancestors.[1]
Reflections on the Revolution in France [1790]

Government is a contrivance of human wisdom to provide for human wants. Men have a right that these wants should be provided for by this wisdom.   *Ib.*

The unbought grace of life, the cheap defense of nations, the nurse of manly sentiment and heroic enterprise is gone!   *Ib.*

That chastity of honor, which felt a stain like a wound.   *Ib.*

Vice itself lost half its evil, by losing all its grossness.   *Ib.*

Kings will be tyrants from policy, when subjects are rebels from principle.
Ib.

Learning will be cast into the mire, and trodden down under the hoofs of a swinish multitude.   *Ib.*

Because half-a-dozen grasshoppers under a fern make the field ring with their importunate chink, whilst thousands of great cattle, reposed beneath the shadow of the British oak, chew the cud and are silent, pray do not imagine that those who make the noise are the only inhabitants of the field; that, of course, they are many in number; or that, after all, they are other than the little shriveled, meager, hopping, though loud and troublesome *insects* of the hour.
Reflections on the Revolution in France

Superstition is the religion of feeble minds.   *Ib.*

He that wrestles with us strengthens our nerves, and sharpens our skill. Our antagonist is our helper.   *Ib.*

To execute laws is a royal office; to execute orders is not to be a king. However, a political executive magistracy, though merely such, is a great trust.[1]
Ib.

You can never plan the future by the past.[2]
Letter to a member of the National Assembly [1791]

Old religious factions are volcanoes burnt out.
Speech on the Petition of the Unitarians [1792]

The cold neutrality of an impartial judge.
Preface to Brissot's Address [1794]

The only thing necessary for the triumph of evil is for good men to do nothing.
Letter to William Smith [January 9, 1795]

All men that are ruined, are ruined on the side of their natural propensities.
Letters on a Regicide Peace [1796], no. 1

---

[1] The Democratic Party is like a mule — without pride of ancestry or hope of posterity. — IGNATIUS DONNELLY [1831–1901], *Speech in the Minnesota Legislature*

[1] See Matthew Henry, p. 386b; Jefferson, p. 472b; Clay, p. 538b; and Calhoun, p. 545b, and note.
[2] See Patrick Henry, p. 465a.

Example is the school of mankind, and they will learn at no other.[1]
Letters on a Regicide Peace, no. 1

Mere parsimony is not economy. . . . Expense, and great expense, may be an essential part of true economy.
Letter to a Noble Lord [1796]

Economy is a distributive virtue, and consists not in saving but selection. Parsimony requires no providence, no sagacity, no powers of combination, no comparison, no judgment.   *Ib.*

And having looked to Government for bread, on the very first scarcity they will turn and bite the hand that fed them.
Thoughts and Details on Scarcity [1800]

GOTTHOLD EPHRAIM LESSING
1729–1781

He who doesn't lose his wits over certain things has no wits to lose.
Emilia Galotti [1772], *act IV, sc. 7*

No person must have to.
Nathan der Weise [1779], *act I, sc. 3*

People are not always what they seem.   *Ib. 6*

The true beggar is the true king.
Ib. II, end

Not all are free who scorn their chains.   *Ib. IV, 4*

One can drink too much, but one never drinks enough.   *Lieder*

Who will not praise a Klopstock?
But will anyone read him? No!
Sinngedichte an den Leser

JOHN PARKER
1729–1775

Stand your ground. Don't fire unless fired upon, but if they mean to have a war let it begin here!
To his Minute Men at Lexington [*April* 19, 1775]

[1] See Franklin, p. 422a.

JOHANN GEORG HAMANN
1730–1788

Poetry is the mother tongue of mankind.   *Aesthetica in Nuce* [1762]

THOMAS OSBERT MORDAUNT
1730–1809

Sound, sound the clarion, fill the fife,
Throughout the sensual world proclaim,
One crowded hour of glorious life
Is worth an age without a name.[1]
From The Bee (October 12, 1791). Verses Written During the War [1756–1763]

MOTOORI NORINAGA[2]
1730–1801

Thus our country is the source and fountainhead of all other countries, and in all matters it excels all the others.
Precious Comb-box

Sages are superior to other people only in their cleverness. The fact is that they were all impostors. Among them the least blameworthy was Confucius.   *Arrowroot*

The Tale of Genji [3] is simply a tale of human life which leaves aside and does not profess to take up at all the question of good and bad, and which dwells only upon the goodness of those who are aware of the sorrow of human existence.   *Tama no Ogushi*

JOHN SCOTT
1730–1783

I Hate That Drum's Discordant Sound.
Title of Poem

[1] Quoted by Sir Walter Scott in *Old Mortality* [1816], ch. 34.
See Scott, p. 522a.
[2] From *Sources of Japanese Tradition*, edited by William Theodore de Bary [1960].
[3] See Murasaki Shikibu, pp. 153b-154a.

JOSIAH WEDGWOOD
1730–1795

Am I not a man and a brother?
On a Medallion [1] [1787]

CHARLES CHURCHILL
1731–1764

Genius is of no country.
The Rosciad [1761], *l. 207*

He mouths a sentence as curs mouth a
bone. *Ib. l. 322*

So loud each tongue, so empty was each
head,
So much they talked, so very little said.
Ib. l. 549

Learn'd without sense, and venerably
dull. *Ib. l. 591*

Those who would make us feel — must
feel themselves.[2] *Ib. l. 962*

Apt alliteration's artful aid.
The Prophecy of Famine [1763],
l. 86

With curious art the brain, too finely
wrought,
Preys on herself, and is destroyed by
thought.
Epistle to William Hogarth
[1763], *l. 645*

Just to the windward of the law.
The Ghost [1763], *pt. III, l. 56*

Though by whim, envy, or resentment
led,
They damn those authors whom they
never read.
The Candidate [1764], *l. 57*

Be England what she will,
With all her faults she is my country
still.[3] *The Farewell, l. 27*

---

[1] Representing a Negro in chains, with one
knee on the ground and both hands lifted up
to heaven. This was adopted as a seal by the
Anti-Slavery Society of London.
[2] Si vis me flere, dolendum est
Primum ipsi tibi
[If you wish me to weep, you yourself
Must first feel grief].
HORACE [65–8 B.C.], *Ars Poetica, l. 102*
See Frost, p. 929b.
[3] England, with all thy faults I love thee
still,

WILLIAM COWPER
1731–1800

Oh! for a closer walk with God.
Olney Hymns [1779], *no.* 1

What peaceful hours I once enjoy'd!
How sweet their memory still!
But they have left an aching void
The world can never fill. *Ib.*

God moves in a mysterious way
His wonders to perform;
He plants his footsteps in the sea
And rides upon the storm. *Ib. 35*

Behind a frowning providence
He hides a smiling face. *Ib.*

Happiness depends, as Nature shows,
Less on exterior things than most sup-
pose.
Table Talk [1782], *l. 246*

Freedom has a thousand charms to
show,
That slaves, howe'er contented, never
know. *Ib. l. 260*

Manner is all in all, whate'er is writ,
The substitute for genius, sense, and
wit. *Ib. l. 542*

Low ambition and the thirst of praise.[1]
Ib. l. 591

[Pope] Made poetry a mere mechanic
art. *Ib. l. 656*

Lights of the world, and stars of human
race.
The Progress of Error [1782], *l. 97*

How much a dunce that has been sent
to roam
Excels a dunce that has been kept at
home! *Ib. l. 415*

My country!
COWPER, *The Task* [1784], bk. II,
The Timepiece, l. 206
Our country! In her intercourse with foreign
nations may she always be in the right; but
our country, right or wrong. — STEPHEN DECA-
TUR, *Toast given at Norfolk* [April 1816]
I hope to find my country in the right:
however, I will stand by her, right or wrong.
— JOHN JORDAN CRITTENDEN [1787–1863], *On
the Mexican War*
See Carl Schurz, p. 733a.
[1] See Pope, p. 407b.

A fool must now and then be right, by chance.
> *Conversation* [1782], *l.* 96

He would not, with a peremptory tone,
Assert the nose upon his face his own.
> *Ib. l.* 121

A moral, sensible, and well-bred man
Will not affront me, and no other can.
> *Ib. l.* 193

Pernicious weed! [1] whose scent the fair annoys,
Unfriendly to society's chief joys,
Thy worst effect is banishing for hours
The sex whose presence civilizes ours.
> *Ib. l.* 251

I cannot talk with civet in the room,
A fine puss-gentleman that's all perfume.
> *Ib. l.* 283

Our wasted oil unprofitably burns,
Like hidden lamps in old sepulchral urns.
> *Ib. l.* 357

A business with an income at its heels
Furnishes always oil for its own wheels.
> *Retirement* [1782], *l.* 615

Absence of occupation is not rest,
A mind quite vacant is a mind distress'd.
> *Ib. l.* 623

Built God a church, and laugh'd His word to scorn.[2]
> *Ib. l.* 688

Philologists, who chase
A panting syllable through time and space,
Start it at home, and hunt it in the dark
To Gaul, to Greece, and into Noah's ark.
> *Ib. l.* 691

I praise the Frenchman,[3] his remark was shrewd —
How sweet, how passing sweet, is solitude!
But grant me still a friend in my retreat
Whom I may whisper — solitude is sweet.
> *Ib. l.* 739

[1] Tobacco.
[2] Voltaire, who built a church at Ferney [1760–1761], with the inscription *Deo erexit Voltaire.*
[3] La Bruyère.

I am monarch of all I survey,
My right there is none to dispute.
> *Verses Supposed to be Written by Alexander Selkirk* [1782], *st. 1*

O Solitude! where are the charms
That sages have seen in thy face?
> *Ib.*

There goes the parson, O illustrious spark!
And there, scarce less illustrious, goes the clerk.
> *On Observing Some Names of Little Note* [1782]

Though on pleasure she was bent,
She had a frugal mind.
> *History of John Gilpin* [1785], *st. 8*

A hat not much the worse for wear.
> *Ib. st.* 46

Now let us sing — Long live the king,
And Gilpin, long live he;
And, when he next doth ride abroad,
May I be there to see!
> *Ib. st.* 63

God made the country, and man made the town.[1]
> *The Task* [1785], *bk. I, The Sofa, l.* 749

Oh for a lodge in some vast wilderness,[2]
Some boundless contiguity of shade,
Where rumor of oppression and deceit,
Of unsuccessful or successful war,
Might never reach me more.
> *Ib. II, The Timepiece, l.* 1

Mountains interpos'd
Make enemies of nations, who had else
Like kindred drops, been mingled into one.
> *Ib. l.* 17

Slaves cannot breathe in England; if their lungs
Receive our air, that moment they are free!
They touch our country, and their shackles fall.
> *Ib. l.* 40

[1] See Bacon, p. 209b, and note.
[2] See *Jeremiah* 9:2, p. 34a, and Byron, p. 557b.

Presume to lay their hand upon the
ark [1]
Of her magnificent and awful cause.
*The Task, bk. II, The
Timepiece, l. 231*

Variety's the very spice of life.[2]
Ib. l. 606

His head,
Not yet by time completely silver'd
o'er,
Bespoke him past the bounds of freak-
ish youth,
But strong for service still, and un-
impair'd. *Ib. l. 702*

Guilty splendor.
Ib. III, The Garden, l. 70

I was a stricken deer [3] that left the
herd
Long since. *Ib. l. 108*

Great contest follows, and much
learned dust
Involves the combatants. *Ib. l. 161*

From reveries so airy, from the toil
Of dropping buckets into empty wells,
And growing old in drawing nothing
up.[4] *Ib. l. 188*

Riches have wings,[5] and grandeur is a
dream. *Ib. l. 265*

Who loves a garden loves a greenhouse
too. *Ib. l. 566*

Now stir the fire, and close the shutters
fast,
Let fall the curtains, wheel the sofa
round,
And, while the bubbling and loud-
hissing urn
Throws up a steamy column, and the
cups,
That cheer but not inebriate,[6] wait on
each,

So let us welcome peaceful evening in.
*The Task, bk. IV, The
Winter Evening, l. 36*

'Tis pleasant, through the loopholes of
retreat,
To peep at such a world; to see the
stir
Of the great Babel, and not feel the
crowd. *Ib. l. 88*

O Winter, ruler of the inverted year! [1]
Ib. l. 120

With spots quadrangular of diamond
form,
Ensanguin'd hearts, clubs typical of
strife,
And spades, the emblems of untimely
graves. *Ib. l. 217*

In indolent vacuity of thought.[2]
Ib. l. 297

It seems the part of wisdom.
Ib. l. 336

All learned, and all drunk! *Ib. l. 478*

Gloriously drunk, obey th' important
call. *Ib. l. 510*

Silently as a dream the fabric rose —
No sound of hammer or of saw was
there.[3]
*Ib. V, The Winter Morning
Walk, l. 144*

But war's a game, which, were their
subjects wise,
Kings would not play at. *Ib. l. 187*

There is in souls a sympathy with
sounds;
And as the mind is pitch'd the ear is
pleased
With melting airs or martial, brisk, or
grave:
Some chord in unison with what we
hear

---

[1] Uzzah put forth his hand to the ark of
God, and took hold of it . . . and the anger
of the Lord was kindled against Uzzah. —
II Samuel 6:6
 [2] See Publilius Syrus, p. 126a.
 [3] See Shakespeare, p. 263b.
 [4] See Sydney Smith, p. 523a.
 [5] See *Proverbs 23:5*, p. 25b.
 [6] See Berkeley, p. 399b.

[1] See Thomson, p. 419b.
 [2] See Samuel Johnson, p. 431a.
 [3] So that there was neither hammer nor axe,
nor any tool of iron heard in the house while
it was in building. — *I Kings 6:7*

No hammers fell, no ponderous axes rung,
Like some tall palm the mystic fabric sprung,
Majestic silence!
REGINALD HEBER [1783–1826], *Palestine*

Is touch'd within us, and the heart replies.
> *The Task, bk.* VI, *Winter Walk*
> *at Noon, l. 1*

Here the heart
May give a useful lesson to the head,
And Learning wiser grow without his
books.   *Ib. l. 85*

Knowledge is proud that he has learn'd
     so much;
Wisdom is humble that he knows no
     more.   *Ib. l. 96*

Nature is but a name for an effect,
Whose cause is God.   *Ib. l. 223*

An honest man, close-button'd to the
     chin,
Broadcloth without, and a warm heart
     within.
> *Epistle to Joseph Hill* [1785], *l. 62*

Shine by the side of every path we tread
With such a luster, he that runs may
     read.[1]
> *Tirocinium* [1785], *l. 79*

Toll for the brave —
     The brave! that are no more;
All sunk beneath the wave,
     Fast by their native shore!
> *On the Loss of the Royal*
> *George* [2] [1791], *st. 1*

And still to love, though prest with ill,
In wintry age to feel no chill,
With me is to be lovely still,
     My Mary!
> *To Mary* [1791], *st. 11*

Beware of desp'rate steps! The darkest
     day
(Live till tomorrow) will have pass'd
     away.
> *The Needless Alarm* [1794].
> *Moral*

The British warrior queen,
Bleeding from the Roman rods.
> *Boadicea* [1782]

[1] See *Habakkuk* 2:2, p. 36a.
[2] The *Royal George* was an English man-of-war of 108 guns, which suddenly heeled over, under the strain caused by the shifting of her guns, while being refitted at Spithead, August 29, 1782. The commander, Admiral Kempenfeldt, and eight hundred of the sailors, marines, and visitors on board were drowned.

I shall not ask Jean Jacques Rousseau
If birds confabulate or no.
> *Pairing Time Anticipated* [c. 1794]

Misses! the tale that I relate
     This lesson seems to carry —
Choose not alone a proper mate,
     But proper time to marry.
> *Ib. Moral*

Oh that those lips had language! Life
     has pass'd
With me but roughly since I heard
     thee last.
> *On the Receipt of My Mother's*
> *Picture* [1798]

Misery still delights to trace
Its semblance in another's case.
> *The Castaway* [1799]

ERASMUS DARWIN
1731–1802

Soon shall thy arm, unconquer'd steam!
     afar
Drag the slow barge, or drive the rapid
     car;
Or on wide-waving wings expanded
     bear
The flying-chariot through the fields of
     air.
> *The Botanic Garden, pt. I,*
> [1789], *l. 289*

Would it be too bold to imagine, that in the great length of time, since the earth began to exist, perhaps millions of ages before the commencement of the history of mankind, would it be too bold to imagine, that all warm-blooded animals have arisen from one living filament which the Great First Cause endued with animality . . . and thus possessing the faculty of continuing to improve by its own inherent activity, and of delivering down those improvements by generation to its posterity, world without end! [1]
> *Zoonomia* [1794]

[1] Here the grandfather of Charles Robert Darwin announces *his* early theory of organic evolution.

CHARLES LEE
1731–1782

Beware that your Northern laurels do not change to Southern willows.[1]

> *To General Horatio Gates after the surrender of Burgoyne at Saratoga [October 17, 1777]*

BEILBY PORTEUS
1731–1808

One murder made a villain, Millions, a hero. Princes were privileged To kill, and numbers sanctified the crime.[2]   *Death, l. 154*

War its thousands slays, Peace, its ten thousands.[3]   *Ib. l. 178*

PIERRE DE BEAUMARCHAIS
1732–1799

Judging by the virtues expected of a servant, does your Excellency know many masters who would be worthy valets?

> *Le Barbier de Séville [1775], act I, sc. 2*

I quickly laugh at everything, for fear of having to cry.[4]   *Ib.*

If you assure me that your intentions are honorable.   *Ib. IV, 6*

If you are mediocre and you grovel, you shall succeed.

> *Le Mariage de Figaro [1784], act III, sc. 3*

You went to some trouble to be born, and that's all.[5]   *Ib. V, 3*

If censorship reigns there cannot be

---

[1] Gates was later defeated by Cornwallis at Camden, South Carolina [August 16, 1780], and was relieved of his command.

[2] See Young, p. 398b.

[3] See *I Samuel 18:7*, p. 12a.

[4] Je me presse de rire de tout, de peur d'être obligé d'en pleurer.
See La Bruyère, p. 381b; Byron, p. 561a; and Lincoln, p. 638a.

[5] Vous vous êtes donné la peine de naître, et rien de plus.

sincere flattery, and only small men are afraid of small writings.

> *Le Mariage de Figaro, act V, sc. 3*

JOHN DICKINSON
1732–1808

Then join hand in hand, brave Americans all! By uniting we stand, by dividing we fall.[1]   *The Liberty Song [1768]*

RICHARD HENRY LEE
1732–1794

That these united colonies are, and of right ought to be, free and independent states; that they are absolved from all allegiance to the British crown; and that all political connection between them and the State of Great Britain is, and ought to be, totally dissolved.

> *Resolution moved at the Continental Congress [June 7, 1776; adopted July 2][2]*

JULIE DE LESPINASSE
1732–1776

The logic of the heart is absurd.

> *Lettres à M. Guibert [August 27, 1774]*

GEORGE WASHINGTON[3]
1732–1799

Discipline is the soul of an army. It makes small numbers formidable; procures success to the weak, and esteem to all.

> *Letter of Instructions to the Captains of the Virginia Regiments [July 29, 1759]*

Let us therefore animate and encourage each other, and show the whole world that a Freeman, contending for

---

[1] See Aesop, p. 76b, and George Pope Morris, p. 600a.

[2] See John Adams, p. 463a-b.

[3] The Father of your Country. — HENRY KNOX, *Letter to Washington* [March 19, 1787] See Henry (Light-Horse Harry) Lee, p. 486a.

liberty on his own ground, is superior to any slavish mercenary on earth.

General Orders, Headquarters, New York [July 2, 1776]

The time is now near at hand which must probably determine whether Americans are to be freemen or slaves; whether they are to have any property they can call their own; whether their houses and farms are to be pillaged and destroyed, and themselves consigned to a state of wretchedness from which no human efforts will deliver them. The fate of unborn millions will now depend, under God, on the courage and conduct of this army. Our cruel and unrelenting enemy leaves us only the choice of brave resistance, or the most abject submission. We have, therefore, to resolve to conquer or die.

Address to the Continental Army before the Battle of Long Island [August 27, 1776]

There is nothing that gives a man consequence, and renders him fit for command, like a support that renders him independent of everybody but the State he serves.

Letter to the President of Congress, Heights of Harlem [September 24, 1776]

To place any dependence upon militia, is, assuredly, resting upon a broken staff. *Ib.*

Without a decisive Naval force we can do nothing definitive. And with it, everything honorable and glorious.

To Lafayette [November 15, 1781]

If men are to be precluded from offering their sentiments on a matter which may involve the most serious and alarming consequences that can invite the consideration of mankind, reason is of no use to us; the freedom of speech may be taken away, and dumb and silent we may be led, like sheep to the slaughter.

Address to Officers of the Army [March 15, 1783]

The preservation of the sacred fire of liberty, and the destiny of the republican model of government, are justly considered as deeply, perhaps as finally staked, on the experiment entrusted to the hands of the American people.

First Inaugural Address [April 30, 1789]

Happily the Government of the United States, which gives to bigotry no sanction, to persecution no assistance, requires only that they who live under its protection should demean themselves as good citizens in giving it on all occasions their effectual support.

Letter to the Jewish Congregation of Newport, Rhode Island [1790]

To be prepared for war is one of the most effectual means of preserving peace.[1]

First Annual Address [to both Houses of Congress, January 8, 1790]

The basis of our political system is the right of the people to make and to alter their constitutions of government.

Farewell Address [September 17, 1796]

Let me now . . . warn you in the most solemn manner against the baneful effects of the spirit of party. *Ib.*

Observe good faith and justice toward all nations. Cultivate peace and harmony with all. . . . The Nation which indulges toward another an habitual hatred or an habitual fondness is in some degree a slave. It is a slave to its animosity or to its affection, either of which is sufficient to lead it astray from its duty and its interest. *Ib.*

'Tis our true policy to steer clear of permanent alliances, with any portion of the foreign world. *Ib.*

There can be no greater error than to expect or calculate upon real favors from nation to nation. *Ib.*

[1] See Vegetius, p. 146b, and note.

It is well, I die hard, but I am not afraid to go.

> Last words [December 14, 1799]

Father, I cannot tell a lie, I did it with my little hatchet.[1]

> Attributed remark from MARK TWAIN, *Mark Twain as Washington*

JOSEPH PRIESTLEY
1733–1804

It was ill policy in Leo the Tenth to patronize polite literature. He was cherishing an enemy in disguise. And the English hierarchy (if there be anything unsound in its constitution) has equal reason to tremble even at an air pump or an electrical machine.

> Experiments and Observations on Different Kinds of Air [1775–1786]

In completing one discovery we never fail to get an imperfect knowledge of others of which we could have no idea before, so that we cannot solve one doubt without creating several new ones.   *Ib.*

CHRISTOPH MARTIN WIELAND
1733–1813

To be not as eloquent would be more eloquent.

> The Journal Merkur [January 1774]

An illusion which makes me happy is worth a verity which drags me to the ground.

> Idris und Zenide [1768], canto III

Too much light often blinds gentlemen of this sort. They cannot see the forest for the trees.

> Musarion [1768], canto II

[1] See Weems, p. 499a.

JOHN ADAMS [1]
1735–1826

Facts are stubborn things; and whatever may be our wishes, our inclinations, or the dictates of our passions, they cannot alter the state of facts and evidence.

> Defense of the British soldiers on trial for the Boston Massacre [1770]

The law, in all vicissitudes of government, fluctuations of the passions, or flights of enthusiasm, will preserve a steady undeviating course; it will not bend to the uncertain wishes, imaginations and wanton tempers of men. . . . It does not enjoin that which pleases a weak, frail man, but without any regard to persons, commands that which is good and punishes evil in all, whether rich or poor, high or low — 'tis deaf, inexorable, inflexible. On the one hand it is inexorable to the cries and lamentations of the prisoners; on the other it is deaf, deaf as an adder,[2] to the clamors of the populace.   *Ib.*

This is the most magnificent movement of all! There is a dignity, a majesty, a sublimity, in this last effort of the patriots that I greatly admire. The people should never rise without doing something to be remembered — something notable and striking. This destruction of the tea is so bold, so daring, so firm, intrepid and inflexible, and it must have so important consequences, and so lasting, that I can't but consider it as an epoch in history!

> Diary [on the Boston Tea Party, December 17, 1773]

I have passed the Rubicon;[3] swim or

[1] He is as disinterested as the being who made him: he is profound in his view; and accurate in his judgment, except where knowledge of the world is necessary to form a judgment. — THOMAS JEFFERSON [January 30, 1787]

See Webster, p. 547a, note 2.

[2] See *Psalms 58:4-5*, p. 19b.

[3] See p. 112b, note 1.

sink, live or die, survive or perish with my country — that is my unalterable determination.[1]

> *In conversation with Jonathan Sewall, Falmouth, Maine [July 1774]*

I must study politics and war, that my sons may have liberty to study mathematics and philosophy, geography, natural history and naval architecture, navigation, commerce, and agriculture, in order to give their children a right to study painting, poetry, music, architecture, statuary, tapestry, and porcelain.

> *Letters of John Adams Addressed to his Wife, edited by Charles Francis Adams [1841], vol. II, letter 78 [1780]*

If it be the pleasure of Heaven that my country shall require the poor offering of my life, the victim shall be ready, at the appointed hour of sacrifice, come when that hour may. But while I do live, let me have a country, and that a free country. . . .

Sir, before God, I believe the hour is come. My judgment approves this measure, and my whole heart is in it. All I have, and all that I am, and all that I hope, in this life, I am now ready to stake upon it; and I leave off as I began, that live or die, survive or perish, I am for the Declaration.

> *Speech [1776]*

All great changes are irksome to the human mind, especially those which are attended with great dangers and uncertain effects.

> *Letter to James Warren [April 22, 1776]*

Yesterday, the greatest question was decided which ever was debated in America, and a greater perhaps never was nor will be decided among men. A resolution was passed without one dissenting colony, "that these United Colonies are, and of right ought to be, free and independent States." [1]

> *Letter to Abigail Adams [July 3, 1776]*

The second day of July, 1776,[2] will be the most memorable epoch in the history of America. I am apt to believe that it will be celebrated by succeeding generations as the great anniversary festival. It ought to be commemorated as the day of deliverance, by solemn acts of devotion to God Almighty. It ought to be solemnized with pomp and parade, with shows, games, sports, guns, bells, bonfires, and illuminations, from one end of this continent to the other, from this time forward forevermore. *Ib.*

The happiness of society is the end of government.

> *Thoughts on Government [1776]*

Fear is the foundation of most governments. *Ib.*

When annual elections end, there slavery begins. *Ib.*

The judicial power ought to be distinct from both the legislative and executive, and independent upon both, that so it may be a check upon both. *Ib.*

A government of laws, and not of men.[3]

> *Original draft of Massachusetts Constitution [1779]*

I pray Heaven to bestow the best of blessings on this house and all that shall hereafter inhabit it. May none but honest and wise men ever rule under this roof.[4]

> *Letter to Abigail Adams [November 2, 1800]*

---

[1] See Richard Henry Lee, p. 460b.

[2] On July 2, 1776, the resolution for independence, drafted by Richard Henry Lee of Virginia, was adopted by a committee including John Adams. On July 4 the Declaration of Independence was agreed to, engrossed, signed by John Hancock, and sent to the legislatures of the States.

[3] See Burke, p. 452, and note.

[4] Written the day after Adams moved into the new White House. President Franklin D.

[1] See Daniel Webster, p. 546b-547a.

Thomas Jefferson still lives [or: . . .
surv —].[1]   *Last words [July 4, 1826]*

ISAAC BICKERSTAFFE
c. 1735 – c. 1812

There was a jolly miller once
    Lived on the River Dee;
He worked and sang from morn till
    night
No lark more blithe than he.
        *Love in a Village [1762], act I,
                                    sc. 2*

And this the burthen of his song
    Forever used to be,
"I care for nobody, not I,
    If no one cares for me." [2]   *Ib.*

CHARLES JOSEPH,
PRINCE DE LIGNE
1735–1814

The   Congress   doesn't   run — it
waltzes.[3]
        *Comment to La Garde–
            Chambonacs [1814]*

WILLIAM JULIUS
MICKLE
1735–1788

The dews of summer nights did fall,
    The moon (sweet regent of the
        sky) [4]
Silvered the walls of Cumnor Hall
    And   many   an   oak   that   grew
        thereby.
        Cumnor Hall [1784], st. 1

For there's nae luck about the house,
    There's nae luck at a';
There's little pleasure in the house
    When our gudeman's awa.
        The Mariner's Wife, st. 1

Roosevelt had it inscribed on the mantelpiece
of the State Dining Room.
[1] Jefferson at Monticello died the same day
— the fiftieth anniversary of the adoption of
the Declaration of Independence — murmuring
"This is the Fourth?"
[2] Naebody cares for me,
    I care for naebody.
        ROBERT BURNS [1759–1796], *I Hae a
                    Wife o' My Ain, st. 4*
[3] Le Congrès ne marche pas, il danse [said
of the Congress of Vienna].
[4] Now Cynthia, named fair regent of the
night. — GAY, *Trivia [1716], bk. III*

PAUL REVERE
1735–1818

To the memory of the glorious
Ninety-two: members of the Honorable
House of Representatives of the Massachusetts Bay who, undaunted by the in-
solent menaces of villains in power,
from a strict regard to conscience and
the liberties of their constituents on the
30th of June 1768 voted NOT TO RE-
SCIND.
        *Inscription on Revere's silver
            "Liberty" bowl [1768]*

If the British went out by water, to
show two lanterns in the North Church
steeple; and if by land, one as a signal,
for we were apprehensive it would be
difficult to cross the Charles River or
get over Boston Neck.[1]
        *Signal code arranged with Colo-
            nel Conant of the Charlestown
            Committee of Safety [April 16,
            1775]. Letter to Dr. Jeremy
            Belknap*

PATRICK HENRY
1736–1799

Caesar had his Brutus; Charles the
First his Cromwell; and George the
Third ["Treason!" cried the Speaker]
— *may profit by their example. If this*
be treason, make the most of it.
        *Speech on the Stamp Act,
            House of Burgesses, Williams-
            burg, Virginia [May 29, 1765]*

I am not a Virginian, but an American.[2]
        *Speech in First Continental Con-
            gress, Philadelphia [October 14,
            1774]*

It is natural for man to indulge in
the illusions of hope. We are apt to
shut our eyes against a painful truth,
and listen to the song of that siren till
she transforms us into beasts. Is this the
part of wise men, engaged in a great
and arduous struggle for liberty? Are we
disposed to be the number of those
who, having eyes, see not, and having

---

[1] See Longfellow, p. 624a.
[2] See Socrates, p. 87b, and note.

ears, hear not,[1] the things which so nearly concern their temporal salvation? For my part, whatever anguish of spirit it may cost, I am willing to know the whole truth; to know the worst, and to provide for it.

Speech in Virginia Convention, Richmond [March 23, 1775]. From WILLIAM WIRT, Patrick Henry [1818]

I have but one lamp by which my feet are guided, and that is the lamp of experience. I know no way of judging of the future but by the past.[2]   *Ib.*

We are not weak if we make a proper use of those means which the God of Nature has placed in our power. . . . The battle, sir, is not to the strong alone;[3] it is to the vigilant, the active, the brave.   *Ib.*

If we wish to be free; if we mean to preserve inviolate those inestimable privileges for which we have been so long contending; if we mean not basely to abandon the noble struggle in which we have been so long engaged, and which we have pledged ourselves never to abandon until the glorious object of our contest shall be obtained — we must fight! I repeat it, sir, we must fight! An appeal to arms, and to the God of hosts, is all that is left us.

Ib.

It is vain, sir, to extenuate the matter. The gentlemen may cry, Peace, peace! but there is no peace.[4] The war has actually begun! The next gale that sweeps from the north will bring to our ears the clash of resounding arms! Our brethren are already in the field! Why stand we here idle? What is it that the gentlemen wish? What would they have? Is life so dear or peace so sweet as to be purchased at the price of chains and slavery? Forbid it, Almighty God. I know not what course others may take,

but as for me, give me liberty or give me death! [1]

Speech in Virginia Convention, Richmond [March 23, 1775]

That religion, or the duty which we owe to our Creator, and the manner of discharging it, can be directed only by reason and conviction, not by force or violence; and therefore all men are equally entitled to the free exercise of religion, according to the dictates of conscience; and that it is the mutual duty of all to practice Christian forbearance, love, and charity towards each other.

Virginia Bill of Rights [2]
[June 12, 1776], art. 16

EDWARD GIBBON
1737–1794

The various modes of worship, which prevailed in the Roman world, were all considered by the people as equally true; by the philosopher, as equally false; and by the magistrate, as equally useful.

Decline and Fall of the Roman Empire [1776–1788], ch. 2

The principles of a free constitution are irrevocably lost, when the legislative power is nominated by the executive.
          Ib. 3

His [Antoninus'] reign is marked by the rare advantage of furnishing very few materials for history; which is indeed little more than the register of the crimes, follies, and misfortunes of mankind.[3]   *Ib.*

It has been calculated by the ablest politicians that no State, without being soon exhausted, can maintain above the hundredth part of its members in arms and idleness.   *Ib. 5*

All taxes must, at last, fall upon agriculture.   *Ib. 8*

---

[1] See *Jeremiah 5:21*, p. 34a.
[2] See Burke, p. 454b.
[3] See *Ecclesiastes 9:11*, p. 28b.
[4] See *Jeremiah 6:14*, p. 34a.

[1] See Aeschylus, p. 78b.
[2] See George Mason, p. 446a. Mason drafted Articles 1, 3, and 12.
[3] See Voltaire, p. 417b.

Corruption, the most infallible symptom of constitutional liberty.
Decline and Fall of the Roman Empire, ch. 21

In every deed of mischief he [Comenus] had a heart to resolve, a head to contrive, and a hand to execute.[1]　　　　　*Ib.* 48

Our sympathy is cold to the relation of distant misery.　　　　　*Ib.* 49

The winds and waves are always on the side of the ablest navigators.[2]
Ib. 68

Vicissitudes of fortune, which spares neither man nor the proudest of his works, which buries empires and cities in a common grave.　　　*Ib.* 71

All that is human must retrograde if it does not advance.　　　　　*Ib.*

The successors of Charles the Fifth may disdain their brethren of England; but the romance of *Tom Jones*,[3] that exquisite picture of human manners, will outlive the palace of the Escurial and the imperial eagle of the house of Austria.　　　*Memoirs* [1796]

Decent easy men, who supinely enjoyed the gifts of the founder.　　*Ib.*

It was here [at the age of seventeen] that I suspended my religious inquiries.　　　　　*Ib.*

I saw and loved.　　　　　*Ib.*

I sighed as a lover, I obeyed as a son.　　　　　*Ib.*

[Of London] Crowds without company, and dissipation without pleasure.
Ib.

The captain of the Hampshire grenadiers [4] . . . has not been useless

[1] He [Hampden] had a head to contrive, a tongue to persuade, and a hand to execute any mischief. — EDWARD HYDE, EARL OF CLARENDON [1609–1674], *History of the Rebellion* [1702–1704], *vol. III, bk. VII, sec.* 84
See Junius, p. 1091b.
[2] See Bussy-Rabutin, p. 357a, and note.
[3] See Fielding, p. 424b.
[4] Gibbon was a captain in the Hampshire militia from June 12, 1759, to December 23, 1762.

to the historian of the Roman Empire.
Memoirs

THOMAS PAINE
1737–1809

From the east to the west blow the trumpet to arms!
Through the land let the sound of it flee;
Let the far and the near all unite, with a cheer,
In defense of our Liberty Tree.
The Liberty Tree [*July* 1775], *st. 4*

Society in every state is a blessing, but Government, even in its best state, is but a necessary evil; in its worst state, an intolerable one.
Common Sense [1776]

Suspicion is the companion of mean souls, and the bane of all good society.
Ib.

When we are planning for posterity, we ought to remember that virtue is not hereditary.　　　　　*Ib.*

O! ye that love mankind! Ye that dare oppose not only the tyranny but the tyrant, stand forth! Every spot of the Old World is overrun with oppression. Freedom hath been hunted round the globe. Asia and Africa have long expelled her. Europe regards her as a stranger and England hath given her warning to depart. O! receive the fugitive and prepare in time an asylum for mankind.[1]　　　　　*Ib.*

These are the times that try men's souls. The summer soldier and the sunshine patriot will, in this crisis, shrink from the service of his country; but he that stands it *now*, deserves the love and thanks of man and woman. Tyranny, like hell, is not easily conquered; yet we have this consolation with us, that the harder the conflict, the more glorious the triumph. What we obtain too cheap, we esteem too lightly; 'tis dearness only that gives everything its value. Heaven knows how to put a proper price upon its goods;

[1] See Samuel Adams, p. 444a.

and it would be strange indeed, if so celestial an article as *Freedom* should not be highly rated.

> *The American Crisis, no. 1*
> *[December 23, 1776]*

Panics, in some cases, have their uses; they produce as much good as hurt. Their duration is always short; the mind soon grows through them and acquires a firmer habit than before. But their peculiar advantage is, that they are the touchstone of sincerity and hypocrisy, and bring things and men to light, which might otherwise have lain forever undiscovered. *Ib.*

Not a place upon earth might be so happy as America. Her situation is remote from all the wrangling world, and she has nothing to do but to trade with them. *Ib.*

A bad cause will ever be supported by bad means and bad men.

> *Ib. 2 [January 13, 1777]*

Those who expect to reap the blessings of freedom must, like men, undergo the fatigue of supporting it.

> *Ib. 4 [September 12, 1777]*

It is not a field of a few acres of ground, but a cause, that we are defending, and whether we defeat the enemy in one battle, or by degrees, the consequences will be the same. *Ib.*

We fight not to enslave, but to set a country free, and to make room upon the earth for honest men to live in.

> *Ib.*

It is the object only of war that makes it honorable. And if there was ever a *just* war since the world began, it is this in which America is now engaged.

> *Ib. 5 [March 21, 1778]*

Character is much easier kept than recovered. *Ib. 13 [April 19, 1783]*

War involves in its progress such a train of unforeseen and unsupposed circumstances that no human wisdom can calculate the end. It has but one thing certain, and that is to increase taxes.

> *Prospects on the Rubicon [1787]*

[Burke] is not affected by the reality of distress touching his heart, but by the showy resemblance of it striking his imagination. He pities the plumage, but forgets the dying bird.

> *Rights of Man, pt. I [1791]*

My country is the world and my religion is to do good.[1]

> *Ib. II [1792], ch. 5*

Every religion is good that teaches man to be good. *Ib.*

A thing moderately good is not so good as it ought to be. Moderation in temper is always a virtue; but moderation in principle is always a vice.[2]

> *Ib.*

And the final event to himself [Burke] has been, that, as he rose like a rocket, he fell like a stick.

> *Letter to the Addressers on the*
> *Late Proclamation [1792]*

I believe in one God and no more, and I hope for happiness beyond this life. I believe in the equality of man; and I believe that religious duties consist in doing justice, loving mercy, and endeavoring to make our fellow-creatures happy.

> *The Age of Reason [1793], pt. I*

It is with a pious fraud as with a bad action; it begets a calamitous necessity of going on. *Ib.*

When authors and critics talk of the sublime, they see not how nearly it borders on the ridiculous.[3]

> *Ib. II, note*

RUDOLF ERICH RASPE

1737–1794

What in the dark I had taken to be a stump of a little tree appearing above the snow, to which I had tied my horse,

---

[1] See Socrates, p. 87b, and note.

[2] See W. L. Garrison, p. 615b.

Extremism in the defense of liberty is no vice. And . . . moderation in the pursuit of justice is no virtue. — BARRY GOLDWATER, *Acceptance speech, Republican Presidential nomination* [*July 16, 1964*]

[3] See Napoleon, p. 504a.

proved to have been the weathercock of the church steeple.

> *Travels of Baron Munchausen*
> [1785], *ch. 2*

We all did our duty, which, in the patriot's, soldier's, and gentleman's language, is a very comprehensive word, of great honor, meaning, and import.

> *Ib. 5*

The sprigs took root in my horse's body, grew up, and formed a bower over me.   *Ib.*

His tunes were frozen up in the horn, and came out now by thawing.

> *Ib. 6*

If any of the company entertain a doubt of my veracity, I shall only say to such, I pity their want of faith.   *Ib.*

A traveler has a right to relate and embellish his adventures as he pleases, and it is very impolite to refuse that deference and applause they deserve.

> *Ib. 21*

ETHAN ALLEN
1738–1789

[Captain Delaplace [1]] gazed at Allen in bewildered astonishment. "By whose authority do you act?" exclaimed he. "In the name of the great Jehovah, and the Continental Congress!" replied Allen.

> *From* WASHINGTON IRVING,
> *Life of Washington* [1855–
> 1859], *vol. I, ch. 38*

JACQUES DELILLE
1738–1813

Fate chooses our relatives, we choose our friends.[2]

> *Malheur et Pitié* [1803], *canto 1*

[1] Commandant at Fort Ticonderoga, New York, May 10, 1775.
[2] Le sort fait les parents, le choix fait les amis.

PETER PINDAR
[JOHN WOLCOT]
1738–1819

What rage for fame attends both great and small!
Better be damned than mentioned not at all!

> *To the Royal Academicians*

Care to our coffin adds a nail, no doubt;
And every grin so merry, draws one out.

> *Expostulatory Odes, 15*

HESTER LYNCH
THRALE [PIOZZI]
1739–1821

The tree of deepest root is found
Least willing still to quit the ground:
'Twas therefore said by ancient sages,
That love of life increased with years
So much, that in our latter stages,
When pain grows sharp and sickness rages,
The greatest love of life appears.

> *Three Warnings*

Johnson's conversation was by much too strong for a person accustomed to obsequiousness and flattery; it was *mustard in a young child's mouth!*

> [*May* 1781] *From* BOSWELL, *Life
> of Johnson* [1791]

DANIEL BLISS
1740–1806

God wills us free, man wills us slaves,
I will as God wills, God's will be done.

> *Epitaph on gravestone of John
> Jack, "A Native of Africa, who
> died March 1773, aged about
> 60 years. Tho' born in a land of
> slavery he was born free."* [1]

JAMES BOSWELL [2]
1740–1795

That favorite subject, Myself.

> *Letter to Temple* [*July 26, 1763*]

[1] See Rousseau, p. 435b, and Schiller, p. 497b.
[2] See also excerpts from BOSWELL'S JOHNSON, pp. 429–434.

He who praises everybody, praises nobody.

> *Life of Johnson* [1791], footnote [*March 30, 1778*]

We cannot tell the precise moment when friendship is formed. As in filling a vessel drop by drop, there is at last a drop which makes it run over; so in a series of kindnesses there is at last one which makes the heart run over.

> *Ib.* [*September 1777*]

I think no innocent species of wit or pleasantry should be suppressed; and that a good pun may be admitted among the smaller excellencies of lively conversation.   *Ib.* [*June 1784*]

LOUIS SÉBASTIEN MERCIER
1740–1814

Extremes meet.[1]

> *Tableaux de Paris* [1782], *vol. IV, ch. 348, title*

AUGUSTUS MONTAGUE TOPLADY
1740–1778

Rock of Ages, cleft for me,
Let me hide myself in thee.

> *Rock of Ages* [1775], *st. 1*

SÉBASTIEN R. N. CHAMFORT
1741–1794

The most wasted day of all is that on which we have not laughed.

> *Maxims and Thoughts, 1*

Chance is a nickname for Providence.   *Ib. 62*

Be my brother, or I will kill you.[2]

> *From* CARLYLE, *French Revolution* [1837], *vol. II, pt. 1, ch. 12*

---

[1] "Extremes meet," as the whiting said with its tail in its mouth. — THOMAS HOOD [1799–1845], *The Doves and the Crows*

[2] Sois mon frère ou je te tue.

A paraphrase of the revolutionary watchword: Fraternity or death.

JOHANN KASPAR LAVATER
1741–1801

Say not you know another entirely, till you have divided an inheritance with him.

> *Aphorisms on Man* [1] [*c. 1788*], *no. 157*

He who, when called upon to speak a disagreeable truth, tells it boldly and has done is both bolder and milder than he who nibbles in a low voice and never ceases nibbling.[2]   *Ib. 302*

Trust not him with your secrets, who, when left alone in your room, turns over your papers.   *Ib. 449*

The public seldom forgive twice.

> *Ib. 606*

Venerate four characters: the sanguine who has checked volatility and the rage for pleasure; the choleric who has subdued passion and pride; the phlegmatic emerged from indolence; and the melancholy who has dismissed avarice, suspicion and asperity.

> *Ib. 609*

If you mean to know yourself, interline such of these aphorisms as affect you agreeably in reading, and set a mark to such as left a sense of uneasiness with you; and then shew your copy to whom you please.   *Ib. 643*

GEBHARD LEBERECHT VON BLÜCHER
1742–1819

Ever forward, but slowly.

> *While leading the Russians at Leipzig* [*October 19, 1813*]

May the pens of the diplomats not ruin again what the people have attained with such exertions.

> *After the Battle of Waterloo* [*1813*]

---

[1] These Aphorisms were much admired and privately annotated by William Blake. See the one-volume edition of Blake's *Poetry and Prose*, edited by Geoffrey Keynes [1927].

[2] Blake's marginal comment on this was "Damn such!"

GEORG CHRISTOPH LICHTENBERG
1742–1799

A knife without a blade, for which the handle is missing.

> *Göttingen Pocket Calendar* [1798], *describing an impossible existence*

ANNA LETITIA BARBAULD
1743–1825

Life! we've been long together,
Through pleasant and through cloudy weather;
'Tis hard to part when friends are dear,
Perhaps 'twill cost a sigh, a tear;
Then steal away, give little warning,
 Choose thine own time;
Say not "Good night"; but in some brighter clime
Bid me "Good morning."

> *Ode to Life*, st. 3

This dead of midnight is the noon of thought.

> *A Summer's Evening Meditation*

GAVRIIL DERZHAVIN
1743–1816

I am a czar — a slave, I am a worm — a god. *God* [1784]

WILLIAM HENRY, DUKE OF GLOUCESTER
1743–1805

Another damned, thick, square book! Always scribble, scribble, scribble! Eh! Mr. Gibbon?

> *Upon receiving from* EDWARD GIBBON *volume II of the Decline and Fall of the Roman Empire* [1781]. *From Best's Literary Memorials*

THOMAS JEFFERSON
1743–1826

A lively and lasting sense of filial duty is more effectually impressed on the mind of a son or daughter by reading *King Lear*, than by all the dry volumes of ethics, and divinity, that ever were written.

> *Letter to Robert Skipwith* [*August 3, 1771*]

The God who gave us life, gave us liberty at the same time.[1]

> *Summary View of the Rights of British America* [1774]

When, in the course of human events, it becomes necessary for one people to dissolve the political bands which have connected them with another, and to assume among the powers of the earth the separate and equal station to which the laws of nature and of nature's God[2] entitle them, a decent respect to the opinions of mankind requires that they should declare the causes which impel them to the separation. We hold these truths to be self-evident; that all men are created equal; that they are endowed by their creator with certain unalienable rights;[3] that among these are life, liberty, and the pursuit of happiness; that to secure these rights, governments are instituted among men, deriving their just powers from the consent of the governed; that whenever any form of government becomes destructive to these ends, it is the right of the people to alter or to abolish it, and to institute new government, laying its foundation on such principles, and organizing its powers in such form, as to them shall seem most likely to effect their safety and happiness.

> *Declaration of Independence* [*July 4, 1776*]

We must therefore . . . hold them [the British] as we hold the rest of mankind, enemies in war, in peace friends. *Ib.*

[1] See Patrick Henry, p. 465b.
[2] See Bolingbroke, p. 397b, and Pope, p. 410a.
[3] The phrase is frequently misquoted "inalienable."

All men are born free and equal, and have certain natural, essential and unalienable rights. — *Constitution of Massachusetts* [1778]

And for the support of this declaration, with a firm reliance on the protection of divine providence, we mutually pledge to each other our lives, our fortunes, and our sacred honor.
Declaration of Independence

Ignorance is preferable to error; and he is less remote from the truth who believes nothing, than he who believes what is wrong.
Notes on the State of Virginia [1781–1785]. *Query 6*

A single zealot may commence persecutor, and better men be his victims.
Ib. 17

Indeed, I tremble for my country when I reflect that God is just.
Ib. 18

Those who labor in the earth are the chosen people of God, if ever he had a chosen people, whose breasts He has made His peculiar deposit for substantial and genuine virtue.   *Ib. 19*

He who permits himself to tell a lie once, finds it much easier to do it a second and third time, till at length it becomes habitual; he tells lies without attending to it, and truths without the world's believing him. This falsehood of the tongue leads to that of the heart, and in time depraves all its good dispositions.
Letter to Peter Carr [*August 19, 1785*]

The basis of our government being the opinion of the people, the very first object should be to keep that right; and were it left to me to decide whether we should have a government without newspapers, or newspapers without a government, I should not hesitate a moment to prefer the latter.
Letter to Colonel Edward Carrington [*January 16, 1787*]

Experience declares that man is the only animal which devours his own kind; for I can apply no milder term to the governments of Europe, and to the

general prey of the rich on the poor.
Letter to Colonel Edward Carrington

I hold it, that a little rebellion, now and then, is a good thing, and as necessary in the political world as storms in the physical.
Letter to James Madison [*January 30, 1787*]

What country before ever existed a century and a half without a rebellion? . . . The tree of liberty must be refreshed from time to time with the blood of patriots and tyrants.[1] It is its natural manure.
Letter to William Stevens Smith [*November 13, 1787*]

The republican is the only form of government which is not eternally at open or secret war with the rights of mankind.
Letter to William Hunter [*March 11, 1790*]

We are not to expect to be translated from despotism to liberty in a feather-bed.
Letter to Lafayette [*April 2, 1790*]

Let what will be said or done, preserve your *sang froid* immovably, and to every obstacle, oppose patience, perseverance, and soothing language.
Letter to William Short [*March 18, 1792*]

Delay is preferable to error.
Letter to George Washington [*May 16, 1792*]

We confide in our strength, without boasting of it; we respect that of others, without fearing it.
Letter to William Carmichael and William Short [1793]

Offices are as acceptable here as elsewhere, and whenever a man has cast a longing eye on them, a rottenness begins in his conduct.
Letter to Tench Coxe [*May 21, 1799*]

[1] See Tertullian, p. 143b, and Barère, p. 484a.

471

I have sworn upon the altar of God, eternal hostility against every form of tyranny over the mind of man.

Letter to Dr. Benjamin Rush
[September 23, 1800]

We are all Republicans — we are all Federalists. If there be any among us who would wish to dissolve this Union or to change its republican form, let them stand undisturbed as monuments of the safety with which error of opinion may be tolerated where reason is left free to combat it.

First Inaugural Address
[March 4, 1801]

But would the honest patriot, in the full tide of successful experiment, abandon a government which has so far kept us free and firm, on the theoretic and visionary fear that this government, the world's best hope, may by possibility want energy to preserve itself?   *Ib.*

Sometimes it is said that man cannot be trusted with the government of himself. Can he, then, be trusted with the government of others? Or have we found angels in the forms of kings to govern him? Let history answer this question.   *Ib.*

Still one thing more, fellow citizens — a wise and frugal government, which shall restrain men from injuring one another, which shall leave them otherwise free to regulate their own pursuits of industry and improvement, and shall not take from the mouth of labor the bread it has earned. This is the sum of good government, and this is necessary to close the circle of our felicities.   *Ib.*

Equal and exact justice to all men, of whatever state or persuasion, religious or political; peace, commerce, and honest friendship with all nations, entangling alliances with none. . . . Freedom of religion; freedom of the press, and freedom of person under the protection of the *habeas corpus*, and trial by juries impartially selected. These principles form the bright constellation which

has gone before us, and guided our steps through an age of revolution and reformation. The wisdom of our sages and the blood of our heroes have been devoted to their attainment. They should be the creed of our political faith, the text of civil instruction, the touchstone by which we try the services of those we trust; and should we wander from them in moments of error or alarm, let us hasten to retrace our steps and to regain the road which alone leads to peace, liberty, and safety.

First Inaugural Address

Of the various executive abilities, no one excited more anxious concern than that of placing the interests of our fellow-citizens in the hands of honest men, with understanding sufficient for their stations.

Letter to Elias Shipman and Others of New Haven [July 12, 1801]

If a due participation of office is a matter of right, how are vacancies to be obtained? Those by death are few; by resignation, none.   *Ib.*

Whensoever hostile aggressions . . . require a resort to war, we must meet our duty and convince the world that we are just friends and brave enemies.

Letter to Andrew Jackson
[December 3, 1806]

When a man assumes a public trust, he should consider himself as public property.[1]

Remark to Baron von Humboldt
[1807]

If, in my retirement to the humble station of a private citizen, I am accompanied with the esteem and approbation of my fellow citizens, trophies obtained by the blood-stained steel, or the tattered flags of the tented field, will never be envied. The care of human life and happiness, and not

[1] See Mathew Henry, p. 386b, and note.

472

their destruction, is the first and only legitimate object of good government.[1]
To the Republican Citizens of Washington County, Maryland [March 31, 1809]

Politics, like religion, hold up the torches of martyrdom to the reformers of error.
Letter to James Ogilvie [August 4, 1811]

The earth belongs to the living, not to the dead.
Letter to John W. Eppes [June 24, 1813]

I agree with you that there is a natural aristocracy among men. The grounds of this are virtue and talents.
Letter to John Adams [October 28, 1813]

Merchants have no country. The mere spot they stand on does not constitute so strong an attachment as that from which they draw their gains.
Letter to Horatio G. Spafford [March 17, 1814]

If a nation expects to be ignorant and free, in a state of civilization, it expects what never was and never will be.
Letter to Colonel Charles Yancey [January 6, 1816]

Enlighten the people generally, and tyranny and oppressions of body and mind will vanish like evil spirits at the dawn of day.
Letter to Du Pont de Nemours [April 24, 1816]

I have the consolation to reflect that during the period of my administration not a drop of the blood of a single fellow citizen was shed by the sword of war or of the law.
Letter to Count Dugnani, Papal Nuncio [February 14, 1818]

But this momentous question [the Missouri Compromise], like a firebell in the night awakened and filled me with

[1] See George Mason, p. 446a.

terror. I considered it the knell of the Union.
Letter to John Holmes [April 22, 1820]

I know no safe depository of the ultimate powers of the society but the people themselves; and if we think them not enlightened enough to exercise their control with a wholesome discretion, the remedy is not to take it from them, but to inform their discretion.
Letter to William Charles Jarvis [September 28, 1820]

And even should the cloud of barbarism and despotism again obscure the science and libraries of Europe, this country remains to preserve and restore light and liberty to them. In short, the flames kindled on the 4th of July, 1776, have spread over too much of the globe to be extinguished by the feeble engines of despotism; on the contrary, they will consume these engines and all who work them.
Letter to John Adams [September 12, 1821]

Amplification is the vice of modern oratory. It is an insult to an assembly of reasonable men, disgusting and revolting instead of persuading. Speeches measured by the hour, die by the hour.
Letter to David Harding, president of the Jefferson Debating Society of Hingham [April 20, 1824]

Men by their constitutions are naturally divided into two parties: (1) Those who fear and distrust the people, and wish to draw all powers from them into the hands of the higher classes. (2) Those who identify themselves with the people, have confidence in them, cherish and consider them as the most honest and safe, although not the most wise depository of the public interests. In every country these two parties exist; and in every one where they are free to think, speak, and write, they will declare themselves.
Letter to Henry Lee [August 10, 1824]

Never buy what you do not want, because it is cheap; it will be dear to you.
A Decalogue of Canons for Observation in Practical Life [February 21, 1825]

When angry, count ten before you speak; if very angry, an hundred.[1]
Ib.

The good old Dominion, the blessed mother of us all.
Thoughts on Lotteries [1826]

This is the Fourth?
Last words [July 4, 1826] [2]

WILLIAM PALEY
1743–1805
Who can refute a sneer?
Moral Philosophy [1785], vol. II, bk. V, ch. 9

CONSTITUTION OF THE UNITED STATES
1787
We the people of the United States, in order to form a more perfect Union, establish justice, insure domestic tranquillity, provide for the common defense, promote the general welfare, and secure the blessings of liberty to ourselves and our posterity, do ordain and establish this Constitution for the United States of America.   *Preamble*

Treason against the United States, shall consist only in levying war against them, or in adhering to their enemies, giving them aid and comfort. No person shall be convicted of treason unless on the testimony of two witnesses to the same overt act, or on confession in open court.   *Art. III, sec. 3*

This Constitution, and the laws of the United States, which shall be made in pursuance thereof; and all treaties made, or which shall be made, under the authority of the United States, shall be the Supreme Law of the land; and the judges in every State shall be bound thereby, any thing in the Constitution or laws of any State to the contrary notwithstanding.   *Art. VI, sec. 2*

Congress shall make no law respecting an establishment of religion, or prohibiting the free exercise thereof; or abridging the freedom of speech, or of the press; or the right of the people peaceably to assemble, and to petition the government for a redress of grievances.   *First Amendment [1791]*

ANTOINE LAURENT LAVOISIER
1743–1794
It is impossible to dissociate language from science or science from language, because every natural science always involves three things: the sequence of phenomena on which the science is based; the abstract concepts which call these phenomena to mind; and the words in which the concepts are expressed. To call forth a concept a word is needed; to portray a phenomenon, a concept is needed. All three mirror one and the same reality.[1]
Traité Élémentaire de Chimie [1789]

I shall therefore content myself with saying that if, by the term *elements*, we mean to express the simple and indivisible molecules that compose bodies, it is probable that we know nothing about them; but if, on the contrary, we express by the term *elements* or *principles of bodies* the idea of the last point reached by analysis, all substances that we have not yet been able to decompose by any means are elements to us.[2]
Ib.

[1] See Mark Twain, p. 762a.
[2] John Adams died the same day. See his last words, p. 464a.

[1] Translated by J. LIPETZ, D. E. GERSHENSON, and D. A. GREENBERG.
[2] Translated by D. McKIE.

JOHANN GOTTFRIED HERDER
1744–1803

A gain it is to find a beautiful human soul.
>*Der gerettete Jungling* [1797]

Light, love, life.
>*Herder's Epitaph* [1803]

ROWLAND HILL
1744–1833

He did not see any reason why the devil should have all the good tunes.
>*Sermons. From* E. W. BROOME, *the Reverend Rowland Hill,* p. 93

JEAN BAPTISTE LAMARCK
1744–1829

FIRST LAW. In every animal . . . a more frequent and continuous use of any organ gradually strengthens, develops and enlarges that organ . . . while the permanent disuse of any organ imperceptibly weakens and deteriorates it, and progressively diminishes its functional capacity, until it finally disappears.

SECOND LAW. All the acquisitions or losses wrought by nature in individuals . . . are preserved by reproduction to the new individuals which arise.
>*Philosophie Zoologique* [1809] [1]

JOSIAH QUINCY
1744–1775

Blandishments will not fascinate us, nor will threats of a "halter" intimidate. For, under God, we are determined that wheresoever, whensoever, or howsoever we shall be called to make our exit, we will die free men.
>*Observations on the Boston Port Bill* [1774]

[1] Translated by HUGH ELLIOT.

CHARLES DIBDIN
1745–1814

Did you ever hear of Captain Wattle? He was all for love, and a little for the bottle.
>*Captain Wattle and Miss Roe*

Here, a sheer hulk, lies poor Tom Bowling,
The darling of our crew;
No more he'll hear the tempest howling,
For death has broach'd him to.
>*Tom Bowling*

Faithful below he did his duty,
But now he's gone aloft.   *Ib.*

Spanking Jack was so comely, so pleasant, so jolly,
Though winds blew great guns, still he'd whistle and sing.
>*The Sailor's Consolation*

HANNAH MORE
1745–1833

Since trifles make the sum of human things,
And half our misery from our foibles springs.
>*Sensibility*

Small habits well pursued betimes
May reach the dignity of crimes.
>*Florio and His Friend*

WILLIAM SCOTT, LORD STOWELL
1745–1836

A dinner lubricates business.
>*From* BOSWELL, *Life of Johnson* [1791]

The elegant simplicity of the three per cents.[1]
>*From* CAMPBELL, *Lives of the Lord Chancellors* [1857], *vol. X, ch. 212*

[1] The sweet simplicity of the three per cents. — DISRAELI, *Endymion* [1880], *ch. 96*

SIR WILLIAM JONES
1746–1794

On parent knees, a naked new-born child,
Weeping thou sat'st while all around thee smiled;
So live, that sinking in thy last long sleep,
Calm thou mayst smile, while all around thee weep.

From the Persian [1786]

GOTTFRIED AUGUST BÜRGER
1747–1794

The dead ride swiftly.

Lenore [1773]

JOHN PAUL JONES
1747–1792

I have not yet begun to fight.

Aboard the Bonhomme Richard [1]
[*September 23, 1779*]

JOHN O'KEEFFE
1747–1833

Amo, amas,
I love a lass,
As a cedar tall and slender;
Sweet cowslip's grace
Is her nominative case,
And she's of the feminine gender!

Agreeable Surprise, act II, sc. 2,
Song

Fat, fair and forty [2] were all the toasts of the young men.   *Irish Minnie*

And why I'm so plump the reason I tell —
Who leads a good life is sure to live well.

Merry Sherwood. A Friar of
Orders Gray, st. 1

You should always except the present company.   *London Hermit*

[1] Engaged with the British frigate *Serapis*, off Flamborough Head, England.
[2] I am resolved to grow fat, and look young till forty! — DRYDEN, *Secret Love; or, The Maiden Queen* [1667], *act III, sc. 1.*

SAMUEL PARR [1]
1747–1825

Now that the old lion is dead, every ass thinks he may kick at him.

[*1784*] *While dining with Sir Joshua Reynolds, after the death of Dr. Johnson. From* BOSWELL, *Life of Johnson* [*1791*]

FRANÇOIS ALEXANDRE FRÉDÉRIC, DUC DE LA ROCHEFOUCAULD– LIANCOURT
1747–1827

Louis XVI: Is it a revolt?
La Rochefoucauld-Liancourt: No, Sire, it is a revolution.

Upon learning at Versailles of the fall of the Bastille [1789]

JOHN LOGAN
1748–1788

Thou hast no sorrow in thy song,
No winter in thy year.

To the Cuckoo [*Attributed*][2]

EMMANUEL JOSEPH SIEYÈS
1748–1836

I survived.[3]

Upon being asked what he had done during the Terror

CHARLES JAMES FOX
1749–1806

[On the fall of the Bastille] How much the greatest event it is that ever happened in the world! and how much the best!

Letter to Richard Fitzpatrick [*July 30, 1789*]. *From* LORD JOHN RUSSELL, *Life and Times of C. J. Fox* [*1859–1866*], *vol. II, p. 361*

[1] Dr. Parr composed the Latin epitaph for the monument to Dr. Johnson, placed in St. Paul's Cathedral, London, February 1796.
[2] Also attributed to MICHAEL BRUCE [1746–1767].
[3] J'ai vécu.

JOHANN WOLFGANG VON GOETHE
1749–1832

There is strong shadow where there is much light.
> *Götz von Berlichingen* [1773],
> *act I*

One lives but once in the world.
> *Clavigo* [1774], *act I, sc. 1*

If you inquire what the people are like here,
I must answer, "The same as everywhere!"
> *Die Leiden des jungen Werthers*
> [1774–1787], *May 17*

Radiant misery.   *Ib.* [*December 24*]

The history of science is science itself; the history of the individual, the individual.   *Mineralogy and Geology*

Getting along with women,
Knocking around with men,
Having more credit than money,
Thus one goes through the world.
> *Claudine von Villa Bella* [1776]

Who never ate his bread with tears,
Who never sat weeping on his bed
During care-ridden nights
Knows you not, you heavenly powers.[1]
> *Wilhelm Meisters Lehrjahre*
> [1786–1830], *bk. II, ch. 13*

All guilt is punished upon earth.   *Ib.*

Who longs in solitude to live,
Ah! soon his wish will gain:
Men hope and love, men get and give,
And leave him to his pain.
> *Ib. III, 1*

Knowst thou the land where the lemon trees bloom,[2]
Where the gold orange glows in the deep thicket's gloom,
Where a wind ever soft from the blue heaven blows,
And the groves are of laurel and myrtle and rose? [3]   *Ib.*

---

[1] See Longfellow, p. 621a.
[2] Kennst du das Land, wo die Zitronen blühn?
[3] See Byron, p. 558a.

If I love you, what business is it of yours?
> *Wilhelm Meisters Lehrjahre,*
> *bk. IV, ch. 9*

One ought, every day at least, to hear a little song, read a good poem, see a fine picture, and, if it were possible, to speak a few reasonable words.[1]
> *Ib. V, 1*

To know of someone here and there whom we accord with, who is living on with us, even in silence — this makes our earthly ball a peopled garden.
> *Ib. VII, 5*

Art is long, life short; [2] judgment difficult, opportunity transient.
> *Ib. 9*

Seeking with the soul the land of the Greeks.
> *Iphigenie auf Tauris* [1787],
> *act I, sc. 1*

A useless life is an early death.   *Ib. 2*

One says a lot in vain, refusing;
The other mainly hears the "No."
> *Ib. 3*

Pleasure and love are the pinions of great deeds.   *Ib. II, 1*

The best is good enough.[3]
> *Italian Journey* [*March 3, 1787*]

A noble person attracts noble people, and knows how to hold on to them.
> *Torquato Tasso* [1790], *act I, sc. 1*

A talent is formed in stillness, a character in the world's torrent.
> *Ib. 2*

Three things are to be looked to in a building: that it stand on the right spot; that it be securely founded; that it be successfully executed.
> *Elective Affinities* [4] [1808],
> *bk. I, ch. 9*

The sum which two married people owe to one another defies calculation. It

---

[1] See Charles Eliot Norton, p. 728b.
[2] See Hippocrates, p. 88b, and note.
[3] In der Kunst ist das Beste gut genug.
[4] Translated by JAMES ANTHONY FROUDE [1818–1894].

is an infinite debt, which can only be discharged through all eternity.

> *Elective Affinities, bk. I, ch. 9*

A pretty foot is a great gift of nature.

> *Ib. 11*

One is never satisfied with a portrait of a person that one knows.

> *Ib. II, 2*

The fate of the architect is the strangest of all. How often he expends his whole soul, his whole heart and passion, to produce buildings into which he himself may never enter.

> *Ib. 3*

Let us live in as small a circle as we will, we are either debtors or creditors before we have had time to look round.

> *Ib. 4*

Mediocrity has no greater consolation than in the thought that genius is not immortal.   *Ib. 5*

A teacher who can arouse a feeling for one single good action, for one single good poem, accomplishes more than he who fills our memory with rows on rows of natural objects, classified with name and form.   *Ib. 7*

Who wants to understand the poem
Must go to the land of poetry;
Who wishes to understand the poet
Must go to the poet's land.

> *West-östlicher Diwan*
> *[1819], motto*

For I have been a man, and that means to have been a fighter.

> *Ib. Buch des Paradies*

If I work incessantly to the last, nature owes me another form of existence when the present one collapses.

> *Letter to Eckermann*
> *[February 4, 1829]*

I call architecture frozen music.[1]

> *Ib. [March 23, 1829]*

---

[1] Ich die Baukunst eine erstarrte Musik nenne. Since it [architecture] is music in space, as it were a frozen music. — FRIEDRICH VON SCHELLING [1775–1854], *Philosophie der Kunst, p. 576* See Madame de Staël, p. 502b.

The artist may be well advised to keep his work to himself till it is completed, because no one can readily help him or advise him with it . . . but the scientist is wiser not to withhold a single finding or a single conjecture from publicity.

> *Essay on Experimentation*

Man errs, while his struggle lasts.[1]

> *Faust [1808–1832], pt. I*
> *Prologue in Heaven*

Dear friend, theory is all gray,
And the golden tree of life is green.

> *Ib. Apprentice Scene*

As soon as you trust yourself, you will know how to live.   *Ib.*

He who wishes to uphold the truth and has but one tongue, he will uphold it indeed.   *Ib. Street Scene*

Two souls dwell, alas! in my breast.

> *Ib. Before the Gate*

I am the spirit that always denies.[2]

> *Ib. Study*

My peace is gone,
My heart is heavy.[3]

> *Ib. Gretchen at the Spinning Wheel*

Who can think of something stupid,
Who can think of anything smart
That prior ages haven't thought of? [4]

> *Ib. pt. II. The Gothic Chamber*

Who strives always to the utmost, him can we save.[5]   *Ib.*

He only earns his freedom and existence who daily conquers them anew.[6]

> *Ib.*

I was fair, too, and that was my undoing.   *Ib.*

The Eternal Feminine draws us on.[7]

> *Ib., last line*

---

[1] Es irrt der Mensch, so lang er strebt.
[2] Ich bin der Geist der stets verneint.
[3] Meine Ruh' ist hin,
   Mein Herz ist schwer.
[4] See *Ecclesiastes 1:9*, p. 27a.
[5] Wer immer strebend sich bemüht,
   Den können wir erlösen.
[6] Nur der verdient sich Freiheit wie das Leben der täglich sie erobern muss.
[7] Das Ewig-Weibliche zieht uns hinan.

Do you wish to roam farther and far-
   ther?
See! The Good lies so near.
Only learn to seize good fortune,
For good fortune's always here.
                          Erinnerung

In limitations he first shows himself the
   master,
And the law can only bring us freedom.   *Was wir Bringen* [1802]

Create, artist! Do not talk!
                             Saying

Everything in the world can be borne
Except for a series of beautiful days.
                    Proverb collection

There is peace
O'er all the peaks,
In all the treetops
You feel scarce a breath.
The little birds are silent in the forest.
Just wait, soon
You too will rest.
              Wanderers Nachtlied II

America, you have it better than our
continent, the old one.[1]
      Wendts Musen-Almanach [1831]

Without haste, but without rest.
                              Motto

More light!   *Last words*

PIERRE SIMON DE LAPLACE
1749–1827

Given for one instant an intelligence
which could comprehend all the forces
by which nature is animated and the
respective positions of the beings which
compose it, if moreover this intelligence
were vast enough to submit these data
to analysis, it would embrace in the
same formula both the movements of
the largest bodies in the universe and
those of the lightest atom; to it nothing

[1] *Amerika, du hast es besser — als unser*
Kontinent, das alte.

would be uncertain, and the future as
the past would be present to its eyes.
      Oeuvres, vol. VII, Théorie Ana-
      lytique des Probabilités [1812–
      1820], *introduction*

The theory of probabilities is at bottom nothing but common sense reduced to calculus.   *Ib.*

Sire, I have no need of that hypothesis.[1]

      From ERIC TEMPLE BELL, *Men*
      of Mathematics [1937]

HONORÉ GABRIEL DE RIQUETTI, COMTE DE MIRABEAU
1749–1791

Go and tell those who have sent you
that we are here by the will of the nation and that we shall not leave save at
the point of bayonets.
      Speech in the États-Généraux
      [*June 23, 1789*]

LADY ANNE BARNARD
1750–1825

When the sheep are in the fauld, and
   the kye's come hame,
And a' the weary warld to rest are
   gone.
      Auld Robin Gray [1771], *st. 1*

JOHN PHILPOT CURRAN
1750–1817

The condition upon which God hath
given liberty to man is eternal vigilance; [2] which condition if he break,

[1] Reply to Napoleon Bonaparte's remark upon
receiving a copy of Laplace's *Mécanique Céleste:*
"You have written this huge book on the system
of the world without once mentioning the author
of the universe."
[2] Commonly quoted: Eternal vigilance is the
price of liberty. Attributed also to Jefferson.
   There is one safeguard known generally to
the wise, which is an advantage and security to
all, but especially to democracies as against
despots. What is it? Distrust. — DEMOSTHENES
[c. 385–322 B.C.], *Philippic 2, sec. 24*

servitude is at once the consequence of his crime and the punishment of his guilt.

Speech Upon the Right of Election of Lord Mayor of Dublin [July 10, 1790]

JOHN TRUMBULL
1750–1831

But optics sharp it needs, I ween,
To see what is not to be seen.
McFingal [1782], *canto I, l.* 67

JAMES MADISON
1751–1836

By a faction, understand a number of citizens, whether amounting to a majority or minority of the whole, who are united and actuated by some common impulse of passion, or of interest, adverse to the rights of other citizens, or to the permanent and aggregate interests of the community.
The Federalist [1787], *no.* 10

The latent causes of faction are thus sown in the nature of man; and we see them everywhere brought into different degrees of activity, according to the different circumstances of civil society. A zeal for different opinions concerning religion, concerning government, and many other points, as well of speculation as of practice; an attachment of different leaders ambitiously contending for pre-eminence and power; or to persons of other descriptions whose fortunes have been interesting to the human passions, have, in turn, divided mankind into parties, inflamed them with mutual animosity, and rendered them much more disposed to vex and oppress each other than to cooperate for their common good. . . . But the most common and durable source of factions has been the various and unequal distribution of property.
Ib.

To secure the public good, and private rights, against the danger of . . .

faction, and at the same time to preserve the spirit and form of popular government, is then the great object to which our inquiries are directed.
The Federalist, no. 10

I believe there are more instances of the abridgment of the freedom of the people by gradual and silent encroachments of those in power than by violent and sudden usurpations.
Speech in the Virginia Convention [June 16, 1788]

RICHARD BRINSLEY SHERIDAN
1751–1816

Mrs. Malaprop: Illiterate him, I say, quite from your memory.
The Rivals [1775], *act I, sc.* 2

'Tis safest in matrimony to begin with a little aversion.   *Ib.*

A circulating library in a town is as an evergreen tree of diabolical knowledge! It blossoms through the year!
                                            Ib.

A progeny of learning.   *Ib.*

Never say more than is necessary.
                                         Ib. II, 1

I know you are laughing in your sleeve.   *Ib.*

He is the very pineapple of politeness!   *Ib. III, 3*

If I reprehend anything in this world, it is the use of my oracular tongue, and a nice derangement of epitaphs!   *Ib.*

As headstrong as an allegory on the banks of the Nile.   *Ib.*

Too civil by half.   *Ib. 4*

Our ancestors are very good kind of folks; but they are the last people I should choose to have a visiting acquaintance with.   *Ib. IV, 1*

No caparisons, miss, if you please. Caparisons don't become a young woman.   *Ib. 2*

You are not like Cerberus, three gentlemen at once, are you?
> *The Rivals, act IV, sc. 2*

The quarrel is a very pretty quarrel as it stands; we should only spoil it by trying to explain it.   *Ib. 3*

My valor is certainly going! — it is sneaking off! I feel it oozing out, as it were, at the palm of my hands!
> *Ib. V, 3*

I own the soft impeachment.   *Ib.*

Through all the drama — whether damned or not —
Love gilds the scene, and women guide the plot.   *Ib. Epilogue*

An apothecary should never be out of spirits.
> *St. Patrick's Day* [1775], *act I, sc. 1*

Death's a debt; his mandamus binds all alike — no bail, no demurrer.
> *Ib. II, 4*

I ne'er could any luster see
In eyes that would not look on me.
> *The Duenna* [1775], *act I, sc. 2*

I loved him for himself alone.
> *Ib. 3*

I was struck all of a heap.
> *Ib. II, 2*

A bumper of good liquor
Will end a contest quicker
Than justice, judge, or vicar.[1]   *Ib. 3*

Conscience has no more to do with gallantry than it has with politics.
> *Ib. 4*

Tale-bearers are as bad as the tale-makers.
> *The School for Scandal* [1777], *act I, sc. 1*

You shall see them on a beautiful quarto page, where a neat rivulet of text shall meander through a meadow of margin.   *Ib.*

You had no taste when you married me.
> *The School for Scandal, act I, sc. 2*

Here's to the maiden of bashful fifteen;
Here's to the widow of fifty;
Here's to the flaunting, extravagant quean,
And here's to the housewife that's thrifty.
     Let the toast pass —
     Drink to the lass;
I'll warrant she'll prove an excuse for the glass.   *Ib. III, 3*

An unforgiving eye, and a damned disinheriting countenance.
> *Ib. IV, 1*

Be just before you're generous.
> *Ib.*

There is not a passion so strongly rooted in the human heart as envy.
> *The Critic* [1779], *act I, sc. 1*

The newspapers! Sir, they are the most villainous — licentious — abominable — infernal — Not that I ever read them — no — I make it a rule never to look into a newspaper.   *Ib.*

Egad, I think the interpreter is the hardest to be understood of the two!
> *Ib. 2*

A practitioner in panegyric, or, to speak more plainly, a professor of the art of puffing.   *Ib.*

The number of those who undergo the fatigue of judging for themselves is very small indeed.[1]   *Ib.*

Certainly nothing is unnatural that is not physically impossible.   *Ib. II, 1*

I wish, sir, you would practice this without me. I can't stay dying here all night.   *Ib. III, 1*

An oyster may be crossed in love.[2]
> *Ib.*

The right honorable gentleman is in-

---

[1] The government of a nation is often decided over a cup of coffee, or the fate of empires changed by an extra bottle of Johannisberg. — G. P. R. JAMES, *Richelieu* [1829], *ch. 16*

[1] See J. R. Lowell, p. 694b, and Bryce, p. 778a.
[2] From the interpolated tragedy, *The Spanish Armada.*

debted to his memory for his jests, and to his imagination for his facts.[1]

Sheridaniana. Speech in Reply to Mr. Dundas

You write with ease to show your breeding,
But easy writing's curst hard reading.

Clio's Protest

JOHANN HEINRICH VOSS
1751–1826

Who does not love wine, women, and song
Remains a fool his whole life long.[2]

Attributed

THOMAS CHATTERTON[3]
1752–1770

Mie love ys dedde,
Gon to hys death-bedde,
Al under the wyllowe-tree.

Mynstrelles Songe [4]

PHILIP FRENEAU
1752–1832

An age employed in edging steel
Can no poetic raptures feel . . .
No shaded stream, no quiet grove
Can this fantastic century move.

Poems [1795]. *To an Author, st. 6*

In spite of all the learned have said,
I still my old opinion keep;
The posture that we give the dead
Points out the soul's eternal sleep.

The Indian Burying Ground
[1788], *st. 1*

Then rushed to meet the insulting foe;
They took the spear — but left the shield.[1]

To the Memory of the Brave Americans who Fell at Eutaw Springs, S.C. September 8, 1781 [1786], *st. 5*

FRIEDRICH MAXIMILIAN VON KLINGER
1752–1831

Sturm und Drang [Storm and stress].

Title of a Play [1776]

LEONARD McNALLY
1752–1820

On Richmond Hill there lives a lass
More bright than Mayday morn;
Whose charms all other maids' surpass, —
A rose without a thorn.

The Lass of Richmond Hill,[2] *st. 1*

JOSEPH DE MAISTRE
1753–1821

Every nation has the government it deserves. *Letter to X* [1811]

The sword of justice has no scabbard.

Les Soirées de Saint-Petersbourg [1821]. *Premier Entretien*

ANTOINE DE RIVAROL
1753–1801

What is not clear is not French.

Discours sur l'universalité de la langue française [1784]

---

[1] See Le Sage, p. 391a.

[2] Wer nicht liebt Wein, Weib und Gesang,
Der bleibt ein Narr sein Leben lang.

The couplet has also been attributed to Luther, apparently on no better authority than an eighteenth-century jingle in which "Luther" is needed to rhyme with "Futter." REDLICH ascribes it to Voss in *Die poetischen Beiträge zum Waudsbecker Bothen* [1871].

[3] See Wordsworth, p. 511b.

[4] This is from the poems of "Thomas Rowley," an imaginary fifteenth-century Bristol poet invented by Chatterton. Editions of the poems appeared in 1778 and 1782, and were exposed in 1777-8 by Thomas Tyrwhitt.

[1] When Prussia hurried to the field,
And snatched the spear, but left the shield.
SCOTT, *Marmion* [1808], *canto III, introduction*

[2] Also attributed to J. UPTON [1670–1749] and W. HUDSON.

JOEL BARLOW
1754–1813

I sing the sweets I know, the charms I feel,
My morning incense, and my evening meal —
The sweets of Hasty Pudding.
The Hasty Pudding [1792], *canto I*

E'en in thy native regions, how I blush
To hear the Pennsylvanians call thee *Mush!* **Ib.**

GEORGE CRABBE[1]
1754–1832

What is a church? — Our honest sexton tells,
'Tis a tall building, with a tower and bells.
The Borough [1810]. *Letter 2, The Church*

Habit with him was all the test of truth,
"It must be right: I've done it from my youth." **Ib.** 3, *The Vicar*

Books cannot always please, however good;
Minds are not ever craving for their food. **Ib.** 24, *Schools*

In idle wishes fools supinely stay;
Be there a will, and wisdom finds a way. *The Birth of Flattery*

Cut and come again.
Tales [1812]. VII, *The Widow's Tale*

And took for truth the test of ridicule.[2]
Tales of the Hall [1819], *bk. VIII, The Sisters*

---

[1] See Byron, p. 555a.
[2] How comes it to pass, then, that we appear such cowards in reasoning, and are so afraid to stand the test of ridicule? — ANTHONY COOPER, EARL OF SHAFTESBURY [1671–1713], *Characteristics: A Letter Concerning Enthusiasm, sec. 2*
Truth, 'tis supposed, may bear all lights; and one of those principal lights or natural mediums by which things are to be viewed in order to a thorough recognition is ridicule itself. — SHAFTESBURY, *Essay on the Freedom of Wit and Humor, sec. 1*
'Twas the saying of an ancient sage (Gorgias

The ring, so worn as you behold,
So thin, so pale, is yet of gold.
His Mother's Wedding Ring

WILLIAM DRENNAN
1754–1820

Nor one feeling of vengeance presume to defile
The cause, or the men, of the Emerald Isle.[1] *Erin* [1795], *st. 3*

JOSEPH JOUBERT
1754–1824

I had to grow old to learn what I wanted to know, and I should need to be young to say well what I know.
Pensées [1842]

Ask the young: they know everything! **Ib.**

To teach is to learn twice. **Ib.**

JEANNE MANON ROLAND
1754–1793

O liberty! O liberty! What crimes are committed in thy name!
Last words, before her death on the guillotine. From LAMARTINE, *Histoire des Girondins* [1847]

CHARLES MAURICE DE TALLEYRAND-PÉRIGORD
1754–1838

Black as the devil,
Hot as hell,
Pure as an angel,
Sweet as love.[2] *Recipe for coffee*

Leontinus, *apud* Aristotle's *Rhetoric*, that humor was the only test of gravity, and gravity of humor. For a subject which would not bear raillery was suspicious; and a jest which would not bear a serious examination was certainly false wit. — *Ib. 5*
[1] The first known use of this appellation for Ireland.
[2] Noir comme le diable,
Chaud comme l'enfer,

[Of the Bourbons] They have learned nothing, and forgotten nothing.[1]

> From CHEVALIER DE PANAT, *letter to Mallet du Pan* [*January 1796*]

[Of the battle of Borodino, 1812] It is the beginning of the end.[2]

> From EDOUARD FOURNIER, *L'Esprit dans l'Histoire* [*1857*]

The United States has thirty-two religions but only one dish.

> *Attributed*

Women sometimes forgive a man who forces the opportunity, but never a man who misses one. *Attributed*

[To a young diplomat] Don't be eager![3]

> From SAINT-BEUVE, *Portraits de Femmes: Madame de Staël*

BENJAMIN WATERHOUSE
1754–1846

Tobacco is a filthy weed,
That from the devil does proceed;
It drains your purse, it burns your clothes,
And makes a chimney of your nose.

> From DR. OLIVER WENDELL HOLMES [*1809–1894*], *who was vaccinated by Dr. Waterhouse*

BERTRAND BARÈRE DE VIEUZAC
1755–1841

The tree of liberty only grows when watered by the blood of tyrants.[4]

> *Speech in the National Convention* [*1792*]

Pur comme un ange,
Doux comme l'amour.
This appears as an inscription on many old coffeepots.
[1] Ils n'ont rien appris, ni rien oublié.
[2] Voilà le commencement de la fin.
[3] Pas de zèle!
[4] See Tertullian, p. 143b, and Jefferson, p. 471b.

It is only the dead who do not return. *Speech* [*1794*]

ANTHELME BRILLAT-SAVARIN
1755–1826

Tell me what you eat, and I will tell you what you are.

> *Physiologie du Goût* [*1825*], *ch. 4*

A dessert without cheese is like a beautiful woman with only one eye.

> *Ib. 14*

One can become a cook, but one is born a roaster of meat. *Ib. 15*

A meal without wine is like a day without sunshine. *Ib.*

NATHAN HALE
1755–1776

I only regret that I have but one life to lose for my country.[1]

> *Last words, before being hanged by the British as a spy* [*September 22, 1776*]

ALEXANDER HAMILTON
1755–1804

A national debt, if it is not excessive, will be to us a national blessing.[2]

> *Letter to Robert Morris* [*April 30, 1781*]

I believe the British government forms the best model the world ever produced. . . . This government has for its object public strength and individual security.

> *Federal Convention Debates* [*June 18, 1787*]

All communities divide themselves into the few and the many. The first are the rich and wellborn, the other the mass of the people. . . . The people are

---

[1] See Addison, p. 393b.
[2] At the time we were funding our national debt, we heard much about "a public debt being a public blessing." — THOMAS JEFFERSON, *Letter to John W. Epps* [*November 6, 1813*]
See Daniel Webster, p. 547a.

turbulent and changing; they seldom judge or determine right. Give therefore to the first class a distinct, permanent share in the government. They will check the unsteadiness of the second, and as they cannot receive any advantage by a change, they therefore will ever maintain good government.

Federal Convention Debates

We are now forming a republican government. Real liberty is neither found in despotism or the extremes of democracy, but in moderate governments. *Ib. [June 26, 1787]*

Let Americans disdain to be the instruments of European greatness. Let the thirteen States, bound together in a strict and indissoluble Union, concur in erecting one great American system, superior to the control of all transatlantic force or influence, and able to dictate the terms of the connection between the old and the new world!

The Federalist [1787–1788],
no. 11

Government implies the power of making laws. It is essential to the idea of a law, that it be attended with a sanction; or, in other words, a penalty or punishment for disobedience.

Ib. 15

Why has government been instituted at all? Because the passions of men will not conform to the dictates of reason and justice, without constraint. **Ib.**

Every power vested in a government is in its nature sovereign, and includes by force of the term a right to employ all the means requisite . . . to the attainment of the ends of such power.

Opinion on the Constitutionality of the Bank [February 23, 1791]

If the end be clearly comprehended within any of the specified powers, and if the measure have an obvious relation to that end, and is not forbidden by any particular provision of the Constitution, it may safely be deemed to come within the compass of the national authority.

Opinion on the Constitutionality of the Bank

LOUIS XVIII
1755–1824

Punctuality is the politeness of kings.[1] *A favorite saying*

JOHN MARSHALL
1755–1835

It is emphatically the province and duty of the judicial department to say what the law is. . . . If two laws conflict with each other, the courts must decide on the operation of each. . . . This is of the very essence of judicial duty.

Marbury v. Madison, 1 Cranch,
1317 [1803]

We must never forget that it is a *constitution* we are expounding.

McCulloch v. Maryland, 4 Wheaton 316, 407 [1819]

This provision is made in a constitution, intended to endure for ages to come, and consequently, to be adapted to the various *crises* of human affairs.

Ib. 415

Let the end be legitimate, let it be within the scope of the constitution, and all means which are appropriate, which are plainly adapted to that end, which are not prohibited, but consist with the letter and spirit of the constitution, are constitutional. *Ib. 421*

The power to tax involves the power to destroy.[2] *Ib. 431*

The people made the Constitution, and the people can unmake it. It is the creature of their own will, and lives only by their will.

Cohens v. Virginia, 6 Wheaton (19 U.S.) 264, 389 [1821]

---

[1] L'exactitude est la politesse des rois.
[2] See Oliver Wendell Holmes, Jr., p. 788b.

MARTIN JOSEPH ROUTH
1755–1854

You will find it a very good practice always to verify your references, sir.
> *From* J. W. BURGON, *Memoir of Dr. Routh, Quarterly Review* [*July 1878*]

HENRY LEE
[LIGHT-HORSE HARRY]
1756–1818

To the memory of the Man, first in war, first in peace, and first in the hearts of his countrymen.
> *Resolutions presented to the House of Representatives on the death of Washington* [*December 1799*]

WILLIAM BLAKE[1]
1757–1827

How sweet I roam'd from field to field,
  And tasted all the summer's pride,
Till I the prince of love beheld
  Who in the sunny beams did glide.
> *Poetical Sketches* [*1783*]. *Song, st. 1*

He loves to sit and hear me sing,
  Then, laughing, sports and plays with me;
Then stretches out my golden wing,
  And mocks my loss of liberty.
> *Ib. st. 4*

My silks and fine array,
  My smiles and languish'd air,
By love are driv'n away;
  And mournful lean Despair
Brings me yew to deck my grave:
Such end true lovers have.
> *Ib. Song, st. 1*

Like a fiend in a cloud,
  With howling woe,
After night I do crowd,
  And with night will go;
I turn my back to the east,
From whence comforts have increas'd;

[1] *Poetry and Prose of William Blake,* Geoffrey Keynes, ed. [*1927*]

For light doth seize my brain
With frantic pain.
> *Poetical Sketches. Mad Song, st. 3*

How have you left the ancient love
  That bards of old enjoy'd in you!
The languid strings do scarcely move!
  The sound is forc'd, the notes are few!
> *Ib. To the Muses, st. 4*

Does the Eagle know what is in the pit?
  Or wilt thou go ask the Mole?
Can Wisdom be put in a silver rod?
  Or Love in a golden bowl?
> *The Book of Thel* [*1789*]. *Thel's Motto*

Piping down the valleys wild,
Piping songs of pleasant glee,
On a cloud I saw a child,
And he laughing said to me:
"Pipe a song about a Lamb!"
> *Songs of Innocence* [*1789*]. *Introduction, st. 1, 2*

And I made a rural pen,
And I stain'd the water clear,
And I wrote my happy songs
Every child may joy to hear.
> *Ib. st. 5*

Sing louder around
To the bells' cheerful sound,
While our sports shall be seen
On the echoing green.
> *Ib. The Echoing Green, st. 1*

Little Lamb, who made thee?
Dost thou know who made thee?
Gave thee life, and bid thee feed
By the stream and o'er the mead;
Gave thee clothing of delight,
Softest clothing, wooly, bright.
> *Ib. The Lamb, st. 1*

My mother bore me in the southern wild,
And I am black, but O! my soul is white;
White as an angel is the English child,
But I am black, as if bereav'd of light.
> *Ib. The Little Black Boy, st. 1*

"And we are put on earth a little space,

That we may learn to bear the beams of
love;
And these black bodies and this sun-
burnt face
Is but a cloud, and like a shady grove."
Songs of Innocence. The
Little Black Boy, st. 4

I'll shade him from the heat, till he can
bear
To lean in joy upon our father's knee;
And then I'll stand and stroke his silver
hair,
And be like him, and he will then love
me. *Ib. st. 7*

When my mother died I was very
young,
And my father sold me while yet my
tongue
Could scarcely cry " 'weep! 'weep!
'weep! 'weep!"
So your chimneys I sweep, and in soot I
sleep.
Ib. The Chimney Sweeper, st. 1

To Mercy, Pity, Peace, and Love
All pray in their distress;
And to these virtues of delight
Return their thankfulness.
Ib. The Divine Image, st. 1

For Mercy has a human heart,
Pity a human face,
And Love, the human form divine,[1]
And Peace, the human dress.[2]
Ib. st. 3

The moon like a flower
In heaven's high bower,
With silent delight
Sits and smiles on the night.
Ib. Night, st. 1

And there the lion's ruddy eyes
Shall flow with tears of gold,
And pitying the tender cries,
And walking round the fold,
Saying "Wrath, by his meekness,
And by his health, sickness,
Is driven away
From our immortal day." *Ib. st. 5*

"For, wash'd in life's river,
My bright mane forever

[1] See Milton, p. 344b.
[2] See *A Divine Image*, p. 489b.

Shall shine like the gold
As I guard o'er the fold."
Songs of Innocence. Night, st. 6

When the voices of children are heard
on the green
And laughing is heard on the hill,
My heart is at rest within my breast
And everything else is still.
Ib. Nurse's Song, st. 1

Can I see another's woe,
And not be in sorrow too?
Can I see another's grief,
And not seek for kind relief?
Ib. On Another's Sorrow, st. 1

Rintrah roars and shakes his fires in the
burden'd air;
Hungry clouds swag on the deep.
The Marriage of Heaven and
Hell [c. 1793]. The Argument

The reason Milton wrote in fetters
when he wrote of Angels and God, and
at liberty when of Devils and Hell, is
because he was a true poet and of the
Devil's party without knowing it.
Ib. The Voice of the Devil, note

The busy bee has no time for sorrow. *Ib. Proverbs of Hell*

No bird soars too high, if he soars
with his own wings. *Ib.*

The pride of the peacock is the glory
of God.
The lust of the goat is the bounty of
God.
The wrath of the lion is the wisdom
of God.
The nakedness of woman is the work
of God. *Ib.*

The cistern contains: the fountain
overflows. *Ib.*

Think in the morning. Act in the
noon. Eat in the evening. Sleep in the
night. *Ib.*

You never know what is enough unless you know what is more than
enough. *Ib.*

Improvement makes straight roads;
but the crooked roads without improvement are roads of genius. *Ib.*

Truth can never be told so as to be
understood, and not be believ'd.
*The Marriage of Heaven and
Hell. Proverbs of Hell*

Enough! or Too Much. *Ib.*

Never seek to tell thy love
Love that never told can be;
For the gentle wind does move
Silently, invisibly.

I told my love, I told my love,
I told her all my heart,
Trembling, cold, in ghastly fears —
Ah, she doth depart.

Soon as she was gone from me
A traveler came by
Silently, invisibly —
O, was no deny.
*Miscellaneous Poems and Frag-
ments [1793–1818]. Poem*

I asked a thief to steal me a peach:
He turned up his eyes.
I ask'd a lithe lady to lie her down:
Holy and meek she cries.

As soon as I went an angel came:
He wink'd at the thief
And smil'd at the dame,
And without one word spoke
Had a peach from the tree,
And 'twixt earnest and joke
Enjoy'd the Lady. *Ib. Poem*

Sleep, Sleep, beauty bright
Dreaming o'er the joys of night.
Sleep, Sleep: in thy sleep
Little sorrows sit and weep.
Ib. A Cradle Song, st. 1

Why art thou silent and invisible,
Father of Jealousy?
Ib. To Nobodaddy

Love to faults is always blind,
Always is to joy inclin'd,
Lawless, wing'd, and unconfin'd,
And breaks all chains from every
mind. *Ib. Poem*

The sword sung on the barren heath,
The sickle in the fruitful field:

The sword he sung a song of death,
But could not make the sickle yield.
*Miscellaneous Poems and
Fragments. Poem*

Abstinence sows sand all over
The ruddy limbs and flaming hair,
But Desire Gratified
Plants fruits of life and beauty there.
Ib. Poem

If you trap the moment before it's
ripe,[1]
The tears of repentance you'll certainly
wipe;
But if once you let the ripe moment
go
You can never wipe off the tears of
woe. *Ib. Poem*

He who binds to himself a joy
Does the winged life destroy;
But he who kisses the joy as it flies
Lives in eternity's sunrise.
Ib. Eternity

What is it men in women do require?
The lineaments of Gratified Desire.
What is it women do in men require?
The lineaments of Gratified Desire.
Ib. The Question Answer'd

The look of love alarms
Because 'tis fill'd with fire;
But the look of soft deceit
Shall win the lover's hire. *Ib. Poem*

Hear the voice of the Bard!
Who Present, Past, and Future, sees;
Whose ears have heard
The Holy Word
That walk'd among the ancient trees.
*Songs of Experience [1794].
Introduction, st. 1*

"Turn away no more;
Why wilt thou turn away?
The starry floor,
The wat'ry shore,
Is giv'n thee till the break of day." [2]
Ib. st. 4

"Love seeketh not itself to please,
Nor for itself hath any care,

[1] See Shakespeare, *II Henry IV*, IV, v, 95,
p. 242b.
[2] See Milton, p. 336a.

But for another gives its ease,
And builds a Heaven in Hell's despair."

Songs of Experience. The Clod and the Pebble, st. 1

"Love seeketh only self to please,
To bind another to its delight,
Joys in another's loss of ease,
And builds a Hell in Heaven's despite." *Ib. st. 3*

O Rose, thou art sick!
The invisible worm
That flies in the night,
In the howling storm,

Has found out thy bed
Of crimson joy,
And his dark secret love
Does thy life destroy.

Ib. The Sick Rose.

Little Fly,
Thy summer's play
My thoughtless hand
Has brush'd away.

Am not I
A fly like thee?
Or art not thou
A man like me?

For I dance,
And drink, and sing,
Till some blind hand
Shall brush my wing.

Ib. The Fly

Tiger! Tiger! burning bright
In the forests of the night,
What immortal hand or eye
Could frame thy fearful symmetry?

In what distant deeps or skies
Burnt the fire of thine eyes?
On what wings dare he aspire?
What the hand dare seize the fire?

Ib. The Tiger, st. 1, 2

What the hammer? what the chain?
In what furnace was thy brain?
What the anvil? what dread grasp
Dare its deadly terrors clasp?

When the stars threw down their
spears,
And water'd heaven with their tears,
Did he smile his work to see?

Did he who made the Lamb make
thee?

Songs of Experience. The Tiger, st. 4, 5

In every cry of every man,
In every infant's cry of fear,
In every voice, in every ban,
The mind-forg'd manacles I hear.

Ib. London, st. 2

But most thro' midnight streets I hear
How the youthful harlot's curse
Blasts the newborn infant's tear,
And blights with plagues the marriage
hearse. *Ib. st. 4*

My mother groan'd! my father wept.
Into the dangerous world I leapt:
Helpless, naked, piping loud:
Like a fiend hid in a cloud.

Ib. Infant Sorrow, st. 1

I was angry with my friend:
I told my wrath, my wrath did end.
I was angry with my foe:
I told it not, my wrath did grow.

Ib. A Poison Tree, st. 1

Cruelty has a human heart,
And Jealousy a human face;
Terror the human form divine,[1]
And Secrecy the human dress.[2]

Ib. A Divine Image, st. 1

My specter around me night and day
Like a wild beast guards my way.
My emanation far within
Weeps incessantly for my sin.

Poems from MSS [c. 1800–
1803]. *Poem, st. 1*

And throughout all eternity
I forgive you, you forgive me.

Ib. st. 14

Mock on, mock on,[3] Voltaire, Rousseau:
Mock on, mock on: 'tis all in vain!
You throw the sand against the wind,
And the wind blows it back again.

Ib. Poem, st. 1

Terror in the house does roar,
But Pity stands before the door.

Ib. Fragment

[1] See Milton, p. 344b.
[2] See *The Divine Image*, p. 487a.
[3] See *Job 21:3*, p. 15b.

There is a smile of love,
And there is a smile of deceit,
And there is a smile of smiles
In which these two smiles meet.
           Poems from MSS. The
                    Smile, st. 1

The cabinet is formed of gold
And pearl and crystal shining bright,
And within it opens into a world
And a little lovely moony night.
      Ib. The Crystal Cabinet, st. 2

For a tear is an intellectual thing,
And a sigh is the sword of an Angel
      King,
And the bitter groan of the martyr's
      woe
Is an arrow from the Almighty's bow.[1]
      Ib The Grey Monk, st. 8

To see a world in a grain of sand
And a heaven in a wild flower,
Hold infinity in the palm of your hand
And eternity in an hour.
      Ib. Auguries of Innocence, l. 1

A robin redbreast in a cage
Puts all Heaven in a rage.   *Ib. l. 5*

A dog starv'd at his master's gate
Predicts the ruin of the state.
                              Ib. l. 9

He who shall hurt the little wren
Shall never be belov'd by men.
                              Ib. l. 29

A truth that's told with bad intent
Beats all the lies you can invent.
                              Ib. l. 53

Every tear from every eye
Becomes a babe in eternity.   *Ib. l. 67*

He who shall teach the child to doubt
The rotting grave shall ne'er get out.
                              Ib. l. 77

He who doubts from what he sees
Will ne'er believe, do what you please.
If the sun and moon should doubt,
They'd immediately go out.   *Ib. l. 97*

The harlot's cry from street to street
Shall weave old England's winding
      sheet.   *Ib. l. 105*

[1] Also in *Jerusalem III, preface* [1804–1820]

Some are born to sweet delight.
Some are born to endless night.
           Poems from MSS. Auguries
                    of Innocence, l. 113

And did those feet in ancient time
Walk   upon   England's   mountains
      green?
And was the holy Lamb of God
On England's pleasant pastures seen?

And did the countenance divine
Shine forth upon our clouded hills?
And was Jerusalem builded here
Among those dark Satanic mills?

Bring me my bow of burning gold:
Bring me my arrows of desire:
Bring me my spear: O clouds unfold!
Bring me my chariot of fire.

I will not cease from mental fight,
Nor shall my sword sleep in my hand
Till we have built Jerusalem
In England's green and pleasant land.
      Milton [1804–1808]. *Preface, poem*

Great things are done when men and
      mountains meet;
This is not done by jostling in the
      street.   *Epigrams* [1808–1811]

If you have form'd a circle to go into,
Go into it yourself and see how you
      would do.   *Ib. To God*

Degrade first the arts if you'd mankind
      degrade.
Hire idiots to paint with cold light and
      hot shade.
      Annotations to Sir Joshua Reyn-
           olds's Discourses [c. 1808]

   To generalize is to be an idiot. To
particularize is the alone distinction of
merit. General knowledges are those
knowledges that idiots possess.   *Ib.*

The Angel that presided o'er my birth
Said, "Little creature, form'd of joy and
      mirth,
Go, love without the help of any thing
      on earth."
           Poems from MSS [c. 1810]

Grown old in love from seven till seven
      times seven,
I oft have wish'd for Hell for ease from
      Heaven.   *Ib.*

The vision of Christ that thou dost see
Is my vision's greatest enemy:
Thine has a great hook nose like thine,
Mine has a snub nose like to mine.
     The Everlasting Gospel [c. 1818]

Both read the Bible day and night,
But thou read'st black where I read
    white.   *Ib.*

This life's dim windows of the soul
Distorts the heavens from pole to pole
And leads you to believe a lie
When you see with, not thro', the eye [1]
                 Ib.

I am sure this Jesus will not do
Either for Englishman or Jew.   *Ib.*

    Poetry fettered fetters the human
race. Nations are destroyed or flourish
in proportion as their poetry, painting,
and music are destroyed or flourish.
     Jerusalem [1804–1820], *ch. 1,*
                   preface

He who would do good to another must
    do it in minute particulars:
General good is the plea of the scoun-
    drel, hypocrite and flatterer,
For art and science cannot exist but in
    minutely organized particulars.
          Ib. 3, sec. 55

England! awake! awake! awake!
Jerusalem thy sister calls!
Why wilt thou sleep the sleep of death
And close her from thy ancient
    walls?   *Ib. 4, sec. 77, st. 1*

JAMES GILLRAY
1757–1815

    The Old Lady of Threadneedle
Street.[2]   *Title of cartoon* [1797]

JOHN PHILIP KEMBLE
1757–1823

Perhaps it was right to dissemble your
    love,

---

[1] We are led to believe a lie
   When we see not thro' the eye.
         Auguries of Innocence, l. 112
[2] The Bank of England.

But — why did you kick me down
   stairs?   *The Panel,*[1] *act I, sc. 1*

ROYALL TYLER
1757–1826

Why should our thoughts to distant
    countries roam,
When each refinement may be found
    at home?
      The Contrast [1787], *prologue*

Since General Shays [2] has sneaked
off and given us the bag to hold.
           Ib. act II, sc. 2

I am at the end of my tether.
              Ib. III, 1

FISHER AMES
1758–1808

A monarchy is a merchantman which
sails well, but will sometimes strike on a
rock, and go to the bottom; a republic
is a raft which will never sink, but then
your feet are always in the water.
     Speech in the House of Repre-
         sentatives [1795]

JAMES MONROE
1758–1831

National honor is national property
of the highest value.
      First Inaugural Address
         [*March 4, 1817*]

The American continents . . . are
henceforth not to be considered as subjects for future colonization by any European powers.
     Annual Message to Congress
     [*December 2, 1823*]; *the Mon-*
     roe Doctrine

    In the wars of the European powers
in matters relating to themselves we
have never taken any part, nor does it
comport with our policy so to do.
                   Ib.

---

[1] An adaptation of Isaac Bickerstaffe's *'Tis
Well 'Tis No Worse.*
[2] Tyler was involved in suppressing Shays's
Rebellion.

We owe it, therefore, to candor, and to the amicable relations existing between the United States and those powers to declare that we should consider any attempt on their part to extend their system to any portion of this hemisphere as dangerous to our peace and safety. With the existing colonies or dependencies of any European power we . . . shall not interfere. But with the governments . . . whose independence we have . . . acknowledged, we could not view any interposition for the purpose of oppressing them, or controlling, in any other manner, their destiny, by any European power, in any other light than as a manifestation of an unfriendly disposition towards the United States.

Annual Message to Congress;
the Monroe Doctrine

HORATIO NELSON
1758–1805

Westminster Abbey, or victory!
At the Battle of Cape St.
Vincent [February 14, 1797].
From SOUTHEY, *Life of*
Nelson [1813], ch. 4

I have only one eye, I have a right to be blind sometimes . . . I really do not see the signal.
At the Battle of Copenhagen
[1801]. Ib. 9

Something must be left to chance; nothing is sure in a sea fight beyond all others.
Memorandum to the fleet, off
Cadiz [October 9, 1805]

But, in case signals can neither be seen or perfectly understood, no captain can do very wrong if he places his ship alongside that of the enemy. *Ib.*

England expects every man will do his duty.[1]
At the Battle of Trafalgar [Octo-
ber 21, 1805]. From SOUTHEY,
Life of Nelson [1813], ch. 9

[1] This famous sentence is thus first reported: "Say to the fleet, England confides that every

Thank God, I have done my duty.
At the Battle of Trafalgar. From
SOUTHEY, *Life of Nelson,*
ch. 9

Kiss me, Hardy. *Ib.*

ROBERT BURNS
1759–1796

Wee, sleekit, cow'rin, tim'rous beastie,
O, what a panic's in thy breastie!
Thou need na start awa sae hasty,
    Wi' bickering brattle!
To a Mouse [1785], st. 1

I'm truly sorry man's dominion
Has broken Nature's social union.
Ib. st. 2

The best laid schemes o' mice and men
Gang aft a-gley.[1] *Ib. st. 7*

    Nature's law,
That man was made to mourn.
Man Was Made to Mourn
[1786], st. 4

Man's inhumanity to man.[2]
Makes countless thousands mourn!
Ib. st. 7

He wales a portion with judicious care;
And "Let us worship God" he says, with solemn air.
The Cotter's Saturday Night
[1786], st. 12

From scenes like these, old Scotia's grandeur springs,
That makes her loved at home, revered abroad:
Princes and lords are but the breath of kings,[3]
"An honest man's the noblest work of God." [4] *Ib. st. 19*

man will do his duty." Captain Pasco, Nelson's flag lieutenant, suggested substituting "expects" for "confides," which was adopted. Captain Blackwood, who commanded the *Euryalus*, says that the correction suggested was from "Nelson expects" to "England expects."
[1] See Ihara Saikaku, p. 379a.
[2] See Pliny, p. 132b, and Wordsworth, p. 508b.
[3] See Goldsmith, p. 449a.
[4] See Pope, p. 409b.

Gie me ae spark o' Nature's fire,
That's a' the learning I desire.
     First Epistle to J. Lapraik
      [1786], *st.* 13

The social, friendly, honest man,
 Whate'er he be,
'Tis he fulfills great Nature's plan,
 And none but he!
     Second Epistle to J. Lapraik
      [1786], *st.* 15

On ev'ry hand it will allow'd be,
He's just — nae better than he should
 be.
   A *Dedication to Gavin Hamilton*
      [1786]

It's hardly in a body's pow'r,
To keep, at times, frae being sour.
   Epistle to Davie [1786], *st.* 2

Misled by fancy's meteor ray,
 By passion driven;
But yet the light that led astray
 Was light from heaven.
   The Vision [1786], II, *st.* 18

His lockèd, lettered, braw brass collar
Showed him the gentleman an'
 scholar.
   The Twa Dogs [1786], *st.* 3

An' there began a lang digression
About the lords o' the creation.
     Ib. st. 6

Oh wad some power the giftie gie us
To see oursels as others see us!
It wad frae monie a blunder free us,
 An' foolish notion.
   To a Louse [1786], *st.* 8

Wee, modest, crimson-tippèd flow'r,
Thou's met me in an evil hour;
For I maun crush amang the stoure
 Thy slender stem:
To spare thee now is past my pow'r,
 Thou bonie gem.
  To a Mountain Daisy [1786], *st.* 1

Stern Ruin's plowshare drives elate,
 Full on thy bloom.[1]   *Ib. st.* 9

[1] See Edward Young, p. 399b.

O life! thou art a galling load,
Along a rough, a weary road,
 To wretches such as I!
   Despondency [1786], *st.* 1

Perhaps it may turn out a sang,
Perhaps turn out a sermon.
   Epistle to a Young Friend
     [1786], *st.* 1

I waive the quantum o' the sin,
The hazard of concealing;
But, och! it hardens a' within,
And petrifies the feeling! *Ib. st.* 6

An atheist-laugh's a poor exchange
For Deity offended.   *Ib. st.* 9

There's nought but care on ev'ry han',
In every hour that passes, O:
What signifies the life o' man,
An' 't were nae for the lasses, O.
   Green Grow the Rashes, O
     [1787], *st.* 1

Auld Nature swears, the lovely dears
Her noblest work she classes, O:
Her prentice han' she try'd on man,
An' then she made the lasses, O.
     Ib. st. 5

Green grow the rashes, O;
Green grow the rashes, O;
The sweetest hours that e'er I spend
Are spent among the lasses, O.
     Ib. chorus

I wasna fou, but just had plenty.
   Death and Dr. Hornbook
     [1787], *st.* 3

John Barleycorn got up again,
And sore surpris'd them all.
   John Barleycorn [1787], *st.* 3

The heart benevolent and kind
The most resembles God.
   A *Winter Night* [1787]

Ye're aiblins nae temptation.
   Address to the Unco Guid
     [1787], *st.* 6

Then gently scan your brother man,
Still gentler sister woman;
Tho' they may gang a kennin wrang,
To step aside is human. *Ib. st.* 7

O, my Luve is like a red, red rose,
That's newly sprung in June.
O, my Luve is like the melodie,
That's sweetly play'd in tune.
> *Johnson's Musical Museum*
> [1787–1796]. *A Red, Red*
> *Rose, st. 1*

Contented wi' little and cantie wi'
mair.
> *Ib. Contented wi' Little, st. 1*

Ye banks and braes o' bonny Doon,
How can ye bloom sae fresh and fair?
How can ye chant, ye little birds,
And I sae weary fu' o' care!
Thou'll break my heart, thou warbling
bird,
That wantons thro' the flowering
thorn!
Thou minds me o' departed joys,
Departed never to return.
> *Ib. The Banks o' Doon, st. 1*

Chords that vibrate sweetest pleasure
Thrill the deepest notes of woe.
> *Ib. Sensibility How Charming, st. 4*

Ae fond kiss, and then we sever;
Ae farewell and then forever!
> *Ib. Ae Fond Kiss, st. 1*

But to see her was to love her,
Love but her, and love forever.[1]
Had we never lov'd sae kindly,
Had we never lov'd sae blindly,
Never met — or never parted —
We had ne'er been broken-hearted.
> *Ib. st. 2*

It was a' for our rightfu' King
We left fair Scotland's strand.
> *Ib. It Was A' for Our Rightfu'*
> *King, st. 1*

Now a' is done that men can do,
And a' is done in vain.   *Ib. st. 2*

He turn'd him right and round about
Upon the Irish shore;
And gae his bridle reins a shake,
With adieu forevermore,
     My dear —
And adieu forevermore!   *Ib. st. 3*

[1] See Halleck, p. 565b, and Tennyson, p. 647a.

John Anderson my jo, John,
When we were first acquent,
Your locks were like the raven,
Your bonie brow was brent;
But now your brow is beld, John,
Your locks are like the snaw,
But blessings on your frosty pow,
John Anderson my jo!

John Anderson my jo, John,
We clamb the hill thegither,
And mony a cantie day, John,
We've had wi' ane anither;
Now we maun totter down, John,
And hand in hand we'll go,
And sleep thegither at the foot,
John Anderson, my jo!
> *Johnson's Musical Museum.*
> *John Anderson My Jo, st.*
> *1, 2*

Farewell to the Highlands, farewell to
the North,
The birthplace of valor, the country of
worth!
Wherever I wander, wherever I rove,
The hills of the Highlands for ever I
love.
> *Ib. My Heart's in the Highlands,*
> *st. 1*

My heart's in the Highlands, my heart is
not here,
My heart's in the Highlands a-chasing
the deer;
A-chasing the wild deer, and following
the roe,
My heart's in the Highlands wherever
I go.   *Ib. chorus*

O whistle, and I'll come to you, my
lad:
Tho' father and mither and a' should
gae mad,
O whistle, and I'll come to you, my
lad.
> *Whistle, and I'll Come to You,*
> *My Lad*

Should auld acquaintance be forgot,
And never brought to mind?
Should auld acquaintance be forgot,
And auld lang syne!
> *Auld Lang Syne* [1788], *st. 1*

For auld lang syne, my dear,
For auld lang syne,
We'll tak a cup o' kindness yet
For auld lang syne!
      Auld Lang Syne, chorus

Flow gently, sweet Afton, among thy
   green braes,
Flow gently, I'll sing thee a song in thy
   praise.
My Mary's asleep by thy murmuring
   stream,
Flow gently, sweet Afton, disturb not
   her dream.
      Afton Water [1789,] *st. 1*

This day Time winds th' exhausted
   chain,
To run the twelvemonth's length
   again.
      New Year's Day [1791], *st. 1*

The voice of Nature loudly cries,
And many a message from the skies,
That something in us never dies.
      Ib. st. 3

When Nature her great masterpiece de-
   sign'd,
And fram'd her last, best work, the
   human mind,
Her eye intent on all the wondrous
   plan,
She form'd of various stuff the various
   Man.
      To Robert Graham [1791], *st. 1*

She is a winsome wee thing,
She is a handsome wee thing,
She is a lo'esome wee thing,
   This sweet wee wife o' mine.
      My Wife's a Winsome Wee
      Thing [1792], *chorus*

The golden hours on angel wings
Flew o'er me and my dearie;
For dear to me as light and life
Was my sweet Highland Mary.
      Highland Mary [1792], *st. 2*

But, oh! fell death's untimely frost,
That nipt my flower sae early.
      Ib. st. 3

If there's a hole in a' your coats,
   I rede you tent it;

A child's amang you takin' notes,
   And faith he'll prent it.
      On the Late Captain Grose's
      Peregrinations Thro' Scotland
      [1793], *st. 1*

Some hae meat and canna eat,
And some wad eat that want it;
But we hae meat, and we can eat,
And sae the Lord be thankit.
      The Selkirk Grace [1793]
      (*attributed*)

O Mary, at thy window be!
It is the wish'd, the trysted hour.
      Mary Morison [1793], *st. 1*

The lovely Mary Morison!   *Ib.*

Whare sits our sulky, sullen dame,
Gathering her brows like gathering
   storm,
Nursing her wrath to keep it warm.
      Tam o' Shanter [1793], *l. 10*

Ah, gentle dames! it gars me greet
To think how monie counsels sweet,
How monie lengthened, sage advices,
The husband frae the wife despises.
      Ib. l. 33

His ancient, trusty, drouthy crony;
Tam lo'ed him like a vera brither —
They had been fou for weeks the-
   gither.   *Ib. l. 43*

Kings may be blest, but Tam was glorious,
O'er a' the ills o' life victorious.
      Ib. l. 57

But pleasures are like poppies spread —
You seize the flow'r, its bloom is shed;
Or like the snow falls in the river —
A moment white — then melts forever.
      Ib. l. 59

That hour, o' night's black arch the
   keystane.   *Ib. l. 69*

Inspiring bold John Barleycorn!
What dangers thou canst make us
   scorn!
Wi' tippenny, we fear nae evil;
Wi' usquebae, we'll face the devil!
      Ib. l. 105

As Tammie glow'red, amazed, and curious,
The mirth and fun grew fast and furious. *Tam o' Shanter, l. 143*

Her cutty sark, o' Paisley harn,
That while a lassie she had worn,
In longitude tho' sorely scanty,
It was her best, and she was vauntie.
Ib. l. 171

"Weel done, Cutty Sark!" [1]
Ib. l. 189

Ah, Tam! Ah! Tam! Thou'll get thy fairin!
In hell they'll roast you like a herrin!
Ib. l. 201

Scots wha hae wi' Wallace bled,
Scots wham Bruce has aften led,
Welcome to your gory bed
    Or to victorie.

Now's the day, and now's the hour;
See the front o' battle lour!
See approach proud Edward's power —
    Chains and slaverie!
Scots Wha Hae [1794], *st. 1, 2*

Lay the proud usurpers low!
Tyrants fall in every foe!
Liberty's in every blow!
    Let us do or die! [2] *Ib. st. 6*

The rank is but the guinea's stamp,
The man's the gowd for a' that.
For A' That and A' That [1795], *st. 1*

A prince can mak a belted knight,
A marquis, duke, and a' that;
But an honest man's aboon his might,
Guid faith, he mauna fa' that.
Ib. st. 4

For a' that, and a' that,
An' twice as muckle 's a' that,
I've lost but ane, I've twa behin',
I've wife eneugh for a' that.
Posthumous Pieces [1799].
The Jolly Beggars, chorus

[1] The famous tea clipper *Cutty Sark,* designed by Hercules Linton and built in 1869, had the story of Tam o' Shanter carved upon her bow and counter. Nannie, with flying locks and scanty shift, was the figurehead.
[2] See Fletcher, p. 313b.

God knows, I'm no the thing I should be,
Nor am I even the thing I could be.
Posthumous Pieces. To the Reverend John M'Math, st. 8

If there's another world, he lives in bliss;
If there is none, he made the best of this.
Ib. Epitaph on William Muir

In durance vile here must I wake and weep,
And all my frowsy couch in sorrow steep.
Ib. Epistle from Esopus to Maria

It's guid to be merry and wise,
It's guid to be honest and true,
It's guid to support Caledonia's cause
And bide by the buff and the blue.
Ib. Here's a Health to Them That's Awa', st. 1

GEORGES JACQUES DANTON
1759–1794

Everything belongs to the fatherland when the fatherland is in danger.
Speech to the Legislative Assembly [August 28, 1792]

We must dare, and dare again, and go on daring.[1]
Ib. [September 2, 1792]

Show my head to the people, it is worth seeing.
Last words, addressed to the executioner

WILLIAM PITT
1759–1806

Necessity is the plea for every infringement of human freedom. It is the argument of tyrants; it is the creed of slaves.[2]
Speech, House of Commons [November 18, 1783]

[1] Il nous faut de l'audace, encore de l'audace, toujours de l'audace.
See Spenser. p. 200b, and note.
[2] See Publilius Syrus, p. 126b.

JOHANN CHRISTOPH FRIEDRICH VON SCHILLER

1759–1805

I feel an army in my fist.
> *Die Räuber (The Robbers)*
> [1781], *act II, end*

The lemonade is weak, like your soul.
> *Kabala und Liebe* [1784], *act V,*
> *sc. 7*

Joy, thou spark from Heav'n immortal,
Daughter of Elysium!
Drunk with fire, toward Heaven advancing
Goddess, to thy shrine we come.
Thy sweet magic brings together
What stern Custom spreads afar;
All mankind knows all men brothers
Where thy happy wing-beats are.[1]
> *An die Freude (Ode to Joy)*
> [1785],[2] *st. 1*

O embrace now all you millions,
With one kiss for all the world.
Brothers, high beyond all stars
Surely dwells a loving Father.
> *Ib. st. 5*

There are three lessons I would write,
Three words as with a burning pen,
In tracings of eternal light
Upon the hearts of men.
> *Hope, Faith, and Love* [c. 1786],
> *st. 1*

Thus grave these lessons on thy soul —
Hope, faith, and love; and thou shalt find

[1] Alle Menschen werden Brüder,
     Wo dein sanfter Flügel weilt.
[2] Translated by THEODORE SPENCER for the Boston Symphony Orchestra, for the performance of Beethoven's Ninth Symphony.
It was during his student days in Bonn that Beethoven fastened upon Schiller's poem. . . . The heady sense of liberation in the verses must have appealed to him as they appealed to every German. They were in the spirit of the times, the spirit that had swept Europe and America, and Beethoven belonged to his time. — JOHN N. BURK, *program notes for the Boston Symphony Orchestra* [October 1, 1965]

Strength when life's surges rudest roll,
Light when thou else wert blind!
> *Hope, Faith, and Love, st. 5*

World history is the world's court.[1]
> *Resignation* [1786]

What one refuses in a minute
No eternity will return.
> *Ib.*

O who knows what slumbers in the background of the times?
> *Don Carlos* [1787], *act I, sc. 1*

O the idea was childish, but divinely beautiful.
> *Ib. 2*

Great souls suffer in silence.
> *Ib. 4*

A moment lived in paradise
Is not atoned for too dearly by death.
> *Ib. 5*

The richest monarch in the Christian world;
The sun in my own dominions never sets.[2]
> *Ib. 6*

Honor women! They wreathe and weave
Heavenly roses into earthly life.
> *Würde der Frauen (The Wonder of Women)* [1795], *l. 186*

What the inner voice says
Will not disappoint the hoping soul.
> *Hope, last stanza* [1797]

If you want to know yourself,
Just look how others do it;
If you want to understand others,
Look into your own heart.
> *Tabulae Votivae* [1797]

Man is created free, and is free,
Though he be born in chains.[3]
> *Die Worte des Glaubens (The Word of the Faithful)* [1797],
> *st. 2*

Virtue is no empty echo.
> *Ib. st. 3*

[1] Die Weltgeschichte ist das Weltgericht.
[2] See Scott, p. 522a, and Daniel Webster, p. 548a.
[3] See Rousseau, p. 435b, and Bliss, p. 468b.

Posterity weaves no garlands for imitators.
> Wallensteins Lager (Wallenstein's Camp) [1798], prologue

He who has done his best for his own time has lived for all times. *Ib.*

Life is earnest, art is gay. *Ib.*

Whatever is not forbidden is permitted. *Ib. sc. 6*

Live and let live.[1] *Ib.*

The peasant is also human — in a manner of speaking. *Ib. sc. 10*

Man is made of ordinary things, and habit is his nurse.
> Wallensteins Tod (Wallenstein's Death) [1798], act I, sc. 4

I have only an office here, and no opinion. *Ib. 5*

What is life without the radiance of love? *Ib. IV, 12*

Time is man's angel. *Ib. V, 11*

What is the short meaning of the long speech?
> Piccolomini [1799], act I, sc. 2

In thy breast are the stars of thy fate. *Ib. II, 6*

You say it as you understand it.
> *Ib.*

When the wine goes in, strange things come out. *Ib. 12*

The dictates of the heart are the voice of fate. *Ib. III, 8*

O tender yearning, sweet hoping!
The golden time of first love!
The eye sees the open heaven,
The heart is intoxicated with bliss;
O that the beautiful time of young love
Could remain green forever.
> The Song of the Bell [1799]

---

[1] Also attributed to Wieland in the Goethe-Zelter correspondence.

Quoted in GOETHE, *Faust*, prologue [1808], and in SWINBURNE, Félise [1866], *st. 59*.

Appearance should never attain reality,
And if nature conquers, then must art retire.
> To Goethe, when he put Voltaire's Mahomet on the stage [1800]

Life is only error,
And death is knowledge.
> Cassandra [1802]

I am better than my reputation.
> Maria Stuart [1801], act III, sc. 4

For this should the singer accompany the king:
Both dwell on the heights of mankind.
> Die Jungfrau von Orleans (Joan of Arc) [1801], act I, sc. 2

Against stupidity the very gods
Themselves contend in vain.[1]
> *Ib. III, 6*

Pain is short, and joy is eternal.
> *Ib. last lines*

What are hopes, what are plans?
> Die Braut von Messina (The Bride of Messina) [1803], act III, sc. 5

Don't let your heart depend on things
That ornament life in a fleeting way!
He who possesses, let him learn to lose,
He who is fortunate, let him learn pain. *Ib. IV, 4*

On the mountains there is freedom!
The world is perfect everywhere,
Save where man comes with his torment. *Ib. IV, 7*

Who reflects too much will accomplish little.
> Wilhelm Tell [1804], act III, sc. 1

This feat of Tell, the archer, will be told
While yonder mountains stand upon their base.
By Heaven! The apple's cleft right through the core. *Ib. 3*

---

[1] Against boredom even the gods themselves struggle in vain. — NIETZSCHE [1844–1900], *The Antichrist, 48*

The most pious man can't stay in peace
If it doesn't please his evil neighbor.
> *Wilhelm Tell, act IV, sc.* 3

MASON LOCKE WEEMS
1759–1825

"George," said his father, "do you know who killed that beautiful little cherry tree yonder in the garden?" . . . Looking at his father with the sweet face of youth brightened with the inexpressible charm of all-conquering truth, he bravely cried out. "I can't tell a lie. I did cut it with my hatchet." [1]
> *The Life of George Washington: With Curious Anecdotes, Equally Honorable to Himself and Exemplary to His Young Countrymen* [1800]

JOSEPH ROUGET DE LISLE
1760–1836

Allons, enfants de la patrie,
Le jour de gloire est arrivé! . . .
Aux armes, citoyens!
Formez vos bataillons!
Marchons! Marchons! Qu'un sang impur
Abreuve nos sillons!
> *The Marseillaise* [2] [1792]

AUGUST FRIEDRICH FERDINAND VON KOTZEBUE
1761–1819

There is another and a better world.
> *The Stranger* [1798], *act I, sc.* 1

---

[1] See George Washington, p. 462a.

[2] Forward, sons of France, the day of glory has come! . . . To arms, citizens! Line up in battalions! Let us march on! And let the impure blood [of our enemies] drench our fields.

Composed in the garrison at Strasbourg and originally called *Chant de guerre de l'armée du Rhin,* the *Marseillaise* took its name from the patriots of Marseilles, who first made it known in Paris.

ANTOINE BOULAY DE LA MEURTHE
1761–1840

It is worse than a crime, it is a blunder. [1]
> *On the execution of the Duc d'Enghien* [1804]

WILLIAM LISLE BOWLES [2]
1762–1850

The cause of Freedom is the cause of God!   *Edmund Burke, l. 78*

ANDREW CHERRY
1762–1812

Loud roar'd the dreadful thunder,
The rain a deluge show'rd.
> *The Bay of Biscay*

Till next day,
There she lay,
In the Bay of Biscay, O!   *Ib.*

GEORGE COLMAN THE YOUNGER
1762–1836

Tell 'em Queen Anne's dead. [3]
> *The Heir-at-Law* [1797], *act I, sc.* 1

Not to be sneezed at.   *Ib. II, 1*

Like two single gentlemen rolled into one.
> *Lodgings for Single Gentlemen*

When taken,
To be well shaken.
> *The Newcastle Apothecary*

O Miss Bailey!
Unfortunate Miss Bailey!
> *Love Laughs at Locksmiths, act II, song*

Says he, "I am a handsome man, but I'm a gay deceiver."   *Ib.*

---

[1] C'est pire qu'un crime, c'est une faute.
Attributed also to TALLEYRAND and FOUCHÉ. SAINTE-BEUVE attributes it to DE LA MEURTHE.
[2] See Simonides, *Fragment 92,* p. 70b.
[3] The phrase became proverbial for telling what everybody knows.

His heart runs away with his head.
Who Wants a Guinea?, act I, sc. 1

I had a soul above buttons.
Sylvester Daggerwood; or, New Hay at the Old Market, sc. 1

Mynheer Vandunck, though he never was drunk,
Sipped brandy and water gaily.
Mynheer Vandunck

John Bull,[1] or An Englishman's Fireside. *Title of play* [1803]

DOROTHEA JORDAN
1762–1816

"Oh where, and Oh! where is your Highland laddie gone?"
"He's gone to fight the French, for King George upon the throne,
And it's Oh! in my heart, how I wish him safe at home!"
The Blue Bells of Scotland

JOSEPH FOUCHÉ
1763–1820

Death is an eternal sleep.[2]
Inscription placed by his orders on cemetery gates [1794]

JOHANN PAUL FRIEDRICH RICHTER [JEAN PAUL]
1763–1825

Weltschmerz.[3]
Selena, oder Über die Unsterblichkeit [or Above Immortality], 2

Providence has given to the French the empire of the land; to the English that of the sea; to the Germans that of — the air!
From CARLYLE, *Critical and Miscellaneous Essays. Richter* [1827]

[1] The origin of the supposed type of the British character.
[2] See Catullus, p. 114b.
[3] Literally, world pain.

SAMUEL ROGERS
1763–1855

Think nothing done while aught remains to do.
Human Life, l. 49

Never less alone than when alone.[1]
Ib. l. 756

By many a temple half as old as Time.[2]
Italy. A Farewell

Mine be a cot beside the hill;
A beehive's hum shall soothe my ear;
A willowy brook that turns a mill,
With many a fall shall linger near.[3]
A Wish, st. 1

Go! you may call it madness, folly;
You shall not chase my gloom away!
There's such a charm in melancholy
I would not if I could be gay.
To —— [1814], st. 1

It doesn't much signify whom one marries, for one is sure to find next morning that it was someone else.
Table Talk

Ward has no heart, they say, but I deny it;
He has a heart, and gets his speeches by it. *Epigram*

JOHANN GOTTFRIED SEUME
1763–1810

You can relax peacefully wherever there is singing
Without fear of what is thought in the land;
No man is robbed where there is singing,
For scoundrels have no songs.
Songs [1804], first strophe

ROBERT HALL
1764–1831

Call things by their right names. . . . Glass of brandy and water! That is the current but not the appropriate

[1] See Cicero, p. 111b.
[2] See John William Burgon, p. 675b.
[3] See Yeats, p. 879b.

name: ask for a glass of liquid fire and distilled damnation.

> From OLINTHUS GREGORY, *Brief Memoir of the Life of Hall*

GASTON PIERRE MARC, DUC DE LÉVIS
1764–1830

Noblesse oblige.[1]

> *Maxims and Reflections* [1808]

THOMAS MORTON
1764–1838

Push on — keep moving.

> *A Cure for the Heartache* [1797], *act II, sc. 1*

Approbation from Sir Hubert Stanley is praise indeed. *Ib. V, 2*

What will Mrs. Grundy say? What will Mrs. Grundy think? [2]

> *Speed the Plow* [1798], *act I, sc. 1*

ANN RADCLIFFE
1764–1823

Fate sits on these dark battlements and frowns,
And as the portal opens to receive me,
A voice in hollow murmurs through the courts
Tells of a nameless deed.[3]

> *The Mysteries of Udolpho* [1794], *motto*

CATHERINE MARIA FANSHAWE
1765–1834

'Twas whisper'd in heaven, 'twas mutter'd in hell,
And echo caught faintly the sound as it fell;
On the confines of earth 'twas permitted to rest,
And the depths of the ocean its presence confess'd.

> *Enigma: The Letter H*

[1] See Sophocles, p. 81a, and Euripides, p. 85b.
[2] See Spencer, p. 706a, and Locker-Hampson, p. 710a.
[3] See Shakespeare, *Macbeth IV, i, 49*, p. 285b.

ROBERT GOODLOE HARPER
1765–1825

Millions for defense, but not one cent for tribute.[1]

> *Toast at banquet for John Marshall* [June 18, 1798]

MARY LAMB
1765–1847

Thou straggler into loving arms,
Young climber-up of knees.

> *A Child, st. 3*

SIR JAMES MACKINTOSH
1765–1832

Diffused knowledge immortalizes itself. *Vindiciae Gallicae* [1791]

The Commons, faithful to their system, remained in a wise and masterly inactivity. *Ib.*

The frivolous work of polished idleness.

> *Dissertation on Ethical Philosophy* [1830]. *Remarks on Thomas Brown*

Disciplined inaction.

> *History of the Revolution in England in 1688* [1834], *ch. 7*

ISAAC D'ISRAELI
1766–1848

Whatever is felicitously expressed risks being worse expressed: it is a wretched taste to be gratified with mediocrity when the excellent lies before us.

> *Curiosities of Literature* [1834]. *On Quotation*

[1] In 1797 a secret agent from Talleyrand told Charles Cotesworth Pinckney, Minister to the French Republic, that the American Commissioners in Paris to protest French attacks on U.S. shipping would be received only if they paid a $50,000 bribe and made a large loan to the French government. Pinckney's reply was: "Not a sixpence, sir." Later, Harper's remark was attributed to him.

THOMAS ROBERT MALTHUS
1766–1834

Population, when unchecked, increases in a geometrical ratio. Subsistence increases only in an arithmetical ratio. A slight acquaintance with numbers will show the immensity of the first power in comparison of the second.

An Essay on the Principle of Population [1798]

ERNST F. MÜNSTER[1]
1766–1839

Absolutism tempered by assassination.

Description of the Russian Constitution

CAROLINA, BARONESS NAIRNE
1766–1845

Will ye no come back again?
Better lo'ed ye canna be,
Will ye no come back again?

Life and Songs [1869]. *Bonnie Charlie's Now Awa'*. *Also attributed to* JAMES HOGG [1770–1835]

Charlie is my darling, the young Chevalier.

Ib. Charlie Is My Darling (*also attributed to Hogg*)

Wi' a hundred pipers an' a', an' a',
We'll up an' gie them a blaw, a blaw,
Wi' a hundred pipers an' a', an' a'.

Ib. The Hundred Pipers

Gude nicht, and joy be wi' you a'.

Ib. Gude Nicht

A penniless lass wi' a lang pedigree.

Ib. The Laird o' Cockpen

I'm wearin' awa'
To the land o' the leal.

Ib. The Land o' the Leal

[1] Hanoverian envoy at St. Petersburg.

There's nae sorrow there, John,
There's neither cauld nor care, John,
The day is aye fair,
In the land o' the leal.

Life and Songs. The Land o' the Leal

MADAME DE STAËL [GERMAINE, BARONNE DE STAËL-HOLSTEIN]
1766–1817

Love is the whole history of a woman's life, it is but an episode in a man's.[1]

De l'Influence des Passions [1796]

A man must know how to defy opinion; a woman how to submit to it.

Delphine [1802]

The sight of such a monument is like a continuous and stationary music.[2]

Corinne [1807], bk. IV, ch. 3

To understand everything makes one tolerant.[3]

Ib. XVIII, 5

I would gladly give half of the wit with which I am credited for half of the beauty you possess.

Letter to Madame Récamier

JOHN QUINCY ADAMS
1767–1848

Think of your forefathers! Think of your posterity![4]

Speech at Plymouth [December 22, 1802]

In charity to all mankind, bearing no malice or ill-will to any human being, and even compassionating those who

[1] L'amour est l'histoire de la vie des femmes, c'est un episode dans celle des hommes.
[2] See Goethe, p. 478a.
[3] Tout comprendre rend très indulgent.
Attributed to Madame de Staël are similar phrases: Comprendre c'est pardonner [To understand is to forgive]. Tout comprendre c'est tout pardonner [To know everything is to forgive everything].
[4] Et maiores vestros et posteros cogitate. — TACITUS [*c.* A.D. 55–117], *Agricola 32, 26*

hold in bondage their fellow men, not knowing what they do.[1]

> *Letter to A. Bronson*
> *[July 30, 1838]*

My wants are many, and, if told,
Would muster many a score;
And were each wish a mint of gold,
I still should long for more.

> *The Wants of Man* [1841], *st. 1*

This is the last of earth! I am content.

> *Last words [February 21, 1848]*

ANDREW JACKSON[2]
1767–1845

The individual who refuses to defend his rights when called by his Government, deserves to be a slave, and must be punished as an enemy of his country and friend to her foe.

> *Proclamation to the people of Louisiana from Mobile [September 21, 1814]*

The brave man inattentive to his duty, is worth little more to his country, than the coward who deserts her in the hour of danger.

> *To troops who had abandoned their lines during the battle of New Orleans [January 8, 1815]*

Our Federal Union! it must be preserved!

> *Toast at Jefferson Birthday Celebration* [1830]

Every man is equally entitled to protection by law; but when the laws undertake to add . . . artificial distinctions, to grant titles, gratuities, and exclusive privileges, to make the rich richer and the potent more powerful, the humble members of society — the farmers, mechanics, and laborers — who have neither the time nor the means of securing like favors to themselves, have a right to complain of the injustice of their government.

> *Veto of the Bank Bill*
> *[July 10, 1832]*

There are no necessary evils in government. Its evils exist only in its abuses. If it would confine itself to equal protection, and, as Heaven does its rains, shower its favors alike on the high and the low, the rich and the poor, it would be an unqualified blessing. *Ib.*

One man with courage makes a majority. *Saying*

FRANÇOIS RENÉ DE CHATEAUBRIAND
1768–1848

[On his conversion to Christianity] I wept and I believed.[1]

> *Le Génie du Christianisme* [1802]

Achilles exists only through Homer. Take away the art of writing from this world, and you will probably take away its glory.[2]

> *Les Natchez* [1826], *preface*

ERNST MORITZ ARNDT
1769–1860

The God who made iron grow
Wanted no slaves.

> *Vaterlandslied* [1812]

What is the German Fatherland?
Wherever the German tongue is heard.

> *Was Ist Des Deutschen Vaterland* [1813]

The Rhine: Germany's river, but not Germany's border.

> *Title of a work* [1813]

---

[1] See Abraham Lincoln, p. 640b.
[2] He was the most American of Americans — an embodied Declaration of Independence — the Fourth of July incarnate. — JAMES PARTON, *Life of Andrew Jackson* [1859]

[1] J'ai pleuré et j'ai cru.
[2] See Pindar, p. 79b, and Alexander the Great, p. 102a.

NAPOLEON I [NAPOLEON BONAPARTE]
1769–1821

Soldiers, from the summit of yonder pyramids forty centuries look down upon you.
> *In Egypt [July 21, 1798]*

Go, sir, gallop, and don't forget that the world was made in six days. You can ask me for anything you like, except time.
> *To an aide [1803]. From R. M. JOHNSTON, The Corsican*

A form of government that is not the result of a long sequence of shared experiences, efforts, and endeavors can never take root.
> *[1803] From J. CHRISTOPHER HEROLD, The Mind of Napoleon [1955]*

From the sublime to the ridiculous is but a step.[1]
> *To the Abbé du Pradt, on the return from Russia [1812], referring to the retreat from Moscow*

You write to me that it's impossible; the word is not French.
> *Letter to General Lemarois [July 9, 1813]*

What is the throne? — a bit of wood gilded and covered with velvet. I am the state[2] — I alone am here the representative of the people. Even if I had done wrong you should not have reproached me in public — people wash their dirty linen at home.[3] France has more need of me than I of France.
> *To the Senate [1814]*

France is invaded; I am leaving to take command of my troops, and, with God's help and their valor, I hope soon to drive the enemy beyond the frontier.
> *At Paris [January 23, 1814]*

The bullet that will kill me is not yet cast.
> *At Montereau [February 17, 1814]*

The Allied Powers having proclaimed that the Emperor Napoleon is the sole obstacle to the re-establishment of peace in Europe, he, faithful to his oath, declares that he is ready to descend from the throne, to quit France, and even to relinquish life, for the good of his country.
> *Act of Abdication [April 4, 1814]*

Unite for the public safety, if you would remain an independent nation.
> *Proclamation to the French People [June 22, 1815]*

Wherever wood can swim, there I am sure to find this flag of England.
> *At Rochefort [July 1815]*

Whatever shall we do in that remote spot? Well, we will write our memoirs. Work is the scythe of time.
> *On board H. M. S. Bellerophon [August 1815]*

[Of his relations with the Empress Josephine] I generally had to give in.
> *On St. Helena [May 19, 1816]*

My maxim was, *la carrière est ouverte aux talents*, without distinction of birth or fortune.[1]
> *Ib. [March 3, 1817]*

Our hour is marked, and no one can claim a moment of life beyond what fate has predestined.
> *To Dr. Arnott [April 1821]*

Two o'clock in the morning courage: I mean unprepared courage.[2]
> *[December 4, 5, 1815] From LAS CASES, Mémorial de Ste-Hélène [1823]*

---

[1] Du sublime au ridicule il n'y a qu'un pas.
The saying has been attributed also to Talleyrand.
See Paine, p. 467b.

[2] See Louis XIV, p. 378a.

[3] Il faut laver son linge sale en famille [One should wash one's dirty linen at home]. — *Saying current since about 1720*

[1] See Carlyle, p. 575b.

[2] Le courage de l'improviste.
The three o'clock in the morning courage, which Bonaparte thought was the rarest. — THOREAU, *Walden [1854], ch. 4, Sounds*
See F. Scott Fitzgerald, p. 1036b.

Madame Montholon having inquired what troops he considered the best, "Those which are victorious, Madame," replied the Emperor.

From BOURRIENNE, *Memoirs* [1829]

A silk stocking filled with mud.
Description of Talleyrand; attributed by SAINTE-BEUVE

An army marches on its stomach.
Attributed

Every French soldier carries a marshal's baton in his knapsack.[1]
Attributed

Perfidious Albion.[2] *Attributed*

Chief of the Army.[3] *Last words*

IVAN KRYLOV
1769–1844

The tricksome little monkey,
The goat with tangled hair,
The donkey,
And the clumsy-fingered bear
A great quartet had planned to start;
They got the notes, viola, fiddles, bass,
And sat beneath a lime tree, on the grass,
To charm creation with their art.
Fables [1809],[4] *The Quartet*

It can't go right like that; you don't know how to sit! *Ib.*

We'll play to quite another tune
And make the hills and forest dance for glee. *Ib.*

I'm sure we'll make it go
By sitting in a row. *Ib.*

We've notes, we've instruments; do tell us how to sit!
The nightingale replies: To sit is not enough. *Fables, The Quartet*

Then change your seats, and fiddles too:
For chamber music's not for you! *Ib.*

When partners can't agree
Their business fares disastrously.
Ib. Swan, Pike and Crab

One day, the pike, the crab, the swan
Set out to drag a truck along the road,
All three together harnessed to the load. *Ib.*

It was not that their load was difficult to move;
But upward strained the swan, toward the skies above,
The crab kept stepping back, the pike was for the pond.
And which was right or wrong, I neither know nor care:
I only know the truck's still there.
Ib.

You think I've got the time to count your crimes, you pup?
Your guilt consists in this: I want to eat you up! *Ib. Wolf and Lamb* [1]

The weak against the strong,
Is always in the wrong. *Ib.*

What good from you yourselves has come?
Why, yes, our ancestors in Rome.
Ib. Geese

Than that old cat there's no one stronger. *Ib. Mouse and Rat*

And why not raise the lid? He never tried that way!
This was a box that opened of itself.
Ib. A Little Box

Heaven save you from a foolish friend;
The too officious fool is worse than any foe. *Ib. Hermit and Bear*

---

[1] Tout soldat français porte dans sa giberne le bâton de maréchal de France.

[2] L'Angleterre, ah! la perfide Angleterre. — JACQUES BÉNIGNE BOSSUET [1627–1704], *Sermon sur la Circoncision*

Napoleon used the phrase in 1803, and it became widespread during the French Revolution.

[3] Tête d'armée.

[4] Translated by SIR BERNARD PARES.

[1] See La Fontaine, *Bk. I, Fable 10,* p. 359a.

ARTHUR WELLESLEY, DUKE OF WELLINGTON
1769–1852

Nothing except a battle lost can be half so melancholy as a battle won.
Dispatch [1815]

I used to say of him [Napoleon] that his presence on the field made the difference of forty thousand men.
[*November 2, 1831*] *From* STANHOPE, *Notes of Conversations with the Duke of Wellington* [1888]

The only thing I am afraid of is fear.[1] *Ib.* [*November 3, 1831*]

Ours [our army] is composed of the scum of the earth — the mere scum of the earth. **Ib.**

My rule always was to do the business of the day in the day.
Ib. [*November 2, 1835*]

They wanted this iron fist to command them.
Ib. [*November 8, 1840*]; *of troops sent by Wellington to the Canadian frontier in the war with America*

There is no mistake; there has been no mistake; and there shall be no mistake. *Wellingtoniana* [1832]

I don't care a twopenny damn what becomes of the ashes of Napoleon Buonaparte. **Attributed**

The battle of Waterloo was won on the playing fields of Eton.
From FRASER, *Words on Wellington* [1889]

Publish and be damned.
Attributed; when his mistress threatened to publish her diary and his letters

[1] See Montaigne, p. 189b, and note.

LUDWIG VAN BEETHOVEN
1770–1827

Art! Who comprehends her? With whom can one consult concerning this great goddess?
Letter to Bettina von Arnim [*August 11, 1810*]

The world is a king, and, like a king, desires flattery in return for favor; but true art is selfish and perverse — it will not submit to the mold of flattery.
Conversations [*March 1820*]

GEORGE CANNING
1770–1827

When our perils are past, shall our gratitude sleep?
No — here's to the pilot that weathered the storm.
Song for the Inauguration of the Pitt Club [*May 25, 1802*]

I give thee sixpence! I will see thee damned first.
The Anti-Jacobin, no. 11 [1797]. *The Friend of Humanity and the Knife-Grinder, st. 9*

I think of those companions true
Who studied with me at the U-
-niversity of Göttingen.
Ib. no. 30 [1798]. *The Rovers, song, st. 1*

A steady patriot of the world alone,
The friend of every country but his own.[1]
Ib. no 36 [1798]. *New Morality, l. 113*

And finds, with keen, discriminating sight,
Black's not so black — nor white so very white. *Ib. l. 199*

Give me the avowed, erect, and manly foe,
Firm I can meet, perhaps return the blow;

[1] This refers to the Jacobin.
See Overbury, p. 315b, and note.

But of all plagues, good Heaven, thy
　　wrath can send,
Save, save, oh save me from the candid
　　friend! [1]
　　　　The Anti-Jacobin, no. 36. New
　　　　　　　　　　Morality, l. 207

In matters of commerce the fault of the
　　Dutch
Is offering too little and asking too
　　much.
　　　　Dispatch to Sir Charles Bagot,
　　　　British Minister at The Hague
　　　　[January 31, 1826]

I called the New World into existence to redress the balance of the Old.
　　　　The King's Message [December
　　　　　　　　　　　　12, 1826]

DAVID EVERETT
1770–1813

You'd scarce expect one of my age
To speak in public on the stage;
And if I chance to fall below
Demosthenes or Cicero,
Don't view me with a critic's eye,
But pass my imperfections by.
Large streams from little fountains
　　flow,
Tall oaks from little acorns grow.[2]
　　　　Written for a school declama-
　　　　tion for Ephraim H. Farrar,
　　　　aged seven, New Ipswich, New
　　　　Hampshire [1791]

GEORG WILHELM
FRIEDRICH HEGEL
1770–1831

What is reasonable is real; that
which is real is reasonable.
　　　　Philosophy of Right [1821]

What experience and history teach is
this — that people and governments
never have learned anything from history, or acted on principles deduced
from it.
　　　　Philosophy of History [1832],[1]
　　　　　　　　　　introduction

Amid the pressure of great events, a
general principle gives no help.　　*Ib.*

To him who looks upon the world
rationally, the world in its turn presents
a rational aspect. The relation is mutual.　　　　　　　　　　　　　*Ib.*

The history of the world is none
other than the progress of the consciousness of freedom.　　　　　*Ib.*

We may affirm absolutely that nothing great in the world has been accomplished without passion.　　　　*Ib.*

It is easier to discover a deficiency in
individuals, in states, and in Providence, than to see their real import and
value.　　　　　　　　　　　　*Ib.*

Life has a value only when it has
something valuable as its object.　*Ib.*

Serious occupation is labor that has
reference to some want.
　　　　　　　Ib. pt. I, sec. 2, ch. 1

It is a matter of perfect indifference
where a thing originated; the only question is: "Is it true in and for itself?"
　　　　　　　　　　　　Ib. III, 3, 2

The Few assume to be the *deputies*,
but they are often only the *despoilers* of
the Many.　　　　　　　*Ib. IV, 3, 3*

JAMES HOGG[2]
1770–1835

We'll o'er the water, we'll o'er the sea,
We'll o'er the water to Charlie;
Come weal, come woe, we'll gather and
　　go,
And live and die wi' Charlie.
　　　　O'er the Water to Charlie

---

[1] Defend me from my friends; I can defend
myself from my enemies. — *Attributed to Maré-*
chal Villars, when taking leave of Louis XIV
[2] The lofty oak from a small acorn grows.
— Lewis Duncombe [1711–1730], *De Minimis*
Maxima (translation)
　　See Anonymous, p. 151a.

[1] Translated by J. Sibree. Quoted by G. B.
Shaw in *The Revolutionist's Handbook.*
[2] The Ettrick Shepherd.

For Kilmeny had been she knew not
   where,
And Kilmeny had seen what she could
   not declare. *Kilmeny, l. 38*

Love is like a dizziness,
It winna let a poor body
Gang about his bizziness.
   Love Is Like a Dizziness, st. 1

PIERRE JACQUES
ÉTIENNE,
COUNT CAMBRONNE
1770–1842

The Guards die, but never surrender.[1] *Attributed*

JOSEPH HOPKINSON
1770–1842

Hail, Columbia! happy land!
Hail, ye heroes! heaven-born band!
Who fought and bled in Freedom's
   cause. *Hail, Columbia,[2] st. 1*

Let independence be our boast,
Ever mindful what it cost;
Ever grateful for the prize,
Let its altar reach the skies. *Ib.*

WILLIAM ROBERT
SPENCER
1770–1834

Oh! where does faithful Gêlert roam,
   The flow'r of all his race?
So true, so brave; a lamb at home,
   A lion in the chase!
   Beth-Gêlert, st. 4

JOHN TOBIN
1770–1804

The man that lays his hand upon a
   woman,

---

[1] La Garde meurt, mais ne se rend pas.
  Cambronne denied having said this phrase,
which was invented by Rougemont after the
battle of Waterloo, in the *Indépendant.* —
FOURNIER, *L'Esprit dans l'Histoire* [1857]
[2] The music, generally attributed to Philip
Phile, was Washington's inaugural march. Hopkinson supplied verses at a singer's request, and
the song won instant acclaim.

Save in the way of kindness, is a
   wretch
Whom 'twere gross flattery to name a
   coward.
   The Honeymoon [1805], *act II,
   sc. 1*

WILLIAM
WORDSWORTH[1]
1770–1850

And homeless near a thousand homes I
   stood,
And near a thousand tables pined and
   wanted food.
   Guilt and Sorrow [*written 1791–
   1794*], *pt. II, st. 41*

A simple child,
That lightly draws its breath,
And feels its life in every limb,
What should it know of death?
   We Are Seven [1798], *st. 1*

O Reader! had you in your mind
Such stores as silent thought can
   bring,
O gentle Reader! you would find
A tale in everything.
   Simon Lee [1798], *st. 9*

In that sweet mood when pleasant
   thoughts
Bring sad thoughts to the mind.
   Lines Written in Early Spring
   [1798], *st. 1*

And 'tis my faith, that every flower
Enjoys the air it breathes. *Ib. st. 3*

Have I not reason to lament
What man has made of man? [2]
   Ib. st. 6

Nor less I deem that there are Powers
Which of themselves our minds im-
   press;
That we can feed this mind of ours
In a wise passiveness.
   Expostulation and Reply [1798],
   st. 6

---

[1] Coleridge said to Wordsworth, "Since Milton,
I know of no poet with so many *felicities* and
unforgettable lines and stanzas as you." —
HENRY NELSON COLERIDGE, *Memoir* [1847]
[2] See Burns, p. 492b.

Up! up! my friend, and quit your
   books;
Or surely you'll grow double:
Up! up! my friend, and clear your
   looks;
Why all this toil and trouble?
      The Tables Turned [1798], *st. 1*

Come forth into the light of things,
Let Nature be your teacher.
              Ib. st. 4

One impulse from a vernal wood
May teach you more of man,
Of moral evil and of good,
Than all the sages can.[1]   *Ib. st. 6*

These hedgerows, hardly hedgerows, little lines
Of sportive wood run wild.
      Lines Composed a Few Miles
      Above Tintern Abbey [1798],
      l. 15

    Sensations sweet,
Felt in the blood, and felt along the
   heart.   *Ib. l. 27*

That best portion of a good man's life,
His little, nameless, unremembered acts
Of kindness and of love.   *Ib. l. 33*

    Blessed mood,
In which the burthen of the mystery,
In which the heavy and the weary weight
Of all this unintelligible world,
Is lightened.   *Ib. l. 41*

While with an eye made quiet by the
   power
Of harmony, and the deep power of joy
We see into the life of things.
              Ib. l. 47

    The sounding cataract
Haunted me like a passion; the tall
   rock,
The mountain, and the deep and
   gloomy wood,
Their colors and their forms, were then
   to me
An appetite; a feeling and a love,
That had no need of a remoter charm,
By thoughts supplied, nor any interest
Unborrowed from the eye.   *Ib. l. 76*

[1] See St. Bernard, p. 154a, and Shakespeare,
pp. 247b and 249b.

    I have learned
To look on nature, not as in the hour
Of thoughtless youth; but hearing
   oftentimes
The still, sad music of humanity,
Nor harsh nor grating, though of ample
   power
To chasten and subdue. And I have felt
A presence that disturbs me with the
   joy
Of elevated thoughts; a sense sublime
Of something far more deeply inter-
   fused,
Whose dwelling is the light of setting
   suns,
And the round ocean and the living
   air,
And the blue sky, and in the mind of
   man;
A motion and a spirit, that impels
All thinking things, all objects of all
   thought,
And rolls through all things.[1]
      Lines Composed a Few Miles
      Above Tintern Abbey, l. 88

    All the mighty world
Of eye and ear, both what they half
   create,
And what perceive.   *Ib. l. 105*

Knowing that Nature never did betray
The heart that loved her.   *Ib. l. 122*

Full twenty times was Peter feared,
For once that Peter was respected.
      Peter Bell [written 1798], *pt. I,*
              st. 3

A primrose by a river's brim
A yellow primrose was to him,
And it was nothing more.   *Ib. st. 12*

The soft blue sky did never melt
Into his heart; he never felt
The witchery of the soft blue sky!
             Ib. st. 15

Fair seedtime had my soul, and I grew
   up
Fostered alike by beauty and by fear.
      The Prelude [written 1799–
      1805], *bk. I, l. 301*

[1] See Shelley, p. 568a.

With what strange utterance did the
loud dry wind
Blow through my ear! the sky seemed
not a sky
Of earth — and with what motion
moved the clouds!
The Prelude, bk. I, l. 337

Dust as we are, the immortal spirit
grows
Like harmony in music; there is a dark
Inscrutable workmanship that recon-
ciles
Discordant elements, makes them cling
together
In one society. *Ib. l. 340*

The grim shape
Towered up between me and the stars,
and still,
For so it seemed, with purpose of its
own
And measured motion like a living
thing,
Strode after me. *Ib. l. 381*

Where the statue stood
Of Newton with his prism and silent
face,
The marble index of a mind forever
Voyaging through strange seas of
thought, alone. *Ib. III, l. 61*

When from our better selves we have
too long
Been parted by the hurrying world, and
droop,
Sick of its business, of its pleasures
tired,
How gracious, how benign, is Solitude.
Ib. IV, l. 354

Brothers all
In honor, as in one community,
Scholars and gentlemen.
Ib. IX, l. 227

Bliss was it in that dawn to be alive,
But to be young was very heaven! [1]
Ib. XI, l. 108

There is
One great society alone on earth:
The noble Living and the noble Dead.
Ib. XI, l. 393

[1] Also in *French Revolution as It Appears to
Enthusiasts* [1804].

One of those heavenly days that cannot
die. *Nutting* [1799], *l. 3*

What fond and wayward thoughts will
slide
Into a lover's head!
"O mercy!" to myself I cried,
"If Lucy should be dead!"
*Strange Fits of Passion Have I
Known* [1799], *st. 1*

She dwelt among the untrodden ways
Beside the springs of Dove,
A maid whom there were none to
praise
And very few to love.[1]

A violet by a mossy stone
Half hidden from the eye!
— Fair as a star, when only one
Is shining in the sky.

She lived unknown, and few could
know
When Lucy ceased to be;
But she is in her grave, and, oh,
The difference to me!
*Lucy: She Dwelt Among the Un-
trodden Ways* [1799]

Three years she grew in sun and
shower,
Then Nature said, "A lovelier flower
On earth was never sown;
This Child I to myself will take;
She shall be mine, and I will make
A Lady of my own."
*Lucy: Three Years She Grew in
Sun and Shower* [1799], *st. 1*

I traveled among unknown men,
In lands beyond the sea;
Nor England! did I know till then
What love I bore to thee.
*I Traveled Among Unknown
Men* [1799], *st. 1*

[1] He lived amidst th' untrodden ways
To Rydal Lake that lead;
A bard whom there were none to praise,
And very few to read.
Unread his works — his "Milk White Doe"
With dust is dark and dim;
It's still in Longmans' shop, and oh!
The difference to him!
— *Parody by* HARTLEY COLERIDGE
[1796–1849]

A slumber did my spirit seal;
  I had no human fears:
She seemed a thing that could not feel
  The touch of earthly years.

No motion has she now, no force;
  She neither hears nor sees;
Rolled round in earth's diurnal course,
  With rocks, and stones, and trees.
     A Slumber Did My Spirit Seal
                     [1799]

    A fingering slave,
One that would peep and botanize
Upon his mother's grave.
    A Poet's Epitaph [1799], *st. 5*

A reasoning, self-sufficing thing,
An intellectual All-in-all!   *Ib. st. 8*

And you must love him, ere to you
He will seem worthy of your love.
                 Ib. st. 11

The harvest of a quiet eye.   *Ib. st. 13*

The sweetest thing that ever grew
Beside a human door.
       Lucy Gray [1799], *st. 2*

And sings a solitary song
That whistles in the wind.
                 Ib. st. 16

    A youth to whom was given
So much of earth — so much of heaven,
And such impetuous blood.
        Ruth [1799], *st. 21*

  Poetry is the breath and finer spirit
of all knowledge; it is the impassioned
expression which is in the countenance
of all Science.
    Lyrical Ballads [2nd ed., 1800],
                    preface

  In spite of difference of soil and climate, of language and manners, of laws
and customs — in spite of things silently gone out of mind, and things
violently destroyed, the Poet binds
together by passion and knowledge the
vast empire of human society, as it is
spread over the whole earth, and over
all time.   *Ib.*

  I have said that poetry is the spontaneous overflow of powerful feelings: it
takes its origin from emotion recollected in tranquillity.
          Lyrical Ballads, preface

Something between a hindrance and a
  help.   *Michael* [1800], *l. 189*

Drink, pretty creature, drink!
       The Pet Lamb [1800], *st. 1*

May no rude hand deface it,
And its forlorn *hic jacet!*
       Ellen Irwin [1800], *st. 7*

She gave me eyes, she gave me ears;
And humble cares and delicate fears;
A heart, the fountain of sweet tears;
  And love, and thought, and joy.
     The Sparrows' Nest [1801], *st. 2*

My heart leaps up when I behold
  A rainbow in the sky:
So was it when my life began;
So is it now I am a man;
So be it when I shall grow old.
  Or let me die!
The Child is father of the Man; [1]
And I could wish my days to be
Bound each to each by natural piety.
    My Heart Leaps Up When I
               Behold [1802]

Sweet childish days, that were as long
As twenty days are now.
    To a Butterfly [1802]. *pt. II,*
    I've Watched You Now a Full
    Half-Hour, st. 2

Pleasures newly found are sweet
When they lie about our feet.
    To the Small Celandine [1802],
                   st. 1

I thought of Chatterton, the marvelous
  boy,
The sleepless soul that perished in his
  pride;
Of him who walked in glory and in joy
Following his plow, along the moun-
  tainside:
By our own spirits are we deified:
We Poets in our youth begin in glad-
  ness;

  [1] See Milton, p. 348b.

But thereof come in the end despondency and madness.[1]
Resolution and Independence [1802], *st. 7*

That heareth not the loud winds when they call;
And moveth all together, if it move at all. *Ib. st. 11*

Choice word and measured phrase, above the reach
Of ordinary men. *Ib. st. 14*

And mighty poets in their misery dead. *Ib. st. 17*

Earth has not anything to show more fair:
Dull would he be of soul who could pass by
A sight so touching in its majesty.
Composed Upon Westminster Bridge [September 3, 1802], *l. 1*

Ne'er saw I, never felt, a calm so deep!
The river glideth at his own sweet will;
Dear God! the very houses seem asleep;
And all that mighty heart is lying still! *Ib. l. 11*

Plain living and high thinking are no more:
The homely beauty of the good old cause
Is gone; our peace, our fearful innocence,
And pure religion breathing household laws.
Written in London [September 1802]

It is a beauteous evening, calm and free,
The holy time is quiet as a nun
Breathless with adoration.
It Is a Beauteous Evening [1802], *l. 1*

Thou liest in Abraham's bosom all the year;
And worship'st at the Temple's inner shrine,
God being with thee when we know it not. *Ib. l. 12*

[1] See Robert Lowell, p. 1075b.

Once did she hold the gorgeous east in fee:
And was the safeguard of the west.
On the Extinction of the Venetian Republic [1802], *l. 1*

And, when she took unto herself a mate,
She must espouse the everlasting sea. *Ib. l. 7*

Men are we, and must grieve when even the shade
Of that which once was great, is passed away. *Ib. l. 11*

Thou hast great allies;
Thy friends are exultations, agonies,
And love, and man's unconquerable mind.
To Toussaint L'Ouverture [1802], *l. 11*

Milton! thou should'st be living at this hour:
England hath need of thee; she is a fen
Of stagnant waters.
London [1802], *l. 1*

Thy soul was like a star, and dwelt apart;
Thou hadst a voice whose sound was like the sea:
Pure as the naked heavens, majestic, free,
So didst thou travel on life's common way,
In cheerful godliness. *Ib. l. 8*

We must be free or die, who speak the tongue
That Shakespeare spake; the faith and morals hold
Which Milton held.
It Is Not To Be Thought Of [1802], *l. 11*

Thou unassuming commonplace
Of Nature.
To the Same Flower [1802], *st. 1*

Oft on the dappled turf at ease
I sit, and play with similes,
Loose types of things through all degrees. *Ib. st. 2*

And stepping westward seemed to be
A kind of heavenly destiny.
> *Stepping Westward* [1803], *st.* 2

Old, unhappy, far-off things,
And battles long ago.
> *The Solitary Reaper* [1803], *st.* 3

The music in my heart I bore
Long after it was heard no more.
> *Ib. st.* 4

The good old rule
Sufficeth them, the simple plan,
That they should take, who have the power,
And they should keep who can.
> *Rob Roy's Grave* [1803], *st.* 9

A brotherhood of venerable trees.
> *Sonnet Composed at —— Castle* [1803], *l.* 6

O for a single hour of that Dundee
Who on that day the word of onset gave!
> *In the Pass of Killicranky* [1803], *l.* 11

There was a time when meadow, grove, and stream,
The earth, and every common sight,
To me did seem
Appareled in celestial light,
The glory and the freshness of a dream.
It is not now as it hath been of yore —
Turn wheresoe'er I may,
By night or day,
The things which I have seen I now can see no more.
> *Ode (Intimations of Immortality from Recollections of Early Childhood* [1]*)* [1803–1806], *st.* 1

The Rainbow comes and goes,
And lovely is the Rose.
> *Ib. st.* 2

The sunshine is a glorious birth;
But yet I know, where'er I go,
That there hath passed away a glory
from the earth.
> *Ib.*

[1] The *Ode on Immortality* is the high water mark which the intellect has reached in this age. — EMERSON, *English Traits* [1856]

Whither is fled the visionary gleam?
Where is it now, the glory and the dream?
> *Ode (Intimations of Immortality, st.* 4

Our birth is but a sleep and a forgetting:
The soul that rises with us, our life's star,
Hath had elsewhere its setting,
And cometh from afar:
Not in entire forgetfulness,
And not in utter nakedness,
But trailing clouds of glory do we come
From God, who is our home:
Heaven lies about us in our infancy! [1]
Shades of the prison-house begin to close
Upon the growing boy.
> *Ib. st.* 5

The youth, who daily farther from the east
Must travel, still is Nature's priest,
And by the vision splendid
Is on his way attended;
At length the man perceives it die away,
And fade into the light of common day.
> *Ib.*

As if his whole vocation
Were endless imitation.
> *Ib. st.* 7

O joy! that in our embers
Is something that doth live,
That nature yet remembers
What was so fugitive!
> *Ib. st.* 9

High instincts before which our mortal nature
Did tremble like a guilty thing surprised.
> *Ib.*

Truths that wake,
To perish never.
> *Ib.*

Though inland far we be,
Our souls have sight of that immortal sea
Which brought us hither.
> *Ib.*

[1] See Lowell, p. 692a.

Though nothing can bring back the hour
Of splendor in the grass, of glory in the flower.
> Ode (*Intimations of Immortality*), st. 10

In years that bring the philosophic mind. *Ib.*

The clouds that gather round the setting sun
Do take a sober coloring from an eye
That hath kept watch o'er man's mortality;
Another race hath been, and other palms are won.
Thanks to the human heart by which we live,
Thanks to its tenderness, its joys, and fears,
To me the meanest flower that blows can give
Thoughts that do often lie too deep for tears. *Ib. st. 11*

O blithe newcomer! I have heard,
I hear thee and rejoice.
O Cuckoo! shall I call thee bird,
Or but a wandering voice?
> *To the Cuckoo* [1804], *st. 1*

No bird, but an invisible thing,
A voice, a mystery. *Ib. st. 4*

She was a phantom of delight
When first she gleamed upon my sight;
A lovely apparition, sent
To be a moment's ornament.
> *She Was a Phantom of Delight* [1804], *st. 1*

A spirit, yet a woman too! *Ib. st. 2*

And now I see with eye serene
The very pulse of the machine. *Ib. st. 3*

A perfect woman, nobly planned,
To warn, to comfort, and command. *Ib.*

I wandered lonely as a cloud
That floats on high o'er vales and hills,
When all at once I saw a crowd,
A host, of golden daffodils.
> *I Wandered Lonely as a Cloud* [1804], *st. 1*

Continuous as the stars that shine
And twinkle on the milky way. *Ib. st. 2*

Ten thousand saw I at a glance,
Tossing their heads in sprightly dance. *Ib.*

A poet could not but be gay,
In such a jocund company. *Ib. st. 3*

That inward eye
Which is the bliss of solitude. *Ib. st. 4*

Stern Daughter of the Voice of God! [1]
> *Ode to Duty* [1805], *st. 1*

A light to guide, a rod
To check the erring, and reprove. *Ib.*

Me this unchartered freedom tires;
I feel the weight of chance-desires;
My hopes no more must change their name,
I long for a repose that ever is the same. *Ib. st. 5*

Stern Lawgiver! *Ib. st. 7*

Thou dost preserve the stars from wrong;
And the most ancient heavens, through Thee, are fresh and strong. *Ib.*

The light that never was, on sea or land;
The consecration, and the Poet's dream.
> *Suggested by a Picture of Peele Castle in a Storm* [1805], *st. 4*

Dear Child of Nature, let them rail!
> *To a Young Lady* [1805], *st. 1*

Thou, while thy babes around thee cling,
Shalt show us how divine a thing
A woman may be made. *Ib. st. 2*

[1] See Milton, p. 347b.

But an old age serene and bright,
And lovely as a Lapland night,
Shall lead thee to thy grave.
                To a Young Lady, st. 3

Who is the happy Warrior? Who is
  he
That every man in arms would wish to
  be?
        Character of the Happy Warrior
                [1806], l. 1

Who, doomed to go in company with
  pain,
And fear, and bloodshed, miserable
  train!
Turns his necessity to glorious gain.
                Ib. l. 12

More skillful in self-knowledge, even
  more pure,
As tempted more; more able to endure,
As more exposed to suffering and distress.   *Ib. l. 23*

But who, if he be called upon to face
Some awful moment to which Heaven
  has joined
Great issues, good or bad for human-
  kind,
Is happy as a lover.   *Ib. l. 48*

And, through the heat of conflict, keeps
  the law
In calmness made, and sees what he
  foresaw.   *Ib. l. 53*

Whom neither shape of danger can dismay,
Nor thought of tender happiness betray.   *Ib. l. 77*

Like — but oh how different!
        Yes, It Was the Mountain Echo
                [1806], st. 2

Nuns fret not at their convent's narrow
  room.
        Nuns Fret Not [1806], l. 1

The world is too much with us; late
  and soon,

Getting and spending, we lay waste our
  powers:
Little we see in Nature that is ours;
We have given our hearts away, a sordid boon!
        The World Is Too Much With
                Us [1806], l. 1

Great God! I'd rather be
A Pagan suckled in a creed outworn;
So might I, standing on this pleasant
  lea,
Have glimpses that would make me less
  forlorn;
Have sight of Proteus rising from the
  sea;
Or hear old Triton blow his wreathed
  horn.   *Ib. l. 9*

Where lies the land to which yon Ship
  must go? [1]
Fresh as a lark mounting at break of
  day,
Festively she puts forth in trim array.
        Where Lies the Land
                [1806], l. 1

Blessed barrier between day and day.
        To Sleep [1806], II, A Flock of
                Sheep, l. 13

Maidens withering on the stalk.[2]
        Personal Talk [1806], Sonnet 1

Dreams, books, are each a world; and
  books, we know,
Are a substantial world, both pure and
  good.
Round these, with tendrils strong as
  flesh and blood,
Our pastime and our happiness will
  grow.   *Ib. 3*

A power is passing from the earth.
        Lines on the Expected Dissolu-
                tion of Mr. Fox [1806], st. 5

----

[1] Where lies the land to which the ship would
    go?
  Far, far ahead, is all her seamen know.
        ARTHUR HUGH CLOUGH [1819–1861],
                Songs of Absence
[2] See Shakespeare, *A Midsummer-Night's
Dream I, i, 77*, p. 228b.

Two voices are there: one is of the sea,[1]
One of the mountains; each a mighty
voice.
>*Thought of a Briton on the Sub-*
>*jugation of Switzerland* [1807],
>*l. 1*

The silence that is in the starry sky,
The sleep that is among the lonely
hills.
>*Song at the Feast of Brougham*
>*Castle* [1807] *l. 163*

Every great and original writer, in
proportion as he is great or original,
must himself create the taste by which
he is to be relished.
>*Letter to Lady Beaumont* [*May*
>*21, 1807*]

A few strong instincts, and a few plain
rules.
>*Alas! What Boots the Long*
>*Laborious Quest?* [1809]

Surprised by joy — impatient as the
wind.
>*Surprised by Joy* [1812], *l. 1*

Strongest minds
Are often those of whom the noisy
world
Hears least.
>*The Excursion* [2] [1814], *bk. I*

The imperfect offices of prayer and
praise. *Ib.*

The good die first,[3]
And they whose hearts are dry as sum-
mer dust
Burn to the socket. *Ib.*

Wrongs unredressed, or insults unavenged. *Ib. III*

Society became my glittering bride.
Ib.

There is a luxury in self-dispraise;
And inward self-disparagement affords
To meditative spleen a grateful feast.
>*The Excursion, bk. IV*

I have seen
A curious child, who dwelt upon a
tract
Of inland ground, applying to his ear
The convolutions of a smooth-lipped
shell,
To which, in silence hushed, his very
soul
Listened intensely; and his countenance
soon
Brightened with joy, for from within
were heard
Murmurings, whereby the monitor ex-
pressed
Mysterious union with its native sea.[1]
>*Ib.*

One in whom persuasion and belief
Had ripened into faith, and faith be-
come
A passionate intuition. *Ib.*

Spires whose "silent finger points to
heaven." [2] *Ib. VI*

A man he seems of cheerful yesterdays
And confident tomorrows. *Ib. VII*

The gods approve
The depth, and not the tumult, of the
soul. *Laodamia* [1814], *st. 13*

An ampler ether, a diviner air.
Ib. st. 18

And beauty, for confiding youth,
Those shocks of passion can prepare
That kill the bloom before its time;

---

[1] Two voices are there: one is of the deep;
And one is of an old half-witted sheep
Which bleats articulate monotony,
And indicates that two and one are three.
And, Wordsworth, both art thine.
>Jᴀᴍᴇs Kᴇɴɴᴇᴛʜ Sᴛᴇᴘʜᴇɴ, *Sonnet,*
>*Wordsworth* [1891]

[2] This will never do. — Fʀᴀɴᴄɪs Jᴇꜰꜰʀᴇʏ,
Opening sentence, review of Wᴏʀᴅsᴡᴏʀᴛʜ's *Excursion, Edinburgh Review* [1814]

[3] See Menander, p. 102a, and note.

---

[1] See Landor, p. 536a.
Upon a mountain height, far from the sea,
I found a shell,
And to my listening ear the lonely thing
Ever a song of ocean seemed to sing,
Ever a tale of ocean seemed to tell.
>Eᴜɢᴇɴᴇ Fɪᴇʟᴅ [1850–1895],
>*The Wanderer, st. 1*

[2] An instinctive taste teaches men to build
their churches in flat countries with spire
steeples, which, as they cannot be referred to any
other object, point as with silent finger to the
sky and stars. — Cᴏʟᴇʀɪᴅɢᴇ, *The Friend* [1809],
no. 14

And blanch, without the owner's crime,
The most resplendent hair.
Lament of Mary Queen of Scots
[1817], st. 6

Enough, if something from our hands have power
To live, and act, and serve the future hour.
The River Duddon, Sonnet:
Afterthought [1820], l. 10

We feel that we are greater than we know. *Ib., l. 14*

Habit rules the unreflecting herd.
Ecclesiastical Sonnets [1822],
pt. II, 28

The feather, whence the pen
Was shaped that traced the lives of these good men,
Dropped from an angel's wing.[1]
Ib. III, 5. Walton's Book of Lives

Give all thou canst; high Heaven rejects the lore
Of nicely calculated less or more.
Ib. 43. Inside of King's College
Chapel, Cambridge

But hushed be every thought that springs
From out the bitterness of things.
Elegiac Stanzas, Addressed to
Sir G. H. B. [1824], st. 7

Ethereal minstrel! pilgrim of the sky!
To a Skylark [1825], l. 1

Type of the wise who soar, but never roam,
True to the kindred points of heaven and home! *Ib.*

Scorn not the sonnet. Critic, you have frowned,
Mindless of its just honors; with this key
Shakespeare unlocked his heart.[2]
Scorn Not the Sonnet [1827], l. 1

[1] The pen wherewith thou dost so heavenly sing
Made of a quill from an angel's wing.
HENRY CONSTABLE [1562–1613], *Sonnet*

[2] See Browning, p. 668a.

Small service is true service while it lasts:
Of humblest friends, bright creature! scorn not one:
The daisy, by the shadow that it casts,
Protects the lingering dewdrop from the sun.
To a Child, written in her album
[1834]

How does the meadow flower its bloom unfold?
Because the lovely little flower is free
Down to its root, and, in that freedom, bold.
A Poet! — He Hath Put His
Heart to School [1842], l. 9

Minds that have nothing to confer
Find little to perceive.
Yes, Thou Art Fair [1845], st. 2

MARIE FRANÇOIS XAVIER BICHAT
1771–1802

Life is the totality of those functions which resist death.
Physiological Researches Upon
Life and Death [1800]

THOMAS DIBDIN
1771–1841

Oh, it's a snug little island!
A right little, tight little island.
The Snug Little Island

WILLIAM PITT
d. 1840

A strong nor'wester's blowing, Bill,
Hark! Don't ye hear it roar, now?
Lord help 'em, how I pities all
Unhappy folks on shore now!
The Sailor's Consolation, st. 1

JAMES MONTGOMERY
1771–1854

Tomorrow — oh, 'twill never be,
If we should live a thousand years!
Our time is all today, today.[1] *Today*

[1] See Sydney Smith, p. 523b.

Give me the hand that is honest and
    hearty,
Free as the breeze and unshackled by
    party.   *Give Me Thy Hand, st. 2*

Who, that hath ever been,
    Could bear to be no more?
Yet who would tread again the scene
    He trod through life before?
         The Falling Leaf, st. 7

Here in the body pent,
    Absent from Him I roam,
Yet nightly pitch my moving tent
    A day's march nearer home.
         At Home in Heaven

Prayer is the soul's sincere desire,
    Uttered or unexpressed;
The motion of a hidden fire
    That trembles in the breast.
         What Is Prayer? st. 1

Prayer is the burden of a sigh,
    The falling of a tear;
The upward glancing of an eye,
    When none but God is near.
         Ib. st. 2

SIR WALTER SCOTT
1771–1832

The way was long, the wind was cold,
The Minstrel was infirm and old;
His withered cheek, and tresses gray,
Seem'd to have known a better day.
    The Lay of the Last Minstrel
    [1805], introduction

The unpremeditated lay.   *Ib.*

Such is the custom of Branksome Hall.
         Ib. canto I, st. 7

What shall be the maiden's fate?
Who shall be the maiden's mate?
         Ib. st. 16

Steady of heart, and stout of hand.
         Ib. st. 21

If thou would'st view fair Melrose
    aright,
Go visit it by the pale moonlight.
         Ib. II, st. 1

I cannot tell how the truth may be;
I say the tale as 'twas said to me.
    The Lay of the Last Minstrel,
         canto II, st. 22

In peace, Love tunes the shepherd's
    reed;
In war, he mounts the warrior's steed;
In halls, in gay attire is seen;
In hamlets, dances on the green.
Love rules the court, the camp, the
    grove,
And men below, and saints above;
For love is heaven, and heaven is love.
         Ib. III, st. 2

    For ne'er
Was flattery lost on poet's ear:
A simple race! they waste their toil
For the vain tribute of a smile.
         Ib. IV, conclusion

Call it not vain; they do not err
Who say, that when the Poet dies,
Mute Nature mourns her worshipper,
And celebrates his obsequies.
         Ib. V, st. 1

True love's the gift which God has
    given
To man alone beneath the heaven:
It is not fantasy's hot fire,
    Whose wishes, soon as granted, fly;
It liveth not in fierce desire,
    With dead desire it doth not die;
It is the secret sympathy,
The silver link, the silken tie,
Which heart to heart and mind to
    mind
In body and in soul can bind.
         Ib. st. 13

Breathes there the man, with soul so
    dead,
Who never to himself hath said,
    This is my own, my native land!
Whose heart hath ne'er within him
    burn'd [1]
As home his footsteps he hath turn'd
    From wandering on a foreign strand!
If such there breathe, go, mark him
    well;
For him no Minstrel raptures swell;

---

[1] See *Luke 24:32,* p. 47b.

High though his titles, proud his
name,
Boundless his wealth as wish can
claim;
Despite those titles, power, and pelf,
The wretch, concentered all in self,
Living, shall forfeit fair renown,
And, doubly dying, shall go down
To the vile dust, from whence he
sprung,
Unwept, unhonor'd, and unsung.[1]
> *The Lay of the Last Minstrel,*
> *canto VI, st. 1*

O Caledonia! stern and wild,
Meet nurse for a poetic child!
Land of brown heath and shaggy
wood;
Land of the mountain and the flood!
> *Ib. st. 2*

That day of wrath, that dreadful day,
When heaven and earth shall pass
away.[2]   *Ib. st. 31*

November's sky is chill and drear,
November's leaf is red and sear.
> *Marmion* [1808], *canto I, intro-*
> *duction, st. 1*

Stood for his country's glory fast,
And nail'd her colors to the mast!
> *Ib. st. 10*

But search the land of living men,
Where wilt thou find their like again?
> *Ib. st. 11*

Just at the age 'twixt boy and youth,
When thought is speech, and speech is
truth.
> *Ib. II, introduction, st. 4*

And come he slow, or come he fast,
It is but Death who comes at last.
> *Ib. st. 30*

Oh, young Lochinvar is come out of
the West,
Through all the wide Border his steed
was the best.
> *Ib. V, st. 12 [Lochinvar, st. 1]*

So faithful in love, and so dauntless in
war,

There never was knight like the young
Lochinvar.
> *Marmion, canto V, st. 12*
> *[Lochinvar, st. 1]*

For a laggard in love, and a dastard in
war,
Was to wed the fair Ellen of brave
Lochinvar.
> *Ib. [Lochinvar, st. 2]*

With a smile on her lips, and a tear in
her eye.   *Ib. [Lochinvar, st. 5]*

Heap on more wood! — the wind is
chill;
But let it whistle as it will,
We'll keep our Christmas merry still.
> *Ib. VI, introduction, st. 1*

England was merry England, when
Old Christmas brought his sports
again.
'Twas Christmas broach'd the mightiest
ale;
'Twas Christmas told the merriest
tale;
A Christmas gambol oft could cheer
The poor man's heart through half the
year.   *Ib. st. 4*

> And dar'st thou, then,
To beard the lion in his den,
The Douglas in his hall?   *Ib. st. 14*

Oh, what a tangled web we weave,
When first we practice to deceive!
> *Ib. st. 17*

O Woman! in our hours of ease,
Uncertain, coy, and hard to please,
And variable as the shade [1]
By the light quivering aspen made;
When pain and anguish wring the
brow,
A ministering angel thou! [2]
> *Ib. st. 30*

"Charge, Chester, charge! On, Stanley,
on!"
Were the last words of Marmion.
> *Ib. st. 32*

To all, to each, a fair goodnight,
And pleasing dreams, and slumbers
light!   *Ib. L'Envoy*

---

[1] See Homer, p. 64b, and note.
[2] See Tommaso di Celano, p. 157b.

[1] See Virgil, p. 118b.
[2] See Shakespeare, p. 266a.

The stag at eve had drunk his fill,
Where danced the moon on Monan's rill,
And deep his midnight lair had made
In lone Glenartney's hazel shade.
The Lady of the Lake [1810],
canto I, st. 1

In listening mood she seemed to stand,
The guardian Naiad of the strand.
Ib. st. 17

Forward and frolic glee was there,
The will to do, the soul to dare.
Ib. st. 21

Soldier, rest! thy warfare o'er,
Sleep the sleep that knows not breaking,
Dream of battled fields no more,
Days of danger, nights of waking.
Ib. st. 31

Hail to the Chief who in triumph advances! [1] *Ib. II, st. 19*

Some feelings are to mortals given,
With less of earth in them than heaven. *Ib. st. 22*

Like the dew on the mountain,
  Like the foam on the river,
Like the bubble on the fountain,
  Thou art gone, and forever!
Ib. III, st. 16 [Coronach, st. 3]

And, Saxon, I am Roderick Dhu!
Ib. V, st. 9

Come one, come all! this rock shall fly
From its firm base as soon as I.
Ib. st. 10

Respect was mingled with surprise,
And the stern joy which warriors feel
In foemen worthy of their steel. *Ib*

Where, where was Roderick then!
One blast upon his bugle horn
Were worth a thousand men!
Ib. VI, st. 18

But answer came there none.
The Bridal of Triermain [1813],
canto III, st. 10

---

[1] The verses beginning with this line were set to music by JAMES SANDERSON [1769–c. 1841]. The march has become traditionally attached to the President of the United States.

Still are the thoughts to memory dear.
Rokeby [1813], *canto I, st. 33*

A mother's pride, a father's joy.
Ib. III, st. 15

Oh, Brignall banks are wild and fair,
  And Greta woods are green,
And you may gather garlands there
  Would grace a summer's queen.
Ib. st. 16

O! many a shaft at random sent
Finds mark the archer little meant!
And many a word, at random spoken,
May soothe or wound a heart that's broken!
The Lord of the Isles [1815],
canto V, st. 18

Randolph, thy wreath has lost a rose.[1]
Ib. VI, st. 18

There was — and O! how many sorrows crowd
Into these two brief words!
Ib. conclusion

A lawyer without history or literature is a mechanic, a mere working mason; if he possesses some knowledge of these, he may venture to call himself an architect. *Guy Mannering* [1815], *ch. 37*

Bluid is thicker than water.[2]
Ib. 38

It's no fish ye're buying, it's men's lives.[3] *The Antiquary* [1816], *ch. 11*

Come as the winds come, when
  Forests are rended,
Come as the waves come, when
  Navies are stranded.
Pibroch of Donald Dhu [1816],
st. 4

Time will rust the sharpest sword,
Time will consume the strongest cord;

---

[1] Robert Bruce's censure of Randolph for permitting a body of English cavalry to pass his flank on the day before the battle of Bannockburn [June 24, 1314].
[2] This proverb is found as early as the seventeenth century.
[3] See Thomas Hood, p. 592b.

That which molders hemp and steel,
Mortal arm and nerve must feel.
>   *Harold the Dauntless* [1817],
>   *canto I, st. 4*

Sea of upturned faces.
>   *Rob Roy* [1817], *ch. 20*

Lochow and the adjacent districts formed the original seat of the Campbells. The expression of "a far cry to Lochow" was proverbial.
>   *Ib. 29, note*

There's a gude time coming.
>   *Ib. 32*

My foot is on my native heath, and my name is MacGregor.   *Ib. 34*

Jock, when ye hae naething else to do, ye may be ay sticking in a tree; it will be growing, Jock, when ye're sleeping.[1]
>   *The Heart of Midlothian* [1818],
>   *ch. 8*

Vacant heart, and hand, and eye,
Easy live and quiet die.
>   *The Bride of Lammermoor*
>   [1819], *ch. 3. Lucy Ashton's
>   Song*

There is a Southern proverb — fine words butter no parsnips.
>   *The Legend of Montrose*
>   [1819], *ch. 3*

The happy combination of fortuitous circumstances.[2]
>   *The Monastery* [1820]. *Answer
>   of the Author of Waverley to
>   the Letter of Captain Clutter-
>   buck*

Within that awful volume [3] lies
The mystery of mysteries!   *Ib. ch. 12*

And better had they ne'er been born,
Who read to doubt, or read to scorn.
>   *Ib.*

[1] The dying words of a Highland laird to his son.
[2] See Daniel Webster, p. 547b.
Fortuitous combination of circumstances. — DICKENS, *Our Mutual Friend* [1864–1865], *vol. II, ch. 7*
[3] The Bible.

When we are handfasted, as we term it, we are man and wife for a year and day; that space gone by, each may choose another mate, or, at their pleasure, may call the priest to marry them for life; and this we call handfasting.[1]
>   *The Monastery. Answer of the
>   Author of Waverley to the Let-
>   ter of Captain Clutterbuck 25*

Spur not an unbroken horse; put not your plowshare too deep into new land.   *Ib.*

Oh, poverty parts good company.
>   *The Abbot* [1820], *ch. 7*

Ah! County Guy, the hour is nigh,
The sun has left the lea.
The orange flower perfumes the bower,
The breeze is on the sea.
>   *Quentin Durward* [1823], *ch. 4*

Tell that to the marines — the sailors won't believe it.[2]
>   *Redgauntlet* [1824], *vol. II, ch. 7*

Too much rest is rust.[3]
>   *The Betrothed* [1825], *ch. 13*

The playbill, which is said to have announced the tragedy of Hamlet, the character of the Prince of Denmark being left out.
>   *The Talisman* [1825], *introduction*

Rouse the lion from his lair.
>   *Ib. heading, ch. 6*

Recollect that the Almighty, who gave the dog to be companion of our pleasures and our toils, hath invested him with a nature noble and incapable of deceit.   *Ib. 24*

[1] This custom of handfasting actually prevailed in the upland days. It arose partly from the want of priests. While the convents subsisted, monks were detached on regular circuits through the wilder districts, to marry those who had lived in this species of connection. —ANDREW LANG, *Note in his edition of The Monastery*
[2] "Right," quoth Ben, "that will do for the marines." — BYRON, *The Island* [1823], *canto II, last line*
"That will do for the marines, but the sailors won't believe it" is an old saying.
[3] German proverb: Rast ich, so rost ich [When I rest, I rust].

If you keep a thing seven years, you are sure to find a use for it.
Woodstock [1826], *ch. 28*

The sun never sets on the immense empire of Charles V.[1]
Life of Napoleon [1827]

Come fill up my cup, come fill up my can,
Come saddle your horses, and call up your men;
Come open the West Port, and let me gang free,
And it's room for the bonnets of Bonny Dundee!
The Doom of Devorgoil [1830].
Bonny Dundee, chorus

One hour of life, crowded to the full with glorious action, and filled with noble risks, is worth whole years of those mean observances of paltry decorum.[2]
Count Robert of Paris [1832],
ch. 25

Heaven knows its time; the bullet has its billet. *Ib.*

SYDNEY SMITH
1771–1845

The schoolboy whips his taxed top; the beardless youth manages his taxed horse with a taxed bridle on a taxed road; and the dying Englishman, pouring his medicine, which has paid seven per cent, into a spoon that has paid fifteen per cent, flings himself back upon his chintz bed which has paid twenty-two per cent, and expires in the arms of an apothecary who has paid a license of a hundred pounds for the privilege of putting him to death.
Review of SEYBERT, *Annals of the United States* [1820]

If you choose to represent the various parts in life by holes upon a table, of different shapes — some circular, some triangular, some square, some oblong — and the persons acting these parts by bits of wood of similar shapes, we shall generally find that the triangular person has got into the square hole, the oblong into the triangular, and a square person has squeezed himself into the round hole. The officer and the office, the doer and the thing done, seldom fit so exactly that we can say they were almost made for each other.[1]
Sketches of Moral Philosophy
[1850]

That knuckle-end of England — that land of Calvin, oatcakes, and sulphur.
Lady Holland's Memoir [1855],
vol. I, ch. 2

No one minds what Jeffrey says: . . . it is not more than a week ago that I heard him speak disrespectfully of the equator. *Ib.*

Preaching has become a byword for long and dull conversation of any kind; and whoever wishes to imply, in any piece of writing, the absence of everything agreeable and inviting, calls it a sermon. *Ib. 3*

Avoid shame, but do not seek glory, — nothing so expensive as glory.
Ib. 4

Take short views, hope for the best, and trust in God. *Ib. 6*

Looked as if she had walked straight out of the ark. *Ib. 7*

No furniture so charming as books.
Ib. 9

Not body enough to cover his mind decently with; his intellect is improperly exposed. *Ib.*

---

[1] Why should the brave Spanish soldier brag the sun never sets in the Spanish dominions, but ever shineth on one part or other we have conquered for our king? — CAPTAIN JOHN SMITH, *Advertisements for the Unexperienced, &c.* [1631]

It may be said of them [the Hollanders] as of the Spaniards, that the sun never sets on their dominions. — GAGE, *New Survey of the West Indies* [1648], *Epistle Dedicatory*

See Schiller, p. 497b, and Daniel Webster, p. 548a.

[2] See Mordaunt, p. 455b.

[1] Generally accepted as the origin of the phrase "A square peg in a round hole."

He has spent all his life in letting down empty buckets into empty wells; and he is frittering away his age in trying to draw them up again.[1]

Lady Holland's Memoir, vol. I, ch. 9

Ah, you flavor everything; you are the vanilla of society.   *Ib.*

As the French say, there are three sexes — men, women, and clergymen.[2] *Ib.*

My living in Yorkshire was so far out of the way, that it was actually twelve miles from a lemon.   *Ib.*

Praise is the best diet for us, after all.   *Ib.*

Daniel Webster struck me much like a steam engine in trousers.   *Ib.*

"Heat, ma'am!" I said; "it was so dreadful here, that I found there was nothing left for it but to take off my flesh and sit in my bones."   *Ib.*

Live always in the best company when you read.   *Ib. 10*

Never give way to melancholy; resist it steadily, for the habit will encroach.   *Ib.*

He was a one-book man. Some men have only one book in them; others, a library.   *Ib. 11*

Marriage resembles a pair of shears, so joined that they can not be separated; often moving in opposite directions, yet always punishing anyone who comes between them.[3]   *Ib.*

Macaulay is like a book in breeches . . . He has occasional flashes of silence, that make his conversation perfectly delightful.   *Ib.*

Let onion atoms lurk within the bowl
And, half suspected, animate the whole.   *Ib. Recipe for Salad*

---

[1] See Cowper, p. 458a.
[2] See Lady Mary Wortley Montagu, p. 414a.
[3] We are the two halves of a pair of scissors, when apart, Pecksniff, but together we are something. — DICKENS, *Martin Chuzzlewit* [1843–1844], *ch. 11*

Serenely full, the epicure would say,
Fate cannot harm me, I have dined today.[1]

Lady Holland's Memoir, Recipe for Salad

What you don't know would make a great book.   *Ib.*

In composing, as a general rule, run your pen through every other word you have written; you have no idea what vigor it will give your style.[2]   *Ib.*

Thank God for tea! What would the world do without tea? — how did it exist? I am glad I was not born before tea.   *Ib.*

That sign of old age, extolling the past at the expense of the present.   *Ib.*

We know nothing of tomorrow; our business is to be good and happy today.[3]   *Ib. 12*

SAMUEL TAYLOR COLERIDGE
1772–1834

Poor little Foal of an oppressed race!
I love the languid patience of thy face.
To a Young Ass [1794], *l. 1*

Blest hour! it was a luxury — to be!
Reflections on Having Left a Place of Retirement [1795], *l. 43*

This Lime Tree Bower My Prison.
Title of poem [1797]

In Xanadu did Kubla Khan
A stately pleasure dome decree:
Where Alph, the sacred river, ran
Through caverns measureless to man
Down to a sunless sea.
So twice five miles of fertile ground
With walls and towers were girdled round.   *Kubla Khan* [1798]

A savage place! as holy and enchanted
As e'er beneath a waning moon was haunted
By woman wailing for her demonlover!   *Ib.*

---

[1] See Horace, p. 122a, and note.
[2] See Samuel Johnson, p. 431b.
[3] See James Montgomery, p. 517b.

Five miles meandering with a mazy motion.   *Kubla Khan*

Ancestral voices prophesying war!
                                        Ib.

It was a miracle of rare device,
A sunny pleasure dome with caves of ice!   *Ib.*

A damsel with a dulcimer
In a vision once I saw:
It was an Abyssinian maid,
And on her dulcimer she played,
Singing of Mount Abora.   *Ib.*

That sunny dome! those caves of ice!
And all who heard should see them there,
And all should cry, Beware! Beware!
His flashing eyes, his floating hair!
Weave a circle round him thrice,
And close your eyes with holy dread,
For he on honeydew hath fed,[1]
And drunk the milk of Paradise.
                                        Ib.

Sir Leoline, the Baron rich,
Hath a toothless mastiff bitch.
              Christabel [1797–1800],
                       pt. I, l. 6

And the spring comes slowly up this way.   *Ib. l. 22*

The one red leaf, the last of its clan,
That dances as often as dance it can.
                          Ib. l. 49

And what can ail the mastiff bitch?
                          Ib. l. 149

Her gentle limbs did she undress,
And lay down in her loveliness.
                          Ib. l. 237

A sight to dream of, not to tell!
                          Ib. l. 252

Saints will aid if men will call:
For the blue sky bends over all!
                          Ib. l. 330

And constancy lives in realms above;
And life is thorny; and youth is vain;
And to be wroth with one we love
Doth work like madness in the brain.
                          Ib. II, l. 410

---

[1] See Hesiod, p. 67a.

It is an ancient Mariner,
And he stoppeth one of three.
"By thy long gray beard and glittering eye,
Now wherefore stopp'st thou me?"
          The Ancient Mariner [1798],
                       pt. I, st. 1

The guests are met, the feast is set:
May'st hear the merry din.   *Ib. st. 2*

He holds him with his glittering eye —
The Wedding Guest stood still,
And listens like a three years' child:
The Mariner hath his will.   *Ib. st. 4*

The ship was cheered, the harbor cleared,
Merrily did we drop
Below the kirk, below the hill,
Below the lighthouse top.   *Ib. st. 6*

The Wedding Guest here beat his breast,
For he heard the loud bassoon.
                          Ib. st. 8

The bride hath paced into the hall,
Red as a rose is she.   *Ib. st. 9*

And now there came both mist and snow,
And it grew wondrous cold:
And ice, mast-high, came floating by,
As green as emerald.   *Ib. st. 13*

The ice was here, the ice was there,
The ice was all around:
It cracked and growled, and roared and howled,
Like noises in a swound!   *Ib. st. 15*

"God save thee, ancient Mariner!
From the fiends, that plague thee thus! —
Why look'st thou so?" — "With my crossbow
I shot the Albatross."   *Ib. st. 20*

The fair breeze blew, the white foam flew,
The furrows followed free;
We were the first that ever burst
Into that silent sea.   *Ib. II, st. 5*

As idle as a painted ship
Upon a painted ocean.   *Ib. st. 8*

Water, water, everywhere,
Nor any drop to drink.
> *The Ancient Mariner, pt. II, st. 9*

The very deep did rot: O Christ!
That ever this should be!
Yea, slimy things did crawl with legs
Upon the slimy sea.   *Ib. st. 10*

About, about, in reel and rout
The death-fires danced at night.
> *Ib. st. 11*

I bit my arm, I sucked the blood,
And cried, A sail! a sail!
> *Ib. III, st. 4*

Her lips were red, her looks were free,
Her locks were yellow as gold:
Her skin was white as leprosy,
The nightmare Life-in-Death was she,
Who thicks man's blood with cold.
> *Ib. st. 11*

"The game is done! I've won, I've
     won!"
Quoth she, and whistles thrice.
> *Ib. st. 12*

The sun's rim dips, the stars rush out:
At one stride comes the dark;
With far-heard whisper o'er the sea
Off shot the specter-bark.   *Ib. st. 13*

We listened and looked sideways up!
Fear at my heart, as at a cup,
My lifeblood seemed to sip.
> *Ib. st. 14*

The hornèd Moon, with one bright
     star
Within the nether tip.   *Ib.*

Each turned his face with a ghastly
     pang,
And cursed me with his eye.
> *Ib. st. 15*

I fear thee, ancient Mariner!
I fear thy skinny hand!
And thou art long, and lank, and
     brown,
As is the ribbed sea-sand.[1]
> *Ib. IV, st. 1*

[1] A note by Coleridge in *Sibylline Leaves*
[1817] says: "For [these] lines I am indebted to
Mr. Wordsworth."

Alone, alone, all, all alone;
Alone on a wide, wide sea.
> *The Ancient Mariner, pt. IV, st. 3*

The moving moon went up the sky,
And nowhere did abide;
Softly she was going up,
And a star or two beside.   *Ib. st. 10*

Her beams bemocked the sultry main,
Like April hoarfrost spread;
But where the ship's huge shadow lay,
The charmed water burnt alway
A still and awful red.   *Ib. st. 11*

A spring of love gushed from my
     heart,
And I blessed them unaware.
> *Ib. st. 14*

Oh sleep! it is a gentle thing,
Beloved from pole to pole.
> *Ib. V, st. 1*

We were a ghastly crew.   *Ib. st. 11*

A noise like of a hidden brook
In the leafy month of June,
That to the sleeping woods all night
Singeth a quiet tune.   *Ib. st. 17*

The man hath penance done,
And penance more will do.
> *Ib. st. 25*

Like one that on a lonesome road
Doth walk in fear and dread,
And having once turned round walks
     on,
And turns no more his head;
Because he knows a frightful fiend
Doth close behind him tread.
> *Ib. VI, st. 10*

Is this the hill? is this the kirk?
Is this mine own countree?
> *Ib. st. 14*

No voice; but oh! the silence sank
Like music on my heart.   *Ib. st. 22*

And the owlet whoops to the wolf be-
     low,
That eats the she-wolf's young.
> *Ib. VII, st. 5*

"Ha! ha!" quoth he, "full plain I see,
The Devil knows how to row."
> *Ib. st. 12*

"O shrieve me, shrieve me, holy man!"
        The Ancient Mariner, pt. VII,
                                st. 14

O Wedding Guest! This soul hath
    been
Alone on a wide wide sea:
So lonely 'twas, that God himself
Scarce seemèd there to be.
                            Ib. st. 19

He prayeth well who loveth well
Both man and bird and beast.
                            Ib. st. 22

He prayeth best who loveth best
All things both great and small;
For the dear God who loveth us,
He made and loveth all.[1]   *Ib. st.* 23

A sadder and a wiser man
He rose the morrow morn.
                            Ib. st. 25

With what deep worship I have still
    adored
The spirit of divinest Liberty.
        France: An Ode [1798], *st.* 1

The frost performs its secret ministry,
Unhelped by any wind.
        Frost at Midnight [1798], *l.* 1

Therefore all seasons shall be sweet to
    thee,
Whether the summer clothe the gen-
    eral earth
With greenness, or the redbreast sit
    and sing
Betwixt the tufts of snow on the bare
    branch.   *Ib. l.* 65

Or if the secret ministry of frost
Shall hang them up in silent icicles,
Quietly shining to the quiet moon.
                            Ib. l. 72

Forth from his dark and lonely hiding
    place
(Portentous sight!) the owlet Atheism,
Sailing on obscene wings athwart the
    noon,
Drops his blue-fringèd lids, and holds
    them close,

[1] See Alexander, p. 684b.

And hooting at the glorious sun in
    Heaven,
Cries out, "Where is it?"
        Fears in Solitude [1798], *l.* 81

And the Devil did grin, for his darling
    sin
Is pride that apes humility.[1]
        The Devil's Thoughts [2] [1799],
                                st. 6

Strongly it bears us along in swelling
    and limitless billows,
Nothing before and nothing behind but
    the sky and the ocean.
        The Homeric Hexameter (*trans-
        lated from Schiller*) [1799?]

In the hexameter rises the fountain's
    silvery column;
In the pentameter aye falling in melody
    back.
        The Ovidian Elegiac Metre
            (*from Schiller*) [1799]

All thoughts, all passions, all delights,
Whatever stirs this mortal frame,
All are but ministers of Love,
And feed his sacred flame.
                Love [1799], *st.* 1

Tranquillity! thou better name
Than all the family of Fame!
        Ode to Tranquillity [1801], *st.* 1

Aloof with hermit-eye I scan
The present works of present man —
A wild and dream-like trade of blood
    and guile,
Too foolish for a tear, too wicked for a
    smile!   *Ib. st.* 4

Hast thou a charm to stay the morning
    star
In his steep course?
        Hymn in the Vale of Chamouni
                            [1802], *l.* 1

Earth, with her thousand voices, praises
    God.   *Ib.*

[1] See Robert Burton, p. 311a.
[2] This poem was written in collaboration with
Southey, who also imitated it in *The Devil's
Walk*, p. 533a.

What is an Epigram? A dwarfish
 whole,
Its body brevity, and wit its soul.[1]
> *An Epigram* [1802]

I see, not feel, how beautiful they are!
> *Dejection: An Ode* [1802], *st. 2*

O Lady! we receive but what we give
And in our life alone does Nature live.
> *Ib. st. 4*

A light, a glory, a fair luminous cloud
Enveloping the Earth.   *Ib.*

Joy is the sweet voice, Joy the luminous
 cloud —
We in ourselves rejoice!
And thence flows all that charms or ear
 or sight,
All melodies the echoes of that voice,
All colors a suffusion from that light.
> *Ib. st. 5*

How seldom, friend! a good great man
 inherits
Honor or wealth, with all his worth and
 pains!
It sounds like stories from the land of
 spirits
If any man obtain that which he merits,
Or any merit that which he obtains.
> *The Good Great Man* [1802]

Trochee trips from long to short;
From long to long in solemn sort
Slow Spondee stalks.
> *Metrical Feet* [1806]

The Knight's bones are dust,
And his good sword rust;
His soul is with the saints, I trust.
> *The Knight's Tomb* [c. 1817]

With Donne, whose muse on dromedary trots,
Wreathe iron pokers into true-love
 knots.
> *On Donne's Poetry* [c. 1818]

The Eighth Commandment was not
 made for bards.
> *The Reproof and Reply* [1823]

[1] See Shakespeare, *Hamlet II, ii, 90*, p. 260b.

Nought cared this body for wind or
 weather,
When youth and I lived in 't together.
> *Youth and Age* [1823–1832], *st. 1*

Flowers are lovely; love is flower-like;
Friendship is a sheltering tree;
Oh the joys that came down shower-
 like,
Of friendship, love, and liberty,
 Ere I was old!   *Ib. st. 2*

All Nature seems at work. Slugs leave
 their lair —
The bees are stirring — birds are on the
 wing —
And Winter slumbering in the open
 air,
Wears on his smiling face a dream of
 Spring!
And I the while, the sole unbusy
 thing,
Nor honey make, nor pair, nor build,
 nor sing.
> *Work Without Hope* [Febru-
> ary 21, 1825]

Work without Hope draws nectar in a
 sieve,
And Hope without an object cannot
 live.   *Ib.*

In many ways doth the full heart reveal
The presence of the love it would conceal.
> *Poems Written in Later Life*
> [1826], *motto*

I counted two-and-seventy stenches,
All well defined, and several stinks.
> *Cologne* [1828]

The river Rhine, it is well known,
Doth wash your city of Cologne;
But tell me, nymphs! what power di-
 vine
Shall henceforth wash the river Rhine?
> *Ib.*

Poetry is not the proper antithesis to
prose, but to science. Poetry is opposed
to science, and prose to metre. The
proper and immediate object of science
is the acquirement, or communication,
of truth; the proper and immediate ob-

ject of poetry is the communication of immediate pleasure.
Definitions of Poetry [1811]

Reviewers are usually people who would have been poets, historians, biographers, etc., if they could; they have tried their talents at one or at the other, and have failed; therefore they turn critics.[1]
Lectures on Shakespeare and Milton [1811–1812]

The last speech [Iago's soliloquy], the motive-hunting of a motiveless malignity — how awful!
Notes on Shakespeare [c. 1812]

Taste is the intermediate faculty which connects the active with the passive powers of our nature, the intellect with the senses; and its appointed function is to elevate the *images* of the latter, while it realizes the *ideas* of the former.
On the Principles of Genial Criticism [1814]

The most general definition of beauty . . . Multeity in Unity. *Ib.*

The Good consists in the congruity of a thing with the laws of the reason and the nature of the will, and in its fitness to determine the latter to actualize the former: and it is always discursive. The Beautiful arises from the perceived harmony of an object, whether sight or sound, with the inborn and constitutive rules of the judgment and imagination: and it is always intuitive.
Ib.

The imagination . . . that reconciling and mediatory power, which incorporating the reason in images of the sense and organizing (as it were) the flux of the senses by the permanence and self-circling energies of the reason, gives birth to a system of symbols, har-

monious in themselves, and consubstantial with the truths of which they are the conductors.
The Statesman's Manual [1816]

Not the poem which we have *read*, but that to which we *return*, with the greatest pleasure, possesses the genuine power, and claims the name of *essential poetry.*[1]
Biographia Literaria [1817], *ch.* 1

Experience informs us that the first defense of weak minds is to recriminate. *Ib.* 2

Indignation at literary wrongs I leave to men born under happier stars. I cannot afford it. *Ib.*

Milton had a highly imaginative, Cowley a very fanciful mind. *Ib.* 4

An idea, in the highest sense of that word, cannot be conveyed but by a symbol. *Ib.* 9

Veracity does not consist in saying, but in the intention of communicating truth. *Ib.*

Never pursue literature as a trade. *Ib.* 11

Until you understand a writer's ignorance, presume yourself ignorant of his understanding. *Ib.* 12

During the act of knowledge itself, the objective and subjective are so instantly united, that we cannot determine to which of the two the priority belongs. *Ib.*

The primary imagination I hold to be the living power and prime agent of all human perception, and as a repetition in the finite mind of the eternal act of creation in the infinite I Am.
Ib. 13

The secondary imagination . . . dissolves, diffuses, dissipates, in order to re-create; or where this process is rendered impossible, yet still at all events it struggles to idealize and to unify. It is

---

[1] Reviewers, with some rare exceptions, are a most stupid and malignant race. As a bankrupt thief turns thief-taker in despair, so an unsuccessful author turns critic. — SHELLEY, *Fragments of Adonais* [1821]
See Disraeli, p. 612b, and Lowell, p. 692b.

[1] See Robert Frost, pp. 929b and 930a.

essentially vital, even as all objects (*as objects*) are essentially fixed and dead.
Biographia Literaria, ch. 13

The fancy is indeed no other than a mode of memory emancipated from the order of time and space. *Ib.*

The two cardinal points of poetry, the power of exciting the sympathy of the reader by a faithful adherence to the truth of nature, and the power of giving the interest of novelty by the modifying colors of imagination.
Ib. 14

That willing suspension of disbelief for the moment, which constitutes poetic faith. *Ib.*

The poet, described in *ideal* perfection, brings the whole soul of man into activity, with the subordination of its faculties to each other, according to their relative worth and dignity. He diffuses a tone and spirit of unity, that blends, and (as it were) *fuses*, each into each, by that synthetic and magical power . . , imagination. *Ib.*

[Imagination] reveals itself in the balance or reconciliation of opposite or discordant qualities: of sameness, with difference; of the general, with the concrete; the idea, with the image; the individual, with the representative; the sense of novelty and freshness, with old and familiar objects; a more than usual state of emotion, with more than usual order; judgment ever awake and steady self-possession, with enthusiasm and feeling profound or vehement; and while it blends and harmonizes the natural and the artificial, still subordinates art to nature; the manner to the matter; and our admiration of the poet to our sympathy with the poetry.
Ib.

No man was ever yet a great poet, without being at the same time a profound philosopher. *Ib.* 15

While [Shakespeare] darts himself forth and passes into all the forms of human character and passion, the one Proteus of the fire and the flood, [Milton] attracts all forms and things to himself, into the unity of his own *Ideal*. All things and modes of action shape themselves anew in the being of Milton; while Shakespeare becomes all things, yet ever remaining himself.
Biographia Literaria, ch. 15

Our myriad-minded Shakespeare.[1]
Ib.

The best part of human language, properly so called, is derived from reflection on the acts of the mind itself.[2]
Ib. 17

The organic form, on the other hand, is innate; it shapes, as it develops, itself from within, and the fullness of its development is one and the same with the perfection of its outward form.
Shakespeare's Judgment Equal to His Genius [1818]

Now Art, used collectively for painting, sculpture, architecture and music, is the mediatress between, and reconciler of, nature and man. It is, therefore, the power of humanizing nature, of infusing the thoughts and passions of man into everything which is the object of his contemplation.
On Poesy or Art [1818]

The artist must imitate that which is within the thing, that which is active through form and figure, and discourses to us by symbols. *Ib.*

The heart should have fed upon the truth, as insects on a leaf, till it be tinged with the color, and show its food in every . . . minutest fiber. *Ib.*

Schiller has the material sublime.
Table Talk [December 29, 1822]

---

[1] A phrase which I have borrowed from a Greek monk, who applies it to a patriarch of Constantinople. [Coleridge's footnote.]

[2] The poem of the act of the mind. — WALLACE STEVENS [1879–1965], *Collected Poems. Of Modern Poetry*

I wish our clever young poets would remember my homely definitions of prose and poetry; that is, prose = words in their best order; poetry = the best words in their best order.
Table Talk [July 12, 1827]

The man's desire is for the woman; but the woman's desire is rarely other than for the desire of the man.
Ib. [July 23, 1827]

Poetry is certainly something more than good sense, but it must be good sense at all events; just as a palace is more than a house, but it must be a house, at least.   *Ib.* [May 9, 1830]

That passage is what I call the sublime dashed to pieces by cutting too close with the fiery four-in-hand round the corner of nonsense.   *Ib.*

The happiness of life is made up of minute fractions — the little soon forgotten charities of a kiss or smile, a kind look, a heartfelt compliment, and the countless infinitesimals of pleasurable and genial feeling.
The Friend. The Improvisatore [1828]

Beneath this sod
A poet lies, or that which once seemed he —
Oh, lift a thought in prayer for S.T.C.!
That he, who many a year, with toil of breath,
Found death in life, may here find life in death.
Epitaph written for himself [1833]

JOSIAH QUINCY, JR.
1772–1864

If this bill [for the admission of Orleans Territory as a State] passes, I am compelled to declare it as my deliberate opinion that the bonds of this Union are virtually dissolved; that the States which compose it are free from their moral obligations; and that, as it will be the right of all, so it will be the duty of some, to prepare definitely for a separation — amicably if they can; violently if they must.[1]
Speech in the U. S. House of Representatives [January 14, 1811]

WILLIAM BARNES RHODES
1772–1826

Bombastes: So have I heard on Afric's burning shore
A hungry lion give a grievous roar;
The grievous roar echoed along the shore.
Artaxaminous: So have I heard on Afric's burning shore
Another lion give a grievous roar;
And the first lion thought the last a bore.
Bombastes Furioso [1810], *act I, sc. 4*

DAVID RICARDO
1772–1823

Labor, like all other things which are purchased and sold, and which may be increased or diminished in quantity, has its natural and its market price. The natural price of labor is that price which is necessary to enable the laborers, one with another, to subsist and perpetuate their race, without either increase or diminution.
On the Principles of Political Economy and Taxation [1817]

FRIEDRICH SCHLEGEL
1772–1829

The historian is a prophet in reverse.   *Athenaeum* [1798–1800]

[1] The gentleman [Quincy] cannot have forgotten his own sentiment, uttered even on the floor of this House, "Peaceably if we can, forcibly if we must." — HENRY CLAY, *Speech* [January 8, 1813]

FRANÇOIS HORACE BASTIEN SÉBASTIANI
1772–1851

Order reigns in Warsaw.[1]
Announcement of the fall of
Warsaw [1831]

ÉTIENNE DE GRELLET
1773–1855

I expect to pass through this world but once; any good thing therefore that I can do, or any kindness that I can show to any fellow creature, let me do it now; let me not defer or neglect it, for I shall not pass this way again.[2]
Attributed

WILLIAM HENRY HARRISON
1773–1841

We admit of no government by divine right . . . the only legitimate right to govern is an express grant of power from the governed.
Inaugural Address [March 4, 1841]

Never with my consent shall an officer of the people, compensated for his services out of their pockets, become the pliant instrument of the Executive will. *Ib.*

A decent and manly examination of the acts of government should be not only tolerated, but encouraged.
Inaugural Address

JOHN RANDOLPH
1773–1833

The surest way to prevent war is not to fear it.
Speech, U.S. House of Representatives [March 5, 1806]

[1] Des lettres que je reçois de Pologne m'annoncent que la tranquillité règne à Varsovie. — DUMAS [1802–1870], *Mémoires* [2nd series], vol. IV, ch. 3

[2] This is not found in any of Grellet's writings, and has been attributed to many others. See Addison, p. 394a.

He is a man of splendid abilities, but utterly corrupt. He shines and stinks like rotten mackerel by moonlight.[1]
Of Edward Livingston; from W. CABELL BRUCE, *John Randolph of Roanoke* [1923], *vol. II, p. 197*

He rowed to his object with muffled oars.   *Of Martin Van Buren*

ROBERT SOUTHEY
1774–1843

"You are old, Father William," the young man cried,
"The few locks which are left you are gray;
You are hale, Father William — a hearty old man:
Now tell me the reason, I pray."
The Old Man's Comforts and How He Gained Them,[2] st. 1

"In the days of my youth, I remembered my God,
And he hath not forgotten my age."
Ib. st. 6

And in at the windows, and in at the door,
And through the walls by thousands they pour;
And down from the ceiling and up through the floor,
From the right and the left, from behind and before,
From within and without, from above and below —

[1] 'Tis vain for present fame to wish.
Our persons first must be forgotten;
For poets are like stinking fish,
They never shine until they're rotten.
McDONALD CLARKE [1798–1842], *Epigram*

[2] Of several parodies of this poem, the one by Lewis Carroll is probably better known than the original. See p. 543b.
"You are old, Father William, and though one would think
All the veins in your body were dry,
Yet the end of your nose is red as a pink;
I beg your indulgence, but why?"
LEE O. HARRIS and JAMES WHITCOMB RILEY, *Father William, st. 1*

And all at once to the Bishop they go.
God's Judgment on a Wicked
Bishop,[1] *st. 17*

It was a summer evening;
Old Kaspar's work was done,
And he before his cottage door
Was sitting in the sun;
And by him sported on the green
His little grandchild Wilhelmine.
The Battle of Blenheim [1798],
st. 1

He came to ask what he had found,
That was so large, and smooth, and
round.   *Ib. st. 2*

" 'Tis some poor fellow's skull," said
he,
"Who fell in the great victory."
Ib. st. 3

But what they fought each other for,
I could not well make out.   *Ib. st. 6*

"And everybody praised the Duke,
Who this great fight did win."
"But what good came of it at last?"
Quoth little Peterkin.
"Why, that I cannot tell," said he;
"But 'twas a famous victory."
Ib. st. 11

Blue, darkly, deeply, beautifully blue.[2]
Madoc in Wales [1805], *pt. I, 5*

What will not woman, gentle woman
dare,
When strong affection stirs her spirit
up?   *Ib. II, 2*

And last of all an Admiral came,
A terrible man with a terrible name —
A name which you all know by sight
very well,

---

[1] Hatto, in the time of the great famine of
914, when he saw the poor exceedingly oppressed
by famine, assembled a great company of them
together into a barn at Kaub and burnt them
. . . because he thought the famine would
sooner cease if those poor folks were dispatched
out of the world. . . . But God . . . sent against
him a plague of mice . . . and the prelate retreated to a tower in the Rhine . . . but the
mice chased him continually . . . and at last
he was most miserably devoured. — THOMAS
CORYAT, *Crudities* [1611]
[2] See Byron, p. 561a.

But which no one can speak, and no
one can spell.
The March to Moscow, st. 8

Curses are like young chickens, they always come home to roost.
The Curse of Kehama [1810],
motto

They sin who tell us love can die;
With life all other passions fly,
All others are but vanity.
Ib. canto X, st. 10

Thou hast been called, O sleep! the
friend of woe;
But 'tis the happy that have called thee
so.   *Ib. XV, st. 12*

No stir in the air, no stir in the sea,
The ship was still as she could be.
The Inchcape Rock,[1] *st. 1*

And then they knew the perilous
Rock,
And blessed the Abbot of Aberbrothok.
Ib. st. 4

Till the vessel strikes with a shivering
shock —
"O Christ! It is the Inchcape Rock."
Ib. st. 15

My days among the dead are past;
Around me I behold,
Where'er these casual eyes are cast,
The mighty minds of old.
My Days Among the Dead Are
Past [1818], *st. 1*

Yet leaving here a name, I trust,
That will not perish in the dust.
Ib. st. 4

Agreed to differ.
Life of Wesley [1820]

The Satanic school.
Vision of Judgment [1821],
original preface

So I told them in rhyme,
For of rhymes I had store.
The Cataract of Lodore

---

[1] A rock in the North Sea, off the Firth of Tay,
Scotland, dangerous to navigators because it is
covered with every tide. There is a tradition
that a warning bell was fixed on the rock by the
Abbot of Aberbrothok, which was stolen by a
sea pirate, who perished on the rock a year later.

From his brimstone bed, at break of
   day,
A-walking the Devil is gone,
To look at his little snug farm of the
   World,
And see how his stock went on.
               The Devil's Walk, st. 1

How then was the Devil dressed?
O, he was in his Sunday's best;
His coat was red, and his breeches were
   blue,
And there was a hole where his tail
   came through.   *Ib. st. 3*

He passed a cottage with a double
   coach-house —
A cottage of gentility;
   And he owned with a grin,
   That his favorite sin
Is pride that apes humility.[1]
                          Ib. st. 8

The arts babblative and scribblative.
   *Colloquies on the Progress and
   Prospects of Society* [1829],
   no. 1, pt. 2

The march of Intellect.   *Ib. 14*

As frozen as charity.[2]
               The Soldier's Wife, st. 4

JANE AUSTEN
1775–1817

It is a truth universally acknowledged, that a single man in possession
of a good fortune, must be in want of a
wife.
   Pride and Prejudice [1813], *ch. 1*

She [Mrs. Bennet] was a woman of
mean understanding, little information,
and uncertain temper.   *Ib.*

A lady's imagination is very rapid; it
jumps from admiration to love, from
love to matrimony in a moment.
                                Ib. 6

Mr. Collins had only to change from
Jane to Elizabeth — and it was soon
done — done while Mrs. Bennet was
stirring the fire.   *Ib. 15*

[1] See Coleridge, p. 526b, and note.
[2] See Hood, p. 593a, and O'Reilly, p. 807a.

You have delighted us long enough.
               Pride and Prejudice, ch. 18

Mrs. Bennet was restored to her
usual querulous serenity.   *Ib. 42*

You ought certainly to forgive them,
as a Christian, but never to admit them
in your sight, or allow their names to be
mentioned in your hearing.   *Ib. 57*

For what do we live, but to make
sport for our neighbors, and laugh at
them in our turn?   *Ib.*

I have been a selfish being all my life,
in practice, though not in principle.
                               Ib. 58

One half of the world cannot understand the pleasures of the other.
                Emma [1815], *ch. 9*

It was a delightful visit — perfect, in
being much too short.   *Ib. 13*

Nobody who has not been in the
interior of a family can say what the
difficulties of any individual of that
family may be.   *Ib. 18*

Business, you know, may bring
money, but friendship hardly ever does.
                               Ib. 34

"Only a novel" . . . in short, only
some work in which the greatest powers
of the mind are displayed, in which the
most thorough knowledge of human
nature, the happiest delineation of its
varieties, the liveliest effusions of wit
and humor are conveyed to the world in
the best chosen language.
          Northanger Abbey [1818], *ch. 5*

What dreadful hot weather we have!
It keeps me in a continual state of
inelegance.
          Letters. To her sister Cassandra
               [*September 18, 1796*]

I do not want people to be very
agreeable, as it saves me the trouble of
liking them a great deal.
          Ib. [*December 24, 1798*]

The little bit (two inches wide) of
ivory on which I work with so fine a

brush as produces little effect after much labor.[1]

Letters. *To J. Edward Austen*
[December 16, 1816]

CHARLES LAMB
1775–1834

I have something more to do than feel.

Letter to Coleridge after the
death of Lamb's mother [1796]

The not unpeaceful evening of a day
Made black by morning storms.

Poem-letter to Coleridge [1797]

I have had playmates, I have had companions,
In my days of childhood, in my joyful school-days —
All, all are gone, the old familiar faces.

Old Familiar Faces [1798]

For God's sake (I never was more serious) don't make me ridiculous any more by terming me gentle-hearted in print[2] . . . substitute drunken dog, ragged head, seld-shaven, odd-eyed, stuttering, or any other epithet which truly and properly belongs to the gentleman in question.

Letter to Coleridge [*August* 1800]

Separate from the pleasure of your company, I don't much care if I never see a mountain in my life.

Letter to Wordsworth [1801]

The man must have a rare recipe for

melancholy, who can be dull in Fleet Street.

Letter to Thomas Manning
[February 15, 1802]

Nursed amid her [London's] noise, her crowds, her beloved smoke — what have I been doing all my life, if I have not lent out my heart with usury to such scenes?   **Ib.**

Gone before
To that unknown and silent shore.

Hester [1803], *st. 7*

A good-natured woman, which is as much as you can expect from a friend's wife, whom you got acquainted with a bachelor.   *Letter to Hazlitt* [1805]

Neat, not gaudy.

Letter to Wordsworth [1806]

This very night I am going to leave off tobacco! Surely there must be some other world in which this unconquerable purpose shall be realized.

Letter to Thomas Manning [1815]

Anything awful makes me laugh. I misbehaved once at a funeral.

Letter to Southey [1815]

[Of Coleridge] An archangel a little damaged.

Letter to Wordsworth [1816]

Fanny Kelly's divine plain face.

Letter to Mrs. Wordsworth [1818]

The red-letter days, now become, to all intents and purposes, dead-letter days.

Essays of Elia [1823]. *Oxford in*
the Vacation [1]

The human species, according to the best theory I can form of it, is composed of two distinct races, the men who borrow, and the men who lend.

Ib. The Two Races of Men

Your borrowers of books — those mutilators of collections, spoilers of the

---

[1] [Miss Austen] had a talent for describing the involvements and feelings and characters of ordinary life which is to me the most wonderful I ever met with. The Big Bow-Wow strain I can do myself like any now going; but the exquisite touch, which renders ordinary commonplace things and characters interesting, from the truth of the description and the sentiment, is denied to me. — SCOTT, *Journal* [March 14, 1826]

[2] For thee, my gentle-hearted Charles, to whom
No sound is dissonant which tells of life.
COLERIDGE, *This Lime Tree Bower My Prison* [1797]

[1] Which, it has been pointed out, was actually written at Cambridge. See E. V. LUCAS, *Lamb and the Universities.*

symmetry of shelves, and creators of odd volumes.

> *Essays of Elia. The Two Races of Men*

Of all sound of all bells (bells, the music nighest bordering upon heaven) most solemn and touching is the peal which rings out the Old Year.

> *Ib. New Year's Eve*

A clear fire, a clean hearth, and the rigor of the game.

> *Ib. Mrs. Battle's Opinions on Whist*

I have no ear.

> *Ib. A Chapter on Ears*

Sentimentally I am disposed to harmony; but organically I am incapable of a tune. *Ib.*

Credulity is the man's weakness, but the child's strength.

> *Ib. Witches, and Other Night Fears*

Not many sounds in life, and I include all urban and all rural sounds, exceed in interest a knock at the door.[1] *Ib. Valentine's Day*

The custom of saying grace at meals had, probably, its origin in the early times of the world, and the hunter-state of man, when dinners were precarious things, and a full meal was something more than a common blessing!

> *Ib. Grace Before Meat*

Presents, I often say, endear absents.
Ib. A Dissertation Upon Roast Pig

Nothing is to me more distasteful than that entire complacency and satisfaction which beam in the countenances of a new-married couple.

Ib. The Behavior of Married People

I came home forever!

> *Letter to Bernard Barton* [1825], *on leaving his "33 years' desk" at the East India House*

---

[1] Doorbells are like a magic game,
  Or the grab bag at a fair —
You never know when you hear one ring
  Who may be waiting there.
  RACHEL FIELD [1894–1942], *Doorbells*

Who first invented work, and bound
  the free
And holiday-rejoicing spirit down?

> *Work*

Riddle of destiny, who can show
What thy short visit meant, or know
What thy errand here below?

> *On an Infant Dying as Soon as Born* [1827]

Martin, if dirt was trumps, what hands you would hold!

> *Lamb's Suppers. From* LEIGH HUNT, *Lord Byron and His Contemporaries* [1828]

Some cry up Haydn, some Mozart,
Just as the whim bites. For my part,
I do not care a farthing candle
For either of them, nor for Handel.[1]

> *Letter to Mrs. William Hazlitt* [1830]

For thy sake, Tobacco, I
Would do anything but die.

> *A Farewell to Tobacco*

A poor relation — is the most irrelevant thing in nature.

> *Last Essays of Elia* [1833]. *Poor Relations*

I love to lose myself in other men's minds.

> *Ib. Detached Thoughts on Books and Reading*

Books think for me. *Ib.*

Books which are no books. *Ib.*

Newspapers always excite curiosity. No one ever lays one down without a feeling of disappointment. *Ib.*

How sickness enlarges the dimensions of a man's self to himself.

> *Ib. The Convalescent*

Your absence of mind we have borne, till your presence of body came to be called in question by it.

> *Ib. Amicus Redivivus*

---

[1] See John Byrom, p. 415a.

A pun is a pistol let off at the ear; not a feather to tickle the intellect.
> *Last Essays of Elia. Popular Fallacies: IX, That the Worst Puns are the Best*

A presentation copy . . . is a copy of a book which does not sell, sent you by the author, with his foolish autograph at the beginning of it; for which, if a stranger, he only demands your friendship; if a brother author, he expects from you a book of yours, which does not sell, in return.
> *Ib. XI, That We Must Not Look a Gift Horse in the Mouth*

The good things of life are not to be had singly, but come to us with a mixture.
> *Ib. XIII, That You Must Love Me and Love My Dog*

The greatest pleasure I know is to do a good action by stealth, and to have it found out by accident.
> *Table Talk. In the Athenaeum* [1834]

WALTER SAVAGE LANDOR
1775–1864

But I have sinuous shells of pearly
> hue . . .
Shake one, and it awakens; then apply
Its polished lips to your attentive ear,
And it remembers its august abodes,
And murmurs as the ocean murmurs there.[1] *Gebir, bk. I* [1798]

Ah what avails the sceptered race,
Ah what the form divine!
> *Rose Aylmer* [1806]

Rose Aylmer, whom these wakeful eyes
May weep, but never see,
A night of memories and of sighs
I consecrate to thee. *Ib.*

[1] See Wordsworth, p. 516b.

There are no fields of amaranth on this side of the grave: there are no voices, O Rhodopè! that are not soon mute, however tuneful: there is no name, with whatever emphasis of passionate love repeated, of which the echo is not faint at last.
> *Imaginary Conversations* [1824–1829]. *Aesop and Rhodopè, I*

Of all failures, to fail in a witticism is the worst, and the mishap is the more calamitous in a drawn out and detailed one. *Ib. Chesterfield and Chatham*

'Tis verse that gives
Immortal youth to mortal maids.
> *Verse*

Around the child bend all the three
Sweet Graces; Faith, Hope, Charity.
Around the man bend other faces;
Pride, Envy, Malice, are his Graces.
> *Around the Child*

When we play the fool, how wide
The theatre expands! beside,
How long the audience sits before us!
How many prompters! what a chorus!
> *Plays* [1846], *st. 2*

There is delight in singing, though
> none hear
Beside the singer.
> *To Robert Browning* [1846]

Shakespeare is not our poet, but the
> world's,
Therefore on him no speech! and brief
> for thee,
Browning! Since Chaucer was alive and
> hale,
No man hath walked along our roads
> with step
So active, so inquiring eye, or tongue
So varied in discourse. *Ib.*

I strove with none, for none was worth
> my strife;
Nature I loved; and next to Nature,
> Art.
I warm'd both hands before the fire of
> life;
It sinks, and I am ready to depart.
> *I Strove with None* [1853]

HIRATA ATSUTANE[1]
1776–1843

It was the gods who formed all the lands of the world at the Creation, and these gods were without exception born in Japan. Japan is thus the homeland of the gods, and that is why we call it the Land of the Gods.
Summary of the Ancient Way

With their scientific instruments the Dutch attempt to determine the properties of things. Unlike China, Holland is a splendid country where they do not rely on superficial conjectures. *Ib.*

The ancient Japanese all constantly and correctly practiced what the Chinese called humanity, righteousness, the five cardinal virtues and the rest, without having any need to name them or to teach them. In China . . . there were evil customs from the very outset, and human behavior . . . was extremely licentious. That is the reason why so many sages appeared in ancient times to guide and instruct the Chinese.
Indignant Discussion of Chinese Books [c. 1810]

The art of medicine, though introduced to Japan from abroad, appears originally to have been taught to foreign countries by our own great gods.
Shizu No Iwaya [1811]

THOMAS CAMPBELL
1777–1844

'Tis distance lends enchantment to the view,
And robes the mountain in its azure hue.[2]
Pleasures of Hope [1799], *pt. I, l. 7*

Hope, for a season, bade the world farewell,

And Freedom shriek'd — as Kosciusko fell!
Pleasures of Hope, pt. I, l. 381

Who hath not own'd, with rapture-smitten frame,
The power of grace, the magic of a name? *Ib. II, l. 5*

And muse on Nature with a poet's eye.
Ib. l. 98

Cease, every joy, to glimmer on my mind,
But leave, oh! leave the light of Hope behind!
What though my wingèd hours of bliss have been
Like angel visits, few and far between?[1] *Ib. l. 375*

On the green banks of Shannon, when Sheelah was nigh,
No blithe Irish lad was so happy as I;
No harp like my own could so cheerily play,
And wherever I went was my poor dog Tray.[2] *The Harper* [1799], *st. 1*

Ye mariners of England,
That guard our native seas;
Whose flag has braved, a thousand years,
The battle and the breeze!
Ye Mariners of England [1800], *st. 1*

While the battle rages loud and long, and the stormy winds do blow. *Ib.*

Britannia needs no bulwarks,
No towers along the steep;
Her march is o'er the mountain waves,
Her home is on the deep. *Ib. st. 3*

The meteor flag of England
Shall yet terrific burn,
Till danger's troubled night depart,
And the star of peace return. *Ib. st. 4*

Oh! once the harp of Innisfail
Was strung full high to notes of gladness;

---

[1] From *Sources of Japanese Tradition*, edited by William Theodore de Bary [1960].
[2] The mountains too, at a distance, appear airy masses and smooth, but seen near at hand they are rough. — DIOGENES LAERTIUS [C. A.D. 200], *Pyrrho, sec. 9*

[1] See John Norris, p. 385a.
[2] My Old Dog Tray. — *Title of song by* STEPHEN C. FOSTER [1826–1864]

But yet it often told a tale
Of more prevailing sadness.
O'Connor's Child, st. 1

'Tis the sunset of life gives me mystical
lore,
And coming events cast their shadows
before.[1]
Lochiel's Warning [1802]

The combat deepens. On, ye brave,
Who rush to glory or the grave!
Wave, Munich! all thy banners wave,
And charge with all thy chivalry!

Few, few shall part where many meet!
The snow shall be their winding sheet
And every turf beneath their feet
Shall be a soldier's sepulcher.
Hohenlinden [1802], *st. 7, 8*

There was silence deep as death,
And the boldest held his breath,
For a time.
Battle of the Baltic [1805], *st. 2*

Ye are brothers! ye are men!
And we conquer but to save.
Ib. st. 5

Star that bringest home the bee,
And sett'st the weary laborer free!
Song to the Evening Star
[1822], *st. 1*

Oh, how hard it is to find
The one just suited to our mind!
Song, st. 1

To live in hearts we leave behind
Is not to die.[2]
Hallowed Ground, st. 6

Oh leave this barren spot to me!
Spare, woodman, spare the beechen
tree! [3]
The Beech Tree's Petition, st. 1

---

[1] See Cicero, p. 111a; Shakespeare, p. 268a;
Shelley, p. 573a; and H. G. Wells, p. 888b.
   Often do the spirits
Of great events stride on before the events,
And in today already walks tomorrow.
   COLERIDGE, *Wallenstein* [1799–1800], *pt.
II, act V, sc. 1*

[2] They are not dead who live
  In hearts they leave behind.
   HUGH ROBERT ORR [b. 1887], *They
Softly Walk, st. 1*

[3] See George Pope Morris, p. 600a.

A stoic of the woods — a man without
a tear.
Gertrude of Wyoming [1809],
pt. I, st. 23

HENRY CLAY
1777–1852

How often are we forced to charge
fortune with partiality towards the unjust! *Letter* [*December 4, 1801*]

If you wish to avoid foreign collision,
you had better abandon the ocean.
*Speech, U.S. House of Repre-
sentatives* [*January 22, 1812*]

Government is a trust, and the officers of the government are trustees; and
both the trust and the trustees are created for the benefit of the people.[1]
Speech at Ashland, Kentucky
[*March 1829*]

The arts of power and its minions are
the same in all countries and in all ages.
It marks its victim; denounces it; and
excites the public odium and the public
hatred, to conceal its own abuses and
encroachments.
Speech, U.S. Senate [*March 14,
1834*]

Precedents deliberately established by
wise men are entitled to great weight.
They are evidence of truth, but *only*
evidence. . . . But a solitary precedent . . . which has never been re-
examined, cannot be conclusive.
Speech, U.S. Senate [*February
18, 1835*]

I have heard something said about
allegiance to the South. I know no
South, no North, no East, no West, to
which I owe any allegiance. The Union,
sir, is my country. *Speech* [1848]

The Constitution of the United
States was made not merely for the

---

[1] See Mathew Henry, p. 386b; Burke, p. 454b;
Jefferson, p. 472b; Calhoun, p. 545b; and Cleveland, p. 771a.
   Our government is the potent, the omnipresent teacher. — LOUIS D. BRANDEIS, *Olmstead
v. U.S.* [1928]

generation that then existed, but for posterity — unlimited, undefined, endless, perpetual posterity.

> *Speech in the Senate*
> *[January 29, 1850]*

Sir, I would rather be right than be President.[1] *Speech* [1850]

LORENZO DOW
1777–1834

You will be damned if you do. — And you will be damned if you don't [definition of Calvinism].

> *Reflections on the Love of God*
> *[1836]*

CARL FRIEDRICH GAUSS
1777–1855

It may be true that people who are *merely* mathematicians have certain specific shortcomings; however, that is not the fault of mathematics, but is true of every exclusive occupation.

> *Letter to H. C. Schumacher* [1845]

Mathematics is the queen of the sciences.

> *From* SARTORIUS VON WALTERS-HAUSEN, *Gauss zum Gedächtniss* [1856]

VALENTINE BLACKER
1778–1823

Put your trust in God, my boys, and keep your powder dry!

> *From* HAYES, *Ballads of Ireland, Col. Oliver's Advice*

WILLIAM HAZLITT
1778–1830

One of the pleasantest things in the world is going a journey; but I like to go by myself.

> *Table Talk* [1821–1822].
> *On Going a Journey*

When I am in the country I wish to vegetate like the country. *Ib.*

[1] Said when told that his defense of the Compromise would endanger his chances for the Presidency.

The soul of a journey is liberty, perfect liberty, to think, feel, do just as one pleases.

> *Table Talk. On Going*
> *a Journey*

Give me a clear blue sky over my head, and the green turf beneath my feet, a winding road before me, and a three hours' march to dinner — and then to thinking! It is hard if I cannot start some game on these lone heaths. *Ib.*

Oh! it is great to shake off the trammels of the world and of public opinion — to lose our importunate, tormenting, everlasting personal identity and become the creature of the moment, clear of all ties . . . to be known by no other title than *the gentleman in the parlor!* *Ib.*

What I mean by living to one's self is living in the world, as in it, not of it. . . . It is to be a silent spectator of the mighty scene of things; . . . to take a thoughtful, anxious interest or curiosity in what is passing in the world, but not to feel the slightest inclination to make or meddle with it.

> *Ib. On Living to One's Self*

Even in the common affairs of life, in love, friendship, and marriage, how little security have we when we trust our happiness in the hands of others! *Ib.*

There is not a more mean, stupid, dastardly, pitiful, selfish, spiteful, envious, ungrateful animal than the Public. It is the greatest of cowards, for it is afraid of itself. *Ib.*

When a man is dead, they put money in his coffin, erect monuments to his memory, and celebrate the anniversary of his birthday in set speeches. Would they take any notice of him if he were living? No![1] *Ib.*

Horus non numero nisi serenas[2] is the motto of a sundial near Venice. There is a softness and a harmony in

[1] See Martial, p. 135a, and Thayer, p. 949a.
[2] I count only the sunny hours.

the words and in the thought unparalleled. *Table Talk. On a Sundial*

No young man believes he shall ever die.
*Ib. The Feeling of Immortality
in Youth*

The young are prodigal of life from a superabundance of it; the old are tenacious on the same score, because they have little left, and cannot enjoy even what remains of it. *Ib.*

As we advance in life, we acquire a keener sense of the value of time. Nothing else, indeed, seems of any consequence; and we become misers in this respect. *Ib.*

The love of liberty is the love of others; the love of power is the love of ourselves.
*Political Essays. The Times
Newspaper*

We never do anything well till we cease to think about the manner of doing it.
*Sketches and Essay. On
Prejudice*

It is better to be able neither to read nor write than to be able to do nothing else.
On the Ignorance of the Learned

Men of genius do not excel in any profession because they labor in it, but they labor in it because they excel.
Characteristics

We are not hypocrites in our sleep.
On Dreams

HENRY PETER,
LORD BROUGHAM
1778–1868

What is valuable is not new, and what is new is not valuable.[1]
*From The Edinburgh Review
[c. 1802], The Work of Thomas
Young*

[1] See Daniel Webster, p. 548b.

The schoolmaster is abroad,[1] and I trust to him, armed with his primer, against the soldier in full military array.
*Speech, Opening of Parliament
[January 29, 1828]*

In my mind, he was guilty of no error he — was chargeable with no exaggeration — he was betrayed by his fancy into no metaphor, who once said that all we see about us, Kings, Lords, and Commons, the whole machinery of the State, all the apparatus of the system, and its varied workings, end in simply bringing twelve good men into a box.
*Present State of the Law
[February 7, 1828]*

Pursuit of Knowledge Under Difficulties. *Title of book* [1830]

Education makes a people easy to lead, but difficult to drive; easy to govern but impossible to enslave.
Attributed

The great Unwashed. *Attributed*

THOMAS, LORD DENMAN
1779–1854

Trial by jury, instead of being a security to persons who are accused, will be a delusion, a mockery, and a snare.
*O'Connell v. The Queen
[September 4, 1844]*

FRANCIS SCOTT KEY
1779–1843

Oh, say, can you see by the dawn's
early light,
What so proudly we hailed at the twilight's last gleaming?

[1] At the first meeting of the London Mechanics' Institution, 1825, John Reynolds, head of a school in Clerkenwell, acted as secretary of the meeting. Lord Brougham, who spoke at this meeting, said in the course of his remarks, "Look out, gentlemen, the schoolmaster is abroad." The phrase attracted little attention at that time, but when used in a speech three years later, it at once became popular.

Whose broad stripes and bright stars,
through the perilous fight,
O'er the ramparts we watched were so
gallantly streaming?
And the rockets' red glare, the bombs
bursting in air,
Gave proof through the night that our
flag was still there.
Oh, say, does that star-spangled banner
yet wave
O'er the land of the free and the home
of the brave?
> *The Star-Spangled Banner* [September 14, 1814], *st. 1*

Then conquer we must, for our cause it
is just —
And this be our motto, "In God is our
trust!"   *Ib. st. 4*

WILLIAM LAMB, VISCOUNT MELBOURNE
1779–1848

I wish I was as cocksure of anything
as Tom Macaulay is of everything.
> *From* COWPER, *Melbourne's Papers* [1889], *preface*

CLEMENT CLARKE MOORE
1779–1863

'Twas the night before Christmas,
when all through the house
Not a creature was stirring — not even
a mouse; [1]
The stockings were hung by the chimney with care,
In hopes that St. Nicholas soon would
be there.
> *A Visit from St. Nicholas* [December 1823]

"Happy Christmas to all, and to all a
goodnight!"   *Ib.*

THOMAS MOORE
1779–1852

Faintly as tolls the evening chime,

Our voices keep tune and our oars keep
time.[1]
> *Poems Relating to America. A Canadian Boat Song, st. 1*

Row, brothers, row, the stream runs
fast,
The rapids are near, and the daylight's
past.   *Ib.*

Go where glory waits thee!
But while fame elates thee,
Oh, still remember me!
> *Irish Melodies* [1807–1834]. *Go Where Glory Waits Thee, st. 1*

Oh, breathe not his name! let it sleep
in the shade,
Where cold and unhonor'd his relics
are laid.
> *Ib. Oh Breathe Not His Name, st. 1*

And the tear that we shed, though in
secret it rolls,
Shall long keep his memory green in
our souls.[2]   *Ib. st. 2*

The harp that once through Tara's
halls
The soul of music shed,
Now hangs as mute on Tara's walls
As if that soul were fled.
> *Ib. The Harp That Once Through Tara's Halls, st. 1*

And the heart that is soonest awake to
the flowers
Is always the first to be touch'd by the
thorns.
> *Ib. Oh, Think Not My Spirits Are Always as Light, st. 1*

Rich and rare were the gems she wore,
And a bright gold ring on her wand she
bore.
> *Ib. Rich and Rare Were the Gems She Wore, st. 1*

Ah! little they think who delight in her
strains,
How the heart of the Minstrel is breaking.
> *Ib. She Is Far from the Land, st. 2*

---

[1] See Shakespeare, *Hamlet I, i, 10*, p. 256b.

[1] See Marvell, p. 360b.
[2] See Shakespeare, *Hamlet I, ii, 2*, p. 257a.

Believe me, if all those endearing young charms
  Which I gaze on so fondly today,
Were to change by tomorrow and fleet in my arms,
  Like fairy gifts fading away,
Thou would'st still be adored as this moment thou art,
  Let thy loveliness fade as it will,
And around the dear ruin each wish of my heart
  Would entwine itself verdantly still.
  Irish Melodies. Believe Me, If All Those Endearing Young Charms, st. 1

No, the heart that has truly lov'd never forgets,
  But as truly loves on to the close;
As the sunflower turns on her god, when he sets,
  The same look which she turn'd when he rose. *Ib. st.* 2

But there's nothing half so sweet in life
As love's young dream.
  Ib. Love's Young Dream, st. 1

Eyes of unholy blue.
  Ib. By That Lake Whose Gloomy Shore, st. 2

'Tis the last rose of summer,
  Left blooming alone;
All her lovely companions
  Are faded and gone.
  Ib. The Last Rose of Summer, st. 1

The Minstrel Boy to the war is gone,
In the ranks of death you'll find him.
His father's sword he has girded on,
And his wild harp slung behind him.
  Ib. The Minstrel Boy, st. 1

Then awake! the heavens look bright, my dear;
'Tis never too late for delight, my dear;
  And the best of all ways
  To lengthen our days
Is to steal a few hours from the night, my dear.
  Ib. The Young May Moon, st. 1

You may break, you may shatter the vase, if you will,

But the scent of the roses will hang round it still.[1]
  Irish Melodies. Farewell! But Whenever, st. 3

No eye to watch, and no tongue to wound us,
All earth forgot, and all heaven around us.
  Ib. Come O'er the Sea, st. 2

The light that lies
In woman's eyes,
Has been my heart's undoing.
  Ib. The Time I've Lost in Wooing, st. 1

My only books
Were woman's looks,
And folly's all they've taught me.
  Ib.

A Persian's heaven is easily made:
'Tis but black eyes and lemonade.
  Intercepted Letters; or, The Two-Penny Post Bag [1813], VI

Oft in the stilly night,
Ere Slumber's chain has bound me,
Fond Memory brings the light
Of other days around me;
  The smiles, the tears,
  Of boyhood's years,
The words of love then spoken;
  The eyes that shone
  Now dimmed and gone,
The cheerful hearts now broken.
  National Airs [1815]. *Oft in the Stilly Night, st.* 1

I feel like one,
  Who treads alone
Some banquet hall deserted,
  Whose lights are fled,

---

[1] The jar will long keep the fragrance of what it was once steeped in when new. — HORACE [65–8 B.C.], *Epistles 1, 2, 69*
That flavor, absorbed when new, remains. — QUINTILIAN [A.D. 42–118]
But, somehow of other, though you fill it with water, the jar retains the odor which it acquired when first used. — ST. JEROME [A.D. 342–420]
The image was frequently used in the classical period; unglazed ware is more absorbent than glazed.

Whose garlands dead,
And all but he departed.
> *National Airs. Oft in the Stilly Night, st. 2*

What though youth gave love and roses,
Age still leaves us friends and wine.
> *Ib. Spring and Autumn, st. 1*

Sound the loud timbrel o'er Egypt's dark sea!
Jehovah has triumph'd — his people are free.
> *Sacred Songs. Sound the Loud Timbrel, st. 1*

There was a little Man, and he had a little Soul;
And he said, "Little Soul, let us try, try, try!"
> *Satirical and Humorous Poems. Little Man and Little Soul, st. 1*

Oh, call it by some better name,
For friendship sounds too cold.
> *Ballads and Songs. Oh, Call It by Some Better Name, st. 1*

There's a bower of roses by Bendemeer's stream,
And the nightingale sings round it all the day long.[1]
> *Lalla Rookh* [1817], *pt. II*

One morn a Peri at the gate
Of Eden stood disconsolate.   *Ib. IV*

Some flow'rets of Eden ye still inherit,
But the trail of the serpent is over them all.   *Ib.*

Oh! ever thus, from childhood's hour,
I've seen my fondest hope decay;
I never loved a tree or flower,
But 'twas the first to fade away.
I never nurs'd a dear gazelle
To glad me with its soft black eye,
But when it came to know me well,
And love me, it was sure to die.
> *Ib. V*

Like Dead Sea fruits, that tempt the eye,
But turn to ashes on the lips.[1]
> *Lalla Rookh* [1817], *pt. V*

Paradise itself were dim
And joyless, if not shared with him!
> *Ib. VI*

HORACE [HORATIO] SMITH
1779–1849

Thinking is but an idle waste of thought,
And nought is everything, and everything is nought.
> *Rejected Addresses* [1812]. *Cui Bono?, st. 8*

In the name of the Prophet — figs.
> *Johnson's Ghost*

And hast thou walk'd about (how strange a story!)
In Thebes's streets three thousand years ago,
When the Memnonium was in all its glory?
> *Address to the Mummy at Belzoni's Exhibition, st. 13*

JOSEPH STORY
1779–1849

I will not say with Lord Hale, that "The Law will admit of no rival" . . . but I will say that it is a jealous mistress, and requires a long and constant courtship. It is not to be won by trifling favors, but by lavish homage.[2]
> *The Value and Importance of Legal Studies* [3] [August 5, 1829]

WILLIAM ELLERY CHANNING
1780–1842

We do, then, with all earnestness, though without reproaching our brethren, protest against the irrational and

---

[1] As I recall them the roses bloom again, and the nightingales sing by the calm Bendemeer. — THACKERAY, *The Newcomes* [1853–1855], *ch. 1*

[1] See Byron, p. 556a.
[2] See Emerson, p. 609a.
[3] Inaugural address as Dane Professor of Law at Harvard University.

unscriptural doctrine of the Trinity. "To us," as to the Apostle and the primitive Christians, "there is one God, even the Father." With Jesus, we worship the Father, as the only living and true God. We are astonished, that any man can read the New Testament, and avoid the conviction, that the Father alone is God.

Unitarian Christianity
[Baltimore, 1819]

I see the marks of God in the heavens and the earth, but how much more in a liberal intellect, in magnanimity, in unconquerable rectitude, in a philanthropy which forgives every wrong, and which never despairs of the cause of Christ and human virtue! I do and I must reverence human nature.[1] . . . I bless it for its kind affections, for its strong and tender love. I honor it for its struggles against oppression . . . for its achievements in science and art, and still more for its examples of heroic and saintly virtue. These are marks of a divine origin and the pledges of a celestial inheritance; and I thank God that my own lot is bound up with that of the human race.[2]

Likeness to God [Providence,
Rhode Island, 1828]

There are seasons, in human affairs, of inward and outward revolution, when new depths seem to be broken up in the soul, when new wants are unfolded in multitudes, and a new and undefined good is thirsted for. There are periods when the principles of experience need to be modified, when hope and trust and instinct claim a share with prudence in the guidance of affairs, when, in truth, *to dare*, is the highest wisdom.[3]

Complete Works [1879].
The Union [1829]

It is chiefly through books that we

enjoy intercourse with superior minds. . . . In the best books, great men talk to us, give us their most precious thoughts, and pour their souls into ours. God be thanked for books. They are the voices of the distant and the dead, and make us heirs of the spiritual life of past ages. Books are true levelers. They give to all, who will faithfully use them, the society, the spiritual presence, of the best and greatest of our race.

Self-Culture [Boston, September
1838]

The mind, in proportion as it is cut off from free communication with nature, with revelation, with God, with itself, loses its life, just as the body droops when debarred from the air and the cheering light from heaven.

Remarks on the Character and
Writings of Fénelon [1843]

I call that mind free which jealously guards its intellectual rights and powers, which calls no man master, which does not content itself with a passive or hereditary faith, which opens itself to light whencesoever it may come, which receives new truth as an angel from Heaven.

Spiritual Freedom

The office of government is not to confer happiness, but to give men opportunity to work out happiness for themselves.

The Life and Character of
Napoleon Bonaparte

KARL
VON CLAUSEWITZ
1780–1831

War is not merely a political act, but also a political instrument, a continuation of political relations, a carrying out of the same by other means.[1]

Vom Kriege [1833]

---

[1] See Albert Schweitzer, p. 939a.
[2] Inscription on Channing Memorial, Public Garden, Boston.
[3] See Spenser, p. 200b, and Danton, p. 496b.

[1] See Mao Tse-Tung, p. 1027b.

CHARLES CALEB COLTON
1780–1832

When you have nothing to say, say nothing.
> *Lacon* [1820–1822], *vol. I, no. 183*

Imitation is the sincerest of flattery.
> *Ib. 217*

The debt which cancels all others.
> *Ib. II, 66*

CHARLES MINER
1780–1865

When I see a merchant over-polite to his customers, begging them to taste a little brandy and throwing half his goods on the counter — thinks I, that man has an ax to grind.
> *Essays from the Desk of Poor Robert the Scribe* [1815]. *Who'll Turn Grindstones* [1]

ADELBERT VON CHAMISSO
1781–1838

Peter Schlemihl.
> *From the title: Peter Schlemihls wundersame Geschichte* [1804]

EBENEZER ELLIOTT
1781–1849

Not kings and lords, but nations!
Not thrones and crowns, but men!
> *Corn Law Rhymes* [1828].
> *When Wilt Thou Save the People? st. 1*

God save the people! *Ib.*

What is a communist? One who hath yearnings
For equal division of unequal earnings.
> *Poetical Works* [1846]. *Epigram*

---

[1] First published in *Luzerne Federalist* [September 7, 1810]. Because of the similarity of the title to *Poor Richard*, the phrase "an ax to grind" has often been attributed to Franklin.

CAPTAIN JAMES LAWRENCE
1781–1813

Tell the men to fire faster and not to give up the ship; fight her till she sinks.[1]
> *On board the U.S. frigate Chesapeake* [June 1, 1813]

THOMAS HART BENTON
1782–1858

This new page opened in the book of our public expenditures, and this new departure taken, which leads into the bottomless gulf of civil pensions and family gratuities.
> *Speech in the U.S. Senate against a grant to President Harrison's widow* [April 1841]

JOHN C. CALHOUN
1782–1850

Protection and patriotism are reciprocal.
> *Speech, U.S. House of Representatives* [December 12, 1811]

The very essence of a free government consists in considering offices as public trusts,[2] bestowed for the good of the country, and not for the benefit of an individual or a party.
> *Speech* [February 13, 1835]

A power has risen up in the government greater than the people themselves, consisting of many and various and powerful interests, combined into one mass, and held together by the cohesive power of the vast surplus in the banks.[3] *Speech* [May 27, 1836]

---

[1] Usually quoted as "Don't give up the ship"; Lawrence's final order as he was carried below fatally wounded, before capture of his ship by the British frigate *Shannon*.
[2] See Henry, p. 386b; Burke, p. 454b; Jefferson, p. 472b; Clay, p. 538b; and Cleveland, p. 771a.
[3] From this speech comes the phrase "Cohesive power of public plunder."

The surrender of life is nothing to sinking down into acknowledgment of inferiority.
> *Speech, U.S. Senate [February 19, 1847]*

It is harder to preserve than to obtain liberty.[1]
> *Speech, U.S. Senate [January 1848]*

ANN TAYLOR
1782–1866

JANE TAYLOR
1783–1824

Who ran to help me when I fell,
And would some pretty story tell,
Or kiss the place to make it well?
My mother.
> *Original Poems for Infant Minds* [1804]. *My Mother [by* ANN TAYLOR], *st. 6*

Twinkle, twinkle, little star,
How I wonder what you are,
Up above the world so high,
Like a diamond in the sky![2]
> *Rhymes for the Nursery* [1806]. *The Star, st. 1*

I like little Pussy, her coat is so warm;
And if I don't hurt her she'll do me no harm.
> *Ib. I Like Little Pussy [by* JANE TAYLOR], *st. 1*

I thank the goodness and the grace
Which on my birth have smiled,
And made me, in these Christian days,
A happy English child.
> *Hymns for Infant Minds* [1810]. *A Child's Hymn of Praise, st. 1*

Oh, that it were my chief delight
To do the things I ought!
Then let me try with all my might
To mind what I am taught.
> *Ib. For a Very Little Child*

And willful waste, depend upon 't,
Brings, almost always, woeful want!
> *Ib. The Pin [by* ANN TAYLOR], *st. 6*

[1] See S. E. Morison, p. 997b.
[2] See Lewis Carroll, p. 744a.

DANIEL WEBSTER
1782–1852

It is, sir, as I have said, a small college, and yet there are those who love it.
> *Dartmouth College Case* [1818]

Whatever makes men good Christians, makes them good citizens.
> *Speech at Plymouth, Massachusetts* [1] *[December 22, 1820]*

Labor in this country is independent and proud. It has not to ask the patronage of capital, but capital solicits the aid of labor.[2]
> *Speech [April 2, 1824]*

We wish that this column, rising towards heaven among the pointed spires of so many temples dedicated to God, may contribute also to produce in all minds a pious feeling of dependence and gratitude. We wish, finally, that the last object to the sight of him who leaves his native shore, and the first to gladden his who revisits it, may be something which shall remind him of the liberty and the glory of his country.
> *Address on Laying the Corner-Stone of the Bunker Hill Monument [June 17, 1825]*

Mind is the great lever of all things; human thought is the process by which human ends are ultimately answered.
> *Ib.*

Knowledge, in truth, is the great sun in the firmament. Life and power are scattered with all its beams.
> *Ib.*

Let our object be our country, our whole country, and nothing but our country.
> *Ib.*

Sink or swim, live or die, survive or

[1] This oration will be read five hundred years hence with as much rapture as it was heard. It ought to be read at the end of every century, and indeed at the end of every year, forever and ever. — JOHN ADAMS, *Letter to Webster* [December 23, 1821]
[2] See Lincoln, p. 637b.

perish, I give my hand and my heart to this vote.[1]

> *Discourse in Commemoration of Adams and Jefferson, Faneuil Hall, Boston* [*August 2, 1826*]

It is my living sentiment, and by the blessing of God it shall be my dying sentiment — Independence now and Independence forever.[2]   *Ib.*

Washington is in the clear upper sky.   *Ib.*

The gentleman has not seen how to reply to this, otherwise than by supposing me to have advanced the doctrine that a national debt is a national blessing.[3]

> *Second Speech on Foote's Resolution* [*January 26, 1830*]

I shall enter on no encomium upon Massachusetts; she needs none. There she is.[4] Behold her, and judge for yourselves. There is her history; the world knows it by heart. The past, at least, is secure. There is Boston and Concord and Lexington and Bunker Hill; and there they will remain forever.   *Ib.*

The people's government, made for the people, made by the people, and answerable to the people.[5]   *Ib.*

When my eyes shall be turned to behold for the last time the sun in heaven, may I not see him shining on the broken and dishonored fragments of a once glorious Union; on States dissevered, discordant, belligerent; on a

land rent with civil feuds, or drenched, it may be, in fraternal blood.

> *Second Speech on Foote's Resolution*

Liberty and Union, now and forever, one and inseparable.   *Ib.*

There is no refuge from confession but suicide; and suicide is confession.

> *Argument on the murder of Captain White* [*April 6, 1830*]

There is nothing so powerful as truth — and often nothing so strange.[1]   *Ib.*

Fearful concatenation of circumstances.[2]   *Ib.*

A sense of duty pursues us ever. It is omnipresent, like the Deity. If we take to ourselves the wings of the morning, and dwell in the uttermost parts of the sea, duty performed or duty violated is still with us, for our happiness or our misery. If we say the darkness shall cover us, in the darkness as in the light our obligations are yet with us.[3]   *Ib.*

He smote the rock of the national resources, and abundant streams of revenue gushed forth. He touched the dead corpse of Public Credit, and it sprung upon its feet.[4]

> *Speech on Hamilton* [*March 10, 1831*]

On this question of principle, while actual suffering was yet afar off, they [the Colonies] raised their flag against a power to which, for purposes of foreign conquest and subjugation, Rome in the height of her glory is not to be compared — a power which has dotted over the surface of the whole globe with

---

[1] See John Adams, p. 463a.

Live or die, sink or swim. — GEORGE PEELE, *Edward I* [c. 1584]

[2] On the day of his [John Adams's] death, hearing the noise of bells and cannon, he asked the occasion. On being reminded that it was "Independent Day," he replied, "Independence forever." — DANIEL WEBSTER, *Works* [1903], *vol. I, p. 150*

[3] See Hamilton, p. 484b.

[4] Generally misquoted as "Massachusetts, there she stands."

[5] Our sovereign, the people. — CHARLES JAMES FOX, toast [1798], for which his name was erased from the Privy Council.

See Wycliffe, p. 163b; Garrison, p. 616a; Lincoln, p. 639a; and Theodore Parker, p. 657b.

[1] See Byron, p. 562a.
[2] See Scott, p. 521a.
[3] See *Psalm 139:9*, p. 23a.

[4] And Moses lifted up his hand, and with his rod he smote the rock twice; and the water came out abundantly. — *Numbers 20:11*

He it was that first gave to the law the air of a science. He found it a skeleton, and clothed it with life, color, and complexion; he embraced the cold statue, and by his touch it grew into youth, health, and beauty. — BARRY YELVERTON, LORD AVONMORE [1736–1805], *On Blackstone*

her possessions and military posts, whose morning drumbeat, following the sun,[1] and keeping company with the hours, circles the earth with one continuous and unbroken strain of the martial airs of England.
Speech [May 7, 1834]

God grants liberty only to those who love it, and are always ready to guard and defend it.
Speech [June 3, 1834]

One country, one constitution, one destiny. *Speech [March 15, 1837]*

There are persons who constantly clamor. They complain of oppression, speculation, and pernicious influence of wealth. They cry out loudly against all banks and corporations, and a means by which small capitalists become united in order to produce important and beneficial results. They carry on mad hostility against all established institutions. They would choke the fountain of industry and dry all streams.
Speech, U.S. Senate [March 12, 1838]

When tillage begins, other arts follow. The farmers therefore are the founders of human civilization.
On Agriculture [January 13, 1840]

America has furnished to the world the character of Washington. And if our American institutions had done nothing else, that alone would have entitled them to the respect of mankind.
On the Completion of Bunker Hill Monument [June 17, 1843]

Thank God! I — I also — am an American! *Ib.*

Justice, sir, is the great interest of man on earth.
On Mr. Justice Story [September 12, 1845]

Inconsistencies of opinion, arising

from changes of circumstances, are often justifiable.[1]
Speech [July 25 and 27, 1846]

Liberty exists in proportion to wholesome restraint.
Speech at the Charleston Bar Dinner [May 10, 1847]

The law: It has honored us; may we honor it. *Ib.*

I have read their platform, and though I think there are some unsound places in it, I can stand upon it pretty well. But I see nothing in it both new and valuable. "What is valuable is not new, and what is new is not valuable." [2]
Speech at Marshfield, Massachusetts [September 1, 1848]

I was born an American; I will live an American; I shall die an American.
Speech [July 17, 1850]

Faneuil Hall, the cradle of American liberty. *Letter [April 1851]*

Men hang out their signs indicative of their respective trades: shoemakers hang out a gigantic shoe; jewelers, a monster watch; and the dentist hangs out a gold tooth; but up in the mountains of New Hampshire, God Almighty has hung out a sign to show that there He makes men.
On the Old Man of the Mountain; [3] *attributed*

I still live.
Last words [October 24, 1852]

SIMÓN BOLÍVAR
1783–1830

A state too extensive in itself, or by virtue of its dependencies, ultimately falls into decay; its free government is transformed into a tyranny; it disre-

---

[1] L'homme absurde est celui qui ne change jamais [The absurd man is he who never changes]. — AUGUSTE MARSEILLE BARTHÉLEMY, *Ma Justification* [1832]

[2] See Lord Brougham, p. 540a.

[3] Natural rock formation in the shape of a human profile, in the Presidential Range of the White Mountains. It gave Hawthorne the theme of his story *The Great Stone Face.*

[1] See Schiller, p. 497b, and Scott, p. 522a.

548

gards the principles which it should preserve, and finally degenerates into despotism. The distinguishing characteristic of small republics is stability: the character of large republics is mutability.   *Letter from Jamaica*

Among the popular and representative systems of government I do not approve of the federal system: it is too perfect; and it requires virtues and political talents much superior to our own.   *Ib.*

Let us give to our republic a fourth power with authority over the youth, the hearts of men, public spirit, habits, and republican morality. Let us establish this Areopagus to watch over the education of the children, to supervise national education, to purify whatever may be corrupt in the republic, to denounce ingratitude, coldness in the country's service, egotism, sloth, idleness, and to pass judgment upon the first signs of corruption and pernicious example.
    Address to the Congress of Angostura

Those who have served the cause of the revolution have plowed the sea.
    Attributed

The three greatest dolts in the world: Jesus Christ, Don Quixote, and I.
    Attributed

REGINALD HEBER
1783–1826

Brightest and best of the sons of the morning,
Dawn on our darkness, and lend us thine aid.
    Hymns. Epiphany, st. 1

By cool Siloam's shady rill
How sweet the lily grows!
    Ib. First Sunday after Epiphany, no. 2

The Son of God goes forth to war,
A kingly crown to gain;

His blood-red banner streams afar;
Who follows in His train?
    Hymns. The Son of God Goes Forth to War, st. 1

From Greenland's icy mountains,
From India's coral strand,
Where Afric's sunny fountains
Roll down their golden sand.
    Ib. Missionary Hymn, st. 1

Though every prospect pleases,
And only man is vile.   *Ib. st. 2*

The heathen in his blindness
Bows down to wood and stone.   *Ib.*

Holy, Holy, Holy! Lord God Almighty!
Early in the morning our song shall rise to Thee:
Holy, Holy, Holy! Merciful and Mighty!
God in Three Persons, Blessed Trinity.
    Ib. Holy, Holy, Holy!

WASHINGTON IRVING
1783–1859

How convenient it would be to many of our great men and great families of doubtful origin, could they have the privilege of the heroes of yore, who, whenever their origin was involved in obscurity, modestly announced themselves descended from a god.
    Knickerbocker's History of New York [1809], *bk. II, ch. 3*

His wife "ruled the roast," and in governing the governor, governed the province, which might thus be said to be under petticoat government.[1]
    Ib. IV, 4

They claim to be the first inventors of those recondite beverages, cocktail, stonefence, and sherry cobbler.[2]
    Ib. 241

There is in every true woman's heart a spark of heavenly fire, which lies dormant in the broad daylight of prosperity; but which kindles up, and

[1] See Themistocles, p. 77b.
[2] See Browning, p. 666b.

beams and blazes in the dark hour of adversity.
The Sketch-Book [1819–1820].
The Wife

Those men are most apt to be obsequious and conciliating abroad, who are under the discipline of shrews at home. *Ib. Rip Van Winkle* [1]

A sharp tongue is the only edge tool that grows keener with constant use.
Ib.

That happy age when a man can be idle with impunity. *Ib.*

A woman's whole life is a history of the affections.
Ib. The Broken Heart

Language gradually varies, and with it fade away the writings of authors who have flourished their allotted time.
Ib. The Mutabilities of Literature

There rise authors now and then, who seem proof against the mutability of language, because they have rooted themselves in the unchanging principles of human nature. *Ib.*

His [the author's] renown has been purchased, not by deeds of violence and blood, but by the diligent dispensation of pleasure.
Ib. Westminster Abbey [*The Poets' Corner*]

The sorrow for the dead is the only sorrow from which we refuse to be divorced. *Ib. Rural Funerals*

Whenever a man's friends begin to compliment him about looking young, he may be sure that they think he is growing old.
Bracebridge Hall [1822]. *Bachelors*

---

[1] The theme of Irving's story derives from DIOGENES LAERTIUS, *Epimenides* [c. A.D. 200]. Epimenides was sent by his father into the field to look for a sheep, turned out of the road at midday and lay down in a certain cave and fell asleep, and slept there fifty-seven years; and after that, when awake, he went on looking for the sheep, thinking that he had been taking a short nap.

I am always at a loss to know how much to believe of my own stories.
Tales of a Traveler [1824]. *To the Reader*

The almighty dollar,[1] that great object of universal devotion throughout our land, seems to have no genuine devotees in these peculiar villages.
Wolfert's Roost [1855]. *The Creole Village*

STENDHAL
[HENRI BEYLE]
1783–1842

I call "crystallization" that action of the mind that discovers fresh perfections in its beloved at every turn of events. *De l'Amour* [1822], *ch. 1*

A wise woman never yields by appointment. It should always be an unforeseen happiness. *Ib. 60*

One can acquire everything in solitude — except character.
Ib. Fragments

Prudery is a kind of avarice, the worst of all. *Ib.*

In matters of sentiment, the public has very crude ideas; and the most shocking fault of women is that they make the public the supreme judge of their lives. *Ib.*

There is no such thing as "natural law": this expression is nothing but old nonsense. Prior to laws, what is natural is only the strength of the lion, or the need of the creature suffering from hunger or cold, in short, need.
The Red and the Black [1831]

I see but one rule: to be clear. If I am not clear, all my world crumbles to nothing.
Reply to Balzac [*October 30, 1840*] [2]

Wit lasts no more than two centuries. *Ib.*

---

[1] See Jonson, p. 303a.
[2] In reference to *La Chartreuse de Parme* [1839].

It is the nobility of their style which will make our writers of 1840 unreadable forty years from now.

Manuscript note [1840]

Love has always been the most important business in my life, I should say the only one.

La Vie d'Henri Brulard [1890]

ALLAN CUNNINGHAM
1784–1842

A wet sheet and a flowing sea,
  A wind that follows fast,
And fills the white and rustling sail,
  And bends the gallant mast.

The Songs of Scotland [1825].
A Wet Sheet and a Flowing Sea,
st. 1

The hollow oak our palace is,
Our heritage the sea.   Ib. st. 3

It's hame and it's hame, hame fain wad
  I be —
O, hame, hame, hame to my ain coun-
  tree!

Ib It's Hame and It's Hame,
refrain

LEIGH HUNT
1784–1859

This Adonis in loveliness was a corpulent man of fifty.[1]

The Examiner [March 22, 1812]

Where the light woods go seaward from the town.

The Story of Rimini [1816],
canto I, l. 18

But most he loved a happy human face.   Ib. canto III, l. 110

The world was all forgot, the struggle o'er,
Desperate the joy. — That day they read no more.[2]   Ib. l. 607

---

[1] For this reference to the Prince Regent, Hunt was imprisoned. But he was allowed to redecorate the walls of his prison with a trellis of roses, had his family with him, and visitors were freely admitted — Byron, indeed, gave a dinner party in his honor at the jail.

[2] See Dante, p. 160a.

Green little vaulter in the sunny grass.

To the Grasshopper and the
Cricket [1817]

Abou Ben Adhem (may his tribe increase!)
Awoke one night from a deep dream of peace.

Abou Ben Adhem [1838]

An angel writing in a book of gold.
Ib.

Write me as one that loves his fellow men.   Ib.

And show'd the names whom love of God had bless'd,
And lo! Ben Adhem's name led all the rest.   Ib.

Jenny kissed me when we met,
Jumping from the chair she sat in;
Time, you thief, who love to get
Sweets into your list, put that in:
Say I'm weary, say I'm sad,
Say that health and wealth have missed me,
Say I'm growing old, but add,
Jenny kissed me.[1]   Rondeau [1838]

Stolen sweets are always sweeter,
Stolen kisses much completer,
Stolen looks are nice in chapels,
Stolen, stolen, be your apples.

Song of Fairies Robbing an
Orchard

A Venus grown fat!
Blue-Stocking Revels

"No love," quoth he, "but vanity, sets love a task like that."
The Glove and the Lions,[2] st. 4

Learn the right
Of coining words in the quick mint of joy.

A Rustic Walk and Dinner, l. 33

A fireside is a great opiate.
A Few Thoughts on Sleep

It has been said of ladies when they write letters, that they put their minds

---

[1] Jenny was Jane Welsh Carlyle, who kissed Hunt when he brought Carlyle good news.

[2] Schiller wrote a poem on the same theme, and Browning's The Glove [1845] is a later version of the familiar legend.

in their postscripts — let out the real objects of their writing, as if it were a second thought, or a thing comparatively indifferent. *Anacreon*

ZACHARY TAYLOR
1784–1850

Hurrah for Old Kentuck! That's the way to do it. Give 'em hell, damn 'em.
Shouted to the 2nd Kentucky Regiment on seeing them rally in battle [Buena Vista, Mexico, February 23, 1847]

A little more grape, Captain Bragg.
Attributed [Ib.]

Tell him to go to hell.[1]
Reply to Santa Anna's demand for surrender [Ib.]

THOMAS DE QUINCEY
1785–1859

The burden of the incommunicable.
Confessions of an English Opium-Eater [1822–1856], pt. I

Call for the grandest of all earthly spectacles, what is that? It is the sun going to his rest. Call for the grandest of all human sentiments, what is that? It is that man should forget his anger before he lies down to sleep.[2]   *Ib.*

So, then, Oxford Street, stony-hearted stepmother, thou that listenest to the sighs of orphans, and drinkest the tears of children, at length I was dismissed from thee.   *Ib.*

Everlasting farewells! and again, and yet again reverberated — everlasting farewells!   *Ib. III*

Dyspepsy is the ruin of most things: empires, expeditions, and everything else.   *Letter to Hessey [1823]*

If once a man indulges himself in murder, very soon he comes to think little of robbing; and from robbing he

comes next to drinking and Sabbath-breaking, and from that to incivility and procrastination.
Murder Considered as One of the Fine Arts [1827]

LADY CAROLINE LAMB
1785–1828

[Of Byron] Mad, bad, and dangerous to know.   *Journal*

THOMAS LOVE PEACOCK
1785–1866

A heeltap! a heeltap! I never could bear it!
So fill me a bumper, a bumper of claret!
Headlong Hall [1816], ch. 5, song

Not drunk is he who from the floor
Can rise alone and still drink more;
But drunk is he who prostrate lies,
Without the power to drink or rise.
The Misfortunes of Elphin [1829], ch. 3, heading, translated from the Welsh

The mountain sheep are sweeter,
But the valley sheep are fatter;
We therefore deemed it meeter
To carry off the latter.   *Ib. 11*

Ancient sculpture is the true school of modesty. But where the Greeks had modesty, we have cant; where they had poetry, we have cant; where they had patriotism, we have cant; where they had anything that exalts, delights, or adorns humanity, we have nothing but cant, cant, cant.
Crotchet Castle [1831], ch. 7

A book that furnishes no quotations is, *me judice,* no book — it is a plaything.   *Ib. 9*

He remembered too late, on his thorny green bed,
Much that well may be thought cannot wisely be said.
Ib. The Priest and the Mulberry Tree, st. 5

---

[1] See McAuliffe, p. 1042b.
[2] See *Ephesians 4:26*, p. 54a.

Gotham's three wise men we be.
Whither in your bowl so free?
To rake the moon from out the sea.
The bowl goes trim. The moon doth
shine.
And our ballast is old wine.
> *Three Men of Gotham* [1837],
> *st. 1*

OLIVER HAZARD
PERRY
1785–1819

We have met the enemy, and they
are ours.
> *Dispatch to General William
> Henry Harrison, announcing
> his victory at the battle of
> Lake Erie* [*United States Brig
> Niagara, September 10, 1813,
> 4 P.M.*]

SAMUEL WOODWORTH
1785–1842

How dear to this heart are the scenes of
my childhood,
When fond recollection presents them
to view!
> *The Old Oaken Bucket*

The old oaken bucket, the iron-bound
bucket,
The moss-covered bucket which hung
in the well.　　　　*Ib.*

Pickaxe, shovel, spade, crowbar, hoe,
and barrow,
Better not invade, Yankees have the
marrow.
> *The Patriotic Diggers* [1814], *st. 1*

We'll show him that Kentucky boys
Are Alligator-horses.
> *The Hunters of Kentucky,*[1] *st. 2*

[1] This ballad has the subtitle *Half Horse and
Half Alligator* and celebrates the participation
of Kentuckians, under the command of General
John Coffee, in the Battle of New Orleans
[January 8, 1815]. It was published as a broad-
side in Boston and in 1826 collected in *Melodies,
Duets, Trios, Songs, and Ballads*, by JAMES M.
CAMPBELL.

LUDWIG BÖRNE
1786–1837

Like buttered bread, state ministers
usually fall on the good side.[1]
> *Collected Works, pt. III*

DAVID CROCKETT
1786–1836

I leave this rule for others when I'm
dead,
Be always sure you're right — then go
ahead.[2]　　*Autobiography* [1834]

Don't shoot, Colonel, I'll come
down: I know I'm a gone coon.[3]
> *Story told by Crockett of a treed
> raccoon*

WILLIAM LEARNED
MARCY
1786–1857

They see nothing wrong in the rule
that to the victor belong the spoils of
the enemy.
> *Speech, U.S. Senate* [*January
> 1832*]

WINFIELD SCOTT
1786–1866

The enemy say that Americans are
good at a long shot, but cannot stand
the cold iron. I call upon you instantly
to give a lie to the slander. Charge!
> *Address to the 11th Infantry
> Regiment* [*Chippewa, Canada,
> June 5, 1814*]

Say to the seceded States, "Wayward
sisters, depart in peace."
> *Letter to W. H. Seward
> [March 3, 1861]*

[1] I never had a piece of toast
Particularly long and wide
But fell upon the sanded floor,
And always on the buttered side.
　　　　　　JAMES PAYN [1884]
[2] Crockett's motto in the War of 1812.
[3] The expression "gone coon" was current
during the Revolutionary War, originating in
the plea of a spy, dressed in raccoon skins, to
his discoverer, an English rifleman. — *Century
Cyclopedia of Names*

BARRY CORNWALL
[BRYAN WALLER
PROCTER]
1787–1874

The sea! the sea! the open sea!
The blue, the fresh, the ever free
Without a mark, without a bound,
It runneth the earth's wide regions
    round.　　　　*The Sea, st. 1*

FRANÇOIS GUIZOT
1787–1874

Enrich yourselves! [1]
　　Speech [March 1, 1843]

JOHANN LUDWIG
UHLAND
1787–1862

Let him sing to whom song is given.
　　Des Sängers Fluch [1814]

EMMA WILLARD
1787–1870

Rocked in the cradle of the deep.
　　The Cradle of the Deep [1831]

RICHARD HARRIS
BARHAM
1788–1845

The Lady Jane was tall and slim,
The Lady Jane was fair.
　　Ingoldsby Legends [1840]. The
　　Knight and the Lady

The Devil must be in that little
Jackdaw!
　　Ib. The Jackdaw of Rheims

GEORGE NOEL GORDON,
LORD BYRON
1788–1824

Friendship is Love without his wings.
　　L'Amitié Est l'Amour sans Ailes
　　　　　　　　　　[1806]

[1] Enrichissez-vous!

I only know we loved in vain;
I only feel — farewell! farewell!
　　Farewell! If Ever Fondest
　　　Prayer [1808], st. 2

When we two parted
　In silence and tears,
Half broken-hearted,
　To sever for years.
　　When We Two Parted [1808],
　　　　　　　　　　st. 1

Near this spot are deposited the remains of one who possessed Beauty
without Vanity, Strength without Insolence, Courage without Ferocity, and
all the Virtues of Man, without his
Vices. This Praise, which would be unmeaning Flattery if inscribed over
human ashes, is but a just tribute to the
Memory of Boatswain, a Dog.
　　Inscription on the monument of
　　　a Newfoundland dog [1808]

The poor dog, in life the firmest friend,
The first to welcome, foremost to
　defend.　　　　　　　　*Ib.*

I'll publish right or wrong:
Fools are my theme, let satire be my
　song.
　　English Bards and Scotch Re-
　　　viewers [1809], l. 5

'Tis pleasant, sure, to see one's name in
　print;
A book's a book, although there's noth-
　ing in 't.　　　　　　*Ib. l. 51*

A man must serve his time to every
　trade
Save censure — critics all are ready
　made.　　　　　　　*Ib. l. 63*

With just enough of learning to mis-
　quote.　　　　　　　*Ib. l. 66*

　As soon
Seek roses in December, ice in June;
Hope constancy in wind, or corn in
　chaff;
Believe a woman or an epitaph,
Or any other thing that's false, before
You trust in critics.　　*Ib. l. 75*

Better to err with Pope, than shine with
　Pye.　　　　　　　*Ib. l. 102*

'Twas thine own genius gave the final
blow,
And help'd to plant the wound that
laid thee low:
So the struck eagle, stretch'd upon the
plain,
No more through rolling clouds to soar
again,
View'd his own feather on the fatal
dart,
And wing'd the shaft that quiver'd in
his heart.[1]
       English Bards and Scotch
          Reviewers, l. 826

Though Nature's sternest painter, yet
the best.[2]   *Ib. l. 839*

Maid of Athens, ere we part,
Give, oh give me back my heart!
       Maid of Athens [1810], *st. 1*

Vex'd with mirth the drowsy ear of
night.
       Childe Harold's Pilgrimage,
          canto I [1812], *st. 2*

Had sigh'd to many, though he loved
but one.   *Ib. st. 5*

Maidens, like moths, are ever caught by
glare,
And Mammon wins his way where seraphs might despair.   *Ib. st. 9*

Might shake the saintship of an anchorite.   *Ib. st. 11*

Adieu! adieu! my native shore
Fades o'er the waters blue.
       Ib. st. 13 [*song*]

My native land, good night!   *Ib.*

Still from the fount of joy's delicious
springs
Some bitter o'er the flowers its bubbling venom flings.[3]   *Ib. st. 82*

War, war is still the cry, "War even to
the knife!" [4]   *Ib. st. 86*

[1] See Aesop, p. 766.
[2] Crabbe.
[3] See Lucretius, p. 114a.
[4] "War even to the knife" was the reply of
Palafox, governor of Saragossa, when summoned
to surrender by the French, who besieged that
city in 1808.

Gone — glimmering through the
dream of things that were.
       Childe Harold's Pilgrimage,
          canto II [1812], *st. 2*

A schoolboy's tale, the wonder of an an
hour!   *Ib.*

The dome of thought, the palace of the
soul.[1]   *Ib. st. 6*

Fair Greece! sad relic of departed
worth!
Immortal, though no more; though
fallen, great!   *Ib. st. 73*

Where'er we tread 'tis haunted, holy
ground.   *Ib. st. 88*

What is the worst of woes that wait on
age?
What stamps the wrinkle deeper on the
brow?
To view each loved one blotted from
life's page,
And be alone on earth, as I am now.
       Ib. st. 98

Once more upon the waters, yet once
more!
And the waves bound beneath me as a
steed
That knows his rider!
       Ib. canto III [1816], *st. 2*

       Years steal
Fire from the mind as vigor from the
limb;
And life's enchanted cup but sparkles
near the brim.   *Ib. st. 8*

And Harold stands upon this place of
skulls.   *Ib. st. 18*

There was a sound of revelry by night,
And Belgium's capital had gather'd
then
Her beauty and her chivalry, and
bright
The lamps shone o'er fair women and
brave men.
A thousand hearts beat happily; and
when
Music arose with its voluptuous swell,
Soft eyes look'd love to eyes which
spake again,

[1] See Waller, p. 333a.

And all went merry as a marriage bell.
But hush! hark! a deep sound strikes
like a rising knell!
> *Childe Harold's Pilgrimage,*
> *canto III, st. 21*

Did ye not hear it? — No! 'twas but
the wind,
Or the car rattling o'er the stony
street.
On with the dance! let joy be uncon-
fined;
No sleep till morn, when Youth and
Pleasure meet
To chase the glowing hours with flying
feet. *Ib. st. 22*

Arm! Arm! it is — it is — the cannon's
opening roar! *Ib.*

And there was mounting in hot haste.
> *Ib. st. 25*

Or whispering, with white lips, "The
foe. They come! they come!"
> *Ib.*

Battle's magnificently stern array!
> *Ib. st. 28*

Like to the apples on the Dead Sea's
shore,
All ashes to the taste.[1] *Ib. st. 34*

> Thou fatal Waterloo.
Millions of tongues record thee, and
anew
Their children's lips shall echo them,
and say —
"Here, where the sword united nations
drew,
Our countrymen were warring on that
day!"
And this is much, and all which will
not pass away.[2] *Ib. st. 35*

He who ascends to mountaintops, shall
find
The loftiest peaks most wrapt in clouds
and snow;

---

[1] See Thomas Moore, p. 543b.
[2] This was the passage Sir Winston Churchill
quoted to President Franklin D. Roosevelt when
both agreed to substitute the term United
Nations for Associated Powers in the pact that
the two leaders wished all the free nations to
sign. [In a conference at the White House,
December 1941.]

He who surpasses or subdues mankind
Must look down on the hate of those
below.
> *Childe Harold's Pilgrimage,*
> *canto III, st. 45*

All tenantless, save to the crannying
wind. *Ib. st. 47*

History's purchased page to call them
great. *Ib. st. 48*

The castled crag of Drachenfels
Frowns o'er the wide and winding
Rhine. *Ib. st. 55*

To fly from, need not be to hate, mankind. *Ib. st. 69*

By the blue rushing of the arrowy
Rhone. *Ib. st. 71*

I live not in myself, but I become
Portion of that around me: [1] and to
me
High mountains are a feeling, but the
hum
Of human cities torture. *Ib. st. 72*

Sapping a solemn creed with solemn
sneer. *Ib. st. 107*

Fame is the thirst of youth.
> *Ib. st. 112*

I have not loved the world, nor the
world me; [2]
I have not flatter'd its rank breath, nor
bow'd
To its idolatries a patient knee.
> *Ib. st. 113*

> I stood
Among them, but not of them; in a
shroud
Of thoughts which were not their
thoughts. *Ib.*

I stood in Venice on the Bridge of
Sighs,
A palace and a prison on each hand.
> *Ib. canto IV* [1818], *st. 1*

Where Venice sate in state, throned on
her hundred isles. *Ib.*

---

[1] I am a part of all that I have met. — TENNY-
SON, *Ulysses* [1842]
[2] See Johnson, p. 433b, and Emerson, p. 601b.

She looks a sea Cybele, fresh from
    ocean,
Rising with her tiara of proud towers
At airy distance, with majestic motion,
A ruler of the waters and their powers.
      Childe Harold's Pilgrimage,
                  canto IV, st. 2

'Tis solitude should teach us how to
    die;
It hath no flatterers; vanity can give
No hollow aid; alone — man with his
    God must strive.   *Ib. st. 33*

The Ariosto of the North.[1]   *Ib. st. 40*

Italia! O Italia! thou who hast
The fatal gift of beauty.[2]   *Ib. st. 42*

Let these describe the undescribable.
                      Ib. st. 53

The starry Galileo, with his woes.
                      Ib. st. 54

The poetry of speech.   *Ib. st. 58*

Then farewell, Horace; whom I hated
    so,
Not for thy faults, but mine.
                      Ib. st. 77

O Rome! my country! city of the soul!
                      Ib. st. 78

The Niobe of nations! there she stands,
Childless and crownless, in her voiceless
    woe.   *Ib. st. 79*

Yet, Freedom! yet thy banner, torn, but
    flying,
Streams like the thunderstorm against
    the wind.   *Ib. st. 98*

Alas! our young affections run to waste,
Or water but the desert.   *Ib. st. 120*

Of its own beauty is the mind diseased.
                    Ib. st. 122

Time, the avenger! unto thee I lift
My hands, and eyes, and heart, and
    crave of thee a gift.   *Ib. st. 130*

Butcher'd to make a Roman holiday!
                    Ib. st. 141

[1] Sir Walter Scott
[2] Based on the famous sonnet of VINCENZO
DA FILICAJA [1642–1707]: Italia, Italia! O tu cui
feo la sorte.

"While stands the Coliseum, Rome
    shall stand;
When falls the Coliseum, Rome shall
    fall;
And when Rome falls — the world." [1]
      Childe Harold's Pilgrimage,
             canto IV, st. 145

Oh! that the desert were my dwelling-
    place.[2]   *Ib. st. 177*

There is a pleasure in the pathless
    woods,
There is a rapture on the lonely shore,
There is society, where none intrudes,
By the deep sea, and music in its roar:
I love not man the less, but Nature
    more.   *Ib. st. 178*

Roll on, thou deep and dark blue
    ocean — roll!
Ten thousand fleets sweep over thee in
    vain;
Man marks the earth with ruin — his
    control
Stops with the shore.   *Ib. st. 179*

He sinks into thy depths with bubbling
    groan,
Without a grave, unknell'd, uncoffin'd,
    and unknown.[3]   *Ib.*

Time writes no wrinkle on thine azure
    brow —
Such as creation's dawn beheld, thou
    rollest now.[4]   *Ib. st. 182*

Thou glorious mirror, where the Al-
    mighty's form
Glasses itself in tempests.
                  Ib. st. 183

Dark-heaving — boundless, endless, and
    sublime —
The image of Eternity.   *Ib.*

And I have loved thee, Ocean! and my
    joy

[1] The saying of the ancient pilgrims, quoted
from BEDE by GIBBON, *The Decline and Fall of
the Roman Empire* [1781], ch. 71.
[2] See *Jeremiah 9:2,* p. 34a, and Cowper, p.
457b.
[3] See Homer, p. 64b; Horace, p. 122b; and
Scott, p. 519a.
[4] And thou vast ocean, on whose awful face
Time's iron feet can print no ruin-trace.
    ROBERT MONTGOMERY, *The Omni-*
        presence of the Deity [1830]

Of youthful sports was on thy breast to
  be
Borne, like thy bubbles, onward: from a
  boy
I wanton'd with thy breakers.
> *Childe Harold's Pilgrimage,*
> *canto IV, st. 184*

And trusted to thy billows far and
  near,
And laid my hand upon thy mane,[1] —
  as I do here.　　　　　*Ib.*

  I awoke one morning and found myself famous.
> *Entry in Memoranda after pub-*
> *lication of first two cantos of*
> *Childe Harold's Pilgrimage.*
> *From* THOMAS MOORE, *Life of*
> *Byron* [1830], *ch. 14*

Clime of the unforgotten brave!
> *The Giaour* [1813], *l. 103*

And lovelier things have mercy shown
To every failing but their own;
And every woe a tear can claim,
Except an erring sister's shame.
> *Ib. l. 418*

I die — but first I have possess'd,
And come what may, I have been
  bless'd.　　　　*Ib. l. 1114*

Know ye the land where the cypress
  and myrtle
Are emblems of deeds that are done in
  their clime? [2]
Where the rage of the vulture, the love
  of the turtle,
Now melt into sorrow, now madden to
  crime.
> *The Bride of Abydos* [1813],
> *canto I, st. 1*

Where the virgins are soft as the roses
  they twine,
And all, save the spirit of man, is divine?　　　　　　*Ib.*

Mark! where his carnage and his conquests cease!

---

[1] He laid his hand upon "the Ocean's mane,"
And played familiar with his hoary locks.
> ROBERT POLLOK [1798–1827], *The*
> *Course of Time, bk. IV, l. 689*

[2] See Goethe, p. 477a.

He makes a solitude, and calls it
  — peace! [1]
> *The Bride of Abydos, canto*
> *II, st. 20*

The fatal facility of the octosyllabic
verse.
> *The Corsair* [1814]. *Dedication*

Such hath it been — shall be — beneath the sun
The many still must labor for the one.
> *Ib. canto I, st. 8*

He left a corsair's name to other times,
Link'd with one virtue, and a thousand
  crimes.　　*Ib. canto III, st. 24*

The Cincinnatus of the West,
Whom envy dared not hate,
Bequeathed the name of Washington
To make man blush there was but
  one! [2]
> *Ode to Napoleon Bonaparte*
> [1814], *II*

Lord of himself — that heritage of
  woe.
> *Lara* [1814], *canto I, st. 2*

She walks in beauty, like the night
  Of cloudless climes and starry skies;
And all that's best of dark and bright
  Meet in her aspect and her eyes:
Thus mellow'd to that tender light
  Which heaven to gaudy day denies.
> *Hebrew Melodies* [1815]. *She*
> *Walks in Beauty, st. 1*

The Assyrian came down like the wolf
  on the fold,
And his cohorts were gleaming in purple and gold;
And the sheen of their spears was like
  stars on the sea,
When the blue wave rolls nightly on
  deep Galilee.
> *Ib. The Destruction of*
> *Sennacherib,[3] st. 1*

---

[1] See Tacitus, p. 140b.
[2] See *Don Juan*, p. 561b, and *The Age of Bronze*, p. 563a.
[3] And it came to pass that night, that the angel of the Lord went out, and smote in the camp of the Assyrians an hundred fourscore and five thousand: and when they arose early in the morning, behold, they were all dead corpses. — *II Kings 19:35*

For the Angel of Death spread his
wings on the blast.
> *Hebrew Melodies. The Destruc-
> tion of Sennacherib, st.* 3

And the might of the Gentile, unsmote
by the sword,
Hath melted like snow in the glance of
the Lord! *Ib. st.* 6

The Glory and the Nothing of a
name. *Churchill's Grave, l.* 43

For years fleet away with the wings of
the dove.
> *The First Kiss of Love, st.* 7

Fare thee well! and if forever,
Still forever, fare thee well.
> *Fare Thee Well* [1816], *st.* 1

Sighing that Nature form'd but one
such man,
And broke the die, in molding Sheridan.[1]
> *Monody on the Death of
> Sheridan* [1816], *l.* 117

My hair is gray, but not with years,
Nor grew it white
In a single night,
As men's have grown from sudden
fears.
> *The Prisoner of Chillon* [1816],
> *st.* 1

O God! it is a fearful thing
To see the human soul take wing
In any shape, in any mood. *Ib. st.* 8

A light broke in upon my brain —
It was the carol of a bird;
It ceased, and then it came again,
The sweetest song ear ever heard.
> *Ib. st.* 10

There be none of Beauty's daughters
With a magic like thee;
And like music on the waters
Is thy sweet voice to me.
> *Stanzas for music* [1816], *st.* 1

I had a dream which was not all a
dream. *Darkness* [1816]

Though the day of my destiny's over,
And the star of my fate hath declined.
> *Stanzas to Augusta* [1816], *st.* 1

---

[1] See Ariosto, p. 178a.

My boat is on the shore,
And my bark is on the sea;
But, before I go, Tom Moore,
Here's a double health to thee!

Here's a sigh to those who love me,
And a smile to those who hate;
And, whatever sky's above me,
Here's a heart for every fate.[1]
> *To Thomas Moore* [1817], *st.* 1, 2

So we'll go no more a-roving
So late into the night,
Though the heart be still as loving,
And the moon be still as bright.

For the sword outwears its sheath,
And the soul wears out the breast,
And the heart must pause to breathe,
And love itself have rest.

Though the night was made for loving,
And the day returns too soon,
Yet we'll go no more a-roving
By the light of the moon.
> *So, We'll Go No More A-Roving*
> [1817]

Mont Blanc is the monarch of moun-
tains;
They crowned him long ago
On a throne of rocks, in a robe of
clouds,
With a diadem of snow.
> *Manfred* [1817], *act I, sc.* 1

His heart was one of those which most
enamor us,
Wax to receive, and marble to retain.[2]
> *Beppo* [1818], *st.* 34

Besides, they always smell of bread and
butter. *Ib. st.* 39

I love the language, that soft bastard
Latin,
Which melts like kisses from a female
mouth. *Ib. st.* 44

I wish he [3] would explain his explanation.
> *Don Juan. Dedication* [written
> 1818], *st.* 2

---

[1] See Longfellow, p. 620b.
[2] See Cervantes, p. 197b.
[3] Coleridge.

In virtues nothing earthly could surpass
her,
Save thine "incomparable oil," Macassar!
Don Juan, canto I, st. 17

But — Oh! ye lords of ladies intellectual,
Inform us truly, have they not hen-
peck'd you all? [1] *Ib. st. 22*

Her stature tall — I hate a dumpy
woman. *Ib. st. 61*

What men call gallantry, and gods
adultery,
Is much more common where the
climate's sultry. *Ib. st. 63*

Christians have burnt each other, quite
persuaded
That all the Apostles would have done
as they did. *Ib. st. 83*

A little still she strove, and much repented,
And whispering "I will ne'er consent"
— consented. *Ib. st. 117*

'Tis sweet to hear the watchdog's honest
bark
Bay deep-mouth'd welcome as we draw
near home;
'Tis sweet to know there is an eye will
mark
Our coming, and look brighter when we
come. *Ib. st. 123*

Sweet is revenge — especially to
women.[2] *Ib. st. 124*

Pleasure's a sin, and sometimes sin's a
pleasure. *Ib. st. 133*

Man's love is of man's life a thing
apart,
'Tis woman's whole existence.
Ib. st. 194

There's nought, no doubt, so much the
spirit calms
As rum and true religion.
Ib. canto II [1819], st. 34

A solitary shriek, the bubbling cry

[1] See Addison, p. 395a.
[2] See Shakespeare, *Coriolanus V, iii, 44,* p.
290a.

Of some strong swimmer in his agony.
Don Juan, canto II, st. 53

If this be true, indeed,
Some Christians have a comfortable
creed. *Ib. st. 86*

Let us have wine and women, mirth
and laughter,
Sermons and soda water the day after.[1]
Ib. st. 178

In her first passion woman loves her
lover,
In all the others, all she loves is love.[2]
Ib. canto III [1821], st. 3

Think you, if Laura had been Petrarch's wife,
He would have written sonnets all his
life? *Ib. st. 7*

He was the mildest-manner'd man
That ever scuttled ship or cut a throat.
Ib. st. 41

Even good men like to make the public
stare. *Ib. st. 81*

The isles of Greece, the isles of Greece! [3]
Where burning Sappho loved and
sung. *Ib. st. 86 [song, st. 1]*

Eternal summer gilds them yet,
But all, except their sun, is set. *Ib.*

The mountains look on Marathon,
And Marathon looks on the sea;
And musing there an hour alone,
I dreamed that Greece might still be
free. *Ib. [st. 3]*

And where are they? and where art
thou,
My country? On thy voiceless shore
The heroic lay is tuneless now —
The heroic bosom beats no more!
And must thy lyre, so long divine,
Degenerate into hands like mine?
Ib. [st. 5]

[1] See Dickens, p. 670a, and George Ade,
p. 886b.
[2] See La Rochefoucauld, p. 356b.
[3]   From isles of Greece
The princes orgulous, their high blood chaf'd,
Have to the port of Athens sent their ships.
SHAKESPEARE, *Troilus and Cressida*
[1601–1603], Prologue

Earth! render back from out thy breast
A remnant of our Spartan dead!
Of the three hundred grant but three,
To make a new Thermopylae.
                Don Juan, canto III [*st. 7*]

You have the Pyrrhic dance as yet,
Where is the Pyrrhic phalanx gone?
Of two such lessons, why forget
The nobler and the manlier one?
You have the letters Cadmus gave —
Think ye he meant them for a slave?
                        Ib. [*st. 10*]

Fill high the bowl with Samian wine!
                        Ib. [*st. 11*]

Place me on Sunium's marble steep,
Where nothing save the waves and I
May hear our mutual murmurs sweep;
There, swan-like, let me sing and die.[1]
A land of slaves shall ne'er be mine —
Dash down yon cup of Samian wine!
                        Ib. [*st. 16*]

Milton's the prince of poets — so we
  say;
A little heavy, but no less divine.
                        Ib. st. 91

And if I laugh at any mortal thing,
'Tis that I may not weep.[2]
                Ib. canto IV [*1821*], *st. 4*

    These two hated with a hate
Found only on the stage.   *Ib. st. 93*

"Arcades ambo" — *id est*, blackguards
  both.   *Ib.*

    I've stood upon Achilles' tomb,
And heard Troy doubted; time will
  doubt of Rome.   *Ib. st. 101*

Oh! "darkly, deeply, beautifully blue," [3]
As someone somewhere sings about the
  sky.   *Ib. st. 110*

There's not a sea the passenger e'er
  pukes in,
Turns up more dangerous breakers than
  the Euxine.
                Ib. canto V [*1821*], *st. 5*

And put himself upon his good behavior.
                Don Juan, canto V, st. 47

That all-softening, overpowering knell,
The tocsin of the soul — the dinner
  bell.   *Ib. st. 49*

The women pardon'd all except her
  face.   *Ib. st. 113*

Polygamy may well be held in dread,
Not only as a sin, but as a bore.
                Ib. canto VI [*1823*], *st. 12*

A lady of "a certain age," which
  means
Certainly aged.   *Ib. st. 69*

The drying up a single tear has more
Of honest fame than shedding seas of
  gore.
                Ib. canto VIII [*1823*], *st. 3*

Not so Leonidas and Washington,
Whose every battlefield is holy ground,
Which breathes of nations saved, not
  worlds undone.[1]   *Ib. st. 5*

Half-pay for life makes mankind worth
  destroying.   *Ib. st. 14*

George Washington had thanks and
  nought beside,
Except the all-cloudless glory (which
  few men's is)
To free his country.[1]
                Ib. canto IX [*1823*], *st. 8*

"Gentlemen farmers" — a race worn
  out quite.   *Ib. st. 32*

When Bishop Berkeley said "there was
  no matter,"
And proved it — 'twas no matter what
  he said.
                Ib. canto XI [*1823*], *st. 1*

And, after all, what is a lie? 'Tis but
The truth in masquerade.   *Ib. st. 37*

'Tis strange the mind, that very fiery
  particle,

---

[1] See Plato, p. 93b, and note.
[2] See Beaumarchais, p. 460a, and Lincoln,
p. 638a.
[3] See Southey, p. 532a.

[1] See *Ode to Napoleon*, p. 558b, and *The Age
of Bronze*, p. 563a.

Should let itself be snuff'd out by an article.

*Don Juan, canto XI, st.
60 [of John Keats* [1]*]*

Ready money is Aladdin's lamp.

Ib. canto XII [1823], st. 12

Cervantes smil'd Spain's chivalry away.

Ib. canto XIII [1823], st. 11

The English winter — ending in July,
To recommence in August.

Ib. st. 42

Society is now one polish'd horde,
Formed of two mighty tribes, the Bores
and Bored.   *Ib. st. 95*

All human history attests
That happiness for man — the hungry
sinner! —
Since Eve ate apples, much depends on
dinner.[2]   *Ib. st. 99*

Of all the horrid, hideous notes of woe,
Sadder than owl songs or the midnight
blast,
Is that portentous phrase, "I told you
so."

Ib. canto XIV [1823], st. 50

'Tis strange — but true; for truth is always strange;
Stranger than fiction.[3]   *Ib. st. 101*

The Devil hath not, in all his quiver's
choice,
An arrow for the heart like a sweet
voice.

Ib. canto XV [1824], st. 13

A lovely being, scarcely form'd or
molded,
A rose with all its sweetest leaves yet
folded.   *Ib. st. 43*

---

[1] See Byron, *John Keats*, p. 562b, and Shelley,
p. 571a.

[2] For a man seldom thinks with more earnest-
ness of anything than he does of his dinner. —
JOHNSON, from MRS. PIOZZI, *Anecdotes of Samuel
Johnson* [1786]
See Fanny Fern, p. 658a.

[3] Le vrai peut quelquefois n'être pas vrai-
semblable [Truth may sometimes be improbable].
— BOILEAU [1636–1711], *L'Art Poétique, III, l. 48*
See Daniel Webster, p. 547b.
Truth is stranger than fiction, but not so
popular. — *Anonymous*

The antique Persians taught three useful things —
To draw the bow, to ride, and speak
the truth.

*Don Juan, canto XVI
[1824], st. 1*

In truth he was a noble steed.

Mazeppa [1819], st. 9

Oh, talk not to me of a name great in
story;
The days of our youth are the days of
our glory;
And the myrtle and ivy of sweet two-
and-twenty
Are worth all your laurels, though ever
so plenty.

*Stanzas written on the Road
Between Florence and Pisa
[1821], st. 1*

All farewells should be sudden.

Sardanapalus [1821], act V

The best of prophets of the future is
the past.   *Journal [January 28, 1821]*

The world is a bundle of hay,
Mankind are the asses that pull,
Each tugs in a different way —
And the greatest of all is John Bull!

*Letter to Thomas Moore
[June 22, 1821]*

Because
He is all-powerful, must all-good, too,
follow?
I judge but by the fruits — and they
are bitter —
Which I must feed on for a fault not
mine.   *Cain [1821], act I, sc. 1*

Who killed John Keats?
"I," says the Quarterly,
So savage and Tartarly;
" 'Twas one of my feats." [1]

John Keats [c. 1821]

He seems
To have seen better days, as who has
not
Who has seen yesterday?

Werner [1822], act I, sc. 1

---

[1] See *Don Juan*, p. 562a, and Shelley, p. 571a.

The "good old times" — all times
 when old are good —
Are gone.
> *The Age of Bronze* [1823], *st. 1*

Whose [1] game was empires and whose
 stakes were thrones,
Whose table earth — whose dice were
 human bones.   *Ib. st. 3*

While Franklin's quiet memory climbs
 to heaven,
Calming the lightning which he thence
 had riven,
Or drawing from the no less kindled
 earth
Freedom and peace to that which
 boasts his birth; [2]
While Washington's a watchword,
 such as ne'er
Shall sink while there's an echo left to
 air.[3]   *Ib. st. 5*

Sublime tobacco! which from east to
 west
Cheers the tar's labor or the Turkman's
 rest.[4]
> *The Island* [1823], *canto II, st. 19*

What's drinking?
A mere pause from thinking!
> *The Deformed Transformed*
> [1824], *act III, sc. 1*

My days are in the yellow leaf; [5]
The flowers and fruits of love are gone;
The worm, the canker, and the grief
 Are mine alone!
> *On My Thirty-sixth Year* [1824],
> *st. 2*

Seek out — less often sought than
 found —
A soldier's grave, for thee the best;

Then look around, and choose thy
 ground,
And take thy rest.
> *On My Thirty-sixth Year, st. 10*

Now Barabbas was a publisher.
> *Alleged alteration in the Bible,*
> *John 18:40* [1]

SARAH JOSEPHA HALE
1788–1879

Mary had a little lamb,
 Its fleece was white as snow,
And everywhere that Mary went,
 The lamb was sure to go.

He followed her to school one day;
 That was against the rule;
It made the children laugh and play,
 To see a lamb at school.
> *Mary's Lamb* [2] [*in The Juvenile*
> *Miscellany, September 1830*], *st.*
> *1, 2*

"What makes the lamb love Mary so?"
 The eager children cry.
"Oh, Mary loves the lamb, you know,"
 The teacher did reply.
> *Ib. st. 5*

ARTHUR
SCHOPENHAUER
1788–1860

Hatred comes from the heart; contempt from the head; and neither feeling is quite within our control.
> *Studies in Pessimism.* [3] *Psycho-*
> *logical Observations*

Every man takes the limits of his
own field of vision for the limits of the
world.   *Ib.*

Every parting gives a foretaste of
death; [4] every coming together again a
foretaste of the resurrection.   *Ib.*

---

[1] Napoleon.
[2] See Franklin, p. 421a, note 1.
[3] See *Ode to Napoleon*, p. 558b, and *Don Juan*, p. 561b.
[4] Let Aristotle and all your philosophers say what they like, there is nothing to be compared with tobacco. — MOLIÈRE [1622–1673], *Don Juan; or, Le Festin de Pierre* [1665], act I, sc. 1. Translated by CURTIS HIDDEN PAGE.
 See Anonymous, p. 1085b.
[5] See Shakespeare, pp. 286a and 292b.

[1] The publisher John Murray sent Byron a lavish copy of the Bible in acknowledgment of a favor, and the poet returned it with the word "robber" changed to "publisher."
[2] The first three stanzas are also attributed to John Roulstone [1805–1822], of Sterling, Mass.
[3] Translated by T. BAILEY SAUNDERS.
[4] Partir c'est mourir un peu [To part is to die a little]. — *French proverb*
 See Haraucourt, p. 835a.

The fundamental fault of the female character is that it has no sense of justice.

> *Studies in Pessimism. On Women*

Dissimulation is innate in woman, and almost as much a quality of the stupid as of the clever. *Ib.*

Noise is the most impertinent of all forms of interruption. It is not only an interruption, but also a disruption of thought. *Ib. On Noise*

The most general survey shows us that the two foes of human happiness are pain and boredom.

> *Essays. Personality; or, What a Man Is*

A man who has no mental needs, because his intellect is of the narrow and normal amount, is, in the strict sense of the word, what is called a philistine.[1]

> *Ib.*

Intellect is invisible to the man who has none.[2]

> *Ib. Our Relation to Others, sec. 23*

There is no more mistaken path to happiness than worldliness, revelry, high life.

> *Ib. Our Relation to Ourselves, sec. 24*

Do not shorten the morning by getting up late; look upon it as the quintessence of life, as to a certain extent sacred.

> *Counsels and Maxims, ch. 2*

JAMES FENIMORE COOPER
1789–1851

Few men exhibit greater diversity, or, if we may so express it, greater antithesis of character than the native warrior of North America. In war, he is daring, boastful, cunning, ruthless, self-denying, and self-devoted; in peace, just, generous, hospitable, revengeful,

---

[1] See Matthew Arnold, p. 713b.
[2] See La Rochefoucauld, *Maxim 375*, p. 356a.

superstitious, modest, and commonly chaste.

> *The Last of the Mohicans* [1826]

'Tis grand! 'tis solemn! 'tis an education of itself to look upon!

> *The Deerslayer* [1841], *ch. 2*

Those families, you know, are our upper crust — not upper ten thousand.[1]

> *The Ways of the Hour [1850], ch. 6*

WILLIAM KNOX
1789–1825

Oh why should the spirit of mortal be proud?

> *Songs of Israel* [1824].
> *Mortality, st. 1*

PETER MERE LATHAM
1789–1875

The practice of physic is jostled by quacks on the one side, and by science on the other.

> *Collected Works, bk. I, ch. 25*

There is nothing so captivating as *new* knowledge. *Ib. 51*

Truth in all its kinds is most difficult to win; and truth in medicine is the most difficult of all. *Ib. 60*

Beware of language, for it is often a great cheat. *Ib. 138*

The diagnosis of disease is often easy, often difficult, and often impossible.

> *Ib. 173*

We should always presume the disease to be curable, until its own nature prove it otherwise. *Ib. 174*

Fortunate, indeed, is the man who takes exactly the right measure of himself, and holds a just balance between what he can acquire and what he can use, be it great or be it small!

> *Ib. II, 11*

A bad book is generally a very easy book, having been composed by its au-

---

[1] See Sam Slick, p. 587b.

thor with no labor of mind whatever; whereas a good book, though it be not necessarily a hard one, yet, since it contains important facts, duly arranged, and reasoned upon with care, must require from the reader some portion of the same attention and study to comprehend and profit by it, as it required from the writer to compose it.
Collected Works, bk. II, ch. 43

The way of death is often smoother than the path of life; and great bodily anguish (there is reason to believe) does not often enter largely into the process of dissolution. *Ib. 91*

Common sense is in medicine the master workman. *Ib. 389*

It takes as much time and trouble to pull down a falsehood as to build up a truth. *Ib. 398*

Remedies are our great analyzers of disease. *Ib. 406*

Faith and knowledge lean largely upon each other in the practice of medicine. *Ib. 408*

It is no easy task to pick one's way from truth to truth through besetting errors. *Ib. 415*

Perfect health, like perfect beauty, is a rare thing; and so, it seems, is perfect disease. *Ib. 443*

It would be a great thing to understand pain in all its meanings.
Ib. 474

It is the great mystery of life itself which is at the bottom of all the mysterious language we are obliged to employ concerning it. *Ib. 494*

People in general have no notion of the sort and amount of evidence often needed to prove the simplest matter of fact. *Ib. 525*

FITZ-GREENE HALLECK
1790–1867

Green be the turf above thee,
Friend of my better days!

None knew thee but to love thee,[1]
Nor named thee but to praise.
On the Death of Joseph Rodman Drake [1820], *st. 1*

Strike — till the last armed foe expires,
Strike — for your altars and your fires;
Strike — for the green graves of your sires;
God — and your native land!
Marco Bozzaris [2] [1855], *st. 3*

But to the hero, when his sword
Has won the battle for the free,
Thy voice sounds like a prophet's word,
And in its hollow tones are heard
The thanks of millions yet to be.
Ib. st. 6

One of the few, the immortal names
That were not born to die. *Ib. st. 7*

ALPHONSE DE LAMARTINE
1790–1869

O time, arrest your flight! and you, propitious hours, arrest your course! Let us savor the fleeting delights of our most beautiful days! [3]
The Lake [1820], *st. 6*

I say to this night: "Pass more slowly"; and the dawn will come to dispel the night.[4] *Ib. st. 8*

Limited in his nature, infinite in his desires, man is a fallen god [5] who remembers the heavens.
Méditations Poétiques [1820].
Sermon 2

---

[1] See Burns, p. 494a, and Tennyson, p. 647a.
[2] A Greek patriot, born about 1788, killed in a night attack against the Turks, near Missolonghi, Greece [August 20, 1823].
[3] O temps, suspends ton vol! et vous, heures propices,
Suspendez votre cours!
Laissez-nous savourer les rapides délices
Des plus beaux de nos jours!
[4] Je dis à cette nuit: "Sois plus lente"; et l'aurore
Va dissiper la nuit.
[5] See Emerson, p. 605a.

What is our life but a succession of preludes to that unknown song whose first solemn note is sounded by Death? [1]
Méditations Poétiques. 2nd series. Sermon 15

Experience is the only prophecy of wise men.   *Speech at Mâcon* [1847]

To love for the sake of being loved is human, but to love for the sake of loving is angelic.
Graziella [1849], *pt. IV, ch. 5*

The more I see of the representatives of the people, the more I admire my dogs.
From COUNT D'ORSAY, *Letter to John Forster* [1850]

FERDINAND RAIMUND
1790–1836

No matter how fair the sun shines,
Still it must set.
Das Mädchen aus der Feenwelt (The Maiden from Fairyland) [1826]

SAMUEL GILMAN
1791–1858

Fair Harvard! Thy sons to thy Jubilee throng.
Ode, Bicentennial, Harvard University [September 8, 1836], *st. 1*

First flower of their wilderness, star of their night,
Calm rising through change and through storm.   *Ib.*

HENRY HART MILMAN
1791–1868

And the cold marble leaped to life a god.   *The Belvedere Apollo*

Ride on! ride on in majesty!
In lowly pomp ride on to die.
Hymns. Ride On!

[1] This passage was used by Liszt as a heading for his tone poem *Les Préludes.*

LYDIA HUNTLEY SIGOURNEY
1791–1865

Ye say they all have passed away,
That noble race and brave.
Indian Names, st. 1

But their name is on your waters [1] —
Ye may not wash it out.   *Ib.*

To evil habit's earliest wile
Lend neither ear, nor glance, nor smile —
Choke the dark fountain ere it flows,
Nor e'en admit the camel's nose.
The Camel's Nose, st. 4

CHARLES SPRAGUE
1791–1875

Here lived and loved another race of beings. Beneath the same sun that rolls over your heads the Indian hunter pursued the panting deer. . . . The Indian of falcon glance and lion bearing, the theme of the touching ballad, the hero of the pathetic tale, is gone.
The American Indian

CHARLES WOLFE
1791–1823

Not a drum was heard, not a funeral note,
As his corse to the rampart we hurried.
The Burial of Sir John Moore at Corunna [1817], *st. 1*

But he lay like a warrior taking his rest,
With his martial cloak around him.
Ib. st. 3

We carved not a line, and we raised not a stone —
But we left him alone with his glory.
Ib. st. 8

[1] We will give the names of our fearless race
To each bright river whose course we trace.
FELICIA D. HEMANS [1793–1835], *Song of Emigration*

JOHN BOWRING
1792–1872

Watchman, tell us of the night,[1]
What its signs of promise are.
>>> *Hymn* [1825]

VICTOR COUSIN
1792–1867

We need religion for religion's sake, morality for morality's sake, art for art's sake.   *Cours de Philosophie* [1818]

JOHN FREDERICK WILLIAM HERSCHEL
1792–1871

Science is the knowledge of many, orderly and methodically digested and arranged, so as to become attainable by one. The knowledge of reasons and their conclusions constitutes *abstract*, that of causes and their effects, and of the laws of nature, *natural science*.
>>> *A Preliminary Discourse on the Study of Natural Philosophy* [1830]

JOHN KEBLE
1792–1866

The trivial round, the common task,
Would furnish all we ought to ask.
>>> *The Christian Year* [1827]. *Morning, st.* 10

Abide with me! Fast falls the eventide;
The darkness deepens: Lord, with me abide!
When other helpers fail, and comforts flee,
Help of the helpless, O abide with me!
>>> *Ib. Evening, st.* 1

Abide with me from morn till eve,
For without Thee I cannot live;
Abide with me when night is nigh,
For without Thee I dare not die.
>>> *Ib. st.* 4

---

[1] See *Isaiah 21:11*, p. 31b.

The voice that breath'd o'er Eden
That earliest wedding day.
>>> *Poems* [1869]. *Holy Matrimony, st.* 1

FREDERICK MARRYAT
1792–1848

All zeal, Mr. Easy.
>>> *Midshipman Easy* [1836], *ch.* 9

I haven't the gift of the gab, my sons — because I'm bred to the sea.   *The Old Navy, st.* 1

It's just six of one and half-a-dozen of the other.   *The Pirate, ch.* 4

Every man paddle his own canoe.
>>> *Settlers in Canada* [1844], *ch.* 8

JOHN HOWARD PAYNE
1792–1852

'Mid pleasures and palaces though we may roam,
Be it ever so humble, there's no place like home.[1]
>>> *Home, Sweet Home. From the opera Clari, the Maid of Milan* [1823]

LORD JOHN RUSSELL
1792–1878

If peace cannot be maintained with honor, it is no longer peace.[2]
>>> *Speech, Greenock* [September 19, 1853]

Among the defects of the bill, which were numerous, one provision was conspicuous by its presence and another by its absence.[3]
>>> *Speech to the electors of the City of London* [April 1859]

PERCY BYSSHE SHELLEY
1792–1822

Once, early in the morning,
Beelzebub arose,

---

[1] Home is home, be it never so homely. — *English proverb* [c. 1300]
[2] See Disraeli, p. 613a, and Neville Chamberlain, p. 897a.
[3] See Tacitus, p. 140a.

With care his sweet person adorning,
He put on his Sunday clothes.[1]
The Devil's Walk [1812], *st. 1*

How wonderful is Death,
Death and his brother Sleep![2]
Queen Mab [1813], *I*

Power, like a desolating pestilence,
Pollutes whate'er it touches; and obedience,
Bane of all genius, virtue, freedom, truth,
Makes slaves of men, and, of the human frame,
A mechanized automation.   *Ib. III*

The awful shadow of some unseen Power
Floats though unseen among us[3] — visiting
This various world with as inconstant wing
As summer winds that creep from flower to flower.
Hymn to Intellectual Beauty [1816], *st. 1*

Spirit of Beauty, that dost consecrate
With thine own hues all thou dost shine upon
Of human thought or form.
Ib. st. 2

Some say that gleams of a remoter world
Visit the soul in sleep — that death is slumber,
And that its shapes the busy thoughts outnumber
Of those who wake and live.
Mont Blanc [1816], *st. 3*

Man's yesterday may ne'er be like his morrow;
Nought may endure but Mutability.[4]
Mutability [1816], *I, st. 4*

I met a traveler from an antique land
Who said: "Two vast and trunkless legs of stone
Stand in the desert. Near them, on the sand,

Half sunk, a shattered visage lies, whose frown,
And wrinkled lip, and sneer of cold command,
Tell that its sculptor well those passions read."   *Ozymandias* [1817]

"My name is Ozymandias, king of kings:
Look on my works, ye Mighty, and despair!"
Nothing beside remains. Round the decay
Of that colossal wreck, boundless and bare,
The lone and level sands stretch far away.   *Ib.*

With hue like that when some great painter dips
His pencil in the gloom of earthquake and eclipse.
The Revolt of Islam [1817],
canto V, st. 23

Lift not the painted veil which those who live
Call Life.   *Sonnet* [1818]

I could lie down like a tired child,
And weep away the life of care
Which I have borne and yet must bear,
Till death like sleep might steal on me.
*Stanzas Written in Dejection
near Naples* [1818], *st. 4*

The good want power, but to weep barren tears.
The powerful goodness want: worse need for them.
The wise want love; and those who love want wisdom;
And all best things are thus confused with ill.
Prometheus Unbound [1818-
1819], *act I, l. 625*

Peace is in the grave.
The grave hides all things beautiful and good:
I am a God and cannot find it there.
Ib. l. 638

From the dust of creeds outworn.
Ib. l. 697

[1] See Southey, p. 533a, and note.
[2] See Homer, p. 64a, and note.
[3] See Wordsworth, p. 509b.
[4] See Heraclitus, p. 77b.

Forms more real than living man,
Nurslings of immortality!
      Prometheus Unbound,
         act I, l. 748

To know nor faith, nor love nor law; to
  be
Omnipotent but friendless is to reign.
       Ib. act II, sc. iv, l. 47

    All love is sweet,
Given or returned. Common as light is
  love,
And its familiar voice wearies not
  ever. . . .
They who inspire it most are fortunate,
As I am now; but those who feel it
  most
Are happier still.[1]   *Ib. II, v,* 39

Death is the veil which those who live
  call life:
They sleep, and it is lifted.
       Ib. III, iii, 113

Nor yet exempt, though ruling them
  like slaves,
From chance, and death, and mutabil-
  ity,
The clogs of that which else might
  overscar
The loftiest star of unascended heaven,
Pinnacled dim in the intense inane.
       Ib. III, iv, 200

Familiar acts are beautiful through
  love.   *Ib. act IV, l.* 403

Man, who wert once a despot and a
  slave;
A dupe and a deceiver; a decay;
A traveler from the cradle to the grave
Through the dim light of this immortal
  day.   *Ib. l.* 549

Good, great and joyous, beautiful and
  free;
This is alone Life, Joy, Empire, and
  Victory.   *Ib. closing lines*

    I love all waste
And solitary places; where we taste
The pleasure of believing what we see
Is boundless, as we wish our souls to
  be.
    Julian and Maddalo [1819], *l.* 14

[1] See La Rochefoucauld, p. 356a.

Thou Paradise of exiles, Italy!
      Julian and Maddalo, l. 57

    It is our will
That thus enchains us to permitted
  ill —
We might be otherwise — we might be
  all
We dream of happy, high majestical.
Where is the love, beauty and truth we
  seek,
But in our mind?   *Ib. l.* 170

Me — who am as a nerve o'er which do
  creep
The else unfelt oppressions of this
  earth.   *Ib. l.* 449

    Most wretched men
Are cradled into poetry by wrong;
They learn in suffering what they teach
  in song.[1]   *Ib. l.* 543

Chameleons feed on light and air:
Poets' food is love and fame.
    An Exhortation [1819], *st.* 1

O wild West Wind, thou breath of
  Autumn's being,
Thou, from whose unseen presence the
  leaves dead
Are driven, like ghosts from an enchant-
  er fleeing,
Yellow, and black, and pale, and hectic
  red,
Pestilence-stricken multitudes.
    Ode to the West Wind [1819], *l.* 1

Wild Spirit, which art moving everywhere;
Destroyer and preserver; hear, oh, hear!
       Ib. l. 13

    Thou dirge
Of the dying year, to which this closing
  night
Will be the dome of a vast sepulcher.
       Ib. l. 23

Oh, lift me as a wave, a leaf, a cloud!
I fall upon the thorns of life! I bleed!
       Ib. l. 44

Make me thy lyre, even as the forest
  is:
What if my leaves are falling like its
  own!

[1] See Butler, p. 353b.

The tumult of thy mighty harmonies
Will take from both a deep, autumnal
   tone,
Sweet though in sadness. Be thou,
   Spirit fierce,
My spirit! Be thou me, impetuous one!
       Ode to the West Wind, l. 57

The trumpet of a prophecy! O Wind,
If winter comes, can spring be far behind?   *Ib. l.* 69

Men of England, wherefore plow
For the lords who lay ye low?
     Song to the Men of England
               [1819], st. 1

Nothing in the world is single,
All things by a law divine
In one spirit meet and mingle.
     Love's Philosophy [1819], *st.* 1

I arise from dreams of thee
In the first sweet sleep of night,
When the winds are breathing low,
And the stars are shining bright.
     The Indian Serenade [1819], *st.* 1

Hell is a city much like London —
A populous and smoky city.
     Peter Bell the Third [1819],
              pt. III, st. 1

    Teas,
Where small talk dies in agonies.
             Ib. st. 12

An old, mad, blind, despised and dying
king.[1]
     England in 1819 [written
          1819], *l.* 1

I met Murder on the way —
He had a mask like Castlereagh.
     The Mask of Anarchy [written
          1819], *st.* 2

   One by one, and two by two,
He toss'd them human hearts to chew.
             Ib. st. 3

A lovely lady, garmented in light
From her own beauty.
     The Witch of Atlas [1820], *st.* 5

A Sensitive Plant in a garden grew.
     The Sensitive Plant [1820],
              pt. I, st. 1

[1] George III.

I bring fresh showers for the thirsting
   flowers,
From the seas and the streams.
        The Cloud [1820], *st.* 1

I am the daughter of Earth and Water,
And the nursling of the Sky;
I pass through the pores of the ocean
   and shores,
I change, but I cannot die.   *Ib. st.* 6

Hail to thee, blithe spirit!
   Bird thou never wert,
That from Heaven, or near it,
   Pourest thy full heart
In profuse strains of unpremeditated
   art.   *To a Skylark* [1821], *st.* 1

And singing still dost soar, and soaring
   ever singest.   *Ib. st.* 2

Thou art unseen — but yet I hear thy
   shrill delight.   *Ib. st.* 4

We look before and after,
   And pine for what is not;
Our sincerest laughter
   With some pain is fraught;
Our sweetest songs are those that tell of
   saddest thought.   *Ib. st.* 18

Teach me half the gladness
   That thy brain must know,
Such harmonious madness
   From my lips would flow,
The world should listen then, as I am
   listening now.   *Ib. st.* 21

Kings are like stars — they rise and set,
   they have
The worship of the world, but no repose.[1]   *Hellas* [1821], *l.* 195

The world's great age begins anew,
   The golden years return,[2]
The earth doth like a snake renew
   Her winter weeds outworn.
             Ib. l. 1060

The world is weary of the past,
Oh, might it die or rest at last!
         Ib. final chorus

[1] See Bacon, p. 208b.
[2] See Virgil, p. 116b.

What! alive, and so bold, O earth?
> *Written on Hearing the News of
> the Death of Napoleon* [1821],
> *st. 1*

The fields of immortality.
> *Epipsychidion* [1821], *l. 133*

I never was attached to that great
sect,
Whose doctrine is, that each one
should select
Out of the crowd a mistress or a
friend,
And all the rest, though fair and wise,
commend
To cold oblivion, though 'tis in the
code
Of modern morals, and the beaten
road
Which those poor slaves with weary
footsteps tread
Who travel to their home among the
dead
By the broad highway of the world,
and so
With one chained friend, perhaps a
jealous foe,
The dreariest and the longest journey
go.
> *Ib. l.* 149

I weep for Adonais [1] — he is dead!
Oh, weep for Adonais! though our
tears
Thaw not the frost which binds so dear
a head! *Adonais* [1821], *st. 1*

Till the Future dares
Forget the Past, his fate and fame shall
be
An echo and a light unto eternity!
> *Ib.*

Most musical of mourners, weep
again! *Ib. st. 4*

To that high Capital, where kingly
Death
Keeps his pale court in beauty and de-
cay,
He came. *Ib. st. 7*

Lost Angel of a ruined Paradise!

[1] John Keats.
See Byron, p. 562a-b.

She knew not 't was her own; as with
no stain
She faded, like a cloud which had out-
wept the rain.
> *Adonais, st. 10*

Desires and Adorations,
Winged Persuasions and veiled Desti-
nies,
Splendors, and Glooms, and glimmer-
ing Incarnations
Of hopes and fears, and twilight Fan-
tasies;
And Sorrow, with her family of Sighs,
And Pleasure, blind with tears, led by
the gleam
Of her own dying smile instead of eyes,
Came in slow pomp. *Ib. st. 13*

Ah woe is me! Winter is come and
gone,
But grief returns with the revolving
year. *Ib. st. 18*

The intense atom glows
A moment, then is quenched in a most
cold repose. *Ib. st. 20*

Alas! that all we loved of him should
be,
But for our grief, as if it had not been,
And grief itself be mortal! *Ib. st. 21*

As long as skies are blue, and fields are
green,
Evening must usher night, night urge
the morrow,
Month follow month with woe, and
year wake year to sorrow. *Ib.*

Why didst thou leave the trodden
paths of men
Too soon, and with weak hands though
mighty heart
Dare the unpastured dragon in his den?
Defenseless as thou wert, oh, where was
then
Wisdom the mirrored shield, or scorn
the spear? *Ib. st. 27*

The Pilgrim of Eternity,[1] whose fame
Over his living head like Heaven is
bent,
An early but enduring monument,

[1] Byron.

Came, veiling all the lightnings of his
    song
In sorrow.   *Adonais, st.* 30

A pard-like spirit, beautiful and swift.
                   Ib. st. 32

In mockery of monumental stone.
                   Ib. st. 35

He wakes or sleeps with the enduring
    dead;
Thou canst not soar where he is sitting
    now —
Dust to the dust! but the pure spirit
    shall flow
Back to the burning fountain whence it
    came,
A portion of the Eternal.   *Ib. st.* 38

He hath awakened from the dream of
    life.   *Ib. st.* 39

He has outsoared the shadow of our
    night;
Envy and calumny and hate and pain,
And that unrest which men miscall de-
    light
Can touch him not and torture not
    again;
From the contagion of the world's slow
    stain
He is secure, and now can never mourn
A heart grown cold, a head grown gray
    in vain.   *Ib. st.* 40

He lives, he wakes — 'tis Death is dead,
    not he.   *Ib. st.* 41

He is made one with Nature: there is
    heard
His voice in all her music, from the
    moan
Of thunder to the song of night's sweet
    bird.   *Ib. st.* 42

He is a portion of the loveliness
Which once he made more lovely.
                   Ib. st. 43

The One remains, the many change
    and pass;
Heaven's light forever shines, Earth's
    shadows fly;
Life, like a dome of many-colored glass,
Stains the white radiance of Eternity,
Until Death tramples it to fragments.
                   Ib. st. 52

The soul of Adonais, like a star,
Beacons from the abode where the
    Eternal are.   *Adonais, st.* 55

Music, when soft voices die,
Vibrates in the memory;
Odors, when sweet violets sicken,
Live within the sense they quicken.

Rose leaves, when the rose is dead,
Are heaped for the beloved's bed;
And so thy thoughts, when thou art
    gone,
Love itself shall slumber on.
        To ——: *Music, When Soft*
             Voices Die [1821]

One word is too often profaned
For me to profane it,
One feeling too falsely disdained
For thee to disdain it.
        To ——: *One Word Is Too*
        Often Profaned [1821], *st.* 1

The desire of the moth for the star,
    Of the night for the morrow,
The devotion to something afar
    From the sphere of our sorrow.
                   Ib. st. 2

Swiftly walk o'er the western wave,
    Spirit of Night!
        To Night [1821], *st.* 1

I ask of thee, beloved Night —
Swift be thine approaching flight,
    Come soon, soon!   *Ib. st.* 5

Rarely, rarely, comest thou,
Spirit of Delight!
        Song: Rarely, Rarely, Comest
             Thou [1821], *st.* 1

I love tranquil solitude
And such society
As is quiet, wise, and good.   *Ib. st.* 7

There is no sport in hate when all the
    rage
Is on one side.
        Lines to a Reviewer [1821]

When the lamp is shattered
The light in the dust lies dead —
When the cloud is scattered
The rainbow's glory is shed.
      When the Lamp Is Shattered
             [1822], *st.* 1

Best and brightest, come away!
To Jane: An Invitation [1822]

Away, away, from men and towns,
To the wild wood and the downs. *Ib.*

I am gone into the fields
To take what this sweet hour yields —
Reflection, you may come tomorrow,
Sit by the fireside with Sorrow. —
You with the unpaid bill, Despair —
You, tiresome verse-reciter, Care —
I will pay you in the grave. *Ib.*

Poets are the hierophants of an un-
apprehended inspiration; the mirrors of
the gigantic shadows which futurity
casts upon the present.[1]
A Defense of Poetry [1821]

Poetry is the record of the best and
happiest moments of the happiest and
best minds. *Ib.*

Poets are the unacknowledged legis-
lators of the world. *Ib.*

PETER VYAZEMSKY
1792–1878

He lives in haste and hurries to feel.[2]
First Snow

JOHN CLARE
1793–1864

I am! yet what I am who cares, or
knows?
My friends forsake me like a memory
lost. *I Am*

Untroubling and untroubled where I
lie —
The grass below — above the vaulted
sky. *Ib.*

The wind and clouds, now here, now
there,
Hold no such strange dominion
As woman's cold, perverted will,
And soon estranged opinion.
When Lovers Part

[1] See Cicero, p. 111a; Shakespeare, p. 268a;
and Campbell, p. 538a, and note.
[2] Quoted by Pushkin as epigraph to *Eugene
Onegin.*

Till kicked and torn and beaten out he
lies
And leaves his hold and cackles, groans,
and dies. *Badger*

If life had a second edition, how I
would correct the proofs.[1]
*Letter to a friend. From J. W.
AND ANNE TIBBLE, John Clare:
A Life* [1932]

FELICIA DOROTHEA
HEMANS
1793–1835

The stately homes of England!
How beautiful they stand,
Amidst their tall ancestral trees,
O'er all the pleasant land! [2]
The Homes of England, st. 1

The breaking waves dashed high
On a stern and rock-bound coast,
And the woods, against a stormy sky,
Their giant branches tossed.
*The Landing of the Pilgrim
Fathers, st.* 1

A band of exiles moored their bark
On a wild New England shore.
Ib. st. 2

Ay, call it holy ground,
The soil where first they trod!
They have left unstained what there
they found —
Freedom to worship God.
Ib. st. 10

The boy [3] stood on the burning deck,

[1] See Benjamin Franklin, p. 421a-b.
[2] Those comfortably padded lunatic asylums,
which are known, euphemistically, as the stately
homes of England. — VIRGINIA WOOLF [1882–
1941], *The Common Reader: Lady Dorothy Nevill*

> The stately homes of England,
> How beautiful they stood
> Before their recent owners
> Relinquished them for good.
>   E. V. KNOX [1881–], *The
>   Stately Homes*

[3] Giacomo Casablanca, whose father, Louis, at
the battle of the Nile, 1798, commanded the
flagship *Orient.* It took fire and blew up, the
commander was mortally wounded, and when
most of the crew fled, Giacomo remained aboard,
in an effort to help his gallant father.

Whence all but he had fled.
> *Casabianca, st.* 1

The flames rolled on; he would not go
Without his father's word.
> *Ib. st.* 3

There came a burst of thunder sound;
The boy — oh! where was he?
> *Ib. st.* 9

Come to the sunset tree!
The day is past and gone.
> *Tyrolese Evening Song, st.* 1

Leaves have their time to fall,
And flowers to wither at the north-
wind's breath,
And stars to set — but all,
Thou hast *all* seasons for thine own, O
Death!
> *The Hour of Death, st.* 1

In the busy haunts of men.
> *Tale of the Secret Tribunal, pt.* I

Oh, call my brother back to me!
I cannot play alone:
The summer comes with flower and
bee —
Where is my brother gone?
> *The Child's First Grief, st.* 1

He never smiled again.
> *Title and refrain of poem*

WILLIAM CULLEN
BRYANT
1794–1878

To him who in the love of Nature
holds
Communion with her visible forms, she
speaks
A various language.
> *Thanatopsis* [1817–1821], *l.* 1

Go forth, under the open sky, and list
To Nature's teachings.   *Ib. l.* 14

The hills,
Rock-ribbed, and ancient as the sun.
> *Ib. l.* 37

Old ocean's gray and melancholy waste.
> *Ib. l.* 43

So live, that when thy summons comes
to join

The innumerable caravan which moves
To that mysterious realm, where each
shall take
His chamber in the silent halls of
death,
Thou go not, like the quarry-slave at
night,
Scourged to his dungeon, but, sustained
and soothed
By an unfaltering trust, approach thy
grave,
Like one that wraps the drapery of his
couch
About him, and lies down to pleasant
dreams.[1]   *Thanatopsis, l.* 73

He who, from zone to zone,
Guides through the boundless sky thy
certain flight,
In the long way that I must tread
alone,
Will lead my steps aright.
> *To a Waterfowl* [1818], *st.* 8

The groves were God's first temples.
> *A Forest Hymn*

The melancholy days are come, the
saddest of the year,
Of wailing winds, and naked woods,
and meadows brown and sere.
> *The Death of the Flowers*
> [*1832*], *st.* 1

Loveliest of lovely things are they,
On earth, that soonest pass away.
The rose that lives its little hour
Is prized beyond the sculptured flower.
> *A Scene on the Banks of the*
> *Hudson, st.* 3

These are the gardens of the Desert,
these
The unshorn fields, boundless and
beautiful,
For which the speech of England has
no name —
The Prairies.   *The Prairies*

Truth, crushed to earth, shall rise
again;
The eternal years of God are hers;
But Error, wounded, writhes in pain,
And dies among his worshippers.
> *The Battlefield, st.* 9

[1] See Lucretius, p. 113b, and Horace, p. 120b.

EDWARD EVERETT [1]
1794–1865

The days of palmy prosperity are not those most favorable to the display of public virtue or the influence of wise and good men. In hard, doubtful, unprosperous, and dangerous times, the disinterested and patriotic find their way, by a species of public instinct, unopposed, joyfully welcomed, to the control of affairs.
> *Mount Vernon Papers, no. 14*

WILLIAM WHEWELL
1794–1866

And so no force however great can stretch a cord however fine into an horizontal line which is accurately straight.[2]
> *Elementary Treatise on Mechanics* [1819]. *The Equilibrium of Forces on a Point*

NARCISSE ACHILLE, COMTE DE SALVANDY
1795–1856

We are dancing on a volcano.
> *At a fête given by the Duc d'Orléans to the King of Naples* [1830]

THOMAS CARLYLE
1795–1881

A well-written Life is almost as rare as a well-spent one.
> *Critical and Miscellaneous Essays. Richter* [1827]

The great law of culture is: Let each become all that he was created capable of being.   *Ib.*

The three great elements of modern

---

[1] His best-known wartime oration was delivered at the dedication of the national cemetery at Gettysburg [November 19, 1863], the same occasion on which Lincoln made his famous address.

[2] In a slightly altered form ("line that shall be absolutey straight"), this was reputed to be an example of unconscious but perfect rhyme.

---

civilization, gunpowder, printing, and the Protestant religion.
> *Critical and Miscellaneous Essays. The State of German Literature* [1827]

Literary men are . . . a perpetual priesthood.   *Ib.*

In every man's writings, the character of the writer must lie recorded.
>   *Ib. Goethe* [1828]

A poet without love were a physical and metaphysical impossibility.
>   *Ib. Burns* [1828]

There is no heroic poem in the world but is at bottom a biography, the life of a man; also, it may be said, there is no life of a man, faithfully recorded, but is a heroic poem of its sort, rhymed or unrhymed.
>   *Ib. Sir Walter Scott* [1838]

To the very last, he [Napoleon] had a kind of idea; that, namely, of *La carrière ouverte aux talents*, The tools to him that can handle them.   *Ib.*

No man lives without jostling and being jostled; in all ways he has to elbow himself through the world, giving and receiving offense.   *Ib.*

All greatness is unconscious, or it is little and naught.   *Ib.*

The uttered part of a man's life, let us always repeat, bears to the unuttered, unconscious part a small unknown proportion. He himself never knows it, much less do others.   *Ib.*

It can be said of him, when he departed he took a Man's life along with him. No sounder piece of British manhood was put together in that eighteenth century of Time.   *Ib.*

Nothing that was worthy in the past departs; no truth or goodness realized by man ever dies, or can die.   *Ib.*

The barrenest of all mortals is the sentimentalist.   *Ib.*

Aesop's Fly, sitting on the axle of the

chariot, has been much laughed at for exclaiming: What a dust I do raise!
> On Boswell's Life of Johnson
> [1832]

Whoso belongs only to his own age, and reverences only its gilt Popinjays or soot-smeared Mumbojumbos, must needs die with it.[1] *Ib.*

The stupendous Fourth Estate, whose wide world-embracing influences what eye can take in? [2] *Ib.*

All work is as seed sown; it grows and spreads, and sows itself anew. *Ib.*

No man who has once heartily and wholly laughed can be altogether irreclaimably bad.[3]
> Sartor Resartus [1833–1834],
> bk. I, ch. 4

He who first shortened the labor of copyists by device of movable types was disbanding hired armies, and cashiering most kings and senates, and creating a whole new democratic world: he had invented the art of printing. *Ib. 5*

Man is a tool-using animal. . . . Without tools he is nothing, with tools he is all. *Ib.*

The everlasting No.
> Ib. 7 (chapter title)

Be not the slave of Words. *Ib. 8*

The everlasting Yea.
> Ib. 9 (chapter title)

Man's unhappiness, as I construe, comes of his greatness; it is because there is an Infinite in him, which with all his cunning he cannot quite bury under the Finite. *Ib.*

Close thy Byron; open thy Goethe.
> Ib.

Wonder is the basis of worship.
> Ib. 10

What you see, yet can not see over, is as good as infinite. *Ib. II, 1*

Sarcasm I now see to be, in general,

[1] See Voltaire, p. 418a.
[2] See *Heroes and Hero-Worship,* p. 577b, and Thackeray, p. 660a.
[3] See W. C. Fields, p. 951b.

the language of the Devil; for which reason I have, long since, as good as renounced it.
> Sartor Resartus, bk. II, ch. 4

To consume your own choler, as some chimneys consume their own smoke;[1] to keep a whole Satanic School spouting, if it must spout, inaudibly, is a negative yet no slight virtue, nor one of the commonest in these times. *Ib. 6*

Alas! the fearful Unbelief is unbelief in yourself. *Ib. 7*

As the Swiss inscription says: *Sprechen ist silbern, Schweigen ist golden* — "Speech is silvern, Silence is golden"; or, as I might rather express it, speech is of time, silence is of eternity.[2]
> Ib. III, 3

Trust not the heart of that man for whom old clothes are not venerable.
> Ib. 6

The Public is an old woman. Let her maunder and mumble.
> Journal [1835]

It is now almost my sole rule of life to clear myself of cants [3] and formulas, as of poisonous Nessus shirts.
> Letter to His Wife [1835]

No lie you can speak or act but it will come, after longer or shorter circulation, like a bill drawn on Nature's Reality, and be presented there for payment — with the answer, No effects.
> The French Revolution [1837],
> pt. I, bk. III, ch. 1

To a shower of gold most things are penetrable. *Ib. 7*

[1] See *Heroes and Hero-Worship,* p. 577b.
Consume your own smoke. — BROWNING, *Pacchiarotto* [1876], 25
Would that he consumed his own smoke. — MELVILLE, *Moby Dick* [1851], ch. 96
See Osler, p. 817b.
[2] Silence is deep as Eternity; speech is shallow as Time. — CARLYLE, *Sir Walter Scott* [1838]
[3] See Johnson, p. 433b.

"The people may eat grass": [1] hasty words, which fly abroad irrevocable — and will send back tidings.
> *The French Revolution, pt. I, bk. III, ch. 9*

A whiff of grapeshot.   *Ib. V, 3*

O poor mortals, how ye make this earth bitter for each other.   *Ib. 5*

Battles, in these ages, are transacted by mechanism; with the slightest possible development of human individuality or spontaneity; men now even die, and kill one another, in an artificial manner.   *Ib. VII, 4*

The difference between Orthodoxy or My-doxy and Heterodoxy or Thy-doxy.[2]
> *Ib. pt. II, bk. IV, ch. 2*

Aristocracy of the Moneybag.
> *Ib. VII, 7*

Democracy is, by the nature of it, a self-canceling business; and gives in the long run a net result of zero.
> *Chartism [1839]. Ch. 6, Laissez-Faire*

No sadder proof can be given by a man of his own littleness than disbelief in great men.
> *Heroes and Hero-Worship [1841]. The Hero as Divinity*

The history of the world is but the biography of great men.[3]   *Ib.*

We must get rid of fear.   *Ib.*

A vein of poetry exists in the hearts of all men.   *Ib. The Hero as Poet*

The Age of Miracles is forever here!
> *Ib. The Hero as Priest*

In books lies the soul of the whole Past Time; the articulate audible voice of the Past, when the body and material substance of it has altogether vanished like a dream.
> *Heroes and Hero-Worship. The Hero as Man of Letters*

All that mankind has done, thought, gained or been: it is lying as in magic preservation in the pages of books.   *Ib.*

The true university of these days is a collection of books.   *Ib.*

Burke said there were Three Estates in Parliament; but, in the Reporters' Gallery yonder, there sat a Fourth Estate more important far than they all. It is not a figure of speech, or witty saying; it is a literal fact — very momentous to us in these times.[1]   *Ib.*

The suffering man ought really to consume his own smoke; there is no good in emitting smoke till you have made it into fire.[2]   *Ib.*

Adversity is sometimes hard upon a man; but for one man who can stand prosperity, there are a hundred that will stand adversity.[3]   *Ib.*

"A fair day's wages for a fair day's work": it is as just a demand as governed men ever made of governing. It is the everlasting right of man.
> *Past and Present [1843], bk. I, ch. 3*

Fire is the best of servants; but what a master! [4]   *Ib. II, 9*

All work, even cotton-spinning, is noble; work is alone noble. . . . A life of ease is not for any man, nor for any god.   *Ib. III, 4*

Every noble crown is, and on earth will forever be, a crown of thorns.
> *Ib. 7*

---

[1] The remark of Foullon, when his finance scheme raised the question: What will the people do?
[2] See William Warburton, p. 419a, note.
[3] History is the essence of innumerable biographies. — *On History* [1830]
See Emerson, p. 605b.

[1] The gallery in which the reporters sit has become a fourth estate of the realm. — MACAULAY, *On Hallam's Constitutional History* [1828]
See *On Boswell's Life of Johnson*, p. 576a.
[2] See *Sartor Resartus*, p. 576b.
[3] See Samuel Butler, p. 755b.
[4] Mammon is like fire: the usefulest of all servants, if the frightfulest of all masters! — *Ib. IV, 7*

Blessed is he who has found his work; let him ask no other blessedness.
Past and Present, bk. III, ch. 4

Captains of Industry.
Ib. IV, 4 (chapter title)

There is endless merit in a man's knowing when to have done.
Francia [1845]

He that works and *does* some Poem, not he that merely *says* one, is worthy of the name of Poet.
Introduction to Cromwell's Letters and Speeches [1845]

Respectable Professors of the Dismal Science.[1]
Latter Day Pamphlets, no. 1 [1850]

A Parliament speaking through reporters to Buncombe and the twenty-seven millions, mostly fools.   *Ib. 6*

A healthy hatred of scoundrels.
Ib. 12

"Genius" (which means transcendent capacity of taking trouble, first of all).[2]
Life of Frederick the Great [1858–1865], *bk. IV, ch. 3*

Happy the people whose annals are blank in history books! [3]   *Ib. XVI, 1*

So here hath been dawning
    Another blue day:
Think, wilt thou let it
    Slip useless away?   *Today*

My whinstone house my castle is;
I have my own four walls.
My Own Four Walls

Lord Bacon could as easily have created the planets as he could have written Hamlet.   *Remark in discussion*

[1] Referring to political economy and social science, Carlyle also in his *Occasional Discourse on the Negro Question* [1849] speaks of "What we might call, by way of Eminence, the Dismal Science."

[2] See Buffon, p. 423b, and note.

[3] Carlyle identifies this as "Montesquieu's aphorism."

See George Eliot, p. 689b.

JOSEPH RODMAN DRAKE
1795–1820

When Freedom from her mountain height,
Unfurled her standard to the air,
She tore the azure robe of night,
And set the stars of glory there;
She mingled with its gorgeous dyes
The milky baldric of the skies,
And striped its pure, celestial white
With streakings of the morning light.
Then from his mansion in the sun
She called her eagle bearer down,
And gave into his mighty hand
The symbol of her chosen land.
The American Flag [1819], *st. 1*

JOHN WOODCOCK GRAVES
1795–1886

D' ye ken John Peel with his coat so gay?
D' ye ken John Peel at the break of day?
D' ye ken John Peel when he's far far away
With his hounds and his horn in the morning?

'Twas the sound of his horn brought me from my bed,
And the cry of his hounds, has me oft-times led;
For Peel's view-hollo would waken the dead,
Or the fox from his lair in the morning.   *John Peel* [1832]

ALEXANDER GRIBOYEDOV
1795–1829

The houses are new, but prejudices are old.
Wit Works Woe [1822–1824], *act II, sc. 5*

I'll seek me out a nook for the heart that's tried too sore.   *Ib. IV, 15*

And what will Princess Marya Aleksevna say? [1]
> *Wit Works Woe, act II, sc.* 15

JOHN KEATS
1795–1821

I stood tiptoe upon a little hill.
> *Poems* [1817]. *I Stood Tiptoe, l.* 1

And then there crept
A little noiseless noise among the leaves,
Born of the very sigh that silence heaves.
> *Ib. l.* 10

Open afresh your round of starry folds,
Ye ardent marigolds!
> *Ib. l.* 47

Where swarms of minnows show their little heads,
Staying their wavy bodies 'gainst the streams.
> *Ib. l.* 72

Sometimes goldfinches one by one will drop
From low hung branches; little space they stop;
But sip, and twitter, and their feathers sleek;
Then off at once, as in a wanton freak:
Or perhaps, to show their black, and golden wings,
Pausing upon their yellow flutterings.
> *Ib. l.* 87

Woman! when I behold thee flippant, vain,
Inconstant, childish, proud, and full of fancies.
> *Ib. Woman! When I Behold Thee Flippant, Vain*

To one who has been long in city pent,[2]
'Tis very sweet to look into the fair
And open face of heaven.
> *Sonnets* [1816–1817]. *To One Who Has Been Long in City Pent*

E'en like the passage of an angel's tear
That falls through the clear ether silently.
> *Ib.*

---

[1] Name used as a symbol for idle gossip.
[2] See Milton, p. 347b.

Much have I travel'd in the realms of gold,
And many goodly states and kingdoms seen;
Round many western islands have I been
Which bards in fealty to Apollo hold.
> *Sonnets. On First Looking into Chapman's Homer*

Then felt I like some watcher of the skies
When a new planet swims into his ken;
Or like stout Cortez when with eagle eyes
He star'd at the Pacific — and all his men
Look'd at each other with a wild surmise —
Silent, upon a peak in Darien.
> *Ib.*

Hear ye not the hum
Of mighty workings? —
Listen awhile ye nations, and be dumb.
> *Ib. Addressed to Haydon*

The poetry of earth is never dead.
> *Ib. On the Grasshopper and the Cricket*

My spirit is too weak — mortality
Weighs heavily on me like unwilling sleep,
And each imagin'd pinnacle and steep
Of godlike hardship, tells me I must die
Like a sick Eagle looking at the sky.
> *Ib. On Seeing the Elgin Marbles*

It keeps eternal whisperings around
Desolate shores, and with its mighty swell
Gluts twice ten thousand caverns.
> *Ib. On the Sea*

Life is but a day;
A fragile dewdrop on its perilous way
From a tree's summit.
> *Sleep and Poetry* [1817], *l.* 85

O for ten years, that I may overwhelm
Myself in poesy; so I may do the deed
That my own soul has to itself decreed.
> *Ib. l.* 96

A drainless shower
Of light is poesy; 'tis the supreme of
   power;
'Tis might half slumb'ring on its own
   right arm.
                    Sleep and Poetry, l. 235

But strength alone though of the Muses
   born
Is like a fallen angel: trees uptorn,
Darkness, and worms, and shrouds, and
   sepulchers
Delight it; for it feeds upon the burrs
And thorns of life; forgetting the great
   end
Of poesy, that it should be a friend
To soothe the cares, and lift the
   thoughts of man.   *Ib. l. 241*

In a drear-nighted December
   Too happy, happy tree,
Thy branches ne'er remember
   Their green felicity.
                    Stanzas [written 1817]

But were there ever any
Writh'd not at passing joy?   *Ib.*

Shed no tear — O shed no tear!
The flower will bloom another year.
Weep no more — O weep no more!
Young buds sleep in the root's white
   core.
            Faery Songs, I [written 1818]

There is not a fiercer hell than the
failure in a great object.
            Endymion [1818], *preface*

The imagination of a boy is healthy,
and the mature imagination of a man is
healthy; but there is a space of life between, in which the soul is in a fer-
ment, the character undecided, the way
of life uncertain, the ambition thick-
sighted: thence proceeds mawkishness,
and the thousand bitters which those
men I speak of must necessarily taste in
going over the following pages.   *Ib.*

A thing of beauty is a joy forever:
Its loveliness increases; it will never
Pass into nothingness; but still will keep
A bower quiet for us, and a sleep
Full of sweet dreams, and health, and
   quiet breathing.   *Ib. bk. I, l. 1*

The grandeur of the dooms
We have imagined for the mighty
   dead.   *Endymion, bk. I, l. 20*

O magic sleep! O comfortable bird,
That broodest o'er the troubled sea of
   the mind
Till it is hush'd and smooth!
                                Ib. l. 453

Time, that aged nurse,
Rock'd me to patience.   *Ib. l. 705*

Wherein lies happiness? In that which
   becks
Our ready minds to fellowship divine,
A fellowship with essence; till we
   shine,
Full alchemiz'd, and free of space. Be-
   hold
The clear religion of heaven!
                                Ib. l. 777

The crown of these
Is made of love and friendship, and sits
   high
Upon the forehead of humanity.
                                Ib. l. 800

A hope beyond the shadow of a dream.
                                Ib. l. 857

Pleasure is oft a visitant; but pain
Clings cruelly to us.   *Ib. l. 906*

'Tis the pest
Of love, that fairest joys give most unrest.   *Ib. II, l. 365*

To sorrow,
   I bade good-morrow,
And thought to leave her far away be-
   hind;
But cheerly, cheerly,
   She loves me dearly;
She is so constant to me, and so kind.
                                Ib. IV, l. 173

"For cruel 'tis," said she,
"To steal my Basil-pot away from me."
            Isabella; or, The Pot of Basil
                          [1818], *st. 62*

Blue! Gentle cousin of the forest-green,
Married to green in all the sweetest
   flowers —

Forget-me-not — the blue bell — and
    that Queen
Of secrecy, the violet.
        Sonnets [1818–1819]. *Blue*

When I have fears that I may cease to
    be
Before my pen has glean'd my teeming
    brain.   *Ib. When I Have Fears*

When I behold, upon the night's
    starr'd face,
Huge cloudy symbols of a high ro-
    mance.   *Ib.*

      Then on the shore
Of the wide world I stand alone, and
    think
Till love and fame to nothingness do
    sink.   *Ib.*

Bright star, would I were steadfast as
    thou art —
Not in lone splendor hung aloft the
    night
And watching, with eternal lids apart,
Like nature's patient, sleepless Eremite,
The moving waters at their priest-like
    task
Of pure ablution round earth's human
    shores.   *Ib. Bright Star*

The day is gone, and all its sweets are
    gone!
Sweet voice, sweet lips, soft hand, and
    softer breast.
        Ib. The Day Is Gone

O what can ail thee, knight at arms,
    Alone and palely loitering?
The sedge has withered from the lake,
    And no birds sing!
    La Belle Dame Sans Merci [1] [*first*
        version, 1819], *st. 1*

I met a lady in the meads
    Full beautiful, a faery's child;
Her hair was long, her foot was light,
    And her eyes were wild.   *Ib. st. 4*

She looked at me as she did love,
And made sweet moan.   *Ib. st. 5*

    "La belle dame sans merci
Thee hath in thrall!"   *Ib. st. 10*

[1] The title of a French poem by ALAIN
CHARTIER [c. 1385 – c. 1433]

This living hand, now warm and capa-
    ble
Of earnest grasping, would, if it were
    cold
And in the icy silence of the tomb,
So haunt thy days and chill thy dream-
    ing nights
That thou would wish thine own heart
    dry of blood
So in my veins red life might stream
    again,
And thou be conscience-calm'd — see
    here it is —
I hold it towards you.
      Lines Supposed to Have Been
      Addressed to Fanny Brawne
      [1819]

Love in a hut, with water and a crust,
Is — Love, forgive us! — cinders, ashes,
    dust.
      Poems [1820]. *Lamia, pt. II, l. 1*

There was an awful rainbow once in
    heaven:
We know her woof, her texture; she is
    given
In the dull catalogue of common
    things.
Philosophy will clip an angel's wings.
               Ib. l. 231

St. Agnes' Eve — Ah, bitter chill it
    was!
The owl, for all his feathers, was a-cold.
The hare limp'd trembling through the
    frozen grass,
And silent was the flock in wooly fold
    Ib. The Eve of St. Agnes, st. 1

The silver, snarling trumpets 'gan to
    chide.   *Ib. st. 4*

The music, yearning like a God in pain.
               Ib. st. 7

She sigh'd for Agnes' dreams, the
    sweetest of the year.   *Ib.*

Asleep in lap of legends old.
               Ib. st. 15

Sudden a thought came like a full-
    blown rose,
Flushing his brow, and in his pained
    heart
Made purple riot.   *Ib. st. 16*

A poor, weak, palsy-stricken, church-
    yard thing.
        Poems. The Eve of St. Agnes,
                    st. 18

As though a tongueless nightingale
    should swell
Her throat in vain, and die, heart-stifled
    in her dell.   *Ib. st. 23*

Full on this casement shone the wintry
    moon,
And threw warm gules on Madeline's
    fair breast.   *Ib. st. 25*

Unclasps her warmed jewels one by
    one;
Loosens her fragrant bodice; by de-
    grees
Her rich attire creeps rustling to her
    knees.   *Ib. st. 26*

And still she slept an azure-lidded sleep.
               Ib. st. 30

And the long carpets rose along the
    gusty floor.   *Ib. st. 40*

And they are gone: aye, ages long ago
These lovers fled away into the storm.
               Ib. st. 42

My heart aches, and a drowsy numb-
    ness pains
My sense, as though of hemlock I had
    drunk,
Or emptied some dull opiate to the
    drains
One minute past, and Lethe-wards had
    sunk.[1]
        Ib. Ode to a Nightingale, st. 1

That thou, light-winged Dryad of the
    trees,
  In some melodious plot
Of beechen green, and shadows num-
    berless,
Singest of summer in full-throated ease.
                    Ib.

O, for a draught of vintage! that hath
    been
Cool'd a long age in the deep-delved
    earth,
Tasting of Flora and the country green,
Dance, and Provençal song, and sun-
    burnt mirth!

[1] See Horace, p. 120b.

O, for a beaker full of the warm South,
Full of the true, the blushful Hippo-
    crene,
With beaded bubbles winking at the
    brim,
  And purple-stained mouth.
        Poems. Ode to a Nightingale,
                    st. 2

Fade far away, dissolve, and quite for-
    get
What thou among the leaves hast never
    known,
The weariness, the fever, and the fret
Here, where men sit and hear each
    other groan;
Where palsy shakes a few, sad, last gray
    hairs,
Where youth grows pale, and specter-
    thin, and dies;
Where but to think is to be full of
    sorrow
  And leaden-eyed despairs.
                 Ib. st. 3

Already with thee! tender is the night.
                 Ib. st. 4

I cannot see what flowers are at my
    feet,
Nor what soft incense hangs upon the
    boughs,
But, in embalmed darkness, guess each
    sweet.   *Ib. st. 5*

The murmurous haunt of flies on sum-
    mer eves.   *Ib.*

Darkling I listen; and, for many a time
I have been half in love with easeful
    Death,
Call'd him soft names in many a mused
    rhyme,
To take into the air my quiet breath;
Now more than ever seems it rich to
    die,
To cease upon the midnight with no
    pain,
While thou art pouring forth thy soul
    abroad
  In such an ecstasy!
Still wouldst thou sing, and I have ears
    in vain —
To thy high requiem become a sod.
                 Ib. st. 6

Thou wast not born for death, immortal Bird!
No hungry generations tread thee down;
The voice I hear this passing night was heard
In ancient days by emperor and clown:
Perhaps the self-same song that found a path
Through the sad heart of Ruth, when, sick for home,
She stood in tears amid the alien corn;
The same that oft-times hath
Charm'd magic casements, opening on the foam
Of perilous seas, in faery lands forlorn.
Poems. *Ode to a Nightingale,*
st. 7

Forlorn! the very word is like a bell
To toll me back from thee to my sole self! *Ib. st. 8*

Was it a vision, or a waking dream?
Fled is that music: — Do I wake or sleep? *Ib.*

Thou still unravish'd bride of quietness,
Thou foster-child of silence and slow time,
Sylvan historian, who canst thus express
A flowery tale more sweetly than our rhyme:
What leaf-fring'd legend haunts about thy shape?
Ib. Ode on a Grecian Urn, st. 1

What men or gods are these? What maidens loth?
What mad pursuit? What struggle to escape?
What pipes and timbrels? What wild ecstasy? *Ib.*

Heard melodies are sweet, but those unheard
Are sweeter. *Ib. st. 2*

Forever wilt thou love, and she be fair! *Ib.*

Forever piping songs forever new.
Ib. st. 3

Who are these coming to the sacrifice?
To what green altar, O mysterious priest,

Lead'st thou that heifer lowing at the skies,
And all her silken flanks with garlands drest?
Poems. *Ode on a Grecian Urn, st. 4*

O Attic shape! Fair attitude!
Ib. st. 5

"Beauty is truth, truth beauty," [1] — that is all
Ye know on earth, and all ye need to know. *Ib.*

To make delicious moan
Upon the midnight hours.
Ib. Ode to Psyche, st. 3

A bright torch, and a casement ope at night,
To let the warm Love in! *Ib. st. 5*

Ever let the fancy roam,
Pleasure never is at home.
Ib. Fancy, l. 1

Bards of Passion and of Mirth,
Ye have left your souls on earth!
Have ye souls in heaven too?
Ib. Ode written on the blank page before BEAUMONT AND FLETCHER, *The Fair Maid of the Inn*

Souls of Poets dead and gone,
What Elysium have ye known,
Happy field or mossy cavern,
Choicer than the Mermaid Tavern?
Have ye tippled drink more fine
Than mine host's Canary wine?
Ib. Lines on the Mermaid Tavern

Season of mists and mellow fruitfulness,

[1] See Herbert, p. 323a.
If asked who said "Beauty is truth, truth beauty!" a great many readers would answer "Keats." But Keats said nothing of the sort. It is what he said the Grecian Urn said, his description and criticism of a certain kind of work of art, the kind from which the evils and problems of this life, the "heart high sorrowful and cloyed," are deliberately excluded. The Urn, for example, depicts, among other beautiful sights, the citadel of a hill town; it does not depict warfare, the evil which makes the citadel necessary. — W. H. AUDEN, *The Dyer's Hand* [*1962*]. Robert Frost

Close bosom-friend of the maturing sun.
> Poems. To Autumn, st. 1

Who hath not seen thee oft amid thy store?

Sometimes whoever seeks abroad may find

Thee sitting careless on a granary floor,

Thy hair soft-lifted by the winnowing wind;

Or on a half-reap'd furrow sound asleep,

Drows'd with the fume of poppies while thy hook

Spares the next swath and all its twined flowers.
> Ib. st. 2

Then in a wailful choir the small gnats mourn

Among the river sallows.
> Ib. st. 3

No, no, go not to Lethe, neither twist Wolf's-bane, tight-rooted, for its poisonous wine.
> Ib. Ode on Melancholy, st. 1

Nor let the beetle, nor the death-moth be

Your mournful Psyche.
> Ib.

Then glut thy sorrow on a morning rose.
> Ib. st. 2

She dwells with Beauty — Beauty that must die.
> Ib. st. 3

Ay, in the very temple of Delight

Veil'd Melancholy has her sovran shrine,

Though seen of none save him whose strenuous tongue

Can burst Joy's grape against his palate fine;

His soul shall taste the sadness of her might,

And be among her cloudy trophies hung.
> Ib.

Deep in the shady sadness of a vale

Far sunken from the healthy breath of morn,

Far from the fiery noon, and eve's one star,

Sat gray-hair'd Saturn, quiet as a stone.
> Ib. Hyperion, bk. I, l. 1

That large utterance of the early Gods!
> Ib. l. 51

As when, upon a tranced summer-night,

Those green-rob'd senators of mighty woods,

Tall oaks, branch-charmed by the earnest stars,

Dream, and so dream all night without a stir.
> Poems. Hyperion, bk I, l. 72

For to bear all naked truths,

And to envisage circumstance, all calm,

That is the top of sovereignty.
> Ib. II, l. 203

Knowledge enormous makes a God of me.
> Ib. III, l. 113

I am certain of nothing but the holiness of the heart's affections and the truth of imagination — what the imagination seizes as beauty must be truth — whether it existed before or not.
> Letter to Benjamin Bailey
> [November 22, 1817]

The imagination may be compared to Adam's dream — he awoke and found it truth.
> Ib.

O for a life of Sensations rather than of Thoughts!
> Ib.

I scarcely remember counting upon happiness — I look not for it if it be not in the present hour — nothing startles me beyond the moment. The setting sun will always set me to rights — or if a sparrow come before my window I take part in its existence and pick about the gravel.
> Ib.

At once it struck me what quality went to form a man of achievement, especially in literature, and which Shakespeare possessed so enormously — I mean *negative capability*, that is, when a man is capable of being in uncertainties, mysteries, doubts, without any irritable reaching after fact and reason.
> Letter to George and Thomas
> Keats [December 22, 1817]

We hate poetry that has a palpable design upon us — and if we do not agree, seems to put its hand in its breeches pocket. Poetry should be great and unobtrusive, a thing which enters into one's soul, and does not startle or amaze with itself, but with its subject.

Letter to John Hamilton Reynolds [February 3, 1818]

Poetry should surprise by a fine excess, and not by singularity. It should strike the reader as a wording of his own highest thoughts, and appear almost as a remembrance.

Letter to John Taylor [February 27, 1818]

If poetry comes not as naturally as leaves to a tree it had better not come at all.　　　　*Ib.*

Scenery is fine — but human nature is finer.

Letter to Benjamin Bailey [March 13, 1818]

Axioms in philosophy are not axioms until they are proved upon our pulses: we read fine things but never feel them to the full until we have gone the same steps as the author.

Letter to John Hamilton Reynolds [May 3, 1818]

I compare human life to a large mansion of many apartments, two of which I can only describe, the doors of the rest being as yet shut upon me.　　*Ib.*

There is an awful warmth about my heart like a load of immortality.

Letter to John Hamilton Reynolds [September 22, 1818]

I begin to get a little acquainted with my own strength and weakness. Praise or blame has but a momentary effect on the man whose love of beauty in the abstract makes him a severe critic on his own works.

Letter to James Hessey [October 9, 1818]

The genius of poetry must work out its own salvation in a man; it cannot be matured by law and precept, but by sensation and watchfulness in itself. That which is creative must create itself —

In *Endymion*, I leaped headlong into the sea, and thereby have become bet-

ter acquainted with the soundings, the quicksands, and the rocks, than if I had stayed upon the green shore, and piped a silly pipe, and took tea and comfortable advice.

Letter to James Hessey

I would sooner fail than not be among the greatest.　　　　*Ib.*

I think I shall be among the English Poets after my death.

Letter to George and Georgiana Keats [October 14, 1818]

The poetical character . . . is not itself — it has no self — it is everything and nothing. . . . It has as much delight in conceiving an Iago as an Imogen.

Letter to Richard Woodhouse [October 27, 1818]

A poet is the most unpoetical of anything in existence; because he has no identity — he is continually infor[ming] — and filling some other body.　*Ib.*

A man's life of any worth is a continual allegory — and very few eyes can see the mystery of his life — a life like the Scriptures, figurative. . . . Lord Byron cuts a figure, but he is not figurative. Shakespeare led a life of allegory: his works are the comments on it.

Letter to George and Georgiana Keats [February 14–May 3, 1819]

Nothing ever becomes real till it is experienced — Even a proverb is no proverb to you till your Life has illustrated it.　　　　*Ib.*

I myself am pursuing the same instinctive course as the veriest human animal you can think of — I am, however young, writing at random — straining at particles of light in the midst of a great darkness — without knowing the bearing of any one assertion, of any one opinion. Yet may I not in this be free from sin?

Ib. [March 19, 1819]

Call the world if you please "The vale of soul-making."

Ib. [April 21, 1819]

I have two luxuries to brood over in my walks, your loveliness and the hour of my death. O that I could have possession of them both in the same minute.

> *To Fanny Brawne [July 25, 1819]*

"If I should die," said I to myself, "I have left no immortal work behind me — nothing to make my friends proud of my memory — but I have lov'd the principle of beauty in all things, and if I had had time I would have made myself remember'd."

> *Ib. [c. February 1820]*

You might curb your magnanimity, and be more of an artist, and load every rift of your subject with ore.

> *Letter to Shelley [August 1820]*

I can scarcely bid you good-bye, even in a letter. I always made an awkward bow. God bless you!

> *Letter to Charles Armitage Brown; Keats's last letter [November 30, 1820]*

Here lies one whose name was writ in water.[1]   *Epitaph for himself [1821]*

LEOPOLD VON RANKE
1795–1886

You have reckoned that history ought to judge the past and to instruct the contemporary world as to the future. The present attempt does not yield to that high office. It will merely tell how it actually happened.[2]

> *Geschichten der Romanischen und Germanischen Volker (History of the Romanic and Germanic Peoples) von 1492 bis 1535 [1824], preface*

[1] Among the many things he has requested of me tonight, this is the principal — that on his gravestone shall be this inscription. — *Letter from Severn, in* RICHARD MONCKTON MILNES, *Life, Letters, and Literary Remains of John Keats* [1848]
See Sophocles, p. 83a, and note.
[2] Wie es eigentlich gewesen.
See Thucydides, p. 89a.

FRIEDRICH WILHELM IV
1795–1861

I love an opposition that has convictions.   *Speech [April 11, 1847]*

Henceforth Prussia goes forward as part of Germany.

> *Proclamation: To My People, to the German Nation [March 21, 1848]*

ALFRED BUNN
1796–1860

I dreamt that I dwelt in marble halls,
With vassals and serfs at my side.

> *The Bohemian Girl [1843], act II, song*

HARTLEY COLERIDGE
1796–1849

The soul of man is larger than the sky,
Deeper than ocean, or the abysmal dark
Of the unfathomed center.

> *To Shakespeare*

She is not fair to outward view
  As many maidens be;
Her loveliness I never knew
  Until she smiled on me:
Oh! then I saw her eye was bright,
A well of love, a spring of light.

> *Song, She Is Not Fair*

Her very frowns are fairer far
Than smiles of other maidens are.

> *Ib.*

HORACE MANN
1796–1859

Lost, yesterday, somewhere between sunrise and sunset, two golden hours, each set with sixty diamond minutes. No reward is offered, for they are gone forever.   *Aphorism*

Be ashamed to die until you have won some victory for humanity.

> *Commencement Address, Antioch College [1859]*

JAMES ROBINSON PLANCHÉ
1796–1880

It would have made a cat laugh.
The Queen of the Frogs [1879],
act I, sc. 4

WILLIAM HICKLING PRESCOTT
1796–1859

What, then, must have been the emotions of the Spaniards, when, after working their toilsome way into the upper air, the cloudy tabernacle parted before their eyes, and they beheld these fair scenes [the valley and city of Mexico] in all their pristine magnificence and beauty! It was like the spectacle which greeted the eyes of Moses from the summit of Pisgah, and, in the warm glow of their feelings, they cried out, "It is the promised land!"
The Conquest of Mexico [1843],
bk. III, ch. 8

The surest test of the civilization of a people — at least, as sure as any — afforded by mechanical art is to be found in their architecture, which presents so noble a field for the display of the grand and the beautiful, and which, at the same time, is so intimately connected with the essential comforts of life.
The Conquest of Peru [1847],
bk. I, ch. 5

Drawing his sword he [Pizarro] traced a line with it on the sand from East to West. Then, turning towards the South, "Friends and comrades!" he said, "on that side are toil, hunger, nakedness, the drenching storm, desertion, and death; on this side ease and pleasure.[1] There lies Peru with its riches here, Panama and its poverty. Choose, each man, what best becomes a brave Castilian. For my part, I go to the South." So saying, he stepped across the line.
Ib. II, 4

[1] See Garibaldi, p. 620a, and Churchill, p. 920b.

SAM SLICK [THOMAS CHANDLER HALIBURTON]
1796–1865

I want you to see Peel, Stanley, Graham, Shiel, Russell, Macaulay, Old Joe, and so on. These men are all upper crust here.[1]
Sam Slick in England
[1843 – 1844],[2] *ch. 24*

Circumstances alter cases.
The Old Judge [1849], *ch. 15*

JOSEPH AUGUSTINE WADE
1796–1845

Meet Me by Moonlight Alone.
Title of poem

THOMAS HAYNES BAYLY
1797–1839

I'd be a butterfly; living a rover,
Dying when fair things are fading away!
I'd Be a Butterfly, st. 3

Oh no! we never mention her —
Her name is never heard;
My lips are now forbid to speak
That once familiar word.
Oh No! We Never Mention Her

Why don't the men propose, Mamma?
Why don't the men propose?
Why Don't the Men Propose?

She wore a wreath of roses
The night that first we met.
She Wore a Wreath

Friends depart, and memory takes them
To her caverns, pure and deep.
Teach Me to Forget

[1] See James Fenimore Cooper, p. 564b.
[2] The "Sam Slick" papers first appeared in a weekly paper in Nova Scotia in 1836.

Tell me the tales that to me were so
　dear,
Long, long ago, long, long ago.
Long, Long Ago [1]

Oh pilot, 'tis a fearful night!
There's danger on the deep.
The Pilot

Absence makes the heart grow fonder: [2]
Isle of Beauty, fare thee well!
Isle of Beauty

I'm Saddest When I Sing.[3]
Title of poem

HEINRICH HEINE [4]
1797–1856

Toward France there journeyed two
　grenadiers.
*Nach Frankreich Zogen Zwei
Grenadier'*, st. 1

From grief too great to banish
Come songs, my lyric minions.[5]
*Aus Meinen Grossen
Schmerzen*, st. 1

I know not why it should be that I
am so sad; there is a fairy tale of olden
days that I cannot get out of my head.[6]
Die Lorelei, st. 1

You are like a flower,
So sweet and pure and fair.[7]
Du Bist Wie eine Blume, st. 1

---

[1] A popular temperance song, *Where Are the
Friends That to Me Were So Dear?* was set to
the tune of *Long, Long Ago.*
[2] Distance sometimes endears friendship, and
absence sweeteneth it. — JAMES HOWELL, *Familiar Letters* [1650], *bk. I, sec. 1, no. 6*
[3] See Artemus Ward, p. 750b.
[4] Therefore a secret unrest
　Tortured thee, brilliant and bold.
　　　　MATTHEW ARNOLD, *Heine's Grave*
[1867]
[5] Out of my own great woe
　I make my little songs.
　　　Translated by ELIZABETH BARRETT
BROWNING
[6] Ich weiss nicht, was soll es bedeuten,
　Dass ich so traurig bin;
　Ein Märchen aus alten Zeiten,
　Das kommt mir nicht aus dem Sinn.
[7] Du bist wie eine Blume,
　So hold und schön und rein.

At first I was almost about to despair,
I thought I never could bear it — but I
did bear it. The question remains:
how?
An Karl von U.

Don't make a fool of me, my pretty
child, don't greet me under the lindens;
after we get back home, everything will
be learned.
Poem

A knight of the holy spirit.
Harzreise

Good Luck is a giddy maid,
Fickle and restless as a fawn;
She smooths your hair; and then the
　jade
Kisses you quickly, and is gone.[1]
Das Glück Ist eine Leichte Dirne,
st. 1

But Madame Bad Luck scorns all this,
　She shows no eagerness for flitting;
But with a long and fervent kiss
　Sits by your bed — and brings her
　　knitting.
Ib. st. 2

For Sleep is good, but Death is better
　still —
The best is never to be born at all.[2]
*Gross Ist die Ähnlichkeit der
beiden schönen*

If one has no heart, one cannot write
for the masses.
Letter to Julius Campe
[*March 18, 1840*]

No talent, but a character.
Atta Troll [1843], *ch. 24*

Ordinarily he is insane, but he has
lucid moments when he is only stupid.
*Of Savoye, appointed ambassa-
dor to Frankfurt by Lamartine*
[*1848*]

---

[1] See Dryden, p. 369b.
Good Luck is the gayest of all gay girls,
　Long in one place she will not stay,
Back from your brow she strokes the curls,
　Kisses you quick and flies away.
But Madame Bad Luck soberly comes . . .
　And sits by your bed, and brings her knitting.
　　　JOHN HAY [1838–1905], *Good and Bad
Luck (after Heine)
[2] See Theognis, p. 77a, and note.

SAMUEL LOVER
1797–1868

Reproof on her lip, but a smile in her
eye.
Rory O'More [1836], *st. 1*

For dhrames always go by contrairies,
my dear.   *Ib. st. 2*

"For there's luck in odd numbers," says
Rory O'More.[1]   *Ib. st. 3*

When first I saw sweet Peggy
'Twas on a market day;
A low-backed car she rode, and sat
Upon a tuft of hay.
The Low-Backed Car, st. 1

WILLIAM
MOTHERWELL
1797–1835

I've wandered east, I've wandered west,
  Through many a weary way;
But never, never can forget
  The love o' life's young day!
Jeannie Morrison, st. 1

MARY
WOLLSTONECRAFT
SHELLEY
1797–1851

I beheld the wretch — the miserable
monster whom I had created.
Frankenstein [1818], *ch. 5*

ALFRED DE VIGNY
1797–1863

I love the sound of the horn, at
night, in the depth of the woods.[2]
Le Cor [1826]

God! how sad is the sound of the
horn deep in the woods![3]   *Ib.*

I [Nature] am called a mother, but I
am a grave.
La Maison du Berger [1864]

[1] See Pliny, p. 133a, and Shakespeare, p. 267b.
[2] J'aime le son du cor, le soir, au fond des bois.
[3] Dieu! que le son du cor est triste au fond
des bois!

Love that which will never be seen
twice.   *Ib.*

Silence alone is great; all else is weakness.   *La Mort du Loup* [1864]

WILHELM I
1797–1888

In Germany, Prussia must make
moral conquests through legislation.
Speech to the Cabinet
[November 8, 1858]

The Prussian army is the people in
arms.   *As Prince Regent* [1860]

I now have no time to be tired.
On his deathbed [March 8, 1888]

AUGUSTE COMTE
1798–1857

Love our principle, order our foundation, progress our goal.
Système de Politique Positive
[1851–1854]

Nothing at bottom is real except humanity.[1]   *Ib.*

The dead govern the living.
Catéchisme Positiviste [1852]

HOFFMANN VON
FALLERSLEBEN
1798–1874

Deutschland, Deutschland über al-
les.
Title of poem [September 1, 1841]

GEORGE LINLEY
1798–1865

Among our ancient mountains,
And from our lovely vales,
Oh, let the prayer re-echo:
"God bless the Prince of Wales!"
God Bless the Prince of Wales,
st. 1

[1] Il n'y a, au fond, de réel que l'humanité.

Though lost to sight, to memory dear
Thou ever wilt remain.[1]
Song (attributed)

JULES MICHELET
1798–1874

England is an empire, Germany is a
nation, a race, France is a person.
Histoire de France [1833–1867]

What is the first part of politics?
Education. The second? Education.
And the third? Education.
Le Peuple [1846]

DAVID MACBETH
MOIR
1798–1851

From the lone sheiling of the misty is-
land
Mountains divide us, and the waste of
seas —
Yet still the blood is strong, the heart is
Highland,
And we in dreams behold the Hebrides.[2]
Canadian Boat Song

ROBERT POLLOK
1798–1827

Sorrows remembered sweeten present
joy.[3]
The Course of Time, bk. I, l. 464

[1] Absent or dead, still let a friend be dear. —
ALEXANDER POPE, *Epistle to Robert, Earl of Oxford and Mortimer* [1721]
[2] This poem, now generally called *The Lone
Sheiling*, appeared anonymously in Blackwood's
Edinburgh Magazine in September 1829, in a
section called Noctes Ambrosianae, edited by
John Wilson ("Christopher North"). The poem
has been attributed to him, to John Galt, John
Lockart, Scott, David Macbeth Moir, a Scottish
physician and friend of Galt's, and others. Edward MacCurdy in *A Literary Enigma* [1935]
and G. H. Needler in *The Lone Sheiling* [1941]
produce convincing evidence that establish Moir
as the author.
[3] See Virgil, *Aeneid I, 203*, p. 117b.

AMOS BRONSON
ALCOTT
1799–1888

One must be a wise reader to quote
wisely and well.
Table Talk. Quotation

To be ignorant of one's ignorance is
the malady of the ignorant.
Ib. Discourse

Why are we not within?
*Outside the Courthouse, Boston,
during the abortive attempt to
free Anthony Burns* [May 26,
1854]. *From* THOMAS WENT-
WORTH HIGGINSON, *Cheerful
Yesterdays* [1899]

The true teacher defends his pupils
against his own personal influence. He
inspires self-trust. He guides their eyes
from himself to the spirit that quickens
him. He will have no disciple.
Orphic Sayings [1840]. *The
Teacher*

Who loves a garden still his Eden
keeps,
Perennial pleasures plants, and wholesome harvests reaps.
Tablets [1868]

I press thee to my heart as Duty's faithful child.
Sonnet to Louisa May Alcott
[1822]

HONORÉ DE BALZAC
1799–1850

It is easier to be a lover than a husband for the simple reason that it is
more difficult to be witty every day
than to say pretty things from time to
time.
Physiologie du Mariage [1829]

I am a galley slave to pen and ink.
Lettres [1832]

Fame is the sun of the dead.
La Recherche de l'Absolu [1834]

I believe in the incomprehensibility of God.
> *Letter to Madame de Hanska* [*1837*]

Those sweetly smiling angels with pensive looks, innocent faces, and cash-boxes for hearts.
> *Cousin Bette* [*1846*], *ch. 15*

RUFUS CHOATE
1799–1859

The courage of New England was the "courage of conscience." It did not rise to that insane and awful passion, the love of war for itself.
> *Address at Ipswich Centennial* [*1834*]

The final end of government is not to exert restraint but to do good.
> *Speech, U.S. Senate* [*July 2, 1841*]

There was a state without king or nobles; there was a church without a bishop;[1] there was a people governed by grave magistrates which it had selected, and by equal laws which it had framed.
> *Speech before the New England Society* [*December 22, 1843*]

We join ourselves to no party that does not carry the flag and keep step to the music of the Union.
> *Letter to the Whig Convention, Worcester* [*October 1, 1855*]

Its constitution the glittering and sounding generalities[2] of natural right

[1] See Junius, p. 1091b.
It [Calvinism] established a religion without a prelate, a government without a king. — GEORGE BANCROFT, *History of the United States* [1834–1876], *vol. III, ch. 6*
Oh, we are weary pilgrims; to this wilderness we bring
A church without a bishop, a state without a king.
> *The Puritan's Mistake* [1844]; *anonymous*
[2] Six years earlier, Choate gave a lecture in Providence, a review of which, by FRANKLIN J. DICKMAN, appeared in the *Journal* of December 14, 1849. Dickman wrote: "We fear that the

which make up the Declaration of Independence.
> *Letter to the Maine Whig Committee* [*1856*]

EUGÈNE DELACROIX
1799–1863

O young artist, you search for a subject — everything is a subject. Your subject is yourself, your impressions, your emotions in the presence of nature.
> *Oeuvres Littéraires*

The first virtue of a painting is to be a feast for the eyes.
> *Journal* [*1893–1895*]

Painting is only a bridge linking the painter's mind with that of the viewer.
> *Ib.*

THOMAS HOOD
1799–1845

Ben Battle was a soldier bold,
  And used to war's alarms;
But a cannonball took off his legs,
  So he laid down his arms.
> *Faithless Nellie Gray* [*1826*], *st. 1*

His death, which happened in his berth,
  At forty-odd befell:
They went and told the sexton, and
  The sexton tolled the bell.
> *Faithless Sally Brown* [*1826*], *st. 17*

There is a silence where hath been no sound,
There is a silence where no sound may be,
In the cold grave — under the deep, deep sea,
Or in wide desert where no life is found.   *Silence* [*1827*]

I remember, I remember
The house where I was born,

glittering generalities of the speaker have left an impression more delightful than permanent." It would seem that Dickman must have the credit of inventing the phrase "glittering generalities," unless his report was merely echoing words used by Choate in the lecture.

The little window where the sun
Came peeping in at morn.
　　　　I Remember, I Remember
　　　　[1827], *st. 1*

I remember, I remember
The fir-trees dark and high;
I used to think their slender tops
Were close against the sky:
It was a childish ignorance,
But now 'tis little joy
To know I'm farther off from heaven
Than when I was a boy.　　*Ib. st. 4*

She stood breast-high amid the corn.[1]
　　　　Ruth [1827], *st. 1*

And there is even a happiness
That makes the heart afraid.
　　　　Ode to Melancholy [1827]

There's not a string attuned to mirth
But has its chord in melancholy.　　*Ib.*

But evil is wrought by want of thought,
As well as want of heart.
　　　　The Lady's Dream [1827], *st. 16*

I saw old Autumn in the misty morn
Stand shadowless like silence, listening
To silence.　　*Autumn* [1827], *st. 1*

Straight down the Crooked Lane,
And all round the Square.
　　　　A Plain Direction, st. 1

Two stern-faced men set out from Lynn
　　Through the cold and heavy mist,
And Eugene Aram walked between,
　　With gyves upon his wrist.
　　　　The Dream of Eugene Aram
　　　　[1829], *st. 36*

Never go to France
　　Unless you know the lingo,
If you do, like me,
　　You will repent, by jingo.
　　　　French and English [1839], *st. 1*

No warmth, no cheerfulness, no health-
　　ful ease,
No comfortable feel in any member —
No shade, no shine, no butterflies, no
　　bees,
No fruits, no flowers, no leaves, no
　　birds,
November!　　　　　　　　　　*No*

[1] See Keats, p. 583a.

Seem'd washing his hands with invisible
　　soap
In imperceptible water.
　　　　*Miss Kilmansegg and Her Pre-
　　cious Leg* [1841–1843]. *Her
　　Christening, st. 10*

O bed! O bed! delicious bed!
That heaven upon earth to the weary
　　head.　　*Ib. Her Dream, st. 7*

Homemade dishes that drive one from
　　home.　　*Ib. Her Misery, st. 1*

Another tumble! — that's his precious
　　nose!
　　　　Parental Ode to My Infant Son,
　　　　st. 3

With fingers weary and worn,
　　With eyelids heavy and red,
A woman sat in unwomanly rags
　　Plying her needle and thread —
　　　　Stitch! stitch! stitch!
In poverty, hunger, and dirt.
　　　　The Song of the Shirt [1843], *st. 1*

She sang the Song of the Shirt.　　*Ib.*

Work! work! work!　　　　*Ib. st. 2*

O men, with sisters dear!
　　O men, with mothers and wives!
It is not linen you're wearing out,
　　But human creatures' lives![1]
　　　　　　　　　　Ib. st. 4

O God! that bread should be so dear,
And flesh and blood so cheap!
　　　　　　　　　　Ib. st. 5

A wife who preaches in her gown,
And lectures in her nightdress.
　　　　The Surplice Question, st. 2

One more unfortunate,
　　Weary of breath,
Rashly importunate,
　　Gone to her death!

Take her up tenderly,
　　Lift her with care;
Fashioned so slenderly,
　　Young, and so fair!
　　　　The Bridge of Sighs [1844], *st. 1, 2*

[1] See Scott, p. 520b.

Alas for the rarity
Of Christian charity
  Under the sun! [1]
        The Bridge of Sighs, st. 9

O'er the earth there comes a bloom;
Sunny light for sullen gloom;
Warm perfume for vapor cold —
I smell the rose above the mold!
        Farewell, Life [1845]*, st. 2*

MARY HOWITT
1799–1888

"Will you walk into my parlor?" said
  the spider to the fly;
" 'Tis the prettiest little parlor that
  ever you did spy."
        The Spider and the Fly

Oh! poverty is a weary thing, 'tis full of
  grief and pain;
It keepeth down the soul of man, as
  with an iron chain;
It maketh even the little child with
  heavy sighs complain.
        The Pet Lamb

THOMAS NOEL
1799–1861

Rattle his bones over the stones!
He's only a pauper, whom nobody
  owns!
        The Pauper's Drive, st. 1

ALEXANDER PUSHKIN
1799–1837

The mind's dispassionate notations,
The heart's asides, inscribed in tears.
        Eugene Onegin [2] [1823]*,
            dedication*

For he possessed the happy gift
Of unaffected conversation:
To skim one topic here, one there,
Keep silent with an expert's air
In too exacting disputation.
        Ib. ch. 1, st. 5

Contented ever with his life,
Himself, his dinner, and his wife.
        Ib. st. 12

Rousseau — please pardon this digres-
  sion —
Could not conceive how solemn Grimm
Dared clean his nails in front of him.
        Eugene Onegin, ch. 1, st. 24

Custom is lord of all mankind.
        Ib. st. 25

A malady to whose causation
We have, alas, as yet no clues,
Known as the Spleen to Albion's na-
  tion,
In our parlance just: The Blues.
        Ib. st. 38

Habit is Heaven's own redress:
It takes the place of happiness.[1]
        Ib. 2, st. 31

Pimen [*writing by lamplight*]: One
  more, the final record, and my
  annals
Are ended, and fulfilled the duty laid
By God on me, a sinner. Not in vain
Hath God appointed me for many years
A witness, teaching me the art of let-
  ters;
A day will come when some laborious
  monk
Will bring to light my zealous, name-
  less toil,
Kindle, as I, his lamp, and from the
  parchment
Shaking the dust of ages, will transcribe
My chronicles.
        Boris Godunov [2]
        [*written* 1825]

Like to some magistrate grown gray in
  office
Calmly he contemplates alike the just
And unjust, with indifference he notes
Evil and good, and knows not wrath
  nor pity.   *Ib.*

Ah! heavy art thou, crown of Monomakh!   *Ib.*

Mosalsky: Good folk! Maria Godu-
nov and her son Feodor have poisoned
themselves. We have seen their dead
bodies. [*The people are silent with horror.*] Why are you silent? Cry, Long live
Czar Dimitry Ivanovich! [*The people
are speechless.*]   *Ib.*

---

[1] See Southey, p. 533a, and O'Reilly, p. 807a.
[2] Translated by WALTER AINDT.

[1] See Burke, p. 452a.
[2] Translated by ALFRED HAYES.

And thus he mused: "From here, indeed
Shall we strike terror in the Swede;
And here a city, by our labor
Founded, shall gall our haughty neighbor;
"Here cut" — so Nature gives command —
"Your window through on Europe: [1] stand
Firm-footed by the sea, unchanging!"
The Bronze Horseman [*written 1833*]

JOHN BROWN
1800–1859

Had I so interfered in behalf of the rich, the powerful, the intelligent, the so-called great, or in behalf of any of their friends . . . every man in this court would have deemed it an act worthy of reward rather than punishment.
Last Speech to the Court [*November 2, 1859*]

I am yet too young to understand that God is any respecter of persons. [2] I believe that to have interfered as I have done . . . in behalf of His despised poor, was not wrong, but right. Now, if it is deemed necessary that I should forfeit my life for the furtherance of the ends of justice, and mingle my blood further with the blood of my children, and with the blood of millions in this slave country whose rights are disregarded by wicked, cruel, and unjust enactments, I submit: so let it be done! *Ib.*

[1] Algarotti has somewhere said: Pétersbourg est la fênetre, par laquelle la Russie regarde en Europe. — AUTHOR'S NOTE, *The Bronze Horseman*
I am at length going to give you some account of this new city, of the great window lately opened in the North, through which Russia looks into Europe. — FRANCESCO ALGAROTTI, *Letters About Russia* [*June 30, 1739*]

[2] See *Acts 10:34*, p. 50a.
The Father, who without respect of persons judgeth according to every man's work. — *I Peter 1:17*

This *is* a beautiful country.
Remark as he rode to the gallows, seated on his coffin [*December 2, 1859*]

JULIA CRAWFORD
1800–1885

Kathleen Mavourneen! the gray dawn is breaking,
The horn of the hunter is heard on the hill.
Kathleen Mavourneen [*1835*], *st. 1*

Oh! hast thou forgotten this day we must part?
It may be for years, and it may be forever;
Then why art thou silent, thou voice of my heart? *Ib.*

THOMAS BABINGTON, LORD MACAULAY
1800–1859

That is the best government which desires to make the people happy, and knows how to make them happy.
On Mitford's History of Greece [*1824*]

Free trade, one of the greatest blessings which a government can confer on a people, is in almost every country unpopular. *Ib.*

Press where ye see my white plume shine, amidst the ranks of war,
And be your oriflamme today the helmet of Navarre.
Ivry [*1824*], *l. 29*

Nobles by the right of an earlier creation, and priests by the imposition of a mightier hand. *On Milton* [*1825*]

The dust and silence of the upper shelf. *Ib.*

As civilization advances, poetry almost necessarily declines. *Ib.*

Perhaps no person can be a poet, or even can enjoy poetry, without a certain unsoundness of mind. *Ib.*

Nothing is so useless as a general maxim.

On Niccolò de Machiavelli [1827]

The English Bible — a book which if everything else in our language should perish, would alone suffice to show the whole extent of its beauty and power.

On John Dryden [1828]

His imagination resembled the wings of an ostrich. It enabled him to run, though not to soar.   *Ib.*

Ye diners-out from whom we guard our spoons.[1]   *Political Georgics*

Men are never so likely to settle a question rightly as when they discuss it freely.   *Southey's Colloquies* [1830]

A single breaker may recede; but the tide is evidently coming in.[2]   *Ib.*

We know no spectacle so ridiculous as the British public in one of its periodical fits of morality.

On Moore's Life of Lord Byron [1831]

From the poetry of Lord Byron they drew a system of ethics compounded of misanthropy and voluptuousness — a system in which the two great commandments were to hate your neighbor and to love your neighbor's wife.   *Ib.*

Boswell is the first of biographers.[3]

On Boswell's Life of Johnson [1831]

That wonderful book, while it obtains admiration from the most fastidious critics, is loved by those who are too simple to admire it.

On Bunyan's Pilgrim's Progress [1831]

Reform, that you may preserve.

Debate on the First Reform Bill [March 2, 1831]

The conformation of his mind was such that whatever was little seemed to him great, and whatever was great seemed to him little.

On Horace Walpole [1833]

Such night in England ne'er had been, nor ne'er again shall be.

The Armada [1833], *l.* 34

An acre in Middlesex is better than a principality in Utopia.[1]

On Lord Bacon [1837]

Every schoolboy knows who imprisoned Montezuma, and who strangled Atahualpa.   *On Lord Clive* [1840]

She [the Roman Catholic Church] may still exist in undiminished vigor when some traveler from New Zealand shall, in the midst of a vast solitude, take his stand on a broken arch of London Bridge to sketch the ruins of St. Paul's.[2]

On Ranke's History of the Popes [1840]

She [the Catholic Church] thoroughly understands what no other Church has ever understood, how to deal with enthusiasts.   *Ib.*

---

[1] See Tennyson, p. 647b.

[2] Macaulay used a similar image in his review [1824] of MITFORD, *Greece,* and in his review [1829] of MILL, *Essay on Government.*

Who knows but that hereafter some traveler like myself will sit down upon the banks of the Seine, the Thames, or the Zuyder Zee, where now, in the tumult of enjoyment, the heart and the eyes are too slow to take in the multitude of sensations? Who knows but he will sit down solitary amid silent ruins, and weep a people inurned and their greatness changed into an empty name? — CONSTANTIN DE VOLNEY [1757–1820], *Ruins, ch. II*

See Horace Walpole, p. 442a-b.

In the firm expectation that when London shall be a habitation of bitterns, when St. Paul and Westminster Abbey shall stand shapeless and nameless ruins in the midst of an unpeopled marsh, when the piers of Waterloo Bridge shall become the nuclei of islets of reeds and osiers, and cast the jagged shadows of their broken arches on the solitary stream, some transatlantic commentator will be weighing in the scales of some new and now unimagined system of criticism the respective merits of the Bells and the Fudges and their historians. — SHELLEY, *Peter Bell the Third* [1819], *dedication*

---

[1] The louder he talked of his honor, the faster we counted our spoons. — EMERSON, *Conduct of Life* [1860], *Worship*

[2] See Arthur Hugh Clough, p. 688b.

[3] See p. 429b note 2.

The Chief Justice was rich, quiet, and infamous.

On Warren Hastings [1841]

I shall not be satisfied unless I produce something which shall for a few days supersede the last fashionable novel on the tables of young ladies.

Letter to Macvey Napier
[November 5, 1841]

In order that he might rob a neighbor whom he had promised to defend, black men fought on the coast of Coromandel and red men scalped each other by the great lakes of North America.   *On Frederick the Great* [1842]

We hardly know an instance of the strength and weakness of human nature so striking and so grotesque as the character of this haughty, vigilant, resolute, sagacious blue-stocking, half Mithridates and half Trissotin, bearing up against a world in arms, with an ounce of poison in one pocket and a quire of bad verses in the other.   *Ib.*

Lars Porsena of Clusium
  By the Nine Gods he swore
That the great house of Tarquin
  Should suffer wrong no more.
By the Nine Gods he swore it,
  And named a trysting day,
And bade his messengers ride forth
East and west and south and north,
  To summon his array.

Lays of Ancient Rome [1842].
Horatius, st. 1

To every man upon this earth
  Death cometh soon or late;
And how can man die better
  Than facing fearful odds
For the ashes of his fathers,
  And the temples of his gods?

Ib. st. 27

Those behind cried "Forward!"
And those before cried "Back!"

Ib. st. 50

Oh, Tiber! father Tiber!
  To whom the Romans pray,
A Roman's life, a Roman's arms,
  Take thou in charge this day.

Ib. st. 59

And even the ranks of Tuscany
Could scarce forbear to cheer.

Horatius, st. 60

A man who has never looked on Niagara has but a faint idea of a cataract; and he who has not read Barère's *Memoirs* may be said not to know what it is to lie.

Review of Mémoires de
Bertrand Barère [1843]

The highest proof of virtue is to possess boundless power without abusing it.

Review of AIKIN, *Life of*
Addison [1843]

He [Richard Steele] was a rake among scholars, and a scholar among rakes.   *Ib.*

There you sit,[1] doing penance for the disingenuousness of years.

Speech, House of Commons
[April 14, 1845]

Forget all feuds, and shed one English tear
O'er English dust. A broken heart lies here.

Epitaph on a Jacobite [1845]

Those who compare the age in which their lot has fallen with a golden age [2] which exists only in imagination, may talk of degeneracy and decay; but no man who is correctly informed as to the past will be disposed to take a morose or desponding view of the present.

History of England [1849–1861],
vol. I, ch. 1

I shall cheerfully bear the reproach of having descended below the dignity of history if I can succeed in placing before the English of the nineteenth century a true picture of the life of their ancestors.   *Ib.*

The Puritan hated bear-baiting, not because it gave pain to the bear, but because it gave pleasure to the spectators.[3]   *Ib. 2*

[1] Sir Robert Peel.
[2] See Horace, p. 122b.
[3] Even bear-baiting was esteemed heathenish and unchristian: the sport of it, not the inhumanity, gave offense. — HUME, *History of England* [1754–1757], *vol. I, ch. 62*

There were gentlemen and there were seamen in the navy of Charles II. But the seamen were not gentlemen, and the gentlemen were not seamen.
History of England
vol. I, ch. 3

The ambassador [of Russia] and the grandees who accompanied him were so gorgeous that all London crowded to stare at them, and so filthy that nobody dared to touch them. They came to the court balls dropping pearls and vermin.
Ib. V, 23

Your Constitution is all sail and no anchor.
Letter to H. S. Randall, author of a Life of Thomas Jefferson [May 23, 1857]

Soon fades the spell, soon comes the night;
Say will it not be then the same,
Whether we played the black or white,
Whether we lost or won the game?
Sermon in a Churchyard, st. 8

HELMUTH VON MOLTKE
1800–1891

First ponder, then dare.[1]
Attributed aphorism

The fate of every nation rests in its own power.
To the German Reichstag [March 1, 1880]

A war, even the most victorious, is a national misfortune. *Letter [1880]*

RICHARD BETHELL,
LORD WESTBURY
1800–1873

Take a note of that; his Lordship says he will turn it over in what he is pleased to call his mind.[2]
Nash, *Life of Lord Westbury [1888], vol. I, p. 158*

---

[1] Erst wägen, dann wagen.
[2] Reported to have been spoken in an audible whisper, from the barristers' table, in reference to a presiding judge. According to Nash, Lord Westbury always disclaimed invention of the mot.

DAVID GLASGOW
FARRAGUT
1801–1870

Damn the torpedoes — full speed ahead! [1]
At the Battle of Mobile Bay [August 5, 1864]

JOHN HENRY,
CARDINAL NEWMAN
1801–1890

Time hath a taming hand.
Persecution [1832], st. 3

Lead, kindly Light, amid the encircling gloom;
Lead thou me on!
The night is dark, and I am far from home;
Lead thou me on!
Keep thou my feet: I do not ask to see
The distant scene; one step enough for me.
The Pillar of Cloud [1833].
Lead Kindly Light, st. 1

And with the morn, those angel faces smile
Which I have loved long since, and lost awhile. *Ib. st. 3*

Growth is the only evidence of life.
Apologia pro Vita Sua [1864]

It is thy very energy of thought
Which keeps thee from thy God.
Dream of Gerontius [1866],
pt. III

Who lets his feelings run
In soft luxurious flow,
Shrinks when hard service must be done,
And faints at every woe.
Flowers Without Fruit [1868]

Living Nature, not dull Art
Shall plan my ways and rule my heart.
Nature and Art [1868], st. 12

---

[1] This is the most famous version. The "torpedoes" were mines anchored by the Confederates in Mobile Bay.

O Lord, support us all the day long, until the shadows lengthen and the evening comes, and the busy world is hushed, and the fever of life is over, and our work is done. Then in thy mercy grant us a safe lodging, and a holy rest, and peace at the last.

Sermon [1834]; *included in the Book of Common Prayer, p. 571*

It is almost a definition of a gentleman to say he is one who never inflicts pain.

Idea of a University [1873]. *The Man of the World*

A great memory does not make a philosopher, any more than a dictionary can be called a grammar.[1]

Ib. Knowledge in Relation to Learning

Ex umbris et imaginibus in veritatem [From shadows and symbols into the truth]!

His Own Epitaph at Edgbaston

BRIGHAM YOUNG
1801–1877

This is the place!

On first seeing the valley of the Great Salt Lake [2] [*July 24, 1847*]

LYDIA MARIA CHILD
1802–1880

Over the river and through the wood, To grandfather's house we'll go; The horse knows the way To carry the sleigh, Through the white and drifted snow.

Thanksgiving Day, st. 1

[1] See Confucius, p. 71a; Lao Tzu, p. 75b; and Heraclitus, p. 77b.

[2] Brigham Young and 142 men, three women and two children were the vanguard of Mormon pioneers who explored westward from Nebraska. Mahonri M. Young, noted sculptor and grandson of Brigham Young, designed the "This Is the Place Monument," dedicated July 24, 1947.

DAVID CHRISTY
1802 – c. 1868

Cotton is King; or, The Economical Relations of Slavery.

Title of book [1855] [1]

ALEXANDRE DUMAS THE ELDER
1802–1870

All for one, one for all, that is our device.[2]

The Three Musketeers [1844], *ch. 9*

Nothing succeeds like success.[3]

Ange Pitou [1854], *vol. I, p. 72*

Let us look for the woman.[4]

The Mohicans of Paris [1854–1855], *vol. III, ch. 10, 11*

VICTOR HUGO
1802–1885

These two halves of God, the Pope and the emperor.

Hernani [1830], *act IV, sc. 2*

God became a man, granted. The devil became a woman.[5]

Ruy Blas [1838], *act II, sc. 5*

Popularity? It is glory's small change.

Ib. III, 5

Greater than the tread of mighty armies is an idea whose time has come.[6]

Histoire d'un Crime [*written 1852*], *conclusion*

[1] Take away *time is money,* and what is left of England? take away *cotton is king,* and what is left of America? — VICTOR HUGO, *Les Misérables* [1862]. *Marius, bk. IV, ch. 4*

[2] See Shakespeare, p. 220a.

[3] Rien ne réussit comme le succès. — *French proverb*

[4] The phrase "Cherchez la femme" is attributed to JOSEPH FOUCHÉ [1763–1820].

[5] Dieu s'est fait homme; soit. Le diable s'est fait femme.

[6] On résiste à l'invasion des armées; on ne résiste pas à l'invasion des idées. (Literally, one can resist the invasion of armies, but not the invasion of ideas.)

Waterloo! Waterloo! Waterloo! Dismal plain! [1]

> *Les Châtiments* [1853],
> *L'Expiation*

The eye was in the tomb and stared at Cain.   *La Conscience* [1859]

You have created a new thrill.[2]

> *Letter to Baudelaire* [October 6,
> 1859]

The supreme happiness of life is the conviction that we are loved.

> *Les Misérables* [3] [1862].
> *Fantine, bk. V, ch. 4*

Great grief is a divine and terrible radiance which transfigures the wretched.   *Ib. 13*

Napoleon . . . mighty somnambulist of a vanished dream.

> *Ib. Cosette, bk. I, ch. 13*

Waterloo is a battle of the first rank won by a captain of the second.

> *Ib. 16*

Would you realize what Revolution is, call it Progress; and would you realize what Progress is, call it Tomorrow.   *Ib. 17*

What is that to the Infinite?

> *Ib. 18*

Great blunders are often made, like large ropes, of a multitude of fibers.

> *Ib. V, 10*

Upon the first goblet he read this inscription, *monkey wine;* upon the second, *lion wine;* upon the third, *sheep wine;* upon the fourth, *swine wine.* These four inscriptions expressed the four descending degrees of drunkenness: the first, that which enlivens; the second, that which irritates; the third, that which stupefies; finally the last, that which brutalizes.[4]   *Ib. VI, 9*

A man is not idle because he is absorbed in thought. There is a visible labor and there is an invisible labor.

> *Le Misérables. Cosette,*
> *bk. VII, ch. 8*

No one ever keeps a secret so well as a child.   *Ib. VIII, 8*

The peculiarity of prudery is to multiply sentinels, in proportion as the fortress is less threatened.[1]

> *Ib. Marius, bk. II, ch. 8*

He had the appearance of a caryatid on vacation; he was supporting nothing but his reverie.   *Ib. IV, 2*

Social prosperity means man happy, the citizen free, the nation great.

> *Ib. Saint Denis, bk. I, ch. 4*

Nothing is more dangerous than discontinued labor; it is habit lost. A habit easy to abandon, difficult to resume.

> *Ib. II, 1*

Thought is the labor of the intellect, reverie is its pleasure.   *Ib.*

Where the telescope ends, the microscope begins. Which of the two has the grander view?   *Ib. III, 3*

A compliment is something like a kiss through a veil.   *Ib. VIII, 1*

Great perils have this beauty, that they bring to light the fraternity of strangers.   *Ib. XII, 4*

Philosophy is the microscope of thought.

> *Ib. Jean Valjean, bk. II, ch. 2*

The sublimest song to be heard on earth is the lisping of the human soul on the lips of children.

> *Ninety-Three* [1879], *pt. III,*
> *bk. III, ch. 1*

To rise at six, to dine at ten,
To sup at six, to sleep at ten,
Makes a man live for ten times ten.

> *Inscription over the door of*
> *Hugo's study*

---

[1] Waterloo! Waterloo! Waterloo! Morne plaine!
[2] Vous créez un frisson nouveau.
[3] Translated by CHARLES E. WILBOUR.
[4] See George Herbert, p. 322b.

[1] That is the refuge of all old coquettes; it is hard for them to be deserted by the gallants, and from such a desertion, in their spite, they take refuge in the trade of a prude. — MOLIÈRE, *Tartuffe* [1667], *act I, sc. 1*

I represent a party which does not yet exist: the party of revolution, civilization.

This party will make the twentieth century.

There will issue from it first the United States of Europe, then the United States of the World.
>   *On the wall of the room in which Hugo died, Place des Vosges, Paris*

LETITIA ELIZABETH LANDON
1802–1838

Few, save the poor, feel for the poor.
>   *The Poor*

Were it not better to forget
Than but remember and regret?
>   *Despondency*

GEORGE POPE MORRIS
1802–1864

Woodman, spare that tree!
  Touch not a single bough! [1]
In youth it sheltered me,
  And I'll protect it now.
>   *Woodman, Spare That Tree* [1830], *st. 1*

The iron-armed soldier, the true-hearted soldier,
The gallant old soldier of Tippecanoe.[2]
>   *Campaign song for William Henry Harrison* [1840]

A song for our banner! The watchword recall
Which gave the Republic her station:
"United we stand, divided we fall!" [3]
It made and preserves us a nation! [4]
>   *The Flag of Our Union*

[1] See Campbell, p. 538a.
[2] Morris's words, sung to the tune of *The Old Oaken Bucket,* were immensely popular. — BEN PERLEY POORE, *Reminiscences* [1886]
[3] See John Dickinson, p. 460b.
[4] Bless'd with victory and peace, may our Heaven-rescued land
  Praise the Power that hath made and preserved us a nation.
  FRANCIS SCOTT KEY, *The Star-Spangled Banner* [1814], *st. 4*

WINTHROP MACKWORTH PRAED
1802–1839

His talk was like a stream, which runs
With rapid change from rocks to roses;
It slipped from politics to puns;
It passed from Mahomet to Moses.
>   *The Vicar, st. 5*

Dame Fortune is a fickle gipsy,
And always blind, and often tipsy;
Sometimes for years and years together,
She'll bless you with the sunniest weather,
Bestowing honor, pudding, pence,
You can't imagine why or whence;
Then in a moment — Presto, pass! —
Your joys are withered like the grass.
>   *The Haunted Tree*

FRIEDRICH JULIUS STAHL
1802–1861

Authority, not majority.
>   *Speech before the Erfurt Parliament* [April 11, 1850]

WILLIAM ALLEN
1803–1879

Fifty-four forty, or fight! [1]
>   *Speech, U.S. Senate* [1844]

THOMAS LOVELL BEDDOES
1803–1849

The anchor heaves, the ship swings free,
The sails swell full. To sea, to sea!
>   *Sailor's Song, st. 2*

If there were dreams to sell,
  What would you buy?

[1] Phrase adopted as the slogan of the war party in the presidential election of 1844. At the time, war with England over the Oregon question seemed imminent. The Democratic convention of 1844 demanded the reoccupation of the whole of Oregon up to 54°40', but the new President, James K. Polk, compomised with Great Britain on the forty-ninth parallel.

Some cost a passing-bell;
  Some a light sigh.
                    Dream Pedlary

If thou wilt ease thine heart
Of love and all its smart,
  Then sleep, dear, sleep.

But wilt thou cure thy heart
Of love and all its smart,
  Then die, dear, die.
          Death's Jest Book [1850]

GEORGE BORROW
1803–1881

There's night and day, brother, both
sweet things; sun, moon, and stars,
brother, all sweet things; there's likewise a wind on the heath. Life is very
sweet, brother; who would wish to die?
          Lavengro [1851], *ch. 25*

I learned . . . to fear God, and to
take my own part.   *Ib. 86*

Youth is the only season for enjoyment, and the first twenty-five years of
one's life are worth all the rest of the
longest life of man, even though those
five-and-twenty be spent in penury and
contempt, and the rest in the possession
of wealth, honors, respectability.
          The Romany Rye [1857], *ch. 30*

EDWARD
BULWER-LYTTON
1803–1873

A good heart is better than all the
heads in the world.
          The Disowned [1828], *ch. 33*

The easiest person to deceive is one's
own self.   *Ib. 42*

Rank is a great beautifier.
          The Lady of Lyons [1838],
                    act II, sc. 1

Love, like Death,
Levels all ranks, and lays the shepherd's
    crook
Beside the scepter.   *Ib. III, 2*

Beneath the rule of men entirely great,
The pen is mightier than the sword.[1]
          Richelieu [1839], *act II, sc. 2*

In the lexicon of youth, which fate
    reserves
For a bright manhood, there is no such
    word
As — *fail.*   *Ib.*

Out-babying Wordsworth and out-
    glittering Keats.[2]
          The New Timon [1846], *pt. I*

In science, read, by preference, the
newest works; in literature, the oldest.
The classic literature is always modern.
          Caxtonia. Hints on Mental
                    Culture

In science, address the few, in literature the many. In science, the few must
dictate opinion to the many; in literature, the many, sooner or later, force
their judgment on the few.
          Ib. Readers and Writers

WILLIAM DRIVER
1803–1886

I name thee Old Glory.
          As the flag was hoisted to the
                    masthead of his brig [3]

RALPH WALDO
EMERSON
1803–1882

Good-bye, proud world! I'm going
    home;
Thou art not my friend and I'm not
    thine.[4]
          Poems [1847]. *Good-bye, st. 1*

For what are they all in their high con-
    ceit,

---

[1] See Cervantes, p. 195b, and Burton, p. 311a.
Eloquence a hundred times has turned the
scale of war and peace at will. — EMERSON,
Progress of Culture [1867]
[2] Tennyson.
[3] On August 10, 1831, a large American flag
was presented to Driver, captain of the *Charles
Doggett*, by a band of women in recognition of
his bringing the British mutineers of the ship
Bounty from Tahiti back to their former home,
Pitcairn Island. The flag is now in the Smith-
sonian Institution, Washington, D.C.
[4] See Johnson, p. 433b, and Byron, p. 556b.

When man in the bush with God may
  meet?   *Poems. Good-bye, st.* 4

Nor knowest thou what argument
Thy life to thy neighbor's creed has
  lent.
All are needed by each one;
Nothing is fair or good alone.
      Ib. Each and All, st. 1

I wiped away the weeds and foam,
I fetched my sea-born treasures home;
But the poor, unsightly, noisome
  things
Had left their beauty on the shore,
With the sun and the sand and the
  wild uproar.   *Ib. st.* 3

I like a church; I like a cowl;
I love a prophet of the soul;
And on my heart monastic aisles
Fall like sweet strains or pensive smiles;
Yet not for all his faith can see
Would I that cowlèd churchman be.
      Ib. The Problem, st. 1

Not from a vain or shallow thought
His awful Jove young Phidias brought.
      Ib. st. 2

The hand that rounded Peter's dome,
And groined the aisles of Christian
  Rome,
Wrought in a sad sincerity;
Himself from God he could not free;
He builded better than he knew; —
The conscious stone to beauty grew.
      Ib.

Earth proudly wears the Parthenon
As the best gem upon her zone.
      Ib. st. 3

The passive Master lent his hand
To the vast soul that o'er him planned.[1]
      Ib.

Announced by all the trumpets of the
  sky,
Arrives the snow.   *Ib. The Snowstorm*

  Enclosed
In a tumultuous privacy of storm.
      Ib.

[1] This couplet is inscibed on the boulder
marking Emerson's grave in Sleepy Hollow
Cemetery, Concord, Massachusetts.

The frolic architecture of the snow.
      Poems. The Snowstorm

Life is too short to waste
In critic peep or cynic bark,
Quarrel or reprimand:
'Twill soon be dark;
Up! mind thine own aim, and
God speed the mark!   *Ib. To J.W.*

There's no rood has not a star above
  it.   *Ib. Musketaquid*

      All sorts of things and weather
Must be taken in together,
To make up a year
And a Sphere.
      *Ib. Fable, The Mountain and the
                              Squirrel*

In May, when sea winds pierced our
  solitudes,
I found the fresh Rhodora in the
  woods.   *Ib. The Rhodora*

Rhodora! if the sages ask thee why
This charm is wasted on the earth and
  sky,
Tell them, dear, that if eyes were made
  for seeing,
Then Beauty is its own excuse for
  being.   *Ib.*

For Nature beats in perfect tune,
And rounds with rhyme her every rune,
Whether she work in land or sea,
Or hide underground her alchemy.
Thou canst not wave thy staff in air,
Or dip thy paddle in the lake,
But it carves the bow of beauty there,
And the ripples in rhymes the oar for-
  sake.   *Ib. Woodnotes II*

Things are in the saddle,
And ride mankind.
      *Ib. Ode Inscribed to
                    W. H. Channing*

There are two laws discrete,
Not reconciled —
Law for man, and law for thing.   *Ib.*

Olympian bards who sung
  Divine ideas below,

Which always find us young,
And always keep us so.
                    Poems. Ode to Beauty

Give all to love;
Obey thy heart;
Friends, kindred, days,
Estate, good fame,
Plans, credit and the Muse,
Nothing refuse.
                    Ib. Give All to Love, st. 1

Heartily know,
When half-gods go,
The gods arrive.   *Ib. st. 4*

Love not the flower they pluck, and
    know it not,
And all their botany is Latin names.
                    Ib. Blight

By the rude bridge that arched the
    flood,
Their flag to April's breeze unfurled,
Here once the embattled farmers stood,
And fired the shot heard round the
    world.
                    *Ib. Hymn Sung at the Com-
                    pletion of the Battle Monu-
                    ment, Concord [July 4, 1837],
                    st. 1*

Hast thou named all the birds without
    a gun? [1]
Loved the wood-rose, and left it on its
    stalk? [2]   *Ib. Forbearance*

"Pass in, pass in," the angels say,
"In to the upper doors,
Nor count compartments of the floors,
But mount to paradise
By the stairway of surprise."
                    Ib. Merlin I

God said, I am tired of kings,
I suffer them no more;
Up to my ear the morning brings
The outrage of the poor.
                    *May-Day and Other Pieces
                    [1867]. Boston Hymn,[3] st. 2*

[1] See S. W. Foss, p. 846a.
[2] See Lytton, p. 741b.
[3] Read at a celebration in Boston of Emancipation Day, January 1, 1863.

Today unbind the captive,
So only are ye unbound;
Lift up a people from the dust,
Trump of their rescue, sound!
                    *May-Day and Other Pieces.
                    Boston Hymn, st. 17*

Oh, tenderly the haughty day
Fills his blue urn with fire.
                    Ib. Ode, st. 1

Go put your creed into your deed,
Nor speak with double tongue.
                    Ib. st. 5

I think no virtue goes with size.
                    Ib. The Titmouse

So nigh is grandeur to our dust,
    So near is God to man,
When Duty whispers low, *Thou must,*
    The youth replies, *I can.*
                    Ib. Voluntaries, III

Nor sequent centuries could hit
Orbit and sum of Shakespeare's wit.
                    Ib. Solution

Born for success he seemed,
With grace to win, with heart to hold,
With shining gifts that took all eyes.
                    Ib. In Memoriam E.B.E.

Nor mourn the unalterable Days
That Genius goes and Folly stays.
                    Ib.

Fear not, then, thou child infirm,
There's no god dare wrong a worm.
                    Ib. Compensation, I

He thought it happier to be dead,
To die for Beauty, than live for bread.
                    Ib. Beauty

Wilt thou seal up the avenues of ill?
Pay every debt, as if God wrote the bill.
                    Ib. "Suum Cuique"

Too busied with the crowded hour to
    fear to live or die.   *Ib. Nature*

Daughters of Time, the hypocritic
    Days,
Muffled and dumb like barefoot
    dervishes,
And marching single in an endless file,
Bring diadems and fagots in their
    hands.   *Ib. Days*

I, too late,
Under her solemn fillet saw the scorn.
     May-Day and Other Pieces.
                Days

It is time to be old,
To take in sail.   *Ib. Terminus*

Obey the voice at eve obeyed at prime.
                  Ib.

Though love repine, and reason chafe,
There came a voice without reply —
" 'Tis man's perdition to be safe,
When for the truth he ought to
die."   *Ib. Sacrifice*

For what avail the plow or sail,
Or land or life, if freedom fail?
         Ib. Boston, st. 5

If the red slayer think he slays,
   Or if the slain think he is slain,
They know not well the subtle ways
   I keep, and pass, and turn again.[1]
           Ib. Brahma

They reckon ill who leave me out;
   When me they fly, I am the wings;
I am the doubter and the doubt,
   And I the hymn the Brahmin sings.
                  Ib.

That book is good
Which puts me in a working mood.
Unless to Thought is added Will,
Apollo is an imbecile.
     Ib. Fragments on the Poetic Gift

In the vaunted works of Art
The master stroke is Nature's part.[2]
               Ib. Art

I am the owner of the sphere,
Of the seven stars and the solar year,
Of Caesar's hand, and Plato's brain,
Of Lord Christ's heart, and Shake-
speare's strain.   *Ib. History*

Ever from one who comes tomorrow
Men wait their good and truth to borrow.   *Ib. Merlin's Song*

[1] See *The Upanishads*, p. 62a.

[2] Nature paints the best part of a picture,
carves the best part of the statue, builds the
best part of the house, and speaks the best part
of the oration. — *Society and Solitude* [1870], *Art*

The music that can deepest reach,
And cure all ill, is cordial speech.
     May-Day and Other Pieces.
               Merlin's Song

Some of your hurts you have cured,
And the sharpest you still have sur-
     vived,
But what torments of grief you en-
     dured
From evils which never arrived! [1]
     Ib. Borrowing [from the French]

A ruddy drop of manly blood
   The surging sea outweighs,
The world uncertain comes and goes,
   The lover rooted stays.
          Ib. Friendship

To different minds, the same world is
a hell, and a heaven.
     Journal [December 20, 1822]

Four snakes gliding up and down a
hollow for no purpose that I could see
— not to eat, not for love, but only
gliding.   *Ib. [April 11, 1834]*

I wish to write such rhymes as shall
not suggest a restraint, but contrariwise
the wildest freedom.
         Ib. [June 27, 1839]

You shall have joy, or you shall have
power, said God; you shall not have
both.   *Ib. [October 1842]*

The sky is the daily bread of the
eyes.   *Ib. [May 25, 1843]*

Poetry must be as new as foam, and
as old as the rock.   *Ib. [March 1845]*

I hate quotations. Tell me what you
know.   *Ib. [May 1849]*

Blessed are those who have no talent!
        Ib. [February 1850]

The word *liberty* in the mouth of
Mr. Webster sounds like the word *love*
in the mouth of a courtesan.
     Ib. [February 12 (?), 1851]

[1] Let us be of good cheer, however, remembering that the misfortunes hardest to bear are
those which never come. — JAMES RUSSELL LOW-
ELL, *Democracy and Addresses* [1884]

I trust a good deal to common fame, as we all must. If a man has good corn, or wood, or boards, or pigs, to sell, or can make better chairs or knives, crucibles or church organs, than anybody else, you will find a broad hard-beaten road to his house, though it be in the woods.[1]
Journal [February 1855]

The blazing evidence of immortality is our dissatisfaction with any other solution.   *Ib. [July 1855]*

Undoubtedly we have no questions to ask which are unanswerable. We must trust the perfection of the creation so far as to believe that whatever curiosity the order of things has awakened in our minds, the order of things can satisfy.
Nature [1836], introduction

Nature never wears a mean appearance. Neither does the wisest man extort her secret and lose his curiosity by finding out all her perfection.   *Ib. sec. 1*

Give me health and a day and I will make the pomp of emperors ridiculous.
Ib. sec. 3

Every natural fact is a symbol of some spiritual fact.   *Ib. sec. 4*

We are like Nebuchadnezzar, dethroned, bereft of reason, and eating grass like an ox.   *Ib. sec. 8*

A man is a god in ruins.[2]   *Ib.*

[1] The editors, E. W. EMERSON and W. E. FORBES, appended a footnote: "There has been much inquiry in the newspapers recently as to whether Mr. Emerson wrote a sentence very like the above which has been attributed to him in print. The Editors do not find the latter in his works, but there can be little doubt that it was a memory quotation by some hearer, or, quite probably, correctly reported from one of his lectures, the same image in differing words."
If a man can write a better book, preach a better sermon, or make a better mousetrap than his neighbor, though he builds his house in the woods the world will make a beaten path to his door. — SARAH S. B. YULE AND MARY S. KEENE, *Borrowings* [1889], *reported by Mrs. Yule as having been used by Emerson in an address*
[2] See Lamartine, p. 565b.

He who has mastered any law in his private thoughts, is master to that extent of all men whose language he speaks, and of all into whose language his own can be translated.
The American Scholar [1837], sec. 3

Wherever Macdonald sits, there is the head of the table.[1]   *Ib.*

What would we really know the meaning of? The meal in the firkin; the milk in the pan; the ballad in the street; the news of the boat.   *Ib.*

If the single man plant himself indomitably on his instincts, and there abide, the huge world will come round to him.[2]   *Ib.*

Men grind and grind in the mill of a truism, and nothing comes out but what was put in. But the moment they desert the tradition for a spontaneous thought, then poetry, wit, hope, virtue, learning, anecdote, all flock to their aid.
Literary Ethics [1838]

Time dissipates to shining ether the solid angularity of facts.
Essays: First Series [1841]. History

There is properly no history; only biography.[3]   *Ib.*

Nature is a mutable cloud, which is always and never the same.   *Ib.*

It is the fault of our rhetoric that we cannot strongly state one fact without seeming to belie some other.   *Ib.*

To believe your own thought, to believe that what is true for you in your private heart is true for all men — that is genius.   *Ib. Self-Reliance*

[1] Emerson's sentence is usually quoted with the substitution of "Macgregor" for "Macdonald."
[2] See Disraeli, p. 612a.
All things come round to him who will but wait. — LONGFELLOW, *Tales of a Wayside Inn, The Student's Tale* [1863]
[3] See Carlyle, p. 577a.

We but half express ourselves, and are ashamed of that divine idea which each of us represents.

> *Essays: First Series.*
> *Self Reliance*

Accept the place the divine providence has found for you, the society of your contemporaries. the connection of events. *Ib.*

Society everywhere is in conspiracy against the manhood of every one of its members. . . . The virtue in most request is conformity. Self-reliance is its aversion. It loves not realities and creators, but names and customs. *Ib.*

Whoso would be a man must be a nonconformist. *Ib.*

The doctrine of hatred must be preached, as the counteraction of the doctrine of love, when that pules and whines. I shun father and mother and wife and brother when my genius calls me. *Ib.*

It is easy in the world to live after the world's opinion; it is easy in solitude to live after our own; but the great man is he who in the midst of the crowd keeps with perfect sweetness the independence of solitude. *Ib.*

A foolish consistency is the hobgoblin of little minds adored by little statesmen and philosophers and divines.[1] *Ib.*

To be great is to be misunderstood. *Ib.*

An institution is the lengthened shadow of one man. *Ib.*

I like the silent church before the service begins, better than any preaching. *Ib.*

Discontent is the want of self-reliance: it is infirmity of will. *Ib.*

Traveling is a fool's paradise. . . . My giant goes with me wherever I go. *Ib.*

[1] See William Allen White, p. 896b.

For every Stoic was a Stoic; but in Christendom where is the Christian? [1]

> *Essays: First Series.*
> *Self Reliance*

Nothing can bring you peace but yourself. *Ib.*

Every sweet has its sour; every evil its good. *Ib. Compensation*

For every thing you have missed, you have gained something else; and for every thing you gain, you lose something else. *Ib.*

Everything in Nature contains all the powers of Nature. Everything is made of one hidden stuff. *Ib.*

It is as impossible for a man to be cheated by anyone but himself, as for a thing to be, and not to be, at the same time. *Ib.*

All mankind love a lover.

> *Ib. Love*

Thou art to me a delicious torment.

> *Ib. Friendship*

Almost all people descend to meet.[2] *Ib.*

Happy is the house that shelters a friend. *Ib.*

A friend is a person with whom I may be sincere. Before him, I may think aloud. *Ib.*

A friend may well be reckoned the masterpiece of Nature. *Ib.*

Two may talk and one may hear, but three cannot take part in a conversation of the most sincere and searching sort. *Ib.*

The only reward of virtue is virtue; the only way to have a friend is to be one. *Ib.*

I do then with my friends as I do with my books. I would have them where I can find them, but I seldom use them. *Ib.*

[1] See Melville, p. 695b.
[2] Men descend to meet. — EMERSON, *Essays. First Series. The Over-Soul*

In skating over thin ice our safety is in our speed.
Essays: First Series. Prudence

Heroism feels and never reasons and therefore is always right.
Ib. Heroism

Beware when the great God lets loose a thinker on this planet. *Ib. Circles*

One man's justice is another's injustice; one man's beauty another's ugliness; one man's wisdom another's folly.
Ib.

Nature abhors the old, and old age seems the only disease; [1] all others run into this one. *Ib.*

Nothing great was ever achieved without enthusiasm. *Ib.*

Nothing astonishes men so much as common sense and plain dealing.
Ib. Art

Beauty will not come at the call of a legislature, nor will it repeat in England or America its history in Greece. It will come, as always, unannounced, and spring up between the feet of brave and earnest men. *Ib.*

I fancy I need more than another to speak (rather than write), with such a formidable tendency to the lapidary style. I build my house of boulders.
Letter to Carlyle [October 30, 1841]

A man may love a paradox without either losing his wit or his honesty.
Walter Savage Landor [Dial, 1841], XII

Literature is the effort of man to indemnify himself for the wrongs of his condition. *Ib.*

There is always a certain meanness in the argument of conservatism, joined with a certain superiority in its fact.
The Conservative [1842]

For it is not meters, but a meter-making argument that makes a

poem — a thought so passionate and alive that like the spirit of a plant or an animal it has an architecture of its own, and adorns nature with a new thing.
Essays: Second Series [1844].
The Poet

Nature and books belong to the eyes that see them. *Ib. Experience*

Of what use is genius, if the organ is too convex or too concave and cannot find a focal distance within the actual horizon of human life? *Ib.*

The only gift is a portion of thyself.[1]
Ib. Gifts

The less government we have, the better — the fewer laws, and the less confided power. *Ib. Politics*

We think our civilization near its meridian, but we are yet only at the cock-crowing and the morning star. In our barbarous society the influence of character is in its infancy. *Ib.*

Money, which represents the prose of life, and which is hardly spoken of in parlors without an apology, is, in its effects and laws, as beautiful as roses.
Ib. Nominalist and Realist

Every man is wanted, and no man is wanted much. *Ib.*

The reward of a thing well done, is to have done it. *Ib.*

He is great who is what he is from Nature, and who never reminds us of others.
Representative Men [1850].
Uses of Great Men

When nature removes a great man, people explore the horizon for a successor; but none comes, and none will. His class is extinguished with him. In some other and quite different field, the next man will appear. *Ib.*

Every hero becomes a bore at last.
Ib.

---

[1] Old age is an incurable disease. — SENECA, *Epistulae ad Lucilium, no. 108*

[1] See Lowell, p. 692b, and Whitman, p. 700b.

Great geniuses have the shortest biographies.

> *Representative Men. Plato; or, The Philosopher*

Things added to things, as statistics, civil history, are inventories. Things used as language are inexhaustibly attractive. *Ib.*

Keep cool: it will be all one a hundred years hence.[1]

> *Ib. Montaigne; or, The Skeptic*

Is not marriage an open question, when it is alleged, from the beginning of the world, that such as are in the institution wish to get out, and such as are out wish to get in? [2] *Ib.*

The Pilgrims came to Plymouth in 1620. The plays of Shakespeare were not published until three years later. Had they been published earlier, our forefathers, or the most poetical among them, might have stayed at home to read them. *Ib. Shakespeare*

Self-reliance, the height and perfection of man, is reliance on God.

> *The Fugitive Slave Law* [1854]

Classics which at home are drowsily read have a strange charm in a country inn, or in the transom of a merchant brig. *English Traits* [1856]

Men are what their mothers made them.

> *Conduct of Life* [1860]. *Fate*

Coal is a portable climate.

> *Ib. Wealth*

The world is his, who has money to go over it. *Ib.*

Art is a jealous mistress.[3] *Ib.*

All educated Americans, first or last, go to Europe. *Ib. Culture*

Solitude, the safeguard of mediocrity, is to genius the stern friend. *Ib.*

[1] What matters what anybody thinks? "It will be all the same a hundred years hence." That is the most sensible proverb ever invented. — GEORGE DU MAURIER, *Peter Ibbetson* [1891]
[2] See Montaigne, p. 190b, and note.
[3] See Story, p. 543b.

There is always a best way of doing everything, if it be to boil an egg. Manners are the happy ways of doing things.

> *Conduct of Life. Behavior*

Fine manners need the support of fine manners in others. *Ib.*

The highest compact we can make with our fellow is — "Let there be truth between us two forevermore." *Ib.*

Shallow men believe in luck.[1]

> *Ib. Worship*

Our chief want in life is somebody who shall make us do what we can.

> *Ib. Considerations by the Way*

Make yourself necessary to somebody. *Ib.*

Beauty without grace is the hook without the bait. *Ib. Beauty*

Never read any book that is not a year old. *Ib. In Praise of Books*

The key to the period appeared to be that the mind had become aware of itself. . . . The young men were born with knives in their brain, a tendency to introversion, self-dissection, anatomizing of motives.

> *Life and Letters in New England* [1867]

God may forgive sins, he said, but awkwardness has no forgiveness in heaven or earth.

> *Society and Solitude* [1870], *Society and Solitude*

The most advanced nations are always those who navigate the most.

> *Ib. Civilization*

Hitch your wagon to a star.[2] *Ib.*

The true test of civilization is, not the census, nor the size of cities, nor the crops — no, but the kind of man the country turns out. *Ib.*

[1] Luck is infatuated with the efficient. — *Persian proverb*
[2] See Carl Schurz, p. 733a.

Every genuine work of art has as much reason for being as the earth and the sun.
>   *Society and Solitude. Art*

A masterpiece of art has in the mind a fixed place in the chain of being, as much as a plant or a crystal.   *Ib.*

We boil at different degrees.
>   *Ib. Eloquence*

The best university that can be recommended to a man of ideas is the gauntlet of the mobs.   *Ib.*

The ornament of a house is the friends who frequent it.
>   *Ib. Domestic Life*

Can anybody remember when the times were not hard and money not scarce?   *Ib. Works and Days*

'Tis the good reader that makes the good book; in every book he finds passages which seem confidences or asides hidden from all else and unmistakably meant for his ear; the profit of books is according to the sensibility of the reader; the profoundest thought or passion sleeps as in a mine, until it is discovered by an equal mind and heart.   *Ib. Success*

We do not count a man's years until he has nothing else to count.
>   *Ib. Old Age*

A mollusk is a cheap edition [of man] with a suppression of the costlier illustrations, designed for dingy circulation, for shelving in an oyster-bank or among the seaweed.
>   *Power and Laws of Thought*
>   *[c. 1870]*

Poetry teaches the enormous force of a few words, and, in proportion to the inspiration, checks loquacity.
>   *Parnassus [1874]. Preface*

There are two classes of poets — the poets by education and practice, these we respect; and poets by nature, these we love.   *Ib.*

Life is not so short but that there is always time enough for courtesy.
>   *Letters and Social Aims [1876].*
>   *Social Aims*

I have heard with admiring submission the experience of the lady who declared that the sense of being perfectly well-dressed gives a feeling of inward tranquillity which religion is powerless to bestow.   *Ib.*

Do not say things. What you are stands over you the while, and thunders so that I cannot hear what you say to the contrary.   *Ib.*

Great men are they who see that spiritual is stronger than any material force, that thoughts rule the world.
>   *Ib. Progress and Culture, Phi*
>   *Beta Kappa Address [July 18,*
>   *1876]*

Next to the originator of a good sentence is the first quoter of it.[1]
>   *Ib. Quotation and Originality*

When Shakespeare is charged with debts to his authors, Landor replies, "Yet he was more original than his originals. He breathed upon dead bodies and brought them into life."
>   *Ib.*

By necessity, by proclivity, and by delight, we all quote.   *Ib.*

A good symbol is the best argument, and is a missionary to persuade thousands.   *Ib. Poetry and Imagination*

Wit makes its own welcome, and levels all distinctions.
>   *Ib. The Comic*

The perception of the comic is a tie of sympathy with other men.   *Ib.*

---

[1] There is not less wit nor less invention in applying rightly a thought one finds in a book, than in being the first author of that thought. — BAYLE, *Dictionnaire Historique et Critique* [1697–1702]

Though old the thought and oft exprest, 'Tis his at last who says it best.
>   JAMES RUSSELL LOWELL, *For an Auto-*
>   *graph* [1868]

What is a weed? A plant whose virtues have not yet been discovered.[1]
Fortune of the Republic [1878]

To live without duties is obscene.
Lectures and Biographical Sketches [1883]. *Aristocracy*

Speak the affirmative; emphasize your choice by utter ignoring of all that you reject. *Ib. The Preacher*

Genius has no taste for weaving sand. *Ib. The Scholar*

A poet in verse or prose must have a sensuous eye, but an intellectual co-perception. *Ib. Plutarch*

All thoughts of a turtle are turtles, and of a rabbit, rabbits.
The Natural History of Intellect [1893]

When you strike at a king, you must kill him.
Recollected by OLIVER WENDELL HOLMES, JR. *From* MAX LERNER, *The Mind and Faith of Justice Holmes* [1943]

ROBERT STEPHEN HAWKER
1803–1875

And shall Trelawny die?
Here's twenty thousand Cornish men
Will know the reason why.
The Song of the Western Men [1825],[2] *st. 1*

---

[1] A weed is no more than a flower in disguise. — JAMES RUSSELL LOWELL, *A Fable for Critics* [1848]

A weed is but an unloved flower! — ELLA WHEELER WILCOX [1850–1919], *The Weed, st. 1*

[2] "And shall Trelawny die?" has been a popular phrase throughout Cornwall since the imprisonment in the Tower of London, in 1688, of Sir Jonathan Trelawny [1650–1721] with six other prelates for refusing to recognize the Declaration of Indulgence issued by James II.

RICHARD HENRY HENGIST HORNE
1803–1884

'Tis always morning somewhere in the world.[1]
Orion [1843], *bk. III, canto 2*

DOUGLAS JERROLD
1803–1857

He is one of those wise philanthropists who in a time of famine would vote for nothing but a supply of toothpicks.
Wit and Opinions of Douglas Jerrold [1859]

Dogmatism is puppyism come to its full growth. *Ib.*

That fellow would vulgarize the day of judgment. *Ib. A Comic Author*

The best thing I know between France and England is — the sea.
Ib. The Anglo-French Alliance

Some people are so fond of ill-luck that they run halfway to meet it.
Ib. Meeting Troubles Halfway

Earth is here [Australia] so kind, that just tickle her with a hoe and she laughs with a harvest.
Ib. A Land of Plenty

The ugliest of trades have their moments of pleasure. Now, if I were a gravedigger, or even a hangman, there are some people I could work for with a great deal of enjoyment.
Ib. Ugly Trades

He was so good he would pour rose-water on a toad.
Ib. A Charitable Man

Talk to him of Jacob's ladder, and he would ask the number of the steps.
Ib. A Matter-of-fact Man

---

[1] See Longfellow, p. 625a.

ROBERT SMITH
SURTEES
1803–1864

Full o' beans and benevolence.
Handley Cross [1843], *ch. 27*

Three things I never lends — my 'oss, my wife, and my name.
Hillingdon Hall [1845], *ch. 33*

More people are flattered into virtue than bullied out of vice.
The Analysis of the Hunting Field [1846], *ch. 1*

Better be killed than frightened to death.
Mr. Facey Romford's Hounds [1864], *ch. 32*

FEDOR TIUTCHEV
1803–1873

A thought, once uttered, is a lie.
Silentium [1830]

Like first love, the heart of Russia will not forget you.
Tribute to Pushkin [*January 29, 1837*]

Homeland of patience, land of the Russian people.
These Poor Villages [1855]

BENJAMIN DISRAELI,
EARL OF
BEACONSFIELD
1804–1881

The microcosm of a public school.
Vivian Grey [1826], *bk. I, ch. 2*

I hate definitions.　　*Ib. II, 6*

Experience is the child of Thought, and Thought is the child of Action. We cannot learn men from books.
Ib. V, 1

Variety is the mother of Enjoyment.
Ib. 4

There is moderation even in excess.
Ib. VI, 1

I repeat . . . that all power is a trust; that we are accountable for its exercise; that, from the people, and for the people, all springs, and all must exist.[1]　　*Vivian Grey bk. VI, ch. 7*

Man is not the creature of circumstances. Circumstances are the creatures of men.　　*Ib.*

A *dark* horse, which had never been thought of, and which the careless St. James had never even observed in the list, rushed past the grandstand in sweeping triumph.
The Young Duke [1831], *bk. I, ch. 5*

Yes, I am a Jew, and when the ancestors of the right honorable gentleman were brutal savages in an unknown island, mine were priests in the temple of Solomon.[2]
Reply to a taunt by Daniel O'Connell

What we anticipate seldom occurs; what we least expected generally happens.
Henrietta Temple [1837], *bk. II, ch. 4*

Though I sit down now, the time will come when you will hear me.[3]
Maiden speech in the House of Commons [1837]

Free trade is not a principle, it is an expedient.[4]
Speech on import duties [*April 25, 1843*]

The noble lord [5] is the Rupert of Parliamentary discussion.
Speech [*April 1844*]

[1] See Wycliffe, p. 163b, and note.
[2] The gentleman will please remember that when his half-civilized ancestors were hunting the wild boar in the forests of Silesia, mine were the princes of the earth. — JUDAH P. BENJAMIN [1811–1884], *reply to a Senator; from* BEN PERLEY POORE, *Reminiscences of Sixty Years in the National Metropolis* [1886]
[3] See Garrison, p. 615b.
[4] See Grover Cleveland, p. 771a.
[5] Lord Stanley.

Youth is a blunder; manhood a struggle; old age a regret.
Coningsby [*1844*], *bk. III, ch. 1*

Property has its duties as well as its rights.[1] *Sybil* [*1845*], *bk. II, ch. 11*

Little things affect little minds.
Ib. III, 2

We all of us live too much in a circle.[2] *Ib. 7*

Mr. Kremlin was distinguished for ignorance; for he had only one idea — and that was wrong.[3] *Ib. IV, 5*

I was told that the privileged and the people formed two nations. *Ib. 8*

The right honorable gentleman[4] caught the Whigs bathing and walked away with their clothes.
Speech, House of Commons [*February 28, 1845*]

A conservative government is an organized hypocrisy.
Speech on Agricultural Interests [*March 17, 1845*]

He was fresh and full of faith that "something would turn up."[5]
Tancred [*1847*], *bk. III, ch. 6*

Everything comes if a man will only wait.[6] *Ib. IV, 8*

A precedent embalms a principle.
Speech on the expenditures of the country [*February 22, 1848*]

Justice is truth in action.
Speech [*February 11, 1851*]

This shows how much easier it is to be critical than to be correct.
Speech [*January 24, 1860*]

---

[1] Property has its duties as well as its rights. — CAPTAIN THOMAS DRUMMOND (inventor of the Drummond light), *Letter to the Landlords of Tipperary* [May 22, 1838]
[2] The life of man is a self-evolving circle. — EMERSON, *Essays* [*1st series*, 1841], *Circles*
[3] See Johnson, p. 431a.
[4] Sir Robert Peel.
[5] See Dickens, p. 671a.
[6] See Emerson, p. 605b.

The characteristic of the present age is craving credulity.
Speech at Oxford Diocesan Conference [*November 25, 1864*]

Is man an ape or an angel?[1] I, my lord, I am on the side of the angels. I repudiate with indignation and abhorrence those newfangled theories. *Ib.*

In the character of the victim [Lincoln], and even in the accessories of his last moments, there is something so homely and innocent that it takes the question, as it were, out of all the pomp of history and the ceremonial of diplomacy — it touches the heart of nations and appeals to the domestic sentiment of mankind.
Speech, House of Commons [*May 1, 1865*]

Ignorance never settles a question.
Ib. [*May 14, 1866*]

Individualities may form communities, but it is institutions alone that can create a nation.
Speech at Manchester [*1866*]

However gradual may be the growth of confidence, that of credit requires still more time to arrive at maturity.
Speech [*November 9, 1867*]

When a man fell into his anecdotage, it was a sign for him to retire.
Lothair [*1870*], *ch. 28*

Every woman should marry — and no man. *Ib. 30*

You know who the critics are? The men who have failed in literature and art.[2] *Ib. 35*

"My idea of an agreeable person," said Hugo Bohun, "is a person who agrees with me." *Ib.*

Increased means and increased leisure are the two civilizers of man.
Speech to the Conservatives of Manchester [*April 3, 1872*]

The secret of success is constancy to purpose. *Speech* [*June 24, 1872*]

---

[1] See rascal, p. 363b, and Charles Darwin, p. 628a.
[2] See Coleridge, p. 528a, and Lowell, p. 692b.

A university should be a place of light, of liberty, and of learning.
> *Speech, House of Commons*
> *[March 11, 1873]*

The author who speaks about his own books is almost as bad as a mother who talks about her own children.
> *Speech [November 19, 1873]*

The health of the people is really the foundation upon which all their happiness and all their powers as a state depend.   *Speech [July 24, 1877]*

Lord Salisbury and myself have brought you back peace — but a peace I hope with honor.[1]
> *Speech, House of Commons*
> *[July 16, 1878]*

A series of congratulatory regrets.[2]
> *Speech, Knightsbridge [July 27, 1878]*

A sophistical rhetorician [Gladstone], inebriated with the exuberance of his own verbosity, and gifted with an egotistical imagination that can at all times command an interminable and inconsistent series of arguments to malign an opponent and to glorify himself.   *Ib.*

The harebrained chatter of irresponsible frivolity.
> *Speech, Guildhall, London*
> *[November 9, 1878]*

His Christianity was muscular.
> *Endymion [1880], ch. 14*

The Athanasian Creed is the most splendid ecclesiastical lyric ever poured forth by the genius of man.   *Ib. 52*

"As for that," said Waldershare, "sensible men are all of the same religion." "And pray, what is that?" inquired the prince. "Sensible men never tell."   *Ib. 81*

[1] See Russell, p. 567b, and Chamberlain, p. 897a.
[2] Lord Hartington's Resolution on the Berlin Treaty.

NATHANIEL HAWTHORNE
1804–1864

Amid the seeming confusion of our mysterious world, individuals are so nicely adjusted to a system, and systems to one another and to a whole, that, by stepping aside for a moment, a man exposes himself to a fearful risk of losing his place forever.
> *Wakefield [1835]*

His hour is one of darkness, and adversity, and peril. But should domestic tyranny oppress us, or the invader's step pollute our soil, still may the Gray Champion come, for he is the type of New England's hereditary spirit; and his shadowy march, on the eve of danger, must ever be the pledge, that New England's sons will vindicate their ancestry.
> *The Gray Champion [1835]*

By the sympathy of your human hearts for sin ye shall scent out all the places — whether in church, bedchamber, street, field, or forest — where crime has been committed, and shall exult to behold the whole earth one stain of guilt, one mighty blood spot.
> *Young Goodman Brown [1835]*

As the moral gloom of the world overpowers all systematic gaiety, even so was their home of wild mirth made desolate amid the sad forest.
> *The Maypole of Merrymount [1836]*

"What is the Unpardonable Sin?" asked the lime-burner. . . .
"It is a sin that grew within my own breast," replied Ethan Brand. . . . The sin of an intellect that triumphed over the sense of brotherhood with man and reverence for God."
> *Ethan Brand [1850]*

On the breast of her gown, in red cloth, surrounded with an elaborate embroidery and fantastic flourishes of gold thread, appeared the letter A.
> *The Scarlet Letter [1850], ch. 2*

There is a fatality, a feeling so irresistible and inevitable that it has the force of doom, which almost invariably compels human beings to linger around and haunt, ghostlike, the spot where some great and marked event has given the color to their lifetime; and still the more irresistibly, the darker the tinge that saddens it.
The Scarlet Letter, ch. 5

Wherever there is a heart and an intellect, the diseases of the physical frame are tinged with the peculiarities of these.   *Ib. 9*

Let men tremble to win the hand of woman, unless they win along with it the utmost passion of her heart.
Ib. 15

"Never, never!" whispered she. "What we did had a consecration of its own."   *Ib. 17*

The scarlet letter was her passport into regions where other women dared not tread. Shame, Despair, Solitude! These had been her teachers — stern and wild ones — and they had made her strong, but taught her much amiss.
Ib. 18

No man, for any considerable period, can wear one face to himself, and another to the multitude, without finally getting bewildered as to which may be the true.   *Ib. 20*

Among many morals which press upon us from the poor minister's miserable experience, we put only this into a sentence: "Be true! Be true! Show freely to the world, if not your worst, yet some trait whereby the worst may be inferred."   *Ib. 24*

The book, if you would see anything in it, requires to be read in the clear, brown, twilight atmosphere in which it was written; if opened in the sunshine, it is apt to look exceedingly like a volume of blank pages.
Twice-Told Tales [1851], *preface*

Not to be deficient in this particular, the author has provided himself with a moral — the truth, namely, that the wrongdoing of one generation lives into the successive ones.
The House of the Seven Gables [1851], *preface*

God will give him blood to drink!
Ib. ch. 1

Life is made up of marble and mud.
Ib. 2

What other dungeon is so dark as one's own heart! What jailer so inexorable as one's self!   *Ib. 11*

Of all the events which constitute a person's biography, there is scarcely one . . . to which the world so easily reconciles itself as to his death.
Ib. 21

The greatest obstacle to being heroic is the doubt whether one may not be going to prove one's self a fool; the truest heroism is, to resist the doubt; and the profoundest wisdom, to know when it ought to be resisted, and when to be obeyed.
The Blithedale Romance [1852], *ch. 2*

I am a woman, with every fault, it may be, that a woman ever had — weak, vain, unprincipled (like most of my sex; for our virtues, when we have any, are merely impulsive and intuitive).   *Ib. 25*

It is because the spirit is inestimable that the lifeless body is so little valued.
Ib. 28

In youth men are apt to write more wisely than they really know or feel; and the remainder of life may be not idly spent in realizing and convincing themselves of the wisdom they uttered long ago.
The Snow Image [1852], *preface*

No author, without a trial, can conceive of the difficulty of writing a romance about a country where there is no shadow, no antiquity, no mystery,

no picturesque and gloomy wrong, nor anything but a commonplace prosperity, in broad and simple daylight, as is happily the case with my dear native land. . . . Romance and poetry, ivy, lichens and wallflowers need ruin to make them grow.
The Marble Faun [1860], *preface*

This greatest mortal consolation, which we derive from the transitoriness of all things — from the right of saying, in every conjuncture, "This, too, will pass away." [1]   *Ib. ch. 16*

Nobody, I think, ought to read poetry, or look at pictures or statues, who cannot find a great deal more in them than the poet or artist has actually expressed. [2]   *Ib. 41*

Mountains are earth's undecaying monuments.
Sketches from Memory [1868].
The Notch of the White Mountains

CHARLES AUGUSTIN SAINTE-BEUVE
1804–1869

Vigny, more secret,
As if in his tower of ivory, retired before noon. [3]
Pensées d'Août, à M. Villemain
[1837], *st. 3*

Silence is the sovereign contempt. [4]
Mes Poisons

[1] See Lincoln, p. 636b.
[2] Every book is written with a constant secret reference to the few intelligent persons whom the writer believes to exist in the million. . . . The artist has always the masters in his eye. — EMERSON, *Progress of Culture* [1867]
[3] Vigny, plus secret,
Comme en sa tour d'ivoire, avant midi, rentrait.
The poet, retired in his Tower of Ivory, isolated, according to his desire, from the world of man, resembles, whether he so wishes or not, another solitary figure, the watcher enclosed for months at a time in a lighthouse at the head of a cliff. — JULES DE GAULTIER [b. 1858], *La Guerre et les Destinées de l'Art*
[4] Le silence seul est le souverain mépris.

SARAH FLOWER ADAMS
1805–1848

Yet in my dreams I'd be
Nearer, my God, to Thee,
Nearer to Thee.
Nearer, My God, to Thee, st. 2

He sendeth sun, He sendeth shower.
Hymn, first line and title

WILLIAM LLOYD GARRISON
1805–1879

Our country is the world — our countrymen are all mankind. [1]
Motto of the Liberator [1831]

Let Southern oppressors tremble — let their secret abettors tremble — let their Northern apologists tremble — let all the enemies of the persecuted blacks tremble.
The Liberator, no. 1
[*January 1, 1831*]

I will be as harsh as truth and as uncompromising as justice. On this subject I do not wish to think, or speak, or write, with moderation. No! No! Tell a man whose house is on fire to give a moderate alarm; tell him to moderately rescue his wife from the hands of the ravisher; tell the mother to gradually extricate her babe from the fire into which it has fallen; but urge me not to use moderation. [2]   *Ib.*

I am in earnest — I will not equivocate — I will not excuse — I will not retreat a single inch; and I will be heard! [3]   *Ib.*

The compact which exists between the North and the South is a covenant with death and an agreement with hell. [4]
Resolution adopted by the Anti-Slavery Society [*January 27, 1843*]

[1] See Socrates, p. 87b, and note.
[2] See Paine, p. 467b.
[3] See Disraeli, p. 611b.
[4] See *Isaiah 28:15*, p. 32a.

With reasonable men, I will reason; with humane men I will plead; but to tyrants I will give no quarter, nor waste arguments where they will certainly be lost.

W. P. AND F. J. T. GARRISON, *William Lloyd Garrison* [1885–1889], *vol. I, p. 188*

Since the creation of the world there has been no tyrant like Intemperance, and no slaves so cruelly treated as his.
Ib. p. 268

We may be personally defeated, but our principles never. *Ib. p. 402*

Wherever there is a human being, I see God-given rights inherent in that being, whatever may be the sex or complexion. *Ib. III, p. 390*

You cannot possibly have a broader basis for any government than that which includes all the people, with all their rights in their hands, and with an equal power to maintain their rights.[1]
Ib. IV, p. 224

COLONEL
SIDNEY SHERMAN
1805–1873

Remember the Alamo![2]
Battle cry, San Jacinto [April 21, 1836]; attributed

ALEXIS
DE TOCQUEVILLE
1805–1859

I know of no country, indeed, where the love of money has taken stronger hold on the affections of men and where a profounder contempt is expressed for the theory of the permanent equality of property.
Democracy in America,[1] pt. I [1835], ch. 3

Within these limits the power vested in the American courts of justice of pronouncing a statute to be unconstitutional forms one of the most powerful barriers that have ever been devised against the tyranny of political assemblies. *Ib. 6*

I have never been more struck by the good sense and the practical judgment of the Americans than in the manner in which they elude the numberless difficulties resulting from their Federal Constitution. *Ib. 8*

In this question, therefore, there is no medium between servitude and license; in order to enjoy the inestimable benefits that the liberty of the press ensures, it is necessary to submit to the inevitable evils that it creates. *Ib. 9*

They [the Americans] have all a lively faith in the perfectibility of man, they judge that the diffusion of knowledge must necessarily be advantageous, and the consequences of ignorance fatal; they all consider society as a body in a state of improvement, humanity as a changing scene, in which nothing is, or ought to be, permanent; and they admit that what appears to them today to be good, may be superseded by something better tomorrow. *Ib. 18*

America is a land of wonders, in which everything is in constant motion and every change seems an improvement. The idea of novelty is there indissolubly connected with the idea of amelioration. No natural boundary seems to be set to the efforts of man; and in his eyes what is not yet done is only what he has not yet attempted to do. *Ib.*

Democratic nations care but little for what has been, but they are haunted by

---

[1] See Wycliffe, p. 163b; Webster, p. 547a; Lincoln, p. 639a; and Parker, p. 657b.

[2] On March 6, 1836, five days after Texas declared her independence from Mexico, President Antonio López de Santa Anna attacked the Alamo, the fortified mission at San Antonio; captured it after every Texan had been killed or wounded; and put the wounded to death. He was defeated and captured at San Jacinto [April 21, 1836] by the Texas army under Commander in Chief Samuel Houston.

[1] The Henry Reeve text, as revised by Francis Bowen, corrected and edited by Phillips Bradley [1945].

visions of what will be; in this direction their unbounded imagination grows and dilates beyond all measure. . . . Democracy, which shuts the past against the poet, opens the future before him.
Democracy in America, pt. II
[1840], bk. I, ch. 17

Thus not only does democracy make every man forget his ancestors, but it hides his descendants and separates his contemporaries from him; it throws him back forever upon himself alone and threatens in the end to confine him entirely within the solitude of his own heart. *Ib. bk. II, ch. 2*

If I were asked . . . to what the singular prosperity and growing strength of that people [the Americans] ought mainly to be attributed, I should reply: To the superiority of their women. *Ib. bk. III, ch. 12*

The love of wealth is therefore to be traced, as either a principal or accessory motive, at the bottom of all that the Americans do; this gives to all their passions a sort of family likeness. . . . It may be said that it is the vehemence of their desires that makes the Americans so methodical; it perturbs their minds, but it disciplines their lives.
Ib. 17

SAMUEL WILBERFORCE[1]
1805–1873

If I were a cassowary
  On the plains of Timbuctoo,
I would eat a missionary,
  Cassock, band,[2] and hymnbook,
  too. *Impromptu*

ELIZABETH BARRETT BROWNING
1806–1861

Thou large-brained woman and large-hearted man.
To George Sand, A Desire
[1844]

[1] Bishop of Oxford, and later of Winchester — nicknamed "Soapy Sam."
[2] Variant: Skin and bones.

Or from Browning some "Pomegranate," which, if cut deep down the middle,
Shows a heart within blood-tinctured of a veined humanity.
Lady Geraldine's Courtship
[1844], st. 41

Life treads on life, and heart on heart;
We press too close in church and mart
To keep a dream or grave apart.
A Vision of Poets [1844],
conclusion, l. 1

Knowledge by suffering entereth,
And life is perfected by death.
Ib. last lines

And I smiled to think God's greatness flowed around our incompleteness —
Round our restlessness, His rest.
Rime of the Duchess May
[1844], conclusion, st. 11

Do ye hear the children weeping, O my brothers,
Ere the sorrow comes with years?
The Cry of the Children [1844],
st. 1

The child's sob in the silence curses deeper
Than the strong man in his wrath.
Ib. st. 13

I tell you hopeless grief is passionless.
Grief [1844], l. 1

Therefore to this dog will I,
Tenderly not scornfully,
  Render praise and favor:
With my hand upon his head,
Is my benediction said
  Therefore and forever.
To Flush, My Dog [1844], st. 14

And lips say "God be pitiful,"
Who ne'er said "God be praised."
The Cry of the Human [1844],
st. 1

And kings crept out again to feel the sun.
Crowned and Buried [1844],
st. 11

"Yes," I answered you last night;
"No," this morning, sir, I say:
Colors seen by candlelight
Will not look the same by day.[1]
        The Lady's "Yes" [1844], *st. 1*

By thunders of white silence overthrown.
        Hiram Power's Greek Slave
        [1850], *last line*

Unless you can muse in a crowd all
day
On the absent face that fixed you;
Unless you can love, as the angels
may,
With the breadth of heaven betwixt
you;
Unless you can dream that his faith is
fast,
Through behoving and unbehoving;
Unless you can die when the dream is
past —
Oh, never call it loving!
        A Woman's Shortcomings
        [1850], *st. 5*

"Guess now who holds thee?" —
"Death," I said. But there
The silver answer rang — "Not Death,
but Love."
        Sonnets from the Portuguese
        [1850], *no. 1*

Go from me. Yet I feel that I shall
stand
Henceforward in thy shadow.   *Ib. 6*

If thou must love me, let it be for
naught
Except for love's sake only.   *Ib. 14*

When our two souls stand up erect and
strong,
Face to face, silent, drawing nigh and
nigher.   *Ib. 22*

[1] To say why gals acts so or so,
Or don't, 'ould be presumin';
Mebby to mean *yes* an' say *no*
Comes nateral to women.
    JAMES RUSSELL LOWELL, *The Biglow
        Papers, series II* [1867], *st. 18*
And if I loved you Wednesday,
Well, what is that to you?
I do not love you Thursday —
So much is true.
    EDNA ST. VINCENT MILLAY [1892–1950],
        Thursday

God only, who made us rich, can make
us poor.
        Sonnets from the Portuguese,
        no. 24

Because God's gifts put man's best
dreams to shame.   *Ib. 26*

How do I love thee? Let me count the
ways.
I love thee to the depth and breadth
and height
My soul can reach, when feeling out of
sight
For the ends of Being and ideal Grace.
        Ib. 43

I love thee with a love I seemed to
lose
With my lost saints — I love thee with
the breath,
Smiles, tears, of all my life! — and, if
God choose,
I shall but love thee better after death.
        Ib.

Life, struck sharp on death,
Makes awful lightning.
        Aurora Leigh [1] [1857], *bk. I, l. 210*

As sings the lark when sucked up out of
sight
In vortices of glory and blue air.
        Ib. l. 1055

I should not dare to call my soul my
own.   *Ib. II, l. 786*

God answers sharp and sudden on some
prayers,
And thrusts the thing we have prayed
for in our face,
A gauntlet with a gift in 't.
        Ib. l. 952

How many desolate creatures on the
earth
Have learnt the simple dues of fellowship
And social comfort, in a hospital.
        Ib. III, l. 1122

A little sunburnt by the glare of life.
        Ib. IV, l. 1140

Since when was genius found respectable?   *Ib. VI, l. 275*

[1] See Edward Fitzgerald, p. 631a.

Earth's crammed with heaven,
And every common bush afire with
    God;
But only he who sees takes off his
    shoes;
The rest sit round it and pluck black-
    berries.
      Aurora Leigh, bk. VII, l. 820

What was he doing, the great god Pan,
    Down in the reeds by the river?
Spreading ruin and scattering ban,
Splashing and paddling with hoofs of a
    goat,
And breaking the golden lilies afloat
    With the dragonfly on the river.
      A Musical Instrument [1860]

Grief may be joy misunderstood;
Only the Good discerns the good.
      De Profundis [1862], *st. 21*

FRIEDRICH HALM
[ELIGIUS FRANZ
JOSEF VON MÜNCH-
BELLINGHAUSEN]
1806–1871

Two souls with but a single thought,
Two hearts that beat as one.[1]
    Der Sohn der Wildness [1842],
        act II

JOHN STUART MILL
1806–1873

The sole end for which mankind are
warranted, individually or collectively,
in interfering with the liberty of action of any of their number is self-
protection.
    Liberty [1859], *introduction*

If all mankind minus one, were of
one opinion, and only one person were
of the contrary opinion, mankind
would be no more justified in silencing
that one person, than he, if he had the
power, would be justified in silencing
mankind.   *Ib. ch. 2*

[1] Zwei Sellen und en Gedanke,
  Zwei Herzen und ein Schlag!
  Translated by MARIA LOVELL.

We can never be sure that the opinion we are endeavoring to stifle is a false
opinion; and if we were sure, stifling it
would be an evil still.   *Liberty, ch. 2*

The liberty of the individual must be
thus far limited; he must not make
himself a nuisance to other people.
      Ib. 3

All good things which exist are the
fruits of originality.   *Ib.*

Liberty consists in doing what one
desires.   *Ib. 5*

The worth of a state, in the long run,
is the worth of the individuals composing it.   *Ib.*

Unearned increment.
    Dissertations and Discussions
        [1859]

It is better to be Socrates dissatisfied
than a pig satisfied.
      Utilitarianism [1863]

Ask yourself whether you are happy,
and you cease to be so.
      Autobiography [1873], *ch. 5*

JOHANN BERNHARD
GRAF VON RECHBERG
1806–1899

Guarantees which are not worth the
paper they are written on.
    In a dispatch concerning the
    recognition of Italy [1861]

NATHANIEL PARKER
WILLIS
1806–1867

The sin forgiven by Christ in Heaven
By man is cursed alway.
      Unseen Spirits, st. 5

CHARLES FRANCIS
ADAMS
1807–1886

It would be superfluous in me to
point out to your Lordship that this is
war.

    Dispatch to Earl Russell
    [*September 5, 1863*]

JEAN LOUIS RODOLPHE AGASSIZ
1807–1873

The world has arisen in some way or another. How it originated is the great question, and Darwin's theory, like all other attempts to explain the origin of life, is thus far merely conjectural. I believe he has not even made the best conjecture possible in the present state of our knowledge.

Evolution and Permanence of Type [1874]

GIUSEPPE GARIBALDI
1807–1882

I offer neither pay, nor quarters, nor provisions; I offer hunger, thirst, forced marches, battles and death. Let him who loves his country in his heart, and not with his lips only, follow me.[1]

From G. M. TREVELYAN, *Garibaldi's Defense of the Roman Republic* [1907–1911].

ROBERT EDWARD LEE
1807–1870

It is well that war is so terrible, or we should get too fond of it.[2]

On seeing a Federal charge repulsed at Fredericksburg [December 1862]

Duty is the sublimest word in our language. Do your duty in all things. You cannot do more. You should never wish to do less.

Inscribed beneath his bust in the Hall of Fame

Let the tent be struck.

Last words [October 12, 1870]

HENRY WADSWORTH LONGFELLOW
1807–1882

Music is the universal language of mankind — poetry their universal pastime and delight.

Outre-Mer [1833–1834]

[1] See Prescott, p. 587a, and Churchill, p. 920b.
[2] See William T. Sherman, p. 705a.

I heard the trailing garments of the Night
Sweep through her marble halls.

Hymn to Night [1839], st. 1

Tell me not, in mournful numbers,
Life is but an empty dream!
For the soul is dead that slumbers,
And things are not what they seem.[1]
Life is real! Life is earnest!
And the grave is not its goal;
Dust thou art, to dust returnest,
Was not spoken of the soul.

A Psalm of Life [1839], st. 1, 2

Art is long, and Time is fleeting,[2]
And our hearts, though stout and brave,
Still, like muffled drums, are beating
Funeral marches to the grave.[3]

Ib. st. 4

Trust no Future, howe'er pleasant!
Let the dead Past bury its dead! [4]
Act — act in the living present!
Heart within, and God o'erhead!

Lives of great men all remind us
We can make our lives sublime,
And, departing, leave behind us
Footprints on the sands of time.

Ib. st. 6, 7

Let us, then, be up and doing,
With a heart for any fate; [5]
Still achieving, still pursuing,
Learn to labor and to wait.   *Ib. st. 9*

There is a Reaper whose name is Death,
And, with his sickle keen,
He reaps the bearded grain at a breath,
And the flowers that grow between.

The Reaper and the Flowers [1839], st. 1

The hooded clouds, like friars,
Tell their beads in drops of rain.

Midnight Mass for the Dying Year [1839], st. 4

[1] See Phaedrus, p. 129b, and W. S. Gilbert, p. 766a.
[2] See Hippocrates, p. 88b, and Goethe, p. 477b.
[3] Our lives are but our marches to the grave. — BEAUMONT AND FLETCHER, *The Humorous Lieutenant* [1619], act III, sc. 5
[4] See *Matthew 8:22*, p. 41b.
[5] See Byron, p. 559b.

Who ne'er his bread in sorrow ate,
Who ne'er the mournful midnight
    hours
Weeping upon his bed has sate,
He knows you not, ye Heavenly Pow-
    ers.[1]
    Hyperion [1839], *bk. I, motto*

Look not mournfully into the Past. It
comes not back again. Wisely improve
the Present. It is thine. Go forth to
meet the shadowy Future, without fear,
and with a manly heart.[2] *Ib. IV, ch. 8*

Skoal! to the Northland! skoal!
Thus the tale ended.
    The Skeleton in Armor
        [1841], *st. 20*

It was the schooner Hesperus,
    That sailed the wintry sea;
And the skipper had taken his little
    daughter,
    To bear him company.
    The Wreck of the Hesperus
        [1842], *st. 1*

But the father answered never a word,
    A frozen corpse was he.   *Ib. st. 12*

Christ save us all from a death like this,
    On the reef of Norman's Woe!
        Ib. st. 22

Under the spreading chestnut tree
    The village smithy stands;
The smith a mighty man is he
    With large and sinewy hands.
And the muscles of his brawny arms
Are strong as iron bands.
    The Village Blacksmith [1842],
        st. 1

His brow is wet with honest sweat,
    He earns whate'er he can,

---

[1] Wer nie sein Brod mit Tränen ass,
   Wer nie die kummervollen Nächte
   Auf seinem Bette weinend sass,
   Der kennt euch nicht, ihr himmlischen
   Mächte.
    GOETHE, *Wilhelm Meister's Apprentice-*
       ship [1786–1830], *bk. II, ch. 13*
  See Goethe, p. 477a.
[2] Blicke nicht trauernd in die Vergangenheit,
   Sie kommt nicht wieder, nutze weise die
   Gegenwart,
   Sie ist dein, der düsteren Zukunft geh ohne
   Furcht mit männliche Sinne entgegen.
    Inscription, Chapel of St. Gilgen, near
       Salzburg

And looks the whole world in the face,
    For he owes not any man.
    The Village Blacksmith, st. 2

Something attempted, something done,
Has earned a night's repose.   *Ib. st. 7*

No one is so accursed by fate,
No one so utterly desolate,
But some heart, though unknown,
Responds unto his own.
    Endymion [1842], *st. 8*

Into each life some rain must fall,
Some days must be dark and dreary.
    The Rainy Day [1842], *st. 3*

I like that ancient Saxon phrase, which
    calls
The burial ground God's Acre!
    God's Acre [1842], *st. 1*

Standing with reluctant feet,
Where the brook and river meet,
Womanhood and childhood fleet!
    Maidenhood [1842], *st. 3*

A banner with the strange device,
    Excelsior!   *Excelsior* [1842], *st. 1*

Stars of the summer night!
    Far in yon azure deeps,
Hide, hide your golden light!
    She sleeps!
    My lady sleeps!
    Sleeps!
    The Spanish Student [1843],
       act I, sc. 3 [*serenade*]

She floats upon the river of his
    thoughts.   *Ib. II, 3*

I stood on the bridge at midnight,
    As the clocks were striking the hour.
    The Bridge [1845]

The day is done, and the darkness
    Falls from the wings of Night,
As a feather is wafted downward
    From an eagle in his flight.
    The Day Is Done [1845], *st. 1*

A feeling of sadness and longing,
    That is not akin to pain,
And resembles sorrow only
    As the mist resembles the rain.
    Ib. st. 3

Some simple and heartfelt lay.
> *The Day Is Done, st. 4*

The bards sublime,
Whose distant footsteps echo
Through the corridors of Time.
> *Ib. st. 5*

And the night shall be filled with
     music,
And the cares, that infest the day,
Shall fold their tents, like the Arabs,
And as silently steal away. *Ib. st. 11*

The horologe of Eternity
Sayeth this incessantly —
"Forever — never!
Never — forever!"
> *The Old Clock on the Stairs*
> *[1845], st. 9*

I shot an arrow into the air,
It fell to earth, I knew not where.
> *The Arrow and the Song [1845],*
> *st. 1*

And the song, from beginning to end,
I found in the heart of a friend.
> *Ib. st. 3*

This is the forest primeval. The mur-
     muring pines and the hem-
     locks . . .
Stand like Druids of old.
> *Evangeline [1847], l. 1*

Alike were they free from
Fear, that reigns with the tyrant, and
     envy, the vice of republics.
> *Ib. pt. I, sec. 1*

When she had passed, it seemed like
the ceasing of exquisite music.
> *Ib.*

Silently one by one, in the infinite
     meadows of heaven
Blossomed the lovely stars, the forget-
     me-nots of the angels.   *Ib. 3*

Talk not of wasted affection! affection
     never was wasted;
If it enrich not the heart of another, its
     waters, returning
Back to their springs, like the rain, shall
     fill them full of refreshment:

That which the fountain sends forth re-
     turns again to the fountain.
> *Evangeline, pt. II, sec. 1*

Give what you have. To someone, it
may be better than you dare to think.
> *Kavanagh [1849]*

Build me straight, O worthy Master!
Staunch and strong, a goodly vessel,
That shall laugh at all disaster,
And with wave and whirlwind wrestle!
> *The Building of the Ship*
> *[1849], l. 1*

And see! she stirs!
She starts — she moves — she seems to
     feel
The thrill of life along her keel.
> *Ib. l. 349*

Sail on, O Ship of State!
Sail on, O Union, strong and great!
Humanity with all its fears,
With all the hopes of future years,
Is hanging breathless on thy fate!
> *Ib. l. 378*

Our hearts, our hopes, are all with thee,
Our hearts, our hopes, our prayers, our
     tears,
Our faith triumphant o'er our fears,
Are all with thee — are all with thee!
> *Ib. l. 396*

There is no fireside, howsoe'er de-
     fended,
But has one vacant chair!
> *Resignation [1849], st. 1*

There is no Death! What seems so is
     transition;
This life of mortal breath
Is but a suburb of the life elysian,
Whose portal we call Death.
> *Ib. st. 5*

Nothing useless is, or low;
Each thing in its place is best;
And what seems but idle show
Strengthens and supports the rest.
> *The Builders [1849], st. 2*

God sent his Singers upon earth
With songs of sadness and of mirth.
> *The Singers [1849], st. 1*

But the great Master said, "I see
No best in kind, but in degree;
I gave a various gift to each,
To charm, to strengthen, and to
    teach."   *The Singers, st. 6*

All your strength is in your union.
All your danger is in discord;
Therefore be at peace henceforward,
And as brothers live together.
    The Song of Hiawatha [1855],
        pt. I

By the shores of Gitche Gumee,
By the shining Big-Sea-Water,
Stood the wigwam of Nokomis,
Daughter of the Moon, Nokomis.
    Ib. III

From the waterfall he named her,
Minnehaha, Laughing Water.
    Ib. IV

As unto the bow the cord is,
So unto the man is woman,
Though she bends him, she obeys him,
Though she draws him, yet she fol-
    lows,
Useless each without the other!
    Ib. X

If we could read the secret history of
our enemies, we should find in each
man's life sorrow and suffering enough
to disarm all hostility.
    Driftwood [1857]

If I am not worth the wooing, I surely
    am not worth the winning.
    The Courtship of Miles Standish
        [1858], *pt. III*

"Why don't you speak for yourself,
John?" [1]   *Ib.*

Saint Augustine! well hast thou said,
    That of our vices we can frame
A ladder, if we will but tread
    Beneath our feet each deed of
    shame.[2]
    The Ladder of St. Augustine
        [1858], *st. 1*

The heights by great men reached and
    kept

[1] See Shakespeare, p. 246a.
[2] See St. Augustine, p. 147a, and Tennyson, p. 649b.

Were not attained by sudden flight,
But they, while their companions slept,
Were toiling upward in the night.
    The Ladder of St. Augustine,
        st. 10

The long mysterious Exodus of death.
    The Jewish Cemetery at New-
        port [1858], *st. 1*

A boy's will is the wind's will,
And the thoughts of youth are long,
    long thoughts.
    My Lost Youth [1858], *refrain*

A Lady with a Lamp [1] shall stand
In the great history of the land,
A noble type of good,
Heroic womanhood.
    Santa Filomena [1858], *st. 10*

Ye are better than all the ballads
    That ever were sung or said;
For ye are living poems,
    And all the rest are dead.
    Children [1858], *st. 9*

Between the dark and the daylight,
When the night is beginning to
    lower,
Comes a pause in the day's occupa-
    tions,
That is known as the Children's
    Hour.
    The Children's Hour [1860],
        st. 1

I hear in the chamber above me
The patter of little feet.   *Ib. st. 2*

Grave Alice, and laughing Allegra,
And Edith with golden hair.
    Ib. st. 3

Listen, my children, and you shall
    hear,
Of the midnight ride of Paul Revere,
On the eighteenth of April, in Seventy-
    five;
Hardly a man is now alive
Who remembers that famous day and
    year.
    Tales of a Wayside Inn [1863–
    1874], *pt. I, The Landlord's*
    Tale: Paul Revere's Ride, st. 1

[1] Florence Nightingale [1820–1910].

One if by land, and two if by sea; [1]
And I on the opposite shore will be,
Ready to ride and spread the alarm
Through every Middlesex village and
farm.
> *Tales of a Wayside Inn, pt. I,*
> *Paul Revere's Ride, st. 2*

The fate of a nation was riding that
night.   *Ib. st. 8*

He seemed the incarnate "Well, I told
you so!"
> *Ib. The Poet's Tale: The Birds*
> *of Killingworth, st. 9*

Ships that pass in the night, and speak
each other in passing,
Only a signal shown and a distant voice
in the darkness;
So on the ocean of life we pass and
speak one another,[2]
Only a look and a voice; then darkness
again and a silence.
> *Ib. pt. III, The Theologian's*
> *Tale: Elizabeth, IV*

Time has laid his hand
Upon my heart, gently, not smiting it,
But as a harper lays his open palm
Upon his harp to deaden its vibra-
tions.
> *The Golden Legend* [1872],
> *pt. IV, The Cloisters*

The grave itself is but a covered bridge
Leading from light to light, through a
brief darkness.[3]
> *Ib. V, A Covered Bridge at*
> *Lucerne*

Don't cross the bridge till you come to
it,

[1] See Paul Revere, p. 464b.
[2] And soon, too soon, we part with pain,
   To sail o'er silent seas again.
      THOMAS MOORE [1779–1852], *Meeting*
                    of the Ships
   Two lives that once part are as ships that
divide. — EDWARD BULWER-LYTTON [1803–1873],
A Lament
   As vessels starting from ports thousands of
miles apart pass close to each other in the naked
breadths of the ocean, nay, sometimes even touch
in the dark. — OLIVER WENDELL HOLMES, *Professor at the Breakfast Table* [1860]
   [3] Death seems but a covered way
   Which opens into light.
      WHITTIER [1807–1892], *My Psalm, st. 14*

Is a proverb old, and of excellent wit.
> *The Golden Legend, pt. VI,*
> *The School of Salerno*

Let him not boast who puts his armor
on
As he who puts if off, the battle done.
> *Morituri Salutamus* [1875],
> *st. 9*

Ye, against whose familiar names not
yet
The fatal asterisk of death is set.
> *Ib. st. 11*

The love of learning, the sequestered
nooks,
And all the sweet serenity of books.
> *Ib. st. 21*

Ah, nothing is too late,
Till the tired heart shall cease to palpi-
tate.   *Ib. st. 22*

For age is opportunity no less
Than youth itself.   *Ib. st. 24*

Not in the clamor of the crowded
street,
Not in the shouts and plaudits of the
throng,
But in ourselves, are triumph and defeat.   *The Poets*

Nothing that is can pause or stay;
The moon will wax, the moon will
wane,
The mist and cloud will turn to rain,
The rain to mist and cloud again,
Tomorrow be today.
> *Kéramos* [1878]

Three silences there are: the first of
speech,
The second of desire, the third of
thought;
This is the lore a Spanish monk, distraught
With dreams and visions, was the first
to teach.
> *The Three Silences of Molinos* [1]

In the long, sleepless watches of the
night.
> *The Cross of Snow* [1879]

[1] Miguel Molinos [1640–1696], Spanish mystic,
one of the early Quietists.

The holiest of all holidays are those
Kept by ourselves in silence and apart;
The secret anniversaries of the heart.
Holidays

Your silent tents of green [1]
   We deck with fragrant flowers;
Yours has the suffering been,
   The memory shall be ours.
Decoration Day, st. 6

Great is the art of beginning, but
   greater the art is of ending;
Many a poem is marred by a superfluous verse.
Elegiac Verse, st. 14

There was a little girl
Who had a little curl
Right in the middle of her forehead;
   And when she was good
   She was very, very good,
But when she was bad she was horrid.
There Was a Little Girl [2]

Out of the shadows of night
The world rolls into light;
It is daybreak everywhere.[3]
The Bells of San Blas,[4] *st. 11*

ROBERT MONTGOMERY
1807–1855

The soul aspiring pants its source to
   mount,
As streams meander level with their
   fount.[5]
The Omnipresence of the Deity
[1828], pt. I

[1]   The low green tent
Whose curtain never outward swings.
   WHITTIER, *Snowbound* [1866]
[2] BLANCHE ROOSEVELT TUCKER, in *The Home Life of Henry W. Longfellow* [1882], states that these lines were written by the poet for his children on a day when Edith did not want to have her hair curled.
[3] See Horne, p. 610b.
[4] The last poem written by Longfellow, dated March 15, 1882. He died March 24.
[5] We take this to be, on the whole, the worst similitude in the world. In the first place, no stream meanders or can possibly meander level with the fount. In the next place, if streams did meander level with their founts, no two motions

JOHN GREENLEAF WHITTIER
1807–1892

No fetters in the Bay State — no slave
   upon our land!
Massachusetts to Virginia
[1843], st. 24

What calls back the past, like the rich
   pumpkin pie?
The Pumpkin [1844], *st. 3*

The Present, the Present is all thou
   hast
   For thy sure possessing;
Like the patriarch's angel hold it fast
   Till it gives its blessing.[1]
My Soul and I [1847], *st. 34*

The Night is mother of the Day,
   The Winter of the Spring,
And ever upon old Decay
   The greenest mosses cling.
A Dream of Summer [1847], *st. 4*

So fallen! so lost! the light withdrawn
   Which once he wore!
The glory from his gray hairs gone
   Forevermore!
Ichabod [2] *[1850], st. 1*

From those great eyes
   The soul has fled:
When faith is lost, when honor dies,
   The man is dead!   *Ib. st. 8*

can be less like each other than that of meandering level and that of mounting upwards. — MACAULAY, *Review of Montgomery's Poems* [1830]
   These lines were omitted in the subsequent edition of the poem.
[1] See *Genesis 32:26,* p. 7b, and Cotton, p. 421a.
[2] This poem was the outcome of the surprise and grief and forecast of evil consequences which I felt on reading the seventh of March speech of Daniel Webster in support of the "compromise," and the Fugitive Slave Law. No partisan or personal enmity dictated it. On the contrary my admiration of the splendid personality and intellectual power of the great senator was never stronger than when I laid down his speech, and, in one of the saddest moments of my life, penned my protest. — WHITTIER's *Note*
   And she named the child Ichabod, saying, The glory is departed from Israel. — *I Samuel 4:21*

Search thine own heart. What paineth thee
In others in thyself may be.
The Chapel of the Hermits
[1853], st. 85

Blessings on thee, little man,
Barefoot boy, with cheek of tan!
The Barefoot Boy [1856], st. 1

Health that mocks the doctor's rules,
Knowledge never learned of schools.
Ib. st. 2

The age is dull and mean. Men creep,
Not walk.
Lines Inscribed to Friends under
Arrest for Treason Against the
Slave Power [1856], st. 1

Nature speaks in symbols and in signs.
To Charles Sumner

For of all sad words of tongue or pen,
The saddest are these: "It might have been!"
Maud Muller [1856], st. 53

Old Floyd Ireson, for his hard heart,
Tarred and feathered and carried in a cart
By the women of Marblehead.
Skipper Ireson's Ride [1860],
st. 1

Round the silver domes of Lucknow,
Moslem mosque and Pagan shrine,
Breathed the air to Britons dearest,
The air of Auld Lang Syne.[1]
The Pipes at Lucknow, st. 9

The windows of my soul I throw
Wide open to the sun.
My Psalm, st. 2

Up from the meadows rich with corn,
Clear in the cool September morn.
Barbara Frietchie [1864], st. 1

The clustered spires of Frederick stand
Green-walled by the hills of Maryland.
Ib. st. 2

[1] See Burns, p. 494b.
It was the pipes of the Highlanders,
And now they played "Auld Lang Syne."
ROBERT TRAILL SPENCE LOWELL [1816–1891], *The Relief of Lucknow* [September 25, 1857]

"Shoot, if you must, this old gray head,
But spare your country's flag," she said.
Barbara Frietchie, st. 18

"Who touches a hair of yon gray head
Dies like a dog! March on!" he said.
Ib. st. 21

The sun that brief December day
Rose cheerless over hills of gray,
And, darkly circled, gave at noon
A sadder light than waning moon.
Snowbound [1866], l. 1

Shut in from all the world without,
We sat the clean-winged hearth about.
Ib. l. 155

Angel of the backward look.
Ib. l. 714

I know not where His islands lift
Their fronded palms in air;
I only know I cannot drift
Beyond His love and care.
The Eternal Goodness [1867],
st. 20

Dear Lord and Father of mankind,
Forgive our foolish ways!
Reclothe us in our rightful mind,
In purer lives Thy service find,
In deeper reverence, praise.
The Brewing of Soma [1872]

God is and all is well.[1]
My Birthday, st. 2

He brings cool dew in his little bill,
And lets it fall on the souls of sin:
You can see the mark on his red breast still
Of fires that scorch as he drops it in.[2]
The Robin, st. 4

[1] See Browning, p. 661b.
[2] Far, far away, is a land of woe and darkness, spirits of evil and fire. Day after day a little bird flies there, bearing in his bill a drop of water to quench the flame. So near the burning stream does he fly that his feathers are scorched by it, and hence he is named "Bron-rhuddyn" — breast-burned. — *Carmarthenshire legend of the robin*
Sweet Robin, I have heard them say
That thou wert there upon the day
That Christ was crowned in cruel scorn,
And bore away one bleeding thorn;
That so the blush upon thy breast

SALMON PORTLAND CHASE
1808–1873

The only way to resumption is to resume.

Letter to Horace Greeley
[March 17, 1866]

The Constitution, in all its provisions, looks to an indestructible Union composed of indestructible States.

Decision in Texas v. White, 7
Wallace 725 [1868]

ANDREW JOHNSON
1808–1875

We are swinging round the circle.

On the Presidential Reconstruction Tour [August 1866]

ALPHONSE KARR
1808–1890

The more things change, the more they remain the same.[1]

Les Guêpes [Janvier, 1849]

MAURICE DE MACMAHON
1808–1893

Here I am, and here I stay.[2]

At Sevastopol [September 1855]

THOMAS MILLER
1808–1874

Christmas comes but once a year.

Title of poem

In shameful sorrow was imprest,
And thence thy genial sympathy
With our redeemed humanity.
  WILLIAM CROSWELL DOANE [1832–1913],
Robin Redbreast

[1] Plus ça change, plus c'est la même chose.
[2] J'y suis, j'y reste.

Reply to the commander in chief, from the trenches before Malakoff, in the siege of Sevastopol, when warned to beware of an explosion which might follow the retreat of the Russians.

CAROLINE SHERIDAN NORTON
1808–1877

Love not! love not! ye hapless sons of clay;
Hope's gayest wreaths are made of earthly flowers.

Love Not, st. 1

A soldier of the Legion lay dying in Algiers;
There was lack of woman's nursing, there was dearth of woman's tears.

Bingen on the Rhine, st. 1

GEORGE WASHINGTON PATTEN
1808–1882

If we must perish in the fight,
Oh! let us die like men.

Oh! Let Us Die Like Men, st. 4

SAMUEL FRANCIS SMITH
1808–1895

My country, 'tis of thee,
Sweet land of liberty,
  Of thee I sing:
Land where my fathers died,
Land of the pilgrims' pride,
From every mountainside
  Let freedom ring.

America [1831], st. 1

Long may our land be bright
With freedom's holy light;
Protect us by thy might,
  Great God, our King!   *Ib. st. 4*

CHARLES ROBERT DARWIN
1809–1882

I have called this principle, by which each slight variation, if useful, is preserved, by the term Natural Selection.

The Origin of Species [1859],
ch. 3

The expression often used by Mr. Herbert Spencer, of the Survival of the

Fittest, is more accurate, and is sometimes equally convenient.[1]

The Origin of Species, ch. 3

We will now discuss in a little more detail the Struggle for Existence.[2]

Ib.

It is interesting to contemplate an entangled bank, clothed with many plants of many kinds, with birds singing on the bushes, with various insects flitting about, and with worms crawling through the damp earth, and to reflect that these elaborately constructed forms, so different from each other, and dependent on each other in so complex a manner, have all been produced by laws acting around us.   *Ib.*

The highest possible stage in moral culture is when we recognize that we ought to control our thoughts.

The Descent of Man [1871], *ch. 4*

The presence of a body of well-instructed men, who have not to labor for their daily bread, is important to a degree which cannot be overestimated; as all high intellectual work is carried on by them, and on such work material progress of all kinds mainly depends, not to mention other and higher advantages.   *Ib. 5*

Progress has been much more general than retrogression.   *Ib.*

The Simiadae then branched off into two great stems, the New World and Old World monkeys; and from the latter at a remote period, Man, the wonder and the glory of the universe, proceeded.[3]   *Ib. 6*

---

[1] This survival of the fittest which I have here sought to express in mechanical terms, is that which Mr. Darwin has called "natural selection, or the preservation of favored races in the struggle for life." — HERBERT SPENCER, *Principles of Biology* [1864–1867], *Indirect Equilibration*

[2] The perpetual struggle for room and food. — MALTHUS, *On Population* [1798], *ch. 3*

[3] I confess freely to you, I could never look long upon a monkey, without very mortifying reflections. — CONGREVE, *Letter to Dennis* [1695] See Disraeli, p. 612b.

Man scans with scrupulous care the character and pedigree of his horses, cattle, and dogs before he matches them; but when he comes to his own marriage he rarely, or never, takes any such care.

The Descent of Man, ch. 21

For my own part I would as soon be descended from that heroic little monkey, who braved his dreaded enemy in order to save the life of his keeper; or from that old baboon, who, descending from the mountains, carried away in triumph his young comrade from a crowd of astonished dogs — as from a savage who delights to torture his enemies, offers up bloody sacrifices, practices infanticide without remorse, treats his wives like slaves, knows no decency, and is haunted by the grossest superstitions.   *Ib.*

The plow is one of the most ancient and most valuable of man's inventions; but long before he existed the land was in fact regularly plowed, and still continues to be thus plowed by earthworms. It may be doubted whether there are many other animals which have played so important a part in the history of the world, as have these lowly organized creatures.

The Formation of Vegetable Mold Through the Action of Worms [1881], *ch. 7*

Physiological experiment on animals is justifiable for real investigation, but not for mere damnable and detestable curiosity.

Letter to E. Ray Lankester

As for a future life, every man must judge for himself between conflicting vague probabilities.

From Life and Letters of Charles Darwin, edited by FRANCIS DARWIN [1887]

I love fools' experiments. I am always making them.   *Ib.*

Believing as I do that man in the distant future will be a far more perfect creature than he now is, it is an intolerable thought that he and all other sentient beings are doomed to complete annihilation after such long-continued slow progress. To those who fully admit the immortality of the human soul, the destruction of our world will not appear so dreadful.

From Life and Letters
of Charles Darwin

EDWARD FITZGERALD
1809–1883

Wake! For the Sun who scatter'd into flight
The Stars before him from the Field of night,
Drives Night along with them from Heav'n and strikes
The Sultan's Turret with a Shaft of Light.

The Rubáiyát of Omar
Khayyám,[1] *st. 1*

Awake! for Morning in the Bowl of Night
Has flung the Stone that puts the Stars to flight:
And Lo! the Hunter of the East has caught
The Sultan's Turret in a Noose of Light.   *Ib.* [*first ed.*]

Now the New Year reviving old Desires,
The thoughtful Soul to Solitude retires.   *Ib. st. 4*

Iram indeed is gone with all his Rose.
Ib. st. 5

Come, fill the Cup, and in the fire of Spring
The Winter garment of Repentance fling:
The Bird of Time has but a little way
To fly — and Lo! the Bird is on the Wing.   *Ib. st. 7* [*first ed.*]

The Leaves of Life keep falling one by one.   *Ib. st. 8*

[1] Translated in four editions, 1859, 1868, 1872, and 1879. The fourth edition is used here, unless otherwise stated.

Each Morn a thousand Roses brings, you say:
Yes, but where leaves the Rose of Yesterday?

The Rubáiyát of Omar
Khayyám, st. 9

A Book of Verses underneath the Bough,
A Jug of Wine, a Loaf of Bread — and Thou
Beside me singing in the Wilderness —
Oh, Wilderness were Paradise enow!
Ib. st. 12

Ah, take the Cash, and let the Credit go,
Nor heed the rumble of a distant Drum!   *Ib. st. 13*

The Worldly Hope men set their Hearts upon
Turns Ashes — or it prospers; and anon,
Like Snow upon the Desert's dusty Face,
Lighting a little hour or two — is gone.   *Ib. st. 16*

Think, in this batter'd Caravanserai
Whose Portals are alternate Night and Day,
How Sultan after Sultan with his Pomp
Abode his destin'd Hour, and went his way.   *Ib. st. 17*

They say the Lion and the Lizard keep
The Courts where Jamshyd gloried and drank deep:
And Bahram, that great Hunter — the Wild Ass
Stamps o'er his Head, but cannot break his sleep.   *Ib. st. 18*

I sometimes think that never blows so red
The Rose as where some buried Caesar bled;
That every Hyacinth the Garden wears
Dropt in her Lap from some once lovely Head.[1]   *Ib. st. 19*

[1] See Shakespeare, p. 266a, and Tennyson, p. 650a.

Ah, my Belovèd, fill the Cup that clears
Today of past Regrets and future
Fears:
Tomorrow! — Why, Tomorrow I may
be
Myself with Yesterday's Sev'n thousand
Years.[1]
The Rubáiyát of Omar
Khayyám, st. 21

For some we loved, the loveliest and
the best
That from his Vintage rolling Time
hath prest.   *Ib. st. 22*

Ah, make the most of what we yet may
spend,
Before we too into the Dust descend;
Dust into Dust, and under Dust, to
lie,
Sans Wine, sans Song, sans Singer,
and — sans End!   *Ib. st. 24*

Myself when young did eagerly frequent
Doctor and Saint, and heard great
argument
About it and about: but evermore
Came out by the same door wherein I
went.   *Ib. st. 27*

And this was all the Harvest that I
reap'd —
"I came like Water, and like Wind I
go."   *Ib. st. 28*

There was the Door to which I found
no Key;
There was the Veil through which I
might not see.
Some little talk awhile of Me and
Thee
There was — and then no more of
Thee and Me.   *Ib. st. 32*

"While you live,
Drink! — for, once dead, you never
shall return."   *Ib. st. 35*

And fear not lest Existence closing
your
Account, and mine, should know the
like no more;
The Eternal Saki from that Bowl has
pour'd

[1] See Euripides, p. 84a.

Millions of Bubbles like us, and will
pour.[1]
The Rubáiyát of Omar
Khayyám, st. 46

'Tis all a Checkerboard of Nights and
Days
Where Destiny with Men for Pieces
plays:
Hither and thither moves, and mates,
and slays,
·And one by one back in the Closet
lays.   *Ib. st. 49 [first ed.]*

Striking from the Calendar
Unborn Tomorrow and dead Yesterday.   *Ib. st. 57*

The Moving Finger writes; and, having
writ,
Moves on: nor all your Piety nor Wit
Shall lure it back to cancel half a Line,
Nor all your Tears wash out a Word of
it.   *Ib. st. 71*

That inverted Bowl we call The Sky,
Whereunder crawling coop'd we live
and die.   *Ib. st. 72 [first ed.]*

Ah, Moon of my Delight who know'st
no wane.   *Ib. st. 74 [first ed.]*

One Flash of it within the Tavern
caught
Better than in the Temple lost outright.   *Ib. st. 77*

And He that with his hand the Vessel
made
Will surely not in after Wrath destroy.   *Ib. st. 85*

After a momentary silence spake
Some Vessel of a more ungainly Make;
"They sneer at me for leaning all
awry:
What! did the Hand then of the Potter
shake?"   *Ib. st. 86*

Who *is* the Potter, pray, and who the
Pot?   *Ib. st. 87*

Indeed the Idols I have loved so long
Have done my credit in this World
much wrong:
Have drown'd my Glory in a shallow
Cup,

[1] See Tennyson, p. 644b.

And sold my Reputation for a Song.
The Rubáiyát of Omar Khayyám, st. 93

I wonder often what the Vintners buy
One half so precious as the stuff they
sell. *Ib. st. 95*

Yet Ah, that Spring should vanish with
the Rose!
That Youth's sweet-scented manuscript
should close! *Ib. st. 96*

Ah Love! could you and I with Him
conspire
To grasp this Sorry Scheme of Things
entire,
Would not we shatter it to bits — and
then
Remold it nearer to the Heart's Desire!
Ib. st. 99

And when like her, O Saki, you shall
pass
Among the Guests Star-scatter'd on the
Grass,
And in your joyous errand reach the
spot
Where I made One — turn down an
empty Glass! *Ib. st. 101*

The King in a carriage may ride,
And the Beggar may crawl at his side;
But in the general race,
They are traveling all the same pace.
Chronomoros

Mrs. Browning's death was rather a
relief to me, I must say; no more Aurora Leighs, thank God!
Letter [July 15, 1861] [1]

Taste is the feminine of genius.
*Letter to James Russell Lowell
[October 1877]*

[1] Aye, dead! and were yourself alive, good Fitz,
How to return your thanks would pass my
wits.
Kicking you seems the common lot of curs,
While more appropriate greeting lends you
grace.
Surely to spit there glorifies your face,
Spitting with lips once sanctified by Hers.
ROBERT BROWNING in *The Athenaeum*
[July 13, 1889]

WILLIAM EWART GLADSTONE
1809–1898

Decision by majorities is as much an
expedient as lighting by gas.
*Speech, House of Commons
[1858]*

You cannot fight against the future.
Time is on our side.
Speech on the Reform Bill [1866]

[The Turks] one and all, bag and
baggage, shall, I hope, clear out from
the province they have desolated and
profaned.
*Speech, House of Commons
[May 7, 1877]*

The disease of an evil conscience is
beyond the practice of all the physicians of all the countries in the world.
Speech, Plumstead [1878]

National injustice is the surest road
to national downfall. *Ib.*

Out of the range of practical politics.
*Speech, Dalkeith [November 26,
1879]*

The resources of civilization are not
yet exhausted.
Speech, Leeds [October 7, 1881]

All the world over, I will back the
masses against the classes.
Speech, Liverpool [June 28, 1886]

I have always regarded that Constitution as the most remarkable work
known to me in modern times to have
been produced by the human intellect,
at a single stroke (so to speak), in its
application to political affairs.[1]
*Letter to the committee in
charge of the celebration of
the centennial anniversary
of the American Constitu-
tion [July 20, 1887]*

[1] As the British Constitution is the most subtle
organism which has proceeded from progressive
history, so the American Constitution is the
most wonderful work ever struck off at a given
time by the brain and purpose of man. — GLAD-
STONE, *Kin Beyond the Sea [North American
Review,* September, 1878]

Selfishness is the greatest curse of the human race.
> *Speech, Hawarden* [*May 28, 1890*]

NIKOLAI GOGOL
1809–1852

It is dreary to live in this world, gentlemen!
> *The Tale of How Ivan Ivanovich Quarreled with Ivan Nikiforovich* [1835]

It is no use to blame the looking glass if your face is awry.
> *The Inspector-General* [1836],
> *epigraph*

Of course, Alexander the Great was a hero, but why smash the chairs?   **Ib.**

The more destruction there is everywhere, the more it shows the activity of town authorities.   **Ib. act I, sc. 1**

I tell everyone very plainly that I take bribes, but what kind of bribes? Why, greyhound puppies. That's a totally different matter.   **Ib.**

The sergeant's widow told you a lie when she said I flogged her. I never flogged her. She flogged herself.
> **Ib. IV, 15**

What are you laughing at? You are laughing at yourselves!   **Ib. V, 8**

And for a long time yet, led by some wondrous power, I am fated to journey hand in hand with my strange heroes and to survey the surging immensity of life, to survey it through the laughter that all can see and through the tears unseen and unknown by anyone.
> *Dead Souls* [1842], *vol. I, ch. 11*

Rus! Rus! I see you, from my lovely enchanted remoteness I see you: a country of dinginess, and bleakness and dispersal; no arrogant wonders of nature crowned by the arrogant wonders of art appear within you to delight or terrify the eyes. . . . So what is the incomprehensible secret force driving me towards you? Why do I constantly hear the echo of your mournful song as it is carried from sea to sea through your entire expanse? . . . And since you are without end yourself, is it not within you that a boundless thought will be born? [1]
> *Dead Souls, vol. I, ch. 12*

Oh troika, winged troika, tell me who invented you? Surely, nowhere but among a nimble nation could you have been born: in a country which has taken itself in earnest and has evenly spread far and wide over half of the globe, so that once you start counting the milestones you may count on till a speckled haze dances before your eyes. . . .

Rus, are you not similar in your headlong motion to one of those nimble troikas that none can overtake? The flying road turns into smoke under you, bridges thunder and pass, all falls back and is left behind! . . . And what does this awesome motion mean? What is the passing strange force contained in these passing strange steeds? Steeds, steeds, what steeds! Has the whirlwind a home in your manes? . . . Rus, whither are you speeding so? Answer me. No answer. The middle bell trills out in a dream its liquid soliloquy; the roaring air is torn to pieces and becomes wind; all things on earth fly by and other nations and states gaze askance as they step aside and give her the right of way.[1]
> *Ib. vol. I, concluding paragraphs*

In the course of the reading he [Pushkin] became more and more melancholy and finally became completely gloomy. When the reading was over he uttered in a voice full of sorrow: "Goodness, how sad is our Russia!"
> *Four Letters Concerning Dead Souls* [1843]

I shall laugh my bitter laugh.
> *Epitaph on Gogol's tombstone*

[1] Translated by VLADIMIR NABOKOV in *Nikolai Gogol* [1944].

OLIVER WENDELL HOLMES[1]
1809–1894

Ay, tear her tattered ensign down!
  Long has it waved on high,
And many an eye has danced to see
  That banner in the sky;
Beneath it rung the battle shout,
  And burst the cannon's roar —
The meteor of the ocean air
  Shall sweep the clouds no more.
        Old Ironsides[2] *[1830], st. 1*

One sad, ungathered rose
On my ancestral tree.
        My Aunt, st. 6

And silence, like a poultice, comes
To heal the blows of sound.
        The Music Grinders, st. 10

And since, I never dare to write
As funny as I can.
        The Height of the Ridiculous,
                st. 8

When the last reader reads no more.
        The Last Reader

Age, like distance, lends a double
charm.[3]
        A Rhymed Lesson. Urania

And when you stick on conversation's
  burrs,
Don't strew your pathway with those
  dreadful *urs.*   *Ib.*

Learn the sweet magic of a cheerful
  face;
Not always smiling, but at least serene.
        The Morning Visit

One flag, one land, one heart, one
  hand,
One Nation, evermore!
        Voyage of the Good Ship Union,
                st. 12

Where we love is home,
Home that our feet may leave, but not
  our hearts.
        Homesick in Heaven, st. 5

There is no time like the old time,
  when you and I were young.[1]
        No Time Like the Old Time.
                st. 1

Lean, hungry, savage, anti-everythings.
        A Modest Request. The Speech

A thought is often original, though
you have uttered it a hundred times.
        The Autocrat of the Breakfast
                Table [1858], ch. 1

Everybody likes and respects self-
made men. It is a great deal better to
be made in that way than not to be
made at all.   *Ib.*

Insanity is often the logic of an accurate mind overtaxed.   *Ib. 2*

Man has his will — but woman has
her way!   *Ib.*

Put not your trust in money, but put
your money in trust.   *Ib.*

I find the great thing in this world is
not so much where we stand, as in what
direction we are moving: To reach the
port of heaven, we must sail sometimes
with the wind and sometimes against
it — but we must sail, and not drift,
nor lie at anchor.   *Ib. 4*

Build thee more stately mansions, O
  my soul,
As the swift seasons roll!
Leave thy low-vaulted past!
Let each new temple, nobler than the
  last,
Shut thee from heaven with a dome
  more vast,
Till thou at length art free,

---

[1] The most successful combination the world
has ever seen, of physician and man of letters.
— Sir William Osler. *From* Harvey Cushing,
Life of Sir William Osler [1925], *vol. I, ch. 15*

[2] This poem roused such popular feeling that
it is generally credited with saving the frigate
Constitution from being destroyed as unfit for
service.

[3] See Campbell, p. 537a, and note.

---

[1] The good old times, the grand old times, the
great old times! — Dickens, *The Chimes* [1844],
First Quarter
  There are no days like the good old days,
  The days when we were youthful!
        Eugene Field [1850–1895], *Old Times,*
                Old Friends, Old Love

Leaving thine outgrown shell by life's
  unresting sea!
    *The Autocrat of the Breakfast
    Table,* [*The Chambered Nauti-
    lus, st. 5*]

Sin has many tools, but a lie is the
handle which fits them all.   *Ib. 6*

There is that glorious Epicurean paradox uttered by my friend the Historian,[1] in one of his flashing moments:
"Give us the luxuries of life, and we
will dispense with its necessaries." [2]
                                       Ib.

Boston State-House is the hub of the
solar system. You couldn't pry that out
of a Boston man, if you had the tire of
all creation straightened out for a crowbar.   *Ib.*

The axis of the earth sticks out visibly through the center of each and
every town or city.   *Ib.*

The world's great men have not
commonly been great scholars, nor its
great scholars great men.   *Ib.*

Knowledge and timber shouldn't be
much used till they are seasoned.
                                       Ib.

The hat is the *ultimum moriens* of
respectability.   *Ib. 8*

Have you heard of the wonderful one-
  hoss shay,
That was built in such a logical way
It ran a hundred years to a day?
    Ib. 11. [*The Deacon's Master-
                    piece, st. 1*]

End of the wonderful one-hoss shay.
Logic is logic. That's all I say.
                        Ib. [*st. 12*]

Little I ask; my wants are few,
  I only wish a hut of stone,
(A *very plain* brown stone will do,)
  That I may call my own.[3]
        Ib. [*Contentment, st. 1*]

---

[1] John Lothrop Motley [1814–1877].

[2] Said Scopas of Thessaly, "We rich men count
our felicity and happiness to lie in these super-
fluities, and not in those necessary things." —
PLUTARCH [A.D. 46–120], *On the Love of Wealth*

[3] See Edward Young, p. 339a, and Goldsmith,
p. 448a.

He comes of the Brahmin caste of
New England. This is the harmless, inoffensive, untitled aristocracy.
        *The Brahmin Caste of New
                    England* [1860]

Science is a first-rate piece of furniture for a man's upper chamber, if he
has common sense on the ground floor.
        The Poet at the Breakfast Table
                    [1872], *ch. 5*

And if I should live to be
The last leaf upon the tree
  In the spring,
Let them smile, as I do now,
At the old forsaken bough
  Where I cling.
            The Last Leaf, st. 8

RICHARD MONCKTON MILNES, BARON HOUGHTON

1809–1885

But the beating of my own heart
Was all the sound I heard.
            The Brookside, st. 1

A fair little girl sat under a tree,
Sewing as long as her eyes could see;
Then smoothed her work, and folded it
    right,
And said, "Dear work, good night,
    good night."
        *Good Night and Good Morning,
                                st. 1*

Lady Moon, Lady Moon, where are you
    roving?
Over the sea.
Lady Moon, Lady Moon, whom are
    you loving?
All that love me!   *A Child's Song*

ABRAHAM LINCOLN

1809–1865

If the good people, in their wisdom,
shall see fit to keep me in the background, I have been too familiar with
disappointments to be very much cha-
grined.

    Address, New Salem, Illinois
                [March 9, 1832]

I go for all sharing the privileges of the government who assist in bearing its burdens.

> Letter to Editor, Sangamon Journal, New Salem, Illinois [June 13, 1836]

If destruction be our lot we must ourselves be its author and finisher. As a nation of freemen we must live through all time, or die by suicide.

> Address, Young Men's Lyceum, Springfield, Illinois [January 27, 1838]

There is no grievance that is a fit object of redress by mob law.   *Ib.*

Towering genius disdains a beaten path. It seeks regions hitherto unexplored.   *Ib.*

No man is good enough to govern another man without that other's consent.

> Speech, Peoria, Illinois [October 16, 1854]

I am not a Know-Nothing; that is certain. How could I be? How can anyone who abhors the oppression of Negroes be in favor of degrading classes of white people? Our progress in degeneracy appears to me to be pretty rapid. As a nation we began by declaring that "all men are created equal." We now practically read it "all men are created equal, except Negroes." When the Know-Nothings get control, it will read "all men are created equal, except Negroes and foreigners and Catholics." When it comes to this, I shall prefer emigrating to some country where they make no pretense of loving liberty — to Russia, for instance, where despotism can be taken pure, and without the base alloy of hypocrisy.

> Letter to Joshua F. Speed [August 24, 1855]

The ballot is stronger than the bullet.

> Speech, Bloomington, Illinois [May 19, 1856]

"A house divided against itself cannot stand." [1] I believe this government cannot endure permanently half slave and half free. I do not expect the Union to be dissolved — I do not expect the house to fall — but I do expect it will cease to be divided. It will become all one thing, or all the other. Either the opponents of slavery will arrest the further spread of it, and place it where the public mind shall rest in the belief that it is in the course of ultimate extinction; or its advocates will push it forward till it shall become alike lawful in all the states, old as well as new, North as well as South.

> Speech, Republican State Convention, Springfield, Illinois [June 16, 1858]

Nobody has ever expected me to be President. In my poor, lean, lank face nobody has ever seen that any cabbages were sprouting out.

> Second campaign speech against Douglas,[2] Springfield, Illinois [July 17, 1858]

As I would not be a *slave*, so I would not be a *master*. This expresses my idea of democracy. Whatever differs from this, to the extent of the difference, is no democracy.[3]

> Fragment [August 1, 1858?]. From ROY P. BASLER, The Collected Works of Abraham Lincoln [1953], vol. II, p. 532

When . . . you have succeeded in dehumanizing the Negro; when you have put him down and made it impossible for him to be but as the beasts of the field; when you have extinguished his soul in this world and placed him where the ray of hope is blown out as in the darkness of the damned, are you quite sure that the demon you have

---

[1] See *Mark 3:25*, p. 45a.

[2] They have seen in his [Douglas's] round, jolly, fruitful face, post offices, land offices, marshalships and cabinet appointments, chargé-ships and foreign missions, bursting and sprouting out in wonderful exuberance, ready to be laid hold of by their greedy hands. — *Ib.*

[3] See *Address to Indiana Regiment*, p. 640b.

roused will not turn and rend you? What constitutes the bulwark of our own liberty and independence? It is not our frowning battlements, our bristling sea coasts, our army and our navy. These are not our reliance against tyranny. All of those may be turned against us without making us weaker for the struggle. Our reliance is in the love of liberty which God has planted in us. Our defense is in the spirit which prized liberty as the heritage of all men, in all lands everywhere. Destroy this spirit and you have planted the seeds of despotism at your own doors. Familiarize yourselves with the chains of bondage and you prepare your own limbs to wear them. Accustomed to trample on the rights of others, you have lost the genius of your own independence and become the fit subjects of the first cunning tyrant who rises among you.[1]

Speech, Edwardsville, Illinois
[September 11, 1858]

That is the issue that will continue in this country when these poor tongues of Judge Douglas and myself shall be silent. It is the eternal struggle between these two principles — right and wrong — throughout the world. They are the two principles that have stood face to face from the beginning of time; and will ever continue to struggle. The one is the common right of humanity, and the other the divine right of kings. It is the same principle in whatever shape it develops itself. It is the same spirit that says, "You toil and work and earn bread, and I'll eat it." No matter in what shape it comes, whether from the mouth of a king who seeks to bestride the people of his own nation and live by the fruit of their labor, or from one race of men as an apology for enslaving another race, it is the same tyrannical principle.

Reply, seventh and last joint debate, Alton, Illinois [October 15, 1858]

This is a world of compensation; and

he who would be no slave must consent to have no slave. Those who deny freedom to others deserve it not for themselves, and, under a just God, cannot long retain it.

Letter to H. L. Pierce and others
[April 6, 1859]

It is said an Eastern monarch once charged his wise men to invent him a sentence to be ever in view, and which should be true and appropriate in all times and situations. They presented him the words: "And this, too, shall pass away." [1] How much it expresses! How chastening in the hour of pride! How consoling in the depths of affliction!

Address, Wisconsin State Agricultural Society, Milwaukee [September 30, 1859]

What is conservatism? Is it not adherence to the old and tried, against the new and untried?

Address, Cooper Union, New York [February 27, 1860]

Let us have faith that right makes might, and in that faith let us to the end dare to do our duty as we understand it.   *Ib.*

No one, not in my situation, can appreciate my feeling of sadness at this parting. To this place, and the kindness of these people, I owe everything. Here I have lived a quarter of a century, and have passed from a young to an old man. Here my children have been born, and one is buried. I now leave, not knowing when or whether ever I may return, with a task before me greater than that which rested upon Washington. Without the assistance of that Divine Being who ever attended him, I cannot succeed. With that assistance I cannot fail. Trusting in Him who can go with me, and remain with you, and be everywhere for good, let us confidently hope that all will yet be well.

Farewell Address, Springfield, Illinois [February 11, 1861]

[1] See Einstein, p. 951a.

[1] See Hawthorne, p. 615a.

If we do not make common cause to save the good old ship of the Union on this voyage, nobody will have a chance to pilot her on another voyage.

Address, Cleveland, Ohio [February 15, 1861]

I have never had a feeling, politically, that did not spring from the sentiments embodied in the Declaration of Independence. . . . I have often inquired of myself what great principle or idea it was that kept this Confederacy so long together. It was not the mere matter of separation of the colonies from the motherland, but that sentiment in the Declaration of Independence which gave liberty not alone to the people of this country, but hope to all the world, for all future time. It was that which gave promise that in due time the weights would be lifted from the shoulders of all men, and that all should have an equal chance. This is the sentiment embodied in the Declaration of Independence. . . . I would rather be assassinated on this spot than surrender it.

Speech, Independence Hall, Philadelphia [February 22, 1861]

It is safe to assert that no government proper ever had a provision in its organic law for its own termination.

First Inaugural Address [March 4, 1861]

If by the mere force of numbers a majority should deprive a minority of any clearly written constitutional right, it might, in a moral point of view, justify revolution — certainly would if such a right were a vital one. **Ib.**

This country, with its institutions, belongs to the people who inhabit it. Whenever they shall grow weary of the existing government, they can exercise their constitutional right of amending it, or their revolutionary right to dismember or overthrow it. **Ib.**

Why should there not be a patient confidence in the ultimate justice of the people? Is there any better or equal hope in the world?

First Inaugural Address

While the people retain their virtue and vigilance, no administration, by any extreme of wickedness or folly, can very seriously injure the government in the short space of four years. **Ib.**

We are not enemies, but friends. We must not be enemies. Though passion may have strained, it must not break, our bonds of affection. The mystic chords of memory, stretching from every battlefield and patriot grave to every living heart and hearthstone all over this broad land, will yet swell the chorus of the Union when again touched, as surely they will be, by the better angels of our nature. **Ib.**

I think the necessity of being *ready* increases. Look to it.

Letter (this is the whole message) to Governor Andrew G. Curtin of Pennsylvania [April 8, 1861]

Labor is prior to, and independent of, capital. Capital is only the fruit of labor, and could never have existed if labor had not first existed. Labor is the superior of capital, and deserves much the higher consideration. Capital has its rights, which are as worthy of protection as any other rights.[1]

First Annual Message to Congress [December 3, 1861]

It is difficult to make a man miserable while he feels he is worthy of himself and claims kindred to the great God who made him.

Address on colonization to a Negro deputation at Washington [August 14, 1862]

My paramount object in this struggle is to save the Union, and is not either to save or to destroy slavery. If I could save the Union without freeing any slave, I would do it; and if I could save it by freeing all the slaves, I would do

[1] See Webster, p. 546b.

it; and if I could do it by freeing some and leaving others alone, I would also do that.

Letter to Horace Greeley
[August 22, 1862]

I shall try to correct errors when shown to be errors; and I shall adopt new views so fast as they shall appear to be true views. . . . I intend no modification of my oft-expressed personal wish that all men, everywhere, could be free. *Ib.*

On the first day of January in the year of our Lord, one thousand eight hundred and sixty-three, all persons held as slaves within any state, or designated part of a state, the people whereof shall then be in rebellion against the United States shall be then, thenceforward, and forever free.

Preliminary[1] Emancipation
Proclamation [September 22,
1862]

The President takes the result of the New York elections[2] philosophically, and will, doubtless, profit by the lesson. When Colonel Forney inquired of him how he felt about New York, he replied: "Somewhat like the boy in Kentucky, who stubbed his toe while running to see his sweetheart. The boy said he was too big to cry, and far too badly hurt to laugh."

Frank Leslie's Illustrated Weekly
[November 22, 1862]

A nation may be said to consist of its territory, its people, and its laws. The territory is the only part which is of certain durability.

Second Annual Message to Con-
gress [December 1, 1862]

If there ever could be a proper time for mere catch arguments, that time surely is not now. In times like the

[1] The Emancipation Proclamation was issued one hundred days later, on January 1, 1863.
[2] The election was a victory for Horatio Seymour, Democratic candidate for governor of New York. Moreover, throughout the North the Democrats picked up a number of congressional seats and won a number of state elections.

present, men should utter nothing for which they would not willingly be responsible through time and in eternity.

Second Annual Message
to Congress

The dogmas of the quiet past are inadequate to the stormy present. The occasion is piled high with difficulty, and we must rise with the occasion. As our case is new, so we must think anew and act anew. We must disenthrall ourselves, and then we shall save our country.

Fellow citizens, we cannot escape history. We of this Congress and this administration will be remembered in spite of ourselves. No personal significance or insignificance can spare one or another of us. The fiery trial through which we pass will light us down in honor or dishonor to the last generation. We say we are for the Union. The world will not forget that we say this. We know how to save the Union. The world knows we do know how to save it. We, even we here, hold the power and bear the responsibility. In giving freedom to the slave, we assure freedom to the free — honorable alike in what we give and what we preserve. We shall nobly save or meanly lose the last, best hope of earth. Other means may succeed; this could not fail. The way is plain, peaceful, generous, just — a way which if followed the world will forever applaud and God must forever bless.

Ib.

Beware of rashness, but with energy and sleepless vigilance go forward and give us victories.

Letter to Major General Joseph
Hooker [January 26, 1863]

The Father of Waters again goes unvexed to the sea.

Letter to James C. Conkling
[August 26, 1863]

I have endured a great deal of ridicule without much malice; and have received a great deal of kindness, not quite free from ridicule. I am used to it.

> *Letter to James H. Hackett*
> *[November 2, 1863]*

Fourscore and seven years ago our fathers brought forth on this continent, a new nation, conceived in Liberty, and dedicated to the proposition that all men are created equal.

Now we are engaged in a great civil war, testing whether that nation or any nation so conceived and so dedicated can long endure. We are met on a great battlefield of that war. We have come to dedicate a portion of that field, as a final resting place for those who here gave their lives that that nation might live. It is altogether fitting and proper that we should do this.

But, in a larger sense, we cannot dedicate — we cannot consecrate — we cannot hallow — this ground. The brave men, living and dead, who struggled here, have consecrated it far above our poor power to add or detract. The world will little note nor long remember what we say here, but it can never forget what they did here. It is for us, the living, rather to be dedicated here to the unfinished work which they who fought here have thus far so nobly advanced. It is rather for us to be here dedicated to the great task remaining before us — that from these honored dead we take increased devotion to that cause for which they gave the last full measure of devotion; that we here highly resolve that these dead shall not have died in vain; that this nation, under God, shall have a new birth of freedom; and that government of the people, by the people, for the people, shall not perish from the earth.[1]

> *Address at Gettysburg [November 19, 1863]*

The President last night had a dream. He was in a party of plain people and as it became known who he was they began to comment on his appear-

[1] See Wycliffe, p. 163b; Webster, p. 547a; Garrison, p. 616a; and Theodore Parker, p. 657b.

ance. One of them said, "He is a common-looking man." The President replied, "Common-looking people are the best in the world: that is the reason the Lord makes so many of them."

> *From Letters of John Hay and Extracts from His Diary, edited by C. L. Hay [December 23, 1863]*

I claim not to have controlled events, but confess plainly that events have controlled me.

> *Letter to A. G. Hodges*
> *[April 4, 1864]*

The world has never had a good definition of the word liberty. And the American people just now are much in want of one. We all declare for liberty; but in using the same word we do not mean the same thing. With some, the word liberty may mean for each man to do as he pleases with himself and the product of his labor; while with others the same word may mean for some men to do as they please with other men and the product of other men's labor. Here are two, not only different, but incompatible things, called by the same name, liberty. And it follows that each of the things is by the respective parties called by two different and incompatible names, liberty and tyranny.

The shepherd drives the wolf from the sheep's throat, for which the sheep thanks the shepherd as his liberator, while the wolf denounces him for the same act. . . . Plainly the sheep and the wolf are not agreed upon a definition of liberty.

> *Address, Sanitary Fair, Baltimore [April 18, 1864]*

I do not allow myself to suppose that either the convention or the League have concluded to decide that I am either the greatest or best man in America, but rather they have concluded that it is not best to swap horses while crossing the river, and have further concluded that I am not so poor a horse that they might not make a botch of it in trying to swap.

> Reply to the National Union League [June 9, 1864]

Truth is generally the best vindication against slander.

> Letter to Secretary Stanton, refusing to dismiss Postmaster-General Montgomery Blair [July 18, 1864]

It has long been a grave question whether any government, not too strong for the liberties of its people, can be strong enough to maintain its existence in great emergencies.

> Response to a serenade [November 10, 1864]

Human nature will not change. In any future great national trial, compared with the men of this, we shall have as weak and as strong, as silly and as wise, as bad and as good.   Ib.

I desire so to conduct the affairs of this administration that if at the end, when I come to lay down the reins of power, I have lost every other friend on earth, I shall at least have one friend left, and that friend shall be down inside me.

> Reply to Missouri Committee of Seventy [1864]

Dear Madam, I have been shown in the files of the War Department a statement of the Adjutant-General of Massachusetts that you are the mother of five [1] sons who have died gloriously on the field of battle. I feel how weak and fruitless must be any words of mine which should attempt to beguile you from the grief of a loss so overwhelming. But I cannot refrain from tendering to you the consolation that may be found in the thanks of the Republic they died to save. I pray that our heavenly Father may assuage the anguish of your bereavement, and leave you only the cherished memory of the loved and lost, and the solemn pride that must be yours to have laid so costly a sacrifice upon the altar of freedom.

> Letter to Mrs. Bixby [November 21, 1864]

It may seem strange that any men should dare to ask a just God's assistance in wringing their bread from the sweat of other men's faces,[1] but let us judge not, that we be not judged.[2]

> Second Inaugural Address [March 4, 1865]

The Almighty has His own purposes.   Ib.

Fondly do we hope, fervently do we pray, that this mighty scourge of war may speedily pass away. Yet, if God wills that it continue until all the wealth piled by the bondsman's two hundred and fifty years of unrequited toil shall be sunk, and until every drop of blood drawn with the lash shall be paid by another drawn with the sword, as was said three thousand years ago, so still it must be said, "The judgments of the Lord are true and righteous altogether." [3]

With malice toward none, with charity for all, with firmness in the right as God gives us to see the right,[4] let us strive on to finish the work we are in, to bind up the nation's wounds, to care for him who shall have borne the battle and for his widow and his orphan, to do all which may achieve and cherish a just and lasting peace among ourselves and with all nations.   Ib.

I have always thought that all men should be free; but if any should be slaves, it should be first those who desire it for themselves, and secondly those who desire it for others. Whenever I hear anyone arguing for slavery, I feel a strong impulse to see it tried on him personally.[5]

> Address to an Indiana Regiment [March 17, 1865]

[1] See *Genesis 3:19*, p. 6a.
[2] See *Matthew 7:1*, p. 41a.
[3] See *Psalms 19:9*, p. 17b.
[4] See John Quincy Adams, p. 503a.
[5] See *Fragment*, p. 635b.

[1] Later, the records were revised; the correct number was two.

Important principles may and must be inflexible.

> Last public address, Washington [April 11, 1865]

If you once forfeit the confidence of your fellow citizens, you can never regain their respect and esteem. It is true that you may fool all the people some of the time; you can even fool some of the people all the time; but you can't fool all of the people all the time.

> To a caller at the White House. From ALEXANDER K. MCCLURE, Lincoln's Yarns and Stories [1904], p. 124

If I were to try to read, much less answer, all the attacks made on me, this shop might as well be closed for any other business. I do the very best I know how — the very best I can; and I mean to keep doing so until the end. If the end brings me out all right, what is said against me won't amount to anything. If the end brings me out wrong, ten angels swearing I was right would make no difference.

> Conversation at the White House. From FRANCIS B. CARPENTER, Six Months at the White House with Abraham Lincoln [1866]

EDGAR ALLAN POE [1]
1809–1849

O, human love! thou spirit given,
On Earth, of all we hope in Heaven!
> Tamerlane [1827]

All that we see or seem
Is but a dream within a dream.
> A Dream Within a Dream [1827]

The happiest day — the happiest hour
My sear'd and blighted heart hath known,
The highest hope of pride and power,
I feel hath flown.
> The Happiest Day — The Happiest Hour [1827]

[1] See James Russell Lowell, p. 692b.

From childhood's hour I have not been
As others were — I have not seen
As others saw.
> Alone [1827]

And the cloud that took the form
When the rest of Heaven was blue
Of a demon in my view.
> Ib.

Hast thou not torn the Naiad from her flood,
The Elfin from the green grass, and from me
The summer dream beneath the tamarind tree?
> Sonnet: To Science [1827]

Sound loves to revel in a summer night. Al Aaraaf [1829], pt. II

It is with literature as with law or empire — an established name is an estate in tenure, or a throne in possession.
> Poems [1831]. Preface, Letter to Mr. B——

Helen, thy beauty is to me
Like those Nicean barks of yore,
That gently, o'er a perfumed sea,
The weary, wayworn wanderer bore
To his own native shore.

On desperate seas long wont to roam,
Thy hyacinth hair, thy classic face,
Thy Naiad airs have brought me home
To the glory that was Greece,
And the grandeur that was Rome.
> To Helen [1831], st. 1, 2

If I could dwell
Where Israfel
Hath dwelt, and he where I,
He might not sing so wildly well
A mortal melody,
While a bolder note than this might swell
From my lyre within the sky.
> Israfel [1] [1831], st. 8

Lo! Death has reared himself a throne
In a strange city.
> The City in the Sea [1831], st. 1

[1] And the angel Israfel, whose heartstrings are a lute, and who has the sweetest voice of all God's creatures. — *The Koran*

The viol, the violet, and the vine.
The City in the Sea, st. 2

While from a proud tower in the town
Death looks gigantically down.[1]
Ib. st. 3

And, Guy De Vere, hast *thou* no
tear? — weep now or never more!
Lenore [1831], *st. 1*

A dirge for her the doubly dead in that
she died so young.   *Ib.*

Vastness! and Age! and Memories of
Eld!
Silence! and Desolation! and dim
Night!
The Coliseum [1833], *st. 1*

Thou wast that all to me, love,
For which my soul did pine —
A green isle in the sea, love,
A fountain and a shrine,
All wreathed with fairy fruits and flow-
ers,
And all the flowers were mine.
To One in Paradise [1834], *st. 1*

And all my days are trances,
And all my nightly dreams
Are where thy gray eye glances,
And where thy footstep gleams —
In what ethereal dances,
By what eternal streams.   *Ib. st. 4*

During the whole of a dull, dark, and
soundless day in the autumn of the
year, when the clouds hung oppressively
low in the heavens, I had been passing
alone, on horseback, through a singularly dreary tract of country, and at
length found myself, as the shades of
evening drew on, within view of the
melancholy House of Usher.
The Fall of the House of Usher
[1838]

Those who dream by day are cogni-
zant of many things which escape those
who dream only by night.
Eleonora [1841]

1 See Hart Crane, p. 1043b.

And much of Madness, and more of
Sin,
And Horror the soul of the plot.
The Conqueror Worm [1843],
st. 3

While the angels, all pallid and wan,
Uprising, unveiling, affirm
That the play is the tragedy, "Man,"
And its hero, the Conqueror Worm.
Ib. st. 5

There is something in the unselfish
and self-sacrificing love of a brute,
which goes directly to the heart of him
who has had frequent occasion to test
the paltry friendship and gossamer
fidelity of mere Man.
The Black Cat [1843]

Perverseness is one of the primitive
impulses of the human heart.   *Ib.*

The boundaries which divide Life
from Death are at best shadowy and
vague. Who shall say where the one
ends, and where the other begins?
The Premature Burial [1844]

With me poetry has been not a purpose, but a passion; and the passions
should be held in reverence: they must
not — they cannot at will be excited,
with an eye to the paltry compensations, or the more paltry commenda-
tions, of mankind.
The Raven and Other Poems
[1845], *preface*

Once upon a midnight dreary, while I
pondered, weak and weary,
Over many a quaint and curious volume of forgotten lore —
While I nodded, nearly napping, suddenly there came a tapping,
As of some one gently rapping, rapping
at my chamber door.
The Raven [1845], *st. 1*

Ah, distinctly I remember it was in the
bleak December;
And each separate dying ember
wrought its ghost upon the floor.
Eagerly I wished the morrow; vainly I
had sought to borrow

From my books surcease of sorrow —
    sorrow for the lost Lenore —
For the rare and radiant maiden whom
    the angels name Lenore —
Nameless *here* for evermore.
                    The Raven, st. 2

The silken sad uncertain rustling of
    each purple curtain.   *Ib. st. 3*

Deep into that darkness peering, long
    I stood there, wondering, fearing,
Doubting, dreaming dreams no mortal
    ever dared to dream before.
                            Ib. st. 5

"Ghastly grim and ancient Raven wan-
    dering from the Nightly shore —
Tell me what thy lordly name is on the
    Night's Plutonian shore!"
Quoth the Raven, "Nevermore."
                            Ib. st. 8

    Whom unmerciful Disaster
Followed fast and followed faster.
                        Ib. st. 11

"Prophet!" said I, "thing of evil! —
    prophet still, if bird or devil!"
                        Ib. st. 16

"Take thy beak from out my heart, and
    take thy form from off my door!"
Quoth the Raven, "Nevermore."
                        Ib. st. 17

And the Raven, never flitting, still is
    sitting, *still* is sitting
On the pallid bust of Pallas just above
    my chamber door;
And his eyes have all the seeming of a
    demon's that is dreaming,
And the lamplight o'er him streaming
    throws his shadow on the floor;
And my soul from out that shadow that
    lies floating on the floor
Shall be lifted — nevermore!
                        Ib. st. 18

From a wild weird clime that lieth, sub-
    lime,
Out of Space — out of Time.
            Dreamland [1845], *st. 1*

The Imp of the Perverse.
            Title of story [1845]

The object Truth, or the satisfaction
of the intellect, and the object Passion,
or the excitement of the heart, are, although attainable, to a certain extent,
in poetry, far more readily attainable in
prose.
    The Philosophy of Composition
                        [1846]

I asked myself — "Of all melancholy
topics, what, according to the universal
understanding of mankind, is the most
melancholy?" Death — was the obvious
reply. "And when," I said, "is this most
melancholy of topics most poetical?"
. . . The answer . . . is obvious —
"When it most closely allies itself to
Beauty: the death, then, of a beautiful
woman is, unquestionably, the most
poetical topic in the world — and
equally is it beyond doubt that the lips
best suited for such topic are those of
a bereaved lover."   *Ib.*

The skies they were ashen and sober;
    The leaves they were crispèd and
    sere —
    The leaves they were withering and
    sere;
It was night in the lonesome October
Of my most immemorial year.
            Ulalume [1847], *st. 1*

It was down by the dank tarn of
    Auber,
In the ghoul-haunted woodland of
    Weir.   *Ib.*

Here once, through an alley Titanic,
    Of cypress, I roamed with my
    soul —
    Of cypress, with Psyche, my soul.
                            Ib. st. 2

Thus I pacified Psyche and kissed her,
And tempted her out of her gloom.
                        Ib. st. 8

Can it be fancied that Deity ever vin-
    dictively
Made in his image a mannikin merely
    to madden it? [1]
        The Rationale of Verse [1848]

[1] What! out of senseless Nothing to provoke
A conscious Something to resent the yoke.
        FITZGERALD, *The Rubáiyát of Omar
        Khayyám* [1859–1879], *st. 78*

A Quixotic sense of the honorable
— of the chivalrous.
>> *Letter to Mrs. Whitman*
>> [*October 18, 1848*]

"Over the Mountains
Of the Moon,
Down the Valley of the Shadow,
Ride, boldly ride,"
The shade replied —
"If you seek for Eldorado!"
>> *Eldorado* [1849], *st. 4*

And the fever called "Living"
Is conquered at last.
>> *For Annie* [1849]

And this maiden she lived with no
other thought
Than to love and be loved by me.

She was a child and *I* was a child,
In this kingdom by the sea,
But we loved with a love that was more
than love —
I and my Annabel Lee —
With a love that the wingèd seraphs
of Heaven
Coveted her and me.
>> *Annabel Lee* [1849], *st. 1, 2*

And neither the angels in Heaven
above
Nor the demons down under the
sea,
Can ever dissever my soul from the
soul
Of the beautiful Annabel Lee.
>> *Ib. st. 5*

In her sepulcher there by the sea —
In her tomb by the side of the sea.
>> *Ib. st. 6*

Keeping time, time, time,
In sort of Runic rhyme,
To the tintinnabulation that so musi-
cally wells
From the bells, bells, bells, bells,
Bells, bells, bells.
>> *The Bells* [1849], *st. 1*

Hear the loud alarum bells —
Brazen bells!
What a tale of terror, now, their tur-
bulency tells! *Ib. st. 3*

I would define, in brief, the Poetry of
words as the Rhythmical Creation of
Beauty. Its sole arbiter is Taste.
>> *The Poetic Principle* [1850]

PIERRE JOSEPH PROUDHON
1809–1865

Property is theft.
>> *Qu'est-ce que la Propriété?*

ALFRED, LORD TENNYSON
1809–1892

Dower'd with the hate of hate, the
scorn of scorn,
The love of love.
>> *The Poet* [1830], *st. 1*

For it was in the golden prime
Of good Haroun Alraschid.
>> *Recollections of the Arabian*
>> *Nights* [1830], *st. 2*

She said, "I am aweary, aweary,
I would that I were dead!"
>> *Mariana* [1] [1830], *refrain*

A still small voice [2] spake unto me,
"Thou art so full of misery,
Were it not better not to be?"
>> *The Two Voices* [1832], *st. 1*

This truth within thy mind rehearse,
That in a boundless universe
Is boundless better, boundless worse.
>> *Ib. st. 9*

Though thou wert scattered to the
wind,
Yet is there plenty of the kind.[3]
>> *Ib. st. 11*

I know that age to age succeeds,
Blowing a noise of tongues and deeds,
A dust of systems and of creeds.
>> *Ib. st. 69*

Like glimpses of forgotten dreams.
>> *Ib. st. 127*

No life that breathes with human
breath

---

[1] See Shakespeare, p. 271b.
[2] See *I Kings 19:12*, p. 13b.
[3] See Fitzgerald, p. 630b.

Has ever truly longed for death.
The Two Voices, st. 132

In after-dinner talk,
Across the walnuts and the wine.
The Miller's Daughter [1832],
st. 4

O mother Ida, many-fountained Ida,
Dear mother Ida, hearken ere I die.
Oenone [1832], *l. 22*

Self-reverence, self-knowledge, self-control,
These three alone lead life to sovereign
power. *Ib. l. 142*

I built my soul a lordly pleasure-house,
Wherein at ease for aye to dwell.
The Palace of Art [1832], *st. 1*

The daughter of a hundred Earls,
You are not one to be desired.
Lady Clara Vere de Vere [1832],
st. 1

A simple maiden in her flower
Is worth a hundred coats-of-arms.
Ib. st. 2

The lion on your old stone gates
Is not more cold to you than I.
Ib. st. 3

The gardener Adam and his wife
Smile at the claims of long descent.
Ib. st. 7

'Tis only noble to be good.
Kind hearts are more than coronets,
And simple faith than Norman blood.
Ib.

Oh! teach the orphan boy to read,
Or teach the orphan girl to sew.
Ib. st. 9

You must wake and call me early, call
me early, mother dear;
Tomorrow 'ill be the happiest time of
all the glad New Year;
Of all the glad New Year, mother, the
maddest, merriest day;
For I'm to be Queen o' the May,
mother, I'm to be Queen o' the
May.
The May Queen [1832], *st. 1*

Music that gentlier on the spirit lies,
Than tir'd eyelids upon tir'd eyes.
The Lotos-Eaters [1832]. *Choric
Song, st. 1*

There is no joy but calm! *Ib. st. 2*

Ah, why
Should life all labor be? *Ib. st. 4*

Let us alone. Time driveth onward
fast,
And in a little while our lips are dumb.
Let us alone. What is it that will last?
All things are taken from us, and become
Portions and parcels of the dreadful
Past. *Ib.*

Give us long rest or death, dark death
or dreamful ease. *Ib.*

Live and lie reclined
On the hills like Gods together, careless
of mankind. *Ib. st. 8*

Dan Chaucer, the first warbler, whose
sweet breath
Preluded those melodious bursts that
fill
The spacious times of great Elizabeth
With sounds that echo still.
A Dream of Fair Women [1832]

A daughter of the gods, divinely tall,
And most divinely fair. *Ib. st. 22*

Willows whiten, aspens quiver,
Little breezes dusk and shiver.
The Lady of Shalott [1832],
pt. I, st. 2

But who hath seen her wave her hand?
Or at the casement seen her stand?
Or is she known in all the land,
The Lady of Shalott? *Ib. st. 3*

All in the blue unclouded weather.
Ib. III, st. 3

"Tirra lirra," by the river
Sang Sir Lancelot. *Ib. st. 4*

She left the web, she left the loom,
She made three paces thro' the room,
She saw the water lily bloom,
She saw the helmet and the plume,
She look'd down to Camelot.

Out flew the web and floated wide;
The mirror cracked from side to side.
"The curse has come upon me," cried
　The Lady of Shalott.
　　　　　　The Lady of Shalott,
　　　　　　pt. III, st. 5

But Lancelot mused a little space;
He said, "She has a lovely face;
God in his mercy lend her grace,
　The Lady of Shalott."
　　　　　　Ib. IV, st. 6

God gives us love. Something to love
　He lends us; but when love is grown
To ripeness, that on which it throve
Falls off, and love is left alone.
　　　　　To J.S. [1842], *st. 4*

More black than ashbuds in the front
　of March.
　　　　The Gardener's Daughter
　　　　　　[1842], *l. 28*

　　Half light, half shade,
She stood, a sight to make an old man
young.　　　　　　*Ib. l. 139*

The long mechanic pacings to and fro,
The set gray life, and apathetic end.
　　　Love and Duty [1842], *l. 17*

　　Ah! when shall all men's good
Be each man's rule, and universal
　peace
Lie like a shaft of light across the land,
And like a lane of beams athwart the
　sea,
Through all the circle of the golden
　year?
　　The Golden Year [1842], *l. 47*

It little profits that an idle king,
By this still hearth, among these barren
　crags,
Match'd with an aged wife, I mete and
　dole
Unequal laws unto a savage race.
　　　　　Ulysses [1842], *l. 1*

　　　I will drink
Life to the lees.　　　　*Ib. l. 6*

Much have I seen and known; cities of
　men
And manners, climates, councils, gov-
　ernments,

Myself not least, but honor'd of them
　all;
And drunk delight of battle with my
　peers,
Far on the ringing plains of windy
　Troy.
I am a part of all that I have met;
Yet all experience is an arch where-
　through
Gleams that untravel'd world.[1]
　　　　　　Ulysses, l. 13

How dull it is to pause, to make an
　end,
To rust unburnished, not to shine in
　use,
As though to breathe were life!
　　　　　　Ib. l. 22

And this gray spirit yearning in desire
To follow knowledge like a sinking
　star,
Beyond the utmost bound of human
　thought.　　　　*Ib. l. 30*

This is my son, mine own Telemachus.
　　　　　　Ib. l. 33

Death closes all: but something ere the
　end,
Some work of noble note, may yet be
　done,
Not unbecoming men that strove with
　gods.　　　　*Ib. l. 51*

　　　The deep
Moans round with many voices. Come,
　my friends,
'Tis not too late to seek a newer world.
Push off, and sitting well in order
　smite
The sounding furrows, for my purpose
　holds
To sail beyond the sunset, and the
　baths
Of all the western stars, until I die.
It may be that the gulfs will wash us
　down;
It may be we shall touch the Happy
　Isles,
And see the great Achilles, whom we
　knew.　　　　*Ib. l. 55*

[1] See Henry Adams, p. 776b.

To strive, to seek, to find, and not to yield.[1]   *Ulysses, l.* 70

Comrades, leave me here a little, while as yet 'tis early morn:
Leave me here, and when you want me, sound upon the bugle horn.
     Locksley Hall [1842], *l.* 1

In the spring a young man's fancy lightly turns to thoughts of love.
     Ib. l. 19

He will hold thee, when his passion shall have spent its novel force,
Something better than his dog, a little dearer than his horse.   *Ib. l.* 49

The many-winter'd crow that leads the clanging rookery home.
     Ib. l. 68

Such a one do I remember, whom to look at was to love.[2]   *Ib. l.* 72

    This is the truth the poet sings,
That a sorrow's crown of sorrow is remembering happier things.[3]
     Ib. l. 75

Like a dog, he hunts in dreams.
     Ib. l. 79

With a little hoard of maxims preaching down a daughter's heart.
     Ib. l. 94

But the jingling of the guinea helps the hurt that Honor feels.
     Ib. l. 105

For I dipp'd into the future, far as human eye could see,
Saw the Vision of the world, and all the wonder that would be;
Saw the heavens fill with commerce, argosies of magic sails,
Pilots of the purple twilight, dropping down with costly bales;
Heard the heavens fill with shouting, and there rain'd a ghastly dew
From the nations' airy navies grappling in the central blue.   *Ib. l.* 119

[1] Inscribed on the memorial cross erected to the memory of Captain Robert Falcon Scott [1868–1912] and his men at Hut Point in the Antarctic.

[2] See Burns, p. 494a, and Halleck, p. 565b.

[3] See Pindar, p. 79b, and note.

Till the war drum throbbed no longer and the battle flags were furled
In the Parliament of Man, the Federation of the world.
     Locksley Hall, l. 127

And the kindly earth shall slumber, lapp'd in universal law.
     Ib. l. 130

Yet I doubt not through the ages one increasing purpose runs,
And the thoughts of men are widened with the process of the suns.
     Ib. l. 137

Knowledge comes, but wisdom lingers.
     Ib. l. 141

Woman is the lesser man, and all thy passions, match'd with mine,
Are as moonlight unto sunlight, and as water unto wine.   *Ib. l.* 151

I will take some savage woman, she shall rear my dusky race.
     Ib. l. 168

I the heir of all the ages, in the foremost files of time.   *Ib. l.* 178

Let the great world spin forever down the ringing grooves of change.
     Ib. l. 182

Better fifty years of Europe than a cycle of Cathay.   *Ib. l.* 184

This proverb flashes through his head, "The many fail, the one suceeds."
     The Day Dream [1842]. *The Arrival, st.* 2

And on her lover's arm she leant,
And round her waist she felt it fold,
And far across the hills they went
In that new world which is the old.
     Ib. The Departure, st. 1

And is there any moral shut
Within the bosom of the rose?
     Ib. Moral, st. 1

My strength is as the strength of ten,
Because my heart is pure.
     Sir Galahad [1842], *st.* 1

Or that eternal lack of pence,
Which vexes public men.
     Will Waterproof's Lyrical Monologue, st. 6

Cophetua sware a royal oath;
"This beggar maid shall be my
 queen!"[1]
   The Beggar Maid [1842], st. 2

Break, break, break,
 On thy cold gray stones, O Sea!
And I would that my tongue could
 utter
The thoughts that arise in me.

O well for the fisherman's boy,
 That he shouts with his sister at
 play!
O well for the sailor lad,
 That he sings in his boat on the bay!

And the stately ships go on
 To their haven under the hill;
But O for the touch of a vanish'd
 hand,
 And the sound of a voice that is still!
  Break, Break, Break [1842], st. 1–3

But the tender grace of a day that is
 dead
Will never come back to me.
     Ib. st. 4

With prudes for proctors, dowagers for
 deans,
And sweet girl-graduates in their golden
 hair.
   The Princess [1847]. *Prologue,*
        l. 141

A rosebud set with little willful thorns,
And sweet as English air could make
 her, she.   *Ib. l. 153*

When we fall out with those we love
And kiss again with tears!
   Ib. pt. II [song, *As Through the*
      Land, l. 8]

And quoted odes, and jewels five-words-
 long
That on the stretched forefinger of all
 Time
Sparkle forever.   *Ib. l. 355*

Sweet and low, sweet and low,
 Wind of the western sea,
Low, low, breathe and blow,
 Wind of the western sea!
Over the rolling waters go,

[1] See Shakespeare, p. 223a, and *Ballads,* p.
1087b.

Come from the dying moon, and
 blow,
 Blow him again to me;
While my little one, while my pretty
 one, sleeps.
   The Princess, pt. III [song,
    Sweet and Low, st. 1]

The splendor falls on castle walls
 And snowy summits old in story:
The long light shakes across the lakes,
 And the wild cataract leaps in glory.
Blow, bugle, blow, set the wild echoes
 flying,
Blow, bugle; answer, echoes, dying, dy-
 ing, dying.
   Ib. IV [song, *The Splendor Falls,*
        st. 1]

The horns of Elfland faintly blowing.
       Ib. [st. 2]

O Love, they die in yon rich sky,
 They faint on hill or field or river:
Our echoes roll from soul to soul,
 And grow forever and forever.
       Ib. [st. 3]

Tears, idle tears, I know not what they
 mean,
Tears from the depth of some divine
 despair
Rise in the heart, and gather to the
 eyes,
In looking on the happy autumn fields,
And thinking of the days that are no
 more.
  Ib. [song, *Tears, Idle Tears, st. 1*]

Dear as remember'd kisses after death,
And sweet as those by hopeless fancy
 feign'd
On lips that are for others; deep as love,
Deep as first love, and wild with all re-
 gret;
O Death in Life, the days that are no
 more.   *Ib.* [st. 4]

O Swallow, Swallow, flying, flying
 South,
Fly to her, and fall upon her gilded
 eaves,
And tell her, tell her, what I tell to
 thee.
   Ib. [song, *O Swallow, st. 1*]

Man is the hunter; woman is his game.
　　The Princess, pt. V, l. 147

Man for the field and woman for the
　hearth:
Man for the sword and for the needle
　she:
Man with the head and woman with
　the heart:
Man to command and woman to obey;
All else confusion.　　*Ib. l. 427*

Home they brought her warrior dead.
　She nor swoon'd nor utter'd cry:
All her maidens, watching, said,
　"She must weep or she will die."
　　*Ib. VI [song, Home They
　　Brought Her Warrior,
　　st. 1]*

　The woman is so hard
Upon the woman.　　*Ib. l. 205*

Ask me no more: thy fate and mine are
　seal'd:
I strove against the stream and all in
　vain:
Let the great river take me to the main:
No more, dear love, for at a touch I
　yield;
Ask me no more.
　　*Ib. VII [song, Ask Me No More,
　　st. 3]*

Now sleeps the crimson petal, now the
　white;
Nor waves the cypress in the palace
　walk;
Nor winks the gold fin in the porphyry
　font:
The firefly wakens: waken thou with
　me.
　　*Ib. [song, Now Sleeps the Crim-
　　son Petal, st. 1]*

Now lies the Earth all Danaë to the
　stars,
And all thy heart lies open unto me.
　　Ib. [st. 3]

　Sweet is every sound,
Sweeter thy voice, but every sound is
　sweet;
Myriads of rivulets hurrying through
　the lawn,

The moan of doves in immemorial
　elms,
And murmuring of innumerable bees.
　　The Princess, pt. VII, l. 203

　Happy he
With such a mother! faith in woman-
　kind
Beats with his blood, and trust in all
　things high
Comes easy to him; and though he trip
　and fall,
He shall not blind his soul with clay.
　　Ib. l. 308

Some sense of duty, something of a
　faith,
Some reverence for the laws ourselves
　have made,
Some patient force to change them
　when we will,
Some civic manhood firm against the
　crowd.　　*Ib. Conclusion, l. 54*

Believing where we cannot prove.
　　*In Memoriam [1850]. Prologue,
　　st. 1*

Our little systems have their day.
　　Ib. st. 5

Let knowledge grow from more to
　more,
　But more of reverence in us dwell;
　That mind and soul, according well,
May make one music as before.
　　Ib. st. 7

I held it truth, with him who sings
　To one clear harp in divers tones,
　That men may rise on stepping-
　stones
Of their dead selves to higher things.[1]
　　Ib. 1, st. 1

I sometimes hold it half a sin
　To put in words the grief I feel;
　For words, like Nature, half reveal
And half conceal the Soul within.
　　Ib. 5, st. 2

But, for the unquiet heart and brain
　A use in measured language lies;
　The sad mechanic exercise,

[1] See St. Augustine, p. 147a, and Longfellow,
p. 623a.

Like dull narcotics numbing pain.
In Memoriam, 5, st. 2

Never morning wore
To evening, but some heart did break.
Ib. 6, st. 2

And from his ashes may be made
The violet of his native land.[1]
Ib. 18, st. 1

I do but sing because I must,
And pipe but as the linnets sing.[2]
Ib. 21, st. 6

Who keeps the keys of all the creeds.
Ib. 23, st. 2

And Thought leap'd out to wed with
Thought
Ere Thought could wed itself with
Speech.   *Ib. st. 4*

'Tis better to have loved and lost
Than never to have loved at all.[3]
Ib. 27, st. 4

Her eyes are homes of silent prayer.
Ib. 32, st. 1

Short swallow-flights of song, that dip
Their wings in tears, and skim away.
Ib. 48, st. 4

Be near me when my light is low.
Ib. 50, st. 1

And Time, a maniac scattering dust,
And Life, a Fury slinging flame.
Ib. st. 2

Do we indeed desire the dead
Should still be near us at our side?
Ib. 51, st. 1

---

[1] See Shakespeare, p. 266a, and Fitzgerald, p. 629b.

[2] Ich singe, wie der Vogel singt
    Der in den Zweigen wohnet.
    GOETHE, *Wilhelm Meister's Apprenticeship* [1786–1830], bk. II, ch. 11

[3] Say what you will, 'tis better to be left than never to have been loved. — CONGREVE, *The Way of the World* [1700], act II, sc. 6
Better to love amiss than nothing to have loved. — CRABBE, *Tales* [1812], *XIV, The Struggles of Conscience*
    What voice did on my spirit fall,
    Peschiera, when thy bridge I crost?
    'Tis better to have fought and lost
    Than never to have fought at all.
    ARTHUR HUGH CLOUGH [1819–1861],
    Peschiera

Hold thou the good; define it well;
    For fear divine Philosophy
    Should push beyond her mark, and
        be
Procuress to the Lords of Hell.
In Memoriam, 53, st. 4

Oh yet we trust that somehow good
Will be the final goal of ill.
Ib. 54, st. 1

But what am I?
An infant crying in the night:
An infant crying for the light:
And with no language but a cry.[1]
Ib. st. 5

So careful of the type she seems,
So careless of the single life.
Ib. 55, st. 2

The great world's altar-stairs,
That slope through darkness up to
God.   *Ib. st. 4*

Nature, red in tooth and claw.
Ib. 56, st. 4

The sweetest soul
That ever look'd with human eyes.
Ib. 57, st. 3

Who breaks his birth's invidious bar,
And grasps the skirts of happy chance,
And breasts the blows of circumstance.
Ib. 64, st. 2

So many worlds, so much to do,
So little done, such things to be.[2]
Ib. 73, st. 1

O last regret, regret can die!
Ib. 78, st. 5

God's finger touch'd him, and he slept.
Ib. 85, st. 5

Fresh from brawling courts
And dusty purlieus of the law.
Ib. 89, st. 3

---

[1] See Pliny, p. 132a–b.

[2] How little I have gained,
    How vast the unattained.
    WHITTIER [1807–1892], *My Triumph,
    st. 7*

There lives more faith in honest doubt,[1]
Believe me, than in half the creeds.
In Memoriam, 96, st. 3

He seems so near, and yet so far.
Ib. 97, st. 6

Ring out, wild bells, to the wild sky!
Ib. 106, st. 1

Ring out the old, ring in the new,
  Ring, happy bells, across the snow:
The year is going, let him go;
Ring out the false, ring in the true.
Ib. st. 2

Ring in the nobler modes of life,
With sweeter manners, purer laws.
Ib. st. 4

Ring out old shapes of foul disease,
  Ring out the narrowing lust of gold;
  Ring out the thousand wars of old,
Ring in the thousand years of peace.

Ring in the valiant man and free,
  The larger heart, the kindlier hand;
  Ring out the darkness of the land,
Ring in the Christ that is to be.
Ib. st. 7, 8

The blind hysterics of the Celt.
Ib. 109, st. 4

And thus he bore without abuse
  The grand old name of gentleman,
  Defamed by every charlatan,
And soiled with all ignoble use.
Ib. 111, st. 6

    Wearing all that weight
Of learning lightly like a flower.
Ib. Conclusion, st. 10

One God, one law, one element,
  And one far-off divine event,
To which the whole creation moves.
Ib. st. 36

He clasps the crag with crooked hands;
Close to the sun in lonely lands,
Ring'd with the azure world he stands.

The wrinkled sea beneath him crawls;
He watches from his mountain walls,
And like a thunderbolt he falls.
The Eagle [1851]

This laurel greener from the brows
Of him that utter'd nothing base.[1]
To the Queen [1851], *st. 2*

Broad-based upon her people's will,
And compass'd by the inviolate sea.
Ib. st. 9

Bury the Great Duke
With an empire's lamentation.
Ode on the Death of the Duke of
Wellington [1852], *st. 1*

The last great Englishman is low.
Ib. st. 3

Rich in saving common sense,
And, as the greatest only are,
In his simplicity sublime.
O good gray head which all men knew!
Ib. st. 4

O iron nerve to true occasion true,
O fall'n at length, that tower of
    strength
Which stood four-square to all the
    winds that blew.   **Ib.**

Not once or twice in our rough island
    story
The path of duty was the way to
    glory.   *Ib. st. 8*

Speak no more of his renown.
Lay your earthly fancies down,
And in the vast cathedral leave him.
God accept him, Christ receive him.
Ib. st. 9

And yet, my Lords, not well: there is a
  higher law.
The Third of February, 1852,
st. 2

We are not cotton-spinners all.
Ib. st. 8

Half a league, half a league,
  Half a league onward,

---

[1] Who never doubted never half believed.
Where doubt there truth is — 'tis her shadow.
    P. J. BAILEY [1816–1902], *Festus: A*
    Country Town

[1] Wordsworth, Tennyson's predecessor as poet
laureate.

All in the valley of death
  Rode the six hundred.
        The Charge of the Light Brigade
              [1854],[1] *st. 1*

"Forward, the Light Brigade!"
Was there a man dismay'd?
                        Ib. st. 2

  Someone had blundered:
Theirs not to make reply,
Theirs not to reason why,
Theirs but to do and die.   *Ib.*

Cannon to right of them,
Cannon to left of them,
Cannon in front of them
  Volley'd and thunder'd.   *Ib. st. 3*

Into the jaws of death,
Into the mouth of hell
  Rode the six hundred.   *Ib.*

I come from haunts of coot and hern,
  I make a sudden sally
And sparkle out among the fern,
  To bicker down a valley.
        The Brook [1855], *song, st. 1*

For men may come and men may go,
But I go on forever.   *Ib. st. 6*

Faultily faultless, icily regular, splendidly null,
Dead perfection, no more.
        Maud [1855], *pt. I, sec. ii*

That jeweled mass of millinery,
That oiled and curled Assyrian Bull.
                        Ib. vi, st. 6

One still strong man in a blatant land.
                        Ib. x, st. 5

And ah for a man to arise in me,
That the man I am may cease to be!
                        Ib. st. 6

Gorgonized me from head to foot,
With a stony British stare.
                        Ib. xiii, st. 2

Come into the garden, Maud,
  For the black bat, night, has flown,
Come into the garden, Maud,
  I am here at the gate alone.
                        Ib. xxii, st. 1

[1] See Bosquet, p. 655b.

For a breeze of morning moves,
  And the planet of Love is on high,
Beginning to faint in the light that she
    loves
  On a bed of daffodil sky.
        Maud, pt. I, sec. xxii, st. 2

All night have the roses heard
  The flute, violin, bassoon;
All night has the casement jessamine
  stirr'd
  To the dancers dancing in tune;
Till a silence fell with the waking bird,
  And a hush with the setting moon.
                        Ib. st. 3

Queen rose of the rosebud garden of
  girls.   *Ib. st. 9*

There has fallen a splendid tear
  From the passion-flower at the gate.
She is coming, my dove, my dear;
  She is coming, my life, my fate;
The red rose cries, "She is near, she is
    near";
  And the white rose weeps, "She is
    late";
The larkspur listens, "I hear, I hear";
  And the lily whispers, "I wait."

She is coming, my own, my sweet;
  Were it ever so airy a tread,
My heart would hear her and beat,
  Were it earth in an earthy bed;
My dust would hear her and beat,
  Had I lain for a century dead,
Would start and tremble under her
    feet,
  And blossom in purple and red.
                        Ib. st. 10, 11

Ah Christ, that it were possible
  For one short hour to see
The souls we loved, that they might tell
    us
  What and where they be.
                        Ib. II, iv, st. 3

And after many a summer dies the
  swan.   *Tithonus* [1860], *l. 4*

Here at the quiet limit of the world.
                        Ib. l. 7

Wearing the white flower of a blameless life,

Before a thousand peering littlenesses,
In that fierce light which beats upon a throne,
And blackens every blot.
Idylls of the King [1859–1885],
dedication, l. 24

Man's word is God in man.
Ib. The Coming of Arthur, l. 132

Large divine and comfortable words.[1]
Ib. l. 267

Clothed in white samite, mystic, wonderful.[2]
Ib. l. 284

Live pure, speak true, right wrong, follow the King —
Else, wherefore born?
Ib. Gareth and Lynette, l. 117

Lightly was her slender nose
Tip-tilted like the petal of a flower.
Ib. l. 574

Our hoard is little, but our hearts are great.
*Ib. The Marriage of Geraint,
l.* 352

For man is man and master of his fate.[3]
Ib. l. 355

The useful trouble of the rain.
Ib. Geraint and Enid, l. 770

It is the little rift within the lute,
That by and by will make the music mute,
And ever widening slowly silence all.
Ib. Merlin and Vivien, l. 386

Blind and naked Ignorance
Delivers brawling judgments, unashamed,
On all things all day long. *Ib. l.* 662

For men at most differ as Heaven and Earth,
But women, worst and best, as Heaven and Hell. *Ib. l.* 812

Elaine the fair, Elaine the lovable,
Elaine, the lily maid of Astolat.
Ib. Lancelot and Elaine, l. 1

[1] Hear what comfortable words our Saviour Christ saith unto all who truly turn to him. — *Book of Common Prayer, Holy Communion*
[2] Also *The Passing of Arthur, l.* 199.
[3] See Sallust, p. 116a, and note.

But, friend, to me
He is all fault who hath no fault at all.
For who loves me must have a touch of earth.
*Idylls of the King, Lancelot
and Elaine, l.* 131

In me there dwells
No greatness, save it be some far-off touch
Of greatness to know well I am not great. *Ib. l.* 447

The shackles of an old love straitened him,
His honor rooted in dishonor stood,
And faith unfaithful kept him falsely true. *Ib. l.* 870

Sweet is true love though given in vain, in vain;
And sweet is death who puts an end to pain. *Ib. l.* 1000

He makes no friend who never made a foe. *Ib. l.* 1082

Figs out of thistles.[1]
Ib. The Last Tournament, l. 356

The greater man the greater courtesy.
Ib. l. 628

The vow that binds too strictly snaps itself. *Ib. l.* 652

For courtesy wins woman all as well
As valor may. *Ib. l.* 702

For manners are not idle, but the fruit
Of loyal nature and of noble mind.
Ib. Guinevere, l. 333

To love one maiden only, cleave to her,
And worship her by years of golden deeds. *Ib. l.* 472

No more subtle master under Heaven
Than is the maiden passion for a maid,
Not only to keep down the base in man,
But teach high thought, and amiable words
And courtliness, and the desire of fame,

[1] Ye shall know them by their fruits. Do men gather grapes of thorns, or figs of thistles? — *Matthew 7:16*

And love of truth, and all that makes a man.
> *Idylls of the King,*
> *Guinevere, l. 475*

Let no man dream but that I love thee still.   *Ib. l. 557*

The days will grow to weeks, the weeks to months,
The months will add themselves and make the years,
The years will roll into the centuries,
And mine will ever be a name of scorn.
> *Ib. l. 619*

To where beyond these voices there is peace.   *Ib. l. 692*

I found Him in the shining of the stars,
I mark'd Him in the flowering of His fields,
But in His ways with men I find Him not.
> *Ib. The Passing of Arthur, l. 9*

For why is all around us here
As if some lesser god had made the world,
But had not force to shape it as he would?   *Ib. l. 13*

And slowly answer'd Arthur from the barge:
The old order changeth, yielding place to new;
And God fulfills himself in many ways,
Lest one good custom should corrupt the world.[1]   *Ib. l. 407*

More things are wrought by prayer
Than this world dreams of. Wherefore, let thy voice
Rise like a fountain for me night and day.[1]   *Ib. l. 414*

From the great deep to the great deep he goes.   *Ib. l. 445*

Cast all your cares on God; that anchor holds.
> *Enoch Arden [1864], l. 222*

Insipid as the queen upon a card.
> *Aylmer's Field [1864], l. 28*

The worst is yet to come.[2]
> *Sea Dreams [1864], l. 301*

[1] Also in *Morte d'Arthur [1842]*.
[2] See Browning, p. 666a.

He said likewise
That a lie which is half a truth is ever the blackest of lies,
That a lie which is all a lie may be met and fought with outright,
But a lie which is part a truth is a harder matter to fight.
> *The Grandmother [1864], st. 8*

Dosn't thou 'ear my 'erse's legs, as they canters awaäy?
Proputty, proputty, proputty — that's what I 'ears 'em saäy.
> *Northern Farmer: New Style*
> *[1869], st. 1*

Doänt thou marry for munny, but goä wheer munny is!   *Ib. st. 5*

Speak to Him thou for He hears, and Spirit with Spirit can meet —
Closer is He than breathing, and nearer than hands and feet.
> *The Higher Pantheism [1869],*
> *st. 6*

Flower in the crannied wall,
I pluck you out of the crannies,
I hold you here, root and all, in my hand,
Little flower — but *if* I could understand
What you are, root and all, and all in all,
I should know what God and man is.
> *Flower in the Crannied Wall*
> *[1869]*

At Flores in the Azores Sir Richard Grenville lay,
And a pinnace, like a flutter'd bird, came flying from far away;
"Spanish ships of war at sea! we have sighted fifty-three!"
> *The Revenge [1878], st. 1*

I should count myself the coward if I left them, my Lord Howard,
To these Inquisition dogs and the devildoms of Spain.   *Ib. st. 2*

The little *Revenge* ran on sheer into the heart of the foe.   *Ib. st. 5*

All the charm of all the Muses often flowering in a lonely word.
> *To Virgil [1882], st. 3*

Cleave ever to the sunnier side of
doubt.
> *The Ancient Sage* [1885], *l.* 68

That man's the best Cosmopolite
Who loves his native country best.
> *Hands All Round* [1885], *l.* 3

After it, follow it,
Follow the Gleam.[1]
> *Merlin and the Gleam* [1889], *st.* 9

Sunset and evening star,
  And one clear call for me!
And may there be no moaning of the
  bar,
When I put out to sea,[2]

But such a tide as moving seems
  asleep,
  Too full for sound and foam,
When that which drew from out the
  boundless deep
Turns again home.
> *Crossing the Bar* [1889], *st.* 1, 2

Twilight and evening bell,
And after that the dark. *Ib. st. 3*

I hope to see my Pilot face to face
When I have crossed the bar.
> *Ib. st. 4*

ROBERT CHARLES WINTHROP
1809–1894

Our Country — whether bounded by
the St. John's and the Sabine, or however otherwise bounded [3] or described,
and be the measurements more or less
— still our Country, to be cherished in
all our hearts, to be defended by all our
hands.
> *Toast at Faneuil Hall* [*Fourth of
July, 1845*]

A star for every State, and a State for
every star.
> *Address on Boston Common* [1862]

SAMUEL DODGE
fl. 1868

People Will Talk. *Title of poem*

HENRY ALFORD
1810–1871

Come, ye thankful people, come,
Raise the song of Harvest-home;
All is safely gathered in,
Ere the winter storms begin.
> *Come, Ye Thankful People,
Come* [1844]

PHINEAS TAYLOR BARNUM
1810–1891

There's a sucker born every minute.
> *Attributed*

PIERRE BOSQUET
1810–1861

It is magnificent, but it is not war.[1]
> *On the charge of the Light
Brigade at Balaklava* [*October
25, 1854*]

WILLIAM HENRY CHANNING
1810–1884

To live content with small means; to
seek elegance rather than luxury, and
refinement rather than fashion; to be
worthy, not respectable, and wealthy,
not rich; to study hard, think quietly,
talk gently, act frankly; to listen to stars

---

[1] The Gleam . . . signifies in my poem the
higher poetic imagination. — *From* HALLAM
TENNYSON, *Alfred, Lord Tennyson, A Memoir*
[1897], *vol. II, p. 366*
> Follow, follow, follow the gleam,
> Banners unfurled o'er all the world.
> Follow, follow, follow the gleam
> Of the chalice that is the Grail.
>> SALLIE HUME DOUGLAS [1923],
>> *Follow the Gleam, refrain*

[2] See Ennius, p. 106b.

[3] The United States — bounded on the north
by the Aurora Borealis, on the south by the
precession of the equinoxes, on the east by the
primeval chaos, and on the west by the Day of
Judgment. — JOHN FISKE [1842–1901], *Bounding
the United States*

[1] C'est magnifique, mais ce n'est pas la guerre.
See Tennyson, p. 652a.

and birds, to babes and sages, with open heart; to bear all cheerfully, do all bravely, await occasions, hurry never. In a word, to let the spiritual, unbidden and unconscious, grow up through the common. This is to be my symphony.
My Symphony

SIR FRANCIS HASTINGS DOYLE
1810–1888

Last night, among his fellow roughs,
　He jested, quaffed, and swore;
A drunken private of the Buffs,
　Who never looked before.
Today, beneath the foeman's frown,
　He stands in Elgin's place,
Ambassador from Britain's crown,
　And type of all her race.
The Private of the Buffs, st. 1

Ay, tear his body limb from limb,
　Bring cord, or axe, or flame,
He only knows that not through him
Shall England come to shame.
Ib. st. 2

FERDINAND FREILIGRATH
1810–1876

Oh love, as long as you can love.[1]
Der Liebe Dauer [1830]

MARGARET FULLER
1810–1850

I myself am more divine than any I see.
Letter to Emerson [*March 1, 1838*]

It does not follow because many books are written by persons born in America that there exists an American literature. Books which imitate or represent the thoughts and life of Europe do not constitute an American literature. Before such can exist, an original idea must animate this nation and fresh

[1] See Anonymous, *Pervigilium Veneris*, p. 150a.

currents of life must call into life fresh thoughts along its shores.
In the New York Tribune [*1846*]

For precocity some great price is always demanded sooner or later in life.
Diary. From Thomas Wentworth Higginson, *Life of Margaret Fuller Ossoli* [*1884*], *ch. 18*

Genius will live and thrive without training, but it does not the less reward the watering pot and pruning knife.
Ib.

I accept the universe.[1]　*Attributed*

ELIZABETH CLEGHORN GASKELL
1810–1865

A man is *so* in the way in the house.
Cranford [*1851–1853*], *ch. 1*

A little credulity helps one on through life very smoothly.
Ib. ch. 11

I'll not listen to reason. . . . Reason always means what someone else has got to say.　*Ib. ch. 14*

JAMES SLOAN GIBBONS
1810–1892

We are coming, Father Abraham, three hundred thousand more.
Three Hundred Thousand More [*1862*],[2] *st. 1*

POPE LEO XIII
[GIOACCHINO PECCI]
1810–1903

Every man has by nature the right to possess property as his own.
Rerum Novarum [*encyclical letter on the condition of labor, May 15, 1891*]

[1] By God! she'd better. — Carlyle's *reported comment*
[2] Song to help raise volunteers for the Union Army.

It is impossible to reduce human society to one level.
Rerum Novarum

It is one thing to have a right to the possession of money, and another to have a right to use money as one pleases.   *Ib.*

WILLIAM MILLER
1810–1872

Wee Willie Winkie rins through the town,
Upstairs and downstairs, in his nichtgown,
Tirlin' at the window, cryin' at the lock,
"Are the weans in their bed? for it's now ten o'clock."
Willie Winkie

ALFRED DE MUSSET
1810–1857

Doubt, if you will, the being who loves you,
Woman or dog, but never doubt love itself.
Premières Poésies [1829–1835],
La Coupe et les Lèvres

I have come too late into a century too old.
Poésies Nouvelles [1835–1852],
Rolla

The most despairing songs are the loveliest of all,
I know immortal ones composed only of tears.   *Ib. La Nuit de Mai*

Do not trifle with love.[1]
Title of a comedy [1834]

How glorious it is — and also how painful — to be an exception.
Le Merle Blanc. I

THEODORE PARKER
1810–1860

Truth never yet fell dead in the streets; it has such affinity with the soul

[1] On ne badine pas avec l'amour.

of man, the seed however broadcast will catch somewhere and produce its hundredfold.
A Discourse of Matters Pertaining to Religion [1842]

Truth stood on one side and Ease on the other; it has often been so.   *Ib.*

Man never falls so low that he can see nothing higher than himself.
Essay, A Lesson for the Day

All men desire to be immortal.
A Sermon on the Immortal Life
[*September 20, 1846*]

A democracy — that is a government of all the people, by all the people, for all the people;[1] of course, a government of the principles of eternal justice, the unchanging law of God; for shortness' sake I will call it the idea of Freedom.   *The American Idea*[2] [1850]

EDMUND HAMILTON SEARS
1810–1876

It came upon the midnight clear,
That glorious song of old,
From Angels bending near the earth
To touch their harps of gold;
"Peace on the earth, good will to men
From Heaven's all gracious King."
The world in solemn stillness lay
To hear the angels sing.
The Angel's Song [1850], *st. 1*

[1] See Wycliffe, p. 163b; Webster, p. 547a; Garrison, p. 616a; and Lincoln, p. 639a.
Parker used the same phrase in a speech delivered in Boston [May 31, 1854] and in a sermon in Music Hall, Boston [July 4, 1858]. William H. Herndon visited Boston and on his return to Springfield, Illinois, took with him some of Parker's sermons and addresses. In his *Abraham Lincoln, vol. II, p. 65*, Herndon says that Lincoln marked with pencil the portion of the Music Hall address, "Democracy is direct self-government, over all the people, by all the people, for all the people."
[2] Speech at the New England Anti-Slavery Convention, Boston [May 29, 1850].

MARTIN FARQUHAR TUPPER
1810–1889

Error is a hardy plant: it flourisheth in every soil.
> *Proverbial Philosophy* [*1838–1842*]. *Of Truth in Things False*

Well-timed silence hath more eloquence than speech.
> *Ib. Of Discretion*

A good book is the best of friends, the same today and forever.
> *Ib. Of Reading*

Nature's own Nobleman, friendly and frank,
Is a man with his heart in his hand!
> *Nature's Nobleman* [*1844*], *st. 1*

JOHN BRIGHT
1811–1889

The Angel of Death has been abroad throughout the land; you may almost hear the beating of his wings.
> *Speech, House of Commons* [*February 23, 1855*]

Force is not a remedy.
> *Speech, Birmingham* [*November 16, 1880*]

My opinion is that the Northern States will manage somehow to muddle through.
> *Said during the American Civil War. From* JUSTIN MCCARTHY, *Reminiscences* [*1899*]

FANNY FERN
[SARA PAYSON PARTON]
1811–1872

The way to a man's heart is through his stomach.[1]   *Willis Parton*

THÉOPHILE GAUTIER
1811–1872

Everything passes. Robust art alone is eternal. The bust outlasts the citadel.[2]   *L'Art* [*1832*]

[1] See Byron, p. 562a.
[2] Tout passe. L'art robuste
   Seul a l'éternité;

HORACE GREELEY
1811–1872

A widow of doubtful age will marry almost any sort of a white man.
> *Letter to Dr. Rufus Wilmot Griswold*

If, on a full and final review, my life and practice shall be found unworthy of my principles, let due infamy be heaped on my memory; but let none be thereby led to distrust the principles to which I proved recreant, nor yet the ability of some to adorn them by a suitable life and conversation. To unerring time be all this committed.
> *Statement* [*1846*]. *From* JAMES PARTON, *Life of Horace Greeley* [*1855*]

The best business you can go into you will find on your father's farm or in his workshop. If you have no family or friends to aid you, and no prospect opened to you there, turn your face to the great West,[1] and there build up a home and fortune.
> *To Aspiring Young Men. Ib.*

The illusion that times that were are better than those that are, has probably pervaded all ages.
> *The American Conflict* [*1864–1866*]

Wisdom is never dear, provided the article be genuine.
> *Address on Agriculture, Houston, Texas* [*May 23, 1871*]

WENDELL PHILLIPS
1811–1884

We live under a government of men and morning newspapers.
> *Speech* [*January 28, 1852*]

Revolutions are not made; they come. A revolution is as natural a

Le buste
   Survit à la cité.
See Dobson, p. 782b.
[1] See J. B. L. Soule, p. 678b.

growth as an oak. It comes out of the past. Its foundations are laid far back.
Speech [January 8, 1852]

The best use of laws is to teach men to trample bad laws under their feet.
Speech [April 12, 1852]

What the Puritans gave the world was not thought, but action.
Speech [December 21, 1855]

The rock underlies all America; it only crops out here.   *Ib.*

One on God's side is a majority.[1]
Speech [November 1, 1859]

Every man meets his Waterloo at last.   *Ib.*

Truth is one forever absolute, but opinion is truth filtered through the moods, the blood, the disposition of the spectator.   *Idols [October 4, 1859]*

Difference of religion breeds more quarrels than difference of politics.
Speech [November 7, 1860]

Revolutions never go backward.[2]
Speech [February 17, 1861]

Aristocracy is always cruel.
Address on Toussaint L'Ouverture [1861]

HARRIET BEECHER STOWE[3]
1811–1896

Eliza made her desperate retreat across the river just in the dusk of twilight. The gray mist of evening, rising slowly from the river, enveloped her as she disappeared up the bank, and the swollen current and floundering masses

of ice presented a hopeless barrier between her and her pursuer.
Uncle Tom's Cabin [1852], ch. 8

I [Topsy] 'spect I growed. Don't think nobody never made me.
Ib. ch. 20

I's wicked — I is. I's mighty wicked, anyhow. I can't help it.   *Ib.*

CHARLES SUMNER
1811–1874

There is the National flag. He must be cold, indeed, who can look upon its folds rippling in the breeze without pride of country. If in a foreign land, the flag is companionship, and country itself, with all its endearments.
Are We a Nation? [November 19, 1867]

The phrase, "public office is a public trust," has of late become common property.[1]
Speech, U.S. Senate [May 31, 1872]

WILLIAM MAKEPEACE THACKERAY
1811–1863

This I set down as a positive truth. A woman with fair opportunities, and without a positive hump, may marry whom she likes.[2]
Vanity Fair [1847–1848], vol. I, ch. 4

Them's my sentiments.   *Ib. 21*

Everybody in Vanity Fair must have remarked how well those live who are comfortably and thoroughly in debt;

---

[1] See Knox, p. 186b.

[2] I know, and all the world knows, that revolutions never go backward. — WILLIAM HENRY SEWARD, *Speech at Rochester on the Irrepressible Conflict* [October 1858]

[3] We have seen an American woman write a novel of which a million copies were sold in all languages, and which had one merit, of speaking to the universal heart, and was read with equal interest to three audiences, namely, in the parlor, in the kitchen, and in the nursery of every house. — EMERSON, *Society and Solitude* [1870]. *Success*

[1] See Matthew Henry, p. 386b, and note.

[2] I should like to see any kind of a man, distinguishable from a gorilla, that some good and even pretty woman could not shape a husband out of. — OLIVER WENDELL HOLMES, *The Professor at the Breakfast-Table* [1860]

The whole world is strewn with snares, traps, gins and pitfalls for the capture of men by women. — BERNARD SHAW, *Man and Superman* [1903], *Epistle Dedicatory*

how they deny themselves nothing; how jolly and easy they are in their minds.
Vanity Fair, vol. I, ch. 22

How to Live Well on Nothing a Year.　　　*Ib. 36 [title]*

I think I could be a good woman if I had five thousand a year.[1]　　*Ib. II, 1*

Ah! *Vanitas vanitatum!* Which of us is happy in this world? Which of us has his desire? or, having it, is satisfied? — Come, children, let us shut up the box and the puppets, for our play is played out.　　　*Ib.* 27

He who meanly admires mean things is a Snob.
The Book of Snobs [1848], *ch.* 2

Rake's Progress.[2]
Pendennis [1848–1850], *ch. 19 [title]*

Yes, I am a fatal man, Madame Fribsbi. To inspire hopeless passion is my destiny.　　　*Ib.* 23

Remember, it's as easy to marry a rich woman as a poor woman.　　*Ib.* 28

Of the Corporation of the Goose-quill — of the Press . . . of the fourth estate.[3] . . . There she is — the great engine — she never sleeps. She has her ambassadors in every quarter of the world — her courtiers upon every road. Her officers march along with armies, and her envoys walk into statesmen's cabinets. They are ubiquitous.　*Ib.* 30

'Tis not the dying for a faith that's so hard, Master Harry — every man of every nation has done that — 'tis the living up to it that's difficult.[4]
Henry Esmond [1852], *bk. I, ch.* 6

'Tis strange what a man may do, and a woman yet think him an angel.
Ib. 7

The wicked are wicked, no doubt, and they go astray and they fall, and

[1] See Huxley, p. 725a.
[2] *The Rake's Progress* is the title of one of the famous series of paintings and engravings by William Hogarth [1697–1764].
[3] See Carlyle, p. 576a.
[4] See Adlai E. Stevenson, p. 1048b.

they come by their deserts; but who can tell the mischief which the very virtuous do?
The Newcomes [1853–1855], *ch.* 20

This Bouillabaisse a noble dish is —
A sort of soup, or broth, or brew.
Ballads [1855]. *The Ballad of Bouillabaisse, st.* 2

Christmas is here:
Winds whistle shrill,
Icy and chill.
Little care we;
Little we fear
Weather without,
Sheltered about
The Mahogany Tree.
Ib. The Mahogany Tree, st. 1

Away from the world and its toils and its cares,
I've a snug little kingdom up four pair of stairs.
Ib. The Cane-Bottom'd Chair, st. 1

I sit here,
Alone and merry at forty year,
Dipping my nose in the Gascon wine.
Ib. The Age of Wisdom, st. 6

Werther had a love for Charlotte
Such as words could never utter;
Would you know how first he met her?
She was cutting bread and butter.[1]
Ib. Sorrows of Werther, st. 1

There lived a sage in days of yore,
And he a handsome pigtail wore;
But wondered much and sorrowed more
Because it hung behind him.
Ib. A Tragic Story (from Adelbert von Chamisso), st. 1

There were three sailors of Bristol City
Who took a boat and went to sea.
But first with beef and captain's biscuits
And pickled pork they loaded she.
Ib. Little Billee, st. 1

[1] Charlotte held a brown loaf in her hand, and was cutting slices for the little ones all round in proportion to their age and appetite. — GOETHE, *The Sorrows of Werther* [1774]

And the youngest he was little Billee.
Ballads. Little Billee, st. 2

To gorging Jack says guzzling Jimmy,
"We've nothing left, us must eat we."
Ib. st. 3

A pedigree reaching as far back as the Deluge.
The Rose and the Ring [1855],
ch. 2

The book of female logic is blotted all over with tears, and Justice in their courts is forever in a passion.
The Virginians [1857–1859],
ch. 4

Women like not only to conquer, but to be conquered.   *Ib.*

Next to the very young, I suppose the very old are the most selfish.
Ib. 61

Through all the doubt and darkness, the danger and long tempest of the war, I think it was only the American leader's [1] indomitable soul that remained entirely steady.   *Ib. 90*

To endure is greater than to dare; to tire out hostile fortune; to be daunted by no difficulty; to keep heart when all have lost it; to go through intrigue spotless; to forego even ambition when the end is gained — who can say this is not greatness?   *Ib. 92*

Bravery never goes out of fashion.
The Four Georges [1860],
George II

ROBERT BROWNING
1812–1889

Sun-treader,[2] life and light be thine forever!   *Pauline* [1833]

I go to prove my soul!
I see my way as birds their trackless way.   *Paracelsus* [1835], *pt. I*

In some time, his good time, I shall arrive:
He guides me and the bird. In his good time!   *Ib.*

[1] George Washington.
[2] Shelley.

Measure your mind's height by the shade it casts!   *Paracelsus, pt. III*

Every joy is gain
And gain is gain, however small.
Ib. IV

Over the sea our galleys went.   *Ib.*

I give the fight up: let there be an end,
A privacy, an obscure nook for me.
I want to be forgotten even by God.
Ib. V

Sidney's self, the starry paladin.
Sordello [1] [1840], *pt. I*

Would you have your songs endure?
Build on the human heart.   *Ib. II*

Any nose
May ravage with impunity a rose.
Ib. VI

Day!
Faster and more fast,
O'er night's brim, day boils at last.
Pippa Passes [1841], *introduction*

The year's at the spring
And day's at the morn;
Morning's at seven;
The hillside's dew-pearled;
The lark's on the wing;
The snail's on the thorn:
God's in his heaven —
All's right with the world.[2]   *Ib. pt. I*

Some unsuspected isle in far-off seas.
Ib. II

In the morning of the world,
When earth was nigher heaven than now.   *Ib. III*

All service ranks the same with God:
With God, whose puppets, best and worst,
Are we; there is no last nor first.
Ib. IV

There's a woman like a dewdrop, she's so purer than the purest.
A Blot in the 'Scutcheon
[1842], *act I, st. 3*

[1] See Lombroso, p. 770a, note.
[2] See Voltaire, p. 417a, and Whittier, p. 626b.

When is man strong until he feels
alone? [1]
Colombe's Birthday [1842],
act III

You know, we French stormed Ratisbon.
Incident of the French Camp
[1842], *st. 1*

"You're wounded!" "Nay," the sol-
dier's pride
Touched to the quick, he said:
"I'm killed, Sire!" And his chief beside,
Smiling the boy fell dead.
Ib. st. 5

That's my last Duchess painted on the
wall.
My Last Duchess [1842], *l. 1*

She had
A heart — how shall I say? — too soon
made glad.   *Ib. l. 21*

The lie was dead,
And damned, and truth stood up in-
stead.
Count Gismond [1842], *st. 13*

Marching along, fifty-score strong,
Great-hearted gentlemen, singing this
song.
Cavalier Tunes [1842], *Marching Along, st. 1*

Boot, saddle, to horse, and away!
Ib. Boot and Saddle, refrain

Morning, evening, noon and night,
"Praise God!" sang Theocrite.
The Boy and the Angel [1845],
st. 1

Just my vengeance complete,
The man sprang to his feet,
Stood erect, caught at God's skirts, and
prayed!
— So, I was afraid!
Instans Tyrannus [1845], *st. 7*

Hamelin Town's in Brunswick,
By famous Hanover city.
The Pied Piper of Hamelin
[1845], *st. 1*

Rats!
They fought the dogs and killed the
cats,
And bit the babies in the cradles,
And ate the cheeses out of the vats,
And licked the soup from the cooks'
own ladles.
*The Pied Piper of Hamelin,
st. 2*

With shrieking and squeaking
In fifty different sharps and flats.
Ib.

When the liquor's out, why clink the
cannikin?
The Flight of the Duchess
[1845], *st. 16*

It's a long lane that knows no turnings.
Ib. st. 17

Just for a handful of silver he left us,
Just for a riband to stick in his coat.
The Lost Leader [1] [1845], *st. 1*

We that had loved him so, followed
him, honored him,
Lived in his mild and magnificent eye,
Learned his great language, caught his
clear accents,
Made him our pattern to live and to
die!   *Ib.*

Shakespeare was of us, Milton was for
us,
Burns, Shelley, were with us — they
watch from their graves!   *Ib.*

One more devils'-triumph and sorrow
for angels,
One more wrong to man, one more insult to God!   *Ib. st. 2*

Let him never come back to us!
There would be doubt, hesitation and
pain,
Forced praise on our part — the
glimmer of twilight,
Never glad confident morning again!
Ib.

It was roses, roses all the way.
The Patriot [1845], *st. 1*

I sprang to the stirrup, and Joris, and
he;

---

[1] See Ibsen, p. 729b.

[1] Often assumed to refer to Wordsworth.

I galloped, Dirck galloped, we galloped all three.
> *How They Brought the Good News from Ghent to Aix* [1845], *st. 1*

And into the midnight we galloped abreast. *Ib.*

The gray sea and the long black land;
And the yellow half-moon large and low.
> *Meeting at Night* [1845], *st. 1*

Then a mile of warm, sea-scented beach. *Ib. st. 2*

Round the cape of a sudden came the sea,
And the sun looked over the mountain's rim:
And straight was a path of gold for him,
And the need of a world of men for me. *Parting at Morning* [1845]

Oh, to be in England now that April's there,
And whoever wakes in England sees, some morning, unaware,
That the lowest boughs and the brushwood sheaf
Round the elm-tree bole are in tiny leaf,
While the chaffinch sings on the orchard bough
In England — now!
> *Home Thoughts, from Abroad* [1845], *l. 1*

That's the wise thrush; he sings each song twice over,
Lest you should think he never could recapture
The first fine careless rapture!
> *Ib. l. 12*

Nobly, nobly Cape St. Vincent to the northwest died away;
Sunset ran, one glorious blood-red, reeking into Cadiz Bay.
> *Home Thoughts, from the Sea* [1845], *l. 1*

Let's contend no more, Love,
Strive nor weep:

All be as before, Love,
— Only sleep!
> *A Woman's Last Word* [1855], *st. 1*

Where the apple reddens
Never pry —
Lest we lose our Edens,
Eve and I.
> *Ib. st. 5*

Beautiful Evelyn Hope is dead!
> *Evelyn Hope* [1855], *st. 1*

You will wake, and remember, and understand. *Ib. st. 7*

Where the quiet-colored end of evening smiles.
> *Love Among the Ruins* [1855], *st. 1*

Earth's returns
For whole centuries of folly, noise and sin! *Ib. st. 7*

This world, and the wrong it does.
> *Old Pictures in Florence* [1855], *st. 7*

What's come to perfection perishes.
Things learned on earth, we shall practice in heaven:
Works done least rapidly, Art most cherishes. *Ib. st. 17*

Your ghost will walk, you lover of trees,
(If our loves remain)
In an English lane.
> *De Gustibus* [1855], *st. 1*

Open my heart, and you will see
Graved inside of it, "Italy." [1]
> *Ib. st. 2*

How well I know what I mean to do
When the long dark autumn evenings come.
> *By the Fireside* [1855], *st. 1*

O woman-country! [2] wooed not wed.
> *Ib. st. 6*

Oh, the little more, and how much it is!
And the little less, and what worlds away! *Ib. st. 39*

[1] See Mary Tudor, p. 187b.
[2] Italy.

If two lives join, there is oft a scar.
They are one and one, with a shadowy
    third;
One near one is too far.
By the Fireside, st. 46

Only I discern
Infinite passion, and the pain
Of finite hearts that yearn.
Two in the Campagna [1855],
st. 12

This is a spray the Bird clung to,
Making it blossom with pleasure.
Misconceptions [1855], *st. 1*

Escape me?
Never —
Beloved!
While I am I, and you are you.
Life in a Love [1855], *st. 1*

To dry one's eyes and laugh at a fall,
And baffled, get up and begin again.
Ib. st. 2

Ah, did you once see Shelley plain,
    And did he stop and speak to you,
And did you speak to him again?
    How strange it seems, and new! [1]
Memorabilia [1855], *st. 1*

Who knows but the world may end to-
    night?
The Last Ride Together [1855],
st. 2

Fail I alone, in words and deeds?
Why, all men strive, and who succeeds?
Ib. st. 5

Sing, riding's a joy! For me I ride.
Ib. st. 7

The instant made eternity —
And heaven just prove that I and she
Ride, ride together, forever ride?
Ib. st. 10

That low man seeks a little thing to
    do,
    Sees it and does it;

---

[1] And did you once find Browning plain?
    And did he really seem quite clear?
    And did you read the book again?
      How strange it seems, and queer.
      CHARLES WILLIAM STUBBS [1845–1912],
Parody

This high man, with a great thing to
    pursue,
Dies ere he knows it.
That low man goes on adding one to
    one,
    His hundred's soon hit;
This high man, aiming at a million,
    Misses an unit.
That, has the world here — should he
    need the next,
    Let the world mind him!
This, throws himself on God, and un-
    perplexed
Seeking shall find Him.
A Grammarian's Funeral [1855],
l. 113

And inasmuch as feeling, the East's
    gift,
Is quick and transient — comes, and lo,
    is gone —
While Northern thought is slow and
    durable.   *Luria* [1855], *act V*

Less is more.[1]
Andrea del Sarto [1855], *l. 78*

Ah, but a man's reach should exceed
    his grasp,
Or what's a heaven for?   *Ib. l. 97*

Again the cousin's whistle! Go, my
    love.   *Ib. last line*

How I shall lie through centuries,
And hear the blessed mutter of the
    mass,
And see God made and eaten all day
    long,
And feel the steady candle-flame, and
    taste
Good strong thick stupefying incense
    smoke!
*The Bishop Orders His Tomb at
Saint Praxed's Church* [1855],
l. 80

Truth that peeps
Over the glass's edge when dinner's
    done,

---

[1] See Hesiod, p. 67b.
Not so honest would be more honest. — G. E.
LESSING, *Emilia Galotti* [1722], *act I, sc. 4*
A popular aphorism with the architect Lud-
wig Mies van der Rohe.

And body gets its sop and holds its noise
And leaves soul free a little.
Bishop Blougram's Apology
[1855], *l.* 17

Just when we are safest, there's a sunset-touch,
A fancy from a flower-bell, someone's death,
A chorus-ending from Euripides.
Ib. l. 183

One wise man's verdict outweighs all the fools'. *Ib. l. 373*

Our interest's on the dangerous edge of things.
The honest thief, the tender murderer,
The superstitious atheist, demirep
That loves and saves her soul in new French books. *Ib. l. 396*

You call for faith:
I show you doubt, to prove that faith exists.
The more of doubt, the stronger faith, I say,
If faith o'ercomes doubt. *Ib. l. 601*

When the fight begins within himself,
A man's worth something. *Ib. l. 793*

What of soul was left, I wonder, when the kissing had to stop?
A Toccata of Galuppi's [1855], *st.* 14

Dear dead women, with such hair, too
— what's become of all the gold
Used to hang and brush their bosoms?
I feel chilly and grown old. *Ib. st. 15*

The sin I impute to each frustrate ghost
Is — the unlit lamp and the ungirt loin.
The Statue and the Bust [1855], *st. 82, 83*

How good is man's life, the mere living! how fit to employ
All the heart and the soul and the senses forever in joy!
Saul [1855], *st.* 9

All's love, yet all's law. *Ib. st. 17*

'Tis not what man does which exalts him, but what man would do!
Saul, st. 18

The sprinkled isles,
Lily on lily, that o'erlace the sea.
Cleon [1855], *l.* 1

And I have written three books on the soul,
Proving absurd all written hitherto,
And putting us to ignorance again.
Ib. l. 57

Rafael made a century of sonnets.
One Word More [1855], 2

Does he paint? he fain would write a poem —
Does he write? he fain would paint a picture. *Ib. 8*

Where my heart lies, let my brain lie also. *Ib. 14*

God be thanked, the meanest of his creatures
Boasts two soul-sides, one to face the world with,
One to show a woman when he loves her.[1] *Ib. 17*

Oh, their Rafael of the dear Madonnas,
Oh, their Dante of the dread Inferno,
Wrote one song — and in my brain I sing it,
Drew one angel — borne, see, on my bosom! *Ib. 19*

That out of three sounds he frame, not a fourth sound, but a star.
Abt Vogler [1864],[2] *st.* 7

On the earth the broken arcs; in the heaven, a perfect round.
Ib. st. 9

The high that proved too high, the heroic for earth too hard,
The passion that left the ground to lose itself in the sky. *Ib. st. 10*

Sorrow is hard to bear, and doubt is slow to clear,
Each sufferer says his say, his scheme of the weal and woe:

[1] See Mark Twain, p. 763a.
[2] The Abt or Abbé George Joseph Vogler [1749–1824] was a composer, professor, Kapellmeister, and writer on music.

But God has a few of us whom he
whispers in the ear;
The rest may reason and welcome; 'tis
we musicians know.
Abt Vogler, st. 11

The C Major of this life. *Ib. st.* 12

Grow old along with me!
The best is yet to be,
The last of life, for which the first was
made.
Our times are in his hand.
Rabbi Ben Ezra [1864], *st.* 1

Irks care the crop-full bird? Frets doubt
the maw-crammed beast?
Ib. st. 4

Then welcome each rebuff
That turns earth's smoothness rough,
Each sting that bids nor sit nor stand,
but go!
Be our joys three parts pain!
Strive, and hold cheap the strain;
Learn, nor account the pang; dare,
never grudge the throe! *Ib. st.* 6

What I aspired to be,
And was not, comforts me. *Ib. st.* 7

Therefore I summon age
To grant youth's heritage. *Ib. st.* 13

Look not thou down but up!
Ib. st. 30

Such ever was love's way; to rise, it
stoops.
A Death in the Desert [1864],
l. 134

Progress, man's distinctive mark alone,
Not God's, and not the beasts': God is,
they are;
Man partly is, and wholly hopes to be.
Ib. l. 586

Letting the rank tongue blossom into
speech.
Caliban upon Setebos [1864],
l. 23

How sad and bad and mad it was [1] —
But then, how it was sweet!
Confessions [1864], *st.* 9

[1] See Swinburne, p. 776a.

Fear death? — to feel the fog in my
throat,
The mist in my face.
Prospice [1864], *l.* 1

No! let me taste the whole of it, fare
like my peers,
The heroes of old,
Bear the brunt, in a minute pay glad
life's arrears
Of pain, darkness, and cold.
Ib. l. 17

Hold me but safe again within the
bond
Of one immortal look.
Eurydice to Orpheus [1864], *l.* 5

This could but have happened once —
And we missed it, lost it forever.
Youth and Art [1864], *st.* 17

All that I own is a print,
An etching, a mezzotint.
A Likeness [1864], *st.* 4

He never saw, never before today,
What was able to take his breath away.
A face to lose youth for, to occupy age
With the dream of, meet death with.[1]
Ib. st. 6

We find great things are made of little
things,
And little things go lessening till at last
Comes God behind them.
Mr. Sludge, "The Medium"
[1864], *l.* 1112

'Tis because stiffish cock-tail, taken in
time,
Is better for a bruise than arnica.[2]
Ib. l. 1478

Boston's a hole, the herring-pond is
wide,
V-notes are something, liberty still
more.
Beside, is he the only fool in the world?
Ib. l. 1523

It's wiser being good than bad;
It's safer being meek than fierce;
It's fitter being sane than mad.

[1] A face that a man might die for. — SIR
ARTHUR CONAN DOYLE, *The Adventures of Sherlock Holmes: A Scandal in Bohemia* [1892]
[2] See Irving, p. 549b.

My own hope is, a sun will pierce
The thickest cloud earth ever stretched;
That, after Last, returns the First,
Though a wide compass round be
    fetched;
That what began best can't end worst,
Nor what God blessed once, prove
    accurs'd.
         Apparent Failure [*1864*], *st. 7*

O Lyric Love, half angel and half bird,
And all a wonder and a wild desire.
         The Ring and the Book [*1868–*
               1869], *pt. I*

    The truth was felt by instinct here,
— Process which saves a world of trou-
    ble and time.
         Ib. IV, Tertium Quid

'Twas a thief said the last kind word to
    Christ:
Christ took the kindness and forgave
    the theft.
         Ib. VI, Giuseppe Caponsacchi

All poetry is difficult to read,
— The sense of it is, anyhow.
         Ib. VII, Pompilia

No work begun shall ever pause for
    death!   *Ib.*

Faultless to a fault.
         Ib. IX, Juris Doctor Johannes-
              Baptista Bottinius

    The curious crime, the fine
Felicity and flower of wickedness.
         Ib. X, The Pope

    What I call God,
And fools call Nature.[1]   *Ib.*

Why comes temptation, but for man
    to meet
And master and make crouch beneath
    his foot,
And so be pedestaled in triumph?
                      Ib.

White shall not neutralize the black,
    nor good

  [1] Some call it Evolution,
    And others call it God. . . .
  Some of us call it Autumn,
    And others call it God.
      W. H. CARRUTH [*1859–1924*], *Each in*
                     His Own Tongue

Compensate bad in man, absolve him
    so:
Life's business being just the terrible
    choice.
         The Ring and the Book,
              pt. X, The Pope

You never know what life means till
    you die:
Even throughout life, 'tis death that
    makes life live,
Gives it whatever the significance.
         Ib. XI, Guido

Save the squadron, honor France, love
    thy wife the Belle Aurore!
         Hervé Riel [*1871*], *st. 11*

A man in armor is his armor's slave.
         Herakles [*1871*]

    In God's good time,
Which does not always fall on Satur-
    day
When the world looks for wages.[1]
                     Ib.

So absolutely good is truth, truth never
    hurts
The teller.
         Fifine at the Fair [*1872*], *st. 32*

    That far land we dream about,
Where every man is his own architect.
         Red Cotton Nightcap Country
                    [*1873*], *II*

    A secret's safe
'Twixt you, me, and the gatepost!
         The Inn Album [*1875*], *II*

Ignorance is not innocence but sin.
         Ib. V

Have you found your life distasteful?
    My life did and does smack sweet.
Was your youth of pleasure wasteful?
    Mine I saved and hold complete.
Do your joys with age diminish?
    When mine fail me, I'll complain.
Must in death your daylight finish?
    My sun sets to rise again.
         At the "Mermaid" [*1876*], *st. 10*

  [1] The old Tuscan proverb, *Iddio non paga
sabato* [God does not pay Saturdays]. — *Life in
Letters of William Dean Howells* [*1928*], *vol.
II, p. 169, letter to Mrs. James T. Fields*
[*February 23, 1903*]

I find earth not gray but rosy,
Heaven not grim but fair of hue.
Do I stoop? I pluck a posy.
Do I stand and stare? [1] All's blue.
At the "Mermaid," st. 12

"With this same key
Shakespeare unlocked his heart" [2] once
more!
Did Shakespeare? If so, the less
Shakespeare he!
House [1876], *st. 10*

Because a man has shop to mind
In time and place, since flesh must live,
Needs spirit lack all life behind,
All stray thoughts, fancies fugitive,
All loves except what trade can give?
Shop [1876], *st. 20*

Good, to forgive;
Best, to forget!
Living, we fret;
Dying, we live.
La Saisiaz [1877]. *Introduction,*
st. 1

Sky — what a scowl of cloud
Till, near and far,
Ray on ray split the shroud:
Splendid, a star!
The Two Poets of Croisic [1878].
Introduction, st. 2

As if true pride
Were not also humble!
Lines written in an album [1882]

Wanting is — what?
Summer redundant,
Blueness abundant,
— Where is the blot?
Wanting Is — What? [3] [1883]

Out of the wreck I rise.
Ixion [1883]

---

[1] What is this life if, full of care,
We have no time to stand and stare?
WILLIAM HENRY DAVIES [1871–1940],
Leisure

[2] See Wordsworth, p. 517a.

[3] Browning is — what?
Riddle redundant,
Baldness abundant,
Sense, who can spot?
ANONYMOUS, in *Punch* [April 21, 1883]

Never the time and the place
And the loved one all together!
Never the Time and the Place
[1883]

Help me with knowledge — for Life's
Old — Death's New!
Epitaph on Levi Lincoln
Thaxter, 1824–1884

A minute's success pays the failure of
years.
Apollo and the Fates [1886], *st. 42*

One who never turned his back but
marched breast forward,
Never doubted clouds would break,
Never dreamed though right were
worsted, wrong would triumph,
Held we fall to rise, are baffled to fight
better,
Sleep to wake.
Asolando [1889]. *Epilogue, st. 3*

SAMUEL DICKINSON
BURCHARD
1812–1891

We are Republicans, and don't propose to leave our party and identify
ourselves with the party whose ante-
cedents have been Rum, Romanism,
and Rebellion.
Speaking for a deputation of
clergymen calling upon James
G. Blaine, the Republican
Presidential candidate, New
York [October 29, 1884]

CHARLES DICKENS
1812–1870

A smattering of everything, and a
knowledge of nothing.
Sketches by Boz [1836–1837].
Tales, ch. 3

He had used the word [humbug] in
its Pickwickian sense.
Pickwick Papers [1836–1837],
ch. 1

"An observer of human nature, sir,"
said Mr. Pickwick.
Ib. 2

"It wasn't the wine," murmured Mr. Snodgrass, in a broken voice. "It was the salmon."
Pickwick Papers, ch. 8

I wants to make your flesh creep.
Ib.

Can I unmoved see thee dying
    On a log
    Expiring frog!   *Ib. 15*

Tongue; well that's a wery good thing when it an't a woman's. *Ib. 19*

Mr. Weller's knowledge of London was extensive and peculiar. *Ib. 20*

Be wery careful o' vidders all your life. *Ib.*

The wictim o' connubiality, as Blue Beard's domestic chaplain said, with a tear of pity, ven he buried him. *Ib.*

Dumb as a drum vith a hole in it, sir. *Ib. 25*

Eccentricities of genius. *Ib. 30*

Keep yourself *to* yourself. *Ib. 32*

Poetry's unnat'ral; no man ever talked poetry 'cept a beadle on Boxin' Day. *Ib. 33*

She knows wot's wot, she does.
Ib. 37

They don't mind it; it's a regular holiday to them — all porter and skittles.[1] *Ib. 41*

Anythin' for a quiet life, as the man said wen he took the sitivation at the lighthouse. *Ib. 43*

Oliver Twist has asked for more!
Oliver Twist [1837–1838], *ch. 2*

"The artful Dodger." *Ib. 8*

"Hard," replied the Dodger. "As nails," added Charley Bates. *Ib. 9*

There is a passion for hunting something deeply implanted in the human breast. *Ib. 10*

I'll eat my head. *Ib.*

[1] Life ain't all beer and skittles, and more's the pity. — GEORGE DU MAURIER, *Trilby* [1894], *pt. I*. See Hughes, p. 718a.

I only know two sorts of boys. Mealy boys, and beef-faced boys.
Oliver Twist, ch. 10

There's light enough for wot I've got to do. *Ib. 47*

"If the law supposes that," said Mr. Bumble . . . "the law is a ass, a idiot." *Ib. 51*

He had but one eye, and the popular prejudice runs in favor of two.
Nicholas Nickleby [1838–1839], *ch. 4*

Subdue your appetites, my dears, and you've conquered human natur.
Ib. 5

There are only two styles of portrait painting; the serious and the smirk.
Ib. 10

Oh! they're too beautiful to live, much too beautiful! *Ib. 14*

I pity his ignorance and despise him.
Ib. 15

The unities, sir . . . are a completeness — a kind of universal dovetailedness with regard to place and time. *Ib. 24*

The two countesses had no outlines at all, and the dowager's was a demd outline. *Ib. 34*

A demd, damp, moist, unpleasant body! *Ib.*

Bring in the bottled lightning, a clean tumbler, and a corkscrew.
Ib. 49

All is gas and gaiters. *Ib.*

My life is one demd horrid grind.
Ib. 64

He has gone to the demnition bow-wows. *Ib.*

What is the odds so long as the fire of soul is kindled at the taper of conwiviality, and the wing of friendship never moults a feather!
The Old Curiosity Shop [1841], *ch. 2*

She's the ornament of her sex.
The Old Curiosity Shop, ch. 5

In love of home, the love of country has its rise. *Ib.* 38

That vague kind of penitence which holidays awaken next morning.
Ib. 40

"Did you ever taste beer?" "I had a sip of it once," said the small servant. "Here's a state of things!" cried Mr. Swiveller. . . . "She *never* tasted it — it can't be tasted in a sip!"
Ib. 57

It was a maxim with Foxey — our revered father, gentlemen — "Always suspect everybody." *Ib.* 66

Rather a tough customer in argyment.
Barnaby Rudge [1841], *ch.* 1

"There are strings," said Mr. Tappertit, ". . . in the human heart that had better not be wibrated."
Ib. 22

Oh gracious, why wasn't I born old and ugly? *Ib.* 70

Any man may be in good spirits and good temper when he's well dressed. There an't much credit in that.
Martin Chuzzlewit [1843–1844],
ch. 5

With affection beaming in one eye, and calculation shining out of the other. *Ib.* 8

"Do not repine, my friends," said Mr. Pecksniff, tenderly. "Do not weep for me. It is chronic." *Ib.* 9

Keep up appearances whatever you do. *Ib.* 11

"Do other men for they would do you." That's the true business precept.
Ib.

Buy an annuity cheap, and make your life interesting to yourself and everybody else that watches the speculation. *Ib.* 18

Leave the bottle on the chimleypiece, and don't ask me to take none, but let me put my lips to it when I am so dispoged.
Martin Chuzzlewit, ch. 19

"She's the sort of woman now," said Mould . . . "one would almost feel disposed to bury for nothing: and do it neatly, too!" *Ib.* 25

He'd make a lovely corpse. *Ib.*

Our fellow-countryman is a model of a man, quite fresh from Natur's mold!
Ib. 34

Oh Sairey, Sairey, little do we know wot lays afore us! *Ib.* 40

I don't believe there's no sich a person! *Ib.* 49

The words she spoke of Mrs. Harris, lambs could not forgive . . . nor worms forget. *Ib.*

Marley was dead, to begin with. There is no doubt whatever about that. The register of his burial was signed by the clergyman, the clerk, the undertaker, and the chief mourner. Scrooge signed it. And Scrooge's name was good upon 'Change for anything he chose to put his hand to.
Old Marley was as dead as a doornail.
A Christmas Carol [1843], *stave* I

Secret, and self-contained, and solitary as an oyster. *Ib.*

I wear the chain I forged in life.
Ib.

In came a fiddler — and tuned like fifty stomachaches. In came Mrs. Fezziwig, one vast substantial smile.
Ib. stave II

Let's have the shutters up . . . before a man can say Jack Robinson.[1]
Ib.

As good as gold. *Ib. stave* III

[1] I'd do it as soon as say Jack Robinson. — FANNY BURNEY, *Evelina* [1778], *letter* 82
I'd get her off before you could say Jack Robinson. — MARIA EDGEWORTH, *The Absentee* [1812], *ch.* 2

"God bless us every one!" said Tiny Tim, the last of all.
A Christmas Carol, stave III

It *was* a turkey! He could never have stood upon his legs, that bird! He would have snapped 'em off short in a minute, like sticks of sealing wax.
Ib. stave V

O let us love our occupations,
Bless the squire and his relations,
Live upon our daily rations,
And always know our proper stations.
The Chimes [1844], *second quarter*

He's tough, ma'am, tough, is J.B. Tough and devilish sly!
Dombey and Son [1848], *ch.* 7

I want to know what it says. . . . The sea, Floy, what it is that it keeps on saying.[1]   *Ib.* 8

"Wal'r, my boy," replied the Captain, "in the Proverbs of Solomon you will find the following words, 'May we never want a friend in need, nor a bottle to give him!' When found, make a note of."   *Ib.* 15

Cows are my passion.   *Ib.* 21

The bearings of this observation lays in the application on it.   *Ib.* 23

You'll find us rough, sir, but you'll find us ready.
David Copperfield [1849–1850], *ch.* 3

I am a lone lorn creetur . . . and everythink goes contrairy with me.
Ib.

Barkis is willin'.   *Ib.* 5

Experientia does it [2] — as Papa used to say.   *Ib.* 11

"In case anything turned up," which was his [Mr. Micawber's] favorite expression.[3]   *Ib.*

[1] See Carpenter, p. 675b.
[2] A pun on Experientia docet [Experience teaches] — TACITUS [c. 55–c. 117], *History, bk. V, ch.* 6
[3] See Disraeli, p. 612a.

I never will desert Mr. Micawber.
David Copperfield, ch. 12

Annual income twenty pounds, annual expenditure nineteen nineteen six, result happiness. Annual income twenty pounds, annual expenditure twenty pounds ought and six, result misery.   *Ib.*

It's a mad world. Mad as Bedlam.
Ib. 14

I'm a very umble person.[1]   *Ib.* 16

The mistake was made of putting some of the trouble out of King Charles's head into my head.[2]
Ib. 17

I only ask for information.   *Ib.* 20

It was as true . . . as turnips is. It was as true . . . as taxes is. And nothing's truer than them.   *Ib.* 21

What a world of gammon and spinach it is, though, ain't it!
Ib. 22

Nobody's enemy but his own.
Ib. 25

Accidents will occur in the best-regulated families.   *Ib.* 28

Ride on! Rough-shod if need be, smooth-shod if that will do, but ride on! Ride on over all obstacles, and win the race!   *Ib.*

A long pull, and a strong pull, and a pull all together.   *Ib.* 30

He's a-going out with the tide.[3]
Ib.

There wasn't room to swing a cat there.   *Ib.* 35

I ate umble pie with an appetite.
Ib. 39

[1] Not only humble but umble, which I look upon to be the comparative, or, indeed, superlative degree. — ANTHONY TROLLOPE, *Doctor Thorne* [1858], *ch.* 4
[2] "King Charles's head" has passed into common use in the English language as a phrase meaning some whimsical obsession. — G. B. STERN [1890–   ], *Monogram*
[3] See Sir James Frazer, p. 829a.

Let sleeping dogs lie — who wants to rouse 'em?
David Copperfield, ch. 39

Skewered through and through with office pens, and bound hand and foot with red tape. *Ib.* 43

It's only my child-wife. *Ib.* 44

A man must take the fat with the lean. *Ib.* 51

Trifles make the sum of life. *Ib.* 53

The seamen said it blew great guns. *Ib.* 55

This is a London particular. . . . A fog, miss.
Bleak House [1852–1853], *ch.* 3

Not to put too fine a point upon it. *Ib.* 11

Whatever was required to be done, the Circumlocution Office was beforehand with all the public departments in the art of perceiving — HOW NOT TO DO IT.
Little Dorrit [1857–1858], *bk. I, ch.* 10

Papa, potatoes, poultry, prunes, and prism, are all very good words for the lips: especially prunes and prism. *Ib. II,* 5

Once a gentleman, and always a gentleman. *Ib.* 28

It was the best of times, it was the worst of times.
A Tale of Two Cities [1859], *bk. I, ch.* 1

A wonderful fact to reflect upon, that every human creature is constituted to be that profound secret and mystery to every other. *Ib.* 3

It is a far, far better thing that I do, than I have ever done; it is a far, far better rest that I go to, than I have ever known. *Ib. III,* 15

In the little world in which children have their existence, whosoever brings them up, there is nothing so finely per-

ceived and so finely felt, as injustice.
Great Expectations [1860–1861], *ch.* 9

Professionally he declines and falls, and as a friend he drops into poetry [Mr. Boffin on Silas Wegg].
Our Mutual Friend [1864–1865], *bk. I, ch.* 5

My best of wishes for your merry Christmases and your happy New Years, your long lives and your true prosperities. Worth twenty pound good if they are delivered as I send them. Remember? Here's a final prescription added, "To be taken for life."
Doctor Marigold's Prescriptions [1865], *ch.* 1

IVAN GONCHAROV
1812–1891

"And he was as intelligent as other people, his soul was pure and clear as crystal; he was noble and affectionate — and yet he did nothing!"
"But why? What was the reason?"
"The reason . . . what reason was there? Oblomovism!" [1]
Oblomov [1859], *pt. IV, ch.* 12

EDWARD LEAR
1812–1888

There was an Old Man with a beard,
Who said: "It is just as I feared!
Two owls and a hen,
Four larks and a wren
Have all built their nests in my beard."
Book of Nonsense [1846]. *Limerick*

How pleasant to know Mr. Lear!
Who has written such volumes of stuff!

[1] That word is Oblomovism.
Now, when I hear a country squire talking about the rights of man and urging the necessity of developing personality, I know from the first word he utters that he is an Oblomov.
When I hear a government official complaining that the system of administration is too complicated and cumbersome, I know that he is an Oblomov. — NIKOLAI DOBROLIUBOV, *What Is Oblomovism?* [1859]

Some think him ill-tempered and queer,
  But a few think him pleasant
  enough.
      Nonsense Songs [1871]. *Preface,*
      st. 1

His body is perfectly spherical,
He weareth a runcible hat. *Ib. st. 5*

The Owl and the Pussycat went to sea
  In a beautiful pea-green boat,
They took some honey, and plenty of
  money,
  Wrapped up in a five-pound note.
The Owl looked up to the stars above,
  And sang to a small guitar,
"O lovely Pussy! O Pussy, my love,
What a beautiful Pussy you are."
      The Owl and the Pussycat
      [1871], *st. 1*

Pussy said to the Owl, "You elegant
  fowl!
How charmingly sweet you sing!
O let us be married! too long we have
  tarried:
But what shall we do for a ring?"
They sailed away, for a year and a day,
  To the land where the Bong-tree
  grows
And there in a wood a Piggy-wig stood
With a ring at the end of his nose.
      Ib. st. 2

"Dear Pig, are you willing to sell for
  one shilling
Your ring?" Said the Piggy, "I will."
      Ib. st. 3

They dined on mince, and slices of
  quince,
  Which they ate with a runcible
  spoon;
And hand in hand, on the edge of the
  sand,
  They danced by the light of the
  moon. *Ib.*

Far and few, far and few,
  Are the lands where the Jumblies
  live;
Their heads are green, and their hands
  are blue,
  And they went to sea in a sieve.
      The Jumblies [1871], *st. 1*

Calico Pie,
  The little Birds fly
Down to the calico tree,
  Their wings were blue,
  And they sang "Tilly-loo!"
  Till away they flew —
And they never came back to me!
      Calico Pie [1871], *st. 1*

Calico Jam,
  The little Fish swam,
Over the syllabub sea. *Ib. st. 2*

Who, or why, or which, or what,
Is the Akond of Swat?
      The Akond of Swat [1] [1873], *l. 1*

She sate upon her Dobie,
  To watch the Evening Star,
And all the Punkahs as they passed,
  Cried, "My! how fair you are!"
      The Cummerbund [1874], *st. 1*

On the top of the Crumpetty Tree
  The Quangle Wangle sat,
But his face you could not see,
  On account of his Beaver Hat.
      The Quangle Wangle's Hat
      [1877], *st. 1*

On the coast of Coromandel
  Where the early pumpkins blow,
  In the middle of the woods
Lived the Yonghy-Bonghy-Bò.
Two old chairs, and half a candle,
One old jug without a handle —
  These were all his worldly goods.
      The Courtship of the Yonghy-
      Bongy-Bò [1877], *st. 1*

There he heard a Lady talking,
To some milk-white Hens of Dork-
  ing —
'Tis the Lady Jingly Jones!
      Ib. st. 2

"I would be your wife most gladly!"
(Here she twirled her fingers madly),
  "But in England I've a mate!"
      Ib. st. 5

[1] Now the Ahkoond of Swat is a vague sort of
  man
Who lives in a country far over the sea;
Pray tell me, good reader, if tell me you can,
What's the Ahkoond of Swat to you folks or to
  me?
      EUGENE FIELD, *The Ahkoond of Swat*
      [1884]

When awful darkness and silence
reign
Over the great Gromboolian plain,
Through the long, long wintry
nights.
*The Dong with the Luminous
Nose* [1877], *st. 1*

When storm-clouds brood on the
towering heights
Of the hills of the Chankly Bore.
Ib.

The Pobble who has no toes
Had once as many as we;
When they said, "Some day you may
lose them all" —
He replied, "Fish fiddle de-dee!"
The Pobble Who Has No Toes
[1877], *st. 1*

Ploffskin, Pluffskin, Pelican jee!
We think no Birds so happy as we!
Plumpskin, Ploshkin, Pelican jill!
We think so then, and we thought so
still.
The Pelican Chorus [1877],
chorus

SAMUEL SMILES
1812–1904

The spirit of self-help is the root of
all genuine growth in the individual;
and, exhibited in the lives of many, it
constitutes the true source of national
vigor and strength. Help from without
is often enfeebling in its effects, but
help from within invariably invigorates.
Self-Help [1859]

WILLIAM
EDMONDSTOUNE
AYTOUN
1813–1865

News of battle! — news of battle!
Hark! 'tis ringing down the street;
And the archways and the pavement
Bear the clang of hurrying feet.
Edinburgh after Flodden [1849],
st. 1

Nowhere beats the heart so kindly
As beneath the tartan plaid!
*Charles Edward at Versailles on
the Anniversary of Culloden*
[1849], *l. 219*

They bore within their breasts the grief
That fame can never heal —
The deep, unutterable woe
Which none save exiles feel.
The Island of the Scots [1849],
st. 12

HENRY WARD
BEECHER
1813–1887

A thoughtful mind, when it sees a
nation's flag, sees not the flag only, but
the nation itself; and whatever may be
its symbols, its insignia, he reads chiefly
in the flag the government, the principles, the truths, the history which belongs to the nation that sets it forth.
The American Flag

Where is human nature so weak as
in the bookstore!
Star Papers [1855]. *Subtleties of
Book Buyers*

Now comes the mystery.
Last words [March 8, 1887]

CLAUDE BERNARD
1813–1878

Great men may be compared to
torches shining at long intervals, to
guide the advance of science. They
light up their time, either by discovering unexpected and fertile phenomena
which open up new paths and reveal
unknown horizons, or by generalizing
acquired scientific facts and disclosing
truths which their predecessors had not
perceived.
*Introduction à l' Étude de
la Médecine Expérimentale*
[1865] [1]

[1] *An Introduction to the Study of Experimental Medicine*, translated by HENRY COPLEY
GREENE [1926].

We may, of course, strike a balance between what a living organism takes in as nourishment and what it gives out in excretions; but the results would be mere statistics incapable of throwing light on the inmost phenomena of nutrition in living beings. According to a Dutch chemist's phrase, this would be like trying to tell what happens inside a house by watching what goes in by the door and what comes out by the chimney.

> *Introduction à l'Étude de la Médecine Expérimentale*

Observation is a passive science, experimentation an active science.
> *Ib.*

The science of life is a superb and dazzlingly lighted hall which may be reached only by passing through a long and ghastly kitchen.   *Ib.*

Science repulses the indefinite.
> *Ib.*

The stability of the *internal medium* is a primary condition for the freedom and independence of certain living bodies in relation to the environment surrounding them.

> *Leçons sur les Phénomènes de la Vie Communs aux Animaux et aux Végétaux* [1878–1879] [1]

All the vital mechanisms, varied as they are, have only one object, that of preserving constant the conditions of life in the internal environment.   *Ib.*

True science teaches us to doubt and to abstain from ignorance.

> *From Bulletin of New York Academy of Medicine, vol. IV* [1928], *p.* 997

Science increases our power in proportion as it lowers our pride.   *Ib.*

If I had to define life in a word, it would be: Life is creation.   *Ib.*

A modern poet has characterized the personality of art and the impersonality of science as follows: Art is I: Science is We.   *Ib.*

---

[1] *Lessons on Reactions Common to Animals and Plants,* translated by J. M. D. OLMSTEAD.

Man can learn nothing unless he proceeds from the known to the unknown.

> *From Bulletin of New York Academy of Medicine, vol. IV, p.* 997

We must never make experiments to confirm our ideas, but simply to control them.   *Ib.*

GEORG BÜCHNER
1813–1837

The Revolution is like Saturn — it eats its own children.
> *Danton's Death* [1835]

The people are like children; they must smash everything to see what is inside.   *Ib.*

JOHN WILLIAM BURGON
1813–1860

A rose-red city half as old as time.[1]
> *Petra* [*Newdigate Prize Poem,* 1845]

JOSEPH EDWARDS CARPENTER
1813–1885

What are the wild waves saying,[2]
Sister, the whole day long?
> *What Are the Wild Waves Saying? st.* 1

JOHN SULLIVAN DWIGHT
1813–1893

Work, and thou wilt bless the day
    Ere the toil be done;
They that work not, cannot pray,
    Cannot feel the sun.
God is living, working still,
    All things work and move;
Work, or lose the power to will,
    Lose the power to love.   *Working*

---

[1] By many a temple half as old as Time. — SAMUEL ROGERS [1763–1855], *Italy* [1822–1828], *A Farewell*
[2] See Dickens, p. 671a.

SÖREN KIERKEGAARD
1813–1855

Life can only be understood backwards; but it must be lived forwards.
Life

All essential knowledge relates to existence, or only such knowledge as has an essential relationship to existence is essential knowledge.
Concluding Unscientific Postscript

The absurd . . . the fact that with God all things are possible. The absurd is not one of the factors which can be discriminated within the proper compass of the understanding: it is not identical with the improbable, the unexpected, the unforeseen.
Fear and Trembling [1843]. *Problemata: Preliminary Expectoration*

JOHN LOUIS O'SULLIVAN
1813–1895

Our manifest destiny is to overspread the continent allotted by Providence for the free development of our yearly multiplying millions.[1]
United States Magazine and Democratic Review [July–August 1845]

EPES SARGENT
1813–1880

A life on the ocean wave,
A home on the rolling deep;
Where the scattered waters rave,
And the winds their revels keep!
A Life on the Ocean Wave [1847], *st. 1*

RICHARD WAGNER
1813–1883

Say, where didst thou tarry so long?
Tannhäuser [1845]

[1] See Josh Billings, p. 685a.

O thou, my gracious evening star.
Tannhäuser

To be German means to carry on a matter for its own sake.
Deutsche Kunst und Deutsche Politik [1] [1867]

Ride of the Valkyries.
Die Walküre [1876]

The pure fool.
Parsifal [1882]

HENRY STEVENSON WASHBURN
1813–1903

We shall meet, but we shall miss him,
There will be one vacant chair.
The Vacant Chair, st. 1

THOMAS OSBORNE DAVIS
1814–1845

Come in the evening, or come in the morning,
Come when you're looked for, or come without warning.
The Welcome, st. 1

Sheep without a Shepherd, when the snow shuts out the sky —
Oh, why did you leave us, Owen? Why did you die?
Lament for the Death of Eoghan Ruadh O'Neill, st. 7

FREDERICK WILLIAM FABER
1814–1863

Hark! Hark! my soul, angelic songs are swelling
O'er earth's green fields, and ocean's wave-beat shore;
How sweet the truth those blessed strains are telling
Of that new life when sin shall be no more!
Oratory Hymns. Pilgrims of the Night

[1] *German Art and German Politics*

O Paradise! O Paradise!
Who doth not crave for rest?
> *Oratory Hymns. Paradise*

Faith of our fathers! holy faith!
We will be true to thee till death.
> *Ib. A Pledge of Faithfulness*

MIKHAIL LERMONTOV
1814–1841

A *Hero of Our Time*, gentlemen, is indeed a portrait, but not of a single individual; it is a portrait composed of all the vices of our generation in the fullness of their development.
> *A Hero of Our Time* [1840],
> *Author's Introduction*

CHARLES MACKAY
1814–1889

There's a good time coming, boys!
A good time coming.
> *The Good Time Coming, st. 1*

Old Tubal Cain was a man of might,
In the days when earth was young.
> *Tubal Cain, st. 1*

Not alone for the blade was the bright steel made,
And he fashioned the first plowshare.[1]
> *Ib. st. 4*

EDWIN McMASTERS STANTON
1814–1869

Now he [Lincoln] belongs to the ages.
> *On the death of Lincoln*
> *[April 15, 1865]*

OTTO VON BISMARCK
1815–1898

The great questions of the time are not decided by speeches and majority

---

[1] See *Isaiah 2:4*, p. 30a.
Tubal fashioned the hand-flung spears
And showed his neighbors peace.
> KIPLING [1865–1936], *Jubal and Tubal Cain, st. 3*

---

decisions — that was the error of 1848 and 1849 — but by iron and blood.[1]
> *Speech to the Prussian Diet*
> *[September 30, 1862]*

A newspaper writer is one who has failed in his calling.
> *Derived from speech [November 10, 1862]*

Politics is not an exact science.[2]
> *Speech to the Herrenhaus*
> *[December 13, 1863]*

The glass house of German statecraft.
> *Concerning Austro-German power, to a commission of the Prussian Landtag [1864]*

Only a completely ready state can permit the luxury of a liberal government.
> *Speech* [1866]

Let us put Germany in the saddle, so to speak — it already knows how to ride.
> *Speech to the North German Reichstag [March 11, 1867]*

A conquering army on the border will not be halted by the power of eloquence.
> *Ib. [September 24, 1867]*

He who has his thumb on the purse has the power.
> *Ib. [May 21, 1869]*

The luxury of one's own opinion.
> *Speech to the Prussian Diet*
> *[December 17, 1873]*

The right people in the right jobs.
> *Speech to the North German Reichstag [1875]*

Politics ruins the character.
> *Reported by Bernhard Brigl in the Berlin Tägliche Rundschau [1881]*

We Germans fear God, but nothing else in the world.
> *Speech to the Reichstag [February 6, 1888]*

---

[1] Eisen und Blut.
[2] Politics is not a science . . . but an art.
— *Speech* [March 15, 1884]

RICHARD HENRY DANA
1815–1882

Six days shalt thou labor and do all
    thou art able,
And on the seventh — holystone the
decks and scrape the cable.

> *Two Years Before the Mast*
> *[1840], ch. 3*

He seldom went up to town without
coming down "three sheets in the
wind."   *Ib. 20*

Everything was "shipshape and Bristol fashion."   *Ib. 22*

DAVID DAVIS
1815–1886

The Constitution of the United
States is a law for rulers and people,
equally in war and in peace, and covers
with the shield of its protection all
classes of men, at all times, and under
all circumstances. No doctrine, involving more pernicious consequences, was
ever invented by the wit of man than
that any of its provisions can be suspended during any of the great exigen-
cies of government.

> *Ex Parte Milligan, 4 Wallace 2,*
> *120–121 [1866]*

DANIEL DECATUR EMMETT
1815–1904

I wish I was in de land ob cotton,
Old times dar am not forgotten.
    Look away, look away,
    Look away, Dixie Land.

> *Dixie* [1] *[1859], st. 1*

[1] Originally this word [Dixie] applied only
to New Orleans; not until the Civil War,
when D. D. Emmett's famous song . . . became the favorite battle song of the Confederacy, was it in general use to designate
the entire South. It came about in this fashion:
  A few years after Louisiana became a part
of the United States . . . one of the New
Orleans banks began issuing ten-dollar notes,
one side of which was printed in English and
the other in French. On the latter, in large
letters, was the French word for ten, *dix*. . . .

In Dixie's land, we'll took our stand,
To lib an' die in Dixie!

> *Dixie, st. 3*

JOHN BABSONE LANE SOULE
1815–1891

Go west, young man.[1]

> *Article in the Terre Haute,*
> *Indiana, Express [1851]*

ANTHONY TROLLOPE
1815–1882

The tenth Muse who now governs
the periodical press.

> *The Warden [1855], ch. 14*

In these days a man is nobody unless
his biography is kept so far posted up
that it may be ready for the national
breakfast table on the morning after his
demise.

> *Doctor Thorne [1858], ch. 25*

Those who offend us are generally
punished for the offense they give; but
we so frequently miss the satisfaction of
knowing that we are avenged!

> *The Small House at Allington*
> *[1864], ch. 50*

She understood how much louder a
cock can crow in its own farmyard than
elsewhere.

> *The Last Chronicle of Barset*
> *[1867], vol. I, ch. 17*

Always remember that when you go
into an attorney's office door, you will
have to pay for it, first or last.

> *Ib. 20*

One of these notes was known simply as a dix;
collectively they were dixies, a name which
was soon applied to the city of issue as well.
— HERBERT ASBURY, *The French Quarter* [1936],
ch. 3

[1] Horace Greeley [1811–1872] used the expression in an editorial in *The New York Tribune*
(see Greeley, p. 658b). As the saying "Go west,
young man, and grow up with the country"
gained popularity, Greeley printed Soule's article, to show the source of his inspiration.
  Many men have stated that the advice was
given to them by Greeley, among them William
S. Verity [1837–1930], who said Greeley had
given it to him in 1859.

It is a comfortable feeling to know that you stand on your own ground. Land is about the only thing that can't fly away.
> *The Last Chronicle of Barset, vol. II, ch. 58*

It's dogged as does it.   *Ib. 61*

Nothing reopens the springs of love so fully as absence, and no absence so thoroughly as that which must needs be endless.   *Ib. 67*

PHILIP JAMES BAILEY
1816–1902

Let each man think himself an act of God,
His mind a thought, his life a breath of God;
And let each try, by great thoughts and good deeds,
To show the most of Heaven he hath in him.   *Festus [1839]. Proem*

It matters not how long we live, but how.   *Ib. Wood and Water*

We live in deeds, not years; in thoughts, not breaths;
In feelings, not in figures on a dial.
We should count time by heart-throbs.
He most lives
Who thinks most — feels the noblest — acts the best.
          Ib. A Country Town

Envy's a coal comes hissing hot from hell.   *Ib.*

The sole equality on earth is death.
          Ib.

America, thou half-brother of the world;
With something good and bad of every land.   *Ib. The Surface*

There is no disappointment we endure One half so great as that we are to ourselves.[1]   *Ib. The Sun*

[1] Every really able man, if you talk sincerely with him, considers his work, however much admired, as far short of what it should be. — EMERSON, *Immortality* [1875]

CHARLOTTE BRONTË
1816–1855

Life, believe, is not a dream
So dark as sages say; [1]
Oft a little morning rain
Foretells a pleasant day.
          Life [1846], st. 1

The human heart has hidden treasures, In secret kept, in silence sealed.
          Evening Solace [1846], st. 1

Reader, I married him.
          Jane Eyre [1847], ch. 38

An abundant shower of curates has fallen upon the north of England.
          Shirley [1849], ch. 1

JAMES THOMAS FIELDS
1816–1881

"We are lost!" the captain shouted, As he staggered down the stairs.
> *The Captain's Daughter; or, The Ballad of the Tempest [1858], st. 4*

But his little daughter whispered, As she took his icy hand,
"Isn't God upon the ocean, Just the same as on the land?" [2]
          Ib. st. 5

How sweet and gracious, even in common speech,
Is that fine sense which men call Courtesy!   *Courtesy*

"I'm an owl; you're another. Sir Critic, good day!"
And the barber kept on shaving.
          The Owl-Critic, last lines and refrain

GUSTAV FREYTAG
1816–1895

Madness of the Caesars.
> *Die Verlorene Handschrift [1864], concerning the proposition that power is evil per se*

[1] See Longfellow, p. 620b.
[2] See Sir Humphrey Gilbert, p. 192a.

ELLEN STURGIS HOOPER
1816–1841

I slept and dreamed that life was beauty.
I woke — and found that life was duty.
Beauty and Duty

EUGÈNE POTTIER
1816–1887

Arise, ye prisoners of starvation,
  Arise, ye wretched of the earth,
For justice thunders condemnation —
A better world's in birth.
L'Internationale [1871] [1]

JOHN GODFREY SAXE
1816–1887

In battle or business, whatever the game,
In law or in love, it is ever the same;
In the struggle for power, or the scramble for pelf,
Let this be your motto — Rely on yourself!
For, whether the prize be a ribbon or throne,
The victor is he who can go it alone! [2]
The Game of Life, st. 7

"God bless the man who first invented sleep!"
So Sancho Panza said, and so say I.
Early Rising, st. 1

It was six men of Indostan
  To learning much inclined,
Who went to see the Elephant
  (Though all of them were blind),
That each by observation
  Might satisfy his mind.
The Blind Men and the Elephant, st. 1

'Tis wise to learn; 'tis God-like to create.
The Library

[1] Adolphe Degeyter wrote the music for the *International*, which was adopted as the rallying song of Communism.
[2] He travels the fastest who travels alone. — KIPLING [1865–1936], *The Winners*

GEORG HERWEGH
1817–1875

The poor human heart must break piecemeal.
Strophen aus der Fremde [1840], *in Rückert's Musenalmanach*

TOM TAYLOR
1817–1880

You lay a wreath on murdered Lincoln's bier,
You, who with mocking pencil wont to trace,
Broad for the self-complacent British sneer,
His length of shambling limb, his furrowed face.
Abraham Lincoln Foully Assassinated,[1] *st. 1*

HENRY DAVID THOREAU
1817–1862

I am a parcel of vain strivings tied
By a chance bond together.
Sic Vita [1841], *st. 1*

Great God, I ask thee for no meaner pelf
Than that I may not disappoint myself,
That in my action I may soar as high
As I can now discern with this clear eye.
A Prayer [1842], *st. 1*

Talk of mysteries! Think of our life in nature — daily to be shown matter, to come in contact with it — rocks, trees, wind on our cheeks! the *solid* earth! the *actual* world! the *common* sense! Contact! Contact! *Who* are we? *where* are we?
The Maine Woods, Ktaadn [1848]

I think that we should be men first, and subjects afterward. It is not desir-

[1] Printed in *Punch,* London [May 6, 1865]. Taylor became editor of *Punch* in 1874. It was at a performance of Taylor's play, *Our American Cousin,* that Lincoln was shot.

able to cultivate a respect for the law, so much as for the right.

Civil Disobedience [1849]

How does it become a man to behave toward this American government to-day? I answered that he cannot without disgrace be associated with it. *Ib.*

When a sixth of the population of a nation which has undertaken to be the refuge of liberty are slaves, and a whole country [1] is unjustly overrun and conquered by a foreign army, and subjected to military law, I think that it is not too soon for honest men to rebel and revolutionize. What makes this duty the more urgent is the fact that the country so overrun is not our own, but ours is the invading army. *Ib.*

A wise man will not leave the right to the mercy of chance, nor wish it to prevail through the power of the majority. There is but little virtue in the action of masses of men. *Ib.*

I came into this world, not chiefly to make this a good place to live in, but to live in it, be it good or bad. *Ib.*

Any man more right than his neighbors constitutes a majority of one. *Ib.*

Under a government which imprisons any unjustly, the true place for a just man is also a prison . . . the only house in a slave State in which a free man can abide with honor. *Ib.*

I saw that the State was half-witted, that it was timid as a lone woman with her silver spoons, and that it did not know its friends from its foes, and I lost all my remaining respect for it, and pitied it. *Ib.*

My life is like a stroll upon the beach, As near the ocean's edge as I can go.

My Life Is Like a Stroll Upon the Beach [1849], st. 1

Methinks my own soul must be a bright invisible green.

A Week on the Concord and Merrimack Rivers [1849]. *Wednesday*

It takes two to speak the truth — one to speak, and another to hear. *Ib.*

This world is but canvas to our imaginations. *Ib.*

Dreams are the touchstones of our characters. *Ib.*

Go where we will on the *surface* of things, men have been there before us. *Ib. Thursday*

The frontiers are not east or west, north or south, but wherever a man *fronts* a fact. *Ib.*

A true account of the actual is the rarest poetry, for common sense always takes a hasty and superficial view. *Ib.*

As if our birth had at first sundered things, and we had been thrust up through into nature like a wedge, and not till the wound heals and the scar disappears, do we begin to discover where we are, and that nature is one and continuous everywhere. *Ib. Friday*

What are the earth and all its interests beside the deep surmise which pierces and scatters them? *Ib.*

It is so rare to meet with a man out-doors who cherishes a worthy thought in his mind, which is independent of the labor of his hands. *Ib.*

The eye may see for the hand, but not for the mind. *Ib.*

Nothing is so much to be feared as fear.[1]   *Journal* [*September 7, 1851*]

The bluebird carries the sky on his back. *Ib.* [*April 3, 1852*]

The perception of beauty is a moral test. *Ib.* [*June 21, 1852*]

---

[1] Mexico.

[1] See Montaigne, p. 189b, and note.

The youth gets together his materials to build a bridge to the moon, or, perchance, a palace or temple on the earth, and, at length, the middle-aged man concludes to build a woodshed with them.
Journal [July 14, 1852]

Fire is the most tolerable third party.
Ib. [January 2, 1853]

Some circumstantial evidence is very strong, as when you find a trout in the milk.   *Ib. [November 11, 1854]*

That man is the richest whose pleasures are the cheapest.
Ib. [March 11, 1856]

The savage in man is never quite eradicated.
Ib. [September 26, 1859]

The fate of the country . . . does not depend on what kind of paper you drop into the ballot box once a year, but on what kind of man you drop from your chamber into the street every morning.
Slavery in Massachusetts [1854]

I should not talk so much about myself if there were anybody else whom I knew as well.
Walden [1854],[1] 1, Economy

I have traveled a good deal in Concord.   *Ib.*

Public opinion is a weak tyrant compared with our own private opinion. What a man thinks of himself, that is which determines, or rather, indicates, his fate.   *Ib.*

As if you could kill time without injuring eternity.   *Ib.*

The mass of men lead lives of quiet desperation.   *Ib.*

[1] *Walden* is the only book I own, although there are some others unclaimed on my shelves. Every man, I think, reads one book in his life, and this one is mine. It is not the best book I ever encountered, perhaps, but it is for me the handiest, and I keep it about me in much the same way one carries a handkerchief — for relief in moments of defluxion or despair. — E. B. WHITE, *The New Yorker [May 23, 1953]*

It is characteristic of wisdom not to do desperate things.
Walden, 1, Economy

Age is no better, hardly so well, qualified for an instructor as youth, for it has not profited so much as it has lost.   *Ib.*

Most of the luxuries, and many of the so-called comforts, of life are not only not indispensable, but positive hindrances to the elevation of mankind.   *Ib.*

To be a philosopher is not merely to have subtle thoughts, nor even to found a school, but so to love wisdom as to live accordingly to its dictates, a life of simplicity, independence, magnanimity, and trust.   *Ib.*

Beware of all enterprises that require new clothes.   *Ib.*

Our moulting season, like that of the fowls, must be a crisis in our lives.   *Ib.*

In the long run men hit only what they aim at.   *Ib.*

The swiftest traveler is he that goes afoot.   *Ib.*

It is not necessary that a man should earn his living by the sweat of his brow [1] unless he sweats easier than I do.   *Ib.*

The man who goes alone can start today; but he who travels with another must wait till that other is ready.   *Ib.*

When a man dies he kicks the dust.   *Ib.*

As for doing good, that is one of the professions which are full.   *Ib.*

There is no odor so bad as that which arises from goodness tainted.[2]   *Ib.*

There are a thousand hacking at the branches of evil to one who is striking at the root.   *Ib.*

[1] See *Genesis 3:19*, p. 6a.
[2] See Shakespeare, p. 293a.

Philanthropy is almost the only virtue which is sufficiently appreciated by mankind. *Walden, 1, Economy*

A man is rich in proportion to the number of things which he can afford to let alone.
Ib. 2, Where I Lived, and What I Lived For

To him whose elastic and vigorous thought keeps pace with the sun, the day is a perpetual morning. *Ib.*

To be awake is to be alive. *Ib.*

I know of no more encouraging fact than the unquestionable ability of man to elevate his life by a conscious endeavor. *Ib.*

I went to the woods because I wished to live deliberately, to front only the essential facts of life, and see if I could not learn what it had to teach, and not, when I came to die, discover that I had not lived. *Ib.*

Our life is frittered away by detail . . . Simplify, simplify. *Ib.*

We do not ride on the railroad; it rides upon us. *Ib.*

Time is but the stream I go a-fishing in. *Ib.*

Books must be read as deliberately and reservedly as they are written.
Ib. 3, Reading

What is called eloquence in the forum is commonly found to be rhetoric in the study. *Ib.*

The works of the great poets have never yet been read by mankind, for only great poets can read them. *Ib.*

It is not all books that are as dull as their readers. *Ib.*

How many a man has dated a new era in his life from the reading of a book. *Ib.*

I love a broad margin to my life.
Ib. 4, Sounds

Our horizon is never quite at our elbows. *Ib. 5, Solitude*

I never found the companion that was so companionable as solitude. We are for the most part more lonely when we go abroad among men than when we stay in our chambers. A man thinking or working is always alone, let him be where he will.
Walden 5, Solitude

I had three chairs in my house: one for solitude, two for friendship, three for society. *Ib. 6, Visitors*

Ministers who spoke of God as if they enjoyed a monopoly of the subject. *Ib.*

I was determined to know beans.
Ib. 7, The Beanfield

Through want of enterprise and faith men are where they are, buying and selling, and spending their lives like serfs. *Ib. 10, Baker Farm*

There is never an instant's truce between virtue and vice. Goodness is the only investment that never fails.
Ib. 11, Higher Laws

Heaven is under our feet as well as over our heads.
Ib. 16, The Pond in Winter

While men believe in the infinite, some ponds will be thought to be bottomless. *Ib.*

What is man but a mass of thawing clay? *Ib. 17, Spring*

Through our own recovered innocence we discern the innocence of our neighbors. *Ib.*

As if there were safety in stupidity alone. *Ib. 18, Conclusion*

If one advances confidently in the direction of his dreams, and endeavors to live the life which he has imagined, he will meet with a success unexpected in common hours. *Ib.*

If a man does not keep pace with his companions, perhaps it is because he hears a different drummer. Let him step to the music which he hears, however measured or far away. *Ib.*

Love your life, poor as it is. You may perhaps have some pleasant, thrilling, glorious hours, even in a poorhouse. The setting sun is reflected from the windows of the almshouse as brightly as from the rich man's abode,
Walden 18, Conclusion

It is life near the bone where it is sweetest.   *Ib.*

Rather than love, than money, than fame, give me truth.   *Ib.*

He would have left a Greek accent slanting the wrong way, and righted up a falling man.
A Plea for Captain John Brown [1859]

I hear many condemn these men because they were so few. When were the good and the brave ever in a majority?   *Ib.*

It was his peculiar doctrine that a man has a perfect right to interfere by force with the slaveholder, in order to rescue the slave. I agree with him. They who are continually shocked by slavery have some right to be shocked by the violent death of the slaveholder, but no others.   *Ib.*

I speak for the slave when I say that I prefer the philanthropy of Captain Brown to that philanthropy which neither shoots me nor liberates me.
Ib.

So we defend ourselves and our henroosts, and maintain slavery.   *Ib.*

He is not Old Brown any longer; he is an angel of light.   *Ib.*

Men will lie on their backs, talking about the fall of man, and never make an effort to get up.
Life Without Principle [1863]

ALEXEI KONSTANTINOVICH TOLSTOI
1817–1875

His pen is breathing revenge.
Vaska Shibanov [1855–1865]

No one can encompass the unencompassable.
Kosma Prutkov [1884] [1]

If thou hast a fountain, shut it up: let even a fountain have a rest.   *Ib.*

Many men are like unto sausages: whatever you stuff them with, that they will bear in them.   *Ib.*

Should you read, upon an enclosure with an elephant, a sign saying *Buffalo*, believe not your eyes.   *Ib.*

If you want to be happy, be.   *Ib.*

CECIL FRANCES ALEXANDER
1818–1895

All things bright and beautiful,
    All creatures great and small,
All things wise and wonderful,
    The Lord God made them all.[2]
All Things Bright and Beautiful [1848], *st. 1*

The rich man in his castle,
    The poor man at his gate,
God made them, high or lowly,
    And ordered their estate.   *Ib. st. 3*

There is a green hill far away,
    Without a city wall,
Where the dear Lord was crucified,
    Who died to save us all.
There Is a Green Hill [1848], *st. 1*

Once in royal David's city
    Stood a lowly cattle shed,
Where a Mother laid her Baby
    In a manger for his bed:
Mary was that Mother mild,
Jesus Christ her little Child.
Once in Royal David's City [1848], *st. 1*

[1] Kosma Prutkov, a pompous and platitudinous clerk who dabbled in the muses, was invented by Tolstoi and the brothers Zhemchuzhnikov, who supplied him with a biography, a portrait, and *Collected Works*, published in 1884. Individual satirical pieces had been appearing under his name since 1851. He became a classic of Russian satirical humor.
Translated by B. G. GURNEY.
[2] See Coleridge, p. 526a.

JOSH BILLINGS
[HENRY WHEELER SHAW]
1818–1885

A sekret ceases tew be a sekret if it iz once confided — it iz like a dollar bill, once broken, it iz never a dollar agin.
                    Affurisms [1] [1865]

Love iz like the meazles; we kant have it bad but onst, and the later in life we have it the tuffer it goes with us.   *Ib.*

Put an Englishman into the garden of Eden, and he would find fault with the whole blarsted consarn; put a Yankee in, and he would see where he could alter it to advantage; put an Irishman in, and he would want tew boss the thing; put a Dutchman in, and he would proceed tew plant it.   *Ib.*

Better make a weak man your enemy than your friend.   *Ib.*

Nature never makes any blunders; when she makes a fool she means it.
                                        Ib.

I don't care how much a man talks, if he only says it in a few words.
                                        Ib.

As scarce as truth is, the supply has always been in excess of the demand.
                                        Ib.

I never knu a man trubbled with melankolly, who had plenty to dew, and did it.   *Ib.*

Poverty iz the stepmother ov genius.
                                        Ib.

Manifest destiny iz the science ov going tew bust, or enny other place before yu git thare.[2]   *Manifest Destiny*

The wheel that squeaks the loudest
Is the one that gets the grease.
                    The Kicker

---

[1] From *Josh Billings: His Sayings.*
[2] See O'Sullivan, p. 676a.

It is better to know nothing than to know what ain't so.[1]   *Proverb* [1874]

EMILY BRONTË
1818–1848

Sleep not, dream not; this bright day
Will not, cannot last for aye;
Bliss like thine is bought by years
Dark with torment and with tears.
                Sleep Not [1846], *st. 1*

Cold in the earth — and fifteen wild
        Decembers
From those brown hills have melted
        into spring.
            Remembrance [1846], *st. 3*

Once drinking deep of that divinest
        anguish,
How could I seek the empty world
        again?   *Ib. st. 8*

No coward soul is mine,
No trembler in the world's storm-
        troubled sphere:
I see Heaven's glories shine,
And faith shines equal, arming me from
        fear.   *Last Lines* [1846], *st. 1*

There is not room for Death.[2]
                                Ib. st. 7

I lingered round them, under that benign sky: watched the moths fluttering among the heath and harebells; listened to the soft wind breathing through the grass; and wondered how anyone could ever imagine unquiet slumbers for the sleepers in that quiet earth.
        Wuthering Heights [1847], *last words*

WILLIAM ELLERY CHANNING
1818–1901

Habitant of castle gray,
Creeping thing in sober way,

---

[1] Better know nothing than half-know many things. — NIETZSCHE, *Thus Spake Zarathustra* [1883–1891], *pt. IV, 64*
[2] See Dylan Thomas, p. 1070a.

Visible sage mechanician,
Skillfulest arithmetician.
The Spider

I laugh, for hope hath happy place with
me —
If my bark sinks, 'tis to another sea.
A Poet's Hope

Most joyful let the Poet be;
It is through him that all men see.
*The Poet of the Old and New
Times*

The hills are reared, the seas are
scooped in vain
If learning's altar vanish from the plain.
Inscription for the Alcott house [1]

ELIZA COOK
1818–1889

I love it, I love it; and who shall dare
To chide me for loving that old armchair?   *The Old Armchair*

Better build schoolrooms for "the boy"
Than cells and gibbets for "the
man." [2]
*A Song for the Ragged Schools,
st. 12*

How busy we are on Tom Tiddler's
ground
Looking for gold and silver. [3]
Tom Tiddler's Ground, st. 1

GEORGE DUFFIELD
1818–1888

Stand up! — stand up for Jesus!
Hymn

WILLIAM MAXWELL
EVARTS
1818–1901

The pious ones of Plymouth, who,
reaching the Rock, first fell upon their

---

[1] This couplet is painted over the mantel of
the Alcott house, Concord, Massachusetts.
[2] Give them a chance — if you stint them
now, tomorrow you'll have to pay
A larger bill for a darker ill.
     DENIS A. MCCARTHY [1870–1931], *Give
Them a Place to Play, st. 4*
[3] Here we are on Tom Tiddler's ground,
picking up gold and silver. — *Children's game*

---

own knees and then upon the aborigi-
nes. [1]
From HENRY WATTERSON *in
The Louisville Courier-
Journal [July 4, 1913]*

JOHN JAMES ROBERT
MANNERS, DUKE
OF RUTLAND
1818–1906

Let wealth and commerce, laws and
learning die,
But leave us still our old nobility.
England's Trust, pt. III, l. 231

KARL MARX
1818–1883

Religion . . . is the opium of the
people.
*Critique of the Hegelian Phi-
losophy of Right [1844], introduction*

It is not the consciousness of men
that determines their existence, but on
the contrary their social existence determines their consciousness.
*Critique of Political Econ-
omy [1859], preface*

The history of all hitherto existing
society is the history of class struggles.
*Manifesto of the Communist
Party [2] [1848], sec. 1*

Of all the classes that stand face to
face with the bourgeoisie today the
proletariat alone is a really revolutionary class. The other classes decay and
finally disappear in the race of modern
industry; the proletariat is its special
and essential product. [3]   *Ib.*

---

[1] This pun has also been attributed to Oliver
Wendell Holmes, Bill Nye, and George Frisbie
Hoar.
[2] Written in collaboration with FRIEDRICH
ENGELS. Translated by SAMUEL MOORE.
[3] By bourgeoisie is meant the class of modern
capitalists, owners of the means of social production and employers of wage labor. By proletariat, the class of modern wage laborers who,
having no means of production of their own,
are reduced to selling their labor power in
order to live. — FRIEDRICH ENGELS [1820–1895],
footnote to Manifesto of the Communist Party

In proportion as the antagonism between classes within the nation vanishes, the hostility of one nation to another will come to an end.
Manifesto of the Communist Party, sec. 2

The ruling ideas of each age have ever been the ideas of its ruling class.
Ib.

The workers have nothing to lose but their chains. They have a world to win. Workers of the world, unite! *Ib. 4*

Nothing can have value without being an object of utility. If it be useless, the labor contained in it is useless, cannot be reckoned as labor, and cannot therefore create value.
Capital [1] [1867–1883], *pt. II, ch. 3*

The intellectual desolation, artificially produced by converting immature human beings into mere machines.
Ib. 10

Capitalist production begets, with the inexorability of a law of nature, its own negation. *Ib. 15*

When commercial capital occupies a position of unquestioned ascendancy, it everywhere constitutes a system of plunder. *Ib. 21*

From each according to his abilities, to each according to his needs.
Critique of the Gotha Program [2] *[1875]*

[1] Abridged edition prepared by JULIAN BORCHARDT, translated by STEPHEN L. TRASK.
[2] This phrase is in quotation marks, and it is believed that Marx is quoting or paraphrasing either Louis Blanc, or the obscure tutor Morelly.
Let each produce according to his aptitudes and his force; let each consume according to his need. — LOUIS BLANC, *Organisation du Travail* [*1840*]
Nothing in society will belong to anyone, either as a personal possession or as capital goods, except the things for which the person has immediate use, for either his needs, his pleasures, or his daily work. Every citizen will make his particular contribution according to the activities of the community according to his capacity, his talent and his age; it is on this basis that his duties will be determined,

JOHN MASON NEALE
1818–1866

Good King Wenceslas looked out
  On the feast of Stephen,
When the snow lay round about,
  Deep and crisp and even.
Good King Wenceslas, st. 1

In his master's steps he trod,
  Where the snow lay dinted;
Heat was in the very sod
  Which the Saint had printed.
Wherefore, Christian men, be sure,
  Wealth or rank possessing,
Ye who now do bless the poor
  Shall yourselves find blessing.
Ib. st. 5

O come, O come, Emmanuel,
And ransom captive Israel.
O Come, O Come, Emmanuel; translated from the Latin, Veni, Veni, Emmanuel

Jerusalem the golden, with milk and
  honey blest,
Beneath thy contemplation sink heart
  and voice oppressed.
Hymn; translated from the Latin of ST. BERNARD OF CLUNY *[c. 1145]*

Brief life is here our portion. *Ib.*

FRANCIS EDWARD SMEDLEY
1818–1864

You are looking as fresh as paint.
Frank Fairlegh [1850]

IVAN SERGEYEVICH TURGENEV
1818–1883

The Diary of a Superfluous Man. [1]
Title of a story [1851]

in conformity with the distributive laws. — MORELLY, *Code de Nature* [c. *1773*]
And distribution was made unto every man according as he had need. — *Acts 4:35*
[1] The phrase is from Pushkin's *Eugene Onegin.*

A nihilist [1] is a man who does not bow to any authorities, who does not take any principle on trust, no matter with what respect that principle is surrounded.

> *Fathers and Sons* [2] [1862], *ch. 5*

That vague, crepuscular time, the time of regrets that resemble hopes, of hopes that resemble regrets, when youth has passed, but old age has not yet arrived. *Ib. 7*

I share no man's opinions; I have my own. *Ib. 13*

The courage not to believe in anything. *Ib. 14*

A picture shows me at a glance what it takes dozens of pages of a book to expound.[3] *Ib. 16*

Whatever a man prays for, he prays for a miracle. Every prayer reduces itself to this: "Great God, grant that twice two be not four." *Prayer*

In days of doubt, in days of sad brooding on my country's fate, thou alone art my rod and my staff — mighty, true, free Russian speech! But for thee, how not to fall into despair, seeing all that happens at home? Yet who can think that such a tongue is not given to a great people?

> *Senilia* [1882]

ARTHUR HUGH CLOUGH
1819–1861

Grace is given of God, but knowledge is bought in the market.
> *The Bothie of Tober-na-Vuolich* [1848], *pt. IV*

---

[1] Nihilism was first encountered in 1829 in Nadazhdin's article against Pushkin. It was used throughout the 1830's with a variety of meanings, but the meaning which became central was applied by Turgenev to the psychology of the men of the 1860's in *Fathers and Sons*. It was also used by Katknov in the magazine which published *Fathers and Sons* four months before the book appeared.

[2] Translated by HARRY STEVENS.

[3] See Anonymous, p. 149b.

A world where nothing is had for nothing.
> *The Bothie of Toberna-Vuolich, pt. VIII*

As ships, becalmed at eve, that lay
With canvas drooping, side by side,
Two towers of sail, at dawn of day
Are scarce long leagues apart descried.
> *Qua Cursum Ventus* [1849], *st. 1*

It fortifies my soul to know
That, though I perish, Truth is so:
That, howsoe'er I stray and range,
Whate'er I do, Thou dost not change.
I steadier step when I recall
That, if I slip, Thou dost not fall.
> *"With Whom Is No Variableness"* [1] [1862]

And almost everyone when age,
Disease, or sorrows strike him,
Inclines to think there is a God,
Or something very like Him.
> *Dipsychus* [1862], *pt. I, sc. 5*

How pleasant it is to have money!
> *Ib.*

That out of sight is out of mind [2]
Is true of most we leave behind.
> *Songs of Absence* [1862]

Say not the struggle naught availeth,
The labor and the wounds are vain,
The enemy faints not, nor faileth,
And as things have been they remain.
> *Say Not the Struggle Naught Availeth* [1862], *st. 1*

For while the tired waves, vainly breaking,
Seem here no painful inch to gain,
Far back, through creeks and inlets making,
Comes silent flooding in, the main.[3]

And not by eastern windows only,
When daylight comes, comes in the light;

---

[1] See *James 1:17*, p. 56a.

[2] See Thomas à Kempis, p. 170b, and note.

[3] See Macaulay, p. 595a.

In front, the sun climbs slow, how
slowly,
But westward, look, the land is bright.[1]
*Say Not the Struggle Naught
Availeth, st. 3, 4*

Thou shalt not kill; but needst not
strive
Officiously to keep alive.
The Latest Decalogue

GEORGE ELIOT
[MARIAN EVANS CROSS]
1819–1880

'Tis God gives skill,
But not without men's hands: He could
not make
Antonio Stradivari's violins
Without Antonio. *Stradivarius*

O may I join the choir invisible
Of those immortal dead who live again
In minds made better by their presence.
O May I Join the Choir Invisible

Any coward can fight a battle when
he's sure of winning; but give me the
man who has pluck to fight when he's
sure of losing. That's my way, sir; and
there are many victories worse than a
defeat.
Janet's Repentance [1857], *ch. 6*

Opposition may become sweet to a
man when he has christened it persecution. *Ib. 8*

It's but little good you'll do a-water-
ing the last year's crops.
Adam Bede [1859], *ch. 18*

It was a pity he couldna be hatched
o'er again, an' hatched different.
Ib.

A patronizing disposition always has
its meaner side. *Ib. 28*

It's them that take advantage that
get advantage i' this world. *Ib. 32*

He was like a cock who thought the
sun had risen to hear him crow.
Ib. 33

[1] Both Sir Winston Churchill and John F.
Kennedy liked to quote this line.

We hand folks over to God's mercy,
and show none ourselves.
Adam Bede, ch. 42

I'm not denyin' the women are foolish; God Almighty made 'em to match
the men. *Ib. 53*

The law's made to take care o'
raskills.
The Mill on the Floss [1860],
bk. III, ch. 4

In natural science, I have understood, there is nothing petty to the
mind that has a large vision of relations, and to which every single object
suggests a vast sum of conditions. It is
surely the same with the observation of
human life. *Ib. IV, 1*

I've never any pity for conceited people, because I think they carry their
comfort about with them.[1] *Ib. V, 4*

The happiest women, like the happiest nations, have no history.[2]
Ib. VI, 3

Nothing is so good as it seems beforehand.
Silas Marner [1861], *ch. 18*

In our springtime every day has its
hidden growth in the mind, as it has in
the earth when the little folded blades
are getting ready to pierce the ground.
Felix Holt, the Radical [1866],
ch. 18

One way of getting an idea of our
fellow-countrymen's miseries is to go
and look at their pleasures. *Ib. 28*

Prophecy is the most gratuitous form
of error.
Middlemarch [1871–1872], *ch. 10*

If we had a keen vision of all that is
ordinary in human life, it would be like
hearing the grass grow or the squirrel's

[1] There is not enough of love and goodness
in the world to throw any of it away on conceited
people. — NIETZSCHE [1844–1900], *Human, All
Too Human, 129*
[2] See Carlyle, p. 578a, and note.

heart beat, and we should die of that roar which is the other side of silence.
Middlemarch, ch. 22

Hostesses who entertain much must make up their parties as ministers make up their cabinets, on grounds other than personal liking.
Daniel Deronda [1876], *bk. I, ch. 5*

A difference of taste in jokes is a great strain on the affections.
Ib. II, 15

Men's men: gentle or simple, they're much of a muchness.   *Ib. IV, 31*

Blessed is the man who, having nothing to say, abstains from giving in words evidence of the fact.
Impressions of Theophrastus Such [1879]

THOMAS DUNN ENGLISH
1819–1902

Oh! don't you remember sweet Alice, Ben Bolt?
Sweet Alice, whose hair was so brown, Who wept with delight when you gave her a smile,
And trembled with fear at your frown?
Ben Bolt [1]

JOSIAH GILBERT HOLLAND
1819–1881

Heaven is not reached at a single bound;
But we build the ladder by which we rise
From the lowly earth to the vaulted skies,
And we mount to its summit round by round.[2]   *Gradatim* [1872], *st. 1*

[1] First published in the *New York Mirror,* September 2, 1843. It was set to music, an adaptation of an old German melody, by NELSON KNEASS, and sung in the play *The Battle of Buena Vista.* In 1894 GEORGE DU MAURIER used the song in his novel *Trilby* and it at once became popular.

[2] Step after step the ladder is ascended. — GEORGE HERBERT, *Jacula Prudentum* [1640]

God give us men! A time like this demands
Strong minds, great hearts, true faith, and ready hands;
Men whom the lust of office does not kill;
Men whom the spoils of office cannot buy;
Men who possess opinions and a will;
Men who have honor; men who will not lie.   *Wanted* [1872], *l. 1*

JULIA WARD HOWE
1819–1910

Mine eyes have seen the glory of the coming of the Lord;
He is trampling out the vintage where the grapes of wrath are stored; [1]
He hath loosed the fateful lightning of His terrible, swift sword;
His truth is marching on.
Battle Hymn of the Republic [1862], *st. 1*

In the beauty of the lilies Christ was born across the sea,
With a glory in His bosom that transfigures you and me;
As He died to make men holy, let us die to make men free.   *Ib. st. 5*

CHARLES KINGSLEY
1819–1875

Oh! that we two were Maying.
The Saint's Tragedy [1848], *act II, sc. 9*

Oh Mary, go and call the cattle home . . .
Across the sands of Dee.
The Sands of Dee, st. 1

The cruel crawling foam.   *Ib. st. 4*

For men must work, and women must weep,
And there's little to earn and many to keep,
Though the harbor bar be moaning.
The Three Fishers, st. 1

[1] See *Isaiah 63:3,* p. 33b.
He treadeth the winepress of the fierceness and wrath of Almighty God. — *Revelation 19:15*

And the sooner it's over, the sooner to
sleep;
And good-bye to the bar and its moaning. *The Three Fishers, st. 3*

Be good, sweet maid, and let who will
be clever;
Do noble things, not dream them, all
day long;
And so make Life, and Death, and
that For Ever
One grand sweet song.
A Farewell, st. 3

In the light of fuller day,
Of purer science, holier laws.
*On the Death of a Certain
Journal* [1] *[1848–1849], st. 5*

More ways of killing a cat than chok-
ing her with cream.
Westward Ho [1855], ch. 20

Clear and cool, clear and cool,
By laughing shallow, and dreaming
pool.
*Water Babies [1863]. Song I,
st. 1*

When all the world is young, lad,
And all the trees are green;
And every goose a swan, lad,
And every lass a queen;
Then hey for boot and horse, lad,
And round the world away:
Young blood must have its course, lad,
And every dog his day.[2]
Ib. Song II, st. 1

When all the world is old, lad,
And all the trees are brown;
And all the sport is stale, lad,
And all the wheels run down.
Ib. st. 2

God grant you find one face there
You loved when all was young! *Ib.*

I once had a sweet little doll, dears,
The prettiest doll in the world;
Her cheeks were so red and so white,
dears,
And her hair was so charmingly curled.
Ib. Song IV, st. 1

[1] *The Christian Socialist.*
[2] See Shakespeare, *Hamlet V, i, 313,* p. 266a.

The loveliest fairy in the world; and
her name is Mrs. Doasyouwouldbedoneby. *Water Babies, ch. 5*

To be discontented with the divine
discontent, and to be ashamed with the
noble shame, is the very germ and first
upgrowth of all virtue.
*Health and Education [1874].
The Science of Health*

Some say that the age of chivalry is
past, that the spirit of romance is dead.
The age of chivalry is never past, so
long as there is a wrong left unredressed
on earth. *Life [1879], vol. II, ch. 28*

JAMES RUSSELL LOWELL
1819–1891

Be noble! and the nobleness that lies
In other men, sleeping, but never dead,
Will rise in majesty to meet thine own.
Sonnet IV [1840]

No man is born into the world whose
work
Is not born with him; there is always
work,
And tools to work withal, for those who
will;
And blessèd are the horny hands of
toil!
*A Glance Behind the Curtain
[1843]*

They are slaves who fear to speak
For the fallen and the weak.
Stanzas on Freedom [1843], st. 4

They are slaves who dare not be
In the right with two or three. *Ib.*

The nurse of full-grown souls is solitude. *Columbus [1844]*

Once to every man and nation comes
the moment to decide,
In the strife of Truth with Falsehood,
for the good or evil side.
The Present Crisis [1844], st. 5

Truth forever on the scaffold, Wrong
forever on the throne [1] —
Yet that scaffold sways the future, and,
behind the dim unknown,
Standeth God within the shadow, keeping watch above his own.
The Present Crisis, st. 8

Then to side with Truth is noble when
we share her wretched crust.
Ib. st. 11

New occasions teach new duties; time
makes ancient good uncouth;
They must upward still, and onward,
who would keep abreast of Truth.
Ib. st. 18

I first drew in New England's air, and
from her hardy breast
Sucked in the tyrant-hating milk that
will not let me rest;
And if my words seem treason to the
dullard and the tame,
'Tis but my Bay State dialect — our fathers spake the same.
On the Capture of Fugitive
Slaves Near Washington
[1845], st. 2

The birch, most shy and ladylike of
trees.
An Indian Summer Reverie
[1846], st. 8

Not only around our infancy
Doth heaven with all its splendors lie;
Daily, with souls that cringe and plot,
We Sinais climb and know it not.[2]
The Vision of Sir Launfal
[1848], prelude to pt. I,
st. 2

For a cap and bells our lives we pay,
Bubbles we buy with a whole soul's
tasking:
'Tis heaven alone that is given away,
'Tis only God may be had for the ask-
ing. *Ib. st. 4*

And what is so rare as a day in June?
Then, if ever, come perfect days;

Then Heaven tries the earth if it be in
tune,
And over it softly her warm ear lays.
The Vision of Sir Launfal,
prelude to pt. I, st. 5

He gives only the worthless gold
Who gives from a sense of duty.
Ib. pt. I, st. 6

Not what we give, but what we
share —
For the gift without the giver is bare; [1]
Who gives himself with his alms feeds
three —
Himself, his hungering neighbor, and
me. *Ib. pt. II, st. 8*

In creating, the only hard thing's to begin;
A grass-blade's no easier to make than
an oak.
A Fable for Critics [1848]

For though he builds glorious temples,
'tis odd
He leaves never a doorway to get in a
god. *Ib. [of Emerson]*

And I honor the man who is willing to
sink
Half his present repute for the freedom
to think,
And, when he has thought, be his cause
strong or weak,
Will risk t' other half for the freedom
to speak. *Ib.*

There comes Poe, with his raven, like
Barnaby Rudge,
Three fifths of him genius and two
fifths sheer fudge. *Ib.*

Nature fits all her children with something to do,
He who would write and can't write,
can surely review.[2] *Ib.*

Ez fer war, I call it murder —
There you hev it plain an' flat;
I don't want to go no furder
Than my Testyment fer that.
The Biglow Papers. Series I
[1848], no. 1, st. 5

---

[1] Worth on foot, and rascals in the coach. —
DRYDEN, *Art of Poetry* [1685], *l. 376*
Wrong rules the land, and waiting Justice
sleeps! — J. G. HOLLAND [1819–1881], *Wanted*
[2] See Wordsworth, p. 513b.

[1] See Emerson, p. 607b, and Whitman, p.
700b.
[2] See Coleridge, p. 528a, and Disraeli, p. 612b.

You've gut to git up airly
Ef you want to take in God.
*The Bigelow Papers. Series I,
no. 1, st. 5*

This goin' ware glory waits ye haint one
agreeable feetur.[1]　　*Ib. 2, st. 6*

　　But John P.
　　Robinson, he
Sez they didn't know everythin' down
in Judee.　　*Ib. 3, st. 8*

A marciful Providunce fashioned us
holler
O' purpose thet we might our principles
swaller.　　*Ib. 4, st. 2*

　　I should like to shoot
The holl gang, by the gret horn spoon!
　　Ib. 5, st. 2

I du believe with all my soul
　In the gret Press's freedom,
To pint the people to the goal
An' in the traces lead 'em.
　　Ib. 6, st. 7

I *don't* believe in princerple,
But oh I *du* in interest.　　*Ib. st. 9*

It ain't by princerples nor men
　My preudunt course is steadied —
I scent wich pays the best, an' then
　Go into it baldheaded.　　*Ib. st. 10*

　　Of my merit
On thet pint you yourself may jedge;
All is, I never drink no sperit,
Nor I haint never signed no pledge.
　　Ib. 7, st. 9

Ez to my princerples, I glory
In hevin' nothin' o' the sort.
　　Ib. st. 10

God makes sech nights, all white an'
　still,
Fur'z you can look or listen,
Moonshine an' snow on field an' hill,
　All silence an' all glisten.
　　Ib. Series II [1866]. *The
　　Courtin', st. 1*

His heart kep' goin' pity-pat,
But hern went pity-Zekle.　　*Ib. st. 15*

My gran'ther's rule was safer 'n 'tis to
crow:

[1] See Thomas Moore, p. 541b.

Don't never prophesy — onless ye
know.
　　*The Biglow Papers. Series II.
　　The Courtin', No. 2*

It's 'most enough to make a deacon
swear.　　*Ib.*

Folks never understand the folks they
hate.　　*Ib.*

Ef you want peace, the thing you've gut
tu du
Is jes' to show you're up to fightin',
tu.[1]　　*Ib.*

Bad work follers ye ez long's ye live.
　　Ib.

The surest plan to make a Man
Is, think him so.　　*Ib.*

Our papers don't purtend to print on'y
wut Guv'ment choose,
An' thet insures us all to git the very
best o' noose.　　*Ib. 3*

No, never say nothin' without you're
compelled tu,
An' then don't say nothin' thet you can
be held tu.　　*Ib. 5*

They came three thousand miles, and
died,
To keep the Past upon its throne;
Unheard, beyond the ocean tide,
Their English mother made her moan.[2]
　　*Graves of Two English Sol-
　　diers on Concord Battle-
　　ground* [1849], *st. 3*

The snow had begun in the gloaming,
　And busily all the night
Had been heaping field and highway
　With a silence deep and white.
　　The First Snowfall
　　[1849], *st. 1*

There is nothing so desperately
monotonous as the sea, and I no longer
wonder at the cruelty of pirates.
　　Fireside Travels [1864]. *At Sea*

It is by presence of mind in untried
emergencies that the native metal of a
man is tested.

　　Abraham Lincoln [1864]

[1] See Vegetius, p. 146b, and note.
[2] Inscribed on the memorial to the two British
soldiers, Concord, Massachusetts.

What men call treasure and the gods call dross.

> *Ode Recited at the Harvard Commemoration* [1865], 4

They come transfigured back,
Secure from change in their high-hearted ways,
Beautiful evermore, and with the rays
Of morn on their white Shields of Expectation! [1] *Ib. 8*

When I was a beggarly boy,
 And lived in a cellar damp,
I had not a friend nor a toy,
 But I had Aladdin's lamp.

> *Aladdin* [1868], *st. 1*

Safe in the hallowed quiets of the past.

> *The Cathedral* [2] [1869], *st. 9*

The wisest man could ask no more of Fate
Than to be simple, modest, manly, true,
Safe from the many, honored by the few;
To count as naught in world, or church, or state;
But inwardly in secret to be great.

> *Sonnet, Jeffries Wyman* [1874]

For me Fate gave, whate'er she else denied,
A nature sloping to the southern side;
I thank her for it, though when clouds arise
Such natures double-darken gloomy skies.

> *Epistle to George William Curtis* [1874]. *Postscript*

The maple puts her corals on in May.

> *The Maple* [1875]

The soil out of which such men as he are made is good to be born on, good to live on, good to die for and to be buried in.

> *Garfield* [September 24, 1881]

There is no good in arguing with the inevitable. The only argument avail-able with an east wind is to put on your overcoat.

> *Democracy* [October 6, 1884]

In vain we call old notions fudge,
And bend our conscience to our dealing;
The Ten Commandments will not budge,
And stealing *will* continue stealing. [1]

> *International Copyright* [November 20, 1885]

These pearls of thought in Persian gulfs were bred,
Each softly lucent as a rounded moon;
The diver Omar plucked them from their bed,
Fitzgerald strung them on an English thread.

> *In a Copy of Omar Khayyám* [1888], *st. 1*

As life runs on, the road grows strange
With faces new, and near the end
The milestones into headstones change,
'Neath every one a friend.

> *Sixty-eighth Birthday* [1889]

Things always seem fairer when we look back at them, and it is out of that inaccessible tower of the past that Longing leans and beckons.

> *Literary Essays, vol. I* [1864–1890], *A Few Bits of Roman Mosaic*

Mishaps are like knives, that either serve us or cut us, as we grasp them by the blade or the handle.

> *Ib. Cambridge Thirty Years Ago*

What a sense of security in an old book which Time has criticized for us!

> *Ib. A Library of Old Authors*

It is curious how tyrannical the habit of reading is, and what shifts we make to escape thinking. [2] There is no bore we dread being left alone with so much as our own minds.

> *Ib. A Moosehead Journal*

---

[1] See Masefield, p. 947b–948a.
[2] Chartres.

[1] Motto of the American Copyright League.
[2] See Sheridan, p. 481b, and Bryce, p. 778a.

Truly there is a tide in the affairs of men,[1] but there is no gulf stream setting forever in one direction.

> *Literary Essays, vol. II [1870–1890], New England Two Centuries Ago*

There is no better ballast for keeping the mind steady on its keel, and saving it from all risk of crankiness, than business. *Ib.*

Puritanism, believing itself quick with the seed of religious liberty, laid, without knowing it, the egg of democracy. *Ib.*

It was in making education not only common to all, but in some sense compulsory on all, that the destiny of the free republics of America was practically settled. *Ib.*

Talent is that which is in a man's power; genius is that in whose power a man is.

> *Ib. Rousseau and the Sentimentalists*

Every man feels instinctively that all the beautiful sentiments in the world weigh less than a single lovely action. *Ib.*

An umbrella is of no avail against a Scotch mist.

> *Ib. III [1870–1890], On a Certain Condescension in Foreigners*

Solitude is as needful to the imagination as society is wholesome for the character. *Ib. Dryden*

A wise skepticism is the first attribute of a good critic.

> *Ib. Shakespeare Once More*

HERMAN MELVILLE
1819–1891

You must have plenty of sea-room to tell the Truth in.

> *Hawthorne and His Mosses [1850]*

Genius all over the world stands hand in hand, and one shock of recognition runs the whole circle round.

> *Hawthorne and His Mosses*

Many sensible things banished from high life find an asylum among the mob. *White Jacket [1850], ch. 7*

Oh, give me again the rover's life — the joy, the thrill, the whirl! Let me feel thee again, old sea! let me leap into thy saddle once more. I am sick of these terra-firma toils and cares; sick of the dust and reek of towns. Let me hear the clatter of hailstones on icebergs, and not the dull tramp of these plodders, plodding their dull way from their cradles to their graves. Let me snuff thee up, sea breeze! and whinny in thy spray. Forbid it, sea gods! intercede for me with Neptune, O sweet Amphitrite,[1] that no dull clod may fall on my coffin! Be mine the tomb that swallowed up Pharaoh and all his hosts; let me lie down with Drake where he sleeps in the sea. *Ib. 19*

Familiarity with danger makes a brave man braver, but less daring. Thus with seamen: he who goes the oftenest round Cape Horn goes the most circumspectly. *Ib. 23*

In time of peril, like the needle to the lodestone, obedience, irrespective of rank, generally flies to him who is best fitted to command. *Ib. 27*

Are there no Moravians in the Moon, that not a missionary has yet visited this poor pagan planet of ours, to civilize civilization and christianize Christendom? [2] *Ib. 64*

Call me Ishmael.

> *Moby-Dick [1851], ch. 1*

Yes, as everyone knows, meditation and water are wedded forever . . . Why did the old Persians hold the sea holy? Why did the Greeks give it a separate deity, and own brother of Jove? Surely all this is not without meaning.

---

[1] See Shakespeare, *Julius Caesar IV, iii, 217.* p. 256a.

[1] Wife of Neptune.
[2] See Emerson, p. 606b.

And still deeper the meaning of that story of Narcissus, who because he could not grasp the tormenting, mild image he saw in the fountain, plunged into it and was drowned. But that same image, we ourselves see in all rivers and oceans. It is the image of the ungraspable phantom of life; and this is the key to it all. *Moby-Dick, ch.* 1

But oh! shipmates! on the starboard hand of every woe, there is a sure delight; and higher the top of that delight, than the bottom of the woe is deep. Is not the main-truck higher than the kelson is low? Delight is to him — a far, far upward, and inward delight — who against the proud gods and commodores of this earth, ever stands forth his own inexorable self. *Ib.* 9

And eternal delight and deliciousness will be his, who coming to lay him down, can say with his final breath — O Father! — chiefly known to me by Thy rod — mortal or immortal, here I die. I have striven to be Thine, more than to be this world's, or mine own. Yet this is nothing; I leave eternity to Thee; for what is man that he should live out the lifetime of his God? *Ib.*

With the landless gull, that at sunset folds her wings and is rocked to sleep between billows; so at nightfall, the Nantucketer, out of sight of land, furls his sails, and lays him to his rest, while under his very pillow rush herds of walruses and whales. *Ib.* 14

But when a man's religion becomes really frantic; when it is a positive torment to him; and, in fine, makes this earth of ours an uncomfortable inn to lodge in; then I think it high time to take that individual aside and argue the point with him. *Ib.* 17

In one word, Queequeg, said I, rather digressively; hell is an idea first born on an undigested apple dumpling;

and since then perpetuated through the hereditary dyspepsias nurtured by Ramadans. *Moby-Dick, ch.* 17

If, at my death, my executors, or more properly my creditors, find any precious MSS. in my desk, then here I prospectively ascribe all the honor and the glory to whaling; for a whaleship was my Yale College and my Harvard. *Ib.* 24

That immaculate manliness we feel within ourselves, so far within us, that it remains intact though all the outer character seem gone; bleeds with keenest anguish at the undraped spectacle of a valor-ruined man. *Ib.* 26

Thou great democratic God! who didst not refuse to the swart convict, Bunyan, the pale poetic pearl; Thou who didst clothe with doubly hammered leaves of finest gold, the stumped and paupered arm of old Cervantes; Thou who didst pick up Andrew Jackson from the pebbles; who didst hurl him upon a warhorse; who didst thunder him higher than a throne! Thou who, in all Thy mighty, earthly marchings, ever cullest thy selectest champions from the kingly commons! *Ib.*

This it is, that forever keeps God's true princes of the Empire from the world's hustings; and leaves the highest honors that this air can give, to those men who become famous more through their infinite inferiority to the choice hidden handful of the Divine Inert, than through their undoubted superiority over the dead level of the mass. *Ib.* 33

All that most maddens and torments; all that stirs up the lees of things; all truth with malice in it; all that cracks the sinews and cakes the brain; all the subtle demonisms of life and thought; all evil, to crazy Ahab, were visibly personified, and made practically assailable in Moby Dick. He piled upon the whale's white hump the sum of all the general rage and hate felt by his whole race from Adam down; and then, as if his chest had been a mortar, he burst his hot heart's shell upon it.

Moby-Dick, ch. 41

For as this appalling ocean surrounds the verdant land, so in the soul of man there lies one insular Tahiti, full of peace and joy, but encompassed by all the horrors of the half known life.

Ib. 58

O Nature, and O soul of man! how far beyond all utterance are your linked analogies! not the smallest atom stirs or lives on matter, but has its cunning duplicate in mind. *Ib.* 70

So, therefore, that mortal man who hath more of joy than sorrow in him, that mortal man cannot be true — not true, or undeveloped. With books the same. The truest of all men was the Man of Sorrows, and the truest of all books is Solomon's and Ecclesiastes is the fine hammered steel of woe.

Ib. 96

Give me a condor's quill! Give me Vesuvius' crater for an inkstand! . . . To produce a mighty book, you must choose a mighty theme. *Ib.* 104

Seat thyself sultanically among the moons of Saturn, and take high abstracted man alone; and he seems a wonder, a grandeur, and a woe. But from the same point, take mankind in mass, and for the most part, they seem a mob of unnecessary duplicates, both contemporary and hereditary.

Ib. 107

There is, one knows not what sweet mystery about this sea, whose gently awful stirrings seem to speak of some hidden soul beneath; like those fabled undulations of the Ephesian sod over the buried Evangelist St. John. And meet it is, that over these sea pastures, wide-rolling watery prairies and Potters' Fields of all four continents, the waves should rise and fall, and ebb and flow unceasingly; for here, millions of mixed shades and shadows, drowned dreams, somnambulisms, reveries; all that we call lives and souls, lie dreaming,

dreaming, still; tossing like slumberers in their beds; the ever-rolling waves but made so by their restlessness.

Moby-Dick, ch. 111

There is no steady unretracing progress in this life; we do not advance through fixed gradations, and at the last one pause: through infancy's unconscious spell, boyhood's thoughtless faith, adolescence' doubt (the common doom), then skepticism, then disbelief, resting at last in manhood's pondering repose of If. But once gone through, we trace the round again; and are infants, boys, and men, and Ifs eternally. Where lies the final harbor, whence we unmoor no more?

Ib. 114

But if the great sun move not of himself; but is as an errand boy in heaven; nor one single star can revolve, but by some invisible power; how then can this one small heart beat; this one small brain think thoughts; unless God does that beating, does that thinking, does that living, and not I. By heaven, man, we are turned round and round in this world, like yonder windlass, and Fate is the handspike. *Ib.* 132

An old, old sight, and yet somehow so young; aye, and not changed a wink since I first saw it, a boy, from the sandhills of Nantucket! The same! — the same! — the same to Noah as to me. There's a soft shower to leeward. Such lovely leewardings! They must lead somewhere — to something else than common land, more palmy than the palms. *Ib.*

Now small fowls flew screaming over the yet yawning gulf; a sullen white surf beat against its steep sides; then all collapsed, and the great shroud of the sea rolled on as it rolled five thousand years ago. *Ib.*

What we take to be our strongest tower of delight, only stands at the caprice of the minutest event — the falling of a leaf, the hearing of a voice, or the receipt of one little bit of paper

scratched over with a few small characters by a sharpened feather.
Pierre [1852], *bk. IV*

One trembles to think of that mysterious thing in the soul, which seems to acknowledge no human jurisdiction, but in spite of the individual's own innocent self, will still dream horrid dreams, and mutter unmentionable thoughts. *Ib.*

A smile is the chosen vehicle for all ambiguities. *Ib.*

Say what some poets will, Nature is not so much her own ever-sweet interpreter, as the mere supplier of that cunning alphabet, whereby selecting and combining as he pleases, each man reads his own peculiar lesson according to his own peculiar mind and mood.
Ib. XXV

But me they'll lash in hammock, drop me deep.
Fathoms down, fathoms down, how I'll dream fast asleep.
I feel it stealing now. Sentry, are you there?
Just ease these darbies [1] at the wrist,
And roll me over fair.
I am sleepy, and the oozy weeds about me twist.
Billy Budd, Foretopman [published 1924], *Billy in the Darbies* [1]

THOMAS WILLIAM PARSONS
1819–1892

Sorrow and the scarlet leaf,
Sad thoughts and sunny weather;
Ah me, this glory and this grief
Agree not well together!
A Song for September

JOHN RUSKIN
1819–1900

He is the greatest artist who has embodied, in the sum of his works, the greatest number of the greatest ideas.
Modern Painters, vol. I [1843], *pt. I, ch. 2*

[1] Manacles.

A falseness in all our impressions of external things, which I would generally characterize as the "Pathetic Fallacy."
Modern Painters, vol. III [1856], *pt. IV, ch. 12*

In order that people may be happy in their work, these three things are needed: They must be fit for it. They must not do too much of it. And they must have a sense of success in it.
Pre-Raphaelitism [1851]

Remember that the most beautiful things in the world are the most useless; peacocks and lilies for instance.
The Stones of Venice [1851–1853], *vol. I, ch. 2*

Blue color is everlastingly appointed by the Deity to be a source of delight.
Lectures on Architecture and Painting [1853], *I*

There is no wealth but life.
Unto This Last [1862], *sec. 77*

That country is the richest which nourishes the greatest number of noble and happy human beings; that man is richest who, having perfected the functions of his own life to the utmost, has also the widest helpful influence, both personal, and by means of his possessions, over the lives of others. *Ib.*

Life being very short, and the quiet hours of it few, we ought to waste none of them in reading valueless books.
Sesame and Lilies [1865], *preface*

All books are divisible into two classes: the books of the hour, and the books of all time.
Ib. Of Kings' Treasuries, sec. 8

Borrowers are nearly always ill-spenders, and it is with lent money that all evil is mainly done, and all unjust war protracted.
The Crown of Wild Olive [1866]. *Work, sec. 34*

Give a little love to a child, and you get a great deal back. *Ib. 49*

There's no music in a "rest," Katie, that I know of: but there's the making

of music in it. And people are always missing that part of the life-melody.
Ethics of the Dust [1866]. *Lecture 4, The Crystal Orders*

Life without industry is guilt, industry without art is brutality.
Lectures on Art [1870]. *III, The Relation of Art to Morals*

Trust thou thy Love: if she be proud, is she not sweet?
Trust thou thy Love: if she be mute, is she not pure?
Lay thou thy soul full in her hands, low at her feet;
Fail, Sun and Breath! — yet, for thy peace, she shall endure.
Trust Thou Thy Love

MAX SCHNECKENBURGER
1819–1849

Dear Fatherland, no fear be thine,
Firm stands thy guard along the Rhine.
The Watch on the Rhine,[1] *st. 4*

WILLIAM WETMORE STORY
1819–1895

Of every noble work the silent part is best,
Of all expression that which cannot be expressed. *The Unexpressed*

QUEEN VICTORIA
1819–1901

We are not interested in the possibilities of defeat.
To A. J. Balfour [December 1899]

We are not amused.
Upon seeing an imitation of herself by the Honorable Alexander Grantham Yorke, groom-in-waiting to the Queen. From Notebooks of a Spinster Lady [January 2, 1900]

[1] Die Wacht am Rhein.

WILLIAM ROSS WALLACE
1819–1881

The hand that rocks the cradle is the hand that rules the world.
The Hand That Rules the World, st. 1

WALT WHITMAN
1819–1892

The United States themselves are essentially the greatest poem. . . . Here at last is something in the doings of man that corresponds with the broadcast doings of the day and night.
Preface to first edition of Leaves of Grass [1855]

The proof of a poet is that his country absorbs him as affectionately as he has absorbed it. *Ib.*

Me imperturbe, standing at ease in nature.
Leaves of Grass [1855–1892] [1]

I hear America singing, the varied carols I hear.
Ib. I Hear America Singing

I will put in my poems that with you is heroism upon land and sea,
And I will report all heroism from an American point of view.
Ib. Starting from Paumanok, 7

I say the whole earth and all the stars in the sky are for religion's sake.
Ib. 8

I say the real and permanent grandeur of these States must be their religion. *Ib.*

[1] The first edition of *Leaves of Grass* consisted of 94 quarto pages and included the preface which set forth Whitman's faith and his poetic theory. Enlarged and revised editions followed. The tenth edition (from which the text used here is taken) was the last edition supervised by Whitman himself, literally from his deathbed, and hence it is sometimes called the "Deathbed Edition." Whitman wrote of it, "as there are now several editions of *Leaves of Grass*, different texts and dates, I wish to say that I prefer and recommend this present one."

Nothing can happen more beautiful than death.[1]

Leaves of Grass. Starting from Paumanok, 12

I celebrate myself and sing myself,
And what I assume you shall assume.

Ib. Song of Myself, 1

I loafe and invite my soul. *Ib.*

Urge and urge and urge,
Always the procreant urge of the world.

Ib. 3

A kelson of the creation is love.

Ib. 5

A child said *What is the grass?* fetching it to me with full hands. *Ib. 6*

Or I guess it is the handkerchief of the Lord. *Ib.*

And now it seems to me the beautiful uncut hair of graves. *Ib.*

Has anyone supposed it lucky to be born?
I hasten to inform him or her, it is just as lucky to die, and I know it.

Ib. 7

I am he that walks with the tender and growing night,
I call to the earth and sea half-held by the night.
Press close bare-bosom'd night — press close magnetic nourishing night!
Night of south winds! night of the large few stars!
Still nodding night! mad naked summer night. *Ib. 21*

Walt Whitman am I, a Kosmos, of mighty Manhattan the son,
Turbulent, fleshy and sensual, eating, drinking and breeding;

No sentimentalist — no stander above men and women, or apart from them;
No more modest than immodest.

Leaves of Grass. Song of Myself, 24

I dote on myself, there is that lot of me and all so luscious. *Ib.*

I hear the violoncello, ('tis the young man's heart's complaint). *Ib. 26*

I believe a leaf of grass is no less than the journey-work of the stars.

Ib. 31

I think I could turn and live with animals, they are so placid and self-contain'd,
I stand and look at them long and long.
They do not sweat and whine about their condition,
They do not lie awake in the dark and weep for their sins,
They do not make me sick discussing their duty to God,
Not one is dissatisfied, not one is demented with the mania of owning things,
Not one kneels to another, nor to his kind that lived thousands of years ago,
Not one is respectable or unhappy over the whole earth. *Ib. 32*

Behold! I do not give lectures or a little charity,
When I give I give myself.[1] *Ib. 40*

I have said that the soul is not more than the body,
And I have said that the body is not more than the soul,
And nothing, not God, is greater to one than one's self is. *Ib. 48*

In the faces of men and women I see God. *Ib.*

Do I contradict myself?
Very well then I contradict myself,
(I am large, I contain multitudes.)

Ib. 51

---

[1] Why fear death? Death is only a beautiful adventure. — CHARLES FROHMAN [1860–1915], last words to a group of friends as the *Lusitania* was sinking [May 7, 1915]
Why should I fear Death's call? Can there e'er be
In life more beautiful adventure than
To re-embark upon that unknown sea?
JAMES TERRY WHITE [1845–1920], *Why Fear? st. 1*

[1] See Emerson, p. 607b, and Lowell, p. 692b.

I sound my barbaric yawp over the roofs of the world.
Leaves of Grass. Song of Myself, 52

I bequeathe myself to the dirt, to grow from the grass I love;
If you want me again, look for me under your boot-soles. *Ib.*

A woman waits for me, she contains all, nothing is lacking.
Ib. A Woman Waits For Me

If anything is sacred the human body is sacred.
Ib. I Sing the Body Electric, 8

I hear it was charged against me that I sought to destroy institutions,
But really I am neither for nor against institutions.
Ib. I Hear It Was Charged Against Me

When I peruse the conquer'd fame of heroes and the victories of mighty generals, I do not envy the generals.
Ib. When I Peruse the Conquer'd Fame

Afoot and light-hearted I take to the open road,
Healthy, free, the world before me,
The long brown path before me, leading wherever I choose.
Ib. Song of the Open Road, 1

Henceforth I ask not good-fortune, I myself am good-fortune. *Ib.*

The earth, that is sufficient,
I do not want the constellations any nearer,
I know they are very well where they are,
I know they suffice for those who belong to them. *Ib.*

A great city is that which has the greatest men and women.
Ib. Song of the Broad-Axe, 4

Youth, large, lusty, loving — Youth, full of grace, force, fascination,

Do you know that Old Age may come after you, with equal grace, force, fascination?
Leaves of Grass. Youth, Day, Old Age and Night

Come, my tan-faced children,
Follow well in order, get your weapons ready;
Have you your pistols? have you your sharp-edged axes?
Ib. Pioneers! O Pioneers! 1

Through the battle, through defeat, moving yet and never stopping,
Pioneers! O pioneers! *Ib.* 13

Out of the cradle endlessly rocking,
Out of the mocking-bird's throat, the musical shuttle,
Out of the Ninth-month midnight.
Ib. Out of the Cradle Endlessly Rocking

Whereto answering, the sea,
Delaying not, hurrying not,
Whisper'd me through the night, and very plainly before daybreak,
Lisp'd to me the low and delicious word death. *Ib.*

Aboard, at a ship's helm,
A young steersman, steering with care.
Ib. Aboard, at a Ship's Helm

But O the ship, the immortal ship! O ship aboard the ship!
O ship of the body — ship of the soul — voyaging, voyaging, voyaging.
Ib.

Silent and amazed, even when a little boy,
I remember I heard the preacher every Sunday put God in his statements,
As contending against some being or influence. *Ib. A Child's Amaze*

Give me the splendid silent sun, with all his beams full-dazzling!
Ib. Give Me the Splendid Silent Sun, 1

Word over all, beautiful as the sky!
Beautiful that war and all its deeds of carnage must in time be utterly lost,

That the hands of the sisters Death and
    Night incessantly softly wash
    again, and ever again, this soil'd
    world;
For my enemy is dead, a man divine as
    myself is dead.
      Leaves of Grass. Reconciliation

When lilacs last in the dooryard
    bloom'd,
And the great star early droop'd in the
    western sky in the night,
I mourn'd — and yet shall mourn with
    ever-returning spring.
      *Ib. When Lilacs Last in the
      Dooryard Bloom'd,* 1

O sane and sacred death.   *Ib.* 7

Come lovely and soothing death,[1]
Undulate round the world, serenely
    arriving, arriving,
In the day, in the night, to all, to each,
Sooner or later, delicate death.
      Ib. 14

Prais'd be the fathomless universe,
For life and joy, and for objects and
    knowledge curious,
And for love, sweet love — But praise!
    praise! praise!
For the sure-enwinding arms of cool-
    enfolding death.   *Ib.*

O Captain! my Captain! our fearful
    trip is done!
The ship has weather'd every rack, the
    prize we sought is won,
The port is near, the bells I hear, the
    people all exulting.
      Ib. O Captain! My Captain! 1

Exult O shores, and ring O bells!
But I with mournful tread,
Walk the deck my Captain lies,
Fallen cold and dead.   *Ib.* 3

This dust was once the man,
Gentle, plain, just and resolute, under
    whose cautious hand,
Against the foulest crime in history
    known in any land or age,
Was saved the Union of these States.
      Ib. This Dust Was Once the Man

[1] See Shakespeare, p. 236b

The whole theory of the universe is di-
    rected unerringly to one single
    individual — namely to You.
      *Leaves of Grass. By Blue
      Ontario's Shore,* 15

Liberty is to be subserved whatever
    occurs.
      *Ib. To a Foil'd European Revolu-
      tionaire,* 1

What do you suppose will satisfy the
    soul, except to walk free and own
    no superior?
      Ib. Laws for Creations, 3

Not till the sun excludes you do I ex-
    clude you.
      Ib. To a Common Prostitute

O we can wait no longer,
We too take ship O soul,
Joyous we too launch out on trackless
    seas,
Fearless for unknown shores.
      Ib. Passage to India, 8

Passage, immediate passage! the blood
    burns in my veins!
Away, O soul! hoist instantly the an-
    chor!
Cut the hawsers — haul out — shake
    out every sail!
Have we not stood here like trees in the
    ground long enough?
Have we not grovel'd here long enough,
    eating and drinking like mere
    brutes?   *Ib.* 9

Darest thou now O soul,
Walk out with me toward the un-
    known region
Where neither ground is for the feet
    nor any path to follow?
      Ib. Darest Thou Now O Soul

To me every hour of the light and dark
    is a miracle,
Every cubic inch of space is a miracle.
      Ib. Miracles, 2

Today a rude brief recitative,
Of ships sailing the seas, each with its
    special flag or ship-signal.
      Ib. Song for All Seas, All Ships, 1

Of sea captains young or old, and the
    mates — and of all intrepid sail-
    ors . . .

Pick'd sparingly, without noise, by thee,
    old Ocean — chosen by thee,
Thou Sea, that pickest and cullest the
    race, in time, and unitest nations!
Suckled by thee, old husky nurse —
    embodying thee!
Indomitable, untamed as thee.
        Leaves of Grass. Song for
          All Seas, All Ships, 1

Our life is closed — our life begins,
The long, long anchorage we leave,
The ship is clear at last — she leaps!
She swiftly courses from the shore,
Joy! shipmate — joy.
        Ib. Joy, Shipmate, Joy!

Camerado, this is no book,
Who touches this touches a man.
           Ib. So Long!

The world, the race, the soul — in
    space and time the universes,
All bound as is befitting each — all
    surely going somewhere.
        Ib. Going Somewhere

Political democracy, as it exists and
practically works in America, with all
its threatening evils, supplies a training
school for making first-class men. It is
life's gymnasium, not of good only, but
of all.   *Democratic Vistas* [1871]

It is native personality, and that
alone, that endows a man to stand before presidents or generals, or in any
distinguish'd collection, with *aplomb*
— and *not* culture, or any knowledge or
intellect whatever.   *Ib.*

I never see that man [Lincoln] without feeling that he is one to become
personally attach'd to, for his combination of purest, heartiest tenderness, and
native western form of manliness.
    Specimen Days [1882]. *The In-*
      auguration [*March 4, 1865*]

He leaves for America's history and
biography, so far, not only its most
dramatic reminiscence — he leaves, in
my opinion, the greatest, best, most
characteristic, artistic, moral personality.
    Ib. Death of President Lincoln
        [*April 16, 1865*]

The real war will never get in the
books.   *Ib. The Real War*

After you have exhausted what there
is in business, politics, conviviality, and
so on — have found that none of these
finally satisfy, or permanently wear
— what remains? Nature remains.
    Specimen Days. New Themes
          Entered Upon

Hast Thou, pellucid, in Thy azure
depths, medicine for case like mine?
    Ib. The Sky [*October 20, 1876*]

You must not know too much, or be
too precise or scientific about birds and
trees and flowers and watercraft; a certain free margin, and even vagueness
— perhaps ignorance, credulity — helps
your enjoyment of these things.
    Ib. Birds [*May 14, 1881*]

To have great poets, there must be
great audiences, too.
    Notes Left Over. Ventures on
         an Old Theme

No really great song can ever attain
full purport till long after the death of
its singer — till it has accrued and incorporated the many passions, many
joys and sorrows, it has itself aroused.
    November Boughs [1888]. *The*
        Bible as Poetry

No one will ever get at my verses
who insists upon viewing them as a
literary performance.
    A Backward Glance O'er Travel'd
        Roads [1888]

Concluding with two items for the
imaginative genius of the West, when
it worthily rises — First, what Herder
taught to the young Goethe, that really
great poetry is always (like the Homeric
or Biblical canticles) the result of a national spirit, and not the privilege of a
polish'd and select few; Second, that
the strongest and sweetest songs yet remain to be sung.   *Ib.*

There is no week nor day nor hour,
when tyranny may not enter upon this
country, if the people lose their rough-
ness and spirit of defiance — Tyranny
may always enter — there is no charm,

no bar against it — the only bar against it is a large resolute breed of men.

> *Notes for Lecturers on Democracy and "Adhesiveness." From* C. J. Furness, *Walt Whitman's Workshop* [1928]

ALICE CARY
1820–1871

Work, and your house shall be duly fed:
Work, and rest shall be won;
I hold that a man had better be dead
Than alive when his work is done.
> *Work*

LUCRETIA PEABODY HALE
1820–1900

At last Elizabeth Eliza said, "They say that the lady from Philadelphia, who is staying in town, is very wise. Suppose I go and ask her what is best to be done."
> *The Peterkin Papers* [1880]

JEAN INGELOW
1820–1897

But two are walking apart forever,
And wave their hands for a mute farewell.
> *Divided. VI, st. 5*

A sweeter woman ne'er drew breath
Than my son's wife, Elizabeth.
> *High Tide on the Coast of Lincolnshire, 1571, st. 11*

There's no dew left on the daisies and clover,
There's no rain left in heaven:
I've said my "seven times" over and over,
Seven times one are seven.
> *Songs of Seven. Seven Times One, st. 1*

O columbine, open your folded wrapper,
Where two twin turtledoves dwell!
O cuckoopint, toll me the purple clapper
That hangs in your clear green bell!
> *Ib. st. 6*

O land where all the men are stones,
Or all the stones are men.
> *A Land That Living Warmth Disowns*

THEODORE O'HARA
1820–1867

On Fame's eternal camping ground
Their silent tents are spread,
And Glory guards, with solemn round,
The bivouac of the dead.
> *The Bivouac of the Dead* [1] [1847], *st. 1*

Sons of the Dark and Bloody ground.[2]
> *Ib. st. 9*

GEORGE FREDERICK ROOT
1820–1895

Tramp! Tramp! Tramp! the boys are marching,
Cheer up, comrades, they will come,
And beneath the starry flag
We shall breathe the air again
Of the free land in our own beloved home.
> *Tramp! Tramp! Tramp!* [1862]

Yes, we'll rally round the flag, boys, we'll rally once again,
Shouting the battle cry of Freedom,
We will rally from the hillside, we'll gather from the plain,
Shouting the battle cry of Freedom.
> *The Battle Cry of Freedom* [1863]

SIR WILLIAM HOWARD RUSSELL
1820–1907

The Russians dashed on towards that thin red-line streak tipped with a line of steel.[3]

> *To The Times of London from the Crimea, describing the British infantry at Balaklava* [October 25, 1854]

[1] Written to commemorate Americans slain in the battle of Buena Vista, February 22–23, 1847.
[2] Translation of the Indian name Kentucky.
[3] Soon the men of the column began to see that though the scarlet line was slender, it was

WILLIAM TECUMSEH SHERMAN
1820–1891

You cannot qualify war in harsher terms than I will. War is cruelty, and you cannot refine it.
> *Letter [September 12, 1864] to James M. Calhoun, Mayor of Atlanta, and others*

Hold the fort! I am coming! [1]
> *Signal from Kenesaw Mountain to General John Murray Corse in Altoona [October 5, 1864]*

The legitimate object of war is a more perfect peace.
> *Speech [St. Louis, July 20, 1865]*

I am tired and sick of war. Its glory is all moonshine. It is only those who have neither fired a shot nor heard the shrieks and groans of the wounded who cry aloud for blood, more vengeance, more desolation. War is hell.[2]
> *Attributed to a graduation address at Michigan Military Academy [June 19, 1879]; from the National Tribune, Washington, D.C. [November 26, 1914]*

I will not accept if nominated and will not serve if elected.[3]
> *Message to Republican National Convention [June 5, 1884]*

JOHN TYNDALL
1820–1893

Heat Considered as a Mode of Motion.   *Title of treatise [1863]*

Life is a wave, which in no two consecutive moments of its existence is composed of the same particles.[1]
> *Fragments of Science, vol. II, Vitality*

The mind of man may be compared to a musical instrument with a certain range of notes, beyond which in both directions we have an infinitude of silence.   *Ib. Matter and Force*

The brightest flashes in the world of thought are incomplete until they have been proved to have their counterparts in the world of fact.
> *Ib. Scientific Materialism*

It is as fatal as it is cowardly to blink facts because they are not to our taste.   *Ib. Science and Man*

Charles Darwin, the Abraham of scientific men — a searcher as obedient to the command of truth as was the patriarch to the command of God.   *Ib.*

Superstition may be defined as constructive religion which has grown incongruous with intelligence.   *Ib.*

Religious feeling is as much a verity as any other part of human consciousness; and against it, on the subjective side, the waves of science beat in vain.
> *Ib. Professor Virchow and Evolution*

HERBERT SPENCER
1820–1903

Progress, therefore, is not an accident, but a necessity. . . . It is a part of nature.
> *Social Statics [1851], pt. I, ch. 2*

Education has for its object the formation of character.   *Ib. 17*

Opinion is ultimately determined by the feelings, and not by the intellect.
> *Ib. IV, 30*

Morality knows nothing of geographical boundaries or distinctions of race.   *Ib.*

---

very rigid and exact. — A. W. KINGLAKE [1809–1891], *Invasion of the Crimea, vol. III, p. 455*

It's "Thin red line of 'eroes'" when the drums begin to roll. — KIPLING [1865–1936], *Tommy, st. 3*

[1] He actually said: Hold out. Relief is coming. General Corse replied: I am short a cheekbone and an ear, but am able to whip all hell yet. See Philip Bliss, p. 777b.

[2] See Robert E. Lee, p. 620a.

[3] The familiar version is: If nominated I will not run; if elected I will not serve.

[1] See Heraclitus, p. 77a.

No one can be perfectly free till all are free; no one can be perfectly moral till all are moral; no one can be perfectly happy till all are happy.

Social Statics, pt. IV, ch. 30

Architecture, sculpture, painting, music, and poetry, may truly be called the efflorescence of civilized life.

Essays on Education [1861].
Education: What Knowledge Is of Most Worth?

Every cause produces more than one effect.

Ib. On Progress: Its Law and Cause

The tyranny of Mrs. Grundy[1] is worse than any other tyranny we suffer under.

Ib. On Manners and Fashion

Old forms of government finally grow so oppressive that they must be thrown off even at the risk of reigns of terror. *Ib.*

Music must take rank as the highest of the fine arts — as the one which, more than any other, ministers to human welfare.

Ib. On the Origin and Function of Music

We too often forget that not only is there "a soul of goodness in things evil,"[2] but very generally a soul of truth in things erroneous.

First Principles [1861]

The fact disclosed by a survey of the past that majorities have been wrong must not blind us to the complementary fact that majorities have usually not been entirely wrong. *Ib.*

Volumes might be written upon the impiety of the pious. *Ib.*

We have unmistakable proof that throughout all past time, there has been a ceaseless devouring of the weak by the strong. *Ib.*

[1] See Thomas Morton, p. 501a, and Locker-Hampson, p. 710a.
[2] See Shakespeare, *Henry V, IV, i, 4*, p. 244b.

This survival of the fittest.

Principles of Biology [1864–1867], *pt. III, ch. 12*

The Republican form of government is the highest form of government: but because of this it requires the highest type of human nature — a type nowhere at present existing.

Essays [1891]. *The Americans*

The ultimate result of shielding men from the effects of folly is to fill the world with fools.

Ib. State Tamperings with Money Banks

HENRI-FRÉDÉRIC AMIEL
1821–1881

Truth is the secret of eloquence and of virtue, the basis of moral authority; it is the highest summit of art and of life. *Journal* [1883]

An error is the more dangerous the more truth it contains. *Ib.*

Doing easily what others find difficult is talent; doing what is impossible for talent is genius. *Ib.*

If ignorance and passion are the foes of popular morality, it must be confessed that moral indifference is the malady of the cultivated classes. *Ib.*

Pure truth cannot be assimilated by the crowd; it must be communicated by contagion. *Ib.*

CHARLES BAUDELAIRE[1]
1821–1867

Hypocrite reader — my fellow man — my brother![2]

Les Fleurs du Mal [1861]

[1] Baudelaire is the foremost seer, king of poets, a *true God*. Even so, he lived in too artistic a milieu; his so highly praised form is meager. Ventures into the unknown demand new forms. — ARTHUR RIMBAUD [1854–1891], *Lettre à Paul Demeny* [*May 15, 1871*]
[2] Hypocrite lecteur — mon semblable — mon frère! (Quoted by T. S. ELIOT in *The Waste Land*.)

The poet is like the prince of the clouds who haunts the tempest and laughs at the archer; exiled on the ground in the midst of jeers, his giant wings prevent him from walking.[1]
Les Fleurs du Mal.
L'Albatros, st. 4

Perfumes, colors and sounds echo one another.   Ib. Correspondances

Mother of memories, mistress of mistresses.[2]   Ib. Le Balcon, st. 1

There, everything is order and beauty, richness, quiet and pleasure.[3]
Ib. L'Invitation au Voyage, refrain

I have more memories than if I were a thousand years old.[4]
Ib. Spleen, l. 1

I am the wound and the knife!
I am the blow and the cheek!
I am the limbs and the wheel —
The victim and the executioner! [5]
Ib. L'Héautontimoroumenos

O Death, old captain, it is time! raise the anchor!
Ib. Le Voyage, VIII

What do I care that you are good? Be beautiful! and be sad! [6]
Nouvelles Fleurs du Mal [1866–1868]. Madrigal Triste, st. 1

There can be no progress (real, that is, moral) except in the individual and by the individual himself.
Mon Coeur Mis à Nu [1887],
XV

There are in every man, at every hour, two simultaneous postulations, one towards God, the other towards Satan.   Ib. XIX

[1] Le Poète est semblable au prince des nuées
Qui hante la tempête et se rit de l'archer;
Exilé sur le sol au milieu des huées,
Ses ailes de géant l'empêchent de marcher.
[2] Mère des souvenirs, maîtresse des maîtresses.
[3] Là, tout n'est qu'ordre et beauté,
Luxe, calme et volupté.
[4] J'ai plus de souvenirs que si j'avais mille ans.
[5] Je suis la plaie et le couteau!
Je suis le soufflet et la joute!
Je suis les membres et la roue,
Et la victime et le bourreau!
[6] Que m'importe que tu sois sage?
Sois belle! et sois triste!

There exist only three beings worthy of respect: the priest, the soldier, the poet. To know, to kill, to create.
Mon Coeur Mis à Nu XXII

To be a great man and a saint for oneself, that is the one important thing.   Ib. LII

Theory of the true civilization. It is not to be found in gas or steam or table turning. It consists in the diminution of the traces of original sin.   Ib. LIX

SIR RICHARD FRANCIS BURTON
1821–1890

Why meet we on the bridge of Time to 'change one greeting and to part?
The Kasidah of Haji Abdu El-Yazdi, I, 11

Indeed he knows not how to know who knows not also how to un-know.
Ib. VI, 18

Do what thy manhood bids thee do, from none but self expect applause;
He noblest lives and noblest dies who makes and keeps his self-made laws.   Ib. VIII, 37

FËDOR MIKHAILOVICH DOSTOEVSKI
1821–1881

Man is a pliable animal, a being who gets accustomed to everything!
The House of the Dead (Prison Life in Siberia) [1861–1862], pt. I, ch. 2

He [Turgenev] said that he was writing a long article against the Russophiles and Slavophiles. I advised him to order a telescope from Paris for his better convenience. "What do you mean?" he asked. "The distance is somewhat great," I replied; "direct the telescope on Russia, and then you will be able to observe us; otherwise you can't really see anything at all."
Letter to Apollon Maikov
[August 16 (28), 1867]

I want to tell you now about the insects to whom God gave "sensual lust." . . . I am that insect, brother, and it is said of me especially. All we Karamazovs are such insects, and, angel as you are, that insect lives in you too, and will stir a tempest in your blood. Tempests, because sensual lust is a tempest — worse than a tempest! Beauty is a terrible and awful thing! It is terrible because it has not been fathomed, for God sets us nothing but riddles.[1] Here the boundaries meet and all contradictions exist side by side. . . .

Yes, man is broad, too broad, indeed. I'd have him narrower. The devil only knows what to make of it! What to the mind is shameful is beauty and nothing else to the heart. Is there beauty in Sodom? Believe me, that for the immense mass of mankind beauty is found in Sodom. Did you know that secret? The awful thing is that beauty is mysterious as well as terrible. God and devil are fighting there, and the battlefield is the heart of man.

> *The Brothers Karamazov*[2]
> *[1879–1880], bk. III, ch. 3*

And if that is so, if they dare not forgive, what becomes of harmony? Is there in the whole world a being who would have the right to forgive and could forgive? I don't want harmony. From love of humanity I don't want it. I would rather be left with unavenged suffering. I would rather remain with my unavenged suffering and unsatisfied indignation, *even if I were wrong.* Besides, too high a price is asked for harmony; it's beyond our means to pay so much to enter on it. And so I hasten to give back my entrance ticket, and if I am an honest man I am bound to give it back as soon as possible. And that I am doing. It's not God that I don't accept, Alyosha, only I most respectfully return Him the ticket. *Ib. V, 4*

We have corrected Thy work and have founded it upon *miracle, mystery* and *authority.* And men rejoiced that

they were again led like sheep, and that the terrible gift that brought them such suffering, was, at last, lifted from their hearts.

> *The Brothers Karamazov,*
> *bk. V, ch. 5*

"How will you escape it? By what will you escape it? That's impossible with your ideas."

"In the Karamazov way, again."

" 'Everything is lawful,' you mean?"
Ib.

Men reject their prophets and slay them, but they love their martyrs and honor those whom they have slain.
Ib. VI, 3

That was a sign to me at that moment. It's for the babe I'm going. Because we are responsible for all.
Ib. XI, 4

Who doesn't desire his father's death? *Ib. XII, 5*

Our fatal troika dashes on in her headlong flight perhaps to destruction, and in all Russia for long past men have stretched out imploring hands and called a halt to its furious reckless course. And if other nations stand aside from that troika that may be not from respect, as the poet would fain believe, but simply from horror. And well it is that they stand aside, but maybe they will cease one day to do so and will form a firm wall confronting the hurrying apparition and will check the frenzied rush of our lawlessness, for the sake of their own safety, enlightenment and civilization. *Ib. 9*

They have their Hamlets, but we still have our Karamazovs! *Ib.*

But profound as psychology is, it's a knife that cuts both ways.
Ib. 10

For a moment the lie becomes truth. *Ib. Epilogue, ch. 2*

We have all come out of Gogol's *Overcoat.*[1]

Attributed to Dostoevski

---

[1] See Einstein, p. 951a.
[2] Translated by CONSTANCE GARNETT.

MARY BAKER EDDY
1821–1910

Jesus of Nazareth was the most scientific man that ever trod the globe. He plunged beneath the material surface of things, and found the spiritual cause.

Science and Health with Key to the Scriptures [*1875*], *p. 313*

Spirit is the real and eternal; matter is the unreal and temporal.

Ib. p. 468

Sickness, sin and death, being inharmonious, do not originate in God nor belong to His government.

Ib. p. 472

How would you define Christian Science?

As the law of God, the law of good, interpreting and demonstrating the divine Principle and rule of universal harmony.

Rudimental Divine Science [*1891*], *p. 1*

GUSTAVE FLAUBERT
1821–1880

One must not always think that feeling is everything. Art is nothing without form.

Letter to Madame Louise Colet [*August 12, 1846*]

What a horrible invention, the bourgeois, don't you think? [1]

Ib. [*September 22, 1846*]

Eugène Melchior, vicomte de Vogüé [*1848–1910*], *Le Roman Russe* [*1886*], ch. 3: The more I read the Russians, the more I understand the observation one of them made to me . . . "We have all come out of Gogol's *Overcoat.*" We see further how evident the connection is with Dostoevski: the formidable novelist is all in his first book, *Poor People,* and *Poor People* has its origin in the *Overcoat.*

De Vogüé reiterated this statement in the speech he made on the occasion of unveiling a centennial monument to Gogol in Moscow in 1909.

[1] Il faut épater le bourgeois [You must shock the bourgeois]. — BAUDELAIRE

One becomes a critic when one cannot be an artist, just as a man becomes a stool pigeon when he cannot be a soldier.

Letter to Madame Louise Colet [*October 22, 1846*]

Axiom: hatred of the bourgeois is the beginning of wisdom.[1]

Letter to George Sand, May 10, 1867

I call a bourgeois anyone whose thinking is vulgar.[1]

Quoted by Maupassant

What is beautiful is moral, that is all there is to it.

Letter to Maupassant [*October 26, 1880*]

NATHAN BEDFORD FORREST
1821–1872

Get there first with the most men.[2]

Statement reported by General Basil Duke and General Richard Taylor

HERMANN LUDWIG FERDINAND VON HELMHOLTZ
1821–1894

Nature as a whole possesses a store of force which cannot in any way be either increased or diminished . . . therefore, the quantity of force in Nature is just as eternal and unalterable as the quantity of matter. . . . I have named [this] general law "The Principle of the Conservation of Force." [3]

Über die Erhaltung der Kraft [*1847*]

Whoever, in the pursuit of science, seeks after immediate practical utility, may generally rest assured that he will

[1] See note 1 in left column.

[2] Erroneous version usually rendered: Git thar fustest with the mostest.

[3] Translated by E. ATKINSON.

Helmholtz's "force" is equivalent to the modern physicist's "energy."

seek in vain. All that science can achieve is a perfect knowledge and a perfect understanding of the action of natural and moral forces.

Academic discourse, Heidelberg
[1862]

FREDERICK LOCKER-LAMPSON
1821–1895

The world's as ugly, ay, as Sin —
And almost as delightful.

The Jester's Plea

And many are afraid of God —
And more of Mrs. Grundy.[1]   *Ib.*

GEORGE JOHN WHYTE-MELVILLE
1821–1878

In the choice of a horse and a wife, a man must please himself, ignoring the opinion and advice of friends.

Riding Recollections [1878]

NIKOLAI NEKRASOV
1821–1877

You do not have to be a poet, but you are obliged to be a citizen.

Poet and Citizen

Wretched and abundant,
Oppressed and powerful,
Weak and mighty,
Mother Russia!

Who Is Happy in Russia?
[1873–1876]

WILLIAM HENRY VANDERBILT
1821–1885

The public be damned.

Reply to a newspaper reporter
[October 2, 1882]

[1] See Thomas Morton, p. 501a, and Herbert Spencer, p. 706a.

RUDOLF VIRCHOW
1821–1902

I formulate the doctrine of pathological generation . . . in simple terms: *omnis cellula a cellula.*[1]

Cellular Pathology [1858].[2]
Disease, Life and Man

MATTHEW ARNOLD
1822–1888

Be his [3]
My special thanks, whose even-balanced soul,
From first youth tested up to extreme old age,
Business could not make dull, nor passion wild:
Who saw life steadily and saw it whole.   *To a Friend* [1849]

Others abide our question. Thou art free.
We ask and ask: Thou smilest and art still,
Out-topping knowledge.

Shakespeare [1849]

Strong is the soul, and wise, and beautiful:
The seeds of godlike power are in us still:
Gods are we, bards, saints, heroes, if we will.

Written in Emerson's Essays
[1849]

Come, dear children, let us away;
Down and away below!
Now my brothers call from the bay,
Now the great winds shorewards blow,
Now the salt tides seawards flow;
Now the wild white horses play,
Champ and chafe and toss in the spray.

The Forsaken Merman [1849],
st. 1

Sand-strewn caverns, cool and deep,
Where the winds are all asleep.

Ib. st. 4

[1] All cells come from [pre-existing] cells.
[2] Essays translated by LELLAND J. RATHER [1958].
[3] Sophocles.

Where great whales come sailing by,
Sail and sail, with unshut eye,
Round the world forever and aye.
                    The Forsaken Merman, st. 4

Down, down, down!
Down to the depth of the sea!
She sits at her wheel in the humming
    town,
Singing most joyfully.   *Ib. st.* 7

Fate gave, what Chance shall not con-
    trol,
His sad lucidity of soul.
                    Resignation [1849]

We cannot kindle when we will
The fire that in the heart resides,
The spirit bloweth and is still,
In mystery our soul abides.
                    Morality [1852], *st.* 1

Calm Soul of all things! make it mine
    To feel, amid the city's jar,
That there abides a peace of thine,
    Man did not make, and can not
    mar.
            Lines Written in Kensington
            Gardens [1852], *st.* 10

Goethe in Weimar sleeps, and Greece,
Long since, saw Byron's struggle cease,
But one such death remained to come;
The last poetic voice is dumb —
We stand today by Wordsworth's
    tomb.

When Byron's eyes were shut in
    death,
We bowed our head and held our
    breath.
He taught us little; but our soul
Had *felt* him like the thunder's roll.
            Memorial Verses, April 1850
            [1852], *st.* 1, 2

Physician of the Iron Age,
Goethe has done his pilgrimage.
He took the suffering human race,
He read each wound, each weakness
    clear;
And struck his finger on the place,
And said: Thou ailest here, and here!
                    Ib. st. 3

But where will Europe's latter hour
Again find Wordsworth's healing
    power?
Others will teach us how to dare,
And against fear our breast to steel;
Others will strengthen us to bear —
But who, ah! who will make us feel?
The cloud of mortal destiny,
Others will front it fearlessly —
But who, like him, will put it by?
                    Memorial Verses, st. 5

Hither and thither spins
The windborne, mirroring soul;
A thousand glimpses wins,
And never sees a whole.
            Empedocles on Etna [1852],
                    act I, *sc. ii, l.* 82

Be neither saint- nor sophist-led, but be
    a man!   *Ib. l.* 136

We do not what we ought;
What we ought not, we do; [1]
And lean upon the thought
That chance will bring us through.
                    Ib. l. 237

Nature, with equal mind,
Sees all her sons at play;
Sees man control the wind,
The wind sweep man away.
                    Ib. l. 257

Is it so small a thing
To have enjoyed the sun,
To have lived light in the spring,
To have loved, to have thought, to have
    done;
To have advanced true friends, and
    beat down baffling foes?
                    Ib. II, *l.* 397

The day in its hotness,
The strife with the palm;
The night in her silence,
The stars in their calm.   *Ib. l.* 465

The same heart beats in every human
    breast.
            The Buried Life [1852], *st.* 2

But often in the world's most crowded
    streets,
But often, in the din of strife,

[1] See *Book of Common Prayer,* p. 59b.

There rises an unspeakable desire
After the knowledge of our buried life.
        The Buried Life, st. 6

What actions are the most excellent?
Those, certainly, which most powerfully
appeal to the great primary human
affections: to those elementary feelings
which subsist permanently in the race,
and which are independent of time.
These feelings are permanent and the
same; that which interests them is permanent and the same also.
        Preface to Poems [1853]

Go, for they call you, Shepherd, from
   the hill.
        The Scholar Gypsy [1853], *st. 1*

Crossing the stripling Thames at Bablock-hithe,
Trailing in the cool stream thy fingers
   wet,
As the slow punt swings round.
        Ib. st. 8

Thou waitest for the spark from
   heaven: and we,
Light half-believers of our casual
   creeds,
Who never deeply felt, nor clearly
   willed . . .
Who hesitate and falter life away,
And lose tomorrow the ground won to-
   day —
Ah! do not we, wanderer! await it too?
        Ib. st. 18

    And amongst us one
Who most has suffered, takes de-
   jectedly
His seat upon the intellectual throne.
        Ib. st. 19

This strange disease of modern life.
        Ib. st. 21

Still nursing the unconquerable hope,
Still clutching the inviolable shade.
        Ib. st. 22

Strew on her roses, roses,
   And never a spray of yew!
In quiet she reposes;
   Ah, would that I did too!
        Requiescat [1853], *st. 1*

Her cabined, ample spirit,
   It fluttered and failed for breath.
Tonight it doth inherit
   The vasty hall of death.
        Requiescat, st. 4

Hark! ah, the nightingale —
The tawny-throated!
        Philomela [1853], *st. 1*

Eternal passion!
Eternal pain!   *Ib. st. 3*

What shelter to grow ripe is ours?
What leisure to grow wise?
        Stanzas in Memory of the
        Author of "Obermann" [1] [1853],
        st. 18

Truth sits upon the lips of dying men.
        Sohrab and Rustum [1853],
        l. 656

Sanity — that is the great virtue of
the ancient literature; the want of that
is the great defect of the modern, in
spite of its variety and power.
        Preface to Poems [1854]

Wandering between two worlds, one
   dead,
The other powerless to be born.
        Stanzas from the Grande Char-
        treuse [1855], *st. 15*

And we forget because we must
And not because we will.
        Absence [1857], *st. 3*

Peace, peace is what I seek, and public
   calm;
Endless extinction of unhappy hates.
        Merope [1858], *l. 100*

With women the heart argues, not the
   mind.   *Ib. l. 341*

The translator of Homer should
above all be penetrated by a sense of
four qualities of his author: that he is
eminently rapid; that he is eminently
plain and direct, both in the evolution
of his thought and in the expression of
it, that is, both in his syntax and in his
words; that he is eminently plain and

[1] Étienne Pivert de Sénancour [1770–1846],
French author. His most notable work, *Ober-*
mann, was published in 1804.

direct in the substance of his thought, that is, in his matter and ideas; and, finally, that he is eminently noble.

On Translating Homer [1861]

The Iliad has a great master's genuine stamp, and that stamp is *the grand style*. *Ib.*

Of these two literatures [France and Germany], as of the intellect of Europe in general, the main effort, for now many years, has been a *critical* effort; the endeavor, in all branches of knowledge — theology, philosophy, history, art, science — to see the object as in itself it really is. *Ib.*

The grand style arises in poetry, when a noble nature, poetically gifted, treats with simplicity or with severity a serious subject. *Ib.*

Nations are not truly great solely because the individuals composing them are numerous, free, and active; but they are great when these numbers, this freedom, and this activity are employed in the service of an ideal higher than that of an ordinary man, taken by himself. *Democracy* [1861]

It is a very great thing to be able to think as you like; but, after all, an important question remains: *what* you think. *Ib.*

The critical power . . . tends to make an intellectual situation of which the creative power can profitably avail itself . . . to make the best ideas prevail.

The Function of Criticism at the Present Time [1864]

Ideas cannot be too much prized in and for themselves, cannot be too much lived with. *Ib.*

There is the world of ideas and the world of practice; the French are often for suppressing the one and the English the other; but neither is to be suppressed. *Ib.*

Burke is so great because, almost alone in England, he brings thought to bear upon politics, he saturates politics with thought.

The Function of Criticism at the Present Time

His [Burke's] greatness is that he lived in a world which neither English Liberalism nor English Toryism is apt to enter — the world of ideas. *Ib.*

The notion of the free play of the mind upon all subjects being a pleasure in itself, being an object of desire, being an essential provider of elements without which a nation's spirit, whatever compensations it may have for them, must, in the long run, die of inanition, hardly enters into an Englishman's thoughts. *Ib.*

I am bound by my own definition of criticism: a disinterested endeavor to learn and propagate the best that is known and thought in the world.

Ib.

Whispering from her [1] towers the last enchantments of the Middle Age . . . Home of lost causes, and forsaken beliefs, and unpopular names, and impossible loyalties!

Essays in Criticism, first series [1865], *preface*

Poetry is simply the most beautiful, impressive and wisely effective mode of saying things, and hence its importance. *Ib. Heinrich Heine*

Philistine must have originally meant, in the mind of those who invented the nickname, a strong, dogged, unenlightened opponent of the children of the light. *Ib.*

On the breast of that huge Mississippi of falsehood called *History*, a foam-bell more or less is no consequence.[2]

Ib. Literary Influence of Academies [1864]

[1] Oxford.

[2] This passage appeared only in the first appearance of the essay in *Cornhill Magazine* [August 1864].

History never embraces more than a small

The great apostle of the Philistines,
Lord Macaulay.
*Essays in Criticism, first
series, Joubert*

Are ye too changed, ye hills?
See, 'tis no foot of unfamiliar men
Tonight from Oxford up your pathway
    strays!
Here came I often, often, in old days —
Thyrsis [1] and I; we still had Thyrsis
    then.   *Thyrsis* [1866], *st. 1*

That sweet city [2] with her dreaming
    spires.   *Ib. st. 2*

He went; his piping took a troubled
    sound
Of storms that rage outside our happy
    ground;
He could not wait their passing; he is
    dead.   *Ib. st. 5*

The bloom is gone, and with the bloom
    go I.   *Ib. st. 6*

Yes, thou art gone! and round me too
    the night
In ever-nearing circle weaves her shade.
I see her veil draw soft across the day,
I feel her slowly chilling breath invade
The cheek grown thin, the brown hair
    sprent with gray;
  I feel her finger light
Laid pausefully upon life's headlong
    train —
The foot less prompt to meet the morn-
    ing dew,
The heart less bounding at emotion
    new,
And hope, once crushed, less quick to
    spring again.   *Ib. st. 14*

part of reality. — LA ROCHEFOUCAULD [1613–
1680], *Paul Sabatier*
    How oft we sigh
    When histories charm to think
        that histories lie!
            THOMAS MOORE [1780–1852], *The
                Skeptic*
    History is nothing more than the belief in
the senses, the belief in falsehood. — NIETZSCHE
[1844–1900], *The Twilight of the Idols, "Reason"
in Philosophy, I*
    History is more or less bunk. — HENRY
FORD [1863–1947], interview with Charles N.
Wheeler, *Chicago Tribune* [May 25, 1916]
    [1] Arthur Hugh Clough [1819–1861].
    [2] Oxford.

Hear it, O Thyrsis, still our tree is
    there! —
Ah, vain! These English fields, this
    upland dim,
These brambles pale with mist engar-
    landed,
That lone, sky-pointing tree, are not
    for him;
To a boon southern country he is fled,
    And now in happier air,
Wandering with the great Mother's
    train divine . . .
Within a folding of the Apennine.
    Thyrsis, st. 18

Why faintest thou? I wandered till I
    died.
Roam on! The light we sought is shin-
    ing still,
Dost thou ask proof? Our tree yet
    crowns the hill,
Our scholar travels yet the loved hill-
    side.   *Ib. st. 24*

The sea is calm tonight.
The tide is full, the moon lies fair
Upon the straits.
    Dover Beach [1867], *st. 1*

Begin, and cease, and then again be-
    gin,
With tremulous cadence slow, and
    bring
The eternal note of sadness in.   *Ib.*

Sophocles long ago
Heard it on the Aegean.   *Ib. st. 2*

The sea of faith
Was once, too, at the full, and round
    earth's shore
Lay like the folds of a bright girdle
    furled;
But now I only hear
Its melancholy, long, withdrawing
    roar,
Retreating, to the breath
Of the night wind down the vast edges
    drear
And naked shingles of the world.

Ah, love, let us be true
To one another! for the world, which
    seems
To lie before us like a land of dreams,

So various, so beautiful, so new,
Hath really neither joy, nor love, nor
   light,
Nor certitude, nor peace, nor help for
   pain;
And we are here as on a darkling plain
Swept with confused alarms of struggle
   and flight,
Where ignorant armies clash by night.
              Dover Beach, st. 3, 4

It is — last stage of all —
When we are frozen up within, and
   quite
The phantom of ourselves,
To hear the world applaud the hollow
   ghost
Which blamed the living man.
             Growing Old [1867], *st.* 7

Creep into thy narrow bed,
Creep, and let no more be said!
           The Last Word [1867], *st.* 1

Let the long contention cease!
Geese are swans, and swans are geese.[1]
                Ib. st. 2

Charge once more, then, and be
   dumb!
Let the victors, when they come,
When the forts of folly fall,
Find thy body by the wall.
                Ib. st. 4

Cruel, but composed and bland,
Dumb, inscrutable and grand,
So Tiberius might have sat,
Had Tiberius been a cat.
           Poor Matthias [1867]

Coldly, sadly descends
The autumn evening. The field
Strewn with its dank yellow drifts
Of withered leaves, and the elms,
Fade into dimness apace,
Silent; hardly a shout
From a few boys late at their play!
        Rugby Chapel [2] [1867], *st.* 1

O strong soul, by what shore
Tarriest thou now? For that force,

Surely, has not been left vain!
Somewhere, surely, afar,
In the sounding labor-house vast
Of being, is practiced that strength,
Zealous, beneficent, firm!
          Rugby Chapel, st. 4

Most men eddy about
Here and there, eat and drink,
Chatter and love and hate,
Gather and squander, are raised
Aloft, are hurled in the dust,
Striving blindly, achieving
Nothing; and then they die.
               Ib. st. 6

Friends who set forth at our side
Falter, are lost in the storm!
We, we only, are left!   *Ib. st.* 8

Then, in such hour of need
Of your fainting, dispirited race,
Ye, like angels, appear,
Radiant with ardor divine.
Beacons of hope, ye appear!
Languor is not in your heart,
Weakness is not in your word,
Weariness not on your brow.
              Ib. st. 13

Herein lies the reason for giving boys
more of Latin composition than of
Greek, superior though the Greek literature be to the Latin; but the power of
the Latin classic is in *character*, that of
the Greek is in *beauty*. Now character
is capable of being taught, learnt, and
assimilated; beauty hardly.
      Schools and Universities on the
              Continent [1868]

Our society distributes itself into
Barbarians, Philistines, and Populace;
and America is just ourselves, with the
Barbarians quite left out, and the Populace nearly.
       Culture and Anarchy [1869],
                    preface

America, that chosen home of newspapers.   ***Ib.***

I am a Liberal, yet I am a Liberal
tempered by experience, reflection, and
renouncement, and I am, above all, a
believer in culture.   ***Ib.*** *Introduction*

---

[1] See Burton, p. 311a.
[2] Arnold's father, Thomas Arnold, the great
headmaster of Rugby, is buried in Rugby
Chapel.

Culture is then properly described not as having its origin in curiosity, but as having its origin in the love of perfection; it is *a study of perfection.*

Culture and Anarchy,
Sweetness and Light

Not a having and a resting, but a growing and a becoming is the character of perfection as culture conceives it.   *Ib.*

The pursuit of perfection, then, is the pursuit of sweetness and light.[1] . . . He who works for sweetness and light united, works to make reason and the will of God prevail.   *Ib.*

The men of culture are the true apostles of equality.   *Ib.*

The governing idea of Hellenism is spirit of consciousness, that of Hebraism, strictness of conscience.

Ib. Hebraism and Hellenism

Below the surface stream, shallow and light,
Of what we say and feel — below the stream,
As light, of what we think we feel, there flows
With noiseless current, strong, obscure and deep,
The central stream of what we feel indeed.

St. Paul and Protestantism [1870]

Culture, the acquainting ourselves with the best that has been known and said in the world.

Literature and Dogma [1873],
preface

Conduct is three-fourths of our life and its largest concern.   *Ib. ch. 1*

Choose equality.

Mixed Essays [1879]. *Equality*

We have the religion of inequality.
          Ib.

To be humanized is to comply with the true law of our human nature; *servare modum, finemque tenere, Naturamque sequi,* says Lucan; "to keep our

[1] See Swift, p. 388b.

measure, and to hold fast our end, and to follow Nature."

Mixed Essays. Equality

Inequality has the natural and necessary effect, under the present circumstances, of materializing our upper class, vulgarizing our middle class, and brutalizing our lower class.   *Ib.*

For poetry the idea is everything; the rest is a world of illusion, of divine illusion. Poetry attaches its emotion to the idea; the idea *is* the fact. The strongest part of our religion today is its unconscious poetry.

Introduction to WARD, *English*
Poets [1880]

Eutrapelia. "A happy and gracious flexibility," Pericles calls this quality of the Athenians . . . lucidity of thought, clearness and propriety of language, freedom from prejudice and freedom from stiffness, openness of mind, amiability of manners, all these seem to go along with a certain happy flexibility of nature, and to depend upon it.

Irish Essays [1882]. *A Speech at*
Eton

English civilization — the humanizing, the bringing into one harmonious and truly humane life, of the whole body of English society — that is what interests me.

Ib. Ecce, Convertimur ad Gentes

That which in England we call the middle class is in America virtually the nation.

A Word About America [1882]

The American Philistine was a livelier sort of Philistine than ours.

A Word More About America
[1885]

What really dissatisfies in American civilization is the want of the *interesting,* a want due chiefly to the want of those two great elements of the interesting, which are elevation and beauty.

Civilization in the United States
[1888]

Coleridge, poet and philosopher wrecked in a mist of opium.

> *Essays in Criticism, second series*
> *[1888]. Byron*

A beautiful and ineffectual angel,[1] beating in the void his luminous wings in vain. *Ib.*

ULYSSES S. GRANT
1822–1885

The art of war is simple enough. Find out where your enemy is. Get at him as soon as you can. Strike at him as hard as you can and as often as you can, and keep moving on.[2]

> *On the art of war*

No terms except an unconditional and immediate surrender can be accepted. I propose to move immediately upon your works.

> *To General S. B. Buckner, Fort*
> *Donelson [February 16, 1862]*

I propose to fight it out on this line, if it takes all summer.

> *Dispatch to Washington, before*
> *Spottsylvania Court House*
> *[May 11, 1864]*

Wherever the enemy goes let our troops go also.

> *Dispatch to General Henry W.*
> *Halleck from City Point, Vir-*
> *ginia [August 1, 1864]*

The war is over — the rebels are our countrymen again.

> *Upon stopping his men from*
> *cheering after Lee's surrender*
> *at Appomattox Court House*
> *[April 9, 1865]*

Let us have peace.

> *Accepting nomination for the*
> *Presidency [May 29, 1868]*

I know no method to secure the repeal of bad or obnoxious laws so effective as their stringent execution.

> *Inaugural Address [March 4,*
> *1869]*

[1] Shelley.
[2] See Halsey, p. 968a.

Let no guilty man escape, if it can be avoided. No personal considerations should stand in the way of performing a public duty.

> *Indorsement of a letter relating*
> *to the Whiskey Ring [July 29,*
> *1875]*

Leave the matter of religion to the family altar, the church, and the private school, supported entirely by private contributions. Keep the church and the State forever separate.

> *Speech at Des Moines, Iowa*
> *[1875]*

Labor disgraces no man; unfortunately you occasionally find men disgrace labor.

> *Speech at Midland International*
> *Arbitration Union, Birmingham,*
> *England [1877]*

They [the Pilgrim Fathers] fell upon an ungenial climate, where there were nine months of winter and three months of cold weather, and that called out the best energies of the men, and of the women too, to get a mere subsistence out of the soil, with such a climate. In their efforts to do that they cultivated industry and frugality at the same time — which is the real foundation of the greatness of the Pilgrims.

> *Speech at New England Society*
> *Dinner [December 22, 1880]*

EDWARD EVERETT
HALE
1822–1909

I am only one,
But still I am one.
I cannot do everything,
But still I can do something;
And because I cannot do everything
I will not refuse to do the something
that I can do.

> *For the Lend-a-Hand Society*

Behind all these men you have to do with, behind officers, and government, and people even, there is the country herself, your country, and . . . you be-

long to her as you belong to your own
mother. Stand by her, boy, as you
would stand by your mother.
The Man Without a Country
[1863]

He loved his country as no other
man has loved her, but no man deserved less at her hands.
Ib. Epitaph of Philip Nolan

It is not necessary to finish your sentences in a crowd, but by a sort of
mumble, omitting sibilants and dentals.
This, indeed, if your words fail you, answers even in public extempore speech,
but better where other talking is going
on.
*My Double and How He Undid
Me* [1868]

To look up and not down,
To look forward and not back,
To look out and not in, and
To lend a hand.[1]
Ten Times One Is Ten [1870]

RUTHERFORD
BIRCHARD HAYES
1822–1893

He serves his party best who serves
the country best.
Inaugural Address [March 5, 1877]

THOMAS HUGHES
1822–1896

Life isn't all beer and skittles;[2] but
beer and skittles, or something better of
the same sort, must form a good part of
every Englishman's education.
Tom Brown's Schooldays
[1857], *pt. I, ch.* 2

He never wants anything but what's
right and fair; only when you come to
settle what's right and fair, it's everything that he wants and nothing that
you want. *Ib. II,* 2

[1] Rule of the Harry Wadsworth Club.
[2] See Dickens, p. 669a.

WILLIAM PORCHER
MILES
1822–1899

"Vote early and vote often," the advice openly displayed on the election
banners in one of our northern cities.
*Speech, House of Represent-
atives* [March 31, 1858]

LOUIS PASTEUR
1822–1895

No, a thousand times no; there does
not exist a category of science to which
one can give the name applied science.
There are science and the applications
of science, bound together as the fruit
to the tree which bears it.[1]
*Pourquoi la France n'a pas
trouvé d'hommes supérieurs
au moment du péril* [Revue
Scientifique, 1871]

In the fields of observation, chance
favors only the mind that is prepared.
Quoted by RENÉ VALLERY-
RADOT *in The Life of
Pasteur* [1927]

THOMAS BUCHANAN
READ
1822–1872

The terrible grumble, and rumble, and
roar,
Telling the battle was on once more,
And Sheridan twenty miles away.
Sheridan's Ride, st. 1

HEINRICH SCHLIEMANN
1822–1890

I have gazed on the face of Agamemnon.
*Telegram to the King of Greece,
upon excavating the fifth and
last grave at Mycenae* [August
1876]

[1] Translated by I. BERNARD COHEN

THEODORE DE BANVILLE
1823–1891

We'll to the woods no more,
The laurels all are cut.[1]
        Nous n'irons plus aux bois

BERNARD ELLIOTT BEE
1823–1861

There is Jackson, standing like a
stone wall!
        *Of General T. J. Jackson at the
        Battle of Bull Run* [2] *[July 21,
        1861]*

GEORGE HENRY BOKER
1823–1890

Lay him low, lay him low,
In the clover or the snow!
What cares he? he cannot know:
Lay him low.
        Dirge for a Soldier,[3] *st. 1*

MATTHEW BROWNE [WILLIAM BRIGHTY RANDS]
1823–1882

Never do today what you can
Put off till tomorrow.[4]
        Lilliput Levee

Great wide, beautiful, wonderful
    world,
With the wonderful waters round you
    curled,
And the wonderful grass upon your
    breast,
World, you are beautifully dressed.
        The Child's World, st. 1

[1] Nous n'irons plus aux bois, les lauriers
sont coupés.
    From an old nursery rhyme. Translated by
A. E. HOUSMAN, *Last Poems* [*1922*], *epigraph*
    [2] Bee was killed in this battle.
    [3] General Philip Kearny, killed near Chantilly,
Virginia [September 1, 1862].
    [4] No idleness, no laziness, no procrastination;
never put off till tomorrow what you can do
today. — LORD CHESTERFIELD, *Letters* [December
26, 1749]

JULIA A. FLETCHER CARNEY
1823–1908

Little drops of water,
Little grains of sand,
Make the mighty ocean
And the pleasant land.
        Little Things [1845], *st. 1*

Little deeds of kindness,
Little words of love,
Help to make earth happy
Like the heaven above.   *Ib. st. 4*

WILLIAM JOHNSON CORY
1823–1892

All beauteous things for which we live
By laws of time and space decay.
But oh, the very reason why
I clasp them, is because they die.
        Mimnermus in Church, st. 4

They told me, Heraclitus, they told me
    you were dead;
They brought me bitter news to hear
    and bitter tears to shed.
I wept, as I remembered how often you
    and I
Had tired the sun with talking and sent
    him down the sky.
And now that thou art lying, my dear
    old Carian guest,
A handful of gray ashes, long long ago
    at rest,
Still are thy pleasant voices, thy Night-
    ingales,[1] awake,
For Death, he taketh all away, but
    them he cannot take.
        *Heraclitus. Paraphrase from
        Callimachus* [2]

BARTHOLOMEW DOWLING
1823–1863

Then stand to your glasses steady!
    We drink in our comrades' eyes:

[1] *The Nightingales* was the title of the poems
left by Heraclitus. See p. 77a–b.
    [2] See Callimachus, p. 104b.

One cup to the dead already —
Hurrah for the next that dies!
The Revel,[1] *st. 1*

THOMAS WENTWORTH HIGGINSON
1823–1911

When a thought takes one's breath away, a lesson on grammar seems an impertinence.
Preface to EMILY DICKINSON'S
Poems, first series [1890]

An easy thing, O Power Divine,
To thank Thee for these gifts of Thine,
For summer's sunshine, winter's snow,
For hearts that kindle, thoughts that glow;
But when shall I attain to this —
To thank Thee for the things I miss?
The Things I Miss

JOHN KELLS INGRAM
1823–1907

Who fears to speak of Ninety-eight?[2]
Who blushes at the name?
When cowards mock the patriot's fate,
Who hangs his head for shame?
The Memory of the Dead,[3] *st. 1*

LEOPOLD KRONECKER
1823–1891

God made integers, all else is the work of man.
Jahresberichte der Deutschen Mathematiker Vereinigung, bk. 2

---

[1] Commemorating the victims of a cholera epidemic in India.
[2] Struggle for Irish independence led by Wolfe Tone, Napper Tandy and others.
[3] First published anonymously in the *Dublin Nation* [April 1, 1843].

GEORGE MARTIN LANE
1823–1897

The waiter roars it through the hall:
"We don't give bread with one fish ball!"
Lay of the Lone Fish Ball[1]
[1855], *st. 10*

CAROLINE ATHERTON BRIGGS MASON
1823–1890

Do they miss me at home — do they miss me?
'Twould be an assurance most dear,
To know that this moment some loved one
Were saying, "I wish he were here."
Do They Miss Me at Home? st. 1

FRANCIS PARKMAN
1823–1893

The growth of New England was a result of the aggregate efforts of a busy multitude, each in his narrow circle toiling for himself, to gather competence or wealth. The expansion of New France was the achievement of a gigantic ambition striving to grasp a continent. It was a vain attempt.
Pioneers of France in the New World [1865], *introduction*

A boundless vision grows upon us; an untamed continent; vast wastes of forest verdure; mountains silent in primeval sleep; river, lake, and glimmering pool; wilderness oceans mingling with the sky. Such was the domain which France conquered for civilization. Plumed helmets gleamed in the shade of its forests, priestly vestments in its dens and fastnesses of ancient barbarism. Men steeped in antique learning, pale with the close breath of the cloister, here spent the noon and evening of their lives, ruled savage hordes with a mild,

---

[1] Lane was professor of Latin at Harvard; the embarrassment of the "lone fish ball" was an actual experience.

parental sway, and stood serene before the direst shapes of death. Men of courtly nurture, heirs to the polish of a far-reaching ancestry, here, with their dauntless hardihood, put to shame the boldest sons of toil.

> *Pioneers of France in the New World, introduction*

Faithfulness to the truth of history involves far more than a research, however patient and scrupulous, into special facts. Such facts may be detailed with the most minute exactness, and yet the narrative, taken as a whole, may be unmeaning or untrue. The narrator must seek to imbue himself with the life and spirit of the time. He must study events in their bearings near and remote; in the character, habits, and manners of those who took part in them. He must himself be, as it were, a sharer or a spectator of the action he describes.

> *Ib.*

If any pale student, glued to his desk, here seek an apology for a way of life whose natural fruit is that pallid and emasculate scholarship of which New England has had too many examples, it will be far better that this sketch had not been written. For the student there is, in its season, no better place than the saddle, and no better companion than the rifle or the oar.

> *Autobiography* [1868] [1]

The most momentous and far-reaching question ever brought to issue on this continent was: Shall France remain here or shall she not?

> *Montcalm and Wolfe* [1884], *introduction*

Versailles was a gulf into which the labor of France poured its earnings, and it was never full.   *Ib. ch. 1*

The [French] Revolution began at the top — in the world of fashion, birth, and intellect — and propagated itself downwards.   *Ib.*

---

[1] Published in *Proceedings of the Massachusetts Historical Society, vol. VIII, p. 353.*

France built its best colony on a principle of exclusion, and failed: England reversed the system, and succeeded.

> *Montcalm and Wolfe, ch. 1*

COVENTRY PATMORE
1823–1896

Ah, wasteful woman! she who may
On her sweet self set her own price,
Knowing man cannot choose but pay,
How has she cheapened Paradise!
How given for nought her priceless gift,
How spoiled the bread and spilled the wine,
Which, spent with due respective thrift,
Had made brutes men and men divine!

> *The Angel in the House* [1854–1856], *bk. I, canto 3. Prelude 3, Unthrift*

A Woman is a foreign land,
Of which, though there he settle young,
A man will ne'er quite understand
The customs, politics, and tongue.

> *Ib. canto 9. Prelude 2, Woman*

Why, having won her, do I woo?
Because her spirit's vestal grace
Provokes me always to pursue,
But, spirit-like, eludes embrace.

> *Ib. II, canto 12. Prelude 1, The Married Lover*

His mother, who was patient, being dead.

> *The Unknown Eros* [1877], *bk. I, canto 10. The Toys, l. 6*

He had put, within his reach,
A box of counters and a red-veined stone,
A piece of glass abraded by the beach,
And six or seven shells,
A bottle with bluebells,
And two French copper coins, ranged there with careful art,
To comfort his sad heart.   *Ib. l. 15*

For want of me the world's course will
   not fail:
When all its work is done, the lie shall
   rot;
The truth is great, and shall prevail,[1]
When none cares whether it prevail or
   not.
> *The Unknown Eros, bk. I, canto*
> *12. Magna est Veritas*

If I were dead, you'd sometimes say,
   "Poor child!"
> *Ib. canto 14. If I Were Dead*

EDWARD POLLOCK
1823–1858

The one who goes is happier
Than those he leaves behind.
> *The Parting Hour*

ERNEST RENAN
1823–1892

The whole of history is incomprehensible without the Christ.
> *La Vie de Jésus* [1863]

O Lord, if there is a Lord, save my
soul, if I have a soul.
> *Prière d'un Sceptique*

Religion is not a popular error; it is a
great instinctive truth, sensed by the
people, expressed by the people.
> *Les Apôtres* [1866]

An immense river of oblivion is
sweeping us away into a nameless
abyss.
> *Souvenirs d'Enfance et de*
> *Jeunesse* [1883]

Immortality is to labor at an eternal
task.
> *L'Avenir de la Science* [1890],
> *preface*

Nothing great is achieved without
chimeras.   *Ib. ch. 19*

---

[1] See *I Esdras 4:14*, p. 36b.
For great is truth, and shall prevail [Magna
est Veritas et praevalebit]. — THOMAS BROOKS,
The Crown and Glory of Christianity [*1662*]

JOHN SHERMAN
1823–1900

I have come home to look after my
fences.[1]
> *Speech to his neighbors,*
> *Mansfield, Ohio*

WILLIAM MARCY TWEED
1823–1878

As long as I count the votes, what are
you going to do about it?
> *Statement by the "Boss" of*
> *Tammany Hall on the bal-*
> *lot in New York City* [*No-*
> *vember 1871*]

PHOEBE CARY
1824–1871

Sometimes, I think, the things we see
Are shadows of the things to be;
   That what we plan we build;
That every hope that hath been crossed,
And every dream we thought was lost,
   In heaven shall be fulfilled.
> *Dreams and Realities, st. 7*

And though hard be the task,
"Keep a stiff upper lip."
> *Keep a Stiff Upper Lip*

One sweetly solemn thought
   Comes to me o'er and o'er;
I am nearer home today
   Than I ever have been before.
> *Nearer Home, st. 1*

For of all the hard things to bear and
   grin,
The hardest is being taken in.
> *Kate Ketcham (parody of*
> WHITTIER's *Maud Muller*

GEORGE WILLIAM CURTIS
1824–1892

While we read history we make history.   *The Call of Freedom*

---

[1] Senator Sherman referred to the fences
around his farm. Said to be the origin of the
political phrase often rendered "to mend
fences."

Every great crisis of human history is a pass of Thermopylae, and there is always a Leonidas and his three hundred to die in it, if they cannot conquer.

The Call of Freedom

ALEXANDRE DUMAS THE YOUNGER
1824–1895

Business? It's quite simple. It's other people's money.

La Question d'Argent [1857], act II, sc. vii

THOMAS JONATHAN [STONEWALL] JACKSON [1]
1824–1863

My duty is to obey orders.

A favorite aphorism

Let us cross over the river, and rest under the trees.

Last words [May 10, 1863]

WILLIAM THOMSON, LORD KELVIN
1824–1907

When you can measure what you are speaking about, and express it in numbers, you know something about it; but when you cannot measure it, when you cannot express it in numbers, your knowledge is of a meager and unsatisfactory kind: it may be the beginning of knowledge, but you have scarcely, in your thoughts, advanced to the stage of *science.*

Popular Lectures and Addresses [1891–1894]

GUSTAV ROBERT KIRCHOFF
1824–1887

The highest object at which the natural sciences are constrained to aim, but which they will never reach, is the determination of the forces which are present in nature, and of the state of

[1] See Bee, p. 719a.

matter at any given moment — in one word, the reduction of all the phenomena of nature to mechanics.[1]

Über das Ziel der Naturwissenschaften [1865]

CHARLES GODFREY LELAND
1824–1903

Hans Breitmann gife a barty —
Where ish dat barty now?

Hans Breitmann's Barty [1857], st. 6

GEORGE MACDONALD
1824–1905

Corage. God mend al.

His anagram motto

Alas! how easily things go wrong!
A sigh too much or a kiss too long,
And there follows a mist and a weeping rain,
And life is never the same again.

Phantastes [1858]. *Song*

Where did you come from, baby dear?
Out of the everywhere into the here.

At the Back of the North Wind. Baby, st. 1, 2

They were all looking for a king
   To slay their foes and lift them high;
Thou cam'st, a little baby thing
   That made a woman cry.

That Holy Thing, st. 1

Said the Wind to the Moon, "I will blow you out!"

The Wind and the Moon, st. 1

There is no feeling in a human heart which exists in that heart alone — which is not, in some form or degree, in every heart.

Unspoken Sermons, second series [1885]

You will be dead so long as you refuse to die.

What's Mine's Mine [1886], ch. 31

[1] Translated by J. B. STALLO.

The world and my being, its life and mine, were one. The microcosm and macrocosm were at length atoned, at length in harmony. I lived in everything; everything entered and lived in me.

Lilith [1895], *ch. 45*

JOHN WHITTAKER WATSON
1824–1890

Oh! the snow, the beautiful snow,
Filling the sky and the earth below.
Beautiful Snow [1869], *st. 1*

HENRY DE LAFAYETTE WEBSTER
1824–1896

The years creep slowly by, Lorena,
The snow is on the grass again.
Lorena, st. 1

WILLIAM ALLEN BUTLER
1825–1902

This same Miss McFlimsey of Madison Square,
The last time we met was in utter despair,
Because she had nothing whatever to wear!
Nothing to Wear [1857], *st. 3*

THOMAS HENRY HUXLEY
1825–1895

I cannot but think that he who finds a certain proportion of pain and evil inseparably woven up in the life of the very worms, will bear his own share with more courage and submission.
On the Educational Value of the Natural History Sciences [1854]

To a person uninstructed in natural history, his country or seaside stroll is a walk through a gallery filled with wonderful works of art, nine-tenths of which have their faces turned to the wall.
On the Educational Value of the Natural History Sciences

Extinguished theologians lie about the cradle of every science as the strangled snakes beside that of Hercules.
Darwiniana. The Origin of Species [1860]

The method of scientific investigation is nothing but the expression of the necessary mode of working of the human mind.
Our Knowledge of the Causes of the Phenomena of Organic Nature [1863]

Let us have "sweet girl graduates" by all means. They will be none the less sweet for a little wisdom; and the "golden hair" will not curl less gracefully outside the head by reason of there being brains within.
Emancipation — Black and White [1865]

For every man the world is as fresh as it was at the first day, and as full of untold novelties for him who has the eyes to see them.
A Liberal Education [1868]

The chess board is the world, the pieces are the phenomena of the universe, the rules of the game are what we call the laws of Nature. The player on the other side is hidden from us. We know that his play is always fair, just, and patient. But also we know, to our cost, that he never overlooks a mistake, or makes the smallest allowance for ignorance.
Ib.

M. Comte's philosophy in practice might be compendiously described as Catholicism *minus* Christianity.
On the Physical Basis of Life [1868]

If some great Power would agree to make me always think what is true and do what is right, on condition of being turned into a sort of clock and wound up every morning before I got out of bed, I should instantly close with the offer.

> On Descartes' Discourse on Method [1870]. Method and Results

There is the greatest practical benefit in making a few failures early in life.
> On Medical Education [1870]

That mysterious independent variable of political calculation, Public Opinion.
> Universities, Actual and Ideal [1874]

Veracity is the heart of morality.
> *Ib.*

Becky Sharp's acute remark that it is not difficult to be virtuous on ten thousand a year [1] has its application to nations; and it is futile to expect a hungry and squalid population to be anything but violent and gross.
> *Joseph Priestley* [1874]

Logical consequences are the scarecrows of fools and the beacons of wise men.   *Animal Automatism* [1874]

Size is not grandeur, and territory does not make a nation.
> On University Education [1876]

Perhaps the most valuable result of all education is the ability to make yourself do the thing you have to do, when it ought to be done, whether you like it or not; it is the first lesson that ought to be learned; and however early a man's training begins, it is probably the last lesson that he learns thoroughly.
> Technical Education [1877]

The great end of life is not knowledge but action.   *Ib.*

If a little knowledge is dangerous, where is the man who has so much as to be out of danger?
> On Elemental Instruction in Physiology [1877]

[1] See Thackeray, p. 66a.

Irrationally held truths may be more harmful than reasoned errors.
> The Coming of Age of The Origin of Species [1880]

It is the customary fate of new truths to begin as heresies and to end as superstitions.   *Ib.*

I asserted — and I repeat — that a man has no reason to be ashamed of having an ape for his grandfather. If there were an ancestor whom I should feel shame in recalling it would rather be a man — a man of restless and versatile intellect — who, not content with an equivocal success in his own sphere of activity, plunges into scientific questions with which he has no real acquaintance, only to obscure them by an aimless rhetoric, and distract the attention of his hearers from the real point at issue by eloquent digressions and skilled appeals to religious prejudice.
> Reply to Wilberforces's question.[1] From LEONARD HUXLEY, Life and Letters of Thomas Henry Huxley [1900], vol. I

GEORGE EDWARD PICKETT
1825–1875

Up, men, and to your posts! Don't forget today that you are from Old Virginia.

> Command at the beginning of his division's charge at Gettysburg [July 3, 1863]

ADELAIDE ANNE PROCTER
1825–1864

Seated one day at the organ,
  I was weary and ill at ease,
And my fingers wandered idly
  Over the noisy keys.
> *A Lost Chord*, st. 1

[1] If anyone were to be willing to trace his descent through an ape as his *grandfather,* would he be willing to trace his descent similarly on the side of his *grandmother?* — BISHOP SAMUEL WILBERFORCE [1805–1873], at the British Association for the Advancement of Science [1860]

But I struck one chord of music
Like the sound of a great Amen.
A Lost Chord, st. 2

BAYARD TAYLOR
1825–1878

Till the sun grows cold,
And the stars are old,
And the leaves of the Judgment Book
unfold.
Bedouin Song, refrain

They sang of love, and not of fame;
   Forgot was Britain's glory;
Each heart recalled a different name,
   But all sang "Annie Laurie."
The Song of the Camp, st. 5

WILLIAM WHITING
1825–1878

Eternal Father, strong to save,
Whose arm doth bind the restless
   wave,
Who bidd'st the mighty ocean deep
Its own appointed limits keep,
O, hear us when we cry to Thee
For those in peril on the sea!
*The Hymn of the U.S. Navy
[1860], Eternal Father, Strong
to Save, st. 1*

CHARLES HAMILTON
AÏDÉ
1826–1906

I sit beside my lonely fire
   And pray for wisdom yet:
For calmness to remember
   Or courage to forget.
Remember or Forget

GROSS HERZOG
FRIEDRICH VON BADEN
1826–1907

Unity makes strength, and, since we
must be strong, we must also be one.
*On German unity under Prus-
sian hegemony, Versailles [Janu-
ary 18, 1871]*

WALTER BAGEHOT
1826–1877

To a great experience one thing is
essential — an experiencing nature.
*Literary Studies. Shakespeare
[1853]*

The reason why so few good books
are written is, that so few people that
can write know anything. In general an
author has always lived in a room, has
read books, has cultivated science, is acquainted with the style and sentiments
of the best authors, but he is out of the
way of employing his own eyes and
ears. He has nothing to hear and nothing to see. His life is a vacuum. *Ib.*

A constitutional statesman is in general a man of common opinions and
uncommon abilities.
*Biographical Studies. The Char-
acter of Sir Robert Peel [1856]*

It is good to be without vices, but it
is not good to be without temptations.
*Ib. Sir George Cornewall Lewis
[1863]*

[Of Guizot] A Puritan born in
France by mistake.
Ib. M. Guizot [1874]

One of the greatest pains to human
nature is the pain of a new idea.
Physics and Politics [1869], ch. 5

An inability to stay quiet . . . is one
of the most conspicuous failings of
mankind.[1] *Ib.*

The most melancholy of human reflections, perhaps, is that on the whole
it is a question whether the benevolence
of mankind does most good or harm.
Ib.

The best reason why monarchy is a
strong government is, that it is an intelligible government: the mass of mankind understand it, and they hardly
anywhere in the world understand any
other.
*The English Constitution
[1872]. The Monarchy*

[1] See Pascal, p. 363b; quoted by Bagehot in
the same chapter.

But of all nations in the world, the English are perhaps the least a nation of pure philosophers.

> *The English Constitution.*
> *The Monarchy*

G. W. HUNT
fl. 1878

We don't want to fight, but, by jingo, if we do,
We've got the ships, we've got the men, we've got the money, too.
We've fought the Bear before, and while Britons shall be true,
The Russians shall not have Constantinople.   *Song* [1] [1878]

DINAH MARIA MULOCK CRAIK
1826–1887

Douglas, Douglas, tender and true!
> *Douglas, Tender and True,* [2]
> *refrain*

Oh, my son's my son till he gets him a wife,
But my daughter's my daughter all her life.   *Young and Old*

JOHN ELLERTON
1826–1893

Now the laborer's task is o'er;
Now the battle day is past;
Now upon the farther shore
Lands the voyager at last.
> *Hymn, st. 1*

Father, in Thy gracious keeping
Leave we now Thy servant sleeping.
> *Ib. refrain*

[1] Sung by Gilbert Hastings Macdermott (Farrell) [1845–1901], "the great Macdermott." The song gave the terms "jingo" and "jingoism" to the political vocabulary, though the phrase "by jingo" had been used earlier by Goldsmith and Thomas Hood.

[2] O Douglas, O Douglas!
Tendir and trewe!
> Sir Richard Holland, *The Buke of the Howlat* [c. 1450], *st. 31*

STEPHEN COLLINS FOSTER
1826–1864

Weep no more, my lady,
Oh! weep no more today!
We will sing one song for the old Kentucky home,
For the old Kentucky home far away.
> *My Old Kentucky Home, chorus*

Way down upon the Swanee River,
Far, far away,
There's where my heart is turning ever;
There's where the old folks stay.
> *The Old Folks at Home, st. 1*

All the world is sad and dreary
Ev'rywhere I roam,
Oh! darkies, how my heart grows weary,
Far from the old folks at home.
> *Ib. chorus*

Down in de cornfield
Hear dat mournful sound:
All de darkies am a-weeping —
Massa's in de cold, cold ground.
> *Massa's in de Cold, Cold Ground, st. 1*

He's gone whar de good niggers go.
> *Uncle Ned, last stanza*

I'm coming, I'm coming, for my head is bending low;
I hear those gentle voices calling, "Old Black Joe."
> *Old Black Joe, st. 3*

O, Susanna! O, don't you cry for me,
I've come from Alabama, wid my banjo on my knee.
> *O, Susanna,* [1] *chorus*

Gwine to run all night!
Gwine to run all day!
I'll bet my money on de bobtail nag —
Somebody bet on de bay.
> *Camptown Races, chorus*

I dream of Jeanie with the light brown hair,

[1] Sung for the first time by Nelson Kneass in Andrews' Eagle Ice Cream Saloon, Pittsburgh, Pennsylvania [September 11, 1847]. It shortly became a world-wide hit.

Floating, like a vapor, on the soft sum-
mer air.
*Jeanie with the Light Brown
Hair, st. 1*

Beautiful dreamer, wake unto me,
Starlight and dewdrop are waiting for
thee.
Beautiful Dreamer, st. 1

GEORGE BRINTON
McCLELLAN
1826–1885

All quiet along the Potomac.[1]
*Frequent report from his Union
headquarters [1861]*

EDWARD STUYVESANT
BRAGG
1827–1912

They love him most for the enemies
he has made.[2]
*Speech seconding presidential
nomination of Grover Cleveland
[July 9, 1884]*

MORTIMER COLLINS
1827–1876

A man is as old as he's feeling,
A woman as old as she looks.
The Unknown Quantity

ALICE HAWTHORNE
[SEPTIMUS WINNER]
1827–1902

Listen to the mockingbird, listen to the
mockingbird,
Still singing where the weeping willows
wave.
Listen to the Mockingbird [1855]

[1] All quiet along the Potomac tonight,
No sound save the rush of the river,
While soft falls the dew on the face of the
dead —
The picket's off duty forever.
ETHEL LYNN BEERS [1827–1879], *The
Picket Guard [1861], st. 6*
[2] An adaptation of Governor Bragg's expres-
sion became a Cleveland campaign slogan: "We
love him for the enemies he has made."

CHARLES ELIOT
NORTON
1827–1908

I think that a knowledge of Greek
thought and life, and of the arts in
which the Greeks expressed their
thought and sentiment, is essential to
high culture. A man may know everything else, but without this knowledge
he remains ignorant of the best intellectual and moral achievements of his own
race. *Letter to F. A. Tupper [1885]*

Whatever your occupation may be
and however crowded your hours with
affairs, do not fail to secure at least a
few minutes every day for refreshment
of your inner life with a bit of poetry.
*Used by a Boston newspaper as
a heading for a column of reprinted poems*

The voice of protest, of warning, of
appeal is never more needed than when
the clamor of fife and drum, echoed by
the press and too often by the pulpit, is
bidding all men fall in and keep step
and obey in silence the tyrannous word
of command. Then, more than ever, it
is the duty of the good citizen not to be
silent. *True Patriotism [1898]*

The old America, the America of our
hopes and our dreams, has come to an
end, and a new America is entering on
the false course which has been tried so
often and which has often led to calamity. This war will in the long run result
in far more evil to the United States
than to Spain. We shall nominally win,
but at the cost of what infinite loss!
*Letter to Edward Lee-Childe
[1898]*

LEW [LEWIS] WALLACE
1827–1905

A man is never so on trial as in
the moment of excessive good fortune.
*Ben Hur: A Tale of the Christ
[1880], bk. V, ch. 7*

Would you hurt a man keenest,
strike at his self-love. *Ib. VI, 2*

Beauty is altogether in the eye of the beholder.[1]

> *The Prince of India* [1893], *bk. III, ch. 6*

WILLIAM ALLINGHAM
1828–1889

Up the airy mountain,
  Down the rushy glen,
We daren't go a-hunting
  For fear of little men.

> *The Fairies, st. 1*

Four ducks on a pond,
A grass bank beyond,
A blue sky of spring,
White clouds on the wing;
What a little thing
To remember for years —
To remember with tears!

> *Four Ducks on a Pond*

HENRIK IBSEN
1828–1906

All or nothing.   *Brand* [1866]

Out yonder under the skies, men have a common saying: "Man, to thyself be true!" But here, 'mongst Trolls, "Troll, to thyself be — enough!" it runs.

> *Peer Gynt* [1867], *act I*

Go round about, Peer! Room enough on the mountain.   *Ib.*

Look into any man's heart you please, and you will always find, in every one, at least one black spot which he has to keep concealed.

> *Pillars of Society* [1877], *act III*

The spirit of truth and the spirit of freedom — they are the pillars of society.   *Ib. IV*

There can be no freedom or beauty about a home life that depends on borrowing and debt.

> *A Doll's House* [1879], *act I*

To crave for happiness in this world is simply to be possessed by a spirit of

---

[1] See Hume, p. 434b, and Hungerford, p. 831b.

revolt. What right have we to happiness?   *Ghosts* [1881], *act I*

I am half inclined to think we are all ghosts, Mr. Manders. It is not only what we have inherited from our fathers that exists again in us, but all sorts of old dead ideas and all kinds of old dead beliefs and things of that kind. They are not actually alive in us; but there they are dormant, all the same, and we can never be rid of them. Whenever I take up a newspaper and read it, I fancy I see ghosts creeping between the lines. There must be ghosts all over the world. They must be as countless as grains of the sands, it seems to me. And we are so miserably afraid of the light, all of us.   *Ib. II*

Mother, give me the sun.   *Ib. III*

I hold that man is in the right who is most closely in league with the future.

> *Letter to Georg Brandes* [*January 3, 1882*]

A community is like a ship; everyone ought to be prepared to take the helm.

> *An Enemy of the People* [1882], *act I*

The minority is always right.

> *Ib. IV*

You should never wear your best trousers when you go out to fight for freedom and truth.   *Ib. V*

The strongest man in the world is he who stands most alone.[1]   *Ib.*

Rob the average man of his life illusion, and you rob him of his happiness at the same stroke.

> *The Wild Duck* [1884], *act V*

Vine leaves in his hair.

> *Hedda Gabler* [1890], *act II*

The younger generation will come knocking at my door.

> *The Master Builder* [1892], *act I*

---

[1] See Browning, p. 662a.

GEORGE MEREDITH
1828–1909

I expect that Woman will be the last thing civilized by Man.
> *The Ordeal of Richard Feverel* [1859], *ch. 1*

Who rises from prayer a better man, his prayer is answered.   *Ib. 12*

The sun is coming down to earth, and the fields and the waters shout to him golden shouts.   *Ib. 19*

Kissing don't last; cookery do!
> *Ib. 28*

See ye not, courtesy
Is the true alchemy,
Turning to gold all it touches and tries?
> *The Song of Courtesy* [1859], *IV*

I've studied men from my topsy-turvy
Close, and, I reckon, rather true.
Some are fine fellows: some, right scurvy:
Most, a dash between the two.
> *Juggling Jerry* [1859], *VII*

Two of a trade, lass, never agree.[1]
> *Ib. IX*

Not till the fire is dying in the grate,
Look we for any kinship with the stars.
Oh, wisdom never comes when it is gold,
And the great price we pay for it full worth;
We have it only when we are half earth.
> *Modern Love* [1862], *IV*

And if I drink oblivion of a day,
So shorten I the stature of my soul.
> *Ib. XII*

That rarest gift
To Beauty, common sense.
> *Ib. XXXII*

In tragic life, God wot,
No villain need be! Passions spin the plot:
We are betrayed by what is false within.   *Ib. XLIII*

[1] See Hesiod, p. 67b.

Their sense is with their senses all mixed in,
Destroyed by subtleties these women are!   *Modern Love, XLVIII*

Ah, what a dusty answer gets the soul
When hot for certainties in this our life!   *Ib. L*

Into the breast that gives the rose
Shall I with shuddering fall?
> *The Spirit of Earth in Autumn* [1862], *st. 1*

Cynicism is intellectual dandyism.
> *The Egoist* [1879], *ch. 7*

In . . . the book of Egoism, it is written, possession without obligation to the object possessed approaches felicity.   *Ib. 14*

On a starred night Prince Lucifer uprose.
Tired of his dark dominion swung the fiend.
> *Lucifer in Starlight* [1883]

Around the ancient track marched, rank on rank,
The army of unalterable law.   *Ib.*

Enter these enchanted woods,
You who dare.
> *The Woods of Westermain* [1883], *st. 1*

She whom I love is hard to catch and conquer,
Hard, but O the glory of the winning were she won!
> *Love in the Valley* [1883], *st. 2*

Darker grows the valley, more and more forgetting:
So were it with me if forgetting could be willed.
Tell the grassy hollow that holds the bubbling well-spring,
Tell it to forget the source that keeps it filled.   *Ib. st. 5*

Love that so desires would fain keep her changeless;
Fain would fling the net, and fain have her free.   *Ib. st. 6*

Thence had he the laugh . . .
Broad as ten thousand beeves
At pasture.
> *The Spirit of Shakespeare* [1883]

Civil limitation daunts
His utterance never; the nymphs blush,
    not he.
> *An Orson of the Muse* [*Walt
> Whitman*] [1883]

A witty woman is a treasure; a witty
beauty is a power.
> *Diana of the Crossways* [1885],
> *ch. 1*

The well of true wit is truth itself.
> *Ib.*

Ireland gives England her soldiers,
her generals too.   *Ib. 2*

With patient inattention hear him
    prate.
> *Bellerophon* [1887], *st. 4*

Full lasting is the song, though he,
The singer, passes.
> *The Thrush in February* [1888],
> *st. 17*

Cannon his name,
Cannon his voice, he came.
> *Napoléon* [1891], *I*

DANTE GABRIEL ROSSETTI
1828–1882

The blessed damozel leaned out
    From the gold bar of Heaven;
Her eyes were deeper than the depth
    Of waters stilled at even;
She had three lilies in her hand,
    And the stars in her hair were seven.
> *The Blessed Damozel* [1850],
> *st. 1*

And the souls mounting up to God
Went by her like thin flames.
> *Ib. st. 7*

The Stealthy School of Criticism.
> *Letter to the Athenaeum* [1871]

I have been here before,
    But when or how I cannot tell;
I know the grass beyond the door,

The sweet keen smell,
The sighing sound, the lights around
    the shore.
> *Sudden Light* [1881], *st. 1*

Still we say as we go —
    "Strange to think by the way,
Whatever there is to know,
    That shall we know one day."
> *The Cloud Confines* [1881], *st. 1*

Was it a friend or foe that spread these
    lies?
Nay, who but infants question in such
    wise?
'Twas one of my most intimate ene-
    mies.   *Fragment* [1881]

A sonnet is a moment's monu-
    ment —
Memorial from the soul's eternity
To one dead deathless hour.
> *Sonnets from the House of
> Life* [1881]. *Proem*

And though thy soul sail leagues and
    leagues beyond —
Still, leagues beyond those leagues,
    there is more sea.
> *Ib. no. 73. The Choice* — III

My name is Might-have-been;
I am also called No-more, Too-late,
    Farewell.
> *Ib. no. 97. A Superscription*

LEO NIKOLAEVICH TOLSTOI[1]
1828–1910

"What's this? am I falling? my legs
are giving way under me," he thought,
and fell on his back. He opened his
eyes, hoping to see how the struggle of
the French soldiers with the artilleryman was ending, and eager to know

[1] Of course you have read Tolstoi's *War and
Peace* and *Anna Karenina*. I never had that
exquisite felicity before the summer, and now
I feel as if I knew the *perfection* in the representation of human life. Life indeed seems less
real than his tale of it. Such infallible veracity!
The impression haunts me as nothing literary
ever haunted me before. — WILLIAM JAMES,
letter to Henry James [1872], *Letters of William
James, vol. II* [1896], *p. 48*

whether the red-haired artilleryman was killed or not, whether the cannons had been taken or saved. But he saw nothing of all that. Above him there was nothing but the sky — the lofty sky, not clear, but still immeasurably lofty, with gray clouds creeping quietly over it.

> *War and Peace* [1865–1869],[1]
> *pt. III, ch. 16*

Three days afterwards the little princess was buried, and Prince Andrey went to the steps of the tomb to take his last farewell of her. Even in the coffin the face was the same, though the eyes were closed. "Ah, what have you done to me?" it still seemed to say. *Ib. IV, 9*

In historical events great men — so called — are but the labels that serve to give a name to an event, and like labels, they have the least possible connection with the event itself. Every action of theirs, that seems to them an act of their own free will, is in an historical sense not free at all, but in bondage to the whole course of previous history, and predestined from all eternity.

> *Ib. IX, 1*

He [Platon Karataev] did not understand, and could not grasp the significance of words taken apart from the sentence. Every word and every action of his was the expression of a force uncomprehended by him, which was his life. *Ib. XII, 13*

For us, with the rule of right and wrong given us by Christ, there is nothing for which we have no standard. And there is no greatness where there is not simplicity, goodness, and truth.

> *Ib. XIV, 18*

The subject of history is the life of peoples and of humanity. To catch and pin down in words — that is, to describe directly the life, not only of hu-

manity, but even of a single people, appears to be impossible.[1]

> *War and Peace, epilogue,*
> *pt. II, ch. 1*

Happy families are all alike; every unhappy family is unhappy in its own way.

> *Anna Karenina* [1875–1877],
> *pt. I, ch. 1*

Ivan Ilych's life had been most simple and most ordinary and therefore most terrible.

> *The Death of Ivan Ilych* [2]
> [1886]

Ivan Ilych saw that he was dying, and he was in continuous despair.

In the depth of his heart he knew he was dying, but not only was he not accustomed to the thought, he simply did not and could not grasp it.

The syllogism he had learned from Kiezewetter's Logic: "Caius is a man, men are mortal, therefore Caius is mortal," had always seemed to him correct as applied to Caius, but certainly not as applied to himself. That Caius — man in the abstract — was mortal, was perfectly correct, but he was not Caius, not an abstract man, but a creature quite, quite separate from all others.

> *Ib.*

Six feet of land was all that he needed.

> *How Much Land Does a Man*
> *Need?* [1886]

The more is given the less the people will work for themselves, and the less they work the more their poverty will increase.[3]

> *Help for the Starving, pt. III*
> [January 1892]

Art is a human activity having for its purpose the transmission to others of the highest and best feelings to which men have risen.

> *What Is Art?* [1898], *ch. 8*

---

[1] See Francis Parkman, p. 721a.

[2] Translated by AYLMER MAUDE.

[3] If you stop supporting that crowd, it will support itself. — SENECA [8 B.C.–A.D. 65], *Epistle 20, 7*

---

[1] Translated by CONSTANCE GARNETT.

ROSCOE CONKLING
1829–1888

He will hew to the line of right, let the chips fall where they may.
> *Speech nominating General Grant for a third term as President, Chicago [June 5, 1880]*

CARL SCHURZ
1829–1906

Ideals are like stars; you will not succeed in touching them with your hands. But like the seafaring man on the desert of waters, you choose them as your guides, and following them you will reach your destiny.[1]
> *Address, Faneuil Hall, Boston [April 18, 1859]*

I will make a prophecy that may now sound peculiar. In fifty years Lincoln's name will be inscribed close to Washington's on this Republic's roll of honor.
> *Letter to Theodore Petrasch [October 12, 1864]*

Our country, right or wrong.[2] When right, to be kept right; when wrong, to be put right.
> *Address, Anti-Imperialistic Conference, Chicago [October 17, 1899]*

CHARLES DUDLEY WARNER[3]
1829–1900

To own a bit of ground, to scratch it with a hoe, to plant seeds, and watch the renewal of life — this is the commonest delight of the race, the most satisfactory thing a man can do.
> *My Summer in a Garden [1870]. Preliminary*

Broad acres are a patent of nobility; and no man but feels more of a man in the world if he have a bit of ground that he can call his own. However small it is on the surface, it is four thousand miles deep; and that is a very handsome property.
> *My Summer in a Garden. Preliminary*

What a man needs in gardening is a cast-iron back, with a hinge in it.
> *Ib. Third Week*

The toad, without which no garden would be complete.
> *Ib. Thirteenth Week*

Politics makes strange bedfellows.
> *Ib. Fifteenth Week*

What small potatoes we all are, compared with what we might be!   *Ib.*

Public opinion is stronger than the legislature, and nearly as strong as the Ten Commandments.
> *Ib. Sixteenth Week*

The thing generally raised on city land is taxes.   *Ib.*

Everybody talks about the weather, but nobody does anything about it.[1]
> *Editorial, The Hartford Courant [August 24, 1897]*

CHARLOTTE ALINGTON BARNARD ["CLARIBEL"]
1830–1869

I cannot sing the old songs I sang long years ago.
> *I Cannot Sing the Old Songs* [2]

Take back the heart that thou gavest,
What is my anguish to thee?
Take back the freedom thou cravest,
Leaving the fetters to me.
> *Take Back the Heart*

---

[1] See Emerson, p. 608b.
[2] See Charles Churchill, p. 456a.
[3] Warner collaborated with Mark Twain on *The Gilded Age*. See p. 759a.

[1] The phrase is commonly attributed to Mark Twain, but the *Hartford Courant* has the exact statement in the aforementioned editorial, which is of course unsigned. Warner was associate editor of the paper (1867–1900).
See Mark Twain, p. 759b.
[2] I cannot sing the old songs now!
   It is not that I deem them low;
'Tis that I can't remember how
   They go.
> C. S. CALVERLEY [1831–1884], *Changed*

THOMAS EDWARD BROWN
1830–1897

A Garden is a lovesome thing, God wot!
My Garden

Not God! in Gardens! when the eve is
    cool?
Nay, but I have a sign:
'Tis very sure God walks in mine.
Ib.

PORFIRIO DÍAZ
1830–1915

Poor Mexico, so far from God and so
close to the United States.
Attributed

EMILY DICKINSON[1]
1830–1886

I never lost as much but twice,
And that was in the sod.
Twice have I stood a beggar
Before the door of God!

Angels – twice descending
Reimbursed my store –
Burglar! Banker! – Father!
I am poor once more!
No. 49 [c. 1858]

Surgeons must be very careful
When they take the knife!
Underneath their fine incisions
Stirs the Culprit – *Life!*
No. 108 [c. 1859]

Our share of night to bear –
Our share of morning –
Our blank in bliss to fill
Our blank in scorning –

Here a star, and there a star,
Some lose their way!
Here a mist, and there a mist,
Afterwards – Day!
No. 113 [c. 1859]

For each ecstatic instant
We must an anguish pay

[1] *The Complete Poems of Emily Dickinson*,
edited by Thomas H. Johnson [1960]. Dates are
of composition, not publication.

In keen and quivering ratio
To the ecstasy.
No. 125 [c. 1859], st. 1

To fight aloud, is very brave —
But *gallanter,* I know
Who charge within the bosom
The Cavalry of Woe –
No. 126 [c. 1859], st. 1

Who counts the wampum of the night
To see that none is due?
No. 128 [c. 1859], st. 3

These are the days when Birds come
    back –
A very few – a Bird or two –
To take a backward look.

These are the days when skies resume
The old – old sophistries of June –
A blue and gold mistake.
No. 130 [c. 1859], st. 1, 2

Oh Sacrament of summer days,
Oh Last Communion in the Haze –
Permit a child to join.

Thy sacred emblems to partake –
Thy consecrated bread to take
And thine immortal wine!
Ib. st. 5, 6

Besides the Autumn poets sing
A few prosaic days
A little this side of the snow
And that side of the Haze –
No. 131 [c. 1859], st. 1

Just lost when I was saved!
Just felt the world go by!
Just girt me for the onset with Eternity,
When breath blew back,
And on the other side
I heard recede the disappointed tide!
No. 160 [c. 1860], st. 1

The thought beneath so slight a film –
Is more distinctly seen –
As laces just reveal the surge –
Or Mists – the Apennine –
No. 210 [c. 1860]

I taste a liquor never brewed,
From Tankards scooped in Pearl –
No. 214 [c. 1860], st. 1

Inebriate of Air – am I –
And Debauchee of Dew –
Reeling – through endless summer
    days –
From inns of Molten Blue –
    No. 214, st. 2

Till Seraphs swing their snowy Hats –
And Saints – to windows run –
To see the little Tippler
Leaning against the – Sun –
    Ib. st. 4

"Hope" is the thing with feathers –
That perches in the soul –
And sings the tune without the
    words –
And never stops – at all –
    No. 254 [c. 1861], st. 1

There's a certain Slant of light,
Winter Afternoons –
That oppresses, like the Heft
Of Cathedral Tunes –
    No. 258 [c. 1861], st. 1

I'm Nobody! Who are you?
Are you – Nobody – too?
Then there's a pair of us!
Don't tell! they'd advertise – you know!

How dreary – to be – Somebody!
How public – like a Frog –
To tell one's name – the livelong
    June –
To an admiring Bog!
    No. 288 [c. 1861]

I tasted – careless – then –
I did not know the Wine
Came once a World – Did you?
Oh, had you told me so –
This Thirst would blister – easier –
    now –
    No. 296 [c. 1861], st. 3

The Soul selects her own Society –
Then – shuts the Door –
To her divine Majority –
Present no more –
    No. 303 [c. 1862], st. 1

I'll tell you how the Sun rose –
A Ribbon at a time –

The Steeples swam in Amethyst –
The news, like Squirrels, ran.
    No. 318 [1862]

Some keep the Sabbath going to
    Church –
I keep it, staying at Home –
With a bobolink for a Chorister –
And an Orchard, for a Dome –
    No. 324 [1862], st. 1

So instead of getting to Heaven, at
    last –
I'm going, all along.   *Ib. st. 3*

After great pain, a formal feeling
    comes.
    No. 341 [c. 1862], st. 1

Of Course – I prayed –
And did God Care?
He cared as much as on the Air
A Bird – had stamped her foot –
And cried "Give Me" –
    No. 376 [c. 1862]

No Rack can torture me –
My Soul – at Liberty –
Behind this mortal Bone
There knits a bolder One –
    No. 384 [c. 1862], st. 1

Except Thyself may be
Thine Enemy –
Captivity is Consciousness –
So's Liberty.   *Ib. st. 4*

Much Madness is divinest Sense –
To a discerning Eye –
Much Sense – the starkest Madness –
'Tis the Majority
In this, as All, prevail –
Assent – and you are sane –
Demur – you're straightway dangerous –
And handled with a Chain.
    No. 435 [c. 1862]

The Wind – tapped like a tired
    Man.
    No. 436 [c. 1862], st. 1

This is my letter to the World
That never wrote to Me –
The simple News that Nature told –
With tender Majesty.
    No. 441 [c. 1862], st. 1

I died for Beauty – but was scarce
Adjusted in the Tomb
When One who died for Truth, was
    lain
In an adjoining Room –
        No. 449 [c. 1862], st. 1

And so, as Kinsmen, met a Night –
We talked between the Rooms –
Until the Moss had reached our lips –
And covered up – our names –
        Ib. st. 3

It was not Death, for I stood up,
And all the Dead, lie down –
        No. 510 [c. 1862], st. 1

It was not Frost, for on my Flesh
I felt Siroccos – crawl –   *Ib. st. 2*

I reckon – when I count at all –
First – Poets – Then the Sun –
Then Summer – Then the Heaven of
    God –
And then – the List is done –

But, looking back – the First so seems
To Comprehend the Whole –
The Others look a needless Show –
So I write – Poets – All –
        No. 569 [c. 1862], st. 1, 2

I like to see it lap the Miles –
And lick the Valleys up –
        No. 585 [c. 1862], st. 1

And neigh like Boanerges –
Then punctual as a Star
Stop – docile and omnipotent
At its own stable door –   *Ib. st. 4*

Afraid! Of whom am I afraid?
Not Death – for who is He?
The Porter of my Father's Lodge
As much abasheth me!
        No. 608 [c. 1862], st. 1

I asked no other thing –
No other – was denied –
I offered Being – for it –
The Mighty Merchant sneered —

Brazil? He twirled a Button –
Without a glance my way –
"But – Madam – is there nothing else –
That We can show – Today?"
        No. 621 [c. 1862]

The Brain – is wider than the Sky –
For – put them side by side –
The one the other will contain
With ease – and You – beside.
        No. 632 [1862], st. 1

I cannot live with You –
It would be Life –
And Life is over there –
Behind the Shelf.
        No. 640 [c. 1862], st. 1

And that White Sustenance –
Despair –   *Ib. st. 12*

Pain – has an Element of Blank –
It cannot recollect
When it begun – or if there were
A time when it was not –
        No. 650 [c. 1862], st. 1

I dwell in Possibility –
A fairer House than Prose –
More numerous of Windows –
Superior – for Doors.
        No. 657 [c. 1862], st. 1

The Soul unto itself
Is an imperial friend –
Or the most agonizing Spy –
An Enemy – could send –
        No. 683 [c. 1862], st. 1

Because I could not stop for Death,
He kindly stopped for me –
The Carriage held but just Ourselves
And Immortality.
        No. 712 [c. 1863], st. 1

Alter! When the Hills do –
Falter! When the Sun
Question if His Glory
Be the Perfect One –

Surfeit! When the Daffodil
Doth of the Dew –
Even as Herself – Sir –
I will – of You –   *No. 729 [c. 1863]*

God gave a Loaf to every Bird –
But just a Crumb – to Me –
        No. 791 [c. 1863], st. 1

This quiet Dust was Gentlemen and
    Ladies
And Lads and Girls – [1]

[1] See Shakespeare, p. 291a.

Was laughter and ability and Sighing,
And Frocks and Curls.
                    No. 813 [c. 1864], st. 1

Adventure most unto itself
The Soul condemned to be –
Attended by a single Hound
Its own identity.
                    No. 822 [c. 1864], st. 4

Dying! To be afraid of thee
One must to thine Artillery
Have left exposed a Friend –
Than thine old Arrow is a Shot
Delivered straighter to the Heart
The leaving Love behind.
                    No. 831 [c. 1864], st. 1

Truth – is as old as God –
His Twin identity
And will endure as long as He
A Co-Eternity –
                    No. 836 [c. 1864], st. 1

The Poets light but Lamps –
Themselves – go out –
The Wicks they stimulate –
If vital Light

Inhere as do the Suns –
Each Age a Lens
Disseminating their
Circumference –   *No. 883 [c. 1864]*

Love – is anterior to Life –
Posterior – to Death –
Initial of Creation, and
The Exponent of Earth.
                    No. 917 [c. 1864]

If I can stop one Heart from breaking
I shall not live in vain
If I can ease one Life the Aching
Or cool one Pain

Or help one fainting Robin
Unto his Nest again
I shall not live in Vain.
                    No. 919 [c. 1864]

Partake as doth the Bee
Abstemiously.
The Rose is an Estate –
In Sicily.   *No. 994 [c. 1865]*

Too scanty 'twas to die for you,
The merest Greek could that.

The living, Sweet, is costlier –
I offer even that –

The Dying, is a trifle, past
But living, this include
The dying multifold – without
The Respite to be dead.
                    No. 1013 [c. 1865]

'Twas my one Glory –
Let it be
Remembered
I was owned of Thee –
                    No. 1028 [c. 1865]

I never saw a Moor –
I never saw the Sea –
Yet know I how the Heather looks
And what a Billow be.

I never spoke with God
Nor visited in Heaven –
Yet certain am I of the spot
As if the Checks were given –
                    No. 1052 [c. 1865]

Not to discover weakness is
The Artifice of strength –
                    No. 1054 [c. 1865], st. 1

Experiment to me
Is every one I meet
If it contain a Kernel?
The Figure of a Nut

Presents upon a Tree
Equally plausibly,
But Meat within, is requisite
To Squirrels, and to Me.
                    No. 1073 [c. 1865]

Nature, like Us is sometimes caught
Without her Diadem.
                    No. 1075 [c. 1866], st. 2

The Sweeping up the Heart,
And putting Love away
We shall not want to use again
Until Eternity.
                    No. 1078 [c. 1866], st. 2

We never know how high we are
Till we are called to rise
And then, if we are true to plan
Our statures touch the skies.[1]
                    No. 1176 [c. 1870], st. 1

[1] See William James, p. 792b.

A word is dead
When it is said,
Some say.
I say it just
Begins to live
That day. *No. 1212 [c. 1872]*

There is no Frigate like a Book
To take us Lands away
Nor any Coursers like a Page
Of prancing Poetry –
This Traverse may the poorest take
Without oppress of Toll –
How frugal is the Chariot
That bears the Human Soul!
  No. 1263 [c. 1873]

I thought that nature was enough
Till Human nature came
But that the other did absorb
As Parallax a Flame –
  No. 1286 [c. 1873], st. 1

Until the Desert knows
That Water grows
His Sands suffice
But let him once suspect
That Caspian Fact
Sahara dies.
  No. 1291 [c. 1873], st. 1

Not with a Club, the Heart is broken
Nor with a Stone –
A Whip so small you could not see it
I've known
To lash the Magic Creature
Till it fell.
  No. 1304 [c. 1874], st. 1

That short – potential stir
That each can make but once –
That Bustle so illustrious
'Tis almost Consequence –

Is the éclat of Death.
Oh, thou unknown Renown
That not a Beggar would accept
Had he the power to spurn –
  No. 1307 [c. 1874]

A little Madness in the Spring
Is wholesome even for the King.
  No. 1333 [c. 1875]

Love's stricken "why"
Is all that love can speak –

Built of but just a syllable
The hugest hearts that break.
  No. 1368 [c. 1876]

Bees are Black, with Gilt Surcingles –
Buccaneers of Buzz.
  No. 1405 [c. 1877], st. 1

A Route of Evanescence
With a revolving Wheel –
A Resonance of Emerald –
A Rush of Cochineal –
And every Blossom on the Bush
Adjusts its tumbled Head –
The mail from Tunis, probably,
An easy Morning's ride.
  No. 1463 [c. 1879]

He ate and drank the precious
    Words –
His Spirit grew robust –
He knew no more that he was poor,
Nor that his frame was Dust –

He danced along the dingy Days
And this Request of Wings
Was but a Book – What Liberty
A loosened spirit brings –
  No. 1587 [c. 1883]

The Pedigree of Honey
Does not concern the Bee –
A Clover, any time, to him,
Is Aristocracy.
  No. 1627 [c. 1884], version II

A Drunkard cannot meet a Cork
Without a Revery –
And so encountering a Fly
This January Day
Jamaicas of Remembrance stir
That send me reeling in.
  No. 1628 [c. 1884]

Beauty crowds me till I die
Beauty mercy have on me
But if I expire today
Let it be in sight of thee –
  No. 1654 [n.d.]

Eden is that old-fashioned House
We dwell in every day
Without suspecting our abode
Until we drive away.
  No. 1657 [n.d.], st. 1

Glory is that bright tragic thing
That for an instant
Means Dominion –
Warms some poor name
That never felt the Sun,
Gently replacing
In oblivion –   *No. 1660 [n.d.]*

I took one Draught of Life –
I'll tell you what I paid –
Precisely an existence –
The market price, they said.

They weighed me, Dust by Dust –
They balanced Film with Film,
Then handed me my Being's worth –
A single Dram of Heaven!
                          No. 1725 [n.d.]

My life closed twice before its close –
It yet remains to see
If Immortality unveil
A third event to me

So huge, so hopeless to conceive
As these that twice befell.
Parting is all we know of heaven,
And all we need of hell.
                          No. 1732 [n.d.]

That it will never come again
Is what makes life so sweet.
                   No. 1741 [n.d.], st. 1

To make a prairie it takes a clover and
        one bee,
One clover, and a bee,
And revery.
The revery alone will do,
If bees are few.   *No. 1755 [n.d.]*

Elysium is as far as to
The very nearest Room
If in that Room a Friend await
Felicity or Doom –

What Fortitude the Soul contains,
That it can so endure
The accent of a coming Foot –
The opening of a Door –
                          No. 1760 [n.d.]

That Love is all there is,
Is all we know of Love;

It is enough, the freight should be
Proportioned to the groove.
                          No. 1765 [n.d.]

If I read a book and it makes my
whole body so cold no fire can ever
warm me, I know that is poetry. If I
feel physically as if the top of my head
were taken off, I know that is poetry.
These are the only ways I know it. Is
there any other way?

From MARTHA GILBERT DICK-
INSON BIANCHI, *Life and Letters
of Emily Dickinson* [1924]

CHRISTINA GEORGINA ROSSETTI
1830–1894

Who has seen the wind?
    Neither you nor I:
But when the trees bow down their
        heads,
    The wind is passing by.
            Who Has Seen the Wind?, st. 2

Does the road wind up-hill all the
        way?
Yes, to the very end.
Will the day's journey take the whole
        long day?
From morn to night, my friend.
                    Up-Hill [1861], st. 1

My heart is like a singing bird.
                A Birthday [1861], st. 1

        The birthday of my life
Is come, my love is come to me.
                          Ib. st. 2

When I am dead, my dearest,
    Sing no sad songs for me;
Plant thou no roses at my head,
    Nor shady cypress tree.
Be the green grass above me
    With showers and dewdrops wet;
And if thou wilt, remember
    And if thou wilt, forget.
                      Song [1862], st. 1

Remember me when I am gone away,
Gone far away into the silent land.
                  Remember [1862], l. 1

Better by far you should forget and
   smile
Than that you should remember and be
   sad.   *Remember, l. 13*

For there is no friend like a sister
In calm or stormy weather;
To cheer one on the tedious way,
To fetch one if one goes astray,
To lift one if one totters down,
To strengthen whilst one stands.
         Goblin Market [1862], *last lines*

In the bleak mid-winter
   Frosty wind made moan,
Earth stood hard as iron,
   Water like a stone;
Snow had fallen, snow on snow,
   Snow on snow,
In the bleak mid-winter,
   Long ago.   *Mid-Winter*

YOSHIDA SHOIN [1]
1830–1859

   To consider oneself different from
ordinary men is wrong, but it is right to
hope that one will not remain like ordinary men.
   Yoshida Shoin Zenshu, vol. II

   The mind of the superior man is like
Heaven. When it is resentful or angry,
it thunders forth its indignation. But
once having loosed its feelings, it is like
a sunny day with a clear sky: within the
heart there remains not the trace of a
cloud. Such is the beauty of true manliness.   *Ib. III*

   Neither the lords nor the shogun can
be depended upon [to save the coun-
try], and so our only hope lies in grass-
roots heroes.   *Ib. V*

ALEXANDER SMITH
1830–1867

In winter, when the dismal rain
   Came down in slanting lines,

[1] From *Sources of Japanese Tradition,* edited
by William de Bary [1960].

And Wind, that grand old harper,
   smote
His thunder-harp of pines.
         A Life Drama [1853], *sc. 2*

   It is not of so much consequence
what you say, as how you say it. Memorable sentences are memorable on account of some single irradiating word.
   Dreamthorp [1863]. *On the
               Writing of Essays*

   Death is the ugly fact which Nature
has to hide, and she hides it well.
      *Ib. Of Death and the Fear
               of Dying*

CHARLES STUART
CALVERLEY
1831–1884

I have a liking old
For thee, though manifold
Stories, I know, are told,
   Not to thy credit!
         Ode to Tobacco, st. 2

The farmer's daughter hath soft brown
   hair
(*Butter and eggs and a pound of
   cheese*)
And I met with a ballad, I can't say
   where,
That wholly consisted of lines like
   these.
      *Ballad, after William Morris
      [The Auld Wife], pt. I, st. 6*

And this song is considered a perfect
   gem,
And as to the meaning, it's what you
   please.   *Ib. II, st. 4*

MARY MAPES DODGE
1831–1905

Life is a mystery as deep as ever death
   can be;
Yet oh, how sweet it is to us, this life
   we live and see!
         The Two Mysteries, st. 3

And as life is to the living, so death is
   to the dead.   *Ib. st. 5*

JAMES ABRAM GARFIELD
1831–1881

Fellow citizens! God reigns, and the Government at Washington still lives!
Speech on assassination of Lincoln, New York [April 15, 1865]

For mere vengeance I would do nothing. This nation is too great to look for mere revenge. But for the security of the future I would do everything.
Ib.

I am not willing that this discussion should close without mention of the value of a true teacher. Give me a log hut, with only a simple bench, Mark Hopkins [1] on one end and I on the other, and you may have all the buildings, apparatus and libraries without him.
Address to Williams College Alumni, New York [December 28, 1871] [2]

HELEN HUNT JACKSON
1831–1885

O suns and skies and clouds of June,
　And flowers of June together,
Ye cannot rival for one hour
　October's bright blue weather.
October's Bright Blue Weather, st. 1

Find me the men on earth who care
　Enough for faith or creed today
To seek a barren wilderness
　For simple liberty to pray.
The Pilgrim Forefathers, st. 5

---

[1] Mark Hopkins [1802–1887], president of Williams College [1836–1872], and president of the American Board of Commissioners for Foreign Missions [1857–1881].
　　For Education is Making Men;
　　So is it now, so was it when
　　Mark Hopkins sat on one end of a log
　　And James Garfield sat on the other.
　　　　ARTHUR GUITERMAN [1871–1943],
　　　　　　　Education
[2] In BURKE A. HINSDALE, *President Garfield and Education* [1882], *p. 43.*

Oh, write of me, not "Died in bitter pains,"
But "Emigrated to another star!"
Emigravit

EDWARD ROBERT BULWER-LYTTON, EARL OF LYTTON [OWEN MEREDITH]
1831–1891

Love thou the rose, yet leave it on its stem.[1]
The Wanderer [1857]. Prologue, pt. I, 19

We may live without poetry, music and art;
We may live without conscience, and live without heart;
We may live without friends; we may live without books;
But civilized man cannot live without cooks.
Lucile [2] [1860], pt. I, canto 2, st. 19

Genius does what it must, and talent does what it can.
Last Words of a Sensitive Second-Rate Poet

JAMES CLERK MAXWELL
1831–1879

For the sake of persons of . . . different types, scientific truth should be presented in different forms, and should be regarded as equally scientific, whether it appears in the robust form and the vivid coloring of a physical illustration, or in the tenuity and paleness of a symbolic expression.
Address to the Mathematics and Physics Section, British Association for the Advancement of Science [1870]

---

[1] See Emerson, p. 603a.
[2] Lord Lytton, the Viceroy, who still lives in the literary hall of fame as the author of *Lucile* — a vast, stale Victorian piece of poetry. — WILLIAM E. WOODWARD, *Meet General Grant* [1928], *pt. IV, ch. 30*

When at last this little instrument appeared, consisting, as it does, of parts every one of which is familiar to us, and capable of being put together by an amateur, the disappointment arising from its humble appearance was only partially relieved on finding that it was really able to talk.

> *The Telephone* [1878]

PHILIP HENRY SHERIDAN
1831–1888

The only good Indians I ever saw were dead.[1]

> *Remark at Fort Cobb, Indian Territory* [*January* 1869]

LOUISA MAY ALCOTT
1832–1888

Christmas won't be Christmas without any presents.

> *Little Women* [1868], *ch.* 1

A little kingdom I possess,
  Where thoughts and feelings dwell;
And very hard the task I find
  Of governing it well.

> *From* EDNAH D. CHENEY, *Louisa May Alcott, Her Life, Letters, and Journals* [1889], *ch.* 3 [*My Kingdom,*[2] *st.* 1]

Resolved to take Fate by the throat and shake a living out of her.   *Ib.* 5

Above man's aims his nature rose.
The wisdom of a just content
Made one small spot a continent,
And tuned to poetry Life's prose.[3]

> *Ib.* 7. [*Thoreau's Flute,*[4] *st.* 2]

[1] EDWARD SYLVESTER ELLIS [1840–1916] reported that after Custer's fight with Black Kettle's band of Cheyenne Indians, the Comanche Chief Toch-a-way (Turtle Dove) was presented to General Sheridan. The Indian said: "Me Toch-a-way, me good Indian." The General's reply, as reported by Ellis, is given in the text; the phrase is more often heard in the version: The only good Indian is a dead Indian.

[2] Written at the age of thirteen.

[3] The word "tuned" is frequently misprinted as "turned."

[4] In *The Atlantic Monthly* [September 1863].

My definition [of a philosopher] is of a man up in a balloon, with his family and friends holding the ropes which confine him to earth and trying to haul him down.

> *Life, Letters, and Journals, ch.* 10

ELIZABETH AKERS ALLEN
1832–1911

Backward, turn backward, O Time, in your flight,
Make me a child again just for tonight!

> *Rock Me to Sleep* [1860], *st.* 1

SIR EDWIN ARNOLD
1832–1904

Shall any gazer see with mortal eyes,
Or any searcher know by mortal mind?
Veil after veil will lift — but there must be
Veil upon veil behind.

> *The Light of Asia* [1879], *bk.* VIII

Nor ever once ashamed
So we be named
Pressmen; Slaves of the Lamp; Servants of Light.

> *The Tenth Muse, st.* 18

WILHELM BUSCH
1832–1908

Diogenes the wise crept into his vat
And spoke: "Yes, yes, this comes from that."

> *Diogenes und die bösen Buben von Korinth* [1856]

This thesis remains firm: Good is the Evil which is permitted.

> *Fromme Helene* [1872]

In general his principle is this:
Whatever is popular is permitted.

> *Julchen* [1877]

To become a father is not hard,
To be a father is, however.   *Ib.*

Temperance is the pleasure
In things we can't get.
Thus live moderately and think intelligently —
He has enough who uses nothing.
Julchen

A true painter, smart and busy,
Always carries a sharp pencil with him.
Maler Klecksel [1884]

WILLIAM CROSWELL DOANE
1832–1913

Ancient of Days, who sittest throned in glory,
To thee all knees are bent, all voices pray.   *Hymn* [1886], *st. 1*

LEWIS CARROLL
[CHARLES LUTWIDGE DODGSON]
1832–1898

All in the golden afternoon
   Full leisurely we glide,
For both our oars with little skill
   By little arms are plied
While little hands make vain pretense
   Our wanderings to guide.
      Alice's Adventures in Wonderland [1865], *introduction, st. 1*

"What is the use of a book," thought Alice, "without pictures or conversations?"   *Ib. ch. 1*

Do cats eat bats? . . . Do bats eat cats?   *Ib.*

Curiouser and curiouser!   *Ib. 2*

How doth the little crocodile
Improve his shining tail,
And pour the waters of the Nile
On every golden scale! [1]

How cheerfully he seems to grin,
How neatly spreads his claws,
And welcomes little fishes in
With gently smiling jaws!
                                    Ib.

"I'll be judge, I'll be jury," said cunning old Fury; "I'll try the whole cause, and condemn you to death."
      Alice's Adventures in Wonderland. ch. 3

Oh my fur and whiskers!   *Ib. 4*

"I can't explain *myself*, I'm afraid, sir," said Alice, "because I'm not myself, you see."
"I don't see," said the Caterpillar.
                                    Ib. 5

"You are old, Father William," the
      young man said,
"And your hair has become very white;
And yet you incessantly stand on your
      head —
Do you think, at your age, it is right?" [1]
      Ib. [*You are old, Father William, st. 1*]

"In my youth," said his father, "I took
      to the law,
And argued each case with my wife;
And the muscular strength, which it
      gave to my jaw,
Has lasted the rest of my life."
                              Ib. [*st. 6*]

"I have answered three questions, and
      that is enough,"
Said his father. "Don't give yourself
      airs!
Do you think I can listen all day to
      such stuff?
Be off, or I'll kick you downstairs!"
                              Ib. [*st. 8*]

"I shall sit here," he said, "on and off, for days and days."   *Ib. 6*

"If everybody minded their own business," said the Duchess in a hoarse growl, "the world would go round a deal faster than it does."   *Ib.*

"Talking of axes," said the Duchess, "chop off her head!"   *Ib.*

Speak roughly to your little boy,
   And beat him when he sneezes:
He only does it to annoy,
   Because he knows it teases.
                                    Ib.

[1] See Isaac Watts, p. 396b.

[1] See Southey, p. 531b.

"All right," said the [Cheshire] Cat; and this time it vanished quite slowly, beginning with the end of the tail, and ending with the grin, which remained some time after the rest of it had gone.

Alice's Adventures in Wonderland, ch. 6

"Then you should say what you mean," the March Hare went on.

"I do," Alice hastily replied; "at least — at least I mean what I say — that's the same thing, you know."

"Not the same thing a bit!" said the Hatter. "Why, you might just as well say that 'I see what I eat' is the same thing as 'I eat what I see'!" *Ib.* 7

"It was the *best* butter," the March Hare meekly replied. *Ib.*

Twinkle, twinkle, little bat!
How I wonder what you're at!
Up above the world you fly,
Like a teatray in the sky.[1]

Ib.

"Take some more tea," the March Hare said to Alice, very earnestly.

"I've had nothing yet," Alice replied in an offended tone: "so I can't take more."

"You mean you can't take *less*," said the Hatter: "it's very easy to take *more* than nothing." *Ib.*

They drew all manner of things — everything that begins with an M . . . such as mousetraps, and the moon, and memory, and muchness — you know you say things are "much of a muchness." *Ib.*

The Queen turned crimson with fury, and after glaring at her for a moment like a wild beast, began screaming, "Off with her head![1] Off with — " *Ib.* 8

"Tut, tut, child," said the Duchess. "Everything's got a moral if only you can find it." *Ib.* 9

And the moral of that is — "Oh, 'tis love, 'tis love, that makes the world go round!" [1]

Alice's Adventures in Wonderland, ch. 9

Take care of the sense and the sounds will take care of themselves.
Ib.

"We called him Tortoise because he taught us," said the Mock Turtle angrily. "Really you are very dull!"
Ib.

"Reeling and Writhing, of course, to begin with," the Mock Turtle replied, "and the different branches of Arithmetic — Ambition, Distraction, Uglification, and Derision." *Ib.*

"Will you walk a little faster?" said a whiting to a snail,
"There's a porpoise close behind us, and he's treading on my tail."
Ib. 10 [*The Lobster-Quadrillle, st.* 1]

Will you, won't you, will you, won't you, will you join the dance?
Ib.

The further off from England the nearer is to France —
Then turn not pale, beloved snail, but come and join the dance.
Ib. [*st.* 3]

'Tis the voice of the Lobster: I heard him declare
"You have baked me too brown, I must sugar my hair." [2]
Ib. ['*Tis the Voice of the Lobster*]

Soup of the evening, beautiful soup!
Ib. [*Turtle Soup*]

Sentence first — verdict afterwards.
Ib. 12

Child of the pure, unclouded brow
And dreaming eyes of wonder!
Though time be fleet and I and thou
Are half a life asunder,

---

[1] See Ann and Jane Taylor, p. 546a.
[2] See Shakespeare, p. 217b, and Cibber, p. 392b.

[1] See W. S. Gilbert, p. 768a, and Anonymous, p. 1105b.
[2] See Isaac Watts, p. 396b.

Thy loving smile will surely hail
The love-gift of a fairy tale.
>*Through the Looking-Glass*
>*[1872], introduction, st. 1*

"The horror of that moment," the King went on, "I shall never, *never* forget!"
"You will, though," the Queen said, "if you don't make a memorandum of it." *Ib. ch. 1*

'Twas brillig, and the slithy toves
Did gyre and gimble in the wabe;
All mimsy were the borogoves,
And the mome raths outgrabe.

Beware the Jabberwock, my son!
The jaws that bite, the claws that catch!
Beware the Jubjub bird, and shun
The frumious Bandersnatch!
>*Ib. [Jabberwocky, st. 1, 2]*

And, as in uffish thought he stood,
The Jabberwock, with eyes of flame,
Came whiffling through the tulgey wood,
And burbled as it came!

One, two! One, two! And through and through
The vorpal blade went snicker-snack!
He left it dead, and with its head
He went galumphing back.

"And hast thou slain the Jabberwock?
Come to my arms, my beamish boy!
O frabjous day! Callooh! Callay!"
He chortled in his joy.
>*Ib. [st. 4–6]*

Curtsy while you're thinking what to say. It saves time. *Ib. 2*

"Now! Now!" cried the Queen. "Faster! Faster!" *Ib.*

"A slow sort of country!" said the Queen. "Now, *here*, you see, it takes all the running you can do, to keep in the same place. If you want to get somewhere else, you must run at least twice as fast as that!" *Ib.*

Speak in French when you can't think of the English for a thing — turn out your toes when you walk — and remember who you are!
>*Through the Looking-Glass, ch. 2*

"If you think we're waxworks," he said, "you ought to pay, you know. Waxworks weren't made to be looked at for nothing. Nohow!" *Ib. 4*

"Contrariwise," continued Tweedledee, "if it was so, it might be; and if it were so, it would be; but as it isn't, it ain't. That's logic." *Ib.*

The sun was shining on the sea,
Shining with all his might:
He did his very best to make
The billows smooth and bright —
And this was odd, because it was
The middle of the night.
>*Ib. [The Walrus and the Car-*
>*penter, st. 1]*

The Walrus and the Carpenter
Were walking close at hand:
They wept like anything to see
Such quantities of sand:
"If this were only cleared away,"
They said, "it would be grand!"

"If seven maids with seven mops
Swept it for half a year,
Do you suppose," the Walrus said,
"That they could get it clear?"
"I doubt it," said the Carpenter,
And shed a bitter tear.
>*Ib. [st. 4, 5]*

"O Oysters, come and walk with us!"
The Walrus did beseech.
"A pleasant walk, a pleasant talk,
Along the briny beach."
>*Ib. [st. 6]*

And thick and fast they came at last,
And more, and more, and more —
All hopping through the frothy waves,
And scrambling to the shore.
>*Ib. [st. 9]*

"The time has come," the Walrus said,
"To talk of many things:
Of shoes — and ships — and sealing-wax —

Of cabbages — and kings —
And why the sea is boiling hot —
And whether pigs have wings."
>   *Through   the   Looking-Glass,*
>   *ch. 4* [*The Walrus and the Car-*
>   *penter, st. 11*]

"But wait a bit," the Oysters cried,
"Before we have our chat;
For some of us are out of breath,
And all of us are fat!"   *Ib.* [*st. 12*]

The Carpenter said nothing but
"The butter's spread too thick!"
>   *Ib.* [*st. 16*]

"I weep for you," the Walrus said:
"I deeply sympathize."
With sobs and tears he sorted out
Those of the largest size,
Holding his pocket-handkerchief
Before his streaming eyes.
>   *Ib.* [*st. 17*]

But answer came there none —
And this was scarcely odd, because
They'd eaten every one.
>   *Ib.* [*st. 18*]

Twopence a week, and jam every
other day.   *Ib. 5*

"The rule is, jam tomorrow, and jam
yesterday — but never jam today."
"It must come sometimes to 'jam today,' " Alice objected.
"No, it can't," said the Queen. "It's
jam every other day: today isn't any
other day, you know."   *Ib.*

"It's a poor sort of memory that only
works backwards," the Queen remarked.   *Ib.*

Consider anything, only don't cry!
>   *Ib.*

"There's no use trying," she said:
"one *can't* believe impossible things."
"I daresay you haven't had much
practice," said the Queen. "When I
was your age, I always did it for half-an-
hour a day. Why, sometimes I've believed as many as six impossible things
before breakfast."   *Ib.*

They gave it me — for an unbirthday
present.   *Ib. 6*

"But 'glory' doesn't mean 'a nice
knockdown argument,' " Alice objected.
"When *I* use a word," Humpty
Dumpty said, in rather a scornful tone,
"it means just what I choose it to
mean — neither more nor less."
"The question is," said Alice,
"whether you *can* make words mean so
many different things."
"The question is," said Humpty
Dumpty, "which is to be master —
that's all."
>   *Through the Looking-Glass,*
>   *ch. 6*

It's as large as life and twice as natural.   *Ib. 7*

His answer trickled through my head,
Like water through a sieve.   *Ib. 8*

What's the French for fiddle-de-
dee?   *Ib. 9*

It isn't etiquette to cut anyone
you've been introduced to. Remove the
joint!   *Ib.*

He would answer to "Hi!" or to any
      loud cry
Such as "Fry me!" or "Fritter my
      wig!"
To "What-you-may-call-um!" or
      "What-was-his-name!"
But especially "Thing-um-a-jig!"
>   *The Hunting of the Snark*
>   [*1876*]. *Fit I, st. 9*

"What's the good of Mercator's North
      Poles and Equators,
Tropics, Zones and Meridian Lines?"
So the Bellman would cry: and the
      crew would reply,
"They are merely conventional signs!"
>   *Ib. Fit II, st. 3*

It frequently breakfasts at five-o'clock
      tea,
And dines on the following day.
>   *Ib. st. 17*

There was silence supreme! Not a
      shriek, not a scream,
Scarcely even a howl or a groan,

As the man they called "Ho!" told his
story of woe
In an antediluvian tone.
The Hunting of the Snark.
Fit III, st. 3

It is this, it is this that oppresses my
soul.   *Ib. st. 11*

And my heart is like nothing so much
as a bowl
Brimming over with quivering curds.
Ib.

You may charge me with murder — or
want of sense —
(We are all of us weak at times):
But the slightest approach to a false
pretense
Was never among my crimes!
Ib. Fit IV, st. 4

They sought it with thimbles, they
sought it with care;
They pursued it with forks and hope;
They threatened its life with a railway
share;
They charmed it with smiles and soap.
Ib. Fit V, st. 1

For the Snark *was* a Boojum, you see.
Ib. Fit VIII, st. 9

He thought he saw an Elephant,
That practiced on a fife:
He looked again, and found it was
A letter from his wife.
"At length I realize," he said,
"The bitterness of Life!"
Sylvie and Bruno [1889], *ch. 5*

He thought he saw a Buffalo
Upon the chimneypiece:
He looked again, and found it was
His sister's husband's niece.
Ib. 6

He thought he saw an Albatross
That fluttered round the lamp:
He looked again, and found it was
A penny postage stamp.
"You'd best be getting home," he said,
"The nights are very damp."
Ib. 12

BENJAMIN HARVEY HILL
1832–1882

He was a foe without hate, a friend
without treachery, a soldier without
cruelty, and a victim without murmuring. He was a public officer without
vices, a private citizen without wrong, a
neighbor without reproach, a Christian
without hypocrisy, and a man without
guile. He was a Caesar without his ambition, a Frederick without his tyranny,
a Napoleon without his selfishness, and
a Washington without his reward.
Tribute to Robert E. Lee; from
THOMAS NELSON PAGE, *Robert
E. Lee* [1911]

JUAN MONTALVO
1832–1889

Old age is an island surrounded by
death.   *On Beauty*

Beauty is harmony, grace is melody.
Ib.

The soul does not hunger for flesh, it
is horrified by it; it does not thirst for
wine, it is killed by it.   *On Genius*

Sensibility is most strong among our
young nations who outdistance the
older ones in science and culture by
means of their imagination.
Chapters Forgotten by Cervantes. Epilogue

There is nothing harder than the
softness of indifference.   *Ib.*

HENRY CLAY WORK
1832–1884

Father, dear father, come home with
me now,
The clock in the belfry strikes one;
You said you were coming right home
from the shop
As soon as your day's work was done.
Come Home, Father [1864], *st. 1*

Bring the good old bugle, boys, we'll
sing another song;

Sing it with a spirit that will start the world along,

Sing it as we used to sing it — fifty thousand strong,

While we were marching through Georgia.

> *Marching Through Georgia*
> *[1865], st. 1*

"Hurrah! hurrah! we bring the Jubilee! Hurrah! Hurrah! the flag that makes you free!"

So we sang the chorus from Atlanta to the sea,

While we were marching through Georgia.　　　　*Ib. chorus*

ISAAC HILL BROMLEY
1833–1898

Conductor, when you receive a fare, Punch in the presence of the passen-jare! . . .

Punch, brothers! Punch with care! Punch in the presence of the passen-jare!

> *Punch, Brother, Punch* [1] *[1875]*

MARY ABIGAIL
DODGE
[GAIL HAMILTON]
1833–1896

Whatever an author puts between the two covers of his book is public property; whatever of himself he does not put there is his private property, as much as if he had never written a word.

> *Country Living and Country*
> *Thinking [1862], preface*

What's virtue in man can't be vice in a cat.　　　　　　*Both Sides*

ADAM LINDSAY GORDON
1833–1870

A little season of love and laughter, Of light and life, and pleasure and pain,

And a horror of outer darkness after, And dust returneth to dust again.[1]

> *The Swimmer*

JOHN MARSHALL
HARLAN
1833–1911

In view of the Constitution, in the eye of the law, there is in this country no superior, dominant, ruling class of citizens. There is no caste here. Our Constitution is color-blind, and neither knows nor tolerates classes among citizens. In respect of civil rights, all citizens are equal before the law. The humblest is the peer of the most powerful.

> *Dissenting opinion, Plessy v.*
> *Ferguson 163 U.S. 537, 559*
> *[1896]*

JOHN JAMES INGALLS
1833–1900

Every man is the center of a circle, whose fatal circumference he cannot pass.

> *Eulogy on Benjamin Hill, U.S.*
> *Senate [January 23, 1882]*

The purification of politics is an iridescent dream. Government is force.

> *Article in the New York World*
> *[1890]*

Next in profusion to the divine profusion of water, light and air, those three physical facts which render existence possible, may be reckoned the universal beneficence of grass.

> *Blue Grass*

I knock unbidden once at every gate! If sleeping, wake; if feasting, rise before

I turn away. It is the hour of fate.

> *Opportunity [1891]*

---

[1] Based on a New York streetcar sign. Erroneously attributed to Mark Twain, who wrote about the verse in *A Literary Nightmare [1876]*.

[1] See Du Maurier, p. 751b, and Marston, p. 821b.

ROBERT GREEN INGERSOLL

1833–1899

Like an armed warrior, like a plumed knight, James G. Blaine marched down the halls of the American Congress and threw his shining lance full and fair against the brazen forehead of every traitor to his country and every maligner of his fair reputation.

> *Speech nominating Blaine for President, National Republican Convention [June 15, 1876]*

I am the inferior of any man whose rights I trample under foot. Men are not superior by reason of the accidents of race or color. They are superior who have the best heart — the best brain.

> *Liberty*

The superior man is the providence of the inferior. He is eyes for the blind, strength for the weak, and a shield for the defenseless. He stands erect by bending above the fallen. He rises by lifting others. ***Ib.***

Every cradle asks us, "Whence?" and every coffin, "Whither?" The poor barbarian, weeping above his dead, can answer these questions as intelligently as the robed priest of the most authentic creed.

> *Address at a child's grave*

We, too, have our religion, and it is this: Help for the living, hope for the dead. ***Ib.***

Few rich men own their own property. The property owns them.[1]

> *Address to the McKinley League, New York [October 29, 1896]*

An honest God is the noblest work of man. *The Gods* [1876]

In nature there are neither rewards nor punishments — there are consequences. *Some Reasons Why* [1896]

Justice is the only worship.
Love is the only priest.
Ignorance is the only slavery.

[1] See Bion, p. 104b.

Happiness is the only good.
The time to be happy is now,
The place to be happy is here,
The way to be happy is to make others so. *Creed*

PETROLEUM V. NASBY [DAVID ROSS LOCKE]

1833–1888

The contract 'twixt Hannah, God and me,
Was not for one or twenty years, but for eternity.

> *Hannah Jane* [1871], *st. 29*

EDMUND CLARENCE STEDMAN

1833–1908

Prison mate and dockyard fellow,
   Blades to Meg and Molly dear,
Off to capture Porto Bello
   Sailed with Morgan the Buccaneer!

> *Morgan,*[1] *st. 1*

JULIA LOUISE MATILDA WOODRUFF

1833–1909

Out of the strain of the Doing,
Into the peace of the Done.

> *Harvest Home* [1910]

JOHN EMERICH EDWARD DALBERG-ACTON, LORD ACTON

1834–1902

There is no error so monstrous that it fails to find defenders among the ablest men. Imagine a congress of eminent celebrities such as More, Bacon, Grotius, Pascal, Cromwell, Bossuet, Montesquieu, Jefferson, Napoleon, Pitt, etc. The result would be an Encyclopedia of Error.

> *Letter to Mary Gladstone [April 24, 1881]*

[1] The old bold mate of Henry Morgan. — JOHN MASEFIELD [1878–1967], *Captain Stratton's Fancy*

Power tends to corrupt and absolute power corrupts absolutely.

> *Letter to Bishop Mandell Creighton [April 5, 1887]*

Advice to Persons About to Write History — Don't.   *Ib. postscript*

Liberty is not a means to a higher political end. It is itself the highest political end.

> *The History of Freedom and Other Essays [1907], ch. 1*

It was from America that the plain ideas that men ought to mind their business, and that the nation is responsible to Heaven for the acts of the State — ideas long locked in the breast of solitary thinkers, and hidden among Latin folios — burst forth like a conqueror upon the world they were destined to transform, under the title of the Rights of Man . . . and the principle gained ground, that a nation can never abandon its fate to an authority it cannot control.   *Ib. 2*

The one pervading evil of democracy is the tyranny of the majority, or rather of that party, not always the majority, that succeeds, by force or fraud, in carrying elections.   *Ib. 3*

Truth is the only merit that gives dignity and worth to history.   *Ib. 4*

Writers the most learned, the most accurate in details, and the soundest in tendency, frequently fall into a habit which can neither be cured nor pardoned — the habit of making history into the proof of their theories.
                                    Ib. 8

GEORGE ARNOLD
1834–1865

Life for the living, and rest for the dead!

> *The Jolly Old Pedagogue, st. 2*

The living need charity more than the dead.   *Ib. st. 3*

SABINE BARING-GOULD
1834–1924

Onward, Christian soldiers,
  Marching as to war,
With the Cross of Jesus
  Going on before!

> *Onward, Christian Soldiers [1864], st. 1*

Now the day is over,
  Night is drawing nigh;
Shadows of the evening
  Steal across the sky.

> *Now the Day Is Over [1865], st. 1*

Through the night of doubt and sorrow
Onward goes the pilgrim band,
Singing songs of expectation,
  Marching to the promised land.

> *Through the Night of Doubt and Sorrow, st. 1; translated [1867] from the Danish of B. S. Ingemann [1825]*

CHARLES FARRAR BROWNE
[ARTEMUS WARD]
1834–1867

I now bid you a welcome adoo.

> *Artemus Ward, His Book [1862]*

My pollertics, like my religion, being of an exceedin' accommodatin' character.   *Ib. The Crisis*

N.B. This is rote sarcastikul.

> *Ib. A Visit to Brigham Young*

The female woman is one of the greatest institooshuns of which this land can boste.

> *Ib. Woman's Rights*

I am not a politician, and my other habits are good.

> *Fourth of July Oration*

The prevailin' weakness of most public men is to Slop over. G. Washington never slopt over.   *Ib.*

I can't sing. As a singist I am not a success. I am saddest when I sing. So are those who hear me. They are sadder even than I am.[1]

Artemus Ward, His Travels [1865].
Lecture

Did you ever have the measels, and if so, how many? *Ib. The Census*

The Puritans nobly fled from a land of despotism to a land of freedim, where they could not only enjoy their own religion, but could prevent everybody else from enjoyin *his.*

London Punch Letters,[2] *no. 5*
[1866]

Why is this thus? What is the reason of this thusness? *Moses, the Sassy*

He [Brigham Young] is dreadfully married. He's the most married man I ever saw in my life. *Ib.*

Let us all be happy and live within our means, even if we have to borrow the money to do it with.
Natural History

The sun has a right to "set" where it wants to, and so, I may add, has a hen. *A Mormon Romance, ch. 4*

They cherish his mem'ry, and them as sell picturs of his birthplace, etc., make it prof'tible cherishin' it.
At the Tomb of Shakespeare

GEORGE LOUIS PALMELLA BUSSON DU MAURIER
1834–1896

The wretcheder one is, the more one smokes; and the more one smokes, the wretcheder one gets — a vicious circle!
Peter Ibbetson [1891]

Songs without words are best. *Ib.*

All will be well for us all, and of such a kind that all who do not sigh for the moon will be well content. *Ib.*

Lovely female shapes are terrible complicators of the difficulties and dangers of this earthly life, especially for their owner. *Trilby* [1894], *pt. I*

That is the worst of those dear people who have charm; they are so terrible to do without, when once you have got accustomed to them and all their ways.
Ib. V

A little work, a little play,
To keep us going — and so, good day!

A little warmth, a little light,
Of love's bestowing — and so, good night! [1]

A little fun, to match the sorrow
Of each day's growing — and so, good morrow!

A little trust that when we die
We reap our sowing! and so — goodby!
Ib. VIII

CHARLES WILLIAM ELIOT
1834–1926

In the modern world the intelligence of public opinion is the one indispensable condition of social progress.
Inaugural address as president of Harvard [1869]

Enter to grow in wisdom.
Depart better to serve thy country and mankind.
Inscriptions on the 1890 Gate to Harvard Yard

To the Fifty-fourth Regiment of Massachusetts Infantry:

[1] La vie est vaine:
   Un peu d'amour,
   Un peu de haine . . .
   Et puis — bonjour!

  La vie est brève:
   Un peu d'espoir,
   Un peu de rêve
   Et puis — bonsoir!
LEON MONTENAEKEN [b. 1859], *Peu de Chose*

See A. L. Gordon, p. 748b, and Marston, p. 821b.

---

[1] See T. H. Bayly, p. 588a.
[2] The Puritan's idea of Hell is a place where everybody has to mind his own business. — *Attributed to* WENDELL PHILLIPS [1811–1884]

The white officers, taking life and honor in their hands, cast in their lot with men of a despised race unproved in war, and risked death as inciters of servile insurrection if taken prisoners, besides encountering all the common perils of camp march and battle.

The black rank and file volunteered when disaster clouded the Union cause, served without pay for eighteen months till given that of white troops, faced threatened enslavement if captured, were brave in action, patient under heavy and dangerous labors, and cheerful amid hardships and privations.

Together they gave to the nation and the world undying proof that Americans of African descent possess the pride, courage, and devotion of the patriot soldier. One hundred and eighty thousand such Americans enlisted under the Union flag in 1863–1865.

> *Inscription on the back of the Robert Gould Shaw Monument, Boston Common* [1897] [1]

Carrier of news and knowledge, instrument of trade and commerce, promoter of mutual acquaintance among men and nations and hence of peace and good will.

Carrier of love and sympathy, messenger of friendship, consoler of the lonely, servant of the scattered family, enlarger of the public life.

> *Inscriptions for the East and West Pavilions, Post Office, Washington, D.C.*[2]

FUKUZAWA YUKICHI[3]
1834–1901

The final purpose of all my work was to create in Japan a civilized nation as

[1] See Robert Lowell, p. 1076b.

[2] These inscriptions were edited by Woodrow Wilson, to read:

Carrier of news and knowledge, instrument of trade and promoter of mutual acquaintance, of peace and good will among men and nations.

Messenger of sympathy and love, servant of parted friends, consoler of the lonely, bond of the scattered family, enlarger of the common life.

[3] From *Sources of Japanese Tradition*, edited by William Theodore de Bary [1960].

well equipped in both the arts of war and peace as those of the Western world.   *Autobiography* [1898]

As long as I remain in private life, I can watch and laugh. But joining the government would draw me into the practice of those ridiculous pretensions which I cannot allow myself to do.

Ib.

ERNST HEINRICH HAECKEL
1834–1919

Ontogenesis, or the development of the individual, is a short and quick recapitulation of phylogenesis,[1] or the development of the tribe to which it belongs, determined by the laws of inheritance and adaptation.

> *The History of Creation* [2] [1868]

The general theory of evolution . . . assumes that in nature there is a great, unital, continuous and everlasting process of development, and that all natural phenomena without exception, from the motion of the celestial bodies and the fall of the rolling stone up to the growth of the plant and the consciousness of man, are subject to the same great law of causation — that they are ultimately to be reduced to atomic mechanics.

> *Freie Wissenschaft und Freie Lehre* [1878] [3]

WALTER KITTREDGE
1834–1905

We're tenting tonight on the old
     campground,
Give us a song to cheer
Our weary hearts, a song of home
And friends we love so dear.

> *Tenting Tonight*, st. 1

[1] Frequently quoted as "Ontogeny recapitulates phylogeny."
See Freud, p. 833b.

[2] Translated by E. R. LANKESTER.

[3] Translated by J. B. STALLO.

WILLIAM MORRIS
1834–1896

I know a little garden close,
Set thick with lily and red rose,
Where I would wander if I might
From dewy morn to dewy night.
> *The Life and Death of Jason*
> [1867]. *A Garden by the Sea,*
> *st. 1*

The idle singer of an empty day.
> *The Earthly Paradise* [1868–
> 1870]. *An Apology, st. 1*

Dreamer of dreams, born out of my due
time,
Why should I strive to set the crooked
straight?　　　　　　　　*Ib. st. 4*

Love is enough, though the world be a-
waning,
And the woods have no voice but the
voice of complaining.
> *Love Is Enough* [1872]

If you want a golden rule that will
fit everybody, this is it: Have nothing
in your houses that you do not know
to be useful, or believe to be beautiful.
> *The Beauty of Life* [1880]

What I mean by Socialism is a condition of society in which there should
be neither rich nor poor, neither master
nor master's man, neither idle nor over-
worked, neither brain-sick brain workers nor heart-sick hand workers, in a
word, in which all men would be living in equality of condition, and would
manage their affairs unwastefully, and
with the full consciousness that harm
to one would mean harm to all — the
realization at last of the meaning of
the word *commonwealth.*
> *Written for "Justice"* [1884]

FRANK RICHARD
STOCKTON
1834–1902

He could open either door he
pleased. . . . If he opened the one,
there came out of it a hungry tiger, the
fiercest and most cruel that could be
procured, which immediately sprang
upon him, and tore him to pieces, as a
punishment for his guilt. . . . But if
the accused person opened the other
door, there came forth from it a lady,
the most suitable to his years and station that his Majesty could select
among his fair subjects. . . . So I leave
it with all of you: Which came out of
the opened door — the lady or the
tiger?
> *The Lady or the Tiger?* [1884]

The board money is in the ginger jar
and our conscience is clear.
> *The Casting Away of Mrs. Lecks*
> *and Mrs. Aleshine* [1886]

JAMES THOMSON
1834–1882

Give a man a pipe he can smoke,
　Give a man a book he can read:
And his home is bright with a calm
　delight,
Though the room be poor indeed.
> *Sunday Up the River* [1869],
> *XV, st. 2*

The City is of Night; perchance of
　Death,
But certainly of Night.
> *The City of Dreadful Night*
> [1874]. *Proem*

CHARLES HENRY
WEBB
1834–1905

Friends I have had both old and
　young,
And ale we drank and songs we sung:
Enough you know when this is said,
That, one and all — they died in bed.
In bed they died and I'll not go
Where all my friends have perished so.
> *Dum Vivimus Vigilamus, st. 1*

That 'tis well to be off with the old
　love
Before one is on with the new
Has somehow passed into a proverb,[1]

[1] It's gude to be merry and wise,
　It's gude to be honest and true;

But who follows its teaching may rue.
Proverbum Sap, st. 1

Were the proverb not wiser if mended,
And the fickle and wavering told
To be sure that they're on with the new
love
Before being off with the old?
Ib. st. 3

JAMES McNEILL WHISTLER
1834–1903

Two and two continue to make four,
in spite of the whine of the amateur for
three, or the cry of the critic for five.
Whistler v. Ruskin [1] [1878]

The rare few, who, early in life, have
rid themselves of the friendship of the
many.
*The Gentle Art of Making
Enemies* [1890], *dedication*

To say of a picture, as is often said in
its praise, that it shows great and earnest labor, is to say that it is incomplete
and unfit for view.
Ib. Propositions, 2

Industry in art is a necessity — not a
virtue — and any evidence of the same,
in the production, is a blemish, not a
quality; a proof, not of achievement,
but of absolutely insufficient work, for
work alone will efface the footsteps of
work.[2] *Ib.*

The masterpiece should appear as the
flower to the painter — perfect in its
bud as in its bloom — with no reason

to explain its presence — no mission to
fulfill — a joy to the artist, a delusion
to the philanthropist — a puzzle to the
botanist — an accident of sentiment
and alliteration to the literary man.
*The Gentle Art of Making
Enemies, Propositions, 2*

Art should be independent of all
claptrap — should stand alone, and appeal to the artistic sense of eye and ear,
without confounding this with emotions entirely foreign to it, as devotion,
pity, love, patriotism, and the like. All
these have no kind of concern with it.
Ib.

The imitator is a poor kind of creature. If the man who paints only the
tree, or flower, or other surface he sees
before him were an artist, the king of
artists would be the photographer. It is
for the artist to do something beyond
this: in portrait painting to put on canvas something more than the face the
model wears for that one day; to paint
the man, in short, as well as his features. *Ib.*

One cannot continually disappoint a
Continent.[1] *Ib.*

I am not arguing with you — I am
telling you. *Ib.*

Wilde: I wish I'd said that.
Whistler: You will, Oscar, you will.
From L. C. INGLEBY, *Oscar
Wilde* [1907]

"I only know of two painters in the
world," said a newly introduced femi-
nine enthusiast to Whistler, "yourself
and Velasquez." "Why," answered
Whistler in dulcet tones, "why drag in
Velasquez?"
From D. C. SEITZ, *Whistler
Stories* [1913]

ALFRED AUSTIN
1835–1913

An earl by right, by courtesy a man.
The Season

It's gude to be off with the old love,
Before you are on with the new.
ANONYMOUS [1816]. Quoted by AN-
THONY TROLLOPE in *Barchester
Towers* [1857], *ch. 46.*
See G. B. Shaw, p. 836a.
[1] In Whistler's lawsuit for libel. Ruskin had
written of Whistler's *Nocturne in Black and
Gold,* "I have seen, and heard, much of Cockney
impudence before now; but never expected to
hear a coxcomb ask two hundred guineas for
flinging a pot of paint in the public's face." —
JOHN RUSKIN, *Fors Clavigera, Letter 79* [1877]
[2] Ars est celare artem [Art lies in concealing
art]. — *Latin proverb*

[1] Referring to a contemplated visit to the
United States.

THOMAS BRIGHAM BISHOP
1835–1905

John Brown's body lies a-moldering in
   the grave,
His soul is marching on.
> *John Brown's Body, st. 1*

Shoo, fly! don't bodder me! I belong to
   Company G,
I feel like a morning star.
> *Shoo, Fly. Refrain*

PHILLIPS BROOKS
1835–1893

O little town of Bethlehem!
   How still we see thee lie;
Above thy deep and dreamless sleep
   The silent stars go by;
Yet in thy dark streets shineth
   The everlasting Light;
The hopes and fears of all the years
   Are met in thee tonight.
> *O Little Town of Bethlehem*
> *[1867], st. 1*

Life comes before literature, as the
material always comes before the work.
The hills are full of marble before the
world blooms with statues.
> *Literature and Life*

Do not pray for easy lives. Pray to be
stronger men! Do not pray for tasks
equal to your powers. Pray for powers
equal to your tasks.
> *Sermons. Going up to Jerusalem*

Greatness after all, in spite of its
name, appears to be not so much a certain size as a certain quality in human
lives. It may be present in lives whose
range is very small.
> *Ib. Purpose and Use of Comfort*

SAMUEL BUTLER
1835–1902

The man who lets himself be bored
is even more contemptible than the
bore.
> *The Fair Haven* [1873]. *Memoir,*
> *ch. 3*

A hen is only an egg's way of making
another egg.
> *Life and Habit* [1877], *ch. 8*

Stowed away in a Montreal lumber
   room
The Discobolus standeth and turneth
   his face to the wall;
Dusty, cobweb-covered, maimed and
   set at naught,
Beauty crieth in an attic and no man
   regardeth.
O God! O Montreal!
> *A Psalm of Montreal* [1884],
> *st. 1*

The Discobolus is put here because he
   is vulgar —
He has neither vest nor pants with
   which to cover his limbs;
I, Sir, am a person of most respectable
   connections —
My brother-in-law is haberdasher to
   Mr. Spurgeon.
O God! O Montreal!   *Ib. st. 5*

It is far safer to know too little than
too much. People will condemn the
one, though they will resent being
called upon to exert themselves to follow the other.
> *The Way of All Flesh* [1] [1903],
> *ch. 5*

Adversity, if a man is set down to it
by degrees, is more supportable with
equanimity by most people than any
great prosperity arrived at in a single
lifetime.[2]   *Ib.*

It is our less conscious thoughts and
our less conscious actions which mainly
mold our lives and the lives of those
who spring from us.   *Ib.*

To me it seems that youth is like
spring, an over-praised season — delightful if it happen to be a favored
one, but in practice very rarely favored
and more remarkable, as a general rule,
for biting east winds than genial
breezes.   *Ib. 6*

---

[1] See John Webster, p. 314b.
[2] See Carlyle, p. 577b.

Taking numbers into account, I should think more mental suffering had been undergone in the streets leading from St. George's, Hanover Square, than in the condemned cells of Newgate.

The Way of All Flesh, 13

Every man's work, whether it be literature or music or pictures or architecture or anything else, is always a portrait of himself.   *Ib.* 14

One great reason why clergymen's households are generally unhappy is because the clergyman is so much at home and close about the house.

Ib. 24

The advantage of doing one's praising for oneself is that one can lay it on so thick and exactly in the right places.

Ib. 34

The best liar is he who makes the smallest amount of lying go the longest way.   *Ib.* 39

An empty house is like a stray dog or a body from which life has departed.[1]

Ib. 72

A man's friendships are, like his will, invalidated by marriage — but they are also no less invalidated by the marriage of his friends.   *Ib.* 75

Life is the art of drawing sufficient conclusions from insufficient premises.

Notebooks [1912]. *Life*

All progress is based upon a universal innate desire on the part of every organism to live beyond its income.

Ib.

---

[1] I suppose I've passed it a hundred times,
    but I always stop for a minute
And look at the house, the tragic house, the
    house with nobody in it.
     JOYCE KILMER [1886–1918], *The House
                 With Nobody In It*

Though analogy is often misleading, it is the least misleading thing we have.

*Notebooks. Music, Pictures,
and Books*

The phrase "unconscious humor" is the one contribution I have made to the current literature of the day.

Ib. Homo Unius Libri

Ideas and opinions, like living organisms, have a normal rate of growth which cannot be either checked or forced beyond a certain point. The more unpopular an opinion is, the more necessary is it that the holder should be somewhat punctilious in his observance of conventionalities generally.

*Ib. The Art of Propagating
Opinion*

Genius . . . has been defined as a supreme capacity for taking trouble.[1] . . . It might be more fitly described as a supreme capacity for getting its possessors into trouble of all kinds and keeping them therein so long as the genius remains.   *Ib. Genius*

I am the *enfant terrible* of literature and science.

Ib. Enfant Terrible: Myself

An apology for the Devil: It must be remembered that we have only heard one side of the case. God has written all the books.

*Ib. Higgledy-Piggledy: An
Apology for the Devil*

God is Love — I dare say. But what a mischievous devil Love is!

Ib. God Is Love

To live is like to love — all reason is against it, and all healthy instinct for it.   *Ib. Life and Love*

The Ancient Mariner would not have taken so well if it had been called *The Old Sailor.*   *Ib. Titles and Subjects*

The public buys its opinions as it buys its meat, or takes in its milk, on the principle that it is cheaper to do

---

[1] See Buffon, p. 423b, and note.

this than to keep a cow. So it is, but the milk is more likely to be watered.

Notebooks. Sequel to "Alps and Sanctuaries"

I do not mind lying, but I hate inaccuracy.

Ib. Truth and Convenience: Falsehood

ANDREW CARNEGIE
1835–1919

The problem of our age is the proper administration of wealth, so that the ties of brotherhood may still bind together the rich and poor in harmonious relationship.

Wealth [North American Review, June 1889]

While the law [of competition] may be sometimes hard for the individual, it is best for the race, because it insures the survival of the fittest in every department. We accept and welcome, therefore, as conditions to which we must accommodate ourselves, great inequality of environment, the concentration of business, industrial and commercial, in the hands of a few, and the law of competition between these, as being not only beneficial, but essential for the future progress of the race.

Ib.

Upon the sacredness of property civilization itself depends — the right of the laborer to his hundred dollars in the savings bank, and equally the legal right of the millionaire to his millions.

Ib.

Surplus wealth is a sacred trust which its possessor is bound to administer in his lifetime for the good of the community.

Ib.

Those who would administer wisely must, indeed, be wise, for one of the serious obstacles to the improvement of our race is indiscriminate charity.

Ib.

Thus is the problem of Rich and Poor to be solved. The law of accumulation will be left free; the laws of distribution free. Individualism will continue, but the millionaire will be but a trustee of the poor; entrusted for a season with a great part of the increased wealth of the community, but administering it for the community far better than it could or would have done for itself.[1]

Wealth

The man who dies . . . rich dies disgraced.

Ib.

Such, in my opinion, is the true Gospel concerning Wealth, obedience to which is destined some day to solve the problem of the Rich and the Poor, and to bring "Peace on earth, among men Good Will."

Ib.

Three generations from shirtsleeves to shirtsleeves.[2]

Attributed

RICHARD GARNETT
1835–1906

Man and woman may only enter Paradise hand in hand. Together, the myth tells us, they left it and together must they return.

De Flagello Myrteo [1905], preface, 12

Perfect love casts out prudery together with fear.

Ib. 59

When Silence speaks for Love she has much to say.

Ib. 99

Sweet are the words of Love, sweeter his thoughts:
Sweetest of all what Love nor says nor thinks.

Ib. 250

Ascend above the restrictions and conventions of the world, but not so high as to lose sight of them.

Ib. 333

---

[1] See Maimonides, p. 155b; Spinoza, p. 374a; and Johnson, p. 431a.
[2] There's nobbut three generations atween clog and clog. — *Lancashire proverb*, which Carnegie liked to quote.

JOHN LUCKEY McCREERY
1835–1906

There is no death! The stars go down
　To rise upon some other shore,
And bright in heaven's jeweled crown
　They shine forevermore.
There Is No Death [1863], *st. 1*

ADAH ISAACS MENKEN
1835–1868

Where is the promise of my years,
　Once written on my brow?
Ere errors, agonies, and fears
Brought with them all that speaks in
　tears,
Ere I had sunk beneath my peers —
　Where sleeps that promise now?
El Suspiro (Infelix) [1868]

LOUISE CHANDLER MOULTON
1835–1908

Bend low, O dusky Night,
　And give my spirit rest,
　Hold me to your deep breast,
And put old cares to flight.
Give back the lost delight
　That once my soul possessed,
　When Love was loveliest.
Tonight

I hied me off to Arcady —
　The month it was the month of
　　May,
　And all along the pleasant way
The morning birds were mad with
　glee,
And all the flowers sprang up to see,
As I went on to Arcady.   *Arcady*

BISHOP HENRY CODMAN POTTER
1835–1908

We have exchanged the Washingtonian dignity for the Jeffersonian simplicity, which was in truth only another name for the Jacksonian vulgarity.
Address at the Washington Centennial Service in St. Paul's Chapel, New York [April 30, 1889]

HARRIET PRESCOTT SPOFFORD
1835–1921

The awful phantom of the hungry
　poor.   *A Winter's Night*

CELIA LAIGHTON THAXTER
1835–1894

Sad soul, take comfort, nor forget
That sunrise never failed us yet.
The Sunrise Never Failed Us Yet, st. 4

Across the narrow beach we flit,
One little sandpiper and I;
And fast I gather, bit by bit,
The scattered driftwood, bleached and
　dry.
The wild waves reach their hands for
　it,
The wild wind raves, the tide runs
　high,
As up and down the beach we flit,
One little sandpiper and I.
The Sandpiper, st. 1

MARK TWAIN[1]
[SAMUEL LANGHORNE CLEMENS]
1835–1910

I'll resk forty dollars that he can out-jump any frog in Calaveras county.
The Celebrated Jumping Frog [1865]

I don't see no p'ints about that frog that's any better'n any other frog.
Ib.

---

[1] I was a fresh, new journalist, and needed a *nom de guerre*; so I confiscated the ancient mariner's discarded one ["Mark Twain"], and have done my best to make it remain what it was in his hands — a sign and symbol and warrant that whatever is found in its company may be gambled on as being the petrified truth. — *Life on the Mississippi* [1883], ch. 50. The earlier use of the pen name was by Captain Isaiah Sellers, in *The New Orleans Picayune*.
The phrase "mark twain," meaning "two fathoms deep," was employed in making soundings on the Mississippi riverboats.

Soap and education are not as sudden as a massacre, but they are more deadly in the long run.

The Facts Concerning the Recent Resignation [1867]

Tomorrow night I appear for the first time before a Boston audience — 4000 critics.

Letter to Pamela Clemens Moffet [*November 9, 1869*]

They spell it Vinci and pronounce it Vinchy; foreigners always spell better than they pronounce.

The Innocents Abroad [1869], *ch. 19*

I do not want Michael Angelo for breakfast — for luncheon — for dinner — for tea — for supper — for between meals. *Ib. 27*

Lump the whole thing! say that the Creator made Italy from designs by Michael Angelo! *Ib.*

Guides cannot master the subtleties of the American joke. *Ib.*

There's millions in it!

The Gilded Age [1] [1873]

Barring that natural expression of villainy which we all have, the man looked honest enough.

A Mysterious Visit [1875]

This poor little one-horse town.

The Undertaker's Chat [1875]

Tom appeared on the sidewalk with a bucket of whitewash and a long-handled brush. He surveyed the fence, and all gladness left him and a deep melancholy settled down upon his spirit. Thirty yards of board fence nine feet high. Life to him seemed hollow, and existence but a burden.

The Adventures of Tom Sawyer [1876], *ch. 2*

Work consists of whatever a body is *obliged* to do . . . Play consists of whatever a body is not obliged to do. *Ib.*

[1] Written in collaboration with CHARLES DUDLEY WARNER.

The minister gave out his text and droned along monotonously through an argument that was so prosy that many a head by and by began to nod — and yet it was an argument that dealt in limitless fire and brimstone and thinned the predestined elect down to a company so small as to be hardly worth the saving.

The Adventures of Tom Sawyer, ch. 5

There was no getting around the stubborn fact that taking sweetmeats was only "hooking," while taking bacon and hams and such valuables was plain simple *stealing* — and there was a command against that in the Bible. So they inwardly resolved that so long as they remained in the business, their piracies should not again be sullied with the crime of stealing. *Ib. 13*

To promise not to do a thing is the surest way in the world to make a body want to go and do that very thing. *Ib. 22*

She makes me wash, they comb me all to thunder . . . The widder eats by a bell; she goes to bed by a bell; she gits up by a bell — everything's so awful reg'lar a body can't stand it. *Ib. 35*

A baby is an inestimable blessing and bother.

Letter to Annie Webster [*September 1, 1876*]

There is a sumptuous variety about the New England weather that compels the stranger's admiration — and regret. The weather is always doing something there; always attending strictly to business; always getting up new designs and trying them on people to see how they will go. But it gets through more business in spring than in any other season. In the spring I have counted one hundred and thirty-six different kinds of weather inside of twenty-four hours. [1]

New England Weather. Speech to the New England Society [*December 22, 1876*]

[1] See Charles Dudley Warner, p. 733b.

Probable nor'east to sou'west winds, varying to the southard and westard and eastard and points between; high and low barometer, sweeping round from place to place; probable areas of rain, snow, hail, and drought, succeeded or preceded by earthquakes with thunder and lightning.

> *New England Weather. Speech to the New England Society*

We haven't all had the good fortune to be ladies; we haven't all been generals, or poets, or statesmen; but when the toast works down to the babies, we stand on common ground.

> *Answering a toast "To the babies," at a banquet in honor of General U.S. Grant [November 14, 1879]*

Among the three or four million cradles now rocking in the land are some which this nation would preserve for ages as sacred things, if we could know which ones they are. *Ib.*

It is the longest river in the world — four thousand three hundred miles. . . . It is also the crookedest river in the world, since in one part of its journey it uses up one thousand three hundred miles to cover the same ground that the crow would fly over in six hundred and seventy-five.

> *Life on the Mississippi* [1883], *ch. 1*

The world and the books are so accustomed to use, and over-use, the word "new" in connection with our country, that we early get and permanently retain the impression that there is nothing old about it. *Ib.*

Sired by a hurricane, dam'd by an earthquake. *Ib. 3*

When I'm playful I use the meridians of longitude and parallels of latitude for a seine, and drag the Atlantic Ocean for whales. I scratch my head with the lightning and purr myself to sleep with the thunder. *Ib.*

The Child of Calamity. *Ib.*

I was gratified to be able to answer promptly, and I did. I said I didn't know. *Life on the Mississippi, ch. 6*

Your true pilot cares nothing about anything on earth but the river, and his pride in his occupation surpasses the pride of kings. *Ib. 7*

By the Shadow of Death, but he's a lightning pilot! *Ib.*

A limb of Satan.[1] *Ib. 8*

I'll learn him or kill him. *Ib.*

Give an Irishman lager for a month, and he's a dead man. An Irishman is lined with copper, and the beer corrodes it. But whiskey polishes the copper and is the saving of him. *Ib. 23*

All the modern inconveniences.

Ib. 43

The educated Southerner has no use for an *r*, except at the beginning of a word. *Ib. 44*

In the South the war is what A.D. is elsewhere; they date from it. *Ib. 45*

War talk by men who have been in a war is always interesting; whereas moon talk by a poet who has not been in the moon is likely to be dull. *Ib.*

Sir Walter [Scott] had so large a hand in making Southern character as it existed before the war that he is in great measure responsible for the war. *Ib. 46*

It was without a compeer among swindles. It was perfect, it was rounded, symmetrical, complete, colossal.

Ib. 52

Persons attempting to find a motive in this narrative will be prosecuted; persons attempting to find a moral in it will be banished; persons attempting to find a plot in it will be shot.

BY ORDER OF THE AUTHOR.
> *Adventures of Huckleberry Finn* [1884]. *Notice*

You don't know about me without you have read a book by the name of

[1] Also in *The Prince and the Pauper, ch. 13.*

The Adventures of Tom Sawyer; but that ain't no matter. That book was made by Mr. Mark Twain, and he told the truth, mainly. There was things which he stretched, but mainly he told the truth.

Adventures of Huckleberry Finn, ch. 1

Jim was most ruined for a servant, because he got stuck up on account of having seen the devil and been rode by witches. *Ib. 2*

We catched fish and talked, and we took a swim now and then to keep off sleepiness. It was kind of solemn, drifting down the big, still river, laying on our backs looking up at the stars, and we didn't ever feel like talking loud, and it warn't often that we laughed — only a little kind of a low chuckle. We had mighty good weather as a general thing, and nothing ever happened to us at all. *Ib. 12*

It most froze me to hear such talk. . . . Thinks I, this is what comes of my not thinking. Here was this nigger, which I had as good as helped to run away, coming right out flat-footed and saying he would steal his children — children that belonged to a man I didn't even know, a man that hadn't ever done me no harm. *Ib. 16*

Pilgrim's Progress, about a man that left his family, it didn't say why. I read considerable in it now and then. The statements was interesting but tough. *Ib. 17*

There warn't anybody at the church, except maybe a hog or two, for there warn't any lock on the door, and hogs likes a puncheon floor in summertime because it's cool. If you notice, most folks don't go to church only when they've got to; but a hog is different. *Ib. 18*

We said there warn't no home like a raft, after all. Other places do seem so cramped up and smothery, but a raft don't. You feel mighty free and easy and comfortable on a raft. *Ib.*

A monstrous big river.

Adventures of Huckleberry Finn. ch. 19

Hain't we got all the fools in town on our side? And ain't that a big enough majority in any town? [1]

Ib. 26

I was trying to make my mouth *say* I would do the right thing and the clean thing, and go and write to that nigger's owner and tell where he was; but deep down in me I knowed it was a lie, and He knowed it. You can't pray a lie — I found that out. *Ib. 31*

I was a-trembling because I'd got to decide forever betwixt two things, and I knowed it. I studied for a minute, sort of holding my breath, and then says to myself, "All right, then, I'll *go* to hell." *Ib.*

An experienced, industrious, ambitious, and often quite picturesque liar.

The Private History of a Campaign That Failed [1885]

He is now fast rising from affluence to poverty.

Henry Ward Beecher's Farm [1885]

He [George Washington Cable] has taught me to abhor and detest the Sabbath day and hunt up new and troublesome ways to dishonor it.

Letter to William Dean Howells [*February 27, 1885*]

Whenever the literary German dives into a sentence, that is the last you are going to see of him till he emerges on the other side of his Atlantic with his verb in his mouth.

A Connecticut Yankee at King Arthur's Court [1889], *ch. 22*

Weather is a literary speciality, and no untrained hand can turn out a good article on it.

The American Claimant [1892], *foreword*

[1] See *Pudd'nhead Wilson's New Calendar,* p. 763a.

Tell the truth or trump — but get the trick.

Pudd'nhead Wilson [1894]. *Pudd'nhead Wilson's Calendar, ch. 1*

Adam was but human — this explains it all. He did not want the apple for the apple's sake, he wanted it only because it was forbidden. *Ib. 2*

Whoever has lived long enough to find out what life is, knows how deep a debt of gratitude we owe to Adam, the first great benefactor of our race. He brought death into the world. *Ib. 3*

Training is everything. The peach was once a bitter almond; cauliflower is nothing but cabbage with a college education. *Ib. 5*

Habit is habit, and not to be flung out of the window by any man, but coaxed downstairs a step at a time. *Ib. 6*

One of the most striking differences between a cat and a lie is that a cat has only nine lives. *Ib. 7*

The holy passion of Friendship is of so sweet and steady and loyal and enduring a nature that it will last through a whole lifetime, if not asked to lend money. *Ib. 8*

Why is it that we rejoice at a birth and grieve at a funeral? It is because we are not the person involved. *Ib. 9*

All say, "How hard it is that we have to die" — a strange complaint to come from the mouths of people who have had to live. *Ib. 10*

When angry, count four; when very angry, swear.[1] *Ib.*

Courage is resistance to fear, mastery of fear — not absence of fear. *Ib. 12*

Nothing so needs reforming as other people's habits. *Ib. 15*

Put all your eggs in the one basket and — WATCH THAT BASKET. *Ib.*

[1] See Jefferson, p. 474a.

If you pick up a starving dog and make him prosperous, he will not bite you. This is the principal difference between a dog and a man.

Pudd'nhead Wilson. Pudd'nhead Wilson's Calendar, ch. 16

Few things are harder to put up with than the annoyance of a good example. *Ib. 19*

It were not best that we should all think alike; it is difference of opinion that makes horse races. *Ib.*

Be good and you will be lonesome.

Following the Equator [1897]. *Caption for author's photograph on shipboard, frontispiece of first edition*

When in doubt tell the truth.

Ib. vol. I, Pudd'nhead Wilson's New Calendar, ch. 2

Truth is the most valuable thing we have. Let us economize it. *Ib. 7*

It could probably be shown by facts and figures that there is no distinctly native American criminal class except Congress. *Ib. 8*

Everything human is pathetic. The secret source of Humor itself is not joy but sorrow. There is no humor in heaven. *Ib. 10*

We should be careful to get out of an experience only the wisdom that is in it — and stop there; lest we be like the cat that sits down on a hot stove lid. She will never sit down on a hot stove lid again — and that is well; but also she will never sit down on a cold one any more. *Ib. 11*

We can secure other people's approval, if we do right and try hard; but our own is worth a hundred of it, and no way has been found out of securing that. *Ib. 14*

It is easier to stay out than get out. *Ib. 18*

Pity is for the living, envy is for the dead. *Ib. 19*

It is by the goodness of God that in our country we have those three unspeakably precious things: freedom of speech, freedom of conscience, and the prudence never to practice either of them.

> *Following the Equator, vol. I, Pudd'nhead Wilson's New Calendar, ch. 20*

"Classic." A book which people praise and don't read. *Ib. 25*

Man is the only animal that blushes. Or needs to. *Ib. 27*

Let us be thankful for the fools. But for them the rest of us could not succeed.[1] *Ib. 28*

There are several good protections against temptations, but the surest is cowardice.[2] *Ib. 36*

There is an old-time toast which is golden for its beauty. "When you ascend the hill of prosperity may you not meet a friend." *Ib. II, 5*

Each person is born to one possession which outvalues all his others — his last breath. *Ib. 6*

It takes your enemy and your friend, working together, to hurt you to the heart; the one to slander you and the other to get the news to you. *Ib. 9*

Grief can take care of itself, but to get the full value of a joy you must have somebody to divide it with.
> *Ib. 12*

In statesmanship get the formalities right, never mind about the moralities. *Ib. 29*

Everyone is a moon, and has a dark side which he never shows to anybody.[3] *Ib. 30*

The reports of my death are greatly exaggerated.
> *Cable from London to the Associated Press* [1897]

[1] See *Huckleberry Finn*, p. 761b.
[2] See Wilde, p. 839a.
[3] See Robert Browning, p. 665b.

A round man cannot be expected to fit in a square hole right away. He must have time to modify his shape.
> *More Tramps Abroad* [1897]

In Boston they ask, How much does he know? In New York, How much is he worth? In Philadelphia, Who were his parents?
> *What Paul Bourget Thinks of Us* [1899]

The silent colossal National Lie that is the support and confederate of all the tyrannies and shams and inequalities and unfairnesses that afflict the peoples — that is the one to throw bricks and sermons at.
> *My First Lie, and How I Got Out of It* [1900]

The blessings-of-civilization trust, wisely and cautiously administered, is a daisy. There is more money in it, more territory, more sovereignty, and other kinds of emolument, than there is in any other game that is played. But Christendom . . . has been so eager to get every stake that appeared on the green cloth, that the people who sit in darkness [1] have noticed it . . . and have become suspicious of the blessings of civilization.
> *To the Person Sitting in Darkness* [1901]

Always do right. This will gratify some people, and astonish the rest.[2]
> *To the Young People's Society, Greenpoint Presbyterian Church, Brooklyn* [February 16, 1901]

A powerful agent is the right word. Whenever we come upon one of those intensely right words in a book or a newspaper the resulting effect is physical as well as spiritual, and electrically prompt.
> *Essay on William Dean Howells* [1906]

[1] See *Psalms 107:10*, p. 21b.
The people which sat in darkness saw great light. — *Matthew 4:16*
[2] President Truman kept this saying on his desk in the White House.

It may be called the Master Passion, the hunger for self-approval.
What Is Man? [1906], *ch. 6*

The fact that man knows right from wrong proves his *intellectual* superiority to the other creatures; but the fact that he can *do* wrong proves his *moral* inferiority to any creature that *cannot*.
Ib.

Thunder is good, thunder is impressive; but it is lightning that does the work.
Letter to an Unidentified Person [1908]

As out of place as a Presbyterian in Hell.
From ALBERT BIGELOW PAINE, *Mark Twain* [1912]

You tell me whar a man gits his corn pone, en I'll tell you what his 'pinions is.
Europe and Elsewhere [1925]. *Corn Pone Opinions*

Its name is Public Opinion. It is held in reverence. It settles everything. Some think it is the voice of God.   *Ib.*

Biographies are but the clothes and buttons of the man — the biography of the man himself cannot be written.
Autobiography [1924], *vol. I, p. 2*

Of all the creatures that were made he [man] is the most detestable. Of the entire brood he is the only one — the solitary one — that possesses malice. That is the basest of all instincts, passions, vices — the most hateful. . . . He is the only creature that inflicts pain for sport, knowing it to *be* pain. . . . Also — in all the list he is the only creature that has a nasty mind.   *Ib. II, p. 7*

The trade of critic, in literature, music, and the drama, is the most degraded of all trades.   *Ib. p. 69*

I believe that our Heavenly Father invented man because he was disappointed in the monkey.
From BERNARD DE VOTO, *Mark Twain in Eruption* [1940]

Familiarity breeds contempt — and children.[1]   *Notebooks*

Good breeding consists in concealing how much we think of ourselves and how little we think of the other person.   *Ib.*

Death, the only immortal who treats us all alike, whose pity and whose peace and whose refuge are for all — the soiled and the pure, the rich and the poor, the loved and the unloved.
Ib. Memorandum written on his deathbed

Loyalty to petrified opinion never yet broke a chain or freed a human soul.
Inscription beneath his bust in the Hall of Fame

The calm confidence of a Christian with four aces.   *Attributed*

THOMAS BAILEY ALDRICH
1836–1907

"Root Beer Sold Here." It seemed to me the perfection of pith and poetry.
The Story of a Bad Boy [1870]

Somewhere — in desolate windswept space —
In Twilight land — in No-man's land —
Two hurrying Shapes met face to face,
And bade each other stand.

"And who are you?" cried one agape,
Shuddering in the gloaming light.
"I know not," said the second Shape,
"I only died last night!"
Identity [1877]

We knew it would rain, for the poplars showed
The white of their leaves.
Before the Rain, st. 3

Some weep because they part,
And languish brokenhearted,
And others — O my heart! —
Because they never parted.
The Difference

[1] See Aesop, p. 76a.

My mind lets go a thousand things,
Like dates of wars and deaths of kings.
Memory

It was very pleasant to me to get a letter from you the other day. Perhaps I should have found it pleasanter if I had been able to decipher it. I don't think that I mastered anything beyond the date (which I knew) and the signature (which I guessed at). There's a singular and a perpetual charm in a letter of yours; it never grows old, it never loses its novelty. . . . Other letters are read and thrown away and forgotten, but yours are kept forever — unread. One of them will last a reasonable man a lifetime.
*Letter to Edward Sylvester
Morse*

So take him, Earth, and this his mortal part
With that shrewd alchemy thou hast, transmute
To flower and leaf in thine unending springs!
Inscription on his gravestone

ISABELLA MARY BEETON
1836–1865

A place for everything and everything in its place.
The Book of Household Management [1861]

Clear as you go. *Ib.*

EDWARD ERNEST BOWEN
1836–1901

Forty years on, when afar and asunder
Parted are those who are singing today.
Forty Years On, Harrow football song [1872]

JOSEPH CHAMBERLAIN
1836–1914

I never like being hit without striking back.
Speech on tariff reform, Greenock, Scotland [October 7, 1903]

Provided that the City of London remains as it is at present, the clearing-house of the world.
Speech, Guildhall, London
[January 19, 1904]

The day of small nations has long passed away. The day of Empires has come.
Speech, Birmingham [May 12, 1904]

WILLIAM SCHWENCK GILBERT [1]
1836–1911

Of all the ships upon the blue,
No ship contain'd a better crew
Than that of worthy Captain Reece,
Commanding of the Mantelpiece.
The "Bab" Ballads [1866–1871].
Captain Reece, st. 1

The *Times* and *Saturday Review*
Beguiled the leisure of the crew.
Ib. st. 7

I write the pretty mottoes which you find inside the crackers.
Ib. Ferdinando and Elvira

And down in fathoms many went the captain and the crew;
Down went the owners — greedy men whom hope of gain allured:
Oh, dry the starting tear, for they were heavily insured.
Ib. Etiquette, st. 1

Oh, I am a cook and a captain bold
And the mate of the *Nancy* brig,
And a bo'sun tight, and a midshipmite,
And the crew of the captain's gig.
The "Bab" Ballads. The Yarn of the "Nancy Bell," st. 3

As innocent as a new-laid egg.
Engaged [1877], *act I*

I'm called Little Buttercup — dear little Buttercup,
Though I could never tell why.
H.M.S. Pinafore [1878], *act I*

[1] His foe was folly and his weapon wit. — ANTHONY HOPE HAWKINS, *inscription on Gilbert Memorial, Victoria Embankment, London*

I am the Captain of the *Pinafore*;
And a right good captain too!
H.M.S. Pinafore, act I

And I'm never, never sick at sea!
  What, never?
  No, never!
  What, *never*?
  Hardly ever!
He's hardly ever sick at sea!
Then give three cheers, and one cheer
  more
For the hardy Captain of the *Pinafore*!
Ib.

I never never use a big, big D.   *Ib*

And so do his sisters, and his cousins,
  and his aunts!
His sisters and his cousins,
Whom he reckons up by dozens,
And his aunts!   *Ib.*

When I was a lad I served a term
As office boy to an Attorney's firm.
I cleaned the windows and I swept the
  floor
And I polished up the handle of the big
  front door.
I polished up that handle so carefullee
That now I am the Ruler of the
  Queen's Navee!   *Ib.*

Stick close to your desks and *never go
  to sea*,
And you all may be Rulers of the
  Queen's Navee!   *Ib.*

Things are seldom what they seem,
Skim milk masquerades as cream.[1]
Ib. II

He is an Englishman!
  For he himself has said it,
  And it's greatly to his credit,
That he is an Englishman!   *Ib.*

  For he might have been a Roosian,
  A French or Turk or Proosian,
Or perhaps Itali-an.
  But in spite of all temptations
  To belong to other nations,
He remains an Englishman.   *Ib.*

[1] See Phaedrus, p. 129b, and Longfellow, p.
620b.

It is, it is a glorious thing
To be a Pirate King.
Pirates of Penzance [1879], *act I*

I am the very model of a modern Major-
  General.   *Ib.*

I know the Kings of England, and I
  quote the fights historical,
From Marathon to Waterloo, in order
  categorical.   *Ib.*

When the foeman bares his steel,
  Tarantara, tarantara!
We uncomfortable feel,
  Tarantara.   *Ib. II*

When constabulary duty's to be done,
The policeman's lot is not a happy
  one.   *Ib.*

Come, friends, who plow the sea,
  Truce to navigation,
  Take another station;
Let's vary piracee
With a little burglaree.[1]   *Ib.*

Twenty love-sick maidens we,
Love-sick all against our will.
Patience [1881], *act I*

You must lie upon the daisies and discourse in novel phrases of your
  complicated state of mind,
The meaning doesn't matter if it's only
  idle chatter of a transcendental
  kind.
And everyone will say,
As you walk your mystic way,
"If this young man expresses himself in
  terms too deep for *me*,
Why, what a very singularly deep young
  man this deep young man must
  be!"   *Ib.*

Then a sentimental passion of a vegetable fashion must excite your languid spleen,
An attachment à la Plato for a bashful
  young potato, or a not too French
  French bean!
Though the Philistines may jostle, you
  will rank as an apostle in the high
  aesthetic band,

[1] The roistering chorus "Hail, hail, the gang's
all here" is sung to Sir Arthur Sullivan's music
for these lines.

If you walk down Piccadilly with a poppy or a lily in your medieval hand.
And everyone will say,
As you walk your flowery way,
"If he's content with a vegetable love, which would certainly not suit *me*,
Why, what a most particularly pure young man this pure young man must be!" *Patience, act I*

Prithee, pretty maiden, will you marry me?
(Hey, but I'm hopeful, willow, willow, waly!) *Ib.*

While this magnetic,
Peripatetic
Lover, he lived to learn,
By no endeavor,
Can magnet ever
Attract a silver churn! *Ib. II*

Sing "Hey to you — good day to you" —
Sing "Bah to you — ha! ha! to you" —
Sing "Booh to you — pooh, pooh to you." *Ib.*

Francesca di Rimini, miminy, piminy,
Je-ne-sais-quoi young man! *Ib.*

A greenery-yallery, Grosvenor Gallery,
Foot-in-the-grave young man! *Ib.*

I see no objection to stoutness, in moderation. *Iolanthe* [1882], *act I*

None shall part us from each other,
One in life and death are we:
All in all to one another —
I to thee and thou to me!
Thou the tree and I the flower —
Thou the idol; I the throng —
Thou the day and I the hour —
Thou the singer; I the song! *Ib.*

Bow, bow, ye lower middle classes!
Bow, bow, ye tradesmen, bow, ye masses. *Ib.*

The Law is the true embodiment
Of everything that's excellent.
It has no kind of fault or flaw,
And I, my Lords, embody the Law.
Ib.

Pretty young wards in Chancery.
Iolanthe, act I

A pleasant occupation for
A rather susceptible Chancellor! *Ib.*

For I'm not so old, and not so plain,
And I'm quite prepared to marry again. *Ib.*

Spurn not the nobly born
With love affected,
Nor treat with virtuous scorn
The well-connected. *Ib.*

Hearts just as pure and fair
May beat in Belgrave Square
As in the lowly air
Of Seven Dials. *Ib.*

Here's a pretty kettle of fish! *Ib. II*

When I went to the Bar as a very young man
(Said I to myself, said I). *Ib.*

I am an intellectual chap,
And think of things that would astonish you.
I often think it's comical
How nature always does contrive
That every boy and every gal,
That's born into the world alive,
Is either a little Liberal,
Or else a little Conservative! *Ib.*

The House of Peers, throughout the war,
Did nothing in particular,
And did it very well. *Ib.*

Oh, Captain Shaw!
Type of true love kept under!
Could thy Brigade
With cold cascade
Quench my great love, I wonder!
Ib.

When you're lying awake with a dismal headache, and repose is tabooed by anxiety,
I conceive you may use any language you choose to indulge in, without impropriety. *Ib.*

For you dream you are crossing the Channel, and tossing about in a steamer from Harwich —
Which is something between a large

bathing machine and a very small
second class carriage.
Iolanthe, act II

Faint heart never won fair lady!
Nothing venture, nothing win [1] —
Blood is thick, but water's thin —
In for a penny, in for a pound —
It's Love that makes the world go
     round! [2]   *Ib.*

Politics we bar,
     They are not our bent:
On the whole we are
     Not intelligent.
Princess Ida [1884], *act I*

I love my fellow creatures — I do all
     the good I can —
Yet everybody says I'm such a disagree-
     able man!
And I can't think why!   *Ib.*

Darwinian Man, though well-behaved,
At best is only a monkey shaved!
         Ib. II

A wandering minstrel I —
     A thing of shreds and patches,
     Of ballads, songs and snatches,
And dreamy lullaby!
The Mikado [1885], *act I*

I can't help it. I was born sneering.
         Ib.

As some day it may happen that a vic-
     tim must be found,
I've got a little list — I've got a little
     list.
Of society offenders who might well be
     underground,
And who never would be missed —
     who never would be missed.   *Ib.*

The idiot who praises, with enthusiastic
     tone,
All centuries but this, and every coun-
     try but his own.[3]   *Ib.*

Three little maids from school are we,
Pert as a schoolgirl well can be,
Filled to the brim with girlish glee.
         Ib.

---

[1] See Heywood, p. 184b.
[2] See Lewis Carroll, p. 744b, and Anonymous.
p. 1105b.
[3] See Overbury, p. 315b, and Canning, p.
506b.

Ah, pray make no mistake,
     We are not shy;
We're very wide awake,
     The moon and I!
The Mikado, act I

Here's a pretty state of things!
Here's a pretty how-de-do.   *Ib.*

My object all sublime
I shall achieve in time —
To make the punishment fit the crime.
         Ib. II

A source of innocent merriment!   *Ib.*

     On a cloth untrue
     With a twisted cue
And elliptical billiard balls.   *Ib.*

I drew my snickersnee!   *Ib.*

The flowers that bloom in the spring,
     tra la,
Have nothing to do with the case.
         Ib.

On a tree by a river a little tomtit
Sang "Willow, titwillow, titwillow!"
And I said to him, "Dicky-bird, why do
     you sit
Singing 'Willow, titwillow, titwillow!'
"Is it weakness of intellect, birdie?" I
     cried,
"Or a rather tough worm in your little
     inside?"
With a shake of his poor little head he
     replied,
"Oh, willow, titwillow, titwillow!"
         Ib.

     There's a fascination frantic
     In a ruin that's romantic;
Do you think you are sufficiently de-
     cayed?   *Ib.*

He uses language that would make
your hair curl.
Ruddigore [1887], *act I*

For you are such a smart little craft —
Such a neat little, sweet little craft,
Such a bright little, tight little,
Slight little, light little
Trim little, prim little craft!   *Ib. II*

I have a song to sing O!
Sing me your song, O!
The Yeomen of the Guard
[1888], *act I*

It's a song of a merryman, moping
  mum,
Whose soul was sad, and whose glance
  was glum,
Who sipped no sup, and who craved no
  crumb,
As he sighed for the love of a lady.
The Yeoman of the
Guard, act I

He led his regiment from behind —
He found it less exciting.
The Gondoliers [1889], act I

That celebrated,
Cultivated,
Underrated nobleman,
The Duke of Plaza Toro! **Ib.**

No soldier in that gallant band
  Hid half as well as he did.
He lay concealed throughout the war,
  And this preserved his gore, O!
                              Ib.

Of that there is no manner of
  doubt —
No probable, possible shadow of
  doubt —
No possible doubt whatever. **Ib.**

Life's a pudding full of plums;
Care's a canker that benumbs,
Wherefore waste our elocution
On impossible solution?
Life's a pleasant institution,
Let us take it as it comes! **Ib.**

Life's perhaps the only riddle
That we shrink from giving up. **Ib.**

The gratifying feeling that our duty has
  been done. **Ib.**

Take a pair of sparkling eyes. **Ib.**

When everyone is somebodee,
Then no one's anybody. **Ib.**

The world has joked incessantly for
  over fifty centuries,
And every joke that's possible has long
  ago been made.
His Excellency: The Played-Out
Humorist [1894]

Humor is a drug which it's the fashion
  to abuse. **Ib.**

BRET HARTE [FRANCIS BRETT HARTE]
1836–1902

A smile lit the eyes of the expiring
Kentuck. "Dying!" he repeated. "He's
a-taking me with him — tell the boys
I've got the Luck with me now"; and
the strong man, clinging to the frail
babe as a drowning man is said to cling
to a straw, drifted away into the shadowy river that flows forever to the unknown sea.
The Luck of Roaring Camp [1868]

At the head of the gulch, on one
of the largest pine trees, they found
the deuce of clubs pinned to the bark
with a bowie knife. It bore the following, written in pencil in a firm hand:
"Beneath this tree lies the body of
JOHN OAKHURST, who struck a streak
of bad luck on the 23rd of November,
1850, and handed in his checks on the
7th of December, 1850."
The Outcasts of Poker Flat
[1858]

Which I wish to remark,
  And my language is plain,
That for ways that are dark
  And for tricks that are vain,
The heathen Chinee is peculiar.
Plain Language from Truthful
James [1870], st. 1

Ah Sin was his name. *Ib. st. 2*

With the smile that was childlike and
  bland. *Ib. st. 4*

We are ruined by Chinese cheap
  labor. *Ib. st. 7*

And on that grave where English oak
  and holly
And laurel wreaths entwine,
Deem it not all a too presumptuous
  folly,
This spray of Western pine!
Dickens in Camp [1870], st. 10

I reside at Table Mountain, and my
  name is Truthful James;

I am not up to small deceit, or any
    sinful games.
       The Society Upon the Stanislaus,
                    st. 1

And he smiled a kind of sickly smile,
    and curled up on the floor,
And the subsequent proceedings inter-
    ested him no more.   *Ib. st. 7*

For there be women, fair as she,
Whose verbs and nouns do more
    agree.   *Mrs. Judge Jenkins, st. 19*

Oh, yer's yer good old whiskey,
Drink it down.
    Two Men of Sandy Bar [1876],
                  act IV

One big vice in a man is apt to keep
out a great many smaller ones.   *Ib.*

Give me a man that is capable of a
devotion to anything, rather than a cold,
calculating average of all the virtues!
                         Ib.

JANE ELLICE HOPKINS
1836–1904

Genius is an infinite capacity for taking pains.[1]
    Work Amongst Working Men
                      [1870]

CESARE LOMBROSO
1836–1909

Klopstock was questioned regarding
the meaning of a passage in his poem.
He replied, "God and I both knew
what it meant once; now God alone
knows." [2]
    The Man of Genius, pt. I, ch. 2

The appearance of a single great
genius is more than equivalent to the
birth of a hundred mediocrities.
                      Ib. II, 2

"Lawsuit mania" . . . a continual
craving to go to law against others,
while considering themselves the injured party.   *Ib. III, 3*

[1] See Buffon, p. 423b, and note.
[2] Also attributed to Browning, apropos of his
Sordello.

The ignorant man always adores
what he cannot understand.
        The Man of Genius,
                pt. III, ch. 3

Men in general, but more particularly the insane, love to speak of themselves, and on this theme they even become eloquent.   *Ib. IV, 1*

FITZHUGH LUDLOW
1836–1870

While we wait for the napkin, the soup
    gets cold,
While the bonnet is trimming, the face
    grows old,
When we've matched our buttons, the
    pattern is sold,
And everything comes too late — too
    late.   *Too Late, st. 2*

JOHN BURROUGHS
1837–1921

Serene, I fold my hands and wait,
    Nor care for wind, nor tide, nor sea;
I rave no more 'gainst time or fate,
    For lo! my own shall come to me.
                Waiting, st. 1

I was born with a chronic anxiety
about the weather.
         Is It Going to Rain?

Literature is an investment of genius
which pays dividends to all subsequent
times.   *Literary Fame*

It is always easier to believe than to
deny. Our minds are naturally affirmative.
    *The Light of Day. The Modern
                    Skeptic*

Time does not become sacred to us
until we have lived it.
        The Spell of the Past

Nature teaches more than she
preaches. There are no sermons in
stones. It is easier to get a spark out of
a stone than a moral.
    *Time and Change. The Gospel
                  of Nature*

Life is a struggle, but not a warfare.
    The Summit of the Years

GROVER CLEVELAND
1837–1908

Public officers are the servants and agents of the people, to execute the laws which the people have made.
> *Letter accepting the nomination for Governor of New York [October 1882]*

Your every voter, as surely as your chief magistrate, exercises a public trust.[1]
> *Inaugural Address [March 4, 1885]*

However plenty silver dollars may become, they will not be distributed as gifts among the people.
> *First Annual Message [December 8, 1885]*

The so-called debtor class . . . are not dishonest because they are in debt.
> *Ib.*

After an existence of nearly twenty years of almost innocuous desuetude these laws are brought forth.
> *Message [March 1, 1886]*

When more of the people's sustenance is exacted through the form of taxation than is necessary to meet the just obligations of government and expenses of its economical administration, such exaction becomes ruthless extortion and a violation of the fundamental principles of a free government.
> *Second Annual Message [December 1886]*

It is a condition which confronts us — not a theory.[2]
> *Third Annual Message [December 6, 1887]*

The lessons of paternalism ought to be unlearned and the better lesson taught that while the people should patriotically and cheerfully support their

[1] "Public office is a public trust" was used by the Cleveland administration as its motto. See Matthew Henry, p. 386b; Burke, p. 454b; Jefferson, p. 472b; Clay, p. 538b; and Calhoun, p. 545b.
[2] See Disraeli, p. 611b.

government, its functions do not include the support of the people.
> *Inaugural Address [March 4, 1893]*

I have tried so hard to do the right.
> *Last words*

ADMIRAL GEORGE DEWEY
1837–1917

You may fire when you are ready, Gridley.
> *To the captain of Dewey's flagship at the Battle of Manila Bay [May 1, 1898]*

WILLIAM DEAN HOWELLS
1837–1920

We live, but a world has passed away
With the years that perished to make us men.   *The Mulberries*

Lord, for the erring thought
Not into evil wrought:
Lord, for the wicked will
Betrayed and baffled still:
For the heart from itself kept,
Our thanksgiving accept.
> *A Thanksgiving*

Though I move with leaden feet,
Light itself is not so fleet;
And before you know me gone
Eternity and I are one.   *Time*

He who sleeps in continual noise is wakened by silence.
> *Pordenone, IV*

See how today's achievement is only tomorrow's confusion;
See how possession always cheapens the thing that was precious.   *Ib.*

The wrecks of slavery are fast growing a fungus crop of sentiment.
> *Their Wedding Journey [1872]*

They were Americans, and they knew how to worship a woman.
> *The Lady of the Aroostook [1879]*

The Bostonian who leaves Boston ought to be condemned to perpetual exile.

> *The Rise of Silas Lapham*
> [1885], *ch. 5*

The man of letters must make up his mind that in the United States the fate of a book is in the hands of the women.   *Literature and Life* [1902]

Does it afflict you to find your books wearing out? I mean literally. . . . The mortality of all inanimate things is terrible to me, but that of books most of all.

> *Letter to Charles Eliot Norton*
> [*April 6, 1903*]

I am not sorry for having wrought in common, crude material so much; that is the right American stuff; and perhaps hereafter, when my din is done, if anyone is curious to know what that noise was, it will be found to have proceeded from a small insect which was scraping about on the surface of our life and trying to get into its meaning for the sake of the other insects larger or smaller. That is, such has been my unconscious work; consciously, I was always, as I still am, trying to fashion a piece of literature out of the life next at hand.

> *Ib.* [*April 26, 1903*]

Clemens was sole, incomparable, the Lincoln of our literature.

> *My Mark Twain*

Some people can stay longer in an hour than others can in a week.

> *Attributed*

HORACE PORTER
1837–1921

A mugwump is a person educated beyond his intellect.

> *A slogan of the Cleveland-
> Blaine campaign* [1884]

INNES RANDOLPH
1837–1887

Oh, I'm a good old rebel, that's what I am,

And for this land of freedom, I do not give a damn.
I'm glad I fought agin her, I only wish we'd won,
And I ain't axed any pardon for anything I've done.

> *A Good Old Rebel* [*c. 1870*],
> *st. 1*

I won't be reconstructed, and I don't give a damn.

> *Ib. st. 4*

ALGERNON CHARLES SWINBURNE
1837–1909

Maiden and mistress of the months and stars
Now folded in the flowerless fields of heaven.

> *Atalanta in Calydon* [1865], *l. 1*

When the hounds of spring are on winter's traces,
The mother of months in meadow or plain
Fills the shadows and windy places
With lisp of leaves and ripple of rain;
And the brown bright nightingale amorous
Is half assuaged for Itylus,
For the Thracian ships and the foreign faces,
The tongueless vigil, and all the pain.

> *Ib. chorus, st. 1*

Come with bows bent and with emptying of quivers,
Maiden most perfect, lady of light,
With a noise of winds and many rivers,
With a clamor of waters, and with might;
Bind on thy sandals, O thou most fleet,
Over the splendor and speed of thy feet,
For the faint east quickens, the wan west shivers,
Round the feet of the day and the feet of the night.   *Ib. st. 2*

For winter's rains and ruins are over,
And all the season of snows and sins;

The days dividing lover and lover,
The light that loses, the night that wins;
And time remembered is grief forgotten,
And frosts are slain and flowers begotten,
And in green underwood and cover
Blossom by blossom the spring begins.
Atalanta in Calydon, chorus, st. 4

Before the beginning of years
There came to the making of man
Time, with a gift of tears;
Grief, with a glass that ran;
Pleasure, with pain for leaven;
Summer, with flowers that fell;
Remembrance fallen from heaven,
And madness risen from hell;
Strength without hands to smite;
Love that endures for a breath;
Night, the shadow of light,
And life, the shadow of death.
Ib. chorus, st. 1

Eyesight and speech they wrought
For the veils of the soul therein,
A time for labor and thought,
A time to serve and to sin; [1]
They gave him light in his ways,
And love, and a space for delight,
And beauty and length of days,
And night, and sleep in the night.
His speech is a burning fire;
With his lips he travaileth;
In his heart is a blind desire,
In his eyes foreknowledge of death;
He weaves, and is clothed with derision;
Sows, and he shall not reap;
His life is a watch or a vision
Between a sleep and a sleep.
Ib. st. 3

We have seen thee, O Love, thou art fair; thou art goodly, O Love.
Ib. chorus

For words divide and rend;
But silence is most noble till the end.
Ib.

[1] See *Ecclesiastes* 3:2, p. 27b.

O wise among women, and wisest,
Our Lady of Pain.
Dolores [1866], *st.* 5

Change in a trice
The lilies and languors of virtue
For the raptures and roses of vice.
Ib. st. 9

O splendid and sterile Dolores,
Our Lady of Pain. *Ib.*

Ah beautiful passionate body
That never has ached with a heart!
Ib. st. 11

The delight that consumes the desire,
The desire that outruns the delight.
Ib. st. 14

Despair the twin-born of devotion.
Ib.

I have passed from the outermost portal
To the shrine where a sin is a prayer.
Ib. st. 17

For the crown of our life as it closes
Is darkness, the fruit there of dust;
No thorns go as deep as a rose's,
And love is more cruel than lust.
Time turns the old days to derision,
Our loves into corpses or wives;
And marriage and death and division
Make barren our lives. *Ib. st.* 20

What ailed us, O gods, to desert you
For creeds that refuse and restrain?
Come down and redeem us from virtue,
Our Lady of Pain. *Ib. st.* 35

Lo, this is she that was the world's delight.
Laus Veneris [1866], *st.* 3

Ah, yet would God this flesh of mine might be
Where air might wash and long leaves cover me;
Where tides of grass break into foam of flowers,
Or where the wind's feet shine along the sea. *Ib. st.* 14

O sad kissed mouth, how sorrowful it is! *Ib. st.* 79

To have known love, how bitter a thing
it is.   *Laus Veneris, st. 103*

There will no man do for your sake, I
think,
What I would have done for the least
word said.
I had wrung life dry for your lips to
drink,
Broken it up for your daily bread.
        The Triumph of Time [1866],
                                st. 12

At the door of life, by the gate of breath,
There are worse things waiting for men
than death.   *Ib. st. 20*

I will go back to the great sweet mother,
Mother and lover of men, the sea.
                Ib. st. 33

I shall never be friends again with
roses;
I shall loathe sweet tunes.   *Ib. st. 45*

Marvelous mercies and infinite love.
        Les Noyades [1866], *st. 1*

I am sick of singing; the bays burn deep
and chafe: I am fain
To rest a little from praise and grievous
pleasure and pain.
        *Hymn to Proserpine: After the
        Proclamation in Rome of the
        Christian Faith* [1866]

Thou hast conquered, O pale Galilean; [1]
the world has grown gray from thy
breath;
We have drunken of things Lethean,
and fed on the fullness of death.
Laurel is green for a season, and love is
sweet for a day;
But love grows bitter with treason, and
laurel outlives not May.
Sleep, shall we sleep after all? for the
world is not sweet in the end;
For the old faiths loosen and fall, the
new years ruin and rend.   *Ib.*

I shall die as my fathers died, and sleep
as they sleep; even so.
For the glass of the years is brittle
wherein we gaze for a span.   *Ib.*

[1] See Julian, p. 144b.

For there is no God found stronger
than death; and death is a sleep.
                Hymn to Proserpine

If you loved me ever so little,
I could bear the bonds that gall,
I could dream the bonds were brittle;
You do not love me at all.
        Satia Te Sanguine [1866], *st. 1*

While he lives let a man be glad,
For none hath joy of his death.
        A Lamentation [1866]. *I, st. 4*

If love were what the rose is,
And I were like the leaf,
Our lives would grow together
In sad or singing weather.
        A Match [1866], *st. 1*

If you were April's lady,
And I were lord in May.   *Ib. st. 5*

If you were queen of pleasure,
And I were king of pain,
We'd hunt down love together,
Pluck out his flying feather,
And teach his feet a measure,
And find his mouth a rein.
                Ib. st. 6

For in the time we know not of
Did fate begin
Weaving the web of days that wove
Your doom, Faustine.
        Faustine [1866], *st. 24*

Take hand and part with laughter;
Touch lips and part with tears;
Once more and no more after,
Whatever comes with years.
        Rococo [1866], *st. 1*

Forget that I remember,
And dream that I forget.   *Ib. st. 2*

The burden of long living. Thou shalt
fear
Waking, and sleeping mourn upon thy
bed;
And say at night "Would God the day
were here,"
And say at dawn "Would God the day
were dead." [1]
        A Ballad of Burdens [1866], *st. 4*

[1] See *Deuteronomy 28:67*, p. 10b.

For life is sweet, but after life is death.
This is the end of every man's desire.
    A Ballad of Burdens. L'Envoy

I shall remember while the light lives
    yet
And in the nighttime I shall not for-
    get.   *Erotion* [1866]

Here, where the world is quiet;
  Here, where all trouble seems
Dead winds' and spent waves' riot
  In doubtful dreams of dreams.
    The Garden of Proserpine
    [1866], *st. 1*

I am tired of tears and laughter,
  And men that laugh and weep;
Of what may come hereafter
  For men that sow and reap:
I am weary of days and hours,
Blown buds of barren flowers,
Desires and dreams and powers
  And everything but sleep.
    Ib. st. 2

We are not sure of sorrow,
  And joy was never sure.   *Ib. st. 10*

From too much love of living,
  From hope and fear set free,
We thank with brief thanksgiving
  Whatever gods may be
That no life lives forever;
That dead men rise up never;
That even the weariest river
  Winds somewhere safe to sea.[1]
    Ib. st. 11

Ah that such sweet things should be
  fleet,
Such fleet things sweet!
    Félise [1866], *st. 22*

Those eyes the greenest of things blue,
The bluest of things gray.   *Ib. st. 24*

I remember the way we parted,
  The day and the way we met;
You hoped we were both broken-
  hearted
  And knew we should both forget.
    An Interlude [1866], *st. 11*

[1] No matter how long the river, the river will
reach the sea. — EUGENE FITCH WARE ("IRON-
QUILL") [1841–1911], *The Blizzard*

And the best and the worst of this is
  That neither is most to blame,
If you have forgotten my kisses
  And I have forgotten your name.
    An Interlude, st. 14

And through the trumpet of a child of
  Rome
Rang the pure music of the flutes of
  Greece.
    Song for the Centenary of
    Walter Savage Landor [1866],
    st. 17

I am that which began;
  Out of me the years roll;
Out of me God and man;
  I am equal and whole;
God changes, and man, and the form
  of them bodily; I am the soul.
    Hertha [1871], *st. 1*

Before ever land was,
  Before ever the sea,
Or soft hair of the grass,
  Or fair limbs of the tree,
Or the flesh-colored fruit of my
  branches, I was, and thy soul was
  in me.   *Ib. st. 2*

A creed is a rod,
  And a crown is of night;
But this thing is God,
  To be man with thy might,
To grow straight in the strength of thy
  spirit, and to live out thy life as
  the light.   *Ib. st. 15*

In the gray beginning of years, in the
  twilight of things that began,
The word of the earth in the ears of
  the world, was it God? was it
  man?   *Hymn of Man* [1871]

Ask nothing more of me, sweet,
All I can give you I give;
Heart of my heart, were it more,
More would be laid at your feet:
Love that should help you to live,
Song that should spur you to soar.
    The Oblation [1871], *st. 1*

It is long since Mr. Carlyle expressed
his opinion that if any poet or other
literary creature could really be "killed

off by one critique" or many, the sooner he was so dispatched the better; a sentiment in which I for one humbly but heartily concur.

Under the Microscope [1872]

A blatant Bassarid of Boston, a rampant Maenad of Massachusetts.[1]

Ib.

To wipe off the froth of falsehood from the foaming lips of inebriated virtue, when fresh from the sexless orgies of morality and reeling from the delirious riot of religion, may doubtless be a charitable office. *Ib.*

The tadpole poet will never grow into anything bigger than a frog; not though in that stage of development he should puff and blow himself till he bursts with windy adulation at the heels of the laureled ox. *Ib.*

Poor splendid wings so frayed and soiled and torn!

A Ballad of François Villon [1878], *st. 3*

Villon, our sad bad glad mad brother's name.[2] *Ib. refrain*

In a coign of the cliff between lowland and highland,
At the sea-down's edge between windward and lee,
Walled round with rocks as an inland island,
The ghost of a garden fronts the sea.

A Forsaken Garden [1878], *st. 1*

Sleep; and if life was bitter to thee, pardon,
If sweet, give thanks; thou hast no more to live;
And to give thanks is good, and to forgive.

Ave atque Vale: In Memory of Charles Baudelaire [1878], *st. 17*

[1] Harriet Beecher Stowe, whose accusations against Byron in "The True Story of Lady Byron's Life" [*Atlantic Monthly*, September 1869] and in *Lady Byron Vindicated* [1870] aroused strong protests in England.
[2] See Browning, p. 666a.

Body and spirit are twins: God only knows which is which.

The Higher Pantheism in a Nutshell [1880], *st. 7*

God, whom we see not, is: and God, who is not, we see:
Fiddle, we know, is diddle: and diddle, we take it, is dee. *Ib. st. 12*

HENRY BROOKS ADAMS
1838–1918

Accident counts for much in companionship as in marriage.

The Education of Henry Adams [1907], *ch. 4*

Women have, commonly, a very positive moral sense; that which they will, is right; that which they reject, is wrong; and their will, in most cases, ends by settling the moral. *Ib. 6*

All experience is an arch, to build upon.[1] *Ib.*

Only on the edge of the grave can man conclude anything. *Ib.*

Although the Senate is much given to admiring in its members a superiority less obvious or quite invisible to outsiders, one Senator seldom proclaims his own inferiority to another, and still more seldom likes to be told of it.
Ib. 7

Friends are born, not made. *Ib.*

A friend in power is a friend lost.[2]
Ib.

The effect of power and publicity on all men is the aggravation of self, a sort of tumor that ends by killing the victim's sympathies. *Ib. 10*

Young men have a passion for regarding their elders as senile. *Ib. 11*

Knowledge of human nature is the beginning and end of political education. *Ib. 12*

These questions of taste, of feeling, of inheritance, need no settlement.

[1] See Tennyson, p. 646b.
[2] See *ch. 28*, p. 777b.

Everyone carries his own inch-rule of taste, and amuses himself by applying it, triumphantly, wherever he travels.
The Education of Henry Adams, ch. 12

Intimates are predestined. *Ib. 13*

Chaos often breeds life, when order breeds habit. *Ib.*

At best, the renewal of broken relations is a nervous matter. *Ib.*

Sumner's[1] mind had reached the calm of water which receives and reflects images without absorbing them; it contained nothing but itself. *Ib.*

The difference is slight, to the influence of an author, whether he is read by five hundred readers, or by five hundred thousand; if he can select the five hundred, he reaches the five hundred thousand. *Ib. 17*

The newspaperman is, more than most men, a double personality; and his person feels best satisfied in its double instincts when writing in one sense and thinking in another. *Ib.*

A teacher affects eternity; he can never tell where his influence stops.
Ib. 20

One friend in a lifetime is much; two are many; three are hardly possible. Friendship needs a certain parallelism of life, a community of thought, a rivalry of aim. *Ib.*

What one knows is, in youth, of little moment; they know enough who know how to learn. *Ib. 21*

He had often noticed that six months' oblivion amounts to newspaper death, and that resurrection is rare. Nothing is easier, if a man wants it, than rest, profound as the grave.
Ib. 22

Morality is a private and costly luxury. *Ib.*

Practical politics consists in ignoring facts. *Ib.*

[1] Charles Sumner [1811–1874].

Nothing in education is so astonishing as the amount of ignorance it accumulates in the form of inert facts.
The Education of Henry Adams, ch. 25

Power when wielded by abnormal energy is the most serious of facts.
Ib. 28

Those who seek education in the paths of duty are always deceived by the illusion that power in the hands of friends is an advantage to them.[1] *Ib.*

A certain chronic irritability — a sort of Bostonitis — which, in its primitive Puritan forms, seemed due to knowing too much of his neighbors and thinking too much of himself. *Ib.*

Modern politics is, at bottom, a struggle not of men but of forces.
Ib.

We combat obstacles in order to get repose, and, when got, the repose is insupportable. *Ib. 29*

Simplicity is the most deceitful mistress that ever betrayed man. *Ib. 30*

No one means all he says, and yet very few say all they mean, for words are slippery and thought is viscous.
Ib. 31

Even in America, the Indian summer of life should be a little sunny and a little sad, like the season, and infinite in wealth and depth of tone — but never hustled. *Ib. 35*

PHILIP PAUL BLISS
1838–1876

Hold the fort, for I am coming![2]
Gospel Songs [1874], Hold the Fort, refrain

[1] See *ch. 7*, p. 776b.
[2] Popular version of what General William Tecumseh Sherman signaled to General John Murray Corse from Kenesaw Mountain when Corse was attacked at Allatoona Pass [October 5, 1864]: "Hold out; relief is coming." See Sherman, p. 705a.

JOHN WILKES BOOTH
1838–1865

Sic semper tyrannis! [1] The South is avenged!

> *His words after shooting President Lincoln [April 14, 1865]*

JAMES BRYCE
1838–1922

Law will never be strong or respected unless it has the sentiment of the people behind it. If the people of a state make bad laws, they will suffer for it. They will be the first to suffer. Suffering, and nothing else, will implant that sentiment of responsibility which is the first step to reform.

> *The American Commonwealth [1888], vol. I, p. 352*

To the vast majority of mankind nothing is more agreeable than to escape the need for mental exertion. . . . To most people nothing is more troublesome than the effort of thinking.[2]

> *Studies in History and Jurisprudence [1901]. Obedience*

The greatest liberty that man has taken with Nature.[3]

> *South America [1912]*

Medicine, the only profession that labors incessantly to destroy the reason for its own existence.

> *Address at dinner for General W. C. Gorgas [March 23, 1914]*

GEORGE COOPER
1838–1927

Sweet Genevieve,
The days may come, the days may go,
But still the hands of memory weave
The blissful dreams of long ago.

> *Sweet Genevieve [c. 1877]*

---

[1] Thus always to tyrants. — *Motto of Virginia*
[2] See R. B. Sheridan, p. 481b, and note.
[3] The Panama Canal.

JOHN MILTON HAY
1838–1905

A keerless man in his talk was Jim,
And an awkward hand in a row,
He never flunked, and he never lied —
I reckon he never knowed how.

> *Jim Bludso, st. 2*

I'll hold her nozzle agin the bank
Till the last galoot's ashore.

> *Ib. 5*

And they all had trust in his cussedness,
And knowed he would keep his word.

> *Ib. 6*

He seen his duty, a dead-sure thing —
And went for it thar and then;
And Christ ain't a-going to be too hard
On a man that died for men.

> *Ib. 7*

I don't go much on religion,
I never ain't had no show;
But I've got a middlin' tight grip, sir,
On the handful o' things I know.
I don't pan out on the prophets
And free will, and that sort of thing —
But I b'lieve in God and the angels
Ever sence one night last spring.

> *Little Breeches, st. 1*

And I think that saving a little child,
And fotching him to his own,
Is a derned sight better business
Than loafing around The Throne.

> *Ib. last stanza*

There are three species of creatures who when they seem coming are going,
When they seem going they come:
Diplomats, women, and crabs.

> *Distichs, no. 2*

Who would succeed in the world should be wise in the use of his pronouns.
Utter the You twenty times, where you once utter the I.

> *Ib. 13*

True luck consists not in holding the best of the cards at the table:

Luckiest he who knows just when to rise and go home.

> *Distichs, no. 15*

The open door.

> *To the cabinet regarding completion of negotiations for the "open door" in China [January 2, 1900]*

GEORGE WASHINGTON JOHNSON
1838–1917

And now we are aged and gray, Maggie,
The trials of life nearly done,
Let us sing of the days that are gone, Maggie,
When you and I were young.

> *When You and I Were Young, Maggie [1866], refrain*

WILLIAM EDWARD HARTPOLE LECKY
1838–1903

Offspring of an idle hour,
Whence has come thy lasting power?

> *On an old song*

The stately ship is seen no more,
The fragile skiff attains the shore;
And while the great and wise decay,
And all their trophies pass away,
Some sudden thought, some careless rhyme,
Still floats above the wrecks of Time.

> *Ib.*

ERNST MACH
1838–1916

Physics is experience, arranged in economical order.

> *The Economical Nature of Physical Inquiry [1882]*

Intelligible as it is . . . that the efforts of thinkers have always been bent upon the "reduction of all physical processes to the motions of atoms," it must yet be affirmed that this is a chimerical ideal. This ideal has often

played an effective part in popular lectures, but in the workshop of the serious inquirer it has discharged scarcely the least function.

> *On the Principle of the Conservation of Energy [1894]*

JOHN, VISCOUNT MORLEY OF BLACKBURN
1838–1923

Evolution is not a force but a process; not a cause but a law.

> *On Compromise [1874]*

Those who would treat politics and morality apart will never understand the one or the other.

> *Rousseau [1876]*

You cannot demonstrate an emotion or prove an aspiration.   *Ib.*

It is not enough to do good; one must do it the right way.   *Ib.*

You have not converted a man because you have silenced him.   *Ib.*

A great interpreter of life ought not himself to need interpretation.

> *Emerson [1884]*

The great business of life is to be, to do, to do without, and to depart.

> *Address on Aphorisms [1887]*

Simplicity of character is no hindrance to subtlety of intellect.

> *Life of Gladstone [1903]*

No man can climb out beyond the limitations of his own character.

> *Critical Miscellanies [1908], Robespierre*

There are some books which cannot be adequately reviewed for twenty or thirty years after they come out.

> *Recollections [1917], vol. I, bk. 2, ch. 8*

The proper memory for a politician is one that knows what to remember and what to forget.   *Ib. II, 4, 2*

In my creed, waste of public money is like the sin against the Holy Ghost.

> *Ib. 5, 3*

Success depends on three things: who says it, what he says, how he says it; and of these three things, what he says is the least important.

Recollections, vol. I, bk. 5, ch. 4

Excess of severity is not the path to order. On the contrary, it is the path to the bomb.   *Ib.*

MARGARET ELIZABETH SANGSTER
1838–1912

Never yet was a springtime,
  Late though lingered the snow,
That the sap stirred not at the whisper
  Of the southwind, sweet and low;
Never yet was a springtime
  When the buds forgot to blow.
    Awakening

PHILIPPE AUGUSTE VILLIERS DE L'ISLE-ADAM
1838–1889

Living? We'll leave that to the servants.[1]   *Axel* [1890]

I have thought too much to stoop to action.   *Ib.*

GEORGE LEYBOURNE
d. 1884

He flies through the air with the greatest of ease,
This daring young man on the flying trapeze;
His figure is handsome, all girls he can please,
And my love he purloined her away!
    The Man on the Flying Trapeze
    [1860]

PAUL CÉZANNE
1839–1906

Treat nature in terms of the cylinder, the sphere, the cone, all in perspective.
    From EMILE BERNARD,
    Paul Cézanne [1925]

[1] Vivre? Les serviteurs feront cela pour nous.

There's a minute of life passing! Paint it in its reality and forget everything to do that! Become it itself . . . give the image of what we actually see, forgetting everything that has appeared before us.

    From JOACHIM GASQUET,
    Paul Cézanne [1926]

FRANCIS PHARCELLUS CHURCH
1839–1906

Virginia, your little friends are wrong. They have been affected by the skepticism of a skeptical age. They do not believe except they see. They think that nothing can be which is not comprehensible by their little minds. All minds, Virginia, whether they be men's or children's, are little. In this great universe of ours man is a mere insect, an ant, in his intellect, as compared with the boundless world about him, as measured by the intelligence capable of grasping the whole of truth and knowledge.

    Editorial: Is There a
    Santa Claus? [1]

Not believe in Santa Claus? You might as well not believe in fairies. . . . No Santa Claus! Thank God, he lives, and he lives forever. A thousand years from now, Virginia, nay, ten times ten thousand years from now, he will continue to make glad the heart of childhood.   *Ib.*

HENRY GEORGE
1839–1897

So long as all the increased wealth which modern progress brings goes but to build up great fortunes, to increase luxury and make sharper the contrast between the House of Have and the House of Want, progress is not real and cannot be permanent.

    Progress and Poverty [1879].
    Introductory: The Problem

[1] First published in the *New York Sun* [September 21, 1897] in reply to an inquiry from Virginia O'Hanlon.

WALTER PATER
1839–1894

Every intellectual product must be judged from the point of view of the age and the people in which it was produced.

The Renaissance [1873].
Mirandola

That sweet look of devotion which men have never been able altogether to love, and which still makes the born saint an object almost of suspicion to his earthly brethren. *Ib. Botticelli*

Hers is the head upon which all "the ends of the world are come," and the eyelids are a little weary. It is a beauty wrought out from within upon the flesh, the deposit, little cell by cell, of strange thoughts and fantastic reveries and exquisite passions. Set it for a moment beside one of those white Greek goddesses or beautiful women of antiquity, and how would they be troubled by this beauty, into which the soul with all its maladies has passed?

Ib. Leonardo de Vinci
[Mona Lisa]

She is older than the rocks among which she sits; like the vampire, she has been dead many times, and learned the secrets of the grave; and has been a diver in deep seas, and keeps their fallen day about her; and trafficked for strange webs with Eastern merchants: and as Leda, was the mother of Helen of Troy, and, as Saint Anne, the mother of Mary; and all this has been to her but as the sound of lyres and flutes, and lives only in the delicacy with which it has molded the changing lineaments, and tinged the eyelids and the hands. *Ib.*

All art constantly aspires towards the condition of music.

Ib. The School of Giorgione

To burn always with this hard, gem-like flame, to maintain this ecstasy, is success in life. *Ib. Conclusion*

What we have to do is to be forever curiously testing new opinions and courting new impressions.

The Renaissance. Conclusion

Art comes to you proposing frankly to give nothing but the highest quality to your moments as they pass. *Ib.*

A book, like a person, has its fortunes with one; is lucky or unlucky in the precise moment of its falling in our way, and often by some happy accident counts with us for something more than its independent value.

Marius the Epicurean [1885],
ch. 6

To know when one's self is interested, is the first condition of interesting other people. *Ib.*

We need some imaginative stimulus, some not impossible ideal such as may shape vague hope, and transform it into effective desire, to carry us year after year, without disgust, through the routine work which is so large a part of life. *Ib. 25*

JAMES RYDER RANDALL
1839–1908

Hark to an exiled son's appeal,
  Maryland, my Maryland!
My Mother State to thee I kneel.
  Maryland, My Maryland [1861],
  st. 2

WILFRID SCAWEN BLUNT
1840–1922

He who has once been happy is for
  aye
Out of destruction's reach.
  With Esther

Ay, this is the famed rock, which Hercules
And Goth and Moor bequeathed us. At
  this door
England stands sentry. *Gibraltar*

HENRY BURTON
1840–1930

Have you had a kindness shown?
Pass it on.　　　　*Pass It On, st. 1*

TIMOTHY J. CAMPBELL
1840–1904

What's the Constitution between
friends? [1]　　　*Attributed [c. 1885]*

HENRY AUSTIN DOBSON
1840–1921

Once at the Angelus
　(Ere I was dead),
Angels all glorious
　Came to my bed.
　　　"Good Night, Babette!" st. 1

Time goes, you say? Ah no!
Alas, Time stays, *we* go.
　　　The Paradox of Time, st. 1

The ladies of St. James's!
　They're painted to the eyes;
Their white it stays forever,
　Their red it never dies:
But Phyllida, my Phyllida!
　Her color comes and goes;
It trembles to a lily —
　It wavers to a rose.
　　　The Ladies of St. James's, st. 4

Ah, would but one might lay his lance
　in rest,
And charge in earnest — were it but a
　mill!　　　*Don Quixote*

Form is the cage and sense the bird.
The poet twirls them in his mind,
And wins the trick with both com-
　bined.　　　*The Toyman*

He praised the thing he understood;
'Twere well if every critic would.
　　The 'Squire at Vauxhall. Moral 2

I intended an ode,
　And it turned to a sonnet.
It began à la mode,
I intended an ode;

---

[1] Reported comment to President Cleveland,
who refused to support a bill on the grounds
that it was unconstitutional.

But Rose crossed the road
　In her latest new bonnet;
I intended an ode;
　And it turned to a sonnet.
　　　　Urceus Exit

All passes. Art alone
　Enduring stays to us;
The bust outlasts the throne —
　The coin, Tiberius.[1]
　　　　Ars Victrix, st. 8

Fame is a food that dead men eat —
I have no stomach for such meat.
　　　*Fame Is a Food That Dead
　　　　Men Eat, st. 1*

THOMAS HARDY
1840–1928

These purblind Doomsters had as
　readily strown
Blisses about my pilgrimage as pain.
　　　　Hap [1866]

When I set out for Lyonnesse,
　A hundred miles away,
　The rime was on the spray,
And starlight lit my lonesomeness.
　　*When I Set Out for Lyonnesse
　　　[1870], st. 1*

Good, but not religious-good.
　　*Under the Greenwood Tree
　　　[1872], ch. 2*

The kingly brilliance of Sirius pierced
the eye with a steely glitter, the star
called Capella was yellow, Aldebaran
and Betelgueux shone with a fiery red.
To persons standing alone on a hill during a clear midnight such as this, the
roll of the world eastward is almost a
palpable movement.
　　*Far from the Madding Crowd
　　　[1874], ch. 2*

Like the British Constitution, she
owes her success in practice to her inconsistencies in principle.
　　The Hand of Ethelberta [1876]

A lover without indiscretion is no
lover at all.　　　　*Ib.*

---

[1] See Théophile Gautier, p. 658a.

In fact, precisely at this transitional point of its nightly roll into darkness the great and particular glory of the Egdon waste began, and nobody could be said to understand the heath who had not been there at such a time. It could best be felt when it could not clearly be seen.

> *The Return of the Native*
> [1878], *ch. 1*

The place became full of a watchful intentness now; for when other things sank brooding to sleep the heath appeared slowly to awake and listen.

> *Ib.*

The great inviolate place had an ancient permanence which the sea cannot claim. Who can say of a particular sea that it is old? Distilled by the sun, kneaded by the moon, it is renewed in a year, in a day, or in an hour. The sea changed, the fields changed, the rivers, the villages, and the people changed, yet Egdon remained. *Ib.*

That cold accretion called the world, which, so terrible in the mass, is so unformidable, even pitiable, in its units.

> *Tess of the D'Urbervilles* [1891], *ch. 13*

That shabby corner of God's allotment where He lets the nettles grow, and where all unbaptized infants, notorious drunkards, suicides, and others of the conjecturally damned are laid. *Ib. 14*

The chronic melancholy which is taking hold of the civilized races with the decline of belief in a beneficent power. *Ib. 18*

The debatable land between predilection and love. *Ib. 20*

Patience, that blending of moral courage with physical timidity. *Ib. 43*

"Justice" was done, and the President of the Immortals (in Aeschylean phrase) had ended his sport with Tess. *Ib. 59*

William Dewy, Tranter Reuben, Farmer Ledlow late at plow, Robert's kin, and John's and Ned's, And the Squire, and Lady Susan, lie in Mellstock churchyard now! [1]

> *Friends Beyond* [1898], *st. 1*

I leant upon a coppice gate When Frost was specter-gray, And Winter's dregs made desolate The weakening eye of day.

> *The Darkling Thrush* [1900], *st. 1*

An aged thrush, frail, gaunt, and small, In blast-beruffled plume.   *Ib. st. 3*

So little cause for carolings Of such ecstatic sound Was written on terrestrial things Afar or nigh around, That I could think there trembled through His happy good-night air Some blessed hope, whereof he knew And I was unaware.   *Ib. st. 4*

Yes; quaint and curious war is! You shoot a fellow down You'd treat if met where any bar is, Or help to half-a-crown.

> *The Man He Killed* [1902], *st. 5*

What of the Immanent Will and its designs? It works unconsciously as heretofore, External artistries in circumstance.

> *The Dynasts* [1904–1908], *pt. I,*
> *forescene*

A local cult called Christianity.

> *Ib. Spirit of the Years, sc. vi*

Ere systemed suns were globed and lit The slaughters of the race were writ.

> *Ib. II, v, semichorus*

My argument is that War makes rattling good history; but Peace is poor reading.   *Ib. Spirit Sinister*

[1] From the aisles each window smiles on grave and grass and yew-tree bough —
While Tranter Reuben, Gordon Selfridge, Edna Best and Thomas Hardy lie in Mellstock Churchyard now.
JOHN BETJEMAN, *Dorset* [1937], *st. 3*

A star looks down at me,
And says: "Here I and you
Stand, each in our degree:
What do you mean to do?"
Waiting Both, st. 1

We two kept house, the Past and I,
  The Past and I;
I tended while it hovered nigh,
Leaving me never alone.
The Ghost of the Past, st. 1

I seem but a dead man held on end
To sink down soon. . . . O you could
  not know
That such swift fleeing
No soul foreseeing —
Not even I — would undo me so!
The Going [1912], *st.* 6

Woman much missed, how you call to
  me, call to me,
Saying that now you are not as you
  were
When you had changed from the one
  who was all to me,
But as at first, when our day was fair.
The Voice [1912], *st* 1

What of the faith and fire within us
  Men who march away
  Ere the barn cocks say
  Night is growing gray,
Leaving all that here can win us?
Men Who March Away
[1914], *st.* 1

That night your great guns, unawares,
Shook all our coffins as we lay,
And broke the chancel window-
  squares,
We thought it was the Judgment Day.
Channel Firing [1914], *st.* 1

Only a man harrowing clods
In a slow silent walk
With an old horse that stumbles and
  nods
Half asleep as they stalk.

Only thin smoke without flame
From the heaps of couch grass;
Yet this will go onward the same
Though dynasties pass.

Yonder a maid and her wight
Come whispering by;
War's annals will cloud into night
Ere their story die.
*In Time of "The Breaking of
Nations"* [1915]

When the Present has latched its
  postern behind my tremulous
  stay,
And the May month flaps its glad green
  leaves like wings,
Delicate-filmed as new-spun silk, will
  the neighbors say,
"He was a man who used to notice
  such things"? *Afterwards, st.* 1

Ah, no; the years O!
Down their chiseled names the rain-
  drop plows.
During Wind and Rain, st. 4

This is the weather the shepherd shuns,
  And so do I;
When beeches drip in browns and
  duns,
  And thresh, and ply;
And hill-hid tides throb, throe on
  throe,
And meadow rivulets overflow,
And drops on gate bars hang in a row,
And rooks in families homeward go,
  And so do I. *Weathers* [1922], *st.* 2

ROSSITER JOHNSON
1840–1931

O for a lodge in a garden of cucum-
  bers! [1]
O for an iceberg or two at control!
O for a vale which at midday the dew
  cumbers!
O for a pleasure trip up to the Pole!
Ninety-nine in the Shade, st. 1

ALFRED THAYER
MAHAN
1840–1914

The world has never seen a more impressive demonstration of the influence

[1] See *Isaiah 1:8*, p. 30a.

of sea power upon its history. Those far distant, storm-beaten ships, upon which the Grand Army never looked, stood between it and the dominion of the world.[1]

> *The Influence of Sea Power Upon the French Revolution and Empire, 1793–1812* [1892], *vol. II, p. 118*

Whether they will or no, Americans must begin to look outward.

> *The Interest of America in Sea Power* [1897]

ROSSITER WORTHINGTON RAYMOND
1840–1918

Life is eternal; and love is immortal; and death is only a horizon; and a horizon is nothing save the limit of our sight.　*A Commendatory Prayer*

WILLIAM GRAHAM SUMNER
1840–1910

The Forgotten Man[2] . . . delving away in patient industry, supporting his family, paying his taxes, casting his vote, supporting the church and the school . . . but he is the only one for whom there is no provision in the great scramble and the big divide. Such is the Forgotten Man. He works, he votes, generally he prays — but his chief business in life is to pay. . . . Who and

---

[1] Apart from the accidents of weather and the tides and currents, about which he admits he could not obtain trustworthy information, Julius Caesar saw no difficulty in invading the Island. There was not then that far-off line of storm-beaten ships which about two thousand years later stood between the great Corsican conqueror and the dominion of the world. — SIR WINSTON S. CHURCHILL, *A History of the English-Speaking Peoples. The Birth of Britain* [1956], *p. 5*

Also quoted by Churchill in the same work under *The Age of Revolution, p. 300.*

See Themistocles, p. 78a.

[2] See Franklin D. Roosevelt, p. 970b.

where is the Forgotten Man in this case, who will have to pay for it all?

> *Speech: The Forgotten Man* [1883]

JOHN ADDINGTON SYMONDS
1840–1893

No seed shall perish which the soul hath sown.

> *Sonnet: Versöhnung, A Belief*

Gods fade; but God abides and in man's heart
Speaks with the clear unconquerable cry
Of energies and hopes that cannot die.

> *Sonnet: On the Sacro Monte*

She smiled, and the shadows departed;
　She shone, and the snows were rain;
And he who was frozen-hearted
　Bloomed up into love again.

> *Eyebright*

These things shall be — a loftier race
Than e'er the world hath known shall rise
With flame of freedom in their souls,
And light of knowledge in their eyes.

> *The Days That Are to Be*

HENRY WATTERSON
1840–1921

Things have come to a helluva pass
When a man can't cudgel his own jackass.

> *Reply when rebuked for criticizing the Governor of Kentucky*

ELIZABETH WORDSWORTH
1840–1932

If all the good people were clever,
　And all clever people were good,
The world would be nicer than ever
　We thought that it possibly could.

> *The Clever and the Good* [1890]

ÉMILE ZOLA
1840–1902

I am little concerned with beauty or perfection. I don't care for the great centuries. All I care about is life, struggle, intensity. I am at ease in my generation.
Mes Haines [1866]

My own art is a negation of society, an affirmation of the individual, outside all rules and demands of society.
Ib.

Truth is on the march and nothing can stop it.
Article in Le Figaro [November 25, 1897]

J'accuse.
Title of letter to the President of the République, L'Aurore [January 13, 1898]

JOHN WILSON[1]
d. 1889

Oh for a book and a shady nook, either in door or out.
For a catalogue of secondhand books

ROBERT BUCHANAN
1841–1901

The Fleshly School of Poetry.
Title of article [1871]

The sweet post-prandial cigar.
De Berny

GEORGES CLEMENCEAU
1841–1929

War is much too serious a matter to be entrusted to the military.[2]
From G. SUAREZ, Clemenceau [1886]

The good Lord had only ten.
In reference to Wilson's Fourteen Points[3]

[1] A London bookseller, friend of Austin Dobson.
[2] La guerre! c'est une chose trop grave pour la confier à des militaires.
[3] See Wilson, p. 842b.

America is the only nation in history which miraculously has gone directly from barbarism to degeneration without the usual interval of civilization.
Attributed

There is nothing harder for the human spirit to bear than being cold-shouldered.
Quoted by CHARLES DE GAULLE, *Le Fil de l' Epée [1932], ch. 2*

OLIVER WENDELL HOLMES, JR.
1841–1935

The life of the law has not been logic: it has been experience.
The Common Law [1881]

The law embodies the story of a nation's development through many centuries, and it cannot be dealt with as if it contained only the axioms and corollaries of a book of mathematics. *Ib.*

I think that, as life is action and passion, it is required of a man that he should share the passion and action of his time at peril of being judged not to have lived.
Memorial Day Address [1884]

Through our great good fortune, in our youth our hearts were touched with fire. *Ib.*

The Law, wherein, as in a magic mirror, we see reflected not only our own lives, but the lives of all men that have been! When I think on this majestic theme, my eyes dazzle.[1]
To the Suffolk Bar Association [1885]

I say to you in all sadness of conviction, that to think great thoughts you must be heroes as well as idealists.
The Profession of the Law [1886]

Thus only can you gain the secret isolated joy of the thinker, who knows that, a hundred years after he is dead and forgotten, men who never heard of

[1] See John Webster, p. 315a.

him will be moving to the measure of his thought — the subtle rapture of a postponed power, which the world knows not because it has no external trappings, but which to his prophetic vision is more real than that which commands an army.

The Profession of the Law

The prophecies of what the courts will do in fact, and nothing more pretentious, are what I mean by the law.

The Path of the Law [1897]

Certainty generally is illusion, and repose is not the destiny of man. *Ib.*

The remoter and more general aspects of the law are those which give it universal interest. It is through them that you not only become a great master in your calling, but connect your subject with the universe and catch an echo of the infinite, a glimpse of its unfathomable process, a hint of the universal law. *Ib.*

The rule of joy and the law of duty seem to me all one.

Speech at Bar Association Dinner, Boston [1900]

Life is an end in itself, and the only question as to whether it is worth living is whether you have enough of it.[1] *Ib.*

A great man represents a great ganglion in the nerves of society, or, to vary the figure, a strategic point in the campaign of history, and part of his greatness consists in his being *there*.

John Marshall [1901]

Taxes are what we pay for civilized society.

Compañía de Tabacos v. Collector, 275 U.S. 87, 100 [1904]

Great cases like hard cases make bad law.

Northern Securities Co. v. United States, 193 U.S. 197, 400 [1904]

[1] See William James, p. 794a.

The Fourteenth Amendment does not enact Mr. Herbert Spencer's *Social Statics*.

Lochner v. New York, 198 U.S. 45, 75 [1905]

General propositions do not decide concrete cases. The decision will depend on a judgment or intuition more subtle than any articulate major premise. *Ib.* 78

The great act of faith is when man decides that he is not God.

Letter to William James [1907]

Life is painting a picture, not doing a sum.

The Class of '61 [*Speeches,* 1913]

I learned in the regiment and in the class the conclusion, at least, of what I think the best service that we can do for our country and for ourselves: To see so far as one may, and to feel the great forces that are behind every detail . . . to hammer out as compact and solid a piece of work as one can, to try to make it first rate, and to leave it unadvertised. *Ib.*

The only prize much cared for by the powerful is power. The prize of the general is not a bigger tent, but command. *Law and the Court* [1913]

Judges are apt to be naïf, simpleminded men, and they need something of Mephistopheles. We too need education in the obvious — to learn to transcend our own convictions and to leave room for much that we hold dear to be done away with short of revolution by the orderly change of law. *Ib.*

I do not think the United States would come to an end if we lost our power to declare an Act of Congress void. I do think the Union would be imperiled if we could not make that declaration as to the laws of the several states. *Ib.*

The attacks upon the Court are merely an expression of the unrest that seems to wonder vaguely whether law

and order pay. When the ignorant are taught to doubt, they do not know what they safely may believe.
Law and the Court

I do not think we need trouble ourselves with the thought that my view depends upon differences of degree. The whole law does so as soon as it is civilized.
LeRoy Fibre Co. v. C., M. & St. P. Ry., 232 U.S. 340, 354 [1914]

I recognize without hesitation that judges do and must legislate, but they can do so only interstitially; they are confined from molar to molecular motions.
Southern Pacific Co. v. Jensen, 244 U.S. 205, 221, [1917]

The common law is not a brooding omnipresence in the sky but the articulate voice of some sovereign or quasi-sovereign that can be identified.
Ib. 222

Certitude is not the test of certainty.   *Natural Law [1918]*

The most stringent protection of free speech would not protect a man in falsely shouting fire in a theater and causing a panic. . . . The question in every case is whether the words used are used in such circumstances and are of such a nature as to create a clear and present danger that they will bring about the substantive evils that Congress has a right to prevent.
Schenck v. United States, 249 U.S. 47 [1919]

When men have realized that time has upset many fighting faiths, they may come to believe even more than they believe the very foundations of their own conduct that the ultimate good desired is better reached by free trade in ideas — that the best test of truth is the power of the thought to get itself accepted in the competition of the market, and that truth is the only ground upon which their wishes safely

can be carried out. That at any rate is the theory of our Constitution. It is an experiment, as all life is an experiment.
Abrams v. United States, 250 U.S. 616, 630 [1919]

I dare say that I have worked off my fundamental formula on you that the chief end of man is to frame general propositions and that no general proposition is worth a damn.
Letter to Sir Frederick Pollock [1920]

Upon this point a page of history is worth a volume of logic.
New York Trust Co. v. Eisner, 256 U.S. 345, 349 [1921]

It is said that this manifesto is more than a theory, that it was an incitement. Every idea is an incitement.
Gitlow v. New York, 268 U.S. 652, 673 [1925]

Three generations of imbeciles are enough.
Buck v. Bell, 274 U.S. 200, 207 [1927]

But if we are to yield to fashionable conventions, it seems to me that theaters are as much devoted to public use as anything well can be. We have not that respect for art that is one of the glories of France. But to many the superfluous is the necessary,[1] and it seems to me that Government does not go beyond its sphere in attempting to make life livable for them.
Tyson & Bro. v. Banton, 273 U.S. 418, 447 [1927]

The power to tax is not the power to destroy while this Court sits.[2]
Panhandle Oil Co. v. Knox, 277 U.S. 223 [1928]

For my part I think it a less evil that some criminals should escape than that the government should play an ignoble part. . . . If the existing code does not permit district attorneys to have a hand in such dirty business, it does not permit

[1] See Voltaire, p. 416b.
[2] See John Marshall, p. 485b.

the judge to allow such iniquities to succeed.

> *Olmstead v. United States, 277*
> *U.S. 438, 470 [1928]*

If there is any principle of the Constitution that more imperatively calls for attachment than any other it is the principle of free thought — not free thought for those who agree with us but freedom for the thought that we hate.

> *United States v. Schwimmer,*
> *279 U.S. 644, 653 [1928]*

The riders in a race do not stop short when they reach the goal. There is a little finishing canter before coming to a standstill. There is time to hear the kind voice of friends and to say to one's self: "The work is done." But just as one says that, the answer comes: "The race is over, but the work never is done while the power to work remains." The canter that brings you to a standstill need not be only coming to rest. It cannot be, while you still live. For to live is to function. That is all there is in living.

> *Radio address on his ninetieth*
> *birthday [March 8, 1931]*

Life seems to me like a Japanese picture which our imagination does not allow to end with the margin. We aim at the infinite and when our arrow falls to earth it is in flames.

> *Message to the Federal Bar Asso-*
> *ciation [February 29, 1932]*

WILLIAM HENRY HUDSON
1841–1922

You cannot fly like an eagle with the wings of a wren.

> *Afoot in England [1909], ch. 6*

MARY ARTEMISIA LATHBURY
1841–1913

Children of yesterday, heirs of tomorrow,

What are you weaving? Labor and sorrow?
Look to your looms again; faster and faster
Fly the great shuttles prepared by the Master.
Life's in the loom! Room for it, room!

> *Song of Hope, st. 1*

JOAQUIN[1]
[CINCINNATUS HINER or HEINE] MILLER
c. 1841–1913

That man who lives for self alone
Lives for the meanest mortal known.

> *Walker in Nicaragua. Chant I,*
> *st. 1*

I do not question school nor creed
Of Christian, Protestant, or Priest;
I only know that creeds to me
Are but new names for mystery,
That good is good from east to east,
And more I do not know nor need
To know, to love my neighbor well.

> *The Tale of the Tall Alcalde*

In men whom men condemn as ill
I find so much of goodness still,[2]
In men whom men pronounce divine
I find so much of sin and blot,
I do not dare to draw a line
Between the two, where God has not.[3]

> *Byron*

The bravest battle that ever was fought;

[1] In a paper, *How I Came to Be a Writer of Books [Lippincott's Magazine,* 1886], quoted in STUART P. SHERMAN's introduction to *The Poetical Works of Joaquin Miller* [1923], Miller explains that his first writing was a public letter in defense of Joaquin Murietta, the outlaw. A Sacramento newspaper banteringly identified him with the outlaw and the name Joaquin clung to him. Miller accepted it and used it in the title of his first book and thereafter.

[2] See Shakespeare, *Henry V, IV, i, 4,* p. 244b.

[3] There is so much good in the worst of us,
And so much bad in the best of us,
That it hardly behooves any of us
To talk about the rest of us.

 First printed in the *Marion* (Kansas) *Record,* owned by Governor Edward Wallis Hoch [1849–1925]; assumed to have been written by him

Shall I tell you where and when?
On the maps of the world you will find
  it not;
It was fought by the mothers of men.
            The Bravest Battle, st. 1

The soul that feeds on books alone —
I count that soul exceeding small
That lives alone by book and creed —
A soul that has not learned to read.
            The Larger College, st. 10

The biggest dog has been a pup.
        William Brown of Oregon, st. 5

Behind him lay the gray Azores,
  Behind the Gates of Hercules;
Before him not the ghost of shores,
  Before him only shoreless seas.
                Columbus, st. 1

He gained a world; he gave that world
Its grandest lesson: "On! sail on!" [1]
                    Ib. st. 5

The Lightning reached a fiery rod,
And on Death's fearful forehead wrote
The autograph of God.
        With Love to You and Yours,
                pt. I, canto 3

PIERRE AUGUSTE RENOIR
1841–1919

  I have a predilection for painting
that lends joyousness to a wall.
        From AMBROISE VOLLARD,
                Renoir [1919]

  In a few generations you can breed
a racehorse. The recipe for making a
man like Delacroix is less well known.
        From JEAN RENOIR, *Renoir My*
                Father [1958]

MINOT JUDSON SAVAGE
1841–1918

There comes an hour of sadness
  With the setting of the sun,

Not for the sins committed,
  But the things I have not done.
                Things Not Done

A man's truest monument must be a
  man.
        The Song of a Man [*Phillips*
                Brooks], *st. 8*

CLEMENT WILLIAM SCOTT
1841–1904

Oh, promise me that some day you
  and I
Will take our love together to some
  sky
Where we can be alone and faith renew,
And find the hollows where those flowers grew.
        Oh, Promise Me [1888] [1]

EDWARD ROWLAND SILL
1841–1887

At the punch bowl's brink
Let the thirsty think
  What they say in Japan:
"First the man takes a drink,
Then the drink takes a drink,
  Then the drink takes the man!" [2]
        An Adage from the Orient

No pity, Lord, could change the heart
From red with wrong to white as wool;
The rod must heal the sin: but Lord,
Be merciful to me, a fool!
            The Fool's Prayer

'Tis by our follies that so long
We hold the earth from heaven away.
                    Ib.

The ill-timed truth we might have
  kept —
Who knows how sharp it pierced and
  stung?

---

[1] Actually, it was Martín Alonso Pinzón who said, "Adelante, adelante, I can't hold with turning back without sighting land."
See Columbus, p. 171b.

[1] Reginald De Koven wrote the music for Scott's ballad, which was first sung in Chicago at the second performance of his opera *Robin Hood,* by the famous contralto Jessie Bartlett Davis [June 10, 1890].
[2] See Herbert, p. 322b, and Swift, p. 389a.

The word we had not sense to say —
Who knows how grandly it had rung?
     The Fool's Prayer

Earth bears no balsam for mistakes;
Men crown the knave, and scourge the
  tool
That did his will.[1]   *Ib.*

SIR HENRY MORTON STANLEY
1841–1904

Doctor Livingstone, I presume?
 *On meeting David Livingstone
 in Ujiji, Central Africa* [Novem-
 ber 10, 1871]

IRONQUILL
[EUGENE FITCH WARE]
1841–1911

Human hopes and human creeds
Have their root in human needs.
  The Rhymes of Ironquill, preface

O Dewey was the morning
 Upon the first of May,
And Dewey was the Admiral
 Down in Manila Bay;
And Dewey were the Regent's eyes,
 "Them" orbs of royal blue!
And Dewey feel discouraged?
 I Dew not think we Dew.
  In the Topeka (*Kansas*) *Daily
  Capital* [May 3, 1898]

Work brings its own relief;
He who most idle is
Has most of grief.   *Today*

No evil deed live oN.
    The Palindrome

---

[1] The law locks up both man and woman
Who steals the goose from off the common,
But lets the greater felon loose
Who steals the common from the goose.
  ANONYMOUS. *From* EDWARD POTTS
  CHEYNEY, *Social and Industrial
  History of England* [1901], *intro-
  duction*

AMBROSE BIERCE[1]
1842–c. 1914

Mark how my fame rings out from zone
 to zone:
A thousand critics shouting: "He's unknown!"   *Couplet*

Cynic, perforce, from study of mankind
In the false volume of his single mind,
He damned his fellows for his own un-
 worth,
And, bad himself, thought nothing
 good on earth.
He yearned to squander what he lived
 to save
And did not, for he could not, cheat
 the grave.   *An Epitaph*

Peyton Farquhar was dead; his body,
with a broken neck, swung gently from
side to side beneath the timbers of the
Owl Creek bridge.
  In the Midst of Life [2] [1891],
  *An Occurrence at Owl Creek
  Bridge*

To men a man is but a mind. Who
 cares
What face he carries or what form he
 wears?
But woman's body is the woman. O
Stay thou, my sweetheart, and do never
 go.
  The Devil's Dictionary [3] [1906]

Achievement, n. the death of endeavor and the birth of disgust. *Ib.*

Advice, n. the smallest current coin.
        Ib.

Bore, n. a person who talks when you
wish him to listen.   *Ib.*

Cynic, n. a blackguard whose faulty
vision sees things as they are, not as
they ought to be.   *Ib.*

Edible, adj. good to eat, and wholesome to digest, as a worm to a toad, a

---

[1] In 1913 Bierce wearied of American civilization and disappeared into Mexico, to seek
"the good, kind darkness."
[2] First published as *Tales of Soldiers and
Civilians*, retitled in 1892.
[3] First published as *The Cynic's Word Book*,
retitled in 1911.

toad to a snake, a snake to a pig, a pig to a man, and a man to a worm.[1]

The Devil's Dictionary

Habit, n. a shackle for the free.

Ib.

Labor, n. one of the processes by which A acquires property for B.

Ib.

Lawsuit, n. a machine which you go into as a pig and come out as a sausage.   *Ib.*

Marriage, n. a community consisting of a master, a mistress, and two slaves, making in all, two.   *Ib.*

Prejudice, n. a vagrant opinion without visible means of support.   *Ib.*

Saint, n. a dead sinner revised and edited.   *Ib.*

Woman would be more charming if one could fall into her arms without falling into her hands.   *Epigrams*

You are not permitted to kill a woman who has wronged you, but nothing forbids you to reflect that she is growing older every minute. You are avenged 1440 times a day.   *Ib.*

Self-denial is indulgence of a propensity to forego.   *Ib.*

CHARLES EDWARD CARRYL
1842–1920

A capital ship for an ocean trip
Was the *Walloping Window Blind* —
No gale that blew dismayed her crew
Or troubled the captain's mind.
The man at the wheel was taught to feel
Contempt for the wildest blow,
And it often appeared, when the weather had cleared,
That he'd been in his bunk below.

Davy and the Goblin: A Nautical Ballad, st. 1

[1] See Wallace Stevens, p. 955b.

WILLIAM JAMES
1842–1910

I have often thought that the best way to define a man's character would be to seek out the particular mental or moral attitude in which, when it came upon him, he felt himself most deeply and intensely active and alive. At such moments there is a voice inside which speaks and says: "This is the real me!"

The Letters of William James, vol. I, p. 199, to Mrs. James [1878]

Nothing so fatiguing as the eternal hanging on of an uncompleted task.

Ib. p. 249, to Carl Stumpf [January 1, 1886]

The difference between the first- and second-best things in art absolutely seems to escape verbal definition — it is a matter of a hair, a shade, an inward quiver of some kind — yet what miles away in the point of preciousness!

Ib. II, p. 87, to Henry Rutgers Marshall [February 7, 1899]

Most people live, whether physically, intellectually or morally, in a very restricted circle of their potential being. They *make use* of a very small portion of their possible consciousness, and of their soul's resources in general, much like a man who, out of his whole bodily organism, should get into a habit of using and moving only his little finger. Great emergencies and crises show us how much greater our vital resources are than we had supposed.[1]

Ib. p. 253, to W. Lutoslawski [May 6, 1906]

The moral flabbiness born of the exclusive worship of the bitch-goddess success. That — with the squalid cash interpretation put on the word success — is our national disease.

Ib. Letter to H. G. Wells [September 11, 1906]

Habit is . . . the enormous flywheel of society, its most precious conserva-

[1] See Emily Dickinson, p. 737b.

tive agent. It alone is what keeps us all within the bounds of ordinance.

> *The Principles of Psychology* [1890], *ch. 4*

There is no more miserable human being than one in whom nothing is habitual but indecision. *Ib.*

Keep the faculty of effort alive in you by a little gratuitous exercise every day. That is, be systematically ascetic or heroic in little unnecessary points, do every day or two something for no other reason than that you would rather not do it, so that when the hour of dire need draws nigh, it may find you not unnerved and untrained to stand the test. *Ib.*

The hell to be endured hereafter, of which theology tells, is no worse than the hell we make for ourselves in this world by habitually fashioning our characters in the wrong way. *Ib.*

We are spinning our own fates, good or evil, and never to be undone. Every smallest stroke of virtue or of vice leaves its never so little scar . . . Nothing we ever do is, in strict scientific literalness, wiped out. *Ib.*

Consciousness . . . does not appear to itself chopped up in bits. . . . A "river" or a "stream" are the metaphors by which it is most naturally described. In talking of it hereafter, let us call it the stream of thought, of consciousness, or of subjective life. *Ib. 9*

As we take, in fact, a general view of the wonderful stream of our consciousness, what strikes us first is this different pace of its parts. Like a bird's life, it seems to be made of an alternation of flights and perchings. *Ib.*

As the brain changes are continuous, so do all these consciousnesses melt into each other like dissolving views. Properly they are but one protracted consciousness, one unbroken stream. *Ib.*

The last peculiarity of consciousness to which attention is to be drawn in this first rough description of its stream is that . . . it is always interested more in one part of its object [thought] than in another, and welcomes and rejects, or chooses, all the while it thinks.

> *The Principles of Psychology, ch. 4*

An act has no ethical quality whatever unless it be chosen out of several all equally possible. *Ib.*

In its widest possible sense, however, a man's Self is the sum total of all that he *can* call his, not only his body and his psychic powers, but his clothes and his house, his wife and children, his ancestors and friends, his reputation and works, his lands and horses, and yacht and bank account. All these things give him the same emotions. If they wax and prosper, he feels triumphant; if they dwindle and die away, he feels cast down. *Ib. 10*

So our self-feeling in this world depends entirely on what we *back* ourselves to be and do. *Ib.*

Creatures extremely low in the intellectual scale may have conception. All that is required is that they should recognize the same experience again. A polyp would be a conceptual thinker if a feeling of "Hello! thingumbob again!" ever flitted through its mind. *Ib. 12*

Let anyone try, I will not say to arrest, but to notice or attend to, the *present* moment of time. One of the most baffling experiences occurs. Where is it, this present? It has melted in our grasp, fled ere we could touch it, gone in the instant of becoming. *Ib. 15*

Genius . . . means little more than the faculty of perceiving in an unhabitual way. *Ib. 19*

The impulse to take life strivingly is indestructible in the race. *Ib. 21*

The art of being wise is the art of knowing what to overlook. *Ib. 22*

The more rational statement is that we feel sorry because we cry, angry because we strike, afraid because we tremble, and not that we cry, strike, or tremble, because we are sorry, angry, or fearful, as the case may be. Without the bodily states following on the perception, the latter would be purely cognitive in form, pale, colorless, destitute of emotional warmth.
The Principles of Psychology, ch. 25

A purely disembodied human emotion is a nonentity. *Ib.*

A thing is important if anyone *think* it important. *Ib. 28, note*

In the deepest heart of all of us there is a corner in which the ultimate mystery of things works sadly.
The Will to Believe [1897]. *Is Life Worth Living?*

Need and struggle are what excite and inspire us; our hour of triumph is what brings the void. Not the Jews of the captivity, but those of the days of Solomon's glory are those from whom the pessimistic utterances in our Bible come. *Ib.*

It is only by risking our persons from one hour to another that we live at all. And often enough our faith beforehand in an uncertified result is the only thing that makes the result come true.
Ib.

This life is worth living, we can say, since it is what we make it, from the moral point of view.[1] *Ib.*

If this life be not a real fight, in which something is eternally gained for the universe by success, it is no better than a game of private theatricals from which one may withdraw at will. But it *feels* like a real fight. *Ib.*

Be not afraid of life. Believe that life *is* worth living, and your belief will help create the fact. *Ib. p. 62*

Man's chief difference from the brutes lies in the exuberant excess of

[1] See Oliver Wendell Holmes, Jr., p. 787a, and Santayana, p. 867a.

his subjective propensities — his preeminence over them simply and solely in the number and in the fantastic and unnecessary character of his wants, physical, moral, aesthetic, and intellectual. Had his whole life not been a quest for the superfluous, he would never have established himself as inexpugnably as he has done in the necessary.
The Will to Believe. Reflex Action and Theism

All the higher, more penetrating ideals are revolutionary. They present themselves far less in the guise of effects of past experience than in that of probable causes of future experience.
Ib. The Moral Philosopher and the Moral Life

There is but one unconditional commandment, which is that we should seek incessantly, with fear and trembling, so to vote and to act as to bring about the very largest total universe of good which we can see. *Ib.*

An unlearned carpenter of my acquaintance once said in my hearing: "There is very little difference between one man and another; but what little there is, is very important." This distinction seems to me to go to the root of the matter.
Ib. The Importance of Individuals

Wherever you are it is your own friends who make your world.
From RALPH BARTON PERRY, *The Thought and Character of William James* [1935], *vol. II* [1899], *ch. 91, conclusion*

Tell him to live by yes and no — yes to everything good, no to everything bad. *Ib.*

Religion . . . shall mean for us the feelings, acts, and experiences of individual men in their solitude.
The Varieties of Religious Experience [1902]. *Lecture 2*

Religion . . . is a man's total reaction upon life. *Ib.*

We can act *as if* there were a God; feel *as if* we were free; consider Nature *as if* she were full of special designs; lay plans *as if* we were to be immortal; and we find then that these words do make a genuine difference in our moral life.

> *The Varieties of Religious Experience. Lecture 3*

There is no worse lie than a truth misunderstood by those who hear it.

> *Ib. Lectures 14 and 15*

The philosophy which is so important in each of us is not a technical matter; it is our more or less dumb sense of what life honestly and deeply means. It is only partly got from books; it is our individual way of just seeing and feeling the total push and pressure of the cosmos.

> *Pragmatism* [1907]. *Lecture 1*

I myself believe that the evidence for God lies primarily in inner personal experiences.   *Ib. Lecture 3*

Our minds thus grow in spots; and like grease spots, the spots spread. But we let them spread as little as possible: we keep unaltered as much of our old knowledge, as many of our old prejudices and beliefs, as we can. We patch and tinker more than we renew. The novelty soaks in; it stains the ancient mass; but it is also tinged by what absorbs it.   *Ib. Lecture 5*

Truth *happens* to an idea. It *becomes* true, is *made* true by events. Its verity *is* in fact an event, a process: the process namely of its verifying itself, its veri-*fication*. Its validity is the process of its valid-*ation*.   *Ib. Lecture 6*

Pluralism lets things really exist in the each-form or distributively. Monism thinks that the all-form or collective-unit form is the only form that is rational.

> *A Pluralistic Universe* [1909]. *Lecture 8*

What we really need the poet's and orator's help to keep alive in us is not . . . the common and gregarious

courage which Robert Shaw showed when he marched with you, men of the Seventh Regiment. It is that more lonely courage which he showed when he dropped his warm commission in the glorious Second to head your dubious fortunes, Negroes of the Fifty-fourth. That lonely kind of courage (civic courage, as we call it in times of peace) is the kind of valor to which the monuments of nations should most of all be reared.[1]

> *Memories and Studies* [1911]. *Robert Gould Shaw: Oration Upon the Unveiling of the Shaw Monument* [*May 31, 1897*]

The deadliest enemies of nations are not their foreign foes; they always dwell within their borders. And from these internal enemies civilization is always in need of being saved. The nation blessed above all nations is she in whom the civic genius of the people does the saving day by day, by acts without external picturesqueness; by speaking, writing, voting reasonably; by smiting corruption swiftly; by good temper between parties; by the people knowing true men when they see them, and preferring them as leaders to rabid partisans or empty quacks.   *Ib.*

Democracy is still upon its trial. The civic genius of our people is its only bulwark.   *Ib.*

So long as antimilitarists propose no substitute for war's disciplinary function, no *moral equivalent* of war, analogous, as one might say, to the mechanical equivalent of heat, so long they fail to realize the full inwardness of the situation.

> *Ib. The Moral Equivalent of War*

Our colleges ought to have lit up in us a lasting relish for the better kind of man, a loss of appetite for mediocrities.

> *Ib. The Social Value of the College-Bred*

[1] See Robert Lowell, p. 1076b.

Real culture lives by sympathies and admirations, not by dislikes and disdains; under all misleading wrappings it pounces unerringly upon the human core.

> *Memories and Studies. The Social Value of the College-Bred*

The "through-and-through" universe seems to suffocate me with its infallible impeccable all-pervasiveness. . . . It seems too buttoned-up and white-chokered and clean-shaven a thing to speak for the vast slow-breathing unconscious Kosmos with its dread abysses and its unknown tides.

> *Essays in Radical Empiricism* [1912], *ch.* 12, *Absolutism and Empiricism*

The union of the mathematician with the poet, fervor with measure, passion with correctness, this surely is the ideal.

> *Collected Essays and Reviews* [1920], *ch.* 11, *Clifford's "Lectures and Essays"* [1879]

I wished, by treating Psychology *like* a natural science, to help her to become one.

> *Ib. A Plea for Psychology as a Natural Science* [1892]

JOHN ALEXANDER JOYCE
1842–1915

I shall love you in December
With the love I gave in May! [1]

> *Question and Answer, st.* 8

PRINCE PËTR ALEKSEEVICH KROPOTKIN
1842–1921

Sociability is as much a law of nature as mutual struggle . . . mutual aid is as much a law of animal life as mutual struggle.　　*Mutual Aid* [1902]

[1] Will you love me in December as you do in May? — JAMES J. WALKER; set to music by ERNEST R. BALL [1905]

SIDNEY LANIER
1842–1881

And the sun is a-wait at the ponderous gate of the West.

> *The Marshes of Glynn* [1877], *l.* 22

Ye marshes, how candid and simple and nothing-withholding and free
Ye publish yourselves to the sky and offer yourselves to the sea!

> *Ib. l. 65*

As the marsh hen secretly builds on the watery sod,
Behold I will build me a nest on the greatness of God:
I will fly in the greatness of God as the marsh hen flies
In the freedom that fills all the space 'twixt the marsh and the skies:
By so many roots as the marsh grass sends in the sod
I will heartily lay me a-hold on the greatness of God:
Oh, like to the greatness of God is the greatness within
The range of the marshes, the liberal marshes of Glynn.　　*Ib. l. 71*

Out of the hills of Habersham,
Down the valleys of Hall.

> *Song of the Chattahoochee* [1877], *st.* 1

Downward the voices of Duty call —
Downward, to toil and be mixed with the main.
The dry fields burn, and the mills are to turn.　　*Ib. st. 5*

The incalculable Up-and-Down of Time.　　*Clover* [1877]

Into the woods my Master went,
Clean forspent, forspent.
Into the woods my Master came,
Forspent with love and shame.

> *A Ballad of Trees and the Master* [1877], *st.* 1

'Twas on a tree they slew Him — last
When out of the woods He came.

> *Ib. st. 2*

STÉPHANE MALLARMÉ
1842–1898

The flesh is sad, alas, and I have read all the books.[1]

Poésies. Brise Marine

Such as into himself at last Eternity has changed him.[2]

Ib. Le Tombeau d'Edgar Poe

A throw of the dice will never abolish chance.[3]   *Ib. Title of poem*

To *name* an object is to take away three-fourths of the pleasure given by a poem. This pleasure consists in guessing little by little: to *suggest* it, that is the ideal.

Réponse à une enquête sur l'évolution littéraire [1891]

You don't make a poem with ideas, but with words.[4]

From PAUL VALÉRY, *Degas, Danse, Dessin*

DAVID LAW PROUDFIT [PELEG ARKWRIGHT]
1842–1897

A man sat on a rock and sought
Refreshment from his thumb;
A dinotherium wandered by
And scared him some.
His name was Smith. The kind of rock
He sat upon was shale.
One feature quite distinguished him —
He had a tail.   *Prehistoric Smith*

Nature abhors imperfect work
And on it lays her ban;
And all creation must despise
A tailless man.   *Ib.*

HUGH ANTOINE D'ARCY
1843–1925

"Say, boys! if you give me just another
whiskey I'll be glad,

And I'll draw right here a picture of the
face that drove me mad.
Give me that piece of chalk with which
you mark the baseball score,
You shall see the lovely Madeleine
upon the bar-room floor."

The Face Upon the Floor [1887] [1]

With chalk in hand the vagabond be-gan
To sketch a face that well might buy
the soul of any man.
Then as he placed another lock upon
the shapely head,
With a fearful shriek he leaped and fell
across the picture — dead!   *Ib.*

SARAH DOUDNEY
1843–1926

Oh, the wasted hours of life
That have drifted by!
Oh, the good that might have been,
Lost without a sigh!

The Lesson of the Water Mill
[1864]

But the waiting time, my brothers,
Is the hardest time of all.

*Psalms of Life. The Hardest
Time of All*

HENRY JAMES[2]
1843–1916

The face of nature and civilization in this our country is to a certain point a very sufficient literary field. But it will yield its secrets only to a really *grasping*

---

[1] Often called "The Face on the Barroom Floor."

[2] You know how opposed your whole "third manner" of execution is to the literary ideals which animate my crude and Orson-like breast, mine being to say a thing in one sentence as straight and explicit as it can be made, and then to drop it forever; yours being to avoid naming it straight, but by dint of breathing and sighing all round and round it, to arouse in the reader who may have had a similar perception already . . . the illusion of a solid object, made . . . wholly out of impalpable materials, air, and the prismatic interference of light, ingeniously focused by mirrors upon empty space. But you *do* it, that's the queerness! — WILLIAM JAMES, *letter to his brother Henry James* [1907]
See Guedalla, p. 1011b.

---

[1] La chair est triste, hélas! et j'ai lu tous les livres.

[2] Tel qu'en Lui-Même enfin l'éternité le change.

[3] Un coup de dés n'abolira jamais le hasard.

[4] Ce n'est point avec des idées que l'on fait des vers, c'est avec des mots.

imagination. . . . To write well and worthily of American things one need even more than elsewhere to be a *master*.

*Letter to Charles Eliot Norton
[January 16, 1871]*

It's a complex fate, being an American, and one of the responsibilities it entails is fighting against a superstitious valuation of Europe.

Letter [1872] quoted in PERCY LUBBOCK, *Letters of Henry James [1920], vol. I, Biographical note*

It takes a great deal of history to produce a little literature.

Hawthorne [1879], ch. 1

Whatever question there may be of his [Thoreau's] talent, there can be none, I think, of his genius. It was a slim and crooked one, but it was eminently personal. He was unperfect, unfinished, inartistic; he was worse than provincial — he was parochial.   *Ib. 4*

Cats and monkeys, monkeys and cats — all human life is there.

*The Madonna of the Future
[1879]*

There are few hours in life more agreeable than the hour dedicated to the ceremony known as afternoon tea.
The Portrait of a Lady [1881]

The real offense, as she ultimately perceived, was her having a mind of her own at all. Her mind was to be his — attached to his own like a small garden plot to a deer park.   *Ib.*

You were ground in the very mill of the conventional!   *Ib.*

The only reason for the existence of a novel is that it does attempt to represent life.   *The Art of Fiction [1888]*

The only obligation to which in advance we may hold a novel, without incurring the accusation of being arbitrary, is that it be interesting.   *Ib.*

The advantage, the luxury, as well as the torment and responsibility of the novelist, is that there is no limit to what he may attempt as an executant — no limit to his possible experiments, efforts, discoveries, successes.

The Art of Fiction

The power to guess the unseen from the seen, to trace the implications of things, to judge the whole piece by the pattern, the condition of feeling life in general so completely that you are well on your way to knowing any particular corner of it — this cluster of gifts may almost be said to constitute experience. . . . If experience consists of impressions, it may be said that impressions *are* experience. . . . Therefore, if I should certainly say to a novice, "Write from experience and experience only," I should feel that this was rather a tantalizing monition if I were not careful immediately to add, "Try to be one of the people on whom nothing is lost."   *Ib.*

We must grant the artist his subject, his idea, his *donnée:* our criticism is applied only to what he makes of it. . . . If we pretend to respect the artist at all, we must allow him his freedom of choice, in the face, in particular cases, of innumerable presumptions that the choice will not fructify. Art derives a considerable part of its beneficial exercise from flying in the face of presumptions.   *Ib.*

There are few things more exciting to me . . . than a psychological reason.
Ib.

The practice of "reviewing" . . . in general has nothing in common with the art of criticism.

Criticism [1893]

The critical sense is so far from frequent that it is absolutely rare, and the possession of the cluster of qualities that minister to it is one of the highest distinctions. . . . In this light one sees the critic as the real helper of the artist, a torchbearing outrider, the interpreter, the brother. . . . Just in proportion as he is sentient and restless, just in proportion as he reacts and reciprocates and penetrates, is the critic a valuable instrument. *Criticism*

However incumbent it may be on most of us to do our duty, there is, in spite of a thousand narrow dogmatisms, nothing in the world that anyone is under the least obligation to *like* — not even (one braces one's self to risk the declaration) a particular kind of writing. *Flaubert* [1893]

The time-honored bread sauce of the happy ending.
Theatricals: Second Series [1895]

I caught him, yes, I held him — it may be imagined with what passion; but at the end of a minute I began to feel what it truly was that I held. We were alone with the quiet day, and his little heart, dispossessed, had stopped.
The Turn of the Screw [1898], *ending*

Live all you can; it's a mistake not to. It doesn't so much matter what you do in particular, so long as you have had your life. If you haven't had that what *have* you had? . . . What one loses one loses; make no mistake about that. . . . The right time is *any* time that one is still so lucky as to have. . . . Live!
The Ambassadors [1903], *bk.* V, *ch.* 2

Really, universally, relations stop nowhere, and the exquisite problem of the artist is eternally but to draw, by a geometry of his own, the circle within which they shall happily *appear* to do so.
Prefaces [1907–1909]. *Roderick Hudson*

There is, I think, no more nutritive or suggestive truth . . . than that of the perfect dependence of the "moral" sense of a work of art on the amount of felt life concerned in producing it. The question comes back thus, obviously, to the kind and the degree of the artist's

prime sensibility, which is the soil out of which his subject springs.
Prefaces. The Portrait of a Lady

To see deep difficulty braved is at any time, for the really addicted artist, to feel almost even as a pang the beautiful incentive, and to feel it verily in such sort as to wish the danger intensified. The difficulty most worth tackling can only be for him, in these conditions, the greatest the case permits of.
Ib.

Life being all inclusion and confusion, and art being all discrimination and selection, the latter, in search of the hard latent *value* with which it alone is concerned, sniffs round the mass as instinctively and unerringly as a dog suspicious of some buried bone.
Ib. The Spoils of Poynton

The fatal futility of Fact. *Ib.*

No themes are so human as those that reflect for us, out of the confusion of life, the close connection of bliss and bale, of the things that help with the things that hurt, so dangling before us forever that bright hard medal, of so strange an alloy, one face of which is somebody's right and ease and the other somebody's pain and wrong.
Ib. What Maisie Knew

The effort really to see and really to represent is no idle business in face of the *constant* force that makes for muddlement. The great thing is indeed that the muddled state too is one of the very sharpest of the realities, that it also has color and form and character, has often in fact a broad and rich comicality.
Ib.

To criticize is to appreciate, to appropriate, to take intellectual possession, to establish in fine a relation with the criticized thing and to make it one's own. *Ib.*

The historian, essentially, wants more documents than he can really use;

the dramatist only wants more liberties than he can really take.

Prefaces. The Aspern Papers

The ever importunate murmur, "Dramatize it, dramatize it!"

Ib. The Altar of the Dead

In art economy is always beauty.

Ib.

The terrible *fluidity* of self-revelation.

Ib. The Ambassadors

The anomalous fact is that the theater, so called, can flourish in barbarism, but that any *drama* worth speaking of can develop but in the air of civilization.

Letter to C. E. Wheeler [April 9, 1911]

I'm glad you like adverbs — I adore them; they are the only qualifications I really much respect.

Letter to Miss M. Betham Edwards [January 5, 1912]

We must know, as much as possible, in our beautiful art . . . what we are talking about — and the only way to know is to have lived and loved and cursed and floundered and enjoyed and suffered. I think I don't regret a single "excess" of my responsive youth — I only regret, in my chilled age, certain occasions and possibilities I didn't embrace.

Letter to Hugh Walpole [August 21, 1913]

I still, in presence of life . . . have reactions — as many as possible. . . . It's, I suppose, because I am that queer monster, the artist, an obstinate finality, an inexhaustible sensibility. Hence the reactions — appearances, memories, many things, go on playing upon it with consequences that I note and "enjoy" (grim word!) noting. It all takes doing — and I *do*. I believe I shall do yet again — it is still an act of life.

Letter to Henry Adams [March 21, 1914]

The effect, if not the prime office, of criticism is to make our absorption and our enjoyment of the things that feed the mind as aware of itself as possible, since that awareness quickens the mental demand, which thus in turn wanders further and further for pasture. This action on the part of the mind practically amounts to a reaching out for the reasons of its interest, as only by its ascertaining them can the interest grow more various. This is the very education of our imaginative life.

The New Novel [1914]

It is art that *makes* life, makes interest, makes importance, for our consideration and application of these things, and I know of no substitute whatever for the force and beauty of its process.

Letter to H. G. Wells [July 10, 1915]

The full, the monstrous demonstration that Tennyson was not Tennysonian.

The Middle Years [1917], ch. 6

Summer afternoon — summer afternoon; to me those have always been the two most beautiful words in the English language.

Quoted by Edith Wharton *in A Backward Glance [1934], ch. 10*

To take what there *is*, and use it, without waiting forever in vain for the preconceived — to dig deep into the actual and get something out of *that* — this doubtless is the right way to live. *Notebooks [1948]*

FREDERIC WILLIAM HENRY MYERS
1843–1901

Coldly sublime, intolerably just.

Saint Paul

ROBERT BRIDGES
1844–1930

When first we met we did not guess That Love would prove so hard a master.

Of more than common friendliness
When first we met we did not guess.
> Shorter Poems, bk. I [1873],
> no. 16, l. 1

For beauty being the best of all we
   know
Sums up the unsearchable and secret
   aims
Of nature.
> The Growth of Love [1876].
> Sonnet 8

Whither, O splendid ship, thy white
   sails crowding,
Leaning across the bosom of the urgent
   West,
That fearest nor sea rising, nor sky
   clouding,
Whither away, fair rover, and what thy
   quest?
> Shorter Poems, bk. II [1879],
> no. 2 (A Passer-By), st. 1

I have loved flowers that fade,
Within whose magic tents
Rich hues have marriage made
With sweet unmemoried scents.
> Ib. no. 13, st. 1

Perfect little body, without fault or
   stain on thee,
With promise of strength and manhood full and fair!
> Ib. III [1880–1884], no. 4
> (On a Dead Child), st. 1

So sweet love seemed that April morn,
When first we kissed beside the thorn,
So strangely sweet, it was not strange
We thought that love could never
   change.
> Ib. V [1893], no. 5, st. 1

My delight and thy delight
Walking, like two angels white,
In the gardens of the night.
> New Poems [1899] no. 9

Gird on thy sword, O man, thy
   strength endue,
In fair desire thine earth-born joy renew.
Live thou thy life beneath the making
   sun

Till Beauty, Truth, and Love in thee
   are one.
> Later Poems [1913], no. 19 (A
> Hymn of Nature), VII, st. 1

Wisdom will repudiate thee, if thou
   think to inquire
why things are as they are or whence
   they came: thy task
is first to learn what is, and in pursuant
   knowledge
pure intellect will find pure pleasure
   and the only ground
for a philosophy comfortable to truth.
> The Testament of Beauty [1929]

Man, in the unsearchable darkness,
   knoweth one thing
That as he is, so was he made.   *Ib.*

ROBERT JONES BURDETTE
1844–1914

There are two days in the week about
which and upon which I never worry.
Two carefree days, kept sacredly free
from fear and apprehension. One of
these days is Yesterday. . . . And the
other day I do not worry about is Tomorrow.   *The Golden Day*

It isn't the experience of today that
drives men mad. It is the remorse for
something that happened yesterday,
and the dread of what tomorrow may
disclose.   *Ib.*

ANATOLE FRANCE [JACQUES ANATOLE FRANÇOIS THIBAULT]
1844–1924

I do not know any reading more easy,
more fascinating, more delightful than
a catalogue.
> The Crime of Sylvestre Bon-
> nard [1] [1881]. The Log, De-
> cember 24, 1849

All the historical books which contain no lies are extremely tedious.
    Ib.

[1] Translated by LAFCADIO HEARN.

Lovers who love truly do not write down their happiness.
> *The Crime of Sylvestre Bonnard. November 30, 1859*

To know is nothing at all; to imagine is everything. *Ib. pt. II, ch. 2*

He flattered himself on being a man without any prejudices; and this pretension itself is a very great prejudice.
> *Ib. 4*

Those who have given themselves the most concern about the happiness of peoples have made their neighbors very miserable. *Ib.*

Man is so made that he can only find relaxation from one kind of labor by taking up another. *Ib.*

People who have no weaknesses are terrible; there is no way of taking advantage of them. *Ib.*

The whole art of teaching is only the art of awakening the natural curiosity of young minds for the purpose of satisfying it afterwards. *Ib.*

The good critic is one who tells of his mind's adventures among masterpieces.
> *La Vie Littéraire [1888], preface*

We reproach people for talking about themselves; but it is the subject they treat best.
> *Ib. Journal des Goncourt*

Chance is perhaps the pseudonym of God when He did not want to sign.[1]
> *Le Jardin d'Epicure [1894]*

The law, in its majestic equality, forbids the rich as well as the poor to sleep under bridges, to beg in the streets, and to steal bread. *Le Lys Rouge[1894]*

We have medicines to make women speak; we have none to make them keep silence.
> *The Man Who Married a Dumb Wife [1912],[2] act II, sc. iv*

[1] See Einstein, p. 950b.
[2] Translated by CURTIS HIDDEN PAGE.

A tale without love is like beef without mustard: an insipid dish.
> *La Révolte des Anges [1914], ch. 8*

RICHARD WATSON GILDER
1844–1909

What is a sonnet? 'Tis a pearly shell
That murmurs of the far-off murmuring sea;
A precious jewel carved most curiously;
It is a little picture painted well.
> *The Sonnet*

GERARD MANLEY HOPKINS[1]
1844–1889

And I have asked to be
  Where no storms come,
Where the green swell is in the havens dumb,
  And out of the swing of the sea.
> *Poems,[2] no. 20, Heaven-Haven, st. 2*

Elected Silence, sing to me
And beat upon my whorlèd ear,
Pipe me to pastures still and be
The music that I care to hear.
> *No. 24, The Habit of Perfection, st. 1*

Thou mastering me
  God! giver of breath and bread;
World's strand, sway of the sea;
  Lord of living and dead;
Thou hast bound bones and veins in me, fastened me flesh,
And after it almost unmade, what with dread,
  Thy doing: and dost thou touch me afresh?
Over again I feel thy finger and find thee.
> *No. 28, The Wreck of the Deutschland, st. 1*

[1] He has left us only ninety poems — but so essential that they will color and convert the development of English poetry for many decades to come. — HERBERT READ [1893–   ] in *The Criterion*, April, 1931
[2] First published in 1918, edited by Robert Bridges. Poem numbers are from the third edition [1948], edited by W. H. Gardner.

The world is charged with the grandeur of God.
> No. 31, *God's Grandeur, l. 1*

Look at the stars! look, look up at the skies!
O look at all the fire-folk sitting in the air!
> No. 32, *The Starlight Night, l. 1*

I caught this morning morning's minion, king-
dom of daylight's dauphin, dapple-dawn-drawn Falcon, in his riding
Of the rolling level underneath him steady air, and striding
High there, how he rung upon the rein of a wimpling wing
In his ecstasy!
> No. 36, *The Windhover, l. 1*

The achieve of, the mastery of the thing!
> *Ib. l. 8*

Brute beauty and valor and act, oh, air, pride, plume, here
Buckle!
> *Ib. l. 9*

Glory be to God for dappled things.
> No. 37, *Pied Beauty, l. 1*

All things counter, original, spare, strange;
Whatever is fickle, freckled (who knows how?)
With swift, slow; sweet, sour; adazzle, dim;
He fathers-forth whose beauty is past change:
Praise him.
> *Ib. l. 7*

Summer ends now; now, barbarous in beauty, the stooks arise
Around; up above, what wind-walks! what lovely behavior
Of silk-sack clouds! Has wilder, willful-wavier
Meal-drift molded ever and melted across skies?
> No. 38, *Hurrahing in Harvest, st. 1*

Felix Randal the farrier, O is he dead then? My duty all ended,
Who have watched his mold of man, big-boned and hardy-handsome,
Pining, pining.
> No. 53, *Felix Randal, st. 1*

When thou at the random grim forge, powerful amidst peers,
Didst fettle for the great gray drayhorse his bright and battering sandal!
> No. 53, *Felix Randal, st. 4*

Margaret, are you grieving
Over Goldengrove unleaving?
> No. 55, *Spring and Fall, l. 1*

Nor mouth had, no nor mind, expressed
What heart heard of, ghost guessed:
It is the blight man was born for,
It is Margaret you mourn for.
> *Ib. l. 12*

As kingfishers catch fire, dragonflies draw flame.
> No. 57, *l. 1*

How to keep — is there any any, is there none such, nowhere known some, bow or brooch or braid or brace, lace, latch or catch or key to keep
Back beauty, keep it, beauty, beauty, beauty . . . from vanishing away?
> No. 59, *The Leaden Echo and the Golden Echo, l. 1*

I say that we are wound
With mercy round and round
As if with air.
> No. 60, *The Blessed Virgin Compared to the Air We Breathe, l. 34*

World-mothering air, air wild,
Wound with thee, in thee isled,
Fold home, fast fold thy child.
> *Ib. l. 124*

Not, I'll not, carrion comfort, Despair, not feast on thee;
Not untwist — slack they may be — these last strands of man
In me or, most weary, cry *I can no more.* I can;
Can something, hope, wish day come, not choose not to be.
> No. 64, *Carrion Comfort, l. 1*

That night, that year
Of now done darkness I wretch lay wrestling with (my God!) my God.
> *Ib. l. 13*

No worst, there is none. Pitched past
pitch of grief,
More pangs will, schooled at forepangs,
wilder wring.　　　*No. 65, l. 1*

O the mind, mind has mountains; cliffs
of fall
Frightful, sheer, no-man-fathomed.
　　　　　　Ib. l. 9

I wake and feel the fell of dark, not day.
What hours, O what black hours we
have spent
This night.　　　*No. 69, l. 1*

I am gall, I am heartburn.　*Ib. l. 9*

I am all at once what Christ is, since he
was what I am, and
This Jack, joke, poor potsherd, patch,
matchwood, immortal diamond,
Is immortal diamond.
　　　No. 72, That Nature Is a Hera-
　　　clitean Fire and of the Comfort
　　　of the Resurrection, last lines

No doubt my poetry errs on the side
of oddness. I hope in time to have a
more balanced and Miltonic style. But
as air, melody, is what strikes me most
of all in music, and design in painting,
so design, pattern, or what I am in the
habit of calling *inscape* is what I above
all aim at in poetry. Now it is the virtue
of design, pattern, or inscape to be distinctive, and it is the vice of distinctive-
ness to become queer. This vice I
cannot have escaped.
　　　Letter to Robert Bridges
　　　[February 15, 1879]

The poetical language of an age
should be the current language heightened, to any degree heightened and unlike itself, but not . . . an obsolete
one.　　*Ib. [August 14, 1879]*

ANDREW LANG
1844–1912

You can cover a great deal of country in
books.
　　　To the Gentle Reader, st. 5

Why, why are rhymes so rare to *love*?
　　　Ballade of Difficult Rhymes

There's a joy without canker or cark,
There's a pleasure eternally new,
'Tis to gloat on the glaze and the mark
Of China that's ancient and blue.
　　　Ballade of Blue China, st. 1

The surge and thunder of the Odyssey.
　　　Sonnet, The Odyssey

JAMES HILARY
MULLIGAN
1844–1916

The moonlight is the softest, in Ken-
tucky,
Summer days come oftest, in Kentucky,
　Friendship is the strongest,
　Love's fires glow the longest,
　Yet a wrong is always wrongest,
　　In Kentucky.
　　　In Kentucky, st. 1

Songbirds are sweetest, in Kentucky,
Thoroughbreds the fleetest, in Ken-
tucky;
　The mountains tower proudest,
　Thunder peals the loudest,
　The landscape is the grandest,
　And politics the damnedest,
　　In Kentucky.　　*Ib. st. 7*

FRIEDRICH WILHELM
NIETZSCHE
1844–1900

Our destiny exercises its influence
over us even when, as yet, we have not
learned its nature: it is our future that
lays down the law of our today.
　　　Human, All Too Human [1]
　　　[1878], 7

One must have a good memory to be
able to keep the promises one makes.
　　　Ib. 59

One will rarely err if extreme actions
be ascribed to vanity, ordinary actions
to habit, and mean actions to fear.
　　　Ib. 74

Every tradition grows ever more
venerable — the more remote is its
origin, the more confused that origin is.
The reverence due to it increases from

[1] Translated by ALEXANDER HARVEY.

generation to generation. The tradition finally becomes holy and inspires awe.
Human, All Too Human, 96

I teach you the Superman. Man is something that is to be surpassed.
Thus Spake Zarathustra [1] [1883–1891], *prologue, ch. 3*

Man is a rope stretched between the animal and the Superman — a rope over an abyss.   *Ib. 4*

I want to teach men the sense of their existence, which is the Superman, the lightning out of the dark cloud man.   *Ib. 7*

This is the hardest of all: to close the open hand out of love, and keep modest as a giver.   *Ib. pt. II, ch. 23*

Distrust all in whom the impulse to punish is powerful.   *Ib. 29*

We ought to learn from the kine one thing: ruminating.   *Ib. IV, 68*

If ye would go up high, then use your own legs! Do not get yourselves *carried* aloft; do not seat yourselves on other people's backs and heads!   *Ib. 73*

It is certainly not the least charm of a theory that it is refutable.
Beyond Good and Evil [2] *[1885–1886], I, 18*

No one is such a liar as the indignant man.   *Ib. II, 26*

It is not the strength but the duration of great sentiments that makes great men.   *Ib. IV, 72*

In revenge and in love woman is more barbarous than man.   *Ib. 139*

The thought of suicide is a great consolation: [3] by means of it one gets successfully through many a bad night.
Ib. 157

[1] Translated by THOMAS COMMON.
[2] Translated by HELEN ZIMMERN.
[3] We are in the power of no calamity while death is in our own. — SIR THOMAS BROWNE, *Religio Medici* [1642] (Everyman ed.), *p. 50*

Blessed are the forgetful: for they get the better even of their blunders.
Beyond Good and Evil VII, 217

Is not life a hundred times too short for us to bore ourselves?   *Ib. 227*

One does not know — cannot know — the best that is in one.
Ib. VIII, 249

The melancholia of everything completed!   *Ib. IX, 277*

The masters have been done away with; the morality of the common man has triumphed.
Genealogy of Morals [1887], *essay 1, aphorism 9*

At the core of all these aristocratic races the beast of prey is not to be mistaken, the magnificent *blond beast*, avidly rampant for spoil and victory.
Ib. 11

The broad effects which can be obtained by punishment in man and beast are the increase of fear, the sharpening of the sense of cunning, the mastery of the desires; so it is that punishment tames man, but does not make him "better."   *Ib. 2, 15*

The sick are the greatest danger for the healthy; it is not from the strongest that harm comes to the strong, but from the weakest.   *Ib. 3, 14*

A strong and well-constituted man digests his experiences (deeds and misdeeds all included) just as he digests his meats, even when he has some tough morsels to swallow.   *Ib. 16*

Two great European narcotics, alcohol and Christianity.
The Twilight of the Idols [1888]. *Things the Germans Lack, 2*

What is it: is man only a blunder of God, or God only a blunder of man?
Ib.

If a man have a strong faith he can indulge in the luxury of skepticism.
Ib. 12

Liberal institutions straightway cease

from being liberal the moment they are soundly established: once this is attained no more grievous and more thorough enemies of freedom exist than liberal institutions.

The Twilight of the Idols.
Things the Germans Lack,
38

It is my ambition to say in ten sentences what everyone else says in a whole book — what everyone else does *not* say in a whole book.   *Ib. 51*

Love is the state in which man sees things most widely different from what they are. The force of illusion reaches its zenith here, as likewise the sweetening and transfiguring power. When a man is in love he endures more than at other times; he submits to everything.

The Antichrist [1] [1888],
aphorism 23

God created woman. And boredom did indeed cease from that moment — but many other things ceased as well! Woman was God's *second* mistake.   *Ib. 48*

Life always gets harder toward the summit — the cold increases, responsibility increases.   *Ib. 57*

I call Christianity the one great curse, the one enormous and innermost perversion, the one great instinct of revenge, for which no means are too venomous, too underhand, too underground and too petty — I call it the one immortal blemish of mankind.

Ib. 62

My doctrine is: Live that thou mayest desire to live again — that is thy duty — for in any case thou wilt live again!   *Eternal Recurrence,* [1] *27*

Even a thought, even a possibility, can shatter us and transform us.

Ib. 30

Nothing on earth consumes a man more quickly than the passion of resentment.   *Ecce Homo* [1] [1888]

I believe only in French culture, and regard everything else in Europe which

[1] Translated by ANTHONY M. LUDOVICI.

calls itself "culture" as a misunderstanding. I do not even take the German kind into consideration.

Ecce Homo

Wherever Germany extends her sway, she ruins culture.   *Ib.*

As an artist, a man has no home in Europe save in Paris.   *Ib.*

Simply by being compelled to keep constantly on his guard, a man may grow so weak as to be unable any longer to defend himself.   *Ib.*

My time has not yet come either; some are born posthumously.   *Ib.*

No one can draw more out of things, books included, than he already knows. A man has no ears for that to which experience has given him no access.

Ib.

The Germans are like women, you can scarcely ever fathom their depths — they haven't any. [1]   *Ib.*

All prejudices may be traced back to the intestines. A sedentary life is the real sin against the Holy Ghost. [2]   *Ib.*

One must separate from anything that forces one to repeat No again and again.   *Ib.*

JOHN BOYLE O'REILLY
1844–1890

They who see the Flying Dutchman never, never reach the shore.

The Flying Dutchman

Doubt is brother-devil to Despair.

Prometheus

The world is large when weary leagues
two loving hearts divide
But the world is small when your
enemy is loose on the other side.

Distance

The red rose whispers of passion
And the white rose breathes of love;

[1] Man thinks woman profound — why? Because he can never fathom her depths. Woman is not even shallow. — *The Twilight of the Idols, Maxims and Missiles, 27*

[2] Translated by CLIFTON P. FADIMAN.

O, the red rose is a falcon,
    And the white rose is a dove.
                 A White Rose, st. 1

You may grind their souls in the self-
    same mill,
You may bind them, heart and brow;
But the poet will follow the rainbow
    still,
And his brother will follow the plow.
         The Rainbow's Treasure, st. 5

Be silent and safe — silence never be-
    trays you.   *Ib.*

This truth keep in sight — every man
    on the planet
Has just as much right as yourself to
    the road.   *Ib.*

The organized charity, scrimped and
    iced,
In the name of a cautious, statistical
    Christ.[1]   *In Bohemia, st. 5*

Well blest is he who has a dear one
    dead;
A friend he has whose face will never
    change —
A dear communion that will not grow
    strange;
The anchor of a love is death.
                 Forever, st. 3

ARTHUR WILLIAM EDGAR O'SHAUGHNESSY
1844–1881

We are the music-makers,
    And we are the dreamers of dreams,
Wandering by lone sea breakers,
    And sitting by desolate streams;
World-losers and world-forsakers,
    On whom the pale moon gleams:
Yet we are the movers and shakers
    Of the world forever, it seems.
                 Ode, st. 1

One man with a dream, at pleasure,
    Shall go forth and conquer a crown;

[1] See Southey, p. 533a, and Hood, p. 593a.

And three with a new song's measure
    Can trample an empire down.
                 Ode, st. 2

For each age is a dream that is dying,
Or one that is coming to birth.
                 Ib. st. 3

WILLIAM ARCHIBALD SPOONER[1]
1844–1930

Kinquering Congs their titles take.
    Announcing the hymn in college
                    chapel

You have deliberately tasted two
worms and you can leave Oxford by the
next town drain.
    Dismissing a student (attributed)

This audience of beery wenches.
         At a woman's college

I remember your name perfectly, but
I just can't think of your face.
               A greeting

PAUL VERLAINE
1844–1896

I often have this strange and moving
    dream
Of an unknown woman, whom I love
    and who loves me.
    Poèmes Saturniens [1866]. *Mon*
               Rêve Familier

The long sobbings
Of the violins
Of autumn
Wound my heart
With monotonous
Languor.[2]   *Ib. Chanson d'Automne*

[1] Canon Spooner, for many years warden of New College, Oxford, was famous for unintentional transposition of (usually initial) word sounds, giving rise to the term "spoonerism."
[2] Les sanglots longs
    Des violons
    De l'automne
    Blessent mon coeur
    D'une langueur
    Monotone.

There is weeping in my heart
Like the rain falling on the city.[1]
   Romances sans Paroles [1874], III

Here are fruits, flowers, leaves and
   branches,
And here is my heart which beats only
   for you.[2]   *Ib. Green*

What have you done, you there
   Weeping without cease,
Tell me, yes you, what have you done
   With all your youth? [3]
      Sagesse [1881], III, st. 6

Music above all, and for this
Prefer an uneven rhythm.[4]
      Jadis et Naguère [1884]. *L'Art
                           Poetique*

Take eloquence and wring its neck!
                              Ib.

And all else is literature.   *Ib.*

BREWSTER HIGLEY
fl. 1873

Oh, give me a home where the buffalo
   roam,
Where the deer and the antelope play,
Where seldom is heard a discouraging
   word
And the skies are not cloudy all day.
      Home on the Range [1873]

R. L. SHARPE
fl. 1890

Each is given a bag of tools,
A shapeless mass and a book of rules;

---

[1] Il pleure dans mon coeur
   Comme il pleut sur la ville.
   See Rimbaud, p. 830b.
[2] Voici des fruits, des fleurs, des feuilles et
   des branches,
   Et puis voici mon coeur qui ne bat que pour
   vous.
[3] Qu'as-tu fait, O toi que voilà
   Pleurant sans cesse,
   Dis, qu'as-tu fait, toi que voilà
   De ta jeunesse?
[4] De la musique avant toute chose,
   Et pour cela préfère l'Impair.

And each must make, ere life is flown,
A stumblingblock or a steppingstone.
      *Stumblingblock or Stepping-
                           stone, st.* 2

JOHN B. BOGART [1]
1845–1921

When a dog bites a man, that is not
news, because it happens so often. But
if a man bites a dog, that is news.
   From Frank M. O'Brien, *The
   Story of The* [New York] *Sun*
   [1918]

WILL CARLETON
1845–1912

Worm or beetle — drought or tempest
   — on a farmer's land may fall,
Each is loaded full o' ruin, but a
   mortgage beats 'em all.
            The Tramp's Story

Not a log in this buildin' but its memories has got,
And not a nail in this old floor but
   touches a tender spot.
      *Out of the Old House, Nancy,
                           st.* 17

Draw up the papers, lawyer, and make
   'em good and stout,
For things at home are crossways, and
   Betsey and I are out.
      Betsey and I Are Out, st. 1

So I have talked with Betsey, and
   Betsey has talked with me,
And so we've agreed together that we
   can't never agree.   *Ib. st.* 3

Betsey, like all good women, had a
   temper of her own.   *Ib. st.* 4

The more we arg'ed the question the
   more we didn't agree.   *Ib. st.* 5

To appreciate heaven well
'Tis good for a man to have some fifteen minutes of hell.
      *Gone with a Handsomer Man,
                           st.* 20

---

[1] City editor of *The Sun*, New York, 1873–
1890.

Over the hill to the poorhouse I'm
  trudgin' my weary way.
      Over the Hill to the Poorhouse,
                               st. 1

WILLIAM KINGDON CLIFFORD
1845–1879

Remember, then, that it [science] is
the guide of action; that the truth
which it arrives at is not that which we
can ideally contemplate without error,
but that which we may act upon without fear; and you cannot fail to see that
scientific thought is not an accompani-
ment or condition of human progress,
but human progress itself.
      Aims and Instruments of Scien-
           tific Thought [1872]

CHARLES FLETCHER DOLE
1845–1927

Good will is the mightiest practical
force in the universe.
                Cleveland Address

Democracy is on trial in the world,
on a more colossal scale than ever before.   *The Spirit of Democracy*

EDWARD HARRIGAN
1845–1911

The drums and fifes, how sweetly they
  did play,
As we marched, marched, marched in
  the Mulligan Guard.
      The Mulligan Guard [1873]

DANIEL WEBSTER HOYT
1845–1936

If you have a friend worth loving,
  Love him. Yes, and let him know
That you love him, ere life's evening

Tinge his brow with sunset glow.
Why should good words ne'er be said
Of a friend till he is dead?
     A Sermon in Rhyme [1878], *st. 1*

GEORGE KENNAN
1845–1924

Heroism, the Caucasian mountain-
eers say, is endurance for one moment
more.
      Letter to Henry Munroe Rogers
                 [July 25, 1921]

EUGENE LEE-HAMILTON
1845–1907

Things bygone are the only things that
  last:
The present is mere grass, quick-mown
  away;
The past is stone, and stands forever
  fast.   *Roman Baths*

HAMILTON WRIGHT MABIE
1845–1916

The peculiarity of the New England
hermit has not been his desire to get
near to God, but his anxiety to get
away from man.
      Backgrounds of Literature.
      Emerson and Concord

GEORGE SAINTSBURY
1845–1933

I have never tried to be in the fashion for the sake of being in it, and seldom, I think, to be out of it for the
sake of being out of it.
     Notes on a Cellar Book [1920],
                 preface

I have never yet given a secondhand
opinion of any thing, or book, or person.   *Ib.*

CHARLES WILLIAM STUBBS
1845–1912

To sit alone with my conscience
Will be judgment enough for me.[1]
Conscience and Future Judgment [1876]

JOHN BANISTER TABB
1845–1909

Out of the dusk a shadow,
  Then a spark;
Out of the clouds a silence,
  Then a lark;
Out of the heart a rapture,
  Then a pain;
Out of the dead, cold ashes,
  Life again.   *Evolution*

PUNCH

Advice to persons about to marry.
— "Don't."   *Vol. VIII, p. 1* [1845]

You pays your money and you takes
your choice.   *X, 16* [1846]

What is Matter? — Never mind.
What is Mind? — No matter.
          XXIX, 19 [1855]

It ain't the 'unting as 'urts 'un, it's
the 'ammer, 'ammer, 'ammer along the
'ard 'igh road.   *XXX, 218* [1856]

It appears the Americans have taken
umbrage.
The deuce they have! Whereabouts
is that?   *LXIII, 189* [1872]

Go directly — see what she's doing,
and tell her she mustn't.
          Ib. 202 [1872]

There was an old owl liv'd in an oak,
The more he heard, the less he spoke;
The less he spoke, the more he heard,
O, if men were all like that wise bird!
          LXVIII, 155 [1875]

[1] There's just ae thing I cannae bear,
  An' that's my conscience.
      R. L. STEVENSON [1850–1894], *In Scots,
      XIV, My Conscience*

It's worse than wicked, my dear, it's
vulgar.   *Almanac* [1876]

Don't look at me, sir, with — ah
— in that tone of voice.
          XCVII, 38 [1884]

I'm afraid you've got a bad egg, Mr.
Jones.
Oh no, my Lord, I assure you! Parts
of it are excellent!   *CIX, 222* [1895]

Look here, Steward, if this is coffee,
I want tea; but if this is tea, then I wish
for coffee.   *CXXIII, 44* [1902]

CHARLES DUPEE BLAKE
1846–1903

Rock-a-bye-baby on the tree top,
When the wind blows the cradle will
  rock,
When the bough breaks the cradle will
  fall,
And down will come baby, cradle and
  all.   *Attributed*

JOSEPH IGNATIUS CONSTANTINE CLARKE
1846–1925

"Well, here's to good honest fighting
  blood!"
Said Kelly and Burke and Shea.
          The Fighting Race, st. 4

"Oh, the fighting races don't die out,
If they seldom die in bed."   *Ib. st. 5*

DANIEL HUDSON BURNHAM
1846–1912

Make no little plans; they have no
magic to stir men's blood.
          Attributed [1]

[1] This quotation is now doubted. See HENRY
M. SAYLOR, *"Make No Little Plans": Daniel
Burnham Thought It but Did He Say It?,"
Journal of the American Institute of Architects,
vol. XXVII, p. 3* [1957]

ALEXANDER MacGREGOR ROSE
1846–1898

Der Kaiser auf der Vaterland
Und Gott on high, all dings gom-
　　mand,
Ve two, ach, don'd you understandt?
Meinself — und Gott.
　　　　Hoch! Der Kaiser (Kaiser &
　　　　　　Co.) [1] [1897], *st. 1*

Gott pulls mit me, und I mit him.
　　　　　　　　　Ib. st. 16

CHARLES PRESTWICK SCOTT
1846–1932

The primary office of a newspaper is
the gathering of news . . . comment is
free, but facts are sacred.
　　In the Manchester Guardian
　　　　　　[May 6, 1926] [2]

HENRYK SIENKIEWICZ
1846–1916

The greater philosopher a man is, the
more difficult it is for him to answer the
foolish questions of common people.
　　　　Quo Vadis? [1896] [3] *ch. 19*

EDWARD NOYES WESTCOTT
1846–1898

Do unto the other feller the way he'd
like to do unto you an' do it fust.
　　　　David Harum [1898], *ch. 20*

They say a reasonable number of
fleas is good fer a dog — keeps him
from broodin' over *bein'* a dog.
　　　　　　　　　Ib. 32

The' ain't nothin' truer in the Bible
'n that sayin' thet them that has gits.
　　　　　　　　　Ib. 35

[1] These verses caused an international incident
when recited by Captain Joseph Bullock Coghlan
[1844–1908] at a dinner given in his honor at the
Union League Club, New York [April 21, 1899].
[2] Its one-hundredth anniversary.
[3] Translated by JEREMIAH CURTIN [1838–1906].

JOHN PETER ALTGELD [1]
1847–1902

In writing *Progress and Poverty*,
he dipped his pen into the tears of the
human race, and with celestial clearness
wrote down what he conceived to be
eternal truths.
　　　Memorial Address on Henry
　　　　　　　George [1897]

ALEXANDER GRAHAM BELL
1847–1922

Mr. Watson, come here, I want
you.
　　　　To his assistant [March 10,
　　　　1876]; the first intelligible
　　　　words transmitted by tele-
　　　　phone

THOMAS ALVA EDISON
1847–1931

There is no substitute for hard
work.　　　*Life* [1932], *ch. 24*

Genius is one per cent inspiration
and ninety-nine per cent perspiration.
　　　　　　　　　Ib

EDGAR FAWCETT
1847–1904

At some glad moment was it nature's
　　choice
To dower a scrap of sunset with a
　　voice?　　*To an Oriole, st. 2*

WALTER LEARNED
1847–1915

A lure more strong, a wish more faint,
Makes one a monster, one a saint.
　　　On the flyleaf of Manon Lescaut

JOHN LOCKE
1847–1889

O Ireland, isn't it grand you look —
　　Like a bride in her rich adornin'?

[1] See Vachel Lindsay, p. 952b, *The Eagle
That Is Forgotten* and note 1.

And with all the pent-up love of my
    heart
I bid you the top o' the mornin'!
    The Exile's Return [*Th' an'am*
    an Dhia: My Soul to God], *st. 1*

ALICE MEYNELL
1847–1922

She walks — the lady of my delight —
A shepherdess of sheep.
Her flocks are thoughts. She keeps
    them white;
She guards them from the steep.
    The Shepherdess, st. 1

I must not think of thee; and, tired yet
    strong,
I shun the thought that lurks in all
    delight —
The thought of thee — and in the blue
    heaven's height
And in the sweetest passage of a song.
    Sonnet, Renouncement

With the first dream that comes with
    the first sleep
I run, I run, I am gathered to thy
    heart.   *Ib.*

LLOYD MIFFLIN
1847–1921

Inscrutable, colossal, and alone.
    Sesostris

JULIA A. MOORE[1]
1847–1920

And now, kind friends, what I have
    wrote
I hope you will pass o'er,
And not criticize as some have done
Hitherto herebefore.
    To My Friends and Critics

"Lord Byron" was an Englishman,
    A poet I believe
His first works in old England
    Was poorly received.

[1] "The Sweet Singer of Michigan," of whom
Mark Twain wrote: "The one and unfailing
great quality which distinguishes her poetry
from Shakespeare's and makes it precious to us
is its stern and simple irrelevancy." — *Following
the Equator* [1897], *vol. II, ch. 8*

Perhaps it was "Lord Byron's" fault
And perhaps it was not.
His life was full of misfortunes,
    Ah, strange was his lot.
    A Sketch of Lord Byron's Life

Leave off the agony, leave off style,
Unless you've got money by you all the
    while.
If you look about you you'll often have
    to smile
To see so many poor people putting on
    style.
    Leave Off the Agony in Style

MILTON NOBLES
1847–1924

The villain still pursued her.
    The Phoenix [1875], *act I, sc. iii*

WILLIAM EDWARD
NORRIS
1847–1925

If your lips would keep from slips,
    Five things observe with care:
To whom you speak; of whom you
    speak;
    And how, and when, and where.
    Quoted in Thirlby Hall

JAMES JEFFREY ROCHE
1847–1908

I'd rather be handsome than homely;
I'd rather be youthful than old;
If I can't have a bushel of silver
I'll do with a barrel of gold.
    Contentment

All loved Art in a seemly way
With an earnest soul and a capital A.
    The V-A-S-E

ARCHIBALD PHILIP
PRIMROSE,
EARL OF ROSEBERY
1847–1929

It is beginning to be hinted that we
are a nation of amateurs.
    Rectorial Address, Glasgow
    [*November 16, 1900*]

GEORGE ROBERT SIMS
1847–1922

It was Christmas Day in the work-house.
> *Christmas Day in the Work-*
> *house, st. 1*

MARY DOW BRINE
fl. 1878

She's somebody's mother, boys, you know,
For all she's aged and poor and slow.
> *Somebody's Mother* [1878]

ARTHUR JAMES BALFOUR
1848–1930

The energies of our system will decay, the glory of the sun will be dimmed, and the earth, tideless and inert, will no longer tolerate the race which has for a moment disturbed its solitude. Man will go down into the pit, and all his thoughts will perish.
> *The Foundations of Belief*
> [1895], *pt. I, ch. 1*

Biography should be written by an acute enemy.
> *Quoted by* S. K. RATCLIFFE *in the London Observer* [*January 30, 1927*]

JOHN VANCE CHENEY
1848–1922

Who drives the horses of the sun
   Shall lord it but a day;
Better the lowly deed were done,
   And kept the humble way.
> *The Happiest Heart, st. 1*

The happiest heart that ever beat
   Was in some quiet breast
That found the common daylight sweet,
   And left to Heaven the rest.
> *Ib. st. 3*

JOHN CHURTON COLLINS
1848–1908

Truth is the object of philosophy, but not always of philosophers.
> *From* LOGAN PEARSALL SMITH,
> *A Treasury of English Apho-*
> *risms*

Mistrust a subordinate who never finds fault with his superior.   *Ib.*

The secret of success in life is known only to those who have not succeeded.
> *Ib.*

If men were as unselfish as women, women would very soon become more selfish than men.   *Ib.*

SIR FRANCIS DARWIN
1848–1925

But in science the credit goes to the man who convinces the world, not to the man to whom the idea first occurs.[1]
> *First Galton Lecture before the*
> *Eugenics Society* [1914]

DIGBY MACKWORTH DOLBEN
1848–1867

The world is young today:
   Forget the gods are old,
   Forget the years of gold
When all the months were May.
> *A Song*

SAMUEL MILLER HAGEMAN
1848–1905

Every sound shall end in silence, but the silence never dies.
> *Silence* [1876], *st. 10*

Earth is but the frozen echo of the silent voice of God.   *Ib. st. 19*

JOEL CHANDLER HARRIS
1848–1908

How many po' sinners'll be kotched out late

---

[1] See Zinsser, p. 949a, and Fleming, p. 963a.

813

En fin' no latch ter de golden gate?
No use fer ter wait twell ter-morrer,
De sun mus'n't set on yo' sorrer —
Sin's ez sharp ez a bamboo-brier, —
O Lord! fetch de mo'ners up higher!
> *Uncle Remus: His Songs and*
> *His Sayings* [1881]

Hit look lak sparrer-grass, hit feel lak sparrer-grass, hit tas'e lak sparrer-grass, en I bless ef 'taint sparrer-grass.
> *Nights with Uncle Remus*
> [1883], *ch. 27*

No 'pollygy aint gwine ter make h'ar come back whar de b'iling water hit.
> *Ib. 45*

Tar-baby ain't sayin' nuthin', en Brer Fox, he lay low.
> *Uncle Remus and His Friends*
> [1892]

Ez soshubble ez a baskit er kittens.
> *Ib.*

Bred en bawn in a brier-patch, Brer Fox.   *Ib.*

You do de pullin', Sis Cow, en I'll do de gruntin'.   *Ib.*

W'en ole man Rabbit say "scoot," dey scooted, en w'en old Miss Rabbit say "scat," dey scatted.   *Ib.*

Lazy fokes' stummucks don't git tired.
> *Uncle Remus: Plantation Proverbs*

Jaybird don't rob his own nes'.
> *Ib.*

Licker talks mighty loud w'en it gits loose fum de jug.   *Ib.*

Hongry rooster don't cackle w'en he fine a wum.   *Ib.*

Youk'n hide de fier, but w'at you gwine do wid de smoke?   *Ib.*

Watch out w'en youer gittin' all you want. Fattenin' hogs ain't in luck.
> *Ib.*

Hop light, ladies,
  Oh, Miss Loo!
Oh, swing dat yaller gal!
  Do, boys, do!
> *Plantation Play Song*

When you've got a thing to say,
Say it! Don't take half a day.
When your tale's got little in it,
Crowd the whole thing in a minute!
Life is short — a fleeting vapor —
Don't you fill the whole blamed paper
With a tale which, at a pinch,
Could be cornered in an inch!
Boil her down until she simmers,
Polish her until she glimmers.
> *Advice to Writers for the Daily*
> *Press*

JORIS KARL HUYSMANS
1848–1907

The loveliest tune imaginable becomes vulgar and insupportable as soon as the public begins to hum it and the hurdygurdies make it their own.
> *Against the Grain,*[1] *ch. 9*

Perfumes, in fact, rarely come from the flowers whose names they bear . . . with the exception of the inimitable jasmine, which it is impossible to counterfeit.   *Ib. 10*

Art is the only clean thing on earth, except holiness.
> *Les Foules de Lourdes* [1906]

RICHARD JEFFERIES
1848–1887

It is eternity now. I am in the midst of it. It is about me in the sunshine; I am in it, as the butterfly in the light-laden air. Nothing has to come; it is now. Now is eternity; now is the immortal life.
> *The Story of My Heart* [1883]

VILFREDO PARETO
1848–1923

Give me a fruitful error any time, full of seeds, bursting with its own corrections. You can keep your sterile truth for yourself.
> *Comment on Kepler*

[1] Translated by JOHN HOWARD.

EBEN EUGENE REXFORD
1848–1916

Darling, I am growing old,
Silver threads among the gold
Shine upon my brow today;
Life is fading fast away.
Silver Threads Among the Gold
[1873], st. 1

HENRY AUGUSTUS
ROWLAND
1848–1901

American science is a thing of the
future, and not of the present or past;
and the proper course of one in my
position is to consider what must be
done to create a science of physics in
the country, rather than to call telegrams, electric lights, and such con-
veniences by the name of science.
Address before the American
Association for the Advance-
ment of Science [1883]

FREDERIC EDWARD
WEATHERLY
1848–1929

Always the same, Darby, my own,
Always the same to your old wife Joan.
Darby and Joan,[1] refrain

The sailor's wife the sailor's star shall
be.   *Nancy Lee, refrain*

BERNHARD VON BÜLOW
1849–1929

A place in the sun.
A Promise for Germany. Speech
before the Reichstag [December
6, 1897]

The king in Prussia — forward; Prussia in Germany — forward; Germany in
the world — forward!   *Ib.*

[1] Old Darby with Joan by his side,
You've often regarded with wonder;
He's dropsical, she is sore-ey'd,
Yet they're ever uneasy asunder.
HENRY WOODFALL, *The Gentleman's*
Magazine [March 1735]

LORD RANDOLPH
SPENCER CHURCHILL
1849–1895

The old gang [members of the Con-
servative government].
Speech, House of Commons
[March 7, 1878]

Ulster will fight; Ulster will be right.
Letter [May 7, 1886]

All great men make mistakes. Napoleon forgot Blücher, I forgot Goschen.[1]
Quoted by LADY DOROTHY
NEVILL, *notebooks*

EDMUND GOSSE
1849–1928

The Past is like a funeral gone by,
The Future comes like an unwelcome
guest.   *May Day*

I do not hunger for a well-stored mind,
I only wish to live my life, and find
My heart in unison with all mankind.
Lying in the Grass

WILLIAM ERNEST
HENLEY
1849–1903

Far in the stillness a cat
Languishes loudly.
In Hospital [1888]. VII, Vigil

Bland as a Jesuit, sober as a hymn.
Ib. XVI, House Surgeon

Valiant in velvet, light in ragged luck,
Most vain, most generous, sternly criti-
cal,
Buffoon and poet, lover and sensualist:
A deal of Ariel, just a streak of Puck,
Much Antony, of Hamlet most of all,
And something of the Shorter-
Catechist.
Ib. XXV, Apparition [Robert
Louis Stevenson]

[1] George Joachim Goschen [1831–1907], British statesman who helped form the Liberal
Unionist party [1886].

As dust that drives, as straws that blow,
Into the night go one and all.
> *Ballade of Dead Actors* [1888]

Out of the night that covers me,
Black as the Pit from pole to pole,
I thank whatever gods may be
For my unconquerable soul.

In the fell clutch of circumstance,
I have not winced nor cried aloud;
Under the bludgeonings of chance
My head is bloody, but unbowed.
> *Echoes* [1888]. *IV, In Memoriam R. T. Hamilton Bruce* ["Invictus"], *st. 1, 2*

It matters not how strait the gate,
How charged with punishments the scroll,
I am the master of my fate;
I am the captain of my soul.[1]
> *Ib. st. 4*

Night with her train of stars
And her great gift of sleep.
> *Ib. XXXV, In Memoriam Margaritae Sororis, st. 2*

Or ever the knightly years were gone
  With the old world to the grave,
I was a King in Babylon
And you were a Christian Slave.
> *Ib. XXXVII, To W. A., st. 1*

These poor Might-Have-Beens,
These fatuous, ineffectual Yesterdays!
> *To James McNeill Whistler* [1892]

What have I done for you,
  England, my England?
What is there I would not do,
  England, my own?
> *For England's Sake. Pro Rege Nostro* [1892], *st. 1*

SARAH ORNE JEWETT
1849–1909

A harbor, even if it is a little harbor, is a good thing, since adventures come into it as well as go out, and the life in it grows strong, because it takes something from the world and has something to give in return.
> *Country Byways. River Driftwood*

Captain Littlepage had overset his mind with too much reading.
> *The Country of the Pointed Firs* [1896], *ch. 5*

The old poets little knew what comfort they could be to man. **Ib.**

Wrecked on the lee shore of age.
> *Ib. 7*

We were standing where there was a fine view of the harbor and its long stretches of shore all covered by the great army of the pointed firs, darkly cloaked and standing as if they waited to embark. As we looked far seaward among the outer islands, the trees seemed to march seaward still, going steadily over the heights and down to the water's edge. **Ib.**

Tact is after all a kind of mind-reading. **Ib. 10**

Yes'm, old friends is always best, 'less you can catch a new one that's fit to make an old one out of. **Ib. 12**

In the life of each of us, I said to myself, there is a place remote and is-landed, and given to endless regret or secret happiness. **Ib. 15**

'Tain't worthwhile to wear a day all out before it comes. **Ib. 16**

The road was new to me, as roads always are, going back. **Ib. 19**

So we die before our own eyes; so we see some chapters of our lives come to their natural end. **Ib.**

The thing that teases the mind over and over for years, and at last gets itself put down rightly on paper — whether little or great, it belongs to Literature.
> *Letter to Willa Cather. Quoted in preface to The Country of the Pointed Firs and Other Stories* [1925]

[1] See Sallust, p. 116a, and note.

EMMA LAZARUS
1849–1887

Give me your tired, your poor,
Your huddled masses yearning to breathe free,
The wretched refuse of your teeming shore,
Send these, the homeless, tempest-tossed, to me:
I lift my lamp beside the golden door.
The New Colossus: Inscription for the Statue of Liberty, New York Harbor

SIR WILLIAM OSLER
1849–1919

The greater the ignorance the greater the dogmatism.
Montreal Medical Journal [1902]

The philosophies of one age have become the absurdities of the next, and the foolishness of yesterday has become the wisdom of tomorrow. *Ib.*

The natural man has only two primal passions, to get and to beget.
Science and Immortality [1904], *ch. 2*

Tact is the saving virtue without which no woman can be a success.
Commencement address to nurses, Johns Hopkins University [*May 7, 1913*]

Speck in cornea, 50¢.
Entry in his account book, first fee as a practicing physician. From HARVEY CUSHING, *Life of Sir William Osler* [1925], *vol. I, ch. 6*

The desire to take medicine is perhaps the greatest feature which distinguishes man from animals. *Ib. 14*

This is yet the childhood of the world, and a supine credulity is still the most charming characteristic of man. *Ib.*

We are here to add what we can *to,* not to get what we can *from,* Life.[1]
From HARVEY CUSHING, *Life of Sir William Osler, vol. I, ch. 14*

Humanity has but three great enemies: fever, famine and war; of these by far the greatest, by far the most terrible, is fever. *Ib.*

The master word [work] . . . is the open sesame to every portal, the great equalizer in the world, the true philosopher's stone which transmutes all the base metal of humanity into gold.[2]
Ib. 22

Things cannot always go your way. Learn to accept in silence the minor aggravations, cultivate the gift of taciturnity and consume your own smoke [3] with an extra draught of hard work, so that those about you may not be annoyed with the dust and soot of your complaints. *Ib.*

Take the sum of human achievement in action, in science, in art, in literature — subtract the work of the men above forty, and while we should miss great treasures, even priceless treasures, we would practically be where we are today. . . . The effective, moving, vitalizing work of the world is done between the ages of twenty-five and forty.[4]　　*Ib. 24* [*The Fixed Period*]

My second fixed idea is the uselessness of men above sixty years of age, and the incalculable benefit it would be in commercial, political, and in professional life, if as a matter of course, men stopped work at this age.[5]　　*Ib.*

[1] Also in *Doctor and Nurse*, in *Aequanimitas and Other Addresses* [1904].
[2] Lecture, *The Master Word in Medicine,* Toronto [October 1, 1903]; also in *Aequanimitas.*
[3] See Carlyle, p. 576b, and note.
[4] Address at Johns Hopkins University, Baltimore, February 22, 1905.
[5] This valedictory address caused much discussion and misquotation. It was headlined in the press OSLER RECOMMENDS CHLOROFORM AT

Nothing will sustain you more potently than the power to recognize in your humdrum routine, as perhaps it may be thought, the true poetry of life — the poetry of the commonplace, of the ordinary man, of the plain, toil-worn woman, with their loves and their joys, their sorrows and their griefs.

> From HARVEY CUSHING, *Life of Sir William Osler*, vol. I, ch. 24
> [*The Student Life*]

I have three personal ideals. One, to do the day's work well and not to bother about tomorrow. . . . The second ideal has been to act the Golden Rule, as far as in me lay, toward my professional brethren and toward the patients committed to my care. And the third has been to cultivate such a measure of equanimity as would enable me to bear success with humility, the affection of my friends without pride, and to be ready when the day of sorrow and grief came to meet it with the courage befitting a man.

> *Ib.* [*Farewell Dinner, May 2, 1905*]

Throw all the beer and spirits into the Irish Channel, the English Channel, and the North Sea for a year, and people in England would be infinitely better. It would certainly solve all the problems with which the philanthropists, the physicians, and the politicians have to deal.[1] *Ib. II, 26*

No man is really happy or safe without a hobby, and it makes precious little difference what the outside interest may be — botany, beetles or butterflies, roses, tulips or irises; fishing, mountaineering or antiquities — anything will do so long as he straddles a hobby and rides it hard.[2] *Ib. 29*

SIXTY, and occasioned many columns of letters, caustic cartoons, and the like, until to "Oslerize" became a byword.

[1] Address at Working Men's College, Camden Town [November 17, 1906].

[2] Address, Medical Library Association, Belfast [July 28, 1909].

Nothing in life is more wonderful than faith — the one great moving force which we can neither weigh in the balance nor test in the crucible.

> From HARVEY CUSHING, *Life of Sir William Osler*, vol. II, ch. 30

In the life of a young man the most essential thing for happiness is the gift of friendship. *Ib. 31*

No bubble is so iridescent or floats longer than that blown by the successful teacher. *Ib.*

The quest for righteousness is Oriental, the quest for knowledge, Occidental.[1] *Ib. 34*

Save the fleeting minute; learn gracefully to dodge the bore.

> From W. S. THAYER, *Osler the Teacher, Johns Hopkins Hospital Bulletin* 30:198 [1919]

IVAN PETROVICH PAVLOV
1849–1936

What can I wish to the youth of my country who devote themselves to science?

Firstly, gradualness. About this most important condition of fruitful scientific work I never can speak without emotion. Gradualness, gradualness and gradualness. From the very beginning of your work, school yourselves to severe gradualness in the accumulation of knowledge.

Learn the ABC of science before you try to ascend to its summit.

> *Bequest to the Academic Youth of Soviet Russia* [1936]

Learn, compare, collect the facts! *Ib.*

Secondly, modesty. Never think that you already know all. However highly

---

[1] Address, Jewish Historical Society of England [April 27, 1914].

you are appraised, always have the courage to say to yourself — I am ignorant.

Bequest to the Academic Youth of Soviet Russia

Thirdly, passion. Remember that science claims a man's whole life. Had he two lives they would not suffice. Science demands an undivided allegiance from its followers. In your work and in your research there must always be passion. *Ib.*

JAMES WHITCOMB RILEY
1849–1916

O'er folded blooms
  On swirls of musk,
The beetle booms adown the glooms
  And bumps along the dusk.
The Beetle, st. 7

The ripest peach is highest on the tree.
The Ripest Peach, st. 1

An' all us other children, when the supper things is done,
We set around the kitchen fire an' has the mostest fun
A-list'nin' to the witch-tales 'at Annie tells about,
An' the Gobble-uns 'at gits you
    Ef you
      Don't
        Watch
          Out!
Little Orphant Annie, st. 1

It hain't no use to grumble and complain,
  It's jest as easy to rejoice;
When God sorts out the weather and sends rain,
  Why rain's my choice.
Wet Weather Talk

Heaven holds all for which you sigh —
There! little girl; don't cry!
A Life Lesson, st. 3

  "As surely as the vine
Grew 'round the stump," she loved me
  — that old sweetheart of mine.
An Old Sweetheart of Mine, st. 12

Tell you what I like the best —
'Long about knee-deep in June,
'Bout the time strawberries melts
On the vine — some afternoon
Like to jes' git out and rest,
And not work at nothin' else.
Knee-Deep in June, st. 1

Oh! the old swimmin' hole! When I last saw the place,
The scenes was all changed, like the change in my face.
The Old Swimmin' Hole, st. 5

Work is the least o' my idees
When the green, you know, gits back in the trees!
When the Green Gits Back in the Trees, st. 1

O, the Raggedy Man! He works fer Pa;
An' he's the goodest man ever you saw!
The Raggedy Man, st. 1

O, it sets my heart a-clickin' like the tickin' of a clock,
When the frost is on the punkin and the fodder's in the shock.
When the Frost Is on the Punkin, st. 3

EDWARD BELLAMY[1]
1850–1898

Your system was liable to periodical convulsions, overwhelming alike the wise and unwise, the successful cutthroat as well as his victim. I refer to the business crises at intervals of five to ten years, which wrecked the industries of the nation.

Looking Backward [1887]

AUGUSTINE BIRRELL
1850–1933

Libraries are not made; they grow.
Obiter Dicta. Book Buying

Good as it is to inherit a library, it is better to collect one. *Ib.*

[1] There is at least a fair chance that another fifty years will confirm Edward Bellamy's position as one of the most authentic prophets of our age. — HEYWOOD BROUN [1931]

That great dust heap called "history."   *Obiter Dicta. Carlyle*

EUGENE FIELD
1850–1895

I feel a sort of yearnin' 'nd a chokin' in
    my throat
When I think of Red Hoss Mountain
    'nd of Casey's tabble dote!
        Casey's Table d'Hôte, st. 1

He could whip his weight in wildcats.
        Modjesky as Cameel, st. 10

No matter what conditions
    Dyspeptic come to feaze,
The best of all physicians
    Is apple pie and cheese!
        Apple Pie and Cheese, st. 5

I'm sure no human heart goes wrong
That's told "Good-by — God bless
    you!"
        "Good-by — God Bless You!",
            st. 2

I never lost a little fish — yes, I am free
    to say
It always was the biggest fish I caught
    that got away.
        Our Biggest Fish, st. 2

How gracious those dews of solace that
    over my senses fall
At the clink of the ice in the pitcher
    the boy brings up the hall!
        The Clink of the Ice, st. 1

When one's all right, he's prone to
    spite
The doctor's peaceful mission;
But when he's sick, it's loud and quick
He bawls for a physician.[1]
        Doctors, st. 2

When I demanded of my friend what
    viands he preferred,

[1] Three faces wears the doctor: when first
    sought
    An angel's; and a god's the cure half-
      wrought;
    But when, the cure complete, he seeks his fee,
    The Devil looks less terrible than he.
        ANONYMOUS

He quoth: "A large cold bottle, and a
    small hot bird!"
        The Bottle and the Bird, st. 1

Have you ever heard of the Sugarplum
    Tree?
'Tis a marvel of great renown!
It blooms on the shore of the Lollipop
    Sea
In the garden of Shuteye Town.
        The Sugarplum Tree, st. 1

Wynken, Blynken, and Nod one night
    Sailed off in a wooden shoe —
Sailed on a river of crystal light
    Into a sea of dew.
        Wynken, Blynken, and Nod, st. 1

The little toy dog is covered with dust,
    But sturdy and staunch he stands;
And the little toy soldier is red with
    rust,
    And his musket molds in his hands;
Time was when the little toy dog was
    new,
    And the soldier was passing fair;
And that was the time when our Little
    Boy Blue
    Kissed them and put them there.
        Little Boy Blue, st. 1

The Rock-a-Bye Lady from Hushaby
    street
Comes stealing; comes creeping.
        The Rock-a-Bye Lady, st. 1

Have you ever heard the wind go
    "Yooooo"?
'Tis a pitiful sound to hear!
It seems to chill you through and
    through
    With a strange and speechless fear.
        The Night Wind, st. 1

The Dinkey Bird goes singing
    In the amfalula tree!
        The Dinkey Bird, st. 1

The gingham dog went "Bow-wow-
    wow!"
And the calico cat replied "Mee-ow!"
The air was littered, an hour or so,
With bits of gingham and calico.
        The Duel, st. 2

Father calls me William, sister calls me
    Will,

Mother calls me Willie, but the fellers
call me Bill!
Jest 'Fore Christmas, st. 1

'Most all the time, the whole year
round, there ain't no flies on me,
But jest 'fore Christmas I'm as good as
I kin be! *Ib.*

FRED GILBERT
1850–1903

The Man Who Broke the Bank at
Monte Carlo. *Title of song* [1892]

SAMUEL GOMPERS
1850–1924

The trade unions are the legitimate
outgrowth of modern societary and industrial conditions. . . . They were
born of the necessity of workers to protect and defend themselves from encroachment, injustice and wrong. . . .
To protect the workers in their inalienable rights to a higher and better life;
to protect them, not only as equals before the law, but also in their health,
their homes, their firesides, their liberties as men, as workers, and as citizens;
to overcome and conquer prejudices
and antagonism; to secure to them the
right to life, and the opportunity to
maintain that life; the right to be full
sharers in the abundance which is the
result of their brain and brawn, and the
civilization of which they are the founders and the mainstay; to this the workers
are entitled. . . . The attainment of
these is the glorious mission of the
trade unions. *Speech* [1898]

JOHN CHEEVER
GOODWIN
1850–1912

For that elephant ate all night,
And that elephant ate all day;
Do what he could to furnish him food,
The cry was still *more hay*.
*Wang: The Man with an Ele-
phant on His Hands* [1891]

HENRY CABOT LODGE
1850–1924

Let every man honor and love the
land of his birth and the race from
which he springs and keep their memory green. It is a pious and honorable
duty. But let us have done with British-
Americans and Irish-Americans and
German-Americans, and so on, and all
be Americans. . . . If a man is going
to be an American at all let him be so
without any qualifying adjectives; and
if he is going to be something else, let
him drop the word American from his
personal description.
The Day We Celebrate [Fore-
fathers' Day]. *Address, New England Society of Brooklyn* [De-
cember 21, 1888]

It is the flag just as much of the man
who was naturalized yesterday as of the
man whose people have been here many
generations. *Address* [1915]

He was a great patriot, a great man;
above all, a great American. His country was the ruling, mastering passion of
his life from the beginning even unto
the end.
*Theodore Roosevelt: Address Be-
fore Congress* [February 9, 1919]

PHILIP BOURKE
MARSTON
1850–1887

A little time for laughter,
A little time to sing,
A little time to kiss and cling,
And no more kissing after.[1]
After, st. 1

LAURA ELIZABETH
RICHARDS
1850–1943

Be you clown or be you King,
Still your singing is the thing.
Tirra Lirra [1930], *dedication, l. ;*

[1] See A. L. Gordon, p. 748b, and Du Maurier
p. 751b.

Every little wave had its nightcap on.
Song for Hal, refrain

Once there was an elephant
Who tried to use the telephant —
No! No! I mean an elephone
Who tried to use the telephone.
Eletelephony, l. 1

ROBERT RICHARDSON
1850–1901

Warm summer sun, shine friendly
here;
Warm western wind, blow kindly here;
Green sod above, rest light, rest
light —
Good night, Annette! Sweetheart, good
night.[1] *To Annette*

ROBERT LOUIS
STEVENSON[2]
1850–1894

Mankind was never so happily inspired as when it made a cathedral.
An Inland Voyage [1878]. *Noyon*

Every man is his own doctor of divinity, in the last resort. *Ib.*

For my part, I travel not to go anywhere, but to go. I travel for travel's
sake. The great affair is to move.
Travels with a Donkey [1878]

Marriage is like life in this — that it
is a field of battle, and not a bed of
roses.
Virginibus Puerisque [1881], I,
ch. 1

Times are changed with him who
marries; there are no more bypath

meadows, where you may innocently
linger, but the road lies long and
straight and dusty to the grave.
Virginibus Puerisque, I, ch. 2

Man is a creature who lives not upon
bread alone but principally by catchwords. *Ib.*

The cruelest lies are often told in silence. *Ib. 4, Truth of Intercourse*

Old and young, we are all on our last
cruise.
Ib. II, Crabbed Age and Youth

It is better to be a fool than to be
dead. *Ib.*

Give me the young man who has
brains enough to make a fool of him·
self! *Ib.*

Books are good enough in their own
way, but they are a mighty bloodless
substitute for life.
Ib. III, An Apology for Idlers

Perpetual devotion to what a man
calls his business, is only to be sustained
by perpetual neglect of many other
things. *Ib.*

There is no duty we so much under-
rate as the duty of being happy. *Ib.*

To travel hopefully is a better thing
than to arrive. *Ib. VI, El Dorado*

To be what we are, and to become
what we are capable of becoming, is the
only end of life.
*Familiar Studies of Men and
Books* [1882]

I am in the habit of looking not so
much to the nature of a gift as to the
spirit in which it is offered.
New Arabian Nights [1882].
The Suicide Club

Fifteen men on the Dead Man's
Chest — [1]

---

[1] Mark Twain adapted this verse by the
Australian poet Richardson for the stone mark-
ing the grave of his daughter Olivia Susan
Clemens, who died August 18, 1896, aged twenty-
four:
Warm summer sun, shine kindly here;
Warm southern wind, blow softly here;
Green sod above, lie light, lie light —
Good night, dear heart, good night, good
night.
See Euripides, p. 83b; Anonymous Latin, p.
151b; and Beaumont and Fletcher, p. 316b.
[2] See Henley, p. 815b.

[1] *Treasure Island* came out of Kingsley's *At
Last,* where I got the Dead Man's Chest — and
that was the seed. — R. L. STEVENSON, *Letter
to Sidney Colvin*
We were crawling slowly along, looking out
for Virgin Garda; the first of those numberless
isles which Columbus, so goes the tale, discovered

Yo-ho-ho, and a bottle of rum!
Drink and the devil had done for the
    rest —
Yo-ho-ho, and a bottle of rum!
    Treasure Island [1883], *ch. 1*

Doctors is all swabs.
    Ib. 3 [Billy Bones]

Many's the long night I've dreamed
of cheese — toasted, mostly.
    Ib. 15 [Ben Gunn]

In winter I get up at night
And dress by yellow candlelight.
In summer, quite the other way,
I have to go to bed by day.

I have to go to bed and see
The birds still hopping on the tree,
Or hear the grown-up people's feet
Still going past me on the street.
    A *Child's Garden of Verses*
    [1885]. *Bed in Summer, st. 1, 2*

A child should always say what's true
And speak when he is spoken to,
And behave mannerly at table;
At least as far as he is able.
    Ib. Whole Duty of Children

Whenever the moon and stars are set,
Whenever the wind is high,
All night long in the dark and wet,
A man goes riding by.
Late in the night when the fires are
    out,
Why does he gallop and gallop about?
    Ib. Windy Nights, st. 1

Dark brown is the river,
    Golden is the sand,
It flows along forever,
    With trees on either hand.
    Ib. Where Go the Boats, st. 1

The pleasant land of counterpane.
    Ib. The Land of Counterpane, st. 4

_____

on St. Ursula's day, and named them after the
saint and her eleven thousand mythical virgins.
Unfortunately, English buccaneers have since
given to most of them less poetic names. The
Dutchman's Cap, Broken Jerusalem, The Dead
Man's Chest, Rum Island, and so forth, mark
a time and race more prosaic. — CHARLES KINGS-
LEY, *At Last* [1870], *ch. 1*

I have a little shadow that goes in and
    out with me,
And what can be the use of him is more
    than I can see.
He is very, very like me from the heels
    up to the head;
And I see him jump before me, when I
    jump into my bed.
    A *Child's Garden of Verses.*
    My Shadow, st. 1

The friendly cow all red and white,
    I love with all my heart:
She gives me cream with all her might,
    To eat with apple tart.
    Ib. The Cow, st. 1

The world is so full of a number of
    things,
I'm sure we should all be as happy as
    kings.   *Ib. Happy Thought*

Little Indian, Sioux or Crow,
Little frosty Eskimo,
Little Turk or Japanee,
O! don't you wish that you were me?
    Ib. Foreign Children

    Am I no a bonny fighter?
    Kidnapped [1886], *ch. 10*
    [Alan Breck]

Of all my verse, like not a single line;
But like my title, for it is not mine.
That title from a better man [1] I stole:
Ah, how much better, had I stol'n the
    whole!
    Underwoods [1887], *foreword*

Life is over, life was gay:
We have come the primrose way.
    Ib. Envoy

Dear Andrew, with the brindled hair.[2]
    Ib. To Andrew Lang

Under the wide and starry sky,
Dig the grave and let me lie.
Glad did I live and gladly die,
    And I laid me down with a will.

This be the verse you grave for me:
Here he lies where he longed to be;

[1] Ben Jonson.
[2] Dear Louis of the awful cheek!
    Who told you it was right to speak,
    Where all the world might hear and stare,
    Of other fellows' "brindled hair"?
    ANDREW LANG [1844–1912], *To R. L. S.*

Home is the sailor, home from sea,
And the hunter home from the hill.
Underwoods. Requiem

If I have faltered more or less
In my great task of happiness.
Ib. The Celestial Surgeon

Yet, O stricken heart, remember, O remember
How of human days he lived the better part.
April came to bloom and never dim December
Breathed its killing chills upon the head or heart.
*Ib. In Memoriam F. A.
Stilwell* [1] [1881]

Let first the onion flourish there,
Rose among roots, the maiden-fair
Wine-scented and poetic soul
Of the capacious salad bowl.
Ib. To a Gardener

My body, which my dungeon is,
And yet my parks and palaces.
Ib. XXXVII

I have thus played the sedulous ape to Hazlitt, to Lamb, to Wordsworth, to Sir Thomas Browne, to Defoe, to Hawthorne, to Montaigne, to Baudelaire and to Obermann.
Memories and Portraits [1887].
A College Magazine

A Penny Plain and Twopence Colored.
*Ib. Essay About Skelt's
Juvenile Drama*

Wealth I ask not, hope nor love,
Nor a friend to know me;
All I ask, the heaven above
And the road below me.
*Songs of Travel. The Vagabond,
st. 4*

The untented Kosmos my abode,
I pass, a willful stranger;
My mistress still the open road
And the bright eyes of danger.
Ib. Youth and Love

[1] Lady Colvin's son by her first marriage; he died at the age of eighteen.

I will make you brooches and toys for your delight
Of birdsong at morning and starshine at night.
Songs of Travel. Romance, st. 1

God, if this were enough,
That I see things bare to the buff.
Ib. If This Were Faith

Bright is the ring of words
When the right man rings them.
Ib. XIV

In the highlands, in the country places,
Where the old plain men have rosy faces,
And the young fair maidens
Quiet eyes. *Ib. XV*

Trusty, dusky, vivid, true,
With eyes of gold and bramble dew,
Steel-true and blade-straight
The great artificer
Made my mate.
Ib. XXV, To My Wife, st. 1

Be it granted me to behold you again in dying,
Hills of home!
Ib. XLV, To S. R. Crockett

Not every man is so great a coward as he thinks he is — nor yet so good a Christian.
The Master of Ballantrae [1889].
Mr. Mackellar's Journey

Nothing like a little judicious levity.
The Wrong Box [1889], *ch.* 7

Do you know what the Governor of South Carolina said to the Governor of North Carolina? It's a long time between drinks, observed that powerful thinker.[1] *Ib.* 8

[1] Of the several traditions relating to the origin of this remark, the most reasonable one traces it to John Motley Morehead [1796–1866], who was Governor of North Carolina 1841–1845. He was visited by James H. Hammond [1807–1864], who was Governor of South Carolina 1842–1844. They engaged in discussion and argument, and when the latter waxed hot, Governor Morehead was reported by a servant to have exclaimed: "It's a long time between drinks." — JOHN MOTLEY MOREHEAD, *letter* [November 21, 1934]

So long as we love we serve; so long as we are loved by others, I would almost say that we are indispensable; and no man is useless while he has a friend.
Across the Plains [1892].
Lay Morals

To be honest, to be kind — to earn a little and spend a little less, to make upon the whole a family happier for his presence, to renounce when that shall be necessary and not to be embittered, to keep a few friends, but these without capitulation — above all, on the same grim condition, to keep friends with himself — here is a task for all that a man has of fortitude and delicacy.
A Christmas Sermon

If your morals make you dreary, depend upon it, they are wrong. I do not say give them up, for they may be all you have, but conceal them like a vice lest they should spoil the lives of better and simpler people. *Ib.*

Here lies one who meant well, tried a little, failed much: — surely that may be his epitaph of which he need not be ashamed. *Ib.*

Ice and iron cannot be welded.
Weir of Hermiston [1896]

Give us grace and strength to forbear and to persevere. Give us courage and gaiety and the quiet mind, spare to us our friends, soften to us our enemies.
Prayer [1]

Youth is wholly experimental.
Letter to a Young Gentleman

ROSE HARTWICK THORPE
1850–1939

She breathed the husky whisper —
"Curfew must not ring tonight."
Curfew Must Not Ring Tonight
[1882], *st. 2*

[1] On the bronze memorial to Stevenson in St. Giles Cathedral, Edinburgh, Scotland.

Long, long years I've rung the curfew
from that gloomy, shadowed tower;
Every evening, just at sunset, it has tolled the twilight hour;
I have done my duty ever, tried to do it just and right,
Now I'm old, I will not miss it. Curfew bell must ring tonight!
Curfew Must Not Ring Tonight,
st. 3

Out she swung — far out; the city seemed a speck of light below,
There 'twixt heaven and earth suspended as the bell swung to and fro. *Ib. st. 7*

ELLA WHEELER WILCOX
1850–1919

Talk happiness. The world is sad enough
Without your woe. No path is wholly rough. *Speech, st. 1*

Talk faith. The world is better off without
Your uttered ignorance and morbid doubt. *Ib. st. 2*

One ship drives east and another drives west
With the selfsame winds that blow.
'Tis the set of sails and not the gales
Which tells us the way to go.
Winds of Fate

No! the two kinds of people on earth that I mean
Are the people who lift and the people who lean. *To Lift or to Lean*

It ever has been since time began,
And ever will be, till time lose breath,
That love is a mood — no more — to man,
And love to woman is life or death.[1]
Blind, st. 1

Laugh, and the world laughs with you;
Weep, and you weep alone;

[1] See Byron, p. 560a.

For the sad old earth must borrow its
    mirth,
But has trouble enough of its own.
Solitude, st. 1

So many gods, so many creeds,
    So many paths that wind and wind,
    When just the art of being kind
Is all this sad world needs.
The World's Need

No question is ever settled
Until it is settled right.
Settle the Question Right

FERDINAND FOCH
1851–1929

My center is giving way, my right is
pushed back, situation excellent, I am
attacking.[1]
*Said at the Second Battle of the
Marne* [1918]. *From* B. H. LID-
DELL HART, *Reputations Ten
Years After* [1928]

EDWARD SMITH
UFFORD
1851–1929

Throw out the lifeline across the dark
    wave,
There is a brother whom someone
    should save.
Throw Out the Lifeline
[1884], *st. 1*

Throw out the lifeline, throw out the
    lifeline,
Someone is sinking today.
Ib. refrain

FRANCIS WILLIAM
BOURDILLON
1852–1921

The night has a thousand eyes,[2]
    And the day but one;
Yet the light of the bright world dies
    With the dying sun.

---

[1] Mon centre cède, ma droite recule, situation
excellente, j'attaque.
[2] On the stars thou gazest, my star; would I
were heaven to look at thee with many eyes. —
Greek Anthology, pt. VIII, no. 7. Translated by
J. W. MACKAIL.
    See Lyly, p. 203a.

The mind has a thousand eyes,
    And the heart but one;
Yet the light of a whole life dies
    When love is done.
The Night Has a Thousand Eyes

ROBERT BONTINE
CUNNINGHAME-
GRAHAM
1852–1936

Success, which touches nothing that
it does not vulgarize, should be its own
reward . . . the odium of success is
hard enough to bear, without the added
ignominy of popular applause.
Success [1902]

God forbid that I should go to any
heaven in which there are no horses.
Letter to Theodore Roosevelt
[1917]

EDWIN MARKHAM
1852–1940

Bowed by the weight of centuries he
    leans
Upon his hoe and gazes on the
    ground,
The emptiness of ages in his face,
And on his back the burden of the
    world.
The Man with the Hoe [1] [1899],
st. 1

O masters, lords and rulers in all lands,
Is this the handiwork you give to God?
Ib. st. 3

Here was a man to hold against the
    world,
A man to match the mountains [2] and
    the sea.
Lincoln, the Man of the People
[1901], *st. 1*

---

[1] Inspired by Millet's painting.
[2] A man to match his mountains, not to
    creep
Dwarfed and abased below them.
WHITTIER, *Among the Hills* [1869],
prelude
    Bring me men to match my mountains. —
SAM WALTER FOSS [1858–1911], *The Coming
American*

The color of the ground was in him, the red earth,
The smack and tang of elemental things.
Lincoln, the Man of the People, st. 2

He went down
As when a lordly cedar, green with boughs,
Goes down with a great shout upon the hills,
And leaves a lonesome place against the sky.   *Ib. st. 4*

He drew a circle that shut me out —
Heretic, rebel, a thing to flout.
But Love and I had the wit to win:
We drew a circle that took him in.
Outwitted

ALBERT ABRAHAM MICHELSON
1852–1931

The more important fundamental laws and facts of physical science have all been discovered, and these are now so firmly established that the possibility of their ever being supplanted in consequence of new discoveries is exceedingly remote . . . Our future discoveries must be looked for in the sixth place of decimals.
Address, dedication ceremony, Ryerson Physical Laboratory, University of Chicago [1894]

GEORGE MOORE
1852–1933

After all there is but one race — humanity.
The Bending of the Bough [1900], act III

The difficulty in life is the choice.
Ib. IV

The wrong way always seems the more reasonable.   *Ib.*

English, Scotchmen, Jews, do well in Ireland — Irishmen never; even the patriot has to leave Ireland to get a hearing.   *Ave [1911]. Overture*

A man travels the world over in search of what he needs and returns home to find it.
The Brook Kerith [1916], ch. 11

HENRY VAN DYKE
1852–1933

If all the skies were sunshine,
  Our faces would be fain
To feel once more upon them
  The cooling plash of rain.
If All the Skies, st. 1

Raise the stone, and thou shalt find me;
  cleave the wood and there am I.[1]
The Toiling of Felix [1900], pt. I, prelude

So it's home again, and home again,
  America for me.
My heart is turning home again, and
  there I long to be.
America for Me, st. 2

Oh, London is a man's town, there's
  power in the air;
And Paris is a woman's town, with
  flowers in her hair.   *Ib. st. 3*

Not to the swift, the race:
Not to the strong, the fight:[2]
Not to the righteous, perfect grace:
Not to the wise, the light.
Reliance, st. 1

The lintel low enough to keep out
  pomp and pride:
The threshold high enough to turn deceit aside.
For the Friends at Hurstmont. The Door

Self is the only prison that can ever
  bind the soul.
The Prison and the Angel

[1] *Oxyrhynchus Logia Agrapha, The Unwritten Sayings of Jesus, Fifth Logion.*
Raise ye the stone or cleave the wood to make a path more fair or flat;
Lo, it is black already with blood some Son of Martha spilled for that.
      RUDYARD KIPLING [1865–1936]. *The Sons of Martha*
[2] See *Ecclesiastes 9:11*, p. 28b, and John Davidson, p. 844b.

It is with rivers as it is with people: the greatest are not always the most agreeable nor the best to live with.

Little Rivers, ch. 2

The first day of spring is one thing, and the first spring day is another. The difference between them is sometimes as great as a month.

Fisherman's Luck, ch. 5

EDGAR WATSON HOWE
1853–1937

A really busy person never knows how much he weighs.

Country Town Sayings [1911]

What people say behind your back is your standing in the community. *Ib.*

There is nothing so well known as that we should not expect something for nothing — but we all do and call it Hope. *Ib.*

JOSÉ MARTÍ
1853–1895

A knowledge of different literatures is the best way to free one's self from the tyranny of any of them.

On Oscar Wilde [1882]

To beautify life is to give it an object. *Ib.*

Terrible times in which priests no longer merit the praise of poets and in which poets have not yet begun to be priests.

On "El Poema de Niágara" of Pérez Bonalde [1883]

This is the age in which hills can look down upon the mountains. *Ib.*

Only those who hate the Negro see hatred in the Negro.

Manifesto of Montecristi [1895]

The spirit of a government must be that of the country. The form of a government must come from the makeup of the country. Government is nothing but the balance of the natural elements of a country. *Our America [1891]*

I have lived in the monster [the United States] and I know its insides; and my sling is the sling of David.

Letter to Manuel Mercado [1895]

CECIL JOHN RHODES
1853–1902

I desire to encourage and foster an appreciation of the advantages which will result from the union of the English-speaking peoples throughout the world, and to encourage in the students from the United States of America an attachment to the country from which they have sprung without I hope withdrawing them or their sympathies from the land of their adoption or birth.

Will, establishing the Rhodes Scholarships

Educational relations make the strongest tie. *Ib.*

So little done — so much to do.

Last words

IRWIN RUSSELL
1853–1879

De man what keeps pullin' de grapevine shakes down a few bunches at leas'.

Precepts at Parting [1888], st. 3

You mus' reason with a mule.

Nebuchadnezzar [1888], st. 3

JAMES A. BLAND
1854–1911

Carry me back to old Virginny,
There's where the cotton and the corn and taters grow;
There's where the birds warble sweet in the springtime,
There's where this old darky's heart am long'd to go.

Carry Me Back to Old Virginny [1875], st. 1

SIR JAMES GEORGE FRAZER
1854–1941

Dwellers by the sea cannot fail to be impressed by the sight of its ceaseless ebb and flow, and are apt, on the principles of that rude philosophy of sympathy and resemblance . . . to trace a subtle relation, a secret harmony, between its tides and the life of man. . . . The belief that most deaths happen at ebb tide is said to be held along the east coast of England from Northumberland to Kent.[1]
The Golden Bough,[2] *ch. 3*

The heaviest calamity in English history, the breach with America, might never have occurred if George the Third had not been an honest dullard.
Ib.

By religion, then, I understand a propitiation or conciliation of powers superior to man which are believed to direct and control the course of nature and of human life. *Ib. 4*

It is a common rule with primitive people not to waken a sleeper, because his soul is away and might not have time to get back. *Ib. 18*

The awe and dread with which the untutored savage contemplates his mother-in-law are amongst the most familiar facts of anthropology. *Ib.*

The world cannot live at the level of its great men. *Ib. 37*

THOMAS RILEY MARSHALL
1854–1925

What this country needs is a good five-cent cigar.[3]
Remark to John Crockett, Chief Clerk of the United States Senate

[1] See Shakespeare, *Henry V, II, iii, 11, p. 243b*, and Dickens, p. 671b.
[2] Abridged one-volume edition [1922]. The original appeared in twelve volumes from 1890 to 1915.
[3] What this country needs is a good five-cent nickel. — FRANKLIN P. ADAMS [1932]

BENJAMIN PIERCE
1854–1914

Mathematics is the science which draws necessary conclusions.
Linear Associative Algebra. In the American Journal of Mathematics, vol. IV [1881], p. 97

JULES HENRI POINCARÉ
1854–1912

The advance of science is not comparable to the changes of a city, where old edifices are pitilessly torn down to give place to new, but to the continuous evolution of zoologic types which develop ceaselessly and end by becoming unrecognizable to the common sight, but where an expert eye finds always traces of the prior work of the past centuries.
Valeur de la Science [1] *[1904]*

Science is built up with facts, as a house is with stones. But a collection of facts is no more a science than a heap of stones is a house.
La Science et l'Hypothèse [1] *[1908]*

ARTHUR RIMBAUD
1854–1891

I went out under the sky, Muse! and I was your vassal.
Ma Bohème. Fantaisie

My tavern was the Big Bear. — My stars in the sky rustled softly.
Ib.

My sad heart foams at the stern.
Le Coeur Volé

Lighter than a cork I danced on the waves. *Le Bateau Ivre [1871]*

Sweeter than apples to children
The green water spurted through my wooden hull. *Ib.*

I have bathed in the poem of the sea . . .
Devouring the green azures. *Ib.*

[1] Translated by G. B. HALSTED.

Sometimes I saw what men have only dreamed of seeing.
Le Bateau Ivre

I have seen the sunset, stained with mystic wonders,
Illumine the rolling waves with long purple forms,
Like actors in ancient plays.   *Ib.*

I long for Europe of the ancient parapets.   *Ib.*

I have seen starry archipelagoes! and islands
Whose heavens are opened to the voyager:
Is it in these bottomless nights that you sleep, in exile,
A million golden birds, O future Vigor?
Ib.

Black A, white E, red I, green U, blue O: vowels,
Someday I shall recount your latent births.[1]   *Voyelles* [1871]

It is found again.
What? Eternity.
It is the sea
Gone with the sun.
L'Éternité [1872]

O seasons, O châteaux,
What soul is without flaws? [2]
Bonheur, refrain

One evening, I sat Beauty in my lap. — And I found her bitter. — And I cursed her.
Une Saison en Enfer (1873)

I found I could extinguish all human hope from my soul.   *Ib.*

Baptism enslaved me.
Ib. Nuit de L'Enfer

I am the master of fantasy.   *Ib.*

Old poetics played a large part in my alchemy of the word.   *Ib.*

---

[1] I devised colors for the vowels! — A black, E white, I red, O yellow, U green. — *Une Saison en Enfer* [1873], *Délires II, Alchimie de Verbe*
[2] O saisons, O châteaux
Quelle âme est sans défauts?

I! I who fashioned myself a sorcerer or an angel, who dispensed with all morality, I have come back to the earth.
Une Saison en Enfer. Adieu

One must be absolutely modern.
Ib.

I have embraced the summer dawn.
Illuminations [1874]. *Aube*

It rains softly on the town.[1]
From a lost poem

I say one must be a *seer*, make oneself a *seer*.
The poet makes himself a *seer* by an immense, long, deliberate derangement of all the senses.[2]
Lettre à Paul Demeny [*May* 15, 1871]

EDITH MATILDA THOMAS
1854–1925

The God of Music dwelleth out of doors.   *Music*

WILLARD DUNCAN VANDIVER
1854–1932

I come from a state that raises corn and cotton and cockleburs and Democrats, and frothy eloquence neither convinces nor satisfies me. I am from Missouri. You have got to show me.
Speech at a naval banquet in Philadelphia [1899]

GERALD BRENNAN
fl. 1899

Th' mem'ry comes like a banshee meself an' me wealth between,
An' I long for a mornin's mornin' in Shanahan's ould shebeen.
Shanahan's Ould Shebeen [1899], *st.* 4

---

[1] Il pleut doucement sur la ville.
Verlaine used this as an epigraph for his *Ariettes Oubliées*, III. See Verlaine, p. 808a.
[2] Déréglement de tous les sens.
See Baudelaire, footnote [1], p. 706b.

If you couldn't afford good whiskey,
  he'd take you on trust for beer.
Shanahan's Ould Shebeen, st. 5

WILLIAM COWPER BRANN[1]
1855–1898

Boston runs to brains as well as to beans and brown bread. But she is cursed with an army of cranks whom nothing short of a straitjacket or a swamp elm club will ever control.
From The Iconoclast. Beans and Blood

No man can be a patriot on an empty stomach.
Ib. Old Glory [July 4, 1893]

It has the subtle flavor of an old pair of socks.   *Ib. Godey's Magazine*

The Lydian notes of Andrew Carnegie as he warbles a riant roundelay in praise of poverty, or laments in pathetic spondees the woes of the man with spondulix.   *Ib. Our American Czars*

HENRY CUYLER BUNNER
1855–1896

Off with your hat as the flag goes by!
  And let the heart have its say;
You're man enough for a tear in your
  eye
That you will not wipe away.
      The Old Flag, st. 1

I have a bookcase, which is what
Many much better men have not.
There are no books inside, for books,
I am afraid, might spoil its looks.
But I've three busts, all secondhand,
Upon the top. You understand
I could not put them underneath —
Shake, Mulleary and Go-ethe.
    Shake, Mulleary and Go-ethe, st. 1

---

[1] Known as "The Iconoclast" from the name of his paper, first published in Austin, Texas, and later in Waco.

EUGENE VICTOR DEBS
1855–1926

While there is a lower class I am in it, while there is a criminal element I am of it; while there is a soul in prison, I am not free.   *On labor and freedom*

The savings of many in the hands of one.   *On wealth*

MARGARET WOLFE HUNGERFORD
1855–1897

Beauty is in the eye of the beholder.[1]
      Molly Bawn [1878]

FRANK FRANKFORT MOORE
1855–1931

He knew that to offer a man friendship when love is in his heart is like giving a loaf of bread to one who is dying of thirst.
      The Jessamy Bride, ch. 9

To strike at a serpent that hisses may only cause it to spring.   *Ib. 19*

WALTER HINES PAGE
1855–1918

There is one thing better than good government, and that is government in which all the people have a part.
      Life and Letters [1922–1925], vol. III, p. 31

SIR ARTHUR WING PINERO
1855–1934

From forty till fifty a man is at heart either a stoic or a satyr.
      The Second Mrs. Tanqueray [1893], act I

---

[1] See Hume, p. 434b, and Wallace, p. 729b.

OLIVE SCHREINER
[RALPH IRON]
1855–1920

The barb in the arrow of childhood suffering is this: its intense loneliness, its intense ignorance.
> *The Story of an African Farm*
> *[1884], ch. 1*

There never was a man who said one word for woman but he said two for man and three for the whole human race.   *Ib. 4*

FIONA MACLEOD
[WILLIAM SHARP]
1855–1905

My heart is a lonely hunter that hunts on a lonely hill.
> *The Lonely Hunter, st. 6*

CY WARMAN
1855–1914

Every daisy in the dell knows my secret, knows it well,
And yet I dare not tell, sweet Marie.
> *Sweet Marie [1893], st. 1*

GEORGE EDWARD WOODBERRY
1855–1930

She from old fountains doth new judgment draw,
Till, word by word, the ancient order swerves
To the true course more nigh; in every age
A little she creates, but more preserves.
> *My Country*

JOSEPH TABRAR
fl. 1892

I've got a little cat,
And I'm very fond of that,
But I'd rather have a bow-wow, wow.
> *Daddy Wouldn't Buy Me a Bow-*
> *Wow [1892]*

LYMAN FRANK BAUM
1856–1919

The Wonderful Wizard of Oz.
> *Title of book [1900]*

FRANCIS BELLAMY
1856–1931

I pledge allegiance to the flag of the United States of America and to the republic for which it stands, one nation, under God, indivisible, with liberty and justice for all.[1]
> *The Pledge of Allegiance to the*
> *Flag [1892]*

THEOBALD VON BETHMANN-HOLLWEG
1856–1921

Just for a word — "neutrality," a word which in wartime has so often been disregarded, just for a scrap of paper — Great Britain is going to make war.
> *To Sir Edward Goschen [August*
> *4, 1914]; dispatch from Goschen*
> *to the British Foreign Office*

LOUIS D. BRANDEIS
1856–1941

Those who won our independence believed that the final end of the State was to make men free to develop their faculties; and that in its government the deliberative forces should prevail over the arbitrary. They valued liberty both as an end and as a means. They believed liberty to be the secret of happiness and courage to be the secret of liberty.[2]
> *Whitney v. California, 274 U.S.*
> *357, 375 [1927]*

Fear of serious injury cannot alone justify suppression of free speech and assembly. Men feared witches and burned women. It is the function of speech to free men from the bondage of irrational fears.   *Ib. 376*

[1] In 1888 JAMES B. UPHAM [1845–1905] wrote a rough draft of the pledge which Bellamy, as chairman of a committee for a national school program to celebrate the four-hundredth anniversary of the discovery of America, helped to put into its final form.

The phrase "under God" was added by a joint resolution of Congress approved by the President, June 14, 1954.

[2] See Thucydides, p. 90a.

They [the makers of the Constitution] conferred, as against the Government, the right to be let alone — the most comprehensive of rights and the right most valued by civilized men.

> *Olmstead v. United States,*
> *277 U.S. 438, 478* [1928]

The greatest dangers to liberty lurk in insidious encroachment by men of zeal, well-meaning but without understanding.

> *Ib. 479*

Our Government is the potent, the omnipresent teacher. For good or for ill, it teaches the whole people by its example.   *Ib. 485*

If we would guide by the light of reason, we must let our minds be bold.

> *New State Ice Co. v. Liebmann,*
> *285 U.S. 262, 311* [1932]

Stare decisis is usually the wise policy, because in most matters it is more important that the applicable rule of law be settled than that it be settled right. . . . But in cases involving the Federal Constitution, where correction through legislative action is practically impossible, this Court has often overruled its earlier decisions. The Court bows to the lessons of experience and the force of better reasoning, recognizing that the process of trial and error, so fruitful in the physical sciences, is appropriate also in the judicial function.

> *Burnet v. Coronado Oil and Gas*
> *Co., 285 U.S. 393, 406* [1932]

There is in most Americans some spark of idealism, which can be fanned into a flame. It takes sometimes a divining rod to find what it is; but when found, and that means often, when disclosed to the owners, the results are often extraordinary.

> *The Words of Justice Brandeis*
> [1953]

KENYON COX
1856–1919

Work thou for pleasure — paint, or
sing, or carve
The thing thou lovest, though the body
starve —
Who works for glory misses oft the
goal;
Who works for money coins his very
soul.
Work for the work's sake, then, and it
may be
That these things shall be added unto
thee.

> *The Gospel of Art* [1895]

SIGMUND FREUD[1]
1856–1939

Being entirely honest with oneself is a good exercise.

> *Origins of Psychoanalysis. Letter*
> *to Fliess* [October 15, 1897]

No one who, like me, conjures up the most evil of those half-tamed demons that inhabit the human breast, and seeks to wrestle with them, can expect to come through the struggle unscathed.

> *Complete Psychological Works.*
> *Dora* [1905]

Conscience is the internal perception of the rejection of a particular wish operating within us.

> *Ib. Totem and Taboo* [1912–
> 1913]

At bottom God is nothing more than an exalted father.   *Ib.*

The psychic development of the individual is a short repetition of the course of development of the race.[2]

> *Leonardo da Vinci* [1916]

When the wayfarer whistles in the dark, he may be disavowing his timidity, but he does not see any the more clearly for doing so.

> *The Problem of Anxiety* [1925]

[1] See Auden, p. 1060a, and Whitehead, p. 861b.

[2] See Haeckel, p. 752b.

The poets and philosophers before me discovered the unconscious; what I discovered was the scientific method by which the unconscious can be studied.

On his seventieth birthday [1926]; *from* LIONEL TRIL-LING, *The Liberal Imagination*

The voice of the intellect is a soft one, but it does not rest until it has gained a hearing. Ultimately, after endlessly repeated rebuffs, it succeeds. This is one of the few points in which one may be optimistic about the future of mankind, but in itself it signifies not a little.   *Future of an Illusion* [1928]

Analogies prove nothing, that is quite true, but they can make one feel more at home.

New Introductory Lectures on Psychoanalysis [1932]

One might compare the relation of the ego to the id with that between a rider and his horse. The horse provides the locomotor energy, and the rider has the prerogative of determining the goal and of guiding the movements of his powerful mount towards it. But all too often in the relations between the ego and the id we find a picture of the less ideal situation in which the rider is obliged to guide his horse in the direction in which it itself wants to go.

Ib. The Anatomy of the Mental Personality (Lecture 31)

The poor ego has a still harder time of it; it has to serve three harsh masters, and has to do its best to reconcile the claims and demands of all three. . . . The three tyrants are the external world, the superego and the id.   *Ib.*

Where id was, there shall ego be.   *Ib.*

Thinking is an experimental dealing with small quantities of energy, just as a general moves miniature figures over a map before setting his troops in action.

Ib. Anxiety and Instinctual Life (Lecture 32)

If one wishes to form a true estimate of the full grandeur of religion, one must keep in mind what it undertakes to do for men. It gives them information about the source and origin of the universe, it assures them of protection and final happiness amid the changing vicissitudes of life, and it guides their thoughts and motions by means of precepts which are backed by the whole force of its authority.

New Introductory Lectures on Psychoanalysis. A Philosophy of Life (Lecture 35)

Religion is an attempt to get control over the sensory world, in which we are placed, by means of the wish-world, which we have developed inside us as a result of biological and psychological necessities.   *Ib.*

Religion is an illusion and it derives its strength from the fact that it falls in with our instinctual desires.   *Ib.*

The Mosaic religion had been a Father religion; Christianity became a Son religion. The old God, the Father, took second place; Christ, the Son, stood in His stead, just as in those dark times every son had longed to do.

Moses and Monotheism [1938]

Man found that he was faced with the acceptance of "spiritual" forces, that is to say such forces as cannot be apprehended by the senses, particularly not by sight, and yet having undoubted, even extremely strong, effects. If we may trust to language, it was the movement of the air that provided the image of spirituality, since the spirit borrows its name from the breath of wind (animus, spiritus, Hebrew: ruach = smoke). The idea of the soul was thus born as the spiritual principle in the individual. . . . Now the realm of spirits had opened for man, and he was ready to endow everything in nature with the soul he had discovered in himself.   *Ib.*

A man who has been the indisputable favorite of his mother keeps for life the feeling of a conqueror, that confidence of success that often induces real success.

> *From* ERNEST JONES, *Life and Works of Sigmund Freud, vol. I* [*1953*], *ch. 1*

The great question . . . which I have not been able to answer, despite my thirty years of research into the feminine soul, is "What does a woman want?"

> *Quoted in* CHARLES ROLO, *Psychiatry in American Life* [*1963*]

EDMOND HARAUCOURT
1856–1941

To leave is to die a little;
To die to what we love.
We leave behind a bit of ourselves
Wherever we have been.[1]

> *Choix de Poésies* [*1891*]. *Rondel de l'Adieu*

ELBERT HUBBARD
1856–1915

It is not book learning young men need, nor instruction about this and that, but a stiffening of the vertebrae which will cause them to be loyal to a trust, to act promptly, concentrate their energies, do a thing — "carry a message to Garcia."[2]

> *A Message to Garcia* [*March 1899*]

The man who is anybody and who does anything is surely going to be criticized, vilified, and misunderstood. This is a part of the penalty for greatness, and every great man understands it;

[1] Partir, c'est mourir un peu;
  C'est mourir à ce qu'on aime.
  On laisse un peu de soi-même
  En toute heure et dans tout lieu.
  Translated by NORBERT GUTERMAN.
  See Schopenhauer, p. 563b.
[2] After the declaration of the Spanish-American War, Andrew Summers Rowan, then Lieutenant, United States Bureau of Military Intelligence, was sent to communicate with General Calixto Garcia. He landed in an open boat near Turquino Peak, April 24, 1898, executed the mission, and brought back information regarding the insurgent army.

and understands, too, that it is no proof of greatness. The final proof of greatness lies in being able to endure contumely without resentment.

> *Get Out or Get in Line*

This will never be a civilized country until we expend more money for books than we do for chewing gum.

> *From The Philistine* [*1895–1915*]

The path of civilization is paved with tin cans. *Ib.*

EDWARD SANDFORD MARTIN
1856–1939

A Little Brother of the Rich.

> *Title of poem*

ROBERT EDWIN PEARY
1856–1920

The Eskimo, Ootah, had his own explanation. Said he: "The devil is asleep or having trouble with his wife, or we should never have come back so easily."

> *The North Pole* [*1910*]

HENRI PHILIPPE PÉTAIN
1856–1951

They shall not pass.[1]

> *Attributed. Verdun* [*February 26, 1916*]

LIZETTE WOODWORTH REESE
1856–1935

When I consider life and its few
  years —
A wisp of fog betwixt us and the sun;

[1] Ils ne passeront pas.
  The first official record of the expression appears in General Nivelle's Order of the Day [June 23, 1916] to his troops at the height of battle: *Vous ne les laisserez pas passer* [You will not let them pass]! — ALAN HORNE, *New York Times Magazine* [February 20, 1966]
  The inscription on the Verdun medal is: **On** ne passe pas.

A call to battle, and the battle
  done . . .
I wonder at the idleness of tears.
                              Tears

The burst of music down an unlisten-
  ing street.   *Ib.*

Creeds grow so thick along the way,
Their boughs hide God.   *Doubt*

GEORGE BERNARD SHAW
1856–1950

My method is to take the utmost
trouble to find the right thing to say,
and then to say it with the utmost
levity.   *Answers to Nine Questions*

It's well to be off with the Old
Woman before you're on with the
New.[1]
          The Philanderer [1893], *act II*

The fickleness of the women I love is
only equaled by the infernal constancy
of the women who love me.[2]   *Ib.*

The test of a man or woman's breeding is how they behave in a quarrel.
                              Ib. IV

People are always blaming their circumstances for what they are. I don't
believe in circumstances. The people
who get on in this world are the people
who get up and look for the circumstances they want, and, if they can't
find them, make them.
          Mrs. Warren's Profession
                      [1893], *act II*

There are no secrets better kept than
the secrets that everybody guesses.
                              Ib. III

A great devotee of the Gospel of
Getting On.   *Ib. IV*

We have no more right to consume
happiness without producing it than to
consume wealth without producing it.
          Candida [1898], *act I*

I'm only a beer teetotaler, not a
champagne teetotaler.   *Ib. III*

---

[1] See C. H. Webb, p. 753b.
[2] See Cervantes, p. 194b.

We don't bother much about dress
and manners in England, because as a
nation we don't dress well and we've no
manners.
          You Never Can Tell [1898],
                              act I

The great advantage of a hotel is
that it's a refuge from home life.
                              Ib. II

There is only one religion, though
there are a hundred versions of it.
          Plays Pleasant and Unpleasant
                  [1898], *vol. II, preface*

You're not a man, you're a machine.
          Arms and the Man [1898], *act III*

The worst sin towards our fellow
creatures is not to hate them, but to be
indifferent to them: that's the essence
of inhumanity.
          The Devil's Disciple [1901], *act II*

This is the true joy in life, the being
used for a purpose recognized by yourself as a mighty one; the being thoroughly worn out before you are thrown
on the scrap heap; the being a force of
nature instead of a feverish selfish little
clod of ailments and grievances complaining that the world will not devote
itself to making you happy.
          Man and Superman [1903],
                      epistle dedicatory

A lifetime of happiness! No man
alive could bear it: it would be hell on
earth.   *Ib. act I*

The more things a man is ashamed
of, the more respectable he is.   *Ib.*

Marry Ann; and at the end of a week
you'll find no more inspiration in her
than in a plate of muffins.   *Ib. II*

An Englishman thinks he is moral
when he is only uncomfortable.
                              Ib. III

The golden rule is that there is no
golden rule.
          Ib. Maxims for Revolutionists

He who can, does. He who cannot,
teaches.   *Ib.*

Marriage is popular because it combines the maximum of temptation with the maximum of opportunity.
*Man and Superman, Maxims
for Revolutionists*

If you strike a child, take care that you strike it in anger, even at the risk of maiming it for life. A blow in cold blood neither can nor should be forgiven. **Ib.**

Virtue consists, not in abstaining from vice, but in not desiring it. **Ib.**

Lack of money is the root of all evil.[1]
Ib.

The greatest of evils and the worst of crimes is poverty.
Major Barbara [1907], *preface*

I can't talk religion to a man with bodily hunger in his eyes.[2]
Ib. act II

Blood and fire! **Ib.**

Home life as we understand it is no more natural to us than a cage is natural to a cockatoo.
Getting Married [1908], *preface*

When two people are under the influence of the most violent, most insane, most delusive, and most transient of passions, they are required to swear that they will remain in that excited, abnormal, and exhausting condition continuously until death do them part.
Ib.

A man is like a phonograph with half-a-dozen records. You soon get tired of them all; and yet you have to sit at table whilst he reels them off to every new visitor. *Ib. (The Play)*

The whole strength of England lies in the fact that the enormous majority of the English people are snobs. **Ib.**

You don't learn to hold your own in the world by standing on guard, but by attacking, and getting well hammered yourself. **Ib.**

[1] See *I Timothy 6:10*, p. 55b.
[2] See Conrad, p. 843b.

Religion is a great force — the only real motive force in the world; but what you fellows don't understand is that you must get at a man through his own religion and not through yours.
Getting Married

I like a bit of a mongrel myself, whether it's a man or a dog; they're the best for every day.
Misalliance [1910], *episode I*

If parents would only realize how they bore their children! **Ib.**

He's a gentleman: look at his boots.
Pygmalion [1912], *act I*

Women upset everything. When you let them into your life, you find that the woman is driving at one thing and you're driving at another. *Ib. II*

Not bloody likely. *Ib. III*

I have to live for others and not for myself; that's middle-class morality.
Ib. V

Independence? That's middle-class blasphemy. We are all dependent on one another, every soul of us on earth.
Ib.

All great truths begin as blasphemies.
Annajanska [1919]

The nauseous sham goodfellowship our democratic public men get up for shop use.
Back to Methuselah [1921].
Gospel of the Brothers Barnabas

Everything happens to everybody sooner or later if there is time enough.
Ib. As Far As Thought Can Reach

Silence is the most perfect expression of scorn. **Ib.**

The worst cliques are those which consist of one man. **Ib.**

Assassination is the extreme form of censorship.
The Rejected Statement, pt. I

The Jews generally give value. They make you pay; but they deliver the

goods. In my experience the men who want something for nothing are invariably Christians.
Saint Joan [1923], *sc. iv*

One man that has a mind and knows it can always beat ten men who haven't and don't.
The Apple Cart [1929], *act I*

I have defined the hundred per cent American as ninety-nine per cent an idiot.
Remarks on Sinclair Lewis receiving the Nobel Prize [1930]

An American has no sense of privacy. He does not know what it means. There is no such thing in the country.
Speech, New York [April 11, 1933]

You in America should trust to that volcanic political instinct which I have divined in you. *Ib.*

LOUIS HENRI SULLIVAN
1856–1924

Form ever follows function.
The Tall Office Building Artistically Considered, Lippincott's Magazine [March 1896]

JOSEPH JOHN THOMSON
1856–1940

From the point of view of the physicist, a theory of matter is a policy rather than a creed; its object is to connect or coordinate apparently diverse phenomena, and above all to suggest, stimulate and direct experiment.
The Corpuscular Theory of Matter [1907]

BOOKER TALIAFERRO WASHINGTON
1856–1915

No race can prosper till it learns that there is as much dignity in tilling a field as in writing a poem.
Up from Slavery [1901]

OSCAR FINGAL O'FLAHERTIE WILLS WILDE
1854–1900

Tread lightly, she is near
  Under the snow,
Speak gently, she can hear
  The daisies grow.
Requiescat, st. 1

  And yet, and yet,
These Christs that die upon the barricades,
God knows it I am with them, in some things.
Sonnet to Liberty: Not That I Love Thy Children

And down the long and silent street,
The dawn, with silver-sandaled feet,
Crept like a frightened girl.
The Harlot's House

  Lo! with a little rod
I did but touch the honey [1] of romance —
And must I lose a soul's inheritance?
Hélas [1881], *l. 12*

A poet can survive everything but a misprint.
The Children of the Poets

As for borrowing Mr. Whistler's ideas about art, the only thoroughly original ideas I have ever heard him express have had reference to his own superiority as a painter over painters greater than himself.
Reply to an attack by James McNeill Whistler. In Truth [January 9, 1890]

Meredith is a prose Browning, and so is Browning. He used poetry as a medium for writing in prose.
The Critic as Artist [1891], *pt. I*

It is through art, and through art only, that we can realize our perfection; through art and art only that we can shield ourselves from the sordid perils of actual existence. *Ib. II*

[1] See *I Samuel 14:27*, p. 12a.

As long as war is regarded as wicked, it will always have its fascination. When it is looked upon as vulgar, it will cease to be popular.

The Critic as Artist, pt. II

There is no sin except stupidity.[1]

Ib.

There is no such thing as a moral or an immoral book. Books are well written, or badly written. That is all.

The Picture of Dorian Gray
[1891], *preface*

All art is quite useless. *Ib.*

There is only one thing in the world worse than being talked about, and that is not being talked about. *Ib. ch. 1*

Conscience and cowardice are really the same things.[2] *Ib.*

A man cannot be too careful in the choice of his enemies.[3] *Ib.*

The only way to get rid of a temptation is to yield to it. *Ib. 2*

He knew the precise psychological moment [4] when to say nothing. *Ib.*

The only difference between a caprice and a lifelong passion is that the caprice lasts a little longer. *Ib.*

Children begin by loving their parents; as they grow older they judge them; sometimes they forgive them.

Ib. 5

Conscience makes egotists of us all.[5] *Ib. 8*

When a woman marries again it is because she detested her first husband. When a man marries again, it is because he adored his first wife.[1] Women try their luck; men risk theirs.

The Picture of Dorian Gray,
ch. 15

Over the piano was printed a notice: Please do not shoot the pianist. He is doing his best.

Impressions of America. Leadville

Nowadays we are all of us so hard up that the only pleasant things to pay are compliments. They're the only things we *can* pay.

Lady Windermere's Fan [1892],
act I

I can resist everything except temptation. *Ib.*

We are all in the gutter, but some of us are looking at the stars. *Ib. III*

In this world there are only two tragedies. One is not getting what one wants, and the other is getting it.

Ib.

What is a cynic? A man who knows the price of everything, and the value of nothing. *Ib.*

Experience is the name everyone gives to their mistakes. *Ib.*

I have never admitted that I am more than twenty-nine, or thirty at the most. Twenty-nine when there are pink shades, thirty when there are not.[2]

Ib. IV

Mrs. Allonby: They say, Lady Hunstanton, that when good Americans die they go to Paris.[3]

Lady Hunstanton: Indeed? And

---

[1] See Marlowe, p. 212b.

[2] See Mark Twain, p. 763a.

[3] See Conrad, p. 843a.

[4] In all considerations the psychological momentum or factor must be allowed to play a prominent part, for without its cooperation there is little to be hoped from the work of the artillery. — *Neue Preussische Kreuzzeitung* [December 16, 1870], commenting upon the siege of Paris.

An error in translation gave us "psychological moment" (i.e. the critical moment). The Parisians ridiculed the phrase as an example of German pedantry, but it speedily became universal.

[5] See Shakespeare, p. 262a.

[1] See Samuel Johnson, p. 431a.

[2] When you come to write my epitaph, Charles, let it be in these delicious words, "She had a long twenty-nine." — JAMES M. BARRIE [1860–1937], *Rosalind*

[3] Good Americans, when they die, go to Paris. — THOMAS GOLD APPLETON [1812–1884]; *from* OLIVER WENDELL HOLMES, *The Autocrat of the Breakfast Table* [1858]

when bad Americans die, where do they go to?

Lord Illingworth: Oh, they go to America.
> *A Woman of No Importance* *[1893], act I*

The youth of America is their oldest tradition. It has been going on now for three hundred years.   *Ib.*

Lord Illingworth: The Book of Life begins with a man and a woman in a garden.

Mrs. Allonby: It ends with Revelations.   *Ib.*

I suppose society is wonderfully delightful. To be in it is merely a bore. But to be out of it simply a tragedy.
> *Ib. III*

Really, if the lower orders don't set us a good example, what on earth is the use of them?
> *The Importance of Being* *Earnest [1895], act I*

I have invented an invaluable permanent invalid called Bunbury, in order that I may be able to go down into the country whenever I choose.   *Ib.*

Of course the music is a great difficulty. You see, if one plays good music, people don't listen, and if one plays bad music people don't talk.   *Ib.*

To lose one parent . . . may be regarded as a misfortune; to lose both looks like carelessness.   *Ib.*

Relations are simply a tedious pack of people, who haven't got the remotest knowledge of how to live, nor the smallest instinct about when to die.
> *Ib.*

I never travel without my diary. One should always have something sensational to read in the train.   *Ib. II*

No woman should ever be quite accurate about her age. It looks so calculating.   *Ib. III*

Democracy means simply the bludgeoning of the people by the people for the people.[1]
> *The Soul of Man Under* *Socialism [1895]*

The fact is, that civilization requires slaves. The Greeks were quite right there. Unless there are slaves to do the ugly, horrible, uninteresting work, culture and contemplation become almost impossible. Human slavery is wrong, insecure, and demoralizing. On mechanical slavery, on the slavery of the machine, the future of the world depends.[2]   *Ib.*

Charity creates a multitude of sins.
> *Ib.*

Art is the most intense mode of individualism that the world has known.
> *Ib.*

Now art should never try to be popular. The public should try to make itself artistic.   *Ib.*

The only thing that one really knows about human nature is that it changes. Change is the one quality we can predicate on it.[3]   *Ib.*

Anybody can make history. Only a great man can write it.   *Aphorisms*

I never saw a man who looked
   With such a wistful eye
Upon that little tent of blue
   Which prisoners call the sky.
> *The Ballad of Reading Gaol* *[1898], pt. I, st. 3*

When a voice behind me whispered low,
   "That fellow's got to swing."
> *Ib. st. 4*

Yet each man kills the thing he loves,[4]
   By each let this be heard,
Some do it with a bitter look,
   Some with a flattering word.

[1] See Lincoln, p. 851a.
[2] See Havelock Ellis, p. 639a.
[3] See Heraclitus, p. 77b.
[4] See Shakespeare, p. 234a.

The coward does it with a kiss,
The brave man with a sword!
　　　The Ballad of Reading Gaol,
　　　　　pt. I, st. 7

It is sweet to dance to violins
When Love and Life are fair:
To dance to flutes, to dance to lutes
Is delicate and rare:
But it is not sweet with nimble feet
To dance upon the air!
　　　　　Ib. II, st. 9

Something was dead in each of us,
And what was dead was Hope.
　　　　　Ib. st. 31

And the wild regrets, and the bloody
　　sweats,
None knew so well as I:
For he who lives more lives than one
More deaths than one must die.
　　　　　Ib. st. 37

I know not whether laws be right,
Or whether laws be wrong;
All that we know who lie in gaol
Is that the wall is strong;
And that each day is like a year,
A year whose days are long.
　　　　　Ib. V, st. 1

The vilest deeds like poison weeds
Bloom well in prison air:
It is only what is good in man
That wastes and withers there:
Pale Anguish keeps the heavy gate
And the Warder is Despair.
　　　　　Ib. st. 5

How else but through a broken heart
May Lord Christ enter in?
　　　　　Ib. st. 14

Where there is sorrow there is holy
ground.　　*De Profundis* [1905]

WOODROW WILSON
1856–1924

The United States must be neutral in
fact as well as in name. . . . We must
be impartial in thought as well as in
action.
　　　Message to the U.S. Senate
　　　　[August 19, 1914]

You deal in the raw material of opinion, and, if my convictions have any
validity, opinion ultimately governs the
world.
　　　Address to the Associated Press
　　　　[April 20, 1915]

There is such a thing as a man being
too proud to fight.
　　　Address to Foreign-Born Citizens
　　　　[May 10, 1915]

[The Civil War] created in this
country what had never existed before
— a national consciousness. It was not
the salvation of the Union; it was the
rebirth of the Union.
　　　Memorial Day Address [1915]

The things that the flag stands for
were created by the experiences of a
great people. Everything that it stands
for was written by their lives. The flag
is the embodiment, not of sentiment,
but of history. It represents the experiences made by men and women, the
experiences of those who do and live
under that flag.
　　　Address [*June 14, 1915*]

We have stood apart, studiously
neutral.
　　　Message to Congress [*Decem-
　　　　ber 7, 1915*]

America cannot be an ostrich with its
head in the sand.
　　　Speech, Des Moines [*Feb-
　　　　ruary 1, 1916*]

There must be, not a balance of
power, but a community of power; not
organized rivalries, but an organized
common peace.
　　　Address to the U.S. Senate
　　　　[January 22, 1917]

It must be a peace without victory.
. . . Victory would mean peace forced
upon the loser, a victor's terms imposed
upon the vanquished. It would be accepted in humiliation, under duress, at
an intolerable sacrifice, and would leave
a sting, a resentment, a bitter memory
upon which terms of peace would rest,

not permanently, but only as upon quicksand. Only a peace between equals can last.

Address to the U.S. Senate

A little group of willful men, representing no opinion but their own, have rendered the great Government of the United States helpless and contemptible.

Statement made in reference to certain members of the Senate [1] *[March 4, 1917]*

Armed neutrality is ineffectual enough at best.

Address to Congress, asking for a declaration of war [April 2, 1917]

The world must be made safe for democracy.[2]　　　　　　*Ib.*

It is a fearful thing to lead this great peaceful people into war, into the most terrible and disastrous of all wars, civilization itself seeming to be in the balance. But the right is more precious than peace, and we shall fight for the things which we have always carried nearest our hearts — for democracy, for the right of those who submit to authority to have a voice in their own governments, for the rights and liberties of small nations, for a universal dominion of right by such a concert of free peoples as shall bring peace and safety to all nations and make the world itself at last free. To such a task we can dedicate our lives and our fortunes, everything that we are and everything that we have, with the pride of those who know that the day has come when America is privileged to spend her blood and her might for the principles that gave her birth and happiness and the peace which she has treasured. God helping her, she can do no other.

Ib.

1. Open covenants of peace, openly arrived at.

2. Absolute freedom of navigation upon the seas.

5. A free, open-minded, and absolutely impartial adjustment of all colonial claims.

Address to Congress (The Fourteen Points) [1] *[January 8, 1918]*

14. A general association of nations must be formed . . . for the purpose of affording mutual guarantees of political independence and territorial integrity to great and small states alike.　　　　　　　*Ib.*

Sometimes people call me an idealist. Well, that is the way I know I am an American. America is the only idealistic nation in the world.

Address at Sioux Falls [September 8, 1919]

The highest and best form of efficiency is the spontaneous cooperation of a free people.

From BERNARD BARUCH, *American Industry at War: A Report of the War Industries Board [March 1921]*

EDWARD FRANCIS ALBEE
1857–1930

Never give a sucker an even break.[2]

Remark

ALICE BROWN
1857–1948

Praise not the critic, lest he think
You crave the shelter of his ink;
But pray his halo, when he dies,
May tip the steelyards of the skies.

The Critic

[1] Eleven Senators had conducted a filibuster against a bill authorizing the arming of American merchant vessels.

[2] See James Harvey Robinson, p. 866b.

[1] See Clemenceau, p. 786a.

[2] Often attributed to W. C. Fields.

JOSEPH CONRAD
1857–1924

A work that aspires, however humbly, to the condition of art should carry its justification in every line.

The Nigger of the Narcissus [1898], preface

But the artist appeals to that part of our being which is not dependent on wisdom; to that in us which is a gift and not an acquisition — and, therefore, more permanently enduring. He speaks to our capacity for delight and wonder, to the sense of mystery surrounding our lives: to our sense of pity, and beauty, and pain.   *Ib.*

The ship, a fragment detached from the earth, went on lonely and swift like a small planet.   *Ib. ch. 2*

Goodbye, brothers! You were a good crowd. As good a crowd as ever fisted with wild cries the beating canvas of a heavy foresail; or tossing aloft, invisible in the night, gave back yell for yell to a westerly gale.   *Ib. 5*

I am a great foe of favoritism in public life, in private life, and even in the delicate relationship of an author to his works.

Lord Jim [1900], author's note

There is a weird power in a spoken word. . . . And a word carries far — very far — deals destruction through time as the bullets go flying through space.   *Ib. ch. 15*

That faculty of beholding at a hint the face of his desire and the shape of his dream, without which the earth would know no lover and no adventurer.   *Ib. 16*

You shall judge of a man by his foes as well as by his friends.[1]   *Ib. 34*

Vanity plays lurid tricks with our memory.   *Ib. 41*

Only a moment; a moment of strength, of romance, of glamour — of

[1] See Wilde, p. 839a.

youth! . . . A flick of sunshine upon a strange shore, the time to remember; the time for a sigh, and — goodbye! — Night — Goodbye . . . !

Youth [1902]

She strode like a grenadier, was strong and upright like an obelisk, had a beautiful face, a candid brow, pure eyes, and not a thought of her own in her head.

Tales of Unrest [1902]. The Return

Running all over the sea trying to get behind the weather.

Typhoon [1902], ch. 2

The sea never changes and its works, for all the talk of men, are wrapped in mystery.   *Ib.*

We live, as we dream — alone.

Heart of Darkness [1902],[1] I

I don't like work — no man does — but I like what is in work — the chance to find yourself. Your own reality — for yourself, not for others — what no other man can ever know.   *Ib.*

The mind of man is capable of anything — because everything is in it, all the past as well as all the future.   *Ib. II*

No fear can stand up to hunger, no patience can wear it out, disgust simply does not exist where hunger is; and as to superstition, beliefs, and what you may call principles, they are less than chaff in a breeze.[2]   *Ib.*

[1] "Heart of Darkness" is experience . . . but it is experience pushed a little (and only very little) beyond the actual facts of the case for the perfectly legitimate, I believe, purpose of bringing it home to the minds and bosoms of the readers. . . . That somber theme had to be given a sinister resonance, a tonality of its own, a continued vibration that, I hoped, would hang in the air and dwell on the ear after the last note had been struck. — CONRAD, *Youth: A Narrative, and Two Other Stories, author's preface*

[2] See G. B. Shaw, p. 837a.

Exterminate all the brutes! [1]
Heart of Darkness II

The horror! The horror! *Ib.*

Mistah Kurtz — he dead.[2] *Ib.*

The air of the New World seems favorable to the art of declamation.
Nostromo [1904], *ch. 6*

Efficiency of a practically flawless kind may be reached naturally in the struggle for bread. But there is something beyond — a higher point, a subtle and unmistakable touch of love and pride beyond mere skill; almost an inspiration which gives to all work that finish which is almost art — which *is* art.
The Mirror of the Sea [1906].
The Fine Art

A man's real life is that accorded to him in the thoughts of other men by reason of respect or natural love.
Under Western Eyes [1911], *pt. I*

Let a fool be made serviceable according to his folly. *Ib. 3*

The belief in a supernatural source of evil is not necessary; men alone are quite capable of every wickedness.
Ib. II, 4

All ambitions are lawful except those which climb upward on the miseries or credulities of mankind.
A Personal Record [1912],
preface

Only in men's imagination does every truth find an effective and undeniable existence. Imagination, not invention, is the supreme master of art as of life. *Ib. ch. 1*

---

[1] For two hundred years, the Judges of England sat on the Bench, condemning to the penalty of death every man, woman, and child who stole property to the value of five shillings; and, during all that time, not one Judge ever remonstrated against the law. We English are a nation of brutes, and ought to be exterminated to the last man. — JOHN BRIGHT [1888]; quoted by Henry Adams, *The Education of Henry Adams* [1907], *ch. 12*

[2] Used by T. S. Eliot as an epigraph for *The Hollow Men* [1925]

In plucking the fruit of memory one runs the risk of spoiling its bloom.
The Arrow of Gold [1919],
author's note

Historian of fine consciences.
Notes on Life and Letters [1921]. *Henry James, An Appreciation*

ÉMILE COUÉ
1857–1926

Every day, in every way, I'm getting better and better.
Formula of his faith cures

CLARENCE SEWARD DARROW
1857–1938

I do not consider it an insult, but rather a compliment to be called an agnostic. I do not pretend to know where many ignorant men are sure — that is all that agnosticism means.
Scopes trial, Dayton, Tennessee [*July 13, 1925*]

I don't believe in God because I don't believe in Mother Goose.
Speech, Toronto [1930]

There is no such thing as justice — in or out of court.
Interview, Chicago [*April 1936*]

JOHN DAVIDSON
1857–1909

My feet are heavy now but on I go,
My head erect beneath the tragic years.
I Felt the World A-Spinning

In anguish we uplift
A new unhallowed song:
The race is to the swift;
The battle to the strong.[1]
War Song, st. 1

---

[1] See *Ecclesiastes 9:11*, p. 28b, and Van Dyke, p. 827b.

And blood in torrents pour
In vain — always in vain,
For war breeds war again.
War Song, st. 7

BENJAMIN FRANKLIN KING, JR.
1857–1894

Nothing to do but work,
Nothing to eat but food,
Nothing to wear but clothes
To keep one from going nude.
The Pessimist, st. 1

Nowhere to go but out,
Nowhere to come but back.
Ib. st. 4

KARL PEARSON
1857–1936

Modern science, as training the mind
to an exact and impartial analysis of
facts, is an education specially fitted to
promote sound citizenship.
The Grammar of Science [1892]

EDGAR SMITH
1857–1938

You may tempt the upper classes
With your villainous demitasses,
But Heaven will protect the working
girl.
*Heaven Will Protect the
Working Girl* [1]

FRANK LEBBY STANTON
1857–1927

Jest a-wearyin' fer you —
All the time a-feelin' blue;
Wishin' fer you — wonderin' when
You'll be comin' home again.
Wearyin' for You, st. 1

Sweetes' li'l' feller —
Everybody knows;

[1] Sung by Marie Dressler [1873–1934] in *Tillie's Nightmare.*

Dunno what ter call 'im,
But he's mighty lak' a rose!
Mighty Lak' a Rose, st. 1

THORSTEIN VEBLEN
1857–1929

Conspicuous consumption of valuable goods is a means of reputability to the gentleman of leisure.
The Theory of the Leisure Class
[1899], *ch. 4*

With the exception of the instinct of self-preservation, the propensity for emulation is probably the strongest and most alert and persistent of the economic motives proper. *Ib. 5*

The requirement of conspicuous wastefulness is not commonly present, consciously, in our canons of taste, but it is none the less present as a constraining norm selectively shaping and sustaining our sense of what is beautiful, and guiding our discrimination with respect to what may legitimately be approved as beautiful and what may not. *Ib. 6*

Priestly vestments show, in accentuated form, all the features that have been shown to be evidence of a servile status and a vicarious life. *Ib. 7*

The dog . . . commends himself to our favor by affording play to our propensity for mastery, and as he is also an item of expense, and commonly serves no industrial purpose, he holds a well-assured place in men's regard as a thing of good repute. *Ib.*

The adoption of the cap and gown is one of the striking atavistic features of modern college life. *Ib. 14*

The classics have scarcely lost in absolute value as a voucher of scholastic respectability, since for this purpose it is only necessary that the scholar should be able to put in evidence some learning which is conventionally recognized as evidence of wasted time. *Ib.*

OWEN HALL
[JAMES DAVIS]
d. 1907

O tell me, pretty maiden, are there any more at home like you?
Floradora [1900], *act II*

JOHN BURNS
1858–1943

The St. Lawrence is water, and the Mississippi is muddy water; but that, sir, is liquid history.
Said on the terrace of the House of Commons, to transatlantic visitors who belittled the size of the Thames

SAM WALTER FOSS
1858–1911

And men two centuries and a half
Trod in the footsteps of that calf.
The Calf-Path,[1] *st. 6*

A rodless Walton of the brooks,
A bloodless sportsman, I.[2]
The Bloodless Sportsman

The woods are made for the hunters of dreams,
The brooks for the fishers of song;
To the hunters who hunt for the gunless game
The streams and the woods belong.
Ib.

Let me live in my house by the side of the road
Where the race of men go by;
They are good, they are bad, they are weak, they are strong,
Wise, foolish — so am I.
Then why should I sit in the scorner's seat,
Or hurl the cynic's ban?
Let me live in my house by the side of the road
And be a friend of man.
The House by the Side of the Road,[3] *st. 5*

[1] The reference is to the streets of Boston.
[2] See Emerson, p. 603a.
[3] He held his seat; a friend to human race.
Fast by the road, his ever-open door

REMY DE GOURMONT
1858–1915

Aesthetic emotion puts man in a state favorable to the reception of erotic emotion. Art is the accomplice of love. Take love away and there is no longer art.
Décadence [1]

It is because peoples do not know each other that they hate each other so little.
Ib.

There are too few obscure writers in French. We accustom ourselves like cowards to love only writing that is easy and that will soon be elementary.
Ib.

Man is a successful animal, that's all.
Promenades Philosophiques

JOHN TROTWOOD
MOORE
1858–1929

Only the gamefish swims upstream.[2]
The Unafraid

ADOLPH S. OCHS
1858–1935

All the news that's fit to print.
Motto of the New York Times [3]

MAX PLANCK
1858–1947

We have no right to assume that any physical laws exist, or if they have ex-

Obliged the wealthy, and relieved the poor.
POPE, translation of HOMER's *Iliad*,
bk. VI, l. 18

[1] Translated by W. A. BRADLEY.
[2] Quoted by GRANTLAND RICE [1880–1954] in *The Ballade of the Gamefish* and *Expanding the Theme.*
Only the gamefish swims upstream,
But the sensible fish swims down.
OGDEN NASH [b. 1902], *When You Say That, Smile*

[3] When Adolph Ochs bought the *New York Times* in 1896 he adopted this motto, which has been printed in every issue since.
It is hard to think of any group of seven words that have aroused more newspaper controversy.
— GERALD W. JOHNSON, *An Honorable Titan* [1946]

isted up to now, that they will continue to exist in a similar manner in the future.

The Universe in the Light of Modern Physics [1931]

Anybody who has been seriously engaged in scientific work of any kind realizes that over the entrance to the gates of the temple of science are written the words: *Ye must have faith.* It is a quality which the scientist cannot dispense with.

Where Is Science Going? [1932]

An important scientific innovation rarely makes its way by gradually winning over and converting its opponents: it rarely happens that Saul becomes Paul. What does happen is that its opponents gradually die out and that the growing generation is familiarized with the idea from the beginning.

The Philosophy of Physics [1936]

THEODORE ROOSEVELT
1858–1919

I wish to preach, not the doctrine of ignoble ease,[1] but the doctrine of the strenuous life.

Speech before the Hamilton Club, Chicago [*April 10, 1899*]

Far better it is to dare mighty things, to win glorious triumphs, even though checkered by failure, than to take rank with those poor spirits who neither enjoy much nor suffer much, because they live in the gray twilight that knows not victory nor defeat. *Ib.*

We must remember not to judge any public servant by any one act, and especially should we beware of attacking the men who are merely the occasions and not the causes of disaster. *Ib.*

[1] Me . . . dulcis alebat
Parthenope, studiis florentem ignobilis otii.
[Sweet Parthenope nourished me, flourishing in studies of ignoble ease.]
VIRGIL [70–19 B.C.]. *Georgics, bk. IV, l. 563*
Parthenope: ancient name of Naples.

Death is always and under all circumstances a tragedy, for if it is not, then it means that life itself has become one.

Letter to Cecil Spring-Rice [*March 12, 1900*]

I am as strong as a bull moose and you can use me to the limit.

Letter to Mark Hanna [*June 27, 1900*]

No man is justified in doing evil on the ground of expediency.

The Strenuous Life [1900]

If we seek merely swollen, slothful ease and ignoble peace, if we shrink from the hard contests where men must win at the hazard of their lives and at the risk of all they hold dear, then bolder and stronger peoples will pass us by, and will win for themselves the domination of the world. *Ib.*

There is a homely adage which runs, "Speak softly and carry a big stick; you will go far." If the American nation will speak softly and yet build and keep at a pitch of the highest training a thoroughly efficient navy, the Monroe Doctrine will go far.

Speech at Minnesota State Fair [*September 2, 1901*]

The first requisite of a good citizen in this Republic of ours is that he shall be able and willing to pull his weight.

Speech, New York [*November 11, 1902*]

A man who is good enough to shed his blood for his country is good enough to be given a square deal afterwards. More than that no man is entitled to, and less than that no man shall have.

Speech at Springfield, Illinois [*July 4, 1903*]

No man is above the law and no man is below it; nor do we ask any man's permission when we require him to obey it. Obedience to the law is demanded as a right; not asked as a favor.

Third Annual Message [December 7, 1903]

In the Western Hemisphere the adherence of the United States to the Monroe Doctrine may force the United States, however reluctantly, in flagrant cases of such wrongdoing or impotence, to the exercise of an international police power.

Annual Message to Congress: Corollary to the Monroe Doctrine [December 6, 1904]

Men with the muckrake are often indispensable to the well-being of society, but only if they know when to stop raking the muck.[1]

Address, laying of the cornerstone, House Office Building, Washington [April 14, 1906]

Malefactors of great wealth.

Speech at Provincetown, Massachusetts [August 20, 1907]

Nature-faker.

Everybody's Magazine [September 1907]

To waste, to destroy, our natural resources, to skin and exhaust the land instead of using it so as to increase its usefulness, will result in undermining in the days of our children the very prosperity which we ought by right to hand down to them amplified and developed.

Message to Congress [December 3, 1907]

The object of government is the welfare of the people. The material progress and prosperity of a nation are desirable chiefly so far as they lead to the moral and material welfare of all good citizens.

The New Nationalism [1910]

Every man holds his property subject to the general right of the community

to regulate its use to whatever degree the public welfare may require it.

Speech, Osawatomie [August 31, 1910]

The lunatic fringe in all reform movements. *Autobiography [1913]*

We demand that big business give the people a square deal; in return we must insist that when anyone engaged in big business honestly endeavors to do right he shall himself be given a square deal. *Ib.*

We stand equally against government by a plutocracy and government by a mob. There is something to be said for government by a great aristocracy which has furnished leaders to the nation in peace and war for generations; even a democrat like myself must admit this. But there is absolutely nothing to be said for government by a plutocracy, for government by men very powerful in certain lines and gifted with "the money touch," but with ideals which in their essence are merely those of so many glorified pawnbrokers.

Letter to Sir Edward Grey [November 15, 1913]

There is no room in this country for hyphenated Americanism. . . . The one absolutely certain way of bringing this nation to ruin, of preventing all possibility of its continuing to be a nation at all, would be to permit it to become a tangle of squabbling nationalities.

Speech before the Knights of Columbus, New York [October 12, 1915]

Put out the light.

Last words [January 6, 1919]

LANGDON SMITH
1858–1908

When you were a tadpole and I was a fish,
In the Paleozoic time.

Evolution [1895], st. 1

[1] See John Bunyan, p. 366a.

SIR WILLIAM WATSON
1858–1935

April, April,
Laugh thy girlish laughter;
Then, the moment after,
Weep thy girlish tears. *Song*

To dress, to call, to dine, to break
  No canon of the social code,
The little laws that lackeys make,
  The futile decalogue of Mode —
How many a soul for these things lives,
  With pious passion, grave intent!
While Nature careless-handed gives
  The things that are more excellent.
        The Things That Are More
              Excellent, st. 6

The sense of greatness keeps a nation
  great. *Our Eastern Treasure*

KATHARINE LEE BATES
1859–1929

O beautiful for spacious skies,
  For amber waves of grain,
For purple mountain majesties
  Above the fruited plain!
America! America!
  God shed his grace on thee
And crown thy good with brotherhood
  From sea to shining sea!
        America the Beautiful [1893],
                    st. 1

O beautiful for patriot dream
  That sees beyond the years
Thine alabaster cities gleam
  Undimmed by human tears!
                    Ib. st. 4

HENRI BERGSON
1859–1941

We are free when our actions eman-
ate from our total personality, when
they express it, when they resemble it
in the indefinable way a work of art
sometimes does the artist.
Essai sur les Données Immédiates
        de la Conscience [1889]

The present contains nothing more
than the past, and what is found in the
effect was already in the cause.
        L'Evolution Créatrice [1907] [1]

Intelligence . . . is the faculty of
making artificial objects, especially tools
to make tools. *Ib.*

L'élan vital [the vital spirit]. *Ib.*

HAROLD EDWIN BOULTON
1859–1935

Speed, bonnie boat, like a bird on the
  wing;
Onward, the sailors cry:
Carry the lad that's born to be king
Over the sea to Skye.
        Skye Boat Song, st. 1

SIR ARTHUR CONAN DOYLE
1859–1930

London, that great cesspool into
which all the loungers of the Empire
are irresistibly drained.
        A Study in Scarlet [1887]

When you have eliminated the impossible, whatever remains, *however
improbable*, must be the truth.
        The Sign of Four [1890], *ch. 6*

The Baker Street irregulars. *Ib.*

It is my belief, Watson, founded
upon my experience, that the lowest
and vilest alleys of London do not
present a more dreadful record of sin
than does the smiling and beautiful
countryside.
        *The Adventures of Sherlock
        Holmes* [1891]. *Copper
        Beeches*

To Sherlock Holmes she is always *the*
woman. *Ib. A Scandal in Bohemia*

[1] O my Bergson, you are a magician, and your
book is a marvel, a real wonder in the history
of philosophy. . . . In finishing it I found . . .
such a flavor of persistent *euphony*, as of a
rich river that never foamed or ran thin, but
steadily and firmly proceeded with its banks full
to the brim. — WILLIAM JAMES, *The Letters of
William James, vol. II, p. 290* [1907]

". . . the curious incident of the dog in the nighttime."

"The dog did nothing in the nighttime."

"That was the curious incident," remarked Sherlock Holmes.

> *The Memoirs of Sherlock Holmes* [1894]. *Silver Blaze*

You know my methods, Watson.

> *Ib. The Crooked Man*

"Excellent!" I [Watson] cried.

"Elementary," said he [Holmes].

> *Ib.*

They were the footprints of a gigantic hound!

> *The Hound of the Baskervilles* [1902], *ch. 2*

Come, Watson, come! The game is afoot.[1]

> *The Return of Sherlock Holmes* [1904]. *The Adventure of the Abbey Grange*

The fair sex is your department.

> *Ib. The Second Stain*

It is a great thing to start life with a small number of really good books which are your very own.

> *Through the Magic Door* [1908]

Mediocrity knows nothing higher than itself, but talent instantly recognizes genius.

> *The Valley of Fear* [1914]

The bow was made in England:
Of true wood, of yew wood,
The wood of English bows.

> *The Song of the Bow, st. 1*

HAVELOCK ELLIS
1859–1939

To be a leader of men one must turn one's back on men.

> *Introduction to* HUYSMANS, *Against the Grain*

The text of the Bible is but a feeble symbol of the Revelation held in the text of Men and Women.

> *Impressions and Comments*

God is an Unutterable Sigh in the Human Heart, said the old German mystic.[1] And therefore said the last word.

> *Impressions and Comments*

Without an element of the obscene there can be no true and deep aesthetic or moral conception of life. . . . It is only the great men who are truly obscene. If they had not dared to be obscene they could never have dared to be great.

> *Ib.*

The omnipresent process of sex, as it is woven into the whole texture of our man's or woman's body, is the pattern of all the process of our life.

> *The New Spirit*

Every artist writes his own autobiography.

> *Ib.*

If men and women are to understand each other, to enter into each other's nature with mutual sympathy, and to become capable of genuine comradeship, the foundation must be laid in youth.

> *The Task of Social Hygiene, ch. 1*

There are few among us who have not suffered from too early familiarity with the Bible and the conceptions of religion.

> *Ib. 7*

There has never been any country at every moment so virtuous and so wise that it has not sometimes needed to be saved from itself.

> *Ib. 10*

The family only represents one aspect, however important an aspect, of a human being's functions and activities. . . . A life is beautiful and ideal, or the reverse, only when we have taken into our consideration the social as well as the family relationship.

> *Little Essays of Love and Virtue* [1922], *ch. 1*

One can know nothing of giving aught that is worthy to give unless one also knows how to take.

> *Ib.*

---

[1] See Shakespeare, *Henry V, III, i, 32,* p. 244a.

[1] God is an unutterable sigh, planted in the depths of the soul. — JEAN PAUL RICHTER [1763–1825]

The byproduct is sometimes more valuable than the product.

> *Little Essays of Love and Virtue, ch. 3*

All civilization has from time to time become a thin crust over a volcano of revolution.   *Ib. 7*

The greatest task before civilization at present is to make machines what they ought to be, the slaves, instead of the masters of men.[1]   *Ib.*

The art of dancing stands at the source of all the arts that express themselves first in the human person. The art of building, or architecture, is the beginning of all the arts that lie outside the person; and in the end they unite.

> *The Dance of Life* [1923], *ch. 2*

Dancing is the loftiest, the most moving, the most beautiful of the arts, because it is no mere translation or abstraction from life; it is life itself.

> *Ib.*

The place where optimism most flourishes is the lunatic asylum.

> *Ib. 3*

Thinking in its lower grades is comparable to paper money, and in its higher forms it is a kind of poetry.

> *Ib.*

In philosophy, it is not the attainment of the goal that matters, it is the things that are met with by the way.

> *Ib.*

The mathematician has reached the highest rung on the ladder of human thought.   *Ib.*

A man must not swallow more beliefs than he can digest.   *Ib. 5*

The Promised Land always lies on the other side of a wilderness.   *Ib.*

What we call "morals" is simply blind obedience to words of command.

> *Ib. 6*

The sun and the moon and the stars would have disappeared long ago . . .

---

[1] See Oscar Wilde, p. 840b.

had they happened to be within the reach of predatory human hands.

> *The Dance of Life, ch. 7*

Had there been a lunatic asylum in the suburbs of Jerusalem, Jesus Christ would infallibly have been shut up in it at the outset of his public career. That interview with Satan on a pinnacle of the Temple would alone have damned him, and everything that happened after could but have confirmed the diagnosis.

> *Impressions and Comments,*
> *series 3*

H. W. FOWLER
1859–1933
AND
F. G. FOWLER
1871–1918

Prefer geniality to grammar.

> *The King's English* [1906], *ch. 2*

HACKNEYED PHRASES. . . . The purpose with which these phrases are introduced is for the most part that of giving a fillip to a passage that might be humdrum without them . . . but their true use when they come into the writer's mind is as danger signals; he should take warning that when they suggest themselves it is because what he is writing is bad stuff, or it would not need such help; let him see to the substance of his cake instead of decorating with sugarplums.

> *A Dictionary of Modern English*
> *Usage*[1] [1926]

QUOTATION. . . . A writer expresses himself in words that have been used before because they give his meaning better than he can give it himself, or because they are beautiful or witty, or because he expects them to touch a chord of association in his reader, or because he wishes to show that he is learned and well read. Quotations due to the last motive are invariably ill-advised; the discerning reader detects it and is contemptuous; the undiscern-

---

[1] Written by H. W. Fowler.

ing is perhaps impressed, but even then is at the same time repelled, pretentious quotations being the surest road to tedium.

> A *Dictionary of Modern English Usage*

KENNETH GRAHAME
1859–1932

As a rule, indeed, grown-up people are fairly correct on matters of fact; it is in the higher gift of imagination that they are so sadly to seek.

> *The Golden Age* [1895]. *The Finding of the Princess*

Monkeys, who very sensibly refrain from speech, lest they should be set to earn their livings.   *Ib. "Lusisti Satis"*

There is nothing — absolutely nothing — half so much worth doing as simply messing about in boats . . . or with boats. . . . In or out of 'em, it doesn't matter.

> *The Wind in the Willows* [1908], *ch.* 1

"Glorious, stirring sight!" murmured Toad . . . "The poetry of motion! The *real* way to travel! The *only* way to travel! Here today — in next week tomorrow! Villages skipped, towns and cities jumped — always somebody else's horizons! O bliss! O poop-poop! O my! O my!"   *Ib.* 2

ALFRED EDWARD HOUSMAN[1]
1859–1936

From Clee to heaven the beacon burns, The shires have seen it plain.

> *A Shropshire Lad* [1896] 1, *st.* 1

Oh, God will save her, fear you not: Be you the men you've been, Get you the sons your fathers got, And God will save the Queen.

> *Ib. st.* 8

[1] I am not a pessimist but a pejorist (as George Eliot said she was not an optimist but a meliorist); and that philosophy is founded on my observation of the world, not on anything so trivial and irrelevant as personal history. — *Autobiographical note written for a French translation of his poems*

Loveliest of trees, the cherry now Is hung with bloom along the bough.

> *A Shropshire Lad* 2, *st.* 1

Now, of my threescore years and ten, Twenty will not come again, And take from seventy springs a score, It only leaves me fifty more.

And since to look at things in bloom Fifty springs are little room, About the woodlands I will go To see the cherry hung with snow.

> *Ib. st.* 2, 3

Clay lies still, but blood's a rover; Breath's a ware that will not keep. Up, lad: when the journey's over There'll be time enough to sleep.

> *Ib.* 4 *(Reveille)*

Lovers lying two and two Ask not whom they sleep beside, And the bridegroom all night through Never turns him to the bride.   *Ib.* 12

When I was one-and-twenty I heard a wise man say, "Give crowns and pounds and guineas But not your heart away; Give pearls away and rubies But keep your fancy free." But I was one-and-twenty, No use to talk to me.

When I was one-and-twenty I heard him say again, "The heart out of the bosom Was never given in vain; 'Tis paid with sighs aplenty And sold for endless rue." And I am two-and-twenty, And Oh, 'tis true, 'tis true.   *Ib.* 13

His folly has not fellow Beneath the blue of day That gives to man or woman His heart and soul away.   *Ib.* 14

Oh, when I was in love with you, Then I was clean and brave, And miles around the wonder grew How well I did behave.

And now the fancy passes by, And nothing will remain,

And miles around they'll say that I
  Am quite myself again.
A Shropshire Lad 18

And silence sounds no worse than
  cheers
After earth has stopped the ears.
Ib. 19 (*To an Athlete Dying*
Young), *st. 4*

The bells they sound on Bredon,
  And still the steeples hum.
"Come all to church, good people" —
Oh, noisy bells, be dumb;
I hear you, I will come.
Ib. 21, st. 7

The lads that will die in their glory and
     never be old.   *Ib. 23, st. 4*

The goal stands up, the keeper
  Stands up to keep the goal.
Ib. 27, st. 4

And fire and ice within me fight
Beneath the suffocating night.[1]
Ib. 30, st. 4

There, like the wind through woods in
  riot,
Through him the gale of life blew high;
The tree of man was never quiet:
Then 'twas the Roman, now 'tis I.
Ib. 31, st. 4

Oh tarnish late on Wenlock Edge,
Gold that I never see.
Ib. 39, st. 3

Into my heart an air that kills
  From yon far country blows:
What are those blue remembered hills,
  What spires, what farms are those?

That is the land of lost content,
  I see it shining plain,
The happy highways where I went
  And cannot come again.   *Ib. 40*

Earth and high heaven are fixed of old
  and founded strong.
Ib. 48, st. 1

Far in a western brookland
  That bred me long ago

[1] See Dante, p. 159b, and Frost, p. 927a.

The poplars stand and tremble
  By pools I used to know.
A Shropshire Lad 52, *st.* 1

There, by the starlit fences,
  The wanderer halts and hears
My soul that lingers sighing
  About the glimmering weirs.
Ib. st. 4

With rue my heart is laden
  For golden friends I had,
For many a rose-lipped maiden
  And many a lightfoot lad.
Ib. 54, st. 1

By brooks too broad for leaping
The lightfoot boys are laid.   *Ib. st. 2*

Now hollow fires burn out to black,
  And lights are guttering low:
Square your shoulders, lift your pack,
  And leave your friends and go.

Oh never fear, man, nought's to dread,
  Look not left nor right:
In all the endless road you tread
  There's nothing but the night.
Ib. 60

Oh many a peer of England brews
Livelier liquor than the Muse,
And malt does more than Milton can
To justify God's ways to man.[1]
Ale, man, ale's the stuff to drink
For fellows whom it hurts to think.
Ib. 62

Mithridates, he died old.[2]   *Ib.*

Pass me the can, lad; there's an end of
  May.   *Last Poems* 9, *st.* 1

The troubles of our proud and angry
  dust
Are from eternity, and shall not fail.
Bear them we can, and if we can we
  must.
Shoulder the sky, my lad, and drink
  your ale.   *Ib. st.* 7

[1] See Milton, p. 341b.
[2] Housman's passage is based on the belief of the ancients that Mithridates the Great [c. 135–63 B.C.] had so saturated his body with poisons that none could injure him. When captured by the Romans he tried in vain to poison himself, then ordered a Gallic mercenary to kill him.

But men at whiles are sober
  And think by fits and starts.
And if they think, they fasten
  Their hands upon their hearts.
Last Poems 10, *st.* 2

The laws of God, the laws of man,
He may keep that will and can;
Not I: let God and man decree
  Laws for themselves and not for me.
Ib. 12

And how am I to face the odds
Of man's bedevilment and God's?
I, a stranger and afraid
  In a world I never made.   *Ib.*

He stood, and heard the steeple
Sprinkle the quarters on the morning
  town.
One, two, three, four, to marketplace
  and people
It tossed them down.

Strapped, noosed, nighing his hour,
He stood and counted them and cursed
  his luck;
And then the clock collected in the
  tower
Its strength, and struck.
Ib. 15 (*Eight O'Clock*)

Happy bridegroom, Hesper brings
All desired and timely things.
All whom morning sends to roam,
Hesper loves to lead them home.
Home return who him behold,
Child to mother, sheep to fold,
Bird to nest from wandering wide: [1]
Happy bridegroom, seek your bride.
Ib. 24 (*Epithalamium*), *st.* 3

These, in the day when heaven was fall-
  ing,
The hour when earth's foundations
  fled,
Followed their mercenary calling
And took their wages and are dead.
Ib. 37 (*Epitaph on an Army of
Mercenaries*),[2] *st.* 1

What God abandoned, these defended.
Last Poems 37, *st.* 2

Tell me not here, it needs not saying,
  What tune the enchantress plays
In aftermaths of soft September
  Or under blanching mays,
For she and I were long acquainted
  And I knew all her ways.
Ib. 40, *st.* 1

They say my verse is sad: no wonder;
  Its narrow measure spans
Tears of eternity, and sorrow,
  Not mine, but man's.
More Poems [1936], *foreword*

I to my perils
  Of cheat and charmer
  Came clad in armor
By stars benign.
Hope lies to mortals
  And most believe her,
  But man's deceiver
Was never mine.   *Ib.* 6, *st.* 1

The rainy Pleiads wester,
  Orion plunges prone,
And midnight strikes and hastens,
  And I lie down alone.[1]
Ib. 11, *st.* 1

My kind and foolish comrade
That breathes all night for me.
Ib. 13, *st.* 3

Life, to be sure, is nothing much to
  lose,
But young men think it is, and we were
  young.   *Ib.* 36

We now to peace and darkness
  And earth and thee restore
Thy creature that thou madest
  And wilt cast forth no more.
Ib. 47 (*For My Funeral*), *st.* 3

Good night; ensured release,
Imperishable peace,
  Have these for yours.[2]

---

[1] See Sappho, p. 69b; and Meleager, p. 110a.
[2] The British regulars who made the retreat
from Mons, beginning August 24, 1914.

[1] See Sappho, p. 69b.
[2] These three lines are on the tablet over Housman's grave in the parish church at Ludlow,
Shropshire.

While sky and sea and land
And earth's foundations stand
And heaven endures.
    More Poems 48 (Alta Quies),
        st. 1

Oh they're taking him to prison for the color of his hair.
    Additional Poems [1937], *18, st. 1*

Good literature continually read for pleasure must, let us hope, do some good to the reader: must quicken his perception though dull, and sharpen his discrimination though blunt, and mellow the rawness of his personal opinions.
    The Name and Nature of Poetry [1]

Experience has taught me, when I am shaving of a morning, to keep watch over my thoughts, because, if a line of poetry strays into my memory, my skin bristles so that the razor ceases to act. . . . The seat of this sensation is the pit of the stomach.   *Ib.*

JEROME KLAPKA JEROME
1859–1927

Let your boat of life be light, packed with only what you need — a homely home and simple pleasures, one or two friends, worth the name, someone to love and someone to love you,[2] a cat, a dog, and a pipe or two, enough to eat and enough to wear, and a little more than enough to drink; for thirst is a dangerous thing.
    Three Men in a Boat [1889],
        ch. 3

It is impossible to enjoy idling thoroughly unless one has plenty of work to do.
    Idle Thoughts of an Idle Fellow
    [1889]. *On Being Idle*

[1] The Leslie Stephen Lecture, Cambridge University [May 9, 1933].
[2] Find someone to love . . . and, oh, someone to love you. — SACHA GUITRY, *Deburau* [1918]

Love is like the measles; we all have to go through it.
    Idle Thoughts of an Idle Fel-
        low. On Being in Love

"Nothing, so it seems to me," said the stranger, "is more beautiful than the love that has weathered the storms of life. . . . The love of the young for the young, that is the beginning of life. But the love of the old for the old, that is the beginning of — of things longer."
    The Passing of the Third Floor
        Back [1908]

WILLIAM JAMES LAMPTON
1859–1917

Same old slippers,
    Same old rice,
Same old glimpse of
    Paradise.   *June Weddings, st. 10*

Where the corn is full of kernels
And the colonels full of corn.
    Kentucky

TSUBOUCHI SHOYO [1]
1859–1935

The writers of popular fiction seem to have taken as their guiding principle the dictum that the essence of the novel lies in the expression of the approved moral sentiments. They accordingly erect a framework of morality into which they attempt to force their plots.
    The Essence of the Novel [1885]

The indiscriminate readers throughout the country also must shoulder their share of the blame. It has long been the custom in Japan to consider the novel as an instrument of education . . . In actual practice, however, only stories of bloodthirsty cruelty or else of pornography are welcomed.
        Ib.

[1] From *Modern Japanese Literature*, edited by Donald Keene [1960].

CHARLES E. STANTON[1]
1859–1933

Lafayette, we are here.[2]
> *Address at the Tomb of Lafayette, Picpus Cemetery, Paris [July 4, 1917]*

JAMES KENNETH STEPHEN[3]
1859–1892

When the Rudyards cease from Kipling
And the Haggards ride no more.
> *Lapsus Calami. To R. K.*

Of sentences that stir my bile,
  Of phrases I detest,
There's one beyond all others vile:
  "He did it for the best."
> *Ib. The Malefactor's Plea, st. 1*

FRANCIS THOMPSON
1859–1907

The fairest things have fleetest end,
  Their scent survives their close:
But the rose's scent is bitterness
  To him that loved the rose.
> *Daisy [1893], st. 10*

She went her unremembering way,
  She went and left in me
The pang of all the partings gone,
  And partings yet to be.
> *Ib. st. 12*

Nothing begins, and nothing ends,
  That is not paid with moan;

[1] Chief disbursing officer of the American Expeditionary Forces in France [1917], deputed by General Pershing to speak on behalf of the A.E.F. on this occasion. He used the phrase again on July 14.
[2] The remark has also been attributed to General Pershing, who in *My Experiences in the World War* [1931] says he cannot remember having said "anything so splendid." However Naboth Hedin, one of the uniformed American correspondents present upon the July 4, 1917, occasion, states that he heard Pershing pronounce the phrase three weeks earlier, on June 14, his second day in Paris:
  "Pershing stepped up to it [Lafayette's grave] and saluted in his best manner and then said in a loud voice, 'Lafayette, we are here.' I was about twenty feet away" [*letter from Naboth Hedrin to Samuel Eliot Morison, June 21, 1954*].
[3] See Wordsworth, note 1, p. 516a.

For we are born in other's pain,
  And perish in our own.
> *Daisy, st. 15*

Look for me in the nurseries of Heaven.[1]
> *To My Godchild*

The innocent moon, which nothing does but shine,
Moves all the laboring surges of the world.
> *Sister Songs, pt. II*

I fled Him, down the nights and down the days;
I fled Him, down the arches of the years;
I fled Him, down the labyrinthine ways
Of my own mind; and in the mist of tears
I hid from Him, and under running laughter.
> *The Hound of Heaven [1893], l. 1*

But with unhurrying chase,
And unperturbèd pace,
Deliberate speed, majestic instancy,
They beat — and a Voice beat
More instant than the Feet —
"All things betray thee, who betrayest Me."
> *Ib. l. 10*

Across the margent of the world I fled,
And troubled the gold gateways of the stars.
> *Ib. l. 25*

I said to dawn, Be sudden; to eve, Be soon.
> *Ib. l. 30*

My days have crackled and gone up in smoke.
> *Ib. l. 122*

All which I took from thee I did but take,
Not for thy harms,
But just that thou might'st seek it in My arms.
> *Ib. l. 171*

There is no expeditious road
To pack and label men for God,
And save them by the barrel load.
> *A Judgment in Heaven, epilogue*

Thou canst not stir a flower
Without troubling of a star.
> *The Mistress of Vision*

[1] This line is inscribed on Thompson's tombstone in Kensal Green.

O world invisible, we view thee,
O world intangible, we touch thee,
O world unknowable, we know thee.
> *The Kingdom of God ("In No
> Strange Land")* [1913], *st. 1*

The drift of pinions, would we
hearken,
Beats at our own clay-shuttered doors.
> *Ib. st. 3*

The angels keep their ancient places;
Turn but a stone, and start a wing!
'Tis ye, 'tis your estrangèd faces,
That miss the many-splendored thing.
> *Ib. st. 4*

Upon thy so sore loss
Shall shine the traffic of Jacob's ladder
Pitched betwixt Heaven and Charing
Cross.
> *Ib. st. 5*

Short arm needs man to reach to
Heaven
So ready is Heaven to stoop to him.
> *Grace of the Way, st. 6*

Know you what it is to be a child? It
is to be something very different from
the man of today. It is to have a spirit
yet streaming from the waters of baptism; it is to believe in love, to believe
in loveliness, to believe in belief; it is to
be so little that the elves can reach to
whisper in your ear; it is to turn pumpkins into coaches, and mice into horses,
lowness into loftiness, and nothing into
everything, for each child has its fairy
godmother in its soul.
> *Shelley. In The Dublin Review*
> *[July 1908]*

Few poets were so mated before, and
no poet was so mated afterwards, until
Browning stooped and picked up a fair-
coined soul that lay rusting in a pool of
tears.
> *Ib.*

SIDNEY WEBB
[LORD PASSFIELD]
1859–1947
AND
BEATRICE WEBB
1858–1943

The inevitability of gradualness.
> *Presidential address, British La-
> bour Party Congress* [1923]

JANE ADDAMS
1860–1935

Private beneficence is totally inadequate to deal with the vast numbers of
the city's disinherited.
> *Twenty Years at Hull House* [1910]

The common stock of intellectual enjoyment should not be difficult of access because of the economic position
of him who would approach it.   *Ib.*

JAMES MATTHEW
BARRIE
1860–1937

The most gladsome thing in the
world is that few of us fall very low; the
saddest that, with such capabilities, we
seldom rise high.
> *The Little Minister* [1891], *ch. 3*

It's a weary warld, and nobody bides
in't.
> *Ib. 4*

You canna expect to be baith grand
and comfortable.
> *Ib. 10*

Let no one who loves be called altogether unhappy. Even love unreturned
has its rainbow.
> *Ib. 24*

Them that has china plates themsels
is the maist careful no to break the
china plates of others.
> *Ib. 26*

We never understand how little we
need in this world until we know the
loss of it.
> *Margaret Ogilvy* [1896], *ch. 8*

In dinner talk it is perhaps allowable
to fling on any fagot rather than let the
fire go out.
> *Tommy and Grizel* [1900], *ch. 3*

Shall we make a new rule of life from
tonight: always to try to be a little
kinder than is necessary?
> *The Little White Bird* [1902],
> *ch. 4*

His lordship may compel us to be
equal upstairs, but there will never be
equality in the servants' hall.
> *The Admirable Crichton*
> *[1903], act 1*

When the first baby laughed for the first time, the laugh broke into a thousand pieces and they all went skipping about, and that was the beginning of fairies. *Peter Pan* [1904], *act I*

Every time a child says "I don't believe in fairies" there is a little fairy somewhere that falls down dead. *Ib.*

Do you believe in fairies? . . . If you believe, clap your hands! *Ib. IV*

It's a sort of bloom on a woman. If you have it [charm], you don't need to have anything else, and if you don't have it, it doesn't much matter what else you have. Some women, the few, have charm for all; and most have charm for one. But some have charm for none.[1] *What Every Woman Knows* [1908], *act I*

The tragedy of a man who has found himself out. *Ib. IV*

One's religion is whatever he is most interested in, and yours is Success. *The Twelve-Pound Look* [1910]

JOHN COLLINS BOSSIDY
1860–1928

And this is good old Boston,
The home of the bean and the cod,
Where the Lowells talk to the Cabots
And the Cabots talk only to God.[2]
Toast, Holy Cross Alumni Dinner [1910]

[1] What is charm? It is what the violet has and the camellia has not. — MARION CRAWFORD [1854–1909], *Children of the King, ch. 5*
"Charm" — which means the power to effect work without employing brute force — is indispensable to women. Charm is a woman's strength just as strength is a man's charm. — HAVELOCK ELLIS [1859–1939], *The Task of Social Hygiene, ch. 3*
[2] Patterned on the toast given at the twenty-fifth anniversary dinner of the Harvard Class of 1880, by a Westerner.
Here's to old Massachusetts,
  The home of the sacred cod,
Where the Adamses vote for Douglas,
  And the Cabots walk with God.

WILLIAM JENNINGS BRYAN
1860–1925

The humblest citizen of all the land, when clad in the armor of a righteous cause, is stronger than all the hosts of Error. *Speech at the National Democratic Convention, Chicago* [1896]

You shall not press down upon the brow of labor this crown of thorns. You shall not crucify mankind upon a cross of gold.[1] *Ib.*

ANTON PAVLOVICH CHEKHOV
1860–1904

I feel more contented when I remember that I have two professions, and not one. Medicine is my lawful wife and literature my mistress. When I am bored with one I spend the night with the other. Though this is irregular, it is not monotonous, and besides neither really loses anything through my infidelity. *Letter to A. S. Suvorin* [August 29, 1888]

We shall rest! We shall hear the angels, we shall see the whole sky all diamonds, we shall see how all earthly evil, all our sufferings are drowned in the mercy that will fill the whole world. And our life will grow peaceful, tender, sweet as a caress. I believe, I do believe. *Uncle Vanya* [1897], *act IV*

To Moscow, to Moscow, to Moscow! *Three Sisters* [1901], *act II*

All I wanted was to say honestly to people: "Have a look at yourselves and see how bad and dreary your lives are!" *Letter to Alexander Tikhonov*

[1] I shall not help crucify mankind upon a cross of gold. I shall not aid in pressing down upon the bleeding brow of labor this crown of thorns. — WILLIAM JENNINGS BRYAN, *speech, House of Representatives* [December 22, 1894]

CHARLES TOWNSEND COPELAND
1860–1952

If I had not been there I should have been very much bored.[1]
> *Comment on a tea party. From* WALTER LIPPMANN, *William Bolitho: A Memoir*

HARRY MICAJAH DAUGHERTY
1860–1941

In a smoke-filled room in some hotel.[2]
> *Republican National Convention, Chicago [June 1920]*

HAMLIN GARLAND
1860–1940

A Son of the Middle Border
> *Title of autobiographical narrative [1917]*

CHARLOTTE PERKINS STETSON GILMAN
1860–1935

Cried all, "Before such things can come,
You idiotic child,
You must alter human nature!"
And they all sat back and smiled.
> *Similar Cases*

"I do not want to be a fly!
I want to be a worm!"
> *A Conservative, st. 6*

[1] I quite agree with Alexander Dumas who, when asked how he had enjoyed a fearfully dull party, said, "I should not have enjoyed it if *I* had not been there." — LAURA TENNANT, *letter to Sidney Colvin* [December 1884]; from E. V. Lucas, *The Colvins and Their Friends*

[2] Daugherty, presidential campaign manager for Senator Warren G. Harding, predicted that the convention would be deadlocked and would be decided by a group of men who "will sit down about two o'clock in the morning around a table in a smoke-filled room." The room was in the suite occupied by George Harvey, rooms 804–805 in the Blackstone Hotel.

I ran against a Prejudice
That quite cut off the view.
> *An Obstacle, st. 1*

There's a whining at the threshold —
There's a scratching at the floor —
To work! To work! In Heaven's name!
The wolf is at the door!
> *The Wolf at the Door, st. 6*

The people people have for friends
Your common sense appall,
But the people people marry
Are the queerest folk of all.
> *Queer People*

WILLIAM RALPH INGE
1860–1954

Literature flourishes best when it is half a trade and half an art.
> *The Victorian Age [1922]*

A man may build himself a throne of bayonets, but he cannot sit on it.
> *From Wit and Wisdom of Dean Inge, edited by* MARCHANT, *no. 108*

JAMES BALL NAYLOR
1860–1945

King David and King Solomon
Led merry, merry lives,
With many, many lady friends
And many, many wives;
But when old age crept over them —
With many, many qualms,
King Solomon wrote the Proverbs
And King David wrote the Psalms.
> *Ancient Authors*

OWEN WISTER
1860–1938

When you call me that, *smile!*
> *The Virginian [1902], ch. 2*

WILLIAM BLISS CARMAN
1861–1929

An open hand, an easy shoe,
And a hope to make the day go through.
> *The Joys of the Road, st. 8*

No fidget and no reformer, just
A calm observer of ought and must.
The Joys of the Road, st. 22

The scarlet of the maples can shake me
    like a cry
Of bugles going by.
A Vagabond Song, st. 2

There is something in October sets the
    gypsy blood astir.   *Ib. st. 3*

I took a day to search for God,
And found Him not. But as I trod
By rocky ledge, through woods un-
    tamed,
Just where one scarlet lily flamed,
I saw His footprint in the sod.
Vestigia, st. 1

LOUISE IMOGEN
GUINEY
1861–1920

He has done with roofs and men,
Open, Time, and let him pass.
Ballad of Kenelm

A short life in the saddle, Lord!
Not long life by the fire.
The Knight Errant, st. 2

I hear in my heart, I hear in its ominous
    pulses
All day, on the road, the hoofs of invis-
    ible horses,
All night, from their stalls, the impor-
    tunate pawing and neighing.
The Wild Ride, st. 1 and 6

Quotations (such as have point and
lack triteness) from the great old authors are an act of filial reverence on
the part of the quoter, and a blessing to
a public grown superficial and external.[1]
In Scribner's Magazine [January
1911]

JOHN LUTHER LONG
1861–1927

To die with honor when one can no
longer live with honor.[2]
Madame Butterfly [1897] (in-
scription on Samurai blade)

[1] See Kipling, p. 874a, and note.
[2] One should die proudly when it is no longer
possible to live proudly. — NIETZSCHE [1844–

EDWARD MacDOWELL
1861–1908

A house of Dreams untold
That looks out over the whispering
    treetops
And faces the setting sun.
House of Dreams [1]

BYRON RUFUS NEWTON
1861–1938

Vulgar of manner, overfed,
Overdressed and underbred;
Heartless, Godless, hell's delight,
Rude by day and lewd by night.
Owed to New York [1906]

Purple-robed and pauper-clad,
Raving, rotting, money-mad;
A squirming herd in Mammon's mesh,
A wilderness of human flesh;
Crazed with avarice, lust, and rum,
New York, thy name's Delirium.
Ib.

ALBERT BIGELOW PAINE
1861–1937

The Great White Way.[2]
Title of novel [1901]

SIR WALTER RALEIGH
1861–1922

I wish I loved the human race;
I wish I loved its silly face;
I wish I liked the way it walks;
I wish I liked the way it talks;
And when I'm introduced to one
I wish I thought, *What jolly fun!*
Wishes of an Elderly Man;
wished at a garden party
[June 1914]

RABINDRANATH
TAGORE
1861–1941

When one knows thee, then alien
there is none, then no door is shut. Oh,

1900], *The Twilight of the Idols, Skirmishes in
a War with the Age, 36*
[1] Preface to his composition *From a Log Cabin,*
and inscribed on the memorial tablet near his
grave.
[2] Later a name for Broadway.

grant me my prayer that I may never lose the touch of the one in the play of the many. *Gitanjali* [1913]

When I bring you colored toys, my child, I understand why there is such a play of colors on clouds, on water, and why flowers are painted in tints.
The Crescent Moon [1913].
When and Why

I do not love him because he is good, but because he is my little child.
Ib. The Judge

ALFRED NORTH WHITEHEAD
1861–1947

The study of mathematics is apt to commence in disappointment. . . . We are told that by its aid the stars are weighed and the billions of molecules in a drop of water are counted. Yet, like the ghost of Hamlet's father, this great science eludes the efforts of our mental weapons to grasp it.
An Introduction to Mathematics [1911]

All the world over and at all times there have been practical men, absorbed in irreducible and stubborn facts; all the world over and at all times there have been men of philosophic temperament, who have been absorbed in the weaving of general principles.
Science and the Modern World [1925]

The science of pure mathematics, in its modern developments, may claim to be the most original creation of the human spirit. *Ib.*

The greatest invention of the nineteenth century was the invention of the method of invention. *Ib.*

The human body is an instrument for the production of art in the life of the human soul.
Adventures of Ideas [1933], *ch. 18*

A general definition of civilization: a civilized society is exhibiting the five qualities of truth, beauty, adventure, art, peace.
Adventures of Ideas, ch. 19

The deliberate aim at Peace very easily passes into its bastard substitute, Anesthesia. *Ib. 20*

There are no whole truths; all truths are half-truths. It is trying to treat them as whole truths that plays the devil.
Dialogues of Alfred North Whitehead [1953],[1] *p. 16*

The vitality of thought is in adventure. *Ideas won't keep.* Something must be done about them. When the idea is new, its custodians have fervor, live for it, and, if need be, die for it.
Ib. p. 100

Intelligence is quickness to apprehend as distinct from ability, which is capacity to act wisely on the thing apprehended. *Ib. p. 135*

Our minds are finite, and yet even in these circumstances of finitude we are surrounded by possibilities that are infinite, and the purpose of human life is to grasp as much as we can out of that infinitude. *Ib. p. 163*

A culture is in its finest flower before it begins to analyze itself. *Ib. p. 169*

The ideas of Freud [2] were popularized by people who only imperfectly understood them, who were incapable of the great effort required to grasp them in their relationship to larger truths, and who therefore assigned to them a prominence out of all proportion to their true importance. *Ib. p. 211*

Art is the imposing of a pattern on experience, and our aesthetic enjoyment in recognition of the pattern.
Ib. p. 228

A philosopher of imposing stature doesn't think in a vacuum. Even his most abstract ideas are, to some extent, conditioned by what is or is not known in the time when he lives. *Ib. p. 229*

With the sense of sight, the idea communicates the emotion, whereas,

[1] As recorded by LUCIEN PRICE.
[2] See Freud, p. 833b.

with sound, the emotion communicates the idea, which is more direct and therefore more powerful.
Dialogues of Alfred North Whitehead, p. 231

Intellect is to emotion as our clothes are to our bodies: we could not very well have civilized life without clothes, but we would be in a poor way if we had only clothes without bodies.
Ib. p. 232

No period of history has ever been great or ever can be that does not act on some sort of high, idealistic motives, and idealism in our time has been shoved aside, and we are paying the penalty for it.
Ib. p. 276

The English never abolish anything. They put it in cold storage.
Ib. p. 309

Shakespeare wrote better poetry for not knowing too much; Milton, I think, knew too much finally for the good of his poetry.
Ib. p. 369

JOHN KENDRICK BANGS
1862–1922

I think mankind by thee would be less bored
If only thou wert not thine own reward.
A Hint to Virtue

ARTHUR CHRISTOPHER BENSON
1862–1925

Land of hope and glory, mother of the free,
How shall we extol thee, who are born of thee?
Wider still and wider shall thy bounds be set;
God, who made thee mighty, make thee mightier yet.
Land of Hope and Glory, chorus

ALBERT JEREMIAH BEVERIDGE
1862–1927

This party comes from the grass roots. It has grown from the soil of the people's hard necessities.
Address as temporary chairman of the Bull Moose Convention, Chicago [August 5, 1912]

JAMES W. BLAKE
1862–1935

East Side, West Side, all around the town,
The tots sang "Ring-a-rosie," "London Bridge is falling down";
Boys and girls together, me and Mamie O'Rourke,
Tripped the light fantastic on the sidewalks of New York.
The Sidewalks of New York [1]
[1894]

CARRIE JACOBS BOND
1862–1946

Well, this is the end of a perfect day,
Near the end of a journey, too.
A Perfect Day, st. 2

For mem'ry has painted this perfect day
With colors that never fade,
And we find at the end of a perfect day
The soul of a friend we've made.
Ib.

NICHOLAS MURRAY BUTLER
1862–1947

An expert is one who knows more and more about less and less.
Commencement address, Columbia University

[1] The music of the song was composed by Charles B. Lawlor [1852–1925].

JOHN JAY CHAPMAN
1862–1933

The New Testament, and to a very large extent the Old, *is* the soul of man. You cannot criticize it. It criticizes you.
Letter [March 26, 1898]

The present in New York is so powerful that the past is lost.   *Ib.* [1909]

People who love soft words and hate iniquity forget this, that reform consists in taking a bone away from a dog. Philosophy will not do this.   *Saying*

GOLDSWORTHY LOWES DICKINSON
1862–1932

Dissatisfaction with the world in which we live and determination to realize one that shall be better, are the prevailing characteristics of the modern spirit.
The Greek View of Life [1898], *ch. 5*

Chinese poetry is of all poetry I know the most human and the least symbolic or romantic. It contemplates life just as it presents itself, without any veil of ideas, any rhetoric or sentiment; it simply clears away the obstruction which habit has built up between us and the beauty of things.
An Essay on the Civilizations of India, China, and Japan [1914]

The United States of America — the greatest potential force, material, moral, and spiritual, in the world.
The Choice Before Us [1917], *ch. 1*

Government is everywhere to a great extent controlled by powerful minorities, with an interest distinct from that of the mass of the people.   *Ib. 4*

LUDWIG FULDA
1862–1939

You remain the King — even in your underwear.   *Der Talisman* [1893]

EDWARD, VISCOUNT GREY OF FALLODON
1862–1933

The lamps are going out all over Europe; we shall not see them lit again in our lifetime.
Comment [August 3, 1914],[1] standing at the windows of his room in the Foreign Office, London, as the lamplighters were turning on the lights in St. James Park

O. HENRY
[WILLIAM SYDNEY PORTER]
1862–1910

If men knew how women pass the time when they are alone, they'd never marry.
The Four Million [1906]. *Memoirs of a Yellow Dog*

What a woman wants is what you're out of. She wants more of a thing when it's scarce.
Heart of the West [1907]. *Cupid à la Carte*

Perhaps there is no happiness in life so perfect as the martyr's.
The Trimmed Lamp [1907]. *The Country of Elusion*

Bohemia is nothing more than the little country in which you do not live.   *Ib.*

You're the goods.
The Voice of the City [1908]. *From Each According to His Ability*

It was beautiful and simple as all truly great swindles are.
The Gentle Grafter [1908]. *The Octopus Marooned*

There are two times when you can never tell what is going to happen. One is when a man takes his first drink; and the other is when a woman takes her latest.   *Ib.*

[1] War was declared 11 P.M. August 4, 1914.

Busy as a one-armed man with the nettle-rash pasting on wallpaper.
The Gentle Grafter.
The Ethics of Pig

Bagdad-on-the-Subway.[1]
Roads of Destiny [1909]. *The Discounters of Money*

History is bright and fiction dull with homely men who have charmed women.
Ib. Next to Reading Matter

You can't appreciate home till you've left it, money till it's spent, your wife till she's joined a woman's club, nor Old Glory till you see it hanging on a broomstick on the shanty of a consul in a foreign town.
Ib. The Fourth in Salvador

She plucked from my lapel the invisible strand of lint (the universal act of woman to proclaim ownership).
Strictly Business [1910]. *A Ramble in Aphasia*

East is East, and West is San Francisco, according to Californians. Californians are a race of people; they are not merely inhabitants of a State.
Ib. A Municipal Report

Take of London fog 30 parts; malaria 10 parts; gas leaks 20 parts; dewdrops gathered in a brickyard at sunrise 25 parts; odor of honeysuckle 15 parts. Mix. The mixture will give you an approximate conception of a Nashville drizzle. *Ib.*

It couldn't have happened anywhere but in little old New York.[2]
Whirligigs [1910]. *A Little Local Color*

I was made by a Dago and presented to the American people on behalf of the French Government for the pur-

pose of welcomin' Irish immigrants into the Dutch city of New York.
Sixes and Sevens [1911]. *The Lady Higher Up* [1]

A straw vote only shows which way the hot air blows.
Rolling Stones [1913]. *A Ruler of Men*

Take it from me — he's got the goods. *The Unprofitable Servant*

Turn up the lights — I don't want to go home in the dark.[2]
Last Words [June 5, 1910]

CHARLES EVANS HUGHES
1862–1948

We are under a Constitution, but the Constitution is what the judges say it is, and the judiciary is the safeguard of our liberty and of our property under the Constitution.
Speech at Elmira, New York [May 3, 1907]

How amazing it is that, in the midst of controversies on every conceivable subject, one should expect unanimity of opinion upon difficult legal questions! In the highest ranges of thought, in theology, philosophy and science, we find differences of view on the part of the most distinguished experts — theologians, philosophers and scientists. The history of scholarship is a record of disagreements. And when we deal with questions relating to principles of law and their applications, we do not suddenly rise into a stratosphere of icy certainty.
Speech to the American Law Institute [May 7, 1936]

The greater the importance of safeguarding the community from incitements to the overthrow of our institutions by force and violence, the more imperative is the need to preserve inviolate the constitutional rights of free

---

[1] Also in *A Madison Square Arabian Night, A Night in New Arabia,* and *What You Want.*
[2] Also in *A Midsummer Knight's Dream, Past One at Rooney's* and *The Rubber Plant's Story.*

[1] The Statue of Liberty.
[2] The reference is to a popular song of the day, "I'm Afraid to Go Home in the Dark."

speech, free press and free assembly in order to maintain the opportunity for free political discussion, to the end that government may be responsive to the will of the people and that changes, if desired, may be obtained by peaceful means. Therein lies the security of the Republic, the very foundation of constitutional government.

> *DeJonge v. Oregon, 299 U.S.*
> *353, 365 [1937]*

MAURICE MAETERLINCK
1862–1949

It is always a mistake not to close one's eyes, whether to forgive or to look better into oneself.

> *Pelléas et Mélisande [1892]*

There are no dead.

> *The Blue Bird [1909], act IV, sc. 2*

SIR HENRY NEWBOLT
1862–1938

To set the cause above renown,
To love the game beyond the prize,
To honor, while you strike him down,
The foe that comes with fearless eyes;
To count the life of battle good
And dear the land that gave you birth,
And dearer yet the brotherhood
That binds the brave of all the earth.

> *The Island Race. Clifton*
> *Chapel, st. 2*

Qui procul hinc, the legend's writ,
The frontier grave is far away —
Qui ante diem periit:
Sed miles, sed pro patria.[1]   *Ib. st. 4*

Take my drum to England, hang et by the shore,
Strike et when your powder's runnin' low;
If the Dons sight Devon, I'll quit the port o' Heaven,
An' drum them up the Channel as we drummed them long ago.

> *Drake's Drum, st. 2*

[1] Who died far away, before his time: but as a soldier, for his country.

Drake he's in his hammock till the great Armadas come.
(Capten, art tha sleepin' there below?)   *Drake's Drum, st. 3*

Now the sunset breezes shiver,
And she's fading down the river,
But in England's song forever
    She's the Fighting Téméraire.

> *The Fighting Téméraire, st. 6*

Play up! play up! and play the game!

> *Vitai Lampada*

EDEN PHILLPOTTS
1862–1960

His father's sister had bats in the belfry and was put away.

> *Peacock House*

ROBERT CAMERON ROGERS
1862–1912

The hours I spent with thee, dear heart,
    Are as a string of pearls to me;
I count them over, every one apart,
    My rosary, my rosary.   *My Rosary*

EDITH WHARTON
1862–1937

There are two ways of spreading light: to be
The candle or the mirror that reflects it.   *Vesalius in Zante*

Mrs. Ballinger is one of the ladies who pursue Culture in bands, as though it were dangerous to meet it alone.   *Xingu [1916]*

I was never allowed to read the popular American children's books of my day because, as my mother said, the children spoke bad English *without the author's knowing it*.

> *A Backward Glance [1934],*
> *ch. 3*

To [Henry] James's intimates, however, these elaborate hesitancies, far from being an obstacle, were like a cobweb bridge flung from his mind to theirs, an invisible passage over which one knew that silver-footed ironies, veiled jokes, tiptoe malices, were stealing to explode a huge laugh at one's feet. *A Backward Glance, ch. 8*

REVEREND E. J. HARDY
fl. 1910

How To Be Happy Though Married. *Title of book* [1910]

HENRY HOLCOMB BENNETT
1863–1924

Hats off!
Along the street there comes
A blare of bugles, a ruffle of drums,
A flash of color beneath the sky:
Hats off!
The flag is passing by.
The Flag Goes By, st. 1

GAMALIEL BRADFORD
1863–1932

I sometimes wish that God were back
In this dark world and wide;[1]
For though some virtues he might lack,
He had his pleasant side.
Exit God

DAVID LLOYD GEORGE, EARL OF DWYFOR
1863–1945

What is our task? To make Britain a fit country for heroes to live in.
Speech, Queen's Hall, London [September 19, 1914]

OLIVER HERFORD
1863–1935

Children, behold the Chimpanzee:
He sits on the ancestral tree
From which we sprang in ages gone.
I'm glad we sprang: had we held on,

[1] See Milton, p. 341a.

We might, for aught that I can say,
Be horrid Chimpanzees today.
The Chimpanzee

Ermined and minked and Persian-lambed,
Be-puffed (be-painted, too, alas!)
Be-decked, be-diamonded —
be-damned!
The women of the better class.
The Women of the Better Class, st. 4

SIR ARTHUR THOMAS QUILLER-COUCH
1863–1944

Literature is not an abstract science, to which exact definitions can be applied. It is an art, the success of which depends on personal persuasiveness, on the author's skill to give as on ours to receive.
Inaugural Lecture at Cambridge University [1913]

JAMES HARVEY ROBINSON
1863–1935

Political campaigns are designedly made into emotional orgies which endeavor to distract attention from the real issues involved, and they actually paralyze what slight powers of cerebration man can normally muster.
The Human Comedy [1937], ch. 9

With supreme irony, the war to "make the world safe for democracy"[1] ended by leaving democracy more unsafe in the world than at any time since the collapse of the revolutions of 1848.
Ib.

GEORGE SANTAYANA
1863–1952

O World, thou choosest not the better part!
It is not wisdom to be only wise,
And on the inward vision close the eyes,

[1] See Woodrow Wilson, p. 842a.

But it is wisdom to believe the heart.
Columbus found a world, and had no chart,
Save one that faith deciphered in the skies;
To trust the soul's invincible surmise
Was all his science and his only art.
> *O World, Thou Choosest Not*
> [1894]

Beauty as we feel it is something indescribable: what it is or what it means can never be said.
> *The Sense of Beauty* [1896].
> *Expression*

Beauty is a pledge of the possible conformity between the soul and nature, and consequently a ground of faith in the supremacy of the good.
> *Ib.*

That life is worth living is the most necessary of assumptions, and, were it not assumed, the most impossible of conclusions.[1]
> *The Life of Reason* [1905–1906], *vol. I*

Fanaticism consists in redoubling your efforts when you have forgotten your aim. *Ib.*

Those who cannot remember the past are condemned to repeat it. *Ib.*

The highest form of vanity is love of fame. *Ib. II*

The human race, in its intellectual life, is organized like the bees: the masculine soul is a worker, sexually atrophied, and essentially dedicated to impersonal and universal arts; the feminine is a queen, infinitely fertile, omnipresent in its brooding industry, but passive and abounding in intuitions without method and passions without justice. *Ib.*

Let a man once overcome his selfish terror at his own finitude, and his finitude is, in one sense, overcome.
> *The Ethics of Spinoza* [1910],
> *introduction*

[1] See William James, p. 794a.

Perhaps the only true dignity of man is his capacity to despise himself.
> *The Ethics of Spinoza,*
> *introduction*

Miracles are propitious accidents, the natural causes of which are too complicated to be readily understood. *Ib.*

The Bible is literature, not dogma.
> *Ib.*

American life is a powerful solvent. It seems to neutralize every intellectual element, however tough and alien it may be, and to fuse it in the native good will, complacency, thoughtlessness, and optimism.
> *Character and Opinion in the*
> *United States* [1920]

All his life he [the American] jumps into the train after it has started and jumps out before it has stopped; and he never once gets left behind, or breaks a leg. *Ib.*

England is the paradise of individuality, eccentricity, heresy, anomalies, hobbies, and humors.
> *Soliloquies in England* [1922].
> *The British Character*

The world is a perpetual caricature of itself; at every moment it is the mockery and the contradiction of what it is pretending to be. *Ib. Dickens*

There is no cure for birth and death save to enjoy the interval.
> *Ib. War Shrines*

I like to walk about amidst the beautiful things that adorn the world; but private wealth I should decline, or any sort of personal possessions, because they would take away my liberty.
> *Ib. The Irony of Liberalism*

My atheism, like that of Spinoza, is true piety towards the universe and denies only gods fashioned by men in their own image, to be servants of their human interests.
> *Ib. On My Friendly Critics*

The young man who has not wept is a savage, and the old man who will not laugh is a fool.
> *Dialogues in Limbo* [1925], *III*

There is nothing impossible in the existence of the supernatural: its existence seems to me decidedly probable.

The Genteel Tradition at Bay
[*1931*]

ERNEST LAWRENCE THAYER
1863–1940

There was ease in Casey's manner as he stepped into his place,
There was pride in Casey's bearing, and a smile on Casey's face,
And when, responding to the cheers, he lightly doffed his hat,
No stranger in the crowd could doubt 'twas Casey at the bat.
　　　　　Casey at the Bat,[1] *st. 6*

Oh! somewhere in this favored land the sun is shining bright;
The band is playing somewhere, and somewhere hearts are light;
And somewhere men are laughing and somewhere children shout,
But there is no joy in Mudville — mighty Casey has struck out.
　　　　　Ib. st. 13

HARRY BRAISTED
fl. 1896

You're Not the Only Pebble on the Beach.　　　*Title of song* [*1896*]

JOSEPH HAYDEN
fl. 1896

There'll be a hot time in the old town tonight.
A Hot Time in the Old Town [2]
[*1896*]

---

[1] First printed in the *San Francisco Examiner* [*June 3, 1888*].
　　Yet I'd take my chance with fame,
　　Calmly let it go at that,
　　With the right to sign my name
　　Under "Casey at the Bat."
　　　　　GRANTLAND RICE [1880–1954], *The Masterpiece*
[2] Hayden's text for a march, *A Hot Time in the Old Town Tonight* [1886], by Theodore August Metz [1848–1936], later a favorite of Theodore Roosevelt's Rough Riders in Cuba, and still later Roosevelt's campaign song.

SIR ROGER CASEMENT
1864–1916

Where all your rights become only an accumulated wrong; where men must beg with bated breath for leave to subsist in their own land, to think their own thoughts, to sing their own songs, to garner the fruits of their own labors . . . then surely it is braver, a saner and truer thing, to be a rebel in act and deed against such circumstances as these than tamely to accept it as the natural lot of men.
　　　　　Statement from prison
[June 29, 1916]

RICHARD HOVEY
1864–1900

For it's always fair weather
When good fellows get together
With a stein on the table and a good song ringing clear.
　　　　　A Stein Song [1898], *st. 1*

I do not know beneath what sky
　Nor on what seas shall be thy fate:
I only know it shall be high,
　I only know it shall be great.
　　　　　Unmanifest Destiny [1898], *st. 7*

O, Eleazer Wheelock was a very pious man;
He went into the wilderness to teach the Indian,
With a *Gradus ad Parnassum*, a Bible, and a drum,
And five hundred gallons of New England rum. . . .
Eleazar was the faculty, and the whole curriculum
Was five hundred gallons of New England rum.
　　　　　Eleazer Wheelock [*Dartmouth College song*], *st. 1*

MARK ANTONY DE WOLFE HOWE
1864–1960

Now, thieving Time, take what you must —
Quickness to hear, to move, to see;

When dust is drawing near to dust
Such diminutions needs must be.
Yet leave, O leave exempt from plunder
My curiosity, my wonder!
Thieving Time [*1951*]

ROBERT LOVEMAN
1864–1923

It is not raining rain to me,
  It's raining daffodils;
In every dimpled drop I see
  Wildflowers on the hills.
April Rain [*1901*], *st. 1*

A health unto the happy!
A fig for him who frets! —
It is not raining rain to me,
  It's raining violets.   *Ib. st. 4*

ANDREW BARTON
[BANJO] PATERSON
1864–1941

Once a jolly swagman camped by a billabong,
Under the shade of a coolibar tree,
And he sang as he sat and waited for
  his billy-boil,
"You'll come a-waltzing, Matilda, with
  me." [1]
Waltzing Matilda (*Australian
  soldiers' marching song*)

STEPHEN PHILLIPS
1864–1915

A man not old, but mellow, like good
  wine.   *Ulysses, act III, sc. i*

JULES RENARD
1864–1910

To succeed you must add water to
your wine, until there is no more wine.
                                Journal

There are moments when everything
goes well; don't be frightened, it won't
last.   *Ib.*

[1] Swagman: tramp. Billabong: pool. Coolibar:
gum tree. Billy: tin container used for brewing
tea.

I am not sincere even when I am
saying that I am not sincere.
                                Journal

We don't understand life any better
at forty than at twenty, but we know it
and admit it.   *Ib.*

MIGUEL DE UNAMUNO
1864–1936

The man of flesh and blood; the one
who is born, suffers and dies — above
all, who dies; the man who eats and
drinks and plays and sleeps and thinks
and wills; the man who is seen and is
heard; the brother, the real brother.
The Tragic Sense of Life [*1913*],
                                ch. 1

Man, by the very fact of being
man, by possessing consciousness, is, in
comparison with the ass or the crab, a
diseased animal. Consciousness is a disease.   *Ib.*

Pantheism is said . . . to be merely
atheism in disguise.   *Ib. 5*

Science is a cemetery of dead ideas,
even though life may issue from them.
                                  Ib.

True science teaches, above all, to
doubt and be ignorant.   *Ib.*

To believe in God is to yearn for His
existence and, furthermore, it is to act
as if He did exist.   *Ib. 8*

Martyrs create faith, faith does not
create martyrs.[1]   *Ib. 9*

To fall into a habit is to begin to
cease to be.   *Ib.*

The intellectual world is divided into
two classes — dilettantes, on the one
hand, and pedants, on the other.
                                Ib. 11

Warmth, warmth, more warmth! for
we are dying of cold and not of darkness. It is not the night that kills, but
the frost.   *Ib. Conclusion*

The devil is an angel too.
                           Two Mothers

[1] See Tertullian, p. 143b, and Suarès, p. 896a.

There are pretenses which are very sincere, and marriage is their school.
Two Mothers

And killing time is perhaps the essence of comedy, just as the essence of tragedy is killing eternity.
San Manuel Bueno, prologue

I would say that teleology is theology, and that God is not a "because," but rather an "in order to." *Ib.*

Let us go on committing suicide by working among our people, and let them dream life just as the lake dreams the sky. *Ib.*

One of those leaders of what they call the social revolution has said that religion is the opiate of the people.[1] Opium . . . opium . . . opium, yes. Let us give them opium so that they can sleep and dream. *Ib.*

Use harms and even destroys beauty. The noblest function of an object is to be contemplated. *Mist* [1914]

In Homeric times people and things had two names: the one given them by men and the one given by the gods. I wonder what God calls me? *Ib.*

Isolation is the worst possible counselor. *Civilization Is Civilism*

Every peasant has a lawyer inside of him, just as every lawyer, no matter how urbane he may be, carries a peasant within himself. *Ib.*

It is sad not to be loved, but it is much sadder not to be able to love.
To a Young Writer

These terrible sociologists, who are the astrologers and alchemists of our twentieth century.
Fanatical Skepticism

Faith which does not doubt is dead faith. *The Agony of Christianity*

We never know, believe me, when we have succeeded best.
Essays and Soliloquies

[1] See Marx, p. 686b.

ISRAEL ZANGWILL
1864–1926

Scratch the Christian and you find the pagan — spoiled.
Children of the Ghetto [1892]

America is God's crucible, the great melting pot where all the races of Europe are melting and re-forming!
The Melting Pot [1908], *act I*

FRANK MOORE COLBY
1865–1925

Men will confess to treason, murder, arson, false teeth, or a wig. How many of them will own up to a lack of humor?
The Colby Essays [1926], *vol. I*

Nobody can describe a fool to the life, without much patient self-inspection. *Ib.*

A new movement is not a stampede to some new object, but a stampede away from some old person. *Ib. II*

Were it not for the presence of the unwashed [1] and the half-educated, the formless, queer and incomplete, the unreasonable and absurd, the infinite shapes of the delightful human tadpole, the horizon would not wear so wide a grin. *Imaginary Obligations*

HERBERT ALBERT LAURENS FISHER
1865–1940

All political decisions are taken under great pressure, and if a treaty serves its turn for ten or twenty years, the wisdom of its framers is sufficiently confirmed.[2] *Political Prophecies* [1918]

It is easier for eight or nine elderly men to feel their way towards unanimity if they are not compelled to conduct their converging maneuvers under the microscopes and telescopes of the press,

[1] See Brougham, p. 540b.
[2] Thirty years is the life of most great treaties. — R. B. MOWAT, *A History of Great Britain* [1922]

but are permitted to shuffle about a little in slippers.

> *An International Experiment* [1]
> [*1921*]

Purity of race does not exist. Europe is a continent of energetic mongrels.

> *A History of Europe* [*1934*], *ch. 1*

Politics is the art of human happiness.

> *Ib. 31*

KING GEORGE V
1865–1936

How is the Empire?

> *Last words* [*January 21, 1936*]

FREDERIC WILLIAM
GOUDY
1865–1947

I am the voice of today, the herald of tomorrow. . . . I coin for you the enchanting tale, the philosopher's moralizing, and the poet's visions. . . . I am the leaden army that conquers the world — I am TYPE.

> *The Type Speaks*

LAURENCE HOPE
[ADELA FLORENCE
CORY NICOLSON]
1865–1904

Less than the dust beneath thy chariot wheel,
Less than the rust that never stains thy sword.

> *Indian Love Lyrics. Less Than*
> *the Dust, st. 1*

Less than the weed that grows beside thy door.

> *Ib. st. 2*

For this is wisdom: to love, to live,
To take what Fate, or the Gods, may give.

> *Ib. The Teak Forest*

To have — to hold — and — in time — let go!

> *Ib.*

Pale hands I loved beside the Shalimar,

[1] The League of Nations.

Where are you now? Who lies beneath your spell?

> *Indian Love Lyrics. Kashmiri*
> *Song, st. 1*

RUDYARD KIPLING
1865–1936

I have eaten your bread and salt.
I have drunk your water and wine.
The deaths ye died I have watched beside
And the lives ye led were mine.

> *Departmental Ditties* [*1886*].
> *Prelude, st. 1*

Little Tin Gods on Wheels.

> *Ib. Public Waste, st. 4*

The blush that flies at seventeen
Is fixed at forty-nine.

> *Ib. My Rival, st. 2*

The toad beneath the harrow knows
Exactly where each tooth point goes;
The butterfly upon the road
Preaches contentment to that toad.

> *Ib. Pagett, M.P., prelude*

Cross that rules the Southern Sky!
Stars that sweep, and turn, and fly,
Hear the Lovers' Litany:
"Love like ours can never die!"

> *Ib. The Lovers' Litany, st. 2*

And a woman is only a woman, but a good cigar is a smoke.

> *Ib. The Betrothed, st. 25*

You'll never plumb the Oriental mind,
And if you did, it isn't worth the toil.

> *Ib. One Viceroy Resigns*

It takes a great deal of Christianity to wipe out uncivilized Eastern instincts, such as falling in love at first sight.

> *Plain Tales from the Hills*
> [*1888*]. *Lispeth*

Never praise a sister to a sister, in the hope of your compliments reaching the proper ears.

> *Ib. False Dawn*

Many religious people are deeply suspicious. They seem — for purely religious purposes, of course — to know more about iniquity than the unregenerate.

> *Plain Tales from the Hills.*
> *Watches of the Night*

She was as immutable as the hills.
But not quite so green.
> *Ib. Venus Annodomini*

Youth had been a habit of hers for so long that she could not part with it.
> *Ib.*

Everyone is more or less mad on one point.[1]
> *Ib. On the Strength of a Likeness*

The silliest woman can manage a clever man; but it needs a very clever woman to manage a fool!
> *Ib. Three and — an Extra*

Lalah is a member of the most ancient profession in the world.
> *In Black and White* [1888].
> *On the City Wall*

Steady the Buffs.
> *Soldiers Three* [1888]

Being kissed by a man who didn't wax his moustache was — like eating an egg without salt.
> *The Story of the Gadsbys* [1888]. *Poor Dear Mamma*

Down to Gehenna or up to the Throne,
He travels the fastest who travels alone.[2]
> *Ib. The Winners (L' Envoi:*
> *What Is the Moral?), st. 1*

More men are killed by overwork than the importance of the world justifies.
> *The Phantom 'Rickshaw* [1888]

He became an officer *and* a gentleman, which is an enviable thing.
> *Under the Deodars* [1888].
> *Only a Subaltern*

Tea fights.[1]
> *Ib.*

Oh, East is East, and West is West, and never the twain shall meet,
Till Earth and Sky stand presently at God's great Judgment Seat;
But there is neither East nor West, border, nor breed, nor birth,
When two strong men stand face to face, though they come from the ends of the earth!
> *The Ballad of East and West* [1889]

For all we take we must pay, but the price is cruel high.
> *The Courting of Dinah Shadd,* [1890]

If I were damned of body and soul,
I know whose prayers would make me whole,
Mother o' mine, O mother o' mine.
> *Mother o' Mine* [1891]

And the end of the fight is a tombstone white with the name of the late deceased,
And the epitaph drear: "A Fool lies here who tried to hustle the East."
> *The Naulahka* [1892], *ch. 5*

When Earth's last picture is painted, and the tubes are twisted and dried,
When the oldest colors have faded, and the youngest critic has died,
We shall rest, and, faith, we shall need it — lie down for an eon or two,
Till the Master of All Good Workmen shall put us to work anew.
> *When Earth's Last Picture Is Painted* [1892], *st. 1*

Ever the wide world over, lass,
Ever the trail held true,

[1] Semel insanivimus omnes [We have all once been mad]. — JOHANNES BAPTISTA MANTUANUS [1448–1516], *Eclogues, no. I*
[2] He may well win the race that runs by himself. — BENJAMIN FRANKLIN, *Poor Richard's Almanac* [1757]
Who travels alone, without lover or friend,
But hurries from nothing, to nought at the end.
ELLA WHEELER WILCOX, *Reply to Rudyard Kipling's Poem*

[1] Giggle, gabble, gobble, git. — OLIVER WENDELL HOLMES [1809–1894], *description of a tea party*

Over the world and under the world,
  And back at the last to you.
      The Gipsy Trail [1892], *st.* 2

They rise to their feet as He passes by,
  gentlemen unafraid.
      Ballads and Barrack Room Bal-
      lads [1892, 1893]. *Dedication,*
      st. 5

"What are the bugles blowin' for?"
  said Files-on-Parade.
"To turn you out, to turn you out," the
  Color-Sergeant said.
      Ib. Danny Deever, st. 1

They've taken of his buttons off an' cut
  his stripes away,
An' they're hangin' Danny Deever in
  the mornin'.   *Ib.*

We aren't no thin red 'eroes.[1]
      Ib. Tommy, st. 4

Single men in barricks don't grow into
  plaster saints.   *Ib.*

For it's Tommy this, an' Tommy that,
  an' "Chuck 'im out, the brute!"
But it's "Savior of 'is country" when
  the guns begin to shoot.
      Ib. st. 5

So 'ere's *to* you, Fuzzy-Wuzzy, at your
  'ome in the Soudan;
You're a pore benighted 'eathen but a
  first-class fightin' man.
      Ib. Fuzzy-Wuzzy, st. 1

The uniform 'e wore
Was nothin' much before,
An' rather less than 'arf o' that be'ind.
      Ib. Gunga Din, st. 2

An' for all 'is dirty 'ide
'E was white, clear white, inside
When 'e went to tend the wounded
  under fire!   *Ib. st. 3*

Though I've belted you an' flayed you,
By the livin' Gawd that made you,
You're a better man than I am, Gunga
  Din!   *Ib. st. 5*

'Ave you 'eard o' the Widow at Windsor
With a hairy gold crown on 'er 'ead?
      Ib. The Widow at Windsor, st. 1

[1] See Sir W. H. Russell, p. 704b.

By the old Moulmein Pagoda, lookin'
  eastward to the sea,
There's a Burma girl a-settin', and I
  know she thinks o' me;
For the wind is in the palm trees, and
  the temple bells they say:
"Come you back, you British soldier;
  come you back to Mandalay!"
Come you back to Mandalay,
  Where the old Flotilla lay;
Can't you 'ear their paddles chunkin'
  from Rangoon to Mandalay?
On the road to Mandalay,
  Where the flyin' fishes play,
An' the dawn comes up like thunder
  outer China 'crost the Bay!
      Ballads and Barrack Room
      Ballads. Mandalay, st. 1

I've a neater, sweeter maiden in a
  cleaner, greener land.   *Ib. st. 5*

Ship me somewheres east of Suez,
  where the best is like the worst,
Where there aren't no Ten Commandments, an' a man can raise a
  thirst.   *Ib. st. 6*

The Devil whispered behind the leaves,
"It's pretty, but is it Art?"
      Ib. The Conundrum of the
      Workshops, st. 1

To the legion of the lost ones, to the
  cohort of the damned.
      Ib. Gentlemen Rankers, st. 1

We're poor little lambs who've lost our
  way,
  Baa! Baa! Baa!
We're little black sheep who've gone
  astray,
  Baa — aa — aa!
Gentlemen rankers out on the spree,
Damned from here to Eternity,
God ha' mercy on such as we,
  Baa! Yah! Baa!
      Ib. refrain

We have done with Hope and Honor,
  we are lost to Love and Truth,
We are dropping down the ladder rung
  by rung;
And the measure of our torment is the
  measure of our youth.

God help us, for we knew the worst too
young!
> *Ballads and Barrack Room Bal-*
> *lads. Gentlemen Rankers, st. 4*

And what should they know of England
who only England know?
> *Ib. The English Flag, st. 1*

And the naked soul of Tomlinson grew
white as a rain-washed bone.
> *Ib. Tomlinson, l. 10*

The sin ye do by two and two ye must
pay for one by one.   *Ib. l. 60*

There's a legion that never was 'listed,
That carries no colors or crest.
> *Ib. The Lost Legion, st. 1*

To go and find out and be damned
(Dear boys!).   *Ib.*

There are nine and sixty ways of con-
structing tribal lays,
And every single one of them is right.
> *Ib. In the Neolithic Age, st. 5*

There be triple ways to take, of the
eagle or the snake,
Or the way of a man with a maid; [1]
But the sweetest way to me is a ship's
upon the sea
In the heel of the Northeast Trade.
> *Ib. The Long Trail, st. 5*

He wrapped himself in quotations [2]
— as a beggar would enfold himself in
the purple of emperors.
> *Many Inventions [1893]. The*
> *Finest Story in the World*

But, spite all modern notions, I've
found her first and best —
The only certain packet for the Islands
of the Blest.
> *The Three-Decker [1894], st. 1*

They copied all they could follow, but
they couldn't copy my mind.
> *The Mary Gloster [1894], l. 59*

When 'Omer smote 'is bloomin' lyre,
He'd 'eard men sing by land an' sea;

[1] See *Proverbs 30:19*, p. 26b.
[2] In literature quotation is good only when
the writer whom I follow goes my way, and,
being better mounted than I, gives me a cast.
— EMERSON, *Quotation and Originality* [1876]
See Louise Imogen Guiney, p. 860a.

An' what he thought 'e might require,
'E went an' took — the same as me!
> *When 'Omer Smote 'Is Bloomin'*
> *Lyre [1894], st. 1*

Back to the Army again, sergeant,
Back to the Army again.
Out o' the cold an' the rain.
> *Back to the Army Again*
> *[1894], refrain*

For to admire an' for to see,
For to be'old this world so wide —
It never done no good to me
But I can't drop it if I tried!
> *For to Admire [1894], refrain*

We be of one blood, ye and I.
> *The Jungle Book [1894].*
> *Kaa's Hunting*

Brother, thy tail hangs down behind.
> *Ib. Road Song of the Bandar-Log,*
> *refrain*

When Pack meets with Pack in the
Jungle, and neither will go from
the trail,
Lie down till the leaders have spoken
— it may be fair words shall prevail.
> *The Second Jungle Book [1895].*
> *The Law of the Jungle, st. 6*

Now these are the Laws of the Jungle,
and many and mighty are they;
But the head and the hoof of the Law
and the haunch and the hump
is — Obey!
> *Ib. st. 19*

He who rebukes the world is rebuked
by the world.
> *Ib. The Undertakers*

They change their skies above them,
But not their hearts that roam.[1]
> *The Nativeborn [1895], st. 2*

The Liner she's a lady, an' she never
looks nor 'eeds —
The Man-o'-War's 'er 'usband, an' 'e
gives 'er all she needs,
But, oh, the little cargo boats that sail
the wet seas roun',

[1] See Horace, p. 123b.

They're just the same as you an' me
a-plyin' up and down!
> *The Liner She's a Lady*
> [1895], *st. 1*

I've taken my fun where I've found it.
> *The Ladies* [1895], *st. 1*

An' I learned about women from 'er.
> *Ib. refrain*

For the Colonel's Lady an' Judy
O'Grady
Are sisters under their skins!
> *Ib. st. 8*

Though there's never a wave of all her
waves
But marks our English dead.
> *The Song of the Dead*
> [1896], II, *st. 1*

If blood be the price of admiralty,
Lord God, we ha' paid in full!   *Ib.*

'E's a sort of a bloomin' cosmopolouse
— soldier an' sailor too.
> *Soldier an' Sailor Too*
> [1896], *st. 2*

A fool there was and he made his
prayer
(Even as you and I!)
To a rag and a bone and a hank of
hair
(We called her the woman who did not
care)
But the fool he called her his lady
fair —
(Even as you and I!)
> *The Vampire* [1897], *st. 1*

Make ye no truce with Adam-zad —
the Bear that walks like a Man! [1]
> *The Truce of the Bear*
> [1898], *st. 2*

Daughter am I in my mother's house;
But mistress in my own.
> *Our Lady of the Snows* [2]
> [1898], *st. 1*

God of our fathers, known of old,
Lord of our far-flung battle line,
Beneath whose awful Hand we hold
Dominion over palm and pine —

[1] Russia.
[2] The Dominion of Canada.

Lord God of Hosts, be with us yet,
Lest we forget — lest we forget!
> *Recessional* [1899], *st. 1*

The tumult and the shouting dies;
The captains and the kings depart:
Still stands Thine ancient sacrifice,
An humble and a contrite heart.
> *Ib. st. 2*

Lo, all our pomp of yesterday
Is one with Nineveh and Tyre!
> *Ib. st. 3*

Lesser breeds without the Law.
> *Ib. st. 4*

For heathen heart that puts her trust
In reeking tube and iron shard,
All valiant dust that builds on dust,
And guarding, calls not Thee to guard,
For frantic boast and foolish word —
Thy mercy on Thy People, Lord!
> *Ib. st. 5*

He's an absent-minded beggar, but he
heard his country call,
And his reg'ment didn't need to send to
find him!
> *The Absent-Minded Beggar*
> [1899], *st. 3*

Take up the White Man's burden. [1]
> *The White Man's Burden*
> [1899], *st. 1*

Your new-caught, sullen peoples,
Half devil and half child.   *Ib.*

We have had a jolly good lesson, and it
serves us jolly well right!
> *The Lesson* [1901], *st. 2*

We have forty million reasons for failure, but not a single excuse.
> *Ib. st. 8*

Little Friend of All the World.
> *Kim* [1901], *ch. 1*

Then ye returned to your trinkets; then
ye contented your souls
With the flanneled fools at the wicket
or the muddied oafs at the goals.
> *The Islanders* [1902], *l. 31*

[1] Pile on the brown man's burden
To satisfy your greed.
> *London Truth;* reprinted in *Middle-
> bury* [*Vermont*] *Register* [March 17,
> 1899]

When the ship goes *wop* (with a wig-
gle between)
And the steward falls into the soup
tureen . . .
Why, then you will know (if you
haven't guessed)
You're "Fifty north and forty west!"
> *The Just-So Stories* [1902].
> *How the Whale Got Its
> Throat*

We get the hump —
Cameelious hump —
The hump that is black and blue!
> *Ib. How the Camel Got His
> Hump*

I keep six honest serving men
(They taught me all I knew);
Their names are What and Why and
When
And How and Where and Who.
> *Ib. The Elephant's Child*

The great gray-green, greasy Limpopo River, all set about with fever-
trees. *Ib.*

Yes, weekly from Southampton,
Great steamers, white and gold,
Go rolling down to Rio
(Roll down — roll down to Rio!)
And I'd like to roll to Rio
Some day before I'm old!
> *Ib. The Beginning of the
> Armadilloes, st. 4*

The Cat. He walked by himself, and
all places were alike to him.
> *Ib. The Cat That Walked By
> Himself*

He went through the wet wild
woods, waving his wild tail, and walking by his wild lone. But he never told
anybody. *Ib.*

Who hath desired the sea? — the sight
of salt water unbounded.
> *The Sea and the Hills* [1903], *st. 1*

So and no otherwise — hillmen desire
their hills! *Ib.*

Something hidden. Go and find it. Go
and look behind the Ranges —

Something lost behind the Ranges.
Lost and waiting for you. Go! [1]
> *The Explorer* [1903], *st. 2*

Creation's cry goes up on high
From age to cheated age:
"Send us the men who do the work
For which they draw the wage!"
> *The Wage Slaves* [1903], *st. 3*

Boots — boots — boots — boots —
movin' up and down again!
There's no discharge in the war! [2]
> *Boots* [1903], *st. 1*

If England was what England seems,
An' not the England of our dreams,
But only putty, brass, an' paint,
'Ow quick we'd drop 'er! But she ain't.
> *The Return* [1903], *refrain*

'Tisn't beauty, so to speak, nor good
talk necessarily. It's just It. Some
women'll stay in a man's memory if
they once walked down a street.
> *Traffics and Discoveries* [1904].
> *Mrs. Bathurst*

If once you have paid him the Danegeld
You never get rid of the Dane.
> *Ib. What Dane-Geld Means,
> st. 4*

What say the reeds at Runnymede?
> *Ib. The Reeds of Runnymede,
> st. 1*

When crew and captain understand
each other to the core,
It takes a gale and more than a gale to
put their ship ashore.
> *Ib. Together, st. 2*

Of all the trees that grow so fair,
Old England to adorn,
Greater are none beneath the Sun,
Than oak, and ash, and thorn.[3]
> *Puck of Pook's Hill* [1906]. A
> *Tree Song, st. 1*

---

[1] Because it is there. — GEORGE LEIGH MALLORY
[1886–1924], *when asked why he wanted to climb
Mt. Everest*
[2] See *Ecclesiastes 8:8*, p. 28a.
[3] See *Glasgerion*, p. 1088a.

Land of our birth, we pledge to thee
Our love and toil in the years to be.
> *Puck of Pook's Hill. The
> Children's Song, st. 1*

Teach us delight in simple things,
And mirth that has no bitter springs.
> *Ib. st. 7*

Enough work to do, and strength
enough to do the work.
> *A Doctor's Work. Address at
> Middlesex Hospital* [1] *[October
> 1908]*

Brothers and Sisters, I bid you beware
Of giving your heart to a dog to tear.
> *The Power of the Dog [1909]*

Take of English earth as much
As either hand may rightly clutch.
In the taking of it breathe
Prayer for all who lie beneath.
> *Rewards and Fairies* [2] *[1910].
> A Charm, st. 1*

If you can meet with Triumph and
Disaster
And treat those two impostors just the
same.   *Ib. If, st. 2*

If you can talk with crowds and keep
your virtue,
Or walk with Kings — nor lose the
common touch.   *Ib. st. 4*

Yours is the Earth and everything
that's in it,
And — which is more — you'll be a
Man, my son!   *Ib.*

One man in a thousand, Solomon says,
Will stick more close than a brother. [3]
> *Ib. The Thousandth Man, st. 1*

But the Thousandth Man will stand by
your side
To the gallows foot — and after!
> *Ib. st. 4*

The female of the species is more
deadly than the male.
> *The Female of the Species
> [1911], st. 1*

Our England is a garden, and such gardens are not made

By singing "Oh, how beautiful!" and
sitting in the shade.
> *The Glory of the Garden
> [1911], st. 5*

Oh, Adam was a gardener, [1] and God
who made him sees
That half a proper gardener's work is
done upon his knees.
> *Ib. st. 8*

For all we have and are,
For all our children's fate,
Stand up and take the war.
The Hun is at the gate!
> *For All We Have and Are
> [1914], st. 1*

There is but one task for all —
One life for each to give.
What stands if Freedom fall?
Who dies if England live?
> *Ib. st. 4*

That packet of assorted miseries
which we call a Ship.
> *The First Sailor [1918]*

Hot and bothered.
> *Independence. Rectorial Ad-
> dress, St. Andrew's [October
> 10, 1923]*

Never again will I spend another
winter in this accursed bucketshop of a
refrigerator called England.
> *Letter to Sidney Colvin. From
> E. V. Lucas, The Colvins and
> Their Friends [1928], p. 294*

When your Daemon is in charge, do
not try to think consciously. Drift, wait,
and obey.
> *Something of Myself for My
> Friends Known and Unknown
> [1937], ch. 8*

LOGAN PEARSALL SMITH [2]

1865–1946

What a bore it is, waking up in the
morning always the same person. I wish

---

[1] Where Kipling died in 1936.
[2] See Corbet, p. 315b.
[3] See *Ecclesiastes* 7:28, p. 28a.

[1] See Shakespeare, p. 215a.
[2] Two weeks before his death, a friend asked
him half jokingly if he had discovered any
meaning in life. "Yes," he replied, "there is

I were unflinching and emphatic, and had big, bushy eyebrows and a Message for the Age. I wish I were a deep Thinker, or a great Ventriloquist.
Trivia [1902]. *Green Ivory*

There are two things to aim at in life: first, to get what you want; and, after that, to enjoy it. Only the wisest of mankind achieve the second.
Afterthoughts [1931]

Happiness is a wine of the rarest vintage, and seems insipid to a vulgar taste. *Ib.*

How awful to reflect that what people say of us is true! *Ib.*

Solvency is entirely a matter of temperament and not of income.
Ib.

It is almost always worth while to be cheated; people's little frauds have an interest which more than repays what they cost us. *Ib.*

When they come downstairs from their Ivory Towers, idealists are apt to walk straight into the gutter. *Ib.*

The indefatigable pursuit of an unattainable perfection, even though it consist in nothing more than in the pounding of an old piano, is what alone gives a meaning to our life on this unavailing star. *Ib.*

Eat with the rich, but go to the play with the poor, who are capable of joy.
Ib.

A best seller is the gilded tomb of a mediocre talent. *Ib.*

What I like in a good author is not what he says, but what he whispers.
Ib.

People say that life is the thing, but I prefer reading. *Ib.*

---

a meaning; at least, for me, there is one thing that matters — to set a chime of words tinkling in the minds of a few fastidious people."
— Cyril Connolly [b. 1903], *A Tribute to Logan Pearsall Smith, in The New Statesman*

Thank heavens, the sun has gone in, and I don't have to go out and enjoy it. *Afterthoughts*

ARTHUR SYMONS
1865–1945

Twitched strings, the clang of metal, beaten drums,
Dull, shrill, continuous, disquieting;
And now the stealthy dancer comes
Undulantly with catlike steps that cling. *Javanese Dancers* [1889]

And I would have, now love is over,
An end to all, an end:
I cannot, having been your lover,
Stoop to become your friend!
After Love [1892], *st. 3*

Life is a dream in the night, a fear among fears,
A naked runner lost in a storm of spears.
In the Wood of Finvara [1896], *st. 1*

My life is like a music hall.
Prologue [1895]

The gray-green stretch of sandy grass,
Indefinitely desolate;
A sea of lead, a sky of slate;
Already autumn in the air, alas!

One stark monotony of stone,
The long hotel, acutely white,
Against the after-sunset light
Withers gray-green, and takes the grass's tone.
Color Studies [1895]. *At Dieppe*

My soul is like this cloudy, flaming opal ring. *Opals* [1896]

I broider the world upon a loom,
I broider with dreams my tapestry;
Here in a little lonely room
I am master of earth and sea,
And the planets come to me.
The Loom of Dreams [1900], *st. 1*

He knew that the whole mystery of beauty can never be comprehended by

the crowd, and that while clearness is a virtue of style, perfect explicitness is not a necessary virtue.
> *The Symbolist Movement in Literature* [1899]. *Gérard de Nerval*

Without charm there can be no fine literature, as there can be no perfect flower without fragrance.
> *Ib. Stéphane Mallarmé*

The mystic too full of God to speak intelligibly to the world.
> *Ib. Arthur Rimbaud*

Many excellent writers, very many painters, and most musicians are so tedious on any subject but their own.
> *Ib.*

Criticism is properly the rod of divination: a hazel switch for the discovery of buried treasure, not a birch twig for the castigation of offenders.
> *An Introduction to the Study of Browning* [1906], *preface*

The great things in poetry are song at the core, but externally mere speech.
> *Dramatis Personae* [1923]. *Sir William Watson*

HERBERT TRENCH
1865–1923

A circumnavigator of the soul.
> *Shakespeare, st. 4*

WILLIAM BUTLER YEATS[1]
1865–1939

Down by the salley gardens my love and I did meet;
She passed the salley gardens with little snow-white feet.
She bid me take love easy, as the leaves grow on the tree;

[1] Yeats was the greatest poet of our times . . . certainly the greatest in this language, and so far as I am able to judge, in any language. — T. S. ELIOT

See W. H. Auden, p. 1060a.

But I, being young and foolish, with her would not agree.
> *Down by the Salley Gardens* [1889]

She bid me take life easy, as the grass grows on the weirs;
But I was young and foolish, and now am full of tears.
> *Ib.*

The years like great black oxen tread the world
And God, the herdsman, goads them on behind.
> *The Countess Cathleen* [1892]

Red Rose, proud Rose, sad Rose of all my days!
Come near me, while I sing the ancient ways.
> *To the Rose Upon the Rood of Time* [1893], *st. 1*

When you are old and gray and full of sleep,
And nodding by the fire, take down this book.[1]
> *When You Are Old* [1893]

How many loved your moments of glad grace,
And loved your beauty, with love false or true,
But one man loved the pilgrim soul in you,
And loved the sorrows of your changing face.
> *Ib.*

I will arise and go now, and go to Innisfree,
And a small cabin build there, of clay and wattles made:
Nine bean-rows will I have there, a hive for the honeybee,
And live alone in the bee-loud glade.

And I shall have some peace there, for peace comes dropping slow,
Dropping from the veils of the morning to where the cricket sings;
There midnight's all a glimmer, and noon a purple glow,
And evening full of the linnet's wings.
> *The Lake Isle of Innisfree* [2] [1893], *st. 1, 2*

[1] See Ronsard, p. 187b.
[2] I had still the ambition, formed in Sligo in my teens, of living in imitation of Thoreau on

I hear it in the deep heart's core.
        The Lake Isle of Innisfree, st. 3

A pity beyond all telling
Is hid in the heart of love.
        The Pity of Love [1893]

The brawling of a sparrow in the
    eaves,
The brilliant moon and all the milky
    sky,
And all that famous harmony of
    leaves,
Had blotted out man's image and his
    cry.
        The Sorrow of Love [1893],
                st. 1

        The land of faery,
Where nobody gets old and godly and
    grave,
Where nobody gets old and crafty and
    wise,
Where nobody gets old and bitter of
    tongue.
        The Land of Heart's Desire 1
                [1894]

        Land of Heart's Desire,
Where beauty has no ebb, decay no
    flood,
But joy is wisdom, time an endless
    song.   *Ib.*

And God stands winding His lonely
    horn,
And time and the world are ever in
    flight.
        Into the Twilight [1899]

And pluck till time and times are done
The silver apples of the moon,
The golden apples of the sun.
        The Song of Wandering Aengus
                [1899], st. 3

Innisfree, a little island in Lough Gill, and
when walking through Fleet Street very home-
sick I heard a little tinkle of water and saw a
fountain in a shop window which balanced a
little ball upon its jet, and began to remember
lake water. From the sudden remembrance came
my poem Innisfree. — *The Trembling of the
Veil* [1926]

    See Samuel Rogers, p. 500b.

    1 Excluded by Yeats from his *Collected Poems*
[1933]

All things uncomely and broken, all
    things worn out and old,
The cry of a child by the roadway, the
    creak of a lumbering cart,
The heavy steps of the plowman,
    splashing the wintry mold,
Are wronging your image that blossoms
    a rose in the deeps of my heart.
        *The Lover Tells of the Rose in
                His Heart* [1899], *st. 1*

Had I the heavens' embroidered
    cloths,
Enwrought with gold and silver light.
        *He Wishes for the Cloths of
                Heaven* [1899]

But I, being poor, have only my
    dreams;
I have spread my dreams under your
    feet;
Tread softly because you tread on my
    dreams.   **Ib.**

When I play on my fiddle in Dooney,
Folk dance like a wave of the sea.
        The Fiddler of Dooney [1899],
                st. 1

O heart! O heart! if she'd but turn her
    head,
You'd know the folly of being com-
    forted.
        The Folly of Being Comforted
                [1904]

Never give all the heart, for love
Will hardly seem worth thinking of
To passionate women if it seem
Certain, and they never dream
That it fades out from kiss to kiss;
For everything that's lovely is
But a brief, dreamy kind of delight.
        Never Give All the Heart [1904]

Better go down upon your marrow-
    bones
And scrub a kitchen pavement, or break
    stones
Like an old pauper, in all kinds of
    weather;
For to articulate sweet sounds together
Is to work harder than all these, and
    yet
Be thought an idler by the noisy set

Of bankers, schoolmasters, and clergymen
The martyrs call the world.
        Adam's Curse [1904], *st.* 2

    It's certain there is no fine thing
Since Adam's fall but needs much laboring.   *Ib. st. 4*

I heard the old, old men say,
"All that's beautiful drifts away
Like the waters."
        *The Old Men Admiring Them-
        selves in the Water* [1904]

Why, what could she have done, being
    what she is?
Was there another Troy for her to
    burn?   *No Second Troy* [1910]

The fascination of what's difficult
Has dried the sap out of my veins, and
    rent
Spontaneous joy and natural content
Out of my heart.
        *The Fascination of What's
        Difficult* [1910]

Wine comes in at the mouth
And love comes in at the eye;
That's all we shall know for truth
Before we grow old and die.
        A Drinking Song [1910]

Though leaves are many, the root is
    one;
Through all the lying days of my youth
I swayed my leaves and flowers in the
    sun;
Now I may wither into the truth.
        *The Coming of Wisdom with
        Time* [1910]

In dreams begins responsibility.[1]
        *Old Play. Epigraph, Responsi-
        bilities* [1914]

Was it for this the wild geese spread
The gray wing upon every tide;
For this that all that blood was shed,
For this Edward Fitzgerald died,
And Robert Emmet and Wolfe Tone,
All that delirium of the brave?

[1] In Dreams Begin Responsibilities. — DEL-
MORE SCHWARTZ, *title of book of poems* [1938]

Romantic Ireland's dead and gone,
It's with O'Leary in the grave.
        September 1913 [1914]

Be secret and exult,
Because of all things known
That is most difficult.
        *To a Friend Whose Work Has
        Come to Nothing* [1914]

I made my song a coat
Covered with embroideries
Out of old mythologies
From heel to throat;
But the fools caught it,
Wore it in the world's eyes
As though they'd wrought it.
Song, let them take it,
For there's more enterprise
In walking naked.   *A Coat* [1914]

I know that I shall meet my fate
Somewhere among the clouds above;
Those that I fight I do not hate,
Those that I guard I do not love;
My country is Kiltartan Cross,
My countrymen Kiltartan's poor.
        *An Irish Airman Foresees His
        Death* [1919]

Nor law, nor duty bade me fight,
Nor public men, nor cheering crowds,
A lonely impulse of delight
Drove to this tumult in the clouds.
        Ib.

And I may dine at journey's end
With Landor and with Donne.
        To a Young Beauty [1919],
                st. 3

Lord, what would they say
Did their Catullus walk that way?
        The Scholars [1919], *st.* 2

All the wild witches, those most noble
    ladies,
For all their broomsticks and their
    tears,
Their angry tears, are gone.
        Lines Written in Dejection [1919]

I knew a phoenix in my youth, so let
    them have their day.
        His Phoenix [1919]

Bring the balloon of the mind
That bellies and drags in the wind
Into its narrow shed.
　　　　The Balloon of the Mind [1919]

We have lit upon the gentle, sensitive
　　mind
And lost the old nonchalance of the
　　hand;
Whether we have chosen chisel, pen or
　　brush,
We are but critics, or but half create.
　　　　Ego Dominus Tuus [1919]

All changed, changed utterly:
A terrible beauty is born.
　　　　　　　Easter 1916 [1921]

Nothing that we love overmuch
Is ponderable to our touch.
　　　　Towards Break of Day [1921],
　　　　　　　　　　　　　　st. 3

Turning and turning in the widening
　　gyre
The falcon cannot hear the falconer;
Things fall apart; the center cannot
　　hold;
Mere anarchy is loosed upon the
　　world,
The blood-dimmed tide is loosed, and
　　everywhere
The ceremony of innocence is
　　drowned;
The best lack all conviction, while the
　　worst
Are full of passionate intensity.
　　　　The Second Coming [1921],
　　　　　　　　　　　　　　st. 1

And what rough beast, its hour come
　　round at last,
Slouches towards Bethlehem to be
　　born?　　　　　　　　*Ib. st. 2*

Imagining in excited reverie
That the future years had come,
Dancing to a frenzied drum,
Out of the murderous innocence of the
　　sea.
　　　　A Prayer for My Daughter
　　　　　　　　　　[1921], *st. 2*

　　For such,
Being made beautiful overmuch,
Consider beauty a sufficient end,

Lose natural kindness and maybe
The heart-revealing intimacy
That chooses right, and never find a
　　friend.
　　　　A Prayer for My Daughter,
　　　　　　　　　　　　　　st. 3

It's certain that fine women eat
A crazy salad with their meat.
　　　　　　　　　　Ib. st. 4

In courtesy I'd have her chiefly learned;
Hearts are not had as a gift but hearts
　　are earned.　　　　　*Ib. st. 5*

And many a poor man that has roved,
Loved and thought himself beloved,
From a glad kindness cannot take his
　　eyes.　　　　　　　　　　*Ib.*

If there's no hatred in a mind
Assault and battery of the wind
Can never tear the linnet from the
　　leaf.　　　　　　　　*Ib. st. 7*

An intellectual hatred is the worst,
So let her think opinions are accursed.
Have I not seen the loveliest woman
　　born
Out of the mouth of Plenty's horn,
Because of her opinionated mind
Barter that horn and every good
By quiet natures understood
For an old bellows full of angry wind?
　　　　　　　　　　Ib. st. 8

That is no country for old men. The
　　young
In one another's arms, birds in the
　　trees
— Those dying generations — at their
　　song,
The salmon-falls, the mackerel-crowded
　　seas,
Fish, flesh, or fowl, commend all sum-
　　mer long
Whatever is begotten, born, and dies.
Caught in that sensual music all neg-
　　lect
Monuments of unaging intellect.
　　　　Sailing to Byzantium [1928], *st. 1*

An aged man is but a paltry thing,
A tattered coat upon a stick, unless
Soul clap its hands and sing, and louder
　　sing
For every tatter in its mortal dress.
　　　　　　　　　　Ib. st. 2

Consume my heart away; sick with de-
sire
And fastened to a dying animal
It knows not what it is; and gather
me
Into the artifice of eternity.
Sailing to Byzantium, st. 3

Once out of nature I shall never take
My bodily form from any natural thing,
But such a form as Grecian goldsmiths
make
Of hammered gold and gold enameling
To keep a drowsy Emperor awake;
Or set upon a golden bough to sing
To lords and ladies of Byzantium
Of what is past, or passing, or to
come.[1]   Ib. st. 4

What shall I do with this absurdity —
O heart, O troubled heart — this cari-
cature,
Decrepit age that has been tied to
me
As to a dog's tail?
Never had I more
Excited, passionate, fantastical
Imagination, nor an ear and eye
That more expected the impossible.
The Tower [1928], I

Does the imagination dwell the most
Upon a woman won or a woman lost?
Ib. II, st. 13

Come let us mock at the great
That had such burdens on the mind
And toiled so hard and late
To leave some monument behind,
Nor thought of the leveling wind.
Nineteen Hundred and Nine-
teen [1928], V

Mock mockers after that
That would not lift a hand maybe
To help good, wise or great
To bar that foul storm out, for we
Traffic in mockery.   Ib.

Much did I rage when young,
Being by the world oppressed,
But now with flattering tongue
It speeds the parting guest.
Youth and Age [1928]

[1] I have read somewhere that in the Emperor's palace at Byzantium was a tree made of gold and silver, and artificial birds that sang. — YEATS's note

Everything that man esteems
Endures a moment or a day.
Love's pleasure drives his love away,
The painter's brush consumes his
dreams.
Two Songs from a Play [1928],
II, st. 2

Whatever flames upon the night
Man's own resinous heart has fed.
Ib.

A shudder in the loins engenders
there
The broken wall, the burning roof and
tower
And Agamemnon dead.
Leda and the Swan [1928]

O chestnut tree, great rooted blos-
somer,
Are you the leaf, the blossom or the
bole?
O body swayed to music, O brightening glance,
How can we know the dancer from the
dance?
Among School Children [1928],
st. 8

Never to have lived is best, ancient
writers say;
Never to have drawn the breath of life,
never to have looked into the eye
of day
The second best's a gay goodnight and
quickly turn away.[1]
From "Oedipus at Colonus,"
st. 3

The innocent and the beautiful
Have no enemy but time.
In Memory of Eva Gore-booth
and Con Markiewicz [1933]

My Self: A living man is blind and
drinks his drop.
What matter if the ditches are impure?
What matter if I live it all once more?
Endure that toil of growing up;
The ignominy of boyhood; the distress
Of boyhood changing into man;
The unfinished man and his pain

[1] See Theognis, p. 77a, and note.

Brought face to face with his own
 clumsiness.
 A Dialogue of Self and Soul
 [1933], *II, st. 1*

I am content to live it all again
And yet again, if it be life to pitch
Into the frog-spawn of a blind man's
 ditch. *Ib. st. 3*

When such as I cast out remorse
So great a sweetness flows into the
 breast
We must laugh and we must sing,
We are blest by everything,
Everything we look upon is blest.
 Ib. st. 4

 But what is Whiggery?
A leveling, rancorous, rational sort of
 mind
That never looked out of the eye of a
 saint
Or out of a drunkard's eye.
 The Seven Sages [1933]

No man has ever lived that had enough
Of children's gratitude or woman's
 love. *Vacillation* [1933], *st. 3*

Swift has sailed into his rest;
Savage indignation there
Cannot lacerate his breast,
Imitate him if you dare,
World-besotted traveler; he
Served human liberty.
 Swift's Epitaph [1] [1933]

The intellect of man is forced to
 choose
Perfection of the life, or of the work,
And if it take the second must refuse
A heavenly mansion, raging in the
 dark. *The Choice* [1933], *st. 1*

But Love has pitched his mansion in
The place of excrement.
 *Crazy Jane Talks with the
 Bishop* [1933], *st. 3*

What were all the world's alarms
To mighty Paris when he found
Sleep upon a golden bed
That first dawn in Helen's arms?
 Words for Music Perhaps
 [1933]. *Lullaby, st. 1*

[1] See Swift, p. 391a, and note.

Speech after long silence; it is right,
All other lovers being estranged or
 dead . . .
That we descant and yet again descant
Upon the supreme theme of Art and
 Song:
Bodily decrepitude is wisdom; young
We loved each other and were ig-
 norant.
 *Words for Music Perhaps.
 After Long Silence*

I carry the sun in a golden cup,
The moon in a silver bag.
 *Ib. Those Dancing Days Are
 Gone, refrain*

I gave what other women gave
That stepped out of their clothes,
But when this soul, its body off,
Naked to naked goes,
He it has found shall find therein
What none other knows.
 A Woman Young and Old
 [1933]. *A Last Confession,
 st. 3*

He that sings a lasting song
Thinks in a marrowbone.
 A Prayer for Old Age [1935], *st. 1*

I pray — for fashion's word is out
And prayer comes round again —
That I may seem, though I die old,
A foolish, passionate man. *Ib. st. 3*

All perform their tragic play,
There struts Hamlet, there is Lear.
 Lapis Lazuli [1936–1939]

 Heaven blazing into the head:
Tragedy wrought to its uttermost.
Though Hamlet rambles and Lear
 rages,
And all the drop-scenes drop at once
Upon a hundred thousand stages,
It cannot grow by an inch or an ounce.
 Ib.

If soul may look and body touch,
Which is the more blest?
 The Lady's Second Song [1936–
 1939], *st. 3*

My temptation is quiet.
Here at life's end
Neither loose imagination,

Nor the mill of the mind
Consuming its rat and bone,
Can make the truth known.
An Acre of Grass [1936–1939],
st. 2

Grant me an old man's frenzy,
Myself must I remake
Till I am Timon and Lear
Or that William Blake
Who beat upon the wall
Till Truth obeyed his call. *Ib. st. 3*

Hurrah for revolution and more can-
non-shot!
A beggar upon horseback lashes a beggar on foot.
The Great Day [1936–
1939], *l. 1*

You think it horrible that lust and
rage
Should dance attention upon my old
age;
They were not such a plague when I
was young;
What else have I to spur me into
song? *The Spur* [1936–1939]

Down the mountain walls
From where Pan's cavern is
Intolerable music falls.
Foul goat-head, brutal arm appear,
Belly, shoulder, bum,
Flash fishlike; nymphs and satyrs
Copulate in the foam.
News for the Delphic Oracle
[1936–1939], *st. 3*

What shall I do for pretty girls
Now my old bawd is dead?
*John Kinsella's Lament for
Mrs. Mary Moore* [1936–
1939], *refrain*

Irish poets, learn your trade,
Sing whatever is well made.
Under Ben Bulben [1936–
1939], *V*

Under bare Ben Bulben's head
In Drumcliff churchyard Yeats is laid.
Ib. VI

On limestone quarried near the spot
By his command these words are cut:

Cast a cold eye
On life, on death.
Horseman, pass by! [1]
Under Ben Bulben, V

The friends that have it I do wrong
When ever I remake a song
Should know what issue is at stake,
It is myself that I remake.
*Variorum Edition of the Poems
of W. B. Yeats*

I am still of opinion that only two
topics can be of the least interest to a
serious and studious mood — sex and
the dead.
The Letters of W. B. Yeats

If a poet interprets a poem of his
own he limits its suggestibility. *Ib.*

We poets would die of loneliness but
for women, and we choose our men
friends that we may have somebody to
talk about women with.
Ib. Letter to Olivia Shakespeare
[1936]

In life courtesy and self-possession,
and in the arts style, are the sensible
impressions of the free mind, for both
arise out of a deliberate shaping of all
things and from never being swept
away, whatever the emotion, into confusion or dullness.
Essays and Introductions
[1961]. *Poetry and The
Tradition*

HARRY DACRE
fl. 1892

Daisy, Daisy, give me your answer, do!
I'm half crazy, all for the love of you!
It won't be a stylish marriage,
I can't afford a carriage,
But you'll look sweet upon the seat
Of a bicycle built for two!
Daisy Bell [1892]

[1] The last three lines are inscribed on Yeats's
grave.

HENRY J. SAYERS
d. 1932

Ta-ra-ra-boom-de-ay!
*Title of minstrel show number
[1891], made famous by Lottie
Collins in 1892*

GEORGE W. YOUNG
fl. 1900

The lips that touch liquor must never
touch mine!
*The Lips That Touch Liquor,
st. 5*

GEORGE ADE[1]
1866–1944

A good folly is worth what you pay
for it.
*Fables in Slang [1899]. A Lot
for Three Dollars*

In uplifting, get underneath.
Ib. The Good Fairy

He had been kicked in the head by a
mule when young and believed everything he read in the Sunday papers.
Ib. The Slim Girl

Only the more rugged mortals should
attempt to keep up with current literature.
Ib. Didn't Care for Storybooks

Never put off until tomorrow what
should have been done early in the Seventies.
*Forty Modern Fables [1901].
The Third and Last Call*

To insure peace of mind ignore the
rules and regulations.
Ib. The Crustacean

If it were not for the presents, an
elopement would be preferable.
*Ib. The General Manager of the
Love Affair*

[1] Somehow I always like to think
Of *Georgeade* as a summer drink,
Sparkling and cool, with just a tang
Of pleasant effervescent slang.
OLIVER HERFORD [1863–1935], *Celebrities
I Have Never Met*

Stay with the procession or you will
never catch up.
*Forty Modern Fables. The
Old-Time Pedagogue*

The time to enjoy a European trip is
about three weeks after unpacking.
Ib. The Hungry Man

Draw your salary before spending it.
Ib. The People's Choice

The man was a pinhead in a good
many respects, but he was wise as a
serpent.
Ib. The Wise Piker

For parlor use the vague generality is
a life-saver.
Ib.

Last night at twelve I felt immense,
But now I feel like thirty cents.
*The Sultan of Sulu [1902].
Remorse*

But, R – e – m – o – r – s – e!
The water-wagon is the place for me;
It is no time for mirth and laughter,
The cold, gray dawn of the morning
after! [1]
Ib.

TRISTAN BERNARD
1866–1947

Men are always sincere. They change
sincerities, that's all.
Ce que l'on dit aux femmes

To live happily with other people one
should only ask of them what they can
give.
L'Enfant prodigue du Vesinet

HENRY BLOSSOM
1866–1919

I Want What I Want When I
Want It.
*Mademoiselle Modiste [1905].
Title of song*

GELETT BURGESS
1866–1951

I never saw a purple cow,
I never hope to see one;

[1] See Byron, p. 560b, and Dickens, p. 670a.

But I can tell you, anyhow,
I'd rather see than be one.
The Purple Cow [1895]

Ah, yes, I wrote the "Purple Cow" —
I'm sorry, now, I wrote it!
But I can tell you, anyhow,
I'll kill you if you quote it.
Cinq Ans Après

EDMUND VANCE COOKE
1866–1932

The woman tempted me — and tempts
me still!
Lord God, I pray You that she ever will!
Adam

And it isn't the fact that you're hurt
that counts,
But only how did you take it.
How Did You Die? st. 1

PHILANDER JOHNSON
1866–1939

The world would sleep if things were
run
By men who say, "It can't be done!"
It Can't Be Done

Cheer up, the worst is yet to come.[1]
Shooting Stars

RICHARD LE GALLIENNE
1866–1947

The cry of the Little Peoples goes up to
God in vain,
For the world is given over to the cruel
sons of Cain.
The Cry of the Little Peoples

WALTER MALONE
1866–1915

And if a lowly singer dries one tear,
Or soothes one humble human heart in
pain,
Be sure his homely verse to God is
dear,
And not one stanza has been sung in
vain.
The Humbler Poets, st. 3

[1] See Tennyson, p. 654a.

THOMAS L. MASSON
1866–1934

Obey That Impulse.
Subscription slogan, Life

A Safe and Sane Fourth.   *Slogan*

GEORGE BARR McCUTCHEON
1866–1928

"You brute!" hissed the Countess.
Graustark [1901], *ch. 16*

BEATRIX POTTER
1866–1943

Once upon a time there were four
little Rabbits, and their names were
— Flopsy, Mopsy, Cottontail, and Peter.
They lived with their Mother in a
sandbank underneath the root of a very
big fir tree.
The Tale of Peter Rabbit

But don't go into Mr. McGregor's
garden.   *Ib.*

The water was all slippy-sloppy in the
larder and the back passage. But Mr.
Jeremy liked getting his feet wet; nobody ever scolded him, and he never
caught a cold.
The Tale of Mr. Jeremy Fisher

No more twist!
The Tailor of Gloucester

LINCOLN STEFFENS
1866–1936

"So you've been over into Russia?"
said Bernard Baruch, and I answered
very literally, "I have been over into the
future, and it works." [1]
Autobiography [1931], *ch. 18*

BERT LESTON TAYLOR
1866–1921

When men are calling names and making faces,

[1] On Steffens's return from the Bullitt mission, 1919.

And all the world's ajangle and ajar,
I meditate on interstellar spaces
And smoke a mild seegar.
Canopus

A bore is a man who, when you ask
him how he is, tells you.
The So-Called Human Race [1922]

HERBERT GEORGE
WELLS
1866–1946

The Time Machine.
Title of book [1895]

The past is but the beginning of a
beginning, and all that is and has been
is but the twilight of the dawn.
The Discovery of the Future
[1901]

Nothing could have been more obvious to the people of the early twentieth
century than the rapidity with which
war was becoming impossible. And as
certainly they did not see it. They did
not see it until the atomic bombs burst
in their fumbling hands.
The World Set Free [1914]

The catastrophe of the atomic bombs
which shook men out of cities and businesses and economic relations, shook
them also out of their old-established
habits of thought, and out of the
lightly held beliefs and prejudices that
came down to them from the past.
Ib.

The War That Will End War.
Title of book [1914]

The professional military mind is by
necessity an inferior and unimaginative
mind; no man of high intellectual quality would willingly imprison his gifts in
such a calling.
The Outline of History [1920],
ch. 40

The Great War and the Petty
Peace.　　　　　*Ib.*

Human history is in essence a history
of ideas.
The Outline of History, ch. 40

Every one of these hundreds of millions of human beings is in some form
seeking happiness. . . . Not one is altogether noble nor altogether trustworthy nor altogether consistent; and
not one is altogether vile. . . . Not a
single one but has at some time wept.
Ib.

Our true nationality is mankind.
Ib. ch. 41

Human history becomes more and
more a race between education and
catastrophe.　　　　　*Ib.*

Life begins perpetually. Gathered together at last under the leadership of
man . . . unified, disciplined, armed
with the secret powers of the atom and
with knowledge as yet beyond dreaming, Life, forever dying to be born
afresh, forever young and eager, will
presently stand upon this earth as upon
a footstool, and stretch out its realm
amidst the stars.[1]　　　　　*Ib.*

An artist who theorizes about his
work is no longer artist but critic.
The Temptation of Harringay

In England we have come to rely
upon a comfortable time lag of fifty
years or a century intervening between
the perception that something ought to
be done and a serious attempt to do
it.
*The Work, Wealth and Happi-
ness of Mankind* [1931], *ch.* 11

The Shape of Things to Come.[2]
Title of book [1933]

SUN YAT-SEN[3]
1866–1925

It is only after mature deliberation
and thorough preparation that I have

[1] See *Matthew 5:34–35,* p. 40b; Pope, p. 408a
and Clarence Day, p. 925b.
[2] See Cicero, p. 111a; Shakespeare, *Troilus and
Cressida I, iii, 334,* p. 268a; and Campbell, p.
538a, and note.
[3] From *Sources of Chinese Tradition,* edited by
William Theodore de Bary [1960].

decided upon the Program of Revolution and defined the procedure of the revolution in three stages. The first is the period of military government; the second, the period of political tutelage; and the third, the period of constitutional government.
The Three Phases of National Reconstruction [1918]

The Chinese people have only family and clan solidarity; they do not have national spirit . . . they are just a heap of loose sand. . . . Other men are the carving knife and serving dish; we are the fish and the meat.
China As a Heap of Loose Sand [1924]

China is now suffering from poverty, not from unequal distribution of wealth. Where there are inequalities of wealth, the methods of Marx can, of course, be used; a class war can be advocated to destroy the inequalities. But in China, where industry is not yet developed, Marx's class war and dictatorship of the proletariat are impracticable. *Capital and the State* [1924]

In the construction of a country it is not the practical workers but the idealists and planners that are difficult to find.
Chung-shan Ch'üan-shu, vol. II

STANLEY BALDWIN
1867–1947

When you think about the defense of England you no longer think of the chalk cliffs of Dover. You think of the Rhine. That is where our frontier lies today.
Speech in the House of Commons [July 30, 1934]

ENOCH ARNOLD
BENNETT
1867–1931

The Old Wives' Tale.[1]
Title of novel [1908]

[1] But refuse profane and old wives' fables, and exercise rather unto godliness. — *I Timothy* 4:7

Being a husband is a whole-time job. *The Title* [1918], *act I*

Pessimism, when you get used to it, is just as agreeable as optimism.
Things That Have Interested Me [1918]

The price of justice is eternal publicity. *Ib. Second Series* [1923]

VICENTE
BLASCO-IBÁÑEZ
1867–1928

It was the roar of the real, the only beast [the crowd in the arena].
Blood and Sand [1908]

WILLIAM CECIL
DAMPIER-WHETHAM
1867–1952

Beyond the bright searchlights of science,
Out of sight of the windows of sense,
Old riddles still bid us defiance,
Old questions of Why and of Whence.
The Recent Development of Physical Science [1904]

ERNEST DOWSON
1867–1900

They saw the glory of the world displayed;
They saw the bitter of it, and the sweet;
They knew the roses of the world should fade,
And be trod under by the hurrying feet.
Nuns of the Perpetual Adoration [1891], *st. 5*

Last night, ah, yesternight, betwixt her lips and mine
There fell thy shadow,[1] Cynara! thy breath was shed

A fool he is to believe the tales of an old wife. — ALEXANDER BARCLAY, *The Ship of Fools* [1508]
Old wives' foolish tales of Robin Hood. — NICHOLAS UDALL [1542]
[1] See T. S. Eliot, p. 1003a.

Upon my soul between the kisses and
　　the wine;
And I was desolate and sick of an old
　　passion,
Yea, I was desolate and bowed my
　　head:
I have been faithful to thee, Cynara! in
　　my fashion.
　　　　*Non Sum Qualis Eram Bonae
　　　　Sub Regno Cynarae* [1] [1896],
　　　　st. 1

I have forgot much, Cynara! gone with
　　the wind,[2]
Flung roses, roses riotously with the
　　throng.　　　　　　　*Ib. st. 3*

I cried for madder music and for
　　stronger wine,
But when the feast is finished and the
　　lamps expire,
Then falls thy shadow, Cynara! the
　　night is thine.　　　　*Ib. st. 4*

They are not long, the weeping and the
　　laughter,
Love and desire and hate:
I think they have no portion in us
　　after
We pass the gate.

They are not long, the days of wine and
　　roses;
Out of a misty dream
Our path emerges for a while, then
　　closes
Within a dream.
　　　　*Vitae Summa Brevis Spem Nos
　　　　Vetat Incohare Longam* [3] [1896]

Because I am idolatrous and have be-
　　sought,
With grievous supplication and con-
　　suming prayer,
The admirable image that my dreams
　　have wrought
Out of her swan's neck and her dark,
　　abundant hair:
The jealous gods, who brook no wor-
　　ship save their own,
Turned my live idol marble and her
　　heart to stone.　　*Epigram* [1896]

[1] See Horace, *Odes IV, i, 3*, p. 122b.
[2] See Rutebeuf, p. 158a.
[3] See Horace, p. 120b.

From troublous sights and sounds set
　　free;
In such a twilight hour of breath,
Shall one retrace his life, or see,
Through shadows, the true face of
　　death?
　　　　Extreme Unction [1896], *st. 3*

MR. DOOLEY
[FINLEY PETER DUNNE]
1867–1936

Life'd not be worth livin' if we didn't
keep our inimies.
　　　　Mr. Dooley in Peace and in War
　　　　[1898]. *On New Year's Resolu-
　　　　tions*

Th' dead ar-re always pop'lar. I
knowed a society wanst to vote a monyment to a man an' refuse to help his
fam'ly, all in wan night.
　　　　　　　　Ib. On Charity

"I think," said Mr. Dooley, "that if
th' Christyan Scientists had some science an' th' doctors more Christianity,
it wudden't make anny diff'rence which
ye called in — if ye had a good nurse."
　　　　Mr. Dooley's Opinions [1900].
　　　　　　　　Christian Science

No matther whether th' constitution
follows th' flag or not, th' supreme
coort follows th' iliction returns.
　　　　*Ib. The Supreme Court's
　　　　　　　　Decisions*

I think a lie with a purpose is wan iv
th' worst kind an' th' mos' profitable.
　　　　　　　　Ib. On Lying

Th' dimmycratic party ain't on
speakin' terms with itsilf.
　　　　*Ib. Mr. Dooley Discusses Party
　　　　　　　　Politics*

Th' raypublican party broke ye, but
now that ye're down we'll not turn a
cold shoulder to ye. Come in an' we'll
keep ye — broke.　　　　*Ib.*

Hogan's r-right whin he says: "Justice is blind." Blind she is, an' deef an'
dumb an' has a wooden leg.
　　　　Ib. Cross-Examinations

No wan cares to hear what Hogan calls "Th' short an' simple scandals iv th' poor."

Mr. Dooley's Opinions. Cross-Examinations

'Twas founded be th' Puritans to give thanks f'r bein' presarved fr'm th' Indyans, an' . . . we keep it to give thanks we are presarved fr'm th' Puritans.   *Ib. Thanksgiving*

Vice . . . is a creature of such heejous mien . . . that th' more ye see it th' betther ye like it.

Ib. The Crusade Against Vice

Glory be, whin business gets above sellin' tinpinny nails in a brown paper cornucopy, 't is hard to tell it fr'm murther.   *Ib. On Wall Street*

"D' ye think th' colledges has much to do with th' progress iv th' wurruld?" asked Mr. Hennessy.

"D' ye think," said Mr. Dooley, "'tis th' mill that makes th' wather run?"   *Ib.*

" 'Twill civilize th' Chinnymen," said Mr. Hennessy.

" 'Twill civilize thim stiff," said Mr. Dooley.

Ib. The Future of China (on German intervention in China)

If ye live enough befure thirty ye won't care to live at all afther fifty.

Ib. Casual Observations

Among men, Hinnissy, wet eye manes dhry heart.   *Ib.*

A fanatic is a man that does what he thinks th' Lord wud do if He knew th' facts iv th' case.   *Ib.*

A vote on th' tallysheet is worth two in the box.   *Ib.*

'Tis as hard f'r a rich man to enther th' kingdom iv Hiven as it is f'r a poor man to get out iv Purgatory.   *Ib.*

Thrust ivrybody, but cut th' ca-ards.   *Ib.*

A man that'd expict to thrain lobsters to fly in a year is called a loonytic; but a man that thinks men can be tu-rrned into angels be an iliction is called a rayformer an' remains at large.

Mr. Dooley's Opinions. Casual Observations

Miracles are laughed at be a nation that r-reads thirty millyon newspapers a day an' supports Wall sthreet.   *Ib.*

Th' flag [1] floats free an' well guarded over th' govermint offices, an' th' cheery people go an' come on their errands — go out alone an' come back with th' throops. Iverywhere happiness, contint, love iv th' shtep-mother counthry, excipt in places where there ar-re people.

Observations by Mr. Dooley [1902]. The Philippine Peace

A reg'lar pollytician can't give away an alley without blushin', but a businessman who is in pollytics jus' to see that th' civil sarvice law gets thurly enfoorced, will give Lincoln Park an' th' public libr'y to th' beef thrust, charge an admission price to th' lake front an' make it a felony f'r annywan to buy stove polish outside iv his store, an' have it all put down to public improvemints with a pitcher iv him in th' cornerstone.   *Ib.*

If a man is wise, he gets rich, an' if he gets rich, he gets foolish, or his wife does. That's what keeps the money movin' around.   *Ib. Newport*

"Oh, well," said Mr. Hennessy, "we are as th' Lord made us."

"No," said Mr. Dooley, "lave us be fair. Lave us take some iv th' blame oursilves."   *Ib.*

But th' best thing about a little judicyous swearin' is that it keeps th' temper. 'Twas intinded as a compromise between runnin' away an' fightin'. Befure it was invinted they was on'y th' two ways out iv an argymint.

Ib. Swearing

I don't think we injye other people's sufferin', Hinnissy. It isn't acshally injyement. But we feel betther f'r it.

Ib. Enjoyment

[1] The American flag in the Philippines.

"Ye know a lot about [raising children]," said Mr. Hennessy.

"I do," said Mr. Dooley. "Not bein' an author, I'm a gr-reat critic."

Dissertations by Mr. Dooley [1906]. The Bringing Up of Children

Th' old story iv th' ant an' th' grasshopper — th' ant that ye can step on an' th' grasshopper ye can't catch.

Ib. The Labor Troubles

"If ye had a boy wud ye sind him to colledge?" asked Mr. Hennessy.

"Well," said Mr. Dooley, "at th' age whin a boy is fit to be in colledge I wudden't have him around th' house."

Ib. The Intellectual Life

Th' prisidincy is th' highest office in th' gift iv th' people. Th' vice-prisidincy is th' next highest an' th' lowest. It isn't a crime exactly. Ye can't be sint to jail f'r it, but it's a kind iv a disgrace. It's like writin' anonymous letters.

Ib. The Vice-President

It is his jooty to rigorously enforce th' rules iv th' Sinit. There ar-re none. Th' Sinit is ruled be courtesy, like th' longshoreman's union. *Ib.*

Slug-ye'er-spouse is an internaytional spoort that has niver become pop'lar on our side iv th' wather. An American lady is not th' person that anny man but a thrained athlete wud care to raise his hand again' save be way iv smoothin' her hair.

Ib. Corporal Punishment

Won't [public flogging] be fine? Th' govermint gives us too little amusemint nowadays. Th' fav'rite pastime iv civilized man is croolty to other civilized man. *Ib.*

"Spare th' rod an' spile th' child," said Mr. Hennessy.

"Yes," said Mr. Dooley, "but don't spare th' rod an' ye spile th' rod, th' child, an' th' child's father." *Ib.*

This home iv opporchunity where ivry man is th' equal iv ivry other man befure th' law if he isn't careful.

Dissertations by Mr. Dooley. The Food We Eat

"Ye ra-aly do think dhrink is a nicissry evil?" said Mr. Hennessy.

"Well," said Mr. Dooley, "if it's an evil to a man, it's not nicissry, an' if it's nicissry it's an evil." *Ib. The Bar*

"He made [money]," said Mr. Dooley, "because he honestly loved it with an innocint affiction. He was thrue to it. Th' reason ye have no money is because ye don't love it f'r itsilf alone. Money won't iver surrinder to such a flirt."

Mr. Dooley on Making a Will and Other Evil Necessities [1919]. On Making a Will

JOHN GALSWORTHY
1867–1933

Justice is a machine that, when someone has once given it the starting push, rolls on of itself.

Justice [1910], act II

Public opinion's always in advance of the law. *Windows [1922], act I*

The value of a sentiment is the amount of sacrifice you are prepared to make for it. *Ib. II*

By the cigars they smoke, and the composers they love, ye shall know the texture of men's souls.

Indian Summer of a Forsyte [1920], ch. 1

He ordered himself a dozen oysters; but, suddenly remembering that the month contained no *r*, changed them to a fried sole.[1]

The White Monkey [1924], pt. III, ch. 7

---

[1] It is unseasonable and unwholesome in all months that have not an *r* in their name to eat an oyster. — WILLIAM BUTLER, *Dyet's Dry Dinner* [1599]

Let's sing a song of glory to Themistocles O'Shea,

If you do not think about the future, you cannot have one.
Swan Song [1928], *pt. II, ch. 6*

A man of action forced into a state of thought is unhappy until he can get out of it.
Maid in Waiting [1931], *ch. 3*

There's just one rule for politicians all over the world: Don't say in Power what you say in Opposition; if you do, you only have to carry out what the other fellows have found impossible.
Ib. 7

One's eyes are what one is, one's mouth what one becomes.
Flowering Wilderness [1932], *ch. 2*

The beginnings and endings of all human undertakings are untidy, the building of a house, the writing of a novel, the demolition of a bridge, and, eminently, the finish of a voyage.
Over the River [1933], *ch. 1*

How to save the old that's worth saving, whether in landscape, houses, manners, institutions, or human types, is one of our greatest problems, and the one that we bother least about.
Over the River, ch. 39

LIONEL JOHNSON
1867–1902

The saddest of all kings
Crown'd, and again discrown'd.
By the Statue of King Charles at Charing Cross, st. 2

Vanquished in life, his death
By beauty made amends.   *Ib. st. 8*

I know you: solitary griefs,
Desolate passions, aching hours!
The Precept of Silence, st. 1

Who ate a dozen oysters on the second day of May.
STODDARD KING [1889–1933], *The Man Who Dared*

CHARLES EDWARD MONTAGUE
1867–1928

I was born below par to th' extent of two whiskies.
Fiery Particles [1923]

"A.E." [GEORGE WILLIAM RUSSELL]
1867–1935

Our hearts were drunk with a beauty
Our eyes could never see.
The Unknown God

Twilight, a timid fawn, went glimmering by,
And Night, the dark-blue hunter, followed fast.   *Refuge*

HENRY LEWIS STIMSON
1867–1950

The only way to make a man trustworthy is to trust him; and the surest way to make him untrustworthy is to distrust him and show your distrust.
The Bomb and the Opportunity [*March* 1946]

The only deadly sin I know is cynicism.
On Active Service in Peace and War [1948], *introduction*

HARRY LEON WILSON
1867–1939

I can be pushed just so far.
Ruggles of Red Gap [1915]

ALAIN [ÉMILE CHARTIER]
1868–1951

To think is to say *no.*
Le Citoyen contre les Pouvoirs

Nothing is more dangerous than an idea, when it's the only one we have.
Système des Beaux-Arts

PAUL CLAUDEL
1868–1955

You explain nothing, O poet, but thanks to you all things become explicable. *La Ville* [1892]

The words I use
Are everyday words and yet are not the same!
You will find no rhymes in my verse, no magic.
There are your very own phrases.
La Muse Qui Est la Grace [1910]

When man tries to imagine Paradise on earth, the immediate result is a very respectable Hell.
Conversations dans le Loir-et-Cher [1929]

NORMAN DOUGLAS
1868–1952

You can tell the ideals of a nation by its advertisements.
South Wind [1917], *ch.* 7

Men have lost sight of distant horizons. Nobody writes for humanity, for civilization; they write for their country, their sect; to amuse their friends or annoy their enemies.
Ib. 8

No one can expect a majority to be stirred by motives other than ignoble.
Ib. 10

No great man is ever born too soon or too late. When we say that the time is not ripe for this or that celebrity, we confess by implication that this very man, and no other, is required.
Ib. 13

For three consecutive months they could barely afford the most unnecessary luxuries of life. *Ib.* 20

Many a man who thinks to found a home discovers that he has merely opened a tavern for his friends.
Ib. 24

WILLIAM EDWARD BURGHARDT DuBOIS
1868–1963

Herein lies the tragedy of the age: not that men are poor — all men know something of poverty; not that men are wicked — who is good? Not that men are ignorant — what is truth? Nay, but that men know so little of men.
The Souls of Black Folk [1903]

It is a peculiar sensation, this double-consciousness, this sense of always looking at one's self through the eyes of others. . . . One feels his two-ness — an American, a Negro; two souls, two thoughts, two unreconciled strivings; two warring ideals in one dark body, whose dogged strength alone keeps it from being torn asunder.
Ib.

MAXIM GORKI[1]
[ALEKSEI MAKSIMOVICH PESHKOV]
1868–1936

The brave man's folly — that is life's wisdom.
The Song of the Falcon [1895]

Former people [Creatures that once were men]. *Title of story* [1897]

Let the storm rage ever stronger! [2]
Song of a Stormy Petrel [1901]

Lies — there you have the religion of slaves and taskmasters.[3]
The Lower Depths [1903]

How marvelous is Man! How proud the word rings — Man! *Ib.*

The proletarian state must bring up thousands of excellent "mechanics of culture," "engineers of the soul." [4]
Speech at the Writers' Congress [1934]

[1] Gorki, "the bitter one," was the writer's pseudonym for his first sketch in a Tiflis newspaper [1892].
[2] This became a rallying cry of the revolutionaries.
[3] The censor forbade this line to be spoken on the stage.
[4] Attributed to Stalin in conversation with Gorki [October 26, 1934]. See Stalin, p. 954b.

Life, as asserted by socialist realism, is deeds, creativeness, the aim of which is the uninterrupted development of the priceless individual qualities of man.

Speech at the Writers' Congress

The basic hero of our books should be labor; that is, man organized by the processes of labor.   *Ib.*

ABE MARTIN
[FRANK McKINNEY "KIN" HUBBARD]
1868–1930

Miss Fawn Lippincut says she wouldn' marry th' best man on earth, but we supposed she wuz much younger.

Abe Martin's Sayings and Sketches [1915]

It's no disgrace t' be poor, but it might as well be.   *Ib.*

He was a power politically fer years, but he never got prominent enough t' have his speeches garbled.   *Ib.*

When a fellow says it hain't the money but the principle o' the thing, it's th' money.

Hoss Sense and Nonsense [1926]

Nobuddy ever fergits where he buried a hatchet.

Abe Martin's Broadcast [1930]

If capital an' labor ever do git t'gether it's good night fer th' rest of us.   *Saying*

Knowin' all about baseball is just about as profitable as bein' a good whittler.   *Ib.*

Now and then an innocent man is sent to the legislature.   *Ib.*

EDWARD VERRALL LUCAS
1868–1938

The French never allow a distinguished son of France to lack a statue.

Wanderings and Diversions [1926]. *Zigzags in France*

Americans are people who prefer the Continent to their own country, but refuse to learn its languages.

Wanderings and Diversions. The Continental Dictionary

Ticket collector — the man who never wants to see your ticket unless you are asleep.   *Ib.*

People in hotels strike no roots. The French phrase for chronic hotel guests even says so: they are called dwellers *sur la branche.*   *Ib. To Be Let or Sold*

There can be no defense like elaborate courtesy.

Reading, Writing and Remembering [1932]

WILLIAM TYLER PAGE
1868–1942

I believe in the United States of America as a Government of the people, by the people, for the people; whose just powers are derived from the consent of the governed; a democracy in a republic, a sovereign Nation of many sovereign States; a perfect Union one and inseparable; established upon those principles of freedom, equality, justice and humanity for which American patriots sacrificed their lives and fortunes. I therefore believe it is my duty to my country to love it, to support its Constitution, to obey its laws, to respect its flag, and to defend it against all enemies.

The American's Creed [1]

EDMOND ROSTAND
1868–1918

A great nose indicates a great man —
Genial, courteous, intellectual,
Virile, courageous.

Cyrano de Bergerac [2] [1897],
act I

Free fighters, free lovers, free spenders —

[1] Adopted by the House of Representatives [April 3, 1918].
[2] Translated by BRIAN HOOKER.

The Cadets of Gascoyne — the defenders
Of old homes, old names, and old splendors.
Cyrano de Bergerac, act II

I fall back dazzled at beholding myself all rosy red,
At having, I myself, caused the sun to rise.
Chantecler [1907], *act II, sc. iii*

It is at night that faith in light is admirable. *Ib.*

ROBERT FALCON SCOTT
1868–1912

Had we lived, I should have had a tale to tell of the hardihood, endurance, and courage of my companions which would have stirred the heart of every Englishman. These rough notes and our dead bodies must tell the tale.[1]
Journal.[2] Message to the Public

ANDRÉ SUARÈS
1868–1948

Heresy is the lifeblood of religions. It is faith that begets heretics. There are no heresies in a dead religion.[3]
Péguy

WILLIAM ALLEN WHITE
1868–1944

What's the Matter with Kansas?
Title of editorial, Emporia Gazette [August 15, 1896]

Tinhorn politicians.
Emporia Gazette [October 25, 1901]

All dressed up, with nowhere to go.
Of the Progressive Party in 1916, after Theodore Roosevelt retired from Presidential competition

Put fear out of your heart. This nation will survive, this state will prosper, the orderly business of life will go forward if only men can speak in whatever way given them to utter what their hearts hold — by voice, by posted card, by letter, or by press. Reason never has failed men. Only force and oppression have made the wrecks in the world.
Emporia Gazette [July 27, 1922]

Consistency is a paste jewel that only cheap men cherish.[1]
Ib. [November 17, 1923]

The talent of a meat-packer, the morals of a moneychanger and the manners of an undertaker.
Obituary of Frank A. Munsey [December 23, 1925]

LAURENCE BINYON
1869–1943

They shall grow not old, as we that are left grow old:
Age shall not weary them, nor the years condemn.
At the going down of the sun and in the morning
We will remember them.
For the Fallen, st. 4

ELLIS PARKER BUTLER
1869–1937

Pigs is Pigs. *Title of story* [1906]

NEVILLE CHAMBERLAIN
1869–1940

For the second time in our history, a British Prime Minister has returned

---

[1] Inscribed on the memorial to Captain Scott and his companions, Waterloo Place, London.
[2] Found by searching party, November 1912.
[3] See Tertullian, p. 143b, and Unamuno, p. 869b.

[1] Commenting on an item in the Topeka *Capital:* "The *Emporia Gazette* is the best-loved paper in Kansas because its editor never looks in yesterday's files to see if what he proposes to write today is consistent."
See Emerson, p. 606a.

from Germany bringing peace with honor. I believe it is peace for our time. . . . Go home and get a nice quiet sleep.[1]

> *Address from 10 Downing Street, London* [*September 30, 1938*] *after returning from the Munich Conference*

Hitler has missed the bus.

> *Speech in the House of Commons* [*April 4, 1940*]

MOHANDAS KARAMCHAND [MAHATMA] GANDHI[2]
1869–1948

Nonviolence is the first article of my faith. It is also the last article of my creed.

> *Defense against charge of sedition* [*March 23, 1922*]

The term *Satyagraha* was coined by me . . . in order to distinguish it from the movement then going on . . . under the name of Passive Resistance.

Its root meaning is "holding on to truth," hence "force of righteousness." I have also called it love force or soul force. In the application of *Satyagraha*, I discovered in the earliest stages that pursuit of truth did not permit violence being inflicted on one's opponent, but that he must be weaned from error by patience and sympathy. For what appears truth to the one may appear to be error to the other. And patience means self-suffering. So the doctrine came to mean vindication of truth, not by the infliction of suffering on the opponent, but on one's self.[3] *Ib.*

Nonviolence and truth (*Satya*) are inseparable and presuppose one an-

other. There is no god higher than truth.

> *True Patriotism: Some Sayings of Mahatma Gandhi* [*1939*][1]

ANDRÉ GIDE
1869–1951

Families! I hate you! Shut-in homes, closed doors, jealous possessions of happiness.

> *Les Nourritures Terrestres* [*1897*]

What another would have done as well as you, do not do it. What another would have said as well as you, do not say it; written as well, do not write it. Be faithful to that which exists nowhere but in yourself — and thus make yourself indispensable. *Ib. Envoi*

Sin is whatever obscures the soul.

> *La Symphonie Pastorale* [*1919*]

The most decisive actions of our life . . . are most often unconsidered actions.

> *Les Faux Monnayeurs* [*1925*]

Art begins with resistance — at the point where resistance is overcome. No human masterpiece has ever been created without great labor. *Poétique*

It is with noble sentiments that bad literature gets written.[2]

> *Letter to François Mauriac* [*1928*]

STRICKLAND GILLILAN
1869–1954

Bilin' down 's repoort, wuz Finnigin!
An' he writed this here: "Musther
  Flannigan —
Off agin, on agin,
Gone agin. — FINNIGIN."

> *Finnigin to Flannigan, st. 6*

Adam
Had 'em.

> *Lines on the Antiquity of Microbes* [3]

---

[1] While we endeavor to maintain peace, I certainly should be the last to forget that if peace cannot be maintained with honor, it is no longer peace. — LORD JOHN RUSSELL, *Speech at Greenock, Scotland* [September 19, 1853]

  See Disraeli, p. 613a.

[2] Mahatma — Great Soul.

[3] See Martin Luther King, p. 1082b.

[1] Edited by S. Hobhouse.

[2] C'est avec de beaux sentiments qu'on fait de la mauvaise littérature.

[3] Said to be the shortest poem in the language.

FREDERIC LAWRENCE KNOWLES
1869–1905

Each little lyrical
Grave or satirical
Musical miracle!
On a flyleaf of Burns's songs

Joy is a partnership,
  Grief weeps alone;
Many guests had Cana,
  Gethsemane had one.
Grief and Joy

STEPHEN BUTLER LEACOCK
1869–1944

He flung himself from the room,
flung himself upon his horse and rode
madly off in all directions.
*Gertrude the Governess
[1911]*

The general idea, of course, in any
first-class laundry, is to see that no shirt
or collar ever comes back twice.
Winnowed Wisdom [1926], ch. 6

By American literature in the proper
sense we ought to mean literature written in an American way, with an
American turn of language and an
American cast of thought. The test is
that it couldn't have been written anywhere else.
*Mark Twain as National
Asset [1932]*

EDGAR LEE MASTERS
1869–1950

All, all, are sleeping on the hill.
*Spoon River Anthology [1915].
The Hill, refrain*

Seeds in a dry pod, tick, tick, tick,
Tick, tick, tick, what little iambics,
While Homer and Whitman roar in
   the pines!   *Ib. Petit, the Poet*

Degenerate sons and daughters,
Life is too strong for you —
It takes life to love life.
Ib. Lucinda Matlock

Out of me unworthy and unknown
The vibrations of deathless music.
*Spoon River Anthology.
Anne Rutledge*

I am Anne Rutledge who sleep beneath
   these weeds,
Beloved in life of Abraham Lincoln.
Ib.

Immortality is not a gift,
Immortality is an achievement;
And only those who strive mightily
Shall possess it.
Ib. The Village Atheist

HENRI MATISSE
1869–1954

I want to reach that state of con-
densation of sensations which constitutes a picture.
Notes d'un Peintre [1908]

What interests me most is neither
still life nor landscape, but the human
figure. It is through it that I best succeed in expressing the almost religious
feeling I have towards life.   *Ib.*

WILLIAM VAUGHN MOODY
1869–1910

This earth is not the steadfast place
We landsmen build upon;
From deep to deep she varies pace,
And while she comes is gone.
Gloucester Moors [1901], st. 4

To be out of the moiling street
With its swelter and its sin!
Who has given to me this sweet,
And given my brother dust to eat?
And when will his wage come in?
Ib. st. 8

Then not to kneel, almost
Seemed like a vulgar boast.
Good Friday [1901], st. 9

Gigantic, willful, young,
Chicago sitteth at the northwest gates,

With restless violent hands and casual
    tongue
Molding her mighty fates.
> *An Ode in Time of Hesitation*
> [*1901*], *st. 3*

Now limb doth mingle with dissolvèd
    limb [1]
In nature's busy old democracy.
> *Ib. st. 6*

The spring-laden breeze
Out of the gladdening west is sinister
With sounds of nameless battle over-
    seas.[2] *Ib. st. 7*

Our fluent men of place and conse-
    quence
Fumble and fill their mouths with hol-
    low phrase,
Or for the end-all of deep arguments
Intone their dull commercial liturgies.
> *Ib.*

O ye who lead,
Take heed!
Blindness we may forgive, but baseness
    we will smite. *Ib. st. 9*

EDWIN ARLINGTON ROBINSON
1869–1935

We cannot know how much we learn
From those who never will return,
Until a flash of unforeseen
Remembrance falls on what has been.
> *Flammonde*

To shake the tree
Of life itself and bring down fruit
unheard-of.
> *Ben Jonson Entertains a Man*
> *from Stratford*

I would have rid the earth of him
Once, in my pride. . . .
I never knew the worth of him
Until he died. *An Old Story*

[1] The reference is to the battlefield grave of
Colonel Robert Gould Shaw and the men of the
54th Massachusetts Regiment (the first enlisted
Negro regiment of the Civil War) who fell at
Fort Wagner [July 18, 1863].
[2] The war in the Philippines.

Life is the gamē that must be played:
This truth at least, good friends, we
    know;
So live and laugh, nor be dismayed
As one by one the phantoms go.
> *Ballade by the Fire. Envoy*

The songs of one who strove to play
The broken flutes of Arcady.
> *Ballade of Broken Flutes*

There be two men of all mankind
That I'm forever thinking on:
They chase me everywhere I go —
Melchizedek, Ucalegon. *Two Men*

Like dead, remembered footsteps on
    old floors.
> *The Pity of the Leaves*

And thus we die,
Still searching, like poor old astrono-
    mers
Who totter off to bed and go to sleep
To dream of untriangulated stars.
> *Octaves, XI*

The saddest among kings of earth,
Bowed with a galling crown, this
    man
Met rancor with a cryptic mirth,
Laconic — and Olympian.
> *The Master: Lincoln*

Wearing upon his forehead, with no
    fear,
The laurel of approved iniquity.
> *Uncle Ananias*

Miniver Cheevy, child of scorn,
Grew lean while he assailed the sea-
    sons;
He wept that he was ever born,
And he had reasons.
> *Miniver Cheevy* [*1910*], *st. 1*

Miniver loved the Medici,
Albeit he had never seen one;
He would have sinned incessantly
Could he have been one. *Ib. st. 5*

Miniver Cheevy, born too late,
Scratched his head and kept on think-
    ing;
Miniver coughed and called it fate,
And kept on drinking. *Ib. st. 8*

Who of us, being what he is,
May scoff at others' ecstasies?
However we may shine today,
More-shining ones are on the way.
Atherton's Gambit

I shall have more to say when I am
dead. *John Brown*

Art's long hazard, where no man may
choose
Whether he play to win, or toil to
lose. *Caput Mortuum*

Love that's wise
Will not say all it means.
Tristram [1927], pt. VII

Love must have wings to fly away from
love,
And to fly back again. *Ib. VIII*

Here where the wind is always north-
northeast
And children learn to walk on frozen
toes. *New England*

Are you to pay for all you have
With all you are? *Cassandra, st. 12*

He glittered when he walked.
Richard Cory, st. 2

So on we worked, and waited for the
light,
And went without the meat, and cursed
the bread;
And Richard Cory, one calm summer
night,
Went home and put a bullet through
his head. *Ib. 4*

"Drink to the bird." He raised up to
the light
The jug that he had gone so far to fill,
And answered huskily: "Well, Mr.
Flood,
Since you propose it, I believe I will."
Mr. Flood's Party, st. 2

GEORGE STERLING
1869–1926

Thou art the star for which all evening
waits. *Aldebaran at Dusk*

WILLIAM STRUNK, JR.
1869–1935

Vigorous writing is concise. A sentence should contain no unnecessary
words, a paragraph no unnecessary sentences, for the same reason that a drawing should have no unnecessary lines
and a machine no unnecessary parts.
This requires not that the writer make
all his sentences short, or that he avoid
all detail and treat his subjects only in
outline, but that every word tell.
*The Elements of Style [1918],
ch. 2, sec. 13*

BOOTH TARKINGTON
1869–1946

There are two things that will be believed of any man whatsoever, and one
of them is that he has taken to drink.
Penrod [1914], ch. 10

They were upon their great theme:
"When I get to be a man!" Being
human, though boys, they considered
their present estate too commonplace
to be dwelt upon. So, when the old
men gather, they say: "When I was a
boy!" It really is the land of nowadays
that we never discover. *Ib. 26*

FRANK LLOYD
WRIGHT
1869–1959

No house should ever be *on* any hill
or on anything. It should be *of* the hill,
belonging to it, so hill and house could
live together each the happier for the
other. *An Autobiography [1932]*

BERNARD MANNES
BARUCH
1870–1965

America has never forgotten — and
will never forget — the nobler things
that brought her into being and that
light her path — the path that was en-

tered upon only one hundred and fifty years ago. . . . How young she is! It will be centuries before she will adopt that maturity of custom — the clothing of the grave — that some people believe she is already fitted for.

Address on accepting The Churchman Award, New York [May 23, 1944]

We are here to make a choice between the quick and the dead. That is our business. Behind the black portent of the new atomic age lies a hope which, seized upon with faith, can work out salvation. If we fail, then we have damned every man to be the slave of fear. Let us not deceive ourselves: we must elect world peace or world destruction.

Address to the United Nations Atomic Energy Commission [June 14, 1946]

We are in the midst of a cold war [1] which is getting warmer.

Speech before the Senate Committee [1948]

The role of government and its relationship to the individual has been changed so radically that today government is involved in almost every aspect of our lives.

Political, economic and racial forces have developed which we have not yet learned to understand or control. If we are ever to master these forces, make certain that government will belong to the people, not the people to the government, and provide for the future better than the past, we must somehow learn from the experiences of the past.

Speech on presenting his papers to Princeton University [May 11, 1964]

HILAIRE BELLOC
1870–1953

Child! do not throw this book about;
Refrain from the unholy pleasure

---

[1] The phrase was first used by Baruch in 1947.

Of cutting all the pictures out!
Preserve it as your chiefest treasure.

A Bad Child's Book of Beasts [1896], dedication

When people call this beast to mind,
They marvel more and more
At such a little tail behind,
So large a trunk before.

Ib. The Elephant

I shoot the Hippopotamus
With bullets made of platinum,
Because if I use leaden ones
His hide is sure to flatten 'em.

Ib. The Hippopotamus

The Whale that wanders round the
    Pole
Is not a table fish.
You cannot bake or boil him whole
Nor serve him in a dish.

Ib. The Whale

Here richly, with ridiculous display,
The Politician's corpse was laid away.
While all of his acquaintance sneered
    and slanged,
I wept; for I had longed to see him
    hanged.

Epitaph on the Politician Himself

A smell of burning fills the startled
    air —
The Electrician is no longer there!

Newdigate Poem

Oh, he didn't believe in Adam and
    Eve —
He put no faith therein;
His doubts began with the fall of
    man,
And he laughed at original sin.

Song of the Pelagian Heresy

How slow the shadow creeps: but when
    'tis past
How fast the shadows fall. How fast!
How fast!   *For a Sundial*

Loss and Possession, death and life are
    one,
There falls no shadow where there
    shines no sun.   *Ib.*

And the men that were boys when I
   was a boy
Shall sit and drink with me.
> *The South Country, st.* 10

Of courtesy, it is much less
Than courage of heart or holiness,
Yet in my walks it seems to me
That the Grace of God is in courtesy.
> *Courtesy*

Do you remember an inn,
Miranda?   *Tarantella*

And the fleas that tease in the High
   Pyrenees,
And the wine that tasted of the tar?
> *Ib.*

I said to Heart, "How goes it?" Heart
   replied:
"Right as a Ribstone Pippin!" But it
   lied.   *The False Heart*

Now just imagine how it feels
When first your toes and then your
   heels,
And then by gradual degrees,
Your shins and ankles, calves and
   knees,
Are slowly eaten, bit by bit.
No wonder Jim detested it!
> *Cautionary Tales* [1907]. *Jim*

The chief defect of Henry King
Was chewing little bits of string.
> *Ib. Henry King*

"Oh, my friends, be warned by me,
That breakfast, dinner, lunch and tea
Are all the human frame requires . . ."
With that the wretched child expires.
> *Ib.*

Matilda told such dreadful lies,
It made one gasp and stretch one's
   eyes;
Her aunt, who, from her earliest youth,
Had kept a strict regard for truth,
Attempted to believe Matilda:
The effort very nearly killed her.
> *Ib. Matilda*

It happened that a few weeks later
Her aunt was off to the theater
To see that interesting play
The Second Mrs. Tanqueray.   *Ib.*

For every time she shouted "Fire!"
They only answered "Little liar!"
And therefore when her aunt returned,
Matilda, and the house, were burned.
> *Cautionary Tales. Matilda*

The nicest child I ever knew
Was Charles Augustus Fortescue.
> *Ib. Charles Augustus Fortescue*

Pale Ebenezer thought it wrong to fight,
But Roaring Bill (who killed him)
   thought it right.   *The Pacifist*

When I am dead, I hope it may be
   said:
"His sins were scarlet, but his books
   were read."   *On His Books*

BENJAMIN NATHAN CARDOZO
1870–1938

What has once been settled by a
precedent will not be unsettled over-
night, for certainty and uniformity are
gains not lightly to be sacrificed.
Above all is this true when honest men
have shaped their conduct on the faith
of the pronouncement.
> *The Paradoxes of Legal
> Science* [1928]

As I search the archives of my memory, I seem to discern six types or methods [of judicial writing] which divide
themselves from one another with
measurable distinctness. There is the
type magisterial or imperative; the type
laconic or sententious; the type conversational or homely; the type refined or
artificial, smelling of the lamp,[1] verging
at times upon preciosity or euphuism;
the type demonstrative or persuasive;
and finally the type tonsorial or agglutinative, so called from the shears
and the pastepot which are its imple-
ments and emblem.
> *Law and Literature* [1931]

[The Constitution] was framed
upon the theory that the peoples of the
several states must sink or swim together, and that in the long run pros-

[1] See Pytheas, p. 101b.

perity and salvation are in union and not division.

> *Baldwin v. Seelig, 294 U.S. 511, 523 [1935]*

Freedom of expression is the matrix, the indispensable condition, of nearly every other form of freedom.

> *Palko v. Connecticut, 302 U.S. 319, 327 [1937]*

ARTHUR J. LAMB
1870–1928

Her beauty was sold for an old man's gold,
She's a bird in a gilded cage.

> *A Bird in a Gilded Cage [1900]*

SIR HARRY LAUDER
1870–1950

Oh, it's nice to get up in the mornin',
But it's nicer to lie in bed.   *Song*

Just a wee doch-an'-dorris
Before we gang awa' . . .
If y' can say
It's a braw brecht moonlecht necht,
Yer a' recht, that's a'.   *Song*

Roamin' in the gloamin'.   *Song*

I Love a Lassie.   *Title of song*

NIKOLAI LENIN
[VLADIMIR ILICH ULYANOV]
1870–1924

Political institutions are a superstructure resting on an economic foundation.

> *The Three Sources and Three Constituent Parts of Marxism* [1] *[1913]*

Every cook has to learn how to govern the state.

> *Will the Bolsheviks Retain Government Power [1917]*

The war is relentless: it puts the alternative in a ruthless relief: either to perish, or to catch up with the ad-

[1] Translated by MAX EASTMAN.

vanced countries and outdistance them, too, in economic matters.[1]

> *The Impending Catastrophe and How to Fight It [1917]*

Communism is Soviet government plus the electrification of the whole country.

> *New External and Internal Position and the Problems of the Party [1920]*

When we say "the state," the state it is we, it is the proletariat, it is the advanced guard of the working class.

> *Speech [May 27, 1922]*

It is true that liberty is precious — so precious that it must be rationed.

> *Attributed. Quoted by* SIDNEY AND BEATRICE WEBB *in Soviet Communism: A New Civilization? [1936], p. 1036*

ROSCOE POUND
1870–1964

The law must be stable, but it must not stand still.

> *Introduction to the Philosophy of Law [1922]*

SAKI
[HECTOR HUGH MUNRO]
1870–1916

The cook was a good cook, as cooks go; and as cooks go she went.

> *Reginald [1904]. Reginald on Besetting Sins*

[1] We have caught up with and outdistanced the advanced countries politically by having built the proletarian dictatorship. But this is not enough. We have to catch up with and outdistance the advanced countries also economically. — JOSEPH STALIN, *Speech [November 19, 1928]* When we sent the first Sputniks into cosmos . . . the whole world saw that the Soviet Union has by far outdistanced the United States of America in important branches of science and technology. Even President John Kennedy was forced to admit that the United States are confronted by the difficult problem of catching up with the Soviet Union in this field. As you see, the expression "catch up with" has appeared in the American vocabulary too. — NIKITA KHRUSHCHEV, *Report to the XXII Congress of the Party [October 17, 1961]*

Women and elephants never forget an injury.
> *Reginald. Reginald on Besetting Sins*

I might have been a goldfish in a glass bowl for all the privacy I got.
> *Ib. The Innocence of Reginald*

The Western custom of one wife and hardly any mistresses.
> *Reginald in Russia* [1910]. *A Young Turkish Catastrophe*

Hating anything in the way of ill-natured gossip ourselves, we are always grateful to those who do it for us and do it well.
> *Ib. The Soul of Laploshka*

Poverty keeps together more homes than it breaks up.
> *The Chronicles of Clovis* [1911]. *Esmé*

"After all, it's not my Axminster," was Tobermory's rejoinder.
> *Ib. Tobermory*

Sredni Vashtar went forth,
His thoughts were red thoughts and his teeth were white.
His enemies called for peace, but he brought them death.
Sredni Vashtar the Beautiful.
> *Ib. Sredni Vashtar*

His socks compelled one's attention without losing one's respect.
> *Ib. Ministers of Grace*

Sherard Blaw, the dramatist who had discovered himself, and who had given so ungrudgingly of his discovery to the world.
> *The Unbearable Bassington* [1912]

The sacrifices of friendship were beautiful in her eyes as long as she was not asked to make them.
> *Beasts and Super-Beasts* [1914]. *Fur*

"The man is a common murderer."
"A common murderer, possibly, but a very uncommon cook."
> *Ib. The Blind Spot*

Waldo is one of those people who would be enormously improved by death.
> *Beasts and Super-Beasts. The Feast of Nemesis*

Children with Hyacinth's temperament don't know better as they grow older; they merely know more.
> *The Toys of Peace* [1919]. *Hyacinth*

In baiting a mousetrap with cheese, always leave room for the mouse.
> *The Square Egg* [1924]. *The Infernal Parliament*

A little inaccuracy sometimes saves tons of explanation.
> *Ib. The Comments of Moung Ka*

T. LAURENCE SEIBERT
fl. 1900

Casey Jones! Orders in his hand.
Casey Jones! Mounted to the cabin,
Took his farewell journey to that promised land.
> *Casey Jones* [1900]; *adapted from verses by* WALLACE SAUNDERS,[1] *set to music by* EDDIE NEWTON

STEPHEN CRANE
1871–1900

They were going to look at war, the red animal — war, the blood-swollen god.
> *The Red Badge of Courage* [1895], *ch. 3*

---

[1] Of the many versions of this traditional ballad, the most familiar is printed in CARL SANDBURG'S *The American Songbag* [1927]. It begins:
> Come all you rounders, for I want you to hear
> The story of a brave engineer.
> Casey Jones was the rounder's name,
> On a big eight-wheeler of a mighty fame.

To the memory of the locomotive engineer whose name as "Casey Jones" became a part of folklore and the American language. "For I'm going to run till she leaves the rail—or make it on time with the southbound mail."—*Inscription on monument to* JOHN LUTHER JONES [1864–1900], *in Calvary Cemetery, Jackson, Tennessee*

It was surprising that Nature had gone tranquilly on with her golden process in the midst of so much devilment.

The Red Badge of Courage, ch. 5

At times he regarded the wounded soldiers in an envious way. He conceived persons with torn bodies to be peculiarly happy. He wished that he, too, had a wound, a red badge of courage. *Ib. 9*

The red sun was pasted in the sky like a wafer. *Ib.*

He had fought like a pagan who defends his religion. *Ib. 17*

He had been to touch the great death, and found that, after all, it was but the great death. He was a man. *Ib. 24*

None of them knew the color of the sky. *The Open Boat [1898]*

When it came night, the white waves paced to and fro in the moonlight, and the wind brought the sound of the great sea's voice to the men on shore, and they felt that they could then be interpreters. *Ib. Last line*

A man said to the universe:
"Sir, I exist!"
"However," replied the universe,
"The fact has not created in me
A sense of obligation."
War Is Kind [1899]. Fragment

THOMAS AUGUSTINE DALY
1871–1948

Sing clear, O throstle,
Thou golden-tongued apostle
And little brown-frocked brother
Of the loved Assisian! *To a Thrush*

WILLIAM HENRY DAVIES
1871–1940

What is this life if, full of care,
We have no time to stand and stare? [1]
Leisure

[1] See Browning, p. 668a.

THEODORE DREISER
1871–1945

Our civilization is still in a middle stage, scarcely beast, in that it is no longer wholly guided by instinct; scarcely human, in that it is not yet wholly guided by reason.
Sister Carrie [1900]

I acknowledge the Furies, I believe in them, I have heard the disastrous beating of their wings.
To Grant Richards [1911]

Oh, the moon is fair tonight along the Wabash,
From the fields there comes the breath of new-mown hay;
Through the sycamores the candle lights are gleaming
On the banks of the Wabash, far away.
On the Banks of the Wabash, chorus [1]

ARTHUR GUITERMAN
1871–1943

The finest thing in London is the Bobby; [2]
Benignant information is his hobby.
The Lyric Baedeker. London

Amoebas at the start
Were not complex;
They tore themselves apart
And started Sex. *Sex, st. 1*

Of all cold words of tongue or pen
The worst are these: "I knew him when — " [3]
Prophets in Their Own Country

RALPH HODGSON
1871–1962

'Twould ring the bells of Heaven
The wildest peal for years,

[1] Dreiser's brother, Paul Dreiser, is credited with writing the song, but according to H. L. Mencken, Dreiser wrote the chorus.
[2] The constable with lifted hand
Conducting the orchestral Strand.
STEPHEN PHILLIPS [1864–1915],
The Wife
[3] See Whittier, p. 626a.

If Parson lost his senses
And people came to theirs,
And he and they together
Knelt down with angry prayers
For tamed and shabby tigers
And dancing dogs and bears,
And wretched, blind pit ponies,
And little hunted hares.
                The Bells of Heaven

But oh, the den of wild things in
The darkness of her eyes!
                The Gypsy Girl

God loves an idle rainbow
No less than laboring seas.
                A Wood Song

Time, you old gypsy man,
Will you not stay,
Put up your caravan
Just for one day?
        Time, You Old Gypsy Man, st. 1

Pity him, this fallen chief,
All his splendor, all his strength,
All his beauty's breadth and length
Dwindled down with shame and grief,
Half the bull he was before,
Bones and leather, nothing more.
                The Bull

Oh, had our simple Eve
Seen through the make-believe!
Had she but known the
Pretender he was!
Out of the boughs he came,
Whispering still her name,
Tumbling in twenty rings
Into the grass.   *Eve, st. 5*

How they all pitied
Poor motherless Eve!   *Ib.*

I climbed the hill as light fell short,
And rooks came home in scramble
    sort.   *The Song of Honor*

I stood upon that silent hill
And stared into the sky until
My eyes were blind with stars and still
I stared into the sky.   *Ib.*

Reason has moons, but moons not
    hers
Lie mirrored on her sea,
Confounding her astronomers,
But O! delighting me.   *Reason*

I saw with open eyes
Singing birds sweet
Sold in the shops
For the people to eat,
Sold in the shops of
Stupidity Street.

I saw in vision
The worm in the wheat,
And in the shops nothing
For people to eat;
Nothing for sale in
Stupidity Street.   *Stupidity Street*

JAMES WELDON JOHNSON
1871–1938

We have come over a way that with
    tears has been watered,
We have come, treading our path
    through the blood of the slaugh-
    tered.
        Lift Every Voice and Sing
                [1900], st. 2

O black and unknown bards of long
    ago,
How came your lips to touch the sacred
    fire?
How, in your darkness, did you come to
    know
The power and beauty of the minstrel's
    lyre?
        O Black and Unknown Bards,
                st. 1

And God stepped out on space,
And He looked around and said,
"I'm lonely —
I'll make me a world."
        God's Trombones [1927]. The
                Creation, st. 1

And God smiled again,
And the rainbow appeared,
And curled itself around his shoulder.
                Ib. st. 7

With his head in his hands,
God thought and thought,
Till he thought: I'll make me a man!
                Ib. st. 10

    Find Sister Caroline . . .
And she's tired —

She's weary —
Go down, Death, and bring her to me.
God's Trombones. Go Down,
Death, st. 5

CHARLES RANN
KENNEDY
1871–1950

A peculiar kind of fear they call courage.
The Terrible Meek [1912]

The meek, the terrible meek, the fierce agonizing meek, are about to enter into their inheritance. *Ib.*

WILBUR DICK NESBIT
1871–1927

Each page of them Quotations that
this Bartlett man got out
Is sure to have old Ibid's prose or
poems strung about.
Old Ibid, st. 2

HERBERT GEORGE
PONTING
1871–1935

On the outside grows the furside, on
the inside grows the skinside;
So the furside is the outside, and the
skinside is the inside.[1]
The Sleeping Bag [2]

MARCEL PROUST
1871–1922

When from a long distant past nothing subsists, after the people are dead,

after the things are broken and scattered, still, alone, more fragile, but with more vitality, more unsubstantial, more persistent, more faithful, the smell and taste of things remain poised a long time, like souls, ready to remind us, waiting and hoping for their moment, amid the ruins of all the rest; and bear unfaltering, in the tiny and almost impalpable drop of their essence, the vast structure of recollection.
Remembrance of Things Past [1]
[1913–1926]. *Swann's Way*

In his younger days a man dreams of possessing the heart of the woman whom he loves; later, the feeling that he possesses the heart of a woman may be enough to make him fall in love with her. *Ib.*

What artists call posterity is the posterity of the work of art.
Ib. Within a Budding Grove,
pt. I

Not only does one not retain all at once the truly rare works, but even within such works it is the least precious parts that one perceives first. Less deceptive than life, these great masterpieces do not give us their best at the beginning.[2]
Ib.

The time which we have at our disposal every day is elastic; the passions that we feel expand it, those that we inspire contract it; and habit fills up what remains. *Ib.*

Like everybody who is not in love, he imagined that one chose the person whom one loved after endless deliberations and on the strength of various qualities and advantages.
Ib. Cities of the Plain, pt. I

We passionately long that there may be another life in which we shall be similar to what we are here below. But

---

[1] When he killed the Mudjokivis,
Of the skin he made him mittens,
Made them with the fur side inside,
Made them with the skin side outside,
He, to get the warm side inside,
Put the inside skin side outside;
He, to get the cold side outside,
Put the warm side fur side inside.
That's why he put the fur side inside,
Why he put the skin side outside,
Why he turned them inside outside —
Anonymous, The Modern Hiawatha
[2] For *The South Polar Times,* Midwinter Day [June 22, 1911], prepared by the men of Captain Robert Falcon Scott's last Antarctic expedition.

Ponting was the photographer for the Scott expedition.
[1] *À la Recherche du Temps Perdu,* translated by C. K. Scott Moncrieff, except the last section, *The Past Recaptured,* which was translated by Frederick A. Blossom.
[2] See Daniel Gregory Mason, p. 915b.

we do not pause to reflect that, even without waiting for that other life, in this life, after a few years we are unfaithful to what we have been, to what we wished to remain immortally.

> *Remembrance of Things Past.*
> *Cities of the Plain, pt. II*

It is often simply from want of the creative spirit that we do not go to the full extent of suffering. And the most terrible reality brings us, with our suffering, the joy of a great discovery, because it merely gives a new and clear form to what we have long been ruminating without suspecting it.   *Ib.*

The bonds that unite another person to ourself exist only in our mind. Memory as it grows fainter relaxes them, and notwithstanding the illusion by which we would fain be cheated and with which, out of love, friendship, politeness, deference, duty, we cheat other people, we exist alone. Man is the creature that cannot emerge from himself, that knows his fellows only in himself; when he asserts the contrary, he is lying.   *Ib. The Sweet Cheat Gone*

We do not succeed in changing things according to our desire, but gradually our desire changes. The situation that we hoped to change because it was intolerable becomes unimportant. We have not managed to surmount the obstacle, as we were absolutely determined to do, but life has taken us round it, led us past it, and then if we turn round to gaze at the remote past, we can barely catch sight of it, so imperceptible has it become.   *Ib.*

There is not a woman in the world the possession of whom is as precious as that of the truths which she reveals to us by causing us to suffer.   *Ib.*

We are healed of a suffering only by experiencing it to the full.   *Ib.*

Happiness is beneficial for the body but it is grief that develops the powers of the mind.

> *Ib. The Past Recaptured*

Only through art can we get outside of ourselves and know another's view of the universe which is not the same as ours and see landscapes which would otherwise have remained unknown to us like the landscapes of the moon. Thanks to art, instead of seeing a single world, our own, we see it multiply until we have before us as many worlds as there are original artists. . . . And many centuries after their core, whether we call it Rembrandt or Vermeer, is extinguished, they continue to send us their special rays.

> *The Maxims of Marcel Proust* [1]

ERNEST RUTHERFORD
1871–1937

We cannot control atomic energy to an extent which would be of any value commercially, and I believe we are not likely ever to be able to do so.

> *Speech to the British Association for the Advancement of Science* [1933]

JOHN MILLINGTON SYNGE
1871–1909

What is the price of a thousand horses against a son where there is one son only?   *Riders to the Sea* [1904]

When I was writing *The Shadow of the Glen* I got more aid than any learning could have given me from a chink in the floor of the old Wicklow house where I was staying, that let me hear what was being said by the servant girls in the kitchen.

> *The Playboy of the Western World* [1907], *preface*

Drink a health to the wonders of the Western world, the pirates, preachers, poteen-makers, with the jobbing jockies; parching peelers, and the juries fill their stomachs selling judgments of the English law.   *Ib. act II*

[1] Edited and translated by JUSTIN O'BRIEN [1948].

May I meet him with one tooth and it aching, and one eye to be seeing seven and seventy divils in the twists of the road, and one old timber leg on him to limp into the scalding grave. There he is now crossing the strands, and that the Lord God would send a high wave to wash him from the world.[1]
> *The Playboy of the Western World, act II*

Aid me for to win her, and I'll be asking God to stretch a hand to you in the hour of death, and lead you short cuts through the Meadows of Ease, and up the floor of Heaven to the Footstool of the Virgin's Son.　　*Ib.*

They're cheering a young lad, the champion playboy of the Western World.　　*Ib. III*

A man who is not afraid of the sea will soon be drowned, he said, for he will be going out on a day he shouldn't. But we do be afraid of the sea, and we do only be drownded now and again.
> *The Aran Islands* [1907]

There is no language like the Irish for soothing and quieting.　　*Ib.*

A translation is no translation, he said, unless it will give you the music of a poem along with the words of it.　　*Ib.*

I knew the stars, the flowers, and the birds,
The gray and wintry sides of many glens,
And did but half remember human words,
In converse with the mountains, moors, and fens.　　*Prelude* [1910]

[1] May the grass grow at your door and the fox build his nest on your hearthstone. May the light fade from your eyes, so you never see what you love. May your own blood rise against you, and the sweetest drink you take be the bitterest cup of sorrow. May you die without benefit of clergy; may there be none to shed a tear at your grave, and may the hearthstone of hell be your best bed forever. — *Traditional Wexford curse*

PAUL VALÉRY
1871–1945

The folly of mistaking a paradox for a discovery, a metaphor for a proof, a torrent of verbiage for a spring of capital truths, and oneself for an oracle, is inborn in us.
> *Introduction to the Method of Leonardo da Vinci* [1] [1895]

Collect all the facts that can be collected about the life of Racine and you will never learn from them the art of his verse. All criticism is dominated by the outworn theory that the man is the cause of the work as in the eyes of the law the criminal is the cause of the crime. Far rather are they both the effects.　　*Ib.*

The sea, the ever renewing sea! [2]
> *Charmes* [1922]. *Le Cimitière Marin*

The wind is rising . . . we must attempt to live.[3]　　*Ib.*

Poetry is simply literature reduced to the essence of its active principle. It is purged of idols of every kind, of realistic illusions, of any conceivable equivocation between the language of "truth" and the language of "creation."
> *Littérature* [1930]

An intelligent woman is a woman with whom one can be as stupid as one wants.
> *Mauvaises Pensées et Autres* [1941]

The painter should not paint what he sees, but what will be seen.　　*Ib.*

That which has always been accepted by everyone, everywhere, is almost certain to be false.　　*Tel Quel* [1943]

God created man, and finding him not sufficiently alone, gave him a female companion so that he might feel his solitude more acutely.　　*Ib.*

[1] Translated by Thomas McGreevy.
[2] La mer, la mer toujours recommence!
[3] Le vent se leve . . . il faut tenter de vivre.

The purpose of psychology is to give us a completely different idea of the things we know best. *Tel Quel*

WILBUR WRIGHT
1867–1912
AND
ORVILLE WRIGHT
1871–1948

Success/ four flights Thursday morning/ all against twenty-one-mile wind/ started from level with engine power alone/ average speed through air thirty-one miles/ longest fifty-nine seconds/ inform press/ home Christmas.

Telegram to the Reverend Milton Wright, from Kitty Hawk, N.C. [December 17, 1903]

EVERARD JACK APPLETON
1872–1931

Somewhere she waits to make you win,
  Your soul in her firm white hands;
Somewhere the gods have made for you
The woman who understands.
The Woman Who Understands

SIR MAX BEERBOHM
1872–1956

Most women are not so young as they are painted.
A Defense of Cosmetics

Zuleika, on a desert island, would have spent most of her time in looking for a man's footprint.
Zuleika Dobson [1911], *ch. 2*

She was hardly more affable than a cameo. *Ib. 3*

The dullard's envy of brilliant men is always assuaged by the suspicion that they will come to a bad end. *Ib. 4*

Ordinary saints grow faint to posterity; whilst quite ordinary sinners pass vividly down the ages. *Ib. 6*

She was one of the people who say "I don't know anything about music really, but I know what I like." [1]
Zuleika Dobson, ch. 9

Of all the objects of hatred, a woman once loved is the most hateful.
Ib. 13

I have known no man of genius who had not to pay, in some affliction or defect either physical or spiritual, for what the gods had given him.
No. 2. The Pines

It seems to be a law of nature that no man ever is loth to sit for his portrait. A man may be old, he may be ugly, he may be burdened with grave responsibilities to the nation, and that nation be at a crisis of its history; but none of these considerations, nor all of them together, will deter him from sitting for his portrait.
Quia Imperfectum

To say that a man is vain means merely that he is pleased with the effect he produces on other people. A conceited man is satisfied with the effect he produces on himself. *Ib.*

Strange, when you come to think of it, that of all the countless folk who have lived before our time on this planet not one is known in history or in legend as having died of laughter.
Laughter

The past is a work of art, free of irrelevancies and loose ends.
Comment

LÉON BLUM
1872–1950

Life does not give itself to one who tries to keep all its advantages at once. I

[1] Bromide no. 1. — GELETT BURGESS, *Are You a Bromide?* [1906]
In art I pull no highbrow stuff,
I know what I like, and that's enough.
WILLIAM W. WOOLLCOTT [1877–1949], *I Am a One Hundred Percent American, st. 3*

have often thought morality may perhaps consist solely in the courage of making a choice. *On Marriage*

No government can remain stable in an unstable society and an unstable world.

À l'Échelle Humaine [1945]

JAMES BONE
1872–1962

The mighty fleet of Wren, with their topgallants and mainsails of stone.

The London Perambulator [1925]

PATRICK REGINALD
CHALMERS
1872–1942

"I find," said 'e, "things very much as 'ow I've always found,
For mostly they goes up and down or else goes round and round."

Roundabouts and Swings, st. 2

What's lost upon the roundabouts we pulls up on the swings! *Ib.*

CALVIN COOLIDGE
1872–1933

There is no right to strike against the public safety by anybody, anywhere, any time.

Telegram to Samuel Gompers, president of the American Federation of Labor, on the Boston police strike [September 14, 1919]

One with the law is a majority.

Speech [July 27, 1920]

Inflation is repudiation.

Speech, Chicago [January 11, 1922]

The business of America is business.

Speech to the Society of American Newspaper Editors [January 17, 1925]

They hired the money, didn't they?

Referring to the European war debts [1925]

I do not choose to run for President in 1928.

Statement to reporters [August 2, 1927]

I love Vermont because of her hills and valleys, her scenery and invigorating climate, but most of all because of her indomitable people.

Address from train platform, Bennington, Vermont [September 21, 1928]

If you don't say anything, you won't be called on to repeat it. *Saying*

He said he was against it.

On being asked what a clergyman preaching on sin had said

PAUL LAURENCE
DUNBAR
1872–1906

Folks ain't got no right to censuah otha folks about dey habits;
Him dat giv' de squir'ls de bushtails made de bobtails fu' de rabbits.

Accountability

It's easy 'nough to titter w'en de stew is smokin' hot,
But hit's mighty ha'd to giggle w'en dey's nuffin' in de pot.

Philosophy

LEARNED HAND
1872–1961

You may ask what then will become of the fundamental principles of equity and fair play which our constitutions enshrine; and whether I seriously believe that unsupported they will serve merely as counsels of moderation. I do not think that anyone can say what will be left of those principles; I do not know whether they will serve only as counsels; but this much I think I do know — that a society so riven that the spirit of moderation is gone, no court can save; that a society where that spirit flourishes, no court need save; that in a society which evades its responsibility by thrusting upon the courts the nurture of that spirit, that spirit in the end will perish.

The Contribution of an Independent Judiciary to Civilization [1942]

Justice, I think, is the tolerable accommodation of the conflicting interests of society, and I don't believe there is any royal road to attain such accommodations concretely.

From PHILIP HAMBURGER, *The Great Judge [1946]*

"I beseech ye in the bowels of Christ, think that ye may be mistaken." [1] I should like to have that written over the portals of every church, every school, and every courthouse, and, may I say, of every legislative body in the United States. I should like to have every court begin, "I beseech ye in the bowels of Christ, think that we may be mistaken."

Morals in Public Life [1951]

I had rather take my chance that some traitors will escape detection than spread abroad a spirit of general suspicion and distrust, which accepts rumor and gossip in place of undismayed and unintimidated inquiry.

Speech to the Board of Regents, University of the State of New York [October 24, 1952]

That community is already in the process of dissolution where each man begins to eye his neighbor as a possible enemy, where nonconformity with the accepted creed, political as well as religious, is a mark of disaffection; where denunciation, without specification or backing, takes the place of evidence; where orthodoxy chokes freedom of dissent; where faith in the eventual supremacy of reason has become so timid that we dare not enter our convictions in the open lists, to win or lose. *Ib.*

¹ See Oliver Cromwell, p. 328a.

The mutual confidence on which all else depends can be maintained only by an open mind and a brave reliance upon free discussion.

Speech to the Board of Regents, University of the State of New York

JOHN McCRAE
1872–1918

In Flanders fields the poppies blow
Between the crosses, row on row.
In Flanders Fields [1915], st. 1

Take up our quarrel with the foe:
To you from failing hands we throw
The torch; be yours to hold it high.
If ye break faith with us who die
We shall not sleep, though poppies
    grow
In Flanders fields. *Ib. st. 3*

PATRICK F. O'KEEFE
1872–1934

Say It with Flowers.[1]
Slogan for the Society of American Florists [1917]

JOSÉ ENRIQUE RODÓ
1872–1917

To govern is to populate, assimilating in the beginning, then educating and selecting. *Ariel*

BERTRAND RUSSELL
1872–1970

Thus mathematics may be defined as the subject in which we never know what we are talking about, nor whether what we are saying is true.

Recent Work on the Principles of Mathematics [1901], in International Monthly, vol. 4, p. 84

Mathematics, rightly viewed, posesses not only truth, but supreme beauty — a beauty cold and austere, like that of

¹ Say It with Music. — *Title of song by* IRVING BERLIN [1921]

sculpture, without appeal to any part of our weaker nature, without the gorgeous trappings of painting or music, yet sublimely pure, and capable of a stern perfection such as only the greatest art can show.[1]

The Study of Mathematics [1902]

Mathematics takes us still further from what is human, into the region of absolute necessity, to which not only the actual world, but every possible world, must conform.   *Ib.*

It is preoccupation with possession, more than anything else, that prevents men from living freely and nobly.

Principles of Social Reconstruction [1917]

The psychology of adultery has been falsified by conventional morals, which assume, in monogamous countries, that attraction to one person cannot coexist with a serious affection for another. Everybody knows that this is untrue.

Marriage and Morals [1929], *ch. 16*

To fear love is to fear life, and those who fear life are already three parts dead.   *Ib.*

A good society is a means to a good life for those who compose it; not something having a kind of excellence on its own account.

Authority and the Individual [1949]

Fear is the main source of superstition, and one of the main sources of cruelty. To conquer fear is the beginning of wisdom.

An Outline of Intellectual Rubbish [1950]

ELLERY SEDGWICK
1872–1960

Autobiographies ought to begin with Chapter Two.

The Happy Profession [1946], *ch. 1*

In America, getting on in the world means getting out of the world we have known before.   *Ib.*

[1] See Millay, p. 1023b.

ALBERT PAYSON TERHUNE
1872–1942

He was red-gold-and-snow of coat, a big slender youngster, with the true "look of eagles" in his deepset dark eyes.

The Heart of a Dog [1924], *ch. 8*

CARL LOTUS BECKER
1873–1945

Economic distress will teach men, if anything can, that realities are less dangerous than fancies, that fact-finding is more effective than fault-finding.

Progress and Power [1935]

The significance of man is that he is that part of the universe that asks the question, What is the significance of Man? He alone can stand apart imaginatively and, regarding himself and the universe in their eternal aspects, pronounce a judgment: The significance of man is that he is insignificant and is aware of it.   *Ib.*

Those of us who think that we are a nation of starry-eyed idealists [1] who have been twice tricked by the British into a European war in order to pull their chestnuts out of the fire [2] have read the history of this country to little purpose. . . . The truth is rather that the existence and friendliness of the British Empire and the power of the British Fleet have for more than a century enabled us to roast our own chestnuts at leisure and eat them in security.   *Ib.*

GEORGE BENNARD
1873–

I will cling to the old rugged cross, And exchange it some day for a crown.

The Old Rugged Cross [1913] *refrain*

[1] See Henry Agard Wallace, p. 1010b.
[2] See Molière, p. 360b.

GUY WETMORE CARRYL
1873–1904

Thank God for peace! Thank God for peace, when the great gray ships come in!
> *When the Great Gray Ships Come In [New York Harbor, August 20, 1898], st. 4*

ARTHUR CHAPMAN
1873–1935

Out where the handclasp's a little stronger,
Out where the smile dwells a little longer,
That's where the West begins.
> *Out Where the West Begins, st. 1*

Out where the skies are a trifle bluer,
Out where friendship's a little truer.
> *Ib. st. 2*

Where there's more of singing and less of sighing,
Where there's more of giving and less of buying,
And a man makes friends without half trying.
> *Ib. st. 3*

SIDONIE-GABRIELLE COLETTE
1873–1954

Those pleasures so lightly called physical.
> *Mélanges*

Whether you are dealing with an animal or a child, to convince is to weaken.
> *Le Pur et l'Impur*

WALTER DE LA MARE
1873–1956

Slowly, silently, now the moon
Walks the night in her silver shoon.
> *Silver*

Here lies a most beautiful lady,
Light of step and heart was she;
I think she was the most beautiful lady
That ever was in the West Country.
> *An Epitaph*

"Is there anybody there?" said the Traveler,
Knocking on the moonlit door;
And his horse in the silence champed the grasses
Of the forest's ferny floor.
> *The Listeners*

"Tell them that I came, and no one answered,
That I kept my word," he said.
> *Ib.*

Look thy last on all things lovely,
Every hour — let no night
Seal thy sense in deathly slumber
Till to delight
Thou hast paid thy utmost blessing;
Since that all things thou wouldst praise
Beauty took from those who loved them
In other days.
> *Fare Well, st. 3*

Nought but vast sorrow was there —
The sweet cheat gone.
> *The Ghost*

Who said "Peacock Pie"?
The old king to the sparrow:
Who said "Crops are ripe"?
Rust to the harrow.
> *The Song of the Mad Prince*

Who said, "Ay, mum's the word"?
> *Ib.*

Life's troubled bubble broken.
> *Ib.*

No lovelier hills than thine have laid
My tired thoughts to rest:
No peace of lovelier valleys made
Like peace within my breast.
> *England, st. 1*

Poor Jim Jay
Got stuck fast
In Yesterday.
> *Jim Jay*

It's a very odd thing —
As odd as can be —
That whatever Miss T. eats
Turns into Miss T.
> *Miss T.*

Three jolly gentlemen,
In coats of red,
Rode their horses
Up to bed.
> *The Huntsmen*

Be not too wildly amorous of the far,
Nor lure thy fantasy to its utmost
  scope.
    The Imagination's Pride

Bang! Now the animal
Is dead and dumb and done.
Nevermore to peep again, creep again,
  leap again,
Eat or sleep or drink again, oh, what
  fun!
    Hi!

MARK FENDERSON
1873–1944

What's the use? Yesterday an egg,
tomorrow a feather duster.
    Caption of cartoon: The
    Dejected Rooster

FORD MADOX
[HUEFFER] FORD
1873–1939

This is the saddest story I have ever
heard.
    The Good Soldier [1915],
    first line

Only two classes of books are of universal appeal: the very best and the very
worst.   *Joseph Conrad* [1924]

WILLIAM GREEN
1873–1952

The labor union is an elemental response to the human instinct for group
action in dealing with group problems.
    Speech [1925]

PERCY HAMMOND
1873–1936

The female knee is a joint and not an
entertainment.   *Dramatic review*

ALFRED JARRY
1873–1907

Mother Ubu, you're very ugly today.
Is it because we have company?
    Ubu Roi [1896]

O the despair of Pygmalion, who
might have created a statue and only
made a woman!
    L'Amour Absolu [1899]

DANIEL GREGORY
MASON
1873–1953

The ideal of independence requires
resistance to the herd spirit now so
widespread, to our worship of quantity
and indifference to quality, to our unthinking devotion to organization,
standardization, propaganda, and advertising.   *Artistic Ideals* [1927]

Art of any profundity can be appreciated only slowly, gradually, in
leisurely contemplation.[1]   *Ib.*

GEORGE EDWARD
MOORE
1873–1958

It appears to me that in Ethics, as
in all other philosophical studies, the
difficulties and disagreements, of which
history is full, are mainly due to a very
simple cause: namely to the attempt to
answer questions, without first discovering precisely *what* question it is which
you desire to answer.
    Principia Ethica [1903], *preface*

DWIGHT WHITNEY
MORROW
1873–1931

Any party which takes credit for the
rain must not be surprised if its opponents blame it for the drought.
    Saying

ALBERT JAY NOCK
1873–1945

All Souls College, Oxford, planned
better than it knew when it limited the
number of its undergraduates to four;
four is exactly the right number for any

[1] See Proust, p. 907b.

college which is really intent on getting results.
> *Memoirs of a Superfluous Man [1943], III, ch. 3*

Money does not pay for anything, never has, never will. It is an economic axiom as old as the hills that goods and services can be paid for only with goods and services. *Ib. 13*

As sheer casual reading matter, I still find the English dictionary the most interesting book in our language.
> *Ib. IV, ch. 1*

CHARLES PÉGUY
1873–1914

It's a nuisance, God said. When those French are gone,
No one will be left to understand certain things I do.
> *Les Sept Contre Paris*

Surrender is essentially an operation by means of which we set about explaining instead of acting.
> *Les Cahiers de la Quinzaine [1905]*

Homer is new and fresh this morning, and nothing, perhaps, is as old and tired as today's newspaper.
> *Note sur M. Bergson et la Philosophie Bergsonienne [1914]*

Freedom is a system based on courage.
> *From* HALÉVY, *Life of Charles Péguy*

SIME SILVERMAN[1]
1873–1933

Wall Street Lays An Egg.
> *Headline announcing stock market crash [October 1929]*

[1] Silverman, who founded and edited the famous theatrical trade paper *Variety* [1905], had perhaps more influence on American slang than any man of his time.

Sticks Nix Hicks Pix.
> *Headline, meaning that rural audiences do not care for moving pictures dealing with country themes*

ALFRED EMANUEL SMITH[1]
1873–1944

The kiss of death.
> *Alluding to Hearst's support of Ogden Mills, Smith's unsuccessful opponent for Governor of New York State [1926]*

Let's look at the record.
> *Campaign speeches [1928]*

The Governor of New York State does not have to be an acrobat.
> *Speech in behalf of Franklin D. Roosevelt [1928]*

Nobody shoots at Santa Claus.
> *Campaign speeches [1936]*

No matter how thin you slice it, it's still baloney. *Ib.*

HENRY MAJOR TOMLINSON
1873–1958

The sea is at its best at London, near midnight, when you are within the arms of a capacious chair, before a glowing fire, selecting phases of the voyages you will never make.
> *The Sea and the Jungle [1912]*

The reader who is illuminated is, in a real sense, the poem.
> *Between the Lines [1930]*

Bad and indifferent criticism of books is just as serious as a city's careless drainage. *Ib.*

[1] He is the Happy Warrior of the political battlefield. — FRANKLIN D. ROOSEVELT, *Nominating speech, Democratic National Convention* [June 26, 1924]. See Wordsworth, p. 515a.
Al Smith knew as much as any living man of the art of democratic government. — ELLERY SEDGWICK, *The Happy Profession* [1946], *ch. 17*

LENA GUILBERT FORD
d. 1915

Keep the home fires burning,
While your hearts are yearning;
Though your lads are far away
They dream of home.
There's a silver lining
Through the dark cloud shining;
Turn the dark cloud inside out,
Till the boys come home.
> *Keep the Home Fires Burning*
> [1915]

SIR NORMAN ANGELL
1874–1967

The Great Illusion.
> *Title of book* [1910] *on the*
> *futility of war*

MAURICE BARING
1874–1945

All theories of what a good play is, or how a good play should be written, are futile. A good play is a play which when acted upon the boards makes an audience interested and pleased. A play that fails in this is a bad play.
> *Have You Anything to Declare?*

CHARLES AUSTIN BEARD
1874–1948
AND
MARY RITTER BEARD
1876–1958

At no time, at no place, in solemn convention assembled, through no chosen agents, had the American people officially proclaimed the United States to be a democracy. The Constitution did not contain the word or any word lending countenance to it, except possibly the mention of "We, the people," in the preamble . . . When the Constitution was framed no respecta-ble person called himself or herself a democrat.
> *America in Midpassage* [1939],
> *ch. 17*

GORDON BOTTOMLEY
1874–1948

Many deaths have place in men
Before they come to die;
Joys must be used and spent, and then
Abandoned and passed by.
> *New Year's Eve, 1913*

When you destroy a blade of grass
You poison England at her roots.
> *To Ironfounders and Others*

Your worship is your furnaces,
Which, like old idols, lost obscenes,
Have molten bowels; your vision is
Machines for making more machines.
> *Ib.*

ANNA HEMPSTEAD BRANCH
1874–1937

Order is a lovely thing;
On disarray it lays its wing,
Teaching simplicity to sing.
> *The Monk in the Kitchen*

His screaming stallions maned with
whistling wind.
> *Nimrod Wars with the Angels*

God wove a web of loveliness,
Of clouds and stars and birds,
But made not anything at all
So beautiful as words.
> *Songs for My Mother: Her*
> *Words, st. 5*

ARTHUR HENRY REGINALD BULLER
1874–1944

There was a young lady named Bright,
Whose speed was far faster than light;
She set out one day
In a relative way,
And returned home the previous night.
> *Limerick* [1]

[1] *Punch,* December 19, 1923.

GILBERT KEITH
CHESTERTON
1874–1936

Likelier the barricades shall blare
Slaughter below and smoke above,
And death and hate and hell declare
That men have found a thing to love.
The Napoleon of Notting Hill
[1906]

"The Christian ideal," it is said, "has not been tried and found wanting; it has been found difficult and left untried."
What's Wrong with the World
[1910], pt. I, ch. 5

Nothing sublimely artistic has ever arisen out of mere art, any more than anything essentially reasonable has ever arisen out of pure reason. There must always be a rich moral soil for any great aesthetic growth.
A Defense of Nonsense [1911]

For the great Gaels of Ireland
Are the men that God made mad,
For all their wars are merry,
And all their songs are sad.[1]
The Ballad of the White Horse
[1911], bk. II

And if ever ye ride in Ireland,
The jest may yet be said,
There is the land of broken hearts,
And the land of broken heads.
Ib. V

Every great literature has always been allegorical — allegorical of some view of the whole universe.
Ib.

The whole difference between construction and creation is exactly this: that a thing constructed can only be loved after it is constructed; but a thing created is loved before it exists.
Preface to DICKENS, *Pickwick Papers*

[1] For the Young Gaels of Ireland
Are the lads that drive me mad;
For half their words need footnotes,
And half their rhymes are bad.
ARTHUR GUITERMAN [1871–1943], *The Young Celtic Poets, st. 2*

A good joke is the one ultimate and sacred thing which cannot be criticized. Our relations with a good joke are direct and even divine relations.
Preface to DICKENS, *Pickwick Papers*

The world will never starve for wonders; but only for want of wonder.
Inscription, General Motors Building, Century of Progress Exposition, Chicago

But they that fought for England,
Following a fallen star,
Alas, alas for England
They have their graves afar.
Elegy in a Country Churchyard

Strong gongs groaning as the guns boom far
(Don John of Austria is going to the war);
Stiff flags straining in the night blasts cold
In the gloom black-purple, in the glint old gold;
Torchlight crimson on the copper kettledrums,
Then the tuckets, then the trumpets, then the cannon, and he comes.
Lepanto [1915]

Cervantes on his galley sets the sword back in the sheath
(Don John of Austria rides homeward with a wreath).
And he sees across a weary land a straggling road in Spain,
Up which a lean and foolish knight forever rides in vain.
Ib.

To an open house in the evening
Home shall men come,
To an older place than Eden
And a taller town than Rome.
The House of Christmas

Burn from my brain and from my breast
Sloth, and the cowardice that clings,
And stiffness and the soul's arrest:
And feed my brain with better things.
A Ballade of a Book Reviewer

The strangest whim has seized me
. . . After all
I think I will not hang myself today.
A Ballade of Suicide

Don't ever take a fence down until
you know the reason why it was put
up.[1]
*Ascribed to Chesterton by John
F. Kennedy in a 1945 notebook*

The face of Father Brown . . .
could shine with ignorance as well as
with knowledge.
The Scandal of Father Brown
[1935]

St. George he was for England,
And before he killed the dragon
He drank a pint of English ale
Out of an English flagon.
The Englishman

Step softly, under snow or rain,
To find the place where men can pray;
The way is all so very plain
That we may lose the way.
The Wise Men

And Noah he often said to his wife
when he sat down to dine,
"I don't care where the water goes if it
doesn't get into the wine."
Wine and Water

Before the Roman came to Rye or out
to Severn strode,
The rolling English drunkard made the
rolling English road.
The Rolling English Road

Tea, although an Oriental,
Is a gentleman at least;
Cocoa is a cad and coward,
Cocoa is a vulgar beast.
The Song of Right and Wrong

I also had my hour;
One far fierce hour and sweet:
There was a shout about my ears,
And palms before my feet.
The Donkey

The Yankee is a dab at electricity and
crime,

¹ See Robert Frost, p. 926a.

He tells you how he hustles and it takes
him quite a time,
I like his hospitality that's cordial and
frank,
I do not mind his money but I do not
like his swank.
A Song of Self-Esteem

SIR WINSTON SPENCER CHURCHILL[1]
1874–1965

I pass with relief from the tossing sea
of Cause and Theory to the firm
ground of Result and Fact.
The Malakand Field Force [1898]

It is better to be making the news
than taking it; to be an actor rather
than a critic.   *Ib.*

Nothing in life is so exhilarating as
to be shot at without result.   *Ib.*

There are men in the world who derive as stern an exaltation from the
proximity of disaster and ruin, as others
from success.   *Ib.*

Victory is the beautiful, bright-
colored flower. Transport is the stem
without which it could never have
blossomed.   *The River War* [1899]

Terminological inexactitude.
Speech, House of Commons
[*February 22, 1906*]

The maxim of the British people is
"Business as usual."
Speech, Guildhall [*November 9,
1914*]

Politics are almost as exciting as war,
and quite as dangerous. In war you can
only be killed once, but in politics
many times.   *Remark* [1920]

By being so long in the lowest form
[at Harrow] I gained an immense advantage over the cleverer boys. . . . I
got into my bones the essential structure of the ordinary British sentence
— which is a noble thing. Naturally I

¹ He mobilized the English language and sent
it into battle. — JOHN F. KENNEDY, on conferring
honorary citizenship on Churchill [April 9, 1963]
See Roosevelt and Churchill, p. 974.

am biased in favor of boys learning English; I would make them all learn English: and then I would let the clever ones learn Latin as an honor, and Greek as a treat.

Roving Commission: My Early Life [1930]

It is a good thing for an uneducated man to read books of quotations. Bartlett's *Familiar Quotations* is an admirable work, and I studied it intently. The quotations when engraved upon the memory give you good thoughts. They also make you anxious to read the authors and look for more.   *Ib.*

Come on now, all you young men, all over the world. You are needed more than ever now to fill the gap of a generation shorn by the war. You have not an hour to lose. You must take your places in life's fighting line. Twenty to twenty-five! These are the years! Don't be content with things as they are. "The earth is yours and the fullness thereof." Enter upon your inheritance, accept your responsibilities. Raise the glorious flags again, advance them upon the new enemies, who constantly gather upon the front of the human army, and have only to be assaulted to be overthrown. Don't take no for an answer, never submit to failure. Do not be fobbed off with mere personal success or acceptance. You will make all kinds of mistakes; but as long as you are generous and true, and also fierce, you cannot hurt the world or even seriously distress her. She was made to be wooed and won by youth.   *Ib.*

Decided only to be undecided, resolved to be irresolute, adamant for drift, solid for fluidity, all-powerful to be impotent.[1]

While England Slept [1936]

Dictators ride to and fro upon tigers which they dare not dismount. And the tigers are getting hungry.[2]   *Ib.*

[1] Of Stanley Baldwin's policies.
[2] He who rides a tiger is afraid to dismount. — WILLIAM SCARBOROUGH, *Chinese Proverbs* [1875], *no. 2082*
See Truman, p. 983a.

I have watched this famous island descending incontinently, fecklessly, the stairway which leads to a dark gulf. It is a fine broad stairway at the beginning, but after a bit the carpet ends. A little farther on there are only flagstones, and a little farther on still these break beneath your feet.

While England Slept

The German dictator, instead of snatching the victuals from the table, has been content to have them served to him course by course.

Speech on the Munich agreement, House of Commons [October 5, 1938]

That long [Canadian] frontier from the Atlantic to the Pacific Oceans, guarded only by neighborly respect and honorable obligations, is an example to every country and a pattern for the future of the world.

Speech in honor of R. B. Bennett, Canada Club, London [April 20, 1939]

I cannot forecast to you the action of Russia. It is a riddle wrapped in a mystery inside an enigma.

Radio broadcast [October 1, 1939]

For each and for all, as for the Royal Navy, the watchword should be, "Carry on, and dread nought."

Speech on traffic at sea, House of Commons [December 6, 1939]

I have nothing to offer but blood, toil, tears and sweat.[1]

First Statement as Prime Minister, House of Commons [May 13, 1940]

[1] Mollify it with thy tears, or sweat, or blood. — JOHN DONNE, *An Anatomy of the World* [1611], *I, 430–431*

Year after year they voted cent per cent, Blood, sweat, and tear-wrung millions — why? for rent!

BYRON, *The Age of Bronze* [1823], *XIV*

See Prescott, p. 587a, and Garibaldi, p. 620a.
It [poetry] is forged slowly and patiently, link by link, with sweat and blood and tears. —

Victory at all costs, victory in spite of all terror, victory however long and hard the road may be; for without victory there is no survival.

First Statement as Prime Minister, House of Commons

We shall not flag or fail. We shall go on to the end. We shall fight in France, we shall fight on the seas and oceans, we shall fight with growing confidence and growing strength in the air, we shall defend our island, whatever the cost may be, we shall fight on the beaches, we shall fight on the landing grounds, we shall fight in the fields and in the streets, we shall fight in the hills; we shall never surrender.

Speech on Dunkirk, House of Commons [June 4, 1940]

If we open a quarrel between the past and the present, we shall find that we have lost the future.

Speech, House of Commons [June 18, 1940]

Upon this battle [of Britain] depends the survival of Christian civilization. Upon it depends our own British life, and the long continuity of our institutions and our Empire. The whole fury and might of the enemy must very soon be turned on us. Hitler knows that he will have to break us in this island or lose the war. If we can stand up to him, all Europe may be free and the life of the world may move forward into broad, sunlit uplands. But if we fail, then the whole world, including the United States, including all that we have known and cared for, will sink into the abyss of a new Dark Age made more sinister, perhaps more protracted, by the lights of perverted science. Let

LORD ALFRED DOUGLAS, *Collected Poems* [1919]
Their sweat, their tears, their blood bedewed the endless plain. — WINSTON S. CHURCHILL, *The Unknown War* [1931], referring to the armies of the Czar before the Russian Revolution
Churchill referred to his promise of blood, toil, tears and sweat in subsequent speeches on October 8, 1940, May 7 and December 2, 1941, and January 27 and November 10, 1942.

us therefore brace ourselves to our duties, and so bear ourselves that, if the British Empire and its Commonwealth last for a thousand years, men will still say: "This was their finest hour."

Speech, House of Commons

We shall defend every village, every town and every city. The vast mass of London itself, fought street by street, could easily devour an entire hostile army; and we would rather see London laid in ruins and ashes than that it should be tamely and abjectly enslaved.

Radio broadcast [July 14, 1940]

Never in the field of human conflict was so much owed by so many to so few.

Tribute to the Royal Air Force, House of Commons [August 20, 1940]

The British Empire and the United States will have to be somewhat mixed up together in some of their affairs for mutual and general advantage. For my own part, looking out upon the future, I do not view the process with any misgivings. I could not stop it if I wished; no one can stop it. Like the Mississippi, it just keeps rolling along.[1] Let it roll. Let it roll on full flood, inexorable, irresistible, benignant, to broader lands and better days. *Ib.*

This wicked man Hitler, the repository and embodiment of many forms of soul-destroying hatred, this monstrous product of former wrongs and shame.

Radio broadcast [September 11, 1940]

Death and sorrow will be the companions of our journey; hardship our garment; constancy and valor our only shield. We must be united, we must be undaunted, we must be inflexible.

Report on the war, House of Commons [October 8, 1940]

[1] Ol' Man River [Mississippi] . . . he keeps on rollin' along. — OSCAR HAMMERSTEIN 2ND [1927], *music by* JEROME KERN

We are waiting for the long-promised invasion. So are the fishes.
> *Radio broadcast to the French people* [*October 21, 1940*]

History with its flickering lamp stumbles along the trail of the past, trying to reconstruct its scenes, to revive its echoes, and kindle with pale gleams the passion of former days. What is the worth of all this? The only guide to a man is his conscience; the only shield to his memory is the rectitude and sincerity of his actions. It is very imprudent to walk through life without this shield, because we are so often mocked by the failure of our hopes and the upsetting of our calculations; but with this shield, however the fates may play, we march always in the ranks of honor.
> *Tribute to Neville Chamberlain, House of Commons* [*November 12, 1940*]

To die at the height of a man's career, the highest moment of his effort here in this world, universally honored and admired, to die while great issues are still commanding the whole of his interest, to be taken from us at a moment when he could already see ultimate success in view — is not the most unenviable of fates.[1]
> *Report on the war, House of Commons* [*December 19, 1940*]

I do not resent criticism, even when, for the sake of emphasis, it parts for the time with reality.
> *Speech, House of Commons* [*January 22, 1941*]

Here is the answer which I will give to President Roosevelt. . . . Give us the tools, and we will finish the job.
> *Radio broadcast* [*February 9, 1941*]

[1] Lord Lothian, British Ambassador to the United States, died in Washington, December 12, 1940.
See Lord Lothian, p. 969b.

This is one of those cases in which the imagination is baffled by the facts.
> *Remark in the House of Commons following the parachute descent in Scotland of Rudolf Hess* [*May 13, 1941*]

The British nation is unique in this respect. They are the only people who like to be told how bad things are, who like to be told the worst.
> *Report on the war, House of Commons* [*June 10, 1941*]

A vile race of quislings [1] — to use the new word which will carry the scorn of mankind down the centuries.
> *Speech at St. James's Palace, London* [*June 12, 1941*]

The destiny of mankind is not decided by material computation. When great causes are on the move in the world . . . we learn that we are spirits, not animals, and that something is going on in space and time, and beyond space and time, which, whether we like it or not, spells duty.
> *Radio broadcast to America on receiving an honorary degree of Doctor of Laws from the University of Rochester, New York* [*June 16, 1941*]

Hitler is a monster of wickedness, insatiable in his lust for blood and plunder. Not content with having all Europe under his heel, or else terrorized into various forms of abject submission, he must now carry his work of butchery and desolation among the vast multitudes of Russia and of Asia. The terrible military machine, which we and the rest of the civilized world so foolishly, so supinely, so insensately allowed the Nazi gangsters to build up year by year from almost nothing, cannot stand idle lest it rust or fall to pieces. It must be in continual motion, grinding up

[1] Vidkun Quisling, head of the Nasjonal Samling party in Norway, who cooperated and collaborated with the Nazis when Germany invaded Norway [April 9, 1940]. Quisling was executed [October 23, 1945].

human lives and trampling down the homes and the rights of hundreds of millions of men. Moreover it must be fed, not only with flesh but with oil. So now this bloodthirsty guttersnipe must launch his mechanized armies upon new fields of slaughter, pillage and devastation.

> *Radio broadcast on the German invasion of Russia [June 22, 1941]*

We will have no truce or parley with you [Hitler], or the grisly gang who work your wicked will. You do your worst — and we will do our best.

> *Speech, London County Council [July 14, 1941]*

The V sign is the symbol of the unconquerable will of the occupied territories, and a portent of the fate awaiting the Nazi tyranny.

> *Message to the people of Europe on launching the V for Victory propaganda campaign [July 20, 1941]*

Nothing is more dangerous in wartime than to live in the temperamental atmosphere of a Gallup Poll,[1] always feeling one's pulse and taking one's temperature.

> *Report on the war, House of Commons [September 30, 1941]*

Do not let us speak of darker days; let us speak rather of sterner days. These are not dark days: these are great days — the greatest days our country has ever lived; and we must all thank God that we have been allowed, each of us according to our stations, to play a part in making these days memorable in the history of our race.

> *Address, Harrow School [October 29, 1941]*

In the past we have had a light which flickered, in the present we have a light which flames, and in the future

there will be a light which shines over all the land and sea.

> *Speech on war with Japan, House of Commons [December 8, 1941]*

What kind of people do they [the Japanese] think we are?

> *Speech to United States Congress [December 26, 1941]*

We have not journeyed all this way across the centuries, across the oceans, across the mountains, across the prairies, because we are made of sugar candy.

> *Speech to the Canadian Senate and House of Commons, Ottawa [December 30, 1941]*

This is no time to speak of the hopes of the future, or the broader world which lies beyond our struggles and our victory. We have to win that world for which lies beyond our struggles and our sacrifices. We have not won it yet. The crisis is upon us. . . . In this strange, terrible world war there is a place for everyone, man and woman, old and young, hale and halt; service in a thousand forms is open. There is no room now for the dilettante, the weakling, for the shirker, or the sluggard. The mine, the factory, the dockyard, the salt sea waves, the fields to till, the home, the hospital, the chair of the scientist, the pulpit of the preacher — from the highest to the humblest tasks, all are of equal honor; all have their part to play.

> *Ib.*

When I warned [the French] that Britain would fight on alone whatever they did, their generals told their prime minister and his divided cabinet, "In three weeks England will have her neck wrung like a chicken." Some chicken; some neck.

> *Ib.*

The late M. Venizelos[1] observed that in all her wars England — he

---

[1] Dr. George H. Gallup founded the British Institute of Public Opinion in 1936.

[1] Eleutherios Venizelos [1864–1936], Greek statesman.

should have said Britain, of course — always wins one battle — the last.

Speech at the Lord Mayor's Day Luncheon, London [November 10, 1942]

Now this is not the end. It is not even the beginning of the end.[1] But it is, perhaps, the end of the beginning.

Ib.

I have not become the King's First Minister in order to preside over the liquidation of the British Empire.

Ib.

The soft underbelly of the Axis.

Report on the war, House of Commons [November 11, 1942]

The proud German Army has once again proved the truth of the saying, "The Hun is always either at your throat or at your feet."

Speech to United States Congress [May 19, 1943]

There was a man who sold a hyena skin while the beast still lived and who was killed in hunting it.

Speech on Allied war gains, House of Commons [August 2, 1944]

"Not in vain" may be the pride of those who survived and the epitaph of those who fell.[2]

Speech, House of Commons [September 28, 1944]

The United States is a land of free speech. Nowhere is speech freer — not even here where we sedulously cultivate it even in its most repulsive form.

Ib.

He [President Franklin D. Roosevelt] died in harness, and we may well

say in battle harness, like his soldiers, sailors and airmen who died side by side with ours and carrying out their tasks to the end all over the world. What an enviable death was his.

Speech, House of Commons [April 17, 1945]

In Franklin Roosevelt there died the greatest American friend we have ever known — and the greatest champion of freedom who has ever brought help and comfort from the New World to the Old.

Ib.

I think "No comment" is a splendid expression. I am using it again and again. I got it from Sumner Welles.

To reporters at Washington airport, after conferring with President Truman at the White House [February 12, 1946]

From Stettin in the Baltic to Trieste in the Adriatic an iron curtain[1] has descended across the Continent.

Address, Westminster College, Fulton, Missouri [March 5, 1946]

This address to which I have given the title, "The Sinews of Peace."

Ib.

---

[1] Between them [Germany] and me there is now a bloody iron curtain which has descended forever! — QUEEN ELIZABETH OF BELGIUM [1874–1965], in 1914. Though German-born, she stood staunchly by her adopted country in World War I.

France . . . a nation of forty millions with a deep-rooted grievance and an iron curtain at its frontier. — GEORGE WASHINGTON CRILE, *A Mechanistic View of War and Peace* [1915]

With a rumble and a roar, an iron curtain is descending on Russian history. — VASILY ROZANOV, *Apocalypse of our Time* [1918]

We were behind the "iron curtain" at last. — ETHEL ANNAKIN SNOWDEN, *Through Bolshevik Russia* [1920]

The Nazi Minister of Enlightenment and Propaganda, Dr. Josef Goebbels [1897–1945], used the phrase "iron curtain" in reference to the U.S.S.R. in *Das Reich* [February 23, 1945]. Hitler's Minister of Finance, Count Lutz Schwerin von Krosigk, also used it [May 2, 1945].

Churchill used it — not publicly — in a top-secret telegram to President Truman [May 12, 1945].

---

[1] See Talleyrand, p. 484a.

[2] The eight thousand paratroopers of the First British Airborne Division who landed in Arnhem, Holland, behind the German lines in September 1944 and held the area for nine days and nights, with a loss of six thousand. Major General R. E. Urquhart, the division commander, radioed to Field Marshal Bernard Montgomery: All will be ordered to break out rather than surrender.

In War: Resolution. In Defeat: Defiance. In Victory: Magnanimity. In Peace: Good Will.
The Second World War: Moral of the Work, vol. I, The Gathering Storm [1948]

No one can guarantee success in war, but only deserve it.
Ib. II, Their Finest Hour [1949]

When you have to kill a man it costs nothing to be polite.
Ib. III, The Grand Alliance [1950]

[Clement] Attlee is a very modest man. And with reason.
On Clement Attlee, the Labor Prime Minister

Everyone has his day and some days last longer than others.
House of Commons [*January 1952*]

A fanatic is one who can't change his mind and won't change the subject.
Saying

The inherent vice of capitalism is the unequal sharing of blessings; the inherent virtue of socialism is the equal sharing of miseries. *Ib.*

Short words are best and the old words when short are best of all. *Ib.*

It is hard, if not impossible, to snub a beautiful woman — they remain beautiful and the rebuke recoils. *Ib.*

This is the sort of English up with which I will not put.[1] *Attributed*

CLARENCE DAY
1874–1935

When eras die, their legacies
Are left to strange police.
Professors in New England guard
The glory that was Greece.
Thoughts Without Words

The parting injunctions
Of mothers and wives

[1] See Wolcott Gibbs, p. 1050b.

Are one of those functions
That poison their lives.
Scenes from the Mesozoic

It is possible that our race may be an accident, in a meaningless universe, living its brief life uncared for, on this dark, cooling star: but even so — and all the more — what marvelous creatures we are! What fairy story, what tale from the Arabian Nights of the jinns, is a hundredth part as wonderful as this true fairy story of simians! It is so much more heartening, too, than the tales we invent. A universe capable of giving birth to many such accidents is — blind or not — a good world to live in, a promising universe. . . . We once thought we lived on God's footstool; it may be a throne.[1]
This Simian World [1920]. XIX

Father declared he was going to buy a new plot in the cemetery, a plot all for himself. "And I'll buy one on a corner," he added triumphantly, "where I can get out!"

Mother looked at him, startled but admiring, and whispered to me, "I almost believe he could do it."
Life with Father [1935]

ROBERT FROST
1874–1963

I'm going out to clean the pasture spring;
I'll only stop to rake the leaves away
(And wait to watch the water clear, I may):
I shan't be gone long. — You come too. *The Pasture, st. 1*

They would not find me changed from him they knew —
Only more sure of all I thought was true.
Into My Own [1913], *st. 4*

Ah, when to the heart of man
Was it ever less than a treason
To go with the drift of things,
To yield with a grace to reason,

[1] See *Matthew 5:34*, p. 40b; Pope, p. 408a; and H. G. Wells, p. 888b.

And bow and accept the end
  Of a love or a season? [1]
            Reluctance [1913], st. 4

Something there is that doesn't love a
  wall.   *Mending Wall* [1914]

My apple trees will never get across
And eat the cones under his pines, I tell
  him.
He only says, "Good fences make good
  neighbors."   *Ib.*

Before I built a wall I'd ask to know
What I was walling in or walling out. [2]
                                   Ib.

And nothing to look backward to with
  pride,
And nothing to look forward to with
  hope.
        The Death of the Hired Man
                            [1914]

Home is the place where, when you
  have to go there,
They have to take you in.   *Ib.*

        The nearest friends can go
With anyone to death, comes so far
  short
They might as well not try to go at
  all.   *Home Burial* [1914]

Most of the change we think we see in
  life
Is due to truths being in and out of
  favor.
        The Black Cottage [1914]

The blue's but a mist from the breath
  of the wind,
A tarnish that goes at a touch of the
  hand.   *Blueberries* [1914]

The best way out is always through.
        A Servant to Servants [1914]

This sleep of mine, whatever sleep it is.
Were he not gone,
The woodchuck could say whether it's
  like his
Long sleep, as I describe its coming on,
Or just some human sleep.
        After Apple-Picking [1914]

[1] See Pope, p. 412b.
[2] See Chesterton, p. 919a.

Pressed into service means pressed out
  of shape.
            The Self-Seeker [1914]

I shall be telling this with a sigh
Somewhere ages and ages hence:
Two roads diverged in a wood, and
  I —
I took the one less traveled by,
And that has made all the difference.
        The Road Not Taken [1916], st. 4

        The Hyla breed
That shouted in the mist a month ago,
Like ghost of sleighbells in a ghost of
  snow.   *Hyla Brook* [1916]

We love the things we love for what
  they are.   *Ib.*

I'd like to get away from earth awhile
And then come back to it and begin
  over.
May no fate willfully misunderstand
  me
And half grant what I wish and snatch
  me away
Not to return. Earth's the right place
  for love:
I don't know where it's likely to go better.   *Birches* [1916]

One could do worse than be a swinger
  of birches.   *Ib.*

I wonder about the trees:
Why do we wish to bear
Forever the noise of these
More than another noise
So close to our dwelling place?
        The Sound of the Trees [1916]

I shall set forth for somewhere,
I shall make the reckless choice
Some say when they are in voice
And tossing so as to scare
The white clouds over them on.
I shall have less to say,
But I shall be gone.   *Ib.*

I met a Californian who would
Talk California — a state so blessed,
He said, in climate, none had ever died
  there
A natural death.
            New Hampshire [1923]

Do you know,
Considering the market, there are
      more
Poems produced than any other thing?
No wonder poets sometimes have to
      seem
So much more businesslike than busi-
      nessmen.
Their wares are so much harder to get
      rid of.   *New Hampshire*

Anything I can say about New
      Hampshire
Will serve almost as well about Ver-
      mont,
Excepting that they differ in their
      mountains.
The Vermont mountains stretch ex-
      tended straight;
New Hampshire mountains curl up in a
      coil.   *Ib.*

The snake stood up for evil in the Gar-
      den.   *The Ax-Helve* [1923]

Why make so much of fragmentary
      blue
In here and there a bird, or butterfly,
Or flower, or wearing-stone, or open
      eye,
When heaven presents in sheets the
      solid hue?
      Fragmentary Blue [1923], *st. 1*

Some say the world will end in fire,
Some say in ice.
From what I've tasted of desire
I hold with those who favor fire.
But if it had to perish twice,
I think I know enough of hate
To say that for destruction ice
Is also great
And would suffice.
      Fire and Ice [1] [1923]

The way a crow
Shook down on me
The dust of snow
From a hemlock tree

Has given my heart
A change of mood

[1] See Dante, p. 159b, and Housman, p. 853a.

And saved some part
Of a day I had rued.
      Dust of Snow [1923]

We heard the miniature thunder where
      he fled.   *The Runaway* [1923]

Whose woods these are I think I
      know.
His house is in the village though;
He will not see me stopping here
To watch his woods fill up with snow.
      Stopping by Woods on a Snowy
      Evening [1923], *st. 1*

My little horse must think it queer
To stop without a farmhouse near.
                          Ib. st. 2

He gives his harness bells a shake
To ask if there is some mistake.
                          Ib. st. 3

The woods are lovely, dark and deep.
But I have promises to keep,
And miles to go before I sleep.[1]
                          Ib. st. 4

Love at the lips was touch
As sweet as I could bear;
And once that seemed too much;
I lived on air.
      To Earthward [1923], *st. 1*

Now no joy but lacks salt
That is not dashed with pain
And weariness and fault;
I crave the stain

Of tears, the aftermark
Of almost too much love,
The sweet of bitter bark
And burning clove.   *Ib. st. 5, 6*

Keep cold, young orchard. Goodbye
      and keep cold.
Dread fifty above more than fifty be-
      low.
      Goodbye and Keep Cold [1923]

Heaven gives its glimpses only to those
Not in position to look too close.
      A Passing Glimpse [1928]

[1] The stars look very cold about the sky,
      And I have many miles on foot to fare.
            KEATS, *Keen, fitful gusts are whispering*
                  here and there [*1817*]

Tree at my window, window tree,
My sash is lowered when night comes
    on;
But let there never be curtain drawn
Between you and me.
        Tree at My Window [1928], *st. 1*

That day she put our heads together,
Fate had her imagination about her,
Your head so much concerned with
    outer,
Mine with inner, weather.   *Ib. st. 4*

It looked as if a night of dark intent
Was coming, and not only a night, an
    age.
Someone had better be prepared for
    rage.
There would be more than ocean-water
    broken
Before God's last *Put out the Light* was
    spoken.
        Once by the Pacific [1928]

I have been one acquainted with the
    night.
    Acquainted with the Night [1928]

If, as they say, some dust thrown in my
    eyes
Will keep my talk from getting over-
    wise,
I'm not the one for putting off the
    proof.
Let it be overwhelming.
        Dust in the Eyes [1928]

Don't join too many gangs. Join few if
    any.
Join the United States and join the
    family —
But not much in between unless a col-
    lege.   *Build Soil* [1932]

The sun was warm but the wind was
    chill.
You know how it is with an April day
When the sun is out and the wind is
    still,
You're one month on in the middle of
    May.
But if you so much as dare to speak,
A cloud comes over the sunlit arch,
A wind comes off a frozen peak,

And you're two months back in the
    middle of March.
        Two Tramps in Mud Time
            [1936], *st. 3*

But yield who will to their separation,
My object in living is to unite
My avocation and my vocation
As my two eyes make one in sight.
Only where love and need are one,
And the work is play for mortal stakes,
Is the deed ever really done
For Heaven and the future's sakes.
        Ib. st. 9

No memory of having starred
Atones for later disregard,
Or keeps the end from being hard.

Better to go down dignified
With boughten friendship by your side
Than none at all. Provide, provide! [1]
        Provide, Provide, st. 6, 7

I never dared be radical when young
For fear it would make me conservative
    when old.   *Precaution* [1936]

Never ask of money spent
Where the spender thinks it went.
Nobody was ever meant
To remember or invent
What he did with every cent.
        The Hardship of Accounting
            [1936]

The land was ours before we were the
    land's.
She was our land more than a hundred
    years
Before we were her people.
        The Gift Outright [1941] [2]

Happiness Makes Up in Height for
What It Lacks in Length.
        Title of poem [1942]

Far in the pillared dark
Thrush music went —
Almost like a call to come in
To the dark and lament.

[1] See Samuel Johnson, p. 432b.
[2] Read first before the Phi Beta Kappa Society
at William and Mary College [December 5, 1941],
later at the inauguration of President John
F. Kennedy [January 20, 1961].

But no, I was out for stars:
I would not come in.
I meant not even if asked,
And I hadn't been.
                    Come In [1942], *st. 4, 5*

And were an epitaph to be my story
I'd have a short one ready for my own.
I would have written of me on my
stone:
I had a lover's quarrel with the world.
                The Lesson for Today [1942]

We dance round in a ring and suppose,
But the Secret sits in the middle and
knows.   *The Secret Sits* [1945]

Here are your waters and your watering
place.
Drink and be whole again beyond confusion.
                            Directive [1947]

        Any eye is an evil eye
That looks in on to a mood apart.
                    A Mood Apart [1947]

It asks a little of us here.
It asks of us a certain height,
So when at times the mob is swayed
To carry praise or blame too far,
We may take something like a star
To stay our minds on and be staid.
            Take Something Like a Star [1949]

Forgive, O Lord, my little jokes on
Thee
And I'll forgive Thy great big one on
me.
                From In the Clearing [1962]

Have I not walked without an upward
look
Of caution under stars that very well
Might not have missed me when they
shot and fell?
It was a risk I had to take — and took.
                            Bravado [1962]

I am assured at any rate
Man's practically inexterminate.
Someday I must go into that.
There's always been an Ararat
Where someone someone else begat
To start the world all over at.
                    A-Wishing Well [1962]

It takes all sorts of in and outdoor
schooling
To get adapted to my kind of fooling.
                    It Takes All Sorts [1962]

Unless I'm wrong
I but obey
The urge of a song:
I'm — bound — away! [1]

And I may return
If dissatisfied
With what I learn
From having died.
                    Away! [1962], *st. 5, 6*

It is absurd to think that the only
way to tell if a poem is lasting is to wait
and see if it lasts. The right reader of a
good poem can tell the moment it
strikes him that he has taken an immortal wound — that he will never get
over it.[2]
            The Poetry of Amy Lowell.
            From the Christian Science
            Monitor [May 16, 1925]

A poem . . . begins as a lump in the
throat, a sense of wrong, a homesickness,
a lovesickness. . . . It finds the thought
and the thought finds the words.
            Letter to Louis Untermeyer
                    [January 1, 1916]

Everything written is as good as it is
dramatic. It need not declare itself in
form, but it is drama or nothing.
                A Way Out [1929], *preface*

It should be of the pleasure of a poem
itself to tell how it can. The figure a
poem makes. It begins in delight and
ends in wisdom. The figure is the same
for love.
            The Figure a Poem Makes,
            preface to Collected Poems
            [1939]

No tears in the writer, no tears in the
reader.[3]   *Ib.*

Like a piece of ice on a hot stove
the poem must ride on its own melt-

---

[1] See *Shenandoah* (chantey), p. 1101a.
[2] See Coleridge, p. 528b; also see *The Figure a Poem Makes*, this column.
[3] See Charles Churchill, p. 456a, and note.

ing. . . . Read it a hundred times; it will forever keep its freshness as a metal keeps its fragrance. It can never lose its sense of a meaning that once unfolded by surprise as it went.[1]
> *The Figure a Poem Makes,*
> *preface to Collected Poems*

How many times it thundered before Franklin took the hint! How many apples fell on Newton's head before he took the hint! Nature is always hinting at us. It hints over and over again. And suddenly we take the hint.
> *Comment*

It is only a moment here and a moment there that the greatest writer has. *Ib.*

Love is an irresistible desire to be irresistibly desired. *Ib.*

Poetry is a way of taking life by the throat. *Ib.*

Talking is a hydrant in the yard and writing is a faucet upstairs in the house. Opening the first takes all the pressure off the second. *Ib.*

The greatest thing in family life is to take a hint when a hint is intended — and not to take a hint when a hint isn't intended. *Ib.*

Always fall in with what you're asked to accept. Take what is given, and make it over your way. My aim in life has always been to hold my own with whatever's going. Not against: with.
> *Ib.*

There's absolutely no reason for being rushed along with the rush. Everybody should be free to go very slow. . . . What you want, what you're hanging around in the world waiting for, is for something to occur to you. [*March 21, 1954*]

Education is . . . hanging around until you've caught on.
> [*January 30, 1963*]

[1] See Coleridge, p. 528b, and Frost, *The Poetry of Amy Lowell,* p. 929b.

ELLEN GLASGOW
1874–1945

Preserve, within a wild sanctuary, an inaccessible valley of reveries.
> *A Certain Measure* [*1943*]

Tilling the fertile soil of man's vanity. *Ib.*

HARRY GRAHAM
1874–1936

Billy, in one of his nice new sashes,
Fell in the fire and was burnt to ashes;
Now, although the room grows chilly,
I haven't the heart to poke poor Billy.
> *Ruthless Rhymes for Heartless Homes* [*1899*]. *Tenderheartedness*

HERBERT CLARK HOOVER
1874–1964

I do not favor the repeal of the Eighteenth Amendment. . . . Our country has deliberately undertaken a great social and economic experiment,[1] noble in motive, far-reaching in purpose.   *Speech* [*August 1928*]

The American system of rugged individualism.[2]
> *Campaign speech, New York*
> [*October 22, 1928*]

Conditions are fundamentally sound.
> *Speech* [*December 1929*]

The fundamental strength of the nation's economy is unimpaired.
> *Message to Congress* [*December 2, 1930*]

[1] Hoover used the phrase also in a letter to Senator William E. Borah [February 28, 1928].
[2] While I can make no claim for having introduced the term "rugged individualism," I should be proud to have invented it. It has been used by American leaders for over a half-century in eulogy of those God-fearing men and women of honesty whose stamina and character and fearless assertion of rights led them to make their own way in life. — HOOVER, *The Challenge to Liberty* [1934], *ch. 5*

The grass will grow in the streets of a hundred cities.

> Speech [October 31, 1932]

A good many things go around in the dark besides Santa Claus.

> Address, John Marshall Republican Club, St. Louis, Missouri [December 16, 1935]

Older men declare war. But it is youth that must fight and die. And it is youth who must inherit the tribulation, the sorrow, and the triumphs that are the aftermath of war.[1]

> Speech, Republican National Convention, Chicago [June 27, 1944]

HAROLD L. ICKES
1874–1952

I am against government by crony.

> On resigning as Secretary of the Interior [February 1946]

HEWLETT JOHNSON
1874–1966

Nothing is better calculated to drive men to desperation than when, in attempting to carry out beneficial reform, they find the whole world aligned against them. The more especially so if amongst those so aligned they discover men who had preached the same ideal, but now dreaded its concrete realization.

> The Soviet Power: The Socialist Sixth of the World [1940], bk. II, ch. 3

W. L. MACKENZIE KING[2]
1874–1950

Labor can do nothing without capital, capital nothing without labor, and neither labor nor capital can do anything without the guiding genius of management; and management, however wise its genius may be, can do nothing without the privileges which the community affords.

> Canadian Club Speech, Montreal [March 17, 1919]

Government, in the last analysis, is organized opinion. Where there is little or no public opinion, there is likely to be bad government, which sooner or later becomes autocratic government.

> Message of the Carillon [1927]

AMY LOWELL
1874–1925

A pattern called a war.
Christ! What are patterns for?

> Patterns

Sappho would speak, I think, quite openly,
And Mrs. Browning guard a careful silence,
But Emily would set doors ajar and slam them
And love you for your speed of observation. The Sisters

You are beautiful and faded,
Like an old opera tune
Played upon a harpsichord. A Lady

Heart-leaves of lilac all over New England,[1]
Roots of lilac under all the soil of New England,
Lilac in me because I am New England. Lilacs

WILLIAM SOMERSET MAUGHAM
1874–1965

Like all weak men he laid an exaggerated stress on not changing one's mind.

> Of Human Bondage [1915], ch. 39

People ask you for criticism, but they only want praise. Ib. 50

[1] See Grantland Rice, p. 962a.
[2] See Truman, Joint Declaration, p. 982b.

[1] Stands the lilac bush tall-growing with heart-shaped leaves of rich green.
WALT WHITMAN, When Lilacs Last in the Dooryard Bloomed [1865–1866]

There is nothing so degrading as the constant anxiety about one's means of livelihood. . . . Money is like a sixth sense without which you cannot make a complete use of the other five.
Of Human Bondage, ch. 51

The mystic sees the ineffable, and the psychopathologist the unspeakable.
The Moon and Sixpence [1919], *ch. 1*

I forget who it was that recommended men for their soul's good to do each day two things they disliked [1] . . . it is a precept that I have followed scrupulously; for every day I have got up and I have gone to bed. *Ib. 2*

Impropriety is the soul of wit.[2]
Ib. 4

Conscience is the guardian in the individual of the rules which the community has evolved for its own preservation. *Ib. 14*

Do you know that conversation is one of the greatest pleasures in life? But it wants leisure.
The Trembling of a Leaf [1921], *ch. 3*

The tragedy of love is indifference.
Ib. 4

I would sooner read a timetable or a catalogue than nothing at all. They are much more entertaining than half the novels that are written.
The Summing Up [1938]

If a nation values anything more than freedom, it will lose its freedom; and the irony of it is that if it is comfort or money that it values more, it will lose that too.
Strictly Personal [1941], *ch. 31*

As mean as cat's meat.
From THOMAS F. BRADY, *The Eighty Years of Mr. Maugham, New York Times Magazine* [*January 24, 1954*]

[1] See William James, p. 793a, and T. H. Huxley, p. 725a.
[2] See Shakespeare, p. 260b.

As far as I can judge, with women it is all take and no give. There must be some women who are not liars.
From Time [*October 17, 1960*]

ALICE DUER MILLER
1874–1942

The white cliffs of Dover, I saw rising steeply
Out of the sea that once made her [England] secure.
The White Cliffs [1940]

I am American bred,
I have seen much to hate here — much to forgive,
But in a world where England is finished and dead,
I do not wish to live. *Ib.*

PAUL RICHARD
1874–

The vagabond, when rich, is called a tourist.
The Scourge of Christ [1929]

JOHN DAVISON ROCKEFELLER, JR.
1874–1960

I believe that every right implies a responsibility; every opportunity, an obligation; every possession, a duty.
Ten Principles: Address in behalf of United Service Organizations, New York [*July 8, 1941*]

ROBERT WILLIAM SERVICE
1874–1958

This is the Law of the Yukon, that only the strong shall thrive;
That surely the weak shall perish, and only the fit survive.[1]
Dissolute, damned and despairful, crippled and palsied and slain,

[1] Now this is the Law of the Jungle — as old and as true as the sky;
And the Wolf that shall keep it may prosper, but the Wolf that shall break it must die.
KIPLING, *The Law of the Jungle* [1895]

This is the Will of the Yukon — Lo,
how she makes it plain!
The Law of the Yukon

Back of the bar, in a solo game, sat
Dangerous Dan McGrew,
And watching his luck was his light-o'-
love, the lady that's known as
Lou.
The Shooting of Dan McGrew,
st. 1

The Northern Lights have seen queer
sights,
But the queerest they ever did see
Was that night on the marge of Lake
Lebarge
I cremated Sam McGee.
The Cremation of Sam McGee,
st. 1

A promise made is a debt unpaid.
Ib. st. 8

Fate has written a tragedy; its name is
"The Human Heart."
The theater is the house of life,
Woman the mummer's part;
The Devil enters the prompter's box
and the play is ready to start.
The Harpy, st. 12

When we, the workers, all demand:
"What are we fighting for?" . . .
Then, then we'll end that stupid crime,
that devil's madness — War.
Michael

GERTRUDE STEIN
1874–1946

Rose is a rose is a rose is a rose.
Sacred Emily [written 1913]

You are all a lost generation.[1]
Used by Ernest Hemingway as
an epigraph for The Sun Also
Rises [1926]

Pigeons on the grass alas.
Four Saints in Three Acts
[written 1927]

---

[1] Hemingway states that the remark was originally made by a garage owner in the Midi to
Gertrude Stein in reference to his young mechanics, who were "une génération perdue."

Before the Flowers of Friendship
Faded Friendship Faded.
Title [written 1930]

Remarks are not literature [said to
Hemingway].
The Autobiography of Alice B.
Toklas [written 1930]

America is my country and Paris is
my home town and it is as it has come
to be. After all anybody is as their land
and air is. Anybody is as the sky is low
or high, the air heavy or clear and anybody is as there is wind or no wind
there. It is that which makes them and
the arts they make and the work they
do and the way they eat and the way
they drink and the way they learn and
everything.
And so I am an American and I have
lived half my life in Paris, not the half
that made me but the half in which I
made what I made.
An American and France [1936]

In the United States there is more
space where nobody is than where anybody is.
This is what makes America what it
is.
The Geographical History of
America [1936]

What is the answer? [*I was silent.*]
In that case, what is the question?
Last words. From ALICE B.
TOKLAS, *What Is Remem-*
bered [1963]

TRUMBULL STICKNEY
1874–1904

Be still. The Hanging Gardens were a
dream.   *Be Still [1905]*

It's autumn in the country I remember.
Mnemosyne

The swallows veering skimmed the
golden grain
At midday with a wing aslant and
limber;
And yellow cattle browsed upon the
plain.   *Ib.*

We sang together in the woods at night.　　　*Mnemosyne*

HARRY WILLIAMS
1874–1924

It's a long way to Tipperary, it's a long
　way to go;
It's a long way to Tipperary, to the
　sweetest girl I know!
Goodbye, Piccadilly, farewell, Leicester
　Square,
It's a long, long way to Tipperary, but
　my heart's right there!
　　　Tipperary [1908] [1]

In the Shade of the Old Apple
Tree.　　　*Title of song* [1]

EDMUND CLERIHEW [2]
BENTLEY
1875–1956

Sir Christopher Wren
Said "I am going to dine with some
　men.
If anybody calls
Say I am designing St. Paul's."
　　　*Biography for Beginners. Sir
　　　Christopher Wren*

John Stuart Mill
By a mighty effort of will
Overcame his natural bonhomie
And wrote *Principles of Political Econ-
omy.*　　　*Ib. John Stuart Mill*

George the Third
Ought never to have occurred.
One can only wonder
At so grotesque a blunder.[3]
　　　Ib. George III

---

[1] Set to music by JACK JUDGE [1878–1938]
[2] A quatrain in the form Bentley popularized
is known as a clerihew.
[3] George the First was always reckoned
　Vile, but viler George the Second;
　And what mortal ever heard
　Any good of George the Third?
　When from earth the Fourth descended
　God be praised, the Georges ended!
　　WALTER SAVAGE LANDOR, *Epigram after
　　hearing* THACKERAY'S *lectures on the four
　　Georges* [1855]

What I like about Clive
Is that he is no longer alive.
There is a great deal to be said
For being dead.
　　　Biography for Beginners. Clive

JOHN BUCHAN,
LORD TWEEDSMUIR
1875–1940

We can only pay our debt to the past
by putting the future in debt to ourselves.
　　　*Address to the people of Canada,
　　　on the coronation of George VI
　　　[May 12, 1937]*

He [Raymond Asquith] disliked
emotion, not because he felt lightly but
because he felt deeply. He most sincerely loved his country, but he loved
her too much to identify her with the
pasteboard goddess of the music halls
and the hustings. . . . Austerely self-
respecting, he had been used to hide his
devotions under a mask of indifference,
and would never reveal them except in
deeds.

Our roll of honor is long, but it holds
no nobler figure. He will stand to those
of us who are left as an incarnation of
the spirit of the land he loved. . . .
He loved his youth, and his youth has
become eternal.
　　　Pilgrim's Way [1940]

Democracy — the essential thing as
distinguished from this or that democratic government — was primarily an
attitude of mind, a spiritual testament,
and not an economic structure or a
political machine. The testament involved certain basic beliefs — that the
personality was sacrosanct, which was
the meaning of liberty; that policy
should be settled by free discussion;
that normally a minority should be
ready to yield to a majority, which in
turn should respect a minority's sacred
things.

Public life is regarded as the crown of
a career, and to young men it is the
worthiest ambition. Politics is still the
greatest and the most honorable adventure.　　　*Ib.*

ZANE GREY
1875–1939

We'll use a signal I have tried and found far-reaching and easy to yell. Waa-hoo!
The Last of the Plainsmen, ch. 4

CARL GUSTAV JUNG
1875–1961

The dynamic principle of fantasy is play, which belongs also to the child, and as such it appears to be inconsistent with the principle of serious work. But without this playing with fantasy no creative work has ever yet come to birth. The debt we owe to the play of imagination is incalculable.
Psychological Types [1923], *ch. 1, p. 82*

The great problems of life — sexuality, of course, among others — are always related to the primordial images of the collective unconscious. These images are really balancing or compensating factors which correspond with the problems life presents in actuality. This is not to be marveled at, since these images are deposits representing the accumulated experience of thousands of years of struggle for adaptation and existence. *Ib. ch. 5, p. 271*

We should not pretend to understand the world only by the intellect; we apprehend it just as much by feeling. Therefore the judgment of the intellect is, at best, only the half of truth, and must, if it be honest, also come to an understanding of its inadequacy. *Ib. conclusion, p. 628*

The woman is increasingly aware that love alone can give her her full stature, just as the man begins to discern that spirit alone can endow his life with its highest meaning. Fundamentally, therefore, both seek a psychic relation one to the other, because love needs the spirit, and the spirit love, for their fulfillment.
Contributions to Analytical Psychology [1928], *p. 185*

Seldom, or perhaps never, does a marriage develop into an individual relationship smoothly and without crises; there is no coming to consciousness without pain.
Contributions to Analytical Psychology, p. 193

In studying the history of the human mind one is impressed again and again by the fact that the growth of the mind is the widening of the range of consciousness, and that each step forward has been a most painful and laborious achievement. *Ib. p. 340*

The meeting of two personalities is like the contact of two chemical substances: if there is any reaction, both are transformed.
Modern Man in Search of a Soul [1933], *p. 57*

The great decisions of human life have as a rule far more to do with the instincts and other mysterious unconscious factors than with conscious will and well-meaning reasonableness. The shoe that fits one person pinches another; there is no recipe for living that suits all cases. Each of us carries his own life-form — an indeterminable form which cannot be superseded by any other. *Ib. p. 69*

Aging people should know that their lives are not mounting and unfolding but that an inexorable inner process forces the contraction of life. For a young person it is almost a sin — and certainly a danger — to be too much occupied with himself; but for the aging person it is a duty and a necessity to give serious attention to himself.
Ib. p. 125

All ages before ours believed in gods in some form or other. Only an unparalleled impoverishment in symbolism could enable us to rediscover the gods as psychic factors, which is to say, as archetypes of the unconscious. No doubt this discovery is hardly credible as yet.
The Integration of the Personality [1939], *p. 72*

If there is anything that we wish to change in the child, we should first examine it and see whether it is not something that could better be changed in ourselves.

The Integration of the Personality, p. 285

The conscious mind allows itself to be trained like a parrot, but the unconscious does not — which is why St. Augustine thanked God for not making him responsible for his dreams.

Psychology and Alchemy [1953], *p. 51*

The unconscious is not just evil by nature, it is also the source of the highest good: not only dark but also light, not only bestial, semihuman, and demonic but superhuman, spiritual, and, in the classical sense of the word, "divine."

The Practice of Psychotherapy [1953], *p. 364*

The little world of childhood with its familiar surroundings is a model of the greater world. The more intensively the family has stamped its character upon the child, the more it will tend to feel and see its earlier miniature world again in the bigger world of adult life. Naturally this is not a conscious, intellectual process.

From Psychological Reflections: A Jung Anthology [1] [1953], *p. 83: Collected Works, vol. 4 The Theory of Psychoanalysis* [1913]

This whole creation is essentially subjective, and the dream is the theater where the dreamer is at once scene, actor, prompter, stage manager, author, audience, and critic.

Ib. p. 58: vol. 8, General Aspects of Dream Psychology [1928]

The dream is the small hidden door in the deepest and most intimate sanctum of the soul, which opens into that primeval cosmic night that was soul long before there was a conscious

[1] Edited by Jolande Jacobi.

ego and will be soul far beyond what a conscious ego could ever reach.

From Psychological Reflections: A Jung Anthology, p. 46: vol. 10, The Meaning of Psychology for Modern Man [1934]

Emotion is the chief source of all becoming-conscious. There can be no transforming of darkness into light and of apathy into movement without emotion.

Ib. p. 32: vol. 9, Psychological Aspects of the Modern Archetype [1938]

No one can flatter himself that he is immune to the spirit of his own epoch, or even that he possesses a full understanding of it. Irrespective of our conscious convictions, each one of us, without exception, being a particle of the general mass, is somewhere attached to, colored by, or even undermined by the spirit which goes through the mass. Freedom stretches only as far as the limits of our consciousness.

Ib. p. 143: vol. 15, Paracelsus the Physician [1942]

Where love rules, there is no will to power; and where power predominates, there love is lacking. The one is the shadow of the other.

Ib. p. 87: vol. 7, The Psychology of the Unconscious [1943]

The erotic instinct is something questionable, and will always be so whatever a future set of laws may have to say on the matter. It belongs, on the one hand, to the original animal nature of man, which will exist as long as man has an animal body. On the other hand, it is connected with the highest forms of the spirit. But it blooms only when spirit and instinct are in true harmony. If one or the other aspect is missing, then an injury occurs, or at least there is a one-sided lack of balance which easily slips into the pathological. Too much of the animal disfigures the civilized human being, too much culture makes a sick animal.

Ib. p. 93

THOMAS MANN
1875–1955

We are most likely to get angry and excited in our opposition to some idea when we ourselves are not quite certain of our own position, and are inwardly tempted to take the other side.

Buddenbrooks [1903], *pt. VIII,*
ch. 2

Beauty can pierce one like a pain.
Ib. XI, 2

Space, like time, engenders forgetfulness; but it does so by setting us bodily free from our surroundings and giving us back our primitive, unattached state. . . . Time, we say, is Lethe; but change of air is a similar draught, and, if it works less thoroughly, does so more quickly.

The Magic Mountain [1924],[1]
ch. 1

A man lives not only his personal life, as an individual, but also, consciously or unconsciously, the life of his epoch and his contemporaries.   *Ib. 2*

The only religious way to think of death is as part and parcel of life; to regard it, with the understanding and the emotions, as the inviolable condition of life.   *Ib. 5*

Time has no divisions to mark its passage, there is never a thunderstorm or blare of trumpets to announce the beginning of a new month or year. Even when a new century begins it is only we mortals who ring bells and fire off pistols.   *Ib.*

Order and simplification are the first steps toward the mastery of a subject — the actual enemy is the unknown.
Ib.

Human reason needs only to will more strongly than fate, and she *is* fate.   *Ib. 6*

Opinions cannot survive if one has no chance to fight for them.   *Ib.*

[1] Translated by H. T. Lowe-Porter.

All interest in disease and death is only another expression of interest in life.

The Magic Mountain, ch. 6

The invention of printing and the Reformation are and remain the two outstanding services of central Europe to the cause of humanity.   *Ib.*

Speech is civilization itself. The word, even the most contradictory word, preserves contact — it is silence which isolates.   *Ib.*

A man's dying is more the survivors' affair than his own.   *Ib.*

What we call mourning for our dead is perhaps not so much grief at not being able to call them back as it is grief at not being able to want to do so.   *Ib. 7*

Time cools, time clarifies; no mood can be maintained quite unaltered through the course of hours.   *Ib.*

Seven is a good handy figure in its way, picturesque, with a savor of the mythical; one might say that it is more filling to the spirit than a dull academic half-dozen.   *Ib.*

In the Word is involved the unity of humanity, the wholeness of the human problem, which permits nobody to separate the intellectual and artistic from the political and social, and to isolate himself within the ivory tower of the "cultural" proper.

Letter [1] *to the dean of the Philosophical Faculty, Bonn University* [*January 1937*]

Hold fast the time! Guard it, watch over it, every hour, every minute! Unregarded it slips away, like a lizard, smooth, slippery, faithless, a pixy wife. Hold every moment sacred. Give each clarity and meaning, each the weight of thine awareness, each its true and due fulfillment.

The Beloved Returns [1939]

[1] Mann, who had left Germany in 1933, wrote from Zurich, after being informed that his name had been struck off the list of Honorary Doctors.

HUGHES MEARNS
1875–1965

As I was going up the stair
I met a man who wasn't there.
He wasn't there again today.
I wish, I wish he'd stay away.
The Psychoed

HASEGAWA NYOZEKAN [1]
1875–

We must direct our efforts towards turning in the reverse direction the cultural nature of the Japanese, which hitherto has had a propensity for the intuitive, until it shows instead a propensity for the intellectual.
The Lost Japan [1952]

The war was started as the result of a mistaken intuitive "calculation" which transcended mathematics. We believed with a blind fervor that we could triumph over scientific weapons and tactics by means of our mystic will. . . . The characteristic reliance on intuition by Japanese had blocked the objective cognition of the modern world.   *Ib.*

FRANK WARD O'MALLEY
1875–1932

Life is just one damned thing after another.[2]
Attributed. (Also attributed to Elbert Hubbard)

RAINER MARIA RILKE
1875–1926

Her smile was not meant to be seen by anyone and served its whole purpose in being smiled.
The Journal of My Other Self [3]

He was a poet and hated the approximate.   *Ib.*

[1] From *Sources of Japanese Tradition*, edited by William Theodore de Bary [1960].
[2] The phrase probably precedes both O'Malley and Hubbard.
[3] Translated by JOHN LINTON [1930].

Love consists in this, that two solitudes protect and touch and greet each other.
Letters to a Young Poet [1]

The future enters into us, in order to transform itself in us, long before it happens.   *Ib.*

We're never single-minded, unperplexed, like migratory birds.
The Duino Elegies, 4

The most visible joy can only reveal itself to us when we've transformed it, within.   *Ib.* 7

Death is the side of life which is turned away from us.
Letter to W. von Hulewicz

A good marriage is that in which each appoints the other guardian of his solitude.   *Letters* [2]

Once the realization is accepted that even between the *closest* human beings infinite distances continue to exist, a wonderful living side by side can grow up, if they succeed in loving the distance between them which makes it possible for each to see the other whole against the sky.   *Ib.*

In the difficult are the friendly forces, the hands that work on us.
Ib.

Works of art are indeed always products of having been in danger, of having gone to the very end in an experience, to where man can go no further.   *Ib.*

RAFAEL SABATINI
1875–1950

Born with the gift of laughter and the sense that the world was mad,[3] and that was his only patrimony.
Scaramouche, ch. 1

[1] Translated by M. D. HERTER NORTON [1934].
[2] Translated by JANE BARNARD GREENE and M. D. HERTER NORTON.
[3] Inscribed over a door in the Hall of Graduate Studies, Yale University. The architect, John Donald Tuttle, explained in a letter in *The New Yorker* [December 8, 1934] his recoiling from

ALBERT SCHWEITZER
1875–1965

Late on the third day, at the very moment when, at sunset, we were making our way through a herd of hippopotamuses, there flashed upon my mind, unforeseen and unsought, the phrase, "Reverence for Life."[1] . . . Now I had found my way to the idea in which affirmation of the world and ethics are contained side by side; now I knew that the ethical acceptance of the world and of life, together with the ideals of civilization contained in this concept, has a foundation in thought.
Out of My Life and Thought [1949]

Affirmation of life is the spiritual act by which man ceases to live unreflectively and begins to devote himself to his life with reverence in order to raise it to its true value. To affirm life is to deepen, to make more inward, and to exalt the will to live. **Ib.**

Truth has no special time of its own. Its hour is now — always. **Ib.**

You don't live in a world all alone. Your brothers are here too.
On Receiving the Nobel Prize [1952]

JOEL ELIAS SPINGARN
1875–1939

The gibe of European scholars that there are three sexes in America — men, women, and professors.
Creative Criticism and Other Essays [1931]

RIDGELY TORRENCE
1875–1950

Of all the languages of earth in which the human kind confer

collegiate Gothic, "a type of architecture that had been designed expressly . . . to enable yeomen to pour molten lead through slots on their enemies below. As a propitiatory gift to my gods . . . and to make them forget by appealing to their senses of humor, I carved the inscription over the door."
[1] See W. E. Channing, p. 544a.

The Master Speaker is the Tear: it is the Great Interpreter.
The House of a Hundred Lights. The Conclusion of the Whole Matter

SHERWOOD ANDERSON
1876–1941

Everyone in the world is Christ and they are all crucified.
Winesburg, Ohio [1919]. *The Philosopher*

I am a lover and have not found my thing to love. **Ib.** *Tandy*

WILLA SIBERT CATHER
1876–1947

No one can build his security upon the nobleness of another person.
Alexander's Bridge [1912], *ch. 8*

There are only two or three human stories, and they go on repeating themselves as fiercely as if they had never happened before.
O Pioneers! [1913], *pt. II, ch. 4*

The history of every country begins in the heart of a man or a woman. **Ib.**

I like trees because they seem more resigned to the way they have to live than other things do. **Ib.** 8

I tell you there is such a thing as creative hate!
The Song of the Lark [1915], *pt. I*

Artistic growth is, more than it is anything else, a refining of the sense of truthfulness. The stupid believe that to be truthful is easy; only the artist, the great artist, knows how difficult it is. **Ib.** VI

That is happiness; to be dissolved into something complete and great.[1]
My Antonia [2] [1918], *bk. I, ch. 2*

[1] Inscribed on Willa Cather's grave in Jaffrey, New Hampshire.
[2] It lifts me to all my superlatives. — OLIVER WENDELL HOLMES, JR., *letter to Ferris Greenslet*

Winter lies too long in country towns; hangs on until it is stale and shabby, old and sullen.

My Antonia, bk. II, ch. 7

Art, it seems to me, should simplify. That, indeed, is very nearly the whole of the higher artistic process; finding what conventions of form and what detail one can do without and yet preserve the spirit of the whole — so that all that one has suppressed and cut away is there to the reader's consciousness as much as if it were in type on the page.

On the Art of Fiction [1920]

That irregular and intimate quality of things made entirely by the human hand.

Death Comes for the Archbishop [1927], bk. I, ch. 3

In New Mexico he always awoke a young man. . . . He had noticed that this peculiar quality in the air of new countries vanished after they were tamed by man and made to bear harvests . . . that lightness, that dry aromatic odor . . . one could breathe that only on the bright edges of the world, on the great grass plains or the sagebrush desert. . . . Something soft and wild and free; something that whispered to the ear on the pillow, lightened the heart, softly, softly picked the lock, slid the bolts, and released the prisoned spirit of man into the wind, into the blue and gold, into the morning, into the morning! [1]

Ib. IX, 3

Only solitary men know the full joys of friendship. Others have their family; but to a solitary and an exile his friends are everything.

Shadows on the Rock [1931], bk. III, ch. 5

[1] The moment I saw the brilliant proud morning shine high up over the deserts of Santa Fe, something stood still in my soul, and I started to attend. . . . In the magnificent fierce morning of New Mexico one sprang awake, a new part of the soul woke up suddenly, and the old world gave way to a new. — D. H. LAWRENCE, *New Mexico [Survey Graphic, 1931]*

SARAH NORCLIFFE CLEGHORN
1876–1959

The golf links lie so near the mill
 That almost every day
The laboring children can look out
And watch the men at play.

Quatrain [1915]

IRVIN SHREWSBURY COBB
1876–1944

I hope it's nothing trivial.

Upon hearing that his boss, Charles S. Chapin of the New York World, was ill [c. 1910]

It smells like gangrene starting in a mildewed silo, it tastes like the wrath to come, and when you absorb a deep swig of it you have all the sensations of having swallowed a lighted kerosene lamp. A sudden, violent jolt of it has been known to stop the victim's watch, snap his suspenders and crack his glass eye right across.

Definition of "corn licker" given to the Distillers' Code Authority, NRA

CHARLES FRANKLIN KETTERING
1876–1958

A man must have a certain amount of intelligent ignorance to get anywhere.

On his seventieth birthday [August 29, 1946]

We should all be concerned about the future because we will have to spend the rest of our lives there.

Seed for Thought [1949]

MAXIM MAXIMOVICH LITVINOV
1876–1951

To strengthen the League of Nations is to abide by the principle of collective security . . . to abide by the principle that peace is indivisible.[1]

> *Speech, League of Nations, Geneva, condemning Italian aggression in Ethiopia [July 1, 1936]*

WILSON MIZNER
1876–1933

No opium-smoking in the elevators.
Sign in Hotel Rand, New York, which Mizner managed [1907]

Carry out your own dead.   *Ib.*

Life's a tough proposition, and the first hundred years are the hardest.
Saying

Be nice to people on your way up because you'll meet 'em on your way down.
> *Ib. (Also attributed to Jimmy Durante)*

When you steal from one author, it's plagiarism; if you steal from many, it's research.   *Ib.*

Treat a whore like a lady and a lady like a whore.   *Ib.*

A good listener is not only popular everywhere, but after a while he gets to know something.   *Ib.*

It's a trip through a sewer in a glass-bottomed boat.[2]
> *Comment on Hollywood*

You sparkle with larceny.   *Remark*

You're a mouse studying to be a rat.   *Ib.*

Why should I talk to you? I've just been talking to your boss.
> *On his deathbed, to a priest [1933]*

[1] In an earlier speech at the League [September 5, 1935] during the Italian preparations for the invasion, Litvinov used a similar phrase: "The thesis of the indivisibility of peace. . . . It has now become clear to the whole world that each war is the creation of a preceding war and the generator of new present or future wars."
See Haile Selassie, p. 1020a, and Wendell Willkie, p. 1025a.
[2] This was later adapted by Mayor James J. Walker as "A reformer is a guy who rides through a sewer in a glass-bottomed boat."

POPE PIUS XII
[EUGENIO PACELLI]
1876–1958

Private property is a natural fruit of labor, a product of intense activity of man, acquired through his energetic determination to ensure and develop with his own strength his own existence and that of his family, and to create for himself and his own an existence of just freedom, not only economic, but also political, cultural and religious.
> *Radio broadcast [September 1, 1944]*

If a worker is deprived of hope to acquire some personal property, what other natural stimulus can be offered him that will inspire him to hard work, labor, saving and sobriety today, when so many nations and men have lost everything and all they have left is their capacity for work?   *Ib.*

A. S. W. ROSENBACH
1876–1952

After love, book collecting is the most exhilarating sport of all.
> *A Book Hunter's Holiday [1936]*

GEORGE MACAULAY
TREVELYAN
1876–1962

A man and what he loves and builds have but a day and then disappear; nature cares not — and renews the annual round untired. It is the old law, sad but not bitter. Only when man destroys the life and beauty of nature, there is the outrage.
> *Grey of Fallodon [1937], bk. I, ch. 3*

Disinterested intellectual curiosity is the lifeblood of real civilization.
> *English Social History [1942], preface*

Education . . . has produced a vast population able to read but unable to distinguish what is worth reading.
> *Ib. ch. 18*

GRACE NOLL CROWELL
1877–1969

God wrote His loveliest poem on the day
He made the first tall silver poplar tree.
Silver Poplars, st. 1

ANTHONY EUWER
1877–

As a beauty I'm not a great star.
There are others more handsome, by far,
But my face — I don't mind it
For I am behind it;
It's the people in front get the jar.
Limeratomy [1]

ROSE FYLEMAN
1877–1957

There are fairies at the bottom of our garden!   *The Fairies, st. 1*

The Queen — now can you guess who that could be
(She's a little girl by day, but at night she steals away)?
Well — it's me!   *Ib. st. 3*

GODFREY HAROLD HARDY
1877–1947

A mathematician, like a painter or a poet, is a maker of patterns. If his patterns are more permanent than theirs, it is because they are made with ideas.
A Mathematician's Apology [1940]

SIR JAMES HOPWOOD JEANS
1877–1946

Taking a very gloomy view of the future of the human race, let us suppose that it can only expect to survive for two thousand million years longer, a period about equal to the past age of the earth. Then, regarded as a being des-

[1] Often quoted by Woodrow Wilson.

tined to live for threescore years and ten, humanity, although it has been born in a house seventy years old, is itself only three days old.
The Wilder Aspects of Cosmogony [1928]

All the pictures which science now draws of nature and which alone seem capable of according with observational fact are mathematical pictures. . . . From the intrinsic evidence of his creation, the Great Architect of the Universe now begins to appear as a pure mathematician.
The Mysterious Universe [1930]

Physics tries to discover the pattern of events which controls the phenomena we observe. But we can never know what this pattern means or how it originates; and even if some superior intelligence were to tell us, we should find the explanation unintelligible.
Physics and Philosophy [1942]

RICHARD R. KIRK
1877–

Thrice blessed are our friends: they come, they stay,
And presently they go away.
Thrice Blessed

A book's an inn whose patrons' praise
Depends on seasons and on days,
On dispositions, and — in fine —
Not wholly on the landlord's wine.
A Book's an Inn

DOUGLAS MALLOCH
1877–1938

If it's your Mississippi in dry time,
If it's yours, Uncle Sam, when it's wet,
If it's your Mississippi in fly time,
In flood time it's your Mississippi yet.
Uncle Sam's River, st. 6

Courage is to feel
The daily daggers of relentless steel
And keep on living.   *Courage, st. 2*

ANGELO PATRI
1877–1965

In one sense there is no death. The life of a soul on earth lasts beyond his departure. You will always feel that life touching yours, that voice speaking to you, that spirit looking out of other eyes, talking to you in the familiar things he touched, worked with, loved as familiar friends. He lives on in your life and in the lives of all others that knew him.[1]

Keep Children from Funerals
[November 30, 1938]

CHARLES HANSON TOWNE
1877–1949

Youth, there are countless stories
    spread
By gentlemen whose hair is gray.
Believe them not, but me instead—
The Nineties were not really gay.

Ballade of Gentle Denial

WILLIAM W. WOOLLCOTT
1877–1949

I am a One Hundred Percent American;
I am a superpatriot.

I Am a One Hundred Percent
American, st. 1

EMILIANO ZAPATA
c. 1877–1919

Men of the South! It is better to die on your feet than to live on your knees![2]
Attributed

McLANDBURGH WILSON
fl. 1915

'Twixt the optimist and pessimist
    The difference is droll:

The optimist sees the doughnut
But the pessimist sees the hole.

Optimist and Pessimist

YOSANO AKIKO
1878–1942

Because my songs are brief,
People think I hoarded words.
I have spared nothing in my songs.
There is nothing I can add.
Unlike a fish, my soul swims without
    gills.
I sing on one breath. *My Songs* [1]

LOUIS KAUFMAN ANSPACHER
1878–1947

Marriage is that relation between man and woman in which the independence is equal, the dependence mutual, and the obligation reciprocal.

Address, Boston [December 30,
1934]

KARLE WILSON BAKER
1878–

Let me grow lovely, growing old —
    So many fine things do:
Laces, and ivory, and gold,
    And silks need not be new.
Old Lace: Let Me Grow Lovely

Today I have grown taller from walking
    with the trees. *Good Company*

AMELIA JOSEPHINE BURR
1878–

As one who looks on a face through a
    window, through life I have looked
    on God.
Because I have loved life, I shall have no
    sorrow to die.
A Song of Living, st. 3

[1] Even the death of friends will inspire us as much as their lives. . . . Their memories will be incrusted over with sublime and pleasing thoughts, as their monuments are overgrown with moss. — THOREAU, *A Week on the Concord and Merrimack Rivers* [1849], *Concord River*
[2] See Roosevelt, p. 973a, and note.

[1] From *Modern Japanese Literature,* edited by Donald Keene [1960].

HENRY SEIDEL CANBY
1878–1961

We can put our children on wheels to see the world, but we cannot give them the kind of home that any town provided in the Nineties, not at any price.
> *The Age of Confidence, ch. 14*

Skunk cabbages! a thousand sonnets died in that misnomer.
> *Meditations in the Woods*

GEORGE MICHAEL COHAN
1878–1942

Always Leave Them Laughing When You Say Goodbye. *Title of song*

Give my regards to Broadway,
 Remember me to Herald Square,
Tell all the gang at Forty-second Street
That I will soon be there.
> *Give My Regards to Broadway* [1904]

The Yanks are coming,
The drums rum-tumming everywhere.
> *Over There* [1917]

And we won't come back till it's over over there. *Ib.*

What's all the shootin' for?
> *The Tavern* [1920]

GRACE HAZARD CONKLING
1878–1958

I have an understanding with the hills
At evening when the slanted radiance fills
Their hollows, and the great winds let them be,
And they are quiet and look down at me. *After Sunset*

Invisible beauty has a word so brief
A flower can say it or a shaken leaf,
But few may ever snare it in a song.
> *Ib.*

To build the trout a crystal stair.
> *The Whole Duty of Berkshire Brooks*

He who gives a passion flower
Always asks it back. *Tampico*

ALFRED EDGAR COPPARD
1878–1957

Adam and Eve and Pinch Me.
> *Title of story* [1921]

Truth is truth and love is love,
Give us grace to taste thereof;
But if truth offend my sweet,
Then I will have none of it.
> *Mendacity, st. 1*

Ere this trick of truth undo me,
Little love, my love, come to me.
> *Ib. st. 3*

ADELAIDE CRAPSEY
1878–1914

These be
Three silent things:
The falling snow . . . the hour
Before the dawn . . . the mouth of one
Just dead. *Cinquain: Triad*

EDWARD JOHN MORETON DRAX PLUNKETT, LORD DUNSANY
1878–1957

A new thing came and they could not see,
A new wind blew and they would not feel it.
> *In His Own Country, st. 1*

May you go safe, my friend, across that dizzy way
No wider than a hair, by which your people go
From earth to Paradise; may you go safe today
With stars and space above, and time and stars below.
> *May You Go Safe: On the Death of a Mohammedan Friend, st. 1*

HARRY EMERSON FOSDICK
1878–1969

The Sea of Galilee and the Dead Sea are made of the same water. It flows down, clear and cool, from the heights of Hermon and the roots of the cedars of Lebanon. The Sea of Galilee makes beauty of it, for the Sea of Galilee has an outlet. It gets to give. It gathers in its riches that it may pour them out again to fertilize the Jordan plain. But the Dead Sea with the same water makes horror. For the Dead Sea has no outlet. It gets to keep.

> *The Meaning of Service* [1920]

WILFRID WILSON GIBSON
1878–1962

One song leads on to another,
One friend to another friend,
So I'll travel along
With a friend and a song.

> *The Empty Purse, st. 1*

All life moving to one measure —
Daily bread.

> *All Life Moving to One Measure*

Just what it meant to smile and smile
And let my son go cheerily —
My son . . . and wondering all the
    while
What stranger would come back to me.

> *The Return, st. 2*

OLIVER ST. JOHN GOGARTY
1878–1957

Only the lion and the cock,
As Galen says, withstand love's shock.[1]
So, dearest, do not think me rude
If I yield now to lassitude,
But sympathize with me. I know
You would not have me roar, or crow.

> *After Galen*

If only gladiators died,
Or heroes, death would be his pride;

[1] See Donne, p. 307a.

But have not little maidens gone,
And Lesbia's sparrow,[1] all alone?

> *Per Iter Tenebricosum*

DONALD ROBERT PERRY MARQUIS
1878–1937

My heart hath followed all my days
Something I cannot name.

> *The Name, st. 1*

The saddest ones are those that wear
The jester's motley garb.

> *The Tavern of Despair*

The world hath just one tale to tell,
    and it is very old,
A little tale — a simple tale — a tale
    that's easy told:
"There was a youth in Babylon who
    greatly loved a maid!"

> *News from Babylon*

And similar goddamned phrases.

> *Ballade of Goddamned Phrases* [2]

I pray Thee make my column read,
And give me thus my daily bread.

> *Prayer*

I love you as New Englanders love pie!

> *Sonnets to a Red-Haired Lady*
> [1922], XII

One boob may die, but deathless is
    The royal race of hicks —
When Ahab went to Askelon
    They sold him gilded bricks.

> *Boob Ballad*

There will be no beans in the Almost Perfect State.[3]

> *The Almost Perfect State* [1927]

dedicated to babs
    with babs knows what
    and babs knows why

> *archy* [4] *and mehitabel* [1927]
> *dedication*

[1] See Catullus, p. 114a.
[2] Inspired by a protest from General Ian Hamilton, Commander of the Mediterranean Expeditionary Force [1915], against turning his cables into hackneyed phrases.
[3] See Robert Burton, p. 310b.
[4] archy a cockroach is unable to use the shift key on the typewriter for capitals and punctuation

oh i should worry and fret
death and i will coquette
there is a dance in the old dame yet
toujours gai toujours gai
      archy and mehitabel   the song
            of mehitabel

procrastination is the
art of keeping
up with yesterday
      ib   certain maxims of archy

an optimist is a guy that has never had
    much experience   *ib*

   what in hell
have i done to deserve all these kittens
    ib   mehitabel and her kittens

dance mehitabel dance
caper and shake a leg
what little blood is left
will fizz like wine in a keg
    ib   mehitabel dances with boreas

  i have noticed that when chickens
quit quarreling over their food they
often find that there is enough for all
of them i wonder if it might not be the
same with the human race
    archy's life of mehitabel [1933]
      random thoughts by archy

  so unlucky
that he runs into accidents
which started out to happen
to somebody else   *ib   archy says*

theres life in the old dame yet
    ib   the retreat from hollywood

it is a cheering thought to think
that god is on the side of the best digestion [1]
    archy does his part [1935]
      the big bad wolf

there is bound to be a certain amount
    of
trouble running any country
if you are president the trouble happens
    to you

---

[1] Give me a good digestion, Lord,
  And also something to digest.
    ANONYMOUS, *A Pilgrim's Grace, st. 1*

but if you are a tyrant you can arrange
    things so
that most of the trouble happens to
    other people
      archy's newest deal

there is always
a comforting thought
in time of trouble when
it is not our trouble
    ib   comforting thoughts

too many creatures
both insects and humans
estimate their own value
by the amount of minor irritation
they are able to cause
to greater personalities than themselves
      ib   pride

the females of all species are most
dangerous when they appear to retreat
    ib   a farewell

  To stroke a platitude until it purrs
like an epigram.   *The Sun Dial*

  Publishing a volume of verse is like
dropping a rose petal down the Grand
Canyon and waiting for the echo.
    Ib.

JOHN MASEFIELD
1878–1967

I must down to the seas again, to the
    lonely sea and the sky,
And all I ask is a tall ship and a star to
    steer her by,
And the wheel's kick and the wind's
    song and the white sail's shaking,
And a gray mist on the sea's face and a
    gray dawn breaking.
      Sea Fever [1902], *st. 1*

I must down to the seas again, for the
    call of the running tide
Is a wild call and a clear call that may
    not be denied.   *Ib. st. 2*

I must down to the seas again, to the
    vagrant gypsy life,
To the gull's way and the whale's way
    where the wind's like a whetted
    knife;

And all I ask is a merry yarn from a
laughing fellow rover,
And quiet sleep and a sweet dream
when the long trick's over.
Sea Fever, st. 3

It's a warm wind, the west wind, full of
birds' cries.
The West Wind [1902], *st. 1*

One road leads to London,
One road runs to Wales,
My road leads me seawards
To the white dipping sails.
Roadways, st. 1

The schooners and the merry crews are
laid away to rest,
A little south the sunset in the Islands
of the Blest.
A Ballad of John Silver
[1902], *st. 6*

To get the whole world out of bed
And washed, and dressed, and warmed,
and fed,
To work, and back to bed again,
Believe me, Saul, costs worlds of pain.
The Everlasting Mercy [1911]

And he who gives a child a treat
Makes joy-bells ring in Heaven's street,
And he who gives a child a home
Builds palaces in Kingdom come.
Ib.

O Christ, the plow, O Christ, the
laughter
Of holy white birds flying after.   *Ib.*

The days that make us happy make us
wise.   *Biography*

Quinquireme of Nineveh from distant
Ophir,
Rowing home to haven in sunny Pales-
tine,
With a cargo of ivory,
And apes and peacocks,[1]
Sandalwood, cedarwood, and sweet
white wine.   *Cargoes, st. 1*

Dirty British coaster with a salt-caked
smokestack,
Butting through the Channel in the
mad March days,
With a cargo of Tyne coal,

[1] See *I Kings 10:22,* p. 13a.

Road rail, pig lead,
Firewood, ironware, and cheap tin
trays.   *Cargoes, st. 3*

Oh London Town's a fine town, and
London sights are rare,
And London ale is right ale, and brisk's
the London air.
London Town, st. 1

When Life knocks at the door no one
can wait,
When Death makes his arrest we have
to go.[1]
The Widow in the Bye Street
[1912], *pt. 2*

What good can painting do to anyone?
I don't say never do it; far from that —
No harm in sometimes painting just for
fun.
Keep it for fun, and stick to what
you're at.
Dauber [1913], *pt. II*

Spit brown, my son, and get a hairy
breast.   *Ib.*

What am I, Life? A thing of watery
salt
Held in cohesion by unresting cells,
Which work they know not why, which
never halt,
Myself unwitting where their Master
dwells?   *Sonnets, 14*

Bitter it is, indeed, in human Fate
When Life's supreme temptation
comes too late.
The Woman Speaks

When custom presses on the souls
apart,
Who seek a God not worshiped by the
herd,
Forth, to the wilderness, the chosen
start
Content with ruin, having but the
Word.
*Lines on the Tercentenary of
Harvard College* [1936]

But he has gone,
A nation's memory and veneration,
Among the radiant, ever venturing on,

[1] See Shakespeare, *Hamlet V, ii 350,* p. 266b.

Somewhere, with morning, as such spirits will.[1]
> On the Finish of the Sailing Ship
> Race Lisbon to Manhattan
> [July 1964]

PAUL REYNAUD
1878–1966

We shall win because we are the
stronger.[2]
> Radio Speech [September 10,
> 1939]

CARL SANDBURG
1878–1967

I am the people — the mob — the
crowd — the mass.
Do you know that all the great work of
the world is done through me?
> I Am the People, the Mob
> [1916]

Hog butcher for the world,
Tool maker, stacker of wheat,
Player with railroads and the nation's
freight handler;
Stormy, husky, brawling,
City of the big shoulders.
> Chicago [1916]

The fog comes
on little cat feet.
It sits looking
over the harbor and city
on silent haunches
and then moves on.   Fog [1916]

Pile the bodies high at Austerlitz and
Waterloo.
Shovel them under and let me work —
I am the grass; I cover all.

And pile them high at Gettysburg
And pile them high at Ypres and Ver-
dun.
Shovel them under and let me work.

---

[1] The reference is to the death of John F.
Kennedy [November 22, 1963].
  See James Russell Lowell, p. 694a.
[2] Nous vaincrons parce que nous sommes les
plus forts.
  The phrase became a war slogan.

Two years, ten years, and passengers
ask the conductor:
What place is this?
Where are we now?

I am the grass.
Let me work.   Grass [1918]
I tell you the past is a bucket of ashes.
> Prairie

The republic is a dream.
Nothing happens unless first a dream.
> Washington Monument by Night

When Abraham Lincoln was shoveled
into the tombs, he forgot the copperheads and the assassin . . . in
the dust, in the cool tombs.
> Cool Tombs [1918]

Take any streetful of people buying
clothes and groceries, cheering a
hero or throwing confetti and
blowing tin horns . . . tell me if
the lovers are losers . . . tell me
if any get more than the lovers
. . . in the dust . . . in the cool
tombs.   Ib.

Lay me on an anvil, O God.
Beat me and hammer me into a crow-
bar.
Let me pry loose old walls.
Let me lift and loosen old foundations.
> Prayers of Steel [1920]

Drum on your drums, batter on your
banjos, sob on the long cool winding saxophones.
Go to it, O jazzmen.
> Jazz Fantasia [1920]

Look out how you use proud words.
When you let proud words go, it is not
easy to call them back.
They wear long boots, hard boots.
> Primer Lesson

Man is a long time coming.
Man will yet win.
Brother may yet line up with brother:
This old anvil laughs at many broken
hammers.
There are men who can't be bought.
> The People Will Live On [1936]

Time is a great teacher.
Who can live without hope?
In the darkness with a great bundle of
    grief the people march.
        The People Will Live On

LOUIS EDWIN THAYER
1878–

I fancy when I go to rest someone will
    bring to light
Some kindly word or goodly act long
    buried out of sight;
But, if it's all the same to you, just give
    to me, instead,
The bouquets while I'm living and the
    knocking when I'm dead.[1]
        Of Post-Mortem Praises, st. 1

EDWARD THOMAS
1878–1917

As poetry is a criticism of life by livers, so the epigram is a criticism of life
by those who have not lived.
        Oxford [1903], *p. 195*

JOHN BROADUS WATSON
1878–1958

Give me a dozen healthy infants,
well-formed, and my own specified
world to bring them up in and I'll guarantee to take any one at random and
train him to become any type of spe-
cialist I might select — doctor, lawyer,
artist, merchant chief and, yes, even
beggarman and thief, regardless of his
talents, penchants, tendencies, abilities,
vocations, and race of his ancestors.
        Behaviorism [1925], *p. 104*

HANS ZINSSER
1878–1940

The scientist takes off from the manifold observations of predecessors, and
shows his intelligence, if any, by his
ability to discriminate between the important and the negligible, by selecting
here and there the significant steppingstones that will lead across the difficul-

[1] See Martial, p. 135a, and Hazlitt, p. 539b.

ties to new understanding. The one
who places the last stone and steps
across to the terra firma of accomplished discovery gets all the credit.
Only the initiated know and honor
those whose patient integrity and devotion to exact observation have made the
last step possible.[1]
        As I Remember Him
        [1940], *ch. 20*

ETHEL BARRYMORE
1879–1959

That's all there is, there isn't any
more.
        *Added, with the permission of
        author* THOMAS RACEWARD, *as
        the curtain line of his play
        Sunday* [1906], *starring Miss
        Barrymore*

SIR WILLIAM HENRY BEVERIDGE
1879–1963

Simple effluxion of time.[2]
        Social Insurance [1942]
The object of government in peace
and in war is not the glory of rulers or
of races, but the happiness of the common man.   *Ib.*

JAMES BRANCH CABELL
1879–1958

I shall marry in haste, and repeat at
leisure.[3]   *Jurgen* [1919], *ch. 38*

There is no faith stronger than that
of a bad-tempered woman in her own
infallibility.   *Ib. 39*

The optimist proclaims that we live
in the best of all possible worlds; and
the pessimist fears this is true.
        The Silver Stallion [1926], *ch. 26*

[1] See Sir Francis Darwin, p. 813b, and Sir Alexander Fleming, p. 963a.
[2] The *Oxford English Dictionary* traces the phrase "effluxion of time" to JOHN MOLLE, *The Living Library* [1621].
[3] See Shakespeare, p. 219a, and Congreve, p. 391b.

No lady is ever a gentleman.
Something About Eve [1927]

LEE WILSON DODD
1879–1933

Much that I sought, I could not find;
Much that I found, I could not bind;
Much that I bound, I could not free;
Much that I freed returned to me.
Ronde Macabre

ALBERT EINSTEIN
1879–1955

$E = mc^2$
*Statement of the mass-energy
equivalence relationship* [1]

The most beautiful thing we can experience is the mysterious. It is the source of all true art and science.
"What I Believe," in Forum
[*October 1930*]

It is not enough that you should understand about applied science in order that your work may increase man's blessings. Concern for man himself and his fate must always form the chief interest of all technical endeavors, concern for the great unsolved problems of the organization of labor and the distribution of goods — in order that the creations of our mind shall be a blessing and not a curse to mankind. Never forget this in the midst of your diagrams and equations.
*Address, California Institute of
Technology* [1931]

The whole of science is nothing more than a refinement of everyday thinking.
Physics and Reality [1936]

Physical concepts are free creations of the human mind, and are not, however it may seem, uniquely determined by the external world.
Evolution of Physics [1938]

[1] Energy equals mass times the speed of light squared.
The original statement is: If a body gives off the energy L in the form of radiation, its mass diminishes by L/c². " — *Ist die Tragheit eines Korpers von seinem Energieghalt abhangig?* [*1905*]

Some recent work by E. Fermi and L. Szilard, which has been communicated to me in manuscript, leads me to expect that the element uranium may be turned into a new and important source of energy in the immediate future. Certain aspects of the situation which has arisen seem to call for watchfulness and, if necessary, quick action on the part of the Administration.
*Letter to President Franklin D.
Roosevelt* [*August 2, 1939*] (*the
letter which resulted in assignment of government funds for
development of the atom bomb*)

This new phenomena [atomic energy] would also lead to the construction of bombs. . . . A single bomb of this type, carried by boat and exploded in a port, might very well destroy the whole port, together with some of the surrounding territory. However, such bombs might very well prove to be too heavy for transportation by air. *Ib.*

As long as there are sovereign nations possessing great power, war is inevitable.
*Einstein on the Atomic Bomb
[Atlantic Monthly, November
1945]*

I do not believe that civilization will be wiped out in a war fought with the atomic bomb. Perhaps two thirds of the people of the earth might be killed, but enough men capable of thinking, and enough books, would be left to start again, and civilization could be restored. *Ib.*

Since I do not foresee that atomic energy is to be a great boon for a long time, I have to say that for the present it is a menace. Perhaps it is well that it should be. It may intimidate the human race into bringing order into its international affairs, which, without the pressure of fear, it would not do. *Ib.*

I shall never believe that God plays dice with the world.[1]
From PHILIPP FRANK, *Einstein,
His Life and Times* [1947]

[1] See Anatole France, p. 802a.

The Lord God is subtle, but malicious he is not.[1]
Inscription in Fine Hall, Princeton University

Every intellectual who is called before one of the committees ought to refuse to testify, i.e., he must be prepared . . . for the sacrifice of his personal welfare in the interest of the cultural welfare of his country. . . . This kind of inquisition violates the spirit of the Constitution.

If enough people are ready to take this grave step they will be successful. If not, then the intellectuals of this country deserve nothing better than the slavery which is intended for them.
Letter to William Frauenglass[2] *[May 16, 1953]*

The unleashed power of the atom has changed everything save our modes of thinking, and we thus drift toward unparalleled catastrophes.
From RALPH E. LAPP, *The Einstein Letter That Started It All [New York Times Magazine, August 2, 1964]*

Our defense is not in armaments, nor in science, nor in going underground. Our defense is in law and order.[3]   *Ib.*

Something deeply hidden had to be behind things.
Ib. [autobiographical handwritten note]

JOHN ERSKINE
1879–1951
The Moral Obligation to Be Intelligent.   *Title of book [1915]*

[1] Raffiniert ist der Herr Gott, aber Boshaft ist er nicht.
See Dostoevski, p. 708a.
[2] Einstein's letter was published in the *New York Times* [June 12, 1953]. Mr. Frauenglass had been subpoenaed to testify before the Senate Internal Security Subcommittee.
[3] See Lincoln, p. 636a.

W. C. FIELDS
1879–1946
It ain't a fit night out for man or beast.   *The Fatal Glass of Beer*

Anyone who hates children and dogs can't be all bad.   *Attributed*

On the whole, I'd rather be in Philadelphia.   *His own epitaph*

EDWARD MORGAN FORSTER
1879–1970
When the book of life is opening, our readings are secret.
The Longest Journey [1907]

Nonsense and beauty have close connections.   *Ib.*

Railway termini . . . are our gates to the glorious and the unknown. Through them we pass out into adventure and sunshine, to them, alas! we return. In Paddington all Cornwall is latent and the remoter west; down the inclines of Liverpool Street lie fenlands and the illimitable Broads; Scotland is through the plyons of Euston; Wessex behind the poised chaos of Waterloo.
Howards End [1910], ch. 2

It will be generally admitted that Beethoven's Fifth Symphony is the most sublime noise that has ever penetrated into the ear of man.   *Ib. 5*

Only connect! That was the whole of her sermon. Only connect the prose and the passion, and both will be exalted, and human love will be seen at its height. Live in fragments no longer. Only connect, and the beast and the monk, robbed of the isolation that is life to either, will die.   *Ib. 22*

The echo began in some indescribable way to undermine her hold on life. Coming at a moment when she chanced to be fatigued, it had managed to murmur, "Pathos, piety, courage — they exist, but are identical, and so is filth. Everything exists, nothing has value." If one had spoken vileness in that place,

or quoted lofty poetry, the [echo's] comment would have been the same —
"Ou-boum."

A Passage to India [1924]

The historian must have some conception of how men who are not historians behave.

Abinger Harvest [1936]. *Captain Edward Gibbon*

How rare, how precious is frivolity! How few writers can prostitute all their powers! They are always implying, "I am capable of higher things."

Notes on English Character. Ronald Firbank

EDMUND L. GRUBER
1879–1941

Over hill, over dale,[1] we have hit the dusty trail
And those caissons go rolling along.
Countermarch! Right about! hear those wagon soldiers shout
While those caissons go rolling along.
Oh, it's hi-hi-yee! for the field artilleree,
Shout out your numbers loud and strong,
And where'er we go, you will always know
That those caissons are rolling along.

The Caisson Song [2] [1908]

JOHN HAYNES HOLMES
1879–1964

If Christians were Christians, there would be no anti-Semitism. Jesus was a Jew. There is nothing that the ordinary Christian so dislikes to remember as this awkward historical fact. But it happens, none the less, to be true.

The Sensible Man's View of Religion [1933]

[1] See Shakespeare, p. 229a.
[2] In April 1908 the 1st Battalion of the 5th Field Artillery relieved the 2nd Battalion in the Philippines. Gruber, then a lieutenant in the 5th, was asked to write a song that would symbolize the spirit of the reunited regiment. There are many variant wordings.

Priests are no more necessary to religion than politicians to patriotism.

The Sensible Man's View of Religion

The universe is not hostile, nor yet is it friendly. It is simply indifferent.

Ib.

The life of humanity upon this planet may yet come to an end, and a very terrible end. But I would have you notice that this end is threatened in our time not by anything that the universe may do to us, but only by what man may do to himself.   *Ib.*

VACHEL LINDSAY
1879–1931

Booth died blind and still by faith he trod,
Eyes still dazzled by the ways of God.

General William Booth Enters into Heaven [1913]

Sleep softly . . . eagle forgotten . . . under the stone,
Time has its way with you there, and the clay has its own.
Sleep on, O brave-hearted, O wise man, that kindled the flame —
To live in mankind is far more than to live in a name.

The Eagle That Is Forgotten [1]
[1913], *st. 5*

Factory windows are always broken.
Somebody's always throwing bricks,
Somebody's always heaving cinders,
Playing ugly Yahoo tricks.

Factory Windows, st. 1

Fat black bucks in a wine-barrel room,
Barrel-house kings; with feet unstable,
Sagged and reeled and pounded on the table,
Pounded on the table,

[1] John Peter Altgeld [1847–1902; Governor of Illinois 1893–1897], widely criticized for pardoning, in June 1893, the anarchists who had been serving life terms since the Haymarket riot in Chicago, May 4, 1886. Altgeld, in pardoning them, declared that "the judge conducted the trial with malicious ferocity."

Beat an empty barrel with the handle
of a broom.
                    The Congo [1914], pt. I

Then I saw the Congo, creeping
    through the black,
Cutting through the forest with a gold-
    en track.   *Ib.*

Be careful what you do,
Or Mumbo-Jumbo, God of the Congo,
And all of the other
Gods of the Congo,
Mumbo-Jumbo will hoo-doo you.
                                    Ib.

A bronzed, lank man! His suit of an-
    cient black,
A famous high top-hat and plain worn
    shawl
Make him the quaint great figure that
    men love,
The prairie-lawyer, master of us all.
            Abraham Lincoln Walks at Mid-
                        night [1914], st. 3

They spoke, I think, of perils past.
They spoke, I think, of peace at last.
One thing I remember:
Spring came on forever,
Spring came on forever,
Said the Chinese nightingale.
            The Chinese Nightingale
                        [1917], end

Planting the trees that would march
    and train
On, in his name to the great Pacific,
Like Birnam Wood to Dunsinane,[1]
Johnny Appleseed [2] swept on.
            In Praise of Johnny Appleseed

    The more probable chance for me
will come in some little row where
strikers are being shot down. . . . I
would be with the fool strikers, right or
wrong.
            Letter to Eleanor Dougherty
                        [October 12, 1918]

[1] See Shakespeare, p. 285b.
[2] John Chapman [1774–1847].
    Remember Johnny Appleseed,
    All ye who love the apple;
    He served his kind by word and deed,
    In God's grand greenwood chapel.
            WILLIAM HENRY VENABLE [1836–
            1918], *Johnny Appleseed, st. 25*

ST. JOHN LUCAS
1879–1934

The curate thinks you have no soul;
I know that he has none.[1]   *My Dog*

GEORGE WASHINGTON
LYON
1879–

Worry, the interest paid by those
who borrow trouble.
                    In Judge [March 1, 1924]

DIXON LANIER
MERRITT
1879–

A wonderful bird is the pelican,
His bill will hold more than his belican.
    He can take in his beak
    Food enough for a week,
But I'm damned if I see how the heli-
    can.   *The Pelican [1910]*

HAROLD MONRO
1879–1932

How lonely we shall be!
What shall we do,
You without me,
I without you?
            Midnight Lamentation, st. 1

They are better than stars or water,
Better than voices of winds that sing,
Better than any man's fair daughter,
Your green glass beads on a silver ring.
            Overheard on a Saltmarsh

A long, dim ecstasy holds her life;
Her world is an infinite shapeless white,
Till her tongue has curled the last holy
    drop,
Then she sinks back into the night.
            Milk for the Cat, st. 8

FELIX RIESENBERG
1879–1939

    The sea has always been a seducer, a
careless lying fellow, not feminine, as

[1] There are things that even the youngest
curate cannot explain. — LEONARD MERRICK,
One Man's View [1897]

many writers imagine, but strongly masculine in its allurement. The king of the sea, with his whiskers of weed and his trident and dolphins, truly represents the main and gives it character. The sea, like a great sultan, supports thousands of ships, his lawful wives. These he caresses and chastises as the case may be. This explains the feminine gender of all proper vessels.

Vignettes of the Sea

WILL ROGERS
1879–1935

All I know is just what I read in the papers.   *Prefatory remark*

I tell you folks, all politics is applesauce.
The Illiterate Digest [1924], *p. 30*

Everything is funny as long as it is happening to somebody else.
Ib. p. 131

More men have been elected between sundown and sunup than ever were elected between sunup and sundown.
Ib. p. 152

I never met a man I didn't like.
Address, Boston [*June 1930*]

A comedian can only last till he either takes himself serious or his audience takes him serious.
Syndicated newspaper article
[*June 28, 1931*]

I not only "don't choose to run"[1] [for President] but I don't even want to leave a loophole in case I am drafted, so I won't "choose." I will say "won't run" no matter how bad the country will need a comedian by that time.
Ib.

Politics has got so expensive that it takes lots of money to even get beat with.   *Ib.*

My forefathers didn't come over on the *Mayflower*, but they met the boat.[2]   *Remark*

[1] See Calvin Coolidge, p. 911b.
[2] Rogers was of Indian descent.

JOSEPH STALIN [IOSIF VISSARIONOVICH DZHUGASHVILI]
1879–1953

Print is the sharpest and the strongest weapon of our party.
Speech [*April 19, 1923*]

Dizziness from success.
Speech [*March 2, 1930*]

The most remarkable thing about socialist competition is that it creates a basic change in people's view of labor, since it changes the labor from a shameful and heavy burden into a matter of honor, matter of fame, matter of valor and heroism.
Speech [*June 27, 1930*]

The Hitlerite blackguards have covered Europe with gallows and concentration camps. . . . They have turned Europe into a prison of nations,[1] and this they call the new order in Europe.
Address to the Moscow Soviet
[*November 6, 1942*]

You cannot make a revolution with silk gloves.
From John Gunther, *Soviet Russia Today*

The writer is an engineer of the human soul.[2]   *Ib.*

A single death is a tragedy, a million deaths is a statistic.
Quoted statement

The inevitability of wars between capitalist countries remains in force.
Last public statement [*1952*]

WALLACE STEVENS
1879–1955

I heard them cry — the peacocks.
Was it a cry against the twilight
Or against the leaves themselves
Turning in the wind,

[1] . . . The saying that Russia is a prison of nations. — V. I. Lenin, *On the Question of National Policy* (and elsewhere)
The expression originated in *La Russie en 1839* by Adolphe de Custine [1790–1857].
[2] See Gorki, p. 894b.

Turning as the flames
Turned in the fire,
Turning as the tails of the peacocks
Turned in the loud fire,
Loud as the hemlocks
Full of the cry of the peacocks?
Or was it a cry against the hemlocks?
　　　Domination of Black [1923]

Twenty men crossing a bridge,
Into a village,
Are　twenty　men　crossing　twenty
　　bridges,
Into twenty villages,
Or one man
Crossing a single bridge into a village.
　　Metaphors of a Magnifico [1923]

Poetry is the supreme fiction, madame.
　　**A High-toned Old Christian
　　　　　　Woman** [1923]

Let be be the finale of seem.
The only emperor is the emperor of ice
　　cream.
　　The Emperor of Ice Cream [1923]

Only, here and there, an old sailor,
Drunk and asleep in his boots,
Catches tigers
In red weather.
　　Disillusionment of Ten O'clock
　　　　　　　　　[1923]

Complacencies of the peignoir, and late
Coffee and oranges in a sunny chair.
　　Sunday Morning [1923], st. 1

We live in an old chaos of the sun,
Or old dependency of day and night,
Or island solitude, unsponsored, free,
Of that wide water, inescapable.
Deer walk upon our mountains, and the
　　quail
Whistle about us their spontaneous
　　cries;
Sweet berries ripen in the wilderness;
And, in the isolation of the sky,
At evening, casual flocks of pigeons
　　make
Ambiguous undulations as they sink,
Downward to darkness, on extended
　　wings.　　　　　　　*Ib. st. 8*

Chieftain Iffucan of Azcan in caftan
Of tan with henna hackles, halt!
　　Bantams in Pine Woods [1923]

Damned universal cock, as if the sun
Was blackamoor to bear your blazing
　　tail.　　　*Bantams in Pine Woods*

I placed a jar in Tennessee,
And round it was, upon a hill.
It made the slovenly wilderness
Surround that hill.
　　Anecdote of the Jar [1923], st. 1

Frogs Eat Butterflies. Snakes Eat
Frogs. Hogs Eat Snakes. Men **Eat**
Hogs.[1]　　　*Title of poem* [1923]

I had as lief be embraced by the porter
　　at the hotel
As to get no more from the moonlight
Than your moist hand.
　　*Two Figures in Dense Violet
　　　　　　　Night* [1923]

Just as my fingers on these keys
Make music, so the self-same sounds
On my spirit make a music, too.
　　Peter Quince at the Clavier
　　　　　　　　　[1923], 1

Beauty is momentary in the mind —
The fitful tracing of a portal;
But in the flesh it is immortal.
The body dies; the body's beauty lives.
　　　　　　　　　Ib. 4

Susanna's music touched the bawdy
　　strings
Of those white elders; but, escaping,
Left only Death's ironic scraping.
Now, in its immortality, it plays
On the clear viol of her memory,
And　makes　a　constant　sacrament　of
　　praise.　　　　　　　　*Ib.*

I do not know which to prefer,
The beauty of inflections
Or the beauty of innuendoes,
The blackbird whistling
Or just after.
　　*Thirteen Ways of Looking at a
　　　　　Blackbird* [1923], st. 5

The gongs rang loudly as the windy
　　booms
Hoo-hooed it in the darkened ocean-
　　booms
　　Sea Surface Full of Clouds
　　　　　　　　　[1923], II

　　　[1] See Ambrose Bierce, p. 791b-792a.

Then the sea
And heaven rolled as one and from the
two
Came fresh transfigurings of freshest
blue.
Sea Surface Full of Clouds, V

She sang beyond the genius of the sea,
The water never formed to mind or
voice,
Like a body wholly body, fluttering
Its empty sleeves; and yet its mimic
motion
Made constant cry, caused constantly a
cry,
That was not ours although we under-
stood,
Inhuman, of the veritable ocean.
The Idea of Order at Key West
[1936], st. 1

Oh! Blessed rage for order, pale Ra-
món,
The maker's rage to order words of the
sea,
Words of the fragrant portals, dimly
starred,
And of ourselves and of our origins,
In ghostlier demarcations, keener
sounds. *Ib. st. 7*

Poetry is the subject of the poem.
The Man with the Blue Guitar
[1937], XXII

I am a native in this world
And think in it as a native thinks.
Ib. XXVIII

The prologues are over. It is question,
now,
Of final belief. So, say that final belief
Must be in a fiction. It is time to
choose.
Asides on the Oboe [1942], st. 1

Light
Is the lion that comes down to drink.
The Glass of Water [1942], st. 2

A. A violent order is disorder; and
B. A great disorder is an order. These
Two things are one.
Connoisseur of Chaos [1942], st. 1

One's grand flights, one's Sunday
baths,

One's tootings at the weddings of the
soul
Occur as they occur.
The Sense of the Sleight-of-
Hand Man [1942], st. 1

The motive for metaphor, shrinking
from
The weight of primary noon,
The ABC of being,

The ruddy temper, the hammer
Of red and blue, the hard sound —
Steel against intimation — the sharp
flash,
The vital, arrogant, fatal, dominant X.
The Motive for Metaphor, st. 4, 5

To get at the thing
Without gestures is to get at it as
Idea.
So-and-So Reclining on Her
Couch [1947], st. 6

The President ordains the bee to be
Immortal.
The President Ordains the Bee
to Be [1947], st. 1

The inconceivable idea of the sun.
Notes Toward a Supreme Fiction
[1947], I

You must become an ignorant man
again
And see the sun again with an ignorant
eye
And see it clearly in the idea of it.
Ib.

The death of one god is the death of
all. *Ib.*

There is a project for the sun. The sun
Must bear no name, gold flourisher, but
be
In the difficulty of what it is to be.
Ib.

The monastic man is an artist. The philosopher
Appoints man's place in music, say, today.
But the priest desires. The philosopher
desires.
And not to have is the beginning of
desire. *Ib. II*

We keep coming back and coming back
To the real: to the hotel instead of the
hymns
That fall upon it out of the wind.
> *An Ordinary Evening in New*
> *Haven* [1950], *IX*

The essential gaudiness of poetry.
> *Stevens's note to* The Emperor
> of Ice Cream

The essential thing in form is to be
free in whatever form is used. A free
form does not assure freedom. As a
form, it is just one more form. So that
it comes to this, I suppose, that I believe in freedom regardless of form.
> *A Note on Poetry* [1937]

What makes the poet the potent figure that he is, or was, or ought to be, is
that he creates the world to which we
turn incessantly and without knowing it
and that he gives to life the supreme
fictions without which we are unable to
conceive of it.
> *The Noble Rider and the Sound*
> *of Words* [1942]

Each man resembles all other men,
each woman resembles all other
women, this year resembles last year.
The beginning of time will, no doubt,
resemble the end of time. One world is
said to resemble another.
> *Three Academic Pieces* [1947]

Poetry is poetry, and one's objective
as a poet is to achieve poetry precisely
as one's objective in music is to achieve
music. There are poets who would regard that as a scandal and who would
say that a poem which had no importance except its importance as poetry
had no importance at all, and that a
poet who had no objective except to
achieve poetry was a fribble and something less than a man of reason.
> *On Selecting* Domination of
> Black *as his best poem*

Sentimentality is a failure of feeling.
> *Opus Posthumous* [1957].
> *Adagia*

A poem should be part of one's sense
of life.   *Ib.*

A poet looks at the world as a man
looks at a woman.
> *Opus Posthumous. Adagia*

All history is modern history.   *Ib.*

Poetry is the sum of its attributes.
                                          Ib.

In the world of words, the imagination is one of the forces of nature.
                                          Ib.

God is in me or else is not at all
(does not exist).   *Ib.*

The world is a force, not a presence.
                                          Ib.

Poetry is a search for the inexplicable.   *Ib.*

SIMEON STRUNSKY
1879–1948

No colonization without misrepresentation.
> *No Mean City* [1944], *ch.* 1

Famous remarks are very seldom
quoted correctly.   *Ib.* 38

LEON TROTSKY
1879–1940

The literary "fellow travelers" of the
Revolution.
> *Literature and Revolution*
> [1923], *ch.* 2

The dictatorship of the Communist
Party is maintained by recourse to every
form of violence.
> *Terrorism and Communism*
> [1924], *p.* 71

CH'EN TU-HSIU [1]
1879–1942

The pulse of modern life is economic
and the fundamental principle of economic production is individual independence.
> *The New Youth* [December
> 1916]

[1] From *Sources of Chinese Tradition*, edited
by William Theodore de Bary [1960]. Ch'en was
the founder [1921] of the Chinese Communist
Party.

All religions, laws, moral and political systems are but necessary means to preserve social order. They are not the individual's original purpose of enjoyment in life and can be changed in accordance with the circumstances of the time.

Man's happiness in life is the result of man's own effort and is neither the gift of God nor a spontaneous natural product.

The New Youth [*February 1918*]

During his lifetime, an individual should devote his efforts to create happiness and to enjoy it, and also to keep it in store in society so that individuals of the future may also enjoy it.   *Ib.*

GEORGE ASAF
[GEORGE H. POWELL]
1880–1951

What's the use of worrying?
It never was worthwhile,
So, pack up your troubles in your old
    kit-bag,
And smile, smile, smile.
Pack Up Your Troubles in Your
Old Kit-Bag [1915]

ALEXANDER BLOK
1880–1921

On they march with sovereign tread,
With a starving dog behind,
With a blood-red flag ahead —
In a storm where none can see,
From the rifle bullets free,
Gently walking in the snow,
Where like pearls the snowflakes glow,
Marches rose-crowned in the van
Jesus Christ, the son of man.
The Twelve [1918]

Yes, we are Scythians, yes, we are
    Asians.   *Scythians* [1918]

JOSEPH CLARK GREW
1880–1965

This [sartorial convention] is a real problem with which I shall have to wrestle during the next few days, for of such stuff is diplomacy made.[1]

Ten Years in Japan [1944]
[*July 20, 1932*]

We have a phrase in English, "straight from the horse's mouth."
Ib. [*October 19, 1939*]. *Address,*
America–Japan Society

ROBERT BROWNING
HAMILTON
1880–

I walked a mile with Pleasure.
    She chattered all the way,
But left me none the wiser
    For all she had to say.

I walked a mile with Sorrow,
    And ne'er a word said she;
But, oh, the things I learned from her
    When Sorrow walked with me!
Along the Road

BRIAN HOOKER
1880–1946

O youth foregone, foregoing!
O dream unseen, unsought!
God give you joy of knowing
What life your death has bought.[2]
A.D. 1919, st. 5

HELEN KELLER
1880–1968

Literature is my Utopia. Here I am not disfranchised. No barrier of the senses shuts me out from the sweet, gracious discourse of my book friends. They talk to me without embarrassment or awkwardness.
The Story of My Life [1902]

[1] In a diplomat's soul you may find iron ore, but it is usually oil — and in a whale of a diplomat you'll find the whole equipment — the blubber of charity, the whalebone of flexibility, the oil of commodity. A great diplomat is a regular Moby Dick. — FRANCIS HACKETT, *Review of* ROGER B. MERRIMAN, *Suleiman the Magnificent, New York Times* [January 4, 1945]

[2] On a tablet at Yale University commemorating the Yale men who died in the First World War.

DOUGLAS MacARTHUR
1880–1964

The unfailing formula for production of morale is patriotism, self-respect, discipline, and self-confidence within a military unit, joined with fair treatment and merited appreciation from without. It cannot be produced by pampering or coddling an army, and is not necessarily destroyed by hardship, danger, or even calamity. Though it can survive and develop in adversity that comes as an inescapable incident of service, it will quickly wither and die if soldiers come to believe themselves the victims of indifference or injustice on the part of their government, or of ignorance, personal ambition, or ineptitude on the part of their military leaders.

> *Annual Report of the Chief of Staff, United States Army, for the Fiscal Year Ending June 30, 1933*

I shall return.

> *On leaving Corregidor for Australia* [March 11, 1942]

I have returned. By the grace of Almighty God, our forces stand again on Philippine soil.

> *Upon landing on Leyte* [October 20, 1944]

I see that the old flagpole still stands. Have your troops hoist the colors to its peak, and let no enemy ever haul them down.

> *To Colonel George M. Jones and 503rd Regimental Combat Team, who recaptured Corregidor* [March 2, 1945]

In war there is no substitute for victory.

> *Address, Joint Meeting of Congress* [April 19, 1951]

I still remember the refrain of one of the most popular barracks ballads of that day, which proclaimed most proudly that old soldiers never die; they just fade away. I now close my military career and just fade away.[1] *Ib.*

[1] See Anonymous, p. 1103a.

It is fatal to enter any war without the will to win it.

> *Speech, Republican National Convention* [July 7, 1952]

GEORGE CATLETT MARSHALL
1880–1959

The refusal of the British and Russian peoples to accept what appeared to be inevitable defeat was the great factor in the salvage of our civilization.

> *Biennial Report of the Chief of Staff, United States Army* [September 1, 1945]

If man does find the solution for world peace it will be the most revolutionary reversal of his record we have ever known. *Ib.*

Our policy is directed not against any country or doctrine but against hunger, poverty, desperation and chaos. Its purpose should be the revival of a working economy in the world so as to permit the emergence of political and social conditions in which free institutions can exist.

> *Address, Harvard University* [June 5, 1947], *embodying the European Recovery Plan (Marshall Plan)*

You can have all of the materiel in the world, but without morale it is largely ineffective.

> *Military Review* [October 1948]

It is not enough to fight. It is the spirit which we bring to the fight that decides the issue. It is morale that wins the victory. *Ib.*

Morale is the state of mind. It is steadfastness and courage and hope. It is confidence and zeal and loyalty. It is *élan, esprit de corps* and determination. *Ib.*

HENRY LOUIS MENCKEN
1880–1956

The virulence of the national appetite for bogus revelation.
A Book of Prefaces [1917], *ch. 1*

To the man with an ear for verbal delicacies — the man who searches painfully for the perfect word, and puts the way of saying a thing above the thing said — there is in writing the constant joy of sudden discovery, of happy accident. *Ib. 2*

Poverty is a soft pedal upon all branches of human activity, not excepting the spiritual. *Ib. 4*

Formalism is the hallmark of the national culture. *Ib.*

Time is a great legalizer, even in the field of morals. *Ib.*

The prophesying business is like writing fugues; it is fatal to everyone save the man of absolute genius.
Prejudices, First Series [1919], *ch. 2*

The public . . . demands certainties; it must be told definitely and a bit raucously that this is true and that is false. But there *are* no certainties.
Ib. 3

All successful newspapers are ceaselessly querulous and bellicose. They never defend anyone or anything if they can help it; if the job is forced upon them, they tackle it by denouncing someone or something else. *Ib. 13*

The great artists of the world are never Puritans, and seldom even ordinarily respectable. *Ib. 16*

To be in love is merely to be in a state of perceptual anesthesia — to mistake an ordinary young man for a Greek god or an ordinary young woman for a goddess. *Ib.*

All the more pretentious American authors try to write chastely and elegantly; the typical literary product of the country is still a refined essay in the *Atlantic Monthly*, perhaps gently jocose but never rough — by Emerson, so to speak, out of Charles Lamb.
The American Language [1919]

Philadelphia is the most pecksniffian of American cities, and thus probably leads the world. *Ib.*

It is the dull man who is always sure, and the sure man who is always dull.
Prejudices, Second Series [1920], *ch. 1*

If, after I depart this vale, you ever remember me and have thought to please my ghost, forgive some sinner and wink your eye at some homely girl.
Epitaph. From Smart Set [*December 1921*]

There are no mute, inglorious Miltons,[1] save in the hallucinations of poets. The one sound test of a Milton is that he functions as a Milton.
Prejudices, Third Series
[*1922*], *ch. 3*

Nine times out of ten, in the arts as in life, there is actually no truth to be discovered; there is only error to be exposed. *Ib.*

Injustice is relatively easy to bear; what stings is justice. *Ib.*

The older I grow the more I distrust the familiar doctrine that age brings wisdom. *Ib.*

Faith may be defined briefly as an illogical belief in the occurrence of the improbable. *Ib. 14*

To be happy one must be (*a*) well fed, unhounded by sordid cares, at ease in Zion, (*b*) full of a comfortable feeling of superiority to the masses of one's fellow men, and (*c*) delicately and unceasingly amused according to one's taste. It is my contention that, if this definition be accepted, there is no country in the world wherein a man constituted as I am — a man of my peculiar weakness, vanities, appetites, and aversions — can be so happy as he can be in the United States. Going further, I lay down the doctrine that it is a

---

[1] See Gray, p. 440b.

sheer physical impossibility for such a man to live in the United States and *not* be happy.

> *On Being an American* [1922]

The difference between a moral man and a man of honor is that the latter regrets a discreditable act, even when it has worked and he has not been caught.

> *Prejudices, Fourth Series*
> [1924], *ch. 11*

Nothing can come out of an artist that is not in the man.

> *Ib. Fifth Series* [1926], *ch. 5*

Christian endeavor is notoriously hard on female pulchritude.

> *The Aesthetic Recoil*

The learned are seldom pretty fellows, and in many cases their appearance tends to discourage a love of study in the young.

> *The New Webster International*
> *Dictionary* [1934]

The Gaseous Vertebrata who own, operate and afflict the universe have treated me with excessive politeness.

> *Happy Days* [1940], *preface*

When A annoys or injures B on the pretense of saving or improving X, A is a scoundrel.

> *Newspaper Days: 1899–1906*
> [1941]

I've made it a rule never to drink by daylight and never to refuse a drink after dark.

> *From the New York Post*
> [*September 18, 1945*]

Conscience is the inner voice that warns us somebody may be looking.

> *A Mencken Chrestomathy* [1949]

There are some people who read too much: the bibliobibuli. I know some who are constantly drunk on books, as other men are drunk on whiskey or religion. They wander through this most diverting and stimulating of worlds in a haze, seeing nothing and hearing nothing.

> *Minority Report: H. L. Menck-*
> *en's Notebooks* [1956]

The booboisie.   *Passim*

ALFRED NOYES
1880–1958

Forty singing seamen, who was puzzled for to know
If the grog they dreamed they swallowed made them dream of all that followed.

> *Forty Singing Seamen*

Go down to Kew in lilac time (it isn't far from London!)
And you shall wander hand in hand with love in summer's wonderland.

> *Barrel Organ, st. 5*

The wind was a torrent of darkness among the gusty trees,
The moon was a ghostly galleon tossed upon cloudy seas,
The road was a ribbon of moonlight over the purple moor,
And the highwayman came riding —
Riding — riding —
The highwayman came riding, up to the old inn-door.

> *The Highwayman*

The landlord's black-eyed daughter,
Bess, the landlord's daughter,
Plaiting a dark red love knot into her long black hair.   *Ib.*

I'll come to thee by moonlight, though hell should bar the way.   *Ib.*

Calling as he used to call, faint and far away,
In Sherwood, in Sherwood, about the break of day.   *Sherwood*

GRANTLAND RICE
1880–1954

When the One Great Scorer comes to write against your name —
He marks — not that you won or lost — but how you played the game.[1]

> *Alumnus Football*

[1] But just this line ye grave for me:
"He played the game."
ROBERT WILLIAM SERVICE [1874–1958],
The Lost Master

All wars are planned by old men
   In council rooms apart,
Who plan for greater armament
   And map the battle chart.[1]
> *Two Sides of War, st. 1*

I've noticed nearly all the dead
   Were hardly more than boys.
> *Ib. st. 4*

RICHARD HENRY TAWNEY
1880–1962

Industrialized communities neglect the very objects for which it is worth while to acquire riches in their feverish preoccupation with the means by which riches can be acquired.
> *The Acquisitive Society* [1920]

MARGARET WIDDEMER
1880–

I have shut my little sister in from life and light
(For a rose, for a ribbon, for a wreath
   across my hair).
> *The Factories* [1915], *st. 1*

Round my path they cry to me, little
   souls unborn —
God of Life! Creator! It was I! It was I!
> *Ib. st. 3*

THOMAS RUSSELL YBARRA
1880–

A Christian is a man who feels
   Repentance on a Sunday
For what he did on Saturday
   And is going to do on Monday.
> *The Christian*

ALBERT JAY COOK
fl. 1917

It's Heaven, Hell or Hoboken [2] before next Christmas Day.
> *Heaven, Hell or Hoboken*

[1] See Herbert Hoover, p. 931a.
[2] Port of embarkation and return for the American Expeditionary Forces during World War I.

FRANKLIN PIERCE ADAMS [F.P.A.]
1881–1960

Christmas is over and Business is Business.
> *For the Other 364 Days*

Up, to the office . . . and so to bed.
> *A Ballade of Mr. Samuel Pepys.*
> *Refrain*

Ruthlessly pricking our gonfalon bub-
   ble,
Making a Giant hit into a double,
Words that are weighty with nothing
   but trouble:
"Tinker to Evers to Chance."
> *Baseball's Sad Lexicon*

The rich man has his motor car,
   His country and his town estate.
He smokes a fifty-cent cigar
   And jeers at Fate.
> *The Rich Man, st. 1*

The best you get is an even break.[1]
> *Ballade of Schopenhauer's*
> *Philosophy*

I shot a poem into the air,
It was reprinted everywhere
From Bangor to the Rocky Range
And always credited to — Exchange.
> *Frequently*

O bards of rhyme and meter free,
My gratitude goes out to ye
For all your deathless lines — ahem!
Let's see now . . . What *is* one of
   them?   *To a Vers Librist*

Of making many books there is no
   end —
So Sancho Panza said, and so say I.
Thou wert my guide, philosopher and
   friend
When only one is shining in the sky.
> *Lines on and from Bartlett's*
> *Familiar Quotations*

Go, lovely Rose that lives its little hour!
Go, little booke! and let who will be
   clever!
Roll on! From yonder ivy-mantled tower

[1] See Albee, p. 842b.

The moon and I could keep this up
forever.
> *Lines on and from Bartlett's*
> *Familiar Quotations*

MARY ANTIN
1881–1949

So at last I was going to America!
Really, really going, at last! The boundaries burst. The arch of heaven soared.
A million suns shone out for every star.
The winds rushed in from outer space,
roaring in my ears, "America! America!"   *The Promised Land* [1912]

JOSEPH CAMPBELL
1881–1944

As a white candle
In a holy place,
So is the beauty
Of an aged face.
> *The Old Woman, st. 1*

SIR ALEXANDER
FLEMING
1881–1955

It is the lone worker who makes the
first advance in a subject: the details
may be worked out by a team, but the
prime idea is due to the enterprise,
thought and perception of an individual.[1]
> *Address, Edinburgh University*
> [1951]

PADRAIC COLUM
1881–1972

Years hence, in rustic speech, a phrase,
As in wild earth a Grecian vase!
> *A Poor Scholar of the Forties*

O woman shapely as a swan.
> *I Shall Not Die for Thee*

And I am praying God on high,
And I am praying Him night and day,

[1] See Sir Francis Darwin, p. 813b, and Hans
Zinsser, p. 949b.

For a little house — a house of my
own —
Out of the wind's and the rain's way.
> *An Old Woman of the Roads,*
> *st. 6*

JOHN FREEMAN
1881–1929

Who may regret what was, since it has
made
Himself himself? All that I was I am,
And the old childish joy now lives in
me
At sight of a green field or a green tree.
> *All That I Was I Am*

EDGAR ALBERT GUEST
1881–1959

Somebody said that it couldn't be done,
But he with a chuckle replied
That maybe it couldn't, but he would
be one
Who wouldn't say so till he'd tried.
> *It Couldn't Be Done*

It takes a heap o' livin' in a house t'
make it home,
A heap o' sun an' shadder, an' ye sometimes have t' roam
Afore ye really 'preciate the things ye
lef' behind,
An' hunger fer 'em somehow, with 'em
allus on yer mind.   *Home*

Let me be a little kinder,
Let me be a little blinder
To the faults of those around me,
Let me praise a little more.   *A Creed*

I'd rather see a sermon than hear one
any day;
I'd rather one should walk with me
than merely tell the way.
> *Sermons We See*

In this bright little package, now isn't it
odd?
You've a dime's worth of something
known only to God!
> *The Package of Seeds*

JOHN EDWARD HAZARD
1881–1935

Ain't It Awful, Mabel!

Title of book

POPE JOHN XXIII
[ANGELO GIUSEPPE RONCALLI]
1881–1963

The social progress, order, security and peace of each country are necessarily connected with the social progress, order, security and peace of all other countries.

At the present day no political community is able to pursue its own interests and develop itself in isolation, because the degree of its prosperity and development is a reflection and a component part of the degree of prosperity and development of all other political communities.

Pacem in Terris
[Encyclical letter,
April 11, 1963]

There exists an intrinsic connection between the common good on the one hand and the structure and function of public authority on the other. The moral order, which needs public authority in order to promote the common good in human society, requires also that the authority be effective in attaining that end. . . .

Today the universal common good poses problems of world-wide dimensions, which cannot be adequately tackled or solved except by the efforts of public authorities endowed with a wideness of power, structure and means of the same proportions: that is, of public authorities which are in a position to operate in an effective manner on a world-wide basis. The moral order itself, therefore, demands that such a form of public authority be established. *Ib.*

An act of the highest importance performed by the United Nations Organization was the universal Declaration of Human Rights, approved in the General Assembly of December 10, 1948. . . . The document represents an important step on the path towards the juridical-political organization of the world community. For in it, in most solemn form, the dignity of a person is acknowledged to all human beings; and as a consequence there is proclaimed, as a fundamental right, the right of free movement in search for truth and in the attainment of moral good and of justice, and also the right to a dignified life.

Pacem in Terris

The representative of the highest spiritual authority of the earth is glad, indeed boasts, of being the son of a humble but robust and honest laborer.

Remark to the Mayor of Fleury-sur-Loire. From Wit and Wisdom of Good Pope John, collected by Henri Fesquet [1963]

PABLO PICASSO
1881–1973

For me, a painting is a dramatic action in the course of which reality finds itself split apart. For me, that dramatic action takes precedence over all other considerations. The pure plastic act is only secondary as far as I'm concerned. What counts is the drama of that plastic act, the moment at which the universe comes out of itself and meets its own destruction.

From Françoise Gilot and Carlton Lake, *Life With Picasso [1964], pt. I*

When I was a child, my mother said to me, "If you become a soldier you'll be a general. If you become a monk you'll end up as the Pope." Instead I became a painter and wound up as Picasso. *Ib.*

Painting isn't an aesthetic operation; it's a form of magic designed as a mediator between this strange hostile world and us, a way of seizing the power by giving form to our terrors as well as our desires. *Ib. VI*

I am only a public entertainer who has understood his time.   *Remark*

WILLIAM TEMPLE
1881–1944

There is no structural organization of society which can bring about the coming of the Kingdom of God on earth, since all systems can be perverted by the selfishness of man.
The Malvern Manifesto [1]

Human status ought not to depend upon the changing demands of the economic process.   *Ib.*

PIERRE TEILHARD DE CHARDIN [2]
1881–1955

If there were no internal propensity to unite, even at a prodigiously rudimentary level — indeed in the molecule itself — it would be physically impossible for love to appear higher up, with us, in "hominized" form. . . . Driven by the forces of love, the fragments of the world seek each other so that the world may come into being.
The Phenomenon of Man [1955], *bk. IV, ch. 2, sec. 2*

Love alone is capable of uniting living beings in such a way as to complete and fulfill them, for it alone takes them and joins them by what is deepest in themselves. . . . Does not love every instant achieve all around us, in the couple or the team, the magic feat . . . of "personalizing" by totalizing? And if that is what it can achieve daily on a small scale, why should it not repeat this one day on world-wide dimensions?   *Ib.*

The end of the world: the wholesale internal introversion upon itself of the noosphere, which has simultaneously reached the uttermost limit of its complexity and its centrality . . . the overthrow of equilibrium, detaching the mind, fulfilled at last, from its material matrix, so that it will henceforth rest with all its weight on God-Omega . . . critical point simultaneously of emergence and emersion, of maturation and evasion.
The Phenomenon of Man, bk. IV, ch. 3, sec. 3

We have only to believe. And the more threatening and irreducible reality appears, the more firmly and desperately must we believe. Then, little by little, we shall see the universal horror unbend, and then smile upon us, and then take us in its more than human arms.
The Divine Milieu [1957], *pt. III, ch. 3, sec. B*

PELHAM GRENVILLE WODEHOUSE
1881–1975

He spoke with a certain what-is-it in his voice, and I could see that, if not actually disgruntled, he was far from being gruntled.
The Code of the Woosters

REGINALD ARKELL
1882–1959

Actual evidence I have none,
But my aunt's charwoman's sister's son
Heard a policeman, on his beat,
Say to a housemaid in Downing Street
That he had a brother, who had a friend,
Who knew when the war was going to end.   *All the Rumors* [1916]

BERTON BRALEY
1882–1966

The grammar has a rule absurd
Which I would call an outworn myth:
"A preposition is a word
You mustn't end a sentence with!" [1]
No Rule to Be Afraid Of, st. 1

---

[1] Drawn up by a Conference of the Province of York, January 10, 1941; signed for the Conference by Temple, then Archbishop of York (later Archbishop of Canterbury).

[2] Translated by BERNARD WALL.

[1] See Churchill, p. 925a.

And so they sailed away, these three,
    Mencken,
    Nathan
    And God.[1]
                        Three Minus One, st. 1

Back of the beating hammer
  By which the steel is wrought,
Back of the workshop's clamor
  The seeker may find the thought.
                        The Thinker, st. 1

Back of the job — the dreamer
Who's making the dream come true!
                        Ib. st. 4

GEORGES BRAQUE
1882–1963

Art upsets, science reassures.
                        Pensées sur l'Art

Truth exists, only falsehood has to be
invented.   *Ib.*

PERCY WILLIAMS
BRIDGMAN
1882–1961

To find the length of an object, we
have to perform certain physical operations. The concept of length is therefore fixed when the operations by which
length is measured are fixed: that is, the
concept of length involves as much as
and nothing more than the set of operations by which length is determined.
                        The Logic of Modern Physics
                        [1927]

EDWARD ARTHUR
BURROUGHS,
BISHOP OF RIPON
1882–1934

After all we could get on very happily
if aviation, wireless, television and the
like advanced no further than at present. . . . Dare I even suggest, at the
risk of being lynched by some of my
hearers, that the sum of human happiness would not necessarily be reduced if
for ten years every physical and chemi-

[1] See Eugene Field, p. 820b.

cal laboratory were closed and the patient and resourceful energy displayed
in them transferred to the lost art of
getting on together and finding the formula for making both ends meet in the
scale of human life. Much, of course,
we should lose by this universal scientific holiday . . . but human happiness would not necessarily suffer.
                        Sermon, to the British Associa-
                        tion for the Advancement of
                        Science [Leeds, September 4,
                        1927]

JOHN DRINKWATER
1882–1937

This be my pilgrimage and goal,
  Daily to march and find
The secret phrases of the soul,
  The evangels of the mind.
                        Vocation

And not a girl goes walking
  Along the Cotswold lanes
But knows men's eyes in April
  Are quicker than their brains.
                        Cotswold Love

Grant us the will to fashion as we feel,
Grant us the strength to labor as we
    know,
Grant us the purpose, ribbed and edged
    with steel,
To strike the blow.   *A Prayer, st. 9*

SIR ARTHUR STANLEY
EDDINGTON
1882–1944

It is one thing for the human mind
to extract from the phenomena of nature the laws which it has itself put into
them; it may be a far harder thing to
extract laws over which it has no control. It is even possible that laws which
have not their origin in the mind may
be irrational, and we can never succeed
in formulating them.
                        Space, Time, and Gravitation
                        [1920]

We have found that where science
has progressed the farthest, the mind

has but regained from nature that which the mind put into nature.

We have found a strange footprint on the shores of the unknown. We have devised profound theories, one after another, to account for its origin. At last we have succeeded in reconstructing the creature that made the footprint. And lo! it is our own.

Space, Time, and Gravitation

FELIX FRANKFURTER
1882–1965

The [Fifteenth] Amendment nullifies sophisticated as well as simple-minded modes of discrimination.

*Lane v. Wilson, 307 U.S. 268,
275 [1939]*

The history of liberty has largely been the history of the observance of procedural safeguards.

*McNabb v. United States, 318
U.S. 332, 347 [1943]*

One who belongs to the most vilified and persecuted minority in history is not likely to be insensible to the freedoms guaranteed by our Constitution. . . . But as judges we are neither Jew nor Gentile, neither Catholic nor agnostic.

*Flag Salute Cases, 319 U.S. 624,
646 [1943]*

Courts ought not to enter this political thicket.

*Colegrove v. Green, 328 U.S.
549, 556 [1946]*

After all, this is the Nation's ultimate judicial tribunal, not a super-legal-aid bureau.

*Uveges v. Pennsylvania, 335 U.S.
437, 449 [1948]*

In a democratic society like ours, relief must come through an aroused popular conscience that sears the conscience of the people's representatives.

*Baker v. Carr, 369 U.S. 186, 270
[1962]*

I know of no title that I deem more honorable than that of Professor of the Harvard Law School.

*Of Law and Life and Other
Things [1965]*

JEAN GIRAUDOUX
1882–1944

There are truths which can kill a nation.   *Electra*

Faithful women are all alike, they think only of their fidelity, never of their husbands.

Amphitryon 38 [1929]

SAMUEL GOLDWYN
1882–

Include me out.   *Saying*

In two words: im-possible.

From ALVA JOHNSTON,
The Great Goldwyn

A verbal contract isn't worth the paper it's written on.   *Ib.*

I read part of it all the way through.
Ib.

I would be sticking my head in a moose.   *Ib.*

If you can't give me your word of honor, will you give me your promise?
Ib.

HERMANN HAGEDORN
1882–1964

The bomb that fell on Hiroshima fell on America too.
It fell on no city, no munition plants, no docks.
It erased no church, vaporized no public buildings, reduced no man to his atomic elements.
But it fell, it fell.
It burst. It shook the land.
God have mercy on our children.
God have mercy on America.

The Bomb That Fell on America

967

WILLIAM FREDERICK HALSEY, JR.
1882–1959

Attack — Repeat — Attack.
> *Dispatch to the South Pacific Force (October 26, 1942) before the Battle of Santa Cruz Islands*

Hit hard, hit fast, hit often.[1]
> *Formula for waging war*

Send them our latitude and longitude.
> *Retort to the enemy's question, "Where is the American Fleet?" [October 1944]*

Our ships have been salvaged and are retiring at high speed toward the Japanese fleet.
> *Radio message [October 1944] after Japanese claims that most of the U.S. Third Fleet had either been sunk or had retired*

JAMES JOYCE
1882–1941

He was outcast from life's feast.
> *Dubliners [1916]. A Painful Case*

Snow was general all over Ireland. It was falling on every part of the dark central plain, on the treeless hills, falling softly upon the Bog of Allen and, farther westward, softly falling into the dark mutinous Shannon waves. It was falling, too, upon every part of the lonely churchyard on the hill where Michael Furey lay buried. It lay thickly drifted on the crooked crosses and headstones, on the spears of the little gate, on the barren thorns. His soul swooned slowly as he heard the snow falling faintly through the universe and faintly falling, like the descent of their last end, upon all the living and the dead.
> *Ib. The Dead*

Pity is the feeling which arrests the mind in the presence of whatsoever is

[1] See Grant, p. 717a.

grave and constant in human sufferings and unites it with the human sufferer.
> *A Portrait of the Artist as a Young Man [1916], ch. 5*

Welcome, O life! I go to encounter for the millionth time the reality of experience and to forge in the smithy of my soul the uncreated conscience of my race.

Old father, old artificer, stand me now and ever in good stead.
> *Ib. Concluding words of Stephen Dedalus*

My patience are exhausted [Molly Bloom].
> *Ulysses [1] [1922]*

A man of genius makes no mistakes. His errors are volitional and are the portals of discovery.
> *Ib.*

And yes I said yes I will Yes.
> *Ib. Last words*

Can't hear with bawk of bats, all thim liffeying waters of. Ho, talk save us! My foos won't moos. I feel as old as yonder elm. A tale told of Shaun or Shem? All Livia's daughter-sons. Dark hawks hear us. Night! Night! My ho head halls. I feel as heavy as yonder stone. Tell me of John or Shaun? Who were Shem and Shaun the living sons or daughters of? Night now! Tell me, tell me, tell me, elm! Night night! Telmetale of stem or stone. Beside the rivering waters of, hitherandthithering waters of. Night!
> *Finnegans Wake [1939], pt. I (end)*

I am passing out. O bitter ending! I'll slip away before they're up. They'll never see. Nor know. Nor miss me. And it's old and old it's sad and old it's sad and weary I go back to you, my cold father, my cold mad father, my cold

[1] In respect of the recurrent emergence of the theme of sex in the minds of his characters, it must always be remembered that his locale was Celtic and his season spring . . . whilst in many places the effect of *Ulysses* on the reader undoubtedly is somewhat emetic, nowhere does it tend to be an aphrodisiac. *Ulysses* may, therefore, be admitted into the United States. — JUDGE JOHN M. WOOLSEY, *U.S. v. One Book Called "Ulysses," 5 Federal Supplement 182, 184 [1933]*

mad feary father, till the near sight of the mere size of him, the moyles and moyles of it, moananoaning, makes me seasilt saltsick and I rush, my only, into your arms, I see them rising! Save me from those therrble prongs! Two more. Onetwo moremens more. So. Avelaval. My leaves have drifted from me. All. But one clings still. I'll bear it on me. To remind me of. Lff! So soft this morning, ours. Yes. Carry me along, taddy, like you done through the toy fair! If I seen him bearing down on me now under whitespread wings like he'd come from Arkangels, I sink I'd die down over his feet, humbly dumbly, only to washup. Yes, tid. There's where. First. We pass through grass behush the bush to. Whish! A gull. Gulls. Far calls. Coming, far! End here. Us then. Finn, again! Take. Bussoftlhee, mememormee! Till thousendsthee. Lps. The keys to. Given! A way a lone a last a loved a long the
Finnegans Wake, pt. IV

FIORELLO H. LAGUARDIA
1882–1947

Ticker tape ain't spaghetti.
Speech, United Nations Relief and Rehabilitation Administration [March 29, 1946]

WINIFRED MARY LETTS
1882–

I saw the spires of Oxford
As I was passing by,
The gray spires of Oxford
Against a pearl-gray sky.
My heart was with the Oxford men
Who went abroad to die.
The Spires of Oxford, st. 1

That God once loved a garden
We learn in Holy writ.
And seeing gardens in the spring
I well can credit it.
Stephen's Green, st. 1

PHILIP HENRY KERR, MARQUESS OF LOTHIAN[1]
1882–1940

A limitation of armaments by political appeasement.[2]
Letter to The Times (London)
[May 1934]

JACQUES MARITAIN
1882–1973

In the modern social order, the *person* is sacrificed to the *individual.* The individual is given universal suffrage, equality of rights, freedom of opinion; while the person, isolated, naked, with no social armor to sustain and protect him, is left to the mercy of all the devouring forces which threaten the life of the soul, exposed to relentless actions and reactions of conflicting interests and appetites. . . . It is a homicidal civilization.   *Three Reformers [1925]*

ALAN ALEXANDER MILNE
1882–1956

Hush! Hush! Whisper who dares!
Christopher Robin is saying his prayers.
When We Were Very Young
[1924]. Vespers

They're changing guard at Buckingham
    Palace —
Christopher Robin went down with
    Alice.   *Ib. Buckingham Palace*

The King asked
The Queen, and
The Queen asked
The Dairymaid:
"Could we have some butter for
The Royal slice of bread?"
Ib. The King's Breakfast

Nobody, my darling,
Could call me
A fussy man —
    BUT

---

[1] See Winston Churchill, p. 922a.
[2] One of the most portentous slogans of the period was coined here. — KONRAD HEIDEN, *Der Führer* [1944], *p. 714*

I do like a little bit of butter to my
bread!
> *When We Were Very Young.*
> *The King's Breakfast*

What shall I call my dear little
dormouse?
His eyes are small, but his tail is e-nor-
mouse.   *Ib. The Christening*

Christopher Robin goes
Hoppity, hoppity,
Hoppity, hoppity, hop.
Whenever I tell him
Politely to stop it, he
Says he can't possibly stop.
> *Ib. Hoppity*

James James
Morrison Morrison
Weatherby George Dupree
Took great
Care of his Mother
Though he was only three.
James James
Said to his Mother,
"Mother," he said, said he:
"You must never go down to the end of
the town, if you don't go down
with me."   *Ib. Disobedience*

I am a Bear of Very Little Brain, and
long words Bother me.
> *Winnie-the-Pooh* [1926], *ch.* 4

Time for a little something.   *Ib. 6*

Christopher Robin
Had wheezles
And sneezles.
> *Now We Are Six* [1927]. *Sneezles*

If I were a bear,
And a big bear, too,
I shouldn't much care
If it froze or snew.   *Ib. Furry Bear*

FRANCES PERKINS
1882–1965

Call me Madame.
> *On being asked how she pre-*
> *ferred to be addressed when*
> *she joined the Cabinet* [1933]

SAM RAYBURN
1882–1961

I like to make running water walk.
> *On Conversation. From* VALTON
> J. YOUNG, *The Speaker's Agent*
> [1956]

The greatest domestic problem facing our country is saving our soil and
water. Our soil belongs also to unborn
generations.   *Ib.*

The one thing besides people that I
claim to know is land.   *Ib.*

FRANKLIN DELANO
ROOSEVELT
1882–1945

There is nothing I love as much as a
good fight.
> *Interview, New York Times*
> [*January 22, 1911*]

These unhappy times call for the
building of plans . . . that build from
the bottom up and not from the top
down, that put their faith once more in
the forgotten man [1] at the bottom of
the economic pyramid.
> *Radio address* [*April 7, 1932*]

The country needs and, unless I mistake its temper, the country demands
bold, persistent experimentation. It is
common sense to take a method and try
it. If it fails, admit it frankly and try
another. But above all, try something.
> *Address, Oglethorpe University*
> [*May 22, 1932*]

I pledge you, I pledge myself, to a
new deal for the American people.
> *Speech accepting the Demo-*
> *cratic nomination for the Presi-*
> *dency, Chicago* [*July 2, 1932*]

There is no indispensable man.
> *Campaign speech, New York*
> [*November 3, 1932*]

[1] See William Graham Sumner, p. 785a.
All honor to the one that in this hour
Cries to the world as from a lighted tower —
Cries for the Man Forgotten.
> EDWIN MARKHAM [1852–1940], *The*
> *Forgotten Man*

The only thing we have to fear is fear itself.[1]

First Inaugural Address
[March 4, 1933]

The moneychangers have fled from their high seats in the temple of our civilization.[2] *Ib.*

In the field of world policy I would dedicate this nation to the policy of the good neighbor.[3] *Ib.*

If I were asked to state the great objective which Church and State are both demanding for the sake of every man and woman and child in this country, I would say that that great objective is "a more abundant life."

Address, Federal Council of Churches of Christ [December 6, 1933]

I am not for a return to that definition of liberty under which for many years a free people were being gradually regimented into the service of the privileged few. I prefer and I am sure you prefer that broader definition of liberty under which we are moving forward to greater freedom, to greater security for the average man than he has ever known before in the history of America.

Fireside Chat [September 30, 1934]

We have earned the hatred of entrenched greed.

Message to Congress [January 3, 1936]

The truth is found when men are free to pursue it.

Address, Temple University [February 22, 1936]

Out of this modern civilization economic royalists carved new dynasties. . . . The royalists of the economic order have conceded that political freedom was the business of the Govern-ment, but they have maintained that economic slavery was nobody's business.

Speech accepting renomination [June 27, 1936]

This generation of Americans has a rendezvous with destiny. *Ib.*

I have seen war. . . . I hate war.

Address, Chautauqua [August 14, 1936]

I have not sought, I do not seek, I repudiate the support of any advocate of Communism or of any other alien "ism" which would by fair means or foul change our American democracy.

Address, Syracuse [September 29, 1936]

I should like to have it said of my first Administration that in it the forces of selfishness and of lust for power met their match. I should like to have it said of my second Administration that in it these forces met their master.

Speech, Madison Square Garden [October 31, 1936]

Men with a passion for anonymity.

Report of President's Committee on Administrative Management [January 12, 1937]

We have always known that heedless self-interest was bad morals; we know now that it is bad economics.

Second Inaugural Address [January 20, 1937]

I see one-third of a nation ill-housed, ill-clad, ill-nourished. *Ib.*

The test of our progress is not whether we add more to the abundance of those who have much; it is whether we provide enough for those who have too little. *Ib.*

The epidemic of world lawlessness is spreading. When an epidemic of physical disease starts to spread, the community approves and joins in a quarantine of the patients in order to protect the health of the community against the spread of the disease. . . . The will for peace on the part of peace-loving na-

---

[1] See Montaigne, p. 189b, and note.
[2] See *Matthew 21:12–13*, p. 43b.
[3] I am as desirous of being a good neighbor as I am of being a bad subject. — THOREAU, *Civil Disobedience* [1849]

971

tions must express itself to the end that nations that may be tempted to violate their agreements and the rights of others will desist from such a course. There must be positive endeavors to preserve peace.

Speech, Chicago [1] [*October 5, 1937*]

War is a contagion. *Ib.*

History proves that dictatorships do not grow out of strong and successful governments, but out of weak and helpless ones. If by democratic methods people get a government strong enough to protect them from fear and starvation, their democracy succeeds; but if they do not, they grow impatient. Therefore, the only sure bulwark of continuing liberty is a government strong enough to protect the interests of the people, and a people strong enough and well enough informed to maintain its sovereign control over its government.

Fireside Chat [*April 14, 1938*]

Remember, remember always that all of us, and you and I especially, are descended from immigrants and revolutionists.[2]

Address, Daughters of the American Revolution [*April 21, 1938*]

A program whose basic thesis is not that the system of free private enterprise for profit has failed in this generation, but that it has not yet been tried.

Message on Concentration of Economic Power [*April 29, 1938*]

The Democratic Party will live and continue to receive the support of the majority of Americans just so long as it remains a liberal party.

Address, Denton, Maryland [*September 5, 1938*]

But the future lies with those wise political leaders who realize that the great public is interested more in Government than in politics.

Address, Jackson Day Dinner [*January 8, 1940*]

The Soviet Union, as everybody who has the courage to face the fact knows, is run by a dictatorship as absolute as any other dictatorship in the world.

Address, American Youth Congress [*February 10, 1940*]

On this tenth day of June 1940 the hand that held the dagger has struck it into the back of its neighbor.[1]

Address, University of Virginia, Charlottesville [*June 10, 1940*]

Eternal truths will be neither true nor eternal unless they have fresh meaning for every new social situation.

Address, University of Pennsylvania [*September 20, 1940*]

And while I am talking to you mothers and fathers, I give you one more assurance. I have said this before, but I shall say it again and again and again: Your boys are not going to be sent into any foreign wars.

Campaign speech, Boston [*October 30, 1940*]

That great historic trio . . . Martin, Barton and Fish.[2] *Ib.*

It is an unfortunate human failing that a full pocketbook often groans more loudly than an empty stomach.

Speech, Brooklyn [*November 1, 1940*]

We must be the great arsenal of democracy.

Fireside Chat [*December 29, 1940*]

In the future days, which we seek to make secure, we look forward to a world founded upon four essential human freedoms. The first is freedom of speech and expression — everywhere

[1] Italian Foreign Minister Count Galeazzo Ciano had just notified the French Ambassador that Italy considered herself at war with France beginning June 11.

[2] Joseph Martin, Bruce Barton, and Hamilton Fish.

[1] The "Quarantine the aggressors" speech.
[2] See *Campaign Speech, Boston,* p. 973b-974a.

in the world. The second is freedom of every person to worship God in his own way — everywhere in the world. The third is freedom from want . . . everywhere in the world. The fourth is freedom from fear . . . anywhere in the world.[1]
Message to Congress [January 6, 1941]

One great difference which has characterized this division [between liberal and conservative parties] has been that the liberal party — no matter what its particular name was at the time — believed in the wisdom and efficacy of the will of the great majority of the people, as distinguished from the judgment of a small minority. . . . The other great difference between the two parties has been this: The liberal party is a party which believes that, as new conditions and problems arise beyond the power of men and women to meet as individuals, it becomes the duty of the Government itself to find new remedies with which to meet them. The liberal party insists that the Government has the definite duty to use all its power and resources to meet new social problems with new social controls — to insure to the average person the right to his own economic and political life, liberty, and the pursuit of happiness.
Public Papers and Addresses, 1938 Volume [1941], introduction

We, too, born to freedom, and believing in freedom, are willing to fight to maintain freedom. We, and all others who believe as deeply as we do, would rather die on our feet than live on our knees.[2]
On receiving the degree of Doctor of Civil Law from Oxford University [June 19, 1941]

[1] See *Atlantic Charter*, p. 974a-b.
[2] See Zapata, p. 943a.
The phrase was a watchword with the Republican forces in the Spanish Civil War, 1936–1939, and is especially identified with the celebrated woman leader La Pasionara.

When you see a rattlesnake poised to strike, you do not wait until he has struck before you crush him.
Fireside Chat [September 11, 1941]

Yesterday, December 7, 1941 — a date which will live in infamy — the United States of America was suddenly and deliberately attacked by naval and air forces of the Empire of Japan.
War Message to Congress [December 8, 1941]

Never before have we had so little time in which to do so much.[1]
Fireside Chat [February 23, 1942]

We all know that books burn — yet we have the greater knowledge that books cannot be killed by fire. People die, but books never die. No man and no force can abolish memory. . . . In this war, we know, books are weapons.
Message, American Booksellers Association [April 23, 1942]

It is not a tax bill but a tax relief bill providing relief not for the needy but for the greedy.
Tax bill veto message [February 22, 1944]

These Republican leaders have not been content with attacks on me, or my wife, or on my sons. No, not content with that, they now include my little dog, Fala. Well, of course, I don't resent attacks . . . but Fala *does* resent them. . . . I think I have a right to resent, to object to libelous statements about my dog.[2]
Speech, Teamsters' Dinner, Washington [September 23, 1944]

All of our people all over the country — except the pure-blooded Indians

[1] See Churchill, p. 921b.
[2] It had been charged that the President, at a cost of several million dollars to the taxpayers, had sent a destroyer to the Aleutian Islands to fetch his Scottie, Fala, allegedly stranded there. When Fala heard these baseless stories of government extravagance on his account, "his Scotch soul was furious. He has not been the same dog since."

— are immigrants or descendants of immigrants, including even those who came over here on the Mayflower.[1]

Campaign speech, Boston
[November 4, 1944]

The American people are quite competent to judge a political party that works both sides of a street. *Ib.*

Perfectionism, no less than isolationism or imperialism or power politics, may obstruct the paths to international peace.

State of the Union Message
[January 6, 1945]

We have learned that we cannot live alone, at peace; that our own well-being is dependent on the well-being of other nations, far away. We have learned that we must live as men, and not as ostriches, nor as dogs in the manger. We have learned to be citizens of the world, members of the human community.

Fourth Inaugural Address
[January 20, 1945]

More than an end to war, we want an end to the beginnings of all wars.

Address written for Jefferson Day
[April 13, 1945] broadcast [2]

The only limit to our realization of tomorrow will be our doubts of today. Let us move forward with strong and active faith. *Ib.*

FRANKLIN D. ROOSEVELT AND WINSTON CHURCHILL

First, their countries seek no aggrandizement, territorial or other.
Second, they desire to see no territorial changes that do not accord with

the freely expressed wishes of the peoples concerned.

Atlantic Charter, drawn up aboard U.S.S. Augusta in Argentia Harbor, Newfoundland [issued August 14, 1941]

Sixth, after the final destruction of the Nazi tyranny, they hope to see established a peace which will afford to all nations the means of dwelling in safety within their own boundaries, and which will afford assurance that all the men in all the lands may live out their lives in freedom from fear and want.[1] *Ib.*

Eighth, they believe that all of the nations of the world, for realistic as well as spiritual reasons, must come to the abandonment of the use of force. Since no future peace can be maintained if land, sea or air armaments continue to be employed by nations which threaten, or may threaten, aggression outside of their frontiers, they believe, pending the establishment of a wider and permanent system of general security, that the disarmament of such nations is essential. *Ib.*

JAMES STEPHENS
1882–1950

I hear a sudden cry of pain!
There is a rabbit in a snare.
The Snare

Forgive us all our trespasses,
Little creatures, everywhere!
Little Things, st. 5

In cloud and clod to sing
Of everything and anything.
The Pit of Bliss

I heard a bird at dawn
Singing sweetly on a tree,
That the dew was on the lawn,
And the wind was on the lea;
But I didn't listen to him,
For he didn't sing to me.
The Rivals, st. 1

[1] See *Address to D.A.R.*, p. 972a.
[2] President Roosevelt died April 12, at Warm Springs, Georgia.

[1] See Roosevelt, *Message to Congress, January 6, 1941*, p. 972b-973a.

They fell out over pigs, let them fall in over pigs.
In the Land of Youth [1924]

Women are wiser than men because they know less and understand more.
The Crock of Gold [1930], *ch.* 2

The bad poet is superabundant in all anthologies of verse.
Preface to A Trophy of Arms [1936], *by* RUTH PITTER

VIRGINIA WOOLF[1]
1882–1941

In people's eyes, in the swing, tramp, and trudge; in the bellow and uproar; the carriages, motor cars, omnibuses, vans, sandwich men shuffling and swinging; brass bands; barrel organs; in the triumph and the jingle and the strange high singing of some aeroplane overhead was what she loved; life; London; this moment in June.
Mrs. Dalloway [1925]

Those comfortably padded lunatic asylums which are known, euphemistically, as the stately homes of England.[2]
The Common Reader [1925]. *Lady Dorothy Nevill*

Trivial personalities decomposing in the eternity of print.
Ib. The Modern Essay

There is no room for the impurities of literature in an essay. *Ib.*

That complete statement which is literature.
Ib. How It Strikes a Contemporary

The word-coining genius, as if thought plunged into a sea of words and came up dripping.
Ib. An Elizabethan Play

The beauty of the world has two edges, one of laughter, one of anguish, cutting the heart asunder.
A Room of One's Own [1929]

[1] The talent of this generation which is most certain of survival. — REBECCA WEST, *Ending in Earnest* [1931]
[2] See Felicia D. Hemans, p. 573b.

Women have served all these centuries as looking-glasses possessing the magic and delicious power of reflecting the figure of man at twice its natural size. *A Room of One's Own*

Surely it was time someone invented a new plot, or that the author came out from the bushes.
Between the Acts [1941]

SIR ANDREW BROWNE CUNNINGHAM
1883–1963

We are so outnumbered there's only one thing to do. We must attack.[1]
Before attacking the Italian fleet, Taranto [*November 1940*]

MAX EASTMAN
1883–1969

I don't know why it is we are in such a hurry to get up when we fall down. You might think we would lie there and rest awhile.
The Enjoyment of Laughter [1936], *pt. III, ch.* 4

KAHLIL GIBRAN
1883–1931

Let there be spaces in your togetherness.[2]
The Prophet [1923]. *On Marriage*

You may give them your love but not your thoughts,
For they have their own thoughts.
You may house their bodies but not their souls,
For their souls dwell in the house of tomorrow, which you cannot visit, not even in your dreams.
You may strive to be like them, but seek not to make them like you,
For life goes not backward nor tarries with yesterday.

[1] Quoted in *British Commanders*, published by *British Information Services* [1945].
[2] See Rilke, p. 938b.

You are the bows from which your children as living arrows are sent forth.
The Prophet. On Children

You give but little when you give of your possessions. It is when you give of yourself that you truly give.[1]
Ib. On Giving

Work is love made visible. And if you cannot work with love but only with distaste, it is better that you should leave your work and sit at the gate of the temple and take alms of those who work with joy.
Ib. On Work

You pray in your distress and in your need; would that you might pray also in the fullness of your joy and in your days of abundance.   *Ib. On Prayer*

He who wears his morality but as his best garment were better naked.
Ib. On Religion

I have learned silence from the talkative, toleration from the intolerant, and kindness from the unkind; yet strange, I am ungrateful to those teachers.
Sand and Foam [1926]

We shall never understand one another until we reduce the language to seven words.[2]   *Ib.*

JOHN CEREDIGION JONES
1883–1947

All's well, for over there among his peers
A happy warrior sleeps.[3]
The Returning Man, st. 4

[1] See Emerson, p. 607b; James Russell Lowell, p. 692b, and Whitman, p. 700b.
[2] If we go on explaining we shall cease to understand one another. — TALLEYRAND [*1754–1838*], quoted by B. BERENSON, *Aesthetics and History*
[3] These lines are inscribed over the archway of the Memorial Chamber in the Peace Tower, Parliament Buildings, Ottawa.
See Wordsworth, p. 515a.

HARRY KEMP
1883–1960

I pitied him in his blindness;
But can I boast, "I see"?
Perhaps there walks a spirit
Close by, who pities me.   *Blind, st. 2*

JOHN MAYNARD KEYNES
1883–1946

He [Clemenceau] had one illusion — France; and one disillusion — mankind, including Frenchmen.
Economic Consequences of the Peace [1919], *ch. 3*

Watching the company, with six or seven senses not available to ordinary men, judging character, motive, and subconscious impulse, perceiving what each was thinking and even what each was going to say next, and compounding with telepathic instinct the argument or appeal best suited to the vanity, weakness, or self-interest of his immediate auditor.[1]   *Ib.*

He [Woodrow Wilson] could write Notes from Sinai or Olympus; he could remain unapproachable in the White House or even in the Council of Ten and be safe. But if he once stepped down to the intimate quality of the Four, the game was evidently up.   *Ib.*

To make the defeated Central Empires into good neighbors.   *Ib. 6*

We have been moved already beyond endurance, and need rest.   *Ib. 7*

Marxian Socialism must always remain a portent to the historians of opinion — how a doctrine so illogical and so dull can have exercised so powerful and enduring an influence over the minds of men, and, through them, the events of history.
The End of Laissez-Faire [1925], *ch. 3*

Thrift may be the handmaid and nurse of Enterprise. But equally she

[1] Lloyd George.

may not. . . . For the engine which drives Enterprise is not Thrift, but Profit.   *A Treatise on Money* [1930]

The love of money as a possession — as distinguished from the love of money as a means to the enjoyments and realities of life — will be recognized for what it is, a somewhat disgusting morbidity, one of those semi-criminal, semi-pathological propensities which one hands over with a shudder to the specialists in mental disease.
    Essays in Persuasion [1931], *pt.* V

In the United States, it is almost inconceivable what rubbish a public man has to utter today if he is to keep respectable.
    In the Atlantic Monthly [*May 1932*]

Words ought to be a little wild for they are the assault of thoughts on the unthinking.
    In the New Statesman and Nation [*July 15, 1933*]

His [Newton's] peculiar gift was the power of holding continuously in his mind a purely mental problem until he had seen through it. . . . Anyone who has ever attempted a pure scientific or philosophical thought knows how one can hold a problem momentarily in one's mind and apply all one's power of concentration to piercing through it, and how it will dissolve and escape and you find that what you are surveying is a blank.   *Essays in Biography* [1933]

There is no harm in being sometimes wrong — especially if one is promptly found out.   *Ib.*

Practical men, who believe themselves to be quite exempt from any intellectual influences, are usually the slaves of some defunct economist. . . . It is ideas, not vested interests, which are dangerous for good or evil.
    The General Theory of Employment, Interest and Money [1936]

BENITO MUSSOLINI
1883–1945

The Italian proletariat needs a blood bath for its force to be renewed.
    Editorial, Popolo d'Italia [1920]

War alone brings up to its highest tension all human energy and puts the stamp of nobility upon the peoples who have the courage to face it.
    Written for The Italian Encyclopedia. From GEORGE SELDES, *Sawdust Caesar* [1935]

Fortunately the Italian people is not yet accustomed to eating several times per day.
    Speech [*December 1930*]; *ib.*

We have buried the putrid corpse of liberty.
    Speech. From MAURICE PARMELEE, *Bolshevism, Fascism and the Liberal-Democratic State* [1934]

The Italian race is a race of sheep.
    From the Ciano Diaries [*January 29, 1940*]

To make a people great it is necessary to send them to battle even if you have to kick them in the pants.
    Ib. [*April 11, 1940*]

JOSÉ ORTEGA Y GASSET
1883–1955

Rancor is an outpouring of a feeling of inferiority.
    Meditations on Quixote [1911]

I am myself and what is around me, and if I do not save it, it shall not save me.   *Ib.*

The Mediterraneans, who do not think clearly, do see clearly.   *Ib.*

Culture is not life in its entirety, but just the moment of security, strength, and clarity.   *Ib.*

Nations are formed and are kept alive by the fact that they have a program for tomorrow.
    Invertebrate Spain [1922], *ch.* 2

A society without an aristocracy, without an elite minority, is not a society.   *Invertebrate Spain, ch. 4*

Conversation is the socializing instrument par excellence, and in its style one can see reflected the capacities of a race.   *Ib. 7*

Man was formed by his struggle with exterior forces and it is only easy for him to discern things which are outside of himself.
   The Modern Theme [1923], ch. 2

Rationalism, in order to save truth, renounces life.   *Ib. 3*

The choice of a point of view is the initial act of a culture.   *Ib. 7*

To define is to exclude and negate.
   Ib. appendix

Order is not pressure which is imposed on society from without, but an equilibrium which is set up from within.
   Mirabeau and Politics [1927]

Europe is really a swarm: many bees on a single course.
   The Revolt of the Masses [1930], prologue

America, far from being the future, was in truth a remote past because it was primitivism.   *Ib.*

Minorities are individuals or groups of individuals especially qualified. The masses are the collection of people not specially qualified.   *Ib. ch. 1*

Physical space and time are the absolute stupidity of the universe.   *Ib. 4*

Our life is at all times and before anything else the consciousness of what we can do.   *Ib.*

A revolution only lasts fifteen years, a period which coincides with the effectiveness of a generation.   *Ib. 10*

War is not an instinct but an invention.   *Ib. epilogue*

It is not the material of life which makes up Dostoevski's "realism," but rather the shape of life.
   Notes on the Novel [1948]

The person portrayed and the portrait are two entirely different things.
   The Dehumanization of Art [1948]

The masses feel that it is easy to flee from reality, when it is the most difficult thing in the world.   *Ib.*

The metaphor is probably the most fertile power possessed by man.   *Ib.*

I am a Spaniard, that is to say, a man without imagination.
   Esthetic Essays [1956]

Primitive man is by definition tactile man.   *Ib.*

TAKAMURA KOTARO[1]
1883–1956

Cheekbones protruding, lips thick, eyes triangular,
Face like a netsuke[2] carved by the great Shuzan,
Expression vacant as though the soul were removed,
Ignorant of himself, jumpy,
Cheap-lived,
Show-off,
Small-minded, self-satisfied,
Monkey-like, fox-like, squirrel-like, gudgeon-like, minnow-like, potsherd-like, gargoyle-faced Japanese!
   The Land of Netsuke

HOWARD ARNOLD WALTER
1883–1918

I would be true, for there are those who trust me;
I would be pure, for there are those who care;
I would be strong, for there is much to suffer;

[1] From *Modern Japanese Literature,* edited by Donald Keene [1960].
[2] A carved button.

I would be brave, for there is much to
dare.
My Creed

ANGELA MORGAN
d. 1957

Work!
Thank God for the swing of it,
For the clamoring, hammering ring of
it,
Passion of labor daily hurled
On the mighty anvils of the world.
Work: A Song of Triumph

WILLIAM CARLOS
WILLIAMS
1883–1963

No wreaths please —
especially no hothouse flowers.
Some common memento is better,
something he prized and is known by:
his old clothes — a few books perhaps.
Tract [1917]

Hell take curtains! Go with some show
of inconvenience; sit openly —
to the weather as to grief.
Or do you think you can shut grief in?
Ib.

so much depends
upon

a red wheel
barrow

glazed with rain
water

beside the white
chickens
Spring and All [1923], *no. XXI*

Mothlike in mists, scintillant in the
minute
brilliance of cloudless days, with broad
bellying sails
they glide to the wind tossing green
water
from their sharp prows while over them
the crew crawls.
The Yachts [1935], *st. 1, 2*

It's the anarchy of poverty
delights me.
The Poor [1938], *st. 1*

THESE
are the desolate, dark weeks
when nature in its barrenness
equals the stupidity of man.[1]

The year plunges into night
and the heart plunges
lower than night.
These [1938], *st. 1, 2*

ERNEST BEVIN
1884–1951

There has never been a war yet
which, if the facts had been put calmly
before the ordinary folk, could not have
been prevented. The common man is
the greatest protection against war.
Speech, House of Commons
[*November* 1945]

ÉDOUARD DALADIER
1884–1970

If French and German blood is now
to be spilled, as it was twenty-five years
ago . . . then each of the two peoples
will fight confident of its own victory.
But surely Destruction and Barbarism
will be the real victors.
Letter to Adolf Hitler
[*August 26, 1939*]

The weakness of democracies is that
once a general has been built up in public opinion it becomes impossible to remove him.
From PERTINAX [ANDRÉ GÉ-
RAUD], *Gravediggers of France*
[*1944*]

A phrase has spread from civilians to
soldiers and back again: "This is a
phony war." [2]
Ib. [*Speech to the Deputies, De-*
cember 22, 1939]

---

[1] See William Cullen Bryant, p. 574b.
[2] Une drôle de guerre.

JAMES ELROY FLECKER
1884–1915

West of these out to seas colder than
    the Hebrides
I must go
Where the fleet of stars is anchored
    and the young
Star captains glow.
> *The Dying Patriot*

We who with songs beguile your pil-
    grimage
And swear that Beauty lives though
    lilies die,
We Poets of the proud old lineage
Who sing to find your hearts, we know
    not why.
> *The Golden Journey to Samar-*
> *kand* [1913], *prologue*

When even lovers find their peace at
    last,
And Earth is but a star, that once had
    shone.   *Ib.*

I have seen old ships sail like swans
    asleep.   *The Old Ships* [1915]

A ship, an isle, a sickle moon —
With few but with how splendid stars.[1]
> *A Ship, An Isle, A Sickle Moon*

TEXAS GUINAN
1884–1933

Hello, sucker!
> *Greeting to night club patrons*

A big butter-and-egg man.[2]
> *Describing a lavish spender or*
> *theatrical "angel"*

FRANZ KAFKA
1884–1924

"This village belongs to the Castle,
and whoever lives here or passes the
night here does so in a manner of
speaking in the Castle itself. Nobody
may do that without the Count's permission."
> *The Castle*[3] [1926]

---

[1] See Whitman, p. 700a.
[2] Title of play by George S. Kaufman [1925].
[3] Translated by EDWIN and WILLA MUIR.

The true way goes over a rope which
is not stretched at any great height but
just above the ground. It seems more
designed to make people stumble than
to be walked upon.
> *The Great Wall of China.*
> *Reflections*

You do not need to leave your room.
Remain sitting at your table and listen.
Do not even listen, simply wait. Do not
even wait, be quite still and solitary.
The world will freely offer itself to you
to be unmasked, it has no choice, it will
roll in ecstasy at your feet.   *Ib.*

Only our concept of time makes it
possible for us to speak of the Day of
Judgment by that name; in reality it is
a summary court in perpetual session.
> *Letters. Quoted in* MAX BROD,
> *Franz Kafka*

All human error is impatience, a premature renunciation of method, a delusive pinning down of a delusion.   **Ib.**

There are two cardinal sins from
which all the others spring: impatience
and laziness.   *Ib.*

BRONISLAW MALINOWSKI
1884–1942

Is war a biological necessity? As regards the earliest cultures the answer is
emphatically negative. The blow of the
poisonous dart from behind a bush, to
murder a woman or a child in their
sleep, is not pugnacity. Nor is head-
hunting, body-snatching, or killing for
food instinctive or natural.
> *Address, Phi Beta Kappa, Har-*
> *vard University* [*September 17,*
> *1936*]

The hero of the next war, the man
who from the air destroys a whole
peaceful township in its sleep with
poison gas, is not expressing any biological characteristics of his organism, or
showing any moral virtues.   **Ib.**

SEAN O'CASEY
1884–1964

The whole world is in a state of chassis.

Juno and the Paycock [1] [1924]

One minute with him is all I ask; one minute alone with him, while you're runnin' for th' priest an' th' doctor.

The Plow and the Stars [1926], act II

A few hundhred scrawls o' chaps with a couple o' guns and Rosary beads, again' a hundhred thousand thrained men with horse, fut an' artillery . . . an' he wants us to fight fair!

Ib. IV

A sober black shawl hides her body entirely,
Touch'd be th' sun an' th' salt spray of th' sea;
But deep in th' darkness a slim hand, so lovely,
Carries a rich bunch of red roses for me!

Red Roses for Me [1942], act IV

CHARLES LEO O'DONNELL
1884–1934

I have never been able to school my eyes
Against young April's blue surprise.

Wonder

KEITH PRESTON
1884–1927

Among our literary scenes,
  Saddest this sight to me,
The graves of little magazines
  That died to make verse free.

The Liberators

I am the captain of my soul; [2]
  I rule it with stern joy;
And yet I think I had more fun
  When I was a cabin boy.

An Awful Responsibility

[1] See Aesop, p. 76a.
[2] See Sallust, p. 116a, and note.

ANNA ELEANOR ROOSEVELT [1]
1884–1962

No one can make you feel inferior without your consent.

This Is My Story [1937]

You gain strength, courage and confidence by every experience in which you really stop to look fear in the face. You are able to say to yourself, "I lived through this horror. I can take the next thing that comes along." . . . You must do the thing you think you cannot do.

You Learn by Living [1960]

Life was meant to be lived, and curiosity must be kept alive. One must never, for whatever reason, turn his back on life.

The Autobiography of Eleanor Roosevelt [1961]

GEORGE SARTON
1884–1956

Scientific activity is the only one which is obviously and undoubtedly cumulative and progressive.

The History of Science and the History of Civilization [1930]

SARA TEASDALE
1884–1933

When I am dead and over me bright April
Shakes out her rain-drenched hair,
Though you should lean above me broken-hearted,
I shall not care.

I Shall Not Care, st. 1

Strephon's kiss was lost in jest,
  Robin's lost in play,
But the kiss in Colin's eyes
  Haunts me night and day.

The Look, st. 2

[1] I have lost more than a friend, I have lost an inspiration. She would rather light candles than curse the darkness and her glow has warmed the world. — ADLAI E. STEVENSON [November 7, 1962]
It is better to light one candle than curse the darkness. — *Motto of the Christopher Society*

Alone in the night
  On a dark hill
With pines around me
  Spicy and still.
          Stars [1921], *st. 1*

Let it be forgotten, as a flower is forgotten,
Forgotten as a fire that once was singing gold,
Let it be forgotten forever and ever,
Time is a kind friend, he will make us old.
    Let It Be Forgotten [1921], *st. 1*

Oh better than the minting
  Of a gold-crowned king
Is the safe-kept memory
  Of a lovely thing.
          The Coin [1921]

O beauty, are you not enough?
Why am I crying after love?
          Spring Night

HARRY S. TRUMAN
1884–1972

When they told me yesterday what had happened, I felt like the moon, the stars and all the planets had fallen on me.
    To reporters the day after his accession to the Presidency [April 13, 1945]

The responsibility of the great states is to serve and not to dominate the world.
    First Message to Congress [April 16, 1945]

When Kansas and Colorado have a quarrel over the water in the Arkansas River they don't call out the National Guard in each state and go to war over it. They bring a suit in the Supreme Court of the United States and abide by the decision. There isn't a reason in the world why we cannot do that internationally.
    Speech, Kansas City [April 1945]

You members of the conference are to be the architects of the better world. In your hands rests our future. By your labors at this conference we shall know if suffering humanity is to achieve a just and lasting peace.
    Radio address to delegates at the opening session of the United Nations conference, San Francisco [April 23, 1945]

We must build a new world, a far better world — one in which the eternal dignity of man is respected.　*Ib.*

Sixteen hours ago an American airplane dropped one bomb on Hiroshima. . . . It is a harnessing of the basic power of the universe. The force from which the sun draws its power has been loosed against those who brought war to the Far East.
    First announcement of the atomic bomb [August 6, 1945]

The release of atomic energy constitutes a new force too revolutionary to consider in the framework of old ideas.
    Message to Congress on atomic energy [October 3, 1945]

Means of destruction hitherto unknown, against which there can be no adequate military defense, and in the employment of which no single nation can in fact have a monopoly.
    Declaration on Atomic Energy by President Truman and Prime Ministers Clement Attlee and W. L. Mackenzie King [November 15, 1945]

Effective, reciprocal, and enforceable safeguards acceptable to all nations.
          Ib.

We must embark on a bold new program for making the benefits of our scientific advances and industrial progress available for the improvement and growth of underdeveloped areas. More than half the people of the world are living in conditions approaching misery. Their food is inadequate. They are the victims of disease. Their economic life is primitive and stagnant. Their poverty is a handicap and a threat both to them and to more prosperous areas.

> *Inaugural Address (Point Four Program) [January 20, 1949]*

If you can't stand the heat, get out of the kitchen.   *Saying* [1]

There is enough in the world for everyone to have plenty to live on happily and to be at peace with his neighbors.

> *Memoirs [1955], vol. I, Year of Decisions, preface*

Being a President is like riding a tiger. A man has to keep on riding or be swallowed.[2]

> *Ib. II, Years of Trial and Hope, ch. 1*

A President either is constantly on top of events or, if he hesitates, events will soon be on top of him. I never felt that I could let up for a single moment.   *Ib.*

No one who has not had the responsibility can really understand what it is like to be President, not even his closest aides or members of his immediate family. There is no end to the chain of responsibility that binds him, and he is never allowed to forget that he is President.   *Ib.*

Once a decision was made, I did not worry about it afterward.   *Ib.*

Most of the problems a President has to face have their roots in the past.   *Ib.*

The Marshall Plan will go down in history as one of America's greatest contributions to the peace of the world.   *Ib. 8*

---

[1] President Truman has used variations of the aphorism . . . for many years, both orally and in his writings. For instance, in his book *Mr. Citizen [1960]* in the chapter entitled "Some Thoughts on the Presidency," he states, "Some men can make decisions and some cannot. Some men fret and delay under criticism. I used to have a saying that applies here, and I note that some people have picked it up." — *Letter to editor from* PHILIP D. LAGERQUIST, Harry S. Truman Library, Independence, Missouri [February 11, 1966]

[2] See Churchill, p. 920a, and note.

To me, party platforms are contracts with the people.

> *Memoirs, vol. II, Years of Trial and Hope, ch. 13*

Polk was a positive man . . . and settled every issue before his term of office expired.   *Ib. 14*

A man who is influenced by the polls or is afraid to make decisions which may make him unpopular is not a man to represent the welfare of the country.   *Ib.*

A President cannot always be popular.   *Ib.*

Every great President in our history had a policy of his own, which eventually won the people's support.   *Ib.*

Popularity and glamor are only part of the factors involved in winning presidential elections. One of the most important of all is luck. In my own case, luck was always with me, though there was never any intention on my part to make things work my way. If a man starts out to make himself President, he hardly ever arrives.   *Ib.*

A President needs political understanding to *run* the government, but he may be *elected* without it.   *Ib.*

The convention system has its faults, of course, but I do not know of a better method for choosing a presidential nominee.   *Ib.*

The Point Four program . . . was created and designed to operate on a continuing basis to point the way to better living for more and more of the world's people — and thus the way to a more lasting peace.   *Ib. 16*

All my life I have fought against prejudice and intolerance.   *Ib. 19*

I have little patience with people who take the Bill of Rights for granted. The Bill of Rights, contained in the first ten amendments to the Constitution, is every American's guarantee of freedom.   *Ib.*

It [General Douglas MacArthur's statement on Korea, March 24, 1951] was in open defiance of my orders as President and as Commander in Chief. This was a challenge to the authority of the President under the Constitution. It also flouted the policy of the United Nations. . . . I was deeply shocked.

> *Memoirs, vol. II, Years of Trial and Hope, ch. 19*

If there is one basic element in our Constitution, it is civilian control of the military.   **Ib.**

There is a right kind and wrong kind of victory, just as there are wars for the right thing and wars that are wrong from every standpoint. . . . The kind of victory MacArthur had in mind — victory by the bombing of Chinese cities, victory by expanding the conflict to all of China — would have been the wrong kind of victory.   **Ib.**

The buck stops here.

> *Sign on Truman's desk as President. From* Alfred Steinberg, *The Man from Missouri* [1962]

SOPHIE TUCKER[1]
1884–1966

From birth to age eighteen, a girl needs good parents. From eighteen to thirty-five, she needs good looks. From thirty-five to fifty-five, she needs a good personality. From fifty-five on, she needs good cash.

> *Said at sixty-nine*

NIELS BOHR
1885–1962

In our description of nature the purpose is not to disclose the real essence of the phenomena but only to track down, so far as it is possible, relations

---

[1] Known as "The Last of the Red-Hot Mamas" from the title of a song by Jack Yellen [1892–] which she introduced in 1928.

---

between the manifold aspects of our experience.

> *Atomic Theory and the Description of Nature* [1934]

ARTHUR WALLACE CALHOUN
1885–

Gentlemen of the old régime in the South would say, "A woman's name should appear in print but twice — when she marries and when she dies."

> *Social History of the American Family* [1918], *citing* Myrta Lockett Avary, *Dixie After the War* [1906]

ZECHARIAH CHAFEE, JR.
1885–1957

The press is a sort of wild animal in our midst — restless, gigantic, always seeking new ways to use its strength. . . . The sovereign press for the most part acknowledges accountability to no one except its owners and publishers.

> *The Press Under Pressure* [*Nieman Reports, April 1948*]

Freedom from something is not enough. It should also be freedom for something. Freedom is not safety but opportunity. Freedom ought to be a means to enable the press to serve the proper functions of communication in a free society.   **Ib.**

ISAK DINESEN
[KAREN BLIXEN]
1885–1962

What is man, when you come to think upon him, but a minutely set, ingenious machine for turning, with infinite artfulness, the red wine of Shiraz into urine?

> *Seven Gothic Tales* [1934]

I had seen a herd of elephant traveling through dense native forest . . . pacing along as if they had an appointment at the end of the world.

> *Out of Africa* [1937], *pt. I, ch. 1*

The giraffe, in their queer, inimitable, vegetative gracefulness, as if it were not a herd of animals but a family of rare, long-stemmed, speckled gigantic flowers slowly advancing.
            Out of Africa, pt. I, ch. 1

If I know a song of Africa — I thought — of the giraffe, and the African new moon lying on her back, of the plows in the fields, and the sweaty faces of the coffee-pickers, does Africa know a song of me? Would the air over the plain quiver with a color that I had had on, or the children invent a game in which my name was, or the full moon throw a shadow over the gravel of the drive that was like me, or would the eagles of Ngong look out for me?
            Ib. 4

I have before seen other countries, in the same manner, give themselves to you when you are about to leave them.
            Ib. V, 1

WILL DURANT
1885–

A statesman cannot afford to be a moralist.   *What Is Civilization?*

The finger that turns the dial rules the air.   *Ib.*

The health of nations is more important than the wealth of nations.   *Ib.*

SACHA GUITRY
1885–1957

The little I know, I owe to my ignorance.   *Toutes Réflexions Faites*

KAREN HORNEY
1885–1952

Fortunately [psycho]analysis is not the only way to resolve inner conflicts. Life itself still remains a very effective therapist.
            Our Inner Conflicts [1945]

ISHIKAWA TAKUBOKU [1]
1885–1912

Like a kite
    Cut from the string,
Lightly the soul of my youth
    Has taken flight.
            Song of My Youth

Sickness is the only way we have to obtain peace of mind.
            The Romaji Diary

RING LARDNER
1885–1933

A good many young writers make the mistake of enclosing a stamped, self-addressed envelope, big enough for the manuscript to come back in. This is too much of a temptation to the editor.
            How to Write Short Stories
            [1924]

"Are you lost, daddy?" I arsked tenderly.
"Shut up," he explained.
            The Young Immigrunts

DAVID HERBERT
LAWRENCE
1885–1930

You love me so much, you want to put me in your pocket. And I should die there smothered.
            Sons and Lovers [1913], *ch. 15*

So now it is vain for the singer to burst
        into clamor
With the great black piano appassionato. The glamor
Of childish days is upon me, my manhood is cast
Down in the flood of remembrance, I
        weep like a child for the past.
            Piano [1916], *st. 3*

Not I, not I, but the wind that blows
        through me!
A fine wind is blowing the new direction of Time.
            Song of a Man Who Has Come
            Through [1920]

[1] From *Modern Japanese Literature* edited by Donald Keene [1960].

I never saw a wild thing
Sorry for itself.   *Self-Pity* [1923]

A snake came to my water trough
On a hot, hot day, and I in pajamas for
    the heat,
To drink there.   *Snake* [1923]

For he seemed to me again like a king,
Like a king in exile, uncrowned in the
    underworld,
Now due to be crowned again.   *Ib.*

Necessary, forever necessary, to burn
out false shames and smelt the heaviest
ore of the body into purity.
          Lady Chatterley's Lover [1928]

How beastly the bourgeois is
especially the male of the species.
          How Beastly the Bourgeois Is
                                        [1929]

Now in November nearer comes the
    sun
down the abandoned heaven.
          November by the Sea [1929]

Reach me a gentian, give me a torch!
Let me guide myself with the blue,
    forked torch of a flower
Down the darker and darker stairs,
    where blue is darkened on blueness
Down the way Persephone goes, just
    now, in first-frosted September.
          Bavarian Gentians [*written* 1929]

Beauty is a mystery. You can neither
eat it nor make flannel out of it.
          Sex Versus Loveliness [1930]

Sex and beauty are inseparable, like
life and consciousness. And the intelligence which goes with sex and beauty,
and arises out of sex and beauty, is intuition.   *Ib.*

How the horse dominated the mind
of the early races, especially of the
Mediterranean! You were a lord if you
had a horse. Far back, far back in our
dark soul the horse prances. . . . The
horse, the horse! The symbol of surging
potency and power of movement, of
action, in man.   *Apocalypse* [1931]

For man, the vast marvel is to be
alive. . . . We ought to dance with

rapture that we should be alive and in
the flesh, and part of the living, incarnate cosmos. I am part of the sun as my
eye is part of me. That I am part of the
earth my feet know perfectly, and my
blood is part of the sea. My soul knows
that I am part of the human race, my
soul is an organic part of the great human race, as my spirit is part of my nation. In my own very self, I am part of
my family.   *Apocalypse*

Oh build your ship of death. Oh build
    it!
For you will need it.
For the voyage of oblivion awaits you.
          The Ship of Death [1933]

SINCLAIR LEWIS
1885–1951

His name was George F. Babbitt,
and . . . he was nimble in the calling
of selling houses for more than people
could afford to pay.
          Babbitt [1922], *ch.* 1

A sensational event was changing
from the brown suit to the gray the
contents of his pockets. He was earnest
about these objects. They were of eternal importance, like baseball or the Republican Party.   *Ib.*

Every compulsion is put upon writers
to become safe, polite, obedient, and
sterile. In protest, I declined election to
the National Institute of Arts and Letters some years ago, and now I must
decline the Pulitzer Prize.[1]
          Letter declining the Pulitzer
          Prize for his novel Arrow-
          smith [1926]

To a true-blue professor of literature
in an American university, literature is
not something that a plain human
being, living today, painfully sits down
to produce. No; it is something dead.
          The American Fear of Literature,
          address, Stockholm, on receiving
          the Nobel Prize for Literature
          [*December* 12, 1930]

[1] Lewis became a member of the National
Institute in 1935.

Our American professors like their literature clear and cold and pure and very dead.
> *The American Fear of Literature, address, Stockholm, on receiving the Nobel Prize for Literature*

It Can't Happen Here.
> *Title of book* [1935]

ANDRÉ MAUROIS
1885–1967

The minds of different generations are as impenetrable one by the other as are the monads of Leibniz.
> *Ariel* [1] [1924], *ch. 12*

Modesty and unselfishness — these are virtues which men praise — and pass by.
> *Ib. 24*

There are certain persons for whom pure truth is a poison.
> *Ib. 29*

CHESTER WILLIAM NIMITZ
1885–1966

A ship is always referred to as "she" because it costs so much to keep one in paint and powder.
> *Speech, Society of Sponsors of the United States Navy* [February 13, 1940]

Uncommon valor was a common virtue.
> *Of the Marines at Iwo Jima* [February–May, 1945]

GEORGE SMITH PATTON [2]
1885–1945

Wars may be fought with weapons, but they are won by men. It is the spirit of the men who follow and of the man who leads that gains the victory.
> *In the Cavalry Journal* [September 1933]

To be a successful soldier you must know history. . . . What you must

[1] Translated by ELLA D'ARCY.
[2] Old Blood and Guts.

know is how man reacts. Weapons change but man who uses them changes not at all. To win battles you do not beat weapons — you beat the soul of man of the enemy man.
> *Letter to Cadet George S. Patton IV* [June 6, 1944]

Take calculated risks. That is quite different from being rash.
> *Ib.*

The most vital quality a soldier can possess is self-confidence, utter, complete and bumptious.
> *Ib.*

Never tell people *how* to do things. Tell them *what* to do and they will surprise you with their ingenuity.
> *War As I Knew It* [1947], *p. 357*

In war nothing is impossible, provided you use audacity.
> *Ib. p. 358*

A pint of sweat will save a gallon of blood.
> *Ib. p. 405*

EZRA POUND
1885–1972

Your mind and you are our Sargasso Sea.
> *Portrait d'une Femme* [1916]

Haie! Haie!
    These were the swift to harry;
These the keen-scented;
These were the souls of blood.
Slow on the leash,
    pallid the leash-men!
> *The Return* [1916]

Tree you are,
Moss you are,
You are violets with wind above them.
A child — so high — you are;
And all this is folly to the world.
> *A Girl*

The apparition of these faces in the crowd;
Petals on a wet, black bough.
> *In a Station of the Metro* [1916]

Winter is icumen in,
Lhude sing Goddamm,

Raineth drop and staineth slop,
And how the wind doth ramm!
   Sing: Goddamm.[1]   *Ancient Music*

The leaves fall early this autumn, in
   wind.
The paired butterflies are already yellow
   with August
Over the grass in the West garden;
They hurt me. I grow older.
      The River Merchant's Wife:
      A Letter (After Rihaku)

For three years, out of key with his
   time,
He strove to resuscitate the dead art
Of poetry; to maintain "the sublime"
In the old sense. Wrong from the
   start —
No, hardly, but seeing he had been
  · born
In a half savage country, out of date.
      Hugh Selwyn Mauberley.
      E.P. Ode pour l'élection de
      son sepulchre [1920], *I*

His true Penelope was Flaubert,
He fished by obstinate isles.   *Ib.*

The age demanded an image
Of its accelerated grimace,
Something for the modern stage,
Not, at any rate, an Attic grace.
        Ib. II

Better mendacities
Than the classics in paraphrase!   *Ib.*

Some quick to arm,
some for adventure,
some from fear of weakness,
some from fear of censure,
some for love of slaughter, in imagination,
learning later . . .
some in fear, learning love of slaughter;
Died some, pro patria,
   non "dulce" non "et decor" . . .
walked eye-deep in hell
believing in old men's lies, the unbelieving
came home, home to a lie.   *Ib. IV*

hysterias, trench confessions,
laughter out of dead bellies.   *Ib.*

There died a myriad,
And of the best, among them,
For an old bitch gone in the teeth,
For a botched civilization.

Charm, smiling at the good mouth,
Quick eyes gone under earth's lid,

For two gross of broken statues,
For a few thousand battered books.
      Hugh Selwyn Mauberley. E. P.
      Ode pour l'élection de son sep-
      ulchre, V

   As for literature
It gives no man a sinecure.
And no one knows, at sight, a master-
   piece.
And give up verse, my boy,
There's nothing in it.
      Ib. IX. Mr. Nixon [1]

Hang it all, Robert Browning,
there can but be the one "Sordello".
      Cantos [1925–1959], *II*

And the betrayers of language
   ......n and the press gang
And those who had lied for hire;
The perverts, the perverters of language, the perverts, who have set
   money-lust
Before the pleasures of the senses;
howling, as of a hen-yard in a printing-
   house, the clatter of presses,
the blowing of dry dust and stray paper,
foetor, sweat, the stench of stale oranges.   *Ib. XIV*

With *Usura*
With usura hath no man a house of
   good stone
each block cut smooth and well fitting.
       Ib. XLV

No picture is made to endure nor to
   live with
but it is made to sell and sell quickly
with usura, sin against nature,
is thy bread ever more of stale rags
is thy bread dry as paper.   *Ib.*

Usura slayeth the child in the womb
It stayeth the young man's courting
It hath brought palsey to bed, lyeth

---

[1] See Anonymous, p. 1083b.

[1] Arnold Bennett.

between the young bride and her bride-
groom
CONTRA NATURAM
Cantos, XLV

What thou lovest well remains,
  the rest is dross
What thou lov'st well shall not be reft
  from thee
What thou lov'st well is thy true heritage
Whose world, or mine or theirs
  or is it of none?
First came the seen, then thus the palpable
    Elysium, though it were in the
    halls of hell.
What thou lovest well is thy true heritage.   *Ib. LXXXI*

The ant's a centaur in his dragon
  world.
Pull down thy vanity, it is not man
Made courage, or made order, or made
  grace,
  Pull down thy vanity, I say pull
  down.
Learn of the green world what can be
  thy place
In scaled invention or true artistry,
Pull down thy vanity,
  Paquin pull down!
The green casque has outdone your ele-
  gance.   *Ib.*

The history of an art is the history of
masterwork, not of failures, or mediocrity.
        The Spirit of Romance [1910]

Poetry must be as well written as
prose.
        Letter to Harriet Monroe
        [January 1915]

Objectivity and again objectivity, and
expression: no hindside-before-ness, no
straddled adjectives (as "addled mosses
dank"), no Tennysonianness of speech;
nothing — nothing that you couldn't,
in some circumstance, in the stress of
some emotion, actually say.   *Ib.*

Literature is language charged with
meaning.
        ABC of Reading [1934], *ch. 2*

Literature is news that *stays* news.
        ABC of Reading, ch. 2

Genius . . . is the capacity to see
ten things where the ordinary man sees
one, and where the man of talent sees
two or three, *plus* the ability to register
that multiple perception in the material
of his art.
        Jefferson and/or Mussolini [1935]

America, my country, is almost a
continent and hardly yet a nation.
        Patria Mia

CHARLES SEYMOUR
1885–1963

We seek the truth, and will endure
the consequences.
        Statement made while president
        of Yale University [1937–1950]

LOUIS UNTERMEYER
1885–

God, if You wish for our love,
Fling us a handful of stars!
        Caliban in the Coal Mines,
        st. 4

His are the triumphs till the day
There's no more grass to cut away
And, weary of labor, weary of play,

Having exhausted every whim,
He stretches out each conquering limb.
And then the small grass covers him.
        Long Feud, st. 5, 6

CARL VAN DOREN
1885–1950

The first writers are first and the rest,
in the long run, nowhere but in anthologies.
        What Is American Literature?

HAROLD TUCKER
WEBSTER
1885–1952

Caspar Milquetoast: The Timid
Soul. *Character in series of cartoons*

The Thrill that Comes Once in a Lifetime. *Title of series of cartoons*

HUMBERT WOLFE
1885–1940

Like a small gray
coffee pot
sits the squirrel.
The Gray Squirrel [1924], *st. 1*

Clean as a lady,
cool as glass,
fresh without fragrance
the tulip was.
Tulip [1924], *st. 1*

Listen! the wind is rising,
  and the air is wild with leaves,
We have had our summer evenings,
  now for October eves!
Autumn (Resignation)
[1926], *st. 2*

ELINOR HOYT WYLIE
1885–1928

We shall walk in velvet shoes:
  Wherever we go
Silence will fall like dews
  On white silence below.
Velvet Shoes [1921], *st. 4*

Avoid the reeking herd,
  Shun the polluted flock,
Live like that stoic bird
  The eagle of the rock.
The Eagle and the Mole [1921],
st. 1

If you would keep your soul
  From spotted sight or sound,
Live like the velvet mole;
  Go burrow underground. *Ib. st. 5*

Say not of Beauty she is good,
Or aught but beautiful.
Beauty [1921]

Enshrine her and she dies, who had
The hard heart of a child. *Ib.*

Down to the Puritan marrow of my
  bones
There's something in this richness that
  I hate.

I love the look, austere, immaculate,
Of landscapes drawn in pearly mono-
  tones.
Wild Peaches [1921], *st. 4*

I was, being human, born alone;
I am, being woman, hard beset;
I live by squeezing from a stone
The little nourishment I get.

In masks outrageous and austere
The years go by in single file;
But none has merited my fear,
And none has quite escaped my smile.
Let No Charitable Hope [1923],
st. 2, 3

My soul, be not disturbed
By planetary war;
Remain securely orbed
In this contracted star.
Address to My Soul [1928], *st. 1*

A subtle spirit has my path attended,
In likeness not a lion but a pard;
And when the arrows flew like hail, and
  hard,
He licked my wounds, and all my
  wounds were mended.
One Person [1928]. *Sonnet 9*

My late discovered earth and early sky.
Ib. Sonnet 17

If any have a stone to throw
It is not I, ever or now. *The Pebble*

The worst and best are both inclined
To snap like vixens at the truth;
But, O, beware the middle mind
That purrs and never shows a tooth!
Nonsense Rhyme, st. 2

Honeyed words like bees,
Gilded and sticky, with a little sting.
Pretty Words

Hail, element of earth, receive thy own,
And cherish, at thy charitable breast,
This man, this mongrel beast:
He plows the sand, and, at his hardest
  need,
He sows himself for seed.
Hymn to Earth [1929], *st. 6*

ZOË AKINS
1886–1958

The Greeks Had a Word For It.
Title of play [1930]

KARL BARTH
1886–1968

Conscience is the perfect interpreter of life.
The Word of God and the Word of Man [1957]

We have before us the fiendishness of business competition and the world war, passion and wrongdoing, antagonism between classes and moral depravity within them, economic tyranny above and the slave spirit below. *Ib.*

WILLIAM ROSE BENÉT
1886–1950

Rain, with a silver flail;
    Sun, with a golden ball;
Ocean, wherein the whale
    Swims minnow-small.
Whale, st. 1

And now there is merely silence, silence, silence, saving
All we did not know. *Sagacity*

HUGO LAFAYETTE BLACK
1886–1971

No higher duty, or more solemn responsibility, rests upon this Court than that of translating into living law and maintaining this constitutional shield deliberately planned and inscribed for the benefit of every human being subject to our Constitution — of whatever race, creed or persuasion.
Chambers v. Florida, 309 *U.S.* 227 [1938]

The First Amendment has erected a wall between church and state. That wall must be kept high and impregnable. We could not approve the slightest breach.
Everson v. Board of Education, 330 *U.S.* 1 [1947]

It is my belief that there *are* "absolutes" in our Bill of Rights, and that they were put there on purpose by men who knew what words meant and meant their prohibitions to be "absolutes."
Interview Before the American Jewish Congress [April 14, 1962]

My view is, without deviation, without exception, without any ifs, buts, or whereases, that freedom of speech means that you shall not do something to people either for the views they have or the views they express or the words they speak or write. *Ib.*

I am for the First Amendment from the first word to the last. I believe it means what it says. *Ib.*

An unconditional right to say what one pleases about public affairs is what I consider to be the minimum guarantee of the First Amendment.
New York Times Company v. Sullivan, 376 *U.S.* 254 [1964]

VAN WYCK BROOKS
1886–1963

His wife not only edited his works but edited him.
The Ordeal of Mark Twain [1920], *ch.* 5

FRANCES CORNFORD
1886–1960

Magnificently unprepared
For the long littleness of life.
Rupert Brooke [1915]

O why do you walk through the fields in gloves,
Missing so much and so much?
O fat white woman whom nobody loves,
Why do you walk through the fields in gloves
When the grass is as soft as the breast of doves
And shivering-sweet to the touch?
To a Fat Lady Seen from the Train [1915]

AL JOLSON
1886–1950

You ain't heard nothin' yet, folks.
Ad lib remark introduced in the first talking motion picture, The Jazz Singer [July 1927]

JOYCE KILMER
1886–1918

I think that I shall never see
A poem lovely as a tree.
A tree whose hungry mouth is pressed
Against the earth's sweet flowing breast.
Trees [1] *[1913]*

Poems are made by fools like me,
But only God can make a tree.　*Ib.*

DAVID MORTON
1886–1957

Who walks with Beauty has no need of fear;
The sun and moon and stars keep pace with him;
Invisible hands restore the ruined year,
And time, itself, grows beautifully dim.
Who Walks with Beauty

SHAEMAS O'SHEEL
1886–1954

They went forth to battle, but they always fell; [2]
Their eyes were fixed above the sullen shields;
Nobly they fought and bravely, but not well,
And sank heart-wounded by a subtle spell.
They Went Forth to Battle, st. 1

SIEGFRIED SASSOON
1886–1967

Soldiers are citizens of death's gray land.　*Dreamers*

[1] See Heywood Broun, p. 1000a, and Ogden Nash, p. 1051b.
[2] They came forth to battle, but they always fell. — JAMES MACPHERSON [1736–1796], *Poems of Ossian, Cath-Loda, Duan Second*

Soldiers are dreamers; when the guns begin
They think of firelit homes, clean beds, and wives.　*Dreamers*

And when the war is done and youth stone dead
I'd toddle safely home and die — in bed.　*Base Details*

Who will remember, passing through this gate,
The unheroic dead who fed the guns?
Who shall absolve the foulness of their fate —
Those doomed, conscripted, unvictorious ones?
On Passing the New Menin Gate

TANIZAKI JUNICHIRO
1886–

The Chinese love jade. That strange lump of stone with its faintly muddy light, like the crystallized air of the centuries, melting dimly, dully back, deeper and deeper — are not we Orientals the only ones who know its charm? We cannot say ourselves what it is that we find in this stone. It quite lacks the brightness of a ruby or an emerald or the glitter of a diamond. But this much we can say: when we see that shadowy surface, we think how Chinese it is, we seem to find in cloudiness the accumulated sediment of the long Chinese past, we think how appropriate it is that the Chinese should admire that surface and that shadow.
In Praise of Shadows [1934] [1]

We do not dislike everything that shines, but we prefer a pensive shadow to a thin transparence.　*Ib.*

We Orientals . . . find beauty not only in the thing itself but in the pattern of shadows, the light and the darkness, which that thing produces. A phosphorescent jewel gives off its glow

[1] From Edward Seidensticker's adaptation, *Atlantic Monthly* Supplement. *Perspective of Japan [January 1955]*.

and color in the dark and loses its beauty in the light of day . . .

Our ancestors cut off the brightness on the land from above and created a world of shadows, and far in the depths of it they placed woman, making her the whitest of beings.
> *In Praise of Shadows*

I would call back at least for literature this world of shadows we are losing. In the mansion called literature I would have the eaves deep and the walls dark, I would push back into the shadows the things that come forward too clearly, I would strip away the useless decoration. I do not ask that this be done everywhere, but perhaps we may be allowed at least one mansion where we can turn off the electric lights and see how it is without them.   *Ib.*

ED WYNN
1886–1966

Every radish I ever pulled up seemed to have a mortgage attached to it.
> *Explaining Why He Sold His Farm*

BRUCE BAIRNSFATHER
1887–1959

Well, if you knows of a better 'ole,[1] go to it.
> *Fragments from France* [1915].
> *Caption of cartoon*

RUPERT BROOKE[2]
1887–1915

Breathless, we flung us on the windy hill,
Laughed in the sun, and kissed the lovely grass.   *The Hill* [1910]

And then you suddenly cried, and turned away.   *Ib.*

Unkempt about those hedges blows
An English unofficial rose.
> *The Old Vicarage, Grant-*
> *chester* [1912]

[1] A trench.
[2] See Frances Cornford, p. 991b.

Curates, long dust, will come and go
On lissom, clerical, printless toe.
> *The Old Vicarage, Grant-*
> *chester*

England's the one land, I know,
Where men with Splendid Hearts may go;
And Cambridgeshire, of all England,
The shire for Men who Understand.
> *Ib.*

For Cambridge people rarely smile,
Being urban, squat, and packed with guile.   *Ib.*

Oh! yet
Stands the church clock at ten to three?
And is there honey still for tea?   *Ib.*

Fish say, they have their stream and pond;
But is there anything beyond?
> *Heaven* [1913]

But somewhere, beyond Space and Time,
Is wetter water, slimier slime!   *Ib.*

And in that Heaven of all their wish,
There shall be no more land, say fish.
> *Ib.*

But there's wisdom in women, of more than they have known,
And thoughts go blowing through them, are wiser than their own.
> *There's Wisdom in Women* [1913]

These I have loved:
White plates and cups, clean-gleaming.   *The Great Lover* [1914]

Then, the cool kindliness of sheets, that soon
Smooth away trouble; and the rough male kiss
Of blankets; grainy wood; live hair that is
Shining and free; blue-massing clouds; the keen
Unpassioned beauty of a great machine;
The benison of hot water; furs to touch;
The good smell of old clothes,   *Ib.*

If I should die, think only this of me:
That there's some corner of a foreign
field
That is forever England.
                    The Soldier [1914]

And think, this heart, all evil shed
    away,
A pulse in the eternal mind, no less
Gives somewhere back the thoughts by
    England given.   *Ib.*

Now, God be thanked, Who has
    matched us with His hour,
And caught our youth, and wakened us
    from sleeping.   *Peace*

The worst friend and enemy is but
Death.   *Ib.*

Blow out, you bugles, over the rich
    dead!
There's none of these so lonely and
    poor of old,
But, dying, has made us rarer gifts than
    gold.   *The Dead* [1914], I

Honor has come back, as a king, to
    earth,
And paid his subjects with a royal wage;
And Nobleness walks in our ways again;
And we have come into our heritage.
                              Ib.

ISAAC GOLDBERG
1887–1938

Diplomacy is to do and say
The nastiest thing in the nicest way.
                    The Reflex

SIDNEY HILLMAN
1887–1946

Politics is the science of how who
gets what, when and why.
            *Political Primer for All
                Americans* [1944]

EARNEST A. HOOTON
1887–1954

Up from the Ape.
            Title of book [1931]

Why Men Behave Like Apes, and
Vice Versa.   *Title of book* [1940]

ROBINSON JEFFERS
1887–1962

You make haste on decay: not blameworthy; life is good, be it stub-
bornly long or suddenly
A mortal splendor; meteors are not
needed less than mountains: shine,
perishing republic.
            Shine, Perishing Republic
                    [1924], *st. 3*

Lend me the stone strength of the past
    and I will lend you
The wings of the future, for I have
    them.
        *To the Rock That Will be a
                Cornerstone* [1924]

    The deep dark-shining
Pacific leans on the land,
Feeling his cold strength
To the outmost margins.
                    Night [1925]

    A creature progressively
Thirsty for life will be for death too.
            Age in Prospect [1926]

Happy people die whole, they are all
    dissolved in a moment, they have
    had what they wanted,
No hard gifts; the unhappy
Linger a space, but pain is a thing that
    is glad to be forgotten; but one
    who has given
His heart to a cause or a country,
His ghost may spaniel it a while, dis-
    consolate to watch it.
            Post Mortem [1926]

The world's God is treacherous and full
    of unreason.   *Birth-Dues* [1928]

I'd sooner, except the penalties, kill a
    man than a hawk.
                Hurt Hawks [1928]

    I have grown to believe
A stone is a better pillow than many
    visions.
            Clouds of Evening [1930]

The strong lean upon death as on a
  rock.   *Gale in April* [1930]

Give Your Heart to the Hawks.
          Title of poem [1933]

I hate my verses, every line, every word.
          Love the Wild Swan

Does it matter whether you hate your
  . . . self? At least
Love your eyes that can see, your mind
  that can
Hear the music, the thunder of the
  wings. Love the wild swan.   *Ib.*

Well: the day is a poem but too much
Like one of Jeffers's, crusted with blood
  and barbaric omens,
Painful to excess, inhuman as a hawk's
  cry.
          *The Day Is a Poem (Septem-
          ber 19, 1939)* [1941]

We shall have to perceive that battle is
  a burning flower or like a huge
  music, and the dive-bomber's
  screaming orgasm
As beautiful as other passions; and that
  death and life are not serious alter-
  natives.
          May–June, 1940, st. 2

If millions are born millions must die,
If England goes down and Germany up
The stronger dog will still be on top.
          Ib. st. 3

  As for me, I would rather
Be a worm in a wild apple than a son of
  man.   *Original Sin* [1948]

CHIANG KAI-SHEK [1]
1887–1975

The general psychology of our people
today can be described as spiritless.
What manifests itself in behavior is
this: lack of discrimination between
good and evil, between what is public
and what is private, and between what
is primary and what is secondary.
          *Speech, Nanchang [September
          1934]*

[1] From *Sources of Chinese Tradition*, edited by
William Theodore de Bary [1960].

The main object of the New Life
Movement [1] is to substitute a rational
life for the irrational.
          Speech, Nanchang

The life of our people will be elevated if we live artistically; we will become wealthy if we live productively;
and we will be safe if we lead a military
way of life. When we do this, we will
have a rational life. . . . If we can
achieve [a rational life], we will have rev-
olutionized the daily life of our people
and laid the foundation for the rehabilitation of our nation.   *Ib.*

LE CORBUSIER
[CHARLES ÉDOUARD
JEANNERET]
1887–1965

A house is a machine for living in.[2]
          Vers une Architecture [1923]

EMILIO MOLA
1887–1937

Fifth column.[3]
          Phrase, Spanish Civil War
          [1936–1939]

SIR BERNARD
MONTGOMERY
[VISCOUNT
MONTGOMERY OF
ALAMEIN]
1887–1976

To us is given the honor of striking a
blow for freedom which will live in history, and in the better days that lie
ahead men will speak with pride of our
doings.
          *Message to his troops [June 5,
          1944] on the eve of the Allied
          invasion of Europe*

[1] The New Life Movement, whose beginning
is marked by this speech, was intended to "rally
the . . . people against the Communists," and
further to "tighten discipline and build up morale in the Kuomintang and nation as a whole."
[2] Une maison est une machine-à-habiter.
[3] Mola, one of Franco's generals, boasted that
he had four columns of troops to lead against
Madrid, and a fifth column of sympathizers
inside Madrid.

I am not a bit anxious about my battles. If I am anxious I don't fight them. I wait until I am ready.
> *From British Information Services publication British Commanders* [1945]

MARIANNE MOORE
1887–1972

I, too, dislike it: there are things that are important beyond all this fiddle.   *Poetry* [1935], *st. 1*

nor till the poets among us can be
"literalists of
    the imagination" — above
        insolence and triviality and can present
for inspection, imaginary gardens with
    real toads in them,
        shall we have
it.   *Ib. st. 4, 5*

There is a great amount of poetry in unconscious fastidiousness.
> *Critics and Connoisseurs* [1935]

Literature is a phase of life. If
    one is afraid of it, the situation is
        irremediable; if
one approaches it familiarly
    what one says of it is worthless.
> *Picking and Choosing* [1935]

I wonder what Adam and Eve
think of it by this time.
> *Marriage* [1935]

But one would not be he who has nothing but plenty.[1]
> *The Jerboa* [1935]

My father used to say,
"Superior people never make long visits,"
Have to be shown Longfellow's grave
or the glass flowers at Harvard.
> *Silence* [1935] [2]

---

[1] I Got Plenty o' Nuttin. — IRA GERSHWIN, *Porgy and Bess* [1935], title and refrain of song.
[2] The author's footnote for *Silence:* "My father used to say, 'Superior people never make long visits. When I am visiting, I like to go

The deepest feeling always shows itself
    in silence;
not in silence, but restraint.
Nor was he insincere in saying, "Make
    my house your inn."
Inns are not residences.   *Silence*

What is our innocence,
what is our guilt? All are
    naked, none is safe.
> *What Are Years?* [1941]

I am troubled, I'm dissatisfied, I'm
    Irish.
> *Spenser's Ireland* [1941],
> *last line*

Among animals, one has a sense of
    humor.
Humor saves a few steps, it saves years.
> *The Pangolin* [1941], *st. 8*

As contagion
    of sickness makes sickness,
contagion of trust can make trust.
> *In Distrust of Merits* [1941]

they're fighting that I
may yet recover from the disease, My
Self; some have it lightly; some will die.
    "Man
        wolf to man"; yes. We devour
            ourselves.   *Ib.*

O small dust of the earth
that walks so arrogantly,
    trust begets power and faith is
an affectionate thing.   *Ib.*

Hate-hardened heart, O heart of iron,
    iron is iron till it is rust.
There never was a war that was not
    inward; I must
fight till I have conquered in myself
    what
causes war, but I would not believe it.
    I inwardly did nothing.
    O Iscariotlike crime!

---

about by myself. I never had to be shown Longfellow's grave or the glass flowers at Harvard.' " Miss A. M. Homans. Edmund Burke, in *Burke's Life*, by Prior: "Throw yourself into a coach," said he. "Come down and make my house your inn."

Beauty is everlasting
And dust is for a time.
> *In Distrust of Merits, st.* 8

O to be a dragon
a symbol of the power of Heaven — of
  silkworm
size or immense; at times invisible.
Felicitous phenomenon!
> *Ò To Be a Dragon* [1959]

To wear the arctic fox
you have to kill it.
> *The Arctic Ox (Or Goat)* [1959]

Camels are snobbish
and sheep, unintelligent;
  water buffaloes, neurasthenic —
even murderous.
Reindeer seem over-serious.   *Ib.*

SAMUEL ELIOT
MORISON
1887–1976

A tough but nervous, tenacious but
restless race [the Yankees]; materially
ambitious, yet prone to introspection,
and subject to waves of religious emotion. . . . A race whose typical member is eternally torn between a passion
for righteousness and a desire to get on
in the world.
> *Maritime History of Massachu-*
> *setts* [1921], *ch.* 2

He [Columbus] enjoyed long
stretches of pure delight such as only a
seaman may know, and moments of
high, proud exultation that only a discoverer can experience.
> *Admiral of the Ocean Sea*
> [1942], *ch.* 49

A few hints as to literary craftsmanship may be useful to budding historians. First and foremost, *get writing!*
> *History as a Literary Art. Old*
> *South Leaflets, ser. II, No. 1*
> [1946]

Franklin may . . . be considered
one of the founding fathers of Ameri-

can democracy, since no democratic
government can last long without conciliation and compromise.
> *The Wisdom of Benjamin*
> *Franklin* [1961]

An historian should yield himself to
his subject, become immersed in the
place and period of his choice, standing
apart from it now and then for a fresh
view.
> *Vistas of History* [1964]. *The*
> *Experiences and Principles of an*
> *Historian*

If the European discovery had been
delayed for a century or two, it is possible that the Aztec in Mexico or the
Iroquois in North America would have
established strong native states capable
of adopting European war tactics and
maintaining their independence to this
day, as Japan kept her independence
from China.
> *The Oxford History of the*
> *American People* [1965], *ch.* 1

America was discovered accidentally
by a great seaman who was looking for
something else; when discovered it was
not wanted; and most of the exploration for the next fifty years was done in
the hope of getting through or around
it. America was named after a man who
discovered no part of the New World.
History is like that, very chancy.
> *Ib.* 2

But sea power has never led to despotism. The nations that have enjoyed
sea power even for a brief period —
Athens, Scandinavia, the Netherlands,
England, the United States — are
those that have preserved freedom for
themselves and have given it to others.
Of the despotism to which unrestrained
military power leads we have plenty of
examples from Alexander to Mao.
> *Ib.* 3

Make no mistake; the American Revolution was not fought to *obtain* freedom, but to *preserve* the liberties that
Americans already had as colonials. In-

dependence was no conscious goal, secretly nurtured in cellar or jungle by bearded conspirators, but a reluctant last resort, to preserve "life, liberty and the pursuit of happiness."

The Oxford History of the American People, ch. 12

The freedmen were not really free in 1865, nor are most of their descendants really free in 1965. Slavery was but one aspect of a race and color problem that is still far from solution here, or anywhere. In America particularly, the grapes of wrath have not yet yielded all their bitter vintage.   *Ib. 33*

These clipper ships of the early 1850's were built of wood in shipyards from Rockland in Maine to Baltimore. These architects, like poets who transmute nature's message into song, obeyed what wind and wave had taught them, to create the noblest of all sailing vessels, and the most beautiful creations of man in America. With no extraneous ornament except a figurehead, a bit of carving and a few lines of gold leaf, their one purpose of speed over the great ocean routes was achieved by perfect balance of spars and sails to the curving lines of the smooth black hull; and this harmony of mass, form and color was practiced to the music of dancing waves and of brave winds whistling in the rigging. These were our Gothic cathedrals, our Parthenon; but monuments carved from snow. For a few brief years they flashed their splendor around the world, then disappeared with the finality of the wild pigeon.[1]   *Ib. 36*

No big modern war has been won without preponderant sea power; and, conversely, very few rebellions of maritime provinces have succeeded without acquiring sea power.[2]   *Ib. 40*

[1] A shorter version of this passage appeared in *Maritime History of Massachusetts [1921], ch. 23.*
[2] See Themistocles, p. 78a; Bacon, p. 209b; and Mahan, p. 785b.

FAIRFIELD OSBORN
1887–1969

We do not live to extenuate the miseries of the past nor to accept as incurable those of the present.

The Limits of the Earth, ch. 10

H. I. PHILLIPS
1887–1965

Horse-sense in an atmosphere of
Pomp and glory,
Self-effacement in a generation
Of self-salesmanship,
A Vermont Yankee in
King Ballyhoo's Court!

Calvin Coolidge

JOHN REED
1887–1920

Ten Days That Shook the World.
Title of firsthand account of the outbreak of the Bolshevik Revolution [1919]

DAME EDITH SITWELL
1887–1964

Remember only this of our hopeless love
That never till Time is done
Will the fire of the heart and the fire of the mind be one.

Heart and Mind

Still falls the Rain —
Dark as the world of man, black as our loss —
Blind as the nineteen hundred and forty nails
Upon the Cross.

Still Falls the Rain [1940]

My poems are hymns of praise to the glory of life.

Collected Poems [1957]. Some Notes on My Poetry

Rhythm is one of the principal translators between dream and reality. Rhythm might be described as, to the world of sound, what light is to the world of sight. It shapes and gives new meaning. Rhythm was described by Schopenhauer as melody deprived of its pitch. *Taken Care Of* [1965], *ch. 14*

ALEXANDER WOOLLCOTT
1887–1943

The two oldest professions in the world — ruined by amateurs.
> *The Knock at the Stage Door. The Actor and the Streetwalker*

Ladies, just a little more virginity, if you don't mind.
> *Capsule Criticism. Beerbohm Tree to the Extras*

There is less in this than meets the eye.
> *A companion's comment at a Maeterlinck play (attributed to* TALLULAH BANKHEAD)

I must get out of these wet clothes and into a dry Martini.
> *From Reader's Digest*

Babies in silk hats playing with dynamite.
> *Of diplomats. From* SAMUEL HOPKINS ADAMS, *A. Woollcott* [1945]

Germany was the cause of Hitler just as much as Chicago is responsible for the Chicago *Tribune*.
> *Last words before the microphone* [January 23, 1943], *on People's Platform program*

ROLAND YOUNG
1887–1953

And here's the happy bounding flea —
You cannot tell the he from she.
The sexes look alike, you see;
But she can tell, and so can he.
> *The Flea*

SAM M. LEWIS AND JOE YOUNG
fl. 1919

How You Gonna Keep 'Em Down on the Farm After They've Seen Paree?
> *Title and refrain of song* [1919]

MAXWELL ANDERSON
1888–1959

What Price Glory?
> *Title of play* [1924] *with* LAWRENCE STALLINGS [1894–1968]

IRVING BERLIN
1888–

You've got to get up, you've got to get up,
You've got to get up this morning!
> *Oh! How I Hate to Get Up in the Morning* [1918]

There's No Business Like Show Business.
> *Composition* [1946]

HENRY BESTON
(1888–1968)

The neon glow of the age of comfort and violence.
> *Review of John Burroughs's America, in The Freeman* [February 11, 1952]

For a moment of night we have a glimpse of ourselves and of our world islanded in its stream of stars — pilgrims of mortality, voyaging between horizons across the eternal seas of space and time.
> *The Outermost House: A Year of Life on the Great Beach of Cape Cod* [1928]

HEYWOOD BROUN
1888–1939

In the march up to the heights of fame there comes a spot close to the summit in which man reads "nothing but detective stories."
> *G.K.C.* [1922]

"Trees" (if I have the name right) is one of the most annoying pieces of verse within my knowledge. The other one is Kipling's "If," with third place reserved for Henley's "Invictus."

"Trees" maddens me, because it contains the most insincere line ever written by mortal man. Surely the Kilmer tongue must have been not far from the Kilmer cheek when he wrote, "Poems are made by fools like me."

> *It Seems to Me* [1935]. "*Trees*," "*If*," *and* "*Invictus*"

Life is a copycat and can be bullied into following the master artist who bids it come to heel.

> *Ib. Nature the Copycat*

I have known people to stop and buy an apple on the corner and then walk away as if they had solved the whole unemployment problem.

> *Ib. Chummy Charlie*

The swaggering underemphasis of New England.

> *Heywood Broun: Collected Edition* [1941]

DALE CARNEGIE
1888–1955

How to Win Friends and Influence People. *Title of book* [1938]

RAYMOND CHANDLER
1888–1959

The Big Sleep.[1]
> *Title of novel* [1939]

J. FRANK DOBIE
1888–1964

The average Ph.D. thesis is nothing but a transference of bones from one graveyard to another.

> *A Texan in England* [1945], *ch. 1*

Conform and be dull.

> *The Voice of the Coyote* [1949], *introduction*

[1] A synonym for death.

Putting on the spectacles of science in expectation of finding the answer to everything looked at signifies inner blindness.

> *The Voice of the Coyote, introduction*

JOHN FOSTER DULLES
1888–1959

Local defense will always be important. But there is no local defense which alone will contain the mighty land power of the Communist world. Local defense must be reinforced by the further deterrent of massive retaliatory power.

> *Address to the Council on Foreign Relations* [January 12, 1954]

You have to take chances for peace, just as you must take chances in war. . . . The ability to get to the verge without getting into the war is the necessary art. If you try to run away from it, if you are scared to go to the brink,[1] you are lost.

> *From* JAMES SHEPLEY, *How Dulles Averted War, in Life* [January 16, 1956]

THOMAS STEARNS
ELIOT
1888–1965

Let us go then, you and I,
When the evening is spread out against the sky
Like a patient etherized upon a table.

> *The Love Song of J. Alfred Prufrock* [1917]

In the room the women come and go
Talking of Michelangelo. *Ib.*

There will be time to murder and create. *Ib.*

And indeed there will be time
To wonder, "Do I dare?" and, "Do I dare?" *Ib.*

I have measured out my life with coffee spoons. *Ib.*

[1] From the phrase "to the brink" developed "brinkmanship."

I should have been a pair of ragged claws
Scuttling across the floors of silent seas.
　　　　The Love Song of J. Alfred
　　　　　　　　　　　　Prufrock

Should I, after tea and cakes and ices,
Have the strength to force the moment
　　to its crisis?　　　　　　　　*Ib.*

I have seen the moment of my greatness flicker,
And I have seen the eternal Footman
　　hold my coat, and snicker,
And in short, I was afraid.　　　*Ib.*

No! I am not Prince Hamlet, nor was
　　meant to be;
Am an attendant lord, one that will do
To swell a progress, start a scene or
　　two,
Advise the prince; no doubt, an easy
　　tool,
Deferential, glad to be of use,
Politic, cautious, and meticulous;
Full of high sentence, but a bit obtuse;
At times, indeed, almost ridiculous —
Almost, at times, the Fool.　　　*Ib.*

I grow old . . . I grow old . . .
I shall wear the bottoms of my trousers
　　rolled.　　　　　　　　　　*Ib.*

Shall I part my hair behind? Do I dare
　　to eat a peach?
I shall wear white flannel trousers, and
　　walk upon the beach.
I have heard the mermaids singing,[1]
　　each to each.

I do not think that they will sing to
　　me.　　　　　　　　　　　*Ib.*

Till human voices wake us, and we
　　drown.　　　　　　　　　　*Ib.*

We have been, let us say, to hear the
　　latest Pole
Transmit the Preludes, through his hair
　　and fingertips.
　　　　Portrait of a Lady [1917], I

And I must borrow every changing
　　shape
To find expression.　　　　　*Ib.* III

　　¹ See Donne, p. 304b.

One thinks of all the hands
That are raising dingy shades
In a thousand furnished rooms.
　　　　　　Preludes [1917], II

Twelve o'clock.
Along the reaches of the street
Held in a lunar synthesis.
　　　Rhapsody on a Windy Night
　　　　　　　　　　　　　[1917]

I am aware of the damp souls of housemaids
Sprouting despondently at area gates.
　　　Morning at the Window [1917]

The readers of the *Boston Evening
　　Transcript*
Sway in the wind like a field of ripe
　　corn.
　　　The Boston Evening Transcript
　　　　　　　　　　　　　[1917]

Upon the glazen shelves kept watch
Matthew and Waldo, guardians of the
　　faith,
The army of unalterable law.[1]
　　　　　Cousin Nancy [1917]

His laughter tinkled among the teacups.　　*Mr. Apollinax* [1917]

He laughed like an irresponsible foetus.
　　　　　　　　　　　　　Ib.

Stand on the highest pavement of the
　　stair —
Lean on a garden urn —
Weave, weave the sunlight in your hair.
　　　La Figlia Che Piange [1917]

Simple and faithless as a smile and
　　shake of the hand.　　　　*Ib.*

Here I am, an old man in a dry month,
Being read to by a boy, waiting for rain.
　　　　　　Gerontion [1920]

After such knowledge, what forgiveness? Think now
History has many cunning passages,
　　contrived corridors
And issues, deceives with whispering
　　ambitions,
Guides us by vanities.　　　　*Ib.*

Paint me the bold anfractuous rocks
Faced by the snarled and yelping seas.
　　　Sweeney Erect [1920], *st.* 1

　　¹ See Meredith, p. 730b.

This oval O cropped out with teeth.
         Sweeney Erect, st. 4

The broad-backed hippopotamus
Rests on his belly in the mud;
Although he seems so firm to us
He is merely flesh and blood.
       The Hippopotamus [1920], *st. 1*

Webster was much possessed by death
And saw the skull beneath the skin.
     Whispers of Immortality [1920],
                  st. 1

He knew the anguish of the marrow
The ague of the skeleton;
No contact possible to flesh
Allayed the fever of the bone.
        Ib. st. 4 [*of Donne*]

Uncorseted, her friendly bust
Gives promise of pneumatic bliss.
              Ib. st. 5

Reorganized upon the floor
She yawns and draws a stocking up.
     Sweeney Among the Nightin-
        gales [1920], *st. 4*

And sang within the bloody wood
When Agamemnon cried aloud,
And let their liquid siftings fall
To stain the stiff dishonored shroud.
            Ib. st. 10

April is the cruelest month, breeding
Lilacs out of the dead land, mixing
Memory and desire, stirring
Dull roots with spring rain.
     The Waste Land [1922]. *I, The*
          Burial of the Dead

    You know only
A heap of broken images, where the sun
    beats,
And the dead tree gives no shelter, the
    cricket no relief,
And the dry stone no sound of water.
    Only
There is shadow under this red rock,
(Come in under the shadow of this red
    rock),
And I will show you something differ-
    ent from either
Your shadow at morning striding be-
    hind you

Or your shadow at evening rising to
    meet you;
I will show you fear in a handful of
    dust.
     The Waste Land. I, The
        Burial of the Dead

I had not thought death had undone so
    many.[1]
Sighs, short and infrequent, were ex-
    haled.[2]   *Ib.*

    I think we are in rats' alley
Where the dead men lost their bones.
    Ib. II, The Game of Chess

O O O O that Shakespeherian Rag —
It's so elegant
So intelligent.   *Ib.*

Hurry up please its time.   *Ib.*

But at my back from time to time I
    hear [3]
The sound of horns and motors, which
    shall bring
Sweeney to Mrs. Porter in the spring.
O the moon shone bright on Mrs. Porter
And on her daughter
They wash their feet in soda water.
     Ib. III, The Fire Sermon

   At the violet hour, when the eyes and
    back
Turn upward from the desk, when the
    human engine waits
Like a taxi throbbing waiting,
I Tiresias, though blind, throbbing be-
    tween two lives.[4]   *Ib.*

When lovely woman stoops to folly [5]
    and
Paces about her room again, alone,
She smooths her hair with automatic
    hand,
And puts a record on the gramophone.
                  Ib.

Phlebas the Phoenician, a fortnight
    dead,

[1] DANTE, *Inferno, canto III, ll. 55–57.*
[2] DANTE, *Inferno, canto IV, ll. 25–27.*
[3] See Marvell, p. 360a.
[4] See Matthew Arnold, p. 712b.
[5] See Goldsmith, p. 448b.

Forgot the cry of gulls, and the deep sea swell
And the profit and loss.
The Waste Land. IV, Death by Water

Here is no water but only rock.
Ib. V, What the Thunder Said

Who is the third who walks always beside you? *Ib.*

And voices singing out of empty cisterns and exhausted wells. *Ib.*

Dayadhvam: I have heard the key
Turn in the door once and turn once only
We think of the key, each in his prison
Thinking of the key, each confirms a prison. *Ib.*

These fragments I have shored against my ruins. *Ib.*

We are the hollow men
We are the stuffed men
Leaning together
Headpiece filled with straw. Alas!
The Hollow Men [1925], *I*

Shape without form, shade without color,
Paralyzed force, gesture without motion;

Those who have crossed
With direct eyes, to death's other Kingdom
Remember us — if at all — not as lost
Violent souls, but only
As the hollow men
The stuffed men. *Ib.*

Between the idea
And the reality
Between the motion
And the act
Falls the Shadow.[1] *Ib. V*

This is the way the world ends
Not with a bang but a whimper. *Ib.*

A cold coming we had of it,
Just the worst time of the year.
Journey of the Magi [1927]

[1] See Dowson, p. 889b.

Because I do not hope to turn again [1]
Because I do not hope
Because I do not hope to turn.
Ash-Wednesday [1930], *I*

Because these wings are no longer wings to fly
But merely vans to beat the air
The air which is now thoroughly small and dry
Smaller and dryer than the will
Teach us to care and not to care
Teach us to sit still. *Ib.*

Lady, three white leopards sat under a juniper tree. *Ib. II*

Terminate torment
Of love unsatisfied
The greater torment
Of love satisfied. *Ib.*

Blown hair is sweet, brown hair over the mouth blown,
Lilac and brown hair;
Distraction, music of the flute, stops and steps of the mind over the third stair,
Fading, fading; strength beyond hope and despair
Climbing the third stair. *Ib. III*

Redeem
The time. Redeem
The unread vision in the higher dream
While jeweled unicorns draw by the gilded hearse. *Ib. IV*

Against the Word the unstilled world still whirled
About the center of the silent Word.

O my people, what have I done unto thee.

Where shall the word be found, where will the word
Resound? Not here, there is not enough silence. *Ib. V*

Wavering between the profit and the loss
In this brief transit where the dreams cross

[1] GUIDO CAVALCANTI, *Perch' Io Non Spero.*

The dreamcrossed twilight between
   birth and dying.
Ash-Wednesday, V

The white sails still fly seaward, seaward
   flying
Unbroken wings.

And the lost heart stiffens and rejoices
In the lost lilac and the lost sea voices
And the weak spirit quickens to rebel
For the bent goldenrod and the lost sea
   smell.   *Ib.*

Even among these rocks,
Our peace in His will.[1]   *Ib.*

What seas what shores what gray rocks
   and what islands
What water lapping the bow
And scent of pine and the woodthrush
   singing through the fog
What images return
O my daughter.   *Marina* [1930]

   I'll convert *you!*
Into a stew.
A nice little, white little, missionary
   stew!   *Sweeney Agonistes*

Birth, and copulation, and death.
That's all the facts when you come to
   brass tacks.   *Ib.*

Two live as one
One live as two
Two live as three
Under the bam
Under the boo
Under the bamboo tree.   *Ib.*

Stone, bronze, stone, steel, stone, oak-
   leaves, horses' heels
Over the paving.
Coriolan I. Triumphal March

O hidden under the dove's wing, hid-
   den in the turtle's breast,
Under the palmtree at noon, under the
   running water
At the still point of the turning world.
O hidden.   *Ib.*

How unpleasant to meet Mr. Eliot! [2]
With his features of clerical cut,

[1] See Dante, p. 161b.
[2] See Edward Lear, p. 672b.

And his brow so grim
And his mouth so prim.
Five-Finger Exercises, V

All our knowledge brings us nearer to
   our ignorance,
All our ignorance brings us nearer to
   death,
But nearness to death no nearer to
   God.
Where is the Life we have lost in liv-
   ing?
Where is the wisdom we have lost in
   knowledge?
Where is the knowledge we have lost in
   information?
The cycles of Heaven in twenty cen-
   turies
Bring us farther from God and nearer
   to the Dust.
The Rock [1934], I

Yet we have gone on living,
Living and partly living.
Murder in the Cathedral [1935],
pt. I

They know and do not know, what it is
   to act or suffer.
They know and do not know, that acting is suffering.   *Ib.*

Saint and Martyr rule from the tomb.
Ib.

The last temptation is the greatest treason:
To do the right deed for the wrong reason.   *Ib.*

Human kind cannot bear very much reality.[1]   *Ib. II*

Time present and time past
Are both perhaps present in time fu-
   ture,
And time future contained in time past.
Four Quartets. Burnt Norton
[1935], I

Footfalls echo in the memory
Down the passage which we did not
   take
Towards the door we never opened
Into the rose garden.   *Ib.*

[1] Also in *Four Quartets, Burnt Norton, pt. I.*

Shall we follow
The deception of the thrush? Into our
    first world.
      Four Quartets. Burnt Norton, I

Garlic and sapphires in the mud
Clot the bedded axle-tree.
The trilling wire in the blood
Sings below inveterate scars
And reconciles forgotten wars.
                Ib. II

At the still point of the turning world.
    Neither flesh nor fleshless.   *Ib.*

   Except for the point, the still point,
There would be no dance, and there is
    only the dance.   *Ib.*

Only through time time is conquered.
                  Ib.

Sudden in a shaft of sunlight
Even while the dust moves
There rises the hidden laughter
Of children in the foliage
Quick now, here, now, always —
Ridiculous the waste sad time
Stretching before and after.   *Ib. V*

In my beginning is my end.
      Ib. East Coker [1940], I

    Keeping time,
Keeping the rhythm in their dancing
As in their living in the living seasons
The time of the seasons and the con-
    stellations
The time of milking and the time of
    harvest
The time of the coupling of man and
    woman
And that of beasts. Feet rising and fall-
    ing.
Eating and drinking. Dung and death.
                  Ib.

What is the late November doing
With the disturbance of the spring.
                Ib. II

A periphrastic study in a worn-out
    poetical fashion,
Leaving one still with the intolerable
    wrestle
With words and meanings. The poetry
    does not matter.   *Ib.*

The only wisdom we can hope to ac-
    quire
Is the wisdom of humility: humility is
    endless.
      Four Quartets. East Coker, II

The houses are all gone under the sea.
                  Ib.

The dancers are all gone under the hill.
                  Ib.

O dark dark dark.[1] They all go into the
    dark,
The vacant interstellar spaces, the va-
    cant into the vacant.   *Ib.*

And we all go with them, into the silent
    funeral,
Nobody's funeral, for there is no one to
    bury.

I said to my soul, be still, and let the
    dark come upon you
Which shall be the darkness of God.
                  Ib.

To arrive where you are, to get from
    where you are not,
You must go by a way wherein there is
    no ecstasy.
In order to arrive at what you do not
    know
You must go by the way which is the
    way of ignorance.   *Ib.*

The whole earth is our hospital
Endowed by the ruined millionaire.
                  Ib.

We call this Friday good.   *Ib.*

    And so each venture
Is a new beginning, a raid on the inar-
    ticulate
With shabby equipment always deteri-
    orating
In the general mess of imprecision of
    feeling,
Undisciplined squads of emotion.
                Ib. V

For us, there is only the trying. The
    rest is not our business.   *Ib.*

Home is where one starts from. As we
    grow older

[1] See Milton, p. 349a.

The world becomes stranger, the pat-
tern more complicated
Of dead and living. Not the intense
moment
Isolated, with no before and after,
But a lifetime burning in every moment
And not the lifetime of one man only
But of old stones that cannot be deci-
phered.
> Four Quartets. East Coker, V

Love is most nearly itself
When here and now cease to matter.
Old men ought to be explorers [1]
Here and there does not matter
We must be still and still moving
Into another intensity
For a further union, a deeper commun-
ion
Through the dark cold and the empty
desolation,
The wave cry, the wind cry, the vast
waters
Of the petrel and the porpoise. In my
end is my beginning.[2] *Ib.*

I do not know much about gods; but I
think that the river
Is a strong brown god — sullen, untamed and intractable.
> *Ib. The Dry Salvages* [1941], I

The sea is the land's edge also, the gran-
ite
Into which it reaches, the beaches
where it tosses
Its hints of earlier and other creation:
The starfish, the hermit crab, the
whale's backbone;
The pools where it offers to our curios-
ity
The more delicate algae and the sea
anemone.
It tosses up our losses, the torn seine,
The shattered lobsterpot, the broken
oar
And the gear of foreign dead men. The
sea has many voices.[3] *Ib.*

There is no end of it, the voiceless wailing,

No end to the withering of withered
flowers.
> Four Quartets. The Dry
> Salvages, II

Only the hardly, barely prayable
Prayer of the one Annunciation. *Ib.*

The backward look behind the assurance
Of recorded history, the backward half-
look
Over the shoulder, towards the primitive terror. *Ib.*

Not fare well,
But fare forward, voyagers. *Ib.* III

Music heard so deeply
That it is not heard at all, but you are
the music
While the music lasts. *Ib.* V
Only undefeated
Because we have gone on trying;
We, content at the last
If our temporal reversion nourish
(Not too far from the yew tree)
The life of significant soil. *Ib.*

What the dead had no speech for,
when living,
They can tell you, being dead: the
communication
Of the dead is tongued with fire beyond
the language of the living.
> *Ib. Little Gidding* [1942], I

Water and fire shall rot
The marred foundations we forgot,
Of sanctuary and choir.
This is the death of water and fire.
 Ib. II

In the uncertain hour before the morn-
ing
Near the ending of interminable night
At the recurrent end of the unending
After the dark dove with the flickering
tongue
Had passed below the horizon of his
homing. *Ib.*
Since our concern was speech, and
speech impelled us
To purify the dialect of the tribe.[1]
 Ib.

---

[1] See Roethke, p. 1065b.
[2] See Mary, Queen of Scots, p. 192b.
[3] See Tennyson, p. 646b.

[1] Donner un sens plus pur aux mots de la
tribu. — STÉPHANE MALLARMÉ [1842–1898], Le
Tombeau d'Edgar Poe

Who then devised the torment? Love.
Love is the unfamiliar Name
Behind the hands that wove
The intolerable shirt of flame
Which human power cannot remove.
   We only live, only suspire
Consumed by either fire or fire.
          Four Quartets. Little
                Gidding, IV

So, while the light fails
On a winter's afternoon, in a secluded
   chapel
History is now and England.   *Ib.* V

We shall not cease from exploration
And the end of all our exploring
Will be to arrive where we started
And know the place for the first time.
                     Ib.

A condition of complete simplicity
(Costing not less than everything)
And all shall be well and
All manner of thing shall be well
When the tongues of flame are in-
   folded
Into the crowned knot of fire
And the fire and the rose are one.
                     Ib.

By the delicate, invisible web you
   wove —
The inexplicable mystery of sound.
        To Walter de la Mare [1948]

What is hell? Hell is oneself,
Hell is alone, the other figures in it
Merely projections.[1]
        The Cocktail Party [1950]

It [tradition] cannot be inherited,
and if you want it you must obtain it
by great labor.
    Tradition and the Individual
            Talent [1919]

The progress of an artist is a continual self-sacrifice, a continual extinction
of personality.   *Ib.*

Poetry is not a turning loose of emotion, but an escape from emotion; it is
not the expression of personality, but
an escape from personality. But, of
course, only those who have personality

and emotions know what it means to
want to escape from these things.
     Tradition and the Individual
                Talent

The only way of expressing emotion
in the form of art is by finding an "objective correlative"; in other words, a
set of objects, a situation, a chain of
events which shall be the formula of
that *particular* emotion.
   Hamlet and His Problems [1919]

Immature poets imitate; mature
poets steal.
        Philip Massinger [1920]

Every vital development in language
is a development of feeling as well.
                   Ib.

In the seventeenth century a dissociation of sensibility set in, from which
we have never recovered; and this
dissociation, as is natural, was aggra-
vated by the influence of the two most
powerful poets of the century, Milton
and Dryden.
   The Metaphysical Poets [1921]

Poets in our civilization, as it exists at
present, must be *difficult*. . . . The
poet must become more and more comprehensive, more allusive, more indirect, in order to force, to dislocate if
necessary, language into its meaning.
                   Ib.

Humility is the most difficult of all
virtues to achieve; nothing dies harder
than the desire to think well of oneself.
    Shakespeare and the Stoicism of
             Seneca [1927]

The great poet, in writing himself,
writes his time.[1]   *Ib.*

We know too much, and are convinced of too little. Our literature is a
substitute for religion, and so is our religion.
   A Dialogue on Dramatic Poetry
                    [1928]

---

[1] See Virgil, p. 119a; and Marlowe, p. 213a, and note.

[1] In a footnote, Eliot writes: "Rémy de Gourmont said much the same thing, in speaking of Flaubert."

If I ask myself . . . why I prefer the poetry of Dante to that of Shakespeare, I should have to say, because it seems to me to illustrate a saner attitude towards the mystery of life.
The Sacred Wood, introduction
[1928]

The general point of view may be described as classicist in literature, royalist in politics, and Anglo-Catholic in religion.
For Lancelot Andrews [1928],
preface

We fight for lost causes because we know that our defeat and dismay may be the preface to our successors' victory, though that victory itself will be temporary; we fight rather to keep something alive than in the expectation that anything will triumph.
Ib. Francis Herbert Bradley

The great weakness of Pragmatism is that it ends by being of no *use* to anybody.   *Ib.*

Genuine poetry can communicate before it is understood.
Dante [1929]

More can be learned about how to write poetry from Dante than from any English poet. . . . The language of each great English poet is his own language; the language of Dante is the perfection of a common language.
Ib.

Shakespeare gives the greatest width of human passion; Dante the greatest altitude and greatest depth.   *Ib.*

Sometimes, however, to be a "ruined man" is itself a vocation.
The Use of Poetry and the Use
of Criticism [1933]. Words-
worth and Coleridge

As things are, and as fundamentally they must always be, poetry is not a career, but a mug's game. No honest poet can ever feel quite sure of the permanent value of what he has writ-

ten: he may have wasted his time and messed up his life for nothing.
The Use of Poetry and the Use
of Criticism. Conclusion

Tradition by itself is not enough; it must be perpetually criticized and brought up to date under the supervision of what I call orthodoxy.
After Strange Gods [1934]

WILLIAM L. LAURENCE
1888–

[On the first atom bomb explosion [1]] A great ball of fire about a mile in diameter, changing colors as it kept shooting upward, from deep purple to orange, expanding, growing bigger, rising as it was expanding, an elemental force freed from its bonds after being chained for billions of years.
In the New York Times [Sep-
tember 26, 1945]

At first it was a giant column that soon took the shape of a supramundane mushroom.   *Ib.*

T. E. LAWRENCE [2]
1888–1935

I loved you, so I drew these tides of
    men into my hands and wrote my
    will across the sky in stars.
To earn you Freedom, the seven-pil-
    lared worthy house, that your eyes
    might be shining for me
When we came.
Seven Pillars of Wisdom [3]
[1926], dedication

There could be no honor in a sure success, but much might be wrested from a sure defeat.
Revolt in the Desert [1927],
ch. 19

---

[1] At Alamogordo, New Mexico, July 16, 1945.
[2] Lawrence changed his name to T. E. Shaw in 1927.
[3] See *Proverbs 9:1*, p. 23b.

EUGENE O'NEILL
1888–1953

Dat ole davil, sea.
> *Anna Christie* [1922], *act I*

We's all poor nuts and things happen, and we yust get mixed in wrong, that's all.
> *Ib. IV*

For de little stealin' dey gits you in jail soon or late. For de big stealin' dey makes you emperor and puts you in de Hall o' Fame when you croaks. If dey's one thing I learns in ten years on de Pullman cars listenin' to de white quality talk, it's dat same fact.
> *The Emperor Jones* [1920], *sc. 1*

Poverty — that most deadly and prevalent of all diseases.
> *Ib.*

Yank: Sure! Lock me up! Put me in a cage! Dat's de on'y answer yuh know. G'wan, lock me up!
Policeman: What you been doin'?
Yank: Enough to gimme life for! I was born, see? Sure, dat's de charge. Write it in de blotter. I was born, get me!
> *The Hairy Ape* [1922]

Desire Under the Elms.
> *Title of play* [1924]

He couldn't design a cathedral without it looking like the First Supernatural Bank!
> *The Great God Brown* [1926]

Our lives are merely strange dark interludes in the electrical display of God the Father!
> *Strange Interlude* [1928]

Mourning Becomes Electra.
> *Title of dramatic trilogy* [1931]

A Long Day's Journey into Night.
> *Title of play* [1956]

JOHN CROWE RANSOM
1888–

Two evils, monstrous either one apart,
Possessed me, and were long and loath
    at going:
A cry of Absence, Absence, in the
    heart,

And in the wood the furious winter
    blowing.   *Winter Remembered*

Hands hold much of heat in little storage.   *They Hail the Sunrise*

The lazy geese, like a snow cloud
Dripping their snow on the green grass,
Tricking and stopping, sleepy and
    proud,
Who cried in goose, Alas.
> *Bells for John Whiteside's*
> *Daughter*

Here lies a lady of beauty and high degree.
Of chills and fever she died, of fever
    and chills,
The delight of her husband, her aunts,
    an infant of three,
And of medicos marveling sweetly on
    her ills.   *Here Lies a Lady*

God have mercy on the sinner
Who must write with no dinner,
No gravy and no grub,
No pewter and no pub,
No belly and no bowels,
Only consonants and vowels.
> *Survey of Literature*

Captain Carpenter rose up in his prime
Put on his pistols and went riding out.
> *Captain Carpenter, st. 1*

ROBERT EMMONS
ROGERS
1888–1941

Marry the boss's daughter.
> *Advice to the Class of 1929,*
> *Massachusetts Institute of Technology*

ALAN SEEGER
1888–1916

I have a rendezvous with Death
At some disputed barricade,
When spring comes back with rustling
    shade
And apple blossoms fill the air.
> *I Have a Rendezvous with Death*

When spring trips north again this
    year,

And I to my pledged word am true,
I shall not fail that rendezvous.
    I Have a Rendezvous with Death

BARTOLOMEO VANZETTI
1888–1927

I found myself compelled to fight back from my eyes the tears, and quanch my heart trobling to my throat to not weep before him. But Sacco's name will live in the hearts of the people when your name, your laws, institutions and your false god are but a dim rememoring of a cursed past in which man was wolf to the man.
    Last Speech to the Court [1]

HENRY AGARD WALLACE [2]
1888–1965

Unemployed purchasing power means unemployed labor and unemployed labor means human want in the midst of plenty. This is the most challenging paradox of modern times.
    Address [1934]

The object of this war is to make sure that everybody in the world has the privilege of drinking a quart of milk a day.[3]
    Address, The Price of Free World Victory [May 8, 1942]

The century on which we are entering can be and must be the century of the common man.   *Ib.*

The hair goes with the hide.
    When asked why he had not mentioned Franklin D. Roosevelt's running mate, Harry S. Truman, in his campaign speech in Madison Square Garden, New York [September 21, 1944]

---

[1] Vanzetti and Nicolo Sacco, Italian anarchists, were executed August 23, 1927, by the Commonwealth of Massachusetts on charges, never conclusively proved, of murder and robbery.

[2] See Clare Boothe Luce, p. 1053b.

[3] This statement became twisted into the purported slogan "Milk for Hottentots."

The people who are fighting against me know that they are not fighting a starry-eyed liberal or mystic. If they really thought that, they wouldn't be worried.[1]
    Speech at testimonial dinner [January 29, 1945]

CONRAD AIKEN
1889–1973

Music I heard with you was more than music,
And bread I broke with you was more than bread.
Now that I am without you, all is desolate;
All that was once so beautiful is dead.
    Bread and Music [1914]

Stars in the purple dusk above the rooftops
Pale in a saffron mist and seem to die,
And I myself on a swiftly tilting planet
Stand before a glass and tie my tie.
    Senlin. Morning Song

One by one in the moonlight there,
Neighing far off on the haunted air,
The unicorns come down to the sea.
    Ib. Evening Song

Rock meeting rock can know love better
Than eyes that stare or lips that touch.
All that we know in love is bitter,
And it is not much.
    Annihilation, st. 8

All lovely things will have an ending,
All lovely things will fade and die,
And youth, that's now so bravely spending,
Will beg a penny by and by.
    All Lovely Things Will Have an Ending

The hiss was now becoming a roar — the whole world was a vast moving screen of snow — but even now it said peace, it said remoteness, it said cold, it said sleep.
    Silent Snow, Secret Snow [1932]

---

[1] See C. L. Becker, p. 913b.

O Altitudo in the bloodstream swims.[1]
And in the Human Heart
[1940]. *Sonnet 6*

Ice is the silent language of the peak;
and fire the silent language of the star.
Ib. 10

For brief as water falling will be death,
and brief as flower falling, or a leaf,
brief as the taking, and the giving,
breath;
thus natural, thus brief, my love, is
grief. *Ib.* 18

ROBERT CHARLES
BENCHLEY
1889–1945

I haven't been abroad in so long that
I almost speak English without an accent. *The Old Sea Rover Speaks*

An Austrian scientist has come out
with the announcement that there is no
such thing as a hundred per cent male
or a hundred per cent female. If this is
true, it is really a big step forward.
*Ib. A Talk to Young Men: Grad-
uation Address, The Decline of
Sex*

Tell us your phobias and we will tell
you what you are afraid of. *Phobias*

It took me fifteen years to discover
that I had no talent for writing, but I
couldn't give it up because by that time
I was too famous. *Remark*

CHRISTOPHER DAWSON
1889–

As soon as men decide that all means
are permitted to fight an evil, then their
good becomes indistinguishable from
the evil that they set out to destroy.
The Judgment of the Nations
[1942]

[1] See Sir Thomas Browne, p. 329b.

PHILIP GUEDALLA
1889–1944

Biography, like big game hunting, is
one of the recognized forms of sport,
and it is as unfair as only sport can
be. *Supers and Supermen* [1920]

The work of Henry James has always
seemed divisible by a simple dynastic
arrangement into three reigns: James I,
James II, and the Old Pretender.[1] *Ib.*

Strange that pre-eminence in Germany has more than once been indi-
cated by an eccentric pattern in the
hair upon the upper lip.
The Hundred Years [1936]

The true history of the United States
is the history of transportation . . . in
which the names of railroad presidents
are more significant than those of Presidents of the United States. *Ib.*

There is no plant in the whole world
of more cautious growth than Anglo-
American negotiation.
Mr. Churchill [1942] (*apropos
the wedding of Mr. Churchill's
parents*)

ADOLF HITLER
1889–1945

My adversaries . . . applied the one
means that wins the easiest victory over
reason: terror and force.
Mein Kampf [1933],[2] *vol. I,
ch. 2*

A majority can never replace the
man. . . . Just as a hundred fools do
not make one wise man, an heroic decision is not likely to come from a hundred cowards. *Ib.* 3

Mankind has grown strong in eternal
struggles and it will only perish through
eternal peace. *Ib.* 4

Strength lies not in defense but in
attack. *Ib.*

All propaganda has to be popular
and has to adapt its spiritual level to

[1] See Henry James, p. 797b.
[2] *My Battle.*

the perception of the least intelligent of those towards whom it intends to direct itself. *Mein Kampf vol. I, ch. 6*

The great masses of the people . . . will more easily fall victims to a big lie than to a small one. *Ib.* 10

If an idea is right in itself, and if thus armed it embarks on the struggle in this world, it is invincible and every persecution will lead to its inner strengthening. *Ib.* 12

Germany will be either a world power or will not be at all.
Ib. II, 14

Never tolerate the establishment of two continental powers in Europe.
Ib.

The Sudetenland is the last territorial claim I have to make in Europe.
Address, at Sports Palast, Berlin [September 26, 1938]

After fifteen years of work I have achieved, as a common German soldier and merely with my fanatical will power, the unity of the German nation, and have freed it from the death sentence of Versailles.[1]
Proclamation to the troops on taking over the leadership of the German armed forces [December 21, 1941]

This war no longer bears the characteristics of former inter-European conflicts. It is one of those elemental conflicts which usher in a new millennium and which shake the world once in a thousand years.
Speech to the Reichstag [April 26, 1942]

Whomsoever England allies herself with, she will see her allies stronger

[1] The Allied and Associated Governments affirm and Germany accepts the responsibility of Germany and her Allies for causing all the loss and damage to which the Allied and Associated Governments and their nationals have been subjected as a consequence of the war imposed upon them by the aggression of Germany and her Allies. — *Article 231 (the "war guilt clause"), Treaty of Versailles [June 28, 1919]*

than she is herself at the end of this war. *Speech to the Reichstag*

If the German people despair, they will deserve no better than they get. If they despair, I will not be sorry for them if God lets them down.
Speech at Munich on the twentieth anniversary of the Munich beer hall putsch [broadcast November 8, 1943]

Is Paris burning?[1]
Asked while at the Oberkommando der Wehrmacht, Rastenburg, Germany [August 25, 1944]

GEORGE S. KAUFMAN
1889–1961
You Can't Take It With You.[2]
Title of play [1936]

Satire is what closes Saturday night.
Saying

STODDARD KING
1889–1933
There's a long, long trail a-winding
Into the land of my dreams,
Where the nightingales are singing
And a white moon beams.
The Long, Long Trail [1913]

WALTER LIPPMANN
1889–1974
Surely the task of statesmanship is more difficult today than ever before in history. . . . The distance between what we know and what we need to know appears to be greater than ever. . . . Nor can we keep to the problem within our borders. Whether we wish it or not we are involved in the world's problems, and all the winds of heaven blow through our land.
A Preface to Politics [1913], ch. 4

[1] Brennt Paris?
[2] Lo, no man taketh his goods with him. — *Song of the Harp-Player [c. 2100 B.C.]*

The principles of liberalism . . . are older than all existing constitutions and are more deeply rooted than any formulation of them that can be put into words. . . .

The liberal philosophy holds that enduring governments must be accountable to someone beside themselves; that a government responsible only to its own conscience is not for long tolerable. It holds that since any government is liable to fail, there is needed a method of changing the governors without wrecking the state. It holds that unless there is a method, be it through elections or otherwise, by which the governed can make their views effective in some proportion to their weight, the nation is at the mercy of violence in the form of terrorism, assassination, conspiracy, mass compulsion, and civil war.
In Defense of Liberalism [*Vanity Fair, November 1934*]

The denial that men may be arbitrary in human transactions *is* the higher law. . . . By this higher law all formal laws and all political behavior are judged in civilized societies. . . . If the sovereign himself may not act willfully, arbitrarily, by personal prerogative, then no one may. His ministers may not. The legislature may not. Majorities may not. Individuals may not. Crowds may not. The national state may not. This law which is the spirit of law is the opposite of an accumulation of old precedents and new fiats. By this higher law, that men must not be arbitrary, the old law is continually tested and the new law reviewed.
The Good Society [*1937*], *ch. 15*

In foreign relations, as in all other relations, a policy has been formed only when commitments and power have been brought into balance.
U. S. Foreign Policy [*1943*]

The final test of a leader is that he leaves behind him in other men the conviction and the will to carry on. . . . The genius of a good leader is to leave behind him a situation which

common sense, without the grace of genius, can deal with successfully.
Roosevelt Has Gone [*April 14, 1945*]

The world state is inherent in the United Nations as an oak tree is in an acorn.   *One World or None* [*1946*]

A regime, an established order, is rarely overthrown by a revolutionary movement; usually a regime collapses of its own weakness and corruption and then a revolutionary movement enters among the ruins and takes over the powers that have become vacant.
For Charles de Gaulle [*Today and Tomorrow, June 5, 1958*]

I don't care about the word isolationism, and I don't care about the word appeasement. I'm interested in the rights and needs and responsibilities of the United States. We are not the policeman of mankind. We are not able to run the world, and we shouldn't pretend that we can. Let us tend to our own business, which is great enough as it is. It's very great. We have neglected our own affairs. Our education is inadequate, our cities are badly built, our social arrangements are unsatisfactory. We can't wait another generation. Unless we can surmount this crisis, and work and get going onto the path of a settlement in Asia, and a settlement in Europe, all of these plans of the Great Society here at home, all the plans for the rebuilding of backward countries in other continents will all be put on the shelf, because war interrupts everything like that.
Conversations with Walter Lippmann [*1965*]. *Lippmann and Eric Sevareid, February 22, 1965*

A free press is not a privilege but an organic necessity in a great society. . . . A great society is simply a big and complicated urban society.[1]
Address, International Press Institute Assembly, London [*May 27, 1965*]

[1] See Lyndon Johnson, p. 1064a.

Without criticism and reliable and intelligent reporting, the government cannot govern.
Address, International Press Institute Assembly, London

Responsible journalism is journalism responsible in the last analysis to the editor's own conviction of what, whether interesting or only important, is in the public interest. *Ib.*

As the free press develops, the paramount point is whether the journalist, like the scientist or scholar, puts truth in the first place or in the second.
Ib.

KATHERINE MANSFIELD
1889–1923

Whenever I prepare for a journey I prepare as though for death. Should I never return, all is in order. This is what life has taught me.
Journal [1922]

I want, by understanding myself, to understand others. I want to be all that I am capable of becoming. . . . This all sounds very strenuous and serious. But now that I have wrestled with it, it's no longer so. I feel happy — deep down. *All is well.*
Ib. (end of her journal)

JAWAHARLAL NEHRU
1889–1964

The French Revolution of a hundred and fifty years ago gradually ushered in an age of political equality, but the times have changed, and that by itself is not enough today. The boundaries of democracy have to be widened now so as to include economic equality also. This is the great revolution through which we are all passing.
Glimpses of World History [1939]

The basic fact of today is the tremendous pace of change in human life.
Credo [*reprinted in the New York Times, September 7, 1958*]

Democracy and socialism are means to an end, not the end itself. *Ib.*

The forces of a capitalist society, if left unchecked, tend to make the rich richer and the poor poorer. *Ib.*

I want nothing to do with any religion concerned with keeping the masses satisfied to live in hunger, filth, and ignorance. I want nothing to do with any order, religious or otherwise, which does not teach people that they are capable of becoming happier and more civilized, on this earth, capable of becoming true *man*, master of his fate and captain of his soul.[1]
From EDGAR SNOW, *Journey to the Beginning* [1958]

ANNA AKHMATOVA
1889–1966

Oh, how good the snapping and the crackle
Of the frost that daily grows more keen!
Laden with its dazzling icy roses,
The white-flaming bush is forced to lean.
Oh, How Good [1940], *st. 1*

What hangs in the balance is nowise in doubt;
We know the event and we brave what we know;
Our clocks are all striking the hour of courage. *Courage* [1942]

O great language we love:
It is you, Russian tongue, we must save, and we swear
We will give you unstained to the sons of our sons;
You shall live on our lips, and we promise you — never
A prison shall know you, but you shall be free
Forever. *Ib.*

[1] See Sallust, p. 116a, and note.

VANNEVAR BUSH
1890–

Science: The Endless Frontier.
Title of book [1945]

The scene changes but the aspirations of men of good will persist.
Modern Arms and Free Men
[1949], *foreword*

If democracy loses its touch, then no great war will be needed to overwhelm it. If it keeps and enhances its strength, no great war need come again.
Ib. Conclusion

Fear cannot be banished, but it can be calm and without panic; and it can be mitigated by reason and evaluation.
Ib.

KAREL ČAPEK
1890–1938

Rossum's Universal Robots.[1]
R.U.R. [1920]

MARCUS COOK CONNELLY
1890–

Gangway for de Lawd God Jehovah!
The Green Pastures[2]
[1930]

God: I'll jest r'ar back an' pass a miracle. *Ib.*

Gabriel: How about cleanin' up de whole mess of 'em and sta'tin' all over ag'in wid some new kind of animal?
God: An' admit I'm licked? *Ib.*

Even bein' Gawd ain't a bed of roses.
Ib.

ELMER DAVIS
1890–1958

Atomic warfare is bad enough; biological warfare would be worse; but there is something that is worse than

[1] The term "robot" came into English through Čapek's play.
[2] Suggested by Roark Bradford's stories, *Ol' Man Adam an' His Chillun.*

either. The French can tell you what it is; or the Czechs, or the Greeks, or the Norwegians, or the Filipinos; it is subjection to an alien oppressor.
No World, If Necessary [*in Saturday Review of Literature,* March 30, 1946]

One world or none, say the atomic scientists. Has it occurred to them that if their one world turned out to be totalitarian and obscurantist, we might better have no world at all? *Ib.*

The republic was not established by cowards, and cowards will not preserve it.
Phi Beta Kappa Oration, Harvard [1953]

With a great price our ancestors obtained this freedom, but we were born free . . . But that freedom can be retained only by the eternal vigilance which has always been its price.
But We Were Born Free
[1954], *ch. 1*

The first and great commandment is, Don't let them scare you. *Ib.*

I believe it [the nation] will endure, but only if we stand up for it. *Ib.*

This will remain the land of the free only so long as it is the home of the brave. *Ib.*

What makes Western civilization worth saving is the freedom of the mind, now under heavy attack from the primitives . . . who have persisted among us. If we have not the courage to defend that faith, it won't matter much whether we are saved or not.
Ib. 6

CHARLES ANDRÉ JOSEPH MARIE DE GAULLE
1890–1970

The sword is the axis of the world, and grandeur is indivisible.
Le Fil de l'Épée [1934]

The perfection preached in the Gospels never yet built up an empire. Every man of action has a strong dose of egotism, pride, hardness, and cunning. But all those things will be forgiven him, indeed, they will be regarded as high qualities, if he can make of them the means to achieve great ends.
> *Le Fil de l'Épée*

Nothing great will ever be achieved without great men, and men are great only if they are determined to be so.
> *Ib.*

France has lost a battle. But France has not lost the war.
> *Broadcast from London to the French people after the fall of France [June 18, 1940]*

Since those whose duty it was to hold the sword of France have let it fall, I have picked up its broken point.
> *Radio address [July 13, 1940]*

Then, at the sight of those bewildered people and of those soldiers in rout . . . I felt myself borne up by a limitless fury. Ah! It's too stupid! The war is beginning as badly as it could. Therefore it must go on. For that, the world is wide. If I live, I will fight, wherever I must, as long as I must, until the enemy is defeated and the national stain washed clean. All I have managed to do since was resolved upon that day.
> *Les Mémoires de Guerre, vol. I [1954]*

At this moment, the worst in her history [the fall of France], it was for me to assume the burden of France.   *Ib.*

But there is no France without a sword.   *Ib.*

France cannot be France without greatness.   *Ib.*

I always thought I was Jeanne d'Arc and Bonaparte. How little one knows oneself.
> *Reply to speaker who compared him to Robespierre; from Figaro Littéraire [1958]*

DWIGHT DAVID EISENHOWER
1890–1969

People of Western Europe: A landing was made this morning on the coast of France by troops of the Allied Expeditionary Force. This landing is part of the concerted United Nations plan for the liberation of Europe, made in conjunction with our great Russian allies. . . . I call upon all who love freedom to stand with us now. Together we shall achieve victory.
> *Broadcast [June 6, 1944 — D-Day]*

Humility must always be the portion of any man who receives acclaim earned in the blood of his followers and the sacrifices of his friends.
> *Address at Guildhall, London [July 12, 1945]*

Nothing is easy in war. Mistakes are always paid for in casualties and troops are quick to sense any blunder made by their commanders.
> *Infantry School Quarterly [April 1953]*

This conjunction of an immense military establishment and a large arms industry is new in the American experience. . . . We recognize the imperative need for this development. Yet we must not fail to comprehend its grave implications. . . . In the councils of government, we must guard against the acquisition of unwarranted influence, whether sought or unsought, by the military-industrial complex. The potential for the disastrous rise of misplaced power exists and will persist.
> *Farewell Radio and Television Address to the American People [January 17, 1961]*

SIR ALAN PATRICK HERBERT
1890–1971

I'm not a jealous woman, but I *can't* see what he sees in her,

I can't see *what* he sees in her, I can't see what he *sees* in her!
> *I Can't Think What He Sees in Her*

Holy Deadlock.[1]
> *Title of novel* [1934] *satirizing the paradoxes of British divorce law*

The Common Law of England has been laboriously built upon a mythical figure — the figure of "The Reasonable Man."
> *Uncommon Law* [1935], *p. 1*

The critical period in matrimony is breakfast-time.   *Ib. p. 98*

An Act of God was defined as something which no reasonable man could have expected.   *Ib. p. 316*

SAMUEL HOFFENSTEIN
1890–1947

Babies haven't any hair;
Old men's heads are just as bare;
Between the cradle and the grave
Lies a haircut and a shave.
> *Songs of Faith in the Year after Next, VIII*

The heart's dead
Are never buried.   *Summer Day*

GERALD WHITE JOHNSON
1890–

A man who has tried to play Mozart, and failed, through that vain effort comes into position better to understand the man who tried to paint the Sistine Madonna, and did.
> *A Little Night-Music* [1937]

Nothing changes more constantly than the past; for the past that influences our lives does not consist of what actually happened, but of what men believe happened.
> *American Heroes and Hero-Worship* [1943], *ch. 1*

[1] Monagony — the state of being married to one person. — BROOKS BECK [1963]

Heroes are created by popular demand, sometimes out of the scantiest materials . . . such as the apple that William Tell never shot, the ride that Paul Revere never finished, the flag that Barbara Frietchie never waved.
> *American Heroes and Hero-Worship, ch. 1*

In all the world there is nothing more timorous than a million dollars, except ten million. In revolutionary times the rich are always the people who are most afraid.
> *American Freedom and the Press* [1958]

ROBERT LEY
1890–1945

Strength through joy.[1]
> *Instruction for the German Labor Front* [December 2, 1933]

CHRISTOPHER MORLEY
1890–1957

And of all man's felicities
The very subtlest one, say I,
Is when for the first time he sees
His hearthfire smoke against the sky.
> *A Hallowe'en Memory, st. 5*

If you have to keep reminding yourself of a thing, perhaps it isn't so.
> *Thunder on the Left* [1925], *ch. 9*

April prepares her green traffic light and the world thinks Go.
> *John Mistletoe* [1931], 8

A human being; an ingenious assembly of portable plumbing.
> *Human Being* [1932], *ch. 11*

The enemies of the Future are always the very nicest people.
> *Kitty Foyle* [1939], *ch. 5*

Dancing is wonderful training for girls, it's the first way you learn to guess what a man is going to do before he does it.   *Ib. 11*

[1] Kraft durch Freude.

There was so much handwriting on the
    wall
That even the wall fell down.
        Around the Clock [1943]

Chattering voltage like a broken wire
The wild cicada cried, Six weeks to
    frost!   *End of August*

Why do they put the Gideon Bibles
only in the bedrooms, where it's usually
too late, and not in the barroom downstairs?
    Contribution to a Contribution

ALLAN NEVINS
1890–1971

Too little and too late.
        Current History [1935]

BORIS PASTERNAK
1890–1960

I cherish this, Thy rigorous conception,
And I consent to play this part therein;
But another play is running at this mo-
    ment,
So, for the present, release me from the
    cast.

And yet, the order of the acts has been
    schemed and plotted,
And nothing can avert the final cur-
    tain's fall.
I stand alone. All else is swamped by
    Pharisaism.
To live life to the end is not a childish
    task.
    Doctor Zhivago [1958]. *The
    Poems of Yurii Zhivago,*[1] *Ham-
    let, st. 3, 4*

It snowed and snowed, the whole world
    over,
Snow swept the world from end to end.
A candle burned on the table;
A candle burned.
    Ib. Winter Night, st. 1

A corner draft fluttered the flame
And the white fever of temptation

[1] Translated by BERNARD GUILBERT GUERNEY.

Upswept its angel wings that cast
A cruciform shadow.
    *Doctor Zhivago. The Poems of
    Yurii Zhivago, Winter Night,
    st. 7*

GEORGE SELDES
1890–1970

Sawdust Caesar.[1]
        Title of book [1932]

FRED M. VINSON
1890–1953

Wars are not "acts of God." They
are caused by man, by man-made institutions, by the way in which man has
organized his society. What man has
made, man can change.
    *Speech, Arlington National
    Cemetery* [*Memorial Day,
    1945*]

"RED" ROWLEY
fl. 1915

Mademoiselle from Armenteers,
Hasn't been kissed in forty years,
    Hinky dinky, parley-voo.
    Mademoiselle from Armentières [2]

Mademoiselle from St. Nazaire,
She never heard of underwear.   *Ib.*

AGATHA CHRISTIE
1891–1976

It is completely unimportant. That is
why it is so interesting.
    The Murder of Roger Ackroyd
    [1926]

JEAN COCTEAU
1891–1963

Mirrors should reflect a little before
throwing back images.
        Des Beaux-Arts

[1] Mussolini.
[2] Soldier song of World War I, with innumerable versions. The tune and verse structure were
based on a British Army song composed by
Alfred James Walden ["Harry Wincott," 1867–
1947].

ELY CULBERTSON
1891–1955

The bizarre world of cards . . . a world of pure power politics where rewards and punishments were meted out immediately. A deck of cards was built like the purest of hierarchies, with every card a master to those below it, a lackey to those above it. And there were "masses" — long suits — which always asserted themselves in the end, triumphing over the kings and aces.

Total Peace [1943], ch. 1

Power politics is the diplomatic name for the law of the jungle.

Must We Fight Russia? [1946], ch. 2

We must conquer war, or war will conquer us. *Ib.*

God and the politicians willing, the United States can declare peace upon the world, and win it. *Ib. 5*

KARL KEICHNER DARROW
1891–

One of the things which distinguishes ours from all earlier generations is this, that we have seen our atoms.

The Renaissance of Physics [1936]

HU SHIH[1]
1891–1962

We in China today have not reached the point where we can take concrete steps to create a new literature, and there is no need of talking theoretically about the techniques of creation. Let us first devote our efforts to the first . . . steps of preparatory work.

La Jeunesse Nouvelle [April 1918]

Only when we realize that there is no eternal, unchanging truth or absolute

---

[1] From *Sources of Chinese Tradition,* edited by William Theodore de Bary [1960].

truth can we arouse in ourselves a sense of intellectual responsibility.

La Jeunesse Nouvelle [April 1919]

The Chinese people's philosophy of life has not yet been brought face to face with science. At this moment we painfully feel that science has not been sufficiently promoted, that scientific education has not been developed.

Ib. Hu Shih wen ts'un

At present the most unfounded and most harmful distortion is to ridicule Western civilization as materialistic and worship Eastern civilization as spiritual. . . . Modern civilization of the West, built on the foundation of the search for human happiness, not only has definitely increased material enjoyment to no small degree, but can also definitely satisfy the spiritual demands of mankind. *Ib.*

The most outstanding characteristic of Eastern civilization is to know contentment, whereas that of Western civilization is not to know contentment. Contented Easterners are satisfied with their simple life and therefore do not seek to increase their material enjoyment. . . . They are satisfied with their present lot and environment and therefore do not want to conquer nature but merely be at home with nature and at peace with their lot. *Ib.*

The civilization under which people are restricted and controlled by a material environment from which they cannot escape, and under which they cannot utilize human thought and intellectual power to change environment and improve conditions, is the civilization of a lazy and nonprogressive people. It is a truly materialistic civilization. *Ib.*

DAVID LOW
1891–1963

I have never met anybody who wasn't against war. Even Hitler and

Mussolini were, according to themselves.

In the New York Times
[February 10, 1946]

OSIP MANDELSTAM
1891 – 1938

On every still suburban street
The gatekeepers are shoveling snow.

On Every Still Suburban
Street [1916], st. 1

In teahouses and in home alike
The samovars' red roses glow.

Ib. st. 2

ELLIOT PAUL
1891–1958

The last time I see Paris will be on the day I die. The city was inexhaustible, and so is its memory.

The Last Time I Saw Paris [1]
[1942], pt. II, 23

HAILIE SELASSIE
1891–1975

Outside the kingdom of the Lord there is no nation which is greater than any other. God and history will remember your judgment.

Speech, the League of Nations [2]
[1936]

ARTHUR HAYS
SULZBERGER
1891–1968

Obviously, a man's judgment cannot be better than the information on which he has based it. Give him the truth and he may still go wrong when he has the chance to be right, but give him no news or present him only with distorted and incomplete data, with ig-

norant, sloppy or biased reporting, with propaganda and deliberate falsehoods, and you destroy his whole reasoning processes, and make him something less than a man.

Address, New York State Publishers Association [August 30, 1948]

Freedom cannot be trifled with. You cannot surrender it for security unless in a state of war, and then you must guard carefully the methods of so doing.

Upon receiving the Columbia College award for distinguished service [1952]

There has been dropped upon utterance and thought a smoke screen of intimidation that dims essential thought and essential talk and begets a fog through which we wander uncertainly. Nor is it the superzealots who bother me so much in all this — it is the lack of plain old-fashioned guts on the part of those who capitulate to them.   *Ib.*

There is more fear in this country than the facts warrant. Beset by doubt, the nation listens to those who seem to offer a cure, even though the medicine be more harmful than the disease. Once more we are met upon a battlefield testing whether this nation or any nation similarly dedicated can long endure.[1]   *Ib.*

The vital measure of a newspaper is not its size but its spirit — that is its responsibility to report the news fully, accurately and fairly.

On accepting an award to the New York Times by Temple Israel, Boston [May 9, 1956]

EARL WARREN
1891–1974

To separate [Negro children] from others of similar age and qualifications solely because of their race generates a feeling of inferiority as to their status in

---

[1] The last time I saw Paris, her heart was warm and gay,
   I heard the laughter of her heart in every street café.
   OSCAR HAMMERSTEIN II [1895–1960], *The Last Time I Saw Paris*
[2] He sought sanctions against Italy, which had invaded Ethiopia.

[1] See Lincoln, p. 639a.

the community that may affect their hearts and minds in a way unlikely ever to be undone. . . . We conclude that in the field of public education the doctrine of "separate but equal" [1] has no place. Separate educational facilities are inherently unequal.

Brown v. Board of Education of Topeka, 347 U.S. 483 [1954] [2]

HERBERT V. WILEY
1891–1954

Stand by to crash.

Last command to the crew of the falling U.S. Navy dirigible Akron [April 4, 1933]

STELLA BENSON
1892–1933

Call no man foe, but never love a stranger.   *To the Unborn, st. 3*

PEARL S. BUCK
1892–1973

I feel no need for any other faith than my faith in human beings. Like Confucius of old, I am so absorbed in the wonder of earth and the life upon it that I cannot think of heaven and the angels. I have enough for this life. If there is no other life, then this one has been enough to make it worth being born, myself a human being.

I Believe [1939]

JOHN BURDON
SANDERSON HALDANE
1892–1964

Now, my suspicion is that the universe is not only queerer than we sup-

---

[1] All railway companies carrying passengers in their coaches in the state shall provide equal but separate accommodations for the white and colored races. — *Louisiana Acts of 1890, no. 111, p. 152;* quoted by Mr. Justice HENRY B. BROWN in *Plessy v. Ferguson, 163 U.S. 537* [1896]

[2] In a later implementation of the same case (*349 U.S. 294* [1955]) the Supreme Court asked that desegregation proceed "with all deliberate speed."

---

pose, but queerer than we *can* suppose. . . . I suspect that there are more things in heaven and earth than are dreamed of, in any philosophy.[1] That is the reason why I have no philosophy myself, and must be my excuse for dreaming.   *Possible Worlds* [1927]

ROBERT HOUGHWOUT
JACKSON
1892–1954

If there is any fixed star in our constitutional constellation, it is that no official, high or petty, can prescribe what shall be orthodox in politics, nationalism, religion, or other matters of opinion or force citizens to confess by word or act their faith therein.

Minersville School District v. Gobitis, 319 U.S. 624, 642 [1940]

The first trial in history for crimes against the peace of the world imposes a grave responsibility. The wrongs which we seek to condemn and punish have been so calculated, so malignant and so devastating that civilization cannot tolerate their being ignored because it cannot survive their being repeated.

Opening address before the International Military Tribunal, Nuremberg [1945]

If it is interstate commerce that feels the pinch, it does not matter how local the operation which applies the squeeze.

U.S. v. Women's Sportswear Manufacturers Association 336 U.S. 460, 464 [1949]

There is danger that, if the Court does not temper its doctrinaire logic with a little practical wisdom, it will convert the constitutional Bill of Rights into a suicide pact.

Terminiello v. Chicago, 337 U.S. 1, 37 [1949]

It is not the function of our Government to keep the citizen from falling into error; it is the function of the citi-

---

[1] See Shakespeare, p. 260a.

zen to keep the Government from falling into error.
> American Communications Association v. Douds, 339 U.S. 382, 442 [1950]

The day that this country ceases to be free for irreligion, it will cease to be free for religion.
> Dissenting opinion, Zorach v. Clausor, 343 U.S. 306, 325 [1952]

HOWARD MUMFORD JONES
1892–

They say the forties are the dangerous ages. *The Forties* [1937]

A few unrepentant old sinners wonder if Marx
Also explains the unsocialized pairs in the parks. *Ib. 32*

ARCHIBALD MacLEISH
1892–

Sometimes within the brain's old ghostly house,
I hear, far off, at some forgotten door,
A music and an eerie faint carouse,
And stir of echoes down the creaking floor.
> *Chambers of Imagery, st. 1*

Beauty is that Medusa's head
Which men go armed to seek and sever.
It is most deadly when most dead,
And dead will stare and sting forever.
> *Beauty*

A poem should not mean
But be. *Ars Poetica* [1926]

There with vast wings across the canceled skies,
There in the sudden blackness the black pall
Of nothing, nothing, nothing — nothing at all.
> *The End of the World* [1926]

The world was always yours: you would not take it.
> *Speech to a Crowd*

And here face downward in the sun
To feel how swift how secretly
The shadow of the night comes on.
> *You, Andrew Marvell* [1930]

Christ but this earth goes over to the squall of time!
Hi but she heels to it — rail down: ribs down: rolling
Dakotas under her hull! And the night climbing
Sucking the green from the ferns by these Berkshire boulders!
> *The Sunset Piece*

We were the first that found that famous country:
We marched by a king's name: we crossed the sierras:
Unknown hardships we suffered . . .
We were lords of it all.
> *Conquistador* [1932]. *Bernal Diaz' Preface*

She lies on her left side her flank golden:
Her hair is burned black with the strong sun:
The scent of her hair is of rain in the dust on her shoulders:
She has brown breasts and the mouth of no other country.
> *Frescoes for Mr. Rockefeller's City* [1933]. *Landscape as a Nude*

America was promises . . .
It was Man who had been promised.
> *America Was Promises* [1939]

EDWARD POWYS MATHERS
1892–

A love-sick heart dies when the heart is whole,
For all the heart's health is to be sick with love.
> *Fard. Translation from the Hindustani of* MIYAN JAGNU [*eighteenth century*]

EDNA ST. VINCENT MILLAY
1892–1950

All I could see from where I stood
Was three long mountains and a wood.
Renascence [1912] l. 1

The world stands out on either side
No wider than the heart is wide;
Above the world is stretched the sky, —
No higher than the soul is high.[1]
The heart can push the sea and land
Farther away on either hand;
The soul can split the sky in two,
And let the face of God shine through.
But East and West will pinch the heart
That cannot keep them pushed apart;
And he whose soul is flat — the sky
Will cave in on him by and by.
Ib. last lines

O world, I cannot hold thee close
enough!
God's World [1917], st. 1

Lord, I do fear
Thou'st made the world too beautiful
this year.
My soul is all but out of me — let fall
No burning leaf; prithee, let no bird
call.   Ib. st. 2

I will be the gladdest thing under the
sun!
I will touch a hundred flowers and not
pick one.
Afternoon on a Hill [1917], st. 1

Life goes on forever like the gnawing of
a mouse.
Ashes of Life [1917], st. 3

My candle burns at both ends;
It will not last the night;
But, ah, my foes, and, oh, my friends —
It gives a lovely light.[2]
A Few Figs from Thistles.
[1920]. First Fig

Safe upon the solid rock the ugly
houses stand:

[1] See Hartley Coleridge, p. 586b.
[2] I burned my candle at both ends,
And now have neither foes nor friends.
SAMUEL HOFFENSTEIN [1890–1947],
Songs of Fairly Utter Despair, 8

Come and see my shining palace built
upon the sand!
A Few Figs from Thistles.
Second Fig

I had a little Sorrow,
Born of a little Sin.
Ib. The Penitent, st. 1

Whether or not we find what we are
seeking
Is idle, biologically speaking.
Ib. I Shall Forget You
Presently, l. 13

Death devours all lovely things;
Lesbia with her sparrow
Shares the darkness — presently
Every bed is narrow.
Passer Mortuus Est [1921], st. 1

My heart is warm with the friends I
make,
And better friends I'll not be knowing;
Yet there isn't a train I wouldn't take,
No matter where it's going.
Travel [1921], st. 3

I know I am but summer to your heart,
And not the full four seasons of the
year.
I Know I Am But Summer
[1923], l. 1

I drank at every vine.
The last was like the first.
I came upon no wine
So wonderful as thirst.
Feast [1923], st. 1

I only know that summer sang in me
A little while, that in me sings no more.
What Lips My Lips Have Kissed
[1923], l. 13

Pity me that the heart is slow to learn
What the swift mind beholds at every
turn.
Pity Me Not [1923], l. 13

Euclid alone
Has looked on Beauty bare.[1] Fortunate
they
Who, though once only and then but
far away,

[1] See Russell, p. 913a.

Have heard her massive sandal set on stone.
Euclid Alone Has Looked on Beauty Bare [1923], *l. 11*

If ever I said, in grief or pride,
I tired of honest things, I lied.
The Goose Girl [1923], *l. 5*

Music my rampart, and my only one.
On Hearing a Symphony of Beethoven [1928], *l. 14*

I am not resigned to the shutting away of loving hearts in the hard ground.
So it is, and so it will be, for so it has been, time out of mind:
Into the darkness they go, the wise and the lovely. Crowned
With lilies and with laurel they go; but I am not resigned.
Dirge Without Music [1928], *st. 1*

Love is not all: it is not meat nor drink
Nor slumber nor a roof against the rain;
Nor yet a floating spar to men that sink.
Love Is Not All [1931], *l. 1*

REINHOLD NIEBUHR
1892–1971

O God, give us serenity to accept what cannot be changed, courage to change what should be changed, and wisdom to distinguish the one from the other.   *Prayer* [1934] [1]

[1] This prayer was composed . . . when Niebuhr preached occasionally in the small church near his summer home in Heath, Massachusetts. After the service, Howard Chandler Robbins, a summer neighbor, asked for a copy. He is reported to have been handed the original, with words to the following effect: "Here, take the prayer. I have no further use for it." Other people, it is clear, have felt differently. Robbins published it as part of a pamphlet the following year. Since then it has been adopted as the motto of Alcoholics Anoymous; the U.S.O. distributed millions of copies to servicemen during World War II; the National Council of Churches has reprinted it; and even today it is used commercially on Christmas cards. — JUNE BINGHAM, *Courage to Change: An Introduction to the Life and Thought of Reinhold Niebuhr* [*1961*]

Goodness, armed with power, is corrupted; and pure love without power is destroyed.   *Beyond Tragedy* [1938]

Man's capacity for justice makes democracy possible, but man's inclination to injustice makes democracy necessary.
The Children of Light and the Children of Darkness [1944]

Life has no meaning except in terms of responsibility.
Faith and History [1949]

Nothing worth doing is completed in our lifetime; therefore, we must be saved by hope. Nothing true or beautiful or good makes complete sense in any immediate context of history; therefore, we must be saved by faith. Nothing we do, however virtuous, can be accomplished alone; therefore, we are saved by love. No virtuous act is quite as virtuous from the standpoint of our friend or foe as from our standpoint. Therefore, we must be saved by the final form of love which is forgiveness.
The Irony of American History [1952]

BASIL O'CONNOR
1892–1972

The world cannot continue to wage war like physical giants and to seek peace like intellectual pygmies.
Address, National Conference of Christians and Jews [1945]

HAROLD WALLACE ROSS
1892–1951

The New Yorker will not be edited for the old lady from Dubuque.[1]
Upon founding The New Yorker [1925]

[1] Later this became "the little old lady from Dubuque."

JOHN RONALD REUEL TOLKIEN
1892–1973

In a hole in the ground there lived a hobbit. Not a nasty, dirty, wet hole, filled with the ends of worms and an oozy smell, nor yet a dry, bare, sandy hole with nothing in it to sit down on or to eat: it was a hobbit-hole, and that means comfort.

> *The Hobbit; or There and Back Again* [1937], *ch. 1*

WENDELL LEWIS WILLKIE
1892–1944

Freedom is an indivisible word.[1] If we want to enjoy it, and fight for it, we must be prepared to extend it to everyone, whether they are rich or poor, whether they agree with us or not, no matter what their race or the color of their skin.   *One World, ch. 13*

The Constitution does not provide for first and second class citizens.

> *An American Program* [1944], *ch. 2*

I believe in America because in it we are free —
free to choose our government, to speak our minds,
to observe our different religions.
Because we are generous with our freedom, we share
our rights with those who disagree with us.
Because we hate no people and covet no people's lands.
Because we are blessed with a natural and varied abundance.
Because we have great dreams and because we have the
opportunity to make those dreams come true.

> *His creed, inscribed on a marker by his grave in Rushville, Indiana*

[1] See Litvinov, p. 941a.

DEAN ACHESON
1893–1971

Whatever the outcome of the appeal, I do not intend to turn my back on Alger Hiss.

> *Statement* [*Time, February 6, 1950*]

MORRIS BISHOP
1893–

After the day is over
And the passers-by are rare
The lights burn low in the barber-shop
And the shades are drawn with care
To hide the haughty barbers
Cutting each other's hair.

> *The Tales the Barbers Tell*

OMAR BRADLEY
1893–

We have grasped the mystery of the atom and rejected the Sermon on the Mount.

> *Address* [*Armistice Day, 1948*]

But it [Pearl Harbor], and the subsequent lessons we learned, day by day, until September 1945, should have taught all military men that our military forces are one team — in the game to win regardless of who carries the ball. This is no time for "fancy dans" who won't hit the line with all they have on every play, unless they can call the signals. Each player on this team — whether he shines in the spotlight of the backfield or eats dirt in the line — must be an All-American.

> *Testimony, Committee on Armed Services, House of Representatives* [*October 19, 1949*]

In war there is no second prize for the runner-up.

> *In the Military Review* [*February 1950*]

Red China is not the powerful nation seeking to dominate the world. Frankly, in the opinion of the Joint Chiefs of Staff, this strategy would involve us in the wrong war, at the wrong place, at the wrong time, and with the wrong enemy.

> *Testimony, Committee on Armed Services and Committee on Foreign Affairs, U.S. Senate* [*May 15, 1951*]

Only one military organization can hold and gain ground in war — a ground army supported by tactical aviation with supply lines guarded by the navy.

> *In the Military Review* [*September 1951*]

JAMES BRYANT CONANT
1893–

He who enters a university walks on hallowed ground.

> *Notes on the Harvard Tercentenary* [1936]

Each honest calling, each walk of life, has its own elite, its own aristocracy based on excellence of performance.

> *Our Fighting Faith. "In This Country There Are No Classes"* [1]

Liberty like charity must begin at home.

> *Ib. Our Unique Heritage* [2]

The primary concern of American education today is not the development of the appreciation of the "good life" in young gentlemen born to the purple. . . . Our purpose is to cultivate in the largest possible number of our future citizens an appreciation of both the responsibilities and the benefits which come to them because they are Americans and are free.

> *Annual Report to the Board of Overseers, Harvard University* [3] [*January 11, 1943*]

[1] Baccalaureate sermon [June 16, 1940]. The title is taken from a statement in an address by JAMES A. GARFIELD [1831–1881], *The Future of the Republic: Its Dangers and its Hopes* [1873].

[2] Address, opening of the first wartime summer term, Harvard College [June 30, 1942].

[3] Describing his purpose, as president of Harvard University, in appointing a University Com-

There is only one proved method of assisting the advancement of pure science — that of picking men of genius, backing them heavily, and leaving them to direct themselves.

> *Letter to the New York Times* [*August 13, 1945*]

The stumbling way in which even the ablest of the scientists in every generation have had to fight through thickets of erroneous observations, misleading generalizations, inadequate formulations, and unconscious prejudice is rarely appreciated by those who obtain their scientific knowledge from textbooks.

> *Science and Common Sense* [1951]

JIMMY DURANTE
1893–

Goodnight, Mrs. Calabash, wherever you are.   *Saying*

Dese are de conditions dat prevail.   *Saying*

HANS FALLADA
[RUDOLF DITZEN]
1893–1947

Little Man, What Now?

> *Title of novel* [1932]

HERMANN GOERING
1893–1946

Shoot first and inquire afterwards, and if you make mistakes, I will protect you.

> *Instruction for the Prussian police* [1933]

Guns will make us powerful; butter will only make us fat.[1]

> *Broadcast* [1936]

When I hear anyone talk of culture, I reach for my revolver.   *Attributed*

mittee on the Objectives of a General Education in a Free Society. The committee's report was published [1945] under the title *General Education in a Free Society.*

[1] See Goebbels, p. 1040a.

HAROLD JOSEPH LASKI
1893–1950

We live under a system by which the many are exploited by the few, and war is the ultimate sanction of that exploitation.

Plan or Perish [1945]

We must plan our civilization or we must perish. *Ib.*

It would be madness to let the purposes or the methods of private enterprise set the habits of the age of atomic energy. *Ib.*

ANITA LOOS
1893–

Gentlemen always seem to remember blondes.

Gentlemen Prefer Blondes
[1925], *ch. 1*

She always believed in the old adage, "Leave them while you're looking good." *Ib.*

A girl never really looks as well as she does on board a steamship, or even a yacht. *Ib.*

Kissing your hand may make you feel very, very good, but a diamond and sapphire bracelet lasts forever. *Ib. 4*

JOHN PHILLIPS MARQUAND
1893–1960

It is worthwhile for anyone to have behind him a few generations of honest, hard-working ancestry.

The Late George Apley [1937],
ch. 3

His father watched him across the gulf of years and pathos which always must divide a father from his son.
Ib. 10

Marriage . . . is a damnably serious business, particularly around Boston.
Ib. 11

There is a certain phase in the life of the aged when the warmth of the heart seems to increase in direct proportion with the years. This is a time of life when a solicitous family does well to watch affectionately over the vagaries of its unattached relatives, particularly of those who are comfortably off.
The Late George Apley, ch. 23

MAO TSE-TUNG
1893–1976

The contradiction between imperialism and the Chinese nation, and the contradiction between feudalism and the great masses of the people, are the principal contradictions in modern Chinese society. . . . The great revolutions of modern and contemporary China have emerged and developed on the basis of these fundamental contradictions.

Selected Works,[1] *III, pp. 81–82*

Armament is an important factor in war, but not the decisive factor. . . . Man, not material, forms the decisive factor.[2] *Lecture* [1938]

War cannot be divorced from politics for a single moment.[3] *Ib.*

The people are like water and the army is like fish.
Aspects of China's Anti-Japanese Struggle [1948]

"Let a hundred flowers blossom" and "let a hundred schools of thought contend."

Speech, Peking [*February 27, 1957*]

The policy of letting a hundred flowers blossom and a hundred schools of thought contend is designed to promote the flourishing of the arts and the progress of science; it is designed to en-

[1] From *Sources of Chinese Tradition*, edited by William Theodore de Bary [1960].
[2] There is still one absolute weapon. . . . That weapon is man himself. — MATTHEW B. RIDGWAY, *Address, Cleveland, Ohio* [November 10, 1953]
[3] See von Clausewitz, p. 544b.

able a socialist culture to thrive in our land. Different forms and styles in art can develop freely, and different schools in science can develop freely, and different schools in science can contend freely. We think that it is harmful to the growth of art and science if administrative measures are used to impose one particular style of art or school of thought and to ban another.

Speech, Peking

When the majority of the people have clear-cut criteria to go by, criticism and self-criticism can be conducted along proper lines, and these criteria can be applied to people's words and actions to determine whether they are fragrant flowers or poisonous weeds.

Ib.

VLADIMIR MAYAKOVSKY
1893–1930

If you wish,
I shall be irreproachably tender:
Not a man, but a cloud in pants!

Cloud in Pants [1914–1915]

Citizen!
Consider my traveling expenses:
Poetry —
    all of it —
        is a trip into the unknown.

Conversation with a Tax Collector about Poetry [1926]

Then there is amortization,
                the worst of all:
amortization of heart and soul. *Ib.*

ALBERT SZENT-GYÖRGYI
VON NAGYRAPOLT
1893–

The real scientist . . . is ready to bear privation and, if need be, starvation rather than let anyone dictate to him which direction his work must take.

Science Needs Freedom [World Digest, 1943]

WILFRED OWEN
1893–1918

Above all, this book is not concerned with Poetry,
The subject of it is War, and the pity of War.
The Poetry is in the pity.
All a poet can do is warn.[1]

Preface to the Poems [published 1920]

What passing bells for these who die as cattle?
Only the monstrous anger of the guns.
Only the stuttering rifles' rapid rattle
Can patter out their hasty orisons.

The Anthem for Doomed Youth, st. 1

And bugles calling for them from sad shires. *Ib.*

What candles may be held to speed them all?
Not in the hands of boys, but in their eyes
Shall shine the holy glimmers of goodbyes. *Ib.*

And each slow dusk a drawing-down of blinds. *Ib.*

If anything might rouse him now
The kind old sun will know.

Futility, st. 1

— Oh what made fatuous sunbeams toil
To break earth's sleep at all? *Ib. st. 2*

Red lips are not so red
As the stained stones kissed by the English dead.
Kindness of wooed and wooer
Seems shame to their love pure.

Greater Love

Courage was mine, and I had mystery,
Wisdom was mine, and I had mastery;
To miss the march of this retreating world
Into vain citadels that are not walled.

Strange Meeting

[1] The last three lines serve as the motto for Benjamin Britten's *War Requiem (Op. 66)*, which uses the Latin text of the Mass for the Dead and some of the poems of Wilfred Owen.

DOROTHY PARKER
1893–1967

Where's the man could ease a heart
Like a satin gown?
The Satin Dress, st. 1

Four be the things I am wiser to know:
Idleness, sorrow, a friend, and a foe.
Inventory, st. 1

Four be the things I'd been better
   without: -
Love, curiosity, freckles, and doubt.
Ib. st. 2

Scratch a lover, and find a foe.
*Ballade of a Great Weariness,
st. 1*

Men seldom make passes
At girls who wear glasses.
News Item

Guns aren't lawful;
Nooses give;
Gas smells awful;
You might as well live.   *Résumé*

Why is it no one ever sent me yet
One perfect limousine, do you suppose?
Ah no, it's always just my luck to get
One perfect rose.
One Perfect Rose, st. 3

He lies below, correct in cypress wood,
And entertains the most exclusive
worms.
Epitaph for a Very Rich Man

There was nothing more fun than a
man!
*The Little Old Lady in
Lavender Silk, st. 3*

Excuse my dust.
Epitaph, suggested by herself

Wit has truth in it; wisecracking is
simply calisthenics with words.
In Paris Review [Summer 1956]

SIR HERBERT READ
1893–1968

Poetry can never again become a
popular art until the poet gives himself

wholly to "the cadence of consenting
feet." [1]
Phases of English Poetry [1928]

The no-man's-years between the wars
[1919–1939].
*Annals of Innocence and
Experience [1940]*

JOACHIM
VON RIBBENTROP
1893–1945

The Führer is always right.
*Address, Königsberg [August 24,
1939]*

ROBERT LEROY RIPLEY
1893–1949

Believe It or Not.
*Title of syndicated newspaper
feature*

HAROLD CLAYTON UREY
1893–

We need first of all to be thoroughly
frightened.
*Speech on the atomic bomb
[December 3, 1945]*

The most dangerous situation that
humanity has ever faced in all history.
One World or None [1946], ch. 2

MAE WEST
1893–

Come up and see me sometime.
Diamond Lil [2] [1932]

Beulah, peel me a grape.
I'm No Angel [1933]

FRED ALLEN
1894–1956

Hollywood is a great place if you're
an orange.   *Saying*

---

[1] The quotation is from FRANCIS BARTON
GUMMERE, *The Beginnings of Poetry* [1901].
[2] The play was later made into a movie, *She
Done Him Wrong.*

To a newspaperman a human being is an item with the skin wrapped around it.   *Saying*

DON BLANDING
1894–1957

It's more than just an easy word for casual goodbye;
It's gayer than a greeting, and it's sadder than a sigh.
                    Aloha Oe: Its Meaning

It's said a hundred different ways, in sadness and in joy,
Aloha means "I love you." So I say "Aloha Oe."   *Ib.*

EDWARD ESTLIN CUMMINGS[1]
1894–1962

All in green went my love riding
on a great horse of gold
into the silver dawn.
                    All in green went my love riding
                    [1923]

four lean hounds crouched low and smiling
my heart fell dead before.   *Ib.*

in Just-
spring when the world is mud-
luscious the little
lame balloonman
whistles far and wee
                    Chansons Innocentes [1923], 1

when the world is puddle-wonderful
                    Ib.

Buffalo Bill's
defunct
          who used to
          ride a watersmooth-silver
                              stallion
and break onetwothreefourfive pigeons-
justlikethat
                    Jesus
he was a handsome man
          and what i want to know is

[1] The terror of typesetters, an enigma to book reviewers, and the special target of all the world's literary philistines. — *Publisher's note, Modern Library edition of The Enormous Room*

how do you like your blueeyed boy
Mister Death   *Portraits* [1923], 8

the Cambridge ladies who live in furnished souls
are unbeautiful and have comfortable minds.
                    Sonnets — Realities [1923], I

Humanity i love you because
when you're hard up you pawn your
intelligence to buy a drink.
                    Humanity i love you [1925]

i spill my bright incalculable soul.
                    Sonnets [1925], II

take it from me kiddo
believe me
my country, 'tis of

you, land of the Cluett
Shirt Boston Garter and Spearmint
Girl With The Wrigley Eyes (of you
land of the Arrow Ide
and Earl &
Wilson
Collars) of you i
sing: land of Abraham Lincoln and
          Lydia E. Pinkham,
land above all of Just Add Hot Water
          And Serve —
from every B.V.D.

let freedom ring

amen.
                    Poem, Or Beauty Hurts
                    Mr. Vinal [1926]

          Turn Your Shirttails Into
Drawers and If It Isn't An Eastman It
          Isn't A
Kodak   *Ib.*

          And there're a
hun-dred-mil-lion-oth-ers, like
all of you successfully if
delicately gelded (or spaded)
gentlemen (and ladies)   *Ib.*

a tiny violetflavored nuisance   *Ib.*

next to of course god america i

love you land of the pilgrims' and so
  forth
>*next to of course god america i*
>*[1926]*

thy sons acclaim your glorious name by
  gorry
by jingo by gee by gosh by gum   *Ib.*

for life's not a paragraph
And death i think is no parenthesis.
>*since feeling is first [1926]*

lady through whose profound and fragile lips
the sweet small clumsy feet of April
  came
into the ragged meadow of my soul.
>*if i have made, my lady,*
>*intricate [1926]*

i sing of Olaf glad and big
whose warmest heart recoiled at war
>*i sing of Olaf glad and big [1931]*

"I will not kiss your f.ing flag"   *Ib.*

"there is some s. I will not eat"   *Ib.*

unless statistics lie he was
more brave than me:more blond than
  you.   *Ib.*

somewhere i have never travelled, gladly
  beyond
any experience, your eyes have their
  silence.
>*somewhere I have never*
>*travelled [1931]*

nobody, not even the rain, has such
  small hands   *Ib.*

King Christ, this world is all aleak;
and lifepreservers there are none:
and waves which only He may walk
Who dares to call Himself a man.
>*Jehovah buried, Satan dead [1935]*

Always the beautiful answer who asks
a more beautiful question.
>*Collected Poems [1938],*
>*introduction*

as freedom is a breakfastfood
or truth can live with right and wrong
or molehills are from mountains made

— long enough and just so long
will being pay the rent of seem
and genius please the talentgang
and water most encourage flame
>*as freedom is a breakfastfood*
>*[1940]*

worms are the words but joy's the voice
>*Ib.*

anyone lived in a pretty how town
(with up so floating many bells down)
spring summer autumn winter
he sang his didn't he danced his did.
>*anyone lived in a pretty how*
>*town [1940]*

my father moved through dooms of
  love
through sames of am through haves of
  give,
singing each morning out of each night
my father moved through depths of
  height
>*my father moved through dooms*
>*of love [1940]*

though dull were all we taste as bright,
bitter all utterly things sweet,
maggoty minus and dumb death
all we inherit, all bequeath   *Ib.*

and nothing quite so least as truth
— i say though hate were why men
  breathe —
because my father lived his soul
love is the whole and more than all
>*Ib.*

a politician is an arse upon
which everyone has sat except a man
>*One Times One [1944], 10*

mr u will not be missed
who as an anthologist
sold the many on the few
not excluding mr u   *Ib.* 11

pity this busy monster, manunkind,
not. Progress is a comfortable disease.
>*Ib.* 14

A world of made
is not a world of born   *Ib.*

We doctors know
a hopeless case if — listen: there's a
    hell
of a good universe next door; let's go
                    One Times One, 14

what if a much of a which of a wind
gives the truth to summer's lie.
                            Ib. 20

— when skies are hanged and oceans
    drowned,
the single secret will still be man   *Ib.*

all ignorance toboggans into know
and trudges up to ignorance again
                            Ib. 39

ALDOUS LEONARD HUXLEY
1894–1963

There are not enough *bon mots* in
existence to provide any industrious
conversationalist with a new stock for
every social occasion.
        Point Counter Point [1928], *ch.* 7

A bad book is as much of a labor to
write as a good one; it comes as sincerely from the author's soul.   *Ib. 13*

There is no substitute for talent. Industry and all the virtues are of no
avail.   *Ib.*

Parodies and caricatures are the most
penetrating of criticisms.   *Ib. 28*

Blood of the world, time staunchless
    flows;
The wound is mortal and is mine.
                            Seasons

Over her the swan shook slowly free
The folded glory of his wings, and
    made
A white-walled tent of soft and
    luminous shade.   *Leda*

A poor degenerate from the ape,
Whose hands are four, whose tail's a
    limb,
I contemplate my flaccid shape

And know I may not rival him
Save with my mind.
            First Philosopher's Song

NIKITA SERGEYEVICH KHRUSHCHEV
1894–1971

Cult of personality.
        *Special Report to Twentieth
        Party Congress* [*February
        1956*]

About the capitalist states, it doesn't
depend on you whether or not we exist.
If you don't like us, don't accept our
invitations, and don't invite us to come
and see you. Whether you like it or
not, history is on our side. We will bury
you.[1]
        *Reported statement at reception
        for Wladyslaw Gomulka at the
        Polish Embassy, Moscow* [*No-
        vember 18, 1956*]

Life is short; live it up.
        *Quoted by the New York Times
        Magazine* [*August 3, 1958*]

WESTBROOK PEGLER
1894–1969

The Era of Wonderful Nonsense.[2]
            Mr. Gump Himself

I am a reactionary, that is what I am,
and I would like to see a political reaction get off to a good start in our largest
city.
        *In the New York World-
        Telegram* [*October 31, 1941*]

I am a member of the rabble in good
standing.   *The Lynching Story*

[1] Neither the original nor the translation of
the last two sentences appeared in either *Pravda*
or the *New York Times* which carried the rest
of the text. Another possible translation of the
last sentence is "We shall be present at your
funeral," i.e., we shall outlive you; but the
above is the familiar version.
[2] The period of spending and speculation during the "Coolidge prosperity."

KENNETH CLAIBORNE ROYALL
1894–1971

A "brass hat" is an officer of at least one rank higher than you whom you don't like and who doesn't like you.[1]
> *Speech, Chamber of Commerce, Wilson, North Carolina [February 15, 1946]*

GENEVIEVE TAGGARD
1894–1948

Try tropic for your balm,
Try storm,
And after storm, calm.
Try snow of heaven, heavy, soft, and
    slow,
Brilliant and warm.
Nothing will help, and nothing do
    much harm.
> *Of the Properties of Nature for Healing an Illness, st. 1*

JAMES THURBER
1894–1961

Well, if I called the wrong number, why did you answer the 'phone?
> *Caption for cartoon (The New Yorker)*

I love the idea of there being two sexes, don't you?   *Ib.*

He knows all about art, but he doesn't know what he likes.   *Ib.*

It's a naive domestic Burgundy without any breeding, but I think you'll be amused by its presumption.   *Ib.*

The War Between Men and Women.
> *Series of cartoons*

Is Sex Necessary?
> *Title of book [1929] written with E. B. WHITE*

Let Your Mind Alone.
> *Title of book [1937]*

[1] Some big brass hat from the War Office. — JAMES HILTON, *Goodbye, Mr. Chips* [1934], *ch. 14*

Early to rise and early to bed makes a male healthy and wealthy and dead.
> *Fables for Our Time [1940]. The Shrike and the Chipmunks*

You might as well fall flat on your face as lean over too far backward.
> *Ib. The Bear Who Let It Alone*

Don't count your boobies until they're hatched.
> *Ib. The Unicorn in the Garden*

It is better to know some of the questions than all of the answers.
> *Saying*

MARK VAN DOREN
1894–1972

Wit is the only wall
Between us and the dark.   *Wit, st. 1*

He talked, and as he talked
    Wallpaper came alive;
Suddenly ghosts walked
    And four doors were five.
> *The Storyteller, st. 1*

Grass nibbling inward
Like green fire.
> *Former Barn Lot, st. 3*

NORBERT WIENER
1894–1964

We have decided to call the entire field of control and communication theory, whether in the machine or in the animal, by the name of Cybernetics, which we form from the Greek [for] steersman.   *Cybernetics [1948]*

This new development [automation] has unbounded possibilities for good and for evil.   *Ib.*

The independent scientist who is worth the slightest consideration as a scientist has a consecration which comes entirely from within himself: a vocation which demands the possibility of supreme self-sacrifice.
> *The Human Use of Human Beings [1950]*

DUKE OF WINDSOR
[KING EDWARD VIII]
1894–1972

I have found it impossible to carry the heavy burden of responsibility and to discharge my duties as King as I would wish to do without the help and support of the woman I love.

> *Farewell broadcast after abdication [December 11, 1936]*

RICHARD BUCKMINSTER
FULLER
1895–

We must think of our whole economics in terms of a preventive pathology instead of a curative pathology.

Don't oppose forces; use them.

God is a verb,
Not a noun.

> *No More Secondhand God*

Nature has . . . some sort of arithmetical-geometrical coordinate system, because nature has all kinds of models. What we experience of nature is in models, and all of nature's models are so beautiful. It struck me that nature's system must be a real beauty, because in chemistry we find that the associations are always in beautiful whole numbers — there are no fractions.

> *From In the Outlaw Area; profile by* CALVIN TOMKINS, *The New Yorker [January 8, 1966]*

All nature's structuring, associating, and patterning must be based on triangles, because there is no structural validity otherwise. This is nature's basic structure, and it is modelable. *Ib.*

Either war is obsolete or men are.
Ib.

ROBERT GRAVES
1895–

As you are woman, so be lovely:
As you are lovely, so be various,

Merciful as constant, constant as various,
ous,
So be mine, as I yours for ever.
> *Pygmalion to Galatea*

Hate is a fear, and fear is rot
That cankers root and fruit alike:
Fight cleanly then, hate not, fear not,
Strike with no madness when you
strike. *Hate Not, Fear Not*

"How is your trade, Aquarius,
This frosty night?"
"Complaints is many and various,
And my feet are cold," says Aquarius.
> *Star Talk, st. 5*

I do not love the Sabbath,
The soapsuds and the starch,
The troops of solemn people
Who to Salvation march.
> *The Boy Out of Church*

"Blonde or dark, sir?" says enough
Whether of women, drink, or snuff.
> *Blonde or Dark?*

Goodbye to All That.
> *Title of autobiography [1929]*

A well-chosen anthology is a complete dispensary of medicine for the more common mental disorders, and may be used as much for prevention as cure. *On English Poetry, 29*

The reason why the hairs stand on end, the eyes water, the throat is constricted, the skin crawls and a shiver runs down the spine when one writes or reads a true poem is that a true poem is necessarily an invocation of the White Goddess, or Muse, the Mother of All Living, the ancient power of fright and lust — the female spider or the queen bee whose embrace is death.[1]
> *The White Goddess [1948], ch. 1*

ROBERT HILLYER
1895–1961

Ah, could we know what vogue will be
tomorrow,
What plumes of Paradise our pens
could borrow!
> *A Letter to Robert Frost [1937]*

[1] See Sophocles, p. 83a.

Blest be thy name, O Vogue, that canst embalm
A minor poet with a potted palm;
Make me immortal in thy exegesis —
Or failing that, at least a Doctor's thesis.

A Letter to Robert Frost

BASIL HENRY LIDDELL HART
1895–1972

Keep strong, if possible. In any case, keep cool. Have unlimited patience. Never corner an opponent, and always assist him to save his face. Put yourself in his shoes — so as to see things through his eyes. Avoid self-righteousness like the devil — nothing so self-blinding.

Deterrent or Defense [1960].
Advice to Statesmen

GROUCHO MARX
1895–1977

I never forget a face, but in your case I'll make an exception. *Saying*

LEWIS MUMFORD
1895–

People have hesitated to call Whitman's poems poetry; it is useless to deny that they belong to sacred literature. *The Golden Day* [1926], 5

Layer upon layer, past times preserve themselves in the city until life itself is finally threatened with suffocation; then, in sheer defense, modern man invents the museum.
The Culture of Cities [1938]

EDWARD E. PARAMORE, JR.
1895–

Oh, the North Countree is a hard countree
That mothers a bloody brood;
And its icy arms hold hidden charms

For the greedy, the sinful and lewd.
And strong men rust, from the gold and the lust
That sears the Northland soul.
The Ballad of Yukon Jake [1921]

Oh, tough as a steak was Yukon Jake —
Hard-boiled as a picnic egg. *Ib.*

EDMUND WILSON
1895–1972

As for the aims and ideals of Marxism, there is one feature of them that is now rightly suspect. The taking-over by the state of the means of production and the dictatorship in the interests of the proletariat can by themselves never guarantee the happiness of anybody but the dictators themselves. Marx and Engles, coming out of authoritarian Germany, tended to imagine socialism in authoritarian terms; and Lenin and Trotsky after them, forced as they were to make a beginning among a people who had known nothing but autocracy, also emphasized this side of socialism and founded a dictatorship which perpetuated itself as an autocracy.
To the Finland Station [1940].
Summary as of 1940

I have derived a good deal more benefit of the civilizing as well as of the inspirational kind [of tradition] from the admirable American bathroom than I have from the cathedrals of Europe. . . . I have had a good many more uplifting thoughts, creative and expansive visions — while soaking in comfortable baths or drying myself after bracing showers — in well-equipped American bathrooms than I have ever had in any cathedral.
A Piece of My Mind [1956], *ch. 4*

I attribute such success as I have had to the use of the periodic sentence.
An Interview with Edmund Wilson [1962]

JOHN RODERIGO
DOS PASSOS
1896–1970

The chilly December day [1]
two shivering bicycle mechanics from
　Dayton, Ohio,[2]
first felt their homemade contraption
whittled out of hickory sticks,
gummed together with Arnstein's bicy-
　cle cement,
stretched with muslin they'd sewn on
　their sister's sewingmachine in
　their own backyard on Hawthorn
　Street in Dayton, Ohio,
soar into the air
above the dunes and the wide beach
at Kitty Hawk.
> *The Big Money* [1936]. *The
> Campers at Kitty Hawk*

EDMUND BLUNDEN
1896–

I am for the woods against the world,
But are the woods for me?
> *The Kiss*

Then is not Death at watch
　Within those secret waters?
What wants he but to catch
　Earth's heedless sons and daughters?
With but a crystal parapet
Between, he has his engines set.
> *The Midnight Skaters*

Dance on this ball-floor thin and wan,
　Use him as though you love him;[3]
Court him, elude him, reel and pass,
And let him hate you through the glass.
> *Ib.*

FRANCIS SCOTT
FITZGERALD
1896–1940

The victor belongs to the spoils.
> *The Beautiful and Damned* [1922]

Then wear the gold hat, if that will
　move her;

If you can bounce high, bounce for her
　too,
Till she cry "Lover, gold-hatted, high-
　bouncing lover,
I must have you!"
> *The Great Gatsby* [1925], *epigraph*

Everyone suspects himself of at least
one of the cardinal virtues, and this is
mine: I am one of the few honest people that I have ever known.
> *Ib. ch. 3*

Her voice is full of money.　　*Ib. 7*

Thirty — the promise of a decade of
loneliness, a thinning list of single men
to know, a thinning briefcase of enthusiasm, thinning hair.　　　　　　*Ib.*

They were careless people, Tom and
Daisy — they smashed up things and
creatures and then retreated back into
their money or their vast carelessness, or
whatever it was that kept them together, and let other people clean up
the mess they had made.　　*Ib. 9*

So we beat on, boats against the current, borne back ceaselessly into the
past.　　　　　　　*Ib. last line*

One writes of scars healed, a loose
parallel to the pathology of the skin,
but there is no such thing in the life of
an individual. There are open wounds,
shrunk sometimes to the size of a pin-
prick, but wounds still. The marks of
suffering are more comparable to the
loss of a finger, or of the sight of an
eye. We may not miss them, either, for
one minute in a year, but if we should
there is nothing to be done about it.
> *Tender Is the Night* [1933],
> *bk. III, ch. 13*

The test of a first-rate intelligence is
the ability to hold two opposed ideas in
the mind at the same time, and still
retain the ability to function.
> *The Crack-up* [1936]

In a real dark night of the soul is it
always three o'clock in the morning.[1]
> *Ib.*

---

[1] December 17, 1903.
[2] See Wilbur and Orville Wright, p. 910a.
[3] See Izaak Walton, p. 326b.

[1] See Napoleon, p. 504b, and note.

It was about then [1920] that I wrote a line which certain people will not let me forget: "She was a faded but still lovely woman of twenty-seven."
Early Success [1937]

Egyptian Proverb: The worst things:
To be in bed and sleep not,
To want for one who comes not.
To try to please and please not.
Notebooks [1]

Show me a hero and I will write you a tragedy. *Ib.*

Draw your chair up close to the edge of the precipice and I'll tell you a story.
Ib.

It is in the thirties that we want friends. In the forties we know they won't save us any more than love did.
Ib.

The hangover became a part of the day as well allowed-for as the Spanish siesta. *My Lost City* [1]

All good writing is swimming under water and holding your breath.
Undated letter

HAROLD N. GILBERT
1896–1966

Keep 'em flying.
Slogan of the Air Forces, poster caption, World War II

GRAHAM LEE HEMMINGER
1896–1949

Tobacco is a dirty weed. I like it.
It satisfies no normal need. I like it.
It makes you thin, it makes you lean,
It takes the hair right off your bean.[2]

[1] In *The Crack-up*, edited by Edmund Wilson [1945].
[2] Caution: Cigarette smoking may be hazardous to your health. — *Warning on cigarette packages, required by federal legislation* [July 27, 1965]

It's the worst darn stuff I've ever seen. I like it. *Tobacco* [1] [1915]

JOE JACOBS
1896–1940

We was robbed!
After the heavyweight title fight between Max Schmeling and Jack Sharkey [June 21, 1932], Jacobs, Schmeling's manager, shouted into the microphone this protest against the decision.

I should of stood in bed.
After leaving a sickbed to attend the World's Series in Detroit [October 1935] and betting on the loser

ROBERT EMMET SHERWOOD
1896–1955

The trouble with me is, I belong to a vanishing race. I'm one of the intellectuals. *The Petrified Forest* [1934]

Poor, dear God. Playing Idiot's Delight. The game that never means anything, and never ends.
Idiot's Delight [1936]

LUTHER W. YOUNGDAHL
1896–

When public excitement runs high as to alien ideologies, is the time when we must be particularly alert not to impair the ancient landmarks set up in the Bill of Rights.
United States v. Lattimore, 112 F. Supp. 507, 518 [May 2, 1953]

JOSEPH AUSLANDER
1897–1965

So there are no more words and all is ended;

[1] See Anonymous, p. 1085b.

The timbrel is stilled, the clarion laid
away;
And Love with streaming hair goes un-
attended
Back to the loneliness of yesterday.
So There Are No More Words
[1924]

LOUISE BOGAN
1897–1970

I burned my life that I might find
A passion wholly of the mind,
Thought divorced from eye and bone,
Ecstasy come to breath alone.
The Alchemist

I had found unmysterious flesh —
Not the mind's avid substance — still
Passionate beyond the will. *Ib.*

Women have no wilderness in them,
They are provident instead,
Content in the tight hot cell of their
hearts
To eat dusty bread. *Women*

BERNARD DE VOTO
1897–1955

New England is a finished place. Its
destiny is that of Florence or Venice,
not Milan, while the American empire
careens onward toward its unpredicted
end. . . . It is the first American section to be finished, to achieve stability
in the conditions of its life. It is the
first old civilization, the first permanent
civilization in America.
*New England: There She Stands.
In Harper's Magazine [March
1932]*

The West begins where the average
annual rainfall drops below twenty
inches. When you reach the line which
marks that drop — for convenience, the
one hundredth meridian — you have
reached the West.
*The Plundered Province. In
Harper's Magazine [August
1934]*

Pessimism is only the name that men
of weak nerves give to wisdom.
*Mark Twain: The Ink of His-
tory. Address, University of Missouri [December 1935]*

Art is the terms of an armistice
signed with fate.
Mark Twain at Work [1942]

The achieved West had given the
United States something that no people
had ever had before, an internal, domestic empire.
The Year of Decision [1943]

Between the amateur and the professional . . . there is a difference not
only in degree but in kind. The skillful
man is, within the function of his skill,
a different integration, a different nervous and muscular and psychological
organization. . . . A tennis player or a
watchmaker or an airplane pilot is an
automatism but he is also criticism and
wisdom.
Across the Wide Missouri [1947]

You can no more keep a martini in
the refrigerator than you can keep a kiss
there. The proper union of gin and vermouth is a great and sudden glory; it is
one of the happiest marriages on earth
and one of the shortest-lived.
The Hour [1951]

The water of life was given to us to
make us see for a while that we are
more nearly men and women, more
nearly kind and gentle and generous,
pleasanter and stronger, than without
its vision there is any evidence we are.
Ib.

One of the facts which define the
United States is that its national and its
imperial boundaries are the same. Another is that it is a political unit which
occupies a remarkably coherent geographical unit of continental extent.
*The Course of Empire
[1952], preface*

History abhors determinism but cannot tolerate chance. *Ib.*

The dawn of knowledge is usually the false dawn.
The Course of Empire, ch. 2

SIR ANTHONY EDEN
1897–

Every succeeding scientific discovery makes greater nonsense of old-time conceptions of sovereignty.
Speech, House of Commons
[November 22, 1945]

WILLIAM FAULKNER
1897–1962

Time is dead as long as it is being clicked off by little wheels; only when the clock stops does time come to life.
The Sound and the Fury
[1929], June Second 1910

I've seed de first en de last. . . . I seed de beginnin, en now I sees de endin. *Ib. April Eighth 1928*

Because no battle is ever won he said. They are not even fought. The field only reveals to man his own folly and despair, and victory is an illusion of philosophers and fools. *Ib.*

They [the Negroes] will endure. They are better than we are. Stronger than we are. Their vices are vices aped from white men or that white men and bondage have taught them: improvidence and intemperance and evasion — not laziness: evasion: of what white men had set them to, not for their aggrandizement or even comfort but his own. . . . And their virtues. . . . Endurance . . . and pity and tolerance and forbearance and fidelity and love of children . . . whether their own or not or black or not.
The Bear [1932], pt. IV

Poor man. Poor mankind.
Light in August [1932], ch. 4

Too much happens. . . . Man performs, engenders, so much more than he can or should have to bear. That's

how he finds that he can bear anything. . . . That's what's so terrible.
Light in August, ch. 13

My, my. A body does get around. Here we aint been coming from Alabama but two months, and now it's already Tennessee. *Ib. 21*

It's not when you realize that nothing can help you — religion, pride, anything — it's when you realize that you don't need any aid. *Ib.*

Gettysburg.[1] . . . You cant understand it. You would have to be born there.
Absalom, Absalom! [1936], ch. 9

Why do you hate the South?
I dont hate it. . . . I dont hate it. . . . *I dont hate it* he thought, panting in the cold air, the iron New England dark; *I dont. I dont! I dont hate it! I dont hate it!* *Ib.*

He [the writer] must teach himself that the basest of all things is to be afraid; and, teaching himself that, forget it forever, leaving no room in his workshop for anything but the old verities and truths of the heart, the old universal truths lacking which any story is ephemeral and doomed — love and honor and pity and pride and compassion and sacrifice.
Speech upon receiving the Nobel
Prize [December 10, 1950]

I decline to accept the end of man.
Ib.

I believe that man will not merely endure: he will prevail. *Ib.*

It is the writer's privilege to help man endure by lifting his heart. *Ib.*

JEFFERSON, YOKNAPATAWPHA CO., Mississippi. Area, 2400 Square Miles. Population, Whites, 6298; Negroes, 9313. WILLIAM FAULKNER, Sole Owner & Proprietor.
Caption for map drawn by
author [1951]

[1] Representing, in context, the South.

The writer's only responsibility is to his art. He will be completely ruthless if he is a good one. He has a dream. It anguishes him so much he must get rid of it. He has no peace until then. Everything goes by the board: honor, pride, decency, security, happiness, all, to get the book written. If a writer has to rob his mother, he will not hesitate; the "Ode on a Grecian Urn" is worth any number of old ladies.

> *From an interview with* FAULK-NER [*New York City, 1956*] *by* JEAN STEIN. *From Writers at Work: The Paris Review Interviews* [*1959*]

Really the writer doesn't want success. . . . He knows he has a short span of life, that the day will come when he must pass through the wall of oblivion, and he wants to leave a scratch on that wall — Kilroy was here [1] — that somebody a hundred, or a thousand years later will see.

> *Faulkner in the University* [*1959*], *Session 8*

PAUL JOSEPH GOEBBELS
1897–1945

We can do without butter, but, despite all our love of peace, not without arms. One cannot shoot with butter but with guns.[2]

> *Address, Berlin* [*January 17, 1936*]

DAVID McCORD
1897–

A handful of sand is an anthology of the universe.

> *Once and for All* [*1929*], *introduction*

Call home the child, whose credulous first hours
Burn at the heart of living, and surprise
The better reason with unbidden truth.

> *A Bucket of Bees* [*1934*]

March is outside the door
Flaming some old desire
As man turns uneasily from his fire.

> *The Crows* [*1934*]

By and by
God caught his eye.

> *Epitaphs: The Waiter*

Still for us where Cottons mather
In the spring the Willas cather
As of yore.

> *And What's More: On Stopping at a New Hampshire Inn* [*1941*]

The decent docent doesn't doze;
He teaches standing on his toes.
His student dassn't doze and does,
And that's what teaching is and was.

> *What Cheer* [*1945*]

But man must light for man
The fires no other can,
And find in his own eye
Where the strange crossroads lie.

> *Communion* [*1950*]

Life is the garment we continually alter, but which never seems to fit.

> *Whereas to Mr. Franklin* [*1956*]

Your life will be rich for others only as it is rich for you.

> *On the Frontiers of Understanding* [*1959*]

ERICH MARIA REMARQUE
1897–1970

Monotonously the lorries sway, monotously come the calls, monotonously falls the rain. It falls on our heads and on the heads of the dead up the line, on the body of the little recruit with the wound that is so much too big for his hip; it falls on Kemmerich's grave; it falls in our hearts.

> *All Quiet on the Western Front* [1] [*1929*]

---

[1] See Anonymous, p. 1103b.

[2] Probably the origin of the slogan "Guns or butter." See Goering, p. 1026b.

[1] Im Westen Nichts Neues.

THORNTON NIVEN WILDER
1897–

Even memory is not necessary for love. There is a land of the living and a land of the dead and the bridge is love, the only survival, the only meaning.

The Bridge of San Luis Rey [1927], last lines

A man looks pretty small at a wedding, George. All those good women standing shoulder to shoulder, making sure that the knot's tied in a mighty public way. *Our Town [1938]*

The dead don't stay interested in us living people for very long. Gradually, gradually, they let go hold of the earth . . . and the ambitions they had . . . and the pleasures they had . . . and the things they suffered . . . and the people they loved. They get weaned away from earth — that's the way I put it, weaned away. *Ib.*

That's what it was to be alive. To move about in a cloud of ignorance; to go up and down trampling on the feelings of those about you. To spend and waste time as though you had a million years. To be always at the mercy of one self-centered passion, or another. Now you know — that's the happy existence you wanted to go back to. *Ib.*

I hold that we cannot be said to be aware of our minds save under responsibility. *The Ides of March [1948]*

STEPHEN VINCENT BENÉT
1898–1943

I died in my boots like a pioneer
With the whole wide sky above me.
The Ballad of William Sycamore

He could fiddle all the bugs off a sweet potato vine.
The Mountain Whippoorwill [1923], st. 22

Oh, Georgia booze is mighty fine booze,

The best yuh ever poured yuh,
But it eats the soles right offen yore shoes,
For Hell's broke loose in Georgia.
The Mountain Whippoorwill, st. 48

I have fallen in love with American names,
The sharp names that never get fat,
The snakeskin titles of mining claims,
The plumed war bonnet of Medicine Hat,
Tucson and Deadwood and Lost Mule Flat.
American Names [1927], st. 1

Bury my heart at Wounded Knee.
Ib. st. 7

American Muse, whose strong and diverse heart
So many men have tried to understand
But only made it smaller with their art,
Because you are as various as your land.
John Brown's Body [1928], invocation

And Thames and all the rivers of the kings
Ran into Mississippi and were drowned.
Ib.

Broad-streeted Richmond . . .
The trees in the streets are old trees used to living with people,
Family trees that remember your grandfather's name.
Ib. bk. IV

Stonewall Jackson, wrapped in his beard and his silence. *Ib.*

A great victor, in defeat as great,
No more, no less, always himself in both. *Ib.*

The ant finds kingdoms in a foot of ground. *Ib.*

But all of them are sure they know God's will.
I am the only man who does not know it. *Ib. V*

Sherman's buzzin' along to de sea,
Like Moses ridin' on a bumblebee.
Ib. VIII

We thought we were done with these things but we were wrong.
We thought, because we had power, we had wisdom.
Litany for Dictatorships [1936]

Our fathers and ourselves sowed dragon's teeth.
Our children know and suffer the armed men. **Ib.**

If two New Hampshiremen aren't a match for the devil, we might as well give the country back to the Indians.
The Devil and Daniel Webster [1936]

Even the damned may salute the eloquence of Mr. Webster. **Ib.**

They were half of the first families in Virginia.
Well, where do you start, when you start counting F.F.V.s?
Western Star [1943], bk. I

HORACE GREGORY
1898–

My boyhood saw
Greek islands floating over Harvard Square.[1]
Chorus for Survival [1935], 14

CLIVE STAPLES LEWIS
1898–1963

The safest road to Hell is the gradual one — the gentle slope, soft underfoot, without sudden turnings, without milestones, without signposts.
The Screwtape Letters [1941], 12

The Future is something which everyone reaches at the rate of sixty minutes an hour, whatever he does, whoever he is. **Ib. 25**

The long, dull, monotonous years of middle-aged prosperity or middle-aged adversity are excellent campaigning weather [for the Devil]. **Ib. 28**

[1] The speaker in the poem is Emerson.

ANTHONY CLEMENT McAULIFFE
1898–

Nuts!
Reply [December 23, 1944] *to a German demand for surrender of the* 101st *Airborne Division, which had been trapped for seven days at Bastogne*

DONALD CULROSS PEATTIE
1898–1964

The time to hear bird music is between four and six in the morning. Seven o'clock is not too late, but by eight the fine rapture is over, due, I suspect, to the contentment of the inner man that comes with breakfast; a poet should always be hungry or have a lost love.
An Almanac for Moderns [1935]. *April* 22

AMELIA EARHART PUTNAM
1898–1937

Courage is the price that life exacts for granting peace.
The soul that knows it not, knows no release
From little things;
Knows not the livid loneliness of fear,
Nor mountain heights where bitter joy can hear
The sound of wings. *Courage*

DOROTHY E. REID

A goosegirl ermined is a goosegirl still
And geese will gabble everywhere she goes. *Not in Andersen*

YOKOMITSU RIICHI[1]
1898–1947

Pleasure — indeed there is nothing to compare with the gaiety and trans-

[1] From *Modern Japanese Literature,* edited by Donald Keene [1960]

parency of the pleasure before death. The heart begins to choke from its extremity of pleasure, as if it were licking some luscious piece of fruit.

Jikan [*Time*] [1931]

NOEL COWARD
1899–1973

Mad dogs and Englishmen go out in
   the midday sun;
The Japanese don't care to, the Chinese wouldn't dare to;
Hindus and Argentines sleep firmly
   from twelve to one,
But Englishmen detest a siesta.

Mad Dogs and Englishmen

Dance, dance, dance, little lady,
Life is fleeting
To the rhythm beating
In your mind.

Dance, Dance, Dance, Little Lady [1928]

I'll see you again,
Whenever spring breaks through again.

Bittersweet [1929], *act I sc. 1*

Certain women should be struck
regularly, like gongs.

Private Lives [1930], *act III*

I've got those weary Twentieth-Century Blues.

Cavalcade [1931], *pt. 3, sc. 2*

Don't Let's be Beastly to the Germans.   *Title of song*

HART CRANE
1899–1932

And yet this great wink of eternity,
Of rimless floods, unfettered leewardings.   *Voyages* [1926], *II*

Adagios of islands, O my Prodigal.

Ib.

Bind us in time, O seasons clear, and
   awe.
O minstrel galleons of Carib fire,
Bequeath us to no earthly shore until
Is answered in the vortex of our grave

The seal's wide spindrift gaze toward
   paradise.   *Voyages, II*

It was a kind and northern face
That mingled in such exile guise
The everlasting eyes of Pierrot
And, of Gargantua, the laughter.

*Praise for an Urn: In Memoriam
Ernest Nelson* [1926]

Damp tonnage and alluvial march of
   days . . .
Tortured with history, its one will —
flow.

The Bridge [1930]. *The River
(Mississippi)*

The swift red flesh, a winter king —
Who squired the glacier woman down
   the sky?
She ran the neighing canyons all the
   spring;
She spouted arms; she rose with maize
   — to die.   *Ib. The Dance*

Bunched in mutual glee
The bearings glint — O murmurless
   and shined
In oilrinsed circles of blind ecstasy!

Ib. Power: Cape Hatteras

And why do I often meet your visage
   here,
Your eyes like agate lanterns — on and
   on
Below the toothpaste and the dandruff
   ads?
And did their riding eyes right through
   your side,
And did their eyes like unwashed platters ride?
And Death, aloft — gigantically down [1]
Probing through you toward me, O
   evermore!

Ib. The Tunnel

Compass, quadrant and sextant contrive
No farther tides . . . High in the
   azure steeps
Monody shall not wake the mariner.
This fabulous shadow only the sea
   keeps.

At Melville's Tomb [1933]

[1] See Poe, p. 642a.

ERNEST HEMINGWAY
1899–1961

You and me, we've made a separate peace.

> *In Our Time* [1924]. *A Very Short Story*

It makes one feel rather good deciding not to be a bitch. . . . It's sort of what we have instead of God.

> *The Sun Also Rises* [1926], *ch. 19*

"Oh, Jake," Brett said, "we could have had such a damned good time together." . . .

"Yes," I said. "Isn't it pretty to think so?"   *Ib. last lines*

I was always embarrassed by the words sacred, glorious, and sacrifice and the expression in vain. We had heard them, sometimes standing in the rain almost out of earshot, so that only the shouted words came through . . . now for a long time, and I had seen nothing sacred, and the things that were glorious had no glory and the sacrifices were like the stockyards at Chicago if nothing was done with the meat except to bury it . . . Abstract words such as glory, honor, courage, or hallow were obscene.

> *A Farewell to Arms* [1929], *ch. 27*

If people bring so much courage to this world the world has to kill them to break them, so of course it kills them. The world breaks everyone and afterward many are strong at the broken places. But those that will not break it kills. It kills the very good and the very gentle and the very brave impartially. If you are none of these you can be sure that it will kill you too but there will be no special hurry.   *Ib. 34*

That was what you did. You died. You did not know what it was about. You never had time to learn. They threw you in and told you the rules and the first time they caught you off base they killed you.   *Ib. 41*

It was like saying goodbye to a statue. After a while I went out and left

the hospital and walked back to the hotel in the rain.

> *A Farewell to Arms, ch. 27*

Grace under pressure.

> *Definition of "guts" in The New Yorker* [November 30, 1929]

I know only that what is moral is what you feel good after and what is immoral is what you feel bad after.

> *Death in the Afternoon* [1932], *ch. 1*

I was trying to write then and I found the greatest difficulty, aside from knowing truly what you really felt, rather than what you were supposed to feel, and had been taught to feel, was to put down what really happened in action; what the actual things were which produced the emotion that you experienced . . . the real thing, the sequence of motion and fact which made the emotion and which would be as valid in a year or in ten years or, with luck and if you stated it purely enough, always.   *Ib.*

If he wrote it he could get rid of it. He had gotten rid of many things by writing them.

> *Winner Take Nothing* [1933]. *Fathers and Sons*

All good books are alike in that they are truer than if they had really happened and after you are finished reading one you will feel that all that happened to you and afterwards it all belongs to you: the good and the bad, the ecstasy, the remorse and sorrow, the people and the places and how the weather was. If you can get so that you can give that to people, then you are a writer.

> *Old Newsman Writes* [*Esquire*, December 1934]

All modern American literature comes from one book by Mark Twain called *Huckleberry Finn*.

> *Green Hills of Africa* [1935], *ch. 1*

The rich were dull and they drank too much. . . . He remembered poor Julian [1] and his romantic awe of them and how he had started a story once that began, "The very rich are different from you and me." And how someone [2] had said to Julian, "Yes, they have more money."

> *The Snows of Kilimanjaro*
> [1936]

Kilimanjaro is a snow-covered mountain 19,710 feet high, and is said to be the highest mountain in Africa. Its western summit is called the Masai "Ngàje Ngài," the House of God. Close to the western summit there is the dried and frozen carcass of a leopard. No one has explained what the leopard was seeking at that altitude.

> *Ib. epigraph*

Ezra [Pound] was right half the time, and when he was wrong, he was so wrong you were never in any doubt about it. Gertrude [Stein] was always right.

> *To John Peale Bishop; quoted in his Homage to Hemingway, New Republic* [November 11, 1936]

No matter how a man alone ain't got no bloody f — ing chance.

> *To Have and Have Not* [1937], *ch. 23*

If we win here we will win everywhere. The world is a fine place and worth the fighting for and I hate very much to leave it.

> *For Whom the Bell Tolls* [1940], *ch. 43*

Cowardice, as distinguished from panic, is almost always simply a lack of ability to suspend the functioning of the imagination.

> *Men at War* [1942], *introduction*

Time is the least thing we have of.

> *From The New Yorker, Profile by* LILLIAN ROSS [*May 13, 1950*] [3]

[1] F. Scott Fitzgerald.
[2] Hemingway.
[3] Reprinted in book form, *Portrait of Hemingway* [1961].

A man can be destroyed but not defeated.

> *The Old Man and the Sea* [1952]

If it is any use to know it, I always try to write on the principle of the iceberg. There is seven-eighths of it under water for every part that shows. Anything you know you can eliminate and it only strengthens your iceberg. It is the part that doesn't show. If a writer omits something because he does not know it then there is a hole in the story.

> *Interview, Paris Review* [*Spring 1958*]

If you are lucky enough to have lived in Paris as a young man, then wherever you go for the rest of your life, it stays with you, for Paris is a movable feast.

> *A Movable Feast* [1964], *epigraph*

ROBERT MAYNARD HUTCHINS
1899–

Democracy . . . is the only form of government that is founded on the dignity of man, not the dignity of some men, of rich men, of educated men or of white men, but of all men. Its sanction is not the sanction of force, but the sanction of human nature. Equality and justice, the two great distinguishing characteristics of democracy, follow inevitably from the conception of men, all men, as rational and spiritual beings.

> *Democracy and Human Nature*

The death of democracy is not likely to be an assassination from ambush. It will be a slow extinction from apathy, indifference, and undernourishment.

> *Great Books* [1954]

CHARLES W. MORTON
1899–1967

It was around two decades ago, in the city room of the Boston *Evening Transcript*, that I first became aware of the elongated-yellow-fruit school of writing. The phrase turned up in a story

. . . about some fugitive monkeys and the efforts of police to recapture them by using bananas as bait.

The Elongated Yellow Fruit [1954]

VLADIMIR NABOKOV
1899–1977

Lolita, light of my life, fire of my loins. My sin, my soul. Lo-lee-ta.

Lolita [1955], pt. I, ch. 1

LELAND STOWE
1899–

An American will tinker with anything he can put his hands on. But how rarely can he be persuaded to tinker with an abstract idea.

They Shall Not Sleep [1944]

E. B. WHITE[1]
1899–

All poets who, when reading from their own works, experience a choked feeling, are major. For that matter, all poets who read from their own works are major, whether they choke or not.

How to Tell a Major Poet from a Minor Poet

"It's broccoli, dear."
"I say it's spinach, and I say the hell with it."

Caption for cartoon by Carl Rose in The New Yorker

Commuter — one who spends his life
In riding to and from his wife;
A man who shaves and takes a train
And then rides back to shave again.

Commuter

It is easier for a man to be loyal to his club than to his planet; the bylaws are shorter, and he is personally acquainted with the other members.

One Man's Meat [1944]

The future . . . seems to me no unified dream but a mince pie, long in the baking, never quite done. *Ib.*

[1] See Thoreau, *Walden*, footnote, p. 682a.
See James Thurber, p. 1033a.

Democracy is the recurrent suspicion that more than half of the people are right more than half of the time.

The Wild Flag. In The New Yorker [July 3, 1943]

When Mrs. Frederick C. Little's second son was born, everybody noticed that he was not much bigger than a mouse. The truth of the matter was, the baby looked very much like a mouse in every way. He was only two inches high; and he had a mouse's sharp nose, a mouse's tail, a mouse's whiskers, and the pleasant, shy manner of a mouse. Before he was many days old he was not only looking like a mouse but acting like one, too — wearing a gray hat and carrying a small cane.

Stuart Little [1945], ch. 1

"My name is Margalo," said the bird, softly, in a musical voice. "I come from fields once tall with wheat, from pastures deep in fern and thistle; I come from vales of meadowsweet, and I love to whistle." *Ib. 8*

It was the best place to be, thought Wilbur, this warm delicious cellar, with the garrulous geese, the changing seasons, the heat of the sun, the passage of swallows, the nearness of rats, the sameness of sheep, the love of spiders, the smell of manure, and the glory of everything.

Charlotte's Web [1952], ch. 22

LOUIS ARMSTRONG
1900–1971

If you have to ask what jazz is, you'll never know. *Saying*

HUMPHREY BOGART
1900–1957

Tennis, anyone?

His sole line in his first play

DENIS WILLIAM BROGAN
1900–

The Englishman is interested in contemporary America. It evokes no response to tell him that Boston is like an English town. He has seen quite enough English towns and would rather hear about New York or Chicago, which are not like English towns.

The English People [1943]

American social fences have to be continually repaired; in England they are like wild hedges; they grow if left alone. *Ib.*

A people that has licked a more formidable enemy than Germany or Japan, primitive North America . . . a country whose national motto has been "root, hog, or die."

The American Character [1944]

Any well-established village in New England or the northern Middle West could afford a town drunkard, a town atheist, and a few Democrats. *Ib.*

JOHN MASON BROWN
1900–1969

Brutus seemed no more than a re-sounding set of vocal cords wrapped up in a toga. *Two on the Aisle* [1938]

To many people dramatic criticism must seem like an attempt to tattoo soap bubbles.

Broadway in Review [1940]

Part of the American myth is that people who are handed the skin of a dead sheep at graduation time think that it will keep their minds alive forever. *Remark*

HERBERT BUTTERFIELD
1900–

It [the scientific revolution] out-shines everything since the rise of Christianity and reduces the Renaissance and Reformation to the rank of mere episodes, mere internal displacements, within the system of medieval Christendom. . . . It looms so large as the real origin of the modern world and of the modern mentality that our cus-

tomary periodization of European history has become an anachronism and an encumbrance.

The Origins of Modern Science [1949]

ELIZABETH, QUEEN MOTHER OF ENGLAND
1900–

The children will not leave unless I do. I shall not leave unless their father does, and the King will not leave the country in any circumstances whatever.

Reported reply as to whether the Princesses would leave England after the bombing of Buckingham Palace [1940]

JAMES HILTON
1900–1954

Anno domini — that's the most fatal complaint of all in the end.

Goodbye, Mr. Chips [1934], *ch. 1*

The austere serenity of Shangri-La. Its forsaken courts and pale pavilions shimmered in repose from which all the fret of existence had ebbed away, leaving a hush as if moments hardly dared to pass. *Lost Horizon* [1933], *ch. 5*

When the High Lama asked him whether Shangri-La was not unique in his experience, and if the Western world could offer anything in the least like it, he answered with a smile: "Well, yes — to be quite frank it reminds me very slightly of Oxford." *Ib. 9*

Memory put a red star in the corner like pictures in a gallery that get sold.

Time and Time Again [1953]

If you forgive people enough you belong to them, and they to you, whether either person likes it or not — squatter's rights of the heart. *Ib.*

MARTHA OSTENSO
1900–1963

Pity the Unicorn,
Pity the Hippogriff,

Souls that were never born
Out of the land of If!
The Unicorn and the Hippogriff,
st. 1

LEROY [SATCHEL] PAIGE
c. 1900–

Don't look back. Something may be gaining on you.
How to Keep Young [1953]

ERNIE PYLE
1900–1945

I write from the worm's-eye point of view.   *Here Is Your War* [1943]

If you go long enough without a bath even the fleas will let you alone.   *Ib.*

ANTOINE DE SAINT-EXUPÉRY
1900–1944

Although human life is priceless, we always act as if something had an even greater price than life. . . . But what is that something?   *Vol de Nuit*

Freedom and constraint are two aspects of the same necessity which is to be what one is and no other.
La Citadelle

ADLAI STEVENSON
1900–1965

More important than winning the election, is governing the nation. That is the test of a political party — the acid, final test.
Speech accepting Democratic presidential nomination [*July 26, 1952*]

Let's talk sense to the American people. Let's tell them the truth, that there are no gains without pains.   *Ib.*

What do we mean by patriotism in the context of our times? . . . A patriotism that puts country ahead of self; a patriotism which is not short, frenzied outbursts of emotion, but the tranquil and steady dedication of a lifetime. There are words that are easy to utter, but this is a mighty assignment. For it is often easier to fight for principles than to live up to them.[1]
Speech, New York City [*August 27, 1952*]

When an American says that he loves his country, he means not only that he loves the New England hills, the prairies glistening in the sun, the wide and rising plains, the great mountains, and the sea. He means that he loves an inner air, an inner light in which freedom lives and in which a man can draw the breath of self-respect.
Ib.

A hungry man is not a free man.[2]
Speech, Kasson, Minnesota [*September 6, 1952*]

A wise man does not try to hurry history.
Speech, San Francisco [*September 9, 1952*]

The time to stop a revolution is at the beginning, not the end.   *Ib.*

Your public servants serve you right.
Speech, Los Angeles [*September 11, 1952*]

This is the first time I have ever heard of a party going into battle under the slogan, "Throw the rascals in."
Speech, Phoenix, Arizona, [*September 12, 1952*]

Those who corrupt the public mind are just as evil as those who steal from the public purse.
Speech, Albuquerque, New Mexico [*September 12, 1952*]

Nature is neutral. Man has wrested from nature the power to make the world a desert or to make the deserts bloom. There is no evil in the atom; only in men's souls.[3]
Speech, Hartford, Connecticut [*September 18, 1952*]

[1] See Thackeray, p. 660a.
[2] See Cato, 107a, and note.
[3] See J. Robert Oppenheimer, p. 1055a-b.

Government [in a democracy] cannot be stronger or more tough-minded than its people. It cannot be more inflexibly committed to the task than they. It cannot be wiser than the people.
Speech, Chicago [September 29, 1952]

As citizens of this democracy, you are the rulers and the ruled, the lawgivers and the law-abiding, the beginning and the end.   *Ib.*

Africa for the Africans means Africa for the Africans and not Africa as a hunting ground for alien ambitions.
Speech, United Nations [February 18, 1961]

If total isolationism is no answer, total interventionism is no answer, either. In fact, the clear, quick, definable, measurable answers are ruled out. In this twilight of power, there is no quick path to a convenient light switch.[1]
Speech, Harvard University [June 17, 1965]

The art of government has grown from its seeds in the tiny city-states of Greece to become the political mode of half the world. So let us dream of a world in which all states, great and small, work together for the peaceful flowering of the republic of man.
Ib.

VIOLET ALLEYN STOREY
1900–

I have a small-town soul.
It makes me want to know
Wee, unimportant things
About the folks that go
Past on swift journeyings.   *Ironical*

WILLIAM LINDSAY WHITE
1900–1973

They Were Expendable.
Title of book [1942]

[1] See John F. Kennedy, p. 1073a.

THOMAS WOLFE
1900–1938

A stone, a leaf, an unfound door.
Look Homeward, Angel! [1] *[1929], foreword*

Which of us has known his brother? Which of us has looked into his father's heart? Which of us has not remained forever prison-pent? Which of us is not forever a stranger and alone?
Ib.

O lost, and by the wind grieved, ghost, come back again.   *Ib.*

Most of the time we think we're sick, it's all in the mind.   *Ib. pt. I, ch. 1*

Making the world safe for hypocrisy.
Ib. III, 36

The young men of this land are not, as they are often called, a "lost" race — they are a race that never yet has been discovered. And the whole secret, power, and knowledge of their own discovery is locked within them — they know it, feel it, have the whole thing in them — and they cannot utter it.
The Web and the Rock [1939], ch. 13

If a man has a talent and cannot use it, he has failed. If he has a talent and uses only half of it, he has partly failed. If he has a talent and learns somehow to use the whole of it, he has gloriously succeeded, and won a satisfaction and a triumph few men ever know.   *Ib. 30*

You Can't Go Home Again.
Title of novel [1940]

ROY CAMPBELL
1901–1957

You praise the firm restraint with which they write —
I'm with you there, of course.
They use the snaffle and the curb all right,
But where's the bloody horse?
On Some South African Novelists

[1] See Milton, p. 339a.

The sap is the music, the stem is the
    flute,
And the leaves are the wings of the
    seraph I shape
Who dances, who springs in a golden
    escape,
Out of the dust and the drought of the
    plain,
To sing with the silver hosannas of
    rain.
The Palm [1928]

JAMES MICHAEL KIERAN, JR.
1901–1952

The brains trust.
> *In conversation with Franklin
> D. Roosevelt [August 1932], re-
> ferring to the professors and
> other such advisers who served
> Roosevelt in his first campaign.
> The phrase later became "brain
> trust."*

LINUS CARL PAULING
1901–

Science is the search for truth — it is
not a game in which one tries to beat
his opponent, to do harm to others.
We need to have the spirit of science in
international affairs, to make the conduct of international affairs the effort to
find the right solution, the just solution
of international problems, not the effort
by each nation to get the better of
other nations, to do harm to them
when it is possible.
No More War! [1958]

CORNELIA OTIS SKINNER
1901–

Woman's virtue is man's greatest invention.   *Paris '90*

THOMAS EDMUND DEWEY
1902–1971

That's why it's time for a change.[1]
*Campaign speech, San Francisco
[September 21, 1944]*

STELLA GIBBONS
1902–

The farm was crouched on a bleak
hillside, whence its fields, fanged with
flints, dropped steeply to the village of
Howling a mile away.
Cold Comfort Farm [1932],
ch. 3

Something nasty in the woodshed.
Ib. 8

WOLCOTT GIBBS
1902–1958

Backward ran sentences until reeled
the mind.[2]
More in Sorrow [1958]. *Time
. . . Fortune . . . Life . . .
Luce*

Where it will all end, knows God!
Ib.

Generally speaking, the American
theater is the aspirin of the middle
classes.[3]
*Ib. Shakespeare, Here's Your
Hat*

LANGSTON HUGHES
1902–1967

I swear to the Lord
I still can't see
Why Democracy means
Everybody but me.
The Black Man Speaks

I am the people, humble, hungry,
    mean —
Hungry yet today despite the dream.
Beaten yet today — O Pioneers! [4]
I am the man who never got ahead,

[1] The phrase was used extensively in the
campaigns of 1944, 1948, and 1952.
[2] See Winston Churchill, p. 925a.
[3] See Marx, p. 686b.
[4] See Whitman, p. 701b.

The poorest worker bartered through
the years.
Let America Be America
Again [1938]

O, let America be America again —
The land that never has been yet —
And yet must be.   *Ib.*

Negro blood is sure powerful — because just *one* drop of black blood
makes a colored man. *One* drop — you
are a Negro! . . . Black is powerful.
Simple Takes a Wife [1953]

CHARLES AUGUSTUS LINDBERGH[1]
1902–

We (that's my ship and I) took off
rather suddenly. We had a report
somewhere around 4 o'clock in the afternoon before that the weather would
be fine, so we thought we would try
it.
Lindbergh's Own Story. In the
New York Times [May 23,
1927]

I saw a fleet of fishing boats. . . . I
flew down almost touching the craft
and yelled at them, asking if I was on
the right road to Ireland.
They just stared. Maybe they didn't
hear me. Maybe I didn't hear them. Or
maybe they thought I was just a crazy
fool. An hour later I saw land.   *Ib.*

OGDEN NASH
(1902–1971)

O money, money, money, I'm not
necessarily one of those who think
thee holy,
But I often stop to wonder how thou
canst go out so fast when thou
comest in so slowly.
Hymn to the Thing That Makes
the Wolf Go [January 1934]

[1] In the spring of '27, something bright and
alien flashed across the sky. A young Minnesotan
who seemed to have had nothing to do with his
generation did a heroic thing, and for a moment
people set down their glasses in country clubs
and speakeasies and thought of their old best
dreams. — F. Scott Fitzgerald [*of Lindbergh*]

There are two kinds of people who
blow through life like a breeze,
And one kind is gossipers, and the other
kind is gossipees.
I'm a Stranger Here Myself
[1938]. *I Have It on Good*
Authority

Bankers Are Just Like Anybody Else,
Except Richer.
Ib. Title of poem

Dogs display reluctance and wrath
If you try to give them a bath.
They bury bones in hideaways
And half the time they trot sideaways.
Ib. An Introduction to Dogs,
st. 4

Barmaids Are Diviner Than Mermaids.
Ib. Title of poem

There was a young belle of old Natchez
Whose garments were always in
patchez.
When comment arose
On the state of her clothes,
She drawled, When Ah itchez, Ah
scratchez!   *Ib. Requiem*

There is only one way to achieve happiness on this terrestrial ball,
And that is to have either a clear conscience, or none at all.
Ib. Inter-Office Memorandum

Women would rather be right than rea-
sonable.
Good Intentions [1942]. *Frailty,*
Thy Name Is a Misnomer

Candy
Is dandy
But liquor
Is quicker.
Many Long Years Ago [1945].
Reflections on Ice-Breaking

I think that I shall never see
A billboard lovely as a tree.
Indeed, unless the billboards fall
I'll never see a tree at all.[1]
Ib. Song of the Open Road

One would be in less danger
From the wiles of the stranger

[1] See Joyce Kilmer, p. 1051b.

If one's own kin and kith
Were more fun to be with.
> *Many Long Years Ago.*
> *Family Court*

The turtle lives 'twixt plated decks
Which practically conceal its sex.
I think it clever of the turtle
In such a fix to be so fertile.
> *Ib. The Turtle*

A bit of talcum
Is always walcum.
> *Ib. Reflection on Babies*

The old men know when an old man
dies. *Ib. Old Men*

There is something about a Martini,
A tingle remarkably pleasant;
A yellow, a mellow Martini;
I wish that I had one at present.
There is something about a Martini,
Ere the dining and dancing begin,
And to tell you the truth,
It is not the vermouth —
I think that perhaps it's the gin.
> *Ib. A Drink with Something in It*

Middle age is when you've met so many
people that every new person you
meet reminds you of someone else.
> *Versus* [1949]. *Let's Not*
> *Climb the Washington*
> *Monument Tonight*

I believe a little incompatibility is the
spice of life, particularly if he has
income and she is pattable.
> *Ib. I Do, I Will, I Have*

My garden will never make me famous,
I'm a horticultural ignoramus,
I can't tell a stringbean from a soybean,
Or even a girl bean from a boy bean.
> *Ib. He Digs, He Dug, He Has Dug*

When I remember bygone days
I think how evening follows morn;
So many I loved were not yet dead,
So many I love were not yet born.
> *Ib. The Middle*

He tells you when you've got on too
much lipstick,
And helps you with your girdle when
your hips stick.
> *Ib. The Perfect Husband*

A door is what a dog is perpetually on
the wrong side of.
> *The Private Dining Room*
> [1953]. *A Dog's Best Friend*
> *Is His Illiteracy*

GEORGE GAYLORD
SIMPSON
1902–

The present chaotic stage of humanity is not, as some wishfully maintain,
caused by a lack of faith but by too
much unreasoning faith and too many
conflicting faiths within these boundaries where such faith should have no
place. The chaos is one that only responsible human knowledge can reduce
to order.
> *The Meaning of Evolution* [1949]

THEODORE SPENCER
1902–1949

Eunuchs, abortive Platonists and priests
Speak always very wisely about love.
> *An Act of Life* [1944]

JOHN ERNST STEINBECK
1902–1968

Man, unlike any other thing organic
or inorganic in the universe, grows beyond his work, walks up the stairs of his
concepts, emerges ahead of his accomplishments.
> *The Grapes of Wrath* [1939],
> *ch. 14*

Okie use' ta mean you was from
Oklahoma. Now it means you're scum.
Don't mean nothing itself, it's the way
they say it. *Ib. 18*

ERSKINE CALDWELL
1903–

Tobacco Road.
> *Title of novel* [1] [1932]

[1] The play [1933], adapted by JACK KIRKLAND,
[1903–1969] had one of the longest runs in
American stage history.

COUNT GALEAZZO CIANO
1903–1944

As always, victory finds a hundred fathers but defeat is an orphan.[1]
> *The Ciano Diaries 1939–1943 [1946].* [*September 9, 1942*]

CYRIL CONNOLLY [PALINURUS]
1903–1974

There is no fury like a woman searching for a new lover.
> *The Unquiet Grave* [1945], *pt. I*

Obesity is a mental state, a disease brought on by boredom and disappointment.   *Ib.*

Imprisoned in every fat man a thin one is wildly signaling to be let out.
> *Ib. II*

COUNTEE CULLEN
1903–1946

One three centuries removed
From the scenes his fathers loved,
Spicy grove, cinnamon tree,
What is Africa to me?
> *Heritage* [1925]

WILLIAM THOMAS CUMMINGS[2]
1903–1944

There are no atheists in the foxholes.
> *Field sermon, Bataan* [1942]. *From* CARLOS P. ROMULO, *I Saw the Fall of the Philippines* [1942]

[1] There's an old saying that victory has a hundred fathers and defeat is an orphan. — JOHN F. KENNEDY, *after the debacle at the Bay of Pigs, Cuba, April 21, 1961*

[2] Father Cummings, a chaplain, was aboard an unmarked Japanese ship transporting prisoners from the Philippines to Japan which was sunk by an American submarine [December 15, 1944].

CLARE BOOTHE LUCE
1903–

Much of what Mr. Wallace[1] calls his global thinking is, no matter how you slice it, still Globaloney.
> *Speech, House of Representatives* [*February 9, 1943*]

GEORGE ORWELL [ERIC BLAIR]
1903–1950

All animals are equal, but some animals are more equal than others.
> *Animal Farm* [1945], *ch. 10*

Big Brother is watching you.
> *1984* [1948]

BENJAMIN SPOCK
1903–

The more people have studied different methods of bringing up children the more they have come to the conclusion that what good mothers and fathers instinctively feel like doing for their babies is the best after all.
> *The Common Sense Book of Baby and Child Care* [1946], *ch. 1*

EVELYN WAUGH
1903–1966

That's the public school system all over. They may kick you out, but they never let you down.
> *Decline and Fall* [1929]

PETER ARNO
1904–1968

I consider your conduct unethical and lousy.   *Caption for cartoon*

RICHARD EBERHART
1904–

But the year had lost its meaning,
And in intellectual chains

[1] Vice-President Henry Wallace.

I lost both love and loathing,
Mured up in the wall of wisdom.
Collected Poems 1930–1960
[1960]. *The Groundhog*

I stood there in the whirling summer,
My hand capped a withered heart,
And thought of China and of Greece,
Of Alexander in his tent;
Of Montaigne in his tower,
Of Saint Theresa in her wild lament.
Ib.

It is what man does not know of God
Composes the visible poem of the
world.   *Ib. On a Squirrel*

This fevers me, this sun on green,
On green glowing, this young spring.
Ib. A Bravery of Earth

Not God he'll catch, in the mystery of
space.
He flaunts his own outcast state
As he throws his imperfections outward
bound.
*Ib. On Shooting Particles
Beyond the World*

CLIFTON FADIMAN
1904–

When you reread a classic you do
not see more in the book than you did
before; you see more in *you* than there
was before.
Any Number Can Play [1957]

MARGARET FISHBACK
1904–

The same old charitable lie
Repeated as the years scoot by
Perpetually makes a hit —
"You really haven't changed a bit!"
The Lie of the Land

GRAHAM GREENE
1904–

That whiskey priest, I wish we had
never had him in the house.
The Power and the Glory [1940]

Have you seen a room from which
faith has gone? . . . Like a marriage
from which love has gone. . . . And
patience, patience everywhere like a
fog.   *The Potting Shed* [1957]

Catholics and Communists have
committed great crimes, but at least
they have not stood aside, like an established society, and been indifferent. I
would rather have blood on my hands
than water like Pilate . . . if you have
abandoned one faith, do not abandon
all faith. There is always an alternative
to the faith we lose. Or is it the same
faith under another name?
The Comedians [1966]

CHRISTOPHER WILLIAM BRADSHAW ISHERWOOD
1904–

I am a camera with its shutter open,
quite passive, recording, not thinking.
Recording the man shaving at the window opposite and the woman in the
kimono washing her hair. Some day, all
this will have to be developed, carefully
printed, fixed.
The Berlin Stories [1945].
Goodbye to Berlin [1939],
A Berlin Diary [Autumn
1930]

GEORGE F. KENNAN
1904–

Something which is vitally important
but which, I think, is often lost sight of
in the United States . . . is the fact
that international life normally has in
it strong competitive elements. It did
not take the challenge of Communism
to produce this situation. Just as there
is no uncomplicated personal relationship between individuals, so, I think,
there is no international relationship
between sovereign states which is without its elements of antagonism, its
competitive aspects. Many of the
present relationships of international
life are only the eroded remnants of
ones which, at one time, were relation-

ships of uncompromising hostility. Every government is in some respects a problem for every other government, and it will always be this way so long as the sovereign state, with its supremely self-centered rationale, remains the basis of international life.

> *Russia and the West under Lenin and Stalin* [1961], *ch. 25*

If we are to regard ourselves as a grown-up nation — and anything else will henceforth be mortally dangerous — then we must, as the Biblical phrase goes, put away childish things; and among these childish things the first to go, in my opinion, should be self-idealization and the search for absolutes in world affairs: for absolute security, absolute amity, absolute harmony.

> *Ib.*

CECIL DAY LEWIS

1904–1971

Tempt me no more; for I
Have known the lightning's hour,
The poet's inward pride,
The certainty of power.

> *Tempt Me No More, st. 1*

And if our blood alone
Will melt this iron earth,
Take it. It is well spent
Easing a savior's birth.

> *Ib. st. 7*

Rest from loving and be living.
Fallen is fallen past retrieving.

> *Rest from Loving*

Make us a wind to shake the world!

> *The Magnetic Mountain* [1933], 31

J. ROBERT OPPENHEIMER[1]

1904–1967

In some sort of crude sense which no vulgarity, no humor, no overstatement

[1] For the passage quoted by Oppenheimer at the explosion of the first atom bomb [Alamogordo, New Mexico, July 16, 1945], see *Bhagavad Gita*, p. 106b. He also quoted Vishnu from the *Gita*: I am become death, the destroyer of worlds.

can quite extinguish, the physicists have known sin; and this is a knowledge which they cannot lose.

> *Physics in the Contemporary World, lecture at Massachusetts Institute of Technology* [November 25, 1947]

The open society, the unrestricted access to knowledge, the unplanned and uninhibited association of men for its furtherance — these are what may make a vast, complex, ever growing, ever changing, ever more specialized and expert technological world, nevertheless a world of human community.

> *Science and the Common Understanding* [1953]

JAMES WILLIAM FULBRIGHT

1905–

There is an inevitable divergence, attributable to the imperfections of the human mind, between the world as it is and the world as men perceive it.

> *Speech in the Senate* [March 27, 1964]

We are handicapped by [foreign] policies based on old myths rather than current realities.

> *Ib.*

The character of the cold war has been profoundly altered . . . by the implicit repudiation by both sides of a policy of total victory. . . . The effect has been to commit us to a policy that can be accurately, though perhaps not prudently, defined as one of "peaceful coexistence."

> *Ib.*

There is much cant in American moralism and not a little inconsistency.

> *Ib.*

We are inclined to confuse freedom and democracy, which we regard as moral principles, with the way in which these are practiced in America — with capitalism, federalism and the two-party system, which are not moral principles, but simply the accepted practices of the American people.

> *Ib.*

The master myth of the cold war is that the Communist bloc is a monolith, composed of governments which are not really governments at all, but organized conspiracies . . . all equally resolute and implacable in their determination to destroy the free world.

Speech in the Senate

We must dare to think "unthinkable" thoughts. We must learn to explore all the options and possibilities that confront us in a complex and rapidly changing world. We must learn to welcome and not to fear the voices of dissent. We must dare to think about "unthinkable things" because when things become unthinkable, thinking stops and action becomes mindless. *Ib.*

GRETA GARBO
1905–

I want to be alone.[1] *Attributed*

DAG HAMMARSKJÖLD
1905–1961

Smiling, sincere, incorruptible —
His body disciplined and limber.
A man who had become what he could,
And was what he was —
Ready at any moment to gather everything
Into one simple sacrifice.

Markings [1964]

Never look down to test the ground before taking your next step: only he who keeps his eye fixed on the far horizon will find his right road. *Ib.*

We carry our nemesis within us: yesterday's self-admiration is the legitimate father of today's feeling of guilt. *Ib.*

What gives life its value you can find — and lose. But never possess. This

[1] Garbo maintains that her most famous remark has always been misquoted. . . . "I only said, 'I want to be *let* alone!'" — JOHN BAINBRIDGE, in *Life* [January 24, 1955]

holds good above all for "the Truth about Life." *Markings*

The longest journey [1]
Is the journey inwards
Of him who has chosen his destiny,
Who has started upon his quest
For the source of his being
(Is there a source?). *Ib.*

So! *That* is the way in which you are tempted to overcome your loneliness — by making the ultimate escape from life. — No! It may be that death is to be your ultimate gift to life: it must not be an act of treachery against it. *Ib.*

In the last analysis, what does the word "sacrifice" mean? Or even the word "gift"? He who has nothing can give nothing. The gift is God's — to God. *Ib.*

STANLEY KUNITZ
1905–

Awake!
    My whirling hands stay at the noon,
Each cell within my body holds a heart
And all my hearts in unison strike twelve.

The Science of the Night

When the light falls, it falls on her
In whose rose-gilded chamber
A music strained through mind
Turns everything to measure.

When the Light Falls

Doomsday is the eighth day of the week.

Foreign Affairs

O Magus with the leathern hand,
The wasted heart, the trailing star,
Time is your madness, which I share,
Blowing next winter into mind . . .
And love herself not there, not there.

The Man Upstairs, st. 4

[1] See Shelley, p. 571a.

On the royal road to Thebes
I had my luck, I met a lovely monster,
And the story's this: I made the mon-
ster me.
The Approach to Thebes

We learn, as the thread plays out, that
we belong
Less to what flatters us than to what
scars,
So, freshly turning, as the turn con-
dones,
For her I killed the propitiatory bird,
Kissing her down. Peace to her bitter
bones,
Who taught me the serpent's word, but
yet the word.
The Dark and the Fair

A fine Italian hand,
With its mimosa touch, has made me
feel
Blind-skinned, indelicate, a fool Ameri-
cano
Touring a culture like a grand museum,
People and statues interchangeable
shows,
Perception blunted as one's syntax
fails.
The Thief

I recognize the gods' capricious hand
And write this poem for money, rage,
and love. *Ib.*

I stand on the terrible threshold, and I
see
The end and the beginning in each
other's arms.
Open the Gates, st. 3

An agitation of the air,
A perturbation of the light
Admonished me the unloved year
Would turn on its hinge that night.
End of Summer, st. 1

Already the iron door of the north
Clangs open: birds, leaves, snows
Order their populations forth,
And a cruel wind blows. *Ib. st. 4*

Now, while the antler of the eaves
Liquefies, drop by drop, I brood

On a Christian thing: unless the leaves
Perish, the tree is not renewed.

If all our perishable stuff
Be nourished to its rot, we clean
Our trunk of death, and in our tough
And final growth are evergreen.
Deciduous Branch, st. 4, 5

I wept for my youth, sweet passionate
young thought,
And cozy women dead that by my side
Once lay: I wept with bitter longing,
not
Remembering how in my youth I cried.
I Dreamed That I Was Old, st. 3

The thing that eats the heart is mostly
heart.
*The Thing That Eats the
Heart, last line*

Cities shall suffer siege and some shall
fall,
But man's not taken. What the deep
heart means,
Its message of the big, round, childish
hand,
Its wonder, its simple lonely cry,
The bloodied envelope addressed to
you,
Is history, that wide and mortal pang.
Night Letter

When young I scribbled, boasting, on
my wall,
No Love, No Property, No Wages.
In youth's good time I somehow
bought them all,
And cheap, you'd think, for maybe a
hundred pages.
Now in my prime, disburdened of my
gear,
My trophies ransomed, broken, lost,
I carve again on the lintel of the year
My sign: *Mobility* — and damn the
cost! *The Summing-Up*

If I must build a church,
Though I do not really want one,
Let it be in the wilderness
Out of nothing but nail-holes.
Revolving Meditation

LIU SHAO-CH'I [1]
1905–

Our ethics are great precisely because they are the ethics of Communism and of the proletariat. Such ethics are not built upon the backward basis of safeguarding the interests of individuals or a small number of exploiters. They are built, on the contrary, upon the progressive basis of . . . saving the world from destruction and of building a happy and beautiful Communist world.[2]

How To Be a Good Communist

Inside the Party we must cultivate the practice of submitting to reason.[3]

On Inner-Party Struggle

PHYLLIS McGINLEY
1905–

Meek-eyed parents hasten down the ramps
To greet their offspring, terrible from camps.

Ode to the End of Summer

Always on Monday morning the press reports
God as revealed to His vicars in various guises —
Benevolent, stormy, patient, or out of sorts.
God knows which God is the God God recognizes.

The Day After Sunday

Prince, I warn you, under the rose,
Time is the thief you cannot banish.
These are my daughters, I suppose.
But where in the world did the children vanish?

Ballade of Lost Objects

[1] From *Sources of Chinese Tradition*, edited by William Theodore de Bary [1960].
[2] *Note from the text: How to Be a Good Communist* is a basic text of indoctrination for party members, delivered first as a series of lectures in July 1939 at the Institute of Marxism-Leninism in Yenan. — W. T. DE BARY
[3] *Note from the text:* This essay, delivered by Liu Shao-ch'i in July 1941 as a series of lectures to a Party school is a kind of sequel to *How To Be a Good Communist.* — W. T. DE BARY

JEAN PAUL SARTRE
1905–

Everything is gratuitous, this garden, this city and myself. When you suddenly realize it, it makes you feel sick and everything begins to drift . . . that's nausea.   *La Nausée* [1938]

Man is not the sum of what he has but the totality of what he does not yet have, of what he might have.

Situations [1939], I

This freedom should not be seen as a metaphysical power of human "nature," nor as the right to do whatever one pleases. . . . We do not do what we want and yet we are responsible for what we are — that is the fact.

Ib. II

Because the Nazi venom worked its way even into our thoughts, every accurate thought was a conquest; because an all-powerful police sought to force us into silence, every word became as precious as a declaration of principle; because we were persecuted, each of our gestures carried the weight of a commitment.   *Les Mouches* [1942]

Man can will nothing unless he has first understood that he must count on no one but himself; that he is alone, abandoned on earth in the midst of his infinite responsibilities, without help, with no other aim than the one he sets himself, with no other destiny than the one he forges for himself on this earth.

Le Être et le Néant [1943]

Hell is — other people! [1]

Huis-Clos [1944]

CHARLES PERCY SNOW
1905–

Literary intellectuals at one pole — at the other scientists. . . . Between the two a gulf of mutual incomprehension.

The Two Cultures and the Scientific Revolution [1959]

[1] See Virgil, p. 119a; and Marlowe, p. 213a, and note.

Scientists have it within them to know what a future-directed society feels like, for science itself, in its human aspect, is just that.

Science and Government [1960]

No one is fit to be trusted with power. . . . No one. . . . Any man who has lived at all knows the follies and wickedness he's capable of. If he does not know it, he is not fit to govern others. And if he does know it, he knows also that neither he nor any man ought to be allowed to decide a single human fate.

The Light and the Dark [1961]

Corridors of Power.

Title of novel [1965]

JOHN BETJEMAN
1906–

He rose, and he put down The Yellow
    Book.
He staggered — and, terrible-eyed,
He brushed past the palms on the stair-
    case
And was helped to a hansom outside.

*The Arrest of Oscar Wilde
at the Cadogan Hotel* [1937],
st. 9

Gracious Lord, oh bomb the Germans.
Spare their women for Thy Sake,
And if that is not too easy
We will pardon Thy Mistake.
But, gracious Lord, whate'er shall be,
Don't let anyone bomb me.

In Westminster Abbey [1940]

The sort of girl I like to see
Smiles down from her great height at
   me.   *The Olympic Girl* [1954]

Oh! would I were her racket pressed
With hard excitement to her breast.
                 Ib.

Summoned by Bells.

Title of book [1960]

LEO DUROCHER
1906–

Nice guys finish last.   *Remark*

WYSTAN HUGH AUDEN
1907–1973

Let us honor if we can
The vertical man
Though we value none
But the horizontal one.

Epigraph for Poems [1930]

If we really want to live, we'd better
   start at once to try;
If we don't it doesn't matter, we'd better start to die.

If We Really Want to Live
[1930]

Sir, no man's enemy, forgiving all
But will his negative inversion, be
   prodigal.

Sir, No Man's Enemy [1930]

Harrow the house of the dead; look
   shining at
New styles of architecture, a change of
   heart.   *Ib.*

The greater the love, the more false to
   its object,
   Not to be born is the best for man; [1]
After the kiss comes the impulse to
   throttle,
   Break the embraces, dance while you
   can.

O Who Can Ever Gaze His Fill
[1937]

The stars are dead. The animals will
   not look.
We are left alone with our day, and the
   time short, and History to the defeated
May say Alas but cannot help nor
   pardon.   *Spain* [1937]

About suffering they were never wrong,
The old masters.

Musée des Beaux Arts [1940]

O plunge your hands in water,
   Plunge them in up to the wrist;
Stare, stare in the basin
   And wonder what you've missed.

The glacier knocks in the cupboard,
   The desert sighs in the bed,

¹ See Sophocles, p. 83a.

And the crack in the tea cup opens
A lane to the land of the dead.
                As I Walked Out One Evening
                    [*1940*], *st. 10, 11*

You were silly like us: your gift survived
    it all;
The parish of rich women, physical de-
    cay,
Yourself; mad Ireland hurt you into
    poetry.
                In Memory of W. B. Yeats
                    [*1940*]

To us he is no more a person
Now but a whole climate of opinion.
                In Memory of Sigmund Freud
                    [*1940*]

One rational voice is dumb: over a
    grave
The household of Impulse mourns one
    dearly loved.
    Sad is Eros, builder of cities,
    And weeping anarchic Aphrodite.
                    Ib.

Lay your sleeping head, my love,
Human on my faithless arm.
                *Lay Your Sleeping Head, My
                Love* [*1940*]

At Dirty Dick's and Sloppy Joe's
    We drank our liquor straight,
Some went upstairs with Margery,
And some, alas, with Kate.
                The Sea and the Mirror [*1944*].
                    Master and Boatswain

And children swarmed to him like set-
    tlers. He became a land.
                    Edward Lear [*1945*]

Sob, heavy world,
Sob as you spin,
Mantled in mist, remote from the
    happy.
                The Age of Anxiety [*1947*]

She looked over his shoulder
    For vines and olive trees,
Marble, well-governed cities
    And ships upon wine-dark seas;
But there on the shining metal
    His hands had put instead

An artificial wilderness
    And a sky like lead.
                The Shield of Achilles [*1955*],
                    st. 1

The mass and majesty of this world,
    all
    That carries weight and always
        weighs the same,
Lay in the hands of others; they were
    small
And could not hope for help, and no
    help came;
What their foes liked to do was
    done, their shame
Was all the worst could wish: they lost
    their pride
And died as men before their bodies
    died.   *Ib. st. 6*

Our researchers into Public Opinion are
    content
That he held the proper opinions for
    the time of year;
When there was peace, he was for
    peace; when there was war, he
    went.
                The Unknown Citizen (*To
                JS/07/M/378 This Marble
                Monument Is Erected by
                the State*)

Was he free? Was he happy? The
    question is absurd:
Had anything been wrong, we should
    certainly have heard.   *Ib.*

A culture is no better than its woods.
                    Bucolics. Woods

When a just man dies,
Lamentation and praise,
Sorrow and joy, are one.
                Elegy for John F. Kennedy
                    [*1963*]

Some thirty inches from my nose
The frontier of my Person goes,
And all the untilled air between
Is private *pagus* or demesne.
Stranger, unless with bedroom eyes
I beckon you to fraternize,
Beware of rudely crossing it:
I have no gun, but I can spit.
                About the House [*1965*]

Some books are undeservedly forgotten; none are undeservedly remembered.

The Dyer's Hand [1] [1962]. *Pt. I,*
Reading

It takes little talent to see clearly what lies under one's nose, a good deal of it to know in which direction to point that organ.   *Ib. Writing*

The old lady, quoted by E. M. Forster — "How can I know what I think till I see what I say?"   *Ib.*

Speaking for myself, the questions which interest me most when reading a poem are two. The first is technical: "Here is a verbal contraption. How does it work?" The second is, in the broadest sense, moral: "What kind of a guy inhabits this poem? What is his notion of the good life or the good place? His notion of the Evil One? What does he conceal from the reader? What does he conceal even from himself?"

Ib. II, Making, Knowing and
Judging

Whatever its actual content and overt interest, every poem is rooted in imaginative awe. Poetry can do a hundred and one things, delight, sadden, disturb, amuse, instruct — it may express every possible shade of emotion, and describe every conceivable kind of event, but there is only one thing that all poetry must do; it must praise all it can for being and for happening.

       Ib.

RACHEL LOUISE CARSON
1907–1964

The sea lies all around us. The commerce of all lands must cross it. The very winds that move over the lands have been cradled on its broad expanse and seek ever to return to it. The continents themselves dissolve and pass to the sea, in grain after grain of eroded land. . . . In its mysterious past it encompasses all the dim origins of life and

[1] See Shakespeare, *Sonnet III*, p. 294a.

receives in the end, after, it may be, many transmutations, the dead husks of that same life. For all at last returns to the sea — the beginning and the end.

     The Sea Around Us [1951]

Over increasingly large areas of the United States, spring now comes unheralded by the return of the birds, and the early mornings are strangely silent where once they were filled with the beauty of bird song.

      Silent Spring [1962]

As crude a weapon as the cave man's club, the chemical barrage has been hurled against the fabric of life.   *Ib.*

CHRISTOPHER FRY
1907–

I travel light; as light,
That is, as a man can travel who will
Still carry his body around because
Of its sentimental value.

    The Lady's Not for Burning
       [1950], *act I*

Religion
Has made an honest woman of the
     supernatural,
And we won't have it kicking over the
     traces again.   *Ib. II*

Where in this small-talking world can I
     find
A longitude with no platitude?

       Ib. III

The moon is nothing
But a circumambulatory aphrodisiac
Divinely subsidized to provoke the
     world
Into a rising birth rate.   *Ib.*

Try thinking of love or something.
Amor vincit insomnia.[1]
     A Sleep of Prisoners [1951]

ANNE MORROW
LINDBERGH
1907–

The wave of the future is coming and there is no fighting it.

    The Wave of the Future [1940]

[1] See Virgil, p. 117a.

LOUIS MacNEICE
1907–1963

Holidays should be like this,
Free from overemphasis,
Time for soul to stretch and spit
Before the world comes back on it.
Epilogue, for W. H. Auden
[1936]

It's no go my honey love, it's no go my
     poppet;
Work your hands from day to day, the
     winds will blow the profit.
The glass is falling hour by hour, the
     glass will fall forever,
But if you break the bloody glass you
     won't hold up the weather.
Bagpipe Music, last stanza

The sunlight on the garden
Hardens and grows cold,
We cannot cage the minute
Within its net of gold,
When all is told
We cannot beg for pardon.
The Sunlight on the Garden,
st. 1

PAUL ENGLE
1908–

Wisdom is knowing when you can't be
wise.   *Poems in Praise* [1959]

HOWELL M. FORGY
1908–

Praise the Lord and pass the ammu-
nition.[1]
Said at Pearl Harbor
[December 7, 1941]

JOHN KENNETH
GALBRAITH
1908–

It is told that such are the aero-
dynamics and wing-loading of the bumblebee that, in principle, it cannot
fly. . . . If all this be true . . . life

[1] Forgy was serving as chaplain on a cruiser at
the time of the Japanese attack; the words were
said to a chain of men handling ammunition.
They were used as the title of a song by Frank
Loesser [September 1942].

among bumblebees must bear a remarkable resemblance to life in the
United States.
American Capitalism: The Con-
cept of Countervailing Power
[1952]

Historians and novelists always have
known that tragedy wonderfully reveals
the nature of man. But, while they have
made rich use of war, revolution, and
poverty, they have been singularly neg-
lectful of financial panics. And one can
relish the varied idiocy of human action
during a panic to the full, for, while it
is a time of great tragedy, nothing is
being lost but money.
The Great Crash, 1929 [1955],
ch. 1

Perhaps it was worth being poor for a
long time to be so rich for just a little
while.   *Ib. 3*

The end had come, but it was not
yet in sight.   *Ib. 5*

The stock market is but a mirror
which, perhaps as in this instance, somewhat belatedly, provides an image of
the underlying or *fundamental* economic situation. Cause and effect run
from the economy to the stock market,
never the reverse. In 1929 the economy
was headed for trouble. Eventually that
trouble was violently reflected in Wall
Street.   *Ib. 6*

Men have been swindled by other
men on many occasions. The autumn
of 1929 was, perhaps, the first occasion
when men succeeded on a large scale in
swindling themselves.   *Ib. 7*

At any given time there exists an inventory of undiscovered embezzlement
in — or more precisely not in — the
country's businesses and banks. This
inventory — it should perhaps be called
the bezzle — amounts at any moment
to many millions of dollars. It also
varies in size with the business cycle. In
good times people are relaxed, trusting,
and money is plentiful. But even
though money is plentiful, there are al-

ways many people who need more. Under these circumstances the rate of embezzlement grows, the rate of discovery falls off, and bezzle increases rapidly. In depression all this is reversed. Money is watched with a narrow, suspicious eye. The man who handles it is assumed to be dishonest until he proves himself otherwise. Audits are penetrating and meticulous. Commercial morality is enormously improved. The bezzle shrinks.

> *The Great Crash, 1929, ch. 8*

Illusion is a comprehensive ill. The rich man who deludes himself into behaving like a mendicant may conserve his fortune although he will not be very happy. The affluent country which conducts its affairs in accordance with rules of another and poorer age also foregoes opportunities. And in misunderstanding itself it will, in any time of difficulty, implacably prescribe for itself the wrong remedies.

> *The Affluent Society* [1958], *ch. 1*

. . . the myth that military power is a function of economic output. If peace and survival are to be achieved, the search must almost certainly go beyond the effort to find a balance in thermonuclear terror.   *Ib. 12*

The family which takes its mauve and cerise, air-conditioned, power-steered, and power-braked automobile out for a tour passes through cities that are badly paved, made hideous by litter, blighted buildings, billboards, and posts for wires that should long since have been put underground. They pass on into a countryside that has been rendered largely invisible by commercial art. . . . They picnic on exquisitely packaged food from a portable icebox by a polluted stream and go on to spend the night at a park which is a menace to public health and morals. Just before dozing off on an air mattress, beneath a nylon tent, amid the stench of decaying refuse, they may re-

flect vaguely on the curious unevenness of their blessings. Is this, indeed, the American genius?

> *The Affluent Society, ch. 18*

In a community where public services have failed to keep abreast of private consumption things are very different. Here, in an atmosphere of private opulence and public squalor, the private goods have full sway.   *Ib.*

Nothing so weakens government as persistent inflation.   *Ib.*

People are the common denominator of progress. So . . . no improvement is possible with unimproved people, and advance is certain when people are liberated and educated. It would be wrong to dismiss the importance of roads, railroads, power plants, mills, and the other familiar furniture of economic development. . . . But we are coming to realize . . . that there is a certain sterility in economic monuments that stand alone in a sea of illiteracy. Conquest of illiteracy comes first.

> *Economic Development* [1964], *ch. 2*

LYNDON BAINES JOHNSON
1908–1973

All I have I would have given gladly not to be standing here today.

> *First address to Congress as President* [*November 27, 1963*]

We have talked long enough in this country about equal rights. We have talked for a hundred years or more. It is time now to write the next chapter — and to write in the books of law.   *Ib.*

Unfortunately many Americans live on the outskirts of hope — some because of their poverty, some because of their color, and all too many because of both. Our task is to help replace their despair with opportunity.[1]

First State of the Union Message [January 8, 1964]

The challenge of the next half century is whether we have the wisdom to use [our] wealth to enrich and elevate our national life — and to advance the quality of American civilization — for in your time we have the opportunity to move not only toward the rich society and the powerful society but upward to the Great Society.[2]

Speech, University of Michigan [May 22, 1964]

This nation, this generation, in this hour has man's first chance to build a Great Society, a place where the meaning of man's life matches the marvels of man's labor.

Address, accepting the Presidential nomination [August 1964]

EDWARD ROSCOE MURROW
1908–1965

I am entirely persuaded that the American public is more reasonable, restrained and mature than most of the broadcast industry's planners believe. Their fear of controversy is not warranted by the evidence.

Speech, Radio and Television News Directors Convention, Chicago [October 15, 1958]

In order to progress, radio need only go backward, to the time when singing commercials were not allowed on news reports, when there was no middle commercial on a news report, when radio was rather proud, alert and fast.

Ib.

THEODORE ROETHKE
1908–1963

For something is amiss or out of place
When mice with wings can wear a
  human face.   *The Bat* [1941]

[1] See Michael Harrington, p. 1082a.
[2] See Lippmann, p. 1013b.

My secrets cry aloud.
I have no need for tongue.
My heart keeps open house,
My doors are widely flung.
Open House [1941]

The veins within our hands betrayed
  our fear.
What we had hoped for had not come
  to pass.   *Interlude* [1941]

Thought does not crush to stone.
The great sledge drops in vain.
Truth never is undone;
His shafts remain.
The Adamant [1941]

This urge, wrestle, resurrection of dry
  sticks,
Cut stems struggling to put down feet,
What saint strained so much,
Rose on such lopped limbs to a new
  life?   *Cuttings* [1948]

I study the lives on a leaf: the little
Sleepers, numb nudgers in cold dimen-
  sions,
Beetles in caves, newts, stone-deaf
  fishes,
Lice tethered to long limp subterranean
  weeds,
Squirmers in bogs,
And bacterial creepers.
The Minimal [1948]

Once upon a tree
I came across a time.
Where Knock Is Open Wide
  [1951]

At Woodlawn I heard the dead cry;
I was lulled by the slamming of iron,
A slow drip over stones,
Toads brooding in wells.
All the leaves stuck out their tongues;
I shook the softening chalk of my
  bones,
Saying,
Snail, snail, glister me forward,
Bird, soft-sigh me home.
Worm, be with me.
This is my hard time.
The Lost Son [1951], 1

I feel the slime of a wet nest.
  Beware Mother Mildew.
Nibble again, fish nerves.
                    The Lost Son, 2

A lively understandable spirit
Once entertained you.
It will come again.
Be still.
Wait.   *Ib. 5*

And the new plants, still awkward in
    their soil,
The lovely diminutives.
          A Field of Light [1951]

I could watch! I could watch!
I saw the separateness of all things!
                    Ib.

My meat eats me. Who waits at the
    gate?
Mother of quartz, your words writhe
    into my ear.
    The Shape of the Fire [1951], 2

To follow the drops sliding from a lifted
    oar,
Head up, while the rower breathes,
  And the small boat drifts quietly
  Shoreward;
To know that light falls and fills,
      Often without our knowing.
                    Ib. 5

I remember the neckcurls, limp and
    damp as tendrils,
And her quick look a sidelong pickerel
    smile.
          Elegy for Jane [1951–1953]

I take this cadence from a man named
    Yeats;
I take it, and I give it back again.
    Four for Sir John Davies [1951–
        1953]. *I, The Dance*

Who rise from flesh to spirit know the
    fall:
The word outleaps the world, and light
    is all.   *Ib. 4*

I wake to sleep, and take my waking
    slow.
I feel my fate in what I cannot fear.
I learn by going where I have to go.
          The Waking [1953]

I knew a woman, lovely in her bones,
When small birds sighed, she would
    sigh back at them;
Ah, when she moved, she moved more
    ways than one:
The shapes a bright container can con-
    tain!   *I Knew a Woman* [1959]

I long for the imperishable quiet at the
    heart of form.
          The Longing [1964]

Old men should be explorers? [1]
I'll be an Indian.
Iroquois.   *Ib.*

Now, in this waning of light,
I rock with the motion of morning;
In the cradle of all that is,
I'm lulled into half-sleep
By the lapping of water,
Cries of the sandpiper.
Water's my will, and my way,
And the spirit runs, intermittently,
In and out of the small waves,
Runs with the intrepid shorebirds —
How graceful the small before danger!

In the first of the moon,
All's a scattering,
A shining.
          Meditation at Oyster River
                    [1964], *IV*

What I love is near at hand,
Always, in earth and air.
          The Far Field [1964], *III*

All finite things reveal infinitude.
                    Ib. IV

O what could be more nice
Than her ways with a man?
          Light Listened [1964]

She sang a final song;
Light listened when she sang.   *Ib.*

I am most immoderately married:
The Lord God has taken my heaviness
    away;
I have merged, like the bird, with the
    bright air,
And my thought flies to the place by
    the bo-tree.

[1] See T. S. Eliot, p. 1006a.

Being, not doing, is my first joy.
　　　　The Abyss [1964], V

We end in joy.
　　　　The Moment [1964], *last line*

In a dark time, the eye begins to see.
　　　　In a Dark Time [1964], st. 1

A steady storm of correspondences!
A night flowing with birds, a ragged
　　moon,
And in broad day the midnight come
　　again!　　　　*Ib.* st. 3

Was I too glib about eternal things,
An intimate of air and all its songs?
Pure aimlessness pursued and yet pur-
　　sued
And all wild longings of the insatiate
　　blood
Brought me down to my knees. O who
　　can be
Both moth and flame? The weak moth
　　blundering by.
Whom do we love? I thought I knew
　　the truth;
Of grief I died, but no one knew my
　　death.　　　　*The Sequel* [1964], I

The soul has many motions, body one.
　　　　The Motion [1964], I

Love begets love. This torment is my
　　joy.　　　　*Ib.* II

Rising or falling's all one discipline!
The line of my horizon's growing thin!
Which is the way? I cry to the dread
　　black,
The shifting shade, the cinders at my
　　back.
Which is the way? I ask, and turn to
　　go,
As a man turns to face on-coming
　　snow.　　　*The Decision* [1964], II

What's the worst portion in this mortal
　　life?
A pensive mistress, and a yelping wife.
　　　　The Marrow [1964], I

Brooding on God, I may become a
　　man.
Pain wanders through my bones like a
　　lost fire;
What burns me now? Desire, desire,
　　desire.　　　　*Ib.* II

Lord, hear me out, and hear me out
　　this day:
From me to Thee's a long and terrible
　　way.　　　　*The Marrow*, III

Yea, I have slain my will, and still I
　　live;
I would be near; I shut my eyes to see;
I bleed my bones, their marrow to be-
　　stow
Upon that God who knows what I
　　would know.　　　　*Ib.* IV

The present falls, the present falls
　　away;
How pure the motion of the rising day,
The white sea widening on a farther
　　shore.
The bird, the beating bird, extending
　　wings —
Thus I endure this last pure stretch of
　　joy,
The dire dimension of a final thing.
　　　　The Tree, the Bird [1964]

Let others probe the mystery if they
　　can.
Time-harried prisoners of *Shall* and
　　Will —
The right thing happens to the happy
　　man.

The bird flies out, the bird flies back
　　again;
The hill becomes the valley, and is still;
Let others delve that mystery if they
　　can.
　　　　The Right Thing [1964], st. 1, 2

Now I adore my life
With the Bird, the abiding Leaf,
With the Fish, the questing Snail,
And the Eye altering all;
And I dance with William Blake
For love, for Love's sake.
　　　　Once More, the Round [1964]

W I L L I A M   S A R O Y A N
1908–

The Time of Your Life.
　　　　Title of play [1939]

If you give to a thief he cannot steal from you, and he is then no longer a thief.
The Human Comedy [1943], *ch. 4*

RICHARD WRIGHT
1908–1960

Goddammit, look! We live here and they live there. We black and they white. They got things and we ain't. They do things and we can't. It's just like living in jail.   *Native Son* [1940]

Who knows when some slight shock, disturbing the delicate balance between social order and thirsty aspiration, shall send the skyscrapers in our cities toppling?   *Ib.*

JAMES AGEE
1909–1955

Now is the night one blue dew.
A Death in the Family [1957],
Knoxville: Summer 1915

Sleep, soft smiling, draws me unto her: and those receive me, who quietly treat me, as one familiar and well-beloved in that home: but will not, oh, will not, not now, not ever; but will not ever tell me who I am.   *Ib.*

DAZAI OSAMU
1909–1948

It is true, I suppose, that nobody finds it exactly pleasant to be criticized or shouted at, but I see in the face of the human being raging at me a wild animal in its true colors, one more horrible than any lion. . . . Anger makes them reveal in a flash human nature in all its horror.
No Longer Human [1958] [1]

My definition of a "respected" man was one who had succeeded almost completely in hoodwinking people, but who was finally seen through by some

[1] Translated by DONALD KEENE.

omniscient, omnipotent person who ruined him and made him suffer a shame worse than death.
No Longer Human

My unhappiness was the unhappiness of a person who could not say no.   *Ib.*

STEPHEN SPENDER
1909–

I think continually of those who were truly great —
The names of those who in their lives fought for life,
Who wore at their hearts the fire's center.
I Think Continually of Those

Born of the sun they traveled a short while towards the sun,
And left the vivid air signed with their honor.   *Ib.*

GEORGE CASPAR HOMANS
1910–

Liberty is a beloved discipline.
The Human Group [1950], *ch. 12*

DON K. PRICE
1910–

Science . . . cannot exist on the basis of a treaty of strict nonaggression with the rest of society; from either side, there is no defensible frontier.
Science and Government [1954]

ELIZABETH BISHOP
1911–

Think of the storm roaming the sky uneasily
like a dog looking for a place to sleep in,
listen to it growling.   *Little Exercise*

This iceberg cuts its facets from within.
Like jewelry from a grave
It saves itself perpetually and adorns
Only itself.
The Imaginary Iceberg
[1946], st. 3

Icebergs behoove the soul
(Both being self-made from elements
    least visible)
To see them so: fleshed, fair, erected,
    indivisible.
        The Imaginary Iceberg, st. 3

WILLIAM GOLDING
1911–

"Fancy thinking the Beast was something you could hunt and kill!" said the head. For a moment or two the forest and all the other dimly appreciated places echoed with the parody of laughter. "You knew, didn't you? I'm part of you? Close, close, close! I'm the reason why it's no go? Why things are what they are?"
        The Lord of the Flies [1954], *ch. 8*

CLARK KERR
1911–

The university has become the multiversity and the nature of the presidency has followed this change. . . . The president of the multiversity is leader, educator, wielder of power, pump; he is also officeholder, caretaker, inheritor, consensus seeker, persuader, bottleneck. But he is mostly a mediator.
        The Uses of the University [*The Godkin lectures at Harvard University, 1963*]

GEORGE BARKER
1913–

Fiend behind the fiend behind the fiend
    behind the
Fiend. Mastodon with mastery, monster
    with an ache
At the tooth of the ego, the dead
    drunk judge:
Wheresoever Thou art our agony will
    find Thee
Enthroned on the darkest altar of our
    heartbreak
Perfect. Beast, brute, bastard. O dog
    my God!
        Sacred Elegy V [1943], *iv*

My joy, my jockey, my Gabriel
Who bares his horns above my sleep
Is sleeping now.
        First Cycle of Love Poems [1947], V

ALBERT CAMUS
1913–1960

Mother died today, or maybe it was yesterday.   *L'Étranger* [1942], I

For the first time, the first, I laid my heart open to the benign indifference of the universe. To feel it so like myself, indeed, so brotherly, made me realize that I'd been happy, and that I was happy still.   *Ib.* IV

The absurd is essentially a divorce. It is in neither one nor the other of the compared elements. It is born of their confrontation.
        Le Mythe de Sisyphe [1942]

The absurd is the essential concept and the first truth.   *Ib.*

It is not rebellion itself which is noble but the demands it makes upon us.   *La Peste* [1947]

Can one be a saint if God does not exist? That is the only concrete problem I know of today.   *Ib.*

In the midst of winter, I finally learned that there was in me an invincible summer.
        Actuelles [*January 6, 1960*]

I shall tell you a great secret, my friend. Do not wait for the last judgment. It takes place every day.
        La Chute [1956]

Freedom of the press is perhaps the freedom that has suffered the most from the gradual degradation of the idea of liberty.
        Resistance, Rebellion, and Death [1] [1960]

A free press can of course be good or bad, but, most certainly, without free-

---

[1] Translated by JUSTIN O'BRIEN from selected essays in *Actuelles* [1950, 1953, 1958].

dom it will never be anything but bad.
. . . Freedom is nothing else but a
chance to be better, whereas enslavement is a certainty of the worse.

Resistance, Rebellion, and Death

NATHALIA CRANE

1913–

Oh, I'm in love with the janitor's boy,
 And the janitor's boy loves me;
He's going to hunt for a desert isle
 In our geography.

The Janitor's Boy [1924], *st. 1*

I linger on the flathouse roof, the
 moonlight is divine.
But my heart is all aflutter like the
 washing on the line.

The Flathouse Roof, st. 1

DONALD FRANCIS MASON

1913–

Sighted sub, sank same.

*Radio message to U. S. Navy
Base [January 28, 1942]*

MURIEL RUKEYSER

1913–

Fly down, Death: Call me:
I have become a lost name.

Madboy's Song, refrain

DELMORE SCHWARTZ[1]

1913–1966

Time is the school in which we learn,
Time is the fire in which we burn.

For Rhoda [1938]

That inescapable animal walks with me,
Has followed me since the black womb
 held,
Moves where I move, distorting my
 gesture,

[1] See Robert Lowell, p. 1075b.

A caricature, a swollen shadow,
A stupid clown of the spirit's motive,
Perplexes and affronts with his own
 darkness,
The secret life of belly and bone.

*The Heavy Bear Who Goes
with Me, st. 3*

KARL SHAPIRO

1913–

Haul up the flag, you mourners,
Not half-mast but all the way;
The funeral is done and disbanded;
The devil's had the final say.

Elegy for Two Banjos, st. 1 and 14

JOHN HERSEY

1914–

There was no sound of planes. The
morning was still; the place was cool
and pleasant.

Then a tremendous flash of light cut
across the sky. Mr. Tanimoto has a distinct recollection that it traveled from
east to west, from the city toward the
hills. It seemed a sheet of sun. Both he
and Mr. Matsuo reacted in terror.
. . . Under what seemed to be a local
dust cloud, the day grew darker and
darker.   *Hiroshima* [1946], *ch. 1*

There, in the tin factory, in the first
moment of the atomic age, a human
being was crushed by books.   *Ib.*

ROSS PARKER

1914–
AND

HUGHIE CHARLES

1907–

There'll always be an England
 While there's a busy street,
Wherever there's a turning wheel,
 A million marching feet.

*There'll Always Be an
England* [1939]

DYLAN THOMAS[1]
1914–1953

The force that through the green fuse
drives the flower
Drives my green age; that blasts the
roots of trees
Is my destroyer.
And I am dumb to tell the crooked rose
My youth is bent by the same wintry
fever.
*The Force That Through the
Green Fuse Drives the Flower*
[1934]

Light breaks where no sun shines;
Where no sea runs, the waters of the
heart
Push in their tides.
*Light Breaks Where No
Sun Shines* [1934]

The hand that signed the paper felled a
city;
Five sovereign fingers taxed the breath,
Doubled the globe of dead and halved a
country;
These five kings did a king to death.
*The Hand That Signed the
Paper* [1936]

When all my five and country senses
see,
The fingers will forget green thumbs
and mark
How, through the halfmoon's vegetable
eye,
Husk of young stars and handfull zo-
diac,
Love in the frost is pared and wintered
by.
*When All My Five and Country
Senses See* [1939]

And death shall have no dominion.[2]
Title and refrain of poem [1943]

After the first death there is no other.
*A Refusal to Mourn the Death,
by Fire, of a Child in London*
[1946]

---

[1] The poetry excerpts are from *Collected Poems*
[1953].
[2] See *Romans 6:9*, p. 50b, and Emily Brontë,
p. 685b.

Forgotten mornings when he walked
with his mother
Through the parables
Of sunlight
And the legend of the green chapels.
Poem in October [1946]

Now as I was young and easy under the
apple boughs
About the lilting house and happy as
the grass was green.
Fern Hill, st. 1 [1946]

And the sabbath rang slowly
In the pebbles of the holy streams.
Ib. st. 2

In the sun that is young once only,
Time let me play and be
Golden in the mercy of his means.
Ib.

And honored among foxes and pheas-
ants by the gay house
Under the new-made clouds and happy
as the heart was long,
In the sun born over and over,
I ran my heedless ways.
Ib. st. 5

Time held me green and dying
Though I sang in my chains like the
sea.   *Ib. st.* 6

Do not go gentle into that good night,
Old age should burn and rave at close
of day;
Rage, rage against the dying of the
light.
*Do Not Go Gentle into That
Good Night* [1952]

One Christmas was so much like
another, in those years around the seatown corner now and out of all sound
except the distant speaking of the voices
I sometimes hear a moment before
sleep, that I can never remember
whether it snowed for six days and six
nights when I was twelve or whether it
snowed for twelve days and twelve
nights when I was six.
Quite Early One Morning
[1954]. *A Child's Christmas in Wales*

It is spring, moonless night in the small town, starless and bible-black.
Under Milk Wood [1954]

You can tear a poem apart to see what makes it technically tick. . . . You're back with the mystery of having been moved by words. The best craftsmanship always leaves holes and gaps in the works of the poem so that something that is *not* in the poem can creep, crawl, flash, or thunder in.

The joy and function of poetry is, and was, the celebration of man, which is also the celebration of man.
Dylan Thomas's Poetic Manifesto. In the Texas Quarterly [*Winter 1961*]

HAROLD ADAMSON

Comin' in on a Wing and a Prayer.
Title of song [1943]

JEROME SEYMOUR BRUNER
1915–

The shrewd guess, the fertile hypothesis, the courageous leap to a tentative conclusion — these are the most valuable coin of the thinker at work. But in most schools guessing is heavily penalized and is associated somehow with laziness.
The Process of Education [1960]

ARTHUR MILLER
1915–

I don't say he's a great man. Willy Loman never made a lot of money. His name was never in the paper. He's not the finest character that ever lived. But he's a human being, and a terrible thing is happening to him. So attention must be paid. He's not to be allowed to fall into his grave like an old dog. Attention, attention must be finally paid to such a person.
Death of a Salesman [1949], *act I*

Willy was a salesman. And for a salesman, there is no rock bottom to the life. He don't put a bolt to a nut, he don't tell you the law or give you medicine. He's a man way out there in the blue, riding on a smile and a shoeshine. And when they start not smiling back — that's an earthquake. And then you get yourself a couple of spots on your hat, and you're finished. Nobody dast blame this man. A salesman is got to dream, boy. It comes with the territory.
Death of a Salesman, Requiem

RICHARD ROVERE
1915–

It is now of course conceded by most fair-minded and objective authorities that there is an establishment in America, a more or less closed and self-sustaining institution that holds a preponderance of power in our more or less open society.
The American Establishment [1962]

The Establishment is a general term for those people in finance, business and the professions, mostly from the Northeast, who hold the principal measure of power and influence in this country, regardless of what administration occupies the White House. *Ib.*

The Establishment has very nearly unchallenged power in deciding what is and what is not respectable opinion in this country. *Ib.*

ROBERT CONQUEST
1917–

Pure joy of knowledge rides as high as art.
The whole heart cannot keep alive on either.
Wills as of Drake and Shakespeare strike together;
Cultures turn rotten when they part.
True frontiers march with those in the mind's eye:

— The white sound rising now to fury
In efflux from the hot venturi
As Earth's close down, give us the end-
less sky.[1]
For the 1956 Opposition of Mars
[1961]

JOHN FITZGERALD KENNEDY
1917–1963

It was involuntary. They sank my
boat.
Remark when asked how he be-
came a hero. Quoted in ARTHUR
M. SCHLESINGER, JR., *A Thou-*
sand Days [1965], *ch. 4*

For without belittling the courage
with which men have died, we should
not forget those acts of courage with
which men . . . have *lived*. The courage of life is often a less dramatic spectacle than the courage of a final moment; but it is no less a magnificent
mixture of triumph and tragedy. A man
does what he must — in spite of personal consequences, in spite of obstacles
and dangers and pressures — and that is
the basis of all human morality.
Profiles in Courage [1956], *ch. 11*

It is time for a new generation of
leadership, to cope with new problems
and new opportunities. For there is a
new world to be won.
Television address [*July 4, 1960*]

The New Frontier of which I speak
is not a set of promises — it is a set of
challenges. It sums up not what I intend to offer the American people, but
what I intend to ask of them.
Speech accepting Democratic
presidential nomination [*July*
15, 1960]

Today, the eyes of all people are
truly upon us, and our governments, in
every branch, at every level, national,

[1] These lines were used in the Pacific Science
Center at the Seattle World's Fair in 1962 to
epitomize the interdependence of science and the
humanities.

state, and local, must be as a city upon
a hill,[1] constructed and inhabited by
men aware of their grave trust and their
great responsibilities.
Speech, Massachusetts State
Legislature [*January 9, 1961*]

For of those to whom much is given,
much is required.[2] And when at some
future date the high court of history sits
in judgment on each of us, recording
whether in our brief span of service we
fulfilled our responsibilities to the state,
our success or failure, in whatever office
we hold, will be measured by the answers to four questions: First, were we
truly men of courage . . . Second,
were we truly men of judgment . . .
Third, were we truly men of integrity
. . . Finally, were we truly men of dedication?   *Ib.*

We observe today not a victory of
party but a celebration of freedom,
symbolizing an end as well as a beginning, signifying renewal as well as
change.
Inaugural address [*January 20,*
1961]

Let the word go forth from this time
and place, to friend and foe alike, that
the torch has been passed to a new generation of Americans, born in this century, tempered by war, disciplined by a
hard and bitter peace, proud of our ancient heritage, and unwilling to witness
or permit the slow undoing of those
human rights to which this nation has
always been committed, and to which
we are committed today at home and
around the world.

Let every nation know, whether it
wishes us well or ill, that we shall pay
any price, bear any burden, meet any
hardship, support any friend, oppose
any foe to assure the survival and the
success of liberty.   *Ib.*

If a free society cannot help the
many who are poor, it cannot save the
few who are rich.   *Ib.*

[1] See John Winthrop, p. 318a, whom Kennedy
quoted in the preceding passage, and note.
[2] See *Luke 12:48*, p. 47a.

Let us never negotiate out of fear, but let us never fear to negotiate.

Inaugural address

All this will not be finished in the first one hundred days. Nor will it be finished in the first one thousand days, nor in the life of this Administration, nor even perhaps in our lifetime on this planet. But let us begin. *Ib.*

Now the trumpet summons us again — not as a call to bear arms, though arms we need; not as a call to battle, though embattled we are; but a call to bear the burden of a long twilight struggle,[1] year in and year out, "rejoicing in hope, patient in tribulation," a struggle against the common enemies of man: tyranny, poverty, disease and war itself. *Ib.*

The energy, the faith, the devotion which we bring to this endeavor will light our country and all who serve it, and the glow from that fire can truly light the world. *Ib.*

And so, my fellow Americans, ask not what your country can do for you; ask what you can do for your country.[2] *Ib.*

[1] See Stevenson, p. 1049a.
[2] For, stripped of the temporary associations which gave rise to it, it is now the moment when by common consent we pause to become conscious of our national life and to rejoice in it, to recall what our country has done for each of us, and to ask ourselves what we can do for our country in return. — OLIVER WENDELL HOLMES, JR. *Address Before John Sedwick Post No. 4, Grand Army of the Republic* [May 30, 1884]
 As has often been said, the youth who loves his Alma Mater will always ask, not "What can she do for me?" but "What can I do for her?" — LE BARON RUSSELL BRIGGS, *Routine and Ideals* [1904]. *College Life*
 In the great fulfillment we must have a citizenship less concerned about what the government can do for it and more anxious about what it can do for the nation. — WARREN GAMALIEL HARDING, *Republican National Convention, Chicago* [June 7, 1916]
 This thought had lain in Kennedy's mind for a long time. As far back as 1945 he had noted down in a looseleaf notebook a quotation from Rousseau: "As soon as any man says of the affairs of the state, What does it matter to

It is our task in our time and in our generation to hand down undiminished to those who come after us, as was handed down to us by those who went before, the natural wealth and beauty which is ours.

Address, dedication ceremonies of the National Wildlife Federation Building [March 3, 1961]

For in the development of this organization [the United Nations] rests the only true alternative to war, and war appeals no longer as a rational alternative. Unconditional war can no longer lead to unconditional victory. It can no longer serve to settle disputes. It can no longer be of concern to great powers alone. For a nuclear disaster, spread by winds and waters and fear, could well engulf the great and the small, the rich and the poor, the committed and the uncommitted alike. Mankind must put an end to war or war will put an end to mankind. So let us resolve that Dag Hammarskjöld did not live, or die, in vain. Let us call a truce to terror.

Address, United Nations [September 25, 1961]

However close we sometimes seem to that dark and final abyss, let no man of peace and freedom despair. For he does not stand alone. If we all can persevere, if we can in every land and office look beyond our own shores and ambitions, then surely the age will dawn in which the strong are just and the weak secure and the peace preserved. *Ib.*

Those who make peaceful revolution impossible will make violent revolution inevitable.

Address to Latin American diplomats, the White House [March 12, 1962]

No one can doubt that the wave of the future is not the conquest of the world by a single dogmatic creed but

me? the state may be given up as lost." — ARTHUR M. SCHLESINGER, JR. *A Thousand Days* [1965], *prologue, footnote*

the liberation of the diverse energies of free nations and free men.
> *Address, University of California, Berkeley [March 23, 1962]*

I think this is the most extraordinary collection of talent, of human knowledge, that has ever been gathered together at the White House, with the possible exception of when Thomas Jefferson dined alone.
> *Address, White House dinner and reception honoring Nobel Prize winners [April 1962]*

Let us not be blind to our differences — but let us also direct attention to our common interests and the means by which those differences can be resolved. And if we cannot end now our differences, at least we can help make the world safe for diversity.
> *Address, American University, Washington, D.C. [June 10, 1963]*

Every American ought to have the right to be treated as he would wish to be treated, as one would wish his children to be treated. This is not the case.
> *Television address on civil rights, after the registration of two Negroes at the University of Alabama [June 12, 1963]*

We are confronted primarily with a moral issue. It is as old as the Scriptures and is as clear as the American Constitution.   *Ib.*

No one has been barred on account of his race from fighting or dying for America — there are no "white" or "colored" signs on the foxholes or graveyards of battle.
> *Message to Congress on proposed civil rights bill [June 19, 1963]*

All free men, wherever they may live, are citizens of Berlin. And therefore, as a free man, I take pride in the words "Ich bin ein Berliner."
> *Address at City Hall, West Berlin [June 26, 1963]*

Yesterday, a shaft of light cut into the darkness. . . . For the first time, an agreement has been reached on bringing the forces of nuclear destruction under international control. . . . It offers to all the world a welcome sign of hope. . . . But the achievement of this goal is not a victory for one side; it is a victory for mankind.
> *Television address, Washington [July 26, 1963]* [1]

When power leads man toward arrogance, poetry reminds him of his limitations. When power narrows the areas of man's concern, poetry reminds him of the richness and diversity of his existence. When power corrupts,[2] poetry cleanses, for art establishes the basic human truths which must serve as the touchstone of our judgment.
> *Address, Amherst College [October 26, 1963]*

I look forward to a great future for America, a future in which our country will match its military strength with our moral restraint, its wealth with our wisdom, its power with our purpose. I look forward to an America which will not be afraid of grace and beauty, which will protect the beauty of our natural environment . . . an America which will reward achievement in the arts as we reward achievement in business and statecraft. . . . I look forward to an America which commands respect throughout the world not only for its strength but for its civilization as well. And I look forward to a world which will be safe not only for democracy and diversity but also for personal distinction.   *Ib.*

Washington is a city of southern efficiency and northern charm.
> *Remark quoted in* ARTHUR M. SCHLESINGER, JR., A *Thousand Days* [1965], *ch.* 25

[1] In Moscow on July 25 Averell Harriman, Lord Hailsham, and Chairman Khrushchev initialed the nuclear test ban treaty.
[2] See Lord Acton, p. 750a.

ROBERT TRAILL SPENCE LOWELL
1917–1977

I will catch Christ with a greased
worm.
> *The Drunken Fisherman*
> *[1946], st. 5*

I saw the spiders marching through air,
Swimming from tree to tree that mil-
    dewed day
  In latter August when the hay
  Came creaking to the barn.[1]
> *Mr. Edwards and the Spider*
> *[1946], st. 1*

On Windsor Marsh, I saw the spider
    die
When thrown into the bowels of fierce
    fire:
  There's no long struggle, no desire
  To get up on its feet and fly —
  It stretches out its feet
And dies. This is the sinner's last re-
    treat;
Yes, and no strength exerted on the
    heat
Then sinews the abolished will, when
    sick
And full of burning, it will whistle on a
    brick.   *Ib. st. 4*

This is the Black Widow, death.
> *Ib. st. 5*

Christ walks on the black water. In
    Black Mud
Darts the kingfisher. On Corpus Christi,
    heart,
Over the drum-beat of St. Stephen's
    choir
I hear him, *Stupor Mundi*, and the
    mud
Flies from his hunching wings and
    beak — my heart,
The blue kingfisher dives on you in fire.
> *Colloquy in Black Rock*
> *[1946], st. 5*

[1] Jonathan Edwards [1703–1758], the Calvin-
ist theologian, wrote at the age of twelve a series
of scientific observations on the spider. One of
his most famous sermons was "Sinners in the
Hands of an Angry God."

Our Lady of Babylon, go by, go by,
I was once the apple of your eye;
Flies, flies are on the plane tree, on the
    streets.
> *As a Plane Tree by the Water*
> *[1946], st. 1*

I saw the sky descending, black and
    white,
Not blue, on Boston.
> *Where the Rainbow Ends*
> *[1946], st. 1*

Now Paris, our black classic, breaking
    up
like killer kings on an Etruscan cup.
> *Beyond the Alps [1959]*

Your *Good Soldier*
the best French novel in the language.[1]
> *Ford Madox Ford [1959]*

O divorced, divorced
from the whale-fat of postwar London!
    Boomed,
cut, plucked and booted! In Provence,
    New York . . .
marrying, blowing . . . nearly dying
at Boulder, when the altitude
pressed the world on your heart.   *Ib.*

Fiction! I'm selling short
your lies that made the great your
    equals. Ford,
you were a kind man and you died in
    want.   *Ib.*

There is no God and Mary is His
    Mother.
> *For George Santayana [1959]*

You said:
"We poets in our youth begin in sad-
    ness;
thereof in the end come despondency
    and madness." [2]
> *To Delmore Schwartz (Cam-*
> *bridge 1946) [1959]*

Who asks for me, the Shelley of my
    age,
must lay his heart out for my bed and
    board.
> *Words for Hart Crane [1959]*

[1] See Ford Madox Ford, p. 915a.
[2] See Wordsworth, pp. 511b–512a.

I doodle handlebar
moustaches on the last Russian Czar.
　　　　　　Grandparents [1959]

We are old-timers,
each of us holds a locked razor.
　　　　　Waking in the Blue [1959]

I keep no rank nor station.
Cured, I am frizzled, stale and small.
　　　　　Home After Three Months
　　　　　　　　　　Away [1959]

Only teaching on Tuesdays, bookworm-
　　ing
in pajamas fresh from the washer each
　　morning,
I hog a whole house on Boston's
"hardly passionate Marlborough
　　Street." [1]
　　　　　Memories of West Street and
　　　　　　　　　　Lepke [1959]

These are the tranquillized *Fifties*,
and I am forty. Ought I to regret my
　　seedtime?
I was a fire-breathing Catholic C.O.,
and made my manic statement,
telling off the state and president, and
　　then
sat waiting sentence in the bull pen
beside a Negro boy with curlicues
of marijuana in his hair.　　　　*Ib.*

Flabby, bald, lobotomized,
he drifted in a sheepish calm,
where no agonizing reappraisal
jarred his concentration on the electric
　　chair —
hanging like an oasis in his air
of lost connections.　　　　　　*Ib.*

Tamed by *Miltown*, we lie on Mother's
　　bed.　　　*Man and Wife* [1959]

　　Oh my *Petite*,
clearest of all God's creatures, still all
　　air and nerve.　　　　　　　*Ib.*

your old-fashioned tirade —
loving, rapid, merciless —
breaks like the Atlantic Ocean on my
　　head.　　　　　　　　　　*Ib.*

　　[1] The quotation is from Henry James.

Gored by the climacteric of his want,
he stalls above me like an elephant.
　　　"To Speak of Woe That Is in
　　　　　　　　Marriage" [1959]

My mind's not right.

A car radio bleats,
"Love, O careless Love. . . ." I hear
my ill-spirit sob in each blood cell,
as if my hand were at its throat. . . .
I myself am hell; [1]
nobody's here.
　　　　　Skunk Hour [1959], st. 5, 6

My old flame, my wife!
Remember our lists of birds?
　　　　　The Old Flame [1964], st. 1

Father, forgive me
my injuries,
as I forgive
those I
have injured!

You never climbed
Mount Sion, yet left
dinosaur
death-steps on the crust,
where I must walk.
　　　　　Middle Age [1964], st. 3, 4

We are like a lot of wild
spiders crying together,
but without tears.
　　　　　Fall 1961 [1964], st. 4

I am tired. Everyone's tired of my
　　turmoil.
　　　　　Eye and Tooth [1964], st. 9

Two months after marching through
　　Boston,
half the regiment was dead;
at the dedication,
William James could almost hear the
　　bronze Negroes [2] breathe.

　　[1] See Virgil, p. 119a; and Marlowe, p. 213a,
and note.
　　[2] On the Saint-Gaudens monument to Colonel
Robert Gould Shaw and the 54th Massachusetts
Regiment.
　　There on foot go the dark outcasts, so true
to nature that one can almost hear them breathing as they march. — WILLIAM JAMES, *Oration
at Dedication of the Monument* [*May 31, 1897*]
　　See Charles W. Eliot, p. 752a, and Moody,
p. 899a.

Their monument sticks like a fishbone
in the city's throat.
Its Colonel is as lean
as a compass needle.

He has an angry wrenlike vigilance,
a greyhound's gentle tautness;
he seems to wince at pleasure,
and suffocate for privacy.
> *For the Union Dead*
> *[1964], st. 7–9*

on Boylston Street, a commercial
photograph
shows Hiroshima boiling.   *Ib. st. 14*

When I crouch to my television set,
the drained faces of Negro school children rise like balloons. *Ib. st. 15*

The Aquarium is gone. Everywhere,
giant finned cars nose forward like fish;
a savage servility
slides by on grease.   *Ib. st. 17*

We beg delinquents for our life.
> *Central Park. In the New York*
> *Review [October 1965]*

ARTHUR MEIER SCHLESINGER, JR.
1917–

Above all he [John F. Kennedy]
gave the world for an imperishable moment the vision of a leader who greatly
understood the terror and the hope, the
diversity and the possibility, of life on
this planet and who made people look
beyond nation and race to the future of
humanity.
> *A Thousand Days* [1] *[1965], ch. 37*

HARLAN CLEVELAND
1918–

The Revolution of Rising Expectations. [2]
> *Title of speech, Colgate*
> *University [1949]*

[1] See John F. Kennedy, p. 1073a-b, and 1074b.
[2] Almost fifteen years ago, when I was working for Paul Hoffman in the Marshall Plan, I had to substitute for him in making a speech at Col-

EDWIN O'CONNOR
1918–1968

The Last Hurrah.
> *Title of novel [1956]*

STEWART LEE UDALL
1920–

The most common trait of all primitive peoples is a reverence for the life-
giving earth, and the native American
shared this elemental ethic: the land
was alive to his loving touch, and he, its
son, was brother to all creatures. His
feelings were made visible in medicine
bundles and dance rhythms for rain,
and all of his religious rites and land
attitudes savored the inseparable world
of nature and God, the master of Life.
During the long Indian tenure the land
remained undefiled save for scars no
deeper than the scratches of cornfield
clearings or the farming canals of the
Hohokams on the Arizona desert.
> *The Quiet Crisis* [1] *[1963], ch. 1*

A land ethic for tomorrow should be
as honest as Thoreau's *Walden,* and as
comprehensive as the sensitive science
of ecology. It should stress the oneness
of our resources and the live-and-help-
live logic of the great chain of life. If,
in our haste to "progress," the economics of ecology are disregarded by citizens and policy makers alike, the result
will be an ugly America.   *Ib. 14*

gate University. Remembering Edmund Burke's famous commentary on the turbulence of his time, I called this speech "Reflections on the Revolution of Rising Expectations." The phrase has since been attributed to nearly every literate American of our time, but I think this was the first time that phrase saw the light of day. — HARLAN CLEVELAND, *The Evolution of Rising Responsibility, address before the U.N. [December 13, 1964]*
[1] The race between education and erosion, between wisdom and waste has not run its course. . . . The nation's battle to preserve the common estate is far from won. . . . The crisis may be quiet, but it is urgent. — JOHN F. KENNEDY, *introduction to The Quiet Crisis*

JEROME DAVID SALINGER

1919–

I keep picturing all these little kids in this big field of rye. . . . If they're running and they don't look where they're going I have to come out from somewhere and catch them. That's all I'd do all day. I'd just be the catcher in the rye and all. I know it's crazy.
The Catcher in the Rye [1951]

There isn't anyone *any*where that isn't Seymour's Fat Lady. Don't you know that? Don't you know that goddam secret yet? And don't you know — listen to me, now — *don't you know who that Fat Lady really is?* . . . Ah, buddy. It's Christ Himself. Christ Himself, buddy.
Franny and Zooey [1961]

MAY SWENSON

1919–

Body my house
my horse my hound
what will I do
when you are fallen   *Question* [1963]

Where can I go
without my mount
all eager and quick
How will I know
in thicket ahead
is danger or treasure
when Body my good
bright dog is dead   *Ib.*

SLOAN WILSON

1920–

The Man in the Gray Flannel Suit.
Title of novel [1955]

RICHARD PURDY WILBUR

1921–

We respect
Some scholars' stutters.
Grace [1947], *st.* 5

The beautiful changes as a forest is
changed
By a chameleon's tuning his skin to it.
The Beautiful Changes
[1947], *st.* 2

I dreamt the past was never past
redeeming:
But whether this was false or honest
dreaming
I beg death's pardon now. And mourn
the dead.
The Pardon [1950], *last stanza*

We milk the cow of the world, and as
we do
We whisper in her ear, "You are not
true."   *Epistemology* [1950], II

I never knew the road
From which the whole earth didn't call
away,
With wild birds rounding the hill
crowns,
Haling out of the heart an old dismay.
The Sirens [1950], *st.* 1

He rocked his only world, and everyone's.
Forgive the hero, you who would have
died
Gladly with all you knew; he rode that
tide
To Ararat: all men are Noah's sons.
Still, Citizen Sparrow [1950],
last stanza

Ho-hum. I am for wit and wakefulness,
And love this feigning lady by Bazille.
What's lightly hid is deepest under-
stood,
And when with social smile and formal
dress
She teaches leaves to curtsy and qua-
drille,
I think there are most tigers in the
wood.   *Ceremony* [1950], *st.* 3

The eyes open to a cry of pulleys,
And spirited from sleep, the astounded
soul
Hangs for a moment bodiless and simple.
as false dawn.

Outside the open window
The morning air is all awash with
angels.
Love Calls Us to the Things of
This World [1956]

The soul shrinks
From all that it is about to remember,
From the punctual rape of every blessèd
day,
And cries,
"Oh, let there be nothing on earth
but laundry,
Nothing but rosy hands in the rising
steam
And clear dances done in the sight of
heaven. *Ib.*

Neither pale nor bright,
The turkey-cock parades
Through radiant squalors, darkly auspi-
cious as
The ace of spades,

Himself his own cortège
And puffed with the pomp of death,
Rehearsing over and over with strangled
râle
His latest breath.
A Black November Turkey
[1956], *st. 3, 4*

Mind in its purest play is like some bat
That beats about in caverns all alone,
Contriving by a kind of senseless wit
Not to conclude against a wall of stone.

It has no need to falter or explore;
Darkly it knows what obstacles are
there,
And so may weave and flitter, dip and
soar
In perfect courses through the blackest
air.

And has this simile a like perfection?
The mind is like a bat. Precisely. Save
That in the very happiest intellection
A graceful error may correct the cave.
Mind [1956]

Dear God, let it be with these donkeys
that I come,
And let it be that angels lead us in
peace

To leafy streams where cherries tremble
in air,
Sleek as the laughing flesh of girls; and
there
In that haven of souls let it be that,
leaning above
Your divine waters, I shall resemble
these donkeys,
Whose humble and sweet poverty will
appear
Clear in the clearness of your eternal
love.
Francis Jammes: A Prayer to Go
to Paradise with the Donkeys
[1956]

The werewolf's painful change. Turning his head away
On the sweaty bolster, he tries to remember
The mood of manhood,

But lies at last, as always,
Letting it happen, the fierce fur soft
to his face,
Hearing with sharper ears.
Beasts [1956], *st. 3, 4*

What is our praise or pride
But to imagine excellence, and try to
make it?
What does it say over the door of
Heaven
But *homo fecit?*
For the New Railway Station in
Rome [1956], *last stanza*

When you come, as you soon must, to
the streets of our city,
Mad-eyed from stating the obvious,
Not proclaiming our fall but begging
us
In God's name to have self-pity,

Spare us all word of the weapons, their
force and range,
The long numbers that rocket the
mind;
Our slow, unreckoning hearts will be
left behind,
Unable to fear what is too strange.

Nor shall you scare us with talk of the
death of the race.

How should we dream of this place
  without us? —
The sun mere fire, the leaves untroubled about us,
A stone look on the stone's face?
    Advice to a Prophet [1961], *st. 3*

Ask us, prophet, how we shall call
Our natures forth when that live
  tongue is all
Dispelled, that glass obscured or broken

In which we have said the rose of our
  love and the clean
Horse of our courage, in which beheld
The singing locust of the soul un-
  shelled,
And all we mean or wish to mean.
    Ib. st. 7, 8

Duke, keep your coin. All men are born
  distraught,
And will not for the world be satisfied.
Whether we live in fact, or but in
  thought,
We die of thirst, here at the fountainside.
    *Ballade for the Duke of Or-
    léans* [1] [1961], *who offered a
    prize at Blois* [c. 1457] *for the
    best ballade employing the line
    "Je meurs de soif auprès de la
    fontaine."*

All bitter things conduce to sweet,
  As this example shows;
Without the little spirochete
We'd have no chocolate to eat,
Nor would tobacco's fragrance greet
  The European nose.
    *Pangloss's Song: A Comic
    Opera Lyric* [1961]

What can I do but move
From folly to defeat,
And call that sorrow sweet
That teaches us to see
The final face of love
In what we cannot be?
    Someone Talking to Himself
    [1961], *last stanza*

[1] See Charles d'Orléans, p. 170b.

WILLIAM H. MAULDIN
1921–

I feel like a fugitive from th' law of
averages.
    Up Front [1944]. *Caption
    for cartoon*

Look at an infantryman's eyes and
you can tell how much war he has seen.
    Ib.

He's right, Joe, when we ain't fightin' we should ack like sojers.   *Ib.*

JACK KEROUAC
1922–1969

The beat generation.   *Remark*

But then they danced down the
street like dingledodies, and I shambled
after as I've been doing all my life after
people who interest me, because the
only people for me are the mad ones,
the ones who are mad to live, mad to
talk, mad to be saved, desirous of everything at the same time, the ones who
never yawn or say a commonplace
thing, but burn, burn, burn like fabulous yellow roman candles exploding
like spiders across the stars and in the
middle you see the blue centerlight pop
and everybody goes "Awww!"
    On the Road [1957]

PHILIP LARKIN
1922–

Only one ship is seeking us, a black-
Sailed unfamiliar, towing at her back
A huge and birdless silence. In her wake
No waters breed or break.
    Next, Please [1955]

JAMES DICKEY
1923–

All families lie together, though some
  are burned alive.
The others try to feel
For them. Some can, it is often said.
    The Firebombing [1965]

There,
In the other wood,

The uncornered animal's, running off
Upon instinct. Sails spread, fox wings
Lift him alive over gullies,
Hair tips all over him lightly

Touched with the moon's red silver,
  Back-hearing around
The stream of his body the tongue of
  hounds
  Feather him. In his own animal sun
Made of human moonlight,

He flies like a bolt running home.
                    Fox Blood [1965]

JAMES BALDWIN
1924–

[The Negro past] of rope, fire, torture, castration, infanticide, rape; death
and humiliation; fear by day and night,
fear as deep as the marrow of the bone;
doubt that he was worthy of life, since
everyone around him denied it; sorrow
for his women, for his kinfolk, for his
children, who needed his protection,
and whom he could not protect; rage,
hatred and murder, hatred for white
men so deep that it often turned
against him and his own, and made all
love, all trust, all joy impossible.
          The Fire Next Time [1963] [1]

TRUMAN CAPOTE
1924–

Other Voices, Other Rooms.
                    Title of book [1948]

I didn't want to harm the man. I
thought he was a very nice gentleman.
Soft-spoken. I thought so right up to
the moment I cut his throat.
                    In Cold Blood [1966]

[1] Originally published in *The New Yorker* as
Letter from a Region of My Mind [November
1962]
  See Anonymous, Spiritual, p. 1101a.

MISHIMA YUKIO
1925–1970

My solitude grew more and more
obese, like a pig.
    Temple of the Golden Pavilion [1]
                                [1959]
The first real problem I faced in my
life was that of beauty.   *Ib.*

What made her ugly was — hope.
Incurable hope, like an obstinate case
of scabies, which lodges, damp and red-
dish, in the infected skin, producing a
constant itching, and refusing to yield
to any outer force.   *Ib.*

ALLEN GINSBERG
1926–

I saw the best minds of my generation
    destroyed by madness, starving
    hysterical naked,
dragging themselves through the negro
    streets at dawn looking for an
    angry fix
angelheaded hipsters burning for the
    ancient heavenly connection to the
    starry dynamo in the machinery of
    night.   *Howl* [1956]

WILLIAM D. SNODGRASS
1926–

It was the nature of the thing:
No moon outlives its leaving night,
No sun its day. And I went on
Rich in the loss of all I sing
To the threshold of waking light,
To larksong and the live, gray dawn.
So night by night, my life has gone.
                    Orpheus [1959]

Pale soul, consumed by fear
of the living world you haunt,
have you learned what habits lead you
to hunt what you do not want;
learned who does not need you;
learned you are no one here?
                    Home Town [1959]

Though trees turn bare and girls turn
    wives,

[1] Translated by IVAN MORRIS.

We shall afford our costly seasons;
There is a gentleness survives
That will outspeak and has its reasons.
There is a loveliness exists,
Preserves us, not for specialists.

April Inventory [*1959*]

MICHAEL HARRINGTON
1928–

The millions who are poor in the
United States tend to become increasingly invisible. . . . It takes an effort
of the intellect and will even to see
them.

*The Other America: Poverty in
the United States* [*1962*], *ch. 1*

The other America, the America of
poverty, is hidden today in a way that it
never was before. Its millions are socially invisible to the rest of us. . . .
The very development of American society is creating a new kind of blindness
about poverty. The poor are increasingly slipping out of the very experience
and consciousness of the nation.   *Ib.*

That the poor are invisible is one of
the most important things about them.
They are not simply neglected . . .
they are not seen.   *Ib.*

For the urban poor the police are
those who arrest you. In almost any
slum there is a vast conspiracy against
the forces of law and order.   *Ib.*

ANNE SEXTON
1928–

You, Doctor Martin, walk
from breakfast to madness. Late August,
I speed through the antiseptic tunnel
    where the moving dead still talk
of pushing their bones against the
    thrust
of cure. And I am queen of this sum-
    mer hotel
    or the laughing bee on a stalk
    of death.

You, Doctor Martin [*1960*], *st. 1*

And we are magic talking to itself,
noisy and alone. I am queen of all my
sins

forgotten. Am I still lost?
Once I was beautiful. Now I am my-
    self,
counting this row and that row of
    moccasins
    waiting on the silent shelf.

You, Doctor Martin, last stanza

MARTIN LUTHER KING, JR.
1929–1968

Injustice anywhere is a threat to justice everywhere.

*Letter from the Birmingham
jail. In the Atlantic Monthly*
[*August 1963*]

Unearned suffering is redemptive. *Ib.*

Nonviolence is the answer to the cru-
cial political and moral questions of our
time; the need for man to overcome
oppression and violence without resort-
ing to oppression and violence.
Man must evolve for all human conflict a method which rejects revenge,
aggression and retaliation. The foundation of such a method is love.[1]

Speech accepting Nobel Peace Prize
[*December 11, 1964*]

The tortuous road which has led
from Montgomery to Oslo is a road
over which millions of Negroes are
traveling to find a new sense of dignity.
It will, I am convinced, be widened into
a superhighway of justice.   *Ib.*

I accept this award with an abiding
faith in America and an audacious faith
in the future of mankind. I refuse to
accept the idea that the "isness" of
man's present nature makes him morally incapable of reaching up for the
"oughtness" that forever confronts
him.   *Ib.*

I refuse to accept the cynical notion
that nation after nation must spiral
down a militaristic stairway into the
hell of nuclear destruction. I believe
that unarmed truth and unconditional
love will have the final word in reality.
    Ib.

[1] See Gandhi, p. 897a.

Nonviolent action, the Negro saw, was the way to supplement, not replace, the process of change. It was the way to divest himself of passivity without arraying himself in vindictive force.
Why We Can't Wait [1964]

The Negro was willing to risk martyrdom in order to move and stir the social conscience of his community and the nation . . . he would force his oppressor to commit his brutality openly, with the rest of the world looking on . . . Nonviolent resistance paralyzed and confused the power structures against which it was directed.
Ib.

YEVGENY ALEXANDROVICH YEVTUSHENKO
1933–

There is no Jewish blood in my veins,
But I am hated with a scabby hatred
By all the anti-Semites,
    like a Jew.
And therefore
    I am a true Russian.
Babi Yar [1961]

ANDREI VOZNESENSKY
1933–

I am Goya
of the bare field, by the enemy's beak gouged
till the craters of my eyes gape
I am grief

I am the tongue
of war, the embers of cities

on the snows of the year 1941
I am hunger
    I Am Goya [1] [1960], *st. 1, 2*

The urge to kill, like the urge to beget,
Is blind and sinister. Its craving is set
Today on the flesh of a hare: tomorrow
    it can
Howl the same way for the flesh of a
    man.
    Hunting a Hare [2] [1964], *st. 5*

Does each cell have a soul within it?
If so, fling open all your little doors,
And all your souls shall flutter like the
    linnet
In the cages of my pores.
    Dead Still [3] [1965], *st. 4*

    I am myself
Among the avalanches, like the Abominable
Snowman, absolutely elusive.
    Who Are We? [4] [1959], *st. 7*

Along a parabola life like a rocket flies,
Mainly in darkness, now and then on a
    rainbow.
    Parabolic Ballad [5] [1960]

Worms come through holes and bold
    men on parabolas.   *Ib.*

[1] A good example of his use of assonance: *Ya Goya . . . nagoye . . . ya gore . . . ya golos . . . goda . . . ya golod . . . ya gorlo . . . goloi.* — P. BLAKE and M. HAYWARD, eds., *Antiworlds: Poetry by Andrei Voznesensky* [1966]
  Translated by STANLEY KUNITZ.
[2] Translated by W. H. AUDEN.
[3] Translated by RICHARD WILBUR.
[4] Translated by STANLEY MOSS.
[5] Translated by W. H. AUDEN.

ANONYMOUS [1]

ANONYMOUS
1250–1700

Sumer is icumen in,
  Lhude sing cuccu!
Groweth sed, and bloweth med,
  And springth the wude nu —
Sing cuccu! [2]   *Cuckoo Song* [c. 1250]

[1] See also p. 149.
[2] See Vogelweide, p. 156a, and Pound, p. 987b-988a.

Ich am of Irlonde
Ant of the holy lande
  Of Irlonde.
Gode sire, pray ich the,
For of saynte charite,
Come ant dance wyth me
  In Irlonde.
    Ich Am of Irlonde

When Adam delved and Eve span
Who was then a gentleman?
> Text used by JOHN BALL *for his*
> *speech at Blackheath to the men*
> *in Wat Tyler's Rebellion* [1381]

I sing of a maiden
   That is makeless;
King of all kings
   To her son she ches.
> Carol. *I Sing of a Maiden* [15th
>   century]

For in my mind, of all mankind
I love but you alone.
> *The Nut-Brown Maid* [15th
>   century], *refrain*

For I must to the greenwood go,
Alone, a banished man.   *Ib.*

No burial this pretty pair
   Of any man receives,
Till Robin Redbreast piously
   Did cover them with leaves.
> *The Children in the Wood,*
>   st. 16

A fool's paradise.
> *Paston Letters* [1462], *no.* 457

Everyman, I will go with thee, and be
   thy guide,
In thy most need to go by thy side.
> *Everyman* [*before* 1500], *act I,*
>   *l.* 522

O Western wind, when wilt thou blow,
   That the small rain down can rain?
Christ, that my love were in my arms
   And I in my bed again!   [*c.* 1530]

Why fearest thou thy outward foe,
   When thou thyself thy harm dost
      feed?
Of grief, or hurt, of pain, or woe,
   Within each thing is sown the seed.
> From TOTTEL'S MISCELLANY,
>   *Songs and Sonnets* [1557]

Crabbed age and youth cannot live together.
Youth is full of pleasance, age is full of
   care.
> *The Passionate Pilgrim* [1] [1599]

---

[1] Often attributed to Shakespeare.

Love me little, love me long,
Is the burden of my song.[1]
> *Love Me Little* [1569–1570],
>   *refrain*

Multiplication is vexation,
Division is as bad;
The rule of three doth puzzle me,
And practice drives me mad.
> *Elizabethan MS* [1570]

Greensleeves was all my joy,
   Greensleeves was my delight;
Greensleeves was my heart of gold,
   And who but Lady Greensleeves.

Alas, my Love! ye do me wrong
   To cast me off discourteously:
And I have loved you so long,
   Delighting in your company.
> From *A Handful of Pleasant*
> *Delights* [1584], *refrain and st.* 1

Shall I bid her go? What, and if I do?
Shall I bid her go, and spare not?
O no, no, no, I dare not.[2]
> *Corydon's Farewell to Phillis,*
>   st. 2

Where griping griefs the heart would
   wound
And doleful dumps the mind oppress,
There music with her silver sound
With speed is wont to send redress.[3]
> *A Song to the Lute in Musicke,*
>   st. 1

The blinded boy that shoots so trim,[4]
From heaven down did hie.
> *King Cophetua and the Beggar*
>   *Maid, st.* 2

It was a friar of orders gray [5]
Walked forth to tell his beads.
> *The Friar of Orders Gray,*[6] *st.* 1

---

[1] See Shakespeare, *Romeo and Juliet* II, vi,
14, p. 224b and Herrick, p. 320a.
[2] Paraphrased by Shakespeare in *Twelfth-
Night* [1598–1600], *act II, sc. iii.*
[3] Another version is used by Shakespeare in
Romeo and Juliet [1594–1595], *act IV, sc. v.*
[4] See Shakespeare, *Romeo and Juliet* II, i, 13,
p. 223b.
[5] See Shakespeare, *The Taming of the Shrew*
IV, i, 148, p. 219b.
[6] THOMAS PERCY [1728–1811] composed this
ballad from various fragments of ancient
ballads found in Shakespeare's plays. It appeared

Our joys as wingèd dreams do fly;
  Why then should sorrow last?
Since grief but aggravates thy loss,
  Grieve not for what is past.
    The Friar of Orders Gray, st. 13

King Stephen was a worthy peer,
His breeches cost him but a crown.
    Take Thy Old Cloak About
             Thee,[1] st. 7

It's pride that puts this country down;
Man, take thine old cloak about thee.
                 Ib.

A fool and his money are soon parted.
    Saying current since the 16th
                 century

April is in my mistress' face,
And July in her eyes hath place,
Within her bosom is September,
But in her heart a cold December.
    From THOMAS MORLEY, *Madri-*
    gals to Four Voices . . . the
    First Book [1594]

Lo here a new Aurora!
    From THOMAS MORLEY, *The*
    First Book of Canzonets
    [1595]

Kill then, and bliss me,
But first come kiss me.
    From THOMAS MORLEY, *The*
    First Book of Ballets [1595]

Shoot, false Love, I care not.
Spend thy shafts and spare not.   *Ib.*

I was more true to Love than Love to
  me.
    From JOHN DOWLAND, *The*
    First Book of Songs or Airs
    [1597]

Thulé, the period of cosmography,
  Doth vaunt of Hecla, whose sulphur-
  eous fire
Doth melt the frozen clime and thaw
  the sky;
  Trinacrian Aetna's flames ascend not
  higher.

in his *Reliques of Ancient English Poetry*
[1765].
[1] Quoted in Shakespeare, *Othello II, iii, 93.*

These things seem wondrous, yet more
  wondrous I,
Whose heart with fear doth freeze, with
  love doth fry.
    From THOMAS WEELKES, *Mad-*
    rigals of Six Parts [1600]

Jerusalem, my happy home,
When shall I come to thee?
When shall my sorrows have an end?
Thy joys when shall I see?
    The Song of Mary [1601]

What poor astronomers are they
Take women's eyes for stars!
    From JOHN DOWLAND, *The*
    Third and Last Book of Songs
    or Airs [1603]

O what a plague is love! How shall I
  bear it?
She will inconstant prove, I greatly fear
  it.
     Phillida Flouts Me, st. 1

And let all women strive to be
As constant as Penelope.
    Constant Penelope, st. 18

Fain would I change that note
To which fond Love hath charmed me.
    From TOBIAS HUME, *Musical*
            Humors [1605]

Turn again Whittington,
Lord Mayor of London.[1]
    Refrain of Bow Bells heard by
    Dick Whittington [c. 1605]

O metaphysical tobacco,
Fetched as far as from Morocco,
  Thy searching fume
  Exhales the rheum,
O metaphysical tobacco.[2]
    From MICHAEL EAST, *The*
    Second Set of Madrigals
    [1606]

From the hag and hungry goblin
That into rags would rend ye,
And the spirit that stands by the naked
  man
In the book of Moons defend ye!
    Tom o' Bedlam [17th century],
                  st. 1

[1] Richard Whittington, son of a London
mercer, rose to be mayor of London three times
before his death in 1423.
[2] See Byron, p. 563a, and note.

With an host of furious fancies
Whereof I am commander,
With a burning spear, and a horse of
    air,
To the wilderness I wander.
By a knight of ghosts and shadows
I summoned am to tourney
Ten leagues beyond the wide world's
    end.
Methinks it is no journey.
                        Tom o' Bedlam, st. 8

There is a lady sweet and kind,
Was never face so pleased my mind;
I did but see her passing by,
And yet I love her till I die.
        From THOMAS FORD, *Music of
            Sundry Kinds* [1607], *st. 1*

Cupid is wingèd and doth range,
Her country so my love doth change;
But change she earth, or change she sky,
Yet will I love her till I die.   *Ib. st. 6*

Four arms, two necks, one wreathing;
Two pairs of lips, one breathing;
Two hearts that multiply
Sighs interchangeably.
        From THOMAS WEELKES, *Airs
            or Fantastic Spirits* [1608]

Love not me for comely grace,
For my pleasing eye or face,
Nor for any outward part,
No, nor for a constant heart.
        From JOHN WILBYE, *Second Set
            of Madrigals* [1608]

The silver swan, who living had no note,
When death approached unlocked her
    silent throat;
Leaning her breast against the reedy
    shore,
Thus sung her first and last, and sung
    no more:
Farewell, all joys; O death, come close
    mine eyes;
More geese than swans now live, more
    fools than wise.
        From ORLANDO GIBBONS, *The
            First Set of Madrigals and Mo-
            tets* [1612], *I*

Laïs now old, that erst attempting lass,
To goddess Venus consecrates her glass;
For she herself hath now no use of one,

No dimpled cheeks hath she to gaze
    upon.
She cannot see her springtime damask
    grace,
Nor dare she look upon her winter face.[1]
        From ORLANDO GIBBONS, *The
            First Set of Madrigals and Mo-
            tets, XIII*

Stay, O sweet, and do not rise!
The light that shines comes from thine
    eyes;
The day breaks not: it is my heart,
Because that you and I must part.
    Stay, or else my joys will die,
    And perish in their infancy.[2]
        JOHN DOWLAND, *A Pilgrim's
            Solace* [1612]

If there is a paradise on the face of the
    earth,
It is this, oh! it is this, oh! it is this.[3]
        *Mogul Inscription in the Red
            Fort at Delhi* [1640]

And when with envy Time, transported,
Shall think to rob us of our joys,
You'll in your girls again be courted,
And I'll go wooing in my boys.
                        Winifreda, st. 8

But in vain she did conjure him
To depart her presence so;
Having a thousand tongues to allure
    him,
And but one to bid him go.
                        Dulcina,[4] *st. 2*

Over the mountains and over the waves,
Under the fountains and under the
    graves;
Under floods that are deepest, which
    Neptune obey,
Over rocks that are steepest, Love will
    find out the way.
        Love Will Find Out the Way, st. 1

Begone, dull Care! I prithee begone
    from me!

[1] Imitated from the Greek of Plato, *The
Greek Anthology.*
See Prior, p. 388a.
[2] Attributed also to John Donne, and included
in a variant in the seventh edition of his poems
[1669].
[3] The translation is from Persian in Murray's
Guide to India.
[4] This song is mentioned by IZAAK WALTON
in *The Compleat Angler* [1653]. It has been
ascribed to Raleigh, on very doubtful authority.

Begone, dull Care! Thou and I shall
    never agree.
        From JOHN PLAYFORD, *Musical
            Companion* [1687]

Though little, I'll work as hard as a
    Turk,
If you'll give me employ,
To plow and sow, and reap and mow,
And be a farmer's boy.
        *The Farmer's Boy [before
            1689], st. 2*

Carriages without horses shall go,
And accidents fill the world with woe.
        *Prophecy attributed to Mother
            Shipton* [1] [*17th century*]

Around the world thoughts shall fly
In the twinkling of an eye.   *Ib.*

Under water men shall walk,
Shall ride, shall sleep, and talk;
In the air men shall be seen
In white, in black, and in green.   *Ib.*

Iron in the water shall float
As easy as a wooden boat.   *Ib.*

A swarm of bees in May
Is worth a load of hay;
A swarm of bees in June
Is worth a silver spoon;
A swarm of bees in July
Is not worth a fly.
        Old English saying

    When poverty comes in at the door,
loves flies out the window.
        *Saying current since the 17th
            century*

Please to remember the fifth of No-
    vember,
Gunpowder treason and plot.
        *Guy Fawkes's Rhyme, tradi-
            tional in England since the
            17th century*

BALLADS

The king sits in Dunfermline town
Drinking the blude-red wine.
        Sir Patrick Spens, st. 1

[1] Most of the prophecies attributed to Mother
Shipton — a witch and prophetess, according to
tradition, who lived in Yorkshire in Tudor
times — are fabrications of the seventeenth century and later.

To Noroway, to Noroway,
To Noroway o'er the faem;
The king's daughter o' Noroway,
'Tis thou must bring her hame.

The first word that Sir Patrick read
So loud, loud laughed he;
The neist word that Sir Patrick read
The tear blinded his e'e.   *Ib. st. 4, 5*

I saw the new moon late yestreen
Wi' the auld moon in her arm;
And if we gang to sea, master,
I fear we'll come to harm.   *Ib. st. 10*

O laith, laith were our gude Scots lords
To wet their cork-heel'd shoon;
But lang or a' the play was play'd
They wat their hats aboon.
        Ib. st. 15

Half owre, half owre to Aberdour,
'Tis fifty fathoms deep;
And there lies gude Sir Patrick Spens,
Wi' the Scots lords at his feet!
        Ib. st. 19

"And what will ye leave to your ain
    mither dear,
Edward, Edward?"
        Edward, Edward, st. 7

"The curse of hell frae me sall ye bear,
Sic counsels ye give to me, O!"   *Ib.*

Fight on, my merry men all;
For why, my life is at an end.[1]
        Chevy Chase

A fairer lady there never was seen
Than the blind beggar's daughter of
    Bethnal Green.
        *The Beggar's Daughter of Beth-
            nal Green,*[2] *st. 33*

When captains courageous, whom
    death could not daunt,

[1] Says Johnnie, "Fight on, my merry men all,
    I'm a little wounded, but I am not slain;
    I will lay me down for to bleed a while,
    Then I'll rise and fight with you again."
        *Johnnie Armstrong's Last Goodnight,
        st. 18; from* DRYDEN'S *Miscellanies*
        [1702]
[2] This very house was built by the blind
beggar of Bednall Green, so much talked of
and sung in ballads. — SAMUEL PEPYS, *Diary*
[June 26, 1663]

Did march to the siege of the city of
    Gaunt,
They mustered their soldiers by two and
    by three,
And the foremost in battle was Mary
    Ambree.   *Mary Ambree,*[1] *st.* 1

Then let Jane Shore with sorrow sing,
That was belovèd of a king.
                   Jane Shore, st. 1

"I'll rest," said he, "but thou shalt
    walk";
So doth this wandering Jew
From place to place, but cannot rest
    For seeing countries new.
            The Wandering Jew, st. 9

For thirty pence our Savior was sold [2]
Among the false Jews, as I have been
    told;
And twenty-nine is the worth of thee,
For I think thou art one penny worser
    than he.
        King John and the Abbot of
               Canterbury, st. 21

Glasgerion swore a full great oath,
By oak, and ash and thorn.[3]
              Glasgerion, st. 19

In Scarlet town, where I was born,
There was a fair maid dwellin',
Made every youth cry Well-a-way!
Her name was Barbara Allen.

All in the merry month of May,
When green buds they were swellin',
Young Jemmy Grove on his deathbed
    lay,
For love of Barbara Allen.
       Barbara Allen's Cruelty, st. 1, 2

So slowly, slowly rase she up,
And slowly she came nigh him,
And when she drew the curtain by —
"Young man, I think you're dyin'."
                      Ib. st. 4

True Thomas lay on Huntlie Bank;
A ferlie he spied wi' his e'e;

---

[1] BEN JONSON calls any virago Mary Ambree,
and JOHN FLETCHER alludes to Mary Ambree
in *The Scornful Lady* [1616].
[2] See George Herbert, p. 322b.
[3] See Kipling, p. 876b.

And there he saw a lady bright
Come riding down by the Eildon Tree.
           Thomas the Rhymer, st. 1

"A bed, a bed," Clerk Saunders said,
"A bed for you and me!"
"Fye na, fye na," said may Margaret,
"Till anes we married be!"
              Clerk Saunders, st. 2

There were twa sisters sat in a bour;
    Binnorie, O Binnorie!
There came a knight to be their wooer,
    By the bonnie milldams o' Binnorie.
                 Binnorie, st. 1

There were three ravens sat on a tree,
They were as black as they might be.

The one of them said to his make,
"Where shall we our breakfast take?"
          The Three Ravens, st. 1, 2

Down there came a fallow doe
As great with young as she might go.
                     Ib. st. 6

She buried him before the prime,
She was dead herself ere evensong time.

God send every gentleman
Such hounds, such hawks, and such a
    leman.   *Ib. st.* 9, 10

Mony a one for him maks mane,
But nane sall ken where he is gane:
O'er his white banes, when they are
    bare,
The wind sall blaw for evermair.
              The Twa Corbies, st. 5

Ye Highlands and ye Lawlands,
O where hae ye been?
They hae slain the Earl of Murray,
And hae laid him on the green.
        The Bonny Earl of Murray, st. 1

O waly, waly, up the bank,
And waly, waly, doun the brae,
And waly, waly, yon burnside,
Where I and my Love wont to gae!
                 Waly, Waly, st. 1

O waly, waly, gin love be bonnie,
A little time while it is new!
But when 'tis auld it waxeth cauld,
And fades awa' like morning dew.
                     Ib. st. 2

But had I wist, before I kist,
That love had been sae ill to win,
I had lock'd my heart in a case o' gowd,
And pinn'd it wi' a siller pin.
Waly, Waly, st. 5

"What gat ye to your dinner, Lord
Randal, my son?
What gat ye to your dinner, my hand-
some young man?"
"I gat eels boil'd in broo'; mother, make
my bed soon,
For I'm weary wi' hunting, and fain
wald lie down." *Lord Randal*

A ship I have got in the North Country
And she goes by the name of the
"Golden Vanity,"
O, I fear she will be taken by a Spanish
Gal-la-lee,
As she sails by the Lowlands low.
The Golden Vanity, st. 1

THE NEW ENGLAND
PRIMER[1]

In Adam's fall
We sinned all.

My Book and Heart
Must never part.

Young Obadias,
David, Josias —
All were pious.

Peter denied
His Lord, and cried.

Young Timothy
Learnt sin to fly.

Xerxes did die,
And so must I.

Zaccheus he
Did climb the tree
Our Lord to see.

Our days begin with trouble here,
Our life is but a span,[2]

[1] As early as 1691, Benjamin Harris of Boston
advertised the forthcoming second impression of
the *New England Primer*. The oldest known
copy extant is dated 1737.
[2] See Bacon, p. 209b-210a.

And cruel death is always near,
So frail a thing is man.

Now I lay me down to sleep,[1]
I pray the Lord my soul to keep;
If I should die before I wake,
I pray the Lord my soul to take.

ANONYMOUS
18th century

Sabina has a thousand charms
To captivate my heart;
Her lovely eyes are Cupid's arms,
And every look a dart:
But when the beauteous idiot speaks,
She cures me of my pain;
Her tongue the servile fetters breaks
And frees her slave again.
From Amphion Anglicus [1700]

Who will change old lamps for new?
The Arabian Nights [European
Version, c. 1700], *The History
of Aladdin*

Open sesame!
Ib. The History of Ali Baba

Drive a coach and six through an Act
of Parliament.
*Credited to Sir Stephen Rice
[1637–1715], Chief Baron of
the Exchequer, by* MACAULAY *in
History of England* [1849–1861],
ch. 12

The Campbells are comin', oho, oho.
Song [c. 1715]

For without money, George,
A man is but a beast:
But bringing money, thou shalt be
Always my welcome guest.
George Barnwell,[2] *II, st. 25*

[1] The first record of this prayer is found in
the *Enchiridion Leonis* [A.D. 1160]. The early
editions of the *Primer* give the first line of the
prayer as: "Now I lay me down to take my
sleep." The familiar version of the line appeared in the edition of 1784. In the edition of
1814 the second line reads, "I pray thee, Lord,
my soul to keep."
[2] Inspired by GEORGE LILLO's play, *The London Merchant; or, The History of George
Barnwell*, first acted in 1731.

The Girl I Left Behind Me.
                    Title of song [1759]

The united voice of all His Majesty's
free and loyal subjects in America
— liberty and property, and no stamps.
        Motto of various American co-
        lonial newspapers [1765–1766]

Yankee Doodle came to town
    Upon a little pony,
He stuck a feather in his hat
And called it macaroni.

Yankee Doodle, keep it up,
    Yankee Doodle dandy,
Mind the music and the step,
    And with the girls be handy.
        Yankee Doodle,[1] *st. 1, chorus*

It's all in the day's work.
        Current since the 18th century

Man may work from sun to sun,
But woman's work is never done.
                        Old saying

Count that day lost whose low descend-
    ing sun
Views from thy hand no worthy action
    done.[2]   *Old saying*

In good king Charles's golden days,
When loyalty no harm meant;
A furious High-Churchman I was,
    And so I gain'd preferment.
Unto my flock I daily preach'd,
Kings are by God appointed,

---

[1] This version was sufficiently popular in America in 1767 to be used in the ballad opera *The
Disappointment; or, The Force of Credulity*
by ANDREW BARTON.
        Father and I went up to camp,
            Along with Captain Goodwin;
        And there we saw the men and boys,
            As thick as hasty pudding.
                Yankee doodle do.
                Version used by ROYALL TYLER,
                    in The Contrast [1790]
The origin of *Yankee Doodle* remains as
mysterious as ever, unless it be deemed a positive result to have eliminated definitely every
theory thus far advanced. — OSCAR GEORGE
THEODORE SONNECK, *Report on the Star-Spangled Banner, Hail Columbia, America, Yankee
Doodle* [1909]
[2] An earlier version (signed by JAMES BOBART,
December 8, 1697) begins "Think" rather than
"Count."

And damned are those who dare resist,
Or touch the Lord's Anointed.
And this is law, I will maintain,
Unto my dying day, sir,
That whatsoever king shall reign,
I will be the Vicar of Bray, sir!
        The Vicar of Bray [1734],
                st. 1 and chorus

Don't tread on me.
        Motto of the first official Amer-
        ican flag; first raised by Lieuten-
        ant John Paul Jones in Commo-
        dore Esek Hopkins's flagship
        Alfred [*December 3, 1775*]

Rebellion to tyrants is obedience to
God.[1]
        Motto on Thomas Jefferson's
                seal [*c. 1776*]

Lost is our old simplicity of times,
The world abounds with laws, and
    teems with crimes.
        On the Proceedings Against
                America,[2] *st. 1*

Our cargoes of meat, drink, and clothes
    beat the Dutch.
        Siege of Boston [1775]

There is nothing new except what is
forgotten.
        Attributed to Mademoiselle
        Bertin, milliner to Marie An-
        toinette [*c. 1785*]

O Paddy dear, an' did ye hear the news
    that's goin' round?
The shamrock is by law forbid to grow
    on Irish ground!
No more St. Patrick's Day we'll keep,
    his color can't be seen,
For there's a cruel law agin the wearin'
    o' the Green!
        The Wearing o' the Green; or,
                The Shan-von-Voght

---

[1] The motto of one, I believe, of the regi-
cides of Charles I. — *Letter from Jefferson to
Edward Everett* [February 24, 1823]
Jefferson's reference probably is to John Brad-
shaw [1602–1659].
[2] In the *Pennsylvania Gazette* [February 8,
1775], "from a late London Magazine."

For they're hangin' men an' women
there for wearin' o' the Green.
The Wearing o' the Green; or,
The Shan-von-Voght

JUNIUS[1]

One precedent creates another. They
soon accumulate and constitute law.
What yesterday was fact, today is doctrine.
The Letters of Junius [1769–
1771]. *Dedication to the Eng-*
lish Nation

The liberty of the press is the palla-
dium of all the civil, political, and religious rights of an Englishman.   *Ib.*

These are the gloomy companions of
a disturbed imagination; the melancholy madness of poetry, without the
inspiration.
Ib. 7, to Sir William Draper
[*March 3, 1769*]

There are some hereditary strokes of
character by which a family may be as
clearly distinguished as by the blackest
features of the human face.
Ib. 12, to the Duke of Grafton
[*May 30, 1769*]

I believe there is yet a spirit of resistance in this country, which will not
submit to be oppressed; but I am sure
there is a fund of good sense in this
country, which cannot be deceived.
Ib. 16, to the Printer of the
Public Advertiser (*H. S.*
Woodfall) [*July 19, 1769*]

We owe it to our ancestors to preserve entire those rights, which they
have delivered to our care: we owe it to
our posterity, not to suffer their dearest
inheritance to be destroyed.
Ib. 20, to the Printer of the
Public Advertiser [*August 8,*
1769]

When the constitution is openly invaded, when the first original right of
the people, from which all laws derive
their authority, is directly attacked, inferior grievances naturally lose their
force, and are suffered to pass by without punishment or observation.
The Letters of Junius. 30, to
the Printer of the Public Adver-
tiser [*October 17, 1769*]

There is a moment of difficulty and
danger at which flattery and falsehood
can no longer deceive, and simplicity
itself can no longer be misled.
Ib. 35,[1] to the Printer of the
Public Advertiser [*December 19,*
1769]

They [the Americans] equally detest
the pageantry of a king, and the super-
cilious hypocrisy of a bishop.[2]   *Ib.*

There is a holy mistaken zeal in politics as well as in religion. By persuading
others, we convince ourselves.   *Ib.*

The least considerable man among us
has an interest equal to the proudest
nobleman, in the laws and constitution
of his country, and is equally called
upon to make a generous contribution
in support of them — whether it be the
heart to conceive, the understanding to
direct, or the hand to execute.[3]
Ib. 37, to the Printer of the
Public Advertiser [*March 19,*
1770]

We lament the mistakes of a good
man, and do not begin to detest him
until he affects to renounce his principles.
Ib. 41, to Lord Mansfield [*No-*
vember 14, 1770]

The injustice done to an individual is
sometimes of service to the public.

---

[1] Pseudonym of the author of a series of letters
in the London *Public Advertiser* 1769–1771 published in book form in 1772. They have been
attributed to, among others, Sir Philip Francis,
Lord Shelburne, Lord George Sackville, and
Lord Temple.

[1] This letter is of great significance in the
history of freedom of the press. The publisher
was prosecuted for seditious libel, and the jury
brought in a verdict of "guilty of printing and
publishing only." After a second trial, Woodfall
was freed on payment of costs.
[2] See Rufus Choate, p. 591a.
[3] See Gibbon, p. 466a.

Facts are apt to alarm us more than the most dangerous principles.

The Letters of Junius,
41, to Lord Mansfield

An honest man, like the true religion, appeals to the understanding, or modestly confides in the internal evidence of his conscience. The impostor employs force instead of argument, imposes silence where he cannot convince, and propagates his character by the sword.

Ib.

If individuals have no virtues, their vices may be of use to us.

Ib. 59, to the Printer of the
Public Advertiser [October 5,
1771]

The temple of fame is the shortest passage to riches and preferment.

Ib.

NURSERY RHYMES[1]

A man of words and not of deeds
Is like a garden full of weeds.

A Man of Words and Not of
Deeds

It's like a lion at the door;
And when the door begins to crack,
It's like a stick across your back;
And when your back begins to smart,
It's like a penknife in your heart;
And when your heart begins to bleed,
You're dead, and dead, and dead, indeed.   *Ib.*

Cock a doodle doo!
My dame has lost her shoe;
My master's lost his fiddle stick,
And knows not what to do.

Cock a Doodle Doo

[1] The rhymes of Mother Goose originated with *Mother Goose Tales* as *Contes de ma mère l'Oye* [1697] by CHARLES PERRAULT [1628–1703]. The *Tales* were first translated in 1729, the rhymes as *Mother Goose's Melody* in 1781 by ROBERT SAMBER, and published in London by John Newbery [1713–1767], who originated the publication of children's books. There are many other collections and versions of the rhymes, like *Gammer Gurton's Garland* [1784], which also included older rhymes of English origin.

Three blind mice, see how they run!
They all ran after the farmer's wife,
She cut off their tails with a carving-knife,
Did you ever see such a sight in your life,
As three blind mice?

Three Blind Mice

A frog he would a-wooing go.
Sing heigh-ho says Rowley.

A Frog He Would A-Wooing Go

With a rowley powley gammon and spinach,
Heigh-ho says Anthony Rowley.

Ib. chorus

Old King Cole
Was a merry old soul,
And a merry old soul was he,
He called for his pipe,
And he called for his bowl,
And he called for his fiddlers three.

Old King Cole

The King of France went up the hill
With forty thousand men;
The King of France came down the hill
And ne'er went up again.

The King of France

Jack Sprat could eat no fat,
His wife could eat no lean;
And so betwixt them both,
They licked the platter clean.

Jack Sprat

Rain, rain, go away,
Come again another day.

Rain, Rain

Pat-a-cake, pat-a-cake, baker's man,
Bake me a cake as fast as you can;
Pat it and prick it, and mark it with B,
Put it in the oven for baby and me.

Pat-a-Cake

The lion and the unicorn
Were fighting for the crown;
The lion beat the unicorn
All round about the town.
Some gave them white bread,
And some gave them brown;

Some gave them plum cake,
And sent them out of town.
          The Lion and the Unicorn

Little Jack Horner sat in the corner,
Eating a Christmas pie.
He put in his thumb, and pulled out a
    plum,
And said, "What a good boy am I!"
          Little Jack Horner

London Bridge is broken down,
My fair lady.   *London Bridge*

Tell tale tit,
Your tongue shall be slit,
And all the dogs in our town
Shall have a bit.
          Tell Tale Tit

As I was going to St. Ives,
I met a man with seven wives,
Each wife had seven sacks,
Each sack had seven cats,
Each cat had seven kits:
Kits, cats, sacks, and wives,
How many were there going to St. Ives?
          As I Was Going to St. Ives

The man in the wilderness asked of me
How many strawberries grew in the
    sea.
I answered him as I thought good,
"As many as red herrings grow in the
    wood."
          The Man in the Wilderness

Ladybug, ladybug, fly away home,
Your house is on fire, and your children
    will burn.   *Ladybug, Ladybug*

Hickory dickory dock,
The mouse ran up the clock,
The clock struck one,
The mouse ran down;
Hickory dickory dock.
          Hickory Dickory Dock

Baa, baa, black sheep,
Have you any wool?
Yes, sir, yes, sir,
Three bags full:
One for my master,
And one for my dame,
And one for the little boy
Who lives down the lane.
          Baa, Baa, Black Sheep

Mary, Mary, quite contrary,
How does your garden grow?
With silver bells, and cockleshells,
And pretty maids all in a row.
          Mary, Mary, Quite Contrary

Oranges and lemons,
Say the bells of St. Clement's.
When will you pay me?
Say the bells of Old Bailey.
When I grow rich,
Say the bells of Shoreditch.
          Oranges and Lemons

Here comes a candle to light you to
    bed,
Here comes a chopper to chop off your
    head.   *Ib.*

"Who killed Cock Robin?"
"I," said the sparrow,
"With my bow and arrow,
I killed Cock Robin." [1]
          Who Killed Cock Robin?

"Who saw him die?"
"I," said the fly,
"With my little eye,
I saw him die."   *Ib.*

This little pig went to market;
This little pig stayed home;
This little pig had roast beef;
This little pig had none;
And this little pig cried, Wee, wee,
    wee!
All the way home.   *This Little Pig*

Little boy blue, come blow your horn,
The sheep's in the meadow, the cow's
    in the corn;
But where is the boy who looks after
    the sheep?
He's under the haystack fast asleep.
Will you wake him? No, not I,
For if I do, he'll be sure to cry.
          Little Boy Blue

Simple Simon met a pieman
Going to the fair:
Says Simple Simon to the pieman,
"Let me taste your ware."
          Simple Simon

Ding dong bell,
The cat is in the well.
    [1] See Byron, p. 562b.

Who put her in?
Little Johnny Green.
                    Plato's Song

Little Tom Tucker
Sings for his supper;
What shall he eat?
White bread and butter.
How will he cut it
Without e'er a knife?
How will he be married
Without e'er a wife?
                    Little Tom Tucker

Crosspatch, draw the latch,
Set by the fire and spin:
Take a cup and drink it up,
Then call your neighbors in.
                    Cross Patch

High diddle diddle
The cat and the fiddle,
The cow jumped over the moon;
The little dog laughed
To see such craft
And the dish ran away with the spoon.
                    High Diddle Diddle

Three wise men of Gotham
Went to sea in a bowl:
And if the bowl had been stronger,
My song had been longer.
                    Three Wise Men of Gotham

Jack and Jill went up the hill
To fetch a pail of water;
Jack fell down and broke his crown,
And Jill came tumbling after.
                    Jack and Jill

Seesaw, Margery Daw,
Jacky shall have a new master;
Jacky must have but a penny a day,
Because he can work no faster.
                    Seesaw, Margery Daw

Taffy was a Welshman, Taffy was a
    thief;
Taffy came to my house and stole a
    piece of beef.
I went to Taffy's house, Taffy wasn't in;
Taffy came to my house and stole a
    marrowbone.
                    Taffy Was a Welshman

The Queen of Hearts
She made some tarts,

All on a summer's day;
The Knave of Hearts
He stole the tarts,
And took them clean away.
                    The Queen of Hearts

Bye baby bunting,
Daddy's gone a-hunting,
Gone to get a rabbit skin
To wrap the baby bunting in.
                    Bye Baby Bunting

Come, let's to bed,
Says Sleepyhead;
Tarry awhile, says Slow;
Put on the pot,
Says Greedy-gut,
We'll sup before we go.
                    Let's to Bed

Four and twenty tailors went to kill a
    snail,
The best man among them durst not
    touch her tail.
She put out her horns like a little Kyloe
    cow,
Run, tailors, run, or she'll kill you all
    e'en now.
                    Four and Twenty Tailors

Goosey goosey gander,
Whither shall I wander?
Upstairs and downstairs,
And in my lady's chamber;
There I met an old man who wouldn't
    say his prayers;
I took him by the left leg
And threw him down the stairs.
                    Goosey Goosey Gander

Sing a song of sixpence,
A pocket full of rye,
Four and twenty blackbirds,
Baked in a pie;
When the pie was opened,
The birds began to sing;
Wasn't that a dainty dish
To set before a king?

The king was in his countinghouse
    Counting out his money;
The queen was in the parlor
    Eating bread and honey;
The maid was in the garden
    Hanging out the clothes,

Along came a blackbird,
  And snipped off her nose.
                    Sing a Song of Sixpence

There was an old woman who lived in a
    shoe,
She had so many children she didn't
    know what to do;
She gave them some broth without any
    bread,
She whipped them all soundly and put
    them to bed.
                    There Was an Old Woman

Ride a cockhorse to Banbury Cross,
To see a fine lady upon a white horse;
Rings on her fingers and bells on her
    toes,
She shall have music wherever she goes.
                    Ride a Cockhorse

Tom, Tom, the piper's son,
He learned to play when he was young.
But all the tune that he could play
Was "Over the hills and far away." [1]
                    Tom, Tom, the Piper's Son

Tom, Tom, the piper's son,
Stole a pig, and away he run;
The pig was eat, and Tom was beat,
And Tom went howling down the
    street.   *Ib.*

"Where are you going to, my pretty
    maid?"
"I'm going a-milking, sir," she said.
            *Where Are You Going To, My
                              Pretty Maid?*

"My face is my fortune, sir," she said.
                                        Ib.

"Nobody asked you, sir," she said.
                                        Ib.

One a penny, two a penny, hot cross
    buns;
If you have no daughters, give them to
    your sons.   *Hot Cross Buns*

Pease-porridge hot, pease-porridge cold,
Pease-porridge in the pot, nine days old.
                    Pease-Porridge Hot

Curlylocks, Curlylocks,
Wilt thou be mine?
Thou shalt not wash dishes

[1] See D'Urfey, p. 384a, and Gay, p. 401b.

Nor yet feed the swine,
But sit on a cushion
And sew a fine seam,
And feed upon strawberries,
Sugar and cream.   *Curlylocks*

I had a little nut tree, nothing would it
    bear
But a silver nutmeg and a golden pear;
The king of Spain's daughter came to
    visit me,
And all for the sake of my little nut
    tree.   *I Had a Little Nut Tree*

Humpty Dumpty sat on a wall,
Humpty Dumpty had a great fall;
All the king's horses
And all the king's men
Couldn't put Humpty Dumpty to-
    gether again.   *Humpty Dumpty*

Little Bo-peep has lost her sheep,
And cannot tell where to find them;
Leave them alone, and they'll come
    home,
And bring their tails behind them.
                    Little Bo-peep

Little Polly Flinders
Sat among the cinders,
Warming her pretty little toes.
Her mother came and caught her,
And whipped her little daughter
For spoiling her nice new clothes.
                    Little Polly Flinders

There was an old woman tossed in a
    blanket,
Seventeen times as high as the moon;
But where she was going no mortal
    could tell,
For under her arm she carried a broom.
Old woman, old woman, old woman,
    said I,
Whither, ah whither, ah whither so
    high?
To sweep the cobwebs from the sky,
And I'll be with you by and by.
                    There Was an Old Woman

The north wind doth blow,
And we shall have snow,
And what will poor robin do then,
    Poor thing?
He'll sit in a barn,
To keep himself warm,

And hide his head under his wing,
Poor thing!
The North Wind Doth Blow

Old mother Hubbard
Went to the cupboard,
To fetch her poor dog a bone;
But when she came there
The cupboard was bare,
And so the poor dog had none.
Old Mother Hubbard

Pussy cat, pussy cat, where have you
been?
I've been to London to look at the
queen.
Pussy cat, pussy cat, what did you
there?
I frightened a little mouse under the
chair. *Pussy Cat*

Peter Piper picked a peck of pickled
peppers;
A peck of pickled peppers Peter Piper
picked.
If Peter Piper picked a peck of pickled
peppers,
Where's the peck of pickled peppers
Peter Piper picked?
Peter Piper

Monday's child is fair of face,
Tuesday's child is full of grace,
Wednesday's child is full of woe,
Thursday's child has far to go,
Friday's child is loving and giving,
Saturday's child has to work for its liv-
ing,
But a child that's born on the Sabbath
day
Is fair and wise and good and gay.
Monday's Child Is Fair of Face

Solomon Grundy,
Born on a Monday,
Christened on Tuesday,
Married on Wednesday,
Took ill on Thursday,
Worse on Friday,
Died on Saturday,
Buried on Sunday:
This is the end
Of Solomon Grundy.
Solomon Grundy

What are little boys made of?
Snips and snails, and puppy dogs' tails;
That's what little boys are made of.
What Are Little Boys Made Of?

What are little girls made of?
Sugar and spice, and everything nice;
That's what little girls are made of.
Ib.

Hickety pickety, my black hen,
She lays eggs for gentlemen.
Gentlemen come every day
To see what my black hen doth lay.
Hickety Pickety

Little Miss Muffet
Sat on a tuffet,
Eating some curds and whey.
Along came a spider,
And sat down beside her,
And frightened Miss Muffet away.
Little Miss Muffet

Peter, Peter Pumpkin-Eater,
Had a wife and couldn't keep her.
He put her in a pumpkin shell,
And there he kept her very well.
Peter, Peter Pumpkin-Eater

Jack, be nimble,
Jack, be quick,
Jack, jump over the candlestick.
Jack Be Nimble

There was a crooked man, and he went
a crooked mile,
He found a crooked sixpence against a
crooked stile;
He bought a crooked cat, which caught
a crooked mouse,
And they all lived together in a little
crooked house.
There Was a Crooked Man

Diddle diddle dumpling, my son John,
He went to bed with his stockings on;
One shoe off, one shoe on;
Diddle diddle dumpling, my son John.
Diddle Diddle Dumpling

Rub-a-dub-dub,
Three men in a tub,
And who do you think they be?
The butcher, the baker,

The candlestick-maker;
Turn 'em out, knaves all three!
Rub-a-Dub-Dub

I saw three ships come sailing by,
Come sailing by, come sailing by,
I saw three ships come sailing by,
On New Year's Day in the morning.
I Saw Three Ships

In fir tar is,
In oak none is.
In mud eel is,
In clay none is.
Goats eat ivy.
Mares eat oats. *In Fir Tar Is*

Lucy Locket lost her pocket,
Kitty Fisher found it;
There was not a penny in it,
But a ribbon round it. *Lucy Locket*

There were three jolly huntsmen,
As I have heard them say,
And they would go a-hunting
Upon St. David's Day.
*There Were Three Jolly
Huntsmen*

All day they hunted,
And nothing did they find,
But a ship a-sailing,
A-sailing with the wind. *Ib.*

O do you know the muffin man,
The muffin man, the muffin man,
O do you know the muffin man,
That lives in Drury Lane?
The Muffin Man

To market, to market, to buy a fat pig,
Home again, home again, jiggety-jig.
To Market, To Market

Doctor Foster went to Gloucester
In a shower of rain;
He stepped in a puddle, up to his middle,
And never went there again.
Doctor Foster

There was an old woman
Lived under a hill;
And if she's not gone,
She lives there still.
There Was an Old Woman

There was a little man, and he had a
little gun,
And his bullets were made of lead, lead,
lead;
He went to the brook, and saw a little
duck,
And shot it through the head, head,
head.
There Was a Little Man

Lavender's blue, dilly dilly, lavender's
green;
When I am king, dilly dilly, you shall
be queen. *Lavender's Blue*

A dillar, a dollar,
A ten o'clock scholar,
What makes you come so soon?
You used to come at ten o'clock,
And now you come at noon.
A Dillar, a Dollar

I had a little pony,
His name was Dapple Gray;
I lent him to a lady
To ride a mile away.
She whipped him, she slashed him,
She rode him through the mire;
I would not lend my pony now
For all the lady's hire.
I Had a Little Pony

Polly, put the kettle on,
Polly, put the kettle on,
Polly, put the kettle on,
We'll all have tea.

Sukey, take it off again,
Sukey, take it off again,
Sukey, take it off again,
They've all gone away.
Polly, Put the Kettle On

Little Tommy Tittlemouse
Lived in a little house;
He caught fishes
In other men's ditches.
Little Tommy Tittlemouse

The farmer in the dell, the farmer in
the dell,
Heigho! the derry oh, the farmer in the
dell. *The Farmer in the Dell*

Hark! Hark! The dogs do bark,
The beggars are coming to town;

Some in rags, some in tags,
And some in velvet gowns.
                                    Hark! Hark!

Ten little Indians standing in a line —
One went home, and then there were
    nine.   *Ten Little Indians*

When good King Arthur ruled this
    land,
He was a goodly king,
He bought three pecks of barley meal,
To make a bag pudding.
                                    Good King Arthur

One misty, moisty morning,
When cloudy was the weather,
I chanced to meet an old man
Clothed all in leather;
He began to compliment,
And I began to grin —
"How do you do?" and "How do you
    do?"
And "How do you do?" again!
                        One Misty, Moisty Morning

Bobby Shaftoe's gone to sea,
Silver buckles on his knee;
He'll come back and marry me,
Pretty Bobby Shaftoe.

Bobby Shaftoe's fat and fair,
Combing down his yellow hair;
He's my love forevermore,
Pretty Bobby Shaftoe.
                                    Bobby Shaftoe

Fe fi fo fum!
I smell the blood of an Englishman;
Be he alive or be he dead,
I'll grind his bones to make my bread.
                                    Fe Fi Fo Fum

Sing, sing! What shall I sing?
The cat's run away with the pudding-
    bag string.
                        Sing, Sing! What Shall I Sing?

Shoe the horse, shoe the mare,
But let the little colt go bare.
                                    Shoe the Horse

There was a man in our town,
And he was wondrous wise;
He jumped into a bramble bush
And scratched out both his eyes.
                        There Was a Man in Our Town

There were two blackbirds,
Sitting on a hill,
The one named Jack,
The other named Jill;
Fly away, Jack! Fly away, Jill!
Come again, Jack! Come again, Jill!
                                    Two Blackbirds

This is the farmer sowing the corn,
That kept the cock that crowed in the
    morn,
That waked the priest all shaven and
    shorn,
That married the man all tattered and
    torn,
That kissed the maiden all forlorn,
That milked the cow with the crumpled
    horn,
That tossed the dog
That worried the cat
That killed the rat
That ate the malt
That lay in the house that Jack built.
                        The House That Jack Built

ANONYMOUS
1800–

Christmas is coming, the geese are get-
    ting fat,
Please to put a penny in the old man's
    hat;
If you haven't got a penny, a ha'penny
    will do,
If you haven't got a ha'penny, God
    bless you!   *Beggar's rhyme*

From ghoulies and ghosties and long-
    leggety beasties
And things that go bump in the night,
    Good Lord, deliver us!
                                    Scottish prayer

Rest and be thankful.
        *Inscription on stone seat in the
        Scottish Highlands, and title of
        one of Wordsworth's poems*

The wisdom of many and the wit of
one.   *Definition of a proverb* [1]

_____
[1] Probably based on the definition of a proverb
which Lord John Russell gave one morning at
breakfast at Mardock's: "One man's wit, and all
men's wisdom." — *Memoirs of Sir James Mack-
intosh* [1765–1832], *vol. I, p. 473*

Sister Anne, do you see any one coming?

> *The anxious cry of Fatima, one of the wives of Bluebeard*

The woods are full of them.

> *Quoted by* ALEXANDER WILSON, *American Ornithology* [1808], *preface*

The cunning seldom gain their ends;
The wise are never without friends.

> *The Fox and the Hen, moral. From* JOHN PIERPONT, *Young Reader* [1843]

Oh, ye'll tak' the high road an' I'll tak' the low road,
An' I'll be in Scotland before ye;
But I and my true love will never meet again,
On the bonnie, bonnie banks o' Loch Lomond.

> *Loch Lomond, refrain*

Went out to milk and I didn't know how,
I milked the goat instead of the cow;
A monkey sittin' on a pile of straw
A-winkin' at his mother-in-law.
Turkey in the straw, turkey in the hay,
Roll 'em up and twist 'em up a high tuckahaw,
And hit 'em up a tune called Turkey in the Straw.

> *Turkey in the Straw,[1] st. 1 and refrain*

Sugar in the gourd and honey in the horn,
I never was so happy since the hour I was born. *Ib. st. 6*

God rest you merry, gentlemen,
Let nothing you dismay;
Remember Christ our Savior,
Was born on Christmas Day.   *Carol*

The holly and the ivy,
When they are both full grown,
Of all the trees that are in the wood,
The holly bears the crown:

[1] The classical American rural tune . . . steps around like an apple-faced farmhand . . . as American as Andrew Jackson, Johnny Appleseed, and Corn on the Cob. — CARL SANDBURG, *The American Songbag* [1927]

The rising of the sun
And the running of the deer,
The playing of the merry organ,
Sweet singing in the choir.

> *Carol. The Holly and the Ivy, st. 1 and refrain*

With drums and guns, and guns and drums
The enemy nearly slew ye.
My darling dear, you look so queer,
Oh, Johnny, I hardly knew ye.

> *Irish folk song, st. 1*

Where are the legs with which you run,
When you went to carry a gun?
Indeed your dancing days are done —
Oh, Johnny, I hardly knew ye.

> *Ib. st. 3*

The press lives by disclosures.

> *The London Times* [1851]

Women and children first.

> *The Birkenhead Drill*[1] [*February 26, 1852*]

Up and down the City Road,
In and out the Eagle,
That's the way the money goes —
Pop goes the weasel!

> *Pop Goes the Weasel*[2] [*c. 1853*]

It is a newspaper's duty to print the news and raise hell.

> *The Chicago Times* [1861]

Free soil, free men, free speech, Frémont.[3]

> *Republican party rallying cry* [1856]

Dirty work at the crossroads.

> *Attributed*[4] *to* WALTER MELVILLE'S *melodrama The Girl Who Took the Wrong Turning; or, No Wedding Bells for Him*

[1] The women and children were the first to be removed from the sinking ship *Birkenhead*.
[2] The weasel was a hatter's tool, and "pop" was a term meaning to pawn or "hock." The Eagle was a music hall in the City Road. The song is attributed to W. R. MANDALE.
[3] John Charles Frémont [1813–1890] was the party's candidate for President.
[4] In *Notes and Queries* (London).

The goose hangs high.[1]
Common saying

All I want of you is a little seevility, and that of the commonest goddamnedest kind.[2]
*The New Bedford Classic, as re-
ported in* ZEPHANIAH W. PEASE,
The History of New Bedford
[1918]. *Supposed to be said by
the mate of a whaler to his ill-
humored captain*

You-all means a race or section,
Family, party, tribe, or clan;
You-all means the whole connection
Of the individual man.
*You-All; from The Richmond
Times-Dispatch*

Some talk of Alexander, and some of
Hercules;
Of Hector, and Lysander, and such
great names as these;
But of all the world's brave heroes,
there's none that can compare
With a tow, row, row, row, row, row
for the British Grenadier.
The British Grenadiers

From the halls of Montezuma,
To the shores of Tripoli,
We fight our country's battles
On the land as on the sea.
U.S. Marines' Song, st. 1

There is a tavern in the town,
And there my true love sits him down,
And drinks his wine with laughter and
with glee,
And never, never thinks of me.
*There Is a Tavern in the Town,
st. 1*

Adieu, adieu, kind friends, adieu, adieu,
adieu,
I can no longer stay with you.

I'll hang my harp on a weeping willow-
tree,[1]
And may the world go well with thee.
*There Is a Tavern in the
Town, refrain*

I belong to that highly respectable tribe
Which is known as the Shabby Gen-
teel . . .
Too proud to beg, too honest to steal.
*The Shabby Genteel; sung by
Sol Smith Russell* [1848–1901]
in A Poor Relation

The sons of the prophet are brave men
and bold,
And quite unaccustomed to fear,
But the bravest by far in the ranks of
the Shah
Was Abdullah Bulbul Amir.
Abdullah Bulbul Amir, st. 1

Now the heroes were plenty and well
known to fame
In the troops that were led by the Czar,
And the bravest of these was a man by
the name
Of Ivan Petrofski Skevar.   *Ib. st. 3*

Is that Mr. Reilly, can anyone tell?
Is that Mr. Reilly that owns the hotel?
Well, if that's Mr. Reilly, they speak of
so highly,
Upon me soul, Reilly, you're doin'
quite well.
Is That Mr. Reilly? [2] [1882],
chorus

Sow a thought, and you reap an act;
Sow an act, and you reap a habit;
Sow a habit, and you reap a character;
Sow a character, and you reap a des-
tiny.
Quoted by SAMUEL SMILES
[1812–1904], *Life and La-
bor* [1887]

Now is the time for all good men to
come to the aid of the party.
*Practice sentence used in type-
writing* [3]

---

[1] Originally, perhaps, "the goose *honks* high"
— it cries and flies high. Wild geese fly higher
when the weather is fine or promises to be fine.
Hence, the prospects are bright; everything is
favorable. — *Century Dictionary*
[2] Another traditional version, repudiated by
New Bedford authority, is that the skipper said:
"All I want out of you is silence, and damn
little of that."

[1] See *Psalm 137*, p. 22b.
[2] Assumed to be the origin of "the life of
Riley," meaning an easy time.
[3] Charles Weller, a court reporter, originated
this expression in . . . 1867 to test the efficiency

The quick brown fox jumps over the lazy dog.
> *Practice sentence used in typewriting*

As Maine goes, so goes the nation.[1]
> *American political maxim* [c. 1888]

Slide, Kelly, Slide.
> *Title of song by* J. W. KELLY [1889]

Oh, Shenandoah, I long to hear you.
Away, you rolling river,
Oh Shenandoah, I long to hear you.
Away, I'm bound away
'Cross the wide Missouri.[2]   *Chantey*

Swing low, sweet chariot,
Comin' for to carry me home;
I looked over Jordan, an' what did I see?
A band of angels coming after me,
Comin' for to carry me home.
> *Negro spiritual*

God gave Noah the rainbow sign.
No more water, the fire next time! [3]
> *Negro spiritual*

Ladling the butter from adjacent tubs,
Stubbs butters Freeman, Freeman butters Stubbs.
> *Variously quoted* [c. 1890], *alluding to the mutual praise of two Oxford historians*

Lizzie Borden took an ax
And gave her mother forty whacks;
When she saw what she had done
She gave her father forty-one!
> *Rhyme popular after the murder trial of Lizzie Borden, Fall River, Massachusetts* [June 1893]

The little cares that fretted me,
I lost them yesterday,

Among the fields above the sea,
Among the winds at play.
> *Out in the Fields* [1]

Out in the fields with God!   *Ib.*

Remember the Maine! [2]
> *Slogan, Spanish-American War* [1898]

Frankie and Johnny were lovers, my gawd, how they could love,
Swore to be true to each other, true as the stars above;
He was her man, but he done her wrong.
> *Frankie and Johnny,*[3] *st.* 1

The halls of fame are open wide
And they are always full;
Some go in by the door called "push,"
And some by the door called "pull."
> *Quoted by Stanley Baldwin* [1867–1947] *in a speech in the House of Commons*

The codfish lays ten thousand eggs,
The homely hen lays one.
The codfish never cackles
To tell you what she's done.
And so we scorn the codfish,
While the humble hen we prize,
Which only goes to show you
That it pays to advertise.
> *It Pays to Advertise*

One white foot — try him,
Two white feet — buy him,
Three white feet — look well about him;
Four white feet — go without him.[4]
> *Rhyme for a horse-buyer*

[1] Published in the Boston *Sunday Globe* April 30, 1899, credited to *St. Paul's Magazine* but not discovered there. Erroneously attributed to E. B. Browning and Imogen Guiney.

[2] On February 15, 1898, the American battleship *Maine* was blown up in Havana harbor, Cuba.

[3] Traditional ballad; there are innumerable versions and verses.

See Shakespeare, p. 220b, and note.

[4] Three white feet and a white nose,
  Rip off his skin and throw him to the crows.
> *New Hampshire version of last two lines*

of the first practical typewriter which his friend Christopher Sholes had constructed. — *Life* [April 11, 1955]

[1] As Maine goes, so goes Vermont. — JAMES FARLEY, *statement to press* [November 4, 1936] *after predicting that Roosevelt would carry 46 states in the presidential election.*

[2] See Robert Frost, p. 929b.

[6] See James Baldwin, p. 1081a.

An apple a day keeps the doctor away.
Current since the 19th century

Time is of the essence. *Saying*

The three most beautiful things in the world: a full-rigged ship, a woman with child, and a full moon. *Saying*

All the world is queer save me and thee; and sometimes I think thee is a little queer.
Attributed to a Quaker, speaking to his wife

Everyone has at least one sermon in him. *Saying*

Man is the only animal that eats when he is not hungry, drinks when he is not thirsty, and makes love at all seasons. *Remark*

You can always tell a Harvard man, but you can't tell him much.
Attributed to JAMES BARNES *[1866–1936]*

I seen my duty and I done it.
Current since the 19th century

Keeping up with the Joneses.
Popular saying

Paying through the nose.[1]
Popular phrase for excessive payment

Doesn't amount to Hannah Cook.[2]
Saying common in Maine and on Cape Cod

Hit's a lot worse to be soul-hungry than to be body-hungry.
A Kentucky mountain woman asking for her granddaughter to be admitted to Berea College high school [c. 1900]. Quoted by CARL R. WOODWARD *in The Wonderful World of Books, edited by Alfred Stefferud [1953]*

There ain't no such animal.
Comment of a New Jersey farmer looking at a dromedary at a circus: cartoon in Life, November 7, 1907, credited to Everybody's Magazine

How old is Ann?
Popular saying in the early 20th century [1]

The Pyramids first, which in Egypt were laid;
Next Babylon's Garden, for Amytis made;
Then Mausolos' Tomb of affection and guilt;
Fourth, the Temple of Dian in Ephesus built;
The Colossus of Rhodes, cast in brass, to the Sun;
Sixth, Jupiter's Statue, by Phidias done;
The Pharos of Egypt comes last, we are told,
Or the Palace of Cyrus, cemented with gold.
Seven Wonders of the Ancient World

Use it up, wear it out;
Make it do, or do without.
New England maxim

Earned a precarious living by taking in one another's washing.
Saying

Something old, something new,
Something borrowed, something blue,
And a lucky sixpence in her shoe.[2]
Wedding rhyme

God looks after fools, drunkards, and the United States. *Epigram*

Oh, why don't you work
Like other men do?
How the hell can I work
When there's no work to do?
Hallelujah, I'm a Bum [c. 1907]

---

[1] Grimm says that Odin had a poll tax which was called in Sweden a nose tax; it was a penny per nose, or poll. — *Deutsche Rechts Alterthümer*

[2] Variously explained as a character who once lived on Campobello Island; a corruption of a phrase in Indian dialect; and a comparison with the worthlessness (for navigation) of a cook on board ship.

[1] This question became well known when *The New York Press,* October 16, 1903, printed the problem: "Mary is 24 years old. She is twice as old as Ann was when Mary was as old as Ann is now. How old is Ann?" The answer is that Ann is 18.

[2] There are variants for the less familiar last line, such as "And a silver sixpence in each shoe."

Old soldiers never die;
They only fade away! [1]
> *War song, British Army*
> [1914–1918]

She was poor but she was honest,
And her parents was the same,
Till she met a city feller,
And she lost her honest name.
> *War song* [1914–1918]

It's the same the whole world over,
It's the poor wot gets the blame,
It's the rich wot gets the pleasure,
Ain't it all a bloomin' shame?
> *Ib. chorus*

Fifty million Frenchmen can't be wrong.[2]
> *Saying popular with American soldiers during World War I* [1917–1918]

Don't sell America short.[3]
> *Popular American saying* [1925–1929]

Lord, through this hour
    Be Thou our Guide,
So by Thy power
    No foot shall slide.
> *Westminster Chimes*

Climb high
Climb far
Your goal the sky
Your aim the star.
> *Inscription on Hopkins Memorial Steps, Williams College, Williamstown, Massachusetts*

Mother, may I go out to swim?
Yes, my darling daughter:
Hang your clothes on a hickory limb
And don't go near the water.
> *Rhyme*

[1] See Douglas MacArthur, p. 959a.
[2] Sometimes "forty" or "thirty" is heard instead of "fifty." When Texas Guinan and her troupe were refused entry into France in 1931, she was quoted as saying: "It goes to show that fifty million Frenchmen *can* be wrong." She promptly renamed her show *Too Hot for Paris,* and toured the United States with it.
[3] The phrase may have stemmed from "Never be a bear on the United States," attributed variously to JUNIUS S. MORGAN [1813–1890] and J. P. MORGAN [1837–1913].

See the happy moron,
He doesn't give a damn.
I wish I were a moron —
My God, perhaps I am!
> *Rhyme*

Work and pray, live on hay,
You'll get pie in the sky when you die.
> *The Preacher and the Slave* [1]

The difficult we do immediately. The impossible takes a little longer.
> *Slogan of United States Army Service Forces*

Kilroy was here.[2]
> *Army saying, World War II*

Hurry up and wait.
> *Ib.*

SNAFU (Situation Normal All Fouled Up).
> *Ib.*

G.I. Joe.
> *World War II term for infantryman* [3]

And when he goes to heaven
To Saint Peter he will tell:
Another Marine reporting, sir;
I've served my time in hell!
> *Epitaph on grave of Pfc. Cameron of the Marine Corps, Guadalcanal* [1942]

Stay with me, God. The night is dark,
The night is cold: my little spark
Of courage dies. The night is long;
Be with me, God, and make me strong.
> *A Soldier — His Prayer,* [4] st. 1

[1] Attributed to Joe Hill in the 1927 edition of *I.W.W. Songs.*
[2] See Faulkner, p. 1040a.
[3] This name, chosen for the soldier in Lieutenant DAVE BREGER's comic strip for *Yank,* the Army weekly, first appeared in the issue of June 17, 1942. Writing in *Time* [February 26, 1945], Lieutenant Breger said: "I decided on 'G.I. Joe,' the 'G.I.' [Government Issue] because of its prevalence in Army talk, and the 'Joe' for the alliterative effect."
[4] This poem, found on a scrap of paper in a slit trench in Tunisia during the battle of El Agheila, was printed in *Poems from the Desert,* by members of the British Eighth Army [1944].

We sure liberated the hell out of this place.

> *American soldier in the ruins of a French village, 1944; quoted by* MAX MILLER, *The Far Shore* [1945]

Spartan simplicity must be observed. Nothing will be done merely because it contributes to beauty, convenience, comfort, or prestige.

> *From the Office of the Chief Signal Officer, U.S. Army* [May 29, 1945]

Soldiers who wish to be a hero
Are practically zero,
But those who wish to be civilians,
Jesus, they run into the millions.

> *Army latrine inscription. Quoted by* NORMAN ROSTEN, *The Big Road* [1945]

We, the peoples of the United Nations, determined to save succeeding generations from the scourge of war, which twice in our lifetime has brought untold sorrow to mankind, and to reaffirm faith in fundamental human rights, in the dignity and worth of the human person, in the equal right of men and women and of nations large and small . . .
And for these ends to practice tolerance and live together in peace with one another as good neighbors . . .
Have resolved to combine these efforts to accomplish our aims.

> *Charter of the United Nations* [June 1945], *preamble* [1]

Since wars begin in the minds of men, it is in the minds of men that the defenses of peace must be constructed.

> *Constitution of the United Nations Educational, Scientific and Cultural Organization* [1946]

We are not dealing simply with a military or scientific problem but with a

[1] The preamble is based on a draft by JAN CHRISTIAN SMUTS [1870–1950].

problem in statecraft and the ways of the human spirit.

> *Report on the International Control of Atomic Energy* [1] [March 16, 1946]

Relief from the terrible fear which can do so much to engender the very thing feared. ***Ib.***

Education is what you have left over after you have forgotten everything you have learned. *Saying*

Till Hell freezes over. *Saying*

A club is a place where twenty men pay for the pleasure of one. *Saying*

One man, one vote.
> *Civil rights slogan*

We shall overcome, we shall overcome,
We shall overcome some day
Oh, deep in my heart I do believe
We shall overcome some day.

> *Civil rights song* [1960] [2]

EPITAPHS

A zealous locksmith died of late,
And did arrive at heaven gate,
He stood without and would not knock,
Because he meant to pick the lock.

> *Epitaph upon a Puritanical Locksmith; from* WILLIAM CAMDEN, *Remains Concerning Britain* [1637]

All the brothers were valiant, and all the sisters virtuous.

> *From the inscription on the tomb of the Duchess of Newcastle in Westminster Abbey* [1673]

[1] Prepared for the U.S. Department of State by a board of consultants: Chester I. Barnard, J. Robert Oppenheimer, Charles A. Thomas, Harry A. Winne, and David E. Lilienthal, chairman.
[2] The song originated on slave plantations in pre-Civil War days. It became a formal Baptist hymn around 1900, called "I'll Overcome Some Day" by the adapter, C. Albert Tindley. It became a protest theme when used by colored workers in 1946 on picket lines in Charleston, S.C.

A house she hath, 'tis made of such good fashion,
The tenant ne'er shall pay for reparation,
Nor will the landlord ever raise her rent
Or turn her out of doors for nonpayment;
From chimney tax this cell is free,
To such a house who would not tenant be?
> *For Rebecca Bogess, Folkestone [August 22, 1688]*

It is so soon that I am done for,
I wonder what I was begun for.
> *For a child aged three weeks, Cheltenham Churchyard*

Here lie I, Martin Elginbrodde:
Ha'e mercy o' my soul, Lord God,
As I wad do, were I Lord God
And ye were Martin Elginbrodde.
> *Aberdeen Churchyard. From* GEORGE MACDONALD, *David Elginbrod* [1862], *ch. 13*

Immaturus obi: sed tu felicior annos
Vive meos, Bona Republica! Vive tuos.
[I died young; but thou, O Good Republic, be more fortunate,
Live out my years! Live your own.]
> *Inscription furnished by Nathaniel Cross, classics professor at the University of Nashville, on the tomb of explorer Meriwether Lewis* [1774–1809]

This is the grave of Mike O'Day
Who died maintaining his right of way.

His right was clear, his will was strong,
But he's just as dead as if he'd been wrong.
> *20th century*

FRENCH

Revenons à nos moutons [Let us return to our sheep — i.e., subject].
> *Maître Patnelin* (15th century farce)

Il ne faut pas être plus royaliste que le roi [One must not be more royalist than the king].
> *Saying from the time of Louis XVI*

Ça ira, ça tiendra [That will be, that will last].
> *Revolutionary song, based on a phrase of Benjamin Franklin's*

Liberté! Egalité! Fraternité! [Liberty! Equality! Fraternity!]
> *Phrase dating from before the French Revolution, officially adopted in 1793*

Tout passe, tout casse, tout lasse [Everything passes, everything perishes, everything palls].
> *Proverb*

Ah, les bons vieux temps où nous étions si malheureux! [Oh, the good old times when we were so unhappy!]
> *Saying*

L'amour, l'amour fait tourner le monde [It's love, it's love that makes the world go round].
> *Song*

Index of Authors

INDEX OF AUTHORS

Index

INDEX

Entries are arranged alphabetically, with hyphenated words indexed as one word. Spelling is in general in accordance with Webster, with dialect spellings indexed in both dialect and standard forms.

The order for possessives and plurals of identical spelling is: *author's, authors, authors'.*

The letter *a* after the page number indicates the left column of the text page referred to; the letter *b* indicates the right column.

For fuller discussion of the index, see the section on the index (pages xvi–xviii) in the *Guide to the Use of* FAMILIAR QUOTATIONS in the front of the book.

Age, old a. lacking neither honor nor lyre, 121a
old a. not yet arrived, 688a
old a. only disease, 607a
old a. play's last act, 112a
old a. serene and bright, 515a
old a. should burn, 1070b
old a. time of spending, 351b
olives of endless a., 293b
or grief or sickness, 321a
outworn buried a., 292b
pays us with a. and dust, 199b
perform promises of youth, 428a
philosophies of one a., 817a
physician of Iron A., 711a
prayers which are a. his alms, 204b
preferable to youth, 395b
regret in chilled a., 800a
returns the Golden A., 116b
scarce expect one of my a., 507a
shakes rooted folly of a., 377b
shall be clearer than noonday, 15a
Shelley of my a., 1075b
sign of old a., 523b
smack of a. in you, 241b
soon comes a., 200a
soul of the a., 303b
spirit of a., 418a
tested to extreme old a., 710b
the a. is dull and mean, 626a
the harbor of all ills, 104b
therefore summon a., 666a
think at your a. it is right, 743b
thinks better of gilded fool, 301b
thou hast nor youth nor a., 271a
'tis well an old a. is out, 372a
to age succeeds, 644b
to cheated age, 876b
too late or cold climate, 347b
toys of a., 409a
tragedy of the a., 894b
'twixt boy and youth, 519a
vastness and a., 642a
veracity with old a., 356b
very staff of my a., 232b
view a. of poverty, 235a
war dearth a. agues, 307b
weak evils a. and hunger, 248b
when a. in wit out, 246b
when old a. crept over, 859b
when Thule no more ultimate, 131a
with stealing steps, 187a
without a name, 455b
wives companions for middle a., 208a
world's great a. begins, 570b
worst of woes wait on a., 555b
young whom a. doth chill, 351a
youth and a. equally a burden, 93b
youth passed a. not arrived, 688a
Aged and gray Maggie, 779a
and poor and slow, 813a
beauty of a. face, 963a
certain age means a., 561b
later times more a. than earlier, 206b
man paltry thing, 882b
matched with a. wife, 646a
thrush frail gaunt, 783b

Aged, youth becomes as a., 271a
Agent, actions work good of a., 373b
free a. thou wast before, 142b
imagination a. of perception, 528b
thus the poor a. despised, 269b
trust no a., 246a
Agents, public officers a., 771a
Age's, poison for a. tooth, 236a
Ages, all a. believed in gods, 935b
and a. hence, 926b
before history, 459b
cycle of the a. renewed, 116b
emptiness of a. in face, 826b
famous to all a., 340a
forties the dangerous a., 1022a
God our help in a. past, 396b
gone a. long ago, 582a
heir of all a., 647b
how many a. hence, 255a
now he belongs to the a., 677a
pass vividly down a., 910a
prior a. haven't thought of, 478b
rock of A., 469a
seven a., 249a
thousand a. in Thy sight, 396b
three poets in three a., 370b
through a. one purpose, 647b
value from esteem of a., 366b
ye unborn a., 442a
Agglomeration called Holy Roman Empire, 417a
Agglutinative, tonsorial or a. type, 902b
Aggrandizement, no a. territorial or other, 974a
Aggravate, I will a. my voice, 229a
Aggravation of self, 776b
Aggravations, accept minor a., 817b
Aggregate efforts of busy multitude, 720b
interests of community, 480a
Aggression of Germany, 1012a
threaten a., 974b
Aggressions, when a. require war, 472b
Aggressors, quarantine the a., 972a
Agin, off a. on a., 897b
Agincourt, affright air at A., 243a
Aging people in contraction of life, 935b
person give attention to self, 935b
Agitation of the air, 1057a
A-gley, gang aft a., 492b
Aglow, all a. is the work, 117b
Agnes, world dear A. is strange, 360b
Agnes', St. A. Eve, 581b
Agnosco veteris vestigia flammae, 118b
Agnostic, compliment to be called a., 844b
judges neither Catholic nor a., 967a
Agnosticism, that's all a. means, 844b
Agnus Dei, 59a
A-going out with tide, 671b
Agonies, errors a. and fears, 758a
exultations a., 512b
small talk dies in a., 570a
Agonizing, fierce a. meek, 907a

Agonizing, most a. spy, 736b
reappraisal, 1076a
Agony, charm a. with words, 247a
leave off a., 812b
strong swimmer in a., 560b
will find Thee, 1068a
Agree, agreed we can't never a., 808b
all things differ all a., 405a
birds in little nests a., 396b
free thought for those who a., 789a
how a. kettle and pot, 38a
let mankind a., 372a
music and poetry a., 309a
people have good sense a. with us, 356a
the more we didn't a., 808b
two of a trade never a., 401b, 730a
verbs and nouns more a., 770a
when partners can't a., 505b
whether they a. or not, 1025a
with her would not a., 879b
Agreeable, do not want people a., 533b
greatest not most a., 828a
haint one a. feetur, 693a
in conversation, 394b
person agrees with me, 612b
to escape mental exertion, 778a
what is more a. than home, 111a
Agreeably, affect you a. in reading, 469b
Agreed, except they be a., 35b
to differ, 532b
together we can't agree, 808b
Agreement, living in a. with nature, 103b
love is a., 211a
on nuclear control, 1074b
who does not forget old a., 72a
with hell, 615b
with hell are we at a., 32a
Agreements, nations tempted to violate a., 972a
Agrecs, agreeable person a., 612b
large style a. not with purse, 214b
Agricultural men the bravest, 133a
Agriculture, all taxes fall upon a., 465b
navigation commerce a., 463a
Ague of skeleton, 1002a
Ague's privilege, 227a
Agues, praise doth nourish a., 240a
war dearth age a., 307b
Ah Sin was his name, 769b
Ahab, all evil to crazy A., 696b
he ran before A., 13b
when A. went to Askelon, 945b
Ahead, man who never got a., 1050b
of the world, 75a
sure you're right go a., 553b
Ahkoond of Swat, 673b
A-hunting, daddy's gone a., 1094b
daren't go a., 729a
upon St. David's Day, 1097a
we will go, 424a
Aid, alliteration's artful a., 456a
and comfort, 474a
come to a. of party, 1100b
expletives feeble a. join, 403a

Amiss or out of place, 1064a
  thou shalt never do a., 37b
Amittuntur, non a. sed praemittuntur, 130a
Amity, absolute a., 1055a
'Ammer along 'ard 'igh road,
  810a
Ammiral, mast of some great a.,
  342a
Ammunition, pass a., 1062a
Amo amas, 476a
  odi et a., 115a
Amoebas at start not complex,
  905b
Among them but not of them,
  556b
Amor, and after A. vincit omnia,
  166a
  batallas de a. campo de pluma,
  128b
  l'a. che muove il sole e l'altre
  stelle, 162a
  omnia vincit a., 117a
  vincit insomnia, 1061b
Amorous descant sung, 345b
  excite my a. propensities, 429b
  from a. causes springs, 404a
  nightingale a., 772b
  not too a. of far, 915a
  of their strokes, 287b
  sweet reluctant a. delay, 345a
  tangled in a. nets, 348b
Amorphous, all was vague and a.,
  110a
Amortization of heart and soul,
  1028a
Amount to Hannah Cook, 1102a
Amour, doux comme l'a., 484a
  l'a. fait tourner le monde,
  1105b
  l'a. l'histoire de la vie des
  femmes, 502b
  on ne badine pas avec l'a., 657a
  un peu d'a., 751b
Amphibious ill-born mob, 385a
Amphitrite, O sweet A., 695b
Amphitryon, I am the true A.,
  371a
  true A. gives dinners, 361b
Ample, cabined a. spirit, 712b
  knowledge her a. page, 440b
  room and verge enough, 441b
Ampler ether, 516b
Amplification vice of oratory,
  473b
Amplified, hand prosperity down
  a., 848a
Amuck, too discreet to run a.,
  411b
Amurath, not A. an A. succeeds,
  242a
Amuse his riper stage, 409a
  you with stories, 452b
Amused according to taste,
  960b
  by its presumption, 1033a
  delicately and unceasingly a.,
  960b
  we are not a., 699a
Amusement, let early education
  be a., 94b
Amusements, great friend to public a., 431a
Amusing with numerous errors,
  448a
Amyntas, what if A. is dark, 116b
Amytis, for A. made, 1102b
Anachronism, periodization of
  history a., 1047b

Analogies, linked a., 697a
  make one more at home, 834a
  prove nothing, 834a
Analogy least misleading thing,
  756b
Analysis, last point reached by a.,
  474b
  submit data to a., 479a
Analyze, culture a. itself, 861b
Anarch, thy hand great A., 414a
Anarchic, weeping a. Aphrodite,
  1060a
Anarchy, digest of a., 454a
  freedom cure of a., 453a
  mere a. loosed on world, 882a
  of poverty, 979b
  show me greater evil, 82a
  wild a. of drink, 304a
Anathema Maranatha, 53a
Anatomizing of motives, 608b
Anatomy, learn a. from dissections, 312b
  Pinch a mere a., 218b
Ancestor I feel shame in recalling,
  725b
Ancestors created world of shadows, 993a
  cut off brightness, 993a
  democracy makes man forget a.,
  617a
  glory belongs to our a., 137a
  in Rome, 505b
  look backward to a., 454a
  no need of a., 417a
  of honorable gentleman, 611b
  owe it to a., 1091a
  part of self, 793b
  true picture of a., 596b
  turned savage wilderness, 453b
  very good kind of folks, 480b
  wisdom of our a., 452a
Ancestral, amidst tall a. trees,
  573b
  happy man works a. acres, 120b
  in a. Jove Troy's sons rejoice,
  119b
  on my a. tree, 633a
  sits on a. tree, 866a
  voices prophesying war, 524a
Ancestry, heirs to polish of a.,
  721a
  honest hand-working a., 1027a
  pride of a., 454a
Anchor, all sail no a., 597a
  heaves ship free, 600b
  hoist instantly a., 702b
  holding a. lost, 216b
  it is time raise a., 707a
  of love is death, 807a
  that a. holds, 654a
Anchorage, long a. we leave, 703b
Anchored, fleet of stars a., 980a
Anchoring, yond tall a. bark,
  279b
Anchorite, saintship of an a., 555a
Anchors, moor bark with two a.,
  125a
  sons a. of mother's life, 83a
  weigh thine a., 105a
Ancient, according to a. custom,
  391b
  account a. ordine retrogrado,
  206b
  and fish-like smell, 297a
  and honorable, 31a
  and natural strength, 444b
  angels keep a. places, 857a
  around a. track, 730b
  close her from a. walls, 491a

Ancient, Europe of a. parapets,
  830a
  fear thee a. mariner, 525a
  feed fat the a. grudge, 232a
  feel spark of that a. flame, 118b
  feet in a. time, 490b
  gentlemen, 265b
  good uncouth, 692a
  heavenly connection, 1081b
  heavens fresh and strong, 514b
  hills a. as sun, 574a
  how left the a. love, 486b
  landmark, 25b
  landmarks in Bill of Rights,
  1037b
  like actors in a. plays, 830a
  mariner, 524b, 525a
  Mariner called Old Sailor, 756b
  marry a. people, 333b
  models perpetuated, 148a
  most a. profession, 872a
  of a. race by birth, 368b
  of days, 35a, 743a
  order swerves, 832a
  power of fright, 1034b
  praise of a. authors, 318a
  raven, 643a
  recognize signals of a. flame,
  161b
  remove not the a. landmark,
  25b
  sacrifice, 875b
  sanity in a. literature, 712b
  simplicity is gone, 379a
  sing a. ways, 879b
  suit of a. black, 953a
  these times are a. times, 206b
  trusty drouthy crony, 495b
  walked among a. trees, 488b
  with the a. is wisdom, 15a
  writers say, 883b
Ancients, speak of a. without idolatry, 415a
  we are a. of the earth, 206b
  wisdom of the a., 452a
Andalusia, weather like April in
  A., 172a
Anderson, John A. my jo John,
  494b
Andrew with brindled hair, 823b
Andrey, Prince A. went to tomb,
  732a
Ane, I've lost but a., 496a
Anecdotage, fell into a., 612b
Anemone, delicate algae and sea
  a., 1006a
Anesthesia bastard substitute,
  861b
  perceptual a., 960a
Anew, ruined love when built a.,
  294a
  think a. act a., 638b
Anfractuous rocks, 1001b
Ange, pur comme un a., 484a
Angel and archangel join, 412a
  ape or a., 612b
  appear to each lover, 398a
  as you are insect in you, 708a
  beautiful ineffectual a., 717a
  consideration like a. came, 243a
  curse his better a., 276a
  devil an a. too, 869b
  drew one a., 665b
  ended and in Adam's ear, 347a
  faces smile, 597b
  golden hours on a. wings, 495a
  good and bad a., 310b
  half a. half bird, 667a
  he is a. of light, 684a

Antiseptic tunnel, 1082a
Antithesis, himself one vile a., 411b
Antler of the eaves, 1057a
Antonio, Stradivari violins without A., 689a
Antony brought drunken forth, 289a
  catch another A., 289b
  happy horse to bear A., 287a
  much A. of Hamlet most, 815b
  my A. is away, 287a
  my oblivion is a very A., 287a
  that revels long o' nights, 254b
  who lost A. the world, 383b
Ant's centaur in dragon world, 989a
Ants preserved in amber, 135a
Anulus in digito tenuatur, 113a
Anvil, beats them on his a., 351b
  laughs at hammers, 948b
  lay me on a., 948b
  sword out of stone and a., 175a
  what the a., 489a
  when an a. hold still, 324b
  when you are a. bear, 324b
Anvils, mighty a. of world, 979a
Anxiety about livelihood, 932a
  banquet partaken in a., 76a
  born with a. about weather, 770b
  state of man a., 363b
  tabooed by a., 767b
Anxious, not a. about battles, 996a
  pleasing a. being, 441a
Anybody anywhere any time, 911a
  can make history, 840b
  else I knew as well, 682a
  is as their land is, 933b
  more space where nobody than a., 933b
  no one's a., 769a
  there said Traveler, 914b
Anyone lived in pretty how town, 1031b
  tennis a., 1046b
  who hates children, 951b
Anythin' for quiet life, 66ga
Anything, courage not to believe in a., 688a
  everything and a., 974b
  for a quiet life, 314a, 669a
  for good of country, 398a
  is there a. beyond, 993b
  not a. to show more fair, 512a
  nothing done while a. remained, 134a
Apart, get to be wide a., 72b
  man's love a thing a., 560a
  mood a., 929a
  no stander above or a., 700b
  souls a., 947b
  standing a. from it, 997b
  through hatred borne a., 83b
Apathetic end, 646a
Apathy, extinction from a., 1045b
  no a. into movement without emotion, 936b
Ape, Devil is ever God's a., 179b
  for his grandfather, 725b
  how like to us, 107a
  like an angry a., 271a
  or angel, 612b
  poor degenerate from a., 1032a
  sedulous a., 824a
  up from the a., 994a
Aped, vices a. from white men, 1039a

Apennine, folding of A., 714b
  mists the A., 734b
Apes, ivory a. and peacocks, 13a, 947a
  lead a. in hell, 219a
  why men behave like a., 994b
Aphorisms, interline a., 469b
Aphrodisiac, circumambulatory a., 1061b
  emetic but nowhere a., 968b
Aphrodite on your rich-wrought throne, 69b
  sleep with golden A., 66a
  spoke and loosened girdle, 64a
  weeping anarchic A., 1060a
  what delight without A., 68b
  work of soft A., 69b
Apish, tardy a. nation, 226b
Aplomb, before presidents with a., 703a
A-plyin' up and down, 875a
Apollo, bards in fealty to A., 579b
  harsh after songs of A., 223a
  I swear by A. Physician, 88a
  imbecile, 604a
  nor does A. always stretch bow, 121b
Apollo's, burned is A. laurel bough, 213b
  first, 326b
  musical as A. lute, 222a, 337a
Apollos watered, 52a
Apollyon, foul fiend A., 365b
Apologists, northern a. tremble, 615b
Apology ain't gwine make h'ar come, 814a
  for Devil, 756b
  too prompt, 347b
Apostle, by the a. Paul, 218a
  golden-tongued a., 905a
  of Philistines Macaulay, 714a
  rank as an a., 766b
Apostles, I am least of a., 52b
  true a. of equality, 716a
  would have done as they, 560a
Apostolic blows and knocks, 352a
Apothecary, expires in arms of a., 522a
  never out of spirits, 481a
  ounce of civet good a., 279b
  true a. thy drugs quick, 225b
Appall, common sense a., 859b
Appalled, property was thus a., 267b
Appalling ocean surrounds land, 697a
Apparel, every true man's a., 272a
  fashion wears out more a., 246b
  oft proclaims the man, 258b
Appareled in celestial light, 513a
  like the spring, 290b
Apparent queen unveiled her light, 345b
Apparition, lovely a. sent, 514a
  of these faces, 987b
  wall confronting a., 708b
  who enjoys not life an a., 330a
Apparitions seen and gone, 385a
Appassionato, great piano a., 985b
Appeal best suited to auditor, 976b
  books of universal a., 915a
  hark to exiled son's a., 781b
  I a. to any white man, 445b
  I a. unto Caesar, 50b
  to arms and God of hosts, 465a
Appeals to religious prejudice, 725b

Appear, fishermen a. like mice, 279b
  small vices do a., 279b
  things not what a. to be, 138a
  to be and appear not to be, 95b
  while these visions did a., 231a
  ye like angels a., 715b
Appearance, in a. at friendship, 376a
  judge not according to a., 48b
  looketh on the outward a., 12a
  never attain reality, 498b
  never wears mean a., 605a
  takes on a. of nearby rock, 77a
Appearances, judging people by a., 359b
  keep up a., 670a
  often are deceiving, 75b
  to mind are four kinds, 138a
Appeared, there a. a chariot of fire, 13b
Appears, thine in mine a., 304b
Appeasement, don't care about word a., 1013b
  political a., 969b
Appeaseth strife, 24b
Appendix, idleness an a. to nobility, 310b
Appetite a feeling and a love, 509a
  an universal wolf, 268a
  breakfast with a., 298a
  cloy hungry edge of a., 226a
  comes with eating, 180b
  for bogus revelation, 960a
  good digestion wait on a., 284b
  humble pie with a., 671b
  increase of a., 257b
  loss of a. for mediocrities, 795b
  makes eating a delight, 350b
  man given to a., 25b
  may sicken, 251a
  not meat but a., 350b
  quench a. keep reason under control, 143a
  sharpen with cloyless sauce his a., 287b
  will into a., 268a
  with keen a. he sits down, 232b
Appetites, cloy a. they feed, 287b
  conflicting interests and a., 969b
  man of my a., 960b
  not their a., 274b
  subdue a. my dears, 669b
Appius, that which A. says, 116a
Applaud hollow ghost, 715a
  old people a. it, 195b
  thee to the very echo, 286b
  world forever a., 638b
Applause, deference and a. deserve, 468a
  delight wonder of our stage, 303b
  from none but self a., 707b
  ignominy of popular a., 826b
  joy pleasance revel and a., 274a
  not least in honor or a., 201a
  of single human being, 433a
  sit attentive to own a., 411a
Apple a day, 1102a
  as an a. reddens, 69b
  blossoms fill air, 1009b
  buy a. on corner, 1000a
  cleft through core, 498b
  easy under the a. boughs, 1070b
  for apple's sake, 762a
  my a. trees never eat cones, 926a

Assault and battery of wind, 882b
  of thoughts on unthinking, 977a
Assaults, defend in a. of our enemies, 60a
Assay so hard, 164a
Assayed, thrice he a., 342b
Assayeth, naught n' a. naught n' acheveth, 165a
Assays of bias, 260a
Assemble, peaceably to a., 474b
Assemblies, nails fastened by masters of a., 29a
Assembling, slow in a., 89a
Assembly, club a. of good fellows, 427b
  free speech press a., 864b-865a
  of portable plumbing, 1017b
  suppression of free a., 832b
Assent and you are sane, 735b
  with civil leer, 411a
Assert eternal Providence, 341b
Asserted, plurality not a. without necessity, 162b
Assertions, convince hearers of own a., 93b
Asses, bridge of a., 103b
  made to bear and you, 219a
  mankind a. that pull, 562b
Assimilated, truth not a. by crowd, 706b
Assimilating educating selecting, 912b
Assisian, brother of loved A., 905a
Assist him to save face, 1035a
Assistance, gives persecution no a., 461b
Assisting advancement of science, 1026b
Associate, the good must a., 452a
Associated, cannot be a. with government, 681a
Association, quotations touch a., 851b
  unplanned uninhibited a., 1055b
Ass's, white curd of a. milk, 411a
Assuage anguish of bereavement, 640a
Assuaged, half a. for Itylus, 772b
Assume a virtue, 264b
  honorable style of Christian, 329b
  spirits either sex a., 342a
  what I a. you a., 700a
Assumes, no vice but a. some virtue, 233b
  the god affects to nod, 371a
Assuming, start a. that men are bad, 177b
Assumptions, most necessary of a., 867a
  not admit a. of superiority, 100a
Assurance given by looks, 314b
  make a. double sure, 285b
  most dear, 720b
  of a man, 264a
  of recorded history, 1006b
Assure survival of liberty, 1072b
Assured, crown themselves a., 293b
  ignorant of what he's most a., 270b
Assyrian Bull, 652a
  came down like wolf, 558b
Assyrians, smote in camp of A., 558b
Asterisk of death, 624b
Astern, look a. row ahead, 137b

Astolat, lily maid of A., 653a
Astonish, gratify some a. rest, 763b
  things that would a. you, 767b
Astonished at my own moderation, 445b
Astonishment, thou shalt become an a., 10b
Astra, ad a. per aspera, 150a
  sic itur ad a., 119b
Astray, all likely to go a., 82a
  black sheep gone a., 873b
  if world go a., 161b
  light that led a., 493a
  one that had been led a., 335b
  we like sheep have gone a., 33a
Astride, give both a. a grave, 309b
Astrologers, sociologists a., 870a
Astronomer, undevout a. is mad, 399b
Astronomers, confounding a., 906a
  poor old a., 899b
  what poor a., 1085b
Astronomy compels soul to look upwards, 94b
Astrophil, who knew not A., 314b
Asunder, afar and a., 765a
  half a life a., 744b
  let no man put a., 61b
  let not man put a., 43a
  put this man and woman a., 390a
  villain and he many miles a., 225a
  whirl a. and dismember me, 236b
Asylum among mob, 695b
  Jesus Christ in a., 851b
  lunatic a. in Jerusalem, 851b
  optimism in lunatic a., 851a
  prepare a. for mankind, 466b
  their last a., 444a
Asylums, comfortably padded a., 975a
Ataualpa, who strangled A., 595b
Atavistic, cap and gown a., 845b
Ate and drank precious words, 738b
  bread with tears, 477a
  cheeses out of vats, 662b
  elephant a. all night, 821a
  the malt, 1098b
  when we were not hungry, 389b
  with runcible spoon, 673a
Athanasian Creed splendid lyric, 613a
Atheism like that of Spinoza, 867b
  little philosophy inclineth to a., 208b
  owlet A., 526a
  pantheism a. in disguise, 869b
  religion and not a., 453a
Atheist half believes God, 399a
  superstitious a., 665a
  town a., 1047a
Atheist-laugh's a poor exchange, 493b
Atheists, no a. in foxholes, 1053a
Athena, gray-eyed A., 65a
Athenians commanded by myself, 77b
  crushed gold-bearing Medes, 70b
  quality of A. lucidity, 716b
  war between Peloponnesians and A., 89a
Athens, bringing owls to A., 91a
  divine city, 79b

Athens, fix eyes on greatness of A., 90a
  maid of A., 555a
  nigh to Euboea, 92b
  nurse of men, 83a
  the eye of Greece, 348b
  to A. sent ships, 560b
  weeds of A. he doth wear, 229b
  ye men of A., 50a
Athis, loved you once long ago A., 69b
Athlete, anny man but thrained a., 892a
  crowned in sweat of brow, 145a
Athletes stronger than backers, 146a
Athwart men's noses as asleep, 223a
A-tiptoe, stand a. when day named, 245a
Atlanta to the sea, 748a
Atlantic, dawn on other side of A., 442a
  drag A. for whales, 760a
  frontier from A. to Pacific, 920b
  Ocean on my head, 1076a
  steep A. stream, 336b
  Thule and A. surge, 419b
Atlantic Monthly, refined essay in A., 960a-b
Atlas, Teneriff or A. unremoved, 346a
Atmosphere, clear brown twilight a., 614a
  of Gallup Poll, 923a
Atom changed everything save thinking, 951a
  in matter duplicate in mind, 697a
  intense a. glows, 571b
  movements of lightest a., 479a
  mystery of the a., 1025b
  no evil in a., 1048b
  secret powers of a., 888b
Atomic age, 901a
  bombs burst in hands, 888a
  cannot control a. energy, 908b
  energy a menace, 950b
  energy lead to bombs, 950b
  first moment of a. age, 1069b
  habits of age of a. energy, 1027a
  reduced no man to a. elements, 967b
  reduced to a. mechanics, 752b
  release of a. energy, 982b
  war fought with a. bomb, 950b
  warfare bad enough, 1015a
Atomies, crumbled out again to his a., 307b
  team of little a., 223a
Atoms and compounds of atoms, 113a
  cannot be swamped by force, 113a
  in reality a. and space, 88a
  onion a. lurk in bowl, 523a
  or systems, 408a
  reduction to motions of a., 779a
  we have seen our a., 1019a
Aton, O living A., 3b
  shinest as A. by day, 4a
Atone, pictures for page a., 413b
Atoned, microcosm and macrocosm a., 724a
  not a. too dearly by death, 497b
Atones for later disregard, 928b
Atreus, son of A., 63a

A-wooing, frog a. go, 1092b
Awry, currents turn a., 262a
  leaning all a., 630b
Awww, everybody goes A., 1080b
Ax, cord or a. or flame, 656a
  fitter to bruise, 351b
  laid unto the root, 39b
  Lizzie Borden took a., 1101a
  neither hammer nor a., 458b
  to grind, 545a
Axes, sharp-edged a., 701b
  talking of a., 743b
Axiom hatred of bourgeois, 709b
  old as hills, 916a
Axioms, derives a. from particulars, 207a
  flies from particulars to a., 207a
  of mathematics, 786b
  proved upon our pulses, 585a
Axis of earth sticks out, 634a
  soft underbelly of A., 924a
  sword a. of world, 1015b
Axle, glowing a. doth allay, 336b
Axletree, clot bedded a., 1005a
Axminster, it's not my A., 904a
Ax's edge did try, 359b
Aye, have profferer construe A., 220b
Aylmer, Rose A. whom these eyes, 536a
Azcan, Chieftain Iffucan of A., 955a
Azores, behind lay gray A., 790a
  Flores in the A., 654b
Aztec would have had strong states, 997b
Azure, arose from out a. main, 420a
  far in a. deeps, 621b
  pellucid in a. depths, 703b
  riding o'er a. realm, 441b
  ringed with a. world, 651a
  steeps, 1043b
Azure-lidded sleep, 582a
Azures, devouring green a., 829b

B

B, mark it with B, 1092b
Baa baa baa, 873b
  baa black sheep, 1093a
Baalim, Peor and B., 334a
Babbitt, his name was B., 986b
Babblative, arts b. and scribblative, 533a
Babbled of green fields, 243b
Babbling drunkenness, 253a
  gossip of the air, 251b
Babe, becomes a b. in eternity, 490a
  birth-strangled b., 285a
  clinging to frail b., 769b
  it's for b. I'm going, 708b
  let mighty b. alone, 354b
  love b. that milks me, 282b
  pity like newborn b., 282b
  pretty B. all burning bright, 210b
  whose birth embraves morn, 354b
Babel, name of it called B., 6b
  stir of the great B., 458b
Babes around thee cling, 514b
  out of the mouth of b., 17a
Babies, bit b. in cradles, 662b
  feel like doing for b., 1053b
  haven't hair, 1017a

Babies in silk hats, 999a
  playing with dynamite, 999a
  toast works down to b., 760a
Bablock-hithe, Thames at B., 712a
Baboon who saved comrade, 628b
Babs knows what and babs knows why, 945b
Baby, a little b. thing, 723b
  and me, 1092b
  blessing and bother, 759b
  bunting, 1094b
  down come b. and all, 810b
  figure of giant mass, 268a
  first b. first laughed, 858a
  inestimable blessing and bother, 759b
  looked like mouse, 1046b
  mother laid her B., 684b
  my b. at my breast, 289a
  rockabye b., 810b
  Tar-b. ain't sayin' nuthin', 814a
  where come from b. dear, 723b
Babylon, I was king in B., 816a
  is fallen, 31b, 58b
  king of B. stood at the parting, 35a
  Our Lady of B., 1075b
  youth in B. loved maid, 945b
Babylonish dialect, 352a
Babylon's gardens, 1102b
Bacchus ever fair and ever young, 371a
  that first, 336b
  with pink eyne, 288a
Bachelor, die a b., 246a
  got acquainted with a b., 534b
  see b. of threescore, 245b
Back, African moon lying on b., 985a
  all roads new going b., 816b
  and side go bare, 188b
  at b. from time to time hear, 1002b
  at last to you, 873a
  at my b. I always hear, 360a
  begins to smart, 1092a
  borne me on his b., 265a
  care not who sees your b., 239a
  carries sky on b., 681b
  cast-iron b. with hinge, 733b
  dagger into b. of neighbor, 972b
  die with harness on our b., 286b
  eyes and b. turn upward, 1002b
  far b. in soul horse prances, 986a
  follow and not see its b., 74a
  got over Devil's b., 313b
  I turn my b. to the east, 486a
  look forward not b., 718a
  mermaid on dolphin's b., 229a
  never came b. to me, 673b
  never turn b. on life, 981b
  not turn my b. on Hiss, 1025b
  nowhere to come but b., 845a
  on b. burden of world, 826b
  on bat's b. I do fly, 297b
  showed his b. above element, 289a
  so much upon his b., 309a
  speed today put b. tomorrow, 201a
  those before cried B., 596a
  to army again, 874b
  to loneliness of yesterday, 1038a
  to you cold father, 968b
  unto ladder turns his b., 254a
  wallet at his b., 268b

Back, what we b. ourselves to be, 793b
Backbone, whale's b., 1006a
Backed like a weasel, 263b
  with God and seas, 216a
Backfield, spotlight of the b., 1025b
Back-friend a shoulder-clapper, 218b
Background, if people keep me in b., 634b
  slumbers in b. of the times, 497b
Back-hearing around, 1081a
Backing men of genius, 1026b
  plague upon such b., 239a
Backs, birthrights proudly on b., 236a
  making beast with two b., 272b
  not sit on others' b., 805a
Backward, angel of b. look, 626b
  dark b. and abysm of time, 296a
  goes who toils most, 161a
  half-look over shoulder, 1006b
  I by b. steps move, 362b
  lean over too far b., 1033b
  life goes not b., 975b
  life understood b., 676a
  look b. to ancestors, 454a
  look b. to with pride, 926a
  look behind assurance, 1006b
  memory that only works b., 746a
  radio need only go b., 1064a
  ran sentences, 1050b
  revolutions never go b., 659a
  turn b. O time, 742b
Bacon, celebrities such as B., 749b
  not written Hamlet, 578a
  secretary of Nature and learning, 326b
  taking b. was stealing, 759b
  think how B. shined, 409b
Bacterial creepers, 1064b
Bad Americans die go to America, 840a
  and dreary lives, 858b
  as for b. all theirs dies, 85b
  beginning makes bad ending, 85b
  better b. epitaph, 261b
  better for being a little b., 272a
  bold b. man, 200a, 298a
  book as much labor, 1032a
  breeding, 91a
  by b. women been deceived, 349a
  cause supported by bad means, 467a
  charm to make b. good, 272a
  come to b. end, 910a
  extract yourself from b. ways, 80b
  free press good or b., 1068b
  from b. beginning great friendships, 109a
  fustian's so sublimely b., 410b
  good and b. angel, 310b
  good and b. of every land, 679a
  good b. indifferent, 374a, 438a
  good die early b. late, 385b
  good or b. for humankind, 515a
  great cases make b. law, 787a
  grow into likeness of b. men, 96a
  half their rhymes b., 918a
  hates children can't be all b., 951b

Banish, thief you cannot b., 1058a
  think not king did b. thee, 226a
  understanding from his mind,
    86a
  wisdom, 101b
  with night we b. sorrow, 301b
Banished, alone a b. man, 1084a
  fear cannot be b., 1015a
  find moral in narrative b., 760b
  for my willful crime b., 348b
  yet true-born Englishman, 226b
Banishing for hours, 457a
Banishment, bitter bread of b.,
    227a
Banjo on my knee, 727b
Banjos, batter on your b., 948b
Bank and shoal of time, 282a
  breathes upon b. of violets,
    251a
  broke b. at Monte Carlo, 821a
  contemplate entangled b., 628a
  First Supernatural B., 1009a
  grass b. beyond, 729a
  moonlight sleeps upon this b.,
    235a
  waly up the b., 1088b
  whereon wild thyme blows,
    229b
Banker, Burglar B. Father, 734a
Bankers just like anybody, 1051b
  schoolmates clergymen, 881a
Bankrupt of life, 368a
Banks, allegory on b. of Nile,
    480b
  and braes o' bonny Doon, 494a
  Brignall b., 520b
  o' Loch Lomond, 1099a
  of Wabash far away, 905b
  Tiber trembled underneath b.,
    253a
  vast surplus in b., 545b
Banner, blood-red b. streams,
    549b
  over me was love, 29a
  royal b. and all quality, 275a
  song for our b., 600a
  that b. in sky, 633a
  torn but flying, 557b
  with strange device, 621b
  yet freedom yet thy b., 557a
Banners, all thy b. wave, 538a
  confusion on thy b. wait, 441b
  flout the sky, 281a
  hang b. on outward walls, 286b
  terrible as an army with b., 29b
  unfurled o'er world, 655a
Banquet, behave in life as at b.,
    138b
  hall deserted, 542b
  partaken in anxiety, 76a
  sated with b. of life, 113b
Banqueting upon borrowing, 38a
Banshee, memory comes like b.,
    830b
Baptism enslaved me, 830a
  spirit streaming from b., 857a
Baptist's, John B. head in a
    charger, 42b
Baptizing in name of Father, 45a
Bar against tyranny resolute men,
    703b-704a
  back of b. in solo game, 933a
  birth's invidious b., 650b
  crossed the b., 655a
  foul storm out, 883a
  gold b. of heaven, 731a
  harbor b. moaning, 690b
  no moaning of b., 655a
  politics we b., 768a

Bar, to b. as very young man,
    767b
Barabbas a publisher, 563b
  stock of B., 235a
  was a robber, 49b
Barb in arrow of childhood, 832a
Barbara, name was B. Allen,
    1088a
Barbarian Scythian bond nor free,
    54b
  weeping above dead, 749a
Barbarians, if superior man dwelt
    among, 72a
  Philistines populace, 715b
Barbaric omens, 995a
  pearl and gold, 343a
  yawp, 701a
Barbarism and despotism, 473b
  destruction and b. victors, 979b
  fanaticism to b. one step, 437a
  fastnesses of ancient b., 720b
  from b. to degeneration, 786b
  my native land prey to b., 145a
  theater flourish in b., 800a
Barbarous dissonance, 337a
  in beauty stooks arise, 803a
  multitude, 233a
  triumph o'er her b. foes, 426b
  woman more b. than man, 805a
Barber, imprudently married b.,
    442b
  kept on shaving, 679b
Barbers, hide the haughty b.,
    1025b
Barbershop, lights burn low in b.,
    1025b
Bard, hear voice of the b., 488b
  here dwelt, 420a
  is envious of bard, 67b
  old or modern b., 336b
  whom none to praise, 510b
Bards, black and unknown b.,
    906b
  eighth commandment not for
    b., 527a
  have a share of honor, 66a
  in fealty to Apollo, 579b
  name me among lyric b., 120b
  of old enjoyed in you, 486b
  of passion, 583b
  of rhyme free, 962b
  Olympian b., 602b
  saints heroes, 710b
  sublime, 622a
Bare, back and side go b., 188b
  Ben Bulben's head, 885a
  bodkin, 262a
  cupboard was b., 1096a
  gift without giver b., 692b
  Goya of the b. field, 1083a
  imagination of feast, 226a
  let little colt go b., 1098a
  looked on Beauty b., 1023b
  old men's heads b., 1017a
  on b. earth he lies, 371b
  poor h. forked animal, 278b
  ruined choirs, 292b
  to the buff, 824b
  trees turn b., 1081b
Bare-bosomed night, 700a
Barefaced poverty drove me to
    verses, 124a
Barefoot boy, 626a
  dance b. on wedding day, 219a
  dervishes, 603b
  him that makes shoes go b.,
    184b
Barère's, not read B. Memoirs,
    596b

Bares, foeman b. steel tarantara,
    766b
  his horns above sleep, 1068b
Bargain catch cold and starve,
    290b
  in the way of b., 239b
  necessity never good b., 421b
  never better b. driven, 203b
Barge, Arthur from the b., 654a
  drag the slow b., 459b
  like burnished throne, 287b
Bark and bite, 396a
  attendant sail, 410a
  band of exiles moored b., 573b
  bitter b. burning clove, 927b
  cynic b., 602b
  fatal and perfidious b., 338b
  hark dogs do b., 1097b
  if my b. sinks, 686a
  is on the sea, 559b
  let no dog b., 231b
  moor b. with two anchors,
    125a
  off shot the specter b., 525a
  puts from native bay, 232b
  see they b. at me, 279a
  star to every wandering b., 294a
  watchdog's honest b., 560a
  worse than bite, 325b
  yond tall anchoring b., 279b
Barking, crowing of cocks and b.
    of dogs, 75a
Barkis is willin', 671a
Barks, Hylax b. in doorway, 116b
  Nicean b. of yore, 641b
  sail upstream, 4a
Barley, land of wheat and b., 10a
Barleycorn, inspiring bold John
    B., 495b
  John B. got up again, 493b
Barmaids diviner than mermaids,
    1051b
Barn, hay creaking to b., 1075a
  sit in a b., 1095b
  stack or the b. door, 334b
Barnaby, like B. Rudge, 692b
Barns, neither reap nor gather
    into b., 41a
Barometer, high and low b., 760b
  sweeping around, 760a
Baron, Sir Leoline the b. rich,
    524a
Barracks, single men in b., 873b
Barrage, chemical b. against life,
    1061b
Barred on account of race, 1074a
  recognize good but be b., 79b
Barrel, beat an empty b., 953a
  do with b. of gold, 812b
  of meal wasted not, 13a
  organs, 975a
  save them by b. load, 856b
Barrel-house kings, 952b
Barren, acre of b. ground, 296a
  after summer b. winter, 214b
  among b. crags, 646a
  bosom starves birth, 439b
  bride, 406b
  buds of b. flowers, 775a
  imagination cold and b., 452b
  leave this b. spot, 538a
  live a b. sister all your life,
    228b
  make b. our lives, 773b
  small model of b. earth, 227b
  superfluity of words, 385b
  sword sung on b. heath, 488a
  'tis all b., 438b
  weep b. tears, 568b

Beautiful, so various so b. so
  new, 715a
soup, 744b
Sredni Vashtar the B., 904a
swindles b. and simple, 863b
that war must be lost, 701b
thing raises man, 178a
things adorn world, 867b
this is b. country, 594b
three most b. things, 1102a
time of young love, 498a
too b. to live, 669b
true words are not b., 75a
uncut hair of graves, 700a
upon the mountains, 33a
what is b. is moral, 709b
what may be approved as b.,
  845b
when I was b., 187b
whole numbers, 1034a
wise and b., 710b
woman with one eye, 484b
women indisputably b. or ugly,
  415b
wonderful world, 719a
words are not true, 75a
world too b. this year, 1023a
you are b. and faded, 931b
Beautifully blue, 532a, 561a
time grows b. dim, 992a
Beautify, to b. life give it object,
  828a
Beauty adventure art, 861b
all that b. all that wealth, 440a
America not afraid of b., 1074a
and high degree, 1009b
and length of days, 773a
and virtue rarely together, 163a
and wisdom rarely conjoined,
  133b
are you not enough, 982a
as b. not great star, 942a
as much b. as could die, 303a
as we feel it, 867a
barbarous in b. stooks, 803a
beholding b. with eye of mind,
  93a
bereft of b., 219b
best of all we know, 801a
body's b. lives 955b
bought by judgment of eye,
  221b
brute b. and valor, 803a
by b. and by fear, 509b
by b. made amends, 893a
calls, 384b
carves bow of b., 602b
clad in b. of thousand stars,
  213b
cold and austere, 913a
come near your b. with nails,
  214b
convenience comfort, 1104a
creation of b., 644b
crieth in attic, 755b
crowds me till I die, 738b
daily b. in his life, 276a
dead black chaos, 220a
definition of b., 528a
die for b., 603b
doth of itself persuade, 220a
draws with single hair, 404b
dreamed life b., 680a
ease and speed not give work
  b., 168b
elevation and b., 716b
everything order and b., 707a
exists in mind, 434b
extent of b. and power, 595a

Beauty fare thee well, 588a
fatal gift of b., 557a
first problem was b., 1081b
flattered upon b., 415b
for ashes, 33b
for confiding youth, 516b
fruits of life and b., 488b
gift of God, 97a
gift to b. common sense, 730a
give b. in the inward soul, 92b
good nature more amiable than
  b., 394b
grows familiar to lover, 393b
habit between us and b., 863a
half the b. I possess, 502b
harmony grace melody, 747b
has not been fathomed, 708a
Helen's b. in brow of Egypt,
  230b
her b. and her chivalry, 555b
I died for b., 736a
ill layer-up of b., 245a
images of b., 93a
in all things, 586a
in art economy is b., 800a
in eye of beholder, 729a, 831b
in naked b. more adorned, 345b
in patterns of shadows, 992b
indescribable, 867a
invisible b., 944a
is a mystery, 986a
is everlasting, 997a
is there b. in Sodom, 708a
is there in truth no b., 323a
is truth, 583b
is vain, 27a
isle of b., 588a
keep back b., 803b
know b. as b., 73a
left b. on shore, 602a
light from her own b., 570a
little concerned with b., 786a
lives though lilies die, 980a
looked on B. bare, 1023b
loses b. in light of day, 993b
love b. truth we seek, 569b
love built on b., 307a
lust not after her b., 23b
makes b. because outlet, 945a
making beautiful old rhyme,
  293b
mathematics supreme b., 913a
mercy have on me, 738b
momentary in mind, 955b
most poetical topic, 643b
must be truth, 584b
mystery of b., 878b
Nature's coin, 337b
nature's system a real b., 1034a
ne'er enjoys, 411b
neither heat limb nor b., 271a
no excellent b., 209b
no spring nor summer b., 307a
nonsense and b. close connections, 951b
not lip or eye b. call, 403a
notion of absolute b., 93a
of aged face, 963a
of good old cause, 512a
of great machine, 993b
of holiness, 18a
of inflections, 955b
of innuendoes, 955b
of minstrel's lyre, 906b
of own b. mind diseased, 557a
of the lilies, 690b
of true manliness, 740a
of world has edges, 975a
one's b. another's ugliness, 607a

Beauty, orators dumb when b.
  pleadeth, 220a
our eyes never see, 893b
own excuse for being, 602b
perception of b. moral, 681b
pierce like pain, 937a
pledge of conformity, 867a
power of b. I remember, 372a
power of Greek in b., 715b
principal b. in a building,
  333b
provoketh thieves, 247b
rarest gift to b., 730a
renown which riches or b. confer, 115b
sat B. in my lap, 830a
say not of B., 990a
sense of pity b. pain, 843a
sex and b. inseparable, 986a
she walks in b., 558b
skin deep, 299b
sleep sleep b. bright, 488a
smother up his b., 238a
so ancient yet ever new, 147a
so long as b. shall be, 147b
sold for old man's gold, 903a
source of b. is in itself, 142a
stone to b. grew, 602a
sublimely pure, 913a
such b. as you master, 293b
such seems your b. still, 293b
sufficient end, 882a
take winds of March with b.,
  295b
teaches such b. as woman's eye,
  222a
terrible and awful, 708a
terrible b. is born, 882a
that dost consecrate, 568a
that Medusa's head, 1022a
that must die, 584a
thing of b. joy, 580a
though injurious, 349b
thy b. is to me, 641b
till b. truth love one, 801b
'tisn't b. nor good talk, 876b
to mind shameful to heart b.,
  708a
too rich for use, 223a
took from who loved them,
  914b
troubled by this b., 781a
truly blent, 251b
undiminished natural b., 1073b
unmask her b. to moon, 258a
use harms b., 870a
what b. is cannot be said, 867a
where b. has no ebb, 880a
where perhaps some b. lies,
  335b
who walks with B., 992a
whole mystery of b., 878b
whose b. past change, 803a
will come unannounced, 607a
wit high birth, 269a
with him b. slain, 220a
withdraws mind from love of
  b., 71a
without extravagance, 89b
without grace, 608b
without vanity, 554b
witty b. a power, 731a
worship in b. of holiness, 18a
wrought out from within, 781a
your b. will wither, 188a
Beauty's, blazon of sweet b. best,
  293b
breadth and length, 906a
but skin deep, 299b

Beauty's ensign yet is crimson, 225b
none of B. daughters, 559a
orient deep, 327a
parallels in b. brow, 292b
rose might never die, 291a
thy b. field, 291b
Beaux, where none are b., 434a
Beaver, on account of his b. hat, 673b
young Harry with b. on, 240a
Becalmed, ships b. at eve, 688b
Became, nothing b. him like leaving, 281b
Because, God not a "b.," 870a
I do not hope, 1003b
it is there, 876b
Beckon you to fraternize, 1060b
Beckoning shadows dire, 336b
what b. ghost, 405b
Beckons, Longing leans and b., 694b
Becks, nods and b., 334b
our minds to fellowship, 580b
Become, all that may b. a man, 282b
had b. what he could, 1056b
I have b. lost name, 1069a
ignorant man again, 956b
let each b. all capable of, 575a
man to behave toward government, 681a
not b. king's first minister, 924a
them with half so good grace, 270b
vilest things b. themselves, 287b
what capable of, 822b
Becomes, blessed youth b. as aged, 271a
nothing b. him ill, 221b
throned monarch better, 234b
Becoming, growing and a b., 716a
limit of b. mirth, 221b
present gone in b., 793b
Becoming-conscious, emotion source of b., 936b
Bed, a b. Clerk Saunders said, 1088b
and so to b., 375a, 962b
angels came to my b., 782a
angels guard my b., 396b
back to b. again, 947a
bad luck sits by b., 588b
be blest that I lie on, 357a
be in b. and sleep not, 1037a
book took him out of b., 310a
brimstone b., 533a
by night, 450a
by night on my b. I sought him, 29b
candle to light to b., 1093b
celestial b., 259b
creep into narrow b., 715a
desert sighs in b., 1059b
die in b., 810b, 992b
died in b., 753b
dread grave little as b., 377b
dull stale tired b., 277a
early to b. early to rise, 421b, 1033b
earth in earthy b., 652b
every b. is narrow, 1023b
every day got up and gone to b., 932a
for this huge birth, 354b
four angels to my b., 357a
get whole world out of b., 947a
go to b. by day, 823a
go to b. with lamb, 202b

Bed, goes to b. and does not pray, 323a
goes to b. by bell, 759b
gravity out of his b., 239a
has found out thy b., 489a
heaped for beloved's b., 572b
heart for my b. and board, 1075b
holy angels guard thy b., 396b
horn brought me from b., 578b
I in my b. again, 1084a
I their map lie flat on this b., 308a
in b. laugh in b. cry, 351a
in thy cold b., 321a
laid in b. majestical, 244b
let's to b. says Sleepyhead, 1094b
lie down in b. of sorrow, 351b
lie on Mother's b., 1076a
lies in his b. walks with me, 236b
lovers to b., 231a
made his own b. ere born, 354b
made his pendent b., 282a
make my b. in hell, 23a
make my b. soon, 1089a
manger for his b., 684b
marriage not b. of roses, 822a
mourn upon thy b., 774b
near approach b. may show, 351a
nicer to lie in b., 903a
O b. O delicious b., 592b
of daffodil sky, 652b
on his thorny green b., 552b
on my grave as now my b., 330b
one and all died in b., 753b
outcries call me from naked b., 204a
paid twenty-two percent, 522a
put them to b., 1095a
rode horses up to b., 914b
run into it as to lover's b., 288b
sate itself in celestial b., 259b
seldom die in b., 810b
should of stood in b., 1037b
sleep upon golden b., 884a
take up thy b., 45a
to b. go sober, 312b
toddle home die in b., 992b
warm weather in b., 388b
welcome to your gory b., 496a
went to b. with stockings on, 1096b
what torment not a marriage b., 308b
when I jump into my b., 823b
Zeus's b. of love, 85a
Bedamned, bedecked bediamonded b., 866b
Bedecked bediamonded bedamned, 866b
so b. ornate and gay, 349b
Bedevilment, man's b. and God's, 854a
Bedewed with liquid odors, 120b
Bedfellows, strange b., 297a, 733b
Bediamonded, bedecked b. bedamned, 866b
Bedlam, mad as B., 671b
Tom o' B., 277a
Bedroom eyes, 1060b
Bed's-feet, as to b. life is shrunk, 306a
Beds, bliss not b. of down, 322a
housewives in your b., 273a
make thee b. of roses, 212b

Beds, think of clean b., 992b
Bedtime, would it were b. Hal, 240b
Bee, brisk as a b., 429b
busy as a b., 202b
busy b. improve each hour, 396b
busy b. no time for sorrow, 487b
clover and one b., 739a
had stung it newly, 350b
how doth the busy b., 396b
laughing b. on stalk, 1082a
love in my bosom like a b., 204b
not good for swarm not good for b., 142b
partake as b. abstemiously, 737a
pedigree not concern b., 738b
preserved in amber, 135a
star that bringest home b., 538a
summer with flower and b., 574a
where the b. sucks, 297b
with honeyed thigh, 336a
Beech, sang beneath spreading b., 117b
Beechen green and shadows, 582a
spare the b. tree, 538a
Beeches drip in browns, 784b
Beef and captain's biscuits, 660b
give library to b. trust, 891b
great eater of b., 251a
meals of b. iron steel, 244a
pig had roast b., 1093b
roast b. of old England, 392b
stole piece of b., 1094a
without mustard, 802b
Beef-faced boys, 669b
Beehive's hum soothe ear, 500b
Bee-loud glade, 879b
Beelzebub, early morning B. arose, 567b
Been, it might have b., 626a
what has b. has b., 369b
who that hath ever b., 518a
Beer and skittles, 669a, 718a
chronicle small b., 273b
come my lad and drink b., 429a
corrodes copper, 760b
felony to drink small b., 215a
parson much bemused in b., 410a
questionable superfluity small b., 215a
root b. sold here, 764b
show vilely to desire small b., 215a
take you on trust for b., 831a
teetotaler, 836a
throw b. into Channel, 818a
Beersheba, Dan to B., 11b, 438b
Beery wenches, 807b
Bee's collected treasures, 442a
Bees black with gilt surcingles, 738b
excel the b. for government, 193a
for flies and hornets for bees, 179a
helmet now hive for b., 204b
honeyed words like b., 990b
if b. are few, 739a
innumerable b., 649b
intellectual life like b., 867a
many b. on single course, 978a
stirring birds on wing, 527b
swarm of b. and honey in the carcass, 11b
swarm of b. in May, 1087a

Bleed my bones, 1066b
Bleeding brow of labor, 858b
  from Roman rods, 459a
  piece of earth, 255a
  purple testament of b. war, 227b
Blemish, Christianity immortal b., 806a
  evidence of industry b., 754a
  formed without b., 70b
  lamb shall be without b., 8a
Blent, beauty truly b., 251b
Bless, except thou b. me, 7b
  God b. Prince of Wales, 589b
  God b. the Pretender, 414b
  God b. us every one, 671a
  God b. you, 1098b
  God b. you my dear, 434a
  good-bye God b. you, 820a
  hand that gave blow, 36oa
  her when she is riggish, 287b
  his name, 21a
  hold angel until he b. thee, 421a
  house from wikked wight, 167b
  I b. God in libraries, 444b
  Lord b. and keep thee, 9b
  man who invented sleep, 68oa
  squire and relations, 671a
  thee Bottom, 230a
  them that curse you, 40b
  turf that wraps clay, 443a
  work and b. day, 675b
  ye the Lord, 39a
  ye who now b. poor, 687b
Blessed Abbot of Aberbrothok, 532b
  abodes, 406a, 408a
  all generations call me b., 45b
  always to be b., 408a
  are the dead, 58b
  are the forgetful, 805b
  are the meek, 40a
  are the merciful, 40a
  are the peacemakers, 40a, 214b
  are the poor in spirit, 39b
  are the pure in heart, 40a
  are they that mourn, 40a
  are they that put their trust in him, 17a
  are they which are persecuted, 40a
  are they who hunger and thirst, 40a
  art thou among women, 45b
  barrier between day and day, 515b
  be he that cometh, 22a
  be Lord God of Israel, 46a
  be man that spares these stones, 299b
  be the name of the Lord, 14a
  be thy name Vogue, 1035a
  bed be b. that I lie on, 357a
  by country's wishes b., 443a
  by everything, 884a
  by yonder b. moon, 224a
  candles of night, 235b
  children call her b., 27a
  come what may been b., 558a
  damozel, 731a
  endless sabbaths b. ones see, 154a
  fell upon knees and b. God, 318b-319a
  green groves of the b., 119a
  half part of b. man, 236a
  he who expects nothing, 407b

Blessed he who has dear one dead, 807a
  he who has found his work, 578a
  hope whereof he knew, 783b
  horny hands of toil, 691b
  I had lived a b. time, 284a
  is the fruit of thy womb, 45b
  is the man that trusteth, 34a
  is the man that walketh not in counsel of ungodly, 16b
  Islands of B., 874a, 947a
  judge none b., 38a
  kings may be b., 495b
  little b. with soft phrase, 272b
  Lord b. the latter end of Job, 16b
  love of God had b., 551b
  man who possesses keen mind, 92a
  memory of the just is b., 24a
  mood, 509a
  more b. to give, 50a
  mother of us all, 474a
  mutter of Mass, 664b
  nor what b. prove accursed, 667a
  over whose acres b. feet, 237b
  part to heaven, 299a
  plot this earth, 226b
  rage for order, 956a
  seeming b. they grow, 447b
  so b. in climate, 926b
  soul or body more b., 884b
  sprung from b. abodes, 406a
  them unaware, 525b
  they that have not seen, 49b
  thou fallest a b. martyr, 299a
  thrice b. are friends, 942b
  thrice four times b., 117b
  to put cares away, 114b
  twice b., 234b
  were but as b. as I, 398a
  who have no talent, 604b
  who having nothing to say, 690a
  whom thou blessest is b., 9b
  with milk and honey b., 687b
  with natural abundance, 1025a
  youth becomes as aged, 271a
Blessedness, perfect b. vision of God, 158b
  single b., 228b
Blesses stars and thinks it luxury, 393a
Blessest, whom thou b. is blessed, 9b
Blesseth him that gives and him that takes, 234b
  with two happy hands, 201b
Blessing and cursing, 10b
  ask me b., 280a
  baby b. and bother, 759b
  brother hath taken away thy b., 7a
  full meal more than a b., 535a
  good neighbor is great b., 67b
  hold fast till gives b., 625b
  I had most need of b., 283b
  makes a b. dear, 350b
  money cannot buy, 326b
  national debt b., 484b, 547a
  no harm in b., 414b
  of St. Peter's Master, 326b
  out of God's b. into sun, 185a
  paid thy utmost b., 914b
  public debt a public b., 484b
  science be b. not curse, 950a

Blessing, shall yourselves find b., 687b
  society is a b., 466b
  unequal sharing of b., 925a
  unqualified b., 503b
Blessings, free trade one of b., 594b
  God from whom all b. flow, 377b
  health and intellect the two b., 102b
  of civilization, 763b
  on thee little man, 626a
  on this house, 463b
  on your frosty pow, 494b
  one of evils and another of b., 65a
  reap b. of freedom, 467a
  secure b. of liberty, 474a
  two supreme b., 85a
  unevenness of b., 1063b
  upon head of the just, 24a
  use b. of gods with wisdom, 122b
  without number, 396b
Blessings-of-civilization trust, 763b
Blew, fair breeze b., 524b
  great guns, 672a
  slughorn to my lips and b., 278b
Blicke nicht trauernd, 621a
Blight man was born for, 803b
Blighted buildings, 1063a
  seared and b. heart, 641a
Blights with plagues, 489b
Blind, all of them were b., 68oa
  and drinks his drop, 883b
  and ignorant in all, 301a
  and naked ignorance, 653a
  and often tipsy, 60ob
  as nails upon Cross, 998b
  beggar's daughter, 1087b
  Booth died b., 952b
  causes conspire to b., 402b
  desire, 773a
  ecstasy, 1043b
  eyes b. with stars, 906a
  eyes for the b., 749a
  eyes of the b. shall be opened, 32a
  eyes to the b., 15b
  for being b. God prepare me, 376a
  Fortune painted b. with muffler, 209a
  Fortune though b. not invisible, 209a
  Fury with abhorred shears, 338b
  guides, 43b
  halt and b., 47a
  he was as often seene, 167b
  Homer sing to me, 213a
  hysterics of Celt, 651a
  I was b., 48b
  justice b. deef and dumb, 890b
  leaders of the b., 43a
  leading blind to pit, 145a
  light when else wert b., 497b
  love is b., 168b, 233a
  love needs be b., 228b
  love to faults always b., 488a
  man's ditch, 884a
  mouths, 338b
  none so b., 386b
  not b. soul with clay, 649b
  not to differences, 1074a
  O b. hearts, 113b

Body, marry my b. to that dust, 321a
  mind or b. to prefer, 408b
  my b. a floating weed, 153a
  my b. my dungeon is, 824a
  my b. now an old tree, 380a
  my good bright dog, 1078a
  my house, 1078a
  Nature God soul, 480b
  naught cared b. for wind, 527b
  no riches above sound b., 38b
  not b. enough to cover mind, 522b
  not more than soul, 700b
  of Benjamin Franklin Printer, 421a
  of little recruit, 1040b
  of this death, 51a
  old in b. but never mind, 112a
  one motion, 1066a
  oppressions of b. and mind, 473a
  part of man's self, 793b
  perfect little b., 801a
  perfectly spherical, 673a
  politic like human body, 435b
  power lies in mind and b., 115b
  presence of b. in question, 535b
  pygmy b., 368a
  reading to mind as exercise to b., 395b
  Resurrection of the b., 60a
  ruler having human b. as subject, 93b
  sex woven into whole b., 850b
  ship of the b., 701b
  sickness-broken b., 333a
  so young b. with so old head, 234a
  soul gentle companion of b., 141a
  soul is form and doth b. make, 201b
  soul its b. off, 884b
  soul look b. touch, 884b
  sound mind in sound b., 139b, 373a
  sound of b. and mind, 121a
  sprigs root in horse's b., 468a
  swayed to music, 883b
  swung gently, 791b
  this is my b., 44b
  'tis mind makes b. rich, 219b
  to be buried obscurely, 209b
  whole b. not be cast into hell, 40a
  wholly body, 956a
  without spirit dead, 56b
  woman's b. the woman, 791b
  worms destroy this b., 15b
Body-hungry, soul-hungry worse than b., 1102a
Body's beauty lives, 955b
  casting b. vest aside, 360a
  go Soul the b. quest, 199a
  hardly in a b. power, 493a
Body-snatching not natural, 980b
Bog, snow falling on B. of Allen, 968a
  to an admiring b., 735a
Bogus revelation, 960a
Bohemia little country, 863b
Boil, cannot bake or b. whole, 901b
  her down until simmers, 814b
  maketh the deep b. like a pot, 16b
  we b. at different degrees, 609a

Boilers, parcel of b. and vats, 433a
Boiling, Hiroshima b., 1077a
  why sea b. hot, 746a
Boils, day b. at last, 661b
  round naked isles, 419b
Bois, n'irons plus aux b., 719a
Boisterously, as b. maintained as gained, 236b
Bold, alive and so b. O earth, 571a
  and turbulent of wit, 368a
  anfractuous rocks, 1001b
  bad man, 200a, 298a
  be b., 200b
  be bloody b. and resolute, 285b
  be not too b., 200b
  brave men and b., 1100b
  cook and captain b., 765b
  destruction of tea so b., 462b
  in conscious virtue b., 404b
  in that freedom b., 517b
  inspiring b. John Barleycorn, 495b
  jockey of Norfolk not too b., 200b
  let our minds be b., 833a
  look with favor on b. beginning, 117a
  maiden never b., 272b
  man first eat oyster, 390b
  men are parabolas, 1083b
  peasantry, 449a
  persistent experimentation, 970b
  righteous are b. as a lion, 26b
  story of Cambuscan b., 336a
  too b. to imagine, 459b
  virtue is b., 271b
  what makes robbers b. but lenity, 215b
Bolder and stronger peoples, 847b
  knits a b. one, 735b
  note than this swell, 641b
Boldest held his breath, 538a
  painters cannot trace, 397a
  sons of toil, 721a
Boldly, attack all the more b., 118b
  ride, 644a
  tells disagreeable truth b., 469b
Boldness certain to win praise, 127b
  lends hand to honest b., 102b
Bole, elm tree b., 663a
  leaf blossom or b., 883b
Bolingbroke, this canker B., 238b
Bolster, head on sweaty b., 1079b
Bolt, Ben B., 690a
  fool's b. soon shot, 184b
  of Cupid fell, 229b
  old age coming b. door, 149b
  running home, 1081a
Bolts, something picked lock slid b., 940a
  stronger b. than Aphrodite, 84b
  up change, 288b
Bomb, don't let anyone b. me, 1059a
  Lord b. Germans, 1059a
  might destroy whole port, 950b
  on Hiroshima, 982b, 967b
  severity path to b., 780a
  war fought with atomic b., 950b
Bombast out blank verse, 206a
  second sublime third b., 144a
Bombastiloquent, 92a
Bombing of Chinese cities, 984a

Bombs, atomic b. burst in hands, 888a
  atomic energy lead to b., 950b
  bursting in air, 541a
Bon mots, not enough b., 1032a
Bona Republica, 1105a
Bonaparte, ashes of Napoleon B., 506a
  Jeanne d'Arc and B., 1016a
Bond, break that sole b., 453a
  happy whom unbroken b. unites, 121a
  I'll seal to such a b., 232b
  let him look to his b., 233a
  neither b. nor free, 54b
  of iniquity, 49b
  of one immortal look, 666b
  of scattered family, 752a
  prosperity's very b. of love, 295b
  scatter and unloose from b., 220a
  so nominated in the b., 234b
  take a b. of fate, 285b
  tied by chance b., 680b
  'tis not in the b., 234b
  trust man on oath or b., 290a
  universal and common b., 191a
  which keeps me pale, 284b
  word as good as b., 197a
Bondage, hold fellow men in b., 503a
  of irrational fears, 832b
  out of the house of b., 8b
  to previous history, 732a
Bondman in hand bears power, 254a
Bondman's, in a b. key, 232a
Bonds, bear b. that gall, 774b
  no b. attached him to life, 162b
  of Union dissolved, 530a
  that unite only in mind, 908a
Bondsman's unrequited toil, 640b
Bone, behind mortal b., 735b
  break b. suck out marrow, 180b
  bright hair about the b., 306b
  consuming rat and b., 885a
  divorced from eye and b., 1038a
  fetch poor dog a b., 1096a
  fever of the b., 1002a
  flesh of flesh b. of b., 348a
  life near b. sweetest, 684a
  mouths sentence as curs b., 456a
  of manhood, 452b
  of my bones, 5b
  of thy bone, 193b
  rag and b. and hair, 875a
  reform taking b. from dog, 863b
  secret life of b., 1069b
  vigor of b., 269a
  white as rain-washed b., 874a
Boneless gums, 282b
Bones and leather, 906a
  are dust, 527a
  arise from my b., 118b
  bitter b., 1057a
  bleed my b., 1066b
  bone of my b., 5b
  bound b. and veins in me, 802b
  bury b. in hideaways, 1051b
  can these b. live, 35a
  chalk of my b., 1064b
  cursed be he that moves my b., 299b
  dead men lost b., 1002b
  dice human b., 563a

Brown hills melted into spring, 685b
in b. study, 202b
Jeanie with light b. hair, 727b
long and lank and b., 525a
long b. path before me, 701a
man's burden, 875b
meadows b. and sere, 574b
myrtles b., 338a
not Old B. any longer, 684a
prefer philanthropy of Captain B., 684a
quick b. fox, 1101a
some gave them b., 1092b
spit b. my son, 947b
strong b. god, 1006a
very plain b. stone, 634a
when all trees b., 691a
Browne, sedulous ape to Sir Thomas B., 824a
Brown-frocked brother, 905a
Browning, find B. plain, 664a
from B. some Pomegranate, 617b
hang it all Robert B., 988b
is what, 668a
Meredith prose B., 838b
Mrs. B. guard silence, 931b
picked fair-coined soul, 857a
since Chaucer was alive, 536b
Browning's, Mrs. B. death relief, 631a
Brown's, John B. body, 755a
Browns, beeches in b. and duns, 784b
Brows, bliss in our b. bent, 287a
earned with sweat of b., 194a
greener from b., 651b
like gathering storm, 495b
nightcap decked his b., 447a
nodded with his darkish b., 62b
not seen in either of our b., 211b
of dauntless courage, 342b
Browsed, cattle b. on plain, 933b
Bruce has aften led, 496a
Brüder, alle Menschen werden B., 497a
Bruise, ax fitter to b., 351b
better for b. than arnica, 666b
it shall b. thy head, 6a
thou shalt b. his heel, 6a
Bruised reed shall he not break, 33a
together crushed and b., 405a
Brunswick, Hamelin town's in B., 662a
Brunt, bear b. pay arrears, 666b
stands b. of life, 84b
Brush, blind hand b. my wing, 489a
essential in painting, 153a
painter's b. consumes dreams, 883b
structural basis established by b., 148a
whether chisel pen b., 882a
whitewash and long-handled b., 759a
work with so fine a b., 533b-534a
Brushed, hand has b. away, 489a
past palms on staircase, 1059a
Brushwood sheaf, 663a
Brutal arm appear, 885a
Brutality, industry without art b., 699a
oppressor commit b. openly, 1083a
Brutalizing lower class, 716b

Brute, beast b. bastard, 1068a
beauty and valor, 803a
chuck 'im out the b., 873a
et tu B., 112b, 255a
love of a b., 642b
you b. hissed countess, 887b
Brutes, eating and drinking like b., 702b
exterminate b., 844a
made b. men men divine, 721b
man's difference from b., 794a
nation of b., 844a
not born to live like b., 160b
without you, 383b
Brutish, nasty b. and short, 318a
Brutus and Cassius not displayed, 140a
Caesar had his B., 464b
dear B., 253b
exit B. now she'll read, 135b
is an honorable man, 255b
makes mine greater, 256a
no orator as B. is, 255b
set of vocal cords, 1047a
you also B., 112b
Bubble blown by successful teacher, 818b
fire burn caldron b., 285a
gonfalon b., 962b
honor but an empty b., 371b
life a b., 210a
life's troubled b., 914b
like b. on fountain, 520a
no b. so iridescent, 818b
now b. burst, 408a
reputation, 249a
world's a b., 209b
Bubbles, borne like thy b. onward, 558a
earth hath b., 281a
man and his dwellings as b., 156a
millions of b. like us, 630b
tattoo soap b., 1047a
we buy, 692a
winking at brim, 582b
Bubbling and loud-hissing urn, 458a
cry of swimmer, 560a-b
sinks with b. groan, 557b
venom flings, 555a
wellspring, 730b
Buccaneer, Morgan the B., 749b
Buccaneers of buzz, 738b
Buck stops here, 984a
Bucket down and full of tears am I, 228a
drop of a b., 32b
of whitewash, 759a
old oaken b., 553a
past a b. of ashes, 948b
up doun as b. in a welle, 167b
Buckets into empty wells, 458a, 523a
two b. filling one another, 228a
Bucketshop of refrigerator, 877b
Buckhurst, I would B. choose, 382a
Buckingham, changing guard at B. Palace, 96b
so much for B., 392a
Buckle, pride plume here b., 803a
Buckler, his truth shall be thy shield and b., 20b
Buckles, silver b. on knee, 1098a
Bucks, fat black b., 952b
Bud, canker lives in sweetest b., 292a
in age I b. again, 323b
not as in b. of spring, 308b

Bud, rose is sweeter in b., 203a
this b. of love, 224a
worm in the b., 252b
Buddha, go for refuge to B., 80b
Budding historians, 997a
Buddy, Christ Himself b., 1078a
Budge, I'll not b. an inch, 219a
Ten Commandments not b., 694b
Buds, cankers in musk rose b., 229b
darling b. of May, 291b
forgot to blow, 780a
of barren flowers, 775a
young b. sleep in root, 580a
Buff and the blue, 496b
bare to the b., 824b
Buffalo, elephant with sign saying B., 684b
home where b. roam, 808a
thought he saw b., 747a
Buffalo Bill's defunct, 1030a
Buffaloes, water b. neurasthenic, 997a
Buffet, not wise who b. against love, 82b
Buffets, blows and b. of world, 284a
fortune's b. and rewards, 263a
Buffon, is it Aristotle Pliny B., 436a
Buffoon and poet, 815b
chemist fiddler and b., 368b
Buffs, private of B., 656a
steady the B., 872a
Bug, flap b. with gilded wings, 411a
snug as b. in rug, 422b
Bugle, blow b. blow, 648b
bring good old b. boys, 747b
one blast upon b. horn, 520a
sound upon b. horn, 647a
Bugles, blare of b., 866a
blow out you b., 994a
calling for them, 1028b
cry of b. going by, 860a
what are b. blowin' for, 873a
Build a new world, 982b
beneath stars, 399b
except the Lord b. the house, 22b
experience arch to b. upon, 776b
from bottom up, 970b
Great Society, 1064a
houses and inhabit them, 33b
if I must b. church, 1057b
intending to b. tower, 47a
lofty rhyme, 338a
me nest on greatness of God, 796b
me straight, 622b
middle-aged b. woodshed, 682a
on fortune build on sand, 318b
on human heart, 661b
pair nor b. nor sing, 527b
schoolrooms for boy, 686a
small cabin b. there, 879b
thee more stately mansions, 633b
they labor in vain that b. it, 22b
throne of bayonets, 859b
time to b. up, 27b
trout crystal stair, 944a
upon this rock b. my church, 43a
what we plan we b., 722b
your ship of death, 986b
youth b. bridge to moon, 682a

Cake, let them eat c., 436b
  see to substance of c., 851b
  some gave plum c., 1093a
Cakes, all that c. brain, 696b
  and ale, 251b
  bridegrooms brides and bridal c., 319b
Calabash, goodnight Mrs. C., 1026b
Calais, find C. lying in my heart, 187b
Calamities of life, 385b
  portents and c. to warn men, 109b
  rather be notorious for c., 134b
  reckon benevolence and right-eousness c., 100a
Calamitous in drawn-out witti-cism, 536b
  necessity of going on, 467b
  to the conquered, 90b
Calamity, child of c., 760a
  fortune not satisfied with one c., 125b
  in English history, 829a
  in power of no c., 805a
  makes c. of so long life, 262a
  man's true touchstone, 316b
  morale not destroyed by c., 959a
  no c. greater than lavish de-sires, 74b
  wedded to c., 225a
Calamus, hinc quam sic c. saevior ense patet, 311a
Calaveras County, 758b
Calcaria, de c. in carbonarium, 144a
Calculate, no wisdom can c. end, 467a
Calculated, nicely c. less or more, 517a
  so c. so malignant, 1021b
  take c. risks, 987b
Calculating average of virtues, 770a
  it looks so c., 840a
Calculation shining out of other, 670a
  sum defies c., 477b
Calculations, upset most careful c., 379a
Calculus, common sense reduced to c., 479b
Caldron, fire burn c. bubble, 285a
  of dissolute loves, 146b
Caledonia stern and wild, 519a
Caledonia's, support C. cause, 496b
Calendar, a c. look in almanac, 230a
  striking from c., 630b
Calf and young lion together, 31a
  bring fatted c., 47a
  false as wolf to c., 268b
  killed c. in high style, 365a
  second beast like a c., 57b
  trod in footsteps of c., 846a
Calf's skin on recreant limbs, 236a
Caliban, 'Ban 'Ban Ca-C., 297a
Calico cat replied Meeow, 820b
  pie, 673b
  tree, 673b
California, talk C., 926b
Californian, I met a C., 926b
Californians race of people, 864a
Calisthenics with words, 1029a
Call, almost like c. to come, 928b
  back world of shadows, 993a

Call back yesterday, 227a, 301b
  bawd a bawd, 102b
  brother back to me, 574a
  brothers c. from bay, 710b
  cattle home, 690b
  delicate creatures ours, 274b
  don't c. out National Guard, 982a
  dunno what to c. him, 845b
  fig a fig, 102b
  first to c. philosophy down, 111b
  for robin redbreast, 314b
  forth thundering Aeschylus, 303b
  gods to witness, 290a
  grief at not wanting to c. dead back, 937b
  heard country's c., 875b
  heaven and earth to witness, 290a
  her blessed, 27a
  Himself a man, 1031a
  home the child, 1040a
  how you c. to me c. to me, 784a
  in and invite God, 308b
  in thy death's head, 323b
  it not vain, 518b
  let no bird c., 1023a
  let us c. thee devil, 273b
  loud winds when they c., 512a
  me anything, 390b
  me early mother dear, 645a
  me horse, 239a
  me Ishmael, 695b
  me madame, 970a
  neighbors in, 1094a
  nigh unto them that c., 23a
  no man foe, 1021a
  none dare c. it treason, 210a
  not easy to c. back, 948b
  nothing c. our own but death, 227b
  obey the important c., 458b
  of running tide, 946b
  one clear c. for me, 655a
  please to c. it rush candle, 219b
  saints aid if men c., 524a
  spade a spade, 102b
  spirits from vasty deep, 239b
  that backing your friends, 239a
  that which we c. a rose, 223b
  the fleeting breath, 440b
  things by right names, 500b
  through curtains c. on us, 305a
  to battle and battle done, 836a
  to the earth and sea, 700a
  today his own, 369b
  truce to terror, 1073b
  truth obeyed c., 885a
  try first thyself and after c. God, 76b
  unless they c. signals, 1025b
  up your men, 522a
  upon all who love freedom, 1016b
  upon my soul, 251b
  when you c. me that smile, 859b
  wild c. and clear c., 946b
  will they come when you c., 239b
  you back dear love, 83b
  you c. for faith, 665a
  you c. me misbeliever, 232a
  you Shepherd from hill, 712a
Called brother's father dad, 236a
  fool c. her lady fair, 875a
  for his pipe, 1092b
  him soft names, 582b
  if shape it might be c., 344a

Called it macaroni, 1090a
  many are c., 43b
  neither two nor one c., 267b
  New World into existence, 507a
  out of Egypt c. my son, 39b
  them untaught knaves, 238b
  till we are c. to rise, 737b
Calleth, deep c. unto deep, 19a
  them all by their names, 23a
Callimachus, tomb of C., 104b
Calling, all my c. and all my art, 190a
  bugles c. for them, 1028b
  dignity of high c., 453b
  each honest c., 1026a
  faint and far away, 961b
  followed mercenary c., 854a
Callooh callay, 745a
Calls back lovely April, 291b
  beauty c., 384b
  death c. ye to the crowd, 327b
  far c. coming far, 969a
  fool c. you foolish, 85a
  if anybody c., 934a
  Jerusalem thy sister c., 491a
  me Tom, 301b
  not Thee to guard, 875b
  stated c. to worship, 428b
  who c. me villain, 261b
Calm, after storm c., 1033a
  after storm comes c., 386b
  all c. as it was bright, 362b
  cankers of c. world, 240a
  contending kings, 220b
  day so cool so c., 323a
  drifted in sheepish c., 1076a
  envisage circumstance c., 584b
  escape into c. regions, 434b
  evening c. and free, 512a
  for a c. unfit, 368a
  gloomy c. of idle vacancy, 431a
  he of c. and happy nature, 93b
  in c. sea every man pilot, 366a
  my soul's c. retreat, 362b
  no joy but c., 645b
  peace and public c., 712b
  Peace and Quiet, 335b
  quiet innocent recreation, 326b
  quiet interchange, 431b
  region where no night, 321a
  sea is c. tonight, 714b
  so deep, 512a
  Soul of all things, 711a
  stars in their c., 711b
  thou mayst smile, 476a
Calme, luxe c. et volupté, 707a
Calmer of thoughts, 326a
Calmness, law in c. made, 515a
  to remember, 726a
Calumniating, envious and c. time, 269a
Calumnies answered best with si-lence, 302b
Calumnious strokes, 258a
Calumny, envy c. hate pain, 572a
  thou shalt not escape c., 262b
Calvary, place called C., 47b
Calves, shins ankles c. knees, 902a
Calvin oatcakes and sulphur, 522b
Cambridge ladies, 1030b
  people rarely smile, 993b
  ye fields of C., 358a
Cambridgeshire of all England, 993b
Cambuscan, story of C. bold, 336a
Cambyses', King C. vein, 239a
Came across a time, 1064b
  fear c. upon me, 14b
  forth to see again stars, 160b

Came, I c. I saw I conquered, 112b
I c. like water, 630a
I c. saw. and overcame, **242b**
into woods Master c., 796b
naked c. I out, 14a
once a world, 735a
out from Egypt, 8b
Satan c. also, 14a
tell them I c., 914b
three thousand miles and died, 693b
to dark tower c., 278b
to making of man, 773a
to scoff, 449b
upon midnight clear, 657b
upon no wine, 1023b
Cameelious hump, 876a
Camel, cloud in shape of a c., 263b
easier for c. to go, 43b
swallow a c., 43b
Camellia, what violet has c. not, 858a
Camelot, looked down to C., 645b
Camel's, not e'en admit c. nose, 566b
Camels are snobbish, 997a
Cameo, more affable than c., 910a
Camera, I am a c., 1054b
Camerado this is no book, 703a
Camlet, my fine c. cloak, 375a
Camp, court the c. the grove, 518b
father and I to c., 1090a
Campaigning weather, 1042a
Campaigns are emotional orgies, 866b
Campaspe, Cupid and my C., 203a
Campbells are comin', 1089b
original seat of C., 521a
Camped by billabong, 869a
Campground, tenting on old c., 752b
Camping, Fame's eternal c. ground, 704b
Camps, covered Europe with concentration c., 954b
terrible from c., 1058a
Campus habet lumen auris acumen, 167a
Can, come fill up my c., 522a
cry I c. no more, 803b
guess if you c., 331b
he who c. does, 836b
if poor whenever you c., 96b
if we c. we must, 853b
live as we c., 102a
live we how we c., 216b
make us do what we c., 608b
pass me the c. lad, 853b
something hope wish, 803b
youth replies I c., 603b
Cana, many guests had C. 898a
Canaan, Abram dwelled in C., 6b
Canadian frontier pattern for world, 920b
Canary wine, 583b
Cancel all our vows, 211b
and tear to pieces, 284b
half a line, 630b
power to c. captivity, 254a
Canceled, across c. skies, 1022a
Cancels, end of life c. bands, 240a
time c. young pain, 84a
Candid, be c. where we can, 407b
brow, 843b
save me from c. friend, 507a
ye marshes how c., 796b

Candied, let c. tongue lick pomp, 263a
Candle, bell book and c., 236b
better to light one c., 981b
book bell and c., 175b
burned on table, 1018a
burning while sleeping, 309b
burns at both ends, 1023a
extinguishes natural c., 381a
feel steady c. flame, 664b
hold c. to my shames, 233a
hold farthing c. to sun, 312a
how far c. throws beams, 235b
light c. to the sun, 362a
if you please to call it a rush c., 219b
lights c. to sun, 312a
lights gleaming, 905b
not care a farthing c., 535b
of understanding, 36b
one small c. light a thousand, 319a
out out brief c., 286b
put c. under a bushel, 40a
scarcely fit to hold c., 415a
set a c. in the sun, 312a
this day light such a c., 180a
to be c. or mirror, 865b
to light you to bed, 1093b
two chairs half c., 673b
white c. in holy place, 963a
Candlelight, colors by c., 618a
dress by yellow c., 823a
Candlelit, old at evening c., 187b
Candles are all out, 283a
blessed c. of night, 235b
burn like fabulous c., 1080b
held to speed them, 1028b
night's c. burnt out, 225a
rather light c., 981b
when c. out all women fair, 137b
Candlestick, jump over c., 1096b
put candle on a c., 40a
Candlestick-maker, butcher baker c., 1096b-1097a
Candlesticks, seven golden c., 57b
Candor and amicable relations, 492a
Candy deal of courtesy, 238b
is dandy, 1051b
not made of sugar c., 923b
Cane, carrying a small c., 1046b
Canem, cave c., 150a
Canker, as killing as c. to rose, 338a
galls infants of spring, 258a
joy without c. or cark, 804a
loathesome c., 292a
that benumbs, 769a
this c. Bolingbroke, 238b
worm c. and grief, 563a
Cankers in musk rose buds, 229b
of calm world, 240a
root and fruit, 1034b
Cannibals that each other eat, 272b
Cannikin, why clink c., 662b
Cannon his name c. his voice, 731a
revolution more c. shot, 885a
then c. and he comes, 918b
to right of them, 652a
Cannonball took off legs, 591b
Cannon's, burst c. roar, 633a
opening roar, 556a
seeking reputation in c. mouth, 249a
Cannons taken or saved, 732a
thundering c. roar, 450b

Cannot, he who c. teaches, 836b
Canoe, paddle own c., 128a, 567b
Canon 'gainst self-slaughter, 257b
of social code, 849a
Canopy, most excellent c. the air, 261a
my c. the skies, 408a
who spread its c., 381a
Cans, paved with tin c., 835b
Canst, give all thou c., 517a
Cant, clear your mind of c., 433b
in American moralism, 1055b
nothing but c., 552b
of criticism, 438a
of hypocrites the worst, 438a
of not men but measures, 452a
Cantankerous, small speech c., 101a
Canted in this canting world, 438a
Canter, little finishing c., 789a
Canters, as they c. awaäy, 654b
Canticles, Homeric or Biblical c., 703b
Cantie, mony a c. day John, 494b
wi' mair, 494a
Canting, canted in this c. world, 438a
Cants, clear myself of c., 576b
which are canted, 438a
Canvas drooping side by side, 688b
of heavy foresail, 843a
sail even with c. rent, 130a
sail with all thy c. set, 105a
to our imaginations, 681b
Canyon, dropping petal down Grand C., 946b
Canyons, neighing c., 1043b
Cap and bells, 692a
and gown atavistic, 845b
by night, 447a
feather in his c., 438a
for c. and bells lives pay, 692a
riband in c. of youth, 265b
Capability and godlike reason, 264b
negative c., 584b
Capable, all I am c. of becoming, 1014a
and wide revenge, 275a
become all c. of, 575a
hand now warm and c., 581b
mathematician c. of reasoning, 94b
mind c. of anything, 843b
not all c. of everything, 116b
of being in uncertainties, 584b
of every wickedness, 844a
of greatest vices, 327b
of higher things, 952a
of nothing but dumbshows, 262b
Capacious salad bowl, 824a
Capacity, all men have is c. for work, 941b
by c. is wisdom acquired, 105b
contribution according to c., 687a
for delight and wonder, 843a
for taking pains, 770a
for taking trouble, 424a, 578a, 756b
functional c., 475a
genius is c. to see, 989b
man's c. for justice, 1024b
naught enters thy c., 251a
to despise himself, 867b
Cap-a-pe, 258a

Cast, why art thou c. down, 19a
wilt c. forth no more, 854b
Caste, Brahmin c. of New England, 634b
Castest, why c. thou off my soul, 20a
Casteth, perfect love c. out fear, 57a
Castigation, birch twig for c., 879a
Castile, no prince of C. gained land, 173b
Castilian, choose what becomes C., 587a
Casting body's vest aside, 360a
dim religious light, 336a
Cast-iron back with hinge, 733b
Castle, bores through his c. wall, 227b
contentions like bars of c., 25a
Doubting C., 365b
habitant of c. gray, 685b
hath pleasant seat, 282a
house my c. is, 578a
man's house his c., 198a
rich man in c., 684b
splendor falls on c. walls, 648b
stand in window of c., 113a
village belongs to C., 980a
Castled crag of Drachenfels, 556
Castlereagh, mask like C., 570a
Castle's strength will laugh, 286b
Castles, building c. in Spain, 171a
Castration, Negro past of c., 1081a
Casts, shadow that it c., 517b
to write a living line, 303b
Casual creeds, 712a
flocks of pigeons, 955a
tongue, 899a
Casualties, mistakes paid in c., 1016b
Cat and fiddle, 1094a
bell the c., 76a, 169b
bought crooked c., 1096b
calico c. replied Meeow, 820b
can't be vice in c., 748a
care killed a c., 247a
cat's a c. Rolet a knave, 377a
Cheshire C. vanished slowly, 744a
consider my c. Jeoffrey, 444b
differences between c. and lie, 762a
dog pipe or two, 855a
endow college or c., 407a
fog comes on c. feet, 948a
had seven kits, 1093a
had Tiberius been c., 715a
harmless necessary c., 234a
has only nine lives, 762a
in gloves catches no mice, 422a
is in well, 1093b
I've got a little c., 832a
languishes loudly, 815b
mad if they behold a c., 234a
made a c. laugh, 587a
may look on king, 185a
melancholy as gib c., 237b
mew and dog have day, 266a
more ways of killing c., 691a
my c. Jeoffrey, 444b
nine lives like a c., 185a
owest c. no perfume, 278b
poor c. i' the adage, 282b
room to swing c., 671b
stronger than that c., 505b
that sits on hot stove lid, 762b
walked by himself, 876a

Cat watch mouse, 391a
when I play with my c., 190a
who shall bell the c., 76a
who will bell c., 169b
worried the c., 1098b
would eat fish, 184a
Catalogue, in c. ye go for men, 284a
no reading more fascinating than c., 801b
of common things, 581b
of things necessary, 376b
read c. sooner than nothing, 932a
Cataract, faint idea of c., 596b
leaps in glory, 648b
sounding c. haunted me, 509a
Cataracts and hurricanoes, 278a
Catastrophe, education and c., 888b
of old comedy, 277a
tickle your c., 242a
Catastrophes, unparalleled c., 951a
Catch a falling star, 304b
another Antony, 289b
as catch can, 442b
bargain c. cold and starve, 290b
Christ with worm, 1075a
claws that c., 745a
conscience of the king, 261b
earth's heedless sons, 1036a
ere she change, 406b
hard to c. and conquer, 730b
him once upon hip, 232a
nets to c. the wind, 315b
not God he'll c., 1054a
perdition c. my soul, 274a
perish or c. up, 903a
springes to c. woodcocks, 259a
the driving gale, 409b
the manners living, 407b
the nearest way, 281b
up with advanced countries, 903b
when pleasure can be had c. it, 432a
with his surcease success, 282a
you will never c. up, 886b
Catched fish and talked, 761a
swallow gudgeons ere they're c., 75b
Catcher in the rye, 1078a
Catches, slow man c. up with swift, 65b
Catchwords, man lives by c., 822b
Catechism, so ends my c., 240b
Catechist, something of Shorter C., 815b
Categorical imperative, 445b
order c., 766b
Caterpillar, I don't see said C., 743b
Caterpillars of the commonwealth, 227a
Caters for the sparrow, 247b
Catharsis, tragedy a c., 99a
Cathay, cycle of C., 647b
Cathedral, in vast c. leave him, 651b
looking like bank, 1009a
mankind inspired made c., 822a
tunes, 735a
Cathedrals, more benefit from bathroom than c., 1035b
our Gothic c., 998a
Cather, Willas c., 1040b
Catholic C.O., 1076a
holy C. Church, 60a
judges neither C. nor agnostic, 967a

Catholicism minus Christianity, 724b
Catholics, all equal except C., 635a
and Communists, 1054b
Catiline, how long C., 110b
prodigal of own possessions, 115b
Catins, mes pensées sont mes c., 437a
Catlike, undulantly with c. steps, 878b
Cato, like C. give laws, 411a
vanquished had C., 134a
Cat's a cat and Rolet a knave, 377a
mean as c. meat, 932a
pull chestnuts with c. paw, 360b
run away with string, 1098a
what c. averse to fish, 439b
Cats, all c. gray when candles out, 137b
and monkeys monkeys and c., 798a
do c. eat bats, 743a
fought dogs killed c., 662b
rain c. and dogs, 391a
seven c., 1093b
those who play with c., 195a
Cattle beneath shadow of oak, 454b
browsed on plain, 933b
call c. home, 690b
cursed above all c., 6a
die as c., 1028b
herdman who drives c., 3b
if c. and horses had hands, 70b
lowly c. shed, 684b
pedigree of horses c., 628b
upon a thousand hills, 19a
would draw gods like c., 70b
yellow c. browsed, 933b
Catullus be resolved and firm, 114b
walk that way, 881b
worst of all poets, 114b
you should cease folly, 114b
Caucasus, thinking on frosty C., 226a
Caught at God's skirts, 662a
God c. his eye, 1040b
hanging around till you've c. on, 930a
him yes I held him, 799a
his clear accents, 662b
in that sensual music, 882b
moral man regrets even if not c., 961a
morning's minion, 803a
mother came and c. her, 1095b
my heavenly jewel, 203b
our youth, 994a
she c. him by his garment, 7b
trout c. with tickling, 252b
with his sweet perfections c., 314b
without diadem, 737b
Cauld, when auld waxeth c., 1088b
Cauliflower cabbage with education, 762a
Causa latet vis notissima, 128b
Causation, law of c., 752b
Cause and effect from economy, 1062b
armor of righteous c., 858b
bad c. bad means, 467a
be c. strong or weak, 692b
beauty of good old c., 512a

Cause, calledst me dog before c., 234a
cannot cross c. why born, 222a
common c. decays, 89b
common c. to save Union, 637a
died in virtue's c., 218b
do not kill or c. to kill, 80b
effect defective comes by c., 260b
effect whose c. is God, 459a
evolution not c. but law, 779b
final c. produces motion, 97b
found spiritual c., 709a
full c. of weeping, 278a
Germany the c. of Hitler, 999a
given his heart to c., 994b
good old c. is gone, 512a
Great First C., 459b
griefs we c. ourselves, 81b
hear me for my c., 255a
hidden but result well known, 128b
idea of oneself as c., 373b
if any man show just c., 61a
if astray c. is in you, 161b
is there any c. in nature, 279a
it is just, 541a
laws or kings c. or cure, 428a
little grace my c., 272b
magnificent and awful c., 458a
not a field but a c., 467a
not be judge in own c., 126a
not jealous for the c., 275b
nothing comes without c., 420b
obstinacy in bad c., 329b, 437b
of freedom cause of God, 499b
of this effect, 260b
or men of Emerald Isle, 483b
perseverance in good c., 437b
produces more than one effect, 706a
report me and my c., 266b, 706a
sea of c. and theory, 919b
set c. above renown, 865a
support Caledonia's c., 496b
tenacious of purpose in rightful c., 121b
try c. condemn to death, 743b
turn him to c. of policy, 243a
watercolors to impaint c., 240b
what in effect already in c., 849b
wherein tongue confuted, 333b
wit in other men, 241b
Zeus first c., 78b
Caused the widow's heart to sing, 15b
Causes célèbres, 396a
flowers as in c. sleep, 327a
from amorous c. springs, 404a
great c. on move, 922b
happy man who could search out c., 117a
home of lost c., 713b
investigation of hidden c., 192b
lost c. preface victory, 1008a
of destruction, 435b
of disaster, 847a
which impel separation, 470b
why and wherefore, 245a
Caution in refusing benefits, 374a
scars of others teach c., 145b
upward look of c., 929a
Cautious, plant of c. growth, 1011b
politic c. and meticulous, 1001a
seldom err, 71b
statistical Christ, 807a
under whose c. hand, 702a
Cavalry of woe, 734b

Cave, courts thee in some pleasant c., 120b
error correct c., 1079a
idols of the c., 207a
shadows on opposite wall of c., 94b
sky will c. in on him, 1023a
Stygian c. forlorn, 334b
vacant interlunar c., 349a
Cave ab homine unius libri, 158b
canem, 150a
Caveat emptor, 150a
Cavern, mossy c., 583b
Pan's c., 885a
Caverns cool and deep, 710b
in c. all alone, 1079a
measureless to man, 523b
pure and deep, 587b
sand-strewn c., 710b
twice ten thousand c., 579b
Caves, beetles in c., 1064b
dark unfathomed c., 440b
of ice, 524a
Caviar to the general, 261a
Cavil on ninth part of hair, 239b
Cawdor, Glamis thou art and C., 281b
I am Thane of C., 281a
shall sleep no more, 283b
Cease and then again begin, 714b
Byron's struggle c., 711a
Catullus you should c. folly, 114b
day and night shall not c., 6b
efforts to find where last rose lingers, 121b
every joy, 537b
fears that I may c., 581a
from mental fight, 490b
from thine own wisdom, 25b
grinders c., 28b
hatreds never c. by hatred, 80a
long contention c., 715a
man I am c. to be, 652a
not c. from exploration, 1007a
poor shall never c., 10b
sing or c. to sing, 412b
the wicked c. from troubling, 14b
time c. and midnight never come, 213b
to ask what morrow will bring, 121a
to be free for religion, 1022a
upon the midnight, 582b
weeping without c., 808a
ye from man, 30a
Ceased, God created woman boredom c., 806a
when Lucy c. to be, 510b
Ceaseless devouring of weak by strong, 706a
thoughts of roaming, 380a
turns with c. pain, 447b
Ceases, forbearance c. to be virtue, 452a
happiness c. like dream, 328b
to be free for irreligion, 1022a
Ceasing, O swiftness never c., 204b
of exquisite music, 622a
pray without c., 55a
Cedant arma togae, 111b
Cedar, as c. tall and slender, 476a
grow like a c. in Lebanon, 21a
lordly c. green with boughs, 827a
Cedars of Lebanon, 21b
roots of c. of Lebanon, 945b
Cedarwood, sandalwood c., 947a

Ceiling, down from the c., 531b
Célébrait, Ronsard me c., 187b
Celebrate, I c. myself, 700a
not c. funeral with weeping, 106b
Celebrated cultivated Duke of Plaza Toro, 769a
Saviour's birth c., 257a
Celebrates his obsequies, 518b
pale Hecate's offerings, 283a
Celebration of freedom, 1072b
of man, 1071a
Célèbres, causes c., 396a
Celebrities, congress of c., 749b
Celeriter, sat c. fieri satis bene, 124b
Celerity never more admired, 288a
Celestial, appareled in c. light, 513a
pattern of c. peace, 214b
sate itself in c. bed, 259b
so c. article as freedom, 467a
wisdom calms the mind, 427b
with c. clearness wrote, 811b
Celia, come my C., 302b
has undone me, 439a
Celibacy has no pleasures, 428a
Cell, deposit little c. by c., 781a
does c. have soul, 1083b
dwell on rock or in c., 199a
ill-spirit sob in each c., 1076b
in body holds heart, 1056b
in narrow c. forever laid, 440a
thine eternal c., 266b
tight hot c., 1038a
Cellar, born in a c., 442b
lived in c. damp, 694a
secretly nurtured in c., 998a
warm delicious c., 1046b
Cells, all c. from pre-existing c., 710b
better schoolrooms than c., 686a
condemned c. of Newgate, 756a
held in cohesion by c., 947b
unresting c., 947b
Cellula, omnis c. a c., 710b
Celt, blind hysterics of C., 651a
Celtic, locale was C., 968b
Cement glue and lime of love, 319b
gummed with bicycle c., 1036a
Cemetery, father buy plot in c., 925b
of dead ideas, 869b
Censorship, assassination extreme c., 837b
if c. reigns, 460a
Censure, careless of c., 404a
durst not c., 426b
every trade save c., 554b
fear of c., 988a
folks no right to c., 911b
freely who have written well, 402b
mankind c. injustice, 94a
pardons raven, 139a
take each man's c., 258b
tax for being eminent, 389a
Census, test of civilization not c., 608b
Cent, not one c. for tribute, 501b
what did with every c., 928b
Centaur, cloud that looked like c., 91a
in dragon world, 989a
Center cannot hold, 882a
intention stabs the c., 295a
man c. of circle, 748b
many lines in dial's c., 243a
my c. giving way, 826a

Choosing, long c. and beginning late, 347b
 presidential nominee, 983b
Chop off her head, 743b
 off your head, 1093b
Chopper to chop off your head, 1093b
Chord in melancholy, 592a
 in unison is touched, 458b-459a
 mirth has c. in melancholy, 310a
 struck c. of music, 726a
Chords of memory, 637b
 that vibrate pleasure, 494a
Chorister, bobolink for c., 735b
Chortled in his joy, 745a
Chorus ending from Euripides, 665a
 from Atlanta to sea, 748a
 of Union, 637b
 what a c., 536b
Chose, David c. him five smooth stones, 12a
Chosen, few are c., 43b
 I have c. you, 49a
 Lord hath c. thee, 10a
 old ocean c. by thee, 703a
 people of God, 471a
 to wilderness the c. start, 947b
 vessel, 49b
Choughs that wing air, 279a
Choux, que la mort me trouve plantant mes c., 189b
Christ ain't going to be too hard, 778b
 all at once what C. is, 804a
 born across the sea, 690b
 born in Bethlehem, 425b
 bowels of C., 328a, 912a
 but this earth goes over, 1022b
 came to save sinners, 55a
 catch C. with worm, 1075a
 cautious statistical C., 807a
 deep did rot O C., 525a
 Don Quixote and I, 549a
 everyone in world is C., 939b
 half a drop ah my C., 213b
 Himself buddy, 1078a
 his captain C., 228a
 history incomprehensible without C., 722a
 I believe in Jesus C., 60a
 in C. all made alive, 53a
 is all and in all, 54b
 is C. thy advocate, 381b
 it is the Inchcape Rock, 532b
 Jesus C. her little child, 684b
 Jesus C. son of man, 958a
 Jesus C. the same yesterday, 56a
 joint heirs with C., 51a
 keep your hearts through C. Jesus, 54b
 kingdom and patience of Jesus C., 57a
 kingdoms of his C., 58a
 Lord C. enter in, 841a
 O C. the plow, 947a
 our Savior, 1099a
 receive him, 651b
 redemption by Jesus C., 60b
 risen from dead, 53a
 rule given by C., 732a
 save us all, 621a
 Savior which is C., 46a
 show me dear C. Thy spouse, 308a
 shut up in asylum, 851b
 sin forgiven by C., 619b
 so Judas did to C., 228a
 soldiers of C. arise, 425b

Christ, testimony of Jesus C., 57b
 that is to be, 651a
 that it were possible, 652b
 that my love in my arms, 1084a
 the Lord risen today, 425a
 the Son in Father's stead, 834b
 thief said last word to C., 667a
 this world all aleak, 1031a
 thou art the C., 43a
 to live is C., 54a
 took the kindness, 667a
 vision of C. thou see, 491a
 walks on black water, 1075a
 what are patterns for, 931b
Christendom, christianize C., 695b
 eager to get stake, 763b
 in C. where Christian, 606b
 live in any place in C., 189a
 wisest fool in C., 202a
Christened on Tuesday, 1096a
Christes loore and his apostles, 166b
Christian, any husband rather than C., 235a
 bear other's misfortunes like C., 413a
 charity, 593a
 civilization, 921a
 darkness fell upon C., 366a
 endeavor hard on pulchritude, 961a
 enterprise for glory of C. religion, 172b
 feels repentance on Sunday, 962a
 fled with a C., 233a
 forgive them as C., 533b
 ground, 414a
 hate him for a C., 232a
 honorable style of C., 329b
 I am a C. faithful man, 217a
 ideal difficult, 918a
 if victory I shall become C., 147b
 in what peace a C. can die, 395a
 inconsistent with C. religion, 443a
 made me in C. days, 546a
 men be sure, 687b
 not so good C. as thinks, 824b
 O my C. ducats, 233a
 only C. come to these parts, 172b
 pagan spoiled, 870b
 persuadest me to be C., 50b
 practice C. forbearance, 465b
 Protestant or priest, 789b
 richest in C. world, 497b
 Scientists more science, 890b
 Science, 709a
 scratch C. find pagan, 870b
 soldiers, 750b
 thing, 1057b
 where C. in Christendom, 606b
 with four aces, 764b
 without hypocrisy, 747b
 witness of soul naturally C., 143a
 wonders of C. religion, 387a
 word of gentleman and C., 195a
 you are Ciceronian not C., 145a
 you were a C. slave, 816a
Christianity a son religion, 834b
 blemish of mankind, 806a
 Catholicism minus C., 724b
 cult called C., 783b
 doctors more C., 890b
 enormous perversion, 806a
 muscular C., 613a

Christianity, narcotics alcohol and C., 805b
 one great curse, 806a
 takes great deal of C., 871b
Christianize Christendom, 695b
Christians, all C. agree, 430a-b
 blood of C. is seed, 143b
 good C. good citizens, 546b
 have burnt each other, 560a
 have comfortable creed, 560b
 have little difference, 431a
 if C. were C. no anti-Semitism, 952a
 lord believing C. from sky, 172b
 see how C. love one another, 143b
 three paynims three Jews three C., 174b
 want something for nothing, 838a
Christmas, at C. no more desire rose, 221a
 at C. play, 188a
 born on C. Day, 1099a
 broached mightiest ale, 519b
 brought sports again, 519b
 comes but once a year, 188a, 627a
 Day in workhouse, 813a
 gambol, 519b
 happy C. to all, 541a
 home C., 910a
 is coming, 1098b
 is here, 660b
 it was C. Day, 210b
 jest 'fore C., 821a
 keep our C. merry still, 519b
 night before C., 541a
 one C. much like another, 1070b
 over and business is business, 962b
 pie, 1093a
 told merriest tale, 519b
 won't be Christmas, 742a
Christmases, merry C. long lives, 672b
Christom child, 243b
Christopher Robin goes hoppity, 970a
 Robin had wheezles, 970a
 Robin saying prayers, 969b
Christ's blood streams, 213b
 in C. coach, 381a
 lady of C. College, 365a
 Lord C. heart, 604a
 lore and his apostles twelve, 166b
 progress and His prayer time, 362b
 stamp, 322b
Christs that die upon barricades, 838b
Chromis did not save himself, 62b
Chronic anxiety about weather, 770b
 do not weep it's c., 670a
 hotel guests, 895b
 melancholy of civilized, 783a
Chronicle of wasted time, 293b
 pride his own c., 268a
 small beer, 273b
 wars of kites, 350a
Chronicles, brief c. of the time, 261b
 transcribe my c., 593b
Chrononhotonthologos, 400b
Chrysanthemum, white c. remains immaculate, 380b

Come not near our fairy queen, 229b
  not to steal away hearts, 255b
  nothing will c. of nothing, 276b
  now and let us reason, 30a
  nowhere to c. but back, 845a
  O c. Emmanuel, 687b
  on now young men, 920a
  one come all, 520a
  out of Gogol's Overcoat, 708b
  over into Macedonia, 50a
  over way with tears watered, 906b
  palaces in kingdom c., 947a
  past and to c. seem best, 242a
  past passing or to c., 883a
  primrose way, 823b
  Romeo c. forth, 225a
  season to c. and go, 412b
  see my shining palace, 1023b
  seeling night, 284b
  shan't be gone long you c. too, 925b
  shape of things to c., 888b
  soon soon, 572b
  that it should c. to this, 257b
  that it will never c. again, 739a
  that they might have life, 48b
  the foe they c., 556a
  they c. they stay, 942b
  things past or things to c., 365b
  things to c., 268a
  thou monarch of the vine, 288a
  thou'lt c. no more, 280b
  three corners of world, 237b
  thy kingdom c., 40b
  till boys c. home, 917a
  to aid of party, 1100b
  to bad end, 910a
  to dedicate field, 639a
  to lay weary bones among ye, 299a
  to me my dear Bozzy, 433a
  to my arms, 745a
  to my woman's breasts, 282a
  to pluck your berries, 338a
  to see and be seen, 128b
— to take their ease, 299b
  to thee by moonlight, 961b
  to this favor she must c., 266a
  to this stage of fools, 279b-280a
  treading path through blood, 906b
  unbutton here, 278b
  until I c. in peace, 13b
  unto me ye that labor, 42a
  unto my love, 201b
  unto these yellow sands, 296a
  up and see me, 1029b
  weal come woe, 507b
  what come may, 281b
  what dreams may c., 261b
  what is to c. I know not, 36b
  what may I have been blessed, 558a
  what may Sinon said, 129b
  wheel is c. full circle, 280b
  when shall I c. to thee, 1085b
  whistle and I'll c. to you, 494b
  whistle and she'll c. to you, 316b
  will they c. when you call, 239b
  will ye no c. back again, 502a
  with bows bent, 772b
  with singing unto Zion, 33a
  within a pint of wine, 395b
  within bending sickle's compass c., 294b
  without warning, 676b
  women c. and go, 1000b

Come, won't c. back till it's over, 944a
  worst yet to c., 654a, 887a
  ye thankful people, 655b
  ye to the waters, 33a
  you back British soldier, 873b
  you spirits that tend, 281b
Comedian can last till he takes himself serious, 954a
  no matter if country need c., 954a
Comedy, catastrophe of the old c., 277a
  dressed for this short c., 199b
  killing time essence of c., 870a
  most lamentable c., 228b
  world is a c., 442b
Comely, attire c. not costly, 202b
  black but c., 29a
  bowed his c. head down, 359b
  grace, 1086a
  spanking Jack was so c., 475b
Comer, grasps in the c., 269a
Comers, entertain all c., 63a
Comes apparelled like spring, 290b
  at one stride c. the dark, 525a
  at the last, 227b
  autumn c. jovial on, 419b
  conquering hero c., 420b
  Death who c. at last, 519a
  effect defective c. by cause, 260b
  ever 'gainst that season c., 257a
  everything c. too late, 770b
  fog c. on cat feet, 948a
  God behind them, 666b
  God c. as sun at noon, 308b
  he c. he c., 371a
  here c. the lady, 224b
  hope never c., 342a
  in the sweet o' the year, 295a
  knowledge c. wisdom lingers, 647b
  look who c. here, 236b
  love that c. too late, 270a
  moment to decide, 691b
  nearer c. the sun, 986a
  pat he c., 277a
  rainbow c. and goes, 513a
  silent flooding in the main, 688b
  something wicked this way c., 285a
  stealing comes creeping, 820b
  take it as it c., 769a
  then cannon and he c., 918b
  thrill that c. once in lifetime, 990a
  to me o'er and o'er, 722b
  unlooked for if c. at all, 402b
  want for one who c. not, 1037a
  wear day out before it c., 816b
  while she c. is gone, 898b
  wine c. in at mouth, 881a
Comest in so slowly, 1051a
  in such questionable shape, 259a
  whence c. thou, 14a
Cometh, another generation c., 27a
  behold the day c., 36a
  forth like a flower, 15a
  from afar, 513b
  from whence c. my help, 22a
  hour c. and now is, 48a
  in the name of the Lord, 22a
  joy c. in the morning, 18a
  my help c. from the Lord, 22a
  the night c., 48b
  this dreamer c., 7b

Cometh, whence it c., 48a
Comets, discoverers as c., 425a
  when beggars die no c., 254b
Comfort, age of c. and violence, 999b
  and despair, 294b
  carrion c., 803b
  cold c. I beg, 237b
  cold c. to fill hungry bellies, 319a
  conceited carry c., 689b
  continual c. in a face, 314b
  from New World to Old, 924b
  gives c. in despair, 214b
  giving enemies aid and c., 474a
  his sad heart, 721b
  hobbit-hole and that means c., 1025a
  like cold porridge, 296b
  me with apples, 29a
  no c. to one not sociable, 291a
  of c. no man speak, 227a
  of miserable partners in woes, 127a
  old poets c. to man, 816b
  scholar who cherishes love of c., 72a
  she hath none to c. her, 34a
  so will I c. you, 33b
  social c. in hospital, 618b
  take c. nor forget, 758b
  thy rod and thy staff c. me, 18a
  to my age, 247b
  values money or c. more, 932a
  warn to c. and command, 514a
  what gnashing is not a c., 308b
  ye my people, 32b
Comfortable advice, 585b
  creed, 560b
  easy and c. on raft, 761a
  feeling of superiority, 960b
  minds, 1030b
  no c. feel, 592a
  not both grand and c., 857b
  O c. bird, 580b
  progress a c. disease, 1031b
  words, 653a
Comfortably in debt, 659b
  padded lunatic asylums, 975a
  speak c. to Jerusalem, 32b
Comforted, be c. for him, 38b
  folly of being c., 880b
  they shall be c., 40a
  would not be c., 39b
Comforters, miserable c. are ye all, 15a
Comforteth, love c. like sunshine, 220a
  one whom his mother c., 33b
Comforting thought when not our trouble, 946b
Comfortless, grim-visaged c. Despair, 439b
  not leave you c., 49a
  through c. despairs, 201a
Comforts, adversity not without c., 208a
  creature c., 386a
  essential c. of life, 587a
  flee, 567a
  from whence c. increased, 486a
  of life not indispensable, 682b
  of weary pilgrimage, 433b
  what I aspired c. me, 666a
Comic, perception of c. tie, 609b
  poet paint follies, 391b
Comical how nature contrive, 767b
Comin', Campbells are c., 1089b
  for to carry me home, 1101a

Contains all nothing lacking, 701a
  the cistern c., 487b
  what fortitude soul c., 739a
Contemneth small things, 38a
Contemplate entangled bank, 628a
  my flaccid shape, 1032a
  our forefathers, 444a
Contemplated, object is to be c., 870a
Contemplation, beneath thy c., 687b
  everything object of c., 529b
  he for c. formed, 345a
  her best nurse C., 337a
  leisurely c. of art, 915b
  mind serene for c., 393b
  more than reading, 364b-365a
  sundry c. of my travels, 250a
Contemporaries, man lives life of c., 937a
  society of c., 606a
Contemporary, both c. and hereditary, 697a
Contempt against majesty of heaven, 420b
  and anger of lip, 252b
  comes from head, 563b
  familiarity breeds c., 76a, 764b
  for c. too high, 357b
  for governor who is afraid, 81b
  for wildest blow, 792a
  no weakness no c., 350a
  silence is c., 615a
  speak of moderns without c., 415b
  treating with c. all from God, 180a
Contemptible, bored more c. than bore, 755a
  rendered United States c., 842a
  ridiculous c. animal, 425a
  struggle, 452a
Contemptuous, discerning reader c., 851b
Contend, different schools c. freely, 1028a
  gods c. in vain, 498b
  no more love, 663a
  schools of thought c., 1027b
  seven towns c. for Homer, 301b
  ye powers of heaven, 354b
Contending against some being, 701b
  calm c. kings, 220b
  fierce c. nations, 394a
  for liberty, 460b-461a
  leaders ambitiously c., 480a
  with adversity, 311a
Content at the last, 1006b
  be c. with your lot, 76a
  don't be c., 920a
  farewell c., 275a
  good pleasure ease c., 409b
  humble livers in c., 298a
  I am c., 503a
  if reversion nourish, 1006b
  in health and mind's c., 375b
  in tight hot cell, 1038a
  in whatsoever state to be c., 54b
  land of lost c., 853a
  majority of men c., 177b
  make c. with fortunes fit, 278a
  mind c. both crown and kingdom, 206a
  money means and c., 249b
  my crown is called c., 215b
  natural c., 881a
  not c. with attacks on me, 973b
  not sigh for moon c., 751a

Content, nothing less will c. me, 452b
  poor and c. is rich, 274b
  shut up in measureless c., 283a
  thoughts that savor of c., 206a
  to breathe his native air, 402a
  to entertain lag-end of my life, 240b
  to live it all again, 884a
  travelers must be c., 248a
  wisdom of just c., 742a
  with life retire from world, 120a
  with my harm, 249b
  with ruin, 947b
  with small means, 655b
  with vegetable love, 767a
  with your lot, 76a
Contented, live on little with c. mind, 114a
  men employed best c., 423a
  most enjoy c. least, 292a
  slaves howe'er c., 456b
  then ye c. your souls, 875b
  wi' little, 494a
  with life dinner wife, 593a
Contentedness, procurer of c., 326a
Contention, let long c. cease, 715a
  man of strife and c., 34a
Contentions are like bars of a castle, 25a
  fat c., 340a
  of a wife, 25a
Contentious, petty wisdom c., 101a
Contentment characteristic of East, 1019b
  fails, 447b
  nor poorest receive c., 309a
  preaches c. to toad, 871b
  recover through c. with physician, 88b
  Western not to know c., 1019b
Contents torn out and stripped, 421a
Contest, end a c. quicker, 481a
  great c. follows, 458a
  let fools c., 409b
Contests, hard c. men must win, 847b
  saints in fierce c., 353b
  what mighty c. rise, 404a
Context, immediate c. of history, 1024b
Contiguity, boundless c. of shade, 457b
Continence, give me c. but not now, 147a
Continent allotted by Providence, 676a
  almost a c. hardly a nation, 989b
  American c. not colonization, 491b
  Americans prefer C., 895b
  brought forth on c., 639a
  disappoint a c., 754b
  heart no island but c., 208b
  iron curtain across C., 924b
  man is a piece of the c., 308b
  mighty c. hitherto unknown, 173b
  most momentous question on c., 721a
  one small spot a c., 742a
  our c. the old one, 479a
  striving to grasp c., 720b
  untamed c., 720b

Continental, Jehovah and C. Congress, 468a
  never tolerate two c. powers, 1012a
Continents dissolve into sea, 1061a
  potters' fields of four c., 697a
Continual comfort in a face, 314b
  contentions of wife are c. dropping, 25a
  endeavor in c. motion, 243a
  feast, 24b
  live in c. mortification, 420b
  small have c. plodders won, 221a
Continually, think c. of truly great, 1067b
  times change and move c., 200b
Continue, stealing will c. stealing, 694b
Continued, not one c. faithful until old age, 96a
Continueth, he fleeth and c. not, 15a
Continuing, faculty of c. to improve, 459b
  no c. city, 56a
Continuous and seems always existing, 73b
  and stationary music, 502b
  as stars that shine, 514b
  brain changes c., 793a
  nature one and c., 681b
  use of any organ, 475a
Contra naturam, 989a
Contract, passions we inspire c. time, 907b
  succession bourn none, 296b
  'twixt Hannah God and me, 749b
  verbal c. not worth paper, 967b
Contracted, orbed in this c. star, 990b
Contraction of life, 935b
Contracts with the people, 983b
Contradict, do I c. myself, 700b
Contradiction between imperialism and Chinese, 1027b
  what a c. is man, 364a
  when we risk no c., 401a
  woman's a c. still, 407a
  world a c., 867b
Contradictions exist side by side, 708a
  in Chinese society, 1027b
Contraption, homemade c., 1036a
  verbal c., 1061a
Contraries, by c. execute all things, 296b
  dreams by c., 589a
  life of one another, 330a
Contrariously, work c., 243a
Contrariwise, 745b
Contrary blast proclaims, 349b
  bringeth bliss, 214b
  everythink c. with me, 671a
  facts c. 'z mules, 391b
  hear what you say to c., 609b
  Mary quite c., 1093b
  men of c. character, 71b
  not state things c. to fact, 107b
  runneth not to the c., 444b
  Spirit and flesh c., 53b
  to the c. notwithstanding, 474b
Contribute to diversion or improvement of country, 394a
Contribution according to capacity, 687a
  to current literature, 756b
Contributions to peace of world, 983a

Contrite, broken and c. heart, 19b
 humble and c. heart, 875b
Contrivance of human wisdom, 454a
Contrivances, wisdom of human c., 452b
Contrive, head to c., 466a
 no farther tides, 1043b
 our fees to pilfer, 91a
Contrived corridors, 1001b
 double debt to pay, 450a
Contriving, life a jest of Fate's c., 402a
Control and communication theory, 1033b
 atomic energy, 908b
 authority nation cannot c., 750a
 chance shall not c., 711a
 civilian c. of military, 984a
 experiments to c. ideas, 675b
 forces not learned to c., 901a
 grammar c. even kings, 361b
 lease of my true love c., 293b
 man c. the wind, 711b
 nothing short of club c., 831a
 nuclear c., 1074b
 ought to c. thoughts, 628a
 prison walls cannot c., 359a
 stops at the shore, 557b
Controlled, events c. me, 639b
Controlling intelligence understands, 142b
Controls, love of other sights c., 304b
 new social c., 973a
Controversy, fear of c. not warranted, 1064a
 hearts of c., 253b
Contumely, proud man's c., 262a
 without resentment, 835b
Conturbat, timor mortis c. me, 176a
Convenience comfort prestige, 1104a
 he that for c. takes oath, 353a
Convenient, a c. season, 50b
 light switch, 1049a
 that there be gods, 128b
Convention, by c. there is color, 88a
 is ruler of all, 80a
 sartorial c., 958a
 system has faults, 983b
Conventional, ground in mill of c., 798a
 merely c. signs, 746b
Conventionalities, punctilious in c., 756b
Conventions and restrictions of world, 757b
Convent's narrow room, 515a
 solitary gloom, 405b
Convents, happy c., 414a
Conversation, brisk as bee in c., 429b
 for c. well endued, 389b
 gift of unaffected c., 593a
 good nature in c., 394b
 happiest c. no competition, 431b
 hinges in French c., 438b
 improved for literary c., 310a
 is but carving, 390a
 Johnson's c. was mustard, 468b
 of most searching sort, 606b
 of select companions, 394a
 one of greatest pleasures, 932a
 preaching word for dull c., 522b
 smaller excellences of c., 469a

Conversation socializing instrument, 978a
 three cannot take part in c., 606b
 wants leisure, 932a
 when you fall into a man's c., 395b
 without pictures or c., 743a
 writing name for c., 437b
Conversational or homely type, 902b
Conversationalist, industrious c., 1032a
Conversation's burrs, 633a
Converse and live with ease, 410b
 formed by thy c., 410a
 high c. with mighty dead, 419b
 Hispanic for c. with God, 434b
 with men of unseen generations, 162b
 with mountains and fens, 909a
Conversing I forget all time, 345b
Conversion, refuse till c. of Jews, 359b
Convert Bill of Rights, 1021b
 you into stew, 1004a
Converted and become as children, 43a
 love c. from thing it was, 292a
 silenced man not c., 779b
Converting human beings to machines, 687a
Convex, organ too c. or concave, 607b
Convey the wise it call, 266b
Convict, swart c. Bunyan, 696b
Convicted, Daniel had c. them, 39a
Conviction, do evil from religious c., 364a
 editor's c., 1014a
 faithful to c. to old age, 96a
 sadness of c., 786b
 the best lack all c., 882a
 we are loved, 599a
Convictions, enter c. in open lists, 912a
 opposition with c., 586b
 transcend own c., 787b
Convince hearers of own assertions, 93b
 to c. is to weaken, 914a
Convinced of too little, 1007b
Convinces, man who c. the world, 813b
Convincing while they thought of dining, 451a
Conviviality, taper of c., 669b
Convolutions of smooth-lipped shell, 516b
Convulsions, system liable to c., 819b
Conwiviality, taper of c., 669b
Cook, amount to Hannah C., 1102a
 and captain bold, 765b
 common murderer uncommon c., 904a
 every c. learn to govern, 903a
 good c. as cooks go, 903b
 ill c. that cannot lick fingers, 225b
 makes his c. his merit, 361a
 one can become a c., 484b
Cookery is an art a noble science, 310b
 kissing don't last c. do, 730a
Cooking, ruling like c. small fish, 74b

Cooks, as c. go she went, 903b
 are gentlemen, 310b
 Epicurean c., 287b
 God sends meat Devil sends c., 183a
 guests praise it not c., 210a
 not live without c., 741b
Cooks' own ladles, 662b
Cool as glass, 990a
 caverns c. and deep, 710b
 clear and c. clear and c., 691a
 day so c. so calm, 323a
 glassy c. translucent wave, 337b
 in any case keep c., 1035a
 in dust in c. tombs, 948a
 in gardens when eve c., 734a
 keep c. it will be all one, 608a
 kept breath to c. pottage, 68a
 kindliness of sheets, 993b
 of the day, 5b
 one pain, 737a
 place was c. and pleasant, 1069b
 sequestered vale of life, 440b
 Siloam's shady rill, 549a
 winding saxophones, 948b
Cooled a long age, 582a
Cool-enfolding death, 702a
Coolibar tree, 869a
Cooling, dark c. star, 925b
 plash of rain, 827b
 streams, 384a
Coolness, wind to bring c. to men, 65b
Cools, till husband c., 407a
 time c. time clarifies, 937b
Coon, gone c., 553b
Cooped we live and die, 630b
Cooperation, spontaneous c. of free people, 842b
Coordinate, nature has c. system, 1034a
Coort, supreme c. follows iliction, 890b
Coot, haunts of c., 652a
Cope, starry c. of heaven, 346a
Co-perception, intellectual c., 610a
Cophetua loved the beggarmaid, 223b
 sware oath, 648a
Copied all they could follow, 874a
Copious Dryden, 412a
Copper, Irishman lined with c., 760b
 kettledrums, 918b
 whiskey polishes c., 760b
Copperheads, forgot c. and assassin, 948b
Coppice, leant upon c. gate, 783b
Copulate in the foam, 885a
Copulation, birth c. and death, 1004a
 let c. thrive, 279b
Copy, couldn't c. my mind, 874a
 leave the world no c., 251b
 show c. to whom you please, 469b
Copycat, life is a c., 1000a
Copyists, shortened labor of c., 576a
Coquette, death and i c., 946a
Coquettes, refuge of old c., 599b
Cor lacerare nequit, 391a
Corage God mend al, 723b
Coral is far more red, 294b
 lip admires, 327a
 of his bones c. made, 296b
Corals, maple puts c. on, 694a
Cord, as unto bow c. is, 623a

Creatures, God's c., 641b
  great and small, 684b
  Leviathan hugest of c., 346b
  little c. everywhere, 974b
  love my fellow c., 768a
  make fellow c. happy, 467b
  makes meaner c. kings, 217b
  meanest of c., 665b
  of a day, 79b
  of all c. man most detestable, 764a
  poets c. most absurd, 412b
  praise for all thy c., 157a
  seem coming are going, 778b
  smashed up c., 1036b
  spiritual c. walk unseen, 345b
  that creep swim or fly, 377a
  that once were men, 894b
  weak c. of clay, 91b
  what marvelous c. we are, 925b
  widows most perverse c., 394b
  you dissect, 406a
Creatures', human c. lives, 592b
Credit, an't much c. in that, 670a
  dead corpse of public c., 547b
  done my c. much wrong, 630b
  gradual growth of c., 612b
  greatly to his c. that he is Englishman, 766a
  having more c. than money, 477a
  his own lie, 296a
  I well can c. it, 969a
  let the c. go, 629b
  not to whom idea occurs, 813b
  places last stone gets c., 949b
  plans c. and Muse, 603a
  shadow of authority and c., 453b
  stories not to thy c., 740b
  to man who convinces, 813b
  used my c., 237b
Creditable acquaintance, 388b
Credited, always c. to Exchange, 962b
Creditors, executors or c., 696b
  we are debtors or c., 478a
Credo quia impossibile, 143b
Credulities, ambitions climb on c., 844a
Credulity, a little c. helps, 656b
  craving c., 612b
  helps enjoyment, 703b
  man's weakness, 535a
  supine c. characteristic of man, 817a
  to whispers of fancy, 428a
  youth the season of c., 426a
Credulous first hours, 1040a
  hatred renders votaries, 436b
Creed, Athanasian C. lyric, 613a
  comfortable c., 560b
  faith or c. today, 741a
  is a rod, 775b
  life to neighbor's c., 602a
  lives alone by book and c., 790a
  most authentic c., 749a
  necessity the c. of slaves, 496b
  nonviolence article of c., 897a
  not question school or c., 789b
  of our political faith, 472b
  put c. into your deed, 603b
  sapping solemn c., 556b
  single dogmatic c., 1073b
  suckled in c. outworn, 515b
  theory of matter not c., 838a
  whatever race c. or persuasion, 991a
Creeds, casual c., 712a

Creeds, dust of c. outworn, 568b
  dust of systems and c., 644b
  grow so thick, 836a
  human hopes and c., 791a
  keys of all c., 650a
  new names for mystery, 789b
  so many gods so many c., 826a
  than in half the c., 651a
  that refuse and restrain, 773b
Creeks, through c. and inlets, 688b
Creep and let no more be said, 715a
  beasts of the forest c. forth, 21b
  dwarfed and abased, 826b
  feet like snails did c., 320b
  flesh c., 669a
  for bellies' sake c., 338b
  in one dull line, 403a
  into narrow bed, 715a
  learn to c. ere learn to go, 184a
  let music c. in our ears, 235b
  love will c. in service, 184a
  men c. not walk, 626a
  nevermore to c. again, 915a
  something not in poem c. in, 1071a
  swim or fly, 377a
  where it may not go, 184a
  wit that can c., 411b
Creepers, bacterial c., 1064b
Creeping, gray clouds c. quietly, 732a
  hours of time, 248b
  like snail to school, 249a
  thing in sober way, 685b
  things c. innumerable, 21b
  through the black, 953a
Creeps, how slow shadow c., 901b
  in this petty pace, 286b
Creetur, lone lorn c., 671a
Cremated Sam McGee, 933a
Crepidam, ne supra c. sutor iudi-caret, 102a
Crept into bosom of the sea, 215a
  like frightened girl, 838b
  music c. by upon waters, 296a
  night c. upon our talk, 256a
Crepuscular time, 688a
Cressid, as false as C., 268b
  where C. lay that night, 235a
Crest, no color or c., 874a
Crested, reared arm C. the world, 288b
Cretan, played C. against C., 136b
Crew and captain understand, 876b
  beguiled leisure of c., 765b
  Bellman cry c. reply, 746b
  captain and his c., 765b
  crawls, 979a
  darling of our c., 475b
  dismayed her c., 792a
  ghastly c., 525b
  immediately the cock c., 44b
  Mirth admit me of thy c. 334b
  no ship better c., 765b
  of captain's gig, 765b
Crews, merry c. laid to rest, 947a
Crib, ass knoweth his master's c., 30a
Cribbed, cabined c. confined, 284b
Cricket is to cricket dear, 104a
  merry as c., 184a
  no relief, 1002a
  on the hearth, 335b
  where c. sings, 879b
Cried A sail a sail, 525a
  Agamemnon c. aloud, 1002a
  for madder music, 890a

Cried Give me, 735b
  in goose Alas, 1009b
  in youth I c., 1057b
  mercy to myself I c., 510b
  My how fair you are, 673b
  No more, 323a
  not winced nor c. aloud, 816a
  out of the depths have I c., 22b
  Peter denied Lord c., 1089a
  poor c. Caesar wept, 255b
  you suddenly c., 993a
Crier, good c. of green sauce, 181a
  town c. spoke my lines, 262b
Cries, bootless c., 291b
  damned that c. Hold enough, 287a
  fisted with wild c., 843a
  holy and meek she c., 488a
  man who turnips c., 429a
  my fate c. out, 259b
  of cicadas, 380a
  of sandpiper, 1065b
  out Where is it, 526b
  pitying the tender c., 487a
  rump-fed ronyon c., 281a
  that which world c. up, 375a
  to world from tower, 970b
  voice of Nature loudly c., 495a
  whistle spontaneous c., 955a
  wind full of birds' c., 947a
Crieth, brother's blood c., 6a
  in the wilderness, 32b
  wisdom c. without, 23a
Crime, blanch without owner's c., 517a
  criminal not cause of c., 909b
  curious c. wickedness, 667a
  electricity and c., 919a
  foulest c. in history, 702a
  from single c. know nation, 118a
  Iscariotlike c., 996b
  like virtue has degrees, 378b
  now madden to c., 558a
  numbers sanctified the c., 460a
  of being young man, 425b
  popularity a c., 376b
  prevention of mutual c., 98b
  punishment fit c., 768b
  servitude consequence of c., 480a
  stupid c. war, 933a
  successful c. called virtue, 131a
  this coyness were no c., 359b
  to be nobly born now c., 315b
  to love too well, 406a
  who for my willful c., 348b
  worse than c. it is blunder, 499b
Crimes against peace, 1021b
  and misfortunes, 417b
  broad blown, 264a
  committed c. but not stood aside, 1054b
  committed in thy name, 483b
  history register of c., 465b
  never among my c., 747a
  one virtue thousand c., 558b
  reach the dignity of c., 475b
  teems with c., 1090b
  time to count your c., 505b
  worst of c. is poverty, 837a
Criminal element I am of it, 831b
  judge condemned when c. absolved, 126a
  no c. class except Congress, 762b
  not c. unless intent c., 150a
  not cause of crime, 909b

Criminals, less evil that some c. escape, 788b

Crimson, beauty's ensign yet is c., 225b
conquest's c. wing, 441b
of c. joy, 489a
petal, 649a
torchlight c. on kettledrums, 918b
with fury, 744a

Crimson-tipped flower, 493a

Crines ingenio suo flexi, 134a

Cringe, souls that c. plot, 692a

Crippled palsied and slain, 932b

Crises, business c. wrecked industries, 819b
Constitution adapted to c., 485b
great c. show resources, 792b
marriage seldom develop without c., 935b

Crisis, force moment to its c., 1001a
moulting season c., 682b
quiet but urgent, 1077b

Crisp, deep and c. and even, 687b

Crisped, leaves c. and sere, 643b

Crispian, feast of C., 245a

Criteria, clear-cut c., 1028a

Critic, better be actor than c., 919b
cry of c. for five, 754a
dreamer c. of dream, 936a
dwell upon excellencies, 394b
good c. tells of masterpieces, 802a
helper of artist, 798b
most degraded of trades, 764a
no longer artist but c., 888b
not bein' author gr-reat c., 892a
peep or cynic bark, 602b
praise not c., 842b
severe c. on own works, 585a
Sir C. good day, 679b
unsuccessful author turns c., 528a
valuable instrument, 799a
well if every c. would, 782a
when cannot be artist, 709b
wise skepticism in good c., 695a
you have frowned, 517a
youngest c. died, 872b

Critical, easier c. than correct, 612a
effort, 713a
generous sternly c., 815b
nothing if not c., 273a
power creative power, 713a
readers should be c. of historians, 107b
sense rare, 798b

Criticism, ask c. want praise, 931b
automatism but also c., 1038b
bad c. as serious as careless drainage, 916b
blown by wind of c., 433b
cant of c., 438a
conducted along proper lines, 1028a
definition of c., 713b
dominated by outworn theory, 909b
dramatic c. tattoo soap bubbles, 1047a
easier than craftsmanship, 92b
easy art difficult, 398b
epigram a c. of life, 949a
father of English c., 428b
not govern without c., 1014a
poetry a c. of life, 949a
reviewing not c., 798b

Criticism rod of divination, 879a
stealthy school of c., 731a
to make enjoyment aware, 800b
when c. parts with reality, 922a
work of c. shaped by geometry, 385a

Criticisms, parodies penetrating c., 1032a

Criticize as some hitherto, 812a
cannot c. Testament, 863a
to c. is to appreciate, 799b

Criticized, book Time c. for us, 694b
good joke not c., 918b
not pleasant to be c., 1067a
relation with c. thing, 799b
tradition perpetually c., 1008b

Criticizes, Testament c. you, 863a

Critic's, don't view with c. eye, 507a

Critics, before you trust in c., 554b
Boston audience c., 759a
failed therefore turn c., 528a
go hang yourselves, 181b
in peace ye c. dwell, 405b
men who have failed, 612b
or but half create, 882a
ready made, 554b
shouting He's unknown, 791b
when c. talk of sublime, 467b

Critique, killed off by one c., 775b-776a

Crito I owe a cock, 88a

Croaks fatal entrance of Duncan, 281b
Hall o' Fame when you c., 1009a

Crocodile, how doth little c., 743a
not move underjaw, 323a
tears, 205b

Crocodiles, not be seized by c., 129b

Cromwell, celebrities such as C., 749b
Charles the First his C., 464b
damned to fame, 410a
guiltless of country's blood, 440b
I charge thee, 299a
if thou fallest O C., 299a

Crony, ancient trusty drouthy c., 495b
government by c., 931b

Crook, by hook or by c., 163b
pregnant hinges of knees, 263a
shepherd's c. beside scepter, 601a

Crooked cannot be made straight, 27a-b
close designs c. counsels, 368a
hands, 651a
house, 1096b
lane, 592a
Leviathan that c. serpent, 32a
man went crooked mile, 1096b
roads are roads of genius, 487b
set c. straight, 753a
shall be made straight, 32b
slim and c. genius, 798a
tell the c. rose, 1070a

Crookedest river in world, 760a

Croolty, pastime of civilized man c., 892a

Crop, familiar as c. in summer, 142a
fungus c. of sentiment, 771b
of corn a field of tares, 204a

Crop-full bird, 666a

Crops are ripe, 914b

Crops flowery food, 408a
watering last year's c., 689a

Cross, a sparkling c. she wore, 404a
blind as nails upon C., 998b
cannot c. cause why born, 222a
hot c. buns, 1095a
nailed on bitter c., 237b
no c. no crown, 322a, 380b
of gold,, 858b
of Jesus, 750b
old rugged c., 913b
over river and rest, 723a
that rules southern sky, 871b
transit where dreams c., 1003b

Crossbow, with my c., 524b

Crossed, every hope c., 722b
oyster may be c. in love, 481b
the Sierras, 1022b
when I have c. bar, 655a
with direct eyes, 1003a

Crosses, crooked c. and headstones, 968a
relics crucifixes, 353b
row on row, 912b
to fret thy soul with c., 201a

Cross-gartered, see thee c., 252b

Crossing Channel and tossing, 767b
death is but c. world, 381a
stripling Thames, 712a

Crosspatch draw latch, 1094a

Crossroads, dirty work at c., 1099b
strange c. lie, 1040b

Crossways, things at home c., 808b

Crotchets in thy head, 267a

Crouch, master and make c., 667a
to fawn to c. to wait, 201a
to television set, 1077a

Crow beautified with our feathers, 206a
before the cock c., 44b
Indian Sioux or C., 823b
louder in own farmyard, 678b
lungs c. like chanticleer, 248b
makes wing to rooky wood, 284b
many-wintered c., 647a
not have me roar or c., 945a
safer 'n to c., 693a
shook down on me, 927a
sun risen to hear him c., 689a
think thy swan a c., 223a
we'll pluck c. together, 218a

Crowbar, creation for c., 634a
hammer me into c., 948b
hoe and barrow, 553a

Crowd, after night I do c., 486a
all at once I saw a c., 514b
and buzz and murmurings, 357b
beauty not comprehended by c.. 878b-879a
faces in the c., 987b
firm against c., 649b
fools that c. thee so, 358a
for c. they need interpreters, 79a
great man in c., 606a
how many sorrows c., 520b
I am the c., 948a
into a shade, 402b
into two brief words, 520b
muse in c. all day, 618a
not feel the c., 458b
not on my soul, 442a
of common men, 327b
only beast in arena the c., 889b

Crowd, out of the c. a mistress or friend, 571a
truth not assimilated by c., 706b
whole thing in minute, 814b
will support itself, 732b
you were a good c., 843a
Crowded, for sake of c. audience, 88b
hour of glorious life, 455b
too busied with c. hour, 603b
with glorious action, 522a
world's most c. streets, 711b
Crowd's, madding c. ignoble strife, 440b
Crowds, beauty c. me till I die, 738b
noise c. beloved smoke, 534b
not act arbitrarily, 1013a
public men nor cheering c., 881b
talk with c. keep virtue, 877a
without company, 466a
Crowed, cock that c. in morn, 1098b
Crowing, faded on c. of the cock, 257a
of cocks and barking of dogs, 75a
Crown, allegiance to c., 460b
ambassador from Britain's c., 656a
becomes monarch better than c., 234b
bowed with galling c., 899b
breeches cost a c., 1085a
chance may c. me, 281b
contrary to c. built paper mill, 215b
cross for c., 913b
defiance to forces of C., 426b
emperor without c., 399a
fell down broke c., 1094a
fighting for c., 1092b
fill me from c. to toe, 281b
from c. of head to sole, 246a
golden c. like a deep well, 228a
good with brotherhood, 849a
hairy gold c. on 'ead, 873a
hath worn the c., 38a
have I no bays to c. it, 323b
head that wears a c., 242a
heaven's jeweled c., 758a
hoary head a c. of glory, 24b
hollow c., 227b
holly bears the c., 1099a
immortal c., 420a
is called content, 215b
is in my heart, 215b
is love and friendship, 580b
is of night, 775b
kingly c. to gain, 549a
knave scourge tool, 791a
laurel c. yield to praise, 111b
man with dream conquer c., 807a
mind content both c. and kingdom, 206a
no cross no c., 322a, 380b
not the king's c. nor sword, 270b
of glory, 57a
of life, 56a, 57b
of life as it closes, 773b
of Monomakh, 593b
of thorns on brow of labor, 858b
old age c. of life, 112a
old Winter's head, 354a
ourselves with rosebuds, 36b
quiet mind richer than c., 206a

Crown, sorrow's c. of sorrow, 647a
still the fine's the c., 270a
sweet fruition of earthly c., 212a
sword mace c. imperial, 244b
that seldom kings enjoy, 215b
the watery glade, 439a
themselves assured, 293b
thorns thy only c., 333a
though they possess c., 385b
virtuous woman is a c., 24a
Crowned again discrowned, 893a
due to be c. again, 986a
ghost sitting c. upon grave, 318a
him long ago, 559b
knot of fire, 1007a
Peace c. with smiles, 363a
with lilies, 1024a
with stars, 377b
Crownest year with thy goodness, 19b
Crownets, walked crowns and c., 289a
Crowning, reason God's c. gift, 82a
Crownless in voiceless woe, 557a
Crowns and pounds and guineas, 852b
are empty things, 385b
birds rounding hill c., 1078b
end c. all, 269b
end c. us not fight, 320a
ending c. the work, 150b
if store of c. be scant, 309a
in shades like these, 449a
last act c. play, 322a
not c. but men, 545a
walked c. and crownets, 289a
Crows and choughs that wing air, 279a
throw him to c., 1101b
wars of kites or c., 350a
Crow's-feet, til c. be growen, 164b
Cru j'ai pleuré et j'ai c., 503b
Crucible, God's c., 870b
not test faith in c., 818b
Crucified dead and buried, 60a
everyone Christ and all c., 939b
let him be c., 44b
where dear Lord c., 684b
Crucifixes, crosses relics c., 353b
Cruciform shadow, 1018b
Crucify mankind on cross of gold, 858b
Son of God afresh, 55b
Crude, berries harsh and c., 338a
no c. surfeit reigns, 337a
Cruel and unrelenting enemy, 461a
aristocracy always c., 659a
as death, 419b
but composed and bland, 715a
crawling foam, 690b
death of Pyramus, 228b
doubts more c. than truths, 361a
I must be c. to be kind, 264b
jealousy is c. as the grave, 30a
love more c. than lust, 773b
mother of sweet loves, 122b
price c. high, 872b
savage extreme rude c., 294a
slain by fair c. maid, 252a
sons of Cain, 887a
tender mercies of the wicked are. c., 24a
'tis said she, 580b
wind blows, 1057a
Cruelest, April c. month, 1002a

Cruelest lies told in silence, 822b
she alive, 251b
Cruelly, Fortune c. scratched, 270a
pain clings c. to us, 580b
Cruelty, all the pride c. and ambition, 199b
farewell fair c., 251b
fear source of c., 913a
full of direst c., 281b
has human heart, 489b
Mr. C., 365b
of pirates, 693b
pastime of civilized man c., 892a
soldier without c., 747b
stories of bloodthirsty c., 855b
to load falling man, 298b
war is c., 705a
Cruise, all on our last c., 822b
Crumb, craved no c., 769a
just a c. to me, 736b
Crumbled out again to his atomies, 307b
Crumbs, dogs eat of c., 43a
Crumpetty tree, 673b
Crumpled, cow with c. horn, 1098b
Cruse, little oil in a c., 13a
Crush amang the stoure, 493a
him before he has struck, 973b
the infamous thing, 417b
thought not c. to stone, 1064b
Crushed, hope c. less quick, 714a
human c. by books, 1069b
in winepress of passion, 171b
most fragrant when c., 208a
odors c. sweeter still, 208a
the sweet poison, 336b
to ground diffuse sweets, 208a
together c. and bruised, 405a
truth c. to earth, 574b
Crushes, friend supports whom Fortune c., 134a
Crusoe, Robinson C., 436a
Crust, dinosaur death-steps on c., 1076b
eaten in peace, 76a
of bread and liberty, 411b
over volcano of revolution, 851a
upper c., 564b, 587b
water and c., 581b
wretched c., 692a
Crusted with blood, 995a
Cry against hemlocks, 955a
all should c. Beware, 524a
at a play to laugh or c., 389b
battle c. of freedom, 704b
Bellman c. crew reply, 746b
bubbling c. of swimmer, 560a-b
but behold a c., 30b
caused constantly a c., 956a
cherry-ripe themselves do c., 300a
clear unconquerable c., 785b
consider anything don't c., 746a
couch when owls do c., 297b
creation's c., 876b
don't you c. for me, 727b
every infant's c. of fear, 489b
far c. to Lochow, 521a
feel sorry because c., 794a
for being born, 210a
for restful death I c., 292b
forgot c. of gulls, 1003a
God for Harry, 244a
great c. in Egypt, 8b
harlot's c. from street, 490a
Havoc, 255a
hear us when we c., 726a

Curate thinks you have no soul, 953b
Curates long dust, 993b
  shower of c., 679b
  will come and go, 993b
Curative, economics c. pathology, 1034a
Curb, care's check and c., 362a
  use snaffle and c. all right, 1049b
  your magnanimity, 586a
Curd, white c. of ass's milk, 411a
Curdied by frost from snow, 290a
Curds and whey, 1096b
  quivering c., 747a
Cure, absence c. of love, 195a
  disease kill patient, 209a
  freedom c. of anarchy, 453a
  laws or kings cause or c., 428a
  no c. for birth and death, 867b
  not worth the pain, 125b
  on exercise depend, 372a
  past c. I am, 294b
  past hope past c. past help, 225b
  seem to offer c., 1020b
  tale would c. deafness, 296a
  thrust of c., 1082a
Cured I am frizzled stale, 1076a
  I treated him God c. him, 187b
  more than Galen c., 324b
  of every folly but vanity, 436a
  some hurts you c., 604b
Cures, endure neither evils nor c., 125a
  me of my pain, 1089b
  to fear worst c. worse, 268b
Curfew bell must ring tonight, 825b
  far-off c. sound, 335b
  must not ring tonight, 825a
  tolls knell, 439b
Curiosity, culture origin not in c., 716a
  damnable detestable c., 628b
  do well in closet by way of c., 415b
  intellectual c., 941b
  love c. freckles doubt, 1029a
  must be kept alive, 981b
  my c. my wonder, 86ga
  natural c. of young, 802a
  newspapers excite c., 535b
  offers to our c., 1006a
  order awakened c., 605a
  permanent and certain, 427b
Curious, amazed and c., 496a
  busy c. thirsty fly, 418b
  crime, 667a
  in unnecessary matters, 37a
  incident of dog, 850a
  objects and knowledge c., 702a
  quaint and c. war is, 783b
  seen a c. child, 516b
  volume of forgotten lore, 642b
Curiouser and curiouser, 743a
Curl, had a little c., 625a
  make your hair c., 768b
  New Hampshire mountains c., 927a
  not c. less gracefully, 724b
Curled Assyrian Bull, 652a
  hair so charmingly c., 691a
  last holy drop, 953b
  rainbow c. around shoulder, 906b
  up on the floor, 770a
  wealthy c. darlings, 272b
  wonderful waters c., 719a

Curlicues of marijuana, 1076a
Curls, frocks and c., 737a
  Hyperion's c., 264a
  natural c., 134a
Curlylocks wilt be mine, 1095a
Curr, let me c. to quercine shades, 110b
Current, genial c. of soul, 440b
  icy c. compulsive course, 275a
  noiseless c. strong, 716a
  swollen c. masses of ice, 659a-b
  take c. when it serves, 256a
  time a river of strong c., 142a
Currents, fresh c. of life, 656a-b
  turn awry, 262a
Curriculum was rum, 868b
Curried, short horse soon c., 183b
Currite, lente c. noctis equi, 213b
Curs, mouths sentence as c. bone, 456a
  of low degree, 448b
Curse, began to c., 44b
  bless them that c. you, 40b
  Christianity one great c., 806a
  creations of mind blessing not c., 950a
  God and die, 14a
  has come upon me, 646a
  his better angel, 276a
  I know how to c., 296a
  O c. of marriage, 274b
  of hell frae me, 1087b
  on his virtues, 393b
  primal eldest c., 263b
  selfishness greatest c., 632a
  the darkness, 981b
  with book bell and candle, 175b
  youthful harlot's c., 489b
Cursed above all cattle, 6a
  be he that moves my bones, 299b
  be man trusteth in man, 34a
  be my tribe, 232a
  be the verse, 411a
  Beauty in lap and c. her, 830a
  Boston c. with cranks, 831a
  bread, 900a
  by man c. alway, 619b
  counted and c. luck, 854a
  Fate has c. you, 84a
  floundered enjoyed, 800a
  hard reading, 482a
  me with his eye, 525a
  name to all ages c., 368a
  O c. spite, 260a
  past, 1010a
  plagues with which mankind c., 385b
  sat Beauty and I c. her, 830a
  thoughts, 283a
Curses all Eve's daughters, 267a
  deeper than strong man, 617b
  like young chickens, 532b
  not loud but deep, 286a
  of the firmament, 373a
  rigged with c. dark, 338b
Cursing, blessing and c., 10b
Cursores vitae lampada tradunt, 113b
Curtain, Anarch lets c. fall, 414a
  close his eyes and draw c., 215a
  iron c., 924b
  never c. between you and me, 928a
  never outward swings, 625a
  Priam's c., 241a
  purple c., 643a
  when she drew c. by, 1088a

Curtained, dreams abuse c. sleep, 283a
Curtain's fall, 1018a
Curtains, for whom your c. drawn, 319b
  fringed c. of thine eye, 296b
  hell take c., 979a
  let fall the c., 458a
  of Solomon, 29a
  spread canopy or c. spun, 381a
  through c. call on us, 305a
Curtius Rufus seems descended from himself, 96a
Curtsied when you have, 296a
Curtsy, customs c. to great kings, 245b
  leaves c. and quadrille, 1078b
  while you're thinking, 745a
Cushion, sit on a c., 1095b
Cussedness, trust in his c., 778b
Custodians, new c. have fervor, 861b
Custom, age cannot wither nor c. stale, 287b
  almost second nature, 221a
  conform to tyrant c., 193b
  follow c. of church where you are, 144b
  Fortune more kind than her c., 234a
  gods' c. to bring low greatness, 87a
  guide of human life, 434b
  in all line of order, 267b
  lord of mankind, 593b
  made property of easiness, 265b
  make it their perch, 270b
  maturity of c., 901a
  more honored in breach, 259a
  nature her c. holds, 265b
  of Branksome Hall, 518a
  old c. made life sweet, **247b**
  one good c. corrupt, 654a
  public use and c., 188b
  reconciles to everything, 452a
  sitting at receipt of c., 41b
  stern c. spreads afar, 497a
  to whom c. due, 51b
  when c. presses, 947b
Customary fate of new truths, 725b
  suits of solemn black, 257b
Customer, tough c., 670a
Customers, empire for raising c., 445a
  sign brings c., 359b
Customs curtsy to great kings, 245b
  evil c. in China, 357a
  language manners laws c., 511a
  politics and tongue, 721b
Cut, all one c. away in reader's consciousness, 940a
  and come again, 483a
  anyone introduced to, 746b
  diamond c. diamond, 317b
  features of clerical c., 1004a
  hawsers haul out, 702b
  him out in little stars, 225a
  if thy hand offend thee c. it off, 40a
  in the evening it is c. down, 20a
  is branch that might have grown, 213b
  it is soon c. off and we fly away, 20b
  it without any knife, 1094a
  kite c. from string, 985b
  knives that serve or c., 694b

Damp, lived in cellar d., 694a
 nights are very d., 747a
 souls of housemaids, 1001b
 tonnage, 1043b
 years d. my intended wing, 347b
Damsel lay deploring, 401a
 to every man a d. or two, 11a
 with dulcimer, 524a
Damyata datta dayadhvamiti, 62a
Dan, Dangerous D. McGrew, 933a
 from D. to Beersheba, 116, 438b
 senior-junior D. Cupid, 221b
Danaë to the stars, 649a
Danaos, timeo D. et dona ferentis, 118a
Dance, a god has given the d., 63b
 and drink and sing, 489a
 and Provençal song, 582a
 antic hay, 212b
 as often as d. it can, 524a
 attendance, 299b
 attention on old age, 885a
 barefoot on wedding day, 219a
 dancer from d., 883b
 in old dame yet, 946a
 join the d., 744b
 like wave of sea, 880b
 little lady, 1043a
 maids d. in a ring, 300b
 make hills and forest d., 505a
 mehitabel dance, 946a
 move easiest who learned to d., 403b
 on this ball-floor, 1036a
 on with the d., 556a
 Pyrrhic d. as yet, 561a
 rhythms for rain, 1077b
 round in ring and suppose, 929a
 rouses him up to d., 66b
 sweet to d. to violins, 184a
 the antic hay, 212b
 there is only the d., 1005a
 time to d., 27b
 tipsy d. and jollity, 336b
 to flutes dance to lutes, 841a
 tossing heads in sprightly d., 514b
 upon the air, 841a
 walk before they d., 412a
 when you do d., 295b
 while you can, 1059b
 with rapture that we alive, 986a-b
 with William Blake, 1066b
 wyth me in Irlonde, 1083b
Danced along dingy days, 738b
 by light of moon, 673a
 daughter of Herodias d., 42b
 David d. before the Lord, 12b
 death-fires d., 525a
 his did, 1031b
 lighter than cork, 829b
 like dinglebodies, 1080b
 moon on Monan's rill, 520a
 star d., 246a
 till doomsday, 391b
 to see that banner, 633a
Dancer from the dance, 883b
 stealthy d. comes, 878b
Dancers all gone under hill, 1005b
 dancing in tune, 652b
Dances as often as dance it can, 524a
 he capers he d., 267a
 in golden escape, 1050a
 in hamlets d. on green, 518b
 in sight of heaven, 1079a

Dances, in what ethereal d., 642a
 lulled with d. and delight, 229b
 oh she d. such a way, 350b
 when she d. in the wind, 369b
Dancing and architecture, 851a
 dancers d. in tune, 652b
 days are done, 223a, 1099b
 dining and d. begin, 1052a
 dogs and bears, 906a
 emptier ever d. in air, 228a
 in the checkered shade, 335a
 is life itself, 851a
 keeping rhythm in d., 1005a
 loftiest of arts, 851a
 music of d. waves, 998a
 on volcano, 575a
 past our d. days, 223a
 source of arts, 851a
 to frenzied drum, 882a
 very merry d. drinking, 372a
 wonderful training, 1017b
Dandin, asked for it Georges D., 361b
Dandruff, toothpaste and d. ads, 1043b
Dandy, candy is d., 1051b
 Yankee Doodle d., 1090a
Dandyism, intellectual d., 730b
Dane, more antique Roman than D., 266b
 never rid of D., 876b
Danegeld, once paid him D., 876b
Danger, above noise and d., 363a
 and tempest of war, 661a
 brave man's choice is d., 85a
 bright eyes of d., 824a
 clear and present d., 788a-b
 days of d., 520a
 difficulty and d., 1091b
 familiarity with d., 695b
 feared no d. knew no sin, 370a
 foretold that d. lurks within, 216a
 glory and d. alike, 89b
 graceful the small before d., 1065b
 hackneyed phrases d. signals, 851b
 in view of d. give up life, 72a
 is in discord, 623a
 less d. from stranger, 1051b
 morale not destroyed by d., 959a
 neither shape of d. dismay, 515a
 nettle d., 239a
 of faction, 480a-b
 of violent death, 318a
 on the deep, 588a
 or treasure, 1078a
 pleased with d., 368a
 when fatherland in d., 496b
 where is man out of d., 725a
Dangerous brow by night, 524
 Dan McGrew, 933a
 delays d. in war, 202b, 214a
 delays have d. ends, 214a
 demur you're d., 735b
 edge of things, 665a
 forties the d. ages, 1022a
 guiled shore to d. sea, 233b
 have in me something d., 266a
 idea d. when only one, 893b
 ideas d. for good or evil, 977a
 if a little knowledge d., 725a
 into d. world I leaped, 489b
 little learning d., 402b
 mad bad d. to know, 552b
 most d. situation humanity has faced, 1029b
 politics as d. as war, 919b

Dangerous, realities less d. than fancies, 913b
 say nothing in d. times, 317b
 such men are d., 253b
 temptation in gay colors, 299b
 thirst d. thing, 855a
 to be of no church d., 428b
 to meet culture alone, 865b
 to our peace and safety, 492a
 when appear to retreat, 946b
 who make no noise are d., 359b
Danger's troubled night, 537b
Dangers, defend us from d. of night, 60b
 delays breed d., 202b
 greatest d. to liberty, 833a
 in what great d. ye spend little span, 113b
 no d. fright him, 427a
 of the seas, 328b
 she loved me for the d., 273a
 thorns and d. of world, 237a
 what d. thou make us scorn, 495b
 with d. compassed round, 346b
Daniel, cast D. into the den of lions, 35a
 come to judgment, 234b
 had convicted them, 39a
 second D., 235a
Dank, addled mosses d., 989a
 tarn of Auber, 643b
Danny, hangin' D. Deever, 873a
Dans, no time for fancy d., 1025b
Dante greatest depth of passion, 1008a
 language of D. common language, 1008a
 more learned from D., 1008a
 of dread Inferno, 665b
 saner attitude towards life, 1008a
Daphnis, my songs draw D. home, 116b
Dapple, name was D. Gray, 1097b
Dappled things, 803a
 turf at ease, 512b
Dapple-dawn-drawn Falcon, 803a
Darbies, ease d. at wrist, 698a
Darby, always same D. my own, 815a
Dare and dare again, 496b
 ask just God's assistance, 640b
 bear to live or d. to die, 409b
 call soul my own, 618b
 choose if you d., 331b
 deadly terrors clasp, 489a
 do duty as understand it, 636b
 endure greater than d., 661a
 enter you who d., 730b
 first ponder then d., 597a
 heart would deny and d. not, 286a
 I d. do all, 282b
 I d. yet may not, 192b
 if they d. not forgive, 708a
 imitate him if you d., 884a
 is highest wisdom, 544a
 letting I d. not, 282b
 love that and say so too, 305a
 mighty things, 847a
 more as I grow older, 190b
 never d. utter untruth, 110b
 never grudge throe, 666a
 no no no I d. not, 1084b
 none d. call it treason, 210a
 O what men d. do, 246b
 on what wings d. he aspire, 489a

Dare, others teach how to d., 711b
slaves who d. not be, 691b
soul to d., 520a
there is much to d., 979a
think unthinkable, 1056a
to be ahead of the world, 75a
to be true, 322b
to be wise, 123a
to eat a peach, 1001a
to love country and be poor, 413a
unpastured dragon, 571b
what hand d. seize fire, 489a
what man d. I d., 285a
wonder Do I d., 1000b
Dared be radical young, 928b
determined d. and done, 444b
none d. thou hast, 199b
to be obscene, 850b
Daren't go a-hunting, 729a
Dares, come before swallow d., 295b
life d. send challenge, 354a
to call Himself a man, 1031a
whisper who d., 969b
who d. do more is none, 282b
Darest thou now O soul, 702b
thou then, 519b
Darien, peak in D., 579b
Daring, brave man braver less d., 695b
dare and go on d., 496b
in war d. boastful, 564a
pilot in extremity, 368a
well-doing and d., 430b
young man on trapeze, 780a
Dark, abyss of new D. Age, 921a
abysmal d. of center, 586b
after that the d., 655a
all night in d. and wet, 823a
amid blaze of noon, 349a
and bloody ground, 704b
and his d. secret love, 489a
and lonely hiding place, 526a
as Erebus, 235a
as good in the d., 320a
as sages say, 679b
as world of man, 998b
at one stride comes the d., 525a
backward and abysm of time, 296a
best of d. and bright, 558b
between d. and daylight, 623b
blanket of the d., 282a
blond or d. sir, 1034b
blue ocean roll, 557b
brown is river, 823a
Care sits enthroned, 121b
Chromis did not save himself from d. death, 62b
cold and empty desolation, 1006a
come to d. and lament, 928b
cooling star, 925b
dark dark amid blaze, 349a
dark dark spaces, 1005b
days d. and dreary, 621b
dove with flickering tongue, 1006b
dull d. soundless day, 642a
ever-during d., 344b
every hour of light d., 702b
everyone moon with d. side, 736a
fate sits on d. battlements, 501a
fear death as children fear d., 208a
fell of d. not day, 804a

Dark, go home in d., 864b
great leap in the d., 318a
hawks hear us, 968b
horse, 611b
hour or twain, 284a
hunt it in the d., 457a
in d. time eye begins to see, 1066a
in the d. and silent grave, 199b
inscrutable workmanship, 510a
iron New England d., 1039b
irrecoverably d., 349a
let d. come upon you, 1005b
lie awake in d. weep for sins, 700b
long d. autumn evenings, 663b
Maid and her Lord, 83b
mutinous Shannon waves, 968a
never refuse drink after d., 961a
night is d., 597b, 1103b
night of d. intent, 928a
night of the soul, 1036b
not d. days great days, 923a
o'er d. her mantle threw, 345b
on a d. hill, 982a
on d. theme trace verses of light, 113a
pillared d., 928b
raging in the d., 884a
road whence no one returns, 114b
Satanic mills, 490b
some days d. and dreary, 621b
soul's d. cottage, 333a
sun to me is d., 349a
they all go into d., 1005b
things in d. besides Santa Claus, 931a
to d. tower came, 278b
'twill soon be d., 602b
unconscious not only d. but light, 936a
unfathomed caves, 440b
violets are d. too, 116 b
wall between us and d., 1033b
wandering in d. labyrinth, 211b
ways that are d., 769b
we are for the d., 289a
what in me is d. illumine, 341b
what is Amyntas d., 116b
whistles in d., 833b
who art d. as night, 294b
with excessive bright, 344b
with torment and tears, 685b
wood where straight way lost, 159a
woods lovely d. deep, 927b
world and wide, 341a
Dark-blue, night d. hunter, 893b
Darkened, blue d. on blueness, 986a
hurtles in d. air, 442a
ocean-booms, 955b
sun or light be not d., 28b
windows be d., 28b
Darkeneth, who d. counsel by words, 16a
Darker and darker stairs, 986a
as d. grows the night, 447b
grows the valley, 730b
larger bill for d. ill, 686a
the tinge that saddens, 614a
Darkest altar of heartbreak, 1068a
before day dawneth, 333b
day will have passed, 459a
sun breaks through d. clouds, 219b
Dark-heaving boundless, 557b
Darkies a-weeping, 727b

Darkies how heart grows weary, 727b
Darkling I listen, 582b
plain, 715a
roll d. down torrent, 427a
stand varying shore, 288b
Darkly deeply beautifully blue, 532a, 561a
it knows obstacles, 1079a
see through glass d., 52b
wise and rudely great, 408b
Darkness, absence d. death, 306a
affronts with his own d., 1069b
again and silence, 624a
and light alike to thee, 23a
and shadow of death, 15a, 21b, 46a
as children fear in d., 113b
awful d. silence reign, 674a
blackness of d., 57a
broods, 4a
cast into outer d., 41b
comprehended it not, 47b
crown of our life is d., 773b
curse the d., 981b
dawn on our d., 549a
deep but dazzling d., 362b
deep in d. a slim hand, 981a
deep things out of d., 15a
deepens, 567a
distant voice in d., 624a
downward to d. on wings, 955a
dying of cold not d., 869b
embalmed d., 582b
encounter d. as a bride, 271a
falls from wings, 621b
fell upon Christian, 366a
gives light in d., 214b
good kind d., 791b
horror of outer d., 748b
how great that d., 41a
how in your d. know, 906b
if light in thee be d., 40b-41a
in d. and with dangers, 346b
in d. the people march, 949a
in him is no d., 57a
in what d. of life spend little span, 113a
instruments of d., 281a
into d. peering, 643a
into d. they go, 1024a
into eternal d. fire and ice, 159b
jaws of d. do devour it, 228b
land of d. and shadow, 15a
lead me from d. to light, 62a
leaves world to d., 440a
lest d. come, 49a
light excelleth d., 27b
light shineth in d., 47b
lighten our d., 60b
like death, 3b
love in spite of d., 305b
mainly in d., 1083b
man in unsearchable d., 801b
no d. into light without emotion, 936b
no light but d. visible, 341b
not walk in d., 48b
of God, 1005b
of her eyes, 906a
of the damned, 635b
of the land, 651a
outer d., 41b, 748b
pain d. and cold, 666b
peace and d., 854b
people that walked in d., 31a
people who sit in d., 763b

Darkness, pestilence that walketh in d., 20b
prince of d. a gentleman, 278b
raven down of d., 337a
rulers of the d., 54a
scatters rear of d. thin, 334b
shaft of light in d., 1074b
shares the d., 1023b
sit in d. here, 343b
such as sit in d., 21b
them that sit in d., 46a
thou drivest away d., 4a
thou makest d., 21b
through a brief d., 624a
through d. up to God, 650b
to d. and to me, 440b
universal d. buries all, 414a
upon face of the deep, 5a
we are not of d., 55a
where d. let me sow light, 157b
which may be felt, 8a
wind torrent of d., 961b
works of d., 51b
worms and shrouds, 580a
year of now done d., 803b
Dark-shining Pacific, 994b
Darky's heart longed to go, 828b
Darling buds of May, 291b
Charlie is my d., 502a
daughter, 1103a
I am growing old, 815a
my d. dear, 1099b
my d. from the lions, 18b
Nature's d., 441b
of men and gods, 112b
of my heart, 400b
of our crew, 475b
old man's d., 185b
sin, 526b
Darlings, wealthy curled d., 272b
Dart, every look a d., 1089b
feather on fatal d., 555a
of chance, 752 b
poisonous d. not pugnacity, 980b
time throw a d. at thee, 319b
Darwin Abraham of scientific men, 705b
Darwinian man, 768a
Darwin's theory conjectural, 620a
Dash down yon cup, 561a
most a d. between two, 730a
thy foot against a stone, 20b
Dashed, breaking waves d. high, 573b
in pieces the enemy, 8b
the brains out, 282b
through thick and thin, 369a
with pain, 729b
Dastard in war, 519b
Dastardly pitiful Public, 539b
Dat veniam corvis vexat censura columbas, 139a
Data, distorted incomplete d., 1020a
submit d. to analysis, 479a
Date, in South d. from war, 760b
out of d., 988a
will live in infamy, 973b
Dates of wars deaths of kings, 765a
Daubed with slime and pitch, 8a
Daughter all her life, 727a
am I in mother's house, 875a
any man's fair d., 953b
as mother so her d., 34b
at point of death, 45b
beggar's d. of Bethnal Green, 1087b

Daughter, Bess the landlord's d., 961b
fairer d. of fair mother, 121a
farmer's d. soft brown hair, 740b
harping on my d., 260b
have you a d., 260b
I have a d., 235a
images return O my d., 1004a
king of Spain's d., 1095b
light God's eldest d., 333b
little d. whispered, 679b
marry boss's d., 1009b
marry d. when you can, 324a
Mrs. Porter and d., 1002b
my d. O my ducats, 233a
of a hundred earls, 645a
of debate, 189a
of earth and water, 570b
of Elysium, 497a
of Herodias danced, 42a
of Jove, 439b
of Moon Nokomis, 623a
of the gods, 645b
one fair d., 261a
sole d. of his voice, 347b
stern d. of voice of God, 514b
still harping on my d., 260b
taken his little d., 621a
undaunted d. of desires, 354b
whipped her little d., 1095b
yes my darling d., 1103a
your d. and the Moor, 272b
Daughter's a daughter all her life, 277a
preaching down d. heart, 647a
Daughters, curses all Eve's d., 267a
degenerate sons and d., 898a
earth's heedless sons and d., 1036a
fairest of her d. Eve, 345a
have done virtuously, 27a
horseleach hath two d., 26b
if you have no d., 1095a
my d. I suppose, 1058a
none of Beauty's d., 559a
O d. of Jerusalem, 29a, 29b
of music brought low, 29a
of my father's house, 252b
of time, 603b
prayers are d. of Zeus, 63b
sage d. of Muses, 79b
tigers not d., 279a
who Shem and Shaun d. of, 968b
words are d. of earth, 427b
Daughter-sons, all Livia's d., 968b
Daunt, death could not d., 1087b
Dauntless, brows of d. courage, 342b
Hampden with d. breast, 440b
in war, 519a
slughorn to my lips, 278b
Dauphin, daylight's d., 803a
David, and D. his ten thousands, 12a
danced before the Lord, 12b
died full of days, 14a
in the city of D., 46a
in the midst, 444a
Josias, 1089a
King D. and King Solomon, 859b
my sling the sling of D., 828b
no more behind your scenes D., 429b
played before the Lord, 12b

David prevailed over the Philistine, 12a
the son of Jesse, 12b
David's, once in royal D. city, 684b
upon St. D. Day, 1097a
word with Sibyl's blending, 157b
Davil, ole d. sea, 1009a
Davos, I am D. not Oedipus, 108a
Daw, Margery D., 1094b
no wiser than a d., 214a
Dawn, before d. of day, 446b
bodiless as false d., 1078b
comes up like thunder, 873b
creation's d. beheld, 557b
embraced summer d., 830b
gray d. breaking, 594b, 946b
heard bird at d., 974b
in Helen's arms, 884a
in that d. to be alive, 510a
into silver d., 1030a
live gray d., 1081b
Morning Star herald of d., 110a
of knowledge false dawn, 1039a
of morning after, 886b
on other side of Atlantic, 442a
on our darkness, 549a
past is twilight of d., 888a
rosy-fingered d., 62b
said to d. Be sudden, 856b
speeds a man, 68a
things the bright d. scattered, 69b
will dispel night, 565b
with silver-sandaled feet, 838b
Dawned from Bullen's eyes, 439b
Dawnest, thou d., 4a
thou d. beautifully, 3b
Dawneth, darkest before day d. 333b
Dawning, bird of d., 257a
here hath been d., 578a
not as d. of day, 308b
Dawn's early light, 540b
Daws, for d. to peck at, 272a
Day, a little work and good d., 751b
a summer's d. and with the setting sun, 343a
after d. is over, 1025b
afterwards d., 734a
all d. no road hoofs, 86oa
all days as marriage d., 322a
all on summer's d., 1094b
all things all d. long, 653a
and night shall not cease, 6b
and way we met, 775a
another blue d., 578a
apple a d., 1102a
April d., 928a
as it fell upon a d., 309a
as morning shows the d., 348b
a-tiptoe when d. named, 245a
aye fair in land o' leal, 502b
barrier between d. and d., 515b
battle d. past, 727a
be day never so long, 185b
be she fairer than the d., 318b
behold the d. cometh, 36a
beneath blue of d., 852b
better d. better deed, 313b
better live one d. of energy, 80a
boils at last, 661b
bounded by D. of Judgment, 655a
breaks not it is heart, 1086b
brief December d., 626b
bright d. is done, 289a
bright d. not for aye, 685b

Death, bringeth to light the shadow of d., 15a
brought d. into world, 341b
build your ship of d., 986b
by beauty made amends, 893a
by inches, 290a
by man came d., 53a
by the shadow of d., 760b
Byron's eyes shut in d., 711a
calls ye to the crowd, 327b
came d. into the world, 36b
captain of men of d., 366a
certain is d. for the born, 106a
certain to all, 242a
chance d. and mutability, 569a
chants doleful hymn to d., 237a
Chromis did not save himself from dark d., 62b
city of night perchance d., 753b
clean trunk of d., 1057b
closed in d. attentive eyes, 429a
closes all, 646b
cold hand of d., 241a
come away d., 252a
come close eyes, 1086a
cometh soon or late, 596a
cool-enfolding d., 702a
could not daunt, 1087b
counteracts Devil who is D., 444b
covenant with d., 32a, 615b
crossing the world, 381a
cruel as d., 419b
cruel d. always near, 1089b
cruel d. of Pyramus, 228b
darkness and shadow of d., 15a, 21b, 46a
darkness like d., 3b
daughter at point of d., 45b
dear beauteous d., 363a
defend to d. your right to say it, 418a
delicate d., 702a
desire father's d., 708b
desireth not d. of sinner, 59b
destroyer of worlds, 1055a
devours lovely things, 1023b
die a dry d., 296a
die not poor d., 308a
die the d. of the righteous, 10a
direst shapes of d., 721a
does not end all, 128a
done to d. by slanderous tongues, 247a
doomed to d. though fated not to die, 370a
draw trigger at his d., 430a
dread d., 64b
dread of something after d., 262a
dry d., 296a
dull cold ear of d., 440b
dumb d., 1031b
dung and d., 1005a
dusty d., 286b
easeful d., 582b
eaten to d. with rust, 241b
éclat of d., 738a
eloquent just and mighty D., 199b
embrace is d., 1034b
end of worldly soore, 167a
enviable d. was his, 924b
equal in presence of d., 125a
equal piece of justice D., 329b
ere thou hast slain another, 319b
eternal sleep, 500a
everybody's looks of d., 375b

Death, exodus of d., 623b
face of d., 890b
face to meet d. with, 296a
faithful unto d., 57b
Falstaff sweats to d., 238b
fear and danger of violent d., 318a
fear d. as children fear dark, 208a
fear d. feel fog, 666b
fear of d. hath me in thrall, 176a
fear of d. more dread than d., 126a
fed on fullness of d., 774a
feed on D., 294b
fell sergeant d., 266b
final accounting, 151a
fly down D., 1069a
for restful d. I cry, 292b
for thirty pence my d., 322b
foreknowledge of d., 773a
foretaste of d., 563b
fortune favored him in moment of d., 140b
found d. in life, 530a
fraternity or d., 469a
from d. to immortality, 62a
from d. to life recover, 211b
from sudden d., 60b
fruit threw d., 308a
functions which resist d., 517b
gallop Pegasus to d., 412a
gates of dark D. stand wide, 118b
give me liberty or d., 465b
go down D. bring her, 907a
go with anyone to d., 926a
gods have neither age nor d., 83a
gone to her d., 592b
good d. does honor to whole life, 163a
good thing to escape d., 82a
great d., 905a
grim d., 316a
grim D. my son and foe, 344a
had undone so many, 1002b
half dead a living d., 349a
halls of d., 574b
happened in his berth, 591b
has broached him to, 475b
hath no more dominion, 50b
hath ten thousand doors, 315a
he also to d. must fall, 364b
he brought them d., 904a
he taketh all away, 719b
heaven gives favorites early d., 102a
here find life in d., 530a
hideous storm of terror, 315a
his d. eclipsed gaiety, 428b
how can you know about d., 72a
how little room we take in d., 327b
how they pray for d., 83b
how wonderful is d., 568a
I am near to d., 69b
I here importune d., 288b
idle and who has done much meet d. alike, 63b
if d. knew how to forgive, 117b
immortal d. has taken mortal life, 113b
improved by d., 904b
in d. daylight finish, 667b
in d. they were not divided, 12b

Death, in his d. all things appear fair, 64b
in itself is nothing, 367a
in one sense no d., 943a
in our own power, 805a
in ranks of d. find him, 542a
in stars written d. of every man, 168a
in the midst of life d., 61b
in the pot, 13b
in the shadow of d., 21b, 46a
in vain to wish for d., 82b
interest in d. interest in life, 937b
intricate as d., 308b
is a sleep, 774b
is a debt, 481a
is afraid of him, 149b
is as lover's pinch, 289a
is before me today, 3b
is dead not he, 572a
is knowledge, 498b
is not D. at watch, 1036a
is nothing to us, 103a, 113b
is only a horizon, 785a
is slumber, 568a
is swallowed up, 53a
island surrounded by d., 747b
jaws of d., 193a, 652a
judge none blessed before his d., 38a
just d. kind umpire, 214a
just that distance from d., 69a
keeps D. his court, 227b
keys of hell and d., 57b
kingly D. keeps court, 571a
kings did king to d., 1070a
kiss of d., 916b
land of darkness and shadow of d., 15a
land of the shadow of d., 31a
last enemy is d., 53a
last guerdon of d., 115b
laugh myself to d., 297a
lays icy hand on kings, 327b
leaden d., 405a
leaves body at d., 106b
life d. and that forever, 691a
life mystery deep as d., 740b
life perfected by d., 617b
life shadow of d., 331a, 773a
life that which men call d., 86a
life well used brings happy d., 174b
life your d. bought, 958b
life's old d. new, 668b
like sleep steal on me, 568b
like this, 621a
limbs cold in death, 119b
lively form of d., 204a
long since D. had majority, 330b
looks gigantically, 642a
love better after d., 618b
love is strong as d., 30a
love posterior to d., 737a
love to woman life or d., 825b
lovely and soothing d., 702a
loves shining mark, 399b
low delicious word d., 701b
made d. his ladder, 201a
make d. proud to take us, 288b
makes equal high and low, 182a
makes his arrest, 947b
makes life live, 667b
marriage d. and division, 773b
may be gift to life, 1056b
men at point of d., 225b
men of d., 366a

Deepest feeling in silence, 996b
  loathing to stomach, 230a
  rivers least sound, 199a
  stream smoothest water d., 199a
  thrill d. notes of woe, 494a
Deeply, I d. sympathize, 746a
  music heard so d., 1006b
Deep-mouthed welcome, 560a
Deeps, distant d. or skies, 489a
  far in yon azure d., 621b
Deep-searched, not d. with saucy
  looks, 221a
Deer and antelope play, 808a
  I was a stricken d., 458a
  in Highlands a-chasing d., 494b
  mice and such small d., 278b
  poor d. thou makest testament,
    247b
  running of the d., 1099b
  stricken d. go weep, 263b
  stricken d. that left herd, 458a
  walk upon our mountains, 955a
Deever, hangin' Danny D., 873a
Deface, no rude hand d., 511b
Defaced, by Time's fell hand d.,
  292b
  lost d. deflowered, 348a
Defamed by every charlatan, 651a
Défauts, quelle âme sans d., 830a
Defeat enemy in one battle, 467a
  from folly to d., 1080a
  in d. as great, 1041b
  in d. defiance, 925a
  in ourselves triumph and d.,
    624b
  is orphan, 1053a
  much wrested from sure d.,
    1008b
  night this world's d., 362a
  not interested in d., 699a
  not victory nor d., 847a
  preface to successors' victory,
    1008a
  refusal to accept d., 959b
  through battle through d., 701b
  unkindness may d. my life, 276a
  victories worse than d., 689a
  well borne without d., 243a
Defeated, destroyed but not d.,
  1045b
  history to the d., 1059b
  make d. empires good neigh-
    bors, 976b
  principles never d., 616a
Defect, cause of this d., 260b
  chief d. of Henry King, 902a
  of modern literature, 712b
  pay in affliction or d., 910b
  satire points at no d., 390a
Defective, effect d. comes by
  cause, 260b
Defects, faith for all d. supplying,
  158a
Defend, against side she would d.,
  390a
  book of moons d. ye, 1085b
  country against enemies, 895b
  dog foremost to d., 455b
  every village town city, 921b
  from all perils, 60b
  God d. the right, 214b
  me from friends, 507a
  ministers of grace d. us, 259a
  neighbor he promised to d.,
    596a
  newspapers not d. if can help
    it, 960a
  not ashamed to d. a friend, 38a
  of England on Rhine, 889a

Defend our island whatever cost,
  921a
  ourselves and henroosts, 684a
  ready to d. liberty, 548a
  refuses to d. rights, 503a
  to death your right to say it,
    418a
  us thy humble servants, 60a
  will d. what's mine, 198a
  with their helps only d., 216a
  you from seasons, 278b
  your departed friend, 371a
Defended, country d. by hands
  655b
  God abandoned these d., 854b
Defender, Faith's D., 414b
Defenders, no error fails to find
  d., 749b
  of old homes, 896a
  truth suffers by heat of d., 380b
Defending not field but cause,
  467a
Defense, as well for d. as repose,
  198a
  at one gate to make d., 349a
  cheap d. of nations, 454a
  deaths glorious in thy d., 393a
  die in d. of his country, 64a
  friend is strong d., 37b
  guilty of corruption and re-
    nounce d., 207a
  he is my d., 19b
  immodest words admit no d.,
    374b
  is in law and order, 951a
  local d. important, 1000b
  millions for d., 501b
  navy its greatest d., 444b
  no adequate military d., 982b
  no d. against reproach, 394b
  no d. like courtesy, 895b
  not in armaments, 951a
  of our Liberty Tree, 466a
  provide for common d., 474a
  ready in d., 453a
  vain to look for d. against
    lightning, 127a
Defenseless as thou wert, 571b
  shield for d., 749a
Defensible, no d. frontier, 1067b
Defensive, d. to a house moat,
  226b
Defer, not d. kindness, 531a
  not to be wise, 392a
  'tis madness to d., 399a
Deference, out of d. cheat others,
  908a
Deferential glad to be of use,
  1001a
Deferred, hope d. maketh the
  heart sick, 24a
Defiance, in defeat d., 925a
  in their eye, 447b
  of my orders, 984a
  spirit of d., 703b
  to all forces of Crown, 426b
Deficiency, easier discover d. than
  see value, 507b
Defile, vengeance presume to d.,
  483b
Defiled his father's grave, 124b
  they that touch pitch d., 246b
Defileth, not that which goeth
  into mouth d., 43a
  that which cometh out of
    mouth d., 43a
Define, facts which d. U.S., 1038b
  hold good d. it well, 650b
  how d. Christian Science, 709a

Define life in a word, 675a
  to d. is to exclude, 978a
Definition, difference escapes d.,
  792b
  of a philosopher, 742b
  of criticism, 713b
  of oats meant to vex, 427b
  of style, 389a
  of word liberty, 639b
Definitions, I hate d., 611a
Deflower, age that will pride d.,
  200a
Deflowered and now to Death
  devote, 348a
Defoe, sedulous ape to D., 824a
Defunct, Buffalo Bill's d., 1030a
  economist, 977a
  ghosts of d. bodies fly, 352a
Defy augury, 266b
  man know to d. opinion, 502b
  the Omnipotent to arms, 341b
  tooth of time, 398b
Degeneracy and decay, 596b
  progress in d. rapid, 635a
Degenerate into hands like mine,
  560b
  poor d. from ape, 1032a
  sons and daughters, 898a
Degenerates, extensive state d.,
  548b-549a
  in hands of man, 436a
Degeneration, from barbarism to
  d., 786b
Degradation not to overcome poverty, 89b
  of idea of liberty, 1068b
Degrade first the arts, 490b
Degraded, critic most d. of trades,
  764a
Degrading anxiety about livelihood, 932a
  classes of white people, 635a
Degree, beauty and high d.,
  1009b
  curs of low d., 448b
  exalted them of low d., 45b
  law depends on differences of d.,
    788a
  no best in kind but d., 623a
  only difference lies in d., 377a
  priority and place, 267b
  stand each in our d., 784a
  take but d. away, 267b
  unless d. preserved place not
    safe, 127b
  when d. is shaked, 267b
Degrees, boil at different d., 609a
  crime like virtue has d., 378b
  estates d. and offices, 233a
  grows up by d., 316b
  ill habits by unseen d., 372a
  one battle or by d., 467a
  scorning the base d., 254a
  set down to adversity by d.,
    755b
  then by gradual d., 902a
  things through all d., 512b
  what wound heal but by d.,
    274a
Dehumanizing Negro, 635b
Dei, Agnus D., 59a
Deified, by our own spirits d.,
  511b
Deign on passing world, 427a
Deity ever vindictively, 643b
  everlastingly appointed by D.,
    698b
  Greeks give sea separate d.,
    695b

Die proudly, 860a
regret can d., 650b
remember that we d. all, 37b
resolve to conquer or d., 461a
reverences age d. with it, 576a
rich, 432b
root hog or d., 1047a
rose with maize to d., 1043b
sail until I d., 646b
saw spider d., 1075a
seem though I d. old, 884b
seems rich to d., 582b
seldom d. in bed, 810b
shall never d., 49a
shall Trelawny d., 610a
sink or swim live or d., 546b
soil good to d. for, 694a
some will d., 996b
speeches by hour d. by hour, 473b
spirit d. of inanition, 713b
swanlike sing and d., 561a
swim or sink live or d., 462b-463a
Tamburlaine must d., 212a
taught us how to d., 400b
teach men to d., 189b
teach us how to d., 557a
tells me I must d., 579a
the death of the righteous, 10a
theirs but to do d., 652a
there smothered, 985b
they seemed to d., 36b
thou shalt surely d., 5b
thus d. still searching, 899b
time to d., 27b
to d. is debt we must discharge, 321b
to d. is gain, 54a, 93a
to d. to sleep, 261b
to itself it live and d., 293a
to leave to d. a little, 835a
to make men free, 690b
to part is to d. a little, 563b
to save charges, 310b
toddle home d. in bed, 992b
too scanty to d. for you, 737a
trust that when we d., 751b
unlamented let me d., 402a
unsung noblest deed will d., 80a
unto the Lord, 51b
we about to d. salute you, 141a
we d. only once, 360b
we must, 216b
we must be free or d., 512b
we must needs d., 12b
we shall d. alone, 363b
we will d. free men, 475a
weep or she will d., 649a
went abroad to d., 969a
what it is to d., 330b
when beggars d., 254b
when dream is past, 618a
when eras d., 925a
when good men d., 85b
when he shall d. cut him in stars, 225a
when I came to d., 683a
who saw him d., 1093b
who would wish to d., 601a
wisdom shall d. with you, 15a
with dead desire not d., 518b
with harness on our back, 286b
with honor, 860a
with you be ready to d., 122a
without benefit of clergy, 909a
without Thee dare not d., 567a

Die without visiting one another, 75a
wolf that break it d., 932b
world a place to d. in, 330b
Xerxes did d., 1089a
ye shall d. like men, 20a
youth fight and d., 931a
Died as one studied in death, 281b
as soldier for his country, 865a
before bodies d., 1060b
before god of love born, 306b
Booth d. blind, 952b
came three thousand miles d., 693b
courage with which men d., 1072a
David d. full of days, 14a
deaths ye d., 871b
die as my fathers d., 774a
dog it was that d., 448b
far away before his time, 865a
for beauty, 736a
for this Fitzgerald d., 881a
gloriously on field, 640a
had I d. hour before, 284a
had no poet and d., 412b
he that d. o' Wednesday, 240b
I d. young, 1105a
I only d. last night, 764b
if only gladiators d., 945a
in bed, 753b
in bitter pains, 741b
in boots like pioneer, 1041a
in harness, 924a
in hollow murmurs d., 443b
in virtue's cause, 218b
in want, 1075b
land where fathers d., 627b
last night of my physician, 387b
learn from having d., 929b
like wise one d., 197b
liked it not and d., 301a
maintaining right of way, 1195a
man that d. for men, 778b
men d. but not for love, 250a
Mithridates he d. old, 853b
Mother d. today, 1068b
never knew worth till he d., 899a
no one d. of laughter, 910b
none d. natural death, 926b
of chills and fever d., 1009b
of grief I d., 1066a
of no blast he d., 367b
on Saturday, 1096a
one and all d. in bed, 753b
one who d. for truth, 736a
queens have d. young and fair, 300b
she d. so young, 642a
she d. young, 315a
she should have d. hereafter, 286b
some pro patria, 988a
sonnets d. in misnomer, 944a
there d. a myriad, 988b
these dead not d. in vain, 639a
to have d. once enough, 119b
to make men holy, 690b
to make verse free, 981a
to northwest d. away, 663a
to save us all, 684b
was what you did, 1044a
wandered till I d., 714b
when I d. last, 305b
when my mother d., 487a
withered when my father d., 265a

Died, would I had d. for thee, 12b
would we had d. in the land of Egypt, 8b
you who would have d., 1078b
youngest critic d., 872b
zealous locksmith d., 1104b
Diem adimere aegritudinem hominibus, 108b
carpe d., 121a
Dies, above all man who d., 869b
after many a summer d., 652b
all that was theirs d., 85b
among worshippers, 574b
an honest fellow, 312b
as when a giant d., 271a
at the opening day, 397a
begotten born and d., 882b
bird of wonder d., 299b
body d. body's beauty lives, 955b
cackles groans and d., 573b
cry not when father d., 429a
enshrine her and she d., 990a
ere he knows it, 664b
fling stone giant d., 418b
he d. and makes no sign, 215a
he that d. pays all debts, 297a
hurrah for next that d., 720a
if tree d. plant another, 425b
in single blessedness, 228b
in your fragrant bosom d., 327a
kicks the dust, 682b
light d. before thy word, 414a
light d. with dying sun, 826a
like a dog, 626b
love built on beauty d., 307a
love-sick heart d., 1022b
man born suffers d., 869b
man d. in pain, 381b
ne'er like angels till passion d., 302a
no gossip ever d. away, 68a
noblest lives and d., 707b
not how man d. but lives, 431a
primrose that forsaken d., 339a
reputation d., 404b
reputation d. quickly, 374a
re-resolves then d., 399a
rich d. disgraced, 757b
Sahara d., 738a
silence never d., 813b
something in us never d., 495a
stretches out feet and d., 1075a
swan, 652b
tumult and shouting d., 875b
what an artist with me, 134a
when just man d., 1060b
when old man d., 1052a
when the Poet d., 518b
who d. if England live, 877b
whom gods love d. young, 102a
youth grows pale and d., 582b
Dies irae dies illa, 157b
nulla d. sine linea, 102a
Diet, Doctor D., 390b
oft with gods doth d., 335b
praise best d. for us, 523a
scrip of joy immortal d., 199a
sober in d., 414a
Dieth, how d. the wise man, 27b
man d. and wasteth away, 15a
no man d. to himself, 51b
Dieu a donc oublié, 378a
mesure le froid à la brebis tondue, 188b
Differ, agreed to d., 532b
all things d. all agree, 405a
in their mountains, 927a

Dines on following day, 746b
Ding dong bell, 1093b
  hey d. a d. d., 250b
Dinginess, country of d., 632a
Dingledodies, danced like d.,
  1080b
Dingy, danced along d. days, 738b
  raising d. shades, 1001b
Dining and dancing begin, 1052a
  while they thought of d., 451a
Dinkey Bird goes singing, 820b
Dinner, after d. is after d.,
  388b
  among old soakers, 375a
  better is a d. of herbs, 24b
  breakfast d. lunch tea, 902a
  good d. and feasting, 375b
  in d. talk fling on fagot, 857b
  lubricates business, 475b
  Michelangelo for d., 759a
  much depends on d., 562a
  not a d. to ask a man to, 431a
  seldom thinks more than of d.,
  562a
  three hours' march to d., 539b
  tocsin the d. bell, 561b
  what gat ye to d., 1089a
  write with no d., 1009b
Dinner's, over glass when d. done,
  664b
Dinners, true Amphitryon gives
  d., 361b
  visits his d. not him, 361a
  were precarious, 535a
Dinosaur death-steps, 1076b
Dinotherium wandered by, 797a
Dinted, where snow lay d., 687b
Diogenes crept into vat, 742b
  if not Alexander would be D.,
  102a
  plucked a cock, 96b
  struck father when son swore,
  312a
Diomede, this sodeyn D., 165a
Dip wings in tears, 650a
Diplomacy is to do and say, 994a
  of such stuff d. made, 958b
Diplomat regular Moby Dick,
  958b
  whale of a d., 958b
Diplomat's, in d. soul iron ore,
  958b
Diplomats, pens of d. not ruin,
  469b
  women and crabs, 778b
Dipped into the future, 647a
  Jonathan d. it in honeycomb,
  12a
Dipping nose in Gascon wine,
  660b
  white d. sails, 947a
Dirck galloped, 663a
Dire, beckoning shadows d., 336b
  dimension of final thing, 1066b
  effects from civil discord, 394a
  gorge of salt sea tide, 234a
  offense from amorous causes,
  404a
Direct and honest not safe, 275a
  eminently plain and d., 712b-
  713a
  him where to look for it, 307b
  leaving to d. themselves, 1026b
  lie d., 251a
  relations with good joke, 918b
  understanding to d., 1091b
Directed unerringly to you, 702b
Direction, advances in d. of
  dreams, 83b

Direction, dictate d. work must
  take, 1028a
  great thing is what d., 633b
  guide horse in d. it wants, 834a
  in which education starts, 94a
  new d. of Time, 985b
  of right line, 379b
  which thou canst not see, 408b
Directions, by indirections find
  d., 260b
  rode off in all d., 898a
Directs the storm, 393a, 413b
Direful spring of Grecian woes,
  405a
Direst, full of d. cruelty, 281b
  shapes of death, 721a
Dirge, by forms unseen d. sung,
  443a
  for her doubly dead, 642a
  in marriage, 257a
  of dying year, 569b
Dirt, bequeathe myself to d., 701a
  eats d. in the line, 1025b
  hairs or straws or d., 410b
  if d. was trumps, 535b
  loss of wealth loss of d., 182a
  painted child of d., 411a
Dirty, all d. and wet, 391a
  at his d. work again, 410b
  British coaster, 947a
  business, 788b
  Dick's and Sloppy Joe's, 1060a
  for all 'is d. 'ide, 873a
  tobacco a d. weed, 1037a
  wash d. linen at home, 504a
  work again, 410b
  work at crossroads, 1099b
Dis aliter visum, 118b
  manibus sacrum, 150b
Disable benefits of your country,
  250a
Disabused, by himself abused or
  d., 409a
Disaffection, nonconformity mark
  of d., 912a
Disagree, doctors d., 407a
  in faith and hope world d.,
  409b
  share rights with those who d.,
  1025a
Disagreeable, such a d. man, 768a
  tells d. truth boldly, 469b
Disagreements, scholarship record
  of d., 864b
Disappeared, sun would have d.,
  851a
  with finality of pigeon, 998a
Disappoint continent, 754b
  not d. hoping soul, 497b
  that I may not d. myself, 680b
Disappointed, fury of d. woman,
  392a
  he shall never be d., 407b
  in monkey, 764a
  tide, 734b
  unhouseled d. unaneled, 259b
Disappointment, boredom and d.,
  1053a
  great as ourselves, 679a
  lay down newspaper with d.,
  535b
  mathematics commence in d.,
  861a
Disappointments, too familiar
  with d., 634a
Disappoints, man appoints God
  d., 170b
Disapprove of what you say, 418a
Disarmament is essential, 974b

Disarray, on d. lays wing, 917b
Disaster clouded Union cause,
  752a
  evil gains equivalent of d., 67b
  exaltation from d. and ruin,
  919b
  laugh at all d., 622b
  no greater d. than greed, 74b
  noble spirit raises itself in d.,
  136b
  nuclear d. engulf all, 1073b
  occasions not causes of d., 847a
  triumph and d., 77a
  unmerciful d., 643a
Disasters, day's d. in morning
  face, 449b
  make guilty of our d., 277a
  middle station fewest d., 385b
  weary with d., 284b
Disastrous beating of wings, 905b
  born to d. end, 201a
  spake of d. chances, 272b
  twilight sheds, 342b
Disastrously, business fares d.,
  505b
Disbanded, funeral done and d.,
  1069b
Disbelief in great men, 577a
  suspension of d., 529a
  then skepticism then d., 697b
Disbranch, sliver and d., 279a
Disburdened of my gear, 1057b
Discard knowledge, 101b
Discarded, welcome home d.
  faith, 237a
Discern, as I can now d., 680b
  infinite passion, 664a
  innocence of neighbors, 683b
  what can we d., 301a
  with this clear eye, 680b
Discerner of the thoughts, 55b
Discerning, gives genius better d.,
  450b
  to a d. eye, 735a
Discharge, no d. in war, 28a, 876b
  to die a debt we must d., 321b
Discharged, at once indebted and
  d., 344b
  debt d. through eternity, 478a
  with greater ease, 321b
Discharging less than tenth, 268b
Disciple not above master, 42a
  true teacher has no d., 590b
Disciples, gave bread to d., 44b
  threatening against d., 49b
Discipline, care of d. is love, 37a
  desire of d., 37a
  in military unit, 959a
  liberty a beloved d., 1067b
  organization and d. of war,
  177a
  rising or falling's one d., 1066a
  soul of army, 460b
Disciplined and limber, 1056a
  by peace, 1072b
  inaction, 501b
Disciplines, I know d. of wars,
  244a
Disclose, merits to d., 441a
  not d. essence of phenomena,
  984a
Disclosed, before buttons be d.,
  258b
Disclosures, press lives by d.,
  1099b
Discobolus standeth face to wall,
  755b
Discomforts accompany my being
  blind, 376a

Dish, butter in a lordly d., 11a
  chameleon's d., 263a
  dainty d., 1094b
  feast of joy a d. of pain, 204b
  fit for gods, 254b
  nor serve him in d., 901b
  of meat too good, 326b
  other men serving d., 889a
  ran away with spoon, 1094a
  thirty-two religions one d., 484a
  woman a d. for the gods, 289a
Dishes, homemade d., 592b
  shalt not wash d., 1095a
Dishonest, man assumed to be d.,
  1063a
  not d. because in debt, 771a
Dishonor, by honor and d., 53b
  fears d. worse than death, 122b
  honor rooted in d., 653b
  no d. to halt at second place,
  111a
  vessel unto d., 51a
  ways to d. Sabbath, 761b
  will not trouble me, 84a
Dishonorable graves, 253b
Dishonorably, to speak d. is pardonable, 83a
Dishonored fragments of Union,
  547a
  shroud, 1002a
Disiecti membra poetae, 120a
Disillusion, one d. mankind, 976b
Disingenuousness of years, 596b
Disinherited, city's d., 857b
Disinheriting, damned d. countenance, 481b
Disinterested as being who made
  him, 462b
  commerce between equals, 448b
  endeavor to learn, 713b
  intellectual curiosity, 941b
Disinterestedness, self-interest
  plays d., 355a
Disjoins remorse from power,
  254a
Dislike, hesitate d., 411a
  same things is friendship, 115b
Disliked, each day two things d.,
  932a
  person who d. gravy, 361b
Dislikes, culture not live by d.,
  796a
Dislocate language into meaning,
  1007b
Dismal, at d. treatise rouse, 286b
  headache, 767b
  science, 578a
  tidings when he frowned, 449b
  universal hiss, 348a
  Waterloo d. plain, 599a
Dismay, neither shape or danger
  d., 515a
  nothing you d., 1099a
  old d., 1078b
Dismayed her crew, 792a
  live laugh nor be d., 899b
  neither be d., 10b
  ran d. away, 235a
  was there man d., 652a
Dismember or overthrow it, 637a
  whirl asunder and d. me, 236b
Dismembered poet, 120a
Dismissed, at length d. from thee,
  552a
Dismount, rides tiger afraid to d.,
  920a
Disobedience, discontent disorder
  d., 452a
  of man's first d., 341b

Disobedient, even if d. I shall follow, 103b
Disorder, all prodigality and d.,
  453b
  discontent d. disobedience, 452a
  domestic d., 383a
  great d. is order, 956a
  order and d., 419a
  sweet d. in the dress, 320a
  violent order d., 956a
Disordered, men d. like you, 433a
Disorders, all ruinous d., 277a
  medicine for mental d., 1034b
Dispatch in putting end to it, 99b
  the soul of business, 415b
Dispatched, sooner d. the better,
  776a
Dispatchful looks, 346a
Dispelled, live tongue all d.,
  1080a
  mist d. when woman appears,
  401b
Dispelling, gleams through fog
  without d., 438b
Dispensary, anthology a d., 1034b
Dispensation of pleasure, 550a
Dispense with necessaries, 634a
  with trifles, 267a
Dispensing equality, 94b
Disperse, by spreading d. to
  naught, 214a
Dispersed, Scots d. over whole
  earth, 205a
Dispirited, fainting d. race, 715b
Display, electrical d. of God,
  1009a
  extended to d. its patterns, 78a
  ridiculous d., 901b
Displayed, flower d. doth fall,
  252a
  glory of world d., 889b
Displeasing, misfortune of our
  friends not d., 356b
Dispoged, lips to it when d., 670b
Dispose, men determine gods d.,
  311b
  unsearchable d., 350a
Disposed, tyrant has d. of foreign
  enemies, 95a
Disposer of other men's stuff,
  191b
Disposes, man proposes God d.,
  170a
Disposition, antic d., 260a
  horridly to shake our d., 259a
  I know d. of women, 109a
  patronizing d., 689a
  to be pleased, 432a
  truant d., 258a
  unfriendly d. towards U.S.,
  492a
Dispositions, praise depends on d.,
  942b
Dispossessed, his little heart d.,
  799a
Dispraise, no d. or blame, 350a
  thing you desire to buy, 26ga
Dispraised no small praise, 348b
Dispraises, praising most d., 411a
Disprized, pangs of d. love, 262a
Disputable, dispute upon everything d., 381a
Disputandi pruritus ecclesiarum
  scabies, 301a
Disputants like sportsmen, 413a
  put me in mind of skuttle fish,
  395a
Disputation, feeling d., 239b
  run in debt by d., 352a

Disputation, too exacting d., 593a
Disputations, doubtful d., 51b
Dispute confute change hands,
  352a
  it like a man, 285b
  my right none to d., 457b
  scholars d. and case still before
  courts, 124a .
  'twixt Tweedledum and Tweedledee, 415a
  upon everything disputable,
  381a
Disputed barricade, 1009b
Disputes, equal justice in private
  d., 89b
Disputing, itch of d., 301a
  warmer way of d., 195a
Disquieted, never to be d., 321a
  they are d. in vain, 18b-19a
  why art thou d. in me, 19a
Disquieting, drums continuous d.,
  878b
Disquietly, follow d. to our
  graves, 277a
Disquiets, almighty time d., 83a
Disregard, atones for later d.,
  928b
Disrespectfully, speak d. of equator, 522b
Disruption, noise d. of thought,
  564a
Dissatisfaction with world, 863a
Dissatisfied, I am troubled I'm d.,
  996b
  not one is d., 700b
  Socrates d., 619b
  with what I learn, 929b
Dissatisfies, what d. in American
  civilization, 716b
Dissect, creatures you d., 406a
Dissections, learn anatomy from
  d., 312b
Dissemble, right to d. your love,
  491a
Disseminating their circumference, 737a
Dissension, in d. never judge, 86a
Dissent, dissidence of d., 453a
  in few days I should d., 329b
  orthodoxy chokes d., 912a
  voices of d., 1056a
Dissenting, passed without one d.
  colony, 463a
Dissever my soul from the soul,
  644a
  sacred hair d., 404b
Dissevered discordant belligerent,
  547a
Dissidence of dissent, 453a
Dissimulation innate in women,
  564a
  love without d., 51a
  playing the knave and d., 375a
  without d. no business, 415b
Dissipates to re-create, 528b
  to shining ether, 605b
Dissipation without pleasure, 466a
Dissociate language from science,
  474b
Dissociation of sensibility, 1007b
Dissolute, caldron of d. loves,
  146b
  damned despairful, 932b
Dissolutely spent Tuesday morning, 237b
Dissolution, anguish not often in
  d., 565a
  community in d., 912a
  keep these limbs from d., 306b

Divine Inert, 696b
Love the human form d., 487a
love which graybeards call d., 216b
lyre so long d., 560b
made brutes men men d., 721b
majority, 735a
makes drudgery d., 324a
man d. as myself dead, 702a
marks of a d. origin, 544a
men whom men pronounce d., 789b
Milton's no less d., 561a
moonlight is d., 1069a
no government by d. right, 531a
nor glimpse d., 414a
philosophy, 337a, 650b
plain face, 534b
principle and rule of harmony, 709a
profane no d. ordinances, 450a
profusion, 748b
relations with good joke, 918b
reliance on d. providence, 471a
right d. of kings, 413b
right of kings, 636a
sign indicates future, 87b
superhuman spiritual and d., 936a
tale of Troy d., 336a
terror human form d., 489b
thought thinks of itself, 97b
to forgive d., 403b
tobacco d. nothing equal, 563a
tobacco d. rare, 311b
train d., 714b
truth is precious and d., 353a
what the form d., 536a
whatever poet writes with d. inspiration, 88a
Divinely, childish but d. beautiful, 497b
in the wrong, 398b
subsidized, 1061b
tall, 645b
Divineness, in poesy participation of d., 206b-207a
Diviner air, 516b
barmaids d. than mermaids, 1051b
Diviner's, glad d. theme, 368b
Divinest anguish, 685b
madness d. sense, 735b
Melancholy, 335b
Divining, takes d. rod to find, 833a
Divinities, new d. of his own, 93a
Divinity, all the d. I understand, 196b
doth hedge a king, 265a
dry volumes of d., 470b
gives wealth even to wicked man, 77a
gossip a kind of d., 68a
in odd numbers, 267b
lectures of ethics or d., 383a
man own doctor of d., 822a
piece of d. in us, 330b
stirs within us, 393b
that shapes our ends, 266a
wingy mysteries in d., 329b
Divisa, Gallia est omnis d. in partes tres, 112a
Division, equal d. of unequal earnings, 545a
is as bad, 1084b
marriage death and d., 773b
mirth the music of d., 199b

Division, salvation not in d., 903a
same as creation, 101a
saw d. grow together, 267b
Divorce, absurd essentially a d., 1068b
long d. of steel, 298a
Divorced divorced, 1075b
from eye and bone, 1038a
from whale-fat, 1075b
sorrow from which not d., 550a
war not d. from politics, 1027b
Divulge, I will never d. such things, 88a-b
Dixie Land, 678a
live and die in D., 678b
Dixit, ipse d., 151a
Dizziness from success, 954b
love like a d., 508a
Dizzy, across that d. way, 944a
how fearful and d., 279a
Do, a' is done that men can d., 494a
all the good you can, 421a
as chapmen do, 269a
as I say not as I do, 317b
as you would be done by, 415a
boys do, 814a
damned if you d., 539a
decided on what they will not d., 100a
each day two things disliked, 92a
enough work to d., 877a
go and d. likewise, 46b
great right little wrong, 234b
his arms might d. what this has done, 332b
how not to d. it, 672a
I d. it more natural, 251b
I dare d. all, 282b
if to d. as easy as to know, 231b
it as for thee, 324a
it after high Roman fashion, 288b
it as for thee, 324a
it with thy might, 28b
just as one pleases, 539b
justly and love mercy, 35b
know not what they d., 47b
know what he ought to d., 158b
let us d. or die, 496a
make it d. or d. without, 1102b
nastiest thing in nicest way, 994a
never d. today what can put off, 719a
never tell how to d. things, 987b
no one knows what he can d., 127a
noble things not dream, 691a
not as some pastors, 258b
not do what we want, 1058b
not choose to run, 911b
not d. what another d. as well, 897b
not do thing they most do show, 293a
not do to others, 72b
not go gentle, 1070b
not we wanderer await, 712a
not what we ought, 711b
nothing we d. wiped out, 793a
now I'll d. it, 263b
O what men dare d., 246b
or die, 313b, 496a
other men for they d. you, 670a
reckless what I d., 284b
seeks little thing to d., 664a
she can d. no other, 842a

Do, so much to d., 650b, 828b
that thou doest d. quickly, 49a
the evil I d., 51a
the very best I can, 641a
theirs but to d. and die, 652a
they d. things we can't, 1067a
they know not what they d., 47b
thing I was born to d., 211a
thing that ends other deeds, 288b
thing think you cannot, 981b
thing you have to, 725a
things worth writing, 421b
this in remembrance, 49a
this one thing I d., 54a
this will never d., 516a
thou but thine, 347a
to be to d. to d. without, 779b
to will and to d. his pleasure, 54a
two things is to do neither, 125a
unto other feller fust, 811a
what country d. for you, 1073a
what d. about it, 722b
what d. when you fallen, 1078a
what d. you mean to d., 784a
what have you or I to d. with it, 437b
what he may, 266a
what I will with mine, 43b
what man may d. to himself, 952b
what man would d. exalts, 665b
what manhood bids, 707b
what then thou would'st, 349b
what thou wilt, 181a
what we back ourselves to d., 793b
what you can d. for country, 1073a
what you d. still betters what is done, 295b
whatsoever thy hand findeth to d., 28b
will to d., 520a
without being commanded, 97a
write what men d., 207a
ye even so unto them, 41a
Doasyouwouldbedoneby, Mrs. D., 691b
Dobie, sate upon her d., 673b
Docent, decent d., 1040b
Doch-an'-dorris, wee d., 903a
Docile and omnipotent, 736a
Dockyard fellow, 749b
mine factory d., 923b
Doctor and saint, 630a
apple keeps d. away, 1102a
Diet Quiet Merryman, 390b
every man own d. of divinity, 822a
fee d. for nauseous draught, 372a
Foster went to Gloucester, 1097a
kills more than general, 382a
Livingstone I presume, 791a
silent I. shook his head, 401a
three faces wears d., 820a
train anyone to be d., 949a
while runnin' for d., 981a
Doctor's, failing that D. thesis, 1035a
outlived the d. pill, 401b
peaceful mission, 820a
Doctors, best d. in the world, 390b
is all swabs, 823a

Doctors, if d. had more Christianity, 890b
we d. know hopeless case, 1032a
when d. disagree, 407a
Doctrinaire logic, 1021b
Doctrine, all the winds of d., 340b
every wind of d., 54a
from women's eyes this d., 222a
go for refuge to D., 80b
hidden under strange verses, 160a
involving pernicious consequences, 678a
little difference in d., 431a
not for d. but music, 403a
of pathological generation, 710b
of separate but equal, 1021a
of strenuous life, 847a
or practice or interpretation, 143a
peculiar d., 684a
prove their d. orthodox, 352a
so illogical and dull, 976b
that each select one, 571a
yesterday fact today d., 1091a
Doctrines, makes d. plain and clear, 353a
Documents, historian wants d., 799b
Dodge, gracefully d. bore, 818b
Dodger, artful D., 669a
Doe, came a fallow d., 1088b
Doer, speaker of words and d.
of deeds, 63b
Doers of the word, 56b
talkers no good d., 217a
Does, dogged as d. it, 679a
he who can d., 836b
sees it and d. it, 664a
Doeth, what thy right hand d., 40b
whatsoever he d. shall prosper, 16b
Doff it for shame, 236a
Doffed, lightly d. hat, 868a
Dog, Almighty gave d., 521b
better than his d., 647a
beware of d., 150a
biggest d. has been pup, 790a
bites man not news, 808b
Boatswain a d., 554b
Body my good bright d., 1078a
breed maggots in dead d., 260b
broodin' over bein' a d., 811a
cat d. pipe or two, 855a
circumcised d., 276b
commends himself to favor, 845b
cutthroat d., 232a
did nothing in nighttime, 850a
dies like a d., 626b
difference between d. and man, 762b
door what d. on wrong side of, 1052b
drunken d. ragged head, 534a
empty house like stray d., 756a
every d. his day, 691a
faithful d. bear him company, 408a
fetch poor d. a bone, 1096a
gingham d. went Bowwow, 820b
grim king's d., 83b
hair of d. that bit us, 184b
hath a day, 184b
have his day, 266a, 691a
heart to d. to tear, 877a

Dog, hold-fast the only d., 243b
I am his Highness' d., 412b
in grave like old d., 1071a
in life firmest friend, 554b
in the manger, 76a
is thy servant a d., 13b
it was that died, 448b
jumps over lazy d., 1101a
let no d. bark, 231b
like d. hunts in dreams, 647a
little d. laughed, 1094b
living d. better than dead lion, 28b
looking for place to sleep, 1067b
make starving d. prosperous, 762b
man bites d., 808b
mine enemy's d., 280a
my little d. Fala, 973b
O d. my God, 1068a
offers drowning d. drink, 324a
old d. Tray, 537b
old wife old d. ready money, 421b
poor d. Tray, 537b
rather be d. and bay the moon, 256a
reform taking bone from d., 863a
returneth to his vomit, 26a
since I am a d. beware, 234a
so poor he could not keep a d., 147b
starved at master's gate, 490a
starving d. behind, 958a
stronger d. be on top, 995a
suspicious of buried bone, 799b
this d. my d., 230b
thou calledst me d., 234a
to gain private ends, 448b
to this d. praise, 617b
tossed d. that worried cat, 1098b
toy d. covered with dust, 820b
truth's a d. must to kennel, 277b
turned to his own vomit, 57a
whose d. are you, 412b
why should a d. have life, 280b
will have his day, 266a
woman or d., 657a
wool of bat tongue of d., 285a
Dogged as does it, 679a
strength, 894b
strong d. unenlightened, 713b
Doggedly, set himself d. to it, 429b
Doglike, on bended arm d., 78b
Dogma, Bible literature not d., 867b
Dogmas of past inadequate, 638b
Dogmatism, greater ignorance greater d., 817a
puppyism at full growth, 610b
Dogmatisms, narrow d., 799a
Dog's, more deadly than mad d.
tooth, 218b
walking, 430b
Dogs, all the d. in town, 1093a
as many d. there be, 448b
careful of breed of d., 381a
crowing of cocks and barking of d., 75a
dancing d. and bears, 906a
delight to bark and bite, 396a
display reluctance, 1051b
drink running at the Nile, 129b
eat of crumbs, 43a
fought d. killed cats, 662b

Dogs, hark d. do bark, 1097b
hates children and d., 951b
Inquisition d., 654b
let slip d. of war, 255a
lies with d. riseth with fleas, 324b
little d. and all, 279a
mad d. and Englishmen, 1043a
more I admire my d., 566a
not live as d. in manger, 974a
pedigree of cattle d., 628b
rain cats and d., 391a
shall eat Jezebel, 13b
shame the gray head, 64b
sleeping d. lie, 672a
straw d., 73b
throw physic to the d., 286b
which hath deeper mouth, 214a
Dogs', puppy d. tails, 1096b
Dog-star rages, 410a
Doing, being not d., 1066a
cease to think about d., 540a
difficult easily, 706b
good one of professions which is full, 682b
impossible genius, 706b
is another thing, 190b
it all takes d. and I do, 800a
joy's soul lies in d., 267b
learn by d., 97b
manners happy ways of d., 608b
miserable d. or suffering, 342a
secure friends by d. favors, 90a
strain of the d., 749b
the great god Pan, 619a
up and d., 620b
Doings, amend your ways and your d., 34a
broadcast d. of day night, 699b
child known by his d., 25a
of mankind subject of my book, 139a
something in d. of man, 699b
Dolabella's Cleopatra, 367b
Dolce far niente, 140b
vita, 162a
Dole, happy man be his d., 182b
happy man happy d., 182b
unequal laws, 646a
weighing delight and d., 257a
Doleful, chants d. hymn, 237a
dumps, 218b, 1084b
shades, 341b
Doll, once had sweet little d., 691a
Dollar, a dillar a d., 1097b
almighty d., 550b
broken never dollar again, 685a
Dollars, hours and minutes d. and cents, 422b
million d. timorous, 1017b
silver d., not distributed as gifts, 771a
Dolores, splendid and sterile D., 773b
Dolphin-like, his delights were d., 289a
Dolphin's, mermaid on d. back, 229a
Dolphins, trident and d., 954a
Dolts, three greatest d., 549a
Domain, such d. France conquered, 720b
Dome, fired Ephesian d., 331a
of many-colored glass, 572a
of thought palace of soul, 555b
of vast sepulcher, 569b
orchard for a d., 735b
rounded Peter's dome, 602a
stately pleasure d., 523b

Earth, more things in heaven and e., 260a, 1021b
my footstool e., 408a
new heaven and new e., 58b
new heavens and a new e., 33b
niggard e., 439b
nigher heaven than now, 661b
nightly to listening e., 393a
no less kindled e., 563a
no more a mother, 132a
not gray but rosy, 668a
not sky of e., 510a
not steadfast place, 898b
nothing but hath bound in e., 218a
nothing on e. but laundry, 1079a
of all languages of e., 939a
of the e. earthy, 53a
on bare e. he lies, 371b
on confines of e., 501a
on e. broken arcs, 665b
on e. no sure happiness, 200b
on e. peace and good will, 46a
on e. peace to men, 59a
one mighty blood spot, 613b
only when we are half e., 730a
or air, 257a
or ever thou hadst formed the e., 20a
paradise on e., 894a
peace on e. good will, 657b
peace on e. mercy mild, 425b
peopling e. waters and sky, 377a
pleasant country's e., 227b
plowed before man, 628b
poetry of e. never dead, 579b
power passing from the e., 515b
proudly wears Parthenon, 602a
put on e. a little space, 486b
puts forth sweet flowers, 112b
rain was upon the e., 6b
raises man from e. to God, 178a
receive her King, 397a
render back from breast, 561a
replenish the e., 5a
rest lightly on you, 151b
reverence for e., 1077b
rich stone in bowels of e., 309b
rid e. of him in my pride, 899a
room on e. for honest men, 467a
sad old e. borrow mirth, 826a
saddest among kings of e., 899b
salt of the e., 40a
scum of the e., 506a
sepulcher of famous men, 90a
shall be full of knowledge, 31a
shall not perish from e., 639a
since e. began to exist, 459b
sing ye heavens e. reply, 425a
sleepers in quiet e., 685b
small dust of e., 996b
small model of barren e., 227b
so much of e., 511a
solid e. actual world, 680b
speak to the e., 15a
spirit given on e., 641a
stand at Judgment Seat, 872b
stand on e. as footstool, 888b
stood hard as iron, 740a
suffered to crawl upon e., 389b
sufficient, 701a
summer clothe general e., 526a
sun is lost and the e., 307b
sure and firm-set e., 283a
swear not by heaven nor e., 40b

Earth, table e. dice human bones, 563a
take him e., 765a
that bears thee dead, 241a
the e. that is sufficient, 701a
their proper element, 319a
they shall inherit the e., 40a
thirsty e. soaks up rain, 357b
this blessed plot this e., 226b
this e. of majesty, 226b
this goodly frame the e., 261a
this is the last of e., 503a
those who labor in e., 471a
though the e. be removed, 19a
thy will be done in e., 40b
tideless and inert, 813a
till heaven and e. pass, 40a
to e. and thee restore, 854b
to earth, 61b
touch of e., 653b
tries e. if it in tune, 692b
truth crushed to e., 574b
two kinds of people on e., 825b
unfolds both heaven and e., 228b
upon e. not his like, 16b
walk the earth unseen, 345b
was without form, 5a
weaned away from e., 1041a
what e. and its interests, 681b
what is pomp but e. and dust, 216b
when I am laid in e., 383b
when I laid the foundations of the e., 16a
when religion makes e. uncomfortable, 696a
whether in e. or air, 257a
which made heaven and e., 22a
while the e. remaineth, 6b
whole e. and all time, 511a
whole e. for religion's sake, 699b
whole e. grows rich, 378b
whole e. our hospital, 1005b
with her thousand voices, 526b
wonder of e. and life, 1021a
word of e. in ears of world, 775b
words are daughters of e., 427b
would know no adventurer, 843a
wretched of e., 680a
write sorrow on bosom of the e., 227b
yours and fullness thereof, 920a
yours is the e., 877a
Earthborn joy renew, 801a
Earthen, kettle and e. pot, 38a
Earthlier happy is rose distilled, 228b
Earthly ball a peopled garden, 477b
dignities, 298b
fancies, 651b
godfathers of heaven's lights, 221a
mighty e. marchings, 696b
nothing e. surpass her, 560a
paragon, 291a
power then likest God's, 234b
roses into e. life, 497b
sum of e. bliss, 347a
sweet fruition of e. crown, 212a
things heavenly or things e., 365b
this wisdom is e., 56b
thoughts of e. men, 67a
touch of e. years, 511a

Earthly, very honey of all e. joy, 357b
who mind e. things, 54b
Earthquake, dam'd by e., 760a
gloom of e. and eclipse, 568b
Lord was not in the e., 13b
when not smiling back, 1071b
Earthquakes with thunder lightning, 760a
Earth's, ablution round e. shores, 581a
as e. close down, 1072a
break e. sleep, 1028b
crammed with heaven, 619a
diurnal course, 511a
foundations fled, 854a
foundations stand, 855a
green fields, 676b
heedless sons, 1036a
human shores, 581a
last picture painted, 872b
lid, 988b
returns, 663b
right place for love, 926b
round e. imagined corners, 307b
round e. shore, 714b
shadows fly, 572a
smoothness rough, 666a
sweet flowing breast, 992a
wide regions round, 554a
Earthworm, feeble e., 364a
Earthworms, earth plowed by e., 628b
Earthy and cold hand of death, 241a
earth in e. bed, 652b
of the earth e., 53a
Ease after war, 200a
an age of e., 449a
and speed not give work beauty, 168b
at e. for aye dwell, 645a
at e. in nature, 699b
at e. in own generation, 786a
but for another gives e., 489a
careless e., 398a
dappled turf at e., 512b
darbies at wrist, 698a
death or dreamful e., 645b
done with so much e., 368a
equal e. unto my pain, 327a
for e. from heaven, 490b
full-throated e., 582a
gives happiness or leaves e., 412b
good pleasure e. content, 409b
greater e. than hogs eat, 352a
heart like satin gown, 1029a
ignoble e., 847a
ignoble e. and peaceful sloth, 343b
joys in another's loss of e., 489a
life of e. not for man, 577b
live at home at e., 328b
live with e., 410b
Meadows of E., 909a
Nature bent to e. us, 356b
never desire worldly e., 420b
no healthful e., 592a
one life the aching, 737a
poet's dignity and e., 411a
prodigal of e., 368a
rots in e. on Lethe wharf, 259b
slothful e., 847b
some come to take their e., 299b
somebody's right and e., 799b
take mine e. in mine inn, 183a
take thine e., 46b

Ease, true e. in writing, 403b
  Truth one side E. other, 657b
  virtue can have naught to do
    with e., 190a
  with e. and you beside, 736b
  with the greatest of e., 780a
  woman in hours of e., 519b
  words flow with e., 377a
  write with e. to show breeding,
    482a
Easeful death, 582b
Easier go through eye of needle,
    43b
  grass blade no e. than oak, 692b
  nothing e. than rest, 777a
  nothing e. than self-deceit, 99a
  played on than pipe, 263b
  swallowed than flap-dragon,
    222b
  sweats e. than I., 682b
  thirst blister e., 735a
  to be critical than correct, 612a
  to believe than deny, 770b
  to fight for principles, 1048b
  to get favor from Fortune, 125b
  to get into enemy's toils, 76b
  to stay out than get out, 762b
Easiest, move e. who learned to
    dance, 403b
Easily, by and by e. said, 263b
  doing difficult e., 706b
  how e. things go wrong, 723b
  never have come back so e.,
    835b
Easiness, lend a kind of e., 264b
  property of e., 265b
Easing savior's birth, 1055b
East and West will pinch heart,
    1023a
  argument with e. wind, 694a-b
  blasted with the e. wind, 7b
  cherubims e. of the garden, 6a
  faint e. quickens, 772b
  fill his belly with e. wind, 15a
  from e. to western Ind, 249b
  good is good from e. to e., 789b
  gorgeous e. in fee, 512b
  gorgeous E. with richest hand,
    343a
  I turn my back to the e., 486a
  is E. West San Francisco, 864b
  is E. West West, 872b
  it is the E. Juliet the sun, 223b
  of Suez, 873b
  one ship e. another west, 825b
  or west Phoenix builds, 327a
  Side West Side, 862b
  somewheres e. of Suez, 873b
  star in the e., 39a
  tried to hustle the e., 872b
  west south north, 596a
  wind never blow, 325b
  youth who from e. travel, 513b
Eastard and points between, 760a
Easter, no sun upon an E. day,
    350b
Eastern, blabbing e. scout, 336b
  dew of yon high e. hill, 257a
  not by e. windows, 688b
  wipe out E. instincts, 871b
  worship E. civilization, 1019b
Eastman, If It Isn't An E., 1030b
East's, feeling E. gift, 664b
Eastward, a garden e. in Eden, 5b
  roll of world e., 782b
  to the sea, 873b
Easy, abstinence e. to me, 429b
  all zeal Mr. E., 567b
  and comfortable on raft, 761a

Easy, as e. to marry rich woman,
    660a
  as grass grows on weirs, 879b
  as leaves grow on tree, 879a
  bad book generally e., 564b
  bid me take love e., 879a
  criticism e. art difficult, 398b
  decent e. men, 466a
  evil is e., 363b
  false man does e., 284a
  give throne would be e., 99b
  how e. bush supposed a bear,
    230b
  if to do as e. as to know, 231b
  jolly and e. in minds, 660a
  leap to pluck bright honor,
    238b
  live quiet die, 521a
  morning's ride, 738b
  my yoke is e., 42a
  not e. to call back, 948b
  not pray for e. lives, 755a
  nothing e. in war, 1016b
  nothing so e. but becomes diffi-
    cult, 108b
  open hand e. shoe, 859b
  Rabelais' e. chair, 413b
  road to Hades e. to travel, 104b
  signal e. to yell, 935a
  smooth e. inoffensive down to
    Hell, 104b
  so e. and so plain a stop, 241a
  there life is supremely e., 65b
  thing O Power Divine, 720a
  'tis e. to be true, 378b
  to blow and swallow not e.,
    106a
  to go down into hell, 118b
  word for casual goodbye, 1030a
  words are e. like the wind, 309a
  writing soon elementary, 846b
  writing's cursed hard reading,
    482a
  young and e., 1070b
Eat, birds for people to e., 906b
  bread in sweat of thy face, 6a
  bread without scarceness, 10a
  cake and have it, 185b
  cannibals that each other e.,
    272b
  cannot e. but little meat, 188b
  cones under his pines, 926a
  dare to e. a peach, 1001a
  did e. and were filled, 42b
  dogs shall e. Jezebel, 13b
  drink be merry, 28b, 46b
  drink tomorrow die, 31b
  dust shalt thou e., 6a
  dust to e., 898b
  dusty bread, 1038a
  eat me soul, 381b
  enough to e. and wear, 855a
  fame food dead men e., 782b
  fine women e. crazy salad, 882b
  for tomorrow we die, 31b
  frogs e. butterflies, 955a
  great ones e. up little ones,
    290b
  he hath not e. paper, 221b-222a
  his pleasant fruits, 29b
  I e. and I swear, 245a
  I e. the air, 263a
  I e. what I see, 744a
  I earn that I e., 249b
  I want to e. you up, 505b
  I'll e. my head, 669a
  in orchard enough to e., 400b
  in the evening, 487b
  it in haste, 8b

Eat, let them e. cake, 436b
  like wolves fight like devils,
    244a
  Nebuchadnezzar did e. grass,
    35a
  neither e. it nor make flannel,
    986a
  nevermore to e. again, 915a
  no beans, 310b
  no fat, 1092b
  no onions nor garlic, 230b
  not to dullness, 423b
  not to e. not for love, 604b
  of fish that fed of worm, 264b
  of the habitation, 232a
  of the tree I did e., 6a
  plant vineyards and e. the fruit,
    33b
  poor when anything to e., 96b
  so I did sit and e., 324a
  some hae meat canna e., 495b
  some s. I will not e., 1031a
  strive mightily e. as friends,
    219a
  take e. this is my body, 44b
  tell me what you e., 484b
  that shall ye e., 9b
  that they may live, 87b
  the fat of the land, 7b
  their flesh shall ye not e., 9b
  thou shalt not e. of it, 5b
  to e. thy heart, 201a
  to e. with apple tart, 823b
  to live not live to e., 361a,
    421b
  up himself, 268a
  us must e. we, 661a
  wad e. that want it, 495b
  way they e. drink and every-
    thing, 933b
  we hae meat we can e., 495b
  will not e. with you, 232a
  with the rich, 878a
  worm that e. of a king, 264b
  you earn bread I'll e., 636a
Eaten a sour grape, 34b
  bit by bit, 902a
  crust e. in peace, 76a
  God made and e., 664b
  have we e. on insane root, 281a
  me out of house and home,
    242a
  slowly e. bit by bit, 902a
  thee for a word, 222b
  they'd e. every one, 746a
  to death with rust, 241b
  worms have e. them, 250a
  your bread and salt, 871b
Eater, great e. of beef, 251a
  out of the e. came meat, 11b
Eateth grass as an ox, 16b
'Eathen, pore benighted 'e., 873a
Eating air on promise of supply,
    241b
  and drinking like brutes, 702b
  appetite comes with e., 180b
  appetite makes e. delight, 350b
  bitter bread of banishment,
    227a
  bread and honey, 1094b
  cares, 335a
  Christmas pie, 1093a
  curds and whey, 1096b
  drinking breeding, 700a
  drinking dung death, 1005a
  egg without salt, 872a
  produce of the land, 64b
  proof of pudding in e., 195b
  several times a day, 977b

Emerald, green as e., 524b
  resonance of e., 738b
Emergencies, government in e., 640a
  great e. show resources, 792b
  presence of mind in e., 693b
Emerges ahead of accomplishments, 1052b
  path e. then closes, 890a
  with verb in mouth, 761b
Emerson, by E. out of Charles Lamb, 960b
Emetic but nowhere aphrodisiac, 968b
Emigrated to another star, 741b
Emily set doors ajar, 931b
  up roos sonne and E., 167b
Eminence, raised to that bad e., 343a
Eminent, censure is tax for being e., 389a
Eminently noble, 713a
  plain and direct, 712b-713a
Emits a brighter ray, 447b
Emmanuel, call his name E., 39a
  O come O come E., 687b
Emmet, Robert E. and Wolfe Tone, 881a
Emotion, Asquith disliked e., 934b
  bounding at e. new, 714a
  cannot demonstrate an e., 779b
  communicates idea, 862a
  disembodied e. a nonentity, 794a
  expressing e. in art, 1007b
  formula of that particular e., 1007b
  idea communicates e., 861b
  intellect is to e. as clothes, 862a
  more than usual e., 529a
  no transforming without e., 936b
  poetry escape from e., 1007a
  poetry express every e., 1061a
  real thing that made e., 1044b
  recollected in tranquillity, 511b
  source of becoming-conscious, 936b
  undisciplined squads of e., 1005b
Emotional, destitute of e. warmth, 794a
  orgies, 866b
Emotions, escape from e., 1007b
  foreign to art, 754b
  of the Spaniards, 587a
Empêchent, ailes de géant l'e., 707a
Emperor and clown, 583a
  big stealin' makes you e., 1009a
  in mine own house, 198a
  keep drowsy e. awake, 883a
  of ice cream, 955a
  pope and e., 598b
  subject to no one but God, 155a
  without crown, 399a
  you are E. yet you weep, 378a
Emperor's, she might lie by e. side, 275b
Emperors have died of gout, 364b
  pomp of e. ridiculous, 605a
  purple of e., 874a
  souls of e. and cobblers, 190a
Emphasis of passionate love, 536b
Emphatic, unflinching and e., 878a
Empire, American e. careens onward, 1038a

Empire, British E. and United States, 921b
  course of e., 400a
  England an e., 590a
  entrusted with e., 73b
  for raising customers, 445a
  friendliness of British E., 913b
  God's princes of e., 696b
  great e. and little minds, 453b
  Holy Roman E., 417a
  how is the E., 871a
  institutions and our E., 921a
  internal domestic e., 1038b
  is e. unpossessed, 217b
  last thousand years, 921b
  liquidation of British E., 924a
  loungers of E. drained, 849b
  my mind to me an e., 192a
  neither holy nor e., 417a
  Neptune's e., 257a
  perfection never built e., 1016a
  power in trust, 368b
  preserve unity of e., 453a
  rod of e., 440b
  sun never sets on e., 522a
  this alone e. and victory, 569a
  thy dread e. Chaos, 414a
  to French e. of land, 500a
  trample e. down, 807b
  vast e. of human society, 511a
  westward the course of e., 400a
  wide arch of ranged e. fall, 287a
  wilderness into e., 453b
Empire's lamentation, 651b
Empires, buries e. in common grave, 466a
  changed by bottle, 481a
  day of e. come, 765b
  dyspepsy ruin of e., 552a
  game was e., 563a
  hatching vain e., 343b
  make central e. good neighbors, 976b
  vaster than e. and more slow, 359b
Employ, how fit to e., 665a
  means requisite to ends, 485a
Employed, age e. in edging steel, 482a
  men e. best contented, 423b
Emptied some dull opiate, 582a
Emptier ever dancing in air, 228a
Emptiness, dull privations and lean e., 306a
  eternal smiles e. betray, 411b
  of ages in face, 826b
  produced the universe, 110a
Emptor, caveat e., 150a
Empty, a little louder but as e., 409a
  bag cannot stand, 422a
  beat an e. barrel, 953a
  born e. into modern age, 378b
  buckets into e. wells, 458a, 523a
  cisterns exhausted wells, 1003a
  crowns are e. things, 385b
  go not e. unto thy mother-in-law, 11b
  her e. room is cold, 110a
  honor but an e. bubble, 371b
  house like stray dog, 756a
  idle singer of e. day, 753a
  is the chair e., 217b
  life an e. dream, 402a, 620b
  mirrors on e. space, 797b
  no life moves in e. passageways, 81a
  no patriot on e. stomach, 831a

Empty quacks, 795b
  rich sent e. away, 46a
  room my heart keeps e., 321a-b
  seek e. world again, 685b
  seven e. ears, 7b
  so e. each head, 456a
  solid pudding e. praise, 413b
  stomach, 972b
  tigers or roaring sea, 225b
  to be e. is to be full, 74a
  turn down e. glass, 631a
  vessel greatest sound, 245a
  virtue no e. echo, 497b
  words are e. thanks, 392b
Emptying, bows bent e. of quivers, 772b
Empty-vaulted night, 337a
Emulation, propensity for e., 845b
  shouting their e., 289b
Enable press to serve functions, 984b
  socialist culture to thrive, 1027b-1028a
Enacting laws like drinking songs, 90b
Enactments, wicked cruel e., 594a
Enameled, makes music with e. stones, 220b
  quaint e. eyes, 339a
  snake throws e. skin, 229b
Enameling, hammered gold and gold e., 883a
Enamored, affliction e. of thy parts, 225a
  of an ass, 230a
Encamp, though an host should e., 18a
Enchafed flood, 273a
Enchains us to permitted ill, 569b
Enchant, I will e. thine ear, 219b
  what deceives may be said to e., 94a
Enchanted, enter e. woods, 730b
  holy and e., 523b
  life's e. cup, 555b
  Medea gathered e. herbs, 235a
Enchanter, ghosts from e. fleeing, 569b
Enchantment, distance lends e., 537b
Enchantments, last e. of Middle Age, 713b
Enchantress, tune e. plays, 854b
Enchants my sense, 268a
Enclose, cherries fairly do e., 300a
Enclosed, forbear to dig dust e. here, 299b
Encloseth, thy breast e. my heart, 217a
Enclosing, mistake of e. envelope, 985b
Encompass, poetic fields e. me, 392b
  unencompassable, 684b
Encompassed by horrors, 697a
Encompasseth, my ring e. thy finger, 216b
Encounter darkness as a bride, 271a
  truth in free and open e., 340b
Encountering fly this January day, 738b
Encourage, animate and e., 460b
  no vice, 450a
  to e. the others, 417a
  water most e. flame, 1031b
Encouraged, examination of government e., 531a
  he ought to be e., 433b

Encourager, pour e. les autres, 417a
Encouraging clever pupil, 425a
Encroach, habit will e., 523a
Encroachment, insidious e. by men of zeal, 833a
Encroachments, gradual and silent e., 480b
Encumbers him with help, 429b
Encumbrance, periodization of history e., 1047b
Encyclopedia of Error, 749b
End a contest quicker, 481a
   apathetic e., 646a
   appointment at e. of world, 984b
   at his e. shall be a fool, 34b
   at the e. take your fill, 67b
   at their wit's e., 21b
   attempt the e., 320b
   beauty sufficient e., 882a
   began to draw to our e., 37a
   begin with certainties e. in doubts, 206b
   beginning and the e., 58b
   beginning of the e., 484a
   beginning of time resemble e., 957a
   being's e. and aim, 409b
   better is the e. of a thing, 28a
   blessed the latter e. of Job, 16b
   born to disastrous e., 201a
   bow and accept e., 926a
   by opposing e. them, 261b
   by sleep we e. heartache, 261b
   chapters of lives to natural e., 816b
   come but not in sight, 1062b
   come to bad e., 910a
   crowns all, 269b
   crowns us not the fight, 320a
   death a necessary e., 254b
   decline to accept e. of man, 1039b
   democracy means to e., 1014b
   depends upon beginning, 131b
   despondency and madness, 512a
   dine at journey's e., 881b
   dispatch in putting e. to it, 99b
   even unto e. of world, 45a
   fairest things fleetest e., 856a
   findeth e. in garden, 4b
   go with me to my e., 298a
   God will put an e. to these, 117b
   going forth is from the e. of the heaven, 17b
   good beginning good e., 183b
   good of subjects e. of kings, 385b
   great e. of learning, 100b
   guide original and e., 148a
   hair to stand an e., 259b
   heartache, 261b
   here, 969a
   here at life's e., 884b
   hold fast our e., 716b
   hope to the e., 56b
   humanity come to terrible e., 952b
   if e. brings me out, 641a
   in e. despondency and madness, 1075b
   in joy, 1066a
   in my beginning is my e., 1005a
   in my e. my beginning, 192b, 1006a
   in one purpose, 243a

End, in the e. truth will conquer, 163a
   is bitter as wormwood, 23b
   is not yet, 43b
   is the renown, 270a
   journey's e., 276a, 881b
   journeys e. in lovers meeting, 251b
   justifying means by the e., 145a
   keeps e. from being hard, 928b
   knew when war going to e., 965b
   knocks you with butt e., 451b
   last e. be like his, 10a
   latter e. of a fray, 240b
   laws e. tyranny begins, 426a
   let e. try the man, 242a
   let the e. be legitimate, 485b
   let there be e., 661b
   liberty as e. and means, 832a
   live life to e., 1018a
   long weary day have e., 201b
   losses restored and sorrows e., 292a
   made e. of life with light, 114a
   made finer e. and went away, 243b
   make me to know mine e., 18b
   makes a swanlike e., 233b
   mankind put e. to war, 1073b
   minutes hasten to their e., 292b
   must justify the means, 387b
   my wrath did e., 489b
   naught at the e., 872a
   no e. in wandering mazes, 344a
   no e. of it the voiceless wailing, 1006a
   no e. to chain of responsibility, 983a
   no e. to withering, 1006b
   no prospect of an e., 446b
   not even beginning of e., 924a
   not forsake me in my e., 374b
   of every man's desire, 775a
   of exploring to arrive, 1007a
   of fight tombstone white, 872a
   of journey too, 862b
   of life cancels bands, 240a
   of life is action, 725a
   of love or season, 926a
   of making many books there is no e., 29a, 962b
   of my tether, 491b
   of perfect day, 862b
   of that man is peace, 18b
   of the beginning, 924a
   of the one-hoss shay, 634a
   of the unending, 1006b
   of the world, 17a, 45a, 965a
   of this day's business, 256b
   one must consider the e., 359b
   only when life comes to e., 78b
   pleasure the beginning and e., 103a
   quiet-colored e. of evening, 663b
   recurrent e. of unending, 1006b
   remember the e., 37b
   right true e. of love, 307a
   sans e., 630a
   see the e. and beginning, 1057a
   served no private e., 407a
   sleep itself must e., 331b
   snow swept world e. to e., 1018a
   socialism means to e., 1014b
   some say world e. in fire, 927a
   something ere the e., 646b
   stay awhile e. the sooner, 207b
   such e. true lovers have, 486a
   swan-like e., 93b

End, their words to the e. of the world, 17b
   there's an e. of May, 853b
   there's an e. on 't, 431b
   this is not the e., 924a
   till I e. my song, 201b
   Time will one day e. it, 269b
   to all an e., 878b
   to beginnings of wars, 974a
   to make the e. most sweet, 226a
   to pause to make e., 646b
   to war, 974a
   true beginning of our e., 230b
   true lover therefore had good e., 175b
   truth to the e. of reckoning, 272a
   war put e. to mankind, 1073b
   war that will e. war, 888a
   we shall go on to e., 921a
   where e. knows God, 1050b
   where you begun, 452a
   whole has beginning middle and e., 99a
   whose e. is destruction, 54b
   world without e., 59b, 459b
   yes to the very e., 739b
   you are beginning and e., 1049a
End-all, be-all and e., 282a
   of deep arguments, 899a
Endearing elegance of female friendship, 428a
   with e. wile, 449b
   young charms, 542a
Endearment, each fond e. tries, 449b
Endeavor, achievement death of e., 791b
   by no e. can magnet, 767a
   Christian e. hard on pulchritude, 961a
   disinterested e. to learn, 713b
   elevate life by e., 683a
   in continual motion, 243a
Endeavors to preserve peace, 972a
   to live life imagined, 683b
Ended, God be praised Georges e., 934a
   his cares now all e., 242b
   our revels now are e., 297b
   so e. Sicilian expedition, 90b
Endin', now sees de e., 1039a
Ending, all lovely things have e., 1010b
   art of e., 625a
   bad beginning makes bad e., 85b
   bread sauce of happy e., 799a
   crowns the work, 150b
   hard beginning good e., 183a
   heaven and earth in ashes e., 157b
   is despair, 297b
   never e. still beginning, 371b
   O bitter e., 968b
   of interminable night, 1006b
Endings, beginnings and e. untidy, 893a
Endless, absence which is e., 679a
   extinction of unhappy hates, 712b
   frontier, 1015a
   humility is e., 1005b
   night, 321a, 441b
   in e. error hurled, 409a
   my days of e. doubt, 198b
   olives of e. age, 293b
   perpetual posterity, 539a
   pure and e. light, 362b
   regret or happiness, 816b

Equinox, who knows when was the e., 331a
Equinoxes, precession of e., 655a
Equipment, shabby e. deteriorating, 1005b
Equity according to conscience of Chancellor, 317a
  act against natural e., 446a
  and fair play, 911b
  is a roguish thing, 317a
  law of humanity justice e., 454a
Equivalent, evil gains e. of disaster, 67b
  mechanical e. of heat, 795b
  moral e. of war, 795b
Equivocate, I will not e., 615b
Equivocation, poetry purged of e., 909b
  will undo us, 265b
Era, new e. in life from reading, 683a
  of wonderful nonsense, 1032b
Eradicated, savage in man never e., 682a
Eras, when e. die, 925a
Ercles' vein, 229a
Erebus, dark as E., 235b
Erect, avowed e. and manly foe, 506b
  by bending above fallen, 749a
  godlike e., 345a
  head e. beneath years, 844b
  sprang to feet stood e., 662a
  two souls e. and strong, 618a
Erected, fleshed fair e., 1068a
  least e. spirit, 342b
  with e. look, 369b
Erecting, corrupted youth in e. grammar school, 215b
Eremite, nature's patient E., 581a
Eretria, farewell renowned E., 92b
Erinyes who exact punishment underground, 64b
Eripuit caelo fulmen mox sceptra tyrannis, 131b
  Jovi fulmen viresque tonandi, 131b
Ermined and minked, 866b
  goosegirl e., 1042b
'Eroes, thin red 'e., 873a
  thin red line of 'e., 705a
Eros builder of cities, 1060a
  unarm E., 288b
  Zeus's child, 84b
Erotic instinct questionable, 936b
Err, Art may e., 372a
  better e. with Pope, 554b
  cautious seldom e., 71b
  fifty times to one does e., 382b
  grossly as few, 368b
  mortal and may e., 327b
  reasoning but to e., 408b
  they do not e., 518b
  to e. human forgive divine, 403b
  to e. is human, 137b, 150b
Errand, fool's e., 437b
  joyous e., 631a
  sleeveless e., 183a
  sun e. boy, 697b
  thy e. here below, 535b
Errare humanum est, 150b
Erred, we have e. and strayed, 59b
  wisest men have e., 349a
Erring, blind man's e. judgment, 402b
  extravagant and e. spirit, 257a
  Lord for the e. thought, 771b

Erring, power e. men call Chance, 337b
  reason's spite, 408b
  rod to check the e., 514b
  sister's shame, 558a
Erroneous, thickets of e. observations, 1026b
  truth in things e., 706a
Error, all men liable to e., 372b
  charged the troops of e., 329b
  chokes windows of mind, 301a
  correct cave, 1079a
  delay preferable to e., 471b
  Encyclopedia of E., 749b
  fruitful e., 814b
  guilty of no e., 540b
  hardy plant, 658a
  hosts of e., 858b
  if this be e., 294a
  ignorance preferable to e., 471a
  in endless e. hurled, 409a
  in pride our e. lies, 408a
  is immense, 397b
  is impatience, 980b
  keep citizen from e., 1021b
  keep government from e., 1022a
  life a mist of e., 315a
  life is only e., 498b
  love truth pardon e., 416b
  more dangerous the more truth, 706b
  no e. not find defenders, 749b
  of 1848 and 1849, 677b
  of opinion tolerated, 472a
  old and gray-headed e., 330b
  only e. to be exposed, 960b
  opponent weaned from e., 897a
  prophecy gratuitous e., 689b
  reformers of e., 473a
  religion not popular e., 722a
  show a man he is in e., 372b
  sink of uncertainty and e., 364a
  to expect favors, 461b
  trial and e., 833a
  truth to one e. to other, 897a
  very e. of the moon, 276a
  when e. begins to appear in state, 109b
  wounded writhes, 574b
Errors agonies and fears, 758a
  amusing with numerous e., 448a
  besetting e., 565a
  correct e. when shown e., 638a
  deliver from e. of wise, 351a
  if to her female e. fall, 404a
  reasoned e., 725b
  stratagems which e. seem, 402b
  volitional, 968b
  wanderings mists and tempests, 113a
'Erse's, 'ear 'e. legs, 654b
Errs if he do deed without God's knowledge, 79a
  man e. while struggle lasts, 478b
Erump, evade e., 110b
Erupit, abiit excessit evasit e., 110b
Eruption, strange e. to our state, 256b
Eruptions, strange e., 239b
Esau, hands are hands of E., 7a
  sold his birthright, 7a
  was a cunning hunter, 7a
Escalier, l'esprit de l'e., 437a
Escape, better ten guilty e., 444b
  cannot e. history, 638b

Escape from life, 1056b
  golden e., 1050a
  good thing to e. death, 82a
  how will you e. it, 708b
  immortals cannot e., 82b
  into calm regions, 434b
  less evil that some e., 788b
  let no guilty e., 717b
  me never, 664a
  mental exertion, 778a
  not e. my iambics, 115b
  poetry e. from emotion, 1007a
  shifts to e. thinking, 694b
  those who dream at night, 642a
  thou shalt not e. calumny, 262b
  thought dissolve and e., 977a
  what struggle to e., 583a
  whipping, 261b
Escaped from the deep, 159a
  none quite e. my smile, 990b
  what speech e. your teeth, 63a
  with skin of my teeth, 15a
Escapes, hair-breadth e., 272b
  rarely e. injuring own hands, 75a
  virtue e. not calumnious strokes, 258a
Escaping left Death's scraping, 955b
Eschewed, one that e. evil, 14a
Escurial, thou art to me E., 324b
  Tom Jones will outlive E., 466a
Eskimo, little frosty E., 823b
  Ootah had explanation, 835b
Espagnol, je parle e. à Dieu, 163b
Espoir, un peu d'e., 751b
Espouse everlasting sea, 512b
Espoused, saw my late e. saint, 341b
Esprit de corps, 959b
  l'e. de l'escalier, 437a
  l'e. de son âge, 418a
Essay loose sally of mind, 427b
  no room for impurities in e., 975a
  of arms make short e., 372a
  refined e. in Atlantic Monthly, 960a-b
Essays, my e. come home, 207b
Essence, drop of thing's e., 907b
  fellowship with e., 580b
  his glassy e., 271a
  knows e. of beauty, 93a
  look to e. of thing, 142b
  not disclose e. of phenomena, 984a
  of novel is moral, 855b
  time is of e., 1102a
Essences, combined e. of heaven and earth, 110a
Essential, assistance from fate e., 379a
  concept and first truth, 1068b
  disarmament is e., 974b
  facts of life, 683a
  four e. freedoms, 972b
  gaudiness of poetry, 957a
  give up e. liberty, 422b
  great expense may be e., 455a
  knowledge, 676a
  natural e. rights, 470b
  poetry, 528b
  provider of elements, 713b
  relation to existence, 676a
  service to country, 389b
  thing in form, 957a
  things e. or things circumstantial, 365b

Euripides, all Hellas monument of E., 90b
chorus ending from E., 665a
drew men as they were, 81a
Europa, bull that kidnapped E., 111a
Europe, all E. may be free, 921a
artist no home in E. save Paris, 806b
continent of energetic mongrels, 871a
depravations of E., 387a
educated Americans to E., 608a
fifty years of E., 647b
governments of E., 471a
if clod washed away E. less, 308b
lamps going out over E., 863b
liberation of E., 1016b
libraries of E., 473b
longest kingly line in E., 417a
new order in E., 954b
noblest river in E., 395a
of ancient parapets, 830a
people of Western E., 1016b
prison of nations, 954b
races of E. melting, 870b
really a swarm, 978a
regards her as stranger, 466b
sauntered E. round, 414a
settlement in E., 1013b
superstitious valuation of E., 798a
two continental powers in E., 1012a
under his heel, 922b
United States and E., 492a
United States of E., 600a
window on E., 594a
European, adopting E. war tactics, 997b
colonization by E. powers, 491b
gibe of E. scholars, 939a
if E. discovery delayed, 997b
instruments of E. greatness, 485a
narcotics, 805b
nose, 1080a
periodization of E. history, 1047b
tricked into E. war, 913b
wars of E. powers, 491b
Europe's latter hour, 711b
Eurydice, half-regained E., 335a
Euston, Scotland through pylons of E., 951b
Eutrapelia happy flexibility, 716b
Euxine, more dangerous breakers than E., 561a
Evade erump, 110b
Evaluation, fear mitigated by e., 1015a
Evanescence, route of e., 738b
Evanescent, velocities of e. increments, 399b
Evangelical, things moral or things e., 365b
Evangelist Saint John, 697a
Evangels of the mind, 966b
Evasion of what white men set them, 1039a
Evasit, abiit excessit e. erupit, 110b
Eve, Adam and E. and pinch me, 944b
and I, 663b
believe in Adam and E., 901b
called his wife's name E., 6a

Eve, child of our grandmother E., 221b
fairest of daughters E., 345a
from noon to dewy e., 343a
like toad at ear of E., 346a
motherless E., 906a
obey voice at e., 604a
oh had simple E., 906a
pensive E., 443b
said to e. Be soon, 856b
since E. ate apples, 562a
son of Adam and E., 387b
span, 1084a
St. Agnes' E., 581b
stag at e., 520a
warblest at e., 339b
wonder what Adam and E. think, 996a
Evelyn, beautiful E. Hope, 663b
Even, approach of even or morn, 344b
as you and I, 875a
break, 842b, 962b
deep and crisp and e., 687b
gray-hooded E., 336b
such is time, 199b
waters stilled at e., 731a
would God it were e., 10b
Even-balanced soul, 710b
Even-handed justice, 282a
Evening and morning were first day, 5a
beauteous e. calm free, 512a
Boston E. Transcript, 1001b, 1045b
bright exhalation in the e., 298a
come in the e., 676b
descends autumn e., 715a
dews of e. carefully shun, 416a
die in e. without regret, 71b
eat in the e., 487b
expects his e. prey, 441b
fairer than e. air, 213b
follows morn, 1052a
full of linnet's wings, 879b
gracious e. star, 676b
grateful e. mild, 345b
housewife ply e. care, 440a
in the e. it is cut down, 20a
is come rise up, 115a
isolation of sky at e., 955a
it was a summer e., 532a
life's e., 809a
like an e. gone, 396b
man that was in e. made, 332b
morning e. noon night, 662a
morning incense e. meal, 483a
must usher night, 571b
not unpeaceful e., 534a
now came still e. on, 345b
of their lives, 720b
open house in e., 918b
quickly come as the E. Star, 110a
quiet-colored end of e., 663b
rainy e. to read this discourse, 325b
shades of e. drew on, 642a
shades prevail, 393a
shadow at e. rising, 1002b
shadows of the e., 750b
shut of e. flowers, 347b
soup of the e., 744b
spread out against sky, 1000b
star for which e. waits, 900a
star love's harbinger, 348a
star you bring all things, 69b
sunset and e. star, 655a

Evening, to his labor until e., 21b
twilight and e. bell, 655a
until e. comes, 598a
watch the e. star, 673b
welcome peaceful e. in, 458b
when it is e. fair weather, 43a
when slanted radiance, 944a
withhold not thine hand in the e., 28b
Evenings, long dark autumn e., 663b
we had had summer e., 990a
Evensong, at last ring to e., 185b
at length ringeth to e., 185b
dead ere e., 1088b
Event, caprice of minutest e., 697b
divine e., 651a
greatest e. in war, 90b
haunt spot of great e., 614a
how much the greatest e., 476b
men labels that name e., 732a
one e. happeneth to all, 27b
prophets make sure of e., 442b
thinking too precisely on e., 264b
third e. to me, 739a
unveil third e. to me, 739a
verity is an e., 795a
we know the e., 1014b
Eventful, strange e. history, 249a
Eventide, fast falls e., 567a
Events cast shadows before, 538a
controlled me, 639b
course of human e., 470b
not lead e. but follow them, 138b
President on top of e., 983a
signs should prefigure e., 111a
soon on top of him, 983a
spirits of great e., 538a
study e. in bearings, 721a
three e. in life, 381b
Ever-during dark surrounds me, 344b
sleep one e. night, 300a
Ever-fixed mark, 294a
Evergreen, final growth e., 1057b
tree of diabolical knowledge, 480b
Ever-increasing wonder and awe, 445a
Everlasting, achievements of intellect e., 116a
an e. now, 358a
beauty is e., 997a
bonfire, 283b
composed to be e. possession, 89a
condemned into e. redemption, 246b
damned to e. fame, 410a
deprived of e. bliss, 213a
doors, 18a
espouse e. sea, 512b
eyes of Pierrot, 1043b
farewells, 552a
Father, 31a
first last e. day, 305b
flint, 224b
from e. to e. thou art God, 20a
had not fixed canon, 257b
here set up my e. rest, 225b
hills, 8a
his mercy is e., 21a
life, 48a
no, 576a
open ye e. gates, 347a
personal identity, 539b

Fame, sang of love not of f., 726a
sun of dead, 590b
take my chance with f., 868a
temple of f., 1092a
thirst of youth, 556b
to fortune and f. unknown, 441a
trust to common f., 605a
vain for f. to wish, 531b
was noised throughout the country, 11a
well known to f., 1100b
what's F., 409b
while f. elates thee, 541b
wisdom and prosperity exceedeth the f., 13a
Famed in song famous Athens, 79b
Troy walls f. in battle, 118a
Fame's eternal beadroll, 200b
eternal camping ground, 704b
Familiar acts beautiful, 569a
and well-beloved in home, 1067a
as his garter, 243a
as rose in spring, 142a
be thou f., 258b
beauty grows f. to lover, 393b
new things are made f., 428b
old and f. objects, 529a
old f. faces, 534a
once f. word, 587b
played f. with hoary locks, 558a
style f. but not coarse, 428a
things are made new, 428b
wine a good f. creature, 274a
Familiarity breeds contempt, 76a
breeds contempt and children, 764b
too early f. with Bible, 850b
with danger, 695b
Familiarize yourselves with chains, 636a
Familiarly, if one approaches f., 996a
Families, best-regulated f., 671b
first f. in Virginia, 1042a
God setteth the solitary in f., 19b
great f. of yesterday, 385a
happy f. alike, 732b
I hate you, 897b
lie together, 1080b
rooks in f. go, 784b
Family, all the f. of fame, 526b
character of f., 1091a
children of one f., 396b
church and private school, 717b
father of a f., 140b
greatest thing in f. life, 930a
happier for his presence, 825a
history begins with me, 96a
holding the ropes, 742b
I am part of my f., 986b
is not in residence, 153b
join the f., 928a
nobody not in f., 533b
of rare long-stemmed flowers, 985a
party tribe or clan, 1100a
refuse to help f., 890b
relationship, 850b
represents one aspect, 850b
root of the state, 99b
servant of scattered f., 752a
stamped character on child, 936a

Family, supporting f. paying taxes, 785a
trees remember name, 1041b
unhappy f. unhappy in own way, 732b
word like great f., 382a
Famine, die by f. die by inches, 386a
fever f. and war, 817b
seven years of f., 7b
Fam'ly, refuse to help f., 890b
Famous Athens divine city, 79b
awoke and found myself f., 558a
by my pen, 353b
by my sword, 353b
by their birth, 226b
Chaucer broad f. poet, 314a
day and year, 623b
earth sepulcher of f. men, 90a
forgotten for want of writers, 122b
found that f. country, 1022b
garden never make me f., 1052a
Hanover city, 662a
harmony of leaves, 880a
high top-hat, 953a
island descending, 920b
let us praise f. men, 38b
maiden f. to all time, 122a
make thee f. by my pen, 353b
not give up writing too f., 1011a
remarks seldom quoted correctly, 957b
through infinite inferiority, 696b
to all ages, 340a
victory, 532a
Famoused, painful warrior f. for fight, 291b
Fan, brain him with lady's f., 239a
cool gales f. the glade, 402b
Fanatic can't change mind, 925a
does what Lord wud do, 891a
Fanatical, my f. will power, 1012a
Fanaticism redoubling efforts, 867a
to barbarism one step, 437a
Fancied, can it be f. that Deity, 643b
Fancies, high reason of f., 339b
host of furious f., 1086a
lay earthly f. down, 651b
our f. are more giddy, 252a
proud and full of f., 579a
realities less dangerous than f., 913b
Fanciful, no test which is not f., 82b
Fancy, ever let f. roam, 583b
excellent f., 265b
from flower bell, 665a
full of shapes is f., 251a
hopeless f. feigned, 648b
is mode of memory, 529a
keep f. free, 852b
motives of more f., 270a
my f. flies, 447b
no time for f. dans, 1025b
not expressed in f., 258b
now f. passes by, 852b
sweet and bitter f., 250b
when I go to rest, 949a
where is f. bred, 233b
whispers of f., 428a
work of brain and f., 376b

Fancy, young man's f., 647a
Fancy-free, maiden meditation f., 229a
Fancy's, impediments in f. course, 270a
misled by f. meteor ray, 493a
Shakespeare F. child, 335a
Faneuil Hall cradle of liberty, 548b
Fanged, fields f. with flints, 1050b
Fangs, beware my f., 234a
Fanny's, pretty F. way, 398a
Fantasies, thousand f. begin to throng, 336b
twilight f., 571b
Fantastic century move, 482a
light f. round, 336b
light f. toe, 334b
plays such f. tricks, 271a
reveries, 781a
summer's heat, 226a
tripped light f., 862b
Fantastical, high f., 251a
imagination, 883a
Fantasy, begot of vain f., 223a
dynamic principle of f., 935a
lure f. to utmost, 915a
master of f., 830a
Fantasy's, not f. hot fire, 518b
Far and few, 673a
and near unite, 466b
as angels ken, 341b
as coin would stretch, 237b
be it from God, 16a
brother f. off, 26b
calls coming f., 969a
cry to Lochow, 521a
do not peer too f., 79a
do not set eyes on things f. off, 79a
fair and softly goes f., 165a
far ahead, 515b
fierce hour and sweet, 919a
forward since we have come so f., 219b
from fiery noon, 584a
from madding crowd, 440b
from old folks at home, 727b
from the sun, 441b
green hill f. away, 684b
how f. candle throws beams, 235b
ill news travels f., 137a
in pillared dark, 928b
in western brookland, 853a
not too amorous of f., 915a
not too f. from yew, 1006b
o'er hills and f. away, 384a
on ringing plains of Troy, 646b
one near one too f., 664a
over hills and f. away, 401b, 1095a
peace to him that is f. off, 33b
pushed just so f., 893b
slight what's near by aiming f., 84a
so f. only should we hate, 81a
so f. trust thee Kate, 239a
so near yet so f., 651a
those f. off are attracted, 72a
whistles f. and wee, 1030a
why art thou so f. from helping me, 17b
Far East, those who brought war to F., 982b
Farce is played, 182a
Farced title 'fore king, 244b

Feast of Stephen, 687b
of wines on the lees, 31b
outcast from life's f., 968a
pomp and f. and revelry, 335a
riseth from f. with keen appetite, 232b
sat at good man's f., 248b
small cheer makes merry f., 218a
to spleen a grateful f., 516b
to the Lord, 8b
what f. is toward, 266b
when f. finished, 890a
when I make a f., 210a
Feasting, good dinner and f., 375b
house of f., 28a
if f. rise, 748b
Feasts, movable f., 59a
shown in courts at f., 337b
Feat of Tell the archer, 498b
Feather, a wit's a f., 409b
as f. wafted downward, 621b
birds of a f., 311b
for each wind, 295a
his own f. on dart, 555a
in hand better than bird in air, 137a
in his cap, 438a
never moults f., 669b
pluck out flying f., 774b
pun pistol not f., 536a
sharpened f., 698a
stuck f. in hat, 1090a
tomorrow f. duster, 915a
whence pen was shaped, 517a
Featherbed, despotism to liberty in f., 471b
Feathered, divide into featherless and f., 96b
his nest well, 314a
tarred f. carried in cart, 626a
with eagle's plumes, 76b
Featherless, divide into f. and feathered, 96b
Feathers, beat f. flat as pancakes, 314a
brain of f., 413b
cover thee with his f., 20b
crow beautified with our f., 206a
field of f. for strife of love, 128b
he shall cover thee with his f., 20b
not only fine f. make fine birds, 76a
owl for all f., 581b
plumes her f., 337a
thing with f., 735a
twitter and f. sleek, 579a
with our own f., 76b
Featly, foot it f., 296a
Feats, 'twas one of my f., 562b
Feature, haint one agreeable f., 693a
one f. distinguished him, 797a
show virtue her own f., 262b
Features, homely f. to keep home, 337b
human f. composed of ten parts, 132b
of clerical cut, 1004a
paint man as well as f., 754b
February, excepting F. alone, 187a
Fecit, homo f., 1079b
Fed, bite hand that f., 455a
dead who f. the guns, 992b

Fed, fish that hath f. of worm, 264b
grown by what it f. on, 257b
look up and are not f., 338b
machine f. with flesh and oil, 923a
man's resinous heart f., 883b
of dainties bred of a book, 221b
on fullness of death, 774a
on honeydew hath f., 524a
purely upon ale, 397b
those former bounty f., 371b
to be happy be well f., 960
washed dressed warmed f., 947a
work and house be f., 704a
Federal, not approve of f. system, 549a
our F. Union, 503a
Federalism practice not principle, 1055b
shown in courts at f., 337b
Federalists, we are all F., 472a
Federation of the world, 647b
Fee bestow upon foul disease, 277a
cure complete he seeks f., 820a
doctor for nauseous draught, 372a
gorgeous east in f., 512b
set life at pin's f., 259b
Feeble earthworm, 364a
engines of despotism, 473b
expletives f. aid join, 403a
help f. up, 290a
if Virtue f. were, 338a
most forcible F., 242a
religion of f. minds, 454b
to quote argues f. industry, 88b
Feebler, nothing f. than a man, 66b
Feed among the lilies, 29b
brain with better things, 918b
cloy appetites they f., 287b
cow and bear shall f., 31a
fat the ancient grudge, 232a
gave thee life did thee f., 486b
He that doth ravens f., 247b
him with bread of affliction, 13b
his flock like a shepherd, 32b
his sacred flame, 526b
men in exile f. on dreams, 79a
nor f. the swine, 1095b
on Death, 294b
on for fault not mine, 562b
on her damask cheek, 252b
on hope, 201a
sleep and f., 264b
them with wormwood, 34a
this mind of ours, 508b
thy harm dost f., 1084a
upon strawberries, 1095b
upon what meat Caesar f., 253b
worm shall f. sweetly, 15b, 309a
you cannot f. capons so, 263a
Feeds, Death that f. on men, 294b
mock meat it f. on, 274a
my father f. flocks, 445a
on books alone, 790a
three, 692b
upon burrs of life, 580a
who gives himself f. three, 692b
Feel amid city's jar, 711a
and know we are eternal, 374b
as if top of head off, 739b
as if we were free, 795a
beauty as we f., 867a
by turns bitter change, 344a
can Sporus f., 411b
fashion as we f., 966b

Feel fog in throat, 666b
great forces behind detail, 787b
happier in passion we f., 356a
heavy as yonder stone, 968b
hell within myself, 330a
her finger light, 714a
how swift how secretly, 1022b
I must f. it as a man, 285b
in wintry age f. no chill, 459a
it and am in torment, 115a
it cannot utter it, 1049b
it so like myself, 1068b
let me f. your pulse, 218b
like doing for babies, 1053b
like morning star, 755a
like thirty cents, 886b
might free on a raft, 761a
more to do than I f., 534a
my fate, 1065a
my heart new opened, 298b
new wind blew they not f., 944b
not f. the crowd, 458b
now does he f. his title, 286a
old as yonder elm, 968b
only f. farewell, 554b
paint best who f. most, 405b
passions we f. expand time, 907b
see not f. how beautiful, 527a
slime of wet nest, 1065a
speak what we f., 280b
steady candle flame, 664b
sweets I know charms I f., 483a
thee again old sea, 695b
thing that could not f., 511a
those who would make us f., 456a
thy finger and find thee, 802b
tragedy to those that f., 442b
we are greater, 517a
what we f. indeed, 716a
what we say and f., 716a
what we think we f., 716a
what wretches feel, 278b
who will make us f., 711b
Feeling, a f. and a love, 509a
apprehend by f. as by intellect, 935a
as old as he's f., 728a
blue, 845a
comfortable f. of superiority, 960b
deepest f. in silence, 996b
development of f. in language, 1007b
disputation, 239b
fellow f., 310a
for single good action, 478a
formal f. comes, 735b
gives greater f. to the worse, 226a
gratifying f. duty done, 769a
high mountains a f., 556b
his cold strength, 994b
imprecision of f., 1005b
makes us eloquent, 136a
no f. not in every heart, 723b
no f. of his business, 265b
not always everything, 709a
of sadness and longing, 621b
one f. falsely disdained, 572b
petrifies the f., 493b
profound or vehement, 529a
push of cosmos, 795a
religious f. part of consciousness, 705b
religious f. toward life, 898b
sensible to f. as to sight, 283a

Feeling, sentimentality failure of f., 957a
taste f. inheritance, 776b
the East's gift, 664b
Feelings, art transmission of highest f., 732b
lets f. run, 597b
not figures on dial, 679a
of men in solitude, 794b
opinion determined by f., 705b
overflow of powerful f., 511b
permanently in race, 712a
some f. to mortals given, 520a
trampling on f., 1041a
Feels, heroism f. never reasons, 607a
imagine how it f., 902a
it with great sensibility, 430a
ne'er f. retiring ebb, 275a
never f. wanton stings, 270a
Fees, contrive our f. to pilfer, 91a
flowing f., 340a
Feet, able to draw with their f., 70b
and did those f., 490b
and his f. not be burned, 23b
are always in water, 491b
at her f. he bowed, 11a
at the f. of Gamaliel, 50b
beneath her petticoat, 350b
cadence of consenting f., 1029b
cat would not wet f., 184a
chase hours with flying f., 556a
clang of hurrying f., 674a
die on f. not live on knees, 943a, 973a
die over f. to washup, 969a
dreams under your f., 880b
dust of your f., 42a
earth my f. know, 986b
fell at his f. as dead, 57b
fog comes on cat f., 948a
four white f. go without him, 1101b
get up on f. and fly, 1075a
grown-up people's f., 823a
heaven under our f., 683b
heavy but on I go, 844b
Hun at throat or f., 924a
if it is well with your f., 123b
in ancient time, 490b
keep thou my f., 597b
lamp by which f. guided, 465a
lamp unto my f., 22a
leave but not hearts, 633b
like unto fine brass, 57b
liked getting f. wet, 887b
little snow-white f., 879a
making a tinkling with their f., 30b
million marching f., 1069b
more be laid at your f., 775b
more instant than F., 856b
move with leaden f., 771b
my f. are cold, 1034b
nearer than hands f., 654b
neither ground for f., 702b
nimble f. dance on air, 841a
of clay, 35a
of day and of night, 772b
of him that bringeth good tidings, 33a
old shoes easiest for f., 207b
over whose acres blessed f., 237b
palms before my f., 919a
patter of little f., 623b
pleasures lie about f., 511b
pretty f. like snails, 320b

Feet, regards what is before his f., 107a
rising and falling, 1005a
roll in ecstasy at your f., 980b
Scots lords at his f., 1087b
shalt thou trample under f., 20b
silver-sandaled f., 838b
six f. of land, 732b
splendor and speed of f., 772b
standing with reluctant f., 621b
stretches out f. and dies, 1075a
teach f. a measure, 774b
to the lame, 15b
tremble under her f., 652b
trod under by hurrying f., 889b
unstable, 952
wash f. in soda water, 1002b
what flowers at my f., 582b
wind's f. shine along sea, 773b
with goat f. dance antic hay, 212b
with twain he covered his f., 30b
with your shoes on your f., 8b
Feetur, haint one agreeable f., 693a
Feign thing or fynde wordes new, 167a
Feigned an angry look, 383a
by f. deaths to die, 305b
hopeless fancy f., 648b
necessities, 328a
Feigning lady by Bazille, 1078b
Felicior, sed tu f., 1105a
Felicities, close circle of f., 472a
of all man's f., 1017b
poet with so many f., 508b
Felicitous phenomenon, 997a
Felicitously, whatever is f. expressed, 501b
Felicity, absent thee from f., 266b
and flower of wickedness, 667a
green f., 580a
human f., 423b
or doom, 739a
perfect bliss and sole f., 212a
possession without obligation, 730b
we make or find, 428a
what more f. to creature, 201a
Felix culpa, 59a
qui potuit cognoscere causas, 117a
Fell, all of us f. down, 255b
among thieves, 46b
at his feet as dead, 57b
at one f. swoop, 285b
bolt of Cupid f., 229b
by that sin f. the angels, 299a
clutch of circumstance, 816a
epitaph of those who f., 924a
fiend f. from heaven, 152a
from morn to noon he f., 343a
Great Caesar f., 255b
heart f. dead, 1030a
help me when I f., 546a
house f. not, 41b
I f. as a dead body, 160a
if angels f., 408a
in fire burned to ashes, 930b
in the great victory, 532a
it f. it burst it shook land, 967b
lash magic creature till it f., 738a
like a stick, 467b
like autumn fruit, 367b
love thee Doctor F., 386b
men f. out knew not why, 351b

Fell, mightiest Julius f., 256b
my f. of hair, 286b
of dark not day, 804a
out over pigs, 975a
scales f. from eyes, 49b
seeds f. by wayside, 42b
sergeant death, 266b
shake my f. purpose, 282a
some f. into good ground, 42b
spirits that f. with Lucifer, 213a
the wall f. down flat, 11a
there he f. down dead, 11a
they always f., 992a
thy shadow Cynara, 889b
thy tempests f. all night, 323b
Time's f. hand, 292b
to earth knew not where, 622a
upon his brother Benjamin's neck, 7b
upon knees blessed God, 318b-319a
when stars shot and f., 929a
Felled, hand that signed f. city, 1070a
Feller, do unto other f. fust, 811a
met a city f., 1103a
sweetest little f., 845a
Fellers call me Bill, 821a
Fellow, careless lying f., 953b
covetous sordid f., 415a
damned in fair wife, 272a
dies an honest f., 312b
do unto other f. fust, 811a
dockyard f., 749b
every sword against his f., 12a
fault came to match, 250a
feeling, 310a
folly has not f., 852b
good hay hath no f., 230a
hail f. well met, 391a
has this f. no feeling, 265b
have such a f. whipped, 262b
he was a good f., 166b
hook-nosed f. of Rome, 242b
I shot his f., 231b
laughing rover, 947a
love my f. creatures, 768a
loves his f. men, 551b
make f. creatures happy, 467b
met a city f., 1103a
my f. man my brother, 706b
no f. in firmament, 254b
of infinite jest, 265b
robustious periwig-pated f., 262b
savage-creating f., 92a
sweetest little f., 845a
touchy testy pleasant f., 394a
travelers of revolution, 957a
want of it the f., 409b
with best king, 166b
Fellowman, assist reduced f., 155b
Fellow's got to swing, 84ob
wise enough to play fool, 252b
Fellows call me Bill, 821a
club assembly of good f., 427b
good f. get together, 868b
it hurts to think, 853b
lewd f., 50a
man knows f. in himself, 908a
Nature hath framed strange f., 231a
of infinite tongue, 245a
some are fine f., 730a
such f. as I crawling, 262a
Fellows', other f. brindled hair, 823b
Fellowship divine, 580b
dues of f., 618b

Foul, from f. to fair, 210b
goat-head, 885a
I doubt some f. play, 258a
limbecks f. as hell, 294a
pearl in your f. oyster, 250b
play, 258a
shapes of f. disease, 651a
so f. and fair a day, 281a
Fouler, death aims with f. spite, 321b
Foulest crime in history, 702a
Foulness of their fate, 992b
Found, came to ask what he had f., 532a
common daylight sweet, 813a
crooked sixpence, 1096b
death in life, 530a
dove f. no rest, 6b
empire for raising customers, 445a
favor in thy sight, 7a
fresh rhodora, 602b
fun where I f. it, 875a
has f. out thy bed, 489a
hast thou f. me O mine enemy, 13b
her first and best, 874a
Him in shining of stars, 654a
I could extinguish hope, 830a
I have f. it, 105a
I oft f. both, 231b
in heart of friend, 622a
in that town dog was f., 448b
in whose hand the cup is f., 7b
it is f. again, 830a
left unstained what f., 573b
looked inwards f. Nature, 367a
lost time never f., 422a
man who has f. himself out, 858a
much f. I could not bind, 950a
one man among a thousand, 28a
out the remedy, 270b
promptly f. out, 977a
rebellion in way he f. it, 240b
refinement f. at home, 491b
Rome city of bricks, 124b
sense beneath rarely f., 403a
sheep which was lost, 47a
sought but f. him not, 29b
struggle to f. Roman state, 117b
that famous country, 1022b
the root of the matter is f., 15b
thing to love, 918a
things much as always f., 911a
tree of deepest root is f., 468b
unmysterious flesh, 1038a
was lost and is f., 47a
weighed in the balances and f. wanting, 35a
when f. make note, 671a
where shall wisdom be f., 15b
where word be f., 1003b
who loveliness within hath f., 305a
woman have I not f., 28a
worship he f. in use, 92b
you as a morsel, 288a
Foundation, fear f. of governments, 463b
for rehabilitation of nation, 995b
is love, 1082b
laid in youth, 850b
new government laying f., 470b
no sure f. on blood, 237a
of constitutional government, 865a

Foundations, earth's f. fled, 854a
earth's f. stand, 855a
loosen old f., 948b
marred f. we forgot, 1006b
of states laws and arms, 177a
order our f., 589b
when I laid f. of earth, 16a
Founded, earth and heaven f. strong, 853a
government f. on compromise, 453a
he hath f. it upon the seas, 18a
principle on which society not f., 438b
securely f., 477b
upon a rock, 41b
Founder, supinely enjoyed gifts of f., 466a
true f. of civil society, 435b
Foundest me poor, 450b
Founding, Franklin one of f. fathers, 997a
since the f. of the city, 149b
Fount Bandusian more sparkling than glass, 122a
of joy's delicious springs, 555a
still from the f., 55a
Fountain and a shrine, 642a
back to burning f., 572a
choke dark f. ere flows, 566b
choke f. of industry, 548a
dying of thirst by the f., 170b
even f. have rest, 684b
from f. wells up bitter taste, 114a
like bubble on f., 520a
of sweet tears, 511b
pitcher broken at the f., 29a
returns again to f., 622b
rise like f. for me, 654a
that which f. sends forth, 622b
the f. overflows, 487b
tormenting image in f., 696a
troubled like f. stirred, 269a
woman moved like f. troubled, 219b
Fountain's silvery column, 526b
Fountains, Afric's sunny f., 549b
fraught with tears, 204a
from old f. new judgment, 832a
silver f. have mud, 292a
streams from little f., 507a
under f. and graves, 1086b
Fountainside, die of thirst at f., 1080a
Four, age best in f. things, 207b
and twenty tailors, 1094b
angels to my bed, 357a
doors were five, 1033b
ducks on a pond, 729a
freedoms, 972b
grant that twice two not f., 688a
hands are f., 1032a
intimate quality of the F., 976b
lean hounds, 1030a
not f. friends in world, 363b
Point F. program, 983b
snakes gliding, 604b
spend in prayer, 198b
things better without, 1029a
things which I know not, 26b
things wiser to know, 1029a
two and two make f., 754a
undergraduates right number, 915b
venerate f. characters, 469b
when angry count f., 762a
winds of the heaven, 36a

Fourfold, threefold f. tomb, 319a
Four-in-hand, fiery f., 530a
Fours, crawling on all f., 417b
Fourscore and seven years ago, 639a
and upward, 280a
if by reason of strength they be f., 237b
wind him up for f. years, 367b
Foursquare in hand and foot, 70b
to winds that blew, 651b
Fourteen hundred years ago nailed, 237b
Fourteenth Amendment not enact Spencer, 787b
Fourth estate, 576a, 577b, 660a
generation of them that hate me, 9a
safe and sane F., 887b
this is the F., 474a
Fowl, dominion over f. of the air, 5a
elegant f., 673a
fish flesh or f., 882b
Fowler, snare of the f., 20b
Fowls, May comen I here f. synge, 165b
of the air shall tell, 15a
of the air sow not, 41a
small f. flew screaming, 697b
Fox, Aesop's f., 310b
be f. to recognize traps, 177b
Brer F. he lay low, 814a
false as f. to lamb, 268b
from lair in morning, 578b
has many tricks, 68a
knows many things, 68a
may f. build on hearthstone, 909a
prince imitate f. and lion, 177b
prince must know how to play f., 136b
quick brown f., 1101a
says they are not ripe, 75b
to wear arctic f., 997a
treason trusted like f., 240b
wings lift him, 1081a
Foxes have holes, 41b
honored among f., 1070b
little f. that spoil vines, 29b
Foxey, maxim with F., 670a
Foxholes, no atheists in f., 1053a
no white or colored signs in f., 1074a
Fox's, patch lion's skin with f., 136b
Frabjous day, 745a
Fractions, happiness made of f., 530a
there are no f., 1034a
Fragile but with more vitality, 907b
dewdrop on perilous way, 579b
profound and f. lips, 1031a
Fragment, ship f. detached, 843a
Fragmentary blue, 927a
Fragments, broken dishonored f., 547a
death tramples it to f., 572a
gather up f., 48b
live in f. no longer, 951b
of the f. twelve baskets, 42b
of the world seek each other, 965a
shored against ruins, 1003a
Fragrance, as metal keeps f., 930a
fresh without f., 990a
jar will keep f., 542b

Freedoms, insensible to f. of Constitution, 967a
Freely, different schools contend f., 1028a
give, 42a
lives at ease that f. lives, 163a
offer itself to you, 980b
possession prevents living f., 913a
serve because we f. love, 346b
show f. your worst trait, 614a
too dear for what's given f., 295a
ye have received, 42a
Freeman butters Stubbs, 1101a
contending for liberty, 460b-461a
no f. taken except by legal judgment, 157b
Freemen, Americans f. or slaves, 461a
nation of f., 635a
who rules o'er f., 433b
Freer, nowhere is speech f., 924a
Frees her slave again, 1089b
one word f. us, 83a
Freeze, mountaintops that f., 298a
thy young blood, 259b
with fear f. love fry, 1085b
Freezes, till hell f. over, 1104b
Freight, nation's f. handler, 948a
proportioned to groove, 739b
Freiheit, nur der verdient sich F., 478b
Frémont, free speech F., 1099b
French and German blood spilled, 979b
believe only in F. culture, 806a
best F. novel in language, 1075b
few obscure writers in F., 846b
for converse with friends, 435a
for fiddle-de-dee, 746b
for suppressing one, 713a
gone no one to understand, 916a
gone to fight the F., 500a
hinges in F. conversation, 438b
I speak F. to men, 163b
new F. books, 665a
not to F. bean, 766b
of Parys to hir unknowe, 166a
only accidentally F., 414b
or Turk or Proosian, 766a
phrase for hotel guests, 895b
presented by F. government, 864a
Revolution began at top, 721a
Revolution ushered in equality, 1014a
soldier carries marshal's baton, 505a
spake ful faire and fetisly, 166a
speak F. when can't think of English, 745b
sprightliness of F., 435a
stormed Ratisbon, 662a
struggle of F. soldiers. 731b
tell you what it is, 1015b
to F. empire of land, 500a
what is not clear is not F., 482b
word impossible not F., 504a
Frenchman, embrace Pole as F., 191a
first man then a F., 414b
I praise the F., 457a
in Academy, 430b
must be always talking, 433a

Frenchmen, did march three F., 244a
Englishman beat three F., 395a
fifty million F., 1103a
mankind including F., 976b
Frenzied drum, 882a
rush of our lawlessness, 708b
Frenzy, demoniac f., 348a
eye in fine f. rolling, 230b
not shaken from resolve by f., 121b
of his fellow citizens, 121b-122a
old man's f., 885a
Frequent, eagerly f. doctor, 630a
more f. use of any organ, 475a
practicer of angling, 326a
Frère, mon semblable mon f., 706b
sois mon f. ou je te tue, 469a
Fresh as a bridegroom, 238a
as a lark, 515b
as month of May, 166a
as paint, 687b
complexion and heart together, 295b
dews of night, 338a
from brawling courts, 650b
heavens f. and strong, 514b
how quick and f. art thou, 251a
makes not f. again, 313a
perfection in beloved, 550b
sae f. and fair, 494a
streams meet in salt sea, 243a
suspicions, 274b
transfigurings of blue, 956a
waste not f. tears, 85b
welcome faire f. May, 167a
without fragrance, 990a
woods and pastures new, 339a
world as f. as at first day, 724b
Freshest blue, 956a
Freshness, glory and f. of a dream, 513a
poem forever keep f., 930a
Fret, I should worry and f., 946a
living we f., 668a
nuns f. not, 515a
of existence, 1047b
passage through it, 333b
thy soul with crosses, 201a
weariness fever f., 582b
Fretful, quills upon f. porpentine, 259b
Frets doubt maw-crammed beast, 666a
fig for him who f., 869a
struts and f. his hour, 286b
Fretted, cares that f. me, 1101a
the pygmy body to decay, 368a
vault, 440a
with golden fire, 261a
Freud, ideas of F., 861b
Freude, Kraft durch F., 1017b
Friar of orders gray, 219b, 1084b
there was wantowne and merye, 166a
Friars, clouds like f., 620b
Fribble and less than man of reason, 957a
Fribsbi, fatal man Madame F., 660a
Friday, call this F. good, 1005b
my man F., 385b
worse on F., 1096a
Friday's child, 1096a
Friend, all he wished a f., 441a

Friend, ascend prosperity not meet f., 763a
at least one f. left, 640a
await felicity or doom, 739a
be a f. of man, 846a
best mirror an old f., 324b
bosom f. of sun, 584a
bring death to a f., 82a
cannot be known, 38a
choose author as choose f., 374b
death of f. make man look sad, 230b-231a
defend your departed f., 371a
do a f. service, 81a
dog the firmest f., 554b
down inside me, 640a
every man will be thy f., 309a
forsake not old f., 37b
favorite has no f., 439b
forsake not old f., 37b
found song in heart of f., 622a
from morn to night my f., 739b
good f. for Jesus' sake, 299b
good wine a f. or being dry, 382a
grant f. in my retreat, 457a
greatest American f., 924b
guide philosopher and f., 410a, 962b
had brother who had f., 965b
had not f. nor toy, 694a
happy house shelters f., 606b
heaven save from foolish f., 505b
honor f. who prospered, 78b
house to lodge f., 411b
I was angry with my f., 489b
idleness sorrow f. foe, 1029a
if I had a f. that loved her, 273a
if thou wouldest get a f., 37b
imperial f., 736b
in need friend indeed, 105b
in need nor foolish, 671a
in power friend lost, 776b
indeed help in need, 309a
is a second self, 111b
is medicine of life, 37b
is strong defense, 37b
keep thy f. under own key, 269b
keep tonge and keep f., 169b
knolling departing f., 241b
left exposed a f., 737a
little f. of all world, 875b
loan loses itself and f., 258b
long sought with difficulty kept, 145a
lost every other f., 640a
lost more than a f., 981b
lost no f., 407a
makes no f. never made foe, 653b
masterpiece of nature, 606b
may you go safe my f., 944b
my f. judge not me, 197b
my God my Father and F., 374b
'neath every one a f., 694b
ne'er said till f. dead, 809b
never find a f., 882b
never known till need, 184b
never want f. in need, 671a
new f. fit to make old, 816b
new f. is as new wine, 37b
no f. in misery, 309a
no f. like sister, 740a
no man useless who has f., 825a

Furside is outside, 907a
Further, hitherto shalt thou come but no f., 16a
nearer to church f. from God, 183a
Fury, allaying their f., 296b
blind F. with abhorred shears, 338b
civil f. first grew high, 351b
cunning old F., 743b
full of sound and f., 286b
in your words, 275b
like woman scorned, 392a
limitless f., 1016a
ne'er spend f. on child, 216b
no f. like woman searching, 1053a
of disappointed woman, 392a
of patient man, 368b
provides arms, 117b
Queen crimson with f., 744a
slinging flame, 650a
stronger than afterthoughts, 84b
trample them in my f., 33b
white sound to f., 1072a
whole f. and might of enemy, 921a
Fuse, through green f. drives flower, 1070a
Fussy, nobody call me f. man, 969b
Fust in us unused, 264b
Fustest, git thar f. with mostest, 709b
Fustian's so sublimely bad, 410b
Fustilarian, you rampallian you f., 242a
Futile decalogue of mode, 849a
Futility, fatal f. of fact, 799b
utility of f., 101a
Future a mince pie, 1046a
aid to interpretation of f., 89a
all concerned about f., 940b
all f. in mind of man, 843b
America was past not f., 978a
American science thing of f., 815a
as past would be present, 479b
been into f. and it works, 887b
cannot fight f., 631b
democracy shuts past opens f., 617a
dipped into the f., 647a
discoveries in decimals, 827a
divine sign indicates f., 87b
education will determine f. life, 94a
enemies of f., 1017b
enters into us, 938b
faith in f. of mankind, 1082b
find we have lost f., 921a
flight of f. days, 343b
great f. for America, 1074b
hope to world for f., 637a
hopes of the f., 923b
imagining f. years come, 882a
in f. light will shine, 923a-b
in your hands rests f., 982a
instruct as to f., 586a
lays down law of today, 804b
lies with wise political leaders, 972a
like unwelcome guest, 815b
lively sense of f. favors, 356a
loses past and dead for f., 86a
meet f. without fear, 621a
most in league with f., 729b
never plan f. by past, 454b

Future, no way of judging f., 465a
not think about f., 893a
O f. Vigor, 830a
of human race, 942a
optimistic f. of mankind, 834b
philosophy triumphs over f. evils, 355a
Present Past F. sees, 488b
provide for f. better than past, 901a
put f. in debt, 934b
scaffold sways f., 692a
security for the f., 426a
security of f., 741a
serve the f. hour, 517a
something everyone reaches, 1042a
spend rest of lives in f., 940b
till f. dares forget past, 571a
time f. in time past, 1004b
transforms self in us, 938b
trust no f., 620b
wave of f. is coming, 1061b
wave of f. not conquest, 1073b
wings of the f., 994b
Future-directed society, 1059a
Future's, heaven and f. sakes, 928b
Futurity, shadows f. casts on present, 573a
Fuzzy-Wuzzy, 'ere's to you F., 873a

G

G, belong to company G, 755a
Gab, gift of g., 567b
Gabble, geese g. everywhere, 1042b
giggle g. gobble git, 872b
Gaberdine, Jewish g., 232a
Gabriel who bares his horns, 1068b
Gadding vine, 338a
Gadire, bound for Javan or G., 349b
Gaels of Ireland, 918a
Gage, one for all we g., 220a
Gai, toujours g., 946a
Gaiety before death, 1042b-1043a
courage g. and quiet mind, 825a
eclipsed g. of nations, 428b
Gain advantage on kingdom of shore, 292b
better to incur loss than g., 105b
every joy is g., 661b
every way makes my g., 276a
guile and lust of g., 420a
is gain however small, 661b
little patch of ground, 264b
madness of many for g. of few, 389a, 405a
man who in view of g., 72a
my good vain hope of g., 205a
necessity to glorious g., 515a
painful inch to g., 688b
serves and seeks for g., 277b
set down as g. each day, 121a
spent in conquest of Jerusalem, 172b
strength by experience, 981a
the whole world, 43a
those that covet with g. fond, 220a

Gain timely inn, 284b
to die is g., 54a, 93a
to find beautiful soul, 475a
voyage not for g. honor wealth, 174a
Gained, boisterously maintained as g., 236b
from heaven all he wished, 441a
how little g., 650b
no title lost no friend, 407a
something g. for universe, 794a
this by philosophy, 97a
whatever he may have g., 72b
who g. by it, 110b
Gaining, something g. on you, 1048a
Gains, do not seek evil g., 67b
evil g. equivalent of disaster, 67b
light g. make heavy purses, 205a
no g. without pains, 1048a
spirit that g. victory, 987a
Gait, excessive laughter and g., 38a
forced g. of shuffling nag, 239b
Gaiters, gas and g., 669b
Gal, every g. born into world, 767b
Gale and more than g., 876b
catch the driving g., 409b
no g. that blew, 792a
note that swells g., 441a
of life blew high, 853a
partake g., 410a
sun and summer g., 441b
that sweeps from north, 465a
yell for yell to g., 843a
Galen, more than G. cured, 324b
says withstand love's shock, 945a
Galeotto was the book, 160a
Galère, dans la g. d'un Turc, 361b
que diable allait-il faire dans cette g., 361b
Gales, cool g. fan the glade, 402b
set of sails not g., 825b
Galilean, O pale G., 774a
Pilot of the G. lake, 338b
you have conquered G., 144b
Galilee, Sea of G. and Dead Sea, 945a
wave rolls nightly on deep G., 558b
Galileo with his woes, 557a
Gall, bear bonds that g., 774b
enough in thy ink, 253a
I am g. I am heartburn, 804a
lack g., 261b
of bitterness, 49b
take my milk for g., 282a
water of g. to drink, 34a
Gallant, in g. trim vessel goes, 441b
old soldier, 600a
Gallanter I know, 734b
Gallantly streaming, 541a
Gallantry, conscience no more to do with g., 481a
what men call g., 560a
Galled, let g. jade wince, 263b
Galleon, moon ghostly g., 961b
Galleons of Carib fire, 1043a
Gallery of works turned to wall, 724a
what the devil do you do in that g., 361b
Galley, Cervantes on g., 918b

Gentleman, smooth-faced g. Commodity, 236a
  so stout a g., 241a
  take hym for grettest g., 168b
  tea g. at least, 919a
  that loves to hear himself talk, 224b
  very nice g., 1081a
  who was then a g., 1084a
  word of g. and Christian, 195a
  writes well for a g., 397a
Gentleman-like, lovely g. man, 229a
Gentlemen and seamen in navy, 596b
  born to purple, 1026a
  cooks are g., 310b
  distinctions between g. and common people, 101a
  dust was g. and ladies, 736b
  farmers, 561b
  God Almighty's g., 368b
  God rest you merry g., 1099a
  great-hearted g., 662a
  lays eggs for g., 1096b
  like Cerberus three g., 481a
  may cry Peace, 465a
  no ancient g., 265b
  not to forget we are g., 452a
  of England, 328b
  of old regime, 984b
  of the shade, 237b
  prefer blondes, 1027a
  rankers, 873b
  scholars and g., 510a
  three jolly g., 914b
  two g. rolled into one, 499b
  unafraid, 873a
  unhand me g., 259b
  were not seamen, 597a
  what is it the g. wish, 465a
  who wrote with ease, 412a
  whose hair gray, 943a
Gentleness, angling produce g., 326a
  fruit of Spirit is g., 53b
  let g. my strong enforcement be, 248b
  man of g., 179a
  survives, 1082a
Gentler, still g. sister woman, 493b
Gentlier on spirit lies, 645b
Gently, do my spiriting g., 296a
  faults lie g. on him, 299a
  flow g. sweet Afton, 495a
  o'er perfumed sea, 641b
  replacing in oblivion, 739a
  roar you g. as sucking dove, 229a
  scan brother man, 493b
  smiling jaws, 743a
  speak g. she can hear, 838b
  thou and nature so g. part, 289a
  time laid hand g., 624a
  use all g., 262b
Genuine night admits no ray, 369a
  substantial and g. virtue, 471a
  wisdom never dear if g., 658b
Genus, hoc g. omne, 120a
  irritabile vatum, 124a
Geographers crowd edges of maps, 136a
Geographical boundaries or distinctions of race, 705b
  coherent g. unit, 1038b

Geography, desert idle in our g., 1069a
  that my sons study g., 463a
Geometric, he by g. scale, 352a
Geometrical, increases in g. ratio, 502a
  mind, 385a
  universe in g. figures, 211b
Geometrician, grammarian rhetorician g., 139a
Geometry, geometrical mind not bound to g., 385a
  no royal road to g., 103b
  of artist's own, 799a
  shaped by hand of g., 385a
George, England and Saint G., 244a
  for King G. upon throne, 500a
  said his father, 499a
  Saint G. for England, 919a
  Saint G. that swinged dragon, 236a
  the First vile, 934a
  the Second viler, 934a
  the Third honest dullard, 829a
  the Third ought never to have occurred, 934a
  the Third profit by example, 464b
  when G. the Third was king, 122a
  without money G., 1089b
Georgeade summer drink, 886a
George's, St. G. Hanover Square, 756a
Georges, God be praised G. ended, 934a
Georgia booze mighty fine, 1041a
  hell's broke loose in G., 1041b
  marching through G., 748a
Germ of all virtue, 691b
German, achieved as G. soldier, 1012a
  dictator, 920b
  dives into sentence, 761b
  Fatherland, 503b
  for converse with enemies, 435a
  French and G. blood spilled, 979b
  I speak G. to my horse, 163b
  if G. people despair, 1012b
  not even G. culture, 806b
  proud G. army, 924a
  statecraft, 677b
  sturdiness of G. tongue, 435a
  to be G. means, 676b
  unity of G. nation, 1012a
  wherever G. tongue heard, 503b
German-Americans, have done with G., 821b
Germans and women have no depths, 806b
  are like women, 806b
  beastly to the G., 1043a
  fear God nothing else, 677b
  Lord bomb G., 1059a
  to G. the air, 500a
Germany, aggression of G., 1012a
  authoritarian G., 1035b
  England down G. up, 995a
  in the world forward, 815a
  is a nation, 590a
  preeminence in G., 1011b
  Prussia part of G., 586b
  put G. in saddle, 677b
  ruins culture, 806b
  the cause of Hitler, 999a
  world power or not at all, 1012a

Germany's, Rhine G. river, 503b
Germens, all g. spill at once, 278a
Gertrude always right, 1045a
Gesang, Wein Weib und G., 482a
Gesture, distorting my g., 1069a
  each g. a commitment, 1058b
  without motion, 1003a
Gestures, get at thing without g., 956b
Get and beget, 817a
  at enemy as soon as you can, 717a
  at thing without gestures, 956b
  desire to g. on in world, 997a
  easier stay out than g. out, 762b
  from where you are not, 1005b
  men g. and give, 477a
  men take best they can g., 432b
  money still get money, 123a
  out of kitchen, 983a
  that I wear, 249b
  the trick, 762a
  thee behind me, 43a
  thee glass eyes, 279b
  thee to a nunnery, 262a
  there first with most, 709b
  time to g., 27b
  understanding, 23b
  up begin again, 664a
  up sweet slug-a-bed, 320b
  what you want, 878a
  whole world out of bed, 947a
  with child mandrake root, 304b
  writing, 997a
  you g. no more of me, 211a
  you the sons your fathers got, 852a
  you to my lady's chamber, 265b
  you've got to g. up, 999b
Gethsemane had one, 898a
Gets, Dead Sea g. to keep, 945a
  Galilee g. to give, 945a
  him to rest, 244b
  pleased with what he g., 248a
  them that has g., 811a
  up by bell, 759b
Getting along with women, 477a
  and spending, 515b
  better and better, 844b
  Gospel of G. On, 513a
  not g. what one wants, 839b
  on in world, 913a
  on together, 966b
  out of world known before, 913a
  prevent lower from g. more, 98a
  to heaven at last, 735b
  what one wants, 839b
  with all thy g. get understanding, 23b
  youth is the time of g., 351b
Gettysburg can't understand it, 1039b
  pile high at G., 948a
Gewesen, wie es eigentlich g., 586a
Ghastly crew, 525b
  dew, 647a
  grim ancient Raven, 643a
  long and g. kitchen, 675a
  night full of g. dreams, 217a
  trembling cold in g. fears, 488a
  turned face with g. pang, 525a
Ghost, beckoning, 405b
  before not g. of shores, 790a
  come back again, 1049b
  embrace my mother's g., 66a

Ghost escapes from vanquished
　pyre, 128a
　frustrate g., 665a
　guessed, 803b
　he gave up g., 47b
　hollow g., 715a
　lost and by wind grieved g.,
　　1049b
　make g. of him that lets me,
　　259b
　man giveth up the g., 15a
　may spaniel it, 994b
　of deceased Roman Empire,
　　318a
　of garden fronts sea, 776a
　of Hamlet's father, 861a
　of sleighbells, 926b
　of snow, 926b
　please my g., 960b
　some old lover's g., 306b
　thrice the g. fled, 118b
　vex not his g., 280b
　what beckoning g., 405b
　wrought g. upon floor, 642b
　your g. will walk, 663b
Ghosties, ghoulies and g., 1098b
Ghostlier demarcations, 956a
Ghostlike, haunt g. the spot, 614a
Ghostly, brain's old g. house,
　1022a
　galleon, 961b
Ghosts, driven like g., 569b
　from enchanter fleeing, 569b
　haunted by g. deposed, 227b
　knight of g. and shadows, 1086a
　of defunct bodies fly, 352a
　of departed quantities, 399b
　true love is like g., 355a
　walked, 1033b
　we are all g., 729b
Ghoul-haunted woodland of Weir,
　643b
Ghoulies and ghosties, 1098b
G.I. Joe, 1103b
Giant, as when a g. dies, 271a
　Atlas upholds, 84b
　baby figure of g. mass, 268a
　branches tossed, 573b
　Despair, 365b
　dwarf on shoulders of g., 310a
　fling stone g. dies, 418b
　making G. hit into double,
　　962b
　my g. goes with me, 606a
　race before the flood, 371a
　tyrannous to use it like g., 270b
　wings prevent walking, 707a
Giant-dwarf, senior-junior g.,
　221b
Giant's robe, 286a
　strength, 270b
Giants in the earth, 6b
　pygmies on shoulders of g.,
　　134a
　standing upon shoulders of g.,
　　379b
　strength of the ancient g., 66a
　wage war like physical g., 1024b
Gib, melancholy as g. cat, 237b
Gibber, squeak and g., 256b
Gibbets, better schoolrooms than
　g., 686a
　keep lifted hand in awe, 398b
Gibbon, eh Mr. G., 470a
Gibe, call it humor when they g.,
　390a
　of European scholars, 939a
Gibeon, sun stand still upon G.,
　11a

Gibes, where be your g. now,
　265b
Giddy, fancies are more g., 252a
　habitation g. and unsure, 242a
　I am g., 268a
　thinks world turns round, 219b
Giddy-paced, brisk and g. times,
　252a
Gideon Bibles only in bedrooms,
　1018a
　sword of Lord and of G., 11a
Gie me ae spark, 493a
Gift, beauty the g. of God, 97a
　crave of thee g., 557a
　death g. to life, 1056b
　every good g. and perfect g.,
　　56a
　fatal g. of beauty, 557a
　feeling the East's g., 664b
　gauntlet with g., 618b
　given for naught priceless g.,
　　721b
　God's to God, 1056b
　great love goes with little g.,
　　104a
　greatest g. freedom of will,
　　161b
　have the g. to know it, 248b
　hearts not had as g., 882b
　heavenly g. of poesy, 369b
　heaven's last best g., 346a
　immortality not g., 898b
　it is a god who gave you this
　　g., 62b
　love g. of fairy tale, 745a
　manner of giving worth more
　　than g., 331b
　never look g. horse in mouth,
　　146a
　not so much nature of g., 822b
　of excellence to few men, 77a
　of God eternal life, 51a
　of laughter, 938b
　of martyrdom, 370a
　of sleep, 816a
　of the gab, 567b
　of unaffected conversation, 593a
　only g. portion of thyself, 607b
　pretty foot g. of nature, 478a
　reason God's crowning g., 82a
　skilled poet through natural g.,
　　79a
　spirit in which g. offered, 822b
　tablet a g. of memory, 95b
　terrible g. lifted from hearts,
　　708b
　though small is precious, 65b
　time with g. of tears, 773a
　to be well-favored g. of for-
　　tune, 246b
　true love's the g., 518b
　various g. to each, 623a
　what does g. mean, 1056b
　without giver bare, 692b
　woman's g. to rain shower,
　　219a
　word better than g., 38a
　your g. survived all, 1060a
Gifted, poetically g., 713a
Giftie, some power g. gie us, 493a
Gifts, adore my g. instead of me,
　323b
　benefit in g. of bad man, 84a
　cluster of g. experience, 798b
　enjoyed g. of founder, 466a
　fairy g. fading away, 542a
　fear Greeks even when they
　　bring g., 118a
　glorious g. of the gods, 62b

Gifts, gods do not give all men
　g., 65b
　liberality in g., 381b
　more of his grace than g., 300b
　my lady's admirable g., 159a
　no hard g., 994b
　people I cannot win with g.,
　　364b
　presented unto him g., 39b
　rarer g. than gold, 994a
　rich g. wax poor, 262a
　riches to make g. to friends,
　　85a
　seven hundred pounds goot g.,
　　266b
　shining g., 603b
　spend not then his g. in vain,
　　302b
　thank Thee for g. of Thine,
　　720a
　two jars of the g. he gives, 65a
Gig, crew of captain's g., 765b
Gigantic hound, 850a
　press restless g., 984b
　speckled g. flowers, 985a
　willful young, 898b
Gigantically down, 642a, 1043b
Giggle gabble gobble git, 872b
　ha'd to g. w'en nuffin' in pot,
　　911b
Gild refined gold, 236b
Gilded and sticky, 990b
　bit of wood g., 504a
　bricks, 945b
　cage, 903a
　car of day, 336b
　eaves, 648b
　flap bug with g. wings, 411a
　fly does lecher, 279b
　fool, 301b
　gay g. scenes, 392b
　hearse, 1003b
　laugh at g. butterflies, 280a
　not marble nor g. monuments,
　　292a
　vessel goes, 441b
Gilding, stripped of lettering and
　g., 421a-b
Gilds, eternal summer g. them,
　560b
　love g. the scene, 481a
Gilead, no balm in G., 34a
Gills, soul swims without g., 943b
Gilpin long live he, 457b
Gilt, dust that is a little g., 269a
　more laud than g. o'erdusted,
　　269a
　surcingles, 738b
Gimble, gyre and g., 745a
Gin, perhaps it's the g., 1052a
　union of g. and vermouth,
　　1038b
Ginger, board money in g. jar,
　753b
　hot i' the mouth, 252a
　nutmegs g. cinnamon cloves,
　　322a
Gingham, bits of g. and calico,
　820b
　dog went Bowwow, 820b
Gins, snares traps g. pitfalls, 659b
Gipsy, fortune fickle g., 600b
Giraffe in queer gracefulness,
　985a
Gird on sword O man, 801a
　up thy loins like a man, 16a
Girded, father's sword g. on, 542a
　he g. up his loins, 13b
　let loins be g., 47a

God, my G. Father and Friend, 374b
my G. have mercy, 191b
my G. look not so fierce, 213b
my G. why hast thou forsaken me, 17b, 45a
my soul thirsteth for G., 19a
nakedness of woman work of G., 487b
name of G. upon lips, 436a
name called the mighty G., 31a
Nature and Nature's G., 397b
nature is the art of G., 329b
Nature's G., 397b, 410a
nearer my G. to thee, 615b
nearer to church further from G., 183a
ne'er said G. be praised, 617b
nest on greatness of G., 796b
never made work for man to mend, 372a
never spoke with G., 737b
next to of course g., 1030b
no G. and Mary His Mother, 1075b
no G. but He most merciful, 149a
no g. higher than truth, 897b
no g. stronger than death, 774b
no g. wrong worm, 603b
no man hath seen G., 48a
no more Aurora Leighs thank G., 631a
no nearer to G., 1004b
no society bring kingdom of G., 965a
noblest work of G., 409b, 492b
none but G. is near, 518a
none other but the house of G., 7a
nor what G. blessed accursed, 667a
not alone G. is within, 138a
not G. for father if not Church for mother, 144a
not G. he'll catch, 1054a
not G. in gardens, 734a
not G. of dead, 47b
not pay Saturdays, 667b
not serve G. if devil bid, 272a
not to get near G., 809b
not willing to do everything, 177b
not worshiped by herd, 947b
nothing not G. greater than self, 700b
now G. alone knows, 770a
O dog my G., 1068a
O G. O Montreal, 755b
O G. that bread so dear, 592b
O G. that it were possible, 301b
O Lamb of G., 59a
O sole G., 4a
obligeth no man to more than ability, 149a
of battles, 245a
of Clotilda grant victory, 147b
of fathers known of old, 875a
of God, 60a
of Life Creator, 962a
of music out of doors, 830a
of my idolatry, 224a
of Nature, 323b
of Nature placed in power, 465a
of such is kingdom of G., 45b
of the Congo, 953a
of truth, 10b
Omega, 765b

God, on right hand of G., 60a
on seventh day G. ended his work, 5a
on side of best digestion, 946a
on side of big squadrons, 357a
once loved a garden, 969a
one G. even the Father, 544a
one g. greatest among gods, 70b
one G. law element, 651a
one G. one principle of being, 142b
one nation under G., 832b
one that feared G., 14a
only G. and angels lookers-on, 207a
only G. can make tree, 992a
only G. had for asking, 692a
only knows which is which, 776b
or Mother Goose, 844b
others call it G., 667a
our help in ages past, 396b
out in fields with G., 1101b
out of me G. and man, 775b
owe G. a death, 242b
pairs off like with like, 66b
patriarch obedient to G., 705b
peace of G. passeth understanding, 54b
perfect blessedness vision of G., 158b
plays dice with world, 950b
pleased G. to visit us with death, 319a
poor dear G., 1037b
poverty in hand of G., 4b
praise G. sang Theocrite, 662a
presume G. to scan, 408a
pride of peacock glory of G., 487b
pseudonym of G., 802a
purlieu of g. of love, 306b
put G. in his statements, 701b
put hand to ark of G., 458a
reason in man like G. in world, 158b
rebellion obedience to G., 1090b
reflect that G. is just, 471a
register of G., 331a
reigns government lives, 741a
render unto G., 43b
rest you merry, 1099a
rib which Lord G. had taken, 5b
round fat oily man of G., 420a
sacrifice to G. of devil's leavings, 413a
said I am tired, 603a
said Let Newton be, 412b
said Let there be light, 5a
said Let us make man, 5a
saint if G. does not exist, 1068b
save the king, 12a, 401a
save the king say amen, 228a
save the mark, 238b
save the people, 545a
save thee Ancient Mariner, 524b
saw that it was good, 5a
say first of G. above, 407b
says there is no G., 436a
Scourge of G., 212a
sea of infinite substance, 152a
secluded from sight of G., 308b
see G. made and eaten, 664b
seen G. face to face, 7b
sees G. in clouds, 408a
self-reliance is reliance on G., 608a

God send every gentleman, 1088b
sends meat Devil sends cooks, 183a
servant of G. well done, 346b
servant of living G., 444b
served my G. with half the zeal, 299a
service greater than the g., 268a
sets nothing but riddles, 708a
setteth the solitary in families, 19b
shall any teach G., 15b
shall smite thee, 50b
shall wipe away tears, 58b
she for G. in him, 345a
shed grace on thee, 849a
shield us, 230a
sigh in heart, 850b
smiled again, 906b
so commanded, 347b
so loved the world, 48a
so near G. to man, 603b
some lesser g. made world, 654a
something known only to G., 963b
sometimes wish G. back, 866a
Son of G. goes forth, 549a
Son of the living G., 43a
sons of G. shouted for joy, 16a
sons of the living G., 35a
souls are in the hand of G., 36b
souls mounting up to G., 731a
speed the mark, 602b
Spirit of G. descending, 39b
spirit shall return unto G., 29a
standeth G. within shadow, 692a
stands winding horn, 880a
stay with me G., 1103b
stepped out on space, 906b
stern daughter of voice of G., 514b
strong brown g., 1006a
subject to G. and Justice, 155a
take in G., 693a
tempers wind, 188b, 438b
temple of G. is holy, 52a
thank G. for peace, 914a
thank G. for tea, 523b
thank G. I have done duty, 492b
the Father a school divine, 412a
the Father in second place, 834b
the first garden made, 358a
the herdsman goads, 879b
the most resembles G., 493b
the unknown g., 50a
the word spake it, 189a
these old men, 83b
they shall be called children of G., 40a
they shall see G., 40a
think himself act of G., 679a
think not G. at all, 349a
think public opinion voice of G., 764a
this is the finger of G., 8a
this nation under G., 639a
this thing is G., 775b
those G. loves do not live long, 102a
those whom G. hath joined together, 61b
thou art the Son of G., 42b
thought and thought, 906b
three-personed G., 308a
through darkness up to G., 650b

God, through life looked on G., 943b
throws himself on G., 664b
thy G. shall be my G., 11b
'tis G. gives skill, 689a
to the greater glory of G., 186a
too full of G. to speak, 879a
took day to search for G., 860a
toward G. and toward Satan, 707a
trust in G. hope for best, 522b
trust in G. keep powder dry, 539a
truth as old as G., 737a
two halves of G., 598b
unchanging law of G., 657b
unless G. does that beating living thinking, 697b
unutterable sigh, 850b
up to Nature's G., 410a
very G. of very G., 60a
voice of people is voice of G., 152b
walk humbly with thy G., 35b
wants nothing of a g. but eternity, 290a
war blood-swollen g., 904b
was it G. was it man, 775b
was the holy Lamb of G., 490b
ways of G. justifiable, 349a
ways of G. to man, 407b
ways of G. to men, 341b
were I Lord G., 1105a
what G. hath joined, 43a
what hath G. wrought, 10a
what I call G., 667a
what is G. everything, 80a
what kind of g. art thou, 244b
what man not know of G., 1054a
what we have instead of G., 1044a
when G. sorts out weather, 819a
where end knows G., 1050b
where G. built church, 179b
who brought over ocean, 319a
who G. doth late and early pray, 300b
who gave life gave liberty, 470b
who is able to prevail, 325b
who is not we see, 776b
who is our home, 513b
who knows what I would, 1066b
who made him sees, 877b
who made rich make poor, 618b
who made thee mighty, 862a
who make iron grow, 503b
whole armor of G., 54a
whom we see not is, 776b
whose puppets are we, 661b
why St. Augustine thanked G., 936a
will of G. prevail, 716a
will provide himself a lamb, 7a
will put an end to these, 117b
will save her, 852a
wills it, 150b
wills us free, 468b
winepress of wrath of G., 690b
wisheth none wreck, 303a
with G. nothing impossible, 45b
with strongest battalions, 435a
with thousand voices praises G., 526b
with us, 39a
without me G. cannot live, 364b
wonder what G. calls me, 870a
word of G. is quick, 55b

God, word of our G. shall stand, 32b
Word was with G., 47b
worketh in you, 54a
world of nature and G., 1077b
world's G. is treacherous, 994b
worship G. in own way, 973a
would G. this flesh might be, 773b
would have three sides, 414b
wove web of loveliness, 917b
wrath of G., 690b
wrath of lion wisdom of G., 487b
wrote loveliest poem, 942a
wrote of angels and G., 487b
yearning like g., 581b
your false g. dim rememoring, 1010a
your G. is one G., 149a
Zion city of our G., 446a
Goddamm, lhude sing G., 987b
Goddamned, similar g. phrases, 945b
Goddamnedest, seevility of commonest g. kind, 1100a
Goddess, bitch g. Success, 792b
consult concerning great g., 506b
Demeter or Earth, 85a
excellently bright, 302a
mistake young woman for g., 960a
moves a g., 405a
night sable g., 399a
of Grecian woes O g. sing, 405a
of the silver lake, 337b
pasteboard g. of hustings, 934b
to thy shrine we come, 497a
walk revealed her as true g., 118a
White G., 1034b
write about it G., 413b
Goddesses, even if g. too should be looking, 65b
take hold ye gods and g., 63b
Godfathers of heaven's lights, 221a
God-given rights, 616a
God-intoxicated man, 373a
Godless hell's delight, 86ob
Godlike, capability and g. reason, 264b
erect, 345a
power in us still, 710b
to create, 680a
Godliness, cheerful g., 512b
cleanliness next to g., 421a
Godly, old and g. and grave, 880a
thou art fair thou art g., 773a
Godmother, fairy g. in soul, 857a
God's above all, 273b
abusing of G. patience, 267a
acre, 621b
allotment, 783a
arrest, 381b
Caesar's self is G., 354a
crucible, 870b
dare ask just G., 640b
Devil is ever G. ape, 179b
do deed without G. knowledge, 79a
earthly power then likest G., 234a
finger touched, 650b
first creature light, 344b
first temples, 574b
footstool may be throne, 925b
for G. sake sit upon ground, 227b

God's, gift is G. to God, 1056b
gifts put dreams to shame, 618b
great Judgment Seat, 872b
greatness flowed, 617b
greenwood chapel, 953a
hand folks over to G. mercy, 689b
heaven is G. throne, 40b
help and their valor, 504b
here is G. plenty, 372a
I'm under G. arrest, 381b
in his heaven, 661b
issue is in G. hands, 79a
justify G. ways to man, 853b
last Put out the light, 928a
light G. eldest daughter, 333b
man's bedevilment and G., 854a
mill grinds slow, 325a
mouth knows not falsehood, 78b
my spirit in G. hand, 364b
not G. not beasts', 666a
one on G. side majority, 659a
preaching of G. sacred Word, 5a
reason G. crowning gift, 82a
skirts, 662a
spies, 280a
sure they know G. will, 1041b
things which are G., 43b
thy country's thy G. and truth's, 299a
true princes of empire, 696b
voice of G. creatures, 641b
ways to man, 853b
we are in G. hand, 244a
will be done, 468b
woman G. second mistake, 806a
ye are G. husbandry, 52a
Gods, all ages believed in g., 935b
all men have need of g., 65a
angels would be g., 408a
approve the depth, 516b
are just, 280b
are on side of stronger, 140a
are we, 710b
arrive, 603a
as flies to boys we to g., 279a
as psychic factors, 935b
aspiring to be g., 408a
believe in g. of state, 93a
built against will of g., 63b
by Nine G. he swore, 596a
call in vain, 498b
contend in vain, 498b
convenient that there be g., 128b
darling of men and g., 112b
daughter of g., 645b
dish fit for g., 254b
do not give all men gifts, 65b
dwells with g. above, 268b
even if g. should be looking, 65b
execute judgment against g. of Egypt, 8b
fade God abides, 785b
fashioned by men, 867b
fault of angels and g., 406a
fight against necessity, 68b
forbid it sea g., 695b
forget g. are old, 813b
formed world at creation, 537a
glorious gifts of the g., 62b
go in various disguises, 66b
good g. how he will talk, 384b
grant me this, 115a
graven images of her g., 31b
happy who knows rural g., 117a-b
have neither age nor death, 83a

Gold, scarfs garters g., 409a
shall shine like the g., 487b
shines like fire, 79a
shower of g., 576b
silver and g. have I none, 49b
silver threads among g., 815a
singing g., 982a
so thin so pale yet g., 483b
steamers white and g., 876a
that I never see, 853a
therefore lovede g. in special, 166b
thumb of g., 167a
to airy thinness beat, 306a
trodden g., 343a
truth with g. she weighs, 413b
turning to g. all it touches, 730a
wear the g. hat, 1036a
were each wish mint of g., 503a
what female heart g. despise, 439b
what is. doing in holy place, 133b
what's become of g., 665a
wisdom never comes g., 730a
wonder that g. esteemed, 178b
work transmutes humanity into g., 817b
years of g., 813b
Gold-bearing, crushed the g. Medes, 70b
Gold-crowned king, 982a
Golden age exists in imagination, 596b
age is before us, 122b
all in g. afternoon, 743a
Aphrodite, 66a, 68b
apples of sun, 880a
as they did in g. world, 247a
bindest in wreaths thy g. hair, 120b
bough, 883a
bought g. opinions, 282b
bowl be broken, 29a
care, 242b
chain from heaven, 63b
circle of g. year, 646a
crown like a deep well, 228a
days fruitful of g. deeds, 344b
deeds, 344b, 653b
door, 817a
every g. scale, 743a
father held out g. scales, 64b
fretted with g. fire, 261a
friends I had, 853b
gate, 814a
goose with g. eggs, 76b
graduates in g. hair, 648a
hair curl gracefully, 724b
hanging in a g. chain, 344a
her flank g., 1022b
host of g. daffodils, 514b
hours on angel wings, 495a
in mercy of his means, 1070b
is the sand, 823a
Jerusalem the g., 687b
keep g. mean, 121b
key, 336a
lads and girls, 291a
lamps in a green light, 360a
like untuned g. strings women are, 213a
locks to silver turned, 204b
love in a g. bowl, 486b
mean, 121b
miller hath g. thumb, 167a
million g. birds, 830a
mind stoops not, 233a

Golden, nature with g. process, 905a
ope their g. eyes, 290b
opes the iron shuts, 338b
pear, 1095b
prime, 644b
returns the G. Age, 116b
rule is no golden rule, 836b
rule to fit everybody, 753a
rule toward patients, 818a
sands and crystal brooks, 306a
seven g. candlesticks, 57b
silence g., 576b
sleep with g. Aphrodite, 66a
stretches out my g. wing, 486a
sun in g. cup, 884b
sun with g. ball, 991a
time of first love, 498a
track, 953a
tree of life is green, 478b
two g. hours, 586b
Vanity, 1089a
wear a g. sorrow, 298a
what delight without g. Aphrodite, 68b
years of g. deeds, 653b
years return, 570b
Goldengrove unleaving, 803b
Goldenrod, bent g., 1004a
Golden-tongued apostle, 905a
Goldfinches one by one drop, 579a
Goldfish in glass bowl, 904a
Gold-hatted high-bouncing lover, 1036b
Goldsmith, here lies Nolly G., 439a
poet naturalist historian, 432a
Goldsmiths, Grecian g. make, 883a
Golf links lie so near mill, 940b
Golgotha, place called G., 45a
Gondola, swam in a g., 250a
Gone agin Finnigin, 897b
all all are g., 534a
and never must return, 338a
and past help, 295a
aye ages long ago, 582a
before to unknown shore, 534b
before you know me g., 771b
coon, 553b
dead and g. lady, 265a
down drain of eternity, 84a
far away into silent land, 739b
glimmering, 555b
good old cause g., 512a
goodness lives though they are g., 85b
he has departed withdrawn g. away, 110b
heaviness that's g., 297b
heavy change now thou art g., 338a
here and there, 293b
heroic enterprise g., 454a
home art g., 291a
I am g. like the shadow, 21b
I shall be g., 926b
I shan't be g. long, 925b
I would have thee g., 224a
if she's not g., 1097a
into world of light, 362b
like snow on desert g., 629b
line is g. out through all the earth, 17b
mischief past and g., 273a
my life has g., 1081b
not lost but g. before, 130a
odds is g., 288b

Gone, Othello's occupation's g., 275a
poets dead and g., 583b
romantic Ireland's dead and g., 881b
room from which faith g., 1054b
sea discoverers to new worlds have g., 304b
she's g. forever, 280b
soon as she was g. from me, 488a
sweet cheat g., 914b
these things are past and g., 114b
thou art g. and forever, 520a
Thursday come and week g., 325a
to her death, 592b
under earth's lid, 988b
while she comes is g., 898b
wind passeth over it and it is g., 21a
with all his rose, 629a
with the wind, 890a
yes thou art g., 714a
Gonfalon bubble, 962b
Gongs rang loudly, 955b
strong g. groaning, 918b
women struck like g., 1043a
Good, a little fun and g. morrow, 751b
a little work and g. day, 751b
a thing moderately g., 467b
abroad for g. of country, 398a
all g. men, 1100b
all g. to me is lost, 345a
all that's g. and fair, 332b
Americans die go to Paris, 839b
amiable or sweet, 348a
ancient g. uncouth, 692a
and bad angel, 310b
and bad of every land, 679a
and faithful servant, 44a
and truth borrow, 604a
annoyance of g. example, 762b
any g. thing I can do, 531a
any g. thing out of Nazareth, 48a
apothecary, 279b
appreciation of g. life, 1026a
apprehension of the g., 226a
arrived in a g. harbor, 318b
as g. almost kill man as g. book, 340a
as g. be out of world, 392b
as g. in the dark, 320a
as g. luck would have it, 267a
as gold, 670b
as I can be, 821a
as seems beforehand, 689b
ask not g. fortune, 701a
bad book as much labor as g., 1032a
bad himself thought nothing g., 791b
bad indifferent, 374a, 438a
be g. and happy today, 523b
be g. be lonesome, 762b
be g. sweet maid, 691a
be of g. cheer, 42b, 49a
becomes indistinguishable from evil, 1011a
befriend themselves, 83a
best is enemy of g., 417b
best is g. enough, 477b
better made by ill, 208a
bid me good m., 470a
book best of friends, 658a
book lifeblood of spirit, 340a

Good boy am I, 1093a
bringeth thee into a g. land, 10a
but not religious-good, 782b
by evil and g. report, 53b
by quiet natures understood, 882b
call this Friday g., 1005b
cannot come to g., 257b
captive g. attending captain ill, 292b
charm to make bad g., 272a
cheer is best physician, 79b
chief g. and market, 264b
cigar is a smoke, 871b
club assembly of g. fellows, 427b
commodity of g. names, 238a
common g. and public authority, 964a
communicated more abundant, 346a
company good discourse, 326a
constituted for practice of g., 100b
corn wood boards to sell, 605a
counselors lack no clients, 270a
crown g. with brotherhood, 849a
day's work, 423b
deed in naughty world, 235b
deed to say well, 298a
demean selves as g. citizens, 461b
deny us for our g., 287b
depart from evil and do g., 18b
desires be for what is g., 72a
devil have all g. tunes, 475a
die early bad late, 385b
die first, 516a
digestion wait on appetite, 284b
dinner and feasting, 375b
do after g. leave evil, 175a
do all the g. I can, 768a
do all the g. you can, 421a
do g. the right way, 779b
do g. to them that hate you, 40b
doing g. one of professions full, 682b
end of government to do g., 591a
enough to shed blood, 847b
Epicurus set forth highest g., 114a
errors of g. men, 351a
every creature of God is g., 55a
every evil has g., 606b
every g. gift, 56a
everything in world g. for something, 369a
evil be thou my g., 345a
evil which is permitted, 742b
fair and learned and g. as she, 319b
fair is by nature g., 201b
faith toward nations, 461b
familiar creature, 274a
fell into g. ground, 42b
fellows get together, 868b
fences make good neighbors, 926a
fight of faith, 55b
filches my g. name, 274a
finds g. in everything, 247b
five-cent cigar, 829a
for a man that he bear the yoke, 34b
for sore eyes, 390b

Good fortune is god among men, 79a
fortune may be short-lived, 318b
fortune to be born human, 379a
fought a g. fight, 55b
free press g. or bad, 1068b
friend for Jesus' sake, 299b
full of g. nature as egg of meat, 224b
general g. is plea of scoundrel, 491a
gentle beast of a g. conscience, 230b
gentle into that g. night, 1070b
glad of other men's g., 249b
go please the gentle and g., 165b
go with me like g. angels, 298a
God saw that it was g., 5a
gods do not give all men g. looks, 65b
gray head all knew, 651b
gods how he will talk, 384b
great and joyous, 569a
great man inherits, 527a
great poet so g. friend, 371b
half so g. a grace, 270b
hand that made you g., 271b
hanging too g. for him, 365b
happiness the only g., 749b
hard beginning is ending, 183a
Haroun Alraschid, 644b
have no need of advocate, 96b
hay sweet hay, 230a
he our g. will sever, 302b
he who would do g., 491a
hearkeners seldom hear g., 386b
hell full of g. intentions, 154b
hell full of g. meanings, 324b
hell paved with g. intentions, 154b, 324b
help g. wise great, 883a
highest g., 111b, 114a
him that bringeth g. tidings, 33a
hold fast that which is g., 55a
hold thou the g., 650b
honest painful sermon, 375a
how few know own g., 371a
how g. and how pleasant, 22b
how g. man's life, 665a
I am the g. shepherd, 48b
I have g. eye uncle, 245b
if all g. people clever, 785b
if g. why do I yield, 281a
if he had not been born, 44b
ill wind blows no man g., 185b
in everything, 247b
in which mind at rest, 161b
is good east to east, 789b
it is not nor cannot come to g., 257b
jest forever, 238b
joke cannot be criticized, 918b
jolly g. lesson, 875b
judge men by g. fortune, 355b
keep g. tongue in head, 297a
King Arthur, 1098b
King Charles's golden days, 1090a
King Wenceslas, 687b
kissing carrion, 260b
know g. as g., 73a
know what were g. to do, 231b
knowing g. and evil, 5b
lad of mettle a g. boy, 239a
largest universe of g., 794b

Good, law commands that which is g., 462b
law is g., 55a
law is good order, 98b
law of God law of g., 709a
laws lead to better, 436a
laws where state armed, 177a
leave while looking g., 1027a
leaves aside g. and bad, 455b
left country for country's g., 398a
life is g., 994b
life of battle g., 865a
life or g. place, 1061a
listener popular, 941a
literature must do g., 855a
live in world g. or bad, 681a
Lord deliver us, 60b, 1098b
Lord is g., 21a
lose g. we oft might win, 270a
love as much as g. fight, 97b
love g. pursue the worst, 129a
love sought is g., 252b
loves what he is g. at, 380a
luck gayest, 588b
luck giddy maid, 588b
luck in odd numbers, 267a-b
luxury was doing g., 386a
maintain g. government, 485a
make g. thing too common, 241b
maketh sun rise on evil and g., 40b
man and a just, 47b
man does not argue, 75a
man's fortune, 277b
man's love, 250a
man's sin, 438a
man's treasure, 74b
many g. men are poor, 68b
marriage, 938b
Master of All G. Workmen, 872b
meaning g. or bad, 369a
meaning in saying he is a g. man, 232a
men and true, 246b
men desire the g., 98a
men eat that they may live, 87b
men of g. will, 46a, 59a, 1015a
men of ill judgment ignore g., 81a
men to do nothing, 454b
mingled yarn g. and ill, 269b
moral what you feel g. after, 1044b
morrow to our waking souls, 304b
mothers and fathers, 1053b
mouth-filling oath, 240a
music g. to melancholy, 374a
must associate, 452a
my g. vain report of gain, 205a
my religion is to do g., 467b
name better than precious ointment, 28a
name better than riches, 125a
name in man and woman, 274a
name is rather to be chosen, 25b
name like precious ointment, 208a
nature in conversation, 394b
neighbor is great blessing, 67b
neighbor policy, 971a
neighbors, 1104a
neither honesty nor g. fellowship, 238a
never bad man g. service, 453b

Good, never done no g. to me, 874b
never g. to bring bad news, 288a
never g. war or bad peace, 422b
news baits, 350a
news worthy of acceptation, 386b
no evil can happen to g. man, 93a
no physician considers own g., 93b
noble to be g., 645a
noble type of g., 623b
not enough to do g., 779b
not enough to have g. mind, 327b
not g. for swarm not g. for bee, 142b
not g. that man should be alone, 5b
not g. to be without temptations, 726b
not love because g., 861a
not three g. men unhanged, 239a
not to make world g., 681a
nothing either g. or bad, 261a
nothing g. alone, 602a
nothing g. makes complete sense, 1024b
obstinacy in bad cause constancy in g., 329b
of moral evil and of g., 509a
of subjects end of kings, 385b
oft interred with bones, 255b
old age, 7a
old Boston, 858a
old paths where is the g. way, 34a
old times are gone, 563a
old times grand old times, 633b
old times when unhappy, 1105b
one g. custom corrupt, 654a
one g. knowledge, 87b
one g. turn deserves another, 133b
only g. discerns g., 619a
only what is g. in man, 841a
or bad for humankind, 515a
or evil side, 691b
orator a g. man skilled in speaking, 107b
our courtiers were g., 392b
out of g. find evil, 342a
overcome evil with g., 51b
panics produce as much g., 467a
Parent of g., 346a
partial evil universal g., 408b
people all with one accord, 447a
people's g. the highest law, 111b
perseverance in g. cause, 437b
philosophy a g. horse, 448b
play audience pleased, 917a
pleasure ease content, 409b
poet's made as well as born, 303b
portion of g. man's life, 509a
possibilities for g. and evil, 1033b
poverty parts g. company, 521b
prospect of distant g., 370b
provoke to harm, 272a
public good, 151b
public g. and private rights, 480a

Good pun may be admitted, 469a
put on g. behavior, 561b
quiet wise and g., 572b
recognize g. but be barred, 79b
religion g. that teaches g., 467b
relinquish life for g. of country, 504b
reputation valuable, 125a
return g. for evil, 388a
rewarded evil for g., 7b
rewardeth evil for g., 25a
rich in g. works, 55b
right reader of g. poem, 929b
ripe and g. scholar, 299b
sat at g. man's feast, 248b
say not of Beauty she is g., 990a
scent of g. goes against wind, 80a
Scots lords, 1087b
second class of intellect g., 177b
see your g. works, 40a
seize g. fortune, 479a
sense equally distributed, 327a
sense gift of Heaven, 407a
sense in country, 1091a
seven hundred pounds g. gifts, 266b
shall not see when g. cometh, 34a
share the g. man's smile, 449b
shepherd, 48b
Sir Critic g. day, 679b
smell of old clothes, 993b
so absolutely g. is truth, 667b
so much g. in worst of us, 789b
society good life, 913a
Soldier best novel, 1075b
some g. some so-so, 135a
some said It might do g., 365b
so-so is g., 250b
soul remembering my g. friends, 227a
speed to your youthful valor, 119b
spinning fates g. or evil, 793a
strong and of g. courage, 10b
strong thick stupefying, 664b
substantial world pure and g., 515b
sum of g. government, 472a
supremacy of g., 867a
sustain g. fortune, 355a
taste and see that the Lord is g., 18b
tendency to g. like water, 100b
that horn and every g., 882b
that might have been, 797b
the g. I do not, 51a
the G. lies so near, 479a
the gods provide thee, 371b
them that call evil g., 30b
there is no man so g., 191a
they are g. they are bad, 846a
thing when an't woman's, 669a
things fruits of originality, 619b
things not had singly, 536a
things strive to dwell, 296b
things which belong to prosperity, 208a
third glass for g. humor, 394b
this world's g., 57a
thought to aim at some g., 97b
time coming, 521a, 677a
to be born on, 694a
to be merry and wise, 182a, 496b, 753a

Good, to do g. and to communicate, 56a
to forgive, 668a
today better tomorrow, 616b
too g. for any but anglers, 326b
too g. to be true, 386b
too much of g. thing, 194a
traced lives of g. men, 517a
tree of knowledge of g. and evil, 5b
trust that somehow g., 650b
two nations g. bad, 360a
unconscious the source of g., 936a
undefined g. thirsted for, 544a
universal common g., 964a
value it next to g. conscience, 326b
vote and act to bring g., 794b
want power, 568b
war slays g. man always, 82b
wastes and withers there, 841a
we know the g., 84b
week's labor, 314a
what do I care you are g., 707a
what a g. boy am I, 1093a
what g. came of it, 532a
what g. can painting do, 947b
what g. from you has come, 505b
whatsoever things are of g. report, 54b
when all men's g., 646a
when Fortune means most g., 236b
when g. men die, 85b
when she was g., 625a
when were g. in majority, 684a
whether benevolence g., 726b
whether it be g. or evil, 29a
why g. words ne'er said, 809b
wine a good creature, 274a
wine needs no bush, 127a
wiser being g. than bad, 666b
without three g. friends, 249b
wits jump, 197a
woman if five thousand a year, 660a
words worth much, 324a
work together for g., 51a
world kills the g., 1044b
write g. in dust, 178b
writing as g. as it is dramatic, 929b
yes to everything g., 794b
Good-bye and keep cold, 927b
brothers, 843a
can scarcely bid g., 586a
God bless you, 820a
leave them laughing when say g., 944a
like g. to statue, 1044a
more than word for g., 1030a
night g., 843b
Piccadilly, 934a
proud world, 601b
reap sowing and so g., 751b
to all that, 1034b
to bar and moaning, 691a
Goodbyes, holy glimmers of g., 1028b
Goodest man ever you saw, 819b
Goodfellowship, nauseous sham g., 837b
Good-humored stomach, 130b
Goodliest, Adam the g. man, 345a
among press of knights, 176a
Goodliness is as the flower of the field, 32b

Grievous pleasure and pain, 774a
  remembrance of them is g., 61a
  roar, 530b
Grievously, sins most g. committed, 61a
Griffith, met by Mr. G., 395a
Grim and ancient Raven, 643a
  brow g. mouth prim, 1004b
  death, 316a
  Death my son and foe, 344a
  heaven not g., 668a
  hushed in g. repose, 441b
  king's dog, 83b
  shape towered up, 510a
  wolf with privy paw, 338b
Grimace, accelerated g., 988a
Grimaces called laughter, 318a
Grimm, Rousseau conceive how G., 593b
Grimness, no graveyard g. when I am gone, 107a
Grim-visaged comfortless Despair, 439b
  war smoothed his front, 216b
Grin, all Nature wears one g., 424a
  bear and g., 722b
  devil did g., 526b
  draws out coffin nail, 468b
  ending with the g., 744a
  how cheerfully seems to g., 743a
  owned with a g., 533a
  remained after rest gone, 744a
  universal g., 424a
Grind, ax to g., 545a
  bones to make bread, 1098a
  demd horrid g., 669b
  exceeding small, 329a
  faces of the poor, 30a
  in mill of truism, 605b
  laws g. the poor, 448a
  mills of God g. slowly, 329a
  souls in self-same mill, 807a
  with water that's past, 324a
Grinders cease, 28b
Grinding, sound of the g. is low, 29a
  up lives, 922b-923a
Grinds, God's mill g. slow, 325a
Grindstone, hold noses to g., 183a
Grinning, mock your own g., 265b
Grip, got a middlin' tight g., 778b
Griping griefs heart wound, 1084b
Grisilda, in trust to fynde G., 168b
Grisly gang, 923a
Gristle, a people still in the g., 452b
Grizzled, his beard was g., 258a
  his hair just g., 367b
Groan, condemned alike to g., 439b
  hear each other g., 582b
  of martyr's woe, 490a
  scarcely howl or g., 746b
  sinks with bubbling g., 557b
  spirit fled with g., 119b
  weep no more nor g., 313a
Groaned, my mother g., 489b
Groaneth, whole creation g., 51a
Groaning, strong gongs g., 918b
Groans, cackles g. and dies, 573b
  more loudly than empty stomach, 972b
  shrieks and g. of wounded, 705a
  sovereign of sighs and g., 221b
Groceries, buying clothes and g., 948b

Grog they dreamed they swallowed, 961b
Groined aisles of Rome, 602a
Gromboolian, great G. plain, 674a
Groove, freight proportioned to g., 739b
Grooves, ringing g. of change, 647b
Gross and scope of my opinion, 256b
  flesh sinks downward, 228b
  gratitude among g. people, 429a
  not g. to sink but light, 220a
  population violent and g., 725a
  scarce so g. as beetles, 279b
  things rank and g., 257b
  two g. broken statues, 988a
Grossest superstitions, 628b
Grossly, decay doth g. close it in, 235b
  err as g. as the few, 368b
Grossness, lost evil by losing g., 454a
Grosvenor Gallery young man, 767a
Grotesque, so striking and g., 596a
Grotius, celebrities such as G., 749b
Ground, acre of barren g., 296a
  all seated on the g., 384a
  another man's g., 267a
  army supported by aviation, 1026a
  as water spilt on the g., 12b
  beat the g., 336b
  betwixt stirrup and g., 197b
  bit of g. to call own, 733b
  Cain was tiller of g., 6a
  call it holy g., 573b
  cannot dedicate this g., 639a
  choose g. take thy rest, 563b
  Christian g., 414a
  color of g. in him, 827a
  crushed to g. diffuse sweets, 208a
  dark and bloody g., 704b
  drops earliest to g., 234a
  exiled on g. in jeers, 707a
  fallen unto me in a fair g., 17a
  Fame's camping g., 704b
  fell into good g., 42b
  four thousand miles deep, 733b
  gain little patch of g., 264b
  gazes on the g., 826b
  grow on Irish g., 1090b
  hallowed g., 1026a
  haunted holy g., 555b
  holy g. where they trod, 573b
  hunting g. for ambitions, 1049a
  in mill of conventional, 798a
  into the sea upon dry g., 8b
  kings sat down upon the g., 38a
  look down to test g., 1056a
  lose g. won today, 712a
  massa's in cold g., 727b
  miles of fertile g., 523b
  more malign with bad seed, 161b
  my lodging is on cold g., 401a
  my tail go to the g., 182b
  neither g. for feet, 702b
  on g. between two stools, 182b
  on the g. the purple flower, 69b
  passion that left g., 665b
  place whereon thou standest is holy g., 8a
  plat of rising g., 335b
  rage outside happy g., 714a
  rope just above g., 980b

Ground, sorrow holy g., 841a
  stand on own g., 679a
  stand your g., 455a
  stood firm on dry g., 10b
  stood like trees in g., 702b
  swalloweth g. with fierceness, 16b
  till thou return unto the g., 6a
  to own a bit of g., 733a
  Tom Tiddler's g., 686a
  tract of inland g., 516b
  tread on classic g., 393a
  vantage g. of truth, 113a
  willing to quit g., 468b
Groundlings, split ears of g., 262b
Grounds, fight on landing g., 921a
Group action in g. problems, 915a
  of willful men, 842a
Grove, but cloud and like shady g., 487a
  court the camp the g., 518b
  meadow g. and stream, 513a
  no quiet g., 482a
  olive g. of Academe, 348b
  shade which g. of myrtles made, 309a
  spicy g. cinnamon tree, 1053a
Grovel, mediocre and you g., 460a
Groveled here long enough, 702b
Groves are of laurel, 477a
  forsake her Cyprian g., 371a
  God's first temples, 574b
  green g. of the blest, 119a
  o'er shady g. they hover, 315a
  of Academe, 124a
  valleys g. hills fields, 212a
Grow, all things g. old, 97a
  asked how pearls did g., 320a
  cannot g. by inch, 884b
  consider lilies how they g., 41a
  corn and taters g., 828b
  enter to g. in wisdom, 751b
  forever and forever, 648b
  from grass I love, 701a
  grass will g. in streets, 931a
  green g. the rashes O, 493b
  hatched would g. mischievous, 254a
  heads g. beneath shoulders, 272b
  in place of one, 389b
  into likeness of bad men, 96a
  learn but not wiser g., 388a
  liberties not made but g., 819b
  like a cedar in Lebanon, 21a
  like savages, 245a
  lopped tree may g. again, 80b
  love's mysteries in souls g., 306b
  makes not fresh nor g. again, 313a
  my wrath did g., 489b
  oaks from acorns g., 151a, 507a
  old along with me, 666a
  on Irish ground, 1090b
  out at heels, 277b
  pastime and happiness g., 515b
  pinks that g., 271b
  poets by sufferings g., 353b
  riches g. in hell, 343a
  roses and white lilies g., 300a
  ruin to make them g., 615a
  say which grain will g., 281a
  she can hear daisies g., 838b
  so be it when I g. old, 511b
  straight in strength of spirit, 775b
  to what they seem, 447b
  trees g. up again quickly, 80b
  trees that g. fair, 876b

Hand that is honest and hearty, 518a
　that made us is divine, 393a
　that made you fair, 271b
　that rocks cradle, 699b
　that rounded Peter's dome, 602a
　that signed the paper, 1070a
　there shall thy h. lead me, 23a
　things made by human h., 940a
　this living h., 581b
　thou openest thine h., 23a
　three lilies in her h., 731a
　thy h. great Anarch, 414a
　thy h. presseth me sore, 18b
　thy right h. shall hold me, 23a
　till some blind h., 489a
　time hath taming h., 597b
　Time's fell h., 292b
　to execute, 466a, 1091b
　took his icy h., 679b
　touch of vanished h., 648a
　tricks by sleight of h., 391b
　under whose cautious h., 702a
　unfriendly to tyrants, 362a
　Uzzah put forth his h., 458a
　vacant heart h. eye, 521a
　wash blood from my h., 283b
　waved her lily h., 401a
　we are in God's h., 244a
　what h. dare seize fire, 489a
　what immortal h. or eye, 489a
　what thy right h. doeth, 40b
　whatsoever thou takest in h., 37b
　with my h. on his head, 617b
　with your staff in your h., 8b
　withhold not thine h. in the evening, 28b
　work of thy h., 33b
Handclasp's a little stronger, 914a
Handed in his checks, 769b
　me my being's worth, 739a
Handel, not care candle for H., 535b
　scarcely fit to hold candle, 415a
Handfasting, this we call h., 521b
Hand-flung spears, 677a
Handful o' things I know, 778b
　of divine inert, 696b
　of dust, 1002b
　of gray ashes, 719b
　of meal in a barrel, 13a
　of sand, 1040a
　of silver, 662b
　of stars, 989b
　with quietness, 27b
　zodiac, 1070a
Handfuls, give me h. of lilies, 119a
Handicap, poverty is h., 982b-983a
Handiwork, firmament showeth his h., 17b
　you give to God, 826b
Handkerchief, holding pocket h., 746a
　of the Lord, 700a
Handle, grasp by blade or h., 694b
　jug without h., 673b
　knife for which h. missing, 470a
　lie a h. fits all tools, 634a
　of big front door, 766a
　right and wrong h. to everything, 139a
　such as h. harp and organ, 6b
　touch not h. not, 54b
　toward my hand, 283a

Handlebar moustaches on Czar, 1076a
Handled, vessels oft h. brightly shine, 213a
　with a chain, 735b
Handler, nation's freight h., 948a
Handles, everything has two h., 139a
Handling, tuning lyre and h. harp, 77b
Handmaid, Nature's h. Art, 367a
　philosophy h. to religion, 207a
　riches good h. worst mistress, 207b
　thrift h. of enterprise, 976b
Handmaiden, low estate of his h., 45b
Hands and eyes and heart, 557a
　and hearts, 216a
　and then take h., 296a
　are four, 1032a
　as bands, 28a
　bear thee up in their h., 20b
　believe in fairies clap h., 858a
　blesseth with two happy h., 201b
　blue, 673a
　by fairy h. knell rung, 443a
　by foreign h. eyes closed, 406a
　clasps with crooked h., 651a
　clean h. and pure heart, 18a
　come knit h., 336b
　country defended by h., 655b
　degenerate into h. like mine, 560b
　diadems and fagots in h., 603b
　entergraft our h., 306b
　establish the work of our h., 20b
　failing h., 912b
　fasten h. upon hearts, 854a
　Father into thy h., 47b
　fetching with full h., 700a
　fold h. and wait, 770b
　folding of the h. to sleep, 23b
　fruit of her h., 27a
　greedy h., 635b
　had put instead, 1060a
　hath not a Jew h., 233b
　his h. formed the dry land, 21a
　hold much of heat, 1009b
　horny h. of toil, 691b
　idle h., 396b
　in h. not of few but many, 89b
　in your h. rests future, 982a
　into thy h. I commend my spirit, 47b
　invisible h. restore year, 992a
　issue is in God's h., 79a
　kills Scots washes his h., 239a
　large and sinewy h., 621a
　lay soul in her h., 699a
　little h. make pretense, 743a
　little h. never made, 396b
　made before knives, 390b
　many h. make light work, 185a
　musket molds in his h., 820b
　my own fair h., 388b
　nearer than h. and feet, 654b
　nobody has such small h., 1031a
　not hearts, 275a
　not in h. of boys, 1028b
　not without men's h., 689a
　of Esau, 7a
　of memory weave, 778a
　of sisters Death and Night, 702a
　one thinks of all the h., 1001b
　oozing out at palm of h., 481a

Hands, pale h. I loved, 871a
　Pilate washed h., 44b
　plunge h. in water, 1059b
　predatory human h., 851b
　rarely escapes injuring own h., 75a
　restless violent h., 899a
　right h. of fellowship, 53b
　rosy h. in steam, 1079a
　savings in h. of one, 831b
　shake h. forever, 211b
　something from our h., 517a
　soul clap h. and sing, 882b
　soul in firm white h., 910a
　speak h. for me, 254b
　strength without h. to smite, 773a
　temples made with h., 50a
　that rod of empire, 440b
　that work on us, 938b
　that wove shirt of flame, 1007a
　true faith ready h., 690b
　union of h. and hearts, 356b
　wave h. for mute farewell, 704a
　weak h. mighty heart, 571b
　what h. you would hold, 535b
　whirling h. at noon, 1056b
　with Pilate wash your h., 228a
　work h. from day to day, 1062a
　wounds in thine h., 36a
Handsaw, know hawk from h., 261a
Handsome as bull that kidnapped Europa, 111a
　big-boned and hardy-h., 803a
　his figure is h., 780a
　house to lodge friend, 411b
　in three hundred pounds, 267a
　is that handsome does, 448a
　Jesus a h. man, 1030a
　man but gay deceiver, 499b
　not h. at twenty, 324b
　others more h. by far, 942a
　property, 733b
　rather be h. than homely, 812b
　some women h. without adornment, 111a
　strong rich or wise, 324b
　ugly thinks herself h., 415b
　wee thing, 495a
　with my mourning very h., 376a
Handsomely, have merit h. allowed, 433b
Handspike, fate is the h., 697b
Handwriting on the wall, 1018a
Handy, with girls be h., 1090a
Handy-dandy which is the justice, 279b
Hang calf's skin on limbs, 236a
　clothes on hickory limb, 1103a
　feel his title h. loose, 286a
　go h. yourselves critics, 181b
　in their own straps, 251a
　it all Robert Browning, 988b
　like icicle on beard, 252b
　loop to h. doubt on, 275a
　my harp on willow-tree, 1100b
　not h. myself today, 919a
　out our banners, 286b
　pearl in cowslip's ear, 229a
　rope enough h. yourselves, 181b
　she would h. on him, 257b
　sorrow, 247a
　that jurymen may dine, 404b
　them on horns of the moon, 289b
　them up in silent icicles, 526a

Hang themselves in hope one will cut halter, 333b
there like fruit my soul, 291a
together or hang separately, 423a
up philosophy, 225a
upon his penthouse lid, 281a
us every mother's son, 229a
when icicles h. by the wall, 222b
yellow leaves do h., 29b
Hanged, house of a man h., 195a
I'll be h., 238b
knows he is to be h., 432b
longed to see him h., 901b
millstone h. about neck, 47a
my poor fool is h., 280b
our harps upon willows, 22b
that horses not be stolen, 376b
they h. Haman, 14a
when skies are h., 1032a
Hangin' Danny Deever, 873a
men and women there, 1091a
Hanging and wiving by destiny, 182b
around in world, 930a
around till you've caught on, 930a
breathless on thy fate, 622b
Danny Deever, 873a
Gardens were dream, 933b
in a golden chain, 344a
likewise destiny, 182b
men and women there, 1091a
not deserve h., 191a
too good for him, 365b
worst use for man, 301a
Hangman, if I were a h., 610b
Hangman's, fear of hell's a h. whip, 312a
Hangover became part of day, 1037a
Hangs as mute on Tara's walls, 541b
blossom that h. on bough, 297b
bodiless as false dawn, 1078b
goose h. high, 1100a
he h. between in doubt, 408b
head for shame, 720a
in clear green bell, 704a
in uncertain balance, 206a
on Dian's temple, 290a
on princes' favors, 298b
tail h. down behind, 874b
thereby h. a tale, 181b, 219b, 248b
upon cheek of night, 223a
what h. in balance nowise in doubt, 1014b
Hank of hair, 875a
Hannah, amount to H. Cook, 1102a
God and me, 749b
Hannibal is at the gates, 151a
know how to win victory H., 106a
put H. in the scales, 139b
Hanover, famous H. city, 662a
St. George's H. Square, 756a
Hans Breitman gife a barty, 723b
Hansom, helped to h. outside, 1059a
Hap, from better h. to worse, 210b
my hope my h. my love, 193b
Ha'penny will do, 1098b
Hapless sons of clay, 627b
Haply I think on thee, 292a

Happen, accidents which started to h. to somebody else, 946a
cannot tell what will h., 863b
it can't h. here, 987a
lies at last letting it h., 1079b
things you do not hope h., 106a
we's nuts and things h., 1009a
Happened, good book h. to you, 1044b
history tell how it h., 386a
nothing ever h. at all, 761a
put down what really h., 1044b
this could have h. once 666b
what men believe h., 1017a
Happening, being and h., 1061a
funny if h. to somebody else, 954a
Happens, future in us before it h., 938b
nothing h. unless first a dream, 948b
too much h., 1039a
trouble h. to others, 946b
trouble h. to you, 946a
truth h. to idea, 795a
unexpected always h., 106a
whatever h. h. as it should, 141b
Happier air, 714b
envy of less h. lands, 226b
family h. for his presence, 825a
I am h. than I know, 347a
in passion we feel, 356a
people capable of being h., 1014b
remembering h. things, 647a
the one who goes is h., 722a
those who feel love most are h., 569a
to be dead, 603b
Happiest conversation no competition, 431b
day happiest hour, 641a
heart that ever beat, 813a
intellection, 1079a
martini one of h. marriages, 1038b
nations no history, 689b
of mortals, 417a
time of New Year, 645a
treatise of natural education, 436a
women have no history, 689b
Happily, plenty to live on h., 983a
Happiness activity in accordance with excellence, 98a
avarice and h., 421b
being's end and aim, 409b
beneficial for body, 908a
care of life and h., 472b
ceases like dream, 328b
consume h., 836a
counting upon h., 584b
depends less on exterior things, 456b
efforts to create h., 958a
envy no man's h., 249b
eternal h. above in heaven, 5a
every human seeking h., 888b
freedom secret of h., 90a
friendship essential for h., 818b
great task of h., 824a
greatest degree of h., 446a
greatest h. for greatest numbers, 416b
habit takes place of h., 593b
hairbreadth missings of h., 424b

Happiness, health foundation of h., 613a
hope for h. beyond life, 467b
in hands of others, 539b
in married estate, 333b
is of retired nature, 394a
ivrywhere excipt where people, 891b
jealous possessions of h., 897b
keep h. in store for society, 958a
liberty secret of h., 832b
lifetime of h. hell, 836b
look into h. through another's eyes, 250b
made of minute fractions, 530a
make ourselves worthy of h., 445b
makes up in height, 928b
mistaken path to h., 564a
no h. perfect as martyr's, 863b
no h. where no wisdom, 82b
no man bear lifetime of h., 836b
not in multitude of friends, 302a
not suffer from scientific holiday, 966b
not write down h., 802a
object of government h., 949b
of common man, 949b
of human race, 453b
of nobody but dictators, 1035b
of peoples, 802a
of society end of government, 463b
on earth no sure h., 200b
on terrestrial ball, 1051b
pastime and our h., 515b
politics art of human h., 871a
principles to effect h., 470b
produced by good tavern, 432a
pursuing and obtaining h., 446a
pursuit of h., 470b, 973a
regret or secret h., 816b
religion assures final h., 834b
result h., 671b
result of man's effort, 958a
rhyming gives men h., 412b
rob of illusion rob of h., 729b
search for human h., 1019b
secret of h. freedom, 90a
she does not find, 427b
sum of human h., 966a
supreme h. of life, 599a
talk h., 825b
tender h. betray, 515a
that makes heart afraid, 592a
the only good, 749b
thirst after h., 436b
to be dissolved into something great, 939b
to crave h. is revolt, 729a-b
too swiftly flies, 439b
two foes of human h., 564a
what right have we to h., 729b
wherein lies h., 580b
wine of rarest vintage, 878a
work out h. for selves, 544b
Happy a health unto the h., 869a
a man as any in world, 375a
accident, 314a, 960a
age when idle with impunity, 550a
alchemy of mind, 418b
and I wrote my h. songs, 486b
as a lover, 515a
as grass was green, 1070b
as heart was long, 1070b

Hard, when h. up pawn intelligence, 1030b
Hard-boiled as picnic egg, 1035b
Hardened, he h. Pharaoh's heart, 8a
Hardens and grows cold, 1062a
  it h. a' within, 493b
Harder, heart h. than stone, 67a
  nothing h. than indifference, 747b
Hardest, first hundred years h., 941a
  first step is h., 418b
  is being taken in, 722b
  knife ill-used, 293a
  of all to close hand, 805a
  softest things overcome h., 74a-b
Hard-favored rage, 243b
Hardihood, dauntless h., 721a
  endurance courage, 896a
Hardiness, herein friendliness h. love, 174b-175a
Hardship, godlike h., 579b
  meet any h., 1072b
  morale not destroyed by h., 959a
  our garment, 921b
Hardships, to stars through h., 150a
  unknown h. we suffered, 1022b
Hard-working ancestry, 1027a
Hardy as Nemean lion's nerve, 259b
  breast, 692a
  kiss me H., 492b
  Thomas H. lie in Mellstock now, 783b
Hardy-handsome, big-boned and h., 803a
Hare and tortoise, 75b
  hold with h. run with hound, 183b
  limped trembling, 581b
  mad March h., 176a
  March H. went on, 744a
  of whom proverb goes, 236a
  rouse lion than start h., 238b
  today on the flesh of a h., 1083b
Harebells, heath and h., 685b
Harebrained chatter, 613a
Hares, little hunted h., 906a
  pull dead lions by beard, 236a
Hark ah the nightingale, 712b
  deep sound strikes, 556a
  don't ye hear it, 517b
  hark dogs do bark, 1097b
  hark my soul, 676b
  hark the lark, 290b
  the herald angels sing, 425b
  to exiled son's appeal, 781b
Harlot's cry, 490a
  youthful h. curse, 489b
Harlots, ye h. sleep at ease, 405b
Harm, content with my h., 249b
  didn't want to h. the man, 1081a
  do h. to other nations, 1050a
  do me no h., 546a
  do not h. subtle wreath of hair, 306b
  does h. to another, 67b
  does h. to my wit, 251a
  fate cannot h. me, 523b
  flea does all h. he can, 308a
  good provoke to h., 272a
  no h. in being wrong, 977a
  no h. in painting for fun, 947b
  no one h. man who does self no wrong, 144b

Harm, none shall h. Macbeth, 285b
  nothing do much h., 1033a
  once h. has been done, 64a
  thy h. dost feed, 1084a
  to one harm to all, 753a
  whether benevolence good or h., 726b
  win us to our harm, 281a
Harmful, more h. than reasoned errors, 725b
  to growth of art and science, 1028a
Harmless as doves, 42a
  drudge, 427b
  entertains the h. day, 300b
  inoffensive aristocracy, 634b
  necessary cat, 234a
  pleasure, 428b
Harmonies, tumult of mighty h., 570a
Harmonious and humane life, 716b
  dulcet and h. breath, 229a
  madness from my lips, 570b
Harmoniously confused, 405a
Harmonizes natural and artificial, 529a
Harmony, absolute h., 1055a
  attention like deep h., 226b
  beauty is h., 747b
  between tides and life, 829a
  cultivate peace and h., 461b
  disposed to h., 535a
  famous h. of leaves, 880a
  for thee O Universe, 142a
  from h. from heavenly h., 370a
  hidden soul of h., 335b
  I don't want h., 708a
  in discord, 123b
  is pure love, 211a
  like h. in music, 510a
  makes heaven drowsy with h., 222a
  more h. in her bright eye, 358b
  music wherever there is h., 330a
  not understood, 408a
  of leaves, 880a
  of the whole universe, 178a
  order proportion, 330a
  perceived h. of object, 528a
  power of h., 509a
  spirit and instinct in h., 936b
  such h. in immortal souls, 235b
  too high a price for h., 708a
  touches of sweet h., 235b
  universal h., 709a
  what becomes of h., 708a
Harms, beg often our own h., 287b
  himself who does harm, 67b
  took not for thy h., 856b
Harness, battle h., 924b
  die with h. on our back, 286b
  died in h., 924a
  gives h. bells shake, 927b
  him that girdeth on his h., 13b
Harnessed, three together h., 505b
Harnessing power of universe, 982b
Harold stands on place of skulls, 555b
Haroun, good H. Alraschid, 644b
Harp, as harper lays palm on h., 624a
  hang h. on willow-tree, 1100b
  no h. like my own, 537b
  not on that string, 217b
  once the h. of Innisfail, 537b

Harp, one clear h., 649b
  such as handle h., 6b
  that once through Tara's halls, 541b
  thunder h. of pines, 740b
  tuning lyre and handling h., 77b
  wild h. slung behind him, 542a
Harper, as h. lays palm on harp, 624a
  wind grand old h., 740b
Harping, still h. on my daughter, 260b
Harps, hanged h. upon willows, 22b
  of gold, 657b
  played before the Lord on h., 12b
Harpsichord, old tune on h., 931b
Harris, words she spoke of Mrs. H., 670b
Harrow house of dead, 1059b
  rust to the h., 914b
  toad beneath h., 871b
  up thy soul, 259b
Harrowing clods, 784a
Harry, cry God for H., 244a
  Harry succeeds, 242b
  little touch of H., 244b
  such as King H., 211a
  these were swift to h., 987b
  young H. with beaver on, 240a
Harsh as truth, 615b
  berries h. and crude, 338a
  cadence of a rugged line, 369b
  ego serves three h. masters, 834a
  in this h. world, 266b
  nor h. nor grating, 509b
  out of tune and h., 262b
  philosophy not h., 337a
  school in which nothing h., 148b
  words of Mercury are h., 223a
Harsher, qualify war in h. terms, 705a
Harshly, strings untouched will h. jar, 213a
Harshness is for good of boy, 379a
  no h. gives offense, 403b
Hart, as h. panteth after water brooks, 19a
  as pants the h., 384a
  be thou like to a young h., 30a
  lame man leap as an h., 32a
  ungalled play, 263b
Harvard, always tell H. man, 1102a
  fair H., 566a
  Greek islands over H. Square, 1042a
  Law School, 967b
  whaleship my H., 696b
Harvest, earth laughs with h., 610b
  gathereth her food in the h., 23b
  God comes as sheaves in h., 308b
  home, 238a, 655b
  is past, 34a
  moon, 386a
  no h. but a thorn, 323a
  of a quiet eye, 511a
  reap the h. of your land, 9b
  seedtime and h., 6b
  shalt not gather the gleanings of h., 9b
  this was all the h. I reaped, 630a

Hearts, while your h. are yearning, 917a
wine unto those of heavy h., 26b
with your hands your h., 216a
wore at h. the fire's center, 1067b
write upon h. of men, 497a
Heartsease, infinite h., 244b
Heart-shaped leaves of green, 931b
Heartsick hand workers, 753a
Heart-stifled, die h., 582a
Heartstrings are a lute, 641b
though jesses my dear h., 274b
Heartthrobs, count time by h., 679a
Heart-whole, warrant him h., 250a
Heart-wounded, sank h., 992a
Hearty, hand that is honest and h., 518a
humble and h. thanks, 60b
old man, 531b
Heat as mode of motion, 705a
burden and h. of day, 43b
cold and h., 6b
fantastic summer's h., 226a
fear no more h. o' the sun, 291a
hands hold much of h., 1009b
if you can't stand h., 983a
I'll shade him from h., 487a
in very sod, 687b
makes h. when he desires, 3b
mechanical equivalent of h., 795b
neither h. affection limb, 271a
neither h. nor light, 315a
neither sun light on them nor h., 58a
no strength exerted on h., 1075a
not furnace for foe, 298a
not see when h. cometh, 34a-b
not snow nor rain nor h., 87a
of conflict, 515a
one draught above h., 251a
one h. drive out another, 205b
Promethean h., 276a
race not without h., 340a
surprised was I with sudden h., 210b
there is nothing hid from the h., 17b
which made my heart to glow, 210b
Heated in the chase, 384a
Heath and harebells, 685b
best felt not clearly seen, 783a
brown h. and shaggy wood, 519a
foot on my native h., 521a
in airy rings skim h., 405a
in the desert, 34a
sword sung on barren h., 488a
Heathen Chinee, 769b
heart that puts trust, 875b
in his blindness, 549b
pore benighted h., 873a
virtues of h. splendid vices, 143b
why do the h. rage, 17a
Heather, know how h. looks, 737b
Heaths, game on these lone h., 539b
Heating, warm without h., 399b
Heat-oppressed brain, 283a

Heaven about to confer great office, 100b
above road below, 824a
all h. around us, 542b
all h. before mine eyes, 336a
all hell that is not h., 213a
all I ask h. above, 824a
all places distant from h. alike, 311b
all things in h., 54b
all this and h. too, 386b
all we hope in h., 641a
alone given away, 692a
and Charing Cross, 857a
and earth in ashes, 157b
and earth pass away, 44a, 519a
and future's sakes, 928b
and home, 517a
and nature sing, 397a
angels in h. above, 644a
as it is in h., 40b
as the h. is high, 21a
ascended into h., 60a
awful rainbow in h., 581b
blazing into head, 884b
breadth of h. betwixt, 618a
brightest h. of invention, 243a
by h. I do love, 222a
call h. and earth to witness, 290a
care of h., 409a
clear religion of h., 580b
combined essences of h. and earth, 110a
commences ere world past, 449a
confess yourself to h., 264a
court it in shape of h., 259b
crawling between h. and earth, 262a
dances in sight of h., 1079a
did recompense send, 441a
differ as h. and hell, 653a
down the abandoned h., 986a
each goes own byway to h., 385b
earth and high h., 853a
earth nigher h. than now, 661b
earth's crammed with h., 619a
endures, 855a
enter into kingdom of h., 41b, 43a
eye of h. to garnish, 237a
eye sees open h., 498a
farewells as stars in h., 269a
finds means to kill joys, 225b
floor of h., 909a
floor of h. is inlaid, 235b
flowerless fields of h., 772b
follies hold earth from h., 790b
four winds of the h., 36a
from Clee to h., 852a
from h. did hie, 1084b
gained from h., 441a
gate of h., 7a
gates not so arched, 315a
gems of h. starry train, 345b
gentle rain from h., 234b
getting to h. at last, 735b
gives glimpses, 927b
gives its favorites, 102a
glance from h. to earth, 230b
God created h. and earth, 5a
God is in h., 28a
God's in his h., 661b
going forth is from the end of the h., 17b
gold bar of heaven, 731a
great eye of h., 200a
had made her such a man, 273a
harbingers to h., 333a

Heaven has joined great issues, 515a
have ye souls in h., 583b
hell I suffer seems a h., 345a
hell or Hoboken, 962a
helps not men who will not act, 76b
hills whose heads touch h., 272b
his blessed part to h., 299a
holds all, 819a
hours to which h. chime, 362b
how long permit to h., 348a
humbler h., 408a
husbandry in h., 283a
if earth be shadow of h., 346b
if h. looked on riches, 389a
if I ascend up into h., 23a
if I cannot bend h., 119b
in h. dream fulfilled, 722b
in h. perfect round, 665b
in heart a little h., 387b
in hell's despair, 489a
in which no horses, 826b
is above all yet, 298a
is love, 518b
it smells to h., 263b
itself points out hereafter, 393b
itself we seek in our folly, 120b
itself would stoop to h., 338a
keys of kingdom of h., 43a
kingdom of h. is at hand, 39b
kingdom of h. like a net, 75a
kingdom of h. like mustard seed, 42b
kiss h. gives earth, 329a
knows how to put price, 466b
knows its time, 522a
lay up treasures in h., 40b
leave her to h., 260a
leave the rest to h., 331b
leaving mercy to h., 424b
left to h. the rest, 813a
less of earth than h., 520a
lies about us in infancy, 513b
lift my soul to h., 298a
light from h., 493a
like egg earth like yolk, 141a
like the h. above, 719b
Lord of h. and earth, 50a
love is h., 518b
made heaven and earth, 22a
majesty of H., 420b
make a h. of hell, 342a
make face of h. so fine, 225a
Maker of h. and earth, 60a
makes h. drowsy with harmony, 222a
man alone beneath h., 518b
man is as H. made him, 196a
marriages made in h., 203a
matches made in h., 182b
meadows of h., 622a
measuring earth and h., 95b
met my dearest foe in h., 258a
mild h. a time ordains, 340b
mind of superior man like h., 740a
more things in h. and earth, 260a, 1021b
most of h. he hath, 679a
mount up to h., 21b
near h. by sea as by land, 192a
never to h. go, 264a
new h. and new earth, 58b
no humor in h., 762b
no rain left in h., 704a
not at single bound, 690a
not beteem winds of h., 257b

Heritage, what thou lovest thy
  true h., 989a
  youth's h., 666a
Hermit, aloof with h. eye, 526b
  crab whale's backbone, 1006a
  dwell a weeping h., 443a
  New England h., 809b
  old h. of Prague, 253a
  poor in place obscure, 198b
  shall I like a h, dwell, 199a
Hermitage, take that for h., 358b
Hermon, heights of H., 945a
Hern, coot and h., 652a
Hero, A H. of Our Time, 677a
  basic h. of books labor, 895a
  cheering h. or throwing confet-
    ti, 948b
  conquering h. comes, 420b
  conqueror Worm, 642b
  every h. becomes bore, 607b
  forgive the h., 1078b
  millions a h., 460a
  must drink brandy, 433a
  of course Alexander h., 632a
  of next war, 980b
  perish or sparrow fall, 408a
  show me a h., 1037a
  soldiers who wish to be h.,
    1104a
  to his valet, 99b
  when his sword has won, 565b
Herod, born in the days of H.,
    39a
  daughter of Herodias pleased
    H., 42b
  out-herods H., 262b
  should not return to H., 39b
Herodias, daughter of H. danced,
    42b
Heroes as well as idealists, 786b
  blood of our h., 472b
  conquered fame of h., 701a
  created by demand, 1017b
  fit country for h., 866a
  gladiators died or h., 945a
  grass-roots h., 740a
  hail ye h., 508a
  hand in hand with my h.,
    632a
  if we will, 710b
  many valiant souls of h., 62a
  peers h. of old, 666b
  seeds of patriots and h., 446a
  thin red h., 873a
  thin red line of h., 705a
  to think great thoughts be h.,
    786b
  were plenty, 1100b
  world's brave h., 1100a
Heroic decision not from cowards,
    1011b
  enterprise is gone, 454a
  for earth too hard, 665b
  lay tuneless now, 560b
  little monkey, 628b
  obstacle to being h., 614b
  pleasures of h. poesy, 332a
  poem a biography, 575b
  sires, 377a
  systematically h., 793a
  womanhood, 623b
Heroically mad, 369a
Heroism endurance for moment
    more, 809b
  feels never reasons, 607a
  labor matter of h., 954b
  truest h. to resist doubt, 614b
  upon land and sea, 699b
  with you is h., 699b

Herons, brood like decrepit h.,
    80b
Herostratus lives that burned
    temple, 331a
Herrin, in hell roast like h., 496a
Herring, fish nor flesh nor good
    red h., 183b
  pond is wide, 666b
Herrings, red h., 1093a
Herveys, men women and H.,
    414a
Herz, mein H. ist schwer, 478b
Hesiod, Homer and H. attributed
    to gods, 70a
  might have kept his breath, 68a
  taught H. beauteous song, 67a
Hesitancies, elaborate h., 865b
Hesitate and falter life away, 712a
  dislike, 411a
Hesitates, if President h., 983a
Hesitation, doubt h. pain, 662b
Hesper loves to lead home, 854a
Hesperian,   apple-bearing   H.
    coast, 84b
Hesperus entreats thy light, 302a
  it was schooner H., 621a
  that led the starry host, 345b
Hessians, yonder are the H.,
    451b
Heterodoxy another man's doxy,
    419a
  thy-doxy, 577a
Hew, not h. as carcass, 254b
  somebody to h. and hack,
    352b
  to line of right, 733a
Hewers of wood, 11a
Hewing wood for master carpen-
    ter, 75a
Hewn on Norwegian hills, 342a
  tree is h. down, 39b
  wisdom hath h. out her seven
    pillars, 23b
Hexameter, in the h. rises, 526b
Hey for boot and horse, 691a
  ho the wind and the rain, 253a,
    278a
  nonino, 250b
  to you good day to you, 767a
Heyday in the blood is tame, 264a
Hi, answer to h. or loud cry, 746b
  but she heels to it, 1022b
  diddle diddle, 1094a
  hi yee, 952a
Hic jacet, forlorn h., 511b
Hickety pickety, 1096b
Hickory, clothes on h. limb, 1103a
  dickory dock, 1093a
  whittled out of h., 1036a
Hicks, royal race of h., 945b
  sticks nix h. pix, 916b
Hid, city set on hill cannot be h.,
    40a
  fiend h. in a cloud, 489b
  half as well as he did, 769a
  hallowed relics h., 334a
  himself among women, 331a
  I h. from Him, 856b
  in heart of love, 880a
  in her interlunar cave, 349a
  lightly h. deepest understood,
    1078b
  love and a cough cannot be h.,
    324a
  Moses h. his face, 8a
  Nature and Nature's laws h.,
    412b
  there is nothing h. from the
    heat, 17b

Hid, wheat h. in two bushels of
    chaff, 231b
  wherefore these things h., 251a
  which is to keep that h., 305a
Hidden, America of poverty is h.,
    1082a
  cause h. result well known,
    128b
  growth in mind, 689b
  half h. from the eye, 510b
  handful of divine inert, 696b
  investigation of h. causes, 192b
  like h. lamps, 457a
  motion of h. fire, 518a
  nature often h., 209a
  noise like h. brook, 525b
  O h. under dove's wing, 1004a
  player on other side h., 724b
  something h. behind things,
    951a
  something h. go and find, 876a
  soul of harmony, 335a
  thy works h. before men, 4a
  treasures, 679b
  under dove's wing, 1004a
Hide, for all 'is dirty h., 873a
  furred gowns h. all, 279b
  hair goes with h., 1010a
  head under his wing, 1096a
  is sure to flatten 'em, 901b
  it under his tongue, 15b
  let me h. myself in thee, 469a
  lies to h. it, 322b
  me from day's garish eye, 336a
  me O my Savior, 425b
  me under the shadow of thy
    wings, 17a
  one talent death to h., 341a
  owest beast no h., 278b
  rude stream that must forever
    h. me, 298b
  shame from every eye, 448b
  stars h. their diminished heads,
    901b
  the fault I see, 412b
  the haughty barbers, 1025b
  their diminished heads, 344b
  those hills of snow, 271b
  thou wear lion's h., 236a
  thyself for a little moment, 32a
  tiger's heart in player's h.,
    206a
  tiger's heart in woman's h.,
    215b
  underground alchemy, 602b
  us from each other's sight, 321a
  what false heart know, 283a
  what may man within h., 271b
  world to h. virtues in, 251b
  your diminished rays, 344b
  your golden light, 621b
Hideaways, bones in h., 1051b
Hideous, making night h., 259a
  more h. in a child, 277b
  notes of woe, 562a
  phantasma or h. dream, 254a
  ruin and combustion, 341b
  storm of terror, 315a
  vice a creature of h. mien,
    891a
Hides, death fact nature h., 740b
  night that h. things from us,
    162a
  not visage from cottage, 295b
  one thing speaks another, 63b
  smiling face, 456b
  what plighted cunning h., 277a
Hidest, why h. thou thy face from
    me, 20a

Human, being h. though boys, 900b
being item with skin wrapped around, 1030a
being portable plumbing, 1017b
being raging at me, 1067a
beings in underground den, 94b
beings into machines, 687a
benefit and enjoyment, 453a
beside a h. door, 511a
best work the h. mind, 495a
body a watch, 434a
body is sacred, 701a
body politic like h. body, 435b
build on h. heart, 661b
chariot that bears h. soul, 738a
Chinese poetry most h., 863a
civilization scarcely h., 905b
civilized h. being, 936b
combination or society, 329a
community, 974a, 1055b
condition, 190b
constant in h. sufferings, 968b
contrivance of h. wisdom, 454a
course of h. events, 470b
creatures' lives, 592b
creeds root in h. needs, 791a
crises of h. affairs, 485b
Cruelty has h. heart, 489b
custom guide of h. life, 434b
Declaration of H. Rights, 964a-b
delightful h. tadpole, 870b
distances between h. beings, 938b
earth's h. shores, 581a
enemies of h. army, 920a
engine waits, 1002b
error is impatience, 980b
everything h. pathetic, 762b
face divine, 344b
faith in h. beings, 1021a
features composed of ten parts, 132b
felicity produced by little advantages, 423b
field of h. conflict, 921b
figure interests me most, 898b
find beautiful h. soul, 475a
four essential h. freedoms, 972b
free the h. will, 412b
functions and activities, 850b
fundamental h. rights, 1104a
future of h. race, 942a
good fortune to be born h., 379a
happiness of h. race, 453b
he served h. liberty, 884a
heart break piecemeal, 680b
heart by which we live, 514a
heart has treasures, 679b
hearts to chew, 570a
highest type of h. nature, 706b
hope springs in h. breast, 408a
hopes and h. creeds, 791a
hum of h. cities, 556b
I had no h. fears, 511a
in h. life much endured, 428a
infringement of h. freedom, 496b
Jealousy has a h. face, 489b
just some h. sleep, 926a
kind not bear much reality, 1004b
king's might greater than h., 87a
knowledge of h. nature, 533b, 776b
life a mansion, 585a

Human, Love the h. form divine, 487a
march of h. mind slow, 453a
Mercy has a h. heart, 487a
mice with wings wear h. face, 1064a
milk of h. kindness, 281b
millions of h. beings, 888b
moonlight, 1081a
more than h. arms, 965b
music ministers to h. welfare, 706a
my Treatise of H. Nature, 434b
nature changes, 840b
nature in its horror, 1067a
nature made arrogant by consideràtion, 90a
nature not change, 640a
nature weak in bookstore, 674b
no h. things of importance, 95a
no themes so h., 799b
noble happy h. beings, 698b
nor h. spark is left, 414a
nothing h. is alien, 108b
O h. love, 641a
observation of h. life, 689b
observer of h. nature, 668b
of h. bliss to h. woe, 351a
of h. days, 824a
on my faithless arm, 1060a
part of the h. race, 986b
Peace the h. dress, 487a
peasant is also h., 498a
Pity has a h. face, 487a
politics art of h. happiness, 871a
pounces on h. core, 796a
power cannot remove, 1007a
predatory h. hands, 851b
primary h. affections, 712a
principles of h. nature, 550a
provide for h. wants, 454a
pursuit of h. glory, 327a
race born to fly upward, 161a
race organized like bees, 867a
relations perfectly exhibited, 99b
reverence h. nature, 544a
rights, 1104a
rights to which committed, 1072b
ruler having h. body as subject, 93b
same heart in every h. breast, 711b
same with h. race, 946a
sanction of h. nature, 1045b
scientific thought h. progress, 809a
Secrecy the h. dress, 489b
see h. soul take wing, 559a
sorrow of h. existence, 455a
species of two races, 534b
stars of h. race, 456b
status not depend on economics, 965a
stories repeat themselves, 939b
suffering h. race, 711a
sum of h. things, 475b
tale of h. life, 455b
tamer of h. breast, 439b
Terror the h. form divine, 489b
things subject to decay, 369a
thought or form, 568a
three words for h. race, 832a
till h. nature came, 738a
to err is h., 137b, 150b, 403b
to love for being loved, 566a
to step aside is h., 493b

Human, tragedy The H. Heart, 933a
undimmed by h. tears, 849a
vanity of h. hopes, 427b
vast empire of h. society, 511a
voices wake us, 1001a
weakness of h. mind, 373b
wholeness of h. problem, 937b
wisdom of h. contrivances, 452b
wish I loved h. race, 86ob
Humane, harmonious and h. life, 716b
heaven and earth are not h., 73b
Humani nil a me alienum puto, 108b
Humanity achieve lasting peace, 982b
base metal of h., 817b
chaotic stage of h., 1052b
common right of h., 636a
exalts delights adorns h., 552b
forehead of h., 580b
has three enemies, 817b
herein chivalry courtesy h., 174b
history life of h., 732a
i love you, 1030b
imitated h. so abominably, 263a
justice and h., 895b
justice equity, 454a
law of h., 454a
may come to end, 952b
nobody writes for h., 894a
nothing real but h., 589b
one race, 827a
only three days old, 942b
reason and justice, 453a
still sad music of h., 509b
veined h., 617b
victory for h., 586b
violence and injury to h., 100a
wearisome condition of h., 202a
with all its fears, 622b
Humanized, to be h. to comply with law, 716a
Humanizes, liberal arts study h., 129a
Humanizing, power of h. nature, 529b
whole body of society, 716b
Humankind, good or bad for h., 515a
lords of h. pass by, 447b
not bear much reality, 1004b
of all tyrannies on h., 370a
porcelain clay of h., 370b
vices and follies of h., 391b
Humans, creatures both insects and h., 946b
Humble Allen, 412a
and contrite heart, 875b
and hearty thanks, 6ob
and sweet poverty, 1079b
appearance of telephone, 742a
are usually envious, 374a
as if pride not h., 668a
be it ever so h., 567b
cares delicate fears, 511b
frowned not on h. birth, 441a
grave adorned, 406a
heart in pain, 887a
heyday in blood is h., 264a
himself shall be exalted, 43b
honor shall uphold the h., 26b
hungry mean, 1050b
kept the h. way, 813a
livers in content, 298a
members of society, 503a

Inhumanity, indifferent is essence of i., 836b
man's i. to man, 492b
Inimies, livin' without i., 890b
Inimitable vegetative gracefulness, 985a
Iniquities, judge allow i., 789a
Iniquity, approved i., 899b
bond of i., 49b
draw i. with cords of vanity, 30b
gray i., 239b
him that doeth i., 3a
I was shapen in i., 19a
is pardoned, 32b
love soft words hate i., 863a
of oblivion, 331b
punish wicked for their i., 31b
reaped i., 35b
religious know more about i., 871b-872a
visiting the i. of the fathers, 9a
Initial of creation, 737a
Iniuria, volenti non fit i., 152a
Injunctions, parting i., 925a
Injure, to benefit and not i., 75b
Injured, forgiveness to i. does belong, 130b
lover's hell, 346a
minds i. by hunger and thirst, 100b
no one i. save by himself, 144b
party, 770a
those I have i., 1076b
whom they have i. they hate, 130b
Injures, never pardons those he i., 130b
Injuries, forgive me my i., 1076b
saints in your i., 273a
Injuring, at expense of i. their virtue, 72b
kill time without i. eternity, 682a
rarely escapes i. own hands, 75a
restrain men from i., 472a
Injurious, beauty though i., 349b
Injury, add insult to i., 129b, 435b
engraved in metal, 179a
fear of i., 832b
greatest service or greatest i., 93b
never forget i., 904a
never use treatment with view to i., 88a
recompense i. with justice, 72b
sooner than insult, 415a
such i. vex a saint, 219a
violence and i. to humanity, 100a
violence and i. to willow, 100a
where i. let me sow pardon, 157a
Injustice, bear with patience i., 361a
complain of i. of government, 503b
conscience with i. corrupted, 215a
easy to bear, 960b
extreme justice extreme i., 151b
extreme justice often i., 108b
extreme law is extreme i., 108b
fear of suffering i., 355a
inclination to i., 1024b
jealousy i., 400a
makes democracy necessary, 1024b

Injustice, mankind censure i., 94a
no i. to person who consents, 152a
nothing so felt as i., 672a-b
on part of government, 959a
one man's justice another's i., 607a
road to downfall, 631b
sometimes public service, 1091b
threat to justice, 1082b
Injye other people's sufferin', 891b
Ink, crave shelter of i., 842b
effusion of i., 444b
essential in painting, 153a
every drop of i. ran cold, 442a
gall enough in thy i., 253a
galley slave to i., 590b
hath not drunk i., 222a
never saw pen and i., 253a
seated livelong day before i. slab, 162a
Inkstand, Vesuvius' crater for i., 697a
Inky, not alone my i. cloak, 257b
Inlaid with patines of bright gold, 235b
Inland island, 776a
though i. far we be, 513b
tract of i. ground, 516b
Inlets, through creeks and i. making, 688b
Inn, book's an i., 942b
classics have charm in i., 608a
gain timely i., 284b
happiness produced by i., 432a
make my house your i., 996b
no room in the i., 46a
remember i. Miranda, 902a
take mine ease in mine i., 183a
up to old i. door, 961b
warmest welcome at an i., 432a
world not i. but hospital, 330a
Inner air i. light, 1048b
blindness, 1000b
man, 54a
mine with i. weather, 928a
resolve i. conflicts, 985a
temple's i. shrine, 512a
weather, 928a
what i. voice says, 497b
Innisfail, harp of I., 537b
Innisfree, go to I., 879b
Innocence and health, 449a
ceremony of i., 882a
changed i. for i., 295a
closing up his eyes, 211b
confession next thing to i., 127b
fearful i., 512a
has nothing to dread, 378b
her i. a child, 369b
ignorance not i., 667b
murderous i. of sea, 882a
never blossom into license, 378b
of love, 252a
of our neighbors, 683b
our peace our i., 512a
recovered i., 683b
silence often of pure i., 295a
what is our i., 996b
Innocent and beautiful, 883b
armed without i. within, 412a
as new-laid egg, 765a
calm quiet i. recreation, 326b
children's souls not i., 146b
condemn an i. person, 417a
coursed down his i. nose, 247b
he that maketh haste to be rich not i., 894a

Innocent, look like i. flower, 282a
man sent to legislature, 895a
merriment, 768b
minds i. and quiet, 358b
moon, 856b
no i. wit be suppressed, 469a
of the blood, 45a
officious i. sincere, 433b
skin of i. lamb parchment, 215a
sleep, 283b
than one i. suffer, 444b
who perished being i., 14b
women i. and pure, 296b
Innocently, live i. God here, 425a
Innocuous desuetude, 771a
Innovation, opponents of i. die out, 847a
scientific i. rarely converts opponents, 847a
Inns not residences, 996b
of molten blue, 735a
Innuendoes, beauty of i., 955b
Innumerable bees, 649b
caravan which moves, 574b
things creeping i., 21b
Inoffensive, smooth easy i. down to Hell, 104b
untitled aristocracy, 634b
Inquire, shoot first i. afterwards, 1026b
why things as they are, 801b
Inquirer, workshop of serious i., 779b
Inquiries, suspended religious i., 466a
Inquiring eye or tongue, 536b
Inquiry thought to aim at some good, 97b
undismayed unintimidated i., 912a
Inquisition, committee i., 951a
dogs, 654b
Inquisitive, acute i. dexterous, 453a
Insane love to speak of selves, 770b
most i. of passions, 837a
ordinarily he is i., 588b
root, 281a
Insanity often logic, 633b
Insatiate blood, 1066a
to pursue war with heaven, 343a
Inscape is what I aim at, 804a
Inscription, altar with i., 50a
Inscriptions, lapidary i., 431b
Inscrutable colossal and alone, 812a
dark i. workmanship, 510a
dumb i. grand, 715a
jest unseen i., 220b
Insect carries impress of Maker, 383a
I am that i. brother, 708a
man mere i., 780b
scraping on surface of life, 772a
vile i. that has risen up, 420b
Insects, creatures both i. and humans, 946b
get meaning for other i., 772a
loud and troublesome i., 454b
of the hour, 454b
to whom God gave lust, 708a
Insensate care of mortals, 113b
Insensibility, stark i., 429b
Insensible, honor i. then, 240b
to freedoms of Constitution, 967a
Inseparable, nonviolence and truth i., 897a

Items for imaginative genius of west, 703b
Iteration, damnable i., 238a
Ithaca, fill I. full of moths, 289b
Itself, is it true in and for i., 507b
    love is most nearly i., 1006a
    thou art the thing i., 278b
Itylus, half assuaged for I., 772b
Iucundior, quae set domestica sede i., 111a
Iudex damnatur ubi nocens absolvitur, 126a
Iudicaret, ne supra crepidam sutor i., 102a
Iura, sunt superis sua i., 129a
Ius est ars boni et aequi, 151a
    summum saepe summa est malitia, 108b
Institia, fiat i. et ruant coeli, 330b
Ivan Ilych's life most simple, 732b
    Petrofski Skevar, 1100b
Ives, going to St. I., 1093a
Ivory apes and peacocks, 13a, 947a
    bit of i. on which I work, 533b
    gate of i., 67a, 119a
    laces i. and gold, 943b
    neck is as a tower of i., 29b
    tower, 615a, 937b
    towers, 878a
Ivy, goats eat i., 1097a
    holly and the i., 1099a
    myrtle and i., 562b
    not hang i. over wine, 127a
    with i. never sere, 338a
Ivy-mantled tower, 440a, 962b

J

Jabal father of such as dwell in tents, 6a
Jabberwock, beware J., 745a
J'accuse, 786a
Jack and Jill, 1094a
    banish plump J., 239b
    be nimble, 1096b
    before say J. Robinson, 670b
    fly away J., 1098b
    gorging J., 661a
    house that J. built, 1098b
    joke poor potsherd, 804a
    little J. Horner, 1093a
    one named J., 1098b
    spanking J. so comely, 475b
    Sprat eat no fat, 1092b
Jackass, cudgel his own j., 785b
Jackdaw, devil must be in j., 554a
Jackson, pick Andrew J. from pebbles, 696b
    standing like stone wall, 719a
    Stonewall J. wrapped in beard, 1041b
Jacksonian vulgarity, 758a
Jacky have new master, 1094a
Jacob called the place Peniel, 7b
    gave Esau bread and pottage, 7a
    God of J. not philosophers, 364a
    served seven years, 7a
    sold his birthright unto J., 7a
    thy tents O J., 10a
    was a plain man, 7a
    was left alone, 7b
    wrestled as angel with J., 325b
Jacob's ladder, 857a

Jacob's, talk of J. ladder, 610b
    voice is J. voice, 7a
Jade, arrant j. on a journey, 448b
    Chinese love j., 992b
    kisses you quickly, 588b
    let galled j. wince, 263b
Jael took a nail, 11a
Jail, all we know who lie in j., 841a
    like living in j., 1067a
    little stealin' gets you in j., 1009a
    patron and the j., 427a
    with chance of being drowned, 430a
Jailer inexorable as self, 614b
Jake, Yukon J., 1035b
Jam, calico j., 673b
    tomorrow j. yesterday, 746a
Jamaicas of remembrance, 738b
James could almost hear the bronze Negroes, 1076a
    First Second and Old Pretender, 1011b
    James Morrison Morrison, 970a
    let J. rejoice, 444b
    Truthful J., 769b
    work of Henry J., 1011b
James's elaborate hesitancies, 865b
    ladies of St. J., 782a
Jamshyd gloried drank deep, 629b
Jane, from J. to Elizabeth, 533a
    Lady J. tall and slim, 554a
Jangled, sweet bells j., 262b
Janitor's, in love with j. boy, 1069a
January, a fly this J. day, 738b
Japan, as J. kept her independence, 997b
    create in J. civilized nation, 752a
    forces of Empire of J., 973b
    from Paris to J., 377a
    gods born in J., 537a
    what they say in J., 790b
Japanee, little Turk or J., 823b
Japanese, cultural nature of J., 938a
    don't care to, 1043a
    gargoyle-faced J., 978b
    heart subject of J. poetry, 419a
    life like J. picture, 789a
    practiced virtues, 537a
    reliance on intuition, 938a
Japheth, Noah begat J., 6b
Jar, feel amid city's j., 711a
    in Tennessee, 955b
    people in front get j., 942a
    strings untouched will harshly j., 213a
    wine j. when molding began, 124a
Jardin, il faut cultiver notre j., 417a
Jargon of the schools, 387a
Jars, two j. on floor of Zeus, 65a
Jasmine impossible to counterfeit, 814b
    inimitable j., 814b
Jasper of jocundity, 176a
Jaundice, jealousy j. of the soul, 370b
Jaundiced eye, 403b
Javan, bound for J. or Gadire, 349b
Jaw, muscular strength to j., 743b
Jawbone of an ass, 11b
Jaws, gently smiling j., 743a
    of darkness do devour it, 228b

Jaws of death, 193a, 652a
    that bite, 745a
Jay, poor Jim J., 914b
Jaybird don't rob own nes', 814a
Jazz, ask what j. is, 1046b
Jazzmen, go to it O j., 948b
Je connais tout fors moi-même, 171b
Jealous, art j. mistress, 608a
    confirmations, 274b
    for they are jealous, 275b
    gods who brook no worship, 890a
    I am a j. God, 9a
    in honor, 249a
    law a j. mistress, 543b
    not a j. woman, 1016b
    not j. for the cause, 275b
    one not easily j., 276b
    possessions of happiness, 897b
    scornful yet j. eyes, 410b
    souls not answered, 275b
    venom clamors of j. woman, 218b
Jealousies, surmises j. conjectures, 241a
Jealousy, beware my lord of j., 274a
    born with love, 356a
    ear of j. heareth all, 36b
    Father of J., 488a
    feeds upon suspicion, 355a
    full of artless j., 265a
    green-eyed j., 233b
    has a human face, 489b
    in j. more self-love, 356a
    injured lover's hell, 346a
    injustice, 400a
    is cruel as the grave, 30a
    is the rage of a man, 23b
    jaundice of the soul, 370b
    life of j., 274b
Jean, farewell to my J., 400b
Jeanie with light brown hair, 727b
Jeanne d'Arc and Bonaparte, 1016a
Jedge, of my merit you j., 693a
Jeers at fate, 962b
    exiled on ground in j., 707a
Jefferson, celebrities such as J., 749b
    Thomas J. still lives, 464a
    when J. dined alone, 1074a
    Yoknapatawpha County, 1039b
Jeffersonian simplicity, 758a
Jeffers's, too much like one of J., 995a
Jeffrey, no one minds J., 522b
Jehovah has triumphed, 543a
    in name of great J., 468a
    is my strength, 31a
    Jove or Lord, 412b
    Lawd God J., 1015a
    tell them I am J. said, 444a
Jehu, the driving of J., 13b
Jelly, distilled almost to j., 258a
    out vile j., 279a
Je-ne-sais-quoi young man, 767a
Jenny kissed me, 551b
Jeoffrey, consider my cat J., 444b
Jeopardy, went in j. of their lives, 12b
Jeremy, Mr. J. liked feet wet, 887b
Jericho, from Jerusalem to J., 46b
    tarry at J. until beards be grown, 12b
Jerusalem, daughters of J., 29a,b

Joy, poor capable of j., 878a
  pray in j. and abundance, 976a
  pure j. of knowledge, 1071b
  reveal itself when transformed in us, 938b
  riding's a j., 664a
  rule it with stern j., 981a
  scrip of j. immortal diet, 199a
  secret j. of thinker, 786b
  senses forever in j., 665a
  shall reap in j., 22b
  shipmate joy, 703a
  silence perfectest herald of j., 246a
  silly j. at silly things, 449a
  snatch a fearful j., 439a
  somebody to divide j. with, 763a
  sons of God shouted for j., 16a
  sorrow and j. are one, 1060b
  source of humor not j., 762b
  spontaneous j., 881a
  stern j. warriors feel, 520a
  strength through j., 1017b
  surprised by j., 516a
  sweeten present j., 590a
  that your j. be full, 49a
  the luminous cloud, 527a
  the thrill the whirl, 695b
  thing of beauty j. forever, 580a
  this alone life j. empire, 569a
  this torment my j., 1066a
  thou spark from heaven, 497a
  to pass to world below, 118b
  to the world, 397a
  to their friends, 65b
  walked in glory and j., 511b
  was never sure, 775a
  we end in j., 1066a
  weep at j., 245a
  where poverty and j., 157a
  with j. and love triumphing, 344b
  without canker or cark, 804b
  work with j., 976a
  writhed not at passing j., 580a
Joybells ring in heaven's street, 947a
Joyful all ye nations rise, 425b
  births, 245a
  in day of prosperity be j., 28a
  let poet be, 686a
  make a j. noise, 19b, 21a
  shall my j. temples bind, 332b
Joyfully, singing most j., 711a
Joyfulness prolongeth his days, 38b
Joyous, good great and j., 569a
  loaves when heart j., 4b
  we too launch out, 702b
Joyously, flowers through grass j. sprang, 156a
Joyousness, lends j. to a wall, 790a
Joy's delicious springs, 555a
  grape, 584a
  soul lies in doing, 267b
  the voice, 1031b
Joys abound as seasons fleet, 214a
  and sorrows song aroused, 703b
  as winged dreams, 1085a
  be j. three parts pain, 666a
  blest with some new j., 367b
  dreaming o'er j. of night, 488a
  fading j. we dote upon, 385a
  fairest j. give unrest, 580b
  fall not to rich alone, 123b

Joys, homely j., 440a
  in another's loss of ease, 489a
  kill your j. with love, 225b
  let j. be as May, 322a
  minds me o' departed j., 494a
  mingle j. with occupation, 425a
  must be used, 917b
  nakedness all j. are due to thee, 307a
  only solitary know j. of friendship, 940a
  our youth our j. our all, 199b
  perish in infancy, 1086b
  present j. more to flesh and blood, 370b
  raise j. and triumphs high, 425a
  rob us of our j., 1086b
  society's chief j., 457a
  summer hath his j., 300a
  taste whole j., 307b
  tasted eternal j. of Heaven, 213a
  tenderness its j. and fears, 514a
  that came down showerlike, 527b
  thy j. when shall I see, 1085b
  to this are folly, 310a
  vain deluding j., 335b
  with age diminish, 667b
  withered like grass, 600b
  youth's season for j., 401b
Jubal father of such as handle harp, 6b
Jubilant, bright pomp ascended j., 347a
Jubilee, bring the j., 748a
  sons to thy j. throng, 566a
Jubjub bird, 745a
Judah and Israel dwelt safely, 13a
  say unto the cities of J., 32b
  sin of J., 34a
Judas had given them the slip, 386b
  so J. did to Christ, 228a
Judea, Bethlehem of J., 39a
Judee, didn't know everythin' in J., 693a
Judge above his last, 102a
  allow iniquities, 789a
  amongst fools a j., 136a
  by sample we j. whole, 194a
  children j. parents, 839a
  condemned when criminal absolved, 126a
  dead drunk j., 1068a
  fitter to invent than j., 209a
  forbear to j., 215a
  I j. not thee, 197b
  I'll be j. I'll be jury, 743b
  impartial j., 454b
  justice j. or vicar, 481a
  man by foes, 843a
  mind proper j. of man, 130b
  my friend j. not me, 197b
  never j. until other side heard, 86a
  no king can corrupt, 298a
  no one should j. own case, 126a
  none blessed, 38a
  not according to appearance, 48b
  not j. by one act, 847a
  not play before done, 321b
  not that ye be not judged, 41a, 640b
  of all things, 364a
  of authors' names, 403b
  of my merit you j., 693a
  out of thy mouth will I j., 47a

Judge, people j. men by success, 355b
  people seldom j. right, 485a
  quick and the dead, 60a
  rain influence and j. prize, 335a
  right j. judges wrong, 82a
  setting yourself up as j., 96a
  should not be young, 94a
  sober as j., 424a
  sole j. of truth, 409a
  the fatherless, 30a
  upright j. learned j., 235a
  whole piece by pattern, 798b
  you as you are, 270b
Judged according to lies, 156b
  in light of final issue, 99a
  intellectual product j. by age, 781a
  judge not that ye be not j., 41a, 640b
  not to have lived, 786b
  should be j. as a captain, 173b
Judge's robe, 270b
Judges, a fool with j., 136a
  all ranged, 402a
  as j. neither Jew nor Gentile, 967a
  common j. of property, 427b
  constitution what j. say, 864b
  do and must legislate, 788a
  hungry j. sentence sign, 404b
  in every state bound thereby, 474b
  naïf simple-minded, 787b
  of facts not laws, 399b
  right judge j. wrong, 82a
Judgest, thou j. another, 50b
Judging character motive impulse, 976b
  for themselves, 481b
  no way of j. future, 465a
  people by appearances, 359b
Judgment, accurate in his j., 462b
  and imagination, 528a
  beauty bought by j. of eye, 221b
  bounded by Day of J., 655a
  bring every work into j., 29a
  commonly we say j. falls, 317a
  complains of his j., 355b
  Daniel come to j., 234b
  defend against your j., 371a
  difficult, 88b, 477b
  do not wait for last j., 1068b
  enough for me, 810a
  ever awake, 529a
  execute j. against gods of Egypt, 8b
  fled to brutish beasts, 255b
  from old fountains new j., 832a
  God and history remember j., 1020a
  God's great J. Seat, 872b
  good j. of Americans, 616b
  green in j., 287b
  he looked for j., 30b
  He which is top of j., 270b
  his ways are j., 10b
  leaves of J. Book unfold, 726a
  man's erring j., 402b
  men of ill j. ignore good, 81a
  my j. approves measure, 463a
  no comparison no j., 455a
  nor people's j. always true, 368b
  not better than information, 1020a
  not industry only but j., 452b
  of intellect half truth, 935a
  or intuition more subtle, 787b

L

Leader, philosophy you l. of life, 111b
test of l., 1013a
that people may require l., 95a
to be l. turn one's back, 850a
who understood terror, 1077a
Leader's indomitable soul, 661a
Leaders, ambition of military l., 959a
ambitiously contending, 480a
blind l. of the blind, 43a
lie down till l. have spoken, 874b
Leadership, new generation of l., 1072a
Leadest thou that heifer, 583b
Leadeth me beside still waters, 17b
me in paths of righteousness, 17b
Leads, astronomy l. from this world, 94b
clanging rookery, 647a
heaven that l. men to hell, 294b
highroad l. to England, 430b
on to fortune, 256a
spirit of man who l., 987a
who l. a good life, 476a
you to believe a lie, 491a
Leaf, abiding l., 1066b
are you the l. blossom, 883b
cut a cabbage l., 442b
fade as a l., 33b
falling of a l., 697b
falls with l. in October, 312b
flower falling or l., 1011a
flower say it or l., 944a
his l. shall not wither, 16b
I were like the l., 774b
in her mouth was an olive l., 6b
last l. upon tree, 634b
let fall no burning l., 1023a
lift me as wave l. cloud, 569b
lives on a l., 1064b
my days in yellow l., 563a
never tear linnet from l., 882b
November's l., 519a
of grass no less than stars, 700b
olive l. pacific sign, 348a
one red l., 524a
round elm tree bole in tiny l., 663a
sere yellow l., 286a
shall be green, 34b
sorrow and scarlet l., 698a
stone l. unfound door, 1049b
transmute to flower and l., 765a
turn over a new l., 196a
Leaf-fringed legend, 583a
Leafy month of June, 525b
roll up l. Olympus, 117a
streams where cherries, 1079b
League, half a l. onward, 651b
in l. with future, 729b
in l. with the stones, 14b
of Nations, 940b
Leagues beyond those leagues, 731b
land appeared at two l., 172a
scarce l. apart descried, 688b
ten l. beyond world's end, 1086a
thousand l. a thousand years, 423a
world large when weary l., 806b
Leaks, gas l. twenty parts, 864a
Leal, land o' the l., 502a,b
Lean above me broken-hearted, 981b

Lean and foolish knight, 918b
and hungry look, 253b
and low ability, 253a
and sallow abstinence, 337b
and slippered pantaloon, 249a
as compass needle, 1077a
body and visage, 333a-b
dull privations and l. emptiness, 306a
four l. hounds, 1030a
grew l. assailed seasons, 899b
horse l. as is a rake, 166b
hungry savage, 633b
in joy upon father's knee, 487a
lard their l. books, 310a
lards the l. earth, 238b
makes you l., 1037a
mournful l. Despair, 486a
on garden urn, 1001b
over too far backward, 1033b
people who l., 825b
Pharaoh's l. kine loved, 239b
poor l. lank face, 635b
rent and beggared, 233a
strong l. upon death, 995a
take fat with l., 672a
unwashed artificer, 237a
white-flaming bush l., 1014b
wife eat no l., 1092b
Lean-faced, Pinch a hungry l. villain, 218b
Leaning across bosom of west, 801a
against the sun, 735a
on reedy shore, 1086a
stuffed men l. together, 1003a
Leanness, style agrees not with l. of purse, 214b
Leans against the land, 447b
elephant l. or stands, 323a
her cheek upon her hand, 223b
Longing l. and beckons, 694b
Pacific l. on the land, 994b
upon his hoe and gazes, 826b
Leant, on lover's arm l., 647b
Lean-witted, lunatic l. fool, 227a
Leap, excepting l. year, 187a
I'll l. up to my God, 213b
in order to stations l., 370a
in the dark, 318a
into thy saddle once more, 695b
lame man l. as an hart, 32a
look before you l., 353a
look ere ye l., 182a
nevermore to l. again, 915a
of whale up Niagara, 422b
to pluck bright honor, 238b
to tentative conclusion, 1071a
Leaped, in Endymion I l., 585a
into dangerous world I l., 489b
out to wed with thought, 650a
Leaping, brooks too broad for l., 853b
frog l. in, 380b
signs of l. houses, 237b
Leaps, cataract l. in glory, 648b
my heart l. up, 511b
nature not proceed by l., 425a
ship clear she l., 703a
Lear, Hamlet rambles L. rages, 884b
pleasant to know Mr. L., 672b
there Hamlet there L., 884b
till I am Timon and L., 885a
Learn and propagate best, 713b
as thread plays out, 1057a
at no other, 455a
by doing, 97b
by going, 1065a

Learn compare collect facts, 818b
fools l. in no other, 422a
from having died, 929b
from our enemies, 129a
from those who teach, 82a
from those who never will return, 899a
gladly he l. and gladly teche, 166b
had to grow old to l., 483b
heart is slow to l., 1023b
him or kill him, 760b
in suffering teach in song, 569b
Irish poets l. trade, 885a
know enough know how to l., 777a
live and l., 388a
man l. nothing without being taught, 132a
neither shall they l. war, 30a
never had time to l., 1044a
nor account pang, 666a
not yet so old but she may l., 234a
of nautilus to sail, 409b
of the green world, 989a
read mark l., 61a
sooner than a song, 412a
task first to l. what is, 801b
they l. to be idle, 55a
to bear beams of love, 487a
to do well, 30a
to hold your own, 837a
to labor and wait, 620b
to read slow, 364a
to teach is to l. twice, 483b
way they eat drink l. and everything, 933b
what life had to teach, 683a
wise l. from enemies, 91a
with view to approbation, 72b
Learned about women from 'er, 875a
all l. all drunk, 458b
although men say he has not l., 71a
and conned by rote, 256a
angling never fully l., 325b
are seldom pretty, 961a
fair and l. and good as she, 319b
fool more foolish, 362a
forgotten everything l., 1104b
grew within this l. man, 213b
his great language, 662b
in courtesy have her l., 882b
Jonson's l. sock, 335a
judge should have l. to know evil, 94a
know best things not l., 439a
libraries of the l., 444b
loads of l. lumber, 404a
love first l. in lady's eyes, 222a
love trade thou hast l., 142a
make the l. smile, 403a
more l. from Dante, 1008a
much l. dust, 458a
nothing forgotten nothing, 484a
on earth practice in heaven, 663b
root of Homer, 301b
thoughts of many men, 65a
to look on nature, 509b
to melt at others' woe, 439b
upright judge l. judge, 235a
what habits lead you, 1081b
when Sorrow walked, 958b
who does not need you, 1081b
with view to improvement, 72a

Lightning reached fiery rod, 790a
 Satan as l. fall, 46b
 scratch head with l., 760a
 strikes mountaintop, 121b
 Superman the l., 805a
 too like the l., 224a
 vain to look for defense against l., 127a
Lightning's hour, 1055a
Lightnings, veiling l. of song 572a
Light-o'-love lady known as Lou, 933a
Lights around the shore, 731b
 burn low in barbershop, 1025b
 candle to sun, 312a
 electric l. not science, 815a
 Father of l., 56a
 fled garlands dead, 542b
 godfathers of heaven's l., 221a
 guttering low, 853b
 keeper of warm l., 82a
 mansion where we can turn off l., 993a
 moon l. up the earth, 69b
 northern l. seen sights, 933a
 of the world, 456b
 ridicule one of principal l., 483a
 see how it is without l., 993a
 that do mislead the morn, 271b
 truth may bear all l., 416a
 turn up l., 864b
 your l. burning, 47a
Light-winged dryad, 582a
Like a small gray coffeepot, 990a
 a winter my absence, 293a
 ape how l. to us, 107a
 but oh how different, 515a
 find l. again, 519a
 God pairs l. with l., 66b
 how do you l. your blueeyed boy, 1030b
 I don't l. you Sabidius, 135a
 I know what I l., 910b
 look upon his l. again, 258a
 me from heels to head, 823b
 more ye see better l. it, 891a
 never met man I didn't l., 954a
 not fair terms, 232b
 nothing anyone obliged to l., 799a
 of each thing, 221a
 one that stands on promontory, 216a
 people like priest, 35a
 poor cat i' the adage, 282b
 same things is friendship, 115b
 those who admire us, 356a
 to an hermit poor, 198b
 to see it lap miles, 736a
 upon earth there is not his l., 16b
 very l. a whale, 263a
 very very l. me, 823b
 want it most l. it least, 415b
 what he loves never l. too much, 302b
 will to like, 183a
Liked book the better, 450b
 it not and died, 301a
 several women, 297a
 way it walks, 86ob
Likely impossibility preferable, 99a
 man in preference to rich, 78a
 not bloody l., 837b
 we are all l. to go astray, 82a
Likeness, gods in l. of men, 50a

Likeness, grow into l. of bad men, 96a
 in l. not lion, 990b
 let us make man after our l., 5a
 of filly foal, 229a
 very l. of roasted crab, 29a
Likenesses, representation should give l., 148a
Likes, doesn't know what he l., 1033a
 nobody l. man who brings bad news, 82a
Likewise, go and do l., 46b
Liking, all love all l. all delight, 320b
 grounds other than l., 690a
 happy l. what they do, 438b
 I have a l. old, 740b
 saves me trouble of l., 533b
Lilac and brown hair, 1003b
 bush tall-growing, 931b
 heart-leaves of l., 931b
 in me, 931b
 lost l., 1004a
 time, 961b
Lilacs last in dooryard bloomed, 702a
 out of dead land, 1002a
Lilies and languors of virtue, 773b
 Beauty lives though l. die, 980a
 beauty of the l., 690b
 breaking golden l., 619a
 crowned with l., 1024a
 feed among the l., 29b
 handfuls of l. to scatter, 119a
 of the field, 41a
 peacocks and l., 698b
 roses and white l. grow, 300a
 silent war of l., 220a
 that fester, 293a
 three l. in her hand, 731a
 twisted braids of l., 337b
 wheat set about with l., 29b
Lilting house, 1070b
 I've heard them l., 446b
Lily, how sweet the l. grows, 549a
 maid of Astolat, 653a
 of the valleys, 29a
 on l. o'erlace sea, 665b
 paint the l., 236b
 poppy or a l., 767a
 scarlet l. flamed, 860a
 thick with l. and rose, 753a
 trembles to a l., 782a
 water l. bloom, 645b
 whispers, 652b
Lily-livered boy, 286a
Lima, curious traveler from L., 442a
Limb, feels life in every l., 508b
 length of shambling l., 680b
 mingle with dissolved limb, 899a
 neither heat affection l., 271a
 of Satan, 760b
 sound wind and l., 196b
 stretches out conquering l., 989b
 tail's a l., 1032a
 tear body l. from l., 656a
Limbecks foul as hell, 294a
Limber, disciplined and l., 1056a
 wing aslant and l., 933b
Limbo large and broad, 344b
Limbs, fair l. of the tree, 775b
 gentle l. undress, 524a
 his l. cold in death, 119b
 I the l. and wheel, 707a

Limbs, lopped l., 1064b
 melter of l., 67b
 of a dismembered poet, 120a
 recreant l., 236a
 ruddy l. flaming hair, 488b
 these l. her provinces, 306b
 thy decent l. composed, 406a
 young in l. judgment old, 233a
Lime of love, 319b
 sat beneath a l. tree, 505a
 tree bower my prison, 523b
Limestone quarried near spot, 885a
Limit, fixes solemn l. of Heaven, 84b
 horizon l. of sight, 785a
 no l. to what novelist attempt, 798b
 of becoming mirth, 221b
 quiet l. of world, 652b
 to realization of tomorrow, 974a
 use me to the l., 847b
 what l. to grief for one so dear, 121a
Limitation, civil l. daunts utterance, 731a
 of armaments, 969b
Limitations, in l. the master, 479a
 no man climb beyond l., 779b
Limitless fire and brimstone, 759b
 fury, 1016a
 swelling and l. billows, 526b
Limits, hell hath no l., 213a
 no l. but sky, 194a
 of own field l. of world, 563b
 own appointed l. keep, 726a
 stony l. cannot hold love, 223b
Limns on water writes in dust, 210a
Limousine, one perfect l., 1029a
Limp and damp as tendrils, 1065a
 into scalding grave, 909a
 live with lame man learn to l., 137a
Limped, hare l. trembling, 581b
Limping with duty, 101a
Limpopo, greasy L. River, 876a
Limps after in base imitation, 226b
Lincoln, beloved of Abraham L., 898b
 in L. something homely, 621b
 land of L. and Pinkham, 1030b
 man to become attached to, 703a
 of our literature, 772a
 shoveled into tombs, 948b
Lincoln's, murdered L. bier, 680b
 name close to Washington's, 733a
Lindens, under the l., 588b
Line, cadence of a rugged l., 369b
 cancel half a l., 630b
 creep in one dull l., 403a
 custom in all l. of order, 267b
 draw l. where God has not, 789b
 eats dirt in the l., 1025b
 embroil about fancied l., 377b
 far-flung battle l., 875a
 fathom l. could never touch, 238b
 fight it out on this l., 717a
 horizontal l. straight, 575a
 in the very first l., 451
 in which force impressed, 379b
 is gone out through all the earth, 17b
 life's fighting l., 920a

Look, my God l. not so fierce, 213b
ne'er l. back, 275a
not down but up, 666a
not left or right, 853b
not thou upon the wine, 26a
of eagles, 913b
of love alarms, 488b
of soft deceit, 488b
on both indifferently, 253b
on my works ye mighty, 568b
on you when last hour comes, 128a
only a l. and voice, 624a
or listen, 693a
out how use proud words, 948b
out not in, 718a
position to l. close, 927b
reader l., 303b
round habitable world, 371a
same l. she turned when he rose, 542a
see monument l. around, 374b
sexes l. alike, 999a
soul l. body touch, 884b
take a backward l., 734b
things fairer when we l. back, 694b
through a millstone, 203a
thy last on things lovely, 914b
to essence of a thing, 142b
to it, 637b
to your looms again, 789b
up at the skies, 803a
up not down, 718a
upon a little child, 425b
upon his life again, 258a
upon world as parish, 420b
upward l. of caution, 929a
we l. before and after, 570b
westward l. land bright, 689a
who comes here, 236b
with favor on bold beginning, 117a
with thine ears, 279b
ye there, 424a
Looked again found it was, 747a
and sighed again, 371b
as she did love, 581a
before thou leaped, 182a
come when l. for, 676b
down to Camelot, 645a
God l. around and said, 906b
into eye of day, 883b
Lot's wife l. back, 7a
love to eyes which spake, 555b
no sooner l. but loved, 250b
on Beauty bare, 1023b
on better days, 248b
out of eye of saint, 884a
over his shoulder, 1060a
sideways up, 525a
through life l. on God, 943b
to government for bread. 455a
unutterable things, 419b
with such a wistful eye, 840b
with wild surmise, 579b
Looker-on, patient l., 321b
Lookers-on, only God and angels l., 207a
Looketh, Lord l. on the heart, 12a
on the outward appearance, 12a
well to ways of her household, 27a
Lookin' eastward to sea, 873b
Looking, all l. for a king, 723b
as like as peas, 181b
at self through others, 894b

Looking, conscience warns somebody l., 961a
eastward to sea, 873b
even if gods should be l., 65b
for gold and silver, 686a
for honest man, 96b
for something to do, 439a
fresh as paint, 687b
hand to plow and l. back, 46b
leave them while l. good, 1027a
on happy fields, 648b
one way rowing another, 365b
over harbor and city, 948a
seaman l. for something else, 997b
see without l. through windows, 74b
well can't move her, 350a
Looking-glass, no use to blame l., 632a
Looking-glasses, women l. reflecting man, 975b
Looks as well as on steamship, 1027a
assurance given by l., 314b
commercing with the skies, 335b
dispatchful l., 346a
everybody's l. of death, 375b
gigantically down, 642a
gods do not give all men good l., 65b
in the clouds, 254a
kindness not beauteous l., 219b
love l. not with eyes, 228b
modest l. cottage adorn, 450b
more elder than thy l., 234b
never l. nor 'eeds, 874b
not deep-searched with saucy l., 221a
old man l. before and after, 62b-63a
on alike, 295b
on tempests, 294a
patron l. with unconcern, 429b
poet l. at world as man at woman, 957a
puts on his pretty l., 236b
quite through deeds of men, 253b
she l. with threatening eye, 236b
she needs good l., 984a
sidelong l. of love, 449a
stolen l. nice, 551b
through Nature up, 410a
toward school with heavy l., 224a
up friend clear your l., 509a
war of l. between them, 220a
were free, 525a
whole world in face, 621b
Loom, broider world upon l., 878b
I can't ply the l., 69b
left the web left the l., 645b
life's in the l., 789b
Looms, look to l. again, 789b
Loon, thou cream-faced l., 286a
Loop to hang doubt on, 275a
Looped and windowed raggedness, 278b
Loophole, from her cabined l. peep, 336b
no l. in case drafted, 954a
Loopholes of retreat, 458b
Loose, all hell broke l., 346a
as the wind, 323a
feel his title hang l., 286a

Loose, hell's broken l., 206a
imagination, 884b
past free of l. ends, 901b
the bands of Orion, 16a
type of things, 512b
w'en it gits l. fum jug, 814a
Loosed, arrows l. several ways, 243a
blood-dimmed tide l., 882a
fateful lightning, 690b
silver cord be l., 29a
Loosen, old faiths l. and fall, 774a
old foundations, 948b
Loosened spirit brings, 738b
Loosens fragrant bodice, 582a
Lopped limbs, 1064b
tree may grow again, 80b
Loquacious, light griefs l., 131b
Loquacity, poetry checks l., 609a
Lord, abideth in presence of l., 4b
all ye works of the L., 39a
am an attendant l., 1001a
among wits, 430a
and Father of mankind, 626b
angel of L. came down, 384a
angel of L. came upon them, 46a
anger of L. kindled, 458a
answered Job out of the whirlwind, 16a
be thankit, 495b
be with you, 59a
believing Christians from sky, 172b
better is little with the fear of the L., 24b
bless thee and keep thee, 9b
bless ye the L., 39a
blessed be L. God, 46a
blessed the latter end of Job, 16b
blot out his name, 373a
bringeth thee into good land, 10a
Cain went out from presence of the L., 6a
Christ the L. risen today, 425a
Christ's heart, 604a
climb tree L. to see, 1089a
coming of the L., 690b
custom l. of mankind, 593b
Dark Maid and her Lord, 83b
day of the L., 54b
day which the L. hath made, 22a
dead which die in the L., 58b
died by the hand of the L., 8b
directeth his steps, 24b
disciples of the L., 49b
do if He knew facts, 891a
fear of the L. is beginning of wisdom, 21b
fear of the L. is wisdom, 15b
feast to the L., 8b
fetch mo'ners up higher, 814a
for the erring thought, 771b
for the L. is good, 21a
forbade me to put off my hat, 364a
forgive O L. my jokes, 929a
from winter plague L. deliver us, 300b
gangway for L., 1015a
gave and hath taken away, 14a
glory of the L. is risen, 33b
go and the L. be with thee, 12a
God Almighty, 58a
God caused a deep sleep, 5b
God formed man, 5a

Lycidas, for L. sorrow not dead, 339a
  sunk low but mounted high, 339a
Lydian measures, 371b
  notes of Andrew Carnegie, 831a
  soft L. airs, 335a
Lyeth between bride and bridegroom, 988b-989a
Lying, African moon l. on back, 985a
  awake with headache, 767b
  days of my youth, 881a
  let me have no l., 295b
  lovers l. two and two, 852b
  mighty heart l. still, 512a
  not mind l. hate inaccuracy, 757a
  now on his side now on back, 64b
  sea careless lying fellow, 953b
  smallest amount of l., 756a
  till noon, 428b
  vainness drunkenness, 253a
  when asserts contrary is l., 908a
  world given to l., 241a
Lynn, set out from L., 592a
Lyonnesse, set out for L., 782b
Lyre, a god has given l. and song, 63b
  bloomin' l., 874a
  idle to play l. for ass, 145a
  lacking neither honor nor l., 121a
  living l., 440b
  make me thy l., 569b
  minstrel's l., 906b
  so long divine, 560b
  tuning l. and handling harp, 77b
  within the sky, 641b
Lyres, sound of l. and flutes, 781a
Lyric love half angel, 667a
  minions, 588a
  name me among l. bards, 120b
Lyrical grave or satirical, 898a

M

M, drew everything begins with M, 744a
Mab, Queen M. hath been with you, 223a
Mabel, ain't it awful M., 964a
Macaroni, called it m., 1090a
MacArthur, victory M. had in mind, 984a
Macassar, incomparable oil M., 560a
Macaulay, apostle of Philistines M., 714a
  book in breeches, 523a
  sure of everything, 541a
Macbeth does murder sleep, 283b
  none shall harm M., 285b
  shall never vanquished be, 285b
  shall sleep no more, 283b
Macdonald, wherever M. sits, 605b
Macduff, lay on M., 287a
Mace, sword the m. the crown, 244b
Macedonia, come into M., 50a
MacGregor, my name is M., 521a
  wherever M. sits, 605b
MacGregor's, Mr. M. garden, 887b
Machiavel, every country hath its M., 176b

Machiavel, much beholden to M., 207a
  Nick M. had ne'er trick, 353a
Machina, deus ex m., 102b
Machinations hollowness treachery, 277a
Machine, air pump or electrical m., 462a
  bathing m., 768a
  beauty of great m., 993b
  for living in, 995b
  for turning wine into urine, 984b
  god from the m., 102b
  justice is a m., 892b
  military m., 922b
  no unnecessary parts, 900b
  not man you're a m., 836b
  pulse of the m., 514a
  slavery of the m., 840b
  time m., 888a
  you're not man you're m., 836b
Machine-à-habiter, 995b
Machines for making m., 917b
  human beings into m., 687a
  slaves not masters, 851a
Machinery of night, 1081b
Mackerel, stinks like rotten m., 531b
Mackerel-crowded seas, 882b
Macrocosm, microcosm and m. atoned, 724a
Macte nova virtute puer, 119b
Mad, all poets are m., 310b
  am m. and am not m., 70a
  as Bedlam, 671b
  as March hare, 176a
  bad and dangerous, 552b
  birds m. with glee, 758a
  cold m. father, 968b
  dogs and Englishmen, 1043a
  don't call a man m., 438b
  everyone m. on one point, 872a
  face that drove me m., 797b
  father and mither gae m., 494b
  fitter sane than m., 666b
  go m. or unstable, 86b
  he first makes m., 86a
  heroically m., 369a
  Hieronymo's m. againe, 204a
  I am not m., 50b
  idolatry, 268a
  if they behold a cat, 234a
  in pursuit, 294b
  Ireland hurt you, 1060a
  lads that drive me m., 918a
  laid to make taker m., 294b
  makes men m., 276a
  man certainly stark m., 190a
  March days, 947a
  March hare, 176a
  men God made m., 918a
  more deadly than m. dog's tooth, 218b
  much learning make m., 50b
  naked summer night, 700a
  nobly wild not m., 320b
  north-northwest, 261a
  O fool I shall go m., 278a
  old m. blind despised king, 570a
  pleasure in being m., 369a
  practice drives me m., 1084b
  prose run m., 410b
  provided man not m., 436a
  pursuit, 583a
  sad and m. and bad, 666a
  sad m. brother's name, 776a
  saint run m., 412b

Mad, sense that world m., 938b
  that he is m. 'tis true, 260b
  that trusts in wolf, 279a
  to live m. to be saved, 1080b
  undevout astronomer is m., 399b
  we are m. nationally, 130b
  we have all been m., 872a
  went m. and bit the man, 448b
  world, 671b
  world mad kings, 236a
Madam Bad Luck, 588b
  call me m., 970a
  is there nothing else, 736a
  poetry the supreme fiction m., 955a
Madden, made mannikin to m. it, 643b
  rave recite and m., 410a
  to crime, 558a
Maddens, all that most m., 656b
  "Trees" m. me, 1000a
Madder music stronger wine, 890a
Maddest merriest day, 645a
Madding, far from m. crowd's strife, 440b
Made a rural pen, 486b
  and loveth all, 526a
  annihilating all that's m., 360a
  as he is so was he m., 801b
  begotten not m., 60a
  better self-m. than not m., 633b
  by whom all things m., 60a
  confusion m. masterpiece, 284a
  critics all ready m., 554b
  day which the Lord hath m., 22a
  did he who m. Lamb, 489b
  dost know who m. thee, 486b
  fearfully and wonderfully m., 23a
  for each other, 522b
  friends born not m., 776b
  God m. and eaten, 664b
  God m. him let him pass for man, 231b
  him a little lower than angels, 17a
  his pendent bed, 282a
  in wisdom hast thou m. all, 21b
  incarnate and was m. man, 60a
  it is he that hath m. us, 21a
  little Lamb who m. thee, 486b
  Lord God m. them all, 684b
  man was m. to mourn, 492b
  marriages m. in heaven, 203a
  men and not made them well, 263a
  mouths in a glass, 278a
  my song a coat, 881b
  myself a motley, 294a
  of sterner stuff, 255b
  poet's m. as well as born, 303b
  sea is his and he m. it, 21a
  stuff as dreams are m. on, 297b
  swears she is m. of truth, 294b
  the best of this, 496b
  this parting well m., 256b
  to sell and quickly, 988b
  us with large discourse, 264b
  what man has m. of man, 508b
  when or you or I are m., 320b
  without fear, 16b
  world I never m., 854a
  world of m. is not world of born, 1031b
Madeleine upon barroom floor, 797b

Main, toil and be mixed with m., 796b
watery m., 292b
Maine, as M. so goes nation, 1101a
remember the M., 1101b
Mainsails of stone, 911a
Mainstay, workers m. of civilization, 821a
Maintain, fuel to m. his fires, 327a
his argument, 244a
it before whole world, 361b
no ill opinions, 450a
poet's dignity and ease, 411a
the sublime, 988a
Maintained, boisterously m. as gained, 236b
Maintaining constitutional shield, 991a
independence to this day, 997b
Main-truck higher than kelson low, 696a
Mair, cantie wi' m., 494a
Maître, qui que tu sois voici ton m., 418a
tel m. tel valet, 188a
Maize, rose with m. to die, 1043b
Majestic free, 512b
instancy, 856b
law in m. equality, 802a
motion, 557a
silence, 458b
theme, 786b
though in ruin, 343b
Majestical, happy high m., 569b
laid in bed m., 244b
roof, 261a
Majesties, purple mountain m., 849a
Majesty, against thy Divine M., 61a
attribute to awe and m., 234b
clad in naked m., 345a
dignity m. sublimity, 462b
moon rising in clouded m., 345b
next in m. surpassed, 370b
of gods is revealed, 65b
of heaven, 420b
of this world, 1060b
rayless m., 399a
ride on in m. to meet thine, 691b
sight so touching in m., 512a
tender m., 735b
this earth of m., 226b
Major, model of m. general, 766b
poets read from own works, 1046a
Majorities, decision by m. expedient, 631b
not act arbitrarily, 1013a
not entirely wrong, 706a
Majority as distinguished from minority, 973a
authority not m., 600b
big enough m. in any town, 761b
deprive minority of right, 637a
divine m., 735a
fools big enough m., 761b
have clear-cut criteria, 1028a
he has joined great m., 133b
long since Death had m., 330b
man with God always in m., 186b
minority yield to m., 934b
never replace man, 1011b

Majority, not leave right to m., 681a
of one, 681a
one man with courage a m., 503b
one on God's side m., 659a
one with law m., 911a
questions not decided by m. 677a
respect minority, 934b
stirred by motives, 894a
'tis m. prevail, 735b
tyranny of m., 750a
when were good and brave in m., 684a
wisdom of m., 973a
Majors, make m. but not scholars, 311a
Make a joyful noise, 19b, 21a
angels weep, 271a
be and m. new nations, 299b
Britain country for heroes, 866a
conscience m. cowards, 262a
content with his fortunes, 278a
fault worse by excuse, 237a
fears m. us traitors, 285b
felicity we m. or find, 428a
ghost of him that lets me, 259b
haste better foot before, 237a
he himself his quietus m., 262a
her laugh at that, 266a
I could not well m. out, 532a
I shall m. reckless choice, 926b 1102b
it do or do without, 1102b
it over your way, 930a
lady of my own, 510b
life what we m. it, 794a
me a child again, 742b
me a fixed figure, 275b
me a willow cabin, 251b
me immortal with a kiss, 213a
me sick discussing duty, 700b
me that to thee, 405b
me to know mine end, 18b
men m. the city, 90b
mighty ocean, 719b
money by any means, 123a
most of what we yet may spend, 630a
my bed in hell, 23a
my bed soon, 1089a
my house your inn, 996b
my seated heart knock, 281b
my small elves coats, 229b
no truce with Adam-zad, 875a
not m. cannot mar, 711a
not m. scarecrow of law, 270a
of your prayers one sacrifice, 298a
only God can m. tree, 992a
our lives sublime, 620b
right to m. government, 461b
shalt not m. any graven image, 9a
so much of fragmentary blue, 927a
soul is form and doth body m., 201b
straight a highway for our God, 32b
sudden sally, 652a
the Lord m. his face shine upon thee, 9b
the most of it, 464b
thee an ark, 6b
thee mightier yet, 862a
thick my blood, 281b
things work my way, 983b

Make, unless philosophy m. a Juliet, 225a
up my sum, 266a
us do what we can, 608b
us heirs of all eternity, 221a
war to live in peace, 98a
waves m. towards pebbled shore, 292b
wind to shake world, 1055a
world safe for democracy, 842a
world safe for diversity, 1074a
worse appear the better, 91a
yourself do thing you have to, 725a
yourselves another face, 262b
Make-believe, Eve seen through m., 906a
Makeless, maiden that is m., 1084a
Maker, flower carries impress of M., 383a
more pure than his m., 14b
of Heaven and earth, 60a
reproacheth his M., 24b
tool m., 948a
Maker's rage, 956a
Makers, abhor m. and their laws approve, 370b
Makes, another which m., 95a
figure a poem m., 929b
heaven drowsy with harmony, 222a
heretic that m. the fire, 295a
me or fordoes me quite, 276b
me poor indeed, 274a
men mad, 276a
night hideous, 259a
one little room an everywhere, 304b
or mars us, 276a
swanlike end, 233b
sweet music with stones, 220b
them and arts and work, 933b
thinking m. it so, 261a
tongue of him that m. it, 222b
whole world kin, 269a
you thin, 1037a
Makest, thou m. darkness, 21b
what m. thou, 33a
Maketh clouds his chariot, 21a
he m. me to lie down, 17b
the deep to boil, 16b
Making green one red, 283b
it blossom with pleasure, 664a
machines for m. machines, 917b
many books, 29a, 962b
news better than taking it, 919b
night hideous, 259a
through creeks and inlets m., 688b
Mal, honi soit qui m. y pense, 163a
Maladies, soul with all its m., 781a
Maladministration, secured against m., 446a
Malady, greatest m. is poverty, 379a
he smiles it is a m., 114b
medicine worse than m., 125b
of cultivated classes, 706b
of not marking, 241b
to whose causation, 593b
Malaria ten parts, 864a
Malcontents, liege of m., 221b
Mars of m., 267a
Male and female created he, 5a
especially m. of species, 986a

Man, doubts began with fall of m., 901b
dream past wit of m., 230a
drest in brief authority, 270b
drink takes m., 790b
drove out the m., 6a
dull ear of drowsy m., 236b
dull m. always sure, 960b
each m. act of God, 679a
each m. kills thing he loves, 840b
each m. resembles other men, 957a
ear of m. hath not seen, 230a
eats when not hungry, 1102a
end of that m. is peace, 18b
enough for tear in eye, 831a
errs while struggle lasts, 478b
Esau was a m. of the field, 7a
escape from rope and gun, 401b
even such a m. so faint, 241a
every cry of every m., 489b
every m. a piece of the continent, 308b
every m. architect of his fortune, 116a
every m. at his best state, 18b
every m. for himself, 185b
every m. has his fault, 290a
every m. hath a good and bad angel, 310b
every m. his greatest enemy, 330a
every m. is wanted, 607b
every m. own architect, 667b
every m. to do duty, 492a
every m. under his vine, 13a
every m. was God or Devil, 368b
expatiate o'er scene of m., 407b
eye of m. hath not heard, 230a
faced with spiritual, 834b
fallen god, 565b
false m., 384b
false m. does easy, 284a
false to any m., 259a
fashion wears out more than m., 246b
favor with God and m., 46b
favorite of mother, 834b
first m. among these than second in Rome, 112a
first m. takes drink, 790b
first-class fightin' m., 873a
fit night for m. or beast, 951b
foolish fond old m., 280a
foolish passionate m., 884b
foot-in-the-grave young m., 767a
for all seasons, 179a
for m. marvel to be alive, 986a
for the field, 649a
for the sword, 649a
forgotten as a dead m. out of mind, 18a
forgotten m., 785a, 970b
formed by struggle, 978a
formed for society, 444b
formed m. of dust, 5a
free as Nature made m., 367a
fresh from natur's mold, 670b
fribble and less than m. of reason, 957a
Friday, 385b
frontiers where m. fronts fact, 681b
fury of patient m., 368b
gently scan brother m., 493b
get a new m., 297a

Man, get away from m., 809b
gird up thy loins like a m., 16a
give every m. thy ear, 258b
giveth up the ghost, 15a
go west young m., 678b
God above or m. below, 407b
God and m. decree, 854a
God became m. devil woman, 598b
god in ruins, 605a
God is not a m., 10a
God's ways to m., 853b
goes riding by, 823a
goeth forth unto his work, 21b
goeth to his long home, 29a
good for a m. that he bear the yoke, 34b
good great m. inherits, 527a
good m. and just, 47b
good m. does not argue, 75a
good m. wafted to all quarters, 80a
good name in m. and woman, 274a
great m. great ganglion, 787a
great nose great m., 895b
greater m. greater courtesy, 653b
greatest fool is m., 377a
greatest m. ever seen, 451b
grew within this learned m., 213b
grows beyond his work, 1052b
guess what m. going to do, 1017b
half part of blessed m., 236a
hand of a mighty m., 22b
hand will be against every m., 7a
happiness of common m., 949b
happy citizen free, 599b
happy m. be his dole, 182b
happy m. happy dole, 182b
happy m. works ancestral acres, 120b
happy old m., 116a
happy the m. and he alone, 369b
hardly a m. now alive, 623b
harrowing clods, 784a
has two primal passions, 817a
has will woman way, 633b
hath penance done, 525b
having put hand to plow, 46b
he was a m., 905a
he was a m. take him for all in all, 258a
he was her m., 1101b
heard wise m. say, 852b
heart of m. place devils dwell in, 330a
hearty old m., 531b
height of m. equal to tips of hands, 132b
her ways with a m., 1065b
her wit was more than m., 369b
high abstracted m. alone, 697a
his greatest enemy, 330a
his own executioner, 330a
honest exceeding poor m., 232b
honest m. appeals to understanding, 1092a
honest m. close-buttoned, 459a
honest m. noblest work of God, 409b, 492b
honest m. sent to lie abroad, 301a
horizontal m., 1059b

Man, horse noblest conquest of m., 423b
how dieth the wise m., 27b
how marvelous is m., 894b
how poor a thing is m., 211a
how proud word M. rings, 894b
howl for flesh of m., 1083b
hungry m. not free, 1048b
hungry sinner, 562a
I am cease to be, 652a
I am first a m., 414b
I appeal to any white m., 445b
I have been a m., 478a
I know myself a m., 301a
I loved the m. and honor memory, 304a
I must feel it as a m., 285b
I never writ nor no m. loved, 294a
I the m. in the moon, 230b
if a m. die shall he live, 15a
if a m. has talent, 1049b
if not wedding day is fixed on, 424b
if such a m. there be, 411a
if superior m. dwelt among Barbarians, 72a
I'll make me a m., 906b
in armor slave, 667b
in arms wish to be, 515a
in bush God meet, 602a
in every m. two postulations, 707a
in gray flannel suit, 1078a
in love endures more, 806a
in mind of m. a motion, 509b
in our town, 1098a
in soul of m. one Tahiti, 697a
in unsearchable darkness, 801b
in whose hand cup is found, 7b
in wilderness, 1093a
in wit a m., 369b
incarnate and was made m., 60a
indispensable m., 970b
inflicts pain for sport, 764a
influenced by polls, 983b
ingrateful m., 278a
inner m., 54a
insignificant and aware of it, 913b
intellect of m. choose, 884a
intellectual superiority of m., 764a
intimates eternity to m., 393b
invented m. because disappointed in monkey, 764a
is a prisoner, 93a
is a reasoning animal, 130a
is a thinking reed, 363b
is alone, 1058b
is as Heaven made him, 196a
is born for uprightness, 71b
is born free, 435b
is born unto trouble, 14b
is created free, 497b
is God blunder of m., 805b
is his own star, 313a
is m. blunder of God, 805b
is m. no more than this, 278b
is man and master, 653a
is not so good Christian, 824b
is not so great a coward, 824b
is one soul many tongues, 143b
is origin of his action, 98a
is something to be surpassed, 805a
is the hunter, 649a
je-ne-sais-quoi young m., 767a
judge m. by foes, 843a

Mediocre passions, 356a
  tomb of m. talent, 878a
Mediocrities, loss of appetite for
  m., 795b
  single genius hundred m., 770a
Mediocrity, gratified with m.,
  501b
  has no greater consolation, 478a
  history of masterwork not m.,
  989a
  knows nothing higher, 850a
  solitude safeguard of m., 608a
Meditate, in his law doth he m.,
  16b
  on blood, 244a
  on interstellar spaces, 888a
  thankless Muse, 338a
Meditating upon whatsoever state,
  106b
Meditation and water wedded,
  695b
  let us all to m., 215a
  maiden m. fancy-free, 229a
  of my heart, 17b
  where m. neither anxiety nor
  doubt, 157a
Meditative spleen. 516b
Mediterraneans see clearly, 977b
Medium, internal m., 675a
Medusa's, beauty that M. head,
  1022a
Meed of some melodious tear,
  338a
Meek and gentle with these
  butchers, 255a
  blessed are the m., 40a
  borne his faculties so m., 282b
  enter inheritance, 907a
  gentle Jesus m. and mild, 425b
  holy and m. she cries, 488a
  I am m. and lowly, 42a
  mysteries revealed unto m., 37a
  ornament of m. spirit, 57a
  safer m. than fierce, 666b
  shall inherit the earth, 18b
  soft m. patient humble, 301b
  terrible m., 907a
Meek-eyed parents, 1058a
Meekness, fruit of Spirit is m.,
  53b
  wrath by his m., 487a
Meet, beauteous flower when next
  we m., 224a
  descend to m., 606b
  experiment to me is everyone
  I m., 737b
  extremes m., 469a
  firm I can m., 506b
  goeth on to m. the armed men,
  16b
  him with one tooth, 909a
  if we do m. again, 256a
  in her aspect and eyes, 558b
  in one spirit m. mingle, 570a
  it and not see its head, 74a
  many ways m. in one town,
  243a
  me by moonlight, 587b
  methinks they are not m., 187a
  morning dew, 714a
  Mr. Eliot, 1004a
  never twain m., 872b
  on bridge of time, 707b
  political greatness and wisdom
  m., 94a
  shadow rising to m. you, 1002b
  spirit with spirit m., 654b
  thee in that hollow vale, 321b
  though infinite never m., 360a

Meet, two smiles m., 490a
  we shall m. but miss him, 676b
  we three m. again, 280b
  when men and mountains m.,
  490b
  where brook and river m., 621b
  with champagne and chicken,
  414a
  with joy in sweet Jerusalem,
  216b
  your visage here, 1043b
Meeter to carry off latter, 552b
Meeting, journeys end in lovers
  m., 251b
  soul may pierce, 335a
Meets in oppugnancy, 267b-268a
  less than m. the eye, 999a
  more meant than m. ear, 336a
Meg and Molly dear, 749b
Mehitabel, dance m. dance, 946a
Meilleur, le m. des mondes possibles, 417a
Meinself und Gott, 811a
Melancholia of everything completed, 805b
Melancholy as battle won, 506a
  as gib cat, 237b
  bait, 231b
  charm in m., 500b
  chord in m., 592a
  chronic m. of civilized, 783a
  days are come, 574b
  divinest M., 335b
  dull-eyed m., 290b
  green and yellow m., 252b
  House of Usher, 642a
  loathed M., 334b
  long withdrawing roar, 714b
  madness, 1091a
  marked him for her own,
  441a
  men eat no beans, 310b
  men most witty, 311a
  mirth has chord in m., 310a
  moping m., 348a
  most m. of reflections, 726b
  most musical most m., 335b
  music is good to the m., 374a
  naked m. isles, 419b
  naught so sweet as m., 310a
  never give way to m., 523a
  no m. if plenty to do, 685a
  O sweetest m., 313b
  ocean's gray m. waste, 574a
  of mine own, 250a
  pale M. sate retired, 443b
  purge m., 295b
  rare recipe for m., 534b
  rhyme and be m., 222a
  shade of m. boughs, 248b
  slow, 447b
  such charm in m., 500b
  suck m. out of song, 248a
  veiled M., 584a
  villainous m., 277a
  what charm soothe m., 448b
  what is most m., 643b
  who dismissed avarice, 469b
Melchizedek Ucalegon, 899b
Meliorist, not optimist but m.,
  852a
Mellow, fruit too m. for me, 414a
  he who goes to bed m., 312b
  humors grave or m., 394a
  like good wine, 869a
  rawness of opinion, 855a
Mellowed, fruit that m. long,
  367b
  to tender light, 558b

Mellowing, delivered upon m. of
  occasion, 222a
  year, 338a
Mellstock, lie in M. churchyard
  now, 783b
Melodies echoes of that voice,
  527a
  heard m. sweet, 583a
Melodious birds sing madrigals,
  212b
  bursts that fill, 645b
  meed of some m. tear, 338a
  plot, 582a
Melody, blundering kind of m.,
  369a
  could you view the m., 358b
  deprived of pitch, 999a
  falling in m. back, 526b
  grace is m., 747b
  life m., 699a
  mortal m., 641b
  my luve is like the m.,
  494a
  singing and making m., 54a
  small foweles maken m., 166a
Melrose, view fair M., 518a
Melt at others' woe, 439b
  butter not m. in mouth, 183b
  in her own fire, 264a
  into his heart, 509b
  let Rome in Tiber m., 287a
  this iron earth, 1055a
  too solid flesh would m., 257b
  with ruth, 339a
Melted, brown hills m. into
  spring, 685b
  fortune m. to water, 379a
  into air, 297b
  like snow, 559a
Melter of limbs, 67b
Melting airs, 458b
  mood, 276b
  poem ride on own m., 929b-
  930a
  pot, 87ob
  sweet music's m. fall, 442a
Melts, grief m. away, 323b
  like kisses, 559b
  pity m. mind to love, 313a
  then m. forever, 495b
Member of the rabble, 1032b
Members in arms and idleness,
  465b
  of human community, 974a
  one of another, 54a
  that one of thy m. should perish, 40a
Même, plus ça change plus la m.,
  627a
Mememormee, bussoftlhee m.,
  969a
Memento, some common m. better, 979a
Memnonium was in all its glory,
  543b
Mémoire, il faut bonne m. après
  qu'on a menti, 136a
Memoirs, not read Barère's M.,
  596b
  we will write our m., 504b
Memorable, days m. in history,
  923a
  sentences, 740b
Memorandum, make a m. of it,
  745a
Memorial, passover shall be for a
  m., 8b
  some have no m., 39a
  to soul's eternity, 731b

Memories encrusted with sublime thoughts, 943a
liars ought to have good m., 331b
more m. than if thousand years old, 707a
mother of m., 707a
night of m. and sighs, 536a
of eld, 642a
Memory, adduces authority uses m., 174a
archives of m., 902b
be green, 257a
cherish his m., 751a
chords of m., 637b
comes like a banshee, 830b
complains of his m., 355b
dear son of m., 334a
emancipated from time, 529a
fills m. with natural objects, 478a
fond m. brings light, 542b
footfalls echo in m., 1004b
Franklin's quiet m., 563a
from false to false, 268b
good m. needed after one has lied, 331b
good m. to keep promises, 804b
green, 257a, 541b
grows fainter relaxes bonds, 908a
hands of m. weave, 778a
he shall have a noble m., 290a
history vitalizes m., 110b
honor his m., 304a
how sweet their m. still, 456b
how vast a m. has Love, 402b
illiterate him from your m., 480b
in book of my m. a rubric, 159a
indebted to m. for jests, 482a
keep m. green, 541b
liar should have good m., 136a
life a m. without pain, 81b
mixing in m. and desire, 1002a
mousetraps moon m. muchness, 744a
my name and m, I leave, 209b
nation's m. and veneration, 947b
no force abolish m., 973b
no m. of having starred, 928b
not make philosopher, 598a
not necessary for love, 1041a
note you in book of m., 214a
of a lovely thing, 982a
of all he stole, 413b
of benefits fades, 81a
of Boatswain a dog, 554b
of loved and lost, 640a
of Paris inexhaustible, 1020a
of the just is blessed, 24a
of them is forgotten, 28b
only shield in war, 922a
outlive his life, 263a
painted perfect day, 862b
pluck from m. rooted sorrow, 286a
plucking fruit of m., 844b
poor m. that only works backwards, 746a
pray bring me to men's m., 160a
profitable cherishing m., 751a
proper m. for politician, 779b
put red star in corner, 1047a
shall be ours, 625a
sinner of his m., 296a
some women stay in m., 876b

Memory, table of my m., 260a
tablet a gift of m., 95b
takes to caverns, 587b
their very m. is fair, 362b
thou fond deceiver, 447a
thoughts to m. dear, 520b
throng into my m., 336b
'tis in my m. locked, 259a
to m. dear thou remain, 590a
vanity tricks m., 843a
ventricle of m., 222a
vibrates in m., 572b
viol of her m., 955b
warder of the brain, 283a
while m. holds a seat, 260a
wit at expense of m., 391a
Mem'ry, cherish his m., 751a
Men, a few honest m., 327b
about me that are fat, 253a
above reach of ordinary m., 512a
adversity test of strong m., 130a
all are m. condemned, 439b
all honorable m., 255b
all m. are liars, 22a
all m. be free, 640b
all m. born distraught, 1080a
all m. born free, 341a
all m. created equal, 470b, 639a
all m. liable to error, 372b
all m. make faults, 292a
all m. Noah's sons, 1078b
all m. strive, 664a
all m. would be tyrants, 385b
all sorts and conditions of m., 60a
all the king's m., 1095b
all the stones are m., 704b
and boys thick as hasty pudding, 1090a
and women merely players, 248b
animals infuse into trunks of m., 234a
April when they woo, 250b
are men, 273b
are my teachers, 408b
are quick to flare up, 65b
are we and must grieve, 512b
are where they are, 683b
arm and burgonet of m., 287b
as in a theater eyes of m., 228a
aspiring to be angels m. rebel, 408a
at point of death, 225b
at whiles sober, 854a
attend m. and not women, 95b
bad cause bad means bad m., 467a
be read as books too much, 406a
be you the m. you've been, 852a
beacons of wise m., 725a
below and saints above, 518b
best m. molded of faults, 272a
best of m., 287b
best of m. that e'er wore earth, 301b
better m. his victims, 471a
black m. are pearls, 221a
bodies of unburied m., 315a
body of well-instructed m., 628a
books like m., 388b
born under happier stars, 528b
boys and girls level with m., 288b
brave m. and worthy patriots, 340a

Men, brave m. brave from the first, 331b
brave m. lived before Agamemnon, 122b
brave m. living and dead, 639a
busy haunts of m., 574a
busy hum of m., 335a
by nature desire knowledge, 97b
by nature equally free, 445b
call up your m., 522a
cannot learn m. from books, 611a
capable of wickedness, 844a
captain of m. of death, 366a
capture of m. by women, 659b
cause or m. of Emerald Isle, 483b
cheerful ways of m., 344b
children of m. full of wiles, 91a
circumstances rule m., 87a
cities of m. and manners, 646a
condemn m. because few, 684a
Constitution for all m., 678a
creatures that once were m., 894b
creep not walk, 626a
crowd of common m., 327b
cunning m. pass for wise, 209a
darling of m. and gods, 112b
day is for honest m., 85a
dead m. rise up never, 775a
Death that feeds on m., 294b
decay, 449a
deceivers ever, 246a
decent easy m., 466a
desire the good, 98a
destiny with m. for pieces plays, 630b
determine gods dispose, 311b
die like m., 20a, 627b
die to make m. free, 690b
died as m. before their bodies died, 1060b
died to make m. holy, 690b
differ as heaven and earth, 653a
difference of forty thousand m., 506a
different from ordinary m., 740a
dine with some m., 934a
disbelief in great m., 577a
disease of old m. avarice, 314a
disgrace labor, 717b
done with roofs and m., 860a
doors for m. to take their exits, 315a
duration of great sentiments makes great m., 805a
dying m., 712b
dying m. enforce attention, 226b
eat hogs, 955b
education is making m., 741a
eight or nine elderly m., 870b
either war obsolete or m., 1034a
England is purgatory of m., 201b
envy of brilliant m., 910a
equal right of m. and women, 1104a
errors of wise m., 351a
evil m. do lives after them, 255a
evils draw m. together, 98b
fair women and brave m., 555b
fear of little m., 729a
feared witches, 832b
fell out knew not why, 351b

Minds are finite, 861b
  are not ever craving, 483a
  balm of hurt m., 283b
  becks m. to fellowship, 580b
  bore so much as own m., 694b
  can heavenly m. yield, 117b
  comfortable m., 1030b
  free to speak our m., 1025a
  great empire and little m., 453b
  greatest m. capable of greatest
    vices, 327b
  grow in spots, 795a
  hobgoblin of little m., 606a
  home in m. of men, 90a
  injured by hunger and thirst,
    100b
  innocent and quiet, 358b
  intercourse with superior m.,
    544b
  keep m. alive forever, 1047a
  keep your hearts and m., 54b
  let our m. be bold, 833a
  lose self in other m., 535b
  made better by presence, 689a
  marriage of true m., 294a
  me o' departed joys, 494a
  mediocre m., 356a
  men of other m., 447b
  mighty m. of old, 532b
  naturally affirmative, 770b
  not aware of m., 1041a
  O miserable m. of men, 113b
  of different generations, 987a
  of few fastidious people, 878a
  of gods not changed, 65a
  of my generation, 1081b
  of strongest m. hears least, 516a
  peace must be in m., 1104a
  record of best m., 573a
  refuge of weak m., 415b
  religion of feeble m., 454b
  small m. never handle great
    themes, 145b
  so many men so many m., 109a
  stay our m. be staid, 929a
  steadiest m. to waver, 82a
  strong m. great hearts, 690b
  that have nothing, 517b
  themselves our m. impress, 508b
  to different m., 604b
  wars begin in m., 1104a
  weak m. recriminate, 528b
  young men's m. are change-
    able, 62b
Mine, every beast of the forest is
    m., 19a
  eyes have seen glory, 690b
  factory dockyard, 923b
  fatal words m. and thine, 194a
  lives ye led were m., 871b
  mother o' m., 872b
  she shall be m., 510b
  was ever grief like m., 322b
  what is yours is m., 105a
Mine, what's m. is yours, 272a
  why shouldst thou have m.,
    350b
  will defend what's m., 198a
  with my heart in it, 297a
Minerals, poisonous m. and that
    tree, 307b
Mingle blood with blood of chil-
    dren, 594a
  in one spirit meet m., 570a
  joys with occupation, 425a
  letters in m. souls, 307a
  you that m. may, 314b
Mingled, like kindred drops been
    m., 457b

Mingled, respect m. with surprise,
    520a
  yarn good and ill, 269b
Mingles, mind m. with whole
    frame, 119a
  with friendly bowl, 411b
  with her cares sweet bitterness,
    115a
Miniature thunder where he fled,
    927b
Minikin won't set fire to Thames,
    442b
Minimum guarantee of First
    Amendment, 991b
Mining, titles of m. claims, 1041b
Minion, morning's m., 803a
  songs lyric m., 588a
Minister droned monotonously,
    759b
  king's first m., 924a
  patient must m. to himself,
    286b
  thou flaming m., 276a
  to mind diseased, 286a
  touch me and no m. so sore,
    411b
Ministering angel shall my sister
    be, 266a
  angel thou, 519b
Minister's, poor m. experience,
    614a
Ministers fall on good side, 553b
  maketh m. flame of fire, 55b
  not act arbitrarily, 1013a
  of grace defend us, 259a
  of love, 526b
  spoke of God as if a monopoly,
    683b
  you murdering m., 282a
Ministers', my actions are my m.,
    366b
Ministry, by the m. of the proph-
    ets, 35b
  frost performs secret m., 526a
Miniver Cheevy, 899b
Minked and Persian-lambed,
    866b
Minnehaha Laughing Water, 623a
Minnesotan, young M. did heroic
    thing, 1051a
Minnow, whale swims m.-small,
    991a
Minnows, swarms of m. show
    heads, 579a
  Triton of the m., 289b
Minnow-small, whale swims m.,
    991a
Minor, embalm m. poet, 1035a
  pants for twenty-one, 412a
Minorities are qualified individu-
    als, 978a
  government controlled by m.,
    863a
Minority always right, 729b
  as distinguished from majority,
    973a
  elite m., 978a
  judgment of small m., 973a
  majority deprive m., 637a
  majority respect m., 934b
  most vilified m. in history, 967a
  yield to majority, 934b
Minstrel boy to war has gone,
    542a
  ethereal m., 517a
  galleons of fire, 1043a
  heart of m. is breaking, 541b
  infirm and old, 518a

Minstrel, no m. raptures swell,
    518b
  wandering m. I, 768a
Minstrel's, power of m. lyre, 906b
Mint of joy, 551b
  tithe of m., 43b
  were each wish m. of gold, 503a
Minting of gold-crowned king,
    982a
Minus, maggots m., 1031b
Minute, cage the m., 1062a
  crowd whole thing in m., 814b
  Cynthia of this m., 406b
  do good in m. particulars, 491a
  of life passing, 780b
  one m. with him, 981a
  save fleeting m., 818b
  speak more in m., 224b
  sucker born every m., 655b
  too late, 267a
Minutely organized particulars,
    491a
  set ingenious machine, 984b
Minute's success pays failure,
    668b
  who buys a m. mirth, 220a
Minutes, a few m. for poetry,
    728b
  fifteen m. of hell, 808b
  five m. with that man, 451b
  hasten to their end, 292b
  hours and m. dollars and cents,
    422b
  my thoughts are m., 228b
  round earth in forty m., 229b
  sixty diamond m., 586b
  unless m. capons, 237b
  what damned m. tells he, 274a
Miracle, cubic inch of space m.,
    702b
  every hour a m., 702b
  man always prays for m., 688a
  musical m., 898a
  mystery and authority, 708a
  no greater m. than myself, 191b
  no testimony establish m., 434b
  of rare device, 524a
  r'ar back pass m., 1015a
Miracles, age of m., 577a
  are past, 269b
  laughed at, 891b
  many signal m. on voyage, 173a
  propitious accidents, 867b
Miraculous, falsehood more m.
    than fact, 434b
Miranda, remember inn M., 902a
Mire, learning cast into m., 454a
  ne'er left man in m., 290a
  rode him through m., 1097b
Mirror, best m. an old friend,
    324b
  cracked from side to side, 646a
  face the m. of the mind, 145b
  hold m. up to nature, 262b
  in every mind, 428b
  in law as magic m., 786b
  look into lives as into m., 109b
  of all courtesy, 168a, 298a
  speech a m. of soul, 127b
  stock market a m., 1062b
  that reflects candle, 865b
  thou glorious m., 557b
Mirrored on her sea, 906a
Mirroring, windborne m. soul,
    711b
Mirrors, light focused by m., 797b
  of shadows futurity casts, 573a
  on empty space, 797b
  should reflect, 1018b

Moderator of passions, 326a
  reasonable m. Death, 329b
Modern, all history m., 957b
  American literature from one
    book, 1044b
  born empty into m. age, 378b
  characteristics of m. spirit, 863a
  disease of m. life, 712a
  inconveniences, 760b
  life economic, 957b
  man invents museum, 1035a
  old or m. bard, 336b
  one must be absolutely m., 830b
  origin of m. world, 1047a
  something for m. stage, 988a
  spite all m. notions, 874a
  wise saws and m. instances,
    249a
Moderns, speak of m. without
  contempt, 415b
Modes, for m. of faith, 409b
Modest and commonly chaste,
  564b
  coy submission m. pride, 345a
  doubt, 268a
  front of this small floor, 354b
  in speech, 72b
  keep m. as giver, 805a
  looks cottage adorn, 450b
  man with reason, 925a
  no more m. than immodest,
    700b
  quip m., 251a
  simple m. manly true, 694a
  stillness and humility, 243b
  the m. near to virtue, 72a
  wee m. crimson-tipped, 493a
  woman dressed in finery, 450b
Modesty a species of nobility,
  373b
  ancient sculpture true m., 552b
  and unselfishness, 987a
  maids in m. say No., 220b
  mine is blushing m., 128a
  overstep not m. of nature, 262b
  secondly m., 818b
  speaks without m., 72a
Modification, bad plan admits no
  m., 126a
Modify, time to m. shape, 763b
Modifying colors of imagination,
  529a
Modo liceat vivere est spes, 108b
Modum, servare m. finemque tenere, 716a
Modus, est m. in rebus, 120a
Moi, l'état c'est m., 378a
Moiling street, 898b
Moist, cold and hot m. and dry,
  369b
  eye dry hand, 241b
  hot cold m. and dry, 344a
  no more than m. hand, 955b
  star upon whose influence, 257a
  unpleasant body, 669b
Moisty morning, 1098a
Molar to molecular motions, 788a
Mold, emperors and cobblers in
  same m., 190a
  fresh from natur's m., 670b
  made him and then broke m.,
    178a
  of form, 262b
  rose above m., 593a
  splashing wintry m., 880b
Molded, best men m. of faults,
  272a
  changing lineaments, 781a
  heart m. as she pleases, 197b

Molded, scarcely formed or m.,
  562a
  two berries m. on one stem,
    230a
Moldering, a-m. in grave, 755a
Molders hemp and steel, 521a
Molding mighty fates, 899a
  wine jar when m. began, 124a
Molds, crack nature's m., 278a
  musket m. in his hands, 820b
Mole, live like velvet m., 990a
  wilt thou go ask the m., 486b
Molecular motions, 788a
Molecule, propensity to unite
  even in m., 965a
Molecules, by mathematics m.
  counted, 861a
  simple and indivisible m., 474b
Molehills from mountains made,
  1031a
Moles, cast his idols to m., 30a
Molle atque facetum, 120a
Mollify it with tears, 920b
Mollusk cheap edition of man,
  609a
Molly Stark a widow, 451b
Moloch sceptered king, 343a
Molten bowels, 917b
  inns of m. blue, 735a
  tears scald like m. lead, 280a
Mome raths outgrabe, 745a
Moment, courage of final m.,
  1072a
  culture m. of clarity, 977b
  dissolved in a m., 994b
  endurance for m. more, 809b
  endures m. or day, 883b
  eternity was in that m., 391b
  face some awful m., 515a
  first m. of atomic age, 1069b
  force m. to its crisis, 1001a
  great pith and m., 262a
  hide thyself for a little m., 32a
  hold every m. sacred, 937b
  I cut his throat, 1081a
  in a m. of time, 46b
  intense m. isolated, 1006a
  knew m. to say nothing, 839a
  lifetime burning in m., 1006a
  lived in paradise, 497b
  loyal and neutral in m., 284a
  men flourish only for a m., 67a
  never let up for single m., 983a
  not of action or inaction, 106a
  nothing startles beyond m.,
    584b
  of difficulty and danger, 1091b
  of greatness flicker, 1001a
  of strength of romance, 843a
  once let ripe m. go, 488b
  only a m., 843a
  only m. here and m. there,
    930a
  perfection but m., 291b
  precise m. to say nothing, 839a
  psychological m., 839a
  this m. in June, 975a
  this which you deem of no m.,
    96a
  time of death every m., 106a
  to decide, 691b
  trap m. before ripe, 488b
  work of a m., 194a
  worst m. in history of France,
    1016a
Momentary, beauty m. in mind,
  955b
Moment's monument, 731b
  sent to be m. ornament, 514a

Moments, art gives quality to m.,
  781b
  best and happiest m., 573a
  hardly dared pass, 1047b
  lucid m., 588b
  no two m. the same, 705b
  of glad grace, 879b
  of high exultation, 997a
  when everything goes well, 869a
Momentum, psychological m.,
  839a
Monads of Leibniz, 987a
Monagony being married to one
  person, 1017a
Monan's, moon on M. rill, 520a
Monarch, becomes throned m.
  better than crown, 234b
  hears, 371a
  love teach m. to be wise, 439b
  merry m. scandalous and poor,
    382a
  morsel for a m., 287b
  of all I survey, 457b
  of mountains, 559b
  of the vine, 288a
  richest m. in world, 497b
Monarchs, fate summons m. obey,
  369a
  perplexes m., 342b
Monarchy intelligible government,
  726b
  is a merchantman, 491b
  universal m. of wit, 326b
  why m. strong government,
    726b
Monastic aisles, 602a
  man artist, 956b
Monday, betwixt Saturday and
  M., 401a
  born on a M., 1096a
  going to do on M., 962a
  morning press reports, 1058a
  snatched on M. night, 237b
Monday's child fair of face, 1096a
Monde, l'amour fait tourner le
  m., 1105b
Mondes, le meilleur des m. possibles, 417a
Mo'ners, Lord fetch m. up higher, 814a
Money, a little wanton m., 178b
  alone preserves life, 379a
  answereth all things, 28b
  ask of m. spent, 928b
  beautiful in laws, 607a
  bet my m. on bobtail nag, 727b
  blessing m. cannot buy, 326b
  board m. in ginger jar, 753b
  bringing m. be welcome, 1089b
  business may bring m., 533b
  business other people's m., 723a
  by you all the while, 812b
  counting out m., 1094b
  disease called lack of m., 181a
  doänt marry for m., 654b
  fool and his m., 1085a
  friendship last lifetime if not
    asked for m., 762a
  go where m. is, 654b
  government consists in taking
    m., 417b
  hain't the m. but the principle,
    895a
  having more credit than m.,
    477a
  hired m. didn't they, 911a
  honey and plenty of m., 673a
  how painful to keep m., 376a
  how pleasant to have m., 688b

Monuments carved from snow, 998a
economic m., 1063b
mountains earth's m., 615a
not marble nor gilded m., 292a
of safety, 472a
of unaging intellect, 882b
of wit survive monuments of power, 206a
Monumentum, si m. requiris circumspice, 374b
Mony a one for him, 1088b
Monyment, vote m. but refuse help, 890b
Mood apart, 929a
blessed m., 509a
given heart change of m., 927a
in any shape any m., 559a
listening m. seemed to stand, 520a
love is a m. to man, 825b
melting m., 276b
no m. maintained through hours, 937b
puts me in working m., 604a
strain of higher m., 338b
sweet m. when pleasant thoughts, 508b
Moody food of love, 288a
Moon, African m. lying on back, 985a
and I, 768b
and I keep this up forever, 963a
and stars keep pace, 992a
appointeth the m. for seasons, 21b
a-roving by light of m., 559b
be not darkened, 28b
be still as bright, 559b
behold the wandering m., 335b
beneath waning m. was haunted, 523b
brilliant m. milky sky, 880a
by yonder blessed m. I swear, 224a
circumambulatory aphrodisiac, 1061b
close by the m., 344b
cold fruitless m., 228b
come from the dying m., 648b
cow jumped over m., 1094a
danced by light of m., 673a
daughter of M. Nokomis, 623a
do not sigh for m., 751a
ebb and flow by the m., 280b
eclipses of m. and other experiments, 173b
error of the m., 276a
everyone is a m. has dark side, 763a
fair as the m., 29b
fair along Wabash, 905b
follow changes of the m., 274b
full m. throw shadow, 985a
ghostly galleon, 961b
hang them on horns of the m., 289b
harvest m., 386a
has set, 69b
hath her eclipse endured, 293b
horned m. with one star, 525a
hush with setting m., 652b
I the man in the m., 230b
if m. shine full or no, 353a
in first of the m., 1065b
in silver bag, 884b
inconstant m., 224a
innocent m., 856b

Moon is down, 283a
kneaded by the m., 783a
Lady M. where are you roving, 634b
landscapes of m., 908b
lanthorn is the m., 230b
lies fair upon the Straits, 714b
like a flower, 487a
lucent as rounded m., 694b
made of green cheese, 185b
make guilty the m., 277a
minions of the m., 237b
moping owl to m. complain, 440a
mountains of m., 644a
mousetraps m. memory muchness, 744a
moving m. went up sky, 525b
new m. with auld in arm, 1087b
no m. outlives night, 1081b
no Moravians in m., 695b
nor the m. by night, 22a
nothing remarkable beneath visiting m., 288b
of my delight, 630b
on casement wintry m., 582a
on Monan's rill, 520a
on whom pale m. gleams, 807a
one revolving m., 368b
or sun or what you please, 219b
pluck honor from pale-faced m., 238b
poet not been in m., 760b
ragged m., 1066a
rake m. from sea, 553a
rather be dog and bay m., 256a
revisitest glimpses of m., 259a
rising in clouded majesty, 345b
roving by light of m., 559b
sadder light than m., 626b
said wind to m., 723b
seventeen times high as m., 1095b
shines bright, 235a
shining to quiet m., 526a
ship woman and full m., 1102a
shone on Mrs. Porter, 1002b
sickle m., 980a
sigh for m., 751a
silent as the m., 349a
silver apples of m., 880a
slowly silently now the m., 914a
stain both m. and sun, 292a
stand still in the valley, 11a
star planets fallen on me, 982a
stars about the lovely m., 69b
sun and m. in flat sea sunk, 337a
sun and m. should doubt, 490a
swear not by the m., 224a
sweet regent of sky, 464a
takes up wondrous tale, 393a
talk by poet, 760b
this night of no m., 152b
tree etched by m., 384a
unmask her beauty to m., 258a
whenever m. and stars set, 823a
white m. beams, 1012b
whom are you loving, 634b
wide awake the m. and I, 768b
will wax wane, 624b
with how sad steps O M., 203b
would have disappeared, 851a
youth build bridge to m., 682a
Moon-calf, 297a
Moonlecht, braw brecht m. necht, 903a

Moonless night in small town, 1071a
Moonlight, come to thee by m., 961b
ghost along m. shade, 405b
how sweet the m. sleeps, 235a
human m., 1081a
is divine, 1069a
meet me by m., 587b
no more from m., 955b
one by one in m., 1010b
ribbon of m., 961b
softest in Kentucky, 804b
unto sunlight, 647b
visit it by pale m., 518a
white waves in m., 905a
Moonlit door, 914b
Moon's red silver, 1081a
Moons, book of m. defend ye, 1085b
not hers lie mirrored, 906a
of Saturn, 697a
reason has m., 906a
Moonshine an' snow, 693a
find out m., 230a
glory of war m., 705a
Moon-struck madness, 348a
Moony, little lovely m. night, 490a
Moor bark with two anchors, 125a
never saw a m., 737b
over the purple m., 961b
your daughter and the M., 272b
Moore, before I go Tom M., 559b
Moored, in Downs fleet m., 401a
Moors, mountains m. fens, 909a
Moos, my foos won't m., 968b
Moose, bull m., 847b
sticking head in m., 967b
Moping melancholy, 348a
merryman m. mum, 769a
owl to moon complain, 440a
Mops, seven m., 745b
Mopsy Cottontail Peter, 887b
Moral and material welfare, 848a
and political systems, 958a
attitude in which most alive, 792b
author provided with m., 614b
authority, 706b
bad m. character, 423a
conception of life, 850b
confronted with m. issue, 1074a
conquests, 589b
courage physical timidity, 783a
depravity within classes, 991a
difference in m. life, 795a
equivalent of war, 795b
everything's got a m., 744a
flabbiness, 792b
force, 863a
gloom of world, 613b
habits make way into lives, 136b
indifference of cultivated, 706b
inferiority of man, 764a
intellectual wants, 794b
law within me, 445a
man and man of honor, 961a
natural and m. forces, 710a
natural philosophy deep m. grave, 209b
no one m. till all m., 706a
not showing m. virtues, 980b
obligation to be intelligent, 951a
of m. evil and of good, 509a
of that is, 744b
or immoral book, 839a

Morning of the world, 661b
  our share of m., 734a
  penitence next m., 670a
  praise at m. blame at night, 403b
  quintessence of life, 564a
  shadow at m. striding, 1002a
  shining m. face, 249a
  singing each m., 1031b
  so soft this m., 969a
  some m. unaware, 663a
  somewhere with m., 948a
  son of the m., 31b
  sons of the m., 549a
  sorrow makes night m., 217a
  sow thy seed in the m., 28b
  stars sang together, 16a
  they that watch for m., 22b
  think in the m., 487b
  this m. came home cloak, 375a
  top o' the m., 812a
  two o'clock in m. courage, 504b
  uncertain hour before m., 1006b
  veils of m., 879b
  wings of the m., 23a
  woe to them that rise early in m., 30b
  womb of m. dew, 200a
  would God it were m., 10b
Morning's at seven, 661b
  easy m. ride, 738b
  minion, 803a
  mornin', 830b
Mornings, forgotten m., 1070b
  savor of m. great delight, 171b
  strangely silent, 1061b
Morocco, far as from M., 1085b
Moron, happy m., 1103b
Morose, obstinate pliant merry m., 135b
  view of present, 596b
Morrison Morrison, 970a
Morrow, a little fun and good m., 751b
  cease to ask what m. will bring, 121a
  desire of night for the m., 572b
  good m. to our waking souls, 304b
  good night till it be m., 224b
  man's yesterday ne'er like m., 568a
  misty m. a myrie someris day, 164b
  night urge the m., 571b
  put not trust in the m., 121a
  rainy m., 293a
  rash who reckons on m., 82b
  rose the m. morn, 526a
  take no thought for m., 41a
  wished the m., 642b
Mors, nil igitur m. est ad nos, 113b
  ultima ratio, 151a
Morsel for a monarch, 287b
  I found you as a m., 288a
  under tongue sweet m., 386a
Morsels, tough m. to swallow, 805b
Mort, que la m. me trouve plantant mes choux, 189b
Mortal and may err, 327b
  arm and nerve feel, 521a
  behind m. bone, 735b
  cloud of m. destiny, 711b
  coil, 262a
  dreams no m. dared, 643a
  every tatter in m. dress, 882b

Mortal frame, 526b
  genius and m. instruments, 254a
  grief itself be m., 571b
  grows on m. soil, 338b
  I sing with m. voice, 346b
  immortal death has taken m. life, 113b
  immortal youth to m. maids, 536b
  knew my son was m., 92b
  laugh at m. thing, 561a
  locked up from m. eye, 354a
  man who hath more joy, 697a
  meanest m. known, 789b
  melody, 641b
  moon eclipse endured, 293b
  nature did tremble, 513b
  nature of mind m., 113b
  no m. could vie with Zeus, 65a
  not m. what you desire, 128b
  O you m. engines, 275a
  or immortal here I die, 696a
  purest treasure m. times afford, 226a
  put on immortality, 53a
  quit this m. frame, 404a
  raised a m. to the skies, 371b
  shall m. man be more just, 14b
  shuffled off this m. coil, 262a
  sins of commission m., 434a
  spirit of m. be proud, 564a
  splendor, 994b
  stakes, 928b
  struck a deep m. blow, 78b
  sufferest m. griefs, 244b
  temples of king, 227b
  tend on m. thoughts, 281b
  therefore Caius is m., 732b
  things doth sway, 200b
  think all men m. but themselves, 399a
  think m. thoughts, 84a
  this his m. part, 765a
  tree whose m. taste, 341b
  what m. heard good of George the Third, 934a
  wide and m. pang, 1057b
  wound is m. and is mine, 1032a
Mortalem vitam mors cum immortalis, 113b
Mortality, nothing serious in m., 284a
  of inanimate things, 772a
  pilgrims of m., 999b
  to frail m. trust, 210a
  touches the heart, 118a
  watch o'er man's m., 514a
  weighs on me like sleep, 579b
Mortality's strong hand, 237a
  too weak to bear them, 385a
Mortals are blaming the gods, 65a
  changeful mind of m., 80a
  happiest of m., 417a
  Hope lies to m., 854b
  make earth bitter, 577a
  miserable m. like leaves, 64b
  more rugged m., 886a
  no ascent too steep for m., 120b
  not in m. to command success, 393a
  some feelings to m. given, 520a
  what all m. may correct, 390a
  what fools these m. be, 129b, 230a
  when to mischief m. bend, 404b
Mortar, his chest as a m., 697a
Mortgage beats 'em all, 808b

Mortgage, every radish had a m., 993a
Mortification, live in continual m., 420b
Mortify a wit, 412b
Mortifying reflections, 628a
Mortis, timor m. conturbat me, 176a
Mosaic religion a father religion, 834b
Moscow, to M. to M., 858b
Moses, greeted M. from Pisgah, 587a
  hid his face, 8a
  Mahomet to M., 600b
  ridin' on bumblebee, 1041b
  smote rock twice, 547b
  was there forty days, 9b
Moslem mosque and pagan shrine, 626a
Mosquitoes, lets big m. through, 321a
Moss, rolling stone gathers no m., 126a
  until m. reached lips, 736a
  you are, 987b
Moss-covered bucket, 553a
Mosses, addled m. dank, 989a
  greenest m. cling, 625b
Mossy cavern, 583b
  violet by m. stone, 510b
Most enjoy contented least, 292a
  fails where m. it promises, 269b
  make the m. of it, 464b
  may err grossly as few, 368b
  thing they m. do show, 293a
  who is it that says m., 293a
Mostest, git thar fustest with m., 799b
Mote in thy brother's eye, 41a
Motes that people sunbeams, 335b
  thick as m. in sonne-beem, 168a
Moth and rust doth corrupt, 40b
  blundering by, 1066b
  both m. and flame, 1066a
  desire of m. for star, 572b
Mother accursed the night she bore me, 84a
  and lover the sea, 774a
  arose a m. in Israel, 11a
  as m. so her daughter, 34b
  blessed m. of us all, 474a
  bring child back to its m., 69b
  call me early m., 645a
  calls me Willie, 821a
  came and caught her, 1095b
  Charybdis your m., 234a
  child to m. sheep to fold, 854a
  Church, 143b
  cruel m. of sweet loves, 122b
  despise not thy m., 26a
  died today, 1068b
  diligence m. of good fortune, 197a
  earth no more a m., 132a
  English m. made moan, 693b
  experience m. of sciences, 194b
  fairer daughter of fair m., 121a
  father and m. gae mad, 494b
  foolish son the heaviness of his m., 24a
  France m. of arts, 187b
  from one m. both draw breath, 79b
  gave m. forty whacks, 1101a
  give me the sun, 729b
  Goose, 844b
  happy with such a m., 649b

Nonpayment, out of doors for n. 1105a
Nonprogressive, lazy n. people, 1019b
Nonsense and beauty close connections, 951b
  corner of n., 530a
  era of wonderful n., 1032b
  grammar n. and learning, 450b
  through sense and n., 369a
Nonviolence and truth inseparable, 897a
  first article of faith, 897a
  is the answer, 1082b
Nonviolent action supplement change, 1083a
  resistance paralyzed, 1083a
Nook, a privacy an obscure n., 661b
  book and shady n., 786a
  for heart tried too sore, 578b
Nooks, sequestered n., 624b
Noon, act in the n., 487b
  and evening of lives, 720b
  athwart the n., 526a
  dark amid blaze of n., 349a
  far from fiery n., 584a
  from morn to n. he fell, 343a
  from n. to dewy eve, 343a
  lying till n., 428b
  midnight is n. of thought, 470a
  morning evening n. night, 662a
  now you come at n., 1097b
  purple glow, 879b
  riding near her highest n., 335b
  sun at n., 308b
  under the palmtree at n., 1004a
  weight of primary n., 956b
  whirling hands at n., 1056b
Noonday, age clearer than n., 15a
  bird of night at n., 254a
  destruction that wasteth at n., 20b
Noontide, night morning and n. night, 217a
Noose, marriage a n., 196b
  of light, 629a
  very best o' n., 693b
Noosed, strapped n. nighing hour, 854a
Nooses give, 1029a
Noosphere, introversion of n., 965a
Nor'east to sou'west winds, 760a
Norm, constraining n. shaping, 845b
Normal, beyond nature of n. man, 378b
  rate of growth, 756b
  satisfies no n. need, 1037a
  situation n. fouled up, 1103b
Norman blood, 645a
Norman's, reef of N. Woe, 621a
Noroway o'er the faem, 1087b
North, Ariosto of the N., 557b
  awake O n. wind, 29b
  Countree hard countree, 1035a
  elevation of the n. star, 173b
  fair weather cometh out of the n., 16a
  farewell to the n., 494b
  fifty n. forty west, 876a
  Hotspur of the N., 239a
  infect to n. star, 246a
  iron door of n., 1057a
  lanterns in N. Church, 464b
  next gale from n., 465a
  no N. no East no West, 538b
  poles and equators, 746b

North, ship in N. Country, 1089a
  spring trips n. again, 1009b
  unripened beauties of n., 393b
  wind doth blow, 1095b
  without sharp n., 304b
North America, native warrior of N., 564a
North Carolina, said to governor of N.C., 824b
North Sea, throw beer into N., 818a
Northeast, establishment mostly from N., 1071b
  heel of N. Trade, 874a
  to sou'west winds, 760a
Northern charm southern efficiency, 1074b
  constant as n. star, 254b
  kind as n. face, 1043b
  laurels not change, 460a
  lights seen queer sights, 933a
  ocean in vast whirls, 419b
  states muddle through, 658a
  thought slow durable, 664b
Northland, skoal to the N., 621a
  soul, 1035b
North-northeast, wind always n., 900a
North-northwest, but mad n., 261a
Northwest, Chicago at n. gates, 898b
  Passage to intellectual world, 438a
  to n. died away, 663a
Norval, my name is N., 445a
Norwegian, pine hewn on N. hills, 342a
Norwegians or Filipinos, 1015b
Nor'wester's, strong n. blowing Bill, 517b
Nose, any n. ravage rose, 661b
  as n. on man's face, 220b
  as sharp as pen, 243b
  assert n. on face his own, 457a
  blackbird snipped off n., 1095a
  Cleopatra's n., 363b
  dipping my n. in Gascon wine, 660b
  end of n. red as pink, 531b
  entuned in hir n. ful semely, 166a
  European n., 1080a
  gave pouncet box his n., 238a
  great n. great man, 895b
  innocent n., 247b
  jolly red n., 322a
  liberty plucks justice by n., 270a
  makes chimney of your n., 484a
  Marian's n, looks red, 223a
  mine has snub n., 491a
  nor e'en admit camel's n., 566b
  nose nose nose, 322a
  often wipe bloody n., 401b
  paying through n., 1102a
  plain as n. in face, 181b
  red n. makes me ashamed, 376a
  ring at end of n., 673a
  that's his precious n., 592b
  thine has great hook n., 491a
  thirty inches from n., 1060b
  tip-tilted like petal, 653a
  which direction to point n., 1061a
  with spectacles on n., 249a
Nosegay of culled flowers, 191b
Noses, athwart n. as asleep, 223a

Noses, hold n. to grindstone, 183a
Nostrils, breathed into his n., 5a-b
  whose breath is in his n., 30a
Not an Attic grace, 988a
  as I will but thou, 44b
  as the world giveth, 49a
  for love, 250a
  I not I, 985b
  in vain, 924a
  lost but gone before, 130a
  my will but thine, 47b
  that I loved Caesar less, 255a
  thus not thus, 62a
  to eat not for love, 604b
  what we give but share, 692b
Notations, dispassionate n., 593a
Note and enjoy noting, 800a
  bolder n. than this, 641b
  deed of dreadful n., 284b
  dreadful n. of preparation, 244a
  eternal n. of sadness, 714b
  fain would change n., 1085b
  it in a book, 32a
  living had no n., 1086a
  one's own n. still folded exactly as sent, 153b
  silent n. Cupid strikes, 330a
  take a n. of that, 597a
  take n. O world, 275a
  that swells gale, 441a
  to which love charmed, 1085b
  tu-who a merry n., 222b
  when found make n., 671a
  work of noble n., 646b
  world little n., 639a
  wrapped in five-pound n., 673a
  you in book of memory, 214a
Notebook, set in a n., 256a
Notes are few, 486b
  as warbled to the string, 336a
  by distance made sweet, 443b
  child's amang you takin' n., 495b
  flute in dying n., 370a
  he listens well who takes n., 160b
  liquid n. close day, 339b
  Lydian n. of Carnegie, 831a
  of gladness, 537b
  range of n., 705b
  rough n. and dead bodies, 896a
  thrill deepest n. of woe, 494a
  through all compass of n., 370a
  trills thick-warbled n., 348b
  V n. are something, 666b
  viola fiddles bass, 505a
  we've n. we've instruments, 505b
  with many a winding bout, 335a
  write N. from Olympus, 976b
Nothing, a man zealous for n. 433a
  a worm a mere n., 420b
  a year, 660a
  ain't heard n. yet, 992a
  airy n., 230b
  all for love n. for reward, 200a
  all or n., 729a
  and it was n. more, 509b
  avert curtain's fall, 1018a
  becomes him ill, 221b
  before and nothing behind, 526b
  begins and nothing ends, 856a
  begot of n. but vain fantasy 223a

Nothing venture nothing win, 768a
  want something for n., 838a
  we can carry n. out, 55a
  we do is wiped out, 793a
  we love overmuch, 882a
  wears clothes but Man, 323a
  when from past n., 907a
  will come of nothing, 276b
  will help, 1033a
  will remain, 852b
  worth doing completed, 1024b
  yields n. but discontent, 452a
  you couldn't actually say, 989a
Nothingness, death a state of n., 93a
  pass into n., 580a
  quintessence even from n., 306a
  to n. do sink, 581a
Nothingnesses of human beings, 95b
Nothing's so hard but search will find it out, 320b
Nothings, labored n., 403a
Nothing-withholding and free, 796b
Notice, man who used to n. such things, 784b
  would they take n., 539b
  you take of my labors, 429b
Notion, an' foolish n., 493a
  of absolute beauty, 93a
  of good life, 1061a
Notions, call old n. fudge, 694b
  fair practices to fair n., 93a
  spite all modern n., 874a
Notorious, rather be n. for calamities, 134b
Noun, God not a n., 1034a
Nouns, verbs and n. more agree, 770a
Nourish, praise doth n. agues, 240a
  show contain and n. all world, 222a
Nourished, how begot how n., 233b
  in womb of pia mater, 222a
  to its rot, 1057b
Nourisher, chief n. in life's feast, 283b
Nourishes, spirit within n., 119a
Nourishing, magnetic n. night, 700a
Nourishment and excretions, 675a
  Demeter gave n. of grain, 85a
  little n. I get, 990b
  which is called supper, 221b
Nous avons changé tout cela, 361a
Novel, anything that happens subject of n., 153b
  attempt to represent life, 798a
  best French n. in language, 1075b
  essence of n. is moral, 855b
  happens because storyteller moved to passion, 153b
  instrument of education, 855b
  only a n., 533b
  only obligation of n. to be interesting, 798a
  passion spent its n. force, 647a
  supersede fashionable n., 596a
Novelist, no limit to what n. attempt, 798b
Novelties, world full of untold n., 724b

Novels, more entertaining than half the n., 932a
Novelty and freshness with familiar, 529a
  interest of n., 529a
  letter never loses n., 765a
  stains ancient mass, 795a
  what a n. is man, 364a
November, 592a
  fifth of N., 1087a
  now in N. nearer comes, 986a
  thirty days hath N., 187a
  what is late N. doing, 1005a
November's leaf, 519a
  sky chill and drear, 519a
Novus ordo seclorum, 116b
Now, an everlasting n., 358a
  eternal n., 358a
  he is dead should I fast, 12b
  here and n. cease to matter, 1006a
  history is n. and England, 1007a
  if n. 'tis not to come, 266b
  is eternity, 814b
  is immortal life, 814b
  is the accepted time, 53b
  is time for drinking, 121a
  is the winter of our discontent, 216b
  laborer's task o'er, 727a
  little man what n., 1026b
  now cried the Queen, 745a
  or never, 438a
  the day is over, 750b
  there is merely silence, 199a
Nowadays, land of n., 900b
Nowhere but in anthologies, 989b
  did abide, 525b
  dressed up n. to go, 986b
  Eclipse first the rest n., 442b
  to go but out, 845a
  who lives everywhere lives n., 135a
Now's the day, 496a
Nox est perpetua una dormienda, 114b
Nozzle, hold n. agin bank, 778b
Nuclear control, 1074b
Nuclear disaster engulf all, 1073b
  hell of n. destruction, 1082b
Nude, keep one from going n,. 845a
Nudgers, numb n., 1064b
Nuffin' in de pot, 911b
Nuisance, guest a n. after three days, 105b
  it's a n. God said, 916a
  not be n. to others, 619b
  relating exploits a n., 373b
  universal n., 373b
  violetflavored n., 1030b
Null, splendidly n., 652a
Nullifies, amendment n. discrimination, 967a
Numb nudgers, 1064b
Number, god delights in odd n., 133a
  greatest happiness of greatest n., 416b
  he telleth the n. of the stars, 23a
  if I called wrong n., 1033a
  more by your n. than light, 300b
  profitable things without n., 172b
  teach us to n. our days, 20b
  the clouds in wisdom, 16a

Number, wealth arithmetic cannot n., 316a
  wealth n. and happiness, 453b
Numbered, God hath n. thy kingdom, 35a
  hairs of head n., 42a
  that which is wanting cannot be n., 27b
Numbering, time made me n. clock, 228b
Numberless are world's wonders, 82a
  infinities of souls, 307b
  shadows n., 582a
Numbers, a few honest men better than n., 327b
  beautiful whole n., 1034a
  came, 410b
  divinity in odd n., 267b
  express it in n., 72a3
  good luck in odd n., 267a-b
  greatest happiness for greatest n., 416b
  I lisped in n., 410b
  if opposed n. pluck hearts, 245a
  in n. warmly pure, 443b
  long n. rocket mind, 1079b
  luck in odd n., 589a
  magic n., 392a
  makes small n. formidable, 460b
  mournful n., 620b
  odd n. most effectual, 133a
  sanctified the crime, 460a
  shout out your n., 952a
  slight acquaintance with n., 502a
  vast n. of disinherited, 857b
  wise words taught in n., 201a
Numbing, narcotics n. pain, 650a
Numbness diffuses my senses, 120b
  drowsy n. pains, 582a
Numerous free active individuals, 713a
  more n. of windows, 736b
  writers become more n., 447a
Numismate, pro tali n. tales merces, 171b
Nun, holy time quiet as n., 512a
Nunnery, get thee to a n., 262a
  of thy chaste breast, 358b
Nuns fret not, 515a ?
Nurse, Athens n. of men, 83a
  best n. Contemplation, 337a
  habit is his n., 498a
  if ye had a good n., 890b
  into greatness, 95a
  meet n. for poetic child, 519a
  Nature's soft n., 242a
  of arms, 447b
  Peace dear of arts, 245a
  of full-grown souls, 691b
  of manly sentiment, 454a
  old husky n., 703a
  sucks the n. asleep, 289a
  this n. this teeming womb, 226b
  thrift n. of enterprise, 976b
  time that aged n., 580b
Nursed dear gazelle, 543a
Nurseries of heaven, 856b
  schools n. of vice, 424a
Nurse's, mewling in n. arms, 249a
Nurses, wives old men's n., 208a
Nursing, lack of woman's n., 627b
  unconquerable hope, 712a
  wrath to keep it warm, 495a
Nursling of the sky, 570b

Olivia, cry out O., 251b
Olympian bards, 602b
  in wrath the O. Periles, 90b
  is a difficult foe, 62b
  laconic and O., 899b
Olympic, victor in O. games or
  announcer, 78a
Olympus ever unchanging, 65b
  made O. tremble, 62b, 66a
  Notes from O., 976b
  pile Ossa on O., 66a
  roll up leafy O., 117a
  shady O., 66a
Om, 62a
Omar, diver O. plucked from bed,
  694b
Omega, I am Alpha and O., 58b
  mind rest on God-O., 965b
Omen, may it not be an o., 149b
Omens, barbaric o., 995a
  sits watching for o., 91b
'Omer smote bloomin' lyre, 874a
Ominous pulses, 860a
Omission, sins of o. venial, 434a
Omitted all voyage of their life,
  256a
Omne ignotum pro magnifico,
  140a
Omnes eodem cogimur, 121b
  eodem patre nati, 311a
Omnia vincit amor, 117a
Omnibuses, carriages and o., 975a
Omnipotent but friendless, 569a
  defy the O. to arms, 341b
  docile and o., 736a
  Father with his thunder, 66a
Omnipresence, brooding o. in sky,
  788a
Omnipresent, government o.
  teacher, 833a
  process of sex, 850b
Omnis cellula a cellula, 710b
On, off agin o. agin, 897b
  off with old o. with new,
  753b, 754a
  Stanley on, 519b
  with the dance, 556a
  with New Woman, 836a
  ye brave, 538a
Once I was beautiful, 1082b
  in a lifetime, 990a
  man can die but o., 242b
  more unto the breach, 243b
  more upon waters, 555b
  one lives but o., 477a
  to every man and nation, 691b
  to have died o. enough, 119b
  upon a tree, 1064b
One a penny, 1095a
  acquainted with night, 928a
  all for o., 220a, 598b
  all o. a hundred years hence,
  608a
  among a thousand, 16a
  and inseparable, 547b
  and one with shadowy third,
  664a
  and the same thing, 374a
  basic element in Constitution,
  984a
  be strong be also o., 726a
  bell strikes o., 399a
  born in a manger, 363a
  by one in moonlight, 1010b
  by one two by two, 570a
  clear call for me, 655a
  composed of many, 119b
  conceive many without the o.,
  95a

One country one constitution,
  548a
  crowded hour, 455b
  damned thing after another,
  938a
  dead deathless hour, 731b
  each hath o. and is o., 304b
  ear herde at tothir out, 165a
  enemy is too much, 325a
  eternity and I are o., 771b
  fair daughter and no more,
  261a
  fall o. by o., 452a
  far-off divine event, 651a
  fire burns out another's, 223a
  fish ball, 720b
  flag one land one heart, 633b
  food to o. poison to others,
  114a
  foot in sea one on shore, 246a
  for all, 220a, 598b
  for my master, 1093a
  for o. sweet grape vine destroy,
  220a
  found truth in all but o., 228a
  god greatest among gods, 70b
  God law element, 651a
  good knowledge, 87b
  good turn deserves another,
  133b
  grand sweet song, 691a
  hearts that beat as o., 619a
  I am only o., 717b
  if by land, 624a
  if ever two were o., 351b
  in life and death, 767a
  is fat and grows old, 239a
  is or is not, 95b
  less than tenth part of o., 268b
  life to lose, 484b
  little o. shall become a thousand, 33b
  live as two, 1004a
  lost but o. twa behin', 496a
  low man adding o. to o., 664b
  majority of o., 681a
  man among a thousand, 28a
  man of o. book, 158b
  man one vote, 1104b
  man's meat another's poison,
  114a
  man's will all men's misery,
  202b
  minute with him, 981a
  more unfortunate, 592b
  my little o. pretty o., 648b
  nation evermore, 633a
  nation indivisible, 832b
  nature o. and continuous, 681b
  near o. too far, 664a
  never lose touch of the o., 861a
  night o. blue dew, 1067a
  not o. for putting off proof,
  928a
  on God's side majority, 659a
  only o. military organization,
  1026a
  our two souls which are o.,
  306a
  pain lessened by another's, 223a
  parted between twelve and o.,
  243b
  path is o. and the same, 77b
  pay for o. by o., 874a
  people arose o. man, 11b
  perfect limousine, 1029a
  perfect rose, 1029a
  shock of recognition, 695b
  small o. a strong nation, 33b

One, splendor of the Mighty O.,
  106b
  spot where I made O., 631a
  striking at root of evil, 682b
  swallow not a summer, 97b
  sweet sacrifice, 298a
  sweetly solemn thought, 722b
  that loved not wisely, 276b
  the o. and the many, 95a
  the other will contain, 736b
  thinks of all the hands, 1001b
  this o. thing I do, 54a
  third of a nation, 971b
  three centuries removed, 1053a
  to succeed possible only o. way,
  97b
  touch of nature, 269a
  twenty pay for o., 1104b
  two and third in your bosom,
  224b
  two moremens more, 969a
  two o. two, 745a
  two three four, 854a
  twothreefourfive pigeons, 1030a
  we are o. flesh, 348a
  who died for truth, 736a
  with law a majority, 911a
  word frees us, 83a
  world or none, 1015b
  world's life and mine o., 724a
One-and-twenty, when I was o.,
  852b
One-armed man pasting wallpaper, 864a
One-book man, 523a
One-horse town, 759a
One-hoss shay, 634a
Oneness, household in o. of mind,
  65b
One's, nothing greater than o.
  self, 700b
Ones, great o. eat up little o.,
  290b
Oneself, be sufficient unto o.,
  190a
  desire to think well of o., 1007b
  entirely honest with o., 833b
  hell is o., 1007a
  idea of o. as cause, 373b
  little one knows o., 1016a
  look better into o., 865a
  mistaking o. for oracle, 909b
  not live unto o., 102b
  to be saint for o. 707b
One-third of a nation, 971b
Onion atoms lurk in bowl, 523a
  let first o. flourish, 824a
  will do well for such shift,
  219a
Onions, eat no o. nor garlic, 230b
  wel loved he garleek o. lekes,
  167a
Onlie begetter of insuing sonnets,
  291b
Only love sprung from only
  hate, 223b
  that it is your o. one, 98a
Onset, stand aside from enemy's
  o., 90a
  with eternity, 734b
  word of o. gave, 513a
Ontogenesis recapitulation of phylogenesis, 752b
Ontogeny recapitulates phylogeny,
  752b
Onward Christian soldiers, 750b
  goes pilgrim band, 750b
  half a league o., 651b
  sailors cry, 849b

P

Penury, chill p., 440b
  talk tendeth only to p., 24b
People, a few fastidious p., 878a
  a stiffnecked p., 9a
  after p. are dead, 907a
  all exulting, 702a
  all p. and tongues, 58a
  all sorts of p., 282b
  all with one accord, 447a
  and statues interchangeable,
    1057a
  are like children, 675b
  are like water, 1027b
  arose as one man, 11b
  be nice to p. on way up, 941a
  beat my p. to pieces, 30a
  because we hate no p., 1025a
  behind p. the country, 717b
  believe these p. from sky,
    173a
  better living for world's p.,
    983b
  bludgeoning of p. by p. for p.,
    840b
  brave new world that has such
    p., 297b
  bring courage to world, 1044a
  British p. like to be told
    worst, 922b
  buying clothes and groceries,
    948b
  Cambridge p. rarely smile, 993b
  came to theirs, 906a
  capable of becoming happier,
    1014b
  cheerfully support government,
    771a-b
  chosen p. of God, 471a
  come to church good p., 853a
  come ye thankful p., 655b
  comfort ye my p., 32b
  common denominator of prog-
    ress, 1063b
  common p. of the skies, 300b
  common-looking p. best, 639b
  complained of long voyage,
    172a
  conceited p. carry comfort, 689b
  confidence in justice of p.,
    637a-b
  considered by p. equally true,
    465b
  contracts with the p., 983b
  cooperation of free p., 842b
  country belongs to p., 637a
  dangerous who make no noise,
    359b
  dear p. who have charm, 751b
  descend to meet, 606b
  difficult to govern, 74b
  distinctions between gentlemen
    and common p., 101a
  easily becomes prey, 178a
  experiment of American p.,
    461b
  eyes of all p. upon us, 318a,
    1072a
  fear and distrust the p., 473b
  few p. who write know any-
    thing, 726b
  find p. have good sense, 356a
  fool some p., 641a
  former p., 894b
  free p. regimented, 971a
  glory of thy p. Israel, 46a
  God save the p., 545a
  good tidings to all p., 46a
  governed by magistrates, 591a
  government belong to p., 901a

People, government for benefit
    of p., 538b
  government for the p., 547a
  government not stronger than
    p., 1049a
  government not support p.,
    771b
  government of all the p.,
    616a
  government of by for p., 639a,
    657b, 895b
  government of p., 616a
  grown-up p., 852a
  grudge what they cannot enjoy,
    76a
  happiness except where p., 891b
  happy p. die whole, 994b
  have always some champion,
    95a
  hell is other p., 1058b
  his p. are free, 543a
  his p. were his temple, 364b
  how you are to govern p., 452a
  humble hungry mean, 1050b
  I am the p., 948a, 1050b
  if German p. despair, 1012b
  imagine a vain thing, 17a
  in arms, 589b
  in front get the jar, 942a
  in hotels strike no roots, 895b
  indictment against whole p.,
    453a
  indomitable p. of Vermont,
    911b
  is a great beast, 123a
  judging p. by appearances, 359b
  land of Russian p., 611a
  law for rulers and p., 678a
  lazy nonprogressive p., 1019b
  lazy p. look for something to
    do, 439a
  leader and commander to the
    p., 33a
  let go hold of p., 1041a
  let my p. go, 8a
  liberal party believed in p.,
    973a
  lift p. from dust, 603b
  like p. like priest, 35a
  love of British p., 453a
  made the Constitution, 485b
  maintain control of govern-
    ment, 972a
  make bad laws then suffer, 778a
  many-headed beast, 123a
  march, 949a
  marry ancient p., 333b
  masses of p. not qualified, 978a
  may be made to follow path,
    71b
  may grow old without visiting,
    75a
  mercy on my poor p., 191b
  mercy on Thy p. Lord, 875b
  met so many p., 1052a
  more than half p. right, 1046b
  most important element, 100b
  motes that p. sunbeams, 335b
  multitude of the gross p., 123a
  narrow-souled p., 413a
  nation territory p. laws, 638a
  never give up liberties, 453b
  never learned from history,
    507b
  new deal for American p., 970b
  no doubt ye are the p., 15a
  no more give the p. straw, 8a
  not always what seem, 455a
  not belong to government, 901a

People numerous and warlike,
    173b
  O my p. what have I done to
    thee, 1003b
  O stormy p., 168b
  oats supports p., 427b
  of his pasture, 21a
  of p. by p. for p., 639a, 657b,
    895b
  of unclean lips, 30b
  of Western Europe, 1016b
  old trees used to p., 1041b
  on whom nothing lost, 798b
  one man die for p., 49a
  one should like to drop, 433a
  one thing besides p. I know,
    970b
  only p. for me mad, 1080b
  our land before we her p., 928b
  our sovereign the p., 547a
  people have for friends, 859b
  people marry, 859b
  poor p. putting on style, 812b
  power from the p., 611b
  privileged and p. two nations,
    612a
  protection of p., 446a
  public officers servants of p.,
    771a
  religion opiate of p., 870a
  representatives of p., 566a
  resemble wild beast, 177b
  retain virtue and vigilance,
    637b
  right of p. to make govern-
    ment, 461b
  right p. in right jobs, 677b
  Sacco's name in hearts of p.,
    1010a
  safe depository of powers, 473b
  say life is the thing, 878a
  seldom judge right, 485a
  sensed by p. expressed by p.,
    722a
  shouted with a great shout, 11a
  show my head to the p., 496b
  small country with few p., 75a
  so dead to liberty, 426a
  special p. unto himself, 10a
  spoil lives of better p., 825a
  still in the gristle, 452b
  such tongue to great p., 688a
  sum married p. owe, 477b
  take any streetful of p., 948b
  talebearer among thy p., 9b
  talk sense to American p., 1048a
  that once bestowed commands,
    139b
  that p. may require leader, 95a
  there is a p. risen, 364b
  this Bible for government by
    p., 163b
  thy p. shall be my p., 11b
  to all the p. you can, 421a
  to marketplace and p., 854a
  to these p. I owe everything,
    636b
  troops of solemn p., 1034b
  turn to benevolent rule, 100a
  two kinds of p., 825b, 1051b
  two thirds of p. killed, 950b
  tyranny enter if p. lose spirit,
    703b
  under violent passion, 837a
  unimproved p., 1063b
  very nicest p., 1017b
  visited and redeemed his p., 46a
  voice of p. is voice of God, 152b
  we are his p., 21a

Point, still p. of world, 1004a
way to better living, 983b
where tooth p. goes, 871b
Pointed firs, 816b
Points, armed at p. exactly, 258a
beaten at all p., 90b
out soul's eternal sleep, 482a
possession eleven p., 392b
silent finger p. to heaven, 516b
to yonder glade, 406a
true to kindred p., 517a
Poised like souls to remind us, 907b
Poison, all men possess p., 132b
deeds like p. weeds, 841a
destroys township with p. gas, 980b
England at roots, 917b
food to one p. to others, 114a
hold p. in the hand, 80a
if you p. us do we not die, 233b
more deadly than mad dog's tooth, 218b
one man's p., 114a
ounce of p. in pocket, 596a
pure truth is p., 987a
steel nor p., 284b
sweet p. for age's tooth, 236a
sweet p. of misused wine, 336b
their lives, 925b
Poisoned rat in hole, 390a
some p. by their wives, 227b
Poisonous dart not pugnacity, 980b
fragrant flowers or p. weeds, 1028a
minerals and that tree, 307b
Nessus shirts, 576b
wolf's-bane for p. wine, 584a
Poke, drew dial from his p., 248a
pig in a p., 185b
poor Billy, 930b
Pokers into true-love knots, 527a
Pole, beloved from p. to p., 525b
black as pit from p. to p., 816a
embrace P. as Frenchman, 191a
from Indus to p., 405b
hear the latest P., 1001a
heavens from p. to p., 491a
intellectuals at one p., 1058b
pleasure trip to P., 784b
so tall to reach p., 396a
soldier's p. is fallen, 288b
true as needle to p., 353b
truth from p. to p., 393a
Whale that wanders round P., 901b
Poles, north p. and equators, 746b
Police, international p. power, 848a
legacies to strange p., 925a
those who arrest you, 1082a
Policeman, heard p. on beat, 965b
U.S. not p. of mankind, 1013b
Policeman's lot not happy one, 766b
Policies based on myths, 1055b
Policy, Fabian p., 106b
legacies to strange p., 925a
foreign relations p., 1013a
honesty best p., 197a
ill p. in Leo the Tenth, 462a
kings tyrants from p., 454a
of letting flowers blossom, 1027b
of the good neighbor, 971a
of United Nations, 984a
President had p. of his own, 983b

Policy settled by free discussion, 934b
stare decisis wise p., 833a
theory of matter a p., 838a
turn him to cause of p., 243a
Polish, felony to buy stove p., 891b
fitter to bruise than p., 351b
her until glimmers, 814b
Polished handle of big front door, 766a
idleness, 501b
perturbation, 242b
satire like p. razor, 414a
Polite, compulsion to become p., 986b
costs nothing to be p., 925a
learning, 386b
patronize p. literature, 462a
Politeness, out of p. cheat others, 908a
pineapple of p., 480b
punctuality p. of kings, 485b
Politesse, l'exactitude la p. des rois, 485b
Politic, body p. like human body, 435b
cautious and meticulous, 1001a
Political affairs, 631b
and cultural freedom, 941b
appeasement, 969b
beginning and end of p. education, 776b
best p. community, 98b
campaigns emotional orgies, 866b
creed of our p. faith, 472b
democracy training school, 703a
dissolve p. bands, 470b
economic racial forces, 901a
equality, 1014a
executive magistracy, 454b
free p. discussion, 865a
freedom business of government, 971a-b
greatness and wisdom meet, 94a
happy warrior of p. battlefield, 916b
institutions superstructure, 903a
liberty highest p. end, 750a
like to see p. reaction, 1032b
man a p. animal, 98a
mode of half world, 1049a
moral and p. systems, 958a
Principles of P. Economy, 934a
prosperity of p. community, 964a
rather p. than religious, 430b
rebellion in p. world, 471b
society exists for noble actions, 98b
test of p. party, 1048a
thicket, 967a
tutelage, 889a
tyranny of p. assemblies, 616b
understanding to run government, 983b
variable of p. calculation, 725a
volcanic p. instinct, 838a
wise p. leaders, 972a
Politician, characteristics of popular p., 91a
coffee makes p. wise, 404b
give away alley, 891b
I am not a p., 750b
is an arse, 1031b
proper memory for p., 779b

Politician, scurvy p., 279b
under every stone lurks p., 91b
would circumvent God, 265b
Politician's corpse laid away, 901b
Politicians, God and p., 1019a
not necessary to patriotism, 952b
one rule for p., 893a
problems with which p. deal, 818a
tinhorn p., 896a
whole race of p., 389b
Politics almost exciting as war, 919b
applesauce, 954a
art of happiness, 871a
customs p. and tongue, 721b
damnedest in Kentucky, 804b
difference of p., 659a
education part of p., 590a
expensive, 954a
greatest adventure, 934b
I must study p. and war, 463a
killed many times in p., 919b
like ours profess, 418b
like religion, 473a
magnanimity in p., 453b
makes strange bedfellows, 733b
more interested in government than p., 972b
my p. like my religion, 750b
no more with gallantry than p., 481a
not exact science, 677b
of accommodatin' character, 750b
orthodox in p., 1021b
power p. law of jungle, 1019a
power p. obstruct peace, 974a
practical p., 631b, 777a
purification of p., 748b
royalist in p., 1008a
ruins character, 677b
saturates p. with thought, 713b
science of how who gets what, 994a
struggle of forces, 777b
to puns, 600b
understand p. and morality, 779b
war not divorced from p., 1027b
we bar, 768a
work of p. shaped by geometry, 385a
world of power p., 1019a
Polity, ideal p., 94b
Polk was positive man, 983b
Poll, talked like poor P., 439a
Pollertics of accommodatin' character, 750b
Polls, influenced by the p., 983b
Polluted, not p. though it passes among impure, 96b
picnic by p. stream, 1063a
shun the p. flock, 990a
sun not p. by privies, 96b
Pollutes whate'er it touches, 568a
Polly, little P. Flinders, 1095b
put kettle on, 1097b
you might have toyed, 401b
'Pollygy aint gwine make h'ar come, 814a
Pollytician give away alley, 891b
Polygamy, before p. was made a sin, 368a
well held in dread, 561b
Polyp would be conceptual, 793b

Q

Quiet conscience stands brunt of life, 84b
consummation have, 291a
courage gaiety q. mind, 825a
crisis q. but urgent, 1077b
desperation, 682a
Doctor Q., 390b
easy live q. die, 521a
enforced from q. sphere, 242b
entertain lag-end with q. hours, 240b
eye made q. by power, 509a
fie upon this q. life, 239a
grave such a q. place, 360a
harvest of a q. eye, 511a
here where world q., 775a
hills q. look down at me, 944a
holy time q. as nun, 512a
hours few, 698b
imperishable q., 1065b
in q. she reposes, 712a
inability to stay q., 726b
interchange of sentiments, 431b
kiss me and be q., 414a
lain still and been q., 14b
limit of world, 652b
mind richer than crown, 206a
minds innocent and q., 358b
my temptation q., 884b
ornament of q. spirit, 57a
retirement rural q. friendship, 419b
rich q. and infamous, 596a
richness q. and pleasure, 707a
scallop shell of q., 199a
shining to the q. moon, 526a
singeth a q. tune, 525b
sleep when the long trick's over, 947a
sleepers in q. earth, 685b
spirit so still and q., 272b
still and q. conscience, 298b
study to be q., 54b
tree of man never q., 853a
truth hath a q. breast, 226a
wise and good, 572b
young maidens q. eyes, 824b
Quiet-colored end of evening, 663b
Quieting, soothing and q., 909a
Quietly shining to quiet moon, 526a
Quietness, bride of q., 583a
handful with q., 27b
Quietness', king made for q. sake, 317b
Quiets, hallowed q. of past, 694a
Quietus, he himself his q. make, 262a
Quill, condor's q., 697a
from angel's wing, 517a
Quillets, his q. his cases, 265b
nice sharp q. of law, 214a
Quills, stops of various q., 339a
upon fretful porpentine, 259b
Quince, slices of q., 673a
Quinquireme of Nineveh, 947a
Quintessence even from nothingness, 306a
morning q. of life, 564a
of dust, 261a
Quintilian, made Q. stare and gasp, 340b
Quintilius give me back my legions, 124b
Quip modest, 251a
Quippe secundae res sapientium animos fatigant, 115b

Quips and cranks, 334b
and quiddities, 237b
shall q. and sentences awe, 246a
Quire of bad verses, 596a
Quiring to young-eyed cherubins, 235b
Quirks of blazoning pens, 273a
Quis custodiet ipsos custodes, 139b
Quislings, vile race of q., 922b
Quit certainty for uncertainty, 428a
John and I are q., 388a
oh quit this mortal frame, 404a
port o' heaven, 865a
quit for shame, 350a
rats have q. it, 296a
willing to q. ground, 468b
you like men, 53a
your books, 509a
yourselves like men, 12a
Quitter, if faut q. tout cela, 328b
Quiver, air q. with a color, 985a
aspens q., 645b
happy is the man that hath his q. full, 22b
inward q. of some kind, 792b
Quivered in his heart, 555a
Quivering curds, 747a
light q. aspen, 519b
ratio, 734b
Quiver's choice, 562a
Quivers, bows bent emptying of q., 772b
Quixote, Don Q. and I, 549a
Quixotic sense of honorable, 644a
Quo usque Catilina abutere patientia, 110b
vadis, 49a
Quod erat demonstrandum, 103b
semper quod ubique quod ab omnibus, 147b
Quot homines tot sententiae, 109a
Quotation, classical q., 433b
good if writer goes my way, 874a
Quotations, backed opinion with q., 387b
Bartlett man got, 907a
Bartlett's Familiar Q., 920a
book furnishes no q., 552b
each page of them q., 907a
from great old authors, 860a
give meaning better, 851b
good to read books of q., 920a
I hate q., 604b
pretentious q. tedium, 852a
some q. ill-advised, 851b
wrapped himself in q., 874a
Quote fights historical, 766b
grow immortal as they q., 398b
kill you if you q. it, 887a
we all q., 609b
wise reader q. wisely, 590b
Quoted, famous remarks seldom q. correctly, 957b
odes and jewels, 648a
Quoter, filial reverence by q., 860a
first q. next to originator, 609b
Quoth, give me q. I, 281a
Raven Nevermore, 643a

R

R, month contained no r, 892b
Southerner no use for r, 760b

Rabbit in a snare, 974b
ole man R. say scoot, 814a
skin to wrap baby, 1094b
thoughts of r. are rabbits, 610a
Rabbits, bobtails fu' de r., 911b
four little r., 887b
thoughts of rabbit are r. 610a
Rabble, army would be base r., 453b
member of the r., 1032b
Rabelais' easy chair, 413b
Rabid partisans, 795b
Race, a simple r., 518b
all run in r., 52a
and color problem, 998a
another r. hath been, 514a
appointed for my second r., 362b
barred on account of r., 1074a
bound up with human r., 544a
Californians a r., 864a
competition best for r., 757a
conscience of my r., 968b
death of the r., 1079b
despised r., 752a
distinctions of r., 705b
dusky r., 647b
every man honor his r., 821b
fainting dispirited r., 715b
feelings permanently in r., 712a
flower of all his r., 508a
foal of an oppressed r., 523b
friend to human r., 846a
future of human r., 942a
Germany a r., 590a
giant r. before the flood, 371a
happiness of human r., 453b
heavenly r. demands zeal, 420a
here lived another race, 566b
history of our r., 923a
human r. born to fly upward, 161a
in conversation see capacities of r., 978a
individual development repetition of r., 833b
is to the swift, 844b
laborers perpetuate r., 530b
laws unto savage r., 646a
loftier r. than known, 785b
lost r., 1049b
lot bound up with human r., 544a
man's imperial r. ensnare, 404b
mother of Aeneas and his r., 112b
names of fearless r., 566b
no matter what r., 1025a
noble r. and brave, 566b
not similar are r. of gods and men, 63a
not superior by r., 749a
not to the swift the r., 827b
not to the swift, 28b
of ancient r. by birth, 368b
of education and catastrophe, 888b
of glory run, 349b
of shame, 349b
of sheep, 977b
our r. may be accident, 925b
out of one man a r., 346b
over work never done, 78a
part of the human r., 986b
pernicious r. of vermin, 389b
pickest and cullest r., 703a
poetry fettered fetters r., 491a

Read, take up r., 147a
 teach orphan boy to r., 645a
 that day r. no more, 551a
 that day we r. no farther, 160a
 timetable sooner than nothing,
  932a
 to by a boy, 1001b
 to doubt or read to scorn, 521a
 to r. comes by nature, 246b
 very few to r., 510b
 what do you r. my lord, 260b
 whoso that kan r. hem as they
  write, 164b
 will anyone r. him, 455a
 wits to r., 303b
 youngsters r. men understand,
  195b
Reader, arouse illusion in r., 797b
 delighting and instructing r.,
  124b
 delights r. instructs too, 377a
 exciting sympathy of r., 529a
 gentle r., 508b
 good book require from r., 565a
 good r. makes good book, 609a
 hypocrite r., 706b
 I married him, 679b
 illuminated is the poem, 916b
 last r. reads no more, 633a
 look, 303b
 no tears in r., 929b
 right r. of good poem, 929b
 take them not for mine, 165b
 what conceal from r., 1061a
 wise r. quote wisely, 590b
Reader's consciousness, 940a
Readers and hearers like my
  books, 210a
 become more indolent, 447a
 five hundred thousand r., 777a
 indiscriminate r., 855b
 not all books dull as r., 683a
 of Boston Evening Transcript,
  1001b
 should be critical of historians,
  107b
 sleepless to give r. sleep, 413b
Readest, thou r. black, 491a
Readeth, he may run that r. it,
  36a
Readiness is all, 266b
Reading, affect you agreeably in
  r., 469b
 after r. your work, 417b
 contemplation more than r.,
  364b-365a
 cursed hard r., 482a
 digressions sunshine of r., 437b
 English dictionary best r., 916a
 I prefer r., 878a
 maketh a full man, 209b
 new era in life from r., 683a
 no r. more fascinating than catalogue, 801b
 oppression of mind, 381a
 overset mind with r., 816b
 peace makes poor r., 783b
 sheer casual r. matter, 916a
 such r. as never read, 413b
 tact a kind of mind r., 816b
 theologian not born by r., 180a
 to mind as exercise to body,
  395b
 tyrannical habit of r., 694b
 valueless books, 698b
 write things worth r., 421b
Readings, our r. secret, 951b
Reads, all he r. assails, 404a
 as task, 430b

Reads but one book, 325b
 he r. much great observer, 253b
 nothing but detective stories,
  999b
Ready, a God r. to pardon, 14a
 completely r. state, 677b
 conference maketh a r. man,
  209b
 fire when r. Gridley, 771b
 for war way to avoid it, 383a
 get weapons r., 701b
 I wait until I am r., 996a
 in defense, 453a
 minds to fellowship, 580b
 money Aladdin's lamp, 562a
 money makes the man, 397a
 my tongue is the pen of a r.
  writer, 19a
 necessity of being r., 637b
 no r. way to virtue, 330a
 old wife old dog r. money, 421b
 rough sir but r., 671a
 stand to your glasses r., 719b
 to gather everything, 1056a
 to perish in wilderness, 319a
 to ride spread alarm, 624a
 to try our fortunes, 242b
 we always are r., 439a
 when sorrow came, 818a
 with every nod to tumble, 216a
 with you be r. to die, 122a
Real, a man's r. life, 844a
 and permanent grandeur, 699b
 coming back to r., 957a
 dark night of soul, 1036b
 lead me from unreal to r., 62a
 life r. life earnest, 620b
 nothing r. but humanity, 589a
 nothing r. till experienced,
  585b
 Simon Pure, 391a
 spirit r. and eternal, 709a
 that is moral, 707a
 thing that made emotion, 1044b
 this is the r. me, 792b
 war never in books, 703a
 what is r. is reasonable, 507a
Realism, Dostoevski's r., 978b
 socialist r., 895a
Realities and creators, 606a
 less dangerous than fancies,
  913b
 muddled state sharpest of r.,
  799b
 not images of beauty but r., 93a
Reality, appearance never attain
  r., 498b
 between idea and r., 1003a
 final word in r., 1082b
 flee from r., 978b
 history illumines r., 110b
 history small part of r., 714a
 human kind nor bear much r.,
  1004b
 in r. atoms and space, 88a
 of distress, 467b
 of experience, 968b
 regulate imagination by r., 429a
 split apart in painting, 964b
 terrible r., 908a
 the more threatening r. appears, 965b
 three mirror same r., 474b
 translators between dream and
  r., 998b
 when criticism parts with r.,
  922a
 your own r. for yourself, 843b
Realization of tomorrow, 974a

Realization, preach ideal dread
  r., 931a
Realize bitterness of life, 747a
 I'd been happy, 1068b
 you don't need aid, 1039b
Realm, invade borders of my r.,
  189a
 mysterious r., 574b
 riding o'er azure r., 441b
 this r. this England, 226b
 turned out of r. in my petticoat, 189a
Realms above, 524a
 and islands as plates, 289a
 Anna whom three r. obey, 404b
 of gold, 579b
 whatever r. to see, 447b
Reap an act, 1100b
 as you sow ye r., 353a
 blessings of freedom, 467a
 harvest of your land, 9b
 he that regardeth the clouds
  shall not r., 28b
 in joy, 22b
 men that sow and r., 775a
 not wholly r. the corners, 9b
 sow not neither r., 41a
 sows and shall not r., 773a
 that shall he also r., 54a
 the whirlwind, 35b
 we r. our sowing, 751b
Reaped, all the harvest I r., 630a
 iniquity, 35b
 wheat never r. nor sown,
  377b-378a
Reaper whose name is Death,
  620b
Reaping, autumn that grew by r.,
  289a
Reappraisal, agonizing r., 1076a
Reaps bearded grain at breath,
  620b
 wholesome harvests r., 590b
Rear my dusky race, 647b
 tender thought, 419b
 to produce and to r. them, 73b
Reared arm crested the world,
  288b
 hills r. in vain, 686a
 himself a throne, 641b
Rearward of a conquered woe,
  293a
Reason against it instinct for it,
  756b
 and will of God prevail, 716a
 argument needs no r., 70a
 art has r. for being, 609a
 asked one another the r., 250b
 beast that wants discourse of
  r., 257b
 but from what we know, 407b
 by r. of strength, 20b
 capability and godlike r., 264b
 chafe, 604a
 common law nothing but r.,
  198a
 destroys book kills r., 340a
 dethroned bereft of r., 605a
 discourse of r., 257b
 fear mitigated by r., 1015a
 feast of r. flow of soul, 411b
 for giving boys Latin, 715b
 fribble and less than man of r.,
  957a
 give r. on compulsion, 239a
 God's crowning gift, 82a
 greatest enemy faith has, 180a
 guide by light of r., 833a
 has moons, 906a

Rend, new years ruin and r., 774a
the affrighted skies, 404b
time to r., 27b
turn and r. you, 636a
words divide and r., 773a
Rended, forests are r., 520b
Render back from breast, 561a
deeds of mercy, 234b
praise and favor, 617b
to all their dues, 51b
unto Caesar, 43b
Renderest, thou r. to every man according to his work, 19b
Rendezvous, shall not fail r., 1010a
with Death, 1009b
with destiny, 971b
Renew a right spirit within me, 19a
herbs that did r. Aeson, 235a
their strength, 33a
tinker more than r., 795a
unspeakable sorrow you bid me r., 118a
Renewal as well as change, 1072b
lovers' quarrels r. of love, 108a
of relations nervous, 777a
plant seeds watch r., 733a
Renewed, cycle of the ages r., 116b
sum of things ever being r., 113b
to be worn out is to be r., 74a
tree not r., 1057b
Renewing, falling out of friends r. is, 108a
Renounce and not be embittered, 825a
guilty of corruption and r. defense, 207a
the devil, 61a
Renouncement, Liberal tempered by r., 715b
Renown and grace is dead, 284a
end is the r., 270a
forfeit fair r., 519a
in high place and of r., 37a
let me win noble r., 64b
marvel of great r., 820b
men of r., 6b
naught but breath of wind, 161a
oh thou unknown r., 738a
purchased not by violence, 550a
set cause above r., 865a
some for r., 398b
speak no more of his r., 651b
win high r., 65b
Renowned be thy grave, 291a
farewell r. Eretria, 92b
Spenser, 319a
Rent, blood and sweat for rent, 920b
envious Casca made, 255b
is sorrow income tears, 321b
lean r. and beggared, 233a
Mordecai r. his clothes, 14a
pay the r. of seem, 1031b
spontaneous joy, 881a
the rocks r., 45a
veil of temple r., 45a
Rents, what are thy r., 244b
Renunciation of method, 980b
Reorganized upon the floor, 1002a
Repair, Freedom shall awhile r., 443a
keep friendship in r., 430a

Repair, some to church r., 403a
Reparation for rights, 426a
tenant ne'er pay r., 1105a
Repay, I will r., 51b
shut when thou shouldest r., 37b
tomorrow will r., 367b
Repeal of Eighteenth Amendment, 930b
of obnoxious laws, 717a
Repeat at leisure, 949b
condemned to r. past, 867a
don't say anything won't have to r. it, 911b
no again and again, 806b
no grievances, 450a
Repeateth, he that r. a matter, 25a
Repeating, oft r. they believe 'em, 387b
Repeats his words, 236b
Repent at leisure, 391b
at leisure, 391b
restore should I r. me, 276a
we do earnestly r., 61a
what's past, 264a
ye kingdom is at hand, 39b
you will r. by jingo, 592a
Repentance, call sinners to r., 41b
decline to buy r., 99a
fear of consequence, 355b
garment of r., 629a
give r. to her lover, 448b
on a Sunday, 962a
tears of r. you'll wipe, 488b
Repented, strove and much r., 560a
Repenting, mirth that no r. draws, 340b
Repine, do not r. my friends, 670a
love r., 604a
Replace despair with opportunity, 1064a
Replacing, gently r. in oblivion, 739a
Replenish the earth, 5a
Replication of your sounds, 253a
Replied Fish fiddle de-dee, 674a
O Lord Thou art, 444a
shade r., 644a
with chuckle r., 963b
Replies, heart r., 459a
Reply churlish, 251a
pause for a r., 255a
reply, 233b
sing ye heavens earth r., 425a
theirs not to r., 652a
Report, by evil r. and good r., 53b
fully accurately fairly, 1020b
heroism from American view, 699b
ill r. while you live, 261b
me and cause aright, 266b
nor heart to r., 230b
of fashions in proud Italy, 226b
to one that sent him, 4a
vexation only to understand the r., 32a
whatsoever things are of good r., 54b
who knows how he may r., 349b
Reported, their praises might be r., 39a
Reporting, ignorant sloppy r., 1020a-b
intelligent r., 1014a

Reports of my death exaggerated, 763a
Repose, as well for defense as r., 198a
earned night's r., 621b
foster-nurse of nature is r., 279a
hushed in grim r., 441b
in trembling hope r., 441a
leave me to r., 442a
long for a r., 514b
not destiny of man, 787a
placid r. under liberty, 362a
pondering r. of If, 697b
quenched in cold r., 571b
rare and bloodless week of r., 91b
tabooed by anxiety, 767b
that ever is the same, 514b
thoughts nature gives way to in r., 283a
when got r. insupportable, 777b
with heels higher than head, 191b
worship but no r., 570b
Reposes, in quiet she r., 712a
Reposing, sorrow breaks r. hours, 217a
Repository of hatred, 921b
Reprehend, if I r. anything in world, 480b
Represent, effort to see and r., 799b
Representation should give likenesses, 148a
taxation without r., 446a
Representative, individual with r., 529a
of highest spiritual authority, 964b
owes you, 452b
Representatives, conscience of r., 967a
House of R., 464b
more I see r. of people, 566a
Repressed their noble rage, 440b
Reprimand, quarrel or r., 602b
Reproach, cheerfully bear r., 596b
everything that is a r. among men, 70a
mine ways without r., 128a
neighbor without r., 747b
no defense against r., 394b
receives r. of being, 294a
Reproached me in public, 504a
Reproacheth his Maker, 24b
Reproaching, without r. brethren, 543b
Reprobation, fall to r., 276a
Reproduction, preserved by r., 475a
Reproof on her lip, 589a
valiant, 251a
Reprove, check erring and r., 514b
matron's glance r., 449a
not a scorner, 24a
sager sort our deeds r., 300a
Reproved each dull delay, 449b
Republic a raft, 491b
be more fortunate, 1105a
democracy in a r., 895b
for which it stands, 832b
gave R. her station, 600a
give to r. fourth power, 549a
is a dream, 948b
not established by cowards, 1015b
of letters, 424b
of man, 1049a

Retain ability to function, 1036b
  enduring as marble to r., 197b
  marble to r., 559b
  not r. all rare works, 907b
Retaliatory, massive r. power,
  1000b
Retire like guest sated, 113b
  like satisfied guest, 120a
  then must art r., 498b
Retired, happiness of r. nature,
  394a
  Leisure, 335b
  pale Melancholy sate r., 443b
  sweet r. solitude, 337a
Retirement, Plato's, 348b
  rural quiet friendship, 419b
  to private citizen, 472b
  urges sweet return, 347b
Retiring at high speed toward
  Japanese, 968a
  in r. draw hearts after, 348b
  ne'er feels r. ebb, 275a
Retort courteous, 251a
Retrace, shall one r. life, 890b
Retreat, dangerous when appear
  to r., 946b
  friend in my r., 457a
  honorable r., 249b
  loopholes of r., 458b
  my soul's calm r., 362b
  not r. a single inch, 615b
  our principal r. and solitude,
  190a
  sinner's last r., 1075a
Retreated back into money, 1036b
Retreating to the breath, 714b
  world, 1028b
Retrieving, fallen past r., 1055a
Retrograde if not advance, 466a
Retrogression, progress more general than r., 628a
Return, all things r. to thee, 142a
  bid time r., 227a
  departed never to r., 494a
  dust shall r. to earth, 29a
  from following after thee, 11b
  gone and never must r., 338a
  he shall not r. to me, 12b
  I shall r., 959a
  like him that travels I r., 293b
  like prodigal doth she r., 232b
  may r. if dissatisfied, 929b
  naked shall he r., 28a
  naked shall I r. thither, 14a
  no eternity will r., 497b
  no more to his house, 14b
  O Shulamite, 29b
  once dead who do not r., 630a
  only dead who do not r., 484b
  redeemed of the Lord shall r.,
  33a
  report to one that sent him, 4a
  retirement urges sweet r., 347b
  snatch me not to r., 926b
  spirit shall r. unto God, 29a
  their thankfulness, 487a
  those who never r., 899a
  till thou r. unto the ground, 6a
  to what base uses we r., 26a
  unto dust r., 6a
  with the greatest pleasure, 528b
  with the year seasons r., 344b
  ye children of men, 20a
Returned home previous night,
  917b
  I have r., 959a
  much freed r. to me, 950a
  then ye r. to trinkets, 875b
  when her aunt r., 902b

Returneth, dog r. to his vomit,
  26a
  none r. that is gone, 3a
  to dust again, 748b
Returning as tedious as go o'er,
  285a
Returns, all r. to sea, 1061b
  earth's r., 663b
  home to find needs, 827b
  no traveler r., 262a
  not to me r. day, 344b
  road whence no one returns,
  114b
  the Golden Age, 116b
Reuben, Tranter R. Farmer Ledlow, 783b
Réussit, rien ne r. comme le
  succès, 598b
Rêve, un peu de r., 751b
Reveal, full heart r., 527b
  half r. half conceal, 649b
  joy r. itself when transformed
  in us, 938b
  no secrets, 450a
Revealed by fire, 52a
  hath root of wisdom been r.,
  37a
  majesty of gods is r., 65b
  unto the meek, 37a
  walk r. her as true goddess,
  118a
Reveals, time r. all, 130b
  to man own folly, 1039a
Revel, joy pleasance r., 274a
  sound loves to r., 641b
Revelation, bogus r., 960a
  in text of men and women,
  850a
Revelations, ends with R., 840a
Revelry by night, 555b
  midnight shout and r., 336b
  mistaken path to happiness,
  564a
  pomp and feast and r., 335a
Revels long o' nights, 254b
  now are ended, 297b
  winds r. keep, 676b
Revenge a wild justice, 208a
  breathing r., 684a
  by this leek horribly r., 245a
  capable and wide r., 275a
  Christianity instinct of r., 806a
  delight of mean spirit, 139b
  envy and r., 341b
  if not victory is yet r., 343a
  if you wrong us shall we not
  r., 233b
  little R. ran on, 654b
  method which rejects r., 1082b
  nation too great for r., 741a
  pen breathing r., 684a
  spur my dull r., 264b
  study of r. immortal hate, 342a
  sweet as my r., 290a
  sweet is r., 560a
  woman has r. ready, 360b
  woman more barbarous in r.
  805a
Revenged, so I am r., 263b
Revengeful, in peace hospitable
  r., 564a
Revenges, time brings in r., 253a
Revenons à nos moutons, 1105b
Revenue, scheme yields no r.,
  452a
  standing r., 453a
  streams of r. gushed, 547b
  tax where no r. found, 452a
Reverberate hills, 251b

Revere, ride of Paul R., 623b
  ride R. never finished, 1017b
Revered, loved at home r. abroad,
  492b
  name illustrious and r., 134b
Reverence, acknowledge restraint
  of r., 89b
  due tradition increases, 804b
  filial r. by quoter, 860a
  for life, 939a
  for life-giving earth, 1077b
  for parents, 78a
  great r. for his son, 373a
  greatest r. due the young, 140a
  human nature, 544a
  humility sense of r., 85b
  in deeper r. praise, 626b
  more of r. in us, 649b
  none so poor to do him r., 255b
  not r. of dead but envy of living, 318a
  passions held in r., 642b
  some r. for laws, 649b
Reverences gilt popinjays, 576a
Reverend vice, 239b
Reverently, entered into r., 61a
Reverie, excited r., 882a
  pleasure of intellect, 599b
  supporting nothing but r., 599b
Reveries, dreams somnambulisms
  r., 697a
  fantastic r., 781a
  so airy, 458a
  valley of r., 930b
Reverse, time will r. your opinions, 96a
  who prospers one day suffer r.,
  82b
Reversion is the action of Tao,
  74a
  no bright r. in sky, 406a
  temporal r., 1006b
Revery alone will do, 739a
  clover bee and r., 739a
  not meet cork without r., 738b
Review, can't write can r., 692b
  Times and Saturday R., 765b
Reviewed, book r. after thirty
  years, 779b
Reviewers stupid and malignant,
  528a
  would have been poets, 528a
Reviewing not criticism, 798b
Revilest God's high priest, 50b
Revised and corrected by author,
  421b
Revisit in dreams the dear dead,
  83b
Revisitest thus glimpses of moon,
  259a
Revisits, gladden him who r. it,
  546b
Revive, after two days will he r.
  us, 35a
  straight again r., 300a
Reviving old desires, 629a
Revolt, inferiors r. to be equal,
  98b
  is it a r., 476b
  nature falls into r., 242a
Revolted, against r. multitudes,
  346b
Revolting and rebellious heart,
  34a
Revolution and more cannon
  shot, 885a
  and reformation, 472b
  call r. progress, 599a
  civilization crust over r., 851a

Roared, loud r. dreadful thunder, 499b
well r. Lion, 230b
Roaring Bill who killed him, 902b
devil as r. lion, 57a
empty tigers or r. sea, 225b
with hollow blasts, 401a
words of my r., 17b
Roars it through the hall, 720b
Rintrah r., 487b
Roast beef of old England, 392b
in hell r. you like herrin, 496a
our own chestnuts, 913b
rules the r., 176a
set house on fire to r. eggs, 209a
Roasted crabs hiss in bowl, 223a
very likeness of r. crab, 229a
Roaster, born a r. of meat, 484b
Rob, if writer r. mother, 1040a
jaybird don't r. own nes', 814a
lady by marriage, 424b
neighbor he promised to defend, 596a
of illusion r. of happiness, 729b
Peter pay Paul, 184a
starve ere I'll r. further, 238b
us of our joys, 1086b
words r. Hybla bees, 256a
Robbed, he's not r. at all, 274b
no man r. where singing, 500b
not wanting what stolen, 274b
that smiles, 273a
we was r., 1037b
Robber, Barabbas a r., 49b
Robbers, the more r. there will be., 74b
what makes r. bold but lenity, 215b
Robbing, live by sharping and r., 423a
think little of r., 552a
Robe, giant's r., 286a
intertissued r. of gold, 244b
judge's r., 270b
of clouds, 559b
Robert, believe R. who has tried it, 119b
Robes and furred gowns, 279b
garland and singing r., 339b
loosely flowing, 302b
mountain in azure hue, 537a
riche or fithele, 166b
sky r. spun of Iris' woof, 336b
washed r. in blood, 58a
Robin bore away thorn, 626b
call for r. redbreast, 314b
fainting r., 737a
redbreast in a cage, 490a
redbreast piously, 108a
what will poor r. do, 1095b
who killed Cock R., 1093b
Robin's lost in play, 981b
Robinson, before say Jack R., 670b
Crusoe, 436a
John P. R. he, 693a
Robots, Rossum's Universal R., 1015a
Robs me of that which not enriches him, 274a
Robust and vivid illustration, 741b
spirit grew r., 738b
Robustious periwig-pated fellow, 262b
Rock, all on a r. reclined, 401a
ay this is the famed r., 781b

Rock, cradle will r., 810b
dwell on r. or in cell, 199a
eagle of the r., 990a
founded upon r., 41b
he is the R., 10b
he only is my r., 19b
it is the Inchcape R., 532b
knew the perilous r., 532b
lean upon death as on r., 995a
Lord is my r., 12b
man sat on a r., 797a
meeting rock know love, 1010b
no water only r., 1003a
of Ages, 469a
of offense, 31a
poetry old as r., 604b
safe upon solid r., 1023a
sails well but strike r., 491b
shadow under red r., 1002a
shadows of a great r. in a weary land, 32a
small r. holds back great wave, 65a
smote r. twice, 547b
takes on appearance of nearby r., 77a
that is higher than I, 19b
the tall r. the mountain, 509a
this r. shall fly, 520a
towered citadel pendant r., 288b
underlies America, 659a
upon this r. I will build, 43a
way of a serpent upon a r., 26b
which Hercules bequeathed, 781b
with motion of morning, 1065b
Rockabye baby, 810b
Lady, 820b
Rockbound, stern and r. coast, 573b
Rocked in cradle of deep, 554a
me to patience, 580b
only world and everyone's, 1078b
to sleep between billows, 696a
Rocket, life like r. flies, 1083b
numbers r. mind, 1079b
rose like a r., 467b
Rockets' red glare, 541a
Rocking, cradle endlessly r., 701b
cradles now r. in land, 760a
Rock-ribbed, hills r., 574a
Rocks and stones and trees, 511a
bold anfractuous r., 1001b
cries of cicadas sink into r., 380a
even among these r., 1004a
hand that r. cradle, 699b
older than r., 781a
seas laugh when r. near, 315a
soften r. or bend oak, 392a
soundings quicksands r., 585b
that are steepest, 1086b
the r. rent, 45a
throne of r., 559b
to roses, 600b
trees wind, 680b
walled round with r., 776a
what gray r., 1004a
whereon greatest men wrecked, 348b
Rocky ledge woods untamed, 860a
shore beats back siege, 227a
Rod, a chief a r., 409b
Aaron's r., 409a
all tremble at the r., 80b
and blows not much good, 179b
beaten with his own r., 182a

Rod, cast thy r. before Pharaoh, 8a
creed is a r., 775b
criticism r. of divination, 879a
Father chiefly known by r., 696a
for angling r. a sturdy oak, 332a
he that spareth his r., 24a
Jonathan put forth the r., 12a
lightning reached fiery r., 790a
lo with a little r., 838b
must heal the sin, 790b
not pious longer than r. behind, 179b
of empire, 440b
of iron, 57b
out of the stem of Jesse, 31a
spare r. and spoil child, 102b, 353a
spare r. spile child, 892a
thy r. and thy staff, 18a
to check the erring, 514b
wisdom be put in silver r., 486b
Rode by witches, 761a
him through mire, 1097b
horses up to bed, 914b
off in all directions, 898a
the six hundred, 652a
upon a cherub, 17a
Roderick, where was R. then, 520a
Roderick Dhu, Saxon I am R., 520a
Rodless Walton of brooks, 846a
Rods, bleeding from Roman r., 459a
Roe, be thou like to a r., 30a
following the r., 494b
Roes, breasts like two young r., 29b
Roger, Sir R. made reflections, 395a
Rogue and peasant slave, 261b
every inch not fool is r., 369a
Rogues, hear r. talk of court news, 280a
Roguish, equity is a r. thing, 317a
Roi, plus royaliste que le r., 1105b
Rois, l'exactitude la politesse des r., 485b
Roland, a R. for an Oliver, 154b
Child R. to dark tower, 278b
est preux et Oliver est sage, 154b
sound your oliphant, 154b
valorous Oliver wise, 154b
Roles, self-interest plays all r., 355a
Rolet, cat's a cat R. a knave, 377a
Roll, centuries r. back to age of gold, 122b
confirm tidings as they r., 393a
darkling down torrent, 427a
'em up, 1099a
eyes begin to r., 413b
felt him like thunder's r., 711a
from soul to soul, 648b
in ecstasy at your feet, 980b
let it r., 921b
life's surges rudest r., 497b
me over fair, 698a
my log I roll yours, 131a
of common men, 239b
of honor holds no nobler figure, 934b
of world eastward palpable, 782b

Run though not soar, 595a
  through fire and water, 267a
  till she leaves rail, 904b
  time will r. back, 334a
  to ride to r., 201a
  true love never did r. smooth, 228b
  wit enough to r. away, 353b
  with patience, 56a
  yet we will make him r., 360a
Runcible hat, 673a
  spoon, 673a
Rune, rounds with rhyme r., 602b
Rung, by fairy hands knell r., 443a
  curfew from gloomy tower, 825b
  down ladder r. by r., 873b
  how grandly it had r., 791a
  night's yawning peal, 284b
  on ladder of thought, 851a
Runic rhyme, 644a
Runner, naked r. lost in spears, 878b
Runners, like r. hand on torch, 113b
Runner-up, in war no prize for r., 1025b
Runneth earth's wide regions, 554a
  my cup r. over, 18a
  not to the contrary, 444b
Runnin' away and fightin', 891b
  for priest an' doctor, 981a
Running all over the sea, 843b
  away and fightin', 891b
  books in r. brooks, 247b
  call of r. tide, 946b
  farced title r. 'fore king, 244b
  first sprightly r., 367b
  it never runs from us, 305b
  laughter, 856b
  of the deer, 1099b
  off upon instinct, 1081a
  to keep in same place, 745a
  trouble r. any country, 946a
  under r. laughter, 856b
  under r. water, 1004a
  water walk, 970b
  written in r. water, 115a
Runnymede, reeds at R., 876b
Runs, he that r. may read, 459a
  he that r. well r. twice, 135b
  heart r. away with head, 500a
  man who r. may fight again, 102b
  running it never r. from us, 305b
  so r. world away, 263b
  through roughest day, 281b
  time r. the clock will strike, 213b
  win race r. by himself, 872a
  with intrepid shorebirds, 1065b
Rupert of parliamentary discussion, 611b
Rural, and I made a r. pen, 486b
  happy who knows r. gods, 117a-b
  honor taken refuge in r. setting, 316b
  quiet friendship, 419b
  vale of r. life, 441a
Rus I see you, 632a
  in urbe, 135b
  said to people of R., 170a
  similar to troika, 632b
Rush, fools r. in, 404a

Rush herds of walruses and whales, 696a
  into the skies, 408a
  my only into your arms, 969a
  nations shall r. like many waters, 31b
  of cochineal, 738b
  please to call it r. candle, 219b
  rushed along with r., 930a
  to glory or grave, 538a
Rushed along with the rush, 930a
  to meet insulting foe, 482b
Rushing of many waters, 31b
  sound of r. wind, 49b
Russet, morn in r. mantle clad, 257a
Russia, been over into R., 887b
  direct telescope on R., 707b
  heart of R. not forget, 611a
  homeland of patience, 611a
  how sad our R., 632b
  last out night in R., 270b
  Mother R., 710a
  not forecast action of R., 920b
  prison of nations, 954b
  vast multitudes of R., 922b
Russian, great R. allies, 1016b
  looks through window, 594a
  I am true R., 1083a
  might have been R., 766a
  mighty R. speech, 688a
  refusal to accept defeat, 959b
  rugged R. bear, 285a
  tongue to converse with all, 435a
  tongue we must save, 1014b
Russians dashed toward line, 704b
  shall not have Constantinople, 727a
Russians' joy to drink, 170a
Russophiles, article against R., 707b
Rust, better to wear out than r. out, 367a
  dew will r. them, 272b
  eaten to death with r., 241b
  his sword r., 527a
  if gold r. what shal iren do, 166b
  iron till it r., 996b
  military machine r., 922b
  moth and r. doth corrupt, 40b
  strong men r., 1035b
  that never stains sword, 871a
  that which never taketh r., 203b
  time r. sharpest sword, 520b
  to the harrow, 914b
  too much rest is r., 521b
  toy soldier red with r., 820b
  unburnished, 646b
Rustic, in r. speech a phrase, 963a
Rustics, amazed gazing r., 450a
Rusting in pool of tears, 857a
Rustled, stars in sky r. softly, 829b
Rustles, everything r. to him in fear, 83a
Rustling of purple curtain, 643a
  spring with r. shade, 1009b
  to her knees, 582a
Rusts, iron r. from disuse, 174a
Rusty, for want of fighting r., 352b
  mail, 268b
Ruth, melt with r., 339a
  sad heart of R., 583a
Ruthless extortion, 771a
  good writer r., 1040a

Ruthless, in war cunning r., 564a
  nor any wildcat so r., 91b
  ruin seize thee r. king, 441b
Ruthlessly pricking bubble, 962b
Rutledge, I am Anne R., 898b
Rydal, to R. Lake that lead, 510b
Rye, catcher in the r., 1078a
  pocket full of r., 1094b
  Roman came to R., 919a

S

Sabachthani, Eli Eli lama s., 45a
Sabato, iddio non paga s., 667b
Sabbath, abhor and detest S., 761b
  child born on S., 1096a
  do not love the S., 1034b
  eternal S. of his rest, 369a
  keep S. going to church, 735b
  made for man, 45a
  rang slowly, 1070b
  remember the s. day, 9a
Sabbath-breaking, drinking and S., 552b
Sabbaths, endless s. blessed ones see, 154a
Sabidius, I don't like you S., 135a
Sabina has thousand charms, 1089b
Sabine, bounded by S., 655a
  Sabines, life the old S. knew, 117b
Sable cloud, 336b
  it was a s. silvered, 258a
  night s. goddess, 399a
  Sleep son of s. Night, 210b
  underneath this s. hearse, 319b
Sables, suit of s., 263a
Sabrina fair, 337b
Sacco's name will live, 1010a
Sack, each s. had seven cats, 1093a
  if s. and sugar be fault, 239b
  intolerable deal of s., 239b
  leave s. live cleanly, 241a
  unless hours cups of s., 237b
Sackcloth, put on s. with ashes, 14a
Sacked the holy citadel of Troy, 65a
Sacks, seven s., 1093a
Sacrament of praise, 955b
  of summer days, 734b
Sacred, Alph the s. river, 523b
  belong to s. literature, 1035a
  cod, 858a
  facts are s., 811a
  feed his s. flame, 526b
  fire, 906b
  fire of liberty, 461b
  hair dissever, 404b
  head now wounded, 333a
  head of thine, 338b
  history a s. thing, 195b
  hold every moment s., 937b
  human body s., 701a
  let there be s. silence, 121b
  lips touch s. fire, 906b
  nothing s., 1044a
  our s. honor, 471a
  preserve cradles as s., 760a
  sane and s. death, 702a
  source of sympathetic tears, 441b
  they lack a s. poet, 122b
  things s. or things profane, 365b

Science knowledge of many, 567a
 law a hocus-pocus s., 414b
 literature not abstract s., 866b
 mysterious is source of art and
   s., 950a
 natural s. involves three things,
   474b
 no category of s. applied, 718b
 not enough to understand s.,
   950a
 not sufficiently promoted,
   1019b
 object of s. truth, 527b
 observation passive s., 675a
 of going to bust, 685a
 of how who gets what, 994a
 of life superb hall, 675a
 of Nature, 376b
 out of olde bokes newe s., 164a
 outdistance in s., 747b
 perverted s., 921a
 pictures s. draws of nature,
   942b
 poetry antithesis to s., 527b
 politics not exact s., 677b
 promote progress of s., 1027b
 proud S., 408a
 purer s. holier laws, 691a
 pursuit of s., 709b
 quacks one side s. other, 564b
 reassures, 966a
 refinement of everyday thinking, 950a
 repulses indefinite, 675a
 scarcely advanced to s., 723a
 search for truth, 1050a
 spectacles of s., 1000b
 spirit of s. in international affairs, 1050a
 teaches doubt, 675a
 temple of s., 847a
 theologians at cradle of s., 724b
 though no s. worth seven, 407a
 thought to aim at some good,
   97b
 treating psychology like natural
   s., 796a
 true s. teaches doubt, 869b
 waves of s. beat in vain, 705b
 where s. progressed farthest,
   966b
 which draws conclusions, 829b
 without conscience ruin, 181a
 youth who devote to s., 818b
Sciences, books must follow s.,
   210a
 experience mother of s., 194b
 mathematics queen of s., 539a
 natural s. aim never reach, 723a
Scientia potestas est, 206b
Scientific, Abraham of s. men,
   705b
 activity cumulative, 981b
 advances available, 982b
 discovery and sovereignty, 1039a
 education, 1019b
 innovation rarely converts opponents, 847a
 Jesus most s. man, 709a
 knowledge from textbooks,
   1026b
 method for studying, 834a
 method of s. investigation, 724b
 plunges into s. questions, 725b
 pure s. thought, 977a
 revolution, 1047a
 thought is human progress,
   809a
 truth in different forms, 741b

Scientist cannot dispense with
   faith, 847a
 independent s., 1033b
 ready to bear privation, 1028a
 takes off from predecessors,
   949a
 wiser not to withhold, 478b
Scientists at other pole, 1058b
Scintillant in cloudless days, 979a
Scissors, two halves of pair of s.,
   523a
Scoff at others' ecstasies, 900a
 fools who came to s., 449b
Scolded, nobody ever s. him, 887b
Scooped, seas s. in vain, 686a
 tankards s. in pearl, 734b
Scoot, as years s. by, 1054a
 old man Rabbit say s., 814a
Scooted, w'en Rabbit say they s.,
   814a
Scope, fantasy to utmost s., 915a
 had not been so short, 299a
 of my opinion, 256b
 this man's art that man's s.,
   292a
 within s. of Constitution, 485b
Scorch, fires that s., 626b
Score, from seventy springs a s.,
   852b
 give me a kiss and to that a s.,
   320a
 muster many a s., 503a
 no books but s. and tally, 215b
Scored, our days are s. against us,
   135a
Scorer, One Great S., 961b
Scorn, bright creature s. not one,
   517b
 child of s., 899b
 dangers make us s., 495b
 delights, 338b
 figure for time of s., 275b
 foul s. that prince invade, 189a
 her own image, 262b
 I can s. and let her go, 318b
 laugh a siege to s., 286b
 laugh to s. power of man, 285b
 laughed His word to s., 457a
 looks beautiful, 252b
 mine ever name of s., 654a
 not all free who s. chains, 455a
 not the sonnet, 517a
 not thing to laugh to s., 250b
 of mankind down centuries,
   922b
 of scorn, 644b
 read to s., 521a
 silence expression of s., 837b
 sound of public s., 348a
 the codfish, 1101b
 the spear, 571b
 the well-connected, 767b
 to change state with kings, 292a
 to take offense, 403b
 under solemn fillet saw s., 604a
 upright man laughed to s., 15a
Scorned his spirit, 253b
 woman s., 392a
Scorner, reprove not a s., 24a
Scorner's, sit in s. seat, 846a
Scornful, most bitter is s. jest,
   426b
 sitteth in the seat of the s., 16b
 yet jealous eyes, 410b
Scorning base degrees, 254a
 our blank in s., 734a
Scorns, whips and s. of time, 262a
Scorpions, I will chastise with s.,
   13a

Scotch mist, 695a
Scotched, we have s. the snake,
   284b
Scotchman, beggarly S., 430a
 if caught young, 431b
 noblest prospect S. sees, 430b
Scotia's grandeur springs, 492b
Scotland, in S. before ye, 1099a
 in S. supports people, 427b
 through pylons of Euston, 951b
Scotland's, left fair S. strand, 494a
Scots dispersed over whole earth,
   205a
 gude S. lords, 1087b
 kills six or seven dozen S., 239a
 lords at his feet, 1087b
 only a few industrious S., 205a
 wha hae wi' Wallace bled, 496a
Scott hand in Southern character,
   760b
Scoundrel, A is a s., 961a
 and coward, 430a
 hypocrite flatterer, 491a
 patriotism last refuge of s.,
   431b
Scoundrels have no songs, 500b
 healthy hatred of s., 578a
Scoured with perpetual motion,
   241b
Scourge, faith is her own s., 134a
 iron s., 439b
 laid upon your hate, 225b
 mighty s. of war, 640b
 of God, 212a
 of small cords, 48a
 of war, 1104a
 tool that did his will, 791a
Scourged to his dungeon, 574b
Scout, blabbing eastern s., 336b
 flout 'em and s. 'em, 97a
Scowl of cloud, 668a
Scramble, great s. and big divide,
   785a
 rooks in s. sort, 906a
Scrambling to the shore, 745b
Scrap of paper, 832b
 of sunset with voice, 811b
 worn out before on s. heap,
   836b
Scrape cable, 678a
Scraping, Death's ironic s., 955b
Scraps, on s. of learning dote,
   398b
 stolen the s., 222b
Scratch Christian find pagan,
   870b
 head with lightning, 760a
 it with a hoe, 733a
 lover find foe, 1029a
 on wall of oblivion, 1040a
Scratched, expect to be s., 195a
 head kept thinking, 899b
 man whom Fortune s., 270a
 out both eyes, 1098a
Scratchez, Ah itchez Ah scratchez,
   1051b
Scratching at the floor, 859b
Scrawls, few hundhred s., 981a
Scream, not a shriek not a s.,
   746b
Screaming, dive-bomber's s. orgasm, 995a
 over yawning gulf, 697b
 stallions maned, 917b
Screams of horror rend, 404b
Screen, smoke s. of intimidation,
   1020b
 world vast s. of snow, 1010b
Screw your courage, 283a

Sea pastures, 697a
   pearl in bosom of s., 309b
   perfumed s., 641b
   Persians hold s. holy, 695b
   plants footsteps in s., 456b
   plow the s., 766b
   Pontic s., 275a
   pouring oil on the s., 132a
   power never led to despotism, 997b
   praise s. on shore remain, 202a
   precious stone set in silver s., 226b
   Proteus rising from s., 515b
   raging waves of the s., 57a
   re-embark on unknown s., 700a
   righteousness as waves of s., 33a
   rising nor sky clouding, 801a
   river will reach s., 775a
   room to tell truth in, 695a
   round cape sudden came s., 663a
   roving over the s., 634b
   running all over s., 843b
   sailed wintry s., 621a
   sailor home from s., 824a
   sang in my chains like s., 1070b
   see one s. and see all, 311a
   sepulcher there by s., 644a
   served revolution plowed s., 549a
   shadow only s. keeps, 1043b
   Sherman's buzzin' to sea, 1041b
   ship's way on s., 874a
   ships of war at s., 654b
   shows false alluring smile, 113b
   shroud of sea, 697b
   sight of immortal s., 513b
   silent s., 524b
   sing by land and s., 874a
   singing over the wine-dark s., 65a
   sinks to another s., 686a
   sky and s. and land, 855a
   slimy s., 525a
   snuff thee up s. breeze, 695b
   spirit that on life's rough s., 205b
   summers in a s. of glory, 298b
   sun an' salt spryy of s., 981a
   sun was shining on s., 745b
   sunless s., 523b
   surging s. outweighs, 604b
   sweet mystery about s., 697a
   swing of the s., 802b
   syllabub s., 673b
   that pickest and cullest, 703a
   the s. is his, 59b
   the sea the open sea, 554a
   the s. the s., 92b
   there was no more s., 58b
   though the mountains be carried into the s., 19a
   thought jump s. and land, 292a
   thousand furlongs of s., 296a
   thy rays in midst of s., 4a
   to English the s., 500a
   to s. through your expanse, 632b
   to s. to s., 600b
   tomb by side of s., 644a
   tomorrow we sail the Ocean S., 121a
   tossed up in waves, 105a
   troubled s. of mind, 580b
   trunk spouts out a s., 347a
   two if by s., 624a
   under deep deep s., 591b

Sea, unicorns come down to s., 1010b
   union with native s., 516b
   unknown s., 769b
   uttermost parts of the s., 23a
   voice whose sound like s., 512b
   walking on the s., 42b
   waters cover the s., 31a
   way of a ship in the s., 26b
   weariest river winds to s., 775a
   we'll o'er the s., 507b
   went to sea in sieve, 673a
   wet sheet flowing s., 551a
   what is it saying, 671a
   when I put out to s., 655a
   where Drake sleeps in s., 695b
   whether in s. or fire, 257a
   white s. widening, 1066b
   who can say s. is old, 783a
   who commands the s. has command, 78a
   who hath desired s., 876a
   who run across s. do not change disposition, 123b
   why s. boiling hot, 746a
   wind nor tide nor s., 770b
   wind of western s. 648a
   winds pierced solitudes, 602b
   wish you a wave of the s., 295b
   work in land or s., 602b
   wrapped in mystery, 843b
   wrinkled s. beneath, 651b
   your mind and you Sargasso S. 987b
Sea-banks, upon the wild s., 235a
Sea-born treasures, 602a
Sea-change, suffer a s., 296a
Sea-down's edge, 776a
Seafarers, hour that turns back longing of s., 161a
Seafaring man on desert of waters, 733a
Seal, god seem to set his s., 264a
   impression as from s. of ring, 95b
   sense in deathly slumber, 914b
   set me as a s., 30a
   slumber did my spirit s., 511a
   to such a bond, 232b
   up avenues of ill, 603b
   upon thine arm, 30a
Sealed bag of ducats, 233a
   in vain, 271b
   thy fate and mine s., 649a
   with seven seals, 58a
Sealing, come s. night, 284b
   shoes ships s. wax, 745b
   snapped off like s. wax, 671a
Seal's wide spindrift gaze, 1043b
Seals of love sealed in vain, 271b
   sealed with seven s., 58a
Seam, sew a fine s., 1095b
Sea-maid's music, 229a
Seaman, betokened wrack to s., 220a
   delight as only s. may know, 997a
   looking for something else, 997b
Seaman's story is of tempest, 127b
Sea-mark of my utmost sail, 276a
Seamen, all her s. know, 515b
   forty singing s., 961b
   thus with s., 695b
   were not gentlemen, 597a
Sear, leaf red and s., 519a
Search for inexplicable, 957b
   happy man who could s. out causes, 117a

Sea land of living men, 519a
   not worth the s., 231b
   out purposes of gods, 79b
   so painful and so long, 382b
   the scriptures, 48b
   their own glory, 26a
   thine own heart, 626a
   things above thy strength, 37a
   took day to s. for God, 860a
   vain my weary s. to find, 448a
   walked in the s. of the depth, 16a
   will find it out, 320b
Searched me and known me, 23a
Searcher know by mortal mind, 742b
   obedient to truth, 705b
Searches, tent that s., 268a
Searcheth, Lord s. all hearts, 14a
Searching, by s. find out God, 15a
   for new lover, 1053a
   like poor astronomers, 899b
Searchlights of science, 889b
Seared and blighted heart, 641a
   conscience s. with hot iron, 55a
Sears Northland soul, 1035b
Sea's face and gray dawn, 946b
   great s. voice, 905a
Seas, backed with God and s., 216a
   colder than Hebrides, 980a
   dangers of the s., 328b
   desperate s. long wont, 641b
   diver in deep s., 781a
   down to s. again, 946b
   faithless as winds or s., 378b
   fight on s. and oceans, 921a
   floors of silent s., 1001a
   freedom of s., 842b
   from the s. and streams, 570b
   guard our native s., 537b
   half s. over, 390b
   he hath founded it upon the s., 18a
   I must down to s., 946b
   incarnadine, 283b
   laboring s., 906a
   laugh when rocks near, 315a
   launch on trackless s., 702b
   mackerel-crowded s., 882b
   of life like wine, 378a
   of space and time, 999b
   on what s. thy fate, 868b
   perilous s., 583a
   port after stormy s., 200a
   rivers run to s., 372a
   roaring with blasts, 401a
   roll to waft me, 408a
   sail wet s. roun', 874b
   scooped in vain, 686a
   shedding s. of gore, 561b
   ships sailing the s., 702b
   shoreless s., 790a
   snarled and yelping s., 1001b
   strange s. of thought, 510a
   tossed upon cloudy s., 961b
   unsuspected isle in s., 661b
   wandering over many s. to these obsequies, 115b
   waste of s., 590a
   what s. what shores, 1004a
   wine-dark s., 1060a
Sea-scented beach, 663a
Seashore, like boy playing on s., 379b
Seaside stroll a gallery, 724a
Seasilt saltsick, 969a
Season, a convenient s., 50b
   be instant in s. 55b

Season, bringeth forth his fruit in s., 16b
each thing that in s. grows, 221a
end of love or s., 926a
ever 'gainst that s., 257a
little s. of love laughter, 748a
love no s. knows, 305a
meat in due s., 21b
moulting s. crisis, 682b
my scope had not this s., 299a
no s. such delight can bring, 319b
of love and laughter, 748a
of mists, 583b
of snows and sin, 772b
overpraised s., 755b
proportion s. form, 267b
shock of corn cometh in s., 14b
tale out of s., 38a
things by s. seasoned, 235b
to come and go, 412b
to every thing there is a s., 27b
word spoken in due s., 24b
your admiration, 258a
youth's s. for joys, 401b
Seasoned, speech s. with salt, 54b
things by season s., 235b
timber never gives, 323a
with a gracious voice, 233b
with Attic salt, 362a
Seasoning of all enjoyments, 361a
sharp s. of truth, 145a
Seasons, afford costly s., 1082a
all s. sweet to thee, 526a
all s. thine O Death, 574a
all times are his s., 308b
appointeth moon for s., 21b
as swift s. roll, 633b
assailed the s., 899b
defend you from s., 278b
depends on s. and days, 942b
he makes s. by months, 3b
joys abound as s. fleet, 214b
lovers' s. run, 305a
man for all s., 179a
mercy s. justice, 234b
not the full four s., 1023b
O s. clear, 1043a
O s. O châteaux, 830a
sorrow breaks s., 217a
time of s. and constellations, 1005a
vernal s. of year, 340a
with the year s. return, 344b
yin and yang became four s., 110a
Seat, castle hath pleasant s., 282a
God's great Judgment S., 872b
of desolation, 342a
of Mars, 226b
of pleasures and loves, 371a
of sensation stomach, 855a
proud s. of Lucifer, 348a
sit in scorner's s., 846a
sitteth in the s. of the scornful, 16b
thy s. is up on high, 228b
thyself sultanically, 697a
upon intellectual throne, 712a
while memory holds a s., 260a
wild sequestered s., 443b
Seated, all s. on the ground, 384a
grace s. on this brow, 264a
heart knock at my ribs, 281b
in thy silver chair, 302a
one day at organ, 725b
Seatown, years around s. corner, 1070b

Seats, change s. and fiddles, 505b
high s. in temple of civilization, 971a
put down mighty from s., 45b
Seaward flying unbroken wings, 1004a
from the town, 551a
looked s. among islands, 816b
trees seemed to march s., 816b
Seawards, my road leads s., 947a
salt tides s. flow, 719b
Secluded chapel, 1007a
eternally from God, 308b
Second, appointed for my s. race, 362b
best to go back quickly, 83a
best's gay goodnight, 883b
childishness, 249a
children for s. time, 91a
class citizens, 1025a
custom almost s. nature, 221a
Daniel, 235a
first among these than s. in Rome, 112a
friend is a s. self, 111b
great nature's s. course, 283b
in war no s. prize, 1025b
is frugality, 75a
mads him, 251b
Mrs. Tanqueray, 902a
no dishonor to halt at s. place, 111a
Theseus a s. Hercules, 136a
thoughts are best, 84b
wife hateful to children, 83b
Secondary, between primary and s., 995a
imagination, 528b
Seconded with will and power, 268a
Secondhand, never give s. opinion, 809a
three busts all s., 831a
Secrecy, for s. no lady closer, 239a
nature's infinite book of s., 287a
queen of s. violet, 581a
the human dress, 489b
Secret aims of nature, 801a
and his dark s. love, 489a
anniversaries of heart, 625a
as grave, 197a
be s. and exult, 881b
black midnight hags, 285a
book with s. reference, 615a
bread eaten in s., 24a
cleanse me from s. faults, 17b
courage s. of liberty, 832b
death a s. of Nature, 141b
dwelleth in s. place, 20b
every creature s. to other, 672a
every daisy knows my s., 832a
extort s. lose curiosity, 605a
guilt by silence betrayed, 370b
inwardly s. great, 694a
isolated joy of thinker, 786b
keeps s. well as child, 599b
liberty s. of happiness, 832b
life of belly and bone, 1069b
locked within them, 1049b
ministry, 526a
not s. if confided, 685a
nothing is s., 46b
of being a bore, 416b
of freedom a brave heart, 90a
of happiness freedom, 90a
of success constancy, 612b
of success in life, 813b
of their own discovery, 1049b

Secret, open rebuke better than s. love, 26b
our readings s., 951b
phrases of soul, 966b
powers of atom, 888b
self-contained solitary, 670b
single s. will still be man, 1032a
sits in middle and knows, 929a
source of humor, 762b
sympathy, 518b
tell you a great s., 1068b
things belong unto the Lord, 10b
though s. it rolls, 541b
thoughts run over all things, 318a
three keep s. if two dead, 421b
treasures in s. kept, 679b
waters, 1036a
whence this s. dread, 393b
whispers of other's watch, 244a
with every s. thing, 29a
Secretary of Nature, 326b
Secretly, how swift how s., 1022b
nurtured in cellar, 998a
Secret's safe 'twixt you and me, 667b
Secrets cry aloud, 1064b
everybody guesses, 836a
from whom no s. are hid, 60b
holding such things to be holy s., 88b
learned s. of grave, 781a
reveal no s., 450a
trust not him with s., 469b
Sect, know neither s. nor idolatry, 173a
never attached to that s., 571a
slave to no s., 410a
write for country for s., 894a
Section, you-all means s., 1100a
Sects, vicissitude of s. and religions, 209b
Seculo, alteri s., 107b
Secure a few minutes for poetry, 728b
amidst falling world, 393a
and now never mourn, 572a
approval if try hard, 762b
blessings of liberty, 474a
friends by doing favors, 90a
from change, 694b
he who s. within can say, 369b
repeal of bad laws, 717a
strong just weak s., 1073b
you count many friends, 129a
Secured against maladministration, 446a
Securely founded, 477b
orbed, 990b
Security, absolute s., 1055a
against future violations, 426a
collective s., 940b-941a
culture moment of s., 977b
for average man, 971a
for the future, 426a
how little s. we have, 539b
in old book, 694b
no s. in nobleness of another, 939b
of all countries connected, 964a
of future, 741a
of people, 446a
of the Republic, 865a
order s. and peace, 964a
public strength individual s., 484b
system of general s., 974b

Sleeping, some s. killed, 227b
Thy servant s., 727a
tree growing when ye're s., 521a
try by s. what it is to die, 330b
wake and waking sleep, 190b
wakened us from s., 994a
woods all night, 525b
Sleepless Eremite, 581a
soul that perished, 511b
to give readers sleep, 413b
vigilance, 638b
watches of night, 624b
Sleeps, after life's fever s., 284b
creation s., 399a
Goethe in Weimar s., 711a
great engine never s., 660a
happy warrior s., 976a
in continual noise, 771b
in dust, 327b
moonlight s. upon this bank, 235a
now s. crimson petal, 649a
on watch, 452a
remorse s., 436b
she s. my lady s., 621b
there s. Titania, 229b
thinks and wills, 869b
till tired he s., 409b
where Drake s. in sea, 695b
where s. that promise now, 758a
while my little one s., 648b
with enduring dead, 572a
Sleepy and proud, 1009b
I am s. and weeds twist, 698a
Sleepyhead, to bed says S., 1094b
Sleet, iron s., 442a
Sleeve, laughing in your s., 480b
laughing up her s., 360b
raveled s. of care, 283b
wear heart upon my s., 272a
Sleeveless errand, 183a
some shortless others, 413b
Sleeves, fluttering empty s., 956a
Sleigh, carry the s., 598a
Sleighbells, ghost of s., 926b
Sleight, tricks by s. of hand, 391b
Slender, as cedar tall and s., 476a
debt to Nature, 321b
thy s. stem, 493a
tops against sky, 592a
waist confined, 332b
Slenderly, fashioned so s., 592b
Slept azure-lidded sleep, 582a
dreamed life beauty, 680a
I should have s., 14b
in peace, 299a
law not dead though it s., 270b
one wink, 291a
Passion s., 426b
resembled my father as he s., 283b
touched him and he s., 650b
while companions s., 623b
Slew, as ambitious I s. him, 255a
dead which he s. at his death, 11b
Death s. not him, 201a
enemy nearly s. ye, 1099b
on tree they s. Him, 796b
thrice he s. the slain, 371b
Slice, no matter how you s. it, 1053b
no matter how thin s., 916b
royal s. of bread, 969b
Slices of quince, 673a
Slide into lover's head, 510b
Kelly s., 1101a
let world s., 182a
no foot shall s., 1103a

Sliding from lifted bar, 1065a
Slight little light little, 768b
me when I woo, 318b
nor Fame I s., 402b
not what's near, 84a
Slightest approach to false pretense, 747a
rememberest not s. folly, 248a
Slightly shakes parting guest, 268b
Slim hand so lovely, 981a
Slime, daubed with s. and pitch, 8a
of a wet nest, 1065a
wetter water slimier s., 993b
Slimier, wetter water s. slime, 993b
Slimy things did crawl with legs, 525a
Sling, my s. the s. of David, 828b
prevailed with a s. and with a stone, 12a
Slinging, fury s. flame, 650a
Slings and arrows of fortune, 261b
Slinks out of race, 340a
Slip away before they're up, 968b
given them the s., 386b
giving enemies s., 437b
if I s. Thou not fall, 688b
let it s. useless away, 578a
let s. dogs of war, 255a
'twixt cup and lip, 311b
Slipped, thrice it s. through my hands, 66a
Slippered, lean and s. pantaloon, 249a
Slippers, same old s., 855b
shuffle about in s., 871a
Slippery, he that stands on s. place, 236b
words s. thought viscous, 777b
Slippy-sloppy, water s. in larder, 887b
Slips, greyhounds in s., 244a
if lips keep from s., 812b
Slit, tongue be s., 1093b
Slithy toves, 745a
Slits the thin-spun life, 338b
Sliver and disbranch, 279a
Slop over, 750b
staineth s., 988a
Slope through darkness to God, 650b
Slopes, gently s. the way, 449a
Sloping to southern side, 694a
Sloppy biased reporting, 1020b
Joe's, 1060a
Sloth and cowardice that clings, 918b
egotism s. idleness, 549a
finds down pillow hard, 291a
peaceful s., 343b
Slothful ease, 847b
man saith, 26a
Slouches toward Bethlehem, 882a
Slough was Despond, 365b
Slovenliness is no part of religion, 420b
Slovenly unhandsome corpse, 238b
wilderness, 955b
Slow, a God s. to anger, 14a
aged and poor and s., 813a
and moving finger, 275b
and silent stream Lethe, 344a
and steady wins, 75b
as tardy as too s., 224b
be s. to speak s. to wrath, 56a
but sure, 325a

Slow but sure moves might, 85a
cold and to temptation s., 293a
come he s., 519a
confidence plant of s. growth, 426a
drag of days, 83b
drag the s. barge, 459b
drags its s. length along, 403a
drip over stones, 1064b
free to go very s., 930a
he that is s. to anger, 24b
heart is s. to learn, 1023b
how s. shadow creeps, 901b
I am s. of speech, 8a
I am s. of study, 229a
in assembling, 89a
learn to read s., 364a
man catches up with swift, 65b
march of human mind s., 453a
Meander's margent green, 337a
melancholy s., 447b
northern thought s. durable, 664b
of a s. tongue, 8a
on the leash, 987b
punt swings round, 712a
rises worth, 426b
silent walk, 784a
sort of country, 745a
spondee stalks, 527a
sun climbs s. how slowly, 689a
swift s. sweet sour, 803a
tarry awhile says S., 1094b
tremulous cadence s., 714b
unreckoning hearts, 1079b
vaster than empires and more s., 359b
wisely and s., 224b
Slow-breathing unconscious Kosmos, 796a
Slowest, haste of fool s. thing, 380a
Slowly, art appreciated only s., 915b
chilling breath invade, 714a
comest in so s., 1051a
ever forward but s., 469b
follies of town crept s., 450b
lowing herd wind s., 440a
mills of God grind s., 329a
night pass more s., 565b
rase she up, 1088a
run s. horses of night, 213b
silently now moon, 914a
spring comes s., 524a
sun climbs slow how s., 689a
Slug-a-bed, sweet s., 320b
Sluggard, go to the ant thou s., 23b
no room for s., 923b
voice of the s., 396b
Sluggardy, May wol have no s. anyght, 167a
Slughorn to my lips I set, 278b
Slugs leave their lair, 527b
Slug-ye'er-spouse an internaytional spoort, 892a
Slumber, death is s., 568a
did my spirit seal, 511a
he that keepeth thee will not s., 22a
honey-heavy dew of s., 254b
I must s. again, 396b
kindly earth s., 647b
lie still and s., 396b
love itself s. on, 572b
neither s. nor sleep, 22a
nor s. nor a roof, 1024a
ports of s. open, 242b

Snow, fallen s. on s., 740a
  falling faintly through universe, 968a
  falling s. silent, 944b
  farewell s. of ferne yere, 165a
  fleece white as s., 563b
  frolic architecture of s., 602b
  frost from purest s., 290a
  gatekeepers shoveling s., 1020a
  geese like s. cloud, 1009b
  general over Ireland, 968a
  gently walking in s., 958a
  ghost of s., 926b
  had begun in gloaming, 693b
  hide hills of s., 271b
  I shall be whiter than s., 19a
  if s. be white, 294b
  is on grass again, 724a
  late though lingered s., 780a
  lay round about, 687b
  like s. falls in river, 495b
  like s. in May, 323b
  like s. on desert's face, 629b
  locks are like s., 494b
  melted like s., 559a
  mockery king of s., 228a
  monuments carved from s., 998a
  moonshine an' s., 693a
  no s. is there, 65b
  nor does s. come near it, 65b
  not s. nor rain nor heat, 87a
  pure as s., 262b
  raiment white as s., 45a
  rain s. hail and drought, 760a
  rosebuds filled with s., 300a
  said peace cold sleep, 1010b
  she is near under s., 838b
  shuts out sky, 676b
  sins shall be white as s., 30a
  step softly under s., 919a
  stood shivering in s., 210b
  swept world end to end, 1018a
  swooned as he heard s., 968a
  tree appearing above s., 467b
  try s. of heaven, 1033a
  tufts of s. on bare branch, 526a
  wallow naked in December s., 226a
  we shall have s., 1095b
  where s. lay dinted, 687b
  white and drifted s., 598a
  white as driven s., 295b
  winter's s., 720a
  wish s. in May's mirth, 221a
  woods fill with s., 927b
  world vast screen of s., 1010b
  wrapped in clouds and s., 556a
  year rich year, 324a
Snow-broth, man whose blood is s., 270a
Snowed for six days and six nights, 1070b
  it s. of mete amd drynke, 166b
  whole world over, 1018a
Snowflakes, like pearls s. glow, 958a
  words like winter s., 63a
Snowman, like Abominable S., 1083b
Snows and sin, 772b
  birds leaves s., 1057a
  of the year 1941, 1083b
  where are s. of yesteryear, 171a
Snow-white, little s. feet, 879a
Snowy, marble of her s. breast, 332a
  seraphs swing s. hats, 735a
  summits old in story, 648b

Snub, hard to s. beautiful woman, 925a
  mine has s. nose, 491a
Snuff approach of tyranny, 453a
  let me s. sea breeze, 695b
  shifted his trumpet took s., 451a
  women drink or s., 1034b
Snuffbox, fill his s., 386b
Snuffed out by article, 562a
Snug as bug in rug, 422b
  little farm the world, 533a
  little island, 517b
So and no otherwise, 876a
  can any man, 239b
  if it was s. it might be, 745b
  if she be not s. to me, 318b
  it has been, 1024a
  much for him, 257a
  runs world away, 263b
Soakers, old s., 375a
Soaking in comfortable baths, 1035b
Soap and education deadly, 759a
  invisible s., 592b
  smiles and s., 747a
  tattoo s. bubbles, 1047a
  what no s., 442b
Soapsuds and the starch, 1034b
Soar, angels alone that s. above, 359a
  but never roam, 517a
  flitter dip and s., 1079a
  in action s. as high, 680b
  into air above dunes, 1036a
  not s. where he is, 572a
  not too high to fall, 315b
  run though not s., 595a
  singing still dost s., 570b
  spur you to s., 775b
  where he is sitting, 572a
Soaring ever singest, 570b
  in high reason of fancies, 339b
Soars, if he s. with own wings, 487b
  no bird s. too high, 487b
Sob as you spin, 1060a
  child's s. curses deeper, 617b
  heavy world, 1060a
  on the saxophones, 948b
Sobbings of violins of autumn, 807b
Sober as a hymn, 815b
  as a judge, 424a
  be s. be vigilant, 57a
  black shawl, 981a
  certainty of waking bliss, 337a
  creeping thing in s. way, 685b
  healthful and with his wits, 356b
  in s. livery clad, 345b
  men at whiles s., 854a
  plain in dress s. in diet, 414a
  skies ashen and s., 643b
  steadfast and demure, 335b
  studious and s., 405b
  take s. coloring from eye, 514a
  to bed go s., 312b
Soberly, entered into s., 61a
Soberness, speak truth and s., 50b
Sobers, drinking s. again, 403a
Sobriety a species of courage, 373b
  justice peace and s., 329a
  property stimulus to s., 941b
Sobs, with s. and tears sorted out, 746a
Sociability law of nature, 796a
Sociable ez baskit er kittens, 814a

Sociable, no comfort to one not s., 291a
Social and family relationship, 850b
  armor, 969b
  conscience of nation, 1083a
  fences, 1047a
  friendly honest man, 493a
  great s. experiment, 930b
  lived in s. intercourse, 431a
  man is a s. animal, 374a
  nature's s. union, 492b
  new s. problems new s. controls, 973a
  order and thirsty aspiration, 1067a
  our s. arrangements unsatisfactory, 1013b
  progress of each country, 964a
  prosperity, 599b
  self-love and s. the same, 410a
  smile, 439b
  Statics, 787b
Socialism in authoritarian terms, 1035b
  inherent virtue of s., 925a
  Marxian s. portent to historians, 976b
  means to end, 1014b
  what I mean by s., 753a
Socialist competition, 954b
  culture to thrive, 1028a
  realism, 895a
Socializing, conversation s. instrument, 978a
Socially invisible, 1082a
Society, affluent s., 1063a
  care of poor incumbent on s., 374a
  circumstances of civil s., 480a
  cling together in one s., 510a
  communication in free s., 984b
  conflicting interests of s., 912a
  conspiracy against manhood, 606a
  democratic s. like ours, 967a
  distributes itself, 715b
  established s., 1054b
  exists for noble actions, 98b
  free s. cannot help poor, 1072b
  future-directed s., 1059a
  good s. means to good life, 913a
  great s. here at home, 1013b
  great s. on earth, 510a
  happiness of s. end of government, 463b
  human combination or s., 329a
  humanizing body of s., 716b
  humble members of s., 503a
  is a blessing, 466b
  is no comfort, 291a
  keep happiness in store in s., 958a
  man was formed for s., 444b
  my art negation of s., 786a
  my glittering bride, 516a
  nerves of s., 787a
  no arts no letters no s., 318a
  no s. bring kingdom of God, 965a
  of neither rich nor poor, 753a
  offenders, 768a
  one polished horde, 562a
  open s., 1055b, 1071b
  pillars of s., 729a
  principle on which s. not founded, 438b
  reduce s. to one level, 657a

Son, antichrist denieth Father
  and S., 57a
as every s. longed to do, 834b
aunt's charwoman's sister's s.,
  965b
be a man my s., 877a
bring forth a s., 39a
brought forth firstborn s., 46a
crucify S. of God afresh, 55b
David the s. of Jesse, 12b
dear s. of memory, 334a
every wise man's s. doth know,
  251b
every wise man's s. know, 251b
false as stepdame to s., 268b
Father S. and Holy Ghost, 45a,
  377b
foolish s. calamity of father,
  25a
foolish s. the heaviness of his
  mother, 24a
glory be to the S., 59b
greatness of name overwhelms
  s., 304a
grim Death my s. and foe, 344a
hang us every mother's s., 229a
have his s. respect him, 373a
his only s. myself, 445a
if s. ask bread, 41a
in father's stead, 834b
knew my s. was mortal, 92b
let my s. go cheerily, 945a
Lord Randal my s., 1089a
man is s. of own works, 116a
marry s. when you will, 324a
my beloved S., 39b
of a Pharisee, 50b
of Atreus, 63a
of God goes forth to war, 549a
of Heaven's eternal king, 334a
of humble laborer, 964b
of Kronos, 62b
of man, 958a
of man came eating and drinking, 42a
of man coming in cloud, 47b
of man nowhere to lay head,
  41b
of man that thou visitest him,
  17a
of man which is a worm, 15b
of Martha, 827b
of mighty Manhattan s., 700a
of the living God, 43a
of the Middle Border, 859a
of the morning, 31b
of the Sun, 99b
only begotten S., 48a
out of Egypt called my s., 39b
pathos which divide father
  from s., 1027a
prince subject Father S., 307b
rather be worm than s. of man,
  995a
reverence for his s., 373a
safety for my s. brother shipmates, 174a
sighed as lover obeyed as s.,
  466a
spit brown my s., 947b
struck father when s. swore,
  312a
the carpenter's s., 42b
this is my s. Telemachus, 646b
this my s. was dead, 47a
thou art ever with me, 47a
thou art the S. of God, 42b
till he gets wife, 727a
to her s. she ches, 1084a

Son, Tom the piper's s., 1095a
unfeathered thing a s., 368a
unto us a s. is given, 31a
virgin shall bear a s., 30b-31a
Virgin's S., 909a
where one s. only, 908b
wise s. maketh a glad father,
  24a
woman behold thy s., 49b
wrath of Peleus' s., 405a
you are young my s., 96a
Song, a god has given the lyre
  and s., 63b
art and s., 884b
at the core, 879a
burden of his s. 464a
burden of my s., 1084b
considered perfect gem, 740b
dance and Provençal s., 582a
does Africa know s. of me, 985a
echo of mournful s., 632b
fable s. or fleeting shade, 320b
famed in s. famous Athens, 79b
filled thicket with honeyed s.,
  91a
fishers of s., 846a
from beginning to end, 622a
full lasting is s., 731a
gentlemen singing this s., 662a
give us s. to cheer, 752b
glorious s. of old, 657b
good s. ringing clear, 868b
great s. after death of singer,
  703b
had been longer, 1094b
hear a little s., 477b
in England's s. forever, 865b
in thy praise, 495a
Jehovah is my s., 31a
lasting singer passes, 731a
learn sooner than a s., 412a
learn suffering teach in s., 569b
let satire be my s., 554b
let them take it, 881b
listen to s. of siren, 464b
Lord is my strength and s., 8b
loves women wine and s., 180a
made s. a coat, 881b
moralize my s., 200a
nature's message into s., 998a
needless Alexandrine ends s.,
  403a
never heard in tale or s., 336b
new unhallowed s., 844b
no sorrow in thy s., 476b
oaten stop or pastoral s., 443b
of a merryman, 769a
of Africa, 985a
of faithful Penelope, 67a
of harvest home, 655b
of man who has come through,
  985b
of night's sweet bird, 572a
of ocean seemed to sing, 516b
of siren nor voice of hyena,
  205b
of sixpence, 1094b
of songs, 29a
of the shirt, 592b
one grand sweet s., 691a
one immortal s., 368b
one s. leads to another, 945a
perhaps it may turn out s.,
  493b
perhaps self-same s., 583a
pipe s. about a Lamb, 486b
read s. not sermon, 322a
required of us a s., 22b
sans wine s. singer, 630a

Song, sea grew civil at her s., 229a
shall rise to Thee, 549b
she sang final s., 1065b
sing another s., 747b
sing one s. for old Kentucky
  home, 727b
sing the Lord's s., 22b
sing unto him a new s., 18b
sing unto the Lord a new s.
  21a
sings a solitary s., 511a
sings lasting s., 884b
sings s. twice over, 663a
snare it in s., 944a
sold reputation for a s., 631a
sounded by Death, 566a
spur me into s., 885a
suck melancholy out of s., 248a
swallow-flights of s., 650a
swear to truth of s., 387a
sweetest passage of s., 812a
sweetest s. ever heard, 559a
sword sung s. of death, 488b
taught Hesiod beauteous s., 67a
that should spur to soar, 775b
thou singer I s., 767a
till I end my s., 201b
time an endless s., 880a
to sing O, 768b
to whom s. given, 554a
travel with friend and s., 945a
unlike subject frame s., 416a
urge of a s., 929b
what s. the Sirens sang, 331a
when this s. sung and past,
  186b
whenever I remake a s., 885b
whose note sounded by death,
  566a
wind's s. sail's shaking, 946b
wine women and s., 482a
wrote one s., 665b
Songbirds sweetest in Kentucky,
  804b
Song's, three with new s. measure,
  807b
Songs, ale drank s. sung, 753a
all their s. sad, 918a
and I wrote my happy s., 486b
angelic s. swelling, 676b
ballads s. snatches, 768a
because my s. brief, 943b
Book of S. and Sonnets, 266b
cannot sing old s., 733b
composed of tears, 657a
despairing s. loveliest, 657a
forever new, 583a
from grief come s., 588a
harsh after s. of Apollo, 223a
his s. were a thousand and five,
  13a
I who once played shepherds'
  s., 117b
laws which ran like drinking s.,
  90b
leave to sing own s., 868b
make and wel endyte, 166a
muse has taught them s., 66a
my lyric minions, 588a
my s. draw Daphnis home, 116b
no sad s. for me, 739b
of expectation, 750b
of one who strove, 899a
of pleasant glee, 486b
of sadness and mirth, 622b
of Zion, 22b
out of woe, 588a
psalms hymns and spiritual s.,
  54a

Stars might not have missed
me, 929a
mistress of months and s., 772b
morning s. sang together, 16a
move still time runs, 213b
night of large few s., 700a
night with train of s., 816a
no I was out for s., 929a
not fire nor s., 84b
not pure in his sight, 15b
of human race, 456b
of summer night, 621b
of thy fate, 498a
on backs looking at s., 761a
on s. thou gazest my star, 203a
others forecast the rising s.,
119a
owl looked up to s., 673a
preserve s. from wrong, 514b
pure and disposed to mount to
s., 161b
puts s. to flight, 629a
realm amidst s., 888b
rise upon other shore, 758a
rush out, 525a
seven s. solar year, 604a
shining of the s., 654a
shooting s. attend thee, 320b
shot madly from spheres, 229a
silent s. go by, 755a
so shall you scale the s., 119b
some of us looking at s., 839b
strike s. with my exalted head,
120b
strives to touch the s., 199b
that round her burn, 393a
that sweep turn fly, 871b
till s. are old, 726a
time and s. below, 944b
to s. through hardships, 150a
two s. keep not motion, 240b
untriangulated s., 899b
wandering s., 57a
we all gaze at s., 107a
when s. shining bright, 570a
when s. threw down, 489a
whenever moon and s. set, 823a
women's eyes for s., 1085b
would have disappeared, 851a
wrote across sky in s., 1008b
Starshine at night, 824b
Star-spangled banner, 541a
Start a scene or two, 1001a
from their spheres, 259b
play ready to s., 933a
rouse lion than s. hare, 238b
straining upon the s., 244a
world all over at, 929a
world along, 748a
wrong from the s., 988a
Started, arrive where we s., 1007a
jumps in after train s., 867b
like a guilty thing, 257a
Starting, dry the s. tear, 765b
Startle or amaze with subject,
585a
statements that s. like a wound,
72a
Starts, by s. 'twas wild, 443b
direction in which education s.,
94a
everything by s., 368b
home is where one s., 1005b
out to make himself President,
983b
she s. she moves, 622b
think by fits and s., 854a
Starvation, fear and s., 972a
prisoners of s., 680a

Starvation, scientist ready to
bear s., 1028a
Starve, bargain catch cold and s.,
290b
ere I'll rob further, 238b
for want of wonder, 918b
let not poor Nelly s., 366b
neither s. nor stuff, 390a
never s. for wonders, 918b
numerous train below, 382b
they that s. with nothing, 231b
work though body s., 833b
Starved at master's gate, 490a
clean s. for a look, 292b
hackney sonneteer, 403b
Starves her generous birth, 439b
honesty is praised and s., 139a
Starving dog behind, 958a
hysterical naked, 1081b
make s. dog prosperous, 762b
Star-y-pointing pyramid, 334a
Stat magni nominis umbra, 134a
State, almost perfect s., 945b
basis of democratic s., 98b
Bay S. dialect, 692a
beweep my outcast s., 291b
body continues in s. of rest,
379b
by delaying preserved s., 106b
change my s. with kings, 292a
church and s. demand for country, 971a
church and s. separate, 717b
compelled to change s., 379b
completely ready s., 677b
death a s. of nothingness, 93a
done the s. some service, 276b
every man at his best s. is vanity, 18b
faithfully to serve s., 328a
falling with falling s., 405a
flaunts his outcast s., 1054a
for every star, 655b
found s. and give it laws, 177b
free men to develop faculties,
832b
glories of our blood and s.,
327b
gods of the s., 93a
have possibility of life, 94b
high and palmy s. of Rome,
256b
his s. is kingly, 341a
I am the s., 378a, 504a
in whatsoever s. to be content,
54b
in wonted manner keep, 302a
independent of everybody but
s., 461a
is proletariat, 903b
isthmus of a middle s., 408b
mock air with idle s., 441b
my glories and s. depose, 228a
my mother s., 781b
nation responsible for s., 750a
no fetters in Bay S., 625b
no s. maintain members in arms
and idleness, 465b
not a mere society, 98b
not act arbitrarily, 1013a
of chassis, 981a
of Denmark, 259b
of man in divers functions,
243a
of man inconstancy, 363b
of man like kingdom, 254a
peace is a s. of mind, 373a
people's s., 331b
pillar of s., 343b

State, predicts ruin of the s.,
490a
primitive unattached s., 937a
prince first servant of s., 435a
proletarian s., 894b
renders service to s., 389b
roote of kingdom the s., 99b
ruin or rule s., 368b
saw that s. was half-witted, 681a
scandal waits on greatest s.,
220b
ship of s., 69a, 81b, 622b
so blessed in climate, 926b
something rotten in s., 259b
sovereign s. self-centered, 1055a
storms of s., 299a
strange eruption to our s., 256b
struggle to found Roman s.,
117b
such is s. of America, 452a
takes no notice of opinions,
328a
taking-over by the s., 1035b
this is the s. of man, 298b
too extensive falls, 548b
touch no s. matters, 450a
traduced the s., 276b
wall between church and s.,
991a
when error begins to appear in
s., 109b
will prosper, 896b
without s., 591a
world or church or s., 694a
world state inherent in U.N.,
1013b
worth of s. is individuals, 619b
Statecraft, German s., 677b
problem in s., 1104b
Stated calls to worship, 428b
Statehouse, Boston S. the hub,
634a
Stately homes of England, 573b,
975a
pleasure dome decree, 523b
sailing like a s. ship, 349b
ships go on, 648a
Statement, complete s. which is
literature, 975a
manic s., 1076a
Statements interesting but tough,
761a
of nature of universals, 99a
put God in his s., 701b
States, all s. work together, 1049a
dissevered discordant, 547a
foundations of s. laws and
arms, 177a
free and independent s., 460b,
463b
goodly s. and kingdoms, 579b
indestructible s., 627a
laws of the several s., 787b
mighty s. characterless, 268b
responsibility of great s., 982a
saved Union of these S., 702a
set exact wealth of s., 240a
she is all s., 305a
sink or swim together, 902b
sovereign s., 895b
strong native s., 997b
thirteen s. bound together, 485a
unborn and accents yet unknown, 255a
worst of all s. is people's state,
331b
Statesman cannot afford to be
moralist, 985a
chemist s. and buffoon, 368b

Steer right onward, 341a
   star to s. her by, 946b
   too nigh sands, 368a
Steered, boats that are not s., 291a
Steering, young steersman s., 701b
Steersman, cybernetics from Greek s., 1033b
   young s. steering, 701b
Stein, Gertrude S. always right, 1045a
   on table, 868b
Stem is the flute, 1050a
   love rose leave it on s., 741b
   or stone, 968b
   rod out of the s. of Jesse, 31a
   thy slender s., 493a
   two berries on one s., 230a
Stemming with hearts of controversy, 253b
Stems, cut s. struggling, 1064b
Stench of decaying refuse, 1063a
   of stale oranges, 988b
Stenches, two and seventy s., 527b
Stentor, great-hearted S., 63a
Step, fanaticism to barbarism one s., 437a
   first s. is hardest, 418b
   from sublime to ridiculous, 504a
   highest s. of charity's golden ladder, 155b
   if true a big s. forward, 1011a
   keep s. obey in silence, 728b
   light of s. and heart, 914a
   made last s. possible, 949b
   mind music and s., 1090a
   must begin with single s., 74b
   one s. enough for me, 597b
   softly under snow, 919a
   steadier s. when I recall, 688b
   to music he hears, 683b
   to s. aside is human, 493b
   twice into same river, 77b
Stepdame, false as s. to son, 268b
Stephen, feast of S., 687b
   King S. worthy peer, 1085a
Stephen's, St. S. choir, 1075a
Stepmother, nature a merciless s., 132a
   poverty s. of genius, 685a
   stony-hearted s., 552a
Stepped down to the Four, 976b
   in a puddle, 1097b
   in blood s. in so far, 285a
   out of their clothes, 884b
Stepping, crab kept s. back, 505b
   westward, 513a
Steppingstone, stumblingblock or s., 808b
Steppingstones of dead selves, 649b
   to understanding, 949a-b
Steps, age with stealing s., 187a
   beware of desperate s., 459a
   by due s. aspire, 336a
   came forth with pilgrim s., 349a
   foot wear s. of his door, 37b
   hear not my s., 283a
   heavy s. of plowman, 880b
   humor saves few s., 996b
   I by backward s. move, 362b
   in his master's s. trod, 687b
   invites my s. and points, 406a
   lead my s. aright, 574b
   Lord directeth his s., 24b
   same s. as author, 585a
   stops and s. of mind, 1003b

Steps, undulantly with catlike s., 878b
   wandering s. and slow, 348b
   were higher that they took, 369b
   with how sad s. O Moon, 203b
Sterile, compulsion to become s., 986b
   seems to me s. promontory, 261a
   splendid and s. Dolores, 773b
   truth for yourself, 814b
Sterility in economic monuments, 1063b
Sterling, refine her s. page, 377a
Stern, a s. a true-born Englishman, 226b
   and rockbound coast, 573b
   and simple irrelevancy, 812a
   battle's s. array, 556a
   Caledonia s. and wild, 519a
   custom spreads afar, 497a
   daughter of voice of God, 514b
   joy warriors feel, 520a
   Lawgiver, 514b
   man s. to view, 449b
   my sad heart foams at s., 829b
   Ruin's plowshare, 493a
   rule it with s. joy, 981a
Sterner, ambition of s. stuff, 255b
   days not darker days, 923a
Sternest, gives s. good-night, 283b
   knight to foe, 176a
   Nature's s. painter, 555a
Stern-faced men set out, 592a
Stew, convert you into s., 1004a
   missionary s., 1004a
   soup or broth or s., 660b
   w'en s. smokin' hot, 911b
Steward falls into soup tureen, 876a
Stewards of their excellence, 293a
Stewed, longing for s. prunes, 270b
Stick across your back, 1092a
   carry a big s., 847b
   coat upon a s., 882b
   fell like a s., 467b
   heart of falsehood, 268b
   hips s., 1052a
   I am a burr I shall s., 272a
   more close than brother, 877a
   there I'll s., 194b
   thine arrows s. fast in me, 18b
   to what you're at, 947b
   to your last, 102a
   with fist instead of s., 351b
Sticketh closer than a brother, 25a
Sticking, ay s. in a tree, 521a
   head in moose, 967b
Sticking-place, screw your courage to s., 283a
Sticks nix hicks pix, 916b
   resurrection of dry s., 1064b
Sticky, gilded and s., 990b
Stiff, civilize them s., 891a
   dishonored shroud, 1002a
   flags straining, 918b
   in opinions, 368b
   twin compasses, 306a
   upper lip, 722b
Stiffen sinews summon blood, 243b
Stiffening of vertebrae, 835a
Stiffens, heart s. and rejoices, 1004a
Stiffish cocktail, 666b
Stiffnecked, a s. people, 9a
Stiffness and soul's arrest, 918b

Stiffness, freedom from s., 716b
Stifle, opinion we endeavor to s., 619b
Stile, over hedge before s., 194b
Stile-a, merrily hent the s., 295b
Still and awful red, 525b
   and quiet conscience, 298b
   be s. and know that I am God, 19a
   be s. Hanging Gardens a dream, 933b
   be s. wait, 1065a
   beside the s. waters, 17b
   everything else is s., 487b
   falls the rain, 998b
   heart is lying s., 512a
   how s. we see thee lie, 755a
   lute be s. I have done, 186b
   mightest s. the enemy, 17a
   point of turning world, 1004a
   quite s. and solitary, 980b
   sad music of humanity, 509b
   should I have lain s., 14b
   small voice, 13b
   small voice of gratitude, 442a
   sound of voice that is s., 648a
   spicy and s., 982a
   spirit bloweth and is s., 711a
   spirit so s. and quiet, 272b
   suburban street, 1020a
   take heed of s. waters, 199a
   to be neat, 302b
   we must be s. and s. moving, 1006a
   when all woods are s., 339b
   when sun out wind s., 928a
Stillness, air solemn s. holds, 440a
   modest s. and humility, 243b
   soft s. and the night, 235b
   solemn s. lay, 657b
   such s., 380a
   talent formed in s., 477b
Still-vexed Bermoothes, 296a
Stilly, army s. sounds, 244a
Stimulate and direct experiment, 838a
Stimulus, need imaginative s., 781b
   property is s. to work, 941b
Sting, all serpents they s., 3b
   cold doth not s., 300b
   death where is thy s., 53a
   each s. that bids, 666a
   how bitter a s. a little fault, 161a
   prick and s. her, 260a
   serpent s. thee twice, 234a
   stare and s. forever, 1022a
   with a little s., 990b
Stinger, 'tis a s., 314a
Stingeth like an adder, 26a
Stings, stinks and s., 411a
   wanton s. of sense, 270a
   what s. is justice, 960b
   you for your pains, 400a
Stink, stand by the fire and s., 277b
Stinking, poets like s. fish, 531b
Stinks and stings, 411a
   like rotten mackerel, 531b
   several, 527b
Stint, if you s. them now, 686a
Stir, all hell s. for this, 245a
   at dismal treatise rouse and s., 286b
   crown me without my s., 281b
   dream all night without s., 584b
   each make but once, 738a

Stir, Jamaicas of remembrance
  s., 738b
  men's blood, 255b
  no s. in air no s. in sea, 532b
  not s. rice though it sticks, 197a
  now s. the fire, 458a
  of echoes down floor, 1022a
  of the great Babel, 458b
  smoke and s. of this dim spot,
    336a
  without great argument, 264b
Stirred by solitary cloud, 380a
  casement jessamine s., 652b
  heart of Englishman, 896a
  troubled like fountain s., 269a
  up with envy and revenge, 341b
  up with high hopes, 340a
Stirring, always s. up some war,
    95a
  dull roots, 1002a
  not a creature s., 541a
  not a mouse s., 256b
Stirrings, gently awful s., 697a
Stirrup, betwixt s. and ground,
    197b
  sprang to s., 662b
Stirs, blood more s. to rouse lion,
    238b
  culprit life, 734a
  divinity that s. within, 393b
  of discontented strife, 309b
  see she s., 622b
  this mortal frame, 526b
  up lees of things, 696b
Stitch in time saves nine, 133b
  stitch stitch, 592b
Stitches, laugh yourselves into s.,
    253a
Stithy, foul as Vulcan's s., 263a
Stock market a mirror, 1062b
  of Barabbas, 235a
  see how his s. went on, 533a
  words once my s. wanting, 371b
Stocking all the day, 447a
  silk s. filled with mud, 505a
  yawns and draws s. up, 1002a
Stockings, commended yellow s.,
    252b
  hung by chimney, 541a
  silk s. and white bosoms, 429b
  to bed with s. on, 1096b
Stocks, worshiped s. and stones,
    341a
Stockyards, sacrifices like s., 1044a
Stoic, every s. was a s., 606b
  from forty till fifty man is s.,
    831b
  live like s. bird, 990a
  of the woods, 538b
Stoicism, Romans call it s., 393b
Stoic's pride, 408b
Stole, like little mice s. in and
    out, 350b
  man s. the fruit, 322b
  memory of all he s., 413b
  pig and away run, 1095a
  tarts and took them away, 1094b
  thence life o' building, 284a
  title from better man I s., 823b
Stolen by your apples, 551b
  better had I s. whole, 823b
  ducats s. by my daughter, 233a
  enough to be s., 400b
  hanged that horses not s., 376b
  my three-and-twentieth year,
    334b
  not wanting what is s., 274b
  odd old ends s. of holy writ,
    217a

Stolen, steed s. shut stable
  door, 183b
  sweets are best, 392b
  sweets sweeter, 551b
  the scraps, 222b
  waters are sweet, 24a
Stomach, army marches on s.,
    505a
  dispenser of invention, 133b
  full talk of fasting easy, 145b
  goes much against my s., 249b
  good-humored s., 130b
  groans more than empty s.,
    972b
  hungry s. cannot hear, 359b
  is not good, 188b
  loathing to s. brings, 230a
  man of an unbounded s., 299a
  no patriot on empty s., 831a
  no s. for such meat, 782b
  seat of sensation s., 855a
  teacher of arts, 133b
  thought depends on s., 418a
  way to heart through s., 658a
Stomachaches, tuned like fifty s.,
    670b
Stomach's, wine for thy s. sake,
    55a
Stomachs, fill s. selling judg-
    ments, 908b
  lazy folks' s., 814a
  store money in s. of needy, 146a
  who have best s. not best think-
    ers, 418a
Stone, ask bread and give s., 41a
  at his heels a s., 265a
  better pillow than visions, 994b
  bows to wood and s., 549b
  bronze s. steel, 1004a
  cold as any s., 243b
  conscious s. to beauty, 602a
  dash thy foot against a s., 20b
  dripping water hollows s., 113a
  dry s. no water, 1002a
  fling s. giant dies, 418a
  flung s. puts stars to flight,
    629a
  he that rolleth a s., 26a
  head s. of the corner, 22a
  heart harder than s., 67a
  heart turned to s., 275b
  heavy as yonder s., 968b
  house of good s., 988b
  hut of s., 634a
  idol marble heart s., 890a
  if any have s. to throw, 990b
  in one hand a s., 105b
  Jackson like s. wall, 719a
  leaf unfound door, 1049b
  legs of s., 568a
  let him first cast s., 48b
  live by squeezing from s., 990b
  look on stone's face, 1080a
  mainsails of s., 911a
  mark with white or black s.,
    196a
  mockery of monumental s., 572a
  moving others themselves as s.,
    293a
  no bigger than agate s., 223a
  not to conclude against s.,
    1079a
  not with club nor s., 738a
  of stumbling, 31a
  one stark monotony of s., 878b
  past is s. stands forever, 809b
  plain brown s. will do, 634a
  precious s. set in silver sea,
    226b

Stone, pulleth sword out of
  s., 175a
  quiet as s., 584a
  raise s. and find me, 827b
  raise s. cleave wood, 827b
  red-veined s., 721b
  rests on the land, 364b
  rich s. best plain set, 209a
  rich s. in bowels of earth, 309b
  rolling s. gathers no moss, 126a
  shall cry out of wall, 283a
  sleep softly eagle under s., 952b
  spark out of s. not moral, 770b
  stem or s., 968b
  strange lump of s., 992b
  strength of past, 994b
  tell where I lie, 402a
  that puts stars to flight, 629a
  thought not crush to s., 1064b
  to beauty grew, 602a
  turn s. start wing, 857a
  under every s. a politician, 91b
  underneath this s. lie, 303a
  violet by mossy s., 510b
  walls do not prison make, 358b
  water like a s., 740a
  we raised not a s., 566b
  which the builders refused, 22a
  without gout or s., 367a
  work philosopher's s., 817b
  written of me on my s., 929a
  youth s. dead, 992b
Stone-deaf fishes, 1064b
Stone's, stone look on s. face,
    1080a
  within a s. throw, 195a
Stones, all the s. are men, 704b
  are iron, 10a
  blessed man that spares these s.,
    299b
  boys throw s. at frogs, 104b
  chose him five smooth s., 12a
  cold gray s. O sea, 648a
  cry out, 47b
  don't throw s. if your windows
    glass, 421b
  have been known to move, 285a
  heap of s. not house, 829b
  house glass not throw s., 324b
  in league with s. of field, 14b
  kissed by English dead, 1028b
  labor of an age in piled s., 334a
  land where men are s., 704b
  makes music with enameled s.,
    220b
  men of s., 280b
  move s. of home, 256a
  no sermons in s., 770b
  not decked with Indian s., 215b
  of Troy, 268b
  philosopher's s., 311b
  prate of my whereabout, 283a
  rocks and s. and trees, 511a
  scrub pavement or break s.,
    88ob
  sermons in s., 247b
  shows that wood s. are one, 95a
  that cannot be deciphered,
    1006a
  time to cast away s., 27b
  trees and s. will teach you, 154a
  worshiped stocks and s., 341a
  you are men of s., 280b
Stonest them sent unto thee, 43b
Stony British stare, 652a
  limits cannot hold love out,
    223b
Stony-hearted stepmother, 552a
Stood against world, 255b

Straightway, he goeth after her s., 23b
Strain at a gnat, 43b
  continuous unbroken s., 548a
  great s. on affections, 690a
  guardian angels sung this s., 420a
  hold cheap the s., 666a
  I heard of higher mood, 338b
  out of s. of doing, 749b
  prophetic s., 336a
  raise somewhat loftier s., 116b
  Shakespeare's s., 604a
  that s. again, 251a
  that s. once more, 447a
  unpremeditated s., 420a
Strained, music s. through mind, 1056b
  quality of mercy not s., 234b
  upward s. the swan, 505b
Straining at particles of light, 585b
  in night blasts cold, 918b
  upon the start, 244a
Strains as would have won the ear, 335a
  blessed s. telling, 676b
  of unpremeditated art, 570b
  sweet s. pensive smiles, 602a
  that might create a soul, 337a
Strait, honor in s. so narrow, 268b
  is the gate, 41b
  matters not how s. gate, 816a
Straitjacket or club, 831a
Straits, moon fair upon s., 714b
  stranger in financial s., 88b
Strand, conducting orchestral S., 905b
  guardian Naiad of s., 520a
  India's coral s., 549b
  left fair Scotland's s., 494a
  pass to American s., 324a
  walked along the S., 429a
  wandering on foreign s., 518b
  world's s., 802b
Stranded, navies are s., 520b
Strands, last s. of man, 803b
  there he is crossing s., 909a
Strange already said by philosopher, 327b
  and moving dream, 807b
  and well-bred, 392a
  art of necessities s., 278a
  bedfellows. 297a, 733b
  but true, 562a
  capers, 248a
  communion not grow s., 807a
  cozenage, 367b
  crossroads lie, 1040b
  dark interludes, 1009a
  disease of modern life, 712a
  eruption to our state, 256b
  eruptions, 239b
  eventful history, 249a
  fear what is too s., 1079b
  force in s. steeds, 632b
  how s. it seems and new, 664a
  interludes, 1009a
  lips of a s. woman drop as honeycomb, 23b
  lisp and wear s. suits, 250a
  Lord's song in s. land, 22b
  lump of stone, 992b
  more cunning to be s., 224a
  most s. that men fear, 254b
  Nature hath framed s. fellows, 31a
  none wreck on s. shelf, 303a
  nothing so s. as truth, 547b

Strange, object s. and high, 360a
  pair of very s. beasts, 250b
  read s. matters, 282a
  road grows s., 694b
  seas of thought, 510a
  so strangely sweet not s., 801a
  soldier full of s. oaths, 249a
  Solomon loved s. women, 13a
  something rich and s., 296b
  stranger in a s. land, 8a
  stranger in a s. country, 82b
  terrible world war, 923b
  that death should sing, 237a
  that desire outlive performance, 242a
  things come out, 498a
  throne in s. city, 641b
  to think by the way, 731b
  truth always s., 562a
  'twas passing s., 272b
  was his lot, 812b
  world is a s. affair, 360b
Strangely pass, 292a
  so s. sweet not strange, 801a
Strangeness, some s. in proportion, 209b
Stranger and afraid, 854a
  and alone, 1049b
  and ye took me in, 44a
  as we grow older world s., 1005b-1006a
  doth not intermeddle, 24b
  entertain this starry s., 354b
  Europe regards her as s., 466b
  he that is surety for a s., 24a
  I am a s. with thee, 19a
  I pass a willful s., 824a
  in a strange country, 82b
  in a strange land, 8a
  in financial straits, 88b
  leave them for poor and s., 9b
  never love a s., 1021a
  than fiction, 562a
  to sorrow, 84a
  troubled mind be s., 322a
  unless with bedroom eyes, 1060b
  what s. come back to me, 945a
  wiles of s., 1051b
Strangers and beggars are from Zeus, 65b
  by s. honored, 406a
  desire we may be better s., 249b
  entertain s., 56a
  gods likening themselves to s., 66b
  gracious and courteous to s., 208b
Strangest, fate of architect s., 478a
  whim seized me, 919a
Strangle, vapors seem to s. him, 238a
Strangled Atahualpa, 595b
  snakes beside Hercules, 724b
Strapped noosed nighing hour, 854a
Straps, hang in their own s., 251a
Stratagem, take tea without a s., 398b
Stratagems, treasons s. and spoils, 235b
  which errors seem, 402b
Strategy involve us in wrong war, 1025b
Stratford, Shakespeare was born at S., 365a
Stratosphere of icy certainty, 864b
Straw dogs, 73b
  drowning man cling to s., 769b
  find quarrel in a s., 265a

Straw, headpiece filled with s., 1003a
  I don't care one s., 109a
  lion shall eat s., 31a
  no more s. to make brick, 8a
  pigmy's s. does pierce it, 279b
  see which way wind is, 317a
  stumbles at a s., 199b
  tickled with a s., 409a
  turkey in the s., 1099a
  vote, 864b
Strawberries, feed upon s., 1095b
  great s. at mouth of pot, 207b
  how many s. in sea, 1093a
  melts on vine, 819b
  of angling as of s., 326a
Strawberry, like s. wives, 207b
Straws, as s. that blow, 816a
  hairs or s. or dirt, 410b
  oaths are s., 243b
Stray, dry dust and s. paper, 988b
  empty house like s. dog, 756a
  howso'er I s. and range, 688b
  if with me fondly s., 401b
  never taught to s., 408a
  thoughts fancies fugitive, 668a
  wishes never learned to s., 440b
Strayed like lost sheep, 59b
Streak, red-line s., 704b
Streakings of morning light, 578b
Stream, bashful s. hath seen God, 354a
  by s. and o'er mead, 486b
  by thy murmuring s., 495a
  ever-rolling s., 396b
  fish have their s., 993b
  gulf s. setting forever, 695a
  islanded in s. of stars, 999b
  meadow grove and s., 513a
  mercy of a rude s., 298b
  no s. meanders level, 625a
  no shaded s., 482a
  no striving against s., 195b
  of consciousness, 793a
  of his body, 1081a
  of time run, 242b
  of what we feel indeed, 716a
  of what we say and feel, 716a
  red life s. again, 581b
  roses by Bendemeer's s., 543a
  runs fast, 541b
  slow and silent s. Lethe, 344a
  smoothest water deepest, 199a
  steep Atlantic s., 336b
  strove against s. in vain, 649a
  summer eves by haunted s., 335a
  surface s. shallow light, 716a
  talk like s., 600b
  time s. I go a-fishing in, 683a
  trailing in cool s., 712a
  wavy bodies 'gainst s., 579a
Streamed like a meteor to air, 342b
Streamers, sails filled s. waving, 349b
Streaming, before his s. eyes, 746a
  from waters of baptism, 857a
  lamplight s., 643a
  light, 337a
  Love with s. hair, 1038a
  meteor s. to the wind, 342b
Streams and woods belong, 846a
  cooling s., 384a
  flow with ambrosia, 85a
  from little fountains, 507a
  lapse of murmuring s., 347a
  like thunderstorm, 557a
  may valley s. content me, 117a
  meander level, 625a

Strike awe into beholders, 389a
  but hear me, 77b
  clock doth s. by algebra, 352a
  clock will s. Devil will come, 213b
  disease or sorrows s. him, 688b
  flat thick rotundity, 278a
  for altars and fires, 565b
  honor foe while you s., 865a
  it and it hurts my hand, 275b
  it when powder's low, 865a
  mine eyes but not my heart, 302b
  my hearts s. twelve, 1056b
  out fine passage, 431b
  rattlesnake poised to s., 973b
  right to s., 911a
  sails well but s. rock, 491b
  spear to thrust club to s., 180b
  stars with my exalted head, 120b
  take care you s. in anger, 837a
  then no planets s., 257a
  to s. the blow, 966b
  truth may s. out his teeth, 199b
  when a hammer s., 324b
  when iron is hot, 125b
  when you s. at king kill him, 610a
  with no madness, 1034b
Strikers, with s. right or wrong, 953a
Strikes, lightning s. mountaintop, 121b
  like rising knell, 556b
  midnight s. and hastens, 854b
  silent note Cupid s., 330a
Striking blow for freedom, 995b
  clocks s. courage, 1014b
  clocks were s. hour, 621b
  hit without s. back, 765a
  so s. and grotesque, 596a
  sometimes a friend, 322b
String attuned to mirth, 592a
  chewing bits of s., 902a
  eyes upon double s., 306b
  harp not on that s., 217b
  kite cut from s., 985b
  moderation is silken s., 309b
  notes as warbled to the s., 336a
  of pearls to me, 865b
  pudding-bag s., 1098a
  sing in a hempen s., 313a
  untune that s., 267b
Stringbean, tell s. from soybean, 1052a
Stringent execution of bad laws, 717a
  protection of free speech, 788a
Strings, bawdy s. of elders, 955b
  better not wibrated, 670a
  languid s. scarcely move, 486b
  like untuned s. women are, 213a
  many s. to bow, 184a
  twitched s., 878b
Strip away useless decoration, 993a
Stripes, broad s. and bright stars, 541a
  cut his s. away, 873a
  forty s. save one, 53b
Stripling Thames, 712a
Strive, all men s., 664a
  alone man with God s., 557a
  and hold cheap the strain, 666a
  earth and water s. again, 405a
  here for mastery, 344a
  mightily eat as friends, 219a
  nor weep, 663a

Strive, not possible to fight even if you s., 64a
  officiously to keep alive, 689a
  on to finish work, 640b
  seven cities s. for Homer, 301b
  to be like them, 975b
  to grasp what they do not know, 101b
  to s. to seek to find, 647a
  to set crooked straight, 753a
  who s. mightily possess, 898b
Striven to be Thine more than world's, 696a
Strives against stress of necessity, 85b
  sage never s. for the great, 74a
  to touch the stars, 199b
  who s. always to utmost, 478b
Striving blindly, 715b
  my s. eye dazzles, 362b
  no s. against stream, 195b
  to better oft we mar, 277b
  to grasp continent, 720b
Strivingly, take life s., 793b
Strivings, parcel of vain s., 680b
  two unreconciled s., 894b
Strode after me, 510a
Stroke, constitution produced at s., 631b
  his silver hair, 487a
  master s. nature's, 604a
  of death as lover's pinch, 289a
  platitude until it purrs, 946b
  tender-handed s. nettle, 400a
  tune of flutes kept s., 287b
Strokes, amorous of their s., 287b
  calumnious s., 258a
  little s. fell great oaks, 422a
  many s. fell the oak, 202b
  tender s. of art, 404b
Stroll, country s. is a gallery, 724a
  life like s. on beach, 681a
Strong, a few s. instincts, 516a
  and active faith, 974a
  and diverse heart, 1041b
  armed so s. in honesty, 256a
  as a bull moose, 847b
  as flesh and blood, 515b
  as iron bands, 621a
  as proofs of holy writ, 274b
  battle is to the s., 844b
  battle not to the s., 28b, 465a
  be s. and of good courage, 10b
  be s. and quit yourselves, 12a
  be s. be also one, 726a
  be s. stand fast on faith, 53a
  brown god, 1006a
  cause s. or weak, 692b
  corruption inhabits blood, 253a
  devised to keep s. in awe, 218a
  devouring of weak by s., 706a
  dogged opponent of light, 713b
  drink is raging, 25a
  enough to be master, 435b
  fifty score s., 662a
  fifty thousand s., 748a
  follow s. drink, 30b
  for much to suffer, 978b
  for service still, 458a
  founded s., 853a
  friend is a s. defense, 37b
  gentleness my s. enforcement, 248b
  give s. drink unto him that is ready to perish, 26b
  God make me s., 1103b
  gongs groaning, 918b
  harder to be won than a s. city, 25a

Strong, harm to s. from weakest, 805b
  heavens fresh and s., 514b
  is the soul, 710b
  just weak secure, 1073b
  keep s. if possible, 1035a
  know the wall is s., 841a
  lance of justice, 279b
  lean upon death, 995a
  life too s. for you, 898a
  long pull and s. pull, 671a
  love built anew more s., 294a
  love is s., 170b
  lure more s., 811b
  made what is s. just, 363b
  man clinging to babe, 769b
  man digests experiences, 805b
  meat to them of full age, 55b
  men rust, 1035b
  men shall bow themselves, 28b
  mortality's s. hand, 237a
  most exquisite and s., 385a
  native states, 997b
  nor s. at thirty, 324b
  nor'wester's blowing Bill, 517b
  not to s. the fight, 827b
  O s. soul, 715a
  obscure and deep, 716a
  only s. thrive, 932b
  out of the s. came sweetness, 11b
  pull, 671b
  pure and sweetly s., 443b
  rejoiceth as a s. man, 17b
  remedy too s. for disease, 83a
  right chiefly with the s., 377b
  rousing like s. man, 340b
  ruling passion s. in death, 406b
  shadow where much light, 477a
  shout out loud and s., 952a
  small one become a s. nation, 33b
  some circumstantial evidence s., 682a
  stagger but not with s. drink, 32a
  they are weak they are s., 846a
  thick stupefying incense, 664b
  tired yet s., 812a
  to me-wards your affection's s., 320a
  to save, 726a
  toil of grace, 289b
  tricks hath s. imagination, 230b
  two s. men face to face, 872b
  we that are s., 51b
  weak against s. wrong, 505b
  when man s. until alone, 662a
  wise man is s., 26a
  without rage, 357a
  yet I am s. and lusty, 247b
Stronger by weakness, 333a
  dog be on top, 995a
  Fate s. than anything, 84a
  gods are on side of s., 140a
  government not s. than people, 1049a
  handclasp's s., 914a
  if bowl had been s., 1094a
  let storm rage s., 894b
  madder music s. wine, 890a
  more doubt s. faith, 665a
  Negroes s. than we are, 1039a
  no s. than my sex, 254b
  nothing s. than habit, 128b
  pray to be s., 755a
  than all afterthoughts, 84b
  than hosts of error, 858b
  than lions, 12b

Task, long day's t. is done, 288b
my t. is smoothly done, 337b
of fortitude and delicacy, 825a
of pure ablution, 581a
one t. for all, 877b
remaining before us, 639a
sore t., 256b
there's the rub the t., 118b
though hard be t., 722b
trivial round common t., 567a
uncompleted t., 792b
what he reads as t., 430b
worldly t. hast done, 291a
Tasking, whole soul's t., 692a
Taskmaster's, my great T. eye, 334b
Taskmasters, lies religion of t., 894b
Tasks, highest to humblest t., 923b
not t. equal to powers, 755a
Tassel-gentle, lure this t. back, 224a
Taste, all ashes to the t., 556a
and see that the Lord is good, 18b
arbiter of t., 140a
by which relished, 516a
connects active with passive, 528a
dull were all we t., 1031b
feminine of genius, 631a
from fountain wells up bitter t., 114a
good strong thick smoke, 664b
inch rule of t., 777a
last t. of sweets, 226b
liquor never brewed, 734b
loathe t. of sweetness, 240a
man's hand not able to t., 230b
never t. who always drink, 304a
no t. when you married me, 481b
not Pierian spring, 403a
of death but once, 254b
of your quality, 261a
prosperity with more t., 391a
questions of t. and feeling, 776b
sans t. sans everything, 249b
sit down and t. my meat, 324a
smell and t. of things, 907b
sole arbiter is t., 644b
things sweet to t. prove sour, 226a
touch not t. not, 54b
tree whose mortal t., 341b
whole joys, 307b
whole of it, 666b
wild vicissitudes of t., 427a
wretched t., 501b
your ware, 1093b
Tasted all the summer's pride, 486a
can't be t. in sip, 670a
eternal joys of Heaven, 213a
I t. careless then, 735a
of desire, 927a
some books to be t., 209b
two worms, 807b
Tasteless, this age how t., 114b
Tastes like wrath to come, 940b
no accounting for t., 150b
runs against popular t., 380b
wit ne'er t., 411b
woman ruin meets, 402a
Tasting of Flora and country, 582a
Tat, tit for t., 185a

Taters, corn and t. grow, 828b
Tatter in mortal dress, 882b
Tattered coat upon stick, 882b
married man t. and torn, 1098b
through t. clothes, 279b
Tatters, tear a passion to t., 262b
Tattlers and busybodies, 55a
Tattoo soap bubbles, 1047a
Taught as if you taught them not, 403b
character t. learned, 715b
dream t. me this wisdom, 328b
first he wroghte afterward t., 166b
folly's all they t. me, 542b
genius never can be t., 371a
happy is he born and t., 300b
her dazzling fence, 337b
I t. thee to love, 307a
it hath t. me to rhyme, 222a
man never flogged never t., 102a
me all I knew, 876a
me serpent's world, 1057a
mind what I am t., 546a
obeyed what wind had t., 998a
rather be t. than teach, 171b
three useful things, 562b
tortoise because he t. us, 744b
us how to live, 400b
us little but our soul, 711a
wise words t. in numbers, 201a
you t. me language, 296a
Tautness, greyhound's gentle t., 1077a
Tavern, happiness produced by t., 432a
I am come to t. alone, 395a
in the town, 1100a
intend to die in t., 155b
let me in t. die, 154b
Mermaid T., 583b
my t. the Big Bear, 829b
one flash in t. caught, 630b
opened t. for friends, 894a
sweeter wine in t. than bishop decanted, 154b
Taverns, knew t. wel in every toun, 166a
Tawny-throated, nightingale t., 712b
Tax for being eminent, 389a
from chimney t. free, 1105a
heavier than kings, 422b
I t. you not you elements, 278a
just man will pay more income t., 94a
not t. bill but t. relief bill, 973b
power to t. not power to destroy, 788b
power to t. power to destroy, 485b
where no revenue found, 452a
Taxation, more t. than necessary, 771a
without representation, 446a
Taxed, never t. for speech, 269b
schoolboy whips t. top, 522a
without consent, 446b
Taxes, all t. fall upon agriculture, 465b
death and t., 423a
generally raised on city land, 733b
pay for civilized society, 787a
true as t., 671b
war certain to increase t., 467a
Taxi throbbing waiting, 1002b

Te spectem te teneam, 128a
Tea, after t. and cakes and ices, 1001a
although Oriental, 919a
and comfortable advice, 585b
and scandal, 391b
and sometimes t., 404b
breakfast dinner lunch t., 902a
breakfasts at five-o'clock t., 746b
ceremony known as afternoon t., 798a
destruction of t. so bold, 462b
fights, 872b
glad not born before t., 523b
honey still for t., 993b
hot water remain upon t., 328b
if this t. I want coffee, 810b
Michelangelo for t., 759a
sweeteners of t., 424b
take some more t., 744a
thank God for t., 523b
without stratagem, 398b
Teach act of order to kingdom, 243a
aim of oratory to t., 111a
beasts shall t. thee, 15a
charm strengthen and t., 623a
child to doubt, 490b
crab to walk straight, 91a
delight in simple things, 877a
gladly lerne and gladly t., 166b
go and t. all nations, 45a
he who shall t. child, 490a
high thought, 653b
him to tell my story, 273a
himself to be afraid, 1039b
his feet a measure, 774b
I t. you Superman, 805a
learn from those who can t., 82a
learn suffering t. in song, 569b
learn what it had to t., 683a
learning does not t. intelligence, 77b
let such t. others, 402b
me half the gladness, 570b
me my God and King, 323b
me to feel another's woe, 412b
me to hear mermaids singing, 304b
me to live, 377b
men sense of existence, 805a
new occasions t. duties, 692a
noble negligences t., 387b
nothing but to name tools, 352a
order to peopled kingdom, 243a
orphan boy to read, 645a
others t. how to dare, 711b
pleased to t., 404a
rather be taught than t., 171b
same prayer doth t. us all, 234b
shall any t. God, 15b
still pleased to t., 404a
the earth shall t. thee, 15a
them diligently unto thy children, 10a
thy necessity to reason, 226a
to t. is to learn twice, 483b
trees and stones will t. you, 154a
us good Lord to serve Thee, 180b
us how to die, 557a
us to care, 1003b
us to have aspiring minds, 212a
us to number our days, 20b
us to sit still, 1003b
villainy you t. me, 233b

Teach, without sneering t. to
   sneer, 411a
ye how to climb, 337b
you more of man, 509a
young idea to shoot, 419b
Teacher affects eternity, 777a
   bubble blown by successful t.,
   818b
city is t. of the man, 70b
government potent t., 538b,
   833b
hold t. equal to parents, 88a
Nature be your t., 509a
time a great t., 949a
true t. has no disciple, 590b
value of true t., 741a
who can arouse feeling, 478a
Teachers by spherical predominance, 277a
men are my t., 408b
shame despair her t., 614a
ungrateful to these t., 976a
Teaches, experience t., 671a
grief t. to waver, 82a
hard dealing t. them suspect,
   232b
he who cannot t., 836b
leaves to curtsy, 1078b
nature t. beasts to know
   friends, 289b
nature t. more than preaches,
   770b
religion good that t. good, 467b
standing on toes, 1040b
such beauty as woman's eye,
   222a
time t. all things, 78a
us to see, 1080a
Teaching a fish to swim, 151b
is awakening curiosity, 802a
nations how to live, 339b
only t. on Tuesdays, 1076a
simplicity to sing, 917b
thank thee Jew for t. word,
   235a
truth persuades by t., 143b
what t. is and was, 1040b
Teachings, nature's t., 574a
Teacup, crack in t. opens, 1060a
Teacups, tinkled among t., 1001b
Teahouses, in t. and home, 1020a
Team, military forces are one t.,
   1025b
of little atomies, 223a
Teapot, storm in a t., 111b
Tear a passion to tatters, 262b
all he had a t., 441a
angel's t., 579a
blinded his e'e, 1087b
body limb from limb, 656a
cost a sigh a t., 470a
dry starting t., 765b
drying up single t., 561b
each other's eyes, 396b
every t. from every eye, 490a
falling of a t., 518a
from eyelids wiped t., 248b
great interpreter, 939b
hast thou no t., 642a
heart to dog to t., 877a
intellectual thing, 490a
man enough for t. in eye, 831a
man without a t., 538b
melodious t., 338a
never t. linnet from leaf,
   882b
newborn infant's t., 489b
O shed no t., 580a
poem apart, 1071a

Tear, savage indignation t.
   heart, 391a
shed bitter t., 745b
shed one English t., 596b
singer dries one t., 887a
smile on lips t. in eye, 519b
splendid t., 652b
still ushered with t., 405b
sympathetic t., 439b
tattered ensign, 633a
to pieces that great bond, 284b
too foolish for t., 526b
we shed though secret, 541b
Tears, all that speaks in t., 758a
angry t. gone, 881b
are on her cheeks, 34b
ate bread with t., 477a
before my t. did drown it, 323b
big round t. coursed down,
   247b
bitter t. to shed, 719b
blood toil t. sweat, 920b
blotted all over with t., 661a
broomsticks and t., 881b
bucket full of t. am I., 228a
but without t., 1076b
cannot bear a mother's t., 119b
crave stain of t., 927b
crocodile t., 205b
dark with torment and t., 685b
dearth of woman's t., 627b
dip wings in t., 650a
dipped pen into t., 811b
drop t. as fast, 276b
fight from eyes t., 1010a
flow with t. of gold, 487a
fountain of sweet t., 511b
fountains fraught with t., 204a
girlish t., 849a
hence these t., 108a
here are the t. of things, 118a
hired t., 330b
idle tears, 648b
idleness of t., 836a
if you have t., 255b
in silence and t., 554b
in t. amid corn, 583a
inscribed in t., 593a
iron t. down Pluto's cheek, 336a
kiss again with t., 648a
like Niobe all t., 257b
Lord God will wipe away t.,
   31b
mine own t. do scald, 280a
mist of t., 856b
never wipe off t. of woe, 488b
no t. in writer no t. in reader,
   929b
nor all your t. wash out, 630b
not pay honor with t., 106b
nothing is here for t., 350a
now am full of t., 879b
of eternity, 854b
of repentance you'll wipe, 488b
of sky for loss of sun, 416a
pool of t., 857a
rain shower of commanded t.,
   219a
Recording Angel dropped t.,
   438a
remember with t., 729a
rent is sorrow income t., 321b
shall drown the wind, 282b
siren t., 294a
smiles t. of boyhood's years,
   542b
smiling through t., 63b
songs composed of t., 657a
such as angels weep, 342b

Tears sweat or blood, 920b
sympathetic t., 441b
that speak, 358a
thaw not frost, 571a
they that sow in t., 22b
thoughts too deep for t., 514a
time with gift of t., 773a
tired of t. and laughter, 775a
touch lips part with t., 774b
undimmed by human t., 849a
unseen and unknown, 632a
waste not fresh t., 85b
watered heaven with t., 489a
way with t. watered, 906b
weep barren t., 568b
wipe away all t., 58b
with sobs and t. sorted, 746a
wrung me to t., 104b
young foolish full of t., 879b
Tear-wrung millions, 920b
Teas where small talk dies, 570a
Tease, fleas that t. in Pyrenees,
   902a
fools no more I'll t., 405b
the housewife's wool, 337b
Teases, he knows it t., 743b
mind over for years, 816b
Teatray, like t. in sky, 744a
Technological world, 1055b
Tecum vivere amem tecum obeam
   libens, 122a
Tedious as twice-told tale, 236b
historical books t., 801b
old fools, 260b
on subject but own, 879a
relations t. pack, 840a
returning as t. as go o'er, 285a
road will be less t., 116b
shorten t. nights, 300a
sport would be t., 238a
thinking her prattle t., 228a
to tell tales already told, 66b
Tedium, pretentious quotations
   t., 852a
Teeming brain, 581a
mistress barren bride, 406b
refuse of t. shore, 817a
womb of kings, 226b
Teeth, bid them keep t. clean,
   289b
bitch gone in the t., 988b
children's t. set on edge, 34b
dragon's t., 1042a
O cropped out with t., 1002a
red thoughts t. white, 904a
sans t. sans eyes, 249b
truth may strike out his t.,
   199b
weeping and gnashing of t., 41b
what speech escaped your t.,
   63a
who made t. shall give bread,
   183a
with the skin of my t., 15a
Teetotaler, beer t. not champagne
   t., 836a
Tehee quod she, 167b
Tekel, Mene Mene T. Upharsin,
   35a
Telegrams, not call t. science,
   815a
Telemachus, mine own T., 646b
Teleology is theology, 870a
Telepathic instinct, 976b
Telephant, elephant tried to use
   t., 822a
Telephone, elephone tried to use
   t., 822a
humble appearance of t., 742a

Times, in the morning of the
t., 206b
later t. more aged than earlier,
206b
lived for all t., 498a
my t. are in thy hand, 18b
necessity of the t., 444a
O what fine t., 416b
of great Elizabeth, 645b
Oh what t. what standards,
110b
old simplicity of t., 1090b
old t. manners books, 450b
old t. not forgotten, 678a
past t. preserve themselves,
1035a
purest treasure mortal t. afford,
226a
pursy t., 264b
seven t. over and over, 704a
signs of the t., 43a
sun itself which makes t.,
305b
terrible t., 828a
that try men's souls, 466b
these t. are ancient t., 206b
these unhappy t., 970b
thus t. do shift, 320b
tide of t., 255a
till time and t. done, 880a
truth which cunning t. put on,
233b
truths not for all t., 417b
Times', my dear t. waste, 292a
Timetable, read t. sooner than
nothing, 932a
Timid soul, 989b
state t. as lone woman, 681a
Timidity, whistles and disavows
t., 833b
Timing, circumstance and proper
t., 92a
is exact, 88b
is most important factor, 68a
know the right t., 68b
Timon, till I am T. and Lear,
885a
Timor mortis conturbat me, 176a
nil terribile nisi ipse t., 207b
Timorous beastie, 492b
foe, 411a
million dollars t., 1017b
Timothy learned sin to fly, 1089a
Tim'rous beastie, 492b
Tin, blowing t. horns, 948b
cheap t. trays, 947b
in t. factory human being
crushed, 1069b
little t. gods, 871b
path paved with t. cans, 835b
Tincture, best virtue has t. of
vice, 190b
Tinge brow with sunset glow,
809b
Tinged by what absorbs it, 795a
eyelids and hands, 781a
Tingle remarkably pleasant, 1052a
Tinhorn politicians, 896a
Tinker more than renew, 795a
to Evers to Chance, 962b
with abstract idea, 1046a
Tinkled among teacups, 1001b
Tinkling, chime of words t., 878a
cymbal, 52b
with their feet, 30b
Tinklings, drowsy t. lull, 440a
Tinpinny, sellin' t. nails, 891a
Tintinnabulation musically wells,
644a

Tints, why flowers painted in t.,
861a
Tiny, little t. boy, 253a
little t. wit, 278a
round bole in t. leaf, 663a
Tim last of all, 671a
Tiphys disclose new worlds, 131a
Tippecanoe, soldier of T., 600a
Tipped with line of steel, 704b
Tippenny, wi' t. fear nae evil,
495b
Tipperary, long way to T., 934a
Tippled drink more fine, 583b
Tippler, little t. leaning, 735a
violetflavored nuisance, 1030b
Tips with silver fruit-tree tops,
224a
Tipsy, blind and often t., 600b
dance and jollity, 336b
Tip-tilted like petal, 653a
Tiptoe malices, 866a
on misty mountaintops, 225a
religion stands on t., 324a
stand a-t. when day named,
245a
upon a little hill, 579a
Tirade, your old-fashioned t.,
1076a
Tire day in toil, 321b
ear the open vowels t., 403a
night in thought, 321b
of all creation, 634a
speeds too fast 'twill t., 221b
Tired and sick of war, 705a
dull stale t. bed, 277a
eyelids upon tired eyes, 645b
give me your t. your poor, 817a
Jezebel t. her head, 13b
nature's sweet restorer, 398b
no time to be t., 589b
of his dark dominion, 730b
of honest things, 1024a
of its pleasures t., 510a
of kings, 603a
of London tired of life, 432a
of my turmoil, 1076b
of ruling over slaves, 435a
of tears and laughter, 775a
on day of victory no one t.,
149b
Sister Caroline t., 906b
stummucks don't git t., 814a
sun with talking, 719b
till t. he sleeps, 409b
today's newspaper t., 916a
waves vainly breaking, 688b
wind tapped like t. man, 735b
with all these, 292b
yet strong shun thought, 812a
Tirer les marrons du feu, 360b
Tires, sad t. in a mile-a, 295b
unchartered freedom t., 514b
Tiresias, I T. though blind,
1002b
Tiresome verse-reciter Care, 573a
Tiring, mothers' wombs the t.
houses, 199b
Tirlin' at the window, 657a
Tirra lirra by the river, 645b
Tit for tat, 185a
tell tale t., 1093a
Titania, there sleeps T., 229b
Titanic, alley t., 643b
Tithe of mint and anise, 43b
Title and profit I resign, 393b
excels at t. page, 447a
farced t. 'fore king, 244b
feel his t. hang loose, 286a
from better man I stole, 823b

Title, gained no t., 407a
like t. for it not mine, 823b
neither can t. to ocean belong,
188b
no lover of pompous t., 189a
no t. I deem more honorable,
967b
ready my t. clear, 397a
Titles are shadows, 385b
gratuities privileges, 503a
high though his t., 519b
kinquering congs t. take, 807b
of mining claims, 1041b
power and pelf, 519a
Titter w'en stew smokin' hot,
911b
Tittle, jot or t., 40a
Tittlemouse, Tommy T., 1097b
Tityrus, once sang of you T.,
117b
To, going t. and fro on earth, 14a
many shall run t. and fro, 35a
reel t. and fro, 21b
the unknown god, 50a
Toad beneath harrow knows,
871b
glorious sight murmured T.,
852a
I had rather be a t., 274b
like t. at ear of Eve, 346a
like t. ugly and venomous, 247b
preaches contentment to t.,
871b
rosewater on a t., 610b
without which no garden complete, 733b
worm to a t., 791b
Toads brooding in wells, 1064b
imaginary gardens with real t.,
996a
Toast golden for its beauty, 763a
let the t. pass, 481b
particularly long, 553b
works down to babies, 760a
Toasted, dreamed of t. cheese,
823a
Toasts of the young men, 476a
Tobacco, devilish and damned t.,
311b
divine nothing equal it, 563a
divine rare, 311b
for thy sake T., 535b
is a dirty weed, 1037a
is a filthy weed, 484a
metaphysical t., 1085b
Road, 1052b
sublime t., 563a
this night leave off t., 534b
Tobacco's fragrance greet, 1080a
Tobermory's rejoinder, 904a
Toboggans, ignorance t. into
know, 1032a
Toby, my uncle T., 438a
Tocsin of the soul, 561b
Today a king, 38a
be good and happy t., 523b
be wise t., 399a
beaten yet t., 1050b
beneath foeman's frown, 656a
call t. his own, 369b
doubts of t., 974a
flower that smiles t., 320b
friends of t., 3a
future lays law of t., 804b
give me t. take tomorrow, 149b
he puts forth tender leaves,
298b
here t. next week tomorrow,
852a

Touched be th' sun, 981a
  chord in unison t., 458b-459a
  God's finger t. him, 650b
  nothing he did not adorn, 432a
  spirits not finely t., 270a
  things he t. worked with, 943a
  to the quick, 662a
  with fire, 786b
  with moon's red silver, 1081a
Touches, mortality t. the heart, 118a
  of sweet harmony, 235b
  who t. this t. a man, 703a
Touching, not succeed in t. ideals, 733a
  sight so t. in majesty, 512a
Touchstone by which we try services, 472b
  calamity man's true t., 316b
  panics t. of sincerity, 467a
Touchstones, dreams t. of characters, 681b
Touchy, pacify t. tribe of poets, 124a
  testy pleasant fellow, 394a
Tough and devilish sly, 671a
  and final growth, 1057b
  as a steak, 1035b
  but nervous, 997a
  customer, 670a
  interesting but t., 761a
  life t. proposition, 941a
  rack of this t. world, 280b
  wedge for tough log, 127a
  worm in little inside, 768b
Tough-minded, government not more t., 1049a
Toujours gai, 946a
Touring culture like museum, 1057a
Tourist, rich vagabond called t., 932b
Tourney, summoned am to t., 1086a
Tout comprendre t. pardonner, 502b
  est pour le mieux, 417a
  milieu entre rien et t., 363b
  passe, 658a
  passe casse lasse, 1105b
  perdu fors l'honneur, 180b
  rire de t., 460a
Toves, slithy t., 745a
Tower and bells, 483a
  burning roof and t., 883b
  clock collected in t., 854a
  cries as from lighted t., 970b
  gloomy shadowed t., 825b
  inaccessible t. of past, 694b
  intending to build t., 47a
  ivory t., 615a
  ivory t. of cultural, 937b
  ivy-mantled t., 440b, 962b
  king's name a t. of strength, 217b
  Montaigne in his t., 1054a
  neck is as a t. of ivory, 29b
  of ivory, 615a
  of strength, 651b
  proud t., 642a
  stand like a firm t., 161a
  strongest t. of delight, 697b
  to dark t. came, 278b
  Trojans sitting on the t., 63a
  yonder ivy-mantled t., 440a
Towered citadel pendant rock, 288b
  cities please us then, 335a
  grim shape t. up, 510a

Towering confidence of twenty-one, 430a
  hopes like t. falcons, 387a
  in her pride of place, 284a
Towers and battlements it sees, 334b
  cloud-capped t., 297b
  death overtake you though in lofty t., 149a
  elephants endorsed with t., 348b
  ivory t., 878a
  no t. along the steep, 537b
  proud t., 557a
  topless t. of Ilium, 213a
  two t. of sail, 688b
  walls and t. girdled round, 523b
  whispering from her t., 713b
  ye antique t., 439a
Town, all around the t., 862b
  all round t., 1092b
  atheist, 1047a
  consul in foreign t., 864a
  country in t., 135b
  crier spoke my lines, 262b
  dear damned distracting t., 405b
  defend village t. city, 921b
  distressed and forsaken, 375b
  drunkard, 1047a
  end of the t., 970a
  follies of t. crept slowly, 450b
  hot time in old t., 868a
  humming t., 711a
  in Scarlet t., 1088a
  is lighter than vanity, 365b
  it rains softly on t., 830b
  leave by t. drain, 807b
  little t. of Bethlehem, 755a
  London a man's t., 827b
  London Town's fine t., 947b
  man in our t., 1098a
  man made the t., 457b
  many ways meet in one t., 243a
  never go down to t., 970a
  one-horse t., 759a
  Paris a woman's t., 827b
  Paris my home t., 933b
  pretty how t., 1031b
  proud tower in t., 642a
  sent them out of t., 1093a
  Shuteye T., 820b
  sprinkle quarters on t., 854a
  taller t. than Rome, 918b
  tavern in the t., 1100a
  what common talk of t. is, 375a
  woods go seaward from t., 551a
  Yankee Doodle to t., 1090a
Town's, London T. fine town, 947b
Towns, away away from t., 573a
  dust and reek of t., 695b
  seen enough English t., 1047a
  seven t. contend for Homer, 301b
  taken t. with words, 311a
  winter too long in country t., 940a
Township, destroys t. in sleep, 980b
Toy dog covered with dust, 820b
  foolish thing but a t., 253a
  had not friend nor t., 694a
  like through t. fair, 969a
  religion but a childish t., 212b
  sells eternity to get t., 220a
  soldier red with rust, 820b
Toyed and kissed, 401b
Toys, all is but t., 84a

Toys, bring you colored t., 861a
  brooches and t. for delight, 824b
  enemies for t., 310a
  for your delight, 824b
  love and all his pleasures t., 300a
  of age, 409a
Trace, boding tremblers learned to t. 449b
  characters of hell to t., 441b
  misery still delights to t., 459b
  noble dust of Alexander, 266a
  on dark theme t. verses of light, 113a
  painters cannot t., 397a
Traced lives of good men, 517a
Traces, in the t. lead 'em, 693a
  of original sin, 707b
  winter's t., 772b
Tracing, fitful t. of portal, 955b
Tracings of eternal light, 497a
Track, around ancient t., 730b
  down relations of aspects of experience, 984a-b
  golden t. 953a
  narrow t. to highest good, 114a
Trackless, launch on t. seas, 702b
  way, 661a
Tract of inland ground, 516b
Trade, commonly called slave t., 420b
  dreadful t., 279b
  except what t. give, 668a
  food of us that t. in love, 288a
  free t., 594b
  free t. in ideas, 788b
  free t. not principle, 611b
  heel of Northeast t., 874a
  homely slighted shepherd's t., 338a
  how is your t. Aquarius, 1034b
  instrument of t., 752a
  Irish poets learn t., 885a
  literature half t. half art, 859b
  love t. thou hast learned, 142a
  mission of t. unions, 821a
  never pursue literature as t., 528b
  no nation ruined by t., 423a
  nothing to do but t., 467a
  of blood and guile, 526b
  serve time to every t., 554b
  slave t., 420b
  two of a t. never agree, 401b, 730a
  unions outgrowth of conditions, 821a
Trades, critic most degraded of t., 764a
  ugliest t. have pleasure, 610b
Tradesmen, bow ye t., 767a
  lying becomes none but t., 295b
Tradition becomes holy, 805a
  cannot be inherited, 1007a
  desert t., 605b
  finally inspires awe, 805a
  for three hundred years, 840a
  grows more venerable, 804b
  not enough, 1008b
  reverence due t. increases, 804b
  youth of America oldest t., 840a
Traduced the state, 276b
Traffic, green t. light, 1017b
  in mockery, 883a
  no kind of t., 296b
  of Jacob's ladder, 857a
Trafficked for strange webs, 781a
Trafficking, sail to all thy t., 105a

Unaccommodated man, 278b
Unaccustomed to fear, 1100b
  to thought of dying, 732b
Unacquainted, not u. with misfortunes, 66b
Unadorned, when u. adorned most, 419b
Unadvertised, leave it u., 787b
Unadvised, too rash too u., 224a
Unadvisedly, entered into u., 61a
Unaffected, affecting to seem u., 392a
Unafraid, gentlemen u., 873a
Unaging intellect, 88zb
Unalienable, certain u. rights, 470b
  essential and u. rights, 470b
Unalterable, army of u. law, 730b, 1001b
  days, 603b
  quantity of force u., 709b
Unaltered, laws ought not to remain u., 98a
Unaneled, unhouseled disappointed u., 259b
Unanimity, feel way toward u., 870b
  on legal questions, 864b
Unapproachable in White House, 976b
Unarm Eros, 288b
Unarmed, being u. be despised, 177a
  truth, 1082b
Unashamed, brawling judgments u., 653a
Unassisted merit advances slowly, 426b
Unassuming commonplace of Nature, 512b
Unattached, vagaries of u. relatives, 1027b
Unattainable perfection, 878a
Unattained, how vast the u., 650b
Unattempted yet in prose or rhyme, 341b
Unavailing star, 878a
Unavenged, insults u., 516a
  suffering, 708a
Unaware, blessed them u., 525b
  hope he knew and I u., 783b
  some morning u., 663a
Unawares, entertained angels u., 56a
Unbarred gates of light, 346b
Unbeautiful and have comfortable minds, 1030b
Unbecoming, not u. men that strove, 646b
Unbelief, fearful u. in yourself, 576b
  help thou mine u., 45b
Unbelieving came home, 988a
Unbend, sweet to let mind u., 122b
  universal horror u., 965b
Unbidden guests welcomest when gone, 214a
  I knock u. once, 748b
  truth, 1040a
Unbirthday present, 746a
Unbodied, souls u., 307b
Unborn, fate of u. millions, 461a
  generations, 970b
  little souls u., 962a
  millions yet u., 444a
  posterity of those u., 394b
  states u., 255a
  ve u. ages, 442a

Unborrowed, interest u. from the eye, 509a
Unbought grace of life, 454a
  health u., 371b
Unbound, so are ye u., 603b
Unbounded, man of an u. stomach, 299a
  salt water u., 876a
Unbowed, head bloody but u., 816a
Unbreathed, virtue unexercised and u., 340a
Unbroken, seaward flying u. wings, 1004a
  spur not u. horse, 521b
Unburied, bodies of u. men, 315a
  unwept u. Patroclus, 64b
Unburnished, rust u., 646b
Unbusy, sole u. thing, 527b
Unbutton, come u. here, 278b
Uncaught, from world's snare u., 288a
Uncertain balance of proud time, 206a
  coy hard to please, 519b
  glory of April day, 220b
  hour before morning, 1006b
  life's u. voyage, 290b
  rustling of curtain, 643a
  to it nothing u., 479a-b
  trumpet give u. sound, 52b
  world u. comes, 604b
Uncertainties, capable of u., 584b
Uncertainty, quit certainty for u., 428a
  sink of u. and error, 364a
Unchanging, no u. truth, 1019a
  Olympus ever u., 65b
Uncharitable to ourselves, 330a
Uncharitableness, from all u. deliver, 60b
Unchartered freedom tires, 514b
Unchecked, capitalist society u., 1014b
  population u. increases, 502a
Uncircumcision, neither circumcision nor u., 54b
Uncivilized Eastern instincts, 871b
Unclasps her warmed jewels, 582a
Uncle, I have good eye u., 245b
  me no uncle, 227a
  my prophetic soul my u., 259b
  yours U. Sam when it's wet, 942b
Unclean, man of u. lips, 30b
  people of u. lips, 30b
  swine is u., 9b
Unclothed, bodies u. must be, 307b
Unclouded, pure u. brow, 744b
  weather, 645b
Unclubable, very u. man, 431a
Uncoffined and unknown, 557b
Uncomely, things u. and broken, 880b
Uncomfortable feel tarantara, 766b
  inn to lodge in, 696a
  moral when u., 836b
Uncommon, common murderer u. cook, 904a
  common opinions u. abilities, 726b
  valor common virtue, 987a
Uncompleted, hanging on of u. task, 792b
Uncompromising as justice, 615b
  hostility, 1055a
Unconcern, patron looks with u., 429b

Unconcerned hear mighty crack, 393a
Unconditional and immediate surrender, 717a
  love, 1082b
  right to say what one pleases, 991b
  war, 1073b
Unconfined, lawless winged u., 488a
  let all her ways be u., 387b
  let joy be u., 556a
Unconquerable, love u. waster, 82a
  man's u. mind, 512b
  nursing u. hope, 712a
  soul, 816a
  will, 342a, 923a
Unconquered, thy arm u. steam, 459b
Unconscionable time dying, 366b
Unconscious, all greatness u., 575b
  archetypes of u., 935b
  collective u., 935a
  discovered u. before me, 834a
  fastidiousness, 996a
  humor, 756b
  infancy's u. spell, 697b
  Kosmos, 796a
  not only evil by nature, 936a
  part of man's life, 575b
  poetry, 716b
  prejudice, 1026b
  spiritual unbidden u., 656a
  studied, 834a
  the source of good, 936a
  work, 772a
Unconsidered, decisive actions often u., 897b
  snapper-up of u. trifles, 295a
Unconstitutional, power to pronounce u., 616b
Uncontrollable laughter, 62b
Unconvincing, preferable to u. possibility, 99a
Uncornered animal's, 1081a
Uncorseted her friendly bust, 1002a
Uncounted, monster with u. heads, 241a
Uncouth, ancient good u., 692a
  savage men u. manners, 452b
Uncreated conscience of race, 968b
  wide womb of u. night, 343b
Uncreating word, 414a
Uncrowned in the underworld, 986a
Unction, flattering u., 264a
Uncumbered with a wife, 371b
Uncut hair of graves, 700a
Undaunted by villains in power, 464b
  daughter of desires, 354b
  we must be u., 921b
Undazzled, kindling her u. eyes, 340b
Undecided, decided only to be u., 920a
Undefeated because we have gone on trying, 1006b
Undefiled, well of English u., 200b
Under blossom that hangs on bough, 297b
  every stone a politician, 91b
  the greenwood tree, 248a
Underbelly, soft u. of Axis, 924a

Unite, workers of the world u., 687a
United, avoid perils by u. forces, 374a
faction u. by common impulse, 480a
nations, 556a
States of Europe, 600a
States of World, 600a
sword u. nations drew, 556a
we must be u., 921b
we stand, 600a
United Nations alternative to war, 1073b
flouted policy of U.N., 984a
peoples of U.N., 1104a
plan for liberation, 1016b
world state inherent in U.N., 1013b
United States and Europe, 492a
bounded on north, 655a
British Empire and U.S., 921b
Constitution and laws of U.S., 474a
Constitution for U.S., 474a
Constitution of U.S. shield, 678a
declare peace, 1019a
deliberately attacked, 973b
fate of book in U.S., 772a
flag of U.S., 832b
fools drunkards and U.S., 1102b
gives bigotry no sanction, 461b
greatest potential force, 863a
has thirty-two religions, 484a
history of U.S., 1011b
I believe in U.S., 895b
in U.S. more space, 933b
in U.S. utter rubbish, 977a
join U.S., 928a
land of free speech, 924a
life in U.S., 1062b
live in U.S. and not happy, 961a
monster the U.S., 828b
neutral in fact, 841a
not end if we declare Act of Congress void, 787b
not proclaimed democracy, 917a
poor Mexico so close to the U.S., 734a
rendered U.S. helpless, 842a
responsibilities of U.S., 1013b
result in evil to U.S., 728b
so happy as in U.S., 960b
students from U.S., 828b
themselves greatest poem, 699b
treason against the U.S., 474a
Ulysses admitted into U.S., 968b
unfriendly towards U.S., 492a
we the people of the U.S., 474a
Unites, happy whom unbroken bond u., 121a
Unitest nations, 703a
Unities sir are a completeness, 669b
Uniting, by u. we stand, 460b
Unity, confound all u. on earth, 285b
dwell together in u., 22b
give to all nations u., 60b
makes strength, 726a
multeity in u., 528a
of German nation, 1012a
of humanity in word, 937b
preserve u. of empire, 453a
Universal and common bond, 191a

Universal, appetite an u. wolf, 268a
blank, 344b
books of u. appeal, 915a
cock, 955b
darkness buries all, 414a
Declaration of Human Rights, 964a-b
dismal u. hiss, 348a
dovetailedness, 669b
frame without mind, 208b
grin, 424a
harmony, 709a
horror unbend, 965b
lapped in u. law, 647b
law, 445b
made u. shout, 253a
monarchy of wit, 326b
Nature did lament, 338a
nature say, 425b
nuisance, 373b
old age in u. man, 206b
partial evil u. good, 408b
peace like light, 646a
prey, 268a
quality is diversity, 190b
Rossum's U. Robots, 1015a
this u. frame began, 370a
truths, 1039b
uproar the u. peace, 285b
Universally relations stop nowhere, 799a
Universals, statements of nature of u., 99a
Universe, accident in meaningless u., 925b
allegorical of u., 918a
anthology of u., 1040a
benign indifference of u., 1068b
born for the u., 451a
chess pieces phenomena of u., 724b
connect subject with u., 787a
emptiness produced the u., 110a
fathomless u., 702a
Gaseous Vertebrata own u., 961a
glory and shame of u., 364a
glory of the u., 628a
Great Architect of U., 942b
harmony for thee O U., 142a
harnessing power of u., 982b
hell of a good u., 1032a
hints for better ordering of u., 157b
I accept the u., 656b
in boundless u., 644b
information about u., 834b
is change, 141b
know another's view of u., 908a
knows the u. not himself, 359b
largest u. of good, 794b
man said to u., 905a
meets own destruction, 964b
not hostile nor friendly, 952b
one u. made up of all that is, 142b
open to our gaze, 211b
piety towards u., 867b
queerer than we suppose, 1021a-b
snow falling faintly through u., 968a
something gained for u., 794a
sun himself at center of u., 178a
systematic procession of u., 178a
this grand book the u., 211b
through-and-through u., 796a

Universe, true piety towards u., 867b
whole theory of u., 702b
Universes, in space and time u., 703a
University become multiversity, 1068a
best u. gauntlet of mobs, 609a
he who enters u., 1026a
Lomonosov our first u., 434b
place of light, 613a
Unjust, God all mercy is God u., 399a
in least u. in much, 47a
let him be u. still, 58b
peace before just war, 422b
sendeth rain on just and u., 40b
war protracted, 698b
will pay less tax, 94a
Unkempt about those hedges, 993a
Unkind, learned kindness from u., 976a
tell me not I am u., 358b
thou art not so u., 249b
when givers prove u., 262a
Unkindest cut of all, 255b
Unkindness, I tax you not with u., 278a
may defeat my life, 276a
may do much, 276a
Unkissed, unknown u. and lost, 164b
Unknelled uncoffined, 557b
Unknow, knows not also to u., 707b
Unknowable, world u. we know, 857a
Unknown, accents yet u., 255a
affection hath u. bottom, 250b
and silent shore, 534b
behind dim u., 692a
black and u. bards, 906b
critics shouting He's u., 791b
enemy is the u., 937a
fearless for u. shores, 702b
footprint on shores of u., 967a
forms of things u., 230b
from known to u., 675b
hardships we suffered, 1022b
let me live unseen u., 402a
loss no loss, 125a
means of destruction hitherto u., 982b
mighty continent hitherto u., 173b
naked in death on u. shore, 118b
nature is but art u., 408b
not lived ill who passed u., 123b
not to know me argues yourselves u., 346a
out of me unworthy u., 898b
poetry trip into u., 1028a
railway termini gates to u., 951b
region, 702b
renown, 738a
sea, 700a
she lived u., 510b
taken for marvelous, 140a
things standing thus u., 266b
things u. proposed, 404a
to fortune and fame u., 441a
to the u. god, 50a
too early seen u., 223b
traveled among u. men, 510b
unkissed and lost, 164b

W

Wanton, as flies to w. boys, 279a
boys that swim on bladders, 298b
freak, 579a
friar ther was w. and merye, 166a
gods that w. in the air, 358b
her w. spirits look out, 269a
imaginations and w. tempers, 462b
stings of sense, 270a
stretched forth necks and w. eyes, 30b
wiles, 334b
Wantoned with thy breakers, 558a
Wantonness, chambering and w., 51b
kindles in clothes a w., 320a
Wanton's, no further than w. bird, 224a
Wantons thro' flowering thorn, 494a
Wants, everything he w., 718a
fantastic unnecessary w., 794b
getting what one w., 839b
has more than he w., 395a
having fewest w., 87b
man w. but little, 399a, 448a
my w. are many, 503a
my w. few, 634a
nor w. that little long, 399a, 448a
not getting what one w., 839b
nothing but eternity, 290a
provide for human w., 454a
speech not to express w., 376b
the natural touch, 285b
to make flesh creep, 66ga
woman w. scarce thing, 863b
War, a god has given deeds of w., 63b
a just w., 422b, 467a
adopting European w. tactics, 997b
aftermath of w., 931a
alone brings nobility, 977b
always stirring up some w., 95a
amidst ranks of w., 594b
an invention, 978a
and carnage be lost, 701b
armament important in w., 1027b
art of w. simple, 717a
as much and as little of w., 209b
battlefield of that w., 639a
beginning badly, 1016a
begun without money, 181a
Between Men and Women, 1033a
blast of w. in ears, 243b
blood-swollen god, 904b
brazen throat of w., 348a
breeds war again, 845a
chance of w., 267b
check murder but what of w., 130b
circumstance of glorious w., 275a
class w. destroy inequalities, 889a
coin is sinews of w., 181a
cold w. altered, 1055b
cold w. getting warmer, 901a
cold w. master myth, 1056a
concealed throughout w., 769a
condition of man condition of w., 317b
conquer us, 1019a

War, conquered what causes w., 996b
Constitution is law in w. and peace, 678a
contagion, 972a
continuation of political relations, 544b
could have been prevented, 979b
danger and tempest of w., 661a
dastard in w., 519b
dauntless in w., 519a
dearth age agues, 307a
delays dangerous in w., 202b
deserve success in w., 925a
devil's madness w., 933a
disease and w. itself, 1073a
dogs of w., 255a
Don John going to w., 918b
doubt and darkness of w., 661a
drum throbbed no longer, 647b
each w. creation of preceding w., 941a
ease after w., 200a
either w. obsolete or men, 1034a
enemies in w. in peace friends, 470b
engaged in great civil w., 639a
epithets of w., 272a
even to the knife, 555a
everybody against w., 1019b
fever famine and w., 817b
first in w. first in peace, 486a
first invented w., 212a
fought with atomic bomb, 950b
France has not lost w., 1016a
garland of the w., 288b
generation shorn by w., 920a
generator of wars, 941a
get too fond of w., 620a
go forth to w. together in a body, 149a
Great Britain going to w., 832b
great w. petty peace, 888a
has actually begun, 465a
hath smoothed his front, 216b
hero of the next w., 980b
how much w. seen, 1080b
I am the tongue of w., 1083a
I call it murder, 692b
I have seen w. I hate w., 971b
I make w. on the living, 186a
if they mean to have w., 455a
image of w. without guilt, 397a
in heaven, 58a
in his heart, 19b
in peace provided for w., 146b
in peace thinks of w., 311b
in state of w. by nature, 390a
in this w. books weapons, 973b
in w. daring boastful, 564a
in w. mounts warrior's steed, 518b
in w. no second prize, 1025b
in w. no substitute for victory, 959a
in w. nothing impossible, 987b
in w. parents inter children, 86b
in w. resolution, 925a
inevitable, 950b
infection and hand of w., 226b
involves train of circumstances, 467a
is a contagion, 972a
is a game, 458b
is cruelty, 705a
is glorious art, 398b

War is hell, 705a
is still the cry, 555a
is toil and trouble, 371b
is w. biological necessity, 980b
its thousands slays, 460a
killed only once in w., 919b
knew when w. going to end, 965b
lead peaceful into w., 842a
let slip dogs of w., 255a
levying w., 474a
liberty to begin and end w., 209b
Lord is a man of w., 8b
love and w. same thing, 196b
love calls to w., 205a
love of w. for itself, 591a
luxury more deadly than w., 139b
magnificent but not w., 655b
make w. for scrap of paper, 832b
make w. to live in peace, 98a
makes rattling good history, 783b
mankind put end to w., 1073b
marching as to w., 750b
men unproved in w., 752a
money sinews of w., 104b
moral equivalent of w., 795b
my voice is still for w., 393b
national misfortune, 597a
neither shall they learn w., 30a
never a w. not inward, 996b
never good w. or bad peace, 422b
never slays bad man, 82b
no discharge in w., 28a, 876b
no great w. come again, 1015a
no modern w. won without sea power, 998a
no w. or battle's sound, 334b
no will to win w., 959b
noble efforts in last w., 426a
not an instinct, 978a
not disturbed by planetary w., 990b
not divorced from politics, 1027b
not rational alternative, 1073b
nothing easy in w., 1016b
object of w. peace, 705a
object only of w. honorable, 467a
of everyone against everyone, 317b
of looks between them, 220a
older men declare w., 931a
only art necessary, 177a
open or secret w., 471b
outcome of the w. in our hands, 64a
pattern called w., 931b
peace better than most just w., 422b
peace corrupt w. waste, 348a
peace not absence of w., 373a
phony w., 979b
political relations by other means, 544b
politics almost exciting as w., 919b
prepared for w., 461b
prince have no study but w., 177a
prophesying w., 524a
purple testament of bleeding w., 227b
put end to mankind, 1073b

War, quaint and curious w. is, 783b
ready for w. to avoid it, 383a
real w. never in books, 703a
red animal, 904b
regarded as wicked, 839a
relentless, 903a
result of mistaken calculation, 938a
same reason causes w., 190a
Scott responsible for w., 760b
scourge of w., 640b, 1104a
seldom enters but where wealth allures, 370a
sentence is for open w., 343a
silent w. of lilies, 220a
sinews of w., 104b, 181a
some slain in w., 227b
Son of God goes forth to w., 549a
Spanish ships of w., 654D
spares not the brave, 70a
stand up and take w., 877b
strange terrible world w., 923b
study politics and w., 463a
stupid crime, 933a
subject of it is W., 1028b
sweets with sweet w. not, 291b
sword of w. or of law, 473a
talk by men who have been in w., 760b
tempered by w., 1072b
that will end war, 888a
the w. is over, 717a
there was w. in heaven, 58a
this is w., 619b
this w. elemental conflict, 1012a
those who brought w. to Far East, 982b
though w. should rise against me, 18a
Thucydides wrote history of w., 89a
time of w. time of peace, 27b
tired and sick of w., 705a
to make world safe, 866b
to prevent w. not fear it, 531a
to w. and arms I fly, 358b
tongue of w., 1083a
too serious for military, 786a
train of circumstances, 467a
tricked into European w., 913b
ultimate sanction of exploitation, 1027a
unconditional w., 1073b
United Nations alternative to w., 1073b
unjust peace before just w., 422b
unjust w. protracted, 698b
unsuccessful or successful w., 457b
vain w. with heaven, 343a
wage w. like physical giants, 1024b
want an end to w., 974a
warmest heart recoiled at w., 1031a
weapons of w. perished, 12b
well that w. so terrible, 620a
what A.D. is elsewhere, 760b
when aggressions require w., 472b
when I speak they are for w., 22a
when w. he went, 1060b
when w. is done, 992b
who desires peace prepare for w., 146b

War, will to win w., 959b
with reremice, 229b
with rights of mankind, 471b
woman cause of ten years' w., 383b
wrong w. at wrong time, 1025b-1026a
Warble child, 221b
native wood-notes wild, 335a
sweet in springtime, 828b
Warbled to the string, 336a
Warbler, Dan Chaucer first w., 645b
Warblest at eve, 339b
Warbling his Doric lay, 339a
thou w. bird, 494a
Warbonnet of Medicine Hat, 1041a
Ward has no heart they say, 500b
Warder is Despair, 841a
memory the w. of brain, 283a
Wardrobe, dalliance in w. lies, 243b
Wards in Chancery, 767b
pretty young w., 767b
Ware, ill w. is never cheap, 324a
pleasing w. is half sold, 324a
taste your w., 1093b
that will not keep, 852b
wiser than thou art w., 248a
Wares harder to get rid of, 927a
Warfare, atomic w. bad enough, 1015a
biological w. worse, 1015a
is accomplished, 32b
life struggle not w., 770b
love a kind of w., 128b
thy w. o'er, 520a
War-horse, hurl Jackson on w., 696b
Warld, a' the weary w., 479b
it's a weary w., 857b
Warlike, people numerous and w., 173b
Warling, young man's w., 185b
Warm and capable of grasping, 581b
cheek and rising bosom, 441b
heart within, 459a
her coat is so w., 546a
into the w. sun, 185a
keeper of w. lights, 82a
keeps w. her note, 327a
let out to w. air, 389b
man whose blood is w., 231a
now w. in love, 405b
nursing wrath to keep it w., 495b
precincts of cheerful day, 441a
ruddy drops that w. heart, 254b
sea-scented beach, 663a
side inside, 907a
so cold no fire w., 739b
summer sun shine friendly, 822a
sun was w. wind chill, 928a
this sensible w. motion, 271a
virtue keep me w., 369b
weather in bed, 388b
wind the west wind, 947a
without heating, 399b
Warm-blooded animals from one filament, 459b
Warmed, glow has w. the world, 981b
hands before fire of life, 536b
unclasps w. jewels, 582a
washed dressed w. fed, 947a

Warmest heart recoiled at war, 1031a
welcome at an inn, 432a
Warming pretty little toes, 1095b
Warmly, in numbers w. pure, 443b
Warms some poor name, 739a
Warmth, a little w. a little light, 751b
about my heart, 585a
no w. no cheerfulness, 592a
of heart increase with years, 1027b
spring brings back balmy w., 114b
warmth more warmth, 869b
Warn, all poet can do is w., 1028b
to comfort and command, 514a
Warned, friends be w. by me, 902a
in a dream, 39b
Warning, come without w., 676b
give w. to world, 292b
steal away give little w., 470a
voice of w. needed, 728b
Warp, weave the w., 441b
Warrant him heart-whole, 250a
she'll prove an excuse, 481b
truth shall be thy w., 199a
Warred for Homer dead, 301b
Warring within breasts, 212a
Warrior, British w. queen, 459a
every lover a w., 128b
happy w. of politics, 916b
happy w. sleeps, 976a
home brought her w., 649a
lay like w. taking rest, 566b
like an armed w., 749a
of North America, 564a
painful w. famoused for fight, 291b
who is the happy W., 515a
Warrior's, in war mounts w. steed, 518b
Warriors, female w., 417b
stern joy w. feel, 520a
War's a game, 458b
annals cloud into night, 784b
disciplinary functions, 795b
glorious art, 398b
used to w. alarms, 591b
Wars, all skillful in the w., 363a
all their w. merry, 918a
and alarums unto nations, 200b
and rumors of wars, 43b
begin in minds, 1104a
boys not sent into foreign w., 972b
brought nothing about, 372a
caused by man, 1018b
chronicle the 'w. of kites, 350a
dates of w., 765a
disciplines of w., 244a
end to beginnings of w., 974a
fierce w. and faithful loves, 200a
for right thing, 984a
forgotten w., 1005a
inevitability of w., 954b
more pangs than w. or women, 298b
most terrible of all w., 842a
not acts of God, 1018b
of European powers, 491b
planned by old men, 962a
that make ambition virtue, 275a
thousand w. of old, 651a

Water, honest w., 290a
 hot w. to remain upon tea, 328b
 I came like w., 630a
 if British went by w., 464b
 imperceptible w., 592b
 in Arkansas River, 982a
 in w. lives the fish, 364b
 is best, 79a
 is good, 73b
 is my will, 1065b
 Just Add Hot W., 1030b
 know worth of w., 422a
 land rats and w. rats, 232a
 land thieves and w. thieves, 232a
 Laughing W., 623a
 like a stone, 740a
 lily bloom, 645b
 limns on w. writes in dust, 210a
 little drops of w., 719b
 little w. in stream fault of source, 145a
 meditation and w. wedded, 695b
 Mississippi muddy w., 846a
 more than ocean w. broken, 928a
 more w. glideth by mill, 185a
 most encourage flame, 1031b
 much w. goeth by mill, 185a
 never formed to mind, 956a
 never hold w., 392b
 name writ in w., 586a
 never miss w. till well dry, 422a
 no more w. fire next time, 1101a
 no sound of w., 1002a
 no w. only rock, 1003a
 not all w. in rough rude sea, 227a
 o'er the w. to Charlie, 507b
 of affliction, 13b, 32a
 of gall to drink, 34a
 of life given to us, 1038b
 of river never the same, 156a
 on hands like Pilate, 1054b
 people are like w., 1027b
 plunge hands in w., 1059b
 profusion of w. light air, 748b
 quarrel over w., 982a
 reasons made mouth w., 352b
 reflects images, 777a
 rivers of w. in a dry place, 32a
 run through fire and w., 267a
 running w. walk, 970b
 Saint Lawrence is w., 846a
 salt w. unbounded, 876a
 saving soil and w., 970b
 skuttle fish blackens w., 395a
 slippy-sloppy in larder, 887b
 snake came to w. trough, 986a
 sound of w., 380b
 spring of ever-flowing w., 120a
 stagnant w. loses purity, 174a
 stained the w. clear, 486b
 steeds to w. at those springs, 290b
 stream smoothest w. deepest, 199a
 struggling for life in the w., 429b
 tar w. so mild and benign, 399b
 through a sieve, 746b
 through fire and through w., 19b
 to succeed add w. to wine, 869a
 tossing green w., 979a
 tree planted by rivers of w., 16b

Water, under running w., 1004a
 under w. men walk, 1087a
 unstable as w., 8a
 until desert knows w., 738a
 virtue more than w. or fire, 72b
 virtues we write in w., 299a
 wagon place for me, 886b
 wait to watch w. clear, 925b
 was made wine, 48a
 wash feet in soda w., 1002b
 wetter w. slimier slime, 993b
 what w. lapping bow, 1004a
 where b'iling w. hit, 814a
 which they beat, 287b
 whole stay of w., 30a
 wide w. inescapable, 955a
 will flow indifferently, 100b
 with w. to drink, 71b
 written in running w., 115a
Watercolors to impaint his cause, 240b
Watercraft, not be precise about w., 703b
Water-drinkers, no poems by w. please for long, 123b
Waterdrops, soul be changed to w., 213b
 waterpot is filled by w., 80a
 women's weapons w., 278a
 worn stones of Troy, 268b
Watered, Apollos w., 52a
 by blood of tyrants, 484a
 heaven with tears, 489a
 our horses in Helicon, 205b
 with tears w., 906b
Waterfall, from w. named her, 623a
Watering last year's crops, 689a
 pot and pruning knife, 656b
 your waters and w. places, 929a
Waterloo, Austerlitz and W., 948a
 battle of first rank, 599a
 dismal plain, 599a
 every man meets W., 659a
 from Marathon to W., 766b
 thou fatal W., 556a
 Wessex behind chaos of W., 951b
 won on playing fields, 506a
Waterman, great-grandfather was but a w., 365b
Watermen look astern row ahead, 137b
Waterpot is filled by waterdrops, 80a
Water's my will, 1065b
 thin, 768a
Waters and their powers, 557a
 at their priestlike task, 581a
 beams of his chambers in w., 21a
 beautiful drifts like w., 881a
 beside the still w., 17b
 cannot quench love, 30a
 cast thy bread upon the w., 28b
 clamor of w. and might, 772b
 cold w. to a thirsty soul, 26a
 come ye to the w., 33a
 cover the sea, 31a
 desert of w., 733a
 do business in great w., 21b
 dreadful noise of w., 217a
 fades o'er w. blue, 555a
 Father of W. unvexed to sea, 638b
 fen of stagnant w., 512b
 fish in troubled w., 386a
 here are your w., 929a
 hitherandthithering w., 968b

Waters, liffeying w., 968b
 like music on w., 559a
 murmuring, 336a
 music crept by upon w., 296a
 nearer roll, 425b
 no w. breed or break, 1080b
 noise of many w., 21a
 of petrel and porpoise, 1006a
 of the heart, 1070a
 once more upon w., 555b
 over great sea winds trouble w., 113a
 over rolling w. go, 648a
 peopling earth w. and sky, 377a
 pour w. of Nile, 743a
 returning to springs, 622a
 rivering w., 968b
 rushing of many w., 31b
 scattered w. rave, 676a
 secret w., 1036a
 should lift their bosoms, 268a
 shout golden shouts, 730a
 Spirit of God moved upon w., 5a
 stilled at even, 731a
 stolen w. are sweet, 24a
 swine perished in w., 41b
 take heed of still w., 199a
 their name is on your w., 566b
 tree planted by the w., 34a
 turns to perilous w., 159a
 vast w. of petrel, 1006a
 voice as sound of many w., 57b
 were a wall, 8b
 were his winding sheet, 309a
 wonderful w. round you, 719a
 words writ in w., 178b
 your divine w., 1079b
Watersmooth-silver stallion, 1030a
Watery, crown the w. glade, 439a
 envious siege of w. Neptune, 227a
 main, 292b
 nest, 332a
 shore, 488b
 sunk beneath w. floor, 339a
 thing of w. salt, 947b
 wide-rolling w. prairies, 697a
Watson, know my methods W., 850a
 Mr. W. come here, 811b
Wattle, ever hear of Captain W., 475b
Wattles, of clay and w. made, 879b
Wave, across the dark w., 826a
 all sunk beneath the w., 459a
 and whirlwind wrestle, 622b
 as w. succeeds w., 265a
 blue w. rolls nightly, 558b
 cry wind cry vast waters, 1006a
 dance like w. of sea, 880b
 every w. had nightcap, 822a
 glassy cool translucent w., 337b
 hands for mute farewell, 704a
 life is a w., 705b
 life on ocean w., 676a
 lift me as w. leaf cloud, 569b
 never w. of all waves, 875a
 obeyed what w. had taught, 998a
 of the future, 1061b, 1073b
 seen her w. hand, 645b
 small rock holds back great w., 65a
 star-spangled banner w., 541a
 swiftly walk over w., 572b
 to wash him from world, 909a

Westminster Abbey or victory, 492a
thrive at W. on fools, 413a
Westward eastward points between, 760a
ho, 252b
look the land is bright, 689a
stepping w., 513a
the course of empire, 400a
Wet, all dirty and w., 391a
all night in dark and w., 823a
black bough, 987b
eye manes dhry heart, 891a
farmers pray that summers be w., 117a
liked getting feet w., 887b
my mind and say something clever, 91a
nor ever w. with rain, 65b
not nasty dirty w. hole, 1025a
out of these w. clothes, 999a
sail w. seas roun', 874b
sheet and flowing sea, 551a
wild woods, 876a
would not w. her feet, 184a
Wetter water slimier slime, 993b
Whacks, forty w., 1101a
Whale, bob for w., 332a
leap of w. up Niagara, 422b
of a diplomat, 958b
swims minnow-small, 991a
that wanders round Pole, 901b
very like a w., 263b
Whalebone of flexibility, 958b
Whale-fat of postwar London, 1075b
Whale's backbone, 1006a
gull's way and w. way, 946b
white hump, 696b
Whales, drag Atlantic for w., 760a
great w. sailing by, 711a
herds of walruses and w., 696a
talk like w., 451b
Whaleship my Yale and Harvard, 696b
Wharf, rots in ease on Lethe w., 259b
What ain't so, 685b
am I Life, 947b
and Why and When, 876a
are they among many, 48b
are we fighting for, 933a
are you when sun shall rise, 300b
art thou idol ceremony, 244b
can I do for her, 1073a
could she have done being what she is, 881a
did hand of potter shake, 630b
did with every cent, 928b
do I know, 190a
does a woman want, 835a
God hath joined, 43a
hath God wrought, 10a
have I done unto thee, 10a
have I to do with thee, 48a
how who gets w., 994a
I am so shall thou be, 152b
is a man profited, 43a
is Africa to me, 1053a
is city but people, 289b
is left when honor lost, 125b
is love 'tis not hereafter, 251b
is man, 984b
is our life, 199a
is so rare as day in June, 692a
is that something, 1048a
is the grass, 700a
is the night, 285a

What is this quintessence of dust, 261a
is truth, 49b
is truth said jesting Pilate, 207b
is your life, 56b
is yours is mine, 105a
makest thou; 33a
needs my Shakespeare, 334a
news on the Rialto, 232a
no soap, 442b
of the night, 31b
price glory, 999b
say they let them say, 202a
tell them w. to do, 987b
the anvil, 489a
the devil was he doing in that galley, 361b
the hammer, 489a
thou seest write, 57b
we need to know, 1012b
who why which w., 673b
you cannot as you would achieve, 218b
Whatever begotten born and dies, 882b
best administered is best, 409b
comes with years, 774b
gods may be, 775a, 816a
I tried to write was verse, 129a
is fickle freckled, 803a
is is in its causes just, 367b
is is right, 408b
Miss T. eats, 914b
stirs this mortal frame, 526b
you have spend less, 433b
you lose reckon no account, 125b
Whatever's, hold own with w. going, 930a
What-is-it, certain w. in voice, 965b
What's come to perfection, 663b
done is done, 284b
gone and what's past help, 295a
Hecuba to him, 261b
her history, 252a
in a name, 223b
past and what's to come, 269a
past is prologue, 297a
the shootin' for, 944a
use of worrying, 958a
Whatsoever, in w. way any come to Me, 106b
ye would men do, 41a
What-was-his-name, 746b
What-you-may-call-um, 746b
Wheat, belly is like a heap of w., 29b
fields tall with w., 1046b
for this planting, 372b
hid in two bushels of chaff, 231b
immortal w., 377b
land of w. and barley, 10a
stacker of w., 948a
worm in the w., 906b
Wheaten, sickle and w. sheaf, 419b
Wheel, as w. runs why water pitcher, 124a
at w. in humming town, 711a
bound upon w. of fire, 280a
breaks butterfly upon w., 411a
broken at the cistern, 29a
ever-whirling w., 200b
I the limbs and w., 707a
in the middle of a wheel, 34b
is come full circle, 280b
man at w. taught to feel, 792a

Wheel, no place for fifth w., 157a
shoulder to the w., 76b
smile once more turn thy w., 277b
sofa round, 458a
that squeaks gets grease, 685a
wherever a turning w., 1069b
with a revolving w., 738b
Wheelbarrow, red w. glazed with rain, 979a
Wheelock, Eleazer W. pious man, 868b
Wheel's kick and winds' song, 946b
Wheels, all w. run down, 691a
beetle w. droning flight, 440a
clocked off by little w., 1039a
dust beneath chariot w., 871a
little tin gods on w., 871b
of Phoebus' wain, 336b
of weary life, 367b
oil for its own w., 457a
on w. to see world, 944a
why tarry the w. of his chariots, 11a
Wheezles and sneezles, 970a
Whelming, under the w. tide, 339a
Whelp, mongrel puppy w. hound, 448b
When, how and w. and where, 812b
how who gets what w., 994a
I knew him w., 905b
men drink they are rich, 90b
or how I cannot tell, 731a
shall we three meet again, 280b
that I was little tiny boy, 253a
the war is done, 992b
Whence and what art thou, 344a
What and Why and W., 876a
comest thou, 14a
cradle asks w., 749a
Whenever, if poor w. you can if rich w. you please, 96b
Whensoever called to make exit, 475a
Where and oh where, 500a
are snows of yesteryear, 171a
are they where art thou, 560b
are we now, 948b
are you going to, 1095a
cries out W. is it, 526b
did you come from baby, 723b
fear to be we know not w., 367a
go without my mount, 1078a
hell is there must we be, 213a
How and W. and Who, 876a
how and when and w., 812b
I am there ye may be, 49a
is fancy bred, 233b
is it now the glory, 513b
is she now, 286a
not how many but w. they are, 87b
was Roderick then, 520a
wast thou when I laid the foundations, 16a
we are is hell, 213a
who are we w. are we, 680b
your treasure is, 40b
Whereabout, stones prate of my w., 283a
Whereas I was blind, 48b
Where'er she lie, 354a
you walk, 402b
Wherefore are these things hid, 251a

World, busy w. and I ne'er
  agree, 357b
busy w. hushed, 598a
but as the w. Gratiano, 231a
but thoroughfare of woe, 167b
call w. if you please, 585b
came death into the w., 36b
came into w. to live in it, 681a
came once a w., 735a
cankers of calm w., 240a
cannot hold thee close enough,
  1023a
canted in this canting w., 438a
canvas to imaginations, 681b
care of this w., 42b
caricature of itself, 867b
charged with grandeur of God,
  803a
chessboard the w., 724b
childhood of w., 817a
children of w. wiser, 47a
children on wheels see w., 944a
choosest not better part, 866b
citizen of the w., 87b, 208b
citizens of the w., 974a
cognition of modern w., 938a
cold accretion called w., 783a
Columbus found a w., 867a
come round to him, 605b
come three corners of w., 237b
comes back on it, 1062a
Commodity bias of the w., 236a
community, 964b
concepts not uniquely determined by w., 950a
conquest of w. by creed, 1073b
consists of men women and
  Herveys, 414a
contributions to peace of w.,
  983a
count as naught in w., 694a
crumbles to nothing, 550b
cry out vanity of w., 374b
dark as w. of man, 998b
dark w. and wide, 341a, 866a
dead become lumber of w.,
  382b
dear Agnes is strange, 360b
death is but crossing w., 381a
destruction of w. not dreadful,
  629a
determination for better w.,
  863a
did w. become sad for me
  alone, 149b
dissatisfaction with w., 863a
do not grow old at all, 375b
domination of w., 847b
don't live in w. alone, 939a
doth two nations bear, 360a
dragon w., 989a
dreaming on things to come,
  293b
dreams books each a w., 515b
dreary in this w., 632a
drowsy syrups of w., 274b
end in fire, 927a
end of the w., 965a
ends of w. are come, 781a
enough and time, 359b
enough in w. for everyone, 983a
even unto end of w., 45a
ever the wide w. over, 872b
everyone in w. is Christ, 939b
everything in w. borne, 479a
false w. but transitory, 176b
fashion of w. passeth, 52a
federation of the w., 647b

World, fill w. with fools, 706b
fine place worth fighting for,
  1045a
fled from this vile w., 292b
folly to the w., 987b
foolery governs w., 317a
foppery of the w., 277a
forgetting by world forgot, 405b
founded on four freedoms, 972b
fragments seek each other that
  w. come to be, 965a
freedom everywhere in w., 973a
friends make your w., 794b
from all deceits of the w., 60b
full of number of things, 823b
full of untold novelties, 724b
gain whole w., 43a
gained w. gave w. lesson, 790a
gave his honors to the w., 299a
Germany in w. forward, 815a
Germany w. power or not at
  all, 1012a
get whole w. out of bed, 947a
getting on in w., 913a
ghosts all over w., 729b
giddy thinks w. turns round,
  219b
give the w. the lie, 199a
give w. assurance of a man,
  264a
give warning to w., 292b
given over to Cain, 887a
given to lying, 241a
gleams of remoter w., 568a
gleams untraveled w., 646b
glory of w. displayed, 889b
glow from fire light w., 1073a
glow has warmed the w., 981b
go into all the w., 45b
go well with thee, 1100b
God made w., 50a
God plays dice with w., 950b
God so loved w., 48a
golden w., 247a
good deed in naughty w., 235b
good w. to live in, 925b
good-bye proud w., 601b
great w. spin forever, 647b
great wonderful w., 719a
grown gray, 774a
half brother of w., 679a
half the w. living in misery,
  982b
half w. knows not how other
  lives, 325a
half w. not understand pleasures
  of other, 533b
hanging around in w., 930a
happy beautiful communist w.,
  1058a
harbor gives to w., 816a-b
harmoniously confused, 405a
has joked incessantly, 769a
has to kill people, 1044a
hath not sweeter creature, 275b
hath one tale to tell, 945b
healthy free w. before me, 701a
heaven commences ere w. past,
  449a
here where w. quiet, 775a
high shore of this w., 244b
his only w. and everyone's,
  1078b
his six days' work a w., 347a
his who has money to go,
  608a
history is world's court, 497b
history of w. biography, 577a

World, history of w. progress
  of freedom, 507b
hog butcher for w., 948a
hold w. but as w., 231a
honest as w. goes, 260b
hope to w. for future, 637a
how w. originated, 620a
huge w. come to him, 605b
I am in charity with w., 390b
I am light of w., 48b
I have overcome w., 49a
I never made, 854a
I never sought w., 433b
ideas were to transform, 750a
if there's another w., 496b
if w. and love were young, 198b
if w. be worth winning, 371b
if w. go astray, 161b
I'll make me a w., 906b
in arms, 596a
in faith and hope w. disagree,
  409b
in love with night, 225a
in solemn stillness, 657b
in this harsh w., 266b
in w. not of it, 539b
in w. they do work, 4a
incessantly wash w., 702a
infinite shapeless white, 953b
intangible we touch, 857a
intellectual w. divided, 869b
into dangerous w. leaped, 489b
into our first w., 1005a
invisible we view, 857a
is a bubble, 209b
is a comedy, 442b
is a fine place, 1045a
is a force not presence, 957b
is a king, 506b
is a nettle, 400a
is ajangle and ajar, 888a
is all aleak, 1031a
is as ugly as sin, 710a
is but small parenthesis, 331b
is grown so bad, 217a
is in silence, 4a
is in state of chassis, 981a
is mine oyster, 267a
is sad enough, 825b
is so faithless, 188a
is young today, 813b
it is a w. to see, 202b
joy to pass to w. below, 118b
joy to the w., 397a
just felt w. go by, 734b
justice done though w. perish,
  186a
knowledge of w. acquired in w.,
  415a
laboring surges of w., 856b
large when leagues divide, 806b
lash rascals through w., 276a
laugh and w. laughs, 825b
lawlessness, 971b
leaden army that conquers w.,
  871a
learn of green w., 989a
leave the w. no copy, 251b
leaves w. to darkness, 440a
lesser god made w., 654a
let the w. mind him, 664b
let us possess one w., 304b
let w. slide, 182a
let w. wag, 183a
letter to w., 735b
light of bright w. dies, 826a
light of the w., 40a, 48b
lights of the w., 456b

World, limits of vision limits
of w., 563b
  listen then as I now, 570b
  little friend of all w., 875b
  little note nor remember, 639a
  little w. made cunningly, 307b
  little w. of childhood, 936a
  live in w. as spectator, 394a
  London clearinghouse of w.,
765b
  look round habitable w., 371a
  look upon w. as parish, 420b
  looks for wages, 667b
  looks on w. rationally, 507b
  looks whole w. in face, 621b
  losers and world forsakers, 807a
  love beyond w., 381a
  love makes w. go round, 744b,
768a, 1105b
  lover's quarrel with w., 929a
  loves w. as his body, 73b
  mad as Bedlam, 671b
  mad w. mad kings, 236a
  made in six days, 504a
  made safe for democracy, 842a
  made to be won by youth, 920a
  maintain before whole w., 361b
  make w. a desert, 1048b
  make w. safe for democracy,
866b
  makes whole w. kin, 269a
  man to hold against w., 826b
  man who convinces w., 812b
  margent of w., 856b
  mass and majesty of w., 1060b
  mass of public wrongs, 204a
  may end tonight, 664a
  mere anarchy loosed on w.,
882a
  mighty w. of eye and ear, 509b
  milk cow of w., 1078b
  money sets w. in motion, 126b
  more overwork than w. justifies, 872a
  morning of the w., 661b
  move into sunlit uplands, 921a
  movers and shakers of w., 807a
  mud-luscious, 1030a
  must be peopled, 246a
  must conform to necessity, 913a
  my all the w., 193b
  my country is the w., 467b
  my own specified w., 949a
  naked shingles of w., 714b
  native in this w., 956a
  nature too noble for w., 289b
  never enjoy w. aright, 377b
  never starve for wonders, 918b
  New W. favorable to declamation, 844a
  new w. to be won, 1072a
  new w. which is old, 647b
  next w. as closely apprehended,
330b
  no government stable in unstable w., 911a
  no local defense contain Communist w., 1000b
  no world but wrongs, 204a
  noisy set martyrs call w., 880b-
881a
  Northwest Passage to intellectual w., 438a
  not as w. giveth, 49a
  not be queen for all w., 298a
  not inn but hospital, 330b
  not live at level of great, 829a
  not lose sight of conventions of
w., 757b

World, not loved w. nor w.
me, 556b
  not sweet in the end, 774a
  not to live but die in, 330b
  now bubble burst now w., 408a
  O w. intangible, 857a
  O w. invisible, 857a
  O w. thou choosest not, 866b
  O w. unknowable, 857a
  O world world world, 269b
  of adult life, 936a
  of cards, 1019a
  of compensation, 636a
  of eye and ear, 509b
  of fashion birth intellect, 721a
  of happy days, 217a
  of human community, 1055b
  of ideas, 713a, 713b
  of light, 362b
  of made, 1031b
  of men for me, 663a
  of nature and God, 1077b
  of sighs, 272b
  of trouble and time, 667a
  of vile faults, 267a
  of words, 957b
  on back burden of w., 826b
  on w. to turn thine eyes, 427a
  one custom corrupt w., 654a
  one kiss for all the w., 497a
  one soul-side to face w., 665b
  one w. or none, 1015b
  one w. resemble another, 957a
  only fence against the w., 373a
  only fool in w., 666b
  opinion governs w., 841b
  organization of w. community,
964b
  origin of modern w., 1047a
  other w. by which faith advanced, 173b
  our country the w., 615b
  over w. and under w., 873a
  pain, 500a
  part we sadly in troublous w.,
216b
  parted by hurrying w., 510a
  pass through w. once, 531a
  peace or world destruction, 901a
  peace reversal of record, 959b
  peep at such a w., 458b
  pendant w., 271b, 344a
  perfect everywhere, 498b
  playboy of Western w., 909a
  please w. and father, 359a
  pleases w. cannot please himself, 377a
  poet creates w., 957a
  poet looks at w., 957b
  poor w. said I, 354b
  posterity w. without end, 459b
  presents rational aspect, 507b
  prettiest doll in w., 691a
  procreant urge of w., 700a
  provoke w. to rising birthrate,
1061b
  puddle-wonderful, 1030a
  queer save me and thee, 1102a
  quiet limit of w., 652b
  race soul all going somewhere,
703a
  rack of this tough w., 280b
  read that w. was spherical, 173b
  reared arm crested the w., 288b
  rebellion in political w., 471b
  rebukes w. rebuked by w., 874b
  remote from wrangling w., 467a
  retire from w. satisfied, 120a
  retreating w., 1028b

World, rhythm to w. of sound,
998b
  richest monarch in w., 497b
  riddle of the w., 409a
  ringed with azure w., 651a
  rocks cradle rules w., 699b
  roll of w. palpable, 782b
  rolls into light, 625a
  roofs of w., 701a
  roses of w. fade, 889b
  round w. forever and aye, 711a
  sad and dreary, 727b
  safe for democracy, 842a, 866b
  safe for distinction, 1074b
  safe for diversity, 1074a
  safe for hypocrisy, 1049b
  same w. a hell a heaven, 604b
  same whole w. over, 1103a
  saving w. from destruction,
1058a
  say to all the w., 256b
  secure amidst falling w., 393a
  see how w. goes, 279b
  see w. in grain of sand, 490a
  seek a newer w., 646b
  seek empty w. again, 685b
  seem all uses of this w., 257b
  seems to smile upon me, 375a
  sense that w. mad, 938b
  sensory w. and wish w., 834b
  serpent deceiveth whole w., 58a
  serve and not dominate w.,
982a
  shore of the wide w., 581a
  shot heard round w., 603a
  should he need next w., 664b
  show contain and nourish all
w., 222a
  shut in from w. without, 626b
  slumbering w., 399a
  small when enemy loose, 806b
  small-talking w., 1061b
  smother up beauty from w.,
238a
  snow swept w. end to end,
1018a
  snowed whole w. over, 1018a
  snug little farm the w., 533a
  so runs w. away, 263b
  sob heavy w., 1060a
  solid earth actual w., 680b
  spectacle unto w., 52a
  stands out, 1023a
  start w. all over at, 929a
  start w. along, 748a
  starve for want of wonder, 918b
  state inherent in U.N., 1013b
  steady patriot of w. alone, 506b
  still point of turning w., 1004a,
1005a
  stood against w., 255b
  story and byword through w.,
318a
  strange terrible w. war, 923b
  superego and id, 834a
  swiftly passes glory of w., 170a
  sword axis of w., 1015b
  syllables govern the w., 317b
  take note O w., 275a
  taketh away sin of w., 48a
  technological w., 1055b
  tell the w., 240b
  ten days that shook w., 998b
  ten hours to w. allot, 198b
  terms between Old and New
W., 485a
  terrible in mass, 783a
  that few is all the w., 211a
  their words to end of w., 17b

Z